2005

JANUARY

M	T	W	T	F	S	S
					1	2
3	4	5	6	7	8	9
10	11	12	13	14	15	16
17	18	19	20	21	22	23
24	25	26	27	28	29	30
31						

FEBRUARY

M	T	W	T	F	S
	1	2	3	4	5
7	8	9	10	11	12
14	15	16	17	18	19
21	22	23	24	25	26
28					

APRIL

M	T	W	T	F	S	S
				1	2	3
4	5	6	7	8	9	10
11	12	13	14	15	16	17
18	19	20	21	22	23	24
25	26	27	28	29	30	

MAY

M	T	W	T	F	S	
						1
2	3	4	5	6	7	8
9	10	11	12	13	14	15
16	17	18	19	20	21	22
23	24	25	26	27	28	29
30	31					

		1	2	3	4	5
6	7	8	9	10	11	12
13	14	15	16	17	18	19
20	21	22	23	24	25	26
27	28	29	30			

JULY

M	T	W	T	F	S	S
				1	2	3
4	5	6	7	8	9	10
11	12	13	14	15	16	17
18	19	20	21	22	23	24
25	26	27	28	29	30	31

AUGUST

M	T	W	T	F	S	S
1	2	3	4	5	6	7
8	9	10	11	12	13	14
15	16	17	18	19	20	21
22	23	24	25	26	27	28
29	30	31				

SEPTEMBER

M	T	W	T	F	S	S
			1	2	3	4
5	6	7	8	9	10	11
12	13	14	15	16	17	18
19	20	21	22	23	24	25
26	27	28	29	30		

OCTOBER

M	T	W	T	F	S	S
					1	2
3	4	5	6	7	8	9
10	11	12	13	14	15	16
17	18	19	20	21	22	23
24	25	26	27	28	29	30
31						

NOVEMBER

M	T	W	T	F	S	S
	1	2	3	4	5	6
7	8	9	10	11	12	13
14	15	16	17	18	19	20
21	22	23	24	25	26	27
28	29	30				

DECEMBER

M	T	W	T	F	S	S
			1	2	3	4
5	6	7	8	9	10	11
12	13	14	15	16	17	18
19	20	21	22	23	24	25
26	27	28	29	30	31	

2006

JANUARY

M	T	W	T	F	S	S
						1
2	3	4	5	6	7	8
9	10	11	12	13	14	15
16	17	18	19	20	21	22
23	24	25	26	27	28	29
30	31					

FEBRUARY

M	T	W	T	F	S	S
		1	2	3	4	5
6	7	8	9	10	11	12
13	14	15	16	17	18	19
20	21	22	23	24	25	26
27	28					

MARCH

M	T	W	T	F	S	S
		1	2	3	4	5
6	7	8	9	10	11	12
13	14	15	16	17	18	19
20	21	22	23	24	25	26
27	28	29	30	31		

APRIL

M	T	W	T	F	S	S
					1	2
3	4	5	6	7	8	9
10	11	12	13	14	15	16
17	18	19	20	21	22	23
24	25	26	27	28	29	30

MAY

M	T	W	T	F	S	S
1	2	3	4	5	6	7
8	9	10	11	12	13	14
15	16	17	18	19	20	21
22	23	24	25	26	27	28
29	30	31				

JUNE

M	T	W	T	F	S	S
			1	2	3	4
5	6	7	8	9	10	11
12	13	14	15	16	17	18
19	20	21	22	23	24	25
26	27	28	29	30		

JULY

M	T	W	T	F	S	S
					1	2
3	4	5	6	7	8	9
10	11	12	13	14	15	16
17	18	19	20	21	22	23
24	25	26	27	28	29	30
31						

AUGUST

M	T	W	T	F	S	S
	1	2	3	4	5	6
7	8	9	10	11	12	13
14	15	16	17	18	19	20
21	22	23	24	25	26	27
28	29	30	31			

SEPTEMBER

M	T	W	T	F	S	S
				1	2	3
4	5	6	7	8	9	10
11	12	13	14	15	16	17
18	19	20	21	22	23	24
25	26	27	28	29	30	

OCTOBER

M	T	W	T	F	S	S
						1
2	3	4	5	6	7	8
9	10	11	12	13	14	15
16	17	18	19	20	21	22
23	24	25	26	27	28	29
30	31					

NOVEMBER

M	T	W	T	F	S	S
		1	2	3	4	5
6	7	8	9	10	11	12
13	14	15	16	17	18	19
20	21	22	23	24	25	26
27	28	29	30			

DECEMBER

M	T	W	T	F	S	S
				1	2	3
4	5	6	7	8	9	10
11	12	13	14	15	16	17
18	19	20	21	22	23	24
25	26	27	28	29	30	31

CIVIL COURT SERVICE

2005 Reissue

CIVIL COURT SERVICE

2005 Reissue

Published by
Jordan Publishing Limited
21 St Thomas Street
Bristol BS1 6JS

E-mail Address
Your views and ideas on *Civil Court Service* are welcomed. You can e-mail our commissioning editor at tony_hawitt@jordanpublishing.co.uk.

British Library Cataloguing-in-Publication Data
A catalogue record for this book is available from the British Library.

ISSN 1466–2728

ISBN 1 84661 005 2

This volume is typeset by Letterpart, Reigate, Surrey.

MANAGING EDITOR: Achim Bosse Chitty gepr RKand, LLM

COMMISSIONING EDITOR: Anthony Hawitt LLB

PUBLISHER: Caroline Vandridge-Ames LLM

Typeset by Letterpart Ltd, Reigate, Surrey
Printed and bound in Great Britain by William Clowes Ltd, Beccles, Suffolk, England.

CONSULTING EDITOR

The Right Honourable Lord Saville of Newdigate

EDITOR-IN-CHIEF

The Right Honourable Lord Justice Laws

FOUNDING EDITOR

Richard Stevens OBE
Solicitor and former District Judge

GENERAL EDITORS

District Judge Neil Hickman
Milton Keynes County Court

Bill Vincent OBE
Solicitor and former District Judge

CONTRIBUTORS

Richard Arnold QC

District Judge Gordon Ashton
Preston County Court

Stephen Bickford-Smith
Barrister

Andrew Child
Barrister

Jeremy Clarke-Williams
Solicitor

His Honour Judge Paul Collins CBE
Senior Circuit Judge
Central London Civil Justice Centre

District Judge Stephen Gerlis
Barnet County Court

Peter Haworth
Solicitor

His Honour Judge Richard Holman
Designated Civil Judge at
Manchester County Court

Edward Levey
Barrister

Frances McCarthy
Solicitor

District Judge Abbas Mithani
Birmingham County Court

Guy Newey QC

Alan Owens
Solicitor

John Pickering
Solicitor

His Honour Judge John Platt
Ilford County Court

District Judge Monty Trent
The Mayor's and City of London
Court

District Judge Michael Walker
Wandsworth County Court

L J West-Knights QC

Civil Court Service sets out the Civil Procedure Rules, Practice Directions, Protocols (incorporating amendments up to Update 40) and Court Guides as at **21 October 2005**.

Later developments have been taken account of wherever possible.

For subsequent amendments see our website at *www.civilcourtservice.co.uk*

Foreword to the First Edition

This century is ending with a new beginning for our civil justice system. We have long been proud of our tradition of judicial independence and impartiality and the judgments of our courts are admired across the world. But unless we can successfully tackle the twin evils of delay and unnecessary expense, we will not in fact be providing justice; and thus will be failing properly to provide an essential element for a truly democratic society.

Lord Woolf accepted without reservation the principle that justice delayed, or justice that costs too much, is in truth no justice at all. Thus his reforms are designed to deal head on with delay and unnecessary expense. They do so by making fundamental changes to our present system.

For the new reforms to succeed there are three basic requirements.

First, there is and will remain a vital need for all those who work in the civil justice system to be properly educated and trained and to have a proper understanding of the new system, for all human institutions are only as good as the people who operate them.

Secondly, those who wish to use the civil justice system must also have a ready and inexpensive means of learning about it, for otherwise justice will remain largely unavailable to most of our society.

Thirdly, the reforms themselves call for the most efficient means possible for the proper management of justice.

To meet these requirements we can count ourselves truly blessed by Information Technology. The extraordinary development of this technology is to my mind one of the outstanding features of the closing decades of the 20th century. For the first time in human history, we have a way of providing education, training, management and administration, which is not confined by paper or by geographical or temporal considerations (and thus by the concomitant expense of these considerations), nor limited to the methods of the past. In my view, Information Technology provides us with an essential tool for ensuring that the new reforms succeed in providing justice for all.

I have been privileged to know the General Editors of Jordans *Civil Court Service* for many years. I have worked with them on seeking to introduce Information Technology to our justice system. They are wholly convinced, as am I, of the great benefits that Information Technology can bring. To my mind, one of those benefits is that the clear and thorough guidance provided in this work is available not only in paper form but also on CD and is updated regularly for all those who have access to the World Wide Web. This service is thus helping in a very significant way indeed to meet the requirements for the success of the new civil justice system.

LORD SAVILLE OF NEWDIGATE *April 1999*

Preface to the First Edition

The reforms to the English law of civil procedure, whose principal measures will come into effect on 26 April 1999, rank in importance with other far-ranging changes of the past, such as the reorganisation of the courts in the latter part of the nineteenth century. Now, as then, the means by which legal remedies are delivered to the people have become less and less efficacious. Heightened expectation of what the law should provide, an increased resort to litigation, growth in the complexity of the law itself, and economic pressures upon the funding of lawsuits have combined to make access to justice more and more problematic. Cost and delay have taken the oil from the hinges of the court door. Elaborate procedures and recourses, perhaps relating particularly to the disclosure of documents and the use of expert evidence, which may be apt for the adjudication of complex disputes where very large sums are at stake (though by no means always even then) have clogged the process of the simpler, smaller claims. The recovery of costs has too often overshadowed resolution of the initial dispute. More than anything else, the pace and intensity of procedural skirmish and manoeuvre have been driven and controlled, not by the court, but by parties and their advisers, often where one party has the capacity to withstand the resulting attrition of resources but the other has not.

Now we have a new beginning. The Civil Procedure Rules do not merely simplify the process of litigation. They involve a conceptual shift in the idea of justice, so that economy and proportionality are not merely desirable aims but are defining features of justice itself. And it is not merely aspiration; it is law. It is what the Rules themselves require, and enjoin the judges, through active case management, to achieve. But the system cannot work unless practitioners and judiciary alike understand it from its inception. Nothing less than the future of the common law, and its service to the people, is engaged in these reforms.

I hope that this new work will prove an invaluable aid to everyone whose professional duty it will be to participate in litigation governed by the Civil Procedure Rules, the Practice Directions and Pre-Action Protocols. It has been assembled by experts and should prove convenient and easy to use. We shall all have need of a *vade mecum* to the new regime; this one, I am sure, will play its part in the latest chapter of the common law's history.

THE RT HON LORD JUSTICE LAWS *March 1999*

Contents

Introduction

It did not really take me by surprise when Richard Stevens told me that he had decided to retire as a joint General Editor of the *Civil Court Service*. He has struggled with ill-health for some years now and late last year realised that the warmer temperatures of the Spanish coast held a greater attraction for him than the delightful view from a somewhat breezy hillside in Staffordshire. Even so, it was a serious personal blow. Richard and I have been great friends for a long time and have worked on many projects together, not always achieving the degree of success which we hoped for and which, I hope, the Brown Book represents, but always with great enjoyment and mutual respect. All of us, including the authors and the publishing team, wish him a long and happy retirement in the sun.

It gives me great pleasure to introduce Neil Hickman as Richard's replacement. Neil is a District Judge at Milton Keynes and was already one of the authors contributing to the work. He is wasting no time in showing his mettle. His selection was a wise decision as, I am quite sure, time will prove.

You will also see some new names on the spine. It is always invidious to single out individuals, but I am particularly pleased that we have been joined by Richard Holman, the Designated Civil Judge at Manchester. I would also like to thank Richard Arnold QC and Jeremy Clarke-Williams who have performed Herculean tasks on very short notice in enabling us to cover for the first time Intellectual Property and Defamation claims respectively. Both are specialist subjects. We have attempted to provide an introduction to the relevant procedure for conducting claims in these areas and have, out of necessity, touched upon some of the substantive law underpinning them. However, for a detailed treatment of the latter the reader is directed to one of the established textbooks.

These extensions of our coverage may signal the start of a trend. There is, of course, a limit to what can be included in a paper volume but you must not overlook either the CD-ROM (inside the back cover at no extra charge!) or the Online part of our service at *www.civilcourtservice.co.uk*. Both include a large amount of material which the book itself could not contain. Largely, up to now, it is unannotated. In the future we plan to make the book and the CD-ROM more obviously part of the same service, repositioning some material and, where we can, extending annotation. The Online service will benefit accordingly.

This Reissue edition has, of course, taken in Update 38 to the CPR. The revisions to the Personal Injury Pre-Action Protocol will, we hope, already be familiar to practitioners in this field; who should also note the relaxation of the conditions in r 25.7 for making an interim payment order. The remnants of the former rules relating to fixed costs are brought into Pt 45, and not before time. The regime for fixed recoverable costs in small road accident personal injury claims in the same Part is refined and extended. Solicitor and client costs proceedings and Law Society interventions form the subjects of a new Pt 67. The telephone hearings pilot has been extended in time and we hear rumours from our usually reliable source that those arrangements will shortly benefit the nation as a whole, albeit probably in a slightly modified form.

Update 39 made significant changes to the treatment of Asylum and Immigration claims, which was necessary to take account of the new regime introduced by the Asylum and Immigration (Treatment of Claimants, etc) Act 2004. Update 40, promised for August, appeared only on 30 September – some things at least, it seems, do not change – but we have done our best.

BILL VINCENT *October 2005*

Table of Statutes

References are to page numbers.

Table of Statutory Instruments

References are to page numbers.

A chronological list of statutory instruments referred to in this work appears at the end of the alphabetical list below.

Chronological List of Statutory Instruments

Solicitors' (Non-Contentious Business)Remuneration Order 1994, SI 1994/2616

1995 Transfer of Functions (Science) Order 1995, SI 1995/2985

1996 Insolvent Companies (Reports on Conduct of Directors) Rules 1996, SI 1996/1909

High Court and County Courts (Allocation of Arbitration Procedings) Order 1996, SI 1996/3215

1997 Social Security (Recovery of Benefits) Regulations 1997, SI 1997/2205

1998 Late Payment of Commercial Debts (Interest) Act 1998 (Commencement No 1) Order 1998, SI 1998/2479

Civil Procedure (Modification of Enactments) Order 1998, SI 1998/2940

Reserve Forces Act 1996 (Consequential Provisions etc) Regulations, SI 1998/3086

Civil Procedure Rules 1998, SI 1998/3132

1999 Civil Procedure (Amendment) Rules 1999, SI 1999/1008

Family Proceedings (Miscellaneous Amendment) Rules 1999, SI 1999/1012

Insolvency (Amendment) (No 2) Rules 1999, SI 1999/1022

Civil Legal Aid (General) (Amendment) Regulations 1999, SI 1999/1113

County Court Judgments (Amendment) Regulations 1999, SI 1999/1845

2000 Civil Procedure (Amendment) Rules 2000, SI 2000/221

Civil Procedure (Amendment) Rules 2000, SI 2000/221

Community Legal Service (Costs) Regulations 2000, SI 2000/441

Conditional Fee Agreements Regulations 2000, SI 2000/692

Access to Justice (Membership Organisations) Regulations 2000, SI 2000/693

Conditional Fee Agreements Order 2000, SI 2000/823

Community Legal Service (Cost Protection) Regulations 2000, SI 2000/824

Access to Justice Act 1999 (Transitional Provisions) Order 2000, SI 2000/900

Civil Procedure (Amendment No 2) Rules 2000, SI 2000/940

Access to Justice Act 1999 (Destination of Appeals) Order 2000, SI 2000/1071

Civil Procedure (Amendment No 3) Rules 2000, SI 2000/1317

Civil Procedure (Amendment No 4) Rules 2000, SI 2000/2092

Collective Conditional Fee Agreements Regulations 2000, SI 2000/2988

2001 Civil Procedure (Amendment) Rules 2001, SI 2001/256

Companies (Disqualification Orders) Regulations 1986, SI 2001/967

Postal Services Act 2000 (Consequential Modifications No 1) Order 2001, SI 2001/1149

Civil Procedure (Amendment No 2) Rules 2001, SI 2001/1388

Civil Procedure (Amendment No 3) Rules 2001, SI 2001/1769

High Court and County Courts (Amendment No 2) Order 2001, SI 2001/2685

Civil Procedure (Amendment No 4) Rules 2001, SI 2001/2792

Financial Services and Markets Act 2000 (Control of Business Transfers) (Requirements on Applicants) Regulations 2001, SI 2001/3625

Civil Procedure (Amendment No 5) Rules 2001, SI 2001/4015

Civil Procedure (Amendment No 6) Rules 2001, SI 2001/4016

2002 Civil Procedure (Amendment) Rules 2002, SI 2002/2058

Civil Procedure (Amendment No 2) Rules 2002, SI 2002/3219

2003 Civil Procedure (Amendment) Rules 2003, SI 2003/364

Conditional Fee Agreements (Miscellaneous Amendments) Regulations 2003, SI 2003/1240

Access to Justice Act 1999 (Commencement No 10) Order 2003, SI 2003/1241

Civil Procedure (Amendment No 2) Rules 2003, SI 2003/1242

Civil Procedure (Amendment No 3) Rules 2003, SI 2003/1329

Civil Procedure (Amendment No 4) Rules 2003, SI 2003/2113

Regulatory Reform (Business Tenancies) (England and Wales) Order 2003, SI 2003/3096

Civil Procedure (Amendment No 5) Rules 2003, SI 2003/3361

2004 Civil Procedure (Amendment) Rules 2004, SI 2004/1306

Civil Procedure (Amendment No 2) Rules 2004, SI 2004/2072

Civil Proceedings Fees Order 2004, SI 2004/3121

Civil Procedure (Amendment No 3) Rules 2004, SI 2004/3129

Civil Procedure (Amendment No 4) Rules 2004, SI 2004/3419

2005 Civil Procedure (Amendment) Rules2005, SI 2005/352

Civil Procedure (Amendment No 2) Rules 2005, SI 2005/656

Civil Procedure (Amendment No 3) Rules 2005, SI 2005/2292

Table of Cases

References are to page numbers.

Table of Practice Directions

References are to page numbers.

Abbreviations

AA 1950	Arbitration Act 1950
AA 1975	Arbitration Act 1975
AA 1979	Arbitration Act 1979
AA 1996	Arbitration Act 1996
ADR	Alternative dispute resolution
A(IID)A 1966	Arbitration (International Investment Disputes) Act 1966
AJA 1970	Administration of Justice Act 1970
AJA 1973	Administration of Justice Act 1973
AJA 1982	Administration of Justice Act 1982
AJA 1985	Administration of Justice Act 1985
AJA 1999	Access to Justice Act 1999
AEA	Attachment of Earnings Act 1971
ASBA 2003	Anti-Social Behaviour Act 2003
ASBO	Anti-social behaviour order
CA 1985	Companies Act 1985
CA 1989	Children Act 1989
CA 1998	Competition Act 1998
CCA 1974	Consumer Credit Act 1974
CCA 1984	County Courts Act 1984
CCFA	Collective Conditional Fee Agreement
CCFO	County Court Fees Order 1999
CCJO 1981	County Courts Jurisdiction Order 1981
CCR	Rules taken from the County Court Rules 1981 and set out (as amended) in Schedule 2 to CPR
CDDA 1986	Company Directors Disqualification Act 1986
CDF	Clinical Disputes Forum
CDPA 1988	Copyright, Designs and Patents Act 1988
CDPD	Chancery Division Practice Direction
CFA	Conditional Fee Agreement
CFA(MA)R 2003	Conditional Fee Agreements (Miscellaneous Amendments) Regulations 2003
CFAO 2000	Conditional Fee Agreements Order 2000
CFAR 2000	Conditional Fee Agreements Regulations 2000
CJA 1988	Criminal Justice Act 1988
CJJA	Civil Jurisdiction and Judgments Act 1982
CJPOA	Criminal Justice and Public Order Act 1994
CLSA 1990	Courts and Legal Services Act 1990
CMC	Case management conference

COA	Charging Orders Act 1979
CPA	Civil Procedure Act 1997
CPFO	Civil Proceedings Fees Order 2004
CPR	Civil Procedure Rules 1998
CPRC	Civil Procedure Rules Committee
DCA	Department for Constitutional Affairs
DDA 1995	Disability Discrimination Act 1995
EA 2002	Enterprise Act 2002
ECHR	European Convention on Human Rights
FISMA	Financial Services and Markets Act 2000
FLA 1986	Family Law Act 1986
FLRA 1987	Family Law Reform Act 1987
HA 1980	Housing Act 1980
HA 1985	Housing Act 1985
HA 1988	Housing Act 1988
HA 1996	Housing Act 1996
HCCCJO	High Court and County Courts Jurisdiction Order 1991
HCCC(AAP)O	High Court and County Courts (Allocation of Arbitration Proceedings) Order 1996
HGCRA	Housing Grants, Construction and Regeneration Act 1996
HRA 1998	Human Rights Act 1998
IA 1986	Insolvency Act 1986
IA 2000	Insolvency Act 2000
ICA 1982	Insurance Companies Act 1982
I(PFD)A	Inheritance (Provisions for Family and Dependants) Act 1975
IR 1986	Insolvency Rules 1986
JPRA 1995	Judicial Pensions and Retirement Act 1995
LAA 1988	Legal Aid Act 1988
L&TA 1954	Landlord and Tenant Act 1954
MSA 1995	Merchant Shipping Act 1995
OFT	Office of Fair Trading
Part [number]	Part [number] of CPR
PD[number]	Practice direction which supplements Part [number] of CPR
PDAsbo	Practice direction on anti-social behaviour (orders under section 1B(4) of the Crime and Disorder Act 1998)
PDCA	Court of Appeal (Civil Division) Practice Direction
PDCCR[number]	Practice direction which supplements the CCR Order of that number
PDCommittal	Practice direction on applications to commit for contempt
PDCompEC	Practice direction on competition law – claims relating to the application ofArticles 81 and 82 of the EC Treaty

PDCompetition	Practice direction on applications for warrants under CA 1998
PDCosts	Practice direction relating to Parts 43–48
PDCrime	Practice direction on the Proceeds of Crime Act 2002 Parts 5 and 8: civil recovery
PDDev	Practice direction on devolution issues (and Crown Office applications) in Wales
PDDirectors	Practice direction on directors disqualification proceedings
PDExecution	Practice direction on execution
PDInsolvency	Practice direction on insolvency proceedings
PDProt	Practice direction on pre-action protocols
PDRSC[number]	Practice direction which supplements the RSC Order of that number
PDWelsh	Practice direction on the use of the Welsh language in the civil courts in Wales
PHA 1997	Protection from Harassment Act 1997
PTR	Pre-trial review
RCJ	Royal Courts of Justice
RSC	Rules taken from the Rules of the Supreme Court 1965 and set out (as amended) in Schedule 1 to CPR
RTA	Road traffic accident
Rule [number]	Rule [number] in CPR
SCA	Supreme Court Act 1981
SCCO	Supreme Court Costs Office (formerly SCTO, see below)
SCFO	Supreme Court Fees Order 1999
SCTO	Supreme Court Taxing Office (now SCCO, see above)
SJE	Single joint expert
SL(R)A 1986	Statute Law (Repeals) Act 1986
TLATA 1996	Trusts of Land and Appointment of Trustees Act 1996

SECTION 1

Procedural Guides

SECTION 1: Procedural Guides

Contents

COSTS

ENFORCEMENT

TENANCIES AND POSSESSION OF LAND

MISCELLANEOUS

APPEALS AND JUDICIAL REVIEW

1: Issuing Proceedings (General Procedure)

Legal background

Whilst the majority of claims are begun by issuing a claim in accordance with CPR Pt 7, several rules and practice directions vary the procedure and reference need therefore also be made to the following:

Type of Claim	CPR Part/Practice Direction	Procedural Guide
Consumer Credit Act 1974	Rule 7.9/PD7B	Guide 2
Money Claims Online	PD7E	Guide 4
No substantial dispute of fact	Part 8	Guide 3
Parties and group litigation	Part 19/PD19B	
Children or patients	Part 21	Guide 17
Injunctions and other interim remedies	Part 25	Guide 23
Pre-action disclosure of documents	Rule 31.16	Guide 24
Costs-only proceedings	Rule 44.12A	Guide 34
Applications under the Companies Acts 1985–89, the Insurance Companies Act 1982 and Part VII of the Financial Services and Markets Act 2000	PD49B (CG)	
Appeals	Part 52	Guides 58 and 59
Defamation claims	Part 53	
Judicial Review	Part 54	Guide 60
Claim for possession of land by landlord	Part 55	Guide 50
Claim for possession of land by mortgagee	Part 55	Guide 51
Claim for possession of land against trespassers	Part 55	Guide 52
Claim for possession of land against (former) licensees	Part 55	Guide 53
Claim by tenant seeking relief from forfeiture	Part 55	Guide 54
Claim for an accelerated possession order of an assured shorthold tenancy	Rules 55.11–55.19	Guide 46
Claim for an interim possession order	Rules 55.20–55.28	Guide 45
Applications relating to business tenancies	Part 56	Guide 49
Applications for injunctions against anti-social behaviour under the Housing Act 1996, s 152		Guide 48
Probate claims	Part 57 (CG)	
Commercial Court claims	Part 58 (CG)	
Mercantile court claims	Part 59 (CG)	
Technology and Construction Court claims	Part 60	Guide 57
Admiralty Court claims	Part 61 (CG)	

Type of Claim	CPR Part/Practice Direction	Procedural Guide
Arbitration claims	Part 62 (CG)	
Patent claims	Part 63 (CG)	
Applications under the Inheritance (Provision for Family and Dependants) Act 1975	Part 57, Section IV	Guide 55
Estates, Trusts and Charities	Part 64	
Applications to enforce a charging order by sale	Rule 73.10/PD73, paras 4.1–4.5	Guide 47
Applications for writ of habeas corpus	Sch 1, RSC Ord 54	Guide 56

Where indicated (CG), please also make reference to the relevant Court Guide applicable in the court in question. The Court Guides are set out in Section 5 of this work.

Procedure

Which court	The following must be issued in the High Court:	
	any claim where the High Court has exclusive jurisdiction by statute (these include, unless the parties agree in writing that the county court shall have jurisdiction, a claim for damages or other remedy for libel or slander, and a claim in which the title to any toll, fair, market or franchise is in question);	PD7, paras 2.3, 2.9 CCA 1984, s 15(2)
	claims for habeas corpus and judicial review;	PD7, para 2.6
	claims needing to be heard in a High Court specialist list	See the preceding list of cases, CPR Parts/practice directions and Guides
	claims for a declaration of incompatibility under Human Rights Act 1998, s 4	HRA 1998, s 4 Rule 30.3(2)(g)
	The following must be issued in a county court:	
	personal injury claims where the claimant does not expect to recover £50,000 or more,	PD7, para 2.2
	other claims where the claimant does not expect to recover more than £15,000	PD7, para 2.1
	any claim where the county court has exclusive jurisdiction by statute	PD7, para 2.3

	Otherwise, a claim may be issued in either court but if the claimant believes that it should be dealt with by a High Court judge by reason of its value, complexity or general importance, it should be started in that court	PD7, para 1 PD7, para 2.4
General requirements	A claim form is completed and lodged at or sent to the court office. Particulars of claim must either be endorsed or provided separately	Rule 7.2(1) Rule 7.4(1)
	Several claims may be included in one claim form	Rule 7.3
Date of issue	The proceedings are started when the court issues the claim form but for the purposes of the Limitation Act 1980 the claim is 'brought' when the completed claim form is received at the court office if that is earlier	PD7, para 5.1
Contents of claim form	The claim form must be headed with the title of the proceedings which should state the claim number, the court or division, the full name of each party and his status (ie claimant/defendant)	PD7, para 4.1
	The nature of the claim must be stated concisely	Rule 16.2(1)(a)
	The remedy sought must be specified	Rule 16.2(1)(b)
	If money is claimed, the form must state either the amount claimed or that the claimant expects to recover:	Rule 16.3(2)
	not more than £5000; or	
	more than £5000 but not more than £15,000; or	
	more than £15,000; or	
	that the claimant cannot say how much he expects to recover.	
	If personal injury damages are sought, the form must state whether the claimant expects to recover more than or not more than £1000 general damages for pain, suffering and loss of amenity	Rule 16.3(3)

	If the claimant as tenant of residential premises seeks an order that the landlord effect repairs, the form must state (i) whether the cost of the repairs or other work is estimated to be more than or not more than £1000, and (ii) whether the claimant expects to recover more than or not more than £1000 in respect of any claim for damages	Rule 16.3(4)
	The claimant must specify any 'devolution issue' (as defined in Government of Wales Act 1998, Sch 8, para 1, or Northern Ireland Act 1998, Sch 10, para 1 or Scotland Act 1998, Sch 6, para 1) he wishes to raise and the relevant statutory provisions	PDDev, para 16.1
	In the High Court, the basis of the claimant's right to issue there (see above) must be stated	Rule 16.3(5)
	In calculating the figures referred to, interest and costs and any possibility of a finding of contributory negligence, a counterclaim or set-off by the defendant or the recoupment of state benefits is to be disregarded	Rule 16.3(6)
	The claim form is a statement of case and so must be verified by a statement of truth (see below), whether or not particulars of claim so verified are served separately	Rule 2.3(1) Rule 22.1(1)
Description of parties	The person making the claim is the claimant. The person against whom it is made is the defendant	Rule 2.3
	If a party is suing or sued in a representative capacity, this must be stated	Rule 16.2(3), (4)
Chancery business	The claim form must be marked 'Chancery Division' (High Court) or 'Chancery Business' (county court)	PD7, para 2.5
Claimant's address	If not represented by a solicitor, the claimant must give his residence or business address as his address for service	Rule 6.5(3)(a)
	If represented, the solicitor's address will be his address for service (but the claim form itself requires his personal address also to be given)	Rule 6.5(5)

	The address for service must be within England or Wales	Rule 6.5(2)
Parties under 18 years of age or suffering mental disorder	A child's name should be followed by '(a child by ..... his litigation friend)' or, if a litigation friend is dispensed with, then simply '(a child)'	PD21, para 1.5
	The name of a party suffering mental disorder should be followed by '(by ..... his litigation friend)'	PD21, para 1.3
	See Guide 17 as to the appointment of a litigation friend and the other special considerations which apply.	
Firms and other unincorporated bodies	In the county court, the names of individuals and partners suing or sued in their own names may be followed by 'trading as [*firm name*]' and when suing or sued in the names of the firm or body, the name may be followed by '[a trading name]'	CCR Ord 5, r 10(1)
	In the High Court it will be convenient to follow a similar practice, as hitherto.	
Particulars of claim	If particulars of claim are to be served as a separate document subsequently to the claim form, it should be endorsed 'particulars of claim will follow'	Rule 16.2(2)
	The particulars must include a concise statement of the facts on which the claimant relies	Rule 16.4(1)(a)
	They must state any claim for aggravated, exemplary or provisional damages, with the grounds for that claim	Rule 16.4(1)(c), (d)
	If a devolution issue (see above under 'Contents of claim form') is raised, the particulars of claim must contain the facts, circumstances and points of law relied on in sufficient detail for the court to determine whether a devolution issue arises	PDDev, para 16.2
	For additional requirements in particular kinds of case, see below.	
	The particulars of claim must be verified by a statement of truth (see below)	Rule 22.1(1)

	If served separately, the Particulars must show the name of the court, the case number, the title of the proceedings and the claimant's address for service	PD16, para 3.8
Statement of truth	The claim form and, if separate, particulars of claim must be verified by a statement of truth. This is a statement that the party putting forward the document believes the facts stated in it are true. It must, subject to permitted exceptions, be signed by the party or his solicitor and is required to be endorsed on (*inter alia*) every statement of case	Rule 22.1(4) Rule 22.1(6)(a) Rule 22.1(8) PD22, paras 3.1–3.11 Rule 22.1(1)
	To make or cause to be made a false statement in a document so verified, without honest belief in its truth, is contempt of court	Rule 32.14
Claim for interest	If the claimant seeks interest, the particulars of claim must state whether he does so under a contract, under an Act (and if so which) or on some other basis (and if so what basis)	Rule 16.4(2)(a)
	In a claim for a specified sum of money, they must also state the percentage rate, the date from which interest is claimed, the date (no later than the date of issue) to which it is claimed, the amount so calculated and the daily rate claimed thereafter	Rule 16.4(2)(b)
Personal injury claims	The particulars of claim must contain the claimant's date of birth and brief details of his injuries	PD16, para 4.1
	A schedule of special damages (if claimed) must be verified by a statement of truth and attached to the particulars of claim	PD22, para 1.4(3) PD16, para 4.2
	A medical report must be attached if medical evidence is relied on	PD16, para 4.3
	If provisional damages are claimed, the relevant details must be given	PD16, para 4.4

Fatal accident claims	The particulars of claim must state that the claim is brought under the Fatal Accidents Act 1976 and give details of the dependants on whose behalf the claim is made and of the nature of the dependency claim	PD16, para 5.1
Defamation claims	There are detailed requirements for claims in libel and slander	PD53
Claims for injunction or declaration relating to land	The particulars of claim must identify the land (from a plan if necessary) and state whether the claim relates to residential premises	PD16, para 7.1
Claims to recover goods	The particulars of claim must contain a statement showing the value of the goods. See below as to goods the subject of CCA 1974 regulated agreements	PD16, para 7.2
Claims for wrongful interference with goods	The particulars of claim must contain the name and address of every person who, to the claimant's knowledge, has or claims an interest in the goods and who is not a party to the claim	Rule 19.5A
Claims based on agreements	If in writing, a copy of the contract must be attached to the particulars of claim together with any relevant general conditions of sale (or a relevant extract)	PD16, para 7.3
	If oral or based on conduct, full details of the words or the conduct and the circumstances of either must be given	PD16, paras 7.4, 7.5
Claims relating to a CCA 1974 regulated agreement	If issued in the High Court, the particulars of claim must contain a statement that the action is not one to which s 141 of the Act applies	PD16, para 7.6
	As to claims for the recovery of protected goods and for Time Orders, see Guide 2.	
Civil Evidence Act 1968	If the claimant wishes to rely on a conviction or adjudication, details must be included in the particulars of claim	PD16, para 8.1
Particular allegations	If relied on, the following must be set out in the particulars of claim: fraud; illegality;	

	misrepresentation; breach of trust; notice or knowledge of a fact; unsoundness of mind or undue influence; wilful default; facts relating to mitigation of loss or damage	PD16, para 8.2
Foreign currency claims	The particulars of claim must state that the claim is for payment in a specified foreign currency, why that is so, the Sterling equivalent at the date of claim and the source of the exchange rate relied on	PD16, para 9.1
Optional material in particulars of claim	Points of law relied on may be referred to. Names of witnesses may be given. Supporting documents (including an expert's report) may be attached	PD16, para 13.3
Conditional fee agreements	A party who wishes to claim an additional liability in respect of a funding arrangement must give any other party information in Form N251 about that claim if he is to recover the additional liability	PDCosts, paras 19.1 and 19.2(1)
Claim issued for service in Scotland, Northern Ireland and Europe under CJJA 1982	If it is intended to serve the claim, without the need for permission, in Scotland or Northern Ireland or one of the European territories which has ratified the Brussels or Lugano Conventions (listed in Guide 16), the claim form and (if separate) the particulars of claim must contain a statement of the grounds on which the claimant is entitled to serve it out of the jurisdiction, ie a statement that the court has power under CJJA 1982 to deal with the claim, and that no proceedings based on the same claim are pending between the parties in Scotland, Northern Ireland or another Convention territory	Rule 6.19(3) PD6B, paras 1.1–1.5 PD7, para 3.5

Claim issued for service out of jurisdiction under the Council Regulation	Where a claim which is to be served out of the jurisdiction is one which the court has power to deal with under Council Regulation (EC) No 44/2001, the claim form and (if separate) the particulars of claim must contain a statement that the court has power under that Regulation to deal with the claim and that no proceedings based on the same claim are pending between the parties in Scotland, Northern Ireland or any other EU Member State except Denmark	Rule 6.19 PD6B, paras 1.1–1.5 PD7, para 3.5A
Service	Once issued the claim, together with forms for the defendant to use for admitting or defending the claim and for acknowledging service, must be served. See Guides 15 and 16	Rule 7.8
Court fees	There is now a combined Civil Proceedings Fees Order which provides for payment of fees both in the High Court and in the county court.	
	Money claim in the High Court: up to £50,000 – £400 not over £100,000 – £700 not over £150,000 – £900 not over £200,000 – £1,100 not over £250,000 – £1,300 not over £300,000 – £1,500 over £300,000 or unlimited – £1,700	CPFO fee 1.1
	Money claim in the county court: up to £300 – £30 not over £500 – £50 not over £1,000 – £80 not over £5,000 – £120 not over £15,000 – £250 not over £50,000 – £400 not over £100,000 – £700 not over £150,000 – £900 not over £200,000 – £1,100 not over £250,000 – £1,300 not over £300,000 – £1,500 over £300,000 or unlimited – £1,700	CPFO fee 1.2
	Claims Production Centre claims (under £100,000) – fees as above less £10. Claims above £99,999.99 cannot be issued through the CPC. Counterclaim – as claim, but no fee in probate.	

	On the commencement of originating proceedings for any other remedy or relief or where the claim for money is additional or alternative to a claim for recovery of land or goods: in the High Court – £400 in the county court – £150	CPFO fee 1.4
	Where a claim for money is alternative to a non-money claim (other than a claim for recovery of land or goods) the fee payable is calculated by reference to the money claim, subject in the county court to a minimum fee of £150.	
	Where the claim or counterclaim is amended and the fee paid before amendment is less than that which would have been payable if the document, as amended, had been so drawn in the first instance, the party amending the document shall pay the difference.	
	Further fees are payable at the allocation stage in relation to claims exceeding £1,500 and at the pre-trial checklist/listing stage in relation to claims allocated to either of the fast track or the multi-track	See Civil Proceedings Fees Order 2004 in Section 6 of this work
Fixed costs	Applicable in respect of solicitors' charges where the claim is for a specified sum over £25	Rules 45.2 and 45.4
Forms	Claim Form N1 Conditional fee agreements – Form N251	

2: Issuing Proceedings (Consumer Credit Act Procedure)

Legal background

Proceedings for an order under certain sections of CCA 1974 must be brought under this procedure, which is set out in the practice direction to Rule 7.9. On the issue of a claim under this procedure the court will fix a hearing date.

Procedure

Which court	The county court has exclusive jurisdiction to hear any claim:	CCA 1974, s 141(1)

	by a creditor or owner to enforce a regulated agreement or any security relating to it; to enforce any linked transaction against the debtor or hirer or his relative. If a claim is issued in the High Court, it must contain a certificate that CCA 1974, s 141 does not apply	PD16, para 8.6
Claims where the procedure must be used	Except where the claim: relates to recovery of land (see Guides 3, 50, 51, 52, and 53); or	PD7B, para 3.2
	is made by a creditor under CCA 1974, s 141, to enforce a regulated agreement where the agreement relates only to money (where the general procedure should be used – see Guide 1),	PD7B, para 3.3
	this procedure must be used in claims under the following sections of CCA 1974 –	PD7B, para 3.1
	s 141 (claim by the creditor to enforce regulated agreement relating to goods etc); s 129 (claim by debtor or hirer for a time order); s 90 (creditor's claim for an order for recovery of protected goods); s 92(1) (creditor's or owner's claim to enter premises to take possession of goods); s 139(1)(a) (debtor's claim for a credit agreement to be reopened as extortionate); and creditor's or owner's claim for a court order to enforce a regulated agreement relating to goods or money where the court order is required by – s 65(1) (improperly-executed agreement); s 86(2) (death of debtor or hirer where agreement is partly secured or unsecured); s 111(2) (default notice etc not served on surety); s 124(1) or (2) (taking of a negotiable instrument in breach of terms of s 123); or s 105(7)(a) or (b) (security not expressed in writing, or improperly executed).	

Restrictions on venue	A claim which includes a claim to recover goods to which a regulated hire-purchase or conditional sale agreement relates may be started only in the county court for the district in which the debtor, or one of the debtors: resides or carries on business; or resided or carried on business at the date when the defendant last made a payment under the agreement	PD7B, para 4.1
	In any other claim to recover goods, the claim may be started only in the court for the district in which the defendant, or one of the defendants, resides or carries on business; or in which the goods are situated	PD7B, para 4.2
	A claim of a debtor or hirer for an order under s 129(1)(b) (a time order) may only be started in the court where the claimant resides or carries on business	PD7B, para 4.3
General requirements	A claim form is completed and lodged at or sent to the court office	Rule 7.2(1)
	The court office will fix a hearing date on the issue of the claim form	PD7B, para 5.1
	At the hearing the court may: dispose of the claim; if the claim is or is to be defended, allocate to track or give directions to enable it to do so	PD7B, paras 6.1–6.3
	Each party must have at least 28 days' notice of the hearing date	PD7B, para 5.6
	Particulars of claim must be served with the claim form	PD7B, para 5.2
Contents of particulars of claim	The particulars of any claim brought to enforce a right to recover possession of goods must contain a statement of the value of the goods	PD16, para 7.2
	The particulars of claim must state that the claim is a Consumer Credit Act claim	PD7B, para 7.1
	In a claim for the delivery of goods where:	

the agreement to be enforced is a regulated hire-purchase or conditional sale agreement; and

the goods are let to a person other than a company or other corporation,

the particulars of claim must also include (in this order) the following information –

the date of the agreement;

the parties to the agreement;

the number or other identification of the agreement (with enough information to allow the debtor to identify the agreement);

where the claimant was not one of the original parties to the agreement, the means by which the rights and duties of the creditor passed to him ;

the place where the agreement was signed by the defendant (if known);

the goods claimed;

the total price of the goods;

the paid-up sum;

the unpaid balance of the total price;

whether a default notice or a notice under s 76(1) or s 88(1) of the Act has been served on the defendant, and, if it has, the date and the method of service;

the date on which the right to demand delivery of the goods accrued;

the amount (if any) claimed as an alternative to the delivery of goods; and

the amount (if any) claimed in addition to –

the delivery of the goods; or

an amount claimed as an alternative to the delivery of goods,

with the grounds of each such claim — PD7B, para 7.2

Particulars of claim for an order under s 129(1)(b) (a time order) must include (in the following order) the following information:

the date of the agreement;

	the parties to the agreement; the number or other means of identifying the agreement; details of any sureties; if the defendant is not one of the original parties to the agreement then the name of the original party to the agreement; the names and addresses of the persons intended to be served with the claim form; the place where the claimant signed the agreement; details of the notice served by the creditor or owner giving rise to the claim for the time order; the total unpaid balance the claimant admits is due under the agreement; the amount of any arrears (if known); the amount and frequency of the payments specified in the agreement; the claimant's proposals for payments of any arrears and of future instalments together with details of his means; and where the claim relates to a breach of the agreement other than for the payment of money, the claimant's proposals for remedying it	PD7B, para 7.3
	Where a claimant is required to obtain a court order to enforce a regulated agreement by: s 65(1) (improperly executed agreement); s 105(7)(a) or (b) (security not expressed in writing, or improperly executed); s 111(2) (default notice etc not served on surety); s 124(1) or (2) (taking of a negotiable instrument in breach of terms of s 123); or s 86(2) (death of debtor or hirer where agreement is partly secured or unsecured), the particulars of claim must state what the circumstances are that require the claimant to obtain a court order for enforcement	PD7B, para 7.4

Parties	All parties to a regulated agreement and any surety, must be made parties to any proceedings relating to the agreement, except where rules of court provide otherwise	CCA 1974, s 141(5)
	The court may dispense with this requirement if:	
	the claim form has not been served on the debtor or the surety; and	
	the claimant either before or at the hearing makes an application (which may be made without notice) for the court to make such an order	PD7B, para 9.1
	This requirement does not apply in a claim where:	
	the claimant was not one of the original parties to the agreement; and	
	the former creditor's rights and duties under the agreement have passed to him by –	
	operation of law; or	
	assignment,	
	unless the court otherwise orders	PD7B, para 9.3
Service	Once issued the claim will need to be served. See Guide 15.	
Court fees	See Guide 1.	
Fixed costs	Applicable in respect of solicitors' charges where the court gives a fixed date for the hearing and judgment is given for the delivery of goods	Rules 45.2 and 45.4
Forms	Claim Form: for Time Order N440 otherwise N1	

3: Issuing Proceedings (Pt 8 Procedure)

Legal background

Among the procedures that perished with the introduction of the CPR are the originating summons and originating motion procedures in the High Court, and the fixed date summons and originating application procedures in the county court. Part 8 provides an alternative procedure for use where a claimant seeks the court's decision on a question which is unlikely to involve a substantial dispute of fact, or where a rule or practice direction requires or permits it. It also seeks to replace those previous procedures which the CPR have abolished. The procedure may be varied by individual practice directions, the most important of which to date is PD8B, or by Schedule rules.

Practice Direction 8B is divided into two sections, A and B, and sets out where the procedure must be used. Section A applies the procedure as set out in Pt 8 ('the general procedure') to those claims set out in Table 1 to PD8B, while Section B introduces a 'fixed date' variation to the procedure ('the fixed date procedure') and applies it to those claims set out in Table 2 to PD8B.

The Schedule rules vary the requirements for the content of the claim form and the procedure generally. They also provide for the use of different prescribed forms. Table 2 to PD8B indicates where a special prescribed form of claim form must be used.

This Guide explains the general procedure for Pt 8 claims where the Schedule rules do not vary it. It also deals with the taking of depositions in or outside England and Wales for use respectively outside or within England and Wales, where the Pt 8 procedure is varied by practice direction.

The provisions of Pt 7 continue to apply where they are not disapplied by or inconsistent with Pt 8 or the practice directions which supplement it. Reference should therefore be made to Guide 1 for matters of general application.

Procedure

Claims where the general procedure may be used	Any claim where the claimant seeks the court's decision on a question which is unlikely to involve a substantial dispute of fact, for example:	Rule 8.1(2)(a)
	a claim for provisional damages which has been settled before the commencement of proceedings where the sole purpose of the claim is to obtain a consent judgment	PD8, para 1.4(2)
Claims where the procedure must be used	*General procedure* All claims listed in Table 1 to PD8B ('Table 1');	
	where an Act provides that an application in the High Court is to be brought by originating summons;	
	where, prior to 26 April 1999, a claim or application would have been brought in the High Court by originating summons;	PD8B, para A.1
	a claim by or against a child or patient which has been settled before the commencement of proceedings where the sole purpose of the claim is to obtain the approval of the court to the settlement;	PD21, para 6.1

	Fixed date procedure Provided that no other procedure is prescribed in an Act, a Schedule rule or a practice direction, the procedure must be used to commence:	PD8B, para B.1
	all claims listed in Table 2 to PD8B;	PD8B, para B.1(1)
	all claims which, before 26 April 1999 would have been commenced –	
	in the High Court by originating motion;	PD8B, para B.1(3)(a)
	in the county court by –	
	originating application; or	
	petition	PD8B, para B.1(3)(b)
	arbitration claims, except where r 62.3(2) applies	Rule 62.3(1)
Variations to the procedure as set out in Pt 8	*General procedure* The claimant must comply with any Act, Schedule rule or practice direction which makes any provision additional or contrary to the provisions of Pt 8 and modify the Pt 8 procedure accordingly	PD8B, para A.2
	Fixed date procedure The claimant must first comply with any special provision set out in the Schedule rules, practice direction or any Act relating to the claim. Such provision may relate, amongst other things, to:	PD8B, para B.2
	where the claim may be started;	
	the contents of the claim form;	
	whether a hearing is required or the amount of notice required to be given of it;	
	any evidence required to be filed in support of the claim;	
	the method by which, and the persons on whom, service of the claim form and evidence in support is to be effected;	
	the form and content of notices, affidavits, answers or replies and how, when and upon whom they must be served;	
	persons who may apply to be joined to the proceedings; and	
	minimum periods of notice before the final hearing	PD8B, para B.3

Inappropriate use of procedure	A court officer may refer a claim to a judge if he believes that a claimant is using the procedure inappropriately	PD8, para 1.5
	A defendant may also object to the use of the procedure – see Guide 5	Rule 8.8(1)
Contents of claim form	The claim form must state: that Pt 8 applies;	Rule 8.2(a)
	the question which the claimant wants the court to decide, or the remedy which the claimant is seeking and the legal basis for it;	Rule 8.2(b)
	the enactment, if any, under which the claim is made;	Rule 8.2(c)
	if either the claimant claims, or the defendant is sued, in a representative capacity, what that capacity is	Rule 8.2(d), (e)
	The claimant must specify any 'devolution issue' (as defined in Government of Wales Act 1998, Sch 8, para 1, or Northern Ireland Act 1998, Sch 10, para 1 or Scotland Act 1998, Sch 6, para 1) he wishes to raise and the relevant statutory provisions together with the facts, circumstances and points of law relied on in sufficient detail for the court to determine whether a devolution issue arises	PDDev, paras 16.1 and 16.2
	Unless a Guide states to the contrary, the above provisions apply whatever else must be included in the claim form by virtue of any Schedule rule.	
Issue	A claim form is completed and lodged with or sent to the court office	Rule 7.2(1)
	Particulars of claim may be endorsed on it or served with it.	
	The claim form to be used is:	
	the claim form number listed against the particular claim in Table 2 to PD8B; or	
	in every other claim, the Pt 8 claim form N208	PD8B, para B.8
	Written evidence on which the claimant wishes to rely must be filed when the claim form is filed but an extension of time may be obtained	Rule 8.5(1) PD8, para 5.5

	Fixed date procedure Where a Schedule rule makes special provision for the contents of particulars of claim, those particulars must be attached to and served with the claim form	PD8B, para B.4
	A hearing date will be given on the issue of the claim form	PD8B, para B.9(1)
	The court will prepare and serve a notice of the hearing for each party. If the claimant serves the claim form personally, a copy of the notice of hearing must be served at the same time	PD8B, para B.9(2) PD8B, para B.11
	at least 21 days' notice of the hearing must to be given;	PD8B, para B.10
	the defendant is not required to file a reply or an acknowledgment of service or defence	PD8B, para B.12
Which court	*Fixed date procedure* Where the claim is brought in a county court, it must be started:	
	in the county court for the district in which –	
	the defendant or one of them lives or carries on business; or	
	the subject matter of the claim is situated; or	
	if there is no defendant, in the county court for the district in which the claimant or one of them lives or carries on business	PD8B, para B.6
Provisions of CPR which do not apply	The following rules do not apply to Pt 8 claims:	
	Part 16 (contents of statements of case);	
	Part 15 (defence and reply);	
	the requirements in Rule 7.8 to serve on the defendant forms for admitting and defending the claim;	
	Rule 14.4 to 14.7 (special rules applicable only to admitting claims for money only);	Rule 8.9(a), (b)
	Part 12 (default judgment);	Rule 12.2(b)
	Part 26 (procedure for allocation to track) – but see below	Rule 8.9(c)
Managing the claim	*General procedure* All claims are treated as allocated to the multi-track	Rule 8.9(c)
	The court may give directions for the management of the claim:	

	immediately the claim is issued; or on filing of the acknowledgment of service; or when the time for filing the acknowledgment has expired.	
	The court may fix a hearing date on issue, or may convene a directions hearing before giving any directions	PD8, para 4.1
	In some cases, the court may deal with the application without a hearing or giving any directions	PD8, para 4.3
	Fixed date procedure At the hearing, the court may: hear and dispose of the claim; or give case management directions which may include – giving directions to enable the claim to be allocated or allocating it to a track when Rule 26.5(3)–(5) and Rules 26.6–26.10 will apply (see Guide 11)	PD8B, paras B.13–B.15
Statement of truth	The claim form and any particulars of claim served separately must be verified by a statement of truth. This is a statement that the party putting forward the document believes the facts stated in it are true. It must, subject to permitted exceptions, be signed by the party or his solicitor and is required to be endorsed on (*inter alia*) every statement of case	Rule 22.1(1) Rule 22.1(4) Rule 22.1(8) PD22, paras 3.1–3.11 Rule 22.1(6)
	So far as the evidence served consists of witness statements, they must be verified by a statement of truth signed by the witness	Rule 22.1(6)(b)
	To make or cause to be made a false statement in a document so verified, without honest belief in its truth, is contempt of court	Rule 32.14
Conditional fee agreements	A party who wishes to claim an additional liability in respect of a funding arrangement must give any other party information in Form N251 about that claim if he is to recover the additional liability	PDCosts, paras 19.1 and 19.2(1)

Claim issued for service in Scotland, Northern Ireland and Europe under CJJA 1982	If it is intended to serve the claim, without the need for leave, in Scotland or Northern Ireland or one of the European territories which has ratified the Brussels or Lugano Conventions (listed in Guide 16), the claim form and (if separate) the particulars of claim must contain a statement of the grounds on which the claimant is entitled to serve it out of the jurisdiction, ie a statement that the court has power under CJJA 1982 to deal with the claim, and that no proceedings based on the same claim are pending between the parties in Scotland, Northern Ireland or another Convention territory	Rule 6.19(3) PD6B, paras 1.1–1.5 PD7, para 3.5
Claim issued for service out of jurisdiction under the Council Regulation	Where a claim which is to be served out of the jurisdiction is one which the court has power to deal with under Council Regulation (EC) No 44/2001, the claim form and (if separate) the particulars of claim must contain a statement that the court has power under that Regulation to deal with the claim and that no proceedings based on the same claim are pending between the parties in Scotland, Northern Ireland or any other EU Member State except Denmark	Rule 6.19 PD6B, paras 1.1–1.5 PD7, para 3.5A
Service	*General procedure* Where there is a defendant, the claim form must be served together with a copy of the evidence filed and a form for the defendant to acknowledge service (see Guides 15 and 16) *Fixed date procedure* As for the general procedure, save that no form of acknowledgment need be served.	Rule 8.5(2) Rule 7.8(1)(c)
Settlement or compromise on behalf of a child or patient	See Guide 17	
Costs-only proceedings	See Guide 34	
Court fees	See Guide 1	

Forms	The claim form to be used is: the claim form number listed against the particular claim in Table 2 to PD8B; or in every other claim, the Pt 8 claim form N208. In addition, where a conditional fee agreement applies, Form N251.	
Which judge	In proceedings in the Chancery Division, a master or district judge may not determine any question of law or as to the construction of a document in proceedings brought under paragraph A.1(2) or (3) of PD8B without the consent of the Vice-Chancellor	PD2B, para 5.1(d)

4: Issuing Proceedings (Money Claim Online)

Legal background

HM Courts Service has taken the first step in bringing court users an internet-based service. Following a successful pilot scheme, CPR r 7.12 and PD7E continue the Money Claim Online (MCOL) facility, which has been provided at Northampton County Court. The facility enables claimants to start certain types of county court claim by requesting their issue electronically via the HM Courts Service website and, when the claim has been started electronically, to apply online for:

- default judgment;
- judgment on acceptance of admission of the whole of the amount claimed;
- the issue of a warrant of execution;
- an electronic record of the claim's progress.

The service is limited to straightforward money claims of less than £100,000. Some categories of claimant or defendant are excluded. The service discourages prolixity by limiting particulars to 1080 characters (approximately 14 lines of printed text). Only enforcement by bailiff is available online.

Procedure

Help	The MCOL website has an excellent online user guide and there is a helpdesk at Northampton for MCOL customers.	
Contact details	Telephone: 0845 601 5935 Fax: 0845 601 5889 URL: *www.moneyclaim.gov.uk*	

	Address: Money Claim Online, Northampton County Court, St Katherine's House, 21–27 St Katherine's Street, Northampton, NN1 2LH DX 702885 Northampton 7	
Which court	Claims will be issued by Northampton County Court and will proceed there until transferred to another court	PD7E, para 1.4
Filing	All documents, applications or requests should normally be filed electronically through the MCOL website (URL above) Documents not capable of being filed electronically should be filed at Northampton County Court at the address given above, not that court's normal office address.	
Method of payment	Fees paid electronically may be paid for by credit card or debit card (or any other method which HM Courts Service may permit, but none had been approved as this edition went to press)	PD7E, para 3.1
Availability	The service is limited to: (a) a Pt 7 claim; (b) of less than £100,000 (excluding interest or costs); (c) in sterling; (d) for a specified amount of money; (e) against a single defendant; or (f) against two defendants if the claim is for a single amount against each of them; (g) whose address for service is within England and Wales	PD7E, para 4
	The service cannot be used by: (i) vexatious litigants (for an up-to-date list of vexatious litigants see *http://www.hmcourts-service.gov.uk/infoabout/vexatious_litigant/index.htm*)	MCOL website
	(ii) a child or patient within Pt 21	PD7E, para 4(3)(a)
	(iii) a person funded by the Legal Services Commission	PD7E, para 4(3)(b)

	(iv) a person claiming exemption from payment or remission of Court fees	PD7E, para 3.2
	The service cannot be used for claims against: (a) the Crown	PD7E, para 4(5)(a)
	(b) a person known to be a child or patient	PD7E, para 4(5)(b)
	(c) a defendant with an address for service outside England and Wales	PD7E, para 4(6)
Court fees	Normal prescribed fees are payable	Civil Proceedings Fees Order 2004: see Guide 1 and Section 6 of this work
	They are paid electronically by credit card or debit card.	
	Other methods of payment will be permitted by HM Courts Service as the service develops	PD7E, para 3.1
Registration	For security reasons persons using the service are required to register (creating for themselves a customer ID and password), to provide personal information for identification purposes and to comply with any other security measures	PD7E, para 2
Starting a claim	The claimant completes and sends an online claim form and pays the issue fee electronically at the URL given above	PD7E, para 5.1
Particulars of claim	The particulars are limited in size to 1080 characters, including spaces. Incorporated within the electronic claim form, they are not filed separately (PD16, para 7.3 requiring copies of contractual documents to be annexed is excluded)	PD7E, paras 5.2, 5.3
Commencement	Receipt of the electronic claim form by the court's computer system (and not by the website, which sends electronic acknowledgment of receipt of request for claim) constitutes the formal commencement date for the purposes of the Limitation Act 1980, etc	PD7E, para 5.5
	Formal printed notice of issue is sent by the court to the claimant by post	PD7E, para 5.6(2)

Service	The court posts a printed version of the claim form to the defendant. The claim form is deemed to be served on the fifth day after the claim was issued irrespective of whether that day is a business date or not	PD7E, para 5.6(1) PD7E, para 5.8
Acknowledgment of service	The defendant may acknowledge service either by: (a) filing written acknowledgment of service in Form N9 at the address given above; (b) telephoning MCOL customer help desk on 0845 6015935; or (c) sending an e-mail to the e-mail address given above (d) but must not send a hard copy in addition	PD7E, para 6.1 PD7E, para 6.2(1)
Varied requirements for acknowledgment of service	If the court is closed on the last date for filing an acknowledgment of service, time for filing is extended to the next day that the court is open	PD7E, para 6.2(3)
Defence and counterclaim	The defendant may file his defence (and counterclaim, if any, provided it is filed together with the defence) either by post to the court office at the address above or by sending it by e-mail to the e-mail address given above	PD7E, para 1.3(1)
	Any fee payable on a counterclaim is payable to the court to which the case was transferred	PD7E, para 10.1
Statement of truth	Claims or defences (however filed) must be verified by a statement of truth. In the case of online forms the requirement to sign a statement of truth is satisfied by a person typing his name underneath it	PD7E, paras 11.2, 12.1
Request for judgment	Judgment in default of acknowledgment of service or defence or in response to admission of the whole of the claim may be made by completing and sending an online request form at the website (URL above)	PD7E, para 13.1

Enforcement	It is possible to request a warrant of execution online by completing and sending an online request form and paying the appropriate fee electronically. No other methods of enforcement are currently available online	PD7E, para 13.2
Transfer out *– to defendant's home court*	If the defendant is an individual whose home court is not Northampton County Court, the court will transfer the claim to the defendant's home court: (a) on an application to set aside or vary judgment (r 13.4); (b) if there is to be a hearing to determine the time and rate of payment (r 14.2); (c) if a defence is filed (r 26.2); (d) if either party makes an application which will require a hearing	PD7E, para 14.1
Transfer out *– to claimant's home court*	If – (a) the defendant is not an individual; (b) the claimant's address for service is outside the district of Northampton County Court; and (c) one of the events listed above occurs, the claim will be transferred to the claimant's home court	PD7E, para 14.2
Viewing the case record electronically	While the MCOL service is in force the claimants or their representatives can view an electronic claim record (updated daily)	PD7E, paras 15.1, 15.2

5: Responding to Claim (Acknowledgment of Service and Disputing Jurisdiction)

Legal background

Part 9 deals in general with responding to a claim. A defendant may do so by acknowledging service, or by filing an admission (see Guide 6) or a defence (see Guide 7).

Procedure

Use of acknowledgment of service	A defendant may file an acknowledgment of service if: he is unable to file a defence in time; or he wishes to dispute the court's jurisdiction	Rule 10.1(3)
Part 8 claims (see Guide 3 for further detail)	Save in respect of claims issued in accordance with PD8B, a defendant to a Pt 8 claim *must* file an acknowledgment of service if he wishes to defend or be heard	PD8B, para B.12 Rule 8.4(2)
	The acknowledgment of service to a Pt 8 claim should be in Form N210, but can be given in an informal document such as a letter	PD8, para 3.2
	The acknowledgment of service must be verified by a statement of truth	Rule 22.1(1)
	A defendant who wishes to challenge the use of the procedure must state his reasons in writing when he files his acknowledgment of service, and if these reasons include matters of evidence, the acknowledgment, or other writing in which the use of the procedure is challenged, should be verified by a statement of truth	PD8, para 3.6
	A defendant wishing to rely on evidence should normally file it with the acknowledgment.	
	A defendant must specify in his written evidence so filed any 'devolution issue' (as defined in Government of Wales Act 1998, Sch 8, para 1, or Northern Ireland Act 1998, Sch 10, para 1 or Scotland Act 1998, Sch 6, para 1) he wishes to raise and the relevant statutory provisions together with the facts, circumstances and points of law relied on in sufficient detail for the court to determine whether a devolution issue arises	PDDev, paras 16.1 and 16.2
Period for filing	Fourteen days after service of the particulars of claim, unless the claim form is served outside England and Wales when special rules apply (see Guide 16)	Rule 10.3(1) Rules 6.22 and 10.3(2)

	No more than 21 days after the service of a claim form in a case seeking a judicial review	Rule 54.8(2)(a)
	Twenty-eight days after service of the claim form or particulars of claim in probate cases	Rule 57.4(2)
	Fourteen days after service of the claim form in Commercial Court or mercantile court cases	Rule 58.6(2) PD58, para 5 Rule 59.5(2)
Content	The defendant's name should be set out in full	PD10, para 5.1
	Where the defendant's name has been incorrectly set out in the claim form, it should be correctly set out on the acknowledgment of service followed by the words 'described as' and the incorrect name	PD10, para 5.2
	The defendant's address for service, which must be within the jurisdiction, must be stated. This must be the address of the defendant's legal representative if the legal representative signs the acknowledgment of service. Otherwise the address for service must be the defendant's residence or business address unless he does not have one within England and Wales	Rule 10.5 Rule 6.5(2)
Signature	An acknowledgment of service must be signed by the defendant or his legal representative	PD10, para 4.1
	Special rules apply where the defendant is a child or patient (see Guide 17)	Part 21 and PD10, para 4.5
	A person holding a senior position in a defendant company or corporation may sign, but must state the position he holds	PD10, para 4.2
	'Senior position' includes director, treasurer, secretary, chief executive manager or other officer, and, in the case of a corporation (not being a registered company), mayor, chairman, president, town clerk or other similar officer	PD10, para 4.3
	Any partner or person having control or management of the business may sign on behalf of a defendant partnership	PD10, para 4.4

Multiple defendants	If two or more defendants acknowledge service of a claim through the same legal representative at the same time, only one acknowledgment of service need be used	PD10, para 5.3
Amendment or withdrawal	An acknowledgment of service may be withdrawn or amended only with the court's permission	PD10, para 5.4
Counterclaims	A claimant who wishes to defend a counterclaim may not file an acknowledgment of service	Rule 20.4(3)
Conditional fee agreements	A defendant who wishes to claim an additional liability in respect of a funding arrangement must give any other party information in Form N251 about that claim if he is to recover the additional liability	PDCosts, para 19.1
Disputing the court's jurisdiction		
Preliminary	A defendant who wishes to dispute the jurisdiction of the court must first file an acknowledgment of service	Rule 11(2)
	If the claim is brought using the Pt 8 procedure, the acknowledgment of service must be verified by a statement of truth	Rule 22.1(1)
	He does not thereby submit to the jurisdiction of the court	Rule 11(3)
	The defendant must then apply for an order that:	
	the court has no jurisdiction; or	
	the court should not exercise the jurisdiction that it has	Rule 11(1)
Time for applying	The application must be made within 14 days after filing an acknowledgment of service	Rule 11(4)(a)
	If the application is not made within that time, a defendant who has filed an acknowledgment of service is deemed to submit to the jurisdiction of the court	Rule 11(5)
Evidence	The application must be supported by evidence	Rule 11(4)(b)

Defence pending hearing	A defendant who has made an application disputing the court's jurisdiction is not obliged to file a defence before the hearing of the application	Rule 11(9)
If the court grants the application	The court may grant the application and may then also order that: the claim form or its service be set aside any order made before commencement of the proceedings or service of the claim form be discharged the proceedings be stayed	Rule 11(6)
Refusal of application	If the court refuses the application: the acknowledgment of service ceases to have effect;	Rule 11(7)
	the defendant must file a further acknowledgment within 14 days or such other period as the court may direct, and if he does so the defendant is treated as having submitted to the court's jurisdiction;	Rule 11(8)
	rules concerning filing of admission or defence will then apply (see Guides 6 and 7).	
Court fees	On the application: in the High Court – £100 in the county court – £60 No fee payable on filing acknowledgment of service	CPFO fee 2.5
Forms	Form N9 (acknowledgment of service) should be used for Pt 7 claims	PD10, para 2
	Form N210 should be used for Pt 8 claims	PD8, para 3.2
	Form N213 should be used when a party other than a claimant acknowledges service of a Pt 20 claim	PD4, para 1.3 and Table 1
	Form N244 may be used for the application	PD23, para 2.1
	In addition, where a conditional fee agreement applies, Form N251.	

6: Responding to Claim (Admission)

Legal background

Part 14 deals with admitting the whole or part of a claim. Procedure differs depending on whether the claim is for:

- money only and if so whether for –
  - a specified sum; or
  - an unspecified sum,
- any other remedy whether or not there is also a claim for money.

Rule 14.7 introduces the concept of an admission of liability to a claim for an unspecified sum, coupled with an offer in satisfaction.

The defendant's admitting the claim or part of it may allow the claimant to seek judgment either by a *request*, when it will be entered administratively by the court officer, or by an *application* to a judge.

Money Claim Online

The Court Service is presently piloting the electronic issue of certain claims through the bulk issue centre at Northampton County Court. For full details see PD7E 'Pilot Scheme for Money Claims Online' and Guide 4. As regards admissions, only the automatic transfer provisions are affected.

Procedure

Making an admission	A party may admit the whole or any part of another party's case by giving notice in writing	Rule 14.1 and 14.2
	The defendant may also file a defence	PD14, para 3.3
Effect of admission where claim is not for money only	The party whose case (or part thereof) is admitted may apply to the judge for judgment (see Guide 18)	Rule 14.3(1)
	Judgment will be such as appears to the court to be warranted by the admission	Rule 14.3(2)
Claims for money only		
Time for admission	Fourteen days after service of particulars of claim but, provided default judgment has not been entered, will be effective if made at any time	Rule 14.2(1), (3), (4)
Service/filing of admission	Where the defendant admits the whole of a claim for a specified sum of money, the admission must be sent direct to the claimant	Rule 14.4(2)
	Otherwise, the admission is filed in court, which sends a copy to the claimant	Rule 14.5(2), 14.6(2) and 14.7(2)

Form of admission	In claims for a specified sum the form is N9A. In claims for an unspecified sum and non-money claims or claims which include them the form is N9C.	
Claims for specified sum – admission of whole claim		
Entry of judgment by request	The claimant requests judgment by using Form N205A. If the defendant has requested time to pay, see below. If the defendant has not requested time to pay, the claimant may specify the date by which judgment is to be paid or the amount and frequency of any instalments	Rule 14.4(4)
	Judgment will be for: the amount claimed, less any payments made; plus interest (if it has been properly claimed – see below); and fixed costs;	Rule 45.4
	payable by the date or at the rate requested, or immediately if no such request	Rule 14.4(6)
Interest	The judgment will include interest to the date of judgment if: the particulars of claim include a claim for interest in the correct form (see Guide 1); and where the claim is made under CCA, 1984 s 69, or SCA, s 35A, the rate is no higher than that payable on judgment debts current at the date of issue of the claim; and the request for judgment includes a calculation of the interest claimed from the date to which it was stated to be calculated in the claim form to the date of the request for judgment	Rule 14.14(1)
	Otherwise, if interest is requested, judgment will be for an amount of interest to be decided by the court, and the court will give directions	Rule 14.14(2), (3)

Claims for specified sum – admission of part		
General procedure	Court sends to claimant notice of the admission to which the claimant must respond by filing a notice (which incorporates a request for judgment) within 14 days of service	Rule 14.5(3), (4), (5)
	If he does not, the claim will be stayed generally until the notice is filed.	
	The claimant must state in the notice whether or not he:	
	accepts the amount admitted in satisfaction;	
	accepts the terms of any request for time to pay.	
	If the claimant does not accept the amount admitted in satisfaction, the part admission is treated as a defence (see Guide 7)	Rule 26.3(4)(a)
Entry of judgment by request	If he accepts the amount admitted, the claimant requests judgment by using Form N225A.	
	If the defendant has requested time to pay, see below.	
	If the defendant has not requested time to pay, the claimant may specify the date by which judgment is to be paid and the amount and frequency of any instalments.	
	Judgment will be for:	
	the amount admitted, less any payments made; and	
	fixed costs –	Rule 45.4
	payable by the date or at the rate requested, or immediately if no such request	Rule 14.5(6),and (7), (8), (9)
	No interest may be added.	
Automatic transfer	If –	
	the claim is not commenced in the defendant's home court;	
	the defendant is an individual;	
	the claimant files notice that he wishes the claim to continue;	
	then the case will be automatically transferred to the defendant's home court	Rules 2.3 and 26.2(4)

	If the claim has been issued online and the defendant is not an individual, it will be transferred to the court for the district in which the claimant's address for service on the claim form is situated	PD7E, para 10.2
Claims for unspecified sum – bare admission of liability		
General procedure	The court sends to the claimant notice of the admission to which the claimant must respond by filing a request for judgment within 14 days of service. If he does not, the claim will be stayed generally until the request for judgment is filed	Rule 14.6(1)–(5)
Entry of judgment by request	The claimant requests judgment by using Form N205B. Judgment will be for: an amount to be determined by the court, and costs. The court will give directions to lead to deciding the amount of judgment (see Guide 31)	Rules 14.6(7) and 14.8
Claim for unspecified sum – admission of liability with offer in satisfaction		
General procedure	The court sends to the claimant notice of the admission which the claimant must complete and return to the court within 14 days of service If he does not, the claim will be stayed generally until the notice is filed	Rule 14.7(2), (3) Rule 14.7(4)
Entry of judgment by request	The claimant requests judgment by using Form N226. The claimant must state in the notice whether or not he: accepts the amount offered in satisfaction; accepts the terms of any request for time to pay	Rule 14.7(5)

	If the claimant does not accept the amount offered in satisfaction, judgment will be entered for an amount to be decided by the court. and the court will give directions to lead to deciding the amount of judgment (see Guide 31)	Rule 14.7(9)
	Where: the claimant accepts the amount offered in satisfaction; and the defendant has not requested time to pay, the claimant may specify the date by which judgment is to be paid and the amount and frequency of any instalments. Judgment will be for: the amount offered by the defendant; and costs, payable by the date or at the rate requested, or immediately if no such request	Rule 14.7(6)–(8)
	If the defendant has requested time to pay, see below. No interest may be added.	
Requests for time to pay		
When request may be made	A defendant who: admits the whole or part of a claim for a specified sum; or admits a claim for an unspecified sum and makes an offer in satisfaction,	Rule 14.9(1)
	may make a request for time to pay ie a request to pay by a certain date or by instalments at times and rates specified in the request	Rule 14.9(2)
	The request must be made with the admission	Rule 14.9(3)
Entry of judgment by request	Where a defendant makes a request for time to pay which is accepted by the claimant, judgment will be entered for: the amount of the claim (specified sum claim – admission of whole); or the amount admitted (specified sum claim – admission of part); or	

	the amount offered (unspecified sum claim), and in all cases will be for payment at the time or rate specified in the request for time to pay	Rule 14.9(6)
	Where a defendant makes a request for time to pay which is not accepted judgment will be entered as above but for payment at a time or rate to be determined by the court	Rule 14.10(4)
Form of request for judgment	Where the defendant has made a request for time to pay, the claimant requests judgment on Form N205A, N225A or N226 whether or not the defendant's request is accepted	PD14, para 4.2 and 4.3
Determination of request for time to pay which is not accepted	A court officer may determine the request for time to pay in any claim: for a specified sum; and	PD14, para 5.2(2)
	where the amount outstanding does not exceed £50,000	Rule 14.11(1)
	If the court officer determines the request, he must do so without a hearing	Rule 14.11(2)
	If the court officer elects not to, or is otherwise unable to, determine the request, it will be determined by the judge.	
	The judge may determine the request with or without a hearing	Rule 14.12(1)
	Where the judge elects to determine the request at a hearing, 7 days' notice of the hearing must be given and the rules as to automatic transfer may apply – see below under 'Automatic transfer'	Rule 14.12(3)
Matters to be taken into account on determination	In deciding the time and rate of payment the court will take into account: the defendant's statement of means set out in the admission form or in any other written notice of the admission filed; the claimant's objections to the defendant's request set out in the claimant's notice; and any other relevant factors	PD14, para 5.1

Re-determination of request for time to pay	Where a request for time to pay has been determined by: a court officer; or a judge without a hearing, either party may apply for a re-determination by a judge. The application is made by application notice (see Guide 18)	Rule 14.13(1)
	Where the determination was by a court officer, the re-determination may be carried out by the judge without a hearing unless the applicant requests a hearing in his application notice	PD14, para 5.4
	Where the determination was made by a judge, the re-determination must be made at a hearing unless the parties agree otherwise	PD14, para 5.5
	The application must be made within 14 days after service on the applicant of the order giving notice of the determination	Rule 14.13(2)
	Upon such an application being made the rule as to automatic transfer applies – see below under 'Automatic transfer'	Rule 14.13(3)
	If the claim has been issued online and the defendant is not an individual, it will be transferred to the court for the district in which the claimant's address for service on the claim form is situated	PD7E, para 10.2
Automatic transfer	Where the judge elects to have a hearing in order to determine a request for time to pay, or an application for re-determination, the claim will be transferred to the defendant's home court if: the only claim is for a specified sum; and the defendant is an individual; and the claim has not been previously transferred under r 13.4 (application to set aside or vary default judgment) or r 26.2 (on issue of allocation questionnaires); and the claim was not started in the defendant's home court or a specialist list	Rules 14.12(2) and 14.13(3)

	'Home Court' means the county court or district registry for the district where the defendant resides or carries on business; if the claim is in the High Court, and there is no district registry for that district, the defendant's home court will be the Royal Courts of Justice	Rule 2.3(1)
Court fees	On application for re-determination: in the High Court – £50 in the county court – £30	CPFO fee 2.8

7: Responding to Claim (Defence)

Legal background

Parts 15 and 16 deal with filing and content of the defence to a claim. Neither of those parts applies to claims brought under the Pt 8 procedure, where no defence is required.

Electronic filing of a defence

Where a court has published an e-mail address on the Court Service website, it is possible to communicate and file specified documents, including a defence, with the court by e-mail (see generally PD5B).

The defendant is able to file a defence electronically. If a defendant who is an individual does so, and Northampton County Court is not his home court, the court will transfer the claim to the defendant's home court. Where the defendant is not an individual, the court will transfer the claim to the court for the district in which the claimant's address for service on the claim form is situated.

Procedure

Consumer Credit Act procedure	A defendant is not required to file a defence, but if he intends to do so he should file it within 14 days of service of particulars of claim. If the defence is filed later than that, the court may take this into account when deciding what order to make about costs	PD7B, para 5.3(2) PD7B, para 5.4

Part 8 claims	There is no requirement to file a defence. A defendant who wishes to challenge the use of the procedure must state his reasons in writing when he files his acknowledgment of service, and if these reasons include matters of evidence, the acknowledgment, or other writing in which the use of the procedure is challenged, should be verified by a statement of truth	PD8, para 3.6
	The acknowledgment of service must be verified by a statement of truth	Rule 22.1(1)
Time for filing – Part 7 claims	Except where the defendant is served outside the jurisdiction, 14 days after service of the particulars of claim, or, where the defendant has filed an acknowledgment of service, 28 days after service of the particulars of claim	Rule 15.4(1)
	Where the defendant is served outside England and Wales, special rules apply (see Guide 16); in Commercial Court and mercantile court cases, if the claim form is served out of the jurisdiction and if the particulars of claim are served after the defendant has filed an acknowledgment of service, then the period for filing a defence is 28 days from the service of the particulars of claim	Rule 15.4(2)(a) Rule 6.23 Rule 58.10(2) Rule 59.9(2)
	The parties may agree that the period for filing a defence be extended for up to 28 days. The defendant must inform the court in writing of any such agreement	Rule 15.5
Consequences of not filing a defence	Judgment in default of defence may be requested or applied for if permitted by Pt 12 – see Guide 29	Rule 15.3
	It is also possible to obtain judgment in default of a counterclaim	Rule 12.3(2)(b)

Consequences of filing defence	Upon filing of a defence the court will issue allocation questionnaires to the claimant(s) and all defendants who have been served with particulars of the claim and against whom judgment has not been entered (see Guide 11)	Rule 26.3(1), (2)
Automatic transfer	If: the claim is for a specified amount; the claim was commenced other than in the defendant's home court; the claim has not been transferred to another defendant's home court; and the defendant is an individual, then on the filing of a defence the claim is automatically transferred to the defendant's home court	Rule 26.2(1), (3)
Service	See Guide 15 for general rules. A copy of the defence must be served by the defendant on every other party	Rule 15.6
'States paid' defence	In a claim for a specified sum of money only, where the defendant's only defence is that he has paid the amount claimed, the court will send a notice to the claimant asking if he wishes to proceed with the claim. If the claimant does not respond to the notice within 28 days of service of the notice, the claim is stayed generally	Rule 15.10(1) Rule 15.10(3)
	The claimant must serve a copy of his response on the defendant	Rule 15.10(2)
	If the claimant gives notice that he wishes the claim to continue, the proceedings continue treating the 'states paid' defence in the same way as any other defence	Rule 26.3(4)
Contents of defence	The defence must state which allegations in the particulars of claim are: admitted; denied; and neither admitted nor denied but are required to be proved	Rule 16.5(1)

	Reasons for denial of an allegation must be given, and the defendant's version of events if this differs from the version given in the particulars of claim	Rule 16.5(2)
	Allegations not specifically dealt with in the defence are deemed to be admitted *unless*:	Rule 16.5(5)
	the defence sets out the nature of the defendant's case in relation to that issue; or	Rule 16.5(3)
	the allegation relates to an amount of money and the amount is not expressly admitted	Rule 16.5(4)
	If the defendant disputes the claimant's statement of value he must:	
	give reasons; and	
	give his own statement of value if he can	Rule 16.5(6)
	The defendant must specify any 'devolution issue' (as defined in Government of Wales Act 1998, Sch 8, para 1, or Northern Ireland Act 1998, Sch 10, para 1 or Scotland Act 1998, Sch 6, para 1) he wishes to raise and the relevant statutory provisions together with the facts, circumstances and points of law relied on in sufficient detail for the court to determine whether a devolution issue arises	PDDev, paras 16.1 and 16.2
	If the defendant is defending in a representative capacity, he must state what that capacity is	Rule 16.5(7)
	Where the defendant is an individual and the claim form does not contain an address at which he resides or carries on business, or contains an incorrect address, the defendant must provide such an address in the defence	PD16, paras 10.4, 10.5
Defence to personal injury claim	Where the claim is for personal injuries and the claimant has attached a medical report in respect of his alleged injuries, the defendant should:	
	state in his defence whether he agrees, disputes or neither agrees nor disputes but has no knowledge of the matters contained in the medical report;	

	where he disputes any part of the medical report, give in his defence his reasons for doing so; and where he has obtained his own medical report on which he intends to rely, attach it to his defence	PD16, para 12.1
	Where the claim is for personal injuries and the claimant has included a schedule of past and future expenses and losses, the defendant should include in or attach to his defence a counter-schedule stating: which of those items he agrees, disputes or neither agrees nor disputes but has no knowledge of; and where any items are disputed, supplying alternative figures where appropriate	PD16, para 12.2
	Any such counter-schedule, whether or not contained within a statement of case, must be verified by a statement of truth	PD22, para 1.4(3)
Defamation claims	Where in a claim for libel or slander a defendant alleges that the words complained of are true or are fair comment on a matter of public interest he must give specific details in support of that allegation	PD53, paras 2.5(2), 2.6(2)
Limitation	Where the defendant relies on a limitation period, he must give details of the expiry of that period	PD16, para 13.1
Defence of tender	Where a defendant wishes to rely on a defence of tender he must make a payment into court of the amount he says he has tendered before the defence will be available to him (see Guide 26)	Rule 37.3
Optional material	Points of law relied on may be referred to. Names of witnesses may be given. Supporting documents (including an expert's report) may be attached	PD16, para 13.3

Statement of truth	The defence must be verified by a statement of truth. This is a statement that the party putting forward the document believes the facts stated in it are true. It must be signed by the party or his solicitor and is required to be endorsed on (*inter alia*) every statement of case	Rule 22.1(4) Rule 22.1(6)(a) Rule 22.1(1)
	To make or cause to be made a false statement in a document so verified, without honest belief in its truth, is contempt of court	Rule 32.14
Conditional fee agreements	A defendant who wishes to claim an additional liability in respect of a funding arrangement must give any other party information in Form N251 about that claim when filing his first document, ie his acknowledgment of service or his defence or any other document such as an application to set aside judgment	PDCosts, paras 19.1–19.3

8: Making a Counterclaim

Legal background

Part 20 of the Rules provides procedures for claims other than those by the original claimant against the original defendant (see also Guides 9 and 10). A claim by a defendant against a claimant is called a counterclaim.

Procedure

Availability	Subject to special rules where the Crown is a party, the defendant to any claim may make a claim against the claimant. A third party who has been brought into the action by an existing party making a claim against him (see Guide 10) may make a counterclaim against that party	Rule 20.4 Rule 20.5(1)
	Where the case is proceeding under the Pt 8 procedure, permission is needed before a counterclaim can be issued	Rule 8.7
The Crown	Where the Crown is claiming taxes, penalties or duties, no counterclaim can be made	RSC Ord 77, r 6(1) CCR Ord 42, r 9(1)

	In any case, no counterclaim may be made against the Crown for repayment of taxes, penalties or duties	RSC Ord 77, r 6(1) CCR Ord 42, r 9(2)
	Where a particular Department is suing or being sued, no counterclaim which does not relate to that Department can be made, by or against the Crown, without permission	RSC Ord 77, r 6(2)(a) CCR Ord 42, r 9(3)(a)
	Where the Crown is suing or being sued in the name of the Attorney-General, no counterclaim can be made, by or against the Crown, without permission	RSC Ord 77, r 6(2)(b) CCR Ord 42, r 9(3)(b)
Additional defendants to a counterclaim	The court may order the addition of a person as a defendant to the counterclaim. Application for such an order may be made without notice unless the court directs otherwise. It should be accompanied by a copy of the proposed counterclaim and must be supported by evidence stating the stage reached in the action, details of the counterclaim including a summary of the facts on which it is based, the name and address of the proposed added defendant and an explanation of any delay	Rule 20.5(1) Rule 20.5(2) PD20, para 1.2 PD20, paras 2.1, 2.2
Time for making a counterclaim	The counterclaim should normally be filed with the defence	Rule 20.4(2)(a)
	Otherwise, the court's permission must be obtained. The application for permission should be accompanied by a copy of the proposed counterclaim and must be supported by evidence stating the stage reached in the action, details of the counterclaim including a summary of the facts on which it is based and an explanation of the delay. Notice must normally be given	Rule 20.4(2)(b) PD20, para 1.2 PD20, paras 2.1, 2.2 Rule 23.4(1)
Method of making a counterclaim	Particulars of it are filed at the court office	Rule 20.4(1)
	If it is filed with the defence, the defence and counterclaim should form one document, the counterclaim following on from the defence	PD20, para 6.1

Contents of counterclaim	The counterclaim (being a 'Pt 20 claim') is a statement of case. It must comply with the requirements for particulars of claim (see Guide 1) save that the statement to explain why it is issued in the High Court (if the case is proceeding there) is not required	Rule 2.3(1) Rule 20.3(1) Rule 20.3(2)(b)
	It must be verified by a statement of truth	Rule 22.1(1)(a)
Service of counterclaim	If filed with the defence, the counterclaim will be served on the claimant with the defence and on any additional defendant to it as a claim form would be served (see Guides 15, 16 and 20) save that the time-limit for serving a claim form does not apply	Rule 20.8(1)(a) Rule 20.3(1) Rule 20.3(2)(a)
	Otherwise, the order giving permission will give directions as to service	Rule 20.8(3)
	If made against an additional defendant to it, the copy served on that party must be accompanied by forms for admitting and defending the counterclaim and for acknowledging service and copies of all statements of case which have been served in the proceedings, together with any other document which the court directs	Rule 20.12(1)
	If served on an additional defendant, a copy of the counterclaim must also be served on any other existing party, even though it is not made against him	Rule 20.12(2)
Responding to a counterclaim	An additional defendant to a counterclaim must file an acknowledgment of service as if served with a claim form (see Guide 5) but the original claimant does not do so	Rule 20.3(1) Rule 20.4(3)
	Each defendant to a counterclaim may serve or file an admission (see Guide 6) or may file a defence to it (see Guide 7)	Rule 20.3(1)

	The time for filing a defence to the counterclaim (unless extended) is 14 days from service or, in the case of an additional defendant to it who has filed an acknowledgment of service, 28 days. Judgment may be obtained in default (see Guide 29)	Rule 15.4(1)(a) Rule 15.4(1)(b) Rule 20.3(1)
Subsequent procedure	A counterclaim will not be allocated separately to track upon a defence to it being filed. The allocation of the proceedings generally will have taken the counterclaim into account if it was filed with the defence. The court will have given management directions on making an order adding a defendant to the counterclaim. In any event it must consider doing so upon a defence to the counterclaim being filed, ensuring so far as practicable that the claim and counterclaim are managed together	Rule 20.3(2)(c) Rule 26.8(1)(e) Rule 20.5(3) Rule 20.13
	The court may however direct that the counterclaim be dealt with as separate proceedings, taking into account the connection between claim and counterclaim, the remedies being sought by each party and the desire of the counterclaiming defendant to have some question determined between himself and another person as well as the existing parties	Rule 3.1(2)(e) Rule 20.9(2)
Forms	Defence and Counterclaim N9B, N9D. Otherwise Pt 20 Claim Form N211. Application Notice N244.	
Court fees	On filing counterclaim, the same as if issuing fresh proceedings – see Guide 1	CPFO fee 1.6
	On adding a party: *High Court* – £50 *County court* – £30	CPFO fee 1.5
	On application for permission on notice: *High Court* – £100 *County court* – £60	CPFO fee 2.5

	On application for permission without notice: *High Court* – £50 *County court* – £30	CPFO fee 2.6

9: Making a Claim Against a Co-Defendant for Contribution or Indemnity

Legal background

Part 20 of the Rules provides procedures for claims other than those by the original claimant against the original defendant (see also Guides 8 and 10). A defendant may wish to make a claim against a fellow defendant, asserting a right to a contribution towards or to an indemnity against the claimant's claim if it should succeed against him.

Procedure

Availability	Any defendant may make a claim for contribution or indemnity against a co-defendant at any time after he has filed an acknowledgment of service or a defence save that, where the case is proceeding under the Pt 8 procedure, permission is needed before any Pt 20 claim can be issued	Rule 20.6 Rule 8.7
Method of making the claim	The claimant (ie the defendant making the claim for contribution or indemnity) files a notice containing a statement of the nature and grounds of his claim	Rule 20.6(a)
Contents of notice	The notice (being a 'Pt 20 claim') is a statement of case. It must comply with the requirements for particulars of claim (see Guide 1) save that the statement to explain why it is issued in the High Court (if the case is proceeding there) is not required It must be verified by a statement of truth	Rule 2.3(1) Rule 20.3(1) Rule 20.3(2)(b) Rule 22.1(1)(a)
Service of notice	When filing the notice, the claimant serves a copy on his co-defendant (see Guide 15). Service is as for a claim	Rule 20.6(b) Rule 20.3(1)

SECTION 1 Procedural Guides

Responding to the notice	The usual requirements for an acknowledgment of service (see Guide 5) and defence (see Guide 7) apply. However, judgment may not be entered in default	Rule 20.3(1) Rule 20.3(3)
	The respondent defendant may admit in writing the truth of the whole or any part of the notice and if he does so the claimant may apply for judgment on the admission	Rule 20.3(4) Rule 14.1(1) and (2) Rule 14.3
Subsequent procedure	The contribution or indemnity proceedings will not be allocated separately to a track upon a defence to the notice being filed but the court will at that point arrange a hearing to consider giving case management directions, ensuring so far as practicable that the claim and those proceedings are managed together	Rule 20.3(2)(c) Rule 20.13
	The court may however direct that the contribution or indemnity proceedings be dealt with as separate proceedings, taking into account the connection between the claim and those proceedings and the remedies being sought by each party	Rule 3.1(2)(e) Rule 20.9(2)
Forms	None prescribed	
Court fees	None prescribed	

10: Making a Claim Against a Non-Party, etc

Legal background

Part 20 of the Rules provides procedures for claims other than those by the original claimant against the original defendant. Claims by a defendant against the claimant (counterclaims) and claims as between defendants for contribution or indemnity (contribution or indemnity notices) are dealt with in Guides 8 and 9. Other claims, usually made against someone who is not until then a party to a claim by or against the person making them, used to be termed Third Party Notices. It is those claims which are referred to as Pt 20 claims in this Guide.

Procedure

Availability	A defendant may make a claim in the proceedings against a non-party for any remedy or against a co-defendant for a remedy other than contribution or indemnity. A person who is a defendant to such a Pt 20 claim may himself make any claim against any person, whether a party or not	Rule 20.2(1)
	Where the case is proceeding under the Pt 8 procedure, permission is needed before a Pt 20 claim can be issued	Rule 8.7
Time for making a Pt 20 claim	The Pt 20 claim must be made before or at the same time as the defendant files his defence	Rule 20.7(3)(a)
	Otherwise, the court's permission must be obtained. The application for permission should be accompanied by a copy of the proposed Pt 20 claim and must be supported by evidence stating the stage reached in the action, details of the proposed claim including a summary of the facts on which it is based, the name and address of the proposed defendant and an explanation of the delay. The application may be made without notice unless the court directs otherwise	Rule 20.7(3)(b) PD20, para 1.2 PD20, para 2.1 PD20, para 2.2 Rule 20.7(5)
Method of making a Pt 20 claim	The defendant (Pt 20 claimant) files at the court office a Pt 20 claim form which must contain or be accompanied by particulars of the claim made	Rule 20.7(2) and (4)
Contents of claim form and particulars	The Pt 20 claim form and particulars are statements of case. They must comply with the requirements for a claim form and particulars of claim (see Guide 1) save that the statement to explain why the claim is issued in the High Court (if the case is proceeding there) is not required	Rule 2.3(1) Rule 20.3(1) Rule 20.3(2)(b)
	They must be verified by a statement of truth	Rule 22.1(1)(a)

Title of proceedings	The title of the proceedings shown in formal documents will need to be changed to reflect the positions of the several parties in the proceedings. The practice direction to Pt 20 sets out examples	PD20, paras 7.1–7.5
Service of Pt 20 claim	If the claim was issued without the need for permission, the form and particulars must be served on the Pt 20 defendant as a claim (see Guides 15 and 16) within 14 days after the Pt 20 claimant has filed his defence to the claim against him	Rule 20.3(1) Rule 20.8(1)(b)
	Otherwise, the court will have given directions as to service when it gave permission to issue the claim	Rule 20.8(3)
	Unless the person to be served is already a party to the proceedings, the service copy must be accompanied by forms for admitting and defending the Pt 20 claim and for acknowledging service and copies of all statements of case which have been served in the proceedings, together with any other document which the court directs	Rule 20.12(1)
	A copy of the Pt 20 claim must also be served on every (other) existing party	Rule 20.12(2)
Responding to a Pt 20 claim	The usual requirements for an acknowledgment of service (see Guide 5) and defence (see Guide 7) apply	Rule 20.3(1)
	The consequence of default is that the party is deemed to admit the Pt 20 claim and is bound by any judgment in the main proceedings as far as relevant. If default judgment has been entered against the Pt 20 claimant, then provided he has satisfied that judgment and does not seek more than a contribution or indemnity, he may enter default judgment in turn against the Pt 20 defendant (see Guide 29); otherwise he must obtain permission before doing so. The application for permission may be made without notice unless the court directs otherwise	Rule 20.11(2)(a) Rule 20.11(2)(b) Rule 20.11(3) Rule 20.11(4)

	The Pt 20 defendant may admit in writing the truth of the whole or any part of the notice and if he does so the Pt 20 claimant may apply for judgment on the admission	Rule 20.3(4) Rule 14.1(1), (2) Rule 14.3
Subsequent procedure	The proceedings on the Pt 20 claim will not be allocated separately to a track upon a defence to the Pt 20 claim being filed but the court will at that point arrange a hearing to consider giving management directions, ensuring so far as practicable that the claim and those proceedings are managed together. The court may treat that hearing as a summary judgment hearing, order that the Pt 20 claim be dismissed, give directions on how the questions it raises should be dealt with, about the role the Pt 20 defendant should take at the trial and about the extent to which he should be bound by the decision in the main claim The court may on the other hand direct that the proceedings on the Pt 20 claim be dealt with as separate proceedings, taking into account the connection between the claim and those proceedings, the remedies being sought by each party and the desire of the Pt 20 claimant to have some question determined between himself and the Pt 20 defendant as well as the other parties	Rule 20.3(2)(c) PD20, para 5.1 Rule 20.13(1) Rule 20.13(2) PD20, para 5.3 Rule 3.1(2)(e) Rule 20.9(2)
Forms	Part 20 claim form N211 Application Notice N244	
Court fees	On adding a party: *High Court* – £50 *County court* – £30 On application for permission on notice: *High Court* – £100 *County court* – £60 On application for permission without notice: *High Court* – £50 *County court* – £30	CPFO fee 1.5 CPFO fee 2.5 CPFO fee 2.6

11: The Allocation Questionnaire

Legal background

When a case becomes defended, the court is required to allocate it to a procedural track. To acquire the information which it needs for this purpose, the court serves an 'allocation questionnaire' upon the parties. The court may also serve such a questionnaire when it is considering allocating a claim to track on other occasions.

Procedure

When sent out by the court	In a case with one defendant, when he files his defence	Rule 26.3(1)
	In a case with several defendants, when the last of them files his defence or (if sooner) when at least one has done so and the time for the remainder to do so has expired	Rule 26.3(2)
	If, in a claim for a specified sum of money, a defence is filed stating that the defendant has paid the amount claimed to the claimant, the questionnaire will not be sent until the claimant has responded that he wishes the claim to proceed	Rule 26.3(4)
	If, in a claim for a specified sum of money, an admission is filed as to part of the claim accompanied by a defence as to the remainder, the questionnaire will not be sent until the claimant has responded that he does not accept the amount admitted and wishes the proceedings to continue	Rule 26.3(4)
	In either of the above cases, if there is more than one defendant and at least one of the others defends the claim, the questionnaire will presumably be sent out once the claimant has responded to the notice in whatever terms.	
	The court may however decide to dispense with a questionnaire or, upon the application of the claimant, serve a questionnaire at an earlier time	Rule 26.3(1)(b) Rule 26.3(5)
	Where, for example, judgment is entered for an amount to be decided (see Guide 31), the court may allocate the case to a track and may require completion of allocation questionnaires	Rules 12.7(2) and 14.8 PD26, para 12.2(1)(b)

When to be replied to	The questionnaire states the date by which it must be completed and returned. This must be at least 14 days after it is served	Rule 26.3(6)
Consultation	The parties should consult with one another and co-operate in completing the questionnaires, without allowing this to delay their being filed	PD26, para 2.3
	When the case is allocated, the court will send each party a copy of the other's completed allocation questionnaires and any supplementary information filed	Rule 26.9(2)
Form	The allocation questionnaire is Form N150	PD26, para 2.1
Settlement	The party must say whether or not he wishes there to be a one month stay to attempt to settle the case either by informal discussion or alternative dispute resolution	Question A
	The court must order such a stay if all the parties so request. It may do so, if it considers it appropriate, even though all do not	Rule 26.4(2)(a) Rule 26.4(2)(b)
	Where a claim is stayed, unless all the parties have consented to the stay or the court orders otherwise, an earlier interim injunction will be automatically set aside	Rule 25.10
	If a stay is ordered, it may later be ordered to be extended. The application for such an order may be by letter, which should confirm that all parties agree and explain the steps being taken and identify any mediator or expert assisting with the process. In the absence of clear reasons to justify a longer stay, the extension will be for no more than 4 weeks, though more than one extension may be granted	Rule 26.4(3) PD26, para 3.1(1) PD26, para 3.1(2)(b) PD26, para 3.1(3)
	The claimant must tell the court if settlement is reached. If this is done by applying for a consent order or approval of the settlement or by accepting money in court, that will be treated as an application to lift the stay to enable the step to be taken	Rule 26.4(4) PD26, para 3.4

	Any party may apply for a stay to be lifted	PD26, para 3.3
	At the end of the stay, unless the claimant has told the court of a settlement, a judge will proceed to give management directions and may allocate the case to a track, require further information or fix an allocation hearing	Rule 26.4(5) PD26, para 3.2
Track	The party must say which track he considers most suitable for the case	Question D
	The basic criterion is the value (as assessed by the court) of that part of the claimant's claim which is in dispute, disregarding interest, costs and any question of contributory negligence	Rule 26.8(2)
	The small claims track is the normal track for claims whose value is no more than £5000, save that:	Rule 26.6(3)
	it will not be the normal track if the claim includes a personal injury claim in which the value of the damages for pain, suffering and loss of amenity is more than £1000 (disregarding eg special damages); and	Rule 26.6(1)(a) Rule 26.6(2)
	if the claim includes a claim by a residential tenant for an order that the landlord repair the premises, it will be the normal track (irrespective of the claim's total value) if neither the cost of the repairs nor the value of any damages claim exceeds £1000; but will not be the normal track otherwise	Rule 26.6(1)(b)
	The fast track is the normal track for any claim whose value does not exceed £15,000 and for which the small claims track is not the normal track; provided that the court considers that:	Rule 26.6(4)
	the trial is likely to last no longer than one day (taken as 5 hours); and	PD26, para 9.1(3)(a)
	oral expert evidence will be limited to one expert per party in any field and to such evidence in two fields	Rule 26.6(5)
	The multi-track is the normal track for any other claim	Rule 26.6(6)

	A case need not be allocated to its normal track. A case including a claim by a tenant for harassment or unlawful eviction cannot be allocated to the small claims track. The court must take into account not only the value of the claim but the nature of the remedy sought, the likely complexity, the number of parties, the value of any counterclaim and any other Pt 20 claim, the amount of oral evidence, the importance to non-parties, the views of the parties and their circumstances. A case involving a disputed allegation of dishonesty will not usually be suitable for the small claims track	Rule 26.7(4) Rule 26.8(1) PD26, para 8.1(1)(d)
	When considering the value of the claim, the court will disregard any amount not in dispute	Rule 26.8(2)(a)
	When considering a claim for possession of land the matters to which the court must have regard additionally include: (a) the amount of any arrears of rent or mortgage instalments; (b) the importance to the defendant of retaining possession of the land; and (c) the importance to the claimant of obtaining vacant possession of the land	Rule 55.9
	A claim will not be allocated to a track for which the normal value is less than the value of the claim, unless the parties consent to that course	Rule 26.7(3)
	A claim with no financial value will be allocated to the track considered most suitable by reference to the criteria mentioned above	Rule 26.7(2)
	Where a claimant makes several claims against different defendants, their values are not aggregated	Rule 26.8(3)
	The party is asked to say if the case is suitable for a High Court specialist list; and to give reasons if the track indicated would not be the normal track for the case	

Pre-action protocols	The party must say whether and if so which protocol applies and whether it has been complied with. (At the date of publication, protocols existed for clinical negligence claims, other personal injury claims, construction and engineering disputes, professional negligence claims, defamation claims and claims for judicial review. They are set out in Section 4 of this work)	Question C, Part 1 PDProt, para 4
	Where no pre-action protocol applies to the claim, the party must say whether it has exchanged evidence with its opponent to assist in settling the claim	Question C, Part 2
	Any non-compliance or less than complete compliance must be explained and will be taken into account by the court in giving management directions and when making orders as to costs; and may result, when judgment is given, in an increase or reduction as the case may be in the interest awarded	PDProt, paras 2.1, 2.3
Applications	The party must say whether he intends to make any applications in the immediate future (see Guides 18–20 and 30) if he has not already done so. The court will try to deal with allocation at the conclusion of the hearing of such an application if it is practicable to do so. It may also wish to consider exercising its power on its own initiative to dispose of apparently hopeless cases or points in them	Question D PD24, para 10 PD26, para 2.4 Rule 3.4 and PD3
	Details are required and further information that might help the court manage the claim.	
	Any application for a case to be tried with a jury must be made within 28 days of service of the defence	Rule 26.11
Trial or final hearing	The estimated length of trial, the names of witnesses intended to be called at the hearing and the available dates for expert and lay witnesses must be stated	Question E

Expert evidence	The party is asked whether he wishes to use expert evidence at the hearing and for details. The answers to these questions will enable the court to consider whether to give permission for such evidence to be used and if so in what form. The party must state whether it has copied any experts' reports to the other parties, whether the case is suitable for a single joint expert and to identify them with the initials 'S J' after their name(s)	Question D
	Similarly, if it is thought that oral expert evidence will be necessary, the reasons must be given	Question D
Location of trial	The party is asked about any preference as to the court where the trial will take place	Question B
Costs	In cases outside the financial scope of the small claims track, represented parties should include an estimate of costs incurred to date and likely overall costs. In substantial cases these questions should be answered in compliance with Part 43	Question G
	A party who has entered a funding agreement need not reveal the amount of any additional liability	PD26, para 2.1(2)(c)
	Not later than when he files the estimate the solicitor acting for a party must deliver a copy to his client	PD26, para 2.1(2)(d)
Other information	The party is invited to identify attached documents provided for the judge to consider. They should have been copied to the other parties and, if possible, agreed; and this information is sought	Question H
Proposed directions	He must attach a list of suggested directions, which also should be agreed if possible. The practice directions to Pts 27, 28 and 29 give guidance on the directions which may be approved. See Guides 12, 13 and 14	Question F

Failure to return questionnaire	If no party returns a questionnaire within the required period, the judge will usually make a peremptory order that unless one is filed within 3 days the claim and any counterclaim be struck out	PD26, para 2.5(1)
	If one or some but not all questionnaires are returned, the judge may be able to allocate the case and give directions. Alternatively he may: fix an allocation hearing and direct that all or any of the parties attend; or allocate the claim to a track if he considers that he has enough information to do so	PD26, para 2.5(2)
	If he considers the information provided to be inadequate the judge may order that further information be provided	Rule 26.5(3)
Allocation hearing	An allocation hearing will be fixed only if the judge is unable to allocate the case and give appropriate directions on the basis of the allocation questionnaires and written material available	PD26, para 6.1
	At least 7 days' notice will be given. Any legal representative attending must be familiar with the case and have the authority to deal with the issues which may arise	PD26, para 6.2(1) PD26, para 6.5
	If an allocation hearing is fixed because a party failed to return his allocation questionnaire or to provide adequate information, the defaulting party is likely to be ordered to pay the costs of the other parties on the indemnity basis. Such costs may well be assessed at the close of the hearing and be ordered to be paid forthwith or within a limited period; and the court may order that the party's statement of case be struck out if he does not so pay them	PD26, para 6.6(2)(a) PD26, para 6.6(2)(b)
	If the defaulting party fails to attend the hearing, it will usually be directed that he make good his default within a stated time and, if not, that his statement of case be struck out	PD26, para 6.6(3)

Court fees	Payable by the claimant on filing his allocation questionnaire, or within 14 days after allocation if questionnaires are dispensed with: *High Court* – £200 *County court* – £100	CPFO fee 2.1
	Exceptions Note the special provisions and exceptions listed in the CPFO.	
	If the fee is not paid, the court will send a warning notice. Continued failure to pay or to secure exemption from the fee will result in the claim being struck out	Rule 3.7

12: Proceeding on the Small Claims Track

Legal background

The small claims track provides a summary procedure for the resolution of the lower value and simpler claims.

Procedure

Availability	The claim will normally be allocated to this track (see Guide 11) if its value is no more than £5000, save that:	Rule 26.6(3)
	it will not be the normal track if the claim includes a personal injury claim in which the value of the damages for pain, suffering and loss of amenity is more than £1000 (disregarding eg special damages); and	Rule 26.6(1)(a)
	if the claim includes a claim by a residential tenant for an order that the landlord repair the premises, it will be the normal track (irrespective of the claim's total value) if neither the cost of the repairs nor the value of any damages claim exceeds £1000; but will not be the normal track otherwise	Rule 26.6(1)(b)
	When considering the value of the claim, the court will disregard:	
	any amount not in dispute;	
	any claim for interest or costs; and	

	any allegation of contributory negligence	Rule 26.8(2)
	A claim whose normal track is the small claims track may not in the event be allocated to it because the court must take into account not only the value of the claim but also:	
	the nature of the remedy sought;	
	the likely complexity;	
	the number of parties;	
	the value of any counterclaim and any other Pt 20 claim;	
	the amount of oral evidence;	
	the importance to non-parties; and	
	the views of the parties and their circumstances	Rule 26.8(1)
	A case involving a disputed allegation of dishonesty will not usually be suitable for this track	PD26, para 8.1(1)(d)
	Where the parties agree, the court may allocate to this track a claim for which it would not be the normal track. (It may not do so without their agreement)	Rule 26.7(3)
	A case including a claim by a tenant for harassment or unlawful eviction cannot be allocated to this track	Rule 26.7(4)
	A claim proceeding under Pt 8 (see Guide 3) cannot be allocated to this track	Rule 8.9(c)
Rules which do not apply	The following Parts and Rules do not apply to small claims:	
	Part 25 (interim remedies) save as regards interim injunctions – see Guide 23;	
	Part 31 (disclosure and inspection), but see below as to service of copy documents;	
	Parts 32 and 33 (evidence) except r 32.1 (power of court to control evidence) – see below;	
	Part 35 (experts and assessors) except rr 35.1 (duty to restrict expert evidence), 35.3 (expert's overriding duty to the court) and 35.8 (single joint experts) – see below;	
	Part 18 (further information), but see below as to directions which may be given;	

	Part 36 (offers to settle and payments into court); and Part 39 (hearings) except r 39.2 (hearing to be in public)	Rule 27.2
Disposal without a hearing	The court may, if all parties agree, deal with the claim without a hearing If the court is minded to do this, the notice of allocation to the track will ask the parties to indicate in writing by a specified date whether they consent If they do, the court will give such directions as are appropriate – including, no doubt, the date by which any written submissions and evidence must reach the court.	Rule 27.10 Rule 27.4(1)(e)
Directions	Upon allocating the claim to this track, the court will usually give directions, which will be set out in the notice of allocation The court may choose to use any of the sets of standard directions, set out in the relevant practice direction, intended for: road accident claims; contractual claims; claims arising out of a residential tenancy; claims arising out of a holiday or wedding etc arrangements; or other claims. These all include a requirement to file and serve copies of all documents to be relied on at the hearing – including any experts' reports. The court may also give special directions, examples of which are also set out in the relevant practice direction. These may include an order: to provide further information; to allow inspection of a document or object; permitting expert evidence and dealing with the instruction of the expert; requiring witness statements to be filed and served;	PD26, para 8.2(1) Rule 27.4(1)(a) PD27, para 2.2, Appendix A Rule 27.4(1)(b), (c) PD27, Appendix A

	as to the arrangements for video evidence: and;	
	that a party's statement of case be struck out if he fails to comply with a direction.	
	If the court gives special directions, it may (before fixing a hearing) review the position after 28 days in case further directions are needed	Rule 27.4(1)(c)
	The court may add to, vary or revoke directions given	Rule 27.7
Preliminary hearing	The court may fix a preliminary hearing but only:	
	to give special directions which need to be explained personally;	
	to dispose of the case where a party has no real prospect of success; or	
	to strike out a statement of case (or part of one) which discloses no reasonable grounds for claiming or defending	Rule 27.6(1)
	The parties will be given at least 14 days' notice	Rule 27.6(3)
	If they agree, the hearing may be treated as the final hearing	Rule 27.6(4)
	Otherwise the court will give any outstanding directions, estimate the time of the final hearing and fix a date for it	Rule 27.6(5)
The hearing	The hearing will normally be before a district judge. A claim allocated to the small claims track may only be assigned to a circuit judge with his consent	PD27, para 1 PD2B, para 11.2
	The parties will have 21 days' notice of the hearing unless they agree to accept less	Rules 27.4(2)(a) and 27.6(5)(a)
	It will normally take place in the judge's room, though it may be held in a courtroom and can be held at any place the court considers appropriate. It will usually be open to the public to attend but not if held away from the court or if the judge decides to hold it in private, which he may do if:	PD27, para 4.2 Rule 2.7 Rule 39.2(1) PD27, para 4.1(3)
	the parties agree;	
	publicity would defeat the object of the hearing;	

	it involves matters relating to national security; it involves confidential information; the interests of a child or patient need to be protected; or he considers it necessary in the interests of justice	PD27, para 4.1(2)(a) Rule 39.2(3)
Representation	A party may be represented at the hearing by: himself; a barrister, a solicitor or a legal executive employed by a solicitor; an employee; if the party is a company, any officer or employee of the company; any other person, if the party is himself also at the hearing; or any other person if the court gives permission	PD27, paras 3.1, 3.2
Conduct of the hearing	The hearing will be informal. The judge may: adopt any method of proceeding that he considers to be fair; ask questions himself; not allow others to question witnesses until he has done so or until all have given their evidence in chief; and limit cross-examination to a fixed time or to a particular subject or issue or both The proceedings will be recorded either by tape-recording by the court or by the judge making a note of the central points. Parties may obtain a transcript of the tape recording on payment of the transcriber's charges or of the note on payment of the court fee	Rule 27.8(2) Rule 27.8(1) PD27, para 4.3(2) PD27, para 4.3(3) Rule 27.8(5) PD27, para 5.1 PD27, paras 5.3 and 5.4 PD27, para 5.1 PD27, para 5.7
Evidence	The strict rules of evidence do not apply, so that evidence which would otherwise be inadmissible may be admitted. Evidence need not be on oath. Thus a party may rely on a witness statement in the absence of the witness, though it must be verified by a statement of truth or it may be excluded	Rule 27.8(3) Rule 27.8(4) Rule 22.1(1)(c) Rule 22.3

	Neither do the usual provisions in the Rules apply, but the court will usually have directed that documents and any experts' reports be filed and served and may extend that to statements of witnesses of fact	Rule 27.2(1)(c), (d) PD27, Appendix A
	The court may give or have given directions as to the issues on which it requires evidence, the nature of the evidence it requires and the way in which it is to be placed before the court; and in doing so may exclude evidence that would otherwise be admissible	Rule 32.1(1), (2)
	Expert evidence, oral or written, may not be given without permission. The usual direction permitting it will provide for a single expert jointly instructed. See Guide 25, Single Experts. The expert's duty to help the court overrides his duty to the party instructing him	Rule 27.5 PD27, Appendix A Rule 35.3
Non-attendance at the hearing	A party who cannot or does not wish to attend the hearing may, at least 7 days beforehand, give the court written notice that he will not attend and asking the court to decide the claim in his absence. The court will then take his statement of case and any other documents he has filed into account when it decides the claim	Rule 27.9(1)
	If the claimant neither attends nor gives such a notice, the court may strike out the claim	Rule 27.9(2)
	If the defendant neither attends nor gives such a notice, but the claimant either attends or gives the notice, the court may decide the claim on the claimant's evidence alone	Rule 27.9(3)
	If neither party attends or gives the notice, the court may strike out the claim and any defence and counterclaim	Rule 27.9(4)
	In any case, the court has power to adjourn to another day and may do so if a party wishes to attend but cannot do so for good reason	PD27, para 6.2

The judgment	The court can give any judgment and make any order which it could give or make in a case proceeding on either of the other tracks	Rule 27.3
	The court must give reasons for its decision. The judge may give them as briefly and simply as the nature of the case allows and will normally do so orally at the hearing. He may however do so later in writing or at another hearing fixed for the purpose	Rule 27.8(6) PD27, para 5.5(1) PD27, para 5.5(2)
	Where the case was disposed of without a hearing or a party did not attend the hearing but had given the notice mentioned above, the judge will make a note of his reasons and the court will send a copy to each party	PD27, para 5.6
Costs	The court may order the following costs to be paid by one party to another:	
	court fees which he has paid;	Rule 27.14(3)(a)
	in the case of the claimant, the fixed costs attributable to issuing the claim or which would have been attributable to the claim had it been for a specified sum;	Rule 27.14(2)(a) and r 45.2, Table 1
	if the proceedings included a claim for an injunction or an order for specific performance, for legal advice and assistance, up to £260;	Rule 27.14(2)(b) PD27, para 7.2
	if the party against whom the order is made has behaved unreasonably, an amount which the court will assess when making the order;	Rule 27.14(2)(d) Rule 43.3
	the expenses which the party or a witness has reasonably incurred in travelling to and from the hearing or in staying away from home to attend the hearing;	Rule 27.14(3)(b)
	loss of earnings by the party or a witness due to attending the hearing or to staying away from home to attend the hearing, up to £50 each per day;	Rule 27.14(3)(c) PD27, para 7.3(1)
	for experts' fees, up to £200 for each expert	Rule 27.14(3)(d) PD27, para 7.3(2)

	However: if the small claims track was not the normal track for the claim, which was allocated to it by agreement, the provisions relating to claims in the fast track apply – see Guide 13; and	Rule 27.14(5)
	Any order for costs made before the claim is allocated will not be affected by the allocation	Rule 44.11(1) and PDCosts, para 15.1(2)
	if a case is re-allocated to or from the small claims track, costs orders made while it was in another track remain effective and the costs regime applicable to the other track applies in respect of the period during which the case was in it	Rules 44.11(2), 44.11 and 27.15
Setting aside judgment	A party who was not present at the hearing and did not give the notice referred to above may apply that the judgment be set aside and the claim reheard. He must make the application within 14 days after notice of the judgment was served upon him	Rule 27.11
	The court will grant the application only if the applicant had a good reason for not attending or being represented or giving the notice *and* has a reasonable prospect of success at the rehearing	Rule 27.11(3)
	If it grants the application, the court must order a rehearing and may proceed with it immediately after hearing the application	Rule 27.11(4)
	The court may make its order subject to conditions (including a condition that money be paid into court) and may specify the consequences of failing to comply	Rule 3.1(3)
	Where the claim was disposed of without a hearing (see above), no application may be made that the judgment be set aside	Rule 27.11(5)
Appeals	Attention is drawn to Part 52 and PD52; note the reduced requirements for documents to be filed with the appellant's notice	PD27, para 8.1 PD52, para 5.8A
	See also Guide 58.	
	If the court dealt with the claim to which the appellant is a party –	
	without a hearing; or	

	in his absence because he gave notice requesting the court to decide the claim in his absence,	
	then application for permission to appeal must be made to the appeal court	PD27, para 8.2
	Where an appeal is allowed the appeal court will, if possible, dispose of the case at the same time without referring the claim to the lower court or ordering a new hearing. It may do so without hearing further evidence	PD27, para 8.3
	Costs of appeal If the court orders a party to pay another's costs of the appeal it must at the same time assess the amount payable	Rule 27.14(2)(c) Rule 43.3
Court fees	On application to set aside – £60 On notice of appeal – £80	CPFO fee 2.5 CPFO fee 2.4(a)
Forms	Application notice N244 Notice of appeal – none prescribed but N244 may be adapted	PD23, para 2.1

13: Proceeding on the Fast Track

Legal background

The fast track provides the procedure by which most claims of modest size will be resolved.

Procedure

Availability	The claim will normally be allocated to this track (see Guide 11) if its value is no more than £15,000 and it does not fall to be allocated to the small claims track	Rule 26.6(4)

	However the claim will not be allocated to this track if the court considers that the trial is likely to last longer than 5 hours, taking account of the likely case management directions (see below) and the court's powers to control evidence and limit cross-examination (see below). The mere possibility that the trial may last longer than 5 hours or the fact that there is to be a split trial will not prevent allocation to this track	Rule 26.6(5)(a) PD26, para 9.1(3)(a) PD26, para 9.1(3)(b) PD26, para 9.1(3)(c), (d)
	Where a Pt 20 claim (see Guides 8, 9 and 10) is to be tried with the claim, it is the total length of the trial which affects the allocation	PD26, para 9.1(3)(e)
	The claim will not be allocated to this track if the court considers that oral expert evidence will exceed one expert per party in any field or such evidence in two fields	Rule 26.6(5)(b)
	A claim proceeding under Pt 8 (see Guide 3) will not be allocated to this track	Rule 8.9(c)
Directions on allocation	Case management directions will be given upon allocation. The notice of allocation must specify the trial date or trial period which will normally be not more than 30 weeks after the date the directions are given; and will specify the date by which pre-trial check lists (see below) are to be returned by the parties. The directions may be given with or without a hearing. See below as to directions hearings	Rule 28.2(1) Rule 28.2(3), (4) Rule 28.5(1) PD26, para 9.2(1)

	The directions will deal with disclosure of documents (see Guide 24), service of witness statements and expert evidence and may regulate amendments of statements of case (see Guide 19) and the provision of further information. The court's concern will be to ensure that the issues are identified and that the necessary evidence is prepared and disclosed. It will take account of steps already taken by the parties and their compliance or non-compliance with any relevant pre-action protocol. The directions will form a timetable for the steps to be taken through to the trial	Rule 28.3(1) Rules 17.1 and 17.2 Rule 18.1 PD28, para 3.3 PD28, para 3.2 Rule 28.2(1)
	The court will expect the parties to co-operate in the giving of directions and may approve agreed directions which they submit	PD28, paras 2.2 and 3.5
	The relevant practice direction sets out forms of direction upon which the court will base its order, guidance on the agreed directions which may be approved and a 'typical' timetable, viz: disclosure – 4 weeks; witness statements – 10 weeks; experts' reports – 14 weeks; pre-trial check lists sent – 20 weeks; pre-trial check lists filed – 22 weeks; trial – 30 weeks; after the date of the notice of allocation	PD28, Appendix PD28, paras 3.6 and 3.7 PD28, para 3.12

Directions hearings	The court will only fix a hearing if it is not possible to deal with allocation and/or directions without one. The hearing may be an allocation hearing or, if the claim has been allocated, a case management hearing. In either case, the hearing will be listed as promptly as possible and at least 3 days' notice of it given to the parties. If it was made necessary by a party's default, the court will usually impose a sanction, which may take the form of an order for costs assessed on the indemnity basis and payable immediately or an order leading to the party's statement of case being struck out	PD28, para 2.2 PD28, para 3.10(1) PD28, para 3.10(2) PD28, para 2.6 PD28, para 2.3 PD26, para 6.6
Variation of directions	The time by which something is directed to be done may be varied by written agreement but this does not apply to:	Rule 2.11
	the date for return of the pre-trial check list;	
	the trial date or trial period; or	
	any date the variation of which would make it necessary to vary either of them	Rule 28.4
	The parties may agree in writing to dispense with or limit disclosure, that a list or disclosure statement need not be made or that disclosure or inspection take place in stages	Rule 31.5 Rule 31.10(8) Rule 31.13
	The written agreement need not be filed	PD28, para 4.5(1)
	In other cases, the parties may apply for an order by consent by filing a draft of the order sought with an agreed statement of the reasons why the variation is sought. The court may direct a hearing of the application	PD28, para 4.5(2)

	If a party is dissatisfied with a direction then he may apply that it be reconsidered *unless* it was made at a hearing at which he was present or represented or of which he had notice (in which case he may only appeal – see Guide 58). The application will be listed for a hearing before the judge who made the order or another judge of the same level and at least 3 days' notice will be given	PD28, para 4.3(1) and (3) PD28, para 4.3(2) PD28, para 4.3(4)(a) PD28, para 4.3(4)(b)
	If it seems that changed circumstances have made a direction inappropriate, the court may vary it or set it aside on application or on its own initiative	PD28, para 4.4
Disclosure	The court may order standard disclosure (see Guide 24) or it may direct that no disclosure take place or specify the documents or classes of documents which the parties must disclose	Rule 28.3(2)
Witness statements	The court will order each party to serve on the others the statement of any witness on whose evidence as to issues of fact he intends to rely at the trial	Rule 32.4(2)
	It may give directions as to the order in which they are to be served and whether they are to be filed. It will normally direct that they be served simultaneously	Rule 32.4(3) PD28, para 3.9(3)
	The statement must contain the evidence which the witness would be allowed to give orally, must be signed and must be verified by a statement of truth	Rule 32.4(1) Rule 22.1(1)(c)
Expert evidence	No party may use expert evidence without the court's permission. See Guide 25	Rule 35.4(1)
Failure to comply with directions	Any party may apply either for an order compelling another to comply or for a sanction to be imposed or for both	PD28, para 5.1
	The application must be made without delay but the other party should first be given a warning	PD28, para 5.2

	The court will not postpone the trial, if that can be avoided, but will make orders backed by sanctions with a view to the case being prepared in time. A sanction, if it takes effect, may prevent the defaulting party from raising or contesting an issue or relying on certain evidence at the trial. The court may order trial of those issues which can be prepared, the remainder being left to be tried later at the expense of the defaulting party. If postponement of the trial is inevitable, the court will order the shortest postponement possible and may require a party personally (though he has representation) to attend a hearing at which such an order may be made	PD28, para 5.4
Pre-trial check lists	The court will send the check lists to the parties no later than 2 weeks before they are to be returned (unless it considers them unnecessary)	PD28, para 6.1(2)
	The check list (inter alia):	
	requires the party to confirm compliance with directions already given, identify any directions still to be complied with and the date by which this will be done, as well as identify any further directions necessary before a trial within the trial period already fixed (and attach an application for such directions and a draft order, see also below);	
	addresses the question of expert evidence, whether the report(s) are agreed, discussed or summarised in a joint statement signed by the experts (the parties can no longer ask permission to call oral expert evidence in the check list but must make a separate application);	
	seeks details of the evidence of fact that the party intends to adduce, any special requirements and whether an interpreter will be provided;	

	requires parties to update their time estimates for trial and, if different from the original estimate, give a new total time estimate for the trial agreed with the other party/parties; obliges parties to attach the following documents: (1) any application and fee for additional directions; (2) a draft order; (3) any listing fee; (4) a proposed timetable for the trial; (5) a costs estimate	PDCosts, Section 6
	requires updated information on representation and the length of hearing. Represented parties should file with the check list and serve on the other parties an estimate of costs incurred and to be incurred in the form illustrated in Precedent H, Schedule of Costs Precedents	PDCosts, para 2.2 PDCosts, para 6.2 PDCosts, para 6.4
	The parties are encouraged to exchange copies of their check lists before filing them, to avoid the court being given conflicting or incomplete information	PD28, para 6.1(4)
	On the basis of the information provided, the court will: fix or confirm the trial date; specify any further steps that need to be taken before trial; and give any directions for the trial itself (including a trial timetable) which it considers appropriate	Rule 28.6(1)
Failure to file pre-trial check list	Where no party files a check list, the court will normally order that if none is filed within 3 days, the claim and any counterclaim be struck out	PD28, para 6.5(1)
	Otherwise, if a party fails to file his check list, the court will normally give listing directions regardless – but without being able to take into account his wishes or requirements – or may fix a listing hearing	PD28, para 6.5(2) Rule 28.5(3)

Listing hearing	If a listing hearing is directed, the court will fix a date which is as early as possible, giving the parties at least 3 days' notice. For the possible consequences of such a hearing being made necessary by a party's default, see 'Directions hearings' above	PD28, para 6.3
Listing directions	The court may give directions as to the issues on which evidence is to be given, the nature of the evidence it requires on those issues and the way in which it is to be placed before the court, and may thereby exclude evidence which would otherwise be admissible	Rule 32.1
	A direction giving permission to use expert evidence will say whether it is to be by report or oral and will name the experts whose evidence is permitted. Permission may be made conditional on the experts discussing their differences and filing a report on the discussion	PD28, para 7.2(4)
	The court may set a timetable for the trial and will confirm or vary the time estimate for the trial	Rule 28.6(1)(b) PD28, para 7.2(2)(b)
	Directions will usually be given for the preparation of a trial bundle	PD28, para 7.2(2)(c)
	The parties should seek to agree the directions and file the proposed order (which will not bind the court), making provision for the matters referred to above	PD28, para 7.2(1)
Variation of directions	See above. The same considerations apply to Listing directions as to others	PD28, para 7.3
The trial	The court will give at least 3 weeks' notice of the date fixed for trial unless the parties have agreed to accept shorter notice or, exceptionally, the court has ordered that shorter notice be given	Rule 28.6(2) PD28, para 7.1(2)
	The trial will normally take place at the court where the case is being managed but it may be at another court if appropriate having regard to the needs of the parties and the availability of court resources. It may be held away from court if need be	PD28, para 8.1 Rule 2.7

	The judge may dispense with an opening address. He may vary the timetable or set his own, but unless he does so, the trial will be conducted in accordance with any order made previously. A witness's statement will stand as evidence in chief unless the court otherwise orders and the court may limit cross-examination	PD28, para 8.2 PD28, para 8.3 Rule 28.7 Rule 32.5(2) Rule 32.1(3)
	If the trial is not finished on the day on which it is listed, the judge will normally sit on the next court day to complete it	PD28, para 8.6
Costs	At the conclusion of the trial, if ordering one party to pay costs to another, the judge will normally assess them summarily	PD28, para 8.5
	The costs of advocacy at the trial (including preparation for the trial) will be fixed according to, in the case of a claimant, the amount awarded (excluding interest, costs and any reductions for contributory negligence) or, in the case of a defendant, the amount claimed (excluding interest and costs) or specified in the claimant's statement of value (taken as over £10,000 if the claimant was not able to give one). If there is no money claim, the amount is taken as between £3000 and £10,000. If there are both a money claim and a non-money claim, the higher of the two amounts will usually be taken	Rule 46.2(3) Rule 46.2(4) Rule 46.2(5)
	If a counterclaim fails, the claimant's costs are based on the higher of the amounts applicable to his claim and the counterclaim	Rule 46.2(6)
	Where the amount is up to £3000, the fixed costs are £350; over £3000 but not more than £10,000 they are £500; and over £10,000 they are £750. If the court awards trial costs, it will normally apply these figures but may apportion costs between the parties according to their degree of success	Rule 46.2(1) Rule 46.2(2)
	If it was necessary for a legal representative to attend to assist the advocate, a further £250 may be allowed	Rule 46.3(2)

	If there are split trials, up to two-thirds of the costs figures above (or £350 if greater) may be allowed for the second trial	Rule 46.3(3), (4)
	A litigant in person will be awarded two-thirds of the figures above, if he can prove financial loss. Otherwise he will be awarded £9.25 per hour for time reasonably spent	Rule 46.3(5) PDCosts, para 52.4
	If a claim and counterclaim both succeed, both parties' costs will be assessed without reference to the other's claim and an order will be made for payment of the difference	Rule 46.3(6)
	Special provision is made for where there is more than one claimant or defendant	Rule 46.4
	The court may also assess summarily costs prior to the trial costs. Parties must, at least 24 hours before the hearing file and serve written statements of costs claimed as closely as possible following Form N260 and should endeavour to agree them before the trial starts	PDCosts, paras 13.2, 13.5
Court fees	On filing the pre-trial check list; or, if the case is listed without such check list, then within 14 days after notice is given of the trial date or trial period.	
	High Court – £600 County court – £275	CPFO fee 2.2
	If the court is informed before a trial date is appointed or at least 7 days before the appointed day that the case is settled, the fee is refunded	
Forms	Form N260	

14: Proceeding on the Multi-Track

Legal background

The multi-track provides the procedure by which not only the more substantial claims will be resolved, but also those proceeding in specialist lists and those others (which may be relatively small or straightforward) which, for one reason or another, have not been allocated to the small claims track or the fast track. The need to deal with cases of widely differing values and complexity means that the court has considerable flexibility in the way it can manage a case appropriately to its particular needs.

Procedure

Availability	The claim will be allocated to this track (see Guide 11) if it is not allocated to the small claims track or the fast track	Rule 26.6(6)
Venue	*Claim issued in the Royal Courts of Justice*	
	If the claim has an estimated value under £50,000, it will normally be transferred to a county court at a civil trial centre unless it is:	PD29, paras 2.2 and 3.1(2)(a)
	required by an enactment to be tried in the High Court;	PD29, para 2.2(a)
	a claim falling within a specialist list, ie –	PD29, para 2.2(b)
	admiralty proceedings;	
	arbitration proceedings;	
	commercial actions;	
	Patents Court business;	
	Technology and Construction Court business; and	
	proceedings under the Companies Act 1985;	Rule 49(2)
	or unless it is important and, in particular, raises questions of importance to persons who are not parties or questions of general public interest; or	HCCCJO, art 7(5)(b)
	is such as to involve complexity of facts, legal issues, remedies or procedures	HCCCJO, art 7(5)(c)
	Suitable claims for trial in the Royal Courts of Justice include:	
	a professional negligence claim;	
	a Fatal Accidents Act claim;	
	a fraud or undue influence claim;	
	a defamation claim;	
	a claim for malicious prosecution or false imprisonment;	
	a claim against the police;	
	a contentious probate claim	PD29, para 2.6
	The court also has a general power to transfer to a county court cases falling outside these categories	CCA 1984, s 40(2)
	The court will consider whether transfer would provide a speedier trial but will not order transfer for this reason alone	HCCCJO, art 7(5)(d)

	Claim issued elsewhere but not at a civil trial centre	
	Any claim in a specialist list will be transferred to a civil trial centre before allocation	PD26, para 10.2(2)
	Otherwise, the court will normally give any directions appropriate upon allocation and then transfer the case to a civil trial centre; though it may either transfer to such a centre to deal with allocation. Alternatively, if it seems that there will be more than one case management conference, and the parties are inconveniently far from the civil trial centre, then the district judge may, with the agreement of the designated civil judge, retain the case for the time being for further management	PD26, para 10.2(5) PD26, para 10.2(8) PD26, para 10.2(10)
	Any allocation hearing and the hearing of any pre-allocation application will be at the original court	PD26, para 10.2(6)
Directions on allocation	Case management directions may be given upon allocation, without a hearing, to form a timetable for the steps to be taken through to the trial. The notice of allocation may specify the trial date or trial period (which the court must fix as soon as practicable). In that case it will specify the date by which pre-trial check lists (see below) are to be returned by the parties	Rule 29.2(1)(a) Rule 29.2(2), (3)(a) Rule 29.2(3)(b)
	Instead of or as well as giving directions, the court may fix a case management conferencem or a pre-trial review. It may fix such a conference or review at any time after allocation	Rule 29.2(1)(b) PD29, para 4.5 Rule 29.3(1)
	Directions, given at or without a hearing, will be tailored to the needs of the case and the steps already taken by the parties. The court will have regard to their compliance or non-compliance with any relevant pre-action protocol. Its concern will be to ensure that the issues are identified and that the necessary evidence is prepared and disclosed	PD29, para 4.2 PD29, para 4.3

	The court will expect the parties to co-operate in the giving of directions and may approve agreed directions which they submit. The relevant practice direction sets out guidance on the agreed directions which may be approved	PD29, para 4.6 PD29, paras 4.7 and 4.8
	The directions will deal with disclosure of documents (see Guide 24), service of witness statements and expert evidence and may regulate amendments of statements of case (see Guide 19) and the provision of further information. They should form a timetable for the steps to be taken through to the trial and make provision for the trial date or trial period (if not already fixed).	
	In the absence of indications to the contrary, the court's general approach will be to direct:	
	filing and service of any further information needed to clarify a party's case;	
	standard disclosure (see Guide 24);	
	simultaneous exchange of witness statements;	
	the instruction of a single joint expert on any appropriate issue;	
	otherwise, simultaneous exchange of experts' reports (unless it is appropriate for reports on the amount of damages to be disclosed subsequently to those on liability);	
	discussion between experts and a statement thereon, if they are not agreed;	
	a case management conference after the time for compliance; and	
	the fixing of a trial period	PD29, para 4.10
	The court will not however (save by agreement) require instruction of a single expert nor appoint an assessor without fixing a case management conference	PD29, para 4.13

Case management conference	The court will fix a case management conference if it appears that it cannot properly give directions on its own initiative and no agreed directions have been filed which it can approve. It will be listed as promptly as possible and at least 3 days' notice will be given	PD29, para 4.12 PD29, para 3.7
	As well as the matters referred to above, the court may consider ordering a split trial or the trial of a preliminary issue; and whether the case should be tried by a High Court judge or a specialist judge	PD29, para 5.3(7) PD29, para 5.9
	If a party intends to apply for a particular direction which may be opposed, he should serve notice and, if the time allowed may thus be insufficient, warn the court of that	PD29, para 5.8
	If a party has legal representation, a representative familiar with the case and with sufficient authority to deal with any issues which may arise must attend. That must be someone personally involved with the conduct of the case, able to deal with fixing the timetable, identification of issues and matters of evidence. A wasted costs order will usually be made if the inadequacy of the person attending or his instructions leads to an adjournment	Rule 29.3(2) PD29, para 5.2(2) PD29, para 5.2(3)
	Parties must ensure that all relevant documents (including witness statements and experts' reports) are available to the judge and that all of them know what directions each seeks. They should consider whether parties personally should attend and whether it would be useful to provide a case summary (prepared by the claimant and agreed with the other parties if possible) setting out in 500 words a brief chronology, facts agreed and in dispute, and evidence needed	PD29, para 5.6 PD29, para 5.7

	If the conference was fixed because of a party's default in completing an allocation questionnaire, the court will usually impose a sanction, which may take the form of an order for costs assessed on the indemnity basis and payable immediately or an order leading to the party's statement of case being struck out	PD26, para 6.6
Variation of directions	The time by which something is directed to be done may be varied by written agreement but this does not apply to:	Rule 2.11
	the date fixed for a case management conference or pre-trial review;	
	the date for return of the pre-trial check list;	
	the trial date or trial period; or	
	any date the variation of which would make it necessary to vary either the trial date or trial period	Rule 29.5
	The parties may agree in writing to dispense with or limit disclosure, that a list or disclosure statement need not be made or that disclosure or inspection take place in stages	Rule 31.5(3) Rule 31.10(8) Rule 31.13
	The written agreement need not be filed	PD29, para 6.5(1)
	In other cases, the parties may apply for an order by consent by filing a draft of the order sought with an agreed statement of the reasons why the variation is sought. The court may direct a hearing of the application	PD29, para 6.5(2)
	If a party is dissatisfied with a direction then he may apply that it be reconsidered *unless* it was made at a hearing at which he was present or represented or of which he had notice (in which case he may only appeal – see Guide 58). The application will be listed for a hearing before the judge who made the order or another judge of the same level and at least 3 days' notice will be given	PD29, para 6.3(1) and (3) PD29, para 6.3(2) PD29, para 6.3(4)(a) PD29, para 6.3(4)(b)

	If it seems that changed circumstances have made a direction inappropriate, the court may vary it or set it aside on application or on its own initiative	PD29, para 6.4
Witness statements	The court will order each party to serve on the others the statement of any witness on whose evidence as to issues of fact he intends to rely at the trial	Rule 32.4(2)
	It may give directions as to the order in which they are to be served and whether they are to be filed. It will normally direct that they be served simultaneously	Rule 32.4(3) PD29, para 4.10(3)
	The statement must contain the evidence which the witness would be allowed to give orally, must be signed and must be verified by a statement of truth	Rule 32.4(1) Rule 22.1(1)(c)
Expert evidence	No party may use expert evidence without the court's permission See Guide 25	Rule 35.4(1)
Failure to comply with directions	Any party may apply for an order compelling another to comply	PD29, para 7.1
	The application must be made without delay but the other party should first be given a warning	PD29, para 7.2
	The court will not postpone the trial, if that can be avoided, but will make orders backed by sanctions with a view to the case being prepared in time. A sanction, if it takes effect, may prevent the defaulting party from raising or contesting an issue or relying on certain evidence at the trial. The court may order trial of those issues which can be prepared, the remainder being left to be tried later at the expense of the defaulting party. If postponement of the trial is inevitable, the court will order the shortest postponement possible and may require a party personally (though he has representation) to attend a hearing at which such an order is to be sought. A hearing other than a trial will not be postponed without a very good reason and late compliance with directions will not be a good reason	PD29, para 7.4

Pre-trial check lists	The court will (unless it considers them unnecessary) send the check lists to the parties no later than 2 weeks before they are to be returned, which will be no later than 8 weeks before the trial date or trial period	Rule 29.6(1) PD29, para 8.1(4) PD29, para 8.1(3)
	The check list (inter alia):	
	requires the party to confirm compliance with directions already given, identify any directions still to be complied with and the date by which this will be done, as well as identify any further directions necessary before a trial within the trial period already fixed (and attach an application for such directions and a draft order, see also below);	
	addresses the question of expert evidence, whether the report(s) are agreed, discussed or summarised in a joint statement signed by the experts (the parties can no longer ask permission to call oral expert evidence in the check list but must make a separate application);	
	seeks details of the evidence of fact that the party intends to adduce, any special requirements and whether an interpreter will be provided;	
	requires parties to update their time estimates for trial and, if different from the original estimate, give a new total time estimate for the trial agreed with the other party/parties;	
	obliges parties to attach the following documents: 1) any application and fee for additional directions; 2) a draft order; 3) any listing fee; 4) a proposed timetable for the trial; 5) a costs estimate	PDCosts, Section 6
	requires updated information on representation and the length of hearing.	

	Represented parties should file with the check list and serve on the other parties an estimate of costs incurred and to be incurred in the form illustrated in Precedent H, Schedule of Costs Precedents	PDCosts, para 2.2 PDCosts, para 6.2 PDCosts, para 6.4
	The parties are encouraged to exchange copies of their check lists before filing them, to avoid the court being given conflicting or incomplete information	PD29, para 8.1(5)
	On the basis of the information provided, the court will:	
	fix a pre-trial review (giving at least 7 days' notice);	Rule 29.7
	cancel a previously fixed pre-trial review;	
	give listing directions;	
	fix or confirm the trial date; and/or	
	give any directions for the trial itself (including a trial timetable) which it considers appropriate	Rule 29.8
Failure to file pre-trial check list	Where no party files a check list, the court will normally order that if none is filed within 3 days, the claim and any counterclaim be struck out	PD29, para 8.3(1)
	Otherwise, if a party fails to file his check list the court will fix a listing hearing on a date which is as early as possible, giving the parties at least 3 days' notice. It will then normally fix or confirm the trial date and make other orders about steps to be taken to prepare the case for trial whether or not the defaulting party attends	PD29, para 8.3(2) PD29, para 8.4
Listing directions	The court may give directions as to the issues on which evidence is to be given, the nature of the evidence it requires on those issues and the way in which it is to be placed before the court, and may thereby exclude evidence which would otherwise be admissible	Rule 32.1
	A direction giving permission to use expert evidence will say whether it is to be by report or oral and will name the experts whose evidence is permitted	PD29, para 9.2(4)

	The court may set or confirm a timetable for the trial and will confirm or vary trial date or week, the time estimate for the trial and the place of trial	Rule 29.8(c)(i) PD29, para 9.1
	Directions will usually be given for the preparation of a trial bundle	PD29, para 9.2(2)(c)
	The parties should seek to agree the directions and file the proposed order (which will not bind the court), making provision for the matters referred to above and any other matter needed to prepare for the trial	PD29, para 9.2(1), (2)
Variation of directions	See above. The same considerations apply to listing directions as to others	PD29, para 9.3
The trial	The trial will normally take place at the court where the case is being managed but it may be at another court if appropriate having regard to the needs of the parties and the availability of court resources. It may be held away from court if need be	PD29, para 10.1 Rule 2.7
	The judge may dispense with an opening address. He may vary the timetable or set his own, but unless he does so, the trial will be conducted in accordance with any order made previously. He will usually allow a witness's statement to stand as evidence in chief and may limit cross-examination	PD29, para 10.2 PD29, para 10.3 Rule 29.9 Rule 32.5(2) Rule 32.1(3)
	Once the trial has begun, the judge will normally sit on consecutive court days until it has been concluded	PD29, para 10.6
	In the High Court, a master or district judge may not hear the case unless:	
	the parties consent; or	
	subject to the exceptions set out in the Appendix to Guide 3, the case is proceeding under Pt 8	PD2B, para 4.1
	In the county court, a district judge may hear the case if:	
	the parties and the designated civil judge consent;	PD2B, para 11.1(d)
	the proceedings are for the recovery of land	PD2B, para 11.1(b)

SECTION 1 Procedural Guides

	subject to the exceptions set out in the Appendix to Guide 3, the case is proceeding under Pt 8;	PD2B, para 11.1(a)
Costs	At the conclusion of the trial, if ordering one party to pay costs to another, the judge may order them to be determined by detailed assessment (see Guide 32). Alternatively he may assess them summarily; and parties should therefore bring to the trial a schedule of the costs incurred and endeavour to agree them before the trial starts	Rule 44.7
Court fees	On filing the pre-trial check list; or, if the case is listed without such check list then within 14 days after notice is given of the trial date or trial period *High Court* – £600 *County court* – £500 If the court is informed before a trial date is appointed or at least 14 days before the appointed day that the case is settled, the fee is refunded	CPFO fee 2.2
Forms	Form N260	

15: Serving Documents

Legal background

Notice is given to parties of the existence of proceedings and of steps taken in them by sending or delivering the relevant documents to them. Part 6 of the Rules sets out general provisions as to the service of documents as well as special provisions dealing with the service of claim forms.

For service outside England and Wales, see Guide 16.

Procedure

Methods of service generally available		
Personal service	Effected by leaving the document with the party (if an individual), a person holding a senior position (if the party is a company or other corporation) or a partner or person having control or management of the partnership business at its principal place of business (if partners sued in the name of their firm)	Rule 6.4(3) Rule 6.4(4) Rule 6.4(5)

	Unless some provision or order requires personal service, it is not to be used where a solicitor is authorised to accept service and has so informed the party seeking to effect service in writing	Rule 6.4(2)
First-class post	Deemed effective the second day after the document was posted to the address for service (see below) of the person to be served	Rule 6.7(1)
	Saturdays and Sundays are not excluded from the calculation and the note in r 6.7 referring to r 2.8 has been held to be erroneous	*Anderton v Clwyd County Council* [2002] EWCA Civ 933
Leaving the document	Deemed effective the day after the document was left at the address for service (see below) of the person to be served	Rule 6.7(1)
Through a document exchange	Deemed effective the second day after it was left at the document exchange. The address for service of the party to be served must include a document exchange box number on his writing paper or that of his solicitor must set one out. This method of service cannot be used if the party has indicated in writing that he is unwilling to be served by it	Rule 6.7(1) PD6, para 2.1
By fax	Deemed effective the day of transmission if transmitted before 4.00 pm on a business day (or the next business day if transmitted otherwise) to a fax number indicated in writing for the purpose by the party to be served or his solicitor. A fax number set out on solicitors' writing paper is assumed so to indicate, as is one set out on a statement of case or a response to a claim filed with the court. It is not mandatory also to send a hard copy but it is advisable to do so in case the fax was not received	Rule 6.7(1) PD6, para 3.1(1) PD6, para 3.1(2) PD6, para 3.4

By other electronic means	Permitted only when both the party serving and the party to be served are legally represented and the latter's solicitors have agreed in writing to the method of service and have provided an e-mail address or other electronic identification	PD6, para 3.3(1) PD6, para 3.3(3)
	Effective the second day after the day on which it was transmitted	Rule 6.7(1)
	It is not mandatory also to send a hard copy but it is advisable to do so in case the transmission was not received	PD6, para 3.4
Time and place of service		
Time and day of service	A document (*other than a claim form)* served after 5.00 pm on a business day (any day other than a Saturday, Sunday or bank holiday) or served on a non-business day is treated as having been served on the next business day	Rule 6.7(2)
	The Court of Appeal has held that this is strictly limited to documents served personally and not by other methods of service.	
Address for service	A party must give an address for service within England and Wales	Rule 6.5(2)
	If he is represented, his address for service is his solicitor's address (except, usually, as to service of a claim form – see below)	Rule 6.5(5)
	If not, he must give his residence or place of business (unless he does not reside or carry on business in England and Wales, when he may give any address within England and Wales)	Rule 6.5(3)
	If an unrepresented party has not given an address for service, the document must be sent as follows:	
	Individual usual or last known residence;	
	Proprietor of a business usual or last known residence or; place of business or last known place of business;	

	Individual suing or sued in name of firm usual or last known residence; or principal or last known place of business; *Corporation incorporated in England and Wales (other than a company)* principal office; or any place within the jurisdiction where it carries on its activities and which has a real connection with the claim; *Company registered in England and Wales* principal office; any place of business of the company within the jurisdiction which has a real connection with the claim; *Any other company or corporation* any place within the jurisdiction where the corporation carries on its activities; any place of business of the company within the jurisdiction	Rule 6.5(6)
Companies	A company may also be served by post to its registered office or (in the case of an overseas company) address registered for the purpose	Companies Act 1985, ss 725, 694A and 695
Service Personnel	Guidance notes as to service on members of HM Forces and members of the United States Air Force are annexed to the practice direction to Pt 6	PD6, para 5
Other considerations		
Children and patients	Special rules apply. See Guide 17.	
Who is to serve	The court will usually serve a document which it has issued or prepared, unless the party on whose behalf it is to be served wishes to serve it himself. A rule, a practice direction or an order may however provide otherwise	Rule 6.3
	In case of doubt, it is advisable to check whether the court will serve or is expecting the party to effect service.	
	When the court serves, it will normally do so by first-class post	PD6, para 8.1

Alternative method	The court can order service by any other method. The application for such an order must be supported by evidence stating the reason and showing what steps have been taken to serve and may be made without notice	Rule 6.8 PD6, para 9.1
Dispensing with service	The court may dispense with service of a document. The application may be made without notice. There is no formal requirement to provide evidence, but the court will need to be satisfied that proper grounds exist	Rule 6.9
	The court will only dispense with service after the time for service has expired in exceptional circumstances	*Anderton v Clwyd CC* [2002] EWCA Civ 933, [2002] 1 WLR 3174; *Wilkey v BBC* [2002] EWCA Civ 1561, [2002] 4 All ER 1177
Proof of service	A rule, practice direction or order may require a certificate of service to be filed	Rule 6.10
	See 'Service of claim form' below.	
Notice of funding	Where the court serves or delivers a claim form, defence or notice of filing of acknowledgment of service it will also serve or deliver a copy of any notice of funding provided:	
	it was filed at the same time as the claim form, defence, or acknowledgment of service, and	
	copies are provided for service	PD6, para 8.3
Non-service by court	Where the court is to serve but is unable to do so, it will give notice to that effect. It then becomes the party's responsibility to effect service	Rule 6.11 PD6, para 8.2
Service of claim form	The defendant's address for service must be given in the claim form if he is to be served by the court	Rule 6.13(1)
	His solicitor's address should be given as his address for service only if the solicitor is authorised to accept service	Rule 6.13(2)

	When a claim form is or particulars of claim are served on a partner or person having control or management of a partnership business at its principal place of business, notice must also be served as to the capacity in which the person is served	PD6, para 4.2
	If the court effects service, it will provide a notice to this effect	Rule 6.14(1)
	If the party effects service, he must file a certificate of service within 7 days	Rule 6.14(2)
Service of claim by contractually agreed method	Where a contract makes provision for service and the claim is in respect only of that contract, it may be served in accordance with that provision	Rule 6.15(1)
	If the service is to be abroad, the usual conditions continue to apply – see Guide 16	Rule 6.15(2)
Service of claim on overseas defendant's agent	The court may in some circumstances by order authorise service on the agent of a defendant who is abroad. The application must be supported by evidence and may be made without notice	Rule 6.16
Period for service of claim form	A claim form must be served within 4 months after the date of issue	Rule 7.5(2)
	The period may be extended	Rule 3.1(2)(a)
Forms	Certificate of Service N215	
	Notice when service effected on a partnership N218	

16: Service Outside England and Wales

Legal background

A party who wishes to serve a document outside England and Wales must either bring the case within the provisions of the Brussels and Lugano Conventions, implemented by the Civil Jurisdiction and Judgments Act 1982 (as amended), or Council Regulation (EC) No 1348/2000 ('the Service Regulation'), or some other statute, or obtain the permission of the court. The procedure is now based upon the new provisions for service set out in Pt 6, Section III (rr 6.17–6.31) and PD6B which supplements it. This Guide describes the position primarily in terms of serving the claim.

Procedure

Service abroad without permission		
Availability	May be either under CJJA or the Service Regulation, or under some other Act giving the court jurisdiction where the defendant is abroad. The latter is not dealt with in this Guide	Rule 6.19
Which countries	Scotland, Northern Ireland, Austria, Belgium, Cyprus (NB *not* the Turkish Republic of Northern Cyprus), Czech Republic, Denmark, Estonia, Finland, France, Germany, Gibraltar, Greece, Hungary, Iceland, Ireland, Italy, Latvia, Lithuania, Luxembourg, Malta, Netherlands, Norway, Poland, Portugal, Slovakia, Slovenia, Spain, Sweden and Switzerland. (NB *not* the Channel Islands or the Isle of Man.)	
Which claims	Those which the English court has power to hear and determine by virtue of CJJA. The two commonest examples will be claims in contract, where the place for the performance of the contract was within England or Wales, and claims in Tort, where the harmful event occurred within England or Wales	Rule 6.19(1) CJJA, Sch 1, art 5 and CJJA, Sch 4
	Note that a consumer (as defined) must be sued in the courts of his domicile and has the right to sue in those courts, irrespective of any contract term to the contrary. Within the UK the consumer must be sued in the courts of that part of the UK in which he resides	CJJA, Sch 4, arts 13–15
Conditions	There must be no proceedings between the parties concerning the same cause of action pending in any of the territories listed above.	

	The defendant must be domiciled in one of those territories *or* the claim must be one in which the English courts have exclusive jurisdiction (eg the case concerns land in England) or have jurisdiction under an agreement made by the parties	Rule 6.19(1), (1A) CJJA, Sch 1 and 4, art 16 and 17
Formal requirements	The claim form and (if separate) the particulars of claim must contain a statement that the court has power under CJJA or the Service Regulation, as the case may be, to deal with the claim and that no proceedings based on the same claim are pending between the parties in Scotland, Northern Ireland or another Convention territory. Example forms of words are set out in the practice direction	PD7, para 3.5 PD6B, paras 1.1–1.3 or 1.3A–1.3C
Service abroad with permission		
How applied for	Application is made without notice, supported by evidence	Rule 6.21(1)
Availability	Permission will be granted only on one of the specified grounds and then only if it appears that the case is a proper one for service out of the jurisdiction	Rule 6.20
General		
Particulars of claim	If a claim form is to be served out of England and Wales, the particulars of claim must be served with it and may not be left 'to follow'	PD6B, para 2.1
Effecting service	Any of the normal means of service (see Guide 15) may be employed *provided* that it is in accordance with the law of the country where service is to be effected	Rule 6.24(1)
	However service will not be effected by the court office simply posting the document to an address outside England and Wales.	
	The party may effect service himself or by his agent and should do so in the cases of the territories listed above	PD6B, para 3.1

Service in accordance with the Service Regulation	The claimant must file with the court of issue the claim form and any translation required by the Service Regulation	Rule 6.26A(2) Service Regulation, Art 8
	The court will seal the claim form and send the documents to the Senior Master's Department which is the transmitting agency for England and Wales	Service Regulation, Art 2
	If service has not been effected within one month, the receiving agency will inform the Senior Master's Department	Service Regulation, Art 7(2)
	A certificate of service will be sent to the Senior Master's Department. The claimant does not need to file evidence of service	Rule 6.26A(4) Service Regulation, Art 10
Service through foreign governments, judicial authorities and British consuls	Otherwise, he may seek to effect service through the foreign government or judicial authority or through a British consul. Whether such service will be possible and, if so, through which authority, depends upon whether the foreign country is party to a relevant Convention or otherwise permits or is willing to effect service	Rule 6.26(1)
	The claimant files in the Foreign Process Office, Room E219, The Royal Courts of Justice a request for such service together with, for each person to be served, two copies of the sealed claim form and accompanying documents, the particulars of claim, the 'Response Pack' (acknowledgment of service and reply forms) and translations of all of these, as required (see below). The documents are then passed to the Foreign Office to make the arrangements	Rule 6.26(2)–(4)
	The expenses of the Foreign Office are borne by the claimant, who must file an undertaking to that effect with his request	Rule 6.29
Translations	Translations are not required if the (or an) official language of the country of service is English or (unless it is a requirement of the Convention under which service is undertaken) if service is to be by a British Consular Authority upon a British subject.	

	If required, the translation is into the official language of the country (or if it has several, the language appropriate to the place of service)	Rule 6.28
	The translation must be certified by the person making it to be correct and the certificate must give his full name, address and qualifications	Rule 6.28(2)
	The authority effecting service will provide a certificate of service	Rule 6.26(5)
Service on foreign State	Permission must be obtained The documents as above and translation (into an official language of the State if English is not one of them) are filed in the Foreign Process Office	Rule 6.27(1), (2)
	The Foreign Office effects service and provides a certificate of service	Rule 6.27(4)
	The expenses of the Foreign Office are borne by the claimant, who must file an undertaking to that effect with his request	Rule 6.29
Period for service of claim form	A claim form must be served within 6 months after the date of issue	Rule 7.5(3)
	The period may be extended	Rule 3.1(2)(a)
Documents other than claim forms	Similar considerations apply to the service abroad of application notices, orders and other documents	Rule 6.30
Time for response	The periods for filing an acknowledgment of service (see Guide 5) or a defence (see Guide 7) when the claim is served without leave outside England and Wales are:	
	Served in Scotland, Northern Ireland or the European territory of a State listed above – 21 days (35 days for a defence following acknowledgment);	
	Served in a non-European territory of one of those states – 31 days (45 days for a defence following acknowledgment)	Rule 6.22

	In all other cases, reference should be made to the table in the relevant practice direction, which gives the number of days within which the defence must be filed. Fourteen days should be added if an acknowledgment of service is filed	PD6B, para 10.2
	If the document served is an application notice or order which requires a response, the period is 7 days less than the period given in the table	PD6B, para 8.1

17: Proceedings Involving a Child or Patient (General Procedure)

Legal background

Part 21 of the Rules contains special provisions which apply in proceedings involving children and patients (as defined). These are supplemented by a practice direction. Unless the court orders otherwise (in the case of a child) it is necessary for the child or patient to be represented by a *litigation friend*. These special procedures are based upon the former RSC Ord 80 and CCR Ord 10.

Any proceedings commenced or conducted in breach of this requirement will be a nullity (unless the court otherwise orders) and a solicitor who purports to act on the record for a child or patient without a litigation friend may become personally liable for the costs of opposing parties.

Procedure

Who is a child	A person under 18	Rule 21.1(2)(a)
Who is a patient	A person who by reason of mental disorder within the meaning of the Mental Health Act 1983 is incapable of managing and administering his property and affairs	Rule 21.1(2)(b) PD21, para 1.1
What is mental disorder	Mental illness, arrested or incomplete development of mind, psychopathic disorder and any other disorder or disability of mind	Mental Health Act 1983, s 1 (2)
	Nothing in the definition is to be construed as implying that a person may be dealt with as suffering from mental disorder by reason only of promiscuity, immoral conduct, sexual deviancy or dependence on alcohol or drugs	*Ibid* s 1 (3)

Requirement for a litigation friend	A *patient* must have a litigation friend to conduct proceedings on his behalf	Rule 21.2(1) PD21, para 1.2
	A *child* must have a litigation friend to conduct proceedings on his behalf unless the court orders otherwise:	Rule 21.2(2) PD21, para 1.4
	the court may make an order permitting the child to conduct proceedings without a litigation friend (for the procedure see r 21.2(4));	Rule 21.2(3)
	if it subsequently appears to the court that it is desirable for a litigation friend to conduct the proceedings on behalf of the child the court may make that appointment	Rule 21.2(5)
	The litigation friend must take all steps and decisions for the benefit of the child or patient	PD21, para 2.1
When must a litigation friend be appointed	A person may not, without permission of the court (unless an order has been made in respect of a child under rule 21.2(3)):	
	make an application against a child or patient before proceedings have started; or	
	take any step in proceedings except –	
	issuing and serving a claim form; or	
	applying for the appointment of a litigation friend under rule 21.6,	
	until the child or patient has a litigation friend	Rule 21.3(2)
	If a party becomes a patient during proceedings, no party may take any step in the proceedings without the permission of the court until the patient has a litigation friend	Rule 21.3(3)
	Any step taken before a child or patient has a litigation friend, shall be of no effect, unless the court otherwise orders	Rule 21.3(4)
How do you decide if a party is a patient	The Rules assume that it is known whether a party is a patient. In case of uncertainty application should be made to resolve this (see Guide 18)	Part 23

	As to assessment of mental capacity see generally the notes to rule 21.1 below.	
Title to proceedings	A child's name should be followed by '(a child by . . ... his litigation friend)' or, if a litigation friend is dispensed with, then simply '(a child)'	PD21, para 1.5
	The name of a patient should be followed by '(by . . ... his litigation friend)'	PD21, para 1.3
Who is appointed (without a court order)	A person authorised under Mental Health Act 1983, Pt VII to conduct legal proceedings in the name or on behalf of a patient is entitled to be the litigation friend of the patient in any proceedings to which his authority extends	Rule 21.4(2)
	If nobody has been appointed by the court (or authorised as above) a person may act as a litigation friend if he: can fairly and competently conduct proceedings on behalf of the child or patient; and has no interest adverse to that of the child or patient; and (claim or counterclaim) undertakes to pay any costs which the child or patient may be ordered to pay	Rule 21.4(3)
Appointment without a court order	(If the court has not appointed) a person wishing to act as a litigation friend must: (if authorised under Mental Health Act 1983, Pt VII) file an official copy of the order or other authorisation; (otherwise) file a certificate of suitability – (claimant) when making the claim; (defendant) when first taking a step in the proceedings	Rule 21.5 PD21, para 2.3
Certificate of suitability of litigation friend	States that the proposed litigation friend: consents to act; believes the person to be a child or patient (with reasons and medical evidence);	

	can fairly and competently conduct proceedings on behalf of the person; has no adverse interest; (claimant) undertakes to pay any costs which the claimant may be ordered to pay in the proceedings A counterclaim is treated like a claim for the purpose of the costs undertaking	Form N235 Rule 21.4(3) PD21, para 2.4 Rule 20.3
Service of certificate of suitability	The litigation friend must: serve the certificate of suitability on every person on whom the claim form should be served; and file a certificate of service when he files the certificate of suitability	Rule 21.5(6) Rule 6.6
Certificate of service	States (see generally Guide 15): that the document has not been returned undelivered; and required details of method of service	Rule 6.10
Appointment by the court (for applications generally see Guide 18)	An application for an order appointing a litigation friend may be made by: a person who wishes to be the litigation friend; or a party. The claimant must apply where: a person makes a claim against a child or patient; the child or patient has no litigation friend; the court has not made an order that the child can act without a litigation friend (ie under rule 21.2(3)); and either (i) someone who is not entitled files a defence or (ii) the claimant wishes to take some step in the proceedings An application must be supported by evidence and the court must be satisfied that the person appointed is 'suitable'	Rule 21.6 PD21, paras 3.1–3.6 Rule 21.6(4) Rule 21.6(5) Rule 21.4(3)
Change of litigation friend	The court may: direct that a person may not act as a litigation friend; terminate the appointment; appoint a new litigation friend in substitution for an existing one.	

	An application for an order must be supported by evidence and the court may not appoint a litigation friend unless satisfied that the person is suitable	Rule 21.7 PD21, paras 4.1–4.4 Rule 21.4(3)
Who is appointed by the court	On an application the court may appoint: the person proposed, or any other person who complies with the conditions in rule 21.4(3)	Rule 21.8(4)
Appointment of the Official Solicitor	The Official Solicitor may be appointed as litigation friend provided: he consents; and provision is made for payment of his costs	PD21, para 3.6
Appointment ceasing – child	When a child who is not a patient reaches 18 a litigation friend's appointment ceases	Rule 21.9(1)
	The child must file and serve notice: that he has reached full age; that the appointment has ceased; giving an address for service; and stating whether or not he intends to carry on with the proceedings	Rule 21.9(4) PD21, para 5.2
	If he does not do so within 28 days the court may, on application, strike out any claim or defence brought by him	Rule 21.9(5)
	If proceedings continue the party will be described as: 'A.B. (formerly a child but now of full age)'	PD21, para 5.3
	The litigation friend may at any time after the child reaches 18 serve notice that his appointment has ceased	PD21, para 5.4
Appointment ceasing – patient	When a patient recovers, the litigation friend's appointment continues until ended by a court order:	Rule 21.9(2)
	application may be made by former patient, litigation friend or a party;	Rule 21.9(3)
	the application must be supported by evidence	PD21, para 5.7
	The patient must file and serve a notice:	

	that the appointment has ceased; giving his address for service; and stating whether or not he intends to carry on the proceedings	Rule 21.9(4) PD21, para 5.8
	If he does not do so within 28 days the court may, on application, strike out any claim or defence brought by him	Rule 21.9(5)
Service of claim form – child	Service of the claim form is upon: a parent or guardian; or (if none) the person with whom the child resides or in whose care he is	Rule 6.6(1)
	A child who is also a patient is so treated	Rule 6.6(1)
Service of claim form – patient	Service of the claim form is upon: the person authorised under Mental Health Act 1983, Pt VII to conduct the proceedings in the name or on behalf of the patient; or (if none) the person with whom the patient resides or in whose care he is	Rule 6.6(1)
Service generally (see Guide 15)	Once a litigation friend has been appointed, service will be upon him as if he was the party	Rule 6.6(1)
	Where the court has made an order under rule 21.2(3) allowing a child to conduct proceedings without a litigation friend, service will be on the child	Rule 6.6(5)
	The court may by order: permit a document to be served on the child or patient, or on a person other than as specified;	Rule 6.6(2)
	treat a document as if it had been properly served although it has been served on someone other than as specified	Rule 6.6(4)
Service of application relating to a litigation friend	An application for an order appointing or changing a litigation friend must be served on:	Rule 21.8
	every person on whom the claim form should be served; and	Rule 21.8(1)
	(if appointing) the patient unless the court otherwise orders; or	Rule 21.8(2)
	(if changing) the existing and proposed litigation friend	Rule 21.8(3)

Statement of truth	Where a statement of truth is required the litigation friend or his legal representative signs this to verify that the litigation friend believes the facts stated in the document are true	Rule 22.1(6) PD22, paras 3.1(1) and 3.7 Rule 22.1(5)
Default judgment	A claimant may only obtain a default judgment against a child or patient:	Rule 12.10(a)(i) PD12, para 2.3(1)
	on an application supported by evidence that he is entitled to the judgment claimed;	
	after appointment of a litigation friend	Rule 12.11(3) PD12, para 4.2
	A counterclaim is treated like a claim	Rule 20.3
Judgment on an admission	There are restrictions on obtaining a judgment by or against a child or patient based on an admission	Rule 14.1(4)
Hearing	A hearing may be in private if this is necessary to protect the interests of a child or patient:	Rule 39.2(3)(d)
	eg approval of a compromise or settlement, or application for payment of money out of court to such party	PD39, para 1.6
	A hearing of an application under Pt 21 will take place in private unless the court otherwise directs	Rule 39.2(3)
Availability of witness statements	The court may at a trial make a direction that a witness statement which stands as evidence in chief is not open to inspection due to the need to protect the interests of a child or patient	Rule 32.13(3)(e)
Compromise or settlement	Where a claim or counterclaim is made:	
	by or on behalf of a child or patient; or	
	against a child or patient,	
	no settlement, compromise or payment and no acceptance of money paid into court shall be valid, so far as it relates to such claim, without court approval	Rule 21.10(1)
	Where before proceedings in which such a claim is made are begun:	
	an agreement is reached for the settlement of the claim; and	

	the sole purpose of proceedings is to obtain the approval of the court to a settlement or compromise,	
	the claim must be made using the Pt 8 procedure (alternative procedure for claims – see Guide 3) and include a request to the court for approval	Rule 21.10(2) PD21, paras 6.1–6.3 Form N292
	If in the Chancery Division, it will be heard by the judge, rather than the master, if the amount involved exceeds £100,000	PD2B, para 5.1(a)
Structured settlements	A practice direction deals with the procedure where a structured settlement is contemplated	PD40C
Interim payments	The approval of the court must be obtained before making a voluntary interim payment to a child or patient	PD21, para 1.7
Acceptance of offers and payments into court	An offer or payment may only be accepted on behalf of a child or patient with the permission of the court	Rule 36.18(1)(a)
	In such cases a payment out of court requires a court order	Rule 36.18(1)(b)
Fatal Accidents Act claims	An offer of settlement includes a proposal for a sum to be apportioned to a dependent child under the 1976 Act	PD21, para 1.6 PD21, paras 7.1–7.3
Control of money recovered	Where in any proceedings: money is recovered on behalf of or for the benefit of a child or patient; or	
	money paid into court is accepted by or on behalf of a child or patient,	
	the money is dealt with under directions of the court and not otherwise	Rule 21.11(1) PD21, paras 8.1–8.5
	These may provide that the money shall be wholly or partly paid into court and:	Rule 21.11(2)
	invested; or otherwise dealt with (eg paid to or for the benefit of the child or patient); or	PD21, paras 10.1–10.5 PD21, paras 11.1–11.7 PD21, para 8.2
	transferred to another court if more convenient	Rule 30.7 PD21, para 8.2(3)

Payment out of funds in court	Applications are to a master or district judge (a hearing may not be required): for payment out to a child; to vary an investment strategy When the child attains 18 his fund is paid out or transferred to him It is assumed that this procedure also applies to small funds held for patients	PD21, para 12.1 PD21, para 12.2 PD21, para 11.2(2)
Guardian of child's estate	The court may appoint the Official Solicitor as a guardian of a child's estate	Rule 21.12 PD21, para 9
Receiver for a patient	It will usually be necessary for the Court of Protection to appoint a receiver for the estate of a patient: money of a patient will be transferred; applications for payment out of funds are to the Court of Protection	PD21, paras 11.1–11.7 Forms N292; CFO 200 PD21, para 12.3
Costs	Costs payable to the solicitor for a child or patient must be approved by the court Neither: the fast track costs provision, nor the power of a court officer to assess costs (unless under rule 48.5) apply to a hearing for the court's approval of a settlement or compromise of a claim by a child or patient The liability of a litigation friend for costs continues until: the appointment ceases; and the former child or patient serves notice on the other parties; or the litigation friend serves notice	Rule 48.5 Rule 46.1(2)(c)(ii) Rule 47.3(1)(b) Rule 21.9(6) PD21, para 5.5
Conditional fees	The court will not vary a percentage increase where the client is a child or patient other than in accordance with rule 48.9(5)	Rule 48.9(6)

Forms	Certificate of suitability of litigation friend N235 Order approving terms of a settlement or compromise (includes transfer of fund to Court of Protection) N292	
Court fees	No additional fee is prescribed.	

18: Applications Generally

Legal background

Applications made during a claim, after judgment or before a claim is commenced are made in accordance with Pt 23. Part 32 deals with evidence at interim hearings.

Certain specific applications are dealt with in the following Guides:

- to add or substitute a party – Guide 20
- to make other amendments – Guide 19
- for summary judgment – Guide 30
- for further information – Guide 21
- to change solicitor – Guide 22
- for interim remedies – Guide 23
- as to disclosure of documents – Guide 24
- for telephone conferences – Guide 28.

Procedure

Considerations when making an application	Applications should be made: as soon as the need becomes apparent;	PD23, para 2.7
	wherever possible so that they can be considered at any other hearing whether arranged or anticipated, eg case management conferences, allocation and listing hearings and pre-trial reviews fixed by the court;	PD23, para 2.8
	with the knowledge that the court may wish to review the conduct of the case as a whole and give any necessary case management directions	PD23, para 2.9
Making the application	By filing an application notice *unless* a rule or practice direction provides otherwise, or the court dispenses with one	Rule 23.3

	Where a date for a hearing has been fixed and a party wishes to make an application at that hearing but he does not have sufficient time to serve an application notice he should inform the other party and the court (if possible in writing) as soon as he can of the nature of the application and the reason for it. He should then make the application orally at the hearing	PD23, para 2.10
Which court	The court where the claim is proceeding unless a trial date has been fixed, when the application must be made to the court where the trial is to take place	Rule 23.2(1)–(3)
Time of application	An application is made when it is received by the court	Rule 23.5
Parties	The person making the application is 'the applicant' and the person against whom the order is sought is 'the respondent'	Rule 23.1
Contents of application notice	An application notice must state: if it is intended to be made to a High Court or circuit judge. (Subject to exceptions noted below and in Guides where they apply, applications will normally be made to a master or district judge but he may refer an application to a judge, who may deal with it or refer it back);	PD23, para 2.6 PD2B, para 1.2 PD23, para 1
	what order the applicant seeks;	Rule 23.6
	brief reasons for the application;	
	the title of the claim;	PD23, para 2.1
	the reference number of the claim;	
	the full name of the applicant;	
	where the applicant is not already a party, his address for service,	
	and must include a request: for a hearing, or that the application be dealt with without a hearing.	
Requirements as to notice	An application may be made without serving an application notice only:	PD23, para 3

	where there is exceptional urgency; where the overriding objective is best furthered by doing so; by consent of all parties; with the permission of the court; or	
	where a court order, rule or practice direction permits	Rule 23.4(2)
	Where an order is made without notice, a copy of the application notice and any evidence filed in support must be served with the order on any party against whom the order is made or was sought	Rule 23.9(2)
	Such a party may apply within 7 days of service of the order for it to be set aside or varied, and the order made must contain a statement to this effect	Rule 23.10 and 23.9(3)
	Otherwise, a copy of the application notice must be served:	
	on each respondent;	Rule 23.4(1)
	as soon as practicable after it is filed and, in any event,	Rule 23.7(1)(a)
	at least 3 clear days before the hearing, unless another time-limit is prescribed by a rule or practice direction	Rule 23.7(1)(b)
	Where a hearing date has been fixed and a party wishes to make application at that hearing but does not have sufficient time to serve an application notice he should: (a) inform the other party; and (b) inform the court (if possible in writing), of the nature of the application and the reason for it. He will then make the application orally at the hearing	PD23, para 2.10
Evidence	Evidence at interim hearings is given in writing by witness statement unless the court orders otherwise	Rule 32.6(1)
	Affidavit evidence may be used but, unless the court has ordered it, or a rule requires it, any additional costs may not be recovered from another party	Rule 32.15

	Any evidence on which the applicant seeks to rely must be filed and served with the application notice unless it has already been filed and served. Exhibits should not be filed unless the court otherwise directs	Rule 23.7(3) PD23, paras 9.3 and 9.6
	If the application notice is to be served by the court, service copies of any evidence in support (which has not already been served) must be filed with the application notice	Rule 23.7(2)
	If an applicant wishes to rely on matters set out in his application notice or a statement of case as evidence, the application notice or statement of case must be verified by a statement of truth	Rule 32.6(2) PD22, para 1.2 PD23, para 9.7
	A respondent who wishes to rely on evidence which has not been filed or served should file and serve it as soon as possible	Rule 32.2(2)(b)
	If the applicant wishes to rely on evidence in reply, he should file and serve it as soon as possible	PD23, para 9.5
Hearing of the application	At the conclusion of the hearing, if the court wishes to order one party to pay costs to another, it may:	
	assess the costs summarily; or	Rule 44.7
	order a payment on account of costs; and	Rule 44.3(8)
	state, for the guidance of a costs officer conducting a detailed assessment of the costs, whether or not the hearing was fit for the attendance of one or more counsel	PDCosts, para 8.7
	In hearings likely to last not more than one day the parties must, at least 24 hours before the hearing, file and serve written statements of costs claimed as closely as possible following Form N260 and should endeavour to agree them before the hearing starts	PDCosts, para 13.5 PDCosts, para 13.2
Disposal of applications without a hearing	The court may deal with an application without a hearing where: the application is for a consent order;	Rule 23.8

	the parties agree (each party should so inform the court in writing and confirm that all evidence and other material on which he relies has been disclosed);	PD23, para 11.1
	the court considers it appropriate.	
	Where the applicant asks that the application be disposed of without a hearing, the master or district judge will consider the request, and if he agrees, will deal with it	PD23, paras 2.3 and 2.4
	If not, directions may be given and the court will fix a hearing	PD23, para 2.5
	Where the court decides of its own initiative to deal with an application without a hearing, opportunity may be given to any *person* likely to be affected to make representations by a specified time and date	Rule 3.3(2) PD23, para 11.2
	Where the court makes an order without giving the opportunity to make representations, any *party* affected may apply within 7 days of service (or such other period as the court may direct) to have the order set aside, varied or stayed and the order must contain a statement to this effect	Rule 3.3(5), (6)
Telephone hearings	For the procedure to be followed see Guide 28	
Video conferencing	If required, application should be made to a master or district judge	PD23, para 7
Service	The rules as to service in general apply (see Guides 15 and).	
Applications by consent	An agreed order may be made by a court officer if all parties are represented and no rule, practice direction or Act requires it to be approved by the court; and if it is: a money judgment; a judgment for the delivery of goods; an order dismissing all or part of the proceedings; a stay of the proceedings on agreed terms; a stay of enforcement;	

	an order setting aside an unsatisfied default judgment;	
	an order to pay out money in court;	
	the discharge of a party from liability;	
	an order as to costs	Rule 40.6(2), (3)
	Otherwise, any party may apply for an order in the terms agreed by application notice attaching a draft of the proposed order which must be drawn so that the judge's name and title can be inserted. The court may deal with the application without a hearing	PD40B, para 3.3 Rule 40.6(5), (6)
	The agreed order must be signed by the legal representatives of all parties (or by an unrepresented party personally) or accompanied by signed letters and must be expressed to be 'By Consent'; and filed	PD23, para 10.2 Rule 40.6(7)
	The application, if required, must be supported by material to satisfy the court that the order is appropriate. A letter will usually suffice	PD23, para 10.4
Court fees	On application generally: *High Court* – £100 *County court* – £60	CPFO fee 2.5
	On application by consent or without notice: *High Court* – £50 *County court* – £30	CPFO fee 2.6
	On application to vary or set aside judgment or suspend enforcement: *High Court* – £50 *County court* – £30	CPFO fee 2.8
	Other particular cases – see relevant Guide.	
Forms	Form N244 may be used	PD23, para 2.1
Which judge	PD2B makes provision for the allocation of applications to various levels of judiciary –	
	In the High Court	
	Injunctions	PD2B, paras 2.1–2.4
	Other pre trial orders and interim remedies	PD2B, paras 3.1, 3.2
	Trials and assessment of damages	PD2B, paras 4.1, 4.2
	Chancery proceedings	PD2B, paras 5.1–5.3

	Assignment of claims to masters and transfer between masters	PD2B, paras 6.1, 6.2
	Freezing orders: cross examination of deponents about assets	PD2B, para 7
	Human Rights Act 1998	PD2B, para 7A
	In the county courts	
	Injunctions and committal	PD2B, paras 8.1–8.3
	Homelessness appeals	PD2B, para 9
	Other pre-trial orders and interim remedies	PD2B, para 10.1
	Trials and assessment of damages	PD2B, paras 11.1, 11.2
	Freezing orders: cross examination of deponents about assets	PD2B, para 12
	Distribution of business between circuit judge and district judge	PD2B, paras 13, 14.1, 14.2
	Human Rights	PD2B, para 15

19: Amendments to Statements of Case

Legal background

Part 17 and the practice direction to it deal with amendments to statements of case. The general rules about applications also apply (see Guide 18). Special rules apply where the amendment involves the addition, removal or substitution of a party (see Guide 20).

A party applying to amend may expect to have to pay the costs of and arising from it (PD17, preamble).

Procedure

Amendment as of right	A statement of case may be amended if it has not been served. Once served, it may only be amended: if the other parties agree; or with the court's permission	Rule 17.1
	The court may subsequently disallow any such amendment either of its own initiative or on the application of a party made within 14 days of service of the amended statement of case	Rule 17.2(1) Rule 3.3(1) Rule 17.2(2)
Amendment on application	The application for permission is made by filing an application notice and a copy of the proposed amended statement of case	PD17, para 1.2

Applications made after any relevant period of limitation	An amendment whose effect is to substitute or add a new claim will not be allowed unless it arises out of substantially the same facts as the existing claim	Rule 17.4
Additional directions	When granting permission, the court may direct amendments to be made to any other statement of case and service of any amended statement of case	Rule 17.3(1)
Formal requirements	A copy of the order and the amended statement of case must be served on every other party, unless the court orders otherwise	PD17, para 1.5
	The amended statement of case as filed and served must be endorsed: 'Amended [*title of statement of case*] [*either* by order of [*identity of judge*] *or* under CPR, [rule 17.1(1) *or* (2)(a)]] dated	PD17, para 2.1
	The original text need not be shown unless the court directs otherwise. The court may also direct that colour or a numerical code be used. Where colour is used, text to be deleted should be struck through in colour, and new text underlined in the same colour	PD17, para 2.2 PD17, para 2.3
	For successive amendments, the order of colours to be used is red, green, violet and yellow	PD17, para 2.4
	Any substantial change must be verified by a statement of truth	PD17, para 1.4
Court fees	On application for permission: *High Court* – £100 *County court* – £60	CPFO fee 2.5
Forms	Application Notice N244	PD23, para 2.1

20: Adding, Removing or Substituting a Party

Legal background

Part 19 and the practice direction to it make special provisions relating to this type of application. The rules differ if the application is made after the end of a relevant period of limitation. The general rules about application notices (Guide 18) and amendments to statements of case (Guide 19) also apply.

Procedure

The court's powers	The court may add a new party in order to resolve: all issues; or issues involving the new party connected with the issues, in the proceedings	Rule 19.2(2)
	The court may order a new party to be substituted for an existing party in order to resolve all the matters in dispute where a party's interest or liability has passed to the new party	Rule 19.2(4)
	A party may be removed if it is undesirable that he should be a party	Rule 19.2(3)
	Save in probate proceedings, all persons jointly entitled to a remedy must be parties unless the court orders otherwise. Such a person must be made a defendant if he does not agree to being a claimant	Rule 19.2
	The court may exercise its powers of its own initiative or on application	PD19, para 1.1
Who may apply	Any party, or any person who wishes to become a party	Rule 19.3(1)
Evidence	An application to add or substitute a party must be supported by evidence. Where the application is to substitute a party the evidence must show the stage of the proceedings reached and what has occurred to cause the change of interest or liability	Rule 19.3(2) PD19, para 1.3
Making the application	Application is made by filing an application notice (see Guide 18) and any evidence in support	PD19, para 1.4 PD19, para 1.3
	The application may be dealt with without a hearing where all parties and any proposed new party agree	PD19, para 1.2
Adding or substituting a claimant	Where the application is to add or substitute a new claimant, the proposed new claimant must consent.	

	There must be filed, with the application notice, that consent and the proposed amended claim form and particulars of claim	Rule 19.3(3)
	The order will not have effect unless and until the proposed new claimant's consent is filed	PD19, para 2.2
Adding or substituting a defendant	A new defendant does not become a party until the amended claim form has been served on him	PD19, para 3.3
	The CPR will then apply to the new defendant. Parts 9, 10, 11 and 15 will be particularly relevant	PD19, para 3.1
Additional directions	When adding or substituting a party, the court may also direct that the claimant or the party making the application file an amended claim form and particulars of claim and that copies of the statements of case and any documents referred to be served on the new party, together with, in the case of a new defendant, forms for acknowledging service of, admitting and defending the claim	PD19, paras 2.3 and 3.2
	When a party is removed, a copy of the order must be served on all other parties and any other person affected by the order and the claimant must file with the court an amended claim form and particulars of claim	PD19, para 4
Applications made after any relevant period of limitation	The court may add or substitute a party only if: the period of limitation was current when proceedings were started; and	Rule 19.4(2)(a)
	the party who is to be replaced was made a party by mistake; or	
	the addition or substitution is necessary in order to pursue the claim against the original party; or	
	the original party's interest has passed by his death or bankruptcy to the new party	Rule 19.4(3)

	Additionally, a new party may be substituted if the court directs that Limitation Act 1980, s 11 or s 12 shall not apply, or where that issue is to be determined at trial	Rule 19.4(4)
Court fees	On application on notice: *High Court* – £100 *County court* – £60	CPFO fee 2.5
	On application without notice: *High Court* – £50 *County court* – £30	CPFO fee 2.6
	On adding a party: *High Court* – £50 *County court* – £30	CPFO fee 1.5
Forms	Form N244 may be used	PD23, para 2.1

21: Application for Further Information or Clarification

Legal background

Formerly known as an application for 'further and better particulars', this particular type of application is covered by Pt 18 and the practice direction which supplements it. Although Pt 18 is headed 'Further Information', the practice direction makes it clear that the procedure may be used in order to seek clarification of the case that the requesting party has to meet.

Guide 18 deals with the rules that apply to applications in general.

Procedure

How to make a request	A request for information may be made:	
	informally by letter, either in the letter itself, or by means of a document of request which accompanies the letter; or	PD18, paras 1.1 and 1.4
	by application to the court	Rule 18.1
	A written request should be made before applying to the court for an order	PD18, para 1.1
When	The court may at any time order a party to:	
	clarify; or	
	give additional information in relation to,	
	any matter in dispute.	
	A preliminary request may therefore be made at any time during the course of proceedings	Rule 18.1

General requirements	The request must:	
	be in a single, comprehensive document so far as possible;	PD18, para 1.3
	be concise and proportionate to enable the party making the request to understand the case he has to meet;	PD18, para 1.2
	be headed with the name of the court and the title and number of the claim;	
	in its heading state that it is a request made under Pt 18, identify the party seeking the information and the party from whom it is sought;	
	state the date on which it is made;	
	set out in a separate numbered paragraph each request for information or clarification;	
	where a request relates to a document, identify that document and (if relevant) the paragraph or words to which it relates;	
	state the date by which a response is required	PD18, para 1.6(1)
	The request may be in a letter if it is brief and the reply is likely to be brief. The letter should deal with no other matters	PD18, paras 1.4 and 1.5
	If not in a letter, the request may be in such a form as allows the party responding to it to use the same form in order to reply, in which case 2 copies of the request must be served	PD18, para 1.6(2)
Time for response	A party must file and serve a response by the time specified in an order	Rule 18.1(3)
	A party should respond to an informal request by the date specified in the request, which date must allow the party from whom the information is sought a reasonable time to respond	PD18, para 1.1
	If a party considers the date unreasonable, he may object (see below)	PD18, para 4.1(a)
Response to request	Where the request is in a letter, the response may be in a letter which should deal with no other matters	PD18, para 2.2

	A response must:	
	be in writing, signed and dated;	PD18, para 2.1
	contain a heading which shows the name of the court and the case number;	
	identify the document as a response (or, as the case may be, a second or third etc response) to that request;	
	repeat the text of each separate paragraph of the request and set out under each paragraph the response to it;	
	have attached to it any document referred to which is not already in the possession of the requesting party;	PD18, para 2.3(1)
	be served on every other party and filed in court together with a copy of the request	PD18, para 2.4
Objecting to a request	A party who refuses to comply with a request must, within the time for response specified by the requesting party:	
	inform the other party in a letter or separate document setting out his reasons;	
	if the refusal relates to the time by which the response is required, set out the time by which he can respond;	PD18, para 4.1
	state, where appropriate, that he considers the request to be disproportionate and why	PD18, para 4.2
Application to the court – formal requirements	An application notice for an order under Pt 18 must:	
	set out or have attached to it the text of the order required;	
	specify the matter(s) about which further information or clarification is sought; and	PD18, para 5.2
	explain, if appropriate, why no informal request was made; or	
	describe the response to the request;	PD18, para 5.3

	be served on all other *parties to the claim* (cf r 23.4(1)) *unless* the other party has failed to respond at all to a request, in which case that application may be dealt with by the judge without a hearing and without notice to the other party	PD18, para 5.6 PD18, para 5.5
	The order made will be served on all parties	PD18, para 5.7
	Where a party is served with an order made on an application which was not served on him:	
	a copy of the application notice and evidence in support must be served with the order unless the court orders otherwise;	Rule 23.9(2)
	that party may apply within 7 days of service for the order to be set aside; and	Rule 23.10
	the order must state that that party is so entitled	Rule 23.9(3)
Statement of truth	A response must be verified by a statement of truth, whether made in reply to a request or pursuant to an order	Rule 22.1(1)(a), (b)
Costs	The court is likely to assess costs summarily. Parties should therefore be prepared to give the court a written statement of the amount of costs incurred	PDCosts, para 13.1 PDCosts, para 13.5
Court fees	On application on notice: *High Court* – £100 *County court* – £60	CPFO fee 2.5
	On application without notice: *High Court* – £50 *County court* – £30	CPFO fee 2.6
Forms	Application: Form N244 may be used Statement of Costs: N260	PD23, para 2.1

22: Change of Solicitor

Legal background

A solicitor whose business address is the address for service of a party will remain on the court record as acting for that party until removed by one of the ways provided for in Pt 42 and the practice direction to it.

Procedure

Change, removal or appointment of solicitor by notice	A notice, called a 'notice of change' must be filed where a party: changes his solicitor; appoints a solicitor after having acted in person; or having acted through a solicitor, wishes to continue the proceedings acting in person.	
	This does not apply where a solicitor is instructed merely as advocate at a hearing	PD42, para 1.3
	The newly appointed solicitor or the party must first serve and then file in court a notice of change	Rule 42.2(1) and PD42, para 1.2
	The former solicitor will, unless his retainer is terminated on revocation or discharge of a certificate (defined as a certificate issued under the Funding Code by the Legal Services Commission or within the meaning of the Civil Legal Aid (General) Regulations 1989), remain on the court record as acting for the party until the notice is filed	Rule 42.1
Removal of solicitor by revocation or discharge of certificate	A solicitor's retainer to act for an assisted person is terminated by the service on the solicitor of a notice of revocation or discharge of his client's certificate and his then sending to the court notice of the revocation or discharge.	Civil Legal Aid (General) Regs 1989, Reg 83 Community Legal Service (Costs) Regulations 2000, Reg 4
	He must also give notice to the other parties and to counsel	CLA(G)R 1989, Reg 82(2)
	If the former assisted person wishes to continue the proceedings, he must either appoint a solicitor who must file notice of change, or he must give an address for service if he wishes to act in person	Rule 42.2(6)
	Failure to comply with this requirement (as with any rule) may lead to his statement of case being struck out	Rule 3.4(2)(c)
Service of notice of change	The notice must be served on every other party and, unless the change is brought about by the revocation or discharge of the party's legal aid certificate, the former solicitor	Rule 42.2(2)(b) Rule 42.2(6)(b)(i)

Contents of notice of change	The notice must state: the party's new address for service which must be in England and Wales; and that it has been served on all necessary persons	 Rule 42.2(3) Rule 6.5(3) Rule 42.2(4)
Removal of solicitor by his own application	A solicitor may apply for an order declaring that he has ceased to act for a party by filing an application notice which must be supported by evidence The application notice must be served on the party for whom the solicitor is acting, unless the court directs otherwise It is the party who is the respondent to the application. The court may direct other persons to be added as respondents but, unless this occurs, care must be taken not to serve other parties to the claim as the application notice and supporting evidence are likely to contain material confidential between solicitor and client.	Rule 42.3(1) and (2)(b) Rule 42.3(2)(a) Rule 23.1(a) Rule 23.1(b)
Removal of solicitor on application of another party	If a party whose solicitor has died, become bankrupt, ceased to practice or cannot be found does not give notice of change of solicitor, any other party may apply for an order that that solicitor has ceased to act for that party The application notice must be given to the party to whose solicitor the application relates and any other parties the court directs, and must be supported by evidence	Rule 42.4(1) Rule 42.4(2) PD42, para 4.2
Service of order for removal	If the court orders the removal of a solicitor, a copy of the order must be served on every party If an order made under rule 42.3 or 42.4 is served by a solicitor or a party, he must file a certificate of service (see Guide 15)	Rules 42.3(3)(a) and 42.4(3)(a) Rules 42.3(3)(b) and 42.4(3)(b)
Court fees	On application: *High Court* – £100 *County court* – £60	CPFO fee 2.5
Forms	Application Notice N244 Notice of change N434	PD23, para 2.1

23: Injunctions and other Interim Remedies

Legal background

Part 25 and the three practice directions that supplement it make provision for the application for and granting of a wide range of interim remedies including freezing injunctions (Mareva orders) and search orders (Anton Piller orders). Additional provisions are made in other Rules and the practice directions to them in respect of some of the remedies.

This Guide deals with applications for:

- interim remedies between parties in existing proceedings;
- orders relating to property, in existing proceedings, against non-parties; and
- orders relating to property in anticipation of proceedings.

Guide 24 deals with applications for disclosure of documents, whether within an existing claim or before a claim is issued.

Part 23 contains general rules about applications (see Guide 18).

Procedure

General considerations and requirements		
The court's powers	The court may grant the following:	
	an interim injunction;	
	an interim declaration;	
	an order for –	
	the detention, custody or preservation of relevant property;	
	the inspection of relevant property;	
	the taking of a sample of relevant property;	
	the carrying out of an experiment on or with relevant property;	
	the sale of relevant property which is of a perishable nature or which for any other good reason it is desirable to sell quickly;	
	the payment of income from relevant property until a claim is decided; and	
	authorisation of a person to enter any land or building in the possession of a party to the proceedings for the purposes of carrying out any such order;	Rule 25.1(1)
	an order to deliver up goods;	
	an order (a 'freezing injunction') restraining a party from removing assets from the jurisdiction or from dealing with any assets wherever located;	Torts (Interference with Goods) Act 1977, s 4

	an order directing a party to provide information about the location of relevant property or assets, or about relevant property or assets which are or may be the subject of an application for a freezing injunction;	Civil Procedure Act 1997, s 7
	a 'search order' requiring a party to admit another party to premises for the purpose of preserving evidence etc;	SCA, s 33 or CCA 1984, s 52
	an order for disclosure of documents (dealt with in Guide 24) or inspection of property before a claim has been made;	SCA, s 34 or CCA 1984, s 53
	an order for disclosure of documents (dealt with in Guide 24) or inspection of property against a non-party;	
	an order for an interim payment	
	an order for a specified fund to be paid into court or otherwise secured;	
	an order permitting a party seeking to recover personal property to pay money into court pending the outcome of the proceedings and directing that, if he does so, the property shall be given up to him;	
	an order directing a party to prepare and file accounts; and	
	an order requiring an account to be taken or enquiries to be made	PD25C, para 2
	This list is not exhaustive	Rule 25.1(3)
	An interim remedy may be granted irrespective of the final remedy claimed	Rule 25.1(4)
Time for applying	Subject to any rule, practice direction or enactment, an application for an interim remedy may be made:	Rule 25.2(2)(a)
	before the proceedings are started;	
	during proceedings; or	
	after final judgment has been given	Rule 25.2(1)
	but a defendant may not apply without the court's permission before he has filed an acknowledgment of service	Rule 25.2(2)(c)

Applications before proceedings	The court may only grant an interim remedy before the start of proceedings if the matter is urgent or it is otherwise in the interests of justice	Rule 25.2(2)
	When granting such an application, the court may give directions which include a direction that a claim be commenced	Rule 25.2(3)
Applications without notice	An application may be made without notice if there are good reasons not to give notice	Rule 25.3(1)
	Evidence in support of the application must state those reasons	Rule 25.3(3)
Applications where there is no related claim	An application for: an interim remedy relating to a claim or a prospective claim in a foreign court; or	Rule 25.4
	inspection, preservation, custody etc of property before commencement of proceedings under SCA, s 33, or CCA 1984, s 52,	
	is made by application notice (see Guide 18), not by issuing a claim.	
Evidence	An application for an interim remedy must be supported by evidence unless the court orders otherwise	Rule 25.3(2)
	Evidence in respect of an application under SCA, ss 33(1) and 34(3), or CCA 1984, ss 52(1) or 53(3), should show, in addition to any other matters, that the property is or may become the subject matter of, or be relevant to the issues in, proceedings or prospective proceedings	Rule 25.5(2)
Injunctions – including freezing injunctions and search orders		
Which judge	Freezing injunctions and search orders may be made by a High Court judge or any other judge duly authorised	PD25, para 1.1

	Where the court has made a freezing order and has ordered a person to make a witness statement or affidavit about his assets and to be cross-examined on its contents, unless the judge directs otherwise, the cross-examination will take place before a master or a district judge, or if the master or district judge directs, before an examiner of the court	PD2B, para 7
	In the High Court, masters and district judges may grant injunctions:	
	by consent;	
	in connection with charging orders and appointments of receivers;	
	in aid of execution of judgments	PD25, para 1.2
	Otherwise, in the High Court, any judge who has trial jurisdiction in the matter may grant an injunction	PD25, para 1.3
	In the county court, any judge who has jurisdiction to conduct the trial of the action may grant an injunction	PD25, para 1.3
	A district judge may also grant an injunction in a money claim before allocation if the amount claimed does not exceed the fast track limit;	PD2B, para 8.1(b)
	A master or district judge may vary or discharge an injunction granted by any judge with the consent of all the parties	PD2B, paras 2.4 and 8.2 PD25, para 1.4
The application notice	The application notice must state the order sought. Evidence in support and a draft of the order, if possible, should be filed with it	PD25, paras 2.1 and 2.2
	In the Royal Courts of Justice, a disk containing the draft order in WordPerfect 5.1 for DOS format should also be supplied if possible.	
	Enquiry should be made at other courts to ascertain whether this would be of assistance. Not all courts will have the facilities to use such a disk.	
	The document file format used should be that of WordPerfect 5.1 for DOS	PD25, para 2.4

Evidence	Applications for freezing orders and search orders must be supported by affidavit evidence	PD25, para 3.1
	Otherwise the general rules as to evidence apply (see Guide 18).	
Urgent applications	The application notice, evidence in support and draft order should where possible be filed 2 hours before the hearing	PD25, para 4.3(1)
	If the application is heard before issue of the application, a draft order should be produced at the hearing and the application notice and evidence in support should be filed the same day or the next working day, or as the court orders	PD25, para 4.3(2)
	Unless there is a need for secrecy, the applicant should inform the respondent of the application informally	PD25, para 4.3(3)
	In the case of urgent applications made before issue of the claim, where possible, the claim form should be served with any order made	PD25, para 4.4(2)
	If an applicant is legally represented, an urgent application may be made by telephone where a hearing can not be obtained. The practice direction contains details of how this may be arranged. A draft order should be faxed to the judge if possible, and the application and evidence in support must be filed the same or the next working day, or as the judge orders	PD25, para 4.5
What the order must contain	An injunction order must: set out clearly what the respondent must do or not do;	PD25, para 5.3
	unless the court orders otherwise, contain an undertaking by the applicant to the court to pay any damages which the respondent(s) (or any other party served with or notified of the order) sustain which the court considers the applicant should pay	PD25, para 5.1(1)
	An injunction order made before issue of the claim form:	

	should state in the title after the names of the applicant and respondent 'the Claimant and Defendant in an Intended Action';	PD25, para 4.4(3)
	unless the court orders otherwise, must contain *either* an undertaking by the applicant to the court to issue a claim form and pay the appropriate fee immediately *or* directions for the commencement of the claim	PD25, paras 4.4(1) and 5.1(5)
	An injunction order made before the issue of an application notice must, unless the court orders otherwise, contain an undertaking to file and pay the appropriate fee on the same or next working day	PD25, para 5.1(4)
	An order made without notice must unless the court orders otherwise contain:	
	an undertaking by the applicant to the court to serve on the respondent the application notice, evidence in support and any order made as soon as practicable;	PD25, para 5.1(2)
	a return date for a further hearing at which the other party can be present	PD25, para 5.1(3)
	An injunction order which is made in the presence of all parties to be bound may be expressed to be effective until trial or further order	PD25, para 5.2
Effect of a stay	If the claim is stayed while an interim injunction is in force, the injunction is set aside unless the court orders otherwise	Rule 25.10
Effect of claim being struck out for non-payment of fee	If a claim is struck out under r 3.7 an interim injunction ceases to have effect after 14 days unless the claimant applies within that time to re-instate the claim	Rule 25.11
Special provisions relating to search orders	Applications for a search order in intellectual property cases should be made to the Chancery Division	PD25, para 8.4
	Supervising solicitor The affidavit in support of the application must name a supervising solicitor, his firm and its address and his experience	PD25, para 7.3(1)

	He must be experienced in the operation of search orders and must *not* be a member of the applicant's firm of solicitors	PD25, para 7.2 PD25, para 8.1
	A supervising solicitor may be contacted either through the Law Society or, for the London area, through the London Solicitors Litigation Association.	
	The supervising solicitor is responsible for the general conduct of the order, including the listing of any items removed, and must report on the carrying out of the order to the applicant's solicitors. (A copy of the report must be filed and served on the respondent)	PD25, para 7.5(6) PD25, para 7.5(11) PD25, para 7.5(12)
	Service The supervising solicitor must serve the order personally, unless the court orders otherwise, in which case the order should so provide and explain why	PD25, para 7.4(1) PD25, para 8.2
	Search and custody of materials The practice direction makes detailed provision as to what documents should be served with or accompany the order and who may or should accompany the supervising solicitor when he serves	PD25, para 7.4
	The practice direction makes detailed provision as to what may be removed, what may be searched, and as to the custody, safekeeping and insurance of removed items	PD25, para 7.5
	Any items removed must be listed and the respondent must have the opportunity to check the list before removal of any items, unless this is impracticable	PD25, para 7.5(6), (7) PD25, para 7.5(13)
Specimen orders	Examples of freezing and search orders are annexed to the practice direction	PD25, Annex
Interim payments		
Conditions to be satisfied before an order may be made	The court may make an order for an interim payment if: the applicant has obtained judgment for, or the respondent has admitted liability to pay the applicant damages to be assessed or some other sum of money;	Rule 25.7(1)(a), (b)

	it is satisfied that the claimant would obtain judgment for a substantial amount of money against the defendant (or at least one of them if more than one) from whom the payment is sought;	Rule 25.7(1)(c) Rule 25.7(3)(a)
	where the applicant is seeking an order for the protection of land, that at trial the defendant would be ordered to pay the claimant for the use and occupation of the land	Rule 25.7(1)(d)
Additional conditions in personal injury claims	In a claim for damages for personal injuries the court may make an order for an interim payment if:	
	the defendant is insured in respect of the claim; or	Rule 25.7(2)(a)
	the claim will be met by an insurer either under Road Traffic Act 1988, s 151 or the Motor Insurers' Bureau agreement, or by the MIB itself; or	Rule 25.7(2)(b)
	the defendant is a public body; and	Rule 25.7(2)(c)
	in a claim against more than one defendant, the court is satisfied that the claimant will recover substantial damages against at least one of them	Rule 25.7(3)
Matters to be taken into account when making the order	The court must take into account contributory negligence and any relevant set-off or counterclaim, and may only award a reasonable proportion of the amount likely to be awarded on final judgment	Rule 25.7(5) Rule 25.7(4)
Children and patients	The court's permission must be obtained before making a voluntary interim payment to a child or patient	PD25B, para 1.2
The application	The application notice and supporting evidence must be served 14 clear days before the hearing	Rule 25.6(3)
	No application may be made before the time for acknowledging service has expired	Rule 25.6(1)
Evidence	The application must be supported by evidence dealing with:	Rule 25.6(3)(b)

	the amount sought;	
	the items in respect of which it is sought;	
	the likely amount of final judgment;	
	the pre-conditions for the granting of an interim payment (see above);	
	in personal injury claims details of special damages and past and future loss;	
	in claims under the Fatal Accidents Act 1976, details of the person(s) on whose behalf the claim is made and the nature of the claim; and	
	any other relevant matters	PD25B, para 2.1
	Documents in support, including medical reports, should be exhibited	PD25B, para 2.2
	The respondent must file and serve his evidence 7 clear days before the hearing. The applicant must file and serve evidence in reply 3 clear days before the hearing	Rule 25.6(4) Rule 25.6(5)
	Any evidence which has already been filed and served may also be relied upon	Rule 25.6(6)
Instalments	The court may order an interim payment to be paid in instalments. If it does so, the order must set out:	Rule 25.6(7)
	the total amount of the payment;	
	the amount of each instalment;	
	the amount and date for payment of each instalment; and	
	the payee	PD25B, para 3
The court's power to adjust the order	The court has a general power to adjust an interim payment order. The order may be to vary or discharge the payment, or for its repayment in whole or in part	Rule 25.8(1), (2)
	The court may order a defendant to re-imburse, in whole or in part, another defendant who has made an interim payment if:	Rule 25.8(2)(c)
	the latter has made a Pt 20 claim against the former in the proceedings; and	

	if the claim (or part) to which the payment relates is continuing, the pre-conditions set out above are met	Rule 25.8(3)
Social Security (Recovery of Benefits) Act 1997	The respondent must obtain and file a certificate of recoverable benefits in certain circumstances. The order must then set out the gross amount of the interim payment, (which will be the amount for the purposes of any adjustment to be made on final disposal of the claim) and the amount by which the payment will be reduced according to the Act of 1997 and the Social Security (Recovery of Benefits) Regulations 1997. The applicant will receive only the net amount of the interim payment	PD25B, paras 4.1–4.4
No disclosure to trial judge	Unless the defendant agrees, the fact of any interim payment should not be disclosed to the trial judge until liability and quantum have been decided	Rule 25.9
Adjustment on final judgment	The court may make an adjustment order of its own motion when finally disposing of a claim or part of it	Rule 25.8(4)
	Where an interim payment has been made, the final judgment must set out the total amount awarded and the amount(s) and date(s) of the interim payment(s). Judgment should be entered for the amount of the award less any interim payment(s) already paid	PD25B, para 5.2 PD25B, para 5.3
	If the amount of the interim payment(s) exceed(s) the amount of the judgment, the court should then make an adjustment order under rule 25.8(5). The court has power to award interest to the defendant; the power should be exercised	PD25B, para 5.4 Rule 25.8(5) PD25B, para 5.5
Court fees	On application made in existing proceedings (or on undertaking to issue them) *High Court* – on notice – £100 without notice – £50 *County court* – on notice – £60 without notice – £30	CPFO fees 2.6, 2.7

Forms	Form N244 may be used	PD23, para 2.1

24: Disclosure of Documents

Legal background

The court will usually order each party to disclose to the others documents relating to the matters in issue between them.

It may also order disclosure by someone not a party to proceedings.

Note: This Guide is subject to modification in the Commercial Court by reason of the replacement of PD31 in that court by Section E of the Commercial Court Guide, although the provisions of Pt 31 themselves do apply in that court.

Procedure

Definitions	A document is anything in which information of any description is recorded	Rule 31.4
	A copy of a document is anything onto which information recorded in it has been copied by any means, directly or indirectly	Rule 31.4
	Disclosure of a document means stating that it exists	Rule 31.2
Small claims	The procedures described in this Guide do not apply to claims allocated to the small claims track. Instead the court will usually direct the parties to file and serve copies of documents on which a party intends to rely (see Guide 12)	Rule 27.2(1)(b) Rule 31.1(2)
Standard disclosure	Standard disclosure requires a party to disclose:	
	the documents on which he relies. If he fails to disclose these he will be unable to rely on them without the court's permission;	Rule 31.21
	documents which –	
	adversely affect his own case;	
	adversely affect another party's case; or	
	support another party's case; and	
	in claims of particular types, documents specified by practice direction. (None had been so specified when this work went to press.)	Rule 31.6

	If the court orders disclosure without more, standard disclosure is required	Rule 31.5(1)
Limits to standard disclosure	Only documents which are or have been in the party's control need be disclosed. A document is in a party's control if he has physical possession of it, has a right to possession of it or has a right to inspect it or take copies of it	Rule 31.8
	More than one copy of a document need not be disclosed, but a copy is treated as a separate document if it contains a modification, obliteration or other marking or feature on which the party intends to rely or which adversely affects his own or another party's case or supports another party's case	Rule 31.9
Searching for documents	The party must make a reasonable search for documents which he must disclose. Factors affecting what is reasonable include:	Rule 31.7(1)
	the number of documents involved;	
	the nature and complexity of the proceedings;	
	the ease and expense of retrieval of a document; and	
	the significance of any document likely to be located	Rule 31.7(2)
Giving the disclosure	The party makes a list of the documents, identifying them in a convenient order and manner and as concisely as possible, and serves it on the other parties. He must identify documents of which he claims he need not or cannot allow inspection, giving the grounds; and documents no longer in his control, saying what has happened to them	Rule 31.19(3) Rule 31.10(2)–(4)
The disclosure statement	The list must include a 'disclosure statement':	Rule 31.10(5)
	setting out the extent of the search made;	
	certifying that the party understands his duty to disclose;	

	certifying that to the best of his knowledge he has complied with it; and	Rule 31.10(6)
	identifying any category or class of documents (not being documents on which he himself relies) for which he will not search or inspection of which he will not permit on the ground that to do so would be unreasonable or disproportionate to the issues in the case	Rule 31.3(2)(b)
	The form of statement required is set out in the relevant practice direction and in the prescribed form. It must be signed by the party or, if the party is a company or other organisation, an appropriate person whose office or position must be stated. The party's solicitor must try to ensure that the person signing understands the duty of disclosure	PD31, Annex A Rule 31.10(7) PD31, para 4.4
	To make or cause to be made a false statement in a document so verified, without honest belief in its truth, is contempt of court	Rule 31.23
	The parties may agree in writing to dispense with a formal list and/or a disclosure statement	Rule 31.10(8)
Variations from standard disclosure	The court may limit or dispense with standard disclosure; and the parties may agree in writing to limit it or dispense with it	Rule 31.5(2) Rule 31.5(3)
	In the fast track, the court will, if appropriate, direct service of copy documents with a disclosure statement instead of a formal list. There appears to be no reason why it should not do the same in suitable multi-track cases	PD28, para 3.6(4)(b) and Appendix
	The parties may agree in writing or the court may direct that disclosure take place in stages	Rule 31.13
	The court may order disclosure of specified documents or classes of documents including disclosure of documents located as a result of a search which it has ordered	Rule 31.12(2)

Continuing duty to disclose	Any duty of disclosure continues until proceedings are concluded and disclosable documents coming to a party's attention must be disclosed immediately to the other parties	Rule 31.11
The right to inspect	A party to whom a document is disclosed has a right to inspect it unless: it is no longer in the control of the party who disclosed it; the party who disclosed it has a right or a duty to withhold inspection; or to permit inspection would be disproportionate to the issues in the case, as asserted in his disclosure statement by the party giving the disclosure	Rule 31.3
	A party is also entitled to inspect a document mentioned in a statement of case, a witness statement, a witness summary or an affidavit; or one mentioned in an expert's report but this does not extend to one mentioned merely in the expert's statement of the substance of his instructions unless the court is satisfied that there are reasonable grounds to consider that statement inaccurate or incomplete	Rule 31.14 Rule 31.14(e) Rule 35.10(4)
Inspection	The party entitled to inspect a document must give the disclosing party written notice of his wish to inspect it. He may also request a copy of it, undertaking to pay the reasonable copying costs. The disclosing party must permit inspection and/or provide the copy within 7 days of receiving the request	Rule 31.15
Resolving issues – specific disclosure and inspection orders	The court may order a party: to disclose and/or provide inspection of documents or specified classes of documents; to carry out a search to the extent stated in the order; and to disclose and/or provide inspection of any documents located as a result of that search	Rule 31.12

	By applying for one or more of these orders, a party may in effect challenge the disclosing party's position that he has disclosed all documents required by standard disclosure, that the search which he has made for documents is reasonable or that to provide inspection of documents within a category or class would be disproportionate to the issues. Such an order will also be applied for by a party who seeks disclosure which is more extensive than standard disclosure.	
Disputed claim to privilege	Where the disclosing party claims that he has a right or a duty to withhold inspection of a disclosed document, the other party may apply to the court to decide whether the claim should be upheld. Such an application must be supported by evidence. The court may require the document to be produced to the court and may invite any person to make representations	Rule 31.19(5) Rule 31.19(7) Rule 31.19(6)
Withholding disclosure in the public interest	A party may apply, without notice, for permission to withhold disclosure of a document on the ground that it would damage the public interest. Unless the court orders otherwise, if such an order is made that document will not be served nor open to inspection. The application must be supported by evidence. The court may require the document to be produced to the court and may invite any person to make representations	Rule 31.19(1) Rule 31.19(2) Rule 31.19(7) Rule 31.19(6)
Disclosure in existing proceedings by non-party	The court may on application order a person who is not a party but is likely to have in his control documents relevant to an issue arising out of the claim to disclose whether he has such documents in his control and if so to produce them to the applicant's legal, medical or other professional advisers (but not to the applicant personally) The application must be supported by evidence	SCA, s 34 CCA 1984, s 53 (both as amended by The Civil Procedure (Modification of Enactments) Order 1998) Rule 31.17(2)

	The documents sought must be likely to support the case of the applicant or adversely affect that of another party	Rule 31.17(3)(a)
	The disclosure must be necessary in order to dispose fairly of the claim or to save costs	Rule 31.17(3)(b)
	The order will specify the documents or classes of documents to be disclosed and require the respondent to say which (if any) of the specified documents are no longer in his control and in respect of which he claims a right or duty to withhold inspection. It may require him to say what has happened to any no longer in his control and may specify the time and place for disclosure and inspection	Rule 31.17(4) Rule 31.17(5)
Disclosure before proceedings commenced	On the application of a person who is likely to be a party in proceedings, the court may order another person who is likely to be a party and to have or have had in his control documents relevant to an issue arising out of the claim to disclose whether he has such documents in his control and if so to produce them to the applicant's legal, medical or other professional advisers (but not to the applicant personally)	Rule 31.16(3)(b) Rule 31.16(3)(a) SCA, s 33 (as amended) CCA 1984, s 52 (as amended)
	The application is made by application notice (see Guide 18), not by issuing a claim	Rule 25.4
	The application must be supported by evidence	Rule 31.16(2)
	The documents sought must be such as would fall to be disclosed by standard disclosure had the proceedings commenced	Rule 31.16(3)(c)
	The disclosure must be desirable in order to dispose fairly of the anticipated proceedings, to assist the dispute being resolved without proceedings or to save costs	Rule 31.16(3)(d)

	The order will specify the documents or classes of documents to be disclosed and require the respondent to say which (if any) of the specified documents are no longer in his control and in respect of which he claims a right or duty to withhold inspection. It may require him to say what has happened to any no longer in his control and may specify the time and place for disclosure and inspection	Rule 31.16(4) Rule 31.16(5)
	If the court makes the order, it may give directions requiring a claim to be commenced – but need not do so	Rule 25.2(3) Rule 25.2(4)
Court fees	On application made in existing proceedings: *on notice* – in the High Court – £100 in the county court – £60	CPFO fee 2.5
	without notice – in the High Court – £50 in the county court – £30	CPFO fee 2.6
	On application made otherwise: in the High Court – £400 in the county court – £150	CPFO fee 1.4
Forms	List of documents N265 Application Notice N244	

25: Using Expert Evidence

Legal background

A party may wish the court to take account of the opinion of a witness who is expert in a field material to a question in issue in the claim.

Note: This Guide is subject to modification in the Commercial Court and mercantile courts. Those differences are highlighted in the notes to Pt 35, set out in Section 2 of this work.

Procedure

Availability	Expert evidence may not be used at all without the permission of the court	Rules 35.4(1) and 27.5

Obtaining permission	While a party may apply for permission by application notice, the question will be considered by the court in giving case management directions. The forms of allocation questionnaire (see Guide 11) and pre-trial check list (see Guides 13 and 14) enable the party to invite the grant of the permission he seeks	PD27, Appendix A Rule 28.3(1)(c) PD28, paras 3.1–3.13, 7.1–7.3 and Appendix PD29, paras 4.1–4.13, 5.1–5.9 and 9.1–9.3
	The court is required to restrict expert evidence to that which is reasonably required to resolve the proceedings	Rule 35.1
The nature of the permission	*Multi-track and fast track* The permission will relate to a named expert or to a specified field of expertise	Rule 35.4(3)
	The court may limit the amount of the expert's fees and expenses which may be recoverable from another party	Rule 35.4(4)
	The evidence is to be given in a written report unless the court directs otherwise. In the fast track the court will not direct that an expert attend a hearing unless it is *necessary* to do so in the interests of justice	Rule 35.5(1) Rule 35.5(2)
	The court may direct that evidence on an issue be given by a single expert jointly instructed (see below). This will be the court's common approach in the fast track; but in the multi-track it will not do so (unless the parties agree) without fixing a case management conference	Rule 35.7(1) PD28, para 3.9(4) PD29, para 4.13
	Small claims track The sample 'Special Direction' set out in the relevant practice direction provides for evidence by a single expert jointly instructed (see below) . His report will be admissible. It will be a matter for the judge conducting the hearing whether and to what extent the expert's oral evidence will be heard	PD27, Appendix A, Form F Rule 27.8(3) Rule 27.8(1)
Single experts	When the court directs that expert evidence on a particular issue be given by a single expert:	

	each party wishing to submit expert evidence on that issue may give instructions to him;	Rule 35.8(1)
	if the parties cannot agree his identity, the court may select the expert either from a list prepared or identified by the parties or in such other manner as it may direct;	Rule 35.7(3) and PD27, Appendix A, Form F
	the parties' instructions to the expert must be copied to each other;	Rule 35.8(2)
	the court may give directions about any inspection, examination or experiments which the expert wishes to carry out, and about the amount of his fees and expenses and how they are to be paid	Rule 35.8(3)(b) Rule 35.8(3)(a) and (4)
Separate experts	Where parties each instruct an expert:	
	they must disclose his report if they are to rely on his evidence. The common direction will be that the reports be disclosed simultaneously;	Rule 35.13 PD28, para 3.9(5)(a) PD29, para 4.10(5)
	the instructions to the expert will not be confidential in that the substance of them must be set out in the report (see below);	Rule 35.10(3)
	any party may use the report of another's expert as evidence at the trial;	Rule 35.11
	the court may:	
	direct a discussion between experts at any stage requiring them to identify the issues and, if possible, reach agreement on an issue;	Rule 35.12(1)
	specify the issues for discussion;	Rule 35.12(2)
	direct the experts to prepare for the court a statement showing where they agree and where and why they disagree	Rule 35.12(3)
	Such directions will be commonly made	PD28, para 3.9(5)(b) PD29, para 4.10(6)

Questions to experts	The parties may submit written questions to an expert about his report. His reply is treated as part of his report. Unless by agreement or with the court's permission, a party may put questions to an expert once only within 28 days of receiving the report and for the purpose of clarification only	Rule 35.6(1) Rule 35.6(3) Rule 35.6(2)
	Any fee charged by the expert for dealing with a question must be borne initially by the party who instructed them, not (if different) the party asking the question	PD35, para 4.3
	If a separately instructed expert does not answer, the court may order that the party instructing him may not rely on his evidence and/or may not recover his fees and expenses from another party	Rule 35.6(4)
Assistance for the expert	Where a party has access to information which is not reasonably available to another party, the court may order the former to serve on the latter a document recording it	Rule 35.9
	An expert may apply in writing for directions. He need not give notice to the parties. The court, when it gives directions, may direct that its order and the request be served on the parties	Rule 35.14
The expert's duties	The expert's duty is to help the court and this overrides his duty to the party instructing him	Rule 35.3
	His report must be addressed to the court, not to the party, and must:	PD35, para 1.1
	contain a statement that he understands that duty and has complied with it;	Rule 35.10(2)
	state the substance of all material instructions given to him (written and oral), summarising the facts and instructions material to his opinions or on which they are based;	Rule 35.10(3) PD35, para 1.2(8)
	give details of his qualifications;	PD35, para 1.2(1)
	give details of any literature or other material on which he has relied;	PD35, para 1.2(2)

	say who carried out any test or experiment and whether the expert supervised it;	PD35, para 1.2(3)
	give the qualifications of any such person;	PD35, para 1.2(4)
	if there is a range of opinions on the matters in the report, summarise it and give reasons for his own opinion;	PD35, para 1.2(5)
	contain a summary of his conclusions; and	PD35, para 1.2(6)
	be verified by a statement of truth	PD35, para 1.3
	The relevant practice direction sets out the slightly different form of statement of truth for use by an expert	PD35, para 1.4
Instructions to experts not privileged	Although instructions to experts are not privileged from disclosure once the expert's report is disclosed, the court will not order disclosure unless it has reasonable grounds for believing that the statement of the substance of the instructions is inaccurate or incomplete	Rule 35.10(4)

26: Offers to Settle and Payments into Court

Legal background

The rules relating to payments into court and offers to settle are set out in Pts 36 and 37, both of which are supplemented by practice directions. The automatic consequences of a payment into court under Pt 36 (a 'Pt 36 payment') are significantly different from those of an offer made under that Part (a 'Pt 36 offer').

Procedure

When an offer or payment may be made	A Pt 36 payment or offer may be made at any time after the commencement of proceedings and may be made in appeal proceedings	Rule 36.2(4)
	An offer to settle made before commencement of proceedings may be taken into account when making any order as to costs (see below)	Rule 36.10(1)

Money claims	Generally, an offer to settle a money claim will not have the consequences described below ('costs consequences') unless it is made by way of a Pt 36 payment into court	Rule 36.3(1)
	However, where a payment to a claimant following acceptance of a Pt 36 payment would be a recoverable benefit for the purposes of the Social Security (Recovery of Benefits) Act 1997, s 1, if the offeror has applied for but not received a certificate of recoverable benefit when he makes the offer, he must make the payment into court within 7 days of receipt of the certificate	Rule 36.23(2)
Mixed money and non-money claims	A defendant must make a Pt 36 payment in respect of the money claim and a Pt 36 offer in respect of the non-money claim if the offer as a whole is to have costs consequences	Rule 36.4(2)
Defence of tender	A defendant who wishes to rely on the defence of tender before claim must pay into court the amount he says was tendered or the defence will not be available to him. The defendant may treat such a payment (or part of it) as a Pt 36 payment, and if he does so, must file and serve a payment notice	Rule 37.3
Non-disclosure of offer or payment	Save where the defence of tender is raised, or where the fact that there has or has not been a Pt 36 payment may be relevant to the question of costs following a trial of the issue of liability prior to the assessment of quantum, the fact that a Pt 36 payment has been made must not be disclosed to the trial judge until all issues of liability and quantum have been decided	Rule 36.19(3)(a) Rule 36.19(3)(b) Rule 36.19(2)
	A Pt 36 offer is treated as 'without prejudice except as to costs'. The general law thus applies as to the privilege that this status affords	Rule 36.19(1)

General requirements		
Part 36 offer	A Pt 36 offer must be in writing, signed by the offeror or legal representative, and state that:	Rule 36.5(1) PD36, para 5.1(2)
	it is a Pt 36 offer;	PD36, para 5.1(1)
	it relates to the whole of the claim or to one or more specified parts of it or issues arising in it;	Rule 36.5(3)(a)
	(if it be the case) it does not include interest, and if so –	Rule 36.22(1)
	whether interest is offered; and, if so –	
	the amount and the rate(s) and period(s) for which it is offered;	Rule 36.22(2)
	if made 21 days or more before the start of the trial, it remains open for a period of 21 days from the date it is made; and that after that the offeree may only accept it if the parties agree liability for costs or the court gives permission;	Rule 36.5(6)(a) Rule 36.5(6)(b)
	if made less than 21 days before the start of the trial, the offeree may only accept it if the parties agree liability for costs or the court gives permission	Rule 36.5(7)
	The offer may accept a specified proportion of liability	Rule 36.5(4)
	Unless interest is specifically excluded, an offer will be taken to include interest up to the last date on which it could be accepted without needing the permission of the court	Rule 36.22(1)
	The offer must state whether it takes into account any counterclaim and may be made by reference to an interim payment	Rule 36.5(3)(b) Rule 36.5(5)
Part 36 payment	A Pt 36 payment notice must be filed in court. The above provisions apply *mutatis mutandis* to what the notice must contain	Rule 36.6(2)
	Additionally, the notice must state:	
	where the claim is for money and non-money remedies –	
	that a Pt 36 offer has been made in respect of the non-money claim(s) and identify the document; and	

	that acceptance of the Pt 36 payment will be treated as acceptance of the Pt 36 offer;	Rule 36.4(3)
	whether any interim payment that may have been made has been taken into account;	Rule 36.6(2)(d)
	where the claim includes a claim for provisional damages, whether the defendant is offering to agree the making of an award of provisional damages and if so –	Rule 36.7(2)
	that the sum is paid into court on the assumption that the claimant will not develop the disease or suffer the deterioration specified in the notice; and	Rule 36.7(3)(a)
	that the offer is conditional on the claimant making any claim for further damages within the period specified in the notice;	Rule 36.7(3)(b)
	where the Social Security (Recovery of Benefits) Act 1997, s 1 would apply to the payment if accepted –	
	the gross amount of compensation;	
	the name and amount of any benefit by which it is reduced; and	
	that the sum paid in is the net amount after such deduction	Rule 36.23(3)
	Money may be paid into court in a foreign currency where the claim is in that currency, or by court order made on application. The practice direction contains further provisions	PD36, paras 9.1–9.4
Offers made before commencement of proceedings	An offer to settle made before the start of proceedings will be taken into account by the court when making an order for costs if the offer:	Rule 36.10(1)
	is expressed to be open for at least 21 days after the date it is made (see below under 'Time . . . .');	
	if made by the potential defendant, includes an offer to pay the costs of the offeree for the period up to 21 days after it is made; and	
	Otherwise complies with Pt 36	Rule 36.10(2)

	Additionally, if the claim is a money claim, the offeror must make a Pt 36 payment in a sum not less than the offer within 14 days of service of the claim form	Rule 36.10(3)
How the payment in is made	The defendant must file: the Pt 36 payment notice and copy for service if required; the payment (usually a cheque payable to 'Her Majesty's Paymaster General' or, in the Royal Courts of Justice, to 'the Accountant-General of the Supreme Court'); for the Royal Courts of Justice, form CFO 100 with the Court Funds Office	PD36, para 4.1
	All or part of money paid into court by a defendant following an order under r 3.1(3) or r 3.1(5) may be treated by him as a Pt 36 payment, in which case he must file a Pt 36 payment notice	Rule 37.2
Service of notice of Pt 36 payment	The court will serve the notice unless the offeror informs the court when making the payment in, that he will serve it. A certificate of service is required if the offeror serves it	Rule 36.6(3) Rule 36.6(4)
Variation of Pt 36 payment	A Pt 36 payment may not be reduced or withdrawn without the court's permission. Reasons will be required	PD36, para 3.4 PD36, para 3.5
	A notice of increased payment must be filed and served. It will be good practice to state in the notice that the increased payment is made on the same terms as the original notice of payment, or to set out any differences	Rule 36.8(4)
Clarification of a Pt 36 payment or offer	The offeree may apply for clarification of a Pt 36 payment or offer within 7 days of its being made. If the offeror does not comply, the offeree may apply to the court for a clarification order unless the trial has started	Rule 36.9(1) Rule 36.9(2)
	A clarification order must specify the date when the Pt 36 payment or offer is deemed to be made	Rule 36.9(3)

Time of offer and acceptance	A Pt 36 offer, or any variation, is effective when received by the offeree	Rule 36.8(1) and (3)
	A Pt 36 payment, or any increase, is effective when notice of the payment or increased payment is received by the offeree	Rule 36.8(2) and (4)
	Acceptance of a Pt 36 payment or offer is effective when notice of acceptance is received by the offeror	Rule 36.8(5)
Acceptance of offer or payment	The court's permission to accept a Pt 36 payment or offer will always be required where a claim is compromised on behalf of a child or patient (see Guide 17)	Rule 21.10
	Subject to that, where there is one defendant to the claim, a Pt 36 payment or offer may be accepted before the commencement of the trial without the court's permission where:	Rules 36.11(1) and 36.12(1)
	it is made not less than 21 days before trial and accepted not later than 21 days after it was made;	Rule 36.11(2)
	it is made less than 21 days before the trial or not accepted within 21 days provided that the parties agree the liability for costs	Rule 36.12(2)
	In a claim with two or more defendants who are sued jointly or in the alternative, permission will be required unless the above conditions are satisfied and the claimant discontinues his claim against the other defendant(s) who must also give their written consent to the acceptance of the Pt 36 payment or offer	Rule 36.17(2)
	(See Guide 27 as to discontinuance and its consequences, particularly as to costs.)	
	The claimant may continue against other defendants whom the claimant alleges have several liability	Rule 36.17(3)

	A notice of acceptance must be filed in court and served on the offeror. The notice must be properly headed, identify the Pt 36 payment or offer to which it relates and be signed by the offeree or his legal representative. Presumably the consent(s) of other defendants, where necessary, should also be filed and referred to in the notice and copies served	PD36, paras 7.6 and 7.7
	Where the offer relates to part of the claim, the notice of acceptance may accept the offer and abandon the remainder of the claim	Rule 36.13(2)
	Otherwise application for permission must be made, to the trial judge if the trial has started, otherwise by application notice under Pt 23	Rules 36.11(2) and 36.12(2)
	The court will make an order for costs if it gives permission	Rules 36.11(3) and 36.12(3)
Costs consequences	*Acceptance before or during trial* Where:	
	a Pt 36 payment or offer is accepted without the need for the court's permission; and,	Rule 36.13(1)
	if appropriate, the balance of the claim is abandoned and the court does not order otherwise;	Rule 36.13(2)
	the claimant will be entitled to his costs of the proceedings up to the date of service of the notice of acceptance.	
	Such costs will include any costs attributable to the defendant's counterclaim if the Pt 36 payment or offer states that it takes into account the counterclaim	Rule 36.13(3)
	Costs will be payable on the standard basis (see Guide 32) if not agreed	Rule 36.13(4)
	After a trial Where at trial a claimant fails to obtain more than a defendant's Pt 36 payment or a more advantageous judgment than a Pt 36 offer, the claimant will be ordered to pay the defendant's costs incurred after the latest date for acceptance of the Pt 36 payment or offer, unless the court considers this to be unjust	Rule 36.20

	Where at trial a claimant obtains more than a Pt 36 payment or a more advantageous judgment, the court will, unless it considers it unjust to do so, order interest, on the amount of the judgment (excluding interest) and costs, to be paid at no more than 10% above the Bank of England base rate, and that costs be payable on the indemnity basis, in each case for some or all of the period following the latest date on which the claimant could have accepted the Pt 36 payment or offer	Rule 36.21(1)–(4)
	In considering whether it would be unjust to make any of those orders, the court will take into account all the circumstances of the case including the terms of any Pt 36 offer, the stage in the proceedings and the information available to the parties when the offer or payment was made and the conduct of the parties in making or not making available information for the purpose of evaluating the offer	Rule 36.21(5)
	Where the payment to a claimant includes a recoverable benefit for the purposes of the Social Security (Recovery of Benefits) Act 1997, the court will take into account the gross figure in the Pt 36 payment notice when considering whether the claimant has bettered or obtained a more advantageous judgment than the Pt 36 payment or offer	PD36, para 10.5
Other consequences of acceptance	Acceptance by a claimant of a Pt 36 payment which: relates to a mixed money and non-money claim; and is accompanied by an offer to settle the non-money part of the claim; will be deemed to be acceptance of both the offer and the payment. The converse is also the case	Rule 36.4 PD36, para 7.11

	Where the Pt 36 payment or offer relates to the whole or part of a claim, the claim (or the relevant part) is stayed (upon the terms of the offer where applicable) and may be enforced without the need for a new claim	Rule 36.15(1)–(3)
	Alternatively, a party may treat the failure to comply with the terms of an accepted offer as a breach of contract, and pursue a contractual remedy within the same proceedings	Rule 36.15(6)
	In the case of an acceptance relating to part of a claim (the remainder not being abandoned), the claim will be stayed as to that part and the court will decide the liability as to costs unless the parties agree	Rule 36.15(3)
	Where approval of the settlement is required, any such stay will only take effect after obtaining that approval	Rule 36.15(4)
	The stay does not prevent the court from enforcing the terms of a Pt 36 offer, dealing with costs or ordering payment out	Rule 36.15(5)
Provisional damages	A claimant who accepts a Pt 36 payment in a claim which includes a claim for provisional damages must within 7 days apply to the court for an award of provisional damages. Money in court may not be paid out until the application is disposed of	Rule 36.7(5) Rule 36.7(6)
Payment out	An order for payment out is required where the court has to approve the terms of settlement or give permission to accept the Pt 36 payment or offer, or where the defendant has made the payment so that he may rely on the defence of tender. Otherwise, the claimant may obtain payment out by filing the relevant practice form setting out the details referred to in the practice direction. Payment must be made to a legal representative where the claimant has one. The court will wish to make the payment by transfer to a bank account wherever possible	Rule 36.18 Rule 36.16 PD36, paras 8.2–8.5

	Where permission is granted after the trial has started, the court must at the same time deal with the whole of the costs of the proceedings	Rule 36.18(2)(b)
	Where the payment to a claimant following acceptance of a Pt 36 payment includes a recoverable benefit for the purposes of the Social Security (Recovery of Benefits) Act 1997, the claimant will receive the moneys in court which will be net of the recoverable benefits	PD36, para 10.4
Interest	Unless the parties agree otherwise, when making an order for payment out, the court will order that interest accruing up to the date of acceptance will be paid to the offeror, and interest accruing thereafter will be paid to the offeree	PD36, para 7.10
	The Court Funds Office Rules 1987 make provision for the investment of money paid into court as a Pt 36 payment which is not accepted, or under a court order.	
Fatal Accidents Act 1976 and Law Reform (Miscellaneous Provisions) Act 1934	Where a single sum of money is agreed or ordered to be paid in a claim under these Acts, the court must apportion it between the different claims either when it gives directions on an application for approval of a settlement for a child or patient, or when it gives permission for the money to be paid out of court, unless apportionment has already been ordered or agreed	Rule 37.4
Forms	Part 36 payment notice N242A	

27: Discontinuance

Legal background

Discontinuance of a claim, or part of it, is dealt with in Pt 38. It should be distinguished from abandonment of a remedy or remedies, when the claim continues for another remedy, which is considered an amendment to which Pt 17 applies (see Guide 19).

Procedure

The right to discontinue	A claim (or part thereof) may be discontinued at any time, but the court's permission is required if:	Rule 38.2(1)
	the court has granted an interim injunction; or	
	any party has given an undertaking to the court;	Rule 38.2(2)(a)
	(It is assumed that the injunction or the undertaking must be extant.)	
	an interim payment has been made and the defendant who made it does not consent;	Rule 38.2(2)(b)
	there is more than one claimant, and all the other claimants do not consent	Rule 38.2(2)(c)
	A claim may be discontinued against all or any of multiple defendants	Rule 38.2(3)
Procedure	Discontinuance may be effected by filing in court a notice of discontinuance which must:	
	be served on all parties;	
	state that it has been so served;	
	have attached to it any necessary consents; and	
	where appropriate, specify the defendant against whom the claim (or part thereof) is discontinued	Rule 38.3
	Where a party wishes to discontinue, but escape the normal consequences as to costs (see below), he should apply on notice (see Guide 18)	Rule 38.6(1)
Effective date of discontinuance	Discontinuance takes effect against a defendant on the day notice is served, but a defendant may apply within 28 days of service to have the notice set aside	Rule 38.5(1) Rule 38.4
Consequences for costs	Unless the court orders otherwise or the claim has been allocated to the small claims track:	Rule 38.6(3)
	a claimant who discontinues will be liable to pay the costs of the defendant against whom he has discontinued in respect of the claim (or the part discontinued) up to and including the date of service of the notice; and	

	those costs may not be assessed until the conclusion of the rest of the proceedings	Rule 38.6
	Costs will be assessable on the standard basis, and statutory interest on costs will run from the date of service of the notice, as does the time for starting detailed assessment proceedings (see Guide 24)	Rule 44.12(1)(d) Rule 44.12(2) Rule 47.7
	Where proceedings are partly discontinued and the claimant has agreed or been ordered to pay costs as a result, the court may stay the remainder of the proceedings if the costs are not paid for more than 14 days after the date agreed or ordered until those costs are paid	Rule 38.8
Subsequent proceedings	A claimant who discontinues a claim against a defendant who has filed a defence may not make another claim arising out of substantially the same facts without the court's permission	Rule 38.7
Defendant may require discontinuance	A defendant to a claim that has been issued but not served on him may serve a notice on the claimant requiring him to serve the claim form or discontinue the claim within not less than 14 days after service of the notice. If the claimant fails to comply with the notice, the court may, on the application of the defendant dismiss the claim or make any other order it thinks just	Rule 7.7
Court fees	On filing notice – no fee.	
Forms	Notice of discontinuance N279	

28: Telephone Hearing Procedure

Legal background

Rule 3.1(2)(d) provides that the court may hold a hearing and hear evidence by telephone or by using any other method of direct oral communication. This is supplemented by PD23, paras 6.1–6.5 which explain how applications may be dealt with in this way, and para 7 which deals with video conferencing. There is no further guidance at present but practices are developing in the courts and this Guide is based upon a survey of the approach being adopted by district judges.

Procedure

General		
What is a telephone hearing	A hearing where the judge communicates by telephone with – the representative of a party; or a party; or a witness.	
Authority	The court may hold a hearing and hear evidence by telephone or by using any other method of direct oral communication	Rule 3.1(2)(d)
Types	There are two types of telephone hearing – (1) all parties communicate with the judge by telephone in a conference call; (2) at least one party is present and one or more parties communicate by telephone (either directly or via a conference call).	
Conference calls	These are arranged by the British Telecom conference call 'call out' system or some other comparable system. Legal Connect is another regular provider and may be contacted on 0800 953 0405. For BT telephone the BT Legal Call Centre on 0800 028 4194 and book the time and date of the hearing.	
Availability	It is for the judge to decide whether to conduct a hearing (in whole or part) by telephone. Any party may request the judge to do so but there is no right to a telephone hearing and the court has a complete discretion	Rule 3.1(2)(d) PD23, para 6.1
Equipment	No special equipment is required but it is of assistance to use a 'hands-free' telephone which makes use of both a loudspeaker and a microphone (a 'speakerphone') instead of the traditional handset –	

	if the use of a 'speakerphone' by any party causes the judge or any other party any difficulty in hearing what is said, the judge may require that party to use a hand-held telephone;	PD23, para 6.5(8)
	where more than one person will be present a 'conference telephone' enables everyone present to hear and be heard whilst remaining seated.	
Uses	The telephone hearing is particularly valuable for case management conferences as it saves time and expense on travel and enables the judge to communicate personally with the fee earners who have conduct of the case	Survey PD23, para 6.1
	Evidence may be taken in appropriate cases by telephone where a witness is abroad or disabled and unable to attend the hearing.	
Injunctions	These applications are normally dealt with at a court hearing but cases of extreme urgency may be dealt with by telephone –	PD25, para 4.2
	the procedure and telephone numbers are set out in the practice directions;	PD25, para 4.5
	injunction applications will be heard by telephone only where the applicant is acting by counsel or solicitors	PD25, para 4.5(5)
Video conferencing	If desired and if facilities are available, application should be made to the master or district judge	PD23, para 7
Applications – including case management conferences		
Authority	The court may order an application or part of an application to be dealt with by a telephone hearing	Rule 3.1(2)(d) PD23, para 6.1
	Some judges indicate when allocating to multi-track that a case is suitable for a telephone case management conference	Survey

Pre-conditions	A telephone hearing will not normally be ordered unless every party entitled to be given notice of the application and heard has consented	PD23, para 6.2
	The agreement of an absent party is required if the representative of another party will be present	PD23, para 6.4
Requests	Applicants should make the request on the application notice	Form N244
	Respondents should ask the court and the other side as soon as possible.	
	Requests may be made by letter or telephone at any time up to the hearing and will then be referred to a district judge (if possible the one who is to deal with the hearing) who decides whether to accede and gives any necessary direction	Survey
Timing	Many district judges only take conference calls at 10.00 am or 2.00 pm because of the difficulty in fitting them into a busy list (it is possible to put back the start of the call).	
	Experience indicates that a longer time estimate may be needed than for a hearing attended by all parties. Case management conferences may need 45 minutes	Survey
Documentation	The parties should in advance file (ideally in an agreed and paginated bundle) –	
	a summary of issues;	
	all documents to be referred to; draft orders or suggested directions	PD23, para 12.1 PD29, para 5.6
	A fax number for the court should be identified so that documents can be transmitted during the hearing	Survey
Listing procedure	To assist judges, and to provide a pre-reading opportunity, the court should highlight any telephone hearing on the daily listings sheet	Survey

Note of proceedings	The judge should keep, either by way of a note or a tape recording, brief details of the proceedings, including the date and a short statement of the decision taken	PD23, para 8
	When a BT conference call has been used a recording of the hearing will be available from BT.	
Litigants in person	Where a party entitled to be heard acts in person, an order will not be made for a telephone hearing unless he will be accompanied by a 'responsible person' who will identify him to the court.	
	The telephone hearing will not be allowed to proceed unless the litigant in person is so accompanied and identified	PD23, para 6.3(1)
	The 'responsible person' may be a barrister, solicitor, legal executive, doctor, clergyman, police officer, prison officer or other person of comparable status	PD23, para 6.3(2)
Arranging the call	It is the responsibility of the applicant to make the necessary arrangements with British Telecom or other comparable service provider	PD23, para 6.5(1)
	For case management conferences the claimant should arrange the call unless the parties agree otherwise.	
	Other than in small courts the judge should be identified and named	Survey
Procedure for telephone hearings (more than one party by telephone)	Unless any other direction is given the applicant's legal representative must – (1) arrange the telephone conference for the time fixed (the call may be 2 or 3 minutes before the time fixed for the application);	
	(2) ascertain whether other parties have instructed counsel and, if so, their identity and whether on a different telephone number;	
	(3) tell the operator the numbers of all participants and the sequence in which to be called, namely:	

	(a) himself and (if on a different number) his counsel; (b) the legal representative (and counsel) for all other parties; and (c) the judge; (4) arrange for the conference to be recorded by the telecommunications provider and the tape sent to the court; (5) (when the judge has been connected) introduce the parties in the usual way – each speaker should remain on the line after being called by the operator setting up the conference call.	PD23, para 6.5
Procedure for BT conference calls	The applicant's legal representative telephones the BT Legal Call Centre and books the time and date of the hearing. There are a number of other service providers and court users are free to choose any of them provided that the requirements set out in the practice direction are met	PD23, para 6.5
	The solicitor confirms to the court that the necessary arrangements have been made. At the appointed time, the BT Legal Call co-ordinator will telephone the solicitors and other participants to the case first, and then the judge. The co-ordinator will start the tape recorder and connect the judge to the other participants. (BT records the case both digitally and on tape cassette to ensure that proceedings are captured). BT sends the tape cassette to the court labelled with the court case reference number, the date of the hearing and the name of the judge.	Guidance from BT
Procedure for hearings (only one party by telephone)	The judge may communicate with one absent party by telephone when the other party (or parties) are present but not all are prepared to do so. The procedure is –	Survey
	the time for the hearing is fixed in the usual way;	

	the absent party telephones the judge at the appointed time (or the judge telephones this party when ready – and if desired arranges to be called back); the judge takes the call in the presence of the other parties and conducts the hearing in the usual way	Survey
	(Note: this will involve the judge in acting as go-between unless a speaker telephone is available, and even then the absent party may not hear the other parties present unless a conference telephone is used.) Where one party travels a distance to a hearing and the other party does not attend (perhaps in error) the judge may be invited to telephone the absent party in case the hearing may continue by telephone – thereby avoiding an abortive journey and a wasted costs order	Survey
Cost	The type of BT conference call stipulated by the practice direction costs 48p per telephone line per minute plus £10 for the taping	Survey
Costs	The telephone charges debited to the account of the party initiating the conference call will be treated as part of the costs of the application	PD23, para 6.5(9)
Court fee	No additional fee is prescribed.	

28A: E-Mail Procedure (Filing and Applications)

Legal background

The Woolf Reforms contemplated increased use of information technology in the civil courts and two initiatives are now authorised by a practice direction – PD5B – supplementing r 5.5.

1) In February 2001, PREMA (Preston E-Mail Applications) was launched at Preston County Court and District Registry as a pilot scheme in the use of e-mail for applications to district judges by solicitors in the course of proceedings. A protocol was produced that set out the procedures to be adopted. This is now replaced by guidance on the Court Service website. For further information (and to download the PREMA user guide and a simple PowerPoint presentation) access: *www.courtservice.gov.uk/using_courts/court_info/preston/prema.htm.* Enquiry may be made by telephone on 01772 832331 or by e-mail to: enquiries@preston.countycourt.gsi.gov.uk

2) In December 2002, a further pilot scheme at Walsall County Court permitted communication with the court and the filing of documents by e-mail. This has been extended to other specified courts pursuant to the new PD5B.

Practitioners who wish to use these e-mail facilities should obtain guidance and updated information as to the courts offering the service from the Court Service website *www.courtservice.gov.uk*.

Procedure for filing documents – PD5B

General		
Which courts?	Basildon, Coventry, Leicester, Preston and Walsall County Courts and the Commercial Court. For an up to date list refer to the website *www.courtservice.gov.uk/using_courts/email_guidance/courts.htm*	PD5B, para 2.1
What may be filed?	(1) General correspondence and enquiries; and (2) specified documents, in proceedings to which the CPR apply	PD5B, para 1.1
What documents?	Refer to the website for an up-to-date list. At the time of printing these are: – Pre-trial check list (listing questionnaire), provided that no fee is payable by the party filing the check list (N170); – Allocation questionnaire, provided that no fee is payable by the party filing the questionnaire (N150); – Particulars of claim (after filing of claim form); – Notice by solicitor of acting (N434); – List of documents (N265); – Certificate of service (N215); – Notice of change of address; – Request for judgment in default under r 12.4(1), or for judgment upon admission under rr 14.4(3), 14.5(6), 14.6(4) or 14.7(5) (N225); – Acknowledgment of service (N9); – Claimant's response to notice of admission under rr 14.5(3) or 14.7(3); (N225A); – Admission, other than one under r 14.4 (N9C);	PD5B, para 2.1(2)

– Claimant's response to notice under r 15.10, where defence is that money claimed has been paid (N236);

– Defence, provided that no counterclaim is made (N9B);

– Notice of discontinuance, provided that the claimant does not require permission to discontinue, and is not required to attach to the notice the consent of another party (N279);

– Reply to defence;

– Notice of change of solicitor (N434);

– Re-issue/amend process, no hearing (provided that no fee is payable) (N446);

– Re-issue/amend process, hearing (provided that no fee is payable) (N446);

– Admission of liability (unspecified amount) (N226);

– Notice of admission (ROG) (N228);

– Amended defence;

– Part admission not accepted (N225A);

– Intention to proceed with states paid defence;

– Statement of witness (provided the document is no more than 10 pages and the total size of the e-mail does not exceed 2Mb as set out in PD5B, para 3.5);

– Claimant/defendant list of documents (provided documents comply with PD5B, para 3.5) (N265);

– Experts' reports;

– Skeleton arguments/case summaries;

– Draft judgments & editorial suggestions for them;

– Request for interlocutory judgment (provided that no fee is payable) (N227);

– Notice of acceptance and request for payment (N243A);

– Application to claimant to vary judgment (N294);

– Request for certificate of judgment (N293A);

	– Any other document which the court has specifically directed to be filed by e-mail	
Excluded steps	Any step in a claim which requires a fee to be paid. Any document included or attached will not be treated as filed	PD5B, paras 3.2, 3.3
Excluded proceedings	The practice direction does not apply to insolvency, adoption or family proceedings	PD5B, para 1.4
Service	Any rule or practice direction requiring the document to be served on any other person must still be complied with A further practice direction deals with service of a document by e-mail	PD6, paras 3.1–3.4
Security	Correspondence or documents of a confidential or sensitive nature should not be send by e-mail as security cannot be guaranteed	PD5B, para 8.7
Urgent messages	The sender should contact the court by telephone to ensure that the message is dealt with without delay	PD5B, para 8.8
E-mail requirements		
General	A short e-mail message will generally be sent with documents as attachments.	
Reply	The court will normally send any reply to messages by e-mail	PD5B, para 8.6
E-mail Format	Rich text or plain text rather than HTML	PD5B, para 4.1
Attachment format	Generally one of the following – (a) Rich Text (.rtf); (b) Plain/Formatted Text (.txt); (c) Hypertext documents (.htm); (d) Microsoft Word viewer/reader (.doc) in Word97 format; (e) Adobe Acrobat (.pdf) minimum viewer version 4; (f) Lotus Notes Web Access (.nsf)	PD5B, para 4.5 Refer to the website
E-mail content	The message must contain the name, telephone number and e-mail address of the sender Correspondence and documents may be sent either as text or attachments	PD5B, para 4.1 PD5B, para 4.2

	Where proceedings have been commenced, the subject line must contain: (1) the case number (2) the parties names (which may be abbreviated) (3) the date and time of any hearing	PD5B, para 4.8
Practice forms	Documents required to be in a practice form must be sent in that form as attachments. Court forms may be downloaded from the Court Service website *www.courtservice.gov.uk* or from local court websites	PD5B, paras 4.3, 4.4
E-mail size	Attachments must not be more than 10 pages long in aggregate and the total e-mail must not exceed 2Mb	PD5B, para 4.7 Refer to the website
Document filing		
General	A hard copy should not be filed in addition (whether by delivery, post or fax)	PD5B, para 8.1
Timing	The time of receipt is recorded A document is not filed until the e-mail is received by the court, whatever time it is shown to have been sent An e-mail received after 4 pm is treated as filed on the next day the court office is open	PD5B, para 8.3 PD5B, para 8.2 PD5B, para 8.4
Responsibility	Where a time limit applies, it remains the responsibility of the party to ensure that the document is filed in time	PD5B, para 8.5
Online Forms Service	The website contains certain documents which a user may complete online and then submit electronically to a specified court.	PD5B, paras 5.1–6.3
Statement of truth		
Requirement	Certain documents must be verified by a statement of truth	Rule 22.1(6)
E-mail procedure	This requirement is satisfied by the party filing a document retaining the document containing the original signature and either – (a) typing the name of the person signing the statement of truth underneath the statement;	

	(b) applying a facsimile of the signature to that document; or (c) filing a scanned version of the document containing the signature	PD5B, para 9
Service copies	The statement of truth must still be signed in manuscript in any hard copies of the document which are served on other parties	

29: Judgment in Default

Legal background

If the defendant is required to file a defence and fails to do so within the time permitted, the claimant can ask the court to enter judgment against him. The procedure and the availability of judgment by this means vary according to the remedy sought in the claim, the identity of the defendant, where he was served and whether or not he acknowledged service.

Provision is made for such judgments to be set aside in certain circumstances.

Procedure

Non-availability	Default judgment is not available:	
	if the defendant has filed a defence to the claim or any part of it (including any document purporting to be a defence);	Rule 12.3(1)(a) and 12.3(2)(a) PD12, para 1.1
	if the time for the defendant to file a defence has not expired (see Guide 7);	Rule 12.3(1)(b) and 12.3(2)(b)
	on a claim brought under the Pt 8 procedure (see Guide 2);	Rule 12.2(b)
	on a claim between defendants for contribution or indemnity (See Guide 9);	Rule 20.3(3)(a)
	on a claim for delivery of goods subject to an agreement regulated by CCA 1974 (see Guide 2);	Rule 12.2(a)
	on a claim for delivery of goods by one of several persons having an interest in them unless the claim is based on a right to possession or the claimant has the written authority of the other persons interested;	Rule 40.14 Rule 12.5(5)
	if the defendant has applied for summary judgment (see Guide 30) and the application has not been disposed of;	Rule 12.3(3)(a)

	if the defendant has satisfied the claim (including costs);	Rule 12.3(3)(b)
	if the claim form was served by the claimant and he has not filed a certificate of service;	Rule 6.14(2)(b)
	on a claim for money only, if the defendant has filed or served an admission of the claim (see Guide 6);	Rule 12.3(3)(c) Rule 14.4 and 14.7
	any claim in the High Court under a mortgage or any claim in the county court for money secured by a mortgage, unless, in either case, permission is first obtained;	PD12, para 1.2(3)
	on any claim in specialist proceedings (admiralty proceedings, arbitration proceedings, commercial actions, Patents Court business and the like, Technology and Construction Court Business and Companies Act 1985 proceedings), save as provided by practice directions to be made under Pt 49;	PD12, para 1.2(4)
	where any party has specified that a 'devolution issue' (as defined in Government of Wales Act 1998, Sch 8, para 1, or Northern Ireland Act 1998, Sch 10, para 1 or Scotland Act 1998, Sch 6, para 1) arises	PDDev, para 16.5
Part 20 claims	Special provisions apply to a claim under Pt 20 (other than a counterclaim) and are described in Guide 10. Default judgment is not available on a contribution notice (see Guide 9)	Rule 20.11 Rule 20.3(3)
Other provisions	Where default judgment is not available, a party may nevertheless be able to seek judgment:	
	by applying to strike out the statement of case if it discloses no grounds for bringing or defending the claim or is an abuse of the court's process or is otherwise likely to obstruct the just disposal of the proceedings or if the party has failed to comply with a rule, practice direction or order;	Rule 3.4
	by applying for or requesting judgment on the basis of an admission made by the defendant (see Guide 6); or	Part 14

	by applying for summary judgment on the ground that the party has no real prospect of defending or pursuing the claim successfully (see Guide 30)	Part 24
'In default of acknowledgment of service'	This expression is used where the defendant who has failed to file a defence has not filed an acknowledgment of service either	Rule 12.3(1)
Default judgment by request		
Request for default judgment	The more common method of obtaining a default judgment is by filing a request in the prescribed form, whereupon the judgment is entered administratively by the court staff. The procedure is only available where the claim is for: money only; the return of goods where the defendant has the alternative of paying their value; or both	Rule 12.4(1)
	It is not available in every such case, however. See below for exceptions. Where the claim includes a claim for some other remedy, the claimant may still request default judgment if he abandons that claim in his request for judgment	Rule 12.4(3)
Nature of judgment entered on request	*Claim for specified sum of money* Judgment will be for the amount of the claim, less any payments made, together with fixed costs; payable by the date specified in the request or by instalments at the times and rate specified in the request; or if neither is specified then immediately	Rule 12.5(1), (2)
	The judgment will include interest to the date of judgment if: the particulars of claim include a claim for interest in the correct form (see Guide 1); and where the claim is made under CCA 1984, s 69, or SCA, s 35A, the rate is no higher than that payable on judgment debts current at the date of issue of the claim; and	

	the request for judgment includes a calculation of the interest claimed from the date to which it was stated to be calculated in the claim form to the date of the request for judgment	Rule 12.6(1)
	Otherwise, if interest is requested, the judgment will be for an amount of interest to be decided by the court, and the court will give directions	Rule 12.6(2) Rule 12.7
	Claim for unspecified amount of money	
	Judgment will be for an amount to be decided by the court, and the court will give directions	Rule 12.5(3) Rule 12.7
	Claim for delivery of goods	
	The judgment will require the defendant to deliver the goods or, if he does not, to pay their value as decided by the court; and to pay costs. The court will give directions with a view to determining the value	Rule 12.5(4) Rule 12.7
Several defendants	The claimant may request judgment against one or more of several defendants and proceed with his claim against the other(s). However, if the judgment is for the delivery of goods, it will not be enforceable without permission until judgment has been obtained against all the defendants	Rule 12.8(1) Rule 12.8(3)
Judgment for costs only	Judgment may be requested for fixed costs only	Rule 12.9(1)(a)
Default judgment on application		
When application required	Default judgment may not be obtained by request but must be applied for by application notice (see Guide 18) in the following cases:	
	wherever the claim is not solely for money or for delivery of goods, the defendant having the alternative of paying the value; or judgment is sought for costs only, not being fixed costs;	Rule 12.4(2)(a) Rule 12.9(1)(b)
	where the defendant is a child or patient;	Rule 12.10(a)(i)
	where one spouse claims in tort against the other;	Rule 12.10(a)(ii)

	where the defendant is the Crown;	Rule 12.10(a)(iii)
	where the defendant was served outside England and Wales without the court's permission (see Guide 16) and he has not filed an acknowledgment of service;	Rule 12.10(b)(i)
	where the defendant (wherever served) is domiciled in Scotland or Northern Ireland or one of the European countries listed in Guide 16 and he has not filed an acknowledgment of service;	Rule 12.10(b)(ii)
	where the defendant is a State and has not filed an acknowledgment of service;	Rule 12.10(b)(iii)
	where the defendant is a diplomatic agent enjoying immunity under the Diplomatic Privileges Act 1964 and he has not filed an acknowledgment of service; and	Rule 12.10(b)(iv)
	where the defendant is a person or organisation enjoying immunity under the International Organisations Acts 1968 and 1981 and he has not filed an acknowledgment of service	Rule 12.10(b)(v)
Evidence etc	Where the defendant is a child or patient, evidence must be filed to show that the claimant is entitled to the judgment claimed, and a litigation friend for the defendant must have been appointed	Rule 12.11(3) PD12, para 4.2(2) Rule 21.2
	Where one spouse claims in tort against the other, evidence must be filed to support the application	Rule 12.11(3)
	Where either: the defendant was served outside England and Wales without the court's permission and has not filed an acknowledgment of service; or	
	where the defendant (wherever served) is domiciled in Scotland or Northern Ireland or one of the European countries listed in Guide 16 and he has not filed an acknowledgment of service,	

	evidence by affidavit must be filed to show that the case is one which the court would have power to hear, that no other court has exclusive jurisdiction and that the claim has been properly served	PD12, para 4.3 and 4.5
	Where the defendant is a State, evidence by affidavit must be filed to show the grounds of the application, prove that the State is excepted from the immunity conferred by the State Immunity Act 1978, show that the claim was properly served and (if appropriate) show that the extended period for acknowledging service provided by that Act has expired	PD12, para 4.4 and para 4.5
	Where the claim is for the delivery of goods, the defendant not having the alternative of paying the value, evidence must be filed to identify the goods and say where they are and to explain why their specific delivery up is sought	PD12, para 4.6
	In any other case, evidence may be required and may (if desired) be set out in the application notice. See Guide 18	PD23, para 9.1 PD23, para 9.7
Service	Where either: the defendant was served outside England and Wales without the court's permission and has not filed an acknowledgment of service; or where the defendant (wherever served) is domiciled in Scotland or Northern Ireland or one of the European countries listed in Guide 16 and he has not filed an acknowledgment of service, the application notice need not be served unless some other rule so requires in the particular circumstances of the case	Rule 12.11(4)
	Where the defendant is a State and has not filed an acknowledgment of service, the application notice need not be served unless the court so directs, in which case special provisions as to service apply	Rule 12.11(5)

	The application notice must be served in all other cases unless the court orders otherwise	PD12, para 5.1 Rule 23.4
	Where the application notice is to be served, a copy of the evidence in support must be served with it, except where the defendant has failed to acknowledge service	Rule 23.7(3)(a) Rule 12.11(2)
Nature of judgment given on application	Such judgment as it appears to the court that the claimant is entitled to on his statement of case	Rule 12.11(1)
Several defendants	If the claim against the defendant against whom judgment is sought can be dealt with separately from the claims against the other defendants, the court may enter default judgment against him and the claimant may proceed against the other defendants	Rule 12.8(2)(a)
	Otherwise the court will not enter judgment against the defendant in default but must deal with the application at the same time as it disposes of the claims against the other defendants	Rule 12.8(2)(b)
	If default judgment is entered against one of two or more defendants for possession of land or delivery of goods, it may not be enforced without permission unless the claimant obtains a similar judgment against the other defendant(s)	Rule 12.8(3)
Judgment for costs only	If judgment is given for other than fixed costs, it will be for an amount of costs to be decided by the court. In practice, the judge will often assess the amount of costs on the same occasion but he may direct that the costs be determined by detailed assessment (see Guide 32)	Rule 12.11(2) Rule 44.7
Court fees	On application on notice: High Court – £100 County court – £60	CPFO fee 2.5
	On application without notice: (no fee on a request for judgment) High Court – £50 County court – £30	CPFO fee 2.6

Forms	Request – N205A, N205B (lower parts) or N255, N227. Application Notice N244	
Setting aside or varying default judgment		
When mandatory	A default judgment must be set aside if the claimant was not entitled to enter it (see Availability above)	Rule 13.2
When discretionary	Even though the judgment is regular, the court may set it aside or vary it if the defendant has a real prospect of successfully defending the claim or it appears that there is some other good reason why the judgment should be set aside or varied or the defendant should be allowed to defend the claim	Rule 13.3(1)
	However, the court must have regard to whether the application was made promptly	Rule 13.3(1)
Procedure	The application is made by application notice, and must be supported by evidence if made on a discretionary ground	Rule 13.4(3)
	If: the claim is for a specified sum; the judgment was obtained in a court which was not the defendant's home court; the claim has not been transferred to another defendant's home court; the defendant is an individual; and the claim was not commenced in a specialist list, the application will be transferred to the defendant's home court	Rule 13.4(1), (2)
	The 'defendant's home court' means the county court district where the defendant resides or carries on business if it is a county court claim or, in the case of a High Court claim, the district registry covering the defendant's residence or place of business or, if none, the RCJ	Rule 2.3(1)

Conditional orders	The court has a general power to attach a condition (including a condition to pay money into court) to any order and to specify the consequences of failure to comply	Rule 3.1(3)
Abandoned claims	Where the claimant abandoned a claim in order to request default judgment (see above), it is restored if the judgment is set aside	Rule 13.6
Forms	Application to set aside N244 Request to set aside – none prescribed.	
Court fees	On application on notice: *High Court* – £100 *County court* – £60	CPFO fee 2.5
	On application without notice: *High Court* – £50 *County court* – £30	CPFO fee 2.6
	No fee is payable on a claimant's request to set aside.	

30: Summary Judgment and Disposal

Legal background

Part 24 and its practice direction set out the procedure and the rules applicable to this type of application. The general rules as to applications also apply (see Guide 18).

Procedure

Summary judgment		
Grounds for summary judgment and the court's approach	The court may give summary judgment in respect of the whole or part of a claim where:	
	the claimant or defendant has no realistic prospect of success on the issue; and	
	there is no other compelling reason why the case or issue should be disposed of at trial	Rule 24.1
	The court also has powers to make similar orders of its own initiative (see below)	Rule 3.4
	The application may be based either on a point of law or evidence or both	PD24, para 1.3

	The court may make a conditional order where it appears improbable that a claim or defence will succeed	PD24, para 4
Claims where summary judgment not available	An order may be made against a claimant in any proceedings. An order may be made against a defendant in any proceedings other than those for: possession of residential premises against a mortgagor or protected tenant (or one holding over after the end of his tenancy); an admiralty claim *in rem*; or contentious probate proceedings	Rule 24.3
Accounts and enquiries	Where a claim includes or necessarily involves the taking of an account or making an enquiry, an application for such an order may be made under Pt 24	PD24, para 6
Specific performance	Where a claim includes a claim for specific performance or rescission of certain types of contract, or for the forfeiture or return of any deposit made under such a contract, an application may be made under Pt 24	PD24, para 7.1(1)(a)
When the application may be made	An application may not be made against a defendant who has not filed an acknowledgment of service or a defence unless the court or a practice direction permits *except*:	Rule 24.4(1)
	in the case of a claim for specific performance, the application may be made at any time after service of the claim form and even before service of the particulars of claim or expiry of the time for filing acknowledgment of service	PD24, para 7.1(1)(b)
Defence not required	A defendant against whom an application is made need not file a defence before the hearing of the application	Rule 24.4(2)
Notice	At least 14 clear days' notice of the hearing and of the issues must be given, save in a claim for specific performance when only 4 clear days' notice need be given	Rule 24.4(3) PD24, para 7.3

General procedure	The application notice must:	
	state that summary judgment under Pt 24 is sought; and	PD24, para 2(2)
	state briefly why the applicant seeks the order;	Rule 23.6
	identify or be accompanied by any evidence on which the applicant relies;	Rule 23.7(3) PD24, para 2(4)
	draw the attention of the respondent to rule 24.5(1) (see below);	PD24, para 2(5)
	in the case of an application for specific performance, have attached to it the text of the order sought	PD24, para 7.2
	The application notice, or evidence, must:	
	identify any point of law or provision in a document on which the applicant relies; and/or	PD24, para 2(3)(a)
	state that it is made because the applicant believes that on the evidence the respondent has no real prospect of succeeding on the claim or issue or (as the case may be) of successfully defending the claim or issue to which the application relates; and	PD24, para 2(3)(b)
	state that the applicant knows of no other compelling reason why the disposal of the claim or issue should await trial	PD24, para 2(3)
Other rules about evidence	The respondent must file and serve any evidence on which he intends to rely at least 7 clear days before the hearing	Rule 24.5(1)
	The claimant must file and serve any evidence on which he wishes to rely in reply at least 3 clear days before the hearing. (These periods will necessarily be abridged if less than 14 days' notice of the hearing has been given; either when the claim is for specific performance or when the court has exercised its general power to abridge the period of notice.)	Rule 24.5(2)
	Evidence that has already been filed and/or served need not be filed or served again	Rule 24.5(4)

	A party may rely on the contents of any statement of case or application as evidence provided it is verified by a statement of truth	Rule 32.6(2)
Conditional orders	As well as orders granting or dismissing the application, the court may make a conditional order	PD24, para 5.1(d)
	This is an order requiring a party either to pay a sum of money into court or to take a specified step, in default of which the claim will be dismissed or the statement of case struck out	PD24, para 5.2 Rule 3.1(3) and (5)
	The court will no longer grant conditional leave to defend	PD24, para 5.2
Consequential directions	On determining an application for summary judgment the court may give directions for the filing and service of a defence and for the management of the case	Rule 24.6
Proceeding where party not served or in attendance	The court may make an order in a party's absence. Where it does so, the court may re-list the hearing of its own initiative or on application	Rule 23.11(1), (2)
	Where a party is served with an order made on an application which was not served on him:	
	a copy of the application notice and evidence in support must be served with the order unless the court orders otherwise;	Rule 23.9(2)
	that party may apply within 7 days of service for the order to be set aside; and	Rule 23.10
	the order must state that that party is so entitled	Rule 23.9(3)
Summary disposal of claims		
The court's general powers	The court may make any order of its own initiative unless a rule or enactment provides otherwise	Rule 3.3(1)
	The court may:	
	strike out a statement of case if –	
	it discloses no reasonable grounds for bringing or defending a claim;	Rule 3.4(2)(a)

	it is an abuse of process or otherwise likely to obstruct the just disposal of the proceedings; or	Rule 3.4(2)(b)
	there has been a failure to comply with a rule, practice direction or court order	Rule 3.4(2)(c)
	or order that –	
	the claim be stayed until further order;	PD3, para 2.4(1)
	the claim form be retained by the court and not served;	PD3, para 2.4(2)
	the claimant may not apply to lift the stay until he provides further information or documents; and/or	PD3, para 2.4(3)
	the defendant provide further information or otherwise clarify his defence and any such order may be in the form of an 'unless' order	PD3, para 3.4
Consequential provisions	Where a statement of case has been struck out pursuant to an 'unless' order, the other party may obtain judgment with costs by filing a request (ie for an administrative entry of judgment) where:	
	the party seeking judgment is the claimant;	
	the whole of a statement of case is struck out; and	
	the claim is for money only, or for return of goods where the defendant has the option to pay the value of those goods, or a combination of those,	Rule 3.5(1)–(3)
	and by making an application on notice in any other case	Rule 3.5(4)
	The party against whom it was entered may apply for the judgment to be set aside within 14 days of service of the judgment	Rule 3.6(1), (2)
	If the right to enter the judgment had not arisen, the court must set it aside; but if the application is made for any other reason it is treated as an application for relief from sanctions under r 3.9 (see below)	Rule 3.6(3) Rule 3.6(4)

	Where a claimant whose statement of case has been struck out is also ordered to pay costs, the court may stay any subsequent claim by that claimant based on substantially the same facts until those costs have been paid	Rule 3.4(4)
Orders made of the court's own initiative	The court may make an order of its own initiative without giving the parties the opportunity of being heard or making representations. When it does so:	Rule 3.3(4)
	any party affected by the order may apply within 7 clear days of service (or such other period as the court may order) to have it set aside, varied or stayed; and	Rule 3.3(5)(a) and 3.3(6)
	the order must so state	Rule 3.3(5)(b)
	Before making such an order the court may give the parties the opportunity to make representations by the time and in the manner specified by the court and may fix a hearing for this purpose of which 3 clear days' notice must be given	Rule 3.3(2), (3)
Sanctions	A sanction is a penal consequence imposed by a rule, practice direction or the court for failing to comply with a rule, practice direction or court order	Rule 3.8(1)
	A party may apply for relief against sanctions, save where the sanction is an order for the payment of costs when the party may only appeal	Rule 3.9(1) Rule 3.8(2)
	An application for such relief must be supported by evidence	Rule 3.9(2)
	The court will take into account all the circumstances of the case, including:	
	the interests of the administration of justice;	
	whether the application for relief has been made promptly;	
	whether the failure to comply was intentional;	
	whether there is a good explanation for the failure;	
	the extent to which the party in default has complied with other rules;	

	whether the failure to comply was caused by the party or his legal representative; whether the trial date or the likely trial date can still be met if relief is granted; the effect which the failure to comply had on each party; and the effect which the granting of relief would have on each party	Rule 3.9(1)
Costs	Where judgment is given for a specified sum either: on an application made under Pt 24; or after the court strikes out a defence on an application made under r 3.4(2)(a), fixed costs may be awarded – in the sum of £175 where the judgment amount exceeds £25 but does not exceed £5000; in the sum of £210 where the judgment amount exceeds £5000 Where the court does not award fixed costs, it is likely that it will assess them summarily. Parties should therefore be prepared to give the court a written statement of the amount of costs incurred	Rule 45.1(2) Rule 45.4, Table 2 PDCosts, para 4.3 PDCosts, para 4.5
Court fees	Application for judgment: *High Court* – £100 *County court* – £60 Application to set aside: *High Court* – £100 *County court* – £60 Application to vary: *High Court* – £50 *County court* – £30	CPFO fee 2.4 CPFO fee 2.4 CPFO fee 2.7
Forms	Application: N244 may be used Statement of Costs: N260	PD23, para 2.1
Which judge	A master or district judge may hear an application for summary judgment even though he would not be able to try the case	PD2B, para 4.1

31: Deciding the Amount Payable under a Judgment

Legal background

In certain circumstances the court may give judgment or make an order for payment of an amount which remains to be decided. The practice direction to Pt 26 sets out a procedure by which the court's determination can be obtained.

Procedure

Availability	Where there is a claim for an amount of money which is not specified and the claimant obtains judgment by request the defendant having failed to file a defence (see Guide 29) or the defendant admitting liability but making no offer or making an offer which the claimant does not accept (see Guide 6) the judgment will be for an amount to be decided by the court	Rule 12.5(3) Rule 14.6(7) Rule 14.7(10)
	Where the claimant requests default judgment for delivery of goods, the judgment will require the defendant to deliver the goods or pay their value, to be decided by the court	Rule 12.5(4)
	Where there is a claim for a specified amount of money and the claimant requests default judgment or judgment on the defendant's full admission, including interest, but:	
	the particulars of claim do not include a claim for interest in the correct form (see Guide 1); or	
	where the claim is made under CCA, 1984 s 69, or SCA, s 35A, the rate is higher than that payable on judgment debts current at the date of issue of the claim; or	
	the request for judgment does not include a calculation of the interest claimed from the date to which it was stated to be calculated in the claim form to the date of the request for judgment,	
	then the judgment for interest will be judgment for an amount to be decided by the court	Rules 12.6(2) and 14.14(2)

	The court may decide the order in which issues are determined (and may dispose summarily of some). Thus it may decide the principle of liability and leave the amount payable to be decided by the court	Rule 1.4(2)
	A judgment entered following the striking out of a statement of case or given on a summary judgment application (see Guide 30) may be to similar effect	Rule 3.5(2)(b)(ii) Part 24
Directions	When the court makes a judgment or order requiring an amount of money to be paid by one party to the other to be decided by the court, it will give directions which may include:	
	(a) listing the claim for a disposal hearing	PD26, para 12.1(1)(a)
	(b) allocating or re-allocating the claim	PD26, para 12.1(1)(b)
	(c) directing the parties to file allocation questionnaires	PD26, para 12.1(1)(c)
	(d) a stay enabling the parties to settle	PD26, para 12.1(1)(d)
	(e) specifying the level or type of judge before whom a hearing will take place and the nature and purpose of that hearing	PD26, para 12.1(2)
	Orders for the taking of an account or making of an inquiry as to any sum due and any similar order are included in the definition of 'a relevant order' but an order for assessment of costs is excluded	PD26, para 12.1(3)
	Where the parties apply for a consent judgment or order they should, if possible, file with their draft consent order agreed directions for the court's approval	PD26, para 12.1(3)
Allocation	The court will allocate a previously unallocated claim to the small claims track if its financial value so qualified it, had the claim been defended	PD26, para 12.3(1)
	Other claims will normally not be allocated to track unless the amount payable appears to be genuinely disputed on substantial grounds; or	PD26, para 12.3(2)(a)
	the dispute is not suitable to be disposed of at a disposal hearing	PD26, para 12.3(2)(b)

Disposal hearings	A disposal hearing will not normally last longer than 30 minutes or require oral evidence to be taken	PD26, para 12.4(1)
	At the hearing the court may:	
	(a) decide and give judgment for the amount payable; or	PD26, para 12.4(2)(a)
	(b) give directions as to the further conduct of the hearing; and	PD26, para 12.4(2)(b)
	(c) treat the hearing as a final small claims track hearing (allocating it so, if necessary)	PD26, para 12.4(3)
	Evidence will normally be in writing and (unless allocated to the small claims track) must be served on the defendant at least 3 days before the disposal hearing or the court will not give judgment	PD26, para 12.4(4), (5)
	Where the judgment was entered in default without a hearing, the court *will* list a disposal hearing	PD26, para 12.7
	At a disposal hearing the court may give directions as above	PD26, para 12.8(1)
	If the financial value of the claim is such that it would be allocated to the small claims track if defended, the court will normally allocate it to that track and may treat the hearing as a small claims hearing	PD26, para 12.8(2)
	The court may decide the amount payable there and then without allocating the claim to a track, provided any written evidence has been served on the defendant at least 3 days before the hearing	PD26, para 12.8(3) PD26, para 12.8(5)
	Evidence will normally be in writing (witness statement, any application notice, statement of case) verified by a statement of truth	PD26, para 12.8(4) Rule 32.6
Costs	The costs will normally be assessed summarily. Parties should therefore file and serve 24 hours before the hearing a statement of costs incurred and endeavour to agree them before the hearing starts	PD26, 12.5 PDCosts, paras 13.2, 13.5
	If the claim is allocated to the small claims track, the rules applicable to that track (see Guide 12) will apply	PD26, para 12.5(1)(c)

	If the claim is allocated to the fast track, the fixed trial costs applicable to that track will *not* apply	PD26, para 12.5(2)
Court fees	If the claim is allocated to a track: High Court – £120 County court – £100 (save for a money only claim for less than £1,500)	CPFO fee 2.1
Which judge	A master or district judge may decide the amount to be paid under a judgment irrespective of the amount involved	PD2B, paras 4.2 and 11.1(c)

32: Detailed Assessment of Costs

Legal background

This Guide covers the procedure to be followed after an order for costs has been made where the amount of those costs is to be decided by a costs officer. The term 'detailed assessment' is used in place of the old term 'taxation'. An assessment of the amount of costs which is made immediately by the court awarding those costs is called a 'summary assessment'.

This Guide does NOT cover:

(i) the detailed assessment of a bill of costs which is payable only out of the Community Legal Services Fund (as to which see r 47.17 and PDCosts, paras 43.1–43.9);

(ii) the detailed assessment of a bill of costs payable out of a fund other than the Community Legal Services Fund (as to which see r 47.17A and PDCosts, paras 44.1–44.10);

(iii) the detailed assessment of solicitor and client costs (as to which see rr 48.9 and 48.10 and PDCosts, paras 56.1–56.19).

Procedure

Detailed assessment	In any order of the court the words 'taxation' and 'to be taxed' are taken to mean 'detailed assessment' and 'to be decided by detailed assessment' respectively unless in either case the context otherwise requires	PDCosts, para 3.8
	An order for costs is to be treated as an order for the amount of costs to be decided by a detailed assessment unless the order otherwise provides	PDCosts, para 12.2

Basis of assessment	There are two bases of assessment: indemnity basis (all costs except those shown to be unreasonable) and standard basis (only those costs shown to be reasonable and proportionate to the matters in issue)	Rule 44.4
	Costs payable by one party to another will be assessed on the standard basis unless the order for costs specifies the indemnity basis	Rule 44.4
Time for detailed assessment proceedings	Unless the court has ordered immediate assessment, proceedings for detailed assessment should not be commenced until the conclusion of the proceedings which gave rise to the assessment	Rule 47.1 PDCosts, para 28.1
	A costs judge or district judge may permit detailed assessment proceedings to be commenced before the conclusion of proceedings if there is no realistic prospect of the claim continuing	PDCosts, para 28.1(5)
	Detailed assessment is not stayed pending an appeal unless an order to that effect is made by the court appealed from or the court appealed to	Rule 47.2 PDCosts, para 29.1
Venue for assessment	The appropriate office for detailed assessment proceedings is either the district registry or county court in which the case was proceeding, or the Principal Registry of the Family Division, if the case was proceeding there (including appeals from the PRFD, a district registry or county court in family proceedings), or the Supreme Court Costs Office (SCCO) in all other cases	Rule 47.4 PDCosts, para 31.1
	A direction specifying the SCCO as the appropriate office may be made in any case having regard to (amongst other things) the size and complexity of the bill of costs to be assessed	PDCosts, para 31.2

Form of bill	There are no prescribed forms of bills of costs. Precedents A, B, C and D are the model forms and their use is to be encouraged. A party relying upon a bill which departs from the ideal form should include in the bill an explanation justifying the departure	PDCosts, paras 3.5 and 3.7
	A bill of costs must contain such of the certificates set out in Costs Precedent F as are appropriate	PDCosts, para 4.15
	If the bill is capable of being copied onto a computer disk, a paying party may request the receiving party to supply a disk copy free of charge: the disk must be supplied within 7 days of request	PDCosts, para 32.11
Commencement of detailed assessment proceedings	The receiving party must serve on the paying party and all other 'relevant persons' (defined below): a notice of commencement; a copy of the bill of costs; copies of the fee notes of counsel and of any expert in respect of fees claimed in the bill; written evidence as to any other disbursements which are claimed and which exceed £250; a statement giving the name and address for service of any person upon whom the receiving party intends to serve the notice of commencement	Rule 47.6 PDCosts, para 32.3
Commencement of detailed assessment proceedings where additional liability claimed	The receiving party must serve on the paying party and all other relevant persons: (1) a notice of commencement; (2) a copy of the bill of costs; (3) the relevant details of the additional liability which include: (a) in the case of a CFA with success fee: (i) a statement showing the amount of costs which have been summarily assessed or agreed and a percentage increase which has been claimed in respect of those costs;	

	(ii) a statement of the reasons for the percentage increase (CFA Regulations 2000, reg 3); (b) in respect of an insurance premium a copy of the insurance certificate; (c) for claims under AJA 1999, s 30 a statement setting out the basis upon which the receiving party's liability for the additional amount is calculated	PDCosts, para 32.4
	The notice of commencement does not have to be sealed by or produced to the court at this stage. The notice should be in Form N252 and should state (amongst other things): the total amount of the bill as drawn; the extra sum payable if a default costs certificate is obtained (see below);	PDCosts, para 32.8
	the date by which points of dispute must be served by the paying party on the receiving party if the paying party wishes to prevent the issue of a default costs certificate. (As to the date, see further 'Points of dispute' below.)	
Deadline for commencement	Detailed assessment proceedings must be commenced within 3 months of the date of the order for costs or other event giving rise to the entitlement of costs, unless the court otherwise orders and unless the parties otherwise agree	Rule 47.7 PDCosts, para 33.1
	Permission to commence assessment proceedings out of time is not required but, in such a case, the court may make an unless order requiring commencement within a specified time and/or disallow all or part of the interest otherwise payable under Judgments Act 1838, s 17 or under County Courts Act 1984, s 74	PDCosts, para 33.4 Rule 47.8

Relevant persons	This expression means: any person who has taken part in the proceedings which gave rise to the assessment and who is directly liable under an order for costs made against him; any person who has given to the receiving party notice in writing that he has a financial interest in the outcome of the assessment and wishes to be a party accordingly; any other person whom the court orders to be treated as a relevant person	PDCosts, para 32.10
Points of dispute	These should follow as closely as possible Costs Precedent G and should (amongst other things):	
	be short and to the point;	PDCosts, para 35.2
	Where practicable suggest a figure to be allowed for each item in respect of which a reduction is sought; and	PDCosts, para 35.3
	be signed by the party serving them or his solicitor.	
	The points of dispute should be served on the receiving party and on every other party to the detailed assessment proceedings whose name and address for service appears in the statement served with the notice of commencement	Rule 47.9(1) PDCosts, para 35.5
	The normal period for service of points of dispute is within 21 days of the date of service of the notice of commencement. However, if the notice of commencement is served on a party outside England and Wales the deadline for service by that party is to be calculated by reference to Part 6, Section III (r 6.22) as if the notice of commencement was a claim form and as if the period for serving points of dispute were the period for filing a defence	Rule 47.9(2) PDCosts, para 35.4
	The time for service of points of dispute may be extended or shortened by agreement or by court order	PDCosts, para 35.1

	If the points of dispute are capable of being copied onto a computer disk the receiving party may within 14 days of receipt of the points of dispute request the paying party to supply a disk copy free of charge. The disk must be supplied within 7 days of the request	PDCosts, para 35.6
	Where an additional liability is claimed the party who serves points of dispute may include a request for information about other methods of financing costs which were available to the receiving party. Pt 18 applies to such a request	PDCosts, para 35.7
Default costs certificates	The receiving party may file a request for a default costs certificate if:	
	the time for serving points of dispute has expired; and	
	he has not been served with any points of dispute.	
	However, no default costs certificate should be issued if, before issue of the certificate, points of dispute are served, even if they are served late	Rule 47.9
	The request for a default costs certificate must be in Form N254, signed by the receiving party or his solicitor and filed in the court office appropriate for detailed assessment proceedings	PDCosts, paras 37.1 and 37.2
	The default costs certificate may be prepared by the receiving party and must be in Form N254	PDCosts, para 37.4
	The issue of a default costs certificate does not prohibit, govern or affect any detailed assessment of the same costs which is made pursuant to Access to Justice Act 1999, s 11 and/or the Legal Aid Act 1988. Thus, if the receiving party's solicitor wishes to claim payment from the Legal Services Commission he must apply for a detailed assessment, and the court may direct a provisional assessment	PDCosts, paras 37.5 and 43.4

Where costs are agreed	Costs certificates (whether interim or final) can be issued by consent of all parties under rule 40.6 and issued by a court officer. If detailed assessment proceedings have already commenced, the bill of costs in those proceedings may be withdrawn by consent whether or not a detailed assessment hearing has been requested	Rule 47.10 PDCosts, para 36.1 PDCosts, para 36.5
	Applications for a certificate relating to agreed costs which are not made by consent must be made on notice and supported by evidence filed and served at least 2 days before the hearing date	Rule 47.10 PDCosts, paras 36.2 and 36.3
	An application for a certificate relating to agreed costs which is not made by consent must be made: where the right to assessment arises from a judgment or court order – to the court which made the judgment or order if the proceedings have not been transferred since then; or to the court to which the proceedings have been transferred; in any other case, to the court which would be the venue for detailed assessment proceedings	Rule 47.10
Optional reply	The receiving party may serve a reply to points of dispute within 21 days of service of the points of dispute. A copy must be served on every other party to the detailed assessment proceedings. A reply may be in the form of: a separate document prepared by the receiving party; or written comments added to the points of dispute. Any reply must be signed by the party or his solicitor	Rule 47.13 PDCosts, para 39.1

Request for hearing	If points of dispute are served, the receiving party must, within 6 months of the order for costs or other event giving rise to the entitlement to costs, file a request for a detailed assessment hearing in Form N258 (non-LSC funded) or Form N258A (LSC funded), accompanied by a long list of documents as specified in the form	Rule 47.14 PDCosts, paras 40.2 and 43.3
	If the receiving party is LSC funded or an assisted person and the rates payable out of the legal aid fund are prescribed rates, his solicitor must also file a legal aid schedule in Precedent E	PDCosts, paras 49.2, 49.3 and 49.4
	If the request is filed late the court may disallow all or part of the interest which could otherwise be payable for the period of delay or, in exercise of its powers in relation to misconduct, disallow all or part of the costs otherwise payable	Rules 44.14 and 47.14 PDCosts, para 40.7
Fixing the date for hearing	On receipt of the request the court will fix a date for the hearing, or give directions or fix a date for a preliminary appointment	PDCosts, para 40.5
	The court will give parties at least 14 days' notice of the hearing and will give to each person who has served points of dispute a copy of the points of dispute annotated by the receiving party so as to show which items have been agreed and their value and to show which items remain in dispute and their value	PDCosts, para 40.6
	Parties may apply to vary the date given by the court for a detailed assessment hearing but the court may refuse the application even if it was made with the consent of all parties	PDCosts, para 40.9
Interim costs certificates	A receiving party who has filed a request for a detailed assessment hearing may apply for an interim costs certificate for such sum as the court considers appropriate	Rule 47.15 PDCosts, para 41.1

Making amendments	Bills of costs, points of dispute and replies may be amended, or supplementary documents may be filed without permission but the court may later disallow the amendment or supplementary document or permit them only upon conditions	PDCosts, para 40.10
Filing papers in support of the bill	These must be filed not less than 7 nor more than 14 days before the hearing date	PDCosts, para 40.11
	The papers to be filed, and the order in which they are to be arranged are:	
	where no additional liability is claimed	
	instructions and briefs to counsel arranged in chronological order together with all advices, opinions and drafts received in response to such instructions;	
	reports and opinions of medical and other experts;	
	any other relevant papers;	
	a full set of any relevant pleadings to the extent that they have not already been filed in court;	
	correspondence, files and attendance notes;	PDCosts, para 40.12(a)
	where a claim is in relation to an additional liability only	
	such of the papers listed above as are relevant to the issues raised by the claim for the additional liability;	PDCosts, para 40.12(b)
	where a claim is for both base costs and an additional liability	
	the papers listed above including any papers relevant to the issues raised by the claim for the additional liability	PDCosts, para 40.12(c)
	The court may direct the receiving party to produce any document which in the opinion of the court is necessary to enable it to reach its decision	PDCosts, para 40.14
The detailed assessment hearing	Only the receiving party and those who have served points of dispute may be heard and only the items specified in the points of dispute may be raised, unless in either case the court otherwise allows	Rule 47.14

	At the hearing, the court will indicate any disallowance or reduction in the sums claimed in the bill of costs by making an appropriate note on the bill	PDCosts, para 42.1
	The receiving party is entitled to his costs of the detailed assessment unless a statute, rule or practice direction otherwise provides or unless the court otherwise orders, having regard to all the circumstances including the conduct of the parties and the degree of success achieved	Rule 47.18
	If the costs of the detailed assessment are awarded to the receiving party, the sums allowed will be added to the bill. If the costs are awarded to the paying party the court will either assess them summarily or make an order for them to be decided by detailed assessment	PDCosts, para 45.1 PDCosts, para 45.2
	The detailed assessment of any legal aid schedule filed (see 'Request for hearing' above) will take place immediately after the detailed assessment of the bill of costs	PDCosts, para 49.7
	Where any amount of an agreed percentage increase is disallowed on assessment it ceases to be payable under a CFA, unless the court is satisfied that it should continue to be paid. The court may adjourn a hearing at which the legal representative acting for the receiving party applies for an order that a disallowed amount should continue to be paid under the agreement	Rule 44.16 PDCosts, Section 20
Offers to settle	In deciding who should pay the costs of the detailed assessment the court will take into account 'without prejudice' offers to settle made by the other side	Rule 47.19
	Offers to settle which are made more than 14 days after the notice of commencement or points of dispute (as the case may be) will be given less weight than those made earlier	PDCosts, para 46.1

	An offer to settle should specify whether it is intended to be inclusive of the costs of preparation of the bill interest and VAT. Unless the offer states otherwise it will be treated as being inclusive of all these items	PDCosts, para 46.2
	Where the receiving party is an assisted person an offer to settle will not have effect unless the court so orders	PDCosts, para 46.4
Completing the bill	The receiving party must make clear the correct figures agreed or allowed in respect of each item and must recalculate the summary of the bill appropriately	PDCosts, para 42.2
	The completed bill of costs must be filed with the court no later than 14 days after the detailed assessment hearing	PDCosts, para 42.3
	With the completed bill the receiving party must also file receipted fee notes and receipted accounts in respect of all disbursements except those covered by a certificate in Precedent F(5) (Disbursements not exceeding £500).	PDCosts, para 42.4
Final costs certificate	A certificate in Form N256 which will include an order to pay the costs to which it relates (unless the court orders otherwise)	Rule 47.16
	No fee is payable. If the receiving party is an assisted person the court will also issue a legal aid assessment certificate in Form EX80A.	
	If there are two or more receiving parties a separate certificate will be issued for each of them	PDCosts, para 42.9
	An application for an order staying enforcement of a certificate may be made to the court which issued it or to the court (if different) which has general jurisdiction to enforce it	PDCosts, para 42.12
Appeals	*Against decisions of authorised court officers*	
	There is no requirement to obtain permission nor duty to seek reasons	PDCosts, para 47.2
	The time-limit is 14 days after the date of the decision to be appealed against	Rules 47.20–47.24 PDCosts, paras 48.1–48.4

	In all other cases see Part 52	Part 52 and PD52
Court fees	On filing request for Legal Aid assessment only: High Court – £120 County court – £100	CPFO fee 5.1
	On filing request for detailed assessment otherwise: High Court – £600 County court – £300	CPFO fee 5.2
	On request for default costs certificate: High Court – £50 County court – £40	CPFO fee 5.3
	On appeal or on application to set aside default costs certificate: High Court – £200 County court – £100	CPFO fee 5.4
	On application to approve Legal Aid assessment certificate: High Court – £50 County court – £30	CPFO fee 5.5

33: Summary Assessment of Costs

Legal background

This Guide covers the procedure to be followed where costs are to be summarily assessed. The assessment of the amount of costs is made immediately by the court awarding those costs.

Procedure

Summary assessment	This is the procedure by which the court when making an order about costs orders payment of a sum of money instead of fixed costs or detailed assessment	Rule 44.3 PDCosts, para 13.1
Grounds for ordering summary assessment	Summary assessment will generally be ordered: at the conclusion of the trial of a case which has been dealt with on the fast track in which case the order will deal with the costs of the whole claim, or	

	at the conclusion of any other hearing which has lasted not more than one day, in which case the order will deal with the costs of the application or matter to which the hearing related. If this hearing disposes of the claim, the order may deal with the costs of the whole claim; or	Rule 44.7(a) PDCosts, para 13.2
	at hearings in the Court of Appeal to which PD52, paras 14.1 and 14.2 apply	PDCosts, para 13.2
Exceptions	Summary assessment may not be ordered in respect of:	
	mortgagees costs incurred in mortgage possession proceedings or other proceedings relating to a mortgage unless the mortgagee asks the court to make an order for his costs to be paid by another party;	PDCosts, para 13.3
	the costs of a receiving party who is a LSC funded client receiving services funded by the LSC or an assisted person within the meaning of the Legal Aid Act 1988;	PDCosts, para 13.9
	the costs of a receiving party who is a child or patient within Pt 21 unless the solicitor acting for the child or patient has waived the right to further costs	PDCosts, para 13.11
	Where an additional liability is claimed the court is prevented from making a summary assessment before the conclusion of the proceedings or the part of the proceedings to which the funding arrangement relates	Rule 44.3A PDCosts, paras 13.12 and 14.5
	Summary assessment may not be ordered if there is good reason not to do so. Example: where the paying party shows substantial grounds for disputing the sum claimed and that cannot be dealt with summarily or there is insufficient time to carry out a summary assessment	PDCosts, para 13.2
Time for summary assessment proceedings	At the conclusion of a fast track trial or other hearing which has lasted not more than one day;	

	or a hearing in the Court of Appeal to which PD52, paras 14.1 and 14.2 relate	PDCosts, para 13.2
	If summary assessment of costs is appropriate but the court awarding costs is unable to deal with the assessment there and then the court must give directions as to a further hearing	PDCosts, para 13.8
Which judge	The judge hearing the fast track trial or application will summarily assess costs. The trial judge cannot order summary assessment by a costs officer	PDCosts, para 13.8
Statement of costs	The party intending to claim costs must prepare Form N260 of the costs he intends to claim setting out:	
	the number of hours to be claimed;	
	the hourly rate to be claimed;	
	the grade of fee earner;	
	the amount and nature of any disbursement to be claimed other than counsel's fee for appearing at the hearing;	
	the amount of solicitors costs to be claimed for attending or appearing at the hearing;	
	the fees of counsel to be claimed in respect of the hearing;	
	any value added tax (unless the receiving party is able to recoup it as Input Tax).	
	The statement of costs must be signed by the party or his legal representative. Where a litigant is an assisted person or is a LSC funded client or is represented by a solicitor in his employment the certificate at the end of Form N260 need not be included	PDCosts, para 13.5(2) and (3) Form N260
	Where the litigant is entitled to claim an additional liability the statement filed and served need not reveal the amount of that liability	PDCosts, para 13.5(5)

Service	The statement of costs must be filed at court and served on any party, against whom an order for payment of those costs is intended to be sought, not less than 24 hours before the date fixed for the hearing	PDCosts, para 13.5(4)
Failure to comply	Where a party without reasonable excuse fails to comply with the service of a statement of costs the court deciding the application may disallow the costs of the claim hearing or application and may order the defaulting party to pay the costs of any further hearing or detailed assessment hearing that may be necessary as a result of that failure	PDCosts, para 13.6
Order on summary assessment	Where the court makes a summary assessment of the costs at the conclusion of proceedings the court will specify: the base costs and if appropriate the additional liability allowed as solicitor's charges, counsel's fees, other disbursements and VAT; and the amount awarded under Pt 46 (fast track trial costs)	PDCosts, para 13.7
Time for payment	An order for payment of costs summarily assessed must be complied with within 14 days of the date of the order unless the court extends the time	Rules 44.3A, 44.8 and 3.1(2)(a)
	Additional liability The existence of a CFA or other funding arrangement is not of itself sufficient reason for not carrying out a summary assessment of base costs. Where costs have been summarily assessed an order for payment will not be made unless the court is satisfied the receiving party is at the time liable to pay his reasonable representative an amount equal to or greater than the costs claimed. A statement in the form of the certificate to Form N260 may be sufficient proof of liability	PDCosts, paras 14.1 and 14.3

Where costs are agreed	Where the parties have agreed the amount of costs and they are recorded in the form of a consent order submitted to the court it is not necessary to provide the court with Form N260. The court is unlikely to interfere with an agreement between parties who agree over costs. However, the court will not endorse disproportionate and unreasonable costs. The fact that a paying party does not dispute the amount of costs will be taken as an indication that they are proportionate and reasonable	PDCosts, para 13.13
	Where an application is agreed by consent the parties should agree a figure for the amount of costs to be inserted in the consent order or agree no order for costs. If an attendance is required to argue solely about costs no costs will be allowed for that attendance unless good reason can be shown	PDCosts, para 13.4
Appeals	In accordance with the general rules relating to appeals	Part 52 and PD52

34: Costs-Only Proceedings

Legal background

This Guide covers the procedure to be followed where the parties to a dispute have reached an agreement on all issues except the amount of costs to be paid by one party to another. Rule 44.12A, supplemented by PDCosts, Section 17, provides a mechanism for the assessment of costs but only in very specific circumstances.

Procedure

Criteria	The parties to a dispute have reached an agreement on all issues (including which party is to pay the costs); the agreement must be made or confirmed in writing; the parties have failed to agree the amount of those costs; no proceedings have been started	Rule 44.12A

Venue	The claim is to be issued in the court which would have been the appropriate office in accordance with r 47.4 had proceedings been brought in relation to the substantive claim	PDCosts, para 17.1
	High Court Costs-only proceedings should not be commenced in the High Court unless the dispute to which the agreement relates was of such a value or type that had substantive proceedings been begun they would have been commenced in the High Court	PDCosts, para 17.1
	RCJ Where substantive proceedings would have been issued out of the RCJ, a costs claim must be issued in the SCCO	PDCosts, para 17.2
Time for issue	None specified.	
Claim form	Part 8 procedure is to be followed. The claim form must – identify the claim or dispute to which the agreement to pay costs relates; state the date and terms of the agreement on which the claimant relies; set out or have attached to it a draft of the order which the claimant seeks; state the amount of the costs claimed; state whether the costs are claimed on the standard or indemnity basis	PDCosts, para 17.3
	The claim form must contain or be accompanied by the agreement or confirmation that the defendant will pay costs	Rule 44.12A(3) PDCosts, para 17.4
Which judge	A costs judge or district judge irrespective of the amount of costs claimed; a court officer may make an order by consent (subject to r 40.6) or an order dismissing a claim	PDCosts, para 17.5
Acknowledgment/ defence	The defendant may file an acknowledgment of service stating he intends to contest the claim or seek a different order	PDCosts, para 17.6

	If the acknowledgement indicates that the application is not opposed the court will make an order for costs without a hearing.	
	The claim will be treated as opposed if a defendant files an acknowledgment of service intending to contest the proceedings or to seek a different remedy. The court must dismiss the claim as soon as such an acknowledgment is filed	Rule 44.12A(4)(b) PDCosts, para 17.9
	A claim will not be treated as opposed and dismissed if the defendant states in the acknowledgment of service that he disputes the amount of the claim for costs or that the application has been issued in the wrong office.	
	When the time for filing the defendant's acknowledgment of service has expired the claimant may request the court to make an order in the terms of his claim	PDCosts, para 17.6
Order for costs	An order for costs is treated as an order for the amount of costs to be decided by detailed assessment to which Pt 47 applies	PDCosts, para 17.8
	Unless the claimant seeks to the contrary the basis of assessment will be the standard basis	PDCosts, para 17.3(5)
	The court on making an order for costs may give directions as to detailed assessment of those costs including the filing and lodging of a bill of costs and determination of those costs.	
Rules which do not apply	Rules 8.1(3) and 8.9 do not apply. Thus the court may not order some procedure other than Pt 8 to apply, and the claim may be dealt with without being allocated to a track. It is not deemed allocated to the multi-track;	
	Part 24 (Summary judgment) does not apply	PDCosts, para 17.10

Procedure where proceedings opposed	A party may issue a claim form under Pt 7 or Pt 8 to sue on an agreement made in settlement of a dispute where that agreement makes provision for costs. The party may issue another claim under Pt 7 or Pt 8 based on the agreement or alleged agreement to which the proceedings under r 44.12A would have applied	PDCosts, paras 17.9 and 17.11
Determination of costs	An order for costs under this provision will be treated as an order that the amount of costs be decided by detailed assessment	PDCosts, para 17.8
Appeals	For appeals against decisions of costs judges/costs officers see Pt 52 and Guides 58 and 59	Part 52 and PD52
Court fees	On filing Pt 8 claim: High Court – £50 County court – £30	CPFO, fee 1.7(b)

35: Application for an Attachment of Earnings Order

Legal background

Where a judgment debtor is in employment, the court may order his employer to deduct periodic amounts from his earnings and remit them to the court against the amount due under the judgment or order to be enforced.

Where it is sought to enforce a maintenance order, the procedure differs considerably. It is not dealt with in this Guide. For a description of the steps to be taken in proceedings which are 'family proceedings', see the relevant Guide in *The Family Court Practice* (Family Law).

Procedure

Availability	The amount due under the judgment or order must be at least £50 or be the balance due under a judgment or order for at least £50	CCR Ord 27, r 7(9)
	The debtor must be in default under the judgment or order	AEA, s 3(3)
Which court	The county court in whose district the debtor resides	CCR Ord 27, r 3(1)

	If the debtor resides outside England and Wales or the creditor does not know where he resides, the county court for the district in which the judgment or order was obtained	CCR Ord 27, r 3(2)
	If applications are made against two or more debtors jointly liable who reside in different districts, then:	
	if any of them resides in the district of the county court which gave the judgment or order, that court;	CCR Ord 27, r 3(3)
	otherwise, any county court in whose district any of them resides.	
	The High Court's jurisdiction is limited to the enforcement of High Court maintenance orders and is not dealt with here.	
Preliminary	If the judgment or order was obtained in a county court other than that to which the application is to be made, the former should be asked to transfer the case to the latter	CCR Ord 25, r 2
	If a judgment or order of the High Court is to be enforced, application should be made to the High Court for an order transferring it to the relevant county court for enforcement and an office copy of the judgment or order to be enforced and a return to any writ of execution should be obtained	CCR Ord 25, r 11
The application	The form of application is filed in the appropriate county court	CCR Ord 27, r 4(1)
	If interest is claimed, a certificate showing the calculation of the amount must be filed in duplicate	CCR Ord 25, r 5A
	In the case of a High Court judgment it is accompanied by an office copy of the judgment or order to be enforced, a certificate verifying the amount due (this will in fact be given in the application form itself), a copy of the sheriff's return to any writ of execution and a copy of the order transferring the proceedings to the county court	CCR Ord 25, r 11(1)

What happens next	The court serves notice of the application, together with a reply form, on the debtor by first-class post (unless the creditor chooses to effect personal service)	CCR Ord 27, r 5(1) CCR Ord 25, r 3(3)
	The debtor is required to complete and return the reply form (giving details of his means and his employment) within 8 days of service (unless he pays the judgment debt)	CCR Ord 27, r 5(2) CCR Ord 27, r 5(2A)
	A copy of the reply is sent to the creditor	CCR Ord 27, r 5(3)
Failure by debtor	If the debtor fails to comply, the court will make a further order requiring compliance, which will contain a warning of the consequences of disobedience and will be served personally. It will also direct that any future payments be made to the court	CCR Ord 27, r 7A(1)
	If the debtor continues to fail to comply, the court will give him notice to show cause why he should not be imprisoned, giving him at least 5 days' notice of the hearing. Failure to comply is punishable by up to 14 days' imprisonment or a fine of up to £500. Such proceedings may be heard by the district judge. A suspended order may be made, on terms that the debtor provide the information	CCR Ord 27, r 7A(2) AEA 1971, s 23
	If the court has information as to the employer's identity, it may request details of the debtor's pay from the employer. Should it prove necessary, it can order the employer to provide it	CCR Ord 27, r 6 AEA, s 14(1)(b)
The order	On the debtor replying, the proper officer may make an attachment of earnings order, which will be based on the information given by the debtor and the use of a table of allowances similar to that applied to the assessment of income support	CCR Ord 27, r 7(1)
	If the proper officer is unable to make an order, the district judge may deal with the application without a hearing or direct that a hearing be fixed	CCR Ord 27, r 7(4) CCR Ord 27, r 7(5)

	Where an order is made without a hearing, either party may apply that it be reconsidered; and a hearing will be fixed for that application	CCR Ord 27, r 7(2) and (6)
	An attachment of earnings order fixes the amount to be deducted in each period (the normal deduction rate) provided that the debtor's net pay for the period is not reduced below a specified amount (the protected earnings rate). The employer remits the amounts deducted to a central accounting point maintained by the Court Service, which passes them on to the creditor	AEA, s 6(5)
Court fees	On application, in respect of each respondent – £60	CPFO fee 7.7
Form	Request for issue N337	

36: Application for a Charging Order

Legal background

The court may impose a charge on the judgment debtor's interest in land, securities or a fund in court. The effect of the order is provided in two stages; an interim charging order followed by a final charging order. The effect of the order is to provide the judgment creditor with a security for the payment of the judgment debt. Payment may then be enforced in one of two ways. The court may appoint a receiver of the income generated by the property charged (see Guide 42). More commonly, the court may make an order for sale in which case the judgment creditor is entitled to payment out of the sale proceeds after any prior charges have been satisfied (see Guide 47).

Procedure

Availability	The remedy is discretionary and will not be granted if it would be oppressive (eg by reason of delay, the small amount of the debt or the small value of the security which a property would provide).	
	In particular, an order will not be made if the debt is the subject of a county court instalment order which is up to date	*Mercantile Credit Co Ltd v Ellis* (1987) *The Times*, 1 April, CA
Which court – funds in court	If the property to be charged is a fund in court, the court in which the fund is lodged	COA 1979, s 1(2)(a)

Other property, jurisdiction as between High Court and county court	The application may only be made in the High Court if the judgment was originally made in the High Court or has subsequently been transferred to the High Court for enforcement *and* the judgment was for a sum exceeding £5000.	COA 1979, s 1(2)(c)
	Other wise the application must be made in the county court	COA 1979, s 1(2)(d)
	If the application must be made in the county court and relates to a High Court judgment the proceedings must first be transferred to the relevant county court for enforcement	Rule 73.3(1)
Which particular court	*High Court applications* In the High Court or the district registry in which the judgment was entered or to which it has since been transferred for enforcement	Rule 73.3(2)
	County court applications The county court in which the judgment was obtained or to which the proceedings have since been transferred	Rule 73.3(2)
	A judgment debtor who wishes to oppose the making of a final order may apply to transfer the proceedings to a more convenient court	PD73, para 3
Application	The application is made by filing an application notice in Form N 379 (which is not to be served) verified by a statement of truth. The application notice must contain the following information:	Rule 73.3(1) See Part 22
	(a) the name and address of the judgment debtor;	
	(b) details of the judgment or order sought to be enforced;	
	(c) the amount of money remaining due;	
	(d) if the judgment debt is payable by instalments, the amount of any instalments in arrears;	
	(e) the names and (if known) the addresses of any other creditors of the judgment debtor of whom the judgment creditor is aware;	
	(f) the asset or assets which it is sought to be charged;	

SECTION 1 Procedural Guides

	(g) details of the judgment debtor's interest in each asset;	
	(h) the names and addresses of the persons on whom an interim charging order must be served under r 73.5(1)	PD73, para 1.2
	If a charging order is sought over the judgment debtor's interest in registered land office copies entries of the title should be filed with the application notice.	
	If satisfied that the application notice contains the required information and that it is proper to make the order , the master or district judge makes an interim charging order and fixes a date to consider whether a final order should be made	Rule 73.4(2)
Service	A copy of the interim order, the application notice and the documents filed in support shall be served by the creditor not less than 21 days before the day fixed for the hearing	Rule 73.5(1)
	If the judgment creditor serves he must either file a certificate of service not less than 2 days before the hearing or produce the certificate at the hearing	Rule 73.5(2)
	Persons to be served: (a) the judgment debtor;	Rule 73.5(1)(a)
	(b) where the order relates to securities not in court, the keeper of the stock register;	Rule 73.5(1)(d)
	(c) where the order relates to a fund in court, the Accountant General at the Court Funds Office;	Rule 73.5(1)(e)
	(d) where the order relates to an interest under a trust, such of the trustees as the court may direct;	Rule 73.5(1)(c)
	(e) any other creditor or interested person as the court may direct	Rule 73.5(1)(b)
	As to the method of service, see Guide 15.	
Objections to the order	Any person who wishes to object to the making of a final charging order must file and serve on the judgment creditor written evidence stating the grounds of his objection not less than 7 days before the hearing	Rule 73.8(1)

The hearing	At the hearing the judge may make a final charging order confirming that the charge should remain in force with or without modifications. The order may be made subject to conditions, for example restricting enforcement	Rule 73.8(2) COA 1979, s 1(2)(c)
Registration	A charging order affecting an interest in land can and should be protected by registration at HM Land Registry or HM Land Charges Registry as appropriate as soon as an interim order is made. If it is discharged on the hearing, the registration must be removed by the creditor.	
Order for sale	See Guide 47	
Court fees	On application: *High Court* – £100 *County court* – £50	 CPFO fee 6.3(b) CPFO fee 7.4(b)
Forms	Application notice N379	

37: Issue of a Writ or Warrant of Delivery

Legal background

In the High Court, a writ of delivery is issued to the sheriff and, in the county court, a delivery warrant is issued to the bailiff, requiring him physically to take the goods from the person against whom an order was made to deliver them up. If the order provides the alternative of payment of the value of the goods, the writ or warrant will require the sheriff or bailiff to levy execution for the value if the goods cannot be uplifted, unless the court has ordered otherwise.

Procedure

Availability	Permission is required to issue the writ or warrant if more than 6 years have elapsed since the order, if there has been a change of parties or (High Court only) if the order was conditional	RSC Ord 46, r 2 CCR Ord 26, r 5
	Permission is required if the judgment was obtained in default against one of several defendants and judgment has not been obtained against all the defendants	Rule 12.8(3)

	Otherwise, the party in whose favour the order was made may issue the writ or warrant as soon as it is made or, if it allows a time for compliance, as soon as that time has expired.	
Issue	*High Court* The applicant files a *præcipe* together with the form of writ for sealing (and produces the order to be enforced and any necessary order giving permission) and then serves the sealed writ on the under-sheriff in whose area the goods are situated	RSC Ord 46, r 6
	County court The applicant files a form of request for the issue of the warrant	CCR Ord 26, rr 1 and 16
Stay of execution	The court has a general power to stay execution of an order on the ground of matters which have occurred since it was made	RSC Ord 45, r 11 CCA 1984, ss 38, 76
Court fees	*High Court* – £50 (NB a further fee is payable to the sheriff)	CPFO fee 6.1
	County court – £90	CPFO fee 7.6
Forms	*High Court* *Præcipe* PF90 Writ Form 64 or 65 *County court* Request N324	

38: Issue of Execution Against Goods

Legal background

In the High Court, a writ of *fieri facias* is issued to the sheriff and, in the county court, a warrant of execution is issued to the bailiff, requiring him to seize and sell the debtor's goods to produce the amount due under the judgment or order. The court may stay or suspend the execution if there are special circumstances or if the debtor is unable to pay.

Procedure

Availability	Permission is required to issue the writ or warrant if more than 6 years have elapsed since the order, if there has been a change of parties, if the order was conditional (High Court only), in certain circumstances if the judgment or order was against the estate of a deceased person or if a receiver or sequestrator has been appointed;	
	otherwise, the party in whose favour the judgment was given or order was made may issue the writ or warrant as soon as it is given or made or, if it allows a time for compliance, as soon as that time has expired	RSC Ord 46, r 2 CCR Ord 26, r 5
	In the county court, if the debt is the subject of an instalment order, the warrant may not be issued so long as the payments are up to date	CCA 1984, s 86
	If the payments are in arrears, a warrant can be issued for all or part of the debt then unpaid (subject to a minimum of £50 or one month's or 4 weeks' instalments)	CCR Ord 26, r 1(2)
Partnerships	Where the judgment was given against a firm in its firm name, permission may be required to issue execution against the goods of individual partners	RSC Ord 81, r 5 CCR Ord 25, r 9
	Where the judgment was given in proceedings between a firm and one or more partners or between two firms with one or more partners in common, permission is required to issue execution to enforce it	RSC Ord 81, r 6 CCR Ord 25, r 10
Which court	*High Court judgment or order* Execution may be issued in the High Court or in any county court in the district of which execution is to be levied	CCR Ord 26, r 2(1)
	County court judgment or order Execution may be issued only in the county court if the amount sought to be recovered is less than £1000 or if the judgment was given in proceedings arising out of an agreement regulated by the Consumer Credit Act 1974.	

	Otherwise, execution may be issued only in the High Court if the amount sought to be recovered is £5000 or more.	
	Execution may be issued in the High Court or the county court in all other cases	HCCCJO, art 8
	It is issued in the county court in which the judgment was given or to which the proceedings have since been transferred.	
Preliminary	If it is intended to enforce a county court judgment in the High Court, the creditor should request from the county court in which the judgment was given or to which the proceedings have since been transferred a certificate of the judgment or order, stating that it is intended to enforce it by execution against goods	CCR Ord 22, r 8
	If it is intended to enforce a High Court judgment in a county court, the creditor should apply for the transfer of the judgment to the county court and obtain an office copy of the judgment or order and a copy of the sheriff's return to any writ of execution issued in the High Court	CCR Ord 25, r 11(1)
Issue	*High Court* The applicant files a *præcipe* together with the form of writ for sealing, producing the judgment or order to be enforced (or the certificate of the county court judgment or order) and any necessary order giving permission. He then serves the sealed writ on the under-sheriff in whose area the goods are situated	RSC Ord 46, r 6
	County court The applicant files a form of request for the issue of the warrant together, if a High Court judgment or order is to be enforced, with an office copy of the judgment, a certificate of the amount due (in practice included in the request), an office copy of the sheriff's return to any High Court execution and a copy of the order transferring to the county court	CCR Ord 26, r 1 CCR Ord 25, r 11(1)

Stay of execution	The court has a general power to stay execution of an order on the ground of matters which have occurred since it was made	RSC Ord 45, r 11 CCA 1984, ss 38 and 76
	The county court has a similar power on the ground of inability to pay, whenever arising	CCA 1984, s 71(2), 88
Court fees	*High Court* – £50 (NB a further fee is payable to the Sheriff)	CPFO fee 6.1
	County court Warrant issued for: up to £125 – fee £30 over £125 – fee £50	 CPFO fee 7.1(a) CPFO fee 7.1(b)
	CCBC cases Warrant issued for: up to £125 – fee £25 over £125 – fee £45	 CPFO fee 7.1(c) CPFO fee 7.1(d)
	On a request for a further attempt at execution at a new address re-issue following notice of a reason for non-execution (except not after suspension and CCBC cases) – fee £20	CPFO fee 7.2
Forms	*High Court* *Præcipe* PF 86 Writ Form 53 to 63	
	County court Request N323	

39: Application for a Third Party Debt Order

Legal background

The court may order a person (the third party) who owes money to the debtor to pay it instead to the creditor in satisfaction or reduction of the judgment debt. The debt attached is usually, but is not limited to, a balance in the debtor's bank account. The procedure replaces with important modifications the former garnishee proceedings which have been abolished.

Procedure

Availability	The judgment creditor must have a money judgment against the judgment debtor and money must be owed to the judgment debtor by a third party who is or carries on business within England and Wales. The money judgment must be immediately enforceable, ie one which has not been stayed; where the date for payment has passed; or at least one instalment has not been paid under any instalment order	Rule 72.1(1) Rule 72.1(1)
	There is no longer a requirement that the amount due to the applicant must exceed £50, but the order is discretionary and may be refused, for example if the administrative costs to which the third party is entitled in complying with the order are out of proportion to the judgment debt.	
Which court	The application is made to the court in which the judgment was given or to which the case has since been transferred	Rule 72.3(1)(b)
Application	By filing in the court office, an application notice in Form N349, verified by a statement of truth and containing the following information	Rule 72.3(1) Rule 72.3(2)(b)
	(1) the name and address of the judgment debtor;	
	(2) details of the judgment or order sought to be enforced;	
	(3) the amount of money remaining due under the judgment or order;	
	(4) if the judgment debt is payable by instalments, the amount of any instalments which have fallen due and remain unpaid;	
	(5) the name and address of the third party;	
	(6) if the third party is a bank or building society –	
	(a) its name and the address of the branch at which the judgment debtor's account is believed to be held; and	
	(b) the account number;	

	(7) confirmation that to the best of the judgment creditor's knowledge or belief the third party – (a) is within the jurisdiction; and (b) owes money to or holds money to the credit of the judgment debtor (8) if the judgment creditor knows or believes that any person other than the judgment debtor has any claim to the money owed by the third party – (a) his name and (if known) his address; and (b) such information as is known to the judgment creditor about his claim (9) details of any other applications for third party debt orders issued by the judgment creditor in respect of the same judgment debt; and (10) the source or grounds of the judgment creditor's knowledge or belief of the matters referred to in (7), (8) and (9)	PD72, para 1.2
	The application is not normally served on the judgment debtor.	
Interim third party debt order	The master or district judge may make an interim third party debt order: (a) fixing a hearing date, not less than 28 days ahead, to consider whether to make a final third party debt order ('the final hearing'); and	Rule 72.4(2)(a), (5)
	(b) directing that until the hearing the third party must not make any payment which reduces the amount he owes to the judgment debtor to less than the figure specified in the order	Rule 72.4(2)(b)
	The amount specified will be the amount remaining due under the judgment together with the fixed costs allowable to the judgment creditor for making the application	PD72, para 2
	The order becomes binding on the third party when it is served upon him	Rule 72.4(4)

Service	*On the third party* The order may be served by the court or by the judgment creditor (who might wish to deliver it immediately, rather than wait for the court to post it). It must be served not less than 21 days before the date of the hearing	Rule 72.5(1)(a)
	On the judgment debtor The order may be served by the court or by the judgment creditor. It must be served not less than 7 days after service on the third party and not less than 7 days before the date of the hearing	Rule 72.5(1)(b)
	The order must be served in accordance with Pt 6. See Guide 15 as to service and as to the address for service.	
	If served by the judgment creditor, he must file a certificate of service not less than 2 days before the hearing or produce the certificate at the hearing	Rule 72.5(2)
	If the third party is a company, it may be served by posting it to the registered office	Companies Act 1985, s 725
Obligations of the third party	*Banks or building societies* If the third party is a bank or building society, it must carry out a search immediately to identify any accounts held with it by the judgment debtor	Rule 72.6(1)
	Unless otherwise ordered this will not include accounts where the judgment debtor is not the sole account holder	PD72, paras 3.1–3.2
	In respect of each account identified the bank or building society must within 7 days of service inform the court and the judgment creditor: (a) of the number of each account; (b) whether it is in credit; (c) if it is in credit, whether the balance is sufficient to cover the amount specified in the order; or if the amount is insufficient, the credit balance at the date of service; and (d) if the bank or building society claims to be entitled to retain the money, details of that claim	Rule 72.6(2)

	Alternatively the bank or building society must inform the court and the judgment creditor within 7 days of service: (a) that the judgment debtor does not hold an account with the bank or building society; or (b) that it is unable to comply with the order for any other reason, for example that the information given is insufficient positively to identify the judgment debtor as the holder of a particular account	Rule 72.6(3)
	The rules do not require banks or building societies to give the information in writing.	
	Other third parties Third parties who are not banks or building societies must inform the court and the judgment creditor in writing if they claim – (a) not to owe money to the judgment debtor; or (b) to owe less than the amount specified in the order	Rule 72.6(4)
Hardship payment orders	Pending the final hearing a judgment debtor may apply for a hardship payment order if the following conditions are satisfied: (a) he is an individual; (b) he is prevented from withdrawing money from his bank or building society as a result of an interim third party debt order; and (c) as a result he or his family is suffering hardship in meeting ordinary living expenses	Rule 72.7(1)
	A judgment debtor may only apply to one court for a hardship payment order	Rule 72.7(3)
	If the interim order was made in the High Court, the application may be made either at the Royal Courts of Justice or at any district registry	Rule 72.7(2)(a)
	If the interim order was made in a county court the application may be made at any county court	Rule 72.7(2)(b)

	Application is made by filing an application notice quoting the case number and the court which made the interim order, verified by a statement of truth and setting out detailed evidence explaining why a hardship payment is needed. Documentary evidence, such as bank statements, wage slips, or mortgage statements should be included	PD72, para 5.1 Rule 72.7(4)(a), (b) PD72, para 5.6
	The application will be dealt with at the court to which it is made	PD72, paras 5.2 and 5.3(1)
	The court in which the interim order has been made will send copies of the original application notice for the third party debt order and the interim order to the court dealing with the hardship application	PD72, para 5.3(2)
	Unless the court otherwise orders the judgment creditor must be given 2 days' notice of the hearing but the application need not be served on the third party	Rule 72.7(5)
	In case of exceptional urgency the court may deal with the application without notice. If so, then wherever possible the judgment creditor will be informed of the application and given an opportunity to make representations by telephone, fax or other means of communication	PD72, para 5.5
	A hardship payment order is directed to the third party and will permit one or more payments out of the account and may specify to whom those payments are to be made (for example by honouring standing order mandates)	Rule 72.7(6)
Transfer of proceedings	If the judgment debtor wishes to oppose the application for a final order, he may apply for the application to be transferred to the court for the district in which he resides or carries on business, or another court	PD72, para 4

Objections to the order	If either the third party or the judgment debtor wishes to object to the final order he must file and serve written evidence setting out the grounds of his objection not less than 3 days before the hearing	Rule 72.8(1), (4)
	If either the third party or the judgment debtor knows or believes that any other person has a claim to the money specified in the interim order, he must file and serve written evidence stating his knowledge of that matter not less than 3 days before the hearing	Rule 72.8(4)
	If the judgment creditor wishes to dispute a claim by a third party other than a bank or building society, either that it does not owe money to the judgment debtor or that the amount owing is less than the amount specified in the order, he must file and serve written evidence setting out his grounds for disputing the third party's claim not less than 3 days before the hearing	Rule 72.8(3), (4)
	If the court is notified that some other person may have a claim to the money specified in the interim order it will serve notice on that person of the application and the date of hearing	Rule 72.8(5)
The hearing	The court may, if the third party does not attend or disputes his indebtedness to the debtor, make a final third party debt order	Rule 72.8(6)(a)
	The court may discharge the interim third party debt order and dismiss the application	Rule 72.8(6)(b)
	The court may dispose summarily of issues in dispute between the parties and any other person claiming the money specified in the order and either make a final third party debt order or discharge the interim third party debt order and dismiss the application	Rule 72.8(6)(c)
	If it is unable to dispose of the issues summarily, the court may direct the trial of an issue and give further directions	Rule 72.8(6)(d)

The final third party debt order	The final third party debt order requires the third party to pay to the creditor the lesser of: (a) the amount of the debt due from the garnishee to the debtor (except the last £1 in an account with a Building Society) less any costs allowed to the third party and expenses of £55 if it is a deposit-taking institution; or (b) the amount of the debt due from the debtor to the creditor together with any costs allowed to the creditor	Rule 72.2(1) SCA 1981, s 40A CCA 1984, s 109
	The order is enforceable against the third party as any other order for payment of money may be enforced	Rule 72.9(1)
	To the extent of the payment made or enforced against him (but not enforcement costs) under the terms of the final third party debt order, the third party is discharged from his liability to the debtor	Rule 72.9(2)
Court fee	On application: *High Court* – £100 for each third party against whom the order is sought	CPFO fee 6.3(a)
	County court – £50 for each third party against whom the order is sought	CPFO fee 7.4(a)
Forms	Application for third party debt order – Form N349 Application for hardship payment order – Form N244	
Money in court	If the debtor is entitled to money held in court, third party debt order proceedings may not be taken in respect of it but the creditor may apply to the court holding it for an order for payment out to him	Rule 72.10

40: Application to Obtain Information from Judgment Debtors

Legal background

The new CPR Pt 71 amalgamates and amends provisions in the former Sch 1, RSC Ord 48 and Sch 2, CCR Ord 25, r 3. The court may order and ultimately compel the judgment debtor to attend and provide information as to his means to pay or otherwise comply with the judgment or order against him. Where the judgment debtor is a company or corporation, one of its officers can similarly be compelled to provide information about its means; and in such a case references in this Guide should be construed accordingly.

Procedure

Availability	The application may be made at any time after the judgment or order has become enforceable	Rule 71.1
Which court	*High Court judgment:* To the High Court (district registry if that is where the enforcement proceedings currently are)	Rule 71.2(2)(b)(i)
	If the judgment has been transferred to a county court for enforcement, it is treated as a judgment of that court – see below	Rule 71.3(1) CCA 1984, s 40(6)(b)
	County court judgment: To the county court which made the judgment which it is sought to enforce	Rule 7.1(2)(b)(i)
	Or to the county court to which a High Court judgment has been transferred for enforcement	CCA 1984, s 40(6)(b)
	Or, if the proceedings to enforce the judgment have since been transferred to another county court, to that county court	Rule 30.2(1)(b)(ii) PD70, paras 2.1
	If the judgment has been transferred to The High Court for enforcement, it is treated as a judgment of that court – see above	CCA 1984, s 40(6)(b) CCR Ord 25, r 2(1)
Making the application	By filing an application notice, without notice to the judgment debtor	Rule 71.2(2)(a)
Contents of the notice	The notice must contain the following information: *General requirements* (a) state the name and address of the judgment debtor; (b) identify the judgment which it is sought to enforce; *Judgments against companies or corporations* (c) state the name and address and position in the company or corporation of the individual whose attendance is to be ordered;	

	Money judgments (d) state the amount presently owing under the judgment; *Other judgments* (f) identify the particular matters about which questions are to be asked; *Production of documents* (g) if the judgment creditor wishes particular documents to be produced, identify the documents which the judgment debtor or individual is to be ordered to produce;	PD71, para 1.2
	Conduct of examination (h) if the judgment creditor wishes the questioning to be conducted before a judge, specify that request and set out the reasons why; *Additional questions* (i) where the questioning is to be conducted by a court officer and the judgment creditor wishes specific questions to be asked which are not contained in PD71, Appendix A or B a list of the questions must be attached to the application notice	PD71, para 4.2(2)
Consideration of the application	The application will initially be considered by a court officer, who may refer it to a judge and will refer it to a judge if questioning before a judge has been requested	PD71, para 1.3(1), (2) Rule 3.2
	Only a judge can decide that questioning should take place at a court other than the county court for the district in which the judgment debtor resides or carries on business	PD71, para 2.1
	If the application notice complies with the requirements set out above, an order will be made without a hearing, either by a court officer or a judge	Rule 71.2(4), (5)
The order	Unless a judge has otherwise ordered, the order (whether made by the High Court or a county court) will require the judgment debtor or individual to: (a) attend at the county court for the district in which he resides or carries on business on a specified date and time;	

	(b) produce at court documents in his control which are specified in the order; and	
	(c) answer on oath such questions as the court may require	PD71, para 2.1 Rule 71.2(6)
	The order will only provide for questioning before a judge if the court is satisfied there are compelling reasons for making such an order	PD71, para 2.2
	The order will contain a notice setting out the consequences of failure to comply	Rule 71.2(7)
Service of the order	The order must be served personally on the debtor or the debtor's officer ordered to attend (see Guide 15) not less than 14 days before the hearing	Rule 71.3(1)
	The court may order service by an alternative method. Since failure to attend may render the judgment debtor liable to imprisonment, a judgment creditor may need to present strong evidence both that personal service cannot be achieved without disproportionate expense and that the judgment debtor will become aware of the order in time to comply	Rule 6.8 PD6, para 9.1
	If the proceedings are in a county court and the judgment creditor is an individual litigant in person service will be effected by the court bailiff	PD71, para 3
	In all other cases the responsibility for effecting service rests on the judgment creditor	PD71, para 3
	Within 7 days after service the person ordered to attend may request the judgment creditor to pay him a sum reasonably sufficient to cover his travelling expenses to and from the court. The judgment creditor must comply with any such request	Rule 71.4(1), (2)
Proof of service and pre-hearing requirements	Where the order has been served by the court bailiff, either personally or by an alternative method ordered by the court, no affidavit of service is required. A certificate of service will be made by the court bailiff	Rule 71.4(1) CCA 1984, s 133(1)

	Where the judgment creditor has been responsible for service one or more affidavits must be sworn and filed as follows:	
	(a) evidence by the person who served the order giving details of how and when it was served	Rule 71.4(1)(a)
	(b) evidence by or on behalf of the judgment creditor either that no request for travelling expenses has been received, or if one has been received, that a sum has been paid in accordance with the request	Rule 71.4(1)(b)
	(c) evidence of the amount outstanding under the judgment	Rule 71.4(1)(c)
	The affidavit or affidavits must either be:	
	(a) filed with the court not less than two days before the hearing; or	
	(b) produced at the hearing	Rule 71.4(2)(a), (b)
The first hearing	*Before a judge* Where a hearing before a judge has been ordered, the judgment creditor or his representative must attend and conduct the questioning	Rule 71.6(3)(b)
	The proceedings will be tape-recorded and the court will not make a written record	PD71, para 5.2
	Before a court officer Where the hearing takes place before a court officer, the court officer will ask a standard set of questions. He will also ask any additional questions which the judgment creditor has attached to his application notice	PD71, paras 4.1, 4.2(2) and Apps A, B
	The judgment creditor or his representative may attend and ask questions himself	PD71, para 4.2(1)
	The questioning will either be tape-recorded (presumably only when the judgment creditor attends) or the court will make a written record of the evidence given. At the end of the hearing any written record will be read back to the judgment debtor or individual and he will be invited to sign it. If he refuses to sign his refusal will be noted on the record of evidence	PD71, para 4.3(1), (2), (3)

	The hearing may be adjourned in which case the court will direct how the judgment debtor is to be served with notice of the new hearing date	Rule 71.7
	Where the judgment debtor is present and can be given oral notice of the date and time of the adjourned hearing, formal service may be dispensed with	Rule 1.1(2)(b) Rule 6.9(1)
Judgment debtor's failure to attend or otherwise comply with the order	If the judgment debtor, which expression includes an officer of a company or corporation who has been ordered to attend to answer questions: (a) fails to attend; (b) refuses to take the oath or to answer any questions; or (c) otherwise fails to comply with the order, eg by failing to produce documents which he has been ordered to produce the judge or court officer conducting the hearing will certify in writing the manner in which the order has not been complied with	PD71, para 6
	The matter will then be referred either to a High Court or circuit judge	Rule 71.8(1)
	The judge will consider first whether the order has been properly served and the judgment creditor has complied with the other pre-hearing requirements	Rule 71.8(3) Rules 71.4, 71.5
	If he is satisfied with these matters, the judge will then consider the nature of the breach as certified in writing by the judge or court officer who conducted the hearing. If he is satisfied that the breach is sufficiently serious, he will make a suspended committal order against the judgment debtor or individual concerned	Rule 71.8(2)
	Terms of suspension The order will be suspended on terms that the person named in the order: (a) attends court for a further appointment at the time and place specified in the order	Rule 71.8(4)(a)(i)
	(b) complies with all the terms of that order and the original order	Rule 71.8(4)(a)(ii)

	The order will also direct that if the person fails to attend the further appointment he must be brought before a judge	Rule 71.8(4)(b)
	The further appointment will be before a judge if the first hearing was ordered to take place before a judge, or if the judge making the suspended committal order so directs	PD71, para 7.1(1)(a), (b)
	Otherwise it will take place before a court officer	PD71, para 7.1(2)
Service of suspended committal order	The requirements for service, proof of service and other pre-hearing requirements set out above, except the provisions relating to the request for and payment of travelling expenses, apply equally to any suspended committal order	PD71, para 7.2
Judgment debtor's failure to attend further appointment or otherwise to comply	If the suspended committal order has been duly served and the judgment debtor fails to attend on the further appointment, the judge or court officer conducting the hearing will certify in writing his failure to attend	PD71, para 8.1
	Similarly, if the judgment debtor attends but fails to comply (eg by refusing to be sworn or answer questions), the judge or court officer will so certify in writing	PD71, para 8.2
	In either case, on the basis of that certificate, the court will then issue a warrant for the arrest of the judgment debtor to be brought before a judge, who may be a master or district judge, and who will consider whether the committal order should be discharged or put into effect	PD71, paras 8.3, 8.4 Rule 71.8(4)(b)
	In practice, the person arrested will be offered the opportunity to purge his contempt by complying with the original order to provide information. If he complies, the suspended committal order will be discharged.	
	If he declines the opportunity the court must proceed immediately to consider whether or not the committal order should be discharged or put into effect.	

	At this point, in order to comply with the HRA 1998 the person arrested must be given details in writing of his alleged contempt, and be offered the opportunity both to have legal representation and to challenge the evidence against him. An adjournment may be essential, for example if the person arrested wishes to challenge the evidence of service either of the original order or the suspended committal order or the contents of a certificate of non-attendance	*Newman v Modern Bookbinders* [2000] 2 All ER 814 *King v Read* [1999] 1 FLR 425, CA
	The suspended committal order will be discharged unless the judge is satisfied beyond reasonable doubt: (a) that the judgment debtor has failed to comply with the original order to attend court; (b) that the judgment debtor has failed to comply with the terms of the suspended committal order; and (c) that both orders have been duly served on the judgment debtor	PD71, para 8.5
	If the breach and due service are either admitted or found proved beyond reasonable doubt, the arrested person must be given a chance to put forward any mitigation before being sentenced	*Shoreditch County Court v de Madeiros* (1988) *The Times*, 24 February, CA
	The court retains a discretion either to enforce the suspended order by issuing an immediate warrant, or to deal with the judgment debtor in any other way which is appropriate to the nature and seriousness of any breach which has been committed, taking account of any mitigation	*Re W(B)* [1969] 1 All ER 594
Court fees	On application: *High Court* – £50 *County court* – £40	CPFO fee 6.2 CPFO fee 7.3
Forms	Application to question an individual judgment debtor – Form N316 Application to question an officer of a company or corporation – Form N316A	

41: Issue of a Writ or Warrant of Possession of Land

Legal background

In the High Court, a writ of possession is issued to the sheriff and, in the county court, a warrant of possession is issued to the bailiff, requiring him physically to take possession of the land (and buildings) and give it to the party in whose favour the judgment was given or the order made.

Procedure

Availability	In the High Court, permission is required unless the order for possession was made in mortgage proceedings. The application must be supported by evidence as to the notice received by those in possession and (if applicable) as to the receipt of notice under Landlord and Tenant Act 1954, s 16(2)	RSC Ord 45, r 3(2) RSC Ord 45, r 3(3)
	Permission is in any event required if more than 6 years have elapsed since the date of the judgment or order, if there has been a change in the party entitled to enforce the order or the party liable under it or (in the High Court only) if the order was conditional. The application notice need not be served unless the court so directs. It must be supported by evidence	RSC Ord 46, r 2(1) CCR Ord 26, r 5(1) RSC Ord 46, r 4 CCR Ord 26, r 5(2)
	Otherwise, the party in whose favour the order was made may issue the writ or warrant as soon as it is made or, if it allows a time for compliance, then as soon as that time has expired.	
	The court has a general power to stay execution of an order on the ground of matters which have occurred since it was made	RSC Ord 45, r 11 CCA 1984, ss 38 and 76
Issue	*High Court* The applicant files a *præcipe* together with the form of writ for sealing and then serves the sealed writ on the under-sheriff in whose area the land is situated	RSC Ord 46, r 6
	County court The applicant files a form of request for the issue of the warrant	CCR Ord 26, r 1

Court fees	*High Court* – £50 (NB a further fee is payable to the sheriff.)	CPFO fee 6.1
	County court – £90	CPFO fee 7.6
Forms	*High Court* *Præcipe* PF88 or PF89 Writ Form 66	
	County court Request N325	

42: Application for the Appointment of a Receiver by way of Equitable Execution

Legal background

Where the debtor has assets which cannot be reached by other enforcement methods, the court may appoint a receiver to take them and apply them (or the income from them) to the payment of the amount due under the judgment or order.

Procedure

Availability	A county court has all the necessary powers of the High Court. It also has express powers to appoint a receiver of interests in land	CCA 1984, s 38 CCA 1984, s 107
	The powers of either court are discretionary. The court must have regard to the amount claimed by the creditor, the amount likely to be obtained by the receiver and the probable costs of his appointment	RSC Ord 51, r 1
Application	The application is made by application notice (see Guide 18) and may be made to the master or district judge	RSC Ord 30, r 1 RSC Ord 51, r 2
	In the county court, if interest is claimed, a calculation must be filed in duplicate	CCR Ord 25, r 5A
	No doubt, in either court such a calculation will form part of the evidence which the applicant will wish to file in support of the application.	
Court fee	On application: *High Court* – £100 *County court* – £50	 CPFO fee 6.3(a) CPFO fee 7.4(a)
Form	Application notice – Form N244.	

43: Issue of a Writ of Sequestration

Legal background

In the High Court, the party in whose favour a judgment has been given or an order made may issue a writ requiring the sequestrators named in it to take possession of all the assets of the party against whom it was made (or, if that party is a company, the assets of its directors or other officers) if he has not complied with it. The remedy is appropriate in circumstances where committal for contempt might (in the case of a contemnor who is an individual) be imposed (see Guide 44), save that the restriction on the court's power to commit for non-compliance with an order to pay money does not apply to sequestration. The county court may also exercise this remedy but it is more appropriate to apply to transfer a county court judgment or order to the High Court for enforcement.

Procedure

Availability	Permission is always required and is only granted in large cases, in view of the considerable expense involved	RSC Ord 45, r 5(1)
The application for permission	The application notice is made returnable before a judge and must be supported by evidence. It must be personally served on the person whose property it is sought to sequestrate, unless the court dispenses with service. The application is usually heard in open court	RSC Ord 46, r 5
Subsequent procedure	If permission is granted, the applicant files a *præcipe* together with the form of writ for sealing and serves the writ on the sequestrators named in it	RSC Ord 46, r 6
Court fees	On the application – £100 On the writ – no fee prescribed	CPFO fee 2.5
Forms	Application Notice N244 Writ Form 67	

44: Application to Commit for Breach of an Order or an Undertaking

Legal background

A party entitled to the benefit of an injunctive order directing another party to do an act within a specified time or to abstain from doing an act, or an undertaking to similar effect, which has not been complied with may apply for that other party's committal to prison for contempt of court. The court may fine the contemnor instead of imprisoning him.

A judgment or order to pay money cannot be enforced in this way (save that liabilities for maintenance in Family proceedings and some debts for taxes may be enforceable by the judgment summons procedure under Debtors Act 1869, s 5, not covered in this work).

The procedures described in this Guide do not apply to breaches of orders made under the Attachment of Earnings Act 1971 or of orders made for obtaining information from a judgment debtor, as to which see Guides 35 and 40 respectively.

Where authority from Sch 1 to the Rules ('RSC') but no authority from Sch 2 ('CCR') is shown below, the county court will adopt the High Court procedure (CCA 1984, s 76).

Procedure

Which court	*High Court* If the contempt is committed in connection with proceedings before the Queen's Bench Divisional Court or in connection with proceedings in an inferior court, the application must be made to that divisional court, but may only be made with its permission	RSC Ord 52, r 1(2) RSC Ord 52, rr 2 and 3
	The procedure, not described in this Guide, varies from that described below.	
	Otherwise the application is made to a judge of the Division which made the order (or took the undertaking) breach of which is alleged	RSC Ord 52, r 1(3)
	County court The application may be made to the county court if it made the order (or took the undertaking) breach of which is alleged. It should be made to the court in which the case is proceeding, there being no requirement to secure transfer to another county court	CCA 1984, s 38 CCR Ord 29, r 1(1) PDCommittal, para 1.2
Availability	The general rule is that a copy of the injunctive order, bearing a warning of the consequences of disobedience (usually called 'a penal notice'), must have been served personally on the person to whom it is addressed	PD40B, para 9.1 RSC Ord 45, r 7(2)(a) and (4) CCR Ord 29, r 1(2)(a) and (3)

	Where the order requires the person to do an act, it must have been served before the time for doing it expired. The court may make a fresh order, providing a new time for compliance or imposing such a time where none appeared in the order breach of which is alleged. The application notice for such an order must be served	RSC Ord 45, r 7(2)(b) CCR Ord 29, r 1(2)(b) RSC Ord 45, r 6(1) Rule 3.1(2)(a) RSC Ord 45, r 6(2)–(3)
	Where the order requires the person to abstain from an act, it may be enforced before service if the court is satisfied that he had notice of it by being present when it was made or having been notified of it by telegram, telephone or otherwise	RSC Ord 45, r 7(6) CCR Ord 29, r 1(6)
	The court may dispense with service of the order to be enforced if it thinks it just to do so	RSC Ord 45, r 7(7) CCR Ord 29, r 1(7)
	An undertaking may be enforced as an order to similar effect. For the undertaking to be enforced, the order reciting it need not have been served but this is nevertheless good practice; and is required in the county court (if a copy is not handed to the person at the time) even though not a condition of enforcement. A penal notice must be endorsed. The party giving the undertaking should sign a statement that he understands it and the consequences of breach	*L & Birm Ry v Grand Junction Canal Co* (1835) 1 Ry Ca 224 *Hussain v Hussain* [1986] 2 WLR 801, CA CCR Ord 29, r 1A PD40B, paras 9.2–9.4
	If the order is addressed to a company, it may be enforced by committal proceedings taken against an officer, as may an undertaking given by a company	RSC Ord 45, r 5(1)(ii) *Biba Ltd v Stratford Investments* [1973] 1 Ch 281
The application	The party seeking to enforce may apply by application notice or by issuing a claim form under Pt 8. An application notice will be more appropriate if the application can be made in existing proceedings in which the order was made or undertaking given	RSC Ord 52, r 4(1) CCR Ord 29, r 1(4) PDCommittal, para 2.2

	The notice or claim form must state the grounds of the application, identifying the provisions alleged to have been disobeyed or broken and listing the ways in which they have been disobeyed or broken. It must be supported by an affidavit which must be served and filed – see the note in 'Forms' below	RSC Ord 52, r 4(1), (2) CCR Ord 29, r 1(4A) PDCommittal, paras 2.5 and 2.6
	The notice or claim form and the affidavit must normally be served personally on the respondent (see Guide 15); but the court may dispense with such service if it thinks it just to do so	RSC Ord 52, r 4(2) CCR Ord 29, r 1(4) RSC Ord 52, r 4(3) CCR Ord 29, r 1(7)
	Fourteen clear days' notice of the hearing must be given unless the court otherwise directs	PDCommittal, para 4.2
	Where the application is adjourned, the order or notice giving the new date should be similarly served unless the respondent was present to hear the new date given or was remanded in custody	*Chiltern DC v Keane* [1985] 1 WLR 619, CA
Alternative remedies	The court regards committal as a last resort and will expect the applicant to have used another remedy if it was likely to have been effective. For example: a writ or warrant of delivery may be issued to enforce an order for the delivery of goods (see Guide 37); a writ or warrant of possession may be issued to enforce an order for possession of land or premises (see Guide 41). An order to do an act may, when appropriate, be enforced by the court's authorising the applicant or some other person to do it at the contemnor's expense	*Danchevsky v Danchevsky* [1974] 3 WLR 709, CA RSC Ord 45, r 8
Case management etc	At any stage the court may give directions (including requiring written evidence to be filed) and may hold a directions hearing or treat the hearing notice of which was given as a directions hearing	PDCommittal, para 4.3

	On application or on its own initiative, the court may strike out the application if it appears groundless or an abuse of process or if there has been a failure to comply with a rule, practice direction or order	PDCommittal, para 5
	The CPR provisions as to single joint expert witnesses and as to providing additional information do not apply	PDCommittal, para 6 and para 7
Discontinuance	The application may not be discontinued without the court's permission	PDCommittal, para 8
The hearing	The application will be heard in open court unless:	
	it arises out of proceedings concerning a child or patient;	
	it arises out of proceedings in which a secret process, discovery or invention was in issue; or	
	it should be heard in private in the interests of the administration of justice or for reasons of national security	RSC Ord 52, r 6(1)
	In such a case, if a committal order is made, a statement will be made in open court giving the name of the person committed, the general nature of the contempt proved and the penalty imposed	RSC Ord 52, r 6(2) PDCommittal, para 9
	The criminal standard of proof applies and the procedure adopted will reflect the quasi-criminal nature of the proceedings	*Dean v Dean* [1987] 1 FLR 517, CA
	Only the grounds specified in the notice or claim form may be relied on, unless the court otherwise permits	RSC Ord 52, r 6(3)
	The respondent is entitled to give or call oral evidence even though he has not acknowledged service or filed an affidavit	RSC Ord 52, r 6(4) PDCommittal, paras 2.5(4), 3.3, and 3.4
The order	The respondent may be sentenced to a term or terms of imprisonment not exceeding 2 years in total	Contempt of Court Act 1981, s 14

	A respondent who is under 21 may be sentenced to detention, but a respondent who is under 18 cannot be given any form of custodial sentence	*R v Selby Justices, ex p Frame* [1991] 2 WLR 965, DC
	A fine may be imposed and, in the case of a company, will be the usual form of penalty	RSC Ord 52, r 9
	The sentence may be suspended on terms	RSC Ord 52, r 7(1)
	The breaches found, the penalty imposed and the terms of any adjournment or suspension must be clearly set out	*Nguyen v Phung* [1984] FLR 773, CA
	An order containing terms of suspension must be served by the applicant unless the court orders otherwise	RSC Ord 52, r 7(2)
	In the county court, the order is for the issue of a warrant of committal and must be served before or when the warrant is executed; or within 36 hours thereafter if the judge signs the warrant itself	CCR Ord 29, r 1(5)
Discharge of contemnor	The respondent may apply to purge his contempt	RSC Ord 52, r 8 CCR Ord 29, r 3
	It is the practice of the Official Solicitor to review cases in which a committal order is made. He may make an application on behalf of the person committed	CCR Ord 29, r 3(3)
Court fees	On application: *High Court* – £100 *County court* – £60	CPFO fee 2.5
Forms	It will be useful to adapt the content and layout of the old Form N78 but care must be exercised. There are grave doubts whether that form complies with HRA 1998, Sch 1, Art 6 in giving the appearance of reversing the burden of proof, which in fact rests with the applicant who must prove the breach beyond reasonable doubt	
	It is strongly recommended that those who wish to use Form N78 adapt it:	PDCommittal, para 1.4

	(1) by deleting the heading 'Notice to show good reason why your committal to prison should not be made' and substituting 'Notice of application for committal'; (2) by deleting the words 'to show good reason why you should not be sent to prison' and substituting 'when the application will be heard'; and (3) by deleting the third bullet point under the heading 'Important notes'.	
Which judge	*High Court* The judge	PD2B, para 3.1(a)
	County court Under Housing Act 1996, ss 152–157 or Protection from Harassment Act 1997, s 3 (or in certain Family proceedings), either the circuit judge or the district judge. Otherwise, the circuit judge	PD2B, para 8.3

45: Claims for the Recovery of Possession of Land Against Trespassers Using the Interim Possession Order Procedure

Legal background

With the exception of interim possession orders (IPOs), new procedures relating to possession claims were introduced from 15 October 2001 by virtue of the Civil Procedure (Amendment) Rules 2001, SI 2001/256. The Civil Procedure (Amendment) Rules 2002, SI 2002/2058 added IPOs to CPR Pt 55 with effect from 2 December 2002.

Standard procedure or IPO procedure?

The claimant has a choice of remedy against a trespasser. Proceedings can be commenced using either the CPR Pt 55, Section I procedure set out in Guide 52 'Guide for the Recovery of Possession of Land against Trespassers' or the IPO procedure to be found in CPR Pt 55, Section III and set out below. As an alternative to the IPO procedure, and particularly where the conditions for applying under Pt 55, Section III are not present but where nevertheless there is a real emergency, practitioners may wish to consider the use of the procedure in Pt 55, Section I coupled with an application to abridge time for service (see CPR r 55.5 and r 3.1(2)(a)). Furthermore, under the IPO procedure there is the expense of two court hearings rather than just the one under the standard procedure and the claimant is required to give undertakings in damages as a condition of the grant of an IPO.

Definition

'A possession claim against trespassers' means a claim for the recovery of land which the claimant alleges is occupied only by a person or persons who entered or remained on the land without the consent of a person entitled to possession of that land but does not include a claim against a tenant or sub-tenant whether his tenancy has been terminated or not (CPR r 55.1(b)).

Procedure

Availability	An application may be made for an interim possession order if: the only claim made in the proceedings is for the recovery of premises; the claim is made by a person who – has an immediate right to possession of the premises; and has had such a right throughout the period of unlawful occupation complained of; the claim is made within 28 days of the date on which the claimant first knew, or ought reasonably to have known, that the defendant, or any of the defendants, was in occupation	Rule 55.21(1)
	the claim is not made against a defendant who entered or remained on the premises with the consent of a person who, at the time consent was given, had an immediate right to possession of the premises	Rule 55.21(2)
Which court	The claim must be started in the county court where the land is situated	Rules 55.3(1) and 55.22(1)
Name of defendant	Where the claimant does not know the name of a person in occupation of the land, the claim must be brought against 'persons unknown' in addition to any named defendants	Rules 55.3(4) and 55.22(1)
Issue	The claimant must file: a claim form; and an application notice, both of which must be in the form set out in the practice direction, as well as the claimant's written evidencegiven by the claimant personally or by a duly authorised officer if a body corporate	Rule 55.22(2), (3), (4) PD55, para 9.1
	Upon issue the court will: issue the claim form and the application for the IPO; and	

	set a date for the hearing of the application for the IPO as soon as is practicable, but not less than 3 daysafter the date of issue	Rule 55.22(5), (6)
Service	Within 24 hours of the issue of the application for the IPO the claimant must serve on the defendant: the claim form; the application notice; the claimant's written evidence; and a blank form for the defendant's witness statement, attached to the application notice	Rule 55.23(1) PD55, para 9.1
	Service is effected by attaching the above documents to the main door or some other part of the property so that they are clearly visible and, if practicable, inserting copies of the above documents in a sealed, transparent envelope addressed to 'the occupiers' through the letter box	Rules 55.6(a), 55.23(2)
	At or before the hearing the claimant must file a certificate of service	Rule 55.23(3)
Defendant's response	At any time before the hearing the defendant may file a witness statement. The witness statement must be in the form set out in the practice direction	Rule 55.24 PD55, para 9.1
Hearing of the application for an interim possession order	In deciding whether to grant the IPO, the court will have regard to whether the claimant has given, or is prepared to give, the following undertakings: if after the IPO is made the court decides that the claimant was not entitled to the order, to reinstate the defendant and pay such damages as the court may order; and before the claim for possession is finally decided, not to damage the property, grant a right of occupation to any other person and damage or dispose of the defendant's property	Rule 55.25(1)
	The court will grant the IPO if:	

	the claimant has filed a certificate of service or otherwise proved service of the documents required to be served; the conditions set out under 'Availability' above are met; and any undertakings given by the claimant are adequate	Rule 55.25(2)
The interim possession order	The IPO must follow the prescribed form and will require the defendant to vacate the premises within 24 hours of the service of the order on him	Rule 55.25(3) PD55, para 9.2
	The court will also set a date for the hearing of the claim for possession which will be not less than 7 days after the date the IPO is made	Rule 55.25(4)
	Where the court does not make an IPO, the court will set a date for the hearing of the claim and may give case management directions	Rule 55.25(5)
Further service	An IPO must be served within 48 hours after it is sealed	Rule 55.26(1)
	The claimant must serve the defendant with: the IPO; the claim form; the claimant's written evidence in support	Rule 55.26(1)
	For the manner of service see 'Service' above	Rules 55.26(2)(b), 55.6(a)
Enforcement	An IPO may not be enforced by a warrant of possession	Rule 55.26(3)
	If the defendant does not vacate the premises, the claimant must ask the police for assistance and produce to them a copy of the IPO and a copy of a certificate of service showing that the 24-hour period has expired.	
The date of the hearing of the claim for possession	Before this date the claimant must file a certificate of service	Rule 55.27(1)
	The IPO expires on the final hearing date	Rule 55.27(2)
	At the hearing the court may: make a final order for possession; dismiss the claim for possession;	

	give directions for the claim to continue under Pt 55, Section I; or	
	enforce any of the claimant's undertakings	Rule 55.27(3)
	Any order so made must be served on the defendant. For the manner of service see 'Service' above	Rules 55.27(3), 55.6(a)
	A final order may be enforced by a warrant of possession	Rule 55.27(5)
Setting aside an interim possession order	If the defendant has vacated the premises, he may apply on grounds of urgency for the IPO to be set aside before the date of the hearing of the claim	Rule 55.28(1)
	Any such application:	
	must be supported by a witness statement; and	Rule 55.28(2)
	may only be made under Pt 55. It may not be made under r 39.3	Rule 55.28(4)
	On receipt of an application, the court will give directions as to:	
	the date for the hearing; and	
	the period of notice, if any, to be given to the claimant	Rule 55.28(3)
	Where the court directs that no notice to the claimant is required, the only matters which the court will consider will be whether to:	
	set aside the IPO; and	
	enforce any undertakings to reinstate the defendant	Rule 55.28(5)
	The court will serve on all parties:	
	a copy of the order made; and	
	where no notice was given to the claimant, a copy of the defendant's application and witness statement in support	Rule 55.28(6)
	Where the defendant's application is on notice to the claimant, the court may treat the hearing as the hearing of the claim	Rule 55.28(6)
Forms	Claim Form N5	
	Application Notice for an Interim Possession Order N130	
	Defendant's Witness Statement N133	
	Interim Possession Order N134	
	Order for Possession N136	PD55, paras 9.1, 9.2

Court fees	On the commencement of proceedings: in the High Court – £400 in the county court – £150	CPFO fee 1.4
Which judge	Claims may be heard and determined by a master or district judge	PD2B, paras 1.1, 11.1(b)

46: Applications for Accelerated Possession Orders of Assured Shorthold Tenancies (Housing Act 1988, s 21)

Legal background

New procedures relating to claims for the recovery of land, set out in CPR Pt 55, were introduced on 15 October 2001 by virtue of the Civil Procedure (Amendment) Rules 2001, SI 2001/256. Sch 2, CCR Ord 49, r6A was revoked in its entirety with effect from 15 October 2001 but replicated without significant amendment by new provisions to be found at CPR rr 55.11–55.19.

Where a claim form relates to proceedings to which CPR Pt 55 would apply if it were issued on or after 15 October 2001 but it is issued before that date, Pt 55 does not apply and the rules of court immediately before that date apply as if they had not been amended or revoked (Civil Procedure (Amendment) Rules 2001, SI 2001/256, r 31). For the procedure prior to 15 October 2001, refer to the June 2001 edition of this work.

Procedure

When the application may be made	The procedure may be used to recover possession of a dwelling-house which has been let on an assured shorthold tenancy instead of making a claim in accordance with Pt 55 (claim for recovery of land by claim form) if: the tenancy and any agreement for the tenancy were entered into on or after 15 January 1989; the only purpose of the proceedings is to recover possession of the dwelling-house and no other claim is made in the proceedings (such as for arrears of rent); the tenancy – did not immediately follow an assured tenancy which was not an assured shorthold tenancy; fulfilled the conditions provided by s 19A or s 20(1)(a)–(c) of the 1988 Act;	

	and the tenancy – was the subject of a written agreement; arises by virtue of s 5 of the 1988 Act but follows a tenancy that was the subject of a written agreement; or relates to the same or substantially the same property let to the same tenant and on the same terms (though not necessarily as to rent or duration) as a tenancy which was the subject of a written agreement; and a notice in accordance with s 21(1) or (4) of the 1988 Act was given to the tenant in writing	Rule 55.12
Issue	A claim form in the prescribed form (see below) must be completed and lodged with, or sent to the court office together with, a copy for each defendant. The claim must be issued out of the court for the district in which the dwelling-house is situated	Rule 55.11(2)
Contents of claim form	Its content is dictated by the Claim Form N5B itself	Rule 55.13(1), (2)
Documents required to be attached to claim form	Copies of the following documents must be attached to the application: the first written tenancy agreement and the current (or most recent) written tenancy agreement; where the tenancy and any agreement for the tenancy were entered into before 28 February 1997 the written notice served in accordance with s 20(2) of the 1988 Act; and the notice in writing given in accordance with s 21 of the 1988 Act; and any other documents necessary to prove the claim	Form N5B Rule 55.13(1)(b)(ii)
Verification	The application must be verified by a statement of truth. The attached documents need to be marked 'A', 'A1', etc	Rule 55.13(2) PD22, para 1.6

Service	The court will send the application and attachments, together with a form of reply (see below) by first-class post to the defendant	Rule 55.13(3)
Responding to the claim	A defendant who wishes to oppose the claimant's application or who wishes to apply for a postponement of possession on grounds of exceptional hardship under Housing Act 1980, s 89 must file the completed form of defence within 14 days after the service of the application	Rule 55.14(1), (2)
	On receipt of the defendant's defence form the court must send a copy of it to the claimant	Rule 55.14(1)(a)
Stay of proceedings	Where: 14 days after service of the claim have expired without the defendant filing a defence; and the claimant has not made a request for an order for possession within 3 months after the expiry of that period, the claim will be stayed	Rule 55.15(4)
Consideration by the judge	The court must refer the claimant's application to the judge without delay: on receipt of –	
	the defendant's reply; or	Rule 55.15(1)(b)
	the claimant's written request for an order for possession where no reply is filed within 14 days after service of the application;	Rule 55.15(2)(b)
	where a reply is received later than 14 days after service of the application but before a request for a possession order is filed	Rule 55.15(3)
	The judge must: make an order for possession; or	Rules 55.16(1), 55.17
	if he is not satisfied that the claim form has been served or that the claimant has established that he is entitled to possession under HA 1988, s 21, either – direct that a date be fixed for a hearing; or give any appropriate case management directions.	

	Alternatively, the judge may strike out the claim if the claim form discloses no reasonable grounds for bringing the claim	Rule 55.16(1),(c)
	Where the judge is not so satisfied, he will fix a day for a hearing, of which not less than 14 days' notice must be given, and may give directions regarding the steps to be taken before and at the hearing	Rule 55.16(1)(b), (2), (3)
Reconsidering the order	The court may, on application made on notice in accordance with CPR Pt 23 within 14 days of service of the order or of its own initiative, set aside, vary or confirm any possession order made without requiring the attendance of the parties	Rule 55.19
Restoring the claim	Where a claim is struck out for disclosing no reasonable grounds for bringing the claim – the court will serve its reasons for striking out the claim with the order; and the claimant may apply to restore the claim within 28 days after the date the order was served on him	Rule 55.16(4)
Postponement of possession	Where the defendant seeks postponement of possession on the ground of exceptional hardship under HA 1980, s 89, the judge may direct a hearing of that issue. Where the judge directs a hearing – he must still make an order for possession in no more than 14 days; the hearing must be held before the date on which possession is to be given up; and the judge will direct how many days' notice the parties must be given of that hearing.	

	Where the judge is satisfied on a hearing directed as above that exceptional hardship would be caused by requiring possession to be given up by the date in the order of possession, he may vary the date on which possession must be given up. Any later date for possession cannot be more than 6 weeks after the making of the original order for possession.	Rule 55.18
	Where the judge is satisfied that the defendant has shown that he will suffer exceptional hardship, the judge may only postpone possession without a hearing if: he considers that possession should be given up 6 weeks after the date of the order or, if the defendant has requested postponement to an earlier date, on that date; and the claimant has indicated on his claim form that he would be content for the court to make such an order without a hearing	PD55, para 8.2
Costs	Fixed costs apply unless the court orders otherwise. The court is unlikely to do so unless there has been an oral hearing	Rule 45.4A(2)
Court fees	£150	CPFO fee 1.4
Forms	Claim Form N5B Notes for Claimant N5C Notice of Issue and Request for Possession Order and Costs N206A Defence N11B Order for Possession N26A	
Which judge	Claims may be heard and determined by a district judge	PD2B, para 11.1(b)

47: Applications to Enforce a Charging Order by Sale

Legal background

Where the debtor is the sole beneficial owner of the asset over which the final charging order has been made separate proceedings must be commenced. The standard Pt 8 procedure as modified by CPR r 73.10 and PD73, paras 4.1–4.5 must be used. The provisions of Pt 7 continue to apply where they are not disapplied by or inconsistent with Pt 8 or the practice directions which supplement it. Reference should therefore be made to Guide 1 for matters of general application.

If the interest charged is a beneficial interest under a trust (eg the interest of one joint proprietor of property) application must be made under Trusts of Land and Appointment of Trustees Act 1996, s 14 using the Pt 8 procedure. There is no monetary limit to county court jurisdiction under this Act (HCCCJO, art 2(1)(a)).

Procedure

Which court	*High Court* The application will be assigned to the Chancery Division	RSC Ord 88, r 2
	It must be issued out of Chancery Chambers or a Chancery district registry	PD73, para 4.2
	County court If the debt secured is due under a regulated agreement, as defined by CCA 1974, the county court has exclusive jurisdiction	CCA 1974, s 141
	If the debt exceeds £30,000 the parties may, by agreement in writing, give jurisdiction to a specified county court	CCA 1984, s 24(2)(g)
	If the debt secured does not exceed £30,000, the application may be issued in the county court. If the court which made the final charging order has jurisdiction, the claim should be made in the same court	CCA 1984, s 23 Rule 73.10(2)
Issue	A claim form is completed and lodged with or sent to the court office	Rule 7.2(1)
	A copy of the charging order must be filed with the claim form	Rule 73.10(4)
	Particulars of claim may be endorsed on it or served with it.	
	The application must be supported by written evidence which must:	
	(a) identify the charging order and the property to be sold;	
	(b) state the amount for which the charge was imposed and the amount due at the date of issue;	
	(c) verify, so far as known, the debtor's title to the property charged;	
	(d) state (so far as the claimant is able to identify):	
	– the names and addresses of any other creditors who have a prior charge or other security over the property;	

	– the amount owed to each such creditor; and (e) give an estimate of the expected sale price of the property; (f) if the claim relates to land, give details of every person who is in possession of the property to the best of the claimant's knowledge; (g) if the claim relates to residential property, state: – whether a Class F land charge or a notice under Family Law Act 1996, s 31(10) or the Matrimonial Homes Act 1983 has been registered; and – if so, on whose behalf the registration has been made; and – that the claimant will serve notice of the claim on that person.	Rule 73.11 PD73, para 4.3
	NB: The claimant must take all reasonable steps to obtain the required information before issuing the claim.	PD73, para 4.4
Statement of truth	The claim form (and any particulars of claim) must be verified by a statement of truth	Rule 22.1(1)
General procedure	A hearing date will be given on the issue of the claim form The court will prepare a notice of the hearing for each party and if the claimant serves the claim form personally, a copy of the notice of hearing must be served at the same time. Thereafter the standard Pt 8 procedure will apply, as to which see Guide 3	
General	Where the judgment debtor is the sole beneficial owner the court will have regard to the amount of the debt and the value of the property charged and will be reluctant to make an immediate order where either is small. The application may be adjourned for a short time to allow the judgment debtor an opportunity to discharge the judgment debt, but ultimately the judgment creditor is entitled to enforce his security.	

	Where the application is made under TLATA, s 14 the court has a wide discretion whether or not to order a sale The court has wide powers to give directions as to the manner in which any sale is carried out. A sample order for sale is set out at PD73, App A	TLATA 1996, s 14 HCCCJO, art 2(1)(a) PD40D, paras 2–5
Court fees	On issue of proceedings: *High Court* – £400 *County court* – £150	CPFO fee 1.4
Forms	Claim Form N208	
Which judge	Claims may be heard and determined by a district judge	PD2B, para 4.1 CCR Ord 31, r 4(4)

48: Applications for Injunctions Against Anti-Social Behaviour under Housing Act 1996, ss 153A–158

Legal background

Chapter III of the Housing Act 1996 as amended by the Anti-Social Behaviour Act 2003 sets out a code for the control of anti-social behaviour by social landlords. Sections 152 and 153 of the 1996 Act have been repealed and replaced by new ss 153A–153E. These offer significantly wider opportunities for the court to grant injunctions to control socially unacceptable behaviour. In addition to powers of arrest which may be added to the whole or specific clauses of an injunction, the court now has power to make an exclusion order even where this will have the effect of excluding a respondent from his own home. Although such applications can be made in the High Court using the Pt 8 procedure, they are in practice almost always made in the county court and this guide deals only with county court procedure.

Procedure

Who may apply	Relevant landlords, ie local authorities as defined by Housing Act 1985, registered social landlords and housing action trusts	HA 1996, s 153E(7)
Availability	The court may make an injunction if the defendant is behaving or has or is threatening to behave in an anti-social manner, ie a manner which is capable of causing nuisance or annoyance to any person who falls within the four categories specific by the Act **and** that behaviour also directly or indirectly affects the housing management functions of a relevant landlord	HA 1996, s 153A

	Those categories are – (a) other tenants of the relevant landlord and their families; (b) any other person living in the neighbourhood; (c) any person engaged in lawful activities in the neighbourhood; and (d) any person employed in connection with the housing management functions of the relevant landlord	HA 1996, s 153A(4)
	The court may also make an injunction if the defendant uses or threatens to use the landlord's premises for an unlawful purpose	HA 1996, s 153B
Which court	The proceedings must be issued in the court for the district where the defendant resides or the conduct complained of occurred	Rule 65.3(2)(b)
Issue	The Pt 8 procedure as modified by Pt 65 and the relevant practice direction applies. The application must be made by using Form N16A which is treated as the Pt 8 claim form	PD65, para 1.1
Contents of claim form	The claim form must state:	
	– that the claim is made under the Housing Act 1996; and	Rule 8.2(c)
	– if the defendant is sued in a representative capacity, what that capacity is	Rule 8.2(e)
	It must set out the terms of the injunction applied for	Rule 65.3(3)(b)
Statement of Truth	Although this does not appear in the prescribed form, the form must be verified by a statement of truth	Rule 22.1(1)
Evidence	The application must be supported by a witness statement filed with the claim form	Rule 65.3(2)(c)
	Where the application is made without notice, the witness statement must give the reasons why notice has not been given	Rule 65.3(4)
General procedure	A hearing date will be given on issue of the claim form	PD8B, para B.9(1)
	The court will prepare a notice of hearing for each party	PD8B, para B.9(2)

Service	If the hearing is on notice the claimant must effect personal service on the defendant of the application, the notice of hearing and a copy of the witness statement not less than 2 days before the hearing	Rule 63.3(5), (6)
Application made without notice	If the court makes an injunction following a without-notice hearing, it must give the defendant an opportunity to make representations as soon as practicable	HA 1996, s 153E(5)
The court's powers	If the defendant is, has, or is threatening to behave in an anti-social manner (see above), or uses or threatens to use the landlord's premises for an unlawful purpose, the court may make an anti-social behaviour injunction prohibiting him from behaving in that manner	HA 1996, s 153A HA 1996, s 153B
	If the defendant's behaviour consists of or includes the use or threat of violence or there is a significant risk of harm to any person within any of the four categories mentioned above and the court makes an injunction under s 153A or 153B, it may: – add a power of arrest to any provision of the injunction, or – make an exclusion order	HA 1996, s 153C
	If those conditions are satisfied, the court may also make an exclusion order or attach a power of arrest to any provision of an order made to restrain breaches of a condition of a tenancy agreement	HA 1996, s 153D
Exclusion orders	An exclusion order excludes the defendant from any premises or any area specified in the injunction. It may have the effect of excluding a person from his own place of residence	HA 1996, s 153C HA 1996, s 153E(2)(b)
Powers of arrest	If a power of arrest is attached to an order made at a without notice hearing the court must afford the defendant an opportunity to make representations as soon as just and convenient at a further hearing on notice to the claimant	HA 1996, s 154(2)

	A power of arrest may have effect for a shorter period than the term of the injunction	HA1996, s 157(1)
	Where a power of arrest has been attached to a provision of the injunction, each provision to which the power of arrest is attached must be set out in a separate paragraph	Rule 65.4(2)(a)
	The claimant must deliver a copy of the relevant provisions to a police station for the area where the conduct occurred; but if the order has been made at a without notice hearing the copy must not be delivered to the police until the defendant has been served with the injunction	Rule 65.4(2)(b) Rule 65.4(3)
Which judge	The powers of the court to make injunctions under sections 153A to 158 may be exercised by a district judge (this includes the power to deal with those who have been arrested and brought before the court for any alleged breach and the power to hear committal applications brought under Sch 2, CCR Ord 29, r 1)	HA 1996, s 158(1) Rule 65.6(6)
Warrants of arrest	If the statutory conditions for attaching a power of arrest were satisfied but the court either did not attach a power of arrest or only attached the power of arrest to certain provisions then, if the claimant considers that the defendant has broken the injunction, he may apply to the court for a warrant of arrest	HA 1996, s 155(3)
	The application must be made under Pt 23 and may be made without notice. It must be supported either by an affidavit or by oral evidence on oath at the hearing	HA 1996, s 155(4) Rule 65.6
Procedure on arrest	A police officer may arrest a defendant on reasonable suspicion of breach of any provision of the injunction to which a power of arrest is attached or under the authority of a warrant of arrest issued by the court	HA 1996, s 155(1), (5)

	A person arrested must be brought before the Court within 24 hours of arrest, Christmas Day, Good Friday and Sundays being left out of account	HA 1996, s 155(2)
	The police must inform the claimant immediately after arrest	HA 1996, s 155(1)
	The judge may deal with the arrested person or adjourn the proceedings, but the matter must then be dealt with within 28 days of the date of first appearance in court	Rule 65.6(4)
	If the matter is not concluded within the 28-day period, the claimant may still proceed by way of an application for committal	Rule 65.6(5)
	If the matter is adjourned, the defendant must be given not less than 2 days notice of the adjourned hearing	Rule 65.6(4)(b)
	The defendant may either be released to appear at the next hearing, or remanded in custody or on bail. Since Parliament has omitted to provide any sanctions for breach of bail, the bail provisions are of no practical value.	
	The defendant may be:	
	– remanded to police custody for up to 3 clear days;	HA 1996, Sch 15, para 4(2)
	– remanded in custody for up to 8 clear days;	HA 1996, Sch 15, para 4(1)
	– remanded in custody for medical examination and report for not more than 3 weeks at a time	HA 1996, s 156(3)
Court fees	Claim – £150	CPFO fee 1.4
	Application – £60	CPFO fee 2.5
Forms	Claim Form N16A	
	Power of Arrest N110A	

48A: Applications for Anti-Social Behaviour Orders under the Crime and Disorder Act 1998

Legal background

The Crime and Disorder Act 1998 as amended by the Police Reform Act 2002 and further amended by the Anti-Social Behaviour Act 2003 enables a county court, but not the High Court, to make an Anti-Social Behaviour order (ASBO) in certain cases. However, the essential feature of this jurisdiction is that there must be existing proceedings to which the person against whom an order is sought is either already a party or can be joined as a party. Claimants are not allowed to start free-standing county court proceedings solely for an ASBO. Such applications (not covered in this work) must be made to the Magistrates' Court. It is, therefore, most likely that there will be a significant degree of overlap between the power to grant an ASBO and the similar power to grant an Anti-Social Behaviour Injunction (ASBI) under Housing Act 1996, s 153A. Claimants should consider carefully which (or indeed whether) either order is appropriate, bearing in mind also that the definition of anti-social behaviour under each Act is not the same. Useful guidance can be found in the Court of Appeal judgment in *Moat Housing Group South Ltd v Harris & anor* [2005] EWCA Civ 287, [2005] All ER (D) 259 (Mar).

Procedure

Who may apply	Relevant authorities as defined by the Act, ie local authorities, social landlords and police authorities may apply	CDA 1998, s 1(1A)
Availability	The court may make an order if an adult defendant has acted, since 1 April 1999, in a manner that caused or was likely to cause harassment, alarm or distress to one or more persons not of the same household as the defendant; *and* the order is necessary to protect relevant persons from further anti-social acts by him	CDA 1998, s 1(1)
	Orders against child defendants may only be made in designated pilot courts (see below)	PD65, para 13.3
Which court	There are no special rules for ASBO applications and the appropriate court of issue will, therefore, depend on the nature of the relief claimed in the principal proceedings, eg possession proceedings must be started in the court for the district where the property is situated. Where no special rules apply to the principal proceedings, good practice dictates that the proceedings be issued in the court where the defendant resides.	
Special rules for child defendants	Where the person against whom the order is sought is a child, proceedings may only be brought in one of the pilot courts. These are –	

	Bristol, Central London, Clerkenwell, Dewsbury, Huddersfield, Leicester, Manchester, Oxford, Tameside, Wigan and Wrexham.	PD65, para 13.3(3)
	The pilot scheme runs from 1 October 2004 to 31 March 2006.	
	Children may only be joined in existing proceedings	PD65, para 13.3(1)
Making the claim	An application may be made in one of three situations:	
	(1) The relevant authority and person against whom the order is sought are already parties to the principal proceedings	CDA 1998, s 1B(2)
	If the relevant authority is the claimant, the application must be made in the claim form. If the circumstances arise after issue of proceedings, the application must be made by application notice as soon as possible	Rule 65.22(1)(a) Rule 65.22(2)
	If the relevant authority is the defendant, the application must be made by application notice which must be filed with the defence, unless the circumstances arise after the filing of the defence	Rule 65.22(1)(b)
	(2) The relevant authority is a party to proceedings and wishes to join a person against whom the order is sought as a party	CDA 1998, s 1B(3B)
	There must be a factual nexus between the subject matter of the proceedings and the conduct which gives grounds for the ASBO application. The claimant issues one application under Pt 19, Section 1 to join the new party and for an ASBO against him	CDA 1998, s 1B(3C) Rule 65.23(1)(b)
	(3) The person against whom the order is sought is a party to existing proceedings and the relevant authority wishes to be joined for the purpose of applying for an ASBO	CDA 1998, s 1B(3)
	Although there is no requirement for a factual nexus between the subject matter of the proceedings and the conduct which gives grounds for the ASBO, the court is unlikely to grant the application unless this nexus exists.	

	The applicant issues one application under Pt 19, Section 1 to be joined as a new party and for an ASBO against the existing party	Rule 65.24(1)
Provisions applying to all claims	The application should normally be made on notice	Rules 65.22(3), 65.23(3) and 65.24(2)(b)
Statement of truth	Written evidence must be verified by a statement of truth	Rule 22.1(1)
Evidence	The application must be supported by a witness statement filed with the claim form or application notice, including evidence that the provisions of CDA 1998, s 1E have been complied with	Rule 65.25
	Where the application is made without notice, the witness statement must give the reasons why notice has not been given	Rule 25.3(1)
General procedure	A hearing date will be given on issue of the claim form or application notice	PD8B, para B.9(1)
	The court will prepare a notice of hearing for each party	PD23, para 2.2 PD8B, para B.9(2)
Service of the application	The defendant must be served with the application, the notice of hearing and a copy of the witness statement not less than 3 clear days before the hearing. The ordinary rules as to service apply but in view of the serious consequences of breach of any order made personal service is clearly preferable if this can be achieved	Rule 23.7(1)(b)
Interim orders	The court has power to make an interim order pending the final hearing of the application	CDA 1998, s 1D
Applying for an interim order	The application should normally be made on notice in accordance with Pt 25 and be included in the claim form or application notice seeking the ASBO	Rule 65.26
	Without-notice applications are permitted under the rules but, because of the criminal consequences following from any breach, should be regarded as wholly exceptional	Rule 25.3

	If a without-notice order is made, there must be a very early return date hearing	*R v Lord Chancellor ex parte M* [2004] 2 All ER 531
Terms of the order	The order prohibits the defendant from doing anything described in the order which is necessary for the purpose of protecting persons in England and Wales from further anti-social acts	CDA 1998, s 1(4) and (6)
	The final order must run for at least 2 years, but this does not mean that all its provisions must do so	CDA 1998, s 1(7)
	Interim orders must run for a specified period and cease to have effect when the application is determined	CDA 1998, s 1D(4) *R (Lonergan) v Crown Court at Lewes* [2005] 1 All ER 362
Variation and discharge	Interim orders may be varied or discharged at any time	CDA 1998, s 1D(4)(b)
	Final orders may be varied at any time or discharged but may only be discharged within a 2-year period after service if the relevant authority consents	CDA 1998, s 1B(5) and (6)
Consequences of breach	Breach of the order is a criminal offence and not a contempt of court	CDA 1998, s 1(10)
Service of the order	Orders and interim orders must be served personally	PD65, para 13.1
Which judge	Any application for an ASBO may be determined by a district judge	PD2B, para 8.1A
Court fees	Claim – £150	CPFO, fee 1.4
	Application – £60	CPFO, fee 2.6
Forms	Claim form – as appropriate for the principal proceedings	
	Application notice – general form	

49: Applications relating to Business Tenancies

Legal background

As from 1 June 2004, the requirement for both parties to apply to the court for approval of an agreement to exclude security of tenancy or to surrender a tenancy has been replaced by a non-court procedure involving a notice from the landlord that is countersigned by the tenant (see Schs 1–4, Regulatory Reform (Business Tenancies) (England and Wales) Order 2003, SI 2003/3096).

Articles 3–9 of the Order change the procedures to be followed in order to renew a tenancy or to terminate it without renewal. Both landlords and tenants are permitted to apply to the court for the terms of a new tenancy to be settled.

Landlords are permitted to apply for an order that the tenancy be terminated without renewal if they can make out one of the statutory grounds for opposition. The requirement for a tenant to serve a counter-notice to a landlord's notice of termination is abolished. Articles 10–12 substitute new time limits for applications to the court to renew tenancies and enable the parties to agree to extend these. Article 18 introduces several changes relating to interim rent (rent payable pending renewal of a tenancy). Tenants as well as landlords are enabled to apply to the court for an interim rent to be determined.

Procedure

Which court	Except where under some enactment the county court does not have jurisdiction, the application must be started in the county court for the district in which the land is situated unless there are exceptional circumstances justifying the use of the High Court.	Rule 56.2(2), (3)
	Those reasons are if there are complicated disputes of fact or points of law of public importance. The value of the property or any financial claim will not alone justify the use of the High Court	PD56, paras 2.4, 2.5
	If a claim is started in the High Court which should have been started in the county court, the claim will either be struck out or transferred to the county court, with consequent effects on costs and resulting in delay	PD56, para 2.3
	Part 8 procedure applies (other than rr 8.5 and 8.6) with the exception of: (1) claims for a new tenancy under L&TA 1954, s 24 in circumstances where the grant of a tenancy at all is opposed; and (2) claims for the termination of a tenancy under s 29(2) of the Act. In both those cases the claimant must use the Pt 7 procedure as modified by Pt 56 and PD56	Rule 56.2(1), (1A)
Court fees	£150	CPFO fee 1.4

Application for new tenancy or to terminate a tenancy		
Availability	Either landlord or tenant may apply to the court for the grant of a new tenancy under L&TA 1954. If one of the parties has already applied, the other party may not also apply. Neither party may apply if the landlord has made an application under s 29(2) of the Act for the termination of the tenancy and the application has been served. An application for a new tenancy may not be withdrawn by the landlord unless the tenant consents	L&TA 1954, s 24(1), (2A), (2B), (2C)
	The tenant must, prior to an application to the court for a new tenancy, have served a notice on the landlord requesting one. The landlord in turn must serve a counter-notice if he objects to a new tenancy on one of the grounds in s 30(1) of the Act.	L&TA 1954, ss 26, 29
Time-limits	Landlord's notice: The notice must, usually, be served not more than 12 nor less than 6 months before the termination date specified (being a date when the tenancy would have expired or could have been terminated by the landlord apart from the Act). The tenant must file his application no later than the date specified in the landlord's notice unless the parties have agreed to extend the period	L&TA 1954, s 25(2)–(6) L&TA 1954, s 25(5), and s 29(2) L&TA 1954, ss 29A, 29B
	Tenant's request: The request must specify a commencement date for the new tenancy which is not more than 12 nor less than 6 months ahead (being no earlier than the date when the tenancy would have expired or could have been terminated by the tenant) and the application must be filed no later than the date specified. Both parties may agree to extend the period for making the application. This period may be further extended by a further agreement before expiry of the initial agreement	L&TA 1954, s 26(2) L&TA 1954, ss 29A, 29B(2), (3)

Contents of claim form	The claim form must state:	
	the property to which the claim relates;	PD56, para 3.4(1)
	particulars of the current tenancy (date, parties, duration), the current rent and the date and method of termination;	PD56, para 3.4(2)
	every notice or request given or made under ss 25 or 26; and	PD56, para 3.4(3)
	the expiry date of the statutory period under s 29A(2) or the extended period agreed under ss 29B(1) or 29B(2);	PD56, para 3.4(4)
	In addition, where the tenant is the claimant, the claim form must contain details of:	
	the nature of the business carried on at the property;	
	whether the tenant relies on ss 23(1A), 31A, 41 or 42 and the basis on which he does so;	
	the claimant's prpoposed new terms for the tenancy; and	
	the name and address of anyone who has a reversionary or freehold interest in the property	PD56, para 3.5
	Where the landlord is making a claim for a new tenancy, the claim form must contain:	
	details of the claimant's proposed terms;	
	whether the claimant is aware that the defendant's tenancy is one to which s 32(2) applies and, if so, whether the claimant requires that any new tenancy shall be a tenancy of the whole of the property comprised in the defendant's current tenancy or just of the holding as defined by s 23(3); and	
	the names and addresses of anyone who has a reversionary or freehold interest in the property	PD56, para 3.7
	Where the claimant landlord is making an application under s 29(2) to terminate the tenancy, the claim form must also contain:	
	the claimant's grounds of opposition;	
	full details of those grounds of opposition; and	

	the terms of a new tenancy that the claimant proposes in the event that his claim fails	PD56, para 3.9
Service of claim	The claim must be served within 2 months of issue (whether in or out of England and Wales)	Rule 56.3(3)
	The time for service may be extended by an order but the application must normally be made within the primary 2-month period	Rule 7.6 as modified by rule 56.3(3)
	Where the claim is opposed, the claimant must use the Pt 7 procedure but the 2-month rule as to service still applies	rule 56.3(4)
Acknowledgment of service (tenant claimant; unopposed)	Where the claim is an unopposed claim and the claimant is the tenant, the acknowledgment of service is to be in Form N210 and must state with particulars: (1) whether, if a new tenancy is granted, the defendant objects to any of the terms proposed by the claimant and if so – (a) the terms to which he objects; and (b) the terms that he proposes in so far as they differ from those proposed by the claimant; (2) whether the defendant is a tenant under a lease having less than 15 years unexpired at the date of the termination of the claimant's current tenancy and, if so, the name and address of any person who, to the knowledge of the defendant, has an interest in the reversion in the property expectant (whether immediate or in not more than 15 years from that date) on the termination of the defendant's tenancy; (3) the name and address of any person having an interest in the property who is likely to be affected by the grant of a new tenancy; and (4) if the claimant's current tenancy is one to which s 32(2) applies, whether the defendant requires that any new tenancy shall be a tenancy of the whole of the property comprised in the claimant's current tenancy	PD56, para 3.10

Acknowledgment of service (landlord claimant; unopposed)	Where the claim is an unopposed claim and the claimant is the landlord, the acknowledgment of service is to be in Form N210 and must state with particulars: (1) the nature of the business carried on at the property; (2) if the defendant relies on ss 23(1A), 41 or 42, the basis on which he does so; (3) whether any, and if so what part, of the property comprised in the tenancy is occupied neither by the defendant nor by a person employed by the defendant for the purpose of the defendant's business; (4) the name and address of – (a) anyone known to the defendant who has an interest in the reversion in the property (whether immediate or in not more than 15 years) on the termination of the defendant's current tenancy and who is likely to be affected by the grant of a new tenancy; or (b) if the defendant does not know of such a person, then anyone who has a freehold interest in the property; and (5) whether, if a new tenancy is granted, the defendant objects to any of the terms proposed by the claimant and, if so – (a) the terms to which he objects; and (b) the terms that he proposes in so far as they differ from those proposed by the claimant	PD56, para 3.11
Acknowledgment of service (tenant claimant; opposed)	Where the claim is an opposed claim and the claimant is the tenant: (1) the acknowledgment of service is to be in form N9; and (2) in his defence the defendant must state with particulars – (a) the defendant's grounds of opposition; (b) full details of those grounds of opposition;	

	(c) whether, if a new tenancy is granted, the defendant objects to any of the terms proposed by the claimant and if so – (i) the terms to which he objects; and (ii) the terms that he proposes in so far as they differ from those proposed by the claimant (d) whether the defendant is a tenant under a lease having less than 15 years unexpired at the date of the termination of the claimant's current tenancy and, if so, the name and address of any person who, to the knowledge of the defendant, has an interest in the reversion in the property expectant (whether immediately or in not more than 15 years from that date) on the termination of the defendant's tenancy; (e) the name and address of any person having an interest in the property who is likely to be affected by the grant of a new tenancy; and (f) if the claimant's current tenancy is one to which s 32(2) applies, whether the defendant requires that any new tenancy shall be a tenancy of the whole of the property comprised in the claimant's current tenancy	PD56, para 3.12
Acknowledgment of service (landlord claimant; termination of tenancy)	Where the claim is an opposed claim and the claimant is the landlord – (1) the acknowledgment of service is to be in Form N9; and2) (2) in his defence the defendant must state with particulars – (a) whether the defendant relies on ss 23(1A), 41 or 42 and, if so, the basis on which he does so; (b) whether the defendant relies on s 31A and, if so, the basis on which he does so; and (c) the terms of the new tenancy that the defendant would propose in the event that the claimant's claim to terminate the current tenancy fails	PD56, para 3.13

Evidence	Where the claim is an unopposed claim, no evidence need be filed unless and until the court directs it to be filed. Where the claim is an opposed claim, evidence (including expert evidence) must be filed by the parties as the court directs and the landlord shall be required to file his evidence first. Unless in the circumstances of the case it is unreasonable to do so, any grounds of opposition shall be tried as a preliminary issue	PD56, paras 3.14, 3.15, 3.16
Forms	Claim Form: N208 Acknowledgment of Service: N210 or N9 (see above)	
Applications for interim rent under s 24A to 24D	Where proceedings have already been commenced for the grant of a new tenancy or the termination of an existing tenancy, the claim for interim rent under s 24A shall be made in those proceedings by: the claim form; the acknowledgment of service or defence; or an application on notice under Pt 23	PD56, para 3.17
	Where no other proceedings have been commenced for the grant of a new tenancy or termination of an existing tenancy or where such proceedings have been disposed of, an application for interim rent under s 24A shall be made under the procedure in Pt 8 and the claim form shall include details of: (1) the property to which the claim relates; (2) the particulars of the relevant tenancy (including date, parties and duration) and the current rent (if not the original rent); (3) every notice or request given or made under ss 25 or 26; (4) if the relevant tenancy has terminated, the date and mode of termination; and (5) if the relevant tenancy has been terminated and the landlord has granted a new tenancy of the property to the tenant	

	(a) particulars of the new tenancy (including date, parties and duration) and the rent; and (b) in a case where s 24C(2) applies but the claimant seeks a different rent under s 24C(3), particulars and matters on which the claimant relies as satisfying s 24C(3).	
Claims relating to compensation for improvements		
Availability	A tenant of business premises may apply to the court to determine whether an intended improvement to the premises (not being one he is obliged by the tenancy conditions to make) is a proper one, for a certificate that an approved improvement has been completed and to determine the compensation entitlement	L&TA 1927, Pt I
Contents of claim form	The claim form must state: (1) the nature of the claim or application or matter to be determined; (2) the holding, the trade or business carried on there and details of the term of the lease; (3) the date and mode of termination of the tenancy and the date the tenant left the property, if appropriate; (4) particulars of the improvement or proposed improvement; (5) if a claim for compensation, the amount claimed	PD56, para 5.2
Subsequent procedure	On issue, the court will fix a hearing	PD56, para 5.3
	The claimant need not file his evidence when he issues the claim	PD56, para 5.6
	The defendant must file an acknowledgment of service but need not file his evidence with it.	Rule 8.3 PD56, para 5.6

	If not the freeholder, the defendant must serve a copy of the claim form, any document served with it and his acknowledgment of service on his landlord – and so on	PD56, para 5.5
	On the hearing date fixed the court may dispose of the claim but will usually give case management directions.	
	The claim is treated as allocated to the multi-track	Rule 8.9(c)
Forms	Claim Form N208	

50: Claims for the Recovery of Possession of Land by Landlords

Legal background

New procedures relating to claims for the recovery of land, set out in CPR Pt 55, were introduced on 15 October 2001 by virtue of the Civil Procedure (Amendment) Rules 2001, SI 2001/256. These new procedures only apply to claims issued on or after 15 October 2001. The rules of court immediately before that date continue to apply to claims issued prior to that date (Civil Procedure (Amendment) Rules 2001, SI 2001/256, r 31). For the procedure prior to 15 October 2001, refer to the June 2001 edition of this work.

Demoted tenancies

The following Guide does not deal with –

(i) applications by local housing authorities, housing action trusts and registered social landlords for a demotion order under HA 1985, s 82A, whether sought as an alternative to an order for possession under Pt 55 or as a free-standing application under Pt 65, Section III;

(ii) any subsequent action in the ensuing year for possession of the property the subject matter of the demoted tenancy.

Those seeking guidance on the procedural aspects of either of the above are referred to Pt 55, Section I and Pt 65, Section III.

Procedure

Which court	The claim must normally be started in the *county court* for the district in which the land is situated unless an enactment provides otherwise.	
	In exceptional circumstances only, the claim may be started in the High Court if the claimant files with his claim form a certificate stating the reasons for bringing the claim in that court, verified by a statement of truth	Rule 55.3(1)

	Circumstances which may justify starting a claim in the High Court are if: (a) there are complicated disputes of fact; or (b) there are points of law of general importance The value of the property and the amount of any financial claim may be relevant circumstances, but these factors alone will not normally justify starting the claim in the High Court	Rule 55.3(2) PD55, para 1.3 PD55, para 1.4
Issue	Sufficient copies of the claim form and particulars of claim are completed and lodged with or sent to the court office to enable one copy of each to be served on each defendant and for one copy to be retained by the court. The claimant should also retain a copy for himself. The particulars of claim must be filed and served *with* the claim form	Rules 55.3(5), 55.4
Contents of the particulars of claim	In a possession claim the particulars of claim must: (a) identify the land to which the claim relates; (b) state whether the claim relates to residential property; (c) state the ground on which possession is claimed; (d) give full details about any tenancy agreement; and (e) give details of every person who, to the best of the claimant's knowledge, is in possession of the property. If the claim includes a claim for non-payment of rent the particulars of claim must set out: (1) the amount due at the start of the proceedings; (2) in schedule form, the dates when the arrears of rent arose, all amounts of rent due, the dates and amounts of all payments made and a running total of the arrears; (3) the daily rate of any rent and interest;	

	(4) any previous steps taken to recover the arrears of rent with full details of any court proceedings; and (5) any relevant information about the defendant's circumstances, in particular: (a) whether the defendant is in receipt of social security benefits; and (b) whether any payments are made on his behalf directly to the claimant under the Social Security Contributions and Benefits Act 1992. If the claimant knows of any person (including a mortgagee) entitled to claim relief against forfeiture as underlessee under Law of Property Act 1925, s 146(4) (or in accordance with Supreme Court Act 1981, s 38, or County Courts Act 1984, s 138(9C)): (i) the particulars of claim must state the name and address of that person; and (ii) the claimant must file a copy of the particulars of claim for service on him	Rules 55.3(5), 55.4 PD55, paras 1.5, 2.1, 2.3, 2.4
Hearing date	The court will fix a date for the hearing when it issues the claim form. The hearing date will be not less than 28 days from the date of issue of the claim form; the standard period between the issue of the claim form and the hearing will be not more than 8 weeks; and the defendant must be served with the claim form and particulars of claim not less than 21 days before the hearing date	Rule 55.5(1), (3)
	The court may exercise its powers to shorten the above time periods. This may be appropriate if: (1) the defendant, or a person for whom the defendant is responsible, has assaulted or threatened to assault: (a) the claimant;	Rule 3.1(2)(a) and (b)

	(b) a member of the claimant's staff; or (c) another resident in the locality; (2) there are reasonable grounds for fearing such an assault; or (3) the defendant, or a person for whom the defendant is responsible, has caused serious damage or threatened to cause serious damage to the property or to the home or property of another resident in the locality.	PD55, paras 3.1, 3.2
Service	The general rules as to service of claim forms apply (see Guides 15 and 16)	Part 6
	Where the claimant serves the claim form and particulars of claim, he must produce at the hearing a certificate of service of those documents and r 6.14(2)(a) does not apply	Rule 55.8(6)
Defendant's response	The defendant does not need to file an acknowledgment of service	Rule 55.7(1)
	The defence must be in Form N11 or N11R, as appropriate	PD55, para 1.5
	The defendant should file his defence within 14 days of service of the particulars of claim or within 28 days if the defendant files an acknowledgment of service	Rule 15.4(1)
	If the defendant does not file a defence within the time specified in r 15.4 he may take part in any hearing but the court may take his failure to do so into account when deciding what order to make about costs	
	Any application by the defendant for a time order under Consumer Credit Act 1974, s 129 may be made:	Rule 55.7(3)
	(1) in his defence; or (2) by application notice in the proceedings	PD55, para 7.1
Evidence	Unless the claim has been allocated to the fast track or the multi-track, evidence may normally be given in writing	Rule 55.8(3)

Each party should wherever possible include all the evidence he wishes to present in his statement of case, verified by a statement of truth	PD55, para 5.1 Rule 22.1(1)
All witness statements must be filed and served at least 2 days before the hearing	Rule 55.8(4)
If relevant the claimant's evidence should include the amount of any rent arrears and interest on those arrears. These amounts should, if possible, be up to date to the date of the hearing (if necessary by specifying a daily rate of arrears and interest). However, r 55.8(4) does not prevent such evidence being brought up to date orally or in writing on the day of the hearing if necessary	PD55, para 5.2
Unless exhibited to a witness statement or statement of case, the claimant must at the hearing produce: (a) the original tenancy agreement; (b) the notice seeking possession; (c) evidence of service of the notice seeking possession; (d) the certificate of service on the defendant (if the claimant has served the defendant with the claim form and particulars of claim).	
If relevant the defendant should give evidence of: (1) the amount of any outstanding social security or housing benefit payments relevant to rent arrears; and (2) the status of: (a) any claims for social security or housing benefit about which a decision has not yet been made; and (b) any applications to appeal or review a social security or housing benefit decision where that appeal or review has not yet concluded	PD55, para 5.3
If: (i) the maker of a witness statement does not attend a hearing; and	

	(ii) the other party disputes material evidence contained in his statement, the court will normally adjourn the hearing so that oral evidence can be given	PD55, para 5.4
The hearing	The court may: (1) decide the claim; or (2) give case management directions	Rule 55.8(1)
	Where the claim is genuinely disputed on grounds which appear to be substantial, case management directions will include the allocation of the claim to a track or directions to enable it to be allocated	Rule 55.8(2)
Allocation to track	When the court decides the track for a possession claim, the matters to which it shall have regard include: (1) the matters set out in r 26.8 as modified by the relevant practice direction; (2) the amount of any arrears of rent; (3) the importance to the defendant of retaining possession of the land; and (4) the importance of vacant possession to the claimant. The financial value of the property will not necessarily be the most important factor in deciding the track for a possession claim and the court may direct a possession claim to be allocated to the fast track even though the value of the property is in excess of £15,000	PD55, para 6.1
	The court will only allocate possession claims to the small claims track if all the parties agree	Rule 55.9(2)

	Where a possession claim has been allocated to the small claims track the claim shall be treated, for the purposes of costs, as if it were proceeding on the fast track except that trial costs shall be in the discretion of the court and shall not exceed the amount that would be recoverable under r 46.2 (amount of fast track costs) if the value of the claim were up to £3000. However, where all the parties agree the court may, when it allocates the claim to the small claims track, order that r 27.14 (costs on the small claims track) applies	Rule 55.9(3) and (4)
	Even when allocated to the multi-track, defended cases will not normally be transferred to a Civil Trial Centre	PD26, para 10.1(1)
Costs	Unless the court orders otherwise the recoverable costs are fixed where there has been no denial of liability or counterclaim, whether or not possession is suspended	Rules 45.2A, 45.4A
Court fees	On the commencement of proceedings: in the High Court – £400 in the county court – £150 The above fees apply even if there is a claim for money as well as for possession	CPFO fee 1.4
Forms	*Claimant* Claim Form N5 Particulars of Claim N119 (amended if appropriate to include a claim for interest on any rent arrears) *Defendant* Defence N11 or N11R (which includes provision for an admission and offer), as appropriate	PD4 PD55, para 1.5
	In addition, where a conditional fee agreement applies, N251	PDCosts, paras 19.1, 19.2(1)
Which judge	In the county court a district judge has concurrent jurisdiction with the circuit judge to hear proceedings for the recovery of land	PD2B, para 11.1(b)

51: Claims for the Recovery of Possession of Land by Mortgagees

Legal background

New procedures relating to claims for the recovery of land, set out in CPR Pt 55, were introduced on 15 October 2001 by virtue of the Civil Procedure (Amendment) Rules 2001, SI 2001/256. These new procedures only apply to claims issued on or after 15 October 2001. The rules of court immediately before that date continue to apply to claims issued prior to that date (Civil Procedure (Amendment) Rules 2001, SI 2001/256, r 31). For the procedure prior to 15 October 2001, refer to the June 2001 edition of this work.

Procedure

Which court	The claim must normally be started in the *county court* for the district in which the land is situated unless an enactment provides otherwise.	Rule 55.3(1)
	In exceptional circumstances only, the claim may be started in the High Court if the claimant files with his claim form a certificate stating the reasons for bringing the claim in that court verified by a statement of truth	Rule 55.3(2)
	Circumstances which may justify starting a claim in the High Court are if: (1) there are complicated disputes of fact; or (2) there are points of law of general importance	PD55, para 1.3
	The value of the property and the amount of any financial claim may be relevant circumstances, but these factors alone will not normally justify starting the claim in the High Court	PD55, para 1.4
	Claims in the High Court are assigned to the Chancery Division	PD55, para 1.6
	Where the claim is founded on a mortgage of a dwelling-house outside Greater London it may be heard and determined only in the county court unless the claim also relates to a claim for foreclosure or sale	CCA 1984, s 21

Issue	Sufficient copies of the claim form and particulars of claim are completed and lodged with or sent to the court office to enable one copy of each to be served on each defendant and for one copy to be retained by the court. The claimant should also retain a copy for himself. The particulars of claim must be filed and served *with* the claim form	Rules 55.3(5), 55.4
Contents of the particulars of claim	In a possession claim the particulars of claim must: (1) identify the land to which the claim relates; (2) state whether the claim relates to residential property; (3) state the ground on which possession is claimed; (4) give full details about any mortgage; and (5) give details of every person who, to the best of the claimant's knowledge, is in possession of the property	PD55, para 2.1
	The particulars of claim must also set out: (1) if the claim relates to residential property whether: (a) a land charge of Class F has been registered under Matrimonial Homes Act 1967, s 2(7); (b) a notice registered under Matrimonial Homes Act 1983, ss 2(8) or 8(3) of the has been entered and on whose behalf; or (c) a notice under Family Law Act 1996, s 31(10) of the has been registered and on whose behalf; and (2) if so, that the claimant will serve notice of the claim on the persons on whose behalf the land charge is registered or the notice or caution entered	PD55, para 2.5(1)
	(3) the state of the mortgage account by including: (a) the amount of: (b) the advance; (c) any periodic repayment; and	

(d) any payment of interest required to be made;

(4) the amount which would have to be paid (after taking into account any adjustment for early settlement) in order to redeem the mortgage at a stated date not more than 14 days after the claim started specifying the amount of solicitor's costs and administration charges which would be payable;

(5) if the loan which is secured by the mortgage is a regulated consumer credit agreement, the total amount outstanding under the terms of the mortgage; and

(a) the rate of interest payable:

(b) at the commencement of the mortgage;

(c) immediately before any arrears referred to in PD55, para 2.5(3) accrued; and PD55, para 2.5(2)

(d) at the commencement of the proceedings

(6) if the claim is brought because of failure to pay the periodic payments when due:

(a) in schedule form, the dates when the arrears arose, all amounts due, the dates and amounts of all payments made and a running total of the arrears;

(i) give details of:

– any other payments required to be made as a term of the mortgage (such as for insurance premiums, legal costs, default interest, penalties, administrative or other charges);

– any other sums claimed and stating the nature and amount of each such charge; and

– whether any of these payments is in arrears and whether or not it is included in the amount of any periodic payment PD55, para 2.5(3)

(7) whether or not the loan which is secured by the mortgage is a regulated consumer credit agreement and, if so, specify the date on which any notice required by Consumer Credit Act 1974, ss 76 or 87 was given PD55, para 2.5(4)

	(8) if appropriate (i.e. if the claim is in the High Court) details that show the property is not one to which Consumer Credit Act 1974, s 141 applies	PD55, para 2.5(5)
	(9) any relevant information about the defendant's circumstances, in particular:	PD55, para 2.5(6)
	(a) whether the defendant is in receipt of social security benefits; and	
	(b) whether any payments are made on his behalf directly to the claimant under the Social Security Contributions and Benefits Act 1992	PD55, para 2.5(7)
	(10) give details of any tenancy entered into between the mortgagor and mortgagee (including any notices served); and	
	(11) state any previous steps which the claimant has taken to recover the money secured by the mortgage or the mortgaged property and, in the case of court proceedings, state:	
	(a) the dates when the claim started and concluded; and	
	(b) the dates and terms of any orders made	PD55, para 2.5(8)
Hearing date	The court will fix a date for the hearing when it issues the claim form	Rule 55.5(1)
	The hearing date will be not less than 28 days from the date of issue of the claim form;	
	the standard period between the issue of the claim form and the hearing will be not more than 8 weeks; and	
	the defendant must be served with the claim form and particulars of claim not less than 21 days before the hearing date	Rule 55.5(3)
	The court may exercise its powers to shorten the above time periods. This may be appropriate if:	Rule 3.1(2)(a), (b)
	(1) the defendant, or a person for whom the defendant is responsible, has assaulted or threatened to assault:	
	(a) the claimant;	

	(b) a member of the claimant's staff; or (c) another resident in the locality; (2) there are reasonable grounds for fearing such an assault; or (3) the defendant, or a person for whom the defendant is responsible, has caused serious damage or threatened to cause serious damage to the property or to the home or property of another resident in the locality	PD55, paras 3.1, 3.2
Service	The general rules as to service of claim forms apply (see Guides 15 and 16)	Part 6
	Where the claimant serves the claim form and particulars of claim, he must produce at the hearing a certificate of service of those documents and r 6.14(2)(a) does not apply	Rule 55.8(6)
Notice to occupiers	Where a mortgagee seeks possession of land which consists of or includes residential property, the claimant must send a notice to the property addressed to 'the occupiers' not less than 14 days before the hearing. The notice must: (1) state that a possession claim for the property has started; (2) show the name and address of the claimant, the defendant and the court which issued the claim form; and (3) give details of the hearing. The claimant must produce at the hearing: (a) a copy of the notice; and (b) evidence that he has served it	Rule 55.10
Defendant's response	The defendant does not need to file an acknowledgment of service	Rule 55.7(1)
	The defence must be in Form N11M	PD55, para 1.5

	The defendant should file his defence within 14 days of service of the particulars of claim or within 28 days if the defendant files an acknowledgment of service	Rule 15.4(1)
	If the defendant does not file a defence within the time specified in r 15.4 he may take part in any hearing but the court may take his failure to do so into account when deciding what order to make about costs	Rule 55.7(3)
	Any application by the defendant for a time order under Consumer Credit Act 1974, s 129 may be made: (1) in his defence; or (2) by application notice in the proceedings	PD55, para 7.1
Evidence	Each party should wherever possible include all the evidence he wishes to present in his statement of case, verified by a statement of truth	Rule 22.1(1) Rule 55.8(3) PD55, para 5.1
	All witness statements must be filed and served at least 2 days before the hearing	Rule 55.8(4)
	If relevant the claimant's evidence should include the amount of any mortgage arrears and interest on those arrears. These amounts should, if possible, be up to date to the date of the hearing (if necessary by specifying a daily rate of arrears and interest). However, r 55.8(4) does not prevent such evidence being brought up to date orally or in writing on the day of the hearing if necessary	PD55, para 5.2
	Unless exhibited to a witness statement, the claimant must at the hearing produce: (1) the original mortgage; (2) official copies of the register of title; (3) the certificate of service (if applicable); (4) the certificate of service of notice on the occupiers; (5) the search of HM Land Registry pursuant to Family Law Act 1996, s 31(10).	

	If relevant the defendant should give evidence of: (a) the amount of any outstanding social security or housing benefit payments relevant to the mortgage arrears; and (b) the status of: (c) any claims for social security or housing benefit about which a decision has not yet been made; and (d) any applications to appeal or review a social security or housing benefit decision where that appeal or review has not yet concluded	PD55, para 5.3
	If: (1) the maker of a witness statement does not attend a hearing; and (2) the other party disputes material evidence contained in his statement, the court will normally adjourn the hearing so that oral evidence can be given	PD55, para 5.4
The hearing	The court may: (1) decide the claim; or (2) give case management directions	Rule 55.8(1)
	Where the claim is genuinely disputed on grounds which appear to be substantial, case management directions will include the allocation of the claim to a track or directions to enable it to be allocated	Rule 55.8(2)
Allocation to track	When the court decides the track for a possession claim, the matters to which it shall have regard include: (1) the matters set out in r 26.8 as modified by the relevant practice direction; (2) the amount of any arrears of mortgage instalments; (3) the importance to the defendant of retaining possession of the land; and (4) the importance of vacant possession to the claimant	Rule 55.9(1)

	The financial value of the property will not necessarily be the most important factor in deciding the track for a possession claim and the court may direct a possession claim to be allocated to the fast track even though the value of the property is in excess of £15,000	PD55, para 6.1
	The court will only allocate possession claims to the small claims track if all the parties agree	Rule 55.9(2)
	Where a possession claim has been allocated to the small claims track the claim will be treated, for the purposes of costs, as if it were proceeding on the fast track except that trial costs are in the discretion of the court and may not exceed the amount that would be recoverable under r 46.2 (amount of fast track costs) if the value of the claim were up to £3000. However, where all the parties agree the court may, when it allocates the claim to the small claims track, order that r 27.14 (costs on the small claims track) applies	Rule 55.9(3) and (4)
	Even when allocated to the multi-track, defended cases will not normally be transferred to a Civil Trial Centre	PD26, para 10.1(1)
Costs	The general rule that the court will assess costs summarily at the end of a hearing that lasts for less than one day does not apply to claims by mortgagees, where they are contractually entitled to add their costs to the mortgage debt	PDCosts, Section 50 *Gomba Holdings UK Limited v Minories Finance Limited (No 2)* [1993] Ch 171
Court fees	On the commencement of proceedings: in the High Court – £400 in the county court – £150 The above fees apply even if there is a claim for money as well as for possession	CPFO fee 1.4
Forms	*Claimant* Claim Form N5 Particulars of Claim N120	

	Defendant	
	Defence N11M (which includes provision for an admission and offer)	PD4 PD55, para 1.5
	In addition, where a conditional fee agreement applies, N251	PDCosts, paras 19.1, 19.2(1)
Which judge	In the county court a district judge has concurrent jurisdiction with the circuit judge to hear proceedings for the recovery of land	PD2B, para 11.1(b)

52: Claims for the Recovery of Possession of Land Against Trespassers

Legal background

With the exception of interim possession orders (IPOs), new procedures relating to possession claims were introduced from 15 October 2001 by virtue of the Civil Procedure (Amendment) Rules 2001, SI 2001/256. The new procedures only apply to claims issued on or after that date; the rules of court immediately before that date continue to apply to claims issued prior to that date. For the procedure prior to 15 October 2001, refer to the June 2001 edition of this work.

The Civil Procedure (Amendment) Rules 2002, SI 2002/2058 added IPOs to CPR Pt 55 with effect from 2 December 2002.

Standard procedure or IPO procedure?

The claimant has a choice of remedy against a trespasser. Proceedings can be commenced using either the procedure set out in CPR Pt 55, Section I set out in this Guide, or the IPO procedure to be found in CPR Pt 55, Section III and set out in Guide 45.

As an alternative to the IPO procedure, and particularly where the conditions for applying under Pt 55, Section III do not apply but where nevertheless there is a real emergency, practitioners may wish to consider the use of the procedure on Pt 55, Section I coupled with an application to abridge time for service (see rr 55.5 and 3.1(2)(a)). Furthermore, under the IPO procedure there is the expense of two court hearings rather than just the one under the standard procedure, and the claimant is required to give undertakings in damages as a condition of the grant of an IPO.

Definition

'A possession claim against trespassers' means a claim for the recovery of land which the claimant alleges is occupied only by a person or persons who entered or remained on the land without the consent of a person entitled to possession of that land but does not include a claim against a tenant or sub-tenant whether his tenancy has been terminated or not (r 55.1(b)).

Procedure

Which court	The claim must normally be started in the *county court* for the district in which the land is situated unless an enactment provides otherwise	Rule 55.3(1)

	In exceptional circumstances only, the claim may be started in the High Court if the claimant files with his claim form a certificate stating the reasons for bringing the claim in that court verified by a statement of truth	Rule 55.3(2)
	Circumstances which may justify starting a claim in the High Court are if: (1) there are complicated disputes of fact; or (2) there are points of law of general importance; or (3) there is a substantial risk of public disturbance or of serious harm to persons or property which properly require immediate determination	PD55, para 1.3
	The value of the property and the amount of any financial claim may be relevant circumstances, but these factors alone will not normally justify starting the claim in the High Court	PD55, para 1.4
Issue	Sufficient copies of the claim form and particulars of claim are completed and lodged with or sent to the court office to enable one copy of each to be served on each defendant, for one to be returned to the claimant and for one copy to be retained by the court	
	Where the claimant does not know the name of a person in occupation or possession of the land, the claim must be brought against 'persons unknown' in addition to any named defendants	Rule 55.3(4)
	The claimant must use the appropriate claim form and particulars of claim form set out in PD4, Table 1	Rule 55.3(5)
	The particulars of claim must be filed and served with the claim form	Rule 55.4
Contents of the particulars of claim	The particulars of claim must: (1) identify the land to which the claim relates; (2) state whether the claim relates to residential property;	

	(3) state the ground on which possession is claimed;	
	(4) give full details about any mortgage or tenancy agreement;	
	(5) give details of every person who, to the best of the claimant's knowledge, is in possession of the property;	PD55, para 2.1
	(6) state the claimant's interest in the land or the basis of his right to claim possession and the circumstances in which it has been occupied without licence or consent;	PD55, para 2.6
	(7) contain a statement of truth	Rule 22.1(1)
Hearing date	The court will fix a date for the hearing when it issues the claim form	Rule 55.5(1)
	The defendant must be served with the claim form, particulars of claim and any witness statements:	
	(1) in the case of residential property, not less than 5 days; and	
	(2) in the case of other land, not less than 2 days,	
	before the hearing date	Rule 55.5(2)
	The court may exercise its powers to shorten the above time periods. This may be appropriate if:	Rule 3.1(2)(a), (b)
	(a) the defendant, or a person for whom the defendant is responsible, has assaulted or threatened to assault:	
	(i) the claimant;	
	(ii) a member of the claimant's staff; or	
	(iii) another resident in the locality;	
	(b) there are reasonable grounds for fearing such an assault; or	
	(c) the defendant, or a person for whom the defendant is responsible, has caused serious damage or threatened to cause serious damage to the property or to the home or property of another resident in the locality	PD55, paras 3.1, 3.2

Service	Subject to the following, the general rules as to service of claim forms apply (see Guides 15 and 16)	Part 6
	Where the claim has been issued against 'persons unknown', the claim form, particulars of claim and any witness statements must be served on those persons by:	
	(1) attaching copies of the claim form, particulars of claim and any witness statements to the main door or some other part of the land so that they are clearly visible; and	
	(2) if practicable, inserting copies of those documents in a sealed transparent envelope addressed to 'the occupiers' through the letter box; or	
	(3) placing stakes in the land in places where they are clearly visible and attaching to each stake copies of the claim form, particulars of claim and any witness statements in a sealed transparent envelope addressed to 'the occupiers'	Rule 55.6
	If the claim form is to be served by the court the claimant must provide sufficient stakes and transparent envelopes	PD55, para 4.1
	Where the claimant serves the claim form and particulars of claim, he must produce at the hearing a certificate of service of those documents and r 6.14(2)(a) does not apply	Rule 55.8(6)
Defendant's response	The defendant does not need to file an acknowledgment of service	Rule 55.7(1)
	The defendant need not file a defence; there is no prescribed form of defence save for form N11	Rule 55.7(2)
Evidence	Each party should wherever possible include all the evidence he wishes to present in his statement of case, verified by a statement of truth	Rule 22.1(1) Rule 55.8(3) PD55, para 5.1
	All witness statements on which the claimant intends to rely must be filed and served with the claim form	Rule 55.8(5)

	If: (1) the maker of a witness statement does not attend a hearing; and (2) the other party disputes material evidence contained in his statement, the court will normally adjourn the hearing so that oral evidence can be given	PD55, para 5.4
The hearing	The court may: (1) decide the claim; or (2) give case management directions	Rule 55.8(1)
	Where the claim is genuinely disputed on grounds which appear to be substantial, case management directions will include the allocation of the claim to a track or directions to enable it to be allocated	Rule 55.8(2)
Allocation to track	When the court decides the track for a possession claim, the matters to which it shall have regard include: (1) the matters set out in r 26.8 as modified by the relevant practice direction; (2) the importance to the defendant of retaining possession of the land; and (3) the importance of vacant possession to the claimant	Rule 55.9(1)
	The financial value of the property will not necessarily be the most important factor in deciding the track for a possession claim and the court may direct a possession claim to be allocated to the fast track even though the value of the property is in excess of £15,000	PD55, para 6.1
	The court will only allocate possession claims to the small claims track if all the parties agree	Rule 55.9(2)

	Where a possession claim has been allocated to the small claims track the claim will be treated, for the purposes of costs, as if it were proceeding on the fast track except that trial costs are in the discretion of the court and may not exceed the amount that would be recoverable under r 46.2 (amount of fast track costs) if the value of the claim were up to £3000. However, where all the parties agree the court may, when it allocates the claim to the small claims track, order that r 27.14 (costs on the small claims track) applies	Rule 55.9(3) and (4)
	Even when allocated to the multi-track, defended cases will not normally be transferred to a Civil Trial Centre	PD26, para 10.1(1)
Costs	Unless the fixed costs in Pt 45 are to apply, the costs of any hearing lasting no more than a day will be summarily assessed	PDCosts, Section 13
Court fees	On the commencement of proceedings: in the High Court – £400 in the county court – £150	CPFO fee 1.4
Forms	*Claimant*	
	Claim Form N5	PD4
	Particulars of Claim N121	PD55, para 1.5
	Defendant	
	Defence N11	
	In addition, where a conditional fee agreement applies, N251	PDCosts, paras 19.1, 19.2(1)
Which judge	In the county court a district judge has concurrent jurisdiction with the circuit judge to hear proceedings for the recovery of land	PD2B, para 11.1(b)
Enforcement	Note: a judgment or order of a county court for possession of land against trespassers under Pt 55 may be enforced in the High Court or in the county court	High Court and County Court (Amendment No 2) Order 2001

53: Claims for the Recovery of Possession of Land Otherwise than under a Mortgage or Tenancy or Against Trespassers

Legal background

New procedures relating to claims for the recovery of land, set out in CPR Pt 55, were introduced on 15 October 2001 by virtue of the Civil Procedure (Amendment) Rules 2001, SI 2001/256. These new procedures only apply to claims issued on or after 15 October 2001. The rules of court immediately before that date continue to apply to claims issued prior to that date (see Civil Procedure (Amendment) Rules 2001, SI 2001/256, r 31). For the procedure prior to 15 October 2001, refer to the June 2001 edition of this work.

Specific provisions apply when the claim is made under a tenancy or mortgage and when the claim is 'against trespassers' within the restricted meaning of CPR r 55.1(b). This Guide covers the cases to which those provisions do not apply.

The procedure set out below does not apply to the enforcement of a charging order by sale (see PD55, para 7.2). Refer instead to CPR r 73.10, the draft orders annexed to PD73, and the procedure set out in Guide 47.

Procedure

Which court	The claim must normally be started in the *county court* for the district in which the land is situated unless an enactment provides otherwise.	
	In exceptional circumstances only, the claim may be started in the High Court if the claimant files with his claim form a certificate stating the reasons for bringing the claim in that court verified by a statement of truth	Rule 55.3(1)
	Circumstances which may justify starting a claim in the High Court are if:	
	(1) there are complicated disputes of fact; or	Rule 55.3(2)
	(2) there are points of law of general importance	PD55, para 1.3
	The value of the property and the amount of any financial claim may be relevant circumstances, but these factors alone will not normally justify starting the claim in the High Court	PD55, para1.4

Issue	Sufficient copies of the claim form and particulars of claim are completed and lodged with or sent to the court office to enable one copy of each to be served on each defendant and for one copy to be retained by the court. The claimant should retain a copy for himself. There is no prescribed form of particulars of claim. The particulars of claim must be filed and served with the claim form	Rule 55.4
Contents of the particulars of claim	The particulars of claim must: (1) identify the land to which the claim relates; (2) state whether the claim relates to residential property; (3) state the ground on which possession is claimed; (4) give full details about any (former) tenancy agreement; and (5) give details of every person who, to the best of the claimant's knowledge, is in possession of the property	PD55, para 2.1
Hearing date	The court will fix a date for the hearing when it issues the claim form	Rule 55.5(1)
	The hearing date will be not less than 28 days from the date of issue of the claim form; the standard period between the issue of the claim form and the hearing will be not more than 8 weeks; and the defendant must be served with the claim form and particulars of claim not less than 21 days before the hearing date	Rule 55.5(3)
	The court may exercise its powers to shorten the above time periods. This may be appropriate if: (1) the defendant, or a person for whom the defendant is responsible, has assaulted or threatened to assault: (a) the claimant; (b) a member of the claimant's staff; or	Rule 3.1(2)(a) and (b)

	(c) another resident in the locality; (2) there are reasonable grounds for fearing such an assault; or (3) the defendant, or a person for whom the defendant is responsible, has caused serious damage or threatened to cause serious damage to the property or to the home or property of another resident in the locality	PD55, paras 3.1, 3.2
Service	The general rules as to service of claim forms apply (see Guides 15 and 16)	Part 6
	Where the claimant serves the claim form and particulars of claim, he must produce at the hearing a certificate of service of those documents and r 6.14(2)(a) does not apply	Rule 55.8(6)
Defendant's response	The defendant does not need to file an acknowledgment of service	Rule 55.7(1)
	There is no prescribed form of defence. The defendant should file his defence within 14 days of service of the particulars of claim or within 28 days if the defendant files an acknowledgment of service	Rule 15.4(1)
	If the defendant does not file a defence within the time specified in r 15.4 he may take part in any hearing but the court may take his failure to do so into account when deciding what order to make about costs	Rule 55.7(3)
Evidence	Each party should wherever possible include all the evidence he wishes to present in his statement of case, verified by a statement of truth	Rule 22.1(1) Rule 55.8(3) PD55, para 5.1
	All witness statements must be filed and served at least 2 days before the hearing	Rule 55.8(4)
	If: (1) the maker of a witness statement does not attend a hearing; and (2) the other party disputes material evidence contained in his statement,	

	the court will normally adjourn the hearing so that oral evidence can be given	PD55, para 5.4
The hearing	The court may: (1) decide the claim; or (2) give case management directions	Rule 55.8(1)
	Where the claim is genuinely disputed on grounds which appear to be substantial, case management directions will include the allocation of the claim to a track or directions to enable it to be allocated	Rule 55.8(2)
Allocation to track	When the court decides the track for a possession claim, the matters to which it shall have regard include: (1) the matters set out in r 26.8 as modified by the relevant practice direction; (2) the importance to the defendant of retaining possession of the land; and (3) the importance of vacant possession to the claimant	Rule 55.9(1)
	The financial value of the property will not necessarily be the most important factor in deciding the track for a possession claim and the court may direct a possession claim to be allocated to the fast track even though the value of the property is in excess of £15,000	PD55, para 6.1
	The court will only allocate possession claims to the small claims track if all the parties agree	Rule 55.9(2)

	Where a possession claim has been allocated to the small claims track the claim will be treated, for the purposes of costs, as if it were proceeding on the fast track except that trial costs are in the discretion of the court and may not exceed the amount that would be recoverable under r 46.2 (amount of fast track costs) if the value of the claim were up to £3000. However, where all the parties agree the court may, when it allocates the claim to the small claims track, order that r 27.14 (costs on the small claims track) applies	Rule 55.9(3) and (4)
	Even when allocated to the multi-track, defended cases will not normally be transferred to a Civil Trial Centre	PD26, para 10.1(1)
Costs	Unless the fixed costs in Pt 45 are to apply, the costs of any hearing lasting no more than a day will be summarily assessed	PDCosts, Section 13
Court fees	On the commencement of proceedings: in the High Court – £400 in the county court – £150 The above fees apply even if there is a claim for money as well as for possession.	CPFO fee 1.4
Forms	*Claimant*	
	Claim Form N5	PD4
	Particulars of claim: no prescribed form	
	Defendant	
	Defence: no prescribed form	
	In addition, where a conditional fee agreement applies, N251	PDCosts, paras 19.1, 19.2(1)
Which judge	In the county court a district judge has concurrent jurisdiction with the circuit judge to hear proceedings for the recovery of land	PD2B, para 11.1(b)

54: Claims by Tenants Seeking Relief from Forfeiture

Legal background

New procedures relating to claims for the recovery of land, set out in CPR Pt 55, were introduced on 15 October 2001 by virtue of the Civil Procedure (Amendment) Rules 2001, SI 2001/256. Oddly, the Part also applies to claims by tenants seeking relief from forfeiture. These new procedures only apply to claims issued on or after 15 October 2001; the rules of court immediately before that date continue to apply to claims issued prior to that date (see Civil Procedure (Amendment) Rules 2001, SI 2001/256, r 31). For the procedure prior to 15 October 2001, refer to the June 2001 edition of this work.

Procedure

Which court	The claim must normally be started in the *county court* for the district in which the land is situated unless an enactment provides otherwise	Rule 55.3(2)
	In exceptional circumstances only, the claim may be started in the High Court if the claimant files with his claim form a certificate stating the reasons for bringing the claim in that court verified by a statement of truth	Rule 55.3(1)
	Circumstances which may justify starting a claim in the High Court are if: (1) there are complicated disputes of fact; or (2) there are points of law of general importance	PD55, para 1.3
	The value of the property and the amount of any financial claim may be relevant circumstances, but these factors alone will not normally justify starting the claim in the High Court	PD55, para 4.1
Issue	Sufficient copies of the claim form and particulars of claim are completed and lodged with or sent to the court office to enable one copy of each to be served on each defendant and for one copy to be retained by the court. The claimant should retain a copy for himself. The particulars of claim must be filed and served with the claim form	Rule 55.4

Contents of the particulars of claim	There is no prescribed form. However, the particulars of claim should:	Rule 16.4(1)(a)
	(1) identify the land to which the claim relates;	
	(2) state the ground on which relief from forfeiture is claimed;	
	(3) state the amount of the arrears payable by the claimant;	
	(4) give full details about any tenancy agreement; and	
	(5) give details of every person who, to the best of the claimant's knowledge, is in possession of the property.	
Hearing date	The court will fix a date for the hearing when it issues the claim form	Rule 55.5(1)
	The defendant must be served with the claim form and particulars of claim in good time before the hearing. The requirement in possession claims that he be served not less than 21 days before the hearing date will no doubt be applied by analogy	Rule 55.5(3)
Service	The general rules as to service of claim forms apply (see Guides 15 and 16)	Part 6
	Where the claimant serves the claim form and particulars of claim, he must produce at the hearing a certificate of service of those documents and r 6.14(2)(a) does not apply	Rule 55.8(6)
Defendant's response	The defendant does not need to file an acknowledgment of service	Rule 55.7(1)
	There is no prescribed form of defence.	
	The defendant should file his defence within 14 days of service of the particulars of claim or within 28 days if the defendant files an acknowledgment of service	Rule 15.4(1)
Evidence	Each party should wherever possible include all the evidence he wishes to present in his statement of case, verified by a statement of truth	Rule 22.1(1) Rule 55.8(3) PD55, para 5.1

	All witness statements must be filed and served at least 2 days before the hearing	Rule 55.8(4)
	If: (1) the maker of a witness statement does not attend a hearing; and (2) the other party disputes material evidence contained in his statement, the court will normally adjourn the hearing so that oral evidence can be given	PD55, para 5.4
The hearing	The court may: (1) decide the claim; or (2) give case management directions	Rule 55.8(1)
	Where the claim is genuinely disputed on grounds which appear to be substantial, case management directions will include the allocation of the claim to a track or directions to enable it to be allocated	Rule 55.8(2)
Allocation to track	When the court decides the track for a claim for relief from forfeiture, the matters to which it shall have regard include: (1) the matters set out in r 26.8 as modified by the relevant practice direction; (2) the amount of the arrears payable by the claimant (3) the importance to the claimant of retaining possession of the land; and (4) the importance of vacant possession to the defendant	Rule 55.9(1)
	The financial value of the property will not necessarily be the most important factor in deciding the track and the court may direct the claim be allocated to the fast track even though the value of the property is in excess of £15,000	PD55, para 6.1
Costs	The standard rules for the summary assessment of costs in cases lasting no more than one day apply	PDCosts, Section 13

Court fees	On the commencement of proceedings: High Court – £400 County court – £150 The above fees apply even if there is a claim for money as well as for possession	CPFO fee 1.4
	If the claimant makes a money claim in addition to relief against forfeiture, a further fee is payable in respect of the money claim (as to which see the table in Guides 1). If he makes a money claim as an alternative to relief against forfeiture, then the fee on the money claim is payable in the High Court; in the county court the fee is either that due on the money claim or £150, whichever is the greater	
Forms	*Claimant*	
	Claim Form N5A	PD4
	Particulars of claim: no prescribed form	
	Defendant	
	Defence: no prescribed form	
	In addition, where a conditional fee agreement applies, N251	PDCosts, paras 19.1, 19.2(1)
Which judge	In the county court a district judge has concurrent jurisdiction with the circuit judge to hear a claim for relief from forfeiture save those claims allocated to the multi-track, which a district judge may only hear with the consent of the parties and of the designated civil judge	PD2B, para 11.1(a)

54A: Suspension of Possession Warrants

Legal background

An application to suspend a warrant of possession must be distinguished from an application to set aside a possession order where it is said that the defendant was unaware of the proceedings in question. Different factors are relevant to the determination of an application to set aside an order. Even where the application is to suspend the execution of the warrant of possession, there are different considerations to be taken into account depending on the type of possession proceedings.

Procedure

Which court	The court where the order for possession was made, namely the county court where the property is situated unless the claim were brought in the High Court	Rule 23.2(1) Rule 55.3
Making the application	By application notice *For more information generally on how to bring an application, see Guide 18*	Rule 23.3
Setting aside an order for possession	Possible where the defendant:	
	makes his application promptly;	Rule 39.3(5)(a)
	had a good reason for not attending the hearing when the order was made; and	Rule 39.3(5)(b)
	has a good prospect of success at trial (ie a good prospect of obtaining an order more favourable to him than the order in fact made. An example might be a suspended rather than an outright order for possession)	Rule 39.3(5)(c)
Assured shorthold tenancies	The usual order for possession requires possession within 14 days of the date of the order being made. If exceptional hardship is shown, a judge may postpone possession for up to 42 days from the date of the original order. No further postponement beyond the maximum of 42 days is possible	HA 1980, s 89 Rule 55.18
Introductory tenancies	Unless judicial review proceedings are brought to challenge the decisions of the housing authority, the court has no power to postpone the operation of a warrant of possession	HA 1996, s 127
Secure tenancies	There is no power to suspend a warrant of possession where the order was made under Housing Act 1985, Grounds 9–11. The court may suspend warrants of possession in all other cases under HA 1985 if it thinks fit	HA 1985, s 85(2)

	The suspension may be ordered at any time up to (but not after) the execution of the warrant of possession	*Manchester City Council v Finn* [2002] EWCA 1998
	The court may impose conditions were it to suspend the warrant of possession	HA 1985, s 85(3)
Mortgage cases	The borrower must show that he is likely to be able to discharge the arrears over a reasonable period of time or that the sale of his property is progressing	AJA 1970, s 36 (as amended by AJA 1973, s 8) *Cheltenham & Gloucester BS v Norgan* [1996] 1 All ER 449
	It is not necessary for the applicant to present his evidence formally	*Cheltenham and Gloucester BS v Grant* [1994] 26 HLR 703
Setting aside an eviction	The court may only set aside a possession which has been executed if:	
	the court subsequently sets aside the order for possession; and	
	there is evidence of abuse of process or oppression relating to the manner in which the warrant were either obtained or executed	*Jephson Homes Housing Association v Moisejevs* [2001] 2 All ER 901
Form	N244	
Court fees	On application: *High Court* – £50 *County Court* – £30	CFPO fee 2.8

55: Application under the Inheritance (Provision for Family and Dependants) Act 1975

Legal background

Under the Inheritance (Provision for Family and Dependants) Act 1975 (as amended by the Law Reform (Succession) Act 1995) certain persons may make a claim for financial provision out of the estate of a deceased person, on the ground that the disposition effected by the deceased's will and/or under the laws of intestacy is not such as to make reasonable financial provision for the applicant. Section 2 of the I(PFD)A sets out the court's powers in making an order. The matters which the court must take into account are set out in s 3, and differ depending upon who is making the application. The categories of applicant who are entitled to make a claim are listed in s 1.

The procedure is governed by CPR Pt 57, Section IV, which replaces the former Sch 1, RSC Ord 99.

Procedure

Who may apply	The spouse of the deceased	
	The former spouse of the deceased, if not remarried	
	A cohabitant of the deceased	I(PFD)A, s 1(1A)
	A child of the deceased	
	Any person who was treated as a child of the family	
	Any other person who immediately before the death of the deceased was being maintained by him	I(PFD)A, s 1(1)(e)
Which court	High Court (Chancery Division, or Family Division) or county court.	
Application	*High Court and county court*	
	Part 8 claim form The claim form should state that it is issued under Pt 8 and should be entitled 'In the estate of X, deceased' and 'In the matter of the Inheritance (Provision for Family and Dependants) Act 1975'	Rule 57.16(1) Rule 8.2(a)
	The claim form must normally be issued within 6 months of the date on which representation is take out	I(PFD)A, s 4
	The court may allow an application to be brought out of time but then will not have the power to treat the deceased's severable share of any joint property as part of the net estate. Any application to extend the period should be included in the claim form	I(PFD)A, s 9
Documents	The claimant must file an affidavit or witness statement in support, exhibiting an official copy of the grant of representation to the deceased's estate and of every testamentary document admitted to proof	Rule 57.16(3)
	The claimant's written evidence must be filed and served with the claim form	Rule 8.5(1) and (2)
Defendants	Personal representatives;	
	Beneficiaries who may be affected by any provision ordered by the court;	

	Other persons affected by the claim; Any other person directed by the court to be added	Rule 19.7
Service	Acknowledgment of service must be filed within 14 days and served on the claimant and any other party	Rule 57.16(2), Rule 8.3(1), Rule 10.3
	A failure to file an acknowledgment of service within 2 weeks means that the defendant may only take part in the hearing of the claim with the court's permission	Rule 8.4
	A defendant who is a personal representative who wishes to remain neutral and agrees to abide by the court's decision (as normally he should unless he has a beneficial interest) should state this in Section A of the acknowledgment of service	PD57, para 15
Evidence in answer	A defendant personal representative must, and any other defendant may, file a witness statement or affidavit in answer within 21 days after service of the claim form on him	Rule 57.16(4)–(5)
	The witness statement or affidavit filed by a personal representative must state to the best of the witness's ability:	
	(a) full details of the value of the deceased's net estate;	PD57, para 16(1)
	(b) details of those beneficially interested in the estate and (in the case of those who are not already parties) the addresses of all living beneficiaries and the value of their interests;	PD57, para 16(2)(a), (b)
	(c) whether any living beneficiary is a child or patient, if so naming him	PD57, para 16(3)
	(d) any facts known to the witness which might affect the exercise of the court's powers under the I(PFD)A	PD57, para 16(4)
Service of answer	Every defendant who lodges a witness statement or affidavit shall at the same time serve a copy on the claimant and on every other defendant who is not represented by the same solicitor	Rule 8.5

Further evidence	The claimant may serve further written evidence in reply within 14 days of service of the defendant's evidence on him. If he does so he must also, within the same time-limit, serve a copy of his evidence on the other parties	Rule 8.5(5) and (6)
Directions	A directions hearing may be requested at same time as issuing claim form	PD8, para 4.1
	In other cases the court will give directions as soon as practicable after the defendant has acknowledged service of the claim form or after the period for acknowledgment has expired	PD8, para 4.2
Orders which may be made:	Periodical payments	I(PFD)A, s 2(1)(a)
	Lump sum	I(PFD)A, s 2(1)(b)
	Transfer of property	I(PFD)A, s 2(1)(c)
	Settlement of property	I(PFD)A, s 2(1)(d)
	Acquisition, transfer and settlement of property	I(PFD)A, s 2(1)(e)
	Variation of antenuptial and post-nuptial settlement	I(PFD)A, s 2(1)(f)
	Treatment of deceased's former beneficial interest in joint property as part of his estate and not passing by survivorship (unless the claim was made outside the primary 6-month period)	I(PFD)A, s 9
	Variation or discharge of secured periodical payments	I(PFD)A, s 16
	Variation or revocation of maintenance payments	I(PFD)A, s 17
	Order relating to disposition intended to defeat a claim under the Act	I(PFD)A, ss 10, 11, 12
Court fees	High Court – £400 County court – £150	CPFO fee 1.4

55A: Probate Claims

Legal background

A 'probate claim' is defined by CPR r 57.1(2) as being a claim for the grant of probate of the will or letters of administration of the estate of a deceased person, the revocation of such a grant, or a decree pronouncing for or against the validity of an alleged will.

Procedure

What is a probate claim?	A probate claim is contentious in nature and, therefore, does not include non-contentious or common form probate business. It includes a claim for the grant of probate of the will, or letters of administration of the estate, of a deceased person, the revocation of such a grant or a decree pronouncing for or against the validity of an alleged will	Rule 57.1(2)
Who may apply?	Anyone who is potentially beneficially entitled pursuant to the will or letter of administration	
Which court	The High Court or, if the deceased's net estate does not exceed £30,000, a county court	PD57, para 2.2 CCA 1984, s 32 CCJO 1981, art 2
	Probate claims in the High Court are assigned to the Chancery Division	Rule 57.2(2)
	Probate claims in the county court may only be brought in a court where there is also a Chancery district registry	Rule 57.2(3)
Issuing the claim	The Pt 7 procedure applies	Rule 57.3(b)
	The claim form and all subsequent documents must be marked at the top 'In the estate of X Deceased (Probate)'. Unless the court directs otherwise, the testamentary documents (see below) must be lodged when the claim form is issued	Rule 57.5(2)(a)
	The claimant must also file written evidence describing any testamentary document that he has any knowledge of, using the specimen form provided	Rule 57.5(3) PD57, para 3.2(1) and Annex
	If the claimant knows of any testamentary document that is not in his possession or control, his evidence must include the name and address of the person in whose possession it is	Rule 57.5(3)(b)
Defendant's response	A defendant who is served with a claim form must file an acknowledgment of service 28 days after service of the particulars of claim (if stated in the claim form to be following) and in any other case 28 days after service of the claim form	Rule 57.4(1) Rule 57.4(2)

	Unless the court directs otherwise, a defendant must lodge any testamentary documents (see below) in his possession when he acknowledges service	Rule 57.5(1), (2)
	Every defendant must also file written evidence describing any testamentary document that he has any knowledge of, using the specimen form provided	Rule 57.5(3) PD57, para 3.2(1) and Annex
	If the defendant knows of any testamentary document that is not in his possession or control, his evidence must include the name and address of the person in whose possession it is	Rule 57.5(3)(b)
Failure to acknowledge service or file defence	A default judgment cannot be obtained in a probate claim and neither r 10.2 nor Pt 12 apply If any defendant fails to acknowledge service, the claimant may, after the time for acknowledging service has expired and upon filing written evidence of service, proceed with the probate claim as if the defendant had acknowledged service	Rule 57.10(1) Rule 57.10(2)
	If no defendant acknowledges service or files a defence, then the claimant may apply to the court for an order that the claim is to proceed to trial. He must file written evidence of service of the claim form and particulars of claim on each of the defendants	Rule 57.10(3)
Probate counterclaim in other proceedings	Part 57 applies with the necessary modifications to a probate counterclaim made in any proceedings other than a probate claim	Rule 57.9(1), (2)
Which track?	All probate claims are allocated to the multi-track	Rule 57.2(4)
Lodging of testamentary documents	Any testamentary document of the deceased in the possession of any party must be lodged with the court	Rule 57.5(1)

	A testamentary document is 'a will, a draft of a will, written instructions for a will made by or at the request of, or under the instructions of, the testator, and any document purporting to be evidence of the contents, or to be a copy, of a will which is alleged to have been lost or destroyed'	Rule 57.1(2)(c)
	Except with the permission of the court, a party shall not be allowed to inspect the testamentary documents or written evidence lodged or filed by any other party until he himself has lodged his testamentary documents and filed his evidence	Rule 57.5(5)
Discontinuance and dismissal	Part 38 does not apply to probate claims	Rule 57.11(1)
	At any stage during a probate claim, on application by any party, the court may order that the claim be discontinued or dismissed and a grant of probate of the will or letters of administration of the estate of the deceased person be made to the person entitled to the grant	Rule 57.11(2)

56: Applications for Writ of Habeas Corpus

Legal background

The writ of habeas corpus now takes three forms. *Habeas corpus ad subjiciendum*, the most important of the three, enables the court to rule upon the lawfulness of the applicant's detention. *Habeas corpus ad testificandum* and *habeas corpus ad respondendum* require detainees to be produced to the court to give evidence or answer certain charges. Schedule 1, RSC Ord 54 contains some provisions which are now outdated.

Procedure

Availability	The applicant must be subject to a current restraint on his liberty. Usually he is detained but he may be on bail.	
	The applicant must be in the jurisdiction ie England or Wales (subject to a few exceptions such as the Isle of Man or protectorates)	RSC Ord 54

Which court	The application is made in Queen's Bench Division of the High Court unless it is an application by a parent or guardian for custody care or control of a child in which case it must be made in the Family Division The Court of Appeal has no original jurisdiction to grant the writ. Inferior courts and tribunals cannot issue the writ.	SCA, s 61, Sch 1, para 2(a) RSC Ord 54, r 1 RSC Ord 54, r 11
Notice	The application for the writ is made without notice though it is in fact common for the respondent to be notified	RSC Ord 54, r 1(2)
Court fees	£400	CPFO fee 1.4
Documents	The application must be supported by a witness statement or affidavit by the applicant, if possible, or on his behalf The applicant must supply the respondent on demand with copies of the witness statement or affidavit unless this is not practicable, in which case the deponent must explain why it is not practicable	RSC Ord 54, r 1(2), (3) RSC Ord 54, r 3
Court's powers	The court may order the immediate issue of the writ. This is rare and happens only if there is full argument at the initial hearing and the case is clear. More commonly the court adjourns the application so that the respondent can be notified or file evidence. The court may direct that an application be made by claim form using Form 87 Where the court directs that the application be adjourned on notice to the defendant, notice must be given using Form 88	RSC Ord 54, r 2 PDRSC54, para 3.1 PDRSC54, para 4.1
Powers of single judge	A single judge can now refuse the application, even in a criminal cause or matter	AJA 1960, s 14(1), repealed by AJA 1999, s 65

Releasing the applicant	The court may order the release of the applicant without issuing the writ in which case the master of the Crown Office writes to the respondent directing the discharge of the applicant. Sometimes the writ is issued after the release as a formality. In these cases rr 5–8 are redundant	RSC Ord 54, r 4(1)
Renewed applications	If the application is refused it cannot be renewed on the same grounds unless there is fresh evidence	AJA 1960, s 14(2)
Appeal against refusal of order	If the application is refused the applicant may with permission appeal. In a non-criminal cause or matter the appeal is to the Court of Appeal and then to the House of Lords. In a criminal cause or matter the appeal is directly to the House of Lords	AJA 1960, s 15(1), (3)
Appeal against order	If the application is granted the respondent may appeal. In a criminal cause or matter the successful applicant may be detained or released on bail pending an appeal by the prosecutor. Subject to this a successful appeal by the respondent will not render the applicant liable to be detained again	AJA 1960, s 15(1), (4)
Habeas corpus ad testificandum	This enables a judge of the High Court to order a prisoner to be produced to give evidence in a court. The application is made by witness statement or affidavit to a judge in chambers	Habeas Corpus Act 1804, s 1
Habeas corpus ad respondendum	This enables a judge of the High Court to order a prisoner to be produced for trial or to be examined. The application is made by witness statement or affidavit to a judge in chambers	Habeas Corpus Act 1803, s 1

57: Technology and Construction Court Claims

Legal Background

The Technology and Construction Court (TCC) is a specialist list dealing with building and construction disputes, and other cases that involve issues or questions which are technically complex. From 25 March 2002, by virtue of the Civil Procedure

(Amendment No 5) Rules 2001, SI 2001/4015, the procedure in the TCC is governed by CPR Pt 60 and PD60. For provisions governing TCC cases before that date see PD49C, which is revoked from that date.

Procedure

Where is it?	The address of the TCC in London is – St Dunstan's House 133–137 Fetter Lane London EC4A 1HD The numbers for the court manager are – Tel 0207 947 7429 Fax 020 7947 7428	
Where to start the claim	The claim may be started in – (a) the TCC in London; (b) a district registry of the High Court – where a case is started in a district registry, it should preferably be started in the Birmingham, Bristol, Cardiff, Chester, Exeter, Leeds, Liverpool, Newcastle, Nottingham or Salford District Registry; (c) certain designated county courts namely Birmingham, Bristol, Cardiff, Central London, Chester, Exeter, Leeds, Liverpool, Newcastle, Nottingham or Salford County Court The normal criteria for deciding whether the case should be started in the High Court or county court apply. Claims of less than £15,000 in value cannot be started in the High Court	PD60, paras 3.1–3.4 PD7, para 2.1
Transfer of proceedings	Applications to transfer to or from the TCC must be made to a TCC judge Transfer between the county court and the High Court is governed by normal rules. Where no TCC judge is available in a High Court district registry or a designated county court, the claim may be transferred to another district registry or the High Court or, in the case of a claim issued in a county court, to another county court where a TCC judge would be available	Rule 30.5(3) Rule 30.3 PD60, paras 5.1–5.2

Form of proceedings	All TCC claims are Pt 7 claims, and assigned to the multi-track. Part 26 does not apply. The claim form must be marked in the top right hand corner 'Technology and Construction Court' below the words 'The High Court, Queen's Bench Division' or 'The ___ County Court'	Rule 60.6 PD60, para 3.2
Which judge	TCC claims which are started in or transferred to London will be assessed by the judge in charge of the TCC and assigned either to a High Court judge by being designated 'HCJ' or a circuit judge ('SCJ'). Where cases are designated SCJ they may be initially assigned to a named judge or assigned on a rota basis to the next available TCC judge. The designated TCC judge will be primarily responsible for case management. All documents relating to the claim must be marked in a similar manner to the claim form with the words 'Technology and Construction Court' and the name of the assigned High Court or circuit judge	Statement by Lord Chief Justice, 7 June 2005 and PD60, para 3.2 PD60, para 6.2
Contents of the particulars of claim	Normal rules apply for Pt 7 claims.	
Contents of the defence and other statements of case	Normal rules apply for Pt 7 claims; statements of truth are required.	
Time-limits	Normal rules apply for filing a defence and acknowledgment of service. Any defence is due 14 days after the particulars of claim, or 28 days if the defendant files an acknowledgment of service	Rule 15.4

General procedure	The court will fix a case management conference within 14 days of the earliest of – (a) the filing of an acknowledgment of service; (b) the filing of a defence; (c) the date of an order transferring the claim to the TCC A case management information sheet (PD60, App A) must be completed by each party and filed and served on all other parties 2 days before the case management conference. The same applies to case management directions forms (PD60, App B) Part 29 and PD29 apply generally, except where varied by or inconsistent with PD60 Any application for orders other than those in the case management directions form must be filed and served 2 days before the case management conference Failure to file/serve a case management information sheet and case management directions form may attract sanctions and lead to an adjournment of the case management conference The general provisions of PD29 apply to the case management conference where a party has a legal representative, ie a representative familiar with the case and with sufficient authority to deal with issues likely to arise must attend	PD60, para 8.1 PD60, para 8.3 Rule 60.6(2) PD60, para 8.3(2) PD60, para 8.5 PD29, paras 5.1–5.9 Rule 60.6(2) Rule 29.3(2)
Timetable	A timetable for pleadings, disclosure, witness statements, expert evidence, further case management conferences, pre-trial review, trial of preliminary issues, and trial will be fixed at the case management conference	PD60, para 8.6
Listing	Pre-trial check lists are not required	PD60, para 10

Pre-Trial review	Where a pre-trial review is ordered, each party must complete the questionnaire and directions forms (PD60, Apps C and D) and file and serve them on other parties 2 days before the pre-trial review. Failure to do so can lead to sanctions and an adjournment The parties should endeavour to agree directions to propose to the court	PD60, paras 9.1, 9.4 PD60, para 9.3
Trial judge	The assigned TCC judge will conduct the trial whenever possible.	
Venue	Wherever there is a TCC judge available (in practice, cases proceeding in the TCC in London are invariably tried in London).	

58: Appeals from a District Judge to a Circuit Judge

Legal background

The table below sets out the procedural steps which need to be taken for an appeal from a district judge to a circuit judge in county court proceedings (other than family, insolvency, probate and Mental Health Act proceedings).

Procedure

Step 1		
Application to the district judge for permission to appeal	Permission to appeal should be applied for as soon as the district judge has given judgment (permission to appeal is not required where the appeal is against a committal order, a refusal to grant *habeas corpus* or a secure accommodation order made under Children Act 1989, s 25). If this is not done or if the district judge refuses permission, application for permission must be made to the circuit judge (see Step 3 below)	Rule 52.3(1), (2)(a) PD52, para 4.6

Step 2		
Obtaining a record of the judgment and (where required) the evidence	(1) A record of the reasoned judgment of the court below should be obtained – (a) If available, an official transcript of the district judge's judgment should be ordered	PD52, para 5.6A(1)(f) PD52, para 5.12
	(b) If the district judge gave a written judgment, a copy of it, signed by the district judge, can be used for an appeal	PD52, para 5.12(1)
	(c) Where the judgment was not officially recorded or issued in writing, an advocate's note of judgment must be provided	PD52, para 5.12(2)
	Note that in a claim allocated to the small claims track unless the court orders it to be filed	PD52, para 5.8(4), (5)
	(2) Where permission to appeal has been granted by the district judge (or is not required), then, if any issues of fact are being raised on the appeal, transcripts of the relevant evidence must be ordered. If the evidence was not officially recorded, typed notes of evidence should be obtained	PD52, paras 5.6A(1)(f), 5.15 PD52, para 5.16
	Note: transcripts or notes of evidence are generally not required for an application for permission to appeal. Accordingly where permission to appeal is required and an application for permission is being made to a circuit judge, then (unless the court otherwise directs) transcripts of evidence should not be ordered unless and until permission to appeal has been granted	PD52, para 5.15

Step 3		
Preparation of appellant's notice, bundle and skeleton argument	(1) Prepare appellant's notice (Form N161) If permission to appeal has been refused by the district judge or no application for permission was made to the district judge, an application for permission must be included in the appellant's notice	Rule 52.4 Rule 52.4(1)
	(2) Appellant's solicitor (or the appellant, if acting in person) prepares appeal bundle	PD52, paras 5.6(2), 5.6A

	(3) Appellant's advocate prepares skeleton argument	PD52, para 5.9
Step 4		
Filing of appellant's notice and other documents	(1) Within 14 days after the date on which the district judge gave his/her decision (or such other time-limit as the district judge directed) the appellant's solicitor (or the appellant, if acting in person) must file with the county court office the original of the appellant's notice (together with the documents specified in (2) and (4) or (5) below) and pay the court fee. (If permission to appeal was granted by the district judge, or is not required, the fee is currently £100 unless the claim was allocated to the small claims track, when the fee is £80.)	Rule 52.4(2)
	(2) The following documents must be filed for the use of the court –	PD52, paras 5.6, 5.6A
	(a) the original of the appellant's notice, plus two additional copies for the court and one copy for each respondent;	PD52, para 5.6(2)(a), (b)
	(b) a bound, indexed and paginated appeal bundle;	
	(c) an official copy of the transcript or other record of judgment (if it is not available by then, see note below);	
	(d) a copy of the appellant's advocate's skeleton argument (but see Step 6 below). Litigants in person are not obliged to provide skeleton arguments, but are encouraged to do so;	PD52, para 5.9(3)
	(e) Where the appeal raises issues of fact and permission to appeal has been granted by the lower court or is not required, transcripts of the relevant evidence (or judge's notes, if the evidence was not recorded);	
	(f) a sealed copy of the order being appealed; and	
	(g) a copy of any order granting or refusing permission to appeal and a copy of the reasons for that decision;	

(h) If the appellant's notice also includes any incidental application (eg for a stay pending appeal) any witness statements or affidavits in support of that application	PD52, para 5.6(2)(f)
Note: if it is not possible to file all the above documents with the appellant's notice, the appellant's solicitor (or the appellant, if acting in person) must indicate on the appellant's notice which of the required documents have not been filed, the reasons why they are not currently available and the date when they are expected to be available	PD52, para 5.7
(3) The county court will then issue the appellant's notice. Service of the appellant's notice and the other requisite documents will usually be effected by the county court office. Whether service is effected by the county court, or a sealed copy of the appellant's notice for service on each respondent is given to the appellant's side, service must be effected as soon as practicable and in any event within seven days of the filing of the appellant's notice.	
(4) Where permission to appeal was granted by the district judge, or is not required, copies of the following documents must be lodged with the county court for service on the respondent(s) –	PD52, para 5.24
(a) a sealed copy of the appellant's notice;	
(b) the appeal bundle;	
(c) the other documents listed in (2) above.	
Note: where any of those documents were not available to be filed with the appellant's notice, copies of them must be served on the respondent(s) when they are subsequently filed with the court.	
(5) The court may refer the case to a circuit judge for directions. The circuit judge may –	
(a) deal with the application on paper without a hearing;	PD52, para 4.11

	(b) list it for oral hearing either with or without notice to the respondent(s); (c) list it on notice to the respondent(s) for oral hearing of the application for permission to appeal with the appeal to be heard on the same occasion if permission is granted	PD52, para 4.15
Step 5		
Directions	The appellant's solicitor (or the appellant, if acting in person) must comply with any further directions given by the judge. Exceptionally, the circuit judge may order the appeal to be transferred to the Court of Appeal. He will do this only if he considers that the appeal would raise an important point of principle or practice or that there is some other compelling reason for the Court of Appeal to hear it	Rule 52.14
Step 6		
Lodging and serving of the appellant's skeleton argument, if not filed with the appellant's notice	If it is impracticable for the appellant's skeleton argument to be filed at the same time as the appellant's notice, the appellant's skeleton argument must be lodged with the county court and a copy served on each respondent within 14 days of the filing of the appellant's notice	PD52, para 5.9(2)
	Note: litigants in person are not obliged to provide skeleton arguments, but are encouraged to do so	PD52, para 5.9(3)
Step 7		
Filing any documents which were not available to file with the appellant's notice	Where any of the documents which should have been filed with the appellant's notice were not available at that time (see note to Step 4(2) above), they must be filed with the county court as soon as possible thereafter, and copies served on the respondent(s).	

Step 8		
Where the appellant's notice includes an application to a circuit judge for permission to appeal, determination of that application	(1) The circuit judge may deal with the application on paper without a hearing. If he/she grants permission to appeal on paper, proceed to Step 9 (2) If the circuit judge refuses permission to appeal on paper, the appellant may request reconsideration at an oral hearing, the appellant's solicitor (or the appellant, in person) must file a letter to that effect (and serve a copy on the respondent(s)) within 7 days after receiving notification of the decision given on paper	PD52, para 4.11 PD52, paras 4.13, 4.14
	(3) If the appellant is in receipt of services funded by the Legal Services Commission, the appellant's solicitor must send to the relevant office of the Legal Services Commission a copy of the circuit judge's reasons for refusing permission to appeal on paper. The court will require confirmation that that has been done if a publicly funded appellant requests reconsideration of the application at an oral hearing	PD52, para 4.17
	(4) At least 4 days before a hearing to reconsider refusal of permission the appellant's advocate must inform the court and the respondent of the points he intends to raise, set out his reasons why permission should be given, and confirm compliance with para 4.17	PD52, para 4.14A(2)
	(5) Where a request for reconsideration at an oral hearing has been made, or the circuit judge has directed that the application for permission be listed for oral hearing initially, the appellant's advocate (or the appellant, if acting in person) attends the oral hearing.	

	(6) If the court has directed that notice of the permission to appeal hearing be given to the respondent(s), the appellant must, within 7 days of receiving notification of that (or within such other period as the court has directed), serve on each respondent a copy of the bundle	PD52, para 4.16
	(7) If a hearing on notice to the respondent(s) has been ordered, the appellant's advocate must be prepared to deal with any points relating to summary assessment of costs	PD52, para 14.1(2)
	(8) If the circuit judge grants permission to appeal, proceed to Step 9.	
	If the circuit judge refuses permission to appeal at an oral hearing, that decision cannot be further appealed	AJA 1999, s 54(4)
Step 9		
Service of documents and other action to be taken after permission to appeal has been granted by a circuit judge	(1) The appellant's solicitor (or the appellant, if acting in person) must serve copies of the documents listed in (2) below within 7 days of receiving the order granting permission to appeal	PD52, para 6.2
	(2) The following documents must be served on the respondent(s), insofar as they have not already been served –	PD52, paras 5.6, 6.2
	(a) a sealed copy of the appellant's notice;	
	(b) a copy of the appeal bundle;	
	(c) a copy of the transcript or other record of judgment;	
	(d) a copy of the appellant's advocate's skeleton argument (litigants in person are not obliged to provide skeleton arguments, but are encouraged to do so);	PD52, para 5.9(3)
	(e) a copy of the order being appealed; and	
	(f) a copy of any order granting or refusing permission to appeal and a copy of the reasons for that decision; and	

	(g) if the appellant's notice includes an incidental application, any witness statements or affidavits in support of that application. (3) If the appeal involves any issues of fact, the appellant's solicitor (or the appellant, if acting in person) must order transcripts of the relevant evidence (or, if the evidence was not officially recorded, take steps to obtain a typed text of the judge's notes of evidence) (4) As soon as the transcripts (or notes) of evidence are available, the appellant's solicitor (or the appellant, if in person) must file the official copies with the county court office and serve photocopies on the respondent(s).	PD52, para 5.15
Step 10		
The hearing	(1) The hearing date for the appeal will be notified by the county court to the solicitors and to any party acting in person (2) The advocates attend the appeal hearing. All appeals are listed on notice to the respondent(s) (unless the circuit judge has otherwise directed). (3) Documents extraneous to the issue in the appeal must be excluded from the bundle. The appeal bundle must contain a signed certificate that this has been understood and complied with	PD52, para 6.3(1)(a) PD52, para 5.6A(2), (3)
Step 11		
Judgment	(1) In the majority of cases the court delivers judgment at the conclusion of the hearing. (2) Where judgment is reserved, the parties will be notified by the county court office of the date when the reserved judgment will be given.	

	(3) If it was the hearing of an application for permission to appeal at which the respondent was present, an appeal against a case management decision, or the appeal was listed for one day or less, the court will normally assess costs summarily	PD52, para 14.1(5)
Step 12		
Appeal to the Court of Appeal	(1) If either party wishes to appeal to the Court of Appeal against a circuit judge's decision given on appeal from a district judge, an application for permission to appeal must be made to the Court of Appeal. (The circuit judge has no jurisdiction to grant or refuse permission to appeal in the case of second tier appeals) (2) The Court of Appeal will not grant permission to bring a second tier appeal unless – (a) the appeal would raise an important point of principle or practice; or (b) there is some other compelling reason for the Court of Appeal to hear it.	AJA 1999, s 55 Rule 52.13

59: Appeals to the Court of Appeal

Legal background

The table below sets out the procedural steps which need to be taken for an appeal to the Court of Appeal from a decision of a High Court judge, a circuit judge or (in those cases where the appeal lies directly to the Court of Appeal) a district judge.

References to 'counsel' include a solicitor holding a higher courts advocacy qualification giving a right of audience before the Court of Appeal.

Further details are available at the Court of Appeal's website at *www.civilappeals.gov.uk*.

Procedure

Step 1		
Application to the lower court for permission to appeal	Permission to appeal should be applied for as soon as judgment has been given (permission to appeal is not required where the appeal is against a committal order, a refusal to grant *habeas corpus* or a secure accommodation order made under Children Act 1989, s 25). If this is not done or if permission is refused, application for permission must be made to the Court of Appeal (see Step 3 below)	Rule 52.3(1), (2)(a) PD52, para 4.6
Step 2		
Obtaining a record of the judgment and (where required) the evidence	(1) A record of the reasoned judgment of the court below should be obtained – (a) If the judge handed down a text of his/her judgment, then a copy of the handed-down judgment signed by the judge can be used for the appeal	PD52, para 5.6A(1)(f) PD52, para 5.12(1)
	(b) If the judgment was not handed down, but was officially recorded, then the appellant must order an official transcript of the judgment	PD52, para 5.12
	(c) Where the judgment was not handed down or officially recorded, an advocate's note of judgment must be provided	PD52, para 5.12(2)
	(2) Where permission to appeal has been granted by the court below (or is not required), then, if any issues of fact are being raised on the appeal, transcripts of the relevant evidence should be ordered. If the evidence was not officially recorded, notes of evidence should be obtained	PD52, paras 5.6A(1)(f), 5.15 PD52, para 5.16

	Note: transcripts or notes of evidence are generally not required for an application for permission to appeal. Accordingly, where permission to appeal is required and an application for permission is being made to the Court of Appeal, then unless the court otherwise directs, the transcripts of evidence should not be ordered unless and until permission to appeal has been granted.	PD52, para 5.15
Step 3		
Preparation of appellant's notice, bundle and skeleton argument	(1) The appellant's notice (Form N161) should be prepared If permission to appeal has been refused by the lower court or no application for permission was made to that court, an application for permission must be included in the appellant's notice	Rule 52.4 Rule 52.4(1)
	(2) The appeal bundle should be prepared by the appellant's solicitor (or the appellant if acting in person)	PD52, paras 5.6(7) and 5.6A
	(3) The skeleton argument should be prepared by the appellant's counsel	PD52, para 5.9
Step 4		
Filing of appellant's notice and other documents	(1) The following documents should be filed with the Civil Appeals Registry (RCJ Room E307) –	PD52, para 15.1(1)
	(a) the original of the appellant's notice plus two copies for the use of the court and one copy for each separately represented respondent (and any respondent in person);	PD52, para 5.6(2)
	(b) a bound, indexed and paginated appeal bundle;	
	(c) an official copy of the transcript or other record of judgment (if it is not available by then, see note below);	
	(d) a copy of the appellant's counsel's skeleton argument (but see Step 6 below). Litigants in person are not obliged to provide skeleton arguments, but are encouraged to do so;	PD52, para 5.9(3)

(e) where the appeal raises issues of fact and permission to appeal has been granted by the lower court or is not required, transcripts of the relevant evidence (or judge's notes, if the evidence was not recorded); (f) a copy of the order being appealed; and (g) a copy of any order granting or refusing permission to appeal and a copy of the reasons for that decision. Note: if it is not possible to file all the above documents with the appellant's notice, the appellant's solicitor (or the appellant, if acting in person) must enter on the appellant's notice which of the required documents have not been filed, the reasons why they are not currently available, and when they are expected to be available	PD52, para 5.7
(2) The appellant's solicitor (or appellant in person) must pay the fee on the appellant's notice. If permission to appeal is being sought from the Court of Appeal the fee at this stage will be £200 and, if permission to appeal is granted, a further fee of £400 will have to be paid on the appeal questionnaire. If permission to appeal has been granted by the lower court, or is not required, the fee on the appellant's notice will be £400, and no fee is payable on the appeal questionnaire	CPFO, fee 12.1
(3) If the appellant's notice also includes any incidental application (eg for a stay pending appeal) any witness statements or affidavits in support of that application must be lodged with the appellant's notice	PD52, para 5.6(2)(f)
(4) The appellant's notice and other documents must be filed within 14 days after the date on which the lower court gave its decision (or within such other period as the lower court has directed)	Rule 52.4(2)

	The Civil Appeals Office will then issue the appellant's notice by putting a seal on it recording the date on which it was filed, and return to the appellant's side a sealed copy of the appellant's notice for service on each respondent, together with a letter acknowledging that the notice has been filed, giving the Court of Appeal reference number for the case and setting out what further steps need to be taken. **Where permission to appeal was granted by the lower court, or permission to appeal is not required, proceed directly to Step 11A.** **Where the appellant is applying to the Court of Appeal for permission to appeal, continue with Step 5, et seq.**	
Step 5		
Service of appellant's notice where permission to appeal is being sought from the Court of Appeal	(1) The appellant's solicitor (or appellant in person) puts the Court of Appeal reference number on each sealed copy ready for service on the respondent(s). (That reference number will be on the receipt letter from the Civil Appeals Office; see Step 4 above.)	
	(2) (Subject to any specific direction given by the Court of Appeal in any particular case) service of the appellant's notice must be effected on the respondent(s) as soon as practicable and, in any event, not later than seven days after the appellant's notice was filed	Rule 52.4(3)
	Note: the appellant's solicitor (or the appellant if acting in person) must serve the appellant's notice (and any other requisite documents) on the respondent(s). The Civil Appeals Office, unlike county courts, does not serve any documents	PD52, para 15.1
	The appellant's solicitor (or the appellant in person) must serve the following on each separately represented respondent (and any respondent in person): (a) a sealed copy of the appellant's notice; and	

	(b) copy of the receipt letter from the Civil Appeals Office Note: where the appellant is applying to the Court of Appeal for permission to appeal, no other documents need be served on the respondent unless and until permission to appeal has been granted, or the Court directs that they be served	PD52, para 5.24
Step 6		
Certificate of service and representation details	When the appellant's notice has been entered in the records of the court, the Civil Appeals Office will send a further letter to the appellant's solicitor (or the appellant, if in person) setting out what further action needs to be taken	PD52, para 6.3
	(1) Within 4 days of the receipt of that letter the appellant's solicitor (or appellant in person) must complete the enclosed 'party details' form and return it to the Civil Appeals Office. (2) The appellant's solicitor (or the appellant in person) must complete the Certificate of Service and return it to the Civil Appeals Office by the date stated in that letter.	
Step 7		
Lodging of the appellant's skeleton argument, if not filed with the appellant's notice	If it was impracticable for the appellant's skeleton argument to be filed at the same time as the appellant's notice, the appellant's skeleton argument must be lodged with the Civil Appeals Office Registry (RCJ Room E307) within 14 days of the filing of the appellant's notice	PD52, para 5.9(2)
	Note: litigants in person are not obliged to provide skeleton arguments, but are encouraged to do so	PD52, para 5.9(3)

Step 8		
Filing any documents which were not available to file with the appellant's notice	Where the appeal bundle and/or transcript of judgment were not available to be filed with the appellant's notice, the appellant's solicitor (or appellant in person) must file them by the date specified in the letter from the Civil Appeals Office acknowledging that the case has been entered in the records of the court (ie the letter referred to in Step 6 above). If the bundle and/or transcript will not be available by that date, the appellant's solicitor (or the appellant, if in person) must write to the Civil Appeals Office setting out the reasons and requesting an extension of time for filing them.	

Step 9		
Action following decision re permission to appeal given by the Court of Appeal on paper	Most applications to the Court of Appeal for permission to appeal are initially dealt with by a single Lord Justice on paper without a hearing. (1) If the single Lord Justice grants permission to appeal on paper proceed to Step 11B.	
	(2) If the single Lord Justice refuses permission to appeal on paper, then consideration (after taking counsel's advice) should be given as to whether to exercise the right to have the application reconsidered at an oral hearing	PD52, para 4.13
	(3) If the appellant is in receipt of services funded by the Legal Services Commission, the appellant's solicitor must send to the relevant office of the Legal Services Commission a copy of the single Lord Justice's reasons for refusing permission to appeal on paper. The Court of Appeal will require confirmation that that has been done if a publicly funded appellant requests reconsideration of the application at an oral hearing	PD52, para 4.17

	(4) If the appellant decides to request reconsideration of the permission to appeal application at an oral hearing, a letter requesting that must be filed with the Civil Appeals Office (and a copy served on the respondent(s)) within 7 days after receipt of the notification that the single Lord Justice refused permission to appeal on paper	PD52, para 4.14
	(5) If a request for renewal is not filed with that 7-day time-limit, the single Lord Justice's decision, refusing permission on paper becomes final	PD52, para 4.14
Step 10		
Oral hearing of the permission to appeal application	(1) The Civil Appeals Listing Office will notify the appellant's solicitor (or the appellant, if acting in person) of the hearing date for the reconsideration of the permission application. Unless otherwise indicated in that letter, it will be listed before a single Lord Justice.	
	Note: the application may well be listed before the single Lord Justice who refused the application on paper (or he or she may be a member of a two-judge court hearing the application)	PD52, para 4.13
	(2) If it is listed before a two-judge court the letter will require the appellant to lodge a second copy of the bundle, transcript and skeleton argument. Unless otherwise directed by the Court of Appeal, the hearing will be without attendance by the respondent(s).	
	(3) If the Court of Appeal has requested the attendance of the respondent(s), the appellant must, within 7 days of receiving notification of the request (or within such other period as the court has directed), serve on each respondent a copy of the bundle	PD52, para 4.16
	(4) Counsel should be briefed to appear at the hearing.	

	(5) Where (as will usually be the case) the single Lord Justice has given reasons for refusing permission to appeal on paper, the appellant's advocate must at least 4 days before the hearing inform the court and the respondent(s) of the points it is proposed to raise, set out reasons why permission should be granted, and confirm, where appropriate, that PD52, para 4.17 has been complied with	PD52, para 4.14A(2)
	(6) Counsel attends the hearing and presents oral submissions.	
	(7) If a hearing on notice to the respondent(s) has been ordered, counsel must be prepared to deal with any points relating to summary assessment of costs	PD52, para 14.1(2)
	(8) If the Court of Appeal grants permission to appeal, proceed to Step 11B.	
	Note: if the court (whether a single Lord Justice or a full court) refuses permission to appeal at an oral hearing, that decision is final and cannot be further appealed	AJA 1999, s 54(4)
Step 11A		
Service of appellant's notice (and other documents) where permission to appeal has been granted by the lower court, or is not required	(1) The appellant's solicitor (or appellant in person) puts the Court of Appeal reference number on each sealed copy ready for service on the respondent(s). (That reference number will be on the receipt letter from the Civil Appeals Office: see Step 4 above)	
	(2) Unless the Court of Appeal otherwise directs) the appeal bundle must be served on the respondent(s): The appeal bundle must include –	PD52, para 5.24
	(a) a sealed copy of the appellant's notice;	
	(b) a sealed copy of the order being appealed;	
	(c) a copy of the transcript or other record of judgment;	

(d) a copy of the appellant's advocate's skeleton argument. Litigants in person are not obliged to provide skeleton arguments, but are encouraged to do so;	PD52, para 5.9(3)
(e) where the appeal raises issues of fact, photocopies of the transcripts of the relevant evidence (or, if the evidence was not recorded, a typed version of the judge's notes of evidence);	
(f) the claim form and statements of case or any application notice or case management documentation, if relevant to the appeal;	
(g) a copy of any order granting or refusing permission to appeal and a copy of the reasons for that decision;	
(h) if the appellant's notice includes an incidental application, any witness statements or affidavits in support of that application;	
(i) where the decision was itself made on appeal, the first order, the reasons given and the appellant's notice used in the first appeal;	
(j) in the case of judicial review or a statutory appeal, the original decision;	
(k) where the appeal is from a tribunal, a copy of the tribunal's reasons for the decision, a copy of the decision reviewed by the tribunal and the reasons for the original decision and any document filed with the tribunal setting out the grounds of appeal from that decision;	
(l) any other documents which the appellant reasonably considers necessary to enable the appeal court to reach its decision;	
(m) such other documents as the Court of Appeal may direct	PD52, para 5.6A

	Note: All documents extraneous to the issues to be considered on the appeal must be excluded and the appellant's legal representative must include in the appeal bundle a certificate that he has read understood and complied with this requirement.	
	If any of the above documents were not filed with the appellant's notice because they were not then available, then copies of them must be served on the respondent(s) when they are subsequently filed with the court.	
	(3) Unless the Court of Appeal otherwise orders, service must be effected on each respondent as soon as practicable and, in any event, not later than 7 days after the appellant's notice was filed	Rule 52.4(3)
	Note: the appellant's solicitor (or the appellant if acting in person) must serve the appellant's notice (and any other requisite documents) on the respondent(s). The Civil Appeals Office, unlike county courts, does not serve any documents	PD52, para 15.1(2)
	(4) The appellant's solicitor (or the appellant, if in person) writes to the Civil Appeals Office confirming that service of the appellant's notice and other documents has been effected.	
	(On receipt of that confirmation the Civil Appeals Office will send a further letter to the appellant's side setting out what further steps must be taken (see Step 12 below).	
Step 11B		
Service of documents and other action to be taken after permission to appeal has been granted by the Court of Appeal	The Civil Appeals Associates Office will send to the appellant's side a copy of the order granting permission to appeal with an appeal questionnaire (AQ) and a letter dealing with the future progress of the appeal.	

	The appellant's solicitor (or the appellant, if acting in person) must serve the appeal bundle within 7 days of receiving the order granting permission to appeal. See **Step 11A** for the documents the appeal bundle must contain	PD52, para 6.2
Step 12		
Appeal Questionnaire	(1) The Civil Appeals Office sends to the parties notification by letter of the 'listing window' and 'hear-by date', and encloses with the letter to the appellant's side an appeal questionnaire (AQ)	PD52, paras 6.3, 6.4
	(2) Within 4 days of the date of that letter the appellant's solicitor (or the appellant, if in person) must complete and file the AQ	PD52, para 6.5
	(3) The AQ must contain –	
	(i) if the appellant is legally represented, the advocate's time estimate for the hearing of the appeal. This should exclude the time required by the court to give judgment;	
	(ii) where a transcript of evidence is relevant to the appeal, confirmation as to what parts of the transcript have been ordered where this is not already in the bundle;	
	(iii) confirmation that copies of the appeal bundle are being prepared and will be held ready for use by the Court of Appeal and an undertaking that they will be supplied on request; and	
	(iv) confirmation that a copies of the AQ and the appeal bundle have been served on the respondent with the date of service	PD52, paras 6.5, 6.6
	Note: where permission to appeal was granted by the Court of Appeal a fee of £400 is payable on the AQ (see Step 4(2) above)	

Step 13		
Lodging and service of the appellant's skeleton argument	If it was not practicable to file the appellant's skeleton argument at the same time as the appellant's notice, it must be lodged with the Civil Appeals Office and served on all respondents within 14 days of the date on which the appellant's nootice was filed.	PD52, para 5.9(2)
	Where permission to appeal has been granted by the Court of Appeal it must be served within 7 days of receipt of the order granting permission to appeal (see Step 11A above).	
Step 14		
Lodging of respondent's skeleton argument	The respondent's counsel must provide a skeleton argument in all cases, whether or not a respondent's notice has been filed	PD52, para 7.6
	A skeleton argument from the respondent's counsel must be filed with the Civil Appeals Office Registry (RCJ Room E307) and a copy served on the appellant's solicitor (or the appellant, if in person) within 14 days of filing of a respondent's notice where the skeleton is not included in that notice, or at least 7 days before the appeal hearing where a respondent's notice ehas not been filed	PD52, para 7.7
Step 15		
Filing and service of any documents which were not available to be filed with the appellant's notice	Where the appeal bundle and/or transcripts were not available to be filed with the appellant's notice, the appellant's solicitor (or the appellant, if in person) must – (1) file them by the date specified in the letter from the Civil Appeals Office acknowledging that the appeal has been entered in the records of the court; and (2) serve copies of them on the respondent(s).	

	If the bundle and/or transcripts will not be available by that date, the appellant's solicitor (or the appellant, if in person) must write to the Civil Appeals Office setting out the reasons and requesting an extension of time for filing and serving them.	
Step 16		
Lodging of additional documents	Where the Court of Appeal grants permission to appeal, the appellant must add to the appeal bundle: (i) the respondent's notice and skeleton argument (if any); (ii) those parts of the transcript of evidence which are directly relevant to any question in issue on the appeal; (iii) the order granting permission to appeal and, where permission was granted at an oral hearing, the transcript or note of any judgment which was given; (iv) any document which the appellant and respondent have agreed to add Where permission to appeal has been refused on a particular issue, doucuments relating only to that issue must be removed.	PD52, paras 6.3A and 7.11
Step 17		
Preparation of bundles and core bundles	(1) There are very detailed requirements as to pagination, format, presentation, binding and other matters. (2) Where the appeal bundle comprises more than 500 mpages exclusive of transcripts the requisite number of copies of a core bundle must be filed after consultation with the respondent's solicitors. (3) The core bundle must be filed within 28 days of service of the appellant's notice where permission was granted by the lower court or permission is not required or within 28 days of receipt of the order of the Court of Appeal giving permission to appeal	PD52, paras 15.4, 15.2 and 15.3

	(4) If the appellant wishes to rely on a supplementary skeleton argument, this must be filed at least 14 days before the hearing. For the respondent the period is 7 days	PD52, para 15.11A
	(5) All documents needed for the hearing must be filed at least 7 days before the hearing	PD52, para 15.11B
Step 18		
Obtaining a hearing date for the appeal	(1) If the appeal is assigned to the fixtures list, or the second fixtures list, the Civil Appeals Listing Office will send letters to the parties' solicitors when the case is ready for a date to be fixed. On receipt of that letter solicitors must arrange for counsel's clerks to attend the Listing Office (RCJ Room E306), or if chambers are out of London, to contact the Listing Office by telephone, to fix a date. (2) If the case is assigned to the Short Warned List (SWL), the Civil Appeals Listing Office will notify the parties' solicitors of that by letter. In SWL cases the parties will be given no choice as to the hearing date. They are on call from a given date. When a suitable gap occurs in the list, the Civil Appeals Listing Office will call the appeal on for hearing by telephone calls to counsel's clerks on half a day's notice (or such longer period as the court may direct). Immediately on receipt of the telephone call counsel's clerk should make arrangements for a substitute counsel to be briefed, if the counsel of first choice is not available. Time should not be wasted trying to get the hearing date altered	PD52, para 15.9
Step 19		
Bundles of authorities	(1) Once a hearing date has been fixed, the appellant's counsel must consult with counsel for the respondent(s) concerning the content of a bundle of authorities	PD52, para 15.11

	(2) The appellant's counsel must then file a bundle containing photocopies of the principal authorities upon which each side will rely at the hearing, with the relevant passages marked	PD52, para 15.11
	(3) That authorities bundle should be lodged with the Civil Appeals Registry 7 days before the hearing, or, if less than 7 days' notice of the hearing has been given, immediately	PD52, para 15.11
	(4) If any party intends to refer to authorities not included in the authorities bundle, the parties can agree a second bundle, which must be filed at least 48 hours before the hearing	PD52, para 15.11
	(5) The bundle of authorities must be certified by the advocates that PD52, para 5.10(3)–(5) of have been complied with	
Step 20		
Checking the hearing arrangements	On the working day before an appeal is due to be heard, counsel's clerks should telephone the Civil Appeals Listing Office after 2 pm to check the arrangements for the hearing. The Listing Office will let counsel's clerks know of any time marking which has been given by the Presiding Lord Justice.	
Step 21		
The hearing	(1) Attend at the RCJ with counsel. Unless some other time marking has been given, appeal hearings commence at 10.30 am.	
	(2) The Lord Justices will have pre-read the skeleton arguments, the judgment of the lower court, and the relevant documents in the appeal bundle. Counsel should therefore proceed to make their points straightaway without any opening or preamble.	
Step 22		
Judgment	(1) In the majority of cases the Court of Appeal delivers judgment at the conclusion of the hearing. In some cases the court will assess costs summarily.	

	(2) Where judgment is reserved, the system is as follows – (a) The Court of Appeal will hand down a typed text of the judgment on a date which will be notified to counsel's clerks by the Presiding Lord Justice's clerk. (b) In most cases the text of the judgment is made available to counsel by 4 pm 2 working days before it is due to be handed down. The judgment can be shown in confidenceto the parties but only for the purpose of obtaining instructions and on the strict understanding that the judgment or its effect is not disclosed to any other person. (c) Counsel attend at the RCJ on the date set for the judgment to be handed down, ready to present their arguments on any consequential matters, in particular the form of the order, summary assessment of costs (see (3) below), and permission to appeal to the House of Lords where such an appeal is contemplated.	PD52, paras 15.12–15.14
	(3) If the appeal was listed for one day or less, the Court of Appeal will usually assess the costs summarily	PD52, para 14.1(5)
Step 23		
The Court of Appeal order	Court of Appeal orders are drawn by the court associate and not by the parties. Copies of the sealed Court of Appeal Order will be sent to the parties by the Civil Appeals Associates' Office.	
Step 24		
Appeal to the House of Lords	There is an appeal to the House of Lords only if permission to appeal is granted either by the Court of Appeal or the House of Lords. If a party is contemplating seeking to appeal to the House of Lords, counsel should apply for permission to appeal as soon as the judgment has been delivered or handed down	Administration of Justice (Appeals) Act 1934, s 1

60: Claims for Judicial Review

Legal background

Claims for judicial review are governed by CPR Pt 54, which replaced RSC Ord 53 with effect from 2 October 2000. Where the application for permission to apply for judicial review was filed before 2 October 2000, RSC Ord 53 and not CPR Pt 54 applies.

A claim for judicial review is a means of vindicating rights in public law. It is defined in the CPR as 'a claim to review the lawfulness of (i) an enactment; or (ii) a decision, action or failure to act in relation to the exercise of a public function'. It is sometimes difficult to tell whether a particular complaint involves a matter of public law or of private law. Frequently, the complaint involves elements of both; where it does, the courts are allowing claimants greater flexibility in choosing their forum. But the distinction between public and private law remains important for a number of purposes. Public law is, like much of English law, defined by the remedies which it has created. In the context of judicial review these are the prerogative orders formerly known as orders of mandamus, prohibition and certiorari but now as mandatory, prohibiting and quashing orders respectively. Orders of habeas corpus still have their own regime – see Guide 56. In addition, injunctions and declarations are available in claims for judicial review where this would be just and convenient, having regard to the nature of the matters in respect of which the prerogative orders are available. A claim for damages may be included in a claim for judicial review if they could have been awarded had the claim been a private law claim.

There are a number of respects in which claims for judicial review differ from private law claims –

There are short time-limits.
The claimant requires the permission of the court to bring the proceedings.
The proceedings are generally conducted without oral evidence.
There is rarely disclosure of documents.
Relief is discretionary.

A Practice Direction on Judicial Review accompanies Pt 54. In addition, there is available from the Administrative Court Office a helpful booklet entitled *Notes for Guidance on Applying for Judicial Review*. The new Pre-Action Protocol – Judicial Review – came into force on 4 March 2002 and is set out in Section 4 of this work.

Procedure

Availability	Where the substance of the claim is a matter of public law and the remedy sought is as stated above. Proceedings for judicial review are generally not appropriate where an alternative remedy is available, such as a statutory appeal	Judicial Review Protocol, paras 2–4 SCA, ss 29–31 Rules 54.2, 54.3
	Judicial review is available in criminal proceedings save in matters relating to trial on indictment	SCA, s 29(3)

Letters before action	The prospective claimant should write a detailed letter before action, allowing 14 days for the prospective defendant to respond, save where the nature of the claim precludes this. The prospective defendant should write a similarly detailed response. The letters should be copied to any interested parties	Judicial Review Protocol, paras 8–17, Annexes A and B
Venue	Proceedings must be issued in the High Court. A claim for judicial review cannot be transferred to a county court	CLSA 1990, s 1(10) CCA 1984, s 38(3)
	Proceedings should be issued in the Administrative Court Office in the Royal Courts of Justice, London whenever practicable save that claims for judicial review which raise a devolution issue under the Government of Wales Act 1998, or which involve a Welsh public body, may be filed at the Law Courts, Cathays Park, Cardiff, CF10 3PG	PD54, paras 2.1–2.3 PD54, paras 3.1–3.2
	If, in an urgent case, it is thought necessary to issue proceedings outside London, the Administrative Court Office should be consulted first (Room C315, Tel: 020 7947 6653)	PD54, para 2.4
Permission	A claimant needs the permission of the court to bring a claim for judicial review	SCA, s 31(3) Rule 54.4
	The application for permission is generally made on the papers in the first instance	PD54, para 8.4
	If permission is refused, or is granted subject to conditions or on certain grounds only, the application may be renewed to a judge orally but only if the initial refusal was on the papers	Rule 54.12
	Where a person served with the claim form has not filed an acknowledgment of service in accordance with the rules (see below), he will not be permitted to take part in the renewed permission hearing unless the court allows him to do so, but the defendant may take part in the substantive hearing, providing that he complies with any directions about filing his grounds and evidence	Rule 54.9

	If permission is refused at the oral hearing, the claimant may apply for permission to appeal to the Court of Appeal. Such application must be filed within 7 days of the decision of the High Court. If the Court of Appeal grants permission to apply for judicial review, the case will proceed in the High Court unless the Court of Appeal orders otherwise	Rule 52.15
	If the Court of Appeal refuses permission to appeal, no further appeal lies to the House of Lords	AJA 1999, s 54
	Where permission is given, the court may give directions. The court will serve the order giving permission, and any directions, on the claimant, the defendant and on any interested party who has acknowledged service	Rule 54.10 Rule 54.11
	Neither the defendant nor any other party served with the claim form may apply to set aside the grant of permission to apply for judicial review	Rule 54.13
	There is no pre-action protocol for judicial review but, save in an exceptional case, the claimant should write a letter before action.	
Time-limits	The proceedings must be brought promptly and in any event within 3 months from the date when the grounds for the application first arose	Rule 54.5
	Where the claimant seeks the quashing of a judgment, order or conviction, time begins to run from the date of that judgment, order or conviction	PD54, para 4.1
	If there is undue delay by the claimant, the court may refuse to grant permission or any relief	SCA, s 31(6)
	The claimant must serve the claim form on the defendant and on any interested party within 7 days after the date of issue	Rule 54.7
	An interested party is any other person who is directly affected by the claim	Rule 54.1(2)(f)

	The defendant and any interested party served with the claim form who wishes to take part in the judicial review must file an acknowledgment of service not more than 21 days after the claim form is served on him; and must serve his acknowledgment on the other parties within 7 days after it is filed. It is not served by the court	Rule 54.8
	If the application for permission is refused, or is granted subject to conditions or on certain grounds only, the application to renew the request for permission at an oral hearing must be made within 7 days after the court serves on the claimant its reasons for not (simply) granting permission	Rule 54.12(4)
	An application for permission to appeal to the Court of Appeal against the refusal of permission must be made within 7 days of the decision of the High Court	Rule 52.15
Contents of claim form	The claim form must specify the relief claimed and must include –	Rule 54.6
	the name and address of any interested party;	
	a detailed statement of the claimant's grounds for bringing the claim for judicial review;	
	a statement of the facts relied on;	
	any application to extend the time-limit for filing the claim form;	
	any application for directions; and	
	a time estimate for the hearing	PD54, para 5.6
	It should be accompanied by –	
	any written evidence relied on;	
	a copy of any order that the claimant seeks to have quashed;	
	where the claim relates to a decision of a court or tribunal, an approved copy of the reasons for reaching that decision;	
	copies of any documents on which the claimant proposes to rely;	
	copies of any relevant statutory material;	

	a list of essential documents for advance reading by the court (with page references to the passages relied on); and,	
	insofar as any of the above are not available, reasons why they are unavailable	PD54, paras 5.7, 5.8
	The claim form should also give details of the claimant's solicitors.	
	Where the claimant seeks to raise any issue under HRA 1998, the claim form must give the particulars required by PD16, para 16.1	PD54, para 5.3
	Where the claimant seeks to raise a devolution issue, the claim form must say so and must specify the relevant statutory provision and the relevant facts	PD54, para 5.4
Acknowledgment of service	The acknowledgment of service should state whether the defendant contests the claim and, if so, summarise his grounds for doing so	Rule 54.8(4)
Opposing the claim	The defendant, and any interested party who wishes to oppose or be heard on the claim, must serve detailed grounds and any evidence within 35 days after service of the order giving permission	Rule 54.14(1)
	The claimant must serve any reply within 14 days of service of the defendant's or interested party's evidence	Rule 54.14(2)
	No other evidence is admissible without the court's permission	Rule 54.16
Preparation for hearing	The claimant requires the court's permission to rely on any grounds other than those for which he has been given permission	Rule 54.15
	The claimant must give the other parties 7 clear days' notice of an application to rely on additional grounds	PD54, para 11.1
	Any person wishing to apply to the court for permission to file evidence or to make representations at the hearing of the claim for judicial review should do so promptly	Rule 54.17

	The court may allow such an intervention and may do so subject to conditions	PD54, paras 13.1, 13.2
	Disclosure is not required unless the court orders otherwise	PD54, para 12.1
	The court may order cross-examination but this is rare	
	The claimant must file two copies of a paginated and indexed bundle	PD54, paras 5.9, 5.10
	The bundle, and the claimant's skeleton argument, must be filed 21 working days before the hearing	PD54, para 15.1
	The defendant and any interested party wishing to make representations must file skeleton arguments 14 working days before the hearing date	PD54, para 15.2
	Skeleton arguments must contain – a time estimate for the complete hearing, including judgment; a list of issues; a list of the legal points to be taken (together with any relevant authorities with page references to the passages relied on); a chronology of events (with page references to the bundle of documents); a list of essential documents for the advance reading of the court (with page references to the passages relied on) (if different from that filed with the claim form); a time estimate for that reading; and a list of persons referred to	PD54, para 15.3
Transfer	Proceedings which commenced as a claim for judicial review may be ordered to continue as if they had not been commenced under Pt 54	Rule 54.20
	Proceedings which were commenced other than under Pt 54 may be transferred to the Administrative Court	PD54, paras 14.1, 14.2 Rule 30.5

Agreed final orders	Where the parties agree about the final order to be made in a claim for judicial review, the claimant should file a document (with two copies) signed by all the parties setting out the terms of the proposed order, together with a short statement of the matters relied on as justifying the proposed order and copies of any authorities and provisions relied on	PD54, para 17.1
	If the court is satisfied that the proposed order should be made, it may make it without a hearing	Rule 54.18
	If the court is not so satisfied, a hearing date will be set	PD54, para 17.3
Forms	Claim Form N461	
	Acknowledgment of service N462	
	Application for permission to appeal a refusal of permission to bring claim for judicial review N161	

SECTION 2

Civil Procedure Rules and Practice Directions

Civil Procedure Rules and Practice Directions

Contents

SECTION 2 Civil Procedure Rules and Practice Directions

SCHEDULE 2 – CCR RULES

PART 1
OVERRIDING OBJECTIVE

CONTENTS OF THIS PART

1.1 The overriding objective

(1) These Rules are a new procedural code with the overriding objective of enabling the court to deal with cases justly.

(2) Dealing with a case justly includes, so far as is practicable –

- (a) ensuring that the parties are on an equal footing;
- (b) saving expense;
- (c) dealing with the case in ways which are proportionate –
  - (i) to the amount of money involved;
  - (ii) to the importance of the case;
  - (iii) to the complexity of the issues; and
  - (iv) to the financial position of each party;
- (d) ensuring that it is dealt with expeditiously and fairly; and
- (e) allotting to it an appropriate share of the court's resources, while taking into account the need to allot resources to other cases.

General note—Lord Woolf has said that the answer to most problems arising out of the CPR may be found in the overriding objective. For the first time, the concept of justice in civil litigation has been deconstructed into discrete strands. Notions of equality, economy, proportionality, expedition and the sharing of court resources have been added to that of fairness to make concrete and accessible what was previously instinctive. Litigants, lawyers and judges must measure every step they take and decision they make against these benchmarks. Their importance as the bedrock of the CPR cannot be overemphasised.

'a new procedural code' (r 1.1(1))—The use of these words denotes an intention that in interpreting the CPR, the provisions of earlier rules and authorities on the interpretation of those rules are not to be taken into account (*Biguzzi v Rank Leisure plc* [1999] 1 WLR 1926, CA; *Walsh v Misseldine* [2000] CPLR 201, (2000) Lawtel, 29 February, CA; and *Sweetman v Shepherd* (2000) 97(14) LSG 43). But the principle may not be absolute (*DEG – Deutsche Investitions- und Entwicklungsgesellschaft mbH v Koshy & ors* [2000] TLR 1, Rimer J, where it was considered that *Re Elgindata (No 2)* [1992] 1 WLR 1207 might be referred to for general principles as to costs).

'an equal footing' (r 1.1(2)(a))—The court is not empowered to restrict the resources devoted to litigation by a well-off litigant. See eg *Maltez v Lewis* (2000) 16 Const LJ 65, ChD, where Neuberger J held that this provision did not mean that the court could prevent one party from employing leading counsel where the other could not afford to do so.

'saving expense' (r 1.1(2)(b))—The signal success of the Civil Justice Council in obtaining agreement about predictable costs in low value cases has highlighted the lack of control over high value cases. In these, particularly in substantial multi-party litigation, costs budgeting is likely to become more widely used. In *AB & ors v Leeds Teaching Hospitals (Re Nationwide Organ Group Litigation)* [2003] EWHC 1034 (QB), Gage J sitting with the Senior Costs Judge made a costs budgeting order in a large class action. Other such orders have also been made.

'the court's resources' (r 1.1(2)(e))—The notion that a late application for an adjournment, if successful, might leave a courtroom empty and a judge unoccupied with trial work and subsequently, when the case was relisted, take up other litigants' time, is easy to follow. But the whole thrust of judicial case management is charged with the need to focus on the important issues and the evidence necessary, but no more than necessary, to resolve them, thereby reducing the demand on court resources. In *Arrow Nominees Inc v Blackledge & ors* (2000) *The Times*, 7 July the Court of Appeal, in relation to the judge below, said:

> 'He did not appear to allot to the case an appropriate share of the court's resources while taking into account the need to allot resources to other cases. In this day and age they are elements of case management which must not only be seen to have been placed in the scales but also given due and proper weight when assessing how justice is to be done to the parties and to other litigants. The balance must be struck so that the case is dealt with in a way which is proportionate to the amount of money involved in the case, its importance and complexity and the financial position of the parties.'

1.2 Application by the court of the overriding objective

The court must seek to give effect to the overriding objective when it –

(a) exercises any power given to it by the Rules; or
(b) interprets any rule, subject to rule 76.2.

General note—Precise literal analysis is not the correct approach to construction of the CPR. They are to be interpreted purposively, in a way which advances the overriding objective.

1.3 Duty of the parties

The parties are required to help the court to further the overriding objective.

General note—This duty, imposed as it is by secondary legislation, is a real one, not an aspiration of the rulemakers. 'Required' replaced 'expected' in an early draft. The court may be expected to consider the imposition of a proportionate sanction on those who do not comply with it. And see *Khalili v Bennett* [2000] EMLR 996, CA where it was said that it is unlikely to be appropriate for one party to sit back while the other does nothing. In *Ambrose v Kaye* [2002] EWCA Civ 91, [2002] 15 EG 134, CA Chadwick LJ emphasised that civil litigation is not a game of skill and chance, and that parties are obliged to identify at an early stage any points on which they intend to rely, even if that means giving the opposing party an opportunity to remedy a technical shortcoming. Ambushing the other side by keeping quiet about a technical error is not acceptable (*Hertsmere Primary Care Trust v Rabindra-Anandh* [2005] EWHC 320 (Ch), Lightman J).

1.4 Court's duty to manage cases

(1) The court must further the overriding objective by actively managing cases.

(2) Active case management includes –

(a) encouraging the parties to co-operate with each other in the conduct of the proceedings;
(b) identifying the issues at an early stage;
(c) deciding promptly which issues need full investigation and trial and accordingly disposing summarily of the others;
(d) deciding the order in which issues are to be resolved;
(e) encouraging the parties to use an alternative dispute resolution(GL) procedure if the court considers that appropriate and facilitating the use of such procedure;
(f) helping the parties to settle the whole or part of the case;
(g) fixing timetables or otherwise controlling the progress of the case;
(h) considering whether the likely benefits of taking a particular step justify the cost of taking it;
(i) dealing with as many aspects of the case as it can on the same occasion;
(j) dealing with the case without the parties needing to attend at court;

(k) making use of technology; and
(l) giving directions to ensure that the trial of a case proceeds quickly and efficiently.

General note—Rule 1.4(1) is revolutionary. The court has not just the power, but the duty to manage cases. At a stroke, on 26 April 1999, the legal and practical authority over the conduct of civil litigation passed from litigants and their lawyers to the court. The Court of Appeal has repeatedly emphasised that it will not interfere with firm and positive case management decisions by procedural judges. However, it remains the case that practitioners must expect some judges to have a more proactive approach than others.

'Active case management' (r 1.4(2))—Note, especially, the emphasis on identifying issues in a case and giving them separate treatment if necessary; the emphasis on settlement; and the requirement to deal with a case as a whole, not just that part of it which may be the subject of an application.

'alternative dispute resolution' (r 1.4(2)(e))—It would be hard to exaggerate the focus on alternative dispute resolution in civil jurisdictions all over the world. While the driving factors may be the cost of running a civil justice system and the cost of using it, there can be no doubt that there is far greater recognition that traditional methods of resolving disputes by negotiation within the litigation process echo the cost and delay within that process. The DCA has made wider use of ADR (usually, but not necessarily, mediation) a cornerstone of its policy. The established Mediation Scheme at Central London Civil Justice Centre has been followed by an increasing number of different schemes at courts throughout the country. The Civil Justice Council and Her Majesty's Courts Service (HMCS) have promoted a Mediation Toolkit, available on the HMCS website, to assist courts and others in setting up new schemes. A national Mediation Helpline (0845 60 30 809) has been set up on a pilot basis and has made a significant number of referrals to mediation. The Court of Appeal in *Halsey v Milton Keynes General NHS Trust* [2004] EWCA Civ 576, [2004] All ER (D) 125 (May), [2004] TLR 292, (2004) *The Times*, 27 May, CA has given some important guidance, building on a number of widely publicised cases. Truly unwilling parties cannot be forced to mediate. However, the court is not obliged to take opposition at face value and may encourage parties to mediate where the judge thinks it appropriate. In the light of the court's observation that all members of the legal profession should routinely consider mediation with their clients, it may well be negligent not to do so.

As to costs, the burden is on the unsuccessful party to show that the successful party was unreasonable in refusing ADR. There is no presumption in favour of mediation. Relevant factors will be –

(a) the nature of the dispute;
(b) the merits of the case;
(c) the use of other settlement methods;
(d) whether the cost would have been disproportionate;
(e) whether prejudicial delay would have been caused; and
(f) whether ADR had a reasonable prospect of success.

The fact that the court had encouraged mediation will be a relevant consideration.

'making use of technology' (r 1.4(2)(k))—An example is the growing use of telephone hearings; for the relevant procedure see Guide 28. The DCA is consulting with a view to a substantial general extension of use of telephone hearings for case management. Video conferencing is increasingly available for civil proceedings (see Video Conferencing Guidance – Admiralty and Commercial Courts Guide, App 14). The Central London Civil Justice Centre now uses e-mail for fixing hearing dates in many cases. See also PD5B governing communication and filing of documents by e-mail.

PART 2
APPLICATION AND INTERPRETATION OF THE RULES

CONTENTS OF THIS PART

2.1 Application of the Rules

(1) Subject to paragraph (2), these Rules apply to all proceedings in –

(a) county courts;
(b) the High Court; and
(c) the Civil Division of the Court of Appeal.

(2) These Rules do not apply to proceedings of the kinds specified in the first column of the following Table (proceedings for which rules may be made under the enactments specified in the second column) except to the extent that they are applied to those proceedings by another enactment –

Proceedings	Enactments
1 Insolvency proceedings	Insolvency Act 1986, ss 411 and 412
2 Non-contentious or common form probate proceedings	Supreme Court Act 1981, s 127
3 Proceedings in the High Court when acting as a Prize Court	Prize Courts Act 1894, s 3
4 Proceedings before the judge within the meaning of Part VII of the Mental Health Act 1983	Mental Health Act 1983, s 106
5 Family proceedings	Matrimonial and Family Proceedings Act 1984, s 40
6 Adoption proceedings	Adoption Act 1976, s 66
7 Election petitions in the High Court	Representation of the People Act 1983, s 182

Amendments—SI 1999/1008; SI 2003/1242.

2.2 The glossary

(1) The glossary at the end of these Rules is a guide to the meaning of certain legal expressions used in the Rules, but is not to be taken as giving those expressions any meaning in the Rules which they do not have in the law generally.

(2) Subject to paragraph (3), words in these Rules which are included in the glossary are followed by '(GL)'.

(3) The words 'counterclaim', 'damages', 'practice form' and 'service', which appear frequently in the Rules, are included in the glossary but are not followed by '(GL)'.

2.3 Interpretation

(1) In these Rules –

'child' has the meaning given by rule 21.1(2);

'civil restraint order' means an order restraining a party –

(a) from making any further applications in current proceedings (a limited civil restraint order);

(b) from issuing certain claims or making certain applications in specified courts (an extended civil restraint order); or

(c) from issuing any claim or making any application in specified courts (a general civil restraint order).

'claim for personal injuries' means proceedings in which there is a claim for damages in respect of personal injuries to the claimant or any other person or in respect of a person's death, and 'personal injuries' includes any disease and any impairment of a person's physical or mental condition;

'claimant' means a person who makes a claim;

'CCR' is to be interpreted in accordance with Part 50;

'court officer' means a member of the court staff;

'defendant' means a person against whom a claim is made;

'defendant's home court' means –

(a) if the claim is proceeding in a county court, the county court for the district in which the defendant resides or carries on business; and

(b) if the claim is proceeding in the High Court, the district registry for the district in which the defendant resides or carries on business or, where there is no such district registry, the Royal Courts of Justice;

(Rule 6.5 provides for a party to give an address for service)

'filing', in relation to a document, means delivering it, by post or otherwise, to the court office;

'judge' means, unless the context otherwise requires, a judge, master or district judge or a person authorised to act as such;

'jurisdiction' means, unless the context requires otherwise, England and Wales and any part of the territorial waters of the United Kingdom adjoining England and Wales;

'legal representative' means a barrister or a solicitor, solicitor's employee or other authorised litigator (as defined in the Courts and Legal Services Act 1990) who has been instructed to act for a party in relation to a claim.

'litigation friend' has the meaning given by Part 21;

'patient' has the meaning given by rule 21.1(2);

'RSC' is to be interpreted in accordance with Part 50;

'statement of case' –

(a) means a claim form, particulars of claim where these are not included in a claim form, defence, Part 20 claim, or reply to defence; and

(b) includes any further information given in relation to them voluntarily or by court order under rule 18.1;

'statement of value' is to be interpreted in accordance with rule 16.3;

'summary judgment' is to be interpreted in accordance with Part 24.

(2) A reference to a 'specialist list' is a reference to a list(GL) that has been designated as such by a rule or practice direction.

(3) Where the context requires, a reference to 'the court' means a reference to a particular county court, a district registry, or the Royal Courts of Justice.

Amendments—SI 2000/2092; SI 2001/4015; SI 2004/2072.

'child' (r 2.3(1))—This term means a person who has not yet attained the age of 18 years.

'claimant' (r 2.3(1))—Since r 20.2(1) defines a claim under Pt 20 as any claim other than a claim by a claimant against a defendant, 'claimant' when used on its own must mean the initiator of proceedings only. All others making a claim are to be described as 'Pt 20 claimants'.

'judge' (r 2.3(1))—This definition relies on the authority given by CPA 1997, s 1(2) and Sch 1, para 2 to extend the jurisdiction of the High Court and county courts to masters and district judges – notwithstanding the apparent contrary intention of SCA 1981 and CCA 1984 – unless, of course, the context otherwise requires. PD2B deals with the distribution of business, restricting in some areas the jurisdiction which they may exercise.

'filing' (r 2.3(1))—Putting a document through the court letter box after close of business is to file it on that day (*Van Aken v London Borough of Camden* [2002] EWCA Civ 1724, [2002] TLR 426, CA). Case management orders will normally provide for filing by 4 pm on the specified date.

'practice direction' (r 2.3(2))—Each rule may only be understood when read together with the corresponding practice direction and vice versa. The Rules were drafted so as to provide the skeleton of civil procedure, to be fleshed out by practice directions. The latter need no parliamentary process for their promulgation and have already been frequently amended in response to identified need. County Courts Act 1984, s 74A gives the Lord Chancellor, or a person approved by him, power to give directions as to the practice and procedure of the county courts. The judges of the High Court have an inherent jurisdiction to regulate their own procedure. Civil Procedure Act 1997, Sch 1, para 6 permits rules to refer to practice directions rather than make provision themselves. While it has been suggested that the CPA may not be sufficient authority for the entirety of the practice directions which have been made, it is submitted that the combined effect of the sources of authority mentioned is to make good any deficiency. Local practice directions may only be promulgated with the consent of the Deputy Head of Civil Justice, May LJ. While it is intended that practice and procedure should be uniform throughout the civil justice system, practitioners may find, particularly as between claims proceeding in the Royal Courts of Justice and those proceeding elsewhere, that different approaches nonetheless exist.

'Royal Courts of Justice' (r 2.3(3))—The reference to the Royal Courts of Justice should be understood as a reference to the Central Office of the High Court of Justice, whose administrative offices happen to be at that address.

2.4 Power of judge, master or district judge to perform functions of the court

Where these Rules provide for the court to perform any act then, except where an enactment, rule or practice direction provides otherwise, that act may be performed –

(a) in relation to proceedings in the High Court, by any judge, master or district judge of that Court; and

(b) in relation to proceedings in a county court, by any judge or district judge.

2.5 Court staff

(1) Where these Rules require or permit the court to perform an act of a formal or administrative character, that act may be performed by a court officer.

(2) A requirement that a court officer carry out any act at the request of a party is subject to the payment of any fee required by a fees order for the carrying out of that act.

(Rule 3.2 allows a court officer to refer to a judge before taking any step)

2.6 Court documents to be sealed

(1) The court must seal(GL) the following documents on issue –

(a) the claim form; and
(b) any other document which a rule or practice direction requires it to seal.

(2) The court may place the seal(GL) on the document –

(a) by hand; or
(b) by printing a facsimile of the seal on the document whether electronically or otherwise.

(3) A document purporting to bear the court's seal(GL) shall be admissible in evidence without further proof.

2.7 Court's discretion as to where it deals with cases

The court may deal with a case at any place that it considers appropriate.

'any place that it considers appropriate'—This provision allows judges to hold court, by way of example, at the home of a witness with disability or to conduct all or part of a hearing at the scene of events – even abroad. Also, district judges often hear small claims by serving prisoners at their place of abode rather than incur the expense of an escorted day in court. Where the overriding objective suggests, the rule may be used even more imaginatively.

2.8 Time

(1) This rule shows how to calculate any period of time for doing any act which is specified –

(a) by these Rules;
(b) by a practice direction; or
(c) by a judgment or order of the court.

(2) A period of time expressed as a number of days shall be computed as clear days.

(3) In this rule 'clear days' means that in computing the number of days –

(a) the day on which the period begins; and
(b) if the end of the period is defined by reference to an event, the day on which that event occurs

are not included.

Examples

(i) Notice of an application must be served at least 3 days before the hearing.
An application is to be heard on Friday 20 October.
The last date for service is Monday 16 October.

(ii) The court is to fix a date for a hearing.
The hearing must be at least 28 days after the date of notice.
If the court gives notice of the date of the hearing on 1 October, the earliest date for the hearing is 30 October.

(iii) Particulars of claim must be served within 14 days of service of the claim form.
The claim form is served on 2 October.
The last day for service of the particulars of claim is 16 October.

(4) Where the specified period –

(a) is 5 days or less; and
(b) includes –
(i) a Saturday or Sunday; or
(ii) a Bank Holiday, Christmas Day or Good Friday,

that day does not count.

Example

Notice of an application must be served at least 3 days before the hearing.

An application is to be heard on Monday 20 October.

The last date for service is Tuesday 14 October.

(5) When the period specified –

(a) by these Rules or a practice direction; or
(b) by any judgment or court order,

for doing any act at the court office ends on a day on which the office is closed, that act shall be in time if done on the next day on which the court office is open.

2.9 Dates for compliance to be calendar dates and to include time of day

(1) Where the court gives a judgment, order or direction which imposes a time limit for doing any act, the last date for compliance must, wherever practicable –

(a) be expressed as a calendar date; and
(b) include the time of day by which the act must be done.

(2) Where the date by which an act must be done is inserted in any document, the date must, wherever practicable, be expressed as a calendar date.

'time limit' (r 2.9(1))—The courts, when imposing a time limit, will now whenever possible refrain from any formula such as 'within 21 days' and instead say 'by no later than 4 pm on Friday, the 27 October 2000' (or as the case may be).

There are often delays in processing orders. In affected courts judges often order calendar dates to be inserted into their draft orders when the orders are actually drawn. Solicitors should bear this in mind when submitting proposed directions.

2.10 Meaning of 'month' in judgments, etc

Where 'month' occurs in any judgment, order, direction or other document, it means a calendar month.

2.11 Time limits may be varied by parties

Unless these Rules or a practice direction provide otherwise or the court orders otherwise, the time specified by a rule or by the court for a person to do any act may be varied by the written agreement of the parties.

(Rules 3.8 (sanctions have effect unless defaulting party obtains relief), 28.4 (variation of case management timetable – fast track); 29.5 (variation of case management timetable – multi-track), provide for time limits that cannot be varied by agreement between the parties)

General note—This rule must be read with r 3.8(3) so that where the time for doing something is subject to stated consequences for failure, whether by rule, practice direction or order, the time may not be extended except by order of the court.

Practice Directions

1 The practice directions to the Civil Procedure Rules apply to civil litigation in the Queen's Bench Division and the Chancery Division of the High Court and to litigation in the county courts other than family proceedings. Where relevant they also apply to appeals to the Civil Division of the Court of Appeal.

2 The practice directions are made –

(1) for the Queen's Bench Division by the Lord Chief Justice as president of that Division;
(2) for the Civil Division of the Court of Appeal by the Master of the Rolls as president of that Division;
(3) for the Chancery Division by the Vice-Chancellor as vice-president of that Division; and
(4) for the county courts by the Lord Chancellor or a person authorised to act on his behalf under section 74A of the County Courts Act 1984.

3 From April 1999 to July 2000 the Lord Chancellor authorised the Vice-Chancellor, Sir Richard Scott (as he then was) under section 74A of the 1984 Act. The Vice-Chancellor made all practice directions for county courts during that time.

4 From July 2000 the Lord Chancellor has authorised Lord Justice May to make these practice directions and he has made all practice directions for the county courts since that date.

5 From September 2003 the Lord Chancellor has authorised Lord Justice Dyson to make practice directions for the county courts.

Practice Direction – Court Offices

This Practice Direction supplements CPR Part 2 (PD2)

CENTRAL OFFICE OF THE HIGH COURT AT THE ROYAL COURTS OF JUSTICE

1 The Central Office shall be divided into such departments, and the business performed in the Central Office shall be distributed among the departments in such manner, as is set out in the Queen's Bench Division Guide.

BUSINESS IN THE OFFICES OF THE SUPREME COURT

2.1 (1) The offices of the Supreme Court shall be open on every day of the year except:
- (a) Saturdays and Sundays,
- (b) Good Friday and the day after Easter Monday,
- (c) Christmas Day and, if that day is a Friday or Saturday, then 28 December,
- (d) Bank Holidays in England and Wales under the Banking and Financial Dealings Act 1971, and
- (e) such other days as the Lord Chancellor, with the concurrence of the Lord Chief Justice, the Master of the Rolls, the President of the Family Division and the Vice-Chancellor ('the Heads of Division') may direct.

(2) The hours during which the offices of the Supreme Court at the Royal Courts of Justice and at the Principal Probate Registry at First Avenue House, 42–49 High Holborn, London WC1V 6NP shall be open to the public shall be as follows:
- (a) from 10 am to 4.30 pm;
- (b) such other hours as the Lord Chancellor, with the concurrence of the Heads of Division, may from time to time direct.

(3) Every District Registry shall be open on the days and during the hours that the Lord Chancellor from time to time directs and, in the absence of any such directions, shall be open on the same days and during the same hours as the county court offices of which it forms part are open.

2.2 One of the masters of the Queen's Bench Division (the 'Practice Master') shall be present at the Central Office on every day on which the office is open for the purpose of superintending the business performed there and giving any directions which may be required on questions of practice and procedure.

COUNTY COURTS

3.1 Every county court shall have an office or, if the Lord Chancellor so directs, two or more offices, situated at such place or places as he may direct, for the transaction of the business of the court.

3.2 (1) Every county court office, or if a court has two or more offices at least one of those offices, shall be open on every day of the year except –
- (a) Saturdays and Sundays,
- (b) the day before Good Friday from noon onwards and Good Friday,
- (c) the Tuesday after the Spring bank holiday,

(d) Christmas Day and, if that day is a Friday or Saturday, then the 28 December,
(e) bank holidays and
(f) such other days as the Lord Chancellor may direct.

(2) In this paragraph 'bank holiday' means a bank holiday in England and Wales under the Banking and Financial Dealings Act 1971 and 'Spring holiday' means the bank holiday on the last Monday in May or any day appointed instead of that day under section 1(2) of that Act.

3.3 Subject to paragraph 3.2(1)(b), the hours during which any court office is open to the public shall be from 10 am to 4 pm or such other hours as the Lord Chancellor may from time to time direct.

Practice Direction – Allocation of Cases to Levels of Judiciary

This Practice Direction supplements CPR Part 2 (PD2B)

1.1 Rule 2.4 provides that judges, masters and district judges may exercise any function of the court except where an enactment, rule or practice direction provides otherwise. This practice direction sets out the matters over which masters and district judges do not have jurisdiction or which they may deal with only on certain conditions. It does not affect jurisdiction conferred by other enactments. Reference should also be made to other relevant practice directions (eg Part 24, paragraph 3 and Part 26, paragraphs 12.1–10). References to circuit judges include recorders and assistant recorders and references to masters and district judges include deputies.

1.2 Wherever a master or district judge has jurisdiction, he may refer the matter to a judge instead of dealing with it himself.

The High Court

INJUNCTIONS

2.1 Search orders (rule 25.1(1)(h)), freezing orders (rule 25.1(1)(f)), an ancillary order under rule 25.1(1)(g) and orders authorising a person to enter land to recover, inspect or sample property (rule 25.1(1)(d)) may only be made by a judge.

2.2 Except where paragraphs 2.3 and 2.4 apply, injunctions and orders relating to injunctions, including orders for specific performance where these involve an injunction, must be made by a judge.

2.3 A master or a district judge may only make an injunction:

(a) in terms agreed by the parties;
(b) in connection with or ancillary to a charging order;
(c) in connection with or ancillary to an order appointing a receiver by way of equitable execution; or
(d) in proceedings under RSC Order 77 rule 16 (order restraining person from receiving sum due from the Crown).

2.4 A master or district judge may make an order varying or discharging an injunction or undertaking given to the court if all parties to the proceedings have consented to the variation or discharge.

OTHER PRE-TRIAL ORDERS AND INTERIM REMEDIES

3.1 A master or district judge may not make orders or grant interim remedies:

- (a) relating to the liberty of the subject;
- (b) relating to criminal proceedings or matters except procedural applications in appeals to the High Court (including appeals by case stated) under any enactment;
- (c) relating to a claim for judicial review, except that interim applications in claims for judicial review may be made to masters of the Queen's Bench Division.
- (d) relating to appeals from masters or district judges;
- (e) in appeals against costs assessment under Parts 43 to 48, except on an appeal under rule 47.20 against the decision of an authorised court officer.
- (f) in applications under section 42 of the Supreme Court Act 1981 by a person subject to a Civil or a Criminal or an All Proceedings Order (vexatious litigant) for permission to start or continue proceedings.
- (g) in applications under section 139 of the Mental Health Act 1983 for permission to bring proceedings against a person.

3.2 This practice direction is not concerned with family proceedings. It is also not concerned with proceedings in the Family Division except to the extent that such proceedings can be dealt with in the Chancery Division or the Family Division eg proceedings under the Inheritance (Provision for Family and Dependants) Act 1975 or under section 14 of the Trusts of Land and Appointment of Trustees Act 1996. District judges (including district judges of the Principal Registry of the Family Division) have jurisdiction to hear such proceedings, subject to any Direction given by the President of the Family Division.

TRIALS AND ASSESSMENTS OF DAMAGES

4.1 A master or district judge may, subject to any practice direction, try a case which is treated as being allocated to the multi-track because it is proceeding under Part 8 (see rule 8.9(c)). He may try a case which has been allocated to the multi-track under Part 26 only with the consent of the parties. Restrictions on the trial jurisdiction of masters and district judges do not prevent them from hearing applications for summary judgment or, if the parties consent, for the determination of a preliminary issue.

4.2 A master or a district judge may assess the damages or sum due to a party under a judgment without limit as to the amount.

'without limit' (para 4.2)—In *Sandry v Jones* (2000) *The Times*, 3 August, the Court of Appeal gave guidance to the effect that very complex or substantial assessments in personal injuries cases should be dealt with by a High Court or circuit judge.

CHANCERY PROCEEDINGS

5.1 In proceedings in the Chancery Division, a master or a district judge may not deal with the following without the consent of the Vice-Chancellor –

- (a) approving compromises (other than applications under the Inheritance

(Provision for Family and Dependants) Act 1975) (i) on behalf of a person under disability where that person's interest in a fund, or if there is no fund, the maximum amount of the claim, exceeds £100,000 and (ii) on behalf of absent, unborn and unascertained persons;

(b) making declarations, except in plain cases;

(c) making final orders under section 1(1) of the Variation of Trusts Act 1958, except for the removal of protective trusts where the interest of the principal beneficiary has not failed or determined;

(d) where the proceedings are brought by a Part 8 claim form in accordance with paragraph A.1(2) or (3) of the Part 8 Practice Direction (statutory or other requirement to use originating summons), determining any question of law or as to the construction of a document which is raised by the claim form;

(e) giving permission to executors, administrators and trustees to bring or defend proceedings or to continue the prosecution or defence of proceedings, and granting an indemnity for costs out of the trust estate, except in plain cases;

(f) granting an indemnity for costs out of the assets of a company on the application of minority shareholders bringing a derivative action, except in plain cases;

(g) making an order for rectification, except for –
   (i) rectification of the register under the Land Registration Act 1925; or
   (ii) alteration or rectification of the register under the Land Registration Act 2002,

   in plain cases;

(h) making orders to vacate entries in the register under the Land Charges Act 1972, except in plain cases;

(i) making final orders on applications under section 19 of the Leasehold Reform Act 1967, section 48 of the Administration of Justice Act 1985 and sections 21 and 25 of the Law of Property Act 1969;

(j) making final orders under the Landlord and Tenant Acts 1927 and 1954, except (i) by consent, and (ii) orders for interim rents under sections 24A to 24D of the 1954 Act;

(k) making orders in proceedings in the Patents Court except (i) by consent, (ii) to extend time, (iii) on applications for permission to serve out of the jurisdiction and (iv) on applications for security for costs.

5.2 A master or district judge may only give directions for early trial after consulting the judge in charge of the relevant list.

5.3 Where a winding-up order has been made against a company, any proceedings against the company by or on behalf of debenture holders may be dealt with, at the Royal Courts of Justice, by a registrar and, in a District Registry with insolvency jurisdiction, by a district judge.

ASSIGNMENT OF CLAIMS TO MASTERS AND TRANSFER BETWEEN MASTERS

6.1 The Senior Master, and the Chief Master will make arrangements for proceedings to be assigned to individual masters. They may vary such arrangements generally or in particular cases, for example, by transferring a case from a master to whom it had been assigned to another master.

6.2 The fact that a case has been assigned to a particular master does not prevent another master from dealing with that case if circumstances require, whether at the request of the assigned master or otherwise.

FREEZING ORDERS: CROSS EXAMINATION OF DEPONENTS ABOUT ASSETS

7 Where the court has made a freezing order under rule 25.1(f) and has ordered a person to make a witness statement or affidavit about his assets and to be cross-examined on its contents, unless the judge directs otherwise, the cross-examination will take place before a master or a district judge, or if the master or district judge directs, before an examiner of the court.

HUMAN RIGHTS

7A A deputy High Court judge, a master or district judge may not try –

(1) a case in a claim made in respect of a judicial act under the Human Rights Act 1998, or
(2) a claim for a declaration of incompatibility in accordance with section 4 of the Human Rights Act 1998.

County Courts

INJUNCTIONS, ANTI-SOCIAL BEHAVIOUR ORDERS AND COMMITTAL

8.1 Injunctions which a county court has jurisdiction to make may only be made by a circuit judge, except –

(a) where the injunction is to be made in proceedings which a district judge otherwise has jurisdiction to hear (see paragraph 11.1 below);
(b) where the injunction is sought in a money claim which has not yet been allocated to a track, where the amount claimed does not exceed the fast track financial limit;
(c) in the circumstances provided by paragraph 2.3.
(d) where the injunction is to be made under any of the following provisions –
    (i) section 153A, 153B or 153D of the Housing Act 1996; or
    (ii) section 3 of the Protection from Harassment Act 1997.

8.1A A District Judge has jurisdiction to make an order under section 1B or 1D of the Crime and Disorder Act 1998 (anti-social behaviour).

8.2 A district judge may make orders varying or discharging injunctions in the circumstances provided by paragraph 2.4.

8.3 A district judge may not make an order committing a person to prison except where an enactment authorises this: see section 23 of the Attachment of Earnings Act 1971, sections 14 and 118 of the County Courts Act 1984, sections 152–157 of the Housing Act 1996, and the relevant rules.

HOMELESSNESS APPEALS

9 A district judge may not hear appeals under section 204 or section 204A of the Housing Act 1996.

OTHER PRE-TRIAL ORDERS AND INTERIM REMEDIES

10.1 In addition to the restrictions on jurisdiction mentioned at paragraphs 8.1–3, paragraph 3.1(d) and (e) above applies.

TRIALS AND ASSESSMENTS OF DAMAGES

11.1 A district judge has jurisdiction to hear the following –

(a) any claim which has been allocated to the small claims track or fast track or which is treated as being allocated to the multi-track under rule 8.9(c) and Table 2 of the practice direction to Part 8, except claims –
  (i) under Part I of the Landlord and Tenant Act 1927;
  (ii) for a new tenancy under section 24 or for the termination of a tenancy under section 29(2) of the Landlord and Tenant Act 1954;
  (iii) for an order under section 38 or 40 of the Landlord and Tenant Act 1987;
  (iv) under paragraph 26 or 27 of Schedule 11 to or section 27 of the Agricultural Holdings Act 1986;
  (v) under section 45(2) of the Matrimonial Causes Act 1973 for a declaration of legitimation by virtue of the Legitimacy Act 1976;
  (vi) under section 35, 38 or 40 of the Fair Trading Act 1973;
  (vii) under Part II of the Mental Health Act 1983;

(b) proceedings for the recovery of land, proceedings under section 82A(2) of the Housing Act 1985 or section 6A(2) of the Housing Act 1988 (demotion claims) or proceedings in a county court under Chapter 1A of the Housing Act 1996 (demoted tenancies);

(c) the assessment of damages or other sum due to a party under a judgment without any financial limit;

(d) with the permission of the designated civil judge in respect of that case, any other proceedings.

11.2 A case allocated to the small claims track may only be assigned to a circuit judge to hear with his consent.

'without any financial limit' (para 11.1(c))—See note under para 4.2. Note the enlarged jurisdiction of district judges in relation to ASBOs and anti-social behaviour injunctions. Also, the consent of the parties is no longer required for any designated civil judge to release cases for trial to a district judge. This does not extend to cases (eg homelessness appeals) which district judges are specifically forbidden to hear. Provided the designated civil judge has given consent, that of the parties is no longer required for the district judge to hear a multi-track trial.

FREEZING ORDERS: CROSS EXAMINATION OF DEPONENTS ABOUT ASSETS

12 To the extent that a county court has power to make a freezing order, paragraph 7 applies as appropriate.

DISTRIBUTION OF BUSINESS BETWEEN CIRCUIT JUDGE AND DISTRICT JUDGE

13 Where both the circuit judge and the district judge have jurisdiction in respect of any proceedings, the exercise of jurisdiction by the district judge is subject to any arrangements made by the designated civil judge for the proper distribution of business between circuit judges and district judges.

14.1 In District Registries of the High Court and in the county court, the designated civil judge may make arrangements for proceedings to be assigned to individual district judges. He may vary such arrangements generally or in particular cases.

14.2 The fact that a case has been assigned to a particular district judge does not prevent another district judge from dealing with the case if the circumstances require.

'designated civil judge' (para 13)—This is one of the few references in the rules and practice directions to the 28 designated civil judges, one for each court group. They are all circuit judges appointed by the Lord Chancellor to have considerable administrative responsibility for the despatch of civil business and to provide local leadership in the implementation of the reforms. They are also the first recourse for appeals from district judges in their group for CPR matters.

HUMAN RIGHTS

15 A district judge may not try a case in which an allegation of indirect discrimination is made against a public authority that would, if the court finds that it occurred, be unlawful under section 19B of the Race Relations Act 1976.

PART 3
THE COURT'S CASE MANAGEMENT POWERS

CONTENTS OF THIS PART

3.1 The court's general powers of management

(1) The list of powers in this rule is in addition to any powers given to the court by any other rule or practice direction or by any other enactment or any powers it may otherwise have.

(2) Except where these Rules provide otherwise, the court may –

- (a) extend or shorten the time for compliance with any rule, practice direction or court order (even if an application for extension is made after the time for compliance has expired);
- (b) adjourn or bring forward a hearing;
- (c) require a party or a party's legal representative to attend the court;
- (d) hold a hearing and receive evidence by telephone or by using any other method of direct oral communication;
- (e) direct that part of any proceedings (such as a counterclaim) be dealt with as separate proceedings;
- (f) stay(GL) the whole or part of any proceedings or judgment either generally or until a specified date or event;
- (g) consolidate proceedings;
- (h) try two or more claims on the same occasion;
- (i) direct a separate trial of any issue;
- (j) decide the order in which issues are to be tried;
- (k) exclude an issue from consideration;
- (l) dismiss or give judgment on a claim after a decision on a preliminary issue;
- (ll) order any party to file and serve an estimate of costs;
- (m) take any other step or make any other order for the purpose of managing the case and furthering the overriding objective.

(3) When the court makes an order, it may –

- (a) make it subject to conditions, including a condition to pay a sum of money into court; and
- (b) specify the consequence of failure to comply with the order or a condition.

(4) Where the court gives directions it may take into account whether or not a party has complied with any relevant pre-action protocol[(GL)].

(5) The court may order a party to pay a sum of money into court if that party has, without good reason, failed to comply with a rule, practice direction or a relevant pre-action protocol.

(6) When exercising its power under paragraph (5) the court must have regard to –

(a) the amount in dispute; and

(b) the costs which the parties have incurred or which they may incur.

(6A) Where a party pays money into court following an order under paragraph (3) or (5), the money shall be security for any sum payable by that party to any other party in the proceedings, subject to the right of a defendant under rule 37.2 to treat all or part of any money paid into court as a Part 36 payment.

(Rule 36.2 explains what is meant by a Part 36 payment)

(7) A power of the court under these Rules to make an order includes a power to vary or revoke the order.

Amendments—SI 1999/1008; SI 2005/2292.

'powers of management' (r 3.1)—Rule 3.1(2)(m) dramatically demonstrates the scope and flexibility of the court's powers and is a reminder of the driving force of the overriding objective (Pt 1). It may be appropriate to exercise these powers, eg to strike out or exclude from consideration certain parts of the case, at the outset of a long trial (*Royal Brompton Hospital Trust v Hammond* [2000] 69 Con LR 170, (2000) Lawtel, 4 December, TCC).

'Except where these Rules provide otherwise' (r 3.1(2))—Rule 7.6 is an example. An extension of time for service of a claim form made after expiry of the time for service is subject to that subrule.

'adjourn ... a hearing' (r 3.1(2)(b))—The court is not required by HRA 1998, Sch 1, Pt I, Art 6 to adjourn a hopeless case to allow a party back into the fray simply because there has been some procedural unfairness along the way (*Lloyds Bank plc v Dix & anor* (2000) (unreported) 26 October, CA).

'telephone' (r 3.1(2)(d))—Parties are encouraged to save costs by taking advantage of telephone and video conferencing services (see Guide 28 and, as to applications, PD23 for procedure). The cost of personal attendance at a hearing may not be recoverable if a telephone hearing could have been arranged at more proportionate expense.

'exclude an issue from consideration' (r 3.1(2)(k))—This Delphically expressed power has not been the subject of great attention. It remains to be seen what it adds to the court's power to strike out (r 3.4) and give summary judgment (Pt 24).

'make it subject to conditions' (r 3.1(3)(a))—In *Price v Price (t/a Poppyland Headwear)* [2003] EWCA Civ 888, [2003] 3 All ER 911, CA the court encouraged more flexible use of this power. While allowing an extension of time for service so as not to bar a claim in its entirety, the court did so on condition that the claimant was limited to damages based on an earlier medical report.

'specify the consequences of failure' (r 3.1(3)(b))—Care must be taken by the court to ensure that the consequences are in proportion to the fault (*Tekna Design Ltd v Davenport Properties Ltd* (1999) Lawtel, 3 November, CA and *McCann (Gerard) v Wimpey Construction* (UK) Ltd (1999) Lawtel, 11 November, CA). This does not mean the least sanction need be the most appropriate (*UCB Corporate Services Ltd (Formerly UCB Bank plc) v Halifax (SW) Ltd* [2000] 1 EGLR 87, [2000] 16 EG 137, (1999) *The Times*, December 23, CA).

Concerns have been expressed as to whether the application of sanctions resulting in the striking out of a case might fall foul of HRA 1998, Sch 1, Pt I, Art 6. Although decisions of a single judge of the Court of Appeal are not to be regarded as authoritative, Laws LJ held in *Arogundade (Eniola) v Mayor & Burgess of the London Borough of Brent* (2000) (unreported) 15 November, that a striking out sanction for a failure to comply with a time order was not a breach of Art 6.

'pre-action protocol' (r 3.1(4))—Pre-action protocols have proved themselves to be a powerful agent of change in daily practice. Drafted by groups of practitioners with different perspectives and approved by the Head of Civil Justice by practice direction, they demonstrate the spirit of openness in litigation which is an important element of the Rules. Compelling anecdotal evidence suggests that they have led to the settlement of a very large number of cases without proceedings being brought. Eight protocols are at present in existence, for personal injury claims, for clinical negligence claims, for construction and engineering disputes, for defamation claims, for professional negligence claims, for judicial review claims, for housing disrepair claims and for disease and illness claims. Paragraph 4 of PDProt makes it clear that in other cases the court will expect parties to act in accordance with the same spirit. The sanction of an order to make a payment into court (r 3.1(5)) is therefore available in all cases where a party has not acted reasonably and openly before the commencement of proceedings. The amended Practice Direction Protocols lays down standards of pre-action behaviour in cases not covered by a specific protocol.

'pay a sum of money into court' (r 3.1(5))—The important decision in *Olatawura v Abiloye* [2002] EWCA Civ 998, [2002] 4 All ER 903, CA establishes a general power to make orders for security for costs outside the specific provisions of Pt 25. Simon Brown LJ gave guidance as to the factors to be considered to ensure that justice was done, while adverting to the risk of denying a litigant access to justice. Generally, the discretion will arise where a party has flagrantly failed to comply with orders or otherwise demonstrated a failure to comply with the spirit of the CPR.

'a power to vary or revoke' (r 3.1(7))—See the note to r 40.2. In *Lloyd's Investment (Scandinavia) Ltd v Ager-Hanssen* [2003] EWHC 1740 (Ch), Patten J considered that the power was not confined to procedural orders but should only be exercised where there was a material change of circumstances or the judge had been misled in some way.

3.2 Court officer's power to refer to a judge

Where a step is to be taken by a court officer –

(a) the court officer may consult a judge before taking that step;
(b) the step may be taken by a judge instead of the court officer.

3.3 Court's power to make order of its own initiative

(1) Except where a rule or some other enactment provides otherwise, the court may exercise its powers on an application or of its own initiative.

(Part 23 sets out the procedure for making an application)

(2) Where the court proposes to make an order of its own initiative –

(a) it may give any person likely to be affected by the order an opportunity to make representations and
(b) where it does so it must specify the time by and the manner in which the representations must be made.

(3) Where the court proposes –

(a) to make an order of its own initiative; and
(b) to hold a hearing to decide whether to make the order,

it must give each party likely to be affected by the order at least 3 days' notice of the hearing.

(4) The court may make an order of its own initiative, without hearing the parties or giving them an opportunity to make representations.

(5) Where the court has made an order under paragraph (4) –

(a) a party affected by the order may apply to have it set aside(GL), varied or stayed(GL); and
(b) the order must contain a statement of the right to make such an application.

(6) An application under paragraph (5)(a) must be made –

(a) within such period as may be specified by the court; or

(b) if the court does not specify a period, not more than 7 days after the date on which the order was served on the party making the application.

(7) If the court of its own initiative strikes out a statement of case or dismisses an application (including an application for permission to appeal or for permission to apply for judicial review), and it considers that the claim or application is totally without merit –

(a) the court's order must record that fact; and

(b) the court must at the same time consider whether it is appropriate to make a civil restraint order.

Amendments—SI 2004/2072; SI 2005/2292.

General note—Every case will be placed before a judge for initial scrutiny, allocation to track and directions once a defence is filed (Pt 26). This stage is the start of judicial case management when the orders made will normally be on the judge's own initiative while giving the parties an opportunity to apply not more than 7 days after service or later, if specified (r 3.3(5) and (6)). There will be instances, particularly at later stages of case management or in substantial multi-track cases, when a judge will invite representations (r 3.3(2)) or hold a hearing (r 3.3(3)) before making a contemplated order. It should be noted that the common practice at the Royal Courts of Justice, where only multi-track cases are dealt with, is for the masters not to make initial directions but to order a case management conference. Practitioners have hoped to avoid payment of the court fee by seeking to invite the court to make an order as if of its own initiative. This may have been in a letter to the court or in the listing questionnaire. The new pre-trial check list (replacing the listing questionnaire), in force from 2 December 2002 (see rr 28.5 and 29.6), makes it clear that if further directions are required at that stage, an application should be made. This should apply in any instance where a party actively seeks an order.

'civil restraint order' (r 3.3(7)(b))—See the new PD3C – Civil Restraint Orders – at p 380 and the **'General note'** thereto.

3.4 Power to strike out a statement of case

(1) In this rule and rule 3.5, reference to a statement of case includes reference to part of a statement of case.

(2) The court may strike out(GL) a statement of case if it appears to the court –

(a) that the statement of case discloses no reasonable grounds for bringing or defending the claim;

(b) that the statement of case is an abuse of the court's process or is otherwise likely to obstruct the just disposal of the proceedings; or

(c) that there has been a failure to comply with a rule, practice direction or court order.

(3) When the court strikes out a statement of case it may make any consequential order it considers appropriate.

(4) Where –

(a) the court has struck out a claimant's statement of case;

(b) the claimant has been ordered to pay costs to the defendant; and

(c) before the claimant pays those costs, he starts another claim against the same defendant, arising out of facts which are the same or substantially the same as those relating to the claim in which the statement of case was struck out,

the court may, on the application of the defendant, stay(GL) that other claim until the costs of the first claim have been paid.

(5) Paragraph (2) does not limit any other power of the court to strike out(GL) a statement of case.

(6) If the court strikes out a claimant's statement of case and it considers that the claim is totally without merit –

(a) the court's order must record that fact; and
(b) the court must at the same time consider whether it is appropriate to make a civil restraint order.

Amendments—SI 2004/2072.

Practice Direction—See PD3 at p 376 for a fuller understanding of the court's powers and how it is likely to use them.

'strike out' (r 3.4)—For guidance about the relationship between the power to strike out, where evidence is no longer excluded, and the power to give summary judgment, see the judgment of May LJ in *S v Gloucestershire CC* [2000] 3 All ER 346, CA.

'abuse of the court's process' (r 3.4(2)(b))—In *Securum Finance Ltd v Ashton* [2000] 3 WLR 1400, the Court of Appeal sounded the final death knell for *Birkett v James* [1978] AC 297, [1977] 3 WLR 38, [1977] 2 All ER 801. A litigant now has no general right to commence a second claim, even within a limitation period, where an earlier claim has been struck out for delay or abuse of process – 'an appropriate share of the court's resources' (r 1.1(2)(e)) will be an important factor. The Court of Appeal has made it clear that the old learning on striking out for want of prosecution did not survive the transitional arrangements in PD51 and that a more flexible approach is adopted (see *Biguzzi v Rank Leisure plc* [1999] 1 WLR 1926, CA). Since the court is responsible for the prosecution of all post-26 April 1999 cases, the notion of want of prosecution has virtually disappeared from everyday practice. The Civil Procedure Rules 1998 enable the court to adopt a more flexible approach when considering applications to strike out claims. And see *Axa Insurance Co Ltd v Swire Fraser Ltd (formerly Robert Fraser Insurance Brokers Ltd)* (2000) *The Times*, 19 January, CA. The court's approach to striking out is now firmly rooted in the justice of the case, according to the overriding objective.

'failure to comply' (r 3.4(2)(c))—When considering the exercise of the power to strike out for such a failure, the court should take into account the matters set out in r 3.9 (Relief from sanctions) and make an order proportionate to the default (*Keith v CPM Field Marketing* (2000) *The Times*, 29 August, CA).

3.5 Judgment without trial after striking out

(1) This rule applies where –

(a) the court makes an order which includes a term that the statement of case of a party shall be struck out if the party does not comply with the order; and
(b) the party against whom the order was made does not comply with it.

(2) A party may obtain judgment with costs by filing a request for judgment if –

(a) the order referred to in paragraph (1)(a) relates to the whole of a statement of case; and
(b) where the party wishing to obtain judgment is the claimant, the claim is for –
    (i) a specified amount of money;
    (ii) an amount of money to be decided by the court;
    (iii) delivery of goods where the claim form gives the defendant the alternative of paying their value; or
    (iv) any combination of these remedies.

(3) Where judgment is obtained under this rule in a case to which paragraph (2)(b)(iii) applies, it will be judgment requiring the defendant to deliver the goods, or (if he does not do so) pay the value of the goods as decided by the court (less any payments made).

(4) The request must state that the right to enter judgment has arisen because the court's order has not been complied with.

(5) A party must make an application in accordance with Part 23 if he wishes to obtain judgment under this rule in a case to which paragraph (2) does not apply.

Amendments—SI 2000/221.

3.6 Setting aside judgment entered after striking out

(1) A party against whom the court has entered judgment under rule 3.5 may apply to the court to set the judgment aside.

(2) An application under paragraph (1) must be made not more than 14 days after the judgment has been served on the party making the application.

(3) If the right to enter judgment had not arisen at the time when judgment was entered, the court must set aside(GL) the judgment.

(4) If the application to set aside(GL) is made for any other reason, rule 3.9 (relief from sanctions) shall apply.

General note—The rule, with its 14-day time limit, deals only with judgments entered pursuant to an 'unless' order. If such a judgment was entered without entitlement the court is obliged to set it aside, even if, for example, it might properly have been entered one day later. In such a case the court might well set aside the judgment but give another under rr 3.3 and 24.2. If an application is made for an order setting aside a judgment entered pursuant to an 'unless' order for any reason other than irregularity, the court will consider all the circumstances (r 3.9(1)).

3.7 Sanctions for non-payment of certain fees

(1) This rule applies where –

- (a) an allocation questionnaire or a pre-trial check list (listing questionnaire) is filed without payment of the fee specified by the relevant Fees Order;
- (b) the court dispenses with the need for an allocation questionnaire or a pre-trial check list or both;
- (c) these Rules do not require an allocation questionnaire or a pre-trial check list to be filed in relation to the claim in question; or
- (d) the court has made an order giving permission to proceed with a claim for judicial review.

(Rule 26.3 provides for the court to dispense with the need for an allocation questionnaire and rules 28.5 and 29.6 provide for the court to dispense with the need for a pre-trial check list)

(Rule 54.12 provides for the service of the order giving permission to proceed with a claim for judicial review)

(2) The court will serve a notice on the claimant requiring payment of the fee specified in the relevant Fees Order if, at the time the fee is due, the claimant has not paid it or made an application for exemption or remission.

(3) The notice will specify the date by which the claimant must pay the fee.

(4) If the claimant does not –

- (a) pay the fee; or
- (b) make an application for an exemption from or remission of the fee,

by the date specified in the notice –

- (i) the claim will automatically be struck out without further order of the court; and

(ii) the claimant shall be liable for the costs which the defendant has incurred unless the court orders otherwise.

(Rule 44.12 provides for the basis of assessment where a right to costs arises under this rule)

(5) Where an application for exemption from or remission of a fee is refused, the court will serve notice on the claimant requiring payment of the fee by the date specified in the notice.

(6) If the claimant does not pay the fee by the date specified in the notice –

(a) the claim will automatically be struck out without further order of the court; and
(b) the claimant shall be liable for the costs which the defendant has incurred unless the court orders otherwise.

(7) If –

(a) a claimant applies to have the claim reinstated; and
(b) the court grants relief,

the relief shall be conditional on the claimant either paying the fee or filing evidence of exemption from payment or remission of the fee within the period specified in paragraph (8).

(8) The period referred to in paragraph (7) is –

(a) if the order granting relief is made at a hearing at which a claimant is present or represented, 2 days from the date of the order;
(b) in any other case, 7 days from the date of service of the order on the claimant.

Amendments—SI 2000/2092; SI 2002/2058; SI 2003/1242.

General note—The fee payable when an allocation questionnaire or pre-trial check list (listing questionnaire) is filed is also payable *whether one is filed or not* (subject only to any exemption or remission). If the fee is not paid when the questionnaire is filed, or the case is one in which no questionnaire is to be filed, the court will impose a time limit within which the fee is to be paid. If the claimant does not comply, the claim will be struck out. On an application to reinstate the claim, the court may grant relief, but only on condition that the claimant pay (or prove exemption or remission) *within 2 days*.

3.7A (1) This rule applies where a defendant files a counterclaim without –

(a) payment of the fee specified by the relevant Fees Order; or
(b) making an application for an exemption from or remission of the fee.

(2) The court will serve a notice on the defendant requiring payment of the fee specified in the relevant Fees Order if, at the time the fee is due, the defendant has not paid it or made an application for exemption or remission.

(3) The notice will specify the date by which the defendant must pay the fee.

(4) If the defendant does not –

(a) pay the fee; or
(b) make an application for an exemption from or remission of the fee,

by the date specified in the notice, the counterclaim will automatically be struck out without further order of the court.

(5) Where an application for exemption from or remission of a fee is refused, the court will serve notice on the defendant requiring payment of the fee by the date specified in the notice.

(6) If the defendant does not pay the fee by the date specified in the notice, the counterclaim will automatically be struck out without further order of the court.

(7) If –

(a) the defendant applies to have the counterclaim reinstated; and
(b) the court grants relief,

the relief will be conditional on the defendant either paying the fee or filing evidence of exemption from payment or remission of the fee within the period specified in paragraph (8).

(8) The period referred to in paragraph (7) is –

(a) if the order granting relief is made at a hearing at which the defendant is present or represented, 2 days from the date of the order;
(b) in any other case, 7 days from the date of service of the order on the defendant.

Amendment—Inserted by SI 2005/2292.

3.7B Sanctions for dishonouring cheque

(1) This rule applies where any fee is paid by cheque and that cheque is subsequently dishonoured.

(2) The court will serve a notice on the paying party requiring payment of the fee which will specify the date by which the fee must be paid.

(3) If the fee is not paid by the date specified in the notice –

(a) where the fee is payable by the claimant, the claim will automatically be struck out without further order of the court;
(b) where the fee is payable by the defendant, the defence will automatically be struck out without further order of the court,

and the paying party shall be liable for the costs which any other party has incurred unless the court orders otherwise.

(Rule 44.12 provides for the basis of assessment where a right to costs arises under this rule)

(4) If –

(a) the paying party applies to have the claim or defence reinstated; and
(b) the court grants relief,

the relief shall be conditional on that party paying the fee within the period specified in paragraph (5).

(5) The period referred to in paragraph (4) is –

(a) if the order granting relief is made at a hearing at which the paying party is present or represented, 2 days from the date of the order;
(b) in any other case, 7 days from the date of service of the order on the paying party.

(6) For the purposes of this rule, 'claimant' includes a Part 20 claimant and 'claim form' includes a Part 20 claim.

Amendment—Inserted by SI 2005/2292.

3.8 Sanctions have effect unless defaulting party obtains relief

(1) Where a party has failed to comply with a rule, practice direction or court order, any sanction for failure to comply imposed by the rule, practice direction or court order has effect unless the party in default applies for and obtains relief from the sanction.

(Rule 3.9 sets out the circumstances which the court may consider on an application to grant relief from a sanction)

(2) Where the sanction is the payment of costs, the party in default may only obtain relief by appealing against the order for costs.

(3) Where a rule, practice direction or court order –

(a) requires a party to do something within a specified time, and
(b) specifies the consequence of failure to comply,

the time for doing the act in question may not be extended by agreement between the parties.

General note—The underlying idea is to maintain the momentum of judicial case management by making it unnecessary for the 'innocent' party to have to apply for a sanction imposed against a 'guilty' party to take effect. It will do so automatically, whatever the source of the sanction. Practitioners are reminded of r 3.8(3) – an agreement to extend time in such cases is of no effect and the court is unlikely to take any such agreement into account when considering an application for relief against the sanction imposed.

'payment of costs' (r 3.8(2))—Relief against all other sanctions should, in the first place, be considered at the level at which the sanction was imposed. But if the payment of costs and some other sanction were imposed by the same order, it is suggested that an appeal only is appropriate, if it is desired to seek relief against both. An appeal, of course, would be appropriate in any case where it is alleged that the imposition of the sanction was wrong. And see rr 23.10, 23.11 and 3.3(5) which are not excluded by this provision.

3.9 Relief from sanctions

(1) On an application for relief from any sanction imposed for a failure to comply with any rule, practice direction or court order the court will consider all the circumstances including –

(a) the interests of the administration of justice;
(b) whether the application for relief has been made promptly;
(c) whether the failure to comply was intentional;
(d) whether there is a good explanation for the failure;
(e) the extent to which the party in default has complied with other rules, practice directions, court orders and any relevant pre-action protocol(GL);
(f) whether the failure to comply was caused by the party or his legal representative;
(g) whether the trial date or the likely trial date can still be met if relief is granted;
(h) the effect which the failure to comply had on each party; and
(i) the effect which the granting of relief would have on each party.

(2) An application for relief must be supported by evidence.

General note—In *Bansal v Cheema* [2001] CP Rep 6 the Court of Appeal delivered an influential ruling which has been regularly cited with approval. Brooke LJ emphasised the importance of judges systematically considering the r 3.9 checklist when considering any aspect of relief against sanctions. In (*Woodhouse v Consignia plc* [2002] EWCA Civ 275, [2002] 2 All ER 737, CA his Lordship explained how this applies equally to removing the automatic stay provided by Pt 51. *Hansom v E Rex Makin & anor* [2003] EWCA Civ 1801 is a valuable antidote to the notion sometimes expressed that a Pt 51 stay should always be lifted if a fair trial is possible. In this case, however, it was emphasised that all r 3.9 factors had to be considered. This view was reiterated in *CIBC Mellon Trust Co v Stolzenberg* [2004] EWCA Civ 827. In *RC Residuals (formerly Regent Chemicals Ltd v Linton Fuel Oils Ltd* [2002] All ER (D) 32 (May), CA the court overruled a judge who had refused to allow expert evidence because reports had been served 10 and 20 minutes after expiry of an unless order. Brooke LJ reiterated the importance of r 3.9. Rule 3.9 will guide an application for an extension of time in any complex case, even though no sanction has been applied (*Sayers v Clarke Walker (Practice Note)* [2002] EWCA Civ 645, [2002] 1 WLR 3095, CA). This broad principle does not apply where an application for an extension of time was made before the expiry of the relevant period (*Robert v Momentum Services Ltd* [2003] EWCA Civ 229, [2003] 1 WLR 1577, CA).

'any sanction' (r 3.9(1))—This provision is unrestricted, and applies to applications for relief from any sanction, whether payment for costs or other and however the application is made.

When delay is under consideration, no distinction should be drawn between the litigant and his advisers (*Daryananii v Kumar and Gerry* (2000) (unreported) 12 December, CA).

'evidence' (r 3.9(2))—In particular, the court will need evidence as to the explanation for the failure (r 3.9(1)(d)) and as to who was responsible (r 3.9(1)(f)). In many cases, but not all, the other matters set out in the rule may be capable of being established by argument based on the existing papers.

3.10 General power of the court to rectify matters where there has been an error of procedure

Where there has been an error of procedure such as a failure to comply with a rule or practice direction –

(a) the error does not invalidate any step taken in the proceedings unless the court so orders; and
(b) the court may make an order to remedy the error.

'error'—Technical defects eg the use of an incorrect form, should be looked at in the light of the overriding objective (*Hannigan v Hannigan & ors* [2000] 2 FCR 650, (2000) *The Independent*, 23 May, (2000) Lawtel, 18 May, CA).

3.11 Power of the court to make a civil restraint order

A practice direction may set out –

(a) the circumstances in which the court has the power to make a civil restraint order against a party to proceedings;
(b) the procedure where a party applies for a civil restraint order against another party; and
(c) the consequences of the court making a civil restraint order.

Amendments—Inserted by SI 2004/2072.

Practice Direction – Striking out a Statement of Case

This Practice Direction supplements CPR Rule 3.4 (PD3)

Introduction—As para 1 of this PD makes clear, r 3.4 and Pt 24 are to be read together as providing a flexible regime for disposing summarily of cases which, for a wide variety of reasons, do not require to be tried. Paragraph 1.8 is an invitation to the imaginative. However, what these rules do not do is empower the court to use this regime in other than clear cases.

INTRODUCTORY

1.1 Rule 1.4(2)(c) includes as an example of active case management the summary disposal of issues which do not need full investigation at trial.

1.2 The rules give the court two distinct powers which may be used to achieve this. Rule 3.4 enables the court to strike out the whole or part of a statement of case which discloses no reasonable grounds for bringing or defending a claim (rule 3.4(2)(a)), or which is an abuse of the process of the court or otherwise likely to obstruct the just disposal of the proceedings (rule 3.4(2)(b)). Rule 24.2 enables the court to give summary judgment against a claimant or defendant where that party has no real prospect of succeeding on his claim or defence. Both those powers may be exercised on an application by a party or on the court's own initiative.

1.3 This practice direction sets out the procedure a party should follow if he wishes to make an application for an order under rule 3.4.

1.4 The following are examples of cases where the court may conclude that particulars of claim (whether contained in a claim form or filed separately) fall within rule 3.4(2)(a):

(1) those which set out no facts indicating what the claim is about, for example 'Money owed £5000',
(2) those which are incoherent and make no sense,
(3) those which contain a coherent set of facts but those facts, even if true, do not disclose any legally recognisable claim against the defendant.

1.5 A claim may fall within rule 3.4(2)(b) where it is vexatious, scurrilous or obviously ill-founded.

1.6 A defence may fall within rule 3.4(2)(a) where:

(1) it consists of a bare denial or otherwise sets out no coherent statement of facts, or
(2) the facts it sets out, while coherent, would not even if true amount in law to a defence to the claim.

1.7 A party may believe he can show without a trial that an opponent's case has no real prospect of success on the facts, or that the case is bound to succeed or fail, as the case may be, because of a point of law (including the construction of a document). In such a case the party concerned may make an application under rule 3.4 or Part 24 (or both) as he thinks appropriate.

1.8 The examples set out above are intended only as illustrations.

1.9 Where a rule, practice direction or order states 'shall be struck out or dismissed' or 'will be struck out or dismissed' this means that the striking out or dismissal will be automatic and that no further order of the court is required.

'two distinct powers' (para 1.2)—Attention is drawn to a third, the mysterious CPR r 3.1(2)(k).

CLAIMS WHICH APPEAR TO FALL WITHIN RULE 3.4(2)(A) OR (B)

2.1 If a court officer is asked to issue a claim form which he believes may fall within rule 3.4(2)(a) or (b) he should issue it, but may then consult a judge (under rule 3.2) before returning the claim form to the claimant or taking any other step to serve the defendant. The judge may on his own initiative make an immediate order designed to ensure that the claim is disposed of or (as the case may be) proceeds in a way that accords with the rules.

2.3 The judge may allow the claimant a hearing before deciding whether to make such an order.

2.4 Orders the judge may make include:

(1) an order that the claim be stayed until further order,
(2) an order that the claim form be retained by the court and not served until the stay is lifted,
(3) an order that no application by the claimant to lift the stay be heard unless he files such further documents (for example a witness statement or an amended claim form or particulars of claim) as may be specified in the order.

2.5 Where the judge makes any such order or, subsequently, an order lifting the stay he may give directions about the service on the defendant of the order and any other documents on the court file.

2.6 The fact that a judge allows a claim referred to him by a court officer to proceed does not prejudice the right of any party to apply for any order against the claimant.

DEFENCES WHICH APPEAR TO FALL WITHIN RULE 3.4(2)(A) OR (B)

3.1 A court officer may similarly consult a judge about any document filed which purports to be a defence and which he believes may fall within rule 3.4(2)(a) or (b).

3.2 If the judge decides that the document falls within rule 3.4(2)(a) or (b) he may on his own initiative make an order striking it out. Where he does so he may extend the time for the defendant to file a proper defence.

3.3 The judge may allow the defendant a hearing before deciding whether to make such an order.

3.4 Alternatively the judge may make an order under rule 18.1 requiring the defendant within a stated time to clarify his defence or to give additional information about it. The order may provide that the defence will be struck out if the defendant does not comply.

3.5 The fact that a judge does not strike out a defence on his own initiative does not prejudice the right of the claimant to apply for any order against the defendant.

GENERAL PROVISIONS

4.1 The court may exercise its powers under rule 3.4(2)(a) or (b) on application or on its own initiative at any time.

4.2 Where a judge at a hearing strikes out all or part of a party's statement of case he may enter such judgment for the other party as that party appears entitled to.

APPLICATIONS FOR ORDERS UNDER RULE 3.4(2)

5.1 Attention is drawn to Part 23 (General Rules about Applications) and to the practice direction that supplements it. The practice direction requires all applications to be made as soon as possible and before allocation if possible.

5.2 While many applications under rule 3.4(2) can be made without evidence in support, the applicant should consider whether facts need to be proved and, if so, whether evidence in support should be filed and served.

APPLICATIONS FOR SUMMARY JUDGMENT

6.1 Applications for summary judgment may be made under Part 24. Attention is drawn to that Part and to the practice direction that supplements it.

VEXATIOUS LITIGANTS

7.1 This practice direction applies where a 'civil proceedings order' or an 'all proceedings order' (as respectively defined under section 42(1A) of the Supreme Court Act 1981) is in force against a person ('the litigant').

7.2 An application by the litigant for permission to begin or continue, or to make any application in, any civil proceedings shall be made by application notice issued in the High Court and signed by the litigant.

7.3 The application notice must state:

(1) the title and reference number of the proceedings in which the civil proceedings order or the all proceedings order, as the case may be, was made,
(2) the full name of the litigant and his address,
(3) the order the applicant is seeking, and
(4) briefly, why the applicant is seeking the order.

7.4 The application notice must be filed together with any written evidence on which the litigant relies in support of his application.

7.5 Either in the application notice or in written evidence filed in support of the application, the previous occasions on which the litigant made an application for permission under section 42(1A) of the said Act must be listed.

7.6 The application notice, together with any written evidence, will be placed before a High Court judge who may:

(1) without the attendance of the applicant make an order giving the permission sought,
(2) give directions for further written evidence to be supplied by the litigant before an order is made on the application,
(3) make an order dismissing the application without a hearing; or
(4) give directions for the hearing of the application.]

7.7 Directions given under paragraph 7.6(4) may include an order that the application notice be served on the Attorney General and on any person against whom the litigant desires to bring the proceedings for which permission is being sought.

7.8 Any order made under paragraphs 6 or 7 will be served on the litigant at the address given in the application notice. CPR Part 6 will apply.

7.9 A person may apply to set aside the grant of permission if:

(1) the permission allowed the litigant to bring or continue proceedings against that person or to make any application against him, and
(2) the permission was granted other than at a hearing of which that person was given notice under paragraph 7.

7.10 Any application under paragraph 7.9 must be made in accordance with CPR Part 23.

Practice Direction – Sanctions for Non-Payment of Fees

This Practice Direction supplements CPR Rule 3.7 (PD3B)

General note—See the note to CPR r 3.7 for relevant commentary.

1 If a claim is struck out under rule 3.7, the court will send notice that it has been struck out to the defendant.

2 The notice will also explain the effect of rule 25.11. This provides that any interim injunction will cease to have effect 14 days after the date the claim is struck out under rule 3.7. Paragraph (2) provides that if the claimant applies to reinstate the claim before the interim injunction ceases to have effect, the injunction will continue until the hearing of the application unless the court orders otherwise. If the claimant makes such an application, the defendant will be given notice in the ordinary way under rule 23.4.

Practice Direction – Civil Restraint Orders

This Practice Direction supplements CPR Rule 3.11 (PD3C)

General note—See r 3.7 for the court's duty to consider making an order when striking out a case as totally without merit. A party is not precluded from applying for an order if the court does not act of its own motion. This practice direction is designed to give formal structure to the principles established in *Bhamjee v Forsdick (Practice Note)* [2003] EWCA Civ 1113, [2004] 1 WLR 88, CA. It proposes a stepped progression from an order, available to all judges in a specific case, to a general order which may only be made by the listed judges. It is considered doubtful, however, notwithstanding the words of the practice direction, whether a general civil restraint order requires an extended order to have been made first. Some litigants have a scattergun approach, not limited to a particular issue or group of issues. The prescribed forms of order also contain penal notices, which are often inappropriate in such cases.

INTRODUCTION

1 This practice direction applies where the court is considering whether to make –

(a) a limited civil restraint order;
(b) an extended civil restraint order; or
(c) a general civil restraint order,

against a party who has issued claims or made applications which are totally without merit.

Rules 3.3(7), 3.4(6) and 23.12 provide that where a statement of case or application is struck out or dismissed and is totally without merit, the court order must specify that fact and the court must consider whether to make a civil restraint order. Rule 52.10(6) makes similar provision where the appeal court refuses an application for permission to appeal, strikes out an appellant's notice or dismisses an appeal.

LIMITED CIVIL RESTRAINT ORDERS

2.1 A limited civil restraint order may be made by a judge of any court where a party has made 2 or more applications which are totally without merit.

2.2 Where the court makes a limited civil restraint order, the party against whom the order is made –

(1) will be restrained from making any further applications in the proceedings in which the order is made without first obtaining the permission of a judge identified in the order;
(2) may apply for amendment or discharge of the order provided he has first obtained the permission of a judge identified in the order; and
(3) may apply for permission to appeal the order and if permission is granted, may appeal the order.

2.3 Where a party who is subject to a limited civil restraint order –

(1) makes a further application in the proceedings in which the order is made without first obtaining the permission of a judge identified in the order, such application will automatically be dismissed –
   (a) without the judge having to make any further order; and
   (b) without the need for the other party to respond to it;
(2) repeatedly makes applications for permission pursuant to that order which are totally without merit, the court may direct that if the party makes any further application for permission which is totally without merit, the decision to dismiss the application will be final and there will be no right of appeal, unless the judge who refused permission grants permission to appeal.

2.4 A party who is subject to a limited civil restraint order may not make an application for permission under paragraphs 2.2(1) or 2.2(2) without first serving notice of the application on the other party in accordance with paragraph 2.5.

2.5 A notice under paragraph 2.4 must –

(1) set out the nature and grounds of the application; and
(2) provide the other party with at least 7 days within which to respond.

2.6 An application for permission under paragraphs 2.2(1) or 2.2(2) –

(1) must be made in writing;
(2) must include the other party's written response, if any, to the notice served under paragraph 2.4; and
(3) will be determined without a hearing.

2.7 An order under paragraph 2.3(2) may only be made by –

(1) a Court of Appeal judge;
(2) a High Court judge or master; or
(3) a designated civil judge or his appointed deputy.

2.8 Where a party makes an application for permission under paragraphs 2.2(1) or 2.2(2) and permission is refused, any application for permission to appeal –

(1) must be made in writing; and

(2) will be determined without a hearing.

2.9 A limited civil restraint order –

(1) is limited to the particular proceedings in which it is made;
(2) will remain in effect for the duration of the proceedings in which it is made, unless the court otherwise orders; and
(3) must identify the judge or judges to whom an application for permission under paragraphs 2.2(1), 2.2(2) or 2.8 should be made.

EXTENDED CIVIL RESTRAINT ORDERS

3.1 An extended civil restraint order may be made by –

(1) a judge of the Court of Appeal;
(2) a judge of the High Court; or
(3) a designated civil judge or his appointed deputy in the county court,

where a party has persistently issued claims or made applications which are totally without merit.

3.2 Unless the court otherwise orders, where the court makes an extended civil restraint order, the party against whom the order is made –

(1) will be restrained from issuing claims or making applications in –
   (a) any court if the order has been made by a judge of the Court of Appeal;
   (b) the High Court or any county court if the order has been made by a judge of the High Court; or
   (c) any county court identified in the order if the order has been made by a designated civil judge or his appointed deputy,

   concerning any matter involving or relating to or touching upon or leading to the proceedings in which the order is made without first obtaining the permission of a judge identified in the order;
(2) may apply for amendment or discharge of the order provided he has first obtained the permission of a judge identified in the order; and
(3) may apply for permission to appeal the order and if permission is granted, may appeal the order.

3.3 Where a party who is subject to an extended civil restraint order –

(1) issues a claim or makes an application in a court identified in the order concerning any matter involving or relating to or touching upon or leading to the proceedings in which the order is made without first obtaining the permission of a judge identified in the order, the claim or application will automatically be struck out or dismissed –
   (a) without the judge having to make any further order; and
   (b) without the need for the other party to respond to it;
(2) repeatedly makes applications for permission pursuant to that order which are totally without merit, the court may direct that if the party makes any further application for permission which is totally without merit, the decision to dismiss the application will be final and there will be no right of appeal, unless the judge who refused permission grants permission to appeal.

3.4 A party who is subject to an extended civil restraint order may not make an application for permission under paragraphs 3.2(1) or 3.2(2) without first serving notice of the application on the other party in accordance with paragraph 3.5.

3.5 A notice under paragraph 3.4 must –

(1) set out the nature and grounds of the application; and
(2) provide the other party with at least 7 days within which to respond.

3.6 An application for permission under paragraphs 3.2(1) or 3.2(2) –

(1) must be made in writing;
(2) must include the other party's written response, if any, to the notice served under paragraph 3.4; and
(3) will be determined without a hearing.

3.7 An order under paragraph 3.3(2) may only be made by –

(1) a Court of Appeal judge;
(2) a High Court judge; or
(3) a designated civil judge or his appointed deputy.

3.8 Where a party makes an application for permission under paragraphs 3.2(1) or 3.2(2) and permission is refused, any application for permission to appeal –

(1) must be made in writing; and
(2) will be determined without a hearing.

3.9 An extended civil restraint order –

(1) will be made for a specified period not exceeding 2 years;
(2) must identify the courts in which the party against whom the order is made is restrained from issuing claims or making applications; and
(3) must identify the judge or judges to whom an application for permission under paragraphs 3.2(1), 3.2(2) or 3.8 should be made.

3.10 The court may extend the duration of an extended civil restraint order, if it considers it appropriate to do so, but it must not be extended for a period greater than 2 years on any given occasion.

3.11 If he considers that it would be appropriate to make an extended civil restraint order –

(1) a master or a district judge in a district registry of the High Court must transfer the proceedings to a High Court judge; and
(2) a circuit judge or a district judge in a county court must transfer the proceedings to the designated civil judge.

GENERAL CIVIL RESTRAINT ORDERS

4.1 A general civil restraint order may be made by –

(1) a judge of the Court of Appeal;
(2) a judge of the High Court; or
(3) a designated civil judge or his appointed deputy in a county court,

where the party against whom the order is made persists in issuing claims or making applications which are totally without merit, in circumstances where an extended civil restraint order would not be sufficient or appropriate.

4.2 Unless the court otherwise orders, where the court makes a general civil restraint order, the party against whom the order is made –

(1) will be restrained from issuing any claim or making any application in –
  (a) any court if the order has been made by a judge of the Court of Appeal;
  (b) the High Court or any county court if the order has been made by a judge of the High Court; or
  (c) any county court identified in the order if the order has been made by a designated civil judge or his appointed deputy,

without first obtaining the permission of a judge identified in the order;

(2) may apply for amendment or discharge of the order provided he has first obtained the permission of a judge identified in the order; and

(3) may apply for permission to appeal the order and if permission is granted, may appeal the order.

4.3 Where a party who is subject to a general civil restraint order –

(1) issues a claim or makes an application in a court identified in the order without first obtaining the permission of a judge identified in the order, the claim or application will automatically be struck out or dismissed –
  (a) without the judge having to make any further order; and
  (b) without the need for the other party to respond to it;

(2) repeatedly makes applications for permission pursuant to that order which are totally without merit, the court may direct that if the party makes any further application for permission which is totally without merit, the decision to dismiss that application will be final and there will be no right of appeal, unless the judge who refused permission grants permission to appeal.

4.4 A party who is subject to a general civil restraint order may not make an application for permission under paragraphs 4.2(1) or 4.2(2) without first serving notice of the application on the other party in accordance with paragraph 4.5.

4.5 A notice under paragraph 4.4 must –

(1) set out the nature and grounds of the application; and
(2) provide the other party with at least 7 days within which to respond.

4.6 An application for permission under paragraphs 4.2(1) or 4.2(2) –

(1) must be made in writing;
(2) must include the other party's written response, if any, to the notice served under paragraph 4.4; and
(3) will be determined without a hearing.

4.7 An order under paragraph 4.3(2) may only be made by –

(1) a Court of Appeal judge;
(2) a High Court judge; or
(3) a designated civil judge or his appointed deputy.

4.8 Where a party makes an application for permission under paragraphs 4.2(1) or 4.2(2) and permission is refused, any application for permission to appeal –

(1) must be made in writing; and
(2) will be determined without a hearing.

4.9 A general civil restraint order –

(1) will be made for a specified period not exceeding 2 years;

(2) must identify the courts in which the party against whom the order is made is restrained from issuing claims or making applications; and

(3) must identify the judge or judges to whom an application for permission under paragraphs 4.2(1), 4.2(2) or 4.8 should be made.

4.10 The court may extend the duration of a general civil restraint order, if it considers it appropriate to do so, but it must not be extended for a period greater than 2 years on any given occasion.

4.11 If he considers that it would be appropriate to make a general civil restraint order –

(1) a master or a district judge in a district registry of the High Court must transfer the proceedings to a High Court judge; and

(2) a circuit judge or a district judge in a county court must transfer the proceedings to the designated civil judge.

GENERAL

5.1 The other party or parties to the proceedings may apply for any civil restraint order.

5.2 An application under paragraph 5.1 must be made using the Part 23 procedure unless the court otherwise directs and the application must specify which type of civil restraint order is sought.

5.3 Examples of a limited civil restraint order, an extended civil restraint order and a general civil restraint order are annexed to this practice direction. These examples may be modified as appropriate in any particular case.

****

Forms—Appended to this practice direction are three forms for: limited civil restraint orders (N19); extended civil restraint orders (N19A); and general civil restraint orders (N19B). These forms can be accessed via the *Civil Court Service* Online or CD-ROM services.

PART 4
FORMS

4 (1) The forms set out in a practice direction shall be used in the cases to which they apply.

(2) A form may be varied by the court or a party if the variation is required by the circumstances of a particular case.

(3) A form must not be varied so as to leave out any information or guidance which the form gives to the recipient.

(4) Where these Rules require a form to be sent by the court or by a party for another party to use, it must be sent without any variation except such as is required by the circumstances of the particular case.

(5) Where the court or a party produces a form shown in a practice direction with the words 'Royal Arms', the form must include a replica of the Royal Arms at the head of the first page.

Practice Direction—See generally PD4 at p 386.

'forms set out in a practice direction' (r 4(1))—The new CPR forms to be used in the High Court and county courts can be accessed and completed on the *Civil Court Service* CD-ROM. Alternatively, a large selection of relevant forms is available via the Internet at the Court Service website *http://www.courtservice.gov.uk.*

Variation of forms—The parties are free to alter the wording or appearance of the forms but only if required to do so by the circumstances of the particular case. The mere fact that they think the alterations would be a sensible improvement is not enough. Moreover, nothing essential is to be omitted.

Practice Directions – Forms

This Practice Direction supplements CPR Part 4 (PD4)

General note—See notes to CPR Pt 4 for relevant commentary.

'forms to be used in civil proceedings' (para 1.1)—The new CPR forms to be used in the High Court and county courts can be accessed and completed on the *Civil Court Service* CD-ROM. Alternatively, a large selection of relevant forms is available via the Internet at the Court Service website *http://www.courtservice.gov.uk.*

SCOPE OF THIS PRACTICE DIRECTION:

1.1 This practice directions lists the forms to be used in civil proceedings on or after 26 April 1999, when the Civil Procedure Rules (CPR) come into force.

1.2 The forms may be modified as the circumstances require, provided that all essential information, especially information or guidance which the form gives to the recipient, is included.

1.3 This practice direction contains 3 tables –

- Table 1 lists forms required by CPR Parts 1–75
- Table 2 lists High Court forms in use before 26 April 1999 which have remained in use on or after that date (see paragraph 4 below)
- Table 3 lists county court forms in use before 26 April 1999 that will remain in use on or after that date (see paragraph 5 below)

1.4 Former prescribed forms are shown as 'No 00'. The former practice forms where they are appropriate for use in either the Chancery or Queen's Bench Division (or where no specific form is available for use in the county court, in that court also) are prefixed 'PF' followed by the number. Where the form is used mainly in the Chancery or Queen's Bench Division, the suffix CH or QB follows the form number.

OTHER FORMS:

2.1 Other forms may be authorised by practice directions. For example the forms relating to Part 61 Admiralty claims are authorised by, and annexed to, the Admiralty Claims practice direction.

TABLE 1

'N' FORMS

CONTENTS:

3.1 This table lists the forms that are referred to and required by Rules or practice directions supplementing particular Parts of the CPR. A practice direction and its paragraphs are abbreviated by reference to the Part of the CPR which it supplements and the relevant paragraph of the practice direction, for example PD 34 1.2. For ease of reference, forms required for claims in the Commercial Court, Technology and Construction Court and for Admiralty claims and Arbitration claims, are separately listed.

Table 1

No	Title
N1	Part 7 (general) claim form (PD 7 3.1)
N1A	Notes for claimant
N1C	Notes for defendant
N1(FD)	Notes for defendant (Consumer Credit Act cases)
N2	Claim form (probate claim) (PD 57 2.1)
N2A	Claimant's notes for guidance (probate claim)
N2B	Defendant's notes for guidance (probate claim)
N3	Acknowledgment of service (probate claim) (Rule 57.4(1))
N5	Claim form for possession of property (PD 55 1.5)
N5A	Claim form for relief against forfeiture (PD 55 1.5)
N5B	Claim form for possession of property (accelerated procedure) (assured shorthold tenancy) (PD 55 1.5)
N5C	Notes for the claimant (accelerated possession procedure)
N6	Claim form for demotion of tenancy (PD65, 5.2)
N7	Notes for defendant (mortgaged residential premises)

Table 1

No	Title
N7A	Notes for defendant (rented residential premises)
N7B	Notes for defendant – forfeiture of the lease (residential premises)
N7D	Notes for defendant – demotion claim
N9	Acknowledgment of service/response pack (PD 10.2)
N9A	Admission and statement of means (specified amount) (PD 14 2.1)
N9B	Defence and counterclaim (specified amount) (PD 15 1.3)
N9C	Admission and statement of means (unspecified amount and non money claims) (PD 14 2.1)
N9D	Defence and counterclaim (unspecified amount and non money claims) (PD 15 1.3)
N10	Notice that acknowledgment of service has been filed – Rule 10.4
N11	Defence form (PD 55 1.5)
N11B	Defence form (accelerated possession procedure) (assured shorthold tenancy) (PD 55 1.5)
N11D	Defence form (demotion of tenancy) (PD65, 5.2)
N11M	Defence form (mortgaged residential premises) (PD 55 1.5)
N11R	Defence form (rented residential premises) (PD 55 1.5)
N16	General form of injunction
N16(1)	General form of injunction (formal parts only)
N16(A)	General form of application for injunction
N17	Judgment for claimant (amount to be decided by court)
N19	Limited civil restraint order
N19A	Extended civil restraint order
N19B	General civil restraint order
N20	Witness summons (PD 34 1.2)
N21	Order for Examination of Deponent before the hearing (PD 34 4.1)
N24	Blank form of order or judgment
N26	Order for possession

Table 1

No	Title
N26A	Order for possession (accelerated possession procedure) (assured shorthold tenancy)
N27	Order for possession on forfeiture (for rent arrears)
N27(2)	Order for possession on forfeiture (for rent arrears) (suspended)
N28	Order for possession (rented premises) (suspended)
N30	Judgment for claimant (default HC)
N30	Judgment for claimant (default CC)
N30(1)	Judgment for claimant (acceptance HC)
N30(1)	Judgment for claimant (acceptance CC)
N30(2)	Judgment for claimant (after determination HC)
N30(2)	Judgment for claimant (after determination CC)
N30(3)	Judgment for claimant (after re-determination HC)
N30(3)	Judgment for claimant (after re-determination CC)
N31	Order for possession (mortgaged premises) (suspended)
N32	Judgment for return of goods
N32(1) HP/CCA	Judgment for delivery of goods
N32(2) HP/CCA	Judgment for delivery of goods (suspended)
N32(3) HP/CCA	Judgment for delivery of goods
N32(4)	Variation order (return of goods)
N32(5) HP/CCA	Order for balance of purchase price
N33	Judgment for delivery of goods
N34	Judgment for claimant (after amount decided by court HC)
N34	Judgment for claimant (after amount decided by court CC)
N37	Hardship Payment Order
N39	Order to attend court for questioning
N40A (cc)	Warrant of arrest
N40B (cc)	Warrant of committal

Table 1

No	Title
N40A (HC)	Warrant of arrest
N40B (HC)	Warrant of committal
N54	Notice of eviction
N79A	Suspended committal order (for disobedience)
N84	Interim Third Party debt order
N85	Final Third Party debt order
N86	Interim Charging order
N87	Final Charging order
N110A	Anti-social behaviour injunction – power of arrest sections 153C and 153D of the Housing Act 1996
N113	Anti-social behaviour (Order under section 1B(4) of the Crime and Disorder Act 1998)
N119	Particulars of claim for possession (rented residential premises) (PD 55 2.1)
N119A	Notes for guidance on completing particulars of claim form (rented residential premises)
N120	Particulars of claim for possession (mortgaged residential premises) (PD 55 2.1)
N121	Particulars of claim for possession (trespassers) (PD 55 2.1
N122	Particulars of claim for demotion of tenancy (PD65, 5.2)
N130	Application for an interim possession order
N133	Witness statement of the defendant to oppose the making of an interim possession order
N134	Interim possession order
N136	Order for possession
N142	Guardianship order (Housing Act 1996, Mental Health Act 1983)
N143	(Interim Hospital order (Housing Act 1996, Mental Health Act 1983)
N144	Recognizance of defendant (Housing Act 1996)
N145	Recognizance of surety (Housing Act 1996)
N146	Warrant of arrest (Housing Act 1996)
N147	Remand order (Housing Act 1996) (bail granted)

Table 1

No	Title
N148	Remand order (Housing Act 1996) (bail not granted)
N150	Allocation Questionnaire (PD 26 2.1)
N150A	Master/DJ's directions on allocation
N151	Allocation Questionnaire (amount to be decided by court)
N151A	Master/DJ's directions on allocation
N152	Notice that [defence][counterclaim] has been filed (PD 26 2.5)
N153	Notice of allocation or listing hearing (PD 26 6.2)
N154	Notice of allocation to fast track (PD 26 4.2 and 9)
N155	Notice of allocation to multi track (PD 26 4.2 and 10)
N156	Order for further information (for allocation) (PD 26 4.2(2))
N157	Notice of allocation to small claims track (PD 26 4.2 and 8)
N158	Notice of allocation to small claims track (preliminary hearing) (PD 26 4.2 and 8)
N159	Notice of allocation to small claims track (no hearing) (PD 26 4.2 and 8)
N160	Notice of allocation to small claims track (with parties consent) (PD 26 4.2 and 8)
N161	Appellant's Notice (PD 52 5.1)
N161A	Guidance notes on completing the appellant's notice
N161B	Important notes for respondents
N162	Respondent's Notice (PD 52 7.3)
N162A	Guidance notes for completing the respondent's notice
N163	Skeleton Argument (PD 52 5.9 and 7.10)
N170	Listing questionnaire (Pre-trial checklist) (PD 28 6.1)
N171	Notice of date for return of listing questionnaire (PD 26 6.1 and PD 28 8.1)
N172	Notice of trial date
N173	Notice of non-payment of fee (Rule 3.7)
N205A	Notice of issue (specified amount)
N205B	Notice of issue (unspecified amount)
N205C	Notice of issue (non-money claim)
N205D	Notice of issue (probate claim)

Table 1

No	Title
N206A	Notice of issue (accelerated possession procedure) (assured shorthold tenancy)
N206B	Notice of issue (possession claim)
N206D	Notice of issue (demotion claim)
N208	Part 8 claim form (PD 8 2.2)
N208A	Part 8 notes for claimant
N208C	Part 8 notes for defendant
N209	Part 8 notice of issue
N210	Part 8 acknowledgment of service (PD 8 3.2)
N210A	Part 8 acknowledgment of service (costs-claim only) (PD 43–48 17.9)
N211	Part 20 claim form (Rule 20.7)
N211A	Part 20 notes for claimant
N211C	Part 20 notes for defendant
N212	Part 20 notice of issue
N213	Part 20 acknowledgment of service (Rule 20.12)
N215	Certificate of service (Rule 6.10)
N216	Notice of non-service (Rule 6.11)
N217	Order for substituted service (rule 6.8)
N218	Notice of service on a partner (PD 6 4.2)
N225	Request for judgment and reply to admission (specified amount) (PD 12 3)
N225A	Notice of part admission (specified amount) (Rule 14.5)
N226	Notice of admission (unspecified amount) (Rule 14.7)
N227	Request for judgment by default (amount to be decided by the court) (Rule 12.5)
N228	Notice of admission (return of goods) (PD 7 Consumer Credit Act 8.5)
N235	Certificate of suitability of litigation friend (PD 21 2.3)
N236	Notice of defence that amount claimed has been paid (Rule 15.10)
N242	Notice of payment into court (under order – Part 37)

Table 1

No	Title
N242A	Notice of acceptance and request for payment (Part 36)
N243A	Notice of acceptance of payment into court (PD 36 7.7)
N244	Application notice (PD 23 2.1)
N244A	Notice of hearing of application (PD 23 2.2)
N251	Notice of funding of case or claim
N252	Notice of commencement of assessment (PD 47 2.3)
N253	Notice of amount allowed on provisional assessment (PD 47 6.5)
N254	Request for default costs certificate (PD 47 3.1)
N255	Default costs certificate HC (PD 47 3.3)
N255	Default costs certificate CC (PD 47 3.3)
N256	Final costs certificate HC (PD 47 5.11)
N256	Final costs certificate CC (PD 47 5.11)
N257	Interim costs certificate (PD 47 5.11)
N258	Request for detailed assessment hearing (non-legal aid) (PD 47 4.3)
N258A	Request for detailed assessment hearing (legal aid only)
N258B	Request for detailed assessment (Costs payable out of a fund other than the Community Legal Service Fund)
N258C	Request for detailed assessment hearing pursuant to an order under Part III of the Solicitors Act 1974
N259	Notice of Appeal (PD 47 48.1)
N260	Statement of costs
N260	Statement of costs (summary assessment) (PD 43 3.2)
N265	List of documents (PD 31 3.1)
N266	Notice to admit facts/admission of facts (Rule 32.18)
N268	Notice to prove documents at trial (Rule 32.19)
N271	Notice of transfer of proceedings (Rule 30)
N279	Notice of discontinuance (Rule 38.3)
N292	Order on settlement on behalf of child or patient (PD 21 11.3)
N294	Claimant's application for a variation order

Table 1

No	Title
N316	Application for order that debtor attend court for questioning (PD 71 1.1)
N316A	Application that an officer of a company attend court for questioning (PD 71 1.1)
N322	Order for recovery of an award
N322A	Application to enforce an award (PD 70 4.1)
N322H	Request to register a High Court judgment or order for enforcement
N349	Application for third party debt order (PD 72 1.1)
N367	Notice of hearing to consider why fine should not be imposed (Rule 34.10)
N379	Application for charging order on land or property (PD 73 1.1)
N380	Application for charging order on securities (PD 73 1.1)
N434	Notice of change of solicitor (Rule 42.2)
N446	Request for re-issue of enforcement or an order to obtain information from judgment debtor (not warrant)
N460	Reasons for allowing or refusing permission to appeal
N461	Judicial Review claim form (Pt 54 PD)
N461 (notes)	Guidance notes on completing the Judicial Review claim form
N462	Judicial Review acknowledgment of service (Pt 54 PD)
N463	Judicial Review – application for urgent consideration
No 32	Order for examination within jurisdiction of witness before trial (Rule 34.8)
No 33	Application for issue of letter of request to judicial authority out of jurisdiction (Rule 34.13)
No 34	Order for issue of letter of request to judicial authority out of jurisdiction (Rule 34.13)
No 35	Letter of request for examination of witness out of jurisdiction (Rule 34.13)
No 37	Order for appointment of examiner to take evidence of witness out of jurisdiction (Rule 34.13(4))
No 41	Default judgment in claim relating to detention of goods (Rule 12.4(1)(c))
No 44	Part 24 Judgment for claimant

Table 1

No	Title
No 44A	Part 24 Judgment for defendant
No 45	Judgment after trial before judge without jury (PD 40B 14)
No 46	Judgment after trial before judge with jury (PD 40B 14)
No 47	Judgment after trial before a judge of the Technology & Construction Court or a master or district judge (PD 40B 14)
No 48	Order after trial of issue directed to be tried under rule 3.1(2)(i)
No 49	Judgment against personal representatives (PD 40B 14.3)
No 52	Notice of claim (CPR 19.8A(4)(a))
No 52A	Notice of judgment or order to an interested party
No 82	Application for appointment of a receiver
No 83	Order directing application for appointment of receiver and granting injunction meanwhile
No 84	Order for appointment of receiver by way of equitable execution (S 37 of Supreme Court Act 1981)
No 93	Order under the Evidence (Proceedings in Other Jurisdictions) Act 1975
No 94	Order for production of documents in marine insurance action (PD 49 7)
No 109	Order for reference to the European Court
No 111	Certificate of money provisions contained in a judgment for registration in another part of the United Kingdom (Schedule 6 to the Civil Jurisdiction and Judgments Act 1982)
No112	Certificate issued under Schedule 7 to the Civil Jurisdiction and Judgments Act 1982 in respect of non-money provisions for registration in another part of the United Kingdom
PF 1	Application for time (Rule 3.1(2)(a))
PF 2	Order for time (Rule 3.1(2)(a))
PF 3	Application for an extension of time for serving a claim form (Rule 7.6)
PF 4	Order for an extension of time for serving a claim form (Rule 7.6)
PF 6(A)	Application for permission to serve claim form out of jurisdiction (Rule 6.21)
PF 6(B)	Order for service out of the jurisdiction (Rule 6.21(4))

Table 1

No	Title
PF 7 QB	Request for service of document abroad (Rules 6.26(2)(a) and 6.27(2)(a))
PF 8	Standard 'unless' order (Rule 26.5(5), Part 26 PD para 2.5 and N150A)
PF 11	Application for Part 24 judgment (whole claim) (Rule 24.2)
PF 12	Application for Part 24 judgment (one or some of several claims) (Rule 24.2)
PF 13	Order under Part 24 (No 1)
PF 14	Order under Part 24 (No 2)
PF 15	Order under Part 24 for amount found due upon detailed assessment of solicitor's bill of costs
PF 16	Notice of court's intention to make an order of its own initiative (Rule 3.3(2) and (3))
PF 17	Order made on court's own initiative without a hearing (Rule 3.3(4) and (5))
PF19	Group Litigation Order (Rule 19.1)
PF20	Application for Part 20 directions
PF21	Order for Part 20 directions
PF 21A	Order to add person as defendant to counterclaim (Rule 20.5)
PF22	Notice claiming contribution or indemnity against another defendant (Rule 20.6)
PF43	Application for security for costs (Rule 25.12, also Companies Act 1985 s 726)
PF44	Order for security for costs (Rule 25.12, also Companies Act 1985 s 726)
PF48	Court record available for use before and at hearing
PF49	Request to parties to state convenient dates for hearing of 1st CMC
PF50	Application for directions (Part 29)
PF52	Order for case management directions in the multi-track (Part 29)
PF53	Order for separate trial of an issue (Rule 3.1(2)(i))
PF 56	Request for further information or clarification with provision for response (PD 18 1.6(2))
PF 57	Application for further information or clarification (PD 18 5)

Table 1

No	Title
PF 58	Order for further information or clarification (Rule 18.1)
PF63	Interim order for receiver in pending claim
PF67	Evidence in support of application to make order of House of Lords an order of the High Court (PD 40B 13.2)
PF68	Order making an order of the House of Lords an order of the High Court (PD 40B 13.3)
PF72	List of exhibits handed in at Trial (PD 39 7)
PF74	Order for trial of whole claim or of an issue by Master or District Judge (PD2B 4.1)
PF78 QB	Solicitor's undertaking as to expenses (re letter of request) (Rule 34.13(6)(b) and PD 34 5.3(5))
PF83	Judgment (non attendance of party) (Rule 39.3)
PF84A	Order on application arising from a failure to comply with an order (Rule 3.1(3))
PF84B	Judgment on application arising from a failure to comply with an order (Rule 3.5(1) and (4))
PF85A	Request for judgment (Rule 3.5(2))
PF85B	Judgment on Request arising from a failure to comply with an order (Rule 3.5(2))
PF113	Evidence in support of application for service by an alternative method (PD 6 9.1)
PF130	Form of advertisement (Rule 6.8)
PF147	Application for order declaring solicitor ceased to act (death etc)
PF148	Order declaring solicitor has ceased to act
PF149	Application by solicitor that he has ceased to act
PF150	Order that solicitor has ceased to act
PF152QB	Evidence in support of application for examination of witness under the Evidence (Proceedings in Other Jurisdictions) Act 1975
PF153QB	Certificate witness under the Evidence (Proceedings in Other Jurisdictions) Act 1975
PF154QB	Order for registration of foreign judgment under the Foreign Judgments (Reciprocal Enforcement) Act 1933

Table 1

No	Title
PF155	Certificates under s 10 of the Foreign Judgments (Reciprocal Enforcement) Act 1933
PF156QB	Evidence in support of application for registration of a Community judgment
PF157QB	Order for registration of a Community judgment
PF158QB	Notice of registration of a Community judgment
PF159QB	Evidence in support of application for registration of a judgment of another Contracting State or Regulation State
PF160QB	Order for registration of a judgment of another Contracting State or Regulation State
PF161QB	Notice of registration of a judgment of another Contracting State or Regulation State
PF163QB	Evidence in support of application for certified copy of a judgment for enforcement in another Contracting State or Regulation State
PF164	Evidence in support of application for certificate as to money provisions of a judgment of the High Court for registration elsewhere in the United Kingdom
PF165	Evidence in support of application for registration of a judgment of a court in another part of the United Kingdom containing non-money provisions
PF166QB	Certificate as to finality etc of Arbitration Award for enforcement abroad (Arbitration Act 1996, s 58)
PF167QB	Order to stay proceedings under s 9 of the Arbitration Act 1996 (PD 49G 6)
PF168	Order to transfer claim from the High Court to county court (County Courts Act 1984; High and County Courts Jurisdiction Order 1991; rule 30.3)
PF170(A)	Application for child or patient's settlement in personal injury or Fatal Accident Act claims before proceedings begun (Rule 21.10(2); (PD 21 6 and 7)
PF170(B)	Application for child or patient's settlement in personal injury or fatal accident claims in existing proceedings (Rule 21.10(2); PD 21 6 and 7)
PF172QB	Request for directions in respect of funds in court or to be brought into court (Rule 21.11)

Table 1

No	Title
PF197	Application for order for transfer from the Royal Courts of Justice to a district registry or vice-versa or from one district registry to another (Rule 30.2(4))
PF198	Order under PF197
PF205	Evidence in support of application for permission to execute for earlier costs of enforcement under s 15(3) and (4) of the Courts and Legal Services Act 1990
PF244	Application Notice (RCT only) (Part 23)
PF12CH	Advertisement for creditors
PF13CH	Advertisement for claimants other than creditors)
PF14CH	[Witness statement] [Affidavit] verifying list of creditors' claims
PF15CH	List of claims by persons claiming to be creditors following advertisement (Exhibit A referred to in [witness statement][affidavit] in PF14CH).
PF16CH	List of claims by persons claiming to be creditors other than those sent in following advertisement (Exhibit B referred to in [witness statement][affidavit] in PF14CH)
PF17CH	List of sums of money which may be due in respect of which no claim has been received (Exhibit C referred to in [witness statement][affidavit] in PF14CH)
PF18CH	Notice to creditor to prove claim
PF19CH	Notice to creditor or other claimant to produce documents or particulars in support of claim
PF20CH	Notice to creditor of allowance of claim
PF21CH	Notice to creditor of disallowance of claim in whole or in part
PF22CH	Order for administration: beneficiaries action reconstituted as creditors claim (Van Oppen order)
PF23CH	[Witness statement] [Affidavit] verifying list of claims other than creditors claims
PF24CH	List of claims not being creditors' claims sent following advertisement (Exhibit D referred to in [witness statement][affidavit] in PF23CH)
PF25CH	List of claims not being creditors' claims other than those sent in following advertisement (Exhibit E referred to in [witness statement][affidavit] in PF23CH)
PF26CH	Notice to claimant other than a creditor to prove claim

Table 1

No	Title
PF27CH	[Witness statement][Affidavit] verifying accounts and answering usual enquiries in administration claim (CPR Rules 32.8 and 32.16)
PF28CH	Executors (or administrators account) (account A in PF27CH)
PF29CH	Masters order stating the results of proceedings before him on the usual accounts and inquiries in an administration claim
PF30CH	Security of receiver or administrator pending determination of a probate claim (PD 44)
PF31CH	Consent to act as trustee (Rule 33.8)
PF32CH	[Witness statement][Affidavit] in support of application for appointment of new litigation friend of child claimant (Rule 21.6(4))
PF33CH	Order for distribution of a Lloyds estate
PF34CH	Order in inquiry as to title in proceedings to enforce charging order where the defendant's title is not disclosed
PF36CH	Order appointing administrator pending determination of probate claim (PD 44)
PF38CH	Order in probate claim approving compromise (PD 44)
	Commercial Court Forms (CPR Part 58)
N1(CC)	Claim form (Pt 58 PD 2.4)
N1c(CC)	Notes for defendant
N9(CC)	Acknowledgment of service (Pt 58 PD 5.1)
N208(CC)	Claim form (Part 8) (Pt 58 PD 2.4)
N208c(CC)	Notes for defendant
N210(CC)	Acknowledgment of service (Part 8) (Pt 58 PD 5.2)
N211(CC)	Claim form (Part 20) (Pt 58 PD 12)
N211c(CC)	Notes for defendant (Part 20)
N213(CC)	Acknowledgment of service (Part 20)
N244(CC)	Application Notice (Pt 58 PD 10.7(2))
N265(CC)	List of Documents
	Technology and Construction forms (CPR Part 60)
TCC/FCM1	Case management information sheet (Pt 60 PD 8.2)

Table 1

No	Title
TCC/PTR1	Pre-trial review questionnaire (Pt 60 PD 9.1)
	Admiralty forms (CPR Part 60)
ADM1	Claim form (Admiralty claim in rem) (Pt 61 PD 3.1)
ADM1A	Claim form (Admiralty claim) (Pt 61 PD 12.3)
ADM1C	Notes for defendant on replying to an in rem claim form
ADM2	Acknowledgment of service for admiralty claims in rem (Pt 61 PD 3.4)
ADM3	Collision statement of case (Pt 61 PD 4.1)
ADM4	Application and undertaking for arrest and custody (Pt 61 PD 5.1(1))
ADM5	Declaration in support of an application for warrant of arrest (Pt 61 PD 5.1(2))
ADM6	Notice to consular officer of intention to apply for warrant of arrest (Pt 61 PD 5.4)
ADM7	Request for caution against arrest (Pt 61 PD6.2)
ADM9	Warrant of arrest (Pt 61 PD 5.5(1))
ADM10	Standard directions to Admiralty Marshal (Pt 61 PD 5.6)
ADM11	Request for caution against release (Pt 61 PD 7.1)
ADM12	Request for undertaking for release (Pt 61 PD 7.1)
ADM12a	Request for withdrawal and caution against release (Pt 61 PD 7.5)
ADM13	Application for judgment in default (Pt 61 PD 8.1)
ADM14	Order for sale of ship (Pt 61 PD 9.2)
ADM15	Claim form (Admiralty limitation claim) (Pt 61 PD 10.1(1))
ADM15B	Notes for defendant on replying to an Admiralty limitation claim
ADM16	Notice of admission of right of claimant to limit liability (Pt 61 PD 10.3)
ADM16a	Defence to Admiralty limitation claim
ADM16b	Acknowledgment of service (Admiralty limitation claim) (Pt 61 PD 10.4)
ADM17	Application for restricted decree (Pt 61 PD 10.5)
ADM17a	Application for general limitation decree (Pt 61 PD 10.6)

Table 1

No	Title
ADM18	Restricted limitation decree (Pt 61 PD 10.5)
ADM19	General limitation decree
ADM20	Defendant's claim in limitation (Pt 61 PD 10.14)
ADM21	Declaration as to liability of a defendant to file and serve statement of case under a decree of limitation (Pt 61 PD 10.16)
	Arbitration forms (CPR Part 62)
N8	Claim form (Arbitration) (Pt 62 PD 2.1)
N8A	Notes for claimant (Arbitration)
N8B	Notes for defendant (Arbitration)
N15	Acknowledgment of service (Arbitration claim)]

TABLE 2

PRACTICE FORMS

CONTENTS:

4.1 This table lists the Practice Forms that may be used under this practice direction. It contains forms that were previously –

- Prescribed Forms contained in Appendix A to the Rules of the Supreme Court 1965
- Queen's Bench masters' Practice Forms
- Chancery masters' Practice Forms

4.2 Where a rule permits, a party intending to use a witness statement as an alternative to an affidavit should amend any form in this Table to be used in connection with that rule so that 'witness statement' replaces 'affidavit' wherever it appears in the form.

4.3 The forms in this list are reproduced in an Appendix to the Chancery and Queen's Bench Guides, in practitioners' text books and on the Court Service website (www.courtservice.gov.uk).

Table 2

No	Title
No 53	Writ of fieri facias (Sch 1 – RSC Ord 45 r 12)
No 54	Writ of fieri facias on order for costs (Sch 1 – RSC Ord 45 r 12)

Table 2

No	Title
No 55	Notice of seizure (Sch 1 – RSC Ord 45 r 2)
No 56	Writ of fieri facias after levy of part (Sch 1 – RSC Ord 45 r 12)
No 57	Writ of fieri facias against personal representatives (Sch 1 – RSC Ord 45 r 12)
No 58	Writ of fieri facias de bonis ecclesiasticis (Sch 1 – RSC Ord 45 r 12)
No 59	Writ of sequestrari de bonis ecclesiasticis (Sch 1 – RSC Ord 45 r 12)
No 62	Writ of fieri facias to enforce Northern Irish or Scottish judgment (Sch 1 – RSC Ord 45 r 12 and Ord 71 r 37(1) and (2))
No 63	Writ of fieri facias to enforce foreign registered judgment (Sch 1 – RSC Ord 45 r 12 and Ord 71 rr 10, 21 and 34)
No 64	Writ of delivery: delivery of goods, damages and costs (Sch 1 – RSC Ord 45 r 4)
No 65	Writ of delivery: delivery of goods or value, damages and costs (Sch 1 – RSC Ord 45 r 12(2))
No 66	Writ of possession (Sch 1 – RSC Ord 45 r 12(3))
No 66A	Writ of possession (Sch 1 – RSC Ord 113 r 7)
No 67	Writ of sequestration (Sch 1 – RSC Ord 45 r 12(4), Ord 46 r 5)
No 68	Writ of restitution (Sch 1 – RSC Ord 46 rr 1 and 3)
No 69	Writ of assistance (Sch 1 – RSC Ord 46 rr 1 and 3)
No 71	Notice of renewal of writ of execution (Sch 1 – RSC Ord 46 r 8)
No 85	Order of committal or other penalty upon finding of contempt of court (Sch 1 – RSC Ord 52)
No 87	Claim form for writ of habeas corpus ad subjiciendum
No 88	Notice of adjourned application for writ of habeas corpus
No 89	Writ of habeas corpus ad subjiciendum
No 90	Notice to be served with writ of habeas corpus ad subjiciendum
No 91	Writ of habeas corpus ad testificandum

Table 2

No	Title
No 92	Writ of habeas corpus ad respondendum
No 95	Certificate of order against the Crown (Sch 1 – RSC Ord 77 r 15 and s 25 of the Crown Proceedings Act 1947))
No 96	Certificate of order for costs against the Crown (Sch 1 – RSC Ord 77 r 15 and s 25 of the Crown Proceedings Act 1947)
No 97	Claim form to grant bail (criminal proceedings) (Sch 1 – RSC Ord 79 r 9(1))
No 97A	Claim form to vary arrangements for bail (criminal proceedings) (Sch 1 – RSC Ord 79 r 9(1))
No 98	Order to release prisoner on bail (Sch 1 – RSC Ord 79 r 9(6),(6A) and (6B))
No 98A	Order varying arrangements for bail (Sch 1 – RSC Ord 79 r 9(10))
No 99	Order of Court of Appeal to admit prisoner to bail (Sch 1 – RSC Ord 59 r 20(5))
No 100	Notice of bail Sch 1 – RSC Ord 79 r 9(7))
No 101	Witness summons – Crown Court
No 103	Witness summons – Crown Court
No 104	Attachment of earnings order (Attachment of Earnings Act 1971)
No 105	Notice under s 10(2) of the Attachment of Earnings Act 1971
No 110	Certificate under s 12 of the Civil Jurisdiction and Judgments Act 1982
PF23 QB	Notice by sheriff of claim to goods taken in execution (Sch 1 – RSC Ord 17 r 2(2))
PF24 QB	Notice by execution creditor of admission or dispute of title of interpleader claimant (Sch 1 – RSC Ord 17 r 2(2))
PF25 QB	Interpleader application (Sch 1 – RSC Ord 17 r 3)
PF26 QB	Interpleader application by sheriff (Sch 1 – RSC Ord 17 r 3)
PF27 QB	Evidence in support of interpleader application (Sch 1 – RSC Ord 17 r 3(4))
PF28 QB	Interpleader order (1) claim barred where Sheriff interpleads (Sch 1 – RSC Ord 17)

Table 2

No	Title
PF29 QB	Interpleader order (1a) Sheriff to withdraw (Sch 1 – RSC Ord 17)
PF30 QB	Interpleader order (2) interpleader claimant substituted as defendant (Sch 1 –RSC Ord 17)
PF31 QB	Interpleader order (3) trial of issue (Sch 1 – RSC Ord 17)
PF32 QB	Interpleader order (4) conditional order for Sheriff to withdraw and trial of issue (Sch 1 – RSC Ord 17)
PF34 QB	Interpleader order (6) summary disposal (Sch 1 – RSC Ord 17 r 5(2))
PF86	Praecipe for writ of fieri facias (Sch 1 – RSC Ord 45 r 12(1) and 46 r 6)
PF87	Praecipe for writ of sequestration (Sch 1 – RSC Ord 45 r 12(4) and 46 r 6)
PF88	Praecipe for writ of possession (Sch 1 – RSC Ord 45 r 12(3), 46 r 6 and 113 r 7)
PF89	Praecipe for writ of possession and fieri facias combined (Sch 1 – RSC Ord 45 r 12 and Ord 46 r 6)
PF90	Praecipe for writ of delivery (Sch 1 – RSC Ord 45 r 12(2) and Ord 46 r 6)
PF97 QB	Order for sale by Sheriff by private contract (Sch 1 – RSC Ord 47 r 6)
PF102	Bench warrant (Sch 1 – RSC Ord 52)
PF103	Warrant of committal (general) (Sch 1 – RSC Ord 52)
PF104	Warrant of committal (contempt in face of court) (Sch 1 – RSC Ord 52)
PF105	Warrant of committal (failure of witness to attend) (Sch 1 – RSC Ord 52)
PF106	Warrant of Committal (of prisoner) (Sch 1 – RSC Ord 52)
PF141	Witness statement/affidavit of personal service of judgment or order (Sch 1 – RSC Ord 45 r 7)
PF177	Order for written statement as to partners in firm (Sch 1 – RSC Ord 81 r 2)

Table 2

No	Title
PF179QB	Evidence on registration of a Bill of Sale (Bills of Sale Act 1878; Sch 1 – RSC Ord 95)
PF180QB	Evidence on registration of an Absolute Bill of Sale, Settlement and Deed of Gift (Sch 1 – RSC Ord 95)
PF181QB	Evidence in support of an application for re-registration of a Bill of Sale (s 14 Bills of Sale Act 1878; Sch 1 – RSC Ord 95)
PF182QB	Order for extension of time to register or re-register a Bill of Sale (s 14 Bills of Sale Act 1878; Sch 1 – RSC Ord 95)
PF183QB	Evidence for permission to enter a memorandum of Satisfaction on a Bill of Sale (s 15 Bills of Sale Act 1878; Sch 1 – RSC Ord 95; PD Bills of Sale para 1)
PF184QB	Claim form for entry of satisfaction on a registered Bill of Sale (s 15 Bill of Sale Act 1878; Sch 1 – RSC Ord 95 r 2; Bills of Sale PD para 3)
PF185QB	Order for entry of Satisfaction on a registered Bill of Sale (s 14 Bills of Sale Act 1878; Sch 1 – RSC Ord 95 r 2)
PF186QB	Evidence on registration of Assignment of Book Debts (s 344 Insolvency Act 1986; Sch 1 – RSC Ord 95 r 6(2))
PF187	Claim form for Solicitor's Charging order (s 73 Solicitors Act 1974; Sch 1 – RSC Ord 106 r 2)
PF188	Charging order: Solicitor's costs (s 73 Solicitors Act 1974; Sch 1 – RSC Ord 106 r 2)
PF6CH	Certificate on application for permission to issue execution on suspended order for possession where defendant in default of acknowledgment of service (Sch 1 – RSC Ord 46 r 2 and 4 and CPR Part 23)
PF7CH	Inquiry for persons entitled to the property of an intestate dying on or after 1 January 1926 (Sch 1 – RSC Ord 85)
PF8CH	Application notice after masters findings on kin enquiry (Benjamin order) giving permission to distribute estate upon footing (Sch 1 – RSC Ord 85)
PF9CH	Order giving leave to distribute estate upon footing (re Benjamin) (Sch 1 – RSC Ord 85)
PF10CH	Judgment in beneficiaries administration claim (Sch 1 – RSC Ord 85)

Table 2	
No	**Title**
PF11CH	Judgment in creditors' administration claim (Sch 1 – RSC Ord 85)

TABLE 3

CONTENTS:

5.1 This table lists county court forms in use before 26 April 1999 that will continue to be used on or after that date.

5.2 Where a rule permits, a party intending to use a witness statement as an alternative to an affidavit should amend any form in this Table to be used in connection with that rule so that 'witness statement' replaces 'affidavit' wherever it appears in the form.

Table 3	
No	**Title**
N27	Judgment for claimant in Action of Forfeiture for non payment of rent
N35	Variation Order
N35A	Variation Order (determination)
N41	Order suspending judgment or Order, and/or Warrant of Execution/Committal
N41A	Order suspending warrant (determination)
N42	Warrant of Execution
N46	Warrant of Delivery and Execution for damages and Costs
N48	Warrant of Delivery, where, if goods are not returned, Levy is to be made for their value
N49	Warrant for Possession of Land
N50	Warrant of Restitution (Order 26 rule 17)
N51	Warrant of Restitution (Order 24, rule 6(1))
N52	Warrant of Possession under Order 24
N53	Warrant of Execution or Committal to District Judge of Foreign Court
N55	Notice of Application for Attachment of Earnings Order

Table 3

No	Title
N55A	Notice of application for attachment of earnings order (maintenance)
N56	Form for replying to an attachment of Earnings application (statement of means)
N58	Order for Defendants attendance at an adjourned Hearing of an Attachment of Earnings Application (maintenance)
N59	Warrant of Committal under section 23(1) of the Attachment of Earnings Act 1971
N60	Attachment of Earnings Order (Judgment Debt)
N61	Order for production of Statement of Means
N61A	Order to employer for production of statement of earnings
N62	Summons for Offence under Attachment of Earnings
N63	Notice to show Cause section 23 of the Attachment of Earnings Act 1971
N64	Suspended Attachment of Earnings Order
N64A	Suspended Attachment of Earnings Order (maintenance)
N65A	Attachment of Earnings Arrears Order
N65	Attachment of Earnings Order (Priority Maintenance)
N66	Consolidated Attachment of Earnings Order
N66A	Notice of Application for Consolidated Attachment of Earnings Order
N67	Judgment Summons under the Debtors Act 1869
N68	Certificate of Service (Judgment Summons)
N69	Order for Debtors Attendance at an Adjourned Hearing of Judgment Summons
N70	Order of Commitment under section 110 of the County Courts Act 1984
N71	Order revoking an Order of Commitment under section 110 of the County Courts Act 1984
N72	Notice to Defendant where a Committal Order made but directed to be suspended under Debtors Act

Table 3

No	Title
N73	New Order on Judgment Summons
N74	Warrant of Committal Judgment Summons under the Debtors Act 1869
N75	Indorsement on a warrant of Committal sent to a Foreign Court
N76	Certificate to be indorsed on duplicate Warrant of Committal issued for re-arrest of Debtor
N77	Notice as to consequences of disobedience to Court Order
N78	Notice to show good reason why an order for your committal to prison should not be made (**Family proceedings only**)
N79	Committal of other Order upon proof of disobedience of a court order or breach of undertaking
N80	Warrant for Committal to Prison
N81	Notice to solicitor to show cause why an undertaking should not be enforced by committal to prison
N82	Order for committal for failure by solicitor to carry out undertaking
N83	Order for discharge from custody under warrant of committal
N88	Interpleader Summons to Execution Creditor
N88(1)	Interpleader Summons to Claimant claiming goods or rent under an execution
N89	Interpleader summons to persons making adverse claims to debt
N90	Summons for assaulting an officer of the court or rescuing goods
N91	Order of Commitment and or Imposing a fine for assaulting an officer of the court or rescuing goods
N92	Request for Administration Order
N93	List of Creditors furnished under the Act of 1971
N94	Administration Order
N95	Order revoking an administration order
N95A	Order suspending or varying an administration order

Table 3

No	Title
N110	Power of arrest attached to injunction under section 2 Domestic Violence and Matrimonial Proceedings Act 1976
N110A	Anti social behaviour injunction – power of arrest s 152/153 HA 1996
N112	Order for Arrest under section 110 of County Courts Act 1984
N112A	Power of arrest, section 23 Attachment of Earnings Act 1971
N117	General form of undertaking
N118	Notice to Defendant where committal order made but directed to be suspended
N130	Application for possession including application for interim possession order (*revised with effect from 2/12/02)*
N131	Notice of application for interim possession order (*will become obsolete from 2/12/02)*
N132	Affidavit of Service of notice of application for interim possession order (*will become obsolete from 2/12/02)*
N133	Affidavit to occupier to oppose the making of an interim possession order (*revised with effect from 2/12/02)*
N134	Interim possession order (*revised with effect from 2/12/02)*
N135	Affidavit of Service of interim possession order (*will become obsolete from 2/12/02)*
N136	Order for possession (*revised with effect from 2/12/02)*
N138	Injunction order
N139	Application for warrant of arrest
N140	Warrant of arrest
N206	Notice of Issue of fixed date claim
N207	Plaint note (Adoption freeing for Adoption)
N200	Petition – **Note old number was N208**
N201	Request for entry of appeal – **Note old number was N209**
N202	Order for party to sue or defend on behalf of others having the same interest – **Note old number was N210**

Table 3

No	Title
N203	Notice to persons on whose behalf party has obtained leave to sue or defend – **Note old number was N211**
N204	Notice to person against whom party has obtained leave to sue or defend on behalf of others – **Note old number was N212**
N224	Request for Service out of England and Wales through the court
N245	Application for suspension of a warrant and/or variation of an instalment order
N246	Claimant's Reply to Defendant's application to vary instalment order
N246A	Claimant's reply to Defendant's application to suspend warrant of execution
N270	Notes for guidance (application for administration order)
N276	Notice of Hearing of Interpleader Proceedings transferred from High Court
N277	Notice of Pre Trial Review of Interpleader proceedings transferred from the High Court
N280	Order of reference of proceedings or questions for inquiry and report
N285	General form of affidavit
N288	Order to produce prisoner
N289	Judgment for Defendant
N293	Certificate or judgment or order
N293A	Combined certificate of judgment and request for writ of fi fa
N295	Order for sale of land
N296	Notice of Judgment or order to party directed to be served with notice
N297	Order for accounts and Inquiries in Creditors Administration Action
N298	Order for Administration
N299	Order for foreclosure nisi of legal mortgage of land
N300	Order for sale in action by equitable mortgagee

Table 3

No	Title
N302	Judgment in action for specific performance (vendors action title accepted)
N303	Order for dissolution of partnership
N304	Notice to parties to attend upon taking accounts
N305	Notice to creditor to prove his claim
N306	Notice to creditor of determination of claim
N307	District Judges order (accounts and inquiries)
N309	Order for foreclosure absolute
N310	Partnership order on further consideration
N311	Administrative action order on further consideration
N313	Indorsement on certificate of judgment (transfer)
N317	Bailiffs report
N317A	Bailiff's report to the claimant
N319	Notice of execution of warrant of committal
N320	Request for return of, or to, warrant
N322	Order for recovery of money awarded by tribunal
N323	Request for warrant of execution
N324	Request for warrant of goods
N325	Request for warrant for possession of land
N326	Notice of issue of warrant of execution
N327	Notice of issue of warrant of execution to enforce a judgment or order
N328	Notice of transfer of proceedings to the High Court
N329	Notes for guidance on completion of N79
N330	Notice of sale or payment under execution in respect of a judgment for a sum exceeding £500
N331	Notice of withdrawal from poss. or payment of moneys on notice of receiving or winding up order
N332	Inventory of goods removed

Table 3

No	Title
N333	Notice of time when and where goods will be sold
N334	Request to hold walking possession and authority to re-enter
N336	Request and result of search in the attachment of earnings index
N337	Request for attachment of earnings order
N338	Request for statement of earnings
N339	Discharge of attachment of earnings order
N340	Notice as to payment under attachment of earnings order made by the High Court
N341	Notice of intention to vary attachment of earnings order under section 10(2) of AE Act 1971
N342	Request for judgment summons
N343	Notice of result of hearing of a judgment summons issued on a judgment or order of the High Court
N344	Request for warrant of committal on judgment summons
N345	Certificate of payment under the Debtors Act 1869
N353	Order appointing receiver of real and personal property
N354	Order appointing receiver of partnership
N355	Interim order for appointment of receiver
N356	Order for appointment of receiver by way of equitable execution
N358	Notice of claim to goods taken in execution
N359	Notice to claimant to goods taken in execution to make deposit or give security
N360	Affidavit in support of interpleader summons other than an execution
N361	Notice of application for relief in pending action
N362	Order on interpleader summons under an execution where the claim is not established
N363	Order on interpleader summons under an execution where the claim is established

Table 3

No	Title
N364	Order on interpleader summons (other than execution) where there is an action
N365	Order on interpleader summons (other than execution) where there is no action
N366	Summons for neglect to levy execution
N368	Order fining a witness for non-attendance
N370	Order of commitment or imposing a fine for insult or misbehaviour
N372	Order for rehearing
N373	Notice of application for an administration order
N374	Notice of intention to review an administration order
N374A	Notice of intention to revoke an administration order
N375	Notice of further creditors claim
N376	Notice of hearing administration order (by direction of the court)
N377	Notice of dividend
N388	Notice to probate registry to produce documents
N390	Notice that a claim has been entered against the Crown
N391	Crown Proceedings Act affidavit in support of application directing payment by Crown to judgment creditor
N392	Crown Proceedings Act notice of application for order directing payment by the Crown to the judgment creditor
N432	Affidavit on payment into court under section 63 of the Trustee Act 1925
N436	Order for sale of land under charging order
N437	District Judges report
N438	Notice to charge holder under Matrimonial Homes Act 1983
N440	Notice of application for time order by debtor or hirer – CC Act 1974
N441	Notification of request for certificate of satisfaction or cancellation

Table 3	
No	**Title**
N441A	Certificate of satisfaction or cancellation of judgment debt
N444	Details of sale under a warrant of execution
N445	Request for re-issue of warrant
N447	Notice to claimant of date fixed for adjourned hearing
N448	Request to defendant for employment details, attachment of earnings
N449	Notice to employer, failure to make deductions under attachment of earnings order

PART 5
COURT DOCUMENTS

CONTENTS OF THIS PART

5.1 Scope of this Part

This Part contains general provisions about –

(a) documents used in court proceedings; and
(b) the obligations of a court officer in relation to those documents.

Practice Direction—See generally PD5 at p 419.

Particular regard should be had to PD5, para 5, which details the provisions for filing documents at court; and PD5, para 6, which deals with the enrolment of deeds and other documents in the Supreme Court.

5.2 Preparation of documents

(1) Where under these Rules, a document is to be prepared by the court, the document may be prepared by the party whose document it is, unless –

(a) a court officer otherwise directs; or
(b) it is a document to which –
  (i) (*revoked*)
  (ii) CCR Order 25, rule 8(9) (reissue of warrant where condition upon which warrant was suspended has not been complied with); or
  (iii) CCR Order 28, rule 11(1) (issue of warrant of committal),

applies.

(2) Nothing in this rule shall require a court officer to accept a document which is illegible, has not been duly authorised, or is unsatisfactory for some other similar reason.

Amendments—SI 2001/2792.

Practice Direction—See generally PD5 at p 419.

See particularly para 2 which sets out the requirements for the documents themselves.

'court officer' (r 5.2(1)(a))—For the definition see r 2.3.

'some other similar reason' (r 5.2(2))—Presumably the overriding objective will be applied.

5.3 Signature of documents by mechanical means

Where any of these Rules or any practice direction requires a document to be signed, that requirement shall be satisfied if the signature is printed by computer or other mechanical means.

Practice Direction—See generally PD5 at p 419.

Mechanical signature—This is of particular application to the Claim Production Centre at Northampton and applies to any signature required in proceedings.

Computer signature—The signature must be supplemented with the name of the person whose signature it is, in such a way that the person can be identified (PD5, para 1).

5.4 Supply of documents from court records – general

(1) A court or court office may keep a publicly accessible register of claims which have been issued out of that court or court office.

(2) Any person who pays the prescribed fee may, during office hours, search any available register of claims.

(The practice direction contains details of available registers)

(3) A party to proceedings may, unless the court orders otherwise, obtain from the records of the court a copy of any document listed in paragraph 4.2A of the Practice Direction.

(4) A party to proceedings may, if the court gives permission, obtain from the records of the court a copy of any other document filed by a party or communication between the court and a party or another person.

(5) Any other person may –

(a) unless the court orders otherwise, obtain from the records of the court a copy of –

(i) a claim form but not any documents filed with or attached to or intended by the claimant to be served with such claim form, subject to paragraph (6) and to any order of the court under paragraph (7);

(ii) a judgment or order given or made in public (whether made at a hearing or without a hearing), subject to paragraph (6); and

(b) if the court gives permission, obtain from the records of the court a copy of any other document filed by a party, or communication between the court and a party or another person.

(6) A person may obtain a copy of a claim form or a judgment or order under paragraph (5)(a) only if –

(a) where there is one defendant, the defendant has filed an acknowledgment of service or a defence;

(b) where there is more than one defendant, either –

(i) all the defendants have filed an acknowledgment of service or a defence;

(ii) at least one defendant has filed an acknowledgment of service or a defence, and the court gives permission;

(c) the claim has been listed for a hearing; or

(d) judgment has been entered in the claim.

(7) The court may, on the application of a party or of any person identified in the claim form –

(a) restrict the persons or classes of persons who may obtain a copy of the claim form;

(b) order that persons or classes of persons may only obtain a copy of the claim form if it is edited in accordance with the directions of the court; or

(c) make such other order as it thinks fit.

(8) A person wishing to obtain a copy of a document under paragraph (3), (4) or (5) must pay any prescribed fee and –

(a) if the court's permission is required, file an application notice in accordance with Part 23; or

(b) if permission is not required, file a written request for the document.

(9) An application for permission to obtain a copy of a document, or for an order under paragraph (7), may be made without notice, but the court may direct notice to be given to any person who would be affected by its decision.

(10) Paragraphs (3) to (9) of this rule do not apply in relation to any proceedings in respect of which a rule or practice direction makes different provision.

Amendments—Substituted by SI 2004/2072; amended by SI 2005/2292.

Practice Direction—See generally PD5 at p 419.

Scope of provision—This covers requests for copies of documents either by the parties or any other person. There is also provision for computer searching for documents although, as yet, this facility is not available at county courts (PD5, para 4.1).

'A party' (r 5.4(3))—Any party who becomes *joined* to proceedings is entitled, without charge, to a copy of all relevant statements of case, written evidence and any appended documents to be supplied by the party joining him (PD5, para 3.1).

'Any other person' (r 5.4(5))—This means any member of the public or press. Note, however, that, in relation to statements of case, they are only entitled to a copy of the claim form. The right to inspect includes witness statements under r 32.13 that have been used as evidence in chief (r 32.13). The provision of r 5.4(2) is confined to the Supreme Court as there are not yet computer search facilities in the county court (PD5, para 4.5).

'any other document' (rr 5.4(4), (5)(b))—Note that if a party or any other person wants a copy of any other document they must request permission from the court. Such documents are limited to documents filed by the parties and communications between the court and a party, or any other person. Neither a party nor any other person can demand inspection of the whole file and demand a copy of any document. A person cannot make a general application under this rule: the documents or class of documents sought must be defined with 'reasonable clarity' (*Dian Ao v David Frankel & Mead* (a firm) [2004] EWHC 2662 (Comm), (2004) Lawtel, 11 October, QBD (Comm Ct)). 'Fishing expeditions' will not be permitted.

'a judgment or order given or made in public' (r 5.4(5)(a)(ii))—Thus, judgments etc given in chambers should not be disclosed. See *In re G (Minors) (Celebrities: Publicity)* (1998) *The Times*, October 28, CA where it was held that in certain circumstances freedom of speech takes precedence over the interests of any children involved when the question of the publication of a judge's decision is involved. Where documents are referred to 'in bulk' in a judicial decision, they may be taken to have been read in court in public (*Smithkline Beecham Biologicals v Connaught Labs Inc* [1999] 4 All ER 498, CA).

The definition of a 'judgment or order' has now been extended to the situation where a case settles part way through a trial (*Re: Guardian Newspapers Ltd (Court record: Disclosure)* [2004] TLR 602, (2004) *The Times*, 14 December, ChD). In such circumstances the records of the court are available for inspection under r 5.4(5)(b). It does not appear that the right to inspect is similarly available where a case settles before trial.

'application for permission' (r 5.4(9))—Application must be made under Pt 23 even if without notice. The application notice should identify the document in respect of which permission is sought and the grounds relied upon (PD5, para 4.4).

5.4A Supply of documents to Attorney-General from court records

(1) The Attorney-General may search for, inspect and take a copy of any documents within a court file for the purpose of preparing an application or considering whether to make an application under section 42 of the Supreme Court Act 1981 or section 33 of the Employment Tribunals Act 1996 (restriction of vexatious proceedings).

(2) The Attorney-General must, when exercising the right under paragraph (1) –

(a) pay any prescribed fee; and
(b) file written request, which must –
  (i) confirm that the request is for the purpose of preparing an application or considering whether to make an application mentioned in paragraph (1); and
  (ii) name the person who would be the subject of the application.

Amendments—Inserted by SI 2004/1306.

5.5 Filing and sending documents

(1) A practice direction may make provision for documents to be filed or sent to the court by –

(a) facsimile; or
(b) other electronic means.

(2) Any such practice direction may –

(a) provide that only particular categories of documents may be filed or sent to the court by such means;
(b) provide that particular provisions only apply in specific courts; and
(c) specify the requirements that must be fulfilled for any document filed or sent to the court by such means.

Amendments—Inserted by SI 2002/2058.

Practice Direction – Court Documents

This Practice Direction supplements CPR Part 5 (PD5)

SIGNATURE OF DOCUMENTS BY MECHANICAL MEANS

1 Where, under rule 5.3, a replica signature is printed electronically or by other mechanical means on any document, the name of the person whose signature is printed must also be printed so that the person may be identified. This paragraph does not apply to claim forms issued through the Claims Production Centre.

FORM OF DOCUMENTS

2.1 Statements of case and other documents drafted by a legal representative should bear his/her signature and if they are drafted by a legal representative as a member or employee of a firm they should be signed in the name of the firm.

2.2 Every document prepared by a party for filing or use at the court must:

(1) Unless the nature of the document renders it impracticable, be on A4 paper of durable quality having a margin, not less than 3.5 centimetres wide,
(2) be fully legible and should normally be typed,
(3) where possible be bound securely in a manner which would not hamper filing or otherwise each page should be endorsed with the case number,
(4) have the pages numbered consecutively,
(5) be divided into numbered paragraphs,

(6) have all numbers, including dates, expressed as figures, and
(7) give in the margin the reference of every document mentioned that has already been filed.

2.3 A document which is a copy produced by a colour photostat machine or other similar device may be filed at the court office provided that the coloured date seal of the court is not reproduced on the copy.

Rule 2.2(3)—Note that the requirement that documents must be bound with green tape or the like has now gone.

SUPPLY OF DOCUMENTS TO NEW PARTIES

3.1 Where a party is joined to existing proceedings, the party joined shall be entitled to require the party joining him to supply, without charge, copies of all statements of case, written evidence and any documents appended or exhibited to them which have been served in the proceedings by or upon the joining party which relate to any issues between the joining party and the party joined, and copies of all orders made in those proceedings. The documents must be supplied within 48 hours after a written request for them is received.

3.2 If the party joined is not supplied with copies of the documents requested under paragraph 3.1 within 48 hours, he may apply under Part 23 for an order that they be supplied.

3.3 The party by whom a copy is supplied under paragraph 3.1 or, if he is acting by a solicitor, his solicitor, shall be responsible for it being a true copy.

SUPPLY OF DOCUMENTS FROM COURT RECORDS

4.1 Registers of claims which have been issued are available for inspection at the following offices of the High Court at the Royal Courts of Justice:

(1) the Central Office of the Queen's Bench Division;
(2) Chancery Chambers.
(3) the Admiralty and Commercial Court Registry.

4.2 No registers of claims are at present available for inspection in county courts or in District Registries or other offices of the High Court.

4.2A A party to proceedings may, unless the court orders otherwise, obtain from the records of the court a copy of –

(a) a certificate of suitability of a litigation friend;
(b) a notice of funding;
(c) a claim form or other statement of case together with any documents filed with or attached to or intended by the claimant to be served with such claim form;
(d) an acknowledgment of service together with any documents filed with or attached to or intended by the party acknowledging service to be served with such acknowledgement of service;
(e) a certificate of service, other than a certificate of service of an application notice or order in relation to a type of application mentioned in sub-paragraph (h)(i) or (ii);
(f) a notice of non-service;
(g) an allocation questionnaire;
(h) an application notice, other than in relation to –
    (i) an application by a solicitor for an order declaring that he has ceased to be the solicitor acting for a party; or

(ii) an application for an order that the identity of a party or witness should not be disclosed;

(i) any written evidence filed in relation to an application, other than a type of application mentioned in sub-paragraph (h)(i) or (ii);

(j) a judgment or order given or made in public (whether made at a hearing or without a hearing);

(k) a statement of costs;

(l) a list of documents;

(m) a notice of payment into court;

(n) a notice of discontinuance;

(o) a notice of change; or

(p) an appellant's or respondent's notice of appeal.

4.3 An application under rule 5.4(4), 5.4(5)(b) or 5.4(6)(b)(ii) for permission to obtain a copy of a document, even if made without notice, must be made under CPR Part 23 and the application notice must identify the document or class of document in respect of which permission is sought and the grounds relied upon.

4.4 An application under rule 5.4(7) by a party or a person identified in a claim form must be made –

(1) under CPR Part 23; and

(2) to a Master or district judge, unless the court directs otherwise.

DOCUMENTS FOR FILING AT COURT

5.1 The date on which a document was filed at court must be recorded on the document. This may be done by a seal or a receipt stamp.

5.2 Particulars of the date of delivery at a court office of any document for filing and the title of the proceedings in which the document is filed shall be entered in court records, on the court file or on a computer kept in the court office for the purpose. Except where a document has been delivered at the court office through the post, the time of delivery should also be recorded.

5.3 Filing by Facsimile

(1) Subject to paragraph (6) below, a party may file a document at court by sending it by facsimile ('fax').

(2) Where a party files a document by fax, he must not send a hard copy in addition.

(3) A party filing a document by fax should be aware that the document is not filed at court until it is delivered by the court's fax machine, whatever time it is shown to have been transmitted from the party's machine.

(4) The time of delivery of the faxed document will be recorded on it in accordance with paragraph 5.2.

(5) It remains the responsibility of the party to ensure that the document is delivered to the court in time.

(6) If a fax is delivered after 4 pm it will be treated as filed on the next day the court office is open.

(7) If a fax relates to a hearing, the date and time of the hearing should be prominently displayed.

(8) Fax should not be used to send letters or documents of a routine or non-urgent nature.

SECTION 2 Civil Procedure Rules and Practice Directions

(9) Fax should not be used, except in an unavoidable emergency, to deliver:
  (a) a document which attracts a fee
  (b) a Part 36 payment notice
  (c) a document relating to a hearing less than two hours ahead
  (d) trial bundles or skeleton arguments.

(10) Where (9)(a) or (b) applies, the fax should give an explanation for the emergency and include an undertaking that the fee or money has been dispatched that day by post or will be paid at the court office counter the following business day.

(11) Where courts have several fax machines, each allocated to an individual section, fax messages should only be sent to the machine of the section for which the message is intended.

5.4 Where the court orders any document to be lodged in Court, the document must, unless otherwise directed, be deposited in the office of that Court.

5.5 A document filed, lodged or held in any court office shall not be taken out of that office without the permission of the court unless the document is to be sent to the office of another court (for example under CPR Part 30 (Transfer)), except in accordance with CPR rule 39.7 (impounded documents) or in accordance with paragraph 5.6 below.

5.6 (1) Where a document filed, lodged or held in a court office is required to be produced to any Court, tribunal or arbitrator, the document may be produced by sending it by registered post (together with a Certificate as in paragraph 5.6(8)(b)) to the court, tribunal or arbitrator in accordance with the provisions of this paragraph.

(2) Any Court, tribunal or arbitrator or any party requiring any document filed, lodged or held in any court office to be produced must apply to that court office by sending a completed request (as in paragraph 5.6(8)(a)), stamped with the prescribed fee.

(3) On receipt of the request the court officer will submit the same to a master in the Royal Courts of Justice or to a district judge elsewhere, who may direct that the request be complied with. Before giving a direction the master or district judge may require to be satisfied that the request is made in good faith and that the document is required to be produced for the reasons stated. The master or district judge giving the direction may also direct that, before the document is sent, an official copy of it is made and filed in the court office at the expense of the party requiring the document to be produced.

(4) On the direction of the master or district judge the court officer shall send the document by registered post addressed to the court, tribunal or arbitrator, with:
  (a) an envelope stamped and addressed for use in returning the document to the court office from which it was sent;
  (b) a Certificate as in paragraph 5.6(8)(b);
  (c) a covering letter describing the document, stating at whose request and for what purpose it is sent, referring to this paragraph of the practice direction and containing a request that the document be returned to the court office from which it was sent in the enclosed envelope as soon as the court or tribunal no longer requires it.

(5) It shall be the duty of the court, tribunal or arbitrator to whom the document was sent to keep it in safe custody, and to return it by

registered post to the court office from which it was sent, as soon as the court, tribunal or arbitrator no longer requires it.

(6) In each court office a record shall be kept of each document sent and the date on which it was sent and the court, tribunal or arbitrator to whom it was sent and the date of its return. It shall be the duty of the court officer who has signed the certificate referred to in para 5.6(8)(b) below to ensure that the document is returned within a reasonable time and to make inquiries and report to the master or district judge who has given the direction under paragraph (3) above if the document is not returned, so that steps may be taken to secure its return.

(7) Notwithstanding the preceding paragraphs, the master or district judge may direct a court officer to attend the court, tribunal or arbitrator for the purpose of producing the document.

(8) (a) I, ___ of ___, an officer of the ___ Court/Tribunal at ___/an arbitrator of ___/the Claimant/Defendant/Solicitor for the Claimant/Defendant [*describing the Applicant so as to show that he is a proper person to make the request*] in the case of ___ v ___ [19___ No ___]

REQUEST that the following document [or documents] be produced to the court/tribunal/arbitrator on the ___ day of 19___ [and following days] and I request that the said document [or documents] be sent by registered post to the proper officer of the court/tribunal/arbitrator for production to that Court/tribunal/arbitrator on that day.

(Signed).

Dated the ___ day of 1999/2___ .

(b) I, A.B., an officer of the ___ Court of ___ certify that the document sent herewith for production to the court/tribunal/arbitrator on the ___ day of ___ 1999/2___ in the case of ___ v ___ and marked 'A.B.' is the document requested on the ___ day of ___ 1999/2___ and I FURTHER CERTIFY that the said document has been filed in and is produced from the custody of the court.

(Signed)

Dated the ___ day of ___ 1999/2___ .

Date of receipt (paras 5.3, 5.4)—Noting the date is important because of the consequences that may flow if documents are not filed at court within required time limits.

'Subject to paragraph (6) below' (para 5.3(1))—This should presumably now refer not only to para (6), but also to paras (7)–(11) as well. This appears to have been missed by the draftsman of Update 13 (see below).

Service and filing by fax (para 5.3)—At the very least, practitioners should ensure that a fax arrives in plenty of time for any hearing to which it relates. Note that there is no guarantee that a fax will be before the court even if it is sent in sufficient time for the hearing (see para 5.3(5)).

ENROLMENT OF DEEDS AND OTHER DOCUMENTS

6.1 (1) Any deed or document which by virtue of any enactment is required or authorised to be enrolled in the Supreme Court may be enrolled in the Central Office of the High Court.

(2) Attention is drawn to the Enrolment of Deeds (Change of Name) Regulations 1994 which are reproduced in the Appendix to this practice direction.

6.2 The following paragraph of the practice direction describes the practice to be followed in any case in which a child's name is to be changed and to which the 1994 Regulations apply.

6.3 (1) Where a person has by any order of the High Court, county court or Family Proceedings Court been given parental responsibility for a child and applies to the Central Office, Filing Department, for the enrolment of a Deed Poll to change the surname (family name) of a child who is under the age of 18 years (unless a child who is or has been married or has formed a civil partnership), the application must be supported by the production of the consent in writing of every other person having parental responsibility.

(2) In the absence of that consent, the application will be adjourned generally unless and until permission is given in the proceedings, in which the said order was made, to change the surname of the child and the permission is produced to the Central Office.

(3) Where an application is made to the Central Office by a person who has not been given parental responsibility for a child by any order of the High Court, county court or Family Proceedings Court for the enrolment of a Deed Poll to change the surname of the child who is under the age of 18 years (unless the child is or has been married or has formed a civil partnership), permission of the court to enrol the Deed will be granted if the consent in writing of every person having parental responsibility is produced or if the person (or, if more than one, persons) having parental responsibility is dead or overseas or despite the exercise of reasonable diligence it has not been possible to find him or her for other good reason.

(4) In cases of doubt the Senior Master or, in his absence, the Practice Master will refer the matter to the Master of the Rolls.

(5) In the absence of any of the conditions specified above the Senior Master or the Master of the Rolls, as the case may be, may refer the matter to the Official Solicitor for investigation and report.

APPENDIX

Regulations made by the Master of the Rolls, Sir Thomas Bingham M.R. on March 3, 1994 (SI 1994 No 604) under s 133(1) of the Supreme Court Act 1981.

1 (1) These regulations may be cited as the Enrolment of Deeds (Change of Name) Regulations 1994 and shall come into force on April 1, 1994.

(2) These Regulations shall govern the enrolment in the Central Office of the Supreme Court of deeds evidencing change of name (referred to in these Regulations as 'deeds poll').

2 (1) A person seeking to enrol a deed poll ('the applicant') must be a Commonwealth citizen as defined by section 37(1) of the British Nationality Act 1981.

(2) If the applicant is a British citizen, a British Dependent Territories citizen or a British Overseas citizen, he must be described as such in the deed poll, which must also specify the section of the British Nationality Act under which the relevant citizenship was acquired.

(3) In any other case, the applicant must be described as a Commonwealth citizen.

(4) The applicant must be described in the deed poll as single, married,

widowed, divorced, a civil partner or former civil partner and, if a former civil partner, whether the civil partnership ended on death or dissolution.

3 (1) As proof of the citizenship named in the deed poll, the applicant must produce
(a) a certificate of birth; or
(b) a certificate of citizenship by registration or naturalisation or otherwise; or
(c) some other document evidencing such citizenship.
(2) In addition to the documents set out in paragraph (1), an applicant who is married or a civil partner must
(a) produce his certificate of marriage[or civil partnership certificate]; and
(b) show that the notice of his intention to apply for the enrolment of the deed poll had been given to his spouse or civil partner by delivery or by post to his spouse's or civil partner's last known address; and
(c) show that he has obtained the consent of his spouse or civil partner to the proposed change of name or that there is good reason why such consent should be dispensed with.

4 (1) The deed poll and the documents referred to in regulation 3 must be exhibited to a statutory declaration by a Commonwealth citizen who is a householder in the United Kingdom and who must declare that he is such in the statutory declaration.
(2) The statutory declaration must state the period, which should ordinarily not be less than 10 years, during which the householder has known the applicant and must identify the applicant as the person referred to in the documents exhibited to the statutory declaration.
(3) Where the period mentioned in paragraph (2) is stated to be less than 10 years, the Master of the Rolls may in his absolute discretion decide whether to permit the deed poll to be enrolled and may require the applicant to provide more information before so deciding.

5 If the applicant is resident outside the United Kingdom, he must provide evidence that such residence is not intended to be permanent and the applicant may be required to produce a certificate by a solicitor as to the nature and probable duration of such residence.

6 The applicant must sign the deed poll in both his old and new names.

7 Upon enrolment the deed poll shall be advertised in the London Gazette by the clerk in charge for the time being of the Filing and Record Department at the Central Office of the Supreme Court.

8 (1) Subject to the following provisions of this regulation, these Regulations shall apply in relation to a deed poll evidencing the change of name of a child as if the child were the applicant.
(2) Paragraphs (3) to (8) shall not apply to a child who has attained the age of 16 and is or has been married or a civil partner.
(3) If the child is under the age of 16, the deed poll must be executed by a person having parental responsibility for him.
(4) If the child has attained the age of 16, the deed poll must, except in the case of a person mentioned in paragraph (2), be executed by a person

having parental responsibility for the child and be endorsed with the child's consent signed in both his old and new names and duly witnessed.

(5) The application for enrolment must be supported –
  (a) by a witness statement showing that the change of name is for the benefit of the child, and
    (i) that the application is submitted by all persons having parental responsibility for the child; or
    (ii) that it is submitted by one person having parental responsibility for the child with the consent of every other person; or
    (iii) that it is submitted by one person having parental responsibility for the child without the consent of every other such person, or by some other person whose name and capacity are given, for reasons set out in the affidavit; and
  (b) by such other evidence, if any, as the Master of the Rolls may require in the particular circumstances of the case.

(6) Regulation 4(2) shall not apply but the statutory declaration mentioned in regulation 4(1) shall state how long the householder has known the deponent under paragraph (5)(a) and the child respectively.

(7) Regulation 6 shall not apply to a child who has not attained the age of 16.

(8) In this regulation 'parental responsibility' has the meaning given in section 3 of the Children Act 1989.

9 The Enrolment of Deeds (Change of Name) Regulations 1983 and the Enrolment of Deeds (Change of Name) (Amendment) Regulations 1990 are hereby revoked.

Practice Direction – Electronic Communication and Filing of Documents

This Practice Direction supplements CPR Rule 5.5 (PD5B)

Important—This latest version of the practice direction came into force on 1 May 2004.

GENERAL

1.1 Section I of this practice direction provides for parties to claims in specified courts to –

(1) communicate with the court by e-mail; and
(2) file specified documents by e-mail.

1.2 Section II of this practice direction provides for parties to claims in specified courts to file specified documents electronically via an online forms service.

1.3 Section III of this practice direction contains general provisions which apply to both Section I and Section II.

1.4 This practice direction does not allow –

(1) communication with the court or the filing of documents by e-mail; or
(2) use of the online forms service,

in proceedings to which the Civil Procedure Rules do not apply.

SECTION I – COMMUNICATION AND FILING OF DOCUMENTS BY E-MAIL

INTERPRETATION

2.1 For the purposes of this Section –

(1) a specified court is a court or court office which has published an e-mail address for the filing of documents on the Court Service website *www.courtservice.gov.uk* ('the Court Service website'); and

(2) a specified document is a document listed on the Court Service website as a document that may be sent to or filed in that court by e-mail.

Communications and documents which may be sent by e-mail

3.1 Subject to paragraph 3.2, a party to a claim in a specified court may send a specified document to the court by e-mail.

Service—This practice direction only provides for electronic filing and does not by itself authorise the use of e-mail for service on other parties, as to which see PD6, para 3.

3.2 Subject to paragraph 3.2A, a party must not use e-mail to take any step in a claim for which a fee is payable.

3.2A A party may make an application using e-mail in the Preston Combined Court, where he is permitted to do so by PREMA (Preston E-mail Application Service) User Guide and Protocols.

3.3 Subject to paragraph 3.3A, if –

(a) a fee is payable on the filing of a particular document; and

(b) a party purports to file that document by e-mail,

the court shall treat the document as not having been filed.

3.3A A party may file an application notice by e-mail in the Civil Appeals Office or in the Preston Combined Court where he is permitted to do so by PREMA (Preston E-mail Application Service) User Guide and Protocols.

(Rule 6.2(1)(e) permits service by e-mail in accordance with the relevant practice direction. Paragraph 3 of the Practice Direction accompanying Part 6 sets out the circumstances in which a party may serve a document by e-mail)

Service—The document is merely filed by e-mail and the need to effect service on other parties in the normal way should not be overlooked.

Fees—At this stage the Court Service has not developed a procedure for payment of the court fee electronically and credit is not available for fees.

TECHNICAL SPECIFICATIONS OF E-MAIL

4.1 The e-mail message must contain the name, telephone number and e-mail address of the sender and should be in plain text or rich text format rather than HTML.

Content—It is important that the court staff can identify the sender from the content of the e-mail without having to open any attachments.

Format—Messages in HTML format may be rejected, hence – where this has been set as the default – users will need to change the format when sending a message to the court.

Responses—Whilst any response from the court will normally be by e-mail, it is important that the court staff can readily identify and communicate by telephone with the sender should the need arise.

4.2 Correspondence and documents may be sent as either text in the body of the e-mail, or as attachments, except as mentioned in paragraph 4.3.

Use of attachments—The e-mail message is in effect the communication (or the covering letter when documents are being filed), although a letter may be included as an attachment and this may be appropriate if lengthy.

4.3 Documents required to be in a practice form must be sent in that form as attachments.

4.4 Court forms may be downloaded from the Court Service website.

Court forms—Those in general use are available in electronic form on the Court Service website.

4.5 Attachments must be sent in a format supported by the software used by the specified court to which it is sent. The format or formats which may be used in sending attachments to a particular specified court are listed on the Court Service website.

Format—Although *MS Word* is used on the computers in the court offices,, these have been programmed to read the most common file formats and these may be identified on the Court Service website. One of these must be used, otherwise the attachment may be unreadable and rejected.

Bespoke software—Documents produced by specialist software (eg *Laserforms*, *PeaPod Solutions*, *Oyez*) cannot be read on the court computers, so where available the document should be saved in *MS Word* format. If the software does not allow this the form may be printed and scanned as an image and attached in that form.

4.6 An attachment which is sent to a specified court in a format not listed on the Court Service website as appropriate for that court will be treated as not having been received by the court.

4.7 The length of attachments and total size of e-mail must not exceed the maximum which a particular specified court has indicated that it can accept. This information is listed on the Court Service website.

'the maximum' (para 4.7)—Currently, the largest e-mail which courts can accept is one of 2 Mb. Note that this limit applies to the e-mail including the attachment and, for technical reasons, this will significantly exceed the size of the document file before it was attached. It is unwise to attach a document file which exceeds (or document files which together exceed) 1.3 Mb.

4.8 Where proceedings have been commenced, the subject line of the e-mail must contain the following information –

(1) the case number;
(2) the parties' names (abbreviated if necessary); and
(3) the date and time of any hearing to which the e-mail relates.

SECTION II – ONLINE FORMS SERVICE

SCOPE AND INTERPRETATION

5.1 Reference to an online forms service is reference to a service available at *www.courtservice.gov.uk* ('the forms website'). The forms website contains certain documents which a user may complete online and then submit electronically to a specified court.

5.2 For the purposes of this Section –

(1) a specified court is a court or court office listed on the Court Service website as able to receive documents filed electronically via the online forms service; and
(2) a specified document is a document which is available for completion on the forms website.

FILING OF DOCUMENTS ONLINE

6.1 A party to a claim in a specified court may send a specified document to the court using the online forms service.

6.2 A party may use the online forms service to take a step in a claim for which a fee is payable. The fee must be paid, using the facilities available at the online forms service, before the application, or other document attracting a fee, is forwarded to the specified court.

6.3 The online forms service will assist the user in completing a document accurately but the user is responsible for ensuring that the rules and practice directions relating to the document have been complied with. Transmission by the service does not guarantee that the document will be accepted by the specified court.

SECTION III – GENERAL PROVISIONS

INTERPRETATION

7 In this Section –

(1) filing or sending a document 'electronically', means filing or sending it in accordance with Section I or Section II; and

(2) a reference to 'transmission' means, unless the context otherwise requires –

(a) in relation to Section I, the e-mail sent by the party to the court; and

(b) in relation to Section II, the electronic transmission of the form by the online forms service to the court.

PROVISIONS RELATING TO THE FILING OF DOCUMENTS ELECTRONICALLY

8.1 Where a party files a document electronically, he must not send a hard copy of that document to the court.

Hard copy—Provided that this practice direction is complied with, the document is duly filed when received by e-mail, so filing should not be duplicated in other ways. This would destroy the benefit of the new procedure being offered for the convenience of parties, as does the lodging of a hard copy following filing by fax.

8.2 A document is not filed until the transmission is received by the court, whatever time it is shown to have been sent.

8.3 The time of receipt of a transmission will be recorded electronically on the transmission as it is received.

8.4 If a transmission is received after 4 pm –

(1) the transmission will be treated as received; and

(2) any document attached to the transmission will be treated as filed,

on the next day the court office is open.

Day of receipt—This brings e-mailed documents into line with documents lodged in other ways.

8.5 A party –

(1) sending an e-mail in accordance with Section I; or

(2) using the online forms service in accordance with Section II,

is responsible for ensuring that the transmission or any document attached to it is filed within any relevant time limits.

Filing on time—It is the obligation of the party to ensure that any time-critical document is received on time and, whilst e-mail may be an efficient method of filing, it should not be thought of as a means of circumventing this obligation.

8.6 The court will normally reply by e-mail where –

(1) the response is to a message transmitted electronically; and
(2) the sender has provided an e-mail address.

8.7 Parties are advised not to transmit electronically any correspondence or documents of a confidential or sensitive nature, as security cannot be guaranteed.

Security—Once the e-mail reaches the GSI (Government Secure Intranet) it is secure, but the link between this and the sender is on the public Internet which is vulnerable to access by others. Encryption technology has not yet been made available, so if the sender has any concerns about privacy, then traditional methods of filing documents should be adopted.

8.8 If a document transmitted electronically requires urgent attention, the sender should contact the court by telephone.

8.9 A document that is required by a rule or practice direction to be filed at court is not filed when it is sent to the judge by e-mail.

STATEMENT OF TRUTH IN DOCUMENTS FILED ELECTRONICALLY

9 Where a party wishes to file a document containing a statement of truth electronically, that party should retain the document containing the original signature and file with the court a version of the document satisfying one of the following requirements –

(1) the name of the person who has signed the statement of truth is typed underneath the statement;
(2) the person who has signed the statement of truth has applied a facsimile of his signature to the statement in the document by mechanical means; or
(3) the document that is filed is a scanned version of the document containing the original signature to the statement of truth.

Statement of truth—It is important that the party filing a document required to be verified by a statement of truth should retain the original signed document in case an issue arises about such verification. This is most likely to occur at trial (or other contested hearing) and, therefore, those documents should be available at such a hearing.

'scanned version' (para 9(3))—The limit on size of e-mail will rule out the use of scanned images of documents of any length.

PART 6
SERVICE OF DOCUMENTS

CONTENTS OF THIS PART

Procedural Guide—See Guide 15, set out in Section 1 of this work.

Practice Direction—See generally PD6 at p 462.

Introduction—This Part sets out the general method of serving documents in the course of proceedings. It follows the format of CCR Ord 7 and is divided into three sections. Rules 6.1–6.11 deal with the general principles of service. Rules 6.12–6.16 deal specifically with service of the claim form which may have been started under Pt 7 (How to Start Proceedings), Pt 8 (Alternative Procedure for Claims), or Pt 20 (Counterclaims and other Additional Claims). Rules 6.17–6.31 now integrate provisions about service out of the jurisdiction, in place of RSC Ord 11 which has been revoked.

The rules for service of proceedings, as amended and as interpreted in judgments of the Court of Appeal, set out a new procedural code sweeping aside the pre-CPR practice differentiating between an irregular judgment (which would be set aside as of right) and a regular judgment (where the defendant had to show that he had a defence on the merits before the court would set the judgment aside). The new code:

(i) identifies the place of service at which a document can properly be served (see the table in r 6.5), being the 'usual or last known residence' in the case of an individual;

(ii) provides that a document served in accordance with the CPR or any relevant practice direction is deemed to be served on the day shown in the table in r 6.7;

(iii) no longer provides in r 6.10 that a certificate of service must state that the document has not been returned undelivered;

(iv) makes it clear that the difference between a default judgment wrongly entered (which must be set aside – see r 13.2) and any other default judgment (which may only be set aside if one of the conditions set out in r 13.3(1) is satisfied and the application was made promptly) depends on whether the procedural steps required by r 12.3 were or were not followed (including service as defined by Pt 6); and

(v) in the case of such an 'other' default judgment, leaves the court with a discretion under r 13.3 even if the claim has never come to the attention of the defendant.

There is nothing in the new code which contravenes the European Convention on Human Rights, Art 6 (*Akram v Adam* [2004] EWCA Civ 1601, [2004] TLR 633, at paras [32]–[34]).

I General Rules about Service

6.1 Part 6 rules about service apply generally

The rules in this Part apply to the service of documents, except where –

(a) any other enactment, a rule in another Part, or a practice direction makes a different provision; or

(b) the court orders otherwise.

(For service in possession claims, see Part 55)

Amendments—SI 2005/2292.

Scope of provision—The court may 'order otherwise' by r 6.8 – service by an alternative method.

Related provisions—'Any other enactment'. These include:

(a) Companies Act 1985, ss 694A, 695 and 725;

(b) Crown Proceedings Act 1947, ss 17 and 18;

(c) Immunity Act 1978, s 12.

'a rule in another Part' (r 6.1(a))—Schedule 1: RSC Ord 10, r 4, Possession Proceedings; RSC Ord 30, r 4, Receivers; RSC Ord 52, Committal; RSC Ord 54, Writ of Habeas Corpus; RSC Ord 69, Service of Foreign Process; RSC Ord 77, r 4, Service on the Crown; RSC Ord 97, Landlord & Tenant Acts; RSC Ord 106, Solicitors Act 1974.

Schedule 2: CCR Ord 7, rr 15, 15A, Recovery of Land; CCR Ord 33, Interpleader; CCR Ord 43, Landlord and Tenant Acts; CCR Ord 45, Application for Detailed Assessment of Returning Officers Account; CCR Ord 47, Application for use of Blood Tests; CCR Ord 48B, Order for Enforcement of Parking Penalties; CCR Ord 49, Notice of Repair under Chancel Repairs Act 1932.

Enforcement proceedings—Specific service rules in Schs 1 and 2 deal with these proceedings.

Part 36 offers—Rules for formal service of documents contained in Pt 6 do not apply to the making of a Pt 36 offer. It is sufficient that the offer is communicated in writing to the offeree and that the offeree receives it (*Charles (Denise) v NTL Group Ltd* (2002) Lawtel, 13 December, CA).

6.2 Methods of service – general

(1) A document may be served by any of the following methods –

(a) personal service, in accordance with rule 6.4;
(b) first class post;
(c) leaving the document at a place specified in rule 6.5;
(d) through a document exchange in accordance with the relevant practice direction; or
(e) by fax or other means of electronic communication in accordance with the relevant practice direction.

(Rule 6.8 provides for the court to permit service by an alternative method)

(2) A company may be served by any method permitted under this Part as an alternative to the methods of service set out in –

(a) section 725 of the Companies Act 1985 (service by leaving a document at or posting it to an authorised place);
(b) section 695 of that Act (service on overseas companies); and
(c) section 694A of that Act (service of documents on companies incorporated outside the UK and Gibraltar and having a branch in Great Britain).

Practice Direction—The supplementing practice direction – PD6 – deals in particular with:
(a) 6.2(1)(a) personal service – on partners PD6, para 4 at p 463; companies or other corporations PD6, para 6 at p 464.
(b) 6.2(1)(d) service by document exchange PD6, para 2 at p 462.
(c) 6.2(1)(e) service by fax and other electronic method PD6, para 3 at p 463.

Scope of provision—Rule 6.2(1) sets out the methods by which documents can be served. In general, these methods are well established and similar to RSC Ord 10 and CCR Ord 7. First-class post must be used when postal service is effected (r 6.2(1)(b)). Provision is made by r 6.8 to permit service by an alternative method.

The list of methods of service in this rule is exhaustive, unless the court permits an alternative under r 6.8 (*Anderton v Clwyd County Council* [2002] EWCA Civ 933, [2002] 3 All ER 813, CA at [68]).

'by fax or other means of electronic communication in accordance with the relevant practice direction' (r 6.2(1)(e))—The placement of a fax number on a standard company letterhead did not indicate that the company would accept service of proceedings by fax for the purposes of r 6.2(1)(e) and PD6, para 3.1 (*Molins plc v GD SpA* (2000) *The Times*, 29 March, CA).

Section 725, Companies Act 1985—Service of documents by leaving, sending or posting to the company's registered office.

Section 695, Companies Act 1985—Service of documents on overseas companies. Permits service on a person at the address listed on the file lodged with the Registrar of Companies.

Section 694A, Companies Act 1985—Service on overseas company at the British registered branch.

The position has now reverted to what it was before s 694A was enacted, namely that process can be served on a foreign company with a place of business in, say, London without the necessity for establishing any link between the process and the business being conducted in London (*Saab & anor v Saudi American Bank* [1999] 1 WLR 1861, CA).

Claims for possession of property under Part 55—Normal rules for service apply but note that PD55, para 2.6 sets out additional requirements where the claim is for possession of property against trespassers.

6.3 Who is to serve

(1) The court will serve a document which it has issued or prepared except where –

(a) a rule provides that a party must serve the document in question;
(b) the party on whose behalf the document is to be served notifies the court that he wishes to serve it himself;
(c) a practice direction provides otherwise;
(d) the court orders otherwise; or
(e) the court has failed to serve and has sent a notice of non-service to the party on whose behalf the document is to be served in accordance with rule 6.11.

(2) Where the court is to serve a document, it is for the court to decide which of the methods of service specified in rule 6.2 is to be used.

(3) Where a party prepares a document which is to be served by the court, that party must file a copy for the court, and for each party to be served.

Practice Direction—See PD6, para 8 at p 465.

General note—Paragraph 8 of PD6 provides that the appropriate method of service by the court will be first-class post and that on receipt of notice of non-service the court is under no further duty to effect service.

Scope of provision—In both High Court and county court proceedings service by the court is the general rule. It is for the court to determine which of the methods of service specified in r 6.2 is to be used. Service by first-class post will be the normal method of service. A party must file with the court sufficient copies of the document for the court and for each party to be served (r 6.3(3)). A party who wishes to serve a document in place of the court must notify the court of his intention to do so (r 6.3(1)(b)).

'Notice of non-service' (r 6.3(1)(e))—See r 6.11. For the form of notice, see Form N216. On receipt, the party has the option of:
(a) providing the court with additional information to enable the court to effect service;
(b) arranging service himself – r 6.3(1)(b);
(c) obtaining an order for service by an alternative method – r 6.8.

'Where the court is to serve a document' (r 6.3(2))—Note PD6, para 8.3 requires the court now to serve or deliver a copy of any notice of funding that has been filed, provided it was filed correctly and copies were provided for service.

Bailiff service—Service by county court bailiff is proved by a bailiff's certificate pursuant to County Courts Act 1984, s 133(1).

6.4 Personal service

(1) A document to be served may be served personally, except as provided in paragraphs (2) and (2A).

(2) Where a solicitor –

(a) is authorised to accept service on behalf of a party; and
(b) has notified the party serving the document in writing that he is so authorised,

a document must be served on the solicitor, unless personal service is required by an enactment, rule, practice direction or court order.

(2A) In civil proceedings by or against the Crown, as defined in rule 66.1(2), documents required to be served on the Crown may not be served personally.

(3) A document is served personally on an individual by leaving it with that individual.

(4) A document is served personally on a company or other corporation by leaving it with a person holding a senior position within the company or corporation.

(The service practice direction sets out the meaning of 'senior position')

(5) A document is served personally on a partnership where partners are being sued in the name of their firm by leaving it with –

(a) a partner; or
(b) a person who, at the time of service, has the control or management of the partnership business at its principal place of business.

Amendments—SI 2005/2292.

Party—A person does not become 'a party' until he has been served with the proceedings but see r 6.13 below.

Service on solicitor—Where a party has a solicitor who has notified the serving party that he is authorised to accept service, the only method of service is upon that solicitor. A solicitor will be considered to be acting for a party until an application is made in accordance with Pt 42 or Form N434 (Change of Solicitor) is served. The solicitor's address must be an address for service within the jurisdiction (r 6.5(2)). Examples of situations where the court may order personal service on a party represented by a solicitor are: an Order endorsed with Penal Notice for committal (Sch 1, RSC Ord 52 and Sch 2, CCR Ord 29)

Service on members of HM Forces and United States Airforce—See the PD6, para 5 – the Annex deals with service of process on regular members of Her Majesty's Forces and members of the United States Airforce.

Personal service on a Company—Paragraph 6.2 of PD6 defines who is a 'person holding a senior position'. Paragraph 6.2(2) deals with corporations which are not registered companies.

Partners—Paragraph 4.1 of PD6 relates to partners who are sued in the name of the partnership and allows personal service on:
(a) a partner;
(b) a person who at the time of service has the control or management of the partnership business at its principal place of business.

Change of address—See PD6, para 7 which requires parties or their legal representatives to give notice in writing of the change as soon as possible to the court and to every other party.

6.5 Address for service

(1) Except as provided by Section III of this Part (service out of the jurisdiction) a document must be served within the jurisdiction.

('Jurisdiction' is defined in rule 2.3)

(2) A party must give an address for service within the jurisdiction.

(3) Where a party –

(a) does not give the business address of his solicitor as his address for service; and
(b) resides or carries on business within the jurisdiction,

he must give his residence or place of business as his address for service.

(4) Any document to be served –

(a) by first class post;
(b) by leaving it at the place of service;
(c) through a document exchange;
(d) by fax or by other means of electronic communication,

must be sent or transmitted to, or left at, the address for service given by the party to be served.

(5) Where –

(a) a solicitor is acting for the party to be served; and
(b) the document to be served is not the claim form;

the party's address for service is the business address of his solicitor.

(Rule 6.13 specifies when the business address of a defendant's solicitor may be the defendant's address for service in relation to the claim form)

(6) Where –

(a) no solicitor is acting for the party to be served; and
(b) the party has not given an address for service,

the document must be sent or transmitted to, or left at, the place shown in the following table.

(Rule 6.2(2) sets out the statutory methods of service on a company)

Nature of party to be served	Place of service
Individual	Usual or last known residence.
Proprietor of a business	Usual or last known residence; or Place of business or last known place of business.
Individual who is suing or being sued in the name of a firm	Usual or last known residence; or Principal or last known place of business of the firm.
Corporation incorporated in England and Wales other than a company	Principal office of the corporation; or Any place within the jurisdiction where the corporation carries on its activities and which has a real connection with the claim.
Company registered in England and Wales	Principal office of the company; or Any place of business of the company within the jurisdiction which has a real connection with the claim.
Any other company or corporation	Any place within the jurisdiction where the corporation carries on its activities; or Any place of business of the company within the jurisdiction.

(7) This rule does not apply where an order made by the court under rule 6.8 (service by an alternative method) specifies where the document in question may be served.

(Rule 42.1 provides that if the business address of his solicitor is given that solicitor will be treated as acting for that party)

(8) In civil proceedings by or against the Crown, as defined in rule 66.1(2) –

(a) service on the Attorney General must be effected on the Treasury Solicitor;
(b) service on a government department must be effected on the solicitor acting for that department as required by section 18 of the Crown Proceedings Act 1947.

(The practice direction to Part 66 gives the list published under section 17 of that Act of the solicitors acting for the different government departments on whom service is to be effected, and of their addresses).

Amendments—SI 2000/221; SI 2000/2092; SI 2005/2292.

Prospective amendment—By virtue of the Civil Procedure (Amendment No 3) Rules 2005, SI 2005/2292, in para (2), after 'A party must give an address for service within the jurisdiction.', there is inserted –

> 'Such address must include a full postcode, unless the court orders otherwise.
>
> (Paragraph 2.4 of the Practice Direction to Part 16 contains provision about the content of an address for service).',

with effect from 6 April 2006.

Scope of provision—The rule distinguishes between parties represented by a solicitor and those acting in person.

To effect service on a solicitor, the solicitor must:

(a) be authorised to accept service on behalf of the party; and

(b) have notified the serving party in writing that he is so authorised (r 6.4(2)).

The solicitor's business address must be within the jurisdiction.

Rule 6.13 specifically deals with when the defendant's solicitor can be served with the claim form. A party not acting by a solicitor must given an address for service within the jurisdiction which must be his residential address or place of business.

If a solicitor is not acting for the party to be served or the party has not given an address for service the document should be served at the place shown in the table in r 6.5(6).

'Usual or last known residence' (r 6.5(6) table)—Part 6 has not changed the fundamental rule of English procedure and jurisdiction that a defendant can be served with originating process within the jurisdiction only if he is present in the jurisdiction at the time of service or deemed service. Although Pt 6 contains general rules about service of documents and does not only apply to service of a claim form, r 6.5 has not swept away the general principle so far as it relates to service of the claim form (*Chellaram & anor v Chellaram & ors (No 2)* [2002] EWHC 632 (Ch), [2002] 3 All ER 17, ChD, Lawrence Collins, J).

In *Cranfield Bridgegrove Ltd* [2003] EWCA Civ 656, [2003] 1 WLR 2441 the Court of Appeal clarified any uncertainty where the defendant was no longer residing at his last known residence and had not, in fact, received the claim. Dyson LJ, who gave the judgment of the court said, at paras [101]–[103]:

> 'There are two conditions precedent for the operation of the provisions of rule 6.5(6), namely that (a) no solicitor is acting for the party to be served, and (b) the party has not given an address for service. If those conditions are satisfied, then the rule states that the document to be sent must be sent or transmitted to, or left at, the place shown in the table. In the case of an individual, that means at his or her usual or last known residence. The rule is plain and unqualified. We see no basis for holding that, if the two conditions are satisfied, and the document is sent to that address, that does not amount to good service. The rule does not say that it is not good service if the defendant does not in fact receive the document. If that had been intended to be the position, the rule would have said so in terms. Nor can we see any basis for holding that, if the claimant knows or believes that the defendant is no longer living at his or her last known residence, service may not be effected by sending the claim form, or leaving it at, that address. That would be to fly in the face of the clear words of the rule. The rule is intended to provide a clear and straightforward mechanism for effecting service where the two conditions precedent to which we have referred are satisfied.'

A judgment following service compliant with Pt 6 can only be set aside as a matter of discretion under r 13.3 if the defendant can show that he has a real prospect of defending the claim or there is some other good reason why the court should intervene. That interpretation does not contravene the European Convention on Human Rights, Art 6 (*Akram v Adam* [2004] EWCA Civ 1601, [2004] TLR 633).

'last known place of business' (r 6.6(6) table)—This means the last place of business known to the claimant. To obtain the requisite knowledge, the claimant has to take reasonable steps to ascertain the defendant's current place of business or the last known place of business (*Spade Lane Cool Stores Ltd v Kilgour* (2004) Lawtel, 25 June, QBD).

'any place' (r 6.5(6) table)—The Court of Appeal has approved the lower court's finding that the test for the place where a corporation 'carries on its activities' or a company has 'any place of business' for the purposes of r 6.5(6) is effectively the same, and service on an address with which the company has no more than a transient or irregular connection will not be valid (*(1) Lakah Group (2) Ramy Lakah v (1) Al Jazeera Satellite Channel (2) Ahmed Mansour* [2003] EWCA (Civ) 1781, (2003) Lawtel, 9 December, CA).

Related provision—Part 6, Section III, Special Provisions about Service out of the Jurisdiction. These rules provide for service out of the jurisdiction in both High Court and county court. 'jurisdiction' means England and Wales and any part of the territorial waters of the United Kingdom adjoining England and Wales (r 2.3(1)).

Registered Companies—The addresses for service referred to in r 6.5(6) are alternatives to and not in place of those prescribed by the CA 1985. The statutory methods are usually conclusive as to service: consequently the methods prescribed in r 6.5(6) should be used with caution particularly where the consequences of failing to prove good service of a claim form or document could be serious for the claimant.

Partners—Paragraph 4 of PD6, deals with service on partners sued in the name of a partnership.

Nominating solicitors to accept service—Where, during the period of validity of a claim form, a defendant nominated solicitors to accept service of documents, the claimant was obliged to serve the claim form on those solicitors so that service on the defendant direct was invalid. Moreover, applying *Vinos v Marks & Spencer plc* [2000] 1 WLR 1311, [2000] 2 All ER 801, the court had no power to extend time for service under r 7.6 outside the 4-month validity of the claim form (*Nanglegan (Carmelita) v The Royal Free Hampstead NHS Trust* [2001] EWCA Civ 127, (2001) Lawtel, 23 January, CA).

Late service of a claim form—The court's limited discretion to extend time for service after the period prescribed in r 7.5 has expired is Draconian. Once a claim is issued (especially close to the expiry of any period of limitation) getting it properly and timeously served must have top priority. The tactic of holding back is not recommended.

6.6 Service of documents on children and patients

(1) The following table shows the person on whom a document must be served if it is a document which would otherwise be served on a child or a patient –

Type of document	Nature of party	Person to be served
Claim form	Child who is not also a patient	One of the child's parents or guardians; or if there is no parent or guardian, the person with whom the child resides or in whose care the child is.
Claim form	Patient	The person authorised under Part VII of the Mental Health Act 1983 to conduct the proceedings in the name of the patient or on his behalf; or if there is no person so authorised, the person with whom the patient resides or in whose care the patient is.

Type of document	Nature of party	Person to be served
Application for an order appointing a litigation friend, where a child or patient has no litigation friend	Child or patient	See rule 21.8.
Any other document	Child or patient	The litigation friend who is conducting proceedings on behalf of the child or patient.

(2) The court may make an order permitting a document to be served on the child or patient, or on some person other than the person specified in the table in this rule.

(3) An application for an order under paragraph (2) may be made without notice.

(4) The court may order that, although a document has been served on someone other than the person specified in the table, the document is to be treated as if it had been properly served.

(5) This rule does not apply where the court has made an order under rule 21.2(3) allowing a child to conduct proceedings without a litigation friend.

(Part 21 contains rules about the appointment of a litigation friend)

Scope of provision—The general principle is that a document in proceedings cannot be served on a patient as if he were not a patient, and if it is so served the proceedings based on it are invalid (*Cutbush v Cutbush* (1893) 37 Sol Jo 685). The principle is likely to apply also to a child. This rule makes special provision for service upon a child or a patient. Service is effected in the normal way upon the category of person specified.

'child'; 'patient' (r 6.6 generally)—See the notes to r 21.1.

Person to be served—Where there is no parent or guardian (for a child) or person authorised (for a patient – see r 21.4(2)), the claim form is to be served on 'the person with whom he resides or in whose care he is'. Once a litigation friend has been appointed (r 21.2), service of documents will be on that person, or the solicitor on the record instructed by that person (if any), in the usual way unless it is an application relating to the appointment of the litigation friend (r 21.8).

'the person with whom [the child or patient] resides or in whose care [the child or patient] is' (r 6.6(1))—The purpose of this provision is to reach a responsible adult who will be concerned to ensure that the child or patient is properly represented in the proceedings and will initiate the appointment of a litigation friend. There will seldom be a problem in the case of a child. In cases of difficulty involving a patient, in addition to attempts at formal service it may be prudent to communicate with any person concerned as to the welfare of the patient in the hope that a suitable representative will emerge. A person cannot be in the care of someone who is himself a patient so where several such persons share a home (eg under supervision) it will be necessary to look beyond the occupants of the home (eg to the persons who provide the supervision). Occupants of a residential care or nursing home will be in the care of the registered proprietor who should bring the proceedings to the attention of any concerned person. If such care is funded by the local authority it would be appropriate to involve the social services department which will have carried out a Community Care assessment of need. Service on a proper officer of the local social services authority or other guardian when the patient is under a guardianship order, or the district health authority when the patient has been compulsorily admitted to hospital under Mental Health Act 1983, may be sufficient. Where no-one can be identified, it is possible to resort to the provision for deemed service (see note below) thereby ensuring that the problem is brought before the court. When there is no response to due service the need for a litigation friend will have to be addressed by the court in any event. Reference may be made to the Official Solicitor in case of continuing difficulty as he may need to be appointed (see notes to r 21.4).

Communication to patient—There is no general requirement for service upon the patient, nor for the court to be satisfied that the proceedings have been brought to the attention of that person. This is surprising because this individual may wish to dispute being a patient or alert some particular person to take steps on his behalf (eg seek appointment as litigation friend). The proceedings may be conducted without a solicitor or the knowledge of the party considered to be a patient notwithstanding that little evidence is required of mental disorder or incapacity and the court may not have enquired into this. It seems that the prospect of an indemnity by the litigation friend (and the fact that the proceedings may be of no effect if the party is not a patient) is regarded as sufficient, but this is little reassurance to any of those involved especially as to the uncertainty that so often arises as to whether or not an individual is to be treated as a patient. In cases of doubt it would be prudent to serve that individual also.

The Court of Appeal has recommended a change in the rules so that a person cannot become a patient without knowing what is going on (*Masterman-Lister v Brutton & Co and Jewell & anor* [2002] EWCA Civ 1889, [2002] All ER (D) 297 (Dec)). It would, therefore, be good practice to ensure that the patient is notified and the court may require confirmation of this.

Deemed service—The provision for deemed service enables the court to proceed with the appointment of a litigation friend when service is not otherwise possible.

6.7 Deemed service

(1) A document which is served in accordance with these rules or any relevant practice direction shall be deemed to be served on the day shown in the following table –

Method of service	Deemed day of service
First class post	The second day after it was posted.
Document exchange	The second day after it was left at the document exchange.
Delivering the document to or leaving it at a permitted address	The day after it was delivered to or left at the permitted address.
Fax	If it is transmitted on a business day before 4 pm, on that day; or In any other case, on the business day after the day on which it is transmitted.
Other electronic method	The second day after the day on which it is transmitted.

(2) If a document is served personally –

(a) after 5 pm, on a business day; or

(b) at any time on a Saturday, Sunday or a Bank Holiday,

it will be treated as being served on the next business day.

(3) In this rule –

'business day' means any day except Saturday, Sunday or a bank holiday; and

'bank holiday' includes Christmas Day and Good Friday.

Amendments—SI 2000/221; SI 2005/2292.

Scope of provision—The presumed date of service for any particular method is shown in tabular form (r 6.7(1)). There is now no restriction upon what date or at what time a document can be served.

'Delivering the document to or leaving it at a permitted address' (r 6.7(1))—Note that when this method of service is used, service is deemed the following day. This may present a trap for the unwary who may be tempted merely to deliver a document to an office on the last permitted day for service.

'Rule 2.8' (note to r 6.7(1))—The Court of Appeal has now held that Saturdays and Sundays are not excluded from the calculation of the day of deemed service by first-class post. Neither r 2.8 itself, nor the bracketed summary of its effect inserted in r 6.7 produces that result (*Anderton v Clwyd County Council* [2002] EWCA Civ 933, [2002] 3 All ER 813, CA).

The effect of this rule may be summarised by the following examples:

Date served	Date deemed served under r 6.7 by:					
	First-class post	DX	Delivery	Fax (before 4 pm)	Fax (other case)	Electronic method
Mon	Wed	Wed	Tue	Mon	Tue	Wed
Tue	Thu	Thu	Wed	Tue	Wed	Thu
Wed	Fri	Fri	Thu	Wed	Thu	Fri
Thu	Sat	Mon	Fri	Thu	Fri	Mon
Fri	Sun	Tue	Mon	Fri	Mon	Tue

'a document is served personally' (r 6.7(2))—Before 2 May 2000, this provision did not apply to service of a claim form. Now, all documents will be treated in the same way.

'bank holiday' (r 6.7(3))—Bank holiday or holiday under Banking and Financial Dealings Act 1971 includes Christmas Day and Good Friday.

'business day' (r 6.7(3))—Is defined as any day except Saturday, Sunday or a bank holiday.

Deemed to be served—The deemed day of service of a document under r 6.7(1) is not rebuttable by evidence proving that service has actually been effected on a different day. An extension of time cannot be granted to extricate the claimant from the consequences of late service where r 7.6(3) is unavailable – *Godwin v Swindon Borough Council* [2001] EWCA Civ 1478, [2001] 4 All ER 641, CA; disapproving *Infantino v Maclean* [2001] 3 All ER 802, (2001) *The Times*, 20 July. Per May LJ at [46]:

> '[T]he provision in r 6.7(1) that "a document … shall be deemed to be served on the day shown in the following table" and the heading to the second column in the table "Deemed day of service" clearly mean that, for each of the five methods of service, the day to be derived from the second column is to be treated as the day on which the document is served. It is a fiction in the sense that you do not look to the day on which the document actually arrived, be it earlier or later than the date to be derived from the table.'

Godwin was followed in *Anderton v Clwyd County Council* [2002] EWCA Civ 933, [2002] 3 All ER 813, the Court of Appeal further holding that the position is unaffected by the HRA 1998 and ECHR, Art 6.

Serving Money Claims Online—Claims served electronically under the Pilot Scheme for Money Claims Online (see Guide 4 and PD7E) are deemed to be served on the fifth day after the claim was issued, irrespective of whether that day is a business day or not (PD7E, para 5.7).

Related provisions—For the definition of 'time', see r 2.8 and the examples given.

6.8 Service by an alternative method

(1) Where it appears to the court that there is a good reason to authorise service by a method not permitted by these Rules, the court may make an order permitting service by an alternative method.

(2) An application for an order permitting service by an alternative method –

(a) must be supported by evidence; and
(b) may be made without notice.

(3) An order permitting service by an alternative method must specify –

(a) the method of service; and
(b) the date when the document will be deemed to be served.

Practice Direction—See PD6 at p 462.

General note—Paragraph 9.1 of PD6 deals with the content of evidence required on an application for an order for service by an alternative method.

Scope of provision—This was previously known as 'substituted service' (RSC Ord 65, r 4 and CCR Ord 7, r 8). An application is to be made without notice but must be supported by evidence. The only question to be decided on an application for service by an alternative method is whether service by the prescribed methods (r 6.2) is impracticable.

The order permitting service by an alternative method must specify the method and the date the document will be deemed to be served.

Related provision—Part 23 – Applications; Rule 32.6 – Evidence in Proceedings other than at Trial; PD32, paras 17–20; RSC Ord 10, r 4; CCR Ord 7, r 15.

Correcting past errors—Where the claimant mistakenly served a claim form on the defendant's insurers rather than the defendant and no order under r 6.8 had been made the court had no power to correct the mistake under r 3.10 and the action failed. Rule 6.8 was intended to be used prospectively rather than retrospectively and could not be applied to correct a past error in service (*Elmes v Hygrade Food Products plc* [2001] EWCA Civ 121, [2001] All ER (D) 158, CA).

'good reason to authorise service' (r 6.8(1))—In *Knauf UK GmbH v British Gypsum Ltd* [2001] EWCA Civ 1570 (at [59]), [2001] 2 All ER (Comm) 960, CA postal service on a German company's UK agents was considered speedier and might have pre-empted the commencement of proceedings abroad. The Court of Appeal held that there cannot be a good reason for ordering service in England by an alternative method on a foreign defendant when, in the absence of any difficulty about effecting service, such an order subverts – and is designed to subvert – the principles on which service and jurisdiction are regulated by agreement between the United Kingdom and its Convention partners.

Forms—For an order for substituted service – N217.

6.9 Power of court to dispense with service

(1) The court may dispense with service of a document.

(2) An application for an order to dispense with service may be made without notice.

Scope of provision—This rule gives the court a general power to 'dispense with service' of a document. This is likely to be used where the party to be served is aware of the substance of the document, for example on application to amend the statement of case the court may dispense of service of that document.

Dispensing retrospectively—The Court of Appeal has given guidance on the manner in which the court should exercise its r 6.9 discretion in *Godwin v Swindon Borough* Council [2001] EWCA Civ 1478, [2002] 1 WLR 997, CA, *Anderton v Clwyd County Council* [2002] EWCA Civ 933, [2002] 1 WLR 3174, *Wilkey v British Broadcasting Corporation* [2002] EWCA Civ 1561, [2002] 4 All ER 1177, CA and, most recently *Cranfield & anor v Bridgegrove Ltd; Claussen v Yeates; McManus v Sharif; Murphy v Staples UK Ltd; Smith v Hughes & anor* [2003] EWCA Civ 656, [2003] 1 WLR 2441, CA. The following principles can now be derived from these cases:

(1) The vast majority of applications in which it would be appropriate to make an order to dispense with service will be for prospective orders, sought and granted before the end of the period for service.
(2) There is power under r 6.9 to dispense with service of the claim form retrospectively as well as prospectively. However, it is only exercisable retrospectively, ie after the end of the period for service, in exceptional circumstances.
(3) *'Category 1' cases* – Where a claimant has not even attempted to serve a claim form in time by one of the methods permitted by r 6.2, he will not be excused.
(4) *'Category 2' cases before 3 July 2002* – Where, before the *Anderton* judgment, a claimant has in fact already made an ineffective attempt in time to serve a claim form by one of the methods allowed by r 6.2, and where the defendant does not dispute that he or his legal adviser has in fact received it, the claimant should be excused altogether from the need to prove service of the claim form in accordance with the rules. Nonetheless, the court will not dispense if the defendant can establish prejudice or some other good reason why the power should not be exercised. Avoidable delay in the issue or service of the claim form or that the claim looks unpromising will not generally constitute such good reason.
(5) *'Category 2' cases after 3 July 2002* – In *Anderton* the Court of Appeal closed the door on the further exercise of r 6.9 as a means of avoiding the Draconian effects of failure to observe the rules for service of a claim form, stating at [2]:

'Now that the disputed interpretations of the CPR have been resolved by *Godwin's* case and by this judgment, there will be very few (if any) acceptable excuses for future failures to observe the rules for service of a claim form. The courts will be entitled to adopt a strict approach, even though the consequences may sometimes appear to be harsh in individual cases.'

(6) Thus, where there has been an ineffective attempt at service after the *Anderton* judgment was handed down on 3 July 2002, the dispensing power will not ordinarily be exercised. In such cases a strict approach will generally be adopted and the court will be the readier to reject the claimant's explanation for late service and to criticise his conduct of the proceedings.
(7) Where the real reason why the claim form was not served in time was not the failure of the court, but the failure of the claimant's solicitors to notify the court in time that the defendant's solicitors were willing to accept service and to request the court to serve urgently rather than 'in due course', it is not right to dispense with service under r 6.9 since the facts are not within the exceptional category of cases identified in *Anderton.*
(8) Rule 6.9 cannot be invoked where what was sent to insurers in time was only a draft claim form and the insurers had no authority to accept service.

Related provision—The court's power to dispense with service is closely related to its power to extend time for serving a claim form in r 7.6. See, in particular, r 7.6(3) and the notes thereto.

6.10 Certificate of service

Where a rule, practice direction or court order requires a certificate of service, the certificate must state the details set out in the following table –

Method of service	Details to be certified
Post	Date of posting
Personal	Date of personal service
Document exchange	Date of delivery to the document exchange
Delivery of document to or leaving it at a permitted place	Date when the document was delivered or left at the permitted place
Fax	Date and time of transmission
Other electronic means	Date of transmission and the means used
Alternative method permitted by the court	As required by the court

Amendments—SI 2004/1306.

Scope of provision—Affidavits of service are no longer required in most circumstances. This rule provides the detailed information to be given in a certificate of service where one is required by a rule, practice direction or court order. The rule's requirements do not apply to a county court bailiff's certificate, as this is not required by a rule, practice direction or court order (see County Courts Act 1984, s 133(1)).

Forms—N215 (Certificate of Service); N218 (Notice of service on partner).

6.11 Notification of outcome of postal service by the court

Where –

(a) a document to be served by the court is served by post; and
(b) such document is returned to the court,

the court must send notification to the party who requested service stating that the document has been returned.

Amendments—Substituted by SI 2005/2292.

Related provision—Rule 6.3(1)(b) (service by a party); r 6.2(1) (prescribed methods of service).

6.11A Notice of non-service by bailiff

Where –

(a) the court bailiff is to serve a document; and
(b) the bailiff is unable to serve it,

the court must send notification to the party who requested service.

Amendments—Inserted by SI 2005/2292.

II Special Provisions about Service of the Claim Form

6.12 General rules about service subject to special rules about service of claim form

The general rules about service are subject to the special rules about service contained in rules 6.13 to 6.16.

Related provisions—Schedule 1: RSC Ord 10, r 4, Service of claim form (in certain actions for possession of land); Pt 6, Section III, Special Provisions about Service out of the Jurisdiction; RSC Ord 77, r 4, Proceeding by and against the Crown; RSC Ord 113, r 4, Summary proceedings for the possession of land.

Schedule 2: CCR Ord 7, r 15–15A, Recovery of land/mortgage possession claims; CCR Ord 24, r 3, Summary proceedings for the recovery of land; CCR Ord 42, r 7, Service on the Crown.

Rule 20.8 – Service of Pt 20 claim form.

6.13 Service of claim form by the court – defendant's address for service

(1) Where a claim form is to be served by the court, the claim form must include the defendant's address for service.

(2) For the purposes of paragraph (1), the defendant's address for service may be the business address of the defendant's solicitor if he is authorised to accept service on the defendant's behalf but not otherwise.

(Rule 6.5 contains general provisions about the address for service)

Prospective amendment—By virtue of the Civil Procedure (Amendment No 3) Rules 2005, SI 2005/2292, after r 6.13, there is inserted –

'(Paragraph 2.4 of the Practice Direction to Part 16 contains provision about the content of an address for service).',

with effect from 6 April 2006.

General note—Paragraph 8.1 of PD6 at p 465 states that where the court effects service, the method will normally be first-class post.

Scope of provision—The claimant must provide the defendant's 'address for service' to enable the court to effect service.

'business address of the defendant's solicitor' (r 6.13(2))—This should be included in the claim form only if the solicitor has been authorised to accept service on the defendant's behalf. Rule 6.4(2) deals with the service of documents other than a claim form on a party's solicitor and requires notification of authority to accept service to be 'in writing'. The solicitors address for service must be within the jurisdiction (r 6.5).

Related provisions—Rule 6.3 – service by the court; r 6.5 – general provisions about the address for service.

6.14 Certificate of service relating to the claim form

(1) Where a claim form is served by the court, the court must send the claimant a notice which will include the date when the claim form is deemed to be served under rule 6.7.

(2) Where the claim form is served by the claimant –

(a) he must file a certificate of service within 7 days of service of the claim form; and

(b) he may not obtain judgment in default under Part 12 unless he has filed the certificate of service.

(Rule 6.10 specifies what a certificate of service must show)

Scope of provision—The court will normally serve the claim form in all cases (r 6.3). To enable the claimant to calculate when the next step in the proceedings is due, the court will send a notice indicating the method of service used and the date of deemed service.

Where service effected by the claimant (r 6.3(1)(b))—The claimant must file the appropriate certificate of service within 7 days of service of the claim form (Form N215 – Certificate of Service or N218 – Notice of Service on a Partner). Rule 6.10 deals with the contents of the certificate of service.

Until a certificate of service has been filed with the court, a claimant may not take other steps in the proceedings such as obtaining default judgment under Pt 12.

Related provision—Rule 7.5: service of the claim form. The general rule is that a claim form must be served within 4 months after the date of issue. There is provision in r 7.6 to extend the time for serving the claim form.

6.15 Service of the claim form by contractually agreed method

(1) Where –

(a) a contract contains a term providing that, in the event of a claim being issued in relation to the contract, the claim form may be served by a method specified in the contract; and

(b) a claim form containing only a claim in respect of that contract is issued,

the claim form shall, subject to paragraph (2), be deemed to be served on the defendant if it is served by a method specified in the contract.

(2) Where the claim form is served out of the jurisdiction in accordance with the contract, it shall not be deemed to be served on the defendant unless –

(a) permission to serve it out of the jurisdiction has been granted under rule 6.20; or

(b) it may be served without permission under rule 6.19.

Amendments—SI 2000/940.

Scope of rule—This rule allows there to be good service of a claim form where there is a provision in a contract giving an English court jurisdiction to try the claim. This may be by virtue of a term in the contract or by virtue of Pt 6, Section III, Special Provisions about Service out of the Jurisdiction.

Related provision—If the claim form is served out of the jurisdiction it will not be deemed to be served on the defendant unless permission was obtained pursuant to r 6.20 unless that permission is not required by virtue of r 6.19.

6.16 Service of claim form on agent of principal who is overseas

(1) Where –

(a) the defendant is overseas; and

(b) the conditions specified in paragraph (2) are satisfied,

the court may, on an application only, permit a claim form relating to a contract to be served on a defendant's agent.

(2) The court may not make an order under this rule unless it is satisfied that –

(a) the contract to which the claim relates was entered into within the jurisdiction with or through the defendant's agent; and

(b) at the time of the application either the agent's authority has not been terminated or he is still in business relations with his principal.

(3) An application under this rule –

(a) must be supported by evidence; and

(b) may be made without notice.

(4) An order under this rule must state a period within which the defendant must respond to the particulars of claim.

(Rule 9.2 sets out how a defendant may respond to particulars of claim)

(5) The power conferred by this rule is additional to the power conferred by rule 6.8 (service by an alternative method).

(6) Where the court makes an order under this rule, the claimant must send to the defendant copies of –

(a) the order; and

(b) the claim form.

Practice Direction—Paragraph 9.1 of PD6 at p 465 sets out the evidence required on an application to support service by r 6.16.

Scope of provision—Where a claimant has entered into a contract with a party residing or carrying on business out of the jurisdiction and that contract has been entered into through an agent of the party who is residing or carrying on business within the jurisdiction, service may be effected on the agent without permission having first to be obtained under Pt 6, Section III.

The court will not make an order unless it is satisfied that the two conditions contained in r 6.16(2) are satisfied.

An application can be made without notice but must be supported by evidence. The order must state the period within which the defendant must respond to the 'particulars of claim' not the claim form. If the court makes an order under r 6.16, the claimant must also send to the defendant copies of the order and the claim form.

Related provisions—Part 23 (applications); r 32.6 (Evidence in proceedings other than at trial); PD32, paras 17–20 (witness statements).

III Special Provisions about Service out of the Jurisdiction

Practice Direction—See generally PD6B at p 469.

6.17 Scope of this Section

This Section contains rules about –

(a) service out of the jurisdiction;
(b) how to obtain the permission of the court to serve out of the jurisdiction; and
(c) the procedure for serving out of the jurisdiction.

(Rule 2.3 defines 'jurisdiction')

Amendments—Inserted by SI 2000/221.

6.18 Definitions

For the purposes of this Part –

(a) 'the 1982 Act' means the Civil Jurisdiction and Judgments Act 1982;
(b) 'the Hague Convention' means the Convention on the service abroad of judicial and extra-judicial documents in civil or commercial matters signed at the Hague on November 15, 1965;
(c) 'Contracting State' has the meaning given by section 1(3) of the 1982 Act;
(d) 'Convention territory' means the territory or territories of any Contracting State to which the Brussels or Lugano Conventions (as defined in section 1(1) of the 1982 Act) apply;
(e) 'Civil Procedure Convention' means the Brussels and Lugano Conventions and any other Convention entered into by the United Kingdom regarding service outside the jurisdiction;
(ea) 'the Service Regulation' means Council Regulation (EC) No 1348/2000 of 29 May 2000 on the service in the Member States of judicial and extrajudicial documents in civil or commercial matters;
(f) 'United Kingdom Overseas Territory' means those territories as set out in the relevant practice direction.
(g) 'domicile' is to be determined –
  (i) in relation to a Convention territory, in accordance with sections 41 to 46 of the 1982 Act;
  (ii) in relation to a Regulation State, in accordance with the Judgments Regulation and paragraphs 9 to 12 of Schedule 1 to the Civil Jurisdiction and Judgments Order 2001;
(h) 'claim form' includes petition and application notice;
(i) 'claim' includes petition and application.
(j) 'the Judgments Regulation' means Council Regulation (EC) No. 44/2001 of 22nd December 2000 on jurisdiction and the recognition and enforcement of judgments in civil and commercial matters; and
(k) 'Regulation State' has the same meaning as 'Member State' in the Judgments Regulation, that is all Member States except Denmark.

(Rule 6.30 provides that where an application notice is to be served out of the jurisdiction under this Part, rules 6.21(4), 6.22 and 6.23 do not apply)

Amendments—Inserted by SI 2000/221; amended by SI 2001/1388; SI 2001/4015; SI 2002/2058.

' "Member State" ' (r 6.18(k))—The Member States of the European Union with effect from 1 May 2004 are Austria, Belgium, Cyprus, the Czech Republic, Denmark, Estonia, Finland, France, Germany, Greece, Hungary, Ireland, Italy, Latvia, Lithuania, Luxembourg, Malta, the Netherlands, Poland, Portugal, Slovakia, Slovenia, Spain, Sweden and the United Kingdom.

6.19 Service out of the jurisdiction where the permission of the court is not required

(1) A claim form may be served on a defendant out of the jurisdiction where each claim included in the claim form made against the defendant to be served is a claim which the court has power to determine under the 1982 Act and –

(a) no proceedings between the parties concerning the same claim are pending in the courts of any other part of the United Kingdom or any other Convention territory; and

(b) (i) the defendant is domiciled in the United Kingdom or in any Convention territory;

(ii) Article 16 of Schedule 1 or 3C to the 1982 Act, or paragraph 11 of Schedule 4 to that Act, refers to the proceedings; or

(iii) the defendant is a party to an agreement conferring jurisdiction to which Article 17 of Schedule 1 or 3C to the 1982 Act, or paragraph 12 of Schedule 4 to that Act, refers.]

(1A) A claim form may be served on a defendant out of the jurisdiction where each claim included in the claim form made against the defendant to be served is a claim which the court has power to determine under the Judgments Regulation and –

(a) no proceedings between the parties concerning the same claim are pending in the courts of any other part of the United Kingdom or any other Regulation State; and

(b) (i) the defendant is domiciled in the United Kingdom or in any Regulation State;

(ii) Article 22 of the Judgments Regulation refers to the proceedings; or

(iii) the defendant is a party to an agreement conferring jurisdiction to which Article 23 of the Judgments Regulation refers.

(2) A claim form may be served on a defendant out of the jurisdiction where each claim included in the claim form made against the defendant to be served is a claim which, under any other enactment, the court has power to determine, although –

(a) the person against whom the claim is made is not within the jurisdiction; or

(b) the facts giving rise to the claim did not occur within the jurisdiction.

(3) Where a claim form is to be served out of the jurisdiction under this rule, it must contain a statement of the grounds on which the claimant is entitled to serve it out of the jurisdiction.

Amendments—Inserted by SI 2000/221; amended by SI 2001/4015; SI 2002/2058.

'no proceedings between the parties concerning the same claim are pending' (rr 6.19(1)(a) and (1A)(a))—When the courts of one Convention territory or Regulation State are seised of a matter, the courts of any other such country are generally required to stay any parallel proceedings brought before them. However, this does not apply when the second court has exclusive jurisdiction to deal with the subject matter of the claim (*Speed Investments Ltd v Formula One Holdings Ltd (No 2)*

[2004] EWCA Civ 1512, [2005] 1 WLR 1936). English law regards the courts as seised of a matter when proceedings have been served (*Dresser UK Ltd v Falcongate Freight Management Ltd* [1992] QB 502).

'any other part of the United Kingdom' (r 6.19(1)(a))—Note that this includes only Scotland and Northern Ireland. It does not include, for example, the Isle of Man or the Channel Islands.

'which the court has power to determine under the Judgments Regulation' (r 6.19(1A))—A detailed examination of the provisions of the Judgments Regulation is beyond the remit of this work but a brief, though necessarily incomplete, summary may be helpful. The general rule is that persons domiciled in a member State shall be sued in that State's courts (Art 2). In matters relating to a contract, proceedings may be taken in the courts for the place of performance of the obligation (Art 5(1)); in claims in tort, proceedings may be taken in the courts of the State where the harmful event occurred (Art 5(3)). In cases involving employment, insurance and consumer cases the presumed weaker party has a choice of forum. An insurer may be sued in the courts of its domicile or that of the policyholder (Arts 9 and 10), but the insured must be sued in the courts of his domicile (Art 12). A consumer must be sued in the courts of his domicile but can choose to sue in the courts of the other party's domicile (Arts 15 to 17). An employee must be sued in the courts of his domicile but can choose to sue the employer in the courts of the employer's domicile or where the work is carried out (Arts 18 to 20). In certain cases relating to land, companies, public registers, intellectual property and the enforcement of judgments, exclusive jurisdiction is allotted to one State's courts irrespective of the parties' domicile (Art 22). The parties may agree in writing to confer jurisdiction on a particular State's courts and that agreement will be effective (Art 23); but an agreement cannot override the exclusive jurisdiction granted by Art 22 and cannot be invoked against an employee, consumer, or insured person unless entered into after the dispute has arisen.

The provisions of the Brussels and Lugano Conventions, and the special provisions governing the issue of proceedings against persons resident in other parts of the United Kingdom, are broadly similar to those of the Judgments Regulation.

'court has power to determine' (r 6.19(2))—To fall within the scope of this provision an enactment has to indicate that it expressly contemplates proceedings against persons outwith the jurisdiction of the court, or that it applies where the wrongful act, neglect or default giving rise to the claim has occurred outside the jurisdiction. Section 423 of the Insolvency Act 1986 does not so indicate and a claim for a declaration that a transaction has been entered into at an undervalue for the purpose of putting assets beyond the reach of creditors requires permission (*Banca Carige SpA Cassa Di Risparmio Di Genova E Imperia v Banco Nacional De Cuba & anor* [2001] 1 WLR 2039, [2001] 3 All ER 923, [2001] 2 Lloyd's Rep 147, ChD, per Lightman J at [19]).

'must contain a statement' (r 6.19(3))—This is a mandatory provision and non-compliance is not a trifling irregularity, though not one sufficient to justify the court in concluding that there has been no service of the claim form at all. The primary purpose of the certificate is to provide information to the court, so that it can know whether or not to mark the claim form 'Not for service out of the jurisdiction' (*Trustor AB v Barclays Bank plc & anor* [2000] All ER (D) 1690 (Oct), ChD, per Rimer J at para [44]).

'the grounds on which the claimant is entitled' (r 6.19(3))—The claimant is only required to use one of the forms of words set out in the practice direction, but particularly as he will have to sign a statement of truth he should also consider carefully which of the provisions of the 1982 Act allows him to do so and how.

6.20 Service out of the jurisdiction where the permission of the court is required

In any proceedings to which rule 6.19 does not apply, a claim form may be served out of the jurisdiction with the permission of the court if –

General grounds

(1) a claim is made for a remedy against a person domiciled within the jurisdiction.

(2) a claim is made for an injunction ordering(GL) the defendant to do or refrain from doing an act within the jurisdiction.

(3) a claim is made against someone on whom the claim form has been or will be served (otherwise than in reliance on this paragraph) and –

(a) there is between the claimant and that person a real issue which it is reasonable for the court to try; and
(b) the claimant wishes to serve the claim form on another person who is a necessary or proper party to that claim.

(3A) a claim is a Part 20 claim and the person to be served is a necessary or proper party to the claim against the Part 20 claimant.

Claims for interim remedies

(4) a claim is made for an interim remedy under section 25(1) of the 1982 Act.

Claims in relation to contracts

(5) a claim is made in respect of a contract where the contract –

(a) was made within the jurisdiction;
(b) was made by or through an agent trading or residing within the jurisdiction;
(c) is governed by English law; or
(d) contains a term to the effect that the court shall have jurisdiction to determine any claim in respect of the contract.

(6) a claim is made in respect of a breach of contract committed within the jurisdiction.

(7) a claim is made for a declaration that no contract exists where, if the contract was found to exist, it would comply with the conditions set out in paragraph (5).

Claims in tort

(8) a claim is made in tort where –

(a) damage was sustained within the jurisdiction; or
(b) the damage sustained resulted from an act committed within the jurisdiction.

Enforcement

(9) a claim is made to enforce any judgment or arbitral award.

Claims about property within the jurisdiction

(10) the whole subject matter of a claim relates to property located within the jurisdiction.

Claims about trusts etc

(11) a claim is made for any remedy which might be obtained in proceedings to execute the trusts of a written instrument where –

(a) the trusts ought to be executed according to English law; and
(b) the person on whom the claim form is to be served is a trustee of the trusts.

(12) a claim is made for any remedy which might be obtained in proceedings for the administration of the estate of a person who died domiciled within the jurisdiction.

(13) a claim is made in probate proceedings which includes a claim for the rectification of a will.

(14) a claim is made for a remedy against the defendant as constructive trustee where the defendant's alleged liability arises out of acts committed within the jurisdiction.

(15) a claim is made for restitution where the defendant's alleged liability arises out of acts committed within the jurisdiction.

Claims by HM Revenue and Customs

(16) a claim is made by the Commissioners for HM Revenue and Customs relating to duties or taxes against a defendant not domiciled in Scotland or Northern Ireland.

Claim for costs order in favour of or against third parties

(17) a claim is made by a party to proceedings for an order that the court exercise its power under section 51 of the Supreme Court Act 1981 to make a costs order in favour of or against a person who is not a party to those proceedings.

(Rule 48.2 sets out the procedure where the court is considering whether to exercise its discretion to make a costs order in favour of or against a non-party)

Admiralty claims

(17A) a claim is –

- (a) in the nature of salvage and any part of the services took place within the jurisdiction; or
- (b) to enforce a claim under section 153, 154 or 175 of the Merchant Shipping Act 1995.

Claims under various enactments

(18) a claim is made under an enactment specified in the relevant practice direction.

Amendments—Inserted by SI 2000/221; amended by SI 2000/1317; SI 2001/1388; SI 2001/4015; SI 2004/2072; SI 2005/2292.

'claim form' (r 6.20)—This includes a Pt 20 claim form (*Shahar v Tsitsekkos* [2004] EWHC 2659 (Ch), [2004] TLR 576, (2004) *The Times*, Nov 30, Mann J).

'may be served out of the jurisdiction' (r 6.20)—The fact that a claim may be served out of the jurisdiction does not necessarily mean that it should be. The court will consider whether England and Wales is the proper place to bring the claim (r 6.21(2A); see also *The Spiliada* [1987] AC 460). While the familiar Latin refers to *forum non conveniens*, the doctrine is not concerned with convenience so much as whether the proceedings are in the appropriate forum; if the claimant can serve out of the jurisdiction as of right, it will be for the defendant to show that another forum is clearly more appropriate. Where the Brussels or Lugano Conventions or the Judgments Regulation apply, a stay on the grounds of *forum non conveniens* will generally not be possible (*Mahme Trust v Lloyds TSB Bank plc* [2004] EWHC 1931 (Ch), [2004] 2 Lloyd's Rep 637, [2004] All ER (D) 549 (Jul)) and neither will an anti-suit injunction, even if the claim verges on the vexatious (*Turner v Grovit (C-159/02)* [2005] 1 AC 101) or is brought in breach of an exclusive jurisdiction clause (*J P Morgan Europe Ltd v Primacom AG* [2005] EWHC 508 (Comm), [2005] All ER (D) 03 (Apr)). If the claimant requires permission, the burden of showing that England and Wales is the proper forum rests on him. The claimant should also consider whether any judgment he obtains will be enforceable (*Motorola Credit Corporation v Uzan* [2003] EWCA Civ 752, [2004] 1 WLR 113) and the ability to enforce a judgment is a factor to be taken into account in deciding which forum is appropriate (*Inter-tel v OCIS plc* [2004] EWHC 2269 (QB), [2004] All ER (D) 142 (Oct), QBD, Tugendhat J). Advice should be sought as to the attitude of the foreign court to service of documents and to judgments obtained in default. It should be borne in mind that English law takes a wider view of jurisdiction than many foreign legal systems.

'someone on whom the claim form has been or will be served (otherwise than in reliance on this paragraph) (r 6.20(3))—The Brussels Convention, the Lugano Convention and the Judgments

Regulation all provide that persons domiciled in a signatory State shall normally be sued in that State's courts. If one of several defendants is domiciled and served in England, the English courts may not decline jurisdiction even though the other defendants are domiciled abroad and the cause of action arose there (*Owusu v Jackson* C-281/02 [2005] 2 WLR 942, ECJ).

'a necessary or proper party' (r 6.20(3)(b))—The court's power to permit service out of the jurisdiction under r 6.20(3) is not less wide than the court's wide power to add or substitute a party under r 19.1(2) (*United Film Distribution Ltd & anor v Chhabria & ors* [2001] EWCA Civ 416, (2001) Lawtel, 28 March, (2001) *The Times*, 5 April, CA).

'a claim made in respect of a contract' (r 6.20(5))—A claim for interpleader relief is not a claim made in respect of a contract for the purposes of r 6.20 (*Cool Carriers AB v HSBC Bank USA* [2001] 2 All ER (Comm) 177, [2001] 2 Lloyd's Rep 22, [2001] CP Rep 82, QBD, Tomlinson J).

'a contract ... made within the jurisdiction' (r 6.20(5)(a))—It is possible for a contract to be made in two places at once and it suffices if one of those places is in England (*Apple Corps Ltd v Apple Computer Inc* [2004] EWHC 768 (Ch), [2004] All ER (D) 107 (Apr), Mann J).

'damage was sustained within the jurisdiction' (r 6.20(8)(a))—This refers to financial loss sustained in a claim in tort, such as a loss of dependency, rather than the damage which completes the cause of action (*Booth v Phillips* [2004] EWHC 1437 (Comm), [2004] 2 Lloyd's Rep 457, [2004] All ER (D) 191 (Jun), Nigel Teare QC, where the claimant's husband was killed while working in Egypt).

'the whole subject matter of the claim relates to property' (r 6.20(10))—Construed properly, r 6.20(10) cannot be taken to be confined to claims relating to the ownership or possession of property. Rather, it extends to any claim for relief so long as it relates to property within the jurisdiction. This construction vests in the court a wide jurisdiction, but since it is discretionary the court can and will consider in each case whether the character and closeness of the relationship is such that the exorbitant jurisdiction against foreigners abroad should properly be exercised (*Banca Carige SpA Cassa Di Risparmio Di Genova E Imperia v Banco Nacional De Cuba & anor* [2001] 1 WLR 2039, [2001] 3 All ER 923, [2001] 2 Lloyd's Rep 147, ChD, per Lightman J at [33]).

6.21 Application for permission to serve claim form out of jurisdiction

(1) An application for permission under rule 6.20 must be supported by written evidence stating –

- (a) the grounds on which the application is made and the paragraph or paragraphs of rule 6.20 relied on;
- (b) that the claimant believes that his claim has a reasonable prospect of success; and
- (c) the defendant's address or, if not known, in what place or country the defendant is, or is likely, to be found.

(2) Where the application is made in respect of a claim referred to in rule 6.20(3), the written evidence must also state the grounds on which the witness believes that there is between the claimant and the person on whom the claim form has been, or will be served, a real issue which it is reasonable for the court to try.

(2A) The court will not give permission unless satisfied that England and Wales is the proper place in which to bring the claim.

(3) Where –

- (a) the application is for permission to serve a claim form in Scotland or Northern Ireland; and
- (b) it appears to the court that the claimant may also be entitled to a remedy there, the court, in deciding whether to give permission, shall –
  - (i) compare the cost and convenience of proceeding there or in the jurisdiction; and

(ii) (where relevant) have regard to the powers and jurisdiction of the Sheriff court in Scotland or the county courts or courts of summary jurisdiction in Northern Ireland.

(4) An order giving permission to serve a claim form out of the jurisdiction must specify the periods within which the defendant may –

(a) file an acknowledgment of service;
(b) file or serve an admission; and
(c) file a defence.

(Part 11 sets out the procedure by which a defendant may dispute the court's jurisdiction)

(The second practice direction to this Part sets out how the periods referred to in paragraphs (a), (b) and (c) are calculated)

Amendments—Inserted by SI 2000/221; amended by SI 2000/940; SI 2001/4015.

'application for permission' (r 6.21(1))—An application may be made after the 4 months for service within the jurisdiction have expired and is not governed by the strict criteria set out in r 7.6(3) (*Cummins v Shell International Manning Services Ltd*, sub nom *Anderton v Clwyd CC (No 2)* [2002] 1 WLR 3203).

'written evidence' (r 6.21(1))—Valuable guidance is given by Toulson J in *MRG (Japan) Ltd v Engelhard Metals Japan Ltd* [2003] EWHC 3418 (Comm), [2004] 1 Lloyd's Rep 731, [2003] All ER (D) 343 (Dec). The applicant must show in respect of each claim he seeks to make that he has 'a good arguable case' and that it falls within a relevant subparagraph of r 6.20 (*Seaconsar Far East Ltd v Bank Markazi Jomhouri Islami Iran* [1994] 1 AC 438, [1993] 3 WLR 756, [1993] 4 All ER 456, HL) – this is a less stringent test than proof on a balance of probabilities. Secondly, the applicant must show that there is a serious issue to be tried in respect of each claim, the 'merits threshold' being the same as if the applicant were resisting an application for summary judgment (*De Molestina v Ponton* [2002] 1 Lloyds Rep 271, [2002] 1 All ER (Comm) 587, [2002] CP Rep 1, QBD). Thirdly, the applicant must persuade the court that England (or Wales) is clearly the appropriate forum. There is a continuing duty of disclosure even after the order has been made, so where a claimant who had obtained an order but not yet served proceedings was himself served with proceedings issued abroad, his failure to disclose this led to the order giving permission being set aside (*Network Telecom (Europe) Ltd v Telephone Systems International Inc* [2003] EWHC 2890 (QB), [2004] 1 All ER (Comm) 418, [2003] All ER (D) 350 (Oct), QBD, Burton J). But the court will be reluctant to allow satellite litigation about whether disclosure has been sufficiently full and, in particular, the claimant is not obliged to set out matters which go no further than showing arguable grounds for disputing the claim.

6.22 Period for acknowledging service or admitting the claim where the claim form is served out of the jurisdiction under rule 6.19

(1) This rule sets out the period for filing an acknowledgment of service or filing or serving an admission where a claim form has been served out of the jurisdiction under rule 6.19.

(Part 10 contains rules about the acknowledgment of service and Part 14 contains rules about admissions)

(2) If the claim form is to be served under rule 6.19(1) or (1A) in Scotland, Northern Ireland or in the European territory of another Contracting State or Regulation State the period is –

(a) where the defendant is served with a claim form which states that particulars of claim are to follow, 21 days after the service of the particulars of claim; and
(b) in any other case, 21 days after service of the claim form.

(3) If the claim form is to be served under rule 6.19(1) in any other territory of a Contracting State the period is –

(a) where the defendant is served with a claim form which states that particulars of claim are to follow, 31 days after the service of the particulars of claim; and

(b) in any other case, 31 days after service of the claim form.

(4) If the claim form is to be served under –

(a) rule 6.19(1) or (1A) in a country not referred to in paragraphs (2) or (3); or

(b) rule 6.19(2),

the period is set out in the relevant practice direction.

Amendments—Inserted by SI 2000/221; amended by SI 2001/4015.

6.23 Period for filing a defence where the claim form is served out of the jurisdiction under rule 6.19

(1) This rule sets out the period for filing a defence where a claim form has been served out of the jurisdiction under rule 6.19.

(Part 15 contains rules about the defence)

(2) If the claim form is to be served under rule 6.19(1) or (1A) in Scotland, Northern Ireland or in the European territory of another Contracting State or Regulation State the period is –

(a) 21 days after service of the particulars of claim; or

(b) if the defendant files an acknowledgment of service, 35 days after service of the particulars of claim.

(3) If the claim form is to be served under rule 6.19(1) in any other territory of a Contracting State the period is –

(a) 31 days after service of the particulars of claim; or

(b) if the defendant files an acknowledgment of service, 45 days after service of the particulars of claim.

(4) If the claim form is to be served under –

(a) rule 6.19(1) or (1A) in a country not referred to in paragraphs (2) or (3); or

(b) rule 6.19(2),

the period is set out in the relevant practice direction.

Amendments—Inserted by SI 2000/221; amended by SI 2001/4015.

Disputing jurisdiction—When a claim form is served out of the jurisdiction under r 6.19, the time for issuing an application challenging the jurisdiction of the court under r 11(4)(a) is governed by the time limits in r 6.23 (*USF Ltd (t/a USF Memcor) v Aqua Techology Hanson NV/SA* [2001] All ER (D) 229, QBD (Comm Ct), per Aikens J).

6.24 Method of service – general provisions

(1) Where a claim form is to be served out of the jurisdiction, it may be served by any method –

(a) permitted by the law of the country in which it is to be served;

(b) provided for by –

  (i) rule 6.25 (service through foreign governments, judicial authorities and British Consular authorities);

  (ii) rule 6.26A (service in accordance with the Service Regulation); or

  (iii) rule 6.27 (service on a State); or

(c) permitted by a Civil Procedure Convention.

(2) Nothing in this rule or in any court order shall authorise or require any person to do anything in the country where the claim form is to be served which is against the law of that country.

Amendments—Inserted by SI 2000/221; amended by SI 2001/256; SI 2001/1388.

'permitted by the law of the country in which it is to be served' (r 6.24(1)(a))—Although it has been said that this provision 'should be applied with a reasonable degree of flexibility' (per Collins J in *Arros Invest Ltd v Rafik Nishanov* [2004] EWHC 576 (Ch)) the onus is on the claimant to show, by expert evidence if necessary, that the local rules have been complied with. For instructive instances of claimants failing to do this see *Arros*; *Crédit Agricole Indosuez v Unicof* [2003] EWHC 2676, [2004] 1 Lloyd's Rep 196, [2003] All ER (D) 21 (Feb); *Shiblaq v Sadikoglu* [2004] EWHC 1890 (Comm), [2004] 2 All ER (Comm) 596.

Method of service in Scotland—The legislation covering citation in Scotland is as follows:

– *Section 3 of the Citation Amendment (Scotland) Act 1882*:

> 'In any civil action or proceeding in any court or before any person or body of persons having by law power to cite parties or witnesses, any summons or warrant of citation of a person, whether as a party or a witness, or warrant of service or judicial intimation, may be executed in Scotland by an officer of the court from which such summons, warrant, or judicial intimation was issued, or other officer who according to the present law and practice, might lawfully execute the same, or by an enrolled law agent, by sending to the known residence or place of business of the person upon whom such summons, warrant, or judicial intimation is to be served … a registered letter by post containing the copy summons or petition or other document required by law in the particular case to be served, with the proper citation or notice subjoined thereto … and such posting shall constitute a legal and valid citation, unless the person cited shall prove that such letter was not left or tendered at his known residence or place of business …'.

– *Section 1 of the Recorded Delivery Service Act 1962* provides that recorded delivery service is now an alternative to registered post.

– *Rule 5 of the Small Claims Rules 1988 (SI 1988/1976)* provides that in actions where the sum sued for does not exceed £750, postal citation should be made by first-class recorded delivery post.

– *Rule 10 of the Summary Cause Rules, Sheriff Court 1976 (SI 1976/476)* provides that in actions where the sum sued for does not exceed £1500 postal citation should be made by first-class recorded delivery post.

– *Rule 15 of the First Schedule (as substituted by SI 1993/1956) to the Sheriff Courts (Scotland) Act 1907* provides that in all other actions postal citation should be made by first-class recorded delivery post.

6.25 Service through foreign governments, judicial authorities and British Consular authorities

(1) Where a claim form is to be served on a defendant in any country which is a party to the Hague Convention, the claim form may be served –

(a) through the authority designated under the Hague Convention in respect of that country; or

(b) if the law of that country permits –

(i) through the judicial authorities of that country, or

(ii) through a British Consular authority in that country.

(2) Where –

(a) paragraph (4) (service in Scotland etc, other than under the Hague Convention) does not apply; and

(b) a claim form is to be served on a defendant in any country which is a party to a Civil Procedure Convention (other than the Hague Convention) providing for service in that country,

the claim form may be served, if the law of that country permits –

(i) through the judicial authorities of that country; or
(ii) through a British Consular authority in that country (subject to any provisions of the applicable convention about the nationality of persons who may be served by such a method).

(3) Where –

(a) paragraph (4) (service in Scotland etc, other than under the Hague Convention) does not apply; and
(b) a claim form is to be served on a defendant in any country with respect to which there is no Civil Procedure Convention providing for service in that country,

the claim form may be served, if the law of that country so permits –

(i) through the government of that country, where that government is willing to serve it; or
(ii) through a British Consular authority in that country.

(4) Except where a claim form is to be served in accordance with paragraph (1) (service under the Hague Convention), the methods of service permitted by this rule are not available where the claim form is to be served in –

(a) Scotland, Northern Ireland, the Isle of Man or the Channel Islands;
(b) any Commonwealth State; or
(c) any United Kingdom Overseas Territory.
(d) (*revoked*)

(5) This rule does not apply where service is to be effected in accordance with the Service Regulation.

Amendments—Inserted by SI 2000/221; amended by SI 2001/1388.

6.26 Procedure where service is to be through foreign governments, judicial authorities and British Consular authorities

(1) This rule applies where the claimant wishes to serve the claim form through –

(a) the judicial authorities of the country where the claim form is to be served;
(b) a British Consular authority in that country;
(c) the authority designated under the Hague Convention in respect of that country; or
(d) the government of that country.

(2) Where this rule applies, the claimant must file –

(a) a request for service of the claim form by the method in paragraph (1) that he has chosen;
(b) a copy of the claim form;
(c) any translation required under rule 6.28; and
(d) any other documents, copies of documents or translations required by the relevant practice direction.

(3) When the claimant files the documents specified in paragraph (2), the court officer will –

(a) seal(GL) the copy of the claim form; and
(b) forward the documents to the Senior Master.

(4) The Senior Master will send documents forwarded under this rule –

(a) where the claim form is being served through the authority designated under the Hague Convention, to that authority; or
(b) in any other case, to the Foreign and Commonwealth Office with a request that it arranges for the claim to be served by the method indicated in the request for service filed under paragraph (2) or, where that request indicates alternative methods, by the most convenient method.

(5) An official certificate which –

(a) states that the claim form has been served in accordance with this rule either personally, or in accordance with the law of the country in which service was effected;
(b) specifies the date on which the claim form was served; and
(c) is made by –
(i) a British Consular authority in the country where the claim form was served;
(ii) the government or judicial authorities in that country; or
(iii) any other authority designated in respect of that country under the Hague Convention,

shall be evidence of the facts stated in the certificate.

(6) A document purporting to be an official certificate under paragraph (5) shall be treated as such a certificate, unless it is proved not to be.

(7) This rule does not apply where service is to be effected in accordance with the Service Regulation.

Amendments—Inserted by SI 2000/221; amended by SI 2001/1388.

'the claimant wishes to serve the claim form' (r 6.26(1))—Where service is effected through the Foreign Office, service is not being effected by the court but by the claimant and if there is delay, the onus is on the claimant to show that all reasonable steps have been taken if he seeks an extension of the time for service under r 7.6(3) (*Chare v Fairclough* [2003] All ER (D) 158 (Jan)).

6.26A Service in accordance with the Service Regulation

(1) This rule applies where a claim form is to be served in accordance with the Service Regulation.

(2) The claimant must file the claim form and any translations or other documents required by the Service Regulation.

(3) When the claimant files the documents referred to in paragraph (2), the court officer will –

(a) seal(GL) the copy of the claim form; and
(b) forward the documents to the Senior Master.

(4) Rule 6.31 does not apply.

(The Service Regulation is annexed to the relevant practice direction)

Amendments—Inserted by SI 2001/1388.

'the Service Regulation' (r 6.26A generally)—The Service Regulation is an attempt to establish an efficient system for the service of documents within the European Union. Its use is complicated by the fact that States may opt out of a number of its provisions; Denmark has of course opted out of it altogether. Up-to-date information on its implementation may be found on the Europa website at *http://www.europa.eu.int*.

The European Commission publishes a 'Manual of receiving agencies' and 'Glossary of documents' that may be served under the Service Regulation and also a 'Consolidated version of the communications of the Member States', which contains a convenient summary of the information that a number of Articles of the Regulation require States to communicate to the Commission.

It will often be prudent to seek the advice of a practitioner in the State in which service is to be effected. The Foreign Process Section (Room E02) at the Royal Courts of Justice will also offer guidance.

6.27 Service of claim form on State where court permits service out of the jurisdiction

(1) This rule applies where a claimant wishes to serve the claim form on a State.

(2) The claimant must file in the Central Office of the Royal Courts of Justice –

(a) a request for service to be arranged by the Foreign and Commonwealth Office;
(b) a copy of the claim form; and
(c) any translation required under rule 6.28.

(3) The Senior Master will send documents filed under this rule to the Foreign and Commonwealth Office with a request that it arranges for the claim form to be served.

(4) An official certificate by the Foreign and Commonwealth Office stating that a claim form has been duly served on a specified date in accordance with a request made under this rule shall be evidence of that fact.

(5) A document purporting to be such a certificate shall be treated as such a certificate, unless it is proved not to be.

(6) Where –

(a) section 12(6) of the State Immunity Act 1978 applies; and
(b) the State has agreed to a method of service other than through the Foreign and Commonwealth Office,

the claim may be served either by the method agreed or in accordance with this rule.

(Section 12(6) of the State Immunity Act 1978 provides that section 12(1) of that Act, which prescribes a method for serving documents on a State, does not prevent the service of a claim form or other document in a manner to which the State has agreed)

(7) In this rule 'State' has the meaning given by section 14 of the State Immunity Act 1978.

Amendments—Inserted by SI 2000/221.

6.28 Translation of claim form

(1) Except where paragraph (4) or (5) applies, every copy of the claim form filed under rule 6.26 (service through judicial authorities, foreign governments etc) or 6.27 (service on State) must be accompanied by a translation of the claim form.

(2) The translation must be –

(a) in the official language of the country in which it is to be served; or
(b) if there is more than one official language of that country, in any official language which is appropriate to the place in the country where the claim form is to be served.

(3) Every translation filed under this rule must be accompanied by a statement by the person making it that it is a correct translation, and the statement must include –

(a) the name of the person making the translation;
(b) his address; and
(c) his qualifications for making a translation.

(4) The claimant is not required to file a translation of a claim form filed under rule 6.26 (service through judicial authorities, foreign governments etc) where the claim form is to be served –

(a) in a country of which English is an official language; or
(b) on a British subject,

unless a Civil Procedure Convention expressly requires a translation.

(5) The claimant is not required to file a translation of a claim form filed under rule 6.27 (service on State) where English is an official language of the State where the claim form is to be served.

Amendments—Inserted by SI 2000/221.

'a British subject' (r 6.28(4)(b))—It is not sufficient for the purposes of this subrule that the recipient understands the English language (compare r 6.33(d) and, importantly, Art 8(1)(b) of the Service Regulation).

6.29 Undertaking to be responsible for expenses of the Foreign and Commonwealth Office

Every request for service filed under rule 6.26 (service through judicial authorities, foreign governments etc) or rule 6.27 (service on State) must contain an undertaking by the person making the request –

(a) to be responsible for all expenses incurred by the Foreign and Commonwealth Office or foreign judicial authority; and
(b) to pay those expenses to the Foreign and Commonwealth Office or foreign judicial authority on being informed of the amount.

Amendments—Inserted by SI 2000/221.

6.30 Service of documents other than the claim form

(1) Where an application notice is to be served out of the jurisdiction under this Section of this Part –

(a) rules 6.21(4), 6.22 and 6.23 do not apply; and
(b) where the person on whom the application notice has been served is not a party to proceedings in the jurisdiction in which the application is made, that person may make an application to the court under rule 11(1) as if he were a defendant and rule 11(2) does not apply.

(Rule 6.21(4) provides that an order giving permission to serve a claim form out of the jurisdiction must specify the periods within which the defendant may (a) file an acknowledgment of service, (b) file or serve an admission, and (c) file a defence)

(Rule 6.22 provides rules for the period for acknowledging service or admitting the claim where the claim form is served out of the jurisdiction under rule 6.19)

(Rule 6.23 provides rules for the period for filing a defence where the claim form is served out of the jurisdiction under rule 6.19)

(The practice direction supplementing this Section of this Part provides that where an application notice is to be served out of the jurisdiction in accordance with this Section of this Part, the court must have regard to the country in which the application notice is to be served in setting the date for the hearing of the application and giving any direction about service of the respondent's evidence)

(Rule 11(1) provides that a defendant may make an application to the court to dispute the court's jurisdiction to try the claim or argue that the court should not exercise its jurisdiction. Rule 11(2) provides that a defendant who wishes to make such an application must first file an acknowledgment of service in accordance with Part 10)

(2) Unless paragraph (3) applies, where the permission of the court is required for a claim form to be served out of the jurisdiction the permission of the court must also be obtained for service out of the jurisdiction of any other document to be served in the proceedings.

(3) Where –

- (a) the court gives permission for a claim form to be served out of the jurisdiction; and
- (b) the claim form states that particulars of claim are to follow,

the permission of the court is not required to serve the particulars of claim out of the jurisdiction.

Amendments—Inserted by SI 2000/221.

6.31 Proof of service

Where –

- (a) a hearing is fixed when the claim is issued;
- (b) the claim form is served on a defendant out of the jurisdiction; and
- (c) that defendant does not appear at the hearing,

the claimant may take no further steps against that defendant until the claimant files written evidence showing that the claim form has been duly served.

Amendments—Inserted by SI 2000/221.

IV Service of Foreign Process

Amendments—This Section was added by Civil Procedure (Amendment) Rules 2002, SI 2002/2058, r 5(d) and Sch 1, Pt II. It came into force on 2 December 2002, replacing the former Sch 1, RSC Ord 69.

6.32 Scope and definitions

(1) This Section of this Part –

- (a) applies to the service in England or Wales of any court process in connection with civil or commercial proceedings in a foreign court or tribunal; but
- (b) does not apply where the Service Regulation applies.

(The Service Regulation is annexed to the relevant practice direction)

(2) In this Section –

(a) 'convention country' –

(i) means a foreign country in relation to which there is a civil procedure convention providing for service in that country of process of the High Court; and

(ii) includes a country which is a party to the Convention on the Service Abroad of Judicial and Extra-Judicial Documents in Civil or Commercial Matters signed at the Hague on 15 November 1965; and

(b) 'process server' means –

(i) a process server appointed by the Lord Chancellor to serve documents to which this Section applies, or

(ii) his authorised agent.

Amendments—Inserted by SI 2002/2058.

6.33 Request for service

Process will be served where the Senior Master receives –

(a) a written request for service –

(i) where the foreign court or tribunal is in a convention country, from a consular or other authority of that country; or

(ii) from the Secretary of State for Foreign and Commonwealth Affairs, with a recommendation that service should be effected;

(b) a translation of that request into English;

(c) two copies of the process to be served; and

(d) unless the foreign court or tribunal certifies that the person to be served understands the language of the process, two copies of a translation of it into English.

Amendments—Inserted by SI 2002/2058.

6.34 Method of service

The process must be served as directed by the Senior Master.

Amendments—Inserted by SI 2002/2058.

6.35 After service

(1) The process server must –

(a) send the Senior Master a copy of the process, and

(i) proof of service; or

(ii) a statement why the process could not be served; and

(b) if the Senior Master directs, specify the costs incurred in serving or attempting to serve the process.

(2) The Senior Master will send the following documents to the person who requested service –

(a) a certificate, sealed with the seal of the Supreme Court for use out of the jurisdiction, stating –

(i) when and how the process was served or the reason why it has not been served; and

(ii) where appropriate, an amount certified by a costs judge to be the costs of serving or attempting to serve the process; and

(b) a copy of the process.

Amendments—Inserted by SI 2002/2058.

Practice Direction – Service

This Practice Direction supplements CPR Part 6 (PD6)

Procedural Guide—See Guide 15, set out in Section 1 of this work.

Methods of Service

1.1 The various methods of service are set out in rule 6.2.

1.2 The following provisions apply to the specific methods of service referred to.

Service by Non-Electronic Means

SERVICE BY DOCUMENT EXCHANGE

2.1 Service by document exchange (DX) may take place only where:

(1) the party's address for service[1] includes a numbered box at a DX, or
(2) the writing paper of the party who is to be served or of his legal representative[2] sets out the DX box number, and
(3) the party or his legal representative has not indicated in writing that they are unwilling to accept service by DX.

1 See rule 6.5.
2 See rule 2.3 for the definition of legal representative.

2.2 Service by DX is effected by leaving the document addressed to the numbered box:

(1) at the DX of the party who is to be served, or
(2) at a DX which sends documents to that party's DX every 'business day'.

Designated document exchanges—The following are designated document exchanges approved by the Lord Chancellor:

(a) Britdoc Limited Hays Wharf
Guildford
Surrey;

(b) Northern Document Exchange Limited
9A Middlesbrough Wharf
Depot Road
Middlesbrough
Cleveland.

The deletion of the words 'unless the contrary is proved' in para 2.2 (with effect from 6 October 2003) defeated a defendant's challenge to effective service (*Hashtroodi v Hancock* [2004] EWCA Civ 652, [2004] 1 WLR 3206, [2004] All ER (D) 368 (May), [2004] TLR 305, (2004) *The Times*, 4 June, CA).

Service by Electronic Means

SERVICE BY FACSIMILE

3.1 Subject to the provisions of paragraph 3.3 below, where a document is to be served by electronic means –

(1) the party who is to be served or his legal representative must previously have expressly indicated in writing to the party serving –
  (a) that he is willing to accept service by electronic means; and
  (b) the fax number, e-mail address or electronic identification to which it should be sent; and

(2) the following shall be taken as sufficient written indication for the purposes of paragraph 3.1(1) –
  (a) a fax number set out on the writing paper of the legal representative of the party who is to be served; or
  (b) a fax number, e-mail address or electronic identification set out on a statement of case or a response to a claim filed with the court.

3.2 Where a party seeks to serve a document by electronic means he should first seek to clarify with the party who is to be served whether there are any limitations to the recipient's agreement to accept service by such means including the format in which documents are to be sent and the maximum size of attachments that may be received.

3.3 An address for service given by a party must be within the jurisdiction and any fax number must be at the address for service. Where an e-mail address or electronic identification is given in conjunction with an address for service, the e-mail address or electronic identification will be deemed to be at the address for service.

3.4 Where a document is served by electronic means, the party serving the document need not in addition send a hard copy by post or document exchange.

Service by fax—Documents including a claim form can now be served by fax. Unless an intention is given to the contrary the fact that a legal representative sets out his fax number on his writing paper will be taken to be sufficient indication that he is willing to accept service by fax (para 3.1(3)). A solicitor is not now required to send a 'hard' copy of the document being served by post. Note para 3.4. The court may take into account in relation to an application arising out of non-receipt of a document the fact that a hard copy was not sent.

E-mail or other electronic methods of service—Service by electronic forms such as e-mail are not well catered for by the CPR. Service can only take place when the specific conditions set out in para 3.3 occur and is relevant only where the serving and the served parties are acting by legal representatives. Consequently the fact that a solicitor exhibits his e-mail address on his letterhead is not conclusive of his willingness to accept service of the documents by this means.

Related provisions—CPR r 6.7 (deemed service).

Service on Certain Individuals

PERSONAL SERVICE ON PARTNERS

4.1 Where partners are sued in the name of a partnership, service should be in accordance with rule 6.4(5) and the table set out in rule 6.5(5) where it refers to an 'individual who is suing or being sued in the name of a firm'.

4.2 A claim form or particulars of claim which are served by leaving them with a person at the principal or last known place of business of the partnership, must at the same time have served with them a notice as to whether that person is being served:

(1) as a partner,
(2) as a person having control or management of the partnership business, or
(3) as both.

Scope of provision—Service of documents including the claim form or particulars of claim will be good service if served on:

(a) A partner;
(b) A person having control or management of the partnership business; or
(c) Both.

When serving a partnership with a claim form or particulars of claim, N218 must be completed.

Related provisions—CPR r 6.5(6) – Service table.

SERVICE ON MEMBERS OF HM FORCES AND UNITED STATES AIR FORCE

5 The Lord Chancellor's Office issued a memorandum on 26 July 1979 as to service on members of HM Forces and guidance notes as to service on members of the United States Air Force. The provisions annexed to this practice direction are derived from that memorandum and guidance notes.

Scope of provision—See the separate annex attached to the practice direction which sets out in detail the procedure for serving members of HM Forces and United States Airforce.

Service Generally

PERSONAL SERVICE ON A COMPANY OR OTHER CORPORATION

6.1 Personal service on a registered company or corporation in accordance with rule 6.4(4) service is effected by leaving a document with 'a person holding a senior position'.

6.2 Each of the following persons is a person holding a senior position:

(1) in respect of a registered company or corporation, a director, the treasurer, secretary, chief executive, manager or other officer of the company or corporation, and
(2) in respect of a corporation which is not a registered company, in addition to those persons set out in (1), the mayor, chairman, president, town clerk or similar officer of the corporation.

Scope of provision—The practice direction relates purely to the alternative method of service on a registered company or corporation in accordance with CPR r 6.5(6) and does not relate to service on registered companies or corporations by any of the other statutory methods referred to in CPR r 6.2(2).

Change of Address

7 A party or his legal representative who changes his address for service shall give notice in writing of the change as soon as it has taken place to the court and every other party.

SERVICE BY THE COURT

8.1 Where the court effects service of a document in accordance with rule 6.3(1) and (2), the method will normally be by first class post.

8.2

8.3 Where the court effects service of a claim form, delivers a defence to a claimant or notifies a claimant that the defendant has filed an acknowledgment of service, the court will also serve or deliver a copy of any notice of funding that has been filed provided –

- (a) it was filed at the same time as the claim form, defence or acknowledgment of service, and
- (b) copies were provided for service.

Scope of provision—Practitioners should note that once they receive notice of non-service of a document, including a claim form by the court, they should take steps to effect service. The duty of the Court Service to effect service pursuant to the rule stops at that point (CPR r 6.3(1)(e)).

Related provision—CPR r 7.5 (Time for service of the claim form). CPR r 7.6 (Extension of time for serving of claim form).

Content of Evidence

THE FOLLOWING APPLICATIONS RELATING TO SERVICE REQUIRE EVIDENCE IN SUPPORT

9.1 An application for an order for service by an alternative method[1] should be supported by evidence stating:

- (1) the reason an order for an alternative method of service is sought, and
- (2) what steps have been taken to serve by other permitted means.

1 See rule 6.8.

9.2 An application for service of a claim form relating to a contract on the agent of a principal who is overseas should be supported by evidence setting out:

- (1) full details of the contract and that it was entered into within the jurisdiction with or through an agent who is either an individual residing or carrying on business within the jurisdiction, or is a registered company or corporation having a registered office or a place of business within the jurisdiction,
- (2) that the principal for whom the agent is acting was, at the time the contract was entered into and is at the time of making the application, neither an individual, registered company or corporation as described in (1) above, and
- (3) why service out of the jurisdiction cannot be effected.

Annex

SERVICE ON MEMBERS OF HM FORCES

1 The following information is for litigants and legal representatives who wish to serve legal documents in civil proceedings in the courts of England and Wales on parties to the proceedings who are (or who, at the material time were) regular members of Her Majesty's Forces.

2 The proceedings may take place in the county court or the High Court, and the documents to be served may be both originating claims, interim applications and pre-action applications. Proceedings for divorce or maintenance and proceedings in the Family Courts generally are subject to special rules as to service which are explained in a practice direction issued by the Senior District Judge of the Principal Registry on 26 June 1979.

3 In these instructions, the person wishing to effect service is referred to as the 'claimant' and the person to be served is referred to as the 'serviceman'; the expression 'overseas' means outside the United Kingdom.

ENQUIRIES AS TO ADDRESS

4 As a first step, the claimant's legal representative will need to find out where the serviceman is serving, if he does not already know. For this purpose he should write to the appropriate officer of the Ministry of Defence as specified in paragraph 10, below.

5 The letter of enquiry should in every case show that the writer is a legal representative and that the enquiry is made solely with a view to the service of legal documents in civil proceedings.

6 In all cases the letter should give the full name, service number, rank or rating, and Ship, Arm or Trade, Regiment or Corps and Unit or as much of this information as is available. Failure to quote the service number and the rank or rating may result either in failure to identify the serviceman or in considerable delay.

7 The letter should contain an undertaking by the legal representative that, if the address is given, it will be used solely for the purpose of issuing and serving documents in the proceedings and that so far as is possible the legal representative will disclose the address only to the court and not to his client or to any other person or body. A legal representative in the service of a public authority or private company should undertake that the address will be used solely for the purpose of issuing and serving documents in the proceedings and that the address will not be disclosed so far as is possible to any other part of his employing organisation or to any other person but only to the court. Normally on receipt of the required information and undertaking the appropriate office will give the service address.

8 If the legal representative does not give the undertaking, the only information he will receive will be whether the serviceman is at that time serving in England or Wales, Scotland, Northern Ireland or overseas.

9 It should be noted that a serviceman's address which ends with a British Forces Post Office address and reference (BFPO) will nearly always indicate that he is serving overseas.

10 The letter of enquiry should be addressed as follows:

(a) Royal Navy Officers

The Naval Secretary
Room 161
Victory Building
HM Naval Base
Portsmouth
Hants PO1 3LS

	RN Ratings	Commodore Naval Drafting Centurion Building Grange Road Gosport Hants PO13 9XA
	RN Medical and Dental Officers	The Medical Director General (Naval) Room 114 Victory Building HM Naval Base Portsmouth Hants PO1 3LS
	Officers of Queen Alexandra's Royal Naval Nursing Service	The Matron-in-Chief QARNNS Room 139 Victory Building HM Naval Base Portsmouth Hants PO1 3LS
	Naval Chaplains	Director General Naval Chaplaincy Service Room 201 Victory Building HM Naval Base Portsmouth Hants PO1 3LS
(b)	Royal Marine Officers and Ranks	Personnel Section West Battery Whale Island Portsmouth Hants PO2 8DX
	RM Ranks HQRM	(DRORM) West Battery Whale Island Portsmouth Hants PO2 8DX
(c)	Army Officers and other ranks	Ministry of Defence Army Personnel Centre Secretariat, Public Enquiries RM CD424 Kentigern House 65 Brown Street Glasgow G2 8EH
(d)	Royal Air Force Officers and Other Ranks	Personnel Management Agency (RAF) Building 248 RAF Innsworth Gloucester GL3 1EZ

ASSISTANCE IN SERVING DOCUMENTS ON SERVICEMEN

11 Once the claimant's legal representative has learnt the serviceman's address, he may use that address as the address for service by post, in cases where this method of service is allowed by the Civil Procedure Rules. There are, however, some situations in which service of the proceedings, whether in the High Court or in the county court, has to be effected personally; in these cases an appointment will have to be sought, through the Commanding Officer of the Unit, Establishment or Ship concerned, for the purpose of effecting service. The procedure for obtaining an appointment is described below, and it applies whether personal service is to be effected by the claimant's legal representative or his agent or by a court bailiff, or, in the case of proceedings served overseas (with the leave of the court) through the British Consul or the foreign judicial authority.

12 The procedure for obtaining an appointment to effect personal service is by application to the Commanding Officer of the Unit, Establishment or Ship in which the serviceman is serving. The Commanding Officer may grant permission for the document server to enter the Unit, Establishment or Ship but if this is not appropriate he may offer arrangements for the serviceman to attend at a place in the vicinity of the Unit, Establishment or Ship in order that he may be served. If suitable arrangements cannot be made the legal representative will have evidence that personal service is impracticable, which may be useful in an application for service by an alternative method.

GENERAL

13 Subject to the procedure outlined in paragraphs 11 and 12, there are no special arrangements to assist in the service of process when a serviceman is outside the United Kingdom. The appropriate office will however give an approximate date when the serviceman is likely to return to the United Kingdom.

14 It sometimes happens that a serviceman has left the service by the time that the enquiry is made. If the claimant's legal representative confirms that the proceedings result from an occurrence when the serviceman was in the Forces and he gives the undertaking referred to in paragraph 7, the last known private address after discharge will normally be provided. In no other case however will the Department disclose the private address of a member of HM Forces.

SERVICE ON MEMBERS OF UNITED STATES AIR FORCE

15 In addition to the information contained in the memorandum of the 26 July 1979, the Lord Chancellor's Office, some doubts having been expressed as to the correct procedure to be followed by persons having civil claims against members of the United States Air Force in this country, issued the following notes for guidance with the approval of the appropriate United States authorities:

16 Instructions have been issued by the U.S. authorities to the commanding officers of all their units in this country that every facility is to be given for the service of documents in civil proceedings on members of the U.S. Air Force. The proper course to be followed by a creditor or other person having a claim against a member of the U.S. Air Force is for him to communicate with the commanding officer or, where the unit concerned has a legal officer, with the legal officer of the defendant's unit requesting him to provide facilities for the

service of documents on the defendant. It is not possible for the U.S. authorities to act as arbitrators when a civil claim is made against a member of their forces. It is, therefore, essential that the claim should either be admitted by the defendant or judgment should be obtained on it, whether in the High Court or a county court. If a claim has been admitted or judgment has been obtained and the claimant has failed to obtain satisfaction within a reasonable period, his proper course is then to write to: Office of the Staff Judge Advocate, Headquarters, Third Air Force, R.A.F. Mildenhall, Suffolk, enclosing a copy of the defendant's written admission of the claim or, as the case may be, a copy of the judgment. Steps will then be taken by the Staff Judge Advocate to ensure that the matter is brought to the defendant's attention with a view to prompt satisfaction of the claim.

Practice Direction – Service out of the Jurisdiction

This Practice Direction supplements CPR Part 6, Section III (PD6B)

Procedural Guide—See Guide 16, set out in Section 1 of this work.

SERVICE IN OTHER MEMBER STATES OF THE EUROPEAN UNION

A1.1 Where service is to be effected in another Member State of the European Union, Council Regulation (EC) No 1348/2000 of 29 May 2000 on the service in the Member States of judicial and extrajudicial documents in civil or commercial matters ('the Service Regulation') applies.

A1.2 The Service Regulation is annexed to this practice direction.

(Article 20(1) of the Service Regulation provides that the Regulation prevails over other provisions contained in bilateral or multilateral agreements or arrangements concluded by the Member of States and in particular Article IV of the protocol to the Brussels Convention of 1968 and the Hague Convention of 15 November 1965)

(Originally published in the official languages of the European Community in the *Official Journal of the European Communities* by the Office for Official Publications of the European Communities)

SERVICE OUT OF THE JURISDICTION WHERE PERMISSION OF THE COURT IS NOT REQUIRED

1.1 The usual form of words of the statement required by rule 6.19(3) where the court has power to determine the claim under the 1982 Act should be –

'I state that the High Court of England and Wales has power under the Civil Jurisdiction and Judgments Act 1982 to hear this claim and that no proceedings are pending between the parties in Scotland, Northern Ireland or another Convention territory of any contracting state as defined by section 1(3) of the Act'.

1.2 However, in proceedings to which rule 6.19(1)(b)(ii) applies, the statement should be –

> 'I state that the High Court of England and Wales has power under the Civil Jurisdiction and Judgments Act 1982, the claim having as its object rights in rem in immovable property or tenancies in immovable property (or otherwise in accordance with the provisions of Article 16 of Schedule 1 or 3C to that Act, or paragraph 11 of Schedule 4 to that Act) to which any of those provisions applies, to hear the claim and that no proceedings are pending between the parties in Scotland, Northern Ireland or another Convention territory of any contracting state as defined by section 1(3) of the Act'.

1.3 And in proceedings to which rule 6.19(1)(b)(iii) applies, the statement should be –

> 'I state that the High Court of England and Wales has power under the Civil Jurisdiction and Judgments Act 1982, the defendant being a party to an an agreement conferring jurisdiction to which Article 17 of Schedule 1 or 3C to that Act or paragraph 12 of Schedule 4 to that Act applies, to hear the claim and that no proceedings are pending between the parties in Scotland, Northern Ireland or another Convention territory of any contracting state as defined by section 1(3) of the Act'.

1.3A The usual form of words of the statement required by rule 6.19(3) where the Judgments Regulation applies should be –

> 'I state that the High Court of England and Wales has power under Council Regulation (EC) No 44/2001 of 22 December 2000 (on jurisdiction and the recognition and enforcement of judgments in civil and commercial matters) to hear this claim and that no proceedings are pending between the parties in Scotland, Northern Ireland or any other Regulation State as defined by section 1(3) of the Civil Jurisdiction and Judgments Act 1982.'

1.3B However, in proceedings to which rule 6.19(1A)(b)(ii) applies, the statement should be –

> 'I state that the High Court of England and Wales has power under Council Regulation (EC) No 44/2001 of 22 December 2000 (on jurisdiction and the recognition and enforcement of judgments in civil and commercial matters), the claim having as its object rights *in rem* in immovable property or tenancies in immovable property (or otherwise in accordance with the provisions of Article 22 of that Regulation) to which Article 22 of that Regulation applies, to hear this claim and that no proceedings are pending between the parties in Scotland, Northern Ireland or any other Regulation State as defined by section 1(3) of the Civil Jurisdiction and Judgments Act 1982.'

1.3C And in proceedings to which rule 6.19(1A)(b)(iii) applies, the statement should be –

> 'I state that the High Court of England and Wales has power under Council Regulation (EC) No 44/2001 of 22 December 2000 (on jurisdiction and the recognition and enforcement of judgments in civil and commercial matters), the defendant being a party to an agreement conferring jurisdiction to which Article 23 of that Regulation applies, to hear this claim and that no proceedings are pending between the parties in Scotland, Northern Ireland or any other Regulation State as defined by section 1(3) of the Civil Jurisdiction and Judgments Act 1982.'

1.3D In proceedings to which Rule 6.19(2) applies, the statement should be –

'I state that the High Court of England and Wales has power to hear this claim under [state the provisions of the relevant enactment] which satisfies the requirements of rule 6.19(2), and that no proceedings are pending between the parties in Scotland or Northern Ireland, or in another Contracting State or Regulation State as defined by section 1(3) of the Civil Jurisdiction and Judgments Act 1982.'

1.4 A claim form appearing to be for service on a defendant under the provisions of rule 6.19 which does not include a statement in the form of 1.1, 1.2, 1.3, 1.3A, 1.3B, 1.3C or 1.3D above will be marked on issue 'Not for service out of the jurisdiction'.

1.5 Where a claim form is served without particulars of claim, it must be accompanied by a copy of Form N1C (notes for defendants).

SERVICE OUT OF THE JURISDICTION WHERE PERMISSION IS REQUIRED

Documents to be filed under rule 6.26(2)(d)

2.1 A complete set of the following documents must be provided for each party to be served out of the jurisdiction –

(1) A copy of particulars of claim if not already incorporated in or attached to the claim.
(2) A duplicate of the claim form of the particulars of claim and of any documents accompanying the claim and of any translation required by rule 6.28.
(3) Forms for responding to the claim.
(4) Any translation required under rule 6.28 and paragraphs 4.1 and 4.2, in duplicate.

2.2 The documents to be served in certain countries require legalisation and the Foreign Process Section (Room E02), Royal Courts of Justice will advise on request. Some countries require legislation and some require a formal letter of request, see Form No 34 to Table 2 of Practice Direction to Part 4 which must be signed by the Senior Master of the Queen's Bench Division irrespective of the Division of the High Court or any county court in which the order was made.

SERVICE IN SCOTLAND, NORTHERN IRELAND, THE CHANNEL ISLANDS, THE ISLE OF MAN, COMMONWEALTH COUNTRIES, UNITED KINGDOM OVERSEAS TERRITORIES

3.1 Where Rule 6.25(4) applies, service should be effected by the claimant or his agent direct except in the case of a Commonwealth State where the judicial authorities have required service to be in accordance with Rule 6.24(1)(b)(i). These are presently Malta and Singapore.

3.2 For the purposes of rule 6.25(4)(c), the following countries are United Kingdom Overseas Territories –

(a) Anguilla;
(b) Bermuda;
(c) British Antarctic Territory;
(d) British Indian Ocean Territory;
(e) Cayman Islands;
(f) Falklands Islands;

(g) Gibraltar;
(h) Montserrat;
(i) Pitcairn, Henderson, Ducie and Oeno;
(j) St Helena and Dependencies;
(k) South Georgia and the South Sandwich Islands;
(l) Sovereign Base Areas of Akrotiri and Dhekelia;
(m) Turks and Caicos Islands; and
(n) Virgin Islands.

TRANSLATIONS

4.1 Rule 6.28 applies to particulars of claim not included in a claim form as well as to claim forms.

4.2 Where a translation of a claim form is required under rule 6.28, the claimant must also file a translation of all the forms that will accompany the claim form.

(It should be noted that English is not an official language in the Province of Quebec)

SERVICE WITH THE PERMISSION OF THE COURT UNDER CERTAIN ACTS

5.1 Rule 6.20(18) provides that a claim form may be served out of the jurisdiction with the court's permission if the claim is made under an enactment specified in the relevant practice direction.

5.2 These enactments are:

(1) The Nuclear Installations Act 1965,
(2) The Social Security Contributions and Benefits Act 1992,
(3) The Directive of the Council of the European Communities dated 15 March 1976 No 76/308/EEC, where service is to be effected in a member state of the European Union,
(4) The Drug Trafficking Offences Act 1994,
(5) (*revoked*)
(6) (*revoked*)
(7) Part VI of the Criminal Justice Act 1988,
(8) The Inheritance (Provision for Family and Dependants) Act 1975,
(9) Part II of the Immigration and Asylum Act 1999,
(10) Schedule 2 to the Immigration Act 1971.
(11) The Financial Services and Markets Act 2000.
(12) The Pensions Act 1995,
(13) The Pensions Act 2004.

5.3 Under the State Immunity Act 1978, the foreign state being served is allowed an additional 2 months over the normal period for filing an acknowledgment of service or defence or for filing or serving an admission allowed under paragraphs 7.3 and 7.4.

SERVICE OF PETITIONS, APPLICATION NOTICES AND ORDERS

6.1 The provisions of Section III of Part 6 (special provisions about service out of the jurisdiction) apply to service out of the jurisdiction of a petition, application notice or order.

(Rule 6.30(1) contains special provisions relating to application notices)

6.2 Where an application notice is to be served out of the jurisdiction in accordance with Section III of Part 6 the court must have regard to the country in which the application notice is to be served in setting the date for the hearing of the application and giving any direction about service of the respondent's evidence.

6.3 Where the permission of the court is required for a claim form to be served out of the jurisdiction the permission of the court, unless rule 6.30(3) applies, must also be obtained for service out of the jurisdiction of any other document to be served in the proceedings and the provisions of this practice direction will, so far as applicable to that other document, apply.

6.4 When particulars of claim are served out of the jurisdiction any statement as to the period for responding to the claim contained in any of the forms required by rule 7.8 to accompany the particulars of claim must specify the period prescribed under rule 6.22 or 6.23 or (as the case may be) by the order permitting service out of the jurisdiction (see rule 6.21(4)).

PERIOD FOR RESPONDING TO A CLAIM FORM

7.1 Where a claim form has been served out of the jurisdiction without permission under rule 6.19 –

(1) Rule 6.22 sets out the period for filing an acknowledgment of service or filing or serving an admission; and where rule 6.22(4) applies, the period will be calculated in accordance with paragraph 7.3 having regard to the Table below;

(2) Rule 6.23 sets out the period for filing a defence and where rule 6.23(4) applies, the period will be calculated in accordance with paragraph 7.4 having regard to the Table below.

7.2 Where an order grants permission to serve a claim form out of the jurisdiction, the periods within which the defendant may –

(1) file an acknowledgment of service;
(2) file or serve an admission;
(3) file a defence,

will be calculated in accordance with paragraphs 7.3 and 7.4 having regard to the Table below.

(Rule 6.21(4) requires an order giving permission for a claim form to be served out of the jurisdiction to specify the period within which the defendant may respond to the claim form)

7.3 The period for filing an acknowledgment of service under Part 10 or filing or serving an admission under Part 14 is –

(1) where the defendant is served with a claim form which states that particulars of claim are to follow, the number of days listed in the Table after service of the particulars of claim; and

(2) in any other case, the number of days listed in the Table after service of the claim form.

For example, where a defendant has been served with a claim form (accompanied by particulars of claim) in the Bahamas, the period for acknowledging service or admitting the claim is 22 days after service.

7.4 The period for filing a defence under Part 15 is –

(1) the number of days listed in the Table after service of the particulars of claim; or
(2) where the defendant has filed an acknowledgment of service, the number of days listed in the Table plus an additional 14 days after the service of the particulars of claim.

For example, where a defendant has been served with particulars of claim in Gibraltar and has acknowledged service, the period for filing a defence is 45 days after service of the particulars of claim.

PERIOD FOR RESPONDING TO AN APPLICATION NOTICE

8.1 Where an application notice or order needs to be served out of the jurisdiction, the period for responding to service is 7 days less than the number of days listed in thc Tablc.

ADDRESS FOR SERVICE AND FURTHER INFORMATION

10.1 A defendant is required by rule 6.5(2) to give an address for service within the jurisdiction.

10.2 Further information concerning service out of the jurisdiction can be obtained from the Foreign Process Section, Room E02, Royal Courts of Justice, Strand, London WC2A 2LL (tel: 020 7947 6691).

Table

Place or country	**number of days**
Abu Dhabi	22
Afghanistan	23
Albania	25
Algeria	22
Angola	22
Anguilla	31
Antigua	23
Antilles (Netherlands)	31
Argentina	22
Armenia	21
Ascension	31
Australia	25
Austria	21
Azores	23
Bahamas	22
Bahrain	22
Balearic Islands	21
Bangladesh	23
Barbados	23
Belarus	21
Belgium	21
Belize	23
Benin	25
Bermuda	31
Bhutan	28
Bolivia	23

Table **Place or country**	**number of days**
Bosnia-Hercegovina	21
Botswana	23
Brazil	22
Brunei	25
Bulgaria	23
Burkina Faso	23
Burma	23
Burundi	22
Cameroon	22
Canada	22
Canary Islands	22
Cape Verde Islands	25
Caroline Islands	31
Cayman Islands	31
Central African Republic	25
Chad	25
Chile	22
China	24
Christmas Island	27
Cocos (Keeling) Islands	41
Colombia	22
Comoros	23
Congo (People's Republic)	25
Corsica	21
Costa Rica	23
Croatia	21
Cuba	24
Cyprus	31
Cyrenaica (see Libya)	21
Czech Republic	21
Denmark	21
Djibouti	22
Dominica	23
Dominican Republic	23
Dubai	22
Ecuador	22
Egypt (Arab Republic)	22
El Salvador (Republic of)	25
Equatorial Guinea	23
Estonia	21
Ethiopia	22
Falkland Islands and Dependencies	31
Faroe Islands	31
Fiji	23
Finland	24
France	21
French Guiana	31
French Polynesia	31

Table **Place or country**	**number of days**
French West Indies	31
Gabon	25
Gambia	22
Georgia	21
Germany	21
Ghana	22
Gibraltar	31
Greece	21
Greenland	31
Grenada	24
Guatemala	24
Guernsey	18
Guyana	22
Haiti	23
Holland (Netherlands)	21
Honduras	24
Hong Kong	31
Hungary	22
Iceland	22
India	23
Indonesia	22
Iran	22
Iraq	22
Ireland (Republic of)	21
Ireland (Northern)	21
Isle of Man	18
Israel	22
Italy	21
Ivory Coast	22
Jamaica	22
Japan	23
Jersey	18
Jordan	23
Kampuchea	38
Kazakhstan	21
Kenya	22
Kirgizstan	21
Korea (North)	28
Korea (South)	24
Kuwait	22
Laos	30
Latvia	21
Lebanon	22
Lesotho	23
Liberia	22
Libya	21
Liechtenstein	21
Lithuania	21

Table **Place or country**	**number of days**
Luxembourg	21
Macau	31
Macedonia	21
Madagascar	23
Madeira	31
Malawi	23
Malaya	24
Maldive Islands	26
Mali	25
Malta	21
Mariana Islands	26
Marshall Islands	32
Mauritania	23
Mauritius	22
Mexico	23
Moldova	21
Monaco	21
Montserrat	31
Morocco	22
Mozambique	23
Nauru Island	36
Nepal	23
Netherlands	21
Nevis	24
New Caledonia	31
New Hebrides (now Vanuatu)	29
New Zealand	26
New Zealand Island Territories	50
Nicaragua	24
Niger (Republic of)	25
Nigeria	22
Norfolk Island	31
Norway	21
Oman (Sultanate of)	22
Pakistan	23
Panama (Republic of)	26
Papua New Guinea	26
Paraguay	22
Peru	22
Philippines	23
Pitcairn Island	31
Poland	21
Portugal	21
Portuguese Timor	31
Puerto Rico	23
Qatar	23
Reunion	31

Table **Place or country**	**number of days**
Romania	22
Russia	21
Rwanda	23
Sabah	23
St Helena	31
St Kitts/Nevis	24
St Lucia	24
St Pierre and Miquelon	31
St Vincent and the Grenadines	24
Samoa (USA Territory) (See also Western Samoa)	30
Sarawak	28
Saudi Arabia	24
Scotland	21
Senegal	22
Seychelles	22
Sharjah	24
Sierra Leone	22
Singapore	22
Slovakia	21
Slovenia	21
Society Islands (French Polynesia)	31
Solomon Islands	29
Somali Democratic Republic	22
South Africa (Republic of)	22
South Georgia (Falkland Island Dependencies)	31
South Orkneys	21
South Shetlands	21
Spain	21
Spanish Territories of North Africa	31
Sri Lanka	23
Sudan	22
Suriname	22
Swaziland	22
Sweden	21
Switzerland	21
Syria	23
Taiwan	23
Tajikistan	21
Tanzania	22
Thailand	23
Tibet	34
Tobago	23
Togo	22
Tonga	30

Table Place or country	number of days
Tortola	31
Trinidad & Tobago	23
Tristan Da Cunha	31
Tunisia	22
Turkey	21
Turkmenistan	21
Turks & Caicos Islands	31
Uganda	22
Ukraine	21
United States of America	22
Uruguay	22
Uzbekistan	21
Vanuatu	29
Vatican City State	21
Venezuela	22
Vietnam	28
Virgin Islands – British (Tortola)	31
Virgin Islands – USA	24
Wake Island	25
Western Samoa	34
Yemen (Republic of)	30
Yugoslavia (except for Bosnia-Hercegovina, Croatia, Macedonia and Slovenia)	21
Zaire	25
Zambia	23
Zimbabwe	22

Annex

Council Regulation (EC) No 1348/2000

of 29 May 2000

on the service in the Member States of judicial and extrajudicial documents in civil or commercial matters

THE COUNCIL OF THE EUROPEAN UNION,

Having regard to the Treaty establishing the European Community, and in particular Article 61(c) and Article 67(1) thereof,

Having regard to the proposal from the Commission[1],

1 OJ C 247 E, 31.8.1999, p 11.

Having regard to the opinion of the European Parliament[2],

2 Opinion of 17 November 1999 (not yet published in the Official Journal).

Having regard to the opinion of the Economic and Social Committee[3],

3 OJ C 368, 20.12.1999, p 47.

Whereas:

(1) The Union has set itself the objective of maintaining and developing the Union as an area of freedom, security and justice, in which the free movement of persons is assured. To establish such an area, the Community is to adopt, among others, the measures relating to judicial cooperation in civil matters needed for the proper functioning of the internal market.

(2) The proper functioning of the internal market entails the need to improve and expedite the transmission of judicial and extrajudicial documents in civil or commercial matters for service between the Member States.

(3) This is a subject now falling within the ambit of Article 65 of the Treaty.

(4) In accordance with the principles of subsidiarity and proportionality as set out in Article 5 of the Treaty, the objectives of this Regulation cannot be sufficiently achieved by the Member States and can therefore be better achieved by the Community. This Regulation does not go beyond what is necessary to achieve those objectives.

(5) The Council, by an Act dated 26 May 1997[4], drew up a Convention on the service in the Member States of the European Union of judicial and extrajudicial documents in civil or commercial matters and recommended it for adoption by the Member States in accordance with their respective constitutional rules. That Convention has not entered into force. Continuity in the results of the negotiations for conclusion of the Convention should be ensured. The main content of this Regulation is substantially taken over from it.

4 OJ C 261, 27.8.1997, p 1. On the same day as the Convention was drawn up the Council took note of the explanatory report on the Convention which is set out on page 26 of the aforementioned Official Journal.

(6) Efficiency and speed in judicial procedures in civil matters means that the transmission of judicial and extrajudicial documents is to be made direct and by rapid means between local bodies designated by the Member States. However, the Member States may indicate their intention of designating only one transmitting or receiving agency or one agency to perform both functions for a period of five years. This designation may, however, be renewed every five years.

(7) Speed in transmission warrants the use of all appropriate means, provided that certain conditions as to the legibility and reliability of the document received are observed. Security in transmission requires that the document to be transmitted be accompanied by a pre-printed form, to be completed in the language of the place where service is to be effected, or in another language accepted by the Member State in question.

(8) To secure the effectiveness of this Regulation, the possibility of refusing service of documents is confined to exceptional situations.

(9) Speed of transmission warrants documents being served within days of reception of the document. However, if service has not been effected after one month has elapsed, the receiving agency should inform the transmitting agency. The expiry of this period should not imply that the request be returned to the transmitting agency where it is clear that service is feasible within a reasonable period.

(10) For the protection of the addressee's interests, service should be effected in the official language or one of the official languages of the place where it is to be effected or in another language of the originating Member State which the addressee understands.

(11) Given the differences between the Member States as regards their rules of procedure, the material date for the purposes of service varies from one Member State to another. Having regard to such situations and the possible difficulties that may arise, this Regulation should provide for a system where it is the law of the receiving Member State which determines the date of service. However, if the relevant documents in the context of proceedings to be brought or pending in the Member State of origin are to be served within a specified period, the date to be taken into consideration with respect to the applicant shall be that determined according to the law of the Member State of origin. A Member State is, however, authorised to derogate from the aforementioned provisions for a transitional period of five years, for appropriate reasons. Such a derogation may be renewed by a Member State at five-year intervals due to reasons related to its legal system.

(12) This Regulation prevails over the provisions contained in bilateral or multilateral agreements or arrangements having the same scope, concluded by the Member States, and in particular the Protocol annexed to the Brussels Convention of 27 September 1968[5] and the Hague Convention of 15 November 1965 in relations between the Member States party thereto. This Regulation does not preclude Member States from maintaining or concluding agreements or arrangements to expedite or simplify the transmission of documents, provided that they are compatible with the Regulation.

5 Brussels Convention of 27 September 1968 on Jurisdiction and the Enforcement of Judgments in Civil and Commercial Matters (OJ L 299, 13.12.1972, p 32; consolidated version, OJ C 27, 26.1.1998, p 1).

(13) The information transmitted pursuant to this Regulation should enjoy suitable protection. This matter falls within the scope of Directive 95/46/EC of the European Parliament and of the Council of 24 October 1995 on the protection of individuals with regard to the processing of personal data and on the free movement of such data[6], and of Directive 97/66/EC of the European Parliament and of the Council of 15 December 1997 concerning the processing of personal data and the protection of privacy in the telecommunications sector[7].

6 OJ L 281, 23.11.1995, p 31.
7 OJ L 24, 30.1.1998, p 1.

(14) The measures necessary for the implementation of this Regulation should be adopted in accordance with Council Decision 1999/468/EC of 28 June 1999 laying down the procedures for the exercise of implementing powers conferred on the Commission[8].

8 OJ L 184, 17.7.1999, p 23.

(15) These measures also include drawing up and updating the manual using appropriate modern means.

(16) No later than three years after the date of entry into force of this Regulation, the Commission should review its application and propose such amendments as may appear necessary.

(17) The United Kingdom and Ireland, in accordance with Article 3 of the Protocol on the position of the United Kingdom and Ireland annexed to the

Treaty on European Union and the Treaty establishing the European Community, have given notice of their wish to take part in the adoption and application of this Regulation.

(18) Denmark, in accordance with Articles 1 and 2 of the Protocol on the position of Denmark annexed to the Treaty on European Union and the Treaty establishing the European Community, is not participating in the adoption of this Regulation, and is therefore not bound by it nor subject to its application,

HAS ADOPTED THIS REGULATION:

CHAPTER I
GENERAL PROVISIONS

ARTICLE 1

Scope

1 This Regulation shall apply in civil and commercial matters where a judicial or extrajudicial document has to be transmitted from one Member State to another for service there.

2 This Regulation shall not apply where the address of the person to be served with the document is not known.

ARTICLE 2

Transmitting and receiving agencies

1 Each Member State shall designate the public officers, authorities or other persons, hereinafter referred to as 'transmitting agencies', competent for the transmission of judicial or extrajudicial documents to be served in another Member State.

2 Each Member State shall designate the public officers, authorities or other persons, hereinafter referred to as 'receiving agencies', competent for the receipt of judicial or extrajudicial documents from another Member State.

3 A Member State may designate one transmitting agency and one receiving agency or one agency to perform both functions. A federal State, a State in which several legal systems apply or a State with autonomous territorial units shall be free to designate more than one such agency. The designation shall have effect for a period of five years and may be renewed at five-year intervals.

4 Each Member State shall provide the Commission with the following information:

(a) the names and addresses of the receiving agencies referred to in paragraphs 2 and 3;
(b) the geographical areas in which they have jurisdiction;
(c) the means of receipt of documents available to them; and
(d) the languages that may be used for the completion of the standard form in the Annex.

Member States shall notify the Commission of any subsequent modification of such information.

'transmitting agencies' (Art 2(1))—The transmitting agency for England and Wales is the Senior Master of the Queen's Bench Division.

ARTICLE 3

Central body

Each Member State shall designate a central body responsible for:

(a) supplying information to the transmitting agencies;
(b) seeking solutions to any difficulties which may arise during transmission of documents for service;
(c) forwarding, in exceptional cases, at the request of a transmitting agency, a request for service to the competent receiving agency.

A federal State, a State in which several legal systems apply or a State with autonomous territorial units shall be free to designate more than one central body.

'central body' (Art 3)—The central body designated for England and Wales is The Senior Master, Foreign Process Department (Room E10), Royal Courts of Justice, Strand, London WC2A 2LL, telephone 020 7947 6691, fax 020 7947 6237.

CHAPTER II
JUDICIAL DOCUMENTS

SECTION 1

TRANSMISSION AND SERVICE OF JUDICIAL DOCUMENTS

ARTICLE 4

Transmission of documents

1 Judicial documents shall be transmitted directly and as soon as possible between the agencies designated on the basis of Article 2.

2 The transmission of documents, requests, confirmations, receipts, certificates and any other papers between transmitting agencies and receiving agencies may be carried out by any appropriate means, provided that the content of the document received is true and faithful to that of the document forwarded and that all information in it is easily legible.

3 The document to be transmitted shall be accompanied by a request drawn up using the standard form in the Annex. The form shall be completed in the official language of the Member State addressed or, if there are several official languages in that Member State, the official language or one of the official languages of the place where service is to be effected, or in another language which that Member State has indicated it can accept. Each Member State shall indicate the official language or languages of the European Union other than its own which is or are acceptable to it for completion of the form.

4 The documents and all papers that are transmitted shall be exempted from legalisation or any equivalent formality.

5 When the transmitting agency wishes a copy of the document to be returned together with the certificate referred to in Article 10, it shall send the document in duplicate.

ARTICLE 5

Translation of documents

1 The applicant shall be advised by the transmitting agency to which he or she forwards the document for transmission that the addressee may refuse to accept it if it is not in one of the languages provided for in Article 8.

2 The applicant shall bear any costs of translation prior to the transmission of the document, without prejudice to any possible subsequent decision by the court or competent authority on liability for such costs.

ARTICLE 6

Receipt of documents by receiving agency

1 On receipt of a document, a receiving agency shall, as soon as possible and in any event within seven days of receipt, send a receipt to the transmitting agency by the swiftest possible means of transmission using the standard form in the Annex.

2 Where the request for service cannot be fulfilled on the basis of the information or documents transmitted, the receiving agency shall contact the transmitting agency by the swiftest possible means in order to secure the missing information or documents.

3 If the request for service is manifestly outside the scope of this Regulation or if non-compliance with the formal conditions required makes service impossible, the request and the documents transmitted shall be returned, on receipt, to the transmitting agency, together with the notice of return in the standard form in the Annex.

4 A receiving agency receiving a document for service but not having territorial jurisdiction to serve it shall forward it, as well as the request, to the receiving agency having territorial jurisdiction in the same Member State if the request complies with the conditions laid down in Article 4(3) and shall inform the transmitting agency accordingly, using the standard form in the Annex. That receiving agency shall inform the transmitting agency when it receives the document, in the manner provided for in paragraph 1.

ARTICLE 7

Service of documents

1 The receiving agency shall itself serve the document or have it served, either in accordance with the law of the Member State addressed or by a particular form requested by the transmitting agency, unless such a method is incompatible with the law of that Member State.

2 All steps required for service of the document shall be effected as soon as possible. In any event, if it has not been possible to effect service within one month of receipt, the receiving agency shall inform the transmitting agency by means of the certificate in the standard form in the Annex, which shall be drawn up under the conditions referred to in Article 10(2). The period shall be calculated in accordance with the law of the Member State addressed.

ARTICLE 8

Refusal to accept a document

1 The receiving agency shall inform the addressee that he or she may refuse to accept the document to be served if it is in a language other than either of the following languages:

(a) the official language of the Member State addressed or, if there are several official languages in that Member State, the official language or one of the official languages of the place where service is to be effected; or

(b) a language of the Member State of transmission which the addressee understands.

2 Where the receiving agency is informed that the addressee refuses to accept the document in accordance with paragraph 1, it shall immediately inform the transmitting agency by means of the certificate provided for in Article 10 and return the request and the documents of which a translation is requested.

'understands' (Art 8(1)(b))—This important concept is unclear. What degree of understanding of English must a foreign resident have to be obliged to accept service in English? In the extradition case of *Re Picken* [2003] All ER (D) 387 (Jun), the Divisional Court remarked that the applicant was largely responsible for the delay in his extradition because he had not acted on a summons, written in French. The court said that it was incredible to suggest that if he had not understood it he would not have had it translated. This may imply that the English courts will take a robust view. However, the opportunity to claim not to be fluent in English offers a ready means of evading service. Particularly if the claim is substantial or the defendant likely to be evasive, it is sensible to serve a translation.

ARTICLE 9

Date of service

1 Without prejudice to Article 8, the date of service of a document pursuant to Article 7 shall be the date on which it is served in accordance with the law of the Member State addressed.

2 However, where a document shall be served within a particular period in the context of proceedings to be brought or pending in the Member State of origin, the date to be taken into account with respect to the applicant shall be that fixed by the law of that Member State.

3 A Member State shall be authorised to derogate from the provisions of paragraphs 1 and 2 for a transitional period of five years, for appropriate reasons.

This transitional period may be renewed by a Member State at five-yearly intervals due to reasons related to its legal system. That Member State shall inform the Commission of the content of such a derogation and the circumstances of the case.

ARTICLE 10

Certificate of service and copy of the document served

1 When the formalities concerning the service of the document have been completed, a certificate of completion of those formalities shall be drawn up in

the standard form in the Annex and addressed to the transmitting agency, together with, where Article 4(5) applies, a copy of the document served.

2 The certificate shall be completed in the official language or one of the official languages of the Member State of origin or in another language which the Member State of origin has indicated that it can accept. Each Member State shall indicate the official language or languages of the European Union other than its own which is or are acceptable to it for completion of the form.

ARTICLE 11

Costs of service

1 The service of judicial documents coming from a Member State shall not give rise to any payment or reimbursement of taxes or costs for services rendered by the Member State addressed.

2 The applicant shall pay or reimburse the costs occasioned by:

(a) the employment of a judicial officer or of a person competent under the law of the Member State addressed;
(b) the use of a particular method of service.

SECTION 2

OTHER MEANS OF TRANSMISSION AND SERVICE OF JUDICIAL DOCUMENTS

ARTICLE 12

Transmission by consular or diplomatic channels

Each Member State shall be free, in exceptional circumstances, to use consular or diplomatic channels to forward judicial documents, for the purpose of service, to those agencies of another Member State which are designated pursuant to Article 2 or 3.

ARTICLE 13

Service by diplomatic or consular agents

1 Each Member State shall be free to effect service of judicial documents on persons residing in another Member State, without application of any compulsion, directly through its diplomatic or consular agents.

2 Any Member State may make it known, in accordance with Article 23(1), that it is opposed to such service within its territory, unless the documents are to be served on nationals of the Member State in which the documents originate.

ARTICLE 14

Service by post

1 Each Member State shall be free to effect service of judicial documents directly by post to persons residing in another Member State.

2 Any Member State may specify, in accordance with Article 23(1), the conditions under which it will accept service of judicial documents by post.

Postal service—For the purposes of the Service Regulation, in England and Wales postal service is only acceptable by registered or recorded delivery mail. A signature must be obtained from the addressee, or a person who is prepared to accept receipt on behalf of the addressee, as proof of delivery.

ARTICLE 15

Direct service

1 This Regulation shall not interfere with the freedom of any person interested in a judicial proceeding to effect service of judicial documents directly through the judicial officers, officials or other competent persons of the Member State addressed.

2 Any Member State may make it known, in accordance with Article 23(1), that it is opposed to the service of judicial documents in its territory pursuant to paragraph 1.

CHAPTER III
EXTRAJUDICIAL DOCUMENTS

ARTICLE 16

Transmission

Extrajudicial documents may be transmitted for service in another Member State in accordance with the provisions of this Regulation.

CHAPTER IV
FINAL PROVISIONS

ARTICLE 17

Implementing rules

The measures necessary for the implementation of this Regulation relating to the matters referred to below shall be adopted in accordance with the advisory procedure referred to in Article 18(2):

(a) drawing up and annually updating a manual containing the information provided by Member States in accordance with Article 2(4);
(b) drawing up a glossary in the official languages of the European Union of documents which may be served under this Regulation;
(c) updating or making technical amendments to the standard form set out in the Annex.

ARTICLE 18

Committee

1 The Commission shall be assisted by a committee.

2 Where reference is made to this paragraph, Articles 3 and 7 of Decision 1999/468/EC shall apply.

3 The Committee shall adopt its rules of procedure.

ARTICLE 19

Defendant not entering an appearance

1 Where a writ of summons or an equivalent document has had to be transmitted to another Member State for the purpose of service, under the provisions of this Regulation, and the defendant has not appeared, judgment shall not be given until it is established that:

- (a) the document was served by a method prescribed by the internal law of the Member State addressed for the service of documents in domestic actions upon persons who are within its territory; or
- (b) the document was actually delivered to the defendant or to his residence by another method provided for by this Regulation;

and that in either of these cases the service or the delivery was effected in sufficient time to enable the defendant to defend.

2 Each Member State shall be free to make it known, in accordance with Article 23(1), that the judge, notwithstanding the provisions of paragraph 1, may give judgment even if no certificate of service or delivery has been received, if all the following conditions are fulfilled:

- (a) the document was transmitted by one of the methods provided for in this Regulation;
- (b) a period of time of not less than six months, considered adequate by the judge in the particular case, has elapsed since the date of the transmission of the document;
- (c) no certificate of any kind has been received, even though every reasonable effort has been made to obtain it through the competent authorities or bodies of the Member State addressed.

3 Notwithstanding paragraphs 1 and 2, the judge may order, in case of urgency, any provisional or protective measures.

4 When a writ of summons or an equivalent document has had to be transmitted to another Member State for the purpose of service, under the provisions of this Regulation, and a judgment has been entered against a defendant who has not appeared, the judge shall have the power to relieve the defendant from the effects of the expiration of the time for appeal from the judgment if the following conditions are fulfilled:

- (a) the defendant, without any fault on his part, did not have knowledge of the document in sufficient time to defend, or knowledge of the judgment in sufficient time to appeal; and
- (b) the defendant has disclosed a prima facie defence to the action on the merits.

An application for relief may be filed only within a reasonable time after the defendant has knowledge of the judgment.

Each Member State may make it known, in accordance with Article 23(1), that such application will not be entertained if it is filed after the expiration of a time to be stated by it in that communication, but which shall in no case be less than one year following the date of the judgment.

5 Paragraph 4 shall not apply to judgments concerning status or capacity of persons.

ARTICLE 20

Relationship with agreements or arrangements to which Member States are Parties

1 This Regulation shall, in relation to matters to which it applies, prevail over other provisions contained in bilateral or multilateral agreements or arrangements concluded by the Member States, and in particular Article IV of the Protocol to the Brussels Convention of 1968 and the Hague Convention of 15 November 1965.

2 This Regulation shall not preclude individual Member States from maintaining or concluding agreements or arrangements to expedite further or simplify the transmission of documents, provided that they are compatible with this Regulation.

3 Member States shall send to the Commission:

(a) a copy of the agreements or arrangements referred to in paragraph 2 concluded between the Member States as well as drafts of such agreements or arrangements which they intend to adopt; and
(b) any denunciation of, or amendments to, these agreements or arrangements.

ARTICLE 21

Legal aid

This Regulation shall not affect the application of Article 23 of the Convention on Civil Procedure of 17 July 1905, Article 24 of the Convention on Civil Procedure of 1 March 1954 or Article 13 of the Convention on International Access to Justice of 25 October 1980 between the Member States Parties to these Conventions.

ARTICLE 22

Protection of information transmitted

1 Information, including in particular personal data, transmitted under this Regulation shall be used by the receiving agency only for the purpose for which it was transmitted.

2 Receiving agencies shall ensure the confidentiality of such information, in accordance with their national law.

3 Paragraphs 1 and 2 shall not affect national laws enabling data subjects to be informed of the use made of information transmitted under this Regulation.

4 This Regulation shall be without prejudice to Directives 95/46/EC and 97/66/EC.

ARTICLE 23

Communication and publication

1 Member States shall communicate to the Commission the information referred to in Articles 2, 3, 4, 9, 10, 13, 14, 15, 17(a) and 19.

2 The Commission shall publish in the *Official Journal of the European Communities* the information referred to in paragraph 1.

ARTICLE 24

Review

No later than 1 June 2004, and every five years thereafter, the Commission shall present to the European Parliament, the Council and the Economic and Social Committee a report on the application of this Regulation, paying special attention to the effectiveness of the bodies designated pursuant to Article 2 and to the practical application of point (c) of Article 3 and Article 9. The report shall be accompanied if need be by proposals for adaptations of this Regulation in line with the evolution of notification systems.

ARTICLE 25

Entry into force

This Regulation shall enter into force on 31 May 2001.

This Regulation shall be binding in its entirety and directly applicable in the Member States in accordance with the Treaty establishing the European Community.
Done at Brussels, 29 May 2000.

For the Council
The President
A. Costa

ANNEX

REQUEST FOR SERVICE OF DOCUMENTS

(Article 4(3) of Council Regulation (EC) No 1348/2000 on the service in the Member States of judicial and extrajudicial documents in civil or commercial matters[1])

Reference No: ___

1. TRANSMITTING AGENCY
   - 1.1. Identity:
   - 1.2. Address:
     - 1.2.1. Street and number/PO box:
     - 1.2.2. Place and code:
     - 1.2.3. Country:
   - 1.3. Tel:
   - 1.4. Fax (*):
   - 1.5. E-mail (*)
2. RECEIVING AGENCY
   - 2.1. Identity:
   - 2.2. Address:
     - 2.2.1. Street and number/PO box:
     - 2.2.2. Place and code:
     - 2.2.3. Country:
   - 2.3. Tel:
   - 2.4. Fax (*):
   - 2.5. E-mail (*):
3. APPLICANT
   - 3.1. Identity:
   - 3.2. Address:
     - 3.2.1. Street and number/PO box:
     - 3.2.2. Place and code:
     - 3.2.3. Country:
   - 3.3. Tel (*):
   - 3.4. Fax (*):
   - 3.5. E-mail (*):
4. ADDRESSEE
   - 4.1. Identity:
   - 4.2. Address:
     - 4.2.1. Street and number/PO box:

4.2.2. Place and code:

4.2.3. Country:

4.3. Tel (*):

4.4. Fax (*):

4.5. E-mail (*):

4.6. Identification number/social security number/organisation number/or equivalent (*):

5. METHOD OF SERVICE

5.1. In accordance with the law of the Member State addressed

5.2. By the following particular method:

5.2.1. If this method is incompatible with the law of the Member State addressed, the document(s) should be served in accordance with the law:

5.2.1.1. yes

5.2.1.2. no

6. DOCUMENT TO BE SERVED

(a) 6.1. Nature of the document

6.1.1. judicial

6.1.1.1. writ of summons

6.1.1.2. judgment

6.1.1.3. appeal

6.1.1.4. other

6.1.2. extrajudicial

(b) 6.2. Date or time limit stated in the document (*):

(c) 6.3. Language of document:

6.3.1. original DE, EN, DK, EL, FI, FR, GR, IT, NL, PT, SV, others:

6.3.2. translation (*) DE, EN, DK, ES, FI, FR, EL, IT, NL, PT, SV, others:

6.4. Number of enclosures:

7. A COPY OF DOCUMENT TO BE RETURNED WITH THE CERTIFICATE OF SERVICE (Article 4(5) of the Regulation)

7.1. Yes (in this case send two copies of the document to be served)

7.2. No

1. You are required by Article 7(2) of the Regulation to effect all steps required for service of the document as soon as possible. In any event, if it is not possible for you to effect service within one month of receipt, you must inform this agency by means of the certificate provided for in point 13.
2. If you cannot fulfil this request for service on the basis of the information or documents transmitted, you are required by Article 6(2) of the Regulation to contact this agency by the swiftest possible means in order to secure the missing information or document.

Done at:

Date:

Signature and/or stamp:

1 OJ L 160, 30.6.2000, p 37.

(*) This item is optional.

Reference No of the receiving agency:

ACKNOWLEDGEMENT OF RECEIPT

(Article 6(1) of Council Regulation (EC) No 1348/2000)

This acknowledgement must be sent by the swiftest possible means of transmission as soon as possible after receipt of the document and in any event within seven days of receipt.

8. DATE OF RECEIPT:

Done at:

Date:

Signature and/or stamp:

NOTICE OF RETURN OF REQUEST AND DOCUMENT

(Article 6(3) of Council Regulation (EC) No 1348/2000)

The request and document must be returned on receipt.

9. REASON FOR RETURN:

9.1. The request is manifestly outside the scope of the Regulation:

9.1.1. the document is not civil or commercial

9.1.2. the service is not from one Member State to another Member State

9.2. Non-compliance with formal conditions required makes service impossible:

9.2.1. the document is not easily legible

9.2.2. the language used to complete the form is incorrect

9.2.3. the document received is not a true and faithful copy

9.2.4. other (please give details):

9.3. The method of service is incompatible with the law of that Member State (Article 7(1) of the Regulation)

Done at:

Date:

Signature and/or stamp:

NOTICE OF RETRANSMISSION OF REQUEST AND DOCUMENT TO THE APPROPRIATE RECEIVING AGENCY

(Article 6(4) of Council Regulation (EC) No 1348/2000)

The request and document were forwarded on to the following receiving agency, which has territorial jurisdiction to serve it:

10.1. Identity:

10.2. Address:

10.2.1. Street and number/PO box:

10.2.2. Place and code:

10.2.3. Country:

10.3. Tel:

10.4. Fax (*):

10.5. E-mail (*):

Done at:

Date:

Signature and/or stamp:

(*) This item is optional.

Reference No of the appropriate receiving agency:

NOTICE OF RECEIPT BY THE APPROPRIATE RECEIVING AGENCY HAVING TERRITORIAL JURISDICTION TO THE TRANSMITTING AGENCY

(Article 6(4) of Council Regulation (EC) No 1348/2000)

This notice must be sent by the swiftest possible means of transmission as soon as possible after receipt of the document and in any event within seven days of receipt.

11. DATE OF RECEIPT:

Done at:

Date:

Signature and/or stamp:

CERTIFICATE OF SERVICE OR NON-SERVICE OF DOCUMENTS

(Article 10 of Council Regulation (EC) No 1348/2000)

The service shall be effected as soon as possible. In any event, if it has not been possible to effect service within one month of receipt, the receiving agency shall inform the transmitting agency (according to Article 7(2) of the Regulation)

12. COMPLETION OF SERVICE

(a) 12.1. Date and address of service:

(b) 12.2. The document was

(A) 12.2.1. served in accordance with the law of the Member State addressed, namely

12.2.1.1. handed to

12.2.1.1.1. the addressee in person

12.2.1.1.2. another person

12.2.1.1.2.1. Name:

12.2.1.1.2.2. Address:

12.2.1.1.2.2.1. Street and number/PO box:

12.2.1.1.2.2.2. Place and code:

12.2.1.1.2.2.3. Country:

12.2.1.1.2.3. Relation to the addressee:

family employee others

12.2.1.1.3. the addressee's address

12.2.1.2. served by post

12.2.1.2.1. without acknowledgement of receipt

12.2.1.2.2. with the enclosed acknowledgement of receipt

12.2.1.2.2.1. from the addressee

12.2.1.2.2.2. another person

12.2.1.2.2.2.1. Name:

12.2.1.2.2.2.2. Address

12.2.1.2.2.2.2.1. Street and number/PO box:

12.2.1.2.2.2.2.2. Place and code:

12.2.1.2.2.2.2.3. Country:

12.2.1.2.2.2.3. Relation to the addressee:

family employee others

12.2.1.3. other method (please say how):

(B) 12.2.2. served by the following particular method (please say how):

(c) 12.3. The addressee of the document was informed (orally) (in writing) that he or she may refuse to accept it if it was not in an official language of the place of service or in an official language of the state of transmission which he or she understands.

13. INFORMATION IN ACCORDANCE WITH ARTICLE 7(2)

It was not possible to effect service within one month of receipt.

14. REFUSAL OF DOCUMENT

The addressee refused to accept the document on account of the language used. The documents are annexed to this certificate.

15. REASON FOR NON-SERVICE OF DOCUMENT

15.1. Address unknown

15.2. Addressee cannot be located

15.3. Document could not be served before the date or time limit stated in point 6.2.

15.4. Others (please specify):

The documents are annexed to this certificate.

Done at:

Date:

Signature and/or stamp:

PART 7
HOW TO START PROCEEDINGS – THE CLAIM FORM

CONTENTS OF THIS PART

Practice Direction—See generally PD7 at p 508.

Procedural Guide—See Guides 1, 2 and 4 set out in Section 1 of this work.

Application of this Part—The provisions of this Part (and many others) are modified as regards particular kinds of proceedings and care needs to be paid to particular rules or practice directions:

Type of Claim	CPR Part/Practice Direction
Consumer Credit Act 1974	Rule 7.9/PD7B
Money Claims Online	PD7E
No substantial dispute of fact	Part 8
Parties and group litigation	Part 19/PD19B
Children or patients	Part 21
Pre-action disclosure of documents	Rule 31.16
Costs-only proceedings	Rule 44.12A
Injunctions and other interim remedies	Part 25
Applications under the Companies Acts 1985–89, the Insurance Companies Act 1982 and Part VII of the Financial Services and Markets Act 2000	PD49B
Appeals	Part 52
Defamation claims	Part 53
Judicial review	Part 54
Claim for possession of land	Part 55
Applications relating to business tenancies	Part 56
Probate claims	Part 57

Type of Claim	CPR Part/Practice Direction
Claims under the Inheritance (Provision for Family and Dependants) Act 1975	Part 57, Section IV
Commercial Court claims	Part 58
Mercantile court claims	Part 59
Technology and Construction Court claims	Part 60
Admiralty Court claims	Part 61
Claims or applications under the Arbitration Act 1996	Part 62
Patent claims	Part 63
Claims relating to estates, trusts and charities	Part 64
Proceedings relating to anti-social behaviour and harassment	Part 65
Proceedings relating to solicitors	Part 67
Applications for Writ of Habeas Corpus	Sch 1, RSC Ord 54

Claims or applications under the Arbitration Act 1996—Except where r 62.3(2) applies, such claims must be started by the issue of an arbitration claim form in accordance with the Pt 8 procedure (r 62.3(1)).

Money Claim Online (MCOL)—It is possible to issue most money claims through the bulk issue centre at Northampton. There are, however, certain restrictions on the cases which can be issued via MCOL, namely:

- the claim must be for a specified sum under £100,000 in sterling only, brought using the Pt 7 procedure;
- the particulars of claim must be limited to not more than 1080 characters, including spaces;
- the claimant must not be 'fees exempt' and can pay the issue fee by credit or debit card;
- the claimant must not be a child or patient, or publicly-funded by the LSC;
- there must be a single defendant, or two defendants if the claim is for a single (ie the same) amount against each of them;
- the defendant must not be the Crown, a child or a patient;
- the defendant's address for service must be within England and Wales.

For full details see r 7.12 and PD7E – Pilot Scheme for Money Claim Online – at p 524, and Guide 4.

Alternative Dispute Resolution—In *Cowl v Plymouth City Council* [2001] EWCA Civ 1935, [2002] TLR 9 the Court of Appeal expressed the wish that, wherever possible, disputes should be resolved through ADR rather than by recourse to the courts. Costs sanctions can be imposed where one party, even though ultimately successful, has unreasonably rejected an offer of ADR made by another party.

An unsuccessful party may argue for its costs where the successful party has unreasonably refused to agree to ADR (*Halsey v Milton Keynes General NHS Trust* [2004] EWCA Civ 576, [2004] 1 WLR 3002). Relevant factors might include:

(a) the nature of the dispute;
(b) the merits of the case (it may not be reasonable for a party with a weak case to insist on the use of ADR);
(c) the extent to which other settlement methods have been attempted;
(d) whether the costs of the ADR procedure would be disproportionately high;
(e) whether any delay in setting up and attending the ADR procedure would be prejudicial;
(f) whether it would be just to impose a costs sanction.

Pre-action protocols—Protocols govern the steps parties should take to seek information from and provide information to each other about a prospective claim. There are at present eight approved pre-action protocols (see Section 4 of this work). Paragraphs 3.3–3.5 of PDProt set out the sanctions for breach of a relevant pre-action protocol. Further pre-action protocols may be added to those presently listed in PDProt, para 5.1, although work on a general pre-action protocol is not to be taken forward. In the meanwhile, PDProt, para 4 says that the court will expect similar behaviour between the parties in cases not covered by any approved protocol and expands on the expected content of the initial letters between the parties, the disclosure of documents and the commissioning of expert reports.

Electronic communication with the court—Where a court has published an e-mail address on the HM Courts Service website, it is possible to communicate with the court and file specified documents with the court by e-mail (see generally PD5B at p 426). Special provisions exist in relation to the county courts at Basildon, Birmingham, Bournemouth, Coventry, Dartford, Leicester, Llangefni, Norwich and Preston. For further details see PD5B.

7.1 Where to start proceedings

Restrictions on where proceedings may be started are set out in the relevant practice direction.

Practice Direction—See PD7, para 1 at p 508 and paras 2.1–2.10 at p 509.

Scope of provision—The general provision is that proceedings may be started in either the High Court or in the county courts; however, claims of £15,000 or less, or personal injury damages' claims under £50,000, must be started in the county court. See PD7, para 2 for further details on where to start proceedings.

Commencement in the 'wrong' county court—A court manager has no power to refuse to accept a claim form sent to the wrong county court (*Gwynedd Council v Grunshaw* [1999] 4 All ER 304, CA). Note also r 30.2(2).

7.2 How to start proceedings

(1) Proceedings are started when the court issues a claim form at the request of the claimant.

(2) A claim form is issued on the date entered on the form by the court.

(A person who seeks a remedy from the court before proceedings are started or in relation to proceedings which are taking place, or will take place, in another jurisdiction must make an application under Part 23)

(Part 16 sets out what the claim form must include)

(The costs practice direction sets out the information about a funding arrangement to be provided with the claim form where the claimant intends to seek to recover an additional liability)

('Funding arrangement' and 'additional liability' are defined in rule 43.2)

Amendments—SI 2000/1317.

Practice Direction—See PD7, paras 3.1–3.9 at p 510, paras 4.1–4.2 at p 511, paras 5.1–5.5 at p 512 and paras 7.1–7.3 at p 513.

'A claim form' (r 7.2(1))—Despite the aim to have only one or two claim forms under the CPR, necessity has ensured the use of several different forms. For the correct claim form to use note PD4, PD8B and Pts 52–64. See also the 'Forms' entries in the various Procedural Guides. Set out below are the more commonly used claim forms. Care should always be taken to ascertain which of Pts 7, 8 or 52–64 applies.

Type of Claim	Claim Form
Money (which includes a claim for damages)	N1
Consumer Credit Act or similar return of goods claim under r 7.9	N1 (FD)

Type of Claim	Claim Form
Claim Production Centre claim form	N1 CPC
Probate claim	N2
Claim for possession by landlord or mortgagor	N5 and N119/N120
Claim for relief from forfeiture	N5A
Applications for accelerated possession of assured tenancies	N5B
Claim for demotion of tenancy	N6
Injunction under Housing Act 1996, s 152	N16A
Claim for possession against trespasser	N5 and N121
Application for possession including application for interim possession order	N5 and N130
Claim where there is no substantial dispute of fact or PD8B has applied the Pt 8 procedure	N208
A Pt 20 claim	N211
Time order under Consumer Credit Act 1974	N440
Claims for judicial review	N461

Reference should also be made to PD7, paras 3, 4 and 5. Further information is also set out in Procedural Guide 1, in Section 1 of this work.

Use of the wrong claim form—A Pt 7 claim will not be struck out if proceedings are wrongly commenced using a Pt 8 claim form where the defendant knows what is being claimed (*Hannigan v Hannigan & ors* [2000] 2 FCR 650, (2000) *The Independent*, 23 May). See also *Thurrock Borough Council v Secretary of State for the Environment, Transport and the Regions* (2000) *The Times*, 20 December, where the Court of Appeal adopted the view of the earlier Court of Appeal in *Hannigan v Hannigan* that substance should take precedence over form when interpreting the CPR.

'on the date' (r 7.2(2))—See PD7, para 5.1 where a claim form is received by the court on a date earlier than the date it is issued. In *Canada Trust Co & ors v Stolzenberg & Gambazzi & ors* (No 2) [2000] 3 WLR 1376, the House of Lords held in a case instituted prior to the inception of the CPR that the concept of 'sued' in arts 2 and 6 of the Lugano and Brussels Conventions should be interpreted as referring to the initiation of proceedings which, in England, was when a writ of originating summons was issued. However, the application of PD7, para 5.1 is limited to the provisions of the Limitation Act 1980 and is not of relevance when deciding when proceedings are brought for the purposes of HA 1996, s 130 (*Salford County Council v Garner (Mark)* [2004] EWCA Civ 364, [2004] All ER (D) 465 (Feb), [2004] TLR 160, (2004) *The Times*, 10 March, CA).

'a person who seeks a remedy … before proceedings are started' (r 7.2(2) note)—See r 23.2(4), PD23, para 5, r 25.4 and PD25, para 4.4.

'the claim form must include' (r 7.2(2) note)—Rule 16.2 sets out the matters which the claim form must contain. Where the claim is for money (including a claim for damages) other than for a specified amount, the claim form must also contain a statement of value (r 16.3). If practicable, the claimant's particulars of claim should be set out in the claim form (r 7.4). The claim form must always be verified by a statement of truth (r 22.1).

'the costs practice direction' (r 7.2(2) note)—See generally PDCosts, Section 19 and Form N251 Notice of Funding of Case or Claim.

Rule 44.3B(1)(c) provides that a party may not recover any additional liability for any period during which the information set out in N251 has not been disclosed. However, by applying a combination of PDCosts, para 10.1 and r 3.9 the court may grant relief from the sanction imposed by r 44.3B (see *WASPS Football Club v Lambert Smith Hampton Group Ltd* [2004] EWHC 1503 (Comm), [2004] All ER (D) 61).

Devolution issue—A party wishing to raise a devolution issue must say so in the claim form (see PDDev, especially para 16).

Representative parties and group litigation actions—See Pt 19 and the practice direction supplementing it, PD19B.

Names—For the requirement to state the full name of each party see PD16, para 2.6.

Postcodes—The full postcodes should be stated for both claimant and defendant. A claim form not containing such information will be issued but stayed, and not served, until the postcodes have been provided or the court has dispensed with the requirement to do so (see further PD16, paras 2.4 and 2.5).

Payment of fee—A fee is payable when the claim is issued unless the claimant successfully applies either for an exemption from, or remission of, the fee. For the fee, see the CPFO 2004 (as amended) in Section 6 of this work. For the sanctions for dishonouring a cheque, see r 3.7B.

Fixed costs on commencement of a claim—See generally r 45.2.

7.3 Right to use one claim form to start two or more claims

A claimant may use a single claim form to start all claims which can be conveniently disposed of in the same proceedings.

'conveniently'—Note the overriding objective in r 1.1(2) and the court's general powers of management (r 3.1(2)).

7.4 Particulars of claim

(1) Particulars of claim must –

(a) be contained in or served with the claim form; or

(b) subject to paragraph (2) be served on the defendant by the claimant within 14 days after service of the claim form.

(2) Particulars of claim must be served on the defendant no later than the latest time for serving a claim form.

(Rule 7.5 sets out the latest time for serving a claim form)

(3) Where the claimant serves particulars of claim separately from the claim form in accordance with paragraph (1)(b), he must, within 7 days of service on the defendant, file a copy of the particulars together with a certificate of service.

(Part 16 sets out what the particulars of claim must include)

(Part 22 requires particulars of claim to be verified by a statement of truth)

(Rule 6.10 makes provision for a certificate of service)

Practice Direction—See PD7, paras 6.1–6.2 at p 512 and paras 7.1–7.3 at p 513.

'service of the claim form' (r 7.4(1)(b))—Note generally Pt 6 and PD6 as well as r 7.5.

'Particulars of claim must be served' (r 7.4(2))—Whilst judicial opinion previously differed as to whether the time for service of particulars of claim could be extended *ex post facto* where service is effected outside the period stipulated in r 7.4(2), the issue has been resolved by *Totty v Snowden, Hewitt v Wirral Cheshire Community NHS Trust* [2001] EWCA Civ 1415, [2001] 4 All ER 565, CA. Particulars of claim are not an integral part of the claim form; accordingly courts have a discretion under r 3.10 to remedy a failure to serve the particulars of claim within the time limits set out in r 7.4, unhindered by the much stricter provisions of r 7.6(3) relating to claim forms.

In *Austin v Newcastle Chronicle & Journal Ltd* [2001] EWCA Civ 834, CA the court reviewed the authorities relevant to the court's discretion under r 3.1(2)(a) to extend the time for service of the particulars of claim (see *Biguzzi v Rank Leisure plc* [1999] 1 WLR 1926, CA and *Johnson & anor v Coburn* (1999) (unreported) 24 November, CA), indicating that relevant factors include (i) the possible prejudice to the other party/parties balanced against the detriment to the party seeking the extension of time; (ii) the need to dispose of cases quickly; and (iii) the right under Art 6 ECHR to a determination of a claim by an independent tribunal. Judge LJ said that each case would turn on its own facts; 'the decisions in other cases, whether before or after the introduction of the CPR are likely to obscure, rather than illuminate, the argument and subsequent decision.'

Where an application for an extension of time for the service of particulars of claim is made before the period for service has expired, it is not necessary to go through the checklist contained in r 3.9, as the claimant is not seeking relief from a sanction. Rather, the court may apply its discretion generally under r 3.1(2)(a) to extend time (*Robert v Momentum Services Ltd* [2003] EWCA Civ 229, [2003] 1 WLR 1577, CA). On the other hand, in a case where the claimant sought an order retrospectively extending time for service of the particulars of claim, medical report and schedule of loss due to have been served by April 2001, on the balance of prejudice between the parties and applying the r 3.9 criteria the time for service of particulars etc was extended, but not so as to permit any claim for either general or special damage which could not be substantiated by any medical report before April 2001 (*Price v Price (t/a Poppyland Headware)* [2003] EWCA Civ 888, [2003] TLR 440, CA).

'Particulars of claim must be served' (r 7.4(2))—This provision does not apply to claims proceeding in the Commercial Court (r 58.5(1)(d)) or in a mercantile court (r 59.4(1)(a)).

'certificate of service' (r 7.4(3))—Form N215, which must be verified by a statement of truth (PD22, para 1.1(6).

'statement of truth' (note to r 7.4(3))—Note PD7, para 7.2.

Late service of documents accompanying the particulars of claim—Where particulars of claim are filed at a late stage but nevertheless within the limitation period, the court should usually extend the time for service of a schedule of special damages not also served at the same time if the effect otherwise would be to dismiss the claimant's case (*Bheroo v Camden and Islington NHS Trust* (2000) Lawtel, 30 June, CA, considering *Costellow v Somerset District Council* [1993] 1 WLR 256).

Specialist jurisdictions—When a claim form is issued out of the Commercial Court or a mercantile court, the claimant must serve particulars of claim within 28 days of the filing of an acknowledgment of service which indicates an intention to defend (r 58.5(1)(c) and r 59.4(1)(c)).

In admiralty claims the particulars of claim must be contained in or served with the claim form, or served on the defendant by the claimant within 75 days after service of the claim form (r 61.3(3)).

Rule 7.4 does not apply to admiralty 'collision' claims (r 61.4(2)).

7.5 Service of a claim form

(1) After a claim form has been issued, it must be served on the defendant.

(2) The general rule is that a claim form must be served within 4 months after the date of issue.

(3) The period for service is 6 months where the claim form is to be served out of the jurisdiction.

'The general rule' (r 7.5(2))—Note r 7.6 for extensions of time for service.

However, contrary provisions do occasionally apply and specific reference needs to be made to any relevant Act, schedule, rule or practice direction. For example, see r 56.3(3) for Landlord and Tenant Acts claims, r 61.3(5) for admiralty claims and r 62.4 for arbitration claims.

'within 4 months' (r 7.5(2))—For the computation of time see rr 2.8 and 6.7. For examples of the working of r 6.7 in relation to this rule see *Anderton v Clwyd County Council and other cases* [2002] EWCA Civ 933, [2002] 1 WLR 3174, CA and the notes at r 7.6 below.

'the period for service is 6 months' (r 7.5(3))—The period is 6 months after the date of issue (cf r 7.5(2)).

Service on a fresh defendant—The claim form should be treated for these purposes as issued against that defendant when he is added or substituted and unless the court orders otherwise the 4 (or 6) months mentioned in r 7.5 will run from that date. Where the case has been in existence for any length of time, the order giving permission to add should include a direction under r 19.4(6)(b). See also *Gregson v Channel Four Television Corporation* (2000) Lawtel, 12 July, CA where it was held that if, in all the circumstances, the court decided to allow a new party to be added or substituted, a consequential order for the service of the claim form on the new party did not have to be rigidly confined by r 7.6.

Permission to serve out of the jurisdiction (r 7.5(3))—The discretion to grant permission to serve out of the jurisdiction is not subject to any express or implied requirement or condition that:

- the application must be made before the end of the period of 4 months from the issue of a claim marked 'not for service out of the jurisdiction'; or
- different criteria apply to an application for such permission made after the end of the period of 4 months from the issue of the claim form than apply to an application made within that period; or
- the criteria set out in r 7.6(3) apply directly or indirectly to the exercise of the discretion, whether the application is made before or after the end of the period of 4 months from the issue of such a claim form (*Cummins v Shell International Manning Services* decided together with *Anderton v Clwyd County Council and other cases* [2002] EWCA Civ 933, [2002] 1 WLR 3174, CA).

Rather, the discretion exercisable on an application made before the end of the 6-month period allowed for service of the claim form out of the jurisdiction is governed by Pt 6, Section III.

Where permission to serve the claim form out of England and Wales has been given and the defendant has not received actual notice of proceedings, the onus is on the claimant to show by expert evidence that the method of service is in compliance with the rules applying in the foreign jurisdiction (*Arros Invest Ltd v Rafik Nishanov* [2004] EWHC 576 (Ch)). The case is yet another where the court criticised a claimant for waiting until the last possible moment before effecting service.

Specialist jurisdictions—When a claim form issued out of the Commercial Court or a mercantile court is served, it must be accompanied by the documents specified in r 7.8(1) (see rr 58.5(1)(b) and 59.4(1)(b)).

7.6 Extension of time for serving a claim form

(1) The claimant may apply for an order extending the period within which the claim form may be served.

(2) The general rule is that an application to extend the time for service must be made –

(a) within the period for serving the claim form specified by rule 7.5; or

(b) where an order has been made under this rule, within the period for service specified by that order.

(3) If the claimant applies for an order to extend the time for service of the claim form after the end of the period specified by rule 7.5 or by an order made under this rule, the court may make such an order only if –

(a) the court has been unable to serve the claim form; or

(b) the claimant has taken all reasonable steps to serve the claim form but has been unable to do so; and,

(c) in either case, the claimant has acted promptly in making the application.

(4) An application for an order extending the time for service –

(a) must be supported by evidence; and

(b) may be made without notice.

Practice Direction—See PD7, paras 8.1–8.2 at p 513.

Scope of provision—The rule enables a claimant to apply for an extension of time for service. However, as the court will wish to deal with the case expeditiously (r 1.1(2)(d)) and the claimant is required to help the court to further the overriding objective (r 1.3), a claim form should be served promptly after issue. The consequences of failure to comply with the rules governing service are extremely serious for a claimant and the situation becomes fraught with procedural perils where service is delayed until the last day or two of the period of 4 months allowed by r 7.5(2). The risks can easily be avoided by progressing the proceedings in accordance with the spirit and letter of the CPR (*Anderton v Clwyd County Council and other cases* [2002] EWCA Civ 933, [2002] 1 WLR 3174, CA). Following *Godwin v Swindon Borough Council* [2001] EWCA Civ 1478, [2002] 1 WLR 997, CA and *Anderton* there will be very few (if any) acceptable excuses for future failures to observe the rules for service of a claim form and the courts will be entitled to adopt a strict approach, even though the consequences may sometimes appear to be harsh in individual cases. See also *Hashtroodi v Hancock* [2004] EWCA Civ 652, [2004] All ER (D) 368 (May), [2004] TLR 305, (2004) *The Times*, 4 June, CA, where the Court of Appeal refused permission to extend the time for service, where the only reason for not having served in time was the negligence of the solicitors concerned. The court held that, had it granted permission, r 7.5 would have ceased to be the general rule.

'the claimant may apply' (r 7.6(1))—The use of the N244 application notice will ensure the application is supported by evidence (in the form of a witness statement) verified by a statement of truth.

'The general rule' (r 7.6(2))—There is a difference between the general rule, which states that an application to extend time for service must be made within the period allowed for service, and the more limited provisions of r 7.6(3) which deals with applications to extend the time for service after the time for so doing has expired. Only in the latter case are the criteria in r 7.6(3) relevant. The rule is silent as to the relevant criteria if an application is made under r 7.6(2); the court will no doubt have regard to the overriding objective in Pt 1 although cases decided prior to 26 April 1999 will not be of assistance to the court. In *Commissioners of Customs and Excise v Eastwood Care Homes (Ilkeston) Ltd* (2000) *The Times*, 7 March, QBD, Lightman J, it was held that it was no longer sufficient to apply some rigid formula and that each application to extend time had to be approached by a broad reference to justice; the claimants were granted an extension where the delay was short, there was no prejudice to the defendant and the case itself had both merit and general significance. Any application to extend time for service under r 7.6(2) should expressly refer to an extension of time in relation to the claim form rather than in relation to the particulars of claim (see *Steele v Mooney & ors* [2005] EWCA Civ 96).

'within the period … specified by rule 7.5' (r 7.6(2)(a))—Note the exceptions set out in the note **'The general rule'** to r 7.5 above.

'only if' (r 7.6(3))—The discretion to extend time for service after the period prescribed for service in r 7.5 has expired only arises if the stipulated provisions in r 7.6(3) apply. None of either the discretionary power in r 3.1(2)(a) to extend time periods, the ability to grant relief from sanctions in r 3.9 or the power in r 3.10 to rectify an error of procedure applies (*Vinos v Marks & Spencer plc* [2000] 1 WLR 1311, [2000] 2 All ER 801, (2000) 97(24) LSG 41, CA, as extended by *Kaur (Satwimder) v CTP Coil Ltd* (2000) Lawtel, 11 July, CA).

In *Nanglegan (Carmelita) v The Royal Free Hampstead NHS Trust* [2001] EWCA Civ 127, (2001) *The Times*, 14 February, CA, service of the claim form was effected, at the end of the 4-month period, on the defendants rather than on the nominated solicitors; it was held that there was no discretion under r 7.6(3) to extend time for service to enable the solicitors themselves to be served. Similar views were expressed by the Court of Appeal the following day in *Elmes v Hygrade Food Products plc* [2001] EWCA Civ 121, [2001] All ER (D) 158, when it was held that r 6.8 had prospective rather than retrospective effect and could not therefore be applied *ex post facto* to correct irregular service.

Further evidence of the strict interpretation of this rule by the Court of Appeal was illustrated in *Godwin v Swindon Borough Council* [2001] EWCA Civ 1478, [2002] 1 WLR 997, CA where the actual date of service of a claim form was within time but the deemed date of service under r 6.7(1) was outside the time for service. The Court of Appeal held that the date specified as the deemed date of service had to be treated as the date of service, irrespective of proof of the date of actual service, and an extension of time could not be granted as r 7.6(3) was not available to the claimant.

Alongside *Godwin v Swindon Borough Council* (above), the leading case on r 7.6(3) is now *Anderton v Clwyd County Council and other cases* [2002] EWCA Civ 933, [2002] 1 WLR 3174, CA. In five related appeals their Lordships held *inter alia* that:

(a) Service of a claim form that has been sent by first-class post or fax before the end of the period for service may, as a result of the 'deemed service' provisions under r 6.7, occur after the end of that period.
(b) The fact that the claim form has actually been received by, and come to the attention of, the defendant or his solicitor through the post, by fax or by means other than personal service within the period of 4 months allowed by r 7.5(2) is legally irrelevant to ascertaining the day of service as deemed by r 6.7.
(c) Saturdays, Sundays and Bank Holidays are not excluded from the calculation of the day of deemed service by first-class post under r 6.7.
(d) If an application for an extension of time is issued by the claimant after the end of the period for service, the court will rarely have power under r 7.6(3) to grant it.
(e) Only in the most exceptional circumstances will it be proper for the court to exercise its discretion under r 6.9 to dispense with service, for example where the claim form had come to

the defendant's solicitors' attention before the end of the 4-month period for service, or there had been an admission of liability and a substantial offer in settlement had been made, or where the claim form was served by fax only 3 minutes after the deadline for service.

(f) The vast majority of applications in which it would be appropriate to make an order to dispense with service will be for prospective orders sought and granted before the end of the period for service.

Subsequently, in *Wilkey v British Broadcasting Corporation* [2002] EWCA Civ 1561, [2002] 4 All ER 1177, CA it was held that where service took place on or before 3 July 2002 (the date of the decision of the Court of Appeal in *Anderton v Clwyd County Council*), the discretion under r 6.9(1) to dispense retrospectively with service of the claim form should in 'category 2' cases ordinarily be exercised in favour of the claimant, unless the defendant could show prejudice (which does not include the loss of a limitation defence) or some other good reason for the court to decline to exercise its discretion. On the other hand, where service took place after 3 July 2002, the discretion under r 6.9(1) should usually not be exercised in the claimant's favour. Category 2 cases are those where actual service took place before the end of the period for service but where the irrebuttable deemed date of service, following *Godwin v Swindon Borough Council*, was out of time.

In yet further clarification of the rule, the Court of Appeal in five related appeals *Cranfield & anor v Bridgegrove Ltd; Claussen v Yeates; McManus v Sharif; Murphy v Staples UK Ltd; Smith v Hughes & anor* [2003] EWCA Civ 656, [2003] 3 All ER 129 held that –

1) The court has jurisdiction to extend time for service under r 7.6(3) where the court has failed through neglect to serve in time.
2) Where, however, the real reason why the claim form was not served in time was not the failure of the court but the failure of the claimant's solicitors to notify the court in time that the defendant's solicitors were willing to accept service and to request the court to serve urgently rather than 'in due course', it was not right to dispense with service under r 6.9 since the facts were not within the exceptional category of cases identified in *Anderton.*
3) Also, r 6.9 cannot be invoked where what was sent to insurers in time was only a draft claim form and the insurers had no authority to accept service.
4) Service on a defendant company's registered office is good service under CA 1985, s 725.
5) Rule 6.5(6) is clear. Where the two conditions – that no solicitor is acting for the party to be served and that the party has not given an address for service – are satisfied, the claim form has to be served, in the case of an individual, at his usual or last known address. The rule is unqualified and says nothing about the defendant having to receive the document or the claimant knowing or believing that the defendant is no longer living at the address (as also subsequently applied in *Akram v Adam* [2004] EWCA Civ 1601, [2004] TLR 633).

'reasonable steps' (r 7.6(3)(b))—Where the address for service is the last known place of business (r 6.5(6)), this means the last place of business known to the claimant. To obtain the requisite knowledge, the claimant has to take reasonable steps to ascertain the defendant's current place of business or the last known place of business (*Spade Lane Cool Stores Ltd v Kilgour* (2004) Lawtel, 25 June, QBD). Here, the claimant's failure to take such reasonable steps resulted in a refusal to grant an extension of time for service. See also r 6.5(6).

'unable to serve claim form' (r 7.6(3)(a))—The Court of Appeal, in *Jones & anor v Telford and Wrekin Council* (1999) *The Times*, 30 July, held on the 9 July 1999, in a case decided under the old CCR Ord 7, r 20(2), that a failure to get medical evidence fully in order was not a good reason for not serving proceedings in time. A similar view, when applying the CPR, was expressed in *Mason v First Leisure Corporation plc* [2003] EWHC 1814 (QB), (2003) Lawtel, 26 August, QBD, Tugendhat J: if unable to serve the medical evidence and/or particulars of claim, a claimant should nevertheless serve the claim form in time and apply for an order for an extension of time in relation just to those documents which cannot be served. See also *Amerada Hess & ors v CW Rome & ors* (2000) *The Times*, 15 March, QBD (Comm Ct), Colman J, where an application to extend time for service made after the period for so doing failed, the claimant being unable to satisfy the tests in r 7.6(3)(b) and (c). Also in *Smith v Probyn and PGA European Tour Ltd* (2000) 97(12) LSG 44, QBD, Morland J, it was held that an application for an extension of time for service of the claim form would fail if the claimant had not taken all reasonable steps to serve the claim form. Likewise, in *Chaudhri v The Post Office* (2001) (unreported) 26 April, QBD, Jack J, unsuccessful service using the document exchange was held not to satisfy the tests of r 7.6(3)(a) and (b) and accordingly no extension of time for service of the claim form was granted. Similarly, circumstances where the delay in effecting service abroad clearly lies with the Foreign Office have been held not to fulfil the criteria for an extension of time under r 7.6(3) (*Chare v Fairclough & ors* [2003] All ER (D) 158 (Jan), Treacy J). On the other hand, where an original claim has been served within the initial 4-month period (r 7.5(2)) but on the wrong defendant, the court has a discretion to extend time for service of an amended claim form naming the proper defendant (*Austin v Newcastle Chronicle & Journal Ltd* [2001] EWCA Civ 834, CA). See also *Cranfield v Bridgegrove* (above).

'evidence' (r 7.6(4)(a))—Note the requirements of PD7, para 8.2.

'may be made without notice' (r 7.6(4)(b))—In addition to the requirements of r 23.9(2) as to service of a copy of the application notice and the supporting evidence, the order, if granted, must contain a statement of the right to make an application to set aside or vary the order under r 23.10.

Challenge to the jurisdiction—It is always necessary for the party challenging the court's jurisdiction on the basis that the claim form had expired prior to the time of service to file an acknowledgment of service, ticking the box indicating that he intends to contest jurisdiction. A failure to do so may be held to be a waiver of the right to challenge the jurisdiction of the court (*Uphill v BRB (Residuary) Ltd)* [2005] EWCA Civ 60).

Service on a fresh defendant—See the note to r 7.5 above.

Part 8 claims—This rule (as do many in Pt 7) applies equally to Pt 8 claims (PD8, para 2.1 and *Barker v Casserly* (2000) Lawtel, 25 October, Johnson J).

Service out of the jurisdiction—See note **'Permission to serve out of the jurisdiction'** under r 7.5 above.

7.7 Application by defendant for service of claim form

(1) Where a claim form has been issued against a defendant, but has not yet been served on him, the defendant may serve a notice on the claimant requiring him to serve the claim form or discontinue the claim within a period specified in the notice.

(2) The period specified in a notice served under paragraph (1) must be at least 14 days after service of the notice.

(3) If the claimant fails to comply with the notice, the court may, on the application of the defendant –

- (a) dismiss the claim; or
- (b) make any other order it thinks just.

Scope of provision—The rule enables a defendant to compel a claimant to serve his claim form. Delay in service is ill-advised (see the notes to r 7.6). This rule assists in those limited cases where the defendant wishes to respond to the particulars of claim (r 9.1(2)) or to dispute the court's jurisdiction under Pt 11.

7.8 Form for defence etc must be served with particulars of claim

(1) When particulars of claim are served on a defendant, whether they are contained in the claim form, served with it or served subsequently, they must be accompanied by –

- (a) a form for defending the claim;
- (b) a form for admitting the claim; and
- (c) a form for acknowledging service.

(2) Where the claimant is using the procedure set out in Part 8 (alternative procedure for claims) –

- (a) paragraph (1) does not apply; and
- (b) a form for acknowledging service must accompany the claim form.

'particulars of claim ... must be accompanied by' (r 7.8(1))—The Court Service has produced a Response Pack (N9) which includes all the forms the defendant needs to enable him to respond to a Pt 7 claim and which is served with the claim form.

7.9 Fixed date and other claims

A practice direction –

(a) may set out the circumstances in which the court may give a fixed date for a hearing when it issues a claim;
(b) may list claims in respect of which there is a specific claim form for use and set out the claim form in question; and
(c) may disapply or modify these Rules as appropriate in relation to the claims referred to in paragraphs (a) and (b).

Practice Direction—See PD7B at p 514, PD7D at p 523.

Scope of provision—Part 7 deals with the majority of claims (eg those for money, including damages); Pt 8 deals with cases involving the court's decision on a question which is unlikely to involve a substantial dispute of fact, claims for recovery of land and numerous miscellaneous applications; r 7.9 deals with: (i) those other cases where a fixed date for a hearing is required on the issue of the claim and (ii) claims by the Inland Revenue for the recovery of taxes. Further information is set out in Guide 2, in Section 1 of this work.

'A practice direction' (r 7.9)—Practice Direction 7B applies the fixed date procedure to claims under Consumer Credit Act 1974 other than claims relating to the recovery of land (see PD7B, para 3.2) or those relating to the recovery of money only (which are started under the Pt 7 procedure).

Practice Direction 7D provides that, in cases brought by the Inland Revenue to recover taxes or NIC, the court will fix a hearing on the filing of a defence rather than allocate to track. PD7D, para 3 sets out the evidence the Inland Revenue may produce at that hearing.

'specific claim form' (r 7.9(b))—Under Consumer Credit Act 1974, use N1 (FD); for a time order use Form N440.

7.10 Production Centre for claims

(1) There shall be a Production Centre for the issue of claim forms and other related matters.

(2) The relevant practice direction makes provision for –

(a) which claimants may use the Production Centre;
(b) the type of claims which the Production Centre may issue;
(c) the functions which are to be discharged by the Production Centre;
(d) the place where the Production Centre is to be located; and
(e) other related matters.

(3) The relevant practice direction may disapply or modify these Rules as appropriate in relation to claims issued by the Production Centre.

Practice Direction—See PD7C at p 520.

Money Claim Online—For full details see PD7E – Pilot Schemes for Money Claims Online – and Guide 4.

7.11 Human Rights

(1) A claim under section 7(1)(a) of the Human Rights Act 1998 in respect of a judicial act may be brought only in the High Court.

(2) Any other claim under section 7(1)(a) of that Act may be brought in any court.

Amendments—Inserted by SI 2000/2092.

'section 7(1)(a) of the Human Rights Act 1998' (r 7.11(1), (2))—This section provides that a person who claims that a public authority has acted (or proposes to act) in a way which is made unlawful by s 6(1) of that Act may bring proceedings against the authority under the Act in the appropriate court or tribunal.

Section 6(1) of the Human Rights Act 1998—This section makes it unlawful for a public body to act in a way which is incompatible with a Convention right.

The appropriate court or tribunal—Cases where the court is to be invited to make a declaration of incompatibility under HRA 1998, s 4 should be either brought in or transferred to the High Court (see s 4 of the Act and r 30.3(2)(g)).

Other relevant rules—In addition to the introduction into the CPR of rr 7.11 and r 30.3(2)(g), the Human Rights Act 1998 has also necessitated additional rr 19.4A and 33.9 as well as PD2B para 7A.

7.12 Electronic issue of claims

(1) A practice direction may make provision for a claimant to start a claim by requesting the issue of a claim form electronically.

(2) The practice direction may, in particular –

- (a) specify –
  - (i) the types of claim which may be issued electronically; and
  - (ii) the conditions which a claim must meet before it may be issued electronically;
- (b) specify –
  - (i) the court where the claim will be issued; and
  - (ii) the circumstances in which the claim will be transferred to another court;
- (c) provide for the filing of other documents electronically where a claim has been started electronically;
- (d) specify the requirements that must be fulfilled for any document filed electronically; and
- (e) provide how a fee payable on the filing of any document is to be paid where that document is filed electronically.

(3) The practice direction may disapply or modify these Rules as appropriate in relation to claims started electronically.

Amendments—Inserted by SI 2003/3361.

Procedural Guide—See Guide 4 set out in Section 1 of this work.

Scope of provision—This rule provides for a practice direction to make provision for claims to be started electronically. The practice direction (see PD7E at p 524) provides for the continuation of the service known as Money Claim Online, which until 1 February 2004 operated as a pilot scheme.

Practice Direction – How to Start Proceedings – The Claim Form

This Practice Direction supplements CPR Part 7 (PD7)

Procedural Guide—See Guide 1, set out in Section 1 of this work.

General note—See also the notes to CPR Pt 7 for relevant commentary.

GENERAL

1 Subject to the following provisions of this practice direction, proceedings which both the High Court and the county courts have jurisdiction to deal with may be started in the High Court or in a county court.

WHERE TO START PROCEEDINGS

2.1 Proceedings (whether for damages or for a specified sum) may not be started in the High Court unless the value of the claim is more than £15,000.

2.2 Proceedings which include a claim for damages in respect of personal injuries must not be started in the High Court unless the value of the claim is £50,000 or more (paragraph 9 of the High Court and County Courts Jurisdiction Order 1991 (SI 1991/724 as amended) describes how the value of a claim is to be determined).

2.3 A claim must be issued in the High Court or a county court if an enactment so requires.

2.4 Subject to paragraphs 2.1 and 2.2 above, a claim should be started in the High Court if by reason of:

(1) the financial value of the claim and the amount in dispute, and/or
(2) the complexity of the facts, legal issues, remedies or procedures involved, and/or
(3) the importance of the outcome of the claim to the public in general,

the claimant believes that the claim ought to be dealt with by a High Court judge.

(CPR Part 30 and the practice direction supplementing Part 30 contain provisions relating to the transfer to the county court of proceedings started in the High Court and vice-versa)

2.5 A claim relating to Chancery business (which includes any of the matters specified in paragraph 1 of Schedule 1 to the Supreme Court Act 1981) may, subject to any enactment, rule or practice direction, be dealt with in the High Court or in a county court. The claim form should, if issued in the High Court, be marked in the top right hand corner 'Chancery Division' and, if issued in the county court, be marked 'Chancery Business'.

(For the equity jurisdiction of county courts, see section 23 of the County Courts Act 1984)

2.6 A claim relating to any of the matters specified in sub-paragraphs (a) and (b) of paragraph 2 of Schedule 1 to the Supreme Court Act 1981 must be dealt with in the High Court and will be assigned to the Queen's Bench Division.

2.7 Practice directions applying to particular types of proceedings, or to proceedings in particular courts, will contain provisions relating to the commencement and conduct of those proceedings.

2.8 A claim in the High Court for which a jury trial is directed will, if not already being dealt with in the Queen's Bench Division, be transferred to that Division.

2.9 The following proceedings may not be started in a county court unless the parties have agreed otherwise in writing:

(1) a claim for damages or other remedy for libel or slander, and
(2) a claim in which the title to any toll, fair, market or franchise is in question.

2.10

(1) The normal rules apply in deciding in which court and specialist list a claim that includes issues under the Human Rights Act 1998 should be

started. They also apply in deciding which procedure to use to start the claim; this Part or CPR Part 8 or CPR Part 54 (judicial review).

(2) The exception is a claim for damages in respect of a judicial act, which should be commenced in the High Court. If the claim is made in a notice of appeal then it will be dealt with according to the normal rules governing where the appeal is heard.

(A county court cannot make a declaration of incompatibility in accordance with section 4 of the Human Rights Act 1998. Legislation may direct that such a claim is to be brought before a specified tribunal)

'libel or slander … toll, fair, market or franchise' (para 2.9(1), (2))—See County Courts Act 1984, ss 15(2)(b) and 18.

THE CLAIM FORM

3.1 A claimant must use practice form N1 or practice form N208 (the Part 8 claim form) to start a claim (but see paragraphs 3.2 and 3.4 below).

3.2 Rule 7.9 deals with fixed date claims and rule 7.10 deals with the Production Centre for the issue of claims; there are separate practice directions supplementing rules 7.9 and 7.10.

3.3 If a claimant wishes his claim to proceed under Part 8, or if the claim is required to proceed under Part 8, the claim form should so state. Otherwise the claim will proceed under Part 7. But note that in respect of claims in specialist proceedings (listed in CPR Part 49) and claims brought under the RSC or CCR set out in the Schedule to the CPR (see CPR Part 50) the CPR will apply only to the extent that they are not inconsistent with the rules and practice directions that expressly apply to those claims.

3.4 Other practice directions may require special practice forms to be used to commence particular types of proceedings, or proceedings in particular courts.

3.5 Where a claim which is to be served out of the jurisdiction is one which the court has power to deal with under the Civil Jurisdiction and Judgments Act 1982, the claim form and, when they are contained in a separate document, the particulars of claim should be endorsed with a statement that the court has power under that Act to deal with the claim and that no proceedings based on the same claim are pending between the parties in Scotland, Northern Ireland or another Convention territory[1].

1 'Convention territory' means the territory or territories of any Contracting State as defined by s 1(3) of the Civil Jurisdiction and Judgments Act 1982, to which the Brussels Conventions or Lugano Convention apply.

3.5A Where a claim which is to be served out of jurisdiction is one which the court has power to deal with under Council Regulation (EC) No 44/2001 of 22 December 2000 on jurisdiction and the recognition and enforcement of judgments in civil and commercial matters, the claim form and, when they are contained in a separate document, the particulars of claim must be endorsed with a statement that the court has power under that Regulation to deal with the claim and that no proceedings based on the same claim are pending between the parties in Scotland, Northern Ireland or another Regulation State[1].

1 'Regulation State' means all Member States except Denmark.

3.6 If a claim for damages or for an unspecified sum is started in the High Court, the claim form must:

(1) state that the claimant expects to recover more than £15,000 (or £50,000 or more if the claim is for personal injuries), or
(2) state that some enactment provides that the claim may only be commenced in the High Court and specify that enactment, or
(3) state that the claim is to be in one of the specialist High Court lists (see CPR Parts 49 and 58–62) and specify that list.

3.7 If the contents of a claim form commencing specialist proceedings complies with the requirements of the specialist list in question the claim form will also satisfy paragraph 3.6 above.

3.8 If a claim for damages for personal injuries is started in the county court, the claim form must state whether or not the claimant expects to recover more than £1000 in respect of pain, suffering and loss of amenity.

3.9 If a claim for housing disrepair which includes a claim for an order requiring repairs or other work to be carried out by the landlord is started in the county court, the claim form must state:

(1) whether or not the cost of the repairs or other work is estimated to be more than £1000, and
(2) whether or not the claimant expects to recover more than £1000 in respect of any claim for damages[1].

If either of the amounts mentioned in (1) and (2) is more than £1000, the small claims track will not be the normal track for that claim.

(The Costs Practice Direction supplementing Parts 43 to 48 contains details of the information required to be filed with a claim form to comply with rule 44.15 (providing information about funding arrangements))

1 See rules 16.3(4) and 26.6.

'Civil Jurisdiction and Judgments Act 1982' (para 3.5)—See also CPR r 6.19(3) which states that where the court's permission is not required to serve a claim form out of the jurisdiction, the claim form must contain a statement of the grounds on which the claimant is entitled to serve it out of the jurisdiction. The Brussels and Lugano Conventions, and the Civil Jurisdiction and Judgments Act 1982, now apply only to Denmark and non-EU parties, Switzerland, Norway, Poland and Iceland.

'Where a claim which is to be served out of the jurisdiction' (para 3.5)—See also r 6.19(3) and PD6B, para 1, the latter of which sets out the usual form of words to be used.

'the claim form and … particulars of claim must be endorsed with a statement' (para 3.5A)—For the appropriate wording see PD6B, paras 1.1–1.3C.

TITLE OF PROCEEDINGS

4.1 The claim form and every other statement of case, must be headed with the title of the proceedings. The title should state:

(1) the number of proceedings,
(2) the court or Division in which they are proceeding,
(3) the full name of each party,
(4) his status in the proceedings (ie claimant/defendant).

Prospective amendments—Words prospectively inserted: Supplement 40 (issued 30 September 2005), with effect from 6 April 2006:

'(Paragraph 2.6 of the Practice Direction to Part 16 sets out what is meant by a full name in respect of each type of claimant.)'

4.2 Where there is more than one claimant and/or more than one defendant, the parties should be described in the title as follows:

(1) AB

(2) CD
(3) EF Claimants
and
(1) GH
(2) IJ
(3) KL Defendants

Exceptions—The general rule is that the title of the claim should contain only the names of the parties. However, there are exceptions to this rule. For example, Chancery Guide, para 2.3 contains the following three:

(i) in the Chancery Division proceedings relating to the administration of an estate should be entitled 'In the estate of AB deceased';
(ii) there are rules to be found in Chancery Guide, para 26.52 dealing with the heading of Lloyds' litigation; and
(iii) proceedings under the Inheritance (Provision for Family and Dependants) Act 1975 should be so entitled.

START OF PROCEEDINGS

5.1 Proceedings are started when the court issues a claim form at the request of the claimant (see rule 7.2) but where the claim form as issued was received in the court office on a date earlier than the date on which it was issued by the court, the claim is 'brought' for the purposes of the Limitation Act 1980 and any other relevant statute on that earlier date.

5.2 The date on which the claim form was received by the court will be recorded by a date stamp either on the claim form held on the court file or on the letter that accompanied the claim form when it was received by the court.

5.3 An enquiry as to the date on which the claim form was received by the court should be directed to a court officer.

5.4 Parties proposing to start a claim which is approaching the expiry of the limitation period should recognise the potential importance of establishing the date the claim form was received by the court and should themselves make arrangements to record the date.

5.5 Where it is sought to start proceedings against the estate of a deceased defendant where probate or letters of administration have not been granted, the claimant should issue the claim against 'the personal representatives of A.B. deceased'. The claimant should then, before the expiry of the period for service of the claim form, apply to the court for the appointment of a person to represent the estate of the deceased.

'Proceedings are started' (para 5.1)—See note **'on the date'** under CPR r 7.2.

PARTICULARS OF CLAIM

6.1 Where the claimant does not include the particulars of claim in the claim form, particulars of claim may be served separately:

(1) either at the same time as the claim form, or
(2) within 14 days after service of the claim form provided that the service of the particulars of claim is within 4 months after the date of issue of the claim form[1] (or 6 months where the claim form is to be served out of the jurisdiction[1]).

1 See rules 7.4(2) and 7.5(2).
2 See rule 7.5(3).

6.2 If the particulars of claim are not included in or have not been served with the claim form, the claim form must contain a statement that particulars of claim will follow[1].

(These paragraphs do not apply where the Part 8 procedure is being used. For information on matters to be included in the claim form or the particulars of claim, see Part 16 (statements of case) and the practice direction which supplements it)

1 See rule 16.2(2).

'within 4 months of the date of issue' (para 6.1(2))—This amended wording was introduced with effect from 28 January 2000 to bring the wording of the practice direction into line with CPR r 7.5(2).

STATEMENT OF TRUTH

7.1 Part 22 requires the claim form and, where they are not included in the claim form, the particulars of claim, to be verified by a statement of truth.

7.2 The form of the statement of truth is as follows:

'[I believe][the claimant believes] that the facts stated in [this claim form] [these particulars of claim] are true.'

7.3 Attention is drawn to rule 32.14 which sets out the consequences of verifying a statement of case containing a false statement without an honest belief in its truth.

(For information regarding statements of truth see Part 22 and the practice direction which supplements it)

Statement of truth—As to who should sign a statement of truth, see PD22, para 3. A modified procedure for such statements applies to cases issued through the Production Centre. Statements of truth are not required at all where the claim form includes a jurat for the content to be verified by an affidavit (PD22, para 1.6).

EXTENSION OF TIME

8.1 An application under rule 7.6 (for an extension of time for serving a claim form under rule 7.6(1)) must be made in accordance with Part 23 and supported by evidence.

8.2 The evidence should state:

(1) all the circumstances relied on,
(2) the date of issue of the claim,
(3) the expiry date of any rule 7.6 extension, and
(4) a full explanation as to why the claim has not been served.

(For information regarding (1) written evidence see Part 32 and the practice direction which supplements it and (2) service of the claim form see Part 6 and the practice direction which supplements it)

Practice Direction – Consumer Credit Act Claim

This Practice Direction supplements CPR Rule 7.9 (PD7B)

Procedural Guide—See Guide 2, set out in Section 1 of this work.

General note—See also the notes to CPR r 7.9.

Fixed costs—See generally CPR rr 45.2 and 45.4.

1.1 In this practice direction 'the Act' means the Consumer Credit Act 1974, a section referred to by number means the section with that number in the Act, and expressions which are defined in the Act have the same meaning in this practice direction as they have in the Act.

1.2 'Consumer Credit Act procedure' means the procedure set out in this practice direction.

Scope of provision—The procedure set out in this practice direction must be used when seeking an order for delivery of goods which are the subject of an agreement regulated by CCA 1974 or when making any of the claims set out in para 3 (below). Claims under CCA 1974 relating to money only are made using the standard CPR Pt 7 procedure (see Guide 1, set out in Section 1 of this work).

Forms—For a time order, use N440; otherwise, N1 (CPR Pt 7 claim form); the defendant is served with a copy of the N1 together with Notes for Guidance Form N1(FD), Form of Admission (N9C) and Form of Defence (Form N9D).

WHEN TO USE THE CONSUMER CREDIT ACT PROCEDURE

2.1 A claimant must use the Consumer Credit Act procedure where he makes a claim under a provision of the Act to which paragraph 3 of this practice direction applies.

2.2 Where a claimant is using the Consumer Credit Act procedure the CPR are modified to the extent that they are inconsistent with the procedure set out in this practice direction.

2.3 The court may at any stage order the claim to continue as if the claimant had not used the Consumer Credit Act procedure, and if it does so the court may give any directions it considers appropriate.

2.4 This practice direction also sets out matters which must be included in the particulars of claim in certain types of claim, and restrictions on where certain types of claim may be started.

THE PROVISIONS OF THE ACT

3.1 Subject to paragraph 3.2 and 3.3 this practice direction applies to claims made under the following provisions of the Act:

(1) section 141 (claim by the creditor to enforce regulated agreement relating to goods etc),
(2) section 129 (claim by debtor or hirer for a time order),
(3) section 90 (creditor's claim for an order for recovery of protected goods),
(4) section 92(1) (creditor's or owner's claim to enter premises to take possession of goods),
(5) section 139(1)(a) (debtor's claim for a credit agreement to be reopened as extortionate), and

(6) creditor's or owner's claim for a court order to enforce a regulated agreement relating to goods or money where the court order is required by –
   (a) section 65(1) (improperly-executed agreement),
   (b) section 86(2) of the Act (death of debtor or hirer where agreement is partly secured or unsecured),
   (c) section 111(2) (default notice etc not served on surety),
   (d) section 124(1) or (2) (taking of a negotiable instrument in breach of terms of section 123), or
   (e) section 105(7)(a) or (b) (security not expressed in writing, or improperly executed).

3.2 This practice direction does not apply to any claim made under the provisions listed in paragraph 3.1 above if that claim relates to the recovery of land.

3.3 This practice direction also does not apply to a claim made by the creditor under section 141 of the Act to enforce a regulated agreement where the agreement relates only to money. Such a claim must be started by the issue of a Part 7 claim form.

RESTRICTIONS ON WHERE TO START SOME CONSUMER CREDIT ACT CLAIMS

4.1 Where the claim includes a claim to recover goods to which a regulated hire purchase agreement or conditional sale agreement relates, it may only be started in the county court for the district in which the debtor, or one of the debtors:

(1) resides or carries on business, or
(2) resided or carried on business at the date when the defendant last made a payment under the agreement.

4.2 In any other claim to recover goods, the claim may only be started in the court for the district:

(1) in which the defendant, or one of the defendants, resides or carries on business, or
(2) in which the goods are situated.

4.3 A claim of a debtor or hirer for an order under section 129(1)(b) of the Act (a time order) may only be started in the court where the claimant resides or carries on business.

(Costs rule 45.1(2)(b) allows the claimant to recover fixed costs in certain circumstances where such a claim is made)

(Paragraph 7 sets out the matters the claimant must include in his particulars of claim where he is using the Consumer Credit Act procedure)

THE CONSUMER CREDIT ACT PROCEDURE

5.1 In the types of claim to which paragraph 3 applies the court will fix a hearing date on the issue of the claim form.

5.2 The particulars of claim must be served with the claim form.

5.3 Where a claimant is using the Consumer Credit Act procedure, the defendant to the claim is not required to:

(1) serve an acknowledgment of service, or

(2) file a defence, although he may choose to do so.

5.4 Where a defendant intends to defend a claim, his defence should be filed within 14 days of service of the particulars of claim. If the defendant fails to file a defence within this period, but later relies on it, the court may take such a failure into account as a factor when deciding what order to make about costs.

5.5 Part 12 (default judgment) does not apply where the claimant is using the Consumer Credit Act procedure.

5.6 Each party must be given at least 28 days' notice of the hearing date.

5.7 Where the claimant serves the claim form, he must serve notice of the hearing date at the same time, unless the hearing date is specified in the claim form.

POWERS OF THE COURT AT THE HEARING

6.1 On the hearing date the court may dispose of the claim.

6.2 If the court does not dispose of the claim on the hearing date:

(1) if the defendant has filed a defence, the court will:
  (a) allocate the claim to a track and give directions about the management of the case, or
  (b) give directions to enable it to allocate the claim to a track,
(2) if the defendant has not filed a defence, the court may make any order or give any direction it considers appropriate.

6.3 Rule 26.5(3) to (5) and rules 26.6 to 26.10 apply to the allocation of a claim under paragraph 6.2.

MATTERS WHICH MUST BE INCLUDED IN THE PARTICULARS OF CLAIM

7.1 Where the Consumer Credit Act procedure is used, the claimant must state in his particulars of claim that the claim is a Consumer Credit Act claim.

7.2 A claimant making a claim for the delivery of goods to enforce a hire purchase agreement or conditional sale agreement which is:

(1) a regulated agreement for the recovery of goods, and
(2) let to a person other than a company or other corporation,

must also state (in this order) in his particulars of claim:

(a) the date of the agreement,
(b) the parties to the agreement,
(c) the number or other identification of the agreement (with enough information to allow the debtor to identify the agreement),
(d) where the claimant was not one of the original parties to the agreement, the means by which the rights and duties of the creditor passed to him,
(e) the place where the agreement was signed by the defendant (if known),
(f) the goods claimed,
(g) the total price of the goods,
(h) the paid up sum,
(i) the unpaid balance of the total price,
(j) whether a default notice or a notice under section 76(1) or section

88(1) of the Act has been served on the defendant, and, if it has, the date and the method of service,

(k) the date on which the right to demand delivery of the goods accrued,

(l) the amount (if any) claimed as an alternative to the delivery of goods, and

(m) the amount (if any) claimed in addition to –

(i) the delivery of the goods, or

(ii) any claim under sub paragraph (l) above with the grounds of each such claim.

7.3 A claimant who is a debtor or hirer making a claim for an order under section 129(1)(b) of the Act (a time order) must state (in the following order) in his particulars of claim:

(1) the date of the agreement,

(2) the parties to the agreement,

(3) the number or other means of identifying the agreement,

(4) details of any sureties,

(5) if the defendant is not one of the original parties to the agreement then the name of the original party to the agreement,

(6) the names and addresses of the persons intended to be served with the claim form,

(7) the place where the claimant signed the agreement,

(8) details of the notice served by the creditor or owner giving rise to the claim for the time order,

(9) the total unpaid balance the claimant admits is due under the agreement, and –

(a) the amount of any arrears (if known), and

(b) the amount and frequency of the payments specified in the agreement,

(10) the claimant's proposals for payments of any arrears and of future instalments together with details of his means,

(11) where the claim relates to a breach of the agreement other than for the payment of money the claimant's proposals for remedying it.

7.4 (1) This paragraph applies where a claimant is required to obtain a court order to enforce a regulated agreement by –

(a) section 65(1) (improperly-executed agreement),

(b) section 105(7)(a) or (b) (security not expressed in writing, or improperly-executed),

(c) section 111(2) (default notice etc not served on surety),

(d) section 124(1) or (2) (taking of a negotiable instrument in breach of terms of section 123), or

(e) section 86(2) of the Act (death of debtor or hirer where agreement is partly secured or unsecured).

(2) The claimant must state in his particulars of claim what the circumstances are that require him to obtain a court order for enforcement.

ADMISSION OF CERTAIN CLAIMS FOR RECOVERY OF GOODS UNDER REGULATED AGREEMENTS

8.1 In a claim to recover goods to which section 90(1)[1] applies:

(1) the defendant may admit the claim, and

(2) offer terms on which a return order should be suspended under section 135(1)(b).

1 Section 90(1) provides that:
'At any time when –
(a) the debtor is in breach of a regulated hire-purchase or a regulated conditional sale agreement relating to goods, and
(b) the debtor has paid to the creditor one-third or more of the total price of the goods, and
(c) the property in the goods remains in the creditor, the creditor is not entitled to recover possession of the goods from the debtor except on an order of the court.'

8.2 He may do so by filing a request in practice form N9C.

8.3 He should do so within the period for making an admission specified in rule 14.2(b). If the defendant fails to file his request within this period, and later makes such a request, the court may take the failure into account as a factor when deciding what order to make about costs.

8.4 On receipt of the admission, the court will serve a copy on the claimant.

8.5 The claimant may obtain judgment by filing a request in practice form N228.

8.6 On receipt of the request for judgment, the court will enter judgment in the terms of the defendant's admission and offer and for costs.

8.7 If:

(1) the claimant does not accept the defendant's admission and offer, and
(2) the defendant does not appear on the hearing date fixed when the claim form was issued,

the court may treat the defendant's admission and offer as evidence of the facts stated in it for the purposes of sections 129(2)(a)[1] and 135(2)[2].

1 Section 129(2) provides that –
'A time order shall provide for one or both of the following, as the court considers just –
(a) the payment by the debtor or hirer or any surety of any sum owed under a regulated agreement or a security by such instalments, payable at such times, as the court, having regard to the means of the debtor or hirer and any surety, considers reasonable;
(b) the remedying by the debtor or hirer of any breach of a regulated agreement (other than non-payment of money) within such period as the court may specify.'
2 Section 135(2) provides that –
'The court shall not suspend the operation of a term [in an order relating to a regulated agreement] requiring the delivery up of goods by any person unless satisfied that the goods are in his possession or control.'

ADDITIONAL REQUIREMENTS ABOUT PARTIES TO THE PROCEEDINGS

9.1 The court may dispense with the requirement in section 141(5) (all parties to a regulated agreement and any surety to be parties to any proceedings) in any claim relating to the regulated agreement, if:

(1) the claim form has not been served on the debtor or the surety, and
(2) the claimant either before or at the hearing makes an application (which may be made without notice) for the court to make such an order.

9.2 In a claim relating to a regulated agreement where:

(1) the claimant was not one of the original parties to the agreement, and
(2) the former creditor's rights and duties under the agreement have passed to him by –

(a) operation of law, or
(b) assignment,

the requirement of section 141(5) (all parties to a regulated agreement and any surety to be parties to any proceedings) does not apply to the former creditor, unless the court otherwise orders.

9.3 Where a claimant who is a creditor or owner makes a claim for a court order under section 86(2) (death of debtor or hirer where agreement is partly secured or unsecured) the personal representatives of the deceased debtor or hirer must be parties to the proceedings in which the order is sought, unless no grant of representation has been made to the estate.

9.4 Where no grant of representation has been made to the estate of the deceased debtor or hirer, the claimant must make an application in accordance with Part 23 for directions about which persons (if any) are to be made parties to the claim as being affected or likely to be affected by the enforcement of the agreement.

9.5 The claimant's application under paragraph 9.4:
(a) may be made without notice, and
(b) should be made before the claim form is issued.

NOTICE TO BE GIVEN TO RE-OPEN A CONSUMER CREDIT AGREEMENT

10.1 Where a debtor or any surety intends to apply for a consumer credit agreement to be reopened after a claim on or relating to the agreement has already begun, and:

(1) section 139(1)(b)[1], or
(2) section 139(1)(c),

applies, the debtor or surety must serve written notice of his intention on the court and every other party to the proceedings within 14 days of the service of the claim form on him.

1 Section 139(1) provides that:
(1) A credit agreement may, if the court thinks just, be reopened on the ground that the credit bargain is extortionate –
(a) on an application for the purpose made by the debtor or any surety to the High Court, county court or sheriff court; or
(b) at the instance of the debtor or a surety in any proceedings to which the debtor and creditor are parties, being proceedings to enforce the credit agreement, any security relating to it or any linked transaction; or
(c) at the instance of the debtor or a surety in other proceedings in any court where the amount paid or payable under the credit agreement is relevant.

10.2 If the debtor or surety (as the case may be) serves a notice under paragraph 10.1 he will be treated as having filed a defence for the purposes of the Consumer Credit Act procedure.

'a claim' (para 10.1)—Where such an application is made in response to a mortgage possession claim, the court will consider whether the claim and the application should be tried at the same time (*City Mortgage Corporation Ltd v Baptiste* [1997] CCLR 64).

Practice Direction – Production Centre

This Practice Direction supplements CPR Rule 7.10 (PD7C)

Money Claim Online—Whilst making use of the information technology available at the Production Centre, the electronic issue of money claims online is dealt with by a separate practice direction – PD7E. See also Guide 4.

GENERAL

1.1 In this practice direction:

'the Centre' means the Production Centre.

'Centre user' means a person who is for the time being permitted to issue claims through the Centre, and includes a solicitor acting for such a person.

'officer' means the officer in charge of the Centre or another officer of the Centre acting on his behalf.

'national creditor code' means the number or reference allotted to a Centre user by the officer.

'Code of Practice' means any code of practice which may at any time be issued by the Court Service relating to the discharge by the Centre of its functions and the way in which a Centre user is to conduct business with the Centre.

'data' means any information which is required to be given to the court or which is to be contained in any document to be sent to the court or to any party.

1.2 For any purpose connected with the exercise of its functions, the Centre will be treated as part of the office of the court whose name appears on the claim form to which the functions relate, or in whose name the claim form is requested to be issued, and the officer will be treated as an officer of that court.

1.3 (1) The functions of the Centre include the provision of a facility which, through the use of information technology, enables a Centre user to have claim forms issued and served, whether or not those claim forms are to be treated as issued in the Northampton County Court or in another county court.

(2) If a Centre user issues claim forms in the name of Northampton County Court, the functions of the Centre also include:

(a) the handling of defences and admissions,

(b) the entry of judgment in default, on admission, on acceptance, or on determination,

(c) the registration of judgments,

(d) the issue of warrants of execution,

(e) where the defendant is an individual, the transfer to the defendant's home court of any case that is to continue following the filing of a defence or where a hearing is required before judgment; or, where the defendant is not an individual, the transfer to the court for the area of the claimants, or where he is represented, his solicitors, address; and

(f) the transfer to the defendant's home court of any case for oral examination or where enforcement of a judgment (other than by warrant of execution, charging order or third party debt order) is to follow.

1.4 (1) Where the officer is to take any step, any rule or practice direction which requires a document to be filed before he does so will be treated as complied with if the data which that document would contain is delivered to the Centre in computer readable form in accordance with the Code of Practice.

(2) Data relating to more than one case may be included in a single document or delivery of data.

(3) CPR rule 6.3(3) (copies of documents to be served by court) does not apply to any document which is to be produced by electronic means from data supplied by a Centre user.

(4) Paragraph 7.3 of the practice direction supplementing CPR Part 16 (statements of case), which requires documentation to be attached to the particulars of contract claims, does not apply to claims to be issued by the Centre.

(5) The practice direction supplementing CPR Part 22 (statements of truth) is modified as follows:

(a) a single statement of truth may accompany each batch of requests to issue claim forms and may be in electronic form,

(b) the form of such a statement should be as follows: 'I believe that the facts stated in the attached claim forms are true.', and

(c) the signature of the appropriate person (as to which see section 3 of the practice direction supplementing CPR Part 22) may be in electronic form.

Scope of provision—This practice direction governs the electronic issuing and process of county-court-only claims through the Production Centre. It is a facility available to bulk issuers who have agreed to comply with the code of practice of the Production Centre. Claims may be issued nominally from any county court. Paragraph 2 sets out the types of claim not suitable for issue through the centre.

'the transfer' (para 1.3(2)(e))—This provision was amended with effect from 31 May 2001 to bring it into line with the normal rules for automatic transfer set out in CPR r 26.2.

Statements of truth (para 1.4(5))—It seems unlikely that a false statement, made without an honest belief in its truth, relating to a claim issued through the Production Centre is punishable under CPR r 32.14.

CLAIMS WHICH MAY NOT BE ISSUED THROUGH THE CENTRE

2.1 The Centre will not issue any claim form which is to be issued in the High Court.

2.2 The Centre will only issue a claim form if the claim is for a specified sum of money less than £100,000.

2.3 The Centre will not issue any of the following types of claim:

(1) a claim against more than two defendants,

(2) a claim against two defendants where a different sum is claimed against each of them,

(3) a claim where particulars of claim separate from the claim form are required,

(4) a claim against the Crown,

(5) a claim for an amount in a foreign currency,

(6) a claim where either party is known to be a child or patient within Part 21 of the Civil Procedure Rules,

(7) a claim where the claimant is a legally assisted person within the meaning of the Legal Aid Act 1988,

(8) a claim where the defendant's address for service as it appears on the claim form is not in England or Wales.
(9) a claim which is to be issued under Part 8 of the Civil Procedure Rules.

Scotland—A provision in para 2.3(8) which appeared to suggest that a claim could be issued through the Production Centre for service in Scotland was deleted with effect from 12 July 1999.

CENTRE USERS

3.1 Only a Centre user may issue or conduct claims through the Centre.

3.2 The officer may permit any person to be a Centre user.

3.3 The officer may withdraw the permission for any person to be a Centre user.

3.4 A Centre user must comply with the provisions of the Code of Practice in his dealings with the Centre.

3.5 The officer will allot a national creditor code to each Centre user.

THE CODE OF PRACTICE

4.1 The Code of Practice will contain provisions designed to ensure that the Centre can discharge its functions efficiently, and it may in particular provide for:

(1) the forms of magnetic media that may be used,
(2) the circumstances in which data may or must be supplied in magnetic form,
(3) the circumstances in which data may or must be supplied in a document and the form that such a document must take,
(4) how often data may be supplied,
(5) the numbering of cases and data relating to cases,
(6) data to be given to the Centre by the Centre user about cases which have been settled or paid or are otherwise not proceeding, and
(7) accounting arrangements and the method of payment of fees.

4.2 The Court Service may change the Code of Practice from time to time.

OTHER MODIFICATIONS TO THE CIVIL PROCEDURE RULES

Powers of the officer to make orders –

5.1 The officer may make the following orders:

(1) an order to set aside a default judgment where, after that judgment has been entered, the claim form in the case is returned by the Post Office as undelivered,
(2) an order to set aside a judgment on application by a Centre user,
(3) an order to transfer a case to another county court for enforcement or for a judgment debtor to attend court for questioning.

Procedure on the filing of a defence –

5.2 (1) This paragraph applies where a Centre user has issued a claim in the Northampton County Court and the defendant has filed a defence to the claim or to part of the claim.
(2) On the filing of the defence the officer will serve a notice on the Centre user requiring the Centre user to notify him within 28 days whether he wishes the claim to proceed.

(3) If the Centre user does not notify the officer within the time specified in the notice that he wishes the claim to proceed the claim will be stayed, and the officer will notify the parties accordingly.

(4) The proceedings will not be transferred as provided by paragraph 1.3(2)(e) until the Centre user notifies the officer that he wishes the claim to continue.

'claim will be stayed' (para 5.2(3))—While the stay may no doubt be lifted on the application of either party under CPR Pt 23, the power to make this order is not given to the officer and the application will normally be considered by the district judge. It must be supported by evidence (CPR r 3.9(2)) and the criteria set out in CPR r 3.9(1) will apply.

Practice Direction – Claims for the Recovery of Taxes

This Practice Direction supplements CPR Rule 7.9 (PD7D)

SCOPE

1.1 This practice direction applies to claims by HM Revenue and Customs for the recovery of –

(a) Income Tax,
(b) Corporation Tax,
(c) Capital Gains Tax,
(d) Interest, penalties and surcharges on Income Tax, Corporation Tax or Capital Gains Tax which by virtue of section 69 of the Taxes Management Act 1970 are to be treated as if they are taxes due and payable,
(e) National Insurance Contributions and interest, penalties and surcharges thereon.

Scope of provision—Most defences filed in claims to which this practice direction relates will not disclose a reasonable ground for defending the claim because of the certificates referred to under para 3.1 below. The practice direction envisages that a hearing, which will be in private (CPR r 39.2(3)(c)), is listed and that at the hearing judgment will usually be entered and consideration given to the payment of the judgment debt.

Furthermore, where the Crown is claiming taxes, penalties or duties, no counterclaim can be made (see CPR r 66.4(1)). In any other claim by the Crown, the defendant cannot make a counterclaim or other Pt 20 claim or raise a defence of set-off which is based on a claim for repayment of taxes, duties or penalties (CPR r 66.4(2)).

PROCEDURE

2.1 If a defence is filed, the court will fix a date for the hearing.

2.2 Part 26 (Case management – preliminary stage) apart from CPR rule 26.2 (automatic transfer) does not apply to claims to which this practice direction applies.

Scope of provision—Thus allocation questionnaires will not be sent out on filing of a defence.

AT THE HEARING

3.1 On the hearing date the court may dispose of the claim.

(Section 70 of the Taxes Management Act 1970 and section 118 of the Social Security Administration Act 1992 provide that a certificate of an officer of the Commissioners for HM Revenue and Customs is sufficient evidence that a sum mentioned in such a certificate is unpaid and due to the Crown)

3.2 But exceptionally, if the court does not dispose of the claim on the hearing date it may give case management directions, which may, if the defendant has filed a defence, include allocating the case.

Scope of provision—Having the power to allocate must imply that, if the court elects to do so, CPR rr 26.5–26.10 will then apply, despite the provisions of para 2.2 above.

Practice Direction – Pilot Scheme for Money Claim Online

(PD7E)

Procedural Guide—See Guide 4, set out in Section 1 of this work.

Scope of provision—This practice direction, supplementing r 7.12, provides for claims to be started electronically. It continues the service known as Money Claim Online which until 1 February 2004 operated as a pilot scheme.

GENERAL

1.1 This practice direction provides for a scheme in which, in the circumstances set out in this practice direction, a request for a claim form to be issued and other specified documents may be filed electronically ('Money Claim Online').

1.2 This practice direction enables claimants and their representatives –

- (1) to start certain types of county court claims by requesting the issue of a claim form electronically via the Court Service website; and
- (2) where a claim has been started electronically –
  - (a) to file electronically a request for –
    - (i) judgment in default:
    - (ii) judgment on acceptance of an admission of the whole of the amount claimed; or
    - (iii) the issue of a warrant of execution; and
  - (b) to view an electronic record of the progress of the claim.

1.3 This practice direction also enables defendants and their representatives –

- (1) to file electronically –
  - (a) an acknowledgment of service;
  - (b) a part admission;
  - (c) a defence; or
  - (d) a counterclaim (if filed together with a defence);
- (2) to view an electronic record of the progress of the claim.

1.4 Claims started using Money Claim Online will be issued by Northampton County Court and will proceed in that court unless they are transferred to another court. The address for filing any document, application or request (other than one which is filed electronically in accordance with this practice direction) is Northampton County Court, St Katherine's House, 21–27 St Katherine's Street, Northampton, NN1 2LH, DX 702885 Northampton 7, fax no. 0845 6015889.

Scope of provision—This practice direction governs the electronic issue and processing of county court money claims online ('MCOL') through an Internet website by any person whose claim satisfies the conditions set out in para 4 below. Claims proceed in the Northampton County Court until transferred pursuant to para 10. The system operates for 24 hours a day, 7 days a week and progress can be checked at any time. The system is only updated during normal court working hours.

Hardware/software requirements—Users must:

(a) have either a personal computer (PC) running Windows or a Macintosh Computer;

(b) have a working Internet connection;

(c) use version 4 or 5 of Microsoft Internet Explorer, Netscape Navigator 4.x or Netscape Communicator 4.x (Internet browsers must have JavaScript and cookies enabled and be capable of supporting 56-bit or 128-bit SSL);

(d) have Adobe Acrobat Reader version 4.0 (or later) to save claim forms to computer and print them. A free copy of the Adobe Acrobat Reader is downloadable online from the MCOL website.

SECURITY

2 The Court Service will take such measures as it thinks fit to ensure the security of steps taken or information stored electronically. These may include requiring users of Money Claim Online –

(1) to enter a customer identification and password;

(2) to provide personal information for identification purposes; and

(3) to comply with any other security measures,

before taking any of the steps mentioned in paragraph 1.2 or 1.3.

Registration—Persons using the system must register online. By registering users agree to accept the Court Service privacy policy available online at *http://www.courtservice.gov.uk/mcol/privacy_policy.htm*. The website has a helpful user guide and tutorial and is supported by a customer help desk open Monday to Friday between 9 am and 5 pm. See Guide 4 for contact details. Registration details require users to provide their own customer ID, password and e-mail address.

FEES

3.1 Where this practice direction provides for a fee to be paid electronically, it may be paid by –

(1) credit card;

(2) debit card; or

(3) any other method which the Court Service may permit.

3.2 A step may only be taken using Money Claim Online on payment of the prescribed fee. The County Court Fees Order 1999 provides that parties may, in certain circumstances, be exempt from payment of fees, or may be entitled to apply for fees to be remitted or reduced. The Court Service website contains guidance as to when this entitlement arises. A claimant who wishes to claim exemption from payment of fees, or to apply for remission or reduction of fees, may not use Money Claim Online and should issue his claim at a court office.

Fees—The same fees are payable as if the claim were issued in a court office – see the Table under 'Court fees' in Guide 1.

TYPES OF CLAIMS WHICH MAY BE STARTED USING MONEY CLAIM ONLINE

4 A claim may be started using Money Claim Online if it meets all the following conditions –

(1) the only remedy claimed is a specified amount of money –

(a) less than £100,000 (excluding any interest or costs claimed); and

  - (b) in sterling;
- (2) the procedure under Part 7 of the Civil Procedure Rules (CPR) is used;
- (3) the claimant is not –
  - (a) a child or patient; or
  - (b) funded by the Legal Services Commission;
- (4) the claim is against –
  - (a) a single defendant; or
  - (b) two defendants, if the claim is for a single amount against each of them;
- (5) the defendant is not –
  - (a) the Crown; or
  - (b) a person known to be a child or patient; and
- (6) the defendant's address for service is within England and Wales.

'a child or patient' (para 4(3)(a))—This is defined by CPR r 21.1(2).

'the Crown' (para 4(5)(a))—This is defined in Part II of the Crown Proceedings Act 1947 and see CPR Sch 1, RSC Ord 77 and Sch 2, CCR Ord 42 for provisions regarding claims against the Crown in the High Court and county court respectively.

'defendant's address for service' (para 4(6))—See CPR r 6.5 for provisions regarding address for service.

Limitations—Paragraph 4 of the practice direction limits claims to sterling money claims between limited categories of claimants and defendants. Defendants must have an address for service within England and Wales. Those against whom an order has been made under SCA 1981, s 42 ('vexatious litigants') will not be able to use the facility because the site provides no means for them to produce the order giving the requisite permission to issue.

STARTING A CLAIM

5.1 A claimant may request the issue of a claim form by –

- (1) completing and sending an online claim form; and
- (2) electronically paying the appropriate issue fee,

at www.courtservice.gov.uk/mcol or www.moneyclaim.gov.uk.

5.2 The particulars of claim –

- (1) must be included in the online claim form and may not be filed separately; and
- (2) must be limited in size to not more than 1080 characters (including spaces).

5.3 Paragraph 7.3 of the practice direction supplementing Part 16 (statements of case), which requires documents to be filed with the particulars of claim in contract claims, does not apply to claims started using an online claim form.

5.4 When an online claim form is received by the Money Claim Online website, an acknowledgment of receipt will automatically be sent to the claimant. The acknowledgment of receipt does not constitute a notice that the claim form has been issued.

5.5 When the court issues a claim form following the submission of an online claim form, the claim is 'brought' for the purposes of the Limitation Act 1980 and any other enactment on the date on which the online claim form is received by the court's computer system. The court will keep a record, by electronic or other means, of when online claim forms are received.

5.6 When the court issues a claim form, it will –

- (1) serve a printed version of the claim form on the defendant; and

(2) send the claimant notice of issue by post.

5.7 The claim form shall have printed on it a unique customer identification number or a password by which the defendant may access the claim on the Court Service website.

5.8 The claim form shall be deemed to be served on the fifth day after the claim was issued irrespective of whether that day is a business day or not.

5.9 Where a period of time within which an acknowledgment of service or a defence must be filed ends on a day when the court is closed, the defendant may file his acknowledgment or defence on the next day that the court is open.

'not more than 1080 characters' (para 5.2(2))—Approximately 16 lines of printed text.

'When the court issues a claim form' (para 5.5)—It is receipt of the electronic claim form by the court's computer system (and not by the website, which sends electronic acknowledgment of receipt of request for claim) that constitutes the formal commencement date for the purposes of the Limitation Act 1980, etc. It should be assumed that the court's system will not receive it on days or at times when the court is closed.

'deemed to be served the fifth day after' (para 5.8)—Note that this is quite different from the normal position under CPR r 6.7. The deemed day of service of a document under r 6.7(1) is not rebuttable by evidence proving that service had actually been effected on a different day (*Godwin v Swindon Borough Council* [2001] EWCA Civ 1478, [2001] 4 All ER 641, CA) – see note **'Deemed to be served'** under CPR r 6.7(1). The same principle will apply to service under this paragraph.

'business day' (para 5.8)—This is defined by CPR r 6.7(3) as any day except Saturday, Sunday or a bank holiday.

ONLINE RESPONSE

6.1 A defendant wishing to file –

(1) an acknowledgment of service of the claim form under CPR Part 10;
(2) a part admission under CPR 14.5;
(3) a defence under CPR Part 15; or
(4) a counterclaim (to be filed together with a defence),

may, instead of filing a written form, do so by completing and sending the relevant online form at www.courtservice.gov.uk/mcol or www.moneyclaim.gov.uk.

6.2 Where a defendant files an online form –

(1) he must not send a hard copy in addition;
(2) the form is not filed until it is received by the court, whatever time it is shown to have been sent;
(3) an online form received after 4 pm will be treated as filed on the next day the court office is open; and
(4) where a time limit applies, it remains the responsibility of the defendant to ensure that the online form is filed in time.

Procedural Guide—See Guide 5, set out in Section 1 of this work.

'sending an e-mail' (para 6.1(2))—This e-mail address may change if the website URL is changed (see under para 5 above). If so, details will be given on the site.

ACKNOWLEDGMENT OF SERVICE

7.1 Attention is drawn to CPR Part 10 and its practice direction which contain rules about acknowledgment of service.

ADMISSION

8.1 Attention is drawn to CPR Part 14 and its practice direction which contain rules about admissions.

DEFENCE

9.1 Attention is drawn to CPR Part 15 and its practice direction which contain rules about defences.

COUNTERCLAIM

10.1 Where a counterclaim is filed using an online form, any fee payable shall be taken by the court to which the claim is transferred under paragraph 14.1.

10.2 Attention is drawn to CPR Part 20 and its practice direction, which contain provisions about counterclaims.

'counterclaim' (para 10.1)—Note that a defence and counterclaim cannot be filed online but must be lodged with the court in the normal manner. A counterclaim against a claimant that is not filed with a defence requires leave of the court – see CPR r 20.4(2)(b).

STATEMENT OF TRUTH

11.1 CPR Part 22 requires any statement of case to be verified by a statement of truth. This applies to any online forms.

11.2 The statement of truth in an online statement of case must be in the form –

> '[I believe][The claimant believes] that the facts stated in this claim form are true.'; or
>
> '[I believe][The defendant believes] that the facts stated in this defence are true.'

as appropriate.

11.3 Attention is drawn to –

(1) paragraph 3 of the practice direction supplementing CPR Part 22, which provides who may sign a statement of truth; and
(2) CPR 32.14, which sets out the consequences of making, or causing to be made, a false statement in a document verified by a statement of truth, without an honest belief in its truth.

SIGNATURE

12.1 Any provision of the CPR which requires a document to be signed by any person is satisfied by that person entering his name on an online form.

REQUEST FOR JUDGMENT OR ISSUE OF WARRANT

13.1 If, in a claim started using Money Claim Online –

(1) the claimant wishes to apply for judgment in default in accordance with CPR Part 12; or
(2) the defendant has filed or served an admission of the whole of the claim in accordance with CPR 14.4,

the claimant may request judgment to be entered in default or on the admission (as the case may be) by completing and sending an online request form at www.courtservice.gov.uk/mcol or www.moneyclaim.gov.uk..

13.2 Where –

(1) judgment has been entered following a request under paragraph 13.1; and

(2) the claimant is entitled to the issue of a warrant of execution without requiring the permission of the court,

the claimant may request the issue of a warrant of execution by –

(a) completing and sending an online request form; and

(b) electronically paying the appropriate fee,

at www.courtservice.gov.uk/mcol or www.moneyclaim.gov.uk.

(Order 26 of the County Court Rules ('CCR') contains rules about warrants of execution. Among other matters, CCR Order 26, rule 1 contains restrictions on when a warrant of execution may be issued if the court has made an order for payment of a sum of money by instalments, and CCR Order 26, rule 5 sets out certain circumstances in which a warrant of execution may not be issued without the permission of the court)

13.3 A request under paragraph 13.1 or 13.2 will be treated as being filed –

(1) on the day the court receives the request, if it receives it before 10 am on a working day; and

(2) otherwise, on the next working day after the court receives the request.

'the claimant may request the issue of a warrant of execution' (para 13.2)—Note that it is, currently, only possible to enforce a MCOL judgment by a county court bailiff's levy. A request can accompany a request for default judgment if payment forthwith is sought.

TRANSFER OF CLAIM

14.1 Where the defendant is an individual and Northampton County Court is not his home court, the court will transfer the claim to the defendant's home court –

(1) under CPR 13.4, if the defendant applies to set aside or vary judgment;

(2) under CPR 14.12, if there is to be a hearing for a judge to determine the time and rate of payment;

(3) under CPR 26.2, if a defence is filed to all or part of the claim; or

(4) if either party makes an application which cannot be dealt with without a hearing.

14.2 Where the defendant is not an individual, if –

(1) the claimant's address for service on the claim form is not within the district of Northampton County Court; and

(2) one of the events mentioned in paragraph 14.1 arises,

the court will transfer the claim to the county court for the district in which the claimant's address for service on the claim form is situated.

VIEWING THE CASE RECORD

15.1 A facility will be provided for parties or their representatives to view an electronic record of the status of claims started using Money Claim Online.

15.2 The record of each claim will be reviewed and, if necessary, updated at least once each day until the claim is transferred from Northampton County Court.

PART 8
ALTERNATIVE PROCEDURE FOR CLAIMS

CONTENTS OF THIS PART

Procedural Guide—See Guide 3, set out in Section 1 of this work.

Scope of Part—Numerically, the overwhelming majority of claims are commenced using a Pt 7 claim form (see generally, Pt 7). However, the CPR abolished the originating summons procedures in the High Court and the fixed date summons and originating application procedures in the county court. Bar those matters covered by r 7.9 (see above, as well as PD7B dealing with Consumer Credit Act claims), Pt 8 fills the vacuum by creating an alternative procedure where:

(a) the claimant seeks the court's decision on a question which is unlikely to involve a substantial dispute of fact (r 8.1(2)(a)) of which examples are set out in PD8, para 1.4.

(b) a rule or practice direction requires or permits the use of the Pt 8 procedure (r 8.1(6)). PD8B (see below) sets out cases where use of the Pt 8 procedure is mandatory, and also modifies the general Pt 8 procedure with the introduction (in Section B of the PD) of a fixed date procedure for certain categories of case (mainly in the county court). Reference should also be made to Guide 3 (Issuing Proceedings (Pt 8 procedure)), set out in Section 1 of this work, which summarises the types of case to which sections A and B of PD8B apply.

Pre-action behaviour—Before issuing proceedings, note the comments in Pt 7 in relation to the pre-action protocols and ADR.

Electronic communication with the court—Where a court has published an e-mail address on the HM Courts Service website, it is possible to communicate with the court and file specified documents with the court by e-mail (see generally PD5B at p 426). Special provisions exist in relation to the county courts at Basildon, Birmingham, Bournemouth, Coventry, Dartford, Leicester, Llangefni, Norwich and Preston. For further details see PD5B.

8.1 Types of claim in which Part 8 procedure may be followed

(1) The Part 8 procedure is the procedure set out in this Part.

(2) A claimant may use the Part 8 procedure where –

(a) he seeks the court's decision on a question which is unlikely to involve a substantial dispute of fact; or

(b) paragraph (6) applies.

(3) The court may at any stage order the claim to continue as if the claimant had not used the Part 8 procedure and, if it does so, the court may give any directions it considers appropriate.

(4) Paragraph (2) does not apply if a practice direction provides that the Part 8 procedure may not be used in relation to the type of claim in question.

(5) Where the claimant uses the Part 8 procedure he may not obtain default judgment under Part 12.

(6) A rule or practice direction may, in relation to a specified type of proceedings –

(a) require or permit the use of the Part 8 procedure; and
(b) disapply or modify any of the rules set out in this Part as they apply to those proceedings.

(Rule 8.9 provides for other modifications to the general rules where the Part 8 procedure is being used)

Practice Direction—See generally PD8, paras 1.1–1.6 at p 536 and the content of PD8B at p 539.

Procedural Guide—Further reference should be made to Guide 3, set out in Section 1 of this work.

'the court may give any directions' (r 8.1(3))—If, for instance, it emerges during the conduct of the Pt 8 claim that the court is required to decide a substantial dispute of fact, then the court will give appropriate directions having regard to Pts 27–29. Most such claims will be treated as allocated to the multi-track (r 8.9(c)). However, see also PD8B, paras B.13–B.15 which enables the court to allocate a claim within PD8B, Section B, to another track. The court will not disapply the Pt 8 procedure in cases where its use is mandatory, eg under PD8B.

Inappropriate use of Part 8 procedure—Under PD8, para 1.5 a court officer may refer a claim to a judge for directions where he considers the Pt 8 procedure is being used inappropriately. In extreme cases, such as where the Pt 8 procedure was used in an attempt to avoid the time limits laid down by Pt 54, the case may be struck out as an abuse of process (*Carter Commercial Developments v Bedford BC & anor* [2001] EWHC Admin 669, [2001] 34 EGCS 99, QBD, Jackson J). The provisions of Pt 8 are designed to meet cases where there is no substantial dispute of fact. A dispute over whether the defendant is entitled to the benefit of Land Registration Act 1925, s 70(1)(g) as a person in receipt of the rent payable under a tenancy by estoppel is not such a case and the application in *UCB Group Ltd v Hedworth* (2001) Lawtel, 8 November, ChD was accordingly dismissed by M Kallipetis QC sitting as a deputy High Court judge.

Rule 8.1(3) and PD8, para 1.6 also state that the court may at any stage order a claim to continue otherwise than under the Pt 8 procedure.

'Paragraph 2 does not apply if a practice direction provides that the Part 8 procedure may not be used in relation to the type of claim in question' (r 8.1(4))—See PD8B, paras A.2 and B.2–B.5 inclusive.

'A rule or practice direction may … require … the use of the Part 8 procedure' (r 8.1(6)(a))—The rule may at the same time modufy the procedure. See, for instance, r 56.3(2)r 62.3(2) applies (r 62.3(1)).

Modifications to the general rules—The following is a list of the main modifications made by either Pt 8 or PD8 to the main body of rules:
(a) the content of the claim form must state the matters set out in r 8.2;
(b) the court may fix a date for a hearing when the Pt 8 claim form is issued (PD8, para 4.1). Alternatively some claims may not require a hearing at all (eg s 38 Landlord and Tenant Act 1954 applications; see PD8, para 4.3);
(c) a claimant must file and serve his written evidence at the same time he files and serves his claim form (r 8.5(1), (2) and PD8, paras 5.1, 5.2);
(d) a claimant may not obtain default judgment under Pt 12 (r 8.1(5));
(e) a defendant *must* file an acknowledgment of service (r 8.3(1)(a) and cf r 10.1(3)) which is in a different form (see N210 and r 8.8(1)) and will include a statement of truth (r 22.1(1));
(f) a defendant himself must serve the acknowledgment of service (r 8.3(1)(b), cf r 8.8(1))
(g) however, a defendant may apparently respond informally by, eg a letter (see PD8, para 3.2) rather than by using Form N210;
(h) save where Section B of PD8B applies, a defendant who fails to file an acknowledgment of service within time may not take part in the hearing unless the court gives permission (r 8.4(2));
(i) Pt 11 (disputing the court's jurisdiction) is modified (r 8.3(4));
(j) a claimant serves neither a form of defence nor a form of admission on the defendant (rr 8.9(a)(iv) and 8.9(b)(ii));
(k) a defendant must file and serve any written evidence on which he intends to rely at the same time he files and serves his acknowledgment of service (r 8.5(3),(4));
(l) Pt 16 (statements of case) does not apply (r 8.9(a)(i));
(m) Pt 15 (defence and reply) does not apply (r 8.9(a)(ii));
(n) a claimant may not obtain judgment by request on an admission (r 8.9(b));
(o) whilst the parties may agree in writing on an extension of time for serving and filing evidence the extensions are limited by PD8, para 5.6(2) and (3) in respect of the defendant' evidence and claimant's evidence in reply respectively;
(p) a Pt 20 claim may only be made with the court's permission (r 8.7);

(q) a Pt 8 claim is treated as allocated to the multi-track (r 8.9(c)) so Pt 26 does not apply. However, note the annotation to r 8.9(c) below in respect of claims covered by Section B of PD8B;
(r) if a hearing date was not fixed when the claim was issued then judicial case management is triggered by the filing of the defendant's acknowledgment of service and evidence, if any, (r 8.8(2) and PD8, para 4.2) or by the expiry of the defendant's time for so doing. Any party may apply to vary or set aside any directions made by the court of its own initiative (r 3.3);
(s) allocation questionnaires are not applicable;
(t) Pt 32 dealing with evidence is modified by r 8.6;
(u) Pt 8 may itself be disapplied or modified by r or practice direction (r 8.1(6)(b)). See, for instance, PD8B.

Costs-only proceedings—Rule 44.12A provides for a summary procedure under Pt 8 where parties have, prior to the issue of proceedings, reached an agreement on all issues but have failed to agree the amount of costs payable by one party to the other.

Extension of period for service of a Part 8 claim—In *Barker v Casserly* (2000) Lawtel, 25 October, Johnson J held that there was a power under the CPR to extend the period for service of a Pt 8 claim. It was not relevant that the power to extend the period of service under r 7.6 was not referred to in Pt 8; PD8, para 2.1 confirmed that Pt 7 contained rules and directions applicable to all claims including Pt 8 claims.

Payment of fee—A fee is payable when the claim is issued unless the claimant successfully applies either for an exemption from, or remission of, the fee. For the fee, see the CPFO 2004 (as amended) in Section 6 of this work. For the sanctions for dishonouring a cheque, see r 3.7B

8.2 Contents of the claim form

Where the claimant uses the Part 8 procedure the claim form must state –

(a) that this Part applies;
(b) (i) the question which the claimant wants the court to decide; or
(ii) the remedy which the claimant is seeking and the legal basis for the claim to that remedy;
(c) if the claim is being made under an enactment, what that enactment is;
(d) if the claimant is claiming in a representative capacity, what that capacity is; and
(e) if the defendant is sued in a representative capacity, what that capacity is.

(Part 22 provides for the claim form to be verified by a statement of truth)

(Rule 7.5 provides for service of the claim form)

(The costs practice direction sets out the information about a funding arrangement to be provided with the claim form where the claimant intends to seek to recover an additional liability)

('Funding arrangement' and 'additional liability' are defined in rule 43.2)

Amendments—SI 2000/1317.

Practice Direction—See generally PD8, paras 2.1–2.2 at p 537 and the content of PD8B at p 539.

Claim form—N208. Note that a Pt 8 claim form must be verified by a statement of truth (r 22.1(1)(a)). PD8, para 2.2 sets out further requirements of a Pt 8 claim form.

Also note Form N208A (Notes for Claimant), N208C (Notes for Defendant), N209 (Notice of Issue) and N210 (Acknowledgment of Service).

Issuing the claim—See PD8, para 2.1. Also note generally r 7.2 (How to start proceedings) and PD7, paras 4 and 5 relating to the title and date of commencement of proceedings.

Use of the wrong claim form—A Pt 8 claim will not be struck out if proceedings are wrongly commenced using a Pt 7 claim form where the defendant knows what is being claimed (*Hannigan v Hannigan & ors* [2000] 2 FCR 650, (2000) *The Independent*, 23 May, CA). See also *Thurrock Borough Council v Secretary of State for the Environment, Transport and the Regions* (2000) *The*

Times, 20 December, where the Court of Appeal adopted the view of the earlier Court of Appeal in *Hannigan v Hannigan* that substance should take precedence over form when interpreting the CPR.

'The costs practice direction sets out the information about a funding arrangement to be provided with the claim form' (r 8.2(e) note)—See generally PDCosts, Section 19 and Notice of Funding Form N251.

Claim for judicial review—Note the additional requirements of r 54.6 and PD54, para 5.6–5.8. Also note r 54.4 (permission required), r 54.5 (time limit for filing a claim form seeking a judicial review) and r 54.7 (service of a claim form seeking a judicial review) together with the relevant provisions of PD54.

8.2A Issue of claim form without naming defendants

(1) A practice direction may set out the circumstances in which a claim form may be issued under this Part without naming a defendant.

(2) The practice direction may set out those cases in which an application for permission must be made by application notice before the claim form is issued.

(3) The application notice for permission –

- (a) need not be served on any other person; and
- (b) must be accompanied by a copy of the claim form that the applicant proposes to issue.

(4) Where the court gives permission it will give directions about the future management of the claim.

Amendments—Inserted by SI 2000/221; amended by SI 2001/256.

Scope of provision—This is essentially a reform of the procedure on trustees' applications for directions. The reform applies, but is not limited, to applications in relation to actual or proposed litigation. The court may, in an appropriate case, be able to assess whether to give the directions sought without hearing from any other party other than the trustees. The most usual situation is where a trustee or executor seeks the court's authorisation either to bring or defend a claim (*Re Beddoe, Downes v Cottam* [1893] 1 Ch 547).

The wording of the rule was amended with effect from 26 March 2001 so as to enable claim forms to be issued without naming the defendants and without prior permission being obtained unless a practice direction expressly requires such permission to be obtained, thereby reversing the effect of the previous rule.

8.3 Acknowledgment of service

(1) The defendant must –

- (a) file an acknowledgment of service in the relevant practice form not more than 14 days after service of the claim form; and
- (b) serve the acknowledgment of service on the claimant and any other party.

(2) The acknowledgment of service must state –

- (a) whether the defendant contests the claim; and
- (b) if the defendant seeks a different remedy from that set out in the claim form, what that remedy is.

(3) The following rules of Part 10 (acknowledgment of service) apply –

- (a) rule 10.3(2) (exceptions to the period for filing an acknowledgment of service); and
- (b) rule 10.5 (contents of acknowledgment of service).

(4) (*revoked*)

(The costs practice direction sets out the information about a funding arrangement to be provided with the acknowledgment of service where the defendant intends to seek to recover an additional liability)

('Funding arrangement' and 'additional liability' are defined in rule 43.2)

Amendments—SI 2000/1317; SI 2001/4015.

Practice Direction—See PD8, paras 3.1–3.6 at p 537 and PD8B, para B.12 at p 539, para B.12.

Statement of truth—From 31 May 2001 an acknowledgment of service in a claim begun under the Pt 8 procedure must be verified by a statement of truth (see r 22.1(1)).

'acknowledgment of service' (r 8.3(1)(a))—Form N210. Whilst a defendant may use an informal document such as a letter to give acknowledgment of service (PD8, para 3.2), such a procedure is not encouraged; the N210 covers all matters necessary for a defendant to consider when filing and serving an acknowledgment of service, including the requirements of r 10.5. However, it is not necessary for a defendant to file an acknowledgment of service in a case to which PD8B, Section B applies (see PD8B, para B.12).

'Rule 10.3(2)' (r 8.3(3)(a))—This rule deals with the time for filing an acknowledgment of service where the claim form is served out of the jurisdiction or when it is served on the agent of an overseas principal.

Devolution issue—A defendant to a Pt 8 claim wishing to raise a devolution issue must say so in his written evidence filed with the acknowledgment of service form (see PDDev, especially para 16).

'The costs practice direction sets out the information about a funding arrangement to be provided with the acknowledgment of service' (r 8.3(4) note)—See generally PDCosts, Section 19 and Form N251 Notice of Funding of Case or Claim.

Claim for judicial review—Note the provisions of r 54.8 and PD54, para 7.1.

8.4 Consequence of not filing an acknowledgment of service

(1) This rule applies where –

(a) the defendant has failed to file an acknowledgment of service; and

(b) the time period for doing so has expired.

(2) The defendant may attend the hearing of the claim but may not take part in the hearing unless the court gives permission.

Practice Direction—See PD8, paras 3.1–3.6 at p 537 and PD8B, para B.12 at p 539, para B.12.

Scope of provision—Save where Section B of PD8B applies, a defendant wishing to contest a Pt 8 claim must file and serve both his acknowledgment of service and his evidence not more that 14 days after date of service; otherwise he may contest the hearing only with the permission of the court.

'permission' (r 8.4(2))—The application for permission will presumably be made orally to the court at the commencement of the hearing. Alternatively, the Pt 23 procedure may be used.

Claim for judicial review—Rule 8.4 does not apply: see r 54.9(3).

8.5 Filing and serving written evidence

(1) The claimant must file any written evidence on which he intends to rely when he files his claim form.

(2) The claimant's evidence must be served on the defendant with the claim form.

(3) A defendant who wishes to rely on written evidence must file it when he files his acknowledgment of service.

(4) If he does so, he must also, at the same time, serve a copy of his evidence on the other parties.

(5) The claimant may, within 14 days of service of the defendant's evidence on him, file further written evidence in reply.

(6) If he does so, he must also, within the same time limit, serve a copy of his evidence on the other parties.

(7) The claimant may rely on the matters set out in his claim form as evidence under this rule if the claim form is verified by a statement of truth.

Practice Direction—See PD8, paras 4.1–4.4 at p 538 and paras 5.1–5.6 at p 538.

Variation of the timetable—Any party may seek to vary the stipulated timetable by:
(a) agreement (PD8, para 5.6);
(b) application to the court (under the Pt 23 procedure, relying on r 3.1(2)(a) which gives the court the power to extend the time for compliance with any rule or practice direction).

'evidence' (r 8.5 generally)—Note also PD8, para 5. Note generally the requirements of Pt 32 and PD32.

Claims under Landlord and Tenant Act 1954, s 24—If the claim is unopposed, Pt 8 generally applies save that r 8.5 is disapplied by r 56.3(3).

8.6 Evidence – general

(1) No written evidence may be relied on at the hearing of the claim unless –

(a) it has been served in accordance with rule 8.5; or
(b) the court gives permission.

(2) The court may require or permit a party to give oral evidence at the hearing.

(3) The court may give directions requiring the attendance for cross-examination[(GL)] of a witness who has given written evidence.

(Rule 32.1 contains a general power for the court to control evidence)

Practice Direction—See PD8, paras 4.1–4.4 at p 538 and paras 5.1–5.6 at p 538.

Claims under Landlord and Tenant Act 1954, s 24—If the claim is unopposed, Pt 8 generally applies save that r 8.6 is disapplied by r 56.3(3)r 8.6(2))—If this is necessary, consideration ought to be given to the appropriateness of continuing with the Pt 8 procedure (note r 8.1(3) and PD8, para 1.6).

Claims in the commercial list—A defendant to a Pt 8 claim proceeding in the commercial list who wishes to rely on written evidence must file and serve it within 28 days after filing an acknowledgment of service (r 58.12).

8.7 Part 20 claims

Where the Part 8 procedure is used, Part 20 (counterclaims and other additional claims) applies except that a party may not make a Part 20 claim (as defined by rule 20.2) without the court's permission.

'permission'—Thus a defendant to a possession claim wishing to raise a counterclaim for eg breach of covenant to repair, will need to apply for permission. For applications for permission to issue a Pt 20 claim, see PD20, para 2. Such an application may be made without notice (r 20.7(5)) and will no doubt be dealt with, in the example given, on the first hearing.

8.8 Procedure where defendant objects to use of the Part 8 procedure

(1) Where the defendant contends that the Part 8 procedure should not be used because –

(a) there is a substantial dispute of fact; and

(b) the use of the Part 8 procedure is not required or permitted by a rule or practice direction,

he must state his reasons when he files his acknowledgment of service.

(Rule 8.5 requires a defendant who wishes to rely on written evidence to file it when he files his acknowledgment of service)

(2) When the court receives the acknowledgment of service and any written evidence it will give directions as to the future management of the case.

(Rule 8.1(3) allows the court to make an order that the claim continue as if the claimant had not used the Part 8 procedure)

Practice Direction—See PD8, para 3.6 at p 538.

Scope of provision—Whilst this rule enables a defendant to object to the use of the Pt 8 procedure, a court may also make such an order of its own initiative (r 8.1(3) as well as PD8, paras 1.5 and 1.6).

'acknowledgment of service' (r 8.8(1))—This must be verified by a statement of truth (r 22.1(1)).

8.9 Modifications to the general rules

Where the Part 8 procedure is followed –

(a) provision is made in this Part for the matters which must be stated in the claim form and the defendant is not required to file a defence and therefore –
   (i) Part 16 (statements of case) does not apply;
   (ii) Part 15 (defence and reply) does not apply;
   (iii) any time limit in these Rules which prevents the parties from taking a step before a defence is filed does not apply;
   (iv) the requirement under rule 7.8 to serve on the defendant a form for defending the claim does not apply;

(b) the claimant may not obtain judgment by request on an admission and therefore –
   (i) rules 14.4 to 14.7 do not apply; and
   (ii) the requirement under rule 7.8 to serve on the defendant a form for admitting the claim does not apply; and

(c) the claim shall be treated as allocated to the multi-track and therefore Part 26 does not apply.

Practice Direction—See generally PD8 at p 536, PD8B at p 539.

'Modifications to the general rules' (r 8.9 generally)—See note **'Modifications to the general rules'** under r 8.1 above.

Practice Direction – Alternative Procedure for Claims

This Practice Direction supplements CPR Part 8 (PD8)

Procedural Guide—See Guide 3, set out in Section 1 of this work.

General note—See also the notes to CPR Pt 8.

TYPES OF CLAIM IN WHICH PART 8 PROCEDURE MAY BE USED

1.1 A claimant may use the Part 8 procedure where he seeks the court's decision on a question which is unlikely to involve a substantial dispute of fact.

1.2 A claimant may also use the Part 8 procedure if a practice direction permits or requires its use for the type of proceedings in question.

1.3 The practice directions referred to in paragraph 1.2 above may in some respects modify or disapply the Part 8 procedure and, where that is so, it is those practice directions that must be complied with.

1.4 The types of claim for which the Part 8 procedure may be used include:

(1) a claim by or against a child or patient which has been settled before the commencement of proceedings and the sole purpose of the claim is to obtain the approval of the court to the settlement,
(2) a claim for provisional damages which has been settled before the commencement of proceedings and the sole purpose of the claim is to obtain a consent judgment, … and
(3) provided there is unlikely to be a substantial dispute of fact, a claim for a summary order for possession against named or unnamed defendants occupying land or premises without the licence or consent of the person claiming possession.

1.5 Where it appears to a court officer that a claimant is using the Part 8 procedure inappropriately, he may refer the claim to a judge for the judge to consider the point.

1.6 The court may at any stage order the claim to continue as if the claimant had not used the Part 8 procedure and, if it does so, the court will allocate the claim to a track and give such directions as it considers appropriate[1].

1 Rule 8.1(3).

Scope of provision—See the note 'Scope of Part' relating to CPR r 8.1.

'a claim by or against a child or patient' (para 1.4(1))—Paragraph 6.1 of PD21, makes use of the CPR Pt 8 procedure mandatory.

'The court may at any stage order the claim to continue as if the claimant had not used the Part 8 procedure' (para 1.6)—It must be doubtful whether the court has such a power in those cases where use of the CPR Pt 8 procedure is mandatory.

ISSUING THE CLAIM

2.1 Part 7 and the practice direction which supplements it contain a number of rules and directions applicable to all claims, including those to which Part 8 applies. Those rules and directions should be applied where appropriate.

2.2 Where a claimant uses the Part 8 procedure, the claim form (practice form N208) should be used and must state the matters set out in rule 8.2 and, if paragraphs 1.2 or 1.3 apply, must comply with the requirements of the practice direction in question. In particular, the claim form must state that Part 8 applies; a Part 8 claim form means a claim form which so states.

(The Costs Practice Direction supplementing Parts 43 to 48 contains details of the information required to be filed with a claim form to comply with rule 44.15 (providing information about funding arrangements))

RESPONDING TO THE CLAIM

3.1 The provisions of Part 15 (defence and reply) do not apply where the claim form is a Part 8 claim form.

3.2 Where a defendant who wishes to respond to a Part 8 claim form is required to file an acknowledgment of service, that acknowledgment of service should be in practice form N210[1] but can, alternatively, be given in an informal document such as a letter.

1 Rule 8.3(1)(a).

3.3 Rule 8.3 sets out provisions relating to an acknowledgment of service of a Part 8 claim form.

3.4 Rule 8.4 sets out the consequence of failing to file an acknowledgment of service.

3.5 The provisions of Part 12 (obtaining default judgment) do not apply where the claim form is a Part 8 claim form.

3.6 Where a defendant believes that the Part 8 procedure should not be used because there is a substantial dispute of fact or, as the case may be, because its use is not authorised by any rule or practice direction, he must state his reasons in writing when he files his acknowledgment of service[1]. If the statement of reasons includes matters of evidence it should be verified by a statement of truth.

1 Rule 8.8(1).

MANAGING THE CLAIM

4.1 The court may give directions immediately a Part 8 claim form is issued either on the application of a party or on its own initiative. The directions may include fixing a hearing date where:

(1) there is no dispute, such as in child and patient settlements, or
(2) where there may be a dispute, such as in claims for mortgage possession or appointment of trustees, but a hearing date could conveniently be given.

4.2 Where the court does not fix a hearing date when the claim form is issued, it will give directions for the disposal of the claim as soon as practicable after the defendant has acknowledged service of the claim form or, as the case may be, after the period for acknowledging service has expired.

4.3 Certain applications may not require a hearing.

4.4 The court may convene a directions hearing before giving directions.

'such as in child and patient settlements' (para 4.1(1))—See the note to para 1.4(1) above.

'such as in claims for mortgage possession' (para 4.1(2))—Such claims have since 15 October 2001 been governed by Pt 55.

'The court may convene a directions hearing' (para 4.4)—At least 3 days' notice of the hearing must be given (CPR r 3.3(3)(b)).

EVIDENCE

5.1 A claimant wishing to rely on written evidence should file it when his Part 8 claim form is issued[1] (unless the evidence is contained in the claim form itself).

1 Rule 8.5.

5.2 Evidence will normally be in the form of a witness statement or an affidavit but a claimant may rely on the matters set out in his claim form provided that it has been verified by a statement of truth.

(For information about (1) statements of truth see Part 22 and the practice direction that supplements it, and (2) written evidence see Part 32 and the practice direction that supplements it)

5.3 A defendant wishing to rely on written evidence, should file it with his acknowledgment of service[1].

1 Rule 8.5(3).

5.4 Rule 8.5 sets out the times and provisions for filing and serving written evidence.

5.5 A party may apply to the court for an extension of time to serve and file evidence under rule 8.5 or for permission to serve and file additional evidence under rule 8.6(1).

(For information about applications see Part 23 and the practice direction that supplements it)

5.6 (1) The parties may, subject to the following provisions, agree in writing on an extension of time for serving and filing evidence under rule 8.5(3) or rule 8.5(5).

(2) An agreement extending time for a defendant to file evidence under rule 8.5(3) –

(a) must be filed by the defendant at the same time as he files his acknowledgment of service; and

(b) must not extend time by more than 14 days after the defendant files his acknowledgment of service.

(3) An agreement extending time for a claimant to file evidence in reply under rule 8.5(5) must not extend time to more than 28 days after service of the defendant's evidence on the claimant.

Practice Direction – How to Make Claims in the Schedule Rules and Other Claims

This Practice Direction supplements CPR Part 8, and Schedule 1 and Schedule 2 to the CPR (PD8B)

Procedural Guide—See Guide 3, set out in Section 1 of this work.

Important—As claims which were governed by the Schedule Rules are brought within the main body of the CPR (for example CPR Pts 55 and 56), they cease to be affected by this practice direction. Generally, references in the Tables to the revoked Schedule rules are removed. In the event of any delay in this process, the entries have no point of reference and they should not be taken as referring to 'equivalent' provisions in the new CPR Parts.

General note—See also the notes to CPR Pt 8.

TERMINOLOGY

1.1 In this practice direction 'Schedule rules' means provisions contained in the Schedules to the CPR, which were previously contained in the Rules of the Supreme Court (1965) or the County Court Rules (1981).

Scope of provision—The 'Schedule rules' are those former Rules of the Supreme Court and County Court Rules not yet replaced by relevant provisions of the CPR. They are to be found as Schs 1 and

2 respectively to the CPR. Over time, as the Civil Procedure Rules Committee prepare new rules to be incorporated into the CPR, the volume of the Schedule rules will decrease.

CONTENTS OF THIS PRACTICE DIRECTION

2.1 This practice direction explains –

(1) how to start the claims referred to in Sections A and B;
(2) which form to use as the claim form; and
(3) the procedure which those claims will follow;

(Further guidance about forms other than claim forms can be found in the practice direction supplementing Part 4)

(Form 87 (modified as necessary) should be used when making an application for a writ of habeas corpus under RSC Order 54 (Schedule 1). Attention is drawn to the relevant existing Administrative Court practice directions for further guidance)

HOW TO USE THIS PRACTICE DIRECTION

3.1 This Practice direction is divided into Sections A and B. Only one section will be relevant to how to make a particular claim or appeal.

3.2 If the claim is described in paragraph A.1 – use section A.

3.3 If the claim is described in paragraph B.1 – use section B.

Form where claim is described in para A.1—The CPR Pt 8 claim form must be used.

Form where claim is described in para B.1—See para B.8 for the appropriate claim form.

Section A

APPLICATION

A.1 Section A applies if –

(1) the claim is listed in Table 1 below;
(2) an Act provides that a claim or application in the High Court is to be brought by originating summons; or
(3) before 26 April 1999, a claim or application in the High Court would have been brought by originating summons, and

no other method for bringing the claim or application on and after 26 April 1999 is specified in a rule or practice direction.

A.2 (1) The claimant must use the Part 8 procedure unless an Act, rule, or practice direction, makes any additional or contrary provision.

(2) Where such additional or contrary provision is made the claimant must comply with it and modify the Part 8 procedure accordingly.

CLAIM FORM

A.3 The claimant must use the Part 8 claim form.

Forms—N208

Table 1

RSC Ord 17, r 3(1)	Interpleader (Mode of application)

Table 1	
RSC Ord 77, r 11	Proceedings by and against the Crown (Interpleader: Application for order against Crown)
RSC Ord 77, r 16(2)	Proceedings by and against the Crown (Attachment of debts, etc)
RSC Ord 77, r 17(1)	Proceedings by and against the Crown (Proceedings relating to postal packets)
RSC Ord 77, r 18(1)	Proceedings by and against the Crown (Applications under sections 17 and 29 of Crown Proceedings Act)
RSC Ord 79, r 8(2)	Criminal Proceedings (Estreat of recognizances)
RSC Ord 79, r 9(2)	Criminal Proceedings (Bail)
RSC Ord 81, r 10(1)	Partners (Applications for orders charging partner's interest in partnership property)
RSC Ord 93, r 5(2)	Applications and Appeals to High Court under Various Acts: Chancery Division (Applications under section 2(3) of the Public Order Act 1936)
RSC Ord 93, r 18(2)	Applications and Appeals to High Court under Various Acts: Chancery Division (Proceedings under section 86 of the Civil Aviation Act 1982)
RSC Ord 94, r 5	Applications and Appeals to High Court under Various Acts: Queen's Bench Division (Exercise of jurisdiction under Representation of the People Acts)
RSC Ord 95, r 2(1)	Bills of Sale Acts 1878 and 1882 and the Industrial and Provident Societies Act 1967 (Entry of satisfaction)
RSC Ord 95, r 3	Bills of Sale Acts 1878 and 1882 and the Industrial and Provident Societies Act 1967 (Restraining removal on sale of goods seized)
RSC Ord 96, r 1	The Mines (Working Facilities and Support) Act 1966 etc (Assignment to Chancery Division)
RSC Ord 96, r 3	The Mines (Working Facilities and Support) Act 1966 etc (Issue of claim form)
RSC Ord 109, r 1(3)	Administration Act 1960 (Applications under Act)

Section B

APPLICATION

B.1 Section B applies if the claim –

(1) is listed in Table 2;
(3) would have been brought before 26 April 1999 –
  (a) in the High Court, by originating motion;
  (b) in the county court –
    (i) by originating application; or
    (ii) by petition, and

no other procedure is prescribed in an Act, a rule or a practice direction.

Table 2

Schedule Rule		Claim Form
RSC Ord 77, r 8(2)[1]	Proceedings by and against the Crown (Summary applications to the court in certain revenue matters)	
RSC Ord 93, r 19(1)	Applications and Appeals to High Court under Various Acts: (Proceedings under section 85(7) of the Fair Trading Act 1973 and the Control of Misleading Advertisements Regulations 1988)	
RSC Ord 93, r 22(3)	Applications and Appeals to High Court under Various Acts: Chancery Division (Proceedings under the Financial Services and Markets Act 2000)	
RSC Ord 94, r 1(2)	Applications and Appeals to High Court under Various Acts: Queen's Bench Division (Jurisdiction of High Court to Quash Certain Orders, Schemes etc)	
RSC Ord 94, r 7(2)	Applications and Appeals to High Court under Various Acts: Queen's Bench Division (Reference of Question of Law by Agricultural Land Tribunal)	
RSC Ord 94, r 11(4)	Applications and Appeals to High Court under Various Acts: Queen's Bench Division (Case stated by Mental Health Review Tribunal)	

Table 2

Schedule Rule		Claim Form
RSC Ord 94, r 12(5)(c)	Applications and Appeals to High Court under Various Acts: Queen's Bench Division Applications for permission under section 289(6) of the Town and Country Planning Act 1990 and section 65(5) of the Planning (Listed Buildings and Conservation Areas) Act 1990	
RSC Ord 94, r 13(5)	Applications and Appeals to High Court under Various Acts: Queen's Bench Division Proceedings under sections 289 and 290 of the Town and Country Planning Act 1990 and under section 65 of the Planning (Listed Buildings and Conservation Areas) Act 1990	
RSC Ord 94, r 14(2)	Applications and Appeals to High Court under Various Acts: Queen's Bench Division Applications under section 13 of the Coroners Act 1988	
RSC Ord 94, r 15(2)	Applications and Appeals to High Court under Various Acts: Queen's Bench Division Applications under section 42 of the Supreme Court Act 1981	
RSC Ord 109, r 2(4)	Administration of Justice Act 1960 (Appeals under section 13 of Act)	
RSC Ord 115, r 2B(1)	Confiscation and Forfeiture in Connection with Criminal Proceedings (I. Drug Trafficking Act 1994 and Criminal Justice (International Co-operation) Act 1990 – Application for confiscation Order)	
RSC Ord 115, r 3(1)	Confiscation and Forfeiture in Connection with Criminal Proceedings (I. Drug Trafficking Act 1994 and Criminal Justice (International Co-operation) Act 1990 – Application for restraint order or charging order)	

Table 2

Schedule Rule		Claim Form
RSC Ord 115, r 7(1)	Confiscation and Forfeiture in Connection with Criminal Proceedings (I. Drug Trafficking Act 1994 and Criminal Justice (International Co-operation) Act 1990 – Realisation of property)	
RSC Ord 115, r 26(1)	Confiscation and Forfeiture in Connection with Criminal Proceedings (III. Terrorism Act 2000 – Application for restraint order)	
RSC Ord 116, r 5(1)	The Criminal Procedure and Investigations Act 1996 (Application under section 54(3))	
CCR Ord 44, r 1(1)	The Agricultural Holdings Act 1986 (Special case stated by arbitrator)	
CCR Ord 44, r 3(1)	The Agricultural Holdings Act 1986 (Removal of arbitrator or setting aside award)	
CCR Ord 45, r 1(1)	The Representation of the People Act 1983 (Application for detailed assessment of returning officer's account)	N408
CCR Ord 46, r 1(1)	The Legitimacy Act 1976 (Manner of application)	
CCR Ord 49, r 7(2)	Miscellaneous Statutes: Injunctions to Prevent Environmental Harm: Town and Country Planning Act 1990 etc (Application for injunction)	
CCR Ord 49, r 12(2)	Miscellaneous Statutes: Mental Health Act 1983 (Application)	
CCR Ord 49, r 15(1)	Miscellaneous Statutes: Postal Services Act 2000 (Application under section 92)	

The Local Government Act 1972 (claims under section 92 – proceedings for disqualification)

1 These types of claim may also be brought by the Part 8 procedure.

SPECIAL PROVISIONS TAKE PRECEDENCE

B.2 The claimant must first comply with any special provision set out in the Schedule rules, practice direction or any Act relating to the claim.

(In Schedule 2, CCR Ord 6 makes special provisions about particulars of claim for certain types of claim)

B.3 Special provisions contained in Schedule rules or an Act may set out –

(1) where the claim may be started;
(2) the contents of the claim form;
(3) whether a hearing is required;
(4) the nature of evidence required in support of the claim, and when it must be filed or served;
(5) the method of service of the claim form and evidence;
(6) persons on whom service must or may be effected;
(7) the form and content of Notices, and when they must or may be filed, and on whom served;
(8) the form and content of any affidavit, answer, or reply and when they must or may be filed or served;
(9) persons who may apply to be joined as parties to the claim;
(10) minimum periods of notice before the hearing date.

B.4 Where a Schedule rule makes special provision for the contents of particulars of claim, those particulars must be attached to the claim form and served with it.

B.5 Subject to any special or contrary provision in an Act or Schedule rule, the claimant must use the procedure set out in the remainder of this section.

'Special provisions contained in Schedule rules or an Act may set out' (para B.3)—The word 'may' is not used in the permissive sense; the list is not exhaustive.

'special provision for the contents of particulars of claim' (para B.4)—Particulars of claim will not normally be used in a CPR Pt 8 claim, but where Schedule rules refer to the content of particulars of claim, it is clear that they must be. Note that CPR r 7.4(1)(b), under which particulars may be served separately, is disapplied.

RESTRICTIONS ON WHERE TO START THE CLAIM

B.6 Where the claimant is bringing a claim in a county court that claim may only be started –

(1) in the county court for the district in which –
  (a) the defendants or one of the defendants lives or carries on business; or
  (b) the subject matter of the claim is situated; or
(2) if there is no defendant named in the claim form, in the county court for the district in which the claimant or one of the claimants lives or carries on business.

B.7 Where the claimant is making a claim in the county court for –

(1) enforcing any charge or lien on land;
(2) the recovery of moneys secured by a mortgage or charge on land,

the claim must be started in the court for the district in which the land, or any part of it, is situated.

Venue—This provision is repeated in Sch 2, CCR Ord 4, r 3.

CLAIM FORM

B.8 This paragraph sets out which Form is to be used as the claim form –

(1) where a claim form number is listed against a particular claim in Table 2, the claimant must use that numbered form as the claim form;
(2) in every other claim, the claimant must use the Part 8 claim form.

COURT WILL FIX A DATE

B.9 When the court issues the claim form it will –

(1) fix a date for the hearing; and
(2) prepare a notice of the hearing date for each party.

'fix a date'—Twenty-one days' notice of the hearing must be given under PD8B, para B.10, unless the court exercises its powers under CPR r 3.1(2)(a) and/or (b) to order otherwise.

SERVICE OF THE CLAIM FORM

B.10 The claim form must be served not less than 21 days before the hearing date.

B.11 Where the claimant serves the claim form, he must serve notice of the hearing date at the same time, unless the hearing date is specified in the claim form.

(CPR Rule 3.1(2) (a) and (b) provide for the court to extend or shorten the time for compliance with any rule or practice direction, and to adjourn or bring forward a hearing)

DEFENDANT IS NOT REQUIRED TO RESPOND

B.12 The defendant is not required to serve an acknowledgment of service.

Defence—The CPR Pt 8 procedure does not require a defendant to file and serve a defence (CPR r 8.9(a)).

AT THE HEARING

B.13 The court may on the hearing date –

(1) proceed to hear the case and dispose of the claim; or
(2) give case management directions.

B.14 Case management directions given under paragraph B.13 will, if the defendant has filed a defence, include the allocation of a case to a track, or directions to enable the case to be allocated.

B.15 CPR rule 26.5(3) to (5) and CPR rules 26.6 to 26.10 apply to the allocation of a claim under paragraph B.14.

'allocation of a case to a track' (para B.14)—Claims within Section B of PD8 are an exception to the general rule (CPR r 8.9(c)) that CPR Pt 8 claims are treated as allocated only to the multi-track. Contested Section B claims may be allocated to any of the three tracks (para B.15). The small claim track would generally be inappropriate. The matters set out in CPR r 26.8 (matters relevant to the allocation to a track) will decide which of the fast track or multi-track is more appropriate.

PART 9
RESPONDING TO PARTICULARS OF CLAIM – GENERAL

Procedural Guide—See Guides 5, 6, 7, set out in Section 1 of this work.

9.1 Scope of this Part

(1) This Part sets out how a defendant may respond to particulars of claim.

(2) Where the defendant receives a claim form which states that particulars of claim are to follow, he need not respond to the claim until the particulars of claim have been served on him.

'he need not respond to the claim until the particulars of claim have been served on him' (r 9.1(2))—See rr 7.4 and 7.5 for the time for service.

9.2 Defence, admission or acknowledgment of service

When particulars of claim are served on a defendant, the defendant may –

(a) file or serve an admission in accordance with Part 14;
(b) file a defence in accordance with Part 15,
(or do both, if he admits only part of the claim); or
(c) file an acknowledgment of service in accordance with Part 10.

Prospective amendment—By virtue of the Civil Procedure (Amendment No 3) Rules 2005, SI 2005/2292, after r 9.2, there is inserted –

> '(Paragraph 10.6 of the Practice Direction to Part 16 contains provision about the content of the admission, defence or acknowledgment of service).',

with effect from 6 April 2006.

'file an acknowledgment of service' (r 9.2(c))—A defendant wishing to dispute the court's jurisdiction under Pt 11 may nevertheless file an acknowledgment of service (r 10.1(3)(b)).

Electronic filing of documents—Special provisions apply in relation to Money Claims Online and in relation to courts that have published an e-mail address on the Court Service website; in these instances it is possible to file specified documents by e-mail (see generally r 7.12 and PD5B respectively).

General rule—A defence should be filed within 14 days of service of the particulars of claim (r 15.4(1)(a)) without the need to file an acknowledgment of service.

Forms—The defendant will have been served with a Response Pack (N9) containing the relevant forms for his use.

Failure to respond—If a defendant fails to carry out any of the steps set out in r 9.2 then the claimant may obtain a default judgment (r 12.1) unless the claim falls within the exceptions set out in r 12.2. Following an amendment to r 12.3(2), it has since 2 May 2000 been possible to obtain a default judgment against a defendant to a counterclaim.

Service abroad—See rr 6.21(4), 6.22 and 6.23 where the claim form is served out of the jurisdiction.

PART 10
ACKNOWLEDGMENT OF SERVICE

CONTENTS OF THIS PART

Procedural Guide—See Guide 5, set out in Section 1 of this work.

10.1 Acknowledgment of service

(1) This Part deals with the procedure for filing an acknowledgment of service.

(2) Where the claimant uses the procedure set out in Part 8 (alternative procedure for claims) this Part applies subject to the modifications set out in rule 8.3.

(3) A defendant may file an acknowledgment of service if –

(a) he is unable to file a defence within the period specified in rule 15.4; or
(b) he wishes to dispute the court's jurisdiction.

(Part 11 sets out the procedure for disputing the court's jurisdiction)

Practice Direction—See generally PD10 at p 551.

'filing' (r 10.1(1))—That is to say delivering to the court, and not to the claimant.

'an acknowledgment of service' (r 10.1(1) and (3))—Different forms apply, depending on the type of claim, viz:

Type of claim	Form
Pt 7	N9, following the filing of which, the Court Service will serve a Form N10
Pt 8	N210
Pt 8 costs-only claim under r 44.12A	N210A
Pt 20	N213
Pt 54	N462

No acknowledgment of service is required in possession of land claims (r 55.7(1)), Consumer Credit Act claims (r 7.9 and PD7B, para 5.3(1)) and those cases still set out in PD8B, Section B.

'Part 8' (r 10.1(2))—There is an apparent conflict between r 10.1(2) and r 8.3(3) as to the extent to which Pt 10 applies to Pt 8 claims. See below under r 10.4

'the modifications set out in rule 8.3' (r 10.1(2))—Note that the express provisions of r 8.3 include a requirement for the defendant to a Pt 8 claim both to file *and serve* the acknowledgment of service form. In any event, the acknowledgment of service must be verified by a statement of truth (see r 22.1(1)).

Claim for judicial review—Note the additional requirements of r 54.8 and PD54, para 7.1.

Specialist jurisdictions—Note the variations to Pt 10 relating to claims in the Commercial Court set out in r 58.6 and to claims in a mercantile court set out in r 59.5.

'if [the defendant] is unable to file a defence' (r 10.1(3)(a))—The presumption is in favour of a defendant filing his defence within 14 days of service of the particulars of claim (for the period of 14 days, see r 15.4(1)(a)). The period for filing a defence extends to 28 days after service of the particulars of a claim if a defendant files an acknowledgment of service.

Service of a claim form without particulars of claim—The period for filing the acknowledgment of service is 14 days after the particulars are served (rr 9.1(2) and 10.3)).

'disputes the court's jurisdiction' (r 10.1(3)(b))—A defendant who wishes to dispute the court's jurisdiction under Pt 11 *must* file an acknowledgment of service (r 11(2)), but does not prejudice his position by doing so (r 11(3)).

Money Claim Online—The procedure for filing an acknowledgment of service is somewhat different where the claim has been electronically issued using the Money Claim Online facility. For more information see PD7E, para 6 and Guide 4.

Electronic filing of acknowledgment of service—Special provisions apply in relation to courts which have published an e-mail address on the Court Service website; in these instances it is possible to file specified documents by e-mail (see generally PD5B).

10.2 Consequence of not filing an acknowledgment of service

If –

(a) a defendant fails to file an acknowledgment of service within the period specified in rule 10.3; and

(b) does not within that period file a defence in accordance with Part 15 or serve or file an admission in accordance with Part 14,

the claimant may obtain default judgment if Part 12 allows it.

'if ... a defendant fails ... within the period specified' (r 10.2(a))—A defendant who fails to file an acknowledgment, defence or admission (as the case may be) within the period specified may still do so outside the time periods set out in rr 10.3, 15.4 or 14.2(1) respectively if the claimant has not in the meanwhile obtained a default judgment.

Nevertheless, either the court or the claimant would be entitled to insist on the defendant seeking an extension of time. Where there is an application on notice for judgment, the claimant being unable merely to *request* judgment in default of acknowledgment, the matter becomes one of the court's discretion although the discretion would normally be exercised in favour of extending time (*Coll v Tattum* [2002] 99(03) LSG 26, (2001) *The Times*, 3 December, Neuberger J).

'if Part 12 allows it' (r 10.2)—See r 12.2 for the listed exceptions. See also Guide 29, set out in Section 1 of this work.

Probate claims—A default judgment cannot be obtained in a probate claim and r 10.2 and Pt 12 do not apply (r 57.10).

Claim for judicial review—Note the provisions of r 54.9 and that r 8.4 does not apply.

10.3 The period for filing an acknowledgment of service

(1) The general rule is that the period for filing an acknowledgment of service is –

(a) where the defendant is served with a claim form which states that particulars of claim are to follow, 14 days after service of the particulars of claim; and

(b) in any other case, 14 days after service of the claim form.

(2) The general rule is subject to the following rules –

(a) Rule 6.22 (which specifies how the period for filing an acknowledgment of service is calculated where the claim form is served out of the jurisdiction);

(b) rule 6.16(4) (which requires the court to specify the period for responding to the particulars of claim when it makes an order under that rule); and

(c) rule 6.21(4) (which requires the court to specify the period within which the defendant may file an acknowledgment of service calculated by reference to Practice Direction 6B when it makes an order giving permission to serve a claim form out of the jurisdiction).

Amendments—SI 2000/940; SI 2005/2292.

Time—For the computation of time, see r 2.8.

'The general rule' (r 10.3(1))—Note the following exceptions:

Type of claim	Period for filing the acknowledgment of service	Rule
Judicial review claim	21 days after service of the claim form	r 54.8(2)(a)
Probate claim	28 days after service of the claim form or the particulars of claim if served later	r 57.4(2)
Commercial Court or mercantile courts claim	14 days after service of the claim form	r 58.6(2) or r 59.5(2)

'14 days after service of the particulars of claim' (r 10.3(1)(a))—For the time within which particulars of claim must be served, see r 7.4(2).

'in any other case' (r 10.3(1)(b))—Other cases are where the claim form and the particulars of claim are served either as one composite statement of case or as two documents served at the same time, but see also the note relating to Pt 8 set out below.

Where the claimant uses the procedure under Pt 8—See r 8.3 which obliges the defendant to a Pt 8 claim to file an acknowledgment of service not more than 14 days after service of the claim form. The acknowledgment of service must be verified by a statement of truth (see r 22.1(1)).

'Rule 6.16(4)' (r 10.3(2)(b))—Rule 6.16 relates to service of a claim form on the agent of a principal who is overseas.

PD8B, Section B—Where claims fall within those classes of cases set out in Section B of PD8B then the defendant is not required to serve an acknowledgment of service (PD8B, para B.12).

10.4 Notice to claimant that defendant has filed an acknowledgment of service

On receipt of an acknowledgment of service, the court must notify the claimant in writing.

'the court must notify the claimant'—In the particular case of Pt 8 claims, this appears to be in addition to service of the acknowledgment of service form by the defendant (r 8.3(1)(b)). However, the Court Service takes the sensible view that r 8.3 excludes the application of this rule with regards to Pt 8 claims, and so will not encumber the claimant with a further, unnecessary, notice in those claims.

Forms—N10.

10.5 Contents of acknowledgment of service

An acknowledgment of service must –

(a) be signed by the defendant or his legal representative; and

(b) include the defendant's address for service.

(Rule 6.5 provides that an address for service must be within the jurisdiction)

(Rule 19.8A modifies this Part where a notice of claim is served under that rule to bind a person not a party to the claim)

Amendments—SI 2001/256.

Practice Direction—See PD10, paras 2–5.5 at p 551.

'must … be signed by' (r 10.5(a))—See PD10, para 4 which sets out who may sign on behalf of companies, partnerships, children and patients. The court will normally reject an acknowledgment signed by someone not authorised by this rule or the practice direction supplementing it; such unauthorised individuals would include a claimant's spouse or a company's accountant. Rejection of the acknowledgment of service may result in the claimant obtaining a default judgment whilst the defendant endeavours to correct the irregularity.

If the electronic Money Claim Online facility is being used, r 10.5(a) does not apply where the defendant acknowledges service by telephone or e-mail (PD7E, para 6.3).

'legal representative' (r 10.5(a))—The term means a barrister or a solicitor, a solicitor's employee or other authorised litigator (as defined by Courts and Legal Services Act 1990) who has been instructed to act for the defendant (r 2.3).

'the defendant's address for service' (r 10.5(b))—Note PD10, para 3 and r 6.5(2), (3).

Claim against a firm—Note Sch 1, RSC Ord 81, r 4 relating to the acknowledgment of service in a claim against a firm.

'Rule 19.8A' (r 10.5 second note)—This rule empowers the court to direct that notice of a claim be served on a non-party who may be affected by any judgment made in the claim. Rule 19.8A(8) applies r 10.4 and 10.5 save that references to the defendant are to be read as references to the person served with notice of the claim.

Where the claimant uses the procedure under Pt 8—The acknowledgment of service must be verified by a statement of truth (see r 22.1(1)).

Additional provisions relating to the acknowledgment of service form—See PD10, para 5.

Practice Direction – Acknowledgment of Service

This Practice Direction supplements CPR Part 10 (PD10)

Procedural Guide—See Guide 5, set out in Section 1 of this work.

General note—See also the notes to CPR Pt 10.

RESPONDING TO THE CLAIM

1.1 Part 9 sets out how a defendant may respond to a claim.

1.2 Part 10 sets out the provisions for acknowledging service (but see rule 8.3 for information about acknowledging service of a claim under the Part 8 procedure).

THE FORM OF ACKNOWLEDGMENT OF SERVICE

2 A defendant who wishes to acknowledge service of a claim should do so by using Form N9.

Part 8 claims—The relevant form is N210, not N9.

Part 8 (r 44.12A) costs-only proceedings—The relevant form is N210A.

Part 20 claims—The relevant form is N213.

ADDRESS FOR SERVICE

3.1 The defendant must include in his acknowledgment of service an address for the service of documents[1].

1 See rule 6.5.

3.2 Where the defendant is represented by a legal representative[1] and the legal representative has signed the acknowledgment of service form, the address must be the legal representative's business address; otherwise the address for service that is given should be as set out in rule 6.5 and the practice direction which supplements Part 6.

1 See rule 2.3 for the definition of legal representative.

'address for the service of documents' (para 3.1)—This must be an address in England or Wales (CPR r 6.5(2)).

SIGNING THE ACKNOWLEDGMENT OF SERVICE

4.1 An acknowledgment of service must be signed by the defendant or by his legal representative.

4.2 Where the defendant is a company or other corporation, a person holding a senior position in the company or corporation may sign the acknowledgment of service on the defendant's behalf, but must state the position he holds.

4.3 Each of the following persons is a person holding a senior position:

(1) in respect of a registered company or corporation, a director, the treasurer, secretary, chief executive, manager or other officer of the company or corporation, and
(2) in respect of a corporation which is not a registered company, in addition to those persons set out in (1), the mayor, chairman, president, town clerk or similar officer of the corporation.

4.4 Where the defendant is a partnership, the acknowledgment of service may be signed by:

(1) any of the partners, or
(2) a person having the control or management of the partnership business.

4.5 Children and patients may acknowledge service only by their litigation friend or his legal representative unless the court otherwise orders[1].

1 See Part 21.

'An acknowledgment of service must be signed by the defendant' (para 4.2)—If the electronic Money Claim Online facility is being used, CPR r 10.5(1)(a) does not apply where the defendant acknowledges service by telephone or e-mail (PD7E, para 6.3).

'unless the court otherwise orders' (para 4.5)—See CPR r 21.2(3), (4).

GENERAL

5.1 The defendant's name should be set out in full on the acknowledgment of service.

5.2 Where the defendant's name has been incorrectly set out in the claim form, it should be correctly set out on the acknowledgment of service followed by the words 'described as' and the incorrect name.

5.3 If two or more defendants to a claim acknowledge service of a claim through the same legal representative at the same time, only one acknowledgment of service need be used.

5.4 An acknowledgment of service may be amended or withdrawn only with the permission of the court.

5.5 An application for permission under paragraph 5.4 must be made in accordance with Part 23 and supported by evidence.

(Paragraph 8.3 of the practice direction supplementing Part 6 (Service of documents) makes provision for the service on the claimant of any notice of funding filed with an acknowledgment of service)

'the defendant's name ... should be correctly set out on the acknowledgment of service' (para 5.2)—Unfortunately there is no obvious space on Form N210 for this to be done. The form will have to be adapted by whatever method appears appropriate.

'only one acknowledgment of service need be used' (para 5.3)—Unfortunately, however, the N9 and N213 forms are designed to be completed by one defendant only and will therefore require amendment if completed on behalf of two or more defendants. Each defendant may still, of course, sign a separate form if this is more convenient.

PART 11
DISPUTING THE COURT'S JURISDICTION

Procedural Guide—See Guide 5, set out in Section 1 of this work.

11 Procedure for disputing the court's jurisdiction

(1) A defendant who wishes to –

(a) dispute the court's jurisdiction to try the claim; or
(b) argue that the court should not exercise its jurisdiction,

may apply to the court for an order declaring that it has no such jurisdiction or should not exercise any jurisdiction which it may have.

(2) A defendant who wishes to make such an application must first file an acknowledgment of service in accordance with Part 10.

(3) A defendant who files an acknowledgment of service does not, by doing so, lose any right that he may have to dispute the court's jurisdiction.

(4) An application under this rule must –

(a) be made within 14 days after filing an acknowledgment of service; and
(b) be supported by evidence.

(5) If the defendant –

(a) files an acknowledgment of service; and
(b) does not make such an application within the period specified in paragraph (4),

he is to be treated as having accepted that the court has jurisdiction to try the claim.

(6) An order containing a declaration that the court has no jurisdiction or will not exercise its jurisdiction may also make further provision including –

(a) setting aside the claim form;
(b) setting aside service of the claim form;
(c) discharging any order made before the claim was commenced or before the claim form was served; and
(d) staying(GL) the proceedings.

(7) If on an application under this rule the court does not make a declaration –

(a) the acknowledgment of service shall cease to have effect;
(b) the defendant may file a further acknowledgment of service within 14 days or such other period as the court may direct; and
(c) the court shall give directions as to the filing and service of the defence in a claim under Part 7 or the filing of evidence in a claim under Part 8 in the event that a further acknowledgment of service is filed.

(8) If the defendant files a further acknowledgment of service in accordance with paragraph (7)(b) he shall be treated as having accepted that the court has jurisdiction to try the claim.

(9) If a defendant makes an application under this rule, he must file and serve his written evidence in support with the application notice, but he need not before the hearing of the application file –

(a) in a Part 7 claim, a defence; or
(b) in a Part 8 claim, any other written evidence.

(10) (*revoked*)

Amendments—SI 2001/4015; SI 2005/2292.

Scope of provision—This short rule provides a simple method by which a defendant may dispute the court's jurisdiction. In brief the steps are:

(a) the defendant files an acknowledgment of service;

(b) he then applies for a declaration that the court has no jurisdiction or should not exercise any jurisdiction it may have;

(c) if such a declaration is made the court may set aside the claim form or service of it, or stay proceedings;

(d) if the declaration is not made then the defendant must either file another acknowledgment of service accepting the court's jurisdiction or the claimant may proceed to obtain such default judgment as is appropriate.

It is always prudent for the party challenging the court's jurisdiction on the basis that the claim form had expired prior to the time of service to file an acknowledgment of service, ticking the box indicating that he intends to contest jurisdiction. Certainly, filing an acknowledgment without giving that indication may be held to be a waiver of the right to challenge the jurisdiction of the court (*Uphill v BRB (Residuary) Ltd* [2005] EWCA Civ 60), as may serving a defence.

'A defendant who wishes to ... argue that the court ... should not exercise any jurisdiction which it may have' (r 11(1)(b))—This covers, for instance, a defendant saying that the dispute should be stayed pending a reference to arbitration or on the ground of *forum non conveniens*. The court has jurisdiction to stay proceedings on the basis of *forum non conveniens* if the defendant is domiciled in a Brussels Convention or Lugano Convention country and the parties have agreed to confer jurisdiction on a non-Convention country (*Ace Insurance Co Ltd v Zurich Insurance Co Ltd & ors* [2001] EWCA Civ 173, [2001] 1 All ER (Comm) 802, CA). The English court has tort jurisdiction over a defendant domiciled in another Contracting State if the 'harmful event' occurred within the jurisdiction, but only if the harmful event was the result of some action within the jurisdiction of the defendant (*Dexter Ltd v Harley* (2001) *The Times*, 2 April, ChD, Lloyd J). Equally, English courts will usually be content to exercise jurisdiction where there is a good, arguable case that r 6.20(5)(a) applies (ie the contract in question was made within the jurisdiction) (*Staines v Walsh & Howard* (2003) Lawtel, 14 March, ChD, Goldring J). Where a claim is brought against defendants, some of whom are resident in England and others in non-Contracting States, Art 2 of the Brussels Convention precludes a court of a Contracting State from declining the jurisdiction conferred on it by Art 2 even though the court of the non-Contracting State would be a more appropriate forum (see *Owusu v Jackson & ors* [2005] European Court of Justice C-281/02, [2005] All ER (D) 47 (March), in which most of the defendants were resident in Jamaica where the claimant had suffered his accident whilst on holiday. On the other hand, English proceedings will be stayed under this Part where proceedings are started within the jurisdiction in competition to proceedings already underway abroad, where considerable progress in the foreign litigation has already occurred and when there is considerable overlap between the issues being raised in each jurisdiction (*BP International Ltd v Energy Infrastructure Group Ltd* [2003] EWHC 3028 (Comm)).

Conflict of laws—The CPR have not altered the principle that proceedings are not 'definitely pending' for the purposes of Brussels Convention 1968, Art 21 until the English courts have seised the proceedings (*SDL International Limited v Centre de Co-operation Internationale* (2000) *The Independent*, 30 October, ChD, Nigel Davis QC).

'A defendant ... must first file an acknowledgment of service' (r 11(2))—See Pt 10 and the accompanying annotations. The period for filing an acknowledgment of service is 14 days after particulars of claim are served (rr 9.1(2) and 10.3). Note also r 7.7 under which a defendant may serve a notice on the claimant requiring him to serve the claim form.

Submission to the jurisdiction—Any conduct on the part of a defendant by which it is said that he has submitted to the jurisdiction of the English courts must be wholly unequivocal. Indicating on an acknowledgment of service that the defendant intends both to contest the jurisdiction of the English courts and to defend the claim is not a waiver of the right to challenge the jurisdiction. Neither is obtaining an extension of time for the service of a defence and the attempted discharge of a freezing order (*SMAY Investments Ltd & anor v Sachdev & ors* [2003] EWHC 474, [2003] All ER (D) 25 (Mar), ChD, Patten J). Even indicating on the acknowledgment of service an intention to defend without also indicating an intention to contest the court's jurisdiction does not prevent a challenge to the jurisdiction. This was the situation in a case where the defendant was domiciled in a Convention country and the relevant question was whether the defendant had entered an appearance under Art 18 of the Lugano Convention, rather than whether the defendant had submitted to the jurisdiction under English law (*IBS Technologies (PVT) Ltd v APM Technologies SA & anor (No 1)* (2003) Lawtel, 7 April, Michael Briggs QC). On the other hand, *Burns-Anderson Independent Network plc v Wheeler* [2005] EWHC 575 (QB) demonstrates the importance of specifically pleading the jurisdiction challenge under this rule. In that case, the defendant initially overlooked a problem with service and sought only an extension of time for their defence. They were held to have submitted to the jurisdiction and waived any right to challenge it.

'An application under this rule' (r 11(4))—See Pt 23 for how to make an application. The application is made to the court where the claim was started (r 23.2(1)) unless the claim has been transferred to another court since it was started (r 23.2(2)).

'An application under this rule must ... be made within 14 days after filing an acknowledgment' (r 11.4)—The court has a general discretion to extend the time within which a defendant would otherwise be bound under r 11.4 to dispute the court's jurisdiction to try a claim (r 3.1(2)(a)).

In the Commercial Court or in a mercantile court the period for making the application is 28 days rather than 14 days (r 58.7(2) or r 59.6(2)), whereupon the claimant need not serve particulars of claim before the hearing of the application (r 58.7(3) or r 59.6(3)). In collision claims a party who wishes to dispute the court's jurisdiction must make an application under Pt 11 within 2 months after filing his acknowledgment of service (r 61.4(4)).

Any application must be brought within 14 days after filing an acknowledgment of service. In *R (Shah) v Immigration Appeal Tribunal, Sec of State for the Home Dept., interested party* [2004] TLR 594, (2004) *The Times*, 9 December, CA the court refused to permit a challenge to the court's jurisdiction mounted for the first time before the Court of Appeal.

'be supported by evidence' (r 11(4)(b))—See the requirements generally of Pt 32 and the practice direction supplementing it.

'he is to be treated as having accepted that the court has jurisdiction' (r 11.5)—See *Uphill v BRB (Residuary) Ltd* [2005] EWCA Civ 60 (and note **'Scope of provison'** above).

'An order containing a declaration' (r 11(6))—For the court's powers, note rr 3.1 and 3.4, as well as the express powers set out in r 11(6).

'staying the proceedings' (r 11(6)(d))—Unless the stay is by consent, the effect of r 25.10 on a case stayed under this rule is to set aside any interim injunction which may have been granted unless the court specifically orders otherwise.

Applications of summary judgment—In general, it is not open to a claimant to seek to obtain summary judgment in the face of a challenge to the court's jurisdiction (*Speed Investments Ltd v Formula One Holdings Ltd* [2004] EWHC 1772 (Ch), [2004] TLR 445).

Forms—N244.

PART 12
DEFAULT JUDGMENT

CONTENTS OF THIS PART

Procedural Guide—See Guide 29, set out in Section 1 of this work.

12.1 Meaning of 'default judgment'

In these Rules, 'default judgment' means judgment without trial where a defendant –

(a) has failed to file an acknowledgment of service; or
(b) has failed to file a defence.

(Part 10 contains provisions about filing an acknowledgment of service and Part 15 contains provisions about filing a defence)

Practice Direction—See generally PD12 at p 565.

Scope of provision—A claimant may obtain default judgment by making a request (administrative) under r 12.4(1) or an application (to a judge) under r 12.4(2), when the application will be made in accordance with Pt 23. Pt 12 is applied to counterclaims by r 20.3(3)(a).

Failure to file—That is to say, before judgment has been entered.

'a defence' (r 12.1(b))—The definition includes a document purporting to be a defence (PD12, para 1.1). If the document filed does not satisfy the requirements for a defence, it is liable to be struck out either on an application by the claimant or by the court acting of its own initiative (rr 3.4, 24.2).

12.2 Claims in which default judgment may not be obtained

A claimant may not obtain a default judgment –

(a) on a claim for delivery of goods subject to an agreement regulated by the Consumer Credit Act 1974;
(b) where he uses the procedure set out in Part 8 (alternative procedure for claims); or
(c) in any other case where a practice direction provides that the claimant may not obtain default judgment.

Practice Direction—See generally PD12 at p 565.

'any other case' (r 12.2(c))—See PD12, para 1.2 for a list of cases where default judgment may not be obtained and PD12, para 1.3 for further examples.

Possession claims under Part 55—Rule 12.2 does not apply to Pt 55 claims (r 55.7(4)).

12.3 Conditions to be satisfied

(1) The claimant may obtain judgment in default of an acknowledgment of service only if –

(a) the defendant has not filed an acknowledgment of service or a defence to the claim (or any part of the claim); and
(b) the relevant time for doing so has expired.

[(2) Judgment in default of defence may be obtained only –

(a) where an acknowledgment of service has been filed but a defence has not been filed;
(b) in a counterclaim made under rule 20.4, where a defence has not been filed,

and, in either case, the relevant time limit for doing so has expired.]

(Rule 20.4 makes general provision for a defendant's counterclaim against a claimant, and rule 20.4(3) provides that Part 10 (acknowledgment of service) does not apply to a counterclaim made under that rule)

(3) The claimant may not obtain a default judgment if –

(a) the defendant has applied –
(i) to have the claimant's statement of case struck out under rule 3.4; or
(ii) for summary judgment under Part 24,

and, in either case, that application has not been disposed of;
(b) the defendant has satisfied the whole claim (including any claim for costs) on which the claimant is seeking judgment; or
(c)
(i) the claimant is seeking judgment on a claim for money; and
(ii) the defendant has filed or served on the claimant an admission under rule 14.4 or 14.7 (admission of liability to pay all of the money claimed) together with a request for time to pay.

(Part 14 sets out the procedure where a defendant admits a money claim and asks for time to pay)

(Rule 6.14 provides that, where the claim form is served by the claimant, he may not obtain default judgment unless he has filed a certificate of service)

(Article 19(1) of Council Regulation (EC) No 1348/2000 of 29 May 2000 on the service in the Member States of judicial and extrajudicial documents in civil or commercial matters applies in relation to judgment in default where the claim form is served in accordance with that Regulation)

Amendments—SI 2000/221; SI 2001/1388.

Practice Direction—See generally PD12 at p 565.

Failure of service—Where the acknowledgment of service is not filed because there has been no valid service, the conditions of r 12.3(1)(a) and (b) are not satisfied and the court has to set aside the judgment (*Shiblaq v Sadikoglu* [2003] All ER(D) 428 (Jul) (Comm Ct)).

Counterclaims—The amendment of r 12.3 by Civil Procedure (Amendment) Rules 2000, r 6 has removed the previous technical difficulty which prevented a default judgment from being obtained on a counterclaim. Thus, for the purposes of judgment in default, a defendant who has made a counterclaim is in the same position as a claimant to an action (r 20.3) and references in this Part to 'claimant' and 'defendant' include claimant and defendant to a counterclaim. However, a claimant is not required to acknowledge service of the defendant's counterclaim (r 20.4(3)).

'the relevant time for doing so has expired' (r 12.3(1)(b))—The general period for filing a defence is 14 days after service of the particulars of claim, or, if the defendant files an acknowledgment of service, 28 days after service of the particulars of claim (r 15.4). Note that if the defendant files an acknowledgment (or a defence, having filed an acknowledgment) out of time but before judgment, that will prevent judgment from being entered. Court offices record the receipt of acknowledgments of service and defences immediately on receipt but there may be a delay in their processing requests for default judgment. Thus, although the request may have reached the court while the defendant was in default, the court may in practice decline to enter the judgment. Similarly, the judge may refuse an application for a default judgment under r 12.4(2) even though, technically, the claimant is entitled to the judgment (*Coll v Tattum* (2001) *The Times*, 3 December, ChD (Neuberger, J)). Here, it was held that if the defendant is late in filing an acknowledgment of service or a defence, he should consider applying for an extension of time before judgment in default is obtained, provided he can show a *bona fide* defence.

Application by defendant for strike out (r 12.3(3)(a)(i))—This provision was added by Civil Procedure (Amendment) Rules 2000, r 6.

Summary judgment (r 12.3(3))—Thus the defendant can effectively prevent default judgment being entered against him by issuing an application for summary judgment. Note that where the *claimant* issues an application for summary judgment prior to a defence being served this also relieves the defendant of the obligation to file a defence and therefore prevents a request for default judgment being granted.

Admission under r 14.4 (r 12.3(3)(c)(ii))—This is an admission of the *whole* amount of a claim for a specified sum. However, r 14.4(3) provides that where such an admission is made the claimant may request judgment and the court will proceed to consider the defendant's request for time to pay under r 14.9.

Admission under r 14.7 (r 12.3(3)(c)(ii))—This is an admission of liability to pay a claim for an unspecified sum where the defendant makes an offer in satisfaction. If the offer is accepted the claimant may request judgment under r 14.7(5). If he does not accept the amount offered he may in any event request judgment under r 14.7(9) for an amount to be decided by the court and costs (r 14.7(10)). If no offer is made (r 14.6), the claimant is entitled to ask for default judgment for an amount to be decided by the court (r 12.7).

'request for time to pay' (r 12.3(3)(c)(ii))—Oddly, where an admission is made without a request for time to pay, the claimant has a choice as to whether to apply for judgment under this Part or under Pt 14. Entry of judgment under this rule clearly implies rejection of the offer (r 12.5(3)). Accordingly it is more appropriate to proceed under r 14.7(9). Where the offer is accepted, judgment should be taken under r 14.7(5).

12.4 Procedure for obtaining default judgment

(1) Subject to paragraph (2), a claimant may obtain a default judgment by filing a request in the relevant practice form where the claim is for –

- (a) a specified amount of money;
- (b) an amount of money to be decided by the court;
- (c) delivery of goods where the claim form gives the defendant the alternative of paying their value; or
- (d) any combination of these remedies.

(2) The claimant must make an application in accordance with Part 23 if he wishes to obtain a default judgment –

- (a) on a claim which consists of or includes a claim for any other remedy; or
- (b) where rule 12.9 or rule 12.10 so provides.

(3) Where a claimant –

- (a) claims any other remedy in his claim form in addition to those specified in paragraph (1); but
- (b) abandons that claim in his request for judgment;

he may still obtain a default judgment by filing a request under paragraph (1).

(4) In civil proceedings against the Crown, as defined in rule 66.1(2), a request for a default judgment must be considered by a Master or district judge, who

must in particular be satisfied that the claim form and particulars of claim have been properly served on the Crown in accordance with section 18 of the Crown Proceedings Act 1947 and rule 6.5(8).

Amendments—SI 2005/2292.

Prospective amendment—By virtue of the Civil Procedure (Amendment No 3) Rules 2005, SI 2005/2292, in r 12.4(2), after 'where rule 12.9 or rule 12.10 so provides', there is inserted –

> ', and where the defendant is an individual, the claimant must provide the defendant's date of birth (if known) in Part C of the application notice.',

with effect from 6 April 2006.

Practice Direction—See generally PD12 at p 565.

'a request in the relevant practice form' (r 12.4(1))—Note the reference in r 12.4(1) to 'a request' for the administrative entry of default judgment and compare this to r 12.4(2) which refers to the making of 'an application' ie to the judge. For forms, see below.

'delivery of goods' (r 12.4(1)(c))—Claims under Consumer Credit Act 1974 are not included (r 12.4(2)(a)). Where there is no alternative of paying value, the evidence must identify the goods, state where the claimant believes them to be situated and why specific delivery up is sought (PD12, para 4.6).

Claims which require an application for default judgment (r 12.4(2))—Paragraph 2.3 of PD12, gives examples of these types of claims.

Requirements on request or application for default judgment—The court must be satisfied that: the particulars of claim have been served (certificate of service); no acknowledgment of service or defence has been filed within the required time; the claim has not been satisfied and there is no admission under either r 14.4 or 14.6 (PD12, para 4.1). The request must be made within 6 months after the end of the period for filing a defence, otherwise the claim will be stayed (r 15.11).

Forms—On a request for judgment for (i) a specified sum of money – N205A or N225; (ii) for an amount to be decided by the court – N205B or N227. Where there is a claim for delivery of goods, those forms should be used, the choice depending on whether the value needs to be assessed by the court (PD12, para 3), but they will need to be adapted.

12.5 Nature of judgment where default judgment obtained by filing a request

(1) Where the claim is for a specified sum of money, the claimant may specify in a request filed under rule 12.4(1) –

- (a) the date by which the whole of the judgment debt is to be paid; or
- (b) the times and rate at which it is to be paid by instalments.

(2) Except where paragraph (4) applies, a default judgment on a claim for a specified amount of money obtained on the filing of a request, will be judgment for the amount of the claim (less any payments made) and costs –

- (a) to be paid by the date or at the rate specified in the request for judgment; or
- (b) if none is specified, immediately.

(Interest may be included in a default judgment obtained by filing a request if the conditions set out in Rule 12.6 are satisfied)

(Rule 45.4 provides for fixed costs on the entry of a default judgment)

(3) Where the claim is for an unspecified amount of money a default judgment obtained on the filing of a request will be for an amount to be decided by the court and costs.

(4) Where the claim is for delivery of goods and the claim form gives the defendant the alternative of paying their value, a default judgment obtained on the filing of a request will be judgment requiring the defendant to –

(a) deliver the goods or (if he does not do so) pay the value of the goods as decided by the court (less any payments made); and

(b) pay costs.

(Rule 12.7 sets out the procedure for deciding the amount of a judgment or the value of the goods)

(5) The claimant's right to enter judgment requiring the defendant to deliver goods is subject to rule 40.14 (judgment in favour of certain part owners relating to the detention of goods).

Practice Direction—See generally PD12 at p 565.

Currency—See PD12, para 5.2 for the requirements where the default judgment is given for a claim for a sum of money other than in sterling.

Interest—See r 12.6 below.

Judgment for an unspecified amount (r 12.5(3))—As to the ascertaining of the amount and costs see PD26, para 12 and r 12.7 below. Although the judgment fixes liability, that does not prevent the defendant from raising points as to quantum arising from acts or omissions claimed (*Lunnun v Singh* [1999] CPLR 587, CA).

Judgment in favour of part owners (r 12.5(5))—Any judgment or order given or made in respect of the claim is to be for the payment of damages only, unless the claimant had the written authority of every other part owner of the goods to make the claim on his behalf as well as for himself (r 40.14(2)).

Default judgment and election of defendant—The entry of a default judgment might not amount to the acceptance of a defendant as being solely responsible for a claim where it is not possible to determine the basis on which the default judgment has been arrived at. A default judgment does not in principle bar the continuance of a claim against another defendant (*Pendleton & anor v Westwater & anor* [2001] EWCA Civ 1841).

12.6 Interest

(1) A default judgment on a claim for a specified amount of money obtained on the filing of a request may include the amount of interest claimed to the date of judgment if –

(a) the particulars of claim include the details required by rule 16.4;

(b) where interest is claimed under section 35A of the Supreme Court Act 1981 or section 69 of the County Courts Act 1984, the rate is no higher than the rate of interest payable on judgment debts at the date when the claim form was issued; and

(c) the claimant's request for judgment includes a calculation of the interest claimed for the period from the date up to which interest was stated to be calculated in the claim form to the date of the request for judgment.

(2) In any case where paragraph (1) does not apply, judgment will be for an amount of interest to be decided by the court.

(Rule 12.7 sets out the procedure for deciding the amount of interest)

Practice Direction—See generally PD12 at p 565.

Rate of interest—The maximum rate in a claim for a specified sum of money is that applicable to judgments under the Judgment Debts (Rates of Interest) Order 1985 and is currently 8%. This rate should not be confused with the interest on special damages in personal injury and fatal accident cases, which is based on the rate on the Special Account and which has been at 7% since 1 August 1999.

Particulars of claim (r 12.6(1)(a))—An application to add a claim for interest to particulars of claim is not guaranteed to succeed (*Ward v Chief Constable of Avon and Somerset* (1985) 129 SJ 606, CA).

12.7 Procedure for deciding an amount or value

(1) This rule applies where the claimant obtains a default judgment on the filing of a request under rule 12.4(1) and judgment is for –

- (a) an amount of money to be decided by the court;
- (b) the value of goods to be decided by the court; or
- (c) an amount of interest to be decided by the court.

(2) Where the court enters judgment it will –

- (a) give any directions it considers appropriate; and
- (b) if it considers it appropriate, allocate the case.

Practice Direction—See generally PD12 at p 565.

Procedure—See PD26, para 12, which describes such hearings as 'disposal hearings', and the notes to that paragraph.

'allocate the case' (r 12.7(2)(b))—See the **'General note'** to r 14.8 which also applies to this provision.

12.8 Claim against more than one defendant

(1) A claimant may obtain a default judgment on request under this Part on a claim for money or a claim for delivery of goods against one of two or more defendants, and proceed with his claim against the other defendants.

(2) Where a claimant applies for a default judgment against one of two or more defendants –

- (a) if the claim can be dealt with separately from the claim against the other defendants –
  - (i) the court may enter a default judgment against that defendant; and
  - (ii) the claimant may continue the proceedings against the other defendants;
- (b) if the claim cannot be dealt with separately from the claim against the other defendants –
  - (i) the court will not enter default judgment against that defendant; and
  - (ii) the court must deal with the application at the same time as it disposes of the claim against the other defendants.

(3) A claimant may not enforce against one of two or more defendants any judgment obtained under this Part for possession of land or for delivery of goods unless –

- (a) he has obtained a judgment for possession or delivery (whether or not obtained under this Part) against all the defendants to the claim; or
- (b) the court gives permission.

Practice Direction—See generally PD12 at p 565.

'one of two or more defendants' (r 12.8(2))—The entry of a default judgment might not amount to an election (ie an election to seek judgment against one defendant only) where it is not possible to determine the basis on which the default judgment has been arrived at. A default judgment might not in principle bar the continuance of a claim against another defendant (*Pendleton & anor v Westwater & anor* [2001] EWCA Civ 1841).

12.9 Procedure for obtaining a default judgment for costs only

(1) Where a claimant wishes to obtain a default judgment for costs only –

- (a) if the claim is for fixed costs, he may obtain it by filing a request in the relevant practice form;
- (b) if the claim is for any other type of costs, he must make an application in accordance with Part 23.

(2) Where an application is made under this rule for costs only, judgment shall be for an amount to be decided by the court.

(Part 45 sets out when a claimant is entitled to fixed costs)

Practice Direction—See generally PD12 at p 565.

'costs only' (r 12.9(2))—The court may assess costs summarily or by detailed assessment (see Pt 44).

12.10 Default judgment obtained by making an application

The claimant must make an application in accordance with Part 23 where –

- (a) the claim is –
  - (i) a claim against a child or patient; or
  - (ii) a claim in tort by one spouse or civil partner against the other.
- (b) he wishes to obtain a default judgment where the defendant has failed to file an acknowledgment of service –
  - (i) against a defendant who has been served with the claim out of the jurisdiction under r 6.19(1) or (1A) (service without leave);
  - (ii) against a defendant domiciled in Scotland or Northern Ireland or in any other Convention territory or Regulation State;
  - (iii) against a State;
  - (iv) against a diplomatic agent who enjoys immunity from civil jurisdiction by virtue of the Diplomatic Privileges Act 1964; or
  - (v) against persons or organisations who enjoy immunity from civil jurisdiction pursuant to the provisions of the International Organisations Acts 1968 and 1981.

Amendments—SI 2001/4015; SI 2005/2292.

Practice Direction—See generally PD12 at p 565 and in particular paras 4.2–4.5 at p 567.

'a child or patient' (r 12.10(a)(i))—As defined in r 21.1(2).

'civil partner' (r 12.10(a)(ii))—As defined in Civil Partnership Act 2004, s 1.

12.11 Supplementary provisions where applications for default judgment are made

(1) Where the claimant makes an application for a default judgment, judgment shall be such judgment as it appears to the court that the claimant is entitled to on his statement of case.

(2) Any evidence relied on by the claimant in support of his application need not be served on a party who has failed to file an acknowledgment of service.

(3) An application for a default judgment on a claim against a child or patient or a claim in tort between spouses or civil partners must be supported by evidence.

(4) An application for a default judgment may be made without notice if –

- (a) the claim under the Civil Jurisdiction and Judgments Act 1982 or the Judgments Regulation, was served in accordance with rules 6.19(1) or 6.19(1A) as appropriate;
- (b) the defendant has failed to file an acknowledgment of service; and
- (c) notice does not need to be given under any other provision of these Rules.

(5) Where an application is made against a State for a default judgment where the defendant has failed to file an acknowledgment of service –

- (a) the application may be made without notice, but the court hearing the application may direct that a copy of the application notice be served on the State;
- (b) if the court –
  - (i) grants the application; or
  - (ii) directs that a copy of the application notice be served on the State,

  the judgment or application notice (and the evidence in support) may be served out of the jurisdiction without any further order;
- (c) where paragraph (5)(b) permits a judgment or an application notice to be served out of the jurisdiction, the procedure for serving the judgment or the application notice is the same as for serving a claim form under Section III of Part 6 except where an alternative method of service has been agreed under section 12(6) of the State Immunity Act 1978.

(Rule 23.1 defines 'application notice')

(6) For the purposes of this rule and rule 12.10 –

- (a) 'domicile' is to be determined –
  - (i) in relation to a Convention territory, in accordance with sections 41 to 46 of the Civil Jurisdiction and Judgments Act 1982;
  - (ii) in relation to a Regulation State, in accordance with the Judgments Regulation and paragraphs 9 to 12 of Schedule 1 to the Civil Jurisdiction and Judgments Order 2001;
- (b) 'Convention territory' means the territory or territories of any Contracting State, as defined by section 1(3) of the Civil Jurisdiction and Judgments Act 1982, to which the Brussels Conventions or Lugano Convention apply;
- (c) 'State' has the meaning given by section 14 of the State Immunity Act 1978;
- (d) 'Diplomatic agent' has the meaning given by Article 1(e) of Schedule 1 to the Diplomatic Privileges Act 1964;
- (e) 'the Judgments Regulation' means Council Regulation (EC) No. 44/2001 of 22nd December 2000 on jurisdiction and the recognition and enforcement of judgments in civil and commercial matters; and
- (f) 'Regulation State' has the same meaning as 'Member State' in the Judgments Regulation, that is all Member States except Denmark.

Amendments—SI 2000/940; SI 2001/4015.

Practice Direction—See generally PD12 at p 565.

'such judgment as … the claimant is entitled to' (r 12.11(1))—Except for claims against a child or patient – see note **'child or patient'** below – where an application must be made under Pt 23 and supported by evidence, the evidence does not have to prove the merits of the claim. The particulars of claim must show the necessary facts to establish the claim and the correct procedure must have been followed to serve the particulars of claim, to which the defendant has not responded.

'child or patient' (r 12.11(3))—A litigation friend (see Pt 21) must be appointed on behalf of a child or patient before judgment can be entered and the court must be satisfied that the claimant is entitled to the judgment sought (PD12, para 4.2). In contrast to r 12.11(1), if an application is made for judgment in default against a child or a patient, the claimant must satisfy the court by evidence that he is *entitled* to the judgment claimed (PD12, para 4.2).

Out of jurisdiction (r 12.11(4))—The application must be supported by *affidavit* evidence (PD12, para 4.5) and see PD12, para 4.3 for evidential requirements.

'against a State' (r 12.11(5))—The application must be supported by *affidavit* evidence (PD12, para 4.5) and see PD12, para 4.4 for evidential requirements.

Practice Direction – Default Judgment

This Practice Direction supplements CPR Part 12 (PD12)

Procedural Guide—See Guide 29, set out in Section 1 of this work.

DEFAULT JUDGMENT

1.1 A default judgment is judgment without a trial where a defendant has failed to file either:

(1) an acknowledgment of service, or
(2) a defence.

For this purpose a defence includes any document purporting to be a defence.

(See Part 10 and the practice direction which supplements it for information about the acknowledgment of service, and Parts 15 and 16 and the practice directions which supplement them for information about the defence and what it should contain)

1.2 A claimant may not obtain a default judgment under Part 12 (notwithstanding that no acknowledgment of service or defence has been filed) if:

(1) the procedure set out in Part 8 (Alternative Procedure for Claims) is being used, or
(2) the claim is for delivery of goods subject to an agreement regulated by the Consumer Credit Act 1974, or

1.3 Other rules and practice directions provide that default judgment under Part 12 cannot be obtained in particular types of proceedings. Examples are:

(1) admiralty proceedings,
(2) arbitration proceedings,
(3) contentious probate proceedings,
(4) claims for provisional damages;
(5) possession claims.

'any document purporting to be a defence' (para 1.1)—As this particular part of the procedure is administrative without judicial intervention, it is not for the staff to scrutinise 'defences' to see whether or not they are what they purport to be, other than to refer any doubtful documents to the judge. The provision also applies to a defence to a counterclaim and references to a 'defendant' include a defendant to a counterclaim.

OBTAINING DEFAULT JUDGMENT

2.1 Rules 12.4(1) and 12.9(1) describe the claims in respect of which a default judgment may be obtained by filing a request in the appropriate practice form.

2.2 A default judgment on:

(1) the claims referred to in rules 12.9(1)(b) and 12.10, and
(2) claims other than those described in rule 12.4(1),

can only be obtained if an application for default judgment is made and cannot be obtained by filing a request.

2.3 The following are some of the types of claim which require an application for a default judgment:

(1) against children and patients[1],
(2) for costs (other than fixed costs) only[2],
(3) by one spouse against the other[3] on a claim in tort[4],
(4) for delivery up of goods where the defendant will not be allowed the alternative of paying their value,
(5) against the Crown, and
(6) against persons or organisations who enjoy immunity from civil jurisdiction under the provisions of the International Organisations Acts 1968 and 1981.

Prospective amendments—Words in italics prospectively inserted in 2.3(3) and 2.3(5) prospectively omitted: Supplement 40 (issued 30 September 2005), with effect from 6 April 2006:

'(3) by one spouse [*or civil partner*] against the other on a claim in tort,
(4) for delivery up of goods where the defendant will not be allowed the alternative of paying their value[; and]
(5) …
(6) against persons or organisations who enjoy immunity from civil jurisdiction under the provisions of the International Organisations Acts 1968 and 1981.'

1 See rule 12.10(a)(i).
2 See rule 12.9(b).
3 See rule 12.10(a)(ii).
4 Tort may be defined as an act or a failure to do an act which causes harm or damage to another person and which gives the other person a right to claim compensation without having to rely on a contract with the person who caused the harm or damage.

DEFAULT JUDGMENT BY REQUEST

3 Requests for default judgment:

(1) in respect of a claim for a specified amount of money or for the delivery of goods where the defendant will be given the alternative of paying a specified sum representing their value, or for fixed costs only, must be in Form N205A or N225, and
(2) in respect of a claim where an amount of money (including an amount representing the value of goods) is to be decided by the court, must be in Form N205B or N227.

Prospective amendments—Paragraph 3.2 inserted: Supplement 40 (issued 30 September 2005), with effect from 6 April 2006:

'[3.1] Requests for default judgment:
(1) in respect of a claim for a specified amount of money or for the delivery of goods where the defendant will be given the alternative of paying a specified sum representing their value, or for fixed costs only, must be in Form N205A or [N225] , and
(2) in respect of a claim where an amount of money (including an amount representing the value of goods) is to be decided by the court, must be in Form [N205B] or [N227].

[3.2 The forms require the claimant to provide the date of birth (if known) of the defendant where the defendant is an individual.]'

Form of application—As stated herein. Otherwise on Application Notice N244.

Court fees on application—On notice – £50; without notice – £25 (CCFO fees 2.4 and 2.5, SCFO fees 2.4 and 2.5).

EVIDENCE

4.1 Both on a request and on an application for default judgment the court must be satisfied that:

(1) the particulars of claim have been served on the defendant (a certificate of service on the court file will be sufficient evidence),
(2) either the defendant has not filed an acknowledgment of service or has not filed a defence and that in either case the relevant period for doing so has expired,
(3) the defendant has not satisfied the claim, and
(4) the defendant has not returned an admission to the claimant under rule 14.4 or filed an admission with the court under rule 14.6.

4.2 On an application against a child or patient[1]:

(1) a litigation friend[2] to act on behalf of the child or patient must be appointed by the court before judgment can be obtained, and
(2) the claimant must satisfy the court by evidence that he is entitled to the judgment claimed.

1 As defined in rule 21.1(2).
2 As defined in the practice direction which supplements Part 21.

4.3 On an application where the defendant was served with the claim either:

(1) outside the jurisdiction[1] without leave under the Civil Jurisdiction and Judgments Act 1982, or the Judgments Regulation, or
(2) within the jurisdiction but when domiciled[2] in Scotland or Northern Ireland or in any other Convention territory[3] or Regulation State,

and the defendant has not acknowledged service, the evidence must establish that:

(a) the claim is one that the court has power to hear and decide,
(b) no other court has exclusive jurisdiction under the Act or Judgments Regulation to hear and decide the claim, and
(c) the claim has been properly served in accordance with Article 20 of Schedule 1 or 3C to the Act, paragraph 15 of Schedule 4 to the Act, or Article 26 of the Judgments Regulation.

1 As defined in rule 2.3.
2 As determined in accordance with the provisions of ss 41 to 46 of the Civil Jurisdictions and Judgments Act 1982.
3 Means the territory of a Contracting State as defined in s 1(3) of the Civil Jurisdiction and Judgments Act 1982.

4.4 On an application against a State[1] the evidence must:

(1) set out the grounds of the application,
(2) establish the facts proving that the State is excepted from the immunity conferred by section 1 of the State Immunity Act 1978,

(3) establish that the claim was sent through the Foreign and Commonwealth Office to the Ministry of Foreign Affairs of the State or, where the State has agreed to another form of service, that the claim was served in the manner agreed; and

(4) establish that the time for acknowledging service, (which is extended to 2 months by section 12(2) of the Act when the claim is sent through the Foreign and Commonwealth Office to the Ministry of Foreign Affairs of the State) has expired.

(See rule 40.8 for when default judgment against a State takes effect)

1 As defined in s 14 of the State Immunity Act 1978.

4.5 Evidence in support of an application referred to in paragraphs 4.3 and 4.4 above must be by affidavit.

4.6 On an application for judgment for delivery up of goods where the defendant will not be given the alternative of paying their value, the evidence must identify the goods and state where the claimant believes the goods to be situated and why their specific delivery up is sought.

GENERAL

5.1 On all applications to which this practice direction applies, other than those referred to in paragraphs 4.3 and 4.4 above[1], notice should be given in accordance with Part 23.

5.2 Where default judgment is given on a claim for a sum of money expressed in a foreign currency, the judgment should be for the amount of the foreign currency with the addition of 'or the Sterling equivalent at the time of payment'.

1 See rule 12.11(4) and (5).

PART 13
SETTING ASIDE OR VARYING DEFAULT JUDGMENT

CONTENTS OF THIS PART

13.1 Scope of this Part

The rules in this Part set out the procedure for setting aside or varying judgment entered under Part 12 (default judgment).

(CCR Order 22 r 10 sets out the procedure for varying the rate at which a judgment debt must be paid)

13.2 Cases where the court must set aside judgment entered under Part 12

The court must set aside(GL) a judgment entered under Part 12 if judgment was wrongly entered because –

(a) in the case of a judgment in default of an acknowledgment of service, any of the conditions in rule 12.3(1) and 12.3(3) was not satisfied;
(b) in the case of a judgment in default of a defence, any of the conditions in rule 12.3(2) and 12.3(3) was not satisfied; or
(c) the whole of the claim was satisfied before judgment was entered.

'must set aside'—The court cannot impose conditions (such as payment of a sum into court) when judgment in default must be set aside as of right, even if the defendant does not have a real prospect of successfully defending the claim. The fact that a judgment is set aside under this rule will not prevent a further default judgment being entered if the conditions for it become satisfied, nor prevent (if appropriate) an application for summary judgment being made. In *Crédit Agricole Indosuez v Unicof Ltd & ors* [2003] EWHC 77, a case involving service of proceedings out of the jurisdiction, a defendant was entitled to have judgment set aside as of right where a claim form was not served either by the method claimed or at all. Rule 13.2 is mandatory. If the claim form is not served, time for filing an acknowledgment of service will not expire and the conditions of r 12.3(1) will not be satisfied.

13.3 Cases where the court may set aside or vary judgment entered under Part 12

(1) In any other case, the court may set aside(GL) or vary a judgment entered under Part 12 if –

(a) the defendant has a real prospect of successfully defending the claim; or
(b) it appears to the court that there is some other good reason why –
  (i) the judgment should be set aside or varied; or
  (ii) the defendant should be allowed to defend the claim.

(2) In considering whether to set aside[(GL)] or vary a judgment entered under Part 12, the matters to which the court must have regard include whether the person seeking to set aside the judgment made an application to do so promptly.

(Rule 3.1(3) provides that the court may attach conditions when it makes an order)

(Article 19(4) of Council Regulation (EC) No 1348/2000 of 29 May 2000 on the service in the Member States of judicial and extrajudicial documents in civil or commercial matters applies to applications to appeal a judgment in default when the time limit for appealing has expired)

Amendments—SI 2001/1388.

'a real prospect of successfully defending the claim' (r 13.3(1)(a))—The burden is on the defendant to satisfy the court that there is good reason why judgment regularly obtained ought to be set aside (*ED & F Man Liquid Products Ltd v Patel* [2003] EWCA Civ 472, [2003] All ER (D) 75 (Apr), CA). Although the burden is reversed, the test is the same as for r 24.2, as to which see the notes to that rule.

The test is similar to that used when deciding whether to strike out the claim. Provided a claim has some chance of success, the court should not strike it out merely because it looks weak and unlikely to succeed, if the only way of testing the efficacy of the case is by a trial of the facts (*Chan U Seek v Alvis Vehicles Ltd* [2003] EWHC 1238, [2003] All ER (D) 78 (May), ChD). Where the case concerns a developing area of the law and it is argued that the law may have developed sufficiently for the claim to stand a reasonable chance of success, the court will require to be satisfied that there is at least some real prospect of that occurring. If there is such a prospect, then by definition the claim is not on that ground hopeless; if there is no such prospect, then it is (*Hudson & ors v HM Treasury & anor* [2003] EWCA Civ 1612).

Provided service was regular (see note **'Deemed to be served'** under r 6.7) the test is applicable even though the defendant had no actual notice of the claim. The fair trial guarantees in ECHR, Art 6 must entitle a defendant to be heard, but if he cannot show the court that his defence would have a real prospect of success, or that there is some other compelling reason why a trial should be conducted, it does not require the parties and the court to indulge in an expensive and time-consuming charade (*Akram v Adam* [2004] EWCA Civ 1601).

In reaching its decision the court should avoid making findings concerning disputed facts, as these matters are best left for trial (*CPL Industrial Services Holding Limited v R & L Freeman & Sons* [2005] EWCA Civ 539).

'some other good reason' (r 13.3(1)(b))—This is not defined but is similar to the provisions under r 24.2(b), which stipulates that, when dealing with an application for summary judgment, the court must also consider whether there is any compelling reason why the case or issue should be disposed of at trial. The overriding objective will also be relevant. An example is where default judgment has been entered on a false basis as to service of proceedings (*Crédit Agricole Indosuez v Unicof Ltd* [2003] EWHC 77).

The rule does not enable a claimant to vary or set aside a judgment in circumstances where that variation increases the judgment amount in his favour (*Hertford Management Ltd v Mastorakis* [2001] All ER (D) 277 (Mar), QBD).

Rule 13.3(2)—Similar guidance on making the application promptly may be found in PD23, para 2.7 (applications generally) and r 3.9(1)(b) (application for relief from sanctions). There is nothing in r 13.3 or in the overriding objective in Pt 1 to suggest that if a defendant does not give a reason for delay in applying to set judgment aside, that is somehow a 'knockout' blow in favour of the claimant which removes the court's discretion to set the judgment aside (*Macdonald (Kathleen) & Macdonald (Peter) v Thorn plc* [1999] CPLR 660, (1999) *The Times*, 15 October, CA). 'Promptly' means 'acting with alacrity' (*Regency Rolls Ltd & anor v Carnall* (2000) Lawtel, 16 October, CA). Here, an application to set aside a judgment made 26 days earlier was held to be unacceptable. By contrast, an application made 37 days after the date of the order sought to be set aside was stated to have been made 'with sufficient promptness', but only because the court accepted the applicant's excuse of not having received letters from his solicitors (*BCCI v Zafar* (2001) Lawtel, 2 November, ChD). There comes a point, however, when mere delay causes such prejudice and time so erodes recollection that the application to set aside the judgment should be rejected (*Sahidur Rahman v Rahman & Bose* (1999) Lawtel, 26 November, ChD).

'conditions' (r 13.3 cross-reference)—The court has no discretion to impose conditions when judgment in default is set aside as of right (r 13.2). Some guidance as to the circumstances in which conditions will be attached can be gleaned from PD24, para 4, (which relates to summary judgment).

Setting aside, subject to payment of monies—An order should not be made making it a condition of setting aside a judgment that the defendant should pay monies that he clearly cannot afford (*Chapple (James) v (1) Williams (David) (2) Emmett (Guy) t/a Global Windows & Conservatories (a firm)* (1999) Lawtel, 8 December, CA). There is no general proposition to the effect that a court is required to invite submissions before imposing financial conditions (*Kamal v Redcliffe Close (Old Brompton Road) Management Ltd* [2005] EWHC 858 (Ch)).

Costs—Before making an order for costs on setting aside a judgment in default of attendance, something more than a failure to comply with an unless order is required. However, a costs sanction is a matter for the judge's discretion and the order will only be varied if wrong in law or unjust by virtue of a serious procedural or other irregularity (*Gore v Jones & anor* (2001) *The Times*, 21 February, ChD).

Setting aside judgment where proceedings not received—The court may refuse to set aside judgment even where it is satisfied that the defendant has received no actual notice of proceedings which were nevertheless properly served at the defendant's last known address pursuant to r 6.5(6), if it is clear that, in any event, the defendant has no defence (*Akram v Adam* [2004] EWCA Civ 1601, [2004] TLR 633).

13.4 Application to set aside or vary judgment – procedure

(1) Where –

(a) the claim is for a specified amount of money;
(b) the judgment was obtained in a court which is not the defendant's home court;
(c) the claim has not been transferred to another defendant's home court under rule 14.12 (admission – determination of rate of payment by judge) or rule 26.2 (automatic transfer); and
(d) the defendant is an individual;

the court will transfer an application by a defendant under this Part to set aside(GL) or vary judgment to the defendant's home court.

(1A) (*revoked*)

(2) Paragraph (1) does not apply where the claim was commenced in a specialist list.

(3) An application under rule 13.3 (cases where the court may set aside(GL) or vary judgment) must be supported by evidence.

Amendments—SI 1999/1008; SI 2000/2092.

'an application' (r 13.4(1))—See Pt 23.

'the defendant is an individual' (r 13.4(1)(d))—This reflects the provisions for automatic transfer on the filing of a defence contained in r 26.2. The case will be transferred to the defendant's court where a specified amount is claimed *and* where the defendant is an individual. Thus, if the defendant is a partnership, company or corporation, the case will remain in the claimant's court. For the procedure involved in making the application, see Pt 23.

'the court will transfer' (r 13.4(1))—The transfer is an administrative rather than a judicial act.

'defendant's home court' (r 13.4(1))—Rule 2.3 defines this as follows:

'(a) if the claim is proceeding in a county court, the county court for the district in which the defendant resides or carries on business; and
(b) if the claim is proceeding in the High Court, the district registry for the district in which the defendant resides or carries on business or, if there is no such district registry, the Royal Courts of Justice'.

'a specialist list' (r 13.4(2))—For full details of the specialist lists see r 49(2).

'must be supported by evidence' (r 13.4(3))—See r 36.2.

13.5 (*revoked*)

13.6 Abandoned claim restored where default judgment set aside

Where –

(a) the claimant claimed a remedy in addition to one specified in rule 12.4(1) (claims in respect of which the claimant may obtain default judgment by filing a request);

(b) the claimant abandoned his claim for that remedy in order to obtain default judgment on request in accordance with rule 12.4(3); and

(c) that default judgment is set aside[(GL)] under this Part,

the abandoned claim is restored when the default judgment is set aside.

PART 14
ADMISSIONS

CONTENTS OF THIS PART

Procedural Guide—See Guide 6, set out in Section 1 of this work.

Scope of Part—This Part falls into four separate sections, namely:
(1) how a defendant may make an admission – rr 14.1 and 14.2;
(2) how judgment may be obtained following a written admission – rr 14.3–14.8 inclusive;
(3) how to deal with a request for time to pay – rr 14.9–14.12;
(4) how to deal with an application for a re-determination – r 14.13.

There are similarities to the former procedure in the county court, but also significant differences. As regards the High Court, the procedures prescribed by this Part are almost entirely new.

Procedure by defendant where the only remedy sought is payment of money—

Type of claim	Admitted in whole or in part	Form of admission	Whether form returned to claimant or filed with the court
specified amount of money	in whole (r 14.4)	N9A	to claimant (r 14.4(2) and PD14, para 3.1)
specified amount of money	in part (r 14.5)	N9A	to the court (r 14.5(2) and PD14, para 3.2)
unspecified amount of money	in whole (court to decide the amount) (r 14.6)	N9C	to the court (r 14.6(2) and PD14, para 3.2)
unspecified amount of money	defendant offers a sum in satisfaction (r 14.7)	N9C	to the court (r 14.7(2) and PD14, para 3.2)

Response Pack—The court or the claimant serves forms N9 and either N9A and N9B or N9C and N9D in a Response Pack when serving a claim form. A defendant wishing to defend part of the claim under r 15.2 should use Form N9B or N9D as appropriate, as well as the form of admission.

Fixed costs on entry of judgment—For the amount to be included in any judgment for the claimant's solicitor's charges see generally r 45.4 and Table 3.

Children and patients—Judgment will not be entered on an admission where –
(1) the defendant is a child or patient, or

(2) the claimant is a child or patient and a part admission is made in respect of a specified sum of money or a sum is offered in satisfaction of a claim for an unspecified amount of money (see rr 14.1(4) and 21.10).

Electronic filing of admission—Special provisions apply in relation to Money Claims Online and in relation to courts which have published an e-mail address on the Court Service website; in these instances it is possible to file specified documents, including admissions, by e-mail (see generally r 7.12 and PD5B respectively). The one exception is that it is not possible to file an admission under r 14.1 (admission of whole of claim for specified amount of money) as such an admission is returned by the defendant to the claimant direct.

14.1 Making an admission

(1) A party may admit the truth of the whole or any part of another party's case.

(2) He may do this by giving notice in writing (such as in a statement of case or by letter).

(3) Where the only remedy which the claimant is seeking is the payment of money, the defendant may also make an admission in accordance with –

- (a) rule 14.4 (admission of whole claim for specified amount of money);
- (b) rule 14.5 (admission of part of claim for specified amount of money);
- (c) rule 14.6 (admission of liability to pay whole of claim for unspecified amount of money); or
- (d) rule 14.7 (admission of liability to pay claim for unspecified amount of money where defendant offers a sum in satisfaction of the claim).

(4) Where the defendant makes an admission as mentioned in paragraph (3), the claimant has a right to enter judgment except where –

- (a) the defendant is a child or patient; or
- (b) the claimant is a child or patient and the admission is made under rule 14.5 or 14.7.

(Rule 21.10 provides that, where a claim is made by or on behalf of a child or patient or against a child or patient, no settlement, compromise or payment shall be valid, so far as it relates to that person's claim, without the approval of the court)

(5) The court may allow a party to amend or withdraw an admission.

(Rule 3.1(3) provides that the court may attach conditions when it makes an order)

Practice Direction—See PD14, paras 2.1–4.3 at p 584.

'statement of case' (r 14.1(2))—See r 16.5. Also note forms N9A, N9C (above).

'specified amount of money' (r 14.1(3)(a))—This term includes, for instance, a personal injury claim for 'damages of £20,000' which under the former RSC and CCR would have been treated as an unliquidated claim.

Period for making an admission—See r 14.2.

'the claimant has a right to enter judgment' (r 14.1(4))—See r 14.3.

'except where ... child or patient' (r 14.1(4)(a) and (b))—See generally Pts 21 and 23.

'the court may allow a party to amend or withdraw an admission' (r 14.1(5))—The court when doing so may impose conditions, including a payment into court (r 3.1(3)) or a costs' sanction (r 44.3). The court will also be concerned to further the overriding objective (r 1.1) and to identify the issues between the parties (r 1.4(2)(b)–(d)).

14.2 Period for making an admission

(1) The period for returning an admission under rule 14.4 or for filing it under rules 14.5, 14.6 or 14.7 is –

- (a) where the defendant is served with a claim form which states that particulars of claim will follow, 14 days after service of the particulars; and
- (b) in any other case, 14 days after service of the claim form.

(2) Paragraph (1) is subject to the following rules –

- (a) Rule 6.22 (which specifies how the period for filing or returning an admission is calculated where the claim form is served out of the jurisdiction); and
- (b) rule 6.16(4) (which requires the court to specify the period for responding to the particulars of claim when it makes an order under that rule).

(3) A defendant may return an admission under rule 14.4 or file it under rules 14.5, 14.6 or 14.7 after the end of the period for returning or filing it specified in paragraph (1) if the claimant has not obtained default judgment under Part 12.

(4) If he does so, this Part shall apply as if he had made the admission within that period.

Practice Direction—See PD14, paras 3.1–3.3 at p 584.

Scope of provision—This rule only applies if the defendant wishes to make an admission under any of rr 14.4–14.7 ie where the sole remedy sought by the claimant is for payment of an amount of money, whether specified or not.

'returning an admission ... or filing it' (r 14.2(1))—An admission of the whole of a specified amount of money is returned to the claimant (r 14.4 and PD14, para 3.1); in the three other circumstances of rr 14.5–14.7 inclusive, the admission is filed with the court.

'14 days after service' (r 14.2(1)(a) and (b))—If a defendant has filed an acknowledgment of service, intending to defend (r 9.2), and then decides to admit, then he will in effect have 28 days from service to serve the admission as default judgment cannot have been requested (r 12.3).

'rule 6.16(4)' (r 14.2(2)(b))—This rule requires that when the court permits a claim form relating to a contract to be served on a defendant's agent, the order must specify the period within which the defendant must respond to the particulars of claim.

14.3 Admission by notice in writing – application for judgment

(1) Where a party makes an admission under rule 14.1(2) (admission by notice in writing), any other party may apply for judgment on the admission.

(2) Judgment shall be such judgment as it appears to the court that the applicant is entitled to on the admission.

Scope of provision—The application for judgment by 'any other party' may be made on a general application under Pt 23 or by an application for summary judgment under Pt 24. It cannot be obtained administratively unless the defendant consents to a judgment being entered. However, in an appropriate case, a party may suggest to the court that the judge use his power under Pt 3 of his own initiative to enter judgment, for instance in a tort action where liability is admitted but quantum is disputed; this may be treated by the court not as a defence at all but as an admission of an unspecified amount. The case could then be listed for a disposal hearing under PD26, para 12.

14.4 Admission of whole of claim for specified amount of money

(1) This rule applies where –

(a) the only remedy which the claimant is seeking is the payment of a specified amount of money; and
(b) the defendant admits the whole of the claim.

(2) The defendant may admit the claim by returning to the claimant an admission in the relevant practice form.

(3) The claimant may obtain judgment by filing a request in the relevant practice form and, if he does so –

(a) if the defendant has not requested time to pay, the procedure in paragraphs (4) to (6) will apply;
(b) if the defendant has requested time to pay, the procedure in rule 14.9 will apply.

(4) The claimant may specify in his request for judgment –

(a) the date by which the whole of the judgment debt is to be paid; or
(b) the times and rate at which it is to be paid by instalments.

(5) On receipt of the request for judgment the court will enter judgment.

(6) Judgment will be for the amount of the claim (less any payments made) and costs –

(a) to be paid by the date or at the rate specified in the request for judgment; or
(b) if none is specified, immediately.

(Rule 14.14 deals with the circumstances in which judgment under this rule may include interest)

Practice Direction—See PD14, paras 3.1–3.3 at p 584, paras 4.1–4.3 at p 585 and paras 5.1–5.6 at p 585.

Scope of provision—The rule provides for where a defendant admits the whole of a claim for a specified amount of money.

Form of admission—N9A, which is sent by the defendant direct to the claimant.

'claimant may obtain judgment by filing a request in the relevant practice form' (r 14.4(3))—Form N225 (Form N205A may also be used). Where the defendant has made a request for time to pay which the claimant accepts, the request for judgment must of course follow the terms of the defendant's offer. Where such a request is not accepted, the claimant must file a copy of the admission and request (r 14.10).

'costs' (r 14.4(6))—The amount to be included for the claimant's solicitor's charges is fixed; see r 45.2 and Table 1 for the fixed commencement costs and r 45.4 and Table 3 for the fixed costs on entry of judgment.

'interest' (r 14.4(6) note)—In the absence of any specific contractual right to interest, the current statutory rate is 8% a year. Also note r 14.14 below.

Time to pay and redetermination—See rr 14.9–14.13 inclusive.

14.5 Admission of part of a claim for a specified amount of money

(1) This rule applies where –

(a) the only remedy which the claimant is seeking is the payment of a specified amount of money; and
(b) the defendant admits part of the claim.

(2) The defendant may admit part of the claim by filing an admission in the relevant practice form.

(3) On receipt of the admission, the court will serve a notice on the claimant requiring him to return the notice stating that –

(a) he accepts the amount admitted in satisfaction of the claim;
(b) he does not accept the amount admitted by the defendant and wishes the proceedings to continue; or
(c) if the defendant has requested time to pay, he accepts the amount admitted in satisfaction of the claim, but not the defendant's proposals as to payment.

(4) The claimant must –

(a) file the notice; and
(b) serve a copy on the defendant,

within 14 days after it is served on him.

(5) If the claimant does not file the notice within 14 days after it is served on him, the claim is stayed(GL) until he files the notice.

(6) If the claimant accepts the amount admitted in satisfaction of the claim, he may obtain judgment by filing a request in the relevant practice form and, if he does so –

(a) if the defendant has not requested time to pay, the procedure in paragraphs (7) to (9) will apply;
(b) if the defendant has requested time to pay, the procedure in rule 14.9 will apply.

(7) The claimant may specify in his request for judgment –

(a) the date by which the whole of the judgment debt is to be paid; or
(b) the time and rate at which it is to be paid by instalments.

(8) On receipt of the request for judgment, the court will enter judgment.

(9) Judgment will be for the amount admitted (less any payments made) and costs –

(a) to be paid by the date or at the rate specified in the request for judgment; or
(b) if none is specified, immediately.

(If the claimant files notice under paragraph (3) that he wishes the proceedings to continue, the procedure which then follows is set out in Part 26)

Practice Direction—See PD14, paras 3.1–3.3 at p 584, paras 4.1–4.3 at p 585 and paras 5.1–5.6 at p 585.

Scope of provision—The rule provides for where the defendant admits part of a claim for a specified sum of money.

'This rule applies' (r 14.5(1))—Rule 14.5 does not apply to claims in the commercial list (r 58.9(1)) or to mercantile claims (r 59.8(1)).

'relevant practice form' (r 14.5(2))—The form for admitting is N9A which, together with the defence Form N9B, is filed with the court.

'the court will serve a notice on the claimant' (r 14.5(3))—See Form N225A.

'the claim is stayed' (r 14.5(5))—Under r 14.5 a claim is stayed if the claimant does not return the N225A within 14 days but the stay is then automatically removed on the N225A being filed late. In the meantime the whole case is stayed, including claims against other defendants, counterclaims and other Pt 20 claims; in particular no allocation questionnaires are served (r 26.3(4)) and no case management directions will be given.

'the claimant ... may obtain judgment by filing a request in the relevant practice form' (r 14.5(6))—Form N225A.

'costs' (r 14.5(9))—The amount to be included for the claimant's solicitor's charges is fixed; see r 45.2 and Table 1 for the fixed commencement costs and r 45.4 and Table 3 for the fixed costs on entry of judgment.

Automatic transfer – 'if the claimant ... wishes the proceedings to continue' (note to r 14.5(9))—If:

(i) the claim is not commenced in the defendant's home court (for a definition of which, see r 2.3) (see note to r 26.2);
(ii) the defendant is an individual; and
(iii) the claimant files notice that he wishes the claim to continue,

then the proceedings are automatically transferred to the defendant's home court under r 26.2(4). At the same time, the court in which the proceedings were commenced will serve allocation questionnaires which are to be filed in the defendant's home court (r 26.3(3))

Time to pay and redetermination—See rr 14.9–14.13 inclusive.

14.6 Admission of liability to pay whole of claim for unspecified amount of money

(1) This rule applies where –

(a) the only remedy which the claimant is seeking is the payment of money;
(b) the amount of the claim is not specified; and
(c) the defendant admits liability but does not offer to pay a specified amount of money in satisfaction of the claim.

(2) The defendant may admit the claim by filing an admission in the relevant practice form.

(3) On receipt of the admission, the court will serve a copy on the claimant.

(4) The claimant may obtain judgment by filing a request in the relevant practice form.

(5) If the claimant does not file a request for judgment within 14 days after service of the admission on him, the claim is stayed[(GL)] until he files the request.

(6) On receipt of the request for judgment the court will enter judgment.

(7) Judgment will be for an amount to be decided by the court and costs.

Practice Direction—See PD14, para 3.1 at p 584.

Scope of provision—The rule provides for where the only claim is for an unspecified amount of money and the defendant admits liability but does not offer a specified amount in satisfaction.

'the defendant admits liability' (r 14.6(1)(c))—Frequently in claims for personal injury the defence will admit negligence but not the extent of the injury and loss suffered. Judgment leading to a disposal hearing will be entered. The defendant should not have filed a defence but rather a form of admission as the claimant is entitled to judgment under r 14.6(4). If the defence – wrongly – admits negligence but expressly denies any loss, the procedural judge will again normally direct that judgment be entered, the defence being treated as an admission.

Form of admission—N9C, which the defendant files with the court.

'the court will serve a copy on the claimant' (r 14.6(3))—See Form N226.

'The claimant may obtain judgment by filing a request in the relevant practice form' (r 14.6(4))—Form N226.

'the claim is stayed' (r 14.6(5))—See note to r 14.5(5) above.

Automatic transfer—A claim for an unspecified amount of money is not automatically transferred (cf r 14.5)

'Judgment will be for an amount to be decided by the court' (r 14.6(7))—See Form N17. The procedural judge will at the time judgment is entered also give directions which will be set out on the N17.

A judgment obtained under this rule is a 'relevant order' as defined in PD26, para 12.1(2)(b). Under PD26, para 12.3 the court will not normally allocate the claim to a track (other than the small claims track) but list the claim for a disposal hearing under PD26, para 12.4, which will not normally last longer than 30 minutes and at which the court will not normally hear oral evidence.

Alternatively, where the amount payable appears to be genuinely disputed on substantial grounds the court may allocate the claim to a track and give case management directions.

'costs' (r 14.6(7))—These are not fixed but will be assessed by the court, if not agreed, subsequently. Unless the case has been allocated to the small claims track, the costs of a disposal hearing will be in the discretion of the court (PD26, para 12.5(2)).

Appeal—See note **'allocate the case'** under r 14.8.

14.7 Admission of liability to pay claim for unspecified amount of money where defendant offers a sum in satisfaction of the claim

(1) This rule applies where –

- (a) the only remedy which the claimant is seeking is the payment of money;
- (b) the amount of the claim is not specified; and
- (c) the defendant –
  - (i) admits liability; and
  - (ii) offers to pay a specified amount of money in satisfaction of the claim.

(2) The defendant may admit the claim by filing an admission in the relevant practice form.

(3) On receipt of the admission, the court will serve a notice on the claimant requiring him to return the notice stating whether or not he accepts the amount in satisfaction of the claim.

(4) If the claimant does not file the notice within 14 days after it is served on him, the claim is stayed(GL) until he files the notice.

(5) If the claimant accepts the offer he may obtain judgment by filing a request in the relevant practice form and if he does so –

- (a) if the defendant has not requested time to pay, the procedure in paragraphs (6) to (8) will apply;
- (b) if the defendant has requested time to pay, the procedure in rule 14.9 will apply.

(6) The claimant may specify in his request for judgment –

- (a) the date by which the whole of the judgment debt is to be paid; or
- (b) the times and rate at which it is to be paid by instalments.

(7) On receipt of the request for judgment, the court will enter judgment.

(8) Judgment will be for the amount offered by the defendant (less any payments made) and costs –

- (a) to be paid on the date or at the rate specified in the request for judgment; or
- (b) if none is specified, immediately.

(9) If the claimant does not accept the amount offered by the defendant, he may obtain judgment by filing a request in the relevant practice form.

(10) Judgment under paragraph (9) will be for an amount to be decided by the court and costs.

Practice Direction—See PD14, paras 3.1–3.3 at p 584, paras 4.1–4.3 at p 585 and paras 5.1–5.6 at p 585.

Scope of provision—The rule provides for where the only claim is for an unspecified amount of money and the defendant admits liability and offers to pay a specified amount in satisfaction.

Form of admission—N9C, which the defendant files with the court.

'the court will serve a notice on the claimant' (r 14.7(3))—See Form N226.

'the claim is stayed' (r 14.7(4))—See note to r 14.5(5) above.

'the claimant ... may obtain judgment by filing a request in the relevant practice form' (r 14.7(5))—Form N226.

'if the defendant has not requested time to pay' (r 14.7(5)(a))—Oddly, where an admission is made without a request for time to pay, the claimant has a choice as to whether to apply for judgment under this Part or under r 12.3. Entry of judgment under Pt 12 clearly implies rejection of the offer (r 12.5(3)). Accordingly it is more appropriate to proceed under r 14.7(9) above. Where the offer is accepted judgment should be taken under r 14.7(5).

'the court will enter judgment' (r 14.7(7))—If the claimant accepts the defendant's offer, judgment will be on Form N17. The procedural judge will at the time judgment is entered also give directions which will be set out in the N17.

A judgment under this rule for an amount to be decided by the court will be a relevant order as defined in PD26, para 12.1(2)(b).

'costs' (r 14.7(8))—Where the claimant accepts the defendant's offer, the costs are not fixed under r 45.4, Table 3, and will therefore have to be assessed by the court; a solicitor applying for such a judgment may consider it worthwhile to file at the same time a statement of costs containing the information set out in PDCosts, para 13.5(2).

'if the claimant does not accept the amount' (r 14.7(9))—If the claimant does not accept the defendant's offer then the costs will normally be assessed by the court at the conclusion of a disposal hearing (note PD26, para 12.5).

Time to pay and redetermination—See rr 14.9–14.13 inclusive.

Automatic transfer—A claim for an unspecified amount of money is not automatically transferred to the defendant's home court (see r 14.5).

Appeal—See note **'allocate the case'** under r 14.8.

14.8 Allocation of claims in relation to outstanding matters

Where the court enters judgment under rule 14.6 or 14.7 for an amount to be decided by the court it will –

(a) give any directions it considers appropriate; and
(b) if it considers it appropriate, allocate the case.

General note—This rule must be read in conjunction with PD26, para 12. Allocation to track will not normally be considered unless either the small claims track is appropriate or there are substantial grounds for disputing the amount payable (see PD26, para 12.3).

'directions' (r 14.8(a))—These could involve disclosure of documents (see Pt 31), evidence (see Pt 32) and experts (see Pt 35).

'allocate the case' (r 14.8(b))—Where a district judge decides the amount at a disposal hearing and does not allocate the claim to the multi-track, an appeal will lie to the circuit judge, even though this is a final decision for the purposes of PD52, paras 2A.1–2A.6. The Court of Appeal has no jurisdiction to hear the appeal unless the claim has been allocated to the multi-track (*Jenkins v BP Oil (UK) Ltd & anor* heard together with *Clark (Inspector of Taxes) v Perks* [2000] 1 WLR 17, CA).

14.9 Request for time to pay

(1) A defendant who makes an admission under rules 14.4, 14.5 or 14.7 (admission relating to a claim for a specified amount of money or offering to pay a specified amount of money) may make a request for time to pay.

(2) A request for time to pay is a proposal about the date of payment or a proposal to pay by instalments at the times and rate specified in the request.

(3) The defendant's request for time to pay must be served or filed (as the case may be) with his admission.

(4) If the claimant accepts the defendant's request, he may obtain judgment by filing a request in the relevant practice form.

(5) On receipt of the request for judgment, the court will enter judgment.

(6) Judgment will be –

(a) where rule 14.4 applies, for the amount of the claim (less any payments made) and costs;

(b) where rule 14.5 applies, for the amount admitted (less any payments made) and costs; or

(c) where rule 14.7 applies, for the amount offered by the defendant (less any payments made) and costs; and

(in all cases) will be for payment at the time and rate specified in the defendant's request for time to pay.

(Rule 14.10 sets out the procedure to be followed if the claimant does not accept the defendant's request for time to pay)

Practice Direction—See PD14, paras 4.1–4.3 at p 585 and paras 5.1–5.6 at p 585.

Scope of provision—A request for time to pay may occur:

(a) under r 14.4 – admission of the whole of a claim for a specified amount;

(b) under r 14.5 – acceptance by the claimant of a defendant's offer in satisfaction of a claim for a specified amount;

(c) under r 14.7 – acceptance by the claimant of a defendant's offer in satisfaction of a claim for an unspecified amount.

Rule 14.9 covers the situation where the defendant's offer to pay over time is accepted by the claimant (cf r 14.10 where it is not).

Forms—The relevant forms for the admission and request for time to pay are those referred to in the notes to rr 14.4, 14.5 and 14.7 above.

Judgment is obtained by the claimant filing a request in Form 225A. Judgment is entered for payment at the time and rate specified in the defendant's request.

14.10 Determination of rate of payment

(1) This rule applies where the defendant makes a request for time to pay under rule 14.9.

(2) If the claimant does not accept the defendant's proposals for payment, he must file a notice in the relevant practice form.

(3) Where the defendant's admission was served direct on the claimant, a copy of the admission and the request for time to pay must be filed with the claimant's notice.

(4) When the court receives the claimant's notice, it will enter judgment for the amount admitted (less any payments made) to be paid at the time and rate of payment determined by the court.

Practice Direction—See PD14, paras 4.1–4.3 at p 585 and paras 5.1–5.6 at p 585.

Scope of provision—This rule covers the same three situations as set out in r 14.9(1) but where the defendant's offer to pay over time is not accepted by the claimant.

'Where the defendant's admission was served direct on the claimant' (r 14.10(3))—This should only happen under r 14.4 but in practice can arise otherwise.

Varying the rate of payment—A rate, once determined, may be subsequently varied on an application under Pt 23 (see PD14, para 6).

Forms—The relevant forms for the admission and request for time to pay are those referred to in the notes to rr 14.4, 14.5 and 14.7.

Judgment is obtained by the claimant filing a request in Form 225A. Judgment is entered for the admitted amount to be paid at a time and rate decided by the court.

14.11 Determination of rate of payment by court officer

(1) A court officer may exercise the powers of the court under rule 14.10(4) where the amount outstanding (including costs) is not more than £50,000.

(2) Where a court officer is to determine the time and rate of payment, he must do so without a hearing.

Practice Direction—See PD14, paras 5.1–5.6 at p 585.

Scope of provision—The court officer will normally determine the time and rate of payment where the amount outstanding, which must include interest as well as costs, is not more than £50,000. Either party dissatisfied with the court officer's determination may seek a redetermination by a judge under r 14.13. Exceptionally, if the court officer is unable to determine, he may refer the matter to the master or district judge.

Varying the rate of payment—A rate once determined may be subsequently varied on an application under Pt 23 (see PD14, para 6).

14.12 Determination of rate of payment by judge

(1) Where a judge is to determine the time and rate of payment, he may do so without a hearing.

(2) Where a judge is to determine the time and rate of payment at a hearing, the proceedings must be transferred automatically to the defendant's home court if –

(a) the only claim is for a specified amount of money;
(b) the defendant is an individual;
(c) the claim has not been transferred to another defendant's home court under rule 13.4 (application to set aside(GL) or vary default judgment – procedure) or rule 26.2 (automatic transfer);
(d) the claim was not started in the defendant's home court; and
(e) the claim was not started in a specialist list.

(Rule 2.3 explains which court is a defendant's home court)

(3) If there is to be a hearing to determine the time and rate of payment, the court must give each party at least 7 days' notice of the hearing.

Practice Direction—See PD14, paras 5.1–5.6 at p 585.

Scope of provision—This rule will only apply if the amount outstanding is more than £50,000 or where the court officer declines to determine the time for and the rate of payment.

Automatic transfer to the defendant's home court—This will arise only if:
(a) the master or district judge orders a hearing (see below);
(b) the admission is made under rr 14.4 and 14.5 (where the claim is for a specified amount);
(c) the defendant is an individual; and
(d) the claim was not started in the defendant's home court (see note to r 26.2).

Note the definition of defendant's home court in r 2.3: as from 2 October 2000 the defendant's home court is determined by where he resides or carries on business rather than by any address for service stated in an acknowledgment of service or defence, although that court may in turn transfer the case to another court if that is more convenient. Where the claim form is issued in the Royal Courts of Justice the defendant's home court will be the district registry for the district where the defendant resides or carries on business. If there is no such district registry the case will remain at the Royal Courts of Justice.

'a hearing' (r 14.12(1))—The necessity for a hearing will only arise when the judge is unable to determine the rate of payment on the information before him. This may arise where the information given by the defendant is inadequate or where the claimant significantly disputes the information given by the defendant.

Varying the rate of payment—See the note above to r 14.11.

14.13 Right of re-determination

(1) Where –

- (a) a court officer has determined the time and rate of payment under rule 14.11; or
- (b) a judge has determined the time and rate of payment under rule 14.12 without a hearing,

either party may apply for the decision to be re-determined by a judge.

(2) An application for re-determination must be made within 14 days after service of the determination on the applicant.

(3) Where an application for re-determination is made, the proceedings must be transferred to the defendant's home court if –

- (a) the only claim (apart from a claim for interest or costs) is for a specified amount of money;
- (b) the defendant is an individual;
- (c) the claim has not been transferred to another defendant's home court under rule 13.4 (application to set aside(GL) or vary default judgment – procedure) or rule 26.2 (automatic transfer);
- (d) the claim was not started in the defendant's home court; and
- (e) the claim was not started in a specialist list.

(Rule 2.3 explains which court is a defendant's home court)

Practice Direction—See PD14, paras 6.1–6.2 at p 586.

'defendant's home court' (r 14.13(3))—See the note to r 14.12.

Hearing—If the original determination was made by a court officer, the judge deciding the application may do so without a hearing (see PD14, para 5.4). A redetermination of a judge's decision must involve a hearing unless the parties agree otherwise (PD14, para 5.5).

Evidence—Neither rule nor practice direction state how evidence is to be presented to the court when it is conducting an oral redetermination. Practice in the county courts has been to permit the parties to present oral evidence rather than to require a witness statement. This practice may change with the use of the application notice Form N244. See also r 32.2.

14.14 Interest

(1) Judgment under rule 14.4 (admission of whole of claim for specified amount of money) shall include the amount of interest claimed to the date of judgment if –

- (a) the particulars of claim include the details required by rule 16.4;
- (b) where interest is claimed under section 35A of the Supreme Court Act 1981 or section 69 of the County Courts Act 1984, the rate is no higher than the rate of interest payable on judgment debts at the date when the claim form was issued; and

(c) the claimant's request for judgment includes a calculation of the interest claimed for the period from the date up to which interest was stated to be calculated in the claim form to the date of the request for judgment.

(2) In any case where judgment is entered under rule 14.4 and the conditions in paragraph (1) are not satisfied judgment shall be for an amount of interest to be decided by the court.

(3) Where judgment is entered for an amount of interest to be decided by the court, the court will give directions for the management of the case.

Scope of provision—This rule only applies to judgments entered under r 14.4. It need not apply to those entered under r 14.5 as the interest is either included in any sum acceptable to the claimant or the claimant proceeds with his claim; similarly under r 14.7 the interest is either included in the judgment obtained under r 14.7(8) or judgment is for an amount to be decided by the court pursuant to r 14.7(10).

Rate of interest—In the absence of any specific contractual right to interest, the current statutory rate is 8% a year.

Specialist jurisdictions—Rule 14.14(1)(a) applies to claims issued out of the Commercial Court or a mercantile court with the modification that the reference to the particulars of claim shall be read as if it referred to the claim form (r 58.9(3) and r 59.4(3)).

Practice Direction – Admissions

This Practice Direction supplements CPR Part 14 (PD14)

Procedural Guide—See Guide 6, set out in Section 1 of this work.

General note—See also the notes to CPR Pt 14.

ADMISSIONS GENERALLY

1.1 Rules 14.1 and 14.2 deal with the manner in which a defendant may make an admission of a claim or part of a claim.

1.2 Rules 14.3, 14.4, 14.5, 14.6 and 14.7 set out how judgment may be obtained on a written admission.

FORMS

2.1 When particulars of claim are served on a defendant the forms for responding to the claim that will accompany them will include a form[1] for making an admission.

1 Practice forms N9A (specified amount) or N9C (unspecified amount).

2.2 If the defendant is requesting time to pay he should complete as fully as possible the statement of means contained in the admission form, or otherwise give in writing the same details of his means as could have been given in the admission form.

RETURNING OR FILING THE ADMISSION

3.1 If the defendant wishes to make an admission in respect of the whole of a claim for a specified amount of money, the admission form or other written notice of the admission should be completed and returned to the claimant within 14 days of service of the particulars of claim[1].

1 Rules 14.2 and 14.4.

3.2 If the defendant wishes to make an admission in respect of a part of a claim for a specified amount of money, or in respect of a claim for an unspecified amount of money, the admission form or other written notice of admission should be completed and filed with the court within 14 days of service of the particulars of claim[1].

1 Rules 14.2 14.5, 14.6 and 14.7.

3.3 The defendant may also file a defence under rule 15.2.

'within 14 days of service' (paras 3.1 and 3.2)—If a defendant requires more time to consider whether to defend, he may file an acknowledgment of service (r 9.2). The period of 14 days is extended where the claim form is served outside the jurisdiction (CPR rr 6.21(4) and 6.22).

REQUEST FOR TIME TO PAY

4.1 A defendant who makes an admission in respect of a claim for a specified sum of money or offers to pay a sum of money in respect of a claim for an unspecified sum may, in the admission form, make a request for time to pay[1].

1 Rule 14.9.

4.2 If the claimant accepts the defendant's request, he may obtain judgment by filing a request for judgment contained in practice form N225A[1]; the court will then enter judgment for payment at the time and rate specified in the defendant's request[2].

1 Rule 14.9(4).
2 Rule 14.9(5) and (6).

4.3 If the claimant does not accept the request for time to pay, he should file notice to that effect by completing practice form N225A; the court will then enter judgment for the amount of the admission (less any payments made) at a time and rate of payment decided by the court (see rule 14.10).

DETERMINING THE RATE OF PAYMENT

5.1 In deciding the time and rate of payment the court will take into account:

(1) the defendant's statement of means set out in the admission form or in any other written notice of the admission filed,
(2) the claimant's objections to the defendant's request set out in the claimant's notice[1], and
(3) any other relevant factors.

1 Practice form N225A.

5.2 The time and rate of payment may be decided:

(1) by a judge with or without a hearing, or
(2) by a court officer without a hearing provided that –
   (a) the only claim is for a specified sum of money, and
   (b) the amount outstanding is not more than £50,000 (including costs).

5.3 Where a decision has been made without a hearing whether by a court officer or by a judge, either party may apply for the decision to be re-determined by a judge[1].

1 Rule 14.13(1).

5.4 If the decision was made by a court officer the re-determination may take place without a hearing, unless a hearing is requested in the application notice.

5.5 If the decision was made by a judge the re-determination must be made at a hearing unless the parties otherwise agree.

5.6 Rule 14.13(2) describes how to apply for a re-determination.

'any other relevant factors' (para 5.1(3))—This expression is not defined. Whether the debt was personal or business, the age and amount of the debt and the manner in which the debt was incurred would all be relevant factors.

VARYING THE RATE OF PAYMENT

6.1 Either party may, on account of a change in circumstances since the date of the decision (or redetermination as the case may be) apply to vary the time and rate of payment of instalments still remaining unpaid.

6.2 An application to vary under paragraph 6.1 above should be made in accordance with Part 23.

PART 15
DEFENCE AND REPLY

CONTENTS OF THIS PART

Procedural Guide—See Guide 7, set out in Section 1 of this work.

Money Claim Online—Where the claim has been electronically issued using the Money Claim Online facility, the defendant is able to file a defence electronically. For more information see r 7.12, PD7E and Guide 4. If a defendant who is an individual files a defence, and Northampton County Court is not his home court, the court will transfer the claim to the defendant's home court. Where the defendant is not an individual, the court will transfer the claim to the court for the district in which the claimant's address for service on the claim form is situated (PD7E, para 14).

Electronic filing of defence and reply—Special provisions apply in relation to courts which have published an e-mail address on the Court Service website; in these instances it is possible to file specified documents, including a defence and reply, by e-mail (see generally PD5B). Special provisions exist in relation to the county courts at Basildon, Birmingham, Bournemouth, Coventry, Dartford, Leicester, Llangefni, Norwich and Preston.

15.1 Part not to apply where claimant uses the Part 8 procedure

This Part does not apply where the claimant uses the procedure set out in Part 8 (alternative procedure for claims).

Practice Direction—See PD15, paras 1.1–1.4 at p 592.

Scope of provision—As a defendant is not required to file a defence under the Pt 8 procedure, Pt 15 does not apply (r 8.9(a)(ii)).

15.2 Filing a defence

A defendant who wishes to defend all or part of a claim must file a defence.

(Part 14 contains further provisions which apply where the defendant admits a claim)

Practice Direction—See generally PD15 at p 591.

Forms—Form N9B (specified amount) or N9D (unspecified amount of money or non-money claim) may be used.

Contents of defence—See generally rr 16.5 and 16.6, PD16, paras 10–15 inclusive and Pt 22 (statement of truth). Additionally, a defence should seek to further the overriding objective in r 1.1 and enable the court to identify the relevant issues in the case (r 1.4(2)(b)–(d) inclusive).

Power to strike out a defence—The court may strike out a defence if it discloses no reasonable grounds for defending a claim, is an abuse of the court's process or fails to comply with a rule, practice direction or other order (r 3.4(2) and the practice direction supplementing it, especially PD3, para 3). The court may exercise this power of its own initiative (r 3.3).

Defence coupled with a part admission—See r 14.5.

Possession claims under Pt 55—In a possession claim against trespassers r 15.2 does not apply (r 55.7(2)).

'must file a defence' (r 15.2)—This confirms the previous county court practice where the defence is filed with the court, as opposed to that in the High Court, where the defence was served on the claimant.

15.3 Consequence of not filing a defence

If a defendant fails to file a defence, the claimant may obtain default judgment if Part 12 allows it.

'if Part 12 allows it' (r 15.3)—See the exceptions in rr 12.2 and 12.3 and the notes thereto.

Counterclaims—Following an amendment to r 12.3(2) it has since 2 May 2000 been possible to obtain a default judgment against a defendant to a counterclaim.

15.4 The period for filing a defence

(1) The general rule is that the period for filing a defence is –

- (a) 14 days after service of the particulars of claim; or
- (b) if the defendant files an acknowledgment of service under Part 10, 28 days after service of the particulars of claim.

(Rule 7.4 provides for the particulars of claim to be contained in or served with the claim form or served within 14 days of service of the claim form)

(2) The general rule is subject to the following rules –

- (a) Rule 6.23 (which specifies how the period for filing a defence is calculated where the claim form is served out of the jurisdiction);
- (b) rule 11 (which provides that, where the defendant makes an application disputing the court's jurisdiction, he need not file a defence before the hearing);
- (c) rule 24.4(2) (which provides that, if the claimant applies for summary judgment before the defendant has filed a defence, the defendant need not file a defence before the summary judgment hearing); and
- (d) rule 6.16(4) (which requires the court to specify the period for responding to the particulars of claim when it makes an order under that rule).

Amendments—SI 2000/940.

Practice Direction—See generally PD15 at p 591.

Probate claims—The general rule set out in r 15.4(1)(b) applies in such claims as if the words 'under Part 10' were deleted (r 57.4(4)).

Time—For the computation of time, see r 2.8.

'after service of the particulars of claim' (r 15.4(1)(a))—Note that time runs from service of the particulars and not from service of a claim form, unless it contains or accompanies the particulars of claim themselves. For the time for service of particulars of claim, see r 7.4.

'an acknowledgment of service' (r 15.4(1)(b))—Rule 10.1(3) envisages that a defendant will not file an acknowledgment of service if at that time he is actually able to file his defence.

'Rule 6.16(4)' (r 15.4(2)(d))—This rule specifies that when the court permits a claim form relating to a contract to be served on a defendant's agent the order must specify the period within which the defendant must respond to the particulars.

Extension of time—An application to the court for an extension of time must be made in accordance with Pt 23. The court has a general discretion as to what, if any, extra time to allow; the court should consider a properly arguable defence, however tardy the defendant may be in making his application for further time (*Johnson & anor v Coburn* (1999) (unreported), 24 November, CA). On an application on notice for judgment in default, the claimant being unable merely to *request* such judgment, the matter becomes one of the court's discretion, although the discretion would normally be exercised in favour of extending time (*Coll v Tattum* (2002) 99(03) LSG 26, (2001) *The Times*, 3 December, Neuberger J).

15.5 Agreement extending the period for filing a defence

(1) The defendant and the claimant may agree that the period for filing a defence specified in rule 15.4 shall be extended by up to 28 days.

(2) Where the defendant and the claimant agree to extend the period for filing a defence, the defendant must notify the court in writing.

'shall be extended by up to 28 days' (r 15.5(1))—A combination of r 15.4(1)(b) and r 15.5 means that, at most, a defendant has 56 days from the service of the particulars of claim within which to file a defence. If yet further time is needed an application must be made to the court under Pt 23, supported by evidence, relying on the court's power to extend time in r 3.1(2)(a).

'the defendant must notify the court in writing' (r 15.5(2))—There is no practice form. A letter will suffice.

15.6 Service of copy of defence

A copy of the defence must be served on every other party.

(Part 16 sets out what a defence must contain)

(The costs practice direction sets out the information about a funding arrangement to be provided with the defence where the defendant intends to seek to recover an additional liability)

('Funding arrangement' and 'additional liability' are defined in rule 43.2)

Amendments—SI 2000/1317.

Scope of provision—This rule does not indicate by whom the copy defences are served. Forms N9B and N9D merely direct the defendant to complete the relevant form and return it to the court. Best practice dictates that the defendant file sufficient copies of the defence with the court, for the court then to serve the parties together with the forms of allocation questionnaire for completion. This is the current expectation of the Court Service.

'The costs practice direction sets out the information about a funding arrangement to be provided with the defence' (s 15.6 note)—See generally PDCosts, Section 19 and Form N251 Notice of Funding of Case or Claim.

Production centre—Special provisions apply where a defence is filed to a claim issued in Northampton County Court through its Production Centre (PD7C, para 5.2). Also, more generally, note PD7C, para 1.3(2)(e) for the transfer of a case to an individual's home court when he/she files a defence at the Production Centre and for the transfer of all other defended cases issued out of the Production Centre to the court for the area of the claimant's, or where he is represented his solicitor's, address.

15.7 Making a counterclaim

Part 20 applies to a defendant who wishes to make a counterclaim.

Practice Direction—See PD15, paras 2.1–2.3 at p 592 and paras 3.1–3.4 at p 592.

'Part 20'—Note in particular r 20.4 dealing with a defendant's counterclaim against a claimant and the requirements of PD15, para 3.1.

15.8 Reply to defence

If a claimant files a reply to the defence, he must –

(a) file his reply when he files his allocation questionnaire; and
(b) serve his reply on the other parties at the same time as he files it.

(Rule 26.3(6) requires the parties to file allocation questionnaires and specifies the period for doing so)

(Part 22 requires a reply to be verified by a statement of truth)

Practice Direction—See PD15, paras 2.1–2.3 at p 592 and paras 3.1–3.4 at p 592.

'a reply' (r 15.8)—For the contents of a reply, see r 16.7. Also note PD15, para 3.2, where a claimant serves both a reply and defence to counterclaim,

'when he files his allocation questionnaire' (r 15.8(a))—Under r 26.3(6), a claimant must file a completed allocation questionnaire no later than the date specified in it, which must be at least 14 days after the court served it on the claimant.

Reply and defence to counterclaim—Under r 15.8 a claimant who files a reply to the defence must file his reply with his allocation questionnaire. Paragraph 3.2 of PD15 requires that, where a claimant serves a reply and a defence to counterclaim, these should form one document. The defence to counterclaim is due 14 days after service of the counterclaim but under r 26.3(6) the date for filing a completed allocation questionnaire is *at least* 14 days after the date it is served by the court. Paragraph 3.2A of PD15 seeks to resolve this problem by stipulating that the court in such circumstances will normally order that the defence to counterclaim be filed by the same date as the reply, ie with the allocation questionnaire; where the court does not make such an order the reply and defence to counterclaim may form separate documents.

Specialist jurisdictions—Rule 15.8 is modified in relation to claims in the commercial list (r 58.10(1)), to mercantile claims (r 59.9(1)) and to Technology and Construction Court claims (r 60.5).

Payment of fee—A fee is payable when a counterclaim is filed unless the defendant successfully applies either for an exemption from or remission of the fee. For the fee, see the CPFO 2004 (as amended) in Section 6 of this work. For the consequences of failing to comply with these provisions, see r 3.7A; for the sanctions for dishonouring a cheque, see r 3.7B.

15.9 No statement of case after a reply to be filed without court's permission

A party may not file or serve any statement of case after a reply without the permission of the court.

Scope of provision—This rule prevents service of rejoinders and other pleadings rarely experienced prior to implementation of the CPR. A defendant may, however, wish in such circumstances to consider amending his defence.

15.10 Claimant's notice where defence is that money claimed has been paid

(1) Where –

(a) the only claim (apart from a claim for costs and interest) is for a specified amount of money; and
(b) the defendant states in his defence that he has paid to the claimant the amount claimed,

the court will send notice to the claimant requiring him to state in writing whether he wishes the proceedings to continue.

(2) When the claimant responds, he must serve a copy of his response on the defendant.

(3) If the claimant fails to respond under this rule within 28 days after service of the court's notice on him the claim shall be stayed(GL).

(4) Where a claim is stayed under this rule any party may apply for the stay(GL) to be lifted.

(If the claimant files notice under this rule that he wishes the proceedings to continue, the procedure which then follows is set out in Part 26)

Scope of provision—This rule adopts the former CCR 'states paid' procedure.

'the court will send notice' (r 15.10(1))—See Form N236.

'the claim shall be stayed' (r 15.10(3))—See the note to r 14.5(5) above.

'any party may apply for the stay to be lifted' (r 15.10(4))—If a claimant wishes to restore an action which has been stayed, then an application must be made to lift the stay and the application fee paid. When both parties are aware that a stay has been imposed, both have a right to be heard if any application to lift the stay is made. The presumption is that the application will be on notice.

Allocation questionnaire—Where the defendant files a 'states paid' defence, no allocation questionnaire is served by the court unless and until the claimant indicates he wishes to continue the proceedings (r 26.3(1)(a) and r 26.3(4)).

Transfer to defendant's home court—If the criteria for automatic transfer apply (r 26.2(1)), then the transfer is effected only on receipt by the court of notification from the claimant that he wishes to continue the proceedings.

15.11 Claim stayed if it is not defended or admitted

(1) Where –

(a) at least 6 months have expired since the end of the period for filing a defence specified in rule 15.4;

(b) no defendant has served or filed an admission or filed a defence or counterclaim; and

(c) the claimant has not entered or applied for judgment under Part 12 (default judgment), or Part 24 (summary judgment),

the claim shall be stayed(GL).

(2) Where a claim is stayed(GL) under this rule any party may apply for the stay to be lifted.

Scope of provision—This rule provides for an automatic stay if no defence or admission has been served at least 6 months after they were due to be filed and yet the claimant has not sought a judgment. The rule does not apply to Pt 8 claims (r 15.1).

Application to lift the stay—Such an application will be made under Pt 23, supported by evidence. Whilst PD15, para 3.4 merely says that whichever party is applying should give the reason for the delay in proceeding with or responding to the claim, an applicant would do well to have in mind the specific provisions of r 3.9.

Interim injunctions—As the stay under r 15.11 will not have been by agreement between the parties, the effect of r 25.10 on a case stayed under this rule is to set aside any interim injunction which may have been granted unless the court specifically orders otherwise.

Practice Direction – Defence and Reply

This Practice Direction supplements CPR Part 15 (PD15)

Procedural Guide—See Guide 7, set out in Section 1 of this work.

General note—See also the notes to CPR Pt 15.

Money Claim Online—The procedure for filing a defence is somewhat different where the claim has been electronically issued using the Money Claim Online facility. For more information see PD7E, para 7 and Guide 4.

DEFENDING THE CLAIM

1.1 The provisions of Part 15 do not apply to claims in respect of which the Part 8 procedure is being used.

1.2 In relation to specialist proceedings (see CPR Part 49) in respect of which special provisions for defence and reply are made by the rules and practice directions applicable to those claims, the provisions of Part 15 apply only to the extent that they are not inconsistent with those rules and practice directions.

1.3 Form N9B (specified amount) or N9D (unspecified amount or non-money claims) may be used for the purpose of defence and is included in the response pack served on the defendant with the particulars of claim.

1.4 Attention is drawn to rule 15.3 which sets out a possible consequence of not filing a defence.

(Part 16 (statements of case) and the practice direction which supplements it contain rules and directions about the contents of a defence)

(The Costs Practice Direction supplementing Parts 43 to 48 contains details of the information required to be filed with a claim form to comply with rule 44.15 (providing information about funding arrangements))

'Specialist proceedings' (para 1.2)—With the exception of proceedings under the Companies Acts 1985–1989 and Patent Court business, CPR Pt 49 no longer applies to the specialist jurisdictions and reference instead should be made to CPR Pts 58–62.

Content of defence—In addition to the matters raised in the practice direction, attention is also directed to:

(a) PD7, para 4: the title of proceedings;
(b) CPR r 16.5: the contents of a defence;
(c) CPR r 16.6: the defence of set-off;
(d) PD16, paras 10–15: the content of a defence.

STATEMENT OF TRUTH

2.1 Part 22 requires a defence to be verified by a statement of truth.

2.2 The form of the statement of truth is as follows:

'[I believe][the defendant believes] that the facts stated in this defence are true.'

2.3 Attention is drawn to rule 32.14 which sets out the consequences of verifying a statement of case containing a false statement without an honest belief in its truth.

(For information about statements of truth see Part 22 and the practice direction which supplements it)

GENERAL

3.1 Where a defendant to a claim serves a counterclaim under Part 20, the defence and counterclaim should normally form one document with the counterclaim following on from the defence.

3.2 Where a claimant serves a reply and a defence to counterclaim, the reply and defence to counterclaim should normally form one document with the defence to counterclaim following on from the reply.

3.2A Rule 15.8(a) provides that a claimant must file any reply with his allocation questionnaire. Where the date by which he must file his allocation questionnaire is later than the date by which he must file his defence to counterclaim (because the time for filing the allocation questionnaire under the court will normally order that the defence to counterclaim must be filed by the same date as the reply. Where the court does not make such an order the reply and defence to counterclaim may form separate documents.

3.3 Where a claim has been stayed under rules 15.10(3) or 15.11(1) any party may apply for the stay to be lifted[1].

1 Rules 15.10(4) and 15.11(2).

3.4 The application should be made in accordance with Part 23 and should give the reason for the applicant's delay in proceeding with or responding to the claim.

(Paragraph 8.3 of the practice direction supplementing Part 6 (Service of documents) makes provision for the service on the claimant of any notice of funding filed with an acknowledgment of service)

'the court will normally order that the defence to counterclaim must be filed by the same date as the reply' (para 3.2A)—That is to say with the allocation questionnaire (r 15.8).

PART 16
STATEMENTS OF CASE

CONTENTS OF THIS PART

16.1 Part not to apply where claimant uses Part 8 procedure

This Part does not apply where the claimant uses the procedure set out in Part 8 (alternative procedure for claims).

Practice Direction—See generally PD16 at p 598.

'Part 8'—This Part applies to all claims except those set out in Pt 8, ie where there is unlikely to be a substantial dispute of fact or where Pt 8 procedure is specifically prescribed. See also PD16, para 1.2.

16.2 Contents of the claim form

(1) The claim form must –

(a) contain a concise statement of the nature of the claim;
(b) specify the remedy which the claimant seeks;
(c) where the claimant is making a claim for money, contain a statement of value in accordance with rule 16.3; and
(d) contain such other matters as may be set out in a practice direction.

(1A) In civil proceedings against the Crown, as defined in rule 66.1(2), the claim form must also contain –

(a) the names of the government departments and officers of the Crown concerned; and
(b) brief details of the circumstances in which it is alleged that the liability of the Crown arose.

(2) If the particulars of claim specified in rule 16.4 are not contained in, or are not served with the claim form, the claimant must state on the claim form that the particulars of claim will follow.

(3) If the claimant is claiming in a representative capacity, the claim form must state what that capacity is.

(4) If the defendant is sued in a representative capacity, the claim form must state what that capacity is.

(5) The court may grant any remedy to which the claimant is entitled even if that remedy is not specified in the claim form.

(Part 22 requires a claim form to be verified by a statement of truth)

(The costs practice direction sets out the information about a funding arrangement to be provided with the statement of case where the defendant intends to seek to recover an additional liability)

('Funding arrangement' and 'additional liability' are defined in rule 43.2)

Amendments—SI 2000/1317; SI 2005/2292.

Practice Direction—See generally PD16 at p 598.

General note—Statements of case have never been more important in civil litigation. While no case should ever founder because of a pleading technicality, it should not be assumed that an error of substance can easily be put right. The reason is to be found in Pt 22 and the requirement for statements of case to be verified by a statement of truth (see that Part (and, very importantly, r 32.14) for further guidance). Once a party wishes to alter the factual basis of a claim or defence to the truth of which he has already deposed, his credibility is at stake. Compared with that risk, the cost of making amendments is of secondary significance. Taking full instructions at the outset, accurately setting them out in the statement of case, and having the lay client make the statement of truth wherever practicable, is best practice for lawyers. Otherwise, it is essential to obtain the client's confirmation that the contents are true before the lawyer signs. This Part is to be read closely throughout with PD16.

'nature of the claim' (r 16.2(1))—Read together with r 16.4(1)(a), this rule requires a claimant to set out the basic facts of the case and its nature. These two elements will show whether or not there are reasonable grounds for bringing the claim.

16.3 Statement of value to be included in the claim form

(1) This rule applies where the claimant is making a claim for money.

(2) The claimant must, in the claim form, state –

- (a) the amount of money which he is claiming;
- (b) that he expects to recover –
  - (i) not more than £5000;
  - (ii) more than £5000 but not more than £15,000; or
  - (iii) more than £15,000; or
- (c) that he cannot say how much he expects to recover.

(3) In a claim for personal injuries, the claimant must also state in the claim form whether the amount which he expects to recover as general damages for pain, suffering and loss of amenity is –

- (a) not more than £1000; or
- (b) more than £1000.

[(4) In a claim which includes a claim by a tenant of residential premises against his landlord where the tenant is seeking an order requiring the landlord to carry out repairs or other work to the premises, the claimant must also state in the claim form –

- (a) whether the estimated costs of those repairs or other work is –
  - (i) not more than £1000; or
  - (ii) more than £1000; and
- (b) whether the financial value of any other claim for damages is –
  - (i) not more than £1000; or
  - (ii) more than £1000.]

(5) If the claim form is to be issued in the High Court it must, where this rule applies –

- (a) state that the claimant expects to recover more than £15,000;
- (b) state that some other enactment provides that the claim may be commenced only in the High Court and specify that enactment;

(c) if the claim is a claim for personal injuries state that the claimant expects to recover £50,000 or more; or
(d) state that the claim is to be in one of the specialist High Court lists and state which list.

(6) When calculating how much he expects to recover, the claimant must disregard any possibility –

(a) that he may recover –
  (i) interest;
  (ii) costs;
(b) that the court may make a finding of contributory negligence against him;
(c) that the defendant may make a counterclaim or that the defence may include a set-off; or
(d) that the defendant may be liable to pay an amount of money which the court awards to the claimant to the Secretary of State for Social Security under section 6 of the Social Security (Recovery of Benefits) Act 1997.

(7) The statement of value in the claim form does not limit the power of the court to give judgment for the amount which it finds the claimant is entitled to.

Amendments—SI 1999/1008.

Practice Direction—See generally PD16 at p 598.

16.4 Contents of the particulars of claim

(1) Particulars of claim must include –

(a) a concise statement of the facts on which the claimant relies;
(b) if the claimant is seeking interest, a statement to that effect and the details set out in paragraph (2);
(c) if the claimant is seeking aggravated damages(GL) or exemplary damages(GL), a statement to that effect and his grounds for claiming them;
(d) if the claimant is seeking provisional damages, a statement to that effect and his grounds for claiming them; and
(e) such other matters as may be set out in a practice direction.

(2) If the claimant is seeking interest he must –

(a) state whether he is doing so –
  (i) under the terms of a contract;
  (ii) under an enactment and if so which; or
  (iii) on some other basis and if so what that basis is; and
(b) if the claim is for a specified amount of money, state –
  (i) the percentage rate at which interest is claimed;
  (ii) the date from which it is claimed;
  (iii) the date to which it is calculated, which must not be later than the date on which the claim form is issued;
  (iv) the total amount of interest claimed to the date of calculation; and
  (v) the daily rate at which interest accrues after that date.

(Part 22 requires particulars of claim to be verified by a statement of truth)

Practice Direction—See generally PD16 at p 598.

'the facts' (r 16.4(1)(a))—Artifice is not to be replaced by artlessness. Telling the story is not the same as giving a concise statement of facts to be relied on. Drafting a statement of case still involves a clear understanding of the difference between facts and the evidence which will be used to prove them. Only the former are to be included. An excessively discursive or unfocussed document is liable to be struck out as 'likely to obstruct the just disposal of the proceedings' (r 3.4(2)(b)). But no essential *facts* should be omitted.

'such other matters' (r 16.4(1)(e))—For personal injury, fatal accident, recovery of land and hire purchase claims, see PD16, paras 4, 5, 6, and 7 respectively. See PD16, paras 1, 2, 3, 8 and 9 for general matters.

16.5 Contents of defence

(1) In his defence, the defendant must state –

(a) which of the allegations in the particulars of claim he denies;
(b) which allegations he is unable to admit or deny, but which he requires the claimant to prove; and
(c) which allegations he admits.

(2) Where the defendant denies an allegation –

(a) he must state his reasons for doing so; and
(b) if he intends to put forward a different version of events from that given by the claimant, he must state his own version.

(3) A defendant who –

(a) fails to deal with an allegation; but
(b) has set out in his defence the nature of his case in relation to the issue to which that allegation is relevant,

shall be taken to require that allegation to be proved.

(4) Where the claim includes a money claim, a defendant shall be taken to require that any allegation relating to the amount of money claimed be proved unless he expressly admits the allegation.

(5) Subject to paragraphs (3) and (4), a defendant who fails to deal with an allegation shall be taken to admit that allegation.

(6) If the defendant disputes the claimant's statement of value under rule 16.3 he must –

(a) state why he disputes it; and
(b) if he is able, give his own statement of the value of the claim.

(7) If the defendant is defending in a representative capacity, he must state what that capacity is.

(8) If the defendant has not filed an acknowledgment of service under Part 10, he must give an address for service.

(Part 22 requires a defence to be verified by a statement of truth)

(Rule 6.5 provides that an address for service must be within the jurisdiction)

Practice Direction—See generally PD16 at p 598.

'defence' (r 16.5(1))—A tactical or holding defence is not a permissible document. Nor is a defence which denies all allegations or puts a claimant to proof. As much care and attention is needed as in settling particulars of claim and for the same reason (see general note to r 16.2). A defendant is obliged to state his own version of the facts (r 16.5(2)(b)) and verify its truth under Pt 22. If he asserts (r 16.5(1)(b)) that he is unable to admit or deny facts pleaded by the claimant, that assertion itself must be the subject of the statement of truth and cannot be used to cloak an inadequately prepared defence.

16.6 Defence of set-off

Where a defendant –

(a) contends he is entitled to money from the claimant; and
(b) relies on this as a defence to the whole or part of the claim,

the contention may be included in the defence and set off against the claim, whether or not it is also a Part 20 claim.

Practice Direction—See generally PD16 at p 598.

16.7 Reply to defence

(1) A claimant who does not file a reply to the defence shall not be taken to admit the matters raised in the defence.

(2) A claimant who –

(a) files a reply to a defence; but
(b) fails to deal with a matter raised in the defence,

shall be taken to require that matter to be proved.

(Part 22 requires a reply to be verified by a statement of truth)

Practice Direction—See generally PD16 at p 598.

'A claimant … shall not be taken to admit' (r 16.7(1))—This rule, which makes it unnecessary to file a reply simply for the purpose of stating that the defendant's version of facts is not accepted, does not avoid the need for a reply if the defence calls for some further facts to be stated.

16.8 Court's power to dispense with statements of case

If a claim form has been –

(a) issued in accordance with rule 7.2; and
(b) served in accordance with rule 7.5,

the court may make an order that the claim will continue without any other statement of case.

Practice Direction—See generally PD16 at p 598.

Practice Direction – Statements of Case

This Practice Direction supplements CPR Part 16 (PD16)

General note—See also the notes to CPR Pt 16.

GENERAL

1.1 The provisions of Part 16 do not apply to claims in respect of which the Part 8 procedure is being used.

1.2 Where special provisions about statements of case are made by the rules and practice directions applying to particular types of proceedings, the provisions of Part 16 and of this practice direction apply only to the extent that they are not inconsistent with those rules and practice directions.

1.3 Examples of types of proceedings with special provisions about statements of case include –

(1) defamation claims (Part 53);
(2) possession claims (Part 55); and
(3) probate claims (Part 57).

1.4 If exceptionally a statement of case exceeds 25 pages (excluding schedules) an appropriate short summary must also be filed and served.

THE CLAIM FORM

2.1 Rule 16.2 refers to matters which the claim form must contain. Where the claim is for money, the claim form must also contain the statement of value referred to in rule 16.3.

2.2 The claim form must include an address at which the claimant resides or carries on business. This paragraph applies even though the claimant's address for service is the business address of his solicitor.

2.3 Where the defendant is an individual, the claimant should (if he is able to do so) include in the claim form an address at which the defendant resides or carries on business. This paragraph applies even though the defendant's solicitors have agreed to accept service on the defendant's behalf.

Prospective amendment—Paragraphs prospectively inserted: Supplement 40 (issued 30 September 2005), with effect from 6 April 2005:

'2.4 Any address which is provided for the purpose of these provisions must include a postcode, unless the court orders otherwise. Postcode information may be obtained from www.royalmail.com or the Royal Mail Address Management Guide.

2.5 If the claim form does not show a full address, including postcode, at which the claimant(s) and defendant(s) reside or carry on business, the claim form will be issued but will be retained by the court and will not be served until the claimant has supplied a full address, including postcode, or the court has dispensed with the requirement to do so. The court will notify the claimant.

2.6 The claim form must be headed with the title of the proceedings, including the full name of each party. The full name means, in each case where it is known:

(a) in the case of an individual, his full unabbreviated name and title by which he is known;
(b) in the case of an individual carrying on business in a name other than his own name, the full unabbreviated name of the individual, together with the title by which he is known, and the full trading name (for example, John Smith 'trading as' or 'T/as' 'JS Autos');
(c) in the case of a partnership (other than a limited liability partnership (LLP)) –
   (i) where partners are being sued in the name of the partnership, the full name by which the partnership is known, together with the words '(A Firm)'; or
   (ii) where partners are being sued as individuals, the full unabbreviated name of each partner and the title by which he is known;
(d) in the case of a company or limited liability partnership registered in England and Wales, the full registered name, including suffix (plc, limited, LLP, etc), if any;
(e) in the case of any other company or corporation, the full name by which it is known, including suffix where appropriate.

(RSC O81 contains rules about claims made by or against partners in their firm name).'

(For information about how and where a claim may be started see Part 7 and the practice direction which supplements it)

PARTICULARS OF CLAIM

3.1 If practicable, the particulars of claim should be set out in the claim form.

3.2 Where the claimant does not include the particulars of claim in the claim form, particulars of claim may be served separately:

(1) either at the same time as the claim form, or
(2) within 14 days after service of the claim form[1] provided that the service of the particulars of claim is not later than 4 months from the date of issue of the claim form[2] (or 6 months where the claim form is to be served out of the jurisdiction[3]).

1 See rule 7.4(1)(b).
2 See rules 7.4(2) and 7.5(2).
3 See rule 7.5(3).

3.3 If the particulars of claim are not included in or have not been served with the claim form, the claim form must also contain a statement that particulars of claim will follow[1].

1 See rule 16.2(2).

3.4 Particulars of claim which are not included in the claim form must be verified by a statement of truth, the form of which is as follows:

'[I believe][the claimant believes] that the facts stated in these particulars of claim are true.'

3.5 Attention is drawn to rule 32.14 which sets out the consequences of verifying a statement of case containing a false statement without an honest belief in its truth.

3.6 The full particulars of claim must include:

(1) the matters set out in rule 16.4, and
(2) where appropriate, the matters set out in practice directions relating to specific types of claims.

3.7 Attention is drawn to the provisions of rule 16.4(2) in respect of a claim for interest.

3.8 Particulars of claim served separately from the claim form must also contain:

(1) the name of the court in which the claim is proceeding,
(2) the claim number,
(3) the title of the proceedings, and
(4) the claimant's address for service.

Matters which must be Included in the Particulars of Claim in Certain Types of Claim

PERSONAL INJURY CLAIMS

4.1 The particulars of claim must contain:

(1) the claimant's date of birth, and
(2) brief details of the claimant's personal injuries.

4.2 The claimant must attach to his particulars of claim a schedule of details of any past and future expenses and losses which he claims.

4.3 Where the claimant is relying on the evidence of a medical practitioner the claimant must attach to or serve with his particulars of claim a report from a medical practitioner about the personal injuries which he alleges in his claim.

4.4 In a provisional damages claim the claimant must state in his particulars of claim:

(1) that he is seeking an award of provisional damages under either section 32A of the Supreme Court Act 1981 or section 51 of the County Courts Act 1984,
(2) that there is a chance that at some future time the claimant will develop some serious disease or suffer some serious deterioration in his physical or mental condition, and
(3) specify the disease or type of deterioration in respect of which an application may be made at a future date.

(Part 41 and the practice direction which supplements it contain information about awards for provisional damages)

Medical report (para 4.3)—There is a possible ambiguity in this practice direction, which may be read to suggest that a medical report must be served in any case where medical evidence will be required at trial. A personal injury claimant may be unable to succeed without medical evidence, but may not have complied with the Personal Injuries Protocol as to expert evidence and may wish to ask the court to direct a single joint expert (CPR r 35.7). This may well be the situation, for instance, in a fast track claim which has been launched towards the end of a limitation period, where, in addition, the claimant only has a short report from a general practitioner. There seems to be no obligation to serve any medical report with the particulars of claim unless it is the evidence of *that practitioner* on which the claimant is relying.

FATAL ACCIDENT CLAIMS

5.1 In a fatal accident claim the claimant must state in his particulars of claim:

(1) that it is brought under the Fatal Accidents Act 1976,
(2) the dependants on whose behalf the claim is made,
(3) the date of birth of each dependant, and
(4) details of the nature of the dependency claim.

5.2 A fatal accident claim may include a claim for damages for bereavement.

5.3 In a fatal accident claim the claimant may also bring a claim under the Law Reform (Miscellaneous Provisions) Act 1934 on behalf of the estate of the deceased.

(For information on apportionment under the Law Reform (Miscellaneous Provisions) Act 1934 and the Fatal Accidents Act 1976 or between dependants see Part 37 and the practice direction which supplements it)

HIRE PURCHASE CLAIMS

6.1 Where the claim is for the delivery of goods let under a hire-purchase agreement or conditional sale agreement to a person other than a company or other corporation, the claimant must state in the particulars of claim:

(1) the date of the agreement,
(2) the parties to the agreement,
(3) the number or other identification of the agreement,
(4) where the claimant was not one of the original parties to the agreement, the means by which the rights and duties of the creditor passed to him,
(5) whether the agreement is a regulated agreement, and if it is not a regulated agreement, the reason why,
(6) the place where the agreement was signed by the defendant,
(7) the goods claimed,
(8) the total price of the goods,
(9) the paid-up sum,
(10) the unpaid balance of the total price,

(11) whether a default notice or a notice under section 76(1) or 98(1) of the Consumer Credit Act 1974 has been served on the defendant, and if it has, the date and method of service,
(12) the date when the right to demand delivery of the goods accrued,
(13) the amount (if any) claimed as an alternative to the delivery of goods, and
(14) the amount (if any) claimed in addition to
   (a) the delivery of the goods, or
   (b) any claim under (13) above,

with the grounds of each claim.

(if the agreement is a regulated agreement the procedure set out in the practice direction relating to consumer credit act claims (which supplements Part 7) should be used)

6.2 Where the claim is not for the delivery of goods, the claimant must state in his particulars of claim:

(1) the matters set out in paragraph 6.1(1) to (6) above,
(2) the goods let under the agreement,
(3) the amount of the total price,
(4) the paid-up sum,
(5) the amount (if any) claimed as being due and unpaid in respect of any instalment or instalments of the total price, and
(6) the nature and amount of any other claim and how it arises.

Other Matters to be Included in Particulars of Claim

7.1 Where a claim is made for an injunction or declaration in respect of or relating to any land or the possession, occupation, use or enjoyment of any land the particulars of claim must:

(1) state whether or not the injunction or declaration relates to residential premises, and
(2) identify the land (by reference to a plan where necessary).

7.2 Where a claim is brought to enforce a right to recover possession of goods the particulars of claim must contain a statement showing the value of the goods.

7.3 Where a claim is based upon a written agreement:

(1) a copy of the contract or documents constituting the agreement should be attached to or served with the particulars of claim and the original(s) should be available at the hearing, and
(2) any general conditions of sale incorporated in the contract should also be attached (but where the contract is or the documents constituting the agreement are bulky this practice direction is complied with by attaching or serving only the relevant parts of the contract or documents).

7.4 Where a claim is based upon an oral agreement, the particulars of claim should set out the contractual words used and state by whom, to whom, when and where they were spoken.

7.5 Where a claim is based upon an agreement by conduct, the particulars of claim must specify the conduct relied on and state by whom, when and where the acts constituting the conduct were done.

7.6 In a claim issued in the High Court relating to a Consumer Credit Agreement, the particulars of claim must contain a statement that the action is not one to which section 141 of the Consumer Credit Act 1974 applies.

'written agreement' (para 7.3)—The requirement to serve a copy should not be overlooked.

Matters which must be Specifically set out in the Particulars of Claim if Relied on

8.1 A claimant who wishes to rely on evidence:

(1) under section 11 of the Civil Evidence Act 1968 of a conviction of an offence, or
(2) under section 12 of the above-mentioned Act of a finding or adjudication of adultery or paternity,

must include in his particulars of claim a statement to that effect and give the following details:

(1) the type of conviction, finding or adjudication and its date,
(2) the court or court-martial which made the conviction, finding or adjudication, and
(3) the issue in the claim to which it relates.

8.2 The claimant must specifically set out the following matters in his particulars of claim where he wishes to rely on them in support of his claim:

(1) any allegation of fraud,
(2) the fact of any illegality,
(3) details of any misrepresentation,
(4) details of all breaches of trust,
(5) notice or knowledge of a fact,
(6) details of unsoundness of mind or undue influence,
(7) details of wilful default, and
(8) any facts relating to mitigation of loss or damage.

'must specifically set out' (para 8.2)—The provisions of CPR r 16.2 as to the nature of the case and CPR r 16.4(1)(a) must be followed if any of these eight matters is to be relied on.

General

9.1 Where a claim is for a sum of money expressed in a foreign currency it must expressly state:

(1) that the claim is for payment in a specified foreign currency,
(2) why it is for payment in that currency,
(3) the Sterling equivalent of the sum at the date of the claim, and
(4) the source of the exchange rate relied on to calculate the Sterling equivalent.

9.2 A subsequent statement of case must not contradict or be inconsistent with an earlier one; for example a reply to a defence must not bring in a new claim. Where new matters have come to light the appropriate course may be to seek the court's permission to amend the statement of case.

9.3 In clinical negligence claims, the words 'clinical negligence' should be inserted at the top of every statement of case.

'new matters have come to light' (para 9.2)—This should not be read as restricting the circumstances in which amendment may be permitted: the courts have hitherto never restricted permission to amend to those cases in which new matters have come to light, and are unlikely to do so now. The approach has always been that any change may be made, if such change is necessary to do justice between the parties and if provision can be made for the cost of consequential changes to the pleadings of other parties. But see the **'General note'** to CPR r 16.2. The fact that a statement of case will have been verified by a statement of truth will be an important factor in the justice of making an amendment.

The Defence

GENERAL

10.1 Rule 16.5 deals with the contents of the defence.

10.2 A defendant should deal with every allegation in accordance with rule 16.5(1) and (2).

10.3 Rule 16.5(3), (4) and (5) sets out the consequences of not dealing with an allegation.

10.4 Where the defendant is an individual, and the claim form does not contain an address at which he resides or carries on business, or contains an incorrect address, the defendant must provide such an address in the defence.

10.5 Where the defendant's address for service is not where he resides or carries on business, he must still provide the address required by paragraph 11.4.

Prospective amendments—Paragraphs prospectively inserted: Supplement 40 (issued 30 September 2005), with effect from 6 April 2006:

> '10.6 Any address which is provided for the purpose of these provisions must include a postcode, unless the court orders otherwise. Postcode information may be obtained from www.royalmail.com or the Royal Mail Address Management Guide.
>
> 10.7 Where a defendant to a claim or counterclaim is an individual, he must provide his date of birth (if known) in the acknowledgment of service, admission, defence, defence and counterclaim, reply or other response.'

STATEMENT OF TRUTH

11.1 Part 22 requires a defence to be verified by a statement of truth.

11.2 The form of the statement of truth is as follows:

> '[I believe][the defendant believes] that the facts stated in the defence are true.'

11.3 Attention is drawn to rule 32.14 which sets out the consequences of verifying a statement of case containing a false statement without an honest belief in its truth.

Matters which must be Included in the Defence

PERSONAL INJURY CLAIMS

12.1 Where the claim is for personal injuries and the claimant has attached a medical report in respect of his alleged injuries, the defendant should:

(1) state in his defence whether he –
  (a) agrees,
  (b) disputes, or
  (c) neither agrees nor disputes but has no knowledge of,
  the matters contained in the medical report,
(2) where he disputes any part of the medical report, give in his defence his reasons for doing so, and
(3) where he has obtained his own medical report on which he intends to rely, attach it to his defence.

12.2 Where the claim is for personal injuries and the claimant has included a schedule of past and future expenses and losses, the defendant should include in or attach to his defence a counter-schedule stating:

(1) which of those items he –
  (a) agrees,
  (b) disputes, or
  (c) neither agrees nor disputes but has no knowledge of, and
(2) where any items are disputed, supplying alternative figures where appropriate.

OTHER MATTERS

13.1 The defendant must give details of the expiry of any relevant limitation period relied on.

13.2 Rule 37.3 and paragraph 2 of the practice direction which supplements Part 37 contain information about a defence of tender.

13.3 A party may:

(1) refer in his statement of case to any point of law on which his claim or defence, as the case may be, is based,
(2) give in his statement of case the name of any witness he proposes to call, and
(3) attach to or serve with this statement of case a copy of any document which he considers is necessary to his claim or defence, as the case may be (including any expert's report to be filed in accordance with Part 35).

(The Costs Practice Direction supplementing Parts 43 to 48 contains details of the information required to be filed with a claim form to comply with rule 44.15 (providing information about funding arrangements))

'any point of law' (para 13.3)—This is not an invitation to mount a legal argument in a statement of case. The nature of the case and the facts relied upon may be all that is needed in most cases. In any other instance, what is sought is *a reference* to the point of law, not an exposition of it.

Competition Act 1998

14 A party who wishes to rely on a finding of the Director General of Fair Trading as provided by section 58 of the Competition Act 1998 must include in his statement of case a statement to that effect and identify the Director's finding on which he seeks to rely.

Prospective amendments—Words prospectively substituted for words in italic: Supplement 40 (issued 30 September 2005), with effect from 6 April 2006:

'14 A party who wishes to rely on a finding of the [*Office*] of Fair Trading as provided by section 58 of the Competition Act 1998 must include in his statement of case a statement to that effect and identify the [*Office's*] finding on which he seeks to rely.'

Human Rights

15.1 A party who seeks to rely on any provision of or right arising under the Human Rights Act 1998 or seeks a remedy available under that Act –

(1) must state that fact in his statement of case; and
(2) must in his statement of case –
  (a) give precise details of the Convention right which it is alleged has been infringed and details of the alleged infringement;
  (b) specify the relief sought;
  (c) state if the relief sought includes –
    (i) a declaration of incompatibility in accordance with section 4 of that Act, or
    (ii) damages in respect of a judicial act to which section 9(3) of that Act applies;
  (d) where the relief sought includes a declaration of incompatibility in accordance with section 4 of that Act, give precise details of the legislative provision alleged to be incompatible and details of the alleged incompatibility;
  (e) where the claim is founded on a finding of unlawfulness by another court or tribunal, give details of the finding; and
  (f) where the claim is founded on a judicial act which is alleged to have infringed a Convention right of the party as provided by section 9 of the Human Rights Act 1998, the judicial act complained of and the court or tribunal which is alleged to have made it.

(The practice direction to Part 19 provides for notice to be given and parties joined in the circumstances referred to in (c), (d) and (f))

15.2 A party who seeks to amend his statement of case to include the matters referred to in paragraph 16.1 must, unless the court orders otherwise, do so as soon as possible.

(Part 17 provides for the amendment of a statement of case)

For subsequent amendments, see our website at

PART 17
AMENDMENTS TO STATEMENTS OF CASE

CONTENTS OF THIS PART

Procedural Guide—See Guide 19, set out in Section 1 of this work.

17.1 Amendments to statements of case

(1) A party may amend his statement of case at any time before it has been served on any other party.

(2) If his statement of case has been served, a party may amend it only –

(a) with the written consent of all the other parties; or

(b) with the permission of the court.

(3) If a statement of case has been served, an application to amend it by removing, adding or substituting a party must be made in accordance with rule 19.4.

(Part 22 requires amendments to a statement of case to be verified by a statement of truth unless the court orders otherwise)

Amendments—SI 2000/221.

General note—*Savings & Investment Bank v Fincken (No 2)* [2003] EWCA Civ 1630, [2003] 3 All ER 1091, CA has finally laid to rest the pre-CPR principle that any amendment should be permitted if the other party could be adequately compensated in costs without injustice. Rather, all the elements of the overriding objective have to be considered. A party may not amend so as to put forward inconsistent factual cases, for example adopting his opponent's version (which he denies) as supporting an alternative basis of claim, but he must frame the amendment so that his statement of truth does not verify what he does not believe (*Binks (Justin) v Securicor Omega Express Ltd* [2003] EWCA Civ 993). Further, a case may be based on alternative factual bases, where a party is not in a position to commit himself to one or the other (*Clarke v Marlborough Fine Art (London) Limited* [2002] 1 WLR 1731, ChD).

After an unsuccessful mediation, a party will not be prevented from raising by amendment a claim which might materially have affected the course of the mediation (*Gold v Mincoff Science & Gold* [2002] EWCA Civ 1157). And in *Savings & Investment Bank Ltd v Fincken* [2003] EWCA Civ 1630, [2004] 1 WLR 667 the Court of Appeal held that it was rare that an admission made in the course of without-prejudice discussions would fall within the unambiguous impropriety exception to the privilege rule and be allowed to found an amendment to a statement of case. Judges should not regard deadlines for amendment as set in stone where no prejudice is caused by a late amendment that may be addressed by an order for costs (*Law Debenture Trust Corp v Lexington Insurance* [2002] EWCA Civ 1673, (2003) Lawtel, 6 January, CA).

Increasing the amount claimed—If it is desired to increase substantially the amount claimed and vacate a trial date accordingly, an application should be made promptly and supported by particulars and evidence (*AC Electrical Wholesale plc v IGW Services* (2000) (unreported) 10 October, CA). An amendment of a claim allocated to the fast track to seek damages in excess of £15,000 does not mean that the case ceases to be a fast track case. See also note **'Amended claims'** under r 26.10.

17.2 Power of court to disallow amendments made without permission

(1) If a party has amended his statement of case where permission of the court was not required, the court may disallow the amendment.

(2) A party may apply to the court for an order under paragraph (1) within 14 days of service of a copy of the amended statement of case on him.

17.3 Amendments to statements of case with the permission of the court

(1) Where the court gives permission for a party to amend his statement of case, it may give directions as to –

- (a) amendments to be made to any other statement of case; and
- (b) service of any amended statement of case.

(2) The power of the court to give permission under this rule is subject to –

- (a) rule 19.1 (change of parties – general);
- (b) rule 19.4 (special provisions about adding or substituting parties after the end of a relevant limitation period(GL)); and
- (c) rule 17.4 (amendments of statement of case after the end of a relevant limitation period).

17.4 Amendments to statements of case after the end of a relevant limitation period

(1) This rule applies where –

- (a) a party applies to amend his statement of case in one of the ways mentioned in this rule; and
- (b) a period of limitation has expired under –
  - (i) the Limitation Act 1980;
  - (ii) the Foreign Limitation Periods Act 1984; or
  - (iii) any other enactment which allows such an amendment, or under which such an amendment is allowed.

(2) The court may allow an amendment whose effect will be to add or substitute a new claim, but only if the new claim arises out of the same facts or substantially the same facts as a claim in respect of which the party applying for permission has already claimed a remedy in the proceedings.

(3) The court may allow an amendment to correct a mistake as to the name of a party, but only where the mistake was genuine and not one which would cause reasonable doubt as to the identity of the party in question.

(4) The court may allow an amendment to alter the capacity in which a party claims if the new capacity is one which that party had when the proceedings started or has since acquired.

(Rule 19.5 specifies the circumstances in which the court may allow a new party to be added or substituted after the end of a relevant limitation period(GL))

Amendments—SI 2001/256.

'a new claim' (r 17.4(2))—See Limitation Act 1980, s 35. This is one area where pre-1999 cases will remain authoritative (see *Welsh Development Agency v Redpath Dorman Long Ltd* [1994] 1

WLR 1409, for the correct approach.) It remains impermissible to amend or to add a cause of action which was not in existence at the date the original proceedings were issued (*Eshelby v Federated European Bank Limited* [1932] 1 KB 254). In *Goode v Martin* [2002] EWCA Civ 1899, [2002] 1 WLR 1828, CA the court gave effect to Art 6 ECHR by allowing an amendment, after the expiry of a limitation period, to allege negligence based on the defendant's version of the facts. What is involved is a comparison between the essential facts alleged in the statement of case before and after the proposed amendment, not the issues which might arise (*Savings and Investment Bank (in liquidation) v Fincken* [2001] EWCA Civ 1639, (2001) *The Times*, 15 November, CA). *Furini v Bajwa* [2004] EWCA Civ 412, [2004] 1 WLR 1971, CA was an unusual case where the limitation period expired after the judge had approved amendments in principle but before they were finally formulated. The principle that amendments took effect at the date when the judgment was given, not the date when the order was formally made, had no application and the amendments were not permitted.

'mistake as to the name' (r 17.4(3))—This rule and not r 19.5 is appropriate where there has been a genuine, non-misleading mistake (*Gregson v Channel Four Television Corporation* (2000) *The Times*, 11 August, CA).

'to alter the capacity' (r 17.4(4))—This provision is to be construed narrowly so as to prevent persons without title to a cause of action starting proceedings, taking an assignment from the person entitled, and then seeking to amend outside the limitation period (*Haq v Singh* [2001] EWCA Civ 957, [2001] 1 WLR 1594, CA).

Practice Direction – Amendments to Statements of Case

This Practice Direction supplements CPR Part 17 (PD17)

A party applying for an amendment will usually be responsible for the costs of and arising from the amendment.

General note—See also the notes to CPR Pt 17 for relevant commentary.

APPLICATIONS TO AMEND WHERE THE PERMISSION OF THE COURT IS REQUIRED

1.1 The application may be dealt with at a hearing or, if rule 23.8 applies, without a hearing.

1.2 When making an application to amend a statement of case, the applicant should file with the court:

(1) the application notice, and
(2) a copy of the statement of case with the proposed amendments.

1.3 Where permission to amend has been given, the applicant should within 14 days of the date of the order, or within such other period as the court may direct, file with the court the amended statement of case.

1.4 If the substance of the statement of case is changed by reason of the amendment, the statement of case should be re-verified by a statement of truth[1].

1 See Part 22 for information about the statement of truth.

1.5 A copy of the order and the amended statement of case should be served on every party to the proceedings, unless the court orders otherwise.

GENERAL

2.1 The amended statement of case and the court copy of it should be endorsed as follows:

(1) where the court's permission was required:

'Amended [Particulars of Claim *or as may be*] by Order of [Master . . . .][District Judge . . . . *or as may be*] dated . . . .'

(2) Where the court's permission was not required:

'Amended [Particulars of Claim *or as may be*] under CPR [rule 17.1(1) or (2)(a)] dated . . . .'

2.2 The statement of case in its amended form need not show the original text. However, where the court thinks it desirable for both the original text and the amendments to be shown, the court may direct that the amendments should be shown either:

(1) by coloured amendments, either manuscript or computer generated, or
(2) by use of a numerical code in a monochrome computer generated document.

2.3 Where colour is used, the text to be deleted should be struck through in colour and any text replacing it should be inserted or underlined in the same colour.

2.4 The order of colours to be used for successive amendments is; (1) red, (2) green, (3) violet and (4) yellow.

(For information about changes to parties see Part 19 and the practice direction which supplements it)

PART 18
FURTHER INFORMATION

Procedural Guide—See Guide 21, set out in Section 1 of this work.

18.1 Obtaining further information

(1) The court may at any time order a party to –

(a) clarify any matter which is in dispute in the proceedings; or
(b) give additional information in relation to any such matter,

whether or not the matter is contained or referred to in a statement of case.

(2) Paragraph (1) is subject to any rule of law to the contrary.

(3) Where the court makes an order under paragraph (1), the party against whom it is made must –

(a) file his response; and
(b) serve it on the other parties,

within the time specified by the court.

(Part 22 requires a response to be verified by a statement of truth)

(Part 53 (defamation) restricts requirements for providing further information about sources of information in defamation claims)

Amendments—SI 2000/221.

Practice Direction—See generally PD18 at p 612.

Scope of provision—Part 18 'Obtaining further information' replaces Requests for Further and Better Particulars and Interrogatories. The practice direction provides for a formal request, by document or letter, to be sent first, giving the respondent a reasonable time within which to reply, before any application is made to the court (PD18, para 1). Although the application must usually be made on notice, in accordance with Pt 23 (PD18, para 5.1), where the respondent does not reply to the request (minimum period 14 days) the application may be made without notice (PD18, para 5.5). Consideration should be given carefully as to the efficacy of making a request before disclosure and the exchange of witness statements (*Hall v Selvaco* [1996] PIQR P344, CA).

'subject to any rule of law to the contrary' (r 18.1(2))—The court may sanction non-disclosure of a document (see r 31.19 and the notes thereto).

'statement of truth' (Note to r 18.1(3))—Endorsement of this has the effect of making the response a statement of case.

18.2 Restriction on the use of further information

The court may direct that information provided by a party to another party (whether given voluntarily or following an order made under rule 18.1) must not be used for any purpose except for that of the proceedings in which it is given.

Practice Direction—See generally PD18 at p 612.

'The court may direct'—Note that the power is discretionary.

Practice Direction – Further Information

This Practice Direction supplements CPR Part 18 (PD18)

Attention is also drawn to Part 22 (Statements of Truth).

Procedural Guide—See Guide 21, set out in Section 1 of this work.

PRELIMINARY REQUEST FOR FURTHER INFORMATION OR CLARIFICATION

1.1 Before making an application to the court for an order under Part 18, the party seeking clarification or information (the first party) should first serve on the party from whom it is sought (the second party) a written request for that clarification or information (a Request) stating a date by which the response to the Request should be served. The date must allow the second party a reasonable time to respond.

1.2 A Request should be concise and strictly confined to matters which are reasonably necessary and proportionate to enable the first party to prepare his own case or to understand the case he has to meet.

1.3 Requests must be made as far as possible in a single comprehensive document and not piecemeal.

1.4 A Request may be made by letter if the text of the request is brief and the reply is likely to be brief; otherwise the Request should be made in a separate document.

1.5 If a Request is made in a letter, the letter should, in order to distinguish it from any other that might routinely be written in the course of a case,

(1) state that it contains a Request made under Part 18, and
(2) deal with no matters other than the Request.

1.6 (1) A Request (whether made by letter or in a separate document) must –
- (a) be headed with the name of the court and the title and number of the claim,
- (b) in its heading state that it is a Request made under Part 18, identify the first party and the second party and state the date on which it is made,
- (c) set out in a separate numbered paragraph each request for information or clarification,
- (d) where a Request relates to a document, identify that document and (if relevant) the paragraph or words to which it relates,
- (e) state the date by which the first party expects a response to the Request,

(2) (a) A Request which is not in the form of a letter may, if convenient, be prepared in such a way that the response may be given on the same document.
- (b) To do this the numbered paragraphs of the Request should appear on the left hand half of each sheet so that the paragraphs of the response may then appear on the right.
- (c) Where a Request is prepared in this form an extra copy should be served for the use of the second party.

1.7 Subject to the provisions of paragraphs 3.1 to 3.3 of the Practice Direction to Part 6, a request should be served by e-mail if reasonably practicable.

Preliminary request—Parties should bear in mind the overriding objective and in particular the court's duty to encourage parties to co-operate with each other (CPR r 1.4(2)(a)), and to identify the issues at an early stage (CPR r 1.4(2)(b)). Thus the request must be 'reasonable' and the respondent given a 'reasonable' period within which to answer. Note also that proportionality applies (para 1.2).

Request by letter (para 1.5)—A certain degree of formality is required to bring a request within this provision. A casual request for information in letter which is not specified as a CPR Pt 18 request will not come within this Part.

RESPONDING TO A REQUEST

2.1 A response to a Request must be in writing, dated and signed by the second party or his legal representative.

2.2 (1) Where the Request is made in a letter the second party may give his response in a letter or in a formal reply.
(2) Such a letter should identify itself as a response to the Request and deal with no other matters than the response.

2.3 (1) Unless the Request is in the format described in paragraph 1.6(2) and the second party uses the document supplied for the purpose, a response must:
(a) be headed with the name of the court and the title and number of the claim,
(b) in its heading identify itself as a response to that Request,
(c) repeat the text of each separate paragraph of the Request and set out under each paragraph the response to it,
(d) refer to and have attached to it a copy of any document not already in the possession of the first party which forms part of the response.
(2) A second or supplementary response to a Request must identify itself as such in its heading.

2.4 The second party must when he serves his response on the first party serve on every other party and file with the court a copy of the Request and of his response.

STATEMENTS OF TRUTH

3 Attention is drawn to Part 22 and to the definition of a statement of case in Part 2 of the rules; a response should be verified by a statement of truth.

GENERAL MATTERS

4.1 (1) If the second party objects to complying with the Request or part of it or is unable to do so at all or within the time stated in the Request he must inform the first party promptly and in any event within that time.
(2) He may do so in a letter or in a separate document (a formal response), but in either case he must give reasons and, where relevant, give a date by which he expects to be able to comply.

4.2 (1) There is no need for a second party to apply to the court if he objects to a Request or is unable to comply with it at all or within the stated time. He need only comply with paragraph 4.1(1) above.
(2) Where a second party considers that a Request can only be complied

with at disproportionate expense and objects to comply for that reason he should say so in his reply and explain briefly why he has taken that view.

Further time to respond (para 4.1)—Note that any request for further time to respond must be made within the original time specified. Reasons for any delay or failure to respond must be given.

APPLICATIONS FOR ORDERS UNDER PART 18

5.1 Attention is drawn to Part 23 (Applications) and to the practice direction which supplements that Part.

5.2 An application notice for an order under Part 18 should set out or have attached to it the text of the order sought and in particular should specify the matter or matters in respect of which the clarification or information is sought.

5.3 (1) If a Request under paragraph 1 for the information or clarification has not been made, the application notice should, in addition, explain why not.

(2) If a Request for clarification or information has been made, the application notice or the evidence in support should describe the response, if any.

5.4 Both the first party and the second party should consider whether evidence in support of or in opposition to the application is required.

5.5 (1) Where the second party has made no response to a Request served on him, the first party need not serve the application notice on the second party, and the court may deal with the application without a hearing.

(2) Sub-paragraph (1) above only applies if at least 14 days have passed since the Request was served and the time stated in it for a response has expired.

5.6 Unless paragraph 5.5 applies the application notice must be served on the second party and on all other parties to the claim.

5.7 An order made under Part 18 must be served on all parties to the claim.

5.8 Costs:

(1) Attention is drawn to the Costs Practice Direction and in particular the court's power to make a summary assessment of costs.

(2) Attention is also drawn to rule 44.13(1) which provides that the general rule is that if an order does not mention costs no party is entitled to costs relating to that order.

'evidence in support' (para 5.4)—This must bear a Statement of Truth (PD32). Additional costs of an affidavit are not normally recoverable (CPR r 32.15(2)). Evidence may appear on the application notice itself.

'no response to a Request' (para 5.5)—Note that this entitles the applicant to apply for an order without notice to the other party and without a hearing.

Application form—None is prescribed but Form N244 may be adapted. As to service, see CPR rr 23.9 and 23.10.

Fee on application—On notice – £50; without notice £25 (CCFO fees 2.4 and 2.5, SCFO fees 2.4 and 2.5).

Costs—As this will be an interim application the court is likely to assess costs summarily. Parties should therefore prepare their written statements of costs in accordance with PDCosts, para 13.5. See also PDCosts, para 13.4 concerning consent orders.

PART 19
PARTIES AND GROUP LITIGATION

CONTENTS OF THIS PART

19.1 Parties – general

Any number of claimants or defendants may be joined as parties to a claim.

Amendments—Inserted by SI 2000/221.

Practice Direction—See generally PD19 at p 625.

I Addition and Substitution of Parties

19.2 Change of parties – general

(1) This rule applies where a party is to be added or substituted except where the case falls within rule 19.5 (special provisions about changing parties after the end of a relevant limitation period(GL)).

(2) The court may order a person to be added as a new party if –

(a) it is desirable to add the new party so that the court can resolve all the matters in dispute in the proceedings; or

(b) there is an issue involving the new party and an existing party which is connected to the matters in dispute in the proceedings, and it is desirable to add the new party so that the court can resolve that issue.

(3) The court may order any person to cease to be a party if it is not desirable for that person to be a party to the proceedings.

(4) The court may order a new party to be substituted for an existing one if –

(a) the existing party's interest or liability has passed to the new party; and
(b) it is desirable to substitute the new party so that the court can resolve the matters in dispute in the proceedings.]

Amendments—Inserted by SI 2000/221.

Practice Direction—See generally PD19 at p 625.

Joinder of financial backer (r 19.2)—The fact that a person is funding another's libel action does not entitle him to be joined as a party to the proceedings (*Earl of Portsmouth v Mostyn; Neil Hamilton v Mohammed Al Fayed* (2000) 97(41) LSG 40, CA).

Adding defendants after default judgment—The court has jurisdiction to allow intended defendants to be joined in an action where there is already a judgment in default. There is a discretionary jurisdiction to achieve justice where, under r 19.2, it is desirable in all the circumstances and also by reason of the overriding objective in Pt 1 (*Humber Work Boats Ltd v The Owners of MV Selby Paradigm* [2004] EWHC 1804 (QB)).

19.3 Provisions applicable where two or more persons are jointly entitled to a remedy

(1) Where a claimant claims a remedy to which some other person is jointly entitled with him, all persons jointly entitled to the remedy must be parties unless the court orders otherwise.

(2) If any person does not agree to be a claimant, he must be made a defendant, unless the court orders otherwise.

(3) This rule does not apply in probate proceedings.

Amendments—Inserted by SI 2000/221.

Practice Direction—See generally PD19 at p 625.

19.4 Procedure for adding and substituting parties

(1) The court's permission is required to remove, add or substitute a party, unless the claim form has not been served.

(2) An application for permission under paragraph (1) may be made by –

(a) an existing party; or
(b) a person who wishes to become a party.

(3) An application for an order under rule 19.2(4) (substitution of a new party where existing party's interest or liability has passed) –

(a) may be made without notice; and
(b) must be supported by evidence.

(4) Nobody may be added or substituted as a claimant unless –

(a) he has given his consent in writing; and
(b) that consent has been filed with the court.

(4A) The Commissioners for HM Revenue and Customs may be added as a party to proceedings only if they consent in writing.

(5) An order for the removal, addition or substitution of a party must be served on –

(a) all parties to the proceedings; and
(b) any other person affected by the order.

(6) When the court makes an order for the removal, addition or substitution of a party, it may give consequential directions about –

(a) filing and serving the claim form on any new defendant;
(b) serving relevant documents on the new party; and
(c) the management of the proceedings.

Amendments—Inserted by SI 2000/221; SI 2005/2292.

Practice Direction—See generally PD19 at p 625.

'The court's permission is required' (r 19.4(1))—The importance of a proper, reasoned explanation for a delay in applying to join a party cannot be overemphasised, particularly when there is an imminent trial date. There is a delicate line to be drawn between privilege and candour, and where a party is asking for a special dispensation (such as joinder at a late stage) it should carefully consider how candid it could be to the court (*Borealis AB v Stargas Ltd and M/V 'Berge Sisar'* [2002] EWCA Civ 757, (2002) Lawtel, 9 May, CA).

Application—See Pt 23. The application must be supported by evidence (PD19, para 1.3).

Adding a party after judgment—On the true construction of Pt 19 the relevant question is whether, after judgment has been given, the proceedings are still continuing, namely whether they are 'existing'. Prima facie, the court has the power, in a proper case, to add a party for the purposes of execution. However, the court will not allow a party to amend a cause of action once judgment has been passed by adding fresh parties, since that amounts to an abuse of process (*Kooltrade Ltd v XTS Ltd & ors* [2001] ECDR 11, [2001] FSR 13, ChD (Pat Ct)).

19.4A Human Rights

Section 4 of the Human Rights Act 1998

(1) The court may not make a declaration of incompatibility in accordance with section 4 of the Human Rights Act 1998 unless 21 days' notice, or such other period of notice as the court directs, has been given to the Crown.

(2) Where notice has been given to the Crown a Minister, or other person permitted by that Act, shall be joined as a party on giving notice to the court.

(Only courts specified in section 4 of the Human Rights Act 1998 can make a declaration of incompatibility.)

Section 9 of the Human Rights Act 1998

(3) Where a claim is made under that Act for damages in respect of a judicial act –

(a) that claim must be set out in the statement of case or the appeal notice; and
(b) notice must be given to the Crown.

(4) Where paragraph (3) applies and the appropriate person has not applied to be joined as a party within 21 days, or such other period as the court directs, after the notice is served, the court may join the appropriate person as a party.

(A practice direction makes provision for these notices.)

Amendments—Inserted by SI 2000/2092.

'notice must be given to the Crown' (r 19.4A(3)(b))—The formal notice required by both r 19.4A and the HRA 1998 should always be given by the court. The party intending to raise the issue of compatibility should, nevertheless, give informal notice of its intention to do so to both the court and the Crown at the earliest possible opportunity. Both notices to the Crown should be given to the person named in the list published under Crown Proceedings Act 1947, s 17 (see PD19, para 6.6 and *Poplar Housing & Regeneration Community Association Ltd v Donoghue* [2001] EWCA Civ 595, [2002] QB 48, CA).

19.5 Special provisions about adding or substituting parties after the end of a relevant limitation period

(1) This rule applies to a change of parties after the end of a period of limitation under –

- (a) the Limitation Act 1980;
- (b) the Foreign Limitation Periods Act 1984;
- (c) any such enactment which allows such a change, or under which such a change is allowed.

(2) The court may add or substitute a party only if –

- (a) the relevant limitation period(GL) was current when the proceedings were started; and
- (b) the addition or substitution is necessary.

(3) The addition or substitution of a party is necessary only if the court is satisfied that –

- (a) the new party is to be substituted for a party who was named in the claim form in mistake for the new party;
- (b) the claim cannot properly be carried on by or against the original party unless the new party is added or substituted as claimant or defendant; or
- (c) the original party has died or had a bankruptcy order made against him and his interest or liability has passed to the new party.

(4) In addition, in a claim for personal injuries the court may add or substitute a party where it directs that –

- (a) (i) section 11 (special time limit for claims for personal injuries); or
  - (ii) section 12 (special time limit for claims under fatal accidents legislation), of the Limitation Act 1980 shall not apply to the claim by or against the new party; or
- (b) the issue of whether those sections apply shall be determined at trial.

(Rule 17.4 deals with other changes after the end of a relevant limitation period(GL))

Amendments—Inserted by SI 2000/221; amended by SI 2001/256.

Practice Direction—See generally PD19 at p 625.

Substitution and the limitation period—The fact that an accrued contractual limitation defence is arguable is no reason for refusing to order the substitution of a party to proceedings, since substitution does nothing to deprive that party of the benefit of that defence. There is no conflict or inconsistency between rr 17.4 and 19.4, since – although r 19.4 contains no formal requirement that a mistake as to the identity of a party needs to be genuine and not misleading – nonetheless these criteria will be applied in the determination of substitution applications, as had been the case before the CPR (*International Distillers & Vintners Ltd (t/a Percy Fox & Co) v JF Hillebrand (UK) Ltd & ors* (2000) *The Times*, 25 January, QBD (David Foskett QC)).

Comparison between r 19.5 and r 17.4—Rule 19.5 applies where the application is to substitute a new party where the wrong person was named in the claim form. Rule 17.4(3) (amendments to statements of case after the end of a relevant limitation period) applies where the intended party was named in the claim form but there was a genuine mistake in giving his name and no one was misled. There is no significant conflict between the two rules (*David Gregson v Channel Four Television Corporation* (2000) Lawtel, 12 July, CA).

19.5A Special rules about parties in claims for wrongful interference with goods

(1) A claimant in a claim for wrongful interference with goods must, in the particulars of claim, state the name and address of every person who, to his knowledge, has or claims an interest in the goods and who is not a party to the claim.

(2) A defendant to a claim for wrongful interference with goods may apply for a direction that another person be made a party to the claim to establish whether the other person –

- (a) has a better right to the goods than the claimant; or
- (b) has a claim which might render the defendant doubly liable under section 7 of the Torts (Interference with Goods) Act 1977.

(3) Where the person referred to in paragraph (2) fails to attend the hearing of the application, or comply with any directions, the court may order that he is deprived of any claim against the defendant in respect of the goods.

(Rule 3.1(3) provides that the court may make an order subject to conditions.)

(4) The application notice must be served on all parties and on the person referred to in paragraph (2).

Amendments—Inserted by SI 2001/256.

Wrongful interference claims—This added provision reduces the likelihood of there being more than one set of proceedings.

II Representative Parties

19.6 Representative parties with same interest

(1) Where more than one person has the same interest in a claim –

- (a) the claim may be begun; or
- (b) the court may order that the claim be continued,

by or against one or more of the persons who have the same interest as representatives of any other persons who have that interest.

(2) The court may direct that a person may not act as a representative.

(3) Any party may apply to the court for an order under paragraph (2).

(4) Unless the court otherwise directs any judgment or order given in a claim in which a party is acting as a representative under this rule –

- (a) is binding on all persons represented in the claim; but
- (b) may only be enforced by or against a person who is not a party to the claim with the permission of the court.

(5) This rule does not apply to a claim to which rule 19.7 applies.

Amendments—Inserted by SI 2000/221.

'any judgment … is binding on all persons represented' (r 19.6(4))—A judgment against claimants representing a club is binding against all the members and enforceable against the individual members, whether or not they knew of, or consented to, the litigation (*David Howells and James Kelly (on behalf of themselves and all other members of the Hemel Hempstead Football and Sports Club) v The Dominion Insurance Co Ltd* [2005] EWHC 552 (QB)).

19.7 Representation of interested persons who cannot be ascertained etc

(1) This rule applies to claims about –

(a) the estate of a deceased person;
(b) property subject to a trust; or
(c) the meaning of a document, including a statute.

(2) The court may make an order appointing a person to represent any other person or persons in the claim where the person or persons to be represented –

(a) are unborn;
(b) cannot be found;
(c) cannot easily be ascertained; or
(d) are a class of persons who have the same interest in a claim and –
  (i) one or more members of that class are within sub-paragraphs (a), (b) or (c); or
  (ii) to appoint a representative would further the overriding objective.

(3) An application for an order under paragraph (2) –

(a) may be made by –
  (i) any person who seeks to be appointed under the order; or
  (ii) any party to the claim; and
(b) may be made at any time before or after the claim has started.

(4) An application notice for an order under paragraph (2) must be served on –

(a) all parties to the claim, if the claim has started;
(b) the person sought to be appointed, if that person is not the applicant or a party to the claim; and
(c) any other person as directed by the court.

(5) The court's approval is required to settle a claim in which a party is acting as a representative under this rule.

(6) The court may approve a settlement where it is satisfied that the settlement is for the benefit of all the represented persons.

(7) Unless the court otherwise directs, any judgment or order given in a claim in which a party is acting as a representative under this rule –

(a) is binding on all persons represented in the claim; but
(b) may only be enforced by or against a person who is not a party to the claim with the permission of the court.

Amendments—Inserted by SI 2000/221.

19.7A Representation of beneficiaries by trustees etc

(1) A claim may be brought by or against trustees, executors or administrators in that capacity without adding as parties any persons who have a beneficial interest in the trust or estate ('the beneficiaries').

(2) Any judgment or order given or made in the claim is binding on the beneficiaries unless the court orders otherwise in the same or other proceedings.

Amendments—Inserted by SI 2002/2058.

19.7B Postal Services Act 2000

(1) An application under section 92 of the Postal Services Act 2000 for permission to bring proceedings in the name of the sender or addressee of a postal packet or his personal representative is made in accordance with Part 8.

(2) A copy of the application notice must be served on the universal service provider and on the person in whose name the applicant seeks to bring the proceedings.

Amendments—Inserted by SI 2005/2292.

19.8 Death

(1) Where a person who had an interest in a claim has died and that person has no personal representative the court may order –

(a) the claim to proceed in the absence of a person representing the estate of the deceased; or

(b) a person to be appointed to represent the estate of the deceased.

(2) Where a defendant against whom a claim could have been brought has died and –

(a) a grant of probate or administration has been made, the claim must be brought against the persons who are the personal representatives of the deceased;

(b) a grant of probate or administration has not been made –

(i) the claim must be brought against 'the estate of' the deceased; and

(ii) the claimant must apply to the court for an order appointing a person to represent the estate of the deceased in the claim.

(3) A claim shall be treated as having been brought against 'the estate of' the deceased in accordance with paragraph (2)(b)(i) where –

(a) the claim is brought against the 'personal representatives' of the deceased but a grant of probate or administration has not been made; or

(b) the person against whom the claim was brought was dead when the claim was started.

(4) Before making an order under this rule, the court may direct notice of the application to be given to any other person with an interest in the claim.

(5) Where an order has been made under paragraphs (1) or (2)(b)(ii) any judgment or order made or given in the claim is binding on the estate of the deceased.

Amendments—Inserted by SI 2000/221.

19.8A Power to make judgments binding on non-parties

(1) This rule applies to any claim relating to –

(a) the estate of a deceased person;

(b) property subject to a trust; or

(c) the sale of any property.

(2) The court may at any time direct that notice of –

(a) the claim; or

(b) any judgment or order given in the claim,

be served on any person who is not a party but who is or may be affected by it.

(3) An application under this rule –

(a) may be made without notice; and
(b) must be supported by written evidence which includes the reasons why the person to be served should be bound by the judgment in the claim.

(4) Unless the court orders otherwise –

(a) a notice of a claim or of a judgment or order under this rule must be –
(i) in the form required by the practice direction;
(ii) issued by the court; and
(iii) accompanied by a form of acknowledgment of service with any necessary modifications;
(b) a notice of a claim must also be accompanied by –
(i) a copy of the claim form; and
(ii) such other statements of case, witness statements or affidavits as the court may direct; and
(c) a notice of a judgment or order must also be accompanied by a copy of the judgment or order.

(5) If a person served with notice of a claim files an acknowledgment of service of the notice within 14 days he will become a party to the claim.

(6) If a person served with notice of a claim does not acknowledge service of the notice he will be bound by any judgment given in the claim as if he were a party.

(7) If, after service of a notice of a claim on a person, the claim form is amended so as substantially to alter the relief claimed, the court may direct that a judgment shall not bind that person unless a further notice, together with a copy of the amended claim form, is served on him.

(8) Any person served with a notice of a judgment or order under this rule –

(a) shall be bound by the judgment or order as if he had been a party to the claim; but
(b) may, provided he acknowledges service –
(i) within 28 days after the notice is served on him, apply to the court to set aside or vary the judgment or order; and
(ii) take part in any proceedings relating to the judgment or order.

(9) The following rules of Part 10 (acknowledgment of service) apply –

(a) rule 10.4; and
(b) rule 10.5, subject to the modification that references to the defendant are to be read as references to the person served with the notice.

(10) A notice under this rule is issued on the date entered on the notice by the court.

Amendments—Inserted by SI 2001/256; substituted by SI 2002/2058.

'Power to make judgments binding on non-parties' (r 19.8A generally)—This replaces Sch 1, RSC Ord 15, r 13A.

19.9 Derivative Claims

(1) This rule applies where a company, other incorporated body or trade union is alleged to be entitled to claim a remedy and a claim is made by one or more members of the company, body or trade union for it to be given that remedy (a 'derivative claim').

(2) The company, body or trade union for whose benefit a remedy is sought must be a defendant to the claim.

(3) After the claim form has been issued the claimant must apply to the court for permission to continue the claim and may not take any other step in the proceedings except –

- (a) as provided by paragraph (5); or
- (b) where the court gives permission.

(4) An application in accordance with paragraph (3) must be supported by written evidence.

(5) The –

- (a) claim form;
- (b) application notice; and
- (c) written evidence in support of the application,

must be served on the defendant within the period within which the claim form must be served and, in any event, at least 14 days before the court is to deal with the application.

(6) If the court gives the claimant permission to continue the claim, the time within which the defence must be filed is 14 days after the date on which the permission is given or such period as the court may specify.

(7) The court may order the company, body or trade union to indemnify the claimant against any liability in respect of costs incurred in the claim.

Amendments—Inserted by SI 2000/221.

III Group Litigation

19.10 Definition

A Group Litigation Order ('GLO') means an order made under rule 19.11 to provide for the case management of claims which give rise to common or related issues of fact or law (the 'GLO issues').

Amendments—Inserted by SI 2000/221.

Practice Direction—See generally PD19B at p 629.

19.11 Group Litigation Order

(1) The court may make a GLO where there are or are likely to be a number of claims giving rise to the GLO issues.

(The practice direction provides the procedure for applying for a GLO)

(2) A GLO must –

- (a) contain directions about the establishment of a register (the 'group register') on which the claims managed under the GLO will be entered;
- (b) specify the GLO issues which will identify the claims to be managed as a group under the GLO; and
- (c) specify the court (the 'management court') which will manage the claims on the group register.

(3) A GLO may –

- (a) in relation to claims which raise one or more of the GLO issues –
  - (i) direct their transfer to the management court;
  - (ii) order their stay [(GL)] until further order; and

(iii) direct their entry on the group register;

(b) direct that from a specified date claims which raise one or more of the GLO issues should be started in the management court and entered on the group register; and

(c) give directions for publicising the GLO.

Amendments—Inserted by SI 2000/221.

Practice Direction—See generally PD19B at p 629.

Parallel proceedings—In *Taylor v Nugent Care Society* [2004] EWCA Civ 51, [2004] 1 WLR 1129, [2004] TLR 56, (2004) *The Times*, January 28, CA, the Court of Appeal said that it would not be an abuse of process for a claimant, having been refused permission to join in group litigation, to bring separate proceedings that ran parallel to the group action. It advised that the court, when giving directions in those proceedings, should take account of the directions in the group proceedings.

19.12 Effect of the GLO

(1) Where a judgment or order is given or made in a claim on the group register in relation to one or more GLO issues –

(a) that judgment or order is binding on the parties to all other claims that are on the group register at the time the judgment is given or the order is made unless the court orders otherwise; and

(b) the court may give directions as to the extent to which that judgment or order is binding on the parties to any claim which is subsequently entered on the group register.

(2) Unless paragraph (3) applies, any party who is adversely affected by a judgment or order which is binding on him may seek permission to appeal the order.

(3) A party to a claim which was entered on the group register after a judgment or order which is binding on him was given or made may not –

(a) apply for the judgment or order to be set aside(GL), varied or stayed(GL); or

(b) appeal the judgment or order,

but may apply to the court for an order that the judgment or order is not binding on him.

(4) Unless the court orders otherwise, disclosure of any document relating to the GLO issues by a party to a claim on the group register is disclosure of that document to all parties to claims –

(a) on the group register; and

(b) which are subsequently entered on the group register.

Amendments—Inserted by SI 2000/221.

Practice Direction—See generally PD19B at p 629.

19.13 Case management

Directions given by the management court may include directions –

(a) varying the GLO issues;

(b) providing for one or more claims on the group register to proceed as test claims;

(c) appointing the solicitor of one or more parties to be the lead solicitor for the claimants or defendants;

(d) specifying the details to be included in a statement of case in order to show that the criteria for entry of the claim on the group register have been met;
(e) specifying a date after which no claim may be added to the group register unless the court gives permission; and
(f) for the entry of any particular claim which meets one or more of the GLO issues on the group register.

(Part 3 contains general provisions about the case management powers of the court)

Amendments—Inserted by SI 2000/221.

Practice Direction—See generally PD19B at p 629.

19.14 Removal from the register

(1) A party to a claim entered on the group register may apply to the management court for the claim to be removed from the register.

(2) If the management court orders the claim to be removed from the register it may give directions about the future management of the claim.

Amendments—Inserted by SI 2000/221.

Practice Direction—See generally PD19B at p 629.

19.15 Test claims

(1) Where a direction has been given for a claim on the group register to proceed as a test claim and that claim is settled, the management court may order that another claim on the group register be substituted as the test claim.

(2) Where an order is made under paragraph (1), any order made in the test claim before the date of substitution is binding on the substituted claim unless the court orders otherwise.

Amendments—Inserted by SI 2000/221.

Practice Direction—See generally PD19B at p 629.

Practice Direction – Addition and Substitution of Parties

This Practice Direction supplements CPR Part 19 (PD19)

A party applying for an amendment will usually be responsible for the costs of and arising from the amendment.

Procedural Guide—See Guide 20, set out in Section 1 of this work.

Changes of Parties

GENERAL

1.1 Parties may be removed, added or substituted in existing proceedings either on the court's own initiative or on the application of either an existing party or a person who wishes to become a party.

1.2 The application may be dealt with without a hearing where all the existing parties and the proposed new party are in agreement.

1.3 The application to add or substitute a new party should be supported by evidence setting out the proposed new party's interest in or connection with the claim.

1.4 The application notice should be filed in accordance with rule 23.3 and, unless the application is made under rule 19.2(4) [1], be served in accordance with rule 23.4.

1 See rule 19.4(3)(a).

1.5 An order giving permission to amend will, unless the court orders otherwise, be drawn up. It will be served by the court unless the parties wish to serve it or the court orders them to do so.

'evidence' (para 1.3)—Note that this is mandatory. It may be endorsed on the application notice provided it is verified by a statement of truth. The cost of preparing an affidavit will not be recoverable from other parties because affidavit evidence is not required by the rule.

Application notice—No form is prescribed but N244 may be used.

ADDITION OR SUBSTITUTION OF CLAIMANT

2.1 Where an application is made to the court to add or to substitute a new party to the proceedings as claimant, the party applying must file:

(1) the application notice,
(2) the proposed amended claim form and particulars of claim, and
(3) the signed, written consent of the new claimant to be so added or substituted.

2.2 Where the court makes an order adding or substituting a party as claimant but the signed, written consent of the new claimant has not been filed:

(1) the order, and
(2) the addition or substitution of the new party as claimant,

will not take effect until the signed, written consent of the new claimant is filed.

2.3 Where the court has made an order adding or substituting a new claimant, the court may direct:

(1) a copy of the order to be served on every party to the proceedings and any other person affected by the order,
(2) copies of the statements of case and of documents referred to in any statement of case to be served on the new party,
(3) the party who made the application to file within 14 days an amended claim form and particulars of claim.

ADDITION OR SUBSTITUTION OF DEFENDANT

3.1 The Civil Procedure Rules apply to a new defendant who has been added or substituted as they apply to any other defendant (see in particular the provisions of Parts 9, 10, 11 and 15).

3.2 Where the court has made an order adding or substituting a defendant whether on its own initiative or on an application, the court may direct:

(1) the claimant to file with the court within 14 days (or as ordered) an amended claim form and particulars of claim for the court file,

(2) a copy of the order to be served on all parties to the proceedings and any other person affected by it,
(3) the amended claim form and particulars of claim, forms for admitting, defending and acknowledging the claim and copies of the statements of case and any other documents referred to in any statement of case to be served on the new defendant,
(4) unless the court orders otherwise, the amended claim form and particulars of claim to be served on any other defendants.

3.3 A new defendant does not become a party to the proceedings until the amended claim form has been served on him[1].

1 *Kettleman v Hansel Properties Ltd* [1987] AC 189, HL.

REMOVAL OF PARTY

4 Where the court makes an order for the removal of a party from the proceedings:

(1) the claimant must file with the court an amended claim form and particulars of claim, and
(2) a copy of the order must be served on every party to the proceedings and on any other person affected by the order.

TRANSFER OF INTEREST OR LIABILITY

5.1 Where the interest or liability of an existing party has passed to some other person, application should be made to the court to add or substitute that person[1].

1 See rule 19.2(4).

5.2 The application must be supported by evidence showing the stage the proceedings have reached and what change has occurred to cause the transfer of interest or liability.

(For information about making amendments generally, see the practice direction supplementing Part 17)

'evidence' (para 5.2)—See note to para 1.3.

HUMAN RIGHTS, JOINING THE CROWN

Section 4 of the Human Rights Act

6.1 Where a party has included in his statement of case –

(1) a claim for a declaration of incompatibility in accordance with section 4 of the Human Rights Act 1998, or
(2) an issue for the court to decide which may lead to the court considering making a declaration,

then the court may at any time consider whether notice should be given to the Crown as required by that Act and give directions for the content and service of the notice. The rule allows a period of 21 days before the court will make the declaration but the court may vary this period of time.

6.2 The court will normally consider the issues and give the directions referred to in paragraph 6.1 at the case management conference.

6.3 Where a party amends his statement of case to include any matter referred to in paragraph 6.1, then the court will consider whether notice should be given to the Crown and give directions for the content and service of the notice.

(The practice direction to CPR Part 16 requires a party to include issues under the Human Rights Act 1998 in his statement of case)

6.4 (1) The notice given under rule 19.4A must be served on the person named in the list published under section 17 of the Crown Proceedings Act 1947.

(The list, made by the Minister for the Civil Service, is annexed to the practice direction to Part 66)

(2) The notice will be in the form directed by the court but will normally include the directions given by the court and all the statements of case in the claim. The notice will also be served on all the parties.

(3) The court may require the parties to assist in the preparation of the notice.

(4) In the circumstances described in the National Assembly for Wales (Transfer of Functions) (No 2) Order 2000 the notice must also be served on the National Assembly for Wales.

(Section 5(3) of the Human Rights Act 1998 provides that the Crown may give notice that it intends to become a party at any stage in the proceedings once notice has been given)

6.5 Unless the court orders otherwise, the minister or other person permitted by the Human Rights Act 1998 to be joined as a party must, if he wishes to be joined, give notice of his intention to be joined as a party to the court and every other party. Where the minister has nominated a person to be joined as a party the notice must be accompanied by the written nomination.

(Section 5(2)(a) of the Human Rights Act 1998 permits a person nominated by a minister of the Crown to be joined as a party. The nomination may be signed on behalf of the minister)

Section 9 of the Human Rights Act 1998

6.6 (1) The procedure in paragraphs 6.1 to 6.5 also applies where a claim is made under sections 7(1)(a) and 9(3) of the Human Rights Act 1998 for damages in respect of a judicial act.

(2) Notice must be given to the Lord Chancellor and should be served on the Treasury Solicitor on his behalf, except where the judicial act is of a court-martial when the appropriate person is the Secretary of State for Defence and the notice must be served on the Treasury Solicitor on his behalf.

(3) The notice will also give details of the judicial act, which is the subject of the claim for damages, and of the court or tribunal that made it.

(Section 9(4) of the Human Rights Act 1998 provides that no award of damages may be made against the Crown as provided for in section 9(3) unless the appropriate person is joined in the proceedings. The appropriate person is the minister responsible for the court concerned or a person or department nominated by him (section 9(5) of the Act))

Practice Direction – Group Litigation

This Practice Direction supplements Section III of Part 19 (PD19B)

INTRODUCTION

1 This practice direction deals with group litigation where the multiple parties are claimants. Section III of Part 19 (group litigation orders) also applies where the multiple parties are defendants. The court will give such directions in such a case as are appropriate.

PRELIMINARY STEPS

2.1 Before applying for a Group Litigation Order ('GLO') the solicitor acting for the proposed applicant should consult the Law Society's Multi-Party Action Information Service in order to obtain information about other cases giving rise to the proposed GLO issues.

2.2 It will often be convenient for the claimants' solicitors to form a Solicitors' Group and to choose one of their number to take the lead in applying for the GLO and in litigating the GLO issues. The lead solicitor's role and relationship with the other members of the Solicitors' Group should be carefully defined in writing and will be subject to any directions given by the court under CPR 19.13(c).

2.3 In considering whether to apply for a GLO, the applicant should consider whether any other order would be more appropriate. In particular he should consider whether, in the circumstances of the case, it would be more appropriate for –

(1) the claims to be consolidated; or
(2) the rules in Section II of Part 19 (representative parties) to be used.

APPLICATION FOR A GLO

3.1 An application for a GLO must be made in accordance with CPR Part 23, may be made at any time before or after any relevant claims have been issued and may be made either by a claimant or by a defendant.

3.2 The following information should be included in the application notice or in written evidence filed in support of the application –

(1) a summary of the nature of the litigation;
(2) the number and nature of claims already issued;
(3) the number of parties likely to be involved;
(4) the common issues of fact or law (the 'GLO issues') that are likely to arise in the litigation; and
(5) whether there are any matters that distinguish smaller groups of claims within the wider group.

3.3 A GLO may not be made[–

(1) in the Queen's Bench Division, without the consent of the Lord Chief Justice,
(2) in the Chancery Division, without the consent of the Vice-Chancellor, or
(3) in a county court, without the consent of the Head of Civil Justice.

3.4 The court to which the application for a GLO is made will, if minded to make the GLO, send to the Lord Chief Justice or the Vice-Chancellor, or the Head of Civil Justice, as appropriate –

(1) a copy of the application notice,
(2) a copy of any relevant written evidence, and
(3) a written statement as to why a GLO is considered to be desirable.

These steps may be taken either before or after a hearing of the application.]

High Court in London

3.5 The application for the GLO should be made to the Senior Master in the Queen's Bench Division or the Chief Chancery Master in the Chancery Division. For claims that are proceeding or are likely to proceed in a specialist list, the application should be made to the senior judge of that list.

High Court outside London

3.6 Outside London, the application should be made to a Presiding Judge or a Chancery Supervising Judge of the circuit in which the district registry which has issued the application notice is situated.

County courts

3.7 The application should be made to the designated civil judge for the area in which the county court which has issued the application notice is situated.

3.8 The applicant for a GLO should request the relevant court to refer the application notice to the judge by whom the application will be heard as soon as possible after the application notice has been issued. This is to enable the judge to consider whether to follow the practice set out in paragraph 3.4 above prior to the hearing of the application.

3.9 The directions under paragraphs 3.5, 3.6 and 3.7 above do not prevent the judges referred to from making arrangements for other judges to hear applications for GLOs when they themselves are unavailable.

GLO MADE BY COURT OF ITS OWN INITIATIVE

4 Subject to obtaining the appropriate consent referred to in paragraph 3.3 and the procedure set out in paragraph 3.4, the court may make a GLO of its own initiative.

(CPR 3.3 deals with the procedure that applies when a court proposes to make an order of its own initiative)

THE GLO

5 CPR 19.11(2) and (3) set out rules relating to the contents of GLOs.

THE GROUP REGISTER

6.1 Once a GLO has been made a Group Register will be established on which will be entered such details as the court may direct of the cases which are to be subject to the GLO.

6.1A A claim must be issued before it can be entered on a Group Register.

6.2 An application for details of a case to be entered on a Group Register may be made by any party to the case.

6.3 An order for details of the case to be entered on the Group Register will not be made unless the case gives rise to at least one of the GLO issues.

(CPR 19.10 defines GLO issues)

6.4 The court, if it is not satisfied that a case can be conveniently case managed with the other cases on the Group Register, or if it is satisfied that the entry of the case on the Group Register would adversely affect the case management of the other cases, may refuse to allow details of the case to be entered on the Group Register, or order their removal from the Register if already entered, although the case gives rise to one or more of the Group issues.

6.5 The Group Register will normally be maintained by and kept at the court but the court may direct this to be done by the solicitor for one of the parties to a case entered on the Register.

6.6 (1) Rule 5.4 (supply of documents from court records) applies where the register is maintained by the court. A party to a claim on the group register may request documents relating to any other claim on the group register in accordance with rule 5.4(1) as if he were a party to those proceedings.

(2) Where the register is maintained by a solicitor, any person may inspect the Group Register during normal business hours and upon giving reasonable notice to the solicitor; the solicitor may charge a fee not exceeding the fee prescribed for a search at the court office.

6.7 In this paragraph, 'the court' means the management court specified in the GLO.

ALLOCATION TO TRACK

7 Once a GLO has been made and unless the management court directs otherwise –

(1) every claim in a case entered on the Group Register will be automatically allocated, or re-allocated (as the case may be), to the multi-track;

(2) any case management directions that have already been given in any such case otherwise than by the management court will be set aside; and

(3) any hearing date already fixed otherwise than for the purposes of the group litigation will be vacated.

MANAGING JUDGE

8 A judge ('the managing judge') will be appointed for the purpose of the GLO as soon as possible. He will assume overall responsibility for the management of the claims and will generally hear the GLO issues. A master or a district judge may be appointed to deal with procedural matters, which he will do in accordance with any directions given by the managing judge. A costs judge may be appointed and may be invited to attend case management hearings.

CLAIMS TO BE STARTED IN MANAGEMENT COURT

9.1 The management court may order that as from a specified date all claims that raise one or more of the GLO issues shall be started in the management court.

9.2 Failure to comply with an order made under paragraph 9.1 will not invalidate the commencement of the claim but the claim should be transferred to the management court and details entered on the Group Register as soon as possible. Any party to the claim may apply to the management court for an order under CPR 19.14 removing the case from the Register or, as the case may be, for an order that details of the case be not entered on the Register.

TRANSFER

10 Where the management court is a county court and a claim raising one or more of the GLO issues is proceeding in the High Court, an order transferring the case to the management court and directing the details of the case to be entered on the Group Register can only be made in the High Court.

PUBLICISING THE GLO

11 After a GLO has been made, a copy of the GLO should be supplied –

(1) to the Law Society, 113 Chancery Lane, London WC2A 1PL; and
(2) to the Senior Master, Queen's Bench Division, Royal Courts of Justice, Strand, London WC2A 2LL.

CASE MANAGEMENT

12.1 The management court may give case management directions at the time the GLO is made or subsequently. Directions given at a case management hearing will generally be binding on all claims that are subsequently entered on the Group Register (see CPR 19.12(1)).

12.2 Any application to vary the terms of the GLO must be made to the management court.

12.3 The management court may direct that one or more of the claims are to proceed as test claims.

12.4 The management court may give directions about how the costs of resolving common issues or the costs of claims proceeding as test claims are to be borne or shared as between the claimants on the Group Register.

CUT-OFF DATES

13 The management court may specify a date after which no claim may be added to the Group Register unless the court gives permission. An early cut-off date may be appropriate in the case of 'instant disasters' (such as transport accidents). In the case of consumer claims, and particularly pharmaceutical claims, it may be necessary to delay the ordering of a cut-off date.

STATEMENTS OF CASE

14.1 The management court may direct that the GLO claimants serve 'Group Particulars of Claim' which set out the various claims of all the claimants on the Group Register at the time the particulars are filed. Such particulars of claim will usually contain –

(1) general allegations relating to all claims; and
(2) a schedule containing entries relating to each individual claim specifying which of the general allegations are relied on and any specific facts relevant to the claimant.

14.2 The directions given under paragraph 14.1 should include directions as to whether the Group Particulars should be verified by a statement or statements of truth and, if so, by whom.

14.3 The specific facts relating to each claimant on the Group Register may be obtained by the use of a questionnaire. Where this is proposed, the management court should be asked to approve the questionnaire. The management court may direct that the questionnaires completed by individual claimants take the place of the schedule referred to in paragraph 14.1(2).

14.4 The management court may also give directions about the form that particulars of claim relating to claims which are to be entered on the Group Register should take.

THE TRIAL

15.1 The management court may give directions –

(1) for the trial of common issues; and
(2) for the trial of individual issues.

15.2 Common issues and test claims will normally be tried at the management court. Individual issues may be directed to be tried at other courts whose locality is convenient for the parties.

COSTS

16.1 CPR 48 contains rules about costs where a GLO has been made.

16.2 Where the court has made an order about costs in relation to any application or hearing which involved both –

(1) one or more of the GLO issues; and
(2) an issue or issues relevant only to individual claims;

and the court has not directed the proportion of the costs that is to relate to common costs and the proportion that is to relate to individual costs in accordance with rule 48.6A(5), the costs judge will make a decision as to the relevant proportions at or before the commencement of the detailed assessment of costs.

PART 20
COUNTERCLAIMS AND OTHER ADDITIONAL CLAIMS

CONTENTS OF THIS PART

Procedural Guides—See Guide 8 (Making a Counterclaim), Guide 9 (Making a Claim against a Co-Defendant for Contribution or Indemnity) and Guide 10 (Making a Claim against a Non-Party, etc), set out in Section 1 of this work.

Practice Direction—See generally PD20 at p 640.

20.1 Purpose of Part 20

The purpose of Part 20 is to enable Part 20 claims to be managed in the most convenient and effective manner.

20.2 Meaning of 'Part 20 claim'

(1) A Part 20 claim is any claim other than a claim by a claimant against a defendant and includes –

- (a) a counterclaim by a defendant against the claimant or against the claimant and some other person;
- (b) a claim by a defendant against any person (whether or not already a party) for contribution(GL) or indemnity(GL) or some other remedy; and
- (c) where a Part 20 claim has been made against a person who is not already a party, any claim made by that person against any other person (whether or not already a party).

(2) In this Part 'Part 20 claimant' means a person who makes a Part 20 claim.

Part 20 claims—The object of this procedure is to avoid multiple claims (in the sense of 'actions') by combining and managing issues arising from the main claim. There are three types of claims: counterclaims, claims between parties for contribution or indemnity and claims against non-parties. Part 26 applies different procedures to each type of claim and great care must be taken to untangle the resulting complexities.

Counterclaims against Crown—Note the restrictions carried by Sch 1, RSC Ord 77, r 6 and Sch 2, CCR Ord 42, r 9.

20.3 Part 20 claim to be treated as a claim for the purposes of the Rules

(1) A Part 20 claim shall be treated as if it were a claim for the purposes of these Rules, except as provided by this Part

(2) The following rules do not apply to Part 20 claims –

(a) rules 7.5 and 7.6 (time within which a claim form may be served);
(b) rule 16.3(5) (statement of value where claim to be issued in the High Court); and
(c) Part 26 (case management – preliminary stage).

(3) Part 12 (default judgment) applies to a Part 20 claim only if it is a counterclaim.

(4) With the exception of –

(a) rules 14.1(1) and 14.1(2) (which provide that a party may admit the truth of another party's case in writing); and
(b) rule 14.3(1) (admission by notice in writing – application for judgment),

which apply to all Part 20 claims, Part 14 (admissions) applies to a Part 20 claim only if it is a counterclaim.

(Rule 12.3(2) sets out how to obtain judgment in default of defence where the Part 20 claim is a counterclaim against the claimant, and rule 20.11 makes special provision for default judgment in some categories of Part 20 claims)

Amendments—SI 2000/221.

'A Part 20 claim shall be treated as if it were a claim' (r 20.3(1))—Save for the exceptions in r 20.3(2), a Pt 20 claim is a statement of case. It must comply with the requirements for particulars of claim, be headed with the correct title (see PD20, para 7), comply with r 16(1)–(4) and be verified by a statement of truth in the form set out in PD20, para 4.2)

'Part 12 (default judgment)' (r 20.3(3))—All Pt 20 claims, other than counterclaims, are, here, exempt from default judgment under Pt 12 but are susceptible to summary judgment under Pt 24.

Counterclaims may, however, escape susceptibility to default judgment by the operation of r 20.4(3) which relieves a claimant defending a counterclaim from having to file an acknowledgment of service. A claimant may thus be said to be outside (r 12.3(1) and (2)). Rule 20.4(3) and (4) were substituted for the former para (3) to reflect an amendment to r 12.3. This now enables judgment in default of defence to a counterclaim made under r 20.4, closing an earlier loophole.

'special provision for default judgment' (note to r 20.3(3))—Part 20 claims against non-parties are subject to a special default judgment provision (r 20.11).

Case management – preliminary stage (r 20.3(2)(c))—When the Pt 20 defendant files a defence other than to a counterclaim the court will arrange a case management hearing (r 20.13). Paragraph 5.3 of PD20 sets out the orders that the court is likely to make.

20.4 Defendant's counterclaim against the claimant

(1) A defendant may make a counterclaim against a claimant by filing particulars of the counterclaim.

(2) A defendant may make a counterclaim against a claimant –

(a) without the court's permission if he files it with his defence; or
(b) at any other time with the court's permission.

(Part 15 makes provision for a defence to a claim and applies to a defence to a counterclaim by virtue of rule 20.3)

(3) Part 10 (acknowledgment of service) does not apply to a claimant who wishes to defend a counterclaim.

'without the court's permission' (r 20.4(2)(a))—See the table at r 20.9 and the notes there regarding the procedure on applications for permission.

'acknowledgment of service' (r 20.4(3))—See the notes on default judgment at r 20.3(3)(a) above.

20.5 Counterclaim against a person other than the claimant

(1) A defendant who wishes to counterclaim against a person other than the claimant must apply to the court for an order that that person be added as defendant to the counterclaim.

(2) An application for an order under paragraph (1) may be made without noticc unlcss thc court dirccts othcrwisc.

(3) Where the court makes an order under paragraph (1), it will give directions as to the management of the case.

'must apply to the court' (r 20.5(1))—See the table at r 20.9 and the notes there regarding the procedure on applications for permission.

20.6 Defendant's claim for contribution or indemnity from co-defendant

(1) A defendant who has filed an acknowledgment of service or a defence may make a Part 20 claim for contribution(GL) or indemnity(GL) against another defendant by –

- (a) filing a notice containing a statement of the nature and grounds of his claim; and
- (b) serving that notice on the other defendant.

(2) A defendant may file and serve a notice under this rule –

- (a) without the court's permission, if he files and serves it –
  - (i) with his defence; or
  - (ii) if his claim for contribution or indemnity is against a defendant added to the claim later, within 28 days after that defendant files his defence; or
- (b) at any other time with the court's permission.

Amendments—SI 2001/4015.

'contribution or indemnity against another defendant' (r 20.6)—For example, a defendant liable to pay damages may claim contribution from others who may share liability under the Civil Liability (Contribution) Act 1978 and does not require the court's permission to do so.

20.7 Procedure for making any other Part 20 claim

(1) This rule applies to any Part 20 claim except –

- (a) a counterclaim; and
- (b) a claim for contribution(GL) or indemnity(GL) made in accordance with rule 20.6.

(2) A Part 20 claim is made when the court issues a Part 20 claim form.

(Rule 7.2(2) provides that a claim form is issued on the date entered on the form by the court)

(3) A defendant may make a Part 20 claim –

(a) without the court's permission if the Part 20 claim is issued before or at the same time as he files his defence;
(b) at any other time with the court's permission.

(Rule 15.4 sets out the period for filing a defence)

(4) Particulars of a Part 20 claim must be contained in or served with the Part 20 claim.

(5) An application for permission to make a Part 20 claim may be made without notice, unless the court directs otherwise.

'a Part 20 claim form' (r 20.7(2))—Form N211 is required. Counterclaims should follow on from the defence forming one document (see PD20, para 6 which also sets out the form of a defence to a counterclaim).

'at any other time with the court's permission' (r 20.7(3)(b))—See the table at r 20.9 and the notes there regarding the procedure on applications for permission.

20.8 Service of a Part 20 claim form

(1) Where a Part 20 claim may be made without the court's permission, the Part 20 claim form must –

(a) in the case of a counterclaim against an existing party only, be served on every other party when a copy of the defence is served;
(b) in the case of any other Part 20 claim, be served on the person against whom it is made within 14 days after the date on which the Part 20 claim is issued by the court.

(2) Paragraph (1) does not apply to a claim for contribution(GL) or indemnity(GL) made in accordance with rule 20.6.

(3) Where the court gives permission to make a Part 20 claim it will at the same time give directions as to the service of the Part 20 claim.

Serving Part 20 Claims (r 20.8)—

Type of claim	Rule ref	When served
Counterclaims		
Counterclaim against claimant filed with defence	r 20.8(1)(a)	With the defence
Counterclaim against claimant filed at any other time	r 20.8(3)	As the court directs
Counterclaim against persons other than claimant	r 20.8(3)	As the court directs
Contribution and indemnity claims		
Claim for contribution or indemnity against co-defendant	r 20.6	At or after filing acknowledgment of service or defence
Other Part 20 claims		
If issued before or at same time defence is filed	r 20.8(1)(b)	Within 14 days of filing defence
If issued at any other time	r 20.8(3)	As the court directs

'service' (r 20.8(3))—The court will decide the method of service (r 6.3(2)) and Pt 6 sets out the methods of service by post, document exchange, fax etc and the date service is deemed to have been effected. Sufficient copies should be lodged with the court for service on all necessary parties.

20.9 Matters relevant to question of whether a Part 20 claim should be separate from main claim

(1) This rule applies where the court is considering whether to –

- (a) permit a Part 20 claim to be made;
- (b) dismiss a Part 20 claim; or
- (c) require a Part 20 claim to be dealt with separately from the claim by the claimant against the defendant.

(Rule 3.1(2)(e) and (j) deal respectively with the court's power to order that part of proceedings be dealt with as separate proceedings and to decide the order in which issues are to be tried)

(2) The matters to which the court may have regard include –

- (a) the connection between the Part 20 claim and the claim made by the claimant against the defendant;
- (b) whether the Part 20 claimant is seeking substantially the same remedy which some other party is claiming from him; and
- (c) whether the Part 20 claimant wants the court to decide any question connected with the subject matter of the proceedings –
  - (i) not only between existing parties but also between existing parties and a person not already a party; or
  - (ii) against an existing party not only in a capacity in which he is already a party but also in some further capacity.

When permission is required to make a Part 20 claim—

Type of claim	Rule ref	Permission required
Counterclaims		
Counterclaim against claimant filed with defence	r 20.4(2)(a)	No
Counterclaim against claimant filed at any other time	r 20.4(2)(b)	Yes
Counterclaim against persons other than claimant	r 20.5(1)	Yes
Contribution, etc claims		
Claim for contribution or indemnity against co-defendant	r 20.6	No
All other Part 20 claims		
If issued before or at same time defence is filed	r 20.7(3)(a)	No
If issued at any other time	r 20.7(3)(b)	Yes

Applications for permission (r 20.9)—Applications are normally made without notice and a copy of the proposed Pt 20 claim should be filed with the application. The application is likely to be dismissed if not supported by the mandatory supporting evidence required by PD20, para 2.

'the connection between the Part 20 claim and the claim made by the claimant against the defendant' (r 20.9(2)(a))—In *Royal Brompton Hospital National Health Trust v Watkins Gray International (UK)* [2000] Con LR 145, CA, Pt 20 proceedings were struck out on the grounds that the claims made against the Pt 20 defendant were not in respect of 'the same damage' as that alleged by the claimant against the defendant in the main proceedings. The Pt 20 claim was for liquidated and ascertained damages for delay, and for repayment of loss and expense. The claim against WGI in the main proceedings was that WGI was in breach of duty in that its conduct had weakened the case for the hospital in the arbitration, making it less able to negotiate a proper compromise. In those circumstances the claims were not in respect of 'the same damage', and the Pt 20 proceedings were struck out.

'against an existing party not only in a capacity in which he is already a party but also in some further capacity' (r 20.9(2)(c)(ii))—In *Re a Debtor (No 87 of 1999), sub nom Debtor v P J Johnston* (2000) 97(7) LSG 40, the claimant sued in her personal capacity, and the defendant brought a counterclaim against her in her capacity as the sole executrix of her husband's estate. Rimer J held that there was nothing in Pt 20 that indicated a claimant suing personally could not be made the object of a counterclaim against him in some different capacity. His Lordship accepted that r 20.9 indicated that such a feature of the counterclaim would be a factor to which the court should have regard to in considering whether to dismiss the counterclaim or to require it to be dealt with separately from the main claim. It would be surprising if the CPR were so rigid to be a complete bar on the counterclaim as there was no such rigidity under the former practice.

20.10 Effect of service of a Part 20 claim

(1) A person on whom a Part 20 claim is served becomes a party to the proceedings if he is not a party already.

(2) When a Part 20 claim is served on an existing party for the purpose of requiring the court to decide a question against that party in a further capacity, that party also becomes a party in the further capacity specified in the Part 20 claim.

'becomes a party to the proceedings' (r 20.10(1))—The title of proceedings must be amended and should comply with PD20, para 7.

Cost sharing arrangement—Part 20 defendants brought into a claim made by an insufficiently resourced claimant would be wise to make a costs sharing arrangement or co-operate with the Pt 20 claimant, eg as to how expert evidence is to be obtained. The court will be unlikely to depart from the usual costs order between them even if the Pt 20 claim determines after the main claim by the impecunious claimant collapses. For a salutary lesson see *Arkin v Borchard Lines Ltd (No 3)* [2003] EWHC 3088 (Comm), [2004] 1 Lloyd's Rep 636, (2003) Lawtel, 16 December, QBD, Colman J.

20.11 Special provisions relating to default judgment on a Part 20 claim other than a counterclaim or a contribution or indemnity notice

(1) This rule applies if –

- (a) the Part 20 claim is not –
  - (i) a counterclaim; or
  - (ii) a claim by a defendant for contribution(GL) or indemnity(GL) against another defendant under rule 20.6; and
- (b) the party against whom a Part 20 claim is made fails to file an acknowledgment of service or defence in respect of the Part 20 claim.

(2) The party against whom the Part 20 claim is made –

- (a) is deemed to admit the Part 20 claim, and is bound by any judgment or decision in the main proceedings in so far as it is relevant to any matter arising in the Part 20 claim;
- (b) subject to paragraph (3), if default judgment under Part 12 is given against the Part 20 claimant, the Part 20 claimant may obtain judgment in respect of the Part 20 claim by filing a request in the relevant practice form.

(3) A Part 20 claimant may not enter judgment under paragraph (2)(b) without the court's permission if –

- (a) he has not satisfied the default judgment which has been given against him; or
- (b) he wishes to obtain judgment for any remedy other than a contribution(GL) or indemnity(GL).

(4) An application for the court's permission under paragraph (3) may be made without notice unless the court directs otherwise.

(5) The court may at any time set aside(GL) or vary a judgment entered under paragraph (2)(b).

'deemed to admit' (r 20.11(2)(a))—Part 12 default judgments are inappropriate as liability is conditional on the Pt 20 claimant losing the main claim. A default will prevent the defendant to a Pt 20 claim from disputing a decision in the main claim.

'if he has not satisfied the default judgment' (r 20.11(3(a))—This provision prevents a Pt 20 claimant from gaining a windfall by pocketing a judgment he has not himself satisfied.

20.12 Procedural steps on service of a Part 20 claim form on a non-party

(1) Where a Part 20 claim form is served on a person who is not already a party it must be accompanied by –

- (a) a form for defending the claim;
- (b) a form for admitting the claim;
- (c) a form for acknowledging service; and
- (d) a copy of –
  - (i) every statement of case which has already been served in the proceedings; and
  - (ii) such other documents as the court may direct.

(2) A copy of the Part 20 claim form must be served on every existing party.

20.13 Case management where there is a defence to a Part 20 claim form

(1) Where a defence is filed to a Part 20 claim the court must consider the future conduct of the proceedings and give appropriate directions.

(2) In giving directions under paragraph (1) the court must ensure that, so far as practicable, the Part 20 claim and the main claim are managed together.

Appropriate directions (r 20.13(1))—See PD20, para 5 for case management of Pt 20 claims and the orders that will normally be made.

Practice Direction – Counterclaims and Other Part 20 Claims

This Practice Direction supplements CPR Part 20 (PD20)

A Part 20 claim is any claim other than the claim by the claimant against the defendant.

Procedural Guide—See Guide 8, set out in Section 1 of this work.

General note—See also the notes to CPR Pt 20 for relevant commentary.

CASES WHERE COURT'S PERMISSION TO MAKE A PART 20 CLAIM IS REQUIRED

1.1 Rules 20.4(2)(b), 20.5(1) and 20.7(3)(b) set out the circumstances in which the court's permission will be needed for making a Part 20 claim.

1.2 Where an application is made for permission to make a Part 20 claim the application notice should be filed together with a copy of the proposed Part 20 claim.

APPLICATIONS FOR PERMISSION TO ISSUE A PART 20 CLAIM

2.1 An application for permission to make a Part 20 claim must be supported by evidence stating:

(1) the stage which the action has reached,
(2) the nature of the claim to be made by the Part 20 claimant or details of the question or issue which needs to be decided,
(3) a summary of the facts on which the Part 20 claim is based, and
(4) the name and address of the proposed Part 20 defendant.

(For further information regarding evidence see the practice direction which supplements Part 32)

2.2 Where delay has been a factor contributing to the need to apply for permission to make a Part 20 claim an explanation of the delay should be given in evidence.

2.3 Where possible the applicant should provide a timetable of the action to date.

2.4 Rules 20.5(2) and 20.7(5) allow applications to be made to the court without notice unless the court otherwise directs.

GENERAL

3 The Civil Procedure Rules apply generally to Part 20 claims as if they were claims[1]. Parties should be aware that the provisions relating to failure to respond will apply.

1 Rule 20.3 but note the exceptions set out in rule 20.3(2) and (3).

STATEMENT OF TRUTH

4.1 The contents of a Part 20 claim should be verified by a statement of truth. Part 22 requires a statement of case to be verified by a statement of truth.

4.2 The form of the statement of truth should be as follows:

'[I believe][the [Part 20 claimant]* believes] that the facts stated in this statement of case are true.'

*(For the purpose of this practice direction the Part 20 claimant means any party making a Part 20 claim)

4.3 Attention is drawn to rule 32.14 which sets out the consequences of verifying a statement of case containing a false statement without an honest belief in its truth.

(For information regarding statements of truth see Part 22 and the practice direction which supplements it)

CASE MANAGEMENT WHERE THERE IS A PART 20 DEFENCE

5.1 Where the Part 20 defendant files a defence, other than to a counterclaim, the court will arrange a hearing to consider case management of the Part 20 claim.

5.2 The court will give notice of the hearing to each party likely to be affected by any order made at the hearing.

5.3 At the hearing the court may:

(1) treat the hearing as a summary judgment hearing,
(2) order that the Part 20 proceedings be dismissed,
(3) give directions about the way any claim, question or issue set out in or arising from the Part 20 claim should be dealt with,
(4) give directions as to the part, if any, the Part 20 defendant will take at the trial of the claim,
(5) give directions about the extent to which the Part 20 defendant is to be bound by any judgment or decision to be made in the claim.

5.4 The court may make any of the orders in 5.3(1) to (5) either before or after any judgment in the claim has been entered by the claimant against the defendant.

FORM OF COUNTERCLAIM

6.1 Where a defendant to a claim serves a counterclaim under this Part, the defence and counterclaim should normally form one document with the counterclaim following on from the defence.

6.2 Where a claimant serves a reply and a defence to counterclaim, the reply and the defence to counterclaim should normally form one document with the defence to counterclaim following on from the reply.

TITLES OF PROCEEDINGS WHERE THERE ARE PART 20 CLAIMS

7.1 The title of every Part 20 claim should contain:

(1) the full name of each party, and
(2) his status in the proceedings (eg claimant, defendant, Part 20 claimant, Part 20 defendant etc). For example:

AB	Claimant
CD	Defendant/Part 20 claimant
EF	Part 20 Defendant

7.2 Where a defendant makes a counterclaim not only against the claimant but also against a non-party the title should show this as follows:

AB	Claimant/Part 20 Defendant
CD	Defendant/Part 20 claimant
	and
XY	Part 20 Defendant

7.3 Where there is more than one Part 20 claim, the parties to the first Part 20 claim should be described as 'Part 20 Claimant (1st claim)' and 'Part 20

Defendant (1st claim)', the parties to the second Part 20 claim should be described as 'Part 20 Claimant (2nd claim)' and 'Part 20 Defendant (2nd claim)', and so on. For example:

AB	Claimant and Part 20 Defendant (2nd claim)
CD	Defendant and Part 20 claimant (1st claim)
EF	Part 20 Defendant (1st claim) and Part 20 Claimant (2nd claim)
GH	Part 20 Defendant (2nd claim)

7.4 Where the full name of a party is lengthy it must appear in the title but thereafter in the statement of case it may be identified by an abbreviation such as initials or a recognised shortened name.

7.5 Where a party to proceedings has more than one status eg Claimant and Part 20 Defendant (2nd claim) or Part 20 Defendant (1st claim) and Part 20 claimant (2nd claim) the combined status must appear in the title but thereafter it may be convenient to refer to the party by name, eg Mr Smith or, if paragraph 7.4 applies, by initials or a shortened name.

7.6 Paragraph 4 of the practice direction supplementing Part 7 contains further directions regarding the title to proceedings.

PART 21
CHILDREN AND PATIENTS

CONTENTS OF THIS PART

Procedural Guide—See Guide 17, set out in Section 1 of this work.

21.1 Scope of this Part

(1) This Part –

(a) contains special provisions which apply in proceedings involving children and patients; and

(b) sets out how a person becomes a litigation friend.

(2) In this Part –

(a) 'child' means a person under 18; and

(b) 'patient' means a person who by reason of mental disorder within the meaning of the Mental Health Act 1983 is incapable of managing and administering his property and affairs.

(Rule 6.6 contains provisions about the service of documents on children and patients)

(Rule 48.5 deals with costs where money is payable by or to a child or patient)

Amendments—SI 2003/3361.

Practice Direction—See generally PD21 at p 661.

Scope of provision—This Part replaces RSC Ord 80 and CCR Ord 10 in making special provision for those litigants who were previously described as being 'persons under disability' although that terminology is no longer used. There are two distinct categories:

(a) 'children' who are by reason of age deemed incapable of acting personally unless permitted by the court;

(b) 'patients' who are treated as being incapable of conducting the proceedings.

A representative known as a 'litigation friend' must generally be appointed to conduct the proceedings in the name and on behalf of the child or patient, and any settlement or compromise must be approved by the court.

'child' (r 21.1(2)(a))—Defined as 'a person under 18' by r 21.1(2)(a). The expressions previously used were 'infant' (RSC Ord 80) and 'minor' (CCR Ord 10) but there is no material difference. There is now provision for the child to act personally even before attaining that age (r 21.2(3)) but approval of the court is required and may subsequently be withdrawn (r 21.2(5)).

'child' or 'patient'—It is possible for a child also to be a patient and this may be relevant if that condition will continue to subsist on ceasing to be a child (eg in regard to the disposal of money awarded to the child). Thus a child who has severe learning disabilities will continue to be a patient even after attaining the age of 18.

'litigation friend' (r 21.1(1)(b))—This expression is used for the representative whether the party is a claimant or defendant and replaces both next friend and guardian *ad litem* used in previous rules. Those terms are still used in family proceedings governed by Family Proceedings Rules 1991, Part IX.

'mental disorder' (r 21.1(2)(b))—Defined by Mental Health Act 1983, s 1(2) as 'mental illness, arrested or incomplete development of mind, psychopathic disorder and any other disorder or disability of mind' and 'mentally disordered' is to be construed accordingly. Nothing in the definition is to be construed as implying that a person may be dealt with as suffering from mental disorder by reason only of 'promiscuity or other immoral conduct, sexual deviancy or dependence on alcohol or drugs' (s 1(3)).

This definition is extremely wide and makes no reference to the degree of impairment, but it provides a useful screening process because merely being eccentric is not a basis for being deprived of one's right to conduct litigation. In cases of dispute, medical evidence is required to confirm the diagnosis of a specific mental disorder and there are basically three categories of person who come within the definition, namely those with:

(a) a mental illness. The largest group comprises elderly people who become mentally impaired (eg by senile dementia or Alzheimer's disease);
(b) learning disabilities. The expression 'learning difficulties' is sometimes used and the previous term was 'mental handicap'; and
(c) brain damage. If the damage was caused during the developmental years (eg in childbirth) this will be classed as learning disabilities.

'patient' (r 21.1(2)(b))—For the purpose of the CPR 'patient' means 'a person who, by reason of mental disorder … is incapable of managing and administering his property and affairs'. The same approach was adopted in RSC Ord 80 and CCR Ord 10 (in the latter the term was 'mental patient'). '[A]ffairs' is restricted to financial affairs (*Re W* [1970] 2 All ER 502; *Re F* 2 FLR 376, HL). This test is also used to establish the jurisdiction of the Court of Protection to administer the property and affairs of patients under Part VII (ss 93–113) of Mental Health Act 1983. There are two distinct components, namely being mentally disordered and being incapable. If one of these is present but there is doubt about the other it may be appropriate to resolve the uncertainty as a preliminary issue in the proceedings.

Whilst mental incapacity by itself may result in a transaction being invalid or unenforceable, it is only when the incapacity is by reason of mental disorder that the law takes away personal rights or powers and enables these to be delegated. Incapacity due to other causes, such as being under the influence of drink or drugs, is not sufficient.

Similarly, being mentally disordered (ie within one of the above categories) does not necessarily result in being a patient, and an assessment of capacity must still be made. Thus:

(a) an individual may be sectioned under the provisions of Mental Health Act 1983 yet not be a patient as regards court proceedings because the criteria are different (consider *Re C (Adult: refusal of medical treatment)* [1994] 1 All ER 819);
(b) an individual with learning disabilities may still have the capacity to manage his affairs especially if they are very basic, although the need to participate in proceedings may tip the balance whilst those proceedings are ongoing.

It is suggested that a three-stage test be applied to determine whether a litigant is a patient:

(1) Is he or she mentally disordered (medical evidence should be relied on)?
(2) Is he or she incapable of managing and administering his or her own affairs (which in this context comprise merely the proceedings – see below)?
(3) Does the incapacity result from the mental disorder?

Presumptions as to capacity—There is a legal presumption that adults are competent until the contrary is proved. This presumption is relevant to the burden of proof. In general the person who alleges that an individual lacks capacity must prove this but the standard of proof is the civil standard, namely upon the balance of probabilities rather than beyond reasonable doubt. Capacity, because it can vary, must be assessed at the time that the decision is to be taken. If an individual has previously been found to lack capacity, there is no presumption of continuance, but if there is clear evidence of incapacity for a considerable period, then the burden of proof may be more easily discharged even though it remains on whoever asserts incapacity.

Doubts about capacity may arise for several reasons but these should not be confused with tests of capacity. Thus the status of the individual (being elderly and living in a nursing home), the outcome of a decision (one that no person in his right mind would be expected to reach) or appearance, behaviour or conversation may cause capacity to be questioned, but these factors do not determine capacity. It is not unusual for outward appearances to create a false impression of lack of capacity (eg physical disabilities may obstruct the power of speech or movement) even where mental capacity is not affected. Conversely, a person may appear capable through social training and experience when in reality they lack the understanding needed to make decisions. In all these situations a proper assessment of capacity should be made.

Communication difficulties—Lack of competence may arise through mental incapacity or an inability to communicate. The Rules do not recognise this distinction and only enable proceedings to be conducted by a representative (the litigation friend) in the case of incapacity due to mental disorder (unlike Insolvency Rules 1986, 7.43–7.46). Other methods of communication should always be attempted when necessary and an interpreter may be provided for those with communication difficulties in the same way as for those who do not understand the language used in court.

Physical disabilities—Where the ability of an individual to conduct or participate in proceedings is impaired due to physical disabilities steps can be taken by the court to overcome these. Thus the loop system may be provided for those who are hard of hearing and enlarged print may be used on all documents for those whose sight is impaired. If necessary hearings should be conducted in a courtroom or chambers with disabled access but they may now be conducted elsewhere should the need arise (r 2.7).

Tests of capacity—There is no universal test of capacity. Legal capacity depends on understanding rather than wisdom; the quality of the decision is irrelevant as long as the person understands what he is deciding. Legal tests vary according to the particular transaction or act involved but are generally issue-specific, ie they relate to the matters which the individual is required to understand. As capacity depends on time and context, a decision as to capacity in one context does not bind a court that has to consider the same issue in a different context. It has been stated (in regard to medical treatment though the test is no doubt universal) that the individual must be able to (a) understand and retain information, and (b) weigh that information in the balance to arrive at a choice (per Butler-Sloss LJ in *Re MB* [1997] 2 FCR 541, CA).

A person found to be a patient may nevertheless be capable of getting married, signing an enduring power of attorney (*Re K, Re F* [1988] 1 All ER 358) or consenting to medical treatment (*Re MB* above), because the matters to be taken into account are different. For a full explanation of the various tests that apply for different purposes reference should be made to the joint Law Society and BMA publication *Assessment of Mental Capacity: Guidance for doctors and lawyers* (Second edition 2004).

Ability to rely upon advice—The extent to which an individual with impaired capacity may rely upon the advice of others was considered by Boreham J in *White v Fell* (1987) (unreported) but quoted by Wright J in *Masterman-Lister v Brutton & Co and Jewell & anor* [2002] EWHC 417 (QB), [2002] All ER (D) 247 (Mar), QBD:

> 'Few people have the capacity to manage all their affairs unaided. In matters of law, particularly litigation, medicine, and given sufficient resources, finance professional advice is almost universally needed and sought. For instance, if the plaintiff succeeds in her claim for compensation … then she will need to take, consider and act upon appropriate advice … It may be that she would have chosen, and would choose now, not to take advice, but that is not the question. The question is: is she capable of doing so? To have that capacity she requires first the insight and understanding of the fact that she has a problem in respect of which she needs advice …
>
> Secondly, having identified the problem, it will be necessary for her to seek an appropriate adviser and to instruct him with sufficient clarity to enable him to understand the problem and to advise her appropriately.
>
> Finally, she needs sufficient mental capacity to understand and to make decisions based upon, or otherwise give effect to such advice as she may receive … [S]he may not understand all the intricacies of litigation, or of a settlement, or of a wise investment policy … But if that were the appropriate test then quite a substantial proportion of the adult population might be regarded as under disability.'

Assessment of capacity—There have been relatively few reported cases on the assessment of capacity and until recently none relating to capacity to manage and administer property and affairs, despite the extent to which this test is applied. Mental capacity is a question of fact so any issue of capacity can only be determined by a judge in legal proceedings acting not as a medical expert but as a lay person influenced by personal observation and on the basis of evidence not only from doctors but also those who know the individual. For comprehensive guidance as to the manner in which capacity should be assessed reference should be made to *Assessment of Mental Capacity: Guidance for doctors and lawyers* (above).

Property and affairs—It becomes necessary to consider what property and affairs should be taken into account when applying the test of a 'patient' in different contexts. It has been held that 'affairs' does not extend to physical care and/or treatment, but includes 'only business matters, legal transactions or other dealings of a similar kind' (*Re F (Mental Patient: Sterilisation)* [1990] 2 AC 1, HL).

Despite the wording of the definition of 'patient', the Court of Appeal has now concentrated on the issue-specific nature of tests of capacity and decided that the test relates to the individual and his immediate problems. Unlike for the Court of Protection jurisdiction, it is not necessary to consider the totality of the property and affairs of the alleged patient when contemplating litigation. Thus:

> '[T]he test to be applied … is whether the party to legal proceedings is capable of understanding, with the assistance of such proper explanation from legal advisers and experts in other disciplines as the case may require, the issues on which his consent or decision is likely to be necessary in the course of those proceedings. If he has capacity to understand that which he needs to understand in order to pursue or defend a claim, I can see no reason why the law – whether substantive or procedural – should require the interposition of a next friend or guardian ad litem (or, as such a person is now described in the Civil Procedure Rules, a litigation friend).'

The mental abilities required include: the ability to recognise a problem, obtain and receive, understand and retain relevant information, including advice; the ability to weigh the information (including that derived from advice) in the balance in reaching a decision; and the ability to communicate that decision (*Masterman-Lister v Brutton & Co and Jewell & anor* [2002] EWCA Civ 1889, [2002] All ER (D) 297 (Dec)).

Medical evidence—Legal practitioners and judges should not jump to conclusions about mental disorder without appropriate evidence especially in the case of litigants who may merely be stubborn or eccentric. The evidence of a suitably qualified person is required as to the diagnosis, and this evidence will generally extend to the issue of capacity. In *Masterman-Lister v Brutton & Co and Jewell & anor* (see above), Kennedy LJ said that 'even where the issue does not seem to be contentious, a District Judge who is responsible for case management will almost certainly require the assistance of a medical report before being able to be satisfied that incapacity exists'.

Usually this expert will be a person with medical qualifications and ideally a psychiatrist. However, a psychologist, especially if of an appropriate speciality, may be better qualified in respect of a person with learning disabilities. Such opinion is merely part of the evidence and the factual evidence of a carer or social worker may also be relevant and even more persuasive. The court must decide whether the expert witness has sufficient knowledge and experience in this area and whether his opinion has been formed on sufficient grounds and on the basis of the correct legal test. The typical medical practitioner has little knowledge of mental capacity and the various legal tests that apply, so the appropriate test should be spelt out, and it should be explained that different tests apply to different types of decision.

Any doctor or other medical witness asked to assist in relation to capacity needs to know the area of the alleged patient's activities in relation to which his advice is sought (*Masterman-Lister v Brutton & Co and Jewell & anor* [2002] EWCA Civ 1889, [2002] All ER (D) 297 (Dec)). All relevant information should be provided, so when the test is whether the individual is incapable of managing his affairs the doctor must, if the jurisdiction of the Court of Protection is being considered, be given some idea of the nature and complexity of those affairs. But if this question arises in the context of litigation, the doctor will need to know what decisions the individual will be called upon to make for the conduct of that litigation. Only if the doctor has this information can he express an opinion as to whether the individual is capable of managing his affairs or giving instructions in regard to the litigation.

Issues as to capacity—There is unlikely to be any issue as to whether a party is a child, but issues can arise as to whether a party is a patient and the rules make no express provision for this situation. Such issue may be raised by the court or one of the parties, or by a litigation friend if there is doubt about whether a party has recovered capacity. It will then be necessary for the proceedings to be stayed until the issue is resolved, and the court may order an inquiry to be made in the proceedings to determine the issue. Notice should be given to the party alleged to be a patient in case he wishes to contest this or arrange representation. This inquiry would normally be heard before a district judge who can compel the attendance of witnesses (including medical attendants and the claimant or defendant himself) and the production of documents. Where there are practical difficulties in obtaining medical evidence the Official Solicitor may be consulted. The court can also direct the Official Solicitor to make inquiries and to report about such matters as the court thinks fit (*Harbin v Masterman* [1896] 1 Ch 351, CA).

Although there is no requirement in the rules for a judicial determination of the question of whether or not capacity exists, courts should always, as a matter of practice, at the first convenient opportunity investigate the question of capacity whenever there is any reason to suspect that it may be absent (eg significant head injury) other than in cases where the Court of Protection has already accepted jurisdiction. Although medical evidence will be required (see above), the judge may consider that he would be assisted by seeing the person alleged to lack capacity (*Masterman-Lister v Brutton & Co and Jewell & anor* [2002] EWCA Civ 1889, [2002] All ER (D) 297 (Dec), Kennedy LJ).

For further consideration of this topic, reference may be made to: Law Commission Report No 231 *Mental Incapacity* (1995); the Green Paper *Who Decides? Making Decisions on behalf of Mentally Incapacitated Adults* (December 1997); and the LCD Report *Making Decisions* (October 1999). A Mental Capacity Bill is now before Parliament and, if enacted, would remove these issues from the family courts to the jurisdiction of a new Court of Protection.

Human rights—When a person is treated as a patient, whether or not as a result of an order of the court, he is thereby deprived of important rights, long cherished by English law and now safeguarded by the European Convention on Human Rights. Although the CPR do not contain any requirement for a judicial determination of the question of whether or not capacity exists, courts should always, as a matter of practice, at the first convenient opportunity investigate the question of capacity whenever there is any reason to suspect that it may be absent, other than in cases where the Court of Protection is already involved (*Masterman-Lister v Brutton & Co and Jewell & anor* [2002] EWCA Civ 1889, [2002] All ER (D) 297 (Dec)).

21.2 Requirement for litigation friend in proceedings by or against children and patients

(1) A patient must have a litigation friend to conduct proceedings on his behalf.

(2) A child must have a litigation friend to conduct proceedings on his behalf unless the court makes an order under paragraph (3).

(3) The court may make an order permitting the child to conduct proceedings without a litigation friend.

(4) An application for an order under paragraph (3) –

- (a) may be made by the child;
- (b) if the child already has a litigation friend, must be made on notice to the litigation friend; and
- (c) if the child has no litigation friend, may be made without notice.

(5) Where –

- (a) the court has made an order under paragraph (3); and
- (b) it subsequently appears to the court that it is desirable for a litigation friend to conduct the proceedings on behalf of the child,

the court may appoint a person to be the child's litigation friend.

Practice Direction—See generally PD21 at p 661.

Scope of provision—The general rule is that a child or patient may only conduct proceedings, whether as claimant or defendant, by a litigation friend. This applies equally to 'Part 20 claims' eg where the child or patient is joined as a third party (r 20.3(1)). The rule only refers to 'a litigation friend' so a child or patient may not have more than one in any particular proceedings. There is nothing to prevent that party having a different litigation friend in other proceedings of a different nature, unless a receiver has been appointed in which event he should generally be the only litigation friend for the patient.

Verification that a party is a child or patient—Paragraph 2.3 of PD21 requires the litigation friend to state in the 'certificate of suitability' that he consents to act and knows or believes the party to be a child or patient. The grounds for this belief must be stated and if based upon medical opinion this document must be attached. It is unlikely to be difficult to ascertain the age of a party, but there may be doubt as to whether a party is a patient (see the notes to r 21.1 for the procedure then to be adopted).

Even where the issue does not seem to be contentious, a district judge who is responsible for case management will generally require the assistance of a medical report before being able to be satisfied that incapacity exists. An admission by a person alleged to lack capacity will carry little weight. It may assist for the judge to see the person alleged to lack capacity (*Masterman-Lister v Brutton & Co and Jewell & anor* [2002] EWCA Civ 1889, [2002] All ER (D) 297 (Dec)).

Notification to the child or patient—Neither the Rules nor Practice Directions actually provide that a child or patient must be given notice of the proceedings, unless (in the case of a patient) the court is involved in the appointment of the litigation friend, so it is possible for proceedings in the name of a child or patient to be commenced or defended without the personal knowledge of that party. Reliance is placed on the certificate of suitability (see above) and upon service on the parent or guardian of the child, or the person with whom the patient resides or in whose care he is (see also PD21, para 2.4). It cannot be assumed that this person will inform the patient in every situation where this would be prudent.

The child as a party (r 21.2(3))—An all or nothing approach to age is no longer adopted (*Gillick v West Norfolk & Wisbech Area Health Authority* [1985] 3 All ER 402, HL). The court may now authorise a child to conduct proceedings, but will only do so when satisfied that the child has the required capacity (ie is of sufficient maturity and understanding). It is both prudent and good practice for the litigation friend to consult the child once able to make a meaningful contribution and particularly as the child approaches 18 since on attaining that age the appointment of the litigation friend ceases and the child (now an adult) may take over conduct of the proceedings (r 21.9(1)).

The patient as a party—An adult who has the necessary capacity will not be a patient even if mentally disordered so there is no need for a comparable provision whereby the court may authorise a patient to conduct proceedings. However, unlike the former rules there may now be a departure from the general rule in so far as the court may permit proceedings to continue (to a limited extent) even though a litigation friend has not been appointed and may validate proceedings that have continued in breach of the requirements (r 21.3). If the patient recovers capacity, the appointment of the litigation friend may be terminated by the court order under r 21.9(2), (3).

Duty of litigation friend—The duty of a litigation friend is set out in PD21, para 2.1. It is 'fairly and competently to conduct proceedings on behalf of a child or patient. He must have no interest in the proceedings adverse to that of the child or patient and all steps and decisions he takes in the proceedings must be taken for the benefit of the child or patient'.

Status of litigation friend—The powers of the litigation friend are not expressly set out but as the appointment is to 'conduct proceedings … on behalf' of the child or patient it may be assumed that, subject to the provisions of the rules, any act which in the ordinary conduct of any proceedings is required or authorised to be done by a party shall or may be done by the litigation friend. Unless the litigation friend is also a receiver appointed by the Court of Protection or an attorney under a registered enduring power of attorney he will have no status in regard to the affairs of the patient outside the proceedings in which he is appointed. It follows that if money is awarded to a child or patient the litigation friend has no authority to receive or expend that money. The money may only be dealt with pursuant to the directions of the court and in this respect reference must be made to r 21.11. Similarly any settlement or compromise will have to be approved by the court under r 21.10.

Statement of truth—Part 22 makes provision for certain documents to be verified by a 'statement of truth'. If a party is a child or a patient it will be the litigation friend (or legal representative on his behalf) who makes and signs this statement – r 22.1(5), (6).

Need for a solicitor—Unlike the former RSC (but not CCR), it appears that there is no requirement for a solicitor to act on behalf of a child or patient whose proceedings are being conducted by a litigation friend. Nevertheless, in a complex or high value case the court may consider that the litigation friend who acts without a solicitor is not 'suitable' within r 21.4(3) and appoint someone else under r 21.7(1)(c).

21.3 Stage of proceedings at which a litigation friend becomes necessary

(1) This rule does not apply where the court has made an order under rule 21.2(3).

(2) A person may not, without the permission of the court –

(a) make an application against a child or patient before proceedings have started; or

(b) take any step in proceedings except –

(i) issuing and serving a claim form; or

(ii) applying for the appointment of a litigation friend under rule 21.6,

until the child or patient has a litigation friend.

(3) If a party becomes a patient during proceedings, no party may take any step in the proceedings without the permission of the court until the patient has a litigation friend.

(4) Any step taken before a child or patient has a litigation friend, shall be of no effect unless the court otherwise orders.

Practice Direction—See generally PD21 at p 661.

Scope of provision—The general principle is that a litigation friend must be appointed before any step is taken in proceedings involving a child or patient (unless the child has been authorised to conduct those proceedings under r 21.2(3)).

Exceptions—Under the previous rules, any proceedings conducted in the absence of a next friend or guardian *ad litem* were of no effect if a party was under a disability. This caused problems where the disability was not identified by the parties or their solicitors, or arose during the proceedings without their knowledge, and liabilities could arise in respect of abortive costs. The court now has a discretion to permit specified steps to be taken before a litigation friend is appointed ('without the permission of the court' – r 21.3(2), (3)) or retrospectively to approve any steps that have been taken without such appointment ('unless the court otherwise orders' – r 21.3(4)).

Implications—It is now possible to make urgent orders in proceedings involving a child or patient before the appointment of a litigation friend, but the court should be made fully aware of all relevant circumstances. Where it is realised during the course of proceedings that a party is (and has been) a child or a patient, the court can retrospectively approve the earlier steps which would otherwise be of no effect. Provided everyone has acted in good faith and there has been no manifest disadvantage to the party subsequently found to have been a patient at the relevant time, it is likely that the court will regularise the position retrospectively (*Masterman-Lister v Brutton & Co and Jewell & anor* [2002] EWCA Civ 1889, [2002] All ER (D) 297 (Dec)). This might be the case where the proceedings have effectively been guided throughout by the person now being appointed as litigation friend. Proceedings inappropriately conducted by the child or patient or an unsuitable person on his behalf will be treated as being of no effect and further proceedings may then be commenced in proper form (the Limitation Acts are unlikely to apply). *Query* whether steps should be retrospectively approved when this would cause prejudice to a party not at fault?

Effect on timetable—Until there is a litigation friend no party may take any step in the proceedings so it is assumed that any timetable is suspended. When the court appoints the litigation friend it may be prudent to consider further directions as to the future conduct of the proceedings.

21.4 Who may be a litigation friend without a court order

(1) This rule does not apply if the court has appointed a person to be a litigation friend.

(2) A person authorised under Part VII of the Mental Health Act 1983 to conduct legal proceedings in the name of a patient or on his behalf, is entitled to be the litigation friend of the patient in any proceedings to which his authority extends.

(3) If nobody has been appointed by the court or, in the case of a patient, authorised under Part VII, a person may act as a litigation friend if he –

(a) can fairly and competently conduct proceedings on behalf of the child or patient; and

(b) has no interest adverse to that of the child or patient; and

(c) where the child or patient is a claimant, undertakes to pay any costs which the child or patient may be ordered to pay in relation to the proceedings, subject to any right he may have to be repaid from the assets of the child or patient.

Practice Direction—See generally PD21 at p 661.

Scope of provision—This rule identifies who may act as a litigation friend without an order appointing him.

Authorised person—Any person authorised under Mental Health Act 1983, Pt VII (ie as a receiver appointed by the Court of Protection – see generally s 96(1)) to conduct legal proceedings in the name or on behalf of a patient is entitled to become the litigation friend in accordance with such authority. An office copy of the order or other authorisation sealed with the official seal of the Court of Protection should be filed. Care should be taken to examine this document because simply being appointed receiver does not by itself give authority to conduct proceedings. It is not clear if the court has power to appoint someone else (as under the former rules), but this situation is unlikely to arise and conflict between the court dealing with the litigation and the Court of Protection should be avoided.

Attorneys—An attorney under a registered enduring power of attorney (EPA) is not specifically mentioned but would be an obvious person to act as litigation friend because he will control the financial affairs of the patient (see Enduring Powers of Attorney Act 1985) and there will in consequence be no need for a receiver. An ordinary power of attorney is of no significance because it ceases to have effect upon the incapacity of the donor, but of course the person acting may otherwise be suitable as litigation friend.

Suitability—There can be no doubt as to the suitability of a person authorised by the Court of Protection (if doubt arises the matter should be referred back to that Court). The rule helpfully sets out the criteria whereby other persons may be regarded as suitable to act as litigation friend (r 21.4(3)), but the court may not waive any of these criteria which the proposed person is unable to satisfy (The Queen on the application of Hussain v Birmingham City Council [2002] EWHC 949, [2002] CP Rep 54, QBD (Admin Ct)). These criteria feature throughout Pt 21 as amplified by PD21, para 2.1 and the court must be satisfied that they are complied with before appointing a litigation friend. They may be relied upon where there is a dispute as to who should be appointed. Apart from this there is no restriction on who may be a litigation friend save that the person appointed must not be a child or a patient and (in practice) should normally be within the jurisdiction. If the court becomes aware of the person's unsuitability, it may remove him under r 21.7 and substitute another person as litigation friend, but there is no express duty to monitor the situation.

Undertaking as to costs (r 21.4(3)(c))—This undertaking is required from the litigation friend of a claimant but not that of a defendant, and this is confirmed in PD21 at para 2.3(2)(e). It is contained in Form N235 Certificate of Suitability of Litigation Friend. A mother's undertaking to meet any liability in costs 'if her circumstances were to change, enabling her to afford them' did not satisfy the requirement of r 21.4(3)(c) and she was, accordingly, ineligible for appointment as a litigation friend (The Queen on the application of Hussain v Birmingham City Council [2002] EWHC 949, [2002] CP Rep 54, QBD (Admin Ct)). The requirement imposes a severe limitation upon the ability of a child or patient to bring a claim. *Query* whether it amounts to discrimination against a person with a mental disability contrary to the DDA 1995 or will otherwise be in breach of Human Rights Act 1998. The litigation friend is in effect required to provide an indemnity so may wish to be protected by a Public Funding certificate, after-the-event (ATE) insurance indemnity policy or otherwise in control of adequate funds held by the child or patient. One way of circumventing the undertaking in the case of a patient is to obtain the authority of the Court of Protection to bring the proceedings. The court has a general discretion as to costs and will take into account the role of the litigation friend but may have power to impose a personal costs liability in case of misconduct quite apart from the undertaking. Further difficulties arise in regard to conditional fee arrangements.

Costs order against litigation friend—An order for costs should not be made against a litigation friend personally without giving him a chance to be heard. This probably means adopting the r 48.2 procedure since the litigation friend is not otherwise a party. Such approach will only be appropriate when the litigation friend has misbehaved in the proceedings. The undertaking to pay the child or patient's costs (if given) is quite different from a personal costs order.

Personal liability of solicitor for costs—A solicitor who acts in any proceedings for or on behalf of a person under disability without a litigation friend will be held personally liable to pay any wasted costs of the proceedings incurred by the other party, even though he himself may not have been aware that the person for whom he has been acting is in fact an infant or a patient (*Yonge v Toynbee*

[1910] 1 KB 215, CA). However, provided everyone has acted in good faith and there has been no manifest disadvantage to the party subsequently found to have been a patient at the relevant time it is likely that the court will regularise the position retrospectively (*Masterman-Lister v Brutton & Co and Jewell & anor* [2002] EWCA Civ 1889, [2002] All ER (D) 297 (Dec)).

21.5 How a person becomes a litigation friend without a court order

(1) If the court has not appointed a litigation friend, a person who wishes to act as a litigation friend must follow the procedure set out in this rule.

(2) A person authorised under Part VII of the Mental Health Act 1983 must file an official copy(GL) of the order or other document which constitutes his authorisation to act.

(3) Any other person must file a certificate of suitability stating that he satisfies the conditions specified in rule 21.4(3).

(4) A person who is to act as a litigation friend for a claimant must file –

(a) the authorisation; or
(b) the certificate of suitability,

at the time when the claim is made.

(5) A person who is to act as a litigation friend for a defendant must file –

(a) the authorisation; or
(b) the certificate of suitability,

at the time when he first takes a step in the proceedings on behalf of the defendant.

(6) The litigation friend must –

(a) serve the certificate of suitability on every person on whom, in accordance with rule 6.6 (service on parent, guardian etc), the claim form should be served; and
(b) file a certificate of service when he files the certificate of suitability.

(Rule 6.10 sets out the details to be contained in a certificate of service)

Practice Direction—See generally PD21 at p 661.

Scope of provision—This rule sets out the procedural steps for the appointment of a litigation friend otherwise than by a court order. It will be relied upon in most cases.

No need for court appointment of litigation friend—A litigation friend may be appointed simply by filing the relevant documents. The certificate is a pre-requisite for appointment without a court order, but will not be conclusive in the event of a dispute as to suitability. It is strange that there is no requirement for the child or patient to be personally notified that proceedings are being brought or defended in his name because he may wish to make representations as to who the litigation friend should be or dispute that he is a patient (see generally the provisions as to service in Pt 6). It is now good practice for anyone intending to become a litigation friend to serve upon or draw to the attention of the intended patient the notice of his intention to act as litigation friend and certificate of suitability, unless there is no prospect of a relevant response (see *Masterman-Lister v Brutton & Co and Jewell & anor* [2002] EWCA Civ 1889, [2002] All ER (D) 297 (Dec), Kennedy LJ). The court may require confirmation of this. The Court of Appeal has recommended a change in the rules so that a person cannot become a patient without knowing what is going on.

'certificate of suitability' (r 21.5(3))—This document confirms that the person to be appointed meets the criteria whereby a person may be regarded as suitable for appointment as litigation friend (r 21.4(3)). As to suitability see note to r 21.4. The certificate is not required where the person is authorised by the Court of Protection to conduct the proceedings (see note to r 21.4).

'certificate of service' (r 21.5(6)(b))—Paragraph 2.4 of PD21 clarifies the persons on whom the certificate of suitability (when required) must be served in accordance with this rule. The alleged patient is not included (but see note **'No need for court appointment of next friend'** above).

Forms—Form N235 (Certificate of suitability of litigation friend).

21.6 How a person becomes a litigation friend by court order

(1) The court may make an order appointing a litigation friend.

(2) An application for an order appointing a litigation friend may be made by –

- (a) a person who wishes to be the litigation friend; or
- (b) a party.

(3) Where –

- (a) a person makes a claim against a child or patient;
- (b) the child or patient has no litigation friend;
- (c) the court has not made an order under rule 21.2(3) (order that a child can act without a litigation friend); and
- (d) either –
  - (i) someone who is not entitled to be a litigation friend files a defence; or
  - (ii) the claimant wishes to take some step in the proceedings,

the claimant must apply to the court for an order appointing a litigation friend for the child or patient.

(4) An application for an order appointing a litigation friend must be supported by evidence.

(5) The court may not appoint a litigation friend under this rule unless it is satisfied that the person to be appointed complies with the conditions specified in rule 21.4(3).

Practice Direction—See generally PD21 at p 661.

Scope of provision—This rule sets out the procedural steps for the appointment of a litigation friend by a court order. These provisions will apply where it has not been possible to appoint a litigation friend without an order pursuant to r 21.5. The court must be satisfied that the person to be appointed is suitable for appointment in accordance with the criteria set out in r 21.4(3). Although the rules do not so provide, the application should be served upon or at least brought to the notice of the party unless there is no prospect of a relevant response (see note **'No need for court appointment of litigation friend'** under r 21.5 above).

Official Solicitor—The Official Solicitor should be approached in case of difficulty and may be appointed if he consents but in practice he will only consent if there is no-one else suitable and willing to act. It is not necessary to approach him in all cases and the court will not be concerned to ascertain whether he has declined to consent before appointing someone else. He should not be appointed without his consent which will not usually be forthcoming until provision is made for payment of his costs (PD21, para 3.6). Save in the most urgent of cases it is unlikely that he will be able to complete his enquiries in less than 3 months. Accordingly, a lengthy adjournment of the proceedings might become necessary and a substantive hearing should not be fixed within such period of his initial appointment without consulting him. Where the circumstances of the case justify the involvement of the Official Solicitor a completed questionnaire and copy of the order appointing him (subject to his consent) together with a copy of the court file should be sent to his office. The Official Solicitor to the Supreme Court is provided for by Supreme Court Act 1981, s 90 and may be contacted at 81 Chancery Lane, London WC2A 1DD; Tel 020-7911-7127, Fax 020-7911-7105.

Service—See r 21.8(1) and (2) for the special rules that apply to an application for appointment by the court of a litigation friend. Paragraph 3.3 of PD21 clarifies who should be served and this includes the (alleged) patient unless the court orders otherwise, but there is still no requirement for a child to be notified of proceedings to be conducted in his name and on his behalf even though he may be approaching 18 (see note to r 21.2).

Evidence—Paragraph 3.4 of PD21 clarifies the evidence required. This will presumably include evidence that the party is a child or patient although this is not expressly stated. For rules as to applications for court orders see Pt 23.

Suitability—See note to r 21.4. The court may appoint the person proposed or any other person who complies with the conditions specified in r 21.4(3) (r 21.8(4)). Thus the criteria of suitability in r 21.4(3) must be satisfied even though r 21.4(1) expressly states that the rule does not apply if the court has appointed a person to be a litigation friend.

21.7 Court's power to change litigation friend and to prevent person acting as litigation friend

(1) The court may –

(a) direct that a person may not act as a litigation friend;
(b) terminate a litigation friend's appointment;
(c) appoint a new litigation friend in substitution for an existing one.

(2) An application for an order under paragraph (1) must be supported by evidence.

(3) The court may not appoint a litigation friend under this rule unless it is satisfied that the person to be appointed complies with the conditions specified in rule 21.4(3).

Practice Direction—See generally PD21 at p 661.

Scope of provision—The court has a general power under r 3.1(7) to revoke or vary its own orders but this rule enables the court to prevent a person from being a litigation friend or replace a litigation friend during the course of proceedings whether or not appointed by an order. The court must be satisfied that the person to be appointed is suitable for appointment in accordance with the criteria set out in r 21.4(3). Any dispute as to who should be the litigation friend would be dealt with under this provision.

Service—See r 21.8(1) and (3). Paragraph 4.4 of PD21 clarifies who should be served. See generally note to r 21.6 as to service. Although this does not include the patient, it may be good practice to consult this person as capacity is not an 'all or nothing' concept.

Evidence—Paragraphs 4.2 and 4.3 of PD21 clarify the evidence required.

Suitability—See note to r 21.4 above. The court may appoint the person proposed or any other person who complies with the conditions specified in r 21.4(3) (r 21.8(4)). Thus the criteria of suitability in r 21.4(3) must be satisfied even though r 21.4(1) expressly states that the rule does not apply if the court has appointed a person to be a litigation friend.

Applications—This rule contemplates an application by a party (or presumably a non-party such as an alternative representative for the child or patient) for the removal of a litigation friend or for an individual to be prevented from adopting that role. The court may, as part of its case management powers, initiate the process (see r 3.3, where the procedure to be adopted is set out). The fact that there is concern as to an actual or potential litigation friend does not necessarily mean that there is someone with an interest in making the application. For rules as to applications for court orders see Pt 23.

Termination—The rules express no limit on the power to terminate the appointment and if the litigation friend acts manifestly contrary to the child or patient's best interests, the court will remove him, even though neither his good faith nor his diligence is in issue (*Re A (Conjoined Twins: Medical Treatment) (No 2)* [2001] 1 FLR 267, CA).

21.8 Appointment of litigation friend by court order – supplementary

(1) An application for an order under rule 21.6 or 21.7 must be served on every person on whom, in accordance with rule 6.6 (service on parent, guardian etc), the claim form should be served.

(2) Where an application for an order under rule 21.6 is in respect of a patient, the application must also be served on the patient unless the court orders otherwise.

(3) An application for an order under rule 21.7 must also be served on –

(a) the person who is the litigation friend, or who is purporting to act as the litigation friend, when the application is made; and
(b) the person who it is proposed should be the litigation friend, if he is not the applicant.

(4) On an application for an order under rule 21.6 or 21.7, the court may appoint the person proposed or any other person who complies with the conditions specified in rule 21.4(3).

Practice Direction—See generally PD21 at p 661.

Scope of provision—This rule makes provision for service of applications relating to the appointment or change of a litigation friend where a party is a child or patient and supplements r 6.6 (which deals with service of the proceedings) in that respect. It also provides that on such application the court is not obliged to appoint the person proposed but may appoint any other person who complies with the conditions specified in r 21.4(3) Although the rules do not so provide, the application should be served upon or at least brought to the notice of the party unless there is no prospect of a relevant response (see note **'No need for court appointment of litigation friend'** under r 21.5 above)..

Service—Service of the application on the parent or guardian of the child, or the person with whom the patient resides or in whose care he is, is required in all cases (this is explained in the note to r 6.6). The application under r 21.6 to appoint a litigation friend must actually be served on the patient (unless the court orders otherwise) but this is not a universal provision. Where it is proposed to change the litigation friend both the existing and intended litigation friend must be served (but not apparently the patient). There is no requirement to serve a child in any of these situations but see the note to r 21.2.

Who is appointed—The court may decide to appoint any other person who meets the criteria set out in r 21.4(3) and is willing to act.

21.9 Procedure where appointment of litigation friend ceases

(1) When a child who is not a patient reaches the age of 18, a litigation friend's appointment ceases.

(2) When a party ceases to be a patient, the litigation friend's appointment continues until it is ended by a court order.

(3) An application for an order under paragraph (2) may be made by –

(a) the former patient;
(b) the litigation friend; or
(c) a party.

(4) The child or patient in respect of whom the appointment to act has ceased must serve notice on the other parties –

(a) stating that the appointment of his litigation friend to act has ceased;
(b) giving his address for service; and
(c) stating whether or not he intends to carry on the proceedings.

(5) If he does not do so within 28 days after the day on which the appointment of the litigation friend ceases the court may, on application, strike out(GL) any claim or defence brought by him.

(6) The liability of a litigation friend for costs continues until –

(a) the person in respect of whom his appointment to act has ceased serves the notice referred to in paragraph (4); or
(b) the litigation friend serves notice on the parties that his appointment to act has ceased.

Practice Direction—See generally PD21 at p 661.

Scope of provision—This rule makes provision for a party ceasing to be a child or patient.

Child—There will be no need for a litigation friend when the child attains 18 (unless the child is also a patient) so the appointment then ceases automatically. If this party does not by notice under r 21.9(4) continue the proceedings they may be struck out. There is no express requirement for the child to be notified of the existence of the proceedings up to that point, but notice of an application to strike out under r 21.9(5) must presumably be given to the party formerly a child, and the litigation friend will remain liable for costs unless the child gives notice as aforesaid or the litigation friend gives notice under r 21.9(6)(b) which must also be given to the party formerly a child.

Patient—The position is different in respect of a patient who recovers capacity. This is an unlikely occurrence when the incapacity arises by reason of learning disability, senility or brain damage but it can arise in the case of mental illness. The litigation friend will only be removed by court order following an application under r 21.9(3) and evidence will be required as to capacity. Notice must still be served by the former patient under r 21.9(4) or the proceedings may be struck out, and the litigation friend will remain liable for costs until that notice is served or he serves his own notice under r 21.9(6)(b).

Liability of litigation friend for costs—The litigation friend of a claimant may have had to give an undertaking as to costs pursuant to r 21.4(3)(c). This liability continues until notice is served on the other parties either by the claimant or the former litigation friend as mentioned above. Presumably the reference in r 21.9(6) to 'The liability of a litigation friend for costs …' refers to such undertaking and is not sufficient to create any additional liability. It is not clear whether, when discharged, the litigation friend is released from all liability for costs or only costs incurred from that date, although it is probably the latter.

21.10 Compromise etc by or on behalf of child or patient

(1) Where a claim is made –

(a) by or on behalf of a child or patient; or

(b) against a child or patient,

no settlement, compromise or payment and no acceptance of money paid into court shall be valid, so far as it relates to the claim by, on behalf of or against the child or patient, without the approval of the court.

(2) Where –

(a) before proceedings in which a claim is made by or on behalf of, or against a child or patient (whether alone or with any other person) are begun, an agreement is reached for the settlement of the claim; and

(b) the sole purpose of proceedings on that claim is to obtain the approval of the court to a settlement or compromise of the claim,

the claim must –

(i) be made using the procedure set out in Part 8 (alternative procedure for claims); and

(ii) include a request to the court for approval of the settlement or compromise.

(3) In proceedings to which Section II of Part 45 applies, the court shall not make an order for detailed assessment of the costs payable to the child or patient but shall assess the costs in the manner set out in that Section.

(Rule 48.5 contains provisions about costs where money payable to a child or patient)

Amendments—SI 2004/3419.

Practice Direction—See generally PD21 at p 661.

Scope of provision—This provision ensures that the approval of the court is obtained to any settlement or compromise on behalf of a child or patient, and extends to accepting any payment into court. Unlike the former RSC Ord 80, rr 10 and 11 and CCR Ord 10, r 10 it applies to claims other than for money and where the claim is made against the child or patient. Without this approval the settlement, compromise or payment of any claim is wholly invalid and unenforceable, and is made entirely at the risk of the parties and their solicitors. An unexpected consequence is that the acceptance by a defendant of a Pt 36 offer to settle made by a litigation friend (including a partial settlement relating to liability) may be withdrawn before court approval is obtained (*Drinkall v Whitwood* [2003] EWCA Civ 1547, [2003] TLR 622, (2003) *The Times*, 13 November, CA).

Purpose—There are three distinct reasons for this provision:

(1) to enable defendants to obtain a valid discharge from the claim;
(2) to protect children and patients from any lack of skill and experience on the part of their advisers which might lead to a settlement of a money claim for less than it is worth – *Black v Yates* [1991] 4 All ER 722;
(3) to ensure that solicitors and counsel are paid their proper costs and fees, and no more (this extends to both overcharging and recommending an unfavourable settlement influenced by an attractive costs offer).

Early settlements—Where a compromise or settlement is reached before proceedings are begun the Pt 8 procedure is used to seek approval of the court (r 21.10(2)). This does not prevent the settlement of small claims (eg under £1000) by payment to parents or carers prior to any proceedings on the basis of their indemnity and that may be appropriate to avoid disproportionate costs, but there are risks especially if the true value of the claim was not recognised.

Late settlements—Where the compromise or settlement is reached after the proceedings have been commenced, approval is sought by way of an application in the course of those proceedings. It would be an abuse of the process of the court for the parties and their solicitors in any subsisting proceedings to make or act on any such settlement, compromise or payment without the court's approval.

Hearing—The hearing will usually be before the district judge or master and (except for very small sums when a hearing may be dispensed with) should generally be attended by the litigation friend and child or patient unless there is good reason to the contrary. The court will wish to be satisfied that the settlement or compromise is one that should be approved and may wish to ascertain the views of the litigation friend (and child if of sufficient maturity and understanding) and inspect any scars which feature in a personal injuries claim. A written opinion from counsel or a suitably experienced solicitor as to liability and quantum will be helpful and may be required.

Costs—The requirement for court approval extends to costs – r 48.5, which replaces RSC Ord 62, r 16. There will be a detailed assessment (r 48.5(2)), but in certain circumstances this may be dispensed with (PDCosts, para 50.2). The claimant's solicitor does not usually seek any costs over and above those recovered from the defendant, so that the child or patient receives the full damages without any deduction for costs (this may change if conditional fees apply in these cases). If such further costs are expressly waived approval of costs may not be required where there has been summary assessment or costs can be agreed or are to be paid by an insurer (PDCosts, para 50.2). It is not clear how this impinges on obligations under a Legal Aid certificate, but the former practice may continue of the court being invited to record its approval of an agreement as to costs and dispense with assessment.

Need for a public hearing—Although any hearing should normally be held in public to comply with Art 6(1) ECHR, there are exceptions and hearings involving the interests of a child or patient may be in private (see r 39.2(3)(d) and PD39, para 1.4A). It has been held that the hearing of an application for the approval of a proposed settlement of a personal injury or Fatal Accident Act claim and the basic reasons therefore should be given in open court, although any part of the hearing intended to acquaint the court with the negotiations culminating in the proposed settlement and other details of the claim and the status and medical condition of the claimant should remain private (*Beatham v Carlisle Hospitals NHS Trust* (1999) *The Times*, 20 May, QBD, Buckley J).

Appeals—A decision not to appeal, where permission has been obtained on the express understanding that the possible appellant needs time to consider the matter, and with no consideration moving from the possible respondents, is not a 'compromise' and does not require the approval of the court (*Re A (Conjoined Twins: Medical Treatment) (No 2)* [2001] 1 FLR 267, CA).

Role of the Court of Protection—These provisions apply even where the proceedings are being conducted by the patient's receiver as litigation friend under the authority of the Court of Protection, but in that event the approval of the Court of Protection should first be obtained to proceed with the settlement.

Structured settlement—Where a structured settlement is contemplated reference should be made to PD40C.

Provisional damages—See PD41 – Provisional Damages.

Forms—Form N292 (Order on settlement on behalf of a child or patient).

21.11 Control of money recovered by or on behalf of child or patient

(1) Where in any proceedings –

(a) money is recovered by or on behalf of or for the benefit of a child or patient; or

(b) money paid into court is accepted by or on behalf of a child or patient,

the money shall be dealt with in accordance with directions given by the court under this rule and not otherwise.

(2) Directions given under this rule may provide that the money shall be wholly or partly paid into court and invested or otherwise dealt with.

Practice Direction—See generally PD21 at p 661.

Scope of provision—This rule ensures that there is supervision by the appropriate court of money awarded to or recovered by a child or patient. This fund (or the balance after allowing for any money authorised to be released for the immediate benefit of the child or patient) will be transferred to the Court Funds Office and applied for the benefit of the claimant in such manner as the court thinks fit (see notes below). Small sums (eg up to £500) may be released to the parents or carers of a child or patient if the court is satisfied that they will invest or use the money for the benefit of the child or patient, but the higher than market interest rates that are obtained make it attractive to retain the fund in court.

Procedure—See PD21, paras 8–12. The hearing may be in private under r 39.2(3)(d) but initial indications (at least in the High Court) are that approval should be given in public (*Beatham v Carlisle Hospitals NHS Trust* (1999) *The Times*, 20 May, QBD).

Order—See Form N292.

Investment and other directions—The court should give directions relating to the fund on Form CFO 320 as soon as possible after the award is made or settlement approved. This may be at the hearing before a district judge or master approving the settlement, but if the award is made at a trial these directions are likely to be adjourned to a district judge or master in chambers at a later date. Investment directions basically comprise a choice between high interest or equity investment, or a combination of the two. This will be influenced by the use to be made of the fund (eg if periodic payments are to be made) and the period of time that the fund is likely to remain invested (capital growth may be appropriate if the child is young, but accumulation of interest will be the only safe course for a child approaching 18). There is provision to direct that interest or instalments of capital be paid out at regular intervals for the support or maintenance of the child or patient. In the case of a child, if a birth certificate is produced 'majority directions' can be given to the effect that the fund be paid out on attaining majority (this will not be appropriate if the child is also a patient). The court staff then complete CFO Form 212 which is sent to the Court Funds Office and a local file is created for the fund.

Transfer to another court—Unless reserved to a particular district judge who has knowledge of the family background, it may be helpful for the file in respect of a continuing fund to be transferred to the county court in the area where the child or patient lives so that attendance at hearings relating to the application of the fund will be more convenient.

Powers of litigation friend—The role of the litigation friend is restricted to the conduct of the proceedings and his powers do not extend to dealing with the financial affairs of the child or patient (*Leather v Kirby* [1965] 3 All ER 927). He should, however, ensure that the fund is properly invested by the court and may have a sufficient continuing interest (eg as a parent or carer) to remain involved in the application of the fund by the court on behalf of the child or patient. The person who is the litigation friend may of course also be the patient's receiver or attorney and continue to administer the fund in that capacity.

Control of money: child—The court will normally control funds held on behalf of a child but may appoint the Official Solicitor as guardian of that child's estate under r 21.12(1). Applications can be made from time to time for payments out for the benefit of the child but the general policy is to expect the parents to meet the child's normal requirements and to preserve (and enhance) the fund for the child on attaining 18. If, however, the fund has been provided for a particular purpose then expenditure in furthering that purpose is appropriate (unless, of course, the parents prefer to meet the expense themselves and thereby enhance the fund). But it should never be overlooked that the fund belongs to the child and should be used in his or her best interests so requests can be made for the release of money for the maintenance, education or benefit of the child. Many district judges are receptive to applications relating to expenditure on items such as a computer or school holiday abroad for a mature child when this would otherwise be denied, but careful scrutiny will be exercised and one or more interviews with the child and parent may be required. Quotations or receipts should be produced and the court may authorise payment direct to the supplier or school. Conflicts of interest do arise in these situations and the court will be concerned to ensure that the fund is applied for the benefit of the child and not the family as a whole, although incidental benefit to others may be unavoidable and unobjectionable.

Different considerations apply to Fatal Accidents Act 1976 damages – see PD21, para 7 and r 37.4 (apportionment by court in Fatal Accidents Act 1976 and Law Reform (Miscellaneous Provisions) Act 1934 proceedings).

Control of money: patient—If the fund is substantial (over £30,000), or the patient already has income or assets which need to be administered, the Court of Protection should be left to administer the entire affairs. Subject to any Legal Aid costs provision the fund will be transferred to the Court of Protection to the credit of the patient to be dealt with as the Court of Protection in its discretion thinks fit. The patient's solicitor should approach the Court of Protection at an earlier stage so that there is no delay when the fund becomes available. Where however the fund is under £20,000 and there is no other reason to involve the Court of Protection (state benefits can be dealt with by an appointee), it can remain in court and be dealt with as if the patient were a child (PD21, para 11.2). Between these two figures, the Master of the Court of Protection should be consulted.

If there is a registered enduring power of attorney (in which event there will not be a receiver appointed by the Court of Protection) it would normally be appropriate for the attorney who is managing the affairs to receive the fund. There may be concern about this if the fund is very large in relation to the estate that such attorney was appointed to administer, and in that event reference should be made to the Master of the Court of Protection who may wish to superimpose a receivership.

Need for Court of Protection involvement—Someone who is treated as a patient and has a litigation friend does not necessarily need to become a patient of the Court of Protection as that jurisdiction is only exercised when, after considering medical evidence, a nominated judge is satisfied as to the person's incapacity. That judge must consider the totality of the property and affairs of the alleged patient. In civil proceedings a judge does not have to consider medical evidence or be satisfied as to incapacity before a person can be treated as a patient and it is only the immediate affairs that are considered (*Masterman-Lister v Brutton & Co and Jewell & anor* [2002] EWCA Civ 1889, [2002] All ER (D) 297 (Dec)). Conversely, a patient of the Court of Protection will require a litigation friend for civil proceedings.

Court Funds Office—Until April 2001 the Court Funds Office was a division of the Public Trust Office but from that date it is transferred to the Court Service.

Public Trust Office—This office, which comprised protection, receivership and trustee functions as well as the Court Funds Office, ceased to exist from April 2001. Trustee functions are transferred to the Official Solicitor's Office and a new Public Guardianship Office takes over the protection and receivership roles.

21.11A Expenses incurred by a litigation friend

(1) In proceedings to which rule 21.11 applies, a litigation friend who incurs expenses on behalf of a child or patient in any proceedings is entitled to recover the amount paid or payable out of any money recovered or paid into court to the extent that it –

- (a) has been reasonably incurred; and
- (b) is reasonable in amount.

(2) Expenses may include all or part of –

- (a) an insurance premium, as defined by rule 43.2(1)(m); or
- (b) interest on a loan taken out to pay an insurance premium or other recoverable disbursement.

(3) No application may be made under this rule for expenses that –

(a) are of a type that may be recoverable on an assessment of costs payable by or out of money belonging to a child or patient; but

(b) are disallowed in whole or in part on such an assessment.

(Expenses which are also 'costs' as defined in rule 43.2(1)(a) are dealt with under rule 48.5(2)).

(4) In deciding whether the expense was reasonably incurred and reasonable in amount, the court must have regard to all the circumstances of the case including the factors set out in rule 44.5(3).

(5) When the court is considering the factors to be taken into account in assessing the reasonableness of expenses incurred by the litigation friend on behalf of a child or patient, it will have regard to the facts and circumstances as they reasonably appeared to the litigation friend or child's or patient's legal representative when the expense was incurred.

(6) Where the claim is settled or compromised, or judgment is given, on terms that an amount not exceeding £5,000 is paid to the child or patient, the total amount the litigation friend may recover under paragraph (1) of this rule shall not exceed 25% of the sum so agreed or awarded, unless the Court directs otherwise. Such total amount shall not exceed 50% of the sum so agreed or awarded.

Amendments—Inserted by SI 2005/2292.

21.12 Appointment of guardian of child's estate

(1) The court may appoint the Official Solicitor to be a guardian of a child's estate where –

(a) money is paid into court on behalf of the child in accordance with directions given under rule 21.11 (control of money received by a child or patient);

(b) the Criminal Injuries Compensation Board or the Criminal Injuries Compensation Authority notifies the court that it has made or intends to make an award to the child;

(c) a court or tribunal outside England and Wales notifies the court that it has ordered or intends to order that money be paid to the child;

(d) the child is absolutely entitled to the proceeds of a pension fund; or

(e) in any other case, such an appointment seems desirable to the court.

(2) The court may not appoint the Official Solicitor under this rule unless –

(a) the persons with parental responsibility (within the meaning of section 3 of the Children Act 1989) agree; or

(b) the court considers that their agreement can be dispensed with.

(3) The Official Solicitor's appointment may continue only until the child reaches 18.

Practice Direction—See generally PD21 at p 661.

Scope of provision—This rule enables the court to appoint the Official Solicitor to be responsible for the estate of a child in certain defined circumstances.

Official Solicitor—The expression means the Official Solicitor to the Supreme Court provided for by SCA, s 90. The Official Solicitor may be contacted at 81 Chancery Lane, London WC2A 1DD; Tel 020 7911 7127, Fax 020 7911 7105.

Practice Direction – Children and Patients

This Practice Direction supplements CPR Part 21 (PD21)

Procedural Guide—See Guide 17, set out in Section 1 of this work.

General note—See also the notes to CPR Pt 21 for relevant commentary.

GENERAL

1.1 In this practice direction 'child' means a person under 18 years old and 'patient' means a person who by reason of mental disorder within the meaning of the Mental Health Act 1983 is incapable of managing and administering his property and affairs.[1]

1 See rule 21.1(2).

1.2 A patient must bring or defend proceedings by a litigation friend (see paragraph 2 below for the definition of a litigation friend).

1.3 In the proceedings referred to in paragraph 1.2 above the patient should be referred to in the title as 'A.B. (by C.D. his litigation friend)'.

1.4 A child must bring or defend proceedings by a litigation friend unless the court has made an order permitting the child to do so on his own behalf[1].

1 See rule 21.2(3).

1.5 Where:

(1) the child has a litigation friend, the child should be referred to in the title to proceedings as 'A.B. (a child by C.D. his litigation friend)', and
(2) the child is conducting proceedings on his own behalf, the child should be referred to in the title as 'A.B. (a child)'.

1.6 The approval of the court must be obtained if a settlement of a claim by or against a child or patient[1] is to be valid. A settlement includes an agreement on a sum to be apportioned to a dependent child under the Fatal Accidents Act 1976.

1 See rule 21.10.

1.7 The approval of the court must also be obtained before making a voluntary interim payment to a child or patient.

(Rule 39.2(3) provides for a hearing or part of a hearing to be in private)

THE LITIGATION FRIEND

2.1 It is the duty of a litigation friend fairly and competently to conduct proceedings on behalf of a child or patient. He must have no interest in the proceedings adverse to that of the child or patient and all steps and decisions he takes in the proceedings must be taken for the benefit of the child or patient.

2.2 A person may become a litigation friend:

(1) of a child –
  (a) without a court order under the provisions of rule 21.5, or
  (b) by a court order under rule 21.6, and
(2) of a patient
  (a) by authorisation under Part VII of the Mental Health Act 1983, or
  (b) by a court order under rule 21.6.

2.3 In order to become a litigation friend without a court order the person who wishes to act as litigation friend must:

(1) if he wishes to act on behalf of a patient, file an official copy of the order or other document which constitutes the authorisation referred to in paragraph 2.2(2)(a) above, or
(2) if he wishes to act on behalf of a child, or on behalf of a patient without the authorisation referred to in (1) above, file a certificate of suitability[1] –
   (a) stating that he consents to act,
   (b) stating that he knows or believes that the [claimant] [defendant] is a [child][patient],
   (c) in the case of a patient, stating the grounds of his belief and if his belief is based upon medical opinion attaching any relevant document to the certificate,
   (d) stating that he can fairly and competently conduct proceedings on behalf of the child or patient and has no interest adverse to that of the child or patient,
   (e) where the child or patient is a claimant, undertaking to pay any costs which the child or patient may be ordered to pay in relation to the proceedings, subject to any right he may have to be repaid from the assets of the child or patient, and
   (f) which he has signed in verification of its contents.

1 See rule 21.5(3).

2.4 The litigation friend must serve a certificate of suitability[1]:

(1) in the case of a child (who is not also a patient) on one of the child's parents or guardians or if there is no parent or guardian, on the person with whom the child resides or in whose care the child is, and
(2) in the case of a patient on the person authorised under Part VII of the Mental Health Act 1983 to conduct proceedings on behalf of the patient or if there is no person so authorised, on the person with whom the patient resides or in whose care the patient is.

1 See rule 21.5(6) and rule 6.9 (service).

2.4A The litigation friend is not required to serve the documents referred to in paragraph 2.3(2)(c) when he serves a certificate of suitability on the person to be served under paragraph 2.4.

2.5 The litigation friend must file either the certificate of suitability together with a certificate of service[1] of it, or the authorisation referred to in paragraph 2.3(1) above:

(1) where the litigation friend is acting on behalf of a claimant, when the claim form is issued, and
(2) where the litigation friend is acting on behalf of a defendant, when he first takes a step in the action.

1 See rule 6.10 for the certificate of service.

APPLICATION FOR A COURT ORDER APPOINTING A LITIGATION FRIEND

3.1 Rule 21.6 sets out who may apply for an order appointing a litigation friend.

3.2 An application should be made in accordance with Part 23 and must be supported by evidence[1].

1 See rule 21.6(4).

3.3 The application notice must be served:

(1) on the persons referred to in paragraph 2.4 above, and
(2) where the application is in respect of a patient, on the patient unless the court orders otherwise.

3.4 The evidence in support must satisfy the court that the proposed litigation friend:

(1) consents to act,
(2) can fairly and competently conduct proceedings on behalf of the child or patient,
(3) has no interest adverse to that of the child or patient, and
(4) where the child or patient is a claimant, undertakes to pay any costs which the child or patient may be ordered to pay in relation to the proceedings, subject to any right he may have to be repaid from the assets of the child or patient.

3.5 Where a claimant wishes to take a step in proceedings against a child or patient who does not have a litigation friend he must apply to the court for an order appointing a litigation friend.

3.6 The proposed litigation friend must satisfy the conditions in paragraph 3.4(1), (2) and (3) above and may be one of the persons referred to in paragraph 2.4 above where appropriate, or otherwise may be the Official Solicitor. Where it is sought to appoint the Official Solicitor, provision should be made for payment of his charges.

CHANGE OF LITIGATION FRIEND AND PREVENTION OF PERSON ACTING AS LITIGATION FRIEND

4.1 Rule 21.7(1) states that the court may:

(1) direct that a person may not act as a litigation friend,
(2) terminate a litigation friend's appointment,
(3) substitute a new litigation friend for an existing one.

4.2 Where an application is made for an order under rule 21.7(1), the application notice must set out the reasons for seeking it. The application must be supported by evidence.

4.3 If the order sought is the substitution of a new litigation friend for an existing one, the evidence must satisfy the court of the matters set out in paragraph 3.4 above.

4.4 The application notice must be served:

(1) on the persons referred to in paragraph 2.4 above, and
(2) on the litigation friend or person purporting to act as litigation friend.

PROCEDURE WHERE THE NEED FOR A LITIGATION FRIEND HAS COME TO AN END

5.1 Rule 21.9 deals with the situation where the need for a litigation friend comes to an end during the proceedings because either:

(1) a child who is not also a patient reaches the age of 18 (full age) during the proceedings, or
(2) a patient ceases to be a patient (recovers).

5.2 A child on reaching full age must serve on the other parties to the proceedings and file with the court a notice:

(1) stating that he has reached full age,
(2) stating that his litigation friend's appointment has ceased[1],
(3) giving an address for service[2], and
(4) stating whether or not he intends to carry on with or continue to defend the proceedings.

1 Rule 21.9(4)(a).
2 See rule 6.5

5.3 If the notice states that the child intends to carry on with or continue to defend the proceedings he shall subsequently be described in the proceedings as:

'A.B. (formerly a child but now of full age)'

5.4 Whether or not a child having reached full age serves a notice in accordance with rule 21.9(4)(a) and paragraph 5.2(2) above, a litigation friend may at any time after the child has reached full age serve a notice on the other parties that his appointment has ceased.

5.5 The liability of a litigation friend for costs continues until a notice that his appointment to act has ceased is served on the other parties[1].

1 Rule 21.9(6).

5.6 Where a patient recovers, an application under rule 21.9(3) must be made for an order under rule 21.9(2) that the litigation friend's appointment has ceased.

5.7 The application must be supported by the following evidence:

(1) a medical report indicating that the patient has recovered and that he is capable of managing and administering his property and affairs,
(2) where the patient's affairs were under the control of the Court of Protection, a copy of the order or notice discharging the receiver, and
(3) if the application is made by the patient, a statement whether or not he intends to carry on with or continue to defend the proceedings.

5.8 An order under rule 21.9(2) must be served on the other parties to the proceedings. The patient must file with the court a notice:

(1) stating that his litigation friend's appointment has ceased,
(2) giving an address for service[1], and
(3) stating whether or not he intends to carry on with or continue to defend the proceedings.

1 See rule 6.5.

SETTLEMENT OR COMPROMISE BY OR ON BEHALF OF A CHILD OR PATIENT PRIOR TO THE START OF PROCEEDINGS

6.1 Where a claim by or on behalf of a child or patient has been dealt with by agreement prior to the start of proceedings and only the approval of the court to the agreement is sought, the claim:

(1) must be made using the Part 8 procedure,

(2) must include a request for approval of the settlement or compromise, and

(3) subject to paragraph 6.4 in addition to the details of the claim, must set out the terms of the settlement or compromise or have attached to it a draft consent order in practice form N292.

6.2 In order to approve the settlement or compromise, the information concerning the claim that the court will require will include:

(1) whether and to what extent the defendant admits liability,

(2) the age and occupation (if any) of the child or patient,

(3) the litigation friend's approval of the proposed settlement or compromise, and

(4) in a personal injury case arising from an accident –

(a) the circumstances of the accident,

(b) any medical reports,

(c) where appropriate, a schedule of any past and future expenses and losses claimed and any other relevant information relating to personal injury as set out in the practice direction which supplements Part 16 (statements of case), and

(d) where considerations of liability are raised –

(i) any evidence or police reports in any criminal proceedings or in an inquest, and

(ii) details of any prosecution brought.

6.3 (1) An opinion on the merits of the settlement or compromise given by counsel or solicitor acting for the child or patient should, except in very clear cases, be obtained.

(2) A copy of the opinion and, unless the instructions on which it was given are sufficiently set out in it, a copy of the instructions, must also be supplied to the court.

(3) A copy or record of any financial advice must also be supplied to the court.

6.4 Where in any personal injury case a claim for damages for future pecuniary loss is settled, the provisions in paragraphs 6.4A and 6.4B must in addition be complied with.

6.4A The court must be satisfied that the parties have considered whether the damages should wholly or partly take the form of periodical payments.

6.4B Where the settlement includes provision for periodical payments, the claim must –

(1) set out the terms of the settlement or compromise; or

(2) have attached to it a draft consent order,

which must satisfy the requirements of rules 41.8 and 41.9 as appropriate.

6.5 Applications for the approval of a settlement or compromise will normally be heard by a master or district judge.

(For information about provisional damages claims see Part 41 and the practice direction which supplements it)

SETTLEMENT OR COMPROMISE BY OR ON BEHALF OF A CHILD OR PATIENT AFTER PROCEEDINGS HAVE BEEN COMMENCED

6.6 Where in any personal injury case a claim for damages for future pecuniary loss, by or on behalf of a child or patient, is dealt with by agreement after proceedings have been commenced, an application should be made for the court's approval of the agreement.

6.7 The court must be satisfied that the parties have considered whether the damages should wholly or partly take the form of periodical payments.

6.8 Where the settlement includes provision for periodical payments, an application under paragraph 6.6 must –

(1) set out the terms of the settlement or compromise; or
(2) have attached to it a draft consent order,

which must include the requirements of rules 41.8 and 41.9 as appropriate.

6.9 The court must be supplied with –

(1) an opinion on the merits of the settlement or compromise given by counsel or solicitor acting for the child or patient, except in very clear cases; and
(2) a copy or record of any financial advice.

APPORTIONMENT UNDER THE FATAL ACCIDENTS ACT 1976

7.1 A judgment on or settlement in respect of a claim under the Fatal Accidents Act 1976 must be apportioned between the persons by or on whose behalf the claim has been brought.

7.2 Where a claim is brought on behalf of a dependent child or children, the money apportioned to any child must be invested on his behalf in accordance with rules 21.10 and 21.11 and paragraphs 8 and 9 below.

7.3 In order to approve an apportionment of money to a dependent child, the court will require the following information:

(1) the matters set out in paragraph 6.2(1), (2) above, and
(2) in respect of the deceased –
    (a) where death was caused by an accident, the matters set out in paragraph 6.2(3)(a),(b) and (c) above, and
    (b) his future loss of earnings, and
(3) the extent and nature of the dependency.

CONTROL OF MONEY RECOVERED BY OR ON BEHALF OF A CHILD OR PATIENT

8.1 Money recovered or paid into court on behalf of or for the benefit of a child or patient shall be dealt with in accordance with directions of the court under rule 21.11.

8.2 The court:

(1) may direct the money to be paid into the High Court for investment,
(2) may also direct that certain sums be paid direct to the child or patient, his litigation friend or his legal representative[1] for the immediate benefit of the child or patient or for expenses incurred on his behalf, and

(3) may direct the applications in respect of the investment of the money be transferred to a local district registry.

1 See rule 2.3 for a definition of legal representative.

8.3 The master or district judge will consider the general aims to be achieved for the money in court (the fund) by investment and will give directions as to the type of investment.

8.4 Where a child is also a patient, and likely to remain so on reaching full age, his fund should be administered as a patient's fund.

8.5 Where a child or patient is legally aided the fund will be subject to a first charge under section 16 of the Legal Aid Act 1988 (the legal aid charge) and an order for the investment of money on the child or patient's behalf must contain a direction to that effect.

8A.1 A litigation friend may make a claim for expenses under rule 21.11A(1) –

(a) where the court has ordered an assessment of costs under rule 48.5(2), at the detailed assessment hearing;
(b) where the litigation friend's expenses are not of a type which would be recoverable as costs on an assessment of costs between the parties, to the Master or District Judge at the hearing to approve the settlement or compromise under Part 21 (the Master or District Judge may adjourn the matter to the Costs Judge); or
(c) where an assessment of costs under Part 48.5(2) is not required, and no approval under Part 21 is necessary, by a Part 23 application supported by a witness statement to a Costs Judge or District Judge as appropriate.

8A.2 In all circumstances, the litigation friend shall support a claim for expenses by filing a witness statement setting out –

(i) the nature and amount of the expense;
(ii) the reason the expense was incurred.

GUARDIAN'S ACCOUNTS

9 Paragraph 8 of the practice direction supplementing Part 40 (Judgments and Orders) deals with the approval of the accounts of a guardian of assets of a child.

INVESTMENT ON BEHALF OF A CHILD

10.1 At the hearing of the application for the approval of the agreement the litigation friend or his legal representative should provide a CFO form 320 (request for investment) for completion by the master or district judge.

10.2 On receipt of that form in the Court Funds Office the investment managers of the Public Trust Office will make the appropriate investment.

10.3 Where an award of damages for a child is made at trial the trial judge may direct:

(1) the money to be paid into court and placed in the special investment account, and
(2) the litigation friend to make an application to a master or district judge for further investment directions.

10.4 If the money to be invested is very small the court may order it to be paid direct to the litigation friend to be put into a building society account (or similar) for the child's use.

10.5 If the money is invested in court it must be paid out to the child when he reaches full age.

INVESTMENT ON BEHALF OF A PATIENT

11.1 The Court of Protection is responsible for protecting the property of patients and is given extensive powers to do so under the Mental Health Act 1983. Fees are charged for the administration of funds by the Court of Protection and these should be provided for in any settlement.

11.2 Where the sum to be administered is:

(1) over £30,000, the order approving the settlement will contain a direction to the litigation friend to apply to the Court of Protection for the appointment of a receiver, after which the fund will be transferred to the Court of Protection,

(2) under £20,000, it may be retained in court and invested in the same way as the fund of a child, or

(3) in intermediate cases the advice of the Master of the Court of Protection should be sought.

11.3 A form of order transferring the fund to the Court of Protection is set out in practice form N292.

11.4 In order for the Court Funds Office to release a fund which is subject to the legal aid charge to the Court of Protection the litigation friend or his legal representative should provide the appropriate area office of the Legal Aid Board with an undertaking in respect of a sum to cover their costs, following which the area office will advise the Court Funds Office in writing of that sum, enabling them to transfer the balance to the Court of Protection on receipt of a CFO form 200 payment schedule authorised by the court.

11.5 The CFO form 200 should be completed and presented to the court where the settlement or trial took place for authorisation, subject to paragraphs 11.6 and 11.7 below.

11.6 Where the settlement took place in the Royal Courts of Justice the CFO form 200 should be completed and presented for authorisation:

(1) on behalf of a child, in the Masters' Secretary's Office, Room E214, and

(2) on behalf of a patient, in the Action Department, Room E15.

11.7 Where the trial took place in the Royal Courts of Justice the CFO form 200 is completed and authorised by the court officer.

PAYMENT OUT OF FUNDS IN COURT

12.1 Applications to a master or district judge:

(1) for payment out of money from the fund for the benefit of the child, or

(2) to vary an investment strategy,

may be dealt with without a hearing unless the court directs otherwise.

12.2 When the child reaches full age, his fund in court:

(1) where it is a sum of money will be paid out to him, and

(2) where it is in the form of investments other than money (for example shares or unit trusts), will be transferred into his name.

12.3 An application for payment out of funds being administered by the Court of Protection must be made to the Court of Protection.

(For further information on payments into and out of court see the practice directions supplementing Parts 36 and 37)

PART 22
STATEMENTS OF TRUTH

CONTENTS OF THIS PART

22.1 Documents to be verified by a statement of truth

(1) The following documents must be verified by a statement of truth –

(a) a statement of case;
(b) a response complying with an order under rule 18.1 to provide further information;
(c) a witness statement;
(d) an acknowledgment of service in a claim begun by way of the Part 8 procedure;.
(e) a certificate stating the reasons for bringing a possession claim or a landlord and tenant claim in the High Court in accordance with rules 55.3(2) and 56.2(2);
(f) a certificate of service; and
(g) any other document where a rule or practice direction requires.

(2) Where a statement of case is amended, the amendments must be verified by a statement of truth unless the court orders otherwise.

(Part 17 provides for amendments to statements of case)

(3) If an applicant wishes to rely on matters set out in his application notice as evidence, the application notice must be verified by a statement of truth.

(4) Subject to paragraph (5), a statement of truth is a statement that –

(a) the party putting forward the document;
(b) in the case of a witness statement, the maker of the witness statement; or

(5) If a party is conducting proceedings with a litigation friend, the statement of truth in –
(a) a statement of case;
(b) a response; or
(c) an application notice,

is a statement that the litigation friend believes the facts stated in the document being verified are true.

(6) The statement of truth must be signed by –

(a) in the case of a statement of case, a response or an application –
(i) the party or litigation friend; or
(ii) the legal representative on behalf of the party or litigation friend; and
(b) in the case of a witness statement, the maker of the statement.

(7) A statement of truth which is not contained in the document which it verifies, must clearly identify that document.

(8) A statement of truth in a statement of case may be made by –

(a) a person who is not a party; or
(b) by two parties jointly,

where this is permitted by a relevant practice direction.

Amendments—SI 2001/256; SI 2001/1388; SI 2001/1769; SI 2001/4015; SI 2004/3419.

'documents must be verified' (r 22.1(1))—The following list of the documents which need verification by statement of truth is not intended to be exhaustive:

- statement of case (r 22.1(1)(a)), which expression includes (r 2.3):
  - claim form (including, with modification, those issued at the Production Centre (PD7C, para 1.4(5)) and those issued online (PD7E, para 11));
  - particulars of claim not included in the claim form;
  - defence;
  - Part 20 claim;
  - reply to defence;
  - further information in relation to them given voluntarily or pursuant to an order under r 18.1;
- other further information given pursuant to such an order (r 22.1(1)(b));
- amendment to statement of case, unless otherwise ordered (r 22.1(2));
- schedule or counter-schedule of expenses and losses in a personal injury claim and any amendment of either (whether or not contained in a statement of case) (PD22, para 1.4(3));
- witness statement (r 22.1(1)(c));
- expert's report (PD35, para 2.3);
- acknowledgment of service in a claim brought under Part 8 (r 22.1(1)(d));
- certificate of reasons for bringing a possession claim or landlord and tenant claim in the High Court (r 22.1(1)(e));
- a certificate of service (r 22.1(1)(f)) verifying the belief of the person who signs the certificate;
- application notice, if its contents are relied on as evidence (r 22.1(3));
- notice of objection to an account (PD40, para 3.3);
- appellant's notice (Form N161);
- respondent's notice (Form N162);
- application for third party debt order (r 72.3(2)(b));
- application for a hardship payment order (r 72.7(4)(b));
- application for charging order (r 73.3(4)(b)).

If the document is verified by affidavit, a statement of truth is not required in addition (PD22, para 1.6).

Who may sign a statement of truth—The statement of truth verifying a statement of case, a response or an application notice must be signed by the party, his litigation friend (r 22.1(5)), or the legal representative of the party (for definition of legal representative, see r 2.3). Paragraph 3 of PD22 sets out in detail who may sign the certificate of truth in relation to various legal entities such as companies, corporations and partnerships.

A legal representative signing a statement of truth on behalf of a party should as a matter of practice have written instructions or confirmation from the party of their authority to sign the statement of truth on that party's behalf.

The statement of truth verifying a witness statement must be signed by the maker of the statement.

It is not obvious that r 5.3 (which authorises a signature 'printed by computer or other mechanical means' where a rule etc requires a document to be signed) applies to the signature of a statement of truth, which is not itself a document but a statement verifying a document's contents. Certain types of county court claim may be commenced electronically (see PD7E). Paragraph 12.1 of PD7E provides that, in the case of an online claim form or a defence being filed by e-mail, the requirement of a statement of truth to be signed by the person making it is satisfied by that person typing his name underneath the statement of truth. The purpose of the rule, that the individual making the statement accepts responsibility for its truth, will nonetheless be served if the court is satisfied that that individual personally caused the signature to be applied – by whatever means – with that intention.

Contempt of court—Proceedings for contempt may be brought against a person if he 'makes or causes to be made' a false statement in a document verified by a statement of truth without an honest belief in its truth (r 32.14). Proceedings under this rule can only be brought –

(i) by the Attorney General; or
(ii) with the permission of the court (see the note to r 32.14 referring to *Malgar Ltd v RE Leach (Engineering) Ltd* [2000] 3 CP Rep 39, [2000] FSR 393, (2000) *The Times*, 17 February, ChD, Scott V-C).

The statement of truth does not have to be contained in the document which it verifies. A separate statement of truth can be signed by a party provided that it clearly identifies the document to which it relates.

Related sources—
r 8.2 – Claim form Pt 8 procedure
r 16.2(1) – Contents of the claim form
r 16.5 – Contents of defence
r 16.7 – Reply to defence
r 17.1 – Amendment to statement of case
r 18.1 – Request for further information
Pt 20 – Counterclaims
Pt 21 – Children and patients
r 31.23 – False disclosure statements
r 32.8 – Form of witness statement
r 38.14 – False statements

Signing the statement of truth on behalf of a party—A legal representative is not stating his own belief as to the truth of the facts put forward. He is confirming the party's belief on whose behalf the signing as to the truthfulness of the facts being put forward. To avoid potential disputes with parties for whom they act, practitioners should be cautious of verifying statements of case themselves and should obtain where possible the signature of the party concerned. Where this is not possible, for example, in a limitation case the claim form or particulars of claim can be filed without a statement of truth, which could then be filed separately at a later date. See PD22, para 1.5.

22.2 Failure to verify a statement of case

(1) If a party fails to verify his statement of case by a statement of truth –

(a) the statement of case shall remain effective unless struck out; but

(b) the party may not rely on the statement of case as evidence of any of the matters set out in it.

(2) The court may strike out[(GL)] a statement of case which is not verified by a statement of truth.

(3) Any party may apply for an order under paragraph (2).

Practice Direction—See generally PD22 at p 673.

Consequences of failure to verify a statement of case—If a party fails to verify a statement of case it will remain effective unless struck out by the court either upon its own motion or on application by a party in accordance with r 22.2(3). The fact that it is not verified is an irregularity which can be cured.

Where a statement of truth has been omitted (*Hannigan v Hannigan* [2000] All ER (D) 693) or completed incorrectly (*Law v St Margaret's Insurances Limited* [2001] EWCA Civ 30) the overriding objective allows the party in default to put matters right, rather than requiring the claim to be struck out.

Cost consequences of failure to verify—The cost consequences for failing to verify a statement of case are set out at PD22, para 4.3 and will usually mean that the costs will have to be paid by the party who failed to verify in any event and forthwith.

Where a statement of case remains unverified, a party may not rely on that statement as evidence of any matters set out in it (r 22.2(1)(b)).

Additional grounds for striking out—The court can strike out a statement of case on the grounds stated in r 3.4(2) as well as the additional ground of failing to verify by a statement of truth.

22.3 Failure to verify a witness statement

If the maker of a witness statement fails to verify the witness statement by a statement of truth the court may direct that it shall not be admissible as evidence.

Practice Direction—See generally PD22 at p 673.

Scope of provision—Unlike r 22.2(1)(b), where a party may not rely on an unverified statement of case, an unverified witness statement does not automatically render it inadmissible unless the court so directs.

A witness statement must comply with the requirements of r 32.8 and PD32, paras 17–20.

22.4 Power of the court to require a document to be verified

(1) The court may order a person who has failed to verify a document in accordance with rule 22.1 to verify the document.

(2) Any party may apply for an order under paragraph (1).

Practice Direction—See generally PD22 at p 673.

Practice Direction – Statements of Truth

This Practice Direction supplements CPR Part 22 (PD22)

General note—See also the notes to CPR Pt 22 for relevant commentary.

DOCUMENTS TO BE VERIFIED BY A STATEMENT OF TRUTH

1.1 Rule 22.1(1) sets out the documents which must be verified by a statement of truth. The documents include:

(1) a statement of case,
(2) a response complying with an order under rule 18.1 to provide further information,
(3) a witness statement,
[(4) an acknowledgment of service in a claim begun by the Part 8 procedure,
(5) a certificate stating the reasons for bringing a possession claim or a landlord and tenant claim in the High Court in accordance with rules 55.3(2) and 56.2(2),
(6) a certificate of service.

1.2 If an applicant wishes to rely on matters set out in his application notice as evidence, the application notice must be verified by a statement of truth[1].

1 See rule 22.1(3).

1.3 An expert's report should also be verified by a statement of truth. For the form of the statement of truth verifying an expert's report (which differs from that set out below) see the practice direction which supplements Part 35.

1.4 In addition, the following documents must be verified by a statement of truth:

(1) an application notice for –
  (a) a third party debt order (rule 72.3),
  (b) a hardship payment order (rule 72.7), or
  (c) a charging order (rule 73.3);
(2) a notice of objections to an account being taken by the court, unless verified by an affidavit or witness statement;
(3) a schedule or counter-schedule of expenses and losses in a personal

injury claim, and any amendments to such a schedule or counter-schedule, whether or not they are contained in a statement of case.

1.5 The statement of truth may be contained in the document it verifies or it may be in a separate document served subsequently, in which case it must identify the document to which it relates.

1.6 Where the form to be used includes a jurat for the content to be verified by an affidavit then a statement of truth is not required in addition.

Forms—N244 (Application Notice).

Scope of provision—The documents to be verified by a statement of truth are clearly set out in PD22, paras 1.1–1.6. It should be noted that there is no requirement for a separate statement of truth in the case where a party uses one of the forms listed in PD4, provided that the form includes a jurat for the content of the form to be verified by affidavit (PD22, para 1.6).

FORM OF THE STATEMENT OF TRUTH

2.1 The form of the statement of truth verifying a statement of case, a response, an application notice or a notice of objections should be as follows:

['I believe][the (*claimant or as may be*) believes] that the facts stated in this *name document being verified*] are true.'

2.2 The form of the statement of truth verifying a witness statement should be as follows:

'I believe that the facts stated in this witness statement are true.'

2.3 Where the statement of truth is contained in a separate document, the document containing the statement of truth must be headed with the title of the proceedings and the claim number. The document being verified should be identified in the statement of truth as follows:

(1) claim form: 'the claim form issued on [*date*]',
(2) particulars of claim: 'the particulars of claim issued on [date]',
(3) statement of case: 'the *defence or as may be*] served on the [*name of party*] on [*date*]',
(4) application notice: 'the application notice issued on [*date*] for [*set out the remedy sought*]',
(5) witness statement: 'the witness statement filed on [*date*] or served on [*party*] on [*date*]'.

Scope of provision—The form of the statement of truth varies depending upon whether a party is:
(a) verifying a statement of case PD22, para 2.1.
(b) a witness statement PD22, para 2.2.
(c) an expert's report PD35, para 1.4.

A legal representative is not stating his own belief in the facts stated being true but is confirming the party for whom he acts belief in their truth. Accordingly, practitioners should be cautious of verifying statements of case and should seek where possible to obtain the signature of the party concerned.

WHO MAY SIGN THE STATEMENT OF TRUTH

3.1 In a statement of case, a response or an application notice, the statement of truth must be signed by:

(1) the party or his litigation friend[1], or
(2) the legal representative[2] of the party or litigation friend.

1 See Part 21 (children and patients).
2 See rule 2.3 for the definition of legal representative.

3.2 A statement of truth verifying a witness statement must be signed by the witness.

3.3 A statement of truth verifying a notice of objections to an account must be signed by the objecting party or his legal representative.

3.4 Where a document is to be verified on behalf of a company or other corporation, subject to paragraph 3.7 below, the statement of truth must be signed by a person holding a senior position[1] in the company or corporation. That person must state the office or position he holds.

1 See rule 6.4(4).

3.5 Each of the following persons is a person holding a senior position:

(1) in respect of a registered company or corporation, a director, the treasurer, secretary, chief executive, manager or other officer of the company or corporation, and
(2) in respect of a corporation which is not a registered company, in addition to those persons set out in (1), the mayor, chairman, president or town clerk or other similar officer of the corporation.

3.6 Where the document is to be verified on behalf of a partnership, those who may sign the statement of truth are:

(1) any of the partners, or
(2) a person having the control or management of the partnership business.

3.6A An insurer or the Motor Insurers' Bureau may sign a statement of truth in a statement of case on behalf of a party where the insurer or the Motor Insurers' Bureau has a financial interest in the result of proceedings brought wholly or partially by or against that party.

3.6B If insurers are conducting proceedings on behalf of many claimants or defendants a statement of truth in a statement of case may be signed by a senior person responsible for the case at a lead insurer, but –

(1) the person signing must specify the capacity in which he signs;
(2) the statement of truth must be a statement that the lead insurer believes that the facts stated in the document are true; and
(3) the court may order that a statement of truth also be signed by one or more of the parties.

3.7 Where a party is legally represented, the legal representative may sign the statement of truth on his behalf. The statement signed by the legal representative will refer to the client's belief, not his own. In signing he must state the capacity in which he signs and the name of his firm where appropriate.

3.8 Where a legal representative has signed a statement of truth, his signature will be taken by the court as his statement:

(1) that the client on whose behalf he has signed had authorised him to do so,
(2) that before signing he had explained to the client that in signing the statement of truth he would be confirming the client's belief that the facts stated in the document were true, and
(3) that before signing he had informed the client of the possible consequences to the client if it should subsequently appear that the client did not have an honest belief in the truth of those facts (see rule 32.14).

3.9 The individual who signs a statement of truth must print his full name clearly beneath his signature.

3.10 A legal representative who signs a statement of truth must sign in his own name and not that of his firm or employer.

3.11 The following are examples of the possible application of this practice direction describing who may sign a statement of truth verifying statements in documents other than a witness statement. These are only examples and not an indication of how a court might apply the practice direction to a specific situation.

Managing Agent	An agent who manages property or investments for the party cannot sign a statement of truth. It must be signed by the party or by the legal representative of the party.
Trusts	Where some or all of the trustees comprise a single party one, some or all of the trustees comprising the party may sign a statement of truth. The legal representative of the trustees may sign it.
Insurers and the Motor Insurers' Bureau	If an insurer has a financial interest in a claim involving its insured then, if the insured is the party, the insurer may sign a statement of truth in a statement of case for the insured party. Paragraphs 3.4 and 3.5 apply to the insurer if it is a company. The claims manager employed by the insurer responsible for handling the insurance claim or managing the staff handling the claim may sign the statement of truth for the insurer (see next example). The position for the Motor Insurers' Bureau is similar.
Companies	Paragraphs 3.4 and 3.5 apply. The word manager will be construed in the context of the phrase 'person holding a senior position' which it is used to define. The court will consider the size of the company and the size and nature of the claim. It would expect the manager signing the statement of truth to have personal knowledge of the content of the document or to be responsible for managing those who have that knowledge of the content. A small company may not have a manager, apart from the directors, who holds a senior position. A large company will have many such managers. In a larger company with specialist claims, insurance or legal departments the statement may be signed by the manager of such department if he or she is responsible for handling the claim or managing the staff handling it.

In-house legal representatives	Legal representative is defined in rule 2.3(1). A legal representative employed by a party may sign a statement of truth. However a person who is not a solicitor, barrister or other authorised litigator, but who is employed by the company and is managed by such a person, is not employed by that person and so cannot sign a statement of truth. (This is unlike the employee of a solicitor in private practice who would come within the definition of legal representative.) However such a person may be a manager and able to sign the statement on behalf of the company in that capacity.

'litigation friend' (para 3.1(1))—For the circumstances when a litigation friend is required see CPR r 21.2.

Companies and corporations—A statement of truth must be signed by a person holding a senior position and the statement of truth must state the position he holds. 'senior position' is defined in para 3.5 and accords with CPR r 6.4(4) and PD6, para 6.2. Useful examples are given in para 3.11 of when a 'manager' can sign a statement of truth.

'partnership' (para 3.6(2))—A statement of truth can be signed by any of the partners or a person having the control or management of the partnership business.

'legal representative' (para 3 generally)—See definition in CPR r 2.3. It means the barrister or solicitor, solicitor's employee or other authorised litigator who has been instructed to act for the party in relation to the claim. The legal representative must state the capacity in which he signs and the name of his firm. A statement of truth cannot be verified in the firm's name.

Obligations of the legal representative—Practitioners attention is drawn to PD22, para 3.8 which sets out specifically the obligations that the legal representative assumes in signing the statement of truth on behalf of a party.

Paragraph 3.10 of PD22 make it clear that the legal representative signs in his own name and not in that of his firm or employer.

Managing agents—Particularly in property litigation, such persons may have the conduct of the litigation on behalf of the actual party but cannot sign a statement of truth which must be signed by the party instructing the managing agent or his legal representative.

Insurers or MIB—Litigation is often conducted by insurers and the MIB in the name of the insured party (PD22, paras 3.6A and 3.11). Insurers or the MIB may sign a statement of truth on behalf of a party provided they have a financial interest in the result of the proceedings. If the insurer is a company the statement of truth must be signed by a person in a 'senior position' (PD22, paras 3.4 and 3.5 apply, and see examples in para 3.11). The claims manager may also sign if he or she is responsible for handling the claim or managing the staff responsible for it.

Trustees—Any one or all of the trustees may sign a statement of truth. Alternatively, their legal representative may sign.

In-house lawyers—'legal representative' is defined in CPR r 2.3 to include a 'solicitor's employee'. This does not cover legal executives or non-lawyers working in an in-house legal department who may have day to day conduct of the litigation. The only exception is if the in-house legal representative can come within the definition of a manager (PD22, para 3.11).

The solicitor with overall conduct of the litigation should sign all statements of truth.

Attorneys—Powers of Attorney Act 1971, s 7 only authorises an attorney to carry out an act which the donor can lawfully do by an attorney. See *Clauss v Pir* 1998] Ch 287, where it was held that this did not permit an attorney to swear an affidavit containing the evidence of the donor. Consequently, it is not possible for an attorney to sign a statement of truth.

CONSEQUENCES OF FAILURE TO VERIFY

4.1 If a statement of case is not verified by a statement of truth, the statement of case will remain effective unless it is struck out[1], but a party may not rely on the contents of a statement of case as evidence until it has been verified by a statement of truth.

1 See rule 22.2(1).

4.2 Any party may apply to the court for an order that unless within such period as the court may specify the statement of case is verified by the service of a statement of truth, the statement of case will be struck out.

4.3 The usual order for the costs of an application referred to in paragraph 4.2 will be that the costs be paid by the party who had failed to verify in any event and forthwith.

Scope of provision—A statement of case which is not verified remains effective until struck out. It is an irregularity that can be cured by verification. Any party may apply for an order to strike out an unverified statement of case (CPR r 22.2(3)). The court may strike out an unverified statement of case of its own motion.

Paragraph 4.3 of PD22 draws attention to the usual cost orders in such application. Without a reasonable excuse such orders are likely to be on the indemnity basis, summarily assessed. As such, a costs order is to be paid in 14 days (CPR r 44.8).

PENALTY

5 Attention is drawn to rule 32.14 which sets out the consequences of verifying a statement of case containing a false statement without an honest belief in its truth, and to the procedures set out in paragraph 28 of the practice direction supplementing Part 32.

General note—Proceedings for contempt of court for a false statement verified by a statement of truth without an honest belief in its truth can only be brought by the Attorney-General or with the permission of the court. The rule refers to a 'person' and not a party. It is therefore conceivable that where a legal representative signs the statement of truth the document to which it relates contains a false statement, questions may arise as to whether the legal representative is exposed to liability for contempt.

Maximum penalty—Contempt of Court Act 1981, s 14(1). Fixed term of imprisonment not exceeding 2 years on any occasion.

PART 23
GENERAL RULES ABOUT APPLICATIONS FOR COURT ORDERS

CONTENTS OF THIS PART

Procedural Guide—See Guide 18, set out in Section 1 of this work.

23.1 Meaning of 'application notice' and 'respondent'

In this Part –

'application notice' means a document in which the applicant states his intention to seek a court order; and

'respondent' means –

(a) the person against whom the order is sought; and

(b) such other person as the court may direct.

Practice Direction—See generally PD23 at p 684.

Paragraph 2.1 deals with the matters to be included in an application notice.

'application notice'—Form N244 is suggested by Pt 4 but any document in which the applicant states his intention to seek a court order (eg a letter) will suffice, for example application for an extension of a stay of proceedings (r 26.4), PD26, para 3.1, or for the correction of an accidental slip in a judgment or order (r 40.12), PD40B, para 4.2.

'such other person as the court may direct'—The respondent will usually be a party to the proceedings who is affected by the application. However the court may wish to hear from, for example, a person not a party to the proceedings but against whom an order for disclosure of documents is sought.

23.2 Where to make an application

(1) The general rule is that an application must be made to the court where the claim was started.

(2) If a claim has been transferred to another court since it was started, an application must be made to the court to which the claim has been transferred.

(3) If the parties have been notified of a fixed date for the trial, an application must be made to the court where the trial is to take place.

(4) If an application is made before a claim has been started, it must be made to the court where it is likely that the claim to which the application relates will be started unless there is good reason to make the application to a different court.

(5) If an application is made after proceedings to enforce judgment have begun, it must be made to any court which is dealing with the enforcement of the judgment unless any rule or practice direction provides otherwise.

Practice Direction—See generally PD23 at p 684.

Transfer—See Pt 30 and PD30, para 3. Automatic transfer of proceedings takes place in certain circumstances (r 26.2).

Applications before proceedings are started—For example, pre-action disclosure of documents. In these types of proceedings, a claim form is not issued. A party must make application in accordance with the Pt 23 procedure (r 25.4).

23.3 Application notice to be filed

(1) The general rule is that an applicant must file an application notice.

(2) An applicant may make an application without filing an application notice if –

(a) this is permitted by a rule or practice direction; or
(b) the court dispenses with the requirement for an application notice.

Practice Direction—See generally PD23 at p 684.

'file' (r 23.3(1))—This means delivery by post or otherwise to the court officer (see definition in r 2.3). On the filing of an application notice requesting a hearing, the court will notify the applicant of the date and time for the hearing of the application. (PD23, para 2.2).

'application without filing an application notice' (r 23.3(2))—The court may permit a party to make an application in writing other than by way of Form N244, for example by letter (*Miller v Allied Sainif (UK) Limited* (2000) *The Times*, 31 October, ChD). See also *Ebert v Venvil* [2001] EWCA Civ 209, 2000] Ch 484, CA, Neuberger J where the court required the claimant to make applications in writing in an effort to save costs. The court may also entertain applications for corrections of an accidental slip or omission by letter (PD40B, para 4.2).

23.4 Notice of an application

(1) The general rule is that a copy of the application notice must be served on each respondent.

(2) An application may be made without serving a copy of the application notice if this is permitted by –

(a) a rule;
(b) a practice direction; or
(c) a court order.

(Rule 23.7 deals with service of a copy of the application notice)

Practice Direction—See generally PD23 at p 684.

Service of application notice—Part 6 deals with service of documents. The application notice must be served on the respondent. The term 'respondent' is defined in r 23.1. Informing the respondent that the application is being made is insufficient notice to comply with r 23.4(1) unless the party can come within the provisions of r 23.4(2).

Paragraph 3 of PD23 sets out circumstances in which applications may be made without serving an application notice.

Applications for interim remedies—An application for an interim remedy may be made without notice if there are good reasons for so doing (r 25.3). The evidence in support of an application without giving notice must state the reasons why such notice was not given (r 25.3(3)).

When a court has dealt with an application without notice service of a copy of the application notice and any evidence in support must be given to the party against whom the Order is made unless the court orders otherwise (r 23.9).

For applications for interim injunctions without notice, in cases of urgency, see r 25.3.

Oral applications—Rule 23.3(2) allows a party to make an oral application provided that the court dispenses with the requirement for an application notice.

23.5 Time when an application is made

Where an application must be made within a specified time, it is so made if the application notice is received by the court within that time.

Practice Direction—See generally PD23 at p 684.

Scope of provision—An application is made when the court receives a request for it to be issued. An application should be made to the court as soon as it becomes apparent or desirable to make it (PD23, para 2.7). To calculate the time within which a particular application must be made, it is important to be clear about the point from which time runs: for example, whether it runs from the date of a previous order or event or from the date of the decision of the court (*Sayers v Clarke Walker (Practice Note)* [2002] EWCA Civ 645, [2002] 1 WLR 3095, CA).

23.6 What an application notice must include

An application notice must state –

(a) what order the applicant is seeking; and
(b) briefly, why the applicant is seeking the order.

(Part 22 requires an application notice to be verified by a statement of truth if the applicant wishes to rely on matters set out in his application notice as evidence)

Practice Direction—See generally PD23 at p 684.

Paragraph 2.1 deals with the content of an application notice. Paragraphs 6 and 7 deal with telephone/video conferencing hearings. Paragraph 9 deals with the requirements for evidence in certain types of applications and para 10 with consent orders.

Draft orders—Except in the simplest of cases, an applicant should provide the court with a draft of the order that he is seeking.

Evidence—The hearing of an application is a hearing within r 32.6 'other than at trial'. The general rule is that evidence is by witness statement. In addition a party may support his application by a verified statement of case or a verified application notice (r 22.1(3)). For the form and content of a witness statement, see r 32.8 and PD32, paras 17–20.

Hearings in public—The former distinction for applications to be heard either 'in chambers' or 'in court' has now disappeared. Applications to which the provisions of Pt 23 apply will either be heard 'in public' or 'in private'. As a general rule, they will normally be heard in public (r 39.2), except where the limited exceptions referred to in r 39.2(3) and PD39, para 1.5, which lists those hearings which will initially be held in private, apply.

23.7 Service of a copy of an application notice

(1) A copy of the application notice –

(a) must be served as soon as practicable after it is filed; and
(b) except where another time limit is specified in these Rules or a practice direction, must in any event be served at least 3 days before the court is to deal with the application.

(2) If a copy of the application notice is to be served by the court, the applicant must, when he files the application notice, file a copy of any written evidence in support.

(3) When a copy of an application notice is served it must be accompanied by –

(a) a copy of any written evidence in support; and

(b) a copy of any draft order which the applicant has attached to his application.

(4) If –

(a) an application notice is served; but

(b) the period of notice is shorter than the period required by these Rules or a practice direction,

the court may direct that, in the circumstances of the case, sufficient notice has been given and hear the application.

(5) This rule does not require written evidence –

(a) to be filed if it has already been filed; or

(b) to be served on a party on whom it has already been served.

(Part 6 contains the general rules about service of documents including who must serve a copy of the application notice)

Practice Direction—See generally PD23 at p 684.
See particularly para 9 at p 687 on evidence.

Scope of provision—After filing an application notice with the appropriate court and having received from the court a time and date for the hearing, the applicant must serve a copy of the application notice on each respondent (r 23.4(1)). Service of the application must be effected at least 3 days before the court is to deal with the application (except where another time limit is specified). For computation of time, see r 2.8 and the examples therein given. Service will generally be effected by the court unless the applicant elects to serve.

Service out of the jurisdiction—Part 6, Section III applies to service out of the jurisdiction of an application notice in much the same way as it applies to service of a claim form (rr 6.18(h) and 6.30(1)).

'must be served as soon as practicable' (r 23.7(1)(a))—Where the applicant serves, failure to do so resulting in prejudice to the respondent may lead to costs penalties against the applicant.

'the court may direct that … sufficient notice has been given and hear the application.' (r 23.7(4))—This allows the court to abridge the time for service of an application notice and to hear the application. The court has a duty to deal with as many aspects of the case as it can on any one occasion (PD23, para 2.8), and has power to review the conduct of the case as a whole and give case management directions at any hearing (PD23, para 2.9). If a party wishes to make an application but is unable to give 3 days' notice the other party should be informed of the nature of the application and the reasons for it (PD23, paras 2.10 and 4.2). The application can then be made orally at the hearing.

Costs—On the hearing of an application notice which does not last for more than one day, the court will in the majority of circumstances wish to make a summary assessment of costs (r 44.7). Practitioners should be aware of their duties where a summary assessment of costs is likely to take place and provide the court with a written statement of costs they intend to claim (PDCosts, Section 13). If an order made on the hearing of an application does not refer to costs then there is no entitlement to costs (r 44.13(1)). If a detailed assessment of costs is ordered in accordance with Pt 47, the court has power to order costs to be paid on account (r 44.3(8)) before those costs are assessed. A party must comply with an order for the payment of costs within 14 days of the judgment order if it states the amount of those costs (r 44.8).

23.8 Applications which may be dealt with without a hearing

The court may deal with an application without a hearing if –

(a) the parties agree as to the terms of the order sought;

(b) the parties agree that the court should dispose of the application without a hearing, or

(c) the court does not consider that a hearing would be appropriate.

Practice Direction—See generally PD23 at p 684.

See paras 2.2–2.6 for procedure to be followed by the court in relation to applications to be dealt with without a hearing. See para 11 where a party relies on provision of r 23.8(b) and (c) (agreement that the court should dispose of an application without a hearing or it does not consider that one is appropriate).

Scope of provision—The overriding objective allows the court to deal with the management of case without the parties needing to attend (r 1.4(2)(j)). The application notice must contain either a request for a hearing or a request that the application be dealt with without a hearing.

23.9 Service of application where application made without notice

(1) This rule applies where the court has disposed of an application which it permitted to be made without service of a copy of the application notice.

(2) Where the court makes an order, whether granting or dismissing the application, a copy of the application notice and any evidence in support must, unless the court orders otherwise, be served with the order on any party or other person –

(a) against whom the order was made; and
(b) against whom the order was sought.

(3) The order must contain a statement of the right to make an application to set aside[(GL)] or vary the order under rule 23.10.

Practice Direction—See generally PD23 at p 684.

See particularly para 3 which provides six examples of where an application can be made without serving an application notice:

(1) Where there is exceptional urgency.
(2) Where the overriding objective is best furthered by doing so.
(3) By consent of all parties.
(4) With the permission of the court.
(5) Where a date for a hearing has been fixed and a party wishes to make an application at that hearing but does not have sufficient time to serve an application notice.
(6) Where a court order, rule or practice direction permits.

23.10 Application to set aside or vary order made without notice

(1) A person who was not served with a copy of the application notice before an order was made under rule 23.9, may apply to have the order set aside [(GL)] or varied.

(2) An application under this rule must be made within 7 days after the date on which the order was served on the person making the application.

Amendments—SI 2000/221.

Practice Direction—See generally PD23 at p 684.

'order made without notice' (r 23.10)—An order made without notice must contain a statement of the right of any party served to make an application to set aside or vary (r 23.9(3)).

Normally the court will draw up any judgment or order (r 40.3). As to provisions for service, see r 6.3.

23.11 Power of the court to proceed in the absence of a party

(1) Where the applicant or any respondent fails to attend the hearing of an application, the court may proceed in his absence.

(2) Where –

(a) the applicant or any respondent fails to attend the hearing of an application; and

(b) the court makes an order at the hearing,

the court may, on application or of its own initiative, re-list the application.

(Part 40 deals with service of orders)

Practice Direction—See generally PD23 at p 684.

Scope of provision—The court may proceed in a party's absence in order to give effect to the overriding objective.

Rule 23.11(1). Generally the court will need to be satisfied that there has been good service on the absent party.

Where a court makes an order at a hearing in the absence of a party the court retains the power to re-list the application on its own initiative or on application by either party even though the order made at the original hearing may have been perfected. In effect, this is a power to 're-hear' the application. The court's powers on re-listing the application include, for example, to set aside, vary, discharge or suspend the original order (PD23, para 12.2). For an example of the use of this rule in practice see *Riverpath Properties Ltd v Brammall* (2000) *The Times*, 16 February, Neuberger J.

23.12 Dismissal of totally without merit applications

If the court dismisses an application (including an application for permission to appeal or for permission to apply for judicial review) and it considers that the application is totally without merit –

(a) the court's order must record that fact; and

(b) the court must at the same time consider whether it is appropriate to make a civil restraint order.

Amendments—Inserted by SI 2004/2072; SI 2005/2292.

'civil restraint order' (r 23.12(b))—See the note to r 3.3, the new PD3C – Civil Restraint Orders – at p 380 and the **'General note'** thereto.

Practice Direction – Applications

This Practice Direction supplements CPR Part 23 (PD23)

Procedural Guide—See Guide 18, set out in Section 1 of this work.

General note—See also the notes to CPR Pt 23 for relevant commentary.

REFERENCE TO A JUDGE

1 A master or district judge may refer to a judge any matter which he thinks should properly be decided by a judge, and the judge may either dispose of the matter or refer it back to the master or district judge.

APPLICATION NOTICES

2.1 An application notice must, in addition to the matters set out in rule 23.6, be signed and include:

(1) the title of the claim,

(2) the reference number of the claim,

(3) the full name of the applicant,

(4) where the applicant is not already a party, his address for service, and

(5) either a request for a hearing or a request that the application be dealt with without a hearing.

Prospective amendments—Words in italics prospectively inserted in 2.1(4): Supplement 40 (issued 30 September 2005), with effect from 6 April 2006:

> '(4) where the applicant is not already a party, his address for service, *including a postcode. Postcode information may be obtained from www.royalmail.com or the Royal Mail Address Management Guide* , and'

(Practice Form N244 may be used)

2.2 On receipt of an application notice containing a request for a hearing the court will notify the applicant of the time and date for the hearing of the application.

2.3 On receipt of an application notice containing a request that the application be dealt with without a hearing, the application notice will be sent to a master or district judge so that he may decide whether the application is suitable for consideration without a hearing.

2.4 Where the master or district judge agrees that the application is suitable for consideration without a hearing, the court will so inform the applicant and the respondent and may give directions for the filing of evidence. (Rules 23.9 and 23.10 enable a party to apply for an order made without a hearing to be set aside or varied.)

2.5 Where the master or district judge does not agree that the application is suitable for consideration without a hearing, the court will notify the applicant and the respondent of the time, date and place for the hearing of the application and may at the same time give directions as to the filing of evidence.

2.6 If the application is intended to be made to a judge, the application notice should so state. In that case, paragraphs 2.3, 2.4 and 2.5 will apply as though references to the master or district judge were references to a judge.

2.7 Every application should be made as soon as it becomes apparent that it is necessary or desirable to make it.

2.8 Applications should wherever possible be made so that they can be considered at any other hearing for which a date has already been fixed or for which a date is about to be fixed. This is particularly so in relation to case management conferences, allocation and listing hearings and pre-trial reviews fixed by the court.

2.9 The parties must anticipate that at any hearing the court may wish to review the conduct of the case as a whole and give any necessary case management directions. They should be ready to assist the court in doing so and to answer questions the court may ask for this purpose.

2.10 Where a date for a hearing has been fixed and a party wishes to make an application at that hearing but he does not have sufficient time to serve an application notice he should inform the other party and the court (if possible in writing) as soon as he can of the nature of the application and the reason for it. He should then make the application orally at the hearing.

APPLICATIONS WITHOUT SERVICE OF APPLICATION NOTICE

3 An application may be made without serving an application notice only:

(1) where there is exceptional urgency,
(2) where the overriding objective is best furthered by doing so,
(3) by consent of all parties,
(4) with the permission of the court,

(5) where paragraph 2.10 above applies, or
(6) where a court order, rule or practice direction permits.

GIVING NOTICE OF AN APPLICATION

4.1 Unless the court otherwise directs or paragraph 3 of this practice direction applies the application notice must be served as soon as practicable after it has been issued and, if there is to be a hearing, at least 3 clear days before the hearing date (rule 23.7(1)(b)).

4.2 Where an application notice should be served but there is not sufficient time to do so, informal notification of the application should be given unless the circumstances of the application require secrecy.

PRE-ACTION APPLICATIONS

5 All applications made before a claim is commenced should be made under Part 23 of the Civil Procedure Rules. Attention is drawn in particular to rule 23.2(4).

TELEPHONE HEARINGS

6.1 The court may order that an application or part of an application be dealt with by a telephone hearing.

6.1A The applicant should indicate on his application notice if he seeks a court order under paragraph 6.1. Where he has not done so but nevertheless wishes to seek an order the request should be made as early as possible.

6.2 An order under 6.1 will not normally be made unless every party entitled to be given notice of the application and to be heard at the hearing has consented to the order.

6.3 (1) Where a party entitled to be heard at the hearing of the application is acting in person, the court –
(a) may not make an order under 6.1 except on condition that arrangements will be made for the party acting in person to be attended at the telephone hearing by a responsible person to whom the party acting in person is known and who can confirm to the court the identity of the party; and
(b) may not give effect to an order under 6.1 unless the party acting in person is accompanied by a responsible person who at the commencement of the hearing confirms to the court the identity of the party.
(2) The 'responsible person' may be a barrister, solicitor, legal executive, doctor, clergyman, police officer, prison officer or other person of comparable status.
(3) If the court makes an order under 6.1 it will generally give any directions necessary for the telephone hearing.

6.4 No representative of a party to an application being heard by telephone may attend the judge in person while the application is being heard unless the other party to the application has agreed that he may do so.

6.5 If an application is to be heard by telephone the following directions will apply, subject to any direction to the contrary:

(1) The applicant's legal representative must arrange the telephone conference for precisely the time fixed by the court. The telecommunications provider must be capable of connecting the parties and the court.

(2) He must tell the operator the telephone numbers of all those participating in the conference call and the sequence in which they are to be called.

(3) It is the responsibility of the applicant's legal representative to ascertain from all the other parties whether they have instructed counsel and, if so the identity of counsel, and whether the legal representative and counsel will be on the same or different telephone numbers.

(4) The sequence in which they are to be called will be:
   (a) the applicant's legal representative and (if on a different number) his counsel,
   (b) the legal representative (and counsel) for all other parties, and
   (c) the judge.

(5) The applicant's legal representative must arrange for the conference to be recorded on tape by the telecommunications provider whose system is being used and must send the tape to the court.

(6) Each speaker is to remain on the line after being called by the operator setting up the conference call. The call may be 2 or 3 minutes before the time fixed for the application.

(7) When the judge has been connected the applicant's legal representative (or his counsel) will introduce the parties in the usual way.

(8) If the use of a 'speakerphone' by any party causes the judge or any other party any difficulty in hearing what is said the judge may require that party to use a hand held telephone.

(9) The telephone charges debited to the account of the party initiating the conference call will be treated as part of the costs of the application.

Procedural Guide—See Guide 28 'Telephone Hearing Procedure', set out in Section 1 of this work.

VIDEO CONFERENCING

7 Where the parties to a matter wish to use video conferencing facilities, and those facilities are available in the relevant court, they should apply to the master or district judge for directions.

(Paragraph 29 and Annex 3 of Practice Direction 32 provide guidance on the use of video conferencing in the civil courts)

NOTE OF PROCEEDINGS

8 The procedural judge should keep, either by way of a note or a tape recording, brief details of all proceedings before him, including the dates of the proceedings and a short statement of the decision taken at each hearing.

EVIDENCE

9.1 The requirement for evidence in certain types of applications is set out in some of the rules and practice directions. Where there is no specific requirement to provide evidence it should be borne in mind that, as a practical matter, the court will often need to be satisfied by evidence of the facts that are relied on in support of or for opposing the application.

9.2 The court may give directions for the filing of evidence in support of or opposing a particular application. The court may also give directions for the filing of evidence in relation to any hearing that it fixes on its own initiative. The directions may specify the form that evidence is to take and when it is to be served.

9.3 Where it is intended to rely on evidence which is not contained in the application itself, the evidence, if it has not already been served, should be served with the application.

9.4 Where a respondent to an application wishes to rely on evidence which has not yet been served he should serve it as soon as possible and in any event in accordance with any directions the court may have given.

9.5 If it is necessary for the applicant to serve any evidence in reply it should be served as soon as possible and in any event in accordance with any directions the court may have given.

9.6 Evidence must be filed with the court as well as served on the parties. Exhibits should not be filed unless the court otherwise directs.

9.7 The contents of an application notice may be used as evidence (otherwise than at trial) provided the contents have been verified by a statement of truth[1].

1 See Part 22.

CONSENT ORDERS

10.1 Rule 40.6 sets out the circumstances where an agreed judgment or order may be entered and sealed.

10.2 Where all parties affected by an order have written to the court consenting to the making of the order a draft of which has been filed with the court, the court will treat the draft as having been signed in accordance with rule 40.6(7).

10.3 Where a consent order must be made by a judge (ie rule 40.6(2) does not apply) the order must be drawn so that the judge's name and judicial title can be inserted.

10.4 The parties to an application for a consent order must ensure that they provide the court with any material it needs to be satisfied that it is appropriate to make the order. Subject to any rule or practice direction a letter will generally be acceptable for this purpose.

10.5 Where a judgment or order has been agreed in respect of an application or claim where a hearing date has been fixed, the parties must inform the court immediately. (note that parties are reminded that under rules 28.4 and 29.5 the case management timetable cannot be varied by written agreement of the parties.)

OTHER APPLICATIONS CONSIDERED WITHOUT A HEARING

11.1 Where rule 23.8(b) applies the parties should so inform the court in writing and each should confirm that all evidence and other material on which he relies has been disclosed to the other parties to the application.

11.2 Where rule 23.8(c) applies the court will treat the application as if it were proposing to make an order on its own initiative.

APPLICATIONS TO STAY CLAIM WHERE RELATED CRIMINAL PROCEEDINGS

11A.1 An application for the stay of civil proceedings pending the determination of related criminal proceedings may be made by any party to the civil proceedings or by the prosecutor or any defendant in the criminal proceedings.

11A.2 Every party to the civil proceedings must, unless he is the applicant, be made a respondent to the application.

11A.3 The evidence in support of the application must contain an estimate of the expected duration of the stay and must identify the respects in which the continuance of the civil proceedings may prejudice the criminal trial.

11A.4 In order to make an application under paragraph 11A.1, it is not necessary for the prosecutor or defendant in the criminal proceedings to be joined as a party to the civil proceedings.

MISCELLANEOUS

12.1 Except in the most simple application the applicant should bring to any hearing a draft of the order sought. If the case is proceeding in the Royal Courts of Justice and the order is unusually long or complex it should also be supplied on disk for use by the court office.

12.2 Where rule 23.11 applies, the power to re-list the application in rule 23.11(2) is in addition to any other powers of the court with regard to the order (for example to set aside, vary, discharge or suspend the order).

COSTS

13.1 Attention is drawn to the costs practice direction and, in particular, to the court's power to make a summary assessment of costs.

13.2 Attention is also drawn to rule 44.13(i) which provides that if an order makes no mention of costs, none are payable in respect of the proceedings to which it relates.

Practice Direction – Pilot Scheme for Telephone Hearings

This Practice Direction supplements CPR Part 23 (PD23B)

GENERAL

1.1 This practice direction is made under rule 51.2. It provides for a pilot scheme ('the Telephone Hearings Pilot Scheme') to operate at the courts specified in the Appendix between the dates specified for each court in the Appendix. The purpose of the Telephone Hearings Pilot Scheme is to extend the scope of hearings which may be conducted by telephone.

1.2 During the operation of the Telephone Hearings Pilot Scheme –

(1) paragraphs 6.1 to 6.3 of the practice direction supplementing Part 23 do not apply to hearings conducted under the Telephone Hearings Pilot Scheme; but

(2) paragraphs 6.4 and 6.5 do apply and where –

(a) the hearing is an allocation hearing, a listing hearing, a case management conference or a pre-trial review; or

(b) the court of its own initiative orders a telephone hearing,

references in paragraph 6.5 to the applicant are to be read as references to the claimant or such other party as the court directs to arrange the telephone hearing; and

(3) paragraph 6.4 is modified so that it also applies to unrepresented parties.

HEARINGS TO BE CONDUCTED BY TELEPHONE

2.1 Subject to paragraph 2.2, the following hearings will be conducted by telephone unless the court otherwise orders –

(1) allocation hearings;
(2) listing hearings;
(3) interim applications, case management conferences or pre-trial reviews with a time estimate of no more than 1 hour; and
(4) any other application with the consent of the parties and the court's agreement.

2.2 Paragraph 2.1 does not apply where –

(1) all the parties are unrepresented;
(2) more than four parties may wish to make representations at the hearing (for this purpose where two or more parties are represented by the same person, they are to be treated as one party);
(3) the hearing could result in the final determination of the whole or part of the proceedings.

2.3 An application for an order that a hearing under paragraph 2.1(1), (2) or (3) should not be conducted by telephone –

(1) must be made at least 7 days before the hearing; and
(2) may be made by letter,

and the court shall determine such application without requiring the attendance of the parties.

2.4 The claimant's legal representative (if any), or the legal representative of such other party as the court directs, shall be responsible for arranging the telephone hearing.

DOCUMENTS

3.1 The legal representative responsible for arranging the telephone hearing must file and serve a case summary and draft order no later than 4 pm on the last working day before the hearing –

(1) if the claim has been allocated to the multi-track; and
(2) in any other case, if the court so directs.

3.2 Where a party seeks to rely on any other document at the hearing, he must file and serve the document no later than 4 pm on the last working day before the hearing.

APPENDIX

Newcastle Combined Court Centre	1 September 2003 – 31st March 2006
Bedford County Court	1 February 2004 – 31st March 2006
Luton County Court	1 February 2004 – 31st March 2006

PART 24
SUMMARY JUDGMENT

CONTENTS OF THIS PART

Procedural Guide—See Guide 30, set out in Section 1 of this work.

24.1 Scope of this Part

This Part sets out a procedure by which the court may decide a claim or a particular issue without a trial.

(Part 53 makes special provision about summary disposal of defamation claims in accordance with the Defamation Act 1996)

Amendments—SI 2000/221.

Practice Direction—See generally PD24 at p 697.

Scope of provision—Part 24 replaces the former RSC Ords 14 and 14A and CCR Ord 9, r 14. The application may be based on a point of law, the evidence or lack of it or a combination of these (PD24, para 1.3). Unlike RSC Ord 14 and CCR Ord 9, r 14, Pt 24 is available to both claimants and defendants. Thus an application under this Part may be made instead of, or as well as, an application to strike out a statement of case under r 3.4(2)(a) on the basis that it discloses no reasonable grounds for bringing or defending the claim (*Taylor & ors v Midland Bank Trust Company Limited* [1999] All ER (D) 831). The court can now order summary judgment on its own initiative. Evidence in support is no longer mandatory and the practice of giving conditional or unconditional permission to defend has been discontinued (PD24, para 5). The court may, however, impose conditions on any order (r 3.1(3)).

'a claim'—A claim includes a part of a claim, and an issue on which the claim in whole or part depends (PD24, para 1.2).

'or a particular issue'—Rather than give judgment for part of the amount claimed, which may preclude the defendant from challenging that amount at trial, the court may make an interim payment order under Pt 25 (*Glencot Development and Design Co Ltd v Ben Barrett & Son (Contractors) Ltd* [2001] All ER (D) 384 (Feb), [2001] 80 Con LR 14, [2001] BLR 207, TCC).

Part 36 offers—For the purposes of a Pt 36 offer, a disposal of a matter by way of summary judgment does not amount to a *trial* (*Tanfern Ltd v Cameron-MacDonald & ors* [2000] 1 WLR 1311) so as to give rise to a claim for an enhanced rate under the provisions of r 36.21. However, the court can still award costs on an indemnity basis and interest at an enhanced rate under its general jurisdiction (*Petrotrade Inc v Texaco Ltd* [2002] 1 WLR 947, [2001] 4 All ER 853, CA).

Complex issues—In a highly complex case, where an application relies on inferences of fact, the overriding objective may well require the claim to go on to trial. The same approach also applies in a case where the issues involve mixed questions of fact and law and the application of the law is complex because it depends crucially on detailed findings of fact (*Yeheskel Arkin v Borchard Lines Ltd & ors (No 2)* [2001] CP Rep 108, (2001) 151 NLJ 970, Comm Ct). Similarly, this summary procedure should not be used as a 'mini-trial' where it is clear that cross-examination of witnesses is necessary (*Somerset-Leeke v Kay Trustees Ltd & anor* [2002] All ER (D) 37 (Jul), ChD).

24.2 Grounds for summary judgment

The court may give summary judgment against a claimant or defendant on the whole of a claim or on a particular issue if –

(a) it considers that –
  (i) that claimant has no real prospect of succeeding on the claim or issue; or
  (ii) that defendant has no real prospect of successfully defending the claim or issue; and
(b) there is no other [compelling reason why the case or issue should be disposed of at a trial.

(Rule 3.4 makes provision for the court to strike out(GL) a statement of case or part of a statement of case if it appears that it discloses no reasonable grounds for bringing or defending a claim)

Amendments—SI 2000/1317.

Practice Direction—See generally PD24 at p 697.

'no real prospect of succeeding … successfully defending' (r 24.2(a))—The test is now the same as that which has to be satisfied on an application to set aside judgment (see Pt 13 and the notes thereto) and is based on the decision in *Alpine Bulk Transport Co Inc v Saudi Eagle Shipping Co Inc, The Saudi Eagle* [1986] 2 Lloyd's Rep 221, CA. Thus the 'triable issue' test is no longer appropriate. A judge can summarily dispose of a claim or defence under this rule if it does not have a *realistic*, as opposed to a fanciful prospect of success – the test is not whether the claim is bound to fail (*Peter Robert Krafft v Camden London Borough Council* (2000) The *Daily Telegraph*, 21 November, (2000) Lawtel, 24 October, CA; *Gwladys James v Evans* [2001] CP Rep 36, CA). Provided a claim has some chance of success, the court should not strike it out merely because it looks weak and unlikely to succeed (*Chan U Seek v Alvis Vehicles Ltd* [2003] All ER (D) 78 (May), ChD; *Jordan Grand Prix Limited v Tiger Telematics Inc* [2005] EWHC 76 (QB)) but a claim which is really hopeless should not be allowed to continue (*Harris (Elizabeth) v Bolt Burdon (a firm)* (2000) Lawtel, 2 February, CA).

In deciding whether to dispose of a claim or defence summarily, a judge should not conduct a mini-trial of issues or make findings on disputed matters of fact as these are best left for trial and summary judgment is not the appropriate course (*Swain v Hillman* [2001] 1 All ER 91, [2000] PIQR 51, [2001] CP Rep 16, CA; *Somerset-Leeke v Kay Trustees Ltd & anor* [2002] All ER (D) 37 (Jul), ChD; *CPL Industrial Services Holding Limited v R & L Freeman & Sons* [2005] EWCA Civ 539; *Merchantbridge & Co Ltd (previously known as Safron Advisers (UK) Ltd v Safron General Partner 1 Ltd* [2005] EWCA Civ 158). For an application for summary judgment to succeed where a strike-out application would not succeed, three conditions must be satisfied –

(a) all substantial facts relevant to the claimant's case which are reasonably capable of being before the court, must be before the court;
(b) those facts must be undisputed or there must be no reasonable prospect of successfully disputing them;
(c) and there must be no real prospect of oral evidence affecting the court's assessment of the facts (*S v Gloucestershire County Council and L v Tower Hamlets London Borough Council* (2000) *The Independent*, 24 March, CA).

The burden of proof rests upon the applicant to establish his assertion that the respondent has no real prospect of success (*ED & F Man Liquid Products Ltd v Patel* [2003] EWCA Civ 472, [2003] All ER (D) 75 (Apr), CA).

Judgment will not be entered for the defendant under this rule where, even though the ill-drawn claim form discloses no claim as pleaded, on the facts which he alleges the claimant has an arguable claim (*Kim Munn v (1) North West Water Ltd (2) Preston Borough Council* (2000) Lawtel, 18 June, CA). Misrepresentation or fraud as a defence to a claim for a dishonoured bill of exchange, such as a cheque, may give rise to a finding of a 'reasonable prospect of successfully defending the claim' (*Solo Industries UK Ltd v Canara Bank* [2001] EWCA Civ 1059, [2001] 1 WLR 1800, [2001] 2 All ER (Comm) 217, [2001] 2 Lloyd's Rep 578, CA).

24.3 Types of proceedings in which summary judgment is available

(1) The court may give summary judgment against a claimant in any type of proceedings.

(2) The court may give summary judgment against a defendant in any type of proceedings except –

(a) proceedings for possession of residential premises against –
  (i) a mortgagor; or
  (ii) a tenant or a person holding over after the end of his tenancy whose occupancy is protected within the meaning of the Rent Act 1977 or the Housing Act 1988; and
(b) proceedings for an admiralty claim in rem.
(c) (*revoked*)

Amendments—SI 1999/1008; SI 2000/2092.

Practice Direction—See generally PD24 at p 697.

'any type of proceedings' (r 24.3 generally)—This includes small claims. There is similar power to grant summary judgment in small claims under r 27.6(1)(b). The exceptions set out in r 24.3(2) only apply to the defendant. Whenever the claim form expressly or by implication involves accounts and inquiries, an application may be made under Pt 24 for a summary order so directing (PD24, para 6). Allegations of deceitful, dishonest and unlawful conduct in an action for unjust enrichment and conspiracy are not suitable for summary disposal where the truth of matters in dispute is not capable of being substantiated by inference from the documentary and affidavit evidence (*Esprit Telecoms UK Ltd & ors v Fashion Gossip Ltd* [2000] All ER (D) 1090, CA). Summary judgment in a libel case is not available to a claimant – the defendant has a right to jury trial (*Safeway Stores plc v Tate* [2001] QB 1120, [2001] 2 WLR 1377, [2001] 4 All ER 193, CA), but is available to a defendant (*Clarkson (Petruska) v Gilbert (Maria) & ors* [2001] All ER (D) 317 (Feb), (2001) Lawtel, 26 February, QBD).

Rule 24.3(2)—Notwithstanding the exceptions referred to, an application can be made under Pt 24 in a claim for specific performance of an agreement for the sale, purchase, exchange, mortgage or charge on any property, or for the grant or assignment of a lease or tenancy. Similarly, there may be an application for rescission of such an agreement, or for the forfeiture or return of any deposit made under such agreement (PD24, para 7.1).

24.4 Procedure

(1) A claimant may not apply for summary judgment until the defendant against whom the application is made has filed –

(a) an acknowledgment of service; or
(b) a defence,

unless –

(i) the court gives permission; or
(ii) a practice direction provides otherwise.

(Rule 10.3 sets out the period for filing an acknowledgment of service and rule 15.4 the period for filing a defence)

[(1A) In civil proceedings against the Crown, as defined in rule 66.1(2), a claimant may not apply for summary judgment until after expiry of the period for filing a defence specified in rule 15.4.

(2) If a claimant applies for summary judgment before a defendant against whom the application is made has filed a defence, that defendant need not file a defence before the hearing.

(3) Where a summary judgment hearing is fixed, the respondent (or the parties where the hearing is fixed of the court's own initiative) must be given at least 14 days' notice of –

(a) the date fixed for the hearing; and
(b) the issues which it is proposed that the court will decide at the hearing.

(4) A practice direction may provide for a different period of notice to be given.

(Part 23 contains the general rules about how to make an application)

(Rule 3.3 applies where the court exercises its powers of its own initiative)

Amendments—SI 2000/221; SI 2005/2292.

Practice Direction—See generally PD24 at p 697.

Procedure—Normally, a file will not come to the judge's attention until allocation, unless a vigilant clerk spots something amiss, but on allocation, or possibly earlier, the court will always consider its powers under r 3.4(1) to consider sanctions or to dispose of a claim summarily. If an application for summary judgment is made prior to allocation, allocation will be put back until the application has been determined. Allocation will almost certainly be dealt with at that time, if the application is unsuccessful. The Allocation Questionnaire (Form N150) contains provision for the party completing it to state that he intends to make an application for summary judgment. That indication does not, by itself, operate as an application which must be made according to the procedure set out in this rule. Without an accompanying application the likelihood is that – subject to the above – allocation will proceed.

Evidence—Note that there is no general requirement for the applicant to serve evidence in support of the application, which is a departure from the procedure under the old rules. However, if he does intend to rely on evidence, he must include it or identify it in his application notice (PD24, para 2(4)). As a statement of truth (see Pt 22) is now included with the claim and defence, their contents could stand as evidence, as could any evidence certified with a statement of truth on the application form itself. See also rr 23.7(3) and 32.6(2), the latter of which is referred to in PD24. See also PD24, para 2(4).

Court's own initiative—Even if neither party has applied for summary judgment, the court may consider giving it (r 3.3(1); *Gwladys James v Evans* [2001] CP Rep 36, CA). For example, on an application to strike out a claim under Pt 3, the court may, when refusing the application and where appropriate, consider making an order for summary judgment instead, even where there has been no application for one (*O'Donnell (Peter John) & ors v Charly Holdings Inc (a company incorporated under the laws of Panama) & anor* (2000) Lawtel, March 14, CA; *Taylor & ors v Midland Bank Trust Company Limited* [1999] All ER (D) 831). The trial judge can order summary judgment after hearing the claimant's case if he is of the opinion that the case is bound to fail and that, therefore, the defendant has no case to answer (*Bentley v Jones Harris* & Co [2001] EWCA Civ 1724, CA). See also note **'No case to answer'** under r 32.1.

'need not file a defence' (r 24.4(2))—While the issue of an application by the claimant for summary judgment relieves the defendant from the need to file a defence, this rule makes no similar provision if the application is made by the defendant. Nevertheless, if the defendant makes an application under this Part, the claimant may not obtain default judgment against him until it is disposed of (r 12.3(3)(a)).

'at least 14 days' notice' (r 24.4(3))—The effect, where the hearing is fixed of the court's own initiative, is to extend the 3-day period mentioned in r 3.3(3). The time is reduced to 4 days for a claimant's application in a claim for specific performance (PD24, para 7.3) As a result of PD24, para 7.1 an applicant for specific performance will not be permitted to rely on the provisions in r 24.4(3);; and r 24.5 below will clearly have no application.

'different period of notice' (r 24.4(4))—This has been added by Civil Procedure (Amendment) Rules 2000, r 12 to allow for flexibility in fixing period of notice and to resolve the conflict between this rule prior to its amendment and PD24, paras 7.1–7.3 (specific performance).

The application—For the form of application, see Pt 23 and PD24, para 2(2).

Damages and causation—Where a defendant applies for summary judgment, the court must conclude that the claimant has a real prospect of succeeding in principle (in this case, that there was a breach of contract), before investigating the likelihood of establishing damages and causation (*Kumarth Khalagy & anor v Alliance and Leicester plc* (2000) Lawtel, 23 October, CA).

24.5 Evidence for the purposes of a summary judgment hearing

(1) If the respondent to an application for summary judgment wishes to rely on written evidence at the hearing, he must –

(a) file the written evidence; and

(b) serve copies on every other party to the application,

at least 7 days before the summary judgment hearing.

(2) If the applicant wishes to rely on written evidence in reply, he must –

(a) file the written evidence; and
(b) serve a copy on the respondent,

at least 3 days before the summary judgment hearing.

(3) Where a summary judgment hearing is fixed by the court of its own initiative –

(a) any party who wishes to rely on written evidence at the hearing must –
(i) file the written evidence; and
(ii) unless the court orders otherwise, serve copies on every other party to the proceedings,

at least 7 days before the date of the hearing;

(b) any party who wishes to rely on written evidence at the hearing in reply to any other party's written evidence must –
(i) file the written evidence in reply; and
(ii) unless the court orders otherwise serve copies on every other party to the proceedings,

at least 3 days before the date of the hearing.

(4) This rule does not require written evidence –

(a) to be filed if it has already been filed; or
(b) to be served on a party on whom it has already been served.

Practice Direction—See generally PD24 at p 697.

'evidence' (r 24.5)—This must bear a Statement of Truth (see PD32). Additional costs of an affidavit are not normally recoverable (r 32.15(2)). Note that it is not mandatory to file evidence in support (r 24.5(4)) but is certainly advisable where there is no evidence already before the court which would support the application.

24.6 Court's powers when it determines a summary judgment application

When the court determines a summary judgment application it may –

(a) give directions as to the filing and service of a defence;
(b) give further directions about the management of the case.

(Rule 3.1(3) provides that the court may attach conditions when it makes an order)

Practice Direction—See generally PD24 at p 697.

Conditional order—Guidance as to the circumstances under which conditions should be attached can be gleaned from PD24, para 4. The court may require a party to pay money into court or take a specified step with strike out or dismissal of claim in default (PD24, para 5.2). This is an example of the court's general power to attach conditions to an order under r 3.1(3). On an application for summary judgment the court should not make a conditional order without considering the party's ability to comply with any conditions, including his ability to pay a sum of money (*Chapple (James) v Williams (David) & anor* (1999) Lawtel, 12 December, CA). Any conditional order has to be reasonable in order to comply with the payer's European Convention right to a fair trial (*Anglo-Eastern Trust Ltd v Kermanshahchi; Alliance v Kermanshahchi* [2002] EWCA Civ 198, [2002] CP Rep 36, CA).

Costs—Regard should be had to the fixed costs provisions of Pt 44 and the court's power to assess the costs summarily (PD24, para 9). If no order for costs is made then no party is entitled to any (r 44.13(1)).

Practice Direction – The Summary Disposal of Claims

This Practice Direction supplements CPR Part 24 (PD24)

Procedural Guide—See Guide 30, set out in Section 1 of this work.

General note—See also the notes to CPR Pt 24.

APPLICATIONS FOR SUMMARY JUDGMENT UNDER PART 24

1.1 Attention is drawn to Part 24 itself and to:
Part 3, in particular rule 3.1(3) and (5),
Part 22,
Part 23, in particular rule 23.6,
Part 32, in particular rule 32.6(2).

1.2 In this paragraph, where the context so admits, the word 'claim' includes:

(1) a part of a claim, and
(2) an issue on which the claim in whole or part depends.

1.3 An application for summary judgment under rule 24.2 may be based on:

(1) a point of law (including a question of construction of a document),
(2) the evidence which can reasonably be expected to be available at trial or the lack of it, or
(3) a combination of these.

1.4 Rule 24.4(1) deals with the stage in the proceedings at which an application under Part 24 can be made (but see paragraph 7.1 below).

Paragraph 1.1—The rules referred to relate respectively to:
CPR r 3.1(3) and (5) – attaching conditions to orders including the paying of money into court;
CPR Pt 22 – statements of truth;
CPR r 23.6 – contents of an application notice;
CPR r 32.6(2) – evidence on applications.

PROCEDURE FOR MAKING AN APPLICATION

2 (1) Attention is drawn to rules 24.4(3) and 23.6.

(2) The application notice must include a statement that it is an application for summary judgment made under Part 24.

(3) The application notice or the evidence contained or referred to in it or served with it must –

(a) identify concisely any point of law or provision in a document on which the applicant relies, and/or

(b) state that it is made because the applicant believes that on the evidence the respondent has no real prospect of succeeding on the claim or issue or (as the case may be) of successfully defending the claim or issue to which the application relates,

and in either case state that the applicant knows of no other reason why the disposal of the claim or issue should await trial.

(4) Unless the application notice itself contains all the evidence (if any) on which the applicant relies, the application notice should identify the written evidence on which the applicant relies. This does not affect the applicant's right to file further evidence under rule 24.5(2).

(5) The application notice should draw the attention of the respondent to rule 24.5(1).

(6) Where the claimant has failed to comply with any pre-action protocol,

an action for summary judgment will not normally be entertained before the defence has been filed or, alternatively, the time for doing so has expired.

Application notice—None is prescribed but Form N244 may be used. Non-compliance with the technicalities in para 2(3) is not as likely to be fatal to the application as was the case under the former rules (*Barclays Bank v Piper* (1995) *The Times*, 31 May, CA) but is likely to result in costs sanctions at least.

Court fees—Application for summary judgment – £50 (SCFO and CCFO fee 2.4).

Service—See CPR rr 23.9 and 23.10.

THE HEARING

3 (1) The hearing of the application will normally take place before a master or a district judge.

(2) The master or district judge may direct that the application be heard by a High Court judge (if the case is in the High Court) or a circuit judge (if the case is in a county court).

'a master or district judge' (para 3(1))—He may hear the application even though the case is outside his jurisdiction for a final trial (PD2B, para 4.1).

THE COURT'S APPROACH

4 Where it appears to the court possible that a claim or defence may succeed but improbable that it will do so, the court may make a conditional order, as described below.

ORDERS THE COURT MAY MAKE

5.1 The orders the court may make on an application under Part 24 include:

(1) judgment on the claim,
(2) the striking out or dismissal of the claim,
(3) the dismissal of the application,
(4) a conditional order,

5.2 A conditional order is an order which requires a party:

(1) to pay a sum of money into court, or
(2) to take a specified step in relation to his claim or defence, as the case may be,

and provides that that party's claim will be dismissed or his statement of case will be struck out if he does not comply.

(Note – the court will not follow its former practice of granting leave to a defendant to defend a claim, whether conditionally or unconditionally)

'A conditional order' (para 5.2)—Although granting 'leave to defend' with conditions has gone, it is replaced by the power to attach conditions to an order. The new provisions provide a greater flexibility than the old.

Costs—Fixed costs may be awarded on an application for summary judgment (CPR r 45.1(2)). The amount of costs is dependant on the amount of debt or damages awarded. For details see CPR r 45.4, Table 2.

ACCOUNTS AND INQUIRIES

6 If a remedy sought by a claimant in his claim form includes, or necessarily involves, taking an account or making an inquiry, an application can be made

under Part 24 by any party to the proceedings for an order directing any necessary accounts or inquiries to be taken or made.

(The Accounts practice direction supplementing Part 40 contains further provisions as to orders for accounts and inquiries)

SPECIFIC PERFORMANCE

7.1 (1) If a remedy sought by a claimant in his claim form includes a claim –

(a) for specific performance of an agreement (whether in writing or not) for the sale, purchase, exchange, mortgage or charge of any property, or for the grant or assignment of a lease or tenancy of any property, with or without an alternative claim for damages, or

(b) for rescission of such an agreement, or

(c) for the forfeiture or return of any deposit made under such an agreement,

the claimant may apply under Part 24 for judgment.

(2) The claimant may do so at any time after the claim form has been served, whether or not the defendant has acknowledged service of the claim form, whether or not the time for acknowledging service has expired and whether or not any particulars of claim have been served.

7.2 The application notice by which an application under paragraph 7.1 is made must have attached to it the text of the order sought by the claimant.

7.3 The application notice and a copy of every affidavit or witness statement in support and of any exhibit referred to therein must be served on the defendant not less than 4 days before the hearing of the application. (Note – the 4 days replaces for these applications the 14 days specified in rule 24.4(3). Rule 24.5 cannot, therefore, apply.)

(This paragraph replaces RSC Order 86, rules 1 and 2 but applies to county court proceedings as well as to High Court proceedings)

Time period for service (para 7.3)—With effect from 2 May 2000, the previous conflict between this provision and CPR r 24.4(4) has been resolved by an amendment to that rule.

SETTING ASIDE ORDER FOR SUMMARY JUDGMENT

8.1 If an order for summary judgment is made against a respondent who does not appear at the hearing of the application, the respondent may apply for the order to be set aside or varied (see also rule 23.11).

8.2 On the hearing of an application under paragraph 8.1 the court may make such order as it thinks just.

COSTS

9.1 Attention is drawn to Part 45 (fixed costs).

9.2 Attention is drawn to the Costs Practice Direction and in particular to the court's power to make a summary assessment of costs.

9.3 Attention is also drawn to rule 44.13(1) which provides that if an order does not mention costs no party is entitled to costs relating to that order.

Costs—As this will be an interim application the court is likely to assess costs summarily. Parties should therefore prepare their written statements of costs in accordance with PDCosts, para 13.5. Paragraph 9.3 also serves to remind practitioners, in particular in relation to consent orders, that if costs or quantum of costs are not mentioned in an order, no costs will be allowed. See also PDCosts, para 13.4 with regard to consent orders.

CASE MANAGEMENT

10 Where the court dismisses the application or makes an order that does not completely dispose of the claim, the court will give case management directions as to the future conduct of the case.

PART 25
INTERIM REMEDIES AND SECURITY FOR COSTS

CONTENTS OF THIS PART

Procedural Guide—See Guide 23, set out in Section 1 of this work.

Amendments—SI 2000/221.

I Interim remedies

25.1 Orders for interim remedies

(1) The court may grant the following interim remedies –

- (a) an interim injunction(GL);
- (b) an interim declaration;
- (c) an order –
  - (i) for the detention, custody or preservation of relevant property;
  - (ii) for the inspection of relevant property;
  - (iii) for the taking of a sample of relevant property;
  - (iv) for the carrying out of an experiment on or with relevant property;
  - (v) for the sale of relevant property which is of a perishable nature or which for any other good reason it is desirable to sell quickly; and
  - (vi) for the payment of income from relevant property until a claim is decided;
- (d) an order authorising a person to enter any land or building in the possession of a party to the proceedings for the purposes of carrying out an order under sub-paragraph (c);
- (e) an order under section 4 of the Torts (Interference with Goods) Act 1977 to deliver up goods;
- (f) an order (referred to as a 'freezing injunction(GL)') –
  - (i) restraining a party from removing from the jurisdiction assets located there; or
  - (ii) restraining a party from dealing with any assets whether located within the jurisdiction or not;

(g) an order directing a party to provide information about the location of relevant property or assets or to provide information about relevant property or assets which are or may be the subject of an application for a freezing injunction(GL);

(h) an order (referred to as a 'search order') under section 7 of the Civil Procedure Act 1997 (order requiring a party to admit another party to premises for the purpose of preserving evidence etc);

(i) an order under section 33 of the Supreme Court Act 1981 or section 52 of the County Courts Act 1984 (order for disclosure of documents or inspection of property before a claim has been made);

(j) an order under section 34 of the Supreme Court Act 1981 or section 53 of the County Courts Act 1984 (order in certain proceedings for disclosure of documents or inspection of property against a non-party);

(k) an order (referred to as an order for interim payment) under rule 25.6 for payment by a defendant on account of any damages, debt or other sum (except costs) which the court may hold the defendant liable to pay;

(l) an order for a specified fund to be paid into court or otherwise secured, where there is a dispute over a party's right to the fund;

(m) an order permitting a party seeking to recover personal property to pay money into court pending the outcome of the proceedings and directing that, if he does so, the property shall be given up to him;

(n) an order directing a party to prepare and file accounts relating to the dispute[;

(o) an order directing any account to be taken or inquiry to be made by the court.

(Rule 34.2 provides for the court to issue a witness summons requiring a witness to produce documents to the court at the hearing or on such date as the court may direct)

(2) In paragraph (1)(c) and (g), 'relevant property' means property (including land) which is the subject of a claim or as to which any question may arise on a claim.

(3) The fact that a particular kind of interim remedy is not listed in paragraph (1) does not affect any power that the court may have to grant that remedy.

(4) The court may grant an interim remedy whether or not there has been a claim for a final remedy of that kind.

Amendments—SI 2002/2058.

Practice Direction—See generally PD25 at p 711 and PD25B at p 731.

'interim remedies' (r 25.1(1))—The jurisdiction to grant interim relief in the High Court is derived from SCA, s 37, and in the county courts is derived from CCA 1984, s 38.

'interim injunction' (r 25.1(1)(a))—See *American Cyanamid Co v Ethicon Limited* [1975] AC 396, for the principles upon which the court will grant an interim injunction. These may be summarised as follows:

(a) The claimant must establish that he has a good arguable claim to the right that he seeks to protect.

(b) The court must not attempt to decide this claim on the evidence filed; it is enough for the claimant to show that there is a serious issue to be tried.

(c) If the claimant satisfies these tests, it is for the court to decide on the balance of convenience whether or not to grant an injunction.

To these principles there must now be added consideration of the principles set out in the overriding objective (r 1.1(2)).

The overriding objective may apply equally to well-established exceptions to these general principles. The principal exceptions are:

(a) The court must assess the relative strength of each party's case where the grant or refusal of an interim injunction will effectively dispose of the claim (*Cambridge Nutrition Ltd v BBC* [1990] 3 All ER 523).
(b) Where the claimant seeks an interim injunction to restrain the exercise of statutory powers by a public authority, the claimant must show that he has a real prospect of success at the trial (*Smith v Inner London Education Authority* [1978] 1 All ER 411, CA).
(c) Where the injunction sought is in mandatory terms, ie the defendant will be ordered to do some positive act, the claimant must show a very strong and clear case before an order will be made.
(d) Where a claimant is seeking protection of his rights under European law, the court has no jurisdiction to grant an interim injunction against Crown (Crown Proceedings Act 1947, s 21 and *Factortame Ltd v Secretary of State for Transport (No 2)* [1991] 1 All ER 70, HL).

The factors affecting the balance of convenience will vary from case to case, but will now be subject to the overriding objective. The two most important factors are likely to remain:

(a) whether damages would provide adequate compensation to the claimant, in which case an injunction should be refused. The defendant's ability to meet any award of damages will be relevant. Damages may not provide adequate compensation if they would be at least very difficult to assess (*Birmingham City Council v In Shops* [1992] NPC 71), or the wrong would be irreparable (*Woodford v Smith* [1970] 1 All ER 1091);
(b) whether more harm would be caused by granting than by refusing the injunction. So the court may more readily restrain a new business activity than interfere with an established one (*American Cyanamid Co v Ethicon Limited* [1975] AC 396 at 408).

Discharge of interim injunction—A defendant may apply to discharge an interim injunction. However, where the application is made shortly before trial, the defendant is protected by an undertaking in damages and there is no evidence that additional damage may be suffered, the court may apply the overriding objective and refuse to hear the application (*Stephenson Ltd v Mandy* (1999) NLD, 30 June, CA).

'interim declaration' (r 25.1(1)(b))—This is a new power that may be increasingly used in the developing field of the court's involvement in authorising and supervising emergency medical treatment.

'authorising any person to enter land' (r 25.1(1)(d))—This power is wider than that contained in the old RSC Ord 29 which did not authorise entry for the purpose of selling property.

'section 4 of the Torts (Interference with Goods) Act 1977' (r 25.1(1)(e))—This power is wider than the old RSC Ord 29, r 2A in that it permits an order to be made before commencement of proceedings (r 25.2(1)(a)).

'relevant property' (r 25.1(2))—This now includes land if the conditions set out in r 25.1(1)(c) are satisfied. This power is in addition to that contained in Pt 40, Section II.

25.2 Time when an order for an interim remedy may be made

(1) An order for an interim remedy may be made at any time, including –

(a) before proceedings are started; and
(b) after judgment has been given.

(Rule 7.2 provides that proceedings are started when the court issues a claim form)

(2) However –

(a) paragraph (1) is subject to any rule, practice direction or other enactment which provides otherwise;
(b) the court may grant an interim remedy before a claim has been made only if –
(i) the matter is urgent; or
(ii) it is otherwise desirable to do so in the interests of justice; and

(c) unless the court otherwise orders, a defendant may not apply for any of the orders listed in rule 25.1(1) before he has filed either an acknowledgment of service or a defence.

(Part 10 provides for filing an acknowledgment of service and Part 15 for filing a defence)

(3) Where the court grants an interim remedy before a claim has been commenced, it may give directions requiring a claim to be commenced.

(4) In particular, the court need not direct that a claim be commenced where the application is made under section 33 of the Supreme Court Act 1981 or section 52 of the County Courts Act 1984 (order for disclosure, inspection etc before commencement of a claim).

Practice Direction—See PD25, para 2.1 at p 711.

25.3 How to apply for an interim remedy

(1) The court may grant an interim remedy on an application made without notice if it appears to the court that there are good reasons for not giving notice.

(2) An application for an interim remedy must be supported by evidence, unless the court orders otherwise.

(3) If the applicant makes an application without giving notice, the evidence in support of the application must state the reasons why notice has not been given.

(Part 3 lists general powers of the court)

(Part 23 contains general rules about making an application)

Practice Direction—See PD25, para 2.4 at p 711, PD25, para 3.2 at p 711, and para 4 at p 725.

'made without notice' (r 25.3(1))—See PD25, para 4 for detailed guidance on the procedure for urgent applications.

'supported by evidence' (r 25.3(2))—See PD25, para 3.2. The requirements of this rule and PD25, para 3 are in addition to the general rules in Pt 23.

Draft order—A draft of the order sought should be filed with the application – see PD25, para 2.4.

25.4 Application for an interim remedy where there is no related claim

(1) This rule applies where a party wishes to apply for an interim remedy but –

(a) the remedy is sought in relation to proceedings which are taking place, or will take place, outside the jurisdiction; or
(b) the application is made under section 33 of the Supreme Court Act 1981 or section 52 of the County Courts Act 1984 (order for disclosure, inspection etc before commencement) before a claim has been commenced.

(2) An application under this rule must be made in accordance with the general rules about applications contained in Part 23.

(The following provisions are also relevant –

- Rule 25.5 (inspection of property before commencement or against a non-party)
- Rule 31.16 (orders for disclosure of documents before proceedings start)

– Rule 31.17 (orders for disclosure of documents against a person not a party))

25.5 Inspection of property before commencement or against a non-party

(1) This rule applies where a person makes an application under –

(a) section 33(1) of the Supreme Court Act 1981 or section 52(1) of the County Courts Act 1984 (inspection etc of property before commencement);

(b) section 34(3) of the Supreme Court Act 1981 or section 53(3) of the County Courts Act 1984 (inspection etc of property against a non-party).

(2) The evidence in support of such an application must show, if practicable by reference to any statement of case prepared in relation to the proceedings or anticipated proceedings, that the property –

(a) is or may become the subject matter of such proceedings; or

(b) is relevant to the issues that will arise in relation to such proceedings.

(3) A copy of the application notice and a copy of the evidence in support must be served on –

(a) the person against whom the order is sought; and

(b) in relation to an application under section 34(3) of the Supreme Court Act 1981 or section 53(3) of the County Courts Act 1984, every party to the proceedings other than the applicant.

25.6 Interim payments – general procedure

(1) The claimant may not apply for an order for an interim payment before the end of the period for filing an acknowledgment of service applicable to the defendant against whom the application is made.

(Rule 10.3 sets out the period for filing an acknowledgment of service)

(Rule 25.1(1)(k) defines an interim payment)

(2) The claimant may make more than one application for an order for an interim payment.

(3) A copy of an application notice for an order for an interim payment must –

(a) be served at least 14 days before the hearing of the application; and

(b) be supported by evidence.

(4) If the respondent to an application for an order for an interim payment wishes to rely on written evidence at the hearing, he must –

(a) file the written evidence; and

(b) serve copies on every other party to the application,

at least 7 days before the hearing of the application.

(5) If the applicant wishes to rely on written evidence in reply, he must –

(a) file the written evidence; and

(b) serve a copy on the respondent,

at least 3 days before the hearing of the application.

(6) This rule does not require written evidence –

(a) to be filed if it has already been filed; or
(b) to be served on a party on whom it has already been served.

(7) The court may order an interim payment in one sum or in instalments.

(Part 23 contains general rules about applications)

25.7 Interim payments – conditions to be satisfied and matters to be taken into account

(1) The court may only make an order for an interim payment where any of the following conditions are satisfied –

(a) the defendant against whom the order is sought has admitted liability to pay damages or some other sum of money to the claimant;
(b) the claimant has obtained judgment against that defendant for damages to be assessed or for a sum of money (other than costs) to be assessed;
(c) it is satisfied that, if the claim went to trial, the claimant would obtain judgment for a substantial amount of money (other than costs) against the defendant from whom he is seeking an order for an interim payment whether or not that defendant is the only defendant or one of a number of defendants to the claim;
(d) the following conditions are satisfied –
  (i) the claimant is seeking an order for possession of land (whether or not any other order is also sought); and
  (ii) the court is satisfied that, if the case went to trial, the defendant would be held liable (even if the claim for possession fails) to pay the claimant a sum of money for the defendant's occupation and use of the land while the claim for possession was pending; or
(e) in a claim in which there are two or more defendants and the order is sought against any one or more of those defendants, the following conditions are satisfied –
  (i) the court is satisfied that, if the claim went to trial, the claimant would obtain judgment for a substantial amount of money (other than costs) against at least one of the defendants (but the court cannot determine which); and
  (ii) all the defendants are either –
    (a) a defendant that is insured in respect of the claim;
    (b) a defendant whose liability will be met by an insurer under section 151 of the Road Traffic Act 1988 or an insurer acting under the Motor Insurers Bureau Agreement, or the Motor Insurers Bureau where it is acting itself; or
    (c) a defendant that is a public body.

(2), (3) (*revoked*)

(4) The court must not order an interim payment of more than a reasonable proportion of the likely amount of the final judgment.

(5) The court must take into account –

(a) contributory negligence; and
(b) any relevant set-off or counterclaim.

Amendments—SI 2004/3419.

'possession of land' (r 25.7(1)(d)(i))—The court may order payment direct to the claimant for use and occupation pending final judgment. Use of this rule enables the claimant to avoid the common-law rules that acceptance of such payments may seriously prejudice the position of the claimant landlord. Alternatively, the court may order payment into court for use and occupation (r 3.1(2)(m), 3.1(3), (5)).

'a substantial amount of money' (r 25.7(1)(c))—Although this is not defined, it is likely that separate pre-trial applications in fast-track cases will be actively discouraged by the application of PD28, para 2.2. The principal purpose of an interim payment is to avoid or relieve hardship that the claimant may otherwise suffer by having to wait for trial or final assessment of his damages. So a comparatively small payment may be justified for a specific purpose. Although the means of the parties are not mentioned in the rule, they may be relevant, as the court is obliged to deal with a case in a way which is proportionate to the financial resources of the parties under r 1.1(2)(c)(iv).

25.8 Powers of court where it has made an order for interim payment

(1) Where a defendant has been ordered to make an interim payment, or has in fact made an interim payment (whether voluntarily or under an order), the court may make an order to adjust the interim payment.

(2) The court may in particular –

- (a) order all or part of the interim payment to be repaid;
- (b) vary or discharge the order for the interim payment;
- (c) order a defendant to reimburse, either wholly or partly, another defendant who has made an interim payment.

(3) The court may make an order under paragraph (2)(c) only if –

- (a) the defendant to be reimbursed made the interim payment in relation to a claim in respect of which he has made a claim against the other defendant for a contribution(GL), indemnity(GL) or other remedy; and
- (b) where the claim or part to which the interim payment relates has not been discontinued or disposed of, the circumstances are such that the court could make an order for interim payment under rule 25.7.

(4) The court may make an order under this rule without an application by any party if it makes the order when it disposes of the claim or any part of it.

(5) Where –

- (a) a defendant has made an interim payment; and
- (b) the amount of the payment is more than his total liability under the final judgment or order,

the court may award him interest on the overpaid amount from the date when he made the interim payment.

'made an interim payment' (r 25.8(5)(a))—This will include payments made voluntarily.

25.9 Restriction on disclosure of an interim payment

The fact that a defendant has made an interim payment, whether voluntarily or by court order, shall not be disclosed to the trial judge until all questions of liability and the amount of money to be awarded have been decided unless the defendant agrees.

'made an interim payment'—This rule may prove difficult to apply. First, the system of case management encourages the trial judge wherever practicable to deal personally with many pre-trial applications and secondly, applications will now be heard in public under r 39.2.

25.10 Interim injunction to cease if claim is stayed

If –

(a) the court has granted an interim injunction(GL) [other than a freezing injunction; and

(b) the claim is stayed(GL) other than by agreement between the parties,

the interim injunction(GL) shall be set aside(GL) unless the court orders that it should continue to have effect even though the claim is stayed.

Amendments—SI 2001/4015.

'the interim injunction shall be set aside' (r 25.10)—There is a risk that the claimant with the benefit of an interim injunction may lose it by inadvertence. He should specifically apply to continue the injunction in a proper case, for example where the claim is stayed pending the outcome of criminal proceedings against the defendant.

25.11 Interim Injunction to cease after 14 days if claim struck out

(1) If –

(a) the court has granted an interim injunction(GL); and

(b) the claim is struck out under rule 3.7 (sanctions for non-payment of certain fees),

the interim injunction shall cease to have effect 14 days after the date that the claim is struck out unless paragraph (2) applies.

(2) If the claimant applies to reinstate the claim before the interim injunction ceases to have effect under paragraph (1), the injunction shall continue until the hearing of the application unless the court orders otherwise.

Amendments—Inserted by SI 1999/1008.

II Security for costs

25.12 (1) A defendant to any claim may apply under this Section of this Part for security for his costsf of the proceedings.

(Part 3 provides for the court to order payment of sums into court in other circumstances. Rule 20.3 provides for this Section of this Part to apply to Part 20 claims)

(2) An application for security for costs must be supported by written evidence.

(3) Where the court makes an order for security for costs, it will –

(a) determine the amount of security; and

(b) direct –

(i) the manner in which; and

(ii) the time within which

the security must be given.

Amendments—Inserted by SI 2000/221.

'A defendant' (r 25.12(1))—Under this section, only a claimant may be ordered to give security for costs. As a result of r 20.3(1), 'defendant' includes a Pt 20 defendant. However, there may well be cases in which no Pt 20 claim is made against the claimant, but in which he nonetheless wants to be given security for his costs. In such a case, recourse will doubtless be had to rr 1.2(a) and 3.1(2)(m), and, where a case management order is made, r 3.1(3)(a). See note **'pay a sum of money into court'** under r 3.1 for the decision of the Court of Appeal in *Olatawura v Abiloye* [2002] EWCA Civ 998, [2002] 4 All ER 903, CA. The court must take care, in ordering security and fixing the amount, not to offend HRA 1998, Sch 1, Pt I, Art 6, which guarantees the right to a fair trial.

'Where the court makes an order' (r 25.12(3))—The form of order that is generally used is:

'IT IS ORDERED

(1) That the Claimant do by no later than 4.00 pm on Tuesday, the 16 July, 2002 give security for the Defendant's costs herein until the conclusion of disclosure in the sum of £27,000 by payment into court or otherwise to the satisfaction of the court;
(2) That, until security be given as ordered, the action be stayed FORTHWITH;
(3) That, if security be not given as ordered, the claim be struck out and the action dismissed without further order, and with judgment for the Defendant for costs; and
(4) That the Claimant pay the Defendant's costs of this application, assessed summarily in the amount of £____ .'

25.13 Conditions to be satisfied

(1) The court may make an order for security for costs under rule 25.12 if –

(a) it is satisfied, having regard to all the circumstances of the case, that it is just to make such an order; and
(b) (i) one or more of the conditions in paragraph (2) applies, or
(ii) an enactment permits the court to require security for costs.

(2) The conditions are –

(a) the claimant is –
(i) resident out of the jurisdiction; but
(ii) not resident in a Brussels Contracting State, a Lugano Contracting State, as defined in section 1(3) of the Civil Jurisdiction and Judgments Act 1982;
(b) (*revoked*)
(c) the claimant is a company or other body (whether incorporated inside or outside Great Britain) and there is reason to believe that it will be unable to pay the defendant's costs if ordered to do so;
(d) the claimant has changed his address since the claim was commenced with a view to evading the consequences of the litigation;
(e) the claimant failed to give his address in the claim form, or gave an incorrect address in that form;
(f) the claimant is acting as a nominal claimant, other than as a representative claimant under Part 19, and there is reason to believe that he will be unable to pay the defendant's costs if ordered to do so;
(g) the claimant has taken steps in relation to his assets that would make it difficult to enforce an order for costs against him.

(Rule 3.4 allows the court to strike out a statement of case and Part 24 for it to give summary judgment)

Amendments—Inserted by SI 2000/221; amended by SI 2001/4015; SI 2002/3219.

'ordinarily resident' (r 25.13(2)(a)(i) and (b)(i))—To determine where a person is 'ordinarily' resident, the court identifies the place at which that person habitually and normally resides, even though his 'real' or permanent home may be elsewhere. Pre-CPR authorities should not be cited. In the case of a foreign claimant the sole criterion is what is just in the circumstances of the particular case (*Leyvand v Barasch & ors* (2000) 97(11) LSG 37, (2000) *The Times*, 23 March, ChD, Lightman J).

'Brussels Convention or the Lugano Convention' (r 25.13(2)(a)(ii) and (b)(ii))—In *De Beer v Kanaar & anor* [2001] EWCA Civ 131, (2001) Lawtel, 9 August the Court of Appeal was uncomplimentary about the drafting of r 25.13(2)(a)(ii). It held that a claimant who was not ordinarily resident in the jurisdiction or in a Convention country could be ordered to give security even if he had assets in a Convention State.

'the claimant is a company … unable to pay' (r 25.13(2)(c))—This provision is in the same terms as CA 1985, s 726(1), but with the important differences that (a) it applies to any company, wherever incorporated, and (b) it is not confined to limited companies. The evidence must give reason to believe that the company *will* – not merely *may* – be unable to pay the costs of a successful defendant.

'the claimant has taken steps' (r 25.13(2)(c))—There is no requirement to show that the claimant has taken such steps *in order to* make enforcement difficult, merely that such difficulty is the result (*Aoun v Bahri & anor* [2002] EWHC Comm 29, [2002] 3 All ER 182, QBD (Comm Ct), Moore-Bick J).

25.14 Security for costs other than from the claimant

(1) The defendant may seek an order against someone other than the claimant, and the court may make an order for security for costs against that person if –

(a) it is satisfied, having regard to all the circumstances of the case, that it is just to make such an order; and

(b) one or more of the conditions in paragraph (2) applies.

(2) The conditions are that the person –

(a) has assigned the right to the claim to the claimant with a view to avoiding the possibility of a costs order being made against him; or

(b) has contributed or agreed to contribute to the claimant's costs in return for a share of any money or property which the claimant may recover in the proceedings; and

is a person against whom a costs order may be made.

(Rule 48.2 makes provision for costs orders against non-parties)

Amendments—Inserted by SI 2000/221.

'has assigned the right ... with a view to avoiding' (r 25.14(2)(a))—An impecunious company in which a right of action is vested is obviously vulnerable to an order for security for costs. If the individual controlling the company is eligible for public funding, then the company may choose to assign its right of action to that individual. This provision is intended to ensure that such an assignment will no longer have the effect of making the action invulnerable to such an order.

25.15 Security for costs of an appeal

(1) The court may order security for costs of an appeal against –

(a) an appellant;

(b) a respondent who also appeals,

on the same grounds as it may order security for costs against a claimant under this Part.

(2) The court may also make an order under paragraph (1) where the appellant, or the respondent who also appeals, is a limited company and there is reason to believe it will be unable to pay the costs of the other parties to the appeal should its appeal be unsuccessful.

Amendments—Inserted by SI 2000/221.

General note—See *Nasser v United Bank of Kuwait* [2001] EWCA Civ 556, CA for a useful discussion of the principles.

Practice Direction – Interim Injunctions

This Practice Direction supplements CPR Part 25 (PD25)

Procedural Guide—See Guide 23, set out in Section 1 of this work.

JURISDICTION

1.1 High Court judges and any other judge duly authorised may grant 'search orders'[1] and 'freezing injunctions'[2].

1 [Rule 25.1(1)(h).
2 Rule 25.1(1)(f).

1.2 In a case in the High Court, masters and district judges have the power to grant injunctions:

(1) by consent,
(2) in connection with charging orders and appointments of receivers,
(3) in aid of execution of judgments.

1.3 In any other case any judge who has jurisdiction to conduct the trial of the action has the power to grant an injunction in that action.

1.4 A master or district judge has the power to vary or discharge an injunction granted by any judge with the consent of all the parties.

'High Court'—Judges of both the High Court and the county courts have jurisdiction in relation to injunctions generally. But these two categories are reserved to the judges of the High Court or those sitting as such, save where any other judge is expressly given jurisdiction.

MAKING AN APPLICATION

2.1 The application notice must state:

(1) the order sought, and
(2) the date, time and place of the hearing.

2.2 The application notice and evidence in support must be served as soon as practicable after issue and in any event not less than 3 days before the court is due to hear the application[1].

1 Rule 23.7(1) and (2) and see rule 23.7(4) (short service).

2.3 Where the court is to serve, sufficient copies of the application notice and evidence in support for the court and for each respondent should be filed for issue and service.

2.4 Whenever possible a draft of the order sought should be filed with the application notice and a disk containing the draft should also be available to the court [in a format compatible with the word processing software used by the court. This will enable the court officer to arrange for any amendments to be incorporated and for the speedy preparation and sealing of the order.

EVIDENCE

3.1 Applications for search orders and freezing injunctions must be supported by affidavit evidence.

3.2 Applications for other interim injunctions must be supported by evidence set out in either:

(1) a witness statement, or

(2) a statement of case provided that it is verified by a statement of truth[1], or

(3) the application provided that it is verified by a statement of truth,

unless the court, an Act, a rule or a practice direction requires evidence by affidavit.

1 See Part 22.

3.3 The evidence must set out the facts on which the applicant relies for the claim being made against the respondent, including all material facts of which the court should be made aware.

3.4 Where an application is made without notice to the respondent, the evidence must also set out why notice was not given.

(See Part 32 and the practice direction that supplements it for information about evidence)

URGENT APPLICATIONS AND APPLICATIONS WITHOUT NOTICE

4.1 These fall into two categories:

(1) applications where a claim form has already been issued, and
(2) applications where a claim form has not yet been issued,

and, in both cases, where notice of the application has not been given to the respondent.

4.2 These applications are normally dealt with at a court hearing but cases of extreme urgency may be dealt with by telephone.

4.3 Applications dealt with at a court hearing after issue of a claim form:

(1) the application notice, evidence in support and a draft order (as in 2.4 above) should be filed with the court two hours before the hearing wherever possible,
(2) if an application is made before the application notice has been issued, a draft order (as in 2.4 above) should be provided at the hearing, and the application notice and evidence in support must be filed with the court on the same or next working day or as ordered by the court, and
(3) except in cases where secrecy is essential, the applicant should take steps to notify the respondent informally of the application.

4.4 Applications made before the issue of a claim form:

(1) in addition to the provisions set out at 4.3 above, unless the court orders otherwise, either the applicant must undertake to the court to issue a claim form immediately or the court will give directions for the commencement of the claim[1],
(2) where possible the claim form should be served with the order for the injunction,
(3) an order made before the issue of a claim form should state in the title after the names of the applicant and respondent 'the Claimant and Defendant in an Intended Action'.

1 Rule 25.2(3).

4.5 Applications made by telephone:

(1) where it is not possible to arrange a hearing, application can be made between 10.00 am and 5.00 pm weekdays by telephoning the Royal

Courts of Justice on [020 7947 6000 and asking to be put in contact with a High Court judge of the appropriate Division available to deal with an emergency application in a High Court matter. [The appropriate district registry may also be contacted by telephone. In county court proceedings, the appropriate county court should be contacted,

(2) where an application is made outside those hours the applicant should either –
   (a) telephone the Royal Courts of Justice on [020 7947 6000 where he will be put in contact with the clerk to the appropriate Duty Judge in the High Court (or the appropriate area circuit judge where known), or
   (b) the Urgent Court Business Officer of the appropriate circuit who will contact the local Duty Judge,

(3) where the facility is available it is likely that the judge will require a draft order to be faxed to him,

(4) the application notice and evidence in support must be filed with the court on the same or next working day or as ordered, together with two copies of the order for sealing,

(5) injunctions will be heard by telephone only where the applicant is acting by counsel or solicitors.

ORDERS FOR INJUNCTIONS

5.1 Any order for an injunction, unless the court orders otherwise, must contain:

(1) an undertaking by the applicant to the court to pay any damages which the respondent(s) (or any other party served with or notified of the order) sustain which the court considers the applicant should pay,

(2) if made without notice to any other party, an undertaking by the applicant to the court to serve on the respondent the application notice, evidence in support and any order made as soon as practicable,

(3) if made without notice to any other party, a return date for a further hearing at which the other party can be present,

(4) if made before filing the application notice, an undertaking to file and pay the appropriate fee on the same or next working day, and

(5) if made before issue of a claim form –
   (a) an undertaking to issue and pay the appropriate fee on the same or next working day, or
   (b) directions for the commencement of the claim.

5.2 An order for an injunction made in the presence of all parties to be bound by it or made at a hearing of which they have had notice, may state that it is effective until trial or further order.

5.3 Any order for an injunction must set out clearly what the respondent must do or not do.

Freezing Injunctions

ORDERS TO RESTRAIN DISPOSAL OF ASSETS WORLDWIDE AND WITHIN ENGLAND AND WALES

6.1 An example of a Freezing Injunction is annexed to this practice direction.

6.2 This example may be modified as appropriate in any particular case. In particular, the court may, if it considers it appropriate, require the applicant's solicitors, as well as the applicant, to give undertakings.

'Freezing Injunctions'—These were formerly known as *Mareva* injunctions. It should be noted that:

(a) The purpose of a freezing injunction is to prevent a defendant on an interim basis from thwarting any judgment against him by disposing of assets against which a judgment might be enforced. The jurisdiction is in addition to, and quite distinct from, the jurisdiction to grant an injunction restraining a defendant from disposing of assets to which a claimant makes a proprietary claim.

(b) A freezing injunction is not for the purpose of giving security but for preventing improper dissipation of assets. It is not possible to object to ordinary dealings even if they diminish the value of the injunction (*Halifax plc v Chandler* [2001] EWCA Civ 1750, [2001] NPC 189, CA).

(c) Such an injunction may be granted either before or after judgment.

(d) The claimant must show:
   (i) 'A good arguable case' in relation to his substantive claim – it is not enough to show merely that there is 'a serious question to be tried' (see for example *Derby v Weldon* [1990] Ch 48, CA, per Parker, LJ at p 57).
   (ii) That the defendant has assets, whether in or outside the jurisdiction.
   (iii) That there is a real risk that, if the court does not grant an order, the defendant will take the opportunity to dissipate those assets or otherwise put them beyond the reach of the court.

(e) The difficulty is always to frame an order that will properly protect a claimant from the ingenuity of an evasive defendant, without on the other hand being such as to enable a rapacious or vengeful claimant unfairly to damage a defendant.

(f) Flexibility of approach is essential: the courts will strive to do justice as required by the circumstances, and may approach decided cases with a degree of caution.

(g) In every case, the first order will be sought without giving the defendant notice of the application, and great care must be taken to ensure that the speed and secrecy are not the cause of injustice.

(h) The claimant will therefore be expected to display proper candour to the court; a claimant who fails in that respect in relation to a material matter may be penalised by the discharge of the injunction, even though the want of candour was not necessarily in relation to a matter that the court treated as decisive in granting the injunction.

(i) Similarly, a claimant who has obtained the benefit of such an injunction is assumed to want to prosecute his action with proper dispatch; a failure to do so may be treated as an abuse of process.

(j) In certain circumstances, a claimant pursuing a claim solely in a foreign court may be entitled to a freezing injunction in an English court, even though the latter might not have jurisdiction in relation to the substantive claim (CJJA, s 25(1)).

(k) A freezing injunction binds the person against whom it is given, as opposed to the assets themselves. It therefore gives the claimant no proprietary rights in the assets, but merely ensures that such assets will be available to meet a judgment in his favour.

(l) The standard form of freezing injunction requires the defendant to give disclosure to a certain extent; there will be cases in which the defendant is entitled to make a claim of privilege against self-incrimination (*Arab Monetary Fund v Hashim (No 8)* [1989] 1 WLR 565, CA).

(m) A third party notified of the freezing injunction is bound by it as soon as he is notified of it, even though the defendant may not yet be aware of it. Such a third party, if he does anything to assist the defendant to thwart the injunction, will be guilty of a contempt of court (*Z Ltd v A* [1982] 1 QB 558).

(n) The cross-undertaking in damages may be onerous. In *Johnson Control Systems v Techni-Track Europa* [2002] EWHC 1613 (TCC), where a freezing order had been wrongly obtained and the defendant was forced into receivership, they were assessed at the value of the defendant as a going concern before the injunction.

Search Orders

7.1 The following provisions apply to search orders in addition to those listed above.

'search orders'—These were formerly known as *Anton Piller* orders. It should be noted that:

(a) A search order in this sense compels the respondent to permit the applicant to enter and search his premises. It differs from a search warrant, in that it is directed, not at the premises themselves, but at the respondent or other person appearing to be in control of the premises and having authority to permit the search.

(b) Accordingly if the respondent refuses to obey the order, the applicant is not entitled to brush aside the refusal and proceed with the search, but instead is restricted to bringing proceedings for contempt of court.

(c) Despite the severity of such an order, the European Court of Human Rights has held that the making of such an order in an appropriate case is not a breach of ECHR, Art 8 (*Chappell v United Kingdom* [1989] FSR 617).

(d) As with freezing injunctions, the first order will invariably be sought without giving the defendant notice of the application, and great care must be taken to ensure that the speed and secrecy are not the cause of injustice.

(e) Also as with freezing injunctions, such an order may be made either before or after judgment.

(f) The evidence should strive to be as complete as is reasonably possible, the emphasis being to satisfy the court that, in the absence of an order, material will be concealed, removed or destroyed. If the result is a large volume of material, then the applicant must assist the court to sift out what is relevant.

(g) To obtain such an order, the applicant must show:
  (i) That he has a strong *prima facie* case: the merits of his claim will certainly be scrutinised.
  (ii) That the danger that the order is to avert is serious.
  (iii) That there is a real possibility that the material will be concealed, removed or destroyed if an order is not made.
  (iv) That the harm caused to the respondent by making the order will not be out of proportion to the value of the order to the applicant.

(h) The standard form of search order requires the defendant to give disclosure to a certain extent; there will be cases in which the defendant is entitled to make a claim of privilege against self-incrimination (*Tate Access Floors v Boswell* [1991] Ch 512).

(i) There is no implied undertaking that information obtained via the order will be used solely for purposes of the action (*Sony Corporation v Anand* [1981] FSR 398). However, the standard form of search order includes an undertaking to that effect.

(j) Information obtained via the order and showing wrongs committed by a third party may be used in the same or separate proceedings against the third party, and the question of privilege against self-incrimination will not arise (*Twentieth Century Fox v Tryare* [1991] FSR 58).

(k) The applicant will be expected to display proper candour to the court; a claimant who fails in that respect in relation to a material matter may be penalised by the discharge of the injunction, even though the want of candour was not necessarily in relation to a matter that the court treated as decisive in granting the injunction. However, see *Gadget Shop v Bug.Com Ltd & ors* (2001) *The Times*, 28 June for a case where notwithstanding failure to make full and frank disclosure and a material departure from this practice direction, Rimer J continued interim injunctive relief.

(l) If any matter comes to light that affects the propriety of making a search order, the applicant is under a duty to bring that matter to the attention of the court, whether the order has already been executed or not.

(m) If a respondent wishes to set aside a search order made without notice, he can refuse to obey it while he makes an urgent application to the court to have it set aside (CPR r 23.10). But this course is not without danger: if he fails to justify his refusal, be may be held to be in contempt, the more so if in the interval he has concealed, removed or destroyed the material (*WEA Records v Visions Channel 4* [1983] 1 WLR 721, CA).

(n) A respondent dissatisfied with a search order made without notice must apply to the court of first instance on notice for variation or discharge before he is entitled to raise the matter before the Court of Appeal (same).

The Supervising Solicitor

7.2 The Supervising Solicitor must be experienced in the operation of search orders. A Supervising Solicitor may be contacted either through the Law Society or, for the London area, through the London Solicitors Litigation Association.

7.3 Evidence:

(1) the affidavit must state the name, firm and its address, and experience

of the Supervising Solicitor, also the address of the premises and whether it is a private or business address, and

(2) the affidavit must disclose very fully the reason the order is sought, including the probability that relevant material would disappear if the order were not made.

7.4 Service:

(1) the order must be served personally by the Supervising Solicitor, unless the court otherwise orders, and must be accompanied by the evidence in support and any documents capable of being copied,

(2) confidential exhibits need not be served but they must be made available for inspection by the respondent in the presence of the applicant's solicitors while the order is carried out and afterwards be retained by the respondent's solicitors on their undertaking not to permit the respondent –

(a) to see them or copies of them except in their presence, and

(b) to make or take away any note or record of them,

(3) the Supervising Solicitor may be accompanied only by the persons mentioned in the order,

[(4) the Supervising Solicitor must explain the terms and effect of the order to the respondent in everyday language and advise him –

(a) of his right to take legal advice and to apply to vary or discharge the order; and

(b) that he may be entitled to avail himself of –

(i) legal professional privilege; and

(ii) the privilege against self-incrimination.

(5) where the Supervising Solicitor is a man and the respondent is likely to be an unaccompanied woman, at least one other person named in the order must be a woman and must accompany the Supervising Solicitor, and

(6) the order may only be served between 9.30am and 5.30pm Monday to Friday unless the court otherwise orders.

7.5 Search and custody of materials:

(1) no material shall be removed unless clearly covered by the terms of the order,

(2) the premises must not be searched and no items shall be removed from them except in the presence of the respondent or a person who appears to be a responsible employee of the respondent,

(3) where copies of documents are sought, the documents should be retained for no more than 2 days before return to the owner,

(4) where material in dispute is removed pending trial, the applicant's solicitors should place it in the custody of the respondent's solicitors on their undertaking to retain it in safekeeping and to produce it to the court when required,

(5) in appropriate cases the applicant should insure the material retained in the respondent's solicitors' custody,

(6) the Supervising Solicitor must make a list of all material removed from the premises and supply a copy of the list to the respondent,

(7) no material shall be removed from the premises until the respondent has had reasonable time to check the list,

(8) if any of the listed items exists only in computer readable form, the

respondent must immediately give the applicant's solicitors effective access to the computers, with all necessary passwords, to enable them to be searched, and cause the listed items to be printed out,

(9) the applicant must take all reasonable steps to ensure that no damage is done to any computer or data,

(10) the applicant and his representatives may not themselves search the respondent's computers unless they have sufficient expertise to do so without damaging the respondent's system,

(11) the Supervising Solicitor shall provide a report on the carrying out of the order to the applicant's solicitors,

(12) as soon as the report is received the applicant's solicitors shall –
- (a) serve a copy of it on the respondent, and
- (b) file a copy of it with the court, and

(13) where the Supervising Solicitor is satisfied that full compliance with paragraph 7.5(7) and (8) above is impracticable, he may permit the search to proceed and items to be removed without compliance with the impracticable requirements.

GENERAL

7.6 The Supervising Solicitor must not be an employee or member of the applicant's firm of solicitors.

7.7 If the court orders that the order need not be served by the Supervising Solicitor, the reason for so ordering must be set out in the order.

7.8 The search order must not be carried out at the same time as a police search warrant.

7.9 There is no privilege against self incrimination in:

(1) Intellectual Property cases in respect of a 'related offence' or for the recovery of a 'related penalty' as defined in section 72 Supreme Court Act 1981;

(2) proceedings for the recovery or administration of any property, for the execution of any trust or for an account of any property or dealings with property in relation to offences under the Theft Act 1968 (see section 31 Theft Act 1968); or

(3) proceedings in which a court is hearing an application for an order under Part IV or Part V of the Children Act 1989 (see section 98 Children Act 1989).

However, the privilege may still be claimed in relation to material or information required to be disclosed by an order, as regards potential criminal proceedings outside those statutory provisions.

7.10 Applications in Intellectual Property cases should be made in the Chancery Division.

7.11 An example of a Search Order is annexed to this practice direction. This example may be modified as appropriate in any particular case.

DELIVERY-UP ORDERS

8.1 The following provisions apply to orders, other than search orders, for delivery up or preservation of evidence or property where it is likely that such an order will be executed at the premises of the respondent or a third party.

8.2 In such cases the court shall consider whether to include in the order for the benefit or protection of the parties similar provisions to those specified above in relation to injunctions and search orders.

INJUNCTIONS AGAINST THIRD PARTIES

9.1 The following provisions apply to orders which will affect a person other than the applicant or respondent, who:

(1) did not attend the hearing at which the order was made; and
(2) is served with the order.

9.2 Where such a person served with the order requests –

(1) a copy of any materials read by the judge, including material prepared after the hearing at the direction of the judge or in compliance with the order; or
(2) a note of the hearing,

the applicant, or his legal representative, must comply promptly with the request, unless the court orders otherwise.

Annex

FREEZING INJUNCTION
Before The Honourable Mr Justice

IN THE HIGH COURT OF JUSTICE
[ ] DIVISION
[ ]

Claim No.

Dated

Applicant

Seal

Respondent

Name, address and reference of Respondent

IF YOU [ ][1] DISOBEY THIS ORDER YOU MAY BE HELD TO BE IN CONTEMPT OF COURT AND MAY BE IMPRISONED, FINED OR HAVE YOUR ASSETS SEIZED.

ANY OTHER PERSON WHO KNOWS OF THIS ORDER AND DOES ANYTHING WHICH HELPS OR PERMITS THE RESPONDENT TO BREACH THE TERMS OF THIS ORDER MAY ALSO BE HELD TO BE IN CONTEMPT OF COURT AND MAY BE IMPRISONED, FINED OR HAVE THEIR ASSETS SEIZED.

1 Insert name of Respondent.

THIS ORDER

1 This is a Freezing Injunction made against [ ] ('the Respondent') on [ ] by Mr Justice [ ] on the application of [ ] ('the Applicant'). The Judge read the Affidavits listed in Schedule A and accepted the undertakings set out in Schedule B at the end of this Order.

2 This order was made at a hearing without notice to the Respondent. The Respondent has a right to apply to the court to vary or discharge the order – see paragraph 13 below.

3 There will be a further hearing in respect of this order on [ ] ('the return date').

4 If there is more than one Respondent –

(a) unless otherwise stated, references in this order to 'the Respondent' mean both or all of them; and
(b) this order is effective against any Respondent on whom it is served or who is given notice of it.

FREEZING INJUNCTION

[*For injunction limited to assets in England and Wales*]

5 Until the return date or further order of the court, the Respondent must not remove from England and Wales or in any way dispose of, deal with or diminish the value of any of his assets which are in England and Wales up to the value of £ .

[*For worldwide injunction*]

5 Until the return date or further order of the court, the Respondent must not –

(1) remove from England and Wales any of his assets which are in England and Wales up to the value of £ ; or
(2) in any way dispose of, deal with or diminish the value of any of his assets whether they are in or outside England and Wales up to the same value.

[*For either form of injunction*]

6 Paragraph 5 applies to all the Respondent's assets whether or not they are in his own name and whether they are solely or jointly owned. For the purpose of this order the Respondent's assets include any asset which he has the power, directly or indirectly, to dispose of or deal with as if it were his own. The Respondent is to be regarded as having such power if a third party holds or controls the asset in accordance with his direct or indirect instructions.

7 This prohibition includes the following assets in particular –

(a) the property known as [*title/address*] or the net sale money after payment of any mortgages if it has been sold;
(b) the property and assets of the Respondent's business [known as [*name*]] [carried on at [*address*]] or the sale money if any of them have been sold; and
(c) [any money standing to the credit of any bank account including the amount of any cheque drawn on such account which has not been cleared.

[*For injunction limited to assets in England and Wales*]

8 If the total value free of charges or other securities ('unencumbered value') of the Respondent's assets in England and Wales exceeds £ , the Respondent may remove any of those assets from England and Wales or may dispose of or deal with them so long as the total unencumbered value of his assets still in England and Wales remains above £ .

[*For worldwide injunction*]

8 (1) If the total value free of charges or other securities ('unencumbered value') of the Respondent's assets in England and Wales exceeds £ , the Respondent may remove any of those assets from England and Wales or may dispose of or deal with them so long as the total unencumbered value of the Respondent's assets still in England and Wales remains above £ .

(2) If the total unencumbered value of the Respondent's assets in England and Wales does not exceed £ , the Respondent must not remove any of those assets from England and Wales and must not dispose of or deal with any of them. If the Respondent has other assets outside England and Wales, he may dispose of or deal with those assets outside England and Wales so long as the total unencumbered value of all his assets whether in or outside England and Wales remains above £ .

PROVISION OF INFORMATION

9 (1) Unless paragraph (2) applies, the Respondent must [immediately] [within hours of service of this order] and to the best of his ability inform the Applicant's solicitors of all his assets [in England and Wales] [worldwide] [exceeding £ in value] whether in his own name or not and whether solely or jointly owned, giving the value, location and details of all such assets.

(2) If the provision of any of this information is likely to incriminate the Respondent, he may be entitled to refuse to provide it, but is recommended to take legal advice before refusing to provide the information. Wrongful refusal to provide the information is contempt of court and may render the Respondent liable to be imprisoned, fined or have his assets seized.

10 Within [ ] working days after being served with this order, the Respondent must swear and serve on the Applicant's solicitors an affidavit setting out the above information.

EXCEPTIONS TO THIS ORDER

11 (1) This order does not prohibit the Respondent from spending £ a week towards his ordinary living expenses and also £ [or a reasonable sum] on legal advice and representation. [But before spending any money the Respondent must tell the Applicant's legal representatives where the money is to come from.]

[(2) This order does not prohibit the Respondent from dealing with or disposing of any of his assets in the ordinary and proper course of business.]

(3) The Respondent may agree with the Applicant's legal representatives that the above spending limits should be increased or that this order should be varied in any other respect, but any agreement must be in writing.

(4) The order will cease to have effect if the Respondent –
   (a) provides security by paying the sum of £ into court, to be held to the order of the court; or
   (b) makes provision for security in that sum by another method agreed with the Applicant's legal representatives.

COSTS

12 The costs of this application are reserved to the judge hearing the application on the return date.

VARIATION OR DISCHARGE OF THIS ORDER

13 Anyone served with or notified of this order may apply to the court at any time to vary or discharge this order (or so much of it as affects that person), but they must first inform the Applicant's solicitors. If any evidence is to be relied upon in support of the application, the substance of it must be communicated in writing to the Applicant's solicitors in advance.

INTERPRETATION OF THIS ORDER

14 A Respondent who is an individual who is ordered not to do something must not do it himself or in any other way. He must not do it through others acting on his behalf or on his instructions or with his encouragement.

15 A Respondent which is not an individual which is ordered not to do something must not do it itself or by its directors, officers, partners, employees or agents or in any other way.

PARTIES OTHER THAN THE APPLICANT AND RESPONDENT

16 **Effect of this order**

It is a contempt of court for any person notified of this order knowingly to assist in or permit a breach of this order. Any person doing so may be imprisoned, fined or have their assets seized.

17 **Set off by banks**

This injunction does not prevent any bank from exercising any right of set off it may have in respect of any facility which it gave to the respondent before it was notified of this order.

18 **Withdrawals by the Respondent**

No bank need enquire as to the application or proposed application of any money withdrawn by the Respondent if the withdrawal appears to be permitted by this order.

[*For worldwide injunction*]

19 **Persons outside England and Wales**

(1) Except as provided in paragraph (2) below, the terms of this order do not affect or concern anyone outside the jurisdiction of this court.
(2) The terms of this order will affect the following persons in a country or state outside the jurisdiction of this court –
   (a) the Respondent or his officer or agent appointed by power of attorney;
   (b) any person who –

(i) is subject to the jurisdiction of this court;
(ii) has been given written notice of this order at his residence or place of business within the jurisdiction of this court; and
(iii) is able to prevent acts or omissions outside the jurisdiction of this court which constitute or assist in a breach of the terms of this order; and

(c) any other person, only to the extent that this order is declared enforceable by or is enforced by a court in that country or state.

[*For worldwide injunction*]

20 **Assets located outside England and Wales**

Nothing in this order shall, in respect of assets located outside England and Wales, prevent any third party from complying with –

(1) what it reasonably believes to be its obligations, contractual or otherwise, under the laws and obligations of the country or state in which those assets are situated or under the proper law of any contract between itself and the Respondent; and
(2) any orders of the courts of that country or state, provided that reasonable notice of any application for such an order is given to the Applicant's solicitors.

COMMUNICATIONS WITH THE COURT

All communications to the court about this order should be sent to –

[*Insert the address and telephone number of the appropriate Court Office*]

If the order is made at the Royal Courts of Justice, communications should be addressed as follows –

Where the order is made in the Chancery Division

Room TM 505, Royal Courts of Justice, Strand, London WC2A 2LL quoting the case number. The telephone number is 0207 947 6754.

Where the order is made in the Queen's Bench Division

Room WG034, Royal Courts of Justice, Strand, London WC2A 2LL quoting the case number. The telephone number is 0207 947 6009.

Where the order is made in the Commercial Court

Room E201, Royal Courts of Justice, Strand, London WC2A 2LL quoting the case number. The telephone number is 0207 947 6826.

The offices are open between 10 am and 4.30 pm Monday to Friday.

SCHEDULE A

AFFIDAVITS

The Applicant relied on the following affidavits –

[*name*]	[*number of affidavit*]	[*date sworn*]	[*filed on behalf of*]
(1)			
(2)			

SCHEDULE B

UNDERTAKINGS GIVEN TO THE COURT BY THE APPLICANT

(1) If the court later finds that this order has caused loss to the Respondent, and decides that the Respondent should be compensated for that loss, the Applicant will comply with any order the court may make.

[(2) The Applicant will –

- (a) on or before [*date*] cause a written guarantee in the sum of £   to be issued from a bank with a place of business within England or Wales, in respect of any order the court may make pursuant to paragraph (1) above; and
- (b) immediately upon issue of the guarantee, cause a copy of it to be served on the Respondent.]

(3) As soon as practicable the Applicant will issue and serve a claim form [in the form of the draft produced to the court] [claiming the appropriate relief].

(4) The Applicant will [swear and file an affidavit] [cause an affidavit to be sworn and filed] [substantially in the terms of the draft affidavit produced to the court] [confirming the substance of what was said to the court by the Applicant's counsel/solicitors].

(5) The Applicant will serve upon the Respondent [together with this order] [as soon as practicable] –

- (i) copies of the affidavits and exhibits containing the evidence relied upon by the Applicant, and any other documents provided to the court on the making of the application;
- (ii) the claim form; and
- (iii) an application notice for continuation of the order.

[(6) Anyone notified of this order will be given a copy of it by the Applicant's legal representatives.]

(7) The Applicant will pay the reasonable costs of anyone other than the Respondent which have been incurred as a result of this order including the costs of finding out whether that person holds any of the Respondent's assets and if the court later finds that this order has caused such person loss, and decides that such person should be compensated for that loss, the Applicant will comply with any order the court may make.

(8) If this order ceases to have effect (for example, if the Respondent provides security or the Applicant does not provide a bank guarantee as provided for above) the Applicant will immediately take all reasonable steps to inform in writing anyone to whom he has given notice of this order, or who he has reasonable grounds for supposing may act upon this order, that it has ceased to have effect.

[(9) The Applicant will not without the permission of the court use any information obtained as a result of this order for the purpose of any civil or criminal proceedings, either in England and Wales or in any other jurisdiction, other than this claim.]

[(10) The Applicant will not without the permission of the court seek to enforce this order in any country outside England and Wales [or seek an order of a similar nature including orders conferring a charge or other security against the Respondent or the Respondent's assets].]

NAME AND ADDRESS OF APPLICANT'S LEGAL REPRESENTATIVES

The Applicant's legal representatives are –

[*Name, address, reference, fax and telephone numbers both in and out of office hours and e-mail*]

SEARCH ORDER **Before The Honourable Mr Justice**	**IN THE HIGH COURT OF JUSTICE** **[ ] DIVISION** **[ ]**
	Claim No.
	Dated
Applicant	
	Seal
Respondent	

Name, address and reference of Respondent

IF YOU [ ][1] DISOBEY THIS ORDER YOU MAY BE HELD TO BE IN CONTEMPT OF COURT AND MAY BE IMPRISONED, FINED OR HAVE YOUR ASSETS SEIZED.

ANY OTHER PERSON WHO KNOWS OF THIS ORDER AND DOES ANYTHING WHICH HELPS OR PERMITS THE RESPONDENT TO BREACH THE TERMS OF THIS ORDER MAY ALSO BE HELD TO BE IN CONTEMPT OF COURT AND MAY BE IMPRISONED, FINED OR HAVE THEIR ASSETS SEIZED.

1 Insert name of Respondent.

THIS ORDER

1 This is a Search Order made against [ ] ('the Respondent') on [ ] by Mr Justice [ ] on the application of [ ] ('the Applicant'). The Judge read the Affidavits listed in Schedule F and accepted the undertakings set out in Schedules C, D and E at the end of this order.

2 This order was made at a hearing without notice to the Respondent. The Respondent has a right to apply to the court to vary or discharge the order – see paragraph 27 below.

3 There will be a further hearing in respect of this order on [ ] ('the return date').

4 If there is more than one Respondent –

(a) unless otherwise stated, references in this order to 'the Respondent' mean both or all of them; and
(b) this order is effective against any Respondent on whom it is served or who is given notice of it.

5 This order must be complied with by –

(a) the Respondent;
(b) any director, officer, partner or responsible employee of the Respondent; and
(c) if the Respondent is an individual, any other person having responsible control of the premises to be searched.

THE SEARCH

6 The Respondent must permit the following persons[1] –

(a) [ ] ('the Supervising Solicitor');
(b) [ ], a solicitor in the firm of [ ], the Applicant's solicitors; and
(c) up to [ ] other persons[2] being [*their identity or capacity*] accompanying them,

(together 'the search party'), to enter the premises mentioned in Schedule A to this order and any other premises of the Respondent disclosed under paragraph 18 below and any vehicles under the Respondent's control on or around the premises ('the premises') so that they can search for, inspect, photograph or photocopy, and deliver into the safekeeping of the Applicant's solicitors all the documents and articles which are listed in Schedule B to this order ('the listed items').

7 Having permitted the search party to enter the premises, the Respondent must allow the search party to remain on the premises until the search is complete. In the event that it becomes necessary for any of those persons to leave the premises before the search is complete, the Respondent must allow them to re-enter the premises immediately upon their seeking re-entry on the same or the following day in order to complete the search.

1 Where the premises are likely to be occupied by an unaccompanied woman and the Supervising Solicitor is a man, at least one of the persons accompanying him should be a woman.

2 None of these persons should be people who could gain personally or commercially from anything they might read or see on the premises, unless their presence is essential.

RESTRICTIONS ON SEARCH

8 This order may not be carried out at the same time as a police search warrant.

9 Before the Respondent allows anybody onto the premises to carry out this order, he is entitled to have the Supervising Solicitor explain to him what it means in everyday language.

10 The Respondent is entitled to seek legal advice and to ask the court to vary or discharge this order. Whilst doing so, he may ask the Supervising Solicitor to delay starting the search for up to 2 hours or such other longer period as the Supervising Solicitor may permit. However, the Respondent must –

(a) comply with the terms of paragraph 27 below;

(b) not disturb or remove any listed items; and
(c) permit the Supervising Solicitor to enter, but not start to search.

[11

(1) Before permitting entry to the premises by any person other than the Supervising Solicitor, the Respondent may, for a short time (not to exceed two hours, unless the Supervising Solicitor agrees to a longer period) –
  (a) gather together any documents he believes may be incriminating or privileged; and
  (b) hand them to the Supervising Solicitor for him to assess whether they are incriminating or privileged as claimed.

(2) If the Supervising Solicitor decides that the Respondent is entitled to withhold production of any of the documents on the ground that they are privileged or incriminating, he will exclude them from the search, record them in a list for inclusion in his report and return them to the Respondent.

(3) If the Supervising Solicitor believes that the Respondent may be entitled to withhold production of the whole or any part of a document on the ground that it or part of it may be privileged or incriminating, or if the Respondent claims to be entitled to withhold production on those grounds, the Supervising Solicitor will exclude it from the search and retain it in his possession pending further order of the court.

12 If the Respondent wishes to take legal advice and gather documents as permitted, he must first inform the Supervising Solicitor and keep him informed of the steps being taken.

13 No item may be removed from the premises until a list of the items to be removed has been prepared, and a copy of the list has been supplied to the Respondent, and he has been given a reasonable opportunity to check the list.

14 The premises must not be searched, and items must not be removed from them, except in the presence of the Respondent.

15 If the Supervising Solicitor is satisfied that full compliance with paragraphs 13 or 14 is not practicable, he may permit the search to proceed and items to be removed without fully complying with them.

DELIVERY UP OF ARTICLES/DOCUMENTS

16 The Respondent must immediately hand over to the Applicant's solicitors any of the listed items, which are in his possession or under his control, save for any computer or hard disk integral to any computer. Any items the subject of a dispute as to whether they are listed items must immediately be handed over to the Supervising Solicitor for safe keeping pending resolution of the dispute or further order of the court.

17 The Respondent must immediately give the search party effective access to the computers on the premises, with all necessary passwords, to enable the computers to be searched. If they contain any listed items the Respondent must cause the listed items to be displayed so that they can be read and copied.[1] The Respondent must provide the Applicant's Solicitors with copies of all listed items contained in the computers. All reasonable steps shall be taken by the Applicant and the Applicant's solicitors to ensure that no damage is done to any computer or data. The Applicant and his representatives may not themselves

search the Respondent's computers unless they have sufficient expertise to do so without damaging the Respondent's system.

1 If it is envisaged that the Respondent's computers are to be imaged (i.e. the hard drives are to be copied wholesale, thereby reproducing listed items and other items indiscriminately), special provision needs to be made and independent computer specialists need to be appointed, who should be required to give undertakings to the court.

PROVISION OF INFORMATION

18 The Respondent must immediately inform the Applicant's Solicitors (in the presence of the Supervising Solicitor) so far as he is aware –

(a) where all the listed items are;
(b) the name and address of everyone who has supplied him, or offered to supply him, with listed items;
(c) the name and address of everyone to whom he has supplied, or offered to supply, listed items; and
(d) full details of the dates and quantities of every such supply and offer.

19 Within [ ] working days after being served with this order the Respondent must swear and serve an affidavit setting out the above information[1].

1 The period should ordinarily be longer than the period in paragraph (2) of Schedule D, if any of the information is likely to be included in listed items taken away of which the Respondent does not have copies.

PROHIBITED ACTS

20 Except for the purpose of obtaining legal advice, the Respondent must not directly or indirectly inform anyone of these proceedings or of the contents of this order, or warn anyone that proceedings have been or may be brought against him by the Applicant until 4.30 p.m. on the return date or further order of the court.

21 Until 4.30 p.m. on the return date the Respondent must not destroy, tamper with, cancel or part with possession, power, custody or control of the listed items otherwise than in accordance with the terms of this order.

22 [Insert any negative injunctions.]

23 [Insert any further order]

COSTS

24 The costs of this application are reserved to the judge hearing the application on the return date.

RESTRICTIONS ON SERVICE

25 This order may only be served between [ ] am/pm and [ ] am/pm [and on a weekday][1].

26 This order must be served by the Supervising Solicitor, and paragraph 6 of the order must be carried out in his presence and under his supervision.

1 Normally, the order should be served in the morning (not before 9.30 am) and on a weekday to enable the Respondent more readily to obtain legal advice.

VARIATION AND DISCHARGE OF THIS ORDER

27 Anyone served with or notified of this order may apply to the court at any time to vary or discharge this order (or so much of it as affects that person), but they must first inform the Applicant's solicitors. If any evidence is to be relied upon in support of the application, the substance of it must be communicated in writing to the Applicant's solicitors in advance.

INTERPRETATION OF THIS ORDER

28 Any requirement that something shall be done to or in the presence of the Respondent means –

- (a) if there is more than one Respondent, to or in the presence of any one of them; and
- (b) if a Respondent is not an individual, to or in the presence of a director, officer, partner or responsible employee.

29 A Respondent who is an individual who is ordered not to do something must not do it himself or in any other way. He must not do it through others acting on his behalf or on his instructions or with his encouragement.

30 A Respondent which is not an individual which is ordered not to do something must not do it itself or by its directors, officers, partners, employees or agents or in any other way.

COMMUNICATIONS WITH THE COURT

All communications to the court about this order should be sent to –

[*Insert the address and telephone number of the appropriate Court Office*]

If the order is made at the Royal Courts of Justice, communications should be addressed as follows –

Where the order is made in the Chancery Division

Room TM 505, Royal Courts of Justice, Strand, London WC2A 2LL quoting the case number. The telephone number is 0207 947 6754.

Where the order is made in the Queen's Bench Division

Room WG034, Royal Courts of Justice, Strand, London WC2A 2LL quoting the case number. The telephone number is 0207 947 6009.

Where the order is made in the Commercial Court

Room E201, Royal Courts of Justice, Strand, London WC2A 2LL quoting the case number. The telephone number is 0207 947 6826.

The offices are open between 10 am and 4.30 pm Monday to Friday.

SCHEDULE A

THE PREMISES

SCHEDULE B

THE LISTED ITEMS

SCHEDULE C

UNDERTAKINGS GIVEN TO THE COURT BY THE APPLICANT

(1) If the court later finds that this order or carrying it out has caused loss to the Respondent, and decides that the Respondent should be compensated for that loss, the Applicant will comply with any order the court may make. Further if the carrying out of this order has been in breach of the terms of this order or otherwise in a manner inconsistent with the Applicant's solicitors' duties as officers of the court, the Applicant will comply with any order for damages the court may make.

[(2) As soon as practicable the Applicant will issue a claim form [in the form of the draft produced to the court] [claiming the appropriate relief].]

(3) The Applicant will [swear and file an affidavit] [cause an affidavit to be sworn and filed] [substantially in the terms of the draft affidavit produced to the court] [confirming the substance of what was said to the court by the Applicant's counsel/solicitors].

(4) The Applicant will not, without the permission of the court, use any information or documents obtained as a result of carrying out this order nor inform anyone else of these proceedings except for the purposes of these proceedings (including adding further Respondents) or commencing civil proceedings in relation to the same or related subject matter to these proceedings until after the return date.

[(5) The Applicant will maintain pending further order the sum of £ [ ] in an account controlled by the Applicant's solicitors.]

[(6) The Applicant will insure the items removed from the premises.]

SCHEDULE D

UNDERTAKINGS GIVEN BY THE APPLICANT'S SOLICITORS

(1) The Applicant's solicitors will provide to the Supervising Solicitor for service on the Respondent –

- (i) a service copy of this order;
- (ii) the claim form (with defendant's response pack) or, if not issued, the draft produced to the court;
- (iii) an application for hearing on the return date;
- (iv) copies of the affidavits [*or draft affidavits*] and exhibits capable of being copied containing the evidence relied upon by the applicant;
- (v) a note of any allegation of fact made orally to the court where such allegation is not contained in the affidavits or draft affidavits read by the judge; and
- (vi) a copy of the skeleton argument produced to the court by the Applicant's [counsel/solicitors].

(2) The Applicants' solicitors will answer at once to the best of their ability any question whether a particular item is a listed item.

(3) Subject as provided below the Applicant's solicitors will retain in their own safe keeping all items obtained as a result of this order until the court directs otherwise.

(4) The Applicant's solicitors will return the originals of all documents obtained as a result of this order (except original documents which belong to the Applicant) as soon as possible and in any event within [two] working days of their removal.

SCHEDULE E

UNDERTAKINGS GIVEN BY THE SUPERVISING SOLICITOR

(1) The Supervising Solicitor will use his best endeavours to serve this order upon the Respondent and at the same time to serve upon the Respondent the other documents required to be served and referred to in paragraph (1) of Schedule D.

(2) The Supervising Solicitor will offer to explain to the person served with the order its meaning and effect fairly and in everyday language, and to inform him of his right to take legal advice [(including an explanation that the Respondent may be entitled to avail himself of the privilege against self-incrimination and legal professional privilege) and to apply to vary or discharge this order as mentioned in paragraph 27 above.

(3) The Supervising Solicitor will retain in the safe keeping of his firm all items retained by him as a result of this order until the court directs otherwise.

[(4) Unless and until the court otherwise orders, or unless otherwise necessary to comply with any duty to the court pursuant to this order, the Supervising Solicitor shall not disclose to any person any information relating to those items, and shall keep the existence of such items confidential.

[(5) Within [48] hours of completion of the search the Supervising Solicitor will make and provide to the Applicant's solicitors, the Respondent or his solicitors and to the judge who made this order (for the purposes of the court file) a written report on the carrying out of the order.

SCHEDULE F

AFFIDAVITS

The Applicant relied on the following affidavits –

[*name*] [*number of affidavit*] [*date sworn*] [*filed on behalf of*]
(1)

(2)

NAME AND ADDRESS OF APPLICANT'S SOLICITORS

The Applicant's solicitors are –

[Name, address, reference, fax and telephone numbers both in and out of office hours.]]

Practice Direction – Interim Payments

This Practice Direction supplements CPR Part 25 (PD25B)

Procedural Guide—See Guide 23, set out in Section 1 of this work.

General note—See also the notes to CPR Pt 25 for relevant commentary.

GENERAL

1.1 Rule 25.7 sets out the conditions to be satisfied and matters to be taken into account before the court will make an order for an interim payment.

1.2 The permission of the court must be obtained before making a voluntary interim payment in respect of a claim by a child or patient.

EVIDENCE

2.1 In application for an interim payment of damages must be supported by evidence dealing with the following:

(1) the sum of money sought by way of an interim payment,
(2) the items or matters in respect of which the interim payment is sought,
(3) the sum of money for which final judgment is likely to be given,
(4) the reasons for believing that the conditions set out in rule 25.7 are satisfied,
(5) any other relevant matters,
(6) in claims for personal injuries, details of special damages and past and future loss, and
(7) in a claim under the Fatal Accidents Act 1976, details of the person(s) on whose behalf the claim is made and the nature of the claim.

2.2 Any documents in support of the application should be exhibited, including, in personal injuries claims, the medical report(s).

2.3 If a respondent to an application for an interim payment wishes to rely on written evidence at the hearing he must comply with the provisions of rule 25.6(4).

2.4 If the applicant wishes to rely on written evidence in reply he must comply with the provisions of rule 25.6(5).

INTERIM PAYMENT WHERE ACCOUNT TO BE TAKEN

2A.1 This section of this practice direction applies if a party seeks an interim payment under rule 25.7(b) where the court has ordered an account to be taken.

2A.2 If the evidence on the application for interim payment shows that the account is bound to result in a payment to the applicant the court will, before making an order for interim payment, order that the liable party pay to the applicant 'the amount shown by the account to be due'.

INSTALMENTS

3 Where an interim payment is to be paid in instalments the order should set out:

(1) the total amount of the payment,
(2) the amount of each instalment,
(3) the number of instalments and the date on which each is to be paid, and

(4) to whom the payment should be made.

COMPENSATION RECOVERY PAYMENTS

4.1 Where in a claim for personal injuries there is an application for an interim payment of damages:

(1) which is other than by consent,
(2) which falls under the heads of damage set out in column 1 of Schedule 2 of the Social Security (Recovery of Benefits) Act 1997 in respect of recoverable benefits received by the claimant set out in column 2 of that Schedule, and
(3) where the defendant is liable to pay recoverable benefits to the Secretary of State,

the defendant should obtain from the Secretary of State a certificate of recoverable benefits.

4.2 A copy of the certificate should be filed at the hearing of the application for an interim payment.

4.3 The order will set out the amount by which the payment to be made to the claimant has been reduced according to the Act and the Social Security (Recovery of Benefits) Regulations 1997.

4.4 The payment made to the claimant will be the net amount but the interim payment for the purposes of paragraph 5 below will be the gross amount.

ADJUSTMENT OF FINAL JUDGMENT FIGURE

5.1 In this paragraph 'judgment' means:

(1) any order to pay a sum of money,
(2) a final award of damages,
(3) an assessment of damages.

5.2 In a final judgment where an interim payment has previously been made which is less than the total amount awarded by the judge, the order should set out in a preamble:

(1) the total amount awarded by the judge, and
(2) the amounts and dates of the interim payment(s).

5.3 The total amount awarded by the judge should then be reduced by the total amount of any interim payments, and an order made for entry of judgment and payment of the balance.

5.4 In a final judgment where an interim payment has previously been made which is more than the total amount awarded by the judge, the order should set out in a preamble:

(1) the total amount awarded by the judge, and
(2) the amounts and dates of the interim payment(s).

5.5 An order should then be made for repayment, reimbursement, variation or discharge under rule 25.8(2) and for interest on an overpayment under rule 25.8(5).

5.6 A practice direction supplementing Part 40 provides further information concerning adjustment of the final judgment sum.

PART 26
CASE MANAGEMENT – PRELIMINARY STAGE

CONTENTS OF THIS PART

Procedural Guides—See Guides 11 (The Allocation Questionnaire), 12 (Proceeding on the Small Claims Track), 13 (Proceeding on the Fast Track) and 14 (Proceeding on the Multi-Track), set out in Section 1 of this work.

Practice Direction—See generally PD26 at p 742.

26.1 Scope of this Part

(1) This Part provides for –

(a) the automatic transfer of some defended cases between courts; and
(b) the allocation of defended cases to case management tracks.

(2) There are three tracks –

(a) the small claims track;
(b) the fast track; and
(c) the multi-track.

(Rule 26.6 sets out the normal scope of each track. Part 27 makes provision for the small claims track. Part 28 makes provision for the fast track. Part 29 makes provision for the multi-track)

Scope of provision—The old rules provided automatic directions in most cases. Now the court's primary duty is to further the overriding objective by actively managing cases assisted by the parties (Pt 1). That includes: encouraging the parties to co-operate with each other in the conduct of the proceedings; identifying the issues at an early stage; deciding promptly which issues need full investigation and trial and accordingly disposing summarily of the others; and deciding the order in which issues are to be resolved.

Part 26, which should be read together with Pts 27, 28 and 29, is the filter through which all defended cases (and undefended ones where damages and interest are still to be quantified if allocation to track is warranted) have to pass for preliminary case management. All four Parts are supplemented by their own comprehensive practice directions.

The only automatic process is the transfer of certain cases to defendants' home courts. Part 26 provides for cases, by judicial decision, to be:

(a) allocated or re-allocated (with or without an allocation hearing) to one of three tracks, small claims track, fast track and multi-track according to criteria set out in (in particular) r 26.6;
(b) case managed according to the principles of active case management;
(c) stayed for settlement;
(d) struck out wholly or partially;
(e) disposed of summarily, in whole or in part;
(f) clarified by the court by ordering the parties to provide further information.

26.2 Automatic transfer

(1) This rule applies to proceedings where –

- (a) the claim is for a specified amount of money;
- (b) the claim was commenced in a court which is not the defendant's home court;
- (c) the claim has not been transferred to another defendant's home court under rule 13.4 (application to set aside(GL) or vary default judgment – procedure) or rule 14.12 (admission – determination of rate of payment by judge); and
- (d) the defendant is an individual.

(2) This rule does not apply where the claim was commenced in a specialist list(GL).

(3) Where this rule applies, the court will transfer the proceedings to the defendant's home court when a defence is filed, unless paragraph (4) applies.

(Rule 2.3 defines 'defendant's home court')

(4) Where the claimant notifies the court under rule 15.10 or rule 14.5 that he wishes the proceedings to continue, the court will transfer the proceedings to the defendant's home court when it receives that notification from the claimant.

(Rule 15.10 deals with a claimant's notice where the defence is that money claimed has been paid)

(Rule 14.5 sets out the procedure where the defendant admits part of a claim for a specified amount of money)

(5) Where –

- (a) the claim is against two or more defendants with different home courts; and
- (b) the defendant whose defence is filed first is an individual,

proceedings are to be transferred under this rule to the home court of that defendant.

(6) The time when a claim is automatically transferred under this rule may be varied by a practice direction in respect of claims issued by the Production Centre.

(Rule 7.10 makes provision for the Production Centre)

Scope of provision—Rule 26.2 provides for the automatic transfer of defended proceedings to the defendant's home court if they meet the four qualifications set out in subpara (1).

'defendant's home court' (r 26.2(3))—Rule 2.3(1) (since 2 October 2000) defines the defendant's home court (in the county court) as the court for the district in which the defendant resides or carries on business. In the High Court the defendant's home court is either the district registry where the defendant resides or carries on business or, if there is no such district registry, then the Royal Courts of Justice. The amendment eliminates the case being automatically transferred to the defendant's solicitor's local court where he puts his professional address on the defence.

'a specialist list' (r 26.2(2))—The expression is defined in Pt 49.

'Claims issued by the Production Centre' (r 26.2(6))—The time for transfer is varied for claims originating in the Production Centre and issued as in the Northampton County Court. On the filing of a defence the proceedings will not be transferred to the defendant's home court until the Centre user notifies the officer that he wishes the claim to continue (PD7C).

26.3 Allocation questionnaire

(1) When a defendant files a defence the court will serve an allocation questionnaire on each party unless –

(a) rule 15.10 or rule 14.5 applies; or
(b) the court dispenses with the need for a questionnaire.

(2) Where there are two or more defendants and at least one of them files a defence, the court will serve the allocation questionnaire under paragraph (1) –

(a) when all the defendants have filed a defence; or
(b) when the period for the filing of the last defence has expired,

whichever is the sooner.

(Rule 15.4 specifies the period for filing a defence)

(3) Where proceedings are automatically transferred to the defendant's home court under rule 26.2, the court in which the proceedings have been commenced will serve an allocation questionnaire before the proceedings are transferred.

(4) Where –

(a) rule 15.10 or rule 14.5 applies; and
(b) the proceedings are not automatically transferred to the defendant's home court under rule 26.2,

the court will serve an allocation questionnaire on each party when the claimant files a notice indicating that he wishes the proceedings to continue.

(5) The court may, on the application of the claimant, serve an allocation questionnaire earlier than it would otherwise serve it under this rule.

(6) Each party must file the completed allocation questionnaire no later than the date specified in it, which shall be at least 14 days after the date when it is deemed to be served on the party in question.

(6A) The date for filing the completed allocation questionnaire may not be varied by agreement between the parties.

(7) The time when the court serves an allocation questionnaire under this rule may be varied by a practice direction in respect of claims issued by the Production Centre.

(Rule 7.10 makes provision for the Production Centre)

(Rule 6.7 specifies when a document is deemed to be served)

Amendments—SI 2001/4015.

Procedural Guide—See Guide 11 (The Allocation Questionnaire) and, in particular, the guidance as to its completion.

Allocation questionnaire—The object of the questionnaire, in conjunction with the parties' statements of case, is to give the procedural judge sufficient information to determine what the relevant issues are likely to be in order to give each case preliminary trial management and allocate it to track. When required, the court will send an allocation questionnaire (Form N150) to all parties. Form N150 has been redesigned and a shorter, improved version came into effect on 29 January 2001. The form can also be accessed/completed on the *Civil Court Service* CD-ROM or via the Internet at the Court Service website *http://www.courtservice.gov.uk/fandl/forms/n150.pdf*. Using the free Adobe Acrobat reader software, the blank form can be completed on screen and then printed ready for submission to the court.

'Each party must file' (r 26.3(6))—Though the parties have a duty to consult and co-operate with each other (see below), surprisingly, they are not required by either the rule or the practice direction to serve their completed questionnaires on each other. (This the court does but only, under r 26.9(2), when the case is allocated.) They may be unaware of conflicts (eg as to suggested track) that might lead to the expense and inconvenience of an allocation hearing which could have been resolved by agreement. It is good practice to serve questionnaires when filing them with the court (the Rule Committee is considering an amendment which would make it a requirement).

Consultation and co-operation—Parties are, by r 1.3, required to help the court to further the overriding objective. Allocation is a prime example. The parties must consult, co-operate in completing the questionnaire, try to agree case management directions and all without delay (see PD26, para 2.3 for the details).

Provision of extra information—Paragraph 2.2 of PD26 and the examples set out there should be considered carefully when providing additional information with the allocation questionnaire. Only information relevant to allocation and case management directions should be filed and the information must be delivered to all other parties and carry confirmation that all parties agree that the information is correct and that it should be put before the court, see PD26, paras 2.2(2)(a) and (b).

Dispensing with the allocation questionnaire (r 26.3(1)(b))—The court has power to dispense with a questionnaire before allocating and, for example, may do so:

(a) when a judge allocates to a track at a hearing in proceedings existing before 26 April 1999 (see PD51, para 15);

(b) where a court hearing takes place (for example on an application for an interim injunction or for summary judgment under Pt 24) before the claim is allocated to a track (see PD26, para 2.4);

(c) on a disposal hearing following default judgment under r 12.7(2) when the amount of damages, interest or value of goods has to be decided by the court (see PD26, para 12).

Claims issued by the Production Centre (r 26.3(7))—Where the claim was issued as in the Northampton County Court, no allocation questionnaires will be served until the Centre user notifies the officer that he wishes the claim to continue (PD7C, para 5.2(4)).

Costs estimate—The requirements for costs estimates are altered from 3 July 2000. Paragraph 2.1 of PD26 is new and follows the changes to the costs rules. See notes on 'Costs' in Guide 11 in Section 1 of this work for a more detailed summary.

26.4 Stay to allow for settlement of the case

(1) A party may, when filing the completed allocation questionnaire, make a written request for the proceedings to be stayed(GL) while the parties try to settle the case by alternative dispute resolution(GL) or other means.

(2) Where –

(a) all parties request a stay(GL) under paragraph (1); or

(b) the court, of its own initiative, considers that such a stay would be appropriate,

the court will direct that the proceedings, either in whole or in part, be stayed for one month, or for such specified period as it considers appropriate.

(3) The court may extend the stay(GL) until such date or for such specified period as it considers appropriate.

(4) Where the court stays(GL) the proceedings under this rule, the claimant must tell the court if a settlement is reached.

(5) If the claimant does not tell the court by the end of the period of the stay(GL) that a settlement has been reached, the court will give such directions as to the management of the case as it considers appropriate.

Amendments—SI 2005/2292.

General note—This rule flows from r 1.4(2)(e) and (f). Active case management includes encouraging and facilitating the use of Alternative Dispute Resolution ('ADR') procedures and helping parties to settle their case.

'the court will direct' (r 26.4(2))—If both parties apply for a stay when completing Section A of the allocation questionnaire, the court will automatically stay proceedings for one month. The court can also order a stay of its own initiative even if not all parties so request or may fix an allocation hearing to decide whether to order one. Unless the claimant tells the court by the end of the period of the stay that settlement is reached the court will give 'appropriate' further case management directions. The parties will be expected to use the time genuinely to explore settlement though the court will not dictate by what means. Those who abuse the system or unjustifiably refuse to co-operate in negotiations or mediation are likely to be met by a district judge purposively applying r 1.4.

'of its own initiative' (r 26.4(2)(b))—The court may direct a stay for the purposes of ADR whether or not the parties apply for one. The factors set out by the Court of Appeal in *Halsey v Milton Keynes General NHS Trust* 2004] EWCA Civ 576, 2004] 1 WLR 3002, 2004] All ER (D) 125 (May), will be relevant.

Sanctions for breach of duty—The Court of Appeal in *Halsey v Milton Keynes General NHS Trust* (see above) gave important guidance on the duty always to consider ADR, building on a number of widely publicised cases. See further the note **'alternative dispute resolution'** under r 1.4, where the guidance is summarised. The likely sanction will sound in costs or higher interest. Costs may be awarded on the indemnity basis. Rule 44.3 sets out the court's discretion and circumstances to be taken into account when exercising its discretion as to costs. The court must have regard to conduct, see r 44.3(4)(a), and conduct includes the manner in which a party has pursued or defended his case or a particular allegation or issue (r 44.3(5)(c)).

In *Dyson (Robert Alan) (1) Field (John Watson) (2) (Executors of the Estate of Lawrence Twohey, Deceased) v Leeds City Council* (1999) Lawtel, 22 November, CA, Lord Woolf MR stated:

> 'Since damages had been substantially agreed, it seemed to the court that the instant case was pre-eminently of the category of cases in which Alternative Dispute Resolution ("ADR") process should be adopted. The defendant was reminded of the court's power to take a strong view about rejecting the court's suggestion of ADR by implementing an order for costs on an indemnity basis or possibly awarding a higher rate of interest to be paid on any damages recoverable.'

ADR—What is ADR and in which cases might it be appropriate? Here the CPR are less than helpful. The Glossary merely defines ADR as 'Collective description of methods of resolving disputes otherwise than through the normal trial process.' This covers a vast range of activities. One can think of it as an arch of processes with negotiation and mediation (where the parties themselves can resolve disputes flexibly) at one end and neutral evaluation, mini-trial or ombudsmen and arbitration (where third parties impose solutions) at the other. Court offices have lists of ADR providers. For further reading see *Mediation in Action* by Hazel Genn distributed by Turnaround Publisher Services Ltd, Tel 0208-829-3000. This is a lively, small book with a helpful list of the main mediation organisations. For a comprehensive and authoritative text see Brown and Marriott *ADR Principles and Practice*, Sweet & Maxwell.

Effect on interim injunction—Where a claim is stayed, save by consent, an earlier interim injunction will be automatically set aside under r 25.10 unless the court orders that it should continue to have effect.

'If the claimant does not tell the court' (r 26.4(5))—It is the claimant's duty to inform the court whether settlement is reached and the court will never permit the action to drift. PD26, para 3.2 provides for the court's approach if the case is not settled.

26.5 Allocation

(1) The court will allocate the claim to a track –

(a) when every defendant has filed an allocation questionnaire, or

(b) when the period for filing the allocation questionnaires has expired,

whichever is the sooner, unless it has –

(i) stayed(GL) the proceedings under rule 26.4; or

(ii) dispensed with the need for allocation questionnaires.

(Rules 12.7 and 14.8 provide for the court to allocate a claim to a track where the claimant obtains default judgment on request or judgment on admission for an amount to be decided by the court)

(2) If the court has stayed(GL) the proceedings under rule 26.4, it will allocate the claim to a track at the end of the period of the stay.

(3) Before deciding the track to which to allocate proceedings or deciding whether to give directions for an allocation hearing to be fixed, the court may order a party to provide further information about his case.

(4) The court may hold an allocation hearing if it thinks it is necessary.

(5) If a party fails to file an allocation questionnaire, the court may give any direction it considers appropriate.

'allocation hearing' (r 26.5(3) and (4))—See PD26, para 6 for general principles, procedures and sanctions.

'the court may order a party to provide further information about his case' (r 26.5(3))—See r 18.1 and note, too, the court's wide case management powers under Pt 24 and rr 3.3 and 3.4.

'If a party fails to file an allocation questionnaire' (r 26.5(5))—

(a) failure by both parties – a judge will normally order that unless an allocation questionnaire is filed within 3 days from service of that order the claim and/or counterclaim will be struck out (PD26, para 2.5(1)(b)).

(b) failure by one party – the judge may allocate the claim to track if there is enough information to do so or order an allocation hearing (PD26, para 2.5(2)). On the other hand, judges will be anxious to ensure that the court's resources are concentrated on genuinely opposed claims and may propose to strike out the defaulting party's statement of case, as above, if it seems that the claim or defence is not actively and sincerely pursued.

(c) default resulting in allocation hearing – if an allocation hearing takes place due to a party's failure to file a questionnaire, the sanction will usually be costs on an indemnity basis paid immediately with a strike out in default of payment (PD26, para 6.6).

26.6 Scope of each track

(1) The small claims track is the normal track for –

- (a) any claim for personal injuries where –
  - (i) the financial value of the claim is not more than £5000; and
  - (ii) the financial value of any claim for damages for personal injuries is not more than £1000;
- (b) any claim which includes a claim by a tenant of residential premises against his landlord where –
  - (i) the tenant is seeking an order requiring the landlord to carry out repairs or other work to the premises (whether or not the tenant is also seeking some other remedy);
  - (ii) the cost of the repairs or other work to the premises is estimated to be not more than £1000; and
  - (iii) the financial value of any other claim for damages is not more than £1000.

(Rule 2.3 defines 'claim for personal injuries' as proceedings in which there is a claim for damages in respect of personal injuries to the claimant or any other person or in respect of a person's death)

(2) For the purposes of paragraph (1) 'damages for personal injuries' means damages claimed as compensation for pain, suffering and loss of amenity and does not include any other damages which are claimed.

(3) Subject to paragraph (1), the small claims track is the normal track for any claim which has a financial value of not more than £5000.

(Rule 26.7(4) provides that the court will not allocate to the small claims track certain claims in respect of harassment or unlawful eviction)

(4) Subject to paragraph (5), the fast track is the normal track for any claim –

(a) for which the small claims track is not the normal track; and
(b) which has a financial value of not more than £15,000.

(5) The fast track is the normal track for the claims referred to in paragraph (4) only if the court considers that –

(a) the trial is likely to last for no longer than one day; and
(b) oral expert evidence at trial will be limited to –
   (i) one expert per party in relation to any expert field; and
   (ii) expert evidence in two expert fields.

(6) The multi-track is the normal track for any claim for which the small claims track or the fast track is not the normal track.

General note—This rule defines the 'normal' criteria for each of the three tracks which are broadly; small claims track – claims of not more than £5000, fast track – claims of over £5000 and not more than £15,000 and multi-track – claims of over £15,000. The special provisions about small claims for personal injuries and housing disrepair and the fast track limitations should be carefully noted. Note also that claims for harassment and unlawful eviction are excluded from small claims track by r 26.7(4).

'The small claims track' (r 26.6(1))—While similar to the former CCR Ord 19, the procedure (set out in Pt 27) has been refined, not least in the discontinuance of the misplaced term 'arbitration'.

'does not include any other damages which are claimed' (r 26.6(2))—Loss of earnings claims or other heads of loss do not exclude a modest personal injuries claim from the small claims track, provided the value of the whole claim does not exceed £5000.

'no longer than one day' (r 26.6(5)(a))—A hearing day is normally regarded as 5 hours (PD26, para 9.1(3)(a)).

Transfer to Trial Centre—Claims allocated to the multi-track (except for a defended county court claim for possession of land) will normally be transferred to the Civil Trial Centre: see PD26, para 10.1(1). This amendment was introduced in Update 9.

26.7 General rule for allocation

(1) In considering whether to allocate a claim to the normal track for that claim under rule 26.6, the court will have regard to the matters mentioned in rule 26.8(1).

(2) The court will allocate a claim which has no financial value to the track which it considers most suitable having regard to the matters mentioned in rule 26.8(1).

(3) The court will not allocate proceedings to a track if the financial value of the claim, assessed by the court under rule 26.8, exceeds the limit for that track unless all the parties consent to the allocation of the claim to that track.

(4) The court will not allocate a claim to the small claims track, if it includes a claim by a tenant of residential premises against his landlord for a remedy in respect of harassment or unlawful eviction.

Amendments—SI 2000/221.

'if the financial value of any claim in those proceedings' (r 26.7(3))—This prevents a claim being apportioned into different tracks eg with a fast track trial on liability followed by a multi-track trial on quantum.

While the court cannot allocate a claim with a higher financial value to a lower track unless the parties consent, it is the court and not the parties which will assess the value (r 26.8(2)).

A straightforward case of a value qualifying it for the multi-track is very likely be case managed as if it were fast track.

A judge has discretion to keep a matter within the small claims track even if the counterclaim exceeds the limit (*Berridge (Paul) (t/a EAB Builders) v RM Bayliss* (1999) Lawtel, 23 November, CA).

Rule 26.7(3) was amended in May 2000 to exclude the financial value of a Pt 20 claim from the operation of r 26.7(3). The financial value of the original claim is the only financial value to be considered under this rule.

'harassment or unlawful eviction' (r 26.7(4))—This exception was incorporated to avoid disqualifying a tenant from Legal Aid, reflecting the overriding objective of ensuring the parties are on an equal footing.

26.8 Matters relevant to allocation to a track

(1) When deciding the track for a claim, the matters to which the court shall have regard include –

(a) the financial value, if any, of the claim;
(b) the nature of the remedy sought;
(c) the likely complexity of the facts, law or evidence;
(d) the number of parties or likely parties;
(e) the value of any counterclaim or other Part 20 claim and the complexity of any matters relating to it;
(f) the amount of oral evidence which may be required;
(g) the importance of the claim to persons who are not parties to the proceedings;
(h) the views expressed by the parties; and
(i) the circumstances of the parties.

(2) It is for the court to assess the financial value of a claim, and in doing so it will disregard –

(a) any amount not in dispute;
(b) any claim for interest;
(c) costs; and
(d) any contributory negligence.

(3) Where –

(a) two or more claimants have started a claim against the same defendant using the same claim form; and
(b) each claimant has a claim against the defendant separate from the other claimants,

the court will consider the claim of each claimant separately when it assesses financial value under paragraph (1).

'include' (r 26.8(1))—The check-list is not exhaustive.

'any amount not in dispute' (r 26.8(2)(a))—Paragraph 7.4 of PD26 sets out the principles to be applied.

'the views expressed by the parties' (r 26.8(1)(h))—The parties' views are persuasive but the court is not bound by them (PD26, para 7.5).

'It is for the court to assess the financial value of the claim' (r 26.8(2))—Conduct, including whether a party exaggerated his claim, will be taken into account when assessing costs (r 44.3(5)(d)) and a party who deliberately exaggerates a claim to force it into a higher track is likely to face a costs sanction following an allocation hearing or after trial following the principles explained by the Court of Appeal in *Afzal v Ford Motor Co Ltd* 1994] 4 All ER 720, CA.

'the claim of each claimant separately' (r 26.8(3))—It is the largest of the values, not the cumulative value, which will affect allocation.

Allocation of claims for possession of land to a track—The financial value of the property will not necessarily be the primary factor in deciding the appropriate track for possession claims. The court may direct a possession claim to be allocated to the fast track even though the value of the property is in excess of £15,000 (PD55, para 6.1). A claim realistically estimated to take more than one day to try will likely be allocated to the multi-track. Rule 55.9 further modifies the matters to which the court must have regard by including –

(a) the amount of any arrears of rent or mortgage instalments;
(b) the importance to the defendant of retaining possession of the land; and
(c) to the claimant of obtaining vacant possession of the land.

Under r 55.9(2) possession cases allocated to the small claims track are treated for the purposes of costs, as if they were proceeding on the fast track except that trial costs shall be in the discretion of the court. They shall not exceed the amount that would be recoverable under r 46.2 (amount of fast track costs) if the value of the claim were up to £3000. However, in accordance with r 55.9(4) the parties can agree to ask the court to exclude r 55.9(3) and order, when it allocates the claim, the normal small claims costs regime to apply.

26.9 Notice of allocation

(1) When it has allocated a claim to a track, the court will serve notice of allocation on every party.

(2) When the court serves notice of allocation on a party, it will also serve –

(a) a copy of the allocation questionnaires filed by the other parties; and
(b) a copy of any further information provided by another party about his case (whether by order or not).

(Rule 26.5 provides that the court may, before allocating proceedings, order a party to provide further information about his case)

General note—This rule may well be amended shortly. See note **'each party must file'** to r 26.3.

26.10 Re-allocation

The court may subsequently re-allocate a claim to a different track.

Re-allocation—This is most likely to occur:
(a) by agreement between parties and with the court's approval; or
(b) after a successful appeal or application to the court to re-allocate the claim; or
(c) after a change in circumstances since an allocation order was made (eg after a split trial or determination of a preliminary issue leaving issues that could be determined on another track).

Amended claims—A claim does not cease to be in the fast track simply because its financial value has been increased beyond the £15,000 limit. In *Maguire v Molin* 2002] EWCA Civ 1083, 2002] 4 All ER 325 the Court of Appeal gave guidance in cases where financial claims were revised upward at the eleventh hour, holding –
(1) Rule 26.10 gives the court an apparently unfettered discretion.
(2) The question of reallocation of a claim from one track to another does not necessarily raise the same issues as those which arise when the initial allocation decision is made.
(3) Once a claim has been allocated to a track, there needs to be a good reason to reallocate it to a different track.
(4) If a fast track claim is amended so that its financial value exceeds £15,000, a district judge may allow the amendment and continue with the hearing of the issue of liability on the fast track. So long as a claim remains in the fast track, the district judge has jurisdiction to hear it (PD2B, para 11.1(a)).
(5) If the revised financial value exceeds £15,000 by a small amount, it will usually be wrong to reallocate if that will cause substantial disruption to the progress of the litigation.
(6) Where the excess is substantial there should usually be a reallocation, even if that means causing considerable delay to the completion of the litigation.
(7) Once reallocated to the multi-track the case must be tried by a circuit judge.
(8) In *Maguire v Molin* the application to amend was only made at the trial. There had been an obvious but unexplained error on the part of the claimant's solicitor. The district judge was entitled to take the view that the application was too late and that the delays and additional costs of aborting the trial on liability were such that, in the interests of justice, the amendment should be refused.

26.11 Trial with a jury

An application for a claim to be tried with a jury must be made within 28 days of service of the defence.

(Section 69 of the Supreme Court Act 1981 and section 66 of the County Courts Act 1984 specify when a claim may be tried with a jury.)

Amendments—Inserted by SI 2000/2092.

Trial with a jury—The requirement that any application for a case to be tried with a jury must be made within 28 days of service of the defence took effect from 2 October 2000.

Practice Direction – Case Management – Preliminary Stage: Allocation and Re-Allocation

This Practice Direction supplements CPR Part 26 (PD26)

Procedural Guide—See Guide 11, set out in Section 1 of this work.

REMINDERS OF IMPORTANT RULE PROVISIONS OTHER THAN PARTS 26–29

Attention is drawn in particular to the following provisions of the Civil Procedure Rules:

Part 1	The Overriding Objective (defined in Rule 1.1). The duty of the court to further that objective by actively managing cases (set out in Rule 1.4). The requirement that the parties help the court to further that objective (set out in Rule 1.3).
Part 3	The court's case management powers (which may be exercised on application or on its own initiative) and the sanctions which it may impose.
Part 24	The court's power to grant summary judgment.
Parts 32–35	Evidence, especially the court's power to control evidence.

Attention is also drawn to the practice directions which supplement those Parts and Parts 27–29, and to those which relate to the various specialist jurisdictions.

THE ALLOCATION QUESTIONNAIRE

2.1 FORM

(1) The allocation questionnaire referred to in Part 26 will be in Form N150.

(2) (a) Attention is drawn to Section 6 of the Costs Practice Direction supplementing Parts 43 to 48, which requires an estimate of costs to be filed and served when an allocation questionnaire is filed by a party to a claim which is outside the limits for the small claims track.

(b) A party will comply with that obligation if the costs estimate he files and serves states the figures for the base costs, incurred and to be incurred, which he expects, if he is successful, to recover from the other party. The estimate should show an itemised breakdown of how it is calculated, showing separately the amounts included for profit costs, disbursements and VAT. It should be substantially in the form illustrated in Precedent H in the schedule to the Costs Practice Direction.

(Paragraph 2.2 of the Costs Practice Direction defines 'base costs')

(c) Any party who has entered into a funding arrangement need not reveal the amount of any additional liability.

(CPR rule 43.2 defines 'funding arrangement' and 'additional liability')

(d) No later than when he files the estimate the solicitor acting for that party must deliver a copy to his client.

Costs estimate—The requirements for costs estimates are altered from 3 July 2000. Paragraph 2.1 is new and follows the changes to the costs rules.

2.2 PROVISION OF EXTRA INFORMATION

(1) This paragraph sets out what a party should do when he files his allocation questionnaire if he wishes to give the court information about matters which he believes may affect its decision about allocation or case management.

(2) The general rule is that the court will not take such information into account unless the document containing it either:

(a) confirms that all parties have agreed that the information is correct and that it should be put before the court, or
(b) confirms that the party who has sent the document to the court has delivered a copy to all the other parties.

(3) The following are examples of information which will be likely to help the court:

(a) a party's intention to apply for summary judgment or some other order that may dispose of the case or reduce the amount in dispute or the number of issues remaining to be decided,
(b) a party's intention to issue a Part 20 claim or to add another party,
(c) the steps the parties have taken in the preparation of evidence (in particular expert evidence), the steps they intend to take and whether those steps are to be taken in co-operation with any other party,
(d) the directions the party believes will be appropriate to be given for the management of the case,
(e) about any particular facts that may affect the timetable the court will set,
(f) any facts which may make it desirable for the court to fix an allocation hearing or a hearing at which case management directions will be given.

2.3 CONSULTATION

(1) The parties should consult one another and co-operate in completing the allocation questionnaires and giving other information to the court.

(2) They should try to agree the case management directions which they will invite the court to make. Further details appear in the practice directions which supplement Parts 28 and 29.

(3) The process of consultation must not delay the filing of the allocation questionnaires.

2.4 HEARINGS BEFORE ALLOCATION

Where a Court hearing takes place (for example on an application for an interim injunction or for summary judgment under Part 24) before the claim is allocated to a track, the court may at that hearing:

(1) dispense with the need for the parties to file allocation questionnaires, treat the hearing as an allocation hearing, make an order for allocation and give directions for case management, or
(2) fix a date for allocation questionnaires to be filed and give other directions.

2.5 CONSEQUENCES OF FAILURE TO FILE AN ALLOCATION QUESTIONNAIRE

(1) If no party files an allocation questionnaire within the time specified by Form N152, the court will order that unless an allocation questionnaire is filed within 7 days from service of that order, the claim, defence and any counterclaim will be struck out without further order of the court.

(2) Where a party files an allocation questionnaire but another party does not, the file will be referred to a judge for his directions and the court may:

(a) allocate the claim to a track if it considers that it has enough information to do so, or
(b) order that an allocation hearing is listed and that all or any parties must attend.

STAY TO ALLOW FOR SETTLEMENT OF THE CASE

3.1 PROCEDURE FOR THE PARTIES TO APPLY TO EXTEND THE STAY

(1) (a) The court will generally accept a letter from any party or from the solicitor for any party as an application to extend the stay under rule 26.4.
(b) The letter should –
(i) confirm that the application is made with the agreement of all parties, and
(ii) explain the steps being taken and identify any mediator or expert assisting with the process.

(2) (a) An order extending the stay must be made by a judge.
(b) The extension will generally be for no more than four weeks unless clear reasons are given to justify a longer time.

(3) More than one extension of the stay may be granted.

3.2 POSITION AT THE END OF THE STAY IF NO SETTLEMENT IS REACHED

(1) At the end of the stay the file will be referred to a judge for his directions.

(2) He will consider whether to allocate the claim to a track and what other directions to give, and may require any party to give further information or fix an allocation hearing.

3.3 Any party may apply for a stay to be lifted.

3.4 POSITION WHERE SETTLEMENT IS REACHED DURING A STAY

Where the whole of the proceedings are settled during a stay, the taking of any of the following steps will be treated as an application for the stay to be lifted:

(1) an application for a consent order (in any form) to give effect to the settlement,
(2) an application for the approval of a settlement where a party is a person under a disability,
(3) giving notice of acceptance of money paid into Court in satisfaction of the claim or applying for money in Court to be paid out.

ALLOCATION, RE-ALLOCATION AND CASE MANAGEMENT

4.1 THE COURT'S GENERAL APPROACH

The Civil Procedure Rules lay down the overriding objective, the powers and duties of the court and the factors to which it must have regard in exercising them. The court will expect to exercise its powers as far as possible in co-operation with the parties and their legal representatives so as to deal with the case justly in accordance with that objective.

4.2 ALLOCATION TO TRACK

(1) In most cases the court will expect to have enough information from the statements of case and allocation questionnaires to be able to allocate the claim to a track and to give case management directions.

(2) If the court does not have enough information to allocate the claim it will generally make an order under rule 26.5(3) requiring one or more parties to provide further information within 14 days.

(3) Where there has been no allocation hearing the notice of allocation will be in Forms N154 (fast track), N155 (multi-track) or N157–160 (small claims).

(4) (a) The general rule is that the court will give brief reasons for its allocation decision, and these will be set out in the notice of allocation.
(b) The general rule does not apply where all the allocation questionnaires which have been filed have expressed the wish for the claim to be allocated to the track to which the court has allocated it.

(5) Paragraph 6 of this practice direction deals with allocation hearings and Paragraph 7 deals with allocation principles.

(6) Paragraph 11 of this practice direction deals with re-allocation.

4.3 The practice directions supplementing Parts 27, 28 and 29 contain further information about the giving of case management directions at the allocation stage.

SUMMARY JUDGMENT OR OTHER EARLY TERMINATION

5.1 Part of the court's duty of active case management is the summary disposal of issues which do not need full investigation and trial (rule 1.4(2)(c)).

5.2 The court's powers to make orders to dispose of issues in that way include:

(a) under rule 3.4, striking out a statement of case, or part of a statement of case, and

(b) under Part 24, giving summary judgment where a claimant or a defendant has no reasonable prospect of success.

The court may use these powers on an application or on its own initiative. The practice direction 'Summary Disposal of Claims' contains further information.

5.3 (1) A party intending to make such an application should do so before or when filing his allocation questionnaire.
(2) Where a party makes an application for such an order before a claim has been allocated to a track the court will not normally allocate the claim before the hearing of the application.
(3) Where a party files an allocation questionnaire stating that he intends to make such an application but has not done so, the judge will usually direct that an allocation hearing is listed.
(4) The application may be heard at that allocation hearing if the application notice has been issued and served in sufficient time.

5.4 (1) This paragraph applies where the court proposes to make such an order of its own initiative.
(2) The court will not allocate the claim to a track but instead it will either:
(a) fix a hearing, giving the parties at least 14 days notice of the date of the hearing and of the issues which it is proposed that the court will decide, or
(b) make an order directing a party to take the steps described in the order within a stated time and specifying the consequence of not taking those steps.

5.5 Where the court decides at the hearing of an application or a hearing fixed under paragraph 5.4(2)(a) that the claim (or part of the claim) is to continue it may:

(1) treat that hearing as an allocation hearing, allocate the claim and give case management directions, or
(2) give other directions.

ALLOCATION HEARINGS

6.1 GENERAL PRINCIPLE

The court will only hold an allocation hearing on its own initiative if it considers that it is necessary to do so.

6.2 PROCEDURE

Where the court orders an allocation hearing to take place:

(1) it will give the parties at least 7 days notice of the hearing in Form N153, and
(2) Form N153 will give a brief explanation of the decision to order the hearing.

6.3 POWER TO TREAT ANOTHER HEARING AS AN ALLOCATION HEARING

Where the court may treat another hearing as an allocation hearing it does not need to give notice to any party that it proposes to do so.

6.4 The notice of allocation after an allocation hearing will be in Forms N154, N155 or N157.

6.5 REPRESENTATION

A legal representative who attends an allocation hearing should, if possible, be the person responsible for the case and must in any event be familiar with the case, be able to provide the court with the information it is likely to need to take its decisions about allocation and case management, and have sufficient authority to deal with any issues that are likely to arise.

6.6 SANCTIONS

(1) This paragraph sets out the sanctions that the court will usually impose for default in connection with the allocation procedure, but the court may make a different order.

(2) (a) Where an allocation hearing takes place because a party has failed to file an allocation questionnaire or to provide further information which the court has ordered, the court will usually order that party to pay on the indemnity basis the costs of any other party who has attended the hearing, summarily assess the amount of those costs, and order them to be paid forthwith or within a stated period.

(b) The court may order that if the party does not pay those costs within the time stated his statement of case will be struck out.

(3) Where a party whose default has led to a fixing of an allocation hearing is still in default and does not attend the hearing the court will usually make an order specifying the steps he is required to take and providing that unless he takes them within a stated time his statement of case will be struck out.

ALLOCATION PRINCIPLES

7.1 RULES 26.6, 26.7 AND 26.8

(1) Rule 26.6 sets out the scope of each track,

(2) Rule 26.7 states the general rule for allocation, and

(3) Rule 26.8 sets out the matters relevant to allocation to a track.

7.2 OBJECTIVE OF THIS PARAGRAPH

The object of this paragraph is to explain what will be the court's general approach to some of the matters set out in Rule 26.8.

7.3 'THE FINANCIAL VALUE OF THE CLAIM'

(1) Rule 26.8(2) provides that it is for the court to assess the financial value of a claim.

(2) Where the court believes that the amount the claimant is seeking exceeds what he may reasonably be expected to recover it may make an order under rule 26.5(3) directing the claimant to justify the amount.

7.4 'ANY AMOUNT NOT IN DISPUTE'

In deciding, for the purposes of rule 26.8(2), whether an amount is in dispute the court will apply the following general principles:

(1) Any amount for which the defendant does not admit liability is in dispute,
(2) Any sum in respect of an item forming part of the claim for which judgment has been entered (for example a summary judgment) is not in dispute,
(3) Any specific sum claimed as a distinct item and which the defendant admits he is liable to pay is not in dispute,
(4) Any sum offered by the defendant which has been accepted by the claimant in satisfaction of any item which forms a distinct part of the claim is not in dispute.

It follows from these provisions that if, in relation to a claim the value of which is above the small claims track limit of £5000, the defendant makes, before allocation, an admission that reduces the amount in dispute to a figure below £5000 (see CPR Part 14), the normal track for the claim will be the small claims track. As to recovery of pre-allocation costs, the claimant can, before allocation, apply for judgment with costs on the amount of the claim that has been admitted (see CPR rule 14.3 but see also (paragraph 15.1(3) of the Costs Practice Direction supplementing CPR Parts 43–48 under which the court has a discretion to allow pre-allocation costs).

7.5 'THE VIEWS EXPRESSED BY THE PARTIES'

The court will treat these views as an important factor, but the allocation decision is one for the court, to be taken in the light of all the circumstances, and the court will not be bound by any agreement or common view of the parties.

7.6 'THE CIRCUMSTANCES OF THE PARTIES'

See paragraph 8.

7.7 'THE VALUE OF ANY COUNTERCLAIM OR OTHER PART 20 CLAIM'

Where the case involves more than one money claim (for example where there is a Part 20 claim or there is more than one claimant each making separate claims) the court will not generally aggregate the claims. Instead it will generally regard the largest of them as determining the financial value of the claims.

THE SMALL CLAIMS TRACK – ALLOCATION AND CASE MANAGEMENT

8.1 ALLOCATION

(1) (a) The Small Claims Track is intended to provide a proportionate procedure by which most straightforward claims with a financial value of not more than £5000 can be decided, without the need for substantial pre-hearing preparation and the formalities of a traditional trial, and without incurring large legal costs. (Rule 26.6 provides for a lower financial value in certain types of case.)
(b) The procedure laid down in Part 27 for the preparation of the case and the conduct of the hearing are designed to make it possible for a litigant to conduct his own case without legal representation if he wishes.

(c) Cases generally suitable for the small claims track will include consumer disputes, accident claims, disputes about the ownership of goods and most disputes between a landlord and tenant other than [opposed claims under Part 56, disputed claims for possession under Part 55 and demotion claims whether in the alternative to possession claims or under Part 65.

(d) A case involving a disputed allegation of dishonesty will not usually be suitable for the small claims track.

(2) Rule 26.7(3) and rule 27.14(5)

(a) These rules allow the parties to consent to the allocation to the small claims track of a claim the value of which is above the limits mentioned in Rule 26.6(2) and, in that event, the rules make provision about costs.

(b) The court will not allocate such a claim to the small claims track, notwithstanding that the parties have consented to the allocation, unless it is satisfied that it is suitable for that track.

(c) The court will not normally allow more than one day for the hearing of such a claim.

(d) The court will give case management directions to ensure that the case is dealt with in as short a time as possible. These may include directions of a kind that are not usually given in small claim cases, for example, for Scott Schedules.

8.2 CASE MANAGEMENT

(1) Directions for case management of claims allocated to the small claims track will generally be given by the court on allocation.

(2) Rule 27.4 contains further provisions about directions and the practice direction supplementing Part 27 sets out the standard directions which the court will usually give.

THE FAST TRACK

9.1 ALLOCATION

(1) Where the court is to decide whether to allocate to the fast track or the multi-track a claim for which the normal track is the fast track, it will allocate the claim to the fast track unless it believes that it cannot be dealt with justly on that track.

(2) The court will, in particular, take into account the limits likely to be placed on disclosure, the extent to which expert evidence may be necessary and whether the trial is likely to last more than a day.

(3) (a) When it is considering the likely length of the trial the court will regard a day as being a period of 5 hours, and will consider whether that is likely to be sufficient time for the case to be heard.

(b) The court will also take into account the case management directions (including the fixing of a trial timetable) that are likely to be given and the court's powers to control evidence and to limit cross-examination.

(c) The possibility that a trial might last longer than one day is not necessarily a conclusive reason for the court to allocate or to re-allocate a claim to the multi-track.

(d) A claim may be allocated to the fast track or ordered to remain on that track although there is to be a split trial.
(e) Where the case involves a counterclaim or other Part 20 claim that will be tried with the claim and as a result the trial will last more than a day, the court may not allocate it to the fast track.

9.2 CASE MANAGEMENT

(1) Directions for the case management of claims which have been allocated to the fast track will be given at the allocation stage or at the listing stage (in either case with or without a hearing) or at both, and if necessary at other times. The trial judge may, at or before the trial, give directions for its conduct.

(2) The practice direction supplementing Part 28 contains further provisions and contains standard directions which the court may give.

THE MULTI-TRACK

10.1 Paragraph 10.2 does not apply to –

(1) a claim for possession of land in the county court, or a demotion claim whether in the alternative to a possession claim or under Part 65;
(2) any claim which is being dealt with at the Royal Courts of Justice.

10.2 VENUE FOR ALLOCATION AND CASE MANAGEMENT

(1) The case management of a claim which is allocated to the multi-track will normally be dealt with at a Civil Trial Centre.

(2) In the case of a claim to which any of Parts 49 or 58–62 apply, case management must be dealt with at a Civil Trial Centre. Sub-paragraphs (4) to (10) do not apply to such a claim. The claim will be allocated to the multi-track irrespective of its value, and must be transferred to a Civil Trial Centre for allocation and case management if not already there.

(3) Where a claim is issued in or automatically transferred to a Civil Trial Centre it will be allocated and managed at that Court.

(4) The following *sub-paragraphs* apply to a claim which is issued in or automatically transferred to a Court which is not a Civil Trial Centre. Such a Court is referred to as a 'feeder court'.

(5) Where a judge sitting at a feeder court decides, on the basis of the allocation questionnaires and any other documents filed by the parties, that the claim should be dealt with on the multi-track he will normally make an order:

(a) allocating the claim to that track,
(b) giving case management directions, and
(c) transferring the claim to a Civil Trial Centre.

(6) If he decides that an allocation hearing or some pre-allocation hearing is to take place (for example to strike out a statement of case under Part 3 of the Rules) that hearing will take place at the feeder court.

(7) If, before allocation, a hearing takes place at a feeder court and in exercising his powers under paragraph 2.4(1) above the judge allocates the claim to the multi-track, he will also normally make an order transferring the claim to a Civil Trial Centre.

(8) A judge sitting at a feeder court may, rather than making an allocation order himself, transfer the claim to a Civil Trial Centre for the decision about allocation to be taken there.

(9) When, following an order for transfer, the file is received at the Civil Trial Centre, a judge sitting at that Centre will consider it and give any further directions that appear necessary or desirable.

(10) Where there is reason to believe that more than one case management conference may be needed and the parties and their legal advisers are located inconveniently far from the Civil Trial Centre, a judge sitting at a feeder court may, with the agreement of the designated civil judge and notwithstanding the allocation of the case to the multi-track, decide that in the particular circumstances of the case it should not be transferred to a Civil Trial Centre, but should be case managed for the time being at the feeder court.

(11) A designated civil judge may at any time make an order transferring a claim from a feeder court to a Civil Trial Centre and he may do so irrespective of the track, if any, to which it has been allocated. He may also permit a feeder court to keep for trial a claim or (subject to review from time to time) a category of claims. Any such permission should take into account the ability of the feeder court in relation to the Civil Trial Centre to provide suitable and effective trial within an appropriate trial period.

(12) No order will be made by a feeder court fixing a date for a hearing at a Civil Trial Centre unless that date has been given or confirmed by a judge or listing officer of that Centre.

'Parts 49 or 58–62 apply' (para 10.2(2))—This provision has been amended with effect from 2 December 2002 so as to add Commercial, Mercantile, TCC, Admiralty and Arbitration proceedings – these are governed by CPR Pts 58–62 – to the existing specialist proceedings, to which Pt 49 applies.

'transferring the claim to a Civil Trial Centre' (para 10.2(5)(c))—The practice of requiring multi-track cases to be transferred automatically from feeder courts to Civil Trial Centres has been relaxed. Many more cases (estimated to take up to 2 days) are being retained by feeder courts for either or both case management directions and trial. The practice is dependent on the feeder court's resources and local arrangements with the Trial Centre: it is necessary to check.

Defended possession actions—A defended county court claim for possession of land allocated to the multi-track will not now normally be transferred to the Civil Trial Centre. This amendment was introduced by Update 9.

General power for feeder courts to retain certain categories of claim (para 10.2(11))—With effect from 2 October 2000, a designated civil judge may permit a feeder court to keep for trial a claim or (subject to review from time to time) a category of claims. Any such permission should take into account the ability of the feeder court in relation to the Civil Trial Centre to provide a suitable and effective trial within an appropriate trial period.

10.3 CASE MANAGEMENT

Part 29 of the Rules and the practice direction supplementing that Part set out the procedure to be adopted.

RE-ALLOCATION OF CLAIMS AND THE VARIATION OF DIRECTIONS

11.1(1) Where a party is dissatisfied with an order made allocating the claim to a track he may appeal or apply to the court to re-allocate the claim.

(2) He should appeal if the order was made at a hearing at which he was present or represented, or of which he was given due notice.

(3) In any other case he should apply to the court to re-allocate the claim.

11.2 Where there has been a change in the circumstances since an order was made allocating the claim to a track the court may re-allocate the claim. It may do so on application or on its own initiative.

The practice directions supplementing Parts 28 and 29 contain provisions about the variation of case management directions.

DETERMINING THE AMOUNT TO BE PAID UNDER A JUDGMENT OR ORDER

General note—Paragraph 12 of PD26, creates a new procedure, a disposal hearing, enabling the court to determine the amount payable under a judgment for an amount of money which is not specified. Straightforward, or unopposed, cases can be listed for a disposal hearing (PD26, para 12.8). More complex or disputed cases will be allocated to track. See Guide 31 (Deciding the Amount Payable under a Judgment).

The practice direction has now been extensively revised by amendment with effect from 2 December 2002. The new provisions include –

(1) A disposal hearing is not appropriate:
- (a) in claims, if defended, that would normally be allocated to the small claims track (para 12.3(1)); or
- (b) where the amount payable appears to be genuinely disputed on substantial grounds (para 12.3(2)).

(2) A disposal hearing is appropriate:
- (a) where the hearing will not normally last longer than 30 minutes;
- (b) where oral evidence is not to be received.

12.1 SCOPE

(1) In the following paragraphs –
- (a) a 'relevant order' means a judgment or order of the court which requires the amount of money to be paid by one party to another to be decided by the court; and
- (b) a 'disposal hearing' means a hearing in accordance with paragraph 12.4.

(2) A relevant order may have been obtained:
- (a) by a judgment in default under Part 12;
- (b) by a judgment on an admission under Part 14;
- (c) on the striking out of a statement of case under Part 3;
- (d) on a summary judgment application under Part 24;
- (e) on the determination of a preliminary issue or on a trial as to liability; or
- (f) at trial.

(3) A relevant order includes any order for the amount of a debt, damages or interest to be decided by the court (including an order for the taking of an account or the making of an inquiry as to any sum due, and any similar order), but does not include an order for the assessment of costs.

'an order for the taking of an account' (para 12.1(3))—See PD40 (Accounts, Inquiries etc) for provisions relating to the taking of accounts under a judgment or order.

12.2 DIRECTIONS

(1) When the court makes a relevant order it will give directions, which may include –
- (a) listing the claim for a disposal hearing;

(b) allocating or re-allocating the claim (but see paragraph 12.3);
(c) directing the parties to file allocation questionnaires by a specified date; and
(d) staying the claim while the parties try to settle the case by alternative dispute resolution or other means.

(2) Directions may specify the level or type of judge before whom a hearing or a further hearing will take place and the nature and purpose of that hearing.

(3) Where the parties apply for a relevant order by consent, they should if possible file with their draft consent order agreed directions for the court's approval.

'the parties ... should ... file ... agreed directions for the court's approval' (para 12.2(3))—It is all too common to see complex consent directions in heavily defended quantum or causation cases leading to a 'disposal hearing'. Note that the court will not approve such orders unless the issues are straightforward and capable of being resolved at a hearing normally lasting no longer than 30 minutes.

12.3 ALLOCATION

(1) If, when the court makes a relevant order –

(a) the claim has not previously been allocated to a track; and
(b) the financial value of the claim (determined in accordance with Part 26) is such that the claim would, if defended be allocated to the small claims track,

the court will normally allocate it to that track.

(2) Where paragraph (1)(b) does not apply, the court will not normally allocate the claim to a track (other than the small claims track) unless –

(a) the amount payable appears to be genuinely disputed on substantial grounds; or
(b) the dispute is not suitable to be dealt with at a disposal hearing.

12.4 DISPOSAL HEARINGS

(1) A disposal hearing is a hearing –

(a) which will not normally last longer than 30 minutes, and
(b) at which the court will not normally hear oral evidence.

(2) At a disposal hearing the court may –

(a) decide the amount payable under or in consequence of the relevant order and give judgment for that amount; or
(b) give directions as to the future conduct of the proceedings.

(3) If the claim has been allocated to the small claims track, or the court decides at the disposal hearing to allocate it to that track, the court may treat the disposal hearing as a final hearing in accordance with Part 27.

(4) Rule 32.6 applies to evidence at a disposal hearing unless the court directs otherwise.

(5) Except where the claim has been allocated to the small claims track, the court will not exercise its power under sub-paragraph (2)(a) unless any written evidence on which the claimant relies has been served on the defendant at least 3 days before the disposal hearing.

'the court will not normally hear oral evidence' (para 12.4(1)(b))—There are important differences between a disposal hearing and a hearing following allocation to track. Unless the judge allocates the matter to a track, evidence is not given orally but by witness statement. A party giving evidence cannot give oral evidence without a direction under para 12.4(4). Thus, a party wishing to cross-examine a witness at a disposal hearing must first apply to the court for a direction to that effect. Once a claim is allocated to a track the hearing will not proceed as a disposal hearing but a trial will be directed, para 12.4(1) will no longer apply and evidence must be given orally in accordance with CPR r 32.2(1)(a).

12.5 COSTS

(1) Attention is drawn to –

- (a) the costs practice direction and in particular to the court's power to make a summary assessment of costs;
- (b) rule 44.13(1) which provides that if an order makes no mention of costs, none are payable in respect of the proceedings to which it relates; and
- (c) rule 27.14 (special rules about costs in cases allocated to the small claims track).

(2) Part 46 (fast track trial costs) will not apply to a case dealt with at a disposal hearing whatever the financial value of the claim. So the costs of a disposal hearing will be in the discretion of the court.

'the costs of a disposal hearing will be in the discretion of the court' (para 12.5(2))—Paragraph 12.5(2) makes it clear that, whatever the value of the case might be, costs are in the court's discretion and not fixed under CPR Pt 46. However, if the court chooses to allocate the matter to the fast track, the Pt 46 costs regime is no longer excluded. Conversely, if the court decides the matter without allocating the claim to the small claims track under para 12.3(1), it must also follow that CPR r 27.14 does not apply the limited small claims costs regime.

12.6 JURISDICTION OF MASTERS AND DISTRICT JUDGES

Unless the court otherwise directs, a Master or a district judge may decide the amount payable under a relevant order irrespective of the financial value of the claim and of the track to which the claim may have been allocated.

Substantial personal injury claims—Where a personal injury claim involves substantial and complex issues on damages, it is not normally appropriate for a district judge to assess damages (*Sandry v Jones* (2000) *The Times*, 3 August, CA).

Appeals from masters and district judges—See &*Tanfern v Cameron-MacDonald & ors* [2000] 1 WLR 1311, [2000] 2 All ER 801, CA for guidance on appeals from district judges trying multi-track cases.

Practice Direction – Pilot Scheme for Mediation in Central London County Court

This Practice Direction supplements CPR Part 26 (PD26B)

GENERAL

1.1 This practice direction provides for a pilot scheme to operate from 1 April 2004 to 31 March 2005 in relation to claims in the Central London County Court.

1.2 This practice direction enables the Central London County Court to –

(1) require the parties to certain types of claims either to attend a mediation appointment or to give reasons for objecting to doing so; and
(2) stay the claim until such an appointment takes place.

1.3 Cases in which a notice of referral to mediation has been served under paragraph 3.1 prior to 31 March 2005 shall remain subject to this practice direction until either –

(1) a mediation appointment has taken place; or
(2) any stay of execution imposed under paragraph 5 has expired or been lifted by the court,

whichever shall be the sooner.

TYPES OF CLAIMS TO WHICH THIS PRACTICE DIRECTION APPLIES

2 This practice direction applies to a claim if it meets all the following conditions –

(1) the small claims track is not the normal track for the claim;
(2) no party to the claim is –
 (a) a child or patient; or
 (b) exempt from payment of court fees; and
(3) the court has not granted an interim injunction in the proceedings.

SERVICE OF MEDIATION NOTICE

3.1 The court may, when it serves the allocation questionnaire under rule 26.3, serve a notice of referral to mediation on each party –

(1) notifying them that the claim is to be referred to mediation; and
(2) requiring them, within 14 days after service of the notice on them, to file and serve a reply to the notice in which they must –
 (a) state whether they agree or object to mediation;
 (b) specify any dates within 3 months of the date of filing the response on which they would not be able to attend a mediation appointment; and
 (c) if they object to mediation, set out their reasons for doing so.

3.2 The cases where a notice of referral to mediation is served on the parties will be chosen at random from those that meet the criteria set out in paragraph 2.

3.3 A party who receives a notice of referral to mediation need not complete and file an allocation questionnaire unless or until directed to do so by the court.

OBJECTION TO MEDIATION

4.1 If one or more of the parties states in his reply that he objects to mediation, the case will be referred to a district judge who may –

(1) direct the case to be listed for a hearing of the objections to mediation;
(2) direct that a mediation appointment should proceed;
(3) order the parties to file and serve completed allocation questionnaires; or
(4) give such directions as to the management of the case as he considers appropriate.

4.2 If a party does not file a reply within the time specified in the notice of referral to mediation, the court and all other parties may proceed as if that party has no objection to the use of mediation in the case.

MEDIATION APPOINTMENT

5.1 If no party objects to mediation, or the court directs that mediation should proceed, the court will direct that the proceedings be stayed for an initial period of 2 months.

5.2 In accordance with the existing Central London County Court Mediation Scheme, the court will fix a date, time and place for the mediation appointment and notify the parties accordingly once all the parties have paid the mediator's charges.

5.3 When the court fixes a mediation appointment it will if necessary extend the stay of proceedings until the date of the appointment.

MEDIATOR'S CHARGES

6.1 A mediator's charge is payable by each party who is to attend a mediation appointment. The court will notify each party of the amount of the charge and request payment of that amount in the notice of referral to mediation.

6.2 A party must pay the mediator's charge to the court within 14 days of being requested to do so or such other period as the court may direct. Any request for further time in which to pay the mediator's charge may be made by letter.

6.3 If any party fails to pay the mediator's charge the court will refer the case to a district judge for directions.

UNSUCCESSFUL MEDIATION

7 If the mediation does not proceed or does not fully resolve the dispute, the mediator will notify the court and the court will –

- (1) either –
  - (a) allocate the claim to a track; or
  - (b) order the parties to file and serve completed allocation questionnaires (if not already filed); and
- (2) give such directions for the further management of the case as it considers appropriate.

PART 27
THE SMALL CLAIMS TRACK

CONTENTS OF THIS PART

Procedural Guide—See Guide 12, set out in Section 1 of this work.

27.1 Scope of this Part

(1) This Part –

(a) sets out the special procedure for dealing with claims which have been allocated to the small claims track under Part 26; and

(b) limits the amount of costs that can be recovered in respect of a claim which has been allocated to the small claims track.

(Rule 27.14 deals with costs on the small claims track)

(2) A claim being dealt with under this Part is called a small claim.

(Rule 26.6 provides for the scope of the small claims track. A claim for a remedy for harassment or unlawful eviction relating, in either case, to residential premises shall not be allocated to the small claims track whatever the financial value of the claim. Otherwise, the small claims track will be the normal track for –

– any claim which has a financial value of not more than £5000 subject to the special provisions about claims for personal injuries and housing disrepair claims;

– any claim for personal injuries which has a financial value of not more than £5000 where the claim for damages for personal injuries is not more than £1000; and

– any claim which includes a claim by a tenant of residential premises against his landlord for repairs or other work to the premises where the estimated cost of the repairs or other work is not more than £1000 and the financial value of any claim for damages in respect of those repairs or other work is not more than £1000)

Practice Direction—See generally PD27 at p 765.

Scope of provision—The term 'arbitration' is no longer used. The financial limit is £5000, with exceptions for personal injury and residential landlord and tenant repair claims. Summary judgment may now be applied for and proceedings will usually be recorded. Provision is made for 'paper disposal' of claims. The grounds for appeal are now the same as for any other final judgment (see

Pt 52). The practice direction provides for specialised directions in particular types of case (PD27, App A). Generally, small claims will be dealt with by the district judge but the functions may be carried out by the circuit judge (PD27, para 1) – this will, however, affect the route of any appeal (see note **'Avenues of appeal'** to r 52.1). Where a case involves fraud it is probably not suitable for the small claims track, even where the amount is within the limit, as a full hearing is more appropriate together with a proper award of costs (*Geoffrey Arnold Wheen v Smithmann European Homes & anor* (2000) Lawtel, 25 September, CA).

'Rule 26.6'—See the notes to that rule.

Financial value of claim (r 27.1(2))—The decision as to the value of the claim is that of the court (r 26.7). Any dispute will be resolved by the court prior to allocation, as it will affect the allocation of the case to track. The intentional overstatement of the amount involved to avoid the claim being referred to the small claims track is a clear abuse of process and may lead to sanctions under Pt 3 (The Court's Case Management Powers) (*Afzal v Ford Motor Co Ltd* [1994] 4 All ER 720, CA). A judge has discretion to keep a claim within the small claims track even if the counterclaim exceeds the limit (r 26.8(1)(e) and *Berridge (Paul) (t/a EAB Builders) v RM Bayliss* (1999) Lawtel, 23 November, CA).

Counterclaim—The financial value for tracking purposes is that of the claim, not the counterclaim. A judge has discretion to keep a matter within the small claims track even if the counterclaim exceeds the limit (*Berridge (Paul) (t/a EAB Builders) v RM Bayliss* (1999) Lawtel, 23 November, CA).

'personal injuries' (r 27.1(2))—'claim for personal injuries' means proceedings in which there is a claim for damages in respect of personal injuries to the claimant or any other person or in respect of a person's death, and 'personal injuries' includes any disease and any impairment of a person's physical or mental condition' (r 2.3(1)). This covers pain, suffering and loss of amenity only – not pecuniary loss (r 26.6(2)).

Residential repairs—If after issue of proceedings but before allocation the landlord carries out repairs which reduce the amount of damages below £1000 this will have the effect of bringing the claim within the small claims track.

Disposal hearings—Under PD26, para 12 the court now has power to allocate proceedings to decide the amount payable under a judgment (now known as a 'disposal hearing') to the small claims track if the financial value of the claim is such that the claim would, if defended, have been allocated to that track. Rule 27.14 below, limiting the court's power to award costs, will then apply.

27.2 Extent to which other Parts apply

(1) The following Parts of these Rules do not apply to small claims –

- (a) Part 25 (interim remedies) except as it relates to interim injunctions(GL);
- (b) Part 31 (disclosure and inspection);
- (c) Part 32 (evidence) except rule 32.1 (power of court to control evidence);
- (d) Part 33 (miscellaneous rules about evidence);
- (e) Part 35 (experts and assessors) except rules 35.1 (duty to restrict expert evidence), 35.3 (experts – overriding duty to the court), 35.7 (court's power to direct that evidence is to be given by single joint expert) and 35.8 (instructions to a single joint expert);
- (f) Subject to paragraph (3), Part 18 (further information);
- (g) Part 36 (offers to settle and payments into court);
- (h) Part 39 (hearings) except rule 39.2 (general rule – hearing to be in public).

(2) The other Parts of these Rules apply to small claims except to the extent that a rule limits such application.

(3) The court of its own initiative may order a party to provide further information if it considers it appropriate to do so.

Amendments—SI 2000/221; SI 2005/2292.

Practice Direction—See generally PD27 at p 765.

Scope of provision—It is only after the case has been allocated to the small claims track that the above provisions do not apply.

Summary judgment—In contrast to the old rules, summary judgment is now available in small claims as it is not one of the provisions excluded by r 27.2. Further, there is power to for the court to grant summary judgment by r 27.6(1)(b) below.

Joint expert (r 27.2(1)(e))—The court's power to direct that evidence be given by a single joint expert (r 35.7) has been added by Civil Procedure (Amendment) Rules 2000, r 15; this resolves the conflict with Form F appended to PD27 (sample 'special directions') which provides for evidence to be given by a single joint expert whereas the previous provisions seemed to exclude it.

27.3 Court's power to grant a final remedy

The court may grant any final remedy in relation to a small claim which it could grant if the proceedings were on the fast track or the multi-track.

Practice Direction—See generally PD27 at p 765.

'final remedy'—This includes, for example, orders for specific performance and injunctions (*Joyce v Liverpool City Corporation; Wynne v Liverpool City Corporation* [1995] 3 All ER 110, CA).

27.4 Preparation for the hearing

(1) After allocation the court will –

- (a) give standard directions and fix a date for the final hearing;
- (b) give special directions and fix a date for the final hearing;
- (c) give special directions and direct that the court will consider what further directions are to be given no later that 28 days after the date the special directions were given;
- (d) fix a date for a preliminary hearing under rule 27.6; or
- (e) give notice that it proposes to deal with the claim without a hearing under rule 27.10 and invite the parties to notify the court by a specified date if they agree the proposal.

(2) The court will –

- (a) give the parties at least 21 days' notice of the date fixed for the final hearing, unless the parties agree to accept less notice; and
- (b) inform them of the amount of time allowed for the final hearing.

(3) In this rule –

- (a) 'standard directions' means –
  - (i) a direction that each party shall, at least 14 days before the date fixed for the final hearing, file and serve on every other party copies of all documents (including any expert's report) on which he intends to rely at the hearing; and
  - (ii) any other standard directions set out in the relevant practice direction; and
- (b) 'special directions' means directions given in addition to or instead of the standard directions.

Practice Direction—See generally PD27 at p 765.

'standard directions' (r 27.4(3)(b))—Appendix A of PD27 contains not only a form of general standard directions (Form A) but also standard directions for use in claims arising out of road accidents (Form B), claims arising out of building disputes, vehicle repairs and similar contractual claims (Form C), tenants' claims for the return of deposits/landlords' claims for damage caused (Form D) and holiday and wedding claims (Form E). Further particular directions may be made from time to time by practice direction.

'without a hearing under rule 27.10' (r 27.4(1)(e))—Rule 27.10 permits a 'paper disposal' of the case without requiring the attendance of the parties. Such a step requires the consent of all parties.

27.5 Experts

No expert may give evidence, whether written or oral, at a hearing without the permission of the court.

(Rule 27.14(3)(d) provides for the payment of an expert's fees)

Practice Direction—See generally PD27 at p 765.

Experts—This provision, which is virtually identical to r 35.4(1), echoes the spirit of Pt 35 notwithstanding that this Part is largely excluded from the small claims track by r 27.2 above.

27.6 Preliminary hearing

(1) The court may hold a preliminary hearing for the consideration of the claim, but only –

- (a) where –
  - (i) it considers that special directions, as defined in rule 27.4, are needed to ensure a fair hearing; and
  - (ii) it appears necessary for a party to attend at court to ensure that he understands what he must do to comply with the special directions; or
- (b) to enable it to dispose of the claim on the basis that one or other of the parties has no real prospect of success at a final hearing; or
- (c) to enable it to strike out[(GL)] a statement of case or part of a statement of case on the basis that the statement of case, or the part to be struck out, discloses no reasonable grounds for bringing or defending the claim.

(2) When considering whether or not to hold a preliminary hearing, the court must have regard to the desirability of limiting the expense to the parties of attending court.

(3) Where the court decides to hold a preliminary hearing, it will give the parties at least 14 days' notice of the date of the hearing.

(4) The court may treat the preliminary hearing as the final hearing of the claim if all the parties agree.

(5) At or after the preliminary hearing the court will –

- (a) fix the date of the final hearing (if it has not been fixed already) and give the parties at least 21 days' notice of the date fixed unless the parties agree to accept less notice;
- (b) inform them of the amount of time allowed for the final hearing; and
- (c) give any appropriate directions.

Practice Direction—See generally PD27 at p 765.

Summary judgment and disposal—Rule 27.6(1)(b) enables the court to award the equivalent of summary judgment (see Pt 24) and similar considerations will apply. Rule 27.6(1)(c) enables the court to exercise case management powers similar to those contained in r 3.4.

27.7 Power of court to add to, vary or revoke directions

The court may add to, vary or revoke directions.

Practice Direction—See generally PD27 at p 765.

27.8 Conduct of the hearing

(1) The court may adopt any method of proceeding at a hearing that it considers to be fair.

(2) Hearings will be informal.

(3) The strict rules of evidence do not apply.

(4) The court need not take evidence on oath.

(5) The court may limit cross-examination(GL).

(6) The court must give reasons for its decision.

Practice Direction—See generally PD27 at p 765.

Representation at hearing—Paragraph 3 of the PD27 contains details of who may present small claims hearings. Basically it will be the parties, a legal representative or a lay representative but in the latter case only if the 'client' is also present. A corporate party may use its officers or employees as its representative or a lay representative who is neither (*Avinue Ltd v Sunrule Ltd* [2003] TLR 677, (2003) All ER (D) 392 (Nov), CA).

The hearing—In contrast to the former position, this will be in public unless the judge orders otherwise (PD27, para 4.1).

Evidence—Paragraph 4.3 of the PD27 gives further details of the extent of the power of the court to adopt any method of proceeding that it considers to be fair including limiting cross-examination. This provision coupled with r 27.8(5) has the effect of overturning the decision in *Chilton v Saga Holidays plc* [1986] 1 All ER, CA.

Recording evidence and decision—Paragraph 5.1 of PD27 provides that the judge may direct proceedings to be tape recorded and district judges' chambers have been provided with equipment to enable them to do so. In any event the judge is required by PD27, para 5.4 to make a note of the central reasons for his judgment unless it is tape recorded (see also PD39, para 6.1). The parties will be entitled to a copy of the transcript of any recording or note of reasons on payment of a charge (PD27,). However, where there is an appeal different provisions apply. See note **'Appeals'** under r 27.11 below. In any event, where there is a 'paper disposal' under r 27.10 below or a party has given notice of non-attendance in accordance with r 27.9 below, a copy of the judge's reasons will be sent by the court to the parties (PD27, para 5.4)

27.9 Non-attendance of parties at a final hearing

(1) If a party who does not attend a final hearing –

- (a) has given written notice to the court and the other party at least 7 days before the hearing date that he will not attend;
- (b) has served on the other party at least 7 days before the hearing date any other documents which he has filed with the court; and
- (c) has, in his written notice, requested the court to decide the claim in his absence and has confirmed his compliance with paragraphs (a) and (b) above,

the court will take into account that party's statement of case and any other documents he has filed and served when it decides the claim.

(2) If a claimant does not –

- (a) attend the hearing; and
- (b) give the notice referred to in paragraph (1),

the court may strike out(GL) the claim.

(3) If –

- (a) a defendant does not –
  - (i) attend the hearing; or
  - (ii) give the notice referred to in paragraph (1); and

(b) the claimant either –
  (i) does attend the hearing; or
  (ii) gives the notice referred to in paragraph (1),

the court may decide the claim on the basis of the evidence of the claimant alone.

(4) If neither party attends or gives the notice referred to in paragraph (1), the court may strike out(GL) the claim and any defence and counterclaim.

Amendments—SI 2005/2292.

Practice Direction—See generally PD27 at p 765.

Adjournment—Nothing in this provision prevents the court from adjourning a hearing where one of the parties has a good reason for not being able to attend on the fixed date (PD27, para 6.2).

27.10 Disposal without a hearing

The court may, if all parties agree, deal with the claim without a hearing.

Practice Direction—See generally PD27 at p 765.

Reasons for decision—See notes to r 27.8 above.

27.11 Setting judgment aside and re-hearing

(1) A party –

  (a) who was neither present nor represented at the hearing of the claim; and
  (b) who has not given written notice to the court under rule 27.9(1),

may apply for an order that a judgment under this Part shall be set aside(GL) and the claim re-heard.

(2) A party who applies for an order setting aside a judgment under this rule must make the application not more than 14 days after the day on which notice of the judgment was served on him.

(3) The court may grant an application under paragraph (2) only if the applicant –

  (a) had a good reason for not attending or being represented at the hearing or giving written notice to the court under rule 27.9(1); and
  (b) has a reasonable prospect of success at the hearing.

(4) If a judgment is set aside(GL) –

  (a) the court must fix a new hearing for the claim; and
  (b) the hearing may take place immediately after the hearing of the application to set the judgment aside and may be dealt with by the judge who set aside(GL) the judgment.

(5) A party may not apply to set aside(GL) a judgment under this rule if the court dealt with the claim without a hearing under rule 27.10.

Practice Direction—See generally PD27 at p 765.

Scope of provision—This is not to be confused with the previous 'setting award aside' which was the equivalent of an appeal under the former rules. Note that not only does the applicant have to give a good reason for not being present at the hearing or giving proper notice under r 27.9(1) but he must also show that he has a reasonable prospect of success, as to which see Pt 24 (Summary Judgment) and the practice direction thereto. This provision is not available to set aside a 'paper disposal' under r 27.10 (r 27.11(5)). If the court does set aside the judgment, it may immediately rehear the small claim (r 27.11(4)(b)), presumably if there is time to do so.

Appeals—Applications under this rule must be distinguished from appeals, which are dealt with by Pt 52.

There, the general procedure is slightly modified for small claim appeals in that the appellant needs to file a record of the reasons for the judgment of the lower court (usually a transcript for which a charge is made) with the notice of appeal only if the court orders it. This is to enable the court to decide if permission to appeal should be granted or, if permission is granted, to enable it to decide the appeal (PD52, paras 5.8C and 5.8D).

27.12

(*revoked*)

27.13

(*revoked*)

27.14 Costs on the small claims track

(1) This rule applies to any case which has been allocated to the small claims track unless paragraph (5) applies.

(Rules 44.9 and 44.11 make provision in relation to orders for costs made before a claim has been allocated to the small claims track)

(2) The court may not order a party to pay a sum to another party in respect of that other party's costs except –

- (a) the fixed costs attributable to issuing the claim which –
  - (i) are payable under Part 45; or
  - (ii) would be payable under Part 45 if that Part applied to the claim;]
- (b) in proceedings which included a claim for an injunction[(GL)] or an order for specific performance a sum not exceeding the amount specified in the relevant practice direction for legal advice and assistance relating to that claim;
- (c) costs assessed by the summary procedure in relation to an appeal; and
- (d) such further costs as the court may assess by the summary procedure and order to be paid by a party who has behaved unreasonably.

(2A) A party's rejection of an offer in settlement will not of itself constitute unreasonable behaviour under paragraph (2)(d) but the court may take it into consideration when it is applying the unreasonableness test.

(Rule 36.2(5) allows the court to order Part 36 costs consequences in a small claim).

(3) The court may also order a party to pay all or part of –

- (a) any court fees paid by another party;
- (b) expenses which a party or witness has reasonably incurred in travelling to and from a hearing or in staying away from home for the purposes of attending a hearing;
- (c) a sum not exceeding the amount specified in the relevant practice direction for any loss of earnings or loss of leave by a party or witness due to attending a hearing or to staying away from home for the purpose of attending a hearing; and
- (d) a sum not exceeding the amount specified in the relevant practice direction for an expert's fees.

(4) The limits on costs imposed by this rule also apply to any fee or reward for acting on behalf of a party to the proceedings charged by a person exercising a right of audience by virtue of an order under section 11 of the Courts and Legal Services Act 1990 (a lay representative).

(5) Where –

- (a) the financial value of a claim exceeds the limit for the small claims track; but
- (b) the claim has been allocated to the small claims track in accordance with rule 26.7(3),

the small claims track costs provisions will apply unless the parties agree that the fast track costs provisions are to apply.

(6) Where the parties agree that the fast track costs provisions are to apply, the claim will be treated for the purposes of costs as if it were proceeding on the fast track except that trial costs will be in the discretion of the court and will not exceed the amount set out for the value of claim in rule 46.2 (amount of fast track trial costs).

Amendments—SI 1999/1008; SI 2000/2092; SI 2005/2292.

Practice Direction—See generally PD27 at p 765.

Costs prior to allocation—The limitation on costs recoverable in small claims matters applies both before and after the matter is allocated to the small claims track unless the court or a practice direction provides otherwise (r 44.9(2)). But note r 44.11(1) – 'Any costs orders made before a claim is allocated will not be affected by allocation'.

'legal advice and assistance' (r 27.14(2)(b))—The maximum is £260 (PD27, para 7.2). Note that it is limited to cases involving injunctions or specific performance only.

Unreasonable behaviour (r 27.14(2)(d))—There is no guidance either in the rules or practice directions as to what amounts to 'unreasonable behaviour'. It might well include making unnecessary applications, refusing to negotiate, failure to comply with pre-action protocols, deliberately mis-stating the value of a claim or failing to attend court. In *Taylor v Ashworth* (1978) 129 NLJ 737, CA, a last-minute decision by a defendant not to proceed with his defence was held to be unreasonable behaviour as was the overstatement of the amount of damages claimed and the raising of a speculative and unsupportable defence in *Afzal v Ford Motor Co Ltd* [1994] 4 All ER 720, CA.

'loss of earnings' (r 27.14(2)(c))—The maximum amount for loss of earnings is £50 per day for each person PD27, para 7.3). The judge may apportion the amount ordered in relation to the length of the hearing. The principle of 'proportionality' would appear to support this.

Expert's fees—The maximum amount is £200 for each expert (PD27, para 7.3). The standard form of directions sent out by the court does not contain a note as to the limit on expert's fees. If the maximum is exceeded it may not be recoverable. Some courts are making this clear in their directions.

Lay representative's fees—Although reference to these is made in r 27.14(4) there is no guidance as to what sums should be allowed.

Small claims costs in unallocated cases—A previous omission to allocate to track does not prevent the court from considering whether it was reasonable to make an assessment in accordance with the small claims costs regime, or to apply the regime to a claim which never was anything more than a small claim (*Voice and Script International Ltd v Alghafar* [2003] EWCA Civ 736).

A party whose personal claim was settled for less than £1000 was entitled to have his costs assessed on the standard basis if the claim, if defended, would have been allocated to either the fast or multi-track due to the extent of technical and medical evidence required, and the defendants had acted unreasonably in dealing with the claim (*(1) Linda Woodings (2) Pauline Abdalla (3) Lesley Noakes (4) Ranjit Kaur Singh (5) Kathleen Riley v British Telecommunications plc* (2003) Lawtel, 17 March (Mayor's & City of London Cty Ct), Marr-Johnson J).

27.15 Claim re-allocated from the small claims track to another track

Where a claim is allocated to the small claims track and subsequently re-allocated to another track, rule 27.14 (costs on the small claims track) will cease to apply after the claim has been re-allocated, and the fast track or multi-track costs rules will apply from the date of re-allocation.

Practice Direction—See generally PD27 at p 765.

Practice Direction – Small Claims Track

This Practice Direction supplements CPR Part 27 (PD27)

Procedural Guide—See Guide 12, set out in Section 1 of this work.

JUDGES

1 The functions of the court described in Part 27 which are to be carried out by a judge will generally be carried out by a district judge but may be carried out by a circuit judge.

CASE MANAGEMENT DIRECTIONS

2.1 Rule 27.4 explains how directions will be given, and rule 27.6 contains provisions about the holding of a preliminary hearing and the court's powers at such a hearing.

2.2 Appendix A sets out details of the case that the court usually needs in the type of case described. Appendix B sets out the Standard Directions that the court may give. Appendix C sets out Special Directions that the court may give.

2.3 Before allocating the claim to the Small Claims Track and giving directions for a hearing the court may require a party to give further information about that party's case.

2.4 A party may ask the court to give particular directions about the conduct of the case.

2.5 In deciding whether to make an order for exchange of witness statements the court will have regard to the following –

(a) whether either or both the parties are represented;
(b) the amount in dispute in the proceedings;
(c) the nature of the matters in dispute;
(d) whether the need for any party to clarify his case can better be dealt with by an order under paragraph 2.3;
(e) the need for the parties to have access to justice without undue formality, cost or delay.

Standard directions (para 2.2)—These are directions suitable for particular cases such as road traffic accidents, building disputes, return of tenant's deposit, holiday and wedding claims as well as some other helpful directions to be used at the discretion of the judge. More are likely to be added in the future. The court may refuse to consider evidence not presented in accordance with the directions. The parties are required to let the court know immediately if the case settles before the hearing date.

REPRESENTATION AT A HEARING

3.1 In this paragraph:

(1) a lawyer means a barrister, a solicitor or a legal executive employed by a solicitor, and

(2) a lay representative means any other person.

3.2 (1) A party may present his own case at a hearing or a lawyer or lay representative may present it for him.

(2) The Lay Representatives (Right of Audience) Order 1999 provides that a lay representative may not exercise any right of audience –

(a) where his client does not attend the hearing;

(b) at any stage after judgment; or

(c) on any appeal brought against the decision made by the district judge in the proceedings.

(3) However the court, exercising its general discretion to hear anybody, may hear a lay representative even in circumstances excluded by this Order.

(4) Any of its officers or employees may represent a corporate party.

'corporate party' (para 3.2(4))—A lay representative is entitled to represent a corporate party in small claims proceedings, notwithstanding he is not an officer or employee of the company (*Avinue Ltd v Sunrule Ltd* [2003] TLR 677, (2003) All ER (D) 392 (Nov), CA).

SMALL CLAIM HEARINGS

4.1 (1) The general rule is that a small claim hearing will be in public.

(2) The judge may decide to hold it in private if:

(a) the parties agree, or

(b) a ground mentioned in rule 39.2(3) applies.

(3) A hearing or part of a hearing which takes place other than at the court, for example at the home or business premises of a party, will not be in public.

4.2 A hearing that takes place at the court will generally be in the judge's room but it may take place in a courtroom.

4.3 Rule 27.8 allows the court to adopt any method of proceeding that it considers to be fair and to limit cross-examination. The judge may in particular:

(1) ask questions of any witness himself before allowing any other person to do so,

(2) ask questions of all or any of the witnesses himself before allowing any other person to ask questions of any witnesses,

(3) refuse to allow cross-examination of any witness until all the witnesses have given evidence in chief,

(4) limit cross-examination of a witness to a fixed time or to a particular subject or issue, or both.

'any method of proceeding' (para 4.3)—This gives the judge very wide power as to the conduct of proceedings and includes an interventionist approach where the judge does most of the questioning of witnesses himself. The normal rules as to evidence do not apply (CPR r 27.2(1)(c)).

RECORDING EVIDENCE AND THE GIVING OF REASONS

5.1 A hearing that takes place at the court will be tape recorded by the court. A party may obtain a transcript of such a recording on payment of the proper transcriber's charges.

5.2 Attention is drawn to section 9 of the Contempt of Court Act 1981 (which deals with the unauthorised use of tape recorders in court) and to the Practice Direction ([1981] 1 WLR 1526) which relates to it.

5.3 (1) The judge may give reasons for his judgment as briefly and simply as the nature of the case allows.

(2) He will normally do so orally at the hearing, but he may give them later at a hearing either orally or in writing.

5.4 Where the judge decides the case without a hearing under rule 27.10 or a party who has given notice under rule 27.9(1) does not attend the hearing, the judge will prepare a note of his reasons and the court will send a copy to each party.

5.5 Nothing in this practice direction affects the duty of a judge at the request of a party to make a note of the matters referred to in section 80 of the County Courts Act 1984.

'section 80 County Courts Act 1984' (para 5.5)—This section requires a note to be made at the hearing, if a party so requests, of any question of law raised at the hearing; facts in evidence on that question; the judge's decision on that question and his determination of the proceedings.

NON-ATTENDANCE OF A PARTY AT A HEARING

6.1 Attention is drawn to rule 27.9 (which enables a party to give notice that he will not attend a final hearing and sets out the effect of his giving such notice and of not doing so), and to paragraph 3 above.

6.2 Nothing in those provisions affects the general power of the court to adjourn a hearing, for example where a party who wishes to attend a hearing on the date fixed cannot do so for a good reason.

COSTS

7.1 Attention is drawn to rule 27.14 which contains provisions about the costs which may be ordered to be paid by one party to another.

7.2 The amount which a party may be ordered to pay under rule 27.14(2)(b) (for legal advice and assistance in claims including an injunction or specific performance) is a sum not exceeding £260.

7.3 The amounts which a party may be ordered to pay under rule 27.14(3)(c) (loss of earnings) and (d) (experts' fees) are:

(1) for the loss of earnings or loss of leave of each party or witness due to attending a hearing or staying away from home for the purpose of attending a hearing, a sum not exceeding £50 per day for each person, and

(2) for expert's fees, a sum not exceeding £200 for each expert.

(As to recovery of pre-allocation costs in a case in which an admission by the defendant has reduced the amount in dispute to a figure below £5000, reference should be made to paragraph 7.4 of the practice direction supplementing CPR Part 26 and to paragraph 5.1(3) of the Costs Directions relating to CPR Part 44)

APPEALS

8.1 Part 52 deals with appeals and attention is drawn to that Part and the accompanying practice direction.

8A An appellant's notice in small claims must be filed and served in Form N164.

8.2 Where the court dealt with the claim to which the appellant is a party:

(1) under rule 27.10 without a hearing; or
(2) in his absence because he gave notice under rule 27.9 requesting the court to decide the claim in his absence,

an application for permission to appeal must be made to the appeal court.

8.3 Where an appeal is allowed the appeal court will, if possible, dispose of the case at the same time without referring the claim to the lower court or ordering a new hearing. It may do so without hearing further evidence.

Fee on appeal—The fee is £100 (CCFO fee 2.3). The fee on an application to set aside a judgment under CPR r 27.11 is £50 (CCFO fee 2.4).

Notice of appeal—None is prescribed but N244 may be adapted.

Costs of appeal—If the court orders a party to pay another's costs of the appeal it must at the same time assess the amount payable (CPR r 27.14(2)(c), r 43.3).

APPENDIX A

INFORMATION AND DOCUMENTATION THE COURT USUALLY NEEDS IN PARTICULAR TYPES OF CASE

ROAD ACCIDENT CASES (where the information or documentation is available)

- witness statements (including statements from the parties themselves);
- invoices and estimates for repairs;
- agreements and invoices for any car hire costs;
- the Police accident report;
- sketch plan which should wherever possible be agreed;
- photographs of the scene of the accident and of the damage.

BUILDING DISPUTES, REPAIRS, GOODS SOLD AND SIMILAR CONTRACTUAL CLAIMS (where the information or documentation is available)

- any written contract;
- photographs;
- any plans;
- a list of works complained of;
- a list of any outstanding works;
- any relevant estimate, invoice or receipt including any relating to repairs to each of the defects;
- invoices for work done or goods supplied;
- estimates for work to be completed;
- a valuation of work done to date.

LANDLORD AND TENANT CLAIMS (where the information or documentation is available)

- a calculation of the amount of any rent alleged to be owing, showing amounts received;

- details of breaches of an agreement which are said to justify withholding any deposit itemised showing how the total is made up and with invoices and estimates to support them.

BREACH OF DUTY CASES (negligence, deficient professional services and the like)

Details of the following:

- what it is said by the claimant was done negligently by the defendant;
- why it is said that the negligence is the fault of the defendant;
- what damage is said to have been caused;
- what injury or losses have been suffered and how any (and each) sum claimed has been calculated;
- the response of the defendant to each of the above.

APPENDIX B

STANDARD DIRECTIONS

(For use where the district judge specifies no other directions)

THE COURT DIRECTS:

1 Each party must deliver to every other party and to the court office copies of all documents on which he intends to rely at the hearing no later than [ ] [14 days before the hearing]. (These should include the letter making the claim and the reply.)

2 The original documents must be brought to the hearing.

3 [Notice of hearing date and time allowed.]

4 The parties are encouraged to contact each other with a view to trying to settle the case or narrow the issues. However the court must be informed immediately if the case is settled by agreement before the hearing date.

5 No party may rely at the hearing on any report from an expert unless express permission has been granted by the court beforehand. Anyone wishing to rely on an expert must write to the court immediately on receipt of this Order and seek permission, giving an explanation why the assistance of an expert is necessary.

NOTE: Failure to comply with the directions may result in the case being adjourned and in the party at fault having to pay costs. The parties are encouraged always to try to settle the case by negotiating which each other. The court must be informed immediately if the case is settled before the hearing.

APPENDIX C

SPECIAL DIRECTIONS

The must clarify his case.	
He must do this by delivering to the court office and to the no later than	
[a list of]	

[details of]	

The must allow the to inspect by appointment within days of receiving a request to do so.

The hearing will not take place at the court but at .

The must bring to court at the hearing the .

Signed statements setting out the evidence of all witnesses on whom each party intends to rely must be prepared and copies included in the documents mentioned in paragraph 1. This includes the evidence of the parties themselves and of any other witness, whether or not he is going to come to court to give evidence.

The court may decide not to take into account a document [or video] or the evidence of a witness if these directions have not been complied with.

If he does not [do so] [ ] his [Claim][Defence] [and Counterclaim] will be struck out and (specify consequence).

It appears to the court that expert evidence is necessary on the issue of and that that evidence should be given by a single expert to be instructed by the parties jointly. If the parties cannot agree about who to choose and what arrangements to make about paying his fee, either party MUST apply to the court for further directions. The evidence is to be given in the form of a written report. Either party may ask the expert questions and must then send copies of the questions and replies to the other party and to the court. Oral expert evidence may be allowed in exceptional circumstances but only after a further order of the court. Attention is drawn to the limit of £200 on expert's fees that may be recovered.

If either party intends to show a video as evidence he must –

(a) contact the court at once to make arrangements for him to do so, because the court may not have the necessary equipment, and

(b) provide the other party with a copy of the video or the opportunity to see it at least days before the hearing.

PART 28
THE FAST TRACK

CONTENTS OF THIS PART

Procedural Guide—See Guide 13, set out in Section 1 of this work.

Practice Direction—See generally PD28 at p 775.

28.1 Scope of this Part

This Part contains general provisions about management of cases allocated to the fast track and applies only to cases allocated to that track.

(Part 27 sets out the procedure for claims allocated to the small claims track)

(Part 29 sets out the procedure for claims allocated to the multi-track)

Fast track claims—This Part is inextricably linked with Pt 26 and should be read in conjunction with it and its practice direction. Rule 26.6 defines the scope of defended cases allocated to the fast track. These include:
(a) defended monetary claims in the range £5000 to £15,000;
(b) smaller claims that fall to be excluded from small claims track either automatically (r 26.6(1)) or by an allocation decision under r 26.8;
(c) trials that are not likely to last for more than 5 hours;
(d) trials in which oral expert evidence will be limited to one expert per party and two expert fields.

28.2 General provisions

(1) When it allocates a case to the fast track, the court will give directions for the management of the case and set a timetable for the steps to be taken between the giving of the directions and the trial.

(2) When it gives directions, the court will –

(a) fix the trial date; or
(b) fix a period, not exceeding 3 weeks, within which the trial is to take place.

(3) The trial date or trial period will be specified in the notice of allocation.

(4) The standard period between the giving of directions and the trial will be not more than 30 weeks.

(5) The court's power to award trial costs is limited in accordance with Part 46.

'the court will give directions for the management of the case and set a timetable' (r 28.2(1))—The procedural judge will scrutinise all the papers and the allocation questionnaires. The court will then simultaneously allocate to the track and set a case management timetable and give directions. The court will ensure that:
(a) the issues have been identified clearly;
(b) pre-action protocols have been properly and fairly complied with (or that the overriding objective is not compromised by any failure to do so);
(c) the necessary evidence will be prepared and disclosed.

The Appendix to PD28 sets out a 'menu' of standard fast track directions and PD28, para 3 sets out detailed guidance on the practice to be followed. It is envisaged that the directions will normally be given without the need for a case management hearing, hence the importance of providing accurate information to the court in the statements of case and allocation questionnaires.

Agreed directions—Note that:
(a) PD26, para 2.2(3)(d) encourages the parties to file appropriate directions for the management of the case;
(b) such directions must comply with PD28, para 3.6 and should, where appropriate comply with para 3.7. The court will take the directions into account in deciding what directions to give even if it does not approve the agreed directions;
(c) if agreed directions are not filed with the allocation questionnaire, the court will make directions of its own initiative when allocating.
(d) in practice, most courts are fixing a three week trial 'window' rather than fixed date.

'not more than 30 weeks' (r 28.2(4))—This is a maximum period and the court is, in a straight forward case, likely to fix a shorter period provided that no directions will be outstanding when the pre-trial check lists must be filed (no more than eight weeks before the trial date or trial period). Note the suggested 'typical timetable' set out in PD28, para 3.12.

Fast track trial costs (r 28.2(5))—The Rule makes reference to Pt 46 which fixes fast track trial costs. Presently, only the costs of an advocate for preparing for and appearing at a fast track trial are fixed. All other costs fall to be assessed by the court. Generally, the court will make a summary assessment of costs after a fast track trial, in which case the order will deal with the costs of the whole claim (see PDCosts, para 13.2(1)). Proportionality will be a crucial factor in assessing fast track costs (r 44.5).

28.3 Directions

(1) The matters to be dealt with by directions under rule 28.2(1) include –

(a) disclosure of documents;
(b) service of witness statements; and
(c) expert evidence.

(2) If the court decides not to direct standard disclosure, it may –

(a) direct that no disclosure take place; or
(b) specify the documents or the classes of documents which the parties must disclose.

(Rule 31.6 explains what is meant by standard disclosure)

(Rule 26.6(5) deals with limitations in relation to expert evidence and the likely length of trial in fast track cases)

'standard disclosure' (r 28.3(2))—Standard disclosure is defined by r 31.6. An order for disclosure implies standard disclosure unless the court otherwise directs (r 31.5)

'service of witness statements' (r 28.3(1)(b))—See Pt 32 for the practice regarding written evidence and the court's power, by r 32.1 to control or exclude admissible evidence. Note PD32, paras 17–25 for the format of witness statements.

'expert evidence' (r 28.3(1)(c))—The court's powers to limit expert evidence and provide for written reports are set out in rr 26.6(5) and 35.5. Note, particularly, r 35.5(2). No party may call an expert or put an expert's report in evidence without the court's permission. The court may direct that evidence is given by a single expert (r 35.7) and this will be the norm in fast track cases (PD28, para 3.9).

28.4 Variation of case management timetable

(1) A party must apply to the court if he wishes to vary the date which the court has fixed for –

(a) the return of a [pre-trial check list under rule 28.5;
(b) the trial; or

(c) the trial period.

(2) Any date set by the court or these Rules for doing any act may not be varied by the parties if the variation would make it necessary to vary any of the dates mentioned in paragraph (1).

(Rule 2.11 allows the parties to vary a date by written agreement except where the rules provide otherwise or the court orders otherwise)

Amendments—SI 2002/2058.

'A party must apply to the court' (r 28.4(1))—Though the parties may agree to vary other timetabling directions they are forbidden to do anything that might vary two 'milestone' dates, the date for the return of a pre-trial check list and the trial date (or trial period). The court will be slow to vary these dates on application (even by consent) and parties must make out a powerful and exceptional case to outweigh the overriding objective that court resources be allocated appropriately. In particular, the court's need to fix trial dates or periods well in advance will be jeopardised were such variations made other than in the rarest of circumstances (r 1.1(2)(e)). The principle is well illustrated in *Matthews v Tarmac Bricks & Tiles Ltd* (1999) 143 SJLB 196, CA, where the Court of Appeal refused to interfere with a Designated Civil Judge's order fixing a trial date despite both parties' wish to defer the trial to meet the convenience of experts. Lord Woolf stated:

> 'I hope the message that will be understood by both the medical profession and the legal profession, is that it is essential that if parties want cases to be fixed for hearing in accordance with the dates which meet their convenience, those dates should be fixed as early as possible. The parties cannot always expect the courts to meet their convenience. If they hold themselves out as practising in the medico-legal field doctors must be prepared to arrange their affairs to meet the commitments of the courts where this is practical. If there is no agreement as to the dates which are acceptable to the court, the lawyers for the parties must be in a position to give the reasons why certain dates are not convenient to doctors…'.

28.5 Pre-trial check list (listing questionnaire)

(1) The court will send the parties a pre-trial check list (listing questionnaire) for completion and return by the date specified in the notice of allocation unless it considers that the claim can proceed to trial without the need for a pre-trial check list.

(2) The date specified for filing a pre-trial check list will not be more than 8 weeks before the trial date or the beginning of the trial period.

(3) If no party files the completed pre-trial checklist by the date specified, the court will order that unless a completed pre-trial checklist is filed within 7 days from service of that order, the claim, defence and any counterclaim will be struck out without further order of the court.

(4) If –

(a) a party files a completed pre-trial checklist but another party does not;
(b) a party has failed to give all the information requested by the pre-trial checklist; or
(c) the court considers that a hearing is necessary to enable it to decide what directions to give in order to complete preparation of the case for trial,

the court may give such directions as it thinks appropriate.

Amendments—Substituted by SI 2002/2058; amended by SI 2005/2292.

Pre-trial check list—Form N170. An editable version of this form is available from the Court Service internet website at *http://www.courtservice.gov.uk/fandl/forms/n170.pdf*. This will be the second and final stage when the court will give case management directions. The court will check that earlier directions have been complied with and then fix or confirm the trial date and trial timetable (r 28.6). Once again, the parties are not obliged to exchange checklists but this is encouraged by PD28, para 6.1(4).

The old-style of listing questionnaire was replaced on 2 December 2002 by a wholly revamped and renamed form, the pre-trial check list (PTC). The change is far from cosmetic. It heralds a completely different approach by the profession – and by the courts – to that period between despatch of the PTC to the solicitors and the commencement of the trial itself.The PTC assumes that the person completing it is himself ready for trial. The opening question seeks confirmation that the party concerned has complied with those directions already given which require action by him. The next asks for the date by which any outstanding directions will be done. If directions are required, then the party seeking them must return the PTC with an application notice, fee and draft order.A pivotal principle embodied within the CPR is that the trial date is only vacated in exceptional circumstances. Another is that judge time is properly utilised: if a case is going to settle, then it should do so sufficiently in advance for the judge to be found other work.

Procedural judges have been encouraged to:

(1) set realistic rather than optimistic directions at allocation or at the case management conference such that they can hold the parties to them later on;
(2) consider the completed PTCs on a fast-tracked basis;
(3) use, where appropriate, the power to make pre-emptory orders based, wherever possible, on the draft order lodged with the other party's PTC, thereby saving the inevitable delay in the court drawing up the order;
(4) resist, even more than at present, unmeritorious applications to vacate the trial date or to move the trial window; and
(5) promote an early settlement, as opposed to one at the doors of the court.

Failure to file the completed pre-trial check list by the date specified (r 28.5(3))—This is a 'milestone' date and delay in filing it is likely to result in costly and Draconian consequences, see PD28, para 6.5.

Court fee on filing the pre-trial check list—The fee is £200 in the county court (CCFO fee 2.2(b)). It is unlikely that a fast track case will have remained in the High Court, but there the fee is £400 (SCFO fee 2.2).

Costs estimate—Section 6 of PDCosts requires a costs estimate to be filed and served at the same time as the pre-trial check list is filed.

28.6 Fixing or confirming the trial date and giving directions

(1) As soon as practicable after the date specified for filing a completed [pre-trial check list the court will –

(a) fix the date for the trial (or, if it has already done so, confirm that date);
(b) give any directions for the trial, including a trial timetable, which it considers appropriate; and
(c) specify any further steps that need to be taken before trial.

(2) The court will give the parties at least 3 weeks' notice of the date of the trial unless, in exceptional circumstances, the court directs that shorter notice will be given.

Amendments—SI 2002/2058.

Directions for the trial—See PD28, paras 7 and 8 and the Menu of Directions in its Appendix.

The trial timetable and time estimate are critical. A hearing day is normally regarded as 5 hours (PD26, para 9.1(3)(a)) with a 10.30 am start. No other business will normally be listed before a one day trial and since there will be no margin for delay the court will require a prompt start. The new regime encourages parties to negotiate long before trial and those who leave it until the last moment should arrive at court with plenty of time to spare *before* the start. Agreed timetables should include sufficient time for the judge to prepare and deliver the judgment (which is likely not to be in the traditional narrative form but may simply identify the issues and then make findings with brief reasons and the result). Time should be included to deal with the summary assessment of costs and consequential orders. Witness statements will stand as evidence in chief and permission will not be given to amplify them or deal with new matters 'without good reason' (r 32.5). Cross-examination will be limited and time should be allocated both for this and for re-examination.

28.7 Conduct of trial

Unless the trial judge otherwise directs, the trial will be conducted in accordance with any order previously made.

The trial—See PD28, para 8 and Pt 32 for the court's approach at trial and to evidence and note in particular, Pt 39 and PD39.

Amendment at trial and reallocation—See note **'Amended claims'** under r 26.10.

Costs—Part 46 deals with Fast Track costs.

Practice Direction – The Fast Track

This Practice Direction supplements CPR Part 28 (PD28)

Procedural Guide—See Guide 13, set out in Section 1 of this work.

GENERAL

1.1 Attention is drawn in particular to the following Parts of the Civil Procedure Rules:

Part 1	The Overriding Objective
Part 3	The Court's Case Management Powers
Part 26	Case Management – Preliminary Stage
Part 31	Disclosure and Inspection of Documents
Parts 32–34	Evidence
Part 35	Experts and Assessors

and to the practice directions which relate to those Parts.

1.2 Attention is also drawn to:

Rule 26.6(5) – which makes provision about limitations on expert evidence and the length of trial in fast track cases.

Part 46 – Fast Track Trial Costs.

Rule 19.4A and the practice direction supplementing it on joining the Crown in certain cases raising Convention rights issues.

CASE MANAGEMENT

2.1 Case management of cases allocated to the fast track will generally be by directions given at two stages in the case:

(1) at allocation to the track, and
(2) on the filing of pre-trial check lists (listing questionnaires).

2.2 The court will seek whenever possible to give directions at those stages only and to do so without the need for a hearing to take place. It will expect to do so with the co-operation of the parties.

2.3 The court will however hold a hearing to give directions whenever it appears necessary or desirable to do so, and where this happens because of the default of a party or his legal representative it will usually impose a sanction.

2.4 The court may give directions at any hearing on the application of a party or on its own initiative.

2.5 When any hearing has been fixed it is the duty of the parties to consider what directions the court should be asked to give and to make any application that may be appropriate to be dealt with at that hearing.

2.6 When the court fixes a hearing to give directions it will give the parties at least 3 days notice of the hearing.

2.7 Appendix A contains forms of directions. When making an order the court will as far as possible base its order on those forms. Agreed directions which the parties file and invite the court to make should also be based on those forms.

2.8 Where a party needs to apply for a direction of a kind not included in the case management timetable which has been set (for example to amend his statement of case or for further information to be given by another party) he must do so as soon as possible so as to minimise the need to change that timetable.

2.9 Courts will make arrangements to ensure that applications and other hearings are listed promptly to avoid delay in the conduct of cases.

DIRECTIONS ON ALLOCATION

3.1 Attention is drawn to the court's duty under rule 28.2(2) to set a case management timetable and to fix a trial date or a trial period, and to the matters which are to be dealt with by directions under rule 28.3(1).

3.2 The court will seek to tailor its directions to the needs of the case and the steps of which it is aware that the parties have already taken to prepare the case. In particular it will have regard to the extent to which any pre-action protocol has or (as the case may be) has not been complied with.

3.3 At this stage the court's first concern will be to ensure that the issues between the parties be identified and that the necessary evidence is prepared and disclosed.

3.4 The court may have regard to any document filed by a party with his allocation questionnaire containing further information provided that the document states either that its contents has been agreed with every other party or that it has been served on every other party and when it was served.

3.5 If:

(1) the parties have filed agreed directions for the management of the case, and
(2) the court considers that the proposals are suitable,

it may approve them and give directions in the terms proposed.

3.6 (1) To obtain the court's approval the agreed directions must:
- (a) set out a timetable by reference to calendar dates for the taking of steps for the preparation of the case,
- (b) include a date or a period (the trial period) when it is proposed that the trial will take place,
- (c) include provision about disclosure of documents, and
- (d) include provision about both factual and expert evidence.

(2) The latest proposed date for the trial or the end of the trial period must be not later than 30 weeks from the date the directions order is made.
(3) The trial period must not be longer than 3 weeks.
(4) The provision in (1)(c) above may:

(a) limit disclosure to standard disclosure between all parties or to less than that, and/or
(b) direct that disclosure will take place by the supply of copy documents without a list, but it must in that case either direct that the parties must serve a disclosure statement with the copies or record that they have agreed to disclose in that way without such a statement.

(5) The provision in (1)(d) may be to the effect that no expert evidence is required.

3.7 Directions agreed by the parties should also where appropriate contain provisions about:

(1) the filing of any reply or amended statement of case that may be required,
(2) dates for the service of requests for further information under the practice direction supplementing Part 18 and questions to experts under rule 35.6 and when they are to be dealt with,
(3) the disclosure of evidence,
(4) the use of a single joint expert, or in cases where the use of a single joint expert has not been agreed the exchange and the agreement of expert evidence (including whether exchange is to be simultaneous or sequential) and without prejudice discussions of the experts).

3.8 If the court does not approve the agreed directions filed by the parties but decides that it will give directions on its own initiative without a hearing, it will take them into account in deciding what directions to give.

3.9 Where the court is to give directions on its own initiative and it is not aware of any steps taken by the parties other than the service of statements of case, its general approach will be:

(1) to give directions for the filing and service of any further information required to clarify either party's case,
(2) to direct standard disclosure between the parties,
(3) to direct the disclosure of witness statements by way of simultaneous exchange,
(4) to give directions for a single joint expert unless there is good reason not to do so,
(5) in cases where directions for a single expert are not given:
    (a) to direct disclosure of experts' reports by way of simultaneous exchange, and
    (b) if experts' reports are not agreed, to direct a discussion between the experts for the purpose set out in rule 35.12(1) and the preparation of a report under rule 35.12(3).

3.10(1) If it appears to the court that the claim is one which will be allocated to the Fast track but that it cannot properly give directions on its own initiative or approve agreed directions that have been filed, the court may either:
    (a) allocate the claim to the Fast track, fix a trial date or trial period and direct that a case management hearing is to be listed and give directions at that hearing, or
    (b) direct that an allocation hearing is to be listed and give directions at that hearing.

(2) In either case the hearing will be listed as promptly as possible.

3.11 Where the court is proposing on its own initiative to make an order under rule 35.15 (which gives the court power to appoint an assessor), the court must, unless the parties have consented in writing to the order, list a directions hearing.

3.12 The table set out below contains a typical timetable the court may give for the preparation of the case.

Disclosure	4 weeks
Exchange of witness statements	10 weeks
Exchange of experts' reports	14 weeks
Sending of [pre-trial check lists (listing questionnaires) by the court	20 weeks
Filing of completed pre-trial check lists	22 weeks
Hearing	30 weeks

These periods will run from the date of the notice of allocation.

3.13(1) Where it considers that some or all of the steps in that timetable are not necessary the court may omit them and direct an earlier trial.

(2) This may happen where the court is informed that a pre-action protocol has been complied with or that steps which it would otherwise order to be taken have already been taken.

(3) It may also happen where an application (for example for summary judgment or for an injunction) has been heard before allocation and little or no further preparation is required. In such a case the court may dispense with the need for a pre-trial check list.

VARIATION OF DIRECTIONS

4.1 This paragraph deals with the procedure to be adopted:

(1) where a party is dissatisfied with a direction given by the court,
(2) where the parties agree about changes they wish made to the directions given, or
(3) where a party wishes to apply to vary a direction.

4.2 (1) It is essential that any party who wishes to have a direction varied takes steps to do so as soon as possible.

(2) The court will assume for the purposes of any later application that a party who did not appeal and who made no application to vary within 14 days of service of the order containing the directions was content that they were correct in the circumstances then existing.

4.3 (1) Where a party is dissatisfied with a direction given or other order made by the court he may appeal or apply to the court for it to reconsider its decision.

(2) He should appeal if the direction was given or the order was made at a hearing at which he was present or represented, or of which he had due notice.

(3) In any other case he should apply to the court to reconsider its decision.

(4) If an application is made for the court to reconsider its decision:

(a) it will usually be heard by the judge who gave the directions or another judge of the same level,
(b) the court will give all parties at least 3 days notice of the hearing, and
(c) the court may confirm its decision or make a different order.

4.4 Where there has been a change in the circumstances since the order was made the court may set aside or vary any direction it has given. It may do so on application or on its own initiative.

4.5 Where the parties agree about changes to be made to the directions given:

(1) If rule 2.11 (variation by agreement of a date set by the court for doing any act other than those stated in the note to that rule) or rule 31.5, 31.10(8) or 31.13 (agreements about disclosure) applied the parties need not file the written agreement.

(2) (a) In any other case the parties must apply for an order by consent.
(b) The parties must file a draft of the order sought and an agreed statement of the reasons why the variation is sought.
(c) The court may make an order in the agreed terms or in other terms without a hearing, but it may direct that a hearing is to be listed.

FAILURE TO COMPLY WITH CASE MANAGEMENT DIRECTIONS

5.1 Where a party has failed to comply with a direction given by the court any other party may apply for an order to enforce compliance or for a sanction to be imposed or both of these.

5.2 The party entitled to apply for such an order must do so without delay but should first warn the other party of his intention to do so.

5.3 The court may take any such delay into account when it decides whether to make an order imposing a sanction or whether to grant relief from a sanction imposed by the rules or any practice direction.

5.4 (1) The court will not allow a failure to comply with directions to lead to the postponement of the trial unless the circumstances of the case are exceptional.
(2) If it is practicable to do so the court will exercise its powers in a manner that enables the case to come on for trial on the date or within the period previously set.
(3) In particular the court will assess what steps each party should take to prepare the case for trial, direct that those steps are taken in the shortest possible time and impose a sanction for non-compliance. Such a sanction may, for example, deprive a party of the right to raise or contest an issue or to rely on evidence to which the direction relates.
(4) Where is appears that one or more issues are or can be made ready for trial at the time fixed while others cannot, the court may direct that the trial will proceed on the issues which are or will then be ready, and order that no costs will be allowed for any later trial of the remaining issues or that those costs will be paid by the party in default.
(5) Where the court has no option but to postpone the trial it will do so for the shortest possible time and will give directions for the taking of the necessary steps in the meantime as rapidly as possible.
(6) Litigants and lawyers must be in no doubt that the court will regard the postponement of a trial as an order of last resort. The court may exercise its power to require a party as well as his legal representative to attend court at a hearing where such an order is to be sought.

'The court will not allow a failure to comply with directions to lead to the postponement of the trial unless the circumstances of the case are exceptional' (para 5.4(1))—The Court of Appeal have supported this robustly. In *Baron v Lovell* (1999) *The Times*, 14 September, the CA approved a trial judge's decision to proceed with a trial on the basis of medical evidence from the claimant only because the defendant had failed to disclose his medical reports until the date of hearing. In *Matthews v Tarmac Bricks & Tiles* (1999) 143 SJLB 196, CA, the trial judge fixed a trial date in a 6-year-old RSI injury case, despite the unparticularised unavailability of the defendants' two experts on that date. On application for leave to appeal it transpired that one expert would be on holiday and the other was subpoenaed to appear elsewhere. The CA refused leave to appeal on grounds that too much delay had occurred already and the court could not always be expected to accommodate the external commitments of experts.

PRE-TRIAL CHECK LISTS (LISTING QUESTIONNAIRES)

6.1 (1) The pre-trial check list (listing questionnaire) will be in Form N170.

(2) Unless it has dispensed with pre-trial check lists, the court will send Forms N170 and N171 (Notice of date for return of the pre-trial check list) to each party no later than 2 weeks before the date specified in the notice of allocation or in any later direction of the court for the return of the completed check lists.

(3) When all the pre-trial check lists have been filed or when the time for filing them has expired and where a party has filed a pre-trial checklist but another party has not done so, the file will be placed before a judge for his directions.

(4) Although the Rules do not require the parties to exchange copies of the check lists before they are filed, they are encouraged to do so to avoid the court being given conflicting or incomplete information.

Attention is drawn to the Costs Practice Direction, Section 6, which requires a costs estimate to be filed and served at the same time as the pre-trial check list is filed.

6.2 Attention is drawn to rule 28.6(1) (which sets out the court's duty at the pre-trial check list stage) and to rule 28.5(4) (which sets out circumstances in which the court may decide to hold a hearing).

6.3 Where the judge decides to hold a hearing under rule 28.5(4) the court will fix a date which is as early as possible and the parties will be given at least 3 days notice of the date.

The notice of a such a hearing will be in Form N153.

6.4 The court's general approach will be as set out in the following paragraphs. The court may however decide to make other orders, and in particular the court will take into account the steps, if any, which the parties have taken to prepare the case for trial.

6.5 (1) Where no party files a pre-trial checklist the court will order that unless a completed pre-trial checklist is filed within 7 days from service of that order, the claim, defence and any counterclaim will be struck out without further order of the court.

(2) Where a party files a pre-trial check list but another party does not do so, the court normally will give directions. These will usually fix or confirm the trial date and provide for steps to be taken to prepare the case for trial.

'Costs Practice Direction' (para 6.1)—Note the requirement to file and serve a costs estimate together with the pre-trial check list.

DIRECTIONS THE COURT WILL GIVE ON LISTING

7.1 Directions the court must give:

(1) The court must confirm or fix the trial date, specify the place of trial

and give a time estimate. The trial date must be fixed and the case listed on the footing that the hearing will end on the same calendar day as that on which it commenced.

(2) The court will serve a notice of hearing on the parties at least 3 weeks before the hearing unless they agree to accept shorter notice or the court authorises shorter service under rule 28.6(2), and

(3) The notice of hearing will be in Form N172.

7.2 Other directions:

(1) The parties should seek to agree directions and may file the proposed order. The court may make an order in those terms or it may make a different order.

(2) Agreed directions should include provision about:
  (a) evidence,
  (b) a trial timetable and time estimate,
  (c) the preparation of a trial bundle,
  (d) any other matter needed to prepare the case for trial.

(3) The court will include such of these provisions as are appropriate in any order that it may make, whether or not the parties have filed agreed directions.

(4) (a) A direction giving permission to use expert evidence will say whether it gives permission for oral evidence or reports or both and will name the experts concerned.
  (b) The court will not make a direction giving permission for an expert to give oral evidence unless it believes it is necessary in the interests of justice to do so.
  (c) Where no 'without prejudice' meeting or other discussion between experts has taken place the court may grant that permission conditionally on such a discussion taking place and a report being filed before the trial.

7.3 The principles set out in paragraph 4 of this practice direction about the variation of directions apply also to directions given at this stage.

THE TRIAL

8.1 The trial will normally take place at the court where the case is being managed, but it may be at another court if it is appropriate having regard to the needs of the parties and the availability of court resources.

8.2 The judge will generally have read the papers in the trial bundle and may dispense with an opening address.

8.3 The judge may confirm or vary any timetable given previously, or if none has been given set his own.

8.4 Attention is drawn to the provisions in Part 32 and the following parts of the Rules about evidence, and in particular –

(1) to rule 32.1 (court's power to control evidence and to restrict cross-examination), and

(2) to rule 32.5(2) (witness statements to stand as evidence in chief).

8.5 At the conclusion of the trial the judge will normally summarily assess the costs of the claim in accordance with rule 44.7 and Part 46 (fast track trial costs). Attention is drawn to the steps the practice directions about costs require the parties to take.

8.6 Where a trial is not finished on the day for which it is listed the judge will normally sit on the next court day to complete it.

APPENDIX

FAST TRACK STANDARD DIRECTIONS

FURTHER STATEMENTS OF CASE

The must file a and serve a copy on no later than .

REQUESTS FOR FURTHER INFORMATION

Any request for clarification or further information based on another party's statement of case shall be served no later than .

[Any such request shall be dealt with no later than]

DISCLOSURE OF DOCUMENTS

[No disclosure of documents is required]
[[Each party] [The] shall give [to the] [to every other party] standard disclosure of documents
[relating to]
by serving copies together with a disclosure statement].
no later than
[Disclosure shall take place as follows:
[Each party shall give standard discovery to every other party by list]
[Disclosure is limited to [standard] [disclosure by the
to the] [of documents relating to damage]
[the following documents]
[The latest date for delivery of the lists is]
[The latest date for service of any request to inspect or for a copy of a document is
]]

WITNESSES OF FACT

Each party shall serve on every other party the witness statements of all witnesses of fact on whom he intends to rely.

There shall be simultaneous exchange of such statements no later than .

EXPERT EVIDENCE

[No expert evidence being necessary, no party has permission to call or rely on expert evidence].

[On it appearing to the court that expert evidence is necessary on the issue of [ ] and that that evidence should be given by the report of a single expert instructed jointly by the parties, the shall no later than inform the court whether or not such an expert has been instructed].

[The expert evidence on the issue of shall be limited to a single expert jointly instructed by the parties.

If the parties cannot agree by who that expert is to be and about the payment of his fees either party may apply for further directions.

Unless the parties agree in writing or the court orders otherwise, the fees and expenses of such an expert shall be paid to him [by the parties equally] [ ] and be limited to £ .

[The report of the expert shall be filed at the court no later than].

[No party shall be entitled to recover by way of costs from any other party more than £ for the fees or expenses of an expert].

The parties shall exchange reports setting out the substance of any expert evidence on which they intend to rely.

[The exchange shall take place simultaneously no later than].

[The shall serve his report(s) no later than the and the shall serve his reports no later than the].

[The exchange of reports relating to [causation] [ ] shall take place simultaneously no later than . The shall serve his report(s) relating to [damage] [ ] no later than and the shall serve his reports relating to it no later than].

Reports shall be agreed if possible no later than [days after service] [ ].

[If the reports are not agreed within that time there shall be a without prejudice discussion between the relevant experts no later than to identify the issues between them and to reach agreement if possible.

The experts shall prepare for the court a statement of the issues on which they agree and on which they disagree with a summary of their reasons, and that statement shall be filed with the court [no later than] [with] [no later than the date for filing] [the [pre-trial check list].

[Each party has permission to use [ ] as expert witness(es) to give [oral] evidence [in the form of a report] at the trial in the field of provided that the substance of the evidence to be given has been disclosed as above and has not been agreed].

[Each party has permission to use in evidence experts' report(s) [and the court will consider when the claim is listed for trial whether expert oral evidence will be allowed].]

QUESTIONS TO EXPERTS

The time for service on another party of any question addressed to an expert instructed by that party is not later than days after service of that expert's report.

Any such question shall be answered within days of service.

REQUESTS FOR INFORMATION ETC

Each party shall serve any request for clarification or further information based on any document disclosed or statement served by another party no later than days after disclosure or service.

Any such request shall be dealt with within days of service.

DOCUMENTS TO BE FILED WITH [PRE-TRIAL CHECK LISTS

The parties must file with their [pre-trial check lists copies of [their experts' reports] [witness statements] [replies to requests for further information]

DATES FOR FILING [PRE-TRIAL CHECK LISTS AND THE TRIAL

Each party must file a completed [pre-trial check list no later than .

The trial of this case will take place [on] [on a date to be fixed between and].

DIRECTIONS FOLLOWING FILING OF [PRE-TRIAL CHECK LIST

Expert evidence

The parties have permission to rely at the trial on expert evidence as follows:

The claimant	Oral evidence Written evidence
The defendant:	Oral evidence Written evidence

Trial timetable

The time allowed for the trial is

[The timetable for the trial may be agreed by the parties, subject to the approval of the trial judge].

[The timetable for the trial (subject to the approval of the trial judge) will be that].

[The evidence in chief for each party will be contained in witness statements and reports, the time allowed for cross-examination by the defendant is limited to and the time allowed for cross-examination by the claimant is limited to].

[The time allowed for the claimant's evidence is . The time allowed for the defendant's evidence is].

The time allowed for the submissions on behalf of each party is .

The remainder of the time allowed for the trial (being) is reserved for the judge to consider and give the judgment and to deal with costs].

Trial bundle etc

[[The claimant shall lodge an indexed bundle of documents contained in a ring binder and with each page clearly numbered at the court not more than 7 days and not less than 3 days before the start of the trial.]

[A case summary (which should not exceed 250 words) outlining the matters still in issue, and referring where appropriate to the relevant documents shall be included in the bundle for the assistance of the judge in reading the papers before the trial].

[The parties shall seek to agree the contents of the trial bundle and the case summary].

Settlement

Each party must inform the court immediately if the claim is settled whether or not it is then possible to file a draft consent order to give effect to their agreement.

PART 29
THE MULTI-TRACK

CONTENTS OF THIS PART

Procedural Guide—See Guide 14, set out in Section 1 of this work.

29.1 Scope of this Part

This Part contains general provisions about management of cases allocated to the multi-track and applies only to cases allocated to that track.

(Part 27 sets out the procedure for claims allocated to the small claims track)

(Part 28 sets out the procedure for claims allocated to the fast track)

Practice Direction—See generally PD29 at p 789.

General note—See PD29 for guidance about case management in multi-track cases in the Royal Courts of Justice and elsewhere. The practice direction contains much invaluable practical advice about the roles of litigants and the court, and should be read and re-read with care.

29.2 Case management

(1) When it allocates a case to the multi-track, the court will –

(a) give directions for the management of the case and set a timetable for the steps to be taken between the giving of directions and the trial; or

(b) fix –

(i) a case management conference; or

(ii) a pre-trial review,

or both, and give such other directions relating to the management of the case as it sees fit.

(2) The court will fix the trial date or the period in which the trial is to take place as soon as practicable.

(3) When the court fixes the trial date or the trial period under paragraph (2), it will –

(a) give notice to the parties of the date or period; and

(b) specify the date by which the parties must file a [pre-trial check list.

Amendments—SI 2002/2058.

'Case management conference ... or pre-trial review' (r 29.2(1)(b))—The case management conference is intended to provide an opportunity to decide the direction the case is to take, after identifying the issues and after investigating the possibility of early settlement, and to lay down the steps needed to progress in that direction. The pre-trial review is intended to ensure that all practical steps needed to make the case ready for trial have been taken or will be taken within a timetable established by the court. It is also intended as an opportunity to lay down a timetable for the trial itself.

'directions' (r 29.2(1))—In most cases of substance, the allocation questionnaires make it obvious that some carefully considered directions must be given: for that purpose, an early directions hearing is almost always indispensable. There are, however, many multi-track cases, particularly those less substantial, where written directions are appropriate in the first instance (PD29, para 3.3). Where a multi-track case is commenced in a feeder court which is not a trial centre, it is common for the case to be allocated to track at the feeder court and transferred to the trial centre for case management (PD29, para 3.1).

29.3 Case management conference and pre-trial review

(1) The court may fix –

(a) a case management conference; or
(b) a pre-trial review,

at any time after the claim has been allocated.

(2) If a party has a legal representative, a representative –

(a) familiar with the case; and
(b) with sufficient authority to deal with any issues that are likely to arise,

must attend case management conferences and pre-trial reviews.

(Rule 3.1(2)(c) provides that the court may require a party to attend the court)

Practice Direction—See PD29, para 5.2 at p 794.

'a representative … familiar with the case' (r 29.3(2))—Failure to observe this requirement runs the risk of attracting a wasted costs order (see PD29, para 5.2(3)).

29.4 Steps taken by the parties

If –

(a) the parties agree proposals for the management of the proceedings (including a proposed trial date or period in which the trial is to take place); and
(b) the court considers that the proposals are suitable,

it may approve them without a hearing and give directions in the terms proposed.

'the court … may approve them' (r 29.4)—It must be emphasised that 'case management' is not a new name for the old 'directions'. The court cannot be expected to rubber-stamp directions agreed by the parties. It will wish in many cases to conduct its own investigation and impose its own views about the direction the case is to take and the way it is to be conducted. It is essential to lodge any agreed minute of order sufficiently far in advance of any hearing to enable the court to consider it. A faxed draft the day before is unlikely to avoid the need to attend.

29.5 Variation of case management timetable

(1) A party must apply to the court if he wishes to vary the date which the court has fixed for –

(a) a case management conference;
(b) a pre-trial review;
(c) the return of a [pre-trial check list under rule 29.6;
(d) the trial; or

(e) the trial period.

(2) Any date set by the court or these Rules for doing any act may not be varied by the parties if the variation would make it necessary to vary any of the dates mentioned in paragraph (1).

(Rule 2.11 allows the parties to vary a date by written agreement except where the rules provide otherwise or the court orders otherwise)

Amendments—SI 2002/2058.

29.6 Pre-trial check list (listing questionnaire)

(1) The court will send the parties a pre-trial check list (listing questionnaire) for completion and return by the date specified in directions given under rule 29.2(3) unless it considers that the claim can proceed to trial without the need for a pre-trial check list.

(2) Each party must file the completed pre-trial check list by the date specified by the court.

(3) If no party files the completed pre-trial checklist by the date specified, the court will order that unless a completed pre-trial checklist is filed within 7 days from service of that order, the claim, defence and any counterclaim will be struck out without further order of the court.

(4) If –

(a) a party files a completed pre-trial checklist but another party does not;
(b) a party has failed to give all the information requested by the pre-trial checklist; or
(c) the court considers that a hearing is necessary to enable it to decide what directions to give in order to complete preparation of the case for trial,

the court may give such directions as it thinks appropriate.

Amendments—Substituted by SI 2002/2058; SI 2005/2292.

'Pre trial check list (listing questionnaire)' (r 29.6 generally)—This provision, substituted with effect from 2 December 2002, now recognises that the document in question has little to do with listing. The trial will have been listed on a fixed date or in a window long before. See also the **'General note'** under r 3.3.

29.7 Pre-trial review

If, on receipt of the parties' pre-trial check lists, the court decides –

(a) to hold a pre-trial review; or
(b) to cancel a pre-trial review which has already been fixed,

it will serve notice of its decision at least 7 days before the date fixed for the hearing or, as the case may be, the cancelled hearing.

Amendments—SI 2002/2058.

29.8 Setting a trial timetable and fixing or confirming the trial date or week

As soon as practicable after –

(a) each party has filed a completed pre-trial check list;
(b) the court has held a listing hearing under rule 29.6(3); or

(c) the court has held a pre-trial review under rule 29.7,

the court will –

(i) set a timetable for the trial unless a timetable has already been fixed, or the court considers that it would be inappropriate to do so;

(ii) fix the date for the trial or the week within which the trial is to begin (or, if it has already done so, confirm that date); and

(iii) notify the parties of the trial timetable (where one is fixed under this rule) and the date or trial period.

Amendments—SI 2002/2058.

'a timetable for the trial' (r 29.8(c)(i))—Experience so far suggests that the courts are not generally insisting on their duty to set a trial timetable. The information supplied in the pre-trial check lists is often insufficient to enable them to do so and the expense of a hearing cannot usually be justified.

29.9 Conduct of trial

Unless the trial judge otherwise directs, the trial will be conducted in accordance with any order previously made.

'in accordance with any order previously made'—The facts of the individual case, measured against the overriding objective, will determine the extent to which a judge may depart from a previous order (*Umm Qarn Management Co Ltd v (1) Bunting (Valerie Anne) (2) Esteem Bloodstock Ltd* [2001] 1 CPLR 20, CA).

Practice Direction – The Multi-Track

This Practice Direction supplements CPR Part 29 (PD29)

Procedural Guide—See Guide 14, set out in Section 1 of this work.

General note—See also the notes to CPR Pt 29 for relevant commentary.

GENERAL

1.1 Attention is drawn in particular to the following Parts of the Civil Procedure Rules:

Part 1	The Overriding Objective
Part 3	The Court's Case Management Powers
Part 26	Case Management – Preliminary Stage
Part 31	Disclosure and Inspection of Documents
Parts 32–34	Evidence
Part 35	Experts and Assessors

and to the practice directions which relate to those Parts.

CASE MANAGEMENT IN THE ROYAL COURTS OF JUSTICE

2.1 This part of the practice direction applies to claims begun by claim form issued in the Central Office or Chancery Chambers in the Royal Courts of Justice.

2.2 A claim with an estimated value of less than £50,000 will generally, unless:

(a) it is required by an enactment to be tried in the High Court,

(b) it falls within a specialist list, or
(c) it falls within one of the categories specified in 2.6 below or is otherwise within the criteria of article 7(5) of the High Court and County Courts Jurisdiction Order 1991,

be transferred to a county court.

2.3 Paragraph 2.2 is without prejudice to the power of the court in accordance with Part 30 to transfer to a county court a claim with an estimated value that exceeds £50,000.

2.4 The decision to transfer may be made at any stage in the proceedings but should, subject to paragraph 2.5, be made as soon as possible and in any event not later than the date for the filing of pre-trial check lists (listing questionnaires).

2.5 If an application is made under rule 3.4 (striking out) or under Part 24 (summary judgment) or under Part 25 (interim remedies), it will usually be convenient for the application to be dealt with before a decision to transfer is taken.

2.6 Each party should state in his allocation questionnaire whether he considers the claim should be managed and tried at the Royal Courts of Justice and, if so, why. Claims suitable for trial in the Royal Courts of Justice include:

(1) professional negligence claims,
(2) Fatal Accident Act claims,
(3) fraud or undue influence claims,
(4) defamation claims,
(5) claims for malicious prosecution or false imprisonment,
(6) claims against the police,
(7) contentious probate claims.

Such claims may fall within the criteria of article 7(5) of the High Court and County Courts Jurisdiction Order 1991.

2.7 Attention is drawn to the practice direction on Transfer (Part 30).

CASE MANAGEMENT – GENERAL PROVISIONS

3.1 (1) Case management of a claim which is proceeding at the Royal Courts of Justice will be undertaken there.
(2) (a) Case management of any other claim which has been allocated to the multi-track will normally be undertaken at a Civil Trial Centre.
(b) The practice direction supplementing Part 26 provides for what will happen in the case of a claim which is issued in or transferred to a court which is not a Civil Trial Centre.

3.2 The hallmarks of the multi-track are:

(1) the ability of the court to deal with cases of widely differing values and complexity, and
(2) the flexibility given to the court in the way it will manage a case in a way appropriate to its particular needs.

3.3 (1) On allocating a claim to the multi-track the court may give directions without a hearing, including fixing a trial date or a period in which the trial will take place,
(2) Alternatively, whether or not it fixes a trial date or period, it may either –

(a) give directions for certain steps to be taken and fix a date for a case management conference or a pre-trial review to take place after they have been taken, or

(b) fix a date for a case management conference.

(3) Attention is drawn to rule 29.2(2) which requires the court to fix a trial date or period as soon as practicable.

3.4 The court may give or vary directions at any hearing which may take place on the application of a party or of its own initiative.

3.5 When any hearing has been fixed it is the duty of the parties to consider what directions the court should be asked to give and to make any application that may be appropriate to be dealt with then.

3.6 The court will hold a hearing to give directions whenever it appears necessary or desirable to do so, and where this happens because of the default of a party or his legal representative it will usually impose a sanction.

3.7 When the court fixes a hearing to give directions it will give the parties at least 3 days notice of the hearing unless rule 29.7 applies (7 days notice to be given in the case of a pre-trial review).

3.8 Where a party needs to apply for a direction of a kind not included in the case management timetable which has been set (for example to amend his statement of case or for further information to be given by another party) he must do so as soon as possible so as to minimise the need to change that timetable.

3.9 Courts will make arrangements to ensure that applications and other hearings are listed promptly to avoid delay in the conduct of cases.

3.10(1) Case management will generally be dealt with by:

(a) a master in cases proceeding in the Royal Courts of Justice,

(b) a district judge in cases proceeding in a District Registry of the High Court, and

(c) a district judge or a circuit judge in cases proceeding in a county court.

(2) A master or a district judge may consult and seek the directions of a judge of a higher level about any aspect of case management.

(3) A member of the court staff who is dealing with the listing of a hearing may seek the directions of any judge about any aspect of that listing.

'a claim ... issued in ... a court which is not a Civil Trial Centre' (para 3.1(2)(b))—Designated civil judges have authority to direct that such courts – 'feeder courts' – may give initial case management directions on paper while at the same time transferring the claims to the Trial Centre for all other purposes. They may also direct that such courts may retain for trial certain multi-track cases, for example (in London) those expected to take up to 2 days to try.

Case management – consideration of periodical payments

3A Attention is drawn to Practice Direction 41B supplementing Part 41 and in particular to the direction that in a personal injury claim the court should consider and indicate to the parties as soon as practicable whether periodical payments or a lump sum is likely to be the more appropriate form for all or part of an award of damages for future pecuniary loss.

DIRECTIONS ON ALLOCATION

4.1 Attention is drawn to the court's duties under rule 29.2.

4.2 The court will seek to tailor its directions to the needs of the case and the steps which the parties have already taken to prepare the case of which it is aware. In particular it will have regard to the extent to which any pre-action protocol has or (as the case may be) has not been complied with.

4.3 At this stage the court's first concern will be to ensure that the issues between the parties are identified and that the necessary evidence is prepared and disclosed.

4.4 The court may have regard to any document filed by a party with his allocation questionnaire containing further information, provided that the document states either that its contents has been agreed with every other party or that it has been served on every other party and when it was served.

4.5 On the allocation of a claim to the multi-track the court will consider whether it is desirable or necessary to hold a case management conference straight away, or whether it is appropriate instead to give directions on its own initiative.

4.6 The parties and their advisers are encouraged to try to agree directions and to take advantage of rule 29.4 which provides that if:

(1) the parties agree proposals for the management of the proceedings (including a proposed trial date or period in which the trial is to take place), and
(2) the court considers that the proposals are suitable,

it may approve them without a hearing and give directions in the terms proposed.

4.7 (1) To obtain the court's approval the agreed directions must –
(a) set out a timetable by reference to calendar dates for the taking of steps for the preparation of the case,
(b) include a date or a period (the trial period) when it is proposed that the trial will take place,
(c) include provision about disclosure of documents, and
(d) include provision about both factual and expert evidence.
(2) The court will scrutinise the timetable carefully and in particular will be concerned to see that any proposed date or period for the trial and (if provided for) for a case management conference is no later than is reasonably necessary.
(3) The provision in (1)(c) above may –
(a) limit disclosure to standard disclosure or less than that, and/or
(b) direct that disclosure will take place by the supply of copy documents without a list, but it must in that case say either that the parties must serve a disclosure statement with the copies or that they have agreed to disclose in that way without such a statement.
(4) The provision in (1)(d) about expert evidence may be to the effect that none is required.

4.8 Directions agreed by the parties should also where appropriate contain provisions about:

(1) the filing of any reply or amended statement of case that may be required,
(2) dates for the service of requests for further information under the practice direction supplementing Part 18 and of questions to experts under rule 35.6 and by when they are to be dealt with,

(3) the disclosure of evidence,
(4) the use of a single joint expert, or in cases where it is not agreed, the exchange of expert evidence (including whether exchange is to be simultaneous or sequential) and without prejudice discussions between experts.

4.9 If the court does not approve the agreed directions filed by the parties but decides that it will give directions of its own initiative without fixing a case management conference, it will take them into account in deciding what directions to give.

4.10 Where the court is to give directions on its own initiative without holding a case management conference and it is not aware of any steps taken by the parties other than the exchange of statements of case, its general approach will be:

(1) to give directions for the filing and service of any further information required to clarify either party's case,
(2) to direct standard disclosure between the parties,
(3) to direct the disclosure of witness statements by way of simultaneous exchange,
(4) to give directions for a single joint expert on any appropriate issue unless there is a good reason not to do so,
(5) unless paragraph 4.11 (below) applies, to direct disclosure of experts' reports by way of simultaneous exchange on those issues where a single joint expert is not directed,
(6) if experts' reports are not agreed, to direct a discussion between experts for the purpose set out in rule 35.12(1) and the preparation of a statement under rule 35.12(3),
(7) to list a case management conference to take place after the date for compliance with those directions, and
(8) to specify a trial period; and
(9) in such cases as the court thinks appropriate, the court may give directions requiring the parties to consider ADR. Such directions may be, for example, in the following terms:

> "The parties shall by date [ ] consider whether the case is capable of resolution by ADR. If any party considers that the case is unsuitable for resolution by ADR, that party shall be prepared to justify that decision at the conclusion of the trial, should the judge consider that such means of resolution were appropriate, when he is considering the appropriate costs order to make.
> The party considering the case unsuitable for ADR shall, not less than 28 days before the commencement of the trial, file with the court a witness statement without prejudice save as to costs, giving reasons upon which they rely for saying that the case was unsuitable."

4.11 If it appears that expert evidence will be required both on issues of liability and on the amount of damages, the court may direct that the exchange of those reports that relate to liability will be exchanged simultaneously but that those relating to the amount of damages will be exchanged sequentially.

4.12(1) If it appears to the court that it cannot properly give directions on its own initiative and no agreed directions have been filed which it can approve, the court will direct a case management conference to be listed.

(2) The conference will be listed as promptly as possible.

4.13 Where the court is proposing on its own initiative to make an order under rule 35.7 (which gives the court power to direct that evidence on a particular issue is to be given by a single expert) or under rule 35.15 (which gives the court power to appoint an assessor), the court must, unless the parties have consented in writing to the order, list a case management conference.

CASE MANAGEMENT CONFERENCES

5.1 The court will at any case management conference:

(1) review the steps which the parties have taken in the preparation of the case, and in particular their compliance with any directions that the court may have given,

(2) decide and give directions about the steps which are to be taken to secure the progress of the claim in accordance with the overriding objective, and

(3) ensure as far as it can that all agreements that can be reached between the parties about the matters in issue and the conduct of the claim are made and recorded.

5.2 (1) Rule 29.3(2) provides that where a party has a legal representative, a representative familiar with the case and with sufficient authority to deal with any issues that are likely to arise must attend case management conferences and pre-trial reviews.

(2) That person should be someone who is personally involved in the conduct of the case, and who has the authority and information to deal with any matter which may reasonably be expected to be dealt with at such a hearing, including the fixing of the timetable, the identification of issues and matters of evidence.

(3) Where the inadequacy of the person attending or of his instructions leads to the adjournment of a hearing, the court will expect to make a wasted costs order.

5.3 The topics the court will consider at a case management conference are likely to include:

(1) whether the claimant has made clear the claim he is bringing, in particular the amount he is claiming, so that the other party can understand the case he has to meet,

(2) whether any amendments are required to the claim, a statement of case or any other document,

(3) what disclosure of documents, if any, is necessary,

(4) what expert evidence is reasonably required in accordance with rule 35.1 and how and when that evidence should be obtained and disclosed,

(5) what factual evidence should be disclosed,

(6) what arrangements should be made about the giving of clarification or further information and the putting of questions to experts, and

(7) whether it will be just and will save costs to order a split trial or the trial of one or more preliminary issues.

5.4 In all cases the court will set a timetable for the steps it decides are necessary to be taken. These steps may include the holding of a case management conference or a pre-trial review, and the court will be alert to perform its duty to fix a trial date or period as soon as it can.

5.5 (1) The court will not at this stage give permission to use expert evidence unless it can identify each expert by name or field in its order and say whether his evidence is to be given orally or by the use of his report.

(2) A party who obtains expert evidence before obtaining a direction about it does so at his own risk as to costs, except where he obtained the evidence in compliance with a pre-action protocol.

5.6 To assist the court, the parties and their legal advisers should:

(1) ensure that all documents that the court is likely to ask to see (including witness statements and experts' reports) are brought to the hearing,

(2) consider whether the parties should attend,

(3) consider whether a case summary will be useful, and

(4) consider what orders each wishes to be made and give notice of them to the other parties.

5.7 (1) A case summary:

(a) should be designed to assist the court to understand and deal with the questions before it,

(b) should set out a brief chronology of the claim, the issues of fact which are agreed or in dispute and the evidence needed to decide them,

(c) should not normally exceed 500 words in length, and

(d) should be prepared by the claimant and agreed with the other parties if possible.

5.8 (1) Where a party wishes to obtain an order not routinely made at a case management conference and believes that his application will be opposed, he should issue and serve the application in time for it to be heard at the case management conference.

(2) If the time allowed for the case management conference is likely to be insufficient for the application to be heard he should inform the court at once so that a fresh date can be fixed.

(3) A costs sanction may be imposed on a party who fails to comply with sub-paragraph (1) or (2).

5.9 At a case management conference the court may also consider whether the case ought to be tried by a High Court judge or by a judge who specialises in that type of claim and how that question will be decided. In that case the claim may need to be transferred to another court.

VARIATION OF DIRECTIONS

6.1 This paragraph deals with the procedure to be adopted:

(1) where a party is dissatisfied with a direction given by the court,

(2) where the parties have agreed about changes they wish made to the directions given, or

(3) where a party wishes to apply to vary a direction.

6.2 (1) It is essential that any party who wishes to have a direction varied takes steps to do so as soon as possible.

(2) The court will assume for the purposes of any later application that a party who did not appeal, and who made no application to vary within 14 days of service of the order containing the directions, was content that they were correct in the circumstances then existing.

6.3 (1) Where a party is dissatisfied with a direction given or other order made by the court he may appeal or apply to the court for it to reconsider its decision.

(2) Unless paragraph 6.4 applies, a party should appeal if the direction was given or the order was made at a hearing at which he was present, or of which he had due notice.

(3) In any other case he should apply to the court to reconsider its decision.

(4) If an application is made for the court to reconsider its decision:

(a) it will usually be heard by the judge who gave the directions or another judge of the same level,

(b) the court will give all parties at least 3 days notice of the hearing, and

(c) the court may confirm its directions or make a different order.

6.4 Where there has been a change in the circumstances since the order was made the court may set aside or vary a direction it has given. It may do so on application or on its own initiative.

6.5 Where the parties agree about changes they wish made to the directions given:

(1) If rule 2.11 (variation by agreement of a date set by the court for doing any act other than those stated in the note to that rule) or rule 31.5, 31.10(8) or 31.13 (agreements about disclosure) applies the parties need not file the written agreement.

(2) (a) In any other case the parties must apply for an order by consent.

(b) The parties must file a draft of the order sought and an agreed statement of the reasons why the variation is sought.

(c) The court may make an order in the agreed terms or in other terms without a hearing, but it may direct that a hearing is to be listed.

FAILURE TO COMPLY WITH CASE MANAGEMENT DIRECTIONS

7.1 Where a party fails to comply with a direction given by the court any other party may apply for an order that he must do so or for a sanction to be imposed or both of these.

7.2 The party entitled to apply for such an order must do so without delay but should first warn the other party of his intention to do so.

7.3 The court may take any such delay into account when it decides whether to make an order imposing a sanction or to grant relief from a sanction imposed by the rules or any other practice direction.

7.4 (1) The court will not allow a failure to comply with directions to lead to the postponement of the trial unless the circumstances are exceptional.

(2) If it is practical to do so the court will exercise its powers in a manner that enables the case to come on for trial on the date or within the period previously set.

(3) In particular the court will assess what steps each party should take to prepare the case for trial, direct that those steps are taken in the shortest possible time and impose a sanction for non-compliance. Such a

sanction may, for example, deprive a party of the right to raise or contest an issue or to rely on evidence to which the direction relates.

(4) Where it appears that one or more issues are or can be made ready for trial at the time fixed while others cannot, the court may direct that the trial will proceed on the issues which are then ready, and direct that no costs will be allowed for any later trial of the remaining issues or that those costs will be paid by the party in default.

(5) Where the court has no option but to postpone the trial it will do so for the shortest possible time and will give directions for the taking of the necessary steps in the meantime as rapidly as possible.

(6) Litigants and lawyers must be in no doubt that the court will regard the postponement of a trial as an order of last resort. Where it appears inevitable the court may exercise its power to require a party as well as his legal representative to attend court at the hearing where such an order is to be sought.

(7) The court will not postpone any other hearing without a very good reason, and for that purpose the failure of a party to comply on time with directions previously given will not be treated as a good reason.

'the court will not allow' (para 7.4(1))—In *Holmes v SGB Services* [2001] EWCA Civ 354 the Court of Appeal drew attention to and emphasised the rigorous nature of this provision.

PRE-TRIAL CHECK LISTS (LISTING QUESTIONNAIRES)

8.1 (1) The pre-trial check list (listing questionnaire) will be in Form N170.

(2) Unless it dispenses with pre-trial check lists and orders an early trial on a fixed date, the court will specify the date for filing completed pre-trial check lists when it fixes the trial date or trial period under rule 29.2(2).

(3) The date for filing the completed pre-trial check lists will be not later than 8 weeks before the trial date or the start of the trial period.

(4) The court will serve the pre-trial check lists on the parties at least 14 days before that date.

(5) Although the rules do not require the parties to exchange copies of the check lists before they are filed they are encouraged to do so to avoid the court being given conflicting or incomplete information.

(6) The file will be placed before a judge for his directions when all the check lists have been filed or when the time for filing them has expired and where a party has filed a checklist but another party has not done so.

8.2 The court's general approach will be as set out in the following paragraphs. The court may however decide to make other orders, and in particular the court will take into account the steps, if any, of which it is aware which the parties have taken to prepare the case for trial.

8.3 (1) Where no party files a pre-trial checklist the court will order that unless a completed pre-trial checklist is filed within 7 days from service of that order, the claim, defence and any counterclaim will be struck out without further order of the court.

(2) Where a party files a pre-trial check list but another party (the defaulting party) does not do so, the court will fix a hearing under rule 29.6(4). Whether or not the defaulting party attends the hearing, the court will normally fix or confirm the trial date and make other orders about the steps to be taken to prepare the case for trial.

8.4 Where the court decides to hold a hearing under rule 29.6(4) the court will fix a date which is as early as possible and the parties will be given at least 3 days notice of the date.

8.5 Where the court decides to hold a pre-trial review (whether or not this is in addition to a hearing under rule 29.6(4)) the court will give the parties at least 7 days notice of the date.

DIRECTIONS THE COURT WILL GIVE ON LISTING

9.1 **Directions the court must give**.

The court must fix the trial date or week, give a time estimate and fix the place of trial.

9.2 **Other directions**

(1) The parties should seek to agree directions and may file an agreed order. The court may make an order in those terms or it may make a different order.
(2) Agreed directions should include provision about:
 (a) evidence especially expert evidence,
 (b) a trial timetable and time estimate,
 (c) the preparation of a trial bundle, and
 (d) any other matter needed to prepare the case for trial.
(3) The court will include such of these provisions as are appropriate in any order that it may make, whether or not the parties have filed agreed directions.
(4) Unless a direction doing so has been given before, a direction giving permission to use expert evidence will say whether it gives permission to use oral evidence or reports or both and will name the experts concerned.

9.3 The principles set out in paragraph 6 of this practice direction about variation of directions applies equally to directions given at this stage.

THE TRIAL

10.1 The trial will normally take place at a Civil Trial Centre but it may be at another court if it is appropriate having regard to the needs of the parties and the availability of court resources.

10.2 The judge will generally have read the papers in the trial bundle and may dispense with an opening address.

10.3 The judge may confirm or vary any timetable given previously, or if none has been given set his own.

10.4 Attention is drawn to the provisions in Part 32 and the following parts of the Rules about evidence, and in particular:

(1) to rule 32.1 (court's power to control evidence and to restrict cross-examination), and
(2) to rule 32.5(2) statements and reports to stand as evidence in chief.

10.5 In an appropriate case the judge may summarily assess costs in accordance with rule 44.7. Attention is drawn to the practice directions about costs and the steps the parties are required to take.

10.6 Once the trial of a multi-track claim has begun, the judge will normally sit on consecutive court days until it has been concluded.

PART 30
TRANSFER

CONTENTS OF THIS PART

30.1 Scope of this Part

(1) This Part deals with the transfer of proceedings between county courts, between the High Court and the county courts and within the High Court.

(2) The practice direction may make provision about the transfer of proceedings between the court and a tribunal.

(Rule 26.2 provides for automatic transfer in certain cases)

Amendments—SI 2003/2113.

Practice Direction—See generally PD30 at p 804.

Scope of provision—This Part deals with transfer of the case by court order (a judicial act) as opposed to automatic transfer provided for in r 14.12(2), r 14.13(3), r 26.2, Sch 2, CCR Ord 22, r 10 or CCR Ord 25, r 2 (an administrative act).

30.2 Transfer between county courts and within the High Court

(1) A county court may order proceedings before that court, or any part of them (such as a counterclaim or an application made in the proceedings), to be transferred to another county court if it is satisfied that –

(a) an order should be made having regard to the criteria in rule 30.3; or
(b) proceedings for –
  (i) the detailed assessment of costs; or
  (ii) the enforcement of a judgment or order,

could be more conveniently or fairly taken in that other county court.

(2) If proceedings have been started in the wrong county court, a judge of the county court may order that the proceedings –

(a) be transferred to the county court in which they ought to have been started;
(b) continue in the county court in which they have been started; or
(c) be struck out.

(3) An application for an order under paragraph (1) or (2) must be made to the county court where the claim is proceeding.

(4) The High Court may, having regard to the criteria in rule 30.3, order proceedings in the Royal Courts of Justice or a district registry, or any part of such proceedings (such as a counterclaim or an application made in the proceedings) to be transferred –

(a) from the Royal Courts of Justice to a district registry; or
(b) from a district registry to the Royal Courts of Justice or to another district registry.

(5) A district registry may order proceedings before it for the detailed assessment of costs to be transferred to another district registry if it is satisfied that the proceedings could be more conveniently or fairly taken in that other district registry.

(6) An application for an order under paragraph (4) or (5) must, if the claim is proceeding in a district registry, be made to that registry.

(7) Where some enactment, other than these Rules, requires proceedings to be started in a particular county court, neither paragraphs (1) nor (2) give the court power to order proceedings to be transferred to a county court which is not the court in which they should have been started or to order them to continue in the wrong court.

(8) Probate proceedings may only be transferred under paragraph (4) to the Chancery Division at the Royal Courts of Justice or to one of the Chancery district registries.

Practice Direction—See generally PD30 at p 804.

'conveniently or fairly' (r 30.2(1))—These words are not defined and mirror those used in the former CCR Ord 16, r 1(a). The court does, however, have full discretion to transfer with which an appellate court will not interfere provided the discretion is used judicially (*Birch v County Motor and Engineering Co Ltd* [1958] 3 All ER 175, CA) and the criteria in r 30.3 are borne in mind as well as the overriding objective.

Costs assessments—In county court cases, assessment may be remitted to the Supreme Court Costs Office without the case being transferred (r 47.4).

30.3 Criteria for a transfer order

(1) Paragraph (2) sets out the matters to which the court must have regard when considering whether to make an order under –

(a) section 40(2), 41(1) or 42(2) of the County Courts Act 1984 (transfer between the High Court and a county court);
(b) rule 30.2(1) (transfer between county courts); or
(c) rule 30.2(4) (transfer between the Royal Courts of Justice and the district registries).

(2) The matters to which the court must have regard include –

(a) the financial value of the claim and the amount in dispute, if different;
(b) whether it would be more convenient or fair for hearings (including the trial) to be held in some other court;
(c) the availability of a judge specialising in the type of claim in question;
(d) whether the facts, legal issues, remedies or procedures involved are simple or complex;
(e) the importance of the outcome of the claim to the public in general;
(f) the facilities available at the court where the claim is being dealt with and whether they may be inadequate because of any disabilities of a party or potential witness;
(g) whether the making of a declaration of incompatibility under section 4 of the Human Rights Act 1998 has arisen or may arise;
(h) in the case of civil proceedings by or against the Crown, as defined in rule 66.1(2), the location of the relevant government department or

officers of the Crown and, where appropriate, any relevant public interest that the matter should be tried in London.

Amendments—SI 2000/2092; SI 2005/2292.

Practice Direction—See generally PD30 at p 804.

'The matters to which the court must have regard' (r 30.3(2))—The express provision of criteria is new, although the criteria themselves are unsurprising and accord with the overriding objective. Examples of the type of factors that the court may consider when deciding which court is the most appropriate for the hearing of a case include:

- the convenience of the parties (as opposed to their solicitors);
- the location of any accident which is the subject of the claim;
- the fact that only damages are in dispute (ie there may be no need for a represented defendant to attend); and
- where a 'view' may be necessary.

The list is not exhaustive.

In *Pepin v Taylor* [2002] EWCA Civ 1522 the Court of Appeal said that there are strong reasons for fixing a venue for the proceedings at a place convenient for the defendant, as the defendant 'does not choose to be sued'. The fact that the defendant may counterclaim does not detract considerably from that principle. However, where the only party giving evidence is the claimant, eg in personal injury cases where only quantum of damages is in dispute, there may be an argument that the claimant's court is the most convenient. In *Fradkina v Network Housing Association* [2002] EWCA Civ 1715 the Court of Appeal ordered proceedings to be transferred away from a county court where the claimant had been 'poorly served by the court' and where 'the court had not adequately dealt with consolidated cases in the past'.

Rule 30.3(2)(a)—The court may disregard any amount admitted when making its decision (cf r 26.8(2)). As to transfer between High Court and county court, note the financial limits set out in High Court and County Courts Jurisdiction Order 1991, as amended, and the provisions of PD29, para 2.

'convenient or fair' (r 30.3(2)(b))—See note to r 30.2(1).

30.4 Procedure

(1) Where the court orders proceedings to be transferred, the court from which they are to be transferred must give notice of the transfer to all the parties.

(2) An order made before the transfer of the proceedings shall not be affected by the order to transfer.

Practice Direction—See generally PD30 at p 804.

Date of transfer—The order takes effect from the date it is made (PD30, para 3).

Procedure for appeal—See PD30, para 5.

Applications to set aside—For example, under r 23.10. The application is made to the court which made the order (PD30, para 6.1) and in accordance with Pt 23 (PD30, para 6.2).

30.5 Transfer between Divisions and to and from a specialist list

(1) The High Court may order proceedings in any Division of the High Court to be transferred to another Division.

(2) The court may order proceedings to be transferred to or from a specialist list.

(3) An application for the transfer of proceedings to or from a specialist list must be made to a judge dealing with claims in that list.

Practice Direction—See generally PD30 at p 804.

'a specialist list' (r 30.5(2),(3))—See r 2.3(2) and Pt 49.

30.6 Power to specify place where hearings are to be held

The court may specify the place (for instance, a particular county court) where the trial or some other hearing in any proceedings is to be held and may do so without ordering the proceedings to be transferred.

Practice Direction—See generally PD30 at p 804.

Scope of provision—This enables a hearing to take place in another court without the proceedings actually being transferred to accommodate the convenience of the parties and to ensure efficiency of trial listing.

In particular, Fast Track cases from several courts are likely to be listed together and, especially in London, to be subject to some last minute re-arranging of venue to ensure that a judge is available to hear a case on the date fixed.

'The court may specify the place'—The court will want to take into account the answers to the question in the allocation questionnaires which invites the parties to suggest which court would be most convenient for them.

30.7 Transfer of control of money in court

The court may order that control of any money held by it under rule 21.11 (control of money recovered by or on behalf of a child or patient) be transferred to another court if that court would be more convenient.

Practice Direction—See generally PD30 at p 804.

30.8 Transfer of competition law claims

(1) This rule applies if, in any proceedings in the Queen's Bench Division (other than proceedings in the Commercial or Admiralty Courts), a district registry of the High Court or a county court, a party's statement of case raises an issue relating to the application of –

- (a) Article 81 or Article 82 of the Treaty establishing the European Community; or
- (b) Chapter I or II of Part I of the Competition Act 1998.

(2) Rules 30.2 and 30.3 do not apply.

(3) The court must transfer the proceedings to the Chancery Division of the High Court at the Royal Courts of Justice.

(4) If any such proceedings which have been commenced in the Queen's Bench Division or a Mercantile Court fall within the scope of rule 58.1(2), any party to those proceedings may apply for the transfer of the proceedings to the Commercial Court, in accordance with rule 58.4(2) and rule 30.5(3). If the application is refused, the proceedings must be transferred to the Chancery Division of the High Court at the Royal Courts of Justice.

Amendments—Revoked by SI 2000/2092; reinserted by SI 2003/3361; substituted by SI 2004/1306; amended by SI 2005/2292.

Practice Direction – Transfer

This Practice Direction supplements CPR Part 30 (PD30)

General note—See also the notes to CPR Pt 30 for relevant commentary.

VALUE OF A CASE AND TRANSFER

1 In addition to the criteria set out in Rule 30.3(2) attention is drawn to the financial limits set out in the High Court and County Courts Jurisdiction Order 1991, as amended.

2 Attention is also drawn to paragraph 2 of the practice direction on Part 29 (The Multi-Track).

DATE OF TRANSFER

3 Where the court orders proceedings to be transferred, the order will take effect from the date it is made by the court.

PROCEDURE ON TRANSFER

4.1 Where an order for transfer has been made the transferring court will immediately send notice of the transfer to the receiving court. The notice will contain:

(1) the name of the case, and
(2) the number of the case.

4.2 At the same time as the transferring court notifies the receiving court it will also notify the parties of the transfer under rule 30.4(1).

PROCEDURE FOR AN APPEAL AGAINST ORDER OF TRANSFER

5.1 Where a district judge orders proceedings to be transferred and both the transferring and receiving courts are county courts, any appeal against that order should be made in the receiving court.]

5.2 The receiving court may, if it is more convenient for the parties, remit the appeal to the transferring court to be dealt with there.]

Appeals—As to appeals from interlocutory orders, see Guide 58, which sets out the distinction between an appeal and an application to set an order aside (para 6 below).

Form of notice of appeal—There is no prescribed form. However, Form PF110 may be used in the High Court and Form N244 in the county courts.

Fees on appeal—On notice – £100 (SCFO and CCFO fee 2.3).

APPLICATIONS TO SET ASIDE

6.1 Where a party may apply to set aside an order for transfer (eg under rule 23.10) the application should be made to the court which made the order.

6.2 Such application should be made in accordance with Part 23 of the Rules and the practice direction which supplements it.

TRANSFER ON THE CRITERION IN RULE 30.3(2)(G)

7 A transfer should only be made on the basis of the criterion in rule 30.3(2)(g) where there is a real prospect that a declaration of incompatibility will be made.

ENTERPRISE ACT 2002

8.1 In this paragraph –

(1) 'the 1998 Act' means the Competition Act 1998;
(2) 'the 2002 Act' means the Enterprise Act 2002; and
(3) 'the CAT' means the Competition Appeal Tribunal.

8.2 Rules 30.1, 30.4 and 30.5 and paragraphs 3 and 6 apply.

TRANSFER FROM THE HIGH COURT OR A COUNTY COURT TO THE COMPETITION APPEAL TRIBUNAL UNDER SECTION 16(4) OF THE ENTERPRISE ACT 2002

8.3 The High Court or a county court may pursuant to section 16(4) of the 2002 Act, on its own initiative or on application by the claimant or defendant, order the transfer of any part of the proceedings before it, which relates to a claim to which section 47A of the 1998 Act applies, to the CAT.

8.4 When considering whether to make an order under paragraph 8.3 the court shall take into account whether –

(1) there is a similar claim under section 47A of the 1998 Act based on the same infringement currently before the CAT;
(2) the CAT has previously made a decision on a similar claim under section 47A of the 1998 Act based on the same infringement; or
(3) the CAT has developed considerable expertise by previously dealing with a significant number of cases arising from the same or similar infringements.

8.5 Where the court orders a transfer under paragraph 8.3 it will immediately –

(1) send to the CAT –
    (a) a notice of the transfer containing the name of the case; and
    (b) all papers relating to the case; and
(2) notify the parties of the transfer.

8.6 An appeal against a transfer order made under paragraph 8.3 must be brought in the court which made the transfer order.

TRANSFER FROM THE COMPETITION APPEAL TRIBUNAL TO THE HIGH COURT UNDER SECTION 16(5) OF THE ENTERPRISE ACT 2002

8.7 Where the CAT pursuant to section 16(5) of the 2002 Act directs transfer of a claim made in proceedings under section 47A of the 1998 Act to the High Court, the claim should be transferred to the Chancery Division of the High Court at the Royal Courts of Justice.

8.8 As soon as a claim has been transferred under paragraph 8.7, the High Court must –

(1) allocate a case number; and
(2) list the case for a case management hearing before a judge.

8.9 A party to a claim which has been transferred under paragraph 8.7 may apply to transfer it to the Commercial Court if it otherwise falls within the scope of rule 58.2(1), in accordance with the procedure set out in rules 58.4(2) and 30.5(3).

PART 31
DISCLOSURE AND INSPECTION OF DOCUMENTS

CONTENTS OF THIS PART

Procedural Guide—See Guide 24, set out in Section 1 of this work.

31.1 Scope of this Part

(1) This Part sets out rules about the disclosure and inspection of documents.

(2) This Part applies to all claims except a claim on the small claims track.

Practice Direction—See generally PD31 at p 819.

Note that PD31 does now apply in the Commercial Court (the former Commercial Court Guide, para E1.4 is no longer included in the February 2002 issue). It is, however, now supplemented in that court by the detailed provisions of Section E of its Guide, and the modified Standard Disclosure Form N265(CC).

'This Part' (r 31.1(1))—The new code, replacing discovery and inspection, limits the normal disclosure obligation to 'standard disclosure' (r 31.6) and subjects the obligation to search for documents to a test of reasonableness and proportionality (r 31.7). The extent of the search made must itself be disclosed and compliance with the duty to disclose must be certified in a 'disclosure statement' (r 31.10(6)). There are new procedures and limitations in respect of inspection. Pre-action and non-party disclosure (rr 31.16 and 31.17) is no longer limited to personal injury and fatal accident claims. Overall, proportionality, and a real appreciation of the issues, are the basic guidelines.

'the small claims track' (r 31.1(2))—See r 27.4 and PD27, App A.

31.2 Meaning of disclosure

A party discloses a document by stating that the document exists or has existed.

'stating'—This means in the list of documents required by r 31.10(2), as opposed to the disclosure statement (r 31.10(5)), since the latter, if fully complying with the rules, may itself list categories of documents amongst which no search has been carried out and it would defeat the object of r 31.7(3) if those documents were to be treated as disclosed within the meaning of this Part. The court may order or the parties may agree to dispense with standard disclosure (r 31.5), and the parties may agree to dispense with lists and disclosure statements (see notes under r 31.10(8)). For an example, see the Annex to PD28 – direction for disclosure by providing copies.

31.3 Right of inspection of a disclosed document

(1) A party to whom a document has been disclosed has a right to inspect that document except where –

(a) the document is no longer in the control of the party who disclosed it;
(b) the party disclosing the document has a right or a duty to withhold inspection of it; or
(c) paragraph (2) applies.

(Rule 31.8 sets out when a document is in the control of a party)

(Rule 31.19 sets out the procedure for claiming a right or duty to withhold inspection)

(2) Where a party considers that it would be disproportionate to the issues in the case to permit inspection of documents within a category or class of document disclosed under rule 31.6(b) –

(a) he is not required to permit inspection of documents within that category or class; but
(b) he must state in his disclosure statement that inspection of those documents will not be permitted on the grounds that to do so would be disproportionate.

(Rule 31.6 provides for standard disclosure)

(Rule 31.10 makes provision for a disclosure statement)

(Rule 31.12 provides for a party to apply for an order for specific inspection of documents)

Practice Direction—See generally PD31 at p 819 and also PD31, Annex A.

'a right to inspect' (r 31.3(1))—This exists unless one of the procedures mentioned in this rule is adopted by the disclosing party. Rule 31.15 deals with that right.

'a right or duty to withhold' (r 31.3(1)(b))—See rr 31.10(4) and 31.19 and the notes to them.

Withholding inspection as disproportionate (r 31.3(2))—Apart from the familiar concepts such as privilege as grounds for withholding inspection, this rule imports a further potential limitation on access to documents on the grounds of proportionality, even in respect of documents falling within the narrow requirements of standard disclosure. For example, the disclosing party may know that amongst a large number of documents in a cluttered and messy (or foreign) archive there will be documents within 'standard disclosure' but take the view that extricating or sorting through or copying them would be disproportionate. In that event, he might disclose them compendiously but object to inspection on this ground. Once the disclosing party asserts in his disclosure statement that permission will not be granted, inspection will not be required in the absence of an order under r 31.12(3). There is no suggested wording, or reference to this type of withholding, in the model disclosure statement, PD31, Annex A, although it is provided for in the disclosure statement part of Practice Form N265.

Note that the procedure differs from that for asserting, and resolving, a claim of right or duty to withhold inspection, as to which see rr 31.10(4) and 31.19 and the notes to them.

31.4 Meaning of document

In this Part –

'document' means anything in which information of any description is recorded; and

'copy', in relation to a document, means anything onto which information recorded in the document has been copied, by whatever means and whether directly or indirectly.

'document'—This includes a surveillance video (*Rall v Hume* [2001] EWCA Civ 146, [2001] CP Rep 58, (2001) *The Times*, 14 March, CA).

31.5 Disclosure limited to standard disclosure

(1) An order to give disclosure is an order to give standard disclosure unless the court directs otherwise.

(2) The court may dispense with or limit standard disclosure.

(3) The parties may agree in writing to dispense with or to limit standard disclosure.

(The court may make an order requiring standard disclosure under rule 28.3 which deals with directions in relation to cases on the fast track and under rule 29.2 which deals with case management in relation to cases on the multi-track)

Practice Direction—See generally PD31 at p 819 and particularly paras 1.1–1.4 at p 820.

'order to give standard disclosure unless the court directs otherwise' (r 31.5(1))—This is the basis of the new, more limited ambit of disclosure. Note the requirement for an order: the old rules on 'automatic discovery' have gone but the requirements of the overriding objective, and the pre-action protocols, are such that preparation for disclosure should start early and in the expectation that an order will be made: in many cases covered by, for instance, the Personal Injury Protocol and that for the Resolution of Clinical Disputes, set out in Section 4 of this work, much of the disclosure will in fact have occurred before proceedings start.

The presumption is that the order will be for standard disclosure or less (if any) (r 31.5(2)).

'may agree in writing to dispense with or to limit' (r 31.5(3))—See generally PD31, para 1, in particular that any such written agreement should be lodged with the court.

31.6 Standard disclosure – what documents are to be disclosed

Standard disclosure requires a party to disclose only –

(a) the documents on which he relies; and

(b) the documents which –

(i) adversely affect his own case;

(ii) adversely affect another party's case; or

(iii) support another party's case; and

(c) the documents which he is required to disclose by a relevant practice direction.

Practice Direction—See generally PD31 at p 819 and particularly paras 1.1–1.4 at p 820.

'requires a party to disclose only'—Note in particular the word 'only'. Costs wasted by reason of the disclosure of other documents – those which are purely 'neutral' for instance, even if relevant under the old familiar rules – may be the subject of adverse costs orders or disallowed on assessment of costs. Set against that must be the higher initial costs of identifying which documents should be included.

Note the three fundamental categories; there is no specific 'relevant practice direction' as referred to at r 31.6(c); the various specialist jurisdictions have their own guidance as set out in the Court

Guides contained in Section 5 of this work, and various of the pre-action protocols identify specific documents that must be disclosed, see for instance Annex B to the Personal Injury Protocol, set out in Section 4 of this work. The purpose of the reference is to include within r 31.6 those documents particular to certain types of proceedings governed by their own practice directions, which might otherwise not obviously fall within the scope of the rule.

Standard disclosure has a particular significance in relation to applications for pre-action disclosure – see the notes under r 31.16.

31.7 Duty of search

(1) When giving standard disclosure, a party is required to make a reasonable search for documents falling within rule 31.6(b) or (c).

(2) The factors relevant in deciding the reasonableness of a search include the following –

- (a) the number of documents involved;
- (b) the nature and complexity of the proceedings;
- (c) the ease and expense of retrieval of any particular document; and
- (d) the significance of any document which is likely to be located during the search.

(3) Where a party has not searched for a category or class of document on the grounds that to do so would be unreasonable, he must state this in his disclosure statement and identify the category or class of document.

(Rule 31.10 makes provision for a disclosure statement)

Practice Direction—See generally PD31 at p 819 and particularly paras 1.1–1.4 at p 820 and para 2 at p 821.

'a reasonable search' (r 31.7(1))—This is a key part of the new rule. The search is to be for documents within r 31.6(b) and (c).

'factors relevant … search include' (r 31.7(2))—This is a non-exhaustive and common-sense list of criteria, and PD31, para 2 contains a further reminder on proportionality under Pt 1, and makes clear that such a decision may be based on matters including dates, location or categories.

'Where a party has not searched … on the grounds that it would be unreasonable, he must state this … and identify the category or class of document' (r 31.7(3))—The extent to which the judgment exercised by the disclosing party must itself be revealed in the disclosure statement seems very clear from these words – positively to identify that which has not been searched (for: 'not searching through' may trigger r 31.3(2)), and the absence of such transparency would lead to an unacceptable level of undisclosed subjectivity. However, subr (3) was a late addition to this Part and other requirements of and under it are now potentially misleading (see the notes under r 31.10). In the Commercial Court the provisions of Admiralty and Commercial Courts Guide, para E3.6 make express the requirement for transparency.

31.8 Duty of disclosure limited to documents which are or have been in party's control

(1) A party's duty to disclose documents is limited to documents which are or have been in his control.

(2) For this purpose a party has or has had a document in his control if –

- (a) it is or was in his physical possession;
- (b) he has or has had a right to possession of it; or
- (c) he has or has had a right to inspect or take copies of it.

Practice Direction—See generally PD31 at p 819 and particularly paras 1.1–1.4 at p 820.

'in his control'—This rule is similar to, but much simpler than, the old rules on 'possession, custody, control'.

31.9 Disclosure of copies

(1) A party need not disclose more than one copy of a document.

(2) A copy of a document that contains a modification, obliteration or other marking or feature –

- (a) on which a party intends to rely; or
- (b) which adversely affects his own case or another party's case or supports another party's case;

shall be treated as a separate document.

(Rule 31.4 sets out the meaning of a copy of a document)

31.10 Procedure for standard disclosure

(1) The procedure for standard disclosure is as follows.

(2) Each party must make, and serve on every other party, a list of documents in the relevant practice form.

(3) The list must identify the documents in a convenient order and manner and as concisely as possible.

(4) The list must indicate –

- (a) those documents in respect of which the party claims a right or duty to withhold inspection; and
- (b) (i) those documents which are no longer in the party's control; and
  - (ii) what has happened to those documents.

(Rule 31.19(3) and (4) require a statement in the list of documents relating to any documents inspection of which a person claims he has a right or duty to withhold)

(5) The list must include a disclosure statement.

(6) A disclosure statement is a statement made by the party disclosing the documents –

- (a) setting out the extent of the search that has been made to locate documents which he is required to disclose;
- (b) certifying that he understands the duty to disclose documents; and
- (c) certifying that to the best of his knowledge he has carried out that duty.

(7) Where the party making the disclosure statement is a company, firm, association or other organisation, the statement must also –

- (a) identify the person making the statement; and
- (b) explain why he is considered an appropriate person to make the statement.

(8) The parties may agree in writing –

- (a) to disclose documents without making a list; and
- (b) to disclose documents without the disclosing party making a disclosure statement.

(9) A disclosure statement may be made by a person who is not a party where this is permitted by a relevant practice direction.

'a list of documents' (r 31.10(2)–(4))—The relevant practice form is N265, and PD31, para 3 amplifies subr (3) in familiar terms.

'claims a right or duty to withhold inspection' (r 31.10(4))—Note the obligatory requirement for such claims to be made in the list itself – there is provision for this in N265 – to be read with the requirement at PD31, para 4.4 and 4.5 that such a statement must normally be made in the disclosure statement: neither the model form nor the disclosure statement part of N265 provide for that).

The requirements as to documents which are no longer in the custody of the disclosing party are unchanged.

Privilege—A claim to withhold inspection on the ground of legal professional privilege falls within r 31.10(4)(a) – see note **'Withholding inspection on the basis of a claim of right or duty'** under r 31.19.

'a disclosure statement' (r 31.10(5)–(7))—The requirements here have not incorporated r 31.7(3). There is no reference here to revealing searches which have not been made and, whilst the model disclosure statement at Annex A to PD31 and the Practice Form N265 include references to dates, places and categories, the purely negative formulation does not enable the other party to exercise any form of check on the subjective decision made by the disclosing party in that respect, and sits unhappily with the final part of the statement both in the form and the model. Paragraph 4 of PD31 deals with disclosure statements generally, and para 4.2 is wider than the bare terms of r 31.10(6), and the forms, but still does not sufficiently identify the positive duty under r 31.7(3). It is a requirement to be transparent about the existence of, especially, places where relevant documents might be but where no search has been conducted. The addition to PD31, para 4.3 made by Update 26 has clarified the status requirements of the signatory of the disclosure statement.

'a statement made by the party' (r 31.10(6))—The statement is to be made by the party himself, or an 'appropriate person' if the party is not an individual (r 31.10(7): that person is *quaere* not to be the legal representative – PD31, para 4.3 requires the maker to be identified, including the office or position he holds in the disclosing party, and para 4.4 sets out that in either case the legal representative must 'endeavour to ensure' that the maker understands the duties under Pt 31).

In the Commercial Court, however, Admiralty and Commercial Courts Guide, para E3.10 sensibly provides that any person can in principle be 'appropriate', including legal representatives. This depends on the particular circumstances, which must be set out in the disclosure statement – a modified version (N265(CC)) – being in use here.

Whilst r 31.10(9) provides for a non-party to make the disclosure statement if a practice direction permits it, there is as yet no such practice direction, save that PD31, para 4.7 permits the MIB to sign the statement in a relevant case.

'certifying that to the best of his knowledge he has carried out that duty' (r 31.10(6)(c))—Since 2 May 2000 there has been in force a rule putting disclosure statements on the same footing as other verifications – see r 31.23 and the note **'Scope of provision'** thereto.

'The parties may agree' (r 31.10(8))—Both lists, and disclosure statements, may be dispensed with by written agreement between the parties: note that under PD28 and PD29, agreed directions for disclosure by copies without lists must also, if they are to be approved by the court, provide either that the parties must serve a disclosure statement with the copies or that they have agreed to disclose in that way without such a statement.

31.11 Duty of disclosure continues during proceedings

(1) Any duty of disclosure continues until the proceedings are concluded.

(2) If documents to which that duty extends come to a party's notice at any time during the proceedings, he must immediately notify every other party.

Practice Direction—See generally PD31 at p 819 and also para 3.3 at p 821.

'immediately notify every other party' (r 31.11(2))—This rule is a welcome clarification, and whilst PD31, para 3.3 requires a party to prepare and serve a supplementary list of documents in this event, the rule requires immediate notification. This should remove the risk of the disclosing party failing in its (not always clearly understood or observed) common law duty not, for instance, to endeavour to complete settlement negotiations where the other party is in ignorance of the new document(s), 'pending' preparation of a supplementary list.

31.12 Specific disclosure or inspection

(1) The court may make an order for specific disclosure or specific inspection.

(2) An order for specific disclosure is an order that a party must do one or more of the following things –

(a) disclose documents or classes of documents specified in the order;
(b) carry out a search to the extent stated in the order;
(c) disclose any documents located as a result of that search.

(3) An order for specific inspection is an order that a party permit inspection of a document referred to in rule 31.3(2).

(Rule 31.3(2) allows a party to state in his disclosure statement that he will not permit inspection of a document on the grounds that it would be disproportionate to do so)

Practice Direction—See generally PD31 at p 819 and also paras 5.1–5.5 at p 822 and paras 6.1–6.2 at p 823.

'an order for specific disclosure' (r 31.12(1) and (2))—The procedure for making an application for specific disclosure, and the test to be applied, are set out at PD31, para 5. The onus is on the applying party to satisfy the court, on evidence, that there has not been adequate compliance with the order in all the circumstances (and bearing in mind the overriding objective); the word 'But' in PD31, para 5.4 may give an indication as to a presumption against entertaining such applications, but if the criteria are met the court will 'usually' make such order as is necessary to ensure proper compliance. The new (as from 25 March 2002, Update 26) PD31, para 5.5 gives an example of an order which may be made; it revives the *Peruvian Guano* concept of 'chain of enquiry' in the appropriate case.

In an appropriate case this rule (and the provisions of Pt 3) empower a court to order a party to sign forms of authority for the disclosure by third parties of, for example, medical records (*Bennett v Compass Group UK and Ireland Ltd & anor* [2002] EWCA Civ 642).

'an order for specific inspection' (r 31.12(1) and (3))—Neither the rule, nor PD31, lays down any procedure or criteria for an application under this rule, which does not deal with claims of right or duty to withhold inspection (governed by r 31.19), nor inspection of documents where the rules provide a right of inspection (under r 31.14, which is dealt with in r 31.15) – it is limited to the proportionality claim under r 31.3(2). Paragraph 6 of PD31 deals only with claims of right or duty notwithstanding its general heading and terms. A party will not go wrong, however, if it uses a procedure analogous to that in respect of specific disclosure.

31.13 Disclosure in stages

The parties may agree in writing, or the court may direct, that disclosure or inspection or both shall take place in stages.

Scope of provision—This is most obviously an appropriate course where liability and the amount of any damages are to be dealt with sequentially, although the rule is not so limited: any issue to be determined separately and first might give rise to such an order, as indeed might a 'case management' judgment that early disclosure of certain documents might lead to early settlement without need for full-scale standard disclosure.

31.14 Documents referred to in statements of case etc

(1) A party may inspect a document mentioned in –

(a) a statement of case;
(b) a witness statement;
(c) a witness summary; or
(d) an affidavit[(GL)].
(e) (*revoked*)

(2) Subject to rule 35.10(4), a party may apply for an order for inspection of any document mentioned in an expert's report which has not already been disclosed in the proceedings.

(Rule 35.10(4) makes provision in relation to instructions referred to in an expert's report)

Amendments—SI 2001/4015.

Practice Direction—See PD31, para 7 at p 823.

Scope of provision—These are rights in addition to those generally given by r 31.3: how to enforce them is set out at r 31.15. The amended (by Update 26, in force from 25 March 2002) PD31, para 7 has new guidance on seeking documents referred to by experts as provided for in the (partly new) r 31.14(2).

31.15 Inspection and copying of documents

Where a party has a right to inspect a document –

(a) that party must give the party who disclosed the document written notice of his wish to inspect it;

(b) the party who disclosed the document must permit inspection not more than 7 days after the date on which he received the notice; and

(c) that party may request a copy of the document and, if he also undertakes to pay reasonable copying costs, the party who disclosed the document must supply him with a copy not more than 7 days after the date on which he received the request.

(Rule 31.3 and 31.14 deal with the right of a party to inspect a document)

Practice Direction—See generally PD31 at p 819.

Scope of provision—The rights dealt with here are those set out at rr 31.3 and 31.14 – the familiar type of right to inspect disclosed documents (unless they are no longer in the control of the disclosing party, or are subject to a claim to withhold inspection of either kind – right/duty or proportionality – r 31.3) and those referred to in other case documents. No express provision is made dealing with a failure to give the inspection after service of the notice and the expiry of 7 days. Such occasions should never arise but if they do an ordinary application under Pt 23 will be appropriate and is likely to result in costs sanctions (at least – continuing default would ultimately lead to a striking out).

31.16 Disclosure before proceedings start

(1) This rule applies where an application is made to the court under any Act for disclosure before proceedings have started.

(2) The application must be supported by evidence.

(3) The court may make an order under this rule only where –

(a) the respondent is likely to be a party to subsequent proceedings;

(b) the applicant is also likely to be a party to those proceedings;

(c) if proceedings had started, the respondent's duty by way of standard disclosure, set out in rule 31.6, would extend to the documents or classes of documents of which the applicant seeks disclosure; and

(d) disclosure before proceedings have started is desirable in order to –

(i) dispose fairly of the anticipated proceedings;

(ii) assist the dispute to be resolved without proceedings; or

(iii) save costs.

(4) An order under this rule must –

(a) specify the documents or the classes of documents which the respondent must disclose; and

(b) require him, when making disclosure, to specify any of those documents –

(i) which are no longer in his control; or

(ii) in respect of which he claims a right or duty to withhold inspection.

(5) Such an order may –

(a) require the respondent to indicate what has happened to any documents which are no longer in his control; and

(b) specify the time and place for disclosure and inspection.

General note—See notes under r 31.17 below.

Exercise of the power under this rule—In *Bermuda International Securities Limited v KPMG (a firm)* [2001] EWCA Civ 269, [2001] CP Rep 73 the Court of Appeal, at [26], expressly declined to lay down guidelines for the exercise of this discretion 'at this early stage in the life of this new rule', stating that:

> 'It will be applicable in a vast range of cases, and it is peculiarly for judges in their case management rôle to work out the circumstances in which pre-action disclosure will be ordered.'

The case nonetheless provides a useful blueprint for and reminder of the basic required elements against which the discretion is to be exercised. Each of the four subrules of r 31.16(3) is a jurisdictional requirement and subrule (d) also imports the discretionary element of desirability. Disclosure is available where appropriate and – as ordered in *Bermuda* – where it might show whether the applicant has any case at all, overall or on any prospective issue. In addition, the court held that the presumption, at r 48.1, that the costs of an application for such disclosure should be borne by the applicant was not irrebuttable. In this case although the costs of the disclosure exercise itself were to be paid by the applicant, the court upheld the judge's refusal to order the applicant to pay the costs of the application, on the grounds that it had been unreasonably resisted. The order was for costs in the case – if there were one – otherwise 'no order'.

'likely to be a party' (r 31.16(3)(a) and (b))—The Court of Appeal held in *Black (Herbert) & ors v Sumitomo Corporation (UK) plc & ors* [2001] EWCA Civ 1819, [2002] 1 WLR 1562, that the judge was wrong, in considering this to be a high initial threshold and therefore, once it was established an order should follow. The statute requires only that the persons are likely to be parties *if* proceedings are issued, and not that it is likely that proceedings will be issued. 'Likely' (to be parties) means 'may well' rather than 'more probably than not'. Although the application was roundly rejected in this case, the decision contains useful statements of principle indicating that, in the right case, the power is a wide one.

'duty by way of standard disclosure … would extend to the documents' (r 31.16(3)(c))—This is a more stringent requirement than under r 31.17 (see also the notes under that rule). So far as it can (sometimes only the respondent will have this information), the court must be satisfied that the documents sought *would* fall within the scope of r 31.6 in relation to the issue in respect of which they are said to be relevant. In *Findel plc & ors v White Arrow Express Ltd & anor* (2002) (unreported) 19 December, Leeds Merc Ct) HHJ McGonigal sitting as a High Court judge held that 'would' means 'more likely than not on a balance of probabilities'.

'disclosure … is desirable' (r 31.16(3)(d))—In *Medisys plc v Arthur Andersen (a firm)* [2002] Lloyd's Rep PN 323, QBD Cooke J upheld the master's refusal to make such an order; in the absence of a clear definition of the issues it could not be said that it would be 'desirable' for the purposes set out in the rule. The requirement for a clear definition of the potential issue(s) is a strand running through all the above cases.

In *Rose v Lynx Express Ltd* [2004] EWCA Civ 447, [2004] 1 BCLC 455, [2004] All ER (D) 43 (Apr), (2004) *The Times*, 22 April, CA the Court of Appeal held that attempting a 'trial' of a preliminary issue at such an application was undesirable; it was enough for the claimant to show that his putative case was properly arguable and had a real prospect of success.

31.17 Orders for disclosure against a person not a party

(1) This rule applies where an application is made to the court under any Act for disclosure by a person who is not a party to the proceedings.

(2) The application must be supported by evidence.

(3) The court may make an order under this rule only where –

(a) the documents of which disclosure is sought are likely to support the case of the applicant or adversely affect the case of one of the other parties to the proceedings; and

(b) disclosure is necessary in order to dispose fairly of the claim or to save costs.

(4) An order under this rule must –

(a) specify the documents or the classes of documents which the respondent must disclose; and

(b) require the respondent, when making disclosure, to specify any of those documents –

(i) which are no longer in his control; or

(ii) in respect of which he claims a right or duty to withhold inspection.

(5) Such an order may –

(a) require the respondent to indicate what has happened to any documents which are no longer in his control; and

(b) specify the time and place for disclosure and inspection.

'application ... under any Act for disclosure' (rr 31.16(1) and 31.17(1))—These rules are a good deal wider than they look. Each is premised upon an application for pre-action (r 31.16) or non-party (r 31.17) disclosure pursuant to (unidentified) statute.

The Acts in question are Supreme Court Act 1981, ss 33 and 34 and County Courts Act 1984, ss 52 and 53 for each rule respectively which provided, amongst other things, for pre-action and non-party disclosure in personal injury and fatal accidents claims. What widens these provisions is not CPR itself but Civil Procedure (Modification of Enactments) Order 1998, the first exercise by the Lord Chancellor of his wide powers under Civil Procedure Act 1997, s 4(2) which came into force on the same day as the CPR. The Order amends each of those sections so that all reference to personal injury or death is removed. Accordingly, such disclosure is now available in principle in all actions of any kind.

In each case, evidence is required on the making of an application, and any order under either rule:

(1) *must* identify the documents or classes to be disclosed and require the respondent to say which documents are no longer in his control or those in respect of which he claims a right or duty to withhold inspection;

(2) *may* require the respondent to say what has happened to any documents no longer in his control and specify a time and place for inspection (subrule (4) in each case).

The differences between rr 31.16 and 31.17 are:

(a) Rule 31.16 –

(i) the respondent and applicants are likely to be parties to subsequent proceedings;

(ii) the documents sought must be ones which would fall within (any part of) r 31.6;

(iii) disclosure at this stage is 'desirable' in order fairly to dispose of the anticipated case, or to assist in settling it or to save costs, (r 31.16(3)).

(b) Rule 31.17 –

(i) the documents sought must be ones which are likely to either support the applicant's case or adversely affect the case of another party;

(ii) disclosure is 'necessary' in order fairly to dispose of the claim or to save costs (r 31.17(3)).

The wide powers under r 31.17 will often make consideration of the principles set out in *Norwich Pharmacal Co v Customs and Excise Commissioners* [1974] AC 133 unnecessary, though they remain an important part of the tools available to trace wrongdoers in a 'chain' (whether or not the respondents are themselves guilty of any wrongdoing, so long as they have in some way 'participated' or been 'involved' in it) – see *Ashworth Hospital Authority v MGN Limited* [2002] UKHL 29, [2002] 1 WLR 2033, HL.

An attempt to persuade the court that this amendment to the principal Acts was *ultra vires* was unsuccessful (*Burrells Wharf Freeholders v Galliard Homes* [2000] CP Rep 4, [2000] TCLR 54, [1999] 2 EGLR 81).

'documents ... sought are likely to support' (r 31.17(3)(a))—Note the differences between this subrule and that at r 31.16(3)(c). In *Three Rivers District Council v Bank of England & ors (No 4)* [2002] EWHC 1118, Comm Ct, Tomlinson J held that 'likely' here, by parity of reasoning with its meaning in r 31.16(3)(a), (b) (see notes above) means 'may well' – something less than the balance of probabilities.

Non-party disclosure – against a competitor owned by a company of which the defendants were shareholders – was ordered in the Commercial Court where the documents required (which included management accounts among other things) were relevant and necessary to resolve the question whether or not new contractual arrangements had been negotiated in good faith and at arm's length (*At the Races Holdings Ltd & anor v Race Course Association & ors* (2005) (unreported) 16 September (Comm Ct) (Christopher Clarke J)).

31.18 Rules not to limit other powers of the court to order disclosure

Rules 31.16 and 31.17 do not limit any other power which the court may have to order –

(a) disclosure before proceedings have started; and
(b) disclosure against a person who is not a party to proceedings.

Scope of provision—Given the above, this saving may have most impact in the context of chasing the identity of further wrongdoers where search orders are appropriate – see Pt 25 and its practice directions, although the provisions of Bankers Books Evidence Act 1879, for instance, remain in force.

31.19 Claim to withhold inspection or disclosure of a document

(1) A person may apply, without notice, for an order permitting him to withhold disclosure of a document on the ground that disclosure would damage the public interest.

(2) Unless the court orders otherwise, an order of the court under paragraph (1) –

(a) must not be served on any other person; and
(b) must not be open to inspection by any person.

(3) A person who wishes to claim that he has a right or a duty to withhold inspection of a document, or part of a document must state in writing –

(a) that he has such a right or duty; and
(b) the grounds on which he claims that right or duty.

(4) The statement referred to in paragraph (3) must be made –

(a) in the list in which the document is disclosed; or
(b) if there is no list, to the person wishing to inspect the document.

(5) A party may apply to the court to decide whether a claim made under paragraph (3) should be upheld.

(6) For the purpose of deciding an application under paragraph (1) (application to withhold disclosure) or paragraph (3) (claim to withhold inspection) the court may –

(a) require the person seeking to withhold disclosure or inspection of a document to produce that document to the court; and
(b) invite any person, whether or not a party, to make representations.

(7) An application under paragraph (1) or paragraph (5) must be supported by evidence.

(8) This Part does not affect any rule of law which permits or requires a document to be withheld from disclosure or inspection on the ground that its disclosure or inspection would damage the public interest.

Practice Direction—See generally PD31 at p 819 and also para 4.6 at p 822 and paras 6.1–6.2 at p 823.

Withholding disclosure—This is an alternative to giving disclosure but claiming to withhold inspection, under rr 31.3(1) and 31.19(3). Since the latter can be tested by the opposing party, but an order under this rule cannot (itself being not disclosed, usually, under r 31.19(2)), the criteria for the making of such an order should accordingly be much stricter.

Withholding inspection on the basis of a claim of right or duty—By subrule (4), this claim must be made in the list, if there is one, and also, according to PD31, para 4.6 but not r 31.19(4)(b) ('to the person wishing to inspect') in the disclosure statement (despite also the terms of N265 and the model statement). The onus is on the party from whom inspection is being withheld to make an application for inspection, which is emphasised by PD31, paras 6.1–6.2. Evidence is required, and the court may inspect the document(s) and invite any interested third party to make representations.

For an example of the flexible exercise of the court's discretion under this rule, where inspection said to be a foreign crime, see *Morris et al v Banque Arabe et Internationale d'Investissement*, sub nom *Re BCCI*, (2000) 97(1) LSG 24, Neuberger J.

Privilege—A claim to withhold inspection on the ground of privilege can properly be made in a wide range of circumstances; the major categories are summarised here, though recourse should be had to more detailed sources in case of doubt. The first category is *legal professional privilege*, which is customarily divided into two different types of communication: those which are privileged in all circumstances, whether or not litigation is involved, and those which are privileged only if they come into existence in contemplation of litigation.

In the former case, in principle all communications which are confidential, and made for the purpose of giving or getting legal advice, are and remain forever (subject to waiver) privileged. Thus, all such letters etc between solicitor and client, whether sent directly or through an agent, between solicitor and counsel, from to or between in-house lawyers and (by statute) between a client and his patent agent or his trademark agent are privileged from production. They need only be listed compendiously as such, sufficiently for the existence of such a category of documents to be identified and for the claim to privilege to be raised (see generally *Three Rivers District Council v Bank of England (No 5)* [2004] UKHL 48, [2004] 3 WLR 1274).

In the latter case, in order for privilege properly to be claimed, the communications must be ones which come into existence once litigation is contemplated, and for the purpose of it in respect of advice or the seeking of information or evidence. Provided that that is the purpose of the creation of such documents, it matters not between whom they pass. Questions can arise where documents come into existence for more than one purpose, or where litigation is merely likely; in that event the court will look at the dominant purpose of the creation of the documents at the time they were made. It is a question of fact.

There is a signal exception to all of the above: documents which come into existence in furtherance of an illegal purpose are not privileged. See, for example, *Walsh Automation (Europe) Ltd v Bridgeman* [2002] EWHC 1344 (QB), but compare *R (Morgan Grenfell) v Special Commissioner of Income Tax* [2002] UKHL 21, [2003] 1 AC 563.

Moreover, criminal or fraudulent conduct for the purposes of acquiring evidence in or for litigation gives rise to the same outcome (*Dubai Aluminium Co Ltd v Al Alawi* [1999] 1 WLR 1964, Rix J. In that case one party obtained material in breach of the Data Protection Act 1998, and it was held that any documents which were generated by, or reported on, such conduct (if relevant to the issues) were discloseable and fell outside the legitimate area of legal professional privilege.

Privilege can be waived. It is the privilege of the client, not the lawyers, so only the client can waive it. Difficulties can arise where the disclosure is accidental. If the mistake is an obvious one, then the party receiving the documents may not use them; in some circumstances the court will intervene and grant injunctive relief (compare *Al Fayed v Metropolitan Police Commissioner* [2002] EWCA Civ 780, *The Times*, 17 June. Disclosure for a limited purpose does not necessarily amount to waiver of privilege for all purposes (see *B v Auckland District Law Society* [2003] UKPC 38, [2003] 2 AC 736). But partial disclosure of a privileged document will waive privilege in the entire document because a party is not entitled to cherry-pick what he discloses (*Dunlop Slazenger International v Joe Bloggs Sports Ltd* [2003] EWCA Civ 901, [2003] All ER (D) 137 (Jun)).

Self-incrimination: A party is not obliged to afford inspection of materials which might expose him to criminal sanctions in the UK, subject to statutory exceptions such as Supreme Court Act 1981, s 72 – intellectual property rights.

Public interest privilege is specifically mentioned at r 31.19(1); it can give rise to an application without notice, and it is a matter for the court rather than one of 'objection' between the parties. The question will be: 'Is it necessary for the proper functioning of the state and its organs and agencies for disclosure to be withheld?', and that test is conducted, now, against the express requirements of the Art 6 right to a fair trial (for both/all parties).

Without prejudice communications: The cardinal rule here is that protection from production is afforded, as a matter of policy, to documents which form part of a genuine exercise in negotiation for the purpose of trying to settle all or part of a dispute between parties (unless both/all parties waive that privilege). Such exchanges are privileged whether or not they are marked 'without prejudice', and such a marking has no effect where the document is in fact not part of such an exercise. The rule, although not absolute, is usually determinative.

Genuine commercial secrets: Plainly, some litigation would be self-defeating if it were necessary to allow the other side to inspect secret manufacturing processes, or lists of customers. Sometimes this can be dealt with by undertakings, sometimes by ordering disclosure which is limited in scope or as to who may see the material. There is no hard and fast rule, and it depends on the circumstances of each case.

'This Part does not affect any rule of law' (r 31.19(8))—These words serve to remind that CPR represents procedural rules only (although the distinction between law and procedure is frequently blurred), and the inference is that matters other than 'public interest' are themselves procedural in character.

31.20 Restriction on use of a privileged document inspection of which has been inadvertently allowed

Where a party inadvertently allows a privileged(GL) document to be inspected, the party who has inspected the document may use it or its contents only with the permission of the court.

Scope of provision—This rule goes some way to resolving the difficulties caused by inadvertent disclosure: permission must be sought and obtained before any use is made of the document or its contents. It leaves entirely open, and subject to existing case law, the circumstances in which permission will be given – confirmed by *Breeze v John Stacy & Sons Ltd* (1999) *The Times*, 8 July, CA.

31.21 Consequence of failure to disclose documents or permit inspection

A party may not rely on any document which he fails to disclose or in respect of which he fails to permit inspection unless the court gives permission.

Scope of provision—In view of the many strictures and sanctions elsewhere in the CPR, this is at first sight a surprisingly anodyne rule, particularly as regards a failure to give disclosure (although it does not cancel the effects of r 3.4, for instance, under which a sufficient failure to give disclosure may result in the striking out of a statement of case). However, a party will not obtain permission to use such an undisclosed document save on terms which make certain that the opposing party suffers no prejudice, so in practice there is an effective sanction.

Failure by both sides to disclose—In what must be an exceptional case, *Gillingham & ors v Gillingham* [2001] EWCA Civ 906, [2001] CPLR 355, CA, the Court of Appeal, in furtherance of the overriding objective and notwithstanding the guiding principles of *Ladd v Marshall* [1954] 1 WLR 1489, CA remitted an action for re-trial after admitting as 'new' evidence a contemporaneous document addressed to the third claimant, signed by the defendant and evidencing the agreement which the claimants sought but failed to prove at trial, which neither side had disclosed (the relevant claimant forgot about it, the defendant offered no explanation). Peter Gibson LJ observed that it was unlikely that such a result could have been achieved prior to the CPR.

Falsification of documents—Although the rules do not expressly say so, it is clear that the court has powers in addition to those under r 31.23. In *Arrow Nominees Inc v Blackledge & ors* (2000) *The Times*, 7 July, CA, the court was faced with documents that had been deliberately tampered with. It was held that ordinarily, default in discovery, so long as it was eventually remedied, would not lead to the denial of a trial, following *Logicrose v Southend United FC* [1988] 1 WLR 1256, but where a party acted so as to put the fairness of a trial in jeopardy and to prevent the court from doing justice or so as to render further proceedings unsatisfactory, the court was bound to refuse to allow that litigant to take any further part and, where appropriate, to determine the proceedings against him. A litigant who showed that he was determined to act with the object of preventing a fair trial forfeited the right to take part in a trial.

31.22 Subsequent use of disclosed documents

(1) A party to whom a document has been disclosed may use the document only for the purpose of the proceedings in which it is disclosed, except where –

- (a) the document has been read to or by the court, or referred to, at a hearing which has been held in public;
- (b) the court gives permission; or
- (c) the party who disclosed the document and the person to whom the document belongs agree.

(2) The court may make an order restricting or prohibiting the use of a document which has been disclosed, even where the document has been read to or by the court, or referred to, at a hearing which has been held in public.

(3) An application for such an order may be made –

- (a) by a party; or
- (b) by any person to whom the document belongs.

Scope of provision—This replaces the complications of implied undertakings in the old rules with a simple rule, sets out express exceptions to the rule against ulterior use and affords locus to a third party who owns a document to apply for an order restricting or prohibiting its use even after a public hearing at which it was aired. None of these provisions is new, and existing case law will continue to be relevant as to what orders the court will make. Permission to use documents read and 'sufficiently referred to' by Laddie J was granted by the Court of Appeal in *Smithkline Beecham Biologicals v Connaught Labs Inc* [1999] 4 All ER 498, CA.

31.23 False disclosure statements

(1) Proceedings for contempt of court may be brought against a person if he makes, or causes to be made, a false disclosure statement, without an honest belief in its truth.

(2) Proceedings under this rule may be brought only –

- (a) by the Attorney-General; or
- (b) with the permission of the court.

Amendments—Inserted by SI 2000/221.

Practice Direction—See since February 2001 (Update 21) PD31, para 8, which draws attention to this provision and also to the guidance on how to operate it in practice, set out at (new) paras 27.1–27.4 of PD32.

Scope of provision—This was new as of 2 May 2000, and was inserted by the Civil Procedure (Amendment) Rules 2000, following criticism that the omission of disclosure statements from the scope of r 32.14 was illogical and potentially harmful, the accuracy of disclosure statements being fundamental to the conduct of litigation. This new rule is in terms identical to r 32.14. See also the notes to r 31.21 for the approach to falsified documents.

Practice Direction – Disclosure and Inspection

This Practice Direction supplements CPR Part 31 (PD31)

Procedural Guide—See Guide 24, set out in Section 1 of this work.

General note—See the notes to CPR Pt 31 for relevant commentary.

Specialist courts—This practice direction is supplemented and amplified by, in particular, Admiralty and Commercial Courts Guide, Section E.

GENERAL

1.1 The normal order for disclosure will be an order that the parties give standard disclosure.

1.2 In order to give standard disclosure the disclosing party must make a reasonable search for documents falling within the paragraphs of rule 31.6.

1.3 Having made the search the disclosing party must (unless rule 31.10(8) applies) make a list of the documents of whose existence the party is aware that fall within those paragraphs and which are or have been in the party's control (see rule 31.8).

1.4 The obligations imposed by an order for standard disclosure may be dispensed with or limited either by the court or by written agreement between the parties. Any such written agreement should be lodged with the court.

THE SEARCH

2 The extent of the search which must be made will depend upon the circumstances of the case including, in particular, the factors referred to in rule 31.7(2). The parties should bear in mind the overriding principle of proportionality (see rule 1.1(2)(c)). It may, for example, be reasonable to decide not to search for documents coming into existence before some particular date, or to limit the search to documents in some particular place or places, or to documents falling into particular categories.

ELECTRONIC DISCLOSURE

2A.1 Rule 31.4 contains a broad definition of a document. This extends to electronic documents, including e-mail and other electronic communications, word processed documents and databases. In addition to documents that are readily accessible from computer systems and other electronic devices and media, the definition covers those documents that are stored on servers and back-up systems and electronic documents that have been 'deleted'. It also extends to additional information stored and associated with electronic documents known as metadata.

2A.2 The parties should, prior to the first Case Management Conference, discuss any issues that may arise regarding searches for and the preservation of electronic documents. This may involve the parties providing information about the categories of electronic documents within their control, the computer systems, electronic devices and media on which any relevant documents may be held, the storage systems maintained by the parties and their document retention policies. In the case of difficulty or disagreement, the matter should be referred to a judge for directions at the earliest practical date, if possible at the first Case Management Conference.

2A.3 The parties should co-operate at an early stage as to the format in which electronic copy documents are to be provided on inspection. In the case of difficulty or disagreement, the matter should be referred to a Judge for directions at the earliest practical date, if possible at the first Case Management Conference.

2A.4 The existence of electronic documents impacts upon the extent of the reasonable search required by Rule 31.7 for the purposes of standard disclosure. The factors that may be relevant in deciding the reasonableness of a search for electronic documents include (but are not limited to) the following: –

(a) The number of documents involved.
(b) The nature and complexity of the proceedings.
(c) The ease and expense of retrieval of any particular document. This includes:
  (i) The accessibility of electronic documents or data including e-mail communications on computer systems, servers, back-up systems and other electronic devices or media that may contain such documents taking into account alterations or developments in hardware or software systems used by the disclosing party and/or available to enable access to such documents.
  (ii) The location of relevant electronic documents, data, computer systems, servers, back-up systems and other electronic devices or media that may contain such documents.
  (iii) The likelihood of locating relevant data.
  (iv) The cost of recovering any electronic documents.
  (v) The cost of disclosing and providing inspection of any relevant electronic documents.
  (vi) The likelihood that electronic documents will be materially altered in the course of recovery, disclosure or inspection.
(d) The significance of any document which is likely to be located during the search.

2A.5 It may be reasonable to search some or all of the parties' electronic storage systems. In some circumstances, it may be reasonable to search for electronic documents by means of keyword searches (agreed as far as possible between the parties) even where a full review of each and every document would be unreasonable. There may be other forms of electronic search that may be appropriate in particular circumstances.

THE LIST

3.1 The list should be in form N265.

3.2 In order to comply with rule 31.10(3) it will normally be necessary to list the documents in date order, to number them consecutively and to give each a concise description (eg letter, claimant to defendant). Where there is a large number of documents all falling into a particular category the disclosing party may list those documents as a category rather than individually eg 50 bank statements relating to account number ___ at ___ Bank, ___20___ to ___20___; or, 35 letters passing between ___ and ___ between ___20___ and ___20___.

3.3 The obligations imposed by an order for disclosure will continue until the proceedings come to an end. If, after a list of documents has been prepared and served, the existence of further documents to which the order applies comes to the attention of the disclosing party, the party must prepare and serve a supplemental list.

DISCLOSURE STATEMENT

4.1 A list of documents must (unless rule 31.10(8)(b) applies) contain a disclosure statement complying with rule 31.10. The form of disclosure statement is set out in Annex A to this practice direction.

4.2 The disclosure statement should:

(1) expressly state that the disclosing party believes the extent of the search to have been reasonable in all the circumstances, and
(2) in setting out the extent of the search (see rule 31.10(6)) draw attention to any particular limitations on the extent of the search which were adopted for proportionality reasons and give the reasons why the limitations were adopted, eg the difficulty or expense that a search not subject to those limitations would have entailed or the marginal relevance of categories of documents omitted from the search.

4.3 Where rule 31.10(7) applies, the details given in the disclosure statement about the person making the statement must include his name and address and the office or position he holds in the disclosing party [or the basis upon which he makes the statement on behalf of the party.

4.4 If the disclosing party has a legal representative acting for him, the legal representative must endeavour to ensure that the person making the disclosure statement (whether the disclosing party or, in a case to which rule 31.10(7) applies, some other person) understands the duty of disclosure under Part 31.

4.5 If the disclosing party wishes to claim that he has a right or duty to withhold a document, or part of a document, in his list of documents from inspection (see rule 31.19(3)), he must state in writing:

(1) that he has such a right or duty, and
(2) the grounds on which he claims that right or duty.

4.6 The statement referred to in paragraph 4.5 above should normally be included in the disclosure statement and must identify the document, or part of a document, to which the claim relates.

[4.7 An insurer or the Motor Insurers' Bureau may sign a disclosure statement on behalf of party where the insurer or the Motor Insurers' Bureau has a financial interest in the result of proceedings brought wholly or partially by or against that party. Rule 31.10(7) and paragraph 4.3 above shall apply to the insurer or the Motor Insurers' Bureau making such a statement.

SPECIFIC DISCLOSURE

5.1 If a party believes that the disclosure of documents given by a disclosing party is inadequate he may make an application for an order for specific disclosure (see rule 31.12).

5.2 The application notice must specify the order that the applicant intends to ask the court to make and must be supported by evidence (see rule 31.12(2) which describes the orders the court may make).

5.3 The grounds on which the order is sought may be set out in the application notice itself but if not there set out must be set out in evidence filed in support of the application.

5.4 In deciding whether or not to make an order for specific disclosure the court will take into account all the circumstances of the case and, in particular, the overriding objective described in Part 1. But if the court concludes that the party from whom specific disclosure is sought has failed adequately to comply with the obligations imposed by an order for disclosure (whether by failing to make a sufficient search for documents or otherwise) the court will usually make such order as is necessary to ensure that those obligations are properly complied with.

5.5 An order for specific disclosure may in an appropriate case direct a party to –

(1) carry out a search for any documents which it is reasonable to suppose may contain information which may –
  (a) enable the party applying for disclosure either to advance his own case or to damage that of the party giving disclosure; or
  (b) lead to a train of enquiry which has either of those consequences; and

(2) disclose any documents found as a result of that search.

CLAIMS TO WITHHOLD DISCLOSURE OR INSPECTION OF A DOCUMENT

6.1 A claim to withhold inspection of a document, or part of a document, disclosed in a list of documents does not require an application to the court. Where such a claim has been made, a party who wishes to challenge it must apply to the court (see rule 31.19(5)).

6.2 Rule 31.19(1) and (6) provide a procedure enabling a party to apply for an order permitting disclosure of the existence of a document to be withheld.

INSPECTION OF DOCUMENTS MENTIONED IN EXPERT'S REPORT (RULE 31.14(2))

7.1 If a party wishes to inspect documents referred to in the expert report of another party, before issuing an application he should request inspection of the document informally, and inspection should be provided by agreement unless the request is unreasonable.

7.2 Where an expert report refers to a large number or volume of documents and it would be burdensome to copy or collate them, the court will only order inspection of such documents if it is satisfied that it is necessary for the just disposal of the proceedings and the party cannot reasonably obtain the documents from another source.

FALSE DISCLOSURE STATEMENT

8 Attention is drawn to rule 31.23 which sets out the consequences of making a false disclosure statement without an honest belief in its truth, and to the procedures set out in paragraphs 28.1–28.3 of the practice direction supplementing Part 32.

Annex A

DISCLOSURE STATEMENT

I, the above named claimant [or defendant] [if party making disclosure is a company, firm or other organisation identify here who the person making the disclosure statement is and why he is the appropriate person to make it] state that I have carried out a reasonable and proportionate search to locate all the documents which I am required to disclose under the order made by the court on day of . I did not search:

(1) for documents predating ,
(2) for documents located elsewhere than ,

(3) for documents in categories other than .

(4) for electronic documents

I carried out a search for electronic documents contained on or created by the following:

[list what was searched and extent of search]

I did not search for the following:

(1) documents created before . . . .,

(2) documents contained on or created by the Claimant's/Defendant's PCs/portable data storage media/databases/servers/back-up tapes/ off-site storage/mobile phones/laptops/notebooks/handheld devices/PDA devices (delete as appropriate),

(3) documents contained on or created by the Claimant's/Defendant's mail files/document files/calendar files/spreadsheet files/graphic and presentation files/web-based applications (delete as appropriate),

(4) documents other than by reference to the following keyword(s)/ concepts . . . . (delete if your search was not confined to specific keywords or concepts).

I certify that I understand the duty of disclosure and to the best of my knowledge I have carried out that duty. I certify that the list above is a complete list of all documents which are or have been in my control and which I am obliged under the said order to disclose.

'I did not search'—As noted under r 31.10 above, this negative formulation does not achieve the intent of r 31.10(5)–(7). It tells the other party nothing about what places or categories might have been searched but were not. The Commercial Court requirement, at para E3.6 of its Guide (see Section 5 of this work) is much clearer and more transparent.

PART 32
EVIDENCE

CONTENTS OF THIS PART

General note to this Part—This Part, amplified by PD32 (Written Evidence) which deals in detail with the form of witness statements and affidavits, should be read with Pt 33 especially as regards hearsay but otherwise covers the procedure on witness statements, witness summaries, affidavits and notices to admit. Rule 32.1 is the major change, in line with other case management provisions. Only r 32.13 of this Part has been amended to date, and PD32 has undergone some minor revisions and a significant change with effect from 25 March 2002 (see notes under r 32.2).

32.1 Power of court to control evidence

(1) The court may control the evidence by giving directions as to –

(a) the issues on which it requires evidence;
(b) the nature of the evidence which it requires to decide those issues; and
(c) the way in which the evidence is to be placed before the court.

(2) The court may use its power under this rule to exclude evidence that would otherwise be admissible.

(3) The court may limit cross-examination[(GL)].

Practice Direction—See generally PD32 at p 834.

Power of court to control evidence—This rule applies to all cases, even small claims (this Part, and Pt 33, are otherwise excluded therefrom by r 27.2(1)(c)). The control here envisaged will apply mostly to the conduct of trials although it could apply at any stage in respect of any evidence or issue. It is an important part of the case management 'toolbox', and facilitates the resolution of issues at all stages. It ranges, in respect of issues, from no evidence at all (in line with Pt 3 powers) to the kind of evidence and what form it should take. Although the rule is not limited in time as to when directions can be given, as regards trial they should ideally be made at a pre-trial review – at any rate so far as possible before the trial itself and in some instances at an early stage of the proceedings especially where issues are not quite fit for summary dismissal but do not merit the full panoply of the traditional approach. However, use of the power at trial will facilitate case management, for example if the case is overburdened with documents.

In *Rall v Hume* [2001] EWCA Civ 146, 2001] CP Rep 58, (2001) *The Times*, 14 March, CA the court held that the intention to deploy video surveillance evidence (whether as part of the defendant's case or by way of cross-examination of the claimant) must be brought to the attention of the court as soon as possible, although the strictures appear to be less strong in respect of the latter type of anticipated use.

'exclude evidence that would otherwise be admissible' (r 32.1(2))—This was brand-new with the advent of the CPR, and enables the court to exclude evidence that, as a matter of law, is relevant to an issue in question. The touchstone will, of course, be the overriding objective and, in particular, proportionality, and this provision is an important addition to the case management regime – see note **'Exercise of this power'** below.

The converse—In *Barings plc & ors v Coopers & Lybrand & ors* [2001] EWCA 1163, (2001) *The Times*, 4 December, CA, the Court of Appeal refused permission to appeal the decision of the trial judge, in an action scheduled to last 30 weeks, to pre-read inadmissible material all of which was in the public domain and would be useful to him in assimilating the issues. It was a matter for the judge's case management discretion, not an issue of principle.

'may limit cross-examination' (r 32.1(3))—Whilst cross-examination has been limited in the past, subrule (3) puts the power beyond doubt – and is likely to occur either on an issue-based footing or by limitation of time.

Exercise of this power—In *GKR Karate Ltd v Yorkshire Post Newspapers Ltd & ors* [2000] 2 All ER 931, CA, the court noted that in libel cases novel and imaginative case management was called for, and that admissible and relevant evidence and cross-examination could be excluded where it was disproportionately expensive or time-consuming, provided that the order made was in accordance with the overriding objective. See also *Watson v Chief Constable of Cleveland Police* [2001] EWCA Civ 1547, where the Court of Appeal upheld, on the basis that the judge had not 'erred' within the meaning of r 52.11(3) and after noting that r 32.1 offered no guidance as to how this discretion should be exercised, a decision to limit cross-examination to some, but not all, of the claimant's previous convictions.

No case to answer—Despite the limitations on acceding to such a submission without putting the applicant to its election as to whether to call evidence, set out by Mance LJ in *Boyce v Wyatt Engineering & ors* [2001] EWCA Civ 692, (2001) *The Times*, 14 June, (2001) Lawtel, 1 May, CA Latham LJ held in *Bentley v Jones Harris & Co* [2001] EWCA Civ 1724, CA that on the rare occasions when a trial judge properly comes to the conclusion at the end of the claimant's evidence that the claim is bound to fail, he can give judgment there and then, either on application or of his own motion, in the same way as if there had been an earlier application for summary judgment under r 24.2.

32.2 Evidence of witnesses – general rule

(1) The general rule is that any fact which needs to be proved by the evidence of witnesses is to be proved –

- (a) at trial, by their oral evidence given in public; and
- (b) at any other hearing, by their evidence in writing.

(2) This is subject –

- (a) to any provision to the contrary contained in these Rules or elsewhere; or
- (b) to any order of the court.

Practice Direction—See generally PD32 at p 834 and below.

Paragraph 1 deals in detail with written materials for use in evidence: the principal vehicles are witness statements, affidavits (which expression includes affirmations) and application notices and statements of case which have been verified in accordance with Pt 22. It should not be assumed that CPR has somehow made a witness statement less rigorous in its requirement for truth than an affidavit, and there ought in principle to be no difference in the weight accorded to statements and affidavits and although the latter are sworn before the witness enters the box, and hence attract the potential consequences of perjury as soon as sworn, the latter attract the analogous consequences of contempt under r 32.14. Affidavits are required by some kinds of proceeding, and may be ordered in aid of foreign proceedings under PD32, para 1.6.

Paragraphs 2–16 of PD32, contain a detailed code on the preparation and form of affidavits, paras 17–24 with witness statements, para 25 with the consequences of defects in either kind of document (they may be ruled inadmissible and/or the costs may be disallowed), and para 26 with the use of statements of case in evidence.

Paragraph 27 – Agreed Bundles for Hearing – (new with effect from 25 March 2002) is not just administrative. The presumption now is that any document in such a bundle is evidence of its contents: a major change.

Commercial Court—By virtue of para F7.2 of the Admiralty and Commercial Courts Guide, PD32, para 13.1 (production of the originals of exhibited documents at a hearing) does not apply in the Commercial Court, unless there is a specific order.

'general rule'—As before, in principle trials will be conducted on the basis of oral evidence and interim hearings on written material.

'This is subject' (r 32.2(2))—The general rules here are subject to the stated exceptions (required not least by reason of written evidence in chief and hearsay at trial, power to permit cross-examination otherwise than at trial and differences of procedure for the types of claim reflected by Pt 8. As for orders of the court, this again preserves full case management under Pt 3 and r 32.1).

32.3 Evidence by video link or other means

The court may allow a witness to give evidence through a video link or by other means.

'by video link or other means'—Note that this is not limited to video links: in principle no 'remote' method is precluded.

For civil cases in the Royal Courts of Justice there exists a *Video-conferencing Protocol* which is referred to at Chancery Guide, para 14.14 and Queen's Bench Guide, para 2.7.4. That protocol has been replaced (as of March 2002) with PD32, Annex 3 'Video Conferencing Guidance', also reproduced as App 14 to the Admiralty and Commercial Courts Guide, which also makes provision for the management of video evidence at para H3. The common strand is that the potential use of video must be raised at the earliest possible moment and at the latest by the time of the pre-trial review.

'may allow'—The House of Lords, in *Roman Polanski v Condé Nast Publications Ltd* [2005] UKHL 10, decided that it was a valid, and potentially sufficient, reason to allow a party to give evidence by video-link where that person was unwilling to appear in person by reason of being a fugitive from justice, and that (contrary to fears expressed by the Court of Appeal) such an order would not tend to bring the administration of justice into disrepute.

32.4 Requirement to serve witness statements for use at trial

(1) A witness statement is a written statement signed by a person which contains the evidence which that person would be allowed to give orally.

(2) The court will order a party to serve on the other parties any witness statement of the oral evidence which the party serving the statement intends to rely on in relation to any issues of fact to be decided at the trial.

(3) The court may give directions as to –

(a) the order in which witness statements are to be served; and
(b) whether or not the witness statements are to be filed.

Practice Direction—See generally PD32 at p 834, also paras 17.1–25.2 at p 839, and particularly para 18.2 at p 840 and paras 23.1–23.2 at p 841.

'witness statement of the oral evidence' (r 32.4(2))—The contents of a witness statement are not limited to first-hand knowledge, in any case to which CEA 1995 applies – which is virtually all (see further under Pt 33) – and accordingly the witness statement may include hearsay, although it should be identified as such, together with its 'degree' and its source(s) set out (PD32, para 18.2). For detail on the form and content of witness statements, see generally PD32, paras 17.1–25.2, Annex 2 thereto and the notes under rr 32.5 and 32.8 below.

'The court will order' (r 32.4(2))—As before, the service of witness statements will always be the subject of an order. For witness summaries, see below at r 32.9. The timing and nature of the order are not dealt with here but form part of the directions to be given under Pts 28 and 29, save for the express power to give directions as to the order in which they are served which will increase the likelihood of sequential service (formerly treated as exceptional) in appropriate cases, especially in light of the general observations of Woolf MR in *McPhilemy v The Times* [1999] 3 All ER 775, CA as to how statements of case and witness statements fit together.

'whether ... the witness statements are to be filed' (r 32.4(3)(b))—The filing provision does not deal with when such an order would be made: filing is required under other Parts (eg Pt 24). Paragraph 23 of PD32, states, unsurprisingly, that filing must be at the court etc where the case is proceeding, and also that where a foreign language statement is to be filed it must be accompanied by a verified translation.

32.5 Use at trial of witness statements which have been served

(1) If –

(a) a party has served a witness statement; and
(b) he wishes to rely at trial on the evidence of the witness who made the statement,

he must call the witness to give oral evidence unless the court orders otherwise or he puts the statement in as hearsay evidence.

(Part 33 contains provisions about hearsay evidence)

(2) Where a witness is called to give oral evidence under paragraph (1), his witness statement shall stand as his evidence in chief[(GL)] unless the court orders otherwise.

(3) A witness giving oral evidence at trial may with the permission of the court –

(a) amplify his witness statement; and
(b) give evidence in relation to new matters which have arisen since the witness statement was served on the other parties.

(4) The court will give permission under paragraph (3) only if it considers that there is good reason not to confine the evidence of the witness to the contents of his witness statement.

(5) If a party who has served a witness statement does not –

(a) call the witness to give evidence at trial; or
(b) put the witness statement in as hearsay evidence,

any other party may put the witness statement in as hearsay evidence.

Practice Direction—See generally PD32 at p 834 and particularly paras 1.1–1.7 at p 834.

Use at trial of witness statements which have been served—The usual rule is that the maker of the statement must be called/tendered for cross-examination, his statement having stood as his evidence in chief.

'shall stand as his evidence in chief' (r 32.5(2))—The first and obvious requirement, amplified by r 32.5(4), is to ensure that the witness statement is complete as to the issues which it is intended to cover. It must also represent, in respect of those issues, 'the truth, the whole truth and nothing but the truth', an obligation which is not always understood. See the detailed notes to r 32.8 below.

'will give permission ... only if ... there is good reason' (r 32.5(4))—The balance between confining a witness to what is in the statement and permitting 'amplification' is (save in respect of genuinely 'new' material) in effect a balance between unnecessarily expensive and elaborate statements on the one hand, and the potential for 'ambush' on the other. Substantial injustice caused by the latter should result in the 'new' evidence simply being excluded, and this is an adjunct to the wide general powers under r 32.1.

'any other party may put the witness statement in as hearsay evidence' (r 32.5(5))—This is entirely new (having an effect opposite to the former RSC Ord 38, r 2A(6)) and puts ordinary witness statements into the same category as that formerly occupied only by experts' reports. However, it being a statement prepared by the opposing party, albeit from a witness they choose not to call, the utility of such a power will ordinarily be limited.

Moreover, *McPhilemy v The Times (No 2)* (2000) (unreported) 10 March, CA has re-affirmed that a party cannot disown the evidence of a witness it puts forward. Accordingly, a party seeking to put in a witness statement served but not used by the other side cannot adopt some parts and invite rejection of the balance – it is all or nothing. The Court of Appeal recognised that this was not entirely satisfactory, but observed that it was a function of the adversarial process.

Where a party does not wish merely to 'put in' statements originally served by the other side (in respect of witnesses the original tendering party chooses not to call or rely upon), but wants to force the tendering party to call or tender those witnesses, the court has no power so to order: the court cannot require any party to tender evidence upon which it does not want to rely (*Society of Lloyds v Jaffray* [2000] 2 All ER (Comm) 181, Cresswell J).

32.6 Evidence in proceedings other than at trial

(1) Subject to paragraph (2), the general rule is that evidence at hearings other than the trial is to be by witness statement unless the court, a practice direction or any other enactment requires otherwise.

(2) At hearings other than the trial, a party may rely on the matters set out in –

(a) his statement of case; or

(b) his application notice,

if the statement of case or application notice is verified by a statement of truth.

Amendments—SI 2000/221.

Practice Direction—See generally PD32 at p 834 and particularly paras 1.1–1.7 at p 834.

Change of wording—As of 2 May 2000, the words formerly in r 32.6(2) ('in support of his application') which arguably (but doubtless unintentionally if so) limited the use of such evidence to applicants in support of applications were removed by Civil Procedure (Amendment) Rules 2000. As always plainly intended, such evidence is available to be deployed by any party for all purposes in the conduct of hearings other than trials.

'hearings otherwise than at trial' (r 32.6(1))—The references to documents, other than witness statements, which have been verified by statements of truth emphasises the status of such documents as evidence, as set out in other Parts dealing with interim applications. However, the basic rule is that the evidence should be in a witness statement (and not an affidavit unless a practice direction or an Act requires it). Affidavits are required in many types of Pt 8 proceedings and, for instance, under PD25 in respect of applications for freezing and search orders.

32.7 Order for cross-examination

(1) Where, at a hearing other than the trial, evidence is given in writing, any party may apply to the court for permission to cross-examine the person giving the evidence.

(2) If the court gives permission under paragraph (1) but the person in question does not attend as required by the order, his evidence may not be used unless the court gives permission.

Order for cross-examination—This extends to all written evidence a power which formerly existed in respect of affidavits. It is unlikely to arise in pre-trial/interim hearings save in exceptional cases, since proportionate case management (indeed consideration of the merits) will usually preclude the desirability of oral testimony. In the case of evidence as to assets filed by a defendant as the result of a freezing order, an application for cross-examination on that material may be granted, albeit in very limited circumstances (*Re Great Futures International Ltd* (2001) (unreported) 22 March, Neuberger J).

32.8 Form of witness statement

A witness statement must comply with the requirements set out in the relevant practice direction.

(Part 22 requires a witness statement to be verified by a statement of truth)

Practice Direction—See generally PD32, paras 17.1–25.2 at p 839.

Forms of witness statements—See PD32, paras 17.1–25.2 and Annex 2 for the complete, formal code. The requirement for marginal note references to documents, often overlooked, in PD32, para 19.1(7) was amended in Update 15 to allow such references to be in the body of the text in bold type. A similar change applies to affidavits (r 32.16 below). There is express power at PD32, para 25.1 to refuse to admit in evidence witness statements which do not comply with Pt 32 and PD32, and to disallow the costs arising from their preparation.

Contents of witness statements—The preparation of witness statements requires great care. They must, of course, reflect the witness's actual recollection. The rules and practice directions do not give guidance on where to draw the line between evidence that would have been given orally 'in chief' and material which might emerge in cross-examination (put another way, evidence which is literally true but potentially misleading through omission on the one hand, and that which goes too far in anticipating cross-examination on the other – both are wrong). The implications of the oath/affirmation, 'the truth, the whole truth and nothing but the truth' are easier to see where the evidence in chief is in response to specific questions than they are where a statement is put into writing. However, both the Chancery and Queen's Bench Guides expressly require a written statement to comply with the 'whole truth' requirement in relation to issues on which it is sought to adduce evidence in chief. Once an issue is selected as appropriate for evidence in chief from a witness, his statement must deal with that issue 'warts and all'. The first thing the witness will be required to do at trial is to swear or affirm on the 'whole truth' basis and confirm the truth of his statement (see Queen's Bench Guide, para 7.10 and Chancery Guide, paras 8.10 onwards and App 4). Wherever a case is proceeding these should be referred to if guidance is needed.

Professional duty—The previous edition of the Commercial Court Guide at para H1.4 stated that 't]he rules of any relevant professional body regarding the drafting of witness statements must also be observed.' Curiously, that reference no longer appears in the new Admiralty and Commercial Court Guide – it may have been considered otiose – although it has been replaced with more general observations on impropriety (see para H1.2). The Bar Code of Conduct, at Pt VII and in the recent new Annex 'Guidance on Preparation of Witness Statements', contains both rules and guidance relating to such drafting. Paragraph 6(iii) of the Annex, in particular, affirms the 'whole truth' requirement and, whilst not placing an *absolute* ban on the exclusion of potentially adverse material, sets out the fundamental approach and highlights the very careful consideration required to be given in the event of any prospective exclusion. The 'bottom line' is almost always going to be: 'if in doubt having considered the guidance, leave it in'.

32.9 Witness summaries

(1) A party who –

  (a) is required to serve a witness statement for use at trial; but
  (b) is unable to obtain one,

may apply, without notice, for permission to serve a witness summary instead.

(2) A witness summary is a summary of –

  (a) the evidence, if known, which would otherwise be included in a witness statement; or
  (b) if the evidence is not known, the matters about which the party serving the witness summary proposes to question the witness.

(3) Unless the court orders otherwise, a witness summary must include the name and address of the intended witness.

(4) Unless the court orders otherwise, a witness summary must be served within the period in which a witness statement would have had to be served.

(5) Where a party serves a witness summary, so far as practicable, rules 32.4 (requirement to serve witness statements for use at trial), 32.5(3) (amplifying witness statements), and 32.8 (form of witness statement) shall apply to the summary.

Witness summaries—This is similar to the old rules about witnesses who were likely to require to be subpoenaed, with the addition of the requirement to treat the summary, so far as possible, as a witness statement.

32.10 Consequence of failure to serve witness statement or summary

If a witness statement or a witness summary for use at trial is not served in respect of an intended witness within the time specified by the court, then the witness may not be called to give oral evidence unless the court gives permission.

No witness statement or summary—This sanction does not literally fall within r 3.8 (it arising out of a rule in respect of breach of an order) but the factors listed in r 3.9 are plainly relevant to any question of permission. Since the avoidance of adjourning a trial date features so strongly in PD28 and PD29, any default which will result in surprise such that the date of a fair trial is jeopardised is highly likely to lead to a refusal of permission to call the witness unless the circumstances are truly exceptional. Where, however, the default is minor (eg slightly late service with no real prejudice to the other side), and the application made promptly (ie before trial) permission is likely to be granted in pursuance of the overriding objective.

For a stark example of the dangers created by disregarding this rule see *Moy v Pettman Smith (a firm) & anor* [2002] EWCA Civ 875, [2002] All ER (D) 126 (Jun), CA.

32.11 Cross-examination on a witness statement

Where a witness is called to give evidence at trial, he may be cross-examined on his witness statement, whether or not the statement or any part of it was referred to during the witness's evidence in chief[(GL)].

'called to give evidence at trial'—A witness's evidence in chief will rarely be given by oral testimony, the usual premise being that the statement is the evidence in chief and that it will be the subject of the witness's oath.

32.12 Use of witness statements for other purposes

(1) Except as provided by this rule, a witness statement may be used only for the purpose of the proceedings in which it is served.

(2) Paragraph (1) does not apply if and to the extent that –

(a) the witness gives consent in writing to some other use of it;
(b) the court gives permission for some other use; or
(c) the witness statement has been put in evidence at a hearing held in public.

Use of witness statements for other purposes—Whilst there is nothing new of itself here, deployment of the statement at any public hearing releases the restriction. Under the old rules witness statements would rarely if ever be 'put in evidence' otherwise than at trial, whereas now they may be used in most interim applications. For public hearings, see r 39.2.

32.13 Availability of witness statements for inspection

(1) A witness statement which stands as evidence in chief[(GL)] is open to inspection during the course of the trial unless the court otherwise directs.

(2) Any person may ask for a direction that a witness statement is not open to inspection.

(3) The court will not make a direction under paragraph (2) unless it is satisfied that a witness statement should not be open to inspection because of –

(a) the interests of justice;
(b) the public interest;
(c) the nature of any expert medical evidence in the statement;
(d) the nature of any confidential information (including information relating to personal financial matters) in the statement; or
(e) the need to protect the interests of any child or patient.

(4) The court may exclude from inspection words or passages in the statement.

Amendments—SI 2001/256.

'during the course of the trial unless the court otherwise directs' (r 32.13(1))—The amended wording of r 32.13(1) (brought in by Update 22, effective 26 March 2001) makes clear – the previous wording having been ambiguous – that it is only during the trial that such a statement is, subject to an order to the contrary, open to inspection.

Inspection of witness statements—The underlying purpose of this rule is to make public proceedings intelligible to the public. The exception is framed in the negative, which shows a presumption against such an order. The power may be exercised in respect of the whole of a statement or any part of it.

32.14 False statements

(1) Proceedings for contempt of court may be brought against a person if he makes, or causes to be made, a false statement in a document verified by a statement of truth without an honest belief in its truth.

(Part 22 makes provision for a statement of truth)

(2) Proceedings under this rule may be brought only –

(a) by the Attorney General; or
(b) with the permission of the court.

Practice Direction—See PD32, paras 28.1–28.4 at p 842 inserted by Update 21 and effective from 12 February 2001 (and subsequently renumbered). This sets out useful practical guidance on the procedure and criteria for the institution of such proceedings.

'False statements'—This represents a new and important codification and express extension of a pre-existing category of contempt (misleading the court), and deals with the situation created by the difference between the swearing of a dishonest affidavit (which would be perjury) and the dishonest 'verifying' of a document, be it a witness statement, statement of case (including further information under Pt 18) or application notice, a wholly new concept. The rule also recognises the grave mischief that can occur by reason of a false verification whether actually deployed in court or not, and is consistent with the underlying notion that all such statements should be treated as being made 'to the court', pursuant to the overriding objective. The offence of perjury is, of course, also committed if a dishonest witness statement is the subject of an oath or affirmation in court.

'Proceedings … may be brought only' (r 32.14(2))—In *Malgar Ltd v RE Leach (Engineering) Ltd* [2000] 3 CP Rep 39, [2000] FSR 393, (2000) *The Times*, 17 February, ChD, Scott V-C, it was held that r 32.14 was governed by the overriding objective as much as any other rule of the CPR: for such an application to succeed it had to be shown that the attempt to interfere with justice was sufficiently serious to warrant contempt proceedings (and in that case the application was refused), and the new paras 28.1–28.4 of PD32, referred to above now include the express requirement that the taking of such proceedings should further the overriding objective.

32.15 Affidavit evidence

(1) Evidence must be given by affidavit[(GL)], instead of or in addition to a witness statement if this is required by the court, a provision contained in any other rule, a practice direction or any other enactment.

(2) Nothing in these Rules prevents a witness giving evidence by affidavit[(GL)] at a hearing other than the trial if he chooses to do so in a case where paragraph (1) does not apply, but the party putting forward the affidavit[(GL)] may not recover the additional cost of making it from any other party unless the court orders otherwise.

Practice Direction—See generally PD32 at p 834 and particularly paras 1.1–16 at p 834 and paras 25.1–25.2 at p 842.

Affidavits—Apart from the compulsory use of affidavits (r 32.6(1)), they *may* be used in place of witness statements although the extra costs will not be recoverable unless the court orders otherwise. This may be useful in cases where, for reasons extraneous to the trial itself, there already exist affidavits containing the requisite material.

32.16 Form of affidavits

An affidavit[(GL)] must comply with the requirements set out in the relevant practice direction.

Practice Direction—See generally PD32, paras 2–16 at p 845 and paras 25.1–25.2 at p 842.

Form of affidavits—See PD32, paras 2–16 which closely mirror the former RSC Ord 41, and PD32, para 25. As with witness statements (see r 32.8 above) the requirement for marginal note references to documents, in PD32, para 6.1(7), was amended in Update 15 to allow such references to be in the body of the text in bold type.

32.17 Affidavit made outside the jurisdiction

A person may make an affidavit[(GL)] outside the jurisdiction in accordance with –

(a) this Part; or
(b) the law of the place where he makes the affidavit[(GL)].

Practice Direction—See generally PD32, paras 2–16 at p 845.

32.18 Notice to admit facts

(1) A party may serve notice on another party requiring him to admit the facts, or the part of the case of the serving party, specified in the notice.

(2) A notice to admit facts must be served no later than 21 days before the trial.

(3) Where the other party makes any admission in response to the notice the admission may be used against him only –

(a) in the proceedings in which the notice to admit is served; and
(b) by the party who served the notice.

(4) The court may allow a party to amend or withdraw any admission made by him on such terms as it thinks just.

Notices to admit facts—Whilst these provisions are familiar for the most part, nevertheless there is no express reference in CPR to the costs consequences of failing to admit a fact which the opposing party subsequently goes to the expense of proving. However, the terms of r 44.3 leave no doubt that where an issue is pursued for no good reason, for instance, the costs of that issue will fall to be paid by the party so behaving, and accordingly notices to admit will continue to be useful tools for parties to reduce the ambit of what is in issue at trial.

32.19 Notice to admit or produce documents

(1) A party shall be deemed to admit the authenticity of a document disclosed to him under Part 31 (disclosure and inspection of documents) unless he serves notice that he wishes the document to be proved at trial.

(2) A notice to prove a document must be served –

(a) by the latest date for serving witness statements; or
(b) within 7 days of disclosure of the document,

whichever is later.

Notice to admit or produce documents—A more appropriate heading for this rule would be 'notice of non-authenticity', since the rule follows the former High Court practice (save that formerly the disclosing party did not have to prove the authenticity of any document unless *either* such a notice had been served *or* the genuineness of the document was put in issue on the pleadings – this latter element has gone and, since there is a prescribed Form N268 for the notice, it is not compliance with the rules for notice to be given in a statement of case). The time limit for serving a notice in respect of a challenged document is 7 days after the later of its disclosure or the latest date for serving witness statements.

32.20 Notarial acts and instruments

A notarial act or instrument may be received in evidence without further proof as duly authenticated in accordance with the requirements of law unless the contrary is proved.

Amendments—Inserted by SI 2005/2292.

Scope of provision—This rule was added by the Civil Procedure (Amendment No 3) Rules 2005 to give probative force to notarial acts.

Practice Direction – Evidence

This Practice Direction supplements CPR Part 32 (PD32)

General note—See also the notes to CPR Pt 32 for relevant commentary.

Specialist courts—This practice direction is of general application, save for part of para 13.1 in the Commercial Court (see note **'Commercial Court'** under para 13.3 below).

EVIDENCE IN GENERAL

1.1 Rule 32.2 sets out how evidence is to be given and facts are to be proved.

1.2 Evidence at a hearing other than the trial should normally be given by witness statement[1] (see paragraph 17 onwards). However a witness may give evidence by affidavit if he wishes to do so[2] (and see paragraph 1.4 below).

1 See rule 32.6(1).
2 See rule 32.15(2).

1.3 Statements of case (see paragraph 26 onwards) and application notices[1] may also be used as evidence provided that their contents have been verified by a statement of truth[2].

(For information regarding evidence by deposition see Part 34 and the practice direction which supplements it)

1 See Part 23 for information about making an application.
2 Rule 32.6(2) and see Part 22 for information about the statement of truth.

1.4 Affidavits must be used as evidence in the following instances:

- (1) where sworn evidence is required by an enactment[1], rule …, order or practice direction,
- (2) in any application for a search order, a freezing injunction, or an order requiring an occupier to permit another to enter his land, and
- (3) in any application for an order against anyone for alleged contempt of court.

1 See, eg, s 3(5)(a) of the Protection from Harassment Act 1997.

1.5 If a party believes that sworn evidence is required by a court in another jurisdiction for any purpose connected with the proceedings, he may apply to the court for a direction that evidence shall be given only by affidavit on any pre-trial applications.

1.6 The court may give a direction under rule 32.15 that evidence shall be given by affidavit instead of or in addition to a witness statement or statement of case:

- (1) on its own initiative, or
- (2) after any party has applied to the court for such a direction.

1.7 An affidavit, where referred to in the Civil Procedure Rules or a practice direction, also means an affirmation unless the context requires otherwise.

AFFIDAVITS

Deponent

2 A deponent is a person who gives evidence by affidavit or affirmation.

Heading

3.1 The affidavit should be headed with the title of the proceedings (see paragraph 4 of the practice direction supplementing Part 7 and paragraph 7 of the practice direction supplementing Part 20); where the proceedings are between several parties with the same status it is sufficient too identify the parties as follows:

	Number:
A.B. (and others)	Claimants/Applicants
C.D. (and others)	Defendants/Respondents
	(as appropriate)

3.2 At the top right hand corner of the first page (and on the backsheet) there should be clearly written:

- (1) the party on whose behalf it is made,
- (2) the initials and surname of the deponent,
- (3) the number of the affidavit in relation to that deponent,
- (4) the identifying initials and number of each exhibit referred to, and
- (5) the date sworn.

Body of affidavit

4.1 The affidavit must, if practicable, be in the deponent's own words, the affidavit should be expressed in the first person and the deponent should:

- (1) commence 'I (*full name*) of (*address*) state on oath ___ ',

(2) if giving evidence in his professional, business or other occupational capacity, give the address at which he works in (1) above, the position he holds and the name of his firm or employer,
(3) give his occupation or, if he has none, his description, and
(4) state if he is a party to the proceedings or employed by a party to the proceedings, if it be the case.

4.2 An affidavit must indicate:

(1) which of the statements in it are made from the deponent's own knowledge and which are matters of information or belief, and
(2) the source for any matters of information or belief.

4.3 Where a deponent:

(1) refers to an exhibit or exhibits, he should state 'there is now shown to me marked "___" the (*description of exhibit*)', and
(2) makes more than one affidavit (to which there are exhibits) in the same proceedings, the numbering of the exhibits should run consecutively throughout and not start again with each affidavit.

Jurat

5.1 The jurat of an affidavit is a statement set out at the end of the document which authenticates the affidavit.

5.2 It must:

(1) be signed by all deponents,
(2) be completed and signed by the person before whom the affidavit was sworn whose name and qualification must be printed beneath his signature,
(3) contain the full address of the person before whom the affidavit was sworn, and
(4) follow immediately on from the text and not be put on a separate page.

Format of affidavits

6.1 An affidavit should:

(1) be produced on durable quality A4 paper with a 3.5 cm margin,
(2) be fully legible and should normally be typed on one side of the paper only,
(3) where possible, be bound securely in a manner which would not hamper filing, or otherwise each page should be endorsed with the case number and should bear the initials of the deponent and of the person before whom it was sworn,
(4) have the pages numbered consecutively as a separate document (or as one of several documents contained in a file),
(5) be divided into numbered paragraphs,
(6) have all numbers, including dates, expressed in figures, and
(7) give the reference to any document or documents mentioned either in the margin or in bold text in the body of the affidavit.

6.2 It is usually convenient for an affidavit to follow the chronological sequence of events or matters dealt with; each paragraph of an affidavit should as far as possible be confined to a distinct portion of the subject.

Inability of deponent to read or sign affidavit

7.1 Where an affidavit is sworn by a person who is unable to read or sign it, the person before whom the affidavit is sworn must certify in the jurat that:

(1) he read the affidavit to the deponent,
(2) the deponent appeared to understand it, and
(3) the deponent signed or made his mark, in his presence.

7.2 If that certificate is not included in the jurat, the affidavit may not be used in evidence unless the court is satisfied that it was read to the deponent and that he appeared to understand it. Two versions of the form of jurat with the certificate are set out at Annex 1 to this practice direction.

Alterations to affidavits

8.1 Any alteration to an affidavit must be initialled by both the deponent and the person before whom the affidavit was sworn.

8.2 An affidavit which contains an alteration that has not been initialled may be filed or used in evidence only with the permission of the court.

Who may administer oaths and take affidavits

9.1 Only the following may administer oaths and take affidavits:

(1) commissioners for oaths[1],
(2) practising solicitors[2],
(3) other persons specified by statute[3],
(4) certain officials of the Supreme Court[4],
(5) a circuit judge or district judge[5],
(6) any justice of the peace[6], and
(7) certain officials of any county court appointed by the judge of that court for the purpose[7].

1 Commissioner for Oaths Act 1889 and 1891.
2 Section 81 of the Solicitors Act 1974.
3 Section 65 of the Administration of Justice Act 1985, s 113 of the Courts and Legal Services Act 1990 and the Commissioners for Oaths (Prescribed Bodies) Regulations 1994 and 1995.
4 Section 2 of the Commissioners for Oaths Act 1889.
5 Section 58 of the County Courts Act 1984.
6 Section 58 as above.
7 Section 58 as above.

9.2 An affidavit must be sworn before a person independent of the parties or their representatives.

Filing of affidavits

10.1 If the court directs that an affidavit is to be filed[1], it must be filed in the court or Division, or Office or Registry of the court or Division where the action in which it was or is to be used, is proceeding or will proceed.

1 Rules 32.1(3) and 32.4(3)(b).

10.2 Where an affidavit is in a foreign language:

(1) the party wishing to rely on it –
  (a) must have it translated, and
  (b) must file the foreign language affidavit with the court, and

(2) the translator must make and file with the court an affidavit verifying the translation and exhibiting both the translation and a copy of the foreign language affidavit.

EXHIBITS

Manner of exhibiting documents

11.1 A document used in conjunction with an affidavit should be:

(1) produced to and verified by the deponent, and remain separate from the affidavit, and
(2) identified by a declaration of the person before whom the affidavit was sworn.

11.2 The declaration should be headed with the name of the proceedings in the same way as the affidavit.

11.3 The first page of each exhibit should be marked:

(1) as in paragraph 3.2 above, and
(2) with the exhibit mark referred to in the affidavit.

Letters

12.1 Copies of individual letters should be collected together and exhibited in a bundle or bundles. They should be arranged in chronological order with the earliest at the top, and firmly secured.

12.2 When a bundle of correspondence is exhibited, the exhibit should have a front page attached stating that the bundle consists of original letters and copies. They should be arranged and secured as above and numbered consecutively.

Other documents

13.1 Photocopies instead of original documents may be exhibited provided the originals are made available for inspection by the other parties before the hearing and by the judge at the hearing.

13.2 Court documents must not be exhibited (official copies of such documents prove themselves).

13.3 Where an exhibit contains more than one document, a front page should be attached setting out a list of the documents contained in the exhibit; the list should contain the dates of the documents.

Commercial Court—That part of para 13.1 which unconditionally requires originals to be produced at the hearing is modified in the Commercial Court by the provisions of Commercial Court Guide, para F6.5.

Exhibits other than documents

14.1 Items other than documents should be clearly marked with an exhibit number or letter in such a manner that the mark cannot become detached from the exhibit.

14.2 Small items may be placed in a container and the container appropriately marked.

General provisions

15.1 Where an exhibit contains more than one document:

(1) the bundle should not be stapled but should be securely fastened in a way that does not hinder the reading of the documents, and
(2) the pages should be numbered consecutively at bottom centre.

15.2 Every page of an exhibit should be clearly legible; typed copies of illegible documents should be included, paginated with 'a' numbers.

15.3 Where affidavits and exhibits have become numerous, they should be put into separate bundles and the pages numbered consecutively throughout.

15.4 Where on account of their bulk the service of exhibits or copies of exhibits on the other parties would be difficult or impracticable, the directions of the court should be sought as to arrangements for bringing the exhibits to the attention of the other parties and as to their custody pending trial.

Affirmations

16 All provisions in this or any other practice direction relating to affidavits apply to affirmations with the following exceptions:

(1) the deponent should commence 'I (*name*) of (*address*) do solemnly and sincerely affirm ___', and
(2) in the jurat the word 'sworn' is replaced by the word 'affirmed'.

WITNESS STATEMENTS

Heading

17.1 The witness statement should be headed with the title of the proceedings (see paragraph 4 of the practice direction supplementing Part 7 and paragraph 7 of the practice direction supplementing Part 20); where the proceedings are between several parties with the same status it is sufficient to identify the parties as follows:

	Number:
A.B. (and others)	Claimants/Applicants
C.D. (and others)	Defendants/Respondents
	(as appropriate)

17.2 At the top right hand corner of the first page there should be clearly written:

(1) the party on whose behalf it is made,
(2) the initials and surname of the witness,
(3) the number of the statement in relation to that witness,
(4) the identifying initials and number of each exhibit referred to, and
(5) the date the statement was made.

Body of witness statement

18.1 The witness statement must, if practicable, be in the intended witness's own words, the statement should be expressed in the first person and should also state:

(1) the full name of the witness,
(2) his place of residence or, if he is making the statement in his professional, business or other occupational capacity, the address at which he works, the position he holds and the name of his firm or employer,
(3) his occupation, or if he has none, his description, and
(4) the fact that he is a party to the proceedings or is the employee of such a party if it be the case.

18.2 A witness statement must indicate:

(1) which of the statements in it are made from the witness's own knowledge and which are matters of information or belief, and
(2) the source for any matters of information or belief.

18.3 An exhibit used in conjunction with a witness statement should be verified and identified by the witness and remain separate from the witness statement.

18.4 Where a witness refers to an exhibit or exhibits, he should state 'I refer to the (*description of exhibit*) marked "___" '.

18.5 The provisions of paragraphs 11.3 to 15.4 (exhibits) apply similarly to witness statements as they do to affidavits.

18.6 Where a witness makes more than one witness statement to which there are exhibits, in the same proceedings, the numbering of the exhibits should run consecutively throughout and not start again with each witness statement.

Format of witness statement

19.1 A witness statement should:

(1) be produced on durable quality A4 paper with a 3.5 cm margin,
(2) be fully legible and should normally be typed on one side of the paper only,
(3) where possible, be bound securely in a manner which would not hamper filing, or otherwise each page should be endorsed with the case number and should bear the initials of the witness,
(4) have the pages numbered consecutively as a separate statement (or as one of several statements contained in a file),
(5) be divided into numbered paragraphs,
(6) have all numbers, including dates, expressed in figures, and
(7) give the reference to any document or documents mentioned either in the margin or in bold text in the body of the statement.

19.2 It is usually convenient for a witness statement to follow the chronological sequence of the events or matters dealt with, each paragraph of a witness statement should as far as possible be confined to a distinct portion of the subject.

Statement of truth

20.1 A witness statement is the equivalent of the oral evidence which that witness would, if called, give in evidence; it must include a statement by the intended witness that he believes the facts in it are true[1].

1 See Part 22 for information about the statement of truth.

20.2 To verify a witness statement the statement of truth is as follows:

'I believe that the facts stated in this witness statement are true'

20.3 Attention is drawn to rule 32.14 which sets out the consequences of verifying a witness statement containing a false statement without an honest belief in its truth.

Inability of witness to read or sign statement

21.1 Where a witness statement is made by a person who is unable to read or sign the witness statement, it must contain a certificate made by an authorised person.

21.2 An authorised person is a person able to administer oaths and take affidavits but need not be independent of the parties or their representatives.

21.3 The authorised person must certify:

(1) that the witness statement has been read to the witness,
(2) that the witness appeared to understand it and approved its content as accurate,
(3) that the declaration of truth has been read to the witness,
(4) that the witness appeared to understand the declaration and the consequences of making a false witness statement, and
(5) that the witness signed or made his mark in the presence of the authorised person.

21.4 The form of the certificate is set out at Annex 2 to this practice direction.

Alterations to witness statements

22.1 Any alteration to a witness statement must be initialled by the person making the statement or by the authorised person where appropriate (see paragraph 21).

22.2 A witness statement which contains an alteration that has not been initialled may be used in evidence only with the permission of the court.

Filing of witness statements

23.1 If the court directs that a witness statement is to be filed[1], it must be filed in the court or Division, or Office or Registry of the court or Division where the action in which it was or is to be used, is proceeding or will proceed.

1 Rule 32.4(3)(b).

23.2 Where the court has directed that a witness statement in a foreign language is to be filed:

(1) the party wishing to rely on it must –
   (a) have it translated, and
   (b) file the foreign language witness statement with the court, and
(2) the translator must make and file with the court an affidavit verifying the translation and exhibiting both the translation and a copy of the foreign language witness statement.

Certificate of court officer

24.1 Where the court has ordered that a witness statement is not to be open to inspection by the public[1] or that words or passages in the statement are not to be open to inspection[2] the court officer will so certify on the statement and make any deletions directed by the court under rule 32.13(4).

1 Rule 32.13(2).
2 Rule 32.13(4).

Defects in affidavits, witness statements and exhibits

25.1 Where:

(1) an affidavit,
(2) a witness statement, or
(3) an exhibit to either an affidavit or a witness statement,

does not comply with Part 32 or this practice direction in relation to its form, the court may refuse to admit it as evidence and may refuse to allow the costs arising from its preparation.

25.2 Permission to file a defective affidavit or witness statement or to use a defective exhibit may be obtained from a judge[1] in the court where the case is proceeding.

1 Rule 2.3(1); definition of judge.

STATEMENTS OF CASE

26.1 A statement of case may be used as evidence in an interim application provided it is verified by a statement of truth[1].

1 See rule 32.6(2)(a).

26.2 To verify a statement of case the statement of truth should be set out as follows:

> 'I believe] the (*party on whose behalf the statement of case is being signed*) believes] that the facts stated in the statement of case are true'.

26.3 Attention is drawn to rule 32.14 which sets out the consequences of verifying a witness statement containing a false statement without an honest belief in its truth.

(For information regarding statements of truth see Part 22 and the practice direction which supplements it)

(Practice directions supplementing Parts 7, 17 provide further information concerning statements of case)

AGREED BUNDLES FOR HEARINGS

27.1 The court may give directions requiring the parties to use their best endeavours to agree a bundle or bundles of documents for use at any hearing.

27.2 All documents contained in bundles which have been agreed for use at a hearing shall be admissible at that hearing as evidence of their contents, unless –

(1) the court orders otherwise; or
(2) a party gives written notice of objection to the admissibility of particular documents.

PENALTY

28.1(1) Where a party alleges that a statement of truth or a disclosure statement is false the party shall refer that allegation to the court dealing with the claim in which the statement of truth or disclosure statement has been made.

(2) The court may –
   (a) exercise any of its powers under the rules;
   (b) initiate steps to consider if there is a contempt of court and, where there is, to punish it;

(The practice direction to RSC Order 52 (Schedule 1) and CCR Order 29 (Schedule 2) makes provision where committal to prison is a possibility if contempt is proved)

   (c) direct the party making the allegation to refer the matter to the Attorney General with a request to him to consider whether he wishes to bring proceedings for contempt of court.

28.2(1) An application to the Attorney General should be made to his chambers at 9 Buckingham Gate London SW1E 6JP in writing. The Attorney General will initially require a copy of the order recording the direction of the judge referring the matter to him and information which –
   (a) identifies the statement said to be false; and
   (b) explains –
      (i) why it is false, and
      (ii) why the maker knew it to be false at the time he made it; and
   (c) explains why contempt proceedings would be appropriate in the light of the overriding objective in Part 1 of the Civil Procedure Rules.

(2) The practice of the Attorney General is to prefer an application that comes from the court, and so has received preliminary consideration by a judge, to one made direct to him by a party to the claim in which the alleged contempt occurred without prior consideration by the court. An application to the Attorney General is not a way of appealing against, or reviewing, the decision of the judge.

28.3 Where a party makes an application to the court for permission for that party to commence proceedings for contempt of court, it must be supported by written evidence containing the information specified in paragraph 28.2(1) and the result of the application to the Attorney General made by the applicant.

28.4 The rules do not change the law of contempt or introduce new categories of contempt. A person applying to commence such proceedings should consider whether the incident complained of does amount to contempt of court and whether such proceedings would further the overriding objective in Part 1 of the Civil Procedure Rules.

VIDEO CONFERENCING

29.1 Guidance on the use of video conferencing in the civil courts is set out at Annex 3 to this practice direction.

A list of the sites which are available for video conferencing can be found on Her Majesty's Courts Service website at www.hmcourts-service.gov.uk.

Video conferencing guidance—The guidance set out at Annex 3 (added by Update 27, March 2002) is derived in part from the work of the Federal Court of Australia and applies to all civil proceedings.

Annex 1

CERTIFICATE TO BE USED WHERE A DEPONENT TO AN AFFIDAVIT IS UNABLE TO READ OR SIGN IT

Sworn at this day of Before me, I having first read over the contents of this affidavit to the deponent *if there are exhibits, add* 'and explained the nature and effect of the exhibits referred to in it'] who appeared to understand it and approved its content as accurate, and made his mark on the affidavit in my presence.

Or, (after, *Before me*) the witness to the mark of the deponent having been first sworn that he had read over etc (*as above*) and that he saw him make his mark on the affidavit. (*Witness must sign*).

CERTIFICATE TO BE USED WHERE A DEPONENT TO AN AFFIRMATION IS UNABLE TO READ OR SIGN IT

Affirmed at this day of Before me, I having first read over the contents of this affirmation to the deponent *if there are exhibits, add* 'and explained the nature and effect of the exhibits referred to in it'] who appeared to understand it and approved its content as accurate, and made his mark on the affirmation in my presence.

Or, (after, *Before me*) the witness to the mark of the deponent having been first sworn that he had read over etc (*as above*) and that he saw him make his mark on the affirmation. (*Witness must sign*).

Annex 2

CERTIFICATE TO BE USED WHERE A WITNESS IS UNABLE TO READ OR SIGN A WITNESS STATEMENT

I certify that I *name and address of authorised person*] have read over the contents of this witness statement and the declaration of truth to the witness *if there are exhibits, add* 'and explained the nature and effect of the exhibits referred to in it'] who appeared to understand (a) the statement and approved its content as accurate and (b) the declaration of truth and the consequences of making a false witness statement, and made his mark in my presence.

Annex 3

General note—This is the same document as the one appended to the Admiralty and Commercial Courts Guide, and it supersedes the former protocol referred to in the Chancery and Queen's Bench Guides.

VIDEO CONFERENCING GUIDANCE

This guidance is for the use of video conferencing (VCF) in civil proceedings. It is in part based, with permission, upon the protocol of the Federal Court of Australia. It is intended to provide a guide to all persons involved in the use of VCF, although it does not attempt to cover all the practical questions which might arise.

Video conferencing generally

1 The guidance covers the use of VCF equipment both (a) in a courtroom, whether via equipment which is permanently placed there or via a mobile unit, and (b) in a separate studio or conference room. In either case, the location at which the judge sits is referred to as the 'local site'. The other site or sites to and from which transmission is made are referred to as 'the remote site' and in any particular case any such site may be another courtroom. The guidance applies to cases where VCF is used for the taking of evidence and also to its use for other parts of any legal proceedings (for example, interim applications, case management conferences, pre-trial reviews).

2 VCF may be a convenient way of dealing with any part of proceedings: it can involve considerable savings in time and cost. Its use for the taking of evidence from overseas witnesses will, in particular, be likely to achieve a material saving of costs, and such savings may also be achieved by its use for taking domestic evidence. It is, however, inevitably not as ideal as having the witness physically present in court. Its convenience should not therefore be allowed to dictate its use. A judgment must be made in every case in which the use of VCF is being considered not only as to whether it will achieve an overall cost saving but as to whether its use will be likely to be beneficial to the efficient, fair and economic disposal of the litigation. In particular, it needs to be recognised that the degree of control a court can exercise over a witness at the remote site is or may be more limited than it can exercise over a witness physically before it.

3 When used for the taking of evidence, the objective should be to make the VCF session as close as possible to the usual practice in a trial court where evidence is taken in open court. To gain the maximum benefit, several differences have to be taken into account. Some matters, which are taken for granted when evidence is taken in the conventional way, take on a different dimension when it is taken by VCF: for example, the administration of the oath, ensuring that the witness understands who is at the local site and what their various roles are, the raising of any objections to the evidence and the use of documents.

4 It should not be presumed that all foreign governments are willing to allow their nationals or others within their jurisdiction to be examined before a court in England or Wales by means of VCF. If there is any doubt about this, enquiries should be directed to the Foreign and Commonwealth Office (International Legal Matters Unit, Consular Division) with a view to ensuring that the country from which the evidence is to be taken raises no objection to it at diplomatic level. The party who is directed to be responsible for arranging the VCF (see paragraph 8 below) will be required to make all necessary inquiries about this well in advance of the VCF and must be able to inform the court what those inquiries were and of their outcome.

5 Time zone differences need to be considered when a witness abroad is to be examined in England or Wales by VCF. The convenience of the witness, the parties, their representatives and the court must all be taken into account. The cost of the use of a commercial studio is usually greater outside normal business hours.

6 Those involved with VCF need to be aware that, even with the most advanced systems currently available, there are the briefest of delays between the receipt of the picture and that of the accompanying sound. If due allowance is not made

for this, there will be a tendency to 'speak over' the witness, whose voice will continue to be heard for a millisecond or so after he or she appears on the screen to have finished speaking.

7 With current technology, picture quality is good, but not as good as a television picture. The quality of the picture is enhanced if those appearing on VCF monitors keep their movements to a minimum.

Preliminary arrangements

8 The court's permission is required for any part of any proceedings to be dealt with by means of VCF. Before seeking a direction, the applicant should notify the listing officer, diary manager or other appropriate court officer of the intention to seek it, and should enquire as to the availability of court VCF equipment for the day or days of the proposed VCF. The application for a direction should be made to the master, district judge or judge, as may be appropriate. If all parties consent to a direction, permission can be sought by letter, fax or e-mail, although the court may still require an oral hearing. All parties are entitled to be heard on whether or not such a direction should be given and as to its terms. If a witness at a remote site is to give evidence by an interpreter, consideration should be given at this stage as to whether the interpreter should be at the local site or the remote site. If a VCF direction is given, arrangements for the transmission will then need to be made. The court will ordinarily direct that the party seeking permission to use VCF is to be responsible for this. That party is hereafter referred to as 'the VCF arranging party'.

9 Subject to any order to the contrary, all costs of the transmission, including the costs of hiring equipment and technical personnel to operate it, will initially be the responsibility of, and must be met by, the VCF arranging party. All reasonable efforts should be made to keep the transmission to a minimum and so keep the costs down. All such costs will be considered to be part of the costs of the proceedings and the court will determine at such subsequent time as is convenient or appropriate who, as between the parties, should be responsible for them and (if appropriate) in what proportions.

10 The local site will, if practicable, be a courtroom but it may instead be an appropriate studio or conference room. The VCF arranging party must contact the listing officer, diary manager or other appropriate officer of the court which made the VCF direction and make arrangements for the VCF transmission. Details of the remote site, and of the equipment to be used both at the local site (if not being supplied by the court) and the remote site (including the number of ISDN lines and connection speed), together with all necessary contact names and telephone numbers, will have to be provided to the listing officer, diary manager or other court officer. The court will need to be satisfied that any equipment provided by the parties for use at the local site and also that at the remote site is of sufficient quality for a satisfactory transmission. The VCF arranging party must ensure that an appropriate person will be present at the local site to supervise the operation of the VCF throughout the transmission in order to deal with any technical problems. That party must also arrange for a technical assistant to be similarly present at the remote site for like purposes.

11 It is recommended that the judge, practitioners and witness should arrive at their respective VCF sites about 20 minutes prior to the scheduled commencement of the transmission.

12 If the local site is not a courtroom, but a conference room or studio, the judge will need to determine who is to sit where. The VCF arranging party must take care to ensure that the number of microphones is adequate for the speakers and that the panning of the camera for the practitioners' table encompasses all legal representatives so that the viewer can see everyone seated there.

13 The proceedings, wherever they may take place, form part of a trial to which the public is entitled to have access (unless the court has determined that they should be heard in private). If the local site is to be a studio or conference room, the VCF arranging party must ensure that it provides sufficient accommodation to enable a reasonable number of members of the public to attend.

14 In cases where the local site is a studio or conference room, the VCF arranging party should make arrangements, if practicable, for the royal coat of arms to be placed above the judge's seat.

15 In cases in which the VCF is to be used for the taking of evidence, the VCF arranging party must arrange for recording equipment to be provided by the court which made the VCF direction so that the evidence can be recorded. An associate will normally be present to operate the recording equipment when the local site is a courtroom. The VCF arranging party should take steps to ensure that an associate is present to do likewise when it is a studio or conference room. The equipment should be set up and tested before the VCF transmission. It will often be a valuable safeguard for the VCF arranging party also to arrange for the provision of recording equipment at the remote site. This will provide a useful back-up if there is any reduction in sound quality during the transmission. A direction from the court for the making of such a back-up recording must, however, be obtained first. This is because the proceedings are court proceedings and, save as directed by the court, no other recording of them must be made. The court will direct what is to happen to the back-up recording.

16 Some countries may require that any oath or affirmation to be taken by a witness accord with local custom rather than the usual form of oath or affirmation used in England and Wales. The VCF arranging party must make all appropriate prior inquiries and put in place all arrangements necessary to enable the oath or affirmation to be taken in accordance with any local custom. That party must be in a position to inform the court what those inquiries were, what their outcome was and what arrangements have been made. If the oath or affirmation can be administered in the manner normal in England and Wales, the VCF arranging party must arrange in advance to have the appropriate holy book at the remote site. The associate will normally administer the oath.

17 Consideration will need to be given in advance to the documents to which the witness is likely to be referred. The parties should endeavour to agree on this. It will usually be most convenient for a bundle of the copy documents to be prepared in advance, which the VCF arranging party should then send to the remote site.

18 Additional documents are sometimes quite properly introduced during the course of a witness's evidence. To cater for this, the VCF arranging party should ensure that equipment is available to enable documents to be transmitted between sites during the course of the VCF transmission. Consideration should be given to whether to use a document camera. If it is decided to use one, arrangements for its use will need to be established in advance. The panel operator will need to know the number and size of documents or objects if their images are to be sent by document camera. In many cases, a simpler and

sufficient alternative will be to ensure that there are fax transmission and reception facilities at the participating sites.

The hearing

19 The procedure for conducting the transmission will be determined by the judge. He will determine who is to control the cameras. In cases where the VCF is being used for an application in the course of the proceedings, the judge will ordinarily not enter the local site until both sites are on line. Similarly, at the conclusion of the hearing, he will ordinarily leave the local site while both sites are still on line. The following paragraphs apply primarily to cases where the VCF is being used for the taking of the evidence of a witness at a remote site. In all cases, the judge will need to decide whether court dress is appropriate when using VCF facilities. It might be appropriate when transmitting from courtroom to courtroom. It might not be when a commercial facility is being used.

20 At the beginning of the transmission, the judge will probably wish to introduce himself and the advocates to the witness. He will probably want to know who is at the remote site and will invite the witness to introduce himself and anyone else who is with him. He may wish to give directions as to the seating arrangements at the remote site so that those present are visible at the local site during the taking of the evidence. He will probably wish to explain to the witness the method of taking the oath or of affirming, the manner in which the evidence will be taken, and who will be conducting the examination and cross-examination. He will probably also wish to inform the witness of the matters referred to in paragraphs 6 and 7 above (co-ordination of picture with sound, and picture quality).

21 The examination of the witness at the remote site should follow as closely as possible the practice adopted when a witness is in the courtroom. During examination, cross-examination and re-examination, the witness must be able to see the legal representative asking the question and also any other person (whether another legal representative or the judge) making any statements in regard to the witness's evidence. It will in practice be most convenient if everyone remains seated throughout the transmission.

PART 33
MISCELLANEOUS RULES ABOUT EVIDENCE

CONTENTS OF THIS PART

General note to this Part—This Part deals mostly with the application of Civil Evidence Act 1995 to Pt 32. This Act came into force, in respect of cases starting after that date, on 1 February 1997. The former transitional provisions, having been doubted by the Court of Appeal as regards the effect of previous directions, were simply repeated by the practice direction under this Part which was first published on 7 May 1999. The practice direction relating to Pt 33 (which deals with nothing else) and which obtains its authority from an amendment to CEA 1995 under the powers in CPA 1997, was amended in Update 9, effective from 13 December 1999, to remove the date lacuna noted in previous editions. It now states that unless directions have been given or orders made *before* 26 April 1999, in respect of the evidence to be given at the trial or hearing, CEA 1995 applies to all cases, whenever started, save where the trial or hearing began before 26 April 1999. Accordingly, there should now be no cases due for trial or hearing under the old Civil Evidence Acts and in respect of which reference will need to be made to former practice (since Pt 33 is entirely premised on CEA 1995). Reference should be made to CEA 1995 itself for substantive questions relating to hearsay.

33.1 Introductory

In this Part –

(a) 'hearsay' means a statement, made otherwise than by a person while giving oral evidence in proceedings, which is tendered as evidence of the matters stated; and

(b) references to hearsay include hearsay of whatever degree.

'hearsay'—The term is here defined for the purposes of this Part: this is a direct quotation from CEA 1995, s 1. The reference to degrees is an important reminder that where PD32, para 18.2(2) requires the source of hearsay to be identified, it will be necessary to set out the whole chain of sources where the hearsay is not first-hand since under CEA 1995 hearsay of whatever degree is permissible (although the weight to be attached is a matter for the court under s 4(2)).

33.2 Notice of intention to rely on hearsay evidence

(1) Where a party intends to rely on hearsay evidence at trial and either –

(a) that evidence is to be given by a witness giving oral evidence; or

(b) that evidence is contained in a witness statement of a person who is not being called to give oral evidence;

that party complies with section 2(1)(a) of the Civil Evidence Act 1995 by serving a witness statement on the other parties in accordance with the court's order.

(2) Where paragraph (1)(b) applies, the party intending to rely on the hearsay evidence must, when he serves the witness statement –

(a) inform the other parties that the witness is not being called to give oral evidence; and

(b) give the reason why the witness will not be called.

(3) In all other cases where a party intends to rely on hearsay evidence at trial, that party complies with section 2(1)(a) of the Civil Evidence Act 1995 by serving a notice on the other parties which –

(a) identifies the hearsay evidence;

(b) states that the party serving the notice proposes to rely on the hearsay evidence at trial; and

(c) gives the reason why the witness will not be called.

(4) The party proposing to rely on the hearsay evidence must –

(a) serve the notice no later than the latest date for serving witness statements; and

(b) if the hearsay evidence is to be in a document, supply a copy to any party who requests him to do so.

Notice of intention to rely on hearsay—This rule deals with three separate situations in which notice is required to be given, and says how to comply with CEA 1995, s 2(1). It should be noted that any failure to comply does not render the evidence inadmissible under the Act (s 2(4)), but will be a breach of the rule, thus giving rise to the whole range of case management options and sanctions, in addition to the court's wide powers to manage evidence under r 32.1.

'hearsay] evidence ... to be given by a witness giving oral evidence' (r 33.2(1)(a))—Here the requirement is complied with by service of a witness statement.

'hearsay] evidence ... contained in a witness statement of a person' (rr 33.2(1)(b) and 33.2(2))—In this instance, in addition to serving a witness statement, *and at the same time*, it is necessary to tell the other parties that the witness is not being called, and why.

'in all other cases' (r 33.2(3) and (4))—Here the hearsay is not in a witness statement at all, and the requirement is to serve a notice identifying the evidence, stating that it is intended to rely on it and why the original maker of the statement will not be called. The time limit for the notice is the latest time for serving witness statements and if any party requests it, a copy of any document containing the hearsay must be provided.

33.3 Circumstances in which notice of intention to rely on hearsay evidence is not required

Section 2(1) of the Civil Evidence Act 1995 (duty to give notice of intention to rely on hearsay evidence) does not apply –

(a) to evidence at hearings other than trials;

(aa) to an affidavit or witness statement which is to be used at trial but which does not contain hearsay evidence;

(b) to a statement which a party to a probate action wishes to put in evidence and which is alleged to have been made by the person whose estate is the subject of the proceedings; or

(c) where the requirement is excluded by a practice direction.

Amendments—SI 1999/1008.

Where notice not required—The rule identifies four situations in which no notice is required: interim hearings, 'first-hand' witness statements/affidavits (added by the first modification to the rules), certain statements in probate actions and where a practice direction excludes the requirement. There is not yet any practice direction which does exclude the requirement.

33.4 Power to call witness for cross-examination on hearsay evidence

(1) Where a party –

(a) proposes to rely on hearsay evidence; and
(b) does not propose to call the person who made the original statement to give oral evidence,

the court may, on the application of any other party, permit that party to call the maker of the statement to be cross-examined on the contents of the statement.

(2) An application for permission to cross-examine under this rule must be made not more than 14 days after the day on which a notice of intention to rely on the hearsay evidence was served on the applicant.

Power to call witness for cross-examination on hearsay—In any situation where a party wishes to rely on hearsay, and is not calling the original maker of the statement, any other party may apply to have the maker there to be cross-examined. Unless the hearsay evidence is at the margin of relevance or any other reason of proportionality militates against it, in principle the maker of a statement should be present to be cross-examined if he is available. The application must be made within 14 days of the notice in whatever form under r 33.2.

33.5 Credibility

(1) Where a party –

(a) proposes to rely on hearsay evidence; but
(b) does not propose to call the person who made the original statement to give oral evidence; and
(c) another party wishes to call evidence to attack the credibility of the person who made the statement,

the party who so wishes must give notice of his intention to the party who proposes to give the hearsay statement in evidence.

(2) A party must give notice under paragraph (1) not more than 14 days after the day on which a hearsay notice relating to the hearsay evidence was served on him.

Credibility—If the recipient of a hearsay notice wishes to call evidence, by way of collateral attack on the original maker of the statement in question, he must give notice, again within 14 days. Whilst the rule does not say so, this is confined to witnesses who are not called to be cross-examined under r 33.4 or who are otherwise unavailable – see CEA 1995, s 5.

33.6 Use of plans, photographs and models as evidence

(1) This rule applies to evidence (such as a plan, photograph or model) which is not –

(a) contained in a witness statement, affidavit[(GL)] or expert's report;
(b) to be given orally at trial; or
(c) evidence of which prior notice must be given under rule 33.2.

(2) This rule includes documents which may be received in evidence without further proof under section 9 of the Civil Evidence Act 1995.

(3) Unless the court orders otherwise the evidence shall not be receivable at a trial unless the party intending to put it in evidence has given notice to the other parties in accordance with this rule.

(4) Where the party intends to use the evidence as evidence of any fact then, except where paragraph (6) applies, he must give notice not later than the latest date for serving witness statements.

(5) He must give notice at least 21 days before the hearing at which he proposes to put in the evidence, if –

- (a) there are not to be witness statements; or
- (b) he intends to put in the evidence solely in order to disprove an allegation made in a witness statement.

(6) Where the evidence forms part of expert evidence, he must give notice when the expert's report is served on the other party.

(7) Where the evidence is being produced to the court for any reason other than as part of factual or expert evidence, he must give notice at least 21 days before the hearing at which he proposes to put in the evidence.

(8) Where a party has given notice that he intends to put in the evidence, he must give every other party an opportunity to inspect it and to agree to its admission without further proof.

Plans, photographs and models—This rule applies to evidence that has its source otherwise than from people who are to be or might be called – the examples given are plans, photographs, models, and the rule includes business and public authority records falling within CEA 1995, s 9.

'evidence of any fact' (r 33.6(4))—In this case the evidence, unless the court orders otherwise, 'shall not be receivable' (r 33.6(3)) unless notice is given either at the latest time for serving witness statements or not less than 21 days before the hearing in a case where either there are no witness statements or the evidence is required to rebut something in a witness statement. There is an exception where the evidence 'forms part of expert evidence' (r 33.6(6)) but, *ex hypothesi*, is not 'contained in … expert's report', otherwise the rule would not apply at all] in which case notice must be given at the same time as service of the report.

'evidence … other than as part of factual or expert evidence' (r 33.6(7))—This strange provision requires notice of the adducing of such evidence to be given not less than 21 days before the hearing.

'opportunity to inspect' (r 33.6(8))—In all cases, it is required not only that there be an opportunity to inspect but also an opportunity to agree the material without further proof.

33.7 Evidence of finding on question of foreign law

(1) This rule sets out the procedure which must be followed by a party who intends to put in evidence a finding on a question of foreign law by virtue of section 4(2) of the Civil Evidence Act 1972.

(2) He must give any other party notice of his intention.

(3) He must give the notice –

- (a) if there are to be witness statements, not later than the latest date for serving them; or
- (b) otherwise, not less than 21 days before the hearing at which he proposes to put the finding in evidence.

(4) The notice must –

- (a) specify the question on which the finding was made; and
- (b) enclose a copy of a document where it is reported or recorded.

33.8 Evidence of consent of trustee to act

A document purporting to contain the written consent of a person to act as trustee and to bear his signature verified by some other person is evidence of such consent.

33.9 Human Rights

(1) This rule applies where a claim is –

(a) for a remedy under section 7 of the Human Rights Act 1998 in respect of a judicial act which is alleged to have infringed the claimant's Article 5 Convention rights; and

(b) based on a finding by a court or tribunal that the claimant's Convention rights have been infringed.

(2) The court hearing the claim –

(a) may proceed on the basis of the finding of that other court or tribunal that there has been an infringement but it is not required to do so, and

(b) may reach its own conclusion in the light of that finding and of the evidence heard by that other court or tribunal.

Amendments—Inserted by SI 2000/2092.

General note—There is as yet no associated change or addition to the practice direction under this Part, but note the deletion of former PD2B, para 15 effected by Update 21 as of 12 February 2001 – see note **'remedy under section 7 of the Human Rights Act 1998'** below.

'remedy under section 7 of the Human Rights Act 1998' (r 33.9(1)(a))—Claims under HRA 1998, s 7(1)(a) in respect of judicial acts, unlike other such claims, may be brought only in the High Court – see new r 7.11 inserted by the same statutory instrument. The deletion referred to above (thus removing reference to what rank of judge can hear matters of this kind in the county court) was made because the paragraph was a pure error on the part of those responsible, and gave rise to the suggestion that although such claims must be *launched* in the High Court, they might be transferred to the county court – otherwise the paragraph would have had no purpose. It might be thought that clearing up the misapprehension caused by the error could have been achieved more transparently, but the position is now intended to be unequivocally that such claims must always be brought, and heard, in the High Court.

'judicial act … infringed … Article 5 Convention rights' (r 33.9(1)(a))—Article 5 rights concern the right to liberty and security of the person. Where a remedy is sought, and there has already been a finding of infringement in respect of a judicial act, the court dealing with that claim may, but is not obliged, simply to accept the finding of infringement; it may adopt the alternative course of coming to its own conclusion as to whether there was an infringement, basing itself on the finding and the evidence before the court that made it. For further guidance on the application of this Rule, reference must be made to textbooks on the Act itself.

Practice Direction – Civil Evidence Act 1995

This Practice Direction supplements CPR Part 33 (PD33)

General note—See the notes to CPR Pt 33 for relevant commentary.

1 Section 16(3A) of the Civil Evidence Act 1995 (c 38) (as amended) provides that transitional provisions for the application of the provisions of the Civil Evidence Act 1995 to proceedings begun before 31 January 1997 may be made by practice direction.

2 Except as provided for by paragraph 3, the provisions of the Civil Evidence Act 1995 apply to claims commenced before 31 January 1997.

3 The provisions of the Civil Evidence Act 1995 do not apply to claims commenced before 31 January 1997 if, before 26 April 1999:

(a) directions were given, or orders were made, as to the evidence to be given at the trial or hearing; or
(b) the trial or hearing had begun.

PART 34
WITNESSES, DEPOSITIONS AND EVIDENCE FOR FOREIGN COURTS

CONTENTS OF THIS PART

General note to this Part—This Part has undergone two very significant revisions.

From 2 December 2002, it contains a simplified version of the former provisions of Sch 1, RSC Ord 70 and deals at rr 34.1–34.7 with securing the attendance of witnesses to give evidence or produce documents (formerly in RSC Ord 38). Rules 34.8–34.15 concern the taking of depositions (formerly in RSC Ord 39) and, at the new Section II, rr 34.16–34.21 pertain to the obtaining of evidence for use in all foreign courts.

From 1 January 2004, by reason of the implementation of Council Regulation (EC) No 1206/2001 of 28 May 2001 (the 'Taking of Evidence Regulation', now set out in full as Annex B to PD34), there are two distinct regimes. One applies to 'Regulation States', ie all EU Member States except Denmark, and the other to all 'other countries'. As a result, r 34.13 is now limited to 'other countries', as is Section II.

The new Section III deals both with taking evidence abroad from persons in Regulation States (r 34.23) and with obtaining evidence for use in courts of Regulation States (r 34.24).

The practice direction relating to Pt 34 has been extensively revised. It now contains detailed provisions as to procedures in respect of both regimes.

The new r 34.13A deals with evidence to be taken abroad for civil recovery under the Proceeds of Crime Act 2002, and it applies irrespective of the country in which the intended deponent is to be found.

PD34B sets out the formula for calculating fees and what expenses are allowable for examiners of the court.

It is expected that the use of depositions will increase. This is not only because of the increased flexibility of approach under the CPR generally, but also because they provide a mechanism for obtaining and testing evidence that does not require public resources to be allocated and, hence, may be available where otherwise the 'resources allocation' criteria in Pt 1 would preclude it.

The Part, subject to the distinctions between Regulation States and others, is clear and requires little commentary and following the two revisions is now the complete code when taken together with PD34 and its Annexes.

I Witnesses and Depositions

34.1 Scope of this Section

(1) This Section of this Part provides –

(a) for the circumstances in which a person may be required to attend court to give evidence or produce a document; and

(b) for a party to obtain evidence before a hearing to be used at the hearing.

(2) In this Section, reference to a hearing includes a reference to the trial.]

Amendments—Substituted by SI 2002/2058.

Practice Direction—See generally PD34 at p 868, PD34B at p 888.

34.2 Witness summonses

(1) A witness summons is a document issued by the court requiring a witness to –

(a) attend court to give evidence; or

(b) produce documents to the court.

(2) A witness summons must be in the relevant practice form.

(3) There must be a separate witness summons for each witness.

(4) A witness summons may require a witness to produce documents to the court either –

(a) on the date fixed for a hearing; or

(b) on such date as the court may direct.

(5) The only documents that a summons under this rule can require a person to produce before a hearing are documents which that person could be required to produce at the hearing.

Practice Direction—See PD34, paras 1.1–1.4 at p 868.

'relevant practice form' (r 34.2(2))—Paragraph 1 of PD34 gives detail on the issue of witness summonses, and specifies the use of Form N20 in duplicate. Neither the practice direction nor the form are helpful where the summons is to be issued in respect of documents held by a company. *Penn-Texas v Murat Anstalt* 1964] 2 All ER 594 is still good law: the summons should be issued against the company itself requiring it, by its proper officer, to give evidence and produce the documents.

'on such date as the court may direct' (r 34.2(4))—This formalises the previous and growing practice, initiated in the Chancery Division, of enabling what was formerly a *subpoena duces tecum* to be returnable on a date prior to the trial.

34.3 Issue of a witness summons

(1) A witness summons is issued on the date entered on the summons by the court.

(2) A party must obtain permission from the court where he wishes to –

(a) have a summons issued less than 7 days before the date of the trial;
(b) have a summons issued for a witness to attend court to give evidence or to produce documents on any date except the date fixed for the trial; or
(c) have a summons issued for a witness to attend court to give evidence or to produce documents at any hearing except the trial.

(3) A witness summons must be issued by –

(a) the court where the case is proceeding; or
(b) the court where the hearing in question will be held.

(4) The court may set aside[(GL)] or vary a witness summons issued under this rule.

Practice Direction—See PD34, paras 1.1–2.4 at p 868.

Permission—Note the three circumstances in which permission is required: otherwise the witness summons will be issued as of right (subject to the entitlement of the witness to apply to have it set aside or varied). The rule is silent as to the application for such permission; it will be without notice to a master or district judge and there is no express requirement for evidence to be adduced. See also PD34, para 1.

'may set aside or vary' (r 34.3(4))—See PD34, para 2 as to the procedure for applying where the summons is in aid of an inferior court, to which it is curiously limited. The same procedures will apply to an 'ordinary' witness summons. In *Harrison v Bloom Camillin* (1999) Lawtel, 14 May, Neuberger J held that pre-CPR authorities, though to be approached with caution, afforded some assistance in the absence of guidance in the CPR as to when to set aside or vary. As always regard must be had to the overriding objective; the position of the witness was not to be ignored under the old rules, and this was more strongly the case under the CPR (and in that case the summons was struck out on the grounds that it was speculative/fishing).

34.4 Witness summons in aid of inferior court or of tribunal

(1) The court may issue a witness summons in aid of an inferior court or of a tribunal.

(2) The court which issued the witness summons under this rule may set it aside.

(3) In this rule, 'inferior court or tribunal' means any court or tribunal that does not have power to issue a witness summons in relation to proceedings before it.

Practice Direction—See PD34, paras 2.1–2.4 at p 868.

General note—See para 2 of PD34 for applications to set aside.

34.5 Time for serving a witness summons

(1) The general rule is that a witness summons is binding if it is served at least 7 days before the date on which the witness is required to attend before the court or tribunal.

(2) The court may direct that a witness summons shall be binding although it will be served less than 7 days before the date on which the witness is required to attend before the court or tribunal.

(3) A witness summons which is –

(a) served in accordance with this rule; and
(b) requires the witness to attend court to give evidence,

is binding until the conclusion of the hearing at which the attendance of the witness is required.

'will be served less than 7 days before' (r 34.5(2))—The reference here, being prospective, reflects the situation where permission to serve 'short' is sought under r 34.3(2)(a).

34.6 Who is to serve a witness summons

(1) A witness summons is to be served by the court unless the party on whose behalf it is issued indicates in writing, when he asks the court to issue the summons, that he wishes to serve it himself.

(2) Where the court is to serve the witness summons, the party on whose behalf it is issued must deposit, in the court office, the money to be paid or offered to the witness under rule 34.7.

General note—As formerly, solicitors may well choose to effect service otherwise than through the court, and in the Commercial Court service of witness summonses is always by the parties and not the court (see the new Admiralty and Commercial Courts Guide, para H1.8(b)). The amount of money to be lodged where court service is available and chosen, or to be tendered with service, is dealt with in the next rule.

34.7 Right of witness to travelling expenses and compensation for loss of time

At the time of service of a witness summons the witness must be offered or paid –

- (a) a sum reasonably sufficient to cover his expenses in travelling to and from the court; and
- (b) such sum by way of compensation for loss of time as may be specified in the relevant practice direction.

Practice Direction—See PD34, paras 3.1–3.4 at p 869.

'such sum … as may be specified in the relevant practice direction' (r 34.7(b))—Paragraph 3 of PD34 sets out that the expenses are those required to travel to court and back home/to work, and that the compensation for lost benefit or earnings is to be calculated in accordance with regulations applicable to witnesses in the Crown Court.

34.8 Evidence by deposition

(1) A party may apply for an order for a person to be examined before the hearing takes place.

(2) A person from whom evidence is to be obtained following an order under this rule is referred to as a 'deponent' and the evidence is referred to as a 'deposition'.

(3) An order under this rule shall be for a deponent to be examined on oath before –

- (a) a judge;
- (b) an examiner of the court; or
- (c) such other person as the court appoints.

(Rule 34.15 makes provision for the appointment of examiners of the court)

(4) The order may require the production of any document which the court considers is necessary for the purposes of the examination.

(5) The order must state the date, time and place of the examination.

(6) At the time of service of the order the deponent must be offered or paid –

- (a) a sum reasonably sufficient to cover his expenses in travelling to and from the place of examination; and

(b) such sum by way of compensation for loss of time as may be specified in the relevant practice direction.

(7) Where the court makes an order for a deposition to be taken, it may also order the party who obtained the order to serve a witness statement or witness summary in relation to the evidence to be given by the person to be examined.

(Part 32 contains the general rules about witness statements and witness summaries)

Practice Direction—See PD34, paras 4.1–4.13 at p 869 and also PD34B at p 888.

'A party may apply' (r 34.8(1))—Neither the rule, nor PD34, offers any guidance as to the circumstances in which such an order will be made (save the reference to examination about assets for use in hearings other than the trial in r 34.12). In the past such orders have usually been made where the witness is too ill or otherwise unable to travel or attend a trial. As stated above, it is anticipated that use of deposition procedure will increase and should be permitted (or indeed ordered by the court under its case management powers) whenever such an order would further the overriding objective.

'an examiner of the court' (r 34.8(3)(b))—Paragraph 4.2 of PD34 sets out how to proceed to obtain an examiner of the court once an order for such an examination has been made. Notwithstanding the reference to the Foreign Process Section of the relevant department, PD34, para 4 is expressly premised on the deposition being taken within the jurisdiction for use within the jurisdiction. See PD34B for the fees of examiners.

'such sum … as may be specified in the relevant practice direction' (r 34.8(6)(b))—Curiously, and despite its dealing with r 34.7(b) above, the practice direction is so worded that it does not contain any provisions relating to the amounts to be tendered under this rule.

'may order … a witness statement' (r 34.8(7))—This rule envisages the situation where the party obtaining the order is causing his 'own' witness to be examined, in which case such an order should normally be made so as to emulate so far as practicable the procedural fairness of examination, and cross-examination, at trial. It is equally open, in principle, to an opposing party to seek an order for examination.

34.9 Conduct of examination

(1) Subject to any directions contained in the order for examination, the examination must be conducted in the same way as if the witness were giving evidence at a trial.

(2) If all the parties are present, the examiner may conduct the examination of a person not named in the order for examination if all the parties and the person to be examined consent.

(3) The examiner may conduct the examination in private if he considers it appropriate to do so.

(4) The examiner must ensure that the evidence given by the witness is recorded in full.

(5) The examiner must send a copy of the deposition –

(a) to the person who obtained the order for the examination of the witness; and

(b) to the court where the case is proceeding.

(6) The party who obtained the order must send each of the other parties a copy of the deposition which he receives from the examiner.

Practice Direction—See PD34, paras 4.3–4.7 at p 869 and para 4.12 at p 870.

General note—Paragraphs 4.3–4.7 and 4.12 of PD34 amplify the procedures to be followed in the ordinary type of examination, in particular as regards objections being raised and recorded for subsequent determination by the court. Note that r 34.9(2) permits any person to be examined, if all parties are present and they, and the potential deponent (and the examiner), agree.

34.10 Enforcing attendance of witness

(1) If a person served with an order to attend before an examiner –

(a) fails to attend; or

(b) refuses to be sworn for the purpose of the examination or to answer any lawful question or produce any document at the examination,

a certificate of his failure or refusal, signed by the examiner, must be filed by the party requiring the deposition.

(2) On the certificate being filed, the party requiring the deposition may apply to the court for an order requiring that person to attend, or to be sworn or to answer any question or produce any document, as the case may be.

(3) An application for an order under this rule may be made without notice.

(4) The court may order the person against whom an order is made under this rule to pay any costs resulting from his failure or refusal.

Practice Direction—See PD34, paras 4.8–4.11 at p 870.

Scope of provision—This rule is amplified by PD34, paras 4.8–4.11, and deals both with failure to attend at all and refusals once present. In particular, the practice direction provides that a failure to comply with an order under Pt 34 is punishable by contempt proceedings.

34.11 Use of deposition at a hearing

(1) A deposition ordered under rule 34.8 may be given in evidence at a hearing unless the court orders otherwise.

(2) A party intending to put in evidence a deposition at a hearing must serve notice of his intention to do so on every other party.

(3) He must serve the notice at least 21 days before the day fixed for the hearing.

(4) The court may require a deponent to attend the hearing and give evidence orally.

(5) Where a deposition is given in evidence at trial, it shall be treated as if it were a witness statement for the purposes of rule 32.13 (availability of witness statements for inspection).

Practice Direction—See generally PD34 at p 868, PD34B at p 888.

General note—Depositions may be used at trial as evidence, unless the court orders otherwise, notice is required not less than 21 days before the trial, and the court may require attendance and oral evidence. If the deposition is admitted, it is as open to inspection as a witness statement, the rule in respect of which (r 32.13) changed in March 2001.

34.12 Restrictions on subsequent use of deposition taken for the purpose of any hearing except the trial

(1) Where the court orders a party to be examined about his or any other assets for the purpose of any hearing except the trial, the deposition may be used only for the purpose of the proceedings in which the order was made.

(2) However, it may be used for some other purpose –

(a) by the party who was examined;

(b) if the party who was examined agrees; or

(c) if the court gives permission.

Practice Direction—See generally PD34 at p 868, PD34B at p 888.

'about his or any other assets for the purpose of any hearing except the trial' (r 34.12(1))—This specifically envisages the deposition procedure being used in respect of identifying assets in the 'freezing order' and tracing jurisdictions, whether before or after judgment, and after judgment in respect of enforcement. The limitations on use are limited to this specific type of examination, it being treated as analogous to compulsory disclosure: in any event once used at trial an 'ordinary' deposition will, in principle, be in the public domain.

34.13 Where a person to be examined is out of the jurisdiction – letter of request

(1) This rule applies where a party wishes to take a deposition from a person who is –

(a) out of the jurisdiction; and

(b) not in a Regulation State within the meaning of Section III of this Part.

(1A) The High Court may order the issue of a letter of request to the judicial authorities of the country in which the proposed deponent is.

(2) A letter of request is a request to a judicial authority to take the evidence of that person, or arrange for it to be taken.

(3) The High Court may make an order under this rule in relation to county court proceedings.

(4) If the government of a country allows a person appointed by the High Court to examine a person in that country, the High Court may make an order appointing a special examiner for that purpose.

(5) A person may be examined under this rule on oath or affirmation or in accordance with any procedure permitted in the country in which the examination is to take place.

(6) If the High Court makes an order for the issue of a letter of request, the party who sought the order must file –

(a) the following documents and, except where paragraph (7) applies, a translation of them –

(i) a draft letter of request;

(ii) a statement of the issues relevant to the proceedings;

(iii) a list of questions or the subject matter of questions to be put to the person to be examined; and

(b) an undertaking to be responsible for the Secretary of State's expenses.

(7) There is no need to file a translation if –

(a) English is one of the official languages of the country where the examination is to take place; or

(b) a practice direction has specified that country as a country where no translation is necessary.

Amendments—SI 1999/1008; SI 2003/2113.

Practice Direction—See PD34, paras 5.1–5.9 at p 871 and paras 6.1–6.8 at p 872 and also Annexes A and B.

Scope of provision—This Rule is otherwise unchanged but is now limited to countries other than 'Regulation States', which means that it applies only to those countries not members of the EU, plus Denmark (see PD34, paras 7.1–7.3).

'a person who is … not in a Regulation State' (r 34.13(1)(b))—Rule 34.13 deals with the taking of depositions in non-Regulation States (see note **'Scope of provision'** above) for use in proceedings within the jurisdiction. The procedural requirements are amplified in detail by PD34, para 5. The application is made under Pt 23 without notice. Once the witness has been deposed, the other rules in this Part of general application to the use of depositions will apply to that deposition. For the procedure relating to deposing persons in Regulation States, see the new r 34.23.

How to deal with depositions to be taken in England and Wales in respect of foreign proceedings (the converse case) is now covered by Section II (for non-Regulation States) and Section III (for Regulation States), see the new r 34.24. Practice Direction 34 deals with non-Regulation States at para 6 and with Regulation States at para 7, which imports the Taking of Evidence Regulation (see above the **'General Note'** under this Part). That Regulation is set out in full as Annex B to PD34.

'draft letter of request' (r 34.13(6)(a)(i))—There is a model letter of request at PD34, Annex A.

Use of ancillary foreign proceedings to obtain depositions for use in English action—In *Omega Group Holdings Ltd & ors v Kozeny & ors* (2001) (unreported) 6 September, QBD (Comm Ct) Peter Gross QC, sitting as a deputy High Court judge, held that it was appropriate to grant an injunction (subject to certain undertakings) to restrain the use of ancillary American proceedings to obtain depositions, on the ground that it would be unconscionable and an abuse of process to subject witnesses to unwarranted double cross-examination and that the English trial would suffer from unnecessary duplication.

34.13A Letter of request – Proceeds of Crime Act 2002

(1) This rule applies where a party to existing or contemplated proceedings in –

(a) the High Court; or

(b) a magistrates' court,

under Part 5 of the Proceeds of Crime Act 2002 (civil recovery of the proceeds etc of unlawful conduct) wishes to take a deposition from a person who is out of the jurisdiction.

(2) The High Court may, on the application of such a party, order the issue of a letter of request to the judicial authorities of the country in which the proposed deponent is.

(3) Paragraphs (4) to (7) of rule 34.13 shall apply irrespective of where the proposed deponent is, and rule 34.23 shall not apply in cases where the proposed deponent is in a Regulation State within the meaning of Section III of this Part.

Amendments—Inserted by SI 2003/3361.

General note—The same procedure is to be followed wherever the intended deponent is to be found.

34.14 Fees and expenses of examiner of the court

(1) An examiner of the court may charge a fee for the examination.

(2) He need not send the deposition to the court unless the fee is paid.

(3) The examiner's fees and expenses must be paid by the party who obtained the order for examination.

(4) If the fees and expenses due to an examiner are not paid within a reasonable time, he may report that fact to the court.

(5) The court may order the party who obtained the order for examination to deposit in the court office a specified sum in respect of the examiner's fees and, where it does so, the examiner will not be asked to act until the sum has been deposited.

(6) An order under this rule does not affect any decision as to the party who is ultimately to bear the costs of the examination.

Amendments—SI 1999/1008.

Practice Direction—See PD34B at p 888.

General note—This rule is supplemented by a separate practice direction under Pt 34 dealing solely with the fees and expenses of examiners of the court, ie PD34B at p 888.

34.15 Examiners of the court

(1) The Lord Chancellor shall appoint persons to be examiners of the court.

(2) The persons appointed shall be barristers or solicitor-advocates who have been practising for a period of not less than three years.

(3) The Lord Chancellor may revoke an appointment at any time.

Amendments—SI 2002/2058.

II Evidence for Foreign Courts

Introduction—This Section, from 1 January 2004, deals with requests from courts in non-Regulation States only and is originally, ie from December 2002, derived from the former Sch 1, RSC Ord 70. This was the only aspect of depositions not then covered by this Part. Any substantive changes – as from December 2002 – to the former practice under RSC Ord 70 are highlighted below.

34.16 Scope and interpretation

(1) This Section applies to an application for an order under the 1975 Act for evidence to be obtained, other than an application made as a result of a request by a court in another Regulation State.

(2) In this Section –

(a) 'the 1975 Act' means the Evidence (Proceedings in Other Jurisdictions) Act 1975, and

(b) 'Regulation State' has the same meaning as in Section III of this Part.

Amendments—Inserted by SI 2002/2058; substituted by SI 2003/2113; amended by SI 2004/1306.

General note—This rule is now relevant only to countries outside the EU and Denmark, these not being Regulation States. It repeats the former Sch 1, RSC Ord 70, r 1(1), excluding a reference to using the 1975 Act for interpretation of the Part. The old RSC Ord 70, r 1(2), giving jurisdiction to a Queen's Bench master, has been removed. However, by reason of the negative wording of r 2.4, and the fact that PD2B does not preclude such matters being dealt with by masters or district judges, the former retain that power and the latter have it expressly for the first time.

'the 1975 Act'—The jurisdiction to make orders of this kind is entirely statutory and the Act, together with this Section and PD34, para 6, provides a complete and comprehensive code in respect of non-Regulation States.

There are limitations on the power to make such orders, set out at ss 2 and 3 of the Act, and reflecting in part an express reservation registered by the United Kingdom when becoming a party to the Hague Convention of 1970, which the Act otherwise enshrines. In particular, there are excluded non-party disclosure (that not then being a feature of English proceedings), evidence for pre-trial purposes, general disclosure of documents (any documents sought must be specified in the request) and any matters which breach UK sovereignty. All rights to claim privilege (both domestic and as regulated by the requesting foreign court) are maintained. The taking of evidence in aid of foreign criminal proceedings is not permitted.

In respect of requests by courts of Regulation States, see now Section III of this Part below. The Taking of Evidence Regulation expressly provides that it prevails over arrangements concluded under the Hague Conventions, which presumably includes the statutory limitations set out above insofar as they are inconsistent with the Regulation.

There have been several recent cases underlining the scope and limitations. Orders under the Act are permissible only in aid of foreign *courts*, as distinct from arbitral tribunals (*Commerce and Industry Insurance Co of Canada v Certain Underwriters at Lloyd's* [2002] 1 Lloyd's Rep 219, Comm Ct). In respect of requests in aid of foreign courts see *Refco Capital Markets Ltd & anor v Credit Suisse (First Boston) Ltd & anor* [2001] EWCA Civ 1733, (2001) *The Times*, 7 December,

CA (regarding unspecified documents and pre-trial evidence) and *SEC v Credit Bancorp Ltd & ors* (2001) (unreported) 20 February, QBD (to the effect that US-style pre-trial discovery is too wide).

34.17 Application for order

An application for an order under the 1975 Act for evidence to be obtained –

(a) must be –
  (i) made to the High Court;
  (ii) supported by written evidence; and
  (iii) accompanied by the request as a result of which the application is made, and where appropriate, a translation of the request into English; and

(b) may be made without notice.

Amendments—Inserted by SI 2002/2058.

'Application for order' (r 34.17 heading)—The provisions of r 34.17 are not to be read in isolation: PD34, para 6.3 gives a list of what is required in making the application. It requires an application form under Pt 23, supported by the materials set out at PD43, para 6.3(1)–(5). The formerly separate regime and different requirements for the Treasury Solicitor (Sch 1, Ord 70, r 3 and old PD34, para 6.4) have been brought into line with 'ordinary' applications and are now referred to only at the new PD34, para 6.4, which reproduces in slightly different language the former rule.

'may be made without notice' (r 34.17(b))—This is a change in practice: under the former Ord 70, r 2(1) it was mandatory that the application be without notice. Otherwise, the rule is effectively unchanged.

Patents Act 1977, s 92—The former reference to examinations under this enactment at Sch 1, RSC Ord 70, r 2(3) has been removed, but reinstated as a separate rule at r 34.21.

34.18 Examination

(1) The court may order an examination to be taken before –

(a) any fit and proper person nominated by the person applying for the order;
(b) an examiner of the court; or
(c) any other person whom the court considers suitable.

(2) Unless the court orders otherwise –

(a) the examination will be taken as provided by rule 34.9; and
(b) rule 34.10 applies.

(3) The court may make an order under rule 34.14 for payment of the fees and expenses of the examination.

Amendments—Inserted by SI 2002/2058.

General note—This rule reproduces in clearer form all of the former Sch 1, RSC Ord 70, r 4.

'as provided by rule 34.9 … and … rule 34.10 applies' (r 34.18(2)(a), (b))—In addition, by virtue of PD34, para 6.8, all of the provisions of paras 4.2–4.12 of that practice direction apply, save as noted under r 34.19 below.

Administrative arrangements are dealt with at PD34, para 6.7; the reference therein to 'the agent referred in paragraph 6.3' is an error and reflects the former para 6.3.

34.19 Dealing with deposition

(1) The examiner must send the deposition of the witness to the Senior Master unless the court orders otherwise.

(2) The Senior Master will –

(a) give a certificate sealed with the seal of the Supreme Court for use out of the jurisdiction identifying the following documents –
   (i) the request;
   (ii) the order of the court for examination; and
   (iii) the deposition of the witness; and
(b) send the certificate and the documents referred to in paragraph (a) to –
   (i) the Secretary of State; or
   (ii) where the request was sent to the Senior Master by another person in accordance with a Civil Procedure Convention, to that other person,

for transmission to the court or tribunal requesting the examination.

Amendments—Inserted by SI 2002/2058.

General note—This rule reproduces in clearer form all of the former Sch 1, RSC Ord 70, r 5. As noted under r 34.18 above, by virtue of PD34, para 6.8, all of the provisions of paras 4.2–4.12 of the practice direction apply, save that the deposition is in all cases to be sent not to any party but to the Senior Master (unless there is an order to the contrary).

34.20 Claim to privilege

(1) This rule applies where –

(a) a witness claims to be exempt from giving evidence on the ground specified in section 3(1)(b) of the 1975 Act; and
(b) that claim is not supported or conceded as referred to in section 3(2) of that Act.

(2) The examiner may require the witness to give the evidence which he claims to be exempt from giving.

(3) Where the examiner does not require the witness to give that evidence, the court may order the witness to do so.

(4) An application for an order under paragraph (3) may be made by the person who obtained the order under section 2 of the 1975 Act.

(5) Where such evidence is taken –

(a) it must be contained in a document separate from the remainder of the deposition;
(b) the examiner will send to the Senior Master –
   (i) the deposition; and
   (ii) a signed statement setting out the claim to be exempt and the ground on which it was made;

(6) On receipt of the statement referred to in paragraph (5)(b)(ii), the Senior Master will –

(a) retain the document containing the part of the witness's evidence to which the claim to be exempt relates; and
(b) send the statement and a request to determine that claim to the foreign court or tribunal together with the documents referred to in rule 34.17.

(7) The Senior Master will –

(a) if the claim to be exempt is rejected by the foreign court or tribunal, send the document referred to in paragraph (5)(a) to that court or tribunal;
(b) if the claim is upheld, send the document to the witness; and

(c) in either case, notify the witness and person who obtained the order under section 2 of the foreign court or tribunal's decision.

Amendments—Inserted by SI 2002/2058.

General note—Save that the application referred to at r 34.20(4) was formerly required to be without notice and no such requirement now exists, this rule reproduces in clearer form all of the former Sch 1, RSC Ord 70, r 6.

Scope of provision—This procedure enables claims of privilege in respect of evidence or documents to be determined by the foreign court without effective waiver or loss of such privilege.

34.21 Order under 1975 Act as applied by Patents Act 1977

Where an order is made for the examination of witnesses under section 1 of the 1975 Act as applied by section 92 of the Patents Act 1977 the court may permit an officer of the European Patent Office to –

(a) attend the examination and examine the witnesses; or
(b) request the court or the examiner before whom the examination takes place to put specified questions to them.

Amendments—Inserted by SI 2002/2058.

General note—As noted above, this replicates the former Sch 1, RSC Ord 70, r 2(3) in clearer form.

III Taking of Evidence – Member States of the European Union

34.22 Interpretation

In this Section –

(a) 'designated court' has the meaning given in the relevant practice direction;
(b) 'Regulation State' has the same meaning as 'Member State' in the Taking of Evidence Regulation, that is all Member States except Denmark;
(c) 'the Taking of Evidence Regulation' means Council Regulation (EC) No 1206/2001 of 28 May 2001 on co-operation between the courts of the Member States in the taking of evidence in civil and commercial matters.

Amendments—Inserted by SI 2003/2113.

Practice Direction—See PD34, paras 7–11 at p 873 and the Regulation itself at PD34, Annex B. Denmark, for the time being, remains subject to the 'old rules' above.

General note—This Section, from. January 2004, relates both to obtaining and supplying evidence where the relevant foreign country is a Regulation State.

'designated court' (r 34.22(a))—See PD34, Annex C for a list.

'Regulation State' (r 34.22(b))—That is, all Member States of the EU except Denmark.

'the Taking of Evidence Regulation' (r 34.22(c))—This is set out in full at PD34, Annex B. It is detailed and, with the new provisions of PD34, comprehensive.

34.23 Where a person to be examined is in another Regulation State

(1) Subject to rule 34.13A, this rule applies where a party wishes to take a deposition from a person who is in another Regulation State.

(2) The court may order the issue of a request to a designated court ('the requested court') in the Regulation State in which the proposed deponent is.

(3) If the court makes an order for the issue of a request, the party who sought the order must file –

(a) a draft Form A as set out in the annex to the Taking of Evidence Regulation (request for the taking of evidence);
(b) except where paragraph (4) applies, a translation of the form;
(c) an undertaking to be responsible for costs sought by the requested court in relation to –
   (i) fees paid to experts and interpreters; and
   (ii) where requested by that party, the use of special procedures or communications technology; and
(d) an undertaking to be responsible for the court's expenses.

(4) There is no need to file a translation if –

(a) English is one of the official languages of the Regulation State where the examination is to take place; or
(b) the Regulation State has indicated, in accordance with the Taking of Evidence Regulation, that English is a language which it will accept.

(5) Where article 17 of the Taking of Evidence Regulation (direct taking of evidence by the requested court) allows evidence to be taken directly in another Regulation State, the court may make an order for the submission of a request in accordance with that article.

(6) If the court makes an order for the submission of a request under paragraph (5), the party who sought the order must file –

(a) a draft Form I as set out in the annex to the Taking of Evidence Regulation (request for direct taking of evidence);
(b) except where paragraph (4) applies, a translation of the form; and
(c) an undertaking to be responsible for the court's expenses.

Amendments—Inserted by SI 2003/2113; amended by SI 2003/3361; SI 2004/1306.

Practice Direction—See PD34, paras 7–10 at p 873 and the Regulation itself at PD34, Annex B.

General note—Annex A to PD34 is not the letter of request to be used in this instance: subject to the brief provisions of this new rule, the whole regime and the forms are all to be found in PD34 and the Regulation at Annex B thereto.

34.24 Evidence for courts of other Regulation States

(1) This rule applies where a court in another Regulation State ('the requesting court') issues a request for evidence to be taken from a person who is in the jurisdiction.

(2) An application for an order for evidence to be taken –

(a) must be made to a designated court;
(b) must be accompanied by –
   (i) the form of request for the taking of evidence as a result of which the application is made; and
   (ii) where appropriate, a translation of the form of request; and
(c) may be made without notice.

(3) Rule 34.18(1) and (2) apply.

(4) The examiner must send –

(a) the deposition to the court for transmission to the requesting court; and
(b) a copy of the deposition to the person who obtained the order for evidence to be taken.

Amendments—Inserted by SI 2003/2113.

Practice Direction—See PD34, paras 7–11 at p 873 and the Regulation itself at PD34, Annex B. The UK has indicated that it will accept requests in English or French.

'designated court' (r 34.24(2)(a))—See PD34, Annex C for a list.

Practice Direction – Depositions and Court Attendance by Witnesses

This Practice Direction supplements CPR Part 34 (PD34)

General note—See the notes to CPR Pt 34 for relevant commentary. In particular, note that paras 6.3 and 6.4 have been completely rewritten as of 2 December 2002.

WITNESS SUMMONSES

Issue of Witness Summons

1.1 A witness summons may require a witness to:

(1) attend court to give evidence,
(2) produce documents to the court, or
(3) both,

on either a date fixed for the hearing or such date as the court may direct[1].

1 Rule 34.2(4).

1.2 Two copies of the witness summons[1] should be filed with the court for sealing, one of which will be retained on the court file.

1 In Practice Form N20.

1.3 A mistake in the name or address of a person named in a witness summons may be corrected if the summons has not been served.

1.4 The corrected summons must be re-sealed by the court and marked 'Amended and Re-Sealed'.

Witness summons issued in aid of an inferior court or tribunal

2.1 A witness summons may be issued in the High Court or a county court in aid of a court or tribunal which does not have the power to issue a witness summons in relation to the proceedings before it[1].

1 Rule 34.4(1).

2.2 A witness summons referred to in paragraph 2.1 may be set aside by the court which issued it[1].

1 Rule 34.4(2).

2.3 An application to set aside a witness summons referred to in paragraph 2.1 will be heard:

(1) in the High Court by a master at the Royal Courts of Justice or by a district judge in a District Registry, and
(2) in a county court by a district judge.

2.4 Unless the court otherwise directs, the applicant must give at least 2 days' notice to the party who issued the witness summons of the application, which will normally be dealt with at a hearing.

Travelling expenses and compensation for loss of time

3.1 When a witness is served with a witness summons he must be offered a sum to cover his travelling expenses to and from the court and compensation for his loss of time[1].

1 Rule 34.7.

3.2 If the witness summons is to be served by the court, the party issuing the summons must deposit with the court:

(1) a sum sufficient to pay for the witness's expenses in travelling to the court and in returning to his home or place of work, and
(2) a sum in respect of the period during which earnings or benefit are lost, or such lesser sum as it may be proved that the witness will lose as a result of his attendance at court in answer to the witness summons.

3.3 The sum referred to in 3.2(2) is to be based on the sums payable to witnesses attending the Crown Court[1].

1 Fixed pursuant to the Prosecution of Offences Act 1985 and the Costs in Criminal Cases General Regulations 1986.

3.4 Where the party issuing the witness summons wishes to serve it himself[1], he must:

(1) notify the court in writing that he wishes to do so, and
(2) at the time of service offer the witness the sums mentioned in paragraph 3.2 above.

1 Rule 34.6(1).

DEPOSITIONS

To be taken in England and Wales for use as evidence in proceedings in courts in England and Wales

4.1 A party may apply for an order for a person to be examined on oath before:

(1) a judge,
(2) an examiner of the court, or
(3) such other person as the court may appoint[1].

1 Rule 34.8(3).

4.2 The party who obtains an order for the examination of a deponent[1] before an examiner of the court[2] must:

(1) apply to the Foreign Process Section of the Masters' Secretary's Department at the Royal Courts of Justice for the allocation of an examiner,
(2) when allocated, provide the examiner with copies of all documents in the proceedings necessary to inform the examiner of the issues, and
(3) pay the deponent a sum to cover his travelling expenses to and from the examination and compensation for his loss of time[3].

1 See rule 34.8(2) for explanation of 'deponent' and 'deposition'.
2 For the appointment of examiners of the court see rule 34.15.
3 Rule 34.8(6).

4.3 In ensuring that the deponent's evidence is recorded in full, the court or the examiner may permit it to be recorded on audiotape or videotape, but the deposition[1] must always be recorded in writing by him or by a competent shorthand writer or stenographer.

1 See rule 34.8(2) for explanation of 'deponent' and 'deposition'.

4.4 If the deposition is not recorded word for word, it must contain, as nearly as may be, the statement of the deponent; the examiner may record word for word any particular questions and answers which appear to him to have special importance.

4.5 If a deponent objects to answering any question or where any objection is taken to any question, the examiner must:

(1) record in the deposition or a document attached to it –
  (a) the question,
  (b) the nature of and grounds for the objection, and
  (c) any answer given, and
(2) give his opinion as to the validity of the objection and must record it in the deposition or a document attached to it.

The court will decide as to the validity of the objection and any question of costs arising from it.

4.6 Documents and exhibits must:

(1) have an identifying number or letter marked on them by the examiner, and
(2) be preserved by the party or his legal representative[1] who obtained the order for the examination, or as the court or the examiner may direct.

1 For the definition of legal representative see rule 2.3.

4.7 The examiner may put any question to the deponent as to:

(1) the meaning of any of his answers, or
(2) any matter arising in the course of the examination.

4.8 Where a deponent:

(1) fails to attend the examination, or
(2) refuses to:
  (a) be sworn, or
  (b) answer any lawful question, or
  (c) produce any document,

the examiner will sign a certificate[1] of such failure or refusal and may include in his certificate any comment as to the conduct of the deponent or of any person attending the examination.

1 Rule 34.10.

4.9 The party who obtained the order for the examination must file the certificate with the court and may apply for an order that the deponent attend for examination or as may be[1]. The application may be made without notice[2].

1 Rule 34.10(2) and (3).
2 Rule 34.10(3).

4.10 The court will make such order on the application as it thinks fit including an order for the deponent to pay any costs resulting from his failure or refusal[1].

1 Rule 34.10(4).

4.11 A deponent who wilfully refuses to obey an order made against him under Part 34 may be proceeded against for contempt of court.

4.12 A deposition must:

(1) be signed by the examiner,

(2) have any amendments to it initialled by the examiner and the deponent,
(3) be endorsed by the examiner with –
  (a) a statement of the time occupied by the examination, and
  (b) a record of any refusal by the deponent to sign the deposition and of his reasons for not doing so, and
(4) be sent by the examiner to the court where the proceedings are taking place for filing on the court file.

4.13 Rule 34.14 deals with the fees and expenses of an examiner.

Depositions to be taken abroad for use as evidence in proceedings before courts in England and Wales where the Taking of Evidence Regulation does not apply

5.1 Where a party wishes to take a deposition from a person outside the jurisdiction, the High Court may order the issue of a letter of request to the judicial authorities of the country in which the proposed deponent is[1].

1 Rule 34.13(1).

5.2 An application for an order referred to in paragraph 5.1 should be made by application notice in accordance with Part 23].

5.3 The documents which a party applying for an order for the issue of a letter of request must file with his application notice are set out in rule 34.13(6). They are as follows:

(1) a draft letter of request in the form set out in Annex A to this practice direction,
(2) a statement of the issues relevant to the proceedings,
(3) a list of questions or the subject matter of questions to be put to the proposed deponent,
(4) a translation of the documents in (1), (2) and (3) above unless the proposed deponent is in a country of which English is an official language, and
(5) an undertaking to be responsible for the expenses of the Secretary of State.

In addition to the documents listed above the party applying for the order must file a draft order.

5.4 The above documents should be filed with the Masters' Secretary in Room E214, Royal Courts of Justice, Strand, London WC2A 2LL.

5.5 The application will be dealt with by the Senior Master of the Queen's Bench Division of the High Court who will, if appropriate, sign the letter of request.

5.6 Attention is drawn to the provisions of rule 23.10 (application to vary or discharge an order made without notice).

5.7 If parties are in doubt as to whether a translation under paragraph 5.3(4) above is required, they should seek guidance from the Foreign Process Section of the Masters' Secretary's Department.

5.8 A special examiner appointed under rule 34.13(4) may be the British Consul or the Consul-General or his deputy in the country where the evidence is to be taken if:

(1) there is in respect of that country a Civil Procedure Convention

providing for the taking of evidence in that country for the assistance of proceedings in the High Court or other court in this country, or
(2) with the consent of the Secretary of State.

5.9 The provisions of paragraphs 4.1 to 4.12 above apply to the depositions referred to in this paragraph.

Depositions to be taken in England and Wales for use as evidence in proceedings before courts abroad pursuant to letters of request where the Taking of Evidence Regulation does not apply

6.1 Section II of Part 34 relating to obtaining evidence for foreign courts applies to letters of request and should be read in conjunction with this part of the practice direction.

6.2 The Evidence (Proceedings in Other Jurisdictions) Act 1975 applies to these depositions.

6.3 The written evidence supporting an application under rule 34.17 (which should be made by application notice – see Part 23) must include or exhibit –

(1) a statement of the issues relevant to the proceedings;
(2) a list of questions or the subject matter of questions to be put to the proposed deponent;
(3) a draft order; and
(4) a translation of the documents in (1) and (2) into English, if necessary.]

6.4 (1) The Senior Master will send to the Treasury Solicitor any request –
(a) forwarded by the Secretary of State with a recommendation that effect should be given to the request without requiring an application to be made; or
(b) received by him in pursuance of a Civil Procedure Convention providing for the taking of evidence of any person in England and Wales to assist a court or tribunal in a foreign country where no person is named in the document as the applicant.
(2) In relation to such a request, the Treasury Solicitor may, with the consent of the Treasury –
(a) apply for an order under the 1975 Act; and
(b) take such other steps as are necessary to give effect to the request.]

6.5 The order for the deponent to attend and be examined together with the evidence upon which the order was made must be served on the deponent.]

6.6 Attention is drawn to the provisions of rule 23.10 (application to vary or discharge an order made without notice).

6.7 Arrangements for the examination to take place at a specified time and place before an examiner of the court or such other person as the court may appoint shall be made by the applicant for the order and approved by the Senior Master.

6.8 The provisions of paragraphs 4.2 to 4.12 apply to the depositions referred to in this paragraph, except that the examiner must send the deposition to the Senior Master.

(For further information about evidence see Part 32 and the practice direction which supplements it)

TAKING OF EVIDENCE BETWEEN EU MEMBER STATES

Taking of Evidence Regulation

7.1 Where evidence is to be taken –

(a) from a person in another Member State of the European Union for use as evidence in proceedings before courts in England and Wales; or
(b) from a person in England and Wales for use as evidence in proceedings before a court in another Member State,

Council Regulation (EC) No 1206/2001 of 28 May 2001 on co-operation between the courts of the Member States in the taking of evidence in civil or commercial matters ('the taking of Evidence Regulation') applies.

7.2 The Taking of Evidence Regulation is annexed to this practice direction as Annex B.

7.3 The Taking of Evidence Regulation does not apply to Denmark. In relation to Denmark, therefore, rule 34.13 and Section II of Part 34 will continue to apply.

(Article 21(1) of the Taking of Evidence Regulation provides that the Regulation prevails over other provisions contained in bilateral or multilateral agreements or arrangements concluded by the Member States and in particular the Hague Convention of 1 March 1954 on Civil Procedure and the Hague Convention of 18 March 1970 on the Taking of Evidence Abroad in Civil or Commercial Matters)

Originally published in the official languages of the European Community in the Official Journal of the European Communities by the Office for Official Publications of the European Communities.

Meaning of 'designated court'

8.1 In accordance with the Taking of Evidence Regulation, each Regulation State has prepared a list of courts competent to take evidence in accordance with the Regulation indicating the territorial and, where appropriate, special jurisdiction of those courts.

8.2 Where Part 34, Section III refers to a 'designated court' in relation to another Regulation State, the reference is to the court, referred to in the list of competent courts of that State, which is appropriate to the application in hand.

8.3 Where the reference is to the 'designated court' in England and Wales, the reference is to the appropriate competent court in the jurisdiction. The designated courts for England and Wales are listed in Annex C to this practice direction.

Central Body

9.1 The Taking of Evidence Regulation stipulates that each Regulation State must nominate a Central Body responsible for –

(a) supplying information to courts;
(b) seeking solutions to any difficulties which may arise in respect of a request; and
(c) forwarding, in exceptional cases, at the request of a requesting court, a request to the competent court.

9.2 The United Kingdom has nominated the Senior Master, Queen's Bench Division, to be the Central Body for England and Wales.

9.3 The Senior Master, as Central Body, has been designated responsible for taking decisions on requests pursuant to Article 17 of the Regulation. Article 17 allows a court to submit a request to the Central Body or a designated competent authority in another Regulation State to take evidence directly in that State.

Evidence to be taken in another Regulation State for use in England and Wales

10.1 Where a person wishes to take a deposition from a person in another Regulation State, the court where the proceedings are taking place may order the issue of a request to the designated court in the Regulation State (Rule 34.23(2)). The form of request is prescribed as Form A in the Taking of Evidence Regulation.

10.2 An application to the court for an order under rule 34.23(2) should be made by application notice in accordance with Part 23.

10.3 Rule 34.23(3) provides that the party applying for the order must file a draft form of request in the prescribed form. Where completion of the form requires attachments or documents to accompany the form, these must also be filed.

10.4 If the court grants an order under rule 34.23 (2), it will send the form of request directly to the designated court.

10.5 Where the taking of evidence requires the use of an expert, the designated court may require a deposit in advance towards the costs of that expert. The party who obtained the order is responsible for the payment of any such deposit which should be deposited with the court for onward transmission. Under the provisions of the Taking of Evidence Regulation, the designated court is not required to execute the request until such payment is received.

10.6 Article 17 permits the court where proceedings are taking place to take evidence directly from a deponent in another Regulation State if the conditions of the article are satisfied. Direct taking of evidence can only take place if evidence is given voluntarily without the need for coercive measures. Rule 34.23(5) provides for the court to make an order for the submission of a request to take evidence directly. The form of request is Form I annexed to the Taking of Evidence Regulation and rule 34.23(6) makes provision for a draft of this form to be filed by the party seeking the order. An application for an order under rule 34.23(5) should be by application notice in accordance with Part 23.

10.7 Attention is drawn to the provisions of rule 23.10 (application to vary or discharge an order made without notice).

Evidence to be taken in England and Wales for use in another Regulation State

11.1 Where a designated court in England and Wales receives a request to take evidence from a court in a Regulation State, the court will send the request to the Treasury Solicitor.

11.2 On receipt of the request, the Treasury Solicitor may, with the consent of the Treasury, apply for an order under rule 34.24.

11.3 An application to the court for an order must be accompanied by the Form of request to take evidence and any accompanying documents, translated if required under paragraph 11.4.

11.4 The United Kingdom has indicated that, in addition to English, it will accept French as a language in which documents may be submitted. Where the form or request and any accompanying documents are received in French they will be translated into English by the Treasury Solicitor.

11.5 The order for the deponent to attend and be examined together with the evidence on which the order was made must be served on the deponent.

11.6 Arrangements for the examination to take place at a specified time and place shall be made by the Treasury Solicitor and approved by the court.

11.7 The court shall send details of the arrangements for the examination to such of –

(a) the parties and, if any, their representatives; or
(b) the representatives of the foreign court,

who have indicated, in accordance with the Taking of Evidence Regulation, that they wish to be present at the examination.

11.8 The provisions of paragraph 4.3 to 4.12 apply to the depositions referred to in this paragraph.

Annex A

DRAFT LETTER OF REQUEST (WHERE THE TAKING OF EVIDENCE REGULATION DOES NOT APPLY)

To the Competent Judicial Authority of

in the of

I [*name*] Senior Master of the Queen's Bench Division of the Supreme Court of England and Wales respectfully request the assistance of your court with regard to the following matters.

1 A claim is now pending in the Division of the High Court of Justice in England and Wales entitled as follows

[*set out full title and claim number*]

in which [*name*] of [*address*] is the claimant and [*name*] of [*address*] is the defendant.

2 The names and addresses of the representatives or agents of [*set out names and addresses of representatives of the parties*].

3 The claim by the claimant is for:

(a) [*set out the nature of the claim*]
(b) [*the relief sought, and*]
(c) [*a summary of the facts.*]

4 It is necessary for the purposes of justice and for the due determination of the matters in dispute between the parties that you cause the following witnesses, who are resident within your jurisdiction, to be examined. The names and addresses of the witnesses are as follows:

5 The witnesses should be examined on oath or if that is not possible within your laws or is impossible of performance by reason of the internal practice and procedure of your court or by reason of practical difficulties, they should be examined in accordance with whatever procedure your laws provide for in these matters.

6 Either/

The witnesses should be examined in accordance with the list of questions annexed hereto.

Or/

The witnesses should be examined regarding [*set out full details of evidence sought*]

NB Where the witness is required to produce documents, these should be clearly identified.

7 I would ask that you cause me, or the agents of the parties (if appointed), to be informed of the date and place where the examination is to take place.

8 Finally, I request that you will cause the evidence of the said witnesses to be reduced into writing and all documents produced on such examinations to be duly marked for identification and that you will further be pleased to authenticate such examinations by the seal of your court or in such other way as is in accordance with your procedure and return the written evidence and documents produced to me addressed as follows:

Senior Master of the Queen's Bench Division

Royal Courts of Justice
Strand
London WC2A 2LL
England

Annex B

Council Regulation (EC) No 1206/2001

of 28 May 2001

on cooperation between the courts of the Member States in the taking of evidence in civil or commercial matters

THE COUNCIL OF THE EUROPEAN UNION,

Having regard to the Treaty establishing the European Community, and in particular Article 61(c) and Article 67(1) thereof,

Having regard to the initiative of the Federal Republic of Germany,

Having regard to the opinion of the European Parliament,

Having regard to the opinion of the Economic and Social Committee,

Whereas:

(1) The European Union has set itself the objective of maintaining and developing the European Union as an area of freedom, security and justice in which the free movement of persons is ensured. For the gradual establishment of

such an area, the Community is to adopt, among others, the measures relating to judicial cooperation in civil matters needed for the proper functioning of the internal market.

(2) For the purpose of the proper functioning of the internal market, cooperation between courts in the taking of evidence should be improved, and in particular simplified and accelerated.

(3) At its meeting in Tampere on 15 and 16 October 1999, the European Council recalled that new procedural legislation in cross-border cases, in particular on the taking of evidence, should be prepared.

(4) This area falls within the scope of Article 65 of the Treaty.

(5) The objectives of the proposed action, namely the improvement of cooperation between the courts on the taking of evidence in civil or commercial matters, cannot be sufficiently achieved by the Member States and can therefore be better achieved at Community level. The Community may adopt measures in accordance with the principle of subsidiarity as set out in Article 5 of the Treaty. In accordance with the principle of proportionality, as set out in that Article, this Regulation does not go beyond what is necessary to achieve those objectives.

(6) To date, there is no binding instrument between all the Member States concerning the taking of evidence. The Hague Convention of 18 March 1970 on the taking of evidence abroad in civil or commercial matters applies between only 11 Member States of the European Union.

(7) As it is often essential for a decision in a civil or commercial matter pending before a court in a Member State to take evidence in another Member State, the Community's activity cannot be limited to the field of transmission of judicial and extrajudicial documents in civil or commercial matters which falls within the scope of Council Regulation (EC) No 1348/2000 of 29 May 2000 on the serving in the Member States of judicial and extrajudicial documents in civil or commercial matters. It is therefore necessary to continue the improvement of cooperation between courts of Member States in the field of taking of evidence.

(8) The efficiency of judicial procedures in civil or commercial matters requires that the transmission and execution of requests for the performance of taking of evidence is to be made directly and by the most rapid means possible between Member States' courts.

(9) Speed in transmission of requests for the performance of taking of evidence warrants the use of all appropriate means, provided that certain conditions as to the legibility and reliability of the document received are observed. So as to ensure the utmost clarity and legal certainty the request for the performance of taking of evidence must be transmitted on a form to be completed in the language of the Member State of the requested court or in another language accepted by that State. For the same reasons, forms should also be used as far as possible for further communication between the relevant courts.

(10) A request for the performance of the taking of evidence should be executed expeditiously. If it is not possible for the request to be executed within 90 days of receipt by the requested court, the latter should inform the requesting court accordingly, stating the reasons which prevent the request from being executed swiftly.

(11) To secure the effectiveness of this Regulation, the possibility of refusing to execute the request for the performance of taking of evidence should be confined to strictly limited exceptional situations.

(12) The requested court should execute the request in accordance with the law of its Member State.

(13) The parties and, if any, their representatives, should be able to be present at the performance of the taking of evidence, if that is provided for by the law of the Member State of the requesting court, in order to be able to follow the proceedings in a comparable way as if evidence were taken in the Member State of the requesting court. They should also have the right to request to participate in order to have a more active role in the performance of the taking of evidence. However, the conditions under which they may participate should be determined by the requested court in accordance with the law of its Member State.

(14) The representatives of the requesting court should be able to be present at the performance of the taking of evidence, if that is compatible with the law of the Member State of the requesting court, in order to have an improved possibility of evaluation of evidence. They should also have the right to request to participate, under the conditions laid down by the requested court in accordance with the law of its Member State, in order to have a more active role in the performance of the taking of evidence.

(15) In order to facilitate the taking of evidence it should be possible for a court in a Member State, in accordance with the law of its Member State, to take evidence directly in another Member State, if accepted by the latter, and under the conditions determined by the central body or competent authority of the requested Member State.

(16) The execution of the request, according to Article 10, should not give rise to a claim for any reimbursement of taxes or costs. Nevertheless, if the requested court requires reimbursement, the fees paid to experts and interpreters, as well as the costs occasioned by the application of Article 10(3) and (4), should not be borne by that court. In such a case, the requesting court is to take the necessary measures to ensure reimbursement without delay. Where the opinion of an expert is required, the requested court may, before executing the request, ask the requesting court for an adequate deposit or advance towards the costs.

(17) This Regulation should prevail over the provisions applying to its field of application, contained in international conventions concluded by the Member States. Member States should be free to adopt agreements or arrangements to further facilitate cooperation in the taking of evidence.

(18) The information transmitted pursuant to this Regulation should enjoy protection. Since Directive 95/46/EC of the European Parliament and of the Council of 24 October 1995 on the protection of individuals with regard to the processing of personal data and on the free movement of such data, and Directive 97/66/EC of the European Parliament and of the Council of 15 December 1997 concerning the processing of personal data and the protection of privacy in the telecommunications sector, are applicable, there is no need for specific provisions on data protection in this Regulation.

(19) The measures necessary for the implementation of this Regulation should be adopted in accordance with Council Decision 1999/468/EC of 28 June 1999 laying down the procedures for the exercise of implementing powers conferred on the Commission.

(20) For the proper functioning of this Regulation, the Commission should review its application and propose such amendments as may appear necessary.

(21) The United Kingdom and Ireland, in accordance with Article 3 of the Protocol on the position of the United Kingdom and Ireland annexed to the Treaty on the European Union and to the Treaty establishing the European Community, have given notice of their wish to take part in the adoption and application of this Regulation.

(22) Denmark, in accordance with Articles 1 and 2 of the Protocol on the position of Denmark annexed to the Treaty on European Union and to the Treaty establishing the European Community, is not participating in the adoption of this Regulation, and is therefore not bound by it nor subject to its application,

HAS ADOPTED THIS REGULATION:

CHAPTER I
GENERAL PROVISIONS

ARTICLE 1

Scope

1 This Regulation shall apply in civil or commercial matters where the court of a Member State, in accordance with the provisions of the law of that State, requests:

(a) the competent court of another Member State to take evidence; or
(b) to take evidence directly in another Member State.

2 A request shall not be made to obtain evidence which is not intended for use in judicial proceedings, commenced or contemplated.

3 In this Regulation, the term 'Member State' shall mean Member States with the exception of Denmark.

ARTICLE 2

Direct transmission between the courts

1 Requests pursuant to Article 1(1)(a), hereinafter referred to as 'requests', shall be transmitted by the court before which the proceedings are commenced or contemplated, hereinafter referred to as the 'requesting court', directly to the competent court of another Member State, hereinafter referred to as the 'requested court', for the performance of the taking of evidence.

2 Each Member State shall draw up a list of the courts competent for the performance of taking of evidence according to this Regulation. The list shall also indicate the territorial and, where appropriate, the special jurisdiction of those courts.

ARTICLE 3

Central body

1 Each Member State shall designate a central body responsible for:

(a) supplying information to the courts;
(b) seeking solutions to any difficulties which may arise in respect of a request;
(c) forwarding, in exceptional cases, at the request of a requesting court, a request to the competent court.

2 A federal State, a State in which several legal systems apply or a State with autonomous territorial entities shall be free to designate more than one central body.

3 Each Member State shall also designate the central body referred to in paragraph 1 or one or several competent authority(ies) to be responsible for taking decisions on requests pursuant to Article 17.

CHAPTER II
TRANSMISSION AND EXECUTION OF REQUESTS

Section 1 – Transmission of the request

ARTICLE 4

Form and content of the request

1 The request shall be made using form A or, where appropriate, form I in the Annex. It shall contain the following details:

(a) the requesting and, where appropriate, the requested court;
(b) the names and addresses of the parties to the proceedings and their representatives, if any;
(c) the nature and subject matter of the case and a brief statement of the facts;
(d) a description of the taking of evidence to be performed;
(e) where the request is for the examination of a person:
 - the name(s) and address(es) of the person(s) to be examined,
 - the questions to be put to the person(s) to be examined or a statement of the facts about which he is (they are) to be examined,
 - where appropriate, a reference to a right to refuse to testify under the law of the Member State of the requesting court,
 - any requirement that the examination is to be carried out under oath or affirmation in lieu thereof, and any special form to be used,
 - where appropriate, any other information that the requesting court deems necessary;
(f) where the request is for any other form of taking of evidence, the documents or other objects to be inspected;
(g) where appropriate, any request pursuant to Article 10(3) and (4), and Articles 11 and 12 and any information necessary for the application thereof.

2 The request and all documents accompanying the request shall be exempted from authentication or any equivalent formality.

3 Documents which the requesting court deems it necessary to enclose for the execution of the request shall be accompanied by a translation into the language in which the request was written.

ARTICLE 5

Language

The request and communications pursuant to this Regulation shall be drawn up in the official language of the requested Member State or, if there are several official languages in that Member State, in the official language or one of the official languages of the place where the requested taking of evidence is to be performed, or in another language which the requested Member State has indicated it can accept. Each Member State shall indicate the official language or languages of the institutions of the European Community other than its own which is or are acceptable to it for completion of the forms.

ARTICLE 6

Transmission of requests and other communications

Requests and communications pursuant to this Regulation shall be transmitted by the swiftest possible means, which the requested Member State has indicated it can accept. The transmission may be carried out by any appropriate means, provided that the document received accurately reflects the content of the document forwarded and that all information in it is legible.

Section 2 – Receipt of request

ARTICLE 7

Receipt of request

1 Within seven days of receipt of the request, the requested competent court shall send an acknowledgement of receipt to the requesting court using form B in the Annex. Where the request does not comply with the conditions laid down in Articles 5 and 6, the requested court shall enter a note to that effect in the acknowledgement of receipt.

2 Where the execution of a request made using form A in the Annex, which complies with the conditions laid down in Article 5, does not fall within the jurisdiction of the court to which it was transmitted, the latter shall forward the request to the competent court of its Member State and shall inform the requesting court thereof using form A in the Annex.

ARTICLE 8

Incomplete request

1 If a request cannot be executed because it does not contain all of the necessary information pursuant to Article 4, the requested court shall inform the requesting court thereof without delay and, at the latest, within 30 days of receipt of the request using form C in the Annex, and shall request it to send the missing information, which should be indicated as precisely as possible.

2 If a request cannot be executed because a deposit or advance is necessary in accordance with Article 18(3), the requested court shall inform the requesting court thereof without delay and, at the latest, within 30 days of receipt of the

request using form C in the Annex and inform the requesting court how the deposit or advance should be made. The requested Court shall acknowledge receipt of the deposit or advance without delay, at the latest within 10 days of receipt of the deposit or the advance using form D.

ARTICLE 9

Completion of the request

1 If the requested court has noted on the acknowledgement of receipt pursuant to Article 7(1) that the request does not comply with the conditions laid down in Articles 5 and 6 or has informed the requesting court pursuant to Article 8 that the request cannot be executed because it does not contain all of the necessary information pursuant to Article 4, the time limit pursuant to Article 10 shall begin to run when the requested court received the request duly completed.

2 Where the requested court has asked for a deposit or advance in accordance with Article 18(3), this time limit shall begin to run when the deposit or the advance is made.

Section 3 – Taking of evidence by the requested court

ARTICLE 10

General provisions on the execution of the request

1 The requested court shall execute the request without delay and, at the latest, within 90 days of receipt of the request.

2 The requested court shall execute the request in accordance with the law of its Member State.

3 The requesting court may call for the request to be executed in accordance with a special procedure provided for by the law of its Member State, using form A in the Annex. The requested court shall comply with such a requirement unless this procedure is incompatible with the law of the Member State of the requested court or by reason of major practical difficulties. If the requested court does not comply with the requirement for one of these reasons it shall inform the requesting court using form E in the Annex.

4 The requesting court may ask the requested court to use communications technology at the performance of the taking of evidence, in particular by using videoconference and teleconference.

The requested court shall comply with such a requirement unless this is incompatible with the law of the Member State of the requested court or by reason of major practical difficulties.

If the requested court does not comply with the requirement for one of these reasons, it shall inform the requesting court, using form E in the Annex.

If there is no access to the technical means referred to above in the requesting or in the requested court, such means may be made available by the courts by mutual agreement.

ARTICLE 11

Performance with the presence and participation of the parties

1 If it is provided for by the law of the Member State of the requesting court, the parties and, if any, their representatives, have the right to be present at the performance of the taking of evidence by the requested court.

2 The requesting court shall, in its request, inform the requested court that the parties and, if any, their representatives, will be present and, where appropriate, that their participation is requested, using form A in the Annex. This information may also be given at any other appropriate time.

3 If the participation of the parties and, if any, their representatives, is requested at the performance of the taking of evidence, the requested court shall determine, in accordance with Article 10, the conditions under which they may participate.

4 The requested court shall notify the parties and, if any, their representatives, of the time when, the place where, the proceedings will take place, and, where appropriate, the conditions under which they may participate, using form F in the Annex.

5 Paragraphs 1 to 4 shall not affect the possibility for the requested court of asking the parties and, if any their representatives, to be present at or to participate in the performance of the taking of evidence if that possibility is provided for by the law of its Member State.

ARTICLE 12

Performance with the presence and participation of representatives of the requesting court

1 If it is compatible with the law of the Member State of the requesting court, representatives of the requesting court have the right to be present in the performance of the taking of evidence by the requested court.

2 For the purpose of this Article, the term 'representative' shall include members of the judicial personnel designated by the requesting court, in accordance with the law of its Member State. The requesting court may also designate, in accordance with the law of its Member State, any other person, such as an expert.

3 The requesting court shall, in its request, inform the requested court that its representatives will be present and, where appropriate, that their participation is requested, using form A in the Annex. This information may also be given at any other appropriate time.

4 If the participation of the representatives of the requesting court is requested in the performance of the taking of evidence, the requested court shall determine, in accordance with Article 10, the conditions under which they may participate.

5 The requested court shall notify the requesting court, of the time when, and the place where, the proceedings will take place, and, where appropriate, the conditions under which the representatives may participate, using form F in the Annex.

ARTICLE 13

Coercive measures

Where necessary, in executing a request the requested court shall apply the appropriate coercive measures in the instances and to the extent as are provided for by the law of the Member State of the requested court for the execution of a request made for the same purpose by its national authorities or one of the parties concerned.

ARTICLE 14

Refusal to execute

1 A request for the hearing of a person shall not be executed when the person concerned claims the right to refuse to give evidence or to be prohibited from giving evidence,

- (a) under the law of the Member State of the requested court; or
- (b) under the law of the Member State of the requesting court, and such right has been specified in the request, or, if need be, at the instance of the requested court, has been confirmed by the requesting court.

2 In addition to the grounds referred to in paragraph 1, the execution of a request may be refused only if:

- (a) the request does not fall within the scope of this Regulation as set out in Article 1; or
- (b) the execution of the request under the law of the Member State of the requested court does not fall within the functions of the judiciary; or
- (c) the requesting court does not comply with the request of the requested court to complete the request pursuant to Article 8 within 30 days after the requested court asked it to do so; or
- (d) a deposit or advance asked for in accordance with Article 18(3) is not made within 60 days after the requested court asked for such a deposit or advance.

3 Execution may not be refused by the requested court solely on the ground that under the law of its Member State a court of that Member State has exclusive jurisdiction over the subject matter of the action or that the law of that Member State would not admit the right of action on it.

4 If execution of the request is refused on one of the grounds referred to in paragraph 2, the requested court shall notify the requesting court thereof within 60 days of receipt of the request by the requested court using form H in the Annex.

ARTICLE 15

Notification of delay

If the requested court is not in a position to execute the request within 90 days of receipt, it shall inform the requesting court thereof, using form G in the Annex. When it does so, the grounds for the delay shall be given as well as the estimated time that the requested court expects it will need to execute the request.

ARTICLE 16

Procedure after execution of the request

The requested court shall send without delay to the requesting court the documents establishing the execution of the request and, where appropriate, return the documents received from the requesting court. The documents shall be accompanied by a confirmation of execution using form H in the Annex.

Section 4 – Direct taking of evidence by the requesting court

ARTICLE 17

1 Where a court requests to take evidence directly in another Member State, it shall submit a request to the central body or the competent authority referred to in Article 3(3) in that State, using form I in the Annex.

2 Direct taking of evidence may only take place if it can be performed on a voluntary basis without the need for coercive measures.

Where the direct taking of evidence implies that a person shall be heard, the requesting court shall inform that person that the performance shall take place on a voluntary basis.

3 The taking of evidence shall be performed by a member of the judicial personnel or by any other person such as an expert, who will be designated, in accordance with the law of the Member State of the requesting court.

4 Within 30 days of receiving the request, the central body or the competent authority of the requested Member State shall inform the requesting court if the request is accepted and, if necessary, under what conditions according to the law of its Member State such performance is to be carried out, using form J.

In particular, the central body or the competent authority may assign a court of its Member State to take part in the performance of the taking of evidence in order to ensure the proper application of this Article and the conditions that have been set out.

The central body or the competent authority shall encourage the use of communications technology, such as videoconferences and teleconferences.

5 The central body or the competent authority may refuse direct taking of evidence only if:

(a) the request does not fall within the scope of this Regulation as set out in Article 1;
(b) the request does not contain all of the necessary information pursuant to Article 4; or
(c) the direct taking of evidence requested is contrary to fundamental principles of law in its Member State.

6 Without prejudice to the conditions laid down in accordance with paragraph 4, the requesting court shall execute the request in accordance with the law of its Member State.

Section 5 – Costs

ARTICLE 18

1 The execution of the request, in accordance with Article 10, shall not give rise to a claim for any reimbursement of taxes or costs.

2 Nevertheless, if the requested court so requires, the requesting court shall ensure the reimbursement, without delay, of:

- - the fees paid to experts and interpreters, and
- the costs occasioned by the application of Article 10(3) and(4).

The duty for the parties to bear these fees or costs shall be governed by the law of the Member State of the requesting court.

3 Where the opinion of an expert is required, the requested court may, before executing the request, ask the requesting court for an adequate deposit or advance towards the requested costs. In all other cases, a deposit or advance shall not be a condition for the execution of a request.

The deposit or advance shall be made by the parties if that is provided for by the law of the Member State of the requesting court.

CHAPTER III
FINAL PROVISIONS

ARTICLE 19

Implementing rules

1 The Commission shall draw up and regularly update a manual, which shall also be available electronically, containing the information provided by the Member States in accordance with Article 22 and the agreements or arrangements in force, according to Article 21.

2 The updating or making of technical amendments to the standard forms set out in the Annex shall be carried out in accordance with the advisory procedure set out in Article 20(2).

ARTICLE 20

Committee

1 The Commission shall be assisted by a Committee.

2 Where reference is made to this paragraph, Articles 3 and 7 of Decision 1999/468/EC shall apply.

3 The Committee shall adopt its Rules of Procedure.

ARTICLE 21

Relationship with existing or future agreements or arrangements between Member States

1 This Regulation shall, in relation to matters to which it applies, prevail over other provisions contained in bilateral or multilateral agreements or arrangements concluded by the Member States and in particular the Hague Convention of 1 March 1954 on Civil Procedure and the Hague Convention of 18 March 1970 on the Taking of Evidence Abroad in Civil or Commercial Matters, in relations between the Member States party thereto.

2 This Regulation shall not preclude Member States from maintaining or concluding agreements or arrangements between two or more of them to further facilitate the taking of evidence, provided that they are compatible with this Regulation.

3 Member States shall send to the Commission:

(a) by 1 July 2003, a copy of the agreements or arrangements maintained between the Member States referred to in paragraph 2;
(b) a copy of the agreements or arrangements concluded between the Member States referred to in paragraph 2 as well as drafts of such agreements or arrangements which they intend to adopt; and
(c) any denunciation of, or amendments to, these agreements or arrangements.

ARTICLE 22

Communication

By 1 July 2003 each Member State shall communicate to the Commission the following:

(a) the list pursuant to Article 2(2) indicating the territorial and, where appropriate, the special jurisdiction of the courts;
(b) the names and addresses of the central bodies and competent authorities pursuant to Article 3, indicating their territorial jurisdiction;
(c) the technical means for the receipt of requests available to the courts on the list pursuant to Article 2(2);
(d) the languages accepted for the requests as referred to in Article 5.

Member States shall inform the Commission of any subsequent changes to this information.

ARTICLE 23

Review

No later than 1 January 2007, and every five years thereafter, the Commission shall present to the European Parliament, the Council and the Economic and Social Committee a report on the application of this Regulation, paying special attention to the practical application of Article 3(1)(c) and 3, and Articles 17 and 18.

ARTICLE 24

Entry into force

1 This Regulation shall enter into force on 1 July 2001.

2 This Regulation shall apply from 1 January 2004, except for Articles 19, 21 and 22, which shall apply from 1 July 2001.

This Regulation shall be binding in its entirety and directly applicable in the Member States in accordance with the Treaty establishing the European Community.
Done at Brussels, 28 May 2001.

For the Council
The President
T. Bodström

(1) OJ C 314, 3.11.2000, p 2.
(2) Opinion delivered on 14 March 2001 (not yet published in the Official Journal).
(3) Opinion delivered on 28 February 2001 (not yet published in the Official Journal).
(4) OJ L 160, 30.6.2000, p 37.
(5) OJ L 281, 23.11.1995, p 31.
(6) OJ L 24, 30.1.1998, p 1.
(7) OJ L 184, 17.7.1999, p 23.

COUNCIL REGULATION (EC) 1206/2001 FORMS ANNEX

Forms—The forms annexed to this Council Regulation can be viewed on the *Civil Court Service* CD-ROM or the Department for Constitutional Affairs' website at *www.dca.gov.uk*.

Annex C

DESIGNATED COURTS IN ENGLAND AND WALES UNDER THE TAKING OF EVIDENCE REGULATION (SEE PARAGRAPH 8 ABOVE)

Area	**Designated court**
London and South Eastern Circuit	Royal Courts of Justice (Queen's Bench Division)
Midland Circuit	Birmingham Civil Justice Centre
Western Circuit	Bristol County Court
Wales and Chester Circuit	Cardiff Civil Justice Centre
Northern Circuit	Manchester County Court
North Eastern Circuit	Leeds County Court

Practice Direction – Fees for Examiners of the Court

This Practice Direction supplements CPR Part 34 (PD34B)

General note—See the notes to CPR Pt 34 for relevant commentary.

SCOPE

1.1 This practice direction sets out –

(1) how to calculate the fees an examiner of the court ('an examiner') may charge; and
(2) the expenses he may recover.

(CPR Rule 34.8(3)(b) provides that the court may make an order for evidence to be obtained by the examination of a witness before an examiner of the court)

1.2 The party who obtained the order for the examination must pay the fees and expenses of the examiner.

(CPR rule 34.14 permits an examiner to charge a fee for the examination and contains other provisions about his fees and expenses, and rule 34.15 provides who may be appointed as an examiner of the court)

THE EXAMINATION FEE

2.1 An examiner may charge an hourly rate for each hour (or part of an hour) that he is engaged in examining the witness.

2.2 The hourly rate is to be calculated by reference to the formula set out in paragraph 3.

2.3 The examination fee will be the hourly rate multiplied by the number of hours the examination has taken. For example –

Examination fee = hourly rate x number of hours.

HOW TO CALCULATE THE HOURLY RATE – THE FORMULA

3.1 Divide the amount of the minimum annual salary of a post within Group 7 of the judicial salary structure as designated by the Review Body on Senior Salaries[1], by 220 to give 'x'; and then divide 'x' by 6 to give the hourly rate. For example–

$$\frac{\text{minimum annual salary}}{220} = x$$

$$\frac{x}{6} = \text{hourly rate}$$

1 The Report of the Review Body on Senior Salaries is published annually by the Stationery Office.

SINGLE FEE CHARGEABLE ON MAKING THE APPOINTMENT FOR EXAMINATION

4.1 An examiner of court is also entitled to charge a single fee of twice the hourly rate (calculated in accordance with paragraph 3 above) as 'the appointment fee' when the appointment for the examination is made.

4.2 The examiner is entitled to retain the appointment fee where the witness fails to attend on the date and time arranged.

4.3 Where the examiner fails to attend on the date and time arranged he may not charge a further appointment fee for arranging a subsequent appointment.

(The examiner need not send the deposition to the court until his fees are paid – see CPR rule 34.14(2))

EXAMINERS' EXPENSES

5.1 The examiner of court is also entitled to recover the following expenses –

(1) all reasonable travelling expenses;
(2) any other expenses reasonably incurred; and
(3) subject to paragraph 5.2, any reasonable charge for the room where the examination takes place.

5.2 No expenses may be recovered under sub-paragraph (3) above if the examination takes place at the examiner's usual business address.

(If the examiner's fees and expenses are not paid within a reasonable time he may report the fact to the court, see CPR Rule 34.14(4) and (5))

PART 35
EXPERTS AND ASSESSORS

CONTENTS OF THIS PART

Procedural Guide—See Guide 25, set out in Section 1 of this work.

General note to this Part—This Part, in respect of experts, is generally regarded, together with Pt 31 (Disclosure), as being at the heart of the civil justice reforms, and has the express aim of reducing the number of expert witnesses, the extent to which they give evidence orally and their tendency to be partisan. It and its practice direction are a complete code (save in some significant respects as regards the Commercial Court and mercantile courts) as to expert evidence save to the extent that restrictive references to expert's directions in Pts 27–29 amplify the underlying policy. The essential thrust is: experts are no longer to be allowed to be 'hired guns', they are to be used only when necessary, and then a presumption in favour of only one (save in the Commercial Court – although express reference to there being no presumption in favour of SJEs in the old Commercial Court Guide has been removed, the general thrust of the new Admiralty and Commercial Courts Guide, para H2.2 is unchanged – and in clinical, and some professional, negligence cases), and in any event only in writing unless the court directs otherwise (on the multi-track) or unless the interests of justice require otherwise (on the fast track) and in principle hardly ever in small claims track cases (given the severe limitations on experts' costs). The duties of experts to the court are set out with crystal clarity, and they are now required not only to address their reports to the court but also sign a comprehensive certificate as to compliance with their duties (modified in some specialist courts). The only suggested reform that was not carried out in full is the complete abrogation of privilege in experts' instructions – instead there is a mildly uneasy compromise (save, curiously, in mercantile courts where the rule about instructions is displaced altogether). Overall the new rules on experts have, save at the level of complex multi-track cases, effected a sea-change in the extent to which they are involved in litigation, although there remains a degree of conflict between the requirements in the Personal Injury Protocol as to the early instructing of experts and the presumptions against their use in this Part. As to that protocol, see further the note **'Pre-Action Protocol for Personal Injury Claims'** to r 35.7 below.

Protocol for the Instruction of Experts to give Evidence in Civil Claims—Finally, after more than 6 years with no one single official Code, Protocol or Guidance, with effect from 5 September 2005, there is annexed to PD35 the June 2005 *Protocol for the Instruction of Experts to give Evidence in Civil Claims*, originally published by the Civil Justice Council. It is wide-ranging and directed to experts as well as the parties.

35.1 Duty to restrict expert evidence

Expert evidence shall be restricted to that which is reasonably required to resolve the proceedings.

Practice Direction—See generally PD35 and particularly its preamble at p 901.

General note—It could be said that this rule is no different from the previous regime: what is different is the whole underlying ethos. The rule should be read with r 32.1.

35.2 Interpretation

A reference to an 'expert' in this Part is a reference to an expert who has been instructed to give or prepare evidence for the purpose of court proceedings.

Employee as expert—Provided that his or her expertise and knowledge of the necessity for objectivity are demonstrated, there is no presumption that an employee of a party cannot be used as an expert under this Part (*Field v Leeds City Council* [1999] CPLR 833, CA).

Compare, however, *Liverpool Roman Catholic Archdiocesan Trust v Goldberg* [2001] 1 WLR 2337, ChD where Evans-Lombe J held that although the evidence of a person having a close personal relationship with the defendant qualified as 'expert' within Civil Evidence Act 1972, s 3 it was inadmissible as a matter of public policy.

See also *The Queen on the application of Factortame & ors v Secretary of State for Transport (No 8)* [2002] EWCA Civ 932, [2002] 3 WLR 1104, CA for observations on the undesirability of experts acting on a contingent fee basis.

35.3 Experts – overriding duty to the court

(1) It is the duty of an expert to help the court on the matters within his expertise.

(2) This duty overrides any obligation to the person from whom he has received instructions or by whom he is paid.

Practice Direction—See PD35, paras 1 (new as at 25 March 2002) and 2 (formerly para 1) at p 901.

General note—Whilst this duty may have been apparent to some experts, and indeed was the common law, prior to CPR, this rule strikes at the undoubted vice of partisanship and leaves, now, no room whatever for reports which are in any way slanted or coloured by the stance of the instructing party. See also *Mutch v Allen* [2001] EWCA Civ 76, (2001) *The Independent*, 5 March, CA at the notes under r 35.6.

Sanction for breach of duty by expert—In *Pearce v Ove Arup & ors* (2001) (unreported) 2 November, ChD, Jacob J noted the absence both of any prescribed sanction in the CPR, and of any comprehensive system of accreditation. Having held that the evidence of an expert was so biased and irrational as to constitute a serious breach of his duty to the court, His Lordship gave the expert time to make representations failing which a copy of the judgment was to be sent to his professional body (RIBA in this case) for them to take whatever disciplinary action they considered appropriate.

35.4 Court's power to restrict expert evidence

(1) No party may call an expert or put in evidence an expert's report without the court's permission.

(2) When a party applies for permission under this rule he must identify –

(a) the field in which he wishes to rely on expert evidence; and
(b) where practicable the expert in that field on whose evidence he wishes to rely.

(3) If permission is granted under this rule it shall be in relation only to the expert named or the field identified under paragraph (2).

(4) The court may limit the amount of the expert's fees and expenses that the party who wishes to rely on the expert may recover from any other party.

Practice Direction—See generally PD35 at p 901.

'without the court's permission' (r 35.4(1))—Again, this was the case before but this rule forms part of the 'sliding scale' of presumptions underlying the Part.

'identify … where practicable the expert in that field' (r 35.4(2)(b))—This is a new requirement: formerly only the expertise was the subject of the leave granted. Given the much tighter case management timetables envisaged on the multi-track as well as the fast track, and indeed the operation of the pre-action protocols, it is likely that the parties will already have identified a specific expert, or will often need to have done so by the time permission is sought if they are to ensure that he or she is going to be available to prepare a report in very short order (compared with the old days) and, if permission for cross-examination is granted, potentially available during the probable trial period.

As to whether a field or issue is one amenable to expert evidence at all, see *Barings plc v Coopers & Lybrand (a firm) & ors* (2001) *The Times*, 7 March, ChD, per Evans-Lombe J, where it was held that expert evidence was admissible where the court accepted that there was a recognised expertise governed by recognised standards and rules of conduct capable of influencing the court's decision on any of the issues which it had to decide – in that case the standards to be observed by reasonably competent managers of a derivatives trading business. Matters of law continue to fall outside the ambit of expert evidence.

In *Hajigeorgiou v Vassiliou* [2005] EWCA 236, the Court of Appeal held that, absent any application of the 'slip rule', where an order merely states the discipline of the expert but not his name, even though the parties had in mind one particular individual, it was open to the party concerned to rely upon a different expert without permission.

However, the party having already had, and rejected, the opinion of 'expert 1', the price of being able to call 'expert 2' would have been, had permission been needed, the requirement to disclose the substance of the opinion of expert 1, even though the report was headed 'draft interim'. In so holding, the court was following an earlier, unreported, decision of the Court of Appeal: *Beck v MOD* [2003] EWCA 1043 and Dyson LJ, giving the judgment of the court in *Hajigeorgiou*, emphasised that 'expert-shopping' was to be discouraged and that such a requirement of disclosure would normally be imposed, as a matter of the exercise of case-management powers, where permission to change experts was sought and granted.

'may limit the amount of expert's fees and expenses' (r 35.4(4))—This is another important manifestation of the drive for proportionality. The court may give permission for experts, but on the basis that whatever the outcome of the case the instructing party can only recover a proportion of the expense. This power is in addition to those relating to the assessment of costs after the event.

35.5 General requirement for expert evidence to be given in a written report

(1) Expert evidence is to be given in a written report unless the court directs otherwise.

(2) If a claim is on the fast track, the court will not direct an expert to attend a hearing unless it is necessary to do so in the interests of justice.

Practice Direction—See PD35, paras 2.1–2.6 at p 904.

'evidence is to be given in a written report unless the court directs otherwise' (r 35.5(1))—This is not merely a requirement for there to be a written report, it is the basic presumption as to how the evidence will be *given*, ie not orally. Paragraph 2 of PD35 amplifies the requirements as to form and content of such a written report, and is noted under r 35.10 below.

Although the Rules are wholly silent on the subject, a single joint expert ('SJE') can be ordered to attend for questioning at trial. If such an order is sought, it may be wise to specify that the purpose is cross-examination by one or more parties. Such orders are likely to be very unusual/disproportionate in small claims (*vide* the costs limit) and in many fast track cases. However, subject to that caveat, SJEs dealing with primary issues, especially if there is an underlying dispute as to the relevant facts, may well be required to attend for cross-examination more frequently than others – in many cases to order otherwise would be unfair to the party whose case is adversely affected by the opinion and/or would hamper the trial court in the fair and proper resolution of the 'expert' issues in the light of all the other evidence before it. Whilst in *Daniels v Walker* [2000] 1 WLR 1382 (see also notes to r 35.7) the Court of Appeal expressly discouraged looking at these provisions from a Human Rights Act perspective, the 'fair and proper resolution' approach to ordering attendance was expressly adopted in *Voaden v Champion & ors* (2000) (unreported) 28 March, Adm Ct, Coleman J, where the relevant facts were in issue and in which it was stated that there would be a presumption, at least in Commercial cases, that SJEs should attend for questioning unless they dealt only with discrete and substantially non-controversial/collateral matters (and note: in that particular case there was doubt as to the kind of questioning to be permitted). It may be that this was not what the rule-makers intended, but it is plainly right in the appropriate type of case.

Whilst the above note remains the view of the editors, the Lord Chief Justice observed in strong terms, albeit *obiter*, in *P v Mid-Kent Area Healthcare NHS Trust* [2001] EWCA Civ 1703, (2001) 98(48) LSG 29, CA at [28] and [29] that although there was a discretion to allow cross-examination it should be 'restricted as far as possible' and 'i]f there is an issue which requires cross-examination, or requires additional evidence, that is one thing. But the court should seek to avoid that situation arising, otherwise the objectives of having a single expert will in many situations be defeated.' This limiting approach was repeated in *Popek v National Westminster Bank plc* [2002] EWCA Civ 42, in which it was held that any intended cross-examination should be the subject of as much advance notice as possible, if not actually obviated, by the asking of those questions in writing. Accordingly, it may be that the approach suggested in the note will be confined to those courts (and types of action) where the full rigours of Pt 35 do not bite.

Fast Track (r 35.5(2))—Note the requirement for necessity in the interests of justice before attendance will be directed, ie cross-examination permitted (though the potential purpose of their presence is not limited to that). However, part of the fast-track allocation process is predicated on such cases lasting no more than a day *and* having no more than a total of four 'live' experts (r 26.6(5)), a fact which will undoubtedly be prayed in aid of a direction under this rule. It is the case that some fast track cases will require experts to be present and some will not, and directions will have to be given that match the overriding objective. One factor will plainly be the procedural judge's perception of the extent to which the trial judge will be unable satisfactorily to resolve the issues reflected by the experts' reports without *either* cross-examination *or* the attendance of the experts in the event (as frequently occurs) the factual matrix which emerges at trial is not that upon which they opined. Accordingly it is not only the nature of the experts' disagreement which falls to be considered but also the soundness of the relevant underlying factual evidence.

35.6 Written questions to experts

(1) A party may put to –

(a) an expert instructed by another party; or
(b) a single joint expert appointed under rule 35.7,

written questions about his report.

(2) Written questions under paragraph (1) –

(a) may be put once only;
(b) must be put within 28 days of service of the expert's report; and
(c) must be for the purpose only of clarification of the report;

unless in any case,

(i) the court gives permission; or
(ii) the other party agrees.

(3) An expert's answers to questions put in accordance with paragraph (1) shall be treated as part of the expert's report.

(4) Where –

(a) a party has put a written question to an expert instructed by another party in accordance with this rule; and
(b) the expert does not answer that question,

the court may make one or both of the following orders in relation to the party who instructed the expert –

(i) that the party may not rely on the evidence of that expert; or
(ii) that the party may not recover the fees and expenses of that expert from any other party.

Practice Direction—See PD35, paras 5.1–5.3 at p 906.

General note—Paragraph 5 of PD35 adds little to r 35.6, save that where questions are sent direct by one party to the expert, a copy of the questions is to be sent to the other side(s). The previous (until Update 24) limitation of such disclosure to parties with solicitors, adversely remarked on in previous editions of this work, has now been removed.

In the first instance, the party who instructed the expert pays for the answers, whichever party puts the question (PD35, para 5.3).

'must be for the purpose only of clarification of the report' (r 35.6(2)(c))—It is to be expected that parties will attempt to go beyond 'clarification'. Admiralty and Commercial Courts Guide, para H2.18, Queen's Bench Guide, para 7.9.9 and Chancery Guide, para 4.18 contain reminders of the limitation on this provision and potential adverse consequences of overstepping the mark without permission. However, the court has power – see below – to permit wider and further questioning and the parties may so agree without a court order. Provided that the parties act in a manner designed to achieve the overriding objective, a certain latitude should be permitted. If issues can be resolved using this process then it will assist in cutting down the need for attendance/cross-examination or go some way to replacing it.

In cases where there is a single joint expert, the questioning procedure still applies and, although the rules and the practice direction are silent on the subject, it can be taken that such questions should be copied to all other parties.

'unless ... the court gives permission' (r 35.6(2)(i))—In *Mutch v Allen* [2001] EWCA Civ 76, (2001) *The Independent*, 5 March, CA the court expressly endorsed the asking of questions (with permission) going beyond clarification. In that case the claimant's experts were asked about the effect which wearing a seatbelt would have had, questions which would have been plainly allowed in cross-examination and the answers to which would have been of the greatest materiality. The court stressed that the new regime was designed to ensure that experts no longer served the exclusive interest of those by whom they were retained but contributed to a just resolution of the dispute, pursuant to the overriding objective, in a cost-effective and expeditious way.

'where ... the expert does not answer that question' (r 35.6(4))—Unless the expert seeks a direction to the contrary under r 35.14, or the party instructing him seeks an order under Pt 23, the expert is bound to answer the questions put, or place those instructing him at risk of the report, and/or its costs, being disallowed. This subrule does not apply to single joint experts.

35.7 Court's power to direct that evidence is to be given by a single joint expert

(1) Where two or more parties wish to submit expert evidence on a particular issue, the court may direct that the evidence on that issue is to given by)one expert only.

(2) The parties wishing to submit the expert evidence are called 'the instructing parties'.

(3) Where the instructing parties cannot agree who should be the expert, the court may –

(a) select the expert from a list prepared or identified by the instructing parties; or

(b) direct that the expert be selected in such other manner as the court may direct.

Practice Direction—See PD35, para 6 at p 904, PD28, para 3.9 at p 777 and PD29, para 4.10 at p 793.

'one expert only' (r 35.7(1))—This is arguably the most radical reform brought in by the CPR. Not only is this permitted by this rule, in addition there are clear presumptions set out at PD28, para 3.9 (fast track) and PD29, para 4.10 (multi-track) that if expert evidence is to be permitted the court is to start from the premise that it should order that it be by way of a single joint expert 'unless there is a good reason not to do so'. This basic premise was strongly reaffirmed by the Lord Chief Justice in *P v Mid-Kent Area Healthcare NHS Trust* [2001] EWCA Civ 1703, (2001) 98(48) LSG 29, CA. Where there are accountancy issues, for instance, a single joint expert should often be acceptable to all parties. Where, however, there are two 'schools of thought' in respect of, eg, medical and causation issues in a personal injury action, the identity of a single joint expert is unlikely to be agreed between the parties and the outcome of the case might be determined by which expert is selected and accordingly each party should be permitted an expert. In *Daniels v Walker* [2000] 1 WLR 1382, the Court of Appeal held that an order for a single joint expert did not necessarily preclude, in the appropriate case where the overriding objective required it, subsequent permission to have an examination conducted by another expert and for use of a report by such expert, although it was stressed that an order for that expert to give oral evidence would not ordinarily be made, if at all, until after an experts' meeting. The Admiralty and Commercial Courts Guide (at para H2.2), the Clinical Disputes Protocol and the new Professional Negligence Protocol (at para B7 and in its Notes for Guidance, para C6) contain material displacing the presumption of a single joint expert, and place the onus of such decisions more on the parties. This approach was affirmed in *S (a Minor) v Birmingham Health Authority* (1999) Lawtel, 23 November, Curtis J, where it was held that the usual CPR restrictions as to experts were inappropriate at the early stages of a complex clinical negligence action as they would hinder the proper pleading of the case. See also *Oxley v Penwarden* (2000) (unreported) 21 July, CA, Kennedy and Mantell LJJ, where the court approved the practice of allowing more than one expert in a clinical negligence case.

The Chancery Guide, at para 4.11, makes this useful observation of general application, having started from the basic presumption:

> 'There remains, however, a body of cases where liability will turn upon expert opinion evidence and where it will be appropriate for the parties to instruct their own experts. For example, in cases where the issue for determination is as to whether a party acted in accordance with proper professional standards, it will often be of value to the court to hear the opinions of more than one expert as to the proper standard in order that the court becomes acquainted with the range of views existing upon the question and in order that the evidence can be tested in cross examination.'

Change of circumstances—Once a direction has been given for a single joint expert, it is not open to the parties to attempt to go behind the order merely by way of subsequent application to a different case management judge later in the proceedings; such a direction stands unless overturned on appeal or set aside if a sufficient change of circumstance can properly be shown (subject, no doubt, to other discretionary factors such as proximity to trial) (see *Jameson v Personal Representatives of Smith (deceased)* [2001] EWCA Civ 1264, 2001] 6 CPLR 489, CA).

'Where the instructing parties cannot agree who should be the expert' (r 35.7(3))—Progress is said to be underway in various fields for organisations representing the interests of claimants on the one hand and those representing defendants on the other to draw up lists of experts in certain disciplines who are likely to be equally acceptable to either side. In default of any agreed list, the final say as to how the expert is to be chosen rests entirely with the court.

Paragraph 6 of PD35 provides that where there has been made an order for a single joint expert in relation to an issue, and that issue involves a number of disciplines, the single expert should be from the dominant discipline and he should collate, and incorporate, the reports of others. This provision, while removing some difficulties in the common law, is likely to be of very infrequent use. However, it should be noted that the statement formerly contained in the Commercial Court the Guide (at para H2.7), to the effect that the court would require to be persuaded before permitting any such expert, has not been reproduced in the new Admiralty and Commercial Courts Guide.

Small claims track—As from 2 May 2000, this rule expressly applies to the small claims track also (see r 27.2 above and the notes thereto).

Pre-Action Protocol for Personal Injury Claims—The joint selection of a medical expert by the parties, after names are put forward by the claimant and pursuant to paras 3.14 and 3.16 of that protocol (set out in Section 4 of this work), is not the same as the joint instruction of that expert. The claimant may instruct such an expert alone and if that does occur the report has the privilege that ordinarily attaches to a medical report prepared for the purposes of litigation. The protocol imposes no requirement for the expert to be jointly instructed and nothing in it requires disclosure merely because it is provided by 'a mutually acceptable expert' (see *Carlson v Townsend* [2001] EWCA Civ 511, *Daily Telegraph*, 24 April, CA).

35.8 Instructions to a single joint expert

(1) Where the court gives a direction under rule 35.7 for a single joint expert to be used, each instructing party may give instructions to the expert.

(2) When an instructing party gives instructions to the expert he must, at the same time, send a copy of the instructions to the other instructing parties.

(3) The court may give directions about –

(a) the payment of the expert's fees and expenses; and
(b) any inspection, examination or experiments which the expert wishes to carry out.

(4) The court may, before an expert is instructed –

(a) limit the amount that can be paid by way of fees and expenses to the expert; and
(b) direct that the instructing parties pay that amount into court.

(5) Unless the court otherwise directs, the instructing parties are jointly and severally liable(GL) for the payment of the expert's fees and expenses.

'each instructing party may give instructions' (r 35.8(1))—In *Daniels v Walker* [2000] 1 WLR 1382 the Court of Appeal held that, whilst ordinarily instructions should be agreed and therefore joint, where there was disagreement there might be a necessity for separate instructions.

Instructions (r 35.8(1) and (2))—Plainly, there can be no communication with the single joint expert which is not completely transparent as between the parties. If any party tries to 'steer' the expert, the others will know (as is the case with 'party' experts, and as will the court in due course, see r 35.10).

Similarly, there are no circumstances in which the court will permit a meeting to take place between a single joint expert and one side in the absence of the other (*P v Mid-Kent Area Healthcare NHS Trust* [2001] EWCA Civ 1703, (2001) 98(48) LSG 29, CA).

Directions about inspection, examination etc (r 35.8(3)(b))—This is premised on what the expert wants to do. He is in charge, not the parties. Any application can be made by the parties or the expert himself under r 35.14.

Fees (rr 35.8(3)(a) and 35.8(4) and (5))—The power to limit fees, unlike r 35.4(4), is on how much is to be paid to the expert. If a direction is made that the fees be paid into court, it will normally be on the basis of equal shares since the purpose of this provision is to ensure that the expert is paid in circumstances where one or both parties may be unhappy as to the appointment (one party is usually going to be unhappy about the product). The fall-back is that normally all parties will be liable for all of the fees.

35.9 Power of court to direct a party to provide information

Where a party has access to information which is not reasonably available to the other party, the court may direct the party who has access to the information to –

(a) prepare and file a document recording the information; and
(b) serve a copy of that document on the other party.

Practice Direction—See PD35, para 3 at p 903.

'information which is not reasonably available'—This novel rule, which is a specific type of order for further information, is part of the 'level playing field' approach of CPR. Paragraph 3 of PD35 specifies that not only must the information be given, but also everything underlying it so that it can be interpreted and its significance assessed.

35.10 Contents of report

(1) An expert's report must comply with the requirements set out in the relevant practice direction.

(2) At the end of an expert's report there must be a statement that –

(a) the expert understands his duty to the court; and
(b) he has complied with that duty.

(3) The expert's report must state the substance of all material instructions, whether written or oral, on the basis of which the report was written.

(4) The instructions referred to in paragraph (3) shall not be privileged(GL) against disclosure but the court will not, in relation to those instructions –

(a) order disclosure of any specific document; or
(b) permit any questioning in court, other than by the party who instructed the expert,

unless it is satisfied that there are reasonable grounds to consider the statement of instructions given under paragraph (3) to be inaccurate or incomplete.

Practice Direction—See PD35, paras 2.1–2.6 at p 904 and PD35, para 4 at p 903.

'must comply with the requirements ... in the relevant practice direction' (r 35.10(1))—Paragraph 2 of PD35 (the structure does not follow that of the rule) sets out detailed requirements which also, together with para 4, repeat the whole rule. The practice direction can thus be read as the complete code as to contents and form subject to the practice in specialist courts – see below. The first requirement is that the report be addressed to the court – an important psychological reinforcement of the duty under r 35.3. Apart from requiring the expert to be transparent about the processes used, he is also required to say whether there is a range of opinion on the matter and the reasons for his particular view.

'a statement that ... the expert understands his duty ... and has complied' (r 35.10(2))—This requirement is repeated verbatim in PD35, para 2.2(7), and the statement is one of the matters which the expert is required to verify under para 2.3. No expert should be instructed without ensuring that he has a copy of Pt 35 and its practice direction. The reference at PD35, para 2.6 to a requirement to comply also with 'any approved expert's protocol' was removed with effect from 2 December 2002; it would appear that any former intention to draft such a protocol has now been abandoned.

This subrule, and the associated paras of PD35 (mentioned above), do now apply in the Commercial Court (previously they did not), but remain excluded in mercantile courts, where instead there is a much more detailed statement which the expert must sign (see Mercantile Courts Guide, paras 11.1, 11.2 and App B, para 12).

However, so outdated has the Mercantile Courts Guide become that its contents must be treated with caution. For instance, its App B says it follows App 12 to the Commercial Court Guide. So it did, but that latter Appendix was amended out of what is now the Admiralty and Commercial Courts Guide in February 2002.

'must state the substance of all material instructions, whether written or oral' (r 35.10(3))—Whilst this is not new in terms of good practice, it is now an express requirement. Paragraph 2.2(8) of PD35 amplifies this a little: the statement should summarise all facts and instructions which are material to the opinions expressed. An expert who is in doubt as to the materiality of any such fact or instruction should disclose it.

This subrule, and the associated PD35, para 2.2(8), do not apply in mercantile courts (see Mercantile Courts Guide, App B, para 4); instead the expert is required to state the facts or assumptions on which his opinion is based. Paragraph 4 of that Appendix provides further that if any of the facts stated are within his own direct knowledge he should make clear which those are, and if a stated assumption is in the opinion of the expert witness unreasonable or unlikely he should state that clearly. Those requirements form part of the more detailed statement referred to above. In the Commercial Court this subrule is not displaced, but rather the new Admiralty and Commercial Courts Guide at para H2.6(a) provides that:

> 'In stating the substance of all material instructions on the basis of which his report is written as required by this subrule and PD35, para 2.2(3)] an expert witness should state the facts or assumptions upon which his opinion is based.'

Although one Guide purports to displace the subrule, and the other to offer guidance on compliance with it, the actual terms of the guidance are identical.

'instructions ... shall not be privileged' (r 35.10(4))—Parties will need to exercise extra judgment in respect of all communications with 'their' experts: there is no privilege in any such matters if they be material to the opinion and it will be for the expert to judge (with or without help from the court under r 35.14) what to disclose.

'but the court will not' (r 35.10(4))—This is the compromise referred to above. Unless the court is satisfied that there are reasonable grounds to consider that the expert has not, despite his certificate, complied with his duty under r 35.10(3), there will be no order for disclosure and no cross-examination on the subject of instructions. Paragraph 4 of PD35 gives some extra guidance in respect of cross-examination: it may be allowed if the instructing party agrees or, if the criteria for apparent non-compliance are met, where the interests of justice appear to require it. This is plainly intended to make such orders very much the exception rather than the rule, and to limit 'satellite' questioning save where it is considered necessary.

35.11 Use by one party of expert's report disclosed by another

Where a party has disclosed an expert's report, any party may use that expert's report as evidence at the trial.

35.12 Discussions between experts

(1) The court may, at any stage, direct a discussion between experts for the purpose of requiring the experts to –

(a) identify and discuss the expert issues in the proceedings; and
(b) where possible, reach an agreed opinion on those issues.]

(2) The court may specify the issues which the experts must discuss.

(3) The court may direct that following a discussion between the experts they must prepare a statement for the court showing –

(a) those issues on which they agree; and
(b) those issues on which they disagree and a summary of their reasons for disagreeing.

(4) The content of the discussion between the experts shall not be referred to at the trial unless the parties agree.

(5) Where experts reach agreement on an issue during their discussions, the agreement shall not bind the parties unless the parties expressly agree to be bound by the agreement.

Amendments—SI 2001/4015.

'for the purpose of requiring the experts to' (r 35.12(1))—In both the Admiralty and Commercial Courts and the Mercantile Courts Guides this description of the purpose of the discussion between experts is replaced by that appearing at para H2.12 and App B, para 16 respectively. Those paragraphs are in identical terms, and the purpose stated is to give the experts the opportunity to discuss the expert issues and to decide, with the benefit of that discussion, on which expert issues they share the same expert opinion and on which expert issues there is a difference of expert opinion between them (and what that difference is). The rule, as amended by SI 2001/4015 (Update 26), is now much closer to what the Court Guides referred to above provide.

Discussions—The essence of this mostly familiar regime is that, while any document which they prepare is 'open', the contents of discussions between experts remain privileged (r 35.12(4)) at trial and any agreement they reach is not binding unless the parties agree to be bound (r 35.12(5)). It is expected that meetings (and joint statements – see below) will, as now, be the usual order.

'the court may direct that ... the experts ... prepare a statement' (r 35.12(3))—In both the Admiralty and Commercial Courts and Mercantile Courts Guides it is provided that the preparation of a joint memorandum, defined with slightly more precision, will be an automatic requirement (see para H2.16 (subject to an order to the contrary) and App B, para 20 respectively).

35.13 Consequence of failure to disclose expert's report

A party who fails to disclose an expert's report may not use the report at the trial or call the expert to give evidence orally unless the court gives permission.

General note—The circumstances in which permission is given to call expert evidence where there has been a failure to disclose a report will be rare indeed.

35.14 Expert's right to ask court for directions

(1) An expert may file a written request for directions to assist him in carrying out his function as an expert.

(2) An expert must, unless the court orders otherwise, provide a copy of any proposed request for directions under paragraph (1) –

(a) to the party instructing him, at least 7 days before he files the request; and

(b) to all other parties, at least 4 days before he files it.

(3) The court, when it gives directions, may also direct that a party be served with a copy of the directions.

(a), (b) (*revoked*)

Amendments—SI 2001/4015.

'An expert may file a written request for directions' (r 35.14(1))—This rule applies to all experts whether 'single joint' or otherwise, and again reinforces the focus of the expert's duty – to the court, and is the corollary of that duty. There is no limitation on the matters which may give rise to such a request. It remains to be seen how frequently and in what circumstances experts will avail themselves of this facility.

'An expert must' (r 35.14(2))—The rule is now (ie since 25 March 2002) the reverse of what it was, and it is now obligatory (subject to a contrary order) for the expert to give advance notice of such a request, thus now following the previously existing practice in the Commercial Court and mercantile courts.

No express provision is made for single joint experts one way or the other.

Mercantile courts—The observation at Mercantile Courts Guide, App B, para 8 to the effect that its provisions displace this rule can safely be ignored: the Guide has fallen behind the amendments to the CPR in this and other respects.

35.15 Assessors

(1) This rule applies where the court appoints one or more persons (an 'assessor') under section 70 of the Supreme Court Act 1981 or section 63 of the County Courts Act 1984.

(2) The assessor shall assist the court in dealing with a matter in which the assessor has skill and experience.

(3) An assessor shall take such part in the proceedings as the court may direct and in particular the court may –

(a) direct the assessor to prepare a report for the court on any matter at issue in the proceedings; and

(b) direct the assessor to attend the whole or any part of the trial to advise the court on any such matter.

(4) If the assessor prepares a report for the court before the trial has begun –

(a) the court will send a copy to each of the parties; and

(b) the parties may use it at trial.

(5) The remuneration to be paid to the assessor for his services shall be determined by the court and shall form part of the costs of the proceedings.

(6) The court may order any party to deposit in the court office a specified sum in respect of the assessor's fees and, where it does so, the assessor will not be asked to act until the sum has been deposited.

(7) Paragraphs (5) and (6) do not apply where the remuneration of the assessor is to be paid out of money provided by Parliament.

Practice Direction—See PD35, paras 7.1–7.4 at p 907.

Scope of provision—Assessors and experts appointed under the above rules are now the only 'third parties' potentially involved in assisting the court: court experts are now a thing of the past, and this rule sets out in expanded terms the statutory basis of the use of assessors. Until County Courts Act

1984, s 63 was modified by Civil Procedure (Modification of Enactments) Order 1998 (the instrument which also extended the ambit of pre-action and non-party disclosure), one signal difference between the county court and the High Court was that in the former, save in respect of taxing costs, assessors could only be appointed on the application of a party whereas the High Court could do it of its own motion. Both courts can now do so.

There does remain, however, one statutory difference: in the County Court Acts, only, are there provisions for parties to object to an assessor. Paragraphs 7.1 and 7.2 of PD35 appear to be couched in terms equally applicable to either court, in respect of taking objection, and yet para 7.3 specifically refers only to the county court. It appears that, notwithstanding the apparently general terms of para 7.2, there is no statutory basis for challenging an assessor in the High Court.

It should be noted that whilst an assessor may be required by the court to produce a report, under no circumstances is he to give oral evidence or be cross-examined, unlike the former court experts.

Practice Direction – Experts and Assessors

This Practice Direction supplements CPR Part 35 (PD35)

Part 35 is intended to limit the use of oral expert evidence to that which is reasonably required. In addition, where possible, matters requiring expert evidence should be dealt with by a single expert. Permission of the court is always required either to call an expert or to put an expert's report in evidence. There is annexed to this Practice Direction a protocol for the instruction of experts to give evidence in civil claims. Experts and those instructing them are expected to have regard to the guidance contained in the protocol.

Procedural Guide—See Guide 25, set out in Section 1 of this work.

General note—See also the notes to CPR Pt 35 for relevant commentary.

Specialist courts—This practice direction is of general application, save for paras 2.2–2.4 which are partly modified in the Commercial Court and modified or excluded in the mercantile courts (see note **'Commercial Court and mercantile courts'** after para 2.6 below).

Protocol for the Instruction of Experts to give Evidence in Civil Claims—This Civil Justice Council publication is now 'official' in that experts and parties are now required to 'have regard' to it. It is annexed to this practice direction.

EXPERT EVIDENCE – GENERAL REQUIREMENTS

1.1 It is the duty of an expert to help the court on matters within his own expertise: rule 35.3(1). This duty is paramount and overrides any obligation to the person from whom the expert has received instructions or by whom he is paid: rule 35.3(2).

1.2 Expert evidence should be the independent product of the expert uninfluenced by the pressures of litigation.

1.3 An expert should assist the court by providing objective, unbiased opinion on matters within his expertise, and should not assume the role of an advocate.

1.4 An expert should consider all material facts, including those which might detract from his opinion.

1.5 An expert should make it clear:

(a) when a question or issue falls outside his expertise; and
(b) when he is not able to reach a definite opinion, for example because he has insufficient information.

1.6 If, after producing a report, an expert changes his view on any material matter, such change of view should be communicated to all the parties without delay, and when appropriate to the court.

FORM AND CONTENT OF EXPERT'S REPORTS

2.1 An expert's report should be addressed to the court and not to the party from whom the expert has received his instructions.

2.2 An expert's report must:

(1) give details of the expert's qualifications;
(2) give details of any literature or other material which the expert has relied on in making the report;
(3) contain a statement setting out the substance of all facts and instructions given to the expert which are material to the opinions expressed in the report or upon which those opinions are based;
(4) make clear which of the facts stated in the report are within the expert's own knowledge;
(5) say who carried out any examination, measurement, test or experiment which the expert has used for the report, give the qualifications of that person, and say whether or not the test or experiment has been carried out under the expert's supervision;
(6) where there is a range of opinion on the matters dealt with in the report –
 (a) summarise the range of opinion, and
 (b) give reasons for his own opinion;
(7) contain a summary of the conclusions reached;
(8) if the expert is not able to give his opinion without qualification, state the qualification; and
(9) contain a statement that the expert understands his duty to the court, and has complied and will continue to comply with that duty.

2.3 An expert's report must be verified by a statement of truth as well as containing the statements required in paragraph 2.2(8) and (9) above.

2.4 The form of the statement of truth is as follows:

'I confirm that insofar as the facts stated in my report are within my own knowledge I have made clear which they are and I believe them to be true, and that the opinions I have expressed represent my true and complete professional opinion.'

2.5 Attention is drawn to rule 32.14 which sets out the consequences of verifying a document containing a false statement without an honest belief in its truth.

(For information about statements of truth see Part 22 and the practice direction which supplements it)

Commercial Court and mercantile courts—The Guides for these courts provide as follows:

The former paras 1.2(7), 1.3 and 1.4 of PD35 are amplified and/or amended – see the notes under r 35.10(2). These paragraphs, now numbered paras 2.2–2.4, have been amended by Update 26 and are now closer to what the Guides provide.

The provisions of the Mercantile Courts Guide should, however, be viewed with caution generally: they were based on the original Commercial Court Guide, which was very substantially amended in February 2002. Moreover, many of the references to the CPR and practice directions have fallen out of date and not been checked or brought into line.

That part of PD35, para 2.2 (formerly para 1.2(8)) which requires the expert to set out the substance of all material instructions is abrogated altogether in the mercantile courts and slightly modified in the Commercial Court (each such court having, probably, the same actual practice) – see the notes to CPR r 35.10(3).

INFORMATION

3 Under Rule 35.9 the court may direct a party with access to information which is not reasonably available to another party to serve on that other party a document which records the information. The document served must include sufficient details of all the facts, tests, experiments and assumptions which underlie any part of the information to enable the party on whom it is served to make, or to obtain, a proper interpretation of the information and an assessment of its significance.

INSTRUCTIONS

4 The instructions referred to in paragraph 2.2(3) will not be protected by privilege (see rule 35.10(4)). But cross-examination of the expert on the contents of his instructions will not be allowed unless the court permits it (or unless the party who gave the instructions consents to it). Before it gives permission the court must be satisfied that there are reasonable grounds to consider that the statement in the report of the substance of the instructions is inaccurate or incomplete. If the court is so satisfied, it will allow the cross-examination where it appears to be in the interests of justice to do so.

QUESTIONS TO EXPERTS

5.1 Questions asked for the purpose of clarifying the expert's report (see rule 35.6) should be put, in writing, to the expert not later than 28 days after receipt of the expert's report (see paragraphs 1.2 to 1.5 above as to verification).

5.2 Where a party sends a written question or questions direct to an expert, a copy of the questions should, at the same time, be sent to the other party or parties.

5.3 The party or parties instructing the expert must pay any fees charged by that expert for answering questions put under rule 35.6. This does not affect any decision of the court as to the party who is ultimately to bear the expert's costs.

General note—Paragraph 4 of PD35 adds little to CPR r 35.6, save that where questions are sent direct by one party to the expert a copy of the questions is to be sent to the other side(s). The previous (until Update 24) limitation of such disclosure to parties with solicitors, adversely remarked on in previous editions of this work, has now been removed.

SINGLE EXPERT

6 Where the court has directed that the evidence on a particular issue is to be given by one expert only (rule 35.7) but there are a number of disciplines relevant to that issue, a leading expert in the dominant discipline should be identified as the single expert. He should prepare the general part of the report and be responsible for annexing or incorporating the contents of any reports from experts in other disciplines.

ORDERS

6A Where an order requires an act to be done by an expert, or otherwise affects an expert, the party instructing that expert must serve a copy of the order on the expert instructed by him. In the case of a jointly instructed expert, the claimant must serve the order.

General note—This paragraph was introduced by Update 38. It is intended to ensure that there can be no doubt in the mind of any expert as to what is required of him or her in orders made as between the parties. It will reinforce the power of the court to make adverse costs orders against experts in appropriate cases (as to which see *Phillips v Symes* [2004] EWHC 2330 (Ch)).

ASSESSORS

7.1 An assessor may be appointed to assist the court under rule 35.15. Not less than 21 days before making any such appointment, the court will notify each party in writing of the name of the proposed assessor, of the matter in respect of which the assistance of the assessor will be sought and of the qualifications of the assessor to give that assistance.

7.2 Where any person has been proposed for appointment as an assessor, objection to him, either personally or in respect of his qualification, may be taken by any party.

7.3 Any such objection must be made in writing and filed with the court within 7 days of receipt of the notification referred to in paragraph 6.1 and will be taken into account by the court in deciding whether or not to make the appointment (section 63(5) of the County Courts Act 1984).

7.4 Copies of any report prepared by the assessor will be sent to each of the parties but the assessor will not give oral evidence or be open to cross-examination or questioning.

ANNEX

PROTOCOL FOR THE INSTRUCTION OF EXPERTS TO GIVE EVIDENCE IN CIVIL CLAIMS

June 2005

1 INTRODUCTION

Expert witnesses perform a vital role in civil litigation. It is essential that both those who instruct experts and experts themselves are given clear guidance as to what they are expected to do in civil proceedings. The purpose of this Protocol is to provide such guidance. It has been drafted by the Civil Justice Council and reflects the rules and practice directions current [in June 2005], replacing the Code of Guidance on Expert Evidence. The authors of the Protocol wish to acknowledge the valuable assistance they obtained by drawing on earlier documents produced by the Academy of Experts and the Expert Witness Institute, as well as suggestions made by the Clinical Dispute Forum. The Protocol has been approved by the Master of the Rolls.

2 AIMS OF PROTOCOL

2.1 This Protocol offers guidance to experts and to those instructing them in the interpretation of and compliance with Part 35 of the Civil Procedure Rules (CPR 35) and its associated Practice Direction (PD35) and to further the objectives of the Civil Procedure Rules in general. It is intended to assist in the interpretation of those provisions in the interests of good practice but it does not replace them. It sets out standards for the use of experts and the conduct of experts and those who instruct them. The existence of this Protocol does not remove the need for experts and those who instruct them to be familiar with CPR35 and PD35.

2.2 Experts and those who instruct them should also bear in mind para 1.4 of the Practice Direction on Protocols which contains the following objectives, namely to:

(a) encourage the exchange of early and full information about the expert issues involved in a prospective legal claim;
(b) enable the parties to avoid or reduce the scope of litigation by agreeing the whole or part of an expert issue before commencement of proceedings; and
(c) support the efficient management of proceedings where litigation cannot be avoided.

3 APPLICATION

3.1 This Protocol applies to any steps taken for the purpose of civil proceedings by experts or those who instruct them on or after 5 September 2005.

3.2 It applies to all experts who are, or who may be, governed by CPR Part 35 and to those who instruct them. Experts are governed by Part 35 if they are or have been instructed to give or prepare evidence for the purpose of civil proceedings in a court in England and Wales (CPR 35.2).

3.3 Experts, and those instructing them, should be aware that some cases may be 'specialist proceedings' (CPR 49) where there are modifications to the Civil Procedure Rules. Proceedings may also be governed by other Protocols. Further, some courts have published their own Guides which supplement the Civil Procedure Rules for proceedings in those courts. They contain provisions affecting expert evidence. Expert witnesses and those instructing them should be familiar with them when they are relevant.

3.4 Courts may take into account any failure to comply with this Protocol when making orders in relation to costs, interest, time limits, the stay of proceedings and whether to order a party to pay a sum of money into court.

LIMITATION

3.5 If, as a result of complying with any part of this Protocol, claims would or might be time barred under any provision in the Limitation Act 1980, or any other legislation that imposes a time limit for the bringing an action, claimants may commence proceedings without complying with this Protocol. In such circumstances, claimants who commence proceedings without complying with all, or any part, of this Protocol must apply, giving notice to all other parties, to the court for directions as to the timetable and form of procedure to be adopted, at the same time as they request the court to issue proceedings. The court may consider whether to order a stay of the whole or part of the proceedings pending compliance with this Protocol and may make orders in relation to costs.

4 DUTIES OF EXPERTS

4.1 Experts always owe a duty to exercise reasonable skill and care to those instructing them, and to comply with any relevant professional code of ethics.

However when they are instructed to give or prepare evidence for the purpose of civil proceedings in England and Wales they have an overriding duty to help the court on matters within their expertise (CPR 35.3). This duty overrides any obligation to the person instructing or paying them. Experts must not serve the exclusive interest of those who retain them.

4.2 Experts should be aware of the overriding objective that courts deal with cases justly. This includes dealing with cases proportionately, expeditiously and fairly (CPR 1.1). Experts are under an obligation to assist the court so as to enable them to deal with cases in accordance with the overriding objective. However the overriding objective does not impose on experts any duty to act as mediators between the parties or require them to trespass on the role of the court in deciding facts.

4.3 Experts should provide opinions which are independent, regardless of the pressures of litigation. In this context, a useful test of 'independence' is that the expert would express the same opinion if given the same instructions by an opposing party. Experts should not take it upon themselves to promote the point of view of the party instructing them or engage in the role of advocates.

4.4 Experts should confine their opinions to matters which are material to the disputes between the parties and provide opinions only in relation to matters which lie within their expertise. Experts should indicate without delay where particular questions or issues fall outside their expertise.

4.5 Experts should take into account all material facts before them at the time that they give their opinion. Their reports should set out those facts and any literature or any other material on which they have relied in forming their opinions. They should indicate if an opinion is provisional, or qualified, or where they consider that further information is required or if, for any other reason, they are not satisfied that an opinion can be expressed finally and without qualification.

4.6 Experts should inform those instructing them without delay of any change in their opinions on any material matter and the reason for it.

4.7 Experts should be aware that any failure by them to comply with the Civil Procedure Rules or court orders or any excessive delay for which they are responsible may result in the parties who instructed them being penalised in costs and even, in extreme cases, being debarred from placing the experts' evidence before the court. In[1] *Phillips v Symes* Peter Smith J held that courts may also make orders for costs (under section 51 of the Supreme Court Act 1981) directly against expert witnesses who by their evidence cause significant expense to be incurred, and do so in flagrant and reckless disregard of their duties to the Court.

1 *Phillips v Symes* [2004] EWHC 2330 (Ch)

5 CONDUCT OF EXPERTS INSTRUCTED ONLY TO ADVISE

5.1 Part 35 only applies where experts are instructed to give opinions which are relied on for the purposes of court proceedings. Advice which the parties do not intend to adduce in litigation is likely to be confidential; the Protocol does not apply in these circumstances[2, 3].

2 *Carlson v Townsend* [2001] 1 WLR 2415

3 *Jackson v Marley Davenport* [2004] 1 WLR 2926

5.2 The same applies where, after the commencement of proceedings, experts are instructed only to advise (eg to comment upon a single joint expert's report) and not to give or prepare evidence for use in the proceedings.

5.3 However this Protocol does apply if experts who were formerly instructed only to advise are later instructed to give or prepare evidence for the purpose of civil proceedings.

6 THE NEED FOR EXPERTS

6.1 Those intending to instruct experts to give or prepare evidence for the purpose of civil proceedings should consider whether expert evidence is appropriate, taking account of the principles set out in CPR Parts 1 and 35, and in particular whether:

(a) it is relevant to a matter which is in dispute between the parties.
(b) it is reasonably required to resolve the proceedings (CPR 35.1);
(c) the expert has expertise relevant to the issue on which an opinion is sought;
(d) the expert has the experience, expertise and training appropriate to the value, complexity and importance of the case; and whether
(e) these objects can be achieved by the appointment of a single joint expert (see section 17 below).

6.2 Although the court's permission is not generally required to instruct an expert, the court's permission is required before experts can be called to give evidence or their evidence can be put in (CPR 35.4).

7 THE APPOINTMENT OF EXPERTS

7.1 Before experts are formally instructed or the court's permission to appoint named experts is sought, the following should be established:

(a) that they have the appropriate expertise and experience;
(b) that they are familiar with the general duties of an expert;
(c) that they can produce a report, deal with questions and have discussions with other experts within a reasonable time and at a cost proportionate to the matters in issue;
(d) a description of the work required;
(e) whether they are available to attend the trial, if attendance is required; and
(f) there is no potential conflict of interest.

7.2 Terms of appointment should be agreed at the outset and should normally include:

(a) the capacity in which the expert is to be appointed (eg party appointed expert, single joint expert or expert advisor);
(b) the services required of the expert (eg provision of expert's report, answering questions in writing, attendance at meetings and attendance at court);
(c) time for delivery of the report;
(d) the basis of the expert's charges (either daily or hourly rates and an estimate of the time likely to be required, or a total fee for the services);
(e) travelling expenses and disbursements;
(f) cancellation charges;

(g) any fees for attending court;
(h) time for making the payment; and
(i) whether fees are to be paid by a third party.
(j) if a party is publicly funded, whether or not the expert's charges will be subject to assessment by a costs officer.

7.3 As to the appointment of single joint experts, see section 17 below.

7.4 When necessary, arrangements should be made for dealing with questions to experts and discussions between experts, including any directions given by the court, and provision should be made for the cost of this work.

7.5 Experts should be informed regularly about deadlines for all matters concerning them. Those instructing experts should promptly send them copies of all court orders and directions which may affect the preparation of their reports or any other matters concerning their obligations.

CONDITIONAL AND CONTINGENCY FEES

7.6 Payments contingent upon the nature of the expert evidence given in legal proceedings, or upon the outcome of a case, must not be offered or accepted. To do so would contravene experts' overriding duty to the court and compromise their duty of independence.

7.7 Agreement to delay payment of experts' fees until after the conclusion of cases is permissible as long as the amount of the fee does not depend on the outcome of the case.

8 INSTRUCTIONS

8.1 Those instructing experts should ensure that they give clear instructions, including the following:

(a) basic information, such as names, addresses, telephone numbers, dates of birth and dates of incidents;
(b) the nature and extent of the expertise which is called for;
(c) the purpose of requesting the advice or report, a description of the matter(s) to be investigated, the principal known issues and the identity of all parties;
(d) the statement(s) of case (if any), those documents which form part of standard disclosure and witness statements which are relevant to the advice or report;
(e) where proceedings have not been started, whether proceedings are being contemplated and, if so, whether the expert is asked only for advice;
(f) an outline programme, consistent with good case management and the expert's availability, for the completion and delivery of each stage of the expert's work; and
(g) where proceedings have been started, the dates of any hearings (including any Case Management Conferences and/or Pre-Trial Reviews), the name of the court, the claim number and the track to which the claim has been allocated.

8.2 Experts who do not receive clear instructions should request clarification and may indicate that they are not prepared to act unless and until such clear instructions are received.

8.3 As to the instruction of single joint experts, see section 17 below.

9 EXPERTS' ACCEPTANCE OF INSTRUCTIONS

9.1 Experts should confirm without delay whether or not they accept instructions. They should also inform those instructing them (whether on initial instruction or at any later stage) without delay if:

- (a) instructions are not acceptable because, for example, they require work that falls outside their expertise, impose unrealistic deadlines, or are insufficiently clear;
- (b) they consider that instructions are or have become insufficient to complete the work;
- (c) they become aware that they may not be able to fulfil any of the terms of appointment;
- (d) the instructions and/or work have, for any reason, placed them in conflict with their duties as an expert; or
- (e) they are not satisfied that they can comply with any orders that have been made.

9.2 Experts must neither express an opinion outside the scope of their field of expertise, nor accept any instructions to do so.

10 WITHDRAWAL

10.1 Where experts' instructions remain incompatible with their duties, whether through incompleteness, a conflict between their duty to the court and their instructions, or for any other substantial and significant reason, they may consider withdrawing from the case. However, experts should not withdraw without first discussing the position fully with those who instruct them and considering carefully whether it would be more appropriate to make a written request for directions from the court. If experts do withdraw, they must give formal written notice to those instructing them.

11 EXPERTS' RIGHT TO ASK COURT FOR DIRECTIONS

11.1 Experts may request directions from the court to assist them in carrying out their functions as experts. Experts should normally discuss such matters with those who instruct them before making any such request. Unless the court otherwise orders, any proposed request for directions should be copied to the party instructing the expert at least seven days before filing any request to the court, and to all other parties at least four days before filing it. (CPR 35.14).

11.2 Requests to the court for directions should be made by letter, containing.

- (a) the title of the claim;
- (b) the claim number of the case;
- (c) the name of the expert;
- (d) full details of why directions are sought; and
- (e) copies of any relevant documentation.

12 POWER OF THE COURT TO DIRECT A PARTY TO PROVIDE INFORMATION

12.1 If experts consider that those instructing them have not provided information which they require, they may, after discussion with those instructing them and giving notice, write to the court to seek directions (CPR 35.14).

12.2 Experts and those who instruct them should also be aware of CPR 35.9. This provides that where one party has access to information which is not readily available to the other party, the court may direct the party who has access to the information to prepare, file and copy to the other party a document recording the information. If experts require such information which has not been disclosed, they should discuss the position with those instructing them without delay, so that a request for the information can be made, and, if not forthcoming, an application can be made to the court. Unless a document appears to be essential, experts should assess the cost and time involved in the production of a document and whether its provision would be proportionate in the context of the case.

13 CONTENTS OF EXPERTS' REPORTS

13.1 The content and extent of experts' reports should be governed by the scope of their instructions and general obligations, the contents of CPR 35 and PD35 and their overriding duty to the court.

13.2 In preparing reports, experts should maintain professional objectivity and impartiality at all times.

13.3 PD 35, para 2 provides that experts' reports should be addressed to the court and gives detailed directions about the form and content of such reports. All experts and those who instruct them should ensure that they are familiar with these requirements.

13.4 Model forms of Experts' Reports are available from bodies such as the Academy of Experts or the Expert Witness Institute.

13.5 Experts' reports must contain statements that they understand their duty to the court and have complied and will continue to comply with that duty (PD35 para 2.2(9)). They must also be verified by a statement of truth. The form of the statement of truth is as follows:

> 'I confirm that insofar as the facts stated in my report are within my own knowledge I have made clear which they are and I believe them to be true, and that the opinions I have expressed represent my true and complete professional opinion.'

This wording is mandatory and must not be modified.

QUALIFICATIONS

13.6 The details of experts' qualifications to be given in reports should be commensurate with the nature and complexity of the case. It may be sufficient merely to state academic and professional qualifications. However, where highly specialised expertise is called for, experts should include the detail of particular training and/or experience that qualifies them to provide that highly specialised evidence.

TESTS

13.7 Where tests of a scientific or technical nature have been carried out, experts should state:

(a) the methodology used; and
(b) by whom the tests were undertaken and under whose supervision, summarising their respective qualifications and experience.

RELIANCE ON THE WORK OF OTHERS

13.8 Where experts rely in their reports on literature or other material and cite the opinions of others without having verified them, they must give details of those opinions relied on. It is likely to assist the court if the qualifications of the originator(s) are also stated.

FACTS

13.9 When addressing questions of fact and opinion, experts should keep the two separate and discrete.

13.10 Experts must state those facts (whether assumed or otherwise) upon which their opinions are based. They must distinguish clearly between those facts which experts know to be true and those facts which they assume.

13.11 Where there are material facts in dispute experts should express separate opinions on each hypothesis put forward. They should not express a view in favour of one or other disputed version of the facts unless, as a result of particular expertise and experience, they consider one set of facts as being improbable or less probable, in which case they may express that view, and should give reasons for holding it.

RANGE OF OPINION

13.12 If the mandatory summary of the range of opinion is based on published sources, experts should explain those sources and, where appropriate, state the qualifications of the originator(s) of the opinions from which they differ, particularly if such opinions represent a well-established school of thought.

13.13 Where there is no available source for the range of opinion, experts may need to express opinions on what they believe to be the range which other experts would arrive at if asked. In those circumstances, experts should make it clear that the range that they summarise is based on their own judgement and explain the basis of that judgement.

CONCLUSIONS

13.14 A summary of conclusions is mandatory. The summary should be at the end of the report after all the reasoning. There may be cases, however, where the benefit to the court is heightened by placing a short summary at the beginning of the report whilst giving the full conclusions at the end. For example, it can assist with the comprehension of the analysis and with the absorption of the detailed facts if the court is told at the outset of the direction in which the report's logic will flow in cases involving highly complex matters which fall outside the general knowledge of the court.

BASIS OF REPORT: MATERIAL INSTRUCTIONS

13.15 The mandatory statement of the substance of all material instructions should not be incomplete or otherwise tend to mislead. The imperative is transparency. The term 'instructions' includes all material which solicitors place in front of experts in order to gain advice. The omission from the statement of 'off-the-record' oral instructions is not permitted. Courts may allow cross-examination about the instructions if there are reasonable grounds to consider that the statement may be inaccurate or incomplete.

14 AFTER RECEIPT OF EXPERTS' REPORTS

14.1 Following the receipt of experts' reports, those instructing them should advise the experts as soon as reasonably practicable whether, and if so when, the report will be disclosed to other parties; and, if so disclosed, the date of actual disclosure.

14.2 If experts' reports are to be relied upon, and if experts are to give oral evidence, those instructing them should give the experts the opportunity to consider and comment upon other reports within their area of expertise and which deal with relevant issues at the earliest opportunity.

14.3 Those instructing experts should keep experts informed of the progress of cases, including amendments to statements of case relevant to experts' opinion.

14.4 If those instructing experts become aware of material changes in circumstances or that relevant information within their control was not previously provided to experts, they should without delay instruct experts to review, and if necessary, update the contents of their reports.

15 AMENDMENT OF REPORTS

15.1 It may become necessary for experts to amend their reports:

(a) as a result of an exchange of questions and answers;
(b) following agreements reached at meetings between experts; or
(c) where further evidence or documentation is disclosed.

15.2 Experts should not be asked to, and should not, amend, expand or alter any parts of reports in a manner which distorts their true opinion, but may be invited to amend or expand reports to ensure accuracy, internal consistency, completeness and relevance to the issues and clarity. Although experts should generally follow the recommendations of solicitors with regard to the form of reports, they should form their own independent views as to the opinions and contents expressed in their reports and exclude any suggestions which do not accord with their views.

15.3 Where experts change their opinion following a meeting of experts, a simple signed and dated addendum or memorandum to that effect is generally sufficient. In some cases, however, the benefit to the court of having an amended report may justify the cost of making the amendment.

15.4 Where experts significantly alter their opinion, as a result of new evidence or because evidence on which they relied has become unreliable, or for any other reason, they should amend their reports to reflect that fact. Amended reports should include reasons for amendments. In such circumstances those instructing experts should inform other parties as soon as possible of any change of opinion.

15.5 When experts intend to amend their reports, they should inform those instructing them without delay and give reasons. They should provide the amended version (or an addendum or memorandum) clearly marked as such as quickly as possible.

16 WRITTEN QUESTIONS TO EXPERTS

16.1 The procedure for putting written questions to experts (CPR 35.6) is intended to facilitate the clarification of opinions and issues after experts' reports have been served. Experts have a duty to provide answers to questions properly put. Where they fail to do so, the court may impose sanctions against the party instructing the expert, and, if, there is continued non-compliance, debar a party from relying on the report. Experts should copy their answers to those instructing them.

16.2 Experts' answers to questions automatically become part of their reports. They are covered by the statement of truth and form part of the expert evidence.

16.3 Where experts believe that questions put are not properly directed to the clarification of the report, or are disproportionate, or have been asked out of time, they should discuss the questions with those instructing them and, if appropriate, those asking the questions. Attempts should be made to resolve such problems without the need for an application to the court for directions.

WRITTEN REQUESTS FOR DIRECTIONS IN RELATION TO QUESTIONS

16.4 If those instructing experts do not apply to the court in respect of questions, but experts still believe that questions are improper or out of time, experts may file written requests with the court for directions to assist in carrying out their functions as experts (CPR 35.14). See Section 11 above.

17 SINGLE JOINT EXPERTS

17.1 CPR 35 and PD35 deal extensively with the instruction and use of joint experts by the parties and the powers of the court to order their use (see CPR 35.7 and 35.8, PD35, para 5).

17.2 The Civil Procedure Rules encourage the use of joint experts. Wherever possible a joint report should be obtained. Consideration should therefore be given by all parties to the appointment of single joint experts in all cases where a court might direct such an appointment. Single joint experts are the norm in cases allocated to the small claims track and the fast track.

17.3 Where, in the early stages of a dispute, examinations, investigations, tests, site inspections, experiments, preparation of photographs, plans or other similar preliminary expert tasks are necessary, consideration should be given to the instruction of a single joint expert, especially where such matters are not, at that stage, expected to be contentious as between the parties. The objective of such an appointment should be to agree or to narrow issues.

17.5 Experts who have previously advised a party (whether in the same case or otherwise) should only be proposed as single joint experts if other parties are given all relevant information about the previous involvement.

17.6 The appointment of a single joint expert does not prevent parties from instructing their own experts to advise (but the costs of such expert advisers may not be recoverable in the case).

JOINT INSTRUCTIONS

17.7 The parties should try to agree joint instructions to single joint experts, but, in default of agreement, each party may give instructions. In particular, all parties should try to agree what documents should be included with instructions and what assumptions single joint experts should make.

17.8 Where the parties fail to agree joint instructions, they should try to agree where the areas of disagreement lie and their instructions should make this clear. If separate instructions are given, they should be copied at the same time to the other instructing parties.

17.9 Where experts are instructed by two or more parties, the terms of appointment should, unless the court has directed otherwise, or the parties have agreed otherwise, include:

(a) a statement that all the instructing parties are jointly and severally liable to pay the experts' fees and, accordingly, that experts' invoices should be sent simultaneously to all instructing parties or their solicitors (as appropriate); and
(b) a statement as to whether any order has been made limiting the amount of experts' fees and expenses (CPR 35.8(4)(a)).

17.10 Where instructions have not been received by the expert from one or more of the instructing parties the expert should give notice (normally at least 7 days) of a deadline to all instructing parties for the receipt by the expert of such instructions. Unless the instructions are received within the deadline the expert may begin work. In the event that instructions are received after the deadline but before the signing off of the report the expert should consider whether it is practicable to comply with those instructions without adversely affecting the timetable set for delivery of the report and in such a manner as to comply with the proportionality principle. An expert who decides to issue a report without taking into account instructions received after the deadline should inform the parties who may apply to the court for directions. In either event the report must show clearly that the expert did not receive instructions within the deadline, or, as the case may be, at all.

CONDUCT OF THE SINGLE JOINT EXPERT

17.11 Single joint experts should keep all instructing parties informed of any material steps that they may be taking by, for example, copying all correspondence to those instructing them.

17.12 Single joint experts are Part 35 experts and so have an overriding duty to the court. They are the parties' appointed experts and therefore owe an equal duty to all parties. They should maintain independence, impartiality and transparency at all times.

17.13 Single joint experts should not attend any meeting or conference which is not a joint one, unless all the parties have agreed in writing or the court has directed that such a meeting may be held[4] and who is to pay the experts' fees for the meeting.

4 *Peet v Mid Kent Area Healthcare NHS Trust* [2002] 1 WLR 210

17.14 Single joint experts may request directions from the court – see Section 11 above.

17.15 Single joint experts should serve their reports simultaneously on all instructing parties. They should provide a single report even though they may have received instructions which contain areas of conflicting fact or allegation. If conflicting instructions lead to different opinions (for example, because the instructions require experts to make different assumptions of fact), reports may need to contain more than one set of opinions on any issue. It is for the court to determine the facts.

CROSS-EXAMINATION

17.16 Single joint experts do not normally give oral evidence at trial but if they do, all parties may cross-examine them. In general written questions (CPR 35.6) should be put to single joint experts before requests are made for them to attend court for the purpose of cross-examination[5].

5 *Daniels v Walker* [2000] 1 WLR 1382

18 DISCUSSIONS BETWEEN EXPERTS

18.1 The court has powers to direct discussions between experts for the purposes set out in the Rules (CPR 35.12). Parties may also agree that discussions take place between their experts.

18.2 Where single joint experts have been instructed but parties have, with the permission of the court, instructed their own additional Part 35 experts, there may, if the court so orders or the parties agree, be discussions between the single joint experts and the additional Part 35 experts. Such discussions should be confined to those matters within the remit of the additional Part 35 experts or as ordered by the court.

18.3 The purpose of discussions between experts should be, wherever possible, to:

(a) identify and discuss the expert issues in the proceedings;
(b) reach agreed opinions on those issues, and, if that is not possible, to narrow the issues in the case;
(c) identify those issues on which they agree and disagree and summarise their reasons for disagreement on any issue; and
(d) identify what action, if any, may be taken to resolve any of the outstanding issues between the parties.

ARRANGEMENTS FOR DISCUSSIONS BETWEEN EXPERTS

18.4 Arrangements for discussions between experts should be proportionate to the value of cases. In small claims and fast-track cases there should not normally be meetings between experts. Where discussion is justified in such cases, telephone discussion or an exchange of letters should, in the interests of proportionality, usually suffice. In multi-track cases, discussion may be face to face, but the practicalities or the proportionality principle may require discussions to be by telephone or video conference.

18.5 The parties, their lawyers and experts should co-operate to produce the agenda for any discussion between experts, although primary responsibility for preparation of the agenda should normally lie with the parties' solicitors.

18.6 The agenda should indicate what matters have been agreed and summarise concisely those which are in issue. It is often helpful for it to include questions to be answered by the experts. If agreement cannot be reached promptly or a party is unrepresented, the court may give directions for the drawing up of the agenda. The agenda should be circulated to experts and those instructing them to allow sufficient time for the experts to prepare for the discussion.

18.7 Those instructing experts must not instruct experts to avoid reaching agreement (or to defer doing so) on any matter within the experts' competence. Experts are not permitted to accept such instructions.

18.8 The parties' lawyers may only be present at discussions between experts if all the parties agree or the court so orders. If lawyers do attend, they should not normally intervene except to answer questions put to them by the experts or to advise about the law[6].

6 *Hubbard v Lambeth, Southwark and Lewisham HA* [2001] EWCA 1455

18.9 The content of discussions between experts should not be referred to at trial unless the parties agree (CPR 35.12(4)). It is good practice for any such agreement to be in writing.

18.10 At the conclusion of any discussion between experts, a statement should be prepared setting out:

(a) a list of issues that have been agreed, including, in each instance, the basis of agreement;
(b) a list of issues that have not been agreed, including, in each instance, the basis of disagreement;
(c) a list of any further issues that have arisen that were not included in the original agenda for discussion;
(d) a record of further action, if any, to be taken or recommended, including as appropriate the holding of further discussions between experts.

18.11 The statement should be agreed and signed by all the parties to the discussion as soon as may be practicable.

18.12 Agreements between experts during discussions do not bind the parties unless the parties expressly agree to be bound by the agreement (CPR 35.12(5)). However, in view of the overriding objective, parties should give careful consideration before refusing to be bound by such an agreement and be able to explain their refusal should it become relevant to the issue of costs.

19 ATTENDANCE OF EXPERTS AT COURT

19.1 Experts instructed in cases have an obligation to attend court if called upon to do so and accordingly should ensure that those instructing them are always aware of their dates to be avoided and take all reasonable steps to be available.

19.2 Those instructing experts should:

(a) ascertain the availability of experts before trial dates are fixed;
(b) keep experts updated with timetables (including the dates and times experts are to attend) and the location of the court;
(c) give consideration, where appropriate, to experts giving evidence via a video-link.
(d) inform experts immediately if trial dates are vacated.

19.3 Experts should normally attend court without the need for the service of witness summonses, but on occasion they may be served to require attendance (CPR 34). The use of witness summonses does not affect the contractual or other obligations of the parties to pay experts' fees.

PART 36
OFFERS TO SETTLE AND PAYMENTS INTO COURT

CONTENTS OF THIS PART

Procedural Guide—See Guide 26, set out in Section 1 of this work.

Practice Direction—See generally PD36 at p 930.

36.1 Scope of this Part

(1) This Part contains rules about –

- (a) offers to settle and payments into court; and
- (b) the consequences where an offer to settle or payment into court is made in accordance with this Part.

(2) Nothing in this Part prevents a party making an offer to settle in whatever way he chooses, but if that offer is not made in accordance with this Part, it will only have the consequences specified in this Part if the court so orders.

(Part 36 applies to Part 20 claims by virtue of rule 20.3)

'if the court so orders' (r 36.1(2))—This Part, in conjunction with the use of pre-action protocols, has had a universally welcomed effect on litigation practice. In particular, the introduction of the claimant's offer to settle, in the knowledge that exaggeration of the claim might be reflected in an unwelcome costs order in due course, has led to a high proportion of settlements before as well as after the commencement of proceedings. This subrule means that the court has a discretion to make suitable costs and interest orders even where offers are made outside the regime prescribed by the Part. However, a defendant will receive no automatic protection as to costs without a payment (see *Amber v Stacey* [2001] 1 WLR 1225, CA). In this respect, the provisions of r 44.3(4)(a) and (c) (factors affecting the exercise of the court's discretion as to the costs order to be made) and r 44.5(3)(a) (factors affecting the court's decision as to the amount of costs) should be noted. But by *Crouch v King's Healthcare NHS Trust* [2005] 1 WLR 2015 and *Trustees of Stokes Pension Fund v Western Power Distribution* (2005) (unreported) 11 July, CA the law has been significantly altered. If an offer is made in clear terms, is open for acceptance for at least 21 days and is otherwise a *Calderbank* offer, is genuine and the defendant was good for the money when offered, it should be treated as a payment into court. To the extent that an offer fulfils none or less than all of these conditions, the cost protection will diminish or disappear. These decisions are of practical value; it remains to be seen whether they give rise to practical problems.

In *Charles (Denise) v NTL Group Ltd* (2002) Lawtel, 13 December, the Court of Appeal emphasised that lack of formality in making an offer was not crucial where the interests of the offeree were not adversely affected. An offer including a term as to costs is not within the scope of Pt 36 and may not be used as such for the purposes of seeking costs on the indemnity basis. It may be taken into account under this discretionary head (*Mitchell v James* [2002] EWCA Civ 997, [2002] CP Rep 72, CA).

36.2 Part 36 offers and Part 36 payments – general provisions

(1) An offer made in accordance with the requirements of this Part is called –

(a) if made by way of a payment into court, 'a Part 36 payment';
(b) otherwise 'a Part 36 offer'.

(Rule 36.3 sets out when an offer has to be made by way of a payment into court)

(2) The party who makes an offer is the 'offeror'.

(3) The party to whom an offer is made is the 'offeree'.

(4) A Part 36 offer or a Part 36 payment –

(a) may be made at any time after proceedings have started; and
(b) may be made in appeal proceedings.

(5) A Part 36 offer or a Part 36 payment shall not have the consequences set out in this Part while the claim is being dealt with on the small claims track unless the court orders otherwise.

(Part 26 deals with allocation to the small claims track)

(Rule 27.2 provides that Part 36 does not apply to small claims)

'after proceedings have started' (r 36.2(4)(a))—An offer made *before* proceedings are started is likely to attract similar orders provided it complies strictly with r 36.10, even though a judicial decision is required. Otherwise, the court's discretion under r 36.1(2) is at large. A Pt 36 offer made to protect the claimant against the costs of first-instance proceedings does not provide protection against the costs of an appeal (*East West Corporation v DKBS 1912* [2003] EWCA Civ 174, [2003] 1 Lloyd's Rep 265, CA).

36.2A Personal injury claims for future pecuniary loss

(1) This rule applies to a claim for damages for personal injury which is or includes a claim for future pecuniary loss.

(2) An offer to settle such a claim will not have the consequences set out in this Part unless it is made by way of a Part 36 offer under this rule, and where such an offer is or includes an offer to pay the whole or part of any damages in the form of a lump sum, it will not have the consequences set out in this Part unless a Part 36 payment of the amount of the lump sum offer is also made.

(3) Where both a Part 36 offer and a Part 36 payment are made under this rule –

- (a) the offer must include details of the payment, and
- (b) rules 36.11(1) and (2) and 36.13(1) and (2) apply as if there were only a Part 36 offer.

(4) A Part 36 offer to which this rule applies may contain an offer to pay, or an offer to accept –

- (a) the whole or part of the damages for future pecuniary loss in the form of –
  - (i) either a lump sum or periodical payments, or
  - (ii) both a lump sum and periodical payments,
- (b) the whole or part of any other damages in the form of a lump sum.

(5) A Part 36 offer to which this rule applies –

- (a) must state the amount of any offer to pay the whole or part of any damages in the form of a lump sum;
- (b) may state what part of the offer relates to damages for future pecuniary loss to be accepted in the form of a lump sum;
- (c) may state, where part of the offer relates to other damages to be accepted in the form of a lump sum, what amounts are attributable to those other damages;
- (d) must state what part of the offer relates to damages for future pecuniary loss to be paid or accepted in the form of periodical payments and must specify –
  - (i) the amount and duration of the periodical payments,
  - (ii) the amount of any payments for substantial capital purchases and when they are to be made, and
  - (iii) that each amount is to vary by reference to the retail prices index (or to some other named index, or that it is not to vary by reference to any index); and
- (e) must state either that any damages which take the form of periodical payments will be funded in a way which ensures that the continuity of payment is reasonably secure in accordance with section 2(4) of the Damages Act 1996 or how such damages are to be paid and how the continuity of their payment is to be secured.

(6) Where a Part 36 payment includes a lump sum for damages for future pecuniary loss, the Part 36 payment notice may state the amount of that lump sum.

(7) Where the defendant makes a Part 36 offer to which this rule applies and which offers to pay damages in the form of both a lump sum and periodical payments, the claimant may only give notice of acceptance of the offer as a whole.

Amendments—Inserted by SI 2004/3129.

General note—This detailed rule supplements the new Pt 41, Section II. From 1 April 2005, it requires the most careful consideration to ensure that the costs consequences are as intended by the party making the offer or payment. Appellate decisions are likely to be necessary to work out the implications. They apply to cases whenever begun. The r 36.2A requirements are onerous.

36.3 A defendant's offer to settle a money claim requires a Part 36 payment

(1) Subject to rules 36.2A(2), 36.5(5) and 36.23, an offer by a defendant to settle a money claim will not have the consequences set out in this Part unless it is made by way of a Part 36 payment.

(2) A Part 36 payment may only be made after proceedings have started.

(Rule 36.5(5) permits a Part 36 offer to be made by reference to an interim payment)

(Rule 36.10 makes provision for an offer to settle a money claim before the commencement of proceedings)

(Rule 36.23 makes provision for where benefit is recoverable under the Social Security (Recovery of Benefit) Act 1997)

Amendments—SI 2004/3129.

36.4 Defendant's offer to settle the whole of a claim which includes both a money claim and a non-money claim

(1) This rule applies where a defendant to a claim which includes both a money claim and a non-money claim wishes –

- (a) to make an offer to settle the whole claim which will have the consequences set out in this Part; and
- (b) to make a money offer in respect of the money claim and a non-money offer in respect of the non-money claim.

(2) The defendant must –

- (a) make a Part 36 payment or Part 36 offer made under rule 36.2A in relation to the money claim; and
- (b) make a Part 36 offer in relation to the non-money claim.

(3) The Part 36 payment notice or Part 36 offer made under rule 36.2A must –

- (a) identify the document which sets out the terms of the Part 36 offer [made under this rule; and
- (b) state that if the claimant gives notice of acceptance of the Part 36 payment or Part 36 offer made under rule 36.2A he will be treated as also accepting the Part 36 offer made under this rule.

(Rule 36.6 makes provision for a Part 36 payment notice)

(4) If the claimant gives notice of acceptance of the Part 36 payment or Part 36 offer made under rule 36.2A, he shall also be taken as giving notice of acceptance of the Part 36 offer in relation to the non-money claim.

Amendments—SI 1999/1008; SI 2004/3129.

36.5 Form and content of a Part 36 offer

(1) A Part 36 offer must be in writing.

(2) A Part 36 offer may relate to the whole claim or to part of it or to any issue that arises in it.

(3) A Part 36 offer must –

(a) state whether it relates to the whole of the claim or to part of it or to an issue that arises in it and if so to which part or issue;
(b) state whether it takes into account any counterclaim; and
(c) if it is expressed not to be inclusive of interest, give the details relating to interest set out in rule 36.22(2).

(4) A defendant may make a Part 36 offer limited to accepting liability up to a specified proportion.

(5) A Part 36 offer may be made by reference to an interim payment.

(Part 25 contains provisions relating to interim payments)

(6) A Part 36 offer made not less than 21 days before the start of the trial must –

(a) be expressed to remain open for acceptance for 21 days from the date it is made; and
(b) provide that after 21 days the offeree may only accept it if –
  (i) the parties agree the liability for costs; or
  (ii) the court gives permission.

(7) A Part 36 offer made less than 21 days before the start of the trial must state that the offeree may only accept it if –

(a) the parties agree the liability for costs; or
(b) the court gives permission.

(Rule 36.8 makes provision for when a Part 36 offer is treated as being made)

(8) If a Part 36 offer is withdrawn it will not have the consequences set out in this Part.

'be expressed to remain open for acceptance for 21 days' (r 36.5(6)(a))—Nonetheless, it may be withdrawn at any time before acceptance (*Scammell v Dicker LTL* [2001] 1 WLR 631, CA). Terms as to costs are not intended to be included in Pt 36 offers (*Mitchell v James* [2002] EWCA Civ 997, [2002] CP Rep 72, CA). This principle also applies to uplift interest (*Ali Reza-Delta Transport v United Arab Shipping Co SAG* (No 2) [2003] EWCA Civ 811, [2003] Lloyd's Rep 455, CA).

36.6 Notice of a Part 36 payment

(1) A Part 36 payment may relate to the whole claim or part of it or to an issue that arises in it.

(2) A defendant who makes a Part 36 payment must file with the court a notice ('Part 36 payment notice') which –

(a) states the amount of the payment;
(b) states whether the payment relates to the whole claim or to part of it or to any issue that arises in it and if so to which part or issue;
(c) states whether it takes into account any counterclaim;
(d) if an interim payment has been made, states that the defendant has taken into account the interim payment; and
(e) if it is expressed not to be inclusive of interest, gives the details relating to interest set out in rule 36.22(2).

(Rule 25.6 makes provision for an interim payment)

(Rule 36.4 provides for further information to be included where a defendant wishes to settle the whole of a claim which includes a money claim and a non-money claim)

(Rule 36.23 makes provision for extra information to be included in the payment notice in a case where benefit is recoverable under the Social Security (Recovery of Benefit) Act 1997)

(3) The offeror must –

(a) serve the Part 36 payment notice on the offeree; and
(b) file a certificate of service of the notice.

(4) (*revoked*)

(Rule 6.10 specifies what must be contained in a certificate of service)

(5) A Part 36 payment may be withdrawn [or reduced only with the permission of the court.

Amendments—SI 1999/1008; SI 2000/2092; SI 2002/3219.

Payment—With effect from 1 April 2003, all payments into court are to the Court Funds Office in London – see PD36, para 4.1 for changes in practice.

'may be withdrawn' (r 36.6(5))—What happens when a claimant gives notice to accept a payment within the time permitted but the defendant makes an application under this rule? In *Flynn v Scougall (Practice Note)* [2004] EWCA Civ 873, [2004] 1 WLR 3069, [2004] 3 All ER 609, [2004] TLR 377, CA the Court of Appeal held that the defendant's application did not automatically deprive the claimant of his right to accept the payment, which was an important factor in determining the defendant's application.

36.7 Offer to settle a claim for provisional damages

(1) A defendant may make a Part 36 payment in respect of a claim which includes a claim for provisional damages.

(2) Where he does so, the Part 36 payment notice must specify whether or not the defendant is offering to agree to the making of an award of provisional damages.

(3) Where the defendant is offering to agree to the making of an award of provisional damages the payment notice must also state –

(a) that the sum paid into court is in satisfaction of the claim for damages on the assumption that the injured person will not develop the disease or suffer the type of deterioration specified in the notice;
(b) that the offer is subject to the condition that the claimant must make any claim for further damages within a limited period; and
(c) what that period is.

(4) Where a Part 36 payment is –

(a) made in accordance with paragraph (3); and
(b) accepted within the relevant period in rule 36.11,

the Part 36 payment will have the consequences set out in rule 36.13, unless the court orders otherwise.

(5) If the claimant accepts the Part 36 payment he must, within 7 days of doing so, apply to the court for an order for an award of provisional damages under rule 41.2.

(Rule 41.2 provides for an order for an award of provisional damages)

(6) The money in court may not be paid out until the court has disposed of the application made in accordance with paragraph (5).

36.8 Time when a Part 36 offer or a Part 36 payment is made and accepted

(1) A Part 36 offer is made when received by the offeree.

(2) A Part 36 payment is made when written notice of the payment into court is served on the offeree.

(3) An improvement to a Part 36 offer will be effective when its details are received by the offeree.

(4) An increase in a Part 36 payment will be effective when notice of the increase is served on the offeree.

(5) A Part 36 offer or Part 36 payment is accepted when notice of its acceptance is received by the offeror.

36.9 Clarification of a Part 36 offer or a Part 36 payment notice

(1) The offeree may, within 7 days of a Part 36 offer or payment being made, request the offeror to clarify the offer or payment notice.

(2) If the offeror does not give the clarification requested under paragraph (1) within 7 days of receiving the request, the offeree may, unless the trial has started, apply for an order that he does so.

(3) If the court makes an order under paragraph (2), it must specify the date when the Part 36 offer or Part 36 payment is to be treated as having been made.

General note—This rule is not intended to allow one party to interrogate another as to the thinking behind an offer or payment but to clarify the basis of it. The power to order disclosure could be used to provide further information in appropriate circumstances (*R v Secretary of State for Transport ex parte Factortame Ltd & ors* (2000) (unreported) 27 July, TCC, Judge Toulmin QC).

36.10 Court to take into account offer to settle made before commencement of proceedings

(1) If a person makes an offer to settle before proceedings are begun which complies with the provisions of this rule, the court will take that offer into account when making any order as to costs.

(2) The offer must –

(a) be expressed to be open for at least 21 days after the date it was made;
(b) if made by a person who would be a defendant were proceedings commenced, include an offer to pay the costs of the offeree incurred up to the date 21 days after the date it was made; and
(c) otherwise comply with this Part.

(3) Subject to paragraph (3A), if the offeror is a defendant to a money claim –

(a) he must make a Part 36 payment within 14 days of service of the claim form; and
(b) the amount of the payment must be not less than the sum offered before proceedings began.

(3A) In a claim to which rule 36.2A applies, if the offeror is a defendant who wishes to offer to pay the whole or part of any damages in the form of a lump sum –

(a) he must make a Part 36 payment within 14 days of service of the claim form; and

(b) the amount of the payment must be not less than the lump sum offered before proceedings began.

(4) An offeree may not, after proceedings have begun, accept –

(a) an offer made under paragraph (2); or

(b) a Part 36 payment made under paragraph (3) or (3A),

without the permission of the court.

(5) An offer under this rule is made when it is received by the offeree.

Amendments—SI 2004/3129.

General note—See notes to rr 36.1(2) and 36.2.

36.11 Time for acceptance of a defendant's Part 36 offer or Part 36 payment

(1) A claimant may accept a Part 36 offer or a Part 36 payment made not less than 21 days before the start of the trial without needing the court's permission if he gives the defendant written notice of acceptance not later than 21 days after the offer or payment was made.

(Rule 36.13 sets out the costs consequences of accepting a defendant's offer or payment without needing the permission of the court)

(2) If –

(a) a defendant's Part 36 offer or Part 36 payment is made less than 21 days before the start of the trial; or

(b) the claimant does not accept it within the period specified in paragraph (1) –

(i) if the parties agree the liability for costs, the claimant may accept the offer or payment without needing the permission of the court;

(ii) if the parties do not agree the liability for costs the claimant may only accept the offer or payment with the permission of the court.

(3) Where the permission of the court is needed under paragraph (2) the court will, if it gives permission, make an order as to costs.

'without needing the court's permission' (r 36.11(1))—The court's permission *will* nonetheless be required if the Pt 36 offer is one to which r 36.10(4) applies, ie an offer made before the commencement of proceedings or a payment made as promised before the commencement of proceedings.

36.12 Time for acceptance of a claimant's Part 36 offer

(1) A defendant may accept a Part 36 offer made not less than 21 days before the start of the trial without needing the court's permission if he gives the claimant written notice of acceptance not later than 21 days after the offer was made.

(Rule 36.14 sets out the costs consequences of accepting a claimant's offer without needing the permission of the court)

(2) If –

(a) a claimant's Part 36 offer is made less than 21 days before the start of the trial; or

(b) the defendant does not accept it within the period specified in paragraph (1) –

(i) if the parties agree the liability for costs, the defendant may accept the offer without needing the permission of the court;

(ii) if the parties do not agree the liability for costs the defendant may only accept the offer with the permission of the court.

(3) Where the permission of the court is needed under paragraph (2) the court will, if it gives permission, make an order as to costs.

36.13 Costs consequences of acceptance of a defendant's Part 36 offer or Part 36 payment

(1) Where a Part 36 offer or a Part 36 payment is accepted without needing the permission of the court the claimant will be entitled to his costs of the proceedings up to the date of serving notice of acceptance.

(2) Where –

(a) a Part 36 offer or a Part 36 payment relates to part only of the claim; and

(b) at the time of serving notice of acceptance the claimant abandons the balance of the claim,

the claimant will be entitled to his costs of the proceedings up to the date of serving notice of acceptance, unless the court orders otherwise.

(3) The claimant's costs include any costs attributable to the defendant's counterclaim if the Part 36 offer or the Part 36 payment notice states that it takes into account the counterclaim.

(4) Costs under this rule will be payable on the standard basis if not agreed.

General note—This rule does not deprive the court of the discretion to make an appropriate costs order where the payment into court has not had the effect of bringing the proceedings to an end (*Clark Goldring v Page* [2001] All ER (D) 353). Where the defendant makes a significant amendment after which the claimant promptly accepts a Pt 36 payment that he declined earlier, it does not follow that the claimant is the successful party (*Factortame Ltd & ors v Secretary of State for the Environment, Transport and the Regions* [2002] EWCA Civ 22, [2002] 2 All ER 838, CA).

36.14 Costs consequences of acceptance of a claimant's Part 36 offer

Where a claimant's Part 36 offer is accepted without needing the permission of the court the claimant will be entitled to his costs of the proceedings up to the date upon which the defendant serves notice of acceptance.

36.15 The effect of acceptance of a Part 36 offer or a Part 36 payment

(1) If a Part 36 offer or Part 36 payment relates to the whole claim and is accepted, the claim will be stayed(GL).

(2) In the case of acceptance of a Part 36 offer which relates to the whole claim –

(a) the stay(GL) will be upon the terms of the offer; and

(b) either party may apply to enforce those terms without the need for a new claim.

(3) If a Part 36 offer or a Part 36 payment which relates to part only of the claim is accepted –

(a) the claim will be stayed(GL) as to that part; and

(b) unless the parties have agreed costs, the liability for costs shall be decided by the court.

(4) If the approval of the court is required before a settlement can be binding, any stay(GL) which would otherwise arise on the acceptance of a Part 36 offer or a Part 36 payment will take effect only when that approval has been given.

(5) Any stay(GL) arising under this rule will not affect the power of the court –

(a) to enforce the terms of a Part 36 offer;
(b) to deal with any question of costs (including interest on costs) relating to the proceedings;
(c) to order payment out of court of any sum paid into court.

(6) Where –

(a) a Part 36 offer has been accepted; and
(b) a party alleges that –
   (i) the other party has not honoured the terms of the offer; and
   (ii) he is therefore entitled to a remedy for breach of contract,

the party may claim the remedy by applying to the court without the need to start a new claim unless the court orders otherwise.

36.16 Payment out of a sum in court on the acceptance of a Part 36 payment

Where a Part 36 payment is accepted the claimant obtains payment out of the sum in court by making a request for payment in the practice form.

36.17 Acceptance of a Part 36 offer or a Part 36 payment made by one or more, but not all, defendants

(1) This rule applies where the claimant wishes to accept a Part 36 offer or a Part 36 payment made by one or more, but not all, of a number of defendants.

(2) If the defendants are sued jointly or in the alternative, the claimant may accept the offer or payment without needing the permission of the court in accordance with rule 36.11(1) if –

(a) he discontinues his claim against those defendants who have not made the offer or payment; and
(b) those defendants give written consent to the acceptance of the offer or payment.

(3) If the claimant alleges that the defendants have a several liability(GL) to him the claimant may –

(a) accept the offer or payment in accordance with rule 36.11(1); and
(b) continue with his claims against the other defendants [if he is entitled to do so.

(4) In all other cases the claimant must apply to the court for –

(a) an order permitting a payment out to him of any sum in court; and
(b) such order as to costs as the court considers appropriate.

Amendments—SI 1999/1008.

36.18 Other cases where a court order is required to enable acceptance of a Part 36 offer or a Part 36 payment

(1) Where a Part 36 offer or a Part 36 payment is made in proceedings to which rule 21.10 applies –

(a) the offer or payment may be accepted only with the permission of the court; and
(b) no payment out of any sum in court shall be made without a court order.

(Rule 21.10 deals with compromise etc by or on behalf of a child or patient)

(2) Where the court gives a claimant permission to accept a Part 36 offer or payment after the trial has started –

(a) any money in court may be paid out only with a court order; and
(b) the court must, in the order, deal with the whole costs of the proceedings.

(3) Where a claimant accepts a Part 36 payment after a defence of tender before claim(GL) has been put forward by the defendant, the money in court may be paid out only after an order of the court.

(Rule 37.3 requires a defendant who wishes to rely on a defence of tender before claim(GL) to make a payment into court)

36.19 Restriction on disclosure of a Part 36 offer or a Part 36 payment

(1) A Part 36 offer will be treated as 'without prejudice(GL) except as to costs'.

(2) The fact that a Part 36 payment has been made shall not be communicated to the trial judge until all questions of liability and the amount of money to be awarded have been decided.

(3) Paragraph (2) does not apply –

(a) where the defence of tender before claim(GL) has been raised;
(b) where the proceedings have been stayed(GL) under rule 36.15 following acceptance of a Part 36 offer or Part 36 payment; or
(c) where –
   (i) the issue of liability has been determined before any assessment of the money claimed; and
   (ii) the fact that there has or has not been a Part 36 payment may be relevant to the question of the costs of the issue of liability.

General note—Despite this rule, it is not necessarily the case that a judge who learns of privileged or inadmissible material, including offers or payments, should recuse himself. The test is whether the judge, subjectively, thinks he cannot continue fairly or whether, objectively, a fair-minded observer would see a real possibility of there not being a fair hearing (*Berg v IML London* [2002] 1 WLR 3271, QBD, Stanley Burnton J). Stanley Burnton J's approach was approved by the Court of Appeal in *Garratt v Saxby (Practice Note)* [2004] EWCA Civ 341, [2004] 1 WLR 2152, (2004) 146 SJLB 237, CA where it was emphasised that a breach of this rule does not necessarily make the proceedings illegitimate. The Court of Appeal considered an awkward question in *HSS Hire Services Group plc v BMB Builders Merchants & anor* [2005] EWCA Civ 626: 'What happens if a preliminary issue on liability is determined in favour of the claimant, and a Pt 36 payment has been made before the order for a split trial?' The court decided that if the judge were unaware of the payment he could exercise his discretion as to the costs of the prelimary issue. If, however, he were aware of the payment, he should except in the most exceptional case reserve the costs until the question of damages was resolved.

36.20 Costs consequences where claimant fails to do better than a Part 36 offer or a Part 36 payment

(1) This rule applies where at trial a claimant –

(a) fails to better a Part 36 payment;
(b) fails to obtain a judgment which is more advantageous than a [defendant's Part 36 offer; or
(c) in a claim to which rule 36.2A applies, fails to obtain a judgment which is more advantageous than the Part 36 offer made under that rule.

(2) Unless it considers it unjust to do so, the court will order the claimant to pay any costs incurred by the defendant after the latest date on which the payment or offer could have been accepted without needing the permission of the court.

(Rule 36.11 sets out the time for acceptance of a defendant's Part 36 offer or Part 36 payment)

Amendments—SI 1999/1008; SI 2004/3129.

General note—When considering whether the claimant has or has not bettered the offer or payment in, like must be compared with like (*Blackham v Entrepose UK* [2004] EWCA Civ 1109, [2004] All ER (D) 478 (Jul)). In that case the claimant recovered more than the payment into court but the damages element was less; the extra award represented interest since the date of the payment. The defendant was entitled to the costs.

36.21 Costs and other consequences where claimant does better than he proposed in his Part 36 offer

(1) This rule applies where at trial –

(a) a defendant is held liable for more; or
(b) the judgment against a defendant is more advantageous to the claimant, than the proposals contained in a claimant's Part 36 offer (including a Part 36 offer made under rule 36.2A).

(2) The court may order interest on the whole or part of any sum of money (excluding interest) awarded to the claimant at a rate not exceeding 10% above base rate (GL) for some or all of the period starting with the latest date on which the defendant could have accepted the offer without needing the permission of the court.

(3) The court may also order that the claimant is entitled to –

(a) his costs on the indemnity basis from the latest date when the defendant could have accepted the offer without needing the permission of the court; and
(b) interest on those costs at a rate not exceeding 10% above base rate (GL).

(4) Where this rule applies, the court will make the orders referred to in paragraphs (2) and (3) unless it considers it unjust to do so.

(Rule 36.12 sets out the latest date when the defendant could have accepted the offer)

(5) In considering whether it would be unjust to make the orders referred to in paragraphs (2) and (3) above, the court will take into account all the circumstances of the case including –

(a) the terms of any Part 36 offer;

(b) the stage in the proceedings when any Part 36 offer or Part 36 payment was made;
(c) the information available to the parties at the time when the Part 36 offer or Part 36 payment was made; and
(d) the conduct of the parties with regard to the giving or refusing to give information for the purposes of enabling the offer or payment into court to be made or evaluated.

(6) Where the court awards interest under this rule and also awards interest on the same sum and for the same period under any other power, the total rate of interest may not exceed 10% above base rate(GL).

Amendments—SI 2000/2092; SI 2004/3129.

'This rule applies where at trial' (r 36.21(1))—Enhanced interest rates are only permitted under *this* provision where there has been a trial (*Petrotrade Inc v Texaco Ltd* [2002] 1 WLR 947, CA). However, in that case the court approved the award of indemnity costs and an enhanced rate of interest under the court's wide discretion as to interest and costs where summary judgment had been entered for better than a claimant's proposal. There is no stigma or moral disapproval implied by an indemnity costs order under this rule (unlike one made under Pt 44) and an order should generally be made (*Kiam v MGN* (No 2) [2002] EWCA Civ 66, [2002] 2 All ER 242).

In *Humpheryes v Nedcon UK & anor* [2004] EWHC 2558 (QB) Roderick Evans J held that this rule applies to a claim with multiple defendants where the claimant is entitled to judgment against all for the whole claim, even if there is apportionment between defendants. When the award equals the Pt 36 offer the claimant is entitled to costs (*Read v Edmed* [2004] TLR 599, (2004) *The Times*, 13 December, Bell J).

'10% above base rate' (r 36.21(2), (3))—This discretionary power is intended to operate as a sanction against the unreasonable conduct of litigation. It is neither a penalty nor ultra vires the Civil Procedure Act 1997 (*All-in-One Design and Build Ltd v Motcomb Estates Ltd & anor* (2000) *The Times*, 4 April, Recorder Michael Black QC).

'will make the orders' (r 36.21(4))—Once the circumstances in r 36.21(1) are found to exist, the onus is on the court to make the order. In such circumstances, the court must justify any decision not to make such an order. In *Huck v Robson* [2002] EWCA Civ 398, [2002] 3 All ER 263, CA it was held that pre-action offers fall within this provision, by virtue of r 36.10. Here, a Pt 36 offer to settle on the basis of a 5% discount as to liability should have attracted indemnity costs when it was bettered.

36.22 Interest

(1) Unless –

(a) a claimant's Part 36 offer which offers to accept a sum of money; or
(b) a Part 36 payment notice,

indicates to the contrary, any such offer or payment will be treated as inclusive of all interest until the last date on which it could be accepted without needing the permission of the court.

(2) Where a claimant's Part 36 offer or Part 36 payment notice is expressed not to be inclusive of interest, the offer or notice must state –

(a) whether interest is offered; and
(b) if so, the amount offered, the rate or rates offered and the period or periods for which it is offered.

36.23 Deduction of benefits

(1) This rule applies where a payment to a claimant following acceptance of a Part 36 offer or Part 36 payment into court would be a compensation payment as defined in section 1 of the Social Security (Recovery of Benefits) Act 1997.

(2) A defendant to a money claim may make an offer to settle the claim which will have the consequences set out in this Part, without making a Part 36 payment if –

(a) at the time he makes the offer he has applied for, but not received, a certificate of recoverable benefit; and
(b) he makes a Part 36 payment not more than 7 days after he receives the certificate.

(Section 1 of the 1997 Act defines 'recoverable benefit')

(3) A Part 36 payment notice must state –

(a) the amount of gross compensation;
(b) the name and amount of any benefit by which that gross amount is reduced in accordance with section 8 and Schedule 2 to the 1997 Act; and
(c) that the sum paid in is the net amount after deduction of the amount of benefit.

(4) For the purposes of rule 36.20(1)(a)claimant fails to better a Part 36 payment if he fails to obtain judgment for more than the gross sum specified in the Part 36 payment notice.

(4A) For the purposes of rule 36.20(1)(c), where the court is determining whether the claimant has failed to obtain a judgment which is more advantageous than the Part 36 offer made under rule 36.2A, the amount of any lump sum paid into court which it takes into account is to be the amount of the gross sum specified in the Part 36 payment notice.

(5) Where –

(a) a Part 36 payment has been made; and
(b) application is made for the money remaining in court to be paid out,

the court may treat the money in court as being reduced by a sum equivalent to any further recoverable benefits paid to the claimant since the date of payment into court and may direct payment out accordingly.

Amendments—SI 2004/3129.

General note—In *Williams v Devon County Council* [2003] EWCA Civ 365, [2003] TLR 172, the Court of Appeal gave important guidance about the application of r 36.23 and the need to make a correct calculation of benefits to avoid unexpected costs consequences.

Practice Direction – Offers to Settle and Payments into Court

This Practice Direction supplements CPR Part 36 (PD36)

Procedural Guide—See Guide 26, set out in Section 1 of this work.

General note—See notes to CPR Pt 36 for relevant commentary.

PART 36 OFFERS AND PART 36 PAYMENTS

1.1 A written offer to settle a claim[1] or part of a claim or any issue that arises in it made in accordance with the provisions of Part 36 is called:

(1) if made by way of a payment into court, a Part 36 payment[2], or

(2) if made otherwise, a Part 36 offer[3] (including an offer under rule 36.2A).

1 Includes Part 20 claims.
2 See rule 36.2(1)(a).
3 See rule 36.2(1)(b).

1.2 A Part 36 offer or Part 36 payment has the costs and other consequences set out in rules 36.13, 36.14, 36.20 and 36.21.

1.3 An offer to settle which is not made in accordance with Part 36 will only have the consequences specified in that Part if the court so orders and will be given such weight on any issue as to costs as the court thinks appropriate[1].

1 See rule 36.1(2).

Prospective amendments—The words above in italics have been inserted by virtue of Update 37 from a date to be appointed.

PARTIES AND PART 36 OFFERS

2.1 A Part 36 offer, subject to paragraph 3 below, may be made by any party.

2.2 The party making an offer is the 'offeror' and the party to whom it is made is the 'offeree'.

2.3 A Part 36 offer may consist of a proposal to settle for a specified sum or for some other remedy.

2.4 A Part 36 offer is made when received by the offeree[1].

1 See rule 36.8(1).

2.5 An improvement to a Part 36 offer is effective when its details are received by the offeree[1].

1 See rule 36.8(3).

PARTIES AND PART 36 PAYMENTS

3.1 An offer to settle for a specified sum made by a defendant[1] must, in order to comply with Part 36, be made by way of a Part 36 payment into court[2].

1 Includes a respondent to a claim or issue.
2 See rule 36.3(1).

3.2 A Part 36 payment is made when the Part 36 payment notice is served on the claimant[1].

1 See rule 36.8(2).

3.3 An increase to a Part 36 payment will be effective when notice of the increase is served on the claimant[1].

(For service of the Part 36 payment notice see rule 36.6(3) and (4))

1 See rule 36.8(4).

3.4 A defendant who wishes to withdraw or reduce a Part 36 payment must obtain the court's permission to do so.

3.5 Permission may be obtained by making an application in accordance with Part 23 stating the reasons giving rise to the wish to withdraw or reduce the Part 36 payment.

MAKING A PART 36 PAYMENT

4.1 Except where paragraph 4.2 applies, to make a Part 36 payment in any court the defendant must –

(1) serve the Part 36 payment notice on the offeree;
(2) file at the court –
  (a) a copy of the payment notice; and
  (b) a certificate of service confirming service on the offeree; and
(3) send to the Court Funds Office –
  (a) the payment, usually a cheque made payable to the Accountant General of the Supreme Court;
  (b) a sealed copy of the claim form; and
  (c) Court Funds Office form 100.

4.2 A litigant in person without a current account may, in a claim proceeding in a county court or District Registry, make a Part 36 payment by –

(1) lodging the payment in cash with the court;
(2) filing at the court –
  (a) the Part 36 payment notice; and
  (b) Court Funds Office form 100.

PART 36 OFFERS AND PART 36 PAYMENTS – GENERAL PROVISIONS

5.1 A Part 36 offer or a Part 36 payment notice must:

(1) state that it is a Part 36 offer or that the payment into court is a Part 36 payment, and
(2) be signed by the offeror or his legal representative[1].

1 For the definition of legal representative see rule 2.3.

5.2 The contents of a Part 36 offer must also comply with the requirements of rule 36.5(3), (5) and (6).

5.3 The contents of a Part 36 payment notice must comply with rule 36.6(2) and, if rule 36.23 applies, with rule 36.23(3).

5.3A The contents of a Part 36 offer to which rule 36.2A applies must comply with the requirements of rule 36.2A(5).

5.4 A Part 36 offer or Part 36 payment will be taken to include interest unless it is expressly stated in the offer or the payment notice that interest is not included, in which case the details set out in rule 36.22(2) must be given.

5.5 Where a Part 36 offer is made by a company or other corporation, a person holding a senior position in the company or corporation may sign the offer on the offeror's behalf, but must state the position he holds.

5.6 Each of the following persons is a person holding a senior position:

(1) in respect of a registered company or corporation, a director, the treasurer, secretary, chief executive, manager or other officer of the company or corporation, and
(2) in respect of a corporation which is not a registered company, in addition to those persons set out in (1), the mayor, chairman, president, town clerk or similar officer of the corporation.

CLARIFICATION OF PART 36 OFFER OR PAYMENT

6.1 An offeree may apply to the court for an order requiring the offeror to clarify the terms of a Part 36 offer or Part 36 payment notice (a clarification order) where the offeror has failed to comply within 7 days with a request for clarification[1].

1 See rule 36.9(1) and (2).

6.2 An application for a clarification order should be made in accordance with Part 23.

6.3 The application notice should state the respects in which the terms of the Part 36 offer or Part 36 payment notice, as the case may be, are said to need clarification.

ACCEPTANCE OF A PART 36 OFFER OR PAYMENT

7.1 The times for accepting a Part 36 offer or a Part 36 payment are set out in rules 36.11 and 36.12.

7.2 The general rule is that a Part 36 offer or Part 36 payment made more than 21 days before the start of the trial may be accepted within 21 days after it was made without the permission of the court. The costs consequences set out in rules 36.13 and 36.14 will then come into effect.

7.2A Where a Part 36 payment is made as part of a Part 36 offer made under rule 36.2A, the payment is ignored for the purposes of determining the times set out in rules 36.11 and 36.13.

7.3 A Part 36 offer or Part 36 payment made less than 21 days before the start of the trial cannot be accepted without the permission of the court unless the parties agree what the costs consequences of acceptance will be.

7.4 The permission of the court may be sought:

(1) before the start of the trial, by making an application in accordance with Part 23, and
(2) after the start of the trial, by making an application to the trial judge.

7.5 If the court gives permission it will make an order dealing with costs and may order that, in the circumstances, the costs consequences set out in rules 36.13 and 36.14 will apply.

7.6 Where a Part 36 offer or Part 36 payment is accepted in accordance with rule 36.11(1) or rule 36.12(1) the notice of acceptance must be sent to the offeror and filed with the court.

7.7 The notice of acceptance:

(1) must set out –
  (a) the claim number, and
  (b) the title of the proceedings,
(2) must identify the Part 36 offer or Part 36 payment notice to which it relates, and
(3) must be signed by the offeree or his legal representative (see paragraphs 5.5 and 5.6 above).

7.8 Where:

(1) the court's approval, or
(2) an order for payment of money out of court, or

(3) an order apportioning money in court –
 (a) between the Fatal Accidents Act 1976 and the Law Reform (Miscellaneous Provisions) Act 1934, or
 (b) between the persons entitled to it under the Fatal Accidents Act 1976,

is required for acceptance of a Part 36 offer or Part 36 payment, application for the approval or the order should be made in accordance with Part 23.

7.9 The court will include in any order made under paragraph 7.8 above a direction for:

(1) the payment out of the money in court, and
(2) the payment of interest.

7.10 Unless the parties have agreed otherwise:

(1) interest accruing up to the date of acceptance will be paid to the offeror, and
(2) interest accruing as from the date of acceptance until payment out will be paid to the offeree.

7.11 A claimant may not accept a Part 36 payment or Part 36 offer made under rule 36.2A which is part of a defendant's offer to settle the whole of a claim consisting of both a money and a non-money claim unless at the same time he accepts the offer to settle the whole of the claim. Therefore:

(1) if a claimant accepts a Part 36 payment which is part of a defendant's offer to settle the whole of the claim, or
(2) if a claimant accepts a Part 36 offer which is part of a defendant's offer to settle the whole of the claim,

the claimant will be deemed to have accepted the offer to settle the whole of the claim[1].

(See paragraph 8 below for the method of obtaining money out of court)

1 See rule 36.4.

PAYMENT OUT OF COURT

8.1 To obtain money out of court following acceptance of a Part 36 payment, the claimant should –

(1) file a request for payment in Court Funds Office form 201 with the Court Funds Office; and
(2) file a copy of form 201 at the court.

8.2 The request for payment should contain the following details:

(1) where the party receiving the payment –
 (a) is legally represented –
  (i) the name, business address and reference of the legal representative, and
  (ii) the name of the bank and the sort code number, the title of the account and the account number where the payment is to be transmitted, and
(2) where the party is acting in person –
 (a) his name and address, and
 (b) his bank account details as in (ii) above.

8.3 Where a trial is to take place at a different court to that where the case is proceeding, the claimant must also file notice of request for payment with the court where the trial is to take place.

8.4 Subject to paragraph 8.5(1) and (2), if a party does not wish the payment to be transmitted into his bank account or if he does not have a bank account, he may send a written request to the Accountant-General for the payment to be made to him by cheque.

8.5 Where a party seeking payment out of court has provided the necessary information, the payment:

(1) where a party is legally represented, must be made to the legal representative,
(2) if the party is not legally represented but is, or has been, in receipt of legal aid in respect of the proceedings and a notice to that effect has been filed, should be made to the Legal Aid Board by direction of the court,
(3) where a person entitled to money in court dies without having made a will and the court is satisfied –
    (a) that no grant of administration of his estate has been made, and
    (b) that the assets of his estate, including the money in court, do not exceed in value the amount specified in any order in force under section 6 of the Administration of Estates (Small Payments) Act 1965,

may be ordered to be made to the person appearing to have the prior right to a grant of administration of the estate of the deceased, eg a widower, widow, child, father, mother, brother or sister of the deceased.

FOREIGN CURRENCY

9.1 Money may be paid into court in a foreign currency:

(1) where it is a Part 36 payment and the claim is in a foreign currency or
(2) under a court order.

9.2 The court may direct that the money be placed in an interest bearing account in the currency of the claim or any other currency.

9.3 Where a Part 36 payment is made in a foreign currency and has not been accepted within 21 days, the defendant may apply for an order that the money be placed in an interest bearing account.

9.4 The application should be made in accordance with Part 23 and should state:

(1) that the payment has not been accepted in accordance with rule 36.11, and
(2) the type of currency on which interest is to accrue.

COMPENSATION RECOVERY

10.1 Where a defendant makes a Part 36 payment in respect of a claim for a sum or part of a sum:

(1) which falls under the heads of damage set out in column 1 of Schedule 2 of the Social Security (Recovery of Benefits) Act 1997 in respect of recoverable benefits received by the claimant as set out in column 2 of that Schedule, and

(2) where the defendant is liable to pay recoverable benefits to the Secretary of State.

the defendant should obtain from the Secretary of State a certificate of recoverable benefits and file the certificate with the Part 36 payment notice.

10.2 If a defendant wishes to offer to settle a claim where he has applied for but not yet received a certificate of recoverable benefits, he may, provided that he makes a Part 36 payment not more than 7 days after he has received the certificate, make a Part 36 offer which will have the costs and other consequences set out in rules 36.13 and 36.20.

10.3 The Part 36 payment notice should state in addition to the requirements set out in rule 36.6(2):

(1) the total amount represented by the Part 36 payment (the gross compensation),
(2) that the defendant has reduced this sum by £ , in accordance with section 8 of and Schedule 2 to the Social Security (Recovery of Benefits) Act 1997, which was calculated as follows:

Name of benefit Amount

and
(3) that the amount paid in, being the sum of £ is the net amount after the deduction of the amount of benefit.

10.4 On acceptance of a Part 36 payment to which this paragraph relates, a claimant will receive the sum in court which will be net of the recoverable benefits.

10.5 In establishing at trial whether a claimant has bettered or obtained a judgment more advantageous than a Part 36 payment to which this paragraph relates, the court will base its decision on the gross sum specified in the Part 36 payment notice.

GENERAL

11.1 Where a party on whom a Part 36 offer, a Part 36 payment notice or a notice of acceptance is to be served is legally represented, the Part 36 offer, Part 36 payment notice and notice of acceptance must be served on the legal representative.

11.2 In a claim arising out of an accident involving a motor vehicle on a road or in a public place:

(1) where the damages claimed include a sum for hospital expenses, and
(2) the defendant or his insurer pays that sum to the hospital under section 157 of the Road Traffic Act 1988,

the defendant must give notice of that payment to the court and all the other parties to the proceedings.

11.3 Money paid into court:

(1) as a Part 36 payment which is not accepted by the claimant, or
(2) under a court order,

will be placed after 21 days in a basic account[1] (subject to paragraph 11.4 below) for interest to accrue.

1 See rule 26 of the Court Funds Office Rules 1987

11.4 Where money referred to in paragraph 11.3 above is paid in in respect of a child or patient it will be placed in a special investment account[1] for interest to accrue.

(A practice direction supplementing Part 21 contains information about the investment of money in court in respect of a child or patient)

(Practice directions supplementing Part 40 contain information about adjustment of the judgment sum in respect of recoverable benefits, and about structured settlements)

(A practice direction supplementing Part 41 contains information about provisional damages awards)

1 See rule 26 as above.

PERSONAL INJURY CLAIMS FOR FUTURE PECUNIARY LOSS

12.1 A Part 36 offer to settle a claim for damages (whether in the form of a lump sum, periodical payments or both) for personal injury which includes a claim for future pecuniary loss must contain the details of the offer which are set out in rule 36.2A.

12.2 Section 2(4) of the Damages Act 1996 sets out the circumstances in which the continuity of periodical payments will be taken to be secure. Section 2(8) and (9) of the Act deal with the index-linking of periodical payments.

12.3 Except where otherwise stated in this Practice Direction, the rules in Part 36 will apply to offers to settle made under rule 36.2A as they apply to other Part 36 payments and to Part 36 offers.

PART 37
MISCELLANEOUS PROVISIONS ABOUT PAYMENTS INTO COURT

CONTENTS OF THIS PART

Procedural Guide—See Guide 26, set out in Section 1 of this work.

Practice Direction—See generally PD37 at p 939.

37.1 Money paid into court under a court order – general

(1) A party who makes a payment into court under a court order must –

(a) serve notice of the payment on every other party; and
(b) in relation to each such notice, file a certificate of service.

(2) Money paid into court under a court order may not be paid out without the court's permission except where –

(a) the defendant treats the money as a Part 36 payment under rule 37.2; and
(b) the claimant accepts the Part 36 payment without needing the permission of the court.

(Rule 36.11 sets out when the claimant can accept a Part 36 payment without needing the permission of the court)

Amendments—SI 2002/3219.

37.2 Money paid into court may be treated as a Part 36 payment

(1) Where a defendant makes a payment into court following an order made under rule 3.1(3) or 3.1(5) he may choose to treat the whole or any part of the money paid into court as a Part 36 payment.

(Rule 36.2 defines a Part 36 payment)

(2) To do this he must file a Part 36 payment notice.

(Rule 36.6 sets out what a Part 36 payment notice must contain and provides for the court to serve it on the other parties)

(3) If he does so Part 36 applies to the money as if he had paid it into court as a Part 36 payment.

37.3 Money paid into court where defendant wishes to rely on defence of tender before claim

(1) Where a defendant wishes to rely on a defence of tender before claim(GL) he must make a payment into court of the amount he says was tendered.

(2) If the defendant does not make a payment in accordance with paragraph (1) the defence of tender before claim[(GL)] will not be available to him until he does so.

(3) Where the defendant makes such payment into court –

(a) he may choose to treat the whole or any part of the money paid into court as a Part 36 payment; and
(b) if he does so, he must file a Part 36 payment notice.

37.4 Proceedings under Fatal Accidents Act 1976 and Law Reform (Miscellaneous Provisions) Act 1934 – apportionment by court

(1) Where –

(a) a claim includes claims arising under –
  (i) the Fatal Accidents Act 1976; and
  (ii) the Law Reform (Miscellaneous Provisions) Act 1934;
(b) a single sum of money is paid into court in satisfaction of those claims; and
(c) the money is accepted,

the court shall apportion the money between the different claims.

(2) The court shall apportion money under paragraph (1) –

(a) when it gives directions under rule 21.11 (control of money received by a child or patient); or
(b) if rule 21.11 does not apply, when it gives permission for the money to be paid out of court.

(3) Where, in an action in which a claim under the Fatal Accidents Act 1976 is made by or on behalf of more than one person –

(a) a sum in respect of damages is ordered or agreed to be paid in satisfaction of the claim; or
(b) a sum of money is accepted in satisfaction of the claim,

the court shall apportion it between the persons entitled to it unless it has already been apportioned by the court, a jury, or agreement between the parties.

37.5 Payment into court under enactments

A practice direction may set out special provisions with regard to payments into court under various enactments.

Amendments—Inserted by SI 2001/4015.

General note—Note that all payments into court are to the Court Funds Office – see the accompanying practice direction. See PD36 for general practice for payment out of court.

Practice Direction – Miscellaneous Provisions about Payments into Court

This Practice Direction supplements CPR Part 37 (PD37)

For information about payments into and out of court in relation to offers to settle see Part 36 and the practice direction which supplements it.

PAYMENTS INTO COURT UNDER AN ORDER

1.1 Except where paragraph 1.2 applies a party paying money into any court under an order must –

(1) send to the Court Funds Office –
  (a) the payment, usually a cheque made payable to the Accountant General of the Supreme Court;
  (b) a sealed copy of the order; and
  (c) a completed Court Funds Office form 100;
(2) serve notice of payment on the other parties; and
(3) file at the court –
  (a) a copy of the notice of payment; and
  (b) a certificate of service confirming service of the notice on each party scrvcd.

1.2 A litigant in person without a current account may, in a claim proceeding in a county court or District Registry, make a payment into court by –

(1) lodging the payment in cash with the court; and
(2) filing at the court –
  (a) a notice of payment; and
  (b) Court Funds Office form 100.

DEFENCE OF TENDER

2.1 Except where paragraph 2.1A applies, a defendant who wishes to pay a sum of money into court in support of a defence of tender should –

(1) send to the Court Funds Office –
  (a) the payment, usually a cheque made payable to the Accountant General of the Supreme Court;
  (b) a sealed copy of the claim form; and
  (c) a completed Court Funds Office form 100;
(2) file at the court with his defence –
  (a) a notice of payment into court; and
  (b) a certificate of service confirming service of the notice on the claimant and his defence; and
(3) serve a copy of the notice of payment into court on the claimant.

2.1A A litigant in person without a current account may, in a claim proceeding in a county court or District Registry, pay a sum of money into court in support of a defence of tender by –

(1) lodging the payment in cash with the court; and
(2) filing with the court –
  (a) a notice of payment with his defence; and
  (b) Court Funds Office form 100.

2.2 A defence of tender will not be available to a defendant until he has complied with paragraph 2.1.

GENERAL

3.1 Where money is paid into court:

(1) under an order permitting a defendant to defend or to continue to defend under rule 37.2(1), or
(2) in support of a defence of tender under rule 37.3,

the party making the payment may, if a defendant, choose to treat the whole or any part of the money as a Part 36 payment[1].

1 Rules 37.2(2) and 37.3(3).

3.2 In order to do so the defendant must file a Part 36 payment notice in accordance with rule 36.6 (see also paragraph 6 of the practice direction which supplements Part 36).

3.3 Rule 37.4 deals with the apportionment of money paid into court in respect of claims arising under:

(1) the Fatal Accidents Act 1976, and
(2) the Law Reform (Miscellaneous Provisions) Act 1934.

(See also paragraph 7.8 of the practice direction supplementing Part 36)

PAYMENT OUT OF COURT

4.1 Except where money which has been paid into court is treated as a Part 36 payment and can be accepted by the claimant without needing the court's permission, the court's permission is required to take the money out of court.

4.2 Permission may be obtained by making an application in accordance with Part 23. The application notice must state the grounds on which the order for payment out is sought. Evidence of any facts on which the applicant relies may also be necessary.

4.3 To obtain the money out of court the applicant must comply with the provisions of paragraph 8 of the practice direction supplementing Part 36 where they apply.

FOREIGN CURRENCY

5 For information on payments into court made in a foreign currency, see paragraph 9 of the practice direction supplementing Part 36.

APPLICATIONS RELATING TO FUNDS IN COURT

6.1 Subject to paragraph 6.2, any application relating to money or securities which have been paid into court, other than an application for the payment out of the money or securities (for example, an application for money to be invested, or for payment of interest to any person) –

(1) must be made in accordance with Part 23; and
(2) may be made without notice, but the court may direct notice to be served on any person.

6.2 Where money paid into court is accepted by or on behalf of a child or patient, rule 21.11(1)(b) provides that the money shall be dealt with in accordance with directions given by the court under that rule and not otherwise. In relation to such cases, reference should be made to paragraphs 8 to 12 of the practice direction supplementing Part 21.

PAYMENT INTO COURT BY LIFE ASSURANCE COMPANY

7.1 A company wishing to make a payment into court under the Life Assurance Companies (Payment into Court) Act 1896 ('the 1896 Act') must file a witness statement or an affidavit setting out –

(1) a short description of the policy under which money is payable;

(2) a statement of the persons entitled under the policy, including their names and addresses so far as known to the company;

(3) a short statement of –

 (a) the notices received by the company making any claim to the money assured, or withdrawing any such claim;

 (b) the dates of receipt of such notices; and

 (c) the names and addresses of the persons by whom they were given;

(4) a statement that, in the opinion of the board of directors of the company, no sufficient discharge can be obtained for the money which is payable, other than by paying it into court under the 1896 Act;

(5) a statement that the company agrees to comply with any order or direction the court may make –

 (a) to pay any further sum into court; or

 (b) to pay any costs;

(6) an undertaking by the company immediately to send to the Accountant General at the Court Funds Office any notice of claim received by the company after the witness statement or affidavit has been filed, together with a letter referring to the Court Funds Office reference number; and

(7) the company's address for service.

7.2 The witness statement or affidavit must be filed at –

(1) Chancery Chambers at the Royal Courts of Justice, or

(2) a Chancery district registry of the High Court.

7.3 The company must not deduct from the money payable by it under the policy any costs of the payment into court, except for any court fee.

7.4 If the company is a party to any proceedings issued in relation to the policy or the money assured by it, it may not make a payment into court under the 1896 Act without the permission of the court in those proceedings.

7.5 If a company pays money into court under the 1896 Act, unless the court orders otherwise it must immediately serve notice of the payment on every person who is entitled under the policy or has made a claim to the money assured.

APPLICATION FOR PAYMENT OUT OF MONEY PAID INTO COURT BY LIFE ASSURANCE COMPANY

8.1 Any application for the payment out of money which has been paid into court under the 1896 Act must be made in accordance with paragraph 4.2 of this practice direction.

8.2 The application must be served on –

(1) every person stated in the written evidence of the company which made the payment to be entitled to or to have an interest in the money;

(2) any other person who has given notice of a claim to the money; and

(3) the company which made the payment, if an application is being made for costs against it, but not otherwise.

PAYMENT INTO COURT UNDER TRUSTEE ACT 1925

9.1 A trustee wishing to make a payment into court under section 63 of the Trustee Act 1925 must file a witness statement or an affidavit setting out –

(1) a short description of –
  (a) the trust; and
  (b) the instrument creating the trust, or the circumstances in which the trust arose;
(2) the names of the persons interested in or entitled to the money or securities to be paid into court, with their address so far as known to him;
(3) a statement that he agrees to answer any inquiries which the court may make or direct relating to the application of the money or securities; and
(4) his address for service.

9.2 The witness statement or affidavit must be filed at –

(1) Chancery Chambers at the Royal Courts of Justice;
(2) a Chancery district registry of the High Court; or
(3) a county court.

9.3 If a trustee pays money or securities into court, unless the court orders otherwise he must immediately serve notice of the payment into court on every person interested in or entitled to the money or securities.

APPLICATION FOR PAYMENT OUT OF FUNDS PAID INTO COURT BY TRUSTEE

10.1 An application for the payment out of any money or securities paid into court under section 63 of the Trustee Act 1925 must be made in accordance with paragraph 4.2 of this practice direction.

10.2 The application may be made without notice, but the court may direct notice to be served on any person.

PAYMENT INTO COURT UNDER VEHICULAR ACCESS ACROSS COMMON AND OTHER LAND (ENGLAND) REGULATIONS 2002

11.1 In this section of this Practice Direction –

(1) expressions used have the meanings given by the Vehicular Access Across Common and Other Land (England) Regulations 2002; and
(2) a regulation referred to by number alone means the regulation so numbered in those Regulations.

11.2 Where the applicant wishes to pay money into a county court under regulation 14 he must file a witness statement or an affidavit when he lodges the money.

11.3 The witness statement or affidavit must –

(1) state briefly why the applicant is making the payment into court; and
(2) be accompanied by copies of –
  (a) the notice served under regulation 6;
  (b) any counter-notice served under regulation 8;
  (c) any amended notice or counter-notice served under regulation 9;
  (d) any determination of the Lands Tribunal of a matter referred to it under regulation 10; and
  (e) any determination of the value of the premises by a chartered surveyor following the service of a valuation notice under regulation 12.

11.4 If an applicant pays money into court under regulation 14, he must immediately serve notice of the payment and a copy of the witness statement or affidavit on the land owner.

11.5 An application for payment out of the money must be made in accordance with paragraph 4 of this practice direction.

PART 38
DISCONTINUANCE

CONTENTS OF THIS PART

Procedural Guide—See Guide 27, set out in Section 1 of this work.

38.1 Scope of this Part

(1) The rules in this Part set out the procedure by which a claimant may discontinue all or part of a claim.

(2) A claimant who –

(a) claims more than one remedy; and
(b) subsequently abandons his claim to one or more of the remedies but continues with his claim for the other remedies,

is not treated as discontinuing all or part of a claim for the purposes of this Part.

(The procedure for amending a statement of case, set out in Part 17, applies where a claimant abandons a claim for a particular remedy but wishes to continue with his claim for other remedies)

Practice Direction—There is no practice direction to Pt 38 but see PD39, para 4 (discontinuance after trial date is fixed). The parties must ensure that the listing officer for the trial court is notified immediately a claim is discontinued. A copy of any order giving effect to a discontinuance should be filed with the listing officer.

General note—A claimant may discontinue all or part of a claim but merely abandoning one or more of the remedies sought does not amount to a discontinuance. The appropriate procedure in such circumstances is for the statement of case to be amended in accordance with Pt 17.

However, in *Isaac v Isaac* (2005) Lawtel, 7 April, Park J held that where claimants had deleted a claim by amendment to the particulars of claim, the claim was in substance discontinued and r 38.6 applied so that the claimants were liable for the defendant's costs of the discontinued claim down to the date of discontinuance. Note the difference between a remedy and a claim. The abandonment of one or more remedies is not a discontinuance unless all remedies are abandoned.

Where a counterclaim is made in response to a claim and the claim is subsequently discontinued, the counterclaim will survive the discontinuance.

Generally speaking, a claimant who discontinues is liable for the defendant's costs unless the court orders otherwise (r 38.6).

There is no provision for discontinuing a defence. Should a defendant not wish to continue to defend the claim, he should make an admission upon which judgment can be entered.

38.2 Right to discontinue claim

(1) A claimant may discontinue all or part of a claim at any time.

(2) However –

(a) a claimant must obtain the permission of the court if he wishes to discontinue all or part of a claim in relation to which –
   (i) the court has granted an interim injunction[(GL)]; or
   (ii) any party has given an undertaking to the court;

(b) where the claimant has received an interim payment in relation to a claim (whether voluntarily or pursuant to an order under Part 25), he may discontinue that claim only if –
   (i) the defendant who made the interim payment consents in writing; or
   (ii) the court gives permission;

(c) where there is more than one claimant, a claimant may not discontinue unless –
   (i) every other claimant consents in writing; or
   (ii) the court gives permission.

(3) Where there is more than one defendant, the claimant may discontinue all or part of a claim against all or any of the defendants.

Scope of provision—Generally, a claimant need not obtain the permission of the court to discontinue except in the special situations provided in r 38.2(2).

Where there is more than one claimant, a claimant cannot discontinue unless every other claimant consents in writing or the court gives permission. However, where there is more than one defendant, a claimant may discontinue all or part of a claim against all or any of the defendants.

An application for permission to discontinue must be made in accordance with Pt 23.

38.3 Procedure for discontinuing

(1) To discontinue a claim or part of a claim, a claimant must –

(a) file a notice of discontinuance; and
(b) serve a copy of it on every other party to the proceedings.

(2) The claimant must state in the notice of discontinuance which he files that he has served notice of discontinuance on every other party to the proceedings.

(3) Where the claimant needs the consent of some other party, a copy of the necessary consent must be attached to the notice of discontinuance.

(4) Where there is more than one defendant, the notice of discontinuance must specify against which defendants the claim is discontinued.

Scope of provision—The discontinuance takes effect upon service of the notice on the other parties to the proceedings (r 38.5).

The claimant must file the notice of discontinuance with the court. The form of notice is N279 in which the claimant certifies he has served a copy of the notice on every other party to the proceedings.

A notice of discontinuance becomes effective on the day that it is served (*Jarvis plc v PriceWaterhouse Coopers* (2000) *The Times*, 10 October, ChD). See also PD39, para 4.1 which provides that the listing officer is to be informed immediately if a claim is discontinued after a trial date or 'window' has been fixed.

If there is more than one claimant the consent of all other claimants must be attached to the notice. If there is more than one defendant, the notice must specify against which defendants the claim is discontinued.

38.4 Right to apply to have notice of discontinuance set aside

(1) Where the claimant discontinues under rule 38.2(1) the defendant may apply to have the notice of discontinuance set aside[(GL)].

(2) The defendant may not make an application under this rule more than 28 days after the date when the notice of discontinuance was served on him.

Scope of provision—This rule allows a defendant 28 days from service of the notice of discontinuance to make application to set aside. He may wish to do so in circumstances where:

(a) he wishes the court to impose conditions on the discontinuance, eg no new proceedings to be brought until the costs of the discontinued proceedings has been determined;
(b) despite discontinuance, the claimant has the intention of commencing proceedings in another jurisdiction;
(c) an abuse of process of the court is alleged.

38.5 When discontinuance takes effect where permission of the court is not needed

(1) Discontinuance against any defendant takes effect on the date when notice of discontinuance is served on him under rule 38.3(1).

(2) Subject to rule 38.4, the proceedings are brought to an end as against him on that date.

(3) However, this does not affect proceedings to deal with any question of costs.

38.6 Liability for costs

(1) Unless the court orders otherwise, a claimant who discontinues is liable for the costs which a defendant against whom he discontinues incurred on or before the date on which notice of discontinuance was served on him.

(2) If proceedings are only partly discontinued –

(a) the claimant is liable under paragraph (1) for costs relating only to the part of the proceedings which he is discontinuing; and
(b) unless the court orders otherwise, the costs which the claimant is liable to pay must not be assessed until the conclusion of the rest of the proceedings.

(3) This rule does not apply to claims allocated to the small claims track.

(Rule 44.12 provides for the basis of assessment where right to costs arises on discontinuance)

Scope of provision—Under r 44.12(1)(d), a defendant's right to costs arises where a claimant discontinues. Costs will be assessed on the standard basis and there will need to be a detailed assessment of the defendant's costs in these circumstances (r 44.7).

A party wishing to avoid the automatic costs consequences may apply under r 38.6(1). Thus, a defendant may apply, on grounds relating to the claimant's conduct, for an order that the costs be assessed on the indemnity basis (see, for an example, *Atlantic Bar & Grill Ltd v Posthouse Hotels Ltd* [2000] CP Rep 32, ChD). A claimant may wish to apply where, having obtained an injunction, he does not wish to pursue a claim for damages. Where an application is made, the burden is on the party making the application.

To show that it is fair to depart from the general rule, it will often be necessary to demonstrate some change in circumstances since the issue of the claim. The fact that the claimant has become alive at a late stage to the commercial effect of factors which were clear at the outset and if properly evaluated could have led to a decision that the proceedings were not worth pursuing is not a good reason (*Walker v Walker* [2005] EWCA Civ 247).

A claimant's liability to pay the defendant's costs pursuant to the rule may be reduced to reflect the defendant's failure to comply with the relevant pre-action protocol (*Aegis Group plc v Inland Revenue* 2005] Lawtel, 13 May).

Where a claimant discontinued a claim because of the fourth defendant's supervening bankruptcy, permission was given to discontinue the claim without liability for costs (*Everton (Clive) v WPBSA (Promotions) Limited & ors* (2001) Lawtel, 18 December, Gray J).

'unless the court orders otherwise' (r 38.6(2)(b))—The court retains its discretion as to costs and may wish to leave all issues relating to costs until the conclusion of the proceedings when it may decide not to make a costs order in accordance with the general rule but in exercise of its discretion under r 44.3(6). See *Ansol Limited v Taylor Joynson Garrett (a firm) & ors* [2002] EWHC 100,

2002] All ER (D) 44, where it was contended by the claimant that the defendants should pay the costs of an interim injunction obtained by the claimant on the ground that the application was necessary to protect the legitimate interests of the claimant. Here, Morritt VC held the appropriate course was to make no order for costs. Nevertheless, the court may order costs on account under r 44.3(8) (see also *PT Bank Negara Indonesia v IBL Trading Ltd* (2002) Lawtel, 13 December).

Generally, for claims allocated to the small claims track, a 'no costs' regime applies. There may be recoverable costs prior to allocation. Discontinuance may also have a bearing on whether a party has behaved unreasonably and should therefore be liable to pay costs in accordance with r 27.14(2)(d).

38.7 Discontinuance and subsequent proceedings

A claimant who discontinues a claim needs the permission of the court to make another claim against the same defendant if –

(a) he discontinued the claim after the defendant filed a defence; and
(b) the other claim arises out of facts which are the same or substantially the same as those relating to the discontinued claim.

Scope of provision—The duty is now on the claimant to seek permission before making another claim against the same defendant arising out of the same facts. Permission to commence fresh proceedings will not be easily given as any new claim could be struck out as an abuse of process. Examples of where the court may give permission are where new evidence has come to light, the claimant was misled by the defendant or where there has been a change in the law.

If permission is granted, the court is likely to attach conditions such as the payment of the costs of the discontinued proceedings or a Pt 36 payment into court.

If the claimant discontinues the first claim before the defendant files a defence, permission to commence another claim is not required.

38.8 Stay of remainder of partly discontinued proceedings where costs not paid

(1) This rule applies where –
(a) proceedings are partly discontinued;
(b) a claimant is liable to pay costs under rule 38.6; and
(c) the claimant fails to pay those costs within 14 days of –
(i) the date on which the parties agreed the sum payable by the claimant; or
(ii) the date on which the court ordered the costs to be paid.

(2) Where this rule applies, the court may stay(GL) the remainder of the proceedings until the claimant pays the whole of the costs which he is liable to pay under rule 38.6

Amendments—SI 2000/1317.

Scope of provision—It is unlikely that the court will order assessment of the costs until the conclusion of the proceedings (r 38.6(2)(b)). Nevertheless, the court may have ordered costs on account (r 44.3(8)) which remain unpaid.

The stay in r 38.8(2) is discretionary and will require an application to the court under Pt 23. See *Stevens v School of Oriental and African Studies & ors* (2001) TLR, 2 February, ChD where it was held a reasonable exercise of the court's power to stay the second proceedings commenced by the claimant until an order for costs in the first proceedings had been satisfied. The court held this did not infringe the right of a litigant to a fair trial pursuant to HRA 1998, Sch 1, Pt I, Art 6.

PART 39
MISCELLANEOUS PROVISIONS RELATING TO HEARINGS

CONTENTS OF THIS PART

Practice Direction—See generally PD39 at p 952, PD39B at p 957.

Putting a party to his election—The Court of Appeal has had to deal with this old chestnut on a surprising number of occasions since 1999. It is no longer necessary to look elsewhere than *Benham Ltd v Kythira Investments Ltd* [2003] EWCA Civ 1794, where the authorities are reviewed. Rarely, if ever, should the judge entertain a submission of no case to answer. If he does, he should then determine, not on the balance of probabilities, but on whether the claim has a reasonable prospect of success. A material consideration may well be that if the submission fails, the defendant may choose to call no evidence, entitling the court to draw adverse inferences which strengthen the claimant's case. In all but exceptional cases the judge should not express a view about the evidence until the evidence is complete and must then decide the case on the evidence, on the balance of probabilities. In other words, he should put the Defendant to his election whether or not to call evidence and decline to entertain the submission if the defendant elects to call it.

39.1 Interpretation

In this Part, reference to a hearing includes a reference to the trial.

39.2 General rule – hearing to be in public

(1) The general rule is that a hearing is to be in public.

(2) The requirement for a hearing to be in public does not require the court to make special arrangements for accommodating members of the public.

(3) A hearing , or any part of it, may be in private if –

- (a) publicity would defeat the object of the hearing;
- (b) it involves matters relating to national security;
- (c) it involves confidential information (including information relating to personal financial matters) and publicity would damage that confidentiality;
- (d) a private hearing is necessary to protect the interests of any child or patient;
- (e) it is a hearing of an application made without notice and it would be unjust to any respondent for there to be a public hearing;
- (f) it involves uncontentious matters arising in the administration of trusts or in the administration of a deceased person's estate; or
- (g) the court considers this to be necessary, in the interests of justice.

(4) The court may order that the identity of any party or witness must not be disclosed if it considers non-disclosure necessary in order to protect the interests of that party or witness.

Practice Direction—See PD39 at p 952 for a more detailed account of the contrast between public and private hearings.

'non-disclosure' (r 39.2(4))—This may provide an alternative to the protection offered by Contempt of Court Act 1981, s 11.

39.3 Failure to attend the trial

(1) The court may proceed with a trial in the absence of a party, but –

- (a) if no party attends the trial, it may strike out(GL) the whole of the proceedings;
- (b) if the claimant does not attend, it may strike out his claim and any defence to counterclaim; and
- (c) if a defendant does not attend, it may strike out his defence or counterclaim (or both).

(2) Where the court strikes out proceedings, or any part of them, under this rule, it may subsequently restore the proceedings, or that part.

(3) Where a party does not attend and the court gives judgment or makes an order against him, the party who failed to attend may apply for the judgment or order to be set aside(GL).

(4) An application under paragraph (2) or paragraph (3) must be supported by evidence.

(5) Where an application is made under paragraph (2) or (3) by a party who failed to attend the trial, the court may grant the application only if the applicant –

- (a) acted promptly when he found out that the court had exercised its power to strike out(GL) or to enter judgment or make an order against him;
- (b) had a good reason for not attending the trial; and
- (c) has a reasonable prospect of success at the trial.

Amendments—SI 2000/2092.

'the court may grant the application only' (r 39.3(5))—The court has no residual discretion. The three criteria have to be met (*Barclays Bank plc v Ellis* (2000) *The Times*, 24 October, CA). The question is whether the applicant has acted with reasonable celerity in the circumstances (*Regency Rolls Ltd & anor v Carnall* (2000) Lawtel, 16 October, CA). A modest claim is as entitled to be reinstated under this rule as a substantial one. If the conditions are met, the whole case should, except in special circumstances, be restored. Part 39 does not allow for selective restoration (*Thakerar v Northwick Park & St Mark's Trust & anor* [2002] EWCA Civ 617). If a defendant knows of the proceedings against him, then he is not entitled to have an order made in his absence set aside as of right simply because he has not been notified of a new hearing date (*Hackney London Borough Council v Driscoll* [2003] EWCA Civ 1037, [2003] 1 WLR 2602, CA). A merits test under r 39.3(5) is appropriate. In *National Westminster Bank v Aaronson* [2004] EWHC 618 (QB), [2004] All ER (D) 178 (Mar) Royce J refused to set aside a judgment in the absence of the defendant where he knew of the date of trial and had failed to obtain an adjournment.

39.4 Timetable for trial

When the court sets a timetable for a trial in accordance with rule 28.6 (fixing or confirming the trial date and giving directions – fast track) or rule 29.8 (setting a trial timetable and fixing or confirming the trial date or week – multi-track) it will do so in consultation with the parties.

39.5 Trial bundles

(1) Unless the court orders otherwise, the claimant must file a trial bundle containing documents required by –

(a) a relevant practice direction; and
(b) any court order.

(2) The claimant must file the trial bundle not more than 7 days and not less than 3 days before the start of the trial.

'must file a trial bundle' (r 39.5(1))—It cannot be emphasised too strongly that a bundle *must* be lodged under this rule whether or not a specific order has been made to that effect. PD39, para 3 explains exactly what is to be done and how. There can be no excuse for non-compliance, for which appropriate sanctions may be expected.

39.6 Representation at trial of companies or other corporations

A company or other corporation may be represented at trial by an employee if –

(a) the employee has been authorised by the company or corporation to appear at trial on its behalf; and
(b) the court gives permission.

'may be represented' (r 39.6)—This rule enables a company to authorise an *employee* to represent it. This should be taken to include authorised *directors* who are not in the strict sense *employees*. In either case, the court will, before deciding whether to give permission, take into account the difficulty of the case and the individual's experience and position in the company and familiarity with the case. (PD39, para 5.3). Moreover, the individual will generally be expected to produce independent evidence of his authority to appear on the company's behalf. *Avinue Ltd v Sunrule Ltd* [2003] EWCA Civ 1942, [2004] 1 WLR 634, CA established that in small claims hearings companies are entitled to appear by lay representatives whether or not duly authorised officers or employees.

39.7 Impounded documents

(1) Documents impounded by order of the court must not be released from the custody of the court except in compliance –

(a) with a court order; or
(b) with a written request made by a Law Officer or the Director of Public Prosecutions.

(2) A document released from the custody of the court under paragraph (1)(b) must be released into the custody of the person who requested it.

(3) Documents impounded by order of the court, while in the custody of the court, may not be inspected except by a person authorised to do so by a court order.

39.8 Claims under the Race Relations Act 1976

In a claim brought under section 57.1 of the Race Relations Act 1976, the court may, where it considers it expedient in the interests of national security –

(a) exclude from all or part of the proceedings –
  (i) the claimant;
  (ii) the claimant's representatives; or
  (iii) any assessors appointed under section 67(4) of that Act;

(b) permit a claimant or representative to make a statement to the court before the start of the proceedings (or part of the proceedings) from which he is to be excluded; or
(c) take steps to keep secret all or part of the reasons for its decision in the claim.

(Section 67A(2) of the Race Relations Act 1976 provides that the Attorney General may appoint a person to represent the interests of a claimant in any proceedings from which he and his representatives are excluded)

Amendments—Inserted by SI 2001/1388.

Practice Direction – Miscellaneous Provisions Relating to Hearings

This Practice Direction supplements CPR Part 39 (PD39)

General note—See also the notes to CPR Pt 39 for relevant commentary.

HEARINGS

1.1 In Part 39, reference to a hearing includes reference to the trial[1].

1 Rule 39.1.

1.2 The general rule is that a hearing is to be in public[1].

1 Rule 39.2(1).

1.3 Rule 39.2(3) sets out the type of proceedings which may be dealt with in private.

1.4 The decision as to whether to hold a hearing in public or in private must be made by the judge conducting the hearing having regard to any representations which may have been made to him.

1.4A The judge should also have regard to Article 6(1) of the European Convention on Human Rights. This requires that, in general, court hearings are to be held in public, but the press and public may be excluded in the circumstances specified in that Article. Article 6(1) will usually be relevant, for example, where a party applies for a hearing which would normally be held in public to be held in private as well as where a hearing would normally be held in private. The judge may need to consider whether the case is within any of the exceptions permitted by Article 6(1).

1.5 The hearings set out below shall in the first instance be listed by the court as hearings in private under rule 39.2(3)(c), namely:

(1) a claim by a mortgagee against one or more individuals for an order for possession of land,
(2) a claim by a landlord against one or more tenants or former tenants for the repossession of a dwelling house based on the non-payment of rent,
(3) an application to suspend a warrant of execution or a warrant of possession or to stay execution where the court is being invited to consider the ability of a party to make payments to another party,
(4) a redetermination under rule 14.13 or an application to vary or suspend the payment of a judgment debt by instalments,
(5) an application for a charging order (including an application to enforce

a charging order), third party debt order, attachment of earnings order, administration order, or the appointment of a receiver,

(6) an order to attend court for questioning,

(7) the determination of the liability of an LSC funded client under regulations 9 and 10 of the Community Legal Service (Costs) Regulations 2000, or of an assisted person's liability for costs under regulation 127 of the Civil Legal Aid (General) Regulations 1989,

(8) an application for security for costs under section 726(1) of the Companies Act 1985, and

(9) proceedings brought under the Consumer Credit Act 1974, the Inheritance (Provision for Family and Dependants) Act 1975 or the Protection from Harassment Act 1997,

(10) an application by a trustee or personal representative for directions as to bringing or defending legal proceedings.

1.6 Rule 39.2(3)(d) states that a hearing may be in private where it involves the interests of a child or patient. This includes the approval of a compromise or settlement on behalf of a child or patient or an application for the payment of money out of court to such a person.

1.7 Attention is drawn to paragraph 5.1 of the practice direction which supplements Part 27 (relating to the hearing of claims in the small claims track), which provides that the judge may decide to hold a small claim hearing in private if the parties agree or if a ground mentioned in rule 39.2(3) applies. A hearing of a small claim in premises other than the court will not be a hearing in public.

1.8 Nothing in this practice direction prevents a judge ordering that a hearing taking place in public shall continue in private, or vice-versa.

1.9 If the court or judge's room in which the proceedings are taking place has a sign on the door indicating that the proceedings are private, members of the public who are not parties to the proceedings will not be admitted unless the court permits.

1.10 Where there is no such sign on the door of the court or judge's room, members of the public will be admitted where practicable. The judge may, if he thinks it appropriate, adjourn the proceedings to a larger room or court.

1.11 When a hearing takes place in public, members of the public may obtain a transcript of any judgment given or a copy of any order made, subject to payment of the appropriate fee.

1.12 When a judgment is given or an order is made in private, if any member of the public who is not a party to the proceedings seeks a transcript of the judgment or a copy of the order, he must seek the leave of the judge who gave the judgment or made the order.

1.13 A judgment or order given or made in private, when drawn up, must have clearly marked in the title:

'Before [*title and name of judge*] sitting in Private'

1.14 References to hearings being in public or private or in a judge's room contained in the Civil Procedure Rules (including the Rules of the Supreme Court and the County Court Rules scheduled to Part 50) and the practice directions which supplement them do not restrict any existing rights of audience or confer any new rights of audience in respect of applications or proceedings which under the rules previously in force would have been heard in court or in chambers respectively.

1.15 Where a court lists a hearing of a claim by a mortgagee for an order for possession of land under paragraph 1.5(1) above to be in private, any fact which needs to be proved by the evidence of witnesses may be proved by evidence in writing.

(CPR rule 32.2 sets out the general rule as to how evidence is to be given and facts are to be proved)

'in public' (para 1.2)—See *Storer v British Gas plc* [2000] 2 All ER 440, CA for an important discussion of the principles by Henry LJ.

FAILURE TO ATTEND THE TRIAL

2.1 Rule 39.3 sets out the consequences of a party's failure to attend the trial.

2.2 The court may proceed with a trial in the absence of a party[1]. In the absence of:

- (1) the defendant, the claimant may –
  - (a) prove his claim at trial and obtain judgment on his claim and for costs, and
  - (b) seek the striking out of any counterclaim,
- (2) the claimant, the defendant may –
  - (a) prove any counterclaim at trial and obtain judgment on his counterclaim and for costs, and
  - (b) seek the striking out of the claim, or
- (3) both parties, the court may strike out the whole of the proceedings.

1 Rule 39.3(1).

2.3 Where the court has struck out proceedings, or any part of them, on the failure of a party to attend, that party may apply in accordance with Part 23 for the proceedings, or that part of them, to be restored and for any judgment given against that party to be set aside[1].

1 Rule 39.3(2) and (3).

2.4 The application referred to in paragraph 2.3 above must be supported by evidence giving reasons for the failure to attend court and stating when the applicant found out about the order against him.

BUNDLES OF DOCUMENTS FOR HEARINGS OR TRIAL

3.1 Unless the court orders otherwise, the claimant must file the trial bundle not more than 7 days and not less than 3 days before the start of the trial.

3.2 Unless the court orders otherwise, the trial bundle should include a copy of:

- (1) the claim form and all statements of case,
- (2) a case summary and/or chronology where appropriate,
- (3) requests for further information and responses to the requests,
- (4) all witness statements to be relied on as evidence,
- (5) any witness summaries,
- (6) any notices of intention to rely on hearsay evidence under rule 32.2,
- (7) any notices of intention to rely on evidence (such as a plan, photograph etc) under rule 33.6 which is not –
  - (a) contained in a witness statement, affidavit or experts report,

(b) being given orally at trial,
(c) hearsay evidence under rule 33.2,

(8) any medical reports and responses to them,
(9) any experts' reports and responses to them,
(10) any order giving directions as to the conduct of the trial, and
(11) any other necessary documents.

3.3 The originals of the documents contained in the trial bundle, together with copies of any other court orders should be available at the trial.

3.4 The preparation and production of the trial bundle, even where it is delegated to another person, is the responsibility of the legal representative[1] who has conduct of the claim on behalf of the claimant.

1 For the definition of legal representative see rule 2.3.

3.5 The trial bundle should be paginated (continuously) throughout, and indexed with a description of each document and the page number. Where the total number of pages is more than 100, numbered dividers should be placed at intervals between groups of documents.

3.6 The bundle should normally be contained in a ring binder or lever arch file. Where more than one bundle is supplied, they should be clearly distinguishable, for example, by different colours or letters. If there are numerous bundles, a core bundle should be prepared containing the core documents essential to the proceedings, with references to the supplementary documents in the other bundles.

3.7 For convenience, experts' reports may be contained in a separate bundle and cross referenced in the main bundle.

3.8 If a document to be included in the trial bundle is illegible, a typed copy should be included in the bundle next to it, suitably cross-referenced.

3.9 The contents of the trial bundle should be agreed where possible. The parties should also agree where possible:

(1) that the documents contained in the bundle are authentic even if not disclosed under Part 31, and
(2) that documents in the bundle may be treated as evidence of the facts stated in them even if a notice under the Civil Evidence Act 1995 has not been served.

Where it is not possible to agree the contents of the bundle, a summary of the points on which the parties are unable to agree should be included.

3.10 The party filing the trial bundle should supply identical bundles to all the parties to the proceedings and for the use of the witnesses.

SETTLEMENT OR DISCONTINUANCE AFTER THE TRIAL DATE IS FIXED

4.1 Where:

(1) an offer to settle a claim is accepted,
(2) or a settlement is reached, or
(3) a claim is discontinued,

which disposes of the whole of a claim for which a date or 'window' has been fixed for the trial, the parties must ensure that the listing officer for the trial court is notified immediately.

4.2 If an order is drawn up giving effect to the settlement or discontinuance, a copy of the sealed order should be filed with the listing officer.

REPRESENTATION AT HEARINGS

5.1 At any hearing, a written statement containing the following information should be provided for the court:

(1) the name and address of each advocate,
(2) his qualification or entitlement to act as an advocate, and
(3) the party for whom he so acts.

5.2 Where a party is a company or other corporation and is to be represented at a hearing by an employee the written statement should contain the following additional information:

(1) The full name of the company or corporation as stated in its certificate of registration.
(2) The registered number of the company or corporation.
(3) The position or office in the company or corporation held by the representative.
(4) The date on which and manner in which the representative was authorised to act for the company or corporation, eg ________19_____: written authority from managing director; or _______ 19_____: Board resolution dated _______19_____.

5.3 Rule 39.6 is intended to enable a company or other corporation to represent itself as a litigant in person. Permission under rule 39.6(b) should therefore be given by the court unless there is some particular and sufficient reason why it should be withheld. In considering whether to grant permission the matters to be taken into account include the complexity of the issues and the experience and position in the company or corporation of the proposed representative.

5.4 Permission under rule 39.6(b) should be obtained in advance of the hearing from, preferably, the judge who is to hear the case, but may, if it is for any reason impracticable or inconvenient to do so, be obtained from any judge by whom the case could be heard.

5.5 The permission may be obtained informally and without notice to the other parties. The judge who gives the permission should record in writing that he has done so and supply a copy to the company or corporation in question and to any other party who asks for one.

5.6 Permission should not normally be granted under Rule 39.6:

(a) in jury trials;
(b) in contempt proceedings.

RECORDING OF PROCEEDINGS

6.1 At any hearing, whether in the High Court or a county court, the proceedings will be tape recorded unless the judge directs otherwise.]

6.2 No party or member of the public may use unofficial recording equipment in any court or judge's room without the permission of the court. To do so without permission constitutes a contempt of court[1].

1 Section 9 of the Contempt of Court Act 1981.

6.3 Any party or person may require a transcript or transcripts of the recording of any hearing to be supplied to him, upon payment of the charges authorised by any scheme in force for the making of the recording or the transcript.

6.4 Where the person requiring the transcript or transcripts is not a party to the proceedings and the hearing or any part of it was held in private under CPR rule 39.2, paragraph 6.3 does not apply unless the court so orders.

6.5 Attention is drawn to paragraph 7.9 of the Court of Appeal (Civil Division) Practice Direction which deals with the provision of transcripts for use in the Court of Appeal at public expense.

EXHIBITS AT TRIAL

7 Exhibits which are handed in and proved during the course of the trial should be recorded on an exhibit list and kept in the custody of the court until the conclusion of the trial, unless the judge directs otherwise. At the conclusion of the trial it is the parties' responsibility to obtain the return of those exhibits which they handed in and to preserve them for the period in which any appeal may take place.

CITATION OF AUTHORITIES

Human Rights

8.1 If it is necessary for a party to give evidence at a hearing of an authority referred to in section 2 of the Human Rights Act 1998 –

(1) the authority to be cited should be an authoritative and complete report; and

(2) the party must give to the court and any other party a list of the authorities he intends to cite and copies of the reports not less than three days before the hearing.

(Section 2(1) of the Human Rights Act 1998 requires the court to take into account the authorities listed there)

(3) Copies of the complete original texts issued by the European Court and Commission either paper based or from the Court's judgment database (HUDOC), which is available on the Internet, may be used.

Practice Direction – Court Sittings

This Practice Direction supplements CPR Part 39 (PD39B)

General note—See also the notes to CPR Pt 39 for relevant commentary.

COURT SITTINGS

1.1 (1) The sittings of the Court of Appeal and of the High Court shall be four in every year, that is to say

(a) the Michaelmas sittings which shall begin on 1 October and end on 21 December;

(b) the Hilary sittings which shall begin on 11 January and end on the Wednesday before Easter Sunday;

(c) the Easter sittings which shall begin on the second Tuesday after Easter Sunday and end on the Friday before the spring holiday; and

(d) the Trinity sittings which shall begin on the second Tuesday after the spring holiday and end on 31 July.

(2) In the above paragraph 'spring holiday' means the bank holiday falling on the last Monday in May or any day appointed instead of that day under section 1(2) of the Banking and Financial Dealings Act 1971.

VACATIONS

The High Court

2.1 (1) One or more judges of each Division of the High Court shall sit in vacation on such days as the senior judge of that Division may from time to time direct, to hear such cases, claims, matters or applications as require to be immediately or promptly heard and to hear other cases, claims, matters or applications if the senior judge of that Division determines that sittings are necessary for that purpose.

(2) Any party to a claim or matter may at any time apply to the court for an order that such claim or matter be heard in vacation and, if the court is satisfied that the claim or matter requires to be immediately or promptly heard, it may make an order accordingly and fix a date for the hearing.

(3) Any judge of the High Court may hear such other cases, claims, matters or applications in vacation as the court may direct.

2.2 The directions in paragraph 3.1 shall not apply in relation to the trial or hearing of cases, claims, matters or applications outside the Royal Courts of Justice.

2.3 (1) Subject to the discretion of the judge, any appeal and any application normally made to a judge may be made in the month of September.

(2) In the month of August, save with the permission of a judge or under arrangements for vacation sittings in courts outside the Royal Courts of Justice, appeals to a judge will be limited to the matters set out in paragraph 3.5 below, and only applications of real urgency will be dealt with, for example urgent applications in respect of injunctions or for possession under RSC Order 113 (Schedule 1 to the CPR).

(3) It is desirable, where this is practical, that applications or appeals are submitted to a master, district judge or judge prior to the hearing of the application or appeal so that they can be marked 'fit for August' or 'fit for vacation.' If they are so marked, then normally the judge will be prepared to hear the application or appeal in August, if marked 'fit for August' or in September if marked 'fit for vacation'. A request to have the papers so marked should normally be made in writing, shortly setting out the nature of the application or appeal and the reasons why it should be dealt with in August or in September, as the case may be.

Chancery Masters

2.4 There is no distinction between term time and vacation so far as business before the Chancery masters is concerned. The masters will deal with all types of business throughout the year, and when a master is on holiday his list will normally be taken by a deputy master.

Queen's Bench Masters

2.5 (1) An application notice may, without permission, be issued returnable before a master in the month of August for any of the following purposes:

to set aside a claim form or particulars of claim, or service of a claim form or particulars of claim;
to set aside judgment; for stay of execution;
for any order by consent;
for judgment or permission to enter judgment;
for approval of settlements or for interim payment;
for relief from forfeiture; for charging order; for garnishee order;
for appointment or discharge of a receiver;
for relief by way of interpleader by a sheriff or High Court enforcement officer;
for transfer to a county court or for trial by master;
for time where time is running in the month of August;

(2) In any case of urgency any other type of application notice (that is other than those for the purposes in (1) above), may, with the permission of a master be issued returnable before a master during the month of August.

Practice Direction – Claims Under the Race Relations Act 1976 (National Security)

This Practice Direction supplements CPR Part 39.8 (PD39C)

1.1 Where a claimant and his representatives have been excluded from all or part of the proceedings under rule 39.8(1)(a), the court will inform the Attorney General of the proceedings.

1.2 The Attorney General may appoint a person (a 'special advocate') under section 67A(2) of the Race Relations Act 1976 to represent the claimant in respect of those parts of the proceedings from which he and his representative have been excluded.

1.3 In exercise of its powers under rule 39.8(c) the court may order the special advocate not to communicate (directly or indirectly) with any persons (including the excluded claimant) –

(1) on any matter discussed or referred to, or
(2) with regard to any material disclosed,

during or with reference to any part of the proceedings from which the claimant and his representative are excluded.

1.4 Where the court makes an order referred to in paragraph 1.3 (or any similar order), the special advocate may apply to the court for directions enabling him to seek instructions from, or otherwise to communicate with an excluded person.

PART 40
JUDGMENTS, ORDERS, SALE OF LAND ETC

CONTENTS OF THIS PART

Amendments—SI 2000/221.

Practice Direction—See generally PD40 at p 968, PD40B at p 972 and PD40D at p 978.

I Judgments and Orders

40.1 Scope of this section

This Section sets out rules about judgments and orders which apply except where any other of these Rules or a practice direction makes a different provision in relation to the judgment or order in question.

Amendments—SI 2000/221; SI 2004/3419.

General note—This Part and its corresponding practice direction is mainly mechanical and standardises the practice of the High Court and county courts in drawing up and serving judgments and orders.

Rates of statutory interest in commercial cases—The CPR give no real guidance as to rates of interest. Previously in commercial cases a rate of 1% over base rate has commonly been used unless for some reason that would be unfair to one party or the other. There is no reason why that measure should not continue to be used, or be used in the county court dealing with a commercial dispute such as a claim under an insurance policy (*Adcock v Co-operative Insurance Society Ltd* [2000] EWCA Civ 117, [2000] All ER (D) 505, [2000] Lloyd's Rep IR 657, *The Times*, 26 April, CA).

40.2 Standard requirements

(1) Every judgment or order must state the name and judicial title of the person who made it, unless it is –

(a) default judgment entered under rule 12.4(1) (entry of default judgment where judgment is entered by a court officer) or a default costs certificate obtained under rule 47.11;
(b) judgment entered under rule 14.4, 14.5, 14.6, 14.7 and 14.9 (entry of judgment on admission where judgment is entered by a court officer);
(c) a consent order under rule 40.6(2) (consent orders made by court officers).
(d) an order made by a court officer under rule 70.5 (orders to enforce awards as if payable under a court order); or
(e) an order made by a court officer under rule 71.2 (orders to obtain information from judgment debtors).

(2) Every judgment or order must –

(a) bear the date on which it is given or made; and
(b) be sealed(GL) by the court.

Amendments—SI 2001/2792.

'the name and judicial title of the person who made it' (r 40.2(1))—It is necessary in dealing with appeals and applications to review or set aside orders to identify the judge of first instance. Judges frequently deal with lists back-to-back and it is advisable to check who the adjudicator was before drawing up an order or judgment. Draft judgments should leave space for the judge's name and title to be inserted (see PD40B, para 3.3(2)).

A judge has jurisdiction to re-consider his decision before an order is drawn up. In *Charlesworth (Willis Arnold) (Claimant) v Relay Roads Ltd (In Liquidation) & ors (No 2)* [1999] 4 All ER 397, Neuberger J stated:

> 'the following principles applied where a party was seeking to call fresh evidence on a new point after judgment had been given but before the order had been drawn up:
> (i) the court had jurisdiction to grant an application to amend the pleadings to raise new points and/or to call fresh evidence and/or to hear fresh argument;
> (ii) the court must clearly exercise its discretion in relation to such an application in a way best designed to achieve justice; and
> (iii) the general rules relating to amendment applied.'

However, it was not appropriate to ask the court to reconsider its decision in an interlocutory matter without strong reasons for doing so, where the parties had acted irrevocably on the basis of the judgment (*Blenheim Leisure (Restaurants) Ltd (No 3), In re* (1999) Lawtel, 28 October, ChD, Neuberger J, declining to follow his earlier decision above). And see note **'a power to vary or revoke'** under r 3.1(7).

40.3 Drawing up and filing of judgments and orders

(1) Except as is provided at paragraph (4) below or by any Practice Direction, every judgment or order will be drawn up by the court unless –

(a) the court orders a party to draw it up;
(b) a party, with the permission of the court, agrees to draw it up;
(c) the court dispenses with the need to draw it up; or
(d) it is a consent order under rule 40.6.

(2) The court may direct that –

(a) a judgment or an order drawn up by a party must be checked by the court before it is sealed(GL); or
(b) before a judgment or an order is drawn up by the court, the parties must file an agreed statement of its terms.

(3) Where a judgment or an order is to be drawn up by a party –

(a) he must file it no later than 7 days after the date on which the court ordered or permitted him to draw it up so that it can be sealed(GL) by the court; and

(b) if he fails to file it within that period, any other party may draw it up and file it.

(4) Except for orders made by the court of its own initiative and unless the court otherwise orders, every judgment or order made in claims proceeding in the Queen's Bench Division at the Royal Courts of Justice, other than in the Administrative Court, will be drawn up by the parties, and rule 40.3 is modified accordingly.

Amendments—SI 2005/2292.

Practice forms for judgment—There is no specific requirement in the final version of this rule that judgments or orders must follow a practice form but PD4 includes mandatory forms of judgments and orders. Note, too, the examples of forms of trial judgment, penal notice and orders requiring an act to be done in PD40B, paras 14.1, 9.1 and 8.

'must file it no later than 7 days' (r 40.3(3)(a))—As this time limit exceeds 5 days, it *includes* weekends and public holidays (r 2.8). It is particularly important to ensure that urgent orders are drawn up and served immediately to ensure that the time limit imposed in the order does not elapse.

40.4 Service of judgments and orders

(1) Where a judgment or an order has been drawn up by a party and is to be served by the court –

(a) the party who drew it up must file a copy to be retained at court and sufficient copies for service on him and on the other parties; and

(b) once it has been sealed(GL), the court must serve a copy of it on each party to the proceedings.

(2) Unless the court directs otherwise, any order made otherwise than at trial must be served on –

(a) the applicant and the respondent; and

(b) any other person on whom the court orders it to be served.

(Rule 6.3 specifies who must serve judgments and orders)

Amendments—SI 2002/2058.

'Service' (r 40.4)—The court will decide the method of service (r 6.3(2)) and Pt 6 sets out the method of service by post, document exchange, fax etc and the date service is deemed to have been effected. Sufficient copies should be lodged with the court for service on all necessary parties.

40.5 Power to require judgment or order to be served on a party as well as his solicitor

Where the party on whom a judgment or order is to be served is acting by a solicitor, the court may order the judgment or order to be served on the party as well as on his solicitor.

'served on the party as well as on his solicitor'—There is currently no guidance as to the circumstances in which such an order will be made. It is likely to be made only in exceptional circumstances, eg to ensure that it is brought to the lay party's attention that an adverse costs order has been made or that an order is penal.

40.6 Consent judgments and orders

(1) This rule applies where all the parties agree the terms in which a judgment should be given or an order should be made.

(2) A court officer may enter and seal(GL) an agreed judgment or order if –

(a) the judgment or order is listed in paragraph (3);
(b) none of the parties is a litigant in person; and
(c) the approval of the court is not required by these Rules, a practice direction or any enactment before an agreed order can be made.

(3) The judgments and orders referred to in paragraph (2) are –

(a) a judgment or order for –
(i) the payment of an amount of money (including a judgment or order for damages or the value of goods to be decided by the court); or
(ii) the delivery up of goods with or without the option of paying the value of the goods or the agreed value.

(b) an order for –
(i) the dismissal of any proceedings, wholly or in part;
(ii) the stay[(GL)] of proceedings on agreed terms, disposing of the proceedings, whether those terms are recorded in a schedule to the order or elsewhere;
(iii) the stay[(GL)] of enforcement of a judgment, either unconditionally or on condition that the money due under the judgment is paid by instalments specified in the order;
(iv) the setting aside under Part 13 of a default judgment which has not been satisfied;
(v) the payment out of money which has been paid into court;
(vi) the discharge from liability of any party;
(vii) the payment, assessment or waiver of costs, or such other provision for costs as may be agreed.

(4) Rule 40.3 (drawing up and filing of judgments and orders) applies to judgments and orders entered and sealed[(GL)] by a court officer under paragraph (2) as it applies to other judgments and orders.

(5) Where paragraph (2) does not apply, any party may apply for a judgment or order in the terms agreed.

(6) The court may deal with an application under paragraph (5) without a hearing.

(7) Where this rule applies –

(a) the order which is agreed by the parties must be drawn up in the terms agreed;
(b) it must be expressed as being 'By Consent';
(c) it must be signed by the legal representative acting for each of the parties to whom the order relates or, where paragraph (5) applies, by the party if he is a litigant in person.

General note—Solicitors not infrequently lodge for sealing a draft consent order without fully appreciating the distinction between the effect of an order of the court and an agreement between the parties scheduled to an order of the court staying proceedings save for the purpose of giving effect to the agreed terms (a *Tomlin* order). A draft which does not make that distinction is likely to be rejected. Common errors include:

(a) asking for an order the court should only make after a hearing, eg if one of the parties is a minor or a patient, or making a possession order against a secure tenant;
(b) failing to use the correct wording for a *Tomlin* order;
(c) forgetting to provide for payment-out of money in court;
(d) putting in the schedule to a *Tomlin* order what should be in the body of the order, eg one of the provisions contained in r 40.6(3)(b)(v);
(e) putting into the body of a *Tomlin* order what should be in the schedule, eg a term outside the powers of the court;

(f) failing to provide specific dates and times for compliance with the order or the scheduled terms;
(g) using absurd or meaningless phrases eg 'the claimant shall be at liberty to accept the sum of £X in settlement', or 'and thereafter the record shall be removed';
(h) creating ambiguity as to other claims, eg claims against other defendants, Part 20 claims and counterclaims;
(i) failing to date the order and/or to obtain the signatures of all parties to the proceedings.

A consent order may be varied by deleting a term which is unenforceable as a matter of law, although the public interest requires a party to be held to an agreed order. The jurisdiction will be sparingly exercised (*Gerrard v Read* [2002] 152 NLJ 22, Blackburne J).

Authority to assess costs—Only an order for costs contained in the body of a *Tomlin* order rather in its Schedule will be accepted by the court as authority to commence an assessment of costs – see PD40B, para 3.5. To remedy such a slip the receiving party should apply to amend the order under the usual 'liberty to apply' provisions.

'if … the approval of the court is not required by these Rules' (r 40.6(2)(c))—Rule 28.4, for example, requires the court to approve a consent order varying a milestone date (eg a trial date). The court, applying its case management powers under Pt 3, is likely to reject a consent order that conflicts with CPR practice or with the overriding objective.

Fees on consent orders—Where no other fee is specified there is a general fee of £30 on filing of a consent order or judgment (SCFO and CCFO, fee 2.5).

40.7 When judgment or order takes effect

(1) A judgment or order takes effect from the day when it is given or made, or such later date as the court may specify.

(2) This rule applies to all judgments and orders except those to which rule 40.10 (judgment against a State) applies.

Compromise after draft judgment handed down—A judge is, in his discretion, entitled to hand down an official judgment despite the parties earlier compromising the action after a draft judgment has been circulated to the lawyers. It is justified to avoid the risk of further costly litigation and where decisions on points of law might be of public interest (*Prudential Assurance Company v McBains Cooper & ors* [2000] All ER (D) 715, CA; *Practice Statement* [1998] All ER (D) 141, considered).

Duty to inform the court of late settlement or negotiations—The Court of Appeal has reminded parties' advisers of their duty to inform the court of negotiations subsequent to judgment being reserved as soon as possible in order to ensure that the court's resources are deployed efficiently (*HFC plc v Midland Bank plc* [2000] FSR 176, (2000) *The Times*, 28 September, ChD).

40.8 Time from which interest begins to run

(1) Where interest is payable on a judgment pursuant to section 17 of the Judgments Act 1838 or section 74 of the County Courts Act 1984, the interest shall begin to run from the date that judgment is given unless –

(a) a rule in another Part or a practice direction makes different provision; or
(b) the court orders otherwise.

(2) The court may order that interest shall begin to run from a date before the date that judgment is given.

'interest shall begin to run from the date that judgment is given' (r 40.8(1))—Formerly, judgment interest ran from the time of entering up the judgment. Note the court's power to order interest to run from a date before the date that judgment is given is in addition to the express provisions of other Parts or practice directions. For examples of the latter, see r 36.21(2) and (3) (consequences where a claimant does better than he proposed in his Pt 36 offer) and r 44.3(6)(g) (interest on costs from or until a date before judgment).

'section 74 of the County Courts Act 1984' (r 40.8(1))—This applies only to judgments exceeding £5000 unless a qualifying debt under Late Payment of Commercial Debts (Interest) Act 1998.

40.9 Who may apply to set aside or vary a judgment or order

A person who is not a party but who is directly affected by a judgment or order may apply to have the judgment or order set aside or varied.

40.10 Judgment against a State in default of acknowledgment of service

(1) Where the claimant obtains default judgment under Part 12 on a claim against a State where the defendant has failed to file an acknowledgment of service, the judgment does not take effect until 2 months after service on the State of –

(a) a copy of the judgment; and
(b) a copy of the evidence in support of the application for permission to enter default judgment (unless the evidence has already been served on the State in accordance with an order made under Part 12).

(2) In this rule, 'State' has the meaning given by section 14 of the State Immunity Act 1978.

40.11 Time for complying with a judgment or order

A party must comply with a judgment or order for the payment of an amount of money (including costs) within 14 days of the date of the judgment or order, unless –

(a) the judgment or order specifies a different date for compliance (including specifying payment by instalments);
(b) any of these Rules specifies a different date for compliance; or
(c) the court has stayed the proceedings or judgment.

(Parts 12 and 14 specify different dates for complying with certain default judgment s and judgments on admissions)

'judgment or order for the payment of an amount of money' (r 40.11)—This provision is limited to an order for the payment of money and will not, thus, affect possession orders where other statutory periods apply (eg the 4-week minimum period for a forfeiture possession order under CCA 1984, s 138).

40.12 Correction of errors in judgments and orders

(1) The court may at any time correct an accidental slip or omission in a judgment or order.

(2) A party may apply for a correction without notice.

'The court may at any time correct an accidental slip or omission' (r 40.12(1))—This re-enacts the former 'slip rule' under RSC Ord 20, r 11 and CCR Ord 15, r 5. It is not limited to errors of the court or its officials but is limited to genuine slips and cannot be used to correct an error of substance, eg an order made without jurisdiction or, rather than dismissing the claim, substituting damages for a nominal sum in favour of a claimant (*Markos v Goodfellow* [2002] EWCA Civ 1542, (2002) 146 SJLB 231, CA). Paragraph 4 of PD40B sets out the mechanics in further detail.

The slip rule cannot enable a court to have second or additional thoughts. Once the order is drawn up any mistakes have to be corrected by an appellate court. However, it is possible under the slip rule to amend an order to give effect to the intention of the court (*Bristol-Myers Squibb Co v (1) Baker Norton Pharmaceuticals Inc (2) Napro Biotherapeutics Inc* [2001] EWCA Civ 414, (2001) Lawtel, 28 March, CA).

40.13 Cases where court gives judgment both on claim and counterclaim

(1) This rule applies where the court gives judgment for specified amounts both for the claimant on his claim and against the claimant on a counterclaim.

(2) If there is a balance in favour of one of the parties, it may order the party whose judgment is for the lesser amount to pay the balance.

(3) In a case to which this rule applies, the court may make a separate order as to costs against each party.

40.14 Judgment in favour of certain part owners relating to the detention of goods

(1) In this rule 'part owner' means one of two or more persons who have an interest in the same goods.

(2) Where –

- (a) a part owner makes a claim relating to the detention of the goods; and
- (b) the claim is not based on a right to possession,

any judgment or order given or made in respect of the claim is to be for the payment of damages only, unless the claimant had the written authority of every other part owner of the goods to make the claim on his behalf as well as for himself.

(3) This rule applies notwithstanding anything in subsection (3) of section 3 of the Torts (Interference with Goods) Act 1977, but does not affect the remedies and jurisdiction mentioned in subsection (8) of that section.

II Sale of Land etc and Conveyancing Counsel

40.15 Scope of this Section

(1) This Section –

- (a) deals with the court's power to order the sale, mortgage, partition or exchange of land; and
- (b) contains provisions about conveyancing counsel.

(Section 131 of the Supreme Court Act 1981 provides for the appointment of the conveyancing counsel of the Supreme Court)

(2) In this Section 'land' includes any interest in, or right over, land.

Amendments—Inserted by SI 2000/221.

40.16 Power to order sale etc

In any proceedings relating to land, the court may order the land, or part of it, to be –

- (a) sold;
- (b) mortgaged;
- (c) exchanged; or
- (d) partitioned.

Amendments—Inserted by SI 2000/221.

SECTION 2 Civil Procedure Rules and Practice Directions

40.17 Power to order delivery up of possession etc

Where the court has made an order under rule 40.16, it may order any party to deliver up to the purchaser or any other person –

(a) possession of the land;
(b) receipt of rents or profits relating to it; or
(c) both.

Amendments—Inserted by SI 2000/221.

40.18 Reference to conveyancing counsel

(1) The court may direct conveyancing counsel to investigate and prepare a report on the title of any land or to draft any document.

(2) The court may take the report on title into account when it decides the issue in question.

(Provisions dealing with the fees payable to conveyancing counsel are set out in the practice direction relating to Part 44)

Amendments—Inserted by SI 2000/221.

40.19 Party may object to report

(1) Any party to the proceedings may object to the report on title prepared by conveyancing counsel.

(2) Where there is an objection, the issue will be referred to a judge for determination.

(Part 23 contains general rules about making an application)

Amendments—Inserted by SI 2000/221.

40.20 Declaratory judgments

The court may make binding declarations whether or not any other remedy is claimed.

Amendments—Inserted by SI 2001/256.

Practice Direction – Accounts, Inquiries etc

This Practice Direction supplements CPR Part 40 (PD40)

General note—See also the notes to CPR Pt 40 for relevant commentary.

ACCOUNTS AND INQUIRIES: GENERAL

1.1 Where the court orders any account to be taken or any inquiry to be made, it may, by the same or a subsequent order, give directions as to the manner in which the account is to be taken and verified or the inquiry is to be conducted.

1.2 In particular, the court may direct that in taking an account, the relevant books of account shall be evidence of their contents but that any party may take such objections to the contents as he may think fit.

1.3 Any party may apply to the court in accordance with CPR Part 23 for directions as to the taking of an account or the conduct of an inquiry or for the variation of directions already made.

1.4 Every direction for the taking of an account or the making of an inquiry shall be numbered in the order so that, as far as possible, each distinct account and inquiry is given its own separate number.

VERIFYING THE ACCOUNT

2 Subject to any order to the contrary:

(1) the accounting party must make out his account and verify it by an affidavit or witness statement to which the account is exhibited,

(2) the accounting party must file the account with the court and at the same time notify the other parties that he has done so and of the filing of any affidavit or witness statement verifying or supporting the account.

OBJECTIONS

3.1 Any party who wishes to contend:

(a) that an accounting party has received more than the amount shown by the account to have been received, or

(b) that the accounting party should be treated as having received more than he has actually received, or

(c) that any item in the account is erroneous in respect of amount, or

(d) that in any other respect the account is inaccurate, must, unless the court directs otherwise, give written notice to the accounting party of his objections.

3.2 The written notice referred to in paragraph 3.1 must, so far as the objecting party is able to do so:

(a) state the amount by which it is contended that the account understates the amount received by the accounting party,

(b) state the amount which it is contended that the accounting party should be treated as having received in addition to the amount he actually received,

(c) specify the respects in which it is contended that the account is inaccurate, and

(d) in each case, give the grounds on which the contention is made.

3.3 The contents of the written notice must, unless the notice contains a statement of truth, be verified by either an affidavit or a witness statement to which the notice is an exhibit.

(Part 22 and the practice direction that supplements it contain provisions about statements of truth)

ALLOWANCES

4 In taking any account all just allowances shall be made without any express direction to that effect.

MANAGEMENT OF PROCEEDINGS

5 The court may at any stage in the taking of an account or in the course of an inquiry direct a hearing in order to resolve an issue that has arisen and for that purpose may order that points of claim and points of defence be served and give any necessary directions.

DELAY

6.1 If it appears to the court that there is undue delay in the taking of any account or the progress of any inquiry the court may require the accounting party or the party with the conduct of the inquiry, as the case may be, to explain the delay and may then make such order for the management of the proceedings (including a stay) and for costs as the circumstances may require.

6.2 The directions the court may give under paragraph 6.1 include a direction that the Official Solicitor take over the conduct of the proceedings and directions providing for the payment of the Official Solicitor's costs.

DISTRIBUTION

7 Where some of the persons entitled to share in a fund are known but there is, or is likely to be, difficulty or delay in ascertaining other persons so entitled, the court may direct, or allow, immediate payment of their shares to the known persons without reserving any part of those shares to meet the subsequent costs of ascertaining the other persons.

GUARDIAN'S ACCOUNTS

8 The accounts of a person appointed guardian of the property of a child (defined in CPR 21.1(2)) must be verified and approved in such manner as the court may direct.

ACCOUNTS AND INQUIRIES TO BE CONDUCTED BEFORE MASTER OR DISTRICT JUDGE

9 Unless the court orders otherwise, an account or inquiry will be taken or made –

(1) by a Master or district judge, if the proceedings are in the High Court; and
(2) by a district judge, if the proceedings are in a county court.

ADVERTISEMENTS

10 The court may –

(1) direct any necessary advertisement; and
(2) fix the time within which the advertisement should require a reply.

EXAMINATION OF CLAIMS

11.1 Where the court orders an account of debts or other liabilities to be taken, it may direct any party, within a specified time, to –

(1) examine the claims of persons claiming to be owed money out of the estate or fund in question.
(2) determine, so far as he is able, which of them are valid; and
(3) file written evidence –

(a) stating his findings and his reasons for them; and
(b) listing any other debts which are or may be owed out of the estate or fund.

11.2 Where the court orders an inquiry for next of kin or other unascertained claimants to an estate or fund, it may direct any party, within a specified time, to –

(1) examine the claims that are made;
(2) determine, so far as he is able, which of them are valid; and
(3) file written evidence stating his findings and his reasons for them.

11.3 If the personal representatives or trustees concerned are not the parties directed by the court to examine claims, the court may direct them to join with the party directed to examine claims in producing the written evidence required by this rule.

CONSIDERATION OF CLAIMS BY THE COURT

12 For the purpose of considering a claim the court may –

(1) direct it to be investigated in any manner;
(2) direct the person making the claim to give further details of it; and
(3) direct that person to –
  (a) file written evidence; or
  (b) attend court to give evidence,
  to support his claim.

NOTICE OF DECISION

13 If –

(1) the court has allowed or disallowed any claim or part of a claim; and
(2) the person making the claim was not present when the decision was made,

the court will serve on that person a notice informing him of its decision.

INTEREST ON DEBTS

14 (1) Where an account of the debts of a deceased person is directed by any judgment, unless the deceased's estate is insolvent or the court orders otherwise, interest shall be allowed –
  (a) on any debt which carries interest, at the rate it carries, and
  (b) on any other debt, from the date of the judgment, at the rate payable on judgment debts at that date.

(2) Where interest on a debt is allowed under paragraph (1)(b), it shall be paid out of any assets of the estate which remain after payment of –
  (a) any costs of the proceedings directed to be paid out of the estate;
  (b) all the debts which have been established; and
  (c) the interest on such of those debts as by law carry interest.

(3) For the purpose of this rule –
  (a) 'debt' includes funeral, testamentary or administration expenses; and
  (b) in relation to any expenses incurred after the judgment, paragraph (1)(b) applies as if, instead of the date of the judgment, it referred to the date when the expenses became payable.

INTEREST ON LEGACIES

15 Where an account of legacies is directed by any judgment, then, subject to –

(a) any directions contained in the will or codicil in question; and
(b) any order made by the court,

interest shall be allowed on each legacy at the basic rate payable for the time being on funds in court or at such other rate as the court shall direct, beginning one year after the testator's death.

Practice Direction – Judgments and Orders

This Practice Direction supplements CPR Part 40 (PD40B)

General note—See also the notes to CPR Pt 40 for relevant commentary.

DRAWING UP AND FILING OF JUDGMENTS AND ORDERS

1.1 Rule 40.2 sets out the standard requirements for judgments and orders and rule 40.3 deals with how judgments and orders should be drawn up.

1.2 A party who has been ordered or given permission to draw up an order must file it for sealing within 7 days of being ordered or permitted to do so[1]. If he fails to do so, any other party may draw it up and file it[2].

1 Rule 40.3(3)(a).
2 Rule 40.3(3)(b).

1.3 If the court directs that a judgment or order which is being drawn up by a party must be checked by the court before it is sealed, the party responsible must file the draft within 7 days of the date the order was made with a request that the draft be checked before it is sealed.

1.4 If the court directs the parties to file an agreed statement of terms of an order which the court is to draw up[1], the parties must do so no later than 7 days from the date the order was made, unless the court directs otherwise.

1 Rule 40.3(2)(b).

1.5 If the court requires the terms of an order which is being drawn up by the court to be agreed by the parties the court may direct that a copy of the draft order is to be sent to all the parties:

(1) for their agreement to be endorsed on it and returned to the court before the order is sealed, or
(2) with notice of an appointment to attend before the court to agree the terms of the order.

PREPARATION OF DEEDS OR DOCUMENTS UNDER AN ORDER

2.1 Where a judgment or order directs any deed or document to be prepared, executed or signed, the order will state:

(1) the person who is to prepare the deed or document, and
(2) if the deed or document is to be approved, the person who is to approve it.

2.2 If the parties are unable to agree the form of the deed or document, any party may apply in accordance with Part 23 for the form of the deed or document to be settled.

2.3 In such case the judge may:

(1) settle the deed or document himself, or
(2) refer it to
  (a) a master, or
  (b) a district judge, or
  (c) a conveyancing counsel of the Supreme Court to settle.

(See also the Sale of Land practice direction supplementing CPR Part 40)

CONSENT ORDERS

3.1 Rule 40.6(3) sets out the types of consent judgments and orders which may be entered and sealed by a court officer. The court officer may do so in those cases provided that:

(1) none of the parties is a litigant in person, and
(2) the approval of the court is not required by the Rules, a practice direction or any enactment[1].

1 Rule 40.6(2).

3.2 If a consent order filed for sealing appears to be unclear or incorrect the court officer may refer it to a judge for consideration[1].

1 Rule 3.2.

3.3 Where a consent judgment or order does not come within the provisions of rule 40.6(2):

(1) an application notice requesting a judgment or order in the agreed terms should be filed with the draft judgment or order to be entered or sealed, and
(2) the draft judgment or order must be drawn so that the judge's name and judicial title can be inserted.

3.4 A consent judgment or order must:

(1) be drawn up in the terms agreed,
(2) bear on it the words 'By Consent', and
(3) be signed by
  (a) solicitors or counsel acting for each of the parties to the order, or
  (b) where a party is a litigant in person, the litigant[1].

1 Rule 40.6(7).

3.5 Where the parties draw up a consent order in the form of a stay of proceedings on agreed terms, disposing of the proceedings[1], and where the terms are recorded in a schedule to the order, any direction for:

(1) payment of money out of court, or
(2) payment and assessment of costs

should be contained in the body of the order and not in the schedule.

1 Rule 40.6(3)(b)(ii).

Authority to assess costs—Only an order for costs contained in the body of a *Tomlin* order rather in its Schedule will be accepted by the court as authority to commence an assessment of costs – see CPR r 40.6(3)(b)(ii). To remedy such a slip the receiving party should apply to amend the order under the usual 'liberty to apply' provisions.

CORRECTION OF ERRORS IN JUDGMENTS AND ORDERS

4.1 Where a judgment or order contains an accidental slip or omission a party may apply for it to be corrected[1].

4.2 The application notice (which may be an informal document such as a letter) should describe the error and set out the correction required. An application may be dealt with without a hearing:

(1) where the applicant so requests,
(2) with the consent of the parties, or
(3) where the court does not consider that a hearing would be appropriate.

4.3 The judge may deal with the application without notice if the slip or omission is obvious or may direct notice of the application to be given to the other party or parties.

4.4 If the application is opposed it should, if practicable, be listed for hearing before the judge who gave the judgment or made the order.

4.5 The court has an inherent power to vary its own orders to make the meaning and intention of the court clear.

1 Rule 40.10.

ADJUSTMENT OF FINAL JUDGMENT FIGURE IN RESPECT OF COMPENSATION RECOVERY PAYMENTS

5.1 In a final judgment[1] where some or all of the damages awarded:

(2) fall under the heads of damage set out in column 1 of Schedule 2 to the Social Security (Recovery of Benefits) Act 1997 in respect of recoverable benefits received by the claimant set out in column 2 of that Schedule and
(3) where the defendant has paid to the Secretary of State the recoverable benefits in accordance with the certificate of recoverable benefits,

there should be stated in a preamble to the judgment or order the amount awarded under each head of damage and the amount by which it has been reduced in accordance with section 8 and Schedule 2 to the Social Security (Recovery of Benefits) Act 1997.

1 In this paragraph, final 'judgment' includes any order to pay a sum of money, a final award of damages and an assessment of damages.

5.2 The judgment or order should then provide for entry of judgment and payment of the balance.

ADJUSTMENT OF FINAL JUDGMENT FIGURE IN RESPECT OF AN INTERIM PAYMENT

6.1 In a final judgment[1] where an interim payment has previously been made which is less than the total amount awarded by the judge, the judgment or order should set out in a preamble:

(1) the total amount awarded by the judge, and
(2) the amount and date of the interim payment(s).

1 As in note above.

6.2 The total amount awarded by the judge should then be reduced by the total amount of any interim payments, and the judgment or order should then provide for entry of judgment and payment of the balance.

6.3 In a final judgment where an interim payment has previously been made which is more than the total amount awarded by the judge, the judgment or order should set out in a preamble;

(1) the total amount awarded by the judge, and
(2) the amount and date of the interim payment(s).

6.4 An order should then be made for repayment, reimbursement, variation or discharge under rule 25.8(2) and for interest on an overpayment under rule 25.8(5).

STATEMENT AS TO SERVICE OF A CLAIM FORM

7.1 Where a party to proceedings which have gone to trial requires a statement to be included in the judgment as to where, and by what means the claim form issued in those proceedings was served, application should made to the trial judge when judgment is given.

7.2 If the judge so orders, the statement will be included in a preamble to the judgment as entered.

ORDERS REQUIRING AN ACT TO BE DONE

8.1 An order which requires an act to be done (other than a judgment or order for the payment of an amount of money) must specify the time within which the act should be done.

8.2 The consequences of failure to do an act within the time specified may be set out in the order. In this case the wording of the following examples suitably adapted must be used:

(1) Unless the [claimant] [defendant] serves his list of documents by 4.00pm on Friday, January 22, 1999 his claim]defence] will be struck out and judgment entered for the [defendant] [claimant]., or
(2) Unless the [claimant] [defendant] serves his list of documents within 14 days of service of this order his [claim] [defence] will be struck out and judgment entered for the [defendant] [claimant].

Example (1) should be used wherever possible.

NON-COMPLIANCE WITH A JUDGMENT OR ORDER

9.1 An order which restrains a party from doing an act or requires an act to be done should, if disobedience is to be dealt with by an application to bring contempt of court proceedings, have a penal notice endorsed on it as follows:

> 'If you the within-named [ ] do not comply with this order you may be held to be in contempt of court and imprisoned or fined, or [in the case of a company or corporation] your assets may be seized.'

9.2 The provisions of paragraph 9.1 above also apply to an order which contains an undertaking by a party to do or not do an act, subject to paragraph 8.3 below.

9.3 The court has the power to decline to:

(1) accept an undertaking, and
(2) deal with disobedience in respect of an undertaking by contempt of court proceedings,

unless the party giving the undertaking has made a signed statement to the effect that he understands the terms of his undertaking and the consequences of failure to comply with it.

9.4 The statement may be endorsed on the court copy of the] order containing the undertaking or may be filed in a separate document such as a letter.

FOREIGN CURRENCY

10 Where judgment is ordered to be entered in a foreign currency, the order should be in the following form: 'It is ordered that the defendant pay the claimant (state the sum in the foreign currency) or the Sterling equivalent at the time of payment.'

COSTS

11.1 Attention is drawn to the costs practice direction and, in particular, to the court's power to make a summary assessment of costs and the provisions relating to interest in detailed assessment proceedings.

11.2 Attention is also drawn to costs rule 44.13(1) which provides that if an order makes no mention of costs, none are payable in respect of the proceedings to which it relates.

JUDGMENTS PAID BY INSTALMENTS

12 Where a judgment is to be paid by instalments, the judgment should set out:

(1) the total amount of the judgment,
(2) the amount of each instalment,
(3) the number of instalments and the date on which each is to be paid, and
(4) to whom the instalments should be paid.

ORDER TO MAKE AN ORDER OF THE HOUSE OF LORDS AN ORDER OF THE HIGH COURT

13.1 Application may be made in accordance with Part 23 for an order to make an order of the House of Lords an order of the High Court. The application should be made to the procedural judge of the Division, District Registry or court in which the proceedings are taking place and may be made without notice unless the court directs otherwise.

13.2 The application must be supported by the following evidence:

(1) details of the order which was the subject of the appeal to the House of Lords,
(2) details of the order of the House of Lords, with a copy annexed, and
(3) a copy annexed of the certificate of the Clerk of Parliaments of the assessment of the costs of the appeal to the House of Lords in the sum of £ . . . .

13.3 The order to make an order of the House of Lords an order of the High Court should be in form no PF68.

EXAMPLES OF FORMS OF TRIAL JUDGMENT

14.1 The following general forms may be used;

(1) judgment after trial before judge without jury – form no 45,
(2) judgment after trial before judge with jury – form no 46,

(3) judgment after trial before a master or district judge – form no 47,
(4) judgment after trial before a judge of the Technology and Construction court – form no 47 but with any necessary modifications.

14.2 A trial judgment should, in addition to the matters set out in paragraphs 5, 6 and 7 above, have the following matters set out in a preamble:

(1) the questions put to a jury and their answers to those questions,
(2) the findings of a jury and whether unanimous or by a majority,
(3) any order made during the course of the trial concerning the use of evidence,
(4) any matters that were agreed between the parties prior to or during the course of the trial in respect of
 (a) liability,
 (b) contribution,
 (c) the amount of the damages or part of the damages, and
(5) the findings of the judge in respect of each head of damage in a personal injury case.

14.3 Form no 49 should be used for a trial judgment against an Estate.

The forms referred to in this practice direction are listed in the practice direction which supplements Part 4 (Forms).

14 On any application or appeal concerning –

(i) a committal order;
(ii) a refusal to grant habeas corpus or
(iii) a secure accommodation order made under section 25 of the Children Act 1989,

if the court ordering the release of the person concludes that his Convention rights have been infringed by the making of the order to which the application or appeal relates, the judgment or order should so state. If the court does not do so, that failure will not prevent another court from deciding the matter.

FOR INFORMATION ABOUT

(1) Orders for provisional damages: see Part 41 and the practice direction which supplements it.
(2) Orders in respect of children and patients: see Part 22 and the practice direction which supplements it.
(3) Orders containing directions for payment of money out of court: see Parts 36 and 37 and the practice directions which supplement them.
(4) Structured settlement orders: see the separate practice direction supplementing Part 40.
(5) Taking accounts and conducting inquiries under a judgment or order: see the separate practice direction supplementing Part 40.

Practice Direction – 1 Court's Powers in Relation to Land, 2 Conveyancing Counsel of the Court

This Practice Direction supplements CPR Part 40 (PD40D)

PART 1
COURT'S POWERS IN RELATION TO LAND

APPLICATION TO THE COURT WHERE LAND SUBJECT TO AN INCUMBRANCE

1.1 In this paragraph 'incumbrance' has the same meaning as it has in section 205(1) of the Law of Property Act 1925.

1.2 Where land subject to any incumbrance is sold or exchanged any party to the sale or exchange may apply to the court for a direction under section 50 of the Law of Property Act 1925 (discharge of incumbrances by the court on sales or exchanges).

1.3 The directions a court may give on such an application include a direction for the payment into court of a sum of money that the court considers sufficient to meet –

(1) the value of the incumbrance; and
(2) further costs, expenses and interest that may become due on or in respect of the incumbrance.

(Section 50(1) of the Law of Property Act 1925 contains provisions relating to the calculation of these amounts)

1.4 Where a payment into court has been made in accordance with a direction under section 50(1) the court may –

(1) declare the land to be freed from the incumbrance; and
(2) make any order it considers appropriate for giving effect to an order made under rule 40.16 or relating to the money in court and the income thereof.

1.5 An application under section 50 should –

(1) if made in existing proceedings, be made in accordance with CPR Part 23;
(2) otherwise, be made by claim form under CPR Part 8.

DIRECTIONS ABOUT THE SALE ETC

2 Where the court has made an order under rule 40.16 it may give any other directions it considers appropriate for giving effect to the order. In particular the court may give directions –

(1) appointing a party or other person to conduct the sale;
(2) for obtaining evidence of the value of the land;
(3) as to the manner of sale;
(4) settling the particulars and conditions of the sale;
(5) fixing a minimum or reserve price;
(6) as to the fees and expenses to be allowed to an auctioneer or estate agent;
(7) for the purchase money to be paid –

(a) into court;
(b) to trustees; or
(c) to any other person;

(8) for the result of a sale to be certified;
(9) under rule 40.18.

APPLICATION FOR PERMISSION TO BID

3.1 Where –

(1) the court has made an order under rule 40.16 for land to be sold; and
(2) a party wishes to bid for the land,

he should apply to the court for permission to do so.

3.2 An application for permission to bid must be made before the sale takes place.

3.3 If the court gives permission to all the parties to bid, it may appoint an independent person to conduct the sale.

3.4 'Bid' in this paragraph includes submitting a tender or other offer to buy.

CERTIFYING SALE RESULT

4.1 If –

(1) the court has directed the purchase money to be paid into court; or
(2) the court has directed that the result of the sale be certified,

the result of the sale must be certified by the person having conduct of the sale.

4.2 Unless the court directs otherwise, the certificate must give details of –

(1) the amount of the purchase price;
(2) the amount of the fees and expenses payable to any auctioneer or estate agent;
(3) the amount of any other expenses of the sale;
(4) the net amount received in respect of the sale;

and must be verified by a statement of truth.

(Part 22 sets out requirements about statements of truth)

4.3 The certificate must be filed –

(1) if the proceedings are being dealt with in the Royal Courts of Justice, in Chancery Chambers;
(2) if the proceedings are being dealt with anywhere else, in the court where the proceedings are being dealt with.

FEES AND EXPENSES OF AUCTIONEERS AND ESTATE AGENTS

5.1 (1) Where the court has ordered the sale of land under rule 40.16, auctioneer's and estate agent's charges may, unless the court orders otherwise, include –

(a) commission;
(b) fees for valuation of the land;
(c) charges for advertising the land;
(d) other expenses and disbursements but not charges for surveys.

(2) The court's authorisation is required for charges relating to surveys.

5.2 If the total amount of the auctioneer's and estate agent's charges authorised under paragraph 5.1(1) –

(1) does not exceed 2.5% of the sale price; and
(2) does not exceed the rate of commission that that agent would normally charge on a sole agency basis,

the charges may, unless the court orders otherwise and subject to paragraph 5.3(3) and (4), be met by deduction of the amount of the charges from the proceeds of sale without the need for any further authorisation from the court.

5.3 If –

(1) a charge made by an auctioneer or estate agent (whether in respect of fees or expenses or both) is not authorised under paragraph 5.1(1);
(2) the total amount of the charges so authorised exceeds the limits set out in paragraph 5.2;
(3) the land is sold in lots or by valuation; or
(4) the sale is of investment property, business property or farm property,

an application must be made to the court for approval of the fees and expenses to be allowed.

5.4 An application under paragraph 5.3 may be made by any party or, if he is not a party, by the person having conduct of the sale, and may be made either before or after the sale has taken place.

PART 2
CONVEYANCING COUNSEL OF THE COURT

REFERENCE TO CONVEYANCING COUNSEL

6.1 When the court refers a matter under rule 40.18, the court may specify a particular conveyancing counsel.

6.2 If the court does not specify a particular conveyancing counsel, references will be distributed among conveyancing counsel in accordance with arrangements made by the Chief Chancery Master.

6.3 Notice of every reference under rule 40.18 must be given to the Chief Chancery Master.

6.4 The court will send a copy of the order, together with all other necessary documents, to conveyancing counsel.

6.5 A court order sent to conveyancing counsel under paragraph 6.4 will be sufficient authority for him to prepare his report or draft the document.

6.6 (1) An objection under rule 40.19 to a report on title prepared by conveyancing counsel must be made by application notice.
(2) The application notice must state –
(a) the matters the applicant objects to; and
(b) the reason for the objection.

Practice Direction – Reserved Judgments

This Practice Direction supplements CPR Part 40 (PD40E)

SCOPE AND INTERPRETATION

1.1 This Practice Direction applies to all judgments given in –

(a) the Court of Appeal (Civil Division); and
(b) the Queen's Bench Division and Chancery Division of the High Court at the Royal Courts of Justice,

including judgments given by Masters, Registrars and Costs Judges.

1.2 In this Practice Direction –

(a) 'relevant court office' means the office of the court in which judgment is to be given; and
(b) 'working day' means any day on which the relevant court office is open.

AVAILABILITY OF RESERVED JUDGMENTS BEFORE HANDING DOWN

2.1 Where judgment is to be reserved the Judge (or Presiding Judge) may, at the conclusion of the hearing, invite the views of the parties' legal representatives as to the arrangements to be made for the handing down of the judgment.

2.2 Unless the Court directs otherwise, the following provisions of this paragraph apply where the Judge or Presiding Judge is satisfied that the judgment will attract no special degree of confidentiality or sensitivity.

2.3 The Court will provide a copy of the draft judgment to the parties' legal representatives by 4 p.m. on the second working day before handing down, or at such other time as the Court may direct.

2.4 A copy of the draft judgment may be shown, in confidence, to the parties provided that:

(a) neither the judgment nor its substance is disclosed to any other person or used in the public domain; and
(b) no action is taken (other than internally) in response to the judgment, before the judgment is handed down.

2.5 Any breach of the obligation of confidentiality prescribed by paragraph 2.4 may be treated as contempt of court.

2.6 The case will be listed for judgment, and the judgment handed down at the appropriate time.

ATTENDANCE AT HANDING DOWN

3.1 Where any consequential orders are agreed, the parties' advocates need not attend on the handing down.

3.2 Where an advocate does attend the Court may, if it considers such attendance was unnecessary, disallow the costs of the attendance.

3.3 If the parties do not indicate that they intend to attend, the judgment may be handed down by a single member of the Court.

AGREED ORDERS FOLLOWING JUDGMENT

4.1 Unless the parties or their legal representatives are told otherwise when the draft judgment is circulated, the parties must, in respect of any draft agreed order –

(a) fax or e-mail a copy to the clerk to the Judge or Presiding Judge (together with any proposed corrections or amendments to the draft judgment); and

(b) file four copies (with completed backsheets) in the relevant court office, by 12 noon on the working day before handing down.

4.2 A copy of a draft order must bear the case reference, the date of handing down and the name of the Judge or Presiding Judge.

CORRECTIONS TO THE DRAFT JUDGMENT

5 Unless the parties or their legal representatives are told otherwise when the draft judgment is circulated, any proposed corrections to the draft judgment should be sent to the clerk to the judge who prepared the draft with a copy to any other party.

(Paragraphs 15.12 to 15.21 of the Practice Direction supplementing Part 52 contain provision about the handing down of reserved judgments in appeals).

PART 41
DAMAGES

CONTENTS OF THIS PART

Amendments—SI 2004/3129.

I – Proceedings to which Section 32A of the Supreme Court Act 1981 or Section 51 of the County Courts Act 1984 applies

41.1 Application and definitions

(1) This Section of this Part applies to proceedings to which SCA s 32A or CCA s 51 applies.

(2) In this Section –

(a) 'SCA s 32A' means section 32A of the Supreme Court Act 1981;
(b) 'CCA s 51' means section 51 of the County Courts Act 1984; and
(c) 'award of provisional damages' means an award of damages for personal injuries under which –
   (i) damages are assessed on the assumption referred to in SCA s 32A or CCA s 51 that the injured person will not develop the disease or suffer the deterioration ; and
   (ii) the injured person is entitled to apply for further damages at a future date if he develops the disease or suffers the deterioration.

Amendments—SI 2004/3129.

Practice Direction—See generally PD41 at p 986.

'proceedings to which SCA s 32A or CCA s 51 applies' (r 41.1(1))—Supreme Court Act 1981, s 32A and County Courts Act 1984, s 51 apply to actions for damages for personal injuries in which there is proved or admitted to be a chance that at some definite or indefinite time in the future the injured person will, as a result of the act or omission which gave rise to the cause of action, develop some serious disease or suffer some serious deterioration in his physical or mental condition.

41.2 Order for an award of provisional damages

(1) The court may make an order for an award of provisional damages if –

(a) the particulars of claim include a claim for provisional damages; and
(b) the court is satisfied that SCA s 32A or CCA s 51 applies.

(Rule 16.4(1)(d) sets out what must be included in the particulars of claim where the claimant is claiming provisional damages)

(2) An order for an award of provisional damages –

(a) must specify the disease or type of deterioration in respect of which an application may be made at a future date;
(b) must specify the period within which such an application may be made; and
(c) may be made in respect of more than one disease or type of deterioration and may, in respect of each disease or type of deterioration, specify a different period within which a subsequent application may be made.

(3) The claimant may make more than one application to extend the period specified under paragraph (2)(b) or (2)(c).

Practice Direction—See generally PD41 at p 986.

41.3 Application for further damages

(1) The claimant may not make an application for further damages after the end of the period specified under rule 41.2(2), or such period as extended by the court.

(2) Only one application for further damages may be made in respect of each disease or type of deterioration specified in the award of provisional damages.

(3) The claimant must give at least 28 days' written notice to the defendant of his intention to apply for further damages.

(4) If the claimant knows –

(a) that the defendant is insured in respect of the claim; and
(b) the identity of the defendant's insurers,

he must also give at least 28 days' written notice to the insurers.

(5) Within 21 days after the end of the 28 day notice period referred to in paragraphs (3) and (4), the claimant must apply for directions.

(6) (*revoked*)

Amendments—SI 2004/3419.

Practice Direction—See generally PD41 at p 986.

II – Periodical Payments under the Damages Act 1996

Amendments—Inserted by SI 2004/3129.

41.4 Scope and interpretation

(1) This Section of this Part contains rules about the exercise of the court's powers under section 2(1) of the 1996 Act to order that all or part of an award of damages in respect of personal injury is to take the form of periodical payments.

(2) In this Section –

(a) 'the 1996 Act' means the Damages Act 1996;
(b) 'damages' means damages for future pecuniary loss; and
(c) 'periodical payments' means periodical payments under section 2(1) of the 1996 Act.

Amendments—Inserted by SI 2004/3129.

41.5 Statement of case

(1) In a claim for damages for personal injury, each party in its statement of case may state whether it considers periodical payments or a lump sum is the more appropriate form for all or part of an award of damages and where such statement is given must provide relevant particulars of the circumstances which are relied on.

(2) Where a statement under paragraph (1) is not given, the court may order a party to make such a statement.

(3) Where the court considers that a statement of case contains insufficient particulars under paragraph (1), the court may order a party to provide such further particulars as it considers appropriate.

Amendments—Inserted by SI 2004/3129.

41.6 Court's indication to parties

The court shall consider and indicate to the parties as soon as practicable whether periodical payments or a lump sum is likely to be the more appropriate form for all or part of an award of damages.

Amendments—Inserted by SI 2004/3129.

41.7 Factors to be taken into account

When considering –

- (a) its indication as to whether periodical payments or a lump sum is likely to be the more appropriate form for all or part of an award of damages under rule 41.6; or
- (b) whether to make an order under section 2(1)(a) of the 1996 Act,

the court shall have regard to all the circumstances of the case and in particular the form of award which best meets the claimant's needs, having regard to the factors set out in the practice direction.

Amendments—Inserted by SI 2004/3129.

41.8 The award

(1) Where the court awards damages in the form of periodical payments, the order must specify –

- (a) the annual amount awarded, how each payment is to be made during the year and at what intervals;
- (b) the amount awarded for future –
  - (i) loss of earnings and other income; and
  - (ii) care and medical costs and other recurring or capital costs;
- (c) that the claimant's annual future pecuniary losses, as assessed by the court, are to be paid for the duration of the claimant's life, or such other period as the court orders; and
- (d) that the amount of the payments shall vary annually by reference to the retail prices index, unless the court orders otherwise under section 2(9) of the 1996 Act.

(2) Where the court orders that any part of the award shall continue after the claimant's death, for the benefit of the claimant's dependants, the order must

also specify the relevant amount and duration of the payments and how each payment is to be made during the year and at what intervals.

(3) Where an amount awarded under paragraph (1)(b) is to increase or decrease on a certain date, the order must also specify –

(a) the date on which the increase or decrease will take effect; and
(b) the amount of the increase or decrease at current value.

(4) Where damages for substantial capital purchases are awarded under paragraph (1)(b)(ii), the order must also specify –

(a) the amount of the payments at current value;
(b) when the payments are to be made; and
(c) that the amount of the payments shall be adjusted by reference to the retail prices index, unless the court orders otherwise under section 2(9) of the 1996 Act.

Amendments—Inserted by SI 2004/3129.

41.9 Continuity of payment

(1) An order for periodical payments shall specify that the payments must be funded in accordance with section 2(4) of the 1996 Act, unless the court orders an alternative method of funding.

(2) Before ordering an alternative method of funding, the court must be satisfied that –

(a) the continuity of payment under the order is reasonably secure; and
(b) the criteria set out in the practice direction are met.

(3) An order under paragraph (2) must specify the alternative method of funding.

Amendments—Inserted by SI 2004/3129.

41.10 Assignment or charge

Where the court under section 2(6)(a) of the 1996 Act is satisfied that special circumstances make an assignment or charge of periodical payments necessary, it shall, in deciding whether or not to approve the assignment or charge, also have regard to the factors set out in the practice direction.

Amendments—Inserted by SI 2004/3129.

Practice Direction – Provisional Damages

This Practice Direction supplements CPR Part 41 (PD41)

CLAIMS FOR PROVISIONAL DAMAGES

1.1 CPR Part 16 and the practice direction which supplements it set out information which must be included in the particulars of claim if a claim for provisional damages is made.

JUDGMENT FOR AN AWARD OF PROVISIONAL DAMAGES

2.1 When giving judgment at trial the judge will:

(1) specify the disease or type of deterioration, or diseases or types of deterioration, which
  (a) for the purpose of the award of immediate damages it has been assumed will not occur, and
  (b) will entitle the claimant to further damages if it or they do occur at a future date,

(2) give an award of immediate damages,

(3) specify the period or periods within which an application for further damages may be made in respect of each disease or type of deterioration, and

(4) direct what documents are to be filed and preserved as the case file in support of any application for further damages.

2.2 The claimant may make an application or applications to extend the periods referred to in paragraph 2.1(3) above[1].

1 See CPR rule 41.2(3).

2.3 A period specified under paragraph 2.1(3) may be expressed as being for the duration of the life of the claimant.

2.4 The documents to be preserved as the case file ('the case file documents') referred to in paragraph 2.1(4) will be set out in a schedule to the judgment as entered.

2.5 Causation of any further damages within the scope of the order shall be determined when any application for further damages is made.

2.6 A form for a provisional damages judgment is set out in the Annex to this practice direction.

THE CASE FILE

3.1 The case file documents must be preserved until the expiry of the period or periods specified or of any extension of them.

3.2 The case file documents will normally include:

(1) the judgment as entered,
(2) the statements of case,
(3) a transcript of the judge's oral judgment,
(4) all medical reports relied on, and
(5) a transcript of any parts of the claimant's own evidence which the judge considers necessary.

3.3 The associate/court clerk will:

(1) ensure that the case file documents are provided by the parties where necessary and filed on the court file,

(2) endorse the court file
  (a) to the effect that it contains the case file documents, and
  (b) with the period during which the case file documents must be preserved, and

(3) preserve the case file documents in the court office where the proceedings took place.

3.4 Any subsequent order:

(1) extending the period within which an application for further damages may be made, or
(2) of the Court of Appeal discharging or varying the provisions of the original judgment or of any subsequent order under sub-paragraph (1) above,

will become one of the case file documents and must be preserved accordingly and any variation of the period within which an application for further damages may be made should be endorsed on the court file containing the case file documents.

3.5 On an application to extend the periods referred to in paragraph 2.1(3) above a current medical report should be filed.

3.6 Legal representatives are reminded that it is their duty to preserve their own case file.

CONSENT ORDERS

4.1 An application to give effect to a consent order for provisional damages should be made in accordance with CPR Part 23. If the claimant is a child or patient[1] the approval of the court must also be sought and the application for approval will normally be dealt with at a hearing.

1 See CPR Part 21 for definitions of child and patient.

4.2 The order should be in the form of a consent judgment and should contain:

(1) the matters set out in paragraph 2.1(1) to (3) above, and
(2) a direction as to the documents to be preserved as the case file documents, which will normally be
    (a) the consent judgment,
    (b) any statements of case,
    (c) an agreed statement of facts, and
    (d) any agreed medical report(s).

4.3 The claimant or his legal representative must lodge the case file documents in the court office where the proceedings are taking place for inclusion in the court file. The court file should be endorsed as in paragraph 3.3(2) above, and the case file documents preserved as in paragraph 3.3(3) above.

DEFAULT JUDGMENT

5.1 Where a defendant:

(1) fails to file an acknowledgment of service in accordance with CPR Part 10, and
(2) fails to file a defence in accordance with CPR Part 15,

within the time specified for doing so, the claimant may not, unless he abandons his claim for provisional damages, enter judgment in default but should make an application in accordance with CPR Part 23 for directions.

5.2 The master or district judge will normally direct the following issues to be decided:

(1) whether the claim is an appropriate one for an award of provisional damages and if so, on what terms, and
(2) the amount of immediate damages.

5.3 If the judge makes an award of provisional damages, the provisions of paragraph 3 above apply.

Annex

(EXAMPLE OF AN AWARD OF PROVISIONAL DAMAGES AFTER TRIAL)

(*TITLE OF PROCEEDINGS*)

THIS CLAIM having been tried before [*title and name of judge*] without a jury at [the Royal Courts of Justice *or as may be*] and [*title and name of judge*] having ordered that judgment as set out below be entered for the claimant

IT IS ORDERED –

(1) that the defendant pay the claimant by way of immediate damages the sum of £. . . . . (being (i) £. . . . . for special damages and £. . . . . [agreed interest][interest at the rate of . . . . . . from . . . . to . . . .] (ii) £. . . . . for general damages and £. . . . . [agreed interest][interest at the rate of 2% from . . . . to . . . .] and (iii) £. . . . . for loss of future earnings and/or earning capacity) on the assumption that the claimant would not at a future date as a result of the act or omission giving rise to the claim develop the following disease/type of deterioration namely [*set out disease or type of deterioration*]

(2) that if the claimant at a further date does develop that [disease][type of deterioration] he should be entitled to apply for further damages provided that the application is made on or before [*set out period*]

(3) that the documents set out in the schedule to this order be filed on the court file and preserved as the case file until the expiry of the period set out in paragraph (2) above or of any extension of that period which has been ordered

(4) (costs)

SCHEDULE

(*list documents referred to in paragraph (3)*)

Practice Direction – Periodical Payments under the Damages Act 1996

This Practice Direction supplements CPR Part 41 (PD41B)

General note—This practice direction has been inserted by virtue of Update 37 with effect from 1 April 2005.

FACTORS TO BE TAKEN INTO ACCOUNT (RULE 41.7)

1 The factors which the court shall have regard to under rule 41.7 include –

(1) the scale of the annual payments taking into account any deduction for contributory negligence;
(2) the form of award preferred by the claimant including –
  (a) the reasons for the claimant's preference; and
  (b) the nature of any financial advice received by the claimant when considering the form of award; and
(3) the form of award preferred by the defendant including the reasons for the defendant's preference.

THE AWARD (RULE 41.8)

2.1 An order may be made under rule 41.8(2) where a dependant would have had a claim under section 1 of the Fatal Accidents Act 1976 if the claimant had died at the time of the accident.

2.2 Examples of circumstances which might lead the court to order an increase or decrease under rule 41.8(3) are where the court determines that –

(1) the claimant's condition will change leading to an increase or reduction in his or her need to incur care, medical or other recurring or capital costs;
(2) gratuitous carers will no longer continue to provide care;
(3) the claimant's educational circumstances will change;
(4) the claimant would have received a promotional increase in pay;
(5) the claimant will cease earning.

CONTINUITY OF PAYMENT (RULE 41.9)

3 Before ordering an alternative method of funding under rule 41.9(1), the court must be satisfied that the following criteria are met –

(1) that a method of funding provided for under section 2(4) of the 1996 Act is not possible or there are good reasons to justify an alternative method of funding;
(2) that the proposed method of funding can be maintained for the duration of the award or for the proposed duration of the method of funding; and
(3) that the proposed method of funding will meet the level of payment ordered by the court.

ASSIGNMENT OR CHARGE (RULE 41.10)

4 The factors which the court shall have regard to under rule 41.10 include –

(1) whether the capitalised value of the assignment or charge represents value for money;
(2) whether the assignment or charge is in the claimant's best interests, taking into account whether these interests can be met in some other way; and
(3) how the claimant will be financially supported following the assignment or charge.

VARIATION

5 The Damages (Variation of Periodical Payments) Order 2004 sets out provisions which enable the court in certain circumstances to provide in an order for periodical payments that it may be varied.

SETTLEMENT

6 Where the parties settle a claim to which rule 36.2A applies, any consent order, whether made under rule 40.6 or on an application under Part 23, must satisfy the requirements of rules 41.8 and 41.9.

SETTLEMENT OR COMPROMISE ON BEHALF OF CHILD OR PATIENT

7 Where a claim for damages for personal injury is made by or on behalf of a child or patient and is settled prior to the start of proceedings or before trial, the provisions of the Practice Direction which supplements Part 21 must be complied with.

PART 42
CHANGE OF SOLICITOR

CONTENTS OF THIS PART

Procedural Guide—See Guide 22, set out in Section 1 of this work.

42.1 Solicitor acting for a party

Where the address for service of a party is the business address of his solicitor, the solicitor will be considered to be acting for that party until the provisions of this Part have been complied with.

(Part 6 contains provisions about the address for service)

Practice Direction—See generally PD42 at p 995.

Scope of provision—The provisions as to service in Pt 6 differentiate between parties represented by solicitors and those who are not. Rule 6.5(2) provides that a party must give an address for service within the jurisdiction. Further, r 6.5(5) establishes that where a solicitor is acting for a party and the document to be served is not the claim form, that party's address for service is the business address of his solicitor. Rule 6.13 relates specifically to service of the claim form and indicates that the defendant's address for service may be the address of his solicitor but only where the solicitor is authorised to accept service on the defendant's behalf.

Consequently, where a party employs a solicitor, the solicitor's business address will be the address for service. All documents served by the court or another party are properly served at that address. The solicitor will be considered to be acting for that party until a notice of change has been filed with the court by the party concerned or his new solicitor and served on every other party (PD42, para 1.2).

42.2 Change of solicitor – duty to give notice

(1) This rule applies where –

(a) a party for whom a solicitor [is acting wants to change his solicitor;
(b) a party, after having conducted the claim in person, appoints a solicitor to act on his behalf (except where the solicitor is appointed only to act as an advocate for a hearing); or
(c) a party, after having conducted the claim by a solicitor, intends to act in person.

(2) Where this rule applies, the party or his solicitor (where one is acting) must –

(a) file notice of the change; and
(b) serve notice of the change on every other party and, where paragraph (1)(a) or (c) applies, on the former solicitor.

(3) The notice must state the party's new address for service.

(4) The notice filed at court must state that notice has been served as required by paragraph (2)(b).

(5) Subject to paragraph (6), where a party has changed his solicitor or intends to act in person, the former solicitor will be considered to be the party's solicitor unless and until –

(a) notice is filed and served in accordance with paragraph (2); or
(b) the court makes an order under rule 42.3 and the order is served as required by paragraph (3) of that rule.

(6) Where the certificate of a LSC funded client or an assisted person is revoked or discharged –

(a) the solicitor who acted for that person will cease to be the solicitor acting in the case as soon as his retainer is determined –
  (i) under regulation 4 of the Community Legal Service (Costs) Regulations 2000; or
  (ii) under regulation 83 of the Civil Legal Aid (General) Regulations 1989; and
(b) if that person wishes to continue –
  (i) where he appoints a solicitor to act on his behalf, paragraph (2) will apply as if he had previously conducted the claim in person; and
  (ii) where he wants to act in person, he must give an address for service.

(Rule 6.5 deals with a party's address for service)

('LSC funded client' and 'assisted person' are defined in rule 43.2)

(7) 'Certificate' in paragraph (6) means –

(a) in the case of a LSC funded client, a certificate issued under the Funding Code (approved under section 9 of the Access to Justice Act 1999), or
(b) in the case of an assisted person, a certificate within the meaning of the Civil Legal Aid (General) Regulations 1989.

Amendments—SI 1999/1008; SI 2000/1317; SI 2004/1306.

Practice Direction—See generally PD42 at p 995.
See particularly paras 2.1–2.7 (Notice of Change of Solicitor) at p 996.

Scope of provision—In the three situations referred to in r 42.2(1) it is mandatory for the party or his solicitor to:
(a) file notice of change; and
(b) serve notice of the change on every other party and (where appropriate) the former solicitor.

See *SMC Engineering (Bristol) Limited v Fraser* (2001) *The Times*, 26 January, CA where a district judge had made an order requiring the claimant to appoint new solicitors. It was held that the court could only forbid solicitors from acting and grant a stay for new solicitors to be appointed. The court could not order the claimant to appoint new solicitors.

No order of the court is required in the circumstances set out in r 42.2(1). Rule 42.2(5) makes it clear that once a solicitor is appointed to act he is considered to be the party's solicitor unless and until the requirements of Pt 42 are complied with.

Notice of change of solicitor is Form N434 and must state the party's new address for service. The notice filed with the court must also state that the notice has been served on every other party and where appropriate the former solicitor.

Revocation or discharge of certificate—From 1 April 2000, the Legal Services Commission has been responsible for funding legal services under the Community Legal Service Fund established by AJA 1999, s 5. Community Legal Service (Costs) Regulations 2000, reg 4 replaces Civil Legal Aid (General) Regulations 1989, reg 83 in respect of the revocation or discharge of a certificate. See *DEG – Deutsche Investitions- und Entwicklungsgesellschaft mbH v Koshy & ors* [2001] EWCA Civ 79, (2001) NLJ, 9 February, (2001) *The Times*, 20 February, CA which confirmed that where a state funding certificate is revoked the court has discretion to revoke the limitation in an order for costs against the previously assisted party provided that no costs attributable to the period after the grant of legal aid are recoverable until a determination in accordance with LAA 1988, s 17 has been carried out. Until all certificates issued under the Civil Legal Aid (General) Regulations 1989 have been discharged or revoked the two systems will operate side by side and CPR makes provision for certificates issued in either case.

A solicitor's retainer under a certificate ends upon receipt by the solicitor of a notice of revocation or discharge of the certificate. The solicitor must serve notice of the revocation or discharge on all other parties and to the court. No further notice or order is required by the solicitor to come off the court record. If the LSC funded client or assisted person wishes to continue with the proceedings and appoints either the solicitor who was acting for him under the certificate or another solicitor he must file notice of change and serve the notice on every other party. Alternatively, if the party who formerly had the benefit of a certificate wishes to act in person then he must give an address for service within the jurisdiction.

42.3 Order that a solicitor has ceased to act

(1) A solicitor may apply for an order declaring that he has ceased to be the solicitor acting for a party.

(2) Where an application is made under this rule –

(a) notice of the application must be given to the party for whom the solicitor is acting, unless the court directs otherwise; and

(b) the application must be supported by evidence.

(3) Where the court makes an order that a solicitor has ceased to act –

(a) a copy of the order must be served on every party to the proceedings; and

(b) if it is served by a party or the solicitor, the party or the solicitor (as the case may be) must file a certificate of service.

Practice Direction—See generally PD42 at p 995.

See specifically para 3 at p 997. Note para 3.3 that an order made under r 42.3 must be served on every party and takes effect only when it is served. If the order is not served by the court the solicitor or person serving the order must file a certificate of service in Practice Form N215.

Scope of provision—A solicitor's retainer is usually an entire contract to conduct or defend the action to the end. Whether it has determined is a matter of fact. It will usually continue until one of the following occurs: the client discharges the solicitor; the solicitor discharges himself; death (but not necessarily – *Donsland Limited v Van Hoogstraten* [2002] EWCA Civ 253, [2002] PNLR 26, CA); incapacity of the party; a change in the solicitor's firm; the final conclusion of the cause or matter. The retainer is subject to implied terms allowing the solicitor to withdraw for good cause, eg where the client fails to provide a reasonable sum of money for disbursements (Solicitors Act 1974, s 65(2)) and upon reasonable notice. The client may end the retainer at any time. If the former client or his new solicitor has not given notice of change under r 42.2, the solicitor whose retainer has determined should apply promptly for an order under this rule. Where solicitors are plainly unwilling to continue to act due to a serious breakdown in the relationship between themselves and their client, they cannot be forced to continue to act and an order removing them from the record should be made (*UCB Bank plc v Hedworth* [2003] EWCA Civ 705).

An application under this rule is made in accordance with Pt 23 and must be supported by evidence setting out the grounds upon which the order is made. It is the party who is the respondent to the application. The court may direct other persons to be added as respondents but, unless this occurs, the other parties to the claim must not be served. See *Miller v Allied Sainif (UK)* (2000) *The Times*, 31 October, Neuberger J where it was held appropriate in a simple case to allow a solicitor to make an application pursuant to r 42.3 in writing. To require their attendance would take up court time and lead to an increase in costs. Solicitors wishing to come off the record in a more complex case would be well advised to attend court. If applying in writing, they will still normally have to file evidence that the application notice has been served on the former client (r 42.3(2)(a)).

The court may direct that notice of the application need not be given to the party for whom the solicitor is or was acting eg where that party has changed address without giving the solicitor details. It is useful practice for the order declaring that the solicitor has ceased to act to set out the address for service of the party concerned. A copy of the order must be served on every party to the claim.

42.4 Removal of solicitor who has ceased to act on application of another party

(1) Where –

(a) a solicitor who has acted for a party –
(i) has died;
(ii) has become bankrupt;
(iii) has ceased to practice; or
(iv) cannot be found; and

(b) the party has not given notice of a change of solicitor or notice of intention to act in person as required by rule 42.2(2),

any other party may apply for an order declaring that the solicitor has ceased to be the solicitor acting for the other party in the case.

(2) Where an application is made under this rule, notice of the application must be given to the party to whose solicitor the application relates unless the court directs otherwise.

(3) Where the court makes an order made under this rule –

(a) a copy of the order must be served on every other party to the proceedings; and

(b) where it is served by a party, that party must file a certificate of service.

Practice Direction—See generally PD42 at p 995.

See specifically para 4 at p 997 which deals with the application and the evidence required in support.

Practice Direction – Change of Solicitor

This Practice Direction supplements CPR Part 42 (PD42)

Procedural Guide—See Guide 22, set out in Section 1 of this work.

General note—See also the notes to CPR Pt 42 for relevant commentary.

SOLICITOR ACTING FOR A PARTY

1.1 Rule 42.1 states that where the address for service of a party is the business address[1] of his solicitor, the solicitor will be considered to be acting for that party until the provisions of Part 42 have been complied with.

1 Rule 6.5 and the practice direction supplementing Part 6 contain information about the business address.

1.2 Subject to rule 42.2(6) (where the certificate of a LSC funded client or assisted person is revoked or discharged), where a party has changed his solicitor or intends to act in person, the former solicitor will be considered to be the party's solicitor unless or until;

(1) a notice of the change is
(a) filed with the court[1], and
(b) served on every other party[2], or

(2) the court makes an order under rule 42.3 and the order is served on every other party[3]. The notice should not be filed until every other party has been served.

1 Rule 42.2(2)(a).
2 Rule 42.2(2)(b).
3 Rule 42.2(5).

1.3 A solicitor appointed to represent a party only as an advocate at a hearing will not be considered to be acting for that party within the meaning of Part 42.

'Solicitor acting for a party'—Paragraphs 1.1 and 1.2 make it plain that where the address for service of a party is the business address of his solicitor, the solicitor will be considered to be acting for that party until the provisions of CPR Pt 42 have been complied with and that to effect a change of solicitor or for the party to act in person, notice of change must be served on all other parties and then filed with the court. Paragraph 1.3 deals with the situation of partial legal services where a solicitor is merely appointed by a party to represent that party as advocate at a hearing. In those circumstances, notice of change is not required.

NOTICE OF CHANGE OF SOLICITOR

2.1 Rule 42.2(1) sets out the circumstances following which a notice of the change must be filed and served.

2.2 A notice of the change giving the last known address of the former assisted person must also be filed and served on every party where, under rule 42.2(6):

(1) the certificate of a LSC funded client or assisted person is revoked or discharged,
(2) the solicitor who acted for that person has ceased to act on determination of his retainer under regulation 83 of those Regulations, and
(3) the LSC funded client or the assisted person wishes either to act in person or appoint another solicitor to act on his behalf.

2.3 In addition, where a party or solicitor changes his address for service, a notice of that change should be filed and served on every party.

2.4 A party who, having conducted a claim by a solicitor, intends to act in person must give in his notice an address for service that is within the jurisdiction[1].

1 See rule 6.5(3).

2.5 Practice form N434 should be used to give notice of any change. The notice should be filed in the court office in which the claim is proceeding.

2.6 Where the claim is proceeding in the High Court the notice should be filed either in the appropriate District Registry or if the claim is proceeding in the Royal Courts of Justice, as follows;

(1) a claim proceeding in the Queen's Bench Division – in the Action Department of the Central Office,
(2) a claim proceeding in the Chancery Division – in Chancery Chambers,
(3) a claim proceeding in the Administrative Court – in the Administrative Court office;
(4) a claim proceeding in the Admiralty and Commercial Registry – in the Admiralty and Commercial Registry, and
(5) a claim proceeding in the Technology and Construction Court – in the Registry of the Technology and Construction Court.

2.7 Where the claim is the subject of an appeal to the Court of Appeal, the notice should also be filed in the Civil Appeals Office.

(The Costs Practice Direction supplementing Part 43 to 48 contains details of the information required to be included when the funding arrangements for the claim change)

Scope of provision—This merely deals with the form of notice and where the notice should be filed in High Court matters. The relevant practice form is N434.

APPLICATION FOR AN ORDER THAT A SOLICITOR HAS CEASED TO ACT

3.1 A solicitor may apply under rule 42.3 for an order declaring that he has ceased to be the solicitor acting for a party.

3.2 The application should be made in accordance with Part 23[1] and must be supported by evidence[2]. Unless the court directs otherwise the application notice must be served on the party[3].

1 See Part 23 and the practice direction which supplements it.
2 See Part 32 and the practice direction which supplements it for information about evidence.
3 Rule 42.3(2).

3.3 An order made under rule 42.3 must be served on every party and takes effect when it is served. Where the order is not served by the court, the person serving must file a certificate of service in practice form N215.

Scope of provision—The order does not take effect until it is served. If service is not by the court the party or person serving must file Certificate of Service in Practice Form N215.

APPLICATION BY ANOTHER PARTY TO REMOVE A SOLICITOR

4.1 Rule 42.4 sets out circumstances in which any other party may apply for an order declaring that a solicitor has ceased to be the solicitor acting for another party in the proceedings.

4.2 The application should be made in accordance with Part 23 and must be supported by evidence. Unless the court directs otherwise the application notice must be served on the party to whose solicitor the application relates.

4.3 An order made under rule 42.4 must be served on every other party to the proceedings. Where the order is not served by the court, the person serving must file a certificate of service in practice form N215.

NEW ADDRESS FOR SERVICE WHERE ORDER MADE UNDER RULES 42.3 OR 42.4

5.1 Where the court has made an order under rule 42.3 that a solicitor has ceased to act or under rule 42.4 declaring that a solicitor has ceased to be the solicitor for a party, the party for whom the solicitor was acting must give a new address for service to comply with rule 6.5(2).

(Rule 6.5(2) provides that a party must give an address for service within the jurisdiction)

(Until such time as a new address for service is given rule 6.5(6) will apply)

PART 43
SCOPE OF COST RULES AND DEFINITIONS

CONTENTS OF THIS PART

Introduction to Costs—Parts 43–48 deal with the provisions as to costs. In particular they deal with the basis upon which the court will award costs at the conclusion of a hearing or case. They also deal with how the court will quantify costs. However, Pts 43–48 do not provide a complete self contained code. In addition the practitioner must have regard to the Cost Practice Directions and CPR Schs 1 and 2. There are many other provisions relating to costs scattered throughout the Rules for example –
- Rule 3.7 (non-payment of fees);
- Rule 27.14 (costs on the small claims track);
- Rule 27.15 (claims re-allocated from the small claims track to another track);
- Rule 28.2 (fast track general provisions);
- Rule 34.14 (fees and expenses of examiner);
- Rule 35.15 (assessors);
- Part 36 (the whole of this Part has cost consequences);
- Rule 38.6 (liability for costs on discontinuance).

The practitioner must also have regard to other sources of material relating to costs for example –
- Solicitors Act 1974;
- Legal Aid Act 1988 (and its associated statutory instruments);
- Access to Justice Act 1999;
- Litigant in Person (Costs and Expenses) Act 1975;
- Conditional Fee Agreements Regulations 2000;
- Collective Conditional Fee Agreements Regulations 2000;
- Judgment Debts (Rate of Interest) Order 1993;
- Solicitors' (Non-Contentious Business) Remuneration Order 1994.

Note—Access to Justice Act 1999, ss 27–31 were implemented on 1 April 2000 and particularly relate to the recovery of 'success fees' and 'insurance premiums' in relation to CFAs entered into after that date. Practitioners should also be aware of the content of –
- Conditional Fee Agreements Regulations 2000;
- Access to Justice (Membership Organisations) Regulations 2000;
- Access to Justice Act 1999 (Transitional Provisions) Order 2000;
- Collective Conditional Fee Agreements Regulations 2000;
- Conditional Fee Agreements (Miscellaneous Amendments) Regulations 2003;
- Civil Procedure (Amendment) Rules 2004.

Transitional provisions—All the provisions of the new costs rules apply from 26 April 1999 both as to the basis upon which costs orders are made and the manner in which those costs are to be quantified or assessed. So far as the practitioner is concerned, litigation may well have been in progress prior to April 26 1999 without a party or their lawyers being aware that the steps they were taking would be viewed differently by a court at the time costs are assessed. The general presumption is that no costs for work undertaken before 26 April 1999 will be disallowed if those costs would have been allowed on a taxation of costs before 26 April 1999 (PD51, para 18(2)).

Any assessment of costs taking place on or after 26 April 1999 will be in accordance with Pts 43–48 (PD51, para 18(1)). The decision to allow costs for work undertaken on or after 26 April 1999 will generally be in accordance with Pts 43–48 (PD51, para 18(3)).

PDCosts, paras 57.2–57.7 deal in more detail with transitional arrangements (see below).

In respect of transitional provisions relating to CFAs entered into before 3 July 2000 see PDCosts, paras 57.8–57.9.

43.1 Scope of this Part

This Part contains definitions and interpretation of certain matters set out in the rules about costs contained in Parts 44 to 48.

(Part 44 contains general rules about costs; Part 45 deals with fixed costs; Part 46 deals with fast track trial costs; Part 47 deals with the detailed assessment of costs and related appeals and Part 48 deals with costs payable in special cases)

Practice Direction—See generally PDCosts at p 1083 and specifically Sections 1–2 at p 1083.

Scope of provision—Family Proceedings: Family Proceedings (Miscellaneous Amendment) Rules 1999 apply Pts 43, 44 (except rr 44.9–44.12), Pts 47 and 48 of Civil Procedure Rules 1998 to the assessment of costs in family proceedings and to proceedings in the Family Division with modifications. The rules apply to any assessment of costs taking place after 26 April 1999 with the proviso that no costs for work done before that date will be disallowed if they would have been allowed on taxation before that date. See also the President's Direction [1999] 3 All ER 192 and the statement from the President of the Family Division (*Law Society Gazette*, 31 August 2000, p 45) applying the costs practice directions and all subsequent editions as and when they are published and come into effect to family proceedings and proceedings in the Family Division to the extent applicable to such proceedings. References to the manner in which legal services are funded pursuant to the Access to Justice Act 1999 are to be disregarded in 'family proceedings' (as defined by the Courts and Legal Services Act 1990, s 58A(2)) and cannot be the subject of an enforceable CFA.

Insolvency: Insolvency (Amendment) (No 2) Rules 1999 provide that CPR Pts 43–48 apply to insolvency proceedings with necessary modifications. They substitute a new Chapter 6 in Pt 7 of Insolvency Rules 1986 dealing with the requirement to assess costs by detailed assessment and the relevant procedure to be adopted.

43.2 Definitions and application

(1) In Parts 44 to 48, unless the context otherwise requires –

- (a) 'costs' includes fees, charges, disbursements, expenses, remuneration, reimbursement allowed to a litigant in person under rule 48.6[, any additional liability incurred under a funding arrangement and any fee or reward charged by a lay representative for acting on behalf of a party in proceedings allocated to the small claims track;
- (b) 'costs judge' means a taxing master of the Supreme Court;
- (c) 'costs officer' means –
  - (i) a costs judge;
  - (ii) a district judge; and
  - (iii) an authorised court officer;
- (d) 'authorised court officer' means any officer of –
  - (i) a county court;
  - (ii) a district registry;
  - (iii) the Principal Registry of the Family Division; or
  - (iv) the Supreme Court Costs Office;

  whom the Lord Chancellor has authorised to assess costs;
- (e) 'fund' includes any estate or property held for the benefit of any person or class of person and any fund to which a trustee or personal representative is entitled in his capacity as such;
- (f) 'receiving party' means a party entitled to be paid costs;
- (g) 'paying party' means a party liable to pay costs;
- (h) 'assisted person' means an assisted person within the statutory provisions relating to legal aid;

(i) 'LSC funded client' means an individual who receives services funded by the Legal Services Commission as part of the Community Legal Service within the meaning of Part I of the Access to Justice Act 1999;
(j) 'fixed costs' means the amounts which are to be allowed in respect of solicitors' charges in the circumstances set out in Section I of Part 45;
(k) 'funding arrangement' means an arrangement where a person has –
  (i) entered into a conditional fee agreement or a collective conditional fee agreement which provides for a success fee within the meaning of section 58(2) of the Courts and Legal Services Act 1990;
  (ii) taken out an insurance policy to which section 29 of the Access to Justice Act 1999 (recovery of insurance premiums by way of costs) applies; or
  (iii) made an agreement with a membership organisation to meet his legal costs;
(l) 'percentage increase' means the percentage by which the amount of a legal representative's fee can be increased in accordance with a conditional fee agreement which provides for a success fee;
(m) 'insurance premiums' means a sum of money paid or payable for insurance against the risk of incurring a costs liability in the proceedings, taken out after the event that is the subject matter of the claim;
(n) 'membership organisation' means a body prescribed for the purposes of section 30 of the Access to Justice Act 1999 (recovery where body undertakes to meet costs liabilities); and
(o) 'additional liability' means the percentage increase, the insurance premium, or the additional amount in respect of provision made by a membership organisation, as the case may be.

(2) The costs to which Parts 44 to 48 apply include –

(a) the following costs where those costs may be assessed by the court –
  (i) costs of proceedings before an arbitrator or umpire;
  (ii) costs of proceedings before a tribunal or other statutory body; and
  (iii) costs payable by a client to his solicitor; and
(b) costs which are payable by one party to another party under the terms of a contract, where the court makes an order for an assessment of those costs.

(3) Where advocacy or litigation services are provided to a client under a conditional fee agreement, costs are recoverable under Parts 44 to 48 notwithstanding that the client is liable to pay his legal representative's fees and expenses only to the extent that sums are recovered in respect of the proceedings, whether by way of costs or otherwise.

(4) In paragraph (3), the reference to a conditional fee agreement is to an agreement which satisfies all the conditions applicable to it by virtue of section 58 of the Courts and Legal Services Act 1990.

Amendments—SI 2000/1317; SI 2001/256; SI 2003/1242; SI 2003/1329; SI 2003/2113.

Practice Direction—See generally PDCosts at p 1083 and specifically Sections 1–2 at p 1083.

Scope of provision—The new approach to costs has resulted in a change in terminology. The word 'taxation' has been abandoned in favour of 'assessment'. Assessment is the process by which the court decides the amount of any costs payable. There are two forms of assessment: summary assessment (r 44.7(a)) and detailed assessment (r 44.7(b)). In the light of the Access to Justice Act 1999 and the ability to recover 'success fees' and 'insurance premiums', the definitions have been expanded to encompass the changes brought about by that Act.

'costs' (r 43.2 generally)—The definition incorporates a similar definition to that contained in the former RSC Ord 62, r 1(4).

'Costs' used in this connection means the costs of conducting litigation and refers to the remuneration of solicitors and disbursements by them (including counsel's fees). The only exception is the fee or reward charged by a lay representative for acting on behalf of a party in proceedings allocated to the small claims track. The costs of a litigant in person are dealt with separately at r 48.6. The definition of costs includes 'any additional liability' incurred under a funding arrangement and relates to the recoverable elements of a success fee which complies with the CFAR 2000, the CCFAR 2000 and the Conditional Fee Agreements (Miscellaneous Amendments) Regulations 2003 (CFA(MA)R 2003); a recoverable insurance premium complying with AJA 1999, s 29 or the relevant element of insurance costs recoverable by a membership organisation (as defined by r 43.2(1)(n)) and which complies with the Access to Justice (Membership Organisations) Regulations 2000).

'LSC funded client' (r 43.2(1)(i))—The AJA 1999 brought about significant changes to the public funding of civil litigation. The Legal Services Commission replaced the Legal Aid Board and is responsible for funding legal services under the Community Legal Service Fund. The LSC's funding code provides for the following levels of service –

- Legal Help: advice and assistance about a legal problem not including representation or advocacy in proceedings;
- Help at Court: advocacy at a specific hearing where the advocate is not formally representing the client in the proceedings;
- Family mediation;
- Legal representation: representation in actual or contemplated proceedings. This can take the form of investigative help (limited to investigating the merits of a potential claim) or full representation;
- Approved family help: this can take the form of help with mediation or general family help;
- Support funding: partial funding in very expensive cases that are primarily being funded privately under or with a view to a CFA. Support funding can take the form of investigative support (equivalent to investigative help) or litigation support (equivalent to full representation).

Certificates (similar to a Legal Aid certificate) are issued for legal representation, approved family help and support funding. The certificate will state which level of service is covered and if proceedings have been issued a copy of the certificate will be lodged with the court.

For some time it will be necessary for the rules relating to Legal Aid and the Community Legal Service to operate side by side until all legal aid certificates granted under the Legal Aid Act 1988 have worked through the system. Consequently the definitions in this rule refer to 'LSC funded client' and 'assisted person' depending under which system the client was funded.

'percentage increase'—Conditional fee agreements entered into before 1 April 2000 referred to 'success fees'. The CFAR 2000 refer to a 'percentage increase'. Only CFAs that comply with those regulations and any subsequent amendment thereto will allow for the recovery of all or part of the percentage increase or success fee from the losing party.

'insurance premium'—To be recoverable from the losing party, an insurance premium must comply with the provisions of AJA 1999, s 29. The main features of such insurance are –

(a) The party taking out the insurance must either have paid or have a liability to pay for the contract of insurance;
(b) The policy must specifically relate to the proceedings in question;
(c) The risk to be covered by the insurance is in respect of a costs liability in the proceedings;
(d) The policy must be taken out after the event which is the subject matter of the claim.

Practitioners should be wary of policy arrangements and/or insurance products that do not impose a direct financial obligation on their client in the event of success or failure in the relevant action.

'Membership Organisation'—For the definition of 'membership organisations' and the ability to recover costs liabilities, see the Access to Justice (Membership Organisations) Regulations 2000.

The Indemnity Principle—A solicitor's costs are initially charged to his client or, where the client is funded by the Community Legal Service Fund, through the Legal Services Commission. An order of the court or a provision in the Rules may entitle the client to recover all or part of his costs from another party. In effect, his right to recover costs is an indemnity against the costs he has incurred with his own solicitor: 'The Indemnity Principle'.

See *Gundry v Sainsbury* [1910] 1 KB 645, CA and *General of Berne v Jardine Reinsurance Management Limited & ors* [1998] 2 All ER 301, CA, May LJ (p 304):

> 'The principle is simply that costs are normally to be paid in compensation for what the receiving party has or is obliged himself to pay. They are not punitive and should not enable the receiving party to make a profit'.

The general presumption is that a client accepts personal liability for his solicitor's costs (*R v Miller* [1993] 1 WLR 1057 and see *Hazlett v South Sefton Magistrates' Court* [2001] EWHC Admin 791; also *Leeds City Council v Carr and Coles and Wells v Barnsley Metropolitan Borough Council* [1999] TLR, 12 November). This presumption is rebuttable for example where there is a *pro bono* arrangement.

Problems have arisen with regard to the indemnity principle and its relationship to contingency fee arrangements. A 'contingency fee' means any sum (whether fixed or calculated either as a percentage of the proceeds or otherwise) payable only in the event of success in the prosecution or defence of any action, suit or other contentious proceedings. Courts have held such agreements to have been contrary to public policy and therefore unenforceable (*British Waterways Board v Norman* (1994) 26 HLR 232, QBD and see *Arata Potato Company Limited v Taylor Joynson Garrett* [1994] 4 All ER 695). In *Thai Trading Co (a firm) v Taylor & anor* [1998] QB 781, CA it was held that it was no longer contrary to public policy for a solicitor to agree not to claim his full fee if the action was lost provided that he did not seek to recover more than his ordinary profit costs and disbursements if he wins. This proposition was called into question by the Queen's Bench Divisional Court in *Hughes v Kingston Borough Council* [1999] QB 1193 and more recently in *Geraghty & Co v Awwad and Gustavon* [1999] All ER (D) 1318, CA where May LJ said:

> '[I]n my judgment where parliament has by what are now successive enactments modified the law by which any arrangement to receive a contingency fee was impermissible there is no present room for the court by an application of what is perceived to be public policy to go beyond that which parliament has provided.'

Solicitors Practice Rules, r 8(1) has been amended with effect from 7 January 1999 to allow contingency fee arrangements provided that they are permitted by statute or by common law.

Access to Justice Act 1999, s 27 replaces CLSA 1990, s 58 and makes all agreements which provide for legal fees to be paid only in certain circumstances subject to the provisions of the new section. It is effective from 1 April 2000 and provides statutory approval for two types of agreement –

- CFAs where a 'success fee' or 'percentage increase' is claimed, or
- CFAs where a solicitor provides for his fees and expenses to be paid only in specified circumstances.

Additionally, from 30 November 2000 the CCFAR 2000 and the CFA(MA)R 2003 permit 'collective conditional fee agreements' (see note **'Collective conditional fee agreements'** below).

Access to Justice Act 1999, s 27 provides statutory approval in the *Thai Trading* or *Bevan Ashford v Geoff Yeandle (Contractors) Ltd* [1999] Ch 239 type of case. The scope of CFAs has now been extended to cover all proceedings except criminal and certain family proceedings (CFAO 2000). However, only CFAs that comply with the CFAR 2000 will be enforceable. Practitioners should be aware that in the light of the *Geraghty* decision (see above) discounted fee arrangements entered into which do not comply with the AJA 1999 and the CFAR 2000 may be unenforceable (see note **'Conditional fee agreements'** below for the requirements for an enforceable CFA).

Exceptions to the Indemnity Principle—

Employed solicitors: see *Lloyds Bank Limited v Eastwood* [1974] 3 All ER 603, CA. See also *Maes Finance Limited & anor v WG Edwards & Partners & anor* [2000] 2 Costs LR 198, QBD, and *Elias J & Cole v British Telecom plc* [2000] All ER (D) 917.

Legal Aid: Civil Legal Aid (General) (Amendment) Regulations 1994 introduced 'prescribed rates' for solicitors. Regulation 107B provides that a solicitor for a successful legally aided client may recover his costs at commercial rates from the party against whom the costs order is made. Civil Legal Aid (General) (Amendment) Regulations 1999 confirm that the Indemnity Principle can be breached even if there is a cost limitation in the Legal Aid certificate.

Law Centres: Where 'free advice' is offered a Law Centre may recover under the terms of a third party costs order (Employed Solicitors Code 1999, r 7 (Law Society's Gazette, 30 March 1994)).

Fast track trial costs: Pt 46 CPR provides fixed rates for fast track trials irrespective of the work carried out, the retainer or commercial rates of charge.

The proper application of the indemnity principle in relation to the assessment of a solicitor's bill of costs requires that the detail of the work done is considered item by item. In particular the recoverable hourly rate as between party and party should never exceed that charged to the client (*General of Berne Insurance Co v Jardine Reinsurance Management Limited & ors* [1998] 1 WLR 1231, CA. Although this case related specifically to a Contentious Business Agreement, the 'item by item' approach was upheld in the case of *Nederlandse Reassurantie Groep Holding NV v Bacon and Woodrow & ors* (1998) (unreported) 21 April, QBD in relation to other types of retainer.

Rule 43.2(3) and (4)—These new provisions have effect only where the CFA in issue was entered into on or after 2 June 2003. See note **'Conditional fee agreements'** below.

Conditional fee agreements—The main requirements for an enforceable CFA are –

1 General requirements for a CFA with or without a success fee

(a) The particular proceedings to which the agreement relates including any counterclaim or proceedings to enforce a judgment must be specified;

(b) The agreement must set out:

   (i) the circumstances in which the lawyers' fees and expenses are payable and whether any payment is due if those circumstances only partly occur;

   (ii) the provisions for termination;

   (iii) the circumstances and cases and the method used to calculate the charges and whether the amount of any charges are limited by reference to the damages.

2 Additional requirements where a percentage increase (success fee) is charged

(a) The reasons for setting the percentage increase at the level stated in the agreement must be specified;

(b) Any percentage increase specifically relating to the costs to the lawyer of postponing the payment of his fees and expenses must be specified.

3 Additional information

The practitioner must also provide the following information to his client before a CFA can be entered into –

(a) The circumstances in which his client may be liable to pay costs;

(b) The circumstances in which his client may seek assessment of the lawyers fees and expenses and the procedure for so doing;

(c) What other methods of financing the costs are available and if so what they are;

(d) If the lawyer considers that any particular method or methods of financing any/all of the costs are appropriate he must say so;

(e) The lawyer must ascertain whether his client is insured against incurring the liability for costs under an existing contract of insurance;

(f) If the lawyer considers that it is appropriate for his client to take out a contract of insurance he must specify:

   (i) his reasons for so doing;

   (ii) whether the lawyer has an interest in that particular product.

4 Additional considerations

(a) The CFA must be in writing and must specify the general and additional requirements referred to above;

(b) The additional information must be given orally to the client except the information concerning insurance which must also be confirmed in writing.

From 2 June 2003, the CFA(MA)R 2003 amend the CFAR 2000 and the CCFAR 2000 and provide that a CFA will be enforceable even though the client is liable to pay his legal representative's fees and expenses only if and to the extent that he recovers damages or costs in the proceedings. These Regulations in effect abrogate the Indemnity Principle in relation to this type of CFA. Practitioners will to this extent be able to agree lawfully with their clients not to seek to recover by way of costs anything in excess of what the court awards or what is agreed will be paid and will no longer be prevented from openly contracting with their clients upon such terms. The Access to Justice Act 1999 (Commencement No 10) Order 2003 brings into force AJA 1999, s 31 which in turn amends SCA 1981, s 51(2), allowing rules of court to be made which limit the Indemnity Principle. As a consequence, r 43.2 has been amended.

The principal differences between the standard CFA and the new 'No win, no fee, no deduction CFA' or 'CFA lite' are that regs 2, 3 and 4 of the CFAR 2000 do not apply. Consequently the general requirements for a 'No win, no fee, no deduction' CFA are those set out in points 1 and 2 above. There is, however, no requirement to provide the additional information referred to at point 3 above. Instead the agreement may specify the circumstances when the client will be liable to pay the legal representative's fees and expenses where:

(a) he fails to co-operate with his lawyer;

(b) he fails to attend any medical or expert examination;

(c) he fails to give instructions; or

(d) withdraws instructions.

Before the agreement is entered into the legal representative must inform his client as to the circumstances in which the client may be liable to pay the lawyer's fees and expenses and provide any further explanation that the client may reasonably require.

There have been a large number of technical challenges to the CFAR 2000. The leading authority is now *Hollins v Russell* [2003] EWCA Civ 718, [2003] All ER (D) 311 (May), CA. Per Brooke LJ:

> '[221] When we turn to matters of law we have explained that a CFA will only be unenforceable if in the circumstances of the particular case the conditions applicable to it by virtue of section 58 have not been sufficiently complied with in the light of their statutory purposes. Cost Judges should ask themselves the following question: "Has the particular departure from a regulation of requirement in section 58 either on its own or in conjunction with any other such departure in this case had a materially adverse effect either upon the protection afforded to the client or upon the proper administration of justice?" … [224] The Court should be watchful when it considers allegations that there have been breaches of the regulations. The parliamentary purpose is to enhance Access to Justice not to impede it and will create better ways of delivering litigation services not worse ones. These purposes will be thwarted if those who render good service to their clients under CFAs are at risk of going unremunerated at the culmination of the bitter trench warfare which has been such an unhappy feature of the recent litigation scene.'

See also *Spencer v Wood & anor* [2004] EWCA Civ 352, [2004] TLR 195, (2004) *The Times*, 30 March, where the court held that the claimant's CFA was unenforceable restating the material breach test set out in *Hollins v Russell.*

In addition to the above requirements the practitioner must, if the success fee and/or insurance premium is to be recovered from the losing party, comply with the notification provisions of r 44.15 and the relevant practice direction, but see *Montlake (as trustees of Wasps Football Club) v Lambert Smith Hampton Group Ltd* [2004] EWHC 938 (Comm), [2004] 20 EG 167, (2004) Lawtel, 19 July, QBD, Langley J. Here, the court allowed recovery of costs in proceedings funded by a CFA where late discovery of that fact had been given on the basis that the defendant had suffered no prejudice.

Collective conditional fee agreements—An agreement which complies with the CFAR 2000 is entered into on an individual basis. Each action is supported by a separate CFA. These Regulations do not sit easily with the practical operation of the mass litigation market. For a practical example of collective conditional fee agreements in practice see *Thornley v Lang* [2003] EWCA Civ 1484, [2004] 1 WLR 378, CA, where the court found on the facts that in relation to the agreement entered into between the parties there was no infringement of the indemnity principle. Legal service providers and funders such as insurers or trade unions undertake routine cases on a bulk basis with the basic terms of the agreement as to funding and costs usually being common to all cases undertaken. An agreement which complies with the CCFAR 2000 does not refer to specific proceedings but provides for fees to be payable on a common basis in relation to a class of proceedings or if it refers to more than one class of proceedings on a common basis in relation to each class. The requirements for the contents of CCFAs are –

1 General requirements for CCFA with or without a success fee

(a) The agreement must specify the circumstances in which the legal representatives fees and expenses are payable;
(b) The agreement must provide that the legal representative inform the recipient of the legal services as to the circumstances in which he may be liable to pay the costs of the legal representative and give any further explanation that may be required;
(c) The CCFA must provide that the legal representative confirm acceptance of instructions specifically with the recipient of legal services.

2 Additional requirements where a percentage increase (success fee) is charged

(a) The legal representative must prepare a written statement setting out –
    (i) a risk assessment;
    (ii) the amount of any percentage increase having regard to the risk assessment; and
    (iii) the reasons for setting the percentage increase at that level.
(b) If the agreement relates to court proceedings the agreement must provide for disclosure of the reasons to the court.

These Regulations have now been amended by the CFA(MA)R 2003, in force from 2 June 2003, which substantially simplify the form of the CCFA in the event that practitioners wish to agree with their clients not to seek to recover by way of costs anything in excess of what the court awards or what it is agreed will be paid.

'lay representative' (r 43.2(1)(a))—Lay representatives may represent a party in cases which have been allocated to the small claims track (Lay Representatives (Rights of Audience) Order 1992). The lay representative may not conduct the litigation for the party but can represent the litigant at any interlocutory or preliminary appointment as well as the hearing itself. His remuneration is a matter of contract with his client. Any recoverable *inter partes* costs are assessed by the court. See *R v Bow County Court ex parte Pelling* (1999) *The Times*, 28 July, regarding attendances of lay representatives at hearings.

'authorised court officer' (r 43.2(1)(d))—Paragraph 30.1 of PDCosts deals with the powers of an authorised court officer.

'fixed costs' (r 43.2(1)(i))—As well as the fixed costs set out in Pt 45, practitioners should be aware that certain fixed costs have been retained in Sch 1, RSC Ord 62, App 3 and Sch 2, CCR Ord 38, App B.

Road traffic accidents—From 6 October 2003, Pt 45 is amended by the addition of rr 45.7–45.14, which provide for fixed recoverable costs of claims arising out of road traffic accidents where the total value of the agreed damages does not exceed £10,000 and no proceedings, other than costs-only proceedings, have been commenced.

From 1 June 2004, Pt 45, Section III (rr 45.15–45.19) applies to all road traffic accidents arising on or after 6 October 2003 and fixes the level of recoverable success fees in cases outside the small claims track and not falling within the costs only provisions of Pt 45, Section II.

'costs which are payable … under the terms of a contract' (r 43.2(2)(b))—See Pt 48.3 and PDCosts, paras 50.1–50.4.

43.3 Meaning of summary assessment

'Summary assessment' means the procedure by which the court, when making an order about costs, orders payment of a sum of money instead of fixed costs or 'detailed assessment'.

Scope of provision—Generally, the court will make a summary assessment of costs:

(a) at the conclusion of the trial of a case which has been dealt with on the fast track. In those cases the order will deal with the costs of the whole claim;
(b) at the conclusion of any other hearing which has lasted less than one day in which case the order will deal with the costs of the application or matter to which the hearing related. If this hearing disposes of the claim, the order may deal with the costs of the whole claim.
(c) at certain hearings in the Court of Appeal (PD52, paras 14.1 and 14.2).

The court will not make a summary assessment of costs if the paying party can show substantial grounds for disputing the sum claimed for costs which cannot be dealt with summarily or there is insufficient time to carry out a summary assessment (PDCosts, para 13.2). Usually summary assessment will only be awarded where the basis of the costs order is 'costs in any event'. The general rule is that no summary assessment of costs will be made if the court has ordered the costs in question to be treated as costs in the case.

Note that r 44.3A prevents a court from making a summary assessment of an additional liability before the conclusion of the proceedings or the part of the proceedings to which the funding arrangement relates. There is no reason why the court should not make a summary assessment of the base costs of the hearing or application unless there is good reason not to do so. In these situations an order for payment will not be made by the court unless it is satisfied that in respect of the costs claimed the receiving party is at the time liable to pay his legal representative an amount equal to or greater than the costs claimed. For example a statement in the form of the certificate appended at the end of Form N260 may be sufficient proof of liability. The mere giving of information which is required under r 44.15 is not sufficient (PDCosts, para 14.3).

For a decision on the principles when it is appropriate for a court to summarily assess, see *Richardson v Desquenne et Giral* [1999] CPLR 744, CA followed in *Picnic at Ascot Incorporated v Derigs & ors* [2001] FSR 2, (2000) Lawtel, 9 February, ChD.

The 'Guide to the Summary Assessment of Costs' (2005 edition), amended from 1 January 2005, provides guideline hourly rates across the country in four distinct bands for solicitors, together with appropriate fees for counsel, which are broad approximations only. Most local Law Societies have agreed guideline hourly rates to be applied in their local courts with their designated civil judges. Practitioners should check with the courts in which they practise to ascertain the local guideline rates.

43.4 Meaning of detailed assessment

'Detailed assessment' means the procedure by which the amount of costs is decided by a costs officer in accordance with Part 47.

Procedural Guide—See Guide 32 (Detailed Assessment of Costs), set out in Section 1 of this work.

Scope of provision—'detailed assessment' is the name given to the procedure formerly known as taxation. The procedure is set out in Pt 47. For the form and content of a bill of costs post-26 April 1999, see PDCosts, Section 4. In any order of the court whether made before or after 26 April 1999 the word 'taxation' will be taken to mean 'detailed assessment' and the words 'to be taxed' will be taken to mean 'to be decided by detailed assessment' (PDCosts, para 3.8).

PART 44
GENERAL RULES ABOUT COSTS

CONTENTS OF THIS PART

44.1 Scope of this Part

This Part contains general rules about costs and entitlement to costs.

(The definitions contained in Part 43 are relevant to this Part)

Practice Direction—See generally PDCosts at p 1083 and specifically Sections 7–23 at p 1097.

44.2 Solicitor's duty to notify client

Where –

(a) the court makes a costs order against a legally represented party; and

(b) the party is not present when the order is made,

the party's solicitor must notify his client in writing of the costs order no later than 7 days after the solicitor receives notice of the order.

Practice Direction—See generally PDCosts at p 1083 and specifically Section 7 at p 1097.

Scope of provision—A solicitor is under a duty to inform his client whenever an adverse costs order is made. 'Client' includes a party for whom a solicitor is acting *and* any other person for example an insurer, trade union or employer who has instructed the solicitor to act or who is liable to pay his fees (PDCosts, para 7.1). Not only must the solicitor notify the client of the order but he must also explain why the order came to be made.

There is no enforcement provision in relation to a breach of this rule but see costs provisions with regard to misconduct, r 44.14 and PDCosts, para 7.3, requiring the solicitor to produce evidence to the court showing that he took reasonable steps to comply with the rule. In default the court may impose sanctions under its general case management powers. In any event if an order is made against a party at a hearing it is likely that the court will summarily assess the costs (r 44.7(a)). Unless the court orders to the contrary, the costs are to be paid within 14 days of the assessment (r 44.8(a)).

Period within which notification should occur—The solicitor must notify his client in writing of the costs order (and the reason why it came to be made) not later than 7 days after the solicitor receives notice of the order, not within 7 days from when the order was made.

44.3 Court's discretion and circumstances to be taken into account when exercising its discretion as to costs

(1) The court has discretion as to –

(a) whether costs are payable by one party to another;
(b) the amount of those costs; and
(c) when they are to be paid.

(2) If the court decides to make an order about costs –

(a) the general rule is that the unsuccessful party will be ordered to pay the costs of the successful party; but
(b) the court may make a different order.

(3) The general rule does not apply to the following proceedings –

(a) proceedings in the Court of Appeal on an application or appeal made in connection with proceedings in the Family Division; or
(b) proceedings in the Court of Appeal from a judgment, direction, decision or order given or made in probate proceedings or family proceedings.

(4) In deciding what order (if any) to make about costs, the court must have regard to all the circumstances, including –

(a) the conduct of all the parties;
(b) whether a party has succeeded on part of his case, even if he has not been wholly successful; and
(c) any payment into court or admissible offer to settle made by a party which is drawn to the court's attention (whether or not made in accordance with Part 36).

(Part 36 contains further provisions about how the court's discretion is to be exercised where a payment into court or an offer to settle is made under that Part)

(5) The conduct of the parties includes –

(a) conduct before, as well as during, the proceedings and in particular the extent to which the parties followed any relevant pre-action protocol;
(b) whether it was reasonable for a party to raise, pursue or contest a particular allegation or issue;
(c) the manner in which a party has pursued or defended his case or a particular allegation or issue; and
(d) whether a claimant who has succeeded in his claim, in whole or in part, exaggerated his claim.

(6) The orders which the court may make under this rule include an order that a party must pay –

(a) a proportion of another party's costs;
(b) a stated amount in respect of another party's costs;
(c) costs from or until a certain date only;
(d) costs incurred before proceedings have begun;

(e) costs relating to particular steps taken in the proceedings;
(f) costs relating only to a distinct part of the proceedings; and
(g) interest on costs from or until a certain date, including a date before judgment.

(7) Where the court would otherwise consider making an order under paragraph (6)(f), it must instead, if practicable, make an order under paragraph (6)(a) or (c).

(8) Where the court has ordered a party to pay costs, it may order an amount to be paid on account before the costs are assessed.

(9) Where a party entitled to costs is also liable to pay costs the court may assess the costs which that party is liable to pay and either –

(a) set off the amount assessed against the amount the party is entitled to be paid and direct him to pay any balance; or
(b) delay the issue of a certificate for the costs to which the party is entitled until he has paid the amount which he is liable to pay.

Practice Direction—See generally PDCosts at p 1083 and specifically Section 8 at p 1097.

Scope of provision—The court's powers in relation to costs are set out in SCA, s 51. Rule 44.3(2)(a) preserves the general rule that the unsuccessful party will be ordered to pay the costs of the successful party. Nevertheless the general rule is subject to the proviso in r 44.3(2)(b) that 'the court may make a different order'. No longer does success either in whole or in part guarantee an order for costs. See *Phonographic Performance v AEI Rediffusion* [1999] 1 WLR 1507, CA, per Woolf MR:

> 'The "follow the event principle" is to be the starting point from which a court can readily depart. The most significant change of emphasis in the new Rules is to require courts to be more ready to make separate orders which reflect the outcome of different issues.'

Prior to the CPR a party who substantially succeeded in an action was entitled to all his costs (*Re Elgindata (No 2)* [1992] 1 WLR 1207, CA). Rule 44.3 now enables the court to do greater justice where a successful party has caused an unsuccessful party to incur costs on an issue which later fails. See *Johnsey v The Secretary of State for the Environment* [2001] EWCA Civ 535, [2001] NPC 79, CA where Chadwick LJ set out the principles to be applied to the determination of costs post-CPR:

(1) Costs cannot be recovered except under an order of the court.
(2) Whether to make a costs order and, if so, what order to make is at the discretion of the trial judge.
(3) The starting point for the exercise of discretion is that costs should follow the event.
(4) The judge may make different orders for costs in relation to discrete issues. In particular, he should consider doing so where a party has been successful on one issue but unsuccessful on another and in that event may make an order for costs against the party who has been generally successful in the litigation.
(5) The judge may deprive a party of costs on an issue on which he has been successful if satisfied that the party acted unreasonably in relation to that issue.
(6) An appellate court should not interfere with the judge's exercise of discretion merely because it takes the view that it would have exercised the discretion differently.

See also *The Estate of Doctor Anandh & anor v Barnet Primary Health Care Trust & ors* [2004] EWCA Civ 05, (2004) Lawtel, 20 February, CA, where the Court of Appeal restated the general rule that costs should follow the event. The submissions in this case did not demonstrate sufficient reason for departing from the general rule.

When making an order for costs, the judge should clearly state his reasons, particularly where the costs incurred are disproportionate or the general rule is departed from (*English v Emery Reimbold and Strick Limited* [2002] EWCA Civ 605; *Verrechia v Commissioner of Police for the Metropolis* [2002] EWCA Civ 605; *Lavelle v Lavelle* [2004] EWCA Civ 223).

'conduct' (r 44.3 generally)—The court has wide power to take into account the conduct of the parties not only during the course of proceedings but *before an action has commenced.* Accordingly, practitioners who ignore any relevant pre-action protocols will not obtain an order in relation to their own costs of the proceedings. In addition they may be ordered to pay the costs of the other party arising out of the non-compliance with the pre-action protocol, probably on an indemnity basis

(PDProt, paras 2.1–3.2). See also r 1.4(2)(a) (parties duty to co-operate with each other) and PDProt, para 4 which deals with pre-action behaviour in cases not covered by a pre-action protocol.

For examples where conduct has been taken into account, see *Liverpool City Council v Rosemary Chavasse Limited and Walton Group plc* [1999] CPLR 802, p 802. The successful claimant only obtained a 50% costs order because of its pre-litigation conduct in failing to negotiate or deal with matters expeditiously. For other examples of conduct which may be taken into account see *Molloy v Shell UK Limited* [2001] EWCA Civ 1272, [2002] PIQR P56, CA, where a claimant exaggerated injuries resulting in judgment of less than payment into court. The normal costs order would be to pay the defendant's costs from the date of payment-in. Here, this was held to be an insufficient remedy for the claimant's conduct. Therefore, the order was made that the claimant pay all of the defendant's costs. Where a claimant intentionally exaggerated her claim, the fact that she beat the defendant's Pt 36 payment was not the guiding factor in awarding costs, the defendant being viewed as the overall winning party taking into account the conduct of the parties, the claimant having shown no intention to settle the matter. The defendant was ordered to pay the claimant's costs down to the date of payment in and the claimant to pay all the defendant's costs thereafter (*Painting v University of Oxford* [2005] EWCA Civ 161). *Cerberus Software Ltd v Rowley* [2001] EWCA Civ 497 was a successful appeal from an EAT where the court declined to award costs because the appellant's behaviour to the claimant had been a 'travesty of good industrial relations'.

Conduct can also relate to the manner in which a party approaches litigation. For an example see *Dunnett v Railtrack plc* [2002] EWCA Civ 303, [2002] 2 All ER 850, CA, where the court held that if a party rejected ADR out of hand when it had been suggested by the court, then it should suffer the consequences when costs came to be decided. In the instant case the court made no order as to costs.

However, in *Halsey v Milton Keynes General NHS Trust* [2004] EWCA Civ 576, [2004] All ER (D) 125 (May), [2004] TLR 292, (2004) *The Times*, 27 May, CA the Court of Appeal held that there is no presumption that a party to a dispute should agree to mediation or other alternative dispute resolution. Refusal to agree to ADR does not justify departure from the general rule that costs follow the event, unless it is shown that the successful party acted unreasonably in refusing to do so.

'offer to settle' (r 44.3(4)(c))—Offers to settle not made in accordance with Pt 36 will only have the consequences specified in that Part if the court so orders and will be given such weight on any issue as to costs as the court thinks appropriate (PD36, para 1.3). There are compelling reasons of both principle and policy why those prepared to make genuine offers of monetary settlement should do so by way of Pt 36 payments rather than by way of written offers alone (*Amber v Stacey* [2001] 1 WLR 1225, CA). See also *Factortame Ltd & ors v Secretary of State for the Environment, Transport and the Regions* [2002] EWCA Civ 22, [2002] 2 All ER 838, CA. Here it was held that the presumption expressed at r 36.20, namely that a claimant who fails to better a payment-in should be treated as the unsuccessful party as from the date fixed for acceptance, can be dislodged in special circumstances, eg where a party has withheld material and has not allowed the other party to make a proper appraisal of that party's case.

See also *Jetoil v Okta* [2003] 1 Lloyds Rep 42, where Aikens J held that although a Pt 36 offer was successful it would be unjust to award indemnity costs and higher than usual interest because until a fairly late stage in the proceedings it was difficult, if not impossible, for the defendant to gauge the proper quantum of the claims being sought.

In *Quorum A/S v Schramm (No 2)* [2002] 2 All ER (Comm) 179, [2002] 2 Lloyd's Rep 72, QBD (CommCt), Thomas J held that where a claimant recovers more than a Pt 36 payment or offer he is entitled to his costs. He should not be deprived of them by reason of a comparison with his Pt 36 offer or payment.

Partial success—The court is entitled to take into account whether a party has succeeded on part of his case even if he has not been wholly successful. A party may be successful on one or the main issue in an application but still find that costs are reduced or even awarded against him where a distinct issue or part of the case has been decided against him. The court also has power to set off any earlier orders for costs against later successful orders (r 44.3(9)(a)).

See *Stocznia Gdanska SA v Latvian Shipping Co & ors* (2001) *The Times*, 25 May, QBD (Comm Ct) where the defendant was successful on two out of three issues the claimant was awarded 38% of its costs. See also *Shirley v Caswell* (2000) Lawtel, 24 July where both claimant and defendant were awarded costs in respect of issues upon which they had succeeded. In respect of abandoned issues the Court of Appeal held that the cost of such issues should be left for determination by the costs judge. However, it is plain that there is jurisdiction to order a paying party to pay only a proportion of a receiving party's costs and *Shirley v Caswell* is not authority to the contrary (*Dooley v Parker & anor* [2002] EWCA Civ 1188).

When determining how to apportion costs between a losing litigant and a partially successful opponent, there are a number of factors to be considered: the successful party's reasonableness in pursuing the issue on which he was defeated; his conduct in relation to that issue and the litigation generally; the extra costs incurred by running that issue in terms of preparation and court time; the extent to which the unsuccessful point was linked to the successful issues in the case; and the fairness of disallowing the successful party some of his costs (*Antonelli v Allen* (2000) *The Times*, 8 December, ChD, Neuberger J).

When deciding what order for costs to make, the court must take into account the level of success in relation to the defence, and the extent to which it has succeeded in respect of its counterclaim. The court will take into account any open offer of settlement that has been made together with the conduct of the parties (*Van Dijk (Dick) v Wilkinson (Anthony) t/a HFF Construction* [2002] EWCA Civ 1780).

In *Carver (Gillian Karen) v Hammersmith & Queen Charlotte's Health Authority* (2000) (unreported) 31 July, QBD, Nelson J reduced the costs of the claimant who had failed to abandon points that she could not have sensibly pursued and that caused substantial delay in the litigation.

In *Summit Property v Pitmans* [2001] EWCA Civ 2020, [2002] 2 CPLR 97, CA, a solicitor's negligence case, the claimant succeeded on the point of a breach of duty of care but lost on the question of damage. Exceptionally, the trial judge ordered: (a) the defendant to pay the unsuccessful claimant's costs of the duty issue; and (b) the claimant to pay the successful defendant's costs on the issue of damage. This was upheld by Court of Appeal. Where a claimant and a defendant who counterclaimed both succeeded, the amount of the claim exceeding the amount of the counterclaim, the defendants were the unsuccessful parties and the claimant was awarded 60% of the costs of the proceedings (*NF Burchall v Bullard* [2005] EWCA Civ 358).

Rule 44.3(6)—The rule provides a non-exhaustive menu of possible orders in descending order of desirability. The court should if practicable make an order for a proportion or percentage of another party's costs. The factors to be considered when applying r 44.3(7) will lead to the conclusion that a trial court should ordinarily not make an order for the costs of issues unless other forms of order could not be made which adequately reflected the justice of the case (*English v Emery Reimbold & Strick Limited* [2002] EWCA Civ 605, [2002] 1 WLR 2409, CA followed in *Budgen v Andrew Gardner Partnership* [2002] EWCA Civ 1125, [2002] TLR 379, CA and in *Gould v Armstrong* [2002] EWCA Civ 1159, [2002] All ER (D) 330 (Jul), CA; *Sykes v Taylor-Rose* [2004] EWCA Civ 99, [2004] All ER (D) 468 (Feb), (2004) *The Independent*, 3 March, CA).

Where there is a real absence of adequate material upon which to form a view, the appropriate order is that there be no order as to costs (*Mayor and Burgesses of the London Borough of Hackney v Campbell Burley & Campbell Lawrence* [2005] EWCA Civ 613).

'amount to be paid on account' (r 44.3(8))—The old regime of 'taxation' often had the effect of depriving the receiving party of his costs for some time. Now, a substantial payment on account should be the norm where a successful party is awarded costs which are to be subject to detailed assessment (*Soliman v Islington Borough Council* (2001) (unreported) 16 July, Crane J). Although the amount is likely to be less than the full amount, when determining the payment on account the judge should consider all the circumstances including the likely result of the detailed assessment, the likelihood of an appeal, the parties respective financial positions and matters such as conduct. But see *Dyson Appliances Ltd v Hoover Ltd* [2003] EWHC 624 (Ch), [2003] All ER (D) 252 (Feb), where an application for an interim payment on account of costs was before Laddie J, who had not had the benefit of hearing the trial and damages enquiry. He concluded there was no presumption that an order for an interim payment should be made. An application under r 44.3(8) was contrasted with the making of an interim certificate under r 47.15, as an application under that rule was preceded by steps that put the costs judge in a position to make an accurate assessment of the costs of the case. A payment on account may be ordered to be made by instalments. See *Mars UK v Teknowledge (No 2)* [1999] 2 Costs LR 44, Jacob J and *Scholes Windows v Magnet (No 2)* [2000] ECDR 266, ChD, where a payment in three instalments was ordered where there was credible evidence that the claimant would be in financial difficulties if it was required to pay the entire sum at once.

Rule 44.3(9)—Where the claimant succeeds in the whole or in part of his claim and the defendant succeeds in the whole or in part of his counterclaim, it is preferable for there to be one order for costs adjusted appropriately, by allowing a proportion or some other partial orders as to costs in favour of one party, instead of making separate orders for costs in favour of the successful claimant and successful defendant on his counterclaim. This will avoid the *Medway Oil & Storage Company Limited v Continental Contractors Limited* [1929] AC 88, HL type of investigation. For an example of the rule in practice, see *Frayling v Premier Upholstery Ltd* (1999) 22(5) IPD 22051, Park J.

Related provisions—Rule 44.3 deals with the court's discretion to award costs. In certain circumstances CPR provide that a party is entitled to costs automatically (unless the court makes some other order). Examples are:

(a) Pt 45 – the fixed costs regime;
(b) r 3.7 – claim struck out for non-payment of fees. Defendant is entitled to his costs;
(c) r 36.13(1) – claimant's right to costs where defendant's offer accepted;

(d) r 36.14 – claimant's rights to costs where defendant accepts claimant's offer;
(e) r 38.6 – discontinuance.

44.3A Costs orders relating to funding arrangements

(1) The court will not assess any additional liability until the conclusion of the proceedings, or the part of the proceedings, to which the funding arrangement relates.

('Funding arrangement' and 'additional liability' are defined in rule 43.2)

(2) At the conclusion of the proceedings, or the part of the proceedings, to which the funding arrangement relates the court may –

- (a) make a summary assessment of all the costs, including any additional liability;
- (b) make an order for detailed assessment of the additional liability but make a summary assessment of the other costs; or
- (c) make an order for detailed assessment of all the costs.

(Part 47 sets out the procedure for the detailed assessment of costs)

Amendments—Inserted by SI 2000/1317.

Practice Direction—See generally PDCosts at p 1083 and specifically Section 9 at p 1100.

Scope of provision—This provision relates to the recovery of 'success fees' and 'insurance premiums' in CFA cases. All questions relating to the recovery of the percentage increase and/or the insurance premium should be determined at the conclusion of the proceedings either by way of summary assessment (for example in a fast track case) or by way of detailed assessment. There is nothing to stop the parties agreeing in writing that although the proceedings are continuing they will nevertheless be treated as concluded for the purpose of assessing costs. Such an agreement may be appropriate where judgment has been given for an amount of damages to be decided by the court and the costs of the claim so far are to be assessed. It is also important that if the court carries out a summary assessment of base costs in a CFA case that it identifies separately the amount allowed in respect of solicitors charges, counsel's fees and other disbursements. Any CFA should specify the consequences of a party winning or losing an interim hearing and its impact on the entitlement to costs, to avoid infringing the indemnity principle (PDCosts, para 14.3; see also PDCosts, paras 14.5–14.9).

Success fees and insurance premiums—In the case of *Callery v Gray* [2001] EWCA Civ 1117, [2001] 1 WLR 2112, CA, the Court of Appeal (upheld by the House of Lords) held:

(a) AJA 1999, s 29 (Recovery of ATE Premiums) does apply to costs only proceedings.
(b) It is reasonable for a solicitor to enter into a CFA with success fee with his client and for the client to purchase an ATE policy at the outset of litigation.
(c) There are three possible types of success fees:
  - (i) Single standard success fees set at the outset: eg in road traffic accident cases the court concluded that the recoverable success fee should not exceed 20%. This was based upon evidence of overall success rates in this type of litigation being in the region of 90%–98%. The court gave no guidance in other types of litigation.
  - (ii) Non-standard single success fees: eg where there are factors at the outset of a case suggesting that the case may fail. In those circumstances a higher success fee than 20% is reasonable. However, the success fee cannot be set until the response from the proposed defendant is known.
  - (iii) Two-stage success fees: if a case is unlikely to settle until at least the end of a protocol period, it may be reasonable to set a higher success fee at the outset allowing for a significant rebate if the case unexpectedly settles within the protocol period. The court gave no guidance as to how the two figures should be calculated, suggesting that they should be set at the outset of the litigation.

(d) In relation to the principles governing the level of recoverable ATE premiums, the focus of attention must be on the benefits purchased by the policy and not the use made of the premium by the insurer.
(e) In relation to an ATE premium certain elements of 'own costs insurance' could be regarded as falling within the description of insuring 'against the risk of liability' within AJA 1999, s 29. In those circumstances the premium of £350 contended for was reasonable.

The Court of Appeal also considered success fees in the conjoined appeals of *Atack v Lee, Ellerton and Harris* [2004] EWCA Civ 1712. The general principles to be applied are:

(1) It is the risk as it appeared to a reasonable solicitor at the time the CFA was entered into which is the vital issue in setting the appropriate success fee. Hindsight is not an option.
(2) Statistical evidence as to the percentage of those types of claim which succeed can be of assistance to a solicitor in setting his success fee.
(3) Factual matrices used by claimants' solicitors to calculate success fees attaching particular percentages when particular factors are present are of no value (see [37]).
(4) The fact a defendant denies liability before a CFA is entered in to does not justify a 100% success fee. The question is what the risk truly was on a proper analysis of the merits and otherwise of the case (see [38}).
(5) The mere fact the case goes all the way to trial on liability does not necessarily mean that 100% success fee is justified as this approach uses hindsight.
(6) The Court encouraged two-stage success fees (ie 100% reducing respectively to a lower percentage if the case settled at a certain point).

Cost judges will be more willing to approve what appear to be high success fees in cases which have gone a long distance towards trial if the maker of the CFA has agreed that a much lower success fee will be payable if the claim settles at an early stage (*Ku v Liverpool City Council* [2005] EWCA Civ 475).

In *Halloran (Thomas) v Delaney (James Francis)* [2002] EWCA Civ 1258, [2002] All ER (D) 30 (Sep) the Court of Appeal held that in all CFAs entered into after 1 August 2001 the appropriate level of success fee recoverable on simple claims settled without court proceedings being issued should be 5%, and that this should include the costs of any costs-only proceedings unless the judge was persuaded that a higher uplift was appropriate in the particular circumstances of the case. However, Brooke LJ qualified his comments in the *Halloran* case when giving judgment in the *Claims Direct Test Cases* [2003] EWCA Civ 136, [2003] All ER (D) 160 (Feb), at para 101:

> 'Subsequent events have shown that I should have expressed myself with greater clarity. The type of case to which I was referring was a case similar to *Callery v Gray* and *Halloran v Delaney* in which, to adopt the "ready reckoner" in *Cook on Costs 2003* at page 545, the prospects of success are virtually 100%. The two-step fee advocated by the court in *Callery v Gray (No 1)* is apt to allow a solicitor in such a case to cater for the wholly unexpected risk lurking below the limpid waters of the simplest of claims. It did not require any research, evidence or submissions from other parties in the industry to persuade the court that in this type of extremely simple claim a success fee of over 5% was no longer tenable in all the circumstances. The guidance given in that judgment was not intended to have any wider application.'

With regard to the various elements of a recoverable ATE policy and the factors which the court should consider in relation to such policies, see the report of Costs Judge O'Hare annexed to the Court of Appeal judgment in *Callery v Gray (No 2)* [2001] EWCA Civ 1246, [2001] 4 All ER 1. The Court of Appeal noted that the views expressed by Costs Judge O'Hare were helpful but were not definitive.

See also *Sharratt v London Central Bus Co (No 2)* (2004) Lawtel, 21 May, CA, where the Court of Appeal upheld an earlier decision of Chief Costs Judge Hurst in connection with the Accident Group Test Cases and gave guidance with regard to recoverable premiums within the meaning of AJA 1999, s 29.

44.3B Limits on recovery under funding arrangements

(1) A party may not recover as an additional liability –

(a) any proportion of the percentage increase relating to the cost to the legal representative of the postponement of the payment of his fees and expenses;
(b) any provision made by a membership organisation which exceeds the likely cost to that party of the premium of an insurance policy against the risk of incurring a liability to pay the costs of other parties to the proceedings;
(c) any additional liability for any period in the proceedings during which he failed to provide information about a funding arrangement in accordance with a rule, practice direction or court order;

(d) any percentage increase where a party has failed to comply with –
(i) a requirement in the costs practice direction; or
(ii) a court order,

to disclose in any assessment proceedings, the reasons for setting the percentage increase at the level stated in the conditional fee agreement.

(2) This rule does not apply in any assessment under rule 48.9 (assessment of a solicitor's bill to his client).

(Rule 3.9 sets out the circumstances the court will consider on an application for the relief from a sanction for the failure to comply with any rule, practice direction or court order)

Amendments—Inserted by SI 2000/1317.

Practice Direction—See generally PDCosts at p 1083 and specifically Section 10 at p 1100.

Scope of provision—Rule 44.3B(1)(a) makes it clear that the percentage increase to be recovered from the losing party relates purely to the risk that the circumstances in which the fees or expenses would be payable might not occur. Regulation 3(1) of the CFAR 2000 provides that the CFA must –

(a) briefly specify the reasons for setting the percentage increase at the level stated in the agreement, and
(b) specify how much of the percentage increase (if any) relates to the cost to the legal representative of postponement of the payment of his fees and expenses.

Consequently, if the legal representative has factored into a CFA a percentage increase to reflect postponement of the payment of his fees or the funding of disbursements this element can only be recovered from his client. This follows from the common law rule that the costs of any proceeding do not extend to an expenditure arising from the need to finance the payment of those fees (*Mann v Eccott* (1994) (unreported), 27 June, CA).

As to the notification by a party of a CFA which seeks to recover a percentage increase from a losing party, see r 44.15 and PDCosts, paras 19.1–19.5. See also the notes to rr 7.2, 8.2, 8.3, 15.6 and 16.6. Where there has been a failure to disclose the existence of a CFA an application for relief from sanctions should be made as soon as the failure is discovered.

Regulation 3(2)(a) of CFAR 2000 and the CFA(MA)R 2003 both provide that where the percentage increase is being assessed by the court, the legal representative or his client may be required to disclose the reasons for setting the percentage increase at the level stated in the agreement. In effect, there is a waiver of legal privilege. Paragraph 32.5 of PDCosts provides that where an additional liability is being sought in detailed assessment a statement of the reasons for the percentage increase given in accordance with CFAR 2000, reg 3 must be provided. Where the additional liability is an insurance premium a copy of the insurance certificate must also be provided. In the absence of these details the receiving party may not recover a percentage increase or insurance premium.

44.4 Basis of assessment

(1) Where the court is to assess the amount of costs (whether by summary or detailed assessment) it will assess those costs –

(a) on the standard basis; or
(b) on the indemnity basis,

but the court will not in either case allow costs which have been unreasonably incurred or are unreasonable in amount.

(Rule 48.3 sets out how the court decides the amount of costs payable under a contract)

(2) Where the amount of costs is to be assessed on the standard basis, the court will –

(a) only allow costs which are proportionate to the matters in issue; and

(b) resolve any doubt which it may have as to whether costs were reasonably incurred or reasonable and proportionate in amount in favour of the paying party.

(Factors which the court may take into account are set out in rule 44.5)

(3) Where the amount of costs is to be assessed on the indemnity basis, the court will resolve any doubt which it may have as to whether costs were reasonably incurred or were reasonable in amount in favour of the receiving party.

(4) Where –

(a) the court makes an order about costs without indicating the basis on which the costs are to be assessed; or

(b) the court makes an order for costs to be assessed on a basis other than the standard basis or the indemnity basis,

the costs will be assessed on the standard basis.

(5) (*revoked*)

(6) Where the amount of a solicitor's remuneration in respect of non-contentious business is regulated by any general orders made under the Solicitors Act 1974, the amount of the costs to be allowed in respect of any such business which falls to be assessed by the court will be decided in accordance with those general orders rather than this rule and rule 44.5.

Amendments—SI 2000/1317.

Practice Direction—See generally PDCosts at p 1083 and specifically Section 11 at p 1101.

Scope of provision—Rule 44.3 sets out the circumstances to be taken into account by a court when deciding an entitlement to costs. Rule 44.4 sets out the basis upon which those costs are to be assessed. The terms 'standard' and 'indemnity' remain but the meaning of those terms is entirely different.

The basic test is that the court will not allow costs which have been unreasonably incurred or are unreasonable in amount. The approach of the Cost Officer to determine questions of reasonableness is set out in *Francis v Francis and Dickerson* [1995] 3 All ER 836:

> 'When considering whether or not an item in a bill is "proper" the correct view point to be adopted by a Taxing Officer is that of a sensible solicitor sitting in his chair and considering what in the light of his then knowledge is reasonable in the interests of his lay client…'

'standard basis' (r 44.4(2))—The court will allow only costs which are proportionate to the matters in issue and will resolve any doubt which it may have as to whether the costs were reasonably incurred or reasonable and proportionate in amount in favour of the paying party.

In applying the test of proportionality the court will have regard to r 1.1(2)(c) where proportionality refers to:

(a) the amount of money involved;
(b) the importance of the case;
(c) the complexity of the issues; and
(d) to the financial position of each party;

Proportionality is not otherwise defined within the CPR. Paragraphs 11.1–11.3 of PDCosts give assistance in applying the test of proportionality. In particular, para 11.1 makes it clear that a fixed percentage cannot be applied in all cases to the value of the claim to ascertain whether or not the costs are proportionate. Reducing proportionality to a formula that costs should not for example exceed 20% or 30% of the claim is erroneous for the reasons referred to in PDCosts, para 11.2. In any proceedings there will be inevitable base costs. The lower the claim the higher are likely to be the base costs proportionate to the amount of that claim. Paragraph 11.3 of PDCosts makes it clear that the time spent in court dealing with a particular issue is not an accurate guide to the amount of time spent by the legal advisers in preparation for the trial of that issue. Solicitors conducting modest litigation 'are under a heavy duty to conduct that litigation in as economic a manner as possible' (*Jefferson v National Freight Carriers plc* [2001] EWCA Civ 2082, [2001] 2 Costs LR 313, CA). 'In modern litigation with the emphasis on proportionality it is necessary for parties to make an assessment at the outset of the likely value of the claim and its importance and complexity and then to plan in advance the necessary work, the appropriate level of person to carry out the work, the overall time which would be necessary and appropriate to spend on the various stages in bringing the action to trial and the likely overall costs' (HHJ Alton, cited with approval by Lord Woolf CJ, in *Jefferson* above).

Guidance has been given by the Court of Appeal on proportionality. See *Lownds v Home Office* [2002] EWCA Civ 365, [2002] All ER (D) 329 (Mar), CA, where Lord Woolf described the principle of proportionality as having a direct bearing on the policy on which the effectiveness of the CPR depends. His Lordship noted:

> 'Because of the central role proportionality should have in the resolution of civil litigation it is essential that Courts should attach the appropriate significance to the requirement of proportionality when making Orders for costs and when assessing the amount of costs. What has however caused practitioners and the members of the judiciary who have to assess costs difficulty is how to give effect to requirements of proportionality. In particular there is uncertainty as to the relationship between the requirement of reasonableness and the requirement of proportionality. Where there is a conflict between reasonableness and proportionality does one requirement prevail over the other, and if so, which requirement is it that takes precedence? There is also the question of whether the proportionality test is to be applied globally or on an item by item basis or both globally and on item by item basis.'

Quantifying costs when proportionality is in issue is a two-stage process:

- Stage 1: the costs officer makes a preliminary judgment on the proportionality of the claim for costs as a whole. He applies for example PDCosts, paras 11.1–11.3.

The costs judge will have regard to whether the appropriate level of fee earner or counsel has been deployed, whether offers to settle have been made, whether unnecessary experts have been instructed and the other matters set out in r 44.5(3).

- Stage 2: item by item consideration of the bill of costs:
  - (i) If the overall costs claimed are proportionate the only test which the costs judge applies is one of reasonableness.
  - (ii) If the overall costs are disproportionate the costs judge should only allow the work which was *necessarily* incurred and should allow a reasonable amount in respect of such work.

  'Necessary' means:
    - (1) a sensible standard which takes fully into account the need to make allowances for different judgments for which those responsible for litigation can sensibly come to as to what is required;
    - (2) using hindsight to set too high a standard is to be avoided;
    - (3) the threshold should be capable of achievement by a competent practitioner without undue difficulty;
    - (4) in assessing what is necessary the costs officer should take into account the conduct of the paying party. An unco-operative opponent can render costs necessary that would otherwise be unnecessary.

In deciding whether the costs of a claim were proportionate the court should look to what it was reasonable for a party to believe might be recovered in the claim. For example:

(a) The proportionality of costs incurred by the claimant should be determined by having regard to the sum that it was reasonable for him to believe he might recover at the time he made his claim.

(b) The proportionality of the costs incurred by the defendant should be determined having regard to the sum that it was reasonable for him to believe the claimant might recover should his claim succeed.

Notwithstanding that a costs judge might have ruled at the outset of a detailed assessment that the bill as a whole was not disproportionate, he may still decide that some items are disproportionate having regard to 'the matters in issue' (*Giambrione (Anita) & ors v JMC Holidays Limited, formerly T/A Sunworld Holidays Ltd* [2002] EWHC 495, (2002) Lawtel, 23 December, QBD, Morland J). In applying the *Lownds* test, it is not necessary for the judge to go through the items in r 44.5 as a checklist (*Ortwein v Rugby Mansions Limited* [2003] EWHC 2077 (Ch), Lloyd J and *Young v J R Smart (Builders) Ltd* [2004] EWHC 103). Failure to consider proportionality on a global basis at the outset of detailed assessment in accordance with *Lownds* is a serious procedural irregularity (*Lloyds TSB v Lampert* [2003] EWHC 249 (Ch), Smith J – appeal allowed).

Additional liability—In deciding whether costs claimed are reasonable and proportionate the court will consider the amount of any additional liability separately from base costs (PDCosts, para 11.5). A hindsight test will not be applied. The court will have regard to the circumstances as they reasonably appeared to the lawyer when the funding arrangement was entered into or at the time of any variation of that arrangement (PDCosts, para 11.7). The court will specifically take into account the matters set out in PDCosts, para 11.8(1). The court has no power to direct that a success fee is recoverable at different rates for different periods of the proceedings. In so far as PDCosts, para 11.8(2) suggests otherwise, it is wrong (*Ku v Liverpool City Council* [2005] EWCA Civ 475). It is understood that PDCosts will be amended shortly. A percentage increase will not be reduced simply on the ground that when added to base costs which the court had determined were reasonable and proportionate, the total appears disproportionate (PDCosts, para 11.9).

'indemnity basis' (r 44.4(3))—Any doubt which the court may have as to whether the costs were reasonably incurred or were reasonable in amount is resolved in favour of the receiving party. There is no reference to proportionality.

The indemnity basis is the appropriate basis for costs in the following cases:

(a) r 48.4(2) – assessment of costs payable to a trustee or personal representative out of a fund;
(b) r 48.8(2) – assessment of costs payable to a solicitor by his own client;
(c) r 48.3 – costs payable pursuant to a contract.

In the past costs have generally been awarded on the indemnity basis where there has been some abuse of process or the presence of 'exceptional circumstances' (*Bowen Jones v Bowen Jones* [1986] 3 All ER 163). To obtain an order for indemnity costs it was necessary to show the presence of factors that would take the case 'outside the run of normal litigation' (*Connaught Restaurants Limited v Indoor Leisure Limited* [1994] 1 WLR 501, CA). Examples of indemnity costs orders are:

(a) the paying party's conduct wholly unmeritorious (*Pritchard v JB Cobden Limited* [1987] 1 All ER 300, CA);
(b) deliberate dishonesty in the conduct of litigation (*Sea Wanderer Limited v Nigel Burgess Limited* (unreported) 1990, CA (May J));
(c) contempt proceedings (*EMI Records Limited v Ian Cameron Wallace Limited* [1982] 2 All ER 1980).

Indemnity costs have also been awarded where there has been deceit or underhandedness, abuse of the court's procedure, tenuous claims, voluminous and unnecessary evidence.

However, the CPR contain a new approach to litigation and 'a new procedural code' (r 1.1) and other provisions indicating a possible change to the old order. See *Biguzzi v Rank Leisure plc* [1999] 1 WLR 1926, CA. In *Excelsior Commercial and Industrial Holdings Ltd v Salisbury Hamer Aspden and Johnson* [2002] EWCA Civ 879, [2002] All ER (D) 39 (Jun), CA Lord Woolf refused to set down guidelines as to when judges should or should not make orders on an indemnity basis. The making of an order on an indemnity basis would be appropriate in circumstances where the facts of the case and/or the conduct of the parties were such as to take the situation away from the norm. An example of when the court has ordered indemnity costs is non-compliance with an order of the court, which may result *inter alia* in costs on the indemnity basis to be paid forthwith. See also *Baron v Lovell* (1999) *The Times*, 14 September, CA. But see *Gore v Jones & anor* (2001) *The Times*, 21 February, ChD, per Pumfrey J where there was a failure by a party to comply with an unless order. It was held that the imposition of costs sanctions was entirely a matter for the discretion of the judge as to whether to apply an indemnity costs order. In addition, the court may order costs to be paid on the indemnity basis where a claimant at trial does better than his own Pt 36 offer (r 36.21(3)) (*Little v George Little Sebire & Co* (1999) *The Times*, 17 November, QBD). It is for the defendant to show that the court should not order indemnity costs in those circumstances (r 36.21(4)). Similarly, where a party has failed to comply with a pre-action protocol and as a result proceedings have been commenced which might not have been, or costs have been increased, the court will consider ordering indemnity costs. Costs on an indemnity basis are not reserved to cases where the court wishes to indicate its disapproval of the conduct of a party. Conduct which falls short of misconduct deserving moral condemnation (but is unreasonable to a high degree and not merely wrong or misguided in hindsight) could justify an order for indemnity costs (*Kiam v MGN Limited* [2002] EWCA Civ 66, [2002] 2 All ER 242, CA). An indemnity costs order under Pt 44 as opposed to Pt 36 does carry some stigma. It is meant to be penal not exhortatory (see also *Reid Minty (a firm) v Taylor* [2001] EWCA Civ 1723, [2002] 2 All ER 150, CA). The purpose of indemnity costs is to redress the injustice of costs which would otherwise accrue to a successful claimant for having had to fight a case for longer than was reasonably necessary (*McPhilemy v Times Newspapers* [2001] EWCA Civ 871, (2001) Lawtel, 21 June, CA). In *ABCI (formerly Arab Business Consortium International) v Banque Franco-Tunisienne & ors* [2002] 1 Lloyd's Rep 511, (2002) Lawtel, 1 May HHJ Chambers ordered indemnity costs against the claimant whose case had constantly changed throughout the course of proceedings and who had produced wholly unacceptable volumes of documentation. Costs may be awarded on the indemnity basis to a publicly funded party to penalise the losing party's unreasonable conduct in a case (*Brawley v Marczynski & anor* [2002] EWCA Civ 1453, [2002] All ER (D) 288, CA).

44.5 Factors to be taken into account in deciding the amount of costs

(1) The court is to have regard to all the circumstances in deciding whether costs were –

- (a) if it is assessing costs on the standard basis –
  - (i) proportionately and reasonably incurred; or
  - (ii) were proportionate and reasonable in amount, or
- (b) if it is assessing costs on the indemnity basis –
  - (i) unreasonably incurred; or
  - (ii) unreasonable in amount.

(2) In particular the court must give effect to any orders which have already been made.

(3) The court must also have regard to –

- (a) the conduct of all the parties, including in particular –
  - (i) conduct before, as well as during, the proceedings; and
  - (ii) the efforts made, if any, before and during the proceedings in order to try to resolve the dispute;
- (b) the amount or value of any money or property involved;
- (c) the importance of the matter to all the parties;
- (d) the particular complexity of the matter or the difficulty or novelty of the questions raised;
- (e) the skill, effort, specialised knowledge and responsibility involved;
- (f) the time spent on the case; and
- (g) the place where and the circumstances in which work or any part of it was done.

(Rule 35.4(4) gives the court power to limit the amount that a party may recover with regard to the fees and expenses of an expert)

Practice Direction—See generally PDCosts at p 1083 and specifically Sections 7–23 at p 1097.

Scope of provision—Rule 44.3 deals with the circumstances to be taken into account when a court decides an entitlement to costs. Rule 44.5 prescribes the factors to be taken into account when considering the amount of those costs. For a discussion as to proportionality see above (r 44.4 and PDCosts, paras 11.1–11.3).

'The court must also have regard' (r 44.5(3))—The factors referred to are akin to the factors which were contained in RSC Ord 62, App 2 save that 'number and importance of documents' has been omitted. In addition, the court will of course take into account proportionality in assessing on the standard basis, but note that value and importance remain relevant to assessment on either basis (paras (b) and (c)).

'conduct' (r 44.5(3)(a))—There is a requirement for the court to take conduct (both before and during the conduct of the proceedings) into account when considering an entitlement to costs (r 44.3(4) and (5)) and again when those costs are quantified. The paying party may firstly argue under r 44.3(5) that because of the receiving party's conduct he should not have to pay the costs either in whole or in part. He can then argue under r 44.5(3) that the amount of costs should be reduced because of the receiving party's conduct or his failure to negotiate. Where a losing party considers that he should not be liable to pay the whole of the costs of the action by reason of the opposing party's conduct, he should make an application to the trial judge when considering what orders as to costs should be made under r 44.3. If he does not do so, it is not open to the paying party when the costs come to be assessed to raise the same matter under r 44.5(3) before the costs judge as a ground for the reduction of the costs he would otherwise have to pay (*Joseph Aaron v Michael Shelton* [2004] EWHC 1162, Jack J).

There is the danger that where detailed assessment of costs is ordered the receiving party may become embroiled in detailed investigations of both allegation and counter-allegation concerning conduct. One way of avoiding this type of investigation is to have costs summarily assessed as the litigation proceeds.

Percentage increase/insurance premium—In deciding whether a percentage increase is reasonable the factors the court will take into account will include:
(1) the risk that the circumstances in which the costs fees or expenses of the lawyer would be payable might or might not occur;
(2) the lawyers liability for disbursements;
(3) what other methods of financing the costs were available to the receiving party for example legal expenses insurance and/or the client's household insurance policy (PDCosts, para 11.8).

When considering whether the cost of insurance cover is reasonable the court will take into account factors such as:
(a) a comparison of cost between a policy purchased to support both sides' legal costs (either in whole or in part) with the likely cost of insurance cover for the losing party's legal costs only;
(b) the level and extent of cover provided;
(c) the availability of pre existing insurance cover such as legal expenses insurance;
(d) any rebate on the premium;
(e) any commission payable to the lawyer (PDCosts, para 11.10).

44.6 Fixed costs

A party may recover the fixed costs specified in Part 45 in accordance with that Part.

Scope of provision—Part 45 sets out the amount to be allowed as fixed costs on commencement of a claim (Table 1), entry of judgment (Table 2) together with miscellaneous fixed costs (Table 3).

Other rules provide for situations where fixed costs may be allowed, generally post-judgment. These can be found in Sch 1, RSC Ord 62 and Sch 2, CCR Ord 38, App B.

Road traffic accidents and employers' liability claims—From 6 October 2003, a fixed-costs regime applies in relation to claims arising from road traffic accidents settled pre-issue, where the agreed damages do not exceed £10,000 (Pt 45, Section II). Fixed success fees in road traffic accident cases funded under CFAs apply from 1 June 2004 in respect of those cases outside the small claims track or not falling within the costs only provisions of Pt 45, Section II (Pt 45, Section III). Fixed success fees apply in employers' liability claims funded under CFAs in respect of those cases not allocated to the small claims track where the injury was sustained after 1 October 2004 (Pt 45, Section IV).

44.7 Procedure for assessing costs

Where the court orders a party to pay costs to another party (other than fixed costs) it may either –

(a) make a summary assessment of the costs; or
(b) order detailed assessment of the costs by a costs officer,

unless any rule, practice direction or other enactment provides otherwise.

(The costs practice direction sets out the factors which will affect the court's decision under this rule)

Practice Direction—See generally PDCosts at p 1083 and specifically Sections 12–14 at p 1103.

Summary assessment—The general rule is that the court will make a summary assessment of the costs at the end of a fast track trial, at the end of any other hearing which has lasted less than a day and certain appeals. However, there is no presumption that a detailed assessment must be ordered where a case lasts for more than a day (see *Q v Q* (2002) Lawtel, 17 July, FD, Wilson J). In relation to a fast track trial the summary assessment will deal with the costs of the whole claim. The summary assessment at the conclusion of a hearing other than a fast track trial will deal with the costs of the application or other matter to which it related, if this hearing disposes of the claim, the order may deal with the costs of the whole claim. A summary assessment must be carried out by the judge hearing the fast track trial or application unless there is good reason why the court should not do so (PDCosts, para 13.2). A trial judge should not summarily assess the costs of a pre-trial application in respect of which a costs order has already been made. Costs could either be summarily assessed by the judge who heard the case or could be referred to a costs judge for detailed assessment (*Mahmood (Maya Alva) and Mahmood (Ziauddin) v Penrose (Rebecca), Penrose (Oliver) and Quay (Stephen)* [2002] EWCA Civ 457). For example, it may not be

SECTION 2 Civil Procedure Rules and Practice Directions

practicable to proceed with summary assessment if the amounts involved are very large; if the paying party shows substantial grounds for disputing the sums claimed; if there are legal arguments relating to the costs which cannot be properly dealt with by summary assessment; or if there is insufficient time. In *R v Cardiff City Council ex parte Brown* (1999) (unreported) 11 June, Harrison J referred costs to detailed assessment when the paying party took a point under the indemnity principle as to the hourly rate properly chargeable by the respondent's in-house legal department. See *Richardson v Desquenne et Giral* [1999] CPLR 744, CA, and *Picnic at Ascot Incorporated v Derigs & ors* [2001] FSR 2, (2000) Lawtel, 9 February, ChD which set out the circumstances when a court should assess costs summarily, particularly with regard to applications for interim relief.

Appeals against summary assessment follow the general rules relating to appeals, set out in Pt 52. There is provision for the Court of Appeal to assess summarily the costs in –

(a) contested hearings directions;
(b) applications for permission to appeal at which the respondent is present;
(c) dismissal list hearings in the Court of Appeal at which the respondent is present;
(d) appeals from case management decisions; and
(e) appeals listed for one day or less.

See PD52, para 14.1. Parties should attend these hearings prepared to deal with summary assessment and comply with the requirements of PDCosts, paras 13.5–13.12.

Additional liability—Generally, the court will not assess the additional liability (defined in r 43.2(1)(o)) to be paid by the losing party until the conclusion of the proceedings (PDCosts, para 13.12). On a summary assessment of the costs of an interim application the court will assess 'base costs' not the recoverable element of any 'percentage increase' and/or 'insurance premium' (r 44.3A).

Detailed assessment—Detailed assessment will not normally be carried out until the proceedings are concluded (r 47.1). Summary assessment of costs may have taken place in relation to the litigation during the course of proceedings. Any summary assessment is not affected by an order for detailed assessment of costs at the conclusion of a claim.

44.8 Time for complying with an order for costs

A party must comply with an order for the payment of costs within 14 days of –

(a) the date of the judgment or order if it states the amount of those costs;
(b) if the amount of those costs (or part of them) is decided later in accordance with Part 47, the date of the certificate which states the amount; or
(c) in either case, such later date as the court may specify.

(Part 47 sets out the procedure for detailed assessment of costs)

Amendments—SI 2000/1317.

Related provisions—Rule 40.8 (time from which interest begins to run); r 40.11 (time for complying with a judgment or order).

Scope of provision—Costs, whether determined by way of summary or detailed assessment, must normally be paid within 14 days of the costs order or costs certificate. A party must within 14 days comply with any order for the payment of costs unless the court specifies a later date (r 44.8). Any application for an extension of time to pay must be supported by adequate evidence (*Pepin v Watts & anor* [2000] All ER (D) 1262, CA). Prior to 26 April 1999 interlocutory costs were generally not assessed until the conclusion of the action. Consequently, many orders for costs had no immediate effect. Now, where a summary assessment of costs is made in the course of litigation a party will have to part with his money at an early stage of the proceedings. Thus the consequences of failure, whether as applicant or respondent to any application before the court for an interim remedy, will immediately become apparent to the client. Practitioners will now have to consider more carefully than ever before making an application or allowing themselves to become subject to one.

If a party is unable to discharge assessed costs within 14 days, he may apply to the court pursuant to r 44.8(c) for an extension of time. Otherwise, an unpaid order for costs is enforceable as a civil debt after the expiration of 14 days. Default in compliance does not automatically prevent the defaulter from continuing with the proceedings but in appropriate circumstances it may found an application to strike out his statement of case (r 3.4(2)(c)).

Note the Register of County Court Judgments (Amendment) Regulations 1999 (in force 26 July 1999), which amend Register of County Court Judgment Regulations 1985, making an order for costs following summary assessment (except one made at a final hearing) exempt from registration.

Conditional fees—Problems sometimes occur where a summary assessment of costs is ordered against a party funded by a CFA. In some circumstances an insurance policy taken out to cover the costs liability in respect of the proceedings may not cover the payment of interim costs. For the present practitioners should refer to 'Guide to the Summary Assessment of Costs' (SCCO, 2005 edition), paras 19–22. See also PDCosts, paras 13.2 and 14.3 which state that courts should nonetheless make summary assessment of base costs leaving any additional liability to be dealt with at the conclusion of proceedings unless there is good reason not to do so. However an order for payment should not be made in CFA cases unless the court is satisfied in respect of the costs claimed that the receiving party is at the time liable to pay his legal representative an amount equal to or greater than the costs claimed. A statement in the form of a certificate at the end to Form N260 may be sufficient proof of liability but notification of the CFA under r 44.15 is not sufficient (PDCosts, para 14.3).

Interest—In the High Court interest on costs is recoverable under Judgments Act 1838, s 17. In the county court, County Courts (Interest on Judgment Debts) Order 1991 (made under CCA 1984, s 74) provides that 'every judgment debt under a relevant judgment' shall carry interest. A relevant judgment is one for the payment of a sum of money not less than £5000 or one in relation to 'qualifying debts' for the purposes of Late Payment of Commercial Debts (Interest) Act 1998. 'Qualifying debts' are those owed to small suppliers by large businesses or public authorities (Late Payment of Commercial Debts (Interest) Act 1998 (Commencement No 1) Order 1998).

Where interest is payable pursuant to Judgments Act 1838, s 17 or CCA 1984, s 74, interest runs from the date that the judgment is given unless a rule or practice direction makes a different provision or the court orders otherwise (r 40.8). See also *Hunt v RM Douglas (Roofing) Limited* [1990] AC 398. Judgments Act 1838, s 17 was amended by Civil Procedure (Modification of Enactments) Order 1998 to give the court a discretion to order interest to begin to run from a date before the date that judgment is given, see r 44.3(6)(g) and *Powell v Herefordshire HA* [2002] EWCA Civ 1786, (2002) *The Times*, 27 December, CA and *Bim Kemi AB v Blackburn Chemicals Limited* (2003) *The Times*, 24 June, CA. However, judgment interest may be barred by lapse of time (see Limitation Act 1980, s 24(2), and *Lowsley v Forbes (t/a LE Design Services)* [1998] 3 WLR 501). The short term interest account rate presently stands at 7%. The Judgment Act rate of interest remains at 8%.

Where a cost order is deemed to have been made, for example on discontinuance or acceptance of a Pt 36 offer, interest begins to run from the date on which the event which gave rise to the entitlement to costs occurred (r 44.12).

Appeals—If the Court of Appeal makes a costs order different from the lower court, the order should be backdated to the date of the judgment of the lower court to allow interest from that date (*Kuwait Airways Co v Iraqi Airways Co (No 2)* [1995] 1 All ER 790, CA).

44.9 Costs on the small claims track and fast track

(1) Part 27 (small claims) and Part 46 (fast track trial costs) contain special rules about –

(a) liability for costs;
(b) the amount of costs which the court may award; and
(c) the procedure for assessing costs.

(2) Once a claim is allocated to a particular track, those special rules shall apply to the period before, as well as after, allocation except where the court or a practice direction provides otherwise.

Amendments—SI 1999/1008.

Practice Direction—See generally PDCosts at p 1083 and specifically Section 15 at p 1108.

Related provisions—The small claims track and fast track have their own costs provisions. Those special rules do not apply until a claim is allocated to a particular track. Any costs orders made before a claim is allocated, for example on a Pt 24 application or injunction application, will not be affected by allocation (r 44.11(1)). But where a case should have been allocated to the small claims track, the small claims costs regime could apply in assessing the basis of an award of costs. The court was not precluded from applying the small claims costs regime to a case which amounted to a small claim even where it had not been allocated to any track (*Voice and Script International Ltd v Alghafar* [2003] EWCA Civ 736, [2003] CP Rep 53, [2003] All ER (D) 86 (May), CA).

A defendant may make an admission of part of a claim thus reducing the amount in dispute and resulting in the allocation of the claim to the small claims track or fast track. In terms of costs this could operate unfairly on the claimant and therefore where judgment is entered for the admitted part of the claim before allocation the court has a discretion to allow costs in respect of the proceedings down to that date (PDCosts, para 15.1(3)).

'before … allocation' (r 44.9(2))—This does not include re-allocation (r 44.11(2)).

44.10 Limitation on amount court may allow where a claim allocated to the fast track settles before trial

(1) Where the court –

(a) assesses costs in relation to a claim which –

(i) has been allocated to the fast track; and

(ii) settles before the start of the trial; and

(b) is considering the amount of costs to be allowed in respect of a party's advocate for preparing for the trial,

it may not allow in respect of those advocate's costs, an amount that exceeds the amount of fast track trial costs which would have been payable in relation to the claim had the trial taken place.

(2) When deciding the amount to be allowed in respect of the advocate's costs, the court shall have regard to –

(a) when the claim was settled; and

(b) when the court was notified that the claim had settled.

(3) In this rule, 'advocate' and 'fast track trial costs' have the meanings given to them by Part 46.

(Part 46 sets out the amount of fast track trial costs which may be awarded)

Practice Direction—See generally PDCosts at p 1083 and specifically Sections 7–23 at p 1097.

Scope of provision—'Fast track trial costs' are dealt with in Pt 46. These are the fixed or capped costs of a party's advocate in preparing for and appearing at trial (r 46.1(2)(b)). These costs are only recoverable if a trial actually takes place. The rule provides for the assessment, of the costs of the successful party's advocate preparing for trial where a fast track case settles before the start of the trial. In addition to these costs the court will of course allow an amount for the preparation work done prior to the actual preparatory work for the trial itself.

44.11 Costs following allocation and re-allocation

(1) Any costs orders made before a claim is allocated will not be affected by allocation.

(2) Where –

(a) a claim is allocated to a track; and

(b) the court subsequently re-allocates that claim to a different track;

then unless the court orders otherwise, any special rules about costs applying –

(i) to the first track, will apply to the claim up to the date of re-allocation; and

(ii) to the second track, will apply from the date of re-allocation.

(Part 26 deals with the allocation and re-allocation of claims between tracks)

Practice Direction—See generally PDCosts at p 1083 and specifically Section 16 at p 1108.

Small claims track—Where the court re-allocates from the small claims track to another track it must consider whether any party is to pay costs down to the date of the order to re-allocate in accordance with the cost rules contained in Pt 27. If it decides to make such an order the court will make a summary assessment of those costs at the time it orders re-allocation (PDCosts, para 16.3).

44.12 Cases where costs orders deemed to have been made

(1) Where a right to costs arises under –

(a) rule 3.7 (defendant's right to costs where claim struck out for non-payment of fees);
(b) rule 36.13(1) (claimant's right to costs where he accepts defendant's Part 36 offer or Part 36 payment);
(c) rule 36.14 (claimant's right to costs where defendant accepts the claimant's Part 36 offer); or
(d) rule 38.6 (defendant's right to costs where claimant discontinues),

a costs order will be deemed to have been made on the standard basis.

(2) Interest payable pursuant to section 17 of the Judgments Act 1838 or section 74 of the County Courts Act 1984 on the costs deemed to have been ordered under paragraph (1) shall begin to run from the date on which the event which gave rise to the entitlement to costs occurred.

'made on the standard basis' (r 44.12(1))—There will have to be a detailed assessment of deemed costs orders in the absence of agreement. Part 47 deals with the way in which a defendant or a claimant may seek assessment of his costs.

Presumably by analogy costs awarded on a judgment under r 14.7(8) (amount offered and accepted in satisfaction of claim for unspecified sum) will also be assessed on the standard basis by detailed assessment.

Interest—Judgments Act 1838, s 17 (amended by Civil Procedure (Modification of Enactments) Order 1998) allows interest to run from the date on which the event which gave rise to the entitlement to costs occurred or from such date as the court may order, which may be earlier (see for example *Bristol Myers Squibb Co v Baker Norton Pharmaceuticals Inc* [2001] EWCA Civ 414, [2001] RPC 45, CA).

44.12A Costs-only proceedings

(1) This rule sets out a procedure which may be followed where –

(a) the parties to a dispute have reached an agreement on all issues (including which party is to pay the costs) which is made or confirmed in writing; but
(b) they have failed to agree the amount of those costs; and
(c) no proceedings have been started.

(1A) (*revoked*)

(2) Either party to the agreement may start proceedings under this rule by issuing a claim form in accordance with Part 8.

(3) The claim form must contain or be accompanied by the agreement or confirmation.

(4) Except as provided in paragraph (4A), in proceedings to which this rule applies the court –

(a) may –
 (i) make an order for costs to be determined by detailed assessment; or
 (ii) dismiss the claim; and
(b) must dismiss the claim if it is opposed.

(4A) In proceedings to which Section II of Part 45 applies, the court shall assess the costs in the manner set out in that Section.

(5) Rule 48.3 (amount of costs where costs are payable pursuant to a contract) does not apply to claims started under the procedure in this rule.

(Rule 7.2 provides that proceedings are started when the court issues a claim form at the request of the claimant)

(Rule 8.1(6) provides that a practice direction may modify the Part 8 procedure)

Amendments—Inserted by SI 2000/1317; amended by SI 2002/2058; SI 2003/2113; SI 2004/3419.

Practice Direction—See generally PDCosts at p 1083 and specifically Section 17 at p 1108.

Scope of provision—Originally, the CPR did not provide a mechanism for the parties to agree costs where they had reached an agreement on all issues except the amount of costs to be paid by one party to another. Rule 44.12A provides such a mechanism but only where –

(a) the parties to a dispute have agreed all issues including which party is to pay the costs;
(b) the agreement is either made or confirmed in writing;
(c) the parties have failed to agree the amount of costs;
(d) no proceedings have been commenced; and (in effect)
(e) the parties agree to the use of the procedure.

The method of commencing costs-only proceedings is by a claim form, in accordance with Pt 8, accompanied by the agreement or confirmation from the paying party. Where the paying party disputes the agreement or his liability to pay costs, the claim will be dismissed. If the paying party does not oppose the application the court will make an order for the costs claimed to be assessed by detailed assessment. The costs of making the application under this rule will be determined in the course of the detailed assessment (see r 47.18 and PDCosts, Section 45). Rule 44.12A(5) makes it clear that costs will be assessed on the standard basis unless the parties otherwise agree. Where the parties apply for an order to be made by consent r 40.6 applies. Rule 8.1(3) and Pt 24 do not apply to proceedings brought under r 44.12A. There is nothing within this rule to prevent a party from issuing a claim form under Pt 7 or Pt 8 to sue on an agreement made in settlement of a dispute where that agreement makes provision for costs, nor from claiming in that case an order for costs or a specified sum in respect of costs.

See *Crosbie v Munroe & anor* [2003] EWCA Civ 350, [2003] 2 All ER 856, CA where the claimant's offer to settle the costs of 'proceedings' subject to assessment under r 47.19(1)(a) covered only the costs of settling the *substantive* claim and not the costs of the *costs-only* proceedings.

44.13 Special situations

(1) Where the court makes an order which does not mention costs –

(a) subject to paragraphs (1A) and (1B), the general rule is that no party is entitled to costs in relation to that order; but
(b) this does not affect any entitlement of a party to recover costs out of a fund held by him as trustee or personal representative, or pursuant to any lease, mortgage or other security.

(1A) Where the court makes –

(a) an order granting permission to appeal;
(b) an order granting permission to apply for judicial review; or
(c) any other order or direction sought by a party on an application without notice,

and its order does not mention costs, it will be deemed to include an order for applicant's costs in the case.

(1B) Any party affected by a deemed order for costs under paragraph (1A) may apply at any time to vary the order.

(2) The court hearing an appeal may, unless it dismisses the appeal, make orders about the costs of the proceedings giving rise to the appeal as well as the costs of the appeal.

(3) Where proceedings are transferred from one court to another, the court to which they are transferred may deal with all the costs, including the costs before the transfer.

(4) Paragraph (3) is subject to any order of the court which ordered the transfer.

Amendments—SI 2001/4015; SI 2005/2292.

'does not mention costs' (r 44.13(1))—Where an order is silent as to costs there is *no entitlement to costs* (namely from another party). This is a change from previous practice where an interlocutory order silent as to costs was treated as an order for 'costs in the cause' at the conclusion of the proceedings (*Friis v Paramount Bagwash Co Limited* [1940] 4 All ER 72).

'application without notice' (r 44.13(1A)(c))—Practitioners should note that from the 1 October 2005 there is something of a halfway house. Where, on an application without notice, the court makes the order or direction sought and the order does not refer to costs, costs are deemed to be the applicant's 'costs in case'. Any party affected by the deemed order for costs may apply 'at any time' to vary the order (the applicant may for example argue that the costs should be his in any event, the respondent that there should be no order). Presumably, such an application might be made when the case was next before the court at a hearing, at the trial or even in costs assessment proceedings.

'as trustee or personal representative, or pursuant to a lease, mortgage or other security' (r 44.13(1)(b))—See rr 48.3 and 48.4.

44.14 Court's powers in relation to misconduct

(1) The court may make an order under this rule where –

- (a) a party or his legal representative, in connection with a summary or detailed assessment, fails to comply with a rule, practice direction or court order; or
- (b) it appears to the court that the conduct of a party or his legal representative, before or during the proceedings which gave rise to the assessment proceedings, was unreasonable or improper.

(2) Where paragraph (1) applies, the court may –

- (a) disallow all or part of the costs which are being assessed; or
- (b) order the party at fault or his legal representative to pay costs which he has caused any other party to incur.

(3) Where –

- (a) the court makes an order under paragraph (2) against a legally represented party; and
- (b) the party is not present when the order is made,

the party's solicitor must notify his client in writing of the order no later than 7 days after the solicitor receives notice of the order.

Amendments—SI 2000/1317.

Practice Direction—See generally PDCosts at p 1083 and specifically Section 18 at p 1110.

Scope of provision—This rule is in addition to the wasted costs jurisdiction under SCA, s 51 which is dealt with in r 48.7. It allows the court to deal with misconduct during the course of summary or detailed assessment proceedings and with conduct before or during the proceedings which gave rise to the assessment proceedings (summary or detailed). The provision extends to the legal representative of a party as well as to the party personally.

'it appears to the court' (r 44.14(1)(b))—The costs officer or the judge assessing costs summarily may at the request of a party or of his own initiative investigate and make orders in respect of any unreasonable or improper conduct by a party or legal representative. Examples are abuse of process (*Burrows v Vauxhall Motors* (1997) *The Times*, 17 December, CA) or procedural failure (*Sasea*

Finance Ltd (in liquidation) (1997) *The Times*, 29 December). See also *Re H (A Minor) (Court bundles: Disallowance of fees)* (2000) *The Times,* 6 June, FD, where there was a failure by the solicitors acting for a paternal grandparent to prepare a bundle of documents for the court. One half of their fees of the hearing was disallowed.

'notify his client' (r 44.14(3))—The provision for notification by a solicitor to his client is similar to that contained in r 44.2.

44.15 Providing information about funding arrangements

(1) A party who seeks to recover an additional liability must provide information about the funding arrangement to the court and to other parties as required by a rule, practice direction or court order.

(2) Where the funding arrangement has changed, and the information a party has previously provided in accordance with paragraph (1) is no longer accurate, that party must file notice of the change and serve it on all other parties within 7 days.

(3) Where paragraph (2) applies, and a party has already filed –

(a) an allocation questionnaire; or
(b) a pre-trial check list (listing questionnaire),

he must file and serve a new estimate of the costs with the notice.

(The costs practice direction sets out –

- the information to be provided when a party issues or responds to a claim form, files an allocation questionnaire, a pre-trial check list, and a claim for costs;
- the meaning of estimate of costs and the information required in it)

(Rule 44.3B sets out situations where the party will not recover a sum representing any additional liability)

Amendments—Inserted by SI 2000/1317; amended by SI 2002/2058.

Practice Direction—See generally PDCosts at p 1083 and specifically Section 19 at p 1110. See also PDProt, paras 4A.1–4A.2.

Scope of provision—For the definition of 'additional liability', see r 43.2(1)(o). To recover an additional liability from a paying party, the receiving party must provide information about the funding arrangements to the court. There is no requirement to specify the amount of the additional liability separately nor to state how it is calculated until it falls to be assessed (PDCosts, para 19.1). Where a person enters into a funding arrangement before the issue of proceedings he should inform other potential parties to the claim that he has done so (PDProt, para 4A1). Section 19 of PDCosts deals specifically with the method by which information about a funding arrangement must be given, the information which must be provided and when notice of change of information must be given. Notice contained in the information is set out in Form N251.

For transitional provisions see PDCosts, para 57.9.

Note that the Access to Justice Act 1999 (Transitional Provisions) Order 2000 provides that no CFA entered into before 1 April 2000 can be a funding arrangement as defined in r 43.2. Consequently, where a CFA or other funding arrangement has been entered into before 1 April 2000 and a new or subsequent funding arrangement is entered into on or after 1 April 2000, the second or subsequent funding arrangement will not give rise to an additional liability recoverable from a paying party. It is only the first CFA or other funding arrangement entered into after 1 April 2000 in relation to an action which will entitle a party to recover an additional liability from another party.

44.16 Adjournment where legal representative seeks to challenge disallowance of any amount of percentage increase

Where –

(a) the court disallows any amount of a legal representative's percentage increase in summary or detailed assessment proceedings; and
(b) the legal representative applies for an order that the disallowed amount should continue to be payable by his client,

the court may adjourn the hearing to allow the client to be –

(i) notified of the order sought; and
(ii) separately represented.

(Regulation 3(2)(b) of the Conditional Fee Agreement Regulations 2000 provides that a conditional fee agreement which provides for a success fee must state that any amount of a percentage increase disallowed on assessment ceases to be payable unless the court is satisfied that it should continue to be so payable. Regulation 5(2)(b) of the Collective Conditional Fee Agreements Regulations 2000 makes similar provision in relation to collective conditional fee agreements)

Amendments—Inserted by SI 2000/1317; amended by SI 2001/256; SI 2002/2058.

Practice Direction—See generally PDCosts at p 1083 and specifically Section 20 at p 1112.

Scope of provision—This provision must be read in conjunction with CFAR 2000, reg 3(2)(b) and CCFAR 2000, reg 5(2)(b), which provide that, on assessment, any amount of a percentage increase disallowed against the paying party retrospectively amends the CFA/CCFA and that the disallowed element of the percentage increase cannot be recovered by the legal representative against his own client, unless the court is satisfied that it should continue to be so payable.

A legal representative may wish to pursue the disallowed element of the percentage increase against his own client. This provision provides the mechanism for carrying out that exercise. Where the paying party is challenging the level of percentage uplift, the prudent practitioner should give his client a clear written explanation of the dispute and of his intention to recover any outstanding balance of the percentage increase from the client and the reasons for so doing. He must also inform his client of his right to attend the detailed assessment hearing when the matter is raised (PDCosts, para 20.5). Once the court has determined the inter partes costs it will adjourn the issue as to whether the disallowed amount should continue to be payable to a future date. An adjournment will not be ordered if (PDCosts, para 20.8(2)):

(a) the receiving party and all parties to the CFA consent to the court deciding the issue without an adjournment;
(b) the receiving party is present in court; and
(c) the court is satisfied the issue can fairly be decided without an adjournment.

The client should also be informed of any hearing and it may well be prudent for him to attend the detailed assessment when the percentage increase is being assessed.

44.17 Application of costs rules

This Part and Part 45 (fixed costs), Part 46 (fast track trial costs, Part 47 (procedure for detailed assessment of costs and default provisions) and Part 48 (special cases), do not apply to the assessment of costs in proceedings to the extent that –

(a) section 11 of the Access to Justice Act 1999, and the provisions made under that Act; or
(b) regulations made under the Legal Aid Act 1988;

make different provision.

(The costs practice direction sets out the procedure to be followed where a party was wholly or partially funded by the Legal Services Commission)

Amendments—Inserted by SI 2000/1317.

Practice Direction—See generally PDCosts at p 1083 and specifically Section 21 at p 1115.

Legal Aid Act 1988—This provision excludes the costs rules to the extent that regulations made under the Legal Aid Act 1988 make different provision. Generally, in those circumstances costs are assessed on the standard basis in accordance with Civil Legal Aid (General) Regulations 1989, reg 107. However, provided that the certificate is issued after 25 February 1994, costs may be awarded against a party in favour of a legally aided party on the indemnity basis pursuant to CLA(G)(A)R 1994, reg 107B. Generally speaking, Legal Aid costs are at prescribed rates (with or without enhancement).

'section 11 Access to Justice Act 1999' (r 44.17(a))—This provides a special mechanism and procedure for assessment of costs where a party is wholly or partially funded by the Legal Services Commission. In these cases, the procedure for determination of costs is set out in PDCosts, Section 22. Access to Justice Act 1999, s 11 provides special protection against liability for costs for litigants who receive funding by the Legal Services Commission as part of the Community Legal Service. Any costs ordered against an 'LSC funded client' must not exceed the amount which it is reasonable to pay having regard to all the circumstances including –

(a) the financial resources of all the parties to the proceedings; and
(b) their conduct in connection with the dispute to which the proceedings relate.

For detailed provisions relating to cost protection, see Community Legal Service (Cost Protection) Regulations 2000. For the procedure for ordering costs against an 'LSC funded client' and/or the LSC, see Community Legal Service (Costs) Regulations, SI 2000/441.

PART 45
FIXED COSTS

CONTENTS OF THIS PART

I Fixed Costs

Note—From 1 April 2005, a new Section I of this Part has replaced the former Section I. It incorporates the provisions of the former Sch 1, RSC Ord 62 and Sch 2, CCR Order 38, extends the fixed costs regime to High Court possession claims under Pt 55 (which were not previously subject to fixed costs) and applies fixed costs to demotion claims under Pt 65.

45.1 Scope of this Section

(1) This Section sets out the amounts which, unless the court orders otherwise, are to be allowed in respect of solicitors' charges in the cases to which this Section applies.

(2) This Section applies where –

- (a) the only claim is a claim for a specified sum of money where the value of the claim exceeds £25 and –
  - (i) judgment in default is obtained under rule 12.4(1);
  - (ii) judgment on admission is obtained under rule 14.4(3);
  - (iii) judgment on admission on part of the claim is obtained under rule 14.5(6);
  - (iv) summary judgment is given under Part 24;
  - (v) the court has made an order to strike out(GL) a defence under rule 3.4(2)(a) as disclosing no reasonable grounds for defending the claim; or
  - (vi) rule 45.3 applies;
- (b) the only claim is a claim where the court gave a fixed date for the hearing when it issued the claim and judgment is given for the delivery of goods, and the value of the claim exceeds £25;
- (c) the claim is for the recovery of land, including a possession claim under Part 55, whether or not the claim includes a claim for a sum of money and the defendant gives up possession, pays the amount claimed, if any, and the fixed commencement costs stated in the claim form;
- (d) the claim is for the recovery of land, including a possession claim under Part 55, where one of the grounds for possession is arrears of rent, for which the court gave a fixed date for the hearing when it issued the claim and judgment is given for the possession of land (whether or not the order for possession is suspended on terms) and the defendant –
  - (i) has neither delivered a defence, or counterclaim, nor otherwise denied liability; or
  - (ii) has delivered a defence which is limited to specifying his proposals for the payment of arrears of rent;
- (e) the claim is a possession claim under Section II of Part 55 (accelerated possession claims of land let on an assured shorthold tenancy) and a possession order is made where the defendant has neither delivered a defence, or counterclaim, nor otherwise denied liability;
- (f) the claim is a demotion claim under Section III of Part 65 or a demotion claim is made in the same claim form in which a claim for possession is made under Part 55 and that demotion claim is successful; or
- (g) a judgment creditor has taken steps under Parts 70 to 73 to enforce a judgment or order.

(The practice direction supplementing rule 7.9 sets out the types of case where a court will give a fixed date for a hearing when it issues a claim)

(3) Any appropriate court fee will be allowed in addition to the costs set out in this Section.

(4) The claim form may include a claim for fixed commencement costs.

Amendments—Substituted by SI 2004/3419.

45.2 Amount of fixed commencement costs in a claim for the recovery of money or goods

(1) The amount of fixed commencement costs in a claim to which rule 45.1(2)(a) or (b) applies –

(a) shall be calculated by reference to Table 1; and
(b) the amount claimed, or the value of the goods claimed if specified, in the claim form is to be used for determining the band in Table 1 that applies to the claim.

(2) The amounts shown in Table 4 are to be allowed in addition, if applicable.

Amendments—Substituted by SI 2004/3419.

45.2A Amount of fixed commencement costs in a claim for the recovery of land or a demotion claim

(1) The amount of fixed commencement costs in a claim to which rule 45.1(2)(c), (d) or (f) applies shall be calculated by reference to Table 2.

(2) The amounts shown in Table 4 are to be allowed in addition, if applicable.

Amendments—Inserted by SI 2004/3419.

TABLE 1

Fixed Costs on Commencement of a Claim

Relevant band	*Where the claim form is served by the court or by any method other than personal service by the claimant*	*Where –* • *the claim form is served personally by the claimant; and* • *there is only one defendant*	*Where there is more than one defendant, for each additional defendant personally served at separate addresses by the claimant*
Where – • the value of the claim exceeds £25 but does not exceed £500	£50	£60	£15
Where – • the value of the claim exceeds £500 but does not exceed £1000	£70	£80	£15

Fixed Costs on Commencement of a Claim

Relevant band	*Where the claim form is served by the court or by any method other than personal service by the claimant*	*Where –* • *the claim form is served personally by the claimant; and* • *there is only one defendant*	*Where there is more than one defendant, for each additional defendant personally served at separate addresses by the claimant*
Where – • the value of the claim exceeds £1000 but does not exceed £5000; or • the only claim is for delivery of goods and no value is specified or stated on the claim form	£80	£90	£15
Where – • the value of the claim exceeds £5000	£100	£110	£15

Amendments—Substituted by SI 2004/3419.

TABLE 2

Fixed Costs on Commencement of a Claim		
Where the claim form is served by the court or by any method other than personal service by the claimant	*Where –* • *the claim form is served personally by the claimant; and* • *there is only one defendant*	*Where there is more than one defendant, for each additional defendant personally served at separate addresses by the claimant*
£69.50	£77	£15

Amendments—Substituted by SI 2004/3419.

45.3 When defendant only liable for fixed commencement costs

(1) Where –

- (a) the only claim is for a specified sum of money; and
- (b) the defendant pays the money claimed within 14 days after service of particulars of claim on him, together with the fixed commencement costs stated in the claim form,

the defendant is not liable for any further costs unless the court orders otherwise.

(2) Where –

- (a) the claimant gives notice of acceptance of a payment into court in satisfaction of the whole claim;
- (b) the only claim is for a specified sum of money; and
- (c) the defendant made the payment into court within 14 days after service of the particulars of claim on him, together with the fixed costs stated in the claim form,

the defendant is not liable for any further costs unless the court orders otherwise.

Amendments—Substituted by SI 2004/3419.

45.4 Costs on entry of judgment in a claim for the recovery of money or goods

Where –

- (a) the claimant has claimed fixed commencement costs under rule 45.2; and
- (b) judgment is entered in a claim to which rule 45.1(2)(a) or (b) applies in the circumstances specified in Table 3, the amount to be included in the judgment for the claimant's solicitor's charges is the total of –
  - (i) the fixed commencement costs; and
  - (ii) the relevant amount shown in Table 3.

Amendments—Substituted by SI 2004/3419.

45.4A Costs on entry of judgment in a claim for the recovery of land or a demotion claim

(1) Where –

- (a) the claimant has claimed fixed commencement costs under rule 45.2A; and
- (b) judgment is entered in a claim to which rule 45.1(2)(d) or (f) applies, the amount to be included in the judgment for the claimant's solicitor's charges is the total of –
  - (i) the fixed commencement costs; and
  - (ii) the sum of £57.25.

(2) Where an order for possession is made in a claim to which rule 45.1(2)(e) applies, the amount allowed for the claimant's solicitor's charges for preparing and filing –

- (a) the claim form;
- (b) the documents that accompany the claim form; and
- (c) the request for possession,

is £79.50.

Amendments—Inserted by SI 2004/3419.

TABLE 3

Fixed Costs on Entry of Judgment in a Claim for the Recovery of Money or Goods

	Where the amount of the judgment exceeds £25 but does not exceed £5000	*Where the amount of the judgment exceeds £5000*
Where judgment in default of an acknowledgment of service is entered under rule 12.4(1) (entry of judgment by request on claim for money only)	£22	£30
Where judgment in default of a defence is entered under rule 12.4(1) (entry of judgment by request on claim for money only)	£25	£35

Fixed Costs on Entry of Judgment in a Claim for the Recovery of Money or Goods

	Where the amount of the judgment exceeds £25 but does not exceed £5000	*Where the amount of the judgment exceeds £5000*
Where judgment is entered under rule 14.4 (judgment on admission), or rule 14.5 (judgment on admission of part of claim) and claimant accepts the defendant's proposal as to the manner of payment	£40	£55
Where judgment is entered under rule 14.4 (judgment on admission), or rule 14.5 (judgment on admission on part of claim) and court decides the date or times of payment	£55	£70
Where summary judgment is given under Part 24 or the court strikes out a defence under rule 3.4(2)(a), in either case, on application by a party	£175	£210
Where judgment is given on a claim for delivery of goods under a regulated agreement within the meaning of the Consumer Credit Act 1974 and no other entry in this table applies	£60	£85

Amendments—Substituted by SI 2004/3419.

45.5 Miscellaneous fixed costs

Table 4 shows the amount to be allowed in respect of solicitor's charges in the circumstances mentioned.

Amendments—Substituted by SI 2004/3419.

TABLE 4

Miscellaneous Fixed Costs	
For service by a party of any document required to be served personally including preparing and copying a certificate of service for each individual served	£15.00
Where service by an alternative method is permitted by an order under rule 6.8 for each individual served	£53.25
Where a document is served out of the jurisdiction – (a) in Scotland, Northern Ireland, the Isle of Man or the Channel Islands; (b) in any other place	£68.25 £77.00

Amendments—Substituted by SI 2004/3419.

45.6 Fixed enforcement costs

Table 5 shows the amount to be allowed in respect of solicitors' costs in the circumstances mentioned. The amounts shown in Table 4 are to be allowed in addition, if applicable.

Amendments—Substituted by SI 2004/3419.

TABLE 5

Fixed Enforcement Costs	
For an application under rule 70.5(4) that an award may be enforced as if payable under a court order, where the amount outstanding under the award:	
exceeds £25 but does not exceed £250	£30.75
exceeds £250 but does not exceed £600	£41.00
exceeds £600 but does not exceed £2,000	£69.50
exceeds £2,000	£75.50
On attendance to question a judgment debtor (or officer of a company or other corporation) who has been ordered to attend court under rule 71.2 where the questioning takes place before a court officer, including attendance by a responsible representative of the solicitor	for each half hour or part, £15.00

Fixed Enforcement Costs	
	(When the questioning takes place before a judge, he may summarily assess any costs allowed.)
On the making of a final third party debt order under rule 72.8(6)(a) or an order for the payment to the judgment creditor of money in court under rule 72.10(1)(b):	
if the amount recovered is less than £150	one-half of the amount recovered
otherwise	£98.50
On the making of a final charging order under rule 73.8(2)(a):	£110
	The court may also allow reasonable disbursements in respect of search fees and the registration of the order.
Where a certificate is issued and registered under Schedule 6 to the Civil Jurisdiction and Judgments Act 1982, the costs of registration	£39.00
Where permission is given under RSC Order 45, rule 3 to enforce a judgment or order giving possession of land and costs are allowed on the judgment or order, the amount to be added to the judgment or order for costs –	
(a) basic costs	£42.50
(b) where notice of the proceedings is to be to more than one person, for each additional person	£2.75
Where a writ of execution as defined in the RSC Order 46, rule 1, is issued against any party	£51.75
Where a request is filed for the issue of a warrant of execution under CCR Order 26, rule 1, for a sum exceeding £25	£2.25
Where an application for an attachment of earnings order is made and costs are allowed under CCR Order 27, rule 9 or CCR Order 28, rule 10, for each attendance on the hearing of the application	£8.50

Amendments—Inserted by SI 2004/3419.

II Road Traffic Accidents – Fixed Recoverable Costs

45.7 Scope and interpretation

(1) This Section sets out the costs which are to be allowed in –

- (a) costs-only proceedings under the procedure set out in rule 44.12A; or
- (b) proceedings for approval of a settlement or compromise under rule 21.10(2),

in cases to which this Section applies.

(2) This Section applies where –

- (a) the dispute arises from a road traffic accident;
- (b) the agreed damages include damages in respect of personal injury, damage to property, or both;
- (c) the total value of the agreed damages does not exceed £10,000; and
- (d) if a claim had been issued for the amount of the agreed damages, the small claims track would not have been the normal track for that claim.

(3) This Section does not apply where the claimant is a litigant in person.

(Rule 2.3 defines 'personal injuries' as including any disease and any impairment of a person's physical or mental condition)

(Rule 26.6 provides for when the small claims track is the normal track)

(4) In this Section –

- (a) 'road traffic accident' means an accident resulting in bodily injury to any person or damage to property caused by, or arising out of, the use of a motor vehicle on a road or other public place in England and Wales;
- (b) 'motor vehicle' means a mechanically propelled vehicle intended for use on roads; and
- (c) 'road' means any highway and any other road to which the public has access and includes bridges over which a road passes.

Amendments—Inserted by SI 2003/2113; amended by SI 2004/3419.

Practice Direction—See PDCosts, paras 25A.1–25A.10 at p 1162A.1.

Scope of provision—This Section provides for fixed recoverable costs in relation to road traffic accident cases, where the accident occurred on or after the 6 October 2003 and the claim is settled for damages not exceeding £10,000.

Court approval of infant settlements—From 1 April 2005, r 45.7(1)(b) clarifies that the fixed recoverable costs regime comprised in Pt 45, Section II should be followed where the court's approval of a settlement in favour of an infant is required. Consequential amendments have also been made to rr 21.10, 44.12A, 45.7, 45.14 and 48.5.

45.8 Application of fixed recoverable costs

Subject to rule 45.12, the only costs which are to be allowed are –

- (a) fixed recoverable costs calculated in accordance with rule 45.9;
- (b) disbursements allowed in accordance with rule 45.10; and
- (c) a success fee allowed in accordance with rule 45.11.

(Rule 45.12 provides for where a party issues a claim for more than the fixed recoverable costs).

Amendments—Inserted by SI 2003/2113.

45.9 Amount of fixed recoverable costs

(1) Subject to paragraphs (2) and (3), the amount of fixed recoverable costs is the total of –

(a) £800;
(b) 20% of the damages agreed up to £5000; and
(c) 15% of the damages agreed between £5000 and £10,000.

(2) Where the claimant –

(a) lives or works in an area set out in the relevant practice direction; and
(b) instructs a solicitor or firm of solicitors who practise in that area,

the fixed recoverable costs shall include, in addition to the costs specified in paragraph (1), an amount equal to 12.5% of the costs allowable under that paragraph.

(3) Where appropriate, value added tax (VAT) may be recovered in addition to the amount of fixed recoverable costs and any reference in this Section to fixed recoverable costs is a reference to those costs net of any such VAT.

Amendments—Inserted by SI 2003/2113.

45.10 Disbursements

(1) The court –

(a) may allow a claim for a disbursement of a type mentioned in paragraph (2); but
(b) must not allow a claim for any other type of disbursement.

(2) The disbursements referred to in paragraph (1) are –

(a) the cost of obtaining –
  (i) medical records;
  (ii) a medical report;
  (iii) a police report;
  (iv) an engineer's report; or
  (v) a search of the records of the Driver Vehicle Licensing Authority;
(b) the amount of an insurance premium or, where a membership organisation undertakes to meet liabilities incurred to pay the costs of other parties to proceedings, a sum not exceeding such additional amount of costs as would be allowed under section 30 in respect of provision made against the risk of having to meet such liabilities;

('membership organisation' is defined in rule 43.2(1)(n))

(c) where they are necessarily incurred by reason of one or more of the claimants being a child or patient as defined in Part 21 –
  (i) fees payable for instructing counsel; or
  (ii) court fees payable on an application to the court;
(d) any other disbursement that has arisen due to a particular feature of the dispute.

('insurance premium' is defined in rule 43.2)

Amendments—Inserted by SI 2003/2113; amended by SI 2003/3361; SI 2004/2072.

45.11 Success fee

(1) A claimant may recover a success fee if he has entered into a funding arrangement of a type specified in rule 43.2(k)(i).

(2) The amount of the success fee shall be 12.5% of the fixed recoverable costs calculated in accordance with rule 45.9(1), disregarding any additional amount which may be included in the fixed recoverable costs by virtue of rule 45.9(2).

(Rule 43.2(k)(i) defines a funding arrangement as including a conditional fee agreement or collective conditional fee agreement which provides for a success fee)

Amendments—Inserted by SI 2003/2113; amended by SI 2003/3361.

Transitional cases—Rule 45.11(2) was substituted with effect from 1 March 2004, up to which date the success fee was to be assessed by the court. It is not clear whether the court's discretion survives in relation to pending cases but, if so, costs judges are likely to exercise it by allowing the specified amount.

45.12 Claims for an amount of costs exceeding fixed recoverable costs

(1) The court will entertain a claim for an amount of costs (excluding any success fee or disbursements) greater than the fixed recoverable costs but only if it considers that there are exceptional circumstances making it appropriate to do so.

(2) If the court considers such a claim appropriate, it may –

(a) assess the costs; or
(b) make an order for the costs to be assessed.

(3) If the court does not consider the claim appropriate, it must make an order for fixed recoverable costs only.

Amendments—Inserted by SI 2003/2113.

45.13 Failure to achieve costs greater than fixed recoverable costs

(1) This rule applies where –

(a) costs are assessed in accordance with rule 45.12(2); and
(b) the court assesses the costs (excluding any VAT) as being an amount which is less than 20% greater than the amount of the fixed recoverable costs.

(2) The court must order the defendant to pay to the claimant the lesser of –

(a) the fixed recoverable costs; and
(b) the assessed costs.

Amendments—Inserted by SI 2003/2113.

45.14 Costs of the costs-only proceedings or the detailed assessment

Where –

(a) the court makes an order for fixed recoverable costs in accordance with rule 45.12(3); or
(b) rule 45.13 applies,

the court must –

(i) make no award for the payment of the claimant's costs in bringing the proceedings under rule 44.12A; and

(ii) order that the claimant pay the defendant's costs of defending those proceedings.

Amendments—Inserted by SI 2003/2113; amended by SI 2004/3419.

III FIXED PERCENTAGE INCREASE IN ROAD TRAFFIC ACCIDENT CLAIMS

Scope of provision—From 1 June 2004, this Section applies to all RTA disputes, where the accident occurred on or after 6 October 2003, which are funded by CFA, are outside the small claims track and do not fall within the costs-only provisions of Section II above. The success fees allowed are as follows:

	Pre-Trial			**Trial**
Solicitor's success fee	12.5%			100%
Counsel's success fee	12.5%	Multi-track: from 21 days pre-trial 75%	Fast track: from 14 days pre-trial 50%	100%

The definition of the term 'trial' is set out in r 44.17. There is a mandatory escape route in catastrophic cases where the damages agreed or ordered exceed £500,000, or would have done so had it not been for a finding of contributory negligence (r 45.18).

45.15 Scope and interpretation

(1) This Section sets out the percentage increase which is to be allowed in the cases to which this Section applies.

(Rule 43.2(1)(l) defines 'percentage increase' as the percentage by which the amount of a legal representative's fee can be increased in accordance with a conditional fee agreement which provides for a success fee)

(2) This Section applies where –

(a) the dispute arises from a road traffic accident; and

(b) the claimant has entered into a funding arrangement of a type specified in rule 43.2(k)(i).

(Rule 43.2(k)(i) defines a funding arrangement as including an arrangement where a person has entered into a conditional fee agreement or collective conditional fee agreement which provides for a success fee).

(3) This Section does not apply if the proceedings are costs only proceedings to which Section II of this Part applies.

(4) This Section does not apply –

(a) to a claim which has been allocated to the small claims track;

(b) to a claim not allocated to a track, but for which the small claims track is the normal track; or

(c) where the road traffic accident which gave rise to the dispute occurred before 6 October 2003.

(5) The definitions in rule 45.7(4) apply to this Section as they apply to Section II.

(6) In this Section –

(a) a reference to 'fees' is a reference to fees for work done under a conditional fee agreement or collective conditional fee agreement;
(b) a reference to 'trial' is a reference to the final contested hearing or to the contested hearing of any issue ordered to be tried separately;
(c) a reference to a claim concluding at trial is a reference to a claim concluding by settlement after the trial has commenced or by judgment; and
(d) 'trial period' means a period of time fixed by the court within which the trial is to take place and where the court fixes more than one such period in relation to a claim, means the most recent period to be fixed.

Amendments—Inserted by SI 2004/1306.

45.16 Percentage increase of solicitors' fees

Subject to rule 45.18, the percentage increase which is to be allowed in relation to solicitors' fees is –

(a) 100% where the claim concludes at trial; or
(b) 12.5% where –
   (i) the claim concludes before a trial has commenced; or
   (ii) the dispute is settled before a claim is issued.

Amendments—Inserted by SI 2004/1306.

45.17 Percentage increase of counsel's fees

(1) Subject to rule 45.18, the percentage increase which is to be allowed in relation to counsel's fees is –

(a) 100% where the claim concludes at trial;
(b) if the claim has been allocated to the fast track –
   (i) 50% if the claim concludes 14 days or less before the date fixed for the commencement of the trial; or
   (ii) 12.5% if the claim concludes more than 14 days before the date fixed for the commencement of the trial or before any such date has been fixed;
(c) if the claim has been allocated to the multi-track –
   (i) 75% if the claim concludes 21 days or less before the date fixed for the commencement of the trial; or
   (ii) 12.5% if the claim concludes more than 21 days before the date fixed for the commencement of the trial or before any such date has been fixed;
(d) 12.5% where –
   (i) the claim has been issued but concludes before it has been allocated to a track; or
   (ii) in relation to costs-only proceedings, the dispute is settled before a claim is issued.

(2) Where a trial period has been fixed, if –

(a) the claim concludes before the first day of that period; and
(b) no trial date has been fixed within that period before the claim concludes,

the first day of that period is treated as the date fixed for the commencement of the trial for the purposes of paragraph (1).

(3) Where a trial period has been fixed, if

(a) the claim concludes before the first day of that period; but
(b) before the claim concludes, a trial date had been fixed within that period,

the trial date is the date fixed for the commencement of the trial for the purposes of paragraph (1).

(4) Where a trial period has been fixed and the claim concludes –

(a) on or after the first day of that period; but
(b) before commencement of the trial,

the percentage increase in paragraph (1)(b)(i) or (1)(c)(i) shall apply as appropriate, whether or not a trial date has been fixed within that period.

(5) For the purposes of this rule, in calculating the periods of time, the day fixed for the commencement of the trial (or the first day of the trial period, where appropriate) is not included.

Amendments—Inserted by SI 2004/1306.

45.18 Application for an alternative percentage increase where the fixed increase is 12.5%

(1) This rule applies where the percentage increase to be allowed –

(a) in relation to solicitors' fees under the provisions of rule 45.16; or
(b) in relation to counsel's fees under rule 45.17,

is 12.5%.

(2) A party may apply for a percentage increase greater or less than that amount if –

(a) the parties agree damages of an amount greater than £500,000 or the court awards damages of an amount greater than £500,000; or
(b) the court awards damages of £500,000 or less but would have awarded damages greater than £500,000 if it had not made a finding of contributory negligence; or
(c) the parties agree damages of £500,000 or less and it is reasonable to expect that if the court had made an award of damages, it would have awarded damages greater than £500,000, disregarding any reduction the court may have made in respect of contributory negligence.

(3) In paragraph (2), a reference to a lump sum of damages includes a reference to periodical payments of equivalent value.

(4) If the court is satisfied that the circumstances set out in paragraph (2) apply it must –

(a) assess the percentage increase; or
(b) make an order for the percentage increase to be assessed.

Amendments—Inserted by SI 2004/1306; amended by SI 2004/3419.

45.19 Assessment of alternative percentage increase

(1) This rule applies where the percentage increase of fees is assessed under rule 45.18(4).

(2) If the percentage increase is assessed as greater than 20% or less than 7.5%, the percentage increase to be allowed shall be that assessed by the court.

(3) If the percentage increase is assessed as no greater than 20% and no less than 7.5% –

(a) the percentage increase to be allowed shall be 12.5%; and
(b) the costs of the application and assessment shall be paid by the applicant.

Amendments—Inserted by SI 2004/1306.

IV – FIXED PERCENTAGE INCREASE IN EMPLOYERS LIABILITY CLAIMS

45.20 Scope and interpretation

(1) Subject to paragraph (2), this Section applies where –

(a) the dispute is between an employee and his employer arising from a bodily injury sustained by the employee in the course of his employment; and
(b) the claimant has entered into a funding arrangement of a type specified in rule 43.2(1)(k)(i).

(2) This Section does not apply –

(a) where the dispute –
(i) relates to a disease;
(ii) relates to an injury sustained before 1 October 2004; or
(iii) arises from a road traffic accident (as defined in rule 45.7(4)(a)); or
(iv) relates to an injury to which Section V of this Part applies; or
(b) to a claim –
(i) which has been allocated to the small claims track; or
(ii) not allocated to a track, but for which the small claims track is the normal track.

(3) For the purposes of this Section –

(a) 'employee' has the meaning given to it by section 2(1) of the Employers' Liability (Compulsory Insurance) Act 1969; and
(b) a reference to 'fees' is a reference to fees for work done under a conditional fee agreement or collective conditional fee agreement.

Amendments—Inserted by SI 2004/2072.

Scope of provision—This section applies to all disputes between employee and employer arising from bodily injury sustained by the employee during the course of employment. It does not relate to industrial disease cases. The accident must have occurred after 1 October 2004 and the claim must be funded by a CFA. The claim must not be proceeding on the small claims track nor (if not allocated to track) be one which, if it were, would be allocated to the small claims track. The success fees allowed are as follows:

	Pre-Trial			Trial
Solicitor's success fee	25%			100%
Counsel's success fee	25%	Multi-track: from 21 days pre-trial 75%	Fast track: from 14 days pre-trial 50%	100%

NB: Where an employee is represented by a 'membership organisation' which has undertaken to meet his legal costs in accordance with AJA 1999, s 30, the 25% referred to above is increased to 27.5%.

45.21 Percentage increase of solicitors' and counsel's fees

In the cases to which this Section applies, subject to rule 45.22 the percentage increase which is to be allowed in relation to solicitors' and counsel's fees is to be determined in accordance with rules 45.16 and 45.17, subject to the modifications that –

- (a) the percentage increase which is to be allowed in relation to solicitors' fees under rule 45.16(b) is –
  - (i) 27.5% if a membership organisation has undertaken to meet the claimant's liabilities for legal costs in accordance with section 30 of the Access to Justice Act 1999; and
  - (ii) 25% in any other case; and
- (b) the percentage increase which is to be allowed in relation to counsel's fees under rule 45.17(1)(b)(ii), (1)(c)(ii) or (1)(d) is 25%.

('membership organisation' is defined in rule 43.2(1)(n))

Amendments—Inserted by SI 2004/2072.

45.22 Alternative percentage increase

(1) In the cases to which this Section applies, rule 45.18(2)–(4) applies where –

- (a) the percentage increase of solicitors' fees to be allowed in accordance with rule 45.21 is 25% or 27.5%; or
- (b) the percentage increase of counsel's fees to be allowed is 25%.

(2) Where the percentage increase of fees is assessed by the court under rule 45.18(4) as applied by paragraph (1) above –

- (a) if the percentage increase is assessed as greater than 40% or less than 15%, the percentage increase to be allowed shall be that assessed by the court; and
- (b) if the percentage increase is assessed as no greater than 40% and no less than 15% –
  - (i) the percentage increase to be allowed shall be 25% or 27.5% (as the case may be); and
  - (ii) the costs of the application and assessment shall be paid by the applicant.

Amendments—Inserted by SI 2004/2072.

V – FIXED RECOVERABLE SUCCESS FEES IN EMPLOYER'S LIABILITY DISEASE CLAIMS

45.23 Scope and Interpretation

(1) Subject to paragraph (2), this Section applies where –

- (a) the dispute is between an employee (or, if the employee is deceased, the employee's estate or dependants) and his employer (or a person alleged to be liable for the employer's alleged breach of statutory or common law duties of care); and
- (b) the dispute relates to a disease with which the employee is diagnosed that is alleged to have been contracted as a consequence of the employer's alleged breach of statutory or common law duties of care in the course of the employee's employment; and

(c) the claimant has entered into a funding arrangement of a type specified in rule 43.2(1)(k)(i).

(2) This Section does not apply where –

(a) the claimant sent a letter of claim to the defendant containing a summary of the facts on which the claim is based and main allegations of fault before 1st October 2005; or

(b) rule 45.20(2)(b) applies.

(3) For the purposes of this Section –

(a) rule 45.15(6) applies;

(b) 'employee' has the meaning given to it by section 2(1) of the Employers' Liability (Compulsory Insurance) Act 1969;

(c) 'Type A claim' means a claim relating to a disease or physical injury alleged to have been caused by exposure to asbestos;

(d) 'Type B claim' means a claim relating to –

(i) a psychiatric injury alleged to have been caused by work-related psychological stress;

(ii) a work-related upper limb disorder which is alleged to have been caused by physical stress or strain, excluding hand/arm vibration injuries; and

(e) 'Type C claim' means a claim relating to a disease not falling within either type A or type B.

(The Table annexed to the Practice Direction supplementing Part 45 contains a non-exclusive list of diseases within Type A and Type B)

Amendments—Inserted by SI 2005/2292.

Scope of provision—From 1 October 2005, this section applies to disputes between an employee and an employer relating to a disease which the employee is diagnosed to have contracted as a consequence of the employer's breach of duty and the employee has entered into a CFA. This Section fixes the level of success fees dependent on the type of industrial disease. The Section does not apply where the facts upon which the claim is based and main allegations of fault occurred before 1 October 2005 or the case is proceeding (or should proceed) on the small claims track.

Industrial diseases are categorised as follows –

(1) Type A – exposure to asbestos.

(2) Type B:

(a) psychiatric injury caused by work related psychological stress;

(b) work related upper limb disorder caused by stress or strain (excluding hand/arm vibration injuries).

(3) Type C – all other disease claims.

The Practice Direction supplementing Pt 45 contains a non exclusive list of the diseases within types A and B. Dependent upon which type of industrial injury is alleged there are varying levels of success fee.

45.24 Percentage increase of solicitors' fees

(1) In the cases to which this Section applies, subject to rule 45.26, the percentage increase which is to be allowed in relation to solicitors' fees is –

(a) 100% if the claim concludes at trial; or

(b) where –

(i) the claim concludes before a trial has commenced; or

(ii) the dispute is settled before a claim is issued,

to be determined by rule 45.24(2).

(2) Where rule 45.24(1)(b) applies, the percentage increase which is to be allowed in relation to solicitors' fees is –

(a) in type A claims –
  (i) 30% if a membership organisation has undertaken to meet the claimant's liabilities for legal costs in accordance with section 30 of the Access to Justice Act 1999; and
  (ii) 27.5% in any other case;
(b) in type B claims, 100%; and
(c) in type C claims –
  (i) 70% if a membership organisation has undertaken to meet the claimant's liabilities for legal costs in accordance with section 30 of the Access to Justice Act 1999; and
  (ii) 62.5% in any other case.

('Membership organisation' is defined in rule 43.2(1)(n))

Amendments—Inserted by SI 2005/2292.

45.25 Percentage increase of counsel's fees

(1) In the cases to which this Section applies, subject to rule 45.26, the percentage increase which is to be allowed in relation to counsel's fees is –

(a) 100% if the claim concludes at trial; or
(b) where –
  (i) the claim concludes before a trial has commenced; or
  (ii) the dispute is settled before a claim is issued,

to be determined by rule 45.25(2).

(2) Where rule 45.25(1)(b) applies, the percentage increase which is to be allowed in relation to counsel's fees is –

(a) if the claim has been allocated to the fast track, the amount shown in Table 6; and
(b) if the claim has been allocated to the multi-track, the amount shown in Table 7.

(3) Where a trial period has been fixed, rules 45.17(2) to 45.17(5) apply for the purposes of determining the date fixed for the commencement of the trial.

Table 6

Claims allocated to the fast track

	If the claim concludes 14 days or less before the date fixed for commencement of the trial	If the claim concludes more than 14 days before the date fixed for commencement of the trial or before any such date has been fixed
Type A claim	50%	27.5%
Type B claim	100%	100%
Type C claim	62.5%	62.5%

Table 7

Claims allocated to the multi-track		
	If the claim concludes 21 days or less before the date fixed for commencement of the trial	If the claim concludes more than 21 days before the date fixed for commencement of the trial or before any such date has been fixed
Type A claim	75%	27.5%
Type B claim	100%	100%
Type C claim	75%	62.5%

Amendments—Inserted by SI 2005/2292.

45.26 Alternative percentage increase

(1) In cases to which this Section applies and subject to paragraph (2) below, rules 45.18(2) to (4) apply where the percentage increase is the amount allowed under rules 45.24 and 45.25.

(2) For the purposes of this section, the sum of £250,000 shall be substituted for the sum of £500,000 in rules 45.18(2)(a) to (c).

(3) Where the percentage increase of fees is assessed by the court under rule 45.18(4), as applied by paragraph 1 above, the percentage increase to be allowed shall be the amount shown in Table 8.

(4) The percentage increase cannot be varied where the case concludes at trial.

Table 8

Type of claim	Amount Allowed	
A	If the percentage increase is assessed as greater than 40% or less than 15%, the percentage increase that is assessed by the court.	If the percentage increase is assessed as no greater than 40% and no less than 15% – (i) 27.5%; and (ii) the costs of the application and assessment shall be paid by the applicant.
B	If the percentage increase is assessed as less than 75%, the percentage increase that is assessed by the court.	If the percentage increase is assessed as no less than 75% – (i) 100%; and (ii) the costs of the application and assessment shall be paid by the applicant.

C	If the percentage increase is assessed as greater than 75% or less than 50%, the percentage increase that is assessed by the court.	If the percentage increase is assessed as no greater than 75% and no less than 50% – (i) 62.5%; and (ii) the costs of the application and assessment shall be paid by the applicant.

Amendments—Inserted by SI 2005/2292.

PART 46
FAST TRACK TRIAL COSTS

CONTENTS OF THIS PART

46.1 Scope of this Part

(1) This Part deals with the amount of costs which the court may award as the costs of an advocate for preparing for and appearing at the trial of a claim in the fast track (referred to in this rule as 'fast track trial costs').

(2) For the purposes of this Part –

- (a) 'advocate' means a person exercising a right of audience as a representative of, or on behalf of, a party;
- (b) 'fast track trial costs' means the costs of a party's advocate for preparing for and appearing at the trial, but does not include –
  - (i) any other disbursements; or
  - (ii) any value added tax payable on the fees of a party's advocate; and
- (c) 'trial' includes a hearing where the court decides an amount of money or the value of goods following a judgment under Part 12 (default judgment) or Part 14 (admissions) but does not include –
  - (i) the hearing of an application for summary judgment under Part 24; or
  - (ii) the court's approval of a settlement or other compromise under rule 21.10.

(Part 21 deals with claims made by or on behalf of, or against, children and patients)

Practice Direction—See generally PDCosts at p 1083 and specifically Section 26 at p 1126.

Scope of provision—In general, CPR makes no distinction between the basis of entitlement and quantification of fast track or multi-track costs. On the fast track, trial costs are fixed (but see r 46.3). Part 46 is long and complex in dealing with this limited provision. Its aim is to provide the parties with a precise figure for recoverable costs for the advocate at trial (including immediate preparation).

'advocate' (r 46.1(2)(a))—This can mean barrister, solicitor or FILEX with appropriate rights of audience.

'fast track trial costs' (r 46.1(2)(b))—These are purely the costs of preparing for and appearing at the trial and exclude disbursements and VAT. Travelling and waiting time may not be claimed in addition. The costs of preparing for and appearing at the trial should be differentiated from general preparation work (attendances on the client, documents and the like) which will be allowed in addition to fast track trial costs.

'trial' (r 46.1(2)(c))—The definition does not include the hearing of a claim which is allocated to the small claims track with the consent of the parties under r 26.7(3) (when costs will be in the discretion of the court but capped at the figures in this Part (r 27.14(5)) or a disposal hearing under PD26, para 12.4 (when costs will be in the discretion of the court, subject to the limits in r 27.14 if the claim has been allocated to the small claims track (PD26, para 12.5 and PDCosts, para 26.3)). An additional liability can be claimed in relation to fast track trial costs. The court has power when considering whether a percentage increase is reasonable to allow different percentages for different items of costs or for different periods during which the costs were incurred (PDCosts, para 27.3).

46.2 Amount of fast track trial costs

(1) The following table shows the amount of fast track trial costs which the court may award (whether by summary or detailed assessment).

Value of the claim	**Amount of fast track trial costs which the court may award**
Up to £3000	£350
More than £3000 but not more than £10,000	£500
More than £10,000	£750

(2) The court may not award more or less than the amount shown in the table except where –

- (a) it decides not to award any fast track trial costs; or
- (b) rule 46.3 applies,

but the court may apportion the amount awarded between the parties to reflect their respective degrees of success on the issues at trial.

(3) Where the only claim is for the payment of money –

- (a) for the purpose of quantifying fast track trial costs awarded to a claimant, the value of the claim is the total amount of the judgment excluding –
  - (i) interest and costs; and
  - (ii) any reduction made for contributory negligence.
- (b) for the purpose of the quantifying fast track trial costs awarded to a defendant, the value of the claim is –
  - (i) the amount specified in the claim form (excluding interest and costs);
  - (ii) if no amount is specified, the maximum amount which the claimant reasonably expected to recover according to the statement of value included in the claim form under rule 16.3; or
  - (iii) more than £10,000, if the claim form states that the claimant cannot reasonably say how much he expects to recover.

(4) Where the claim is only for a remedy other than the payment of money the value of the claim is deemed to be more than £3000 but not more than £10,000, unless the court orders otherwise.

(5) Where the claim includes both a claim for the payment of money and for a remedy other than the payment of money, the value of the claim is deemed to be the higher of –

- (a) the value of the money claim decided in accordance with paragraph (3); or
- (b) the deemed value of the other remedy decided in accordance with paragraph (4),

unless the court orders otherwise.

(6) Where –

- (a) a defendant has made a counterclaim against the claimant;

(b) the counterclaim has a higher value than the claim; and

(c) the claimant succeeds at trial both on his claim and the counterclaim,

for the purpose of quantifying fast track trial costs awarded to the claimant, the value of the claim is the value of the defendant's counterclaim calculated in accordance with this rule.

(Rule 20.4 sets out how a defendant may make a counterclaim)

'counterclaim' (r 46.2(6))—Where a defendant's counterclaim is higher than the claim a successful claimant in relation to both claim and counterclaim is entitled to fast track trial costs based on the value of the defendant's counterclaim.

Adjournment—The amount of fast track trial costs referred to is in respect of 'the trial' irrespective of the length of that trial. The fast track is the normal track only if the trial is likely to last for no longer than one day (r 26.6(5)). In relation to allocation a day is taken as being a period of 5 hours (PD26, para 9.1(3)(a)). Accordingly, practitioners should note that where fast track trial cases are adjourned to another day they will not be able to recover additional fast track trial costs or adjournment fees.

46.3 Power to award more or less than the amount of fast track trial costs

(1) This rule sets out when a court may award –

(a) an additional amount to the amount of fast track trial costs shown in the table in rule 46.2(1); and

(b) less than those amounts.

(2) If –

(a) in addition to the advocate, a party's legal representative attends the trial;

(b) the court considers that it was necessary for a legal representative to attend to assist the advocate; and

(c) the court awards fast track trial costs to that party,

the court may award an additional £250 in respect of the legal representative's attendance at the trial.

(Legal representative is defined in rule 2.3)

(2A) The court may in addition award a sum representing an additional liability.

(The requirements to provide information about a funding arrangement where a party wishes to recover any additional liability under a funding arrangement are set out in the costs practice direction)

('Additional liability' is defined in rule 43.2)

(3) If the court considers that it is necessary to direct a separate trial of an issue then the court may award an additional amount in respect of the separate trial but that amount is limited in accordance with paragraph (4) of this rule.

(4) The additional amount the court may award under paragraph 3 must not exceed two-thirds of the amount payable for that claim, subject to a minimum award of £350.

(5) Where the party to whom fast track trial costs are to be awarded is a litigant in person, the court will award –

(a) if the litigant in person can prove financial loss, two-thirds of the amount that would otherwise be awarded; or

(b) if the litigant in person fails to prove financial loss, an amount in respect of the time spent reasonably doing the work at the rate specified in the costs practice direction.

(6) Where a defendant has made a counterclaim against the claimant, and –

(a) the claimant has succeeded on his claim; and

(b) the defendant has succeeded on his counterclaim,

the court will quantify the amount of the award of fast track trial costs to which –

(i) but for the counterclaim, the claimant would be entitled for succeeding on his claim; and

(ii) but for the claim, the defendant would be entitled for succeeding on his counterclaim,

and make one award of the difference, if any, to the party entitled to the higher award of costs.

(7) Where the court considers that the party to whom fast track trial costs are to be awarded has behaved unreasonably or improperly during the trial, it may award that party an amount less than would otherwise be payable for that claim, as it considers appropriate.

(8) Where the court considers that the party who is to pay the fast track trial costs has behaved improperly during the trial the court may award such additional amount to the other party as it considers appropriate.

Amendments—SI 2000/1317.

Practice Direction—See generally PDCosts at p 1083 and specifically Section 27 at p 1126.

Scope of provision—The scope for increasing fast track trial costs is extremely limited.

'legal representative' (r 46.3(2))—The extra fee is only allowed if it was 'necessary' for a legal representative to attend to assist the advocate. Where counsel is instructed as the 'advocate' a solicitor does not now have a professional obligation in a civil action to attend with counsel.

'Additional liability' (note to r 46.3(2A))—In addition to fast track trial costs, the court has power to award a sum representing an 'additional liability' (r 43.2(1)(o)) defined as a percentage increase in a CFA, a recoverable insurance premium, or recoverable costs incurred by a 'membership organisation' (r 43.2(1)(n)). The maximum permitted increased percentage is 100% (CFAO 2000, SI 2000/823). See also PDCosts, paras 27.1–27.3.

'litigant in person' (r 46.3(5))—Fast track trial costs can be awarded to a litigant in person. If the litigant in person can prove financial loss he will recover two thirds of the amount which would otherwise be awarded in accordance with r 46.2 *irrespective of his loss*. If he fails to prove financial loss he will recover the time reasonably spent in carrying out the work at the rate of £9.25 per hour (PDCosts, para 52.4).

Counterclaims (r 46.3(6))—Where a claimant is successful on his claim and a defendant successful on his counterclaim the court will separately quantify the amount of fast track trial costs to which both claimant and defendant are entitled, ignoring the presence of the other claim. The court will then take one from the other and make an award for the difference to the party with the higher entitlement (if any). *Medway Oil & Storage Company Limited v Continental Contractors Limited* [1929] AC 88, HL does not apply to fast track trial costs.

Unreasonable or improper behaviour (r 46.3(7) and (8))—The court retains the power to award less than fixed fast track trial costs where one or the other party has behaved unreasonably or improperly 'during the trial'. If the offending party is the receiving party the court may award less than would otherwise have been payable; if it is the paying party the court may award an additional amount to the receiving party. No guidance is given by the rules or practice direction relating to the amount of any adjustment in these circumstances. The provisions relate solely to the 'party' and do not refer to the behaviour of a party's legal representative.

46.4 Fast track trial costs where there is more than one claimant or defendant

(1) Where the same advocate is acting for more than one party –

(a) the court may make only one award in respect of fast track trial costs payable to that advocate; and
(b) the parties for whom the advocate is acting are jointly entitled to any fast track trial costs awarded by the court.

(2) Where –

(a) the same advocate is acting for more than one claimant; and
(b) each claimant has a separate claim against the defendant,

the value of the claim, for the purpose of quantifying the award in respect of fast track trial costs is to be ascertained in accordance with paragraph (3).

(3) The value of the claim in the circumstances mentioned in paragraph (2) is –

(a) where the only claim of each claimant is for the payment of money –
(i) if the award of fast track trial costs is in favour of the claimants, the total amount of the judgment made in favour of all the claimants jointly represented; or
(ii) if the award is in favour of the defendant, the total amount claimed by the claimants;

and in either case, quantified in accordance with rule 46.2(3);

(b) where the only claim of each claimant is for a remedy other than the payment of money, deemed to be more than £3000 but not more than £10,000; and
(c) where claims of the claimants include both a claim for the payment of money and for a remedy other than the payment of money, deemed to be –
(i) more than £3000 but not more than £10,000; or
(ii) if greater, the value of the money claims calculated in accordance with sub paragraph (a) above.

(4) Where –

(a) there is more than one defendant; and
(b) any or all of the defendants are separately represented,

the court may award fast track trial costs to each party who is separately represented.

(5) Where –

(a) there is more than one claimant; and
(b) a single defendant,

the court may make only one award to the defendant of fast track trial costs, for which the claimants are jointly and severally liable.[(GL)]

(6) For the purpose of quantifying the fast track trial costs awarded to the single defendant under paragraph (5), the value of the claim is to be calculated in accordance with paragraph (3) of this rule.

PART 47
PROCEDURE FOR DETAILED ASSESSMENT OF COSTS AND DEFAULT PROVISIONS

CONTENTS OF THIS PART

(The definitions contained in Part 43 are relevant to this Part)

Procedural Guide—See Guide 32, set out in Section 1 of this work.

Introduction—To a large extent Pt 47 detailed assessment is based on the former SCTO Practice Direction No 1 of 1995 but there are two major innovations:

(1) a 'default procedure' has been introduced; and
(2) a formal system of appeals has been introduced.

Detailed assessment is commenced by serving the bill and supporting documents on other interested parties. If the bill is not challenged by the paying party serving on the receiving party of 'points of dispute' (r 47.9), the receiving party may apply for a certificate (a Default Costs Certificate) which will entitle him to receive payment of the whole amount claimed (r 47.11). The court is not involved with the proceedings until the receiving party either:

(a) seeks a default costs certificate where the paying party has failed to serve points of dispute; or
(b) requests a detailed assessment hearing.

The court has power to order a payment on account before detailed assessment (r 44.3(8)) and/or issue an interim certificate (r 47.15) at any time after the receiving party has filed a request for a detailed assessment hearing. There is no requirement that the interim certificate should relate to any amount agreed between the parties or decided by detailed assessment but is likely to bear some relationship to the amount of the costs claimed that are not challenged.

A party must comply with an order for the payment of costs contained in a default interim or final costs certificate within 14 days unless the court orders otherwise (r 44.8).

For definition of terms and matters of general application see Pt 43.

Section I – General Rules about Detailed Assessment

47.1 Time when detailed assessment may be carried out

The general rule is that the costs of any proceedings or any part of the proceedings are not to be assessed by the detailed procedure until the conclusion of the proceedings but the court may order them to be assessed immediately.

(The costs practice direction gives further guidance about when proceedings are concluded for the purpose of this rule)

Practice Direction—See generally PDCosts at p 1083 and specifically Section 28 at p 1127.

'assessed immediately'—It will be rare for detailed assessment of the costs of part of proceedings to be ordered to be carried out before the proceedings are concluded, summary assessment being preferred. Any summary assessment of costs which has already taken place within the course of proceedings is unaffected by detailed assessment of costs.

'the conclusion of the proceedings'—Paragraph 28.1 of PDCosts, gives examples of when proceedings are concluded (see *Hicks v Russell Jones and Walker* [2001] CP Rep 25, CA). Application may be made to the court to determine entitlement to commence detailed assessment proceedings or their ability to continue (PDCosts, para 28.1(3) and (4)).

47.2 No stay of detailed assessment where there is an appeal

Detailed assessment is not stayed pending an appeal unless the court so orders.

Practice Direction—See generally PDCosts at p 1083 and specifically Section 29 at p 1127.

Scope of provision—The detailed assessment will proceed unless the court orders otherwise. An application for a stay may be made to the judge whose order is being appealed or from the appellate court or, if appropriate, a costs officer (PDCosts, para 29.1(2)).

47.3 Powers of an authorised court officer

(1) An authorised court officer has all the powers of the court when making a detailed assessment, except –

- (a) power to make a wasted costs order as defined in rule 48.7;
- (b) power to make an order under –
  - (i) rule 44.14 (powers in relation to misconduct);
  - (ii) rule 47.8 (sanction for delay in commencing detailed assessment proceedings);
  - (iii) paragraph (2) (objection to detailed assessment by authorised court officer); and
- (c) power to make a detailed assessment of costs payable to a solicitor by his client, unless the costs are being assessed under rule 48.5 (costs where money is payable to a child or patient).

(2) Where a party objects to the detailed assessment of costs being made by an authorised court officer, the court may order it to be made by a costs judge or a district judge.

(The costs practice direction sets out the relevant procedure)

Practice Direction—See generally PDCosts at p 1083 and specifically Section 30 at p 1127.

Scope of provision—Authorised court officers at present are only to be found in the SCCO where they are authorised (r 43.2(1)(d)) to carry out detailed assessments is limited by the value of the amounts claimed as follows:

Senior Executive Officers	£30,000 (excluding VAT)
Principal Officers	£75,000 (excluding VAT)

'Where a party objects' (r 47.3(2))—The parties may agree that the assessment be not dealt with by an authorised court officer (PDCosts, para 30.1(3)). If one party objects he must make application in accordance with Pt 23 to a costs judge or district judge stating the reasons for objection (PDCosts, para 30.1(4)).

47.4 Venue for detailed assessment proceedings

(1) All applications and requests in detailed assessment proceedings must be made to or filed at the appropriate office.

(The costs practice direction sets out the meaning of 'appropriate office' in any particular case)

(2) The court may direct that the appropriate office is to be the Supreme Court Costs Office.

(3) A county court may direct that another county court is to be the appropriate office.

(4) A direction under paragraph (3) may be made without proceedings being transferred to that court.

(Rule 30.2 makes provision for any county court to transfer the proceedings to another county court for detailed assessment of costs)

Practice Direction—See generally PDCosts at p 1083 and specifically Section 31 at p 1128.

Scope of provision—Detailed assessment will generally take place at the court in which the case was proceeding. However the rule gives considerable scope for the court to direct detailed assessment to take place at another county court or district registry. This may be for the convenience of the parties or the court and a direction under r 47.4(2) or (3) may be made on application by the parties or on the court's own initiative (PDCosts, para 31.2(1)).

'appropriate office' (r 47.4(1))—This is defined in PDCosts, para 31.1.

'another county court' (r 47.4(3))—Only the detailed assessment will be dealt with at that court unless the proceedings as a whole are transferred (r 47.4(4)).

'the Supreme Court Costs Office' (r 47.4(2))—Unless it is the 'appropriate office' within PDCosts, para 31.1, such a direction will only be made if the court is faced with a large complex and high value bill of costs which would be outside that court's general experience and had the potential for taking up a substantial amount of court time and/or resources (PDCosts, para 31.2(3)).

Section II – Costs Payable by One Party to Another – Commencement of Detailed Assessment Proceedings

47.5 Application of this section

This section of Part 47 applies where a costs officer is to make a detailed assessment of costs which are payable by one party to another.

General note—For the practice in relation to costs to be paid out of the Legal Aid Fund, see Pt VI, r 47.17 and PDCosts, paras 49.1–49.8.

47.6 Commencement of detailed assessment proceedings

(1) Detailed assessment proceedings are commenced by the receiving party serving on the paying party –

(a) notice of commencement in the relevant practice form; and
(b) a copy of the bill of costs.

(Rule 47.7 sets out the period for commencing detailed assessment proceedings)

(2) The receiving party must also serve a copy of the notice of commencement and the bill on any other relevant persons specified in the costs practice direction.

(3) A person on whom a copy of the notice of commencement is served under paragraph (2) is a party to the detailed assessment proceedings (in addition to the paying party and the receiving party).

(The costs practice direction deals with –

- other documents which the party must file when he requests detailed assessment;
- the court's powers where it considers that a hearing may be necessary;
- the form of a bill;
- the length of notice which will be given if a hearing date is fixed)

Practice Direction—See generally PDCosts at p 1083 and specifically Section 32 at p 1129.

Forms—Form N252 (Notice of Commencement of Assessment of Bill of Costs).

'serving on the paying party' (r 47.6(1))—It is no longer necessary to commence detailed assessment proceedings by filing papers at court. At this stage the court is not involved. Paragraphs 32.4 and 32.5 of PDCosts set out the additional documents that must accompany a bill of costs.

'other relevant persons' (r 47.6(2))—See PDCosts, para 32.10. Generally speaking any person who has taken part in the proceedings which gave rise to the assessment and is directly liable under an order for costs or who has given notice to the receiving party that he has a financial interest in the outcome of the assessment and wishes to be a party, should be served with the bill of costs. Where a party is unsure whether a person should be served with a copy of the Bill application can be made to the court for directions and if possible joinder as a party (Pt 19). Any such application is made in accordance with Pt 23.

Note that where paying parties are jointly and severally liable for costs all such parties must be served with the documents in accordance with r 47.6(1) or costs will be disallowed even against the party who has been served (*Mainwaring v Goldtech (No 2)* [1999] 1 WLR 745, CA).

Additional liability—Detailed assessment may take place in respect of:
(a) base costs where a claim for an additional liability has not been made or agreed; or
(b) a claim for additional liability only, base costs having been summarily assessed or agreed; or
(c) both base costs and additional liability.

Where detailed assessment is in respect of an additional liability, in addition to the documents to be served with the notice of commencement (PDCosts, para 32.3) the 'relevant details' of the additional liability must also be served (PDCosts, para 32.4). The relevant details of an additional liability are (PDCosts, para 32.5):
(a) In the case of a CFA with success fee:
  (i) a statement showing the amount of costs summarily assessed or agreed and a percentage increase which has been claimed in respect of those costs;
  (ii) a statement of the reasons given in accordance with CFAR 2000, reg 3.
(b) In relation to an insurance premium:

- a copy of the insurance certificate showing the extent of that cover.

(c) In relation to an additional liability under AJA 1999, s 30:

- a statement setting out the basis upon which the receiving party's liability for the additional amount is calculated.

Related provision—For narrative as to the form and content of the bill of costs, see commentary to PDCosts, Section 4.

47.7 Period for commencing detailed assessment proceedings

The following table shows the period for commencing detailed assessment proceedings.

Source of right to detailed assessment	Time by which detailed assessment proceedings must be commenced
Judgment, direction, order, award or other determination	3 months after the date of the judgment etc Where detailed assessment is stayed pending an appeal, 3 months after the date of the order lifting the stay.
Discontinuance under Part 38	3 months after the date of service of notice of discontinuance under rule 38.3; or 3 months after the date of the dismissal of application to set the notice of discontinuance aside under rule 38.4
Acceptance of an offer to settle or a payment into court under Part 36	3 months after the date when the right to costs arose.

Practice Direction—See generally PDCosts at p 1083 and specifically Section 33 at p 1131.

Scope of provision—A party has 3 months from the date of the event giving rise to detailed assessment to commence detailed assessment proceedings. This can be extended by agreement of the parties in accordance with r 2.11. It is not necessary for a party to apply to the court for permission to commence detailed assessment proceedings out of time. It may be appropriate for the receiving party who is unable to comply with the time limit to apply to the court to extend the period of time for commencing detailed assessment proceedings giving reasons for so doing. A successful application will have the effect of preventing the sanction of disallowance of interest referred to in r 47.8(3).

47.8 Sanction for delay in commencing detailed assessment proceedings

(1) Where the receiving party fails to commence detailed assessment proceedings within the period specified –

(a) in rule 47.7; or

(b) by any direction of the court,

the paying party may apply for an order requiring the receiving party to commence detailed assessment proceedings within such time as the court may specify.

(2) On an application under paragraph (1), the court may direct that, unless the receiving party commences detailed assessment proceedings within the time

specified by the court, all or part of the costs to which the receiving party would otherwise be entitled will be disallowed.

(3) If –

(a) the paying party has not made an application in accordance with paragraph (1); and
(b) the receiving party commences the proceedings later than the period specified in rule 47.7,

the court may disallow all or part of the interest otherwise payable to the receiving party under –

(i) section 17 of the Judgments Act 1838; or
(ii) section 74 of the County Courts Act 1984,

but must not impose any other sanction except in accordance with rule 44.14 (powers in relation to misconduct).

(4) Where the costs to be assessed in a detailed assessment are payable out of the [Community Legal Service Fund, this rule applies as if the receiving party were the solicitor to whom the costs are payable and the paying party were the [Legal Services Commission.

Amendments—SI 2000/1317.

Practice Direction—See generally PDCosts at p 1083 and specifically Section 34 at p 1131.

'may disallow … interest' (r 47.8(3))—Judgments Act 1838, s 17 has been amended to give the court a discretion to disallow all or part of any interest to which the receiving party would otherwise be entitled. This is the only sanction available where the receiving party commences detailed assessment proceedings late, unless there has been misconduct entitling the court to exercise its powers under r 44.14.

Disallowance of costs pursuant to r 44.14 is a disproportionate sanction for failure to initiate the procedure for detailed assessment within the three months allowed under r 47.7 (*Botham v Imran Khan* [2005] EWHC 2602, [2005] 2 Costs LR 259 (QB)).

'Legal Services Commission' (r 47.8(4))—The Legal Services Commission is now able to make application under r 47.8(1) where there has been delay by the assisted party's solicitor in commencing detailed assessment proceedings. This is not an infrequent occurrence and may cause difficulties to counsel and in certain circumstances experts who remain unpaid and cannot themselves commence detailed assessment proceedings.

Where practitioners delay in submitting LSC-funded-only bills for assessment in accordance with r 47.17 beyond the 3-month period allowed by r 47.7, the court may disallow all or part of the costs claimed under Civil Legal Aid (General) Regulations 1989, reg 109. For an example of the use of this discretion by the court see *Official Receiver v Dobson & ors, Re Homes Assured Corp plc; Sampson & anor v Wilson & ors* (2001) Lawtel, 3 December, ChD, Park J. Where a bill of costs was assessed 3 years after the event, the claimants recovered 80% of their costs as assessed, which met sufficiently the seriousness of their delay and failure to comply with a court order (*Q v J* (2003) (unreported) 3 March, Sumner J).

47.9 Points of dispute and consequence of not serving

(1) The paying party and any other party to the detailed assessment proceedings may dispute any item in the bill of costs by serving points of dispute on –

(a) the receiving party; and
(b) every other party to the detailed assessment proceedings.

(2) The period for serving points of dispute is 21 days after the date of service of the notice of commencement.

(3) If a party serves points of dispute after the period set out in paragraph (2), he may not be heard further in the detailed assessment proceedings, unless the court gives permission.

(The costs practice direction sets out requirements about the form of points of dispute)

(4) The receiving party may file a request for a default costs certificate if –

(a) the period set out in rule 47.9(2) for serving points of dispute has expired; and
(b) he has not been served with any points of dispute.

(5) If any party (including the paying party) serves points of dispute before the issue of a default costs certificate the court may not issue the default costs certificate.

(Section IV of this Part sets out the procedure to be followed after points of dispute have been filed)

Practice Direction—See generally PDCosts at p 1083 and specifically Section 35 at p 1131.

Forms—For model form of points of dispute, see Precedent G, Schedule of Costs Precedents.

'the period … is 21 days' (r 47.9(2))—The parties may agree an extension of time for the service of points of dispute (PDCosts, para 35.1). The paying party may also apply to the court for an order under r 3.1(2)(a) to extend the time for service of points of dispute. Application is made in accordance with Pt 23. If points of dispute are served after the time laid down in the rule the paying party may not be heard further in the detailed assessment proceedings unless the court gives permission (r 47.9(3)).

Where a default cost certificate is issued, it contains an order for costs which must be complied with within 14 days (r 44.8).

Additional liability—Where the receiving party claims an additional liability the party who serves points of dispute may include a request for information about what other methods of financing the action were available to the receiving party. Part 18 (Further Information) applies to such a request (PDCosts, para 35.7).

47.10 Procedure where costs are agreed

(1) If the paying party and the receiving party agree the amount of costs, either party may apply for a costs certificate (either interim or final) in the amount agreed.

(Rule 47.15 and rule 47.16 contain further provisions about interim and final costs certificates respectively)

(2) An application for a certificate under paragraph (1) must be made to the court which would be the venue for detailed assessment proceedings under rule 47.4.

Amendments—SI 2000/1317.

Practice Direction—See generally PDCosts at p 1083 and specifically Section 36 at p 1133.

Scope of provision—The parties may agree all or part of the costs in relation to proceedings. The rule allows either party to apply for a costs certificate from the court, either an interim certificate if part of the costs are agreed or a final certificate if all the costs are agreed.

There may be circumstances where a party claims that the other party to proceedings has agreed to pay costs but has not done so and will not join in a consent application. In such circumstances the receiving party may apply under Pt 23 for a costs certificate to be issued. An application must be supported by evidence and any evidence in reply must be served at least 2 days before the hearing (PDCosts, para 36.3). Where parties settle an action but do not agree the issue of costs, in all but the most straightforward of cases a judge is entitled to tell the parties that if they have not reached any agreement on costs, they have not settled the dispute (*BCT Software Solutions v Brewer & Sons Ltd* [2003] EWCA Civ 939, [2004] FSR 9, (2003) Lawtel, 14 July, CA).

Section III – Costs Payable by One Party to Another – Default Provisions

47.11 Default costs certificate

(1) Where the receiving party is permitted by rule 47.9 to obtain a default costs certificate, he does so by filing a request in the relevant practice form.

(The costs practice direction deals with the procedure by which the receiving party may obtain a default costs certificate)

(2) A default costs certificate will include an order to pay the costs to which it relates.

(3) Where a receiving party obtains a default costs certificate, the costs payable to him for the commencement of detailed assessment proceedings shall be the sum set out in the costs practice direction.

Amendments—SI 1999/1008.

Practice Direction—See generally PDCosts at p 1083 and specifically Section 37 at p 1133.

Forms—N254 (Request for a Default Costs Certificate); N255 (Default Costs Certificate (county court)); N255HC (Default Costs Certificate (High Court)).

Scope of provision—The default cost certificate is an entirely new concept and entitles the receiving party to obtain a certificate for the full amount of costs due to him where the paying party without good reason fails to respond to the service of a bill of costs.

'an order to pay' (r 47.11(2))—The order will require payment within 14 days and can be enforced as a judgment of the court.

Generally under CPR, it is for the court to draw up every judgment or order (r 40.3). A default costs certificate is an exception. Paragraph 37.4 of PDCosts gives the receiving party permission to draw up a default costs certificate.

Legal Services Commission/Legal Aid—Where a default costs certificate is obtained against a paying party this does not affect detailed assessment of costs in accordance with funding provided by the Legal Services Commission pursuant to AJA 1999, s 11 or at prescribed rates in accordance with the Legal Aid Act 1988 where the receiving party is an assisted person (PDCosts, para 37.5).

Stay of enforcement—See PDCosts, paras 37.6–37.7.

47.12 Setting aside default costs certificate

(1) The court must set aside a default costs certificate if the receiving party was not entitled to it.

(2) In any other case, the court may set aside or vary a default costs certificate if it appears to the court that there is some good reason why the detailed assessment proceedings should continue.

(3) Where –

(a) the receiving party has purported to serve the notice of commencement on the paying party;
(b) a default costs certificate has been issued; and
(c) the receiving party subsequently discovers that the notice of commencement did not reach the paying party at least 21 days before the default costs certificate was issued;

the receiving party must –

(i) file a request for the default costs certificate to be set aside; or
(ii) apply to the court for directions.

(4) Where paragraph (3) applies, the receiving party may take no further step in –

(a) the detailed assessment proceedings; or
(b) the enforcement of the default costs certificate,

until the certificate has been set aside or the court has given directions.

(The costs practice direction contains further details about the procedure for setting aside a default costs certificate and the matters which the court must take into account)

Practice Direction—See generally PDCosts at p 1083 and specifically Section 38 at p 1134.

'if the receiving party was not entitled to it' (r 47.12(1))—The court has no discretion in such a case. The usual case will be that the Notice of Commencement did not reach the paying party at least 21 days before the default costs certificate was issued. The procedure when the receiving party discovers this to be the case is set out in paras (3) and (4).

'request … certificate to be set aside' (r 47.12(3)(i))—A court officer may set aside a default costs certificate in these circumstances (PDCosts, para 38.1(1)).

'In any other case' (r 47.12(2))—Where the default costs certificate was obtained regularly the onus is upon the paying party to establish that there is some good reason why detailed assessment proceedings should continue. The application should be made in accordance with Pt 23 and must be supported by evidence (PDCosts, para 38.2). The court will take into account whether the paying party made the application promptly (PDCosts, para 38.2(2)). The paying party should file with his application a draft of the points of dispute he proposes to serve if his application is granted (PDCosts, para 38.2(3)). If the court sets aside the default cost certificate it can impose conditions (r 3.1(3)). In particular it may order the paying party to pay an amount on account to the receiving party in accordance with r 44.3(8). The court also has the power to stay enforcement of the certificate.

Section IV – Costs Payable by One Party to Another – Procedure where Points of Dispute are Served

47.13 Optional reply

(1) Where any party to the detailed assessment proceedings serves points of dispute, the receiving party may serve a reply on the other parties to the assessment proceedings.

(2) He may do so within 21 days after service on him of the points of dispute to which his reply relates.

(The costs practice direction sets out the meaning of reply)

Amendments—SI 2000/1317.

Practice Direction—See generally PDCosts at p 1083 and specifically Section 39 at p 1135.

Scope of provision—Although the rule refers to an 'optional' reply, in all but the simplest of cases a reply will be appropriate. Failure to serve a reply may be a factor which is taken into account when the court considers the liability for costs of detailed assessment proceedings in accordance with r 47.18.

'may serve a reply' (r 47.13(1))—The time is 21 days after the service of the points of dispute (r 47.13(2)). This may be extended by agreement (r 2.11). Alternatively an application to the court may be made (r 3.1(2)(a)).

47.14 Detailed assessment hearing

(1) Where points of dispute are served in accordance with this Part, the receiving party must file a request for a detailed assessment hearing.

(2) He must file the request within 3 months of the expiry of the period for commencing detailed assessment proceedings as specified –

(a) in rule 47.7; or
(b) by any direction of the court.

(3) Where the receiving party fails to file a request in accordance with paragraph (2), the paying party may apply for an order requiring the receiving party to file the request within such time as the court may specify.

(4) On an application under paragraph (3), the court may direct that, unless the receiving party requests a detailed assessment hearing within the time specified by the court, all or part of the costs to which the receiving party would otherwise be entitled will be disallowed.

(5) If –

(a) the paying party has not made an application in accordance with paragraph (3); and

(b) the receiving party [files a request for a detailed assessment hearing later than the period specified in paragraph (2),

the court may disallow all or part of the interest otherwise payable to the receiving party under –

(i) section 17 of the Judgments Act 1838; or

(ii) section 74 of the County Courts Act 1984,

but must not impose any other sanction except in accordance with rule 44.14 (powers in relation to misconduct).

(6) No party other than –

(a) the receiving party;

(b) the paying party; and

(c) any party who has served points of dispute under rule 47.9,

may be heard at the detailed assessment hearing unless the court gives permission.

(7) Only items specified in the points of dispute may be raised at the hearing, unless the court gives permission.

(The costs practice direction specifies other documents which must be filed with the request for hearing and the length of notice which the court will give when it fixes a hearing date)

Amendments—SI 1999/1008; SI 2002/2058.

Practice Direction—See generally PDCosts at p 1083 and specifically Section 40 at p 1135.

Forms—N258 (Request for Detailed Assessment Hearing (non-legal aid)) or N258A (Request for Detailed Assessment (legal aid only)).

'receiving party must file a request' (r 47.14(1))—Unless there has been application for a default costs certificate the request for a detailed assessment hearing will be the first occasion the court has been involved in the detailed assessment proceedings.

Paragraph 40.2 of PDCosts sets out the documents that must accompany the request.

'3 months of the expiry of the period for commencing detailed assessment proceedings' (r 47.14(2))—Generally speaking, the receiving party has 6 months from the date of judgment, order or other determination to request a detailed assessment hearing. If the receiving party fails to apply for detailed assessment within the time specified, it is open for the paying party to make an application (r 47.14(3)). This may result in the receiving party being disallowed all or part of his costs or interest for the period of delay.

'specified in the points of dispute' (r 47.14(7))—The points of dispute should be marked to show which items have been agreed and their value. The bill of costs or the points of dispute should note which items remain in dispute and their value (PDCosts, para 40.2(d)).

Section V – Interim Costs Certificate and Final Costs Certificate

47.15 Power to issue an interim certificate

(1) The court may at any time after the receiving party has filed a request for a detailed assessment hearing –

(a) issue an interim costs certificate for such sum as it considers appropriate;

(b) amend or cancel an interim certificate.

(2) An interim certificate will include an order to pay the costs to which it relates, unless the court orders otherwise.

(3) The court may order the costs certified in an interim certificate to be paid into court.

Practice Direction—See generally PDCosts at p 1083 and specifically Section 41 at p 1140.

Forms—N257 (Interim Cost Certificate).

Scope of provision—Once a request for detailed assessment hearing has been made in accordance with r 47.14, the court has complete discretion to award an interim certificate. There is no requirement that the costs be assessed or agreed prior to the issue of an interim certificate. The court will award such sum as it considers appropriate. This power is in addition to the court's power to order costs on account (r 44.3(8)).

An interim costs certificate includes an order to pay within 14 days of its date (r 44.8). Nevertheless, the court issuing the certificate has the power to stay enforcement (PDCosts, Section 41).

'The court may … issue'—Application for an interim certificate is in accordance with Pt 23 (PDCosts, para 51.1(1)). There is no express requirement that it be supported by evidence.

47.16 Final costs certificate

(1) In this rule a completed bill means a bill calculated to show the amount due following the detailed assessment of the costs.

(2) The period for filing the completed bill is 14 days after the end of the detailed assessment hearing.

(3) When a completed bill is filed the court will issue a final costs certificate and serve it on the parties to the detailed assessment proceedings.

(4) Paragraph (3) is subject to any order made by the court that a certificate is not to be issued until other costs have been paid.

(5) A final costs certificate will include an order to pay the costs to which it relates, unless the court orders otherwise.

(The costs practice direction deals with the form of a final costs certificate)

Amendments—SI 1999/1008.

Practice Direction—See generally PDCosts at p 1083 and specifically Section 42 at p 1140.

Forms—N256 (Final Costs Certificate (county court)); N256HC (Final Costs Certificate (High Court)).

Scope of provision—The onus is on the receiving party to complete the bill once detailed assessment proceedings have been concluded. He does so by calculating the amounts due and filing the completed bill, together with receipted fee notes and receipted accounts in respect of all disbursements exceeding £500 (PDCosts, para 42.3). The court will not issue a final costs certificate until the receiving party has paid all outstanding court fees (PDCosts, para 42.5).

'order to pay' (r 47.16(5))—This will require payment of the costs within 14 days (r 44.8).

Stay and enforcement—As with interim certificates, the practice direction deals with applications for stay or enforcement of costs certificates which in general must be made to the court which issued the certificate or has jurisdiction to enforce it. Proceedings for enforcement may not be issued in the SCCO.

Section VI – Detailed Assessment Procedure for Costs of a LSC Funded Client or an Assisted Person where Costs are Payable out of the Community Legal Service Fund

47.17 Detailed assessment procedure for costs of a LSC funded client or an assisted person where costs are payable out of the Community Legal Service Fund

(1) Where the court is to assess costs of a LSC funded client or an assisted person which are payable out of the Community Legal Service Fund, that person's solicitor may commence detailed assessment proceedings by filing a request in the relevant practice form.

(2) A request under paragraph (1) must be filed within 3 months after the date when the right to detailed assessment arose.

(3) The solicitor must also serve a copy of the request for detailed assessment on the LSC funded client or the assisted person, if notice of [that person's interest has been given to the court in accordance with community legal service or legal aid regulations.

(4) Where the solicitor has certified that the LSC funded client or the assisted person wishes to attend an assessment hearing, the court will, on receipt of the request for assessment, fix a date for the assessment hearing.

(5) Where paragraph (3) does not apply, the court will, on receipt of the request for assessment provisionally assess the costs without the attendance of the solicitor, unless it considers that a hearing is necessary.

(6) After the court has provisionally assessed the bill, it will return the bill to the solicitor.

(7) The court will fix a date for an assessment hearing if the solicitor informs the court, within 14 days after he receives the provisionally assessed bill, that he wants the court to hold such a hearing.

Amendments—SI 2000/1317; SI 2000/2092.

Practice Direction—See generally PDCosts at p 1083 and specifically Sections 43 at p 1141 and 49 at p 1146.

Forms—N258A (Request for Detailed Assessment (legal aid/LSC only)); N253 (Notice of Amount allowed on Provisional Assessment).

Scope of provision—This rule deals with the assessment of costs of an LSC funded client or assisted person whose costs will be payable out of the Community Legal Services Fund and provides the only situation where there can be a provisional assessment of costs. Practitioners should refer to PDCosts, Section 49.

The procedure is similar to pre-26 April 1999 practice. See Practice Direction (Supreme Court Taxing Office), No 3 of 1994.

A request for detailed assessment must be filed within 3 months after the date when the right to detailed assessment arose. The request for detailed assessment is in Form N258A and must be accompanied by the documents referred to in PDCosts, para 43.3.

Mixed LSC funded/party and party costs—These are cases where costs are recoverable from another party and also from the Community Legal Services Fund. There are no specific provisions within the Costs Rules for dealing with these situations. The claim against the Community Legal Services Fund will depend upon whether a certificate was issued before or after 1 April 2000. If the former, the claim will be limited to prescribed rates in accordance with Legal Aid in Civil

Proceedings (Remuneration) Regulations 1994. If the latter, in accordance with AJA 1999, s 11 and provisions made under that Act. In respect of costs recoverable pursuant to the Legal Aid Act 1988, practitioners should note the requirements of PDCosts, Section 49 which requires a Legal Aid schedule to be filed (PDCosts, para 40.2). A model form of the schedule is set out in Precedent E, Schedule of Costs Precedents. The detailed assessment of the Community Legal Service Fund aspect of a mixed bill will be dealt with separately from the party and party assessment. For example, a receiving party may obtain a default costs certificate against the paying party and the court may direct a separate detailed assessment of the Community Legal Service Fund element of a mixed bill.

47.17A Detailed assessment procedure where costs are payable out of a fund other than the Community Legal Service Fund

(1) Where the court is to assess costs which are payable out of a fund other than the Community Legal Service Fund, the receiving party may commence detailed assessment proceedings by filing a request in the relevant practice form.

(2) A request under paragraph (1) must be filed within 3 months after the date when the right to detailed assessment arose.

(3) The court may direct that the party seeking assessment serve a copy of the request on any person who has a financial interest in the outcome of the assessment.

(4) The court will, on receipt of the request for assessment, provisionally assess the costs without the attendance of the receiving party, unless it considers that a hearing is necessary.

(5) After the court has provisionally assessed the bill, it will return the bill to the receiving party.

(6) The court will fix a date for an assessment hearing if the party informs the court, within 14 days after he receives the provisionally assessed bill, that he wants the court to hold such a hearing.

Amendments—Inserted by SI 2000/1317.

Practice Direction—See generally PDCosts at p 1083 and specifically Section 44 at p 1143.

Forms—Form N258B (Request for detailed assessment (Costs payable out of a fund other than the Community Legal Service Fund)).

Scope of provision—This provision allows the court to assess costs payable out of a fund which is not the Community Legal Service Fund. For example, this provision will allow the court to assess costs in relation to funds held by the Court of Protection or trust funds in general. The rule provides for a form of provisional assessment without the attendance of the receiving party akin to assessment of costs in claims funded by the Community Legal Service Fund. There is provision (r 47.17A(4) and PDCosts, Section 44) for an assessment hearing if the receiving party is unhappy with the provisionally assessed bill.

Section VII – Costs of Detailed Assessment Proceedings

47.18 Liability for costs of detailed assessment proceedings

The receiving party is entitled to his costs of the detailed assessment proceedings except where –

(a) the provisions of any Act, any of these Rules or any relevant practice direction provide otherwise; or

(b) the court makes some other order in relation to all or part of the costs of the detailed assessment proceedings.

(2) In deciding whether to make some other order, the court must have regard to all the circumstances, including –

(a) the conduct of all the parties;
(b) the amount, if any, by which the bill of costs has been reduced; and
(c) whether it was reasonable for a party to claim the costs of a particular item or to dispute that item.

Practice Direction—See generally PDCosts at p 1083 and specifically Section 45 at p 1144.

Scope of provision—In general, the costs of detailed assessment will be dealt with by way of summary assessment. A party is not required to serve a statement of costs of the detailed assessment proceedings unless the court orders him to do so (PDCosts, para 45.3). The court may order detailed assessment (PDCosts, para 45.2) in which case it will give directions for the future conduct of those detailed assessment proceedings. The costs of detailed assessment are dealt with under the provision of this rule and not under r 47.8, even where there has been substantial delay in commencing detailed assessment. Rule 47.18 raises a rebuttable presumption that the receiving party should have his costs of detailed assessment, subject to any different order made by the costs judge (*Bufton v Hill* [2002] EWHC 977 (QB), [2002] Costs LR 381, QBD, Silber J).

47.19 Offers to settle without prejudice save as to costs of the detailed assessment proceedings

(1) Where –

(a) a party (whether the paying party or the receiving party) makes a written offer to settle the costs of the proceedings which gave rise to the assessment proceedings; and
(b) the offer is expressed to be without prejudice[(GL)] save as to the costs of the detailed assessment proceedings,

the court will take the offer into account in deciding who should pay the costs of those proceedings.

(2) The fact of the offer must not be communicated to the costs officer until the question of costs of the detailed assessment proceedings falls to be decided.

(The costs practice direction provides that rule 47.19 does not apply where the receiving party is a LSC funded client oran assisted person, unless the court orders otherwise)

Amendments—SI 2000/1317; SI 2002/2058.

Practice Direction—See generally PDCosts at p 1083 and specifically Section 46 at p 1145.

Scope of provision—Offers to settle the costs of proceedings must be in writing and expressed to be without prejudice save as to the costs of the detailed assessment proceedings. See *Wills v The Crown Estate Commissioners* [2003] EWHC 1718 (Ch), Smith J where the costs judge had been right to consider the only offer which complied with r 47.19 and PDCosts, Section 46 in deciding on the costs of detailed assessment and to ignore other offers which did not comply. There is no longer any time limit for such an offer to be made but it should normally be made by the paying party within 14 days of receipt of the commencement notice, or by the receiving party within 14 days after service of points of dispute. The earlier the offer is made the more weight it is likely to carry (PDCosts, para 46.1). An offer to settle should specify whether or not it is intended to be inclusive of the cost of preparation of the bill, interest and VAT. The offer may include or exclude some or all of these items but the position must be made clear on the face of the offer. Unless the offer states otherwise the offer will be treated as being inclusive of all these items (PDCosts, para 46.2).

If an offer to settle is accepted, r 47.10 applies (PDCosts, para 46.3).

Although the rule indicates that it does not apply where the receiving party is an assisted person, PDCosts, para 46.4 qualifies this with the words 'unless the court so orders'.

Consequently, in the case of a party funded by the Community Legal Services Fund, the court has the power to take the offer into account if it decides that it is appropriate to do so. An offer to settle without prejudice save as to costs is of somewhat less significance in terms of its consequences than a Pt 36 offer relating to the proceedings as a whole or an issue within the proceedings.

'costs of the proceedings which gave rise to the assessment proceedings' (r 47.19(1)(a))—In cases where existing proceedings lead to an order for assessment of costs, a r 47.19 offer will include the costs of preparation of the bill of costs (PDCosts, para 46.2). However, in the context of proceedings under r 44.12A (costs-only proceedings where there have been no prior proceedings) the words in r 47.19(1)(a) 'the costs of the proceedings which gave rise to the assessment proceedings' embrace all letters and negotiations between the parties which led up to the agreement between the parties. Until the time that the substantive claim is settled the 'proceedings' relate to the liability and amount of compensation, but after the substantive claim has been settled the 'proceedings' relate to the assessment of costs that the paying party has to pay. Consequently, the costs of preparing the bill of costs in costs-only proceedings is not included in a r 47.19 offer unless specifically provided for (*Crosbie v Munroe & anor* [2003] EWCA Civ 350, [2003] 2 All ER 856, CA).

Section VIII – Appeals from Authorised Court Officers in Detailed Assessment Proceedings

General note—The former proceedings by way of review or the carrying in of objections are no longer available. Any party to detailed assessment proceedings may appeal any decision of the court in relation to those proceedings. Costs appeals have been assimilated with general provisions for appeal in proceedings brought under CPR. Part 52 deals with appeals. See also PD52, supplementing that Part. However appeals against the decision of an authorised court officer in detailed assessment proceedings are excluded from Part 52. These appeals are dealt with in rr 47.20–47.23.

Generally, an appellant or respondent requires permission to appeal, which may be made –

(a) to the court at the hearing at which the decision to appeal was made; or

(b) to the appeal court in an appeal notice (r 52.3(2)).

Where the appellant seeks permission from the appeal court, such permission must be requested in the appellant's notice and generally, unless the lower court makes any different direction, notice must be filed at the appeal court, within 14 days after the date of the decision of the lower court, that the appellant wishes to appeal.

The destination of appeals is dealt with in the Access to Justice Act 1999 (Destination of Appeals) Order 2000. Appeals from decisions of a costs judge will continue to lie to a judge of the High Court. Similarly, appeals from district judges sitting in their capacity as costs officers of the High Court will lie to a judge of the High Court. Appeals from district judges in their capacity as costs officers in the county court will lie to a judge of a county court. (See PD52).

47.20 Right to appeal

(1) Any party to detailed assessment proceedings may appeal against a decision of an authorised court officer in those proceedings.

(2) For the purposes of this Section, a LSC funded client or an assisted person is not a party to detailed assessment proceedings.

(Part 52 sets out general rules about appeals)

Amendments—SI 2000/940; SI 2000/1317.

Practice Direction—See generally PDCosts at p 1083 and specifically Section 47 at p 1145.

Scope of provision—In respect of appeals from authorised court officers, there is no requirement to obtain permission nor is there a duty to seek reasons.

47.21 Court to hear appeal

An appeal against a decision of an authorised court officer is to a costs judge or a district judge of the High Court.

Amendments—SI 2000/940.

47.22 Appeal procedure

(1) The appellant must file an appeal notice within 14 days after the date of the decision he wishes to appeal against.

(2) On receipt of the appeal notice, the court will –

(a) serve a copy of the notice on the parties to the detailed assessment proceedings; and
(b) give notice of the appeal hearing to those parties.

Amendments—SI 2000/940; SI 2000/1317.

Practice Direction—See generally PDCosts at p 1083 and specifically Section 48 at p 1146.

Scope of provision—The appellant must file a notice (Form 16, Schedule of Costs Forms). The notice must set out the grounds of appeal. The appeal notice should be accompanied by a suitable record of the judgment appealed against. Where the judgment to be appealed has been officially recorded, an approved transcript of that record should accompany the applicant's notice.

47.23 Powers of the court on appeal

On an appeal from an authorised court officer the court will –

(a) re-hear the proceedings which gave rise to the decision appealed against; and
(b) make any order and give any directions as it considers appropriate.

Amendments—SI 2000/940.

47.24 (*revoked*)

47.25 (*revoked*)

47.26 (*revoked*)

PART 48
COSTS – SPECIAL CASES

CONTENTS OF THIS PART

(The definitions contained in Part 43 are relevant to this Part)

Section I – Costs Payable by or to Particular Persons

48.1 Pre-commencement disclosure and orders for disclosure against a person who is not a party

(1) This paragraph applies where a person applies –

(a) for an order under –
(i) section 33 of the Supreme Court Act 1981; or
(ii) section 52 of the County Courts Act 1984,
(which give the court powers exercisable before commencement of proceedings); or

(b) for an order under –
(i) section 34 of the Supreme Court Act 1981; or
(ii) section 53 of the County Courts Act 1984,
(which give the court power to make an order against a non-party for disclosure of documents, inspection of property etc).

(2) The general rule is that the court will award the person against whom the order is sought his costs –

(a) of the application; and
(b) of complying with any order made on the application.

(3) The court may however make a different order, having regard to all the circumstances, including –

(a) the extent to which it was reasonable for the person against whom the order was sought to oppose the application; and
(b) whether the parties to the application have complied with any relevant pre-action protocol.

'The court may however make a different order' (r 48.1(3))—For an example of this rule in practice see *Bermuda International Securities Limited v KPMG (a firm)* [2001] EWCA Civ 269, [2001] CP Rep 73, CA, where it was decided that production of certain documents had been unreasonably resisted and costs were awarded accordingly.

48.2 Costs orders in favour of or against non-parties

(1) Where the court is considering whether to exercise its power under section 51 of the Supreme Court Act 1981 (costs are in the discretion of the court) to make a costs order in favour of or against a person who is not a party to proceedings –

- (a) that person must be added as a party to the proceedings for the purposes of costs only; and
- (b) he must be given a reasonable opportunity to attend a hearing at which the court will consider the matter further.

(2) This rule does not apply –

- (a) where the court is considering whether to –
  - (i) make an order against the Legal Services Commission;
  - (ii) make a wasted costs order (as defined in 48.7); and
- (b) in proceedings to which rule 48.1 applies (pre-commencement disclosure and orders for disclosure against a person who is not a party).

Amendments—SI 2000/1317.

Scope of provision—The basis upon which the court will order costs against non-parties is set out by Goff LJ in *Symphony Group plc v Hodgson* [1993] 4 All ER 143, 151:

(1) an order for the payment of costs by a non-party will always be exceptional. The judge should treat any application for such an order with considerable caution;
(2) it will be even more exceptional for an order for the payment of costs to be made against a non-party, where the applicant has a cause of action against the non-party and could have joined him as a party to the original proceedings;
(3) even if the applicant can provide a good reason for not joining the non-party against whom he has a valid cause of action, he should warn the non-party at the earliest opportunity of the possibility that he may seek to apply for costs against him. At the very least this will give the non-party an opportunity to apply to be joined as a party;
(4) an application for payment of costs by a non-party should normally be determined by the trial judge;
(5) the fact that the trial judge may in the course of his judgment in the action have expressed views on the conduct of the non-party neither constitutes bias nor the appearance of bias;
(6) the procedure for the determination of costs is a summary procedure, not necessarily subject to all the rules that would apply in an action;
(7) the normal rule is that witnesses in either civil or criminal proceedings enjoy immunity from any form of civil action in respect of evidence given during those proceedings;
(8) the fact that an employee, or even a director or the managing director, of a company gives evidence in an action does not normally mean that the company is taking part in that action;
(9) the judge should be alert to the possibility that an application against a non-party is motivated by resentment of an inability to obtain an effective order for costs against a legally aided litigant.

There are two issues that need to be considered in determining whether the court should exercise its power under SCA 1981, s 51(1) and (3); first, whether there are exceptional circumstances to justify an order against a non-party, and secondly, to what extent the conduct of that party has caused loss to the applicant. The court has also to consider whether it would be just to make such an order (*Globe Equities Limited v Globe Legal Services Limited* [1999] BLR 232, CA).

See also *SBJ Stephenson v Mandy (No 2)* [2000] FSR 651, [2000] CP Rep 64, QB where the court ordered the defendant's new employer to pay one half the claimant's costs of the litigation arising from the breach of a restrictive covenant preventing the defendant from soliciting former customers even though the defendant's new employer was not a party to the action.

Note the exceptions in r 48.2(2) for example: orders against the Community Legal Service Fund, wasted costs applications and in applications for pre-commencement disclosure. Any costs orders against the Legal Services Commission are regulated by AJA 1999, s 11. For the nature and type of procedure to be adopted in such applications, see *Robertson Research International Limited v ABG Exploration BV & ors* [1999] CPLR 756; PDCosts, Sections 22–23.

'that person must be added as a party to the proceedings' (r 48.2(1)(a))—As a general principle 'pure funders' are exempt from liability for the successful unfunded party's costs under SCA 1981, s 51:

(1) The position of a professional funder such as a trade union or insurer is very different from the position of a pure funder. It is usually just and reasonable to grant an application under SCA 1981, s 51 against a professional funder. Although costs orders against non-parties are to be regarded as 'exceptional', in this context exceptional means no more than outside the ordinary run of cases where parties pursued or defended claims for their own benefit and at their own expense. Where the non-party not merely funded the proceedings but also substantially controlled them or was to benefit from them, justice would ordinarily require that if the proceedings failed, that person would pay the successful party's costs (*Dymocks Franchise Systems (NSW) Pty Ltd v Todd & ors (No 2) (New Zealand)* [2004] UKPC 39). However, a professional funder should be potentially liable for the costs of the opposing party only to the extent of the funding provided (*Arkin v Borchard Lines Limited* [2005] EWCA Civ 655, where the court observed that professional funders were likely to cap the funds that they provided in order to limit their exposure to a reasonable amount, with the effect that costs would be kept proportionate).

(2) Indiscriminate and unrestricted charitable funding would, however, not always accord with the overriding objective of the CPR. A relevant factor is whether the charitable donor has reasonable grounds for believing that the litigant in question has reasonable prospects of success.

(3) At the same time, a blanket exemption for charitable donors from the risk of a s 51 order would have an inhibiting effect on the freedom of expression and, therefore, be contrary to ECHR, art 10 (*Hamilton v Al Fayed (No 2)* [2002] EWCA Civ 665, [2002] Costs LR 389, CA).

The court has power to make a costs order against an expert who by his evidence causes significant expense to be incurred and did so in flagrant disregard of his duties to the court (*Phillips v Symes* [2005] 2 Costs LR 224).

For a solicitor to defer or limit payment of his charges until after the outcome of a case is not to act as a funder, maintainer or financier. Even though he may be acting irrationally or over-generously, he is not acting outside his role as a solicitor in such a situation.

Per Hale LJ in *Floods of Queensferry Ltd v Shand Construction Ltd & ors* [2002] EWCA Civ 918, [2003] Lloyd's Rep IR 181, CA:

> The solicitors did not engage in an improper no win/no fee arrangement. They simply took a risk and extended credit to their client. It would be a sad day if solicitors could not extend credit, even to their litigation clients, without fear of vulnerability to a Section 51 order.'

See also *Burstein v Times Newspapers Limited (No 2)* [2002] EWCA Civ 1739, (2002) 146 SJLB 277, CA and *Gulf Azov Shipping Company Ltd v Chief Humphrey Irikefe Idisi* [2004] EWCA Civ 292, (2004) Lawtel, 15 March, CA, where the court made costs orders against two funders of the first defendant's litigation on the basis they had both provided sums of money for his defence and had directed the litigation in a manner that had resulted in undue expense or hardship to the successful party.

In respect of costs against an insolvent company, costs will only be recoverable from a third party if the funding provided by the non-party and the costs incurred by the claiming party have a causal link. Such an order would normally be appropriate only where a company officer stood to benefit from the litigation, controlled and directed it, or started and pursued it unreasonably or for an ulterior purpose not connected with the best interest of the company (*Gemma Limited v Gimson & ors* [2005] EWHC 69 (QB)). See also *Goodwood Recoveries Limited v Breen* [2005] EWCA Civ 414 and *CIBC Mellon Trust Company & anor v Wolfgang Otto Stolzenberg & ors* [2005] EWCA Civ 628.

48.3 Amount of costs where costs are payable pursuant to a contract

(1) Where the court assesses (whether by the summary or detailed procedure) costs which are payable by the paying party to the receiving party under the terms of a contract, the costs payable under those terms are, unless the contract expressly provides otherwise, to be presumed to be costs which –

(a) have been reasonably incurred; and
(b) are reasonable in amount;

and the court will assess them accordingly.

(The costs practice direction sets out circumstances where the court may order otherwise)

(2) This rule does not apply where the contract is between a solicitor and his client.

Practice Direction—See generally PDCosts at p 1083 and specifically Section 50 at p 1147.

Scope of provision—There are many contracts which contain provisions regarding the liability of costs incurred pursuant to the contract. Examples are mortgages, leases or guarantees. Rule 48.3 makes it clear that the indemnity basis for assessing costs should be applied unless the contract states otherwise. If the terms of the contract are manifestly unreasonable then the presumption will be rebutted and in those circumstances the court will reduce or disallow some of the costs recovered.

With regard to the principles which apply to costs relating to mortgages, practitioners are referred to PDCosts, paras 50.3 and 50.4 and to *Gomba Holdings UK Limited v Minories Finance Limited (No 2)* [1992] 3 WLR 723 and *Mortgage Funding Corporation plc v Kashef-Hamadani* (1993) (unreported) 26 April, CA.

It should be noted that this rule does not apply in relation to a contract between a solicitor and his client which is governed by Solicitors Act 1974 (r 48.7).

48.4 Limitations on court's power to award costs in favour of trustee or personal representative

(1) This rule applies where –

(a) a person is or has been a party to any proceedings in the capacity of trustee or personal representative; and

(b) rule 48.3 does not apply.

(2) The general rule is that he is entitled to be paid the costs of those proceedings, insofar as they are not recovered from or paid by any other person, out of the relevant trust fund or estate.

(3) Where he is entitled to be paid any of those costs out of the fund or estate, those costs will be assessed on the indemnity basis.

Amendments—SI 1999/1008; SI 2001/4015.

Scope of provision—A trustee or personal representative is entitled to the costs of any proceedings brought in that capacity on an indemnity basis. Normally, unless they can be recovered from the other party, the court will order such costs to be paid out of the trust fund (*Re Beddoe* [1893] 1 Ch 547).

See also *D'Abo v Paget (No 2)* (2000) *The Times*, 10 August where it was held that the claimant's application to bring the proceedings was to enable her to make a claim for costs in the event that the first defendant lost. The court refused the claimant's application for costs out of the fund. The judge observed that a more robust attitude to costs was appropriate under the CPR although the guidelines in *Re Buckton* [1907] 2 Ch 406 have not been superseded.

Pre-emptive costs orders, where for example a beneficiary makes a hostile claim against trustees or other beneficiaries, should only be made where the court hearing the application is satisfied that no other order could properly be made by the court (*Chessels v British Telecommunications plc* [2001] Pens LR 141, Laddie J).

48.5 Costs where money is payable by or to a child or patient

(1) This rule applies to any proceedings where a party is a child or patient and –

(a) money is ordered or agreed to be paid to, or for the benefit of, that party; or

(b) money is ordered to be paid by him or on his behalf.

('Child' and 'patient' are defined in rule 2.3)

(2) The general rule is that –

(a) the court must order a detailed assessment of the costs payable by, or out of money belonging to, any party who is a child or patient; and

(b) on an assessment under paragraph (a), the court must also assess any costs payable to that party in the proceedings, unless –
   (i) the court has issued a default costs certificate in relation to those costs under rule 47.11; or
   (ii) the costs are payable in proceedings to which Section II of Part 45 applies.

(3) The court need not order detailed assessment of costs in the circumstances set out in the costs practice direction.

(4) Where –

(a) a claimant is a child or patient; and
(b) a detailed assessment has taken place under paragraph (2)(a),

the only amount payable by the child or patient is the amount which the court certifies as payable.

(This rule applies to a counterclaim by or on behalf of a child or patient by virtue of rule 20.3)

Amendments—SI 2004/3419; SI 2005/2292.

Practice Direction—See generally PDCosts at p 1083 and specifically Section 51 at p 1149.

Scope of provision—'Child' and 'patient' are defined in r 2.3. Generally, the court has an overriding duty to protect the interests of a child or patient. If, therefore, a child or patient is liable to pay costs (to another party or, as he usually will be, to his solicitor) the court will order detailed assessment of those costs unless one of the circumstances set out in PDCosts, para 51.1 applies. The court must similarly order a detailed assessment of any costs payable out of monies belonging to the child or patient. Accordingly, where solicitors for example seek to recoup from a child or patient the balance of an unrecovered ATE premium or the balance of a success fee not recovered from the paying party, they may only do so after a detailed assessment has taken place.

Where there is an assessment of costs payable by a child or patient, the court must also assess the costs awarded to the child or patient in the proceedings unless:

(1) a default costs certificate has been obtained; or
(2) the solicitor acting for the child or patient has accepted fixed recoverable costs pursuant to Pt 45, Section II (Road traffic accidents – fixed recoverable costs).

Paragraph 51.1 of PDCosts sets out the circumstances in which the court need not order assessment of costs, for example where costs are recovered from a paying party on behalf of the child or patient and the solicitors acting for that party waive any further claim for costs.

48.6 Litigants in person

(1) This rule applies where the court orders (whether by summary assessment or detailed assessment) that the costs of a litigant in person are to be paid by any other person.

(2) The costs allowed under this rule must not exceed, except in the case of a disbursement, two-thirds of the amount which would have been allowed if the litigant in person had been represented by a legal representative.

(3) The litigant in person shall be allowed –

(a) costs for the same categories of –
   (i) work; and
   (ii) disbursements,

which would have been allowed if the work had been done or the disbursements had been made by a legal representative on the litigant in person's behalf;

(b) the payments reasonably made by him for legal services relating to the conduct of the proceedings; and

(c) the costs of obtaining expert assistance in assessing the costs claim.

(4) The amount of costs to be allowed to the litigant in person for any item of work claimed shall be –

(a) where the litigant can prove financial loss, the amount that he can prove he has lost for time reasonably spent on doing the work; or

(b) where the litigant cannot prove financial loss, an amount for the time reasonably spent on doing the work at the rate set out in the practice direction.

(5) A litigant who is allowed costs for attending at court to conduct his case is not entitled to a witness allowance in respect of such attendance in addition to those costs.

(6) For the purposes of this rule, a litigant in person includes –

(a) a company or other corporation which is acting without a legal representative; and

(b) a barrister, solicitor, solicitor's employee or other authorised litigator (as defined in the Courts and Legal Services Act 1990) who is acting for himself.

Amendments—SI 2002/2058.

Practice Direction—See generally PDCosts at p 1083 and specifically Section 52 at p 1149.

Scope of provision—The costs allowed to a litigant in person will be for the same categories of work and disbursements as would have been allowed if the work had been done or the disbursements made by a legal representative on behalf of the litigant in person.

The rule allows for recovery by a litigant in person of 'partial legal services' provided by legal representatives on his behalf.

'two thirds of the amount' (r 48.6(2))—A judge must make an assessment of the sum he would allow the solicitor and then restrict the litigant in person's costs to two thirds of that sum (*Hart v Aga Khan Foundation (UK)* [1984] 2 All ER 429). See *Mealing McLeod v Common Professional Examination Board* (2000) *The Times*, 2 May, (2000) SCCO No 7 which suggests that more time should be allowed to a litigant in person than to a solicitor doing the same task and deals with issues of proportionality where one side is legally represented and the other side is a litigant in person.

A litigant in person is entitled to his time for researching his case at the rate fixed by statute subject to the two-thirds rule. See *The Queen on the application of Wulfsohn v Legal Services Commission* [2002] EWCA Civ 250, [2002] Costs LR 341, CA, where a litigant in person claimed in excess of 1200 hours in researching and preparing his case. Likely solicitors' costs were in excess of £15,000 and the court allowed the litigant in person £10,460.

Contrast *Greville v Sprake* [2001] EWCA Civ 234, CA where it was said that a 'litigant in person is limited to the time which would reasonably have been spent by a solicitor on the preparation of his or her case (CPR rule 48.6(3)(a)). In any event the litigant in person cannot get more than two thirds of what a solicitor would obtain if the solicitor were making the application for costs (see CPR rule 48.6(2)).'

See also *United Building and Plumbing Contractors v Kajla* [2002] EWCA Civ 628, (2002) Lawtel, 29 April, CA, where it was held that a litigant in person who was assisted in the preparation and presentation of his case by a non-legally qualified person could not recover the fees of that person. The phrase 'legal services' contained in r 48.6(3)(b) was held to refer to services that are legal and provided by or under the supervision of a lawyer.

'the costs of obtaining expert assistance' (r 48.6(3)(c))—See PDCosts, para 52.1 for a list of qualified experts.

'financial loss' (r 48.6(4)(a))—The onus is on the litigant in person to prove that he has suffered 'financial loss'. He must produce to the court written evidence to support the claim and must serve a copy of that evidence on any party against whom he seeks costs at least 24 hours before the hearing at which the question of loss may be decided (PDCosts, para 52.2). Where he commences detailed assessment proceedings, written evidence should be served with the notice of commencement (PDCosts, para 52.3).

'the rate set out in the practice direction' (r 48.6(4)(b))—The rate is £9.25 per hour (PDCosts, para 52.4).

'litigant in person includes … a … solicitor' (r 48.6(6)(b))—A solicitor who, instead of acting for himself, is represented in the proceedings by his firm or by himself in his firm's name is not a litigant in person for the purpose of the CPR (PDCosts, para 52.5). See *Malkinson v Trim* [2002] EWCA Civ 1273, [2002] Costs LR 515, CA, where a solicitor recovered costs for work done by one of his partners as well as work done by himself or one of his employees. Rule 48.6(6)(b) must be read subject to PDCosts, para 52.5. See also *Boyd and Hutchinson v Joseph*; sub nom *Joseph v Boyd and Hutchinson (a firm)* [2003] EWHC 413 (Ch), [2003] TLR 252, ChD, Patten J in relation to the definition of a practising solicitor who is able to charge for her time.

'costs for attending at court' (r 48.6(5))—Provided that a litigant in person can show he has suffered financial loss he will recover two thirds of the fast trial costs prescribed by r 46.2, irrespective of the amount of his loss.

***McKenzie* friends**—A litigant in person may have assistance in presenting his case from a person sitting beside him and giving help and advice during the course of the proceedings. Such a person is not an advocate appearing on behalf of the litigant. Section 27(2)(c) of the CLSA 1990 governs the position. In *R v Bow County Court ex parte Pelling* [1999] 1 WLR 1807, CA the Court of Appeal, in giving its reasons for an order declaring a party a vexatious litigant, took the opportunity to restate general principles and give guidance concerning the activities of unqualified persons who from time to time sought to help litigants:

(1) Section 27 of the CLSA 1990 governs rights of audience.
(2) A right of audience ought only to be granted to an unqualified person in exceptional circumstances and the court should pause before granting rights to people who make a practice of seeking to represent otherwise unrepresented litigants.
(3) Three principles apply in relation to *McKenzie* friends:
   (a) they have no right to act as such, only to offer a litigant reasonable assistance;
   (b) if a *McKenzie* friend seeks to address the court he becomes an advocate and requires rights of audience;
   (c) in general a litigant in person is permitted a *McKenzie* friend unless the judge is satisfied fairness and the interests of justice do not so require.

A court may only grant a right of audience to a *McKenzie* friend in exceptional circumstances. An argument that the *McKenzie* friend was better able to put the applicant's case does not amount to an exceptional circumstance. It is important for the court to maintain fairness and parity, particularly where each party appears in person (*Re D (a child)* [2005] EWCA Civ 743).

Cost of legal advice—Where no solicitors have been named on the court record as representing a successful party the costs judge is entitled to find on the evidence that the party has nevertheless been advised by a solicitor and that the costs of those services should be allowed (*Paturel v Marble Arch Services Limited* (2005) Lawtel, 3 June, Cox J).

48.6A Costs where the court has made a Group Litigation Order

(1) This rule applies where the court has made a Group Litigation Order ('GLO').

(2) In this rule –

   (a) 'individual costs' means costs incurred in relation to an individual claim on the group register;
   (b) 'common costs' means –
      (i) costs incurred in relation to the GLO issues;
      (ii) individual costs incurred in a claim while it is proceeding as a test claim; and
      (iii) costs incurred by the lead solicitor in administering the group litigation; and
   (c) 'group litigant' means a claimant or defendant, as the case may be, whose claim is entered on the group register.

(3) Unless the court orders otherwise, any order for common costs against group litigants imposes on each group litigant several liability[(GL)] for an equal proportion of those common costs.

(4) The general rule is that where a group litigant is the paying party, he will, in addition to any costs he is liable to pay to the receiving party, be liable for –

(a) the individual costs of his claim; and
(b) an equal proportion, together with all the other group litigants, of the common costs.

(5) Where the court makes an order about costs in relation to any application or hearing which involved –

(a) one or more GLO issues; and
(b) issues relevant only to individual claims,

the court will direct the proportion that is to relate to common costs and the proportion that is to relate to individual costs.

(6) Where common costs have been incurred before a claim is entered on the group register, the court may order the group litigant to be liable for a proportion of those costs.

(7) Where a claim is removed from the group register, the court may make an order for the costs in that claim which includes a proportion of the common costs incurred up to the date on which the claim is removed from the group register.

(Part 19 sets out the rules about group litigation)

Amendments—Inserted by SI 2000/1317.

Scope of provision—See Part 19, Section III, Group Litigation, rr 19.10–19.15. A Group Litigation Order (GLO) means an order to provide for the case management of claims which give rise to common or related issues of fact or law. GLOs were formally known as Multi-Party Actions. Generally, where a group litigant is the paying party he will, in addition to any costs he is liable to pay to the receiving party, have to pay –

(a) the individual costs of his claim; and
(b) an equal proportion together with all the other group litigants of the 'common costs'.

These are costs incurred in relation to the determination of common issues or the individual costs incurred whilst the claim was proceeding as a test claim or incurred by the Lead Solicitor in administering the group litigation. Such costs may include the convening the meetings of litigants or producing news sheets, bulletins or updates, the rule imposes a several liability against each litigant who has been joined in the GLO Order (r 48.6A(3)). For an example in practice, see *Ochwat v Watson Burton (a firm)* [1999] All ER (D) 1907.

In *Giambrone v JMC Holidays Limited (formerly t/a Sun World Holidays Limited)* [2002] EWHC 2932, [2003] 1 All ER 982 Morland J held that in most GLO cases there will be no need for any detailed assessment of costs until the conclusion of group litigation. Claimants' solicitors are entitled to an adequate cash flow from the defendants once the general issue of liability has been admitted or determined in the claimants' favour. His Lordship expressed the hope that defendants' solicitors would agree to pay at various stages in the group litigation a realistic interim amount on account of final detailed assessment of costs if necessary. If agreement cannot be reached as to an interim payment, it should be dealt with cheaply and shortly by the nominated trial judge under r 44.3(8). If the judge is provided beforehand with a written schedule of costs, together with a succinct skeleton of the issues and the rival contentions of the parties it may be possible for the award of costs on account to be dealt with on paper. In *AB & ors v Leeds Teaching Hospitals (Re Nationwide Organ Group Litigation)* [2003] EWHC 1034 (QB) Gage J capped the costs to be incurred by the publicly funded claimants by way of costs budgeting.

Section II – Costs Relating to Solicitors and Other Legal Representatives

48.7 Personal liability of legal representative for costs – wasted costs orders

(1) This rule applies where the court is considering whether to make an order under section 51(6) of the Supreme Court Act 1981 (court's power to disallow or (as the case may be) order a legal representative to meet, 'wasted costs').

(2) The court must give the legal representative a reasonable opportunity to attend a hearing to give reasons why it should not make such an order.

(3) (*revoked*)

(4) When the court makes a wasted costs order, it must –

(a) specify the amount to be disallowed or paid; or
(b) direct a costs judge or a district judge to decide the amount of costs to be disallowed or paid.

(5) The court may direct that notice must be given to the legal representative's client, in such manner as the court may direct –

(a) of any proceedings under this rule; or
(b) of any order made under it against his legal representative.

(6) Before making a wasted costs order, the court may direct a costs judge or a district judge to inquire into the matter and report to the court.

(7) The court may refer the question of wasted costs to a costs judge or a district judge, instead of making a wasted costs order.

Amendments—SI 2000/1317; SI 2002/2058.

Practice Direction—See generally PDCosts at p 1083 and specifically Section 53 at p 1150.

Scope of provision—Supreme Court Act 1981, s 51(6) sets out the wasted costs provisions. In *Ridehalgh v Horsefield* [1994] 3 All ER 848, CA, the Court of Appeal gave guidance for the exercise by courts of their jurisdiction to make wasted costs orders. In general, lawyers should not be deterred from pursuing their clients interests for fear of incurring personal liability for costs. Such orders should not be made without a fair opportunity for the lawyer to defend the application. The decision must now be read in the context of this rule and PDCosts, paras 53.1–53.10.

'When the court makes a wasted costs order' (r 48.7(4))—A three-stage process is to be applied in connection with such applications:

(1) has the legal representative of whom complaint been made acted improperly, unreasonably or negligently;
(2) if so, did such conduct cause the applicant to incur unnecessary costs;
(3) if so, was it in all the circumstances just to order the legal representative to compensate the applicant for the whole or part of the relevant costs (PDCosts, para 53.4).

'improperly' relates to conduct which would ordinarily lead to disbarment, striking off, suspension from practice or other serious professional penalty (*Ridehalgh v Horsefield* above).

'unreasonably' describes conduct which is designed to harass the opposition rather than advance the resolution of the case. The test is whether the conduct permits a reasonable explanation (*Ridehalgh v Horsefield* above).

'negligent' should be looked at in a non-technical way to denote failure to act with the competence reasonably expected of ordinary members of the legal profession (*Re Sternberg, Reed, Taylor & Gill* (1999) *The Times*, 26 July). See also *Dempsey v Johnstone* [2003] EWCA Civ 1134, [2004] PNLR 2, CA, where the court held that negligence alone would justify the making of a wasted costs order under s 51 of the Act and, in a case where the gist of the complaint was the pursuit of a hopeless case, the test was whether no reasonably competent legal representative would have continued with the action.

Any impropriety should be a very serious one. The cases of *Ridehalgh v Horsefield & anor* (1994) Ch 205 and *Medcalf v Mardell;* sub nom *Medcalf v Weatherill & anor* [2002] UKHL 27, [2002] 3 WLR 172, HL should now be taken to state the law in relation to this area. There has to be something more than negligence – something akin to abuse of process – to make a legal representative subject to a wasted costs order. It is proper to take account of the fact that a client is legally aided: there can be an abuse if that fact forms the basis on which the legal representative proceeds improperly, that is to say in the knowledge that his client will probably not have to pay the other side's costs (*Persaud & anor v Persaud & ors* [2003] EWCA Civ 394, (2003) Lawtel, 7 March, CA).

Generally speaking, applications for wasted costs are best left until the end of the trial (PDCosts, para 53.1).

The court's discretion with regard to a wasted costs application should be exercised in two stages:

(i) The court must be satisfied that it has evidence or material which if unanswered would be likely to lead to a wasted costs order being made and that wasted costs proceedings are justified notwithstanding the likely costs involved.

(ii) The court will consider after giving the legal representative an opportunity to put forward his case whether it is appropriate to make a wasted costs order in all the circumstances.

An applicant seeking a wasted costs order must bear in mind the principles of proportionality. It is not proportionate for the court to spend more time on wasted costs proceedings than it would generally expend on the substantive proceedings (*Re Merc Property Limited* (1999) *The Times*, 19 May, ChD, Lindsay J). See also *White v White* [2003] EWCA Civ 156, where the Court of Appeal was reluctant to interfere with the discretion of a judge in refusing to make a wasted costs order based on issues of proportionality. The fact that the proceedings were compromised by a Tomlin order does not prevent a judge dealing with an application for wasted costs (*Wagstaff v Colls* [2003] EWCA Civ 469, [2003] TLR 222, [2003] PNLR 29, CA).

Solicitors and other legal representatives—This is any person exercising a right to conduct litigation on behalf of a party. See *Byrne v South Sefton Health Authority* [2001] EWCA Civ 1904, [2002] 1 WLR 775, CA, where solicitors who failed to issue proceedings did not fall within the definition of persons exercising a right to conduct litigation in the proceedings. The court has to be satisfied that the conduct of the person against whom the wasted costs order is to be made was causative of the costs that have been incurred.

Public funds/legal aid—Legal representatives acting for publicly funded parties are in a specially vulnerable position with regard to wasted costs applications. Practitioners should bear in mind that their client is not their paymaster and in all probability not liable for the costs of the other side. In *Gandasha v Nandha and Karia* (2001) Lawtel, 23 November, ChD, Jacob J, where the outcome of a case depended on credibility, it could not be said that the solicitors acting for a publicly funded client should have gone so far as to advise the Legal Aid Board that the claim could not succeed. Accordingly a wasted costs order made on that basis was successfully appealed. For the procedure to be adopted where a publicly funded party has been unsuccessful and the receiving party seeks to recover costs against the LSC or Legal Aid Board see *Re O (a minor)* [1997] 1 FLR 465, CA.

Counsel—The liability of a barrister for a wasted costs order is not limited to his conduct of the proceedings in court. He comes within the definition of a person 'exercising a right of audience or a right to conduct litigation (*Brown v Bennett & ors (No 3)* [2002] 1 WLR 713, ChD, where it was held that a barrister could be liable for wasted costs, despite the fact that the conduct complained of did not occur when he was exercising his rights of audience). Liability for wasted costs is to be determined by reference to the question of whether, but for the conduct complained of, on the balance of probabilities the costs in question would have been incurred.

The House of Lords in *Medcalf v Mardell;* sub nom *Medcalf v Weatherill & anor* [2002] UKHL 27, [2002] 3 WLR 172, HL approved *Brown v Bennett* and confirmed that the court has jurisdiction under SCA 1981, s 51 to make a wasted costs order against the legal representative of any opposing party. Furthermore, a barrister could be liable for a wasted costs order in relation to conduct immediately relevant to the exercise of a right of audience although not involving advocacy. Nevertheless, a court considering making a wasted costs order had to make full allowance for the inability of the respondent lawyers to provide a full story to the court because of the privilege of the client. The court should not make an order against a lawyer precluded by legal professional privilege from advancing a full answer to the complaint against him, without satisfying itself that it was in all the circumstances fair to do so.

48.8 Basis of detailed assessment of solicitor and client costs

(1) This rule applies to every assessment of a solicitor's bill to his client except a bill which is to be paid out of the Community Legal Service Fund under the Legal Aid Act 1988 or the Access to Justice Act 1999.

(1A) Section 74(3) of the Solicitors Act 1974 applies unless the solicitor and client have entered into a written agreement which expressly permits payment to the solicitor of an amount of costs greater than that which the client could have recovered from another party to the proceedings.

(2) Subject to paragraph (1A), costs are to be assessed on the indemnity basis but are to be presumed –

- (a) to have been reasonably incurred if they were incurred with the express or implied approval of the client;
- (b) to be reasonable in amount if their amount was expressly or impliedly approved by the client;
- (c) to have been unreasonably incurred if –
  - (i) they are of an unusual nature or amount; and
  - (ii) the solicitor did not tell his client that as a result he might not recover all of them from the other party.

(3) Where the court is considering a percentage increase, whether on the application of the legal representative under rule 44.16 or on the application of the client, the court will have regard to all the relevant factors as they reasonably appeared to the solicitor or counsel when the conditional fee agreement was entered into or varied.

((4) In paragraph (3), 'conditional fee agreement' means an agreement enforceable under section 58 of the Courts and Legal Services Act 1990 at the date on which that agreement was entered into or varied.

Amendments—SI 1999/1008; SI 2000/1317; SI 2001/256.

Practice Direction—See generally PDCosts at p 1083 and specifically Sections 54–55 at p 1151.

Scope of provision—Rule 48.9 (conditional fees) has been revoked and the scope of r 48.8 has been enlarged to enable an assessment to take place of solicitor and client costs in respect of CFAs entered into after 1 April 2000. Generally speaking this rule will apply to all solicitor and client costs except where the bill is to be paid by the Community Legal Service Fund. Detailed assessment of a solicitor and client bill being on the indemnity basis (r 48.8(2)), proportionality is not an issue. The factors which the court takes into account are set out in r 48.8(2). Subparagraphs (a) and (b) provide that costs are reasonably incurred and are reasonable in amount if they were incurred with the express or implied approval of the client. See *Macdougall & ors v Boote Edgar Esterkin* (2000) SCCO Review No 15, QBD where it was held that in order to raise the presumption that costs were incurred with 'the express or implied approval' of the client the approval of the client has to be 'informed'. In order to rely on 'informed approval' the onus lies with the solicitor to ensure that it is secured following a full and fair exposition of all relevant factors so that the lay client can reasonably be bound by it. Attention is drawn to subpara (c) in relation to costs of an 'unusual nature or amount' which are presumed to have been unreasonably incurred unless the solicitor expressly informed the client before they were incurred that they might not be allowed against the other party.

Approval from the client to incur costs and their amount is not yet required in writing but practitioners should be aware of the Solicitors Practice (Costs and Information and Client Care) Amendment Rule 1998, effective from 3 September 1999, amending the existing Solicitors Practice Rule 15.

> 'A solicitor shall:
> (a) give information about costs and other matters; and
> (b) operate a complaints handling procedure,
>
> in accordance with a solicitors costs information and client care code made from time to time by the Council of the Law Society with the concurrence of the Master of the Rolls.'

That code, *inter alia*, provides that solicitors shall give to their clients details of the overall costs 'on the best information possible', the basis of the firms charge and update cost information at regular intervals (at least every 6 months).

'Section 74(3) of the Solicitors Act 1974' (r 48.8(1A))—Section 74(3) states:

> 'The amount which may be allowed on taxation of any costs or bill of costs in respect of any item relating to the proceedings in a county court shall not, except insofar as the rules of court

> may otherwise provide exceed the amount which could have been allowed in respect of that item as between party and party in those proceedings, having regard to the nature of the proceedings and the amount of the claim and of any counterclaim.'

Fast track trial costs are fixed (r 46.2) and s 74(3) precludes a solicitor from recovering any shortfall or difference in relation to this charge on a solicitor/client basis unless the solicitor and client have entered into a written agreement which expressly permits such a payment. The prudent practitioner will provide for this eventuality in his retainer with the client at the outset of the proceedings or obtain the client's signature to an agreement for the solicitor and client charges to exceed those recoverable as between party and party. The relevance of this provision will increase if fast track costs are capped or fixed in the future.

Where the receiving party's costs are reduced on assessment between the parties, they can still be recovered as between solicitor and client. Section 74(3) exists to apply a cap where there are limits under the CPR for the level of recoverable costs between the parties. It does not have the effect of making the assessment between the parties into a cap on the costs as between solicitor and client (*Sarah Jane Lynch v Paul Davidson Taylor (a firm)* [2004] EWCH 89 (QB)).

'costs ... are to be presumed' (r 48.8(2))—The presumption is rebuttable by evidence (PDCosts, para 54.2(2)).

Where the court is considering a percentage increase—This rule repeats the test set out in PDCosts, para 11.7 and requires the court not to adopt a hindsight test in relation to the assessment of an additional liability. The relevant factors to be taken into account by the court are set out in PDCosts, para 11.8 and practitioners are reminded that the court has power when considering whether a percentage increase is reasonable to allow different percentages for different items of costs or for different periods during which costs were incurred (PDCosts, para 11.8(2)).

48.9 (*revoked*)

48.10 Assessment procedure

(1) This rule sets out the procedure to be followed where the court has made an order under Part III of the Solicitors Act 1974 for the assessment of costs payable to a solicitor by his client.

(2) The solicitor must serve a breakdown of costs within 28 days of the order for costs to be assessed.

(3) The client must serve points of dispute within 14 days after service on him of the breakdown of costs.

(4) If the solicitor wishes to serve a reply, he must do so within 14 days of service on him of the points of dispute.

(5) Either party may file a request for a hearing date –

- (a) after points of dispute have been served; but
- (b) no later than 3 months after the date of the order for the costs to be assessed.

(6) This procedure applies subject to any contrary order made by the court.

(Other rules about costs payable in special cases can be found in Schedule 1, in the following RSC – Ord 30 (remuneration of receivers); Ord 49 (costs of garnishee))

Amendments—SI 1999/1008.

Practice Direction—See generally PDCosts at p 1083 and specifically Section 56 at p 1152.

Forms—Precedents J–M, Schedule of Costs Precedents.

Related provision—Part 67.

Scope of provision—Applications for detailed assessment must be made using the Pt 8 procedure (PD8B, para A.1(1) and Table 1. The rule varies the normal Pt 8 procedure.

'points of dispute' (r 48.10(3))—If points of dispute are not served, a default costs certificate cannot be issued by the solicitor (PDCosts, para 56.7). Instead, application should be made in accordance with Pt 23. The practice direction contains detailed provisions as to the operation of the assessment procedure.

Practice Direction About Costs

Supplementing CPR Parts 43–48 (PDCosts)

SECTION 1 – INTRODUCTION

1.1 This practice direction supplements Parts 43 to 48 of the Civil Procedure Rules. It applies to all proceedings to which those Parts apply.

1.2 Paragraphs 57.1 to 57.9 of this practice direction deal with various transitional provisions affecting proceedings about costs.

1.3 Attention is drawn to the powers to make orders about costs conferred on the Supreme Court and any county court by Section 51 of the Supreme Court Act 1981.

1.4 In these Directions –

'counsel' means a barrister or other person with a right of audience in relation to all proceedings in the High Court or in the county courts in which he is instructed to act.

'LSC' means Legal Services Commission.

'solicitor' means a solicitor of the Supreme Court or other person with a right of audience in relation to proceedings, who is conducting the claim or defence (as the case may be) on behalf of a party to the proceedings and, where the context admits, includes a patent agent.

1.5 In respect of any document which is required by these Directions to be signed by a party or his legal representative the practice direction supplementing Part 22 will apply as if the document in question was a statement of truth. (The practice direction supplementing Part 22 makes provision for cases in which a party is a child, a patient or a company or other corporation and cases in which a document is signed on behalf of a partnership).

'Attention is drawn ... Supreme Court Act 1981' (para 1.3)—Supreme Court Act 1981, s 51 was modified by the Courts and Legal Services Act 1990, s 4(1). Section 51 provides the basis of costs in the following courts –

(a) the Civil Division of the Court of Appeal
(b) the High Court
(c) the county court

The general principle is that costs shall be in the discretion of the court. This is subject to the power (now vested in the CPRC) to make rules relating to the costs of proceedings which include prescribing scales of costs to be paid to legal and other representatives (SCA 1981, s 51(2); see also CPR r 44.3(2)).

The court retains the power to determine both the entitlement to and the amount of any costs (SCA 1981, s 51(3)).

Supreme Court Act 1981, s 51(6) and (7) give the statutory basis for 'wasted costs' (see CPR r 48.7).

'In respect of any document ... on behalf of a partnership' (para 1.5)—There are a number of documents relating to costs which require the signature of the party or his legal representative. For example a statement of costs, summary assessment (Form N260) and the certificates for inclusion in bills of costs (Precedent F, Schedule of Costs Precedents) and points of dispute (Precedent G,

Schedule of Costs Precedents). This provision equates signature of any such document to the statement of truth (PD22, paras 3.1–3.11 dealing with who may sign the certificate of truth).

Paragraph 3.8 of PD22 deals with this liability and consequences for a legal representative who has signed a statement of truth. 'Legal representative' is defined in CPR r 2.3.

SECTION 2 – SCOPE OF COSTS RULES AND DEFINITIONS

Rule 43.2 Definitions and Application

2.1 Where the court makes an order for costs and the receiving party has entered into a funding arrangement as defined in rule 43.2, the costs payable by the paying party include any additional liability (also defined in rule 43.2) unless the court orders otherwise.

2.2 In the following paragraphs –

'funding arrangement', 'percentage increase' and 'additional liability' have the meanings given to them by rule 43.2.

A 'conditional fee agreement' is an agreement with a person providing advocacy or litigation services which provides for his fees and expenses, or part of them, to be payable only in specified circumstances, whether or not it provides for a success fee as mentioned in section 58(2)(b) of the Courts and Legal Services Act 1990.

'base costs' means costs other than the amount of any additional liability.

2.3 Rule 44.3A(1) provides that the court will not assess any additional liability until the conclusion of the proceedings or the part of the proceedings to which the funding arrangement relates. (As to the time when detailed assessment may be carried out see Section 27 of this practice direction).

2.4 For the purposes of the following paragraphs of this practice direction and rule 44.3A proceedings are concluded when the court has finally determined the matters in issue in the claim, whether or not there is an appeal. The making of an award of provisional damages under Part 41 will also be treated as a final determination of the matters in issue.

2.5 The court may order or the parties may agree in writing that, although the proceedings are continuing, they will nevertheless be treated as concluded.

SECTION 3 – MODEL FORMS FOR CLAIMS FOR COSTS

Rule 43.3 Meaning of Summary Assessment

3.1 Rule 43.3 defines summary assessment. When carrying out a summary assessment of costs where there is an additional liability the court may assess the base costs alone, or the base costs and the additional liability.

3.2 Form N260 is a model form of Statement of Costs to be used for summary assessments.

3.3 Further details about Statements of Costs are given in paragraph 13.5 below.

Rule 43.4 Meaning of Detailed Assessment

3.4 Rule 43.4 defines detailed assessment. When carrying out a detailed assessment of costs where there is an additional liability the court will assess both the base costs and the additional liability, or, if the base costs have already been assessed, the additional liability alone.

3.5 Precedents A, B, C and D in the Schedule of Costs Precedents annexed to this practice direction are model forms of bills of costs to be used for detailed assessments.

3.6 Further details about bills of costs are given in the next section of these Directions and in paragraphs 27.1 to 48.1, below.

3.7 Precedents A, B, C and D in the Schedule of Costs Precedents and the next section of this practice direction all refer to a model form of bill of costs. The use of a model form is not compulsory, but is encouraged. A party wishing to rely upon a bill which departs from the model forms should include in the background information of the bill an explanation for that departure.

3.8 In any order of the court (whether made before or after 26 April 1999) the word 'taxation' will be taken to mean 'detailed assessment' and the words 'to be taxed' will be taken to mean 'to be decided by detailed assessment' unless in either case the context otherwise requires.

'Precedents A, B, C and D in the Schedule of Costs Precedents' (para 3.5)—There are no prescribed forms for bills of costs. Precedents A, B, C and D are model forms of bill. Whilst their use is not compulsory it is encouraged. A party relying on a bill which departs from the model forms should include in the background information an explanation for that departure.

- *Precedent A* – This form of bill is used where the receiving party's solicitor and counsel are operating on CFA terms. It deals with both base costs and also assessment of additional liability.
- *Precedent B* – This form deals with the detailed assessment of an additional liability only.
- *Precedent C* – This is the form of bill to be used where costs are claimed against the paying party in non-CFA cases and/or the LSC.
- *Precedent D* – An alternative form of bill with single columns only for amounts claimed and separate parts for costs payable by the LSC. In effect this is the old Form 2 produced with the CPR on 26 April 1999.

If a bill is capable of being copied onto a computer disc the paying party may ask the receiving party to supply a disc copy free of charge; the disc must be supplied within 7 days of request (para 32.11).

SECTION 4 – FORM AND CONTENTS OF BILLS OF COSTS

4.1 A bill of costs may consist of such of the following sections as may be appropriate –

(1) title page;
(2) background information;
(3) items of costs claimed under the headings specified in paragraph 4.6;
(4) summary showing the total costs claimed on each page of the bill;
(5) schedules of time spent on non-routine attendances; and
(6) the certificates referred to in paragraph 4.15.

4.2 Where it is necessary or convenient to do so, a bill of costs may be divided into two or more parts, each part containing sections (2), (3) and (4) above. A division into parts will be necessary or convenient in the following circumstances –

(1) Where the receiving party acted in person during the course of the proceedings (whether or not he also had a legal representative at that time) the bill should be divided into different parts so as to distinguish between;
 (a) the costs claimed for work done by the legal representative; and
 (b) the costs claimed for work done by the receiving party in person.
(2) Where the receiving party was represented by different solicitors

during the course of the proceedings, the bill should be divided into different parts so as to distinguish between the costs payable in respect of each solicitor.

(3) Where the receiving party obtained legal aid or LSC funding in respect of all or part of the proceedings the bill should be divided into separate parts so as to distinguish between;
   (a) costs claimed before legal aid or LSC funding was granted;
   (b) costs claimed after legal aid or LSC funding was granted; and
   (c) any costs claimed after legal aid or LSC funding ceased.

(4) Where value added tax (VAT) is claimed and there was a change in the rate of VAT during the course of the proceedings, the bill should be divided into separate parts so as to distinguish between;
   (a) costs claimed at the old rate of VAT; and
   (b) costs claimed at the new rate of VAT.

(5) Where the bill covers costs payable under an order or orders under which there are different paying parties the bill should be divided into parts so as to deal separately with the costs payable by each paying party.

(6) Where the bill covers costs payable under an order or orders, in respect of which the receiving party wishes to claim interest from different dates, the bill should be divided to enable such interest to be calculated.

4.3 Where a party claims costs against another party and also claims costs against the LSC only for work done in the same period, the costs claimed against the LSC only can be claimed either in a separate part of the bill or in additional columns in the same part of the bill. Precedents C and D in the Schedule of Costs Precedents annexed to this Practice Direction show how bills should be drafted when costs are claimed against the LSC only.

4.4 The title page of the bill of costs must set out –

(1) the full title of the proceedings;
(2) the name of the party whose bill it is and a description of the document showing the right to assessment (as to which see paragraph 39.4, below);
(3) if VAT is included as part of the claim for costs, the VAT number of the legal representative or other person in respect of whom VAT is claimed;
(4) details of all legal aid certificates, LSC certificates and relevant amendment certificates in respect of which claims for costs are included in the bill.

4.5 The background information included in the bill of costs should set out –

(1) a brief description of the proceedings up to the date of the notice of commencement;
(2) a statement of the status of the solicitor or solicitor's employee in respect of whom costs are claimed and (if those costs are calculated on the basis of hourly rates) the hourly rates claimed for each such person.

It should be noted that 'legal executive' means a Fellow of the Institute of Legal Executives.

Other clerks, who are fee earners of equivalent experience, may be entitled to similar rates. It should be borne in mind that Fellows of the Institute of Legal Executives will have spent approximately 6 years in practice, and taken both general and specialist examinations. The Fellows have therefore acquired considerable practical and academic experience.

Clerks without the equivalent experience of legal executives will normally be treated as being the equivalent of trainee solicitors and para-legals.

(3) a brief explanation of any agreement or arrangement between the receiving party and his solicitors which affects the costs claimed in the bill.

4.6 The bill of costs may consist of items under such of the following heads as may be appropriate –

(1) attendances on the court and counsel up to the date of the notice of commencement;
(2) attendances on and communications with the receiving party;
(3) attendances on and communications with witnesses including any expert witness;
(4) attendances to inspect any property or place for the purposes of the proceedings;
(5) attendances on and communications with other persons, including offices of public records;
(6) communications with the court and with counsel;
(7) work done on documents: preparing and considering documentation, including documentation relating to pre-action protocols where appropriate, work done in connection with arithmetical calculations of compensation and/or interest and time spent collating documents;
(8) work done in connection with negotiations with a view to settlement if not already covered in the heads listed above;
(9) attendances on and communications with London and other agents and work done by them;
(10) other work done which was of or incidental to the proceedings and which is not already covered in the heads listed above.

4.7 In respect of each of the heads of costs –

(1) 'communications' means letters out and telephone calls;
(2) communications which are not routine communications must be set out in chronological order;
(3) routine communications should be set out as a single item at the end of each head.

4.8 Routine communications are letters out, e-mails out and telephone calls which because of their simplicity should not be regarded as letters or e-mails of substance or telephone calls which properly amount to an attendance.

4.9 Each item claimed in the bill of costs must be consecutively numbered.

4.10 In each part of the bill of costs which claims items under head (1) (attendances on court and counsel) a note should be made of –

(1) all relevant events, including events which do not constitute chargeable items;
(2) any orders for costs which the court made (whether or not a claim is made in respect of those costs in this bill of costs).

4.11 The numbered items of costs may be set out on paper divided into columns. Precedents A, B, C and D in the Schedule of Costs Precedents annexed to this practice direction illustrate various model forms of bills of costs.

4.12 In respect of heads (2) to (10) in paragraph 4.6 above, if the number of attendances and communications other than routine communications is twenty or more, the claim for the costs of those items in that section of the bill of costs should be for the total only and should refer to a schedule in which the full record of dates and details is set out. If the bill of costs contains more than one schedule each schedule should be numbered consecutively.

4.13 The bill of costs must not contain any claims in respect of costs or court fees which relate solely to the detailed assessment proceedings other than costs claimed for preparing and checking the bill.

4.14 The summary must show the total profit costs and disbursements claimed separately from the total VAT claimed. Where the bill of costs is divided into parts the summary must also give totals for each part. If each page of the bill gives a page total the summary must also set out the page totals for each page.

4.15 The bill of costs must contain such of the certificates, the texts of which are set out in Precedent F of the Schedule of Costs Precedents annexed to this practice direction, as are appropriate.

4.16 The following provisions relate to work done by solicitors –

(1) Routine letters out and routine telephone calls will in general be allowed on a unit basis of 6 minutes each, the charge being calculated by reference to the appropriate hourly rate. The unit charge for letters out will include perusing and considering the relevant letters in and no separate charge should be made for incoming letters.

(2) E-mails received by solicitors will not normally be allowed. The court may, in its discretion, allow an actual time charge for preparation of e-mails sent by solicitors which properly amount to attendances provided that the time taken has been recorded. The court may also, in its discretion, allow a sum in respect of routine e-mails sent to the client or others on a unit basis of 6 minutes each, the charge being calculated by reference to the appropriate hourly rate.

(3) Local travelling expenses incurred by solicitors will not be allowed. The definition of 'local' is a matter for the discretion of the court. While no absolute rule can be laid down, as a matter of guidance, 'local' will, in general, be taken to mean within a radius of 10 miles from the court dealing with the case at the relevant time. Where travelling and waiting time is claimed, this should be allowed at the rate agreed with the client unless this is more than the hourly rate on the assessment.

(4) The cost of postage, couriers, out-going telephone calls, fax and telex messages will in general not be allowed but the court may exceptionally in its discretion allow such expenses in unusual circumstances or where the cost is unusually heavy.

(5) The cost of making copies of documents will not in general be allowed but the court may exceptionally in its discretion make an allowance for copying in unusual circumstances or where the documents copied are unusually numerous in relation to the nature of the case. Where this discretion is invoked the number of copies made, their purpose and the costs claimed for them must be set out in the bill.

(6) Agency charges as between a principal solicitor and his agent will be dealt with on the principle that such charges, where appropriate, form part of the principal solicitor's charges. Where these charges relate to

head (1) in paragraph 4.6 (attendances at court and on counsel) they should be included in their chronological order in that head. In other cases they should be included in head (9) (attendances on London and other agents).

4.17

(1) Where a claim is made for a percentage increase in addition to an hourly rate or base fee, the amount of the increase must be shown separately, either in the appropriate arithmetic column or in the narrative column. (For an example see Precedent A or Precedent B.)

(2) Where a claim is made against the LSC only and includes enhancement and where a claim is made in family proceedings and includes a claim for uplift or general care and conduct, the amount of enhancement, uplift and general care and conduct must be shown, in respect of each item upon which it is claimed, as a separate amount either in the appropriate arithmetic column or in the narrative column. (For an example, see Precedent C.)

'Enhancement' means the increase in prescribed rates which may be allowed by a costs officer in accordance with the Legal Aid in Civil Proceedings (Remuneration) Regulations 1994 or the Legal Aid in Family Proceedings Regulations 1991.

'A bill of costs … paragraph 4.15' (para 4.1)—The rules and practice direction do not prescribe the way in which a bill must be drawn other than to specify that it must contain some or all of the sections set out in this paragraph.

'a bill of costs may be divided' (para 4.2)—The bill should be divided into different parts to reflect the fact that a party has acted in person or that different legal representatives have acted for a party during the course of proceedings. The bill should also be divided into different parts if legal aid or LSC funding was granted in respect of all or part of the proceedings to show the costs claimed against another party or recoverable only against the Legal Services Commission. The bill should also be divided to establish when a party has entered into a funding arrangement or CFA (as defined in CPR r 43.2). The bill should also be divided to show any changes in the rate of VAT or where costs payable under an order or orders claim interest from different dates (para 4.2(6)).

'The background information' (para 4.5)—The bill should contain a brief narrative of the history of the matter summarising the issues involved and the steps taken.

It is increasingly common for bills of costs to be challenged on the basis that the indemnity principle has been breached. It is therefore important to include in the background information full details of the retainer between the solicitor and client. Where there is a dispute between paying party and receiving party relating to a breach of the indemnity principle a copy of any client care letter or other form of written retainer must be provided to the court if the matter proceeds to a detailed assessment hearing (para 40.2(i)).

In principle, the terms and conditions of business of a solicitor contained in a letter to his client which does not contain advice cannot be the subject of a claim of legal and professional privilege. Where a document *is* privileged, the receiving party may not rely on it by producing it to the costs judge without also disclosing it (on appropriate terms as to confidentiality) to the paying party or his representative (*Dickinson (t/a Dickinson Equipment Finance) v Rushmer (t/a FJ Associates)* [2002] Costs LR 128, ChD, Rimer J). This implies no breach of HRA 1998; the question of disclosure does not arise when the paying party merely asserts an issue (such as lack of retainer) without having any material upon which it is based (*South Coast Shipping Co Ltd v Havant Borough Council* [2002] 3 All ER 779, [2002] Costs LR 98, ChD, Pumfrey J).

Expense rate/care and conduct—The background information must set out the status of the legal representative who has carried out the work together with his hourly rate and charge-out rate. A solicitor calculates the reasonable charge to be included within the bill of costs by taking into account –

(a) the grade of fee earner reasonably employed carrying out the work;
(b) the time reasonably spent by the fee earner, and
(c) the expense rate of the fee earner concerned.

Only the time spent by fee earners can be charged. As to who is a fee earner see *Smith Graham (a firm) v The Lord Chancellor* (1999) 149 NLJ 1443. The salaries of other staff will be taken into account in calculating the appropriate expense rate. Unlike RSC Ord 62, App 3, Pt II, para 4.6 does not make a distinction between the hourly rate representing the broad average direct costs of the work (factor A) and a percentage mark up for care and conduct (factor B). The B factor was normally applied to all work reasonably done other than travelling and waiting. That item was a variable percentage and was intended to reflect the additional average degree of responsibility and supervision involved in getting an action ready for trial. In the past the amount of such uplift has been a matter for discretion of the costs officer (see *Brush v Bower Cotton and Bower* [1993] All ER 471 regarding the level of uplift to be claimed and allowed in more complex cases).

Recently there has been a move away from the A + B factor approach to a composite rate of charges (see *General of Berne v Jardine Reinsurance Management Limited & ors* [1998] 2 All ER 301, CA where the court indicated that bills of costs should more closely reflect the agreement between the solicitor and the client to show the costs which are payable by the client). This move away from the A + B factor to a composite rate of charge is demonstrated in the model forms of bill of costs.

'The bill of costs may consist of … the following heads' (para 4.6)—This paragraph sets out the categories of work carried out by a solicitor or litigant for which a charge can be made. The twelve categories referred to in the previous Practice Direction (PD43, para 2.5) have been reduced to ten with the former categories of para 2.5(5) (searches and enquiries made at offices of public records, the Companies Registry and similar searches and enquiries) and 2.5(8) (work done in connection with arithmetical calculations of compensation and/or interest) being amalgamated in para 4.6(5) and (7).

Travelling and waiting times—The recoverable rate depends on the agreement between the solicitor and client. Where the retainer does not differentiate between preparation, travel and waiting there will be no difference in the amount claimed. If the agreement provides for a reduced rate for travelling and waiting only the reduced rate will be recoverable from the paying party.

'Routine communications' (para 4.8)—It is not possible to claim for the cost of routine incoming letters or e-mails received.

'paper divided into columns' (para 4.11)—See model form bill of Costs Precedents A, B, C and D, Schedule of Costs Precedents. Model forms A, B and C incorporate separate columns for disbursements made on behalf of clients and VAT thereon.

Paragraph 4.13—The costs of detailed assessment proceedings will generally be dealt with by summary assessment at the conclusion of the detailed assessment hearing. Practitioners should be aware of para 45.3 that no party should file or serve a statement of costs in relation to the detailed assessment proceedings unless the court orders him to do so.

'The bill of costs must contain' (para 4.15)—Precedent F, Schedule of Costs Precedents sets out a number of certificates to be annexed to a bill. In particular attention is drawn to the certificate with regard to the accuracy and completeness of the bill. The purpose of the certificate is to satisfy the court that the indemnity principle has not been breached (note *Bailey v IBC Vehicles Limited* [1998] 3 All ER 570, CA). In signing the bill the solicitor is certifying that the contents of the bill are correct. Per Henry LJ:

> 'The signature of the bill of costs is effectively the certificate by an officer of the court that the receiving party's solicitors are not seeking to recover in relation to any item more than they have agreed to charge their client …
>
> For the avoidance of doubt I also agree that the taxing officer may and should seek further information where some feature of the case raises suspicions that the whole truth may not have been told …
>
> The other side have a presumption of trust afforded by the signature of an officer of the court and a breach of that trust should be treated as a most serious disciplinary offence.'

The certificates on a bill of costs are essentially a statement of truth (para 1.5).

Costs of preparing the bill

4.18 A claim may be made for the reasonable costs of preparing and checking the bill of costs.

'checking the bill of costs'—The reasonable costs of instructing a costs draftsman to prepare the bill of costs may be claimed. The model forms of bill show these costs to be calculated on an hourly basis and not a percentage fee for drawing the bill which may not be allowable on the basis they are neither reasonable nor proportionate. The costs of the solicitor in checking, vouching and certifying the bill may also be claimed.

SECTION 5 – SPECIAL PROVISIONS RELATING TO VAT

5.1 This section deals with claims for value added tax (VAT) which are made in respect of costs being dealt with by way of summary assessment or detailed assessment.

VAT registration number

5.2 The number allocated by HM Revenue and Customs to every person registered under the Value Added Tax Act 1983 (except a Government Department) must appear in a prominent place at the head of every statement, bill of costs, fee sheet, account or voucher on which VAT is being included as part of a claim for costs.

Entitlement to VAT on costs

5.3 VAT should not be included in a claim for costs if the receiving party is able to recover the VAT as input tax. Where the receiving party is able to obtain credit from HM Revenue and Customs for a proportion of the VAT as input tax, only that proportion which is not eligible for credit should be included in the claim for costs.

5.4 The receiving party has responsibility for ensuring that VAT is claimed only when the receiving party is unable to recover the VAT or a proportion thereof as input tax.

5.5 Where there is a dispute as to whether VAT is properly claimed the receiving party must provide a certificate signed by the solicitors or the auditors of the receiving party substantially in the form illustrated in Precedent F in the Schedule of Costs Precedents annexed to this practice direction. Where the receiving party is a litigant in person who is claiming VAT, reference should be made by him to HM Revenue and Customs and wherever possible a Statement to similar effect produced at the hearing at which the costs are assessed.

5.6 Where there is a dispute as to whether any service in respect of which a charge is proposed to be made in the bill is zero rated or exempt, reference should be made to HM Revenue and Customs and wherever possible the view of HM Revenue and Customs obtained and made known at the hearing at which the costs are assessed. Such application should be made by the receiving party. In the case of a bill from a solicitor to his own client, such application should be made by the client.

'VAT should not be included … if the receiving party is able to recover the VAT as input tax' (para 5.3)—This means that in the case of the vast majority of commercial litigants, VAT should not be claimed in bills of costs or schedules of costs for summary assessment. It frequently is claimed in practice and where the paying party is unrepresented it arguably amounts to unprofessional conduct.

'the receiving party must provide a certificate' (para 5.5)—If the assessment is on the standard basis, any doubt as to the recoverability of VAT must of course be resolved in favour of the paying party.

Form of bill of costs where VAT rate changes

5.7 Where there is a change in the rate of VAT, suppliers of goods and services are entitled by ss 88(1) and 88(2) of the VAT Act 1994 in most circumstances to elect whether the new or the old rate of VAT should apply to a supply where the basic and actual tax points span a period during which there has been a change in VAT rates.

5.8 It will be assumed, unless a contrary indication is given in writing, that an election to take advantage of the provisions mentioned in paragraph 5.7 above and to charge VAT at the lower rate has been made. In any case in which an election to charge at the lower rate is not made, such a decision must be justified to the court assessing the costs.

Apportionment

5.9 All bills of costs, fees and disbursements on which VAT is included must be divided into separate parts so as to show work done before, on and after the date or dates from which any change in the rate of VAT takes effect. Where, however, a lump sum charge is made for work which spans a period during which there has been a change in VAT rates, and paragraphs 5.7 and 5.8 above do not apply, reference should be made to paragraphs 8 and 9 of Appendix F of Customs' Notice 700 (or any revised edition of that Notice), a copy of which should be in the possession of every registered trader. If necessary, the lump sum should be apportioned. The totals of profit costs and disbursements in each part must be carried separately to the summary.

5.10 Should there be a change in the rate between the conclusion of a detailed assessment and the issue of the final costs certificate, any interested party may apply for the detailed assessment to be varied so as to take account of any increase or reduction in the amount of tax payable. Once the final costs certificate has been issued, no variation under this paragraph will be permitted.

Disbursements

5.11 Petty (or general) disbursements such as postage, fares etc which are normally treated as part of a solicitor's overheads and included in his profit costs should be charged with VAT even though they bear no tax when the solicitor incurs them. The cost of travel by public transport on a specific journey for a particular client where it forms part of the service rendered by a solicitor to his client and is charged in his bill of costs, attracts VAT.

5.12 Reference is made to the criteria set out in the VAT Guide (Customs and Excise Notice 700 – 1 August 1991 edition paragraph 83, or any revised edition of that Notice), as to expenses which are not subject to VAT. Charges for the cost of travel by public transport, postage, telephone calls and telegraphic transfers where these form part of the service rendered by the solicitor to his client are examples of charges which do not satisfy these criteria and are thus liable to VAT at the standard rate.

Legal Aid/LSC funding

5.13(1) VAT will be payable in respect of every supply made pursuant to a legal aid/LSC certificate where –

- (a) the person making the supply is a taxable person; and
- (b) the assisted person/LSC funded client –
  - (i) belongs in the United Kingdom or another member State of the European Union; and
  - (ii) is a private individual or receives the supply for non-business purposes.

(2) Where the assisted person/LSC funded client belongs outside the European Union, VAT is generally not payable unless the supply relates to land in the United Kingdom.
(3) For the purpose of sub-paragraphs (1) and (2), the place where a person belongs is determined by section 9 of the Value Added Tax Act 1994.
(4) Where the assisted person/LSC funded client is registered for VAT and the legal services paid for by the LSC are in connection with that person's business, the VAT on those services will be payable by the LSC only.

5.14 Any summary of costs payable by the LSC must be drawn so as to show the total VAT on counsel's fees as a separate item from the VAT on other disbursements and the VAT on profit costs.

Tax invoice

5.15 A bill of costs filed for detailed assessment is always retained by the Court. Accordingly if a solicitor waives his solicitor and client costs and accepts the costs certified by the court as payable by the unsuccessful party in settlement, it will be necessary for a short statement as to the amount of the certified costs and the VAT thereon to be prepared for use as the tax invoice.

Vouchers

5.16 Where receipted accounts for disbursements made by the solicitor or his client are retained as tax invoices a photostat copy of any such receipted account may be produced and will be accepted as sufficient evidence of payment when disbursements are vouched.

Certificates

5.17 In a costs certificate payable by the LSC, the VAT on solicitor's costs, counsel's fees and disbursements will be shown separately.

Litigants acting in person

5.18 Where a litigant acts in litigation on his own behalf he is not treated for the purposes of VAT as having supplied services and therefore no VAT is chargeable in respect of work done by that litigant (even where, for example, that litigant is a solicitor or other legal representative).

5.19 Consequently in the circumstances described in the preceding paragraph, a bill of costs presented for agreement or assessment should not claim any VAT which will not be allowed on assessment.

Government Departments

5.20 On an assessment between parties, where costs are being paid to a Government Department in respect of services rendered by its legal staff, VAT should not be added.

SECTION 6 ESTIMATES OF COSTS

6.1 This section sets out certain steps which parties and their legal representatives must take in order to keep the parties informed about their potential liability in respect of costs and in order to assist the court to decide what, if any, order to make about costs and about case management.

6.2

(1) In this section an 'estimate of costs' means –
(a) an estimate of base costs (including disbursements) already incurred; and
(b) an estimate of base costs (including disbursements) to be incurred,
which a party intends to seek to recover from any other party under an order for costs if he is successful in the case.

('Base costs' are defined in paragraph 2.2 of this Practice Direction.)

(2) A party who intends to recover an additional liability (defined in rule 43.2) need not reveal the amount of that liability in the estimate.

6.3 The court may at any stage in a case order any party to file an estimate of costs and to serve copies of the estimate on all other parties. The court may direct that the estimate be prepared in such a way as to demonstrate the likely effects of giving or not giving a particular case management direction which the court is considering, for example a direction for a split trial or for the trial of a preliminary issue. The court may specify a time limit for filing and serving the estimate. However, if no time limit is specified the estimate should be filed and served within 28 days of the date of the order.

6.4

(1) When –
(a) a party to a claim which is outside the financial scope of the small claims track files an allocation questionnaire; or
(b) a party to a claim which is being dealt with on the fast track or the multi track, or under Part 8, files a pre-trial check list (listing questionnaire),

he must also file an estimate of costs and serve a copy of it on every other party, unless the court otherwise directs. Where a party is represented, the legal representative must in addition serve an estimate on the party he represents.

(2) Where a party is required to file and serve a new estimate of costs in accordance with Rule 44.15(3), if that party is represented the legal representative must in addition serve the new estimate on the party he represents.

(3) This paragraph does not apply to litigants in person.

6.5 An estimate of costs should be substantially in the form illustrated in Precedent H in the Schedule of Costs Precedents annexed to the Practice Direction.

6.5A

(1) If there is a difference of 20% or more between the base costs claimed by a receiving party on detailed assessment and the costs shown in an estimate of costs filed by that party, the receiving party must provide a statement of the reasons for the difference with his bill of costs.

(2) If a paying party –
(a) claims that he reasonably relied on an estimate of costs filed by a receiving party; or
(b) wishes to rely upon the costs shown in the estimate in order to dispute the reasonableness or proportionality of the costs claimed,

the paying party must serve a statement setting out his case in this regard in his points of dispute.

('Relevant person' is defined in paragraph 32.10(1) of the Costs Practice Direction)

6.6

(1) On an assessment of the costs of a party, the court may have regard to any estimate previously filed by that party, or by any other party in the same proceedings. Such an estimate may be taken into account as a factor among others, when assessing the reasonableness and proportionality of any costs claimed.

(2) In particular, where –

(a) there is a difference of 20% or more between the base costs claimed by a receiving party and the costs shown in an estimate of costs filed by that party; and

(b) it appears to the court that –

(i) the receiving party has not provided a satisfactory explanation for that difference; or

(ii) the paying party reasonably relied on the estimate of costs;

the court may regard the difference between the costs claimed and the costs shown in the estimate as evidence that the costs claimed are unreasonable or disproportionate.

Scope of provision—Estimates of costs are required in fast track and multi track cases but are not required in claims allocated to the small claims track. They are not required from the litigant in person. A court can call for an estimate of costs from a party at any stage in proceedings. For example the court may call for an estimate of costs from either or both parties before ordering specific disclosure if the court considers that the costs of providing specific disclosure may be disproportionate (para 6.3). With effect from 12 February 2001 there is an apparent conflict between the information required on the allocation questionnaire about the costs of a claim (Form N150) and the practice direction. Strict compliance with PDCosts, para 6.5 is only required in 'substantial cases'. These are not defined in the notes accompanying the allocation questionnaire and it is assumed these relate to multi-track cases. Where Precedent H, Schedule of Costs Precedents is required it is in effect a bill of costs prepared without a narrative or background history. A party must not only file his estimate of costs at court but must serve it on every other party and also his own client. These estimates are in addition to a solicitor's obligation to provide his client with sufficient information about costs to comply with the Solicitors Practice (Costs and Information and Client Care) Amendment Rule 1998. The Law Society's Guide to Professional Conduct of Solicitors makes it clear that the final amount payable by a party should not vary substantially from an estimate given to that party unless the client has been informed of any changed circumstances in writing (see *Wong v Vizards* (1997) 2 Costs LR 46, QBD, Toulson J). See also *Mars UK v Teknowledge* (No 2) [1999] 2 Costs LR 44 where (*inter alia*) Jacob J stated that for a party to run up unforeseeably large bills without warning to the other party was a factor which the court could take into account on detailed assessment (CPR r 44.3(5)).

Costs capping: In *Griffiths v Solutia* [2001] EWCA Civ 736, [2001] Costs LR 247, CA, Sir Christopher Staughton said that, although the CPR did not confer on the court an express power to place an advance limit on the costs which would be recoverable for all or part of the litigation (equivalent to the power of the Arbitration Act 1996, s 65), 'case management powers will allow a judge in the future to exercise the power of limiting costs, either indirectly or even directly so that they are proportionate to the amount involved'.

In *AB v Leeds Teaching Hospitals NHS Trust (Re Nationwide Organ Group Litigation)* [2003] EWHC 1034 (QB) (case management of the *Nationwide Organ Group* litigation) Gage J set a budget in respect of the claimants' publicly funded costs, in order to guide the claimants as to the proportionality of their costs expenditure and to provide a cap on the costs which they will recover if successful (unless the court orders otherwise). See also *Various claimants v TUI UK Limited & ors* (2005) (unreported) 11 August (SCCO), Chief Master Hurst, in relation to the general principles of costs capping in a group litigation order.

The court should consider making a costs capping order only where there is a real and substantial risk that otherwise costs will be disproportionately or unreasonably incurred, which cannot be managed by conventional case management and a detailed assessment of costs after trial, and it is just to make such an order. The application must be supported by evidence showing a *prima facie* case that those conditions can be satisfied. The allocation and listing questionnaires will have attached estimates of the likely overall costs, which would give a good guide, and the court should be able to deal with an application at a comparatively short hearing. The benefit of doubt in respect of the reasonableness of prospective costs should be resolved in favour of the party being capped (*Smart v East Cheshire NHS Trust* [2003] EWHC 2806, (2003) Lawtel, 2 December, QBD, Gage J).

See also *King v Telegraph Group Limited* [2004] EWCA Civ 619, [2004] All ER (D) 242 (May), [2004] TLR 277, (2004) *The Times*, 21 May, CA, where the Court of Appeal laid down a stringent procedure for controlling costs in defamation proceedings funded by CFAs. In future, if the master or district judge dealing with the procedural issues considers that a budget or cap is required, he will refer the issue of imposing a cap to a costs judge. The costs judge will determine what sum is reasonable and proportionate to fix as recoverable costs of the action (see paras [101]–[106]). It is almost inevitable that this approach will be adopted in future in complex and expensive litigation other than defamation.

The Senior Costs Judge, with the approval of the Deputy Head of Civil Justice, has given useful advice about costs capping orders. It is thought that, unless otherwise stated, an order speaks from the date it is made and is not retrospective but, for the sake of clarity, a start date for the costs cap should be stated on the face of the order. In most cases, defendants who are concerned about the level of costs will be content to submit to a cap on their costs, and although all the applications to date have been in respect of the claimants' costs, it appears to be good practice and in accordance with the overriding objective that both sides' costs should be capped.

Estimates of costs: See *Cornerhouse Research (R on the application of) v Secretary of State for Trade and Industry* [2005] EWCA Civ 192 which is the key authority on protective costs orders (PCO's) in public law litigation. It revisits and revamps the criteria set down in *R v Lord Chancellor ex parte CPAG* [1999] 1 WLR 347 bringing the merits threshold in line with the summary judgment test of 'properly arguable' and makes the following additional points:

(1) An applicant must have no private interest in the outcome of the case.
(2) An application is more likely to succeed where the applicant's lawyers are acting *pro bono*.
(3) Where lawyers are not acting *pro bono*, a capping order is likely to be required.
(4) Such an order is likely to restrict the costs to fees for solicitors and junior counsel only, ie the outcome must be modest.

There is further important guidance in respect of the costs of seeking and resisting as PCO and the procedure for doing so.

Costs estimates are an important part of the machinery of case management. In *Leigh v Michelin Tyre plc* [2003] EWCA Civ 1766, [2003] TLR 699, the Court of Appeal held that there were three circumstances in which costs estimates should be taken in to account on an assessment of costs:

(1) Estimates made by solicitors of the overall likely costs should usually provide a useful yardstick by which the reasonableness of the costs finally claimed may be measured. If there is a substantial difference between the estimated costs and the costs claimed, that difference calls for an explanation. In the absence of a satisfactory explanation, the court may conclude that the difference itself is evidence from which it can conclude that the costs claimed are unreasonable.
(2) The court may take the estimated costs into account if the paying party shows that it relied upon the estimate in a certain way.
(3) The court can take the estimate into account in cases where it decides that it would probably have given different case management directions if a realistic estimate had been given.

The court went on to conclude that the costs judge should determine how, if at all, to reflect the costs estimate in the assessment, before going on to decide whether – for reasons unrelated to the estimate – there are elements of the costs claimed that were unreasonably incurred or unreasonable in amount.

Estimates of costs for LSC funded parties are to be prepared on the basis of the proper solicitor and client charge in respect of the costs to be recovered from the paying party and at prescribed rates for costs claimed against the LSC only. Estimates of costs do not limit the amount of costs which may be recovered in proceedings. The court may have regard to any estimate previously filed by that party and take it into account as a factor amongst others when assessing the reasonableness of any costs claimed (para 6.6).

Additional liability—Where a solicitor has entered into a funding arrangement (defined in CPR r 43.2) any estimate of costs relates to the base costs only and need not reveal the amount of any additional liability in the estimate provided to the court or the other party.

Directions Relating to Part 44 – General Rules About Costs

SECTION 7 – SOLICITOR'S DUTY TO NOTIFY CLIENT: RULE 44.2

7.1 For the purposes of rule 44.2 'client' includes a party for whom a solicitor is acting and any other person (for example, an insurer, a trade union or the LSC) who has instructed the solicitor to act or who is liable to pay his fees.

7.2 Where a solicitor notifies a client of an order under that rule, he must also explain why the order came to be made.

7.3 Although rule 44.2 does not specify any sanction for breach of the rule the court may, either in the order for costs itself or in a subsequent order, require the solicitor to produce to the court evidence showing that he took reasonable steps to comply with the rule.

SECTION 8 – COURT'S DISCRETION AND CIRCUMSTANCES TO BE TAKEN INTO ACCOUNT WHEN EXERCISING ITS DISCRETION AS TO COSTS: RULE 44.3

8.1 Attention is drawn to the factors set out in this rule which may lead the court to depart from the general rule stated in rule 44.3(2) and to make a different order about costs.

8.2 In a probate claim where a defendant has in his defence given notice that he requires the will to be proved in solemn form (see paragraph 8.3 of the practice direction supplementing Part 57), the court will not make an order for costs against the defendant unless it appears that there was no reasonable ground for opposing the will. The term 'probate claim' is defined in rule 57.1(2).

8.3

(1) The court may make an order about costs at any stage in a case.

(2) In particular the court may make an order about costs when it deals with any application, makes any order or holds any hearing and that order about costs may relate to the costs of that application, order or hearing.

(3) Rule 44.3A(1) provides that the court will not assess any additional liability until the conclusion of the proceedings or the part of the proceedings to which the funding arrangement relates. (Paras 2.4 and 2.5 above explain when proceedings are concluded. As to the time when detailed assessment may be carried out see paragraphs 28.1, below.)

8.4 In deciding what order to make about costs the court is required to have regard to all the circumstances including any payment into court or admissible offer to settle made by a party which is drawn to the court's attention (whether or not it is made in accordance with Part 36). Where a claimant has made a Part 36 offer and fails to obtain a judgment which is more advantageous than that offer, that circumstance alone will not lead to a reduction in the costs awarded to the claimant under this rule.

8.5 There are certain costs orders which the court will commonly make in proceedings before trial. The following table sets out the general effect of these orders. The table is not an exhaustive list of the orders which the court may make.

Term	Effect
Costs Costs in any event	The party in whose favour the order is made is entitled to the costs in respect of the part of the proceedings to which the order relates, whatever other costs orders are made in the proceedings.
Costs in the case Costs in the application	The party in whose favour the court makes an order for costs at the end of the proceedings is entitled to his costs of the part of the proceedings to which the order relates.
Costs reserved	The decision about costs is deferred to a later occasion, but if no later order is made the costs will be costs in the case.
Claimant's/defendant's costs in the case/application	If the party in whose favour the costs order is made is awarded costs at the end of the proceedings, that party is entitled to his costs of the part of the proceedings to which the order relates. If any other party is awarded costs at the end of the proceedings, the party in whose favour the final costs order is made is not liable to pay the costs of any other party in respect of the part of the proceedings to which the order relates.
Costs thrown away	Where, for example, a judgment or order is set aside, the party in whose favour the costs order is made is entitled to the costs which have been incurred as a consequence. This includes the costs of – (a) preparing for and attending any hearing at which the judgment or order which has been set aside was made; (b) preparing for and attending any hearing to set aside the judgment or order in question; (c) preparing for and attending any hearing at which the court orders the proceedings or the part in question to be adjourned; (d) any steps taken to enforce a judgment or order which has subsequently been set aside.

Term	Effect
Costs of and caused by	Where, for example, the court makes this order on an application to amend a statement of case, the party in whose favour the costs order is made is entitled to the costs of preparing for and attending the application and the costs of any consequential amendment to his own statement of case.
Costs here and below	The party in whose favour the costs order is made is entitled not only to his costs in respect of the proceedings in which the court makes the order but also to his costs of the proceedings in any lower court. In the case of an appeal from a Divisional Court the party is not entitled to any costs incurred in any court below the Divisional Court.
No order as to costs Each party to pay his own costs	Each party is to bear his own costs of the part of the proceedings to which the order relates whatever costs order the court makes at the end of the proceedings.

8.6 Where, under rule 44.3(8), the court orders an amount to be paid before costs are assessed –

(1) the order will state that amount, and
(2) if no other date for payment is specified in the order rule 44.8 (Time for complying with an order for costs) will apply.

Fees of counsel

8.7

(1) This paragraph applies where the court orders the detailed assessment of the costs of a hearing at which one or more counsel appeared for a party.
(2) Where an order for costs states the opinion of the court as to whether or not the hearing was fit for the attendance of one or more counsel, a costs officer conducting a detailed assessment of costs to which that order relates will have regard to the opinion stated.
(3) The court will generally express an opinion only where –
   (a) the paying party asks it to do so;
   (b) more than one counsel appeared for the party or,
   (c) the court wishes to record its opinion that the case was not fit for the attendance of counsel.

Fees payable to conveyancing counsel appointed by the court to assist it

8.8

(1) Where the court refers any matter to the conveyancing counsel of the

court the fees payable to counsel in respect of the work done or to be done will be assessed by the court in accordance with rule 44.3.

(2) An appeal from a decision of the court in respect of the fees of such counsel will be dealt with under the general rules as to appeals set out in Part 52. If the appeal is against the decision of an authorised court officer, it will be dealt with in accordance with rules 47.20 to 47.23.

'Costs thrown away' (para 8.5 table)—This is of limited use bearing in mind the court's powers to summarily assess costs.

'No order as to costs' (para 8.5 table)—This is similar to an order which is silent as to costs. Note CPR r 44.13(1) – where an order is silent as to costs there is no entitlement to costs.

Part 36 offers—Where a claimant fails to beat his own Pt 36 offer at trial, practitioners should note para 8.4 which makes it clear that this will not in itself lead to a reduction in the amount of costs awarded to him.

'Where, under r 44.3(8) … will apply' (para 8.6)—'An order for costs on account' is an order for payment of those costs within 14 days unless the court orders otherwise (CPR r 44.8).

Certificates for counsel (para 8.7)—With limited exceptions the rules do not provide for certificates for counsel. The court should only be asked to express an opinion as to the appropriateness of attendance by counsel in the limited circumstances referred to in para 8.7(3).

Examples of exceptions where certificates for counsel are still required are –

(a) Sch 2, CCR Ord 27, r 9(1)(b) costs allowed to judgment creditor on application for attachment of earnings;

(b) Sch 2, CCR Ord 28, r 10(2)(ii) costs on judgment summons.

SECTION 9 – COSTS ORDERS RELATING TO FUNDING ARRANGEMENTS: RULE 44.3A

9.1 Under an order for payment of 'costs', the costs payable will include an additional liability incurred under a funding arrangement.

9.2

(1) If before the conclusion of the proceedings the court carries out a summary assessment of the base costs it may identify separately the amount allowed in respect of: solicitor's charges; counsels' fees; other disbursements; and any value added tax (VAT). Sections (13 and 14 of this practice direction deal with summary assessment.)

(2) If an order for the base costs of a previous application or hearing did not identify separately the amounts allowed for solicitor's charges, counsel's fees and other disbursements, a court which later makes an assessment of an additional liability may apportion the base costs previously ordered.

SECTION 10 – LIMITS ON RECOVERY UNDER FUNDING ARRANGEMENTS: RULE 44.3B

10.1 In a case to which rule 44.3(B)(1)(c) or (d) applies the party in default may apply for relief from the sanction. He should do so as quickly as possible after he becomes aware of the default. An application, supported by evidence, should be made under Part 23 to a costs judge or district judge of the court which is dealing with the case. (Attention is drawn to rules 3.8 and 3.9 which deal with sanctions and relief from sanctions).

10.2 Where the amount of any percentage increase recoverable by counsel may be affected by the outcome of the application, the solicitor issuing the application must serve on counsel a copy of the application notice and notice of the hearing as soon as practicable and in any event at least 2 days before the hearing. Counsel may make written submissions or may attend and make oral submissions at the hearing. (Paragraph 1.4 contains definitions of the terms 'counsel' and 'solicitor'.)

'In a case to which rule 44.3B(1)(c) or (d) applies'—Rule 44.3B(1)(c) of the CPR applies to any additional liability for any period in the proceedings during which a party has failed to provide information about a funding arrangement in accordance with a rule, practice direction or court order. See CPR r 44.15 and PDCosts, Section 19 about providing information concerning funding arrangements.

Rule 44.3B(1)(d) relates to a party who seeks a percentage increase but who fails to disclose in assessment proceedings the reason for setting the percentage increase at the level stated in the CFA (see Conditional Fee Agreements Regulations 2000, reg 3(2)(a); see also paras 32.5 and 40.14).

SECTION 11 – FACTORS TO BE TAKEN INTO ACCOUNT IN DECIDING THE AMOUNT OF COSTS: RULE 44.5

11.1 In applying the test of proportionality the court will have regard to rule 1.1(2)(c). The relationship between the total of the costs incurred and the financial value of the claim may not be a reliable guide. A fixed percentage cannot be applied in all cases to the value of the claim in order to ascertain whether or not the costs are proportionate.

11.2 In any proceedings there will be costs which will inevitably be incurred and which are necessary for the successful conduct of the case. Solicitors are not required to conduct litigation at rates which are uneconomic. Thus in a modest claim the proportion of costs is likely to be higher than in a large claim, and may even equal or possibly exceed the amount in dispute.

11.3 Where a trial takes place, the time taken by the court in dealing with a particular issue may not be an accurate guide to the amount of time properly spent by the legal or other representatives in preparation for the trial of that issue.

11.4 Where a party has entered into a funding arrangement the costs claimed may, subject to rule 44.3B include an additional liability.

11.5 In deciding whether the costs claimed are reasonable and (on a standard basis assessment) proportionate, the court will consider the amount of any additional liability separately from the base costs.

11.6 In deciding whether the base costs are reasonable and (if relevant) proportionate the court will consider the factors set out in rule 44.5.

11.7 Subject to paragraph 17.8(2), when the court is considering the factors to be taken into account in assessing an additional liability, it will have regard to the facts and circumstances as they reasonably appeared to the solicitor or counsel when the funding arrangement was entered into and at the time of any variation of the arrangement.

11.8

(1) In deciding whether a percentage increase is reasonable relevant factors to be taken into account may include –

- a) the risk that the circumstances in which the costs, fees or expenses would be payable might or might not occur;
- b) the legal representative's liability for any disbursements;
- c) what other methods of financing the costs were available to the receiving party.

(2) (*revoked*)

11.9 A percentage increase will not be reduced simply on the ground that, when added to base costs which are reasonable and (where relevant) proportionate, the total appears disproportionate.

11.10 In deciding whether the cost of insurance cover is reasonable, relevant factors to be taken into account include:

(1) where the insurance cover is not purchased in support of a conditional fee agreement with a success fee, how its cost compares with the likely cost of funding the case with a conditional fee agreement with a success fee and supporting insurance cover;
(2) the level and extent of the cover provided;
(3) the availability of any pre-existing insurance cover;
(4) whether any part of the premium would be rebated in the event of early settlement;
(5) the amount of commission payable to the receiving party or his legal representatives or other agents.

11.11 Where the court is considering a provision made by a membership organisation, rule 44.3B(1)(b) provides that any such provision which exceeds the likely cost to the receiving party of the premium of an insurance policy against the risk of incurring a liability to pay the costs of other parties to the proceedings is not recoverable. In such circumstances the court will, when assessing the additional liability, have regard to the factors set out in paragraph 11.10 above, in addition to the factors set out in rule 44.5.

Scope of provision—Paragraphs 11.1–11.3 are the only provisions within the Rules and Practice Directions that define the test of proportionality to be adopted by courts in relation to costs. The theory that total costs recoverable can in some way be linked strictly to the financial value of a claim is disproved. In any claim it is inevitable that solicitors incur certain base costs in relation to its preparation. For example interviewing witnesses, preparing the statement of case, marshalling documents, instructing counsel, etc. These base costs are likely to be proportionately higher the smaller the claim. The court must have regard to these base costs when arriving at any decision concerning the amount of costs of a case and what is proportionate. The practice direction makes it clear that linking costs to the time taken at trial to determine an issue will not be an accurate guide to the amount of time properly spent in preparing for that issue at trial. For an example of the court applying these principles in practice see *Jefferson v National Freight Carriers plc* [2001] EWCA Civ 2082, [2001] 2 Costs LR 313, CA.

Additional liability—Paragraph 11.5 makes it clear that the court will determine the base costs first and any additional liability separately and subsequently to the base costs. The court when considering the additional liability will not apply a hindsight test but will look at the circumstances as they reasonably appeared to the solicitor or counsel when the funding arrangement was entered into (para 11.7).

'other methods of financing the costs' (para 11.8(1)(c))—Paragraph 4.2(d) of the Conditional Fee Agreements Regulations 2000, SI 2000/692, requires a legal representative to inform his client whether other methods of financing his claim are available and if so how they apply to the proceedings in question. In addition, the Solicitors Costs Information and Client Care Code 1999, para 4(j) provides that solicitors must discuss with their clients how, when and by whom any costs are to be met. In particular, it is incumbent upon the practitioner to ascertain from his client whether the client's liability for costs is covered by pre-existing insurance, for example the client's own household policy or a before the event (BTE) policy. In addition to motor insurance policies, BTE insurance is also commonly available as part of household insurance, an employment package, as membership of a trade union, a credit or chargecard service or a stand-alone policy. The impact of BTE insurance was considered by the Court of Appeal in *Sarwar v Alam* [2001] EWCA Civ 1401, [2001] 4 All ER 541, CA, when Phillips MR set out the proper practice for a solicitor inquiring about BTE cover.

> 'In our judgment proper modern practice dictates that a solicitor should normally invite a client to bring to the first interview any relevant motor insurance policy, any household insurance policy and any standalone BTE insurance policy belonging to the client and/or any spouse or partner living in the same household as the client. It seems desirable for a solicitor to develop

> the practice of sending a standard form letter requesting a sight of these documents to the client in advance of the first interview. At the interview the solicitor will also ask the client as required by paragraph 4(j)(4) of the Client Care Code whether his/her liability for costs may be paid by another person, for example an employer or trade union.'

The solicitor's inquiries should be proportionate to the amount at stake. The solicitor is not obliged to embark on a treasure hunt. However where, before ATE insurance has been taken out and a CFA entered into, proper enquiries have not been made by a claimant's legal representative as to whether the claimant's liability for costs is covered by any pre-existing insurance, there is a material breach of the CFAR 2000, the CFA is unenforceable and, therefore, no costs are recoverable (*Samonini v London General Transport Services Limited* (2005) Lawtel, 2 February, Chief Master Hurst).

'insurance cover' (para 11.10)—This paragraph gives guidance to the court in the factors to be taken into account when considering whether an insurance premium in respect of an insurance policy which complies with AJA 1999, s 29 can be recovered from the paying party.

SECTION 12 – PROCEDURE FOR ASSESSING COSTS: RULE 44.7

12.1 Where the court does not order fixed costs (or no fixed costs are provided for) the amount of costs payable will be assessed by the court. This rule allows the court making an order about costs either –

- (a) to make a summary assessment of the amount of the costs, or
- (b) to order the amount to be decided in accordance with Part 47 (a detailed assessment).

12.2 An order for costs will be treated as an order for the amount of costs to be decided by a detailed assessment unless the order otherwise provides.

12.3 Whenever the court awards costs to be assessed by way of detailed assessment it should consider whether to exercise the power in rule 44.3(8) (Courts Discretion as to Costs) to order the paying party to pay such sum of money as it thinks just on account of those costs.

SECTION 13 – SUMMARY ASSESSMENT: GENERAL PROVISIONS

13.1 Whenever a court makes an order about costs which does not provide for fixed costs to be paid the court should consider whether to make a summary assessment of costs.

13.2 The general rule is that the court should make a summary assessment of the costs –

- (1) at the conclusion of the trial of a case which has been dealt with on the fast track, in which case the order will deal with the costs of the whole claim, and
- (2) at the conclusion of any other hearing, which has lasted not more than one day, in which case the order will deal with the costs of the application or matter to which the hearing related. If this hearing disposes of the claim, the order may deal with the costs of the whole claim;
- (3) in hearings in the Court of Appeal to which paragraph 14 of the practice direction supplementing Part 52 (Appeals) applies

unless there is good reason not to do so, eg where the paying party shows substantial grounds for disputing the sum claimed for costs that cannot be dealt with summarily or there is insufficient time to carry out a summary assessment.

13.3 The general rule in paragraph 13.2 does not apply to a mortgagee's costs incurred in mortgage possession proceedings or other proceedings relating to a mortgage unless the mortgagee asks the court to make an order for his costs to be paid by another party. Paragraphs 50.3 and 50.4 deal in more detail with costs relating to mortgages.

13.4 Where an application has been made and the parties to the application agree an order by consent without any party attending, the parties should agree a figure for costs to be inserted in the consent order or agree that there should be no order for costs. If the parties cannot agree the costs position, attendance on the appointment will be necessary but, unless good reason can be shown for the failure to deal with costs as set out above, no costs will be allowed for that attendance.

13.5

(1) It is the duty of the parties and their legal representatives to assist the judge in making a summary assessment of costs in any case to which paragraph 13.2 above applies, in accordance with the following paragraphs.

(2) Each party who intends to claim costs must prepare a written statement of the costs he intends to claim showing separately in the form of a schedule –

(a) the number of hours to be claimed,

(b) the hourly rate to be claimed,

(c) the grade of fee earner;

(d) the amount and nature of any disbursement to be claimed, other than counsel's fee for appearing at the hearing,

(e) the amount of solicitor's costs to be claimed for attending or appearing at the hearing,

(f) the fees of counsel to be claimed in respect of the hearing, and

(g) any value added tax (VAT) to be claimed on these amounts.

(3) The statement of costs should follow as closely as possible Form N260 and must be signed by the party or his legal representative. Where a litigant is an assisted person or is a LSC funded client or is represented by a solicitor in the litigant's employment the statement of costs need not include the certificate appended at the end of Form N260.

(4) The statement of costs must be filed at court and copies of it must be served on any party against whom an order for payment of those costs is intended to be sought. The statement of costs should be filed and the copies of it should be served as soon as possible and in any event not less than 24 hours before the date fixed for the hearing.

(5) Where the litigant is or may be entitled to claim an additional liability the statement filed and served need not reveal the amount of that liability.

13.6 The failure by a party, without reasonable excuse, to comply with the foregoing paragraphs will be taken into account by the court in deciding what order to make about the costs of the claim, hearing or application, and about the costs of any further hearing or detailed assessment hearing that may be necessary as a result of that failure.

13.7 If the court makes a summary assessment of costs at the conclusion of proceedings the court will specify separately –

(a) the base costs, and if appropriate, the additional liability allowed as solicitor's charges, counsel's fees, other disbursements and any VAT; and

(b) the amount which is awarded under Part 46 (Fast Track Trial Costs).

13.8 The court awarding costs cannot make an order for a summary assessment of costs by a costs officer. If a summary assessment of costs is appropriate but the court awarding costs is unable to do so on the day, the court must give directions as to a further hearing before the same judge.

13.9 The court will not make a summary assessment of the costs of a receiving party who is an assisted person or LSC funded client.

13.10 A summary assessment of costs payable by an assisted person or LSC funded client is not by itself a determination of that person's liability to pay those costs (as to which see rule 44.17 and paragraphs 21.1 to 23.17 of this practice direction).

13.11

(1) The court will not make a summary assessment of the costs of a receiving party who is a child or patient within the meaning of Part 21 unless the solicitor acting for the child or patient has waived the right to further costs (see paragraph 51.1 below).

(2) The court may make a summary assessment of costs payable by a child or patient.

13.12

(1) Attention is drawn to rule 44.3A(1) which prevents the court from making a summary assessment of an additional liability before the conclusion of the proceedings or the part of the proceedings to which the funding arrangement relates. Where this applies, the court should nonetheless make a summary assessment of the base costs of the hearing or application unless there is a good reason not to do so.

(2) Where the court makes a summary assessment of the base costs all statements of costs and costs estimates put before the judge must be retained on the court file.

13.13 The court will not give its approval to disproportionate and unreasonable costs. Accordingly –

(a) When the amount of the costs to be paid has been agreed between the parties the order for costs must state that the order is by consent.

(b) If the judge is to make an order which is not by consent, the judge will, so far as possible, ensure that the final figure is not disproportionate and/or unreasonable having regard to Part 1 of the CPR. The judge will retain this responsibility notwithstanding the absence of challenge to individual items in the make-up of the figure sought. The fact that the paying party is not disputing the amount of costs can however be taken as some indication that the amount is proportionate and reasonable. The judge will therefore intervene only if satisfied that the costs are so disproportionate that it is right to do so.

Summary assessment—See Guide 33 set out in Section 1 of this work.

If there is a genuine argument between the parties on a summary assessment of costs about whether the indemnity principle has been breached the proper course is for the judge to order detailed assessment (see *R v Cardiff City Council ex parte Brown* (1999) (unreported) 11 June where Harrison J referred costs to detailed assessment when the paying party took a point under the indemnity principle as to the hourly rate which could properly be charged by the respondent's in-house legal department).

Summary assessment is to be carried out by the judge who hears the trial or application. He cannot adjourn it to a district judge or a costs judge (see (para 13.8).

'statement of the costs' (para 13.5(2))—The statement of costs must be signed with the appropriate certificate (see Form N260) by the party or his legal representative (defined in CPR r 2.3) unless the party is an LSC funded client or represented by a solicitor in the litigant's employment (para 13. 5(3)). The purpose of the certificate is to establish that the indemnity principle has not been breached. Failure by a party in appropriate circumstances to prepare for summary assessment of costs may be taken into account by a court in deciding entitlement to a costs order, the amount of the costs of any further hearing by way of detailed assessment or otherwise resulting from that failure. It is likely that any such costs order will be on an indemnity basis. Summary assessment of costs in interim applications not lasting more than one day are the norm and not the exception. Where the application disposes of the claim the court may summarily assess the costs of the whole claim. Parties must prepare accordingly. However, a party's failure to serve a schedule of costs 24 hours prior to the hearing does not justify the refusal of an application for summary assessment of that party's costs in the absence of aggravating factors (*Macdonald v Taree Holdings Ltd* [2001] CPLR 439, [2001] 1 Costs LR 147, ChD, Neuberger J). See also *Re Michaelides* (2005) 2 Costs LR 191 where the court reviewed the process of how summary assessment should be carried out by the judge hearing the case.

'disbursements and any VAT' (para 13.7)—Where the fees of experts have been claimed it is good practice to produce a breakdown of fees being claimed to the court with the statement of costs, if practicable. Where there is doubt about the receiving party's entitlement to VAT the court may be prepared to take this into account and make a conditional order requiring the receiving party to file a certificate concerning the recoverability of VAT by a specific date but the safer and correct practice is to have the information available at the hearing.

Amount of costs on summary assessment—Practitioners are referred to the *Guide to the Summary Assessment of Costs* (2005 edition) which is intended to assist both the judiciary and litigants in relation to the summary assessment of costs. The Guide contains guideline hourly rates for solicitors based on four categories of fee earner. From 1 January 2005, new rates have been promulgated replacing the figures set out at pages 63–67 of the Guide (2002 edition). There are now four bands throughout the country instead of each local area setting an individual rate. Appendix 2 of the Guide, showing the new guideline rates, is set out following this practice direction. However, costs and fees exceeding the guideline rates may well be justified in appropriate cases. In *Higgs v Camden and Islington Health Authority* (2003) Costs LR 211, a complex high-value clinical negligence claim involving an unusually intensive level of input from solicitors and counsel, hourly rates much higher than the guideline rates were approved. Practitioners should ascertain whether any local arrangements or guidelines apply to the court where their case or application is proceeding.

Costs summarily assessed are, unless the court orders otherwise, to be paid within 14 days (CPR r 44.8).

Additional liability—Rule 44.3A of the CPR prevents the court from making a summary assessment of an additional liability before the conclusion of the proceedings or the part of the proceedings to which the funding arrangement relates. The court may nonetheless make a summary assessment of the base costs, unless there is good reason not to do so (para 13.12).

Appeal—There is no specific appeal process against summary assessment. Appeals follow the procedure in CPR Pt 52 and PD52 (see *Hosking v Michaelides & anor* (2003) Lawtel, 28 November, Blackburne J).

SECTION 14 – SUMMARY ASSESSMENT WHERE COSTS CLAIMED INCLUDE AN ADDITIONAL LIABILITY

Orders made before the conclusion of the proceedings

14.1 The existence of a conditional fee agreement or other funding arrangement within the meaning of rule 43.2 is not by itself a sufficient reason for not carrying out a summary assessment.

14.2 Where a legal representative acting for the receiving party has entered into a conditional fee agreement the court may summarily assess all the costs (other than any additional liability).

14.3 Where costs have been summarily assessed an order for payment will not be made unless the court has been satisfied that in respect of the costs claimed, the receiving party is at the time liable to pay to his legal representative an amount equal to or greater than the costs claimed. A statement in the form of the certificate appended at the end of Form N260 may be sufficient proof of liability. The giving of information under rule 44.15 (where that rule applies) is not sufficient.

14.4 The court may direct that any costs, for which the receiving party may not in the event be liable, shall be paid into court to await the outcome of the case, or shall not be enforceable until further order, or it may postpone the receiving party's right to receive payment in some other way.

Scope of provision—Where a 'funding arrangement' as defined in CPR r 43.2 is in place, summary assessment can take place of base costs only prior to the conclusion of proceedings. It is important that the CFA provides that the receiving party is at the time of the summary assessment liable to pay to his legal representative an amount of at least equal to or greater than the costs that are being claimed, otherwise the indemnity principle will be breached. Consequently practitioners should ensure that a CFA entered into by them with their client entitles them to the payment of their base costs and disbursements at the interim hearing stage of proceedings. The CFA must also provide for a success fee on the base costs allowed at an interim hearing if the case is successful overall. The court will normally be satisfied that the indemnity principle is not breached if the certificate at the end of Form N260 has been completed and signed (para 14.3). Although the court may summarily assess base costs if a funding arrangement is in place it may postpone the payment of those costs until the conclusion of proceedings (para 14.4).

Orders made at the conclusion of the proceedings

14.5 Where there has been a split trial, (ie the trial of one or more issues separately from other issues), the court will not normally order detailed assessment of the additional liability until all issues have been tried unless the parties agree.

14.6 Rule 44.3A(1)(2) sets out the ways in which the court may deal with the assessment of the costs where there is a funding arrangement. Where the court orders detailed assessment of an additional liability but makes a summary assessment of the base costs –

(1) The order will state separately the base costs allowed as solicitor's charges, counsel's fees, any other disbursements and any VAT.
(2) the statements of costs upon which the judge based his summary assessment must be retained on the court file.

14.7 Where the court makes a summary assessment of an additional liability at the conclusion of proceedings, that assessment must relate to the whole of the proceedings; this will include any additional liability relating to base costs allowed by the court when making a summary assessment on a previous application or hearing.

14.8 Paragraph 13.13 applies where the parties are agreed about the total amount to be paid by way of costs, or are agreed about the amount of the base costs that will be paid. Where they disagree about the additional liability the court may summarily assess that liability or make an order for a detailed assessment.

14.9 In order to facilitate the court in making a summary assessment of any additional liability at the conclusion of the proceedings the party seeking such costs must prepare and have available for the court a bundle of documents which must include –

(1) a copy of every notice of funding arrangement (Form N251) which has been filed by him;
(2) a copy of every estimate and statement of costs filed by him;

(3) a copy of the risk assessment prepared at the time any relevant funding arrangement was entered into and on the basis of which the amount of the additional liability was fixed.

Scope of provision—An 'additional liability' may be summarily assessed at the conclusion of proceedings. This is likely to occur in fast track cases where at the conclusion of the trial the court will summarily assess the entire costs of the action. This may not always be practical or appropriate and in these cases the court may assess the base costs summarily at the conclusion of the action and adjourn the assessment of additional liability for detailed assessment (para 14.8).

SECTION 15 – COSTS ON THE SMALL CLAIMS TRACK AND FAST TRACK: RULE 44.9

15.1

(1) Before a claim is allocated to one of those tracks the court is not restricted by any of the special rules that apply to that track.

(2) Where a claim has been allocated to one of those tracks, the special rules which relate to that track will apply to work done before as well as after allocation save to the extent (if any) that an order for costs in respect of that work was made before allocation.

(3) (i) This paragraph applies where a claim, issued for a sum in excess of the normal financial scope of the small claims track, is allocated to that track only because an admission of part of the claim by the defendant reduces the amount in dispute to a sum within the normal scope of that track.

(See also paragraph 7.4 of the practice direction supplementing CPR Part 26)

(ii) On entering judgment for the admitted part before allocation of the balance of the claim the court may allow costs in respect of the proceedings down to that date.

SECTION 16 – COSTS FOLLOWING ALLOCATION AND RE-ALLOCATION: RULE 44.11

16.1 This paragraph applies where the court is about to make an order to re-allocate a claim from the small claims track to another track.

16.2 Before making the order to re-allocate the claim, the court must decide whether any party is to pay costs to any other party down to the date of the order to re-allocate in accordance with the rules about costs contained in Part 27 (The Small Claims Track).

16.3 If it decides to make such an order about costs, the court will make a summary assessment of those costs in accordance with that Part.

SECTION 17 – COSTS-ONLY PROCEEDINGS: RULE 44.12A

17.1 A claim form under this rule should not be issued in the High Court unless the dispute to which the agreement relates was of such a value or type that had proceedings been begun they would have been commenced in the High Court.

17.2 A claim form which is to be issued in the High Court at the Royal Courts of Justice will be issued in the Supreme Court Costs Office.

17.3 Attention is drawn to rule 8.2 (in particular to paragraph (b)(ii)) and to rule 44.12A(3). The claim form must –

(1) identify the claim or dispute to which the agreement to pay costs relates;
(2) state the date and terms of the agreement on which the claimant relies;
(3) set out or have attached to it a draft of the order which the claimant seeks;
(4) state the amount of the costs claimed; and,
(5) state whether the costs are claimed on the standard or indemnity basis. If no basis is specified the costs will be treated as being on the standard basis.

17.4 The evidence to be filed and served with the claim form under Rule 8.5 must include copies of the documents on which the claimant relies to prove the defendant's agreement to pay costs.

17.5 A costs judge or a district judge has jurisdiction to hear and decide any issue which may arise in a claim issued under this rule irrespective of the amount of the costs claimed or of the value of the claim to which the agreement to pay costs relates. A costs officer may make an order by consent under paragraph 17.7, or an order dismissing a claim under paragraph 17.9 below.

17.6 When the time for filing the defendant's acknowledgment of service has expired, the claimant may by letter request the court to make an order in the terms of his claim, unless the defendant has filed an acknowledgment of service stating that he intends to contest the claim or to seek a different order.

17.7 Rule 40.6 applies where an order is to be made by consent. An order may be made by consent in terms which differ from those set out in the claim form.

17.8

(1) An order for costs made under this rule will be treated as an order for the amount of costs to be decided by a detailed assessment to which Part 47 and the practice directions relating to it apply. Rule 44.4(4) (determination of basis of assessment) also applies to the order.
(2) In cases in which an additional liability is claimed, the costs judge or district judge should have regard to the time when and the extent to which the claim has been settled and to the fact that the claim has been settled without the need to commence proceedings.

17.9(1) For the purposes of rule 44.12A(4)(b) –
(a) a claim will be treated as opposed if the defendant files an acknowledgment of service stating that he intends to contest the making of an order for costs or to seek a different remedy; and
(b) a claim will not be treated as opposed if the defendant files an acknowledgment of service stating that he disputes the amount of the claim for costs.

(2) An order dismissing the claim will be made as soon as an acknowledgment of service opposing the claim is filed. The dismissal of a claim under rule 44.12A(4) does not prevent the claimant from issuing another claim form under Part 7 or Part 8 based on the agreement or alleged agreement to which the proceedings under this rule related.

17.10

(1) Rule 8.9 (which provides that claims issued under Part 8 shall be treated as allocated to the multi-track) shall not apply to claims issued under this rule. A claim issued under this rule may be dealt with without being allocated to a track.

(2) Rule 8.1(3) and Part 24 do not apply to proceedings brought under rule 44.12(A).

17.11 Nothing in this rule prevents a person from issuing a claim form under Part 7 or Part 8 to sue on an agreement made in settlement of a dispute where that agreement makes provision for costs, nor from claiming in that case an order for costs or a specified sum in respect of costs.

Scope of provision—See Guide 34 and the notes to CPR r 44.12A. This procedure is only available where the parties to a dispute have agreed all issues including which party is to pay the costs. If an acknowledgment of service is lodged opposing the claim, the proceedings must be dismissed (para 17.9) and it will be necessary for the receiving party to sue on the claim or any agreement made (para 17.11). The order, if made, is simply an order that the defendant pay the claimant's costs, to be determined by detailed assessment so that the normal procedure under CPR Pt 47 will then follow.

SECTION 18 – COURT'S POWERS IN RELATION TO MISCONDUCT: RULE 44.14

18.1 Before making an order under rule 44.14 the court must give the party or legal representative in question a reasonable opportunity to attend a hearing to give reasons why it should not make such an order.

18.2 Conduct before or during the proceedings which gave rise to the assessment which is unreasonable or improper includes steps which are calculated to prevent or inhibit the court from furthering the overriding objective.

18.3 Although rule 44.14(3) does not specify any sanction for breach of the obligation imposed by the rule the court may, either in the order under paragraph (2) or in a subsequent order, require the solicitor to produce to the court evidence that he took reasonable steps to comply with the obligation.

SECTION 19 – PROVIDING INFORMATION ABOUT FUNDING ARRANGEMENTS: RULE 44.15

19.1

(1) A party who wishes to claim an additional liability in respect of a funding arrangement must give any other party information about that claim if he is to recover the additional liability. There is no requirement to specify the amount of the additional liability separately nor to state how it is calculated until it falls to be assessed. That principle is reflected in rules 44.3A(1) and rule 44.15, in the following paragraphs and in Sections 6, 13, 14 and 31 of this Practice Direction. Section 6 deals with estimates of costs, Sections 13 and 14 deal with summary assessment and Section 31 deals with detailed assessment.

(2) In the following paragraphs a party who has entered into a funding arrangement is treated as a person who intends to recover a sum representing an additional liability by way of costs.

(3) Attention is drawn to paragraph 57.9 of this Practice Direction which sets out time limits for the provision of information where a funding arrangement is entered into between 31 March and 2 July 2000 and proceedings relevant to that arrangement are commenced before 3 July 2000.

Method of giving information

19.2

(1) In this paragraph, 'claim form' includes petition and application notice, and the notice of funding to be filed or served is a notice containing the information set out in Form N251.

(2) (a) A claimant who has entered into a funding arrangement before starting the proceedings to which it relates must provide information to the court by filing the notice when he issues the claim form.

(b) He must provide information to every other party by serving the notice. If he serves the claim form himself he must serve the notice with the claim form. If the court is to serve the claim form, the court will also serve the notice if the claimant provides it with sufficient copies for service.

(3) A defendant who has entered into a funding arrangement before filing any document

(a) must provide information to the court by filing notice with his first document. A 'first document' may be an acknowledgment of service, a defence, or any other document, such as an application to set aside a default judgment.

(b) must provide information to every party by serving notice. If he serves his first document himself he must serve the notice with that document. If the court is to serve his first document the court will also serve the notice if the defendant provides it with sufficient copies for service.

(4) In all other circumstances a party must file and serve notice within 7 days of entering into the funding arrangement concerned.

(5) There is no requirement in this Practice Direction for the provision of information about funding arrangements before the commencement of proceedings. Such provision is however recommended and may be required by a pre-action protocol.

Notice of change of information

19.3

(1) Rule 44.15 imposes a duty on a party to give notice of change if the information he has previously provided is no longer accurate. To comply he must file and serve notice containing the information set out in Form N251. Rule 44.15(3) may impose other duties in relation to new estimates of costs.

(2) Further notification need not be provided where a party has already given notice:

(a) that he has entered into a conditional fee agreement with a legal representative and during the currency of that agreement either of them enters into another such agreement with an additional legal representative; or

(b) of some insurance cover, unless that cover is cancelled or unless new cover is taken out with a different insurer.

(3) Part 6 applies to the service of notices.

(4) The notice must be signed by the party or by his legal representative.

Information which must be provided

19.4

(1) Unless the court otherwise orders, a party who is required to supply information about a funding arrangement must state whether he has –

entered into a conditional fee agreement which provides for a success fee within the meaning of section 58(2) of the Courts and Legal Services Act 1990;
taken out an insurance policy to which section 29 of the Access to Justice Act 1999 applies;
made an arrangement with a body which is prescribed for the purpose of section 30 of that Act;
or more than one of these.

(2) Where the funding arrangement is a conditional fee agreement, the party must state the date of the agreement and identify the claim or claims to which it relates (including Part 20 claims if any).

(3) Where the funding arrangement is an insurance policy, the party must state the name and address of the insurer, the policy number and the date of the policy, and must identify the claim or claims to which it relates (including Part 20 claims if any).

(4) Where the funding arrangement is by way of an arrangement with a relevant body the party must state the name of the body and set out the date and terms of the undertaking it has given and must identify the claim or claims to which it relates (including Part 20 claims if any).

(5) Where a party has entered into more than one funding arrangement in respect of a claim, for example a conditional fee agreement and an insurance policy, a single notice containing the information set out in Form N251 may contain the required information about both or all of them.

19.5 Where the court makes a Group Litigation Order, the court may give directions as to the extent to which individual parties should provide information in accordance with rule 44.15. (Part 19 deals with Group Litigation Orders.)

Scope of provision—Where a funding arrangement (defined in CPR r 43.2) is entered into before proceedings are commenced, PDProt, para 4A.1, provides that the person entering into the funding arrangement should inform other potential parties to the claim that he has done so. No time limit is specified. Paragraph 4A.2 of PDProt makes it clear that this provision applies to all proceedings. There is no requirement to specify in the notice the amount of the additional liability or to state how it is calculated until it falls to be assessed (para 19.1(1)).

Forms—Form N251

SECTION 20 – PROCEDURE WHERE LEGAL REPRESENTATIVE WISHES TO RECOVER FROM HIS CLIENT AN AGREED PERCENTAGE INCREASE WHICH HAS BEEN DISALLOWED OR REDUCED ON ASSESSMENT: RULE 44.16

20.1(1) Attention is drawn to regulation 3(2)(b) of the Conditional Fee Agreements Regulations 2000 and to regulation 5(2)(b) of the Collective Conditional Fee Agreements Regulations 2000, which provide that some or all of a success fee ceases to be payable in certain circumstances.

(2) Rule 44.16 allows the court to adjourn a hearing at which the legal representative acting for the receiving party applies for an order that a disallowed amount should continue to be payable under the agreement.

20.2 In the following paragraphs 'counsel' means counsel who has acted in the case under a conditional fee agreement which provides for a success fee. A reference to counsel includes a reference to any person who appeared as an advocate in the case and who is not a partner or employee of the solicitor or firm which is conducting the claim or defence (as the case may be) on behalf of the receiving party.

Procedure following Summary Assessment

20.3

(1) If the court disallows any amount of a legal representative's percentage increase, the court will, unless sub-paragraph (2) applies, give directions to enable an application to be made by the legal representative for the disallowed amount to be payable by his client, including, if appropriate, a direction that the application will be determined by a costs judge or district judge of the court dealing with the case.

(2) The court that has made the summary assessment may then and there decide the issue whether the disallowed amount should continue to be payable, if:

  (a) the receiving party and all parties to the relevant agreement consent to the court doing so;

  (b) the receiving party (or, if corporate, an officer) is present in court; and

  (c) the court is satisfied that the issue can be fairly decided then and there.

Procedure following Detailed Assessment

20.4

(1) Where detailed assessment proceedings have been commenced, and the paying party serves points of dispute (as to which see Section 34 of this Practice Direction), which show that he is seeking a reduction in any percentage increase charged by counsel on his fees, the solicitor acting for the receiving party must within 3 days of service deliver to counsel a copy of the relevant points of dispute and the bill of costs or the relevant parts of the bill.

(2) Counsel must within 10 days thereafter inform the solicitor in writing whether or not he will accept the reduction sought or some other reduction. Counsel may state any points he wishes to have made in a reply to the points of dispute, and the solicitor must serve them on the paying party as or as part of a reply.

(3) Counsel who fails to inform the solicitor within the time limits set out above will be taken to accept the reduction unless the court otherwise orders.

20.5 Where the paying party serves points of dispute seeking a reduction in any percentage increase charged by a legal representative acting for the receiving party, and that legal representative intends, if necessary, to apply for an order that any amount of the percentage disallowed as against the paying party shall continue to be payable by his client, the solicitor acting for the receiving party must, within 14 days of service of the points of dispute, give to his client a clear written explanation of the nature of the relevant point of dispute and the effect it will have if it is upheld in whole or in part by the court, and of the client's right to attend any subsequent hearings at court when the matter is raised.

20.6 Where the solicitor acting for a receiving party files a request for a detailed assessment hearing it must if appropriate, be accompanied by a certificate signed by him stating:

(1) that the amount of the percentage increase in respect of counsel's fees or solicitor's charges is disputed;
(2) whether an application will be made for an order that any amount of that increase which is disallowed should continue to be payable by his client;
(3) that he has given his client an explanation in accordance with paragraph 20.5; and,
(4) whether his client wishes to attend court when the amount of any relevant percentage increase may be decided.

20.7

(1) The solicitor acting for the receiving party must within 7 days of receiving from the court notice of the date of the assessment hearing, notify his client, and if appropriate, counsel in writing of the date, time and place of the hearing.
(2) Counsel may attend or be represented at the detailed assessment hearing and may make oral or written submissions.

20.8

(1) At the detailed assessment hearing, the court will deal with the assessment of the costs payable by one party to another, including the amount of the percentage increase, and give a certificate accordingly.
(2) The court may decide the issue whether the disallowed amount should continue to be payable under the relevant conditional fee agreement without an adjournment if:
    (a) the receiving party and all parties to the relevant agreement consent to the court deciding the issue without an adjournment,
    (b) the receiving party (or, if corporate, an officer or employee who has authority to consent on behalf of the receiving party) is present in court, and
    (c) the court is satisfied that the issue can be fairly decided without an adjournment.
(3) In any other case the court will give directions and fix a date for the hearing of the application.

Scope of provision—Where a percentage increase is disallowed on assessment the CFA to which it relates is retrospectively amended. The balance of the percentage increase cannot be recovered by the legal representative from his client unless the court is satisfied that it should continue to be so payable. This applies even where a legal representative agrees a lower percentage increase than is specified in the CFA, for example where a claim is compromised prior to the issue of proceedings (Conditional Fee Agreements Regulations 2000, reg 3(2)(b) and (c)). Section 20 provides a complex procedure to enable a legal representative to recover the balance of the percentage increase which has been disallowed by the court, or not agreed by the paying party, directly from his client. Generally speaking the court will first of all deal with an inter partes detailed assessment of the additional liability. Where any element of the percentage increase is disallowed and the legal representative wishes to recover it from his client the court will then adjourn the proceedings to another date. In certain specified circumstances the court will deal with the matter without an adjournment (para 20.8(2)). This provision will also apply in respect of collective conditional fee agreements made pursuant to the Collective Conditional Fee Agreements Regulations 2000.

SECTION 21 – APPLICATION OF COSTS RULES: RULE 44.17

21.1 Rule 44.17(b) excludes the costs rules to the extent that regulations under the Legal Aid Act 1988 make different provision. The primary examples of such regulations are the regulations providing prescribed rates (with or without enhancement).

21.2 Rule 44.17(a) also excludes the procedure for the detailed assessment of costs in cases to which Section 11 of the Access to Justice Act 1999 applies, whether it applies in whole or in part. In these excluded cases the procedure for determination of costs is set out in Section 22 of this practice direction.

21.3 Section 11 of the Access to Justice Act 1999 provides special protection against liability for costs for litigants who receive funding by the LSC (Legal Services Commission) as part of the Community Legal Service. Any costs ordered to be paid by a LSC funded client must not exceed the amount which is reasonable to pay having regard to all the circumstances including –

(a) the financial resources of all the parties to the proceedings, and
(b) their conduct in connection with the dispute to which the proceedings relate.

21.4 In this Practice Direction

'cost protection' means the limit on costs awarded against a LSC funded client set out in Section 11(1) of the Access to Justice Act 1999.

'partner' has the meaning given by the Community Legal Service (Costs) Regulations 2000.

21.5 Whether or not cost protection applies depends upon the 'level of service' for which funding was provided by the LSC in accordance with the Funding Code approved under section 9 of the Access to Justice Act 1999. The levels of service referred to are:

(1) Legal Help – advice and assistance about a legal problem, not including representation or advocacy in proceedings.
(2) Help at Court – advocacy at a specific hearing, where the advocate is not formally representing the client in the proceedings.
(3) Family Mediation.
(4) Legal Representation – representation in actual or contemplated proceedings. Legal Representation can take the form of Investigative Help (limited to investigating the merits of a potential claim) or Full Representation.
(5) Approved Family Help – this can take the form of Help with Mediation (legal advice in support of the family mediation process) or General Family Help (help negotiating a settlement to a family dispute without recourse to adversarial litigation).
(6) Support Funding – partial funding in expensive cases that are primarily being funded privately, under or with a view to a conditional fee agreement. Support Funding can take the form of Investigative Support (equivalent to *Investigative Help*) or Litigation Support (equivalent to *Full Representation*).

21.6 Levels of service (4) (5) and (6) are provided under a certificate (similar to a legal aid certificate). The certificate will state which level of service is covered. Where there are proceedings, a copy of the certificate will be lodged with the court.

21.7 Cost protection does not apply where –

(1) the LSC funded client receives Help at Court;

(2) the LSC funded client receives Litigation Support (but see further, paragraph 21.8);

(3) the LSC funded client receives Investigative Support (except where the proceedings for which Investigative Support was given are not pursued after the certificate is discharged). Investigative Support will not normally cover the issue of proceedings (except for disclosure), but cost protection may be relevant if the defendant seeks an assessment of pre-action costs;

(4) the LSC funded client receives Legal Help only, ie where the solicitor is advising, but not representing a litigant in person. However, where the LSC funded client receives Legal Help, eg to write a letter before action, but later receives Legal Representation or Approved Family Help in respect of the same dispute, cost protection does apply to all costs incurred by the receiving party in the funded proceedings or prospective proceedings.

21.8 Where cost protection does not apply, the court may award costs in the normal way. In the case of Litigation Support, costs that are not covered by the LSC funded client's insurance are usually payable by the LSC rather than the funded client, and the court should order accordingly (see Regulation 6 of the Community Legal Service (Cost Protection) Regulations 2000).

21.9 Where work is done before the issue of a certificate, cost protection does not apply to those costs, except where –

(1) pre-action Legal Help is given and the LSC funded client subsequently receives Legal Representation or Approved Family Help in the same dispute; or

(2) where urgent work is undertaken immediately before the grant of an emergency certificate when no emergency application could be made as the LSC's offices were closed, provided that the solicitor seeks an emergency certificate at the first available opportunity and the certificate is granted.

21.10 If a LSC funded client's certificate is revoked, cost protection does not apply to work done before or after revocation.

21.11 If a LSC funded client's certificate is discharged, cost protection only applies to costs incurred before the date on which funded services ceased to be provided under the certificate. This may be a date before the date on which the certificate is formally discharged by the LSC (*Burridge v Stafford: Khan v Ali* [2000] 1 WLR 927, [1999] 4 All ER 660, CA).

Assessing a LSC Funded Client's Resources

21.12 The first £100,000 of the value of the LSC funded client's interest in the main or only home is disregarded when assessing his or her financial resources for the purposes of S.11 and cannot be the subject of any enforcement process by the receiving party. The receiving party cannot apply for an order to sell the LSC funded client's home, but could secure the debt against any value exceeding £100,000 by way of a charging order.

21.13 The court may only take into account the value of the LSC funded client's clothes, household furniture, tools and implements of trade to the extent that it considers that having regard to the quantity or value of the items, the circumstances are exceptional.

21.14 The LSC funded client's resources include the resources of his or her partner, unless the partner has a contrary interest in the dispute in respect of which funded services are provided.

Party acting in a Representative, Fiduciary or Official Capacity

21.15

(1) Where a LSC funded client is acting in a representative, fiduciary or official capacity, the court shall not take the personal resources of the party into account for the purposes of either a Section 11 order or costs against the Commission, but shall have regard to the value of any property or estate or the amount of any fund out of which the party is entitled to be indemnified, and may also have regard to the resources of any persons who are beneficially interested in the property, estate or fund.

(2) Similarly, where a party is acting as a litigation friend to a client who is a child or a patient, the court shall not take the personal resources of the litigation friend into account in assessing the resources of the client.

(3) The purpose of this provision is to ensure that any liability is determined with reference to the value of the property or fund being used to pay for the litigation, and the financial position of those who may benefit from or rely on it.

Costs against the LSC

21.16 Regulation 5 of the Community Legal Service (Cost Protection) Regulations 2000 governs when costs can be awarded against the LSC. This provision only applies where cost protection applies and the costs ordered to be paid by the LSC funded client do not fully meet the costs that would have been ordered to be paid by him or her if cost protection did not apply.

21.17 In this section and the following two sections of this practice direction 'non-funded party' means a party to proceedings who has not received LSC funded services in relation to these proceedings under a legal aid certificate or a certificate issued under the LSC Funding Code other than a certificate which has been revoked.

21.18 The following criteria set out in Regulation 5 must be satisfied before the LSC can be ordered to pay the whole or any part of the costs incurred by a non-funded party –

(1) the proceedings are finally decided in favour of a non-funded party;

(2) unless there is good reason for delay (and the application for funded services was made on or after 3 December 2001) the non-funded party provides written notice of intention to seek an order against the LSC within 3 months of the making of the Section 11(1) costs order;

(3) the court is satisfied that it is just and equitable in the circumstances that provision for the costs should be made out of public funds; and

(4) where costs are incurred in a court of first instance, the following additional criteria must also be met –

(i) the proceedings were instituted by the LSC funded client;
(ii) the non-funded party is an individual; and
(iii) the non-funded party will suffer severe financial hardship unless the order is made.

('Section 11(1) costs order' is defined in paragraph 22.1, below)

21.19 In determining whether conditions (3) and (4) are satisfied, the court shall take into account the resources of the non-funded party and his partner (unless the partner has a contrary interest).

Effect of Appeals

21.20

(1) An order for costs can only be made against the LSC when the proceedings (including any appeal) are finally decided. Therefore, where a court of first instance decides in favour of a non-funded party and an appeal lies, any order made against the LSC shall not take effect until –
(a) where permission to appeal is required, the time limit for permission to appeal expires, without permission being granted;
(b) where permission to appeal is granted or is not required, the time limit for appeal expires without an appeal being brought.
(2) This means that, if the LSC funded client appeals, any earlier order against the LSC can never take effect. If the appeal is unsuccessful, the court can make a fresh order.

Scope of provision—See Guidance Notes issued by the Senior Costs Judge dated 4 October 2001.

SECTION 22 – ORDERS FOR COSTS TO WHICH SECTION 11 OF THE ACCESS TO JUSTICE ACT 1999 APPLIES

22.1 In this Practice Direction:

'order for costs to be determined' means an order for costs to which Section 11 of the Access to Justice Act 1999 applies under which the amount of costs payable by the LSC funded client is to be determined by a costs judge or district judge under Section 23 of this Practice Direction.

'order specifying the costs payable' means an order for costs to which Section 11 of the Act applies and which specifies the amount which the LSC funded client is to pay.

'full costs' means, where an order to which Section 11 of the Act applies is made against a LSC funded client, the amount of costs which that person would, had cost protection not applied, have been ordered to pay.

'determination proceedings' means proceedings to which paragraphs 22.1 to 22.10 apply.

'Section 11(1) costs order' means an order for costs to be determined or an order specifying the costs payable other than an order specifying the costs payable which was made in determination proceedings.

'statement of resources' means

(1) a statement, verified by a statement of truth, made by a party to proceedings setting out:
(a) his income and capital and financial commitments during the previous year and, if applicable, those of his partner;

(b) his estimated future financial resources and expectations and, if applicable, those of his partner ('partner' is defined in paragraph 21.4, above);

(c) a declaration that he and, if applicable, his partner, has not deliberately foregone or deprived himself of any resources or expectations;

(d) particulars of any application for funding made by him in connection with the proceedings; and,

(e) any other facts relevant to the determination of his resources; or

(2) a statement, verified by a statement of truth, made by a client receiving funded services, setting out the information provided by the client under Regulation 6 of the Community Legal Service (Financial) Regulations 2000, and stating that there has been no significant change in the client's financial circumstances since the date on which the information was provided or, as the case may be, details of any such change.

'Regional Director' means any Regional Director appointed by the LSC and any member of his staff authorised to act on his behalf.

22.2 Regulations 8 to 13 of the Community Legal Service (Costs) Regulations 2000 as amended set out the procedure for seeking costs against a funded client and the LSC. The effect of these Regulations is set out in this section and the next section of this Practice Direction.

22.3 As from 5 June 2000, Regulations 9 to13 of the Community Legal Service (Costs) Regulations 2000 as amended also apply to certificates issued under the Legal Aid Act 1988 where costs against the assisted person fall to be assessed under Regulation 124 of the Civil Legal Aid (General) Regulations 1989. In this section and the next section of this Practice Direction the expression 'LSC funded client' includes an assisted person (defined in rule 43.2).

22.4 Regulation 8 of the Community Legal Service (Costs) Regulations 2000 as amended provides that a party intending to seek an order for costs against a LSC funded client may at any time file and serve on the LSC funded client a statement of resources. If that statement is served 7 or more days before a date fixed for a hearing at which an order for costs may be made, the LSC funded client must also make a statement of resources and produce it at the hearing.

22.5 If the court decides to make an order for costs against a LSC funded client to whom cost protection applies it may either:

(1) make an order for costs to be determined, or
(2) make an order specifying the costs payable.

22.6 If the court makes an order for costs to be determined it may also

(1) state the amount of full costs, or
(2) make findings of facts, eg, concerning the conduct of all the parties which are to be taken into account by the court in the subsequent determination proceedings.

22.7 The court will not make order specifying the costs payable unless:

(1) it considers that it has sufficient information before it to decide what amount is a reasonable amount for the LSC funded client to pay in accordance with Section 11 of the Act, and
(2) either

(a) the order also states the amount of full costs, or
(b) the court considers that it has sufficient information before it to decide what amount is a reasonable amount for the LSC funded client to pay in accordance with Section 11 of the Act and is satisfied that, if it were to determine the full costs at that time, they would exceed the amounts specified in the order.

22.8 Where an order specifying the costs payable is made and the LSC funded client does not have cost protection in respect of all of the costs awarded in that order, the order must identify the sum payable (if any) in respect of which the LSC funded client has cost protection and the sum payable (if any) in respect of which he does not have cost protection.

22.9 The court cannot make an order under Regulations 8 to 13 of the Community Legal Service (Costs) Regulations 2000 as amended except in proceedings to which the next section of this Practice Direction applies.

Scope of provision—See the Guidance Notes issued by the Senior Costs Judge dated 4 October 2001.

SECTION 23 – DETERMINATION PROCEEDINGS AND SIMILAR PROCEEDINGS UNDER THE COMMUNITY LEGAL SERVICE (COSTS) REGULATIONS 2000

23.1 This section of this Practice Direction deals with:

(1) proceedings subsequent to the making of an order for costs to be determined,
(2) variations in the amount stated in an order specifying the amount of costs payable and
(3) the late determination of costs under an order for costs to be determined;
(4) appeals in respect of determination.

23.2 In this section of this Practice Direction 'appropriate court office' means:

(1) the district registry or county court in which the case was being dealt with when the Section 11(1) order was made, or to which it has subsequently been transferred; or
(2) in all other cases, the Supreme Court Costs Office.

23.2A

(1) This paragraph applies where the appropriate office is any of the following county courts:
Barnet, Bow, Brentford, Bromley, Central London, Clerkenwell, Croydon, Edmonton, Ilford, Kingston, Lambeth, Mayors and City of London, Romford, Shoreditch, Uxbridge, Wandsworth, West London, Willesden and Woolwich.
(2) Where this paragraph applies:–
(i) a receiving party seeking an order specifying costs payable by an LSC funded client and/or by the Legal Services Commission under this section must file his application in the Supreme Court Costs Office and, for all purposes relating to that application, the Supreme Court Costs Office will be treated as the appropriate office in that case; and
(ii) unless an order is made transferring the application to the Supreme Court Costs Office as part of the High Court, an appeal from any

decision made by a costs judge shall lie to the Designated Civil Judge for the London Group of County Courts or such judge as he shall nominate. The appeal notice and any other relevant papers should be lodged at the Central London Civil Justice Centre.

23.3

(1) A receiving party seeking an order specifying costs payable by an LSC funded client and/or by the LSC may within 3 months of an order for costs to be determined, file in the appropriate court office an application in Form N244 accompanied by

(a) the receiving party's bill of costs (unless the full costs have already been determined);

(b) the receiving party's statement of resources (unless the court is determining an application against a costs order against the LSC and the costs were not incurred in the court of first instance); and

(c) if the receiving party intends to seek costs against the LSC, written notice to that effect.

(2) If the LSC funded client's liability has already been determined and is less than the full costs, the application will be for costs against the LSC only. If the LSC funded client's liability has not yet been determined, the receiving party must indicate if costs will be sought against the LSC if the funded client's liability is determined as less than the full costs.

(The LSC funded client's certificate will contain the addresses of the LSC funded client, his solicitor, and the relevant Regional Office of the LSC)

23.4 The receiving party must file the above documents in the appropriate court office and (where relevant) serve copies on the LSC funded client and the Regional Director. In respect of applications for funded services made before 3 December 2001 a failure to file a request within the 3 months time limit specified in Regulation 10(2) is an absolute bar to the making of a costs order against the LSC. Where the application for funded services was made on or after 3 December 2001 the court does have power to extend the 3 months time limit, but only if the applicant can show good reason for the delay.

23.5 On being served with the application, the LSC funded client must respond by filing a statement of resources and serving a copy of it on the receiving party (and the Regional Director where relevant) within 21 days. The LSC funded client may also file and serve written points disputing the bill within the same time limit. (Under rule 3.1 the court may extend or shorten this time limit.)

23.6 If the LSC funded client fails to file a statement of resources without good reason, the court will determine his liability (and the amount of full costs if relevant) and need not hold an oral hearing for such determination.

23.7 When the LSC funded client files a statement or the 21 day period for doing so expires, the court will fix a hearing date and give the relevant parties at least 14 days notice. The court may fix a hearing without waiting for the expiry of the 21 day period if the application is made only against the LSC.

23.8 Determination proceedings will be listed for hearing before a costs judge or district judge. The determination of the liability on the LSC funded client will be listed as a private hearing.

23.9 Where the LSC funded client does not have cost protection in respect of all of the costs awarded, the order made by the costs judge or district judge must in addition to specifying the costs payable, identify the full costs in respect of which cost protection applies and the full costs in respect of which cost protection does not apply.

23.10 The Regional Director may appear at any hearing at which a costs order may be made against the LSC. Instead of appearing, he may file a written statement at court and serve a copy on the receiving party. The written statement should be filed and a copy served, not less than 7 days before the hearing.

Variation of an order specifying the costs payable

23.11

(1) This paragraph applies where the amount stated in an order specifying the costs payable plus the amount ordered to be paid by the LSC is less than the full costs to which cost protection applies.
(2) The receiving party may apply to the court for a variation of the amount which the LSC funded client is required to pay on the ground that there has been a significant change in the client's circumstances since the date of the order.

23.12 On an application under paragraph 23.11, where the order specifying the costs payable does not state the full costs.

(1) the receiving party must file with his application the receiving party's statement of resources and bill of costs and copies of these documents should be served with the application.
(2) The LSC funded client must respond to the application by making a statement of resources which must be filed at court and served on the receiving party within 21 days thereafter. The LSC funded client may also file and serve written points disputing the bill within the same time limit.
(3) The court will, when determining the application assess the full costs identifying any part of them to which cost protection does apply and any part of them to which cost protection does not apply.

23.13 On an application under paragraph 23.11 the order specifying the costs payable may be varied as the court thinks fit. That variation must not increase:

(1) the amount of any costs ordered to be paid by the LSC, and
(2) the amount payable by the LSC funded client,

to a sum which is greater than the amount of the full costs plus the costs of the application.

23.14

(1) Where an order for costs to be determined has been made but the receiving party has not applied, within the three month time limit under paragraph 23.2, the receiving party may apply on any of the following grounds for a determination of the amount which the funded client is required to pay:
    (a) there has been a significant change in the funded client's circumstances since the date of the order for costs to be determined; or
    (b) material additional information about the funded client's financial resources is available which could not with reasonable diligence have been obtained by the receiving party at the relevant time; or
    (c) there were other good reasons for the failure by the receiving party to make an application within the time limit.

(2) An application for costs payable by the LSC cannot be made under this paragraph.

23.15

(1) Where the receiving party has received funded services in relation to the proceedings, the LSC may make an application under paragraphs 23.11 and 23.14 above.

(2) In respect of an application under paragraph 23.11 made by the LSC, the LSC must file and serve copies of the documents described in paragraph 23.12(1).

23.16 An application under paragraph 23.11, 23.14 and 23.15 must be commenced before the expiration of 6 years from the date on which the court made the order specifying the costs payable, or (as the case may be) the order for costs to be determined.

23.17 Applications under paragraphs 23.11, 23.14 and 23.15 should be made in the appropriate court office and should be made in Form N244 to be listed for a hearing before a costs judge or district judge.

23.18

(1) Save as mentioned above any determination made under Regulation 9 or 10 of the Costs Regulations is final (Regulation 11(1)). Any party with a financial interest in the assessment of the full costs, other than a funded party, may appeal against that assessment in accordance with CPR Part 52 (Regulation 11(2) and CPR rule 47.20).

(2) The receiving party or the Commission may appeal on a point of law against the making of a costs order against the Commission, against the amount of costs the Commission is required to pay or against the court's refusal to make such an order (Regulation 11(4)).

Scope of provision—See the Guidance Notes issued by the Senior Costs Judge dated 4 October 2001.

Directions Relating to Part 45 – Fixed Costs

SECTION 24 – FIXED COSTS IN SMALL CLAIMS

24.1 Under Rule 27.14 the costs which can be awarded to a claimant in a small claims track case include the fixed costs payable under Part 45 attributable to issuing the claim.

24.2 Those fixed costs shall be the sum of –

(a) the fixed commencement costs calculated in accordance with Table 1 of Rule 45.2 and;

(b) the appropriate court fee or fees paid by the claimant.

SECTION 24A – CLAIMS TO WHICH PART 45 DOES NOT APPLY

24A In a claim to which Part 45 does not apply, no amount shall be entered on the claim form for the charges of the claimant's solicitor, but the words 'to be assessed' shall be inserted.

SECTION 25 – FIXED COSTS ON THE ISSUE OF A DEFAULT COSTS CERTIFICATE

25.1 Unless paragraph 25.2 applies or unless the court orders otherwise, the fixed costs to be included in a default costs certificate are £80 plus a sum equal to any appropriate court fee payable on the issue of the certificate.

25.2 The fixed costs included in a certificate must not exceed the maximum sum specified for costs and court fee in the notice of commencement.

SECTION 25A – ROAD TRAFFIC ACCIDENTS: FIXED RECOVERABLE COSTS IN COSTS-ONLY PROCEEDINGS

Scope

25A.1 Section II of Part 45 ('the Section') provides for certain fixed costs to be recoverable between parties in respect of costs incurred in disputes which are settled prior to proceedings being issued. The Section applies to road traffic accident disputes as defined in rule 45.7(4)(a), where the accident which gave rise to the dispute occurred on or after 6 October 2003.

25A.2 The Section does not apply to disputes where the total agreed value of the damages is within the small claims limit or exceeds £10,000. Rule 26.8(2) sets out how the financial value of a claim is assessed for the purposes of allocation to track.

25A.3 Fixed recoverable costs are to be calculated by reference to the amount of agreed damages which are payable to the receiving party. In calculating the amount of these damages –

(a) account must be taken of both general and special damages and interest;
(b) any interim payments made must be included;
(c) where the parties have agreed an element of contributory negligence, the amount of damages attributed to that negligence must be deducted;
(d) any amount required by statute to be paid by the compensating party directly to a third party (such as sums paid by way of compensation recovery payments and National Health Service expenses) must not be included.

25A.4 The Section applies to cases which fall within the scope of the Uninsured Drivers Agreement dated 13 August 1999. The section does not apply to cases which fall within the scope of the Untraced Drivers Agreement dated 14 February 2003.

Fixed recoverable costs formula

25A.5 The amount of fixed costs recoverable is calculated by totalling the following –

(a) the sum of £800;
(b) 20% of the agreed damages up to £5000; and
(c) 15% of the agreed damages between £5000 and £10,000.
For example, agreed damages of £7523 would result in recoverable costs of £2178.45 ie
£800 + (20% of £5000) + (15% of £2523).

Additional costs for work in specified areas

25A.6 The area referred to in rule 45.9(2) consists of (within London) the county court districts of Barnet, Bow, Brentford, Central London, Clerkenwell, Edmonton, Ilford, Lambeth, Mayors and City of London, Romford, Shoreditch, Wandsworth, West London, Willesden and Woolwich and (outside London) the county court districts of Bromley, Croydon, Dartford, Gravesend and Uxbridge.

Multiple claimants

25A.7 Where there is more than one potential claimant in relation to a dispute and two or more claimants instruct the same solicitor or firm of solicitors, the provisions of the section apply in respect of each claimant.

Information to be included in the claim form

25A.8 Costs only proceedings are commenced using the procedure set out in rule 44.12A. A claim form should be issued in accordance with Part 8. Where the claimant is claiming an amount of costs which exceed the amount of the fixed recoverable costs he must include on the claim form details of the exceptional circumstances which he considers justifies the additional costs.

25A.9 The claimant must also include on the claim form details of any disbursements or success fee he wishes to claim. The disbursements that may be claimed are set out in rule 45.10(1). If the disbursement falls within 45.10(2)(d) (disbursements that have arisen due to a particular feature of the dispute) the claimant must give details of the particular feature of the dispute and why he considers the disbursement to be necessary.

Disbursements and success fee

25A.10 If the parties agree the amount of the fixed recoverable costs and the only dispute is as to the payment of, or amount of, a disbursement or as to the amount of a success fee, then proceedings should be issued under rule 44.12A in the normal way and not by reference to Section II of Part 45.

SECTION 25B FIXED RECOVERABLE SUCCESS FEES IN EMPLOYER'S LIABILITY DISEASE CLAIMS

25B.1 The following table is a non-exclusive list of the conditions that will fall within Type A and Type B claims for the purposes of Rule 45.23.

Claim type	Description
A	Asbestosis
	Mesothelioma
	Bilateral Pleural Thickening
	Pleural Plaques
B	Repetitive Strain Injury/WRULD
	Carpal Tunnel Syndrome caused by Repetitive Strain Injury
	Occupational Stress

SECTION 2 Civil Procedure Rules and Practice Directions

Directions Relating to Part 46 – Fast Track Trial Costs

SECTION 26 – SCOPE OF PART 46: RULE 46.1

26.1 Part 46 applies to the costs of an advocate for preparing for and appearing at the trial of a claim in the fast track.

26.2 It applies only where, at the date of the trial, the claim is allocated to the fast track. It does not apply in any other case, irrespective of the final value of the claim.

26.3 In particular it does not apply to –

- (a) the hearing of a claim which is allocated to the small claims track with the consent of the parties given under rule 26.7(3); or
- (b) a disposal hearing at which the amount to be paid under a judgment or order is decided by the court (see paragraph 12.8 of the practice direction which supplements Part 26 (Case Management – Preliminary Stage)).

Cases which settle before trial

26.4 Attention is drawn to rule 44.10 (limitation on amount court may award where a claim allocated to the fast track settles before trial).

'the trial' (para 26.1)—See note to CPR r 46.1 for the meaning of 'trial'.

'disposal hearing'—(para 26.3(b))—These are hearings where there has not been an allocation to a track, the only issue being the quantification of the amount payable. Examples of disposal hearings are cases where damages are to be assessed following a judgment in default, judgment on admission, the striking out of statement of case or on a summary judgment application. In these circumstances, if the financial value of the claim is such that, if defended, the claim would have been allocated to the small claims track, it is likely that the proceedings to decide the amount will be allocated to that track and therefore that the only recoverable costs will be in accordance with CPR r 27.14 (see PD26, para 12.8(2)). In other circumstances costs are at the discretion of the court. There is no entitlement to fast track trial costs (PD26, para 12.9(4)).

SECTION 27 – POWER TO AWARD MORE OR LESS THAN THE AMOUNT OF FAST TRACK TRIAL COSTS: RULE 46.3

27.1 Rule 44.15 (providing information about funding arrangements) sets out the requirement to provide information about funding arrangements to the court and other parties. Section 19 of this practice direction sets out the information to be provided and when this is to be done.

27.2 Section 11, of this practice direction explains how the court will approach the question of what sum to allow in respect of additional liability.

27.3 The court has the power, when considering whether a percentage increase is reasonable, to allow different percentages for different items of costs or for different periods during which costs were incurred.

Additional liability—The court has power to award a percentage increase/or additional liability in relation to fast track trial costs. The maximum permitted percentage increase is 100%.

Directions Relating to Part 47 – Procedure for Detailed Assessment of Costs and Default Provisions

SECTION 28 – TIME WHEN ASSESSMENT MAY BE CARRIED OUT: RULE 47.1

28.1

(1) For the purposes of rule 47.1, proceedings are concluded when the court has finally determined the matters in issue in the claim, whether or not there is an appeal.

(2) For the purposes of this rule, the making of an award of provisional damages under Part 41 will be treated as a final determination of the matters in issue.

(3) The court may order or the parties may agree in writing that, although the proceedings are continuing, they will nevertheless be treated as concluded.

(4) (a) A party who is served with a notice of commencement (see paragraph 32.3 below) may apply to a costs judge or a district judge to determine whether the party who served it is entitled to commence detailed assessment proceedings.

(b) On hearing such an application the orders which the court may make include: an order allowing the detailed assessment proceedings to continue, or an order setting aside the notice of commencement.

(5) A costs judge or a district judge may make an order allowing detailed assessment proceedings to be commenced where there is no realistic prospect of the claim continuing.

SECTION 29 – NO STAY OF DETAILED ASSESSMENT WHERE THERE IS AN APPEAL: RULE 47.2

29.1

(1) Rule 47.2 provides that detailed assessment is not stayed pending an appeal unless the court so orders.

(2) An application to stay the detailed assessment of costs pending an appeal may be made to the court whose order is being appealed or to the court who will hear the appeal.

SECTION 30 – POWERS OF AN AUTHORISED COURT OFFICER: RULE 47.3

30.1

(1) The court officers authorised by the Lord Chancellor to assess costs in the Supreme Court Costs Office and the Principal Registry of the Family Division are authorised to deal with claims for costs not exceeding £30,000 (excluding VAT) in the case of senior executive officers, or their equivalent, and £75,000 (excluding VAT) in the case of principal officers.

(2) In calculating whether or not a bill of costs is within the authorised amounts, the figure to be taken into account is the total claim for costs including any claim for additional liability.

(3) Where the receiving party, paying party and any other party to the

detailed assessment proceedings who has served points of dispute are agreed that the assessment should not be made by an authorised court officer, the receiving party should so inform the court when requesting a hearing date. The court will then list the hearing before a costs judge or a district judge.

(4) In any other case a party who objects to the assessment being made by an authorised court officer must make an application to the costs judge or district judge under Part 23 (General Rules about Applications for Court Orders) setting out the reasons for the objection and if sufficient reason is shown the court will direct that the bill be assessed by a costs judge or district judge.

SECTION 31 – VENUE FOR DETAILED ASSESSMENT PROCEEDINGS: RULE 47.4

31.1 For the purposes of Rule 47.4(1) the 'appropriate office' means –

(1) the district registry or county court in which the case was being dealt with when the judgment or order was made or the event occurred which gave rise to the right to assessment, or to which it has subsequently been transferred; or

(2) in all other cases, including Court of Appeal cases, the Supreme Court Costs Office.

31.1A

(1) This paragraph applies where the appropriate office is any of the following county courts:
Barnet, Bow, Brentford, Bromley, Central London, Clerkenwell, Croydon, Edmonton, Ilford, Kingston, Lambeth, Mayors and City of London, Romford, Shoreditch, Uxbridge, Wandsworth, West London, Willesden and Woolwich.

(2) Where this paragraph applies: –

(i) the receiving party must file any request for a detailed assessment hearing in the Supreme Court Costs Office and, for all purposes relating to that detailed assessment, the Supreme Court Costs Office will be treated as the appropriate office in that case; and

(ii) unless an order is made under rule 47.4(2) directing that the Supreme Court Costs Office as part of the High Court shall be the appropriate office, an appeal from any decision made by a costs judge shall lie to the Designated Civil Judge for the London Group of County Courts or such judge as he shall nominate. The appeal notice and any other relevant papers should be lodged at the Central London Civil Justice Centre.

31.2

(1) A direction under rule 47.4(2) or (3) specifying a particular court, registry or office as the appropriate office may be given on application or on the court's own initiative.

(2) Before making such a direction on its own initiative the court will give the parties the opportunity to make representations.

(3) Unless the Supreme Court Costs Office is the appropriate office for the purposes of Rule 47.4(1) an order directing that an assessment is to take place at the Supreme Court Costs Office will be made only if it is appropriate to do so having regard to the size of the bill of costs, the

difficulty of the issues involved, the likely length of the hearing, the cost to the parties and any other relevant matter.

SECTION 32 – COMMENCEMENT OF DETAILED ASSESSMENT PROCEEDINGS: RULE 47.6

32.1 Precedents A, B, C and D in the Schedule of Costs Precedents annexed to this practice direction are model forms of bills of costs for detailed assessment. Further information about bills of costs is set out in Section 4.

32.2 A detailed assessment may be in respect of:

(1) base costs, where a claim for additional liability has not been made or has been agreed;

(2) a claim for additional liability only, base costs having been summarily assessed or agreed;
or

(3) both base costs and additional liability.

32.3 If the detailed assessment is in respect of costs without any additional liability, the receiving party must serve on the paying party and all the other relevant persons the following documents:

(a) a notice of commencement;

(b) a copy of the bill of costs;

(c) copies of the fee notes of counsel and of any expert in respect of fees claimed in the bill;

(d) written evidence as to any other disbursement which is claimed and which exceeds £250;

(e) a statement giving the name and address for service of any person upon whom the receiving party intends to serve the notice of commencement.

32.4 If the detailed assessment is in respect of an additional liability only, the receiving party must serve on the paying party and all other relevant persons the following documents:

(a) a notice of commencement;

(b) a copy of the bill of costs;

(c) the relevant details of the additional liability;

(d) a statement giving the name and address of any person upon whom the receiving party intends to serve the notice of commencement.

32.5 The relevant details of an additional liability are as follows:

(1) In the case of a conditional fee agreement with a success fee:

  (a) a statement showing the amount of costs which have been summarily assessed or agreed, and the percentage increase which has been claimed in respect of those costs;

  (b) a statement of the reasons for the percentage increase given in accordance with regulation 3(1)(a) of the Conditional Fee Agreements Regulations or regulation 5(1)(c) of the Collective Conditional Fee Agreements Regulations 2000.

(2) If the additional liability is an insurance premium: a copy of the insurance certificate showing whether the policy covers the receiving party's own costs; his opponents costs; or his own costs and his opponent's costs; and the maximum extent of that cover, and the amount of the premium paid or payable.

(3) If the receiving party claims an additional amount under Section 30 of the Access of Justice Act 1999: a statement setting out the basis upon which the receiving party's liability for the additional amount is calculated.

32.6 Attention is drawn to the fact that the additional amount recoverable pursuant to section 30 of the Access to Justice Act 1999 in respect of a membership organisation must not exceed the likely cost of the premium of an insurance policy against the risk of incurring a liability to pay the costs of other parties to the proceedings as provided by the Access to Justice (Membership Organisation) Regulations 2000 Regulation 4.

32.7 If a detailed assessment is in respect of both base costs and an additional liability, the receiving party must serve on the paying party and all other relevant persons the documents listed in paragraph 32.3 and the documents giving relevant details of an additional liability listed in paragraph 32.5.

32.8

(1) The notice of commencement should be in Form N252.
(2) Before it is served, it must be completed to show as separate items:
  (a) the total amount of the costs claimed in the bill;
  (b) the extra sum which will be payable by way of fixed costs and court fees if a default costs certificate is obtained.

32.9

(1) This paragraph applies where the notice of commencement is to be served outside England and Wales.
(2) The date to be inserted in the notice of commencement for the paying party to send points of dispute is a date (not less than 21 days from the date of service of the notice) which must be calculated by reference to Part 6 Section III as if the notice were a claim form and as if the date to be inserted was the date for the filing of a defence.

32.10

(1) For the purposes of rule 47.6(2) a 'relevant person' means:
  (a) any person who has taken part in the proceedings which gave rise to the assessment and who is directly liable under an order for costs made against him;
  (b) any person who has given to the receiving party notice in writing that he has a financial interest in the outcome of the assessment and wishes to be a party accordingly;
  (c) any other person whom the court orders to be treated as such.
(2) Where a party is unsure whether a person is or is not a relevant person, that party may apply to the appropriate office for directions.
(3) The court will generally not make an order that the person in respect of whom the application is made will be treated as a relevant person, unless within a specified time he applies to the court to be joined as a party to the assessment proceedings in accordance with Part 19 (Parties and Group Litigation).

32.11

(1) This paragraph applies in cases in which the bill of costs is capable of being copied onto a computer disk.
(2) If, before the detailed assessment hearing, a paying party requests a disk copy of a bill to which this paragraph applies, the receiving party

must supply him with a copy free of charge not more than 7 days after the date on which he received the request.

Scope of provision—Detailed assessment proceedings are commenced by serving a notice of commencement in Form N252 together with the documents referred to in paras 32.3–32.4. It is for the receiving party to complete Form N252 with the information referred to in para 32.8. The notice of commencement is served on all 'relevant persons' who are defined in para 32.10. The practice direction makes provision for the service of the Notice of commencement outside England and Wales (para 32.9). It also makes provision for the service of bills of costs capable of being copied on to computer disc (para 32.11).

Additional liability—The practice direction differentiates between commencing detailed assessment proceedings in three different types of case –
(1) where base costs only are claimed without any additional liability (para 32.3)
(2) where an additional liability only is claimed (para 32.4)
(3) where both base costs and an additional liability are claimed.

Where an additional liability is claimed the practice direction requires that 'relevant details' of the additional liability are disclosed to the paying party. A definition of 'relevant details' is set out in full in para 32.5.

Forms—N252

SECTION 33 – PERIOD FOR COMMENCING DETAILED ASSESSMENT PROCEEDINGS: RULE 47.7

33.1 The parties may agree under rule 2.11 (Time limits may be varied by parties) to extend or shorten the time specified by rule 47.7 for commencing the detailed assessment proceedings.

33.2 A party may apply to the appropriate office for an order under rule 3.1(2)(a) to extend or shorten that time.

33.3 Attention is drawn to rule 47.6(1). The detailed assessment proceedings are commenced by service of the documents referred to.

33.4 Permission to commence assessment proceedings out of time is not required.

Scope of provision—Although permission to commence assessment proceedings out of time is not required it may be prudent for a practitioner who will be unable to comply with the period for commencing detailed assessment proceedings set out in CPR r 47.7 to seek an extension of time under CPR r 3.1(2)(a). If such an order is made, the sanctions referred to in CPR r 47.8 will not take effect.

SECTION 34 – SANCTION FOR DELAY IN COMMENCING DETAILED ASSESSMENT PROCEEDINGS: RULE 47.8

34.1

(1) An application for an order under rule 47.8 must be made in writing and be issued in the appropriate office.
(2) The application notice must be served at least 7 days before the hearing.

SECTION 35 – POINTS OF DISPUTE AND CONSEQUENCES OF NOT SERVING: RULE 47.9

35.1 The parties may agree under rule 2.11 (Time limits may be varied by parties) to extend or shorten the time specified by rule 47.9 for service of points of dispute. A party may apply to the appropriate office for an order under rule 3.1(2)(a) to extend or shorten that time.

35.2 Points of dispute should be short and to the point and should follow as closely as possible Precedent G of the Schedule of Costs Precedents annexed to this practice direction.

35.3 Points of dispute must –

(1) identify each item in the bill of costs which is disputed,
(2) in each case state concisely the nature and grounds of dispute,
(3) where practicable suggest a figure to be allowed for each item in respect of which a reduction is sought, and
(4) be signed by the party serving them or his solicitor.

35.4

(1) The normal period for serving points of dispute is 21 days after the date of service of the notice of commencement.
(2) Where a notice of commencement is served on a party outside England and Wales the period within which that party should serve points of dispute is to be calculated by reference to Part 6 Section III as if the notice of commencement was a claim form and as if the period for serving points of dispute were the period for filing a defence.

35.5 A party who serves points of dispute on the receiving party must at the same time serve a copy on every other party to the detailed assessment proceedings, whose name and address for service appears on the statement served by the receiving party in accordance with paragraph 32.3 or 32.4 above.

35.6

(1) This paragraph applies in cases in which points of dispute are capable of being copied onto a computer disk.
(2) If, within 14 days of the receipt of the points of dispute, the receiving party requests a disk copy of them, the paying party must supply him with a copy free of charge not more than 7 days after the date on which he received the request.

35.7

(1) Where the receiving party claims an additional liability, a party who serves points of dispute on the receiving party may include a request for information about other methods of financing costs which were available to the receiving party.
(2) Part 18 (further information) and the Practice Direction Supplementing that part apply to such a request.

'A party may apply … to extend' (para 35.1)—The application must be made in accordance with CPR Pt 23.

'Precedent G of the Schedule of Costs Precedents' (para 35.2 and see also para 35.3)—There has been a tendency in the past for points of dispute to be long-winded, in many cases longer than the bill itself. Precedent G, Schedule of Costs Precedents is the model form of points of dispute and is an attempt to reduce the document to more manageable proportions. It is intended to provide basic information as to the item in dispute, the nature of the dispute and the amount in dispute. This information can be expanded upon at the detailed assessment hearing, should it proceed.

'request for information about other methods of financing costs' (para 35.7)—Legal representatives are under a duty to advise their clients about a wide number of matters before a CFA is entered into. In particular the legal representative must consider whether his client's risk of incurring a liability for costs, in respect of the proceedings to which the CFA will relate, is insured against under an existing contract of insurance (for example legal expenses insurance and/or general household insurance). He must also consider whether there are any other methods of financing any or all of the costs before he recommends a policy of insurance (Conditional Fee Agreements Regulations 2000, para 4(2)(c) and (e)). For a fuller discussion on this topic see *Sarwar v Alam* [2001] EWCA Civ 1401, [2001] 4 All ER 541, CA. See also PDCosts, para 11.10. Paragraph 35.7 allows the paying party to request further information from the receiving party about any other methods of financing the action which were available to the receiving party and which may have been a less expensive option than a CFA with linked insurance (for example, legal expenses insurance or other types of retainer). Any request for further information must comply with CPR Pt 18.

Forms—Precedent G, Schedule of Costs Precedents

SECTION 36 – PROCEDURE WHERE COSTS ARE AGREED: RULE 47.10

36.1 Where the parties have agreed terms as to the issue of a costs certificate (either interim or final) they should apply under rule 40.6 (Consent judgments and orders) for an order that a certificate be issued in terms set out in the application. Such an application may be dealt with by a court officer, who may issue the certificate.

36.2 Where in the course of proceedings the receiving party claims that the paying party has agreed to pay costs but that he will neither pay those costs nor join in a consent application under paragraph 36.1, the receiving party may apply under Part 23 (General Rules about Applications for Court Orders) for a certificate either interim or final to be issued.

36.3 An application under paragraph 36.2 must be supported by evidence and will be heard by a costs judge or a district judge. The respondent to the application must file and serve any evidence he relies on at least 2 days before the hearing date.

36.4 Nothing in rule 47.10 prevents parties who seek a judgment or order by consent from including in the draft a term that a party shall pay to another party a specified sum in respect of costs.

36.5

(1) The receiving party may discontinue the detailed assessment proceedings in accordance with Part 38 (Discontinuance).

(2) Where the receiving party discontinues the detailed assessment proceedings before a detailed assessment hearing has been requested, the paying party may apply to the appropriate office for an order about the costs of the detailed assessment proceedings.

(3) Where a detailed assessment hearing has been requested the receiving party may not discontinue unless the court gives permission.

(4) A bill of costs may be withdrawn by consent whether or not a detailed assessment hearing has been requested.

SECTION 37 – DEFAULT COSTS CERTIFICATE: RULE 47.11

37.1(1) A request for the issue of a default costs certificate must be made in Form N254 and must be signed by the receiving party or his solicitor.

(2) The request must be accompanied by a copy of the document giving the right to detailed assessment. (Section 40.4 of the Costs Practice Direction identifies the appropriate documents.)

37.2 The request must be filed at the appropriate office.

37.3 A default costs certificate will be in Form N255.

37.4 Attention is drawn to rules 40.3 (Drawing up and Filing of Judgments and Orders) and 40.4 (Service of Judgments and Orders) which apply to the preparation and service of a default costs certificate. The receiving party will be treated as having permission to draw up a default costs certificate by virtue of this practice direction.

37.5 The issue of a default costs certificate does not prohibit, govern or affect any detailed assessment of the same costs which are payable out of the Community Legal Service Fund.

37.6 An application for an order staying enforcement of a default costs certificate may be made either –

(1) to a costs judge or district judge of the court office which issued the certificate; or
(2) to the court (if different) which has general jurisdiction to enforce the certificate.

37.7 Proceedings for enforcement of default costs certificates may not be issued in the Supreme Court Costs Office.

37.8 The fixed costs payable in respect of solicitor's charges on the issue of the default costs certificate are £80.

Scope of provision—A request for the issue of a default costs certificate is in Form N254 which is completed by the receiving party, who is treated as having permission to draw it up (para 37.4).

LSC funding—The issue of a default costs certificate in a mixed bill of costs does not affect the detailed assessment of the receiving party's LSC funded costs claimed at prescribed rates. The assessment of costs payable out of the Community Legal Service Fund will continue in accordance with CPR r 47.17. See also Section 43.

Enforcement (paras 37.6–37.7)—All certificates for costs contain an order to pay within 14 days (CPR r 44.8). Applications to stay enforcement or to extend time to pay must be made in accordance with CPR Pt 23.

SECTION 38 – SETTING ASIDE DEFAULT COSTS CERTIFICATE: RULE 47.12

38.1

(1) A court officer may set aside a default costs certificate at the request of the receiving party under rule 47.12(3).
(2) A costs judge or a district judge will make any other order or give any directions under this rule.

38.2

(1) An application for an order under rule 47.12(2) to set aside or vary a default costs certificate must be supported by evidence.
(2) In deciding whether to set aside or vary a certificate under rule 47.12(2) the matters to which the court must have regard include whether the party seeking the order made the application promptly.
(3) As a general rule a default costs certificate will be set aside under rule 47.12(2) only if the applicant shows a good reason for the court to do so and if he files with his application a copy of the bill and a copy of the default costs certificate, and a draft of the points of dispute he proposes to serve if his application is granted.

38.3

(1) Attention is drawn to rule 3.1(3) (which enables the court when making an order to make it subject to conditions) and to rule 44.3(8) (which enables the court to order a party whom it has ordered to pay costs to pay an amount on account before the costs are assessed).
(2) A costs judge or a district judge may exercise the power of the court to

make an order under rule 44.3(8) although he did not make the order about costs which led to the issue of the default costs certificate.

38.4 If a default costs certificate is set aside the court will give directions for the management of the detailed assessment proceedings.

'An application for an order' (para 38.2(1))—Any application for an order under CPR r 47.12 must be made in accordance with CPR Pt 23.

SECTION 39 – OPTIONAL REPLY: RULE 47.13

39.1

(1) Where the receiving party wishes to serve a reply, he must also serve a copy on every other party to the detailed assessment proceedings. The time for doing so is within 21 days after service of the points of dispute.

(2) A reply means –
 (i) a separate document prepared by the receiving party; or
 (ii) his written comments added to the points of dispute.

(3) A reply must be signed by the party serving it or his solicitor.

SECTION 40 – DETAILED ASSESSMENT HEARING: RULE 47.14

40.1 The time for requesting a detailed assessment hearing is within 3 months of the expiry of the period for commencing detailed assessment proceedings.

40.2 The request for a detailed assessment hearing must be in Form N258. The request must be accompanied by –

(a) a copy of the notice of commencement of detailed assessment proceedings;
(b) a copy of the bill of costs,
(c) the document giving the right to detailed assessment (see paragraph 39.4 below);
(d) a copy of the points of dispute, annotated as necessary in order to show which items have been agreed and their value and to show which items remain in dispute and their value;
(e) as many copies of the points of dispute so annotated as there are persons who have served points of dispute;
(f) a copy of any replies served;
(g) a copy of all orders made by the court relating to the costs which are to be assessed;
(h) copies of the fee notes and other written evidence as served on the paying party in accordance with paragraph 32.3 above;
(i) where there is a dispute as to the receiving party's liability to pay costs to the solicitors who acted for the receiving party, any agreement, letter or other written information provided by the solicitor to his client explaining how the solicitor's charges are to be calculated;
(j) a statement signed by the receiving party or his solicitor giving the name, address for service, reference and telephone number and fax number, if any, of –
 (i) the receiving party;
 (ii) the paying party;
 (iii) any other person who has served points of dispute or who has given notice to the receiving party under paragraph 32.10(1)(b) above;

and giving an estimate of the length of time the detailed assessment hearing will take;

(k) where the application for a detailed assessment hearing is made by a party other than the receiving party, such of the documents set out in this paragraph as are in the possession of that party;

(l) where the court is to assess the costs of an assisted person or LSC funded client –

  (i) the legal aid certificate, LSC certificate and relevant amendment certificates, any authorities and any certificates of discharge or revocation.

  (ii) a certificate, in Precedent F(3) of the Schedule of Costs Precedents;

  (iii) if the assisted person has a financial interest in the detailed assessment hearing and wishes to attend, the postal address of that person to which the court will send notice of any hearing;

  (iv) if the rates payable out of the LSC fund are prescribed rates, a schedule to the bill of costs setting out all the items in the bill which are claimed against other parties calculated at the legal aid prescribed rates with or without any claim for enhancement: (further information as to this schedule is set out in Section 48 of this practice direction);

  (v) a copy of any default costs certificate in respect of costs claimed in the bill of costs.

40.3

(1) This paragraph applies to any document described in paragraph 40.2(i) above which the receiving party has filed in the appropriate office. The document must be the latest relevant version and in any event have been filed not more than 2 years before filing the request for a detailed assessment hearing.

(2) In respect of any documents to which this paragraph applies, the receiving party may, instead of filing a copy of it, specify in the request for a detailed assessment hearing the case number under which a copy of the document was previously filed.

40.4 'The document giving the right to detailed assessment' means such one or more of the following documents as are appropriate to the detailed assessment proceedings –

(a) a copy of the judgment or order of the court giving the right to detailed assessment;

(b) a copy of the notice served under rule 3.7 (sanctions for non-payment of certain fees) where a claim is struck out under that rule;

(c) a copy of the notice of acceptance where an offer to settle is accepted under Part 36 (Offers to settle and payments into court);

(d) a copy of the notice of discontinuance in a case which is discontinued under Part 38 (Discontinuance);

(e) a copy of the award made on an arbitration under any Act or pursuant to an agreement, where no court has made an order for the enforcement of the award;

(f) a copy of the order, award or determination of a statutorily constituted tribunal or body;

(g) in a case under the Sheriffs Act 1887, the sheriff's bill of fees and charges, unless a court order giving the right to detailed assessment has been made;

(h) a notice of revocation or discharge under Regulation 82 of the Civil Legal Aid (General) Regulations 1989.

(j) In the county courts certain Acts and Regulations provide for costs incurred in proceedings under those Acts and Regulations to be assessed in the county court if so ordered on application. Where such an application is made, a copy of the order.

40.5 On receipt of the request for a detailed assessment hearing the court will fix a date for the hearing, or, if the costs officer so decides, will give directions or fix a date for a preliminary appointment.

40.6

(1) The court will give at least 14 days notice of the time and place of the detailed assessment hearing to every person named in the statement referred to in paragraph 40.2(j) above.

(2) The court will when giving notice, give each person who has served points of dispute a copy of the points of dispute annotated by the receiving party in compliance with paragraph 40.2(d) above.

(3) Attention is drawn to rule 47.14(6) and 47.14(7): apart from the receiving party, only those who have served points of dispute may be heard on the detailed assessment unless the court gives permission, and only items specified in the points of dispute may be raised unless the court gives permission.

40.7

(1) If the receiving party does not file a request for a detailed assessment hearing within the prescribed time, the paying party may apply to the court to fix a time within which the receiving party must do so. The sanction, for failure to request a detailed assessment hearing within the time specified by the court, is that all or part of the costs may be disallowed (see rule 47.8(2)).

(2) Where the receiving party commences detailed assessment proceedings after the time specified in the rules but before the paying party has made an application to the court to specify a time, the only sanction which the court may impose is to disallow all or part of the interest which would otherwise be payable for the period of delay, unless the court exercises its powers under rule 44.14 (court's powers in relation to misconduct).

40.8 If either party wishes to make an application in the detailed assessment proceedings the provisions of Part 23 (General Rules about Applications for Court Orders) apply.

40.9

(1) This paragraph deals with the procedure to be adopted where a date has been given by the court for a detailed assessment hearing and –

(a) the detailed assessment proceedings are settled; or

(b) a party to the detailed assessment proceedings wishes to apply to vary the date which the court has fixed; or

(c) the parties to the detailed assessment proceedings agree about changes they wish to make to any direction given for the management of the detailed assessment proceedings.

(2) If detailed assessment proceedings are settled, the receiving party must give notice of that fact to the court immediately, preferably by fax.
(3) A party who wishes to apply to vary a direction must do so in accordance with Part 23 (General Rules about Applications for Court Orders).
(4) If the parties agree about changes they wish to make to any direction given for the management of the detailed assessment proceedings –
   (a) they must apply to the court for an order by consent; and
   (b) they must file a draft of the directions sought and an agreed statement of the reasons why the variation is sought; and
   (c) the court may make an order in the agreed terms or in other terms without a hearing, but it may direct that a hearing is to be listed.

40.10
(1) If a party wishes to vary his bill of costs, points of dispute or a reply, an amended or supplementary document must be filed with the court and copies of it must be served on all other relevant parties.
(2) Permission is not required to vary a bill of costs, points of dispute or a reply but the court may disallow the variation or permit it only upon conditions, including conditions as to the payment of any costs caused or wasted by the variation.

40.11 Unless the court directs otherwise the receiving party must file with the court the papers in support of the bill not less than 7 days before the date for the detailed assessment hearing and not more than 14 days before that date.

40.12 The following provisions apply in respect of the papers to be filed in support of the bill;

(a) if the claim is for costs only without any additional liability the papers to be filed, and the order in which they are to be arranged are as follows:
   (i) instructions and briefs to counsel arranged in chronological order together with all advices, opinions and drafts received and response to such instructions;
   (ii) reports and opinions of medical and other experts;
   (iii) any other relevant papers;
   (iv) a full set of any relevant pleadings to the extent that they have not already been filed in court;
   (v) correspondence, files and attendance notes;
(b) where the claim is in respect of an additional liability only, such of the papers listed at (a) above, as are relevant to the issues raised by the claim for additional liability;
(c) where the claim is for both base costs and an additional liability, the papers listed at (a) above, together with any papers relevant to the issues raised by the claim for additional liability.

40.13 The provisions set out in Section 20 of the practice direction apply where the court disallows any amount of a legal representative's percentage increase, and the legal representative applies for an order that the disallowed amount should continue to be payable by the client in accordance with Rule 44.16.

40.14 The court may direct the receiving party to produce any document which in the opinion of the court is necessary to enable it to reach its decision. These documents will in the first instance be produced to the court, but the court may ask the receiving party to elect whether to disclose the particular document to the paying party in order to rely on the contents of the document, or whether to decline disclosure and instead rely on other evidence.

40.15 Costs assessed at a detailed assessment at the conclusion of proceedings may include an assessment of any additional liability in respect of the costs of a previous application or hearing.

40.16 Once the detailed assessment hearing has ended it is the responsibility of the legal representative appearing for the receiving party or, as the case may be, the receiving party in person to remove the papers filed in support of the bill.

Scope of provision—These provisions set out in great detail when a party must request a detailed assessment hearing and deal with fixing the date for the hearing, applications, adjournments and amendments together with the documents which the court requires to be filed in support of the bill of costs.

The points of dispute should be annotated to show items which have been agreed and their value and items which remain in dispute and their value. It is helpful also to annotate the bill of costs itself to show which items are agreed and which remain in dispute. Alternatively an amended bill of costs agreed with the other parties may be filed indicating only the items remaining in dispute.

Solicitor's retainer – dispute as to indemnity principle—Where there is a dispute relating to the receiving party's liability to pay costs to his own solicitor on the indemnity principle, the written form of retainer or client care letter or any other written information to establish the basis of the solicitor's charging rate and the costs must be produced to the court (para 40.2(i)).

'the receiving party to produce any document ... to enable it to reach its decision' (para 40. 14)—The court now has wide powers to require the receiving party to produce 'any document' which in the opinion of the court is necessary to enable it to reach its decision. Where there is a dispute with regard to an additional liability this could include the CFA itself together with any correspondence passing between a legal representative and his client relating to the CFA and how it was entered into.

There may also be a dispute with regard to the operation of the indemnity principal and/or whether the action is being maintained by a third party. The costs judge does not have power to override legal privilege in respect of the documents of the receiving party but:

(1) Where a disputed issue of fact arises in detailed assessment the costs judge may direct production to him of a relevant document (PDCosts, para 40.14). Alternatively, the receiving party may seek to rely upon a privileged document. The costs judge cannot override the receiving party's privilege but he can put that party to its election upon whether to rely on the document or seek to prove the fact by other means, eg by way of oral evidence from the receiving party's solicitor.

(2) The decision to put the receiving party to its election is one for the costs judge having regard to relevance and proportionality. Where a document is of sufficient importance to be taken into account in determining the recoverability of costs, the receiving party must be put to his election.

(3) If the receiving party seeks to prove the fact by other means, the paying party is not automatically entitled to see the relevant document in the possession of the receiving party and upon which that party does not intend to rely (*Dickinson (t/a Dickinson Equipment Finance) v Rushmer (t/a FJ Associates)* [2002] Costs LR 128, ChD, Rimer J; *South Coast Shipping Co Ltd v Havant Borough Council* [2002] 3 All ER 779, [2002] Costs LR 98, ChD, Pumfrey J).

Another possibility is that, in striking a balance between the parties, the costs judge might need to disclose to the paying party all or part of a privileged document without prejudice to the document's owner's right to claim privilege in any subsequent context (*Goldman v Hesper* [1988] 1 WLR 1238, [1988] 3 All ER 97, CA). See also Section 4 – Form and Content of Bill of Costs.

Conditional fee agreements—A costs judge should normally exercise his discretion to require the receiving party – subject to his right of election – to produce a copy of the CFA, edited if necessary to remove confidential information. Attendance notes prepared by the receiving party's solicitors showing compliance with, for example, CFAR 2000, reg 4 should not normally be disclosed (*Hollins v Russell* [2003] EWCA Civ 718, [2003] All ER (D) 311 (May), CA; *Bailey v IBC Vehicles Ltd* (1998) 3 All ER 570 distinguished).

Detailed assessment hearing—The court will give at least 14 days notice of the time and place of the detailed assessment hearing. Only those parties who have served points of dispute may be heard and only items specified in the points of dispute may be raised, unless the court gives permission (para 40.6(3)). The court may penalise a receiving party who requested a detailed assessment hearing after the time specified in CPR r 47.14 but, if the paying party does not make application to the court to request a hearing date, the only sanction which the court may impose is to disallow all or part of the interest otherwise payable in respect of the period of delay.

Papers to be filed in support of the bill—The documents in support of the bill together with the order in which they are to be arranged are set out clearly in para 40.1(2). Where an additional liability is claimed any papers relevant to the issues raised by the claim must also be lodged.

SECTION 41 – POWER TO ISSUE AN INTERIM CERTIFICATE: RULE 47.15

41.1

(1) A party wishing to apply for an interim certificate may do so by making an application in accordance with Part 23 (General Rules about Applications for Court Orders).

(2) Attention is drawn to the fact that the court's power to issue an interim certificate arises only after the receiving party has filed a request for a detailed assessment hearing.

Scope of provision—An interim certificate can be issued at any time after a detailed assessment hearing has been sought. In addition the court can also make an order for payment of costs on account (CPR r 44.3(8)).

See *Dyson Appliances Ltd v Hoover Ltd* [2003] EWHC 624, [2003] All ER (D) 252 (Feb), which explains the difference between an application for payment on account pursuant to CPR r 44.3(8) and an interim payment pursuant to CPR r 47.15. See also *CICB Mellon Trust Company Ltd v Mora Hotel Corp BV* [2002] EWCA Civ 1688, (2003) Lawtel, 20 February, CA in relation to the discretion of the court pursuant to an order under CPR r 47.15.

SECTION 42 – FINAL COSTS CERTIFICATE: RULE 47.16

42.1 At the detailed assessment hearing the court will indicate any disallowance or reduction in the sums claimed in the bill of costs by making an appropriate note on the bill.

42.2 The receiving party must, in order to complete the bill after the detailed assessment hearing make clear the correct figures agreed or allowed in respect of each item and must re-calculate the summary of the bill appropriately.

42.3 The completed bill of costs must be filed with the court no later than 14 days after the detailed assessment hearing.

42.4 At the same time as filing the completed bill of costs, the party whose bill it is must also produce receipted fee notes and receipted accounts in respect of all disbursements except those covered by a certificate in Precedent F(5) in the Schedule of Costs annexed to this practice direction.

42.5 No final costs certificate will be issued until all relevant court fees payable on the assessment of costs have been paid.

42.6 If the receiving party fails to file a completed bill in accordance with rule 47.16 the paying party may make an application under Part 23 (General Rules about Applications for Court Orders) seeking an appropriate order under rule 3.1 (The court's general powers of management).

42.7 A final costs certificate will show –

(a) the amount of any costs which have been agreed between the parties or which have been allowed on detailed assessment;

(b) where applicable the amount agreed or allowed in respect of VAT on the costs agreed or allowed.

This provision is subject to any contrary provision made by the statutory provisions relating to costs payable out of the Community Legal Service Fund.

42.8 A final costs certificate will include disbursements in respect of the fees of counsel only if receipted fee notes or accounts in respect of those disbursements have been produced to the court and only to the extent indicated by those receipts.

42.9 Where the certificate relates to costs payable between parties a separate certificate will be issued for each party entitled to costs.

42.10 Form N257 is a model form of interim costs certificate and Form N256 is a model form of final costs certificate.

42.11 An application for an order staying enforcement of a interim costs certificate or final costs certificate may be made either –

(1) to a costs judge or district judge of the court office which issued the certificate; or
(2) to the court (if different) which has general jurisdiction to enforce the certificate.

42.12 Proceedings for enforcement of interim costs certificates or final costs certificates may not be issued in the Supreme Court Costs Office.

Scope of provision—Once the detailed assessment hearing has taken place it is the duty of the receiving party to complete the bill to show the total amount of costs which have been agreed or allowed in respect of each item. The summary of the bill must also be recalculated (para 42.2). The final costs certificate will in addition to showing the amount to be paid include an order for payment of costs.

Receipted fee notes and accounts—When the completed bill of costs is filed the receiving party must produce receipted fee notes from counsel and receipted accounts in respect of disbursements exceeding £500 (para 42.4).

Fees—Lodgment and taxing fees have been abandoned in favour of a flat fee on the filing of a request for detailed assessment. There are transitional provisions where a bill of costs for detailed assessment is filed pursuant to a judgment or an order made by a court prior to 26 April 1999. The relevant fees are those applicable prior to 26 April 1999. See CCFO and SCFO in Section 6 of this work.

SECTION 43 – DETAILED ASSESSMENT PROCEDURE WHERE COSTS ARE PAYABLE OUT OF THE COMMUNITY LEGAL SERVICE FUND: RULE 47.17

43.1 The provisions of this section apply where the court is to assess costs which are payable only out of the community legal service fund. Paragraphs 39.1 to 40.16 and 49.1 to 49.8 apply in cases involving costs payable by another person as well as costs payable only out of the Community Legal Service Fund.

43.2 The time for requesting a detailed assessment under rule 47.17 is within 3 months after the date when the right to detailed assessment arose.

43.3 The request for a detailed assessment of legal aid costs must be in Form N258A. The request must be accompanied by –

(a) a copy of the bill of costs;
(b) the document giving the right to detailed assessment (for further information as to this document, see paragraph 40.4 above);
(c) a copy of all orders made by the court relating to the costs which are to be assessed;
(d) copies of any fee notes of counsel and any expert in respect of fees claimed in the bill;

(e) written evidence as to any other disbursement which is claimed and which exceeds £250;

(f) the legal aid certificates, LSC certificates, any relevant amendment certificates, any authorities and any certificates of discharge or revocation;

(g) In the Supreme Court Costs Office the relevant papers in support of the bill as described in paragraph 40.12 above; in cases proceeding in district registries and county courts this provision does not apply and the papers should only be lodged if requested by the costs officer;

(h) a statement signed by the solicitor giving his name, address for service, reference, telephone number, fax number and, if the assisted person has a financial interest in the detailed assessment and wishes to attend, giving the postal address of that person, to which the court will send notice of any hearing.

43.4 Rule 47.17 provides that the court will hold a detailed assessment hearing if the assisted person has a financial interest in the detailed assessment and wishes to attend. The court may also hold a detailed assessment hearing in any other case, instead of provisionally assessing a bill of costs, where it considers that a hearing is necessary. Before deciding whether a hearing is necessary under this rule, the court may require the solicitor whose bill it is, to provide further information relating to the bill.

43.5 Where the court has provisionally assessed a bill of costs it will send to the solicitor a notice, in Form N253 annexed to this practice direction, of the amount of costs which the court proposes to allow together with the bill itself. The legal representative should, if the provisional assessment is to be accepted, then complete the bill.

43.6 The court will fix a date for a detailed assessment hearing if the solicitor informs the court within 14 days after he receives the notice of the amount allowed on the provisional assessment that he wants the court to hold such a hearing.

43.7 The court will give at least 14 days notice of the time and place of the detailed assessment hearing to the solicitor and, if the assisted person has a financial interest in the detailed assessment and wishes to attend, to the assisted person.

43.8 If the solicitor whose bill it is, or any other party wishes to make an application in the detailed assessment proceedings, the provisions of Part 23 (General Rules about Applications for Court Orders) applies.

43.9 It is the responsibility of the legal representative to complete the bill by entering in the bill the correct figures allowed in respect of each item, recalculating the summary of the bill appropriately and completing the Community Legal Service assessment certificate (Form EX80A).

'the relevant papers in support of the bill' (para 43.3(g))—For assessments proceeding in District Registries or county courts there is now no requirement for a solicitor to lodge the documents referred to in para 40.12 unless requested to do so by the costs officer.

Costs payable out of the Community Legal Service Fund—These provisions deal with legal aid/LSC only costs. Where a party is seeking detailed assessment of a mixed party and party and costs from the CLSF should refer to Section 49 (Costs payable by the LSC at prescribed rates). CPR r 47.14 allows for a provisional detailed assessment of CLSF costs with provision for the court to fix a date for a detailed assessment hearing if the solicitor of the assisted person/funded party wishes to attend (para 43.6). Detailed assessment proceedings are commenced on Form N258A. The request must be accompanied by the documents referred to in para 43.3.

Fees—See note as to fees under Section 42 above. There is an additional fee of £20 on applying to the court for a Community Legal Service assessment certificate (Form EX80A).

SECTION 44 – COSTS OF DETAILED ASSESSMENT PROCEEDINGS

Where costs are payable out of a fund other than the Community Legal Service Fund: rule 47.17A

44.1 Rule 47.17A provides that the court will make a provisional assessment of a bill of costs payable out of a fund (other than the Community Legal Services Fund) unless it considers that a hearing is necessary. It also enables the court to direct under rule 47.17A(3) that the receiving party must serve a copy of the request for assessment and copies of the documents which accompany it, on any person who has a financial interest in the outcome of the assessment.

44.2

(a) A person has a financial interest in the outcome of the assessment if the assessment will or may affect the amount of money or property to which he is or may become entitled out of the fund.
(b) Where an interest in the fund is itself held by a trustee for the benefit of some other person, that trustee will be treated as having such a financial interest.
(c) 'Trustee' includes a personal representative, receiver or any other person acting in a fiduciary capacity.

44.3 The request for a detailed assessment of costs out of the fund should be in Form N258B, be accompanied by the documents set out at paragraph 43.3(a) to (e) and (g) above and the following;

(a) a statement signed by the receiving party giving his name, address for service, reference, telephone number, fax number and,
(b) a statement of the postal address of any person who has a financial interest in the outcome of the assessment, to which the court may send notice of any hearing; and
(c) in respect of each person stated to have such an interest if such person is a child or patient, a statement to that effect.

44.4 The court will decide, having regard to the amount of the bill, the size of the fund and the number of persons who have a financial interest, which of those persons should be served. The court may dispense with service on all or some of them.

44.5 Where the court makes an order dispensing with service on all such persons it may proceed at once to make a provisional assessment, or, if it decides that a hearing is necessary, give appropriate directions. Before deciding whether a hearing is necessary under this rule, the court may require the receiving party to provide further information relating to the bill.

44.6

(1) Where the court has provisionally assessed a bill of costs, it will send to the receiving party, a notice in Form N253 of the amount of costs which the court proposes to allow together with the bill itself. If the receiving party is legally represented the legal representative should, if the provisional assessment is to be accepted, then complete the bill.
(2) The court will fix a date for a detailed assessment hearing, if the receiving party informs the court within 14 days after he receives the

notice in Form N253 of the amount allowed on the provisional assessment, that he wants the court to hold such a hearing.

44.7 Where the court makes an order that a person who has a financial interest is to be served with a copy of the request for assessment, it may give directions about service and about the hearing.

44.8 The court will give at least 14 days notice of the time and place of the detailed assessment hearing to the receiving party and, to any person who has a financial interest in the outcome of the assessment and has been served with a copy of the request for assessment.

44.9 If the receiving party, or any other party or any person who has a financial interest in the outcome of assessment, wishes to make an application in the detailed assessment proceedings, the provisions of Part 23 (General Rules about Applications for Court Orders) applies.

44.10 If the receiving party is legally represented the legal representative must in order to complete the bill after the assessment make clear the correct figures allowed in respect of each item and must recalculate the summary of the bill if appropriate.

Scope of provision—Rule 47.17A allows the court to assess costs payable out of a fund which is not the Community Legal Service Fund. For example the court may assess costs in relation to funds held by the Court of Protection or trust funds in general. The provisions are akin to the detailed assessment procedure where costs are payable out of the Community Legal Service Fund and allow for the provisional assessment of a bill of costs.

There is provision for the court to decide, having regard to the amount of the bill, the size of the fund and the number of persons who have a financial interest, which of those persons should be served with the bill. The court may dispense with service on some or all of them (para 44.4).

Forms—N258B – Request for a detailed assessment of costs out of the fund.

SECTION 45 – LIABILITY FOR COSTS OF DETAILED ASSESSMENT PROCEEDINGS: RULE 47.18

45.1 As a general rule the court will assess the receiving party's costs of the detailed assessment proceedings and add them to the bill of costs.

45.2 If the costs of the detailed assessment proceedings are awarded to the paying party, the court will either assess those costs by summary assessment or make an order for them to be decided by detailed assessment.

45.3 No party should file or serve a statement of costs of the detailed assessment proceedings unless the court orders him to do so.

45.4 Attention is drawn to the fact that in deciding what order to make about the costs of detailed assessment proceedings the court must have regard to the conduct of all parties, the amount by which the bill of costs has been reduced and whether it was reasonable for a party to claim the costs of a particular item or to dispute that item.

45.5(1) In respect of interest on the costs of detailed assessment proceedings, the interest shall begin to run from the date of the default, interim or final costs certificate as the case may be.

(2) This provision applies only to the costs of the detailed assessment proceedings themselves. The costs of the substantive proceedings are governed by rule 40.8(1).

Scope of provision—Costs in relation to detailed assessment proceedings are generally summarily assessed at the conclusion of the detailed assessment hearing. There is no requirement for practitioners to file or serve a statement of costs of the detailed assessment proceedings prior to that hearing unless the court orders them so to do (para 45.3). The costs of the detailed assessment proceedings (other than the costs of preparing and checking the bill) should not be included in the bill of costs itself.

SECTION 46 – OFFERS TO SETTLE WITHOUT PREJUDICE SAVE AS TO THE COSTS OF THE DETAILED ASSESSMENT PROCEEDINGS: RULE 47.19

46.1 Rule 47.19 allows the court to take into account offers to settle, without prejudice save as to the costs of detailed assessment proceedings, when deciding who is liable for the costs of those proceedings. The rule does not specify a time within which such an offer should be made. An offer made by the paying party should usually be made within 14 days after service of the notice of commencement on that party. If the offer is made by the receiving party it should normally be made within 14 days after the service of points of dispute by the paying party. Offers made after these periods are likely to be given less weight by the court in deciding what order as to costs to make unless there is good reason for the offer not being made until the later time.

46.2 Where an offer to settle is made it should specify whether or not it is intended to be inclusive of the cost of preparation of the bill, interest and value added tax (VAT). The offer may include or exclude some or all of these items but the position must be made clear on the face of the offer so that the offeree is clear about the terms of the offer when it is being considered. Unless the offer states otherwise, the offer will be treated as being inclusive of all these items.

46.3 Where an offer to settle is accepted, an application may be made for a certificate in agreed terms, or the bill of costs may be withdrawn, in accordance with rule 47.10 (Procedure where costs are agreed).

46.4 Where the receiving party is an assisted person or an LSC funded client, an offer to settle without prejudice save as to the costs of the detailed assessment proceedings will not have the consequences specified under rule 47.19 unless the court so orders.

'offer to settle' (para 46.2)—An offer to settle must make clear whether it includes the costs of preparing the bill, interest and VAT. Unless stated otherwise, the offer will be deemed to include these items.

'Where the receiving party is an assisted person or LSC funded client' (para 46.4)—A paying party faced with a legally assisted or LSC funded receiving party should make it clear in any offer to settle that they intend to seek permission from the court to disapply the general rule in accordance with para 46.4.

SECTION 47 – APPEALS FROM AUTHORISED COURT OFFICERS IN DETAILED ASSESSMENT PROCEEDINGS: RIGHT TO APPEAL: RULE 47.20

47.1 This Section and the next Section of this practice direction relate only to appeals from authorised court officers in detailed assessment proceedings. All other appeals arising out of detailed assessment proceedings (and arising out of summary assessments) are dealt with in accordance with Part 52 and the practice direction which supplements that Part. The destination of appeals is dealt with in accordance with the Access to Justice Act 1999 (Destination of Appeals) Order 2000.

47.2 In respect of appeals from authorised court officers, there is no requirement to obtain permission, or to seek written reasons.

General note—See notes to CPR r 47.20.

SECTION 48 – PROCEDURE ON APPEAL FROM AUTHORISED COURT OFFICERS: RULE 47.22

48.1 The appellant must file a notice which should be in Form N161 (an appellant's notice).

48.2 The appeal will be heard by a costs judge or a district judge of the High Court, and is a re-hearing.

48.3 The appellant's notice should, if possible, be accompanied by a suitable record of the judgment appealed against. Where reasons given for the decision have been officially recorded by the court an approved transcript of that record should accompany the notice. Photocopies will not be accepted for this purpose. Where there is no official record the following documents will be acceptable:

(1) The officer's comments written on the bill.
(2) Advocates' notes of the reasons agreed by the respondent if possible and approved by the authorised court officer.

When the appellant was unrepresented before the authorised court officer, it is the duty of any advocate for the respondent to make his own note of the reasons promptly available, free of charge to the appellant where there is no official record or if the court so directs. Where the appellant was represented before the authorised court officer, it is the duty of his/her own former advocate to make his/her notes available. The appellant should submit the note of the reasons to the costs judge or district judge hearing the appeal.

48.4 The appellant may not be able to obtain a suitable record of the authorised court officer's decision within the time in which the appellant's notice must be filed. In such cases the appellant's notice must still be completed to the best of the appellant's ability. It may however be amended subsequently with the permission of the costs judge or district judge hearing the appeal.

SECTION 49 – COSTS PAYABLE BY THE LSC AT PRESCRIBED RATES:

49.1 This section applies to a bill of costs of an assisted person or LSC funded client which is payable by another person where the costs which can be claimed against the LSC are restricted to prescribed rates (with or without enhancement).

49.2 Where this section applies, the solicitor of the assisted person or LSC funded client must file a legal aid/LSC schedule in accordance with paragraph 39.2(1) above. The schedule should follow as closely as possible Precedent E of the Schedule of Costs Precedents annexed to this practice direction.

49.3 The schedule must set out by reference to the item numbers in the bill of costs, all the costs claimed as payable by another person, but the arithmetic in the schedule should claim those items at prescribed rates only (with or without any claim for enhancement).

49.4 Where there has been a change in the prescribed rates during the period covered by the bill of costs, the schedule (as opposed to the bill) should be divided into separate parts, so as to deal separately with each change of rate. The schedule must also be divided so as to correspond with any divisions in the bill of costs.

49.5 If the bill of costs contains additional columns setting out costs claimed against the LSC only, the schedule may be set out in a separate document or, alternatively, may be included in the additional columns of the bill.

49.6 The detailed assessment of the legal aid/LSC schedule will take place immediately after the detailed assessment of the bill of costs.

49.7 Attention is drawn to the possibility that, on occasions, the court may decide to conduct the detailed assessment of the legal aid/LSC schedule separately from any detailed assessment of the bill of costs. This will occur, for example, where a default costs certificate is obtained as between the parties but that certificate is not set aside at the time of the detailed assessment pursuant to the Legal Aid Act 1988 or regulations thereunder.

49.8 Where costs have been assessed at prescribed rates it is the responsibility of the legal representative to enter the correct figures allowed in respect of each item and to recalculate the summary of the legal aid/LSC schedule.

Scope of provision—Civil Legal Aid (General) (Amendment) Regulations 1994 and Legal Aid in Civil Proceedings (Remuneration) Regulations 1994 apply to civil proceedings in respect of which a legal aid certificate is granted on or after 25 February 1994. Remuneration is allowed in accordance with Legal Aid in Civil Proceedings (Remuneration) Regulations 1994 which restrict the costs which can be claimed out of the legal aid fund to prescribed rates. These provisions apply in a mixed detailed assessment where party and party costs and legal aid/LSC costs are claimed. It is possible for solicitors to claim on a party and party basis more than the prescribed rates provided that recovery is made from the paying party in full. If the paying party defaults either wholly or in part or if there are legal aid/LSC only costs the Legal Services Commission will only pay at prescribed rates. Consequently in a mixed assessment of this type it is necessary for the solicitor to file a schedule setting out the party and party costs at prescribed rates with or without any claim for enhancement. The schedule should follow, as closely as possible, Precedent E of the Schedule of Cost Precedents.

Directions Relating to Part 48 – Costs – Special Cases

SECTION 50 – AMOUNT OF COSTS WHERE COSTS ARE PAYABLE PURSUANT TO CONTRACT: RULE 48.3

50.1 Where the court is assessing costs payable under a contract, it may make an order that all or part of the costs payable under the contract shall be disallowed if it is satisfied by the paying party that costs have been unreasonably incurred or are unreasonable in amount.

50.2 Rule 48.3 only applies if the court is assessing costs payable under a contract. It does not –

(1) require the court to make an assessment of such costs; or
(2) require a mortgagee to apply for an order for those costs that he has a contractual right to recover out of the mortgage funds.

50.3 The following principles apply to costs relating to a mortgage –

(1) An order for the payment of costs of proceedings by one party to another is always a discretionary order: section 51 of the Supreme Court Act 1981.
(2) Where there is a contractual right to the costs the discretion should ordinarily be exercised so as to reflect that contractual right.
(3) The power of the court to disallow a mortgagee's costs sought to be added to the mortgage security is a power that does not derive from

section 51, but from the power of the courts of equity to fix the terms on which redemption will be allowed.

(4) A decision by a court to refuse costs in whole or in part to a mortgagee litigant may be –

(a) a decision in the exercise of the section 51 discretion;

(b) a decision in the exercise of the power to fix the terms on which redemption will be allowed;

(c) a decision as to the extent of a mortgagee's contractual right to add his costs to the security; or

(d) a combination of two or more of these things.

The statements of case in the proceedings or the submissions made to the court may indicate which of the decisions has been made.

(5) A mortgagee is not to be deprived of a contractual or equitable right to add costs to the security merely by reason of an order for payment of costs made without reference to the mortgagee's contractual or equitable rights, and without any adjudication as to whether or not the mortgagee should be deprived of those costs.

50.4

(1) Where the contract entitles a mortgagee to –

(a) add the costs of litigation relating to the mortgage to the sum secured by it;

(b) require a mortgagor to pay those costs, or

(c) both,

the mortgagor may make an application for the court to direct that an account of the mortgagee's costs be taken.

(Rule 25.1(1)(n) provides that the court may direct that a party file an account)

(2) The mortgagor may then dispute an amount in the mortgagee's account on the basis that it has been unreasonably incurred or is unreasonable in amount.

(3) Where a mortgagor disputes an amount, the court may make an order that the disputed costs are assessed under rule 48.3.

Scope of provision—Since implementation of the CPR there has been considerable confusion with regard to the meaning of CPR r 48.3 (see notes to that rule). The practice direction attempts to clarify when the rule is to apply and the basis of quantification. The basis of assessment of costs under this rule is the indemnity basis.

Mortgage possession proceedings—Summary assessment of costs does not apply to a mortgagee's costs incurred in mortgage possession proceedings or other proceedings relating to a mortgage unless the mortgagee asks the court to make an order for his costs to be paid by another party. Where the contract entitles a mortgagee to add the costs of litigation relating to the mortgage to the sum secured by it and/or requires a mortgagor to pay those costs the mortgagor may make application to the court to direct an account of the mortgagee's costs be taken (para 50.4 and CPR r 25.1(1)(n)). The court on hearing the application will consider whether the costs have been unreasonably incurred or are unreasonable in amount and may make an order for those costs to be assessed in accordance with para 50.4 and CPR r 48.3.

SECTION 50A – LIMITATION ON COURT'S POWER TO AWARD COSTS IN FAVOUR OF TRUSTEE OR PERSONAL REPRESENTATIVE: RULE 48.4

50A.1 A trustee or personal representative is entitled to an indemnity out of the relevant trust fund or estate for costs properly incurred, which may include costs awarded against the trustee or personal representative in favour of another party.

50A.2 Whether costs were properly incurred depends on all the circumstances of the case, and may, for example, depend on –

(1) whether the trustee or personal representative obtained directions from the court before bringing or defending the proceedings;
(2) whether the trustee or personal representative acted in the interests of the fund or estate or in substance for a benefit other than that of the estate, including his own; and
(3) whether the trustee or personal representative acted in some way unreasonably in bringing or defending, or in the conduct of, the proceedings.

50A.3 The trustee or personal representative is not to be taken to have acted in substance for a benefit other than that of the fund by reason only that he has defended a claim in which relief is sought against him personally.

SECTION 51 – COSTS WHERE MONEY IS PAYABLE BY OR TO A CHILD OR PATIENT: RULE 48.5

51.1 The circumstances in which the court need not order the assessment of costs under rule 48.5(3) are as follows –

(a) where there is no need to do so to protect the interests of the child or patient or his estate;
(b) where another party has agreed to pay a specified sum in respect of the costs of the child or patient and the solicitor acting for the child or patient has waived the right to claim further costs;
(c) where the court has decided the costs payable to the child or patient by way of summary assessment and the solicitor acting for the child or patient has waived the right to claim further costs;
(d) where an insurer or other person is liable to discharge the costs which the child or patient would otherwise be liable to pay to his solicitor and the court is satisfied that the insurer or other person is financially able to discharge those costs.

SECTION 52 – LITIGANTS IN PERSON: RULE 48.6

52.1 In order to qualify as an expert for the purpose of rule 48.6(3)(c) (expert assistance in connection with assessing the claim for costs), the person in question must be a –

(1) barrister,
(2) solicitor,
(3) Fellow of the Institute of Legal Executives,
(4) Fellow of the Association of Law Costs Draftsmen,
(5) law costs draftsman who is a member of the Academy of Experts,
(6) law costs draftsman who is a member of the Expert Witness Institute.

52.2 Where a litigant in person wishes to prove that he has suffered financial loss he should produce to the court any written evidence he relies on to support that claim, and serve a copy of that evidence on any party against whom he seeks costs at least 24 hours before the hearing at which the question may be decided.

52.3 Where a litigant in person commences detailed assessment proceedings under rule 47.6 he should serve copies of that written evidence with the notice of commencement.

52.4 The amount which may be allowed to a litigant in person under rule 46.3(5)(b) and rule 48.6(4) is £9.25 per hour.

52.5 Attention is drawn to rule 48.6(6)(b). A solicitor who, instead of acting for himself, is represented in the proceedings by his firm or by himself in his firm name, is not, for the purpose of the Civil Procedure Rules, a litigant in person.

SECTION 53 – PERSONAL LIABILITY OF LEGAL REPRESENTATIVE FOR COSTS – WASTED COSTS ORDERS: RULE 48.7

53.1 Rule 48.7 deals with wasted costs orders against legal representatives. Such orders can be made at any stage in the proceedings up to and including the proceedings relating to the detailed assessment of costs. In general, applications for wasted costs are best left until after the end of the trial.

53.2 The court may make a wasted costs order against a legal representative on its own initiative.

53.3 A party may apply for a wasted costs order –

(1) by filing an application notice in accordance with Part 23; or
(2) by making an application orally in the course of any hearing.

53.4 It is appropriate for the court to make a wasted costs order against a legal representative, only if –

(1) the legal representative has acted improperly, unreasonably or negligently;
(2) his conduct has caused a party to incur unnecessary costs; and
(3) it is just in all the circumstances to order him to compensate that party for the whole or part of those costs.

53.5 The court will give directions about the procedure that will be followed in each case in order to ensure that the issues are dealt with in a way which is fair and as simple and summary as the circumstances permit.

53.6 As a general rule the court will consider whether to make a wasted costs order in two stages –

(1) in the first stage, the court must be satisfied –
    (a) that it has before it evidence or other material which, if unanswered, would be likely to lead to a wasted costs order being made; and
    (b) the wasted costs proceedings are justified notwithstanding the likely costs involved.
(2) at the second stage (even if the court is satisfied under paragraph (1)) the court will consider, after giving the legal representative an opportunity to give reasons why the court should not make a wasted costs order, whether it is appropriate to make a wasted costs order in accordance with paragraph 53.4 above.

53.7 On an application for a wasted costs order under Part 23 the court may proceed to the second stage described in paragraph 53.6 without first adjourning the hearing if it is satisfied that the legal representative has already had a reasonable opportunity to give reasons why the court should not make a wasted costs order. In other cases the court will adjourn the hearing before proceeding to the second stage.

53.8 On an application for a wasted costs order under Part 23 the application notice and any evidence in support must identify –

(1) what the legal representative is alleged to have done or failed to do; and
(2) the costs that he may be ordered to pay or which are sought against him.

53.9 A wasted costs order is an order –

(1) that the legal representative pay a specified sum in respect of costs to a party; or
(2) for costs relating to a specified sum or items of work to be disallowed.

53.10 Attention is drawn to rule 44.3A(1) and (2) which respectively prevent the court from assessing any additional liability until the conclusion of the proceedings (or the part of the proceedings) to which the funding arrangement relates, and set out the orders the court may make at the conclusion of the proceedings.

Scope of provision—The law relating to wasted costs orders remains unchanged. Paragraph 53.4 gives brief guidance when it is appropriate for a court to make a wasted costs order and para 53.6 sets out the two stage process in relation to an application for wasted costs. Although a two stage process is envisaged the court can, if it satisfied that the legal representative has had reasonable notice, proceed to the second stage without an adjournment (para 53.7). It is now clear that orders for wasted costs can be made in three ways –
(1) on the courts own initiative
(2) on a Pt 23 application
(3) on application made orally at a hearing

An application made in accordance with CPR Pt 23 must comply with the requirements of para 53.8. The court in addition to making the orders referred to in para 53.9 can order a solicitor to indemnify his own client in relation to a costs order made against him.

SECTION 54 – BASIS OF DETAILED ASSESSMENT OF SOLICITOR AND CLIENT COSTS: RULE 48.8

54.1 A client and his solicitor may agree whatever terms they consider appropriate about the payment of the solicitor's charges for his services. If however, the costs are of an unusual nature (either in amount or in the type of costs incurred) those costs will be presumed to have been unreasonably incurred unless the solicitor satisfies the court that he informed the client that they were unusual and, where the costs relate to litigation, that he informed the client they might not be allowed on an assessment of costs between the parties. That information must have been given to the client before the costs were incurred.

54.2

(1) Costs as between a solicitor and client are assessed on the indemnity basis as defined by rule 44.4.
(2) Attention is drawn to the presumptions set out in rule 48.8(2). These presumptions may be rebutted by evidence to the contrary.

54.3 Rule 48.10 and Section 56 of this practice direction deal with the procedure to be followed for obtaining the assessment of a solicitor's bill pursuant to an order under Part III of the Solicitors Act 1974.

54.4 If a party fails to comply with the requirements of rule 48.10 concerning the service of a breakdown of costs or points of dispute, any other party may apply to the court in which the detailed assessment hearing should take place for an order requiring compliance with rule 48.10. If the court makes such an order, it may –

(a) make it subject to conditions including a condition to pay a sum of money into court; and
(b) specify the consequence of failure to comply with the order or a condition.

54.5

(1) A client who has entered into a conditional fee agreement with a solicitor may apply for assessment of the base costs (which is carried out in accordance with rule 48.8(2) as if there were no conditional fee agreement) or for assessment of the percentage increase (success fee) or both.
(2) Where the court is to assess the percentage increase the court will have regard to all the relevant factors as they appeared to the solicitor or counsel when the conditional fee agreement was entered into.

54.6 Where the client applies to the court to reduce the percentage increase which the solicitor has charged the client under the conditional fee agreement, the client must set out in his application notice –

(a) the reasons why the percentage increase should be reduced; and
(b) what the percentage increase should be.

54.7 The factors relevant to assessing the percentage increase include –

(a) the risk that the circumstances in which the fees or expenses would be payable might not occur;
(b) the disadvantages relating to the absence of payment on account;
(c) whether there is a conditional fee agreement between the solicitor and counsel;
(d) the solicitor's liability for any disbursements.

54.8 When the court is considering the factors to be taken into account, it will have regard to the circumstances as they reasonably appeared to the solicitor or counsel when the conditional fee agreement was entered into.

Scope of provision—Detailed assessment of costs between a solicitor and client is on the indemnity basis and as such proportionality is not a relevant factor. Note the presumptions in CPR r 48.8(2) which can be rebutted.

These provisions do not relate to a contentious business agreement entered into in accordance with the Solicitors Act 1974, ss 59–63. CPR r 48.10 sets out the assessment procedure.

SECTION 56 – PROCEDURE ON ASSESSMENT OF SOLICITOR AND CLIENT COSTS: RULE 48.10

56.1 The paragraphs in this section apply to orders made under Part III of the Solicitors Act 1974 for the assessment of costs. In these paragraphs 'client' includes any person entitled to make an application under Part III of that Act.

56.2 The procedure for obtaining an order under Part III of the Solicitors Act 1974 is by the alternative procedure for claims under Part 8, as modified by rule 67.3 and the Practice Direction supplementing Part 67. Precedent J of the Schedule of Costs Precedents annexed to this practice direction is a model form of claim form. The application must be accompanied by the bill or bills in respect of which assessment is sought, and, if the claim concerns a conditional fee agreement, a copy of that agreement. If the original bill is not available a copy will suffice.

56.3 Model forms of order which the court may make are set out in Precedents K, L and M of the Schedule of Costs Precedents annexed to this practice direction.

56.4 Attention is drawn to the time limits within which the required steps must be taken: ie the solicitor must serve a breakdown of costs within 28 days of the order for costs to be assessed, the client must serve points of dispute within 14 days after service on him of the breakdown, and any reply must be served within 14 days of service of the points of dispute.

56.5 The breakdown of costs referred to in rule 48.10 is a document which contains the following information –

(a) details of the work done under each of the bills sent for assessment; and

(b) in applications under Section 70 of the Solicitors Act 1974, an account showing money received by the solicitor to the credit of the client and sums paid out of that money on behalf of the client but not payments out which were made in satisfaction of the bill or of any items which are claimed in the bill.

56.6 Precedent P of the Schedule of Costs Precedents annexed to this practice direction is a model form of breakdown of costs. A party who is required to serve a breakdown of costs must also serve –

(1) copies of the fee notes of counsel and of any expert in respect of fees claimed in the breakdown, and

(2) written evidence as to any other disbursement which is claimed in the breakdown and which exceeds £250.

56.7 The provisions relating to default costs certificates (rule 47.11) do not apply to cases to which rule 48.10 applies.

56.8 Points of dispute should, as far as practicable, be in the form complying with paragraphs 35.1–35.7.

56.9 The time for requesting a detailed assessment hearing is within 3 months after the date of the order for the costs to be assessed.

56.10 The form of request for a hearing date must be in Form N258C. The request must be accompanied by copies of –

(a) the order sending the bill or bills for assessment;

(b) the bill or bills sent for assessment;

(c) the solicitor's breakdown of costs and any invoices or accounts served with that breakdown;

(d) a copy of the points of dispute, annotated as necessary in order to show which items have been agreed and their value and to show which items remain in dispute;

(e) as many copies of the points of dispute so annotated as there are other parties to the proceedings to whom the court should give details of the assessment hearing requested;

(f) a copy of any replies served;

(g) a statement signed by the party filing the request or his legal representative giving the names and addresses for service of all parties to the proceedings.

56.11 The request must include an estimate of the length of time the detailed assessment hearing will take.

56.12 On receipt of the request for a detailed assessment hearing the court will fix a date for the hearing or if the costs judge or district judge so decides, will give directions or fix a date for a preliminary appointment.

56.13

(1) The court will give at least 14 days notice of the time and place of the detailed assessment hearing to every person named in the statement referred to in paragraph 56.10(g) above.

(2) The court will when giving notice, give all parties other than the party who requested the hearing a copy of the points of dispute annotated by the party requesting the hearing in compliance with paragraph 56.10(e) above.

(3) Attention is drawn to rule 47.14(6) and (7): apart from the solicitor whose bill it is, only those parties who have served points of dispute may be heard on the detailed assessment unless the court gives permission, and only items specified in the points of dispute may be raised unless the court gives permission.

56.14

(1) If a party wishes to vary his breakdown of costs, points of dispute or reply, an amended or supplementary document must be filed with the court and copies of it must be served on all other relevant parties.

(2) Permission is not required to vary a breakdown of costs, points of dispute or a reply but the court may disallow the variation or permit it only upon conditions, including conditions as to the payment of any costs caused or wasted by the variation.

56.15 Unless the court directs otherwise the solicitor must file with the court the papers in support of the bill not less than 7 days before the date for the detailed assessment hearing and not more than 14 days before that date.

56.16 Once the detailed assessment hearing has ended it is the responsibility of the legal representative appearing for the solicitor or, as the case may be, the solicitor in person to remove the papers filed in support of the bill.

56.17

(1) Attention is drawn to rule 47.15 (power to issue an interim certificate).

(2) If, in the course of a detailed assessment hearing of a solicitor's bill to his client, it appears to the costs judge or district judge that in any event the solicitor will be liable in connection with that bill to pay money to the client, he may issue an interim certificate specifying an amount which in his opinion is payable by the solicitor to his client. Such a certificate will include an order to pay the sum it certifies unless the court orders otherwise.

56.18

(1) Attention is drawn to rule 47.16 which requires the solicitor to file a completed bill within 14 days after the end of the detailed assessment hearing. The court may dispense with the requirement to file a completed bill.

(2) After the detailed assessment hearing is concluded the court will –

  (a) complete the court copy of the bill so as to show the amount allowed;

  (b) determine the result of the cash account;

  (c) award the costs of the detailed assessment hearing in accordance with Section 70(8) of the Solicitors Act 1974; and

(d) issue a final costs certificate showing the amount due following the detailed assessment hearing.

56.19 A final costs certificate will include an order to pay the sum it certifies unless the court orders otherwise.

Scope of provision—These provisions relate to Solicitors Act 1974 Pt III assessments where there is a dispute between the solicitor and his client with regard to the solicitor's costs (see the provisions of Pt 67, which sets out the jurisdiction and Solicitors Act 1974, Pt III). An application for an order under these provisions is made by using the alternative procedure for claims under CPR Pt 8. There are model forms to accompany any order which the court may make (Precedents J–M, Schedule of Costs Precedents).

SECTION 57 – TRANSITIONAL ARRANGEMENTS:

57.1 In this section 'the previous rules' means the Rules of the Supreme Court 1965 ('RSC') or County Court Rules 1981 ('CCR'), as appropriate.

General Scheme of Transitional Arrangements concerning Costs Proceedings

57.2

(1) Paragraph 18 of the practice direction which supplements Part 51 (Transitional Arrangements) provides that the CPR govern any assessments of costs which take place on or after 26 April 1999 and states a presumption to be applied in respect of costs for work undertaken before 26 April 1999.

(2) The following paragraphs provide five further transitional arrangements –

- (a) to provide an additional presumption to be applied when assessing costs which were awarded by an order made in a county court before 26 April 1999 which allowed costs 'on Scale 1' to be determined in accordance with CCR Appendix A, or 'on the lower scale' to be determined in accordance with CCR Appendix C;
- (b) to preserve the effect of CCR Appendix B Part III, paragraph 2;
- (c) to clarify the approach to be taken where a bill of costs was provisionally taxed before 26 April 1999 and the receiving party is unwilling to accept the result of the provisional taxation;
- (d) to preserve the right to carry in objections or apply for a reconsideration in all taxation proceedings commenced before 26 April 1999;
- (e) to deal with funding arrangements made before 3 July 2000.

Scope of provision—See PD51, para 18. The general presumption is that no costs for work undertaken before 26 April 1999 will be disallowed if those costs would have been allowed in a costs taxation before 26 April 1999.

Scale 1 or lower scale costs

57.3 Where an order was made in county court proceedings before 26 April 1999 under which the costs were allowed on Scale 1 or the lower scale, the general presumption is that no costs will be allowed under that order which would not have been allowed in a taxation before 26 April 1999.

Fixed costs on the lower scale

57.4 The amount to be allowed as fixed costs for making or opposing an application for a rehearing to set aside a judgment given before 26 April 1999 where the costs are on lower scale is £11.25.

Bills provisionally taxed before 26 April 1999

57.5 In respect of bills of costs provisionally taxed before 26 April 1999 –

(1) The previous rules apply on the question who can request a hearing and the time limits for doing so; and
(2) The CPR govern any subsequent hearing in that case.

'The previous rules' (para 57.5(1))—The former RSC Ord 62 and CCR Ord 38 apply in relation to who can request a hearing and the time limits for so doing. Thereafter the CPR govern any subsequent hearing.

Bills taxed before 26 April 1999

57.6 Where a bill of costs was taxed before 26 April 1999, the previous rules govern the steps which can be taken to challenge that taxation.

'the previous rules'—The former RSC Ord 62 and CCR Ord 38 provide the steps that can be taken to challenge the taxation by way of carrying in objections or review.

Other taxation proceedings

57.7

(1) This paragraph applies to taxation proceedings which were commenced before 26 April 1999, were assigned for taxation to a taxing master or district judge, and which were still pending on 26 April 1999.
(2) Any assessment of costs that takes place in cases to which this paragraph applies which is conducted on or after 26 April 1999, will be conducted in accordance with the CPR.
(3) In addition to the possibility of appeal under rules 47.20 to 47.23 and Part 52 any party to a detailed assessment who is dissatisfied with any decision on a detailed assessment made by a costs judge or district judge may apply to that costs judge or district judge for a review of the decision. The review shall, for procedural purposes, be treated as if it were an appeal from an authorised court officer.
(4) The right of review provided by paragraph (3) above, will not apply in cases in which, at least 28 days before the date of the assessment hearing, all parties were served with notice that the rights of appeal in respect of that hearing would be governed by Part 47 Section VIII (Appeals from Authorised Court Officers in Detailed Assessment Proceedings) and Part 52 (Appeals).
(5) An order for the service of notice under sub-paragraph (4) above may be made on the application of any party to the detailed assessment proceedings or may be made by the court of its own initiative.

Scope of provision—Generally these provisions apply only to taxation proceedings prior to 26 April 1999 which had already been assigned to a taxing master or district judge and were pending at 26 April 1999. Any assessment of costs conducted on or after 26 April 1999 will usually be in accordance with the CPR.

Transitional provisions concerning the Access to Justice Act 1999 sections 28 to 31

57.8

(1) Sections 28 to 31 of the Access to Justice Act 1999, the Conditional Fee Agreements Regulations 2000, the Access to Justice (Membership Organisations) Regulations 2000 and the Access to Justice Act 1999 (Transitional Provisions) Order 2000 came into force on 1 April 2000. The Civil Procedure (Amendment No 3) Rules come into force on 3 July 2000.

(2) The Access to Justice Act 1999 (Transitional Provisions) Order 2000 provides that no conditional fee agreement or other arrangement about costs entered into before 1 April 2000 can be a funding arrangement, as defined in rule 43.2. The order also has the effect that where an conditional fee agreement or other funding arrangement has been entered into before 1 April 2000 and a second or subsequent funding arrangement of the same type is entered into on or after 1 April 2000, the second or subsequent funding arrangement does not give rise to a liability which is recoverable from a paying party.

(3) The Collective Conditional Fee Agreements Regulations 2000 came into force on 30 November 2000. The Regulations apply to agreements entered into on or after that date. Agreements entered into before that date are treated as if the Regulations had not come into force.

57.9

(1) Rule 39 of the Civil Procedure (Amendment No 3) Rules 2000 applies where between 1 April and 3 July 2000 (including both dates) –
   - a funding arrangement is entered into, and
   - proceedings are started in respect of a claim, the subject of that agreement.

(2) Attention is drawn to the need to act promptly so as to comply with the requirements of the Rules and the practice directions by 31 July 2000 (ie within the 28 days from 3 July 2000 permitted by Rule 39) if that compliance is to be treated as compliance with the relevant provision. Attention is drawn in particular to Rule 44.15 (Providing Information about Funding Arrangements) and Section 19 of this practice direction.

(3) Nothing in the legislation referred to above makes provision for a party who has entered into a funding arrangement to recover from another party any amount of an additional liability which relates to anything done or any costs incurred before the arrangement was entered into.

Scope of provision—These provisions make it clear that no CFA or other funding arrangement entered into before 1 April 2000 can create an additional liability recoverable from the paying party (see also *Cheshire County Court v Lea* (2003) Lawtel, 5 March). The Access to Justice Act 1999 (Transitional Provisions) Order 2000 makes it clear that where a legal representative has entered into a funding arrangement with his client before 1 April 2000 any subsequent CFA or funding arrangement entered into after 1 April 2000 cannot give rise to an additional liability which is recoverable from a paying party. Consequently it is only a first CFA entered into after 1 April 2000 which will give rise to a recoverable additional liability.

SCHEDULE OF COSTS PRECEDENTS

A: Model form of bill of costs (receiving party's solicitor and counsel on CFA terms)

B: Model form of bill of costs (detailed assessment of additional liability only)

C: Model form of bill of costs (payable by Defendant and the LSC)

D: Model form of bill of costs (alternative form, single column for amounts claimed, separate parts for costs payable by the LSC only)

E: Legal Aid/LSC Schedule of Costs

F: Certificates for inclusion in bill of costs

G: Points of dispute

H: Estimate of costs served on other parties

J: Solicitors Act 1974: Part 8 claim form under Part III of the Act

K: Solicitors Act 1974: order for delivery of bill

L: Solicitors Act 1974: order for detailed assessment (client)

M: Solicitors Act 1974: order for detailed assessment (solicitors)

P: Solicitors Act 1974: breakdown of costs

Costs Precedents—All of the Costs Precedents can be accessed on the *Civil Court Service* CD-ROM or via the Internet at the Court Service website *http://www.courtservice.gov.uk.*

Guide to Summary Assessment of Costs Revised January 2005

FOREWORD

2005 Edition

Since the introduction of the CPR, Judges at all levels are required to assess costs summarily at the end of a trial on the fast track or at the conclusion of any other hearing which has lasted not more than one day. This requirement led to an immediate request from Judges for some guidance as to how to go about summary assessment. A comprehensive Guide was published in 2002 by the Supreme Court Costs Office which contained, at Appendix 2, guideline figures for a large number of places on the circuits. Those guideline figures were revised in 2003, and, in order to avoid having a multiplicity of figures, three separate bands were introduced, each covering areas having broadly similar charging rates. In addition banded rates were also given for the City of London, Central London and Outer London.

The Retail Prices Index has been used on this occasion to arrive at rates for each area to take effect from 1 January 2005 with the intention that those rates should remain in force for 2 years.

Questions have been raised as to the provenance and standing of the Guide. Its provenance is that it was produced at the request of Sir Richard Scott V-C when Deputy Head of Civil Justice (now Lord Scott of Foscotte) in order to assist Judges who were faced for the first time with the task of summary assessment. As to the standing of the Guide it is, as it makes clear, no more than a guide and a starting point for Judges carrying out summary assessment. The figures set out in Appendix 2 to the Guide are broad approximations only. The Guide is intended to be of help and assistance to Judges but is not intended as a substitute for the proper exercise of their discretion having heard argument on the issues to be decided.

Dated 21 December 2004
The Right Honourable
The Lord Phillips of Worth Matravers
Master of the Rolls

INTRODUCTION

1 Sections 13 and 14 of the Costs Practice Direction deal with the general provisions relating to summary assessment. Rule 43.2 defines costs and Rule 44.7 contains the court's power to make a summary assessment. (Appendix 1 contains extracts from the relevant Rules and Practice Directions.)

2 The general rule is that the court should make a summary assessment of the costs:

(a) at the conclusion of the trial of a case which has been dealt with on the fast track, in which case the order will deal with the costs of the whole claim; and
(b) at the conclusion of any other hearing which has lasted not more than one day, in which case the order will deal with the costs of the application or matter to which the hearing related. If this hearing disposes of the claim, the order may deal with the costs of the whole claim.

3 If there is a conditional fee agreement or other funding arrangement, Rule 44.3A prevents the court from making a summary assessment of an additional liability before the conclusion of the proceedings or the part of the proceedings to which the funding arrangement relates. In such a case, the court should nonetheless make a summary assessment of the base costs of the hearing or application unless there is good reason not to do so. Where the court makes a summary assessment of the base costs, all statements of costs and estimates put before the Judge will be retained on the court file and the Judge carrying out a final assessment must be supplied with copies of all the costs orders previously made and, if required, be shown all the previous costs statements and estimates.

4 The court should not make a summary assessment of the costs of a receiving party who is an assisted person or LSC funded client. The court may make a summary assessment of costs payable by an assisted person or by a LSC funded client. Such an assessment is not by itself a determination of that person's liability to pay those costs (as to which see Rule 44.17 and paragraphs 20.1 to 22.33 of the Costs Practice Direction.

5 The court must not make a summary assessment of the costs of a receiving party who is a child or patient within Part 21 unless the solicitor acting for the child or patient has waived the right to further costs. The court may make a summary assessment of costs payable by a child or patient.

6 The court awarding costs cannot make an order for the summary assessment to be carried out by a costs officer. If summary assessment of costs is appropriate but the court awarding costs is unable to carry out the assessment on the day it must give directions as to a further hearing before the same Judge or order detailed assessment.

THE APPROACH TO COSTS

7 General approach to summary and detailed assessment should be the same. For the summary assessment to be accurate the Judge must be informed about

previous summary assessments carried out in the case. This is particularly important where the Judge is assessing all the costs at the conclusion of a case.

8 The court should not be seen to be endorsing disproportionate and unreasonable costs. Accordingly:

(a) When the amount of the costs to be paid has been agreed the court should make this clear by saying that the order is by consent.
(b) If the Judge is to make an order which is not by consent, he will, so far as possible, ensure that the final figure is not disproportionate and/or unreasonable having regard to Part 1 of the CPR. He will retain this responsibility notwithstanding the absence of challenge to individual items comprised in the figure sought.

9 Where a case is simple and straightforward it is obviously easier to decide whether the final figure is disproportionate than where the case is more complex. For this reason, it is impossible to ignore the work on the case which has had to be done.

10 The fact that the paying party is not disputing the amount of costs can be taken as some indication that the amount is proportionate and reasonable. The Judge therefore will intervene only if satisfied that the costs are so disproportionate that it is right to do so.

11 The court can allow a sum which it considers to be proportionate as a payment on account whilst at the same time ordering detailed assessment.

THE BASIS OF ASSESSMENT

THE STANDARD BASIS

12 Rule 44.4(1) and (2) (Appendix 1) provide that where the court assesses the amount of costs on the standard basis it will not allow costs which have been unreasonably incurred or are unreasonable in amount and will only allow costs which are proportionate to the matters in issue. The court will resolve in favour of the paying party any doubt which it may have as to whether the costs were reasonably incurred or were reasonable and proportionate in amount.

THE INDEMNITY BASIS

13 Rule 44.4(1) and (3) (Appendix 1) provide that where the court assesses the amount of costs on the indemnity basis it will not allow costs which have been unreasonably incurred or are unreasonable in amount and it will resolve in favour of the receiving party any doubt which it may have as to whether costs were reasonably incurred or were reasonable in amount. The test of proportionality is not mentioned in the definition of the indemnity basis.

PROPORTIONALITY

14 'Proportionality' is not defined in the rules or the Practice Direction. Section 11 of the Costs Practice Direction indicates, however, that in applying the test of proportionality the court will have regard to rule 1.1(2)(c) by, so far as practicable, dealing with the case in ways which are proportionate:

(i) to the amount of money involved;
(ii) to the importance of the case;
(iii) to the complexity of the issues; and

(iv) to the financial position of each party.

15 Paragraphs 11.1 to 11.3 of the Practice Direction give the following warnings as to the test of proportionality.

(i) The relationship between the total costs incurred and the financial value of the claim may not be a reliable guide. A fixed percentage cannot be applied in all cases to the value of the claim in order to ascertain whether or not the costs are proportionate.

(ii) In any proceedings, there will be costs which will inevitably be incurred and which are necessary for the successful conduct of the case. Solicitors are not required to conduct litigation at rates which are uneconomic. Thus in a modest claim the proportion of costs is likely to be higher than in a large claim and may even equal or possibly exceed the amount in dispute.

(iii) Where a trial takes place the time taken by the court in dealing with the particular issue may not be an accurate guide to the amount of time properly spent by the legal or other representatives in preparation for the trial of that issue.

16 The Court of Appeal has given guidance on the correct approach to proportionality when assessing costs:

> 'what is required is a two stage approach. There has to be a global approach and an item by item approach. The global approach will indicate whether the total sum claimed is or appears to be disproportionate having particular regard to the considerations which Part 44.5(3) states are relevant. If the costs as a whole are not disproportionate according to that test then all that is normally required is that each item should have been reasonably incurred and the costs for that item should be reasonable. If on the other hand the costs as a whole appear disproportionate then the court will want to be satisfied that the work in relation to each item was necessary, and, if necessary, the cost of the item was reasonable'

(*Home Office v Lownds* [2002] EWCA Civ 365; [2002] 1 WLR 2450; [2002] 4 All ER 775 CA).

The text of rule 44.5(3) is included in Appendix 1 to this Guide.

17 The relevant costs for consideration at the first stage are the base costs only before VAT is added (CPD 11.5 and *Giambrone v JMC Holidays* [2003] 2 Costs LR 189).

18 The fact that, at the first stage, the costs as a whole appear to be proportionate does not prevent the court from finding individual items are disproportionate and applying the test of necessity to them alone (Giambrone).

SUMMARY ASSESSMENT WHERE COSTS CLAIMED INCLUDE AN ADDITIONAL LIABILITY

19 Rule 44.3A deals with costs orders relating to funding arrangements. An order for payment of 'costs' includes an additional liability incurred under a funding arrangement. Where the court carries out a summary assessment of base costs before the conclusion of proceedings it is helpful if the order identifies separately the amount allowed in respect of: solicitors charges; Counsel's fees; other disbursements; and any value added tax. If this is not done, the court which later makes an assessment of an additional liability, will have to apportion the base costs previously assessed.

20 Rule 44.3B sets out the limits on recovery under funding arrangements. The court will consider the amount of any additional liability separately from the base costs and when considering the factors to be taken into account under rule 44.5 in assessing an additional liability the court will have regard to the facts and circumstances as they reasonably appeared to the solicitor or Counsel when the funding arrangement was entered into and at the time of any variation of the arrangement.

ORDERS MADE BEFORE THE CONCLUSION OF PROCEEDINGS

21 Where an order for costs is made before the conclusion of the proceedings and a legal representative for the receiving party has entered into a conditional fee agreement the court may summarily assess the base costs. An order for payment of those costs will not be made unless the court is satisfied that the receiving party is at the time liable to pay to his legal representative an amount equal to or greater than the costs claimed. If the court is not so satisfied it may direct that any costs, for which the receiving party may not in the final event be liable, be paid into court to await the outcome of the case or shall not be enforceable until further order, or the court may postpone the receiving party's right to receive payment in some other way.

ORDERS MADE AT THE CONCLUSION OF PROCEEDINGS

22 Where the court makes a summary assessment of an additional liability at the conclusion of the proceedings, that assessment must relate to the whole of the proceedings; this will include any additional liability relating to base costs allowed by the court when making a summary assessment on a previous application or hearing.

FACTORS TO BE TAKEN INTO ACCOUNT IN DECISING THE AMOUNT OF COSTS

23 Rule 44.5 (Appendix 1) sets out the factors to be taken into account. Those factors include: the conduct of all the parties, including in particular, conduct before as well as during the proceedings and the efforts made, if any, before and during the proceedings in order to try to resolve the dispute.

24 In deciding whether the costs claimed are reasonable and (on the standard basis) proportionate, the court will consider the amount of any additional liability separately from the base costs.

25 The Judge, before commencing a summary assessment on the standard basis should, in accordance with the guidance in *Home Office v Lownds* [2002] EWCA Civ 365; [2002] 1 WLR 2450; [2002] 4 All ER 775 CA) (see paragraph 16 above), step back and consider the proportionality of the costs claimed. If the costs claimed overall appear proportionate they may be assessed applying a test of reasonableness. If on the other hand the costs appear to be disproportionate then the more stringent test of necessity should be applied. If previous orders for summarily assessed costs have been made then the Judge should, subject to paragraph 27, consider the proportionality of the total costs of the proceedings.

26 In considering what is necessary, a sensible standard of necessity has to be adopted. This is a standard which takes fully into account the need to make allowances for the different judgements which those responsible for litigation can sensibly come to as to what is required. The danger of setting too high a standard with the benefit of hindsight has to be avoided. The threshold required

to meet 'necessity' is higher than that of 'reasonableness' but it is still a standard that a competent practitioner should be able to achieve without undue difficulty. In deciding what is necessary the conduct of the other party is highly relevant. A party who is unco-operative may render necessary costs which would otherwise be unnecessary. It is acceptable that that party should pay the costs for the expense which he has made necessary.

27 In arriving at a final figure the Judge should not reduce the costs of the receiving party on account of the costs awarded to that party under a previous summary assessment. To do so would impugn the decision of the earlier Judge. Where however the amount of costs previously ordered to be paid has been agreed by the parties with no judicial assessment there is nothing to prevent the court taking these figures into account when considering proportionality.

CONDITIONAL FEE AGREEMENTS WITH A SUCCESS FEE

28 The factors to be taken into account when deciding whether a percentage increase is reasonable may include:

- (a) the risk that the circumstances in which the costs, fees or expenses would be payable might or might not occur;
- (b) the legal representative's liability for any disbursements;
- (c) what other methods of financing the costs were available to the receiving party.

The court has the power to allow different percentages for different items of costs or for different periods during which costs were incurred (CPD 11.8(2)). The court should have regard to the facts and circumstances as they reasonably appeared to the solicitor or Counsel when the funding arrangement was entered into, and at the time of any variation of the agreement (CPD 11.7).

29 A percentage increase should not be reduced simply on the ground that, when added to base costs which are reasonable and (where relevant) proportionate, the total appears disproportionate (CPD 11.9).

In road traffic accident claims where the accident occurred on or after 6 October 2003 the percentage increase to be allowed as a success fee is fixed by rules: see CPR 45 Section 111.

INSURANCE PREMIUMS

30 Relevant factors to be taken into account when deciding whether the cost of insurance cover is reasonable include:

- (a) where the insurance cover is not purchased in support of a conditional fee agreement with a success fee, how its cost compares with the likely cost of funding the case with a conditional fee agreement with a success fee and supporting insurance cover;
- (b) the level and extent of the cover provided;
- (c) the availability of any pre-existing insurance cover;
- (d) whether any part of the premium would be rebated in the event of early settlement;
- (e) the amount of commission payable to the receiving party or his legal representatives or other agents.

MEMBERSHIP ORGANISATION – ADDITIONAL AMOUNT

31 When considering a provision made by a membership organisation the court should not allow a provision which exceeds the likely cost to the receiving party of the premium of an insurance policy against the risk of incurring a liability to pay the costs of other parties to the proceedings. In those circumstances the court will have regard to the factors set out in paragraph 26 above in addition to the factors set out in rule 44.5 (Appendix 1).

SUCCESS FEE DIPUTES BETWEEN LEGAL REPRESENTATIVE AND CLIENT: PROCEDURE FOLLOWING THE SUMMARY ASSESSMENT

32 A court which has made a summary assessment which disallows or reduces a legal representative's percentage increase may then and there decide the issue whether the disallowed amount should continue to be payable. The court may do this if:

- (a) the receiving party and all parties to the relevant agreement consent to the court doing so;
- (b) the receiving party (or, if corporate, a duly authorised officer) is present in court; and
- (c) the court is satisfied that the issue can be fairly decided then and there.

33 In any other case the court will give directions to enable an application to be made by the legal representative for the disallowed amount to be payable by his client, including if appropriate a direction that the application will be determined by a Costs Judge or District Judge of the court dealing with the case.

GENERAL PRINCIPLES TO BE APPLIED IN SUMMARY ASSESSMENT

THE INDEMNITY PRINCIPLE

34 A party in whose favour an order for costs has been made may not recover more than he is liable to pay his own solicitors. See *Harold v Smith* [1865] H&N 381, 385; and *Gundry v Sainsbury* [1910] 1 KB 645 CA. There are exceptions to the principle, notably costs funded by the Legal Services Commission and fees payable under certain types of conditional fee agreement.

35 The statement of costs put before the court for summary assessment must be signed by the party or its legal representative. That form contains the statement:

> 'The costs estimated above do not exceed the costs which the party is liable to pay in respect of the work which this estimate covers.'

36 Following the decision of Lord Justice Henry in *Bailey v IBC Vehicles Ltd* [1998] 3 All ER 570 CA, the signature of a statement of costs (or a bill for detailed assessment) by a solicitor is, in normal circumstances, sufficient to enable the court to be satisfied that the indemnity principle has not been breached. A solicitor is an officer of the court and as Henry LJ stated:

> 'In so signing he certifies that the contents of the bill are correct. That signature is no empty formality. The bill specifies the hourly rates applied … If an agreement between the receiving solicitor and his client … restricted (say) the hourly rate payable by the client that hourly rate is the most that can be claimed or recovered on assessment … The signature of the bill of costs … is effectively the certificate of an officer of the court that

the receiving party's solicitors are not seeking to recover in relation to any item more than they have agreed to charge their client . . .'

DEFERRING PAYMENT OF COSTS

37 As a general rule a paying party should be ordered to pay the amount of any summarily assessed costs within 14 days. Before making such an order the court should consider whether an order for payment of the costs might bring the action to an end and whether this would be just in all the circumstances.

LITIGANTS IN PERSON

38 Where the receiving party is a litigant in person rule 48.6 (Appendix 1) governs the way in which the question of costs should be dealt with. A litigant in person may be allowed a sum in respect of costs at the rate of £9.25 for each hour reasonably spent in preparation and attendance. He may be allowed a reasonable sum in excess of that amount if he can show that his work on the case has caused him financial loss justifying a higher award.

39 In all cases there is an absolute cap on the amount recoverable by a litigant in person, namely the reasonable costs of disbursements plus two thirds of the amount which would have been allowed if the litigant in person had been legally represented. (rule 48.6(2)). The litigant in person is entitled to recover in addition: payments reasonably made for legal services relating to the conduct of the proceedings; and the costs of obtaining expert assistance in connection with assessing the claim for costs. This does mean that a litigant in person may be able to claim both the cost of obtaining legal advice and services as well as the cost of undertaking the litigation in person. Those qualified to give expert assistance in connection with assessing the claim for costs are: a barrister, a solicitor, Fellow of the Institute of Legal Executives, Fellow of the Association of Law Costs Draftsmen, a law costs draftsman who is a member of the Academy of Experts and a law costs draftsman who is a member of the Expert Witness Institute.

40 Although the definition of litigant in person includes a solicitor, a solicitor who instead of acting for himself is represented in the proceedings by his firm, or by himself in his firm name, is not, for the purpose of the Civil Procedure Rules, a litigant in person (see Section 52 of the Costs Practice Direction).

GUIDELINE FIGURES FOR SOLICITORS HOURLY RATES

41 Guideline figures for solicitors charges (as at January 2005) are published in Appendix 2 to this Guide, which also contains some explanatory notes. The guideline rates are not scale figures: they are broad approximations only. In any particular area the Designated Civil Judge may supply more up to date guidelines for rates in that area. Costs and fees exceeding the guidelines may well be justified in an appropriate case and that is a matter for the exercise of discretion by the court.

42 The guideline figures are not intended to replace figures used by those with accurate local knowledge. They are intended to provide a starting point for those faced with summary assessment who do not have that local knowledge.

43 In substantial and complex litigation an hourly rate in excess of the guideline figures may be appropriate for grade A fee earners where other factors, including the value of the litigation, the level of the complexity, the

urgency or importance of the matter, as well as any international element, would justify a significantly higher rate to reflect higher average costs.

SOLICITOR ADVOCATES

44 Remuneration of solicitor advocates is based on the normal principles for remuneration of solicitors. It is not therefore appropriate to seek a brief fee and refreshers as if the advocate were a member of the Bar. If the cost of using a solicitor advocate is more than the cost of instructing Counsel, the higher cost is unlikely to be recovered. The figures properly recoverable by solicitor advocates should reflect the amount of preparation undertaken, the time spent in court and the weight and gravity of the case.

45 Where the solicitor advocate is also the solicitor who does the preparation work, the solicitor is entitled to charge normal solicitors' rates for that preparation, but once the solicitor advocate starts preparation for the hearing itself the fees recoverable should not exceed those which would be recoverable in respect of Counsel.

46 It is clearly wrong for the fees of a solicitor acting as a junior Counsel to exceed the fee appropriate for the leading Counsel.

COUNSEL FEES

47 A proper measure for Counsels' fees is to estimate what fee a hypothetical Counsel, capable of conducting the case effectively, but unable or unwilling to insist on the higher fees sometimes demanded by Counsel of pre-eminent reputation, would be content to take on the brief: but there is no precise standard of measurement and the judge must, using his or her knowledge and experience, determine the proper figure. (Per Pennycuick J in *Simpsons Motor Sales (London) Ltd v Hendon Borough Council* [1965] 1 WLR 112.)

GUIDELINE FIGURES

48 Appendix 2 contains a table of Counsels' fees relating to proceedings in run of the mill cases in the Queen's Bench and Chancery Divisions and in the Administrative Court. These figures are not recommended rates but it is hoped that Judges may find the figures of some help when they are called upon to assess Counsels' fees. It has not been possible to publish more specific guideline figures because of lack of sufficient data.

49 The figures contained in the table in Appendix 2 are based upon figures supplied by the Bar and in broad terms the figures are averages based on the information supplied.

THE TIME SPENT BY SOLICITORS AND COUNSEL

50 There can be no guidance as to whether the time claimed has been reasonably spent, and it is for the Judge in each case to consider the work properly undertaken by Solicitors and Counsel and to arrive at a figure which is in all circumstances reasonable.

A MODEL FORM OF STATEMENT OF COSTS

51 A model form of Statement of Costs is to be found in Appendix 3.

FAST TRACK TRIAL COSTS

52 The amount of fast track trial costs is set out in the table to Rule 46.2. Rule 46.1(2) provides definitions of 'advocate', 'fast track trial costs' and 'trial'. The court may not award more or less than the amount shown in the table except where it decides not to award any fast track trial costs or where rule 46.3 applies. Rule 46.3 sets out the court's power to award more or less than the amount of fast track trial costs (Appendix 1).

SUMMARY ASSESSMENT OF COSTS IN THE COURT OF APPEAL

53 The Practice Direction supplementing CPR Part 52 identifies five types of hearing at which costs are likely to be assessed by way of summary assessment and states that parties attending any of those hearings should be prepared to deal with the summary assessment. The Costs Practice Direction (paragraph 13.5) places a duty on the parties and their legal representatives to file and serve a statement of any costs they intend to claim in respect of such hearings.

55 In this Guide the term 'Counsel' includes a solicitor-advocate who is instructed by another solicitor.

CONTESTED DIRECTIONS HEARINGS; APPLICATIONS FOR PERMISSION TO APPEAL AT WHICH THE RESPONDENT IS PRESENT AND APPEALS FROM CASE MANAGEMENT DECISIONS

56 The guidance given below in relation to contested directions hearings, applications for permission to appeal at which the respondent is present and appeals from case management decisions relates to hearings which, although important, are not difficult or complex and are not of general public importance and are listed either for a hearing not exceeding one hour or for a hearing not exceeding one half day.

57 If these hearings are attended by solicitor and Counsel the number of hours which it is reasonable to presume that the solicitor will undertake (in respect of preparation, attendance, travel in Central London and waiting) is 4 hours for a one hour appointment and 7.5 hours for a half day appointment. It is reasonable to presume that Counsel who has between 5 and 10 years' experience merits a fee of approximately £550 (exclusive of VAT) for a one hour appointment and merits a fee of approximately £880 (exclusive of VAT) for a half day appointment.

58 If these hearings were attended by a solicitor without Counsel it is reasonable to presume that the total number of hours the solicitor will spend (in respect of preparation, attendance, travel in Central London and waiting) is 5 hours for a one hour appointment and 10 hours for a half day appointment.

59 If these hearings are attended by a litigant in person it is reasonable to presume that the total number of hours the litigant in person will spend (in respect of preparation, attendance and waiting) is 9 hours for a one hour appointment and 14 hours for a half day appointment. In each case a further allowance should be made for time and expense in travelling to the appointment.

DISMISSAL LIST HEARING AT WHICH THE RESPONDENT IS PRESENT

60 The guidance given below in relation to dismissal list hearings in the Court of Appeal at which the respondent is present, relates to cases which are listed for

less than one hour and are of significantly less weight than the contested directions hearings, applications for permission to appeal and appeals from case management decisions described above.

61 If the hearing is attended by solicitor and Counsel (for the appellant or the respondent), it is reasonable to presume that the total number of hours to allow the solicitor (in respect of preparation, attendance, travel in Central London and waiting) is 2 hours, and it is reasonable to presume that Counsel who has between 5 and 10 years' experience merits a fee of approximately £385 (exclusive of VAT).

62 If an appeal is dismissed and costs are awarded to the respondent, it will probably be appropriate to allow further costs in respect of work previously done in responding to the appeal. Consideration should be given to whether it is in fact appropriate to carry out a summary assessment, depending on the amount of work done by the respondent.

63 Subject to paragraph 62, if the hearing is attended by a solicitor without Counsel it is reasonable to presume that the total number of hours to allow the solicitor (in respect of preparation, attendance, travel in Central London and waiting) is 3 hours.

64 Subject to paragraph 62, if the hearing is attended by a litigant in person it is reasonable to presume that the total number of hours to allow the litigant in person (in respect of preparation, attendance and waiting) is 6 hours with a further allowance for time and expense in travelling to the appointment.

APPEALS LISTED FOR ONE DAY OR LESS

65 Appeals listed for one day or less vary enormously as to weight, complexity and importance. Thus, it is not at present possible to give guidance as to the number of hours reasonably spent by solicitors (in respect of preparation, attendances, travel and waiting) in such appeals. The following general guidance is given:

(1) It may not be appropriate to carry out a summary assessment if a case lasts more than half a day or involves leading Counsel since in those circumstances the case is likely to be complex and weighty. It will often be unwise for the court summarily to assess costs in a matter which is not simple and straightforward, unless the difference between the parties is comparatively small, or unless the correct allowance appears clear.

(2) Where both Counsel and solicitors have been instructed, the reasonable fees of Counsel are likely to exceed the reasonable fees of the solicitor.

(3) The fact that the same Counsel appeared in the lower court does not greatly reduce the reasonable fee unless, for example, the lower court dealt with a great many more issues than are raised on the appeal. It is reasonable for Counsel to spend as much time preparing issues for the Court of Appeal hearing as he spent preparing those issues for the lower court hearing.

(4) If the case merits leading Counsel it may merit also the instruction of a junior to assist him. The junior's fees should be allowed at one half of the leader's fees unless:
   - the junior is a senior junior and the case merited both a leader and a senior junior.

- The junior took a responsibility which was equal to or larger than that taken by the leader.
- The junior undertook work not covered by the brief.

(5) In many cases the largest element in the solicitors' reasonable fees for work in the Court of Appeal concerns instructing Counsel and preparing the appeal bundles. Time spent by the solicitor in the development of legal submissions will only be allowed where it does not duplicate work done by Counsel and is claimed at a rate the same or lower than the rate Counsel would have claimed.

(6) Although the solicitor may have spent many hours with the client, the client should have been warned that little of this time is recoverable against a losing party. Reasonable time spent receiving instructions and reporting events should not greatly exceed the time spent on attending the opponents.

(7) Given that the case will be presented by a barrister or a solicitor advocate there is usually no reason for any other solicitor to spend many hours perusing papers. A large claim for such perusal probably indicates that a new fee earner was reading in. Reading in fees are not normally recoverable from an opponent.

(8) Although it is usually reasonable to have a senior fee earner sitting with Counsel in the Court of Appeal, it is not usually reasonable to have two fee earners. The second fee earner may be there for training purposes only.

(9) In most appeals it will be appropriate to make an allowance for copy documents. The allowance for copying which is included in the solicitor's hourly rates will have already been used up or exceeded in the lower court. An hourly rate charge is appropriate for selecting and collating documents and dictating the indices. If the paperwork is voluminous much of this should be delegated to a trainee. Note that:

a. for the copying itself, a fair allowance is 10p per page, i.e. £100 per 1,000 sheets. This includes an allowance for checking the accuracy of the copying.

b. Time spent standing at the photocopier and time spent taking the papers to a local photocopy shop is not recoverable. Such work is not fee earner work; it is secretarial.

(10) It must be borne in mind that skeleton arguments will have been lodged at an early stage, and, in respect of floating appeals, the case may have come into and out of the list. In those circumstances it may be necessary to change Counsel which would inevitably increase the costs. New Counsel may decide to submit a different skeleton argument. Where this has occurred, detailed assessment is to be preferred.

SOLICITORS CHARGES IN THE COURT OF APPEAL

66 Although many appointments in the Court of Appeal merit the attendance of a senior fee earner familiar with the case, the most minor appointments may not. For example, on an application in the dismissal list in a case tried in Newcastle, if Counsel who was briefed for the trial attends it may be unreasonable for a solicitor familiar with the case to travel from Newcastle to attend also. In order to arrive at a notional figure to represent the instruction of and costs of an agent, it may be appropriate to disallow most of the travel time and travelling expenses claimed by the solicitor.

67 The Court of Appeal has stated that it is the duty of litigators (particularly trade unions and insurers) to keep down the cost of litigation. This means that if they instruct London solicitors who charge London rates for a case which has no obvious connection with London and which does not require expertise only to be found there, they will, even if successful, recover less than the solicitors have charged (see *Wraith v Sheffield Forgemasters Ltd* [1998] 1 WLR 132 CA).

68 In relation to the first four types of hearing appropriate for summary assessment in the Court of Appeal, some guidance is given above suggesting the number of hours which may be reasonable for the solicitor to spend. That guidance should be used as a starting point only. The court should also have regard to the number of hours actually claimed.

COUNSELS FEES IN THE COURT OF APPEAL

69 Counsel's fees depend upon the seniority of Counsel which it was reasonable to instruct and the market price for the item of work in question. It is not appropriate to specify an hourly rate for Counsel and to remunerate them at a multiple of that rate according to the number of hours reasonably spent. Such an approach would reward the indolent and penalise the expeditious.

70 In previous paragraphs (paragraphs 57 and 61), figures were suggested for brief fees for Counsel who has between 5 and 10 years' experience. For less experienced Counsel it may be appropriate to reduce these figures; for more experienced Counsel it may be appropriate to increase these figures. The guideline figures are a starting point only and the Court has the discretion to allow fees appropriate to the particular circumstances of the appeal.

CONDITIONAL FEE AGREEMENTS WITH SUCCESS FEES

71 Although it is not common for appellants to enter into such agreements, it is common for respondents (the successful party at first instance) whose claim or defence was conducted under a conditional fee agreement: such agreements often cover appeals brought by the opponent.

72 Attention is drawn to paragraph 3 of this Guide dealing with summary assessment of an additional liability at the conclusion of proceedings.

73 Paragraphs 27 and 28 set out the factors to be taken into account when deciding whether a percentage increase is reasonable.

COSTS AWARDED TO LIP

74 Attention is drawn to paragraphs 38 to 40 of this Guide.

P. T. Hurst
Senior Costs Judge
PTH\54\Guide to Summary Assessment of Costs
3.12.04

****

APPENDIX 2

GUIDLINE FIGURES FOR THE SUMMARY ASSESSMENT OF COSTS

SOLICITORS HOURLY RATES

The guideline rates for solicitors provided here are broad approximations only. In any particular area the Designated Civil Judge may supply more exact guidelines for rates in that area. Also the costs estimate provided by the paying party may give further guidance if the solicitors for both parties are based in the same locality.

The following diagram shows guideline figures for each of three bands outside the London area, and a further three bands within the London area with a statement of the localities included in each band. In each band there are four columns specifying figures for different grades of fee earner.

LOCALITIES

The guideline figures have been grouped according to locality by way of general guidance only. Although many firms may be comparable with others in the same locality, some of them will not be. For example, a firm located in the City of London which specialises in fast track personal injury claims may not be comparable with other firms in that locality and vice versa.

In any particular case the hourly rate it is reasonable to allow should be determined by reference to the rates charged by comparable firms. For this purpose the costs estimate supplied by the paying party may be of assistance The rate to allow should not be determined by reference to locality or postcode alone.

GRADES OF FEE EARNER

The grades of fee earner have been agreed between representatives of the Supreme Court Costs Office, the Association of District Judges and the Law Society. The categories are as follows:

1 Solicitors with over eight years post qualification experience including at least eight years litigation experience.

2 Solicitors and legal executives with over four years post qualification experience including at least four years litigation experience.

3 Other solicitors and legal executives and fee earners of equivalent experience.

4 Trainee solicitors, para legals and other fee earners.

'Legal Executive' means a Fellow of the Institute of Legal Executives. Those who are not Fellows of the Institute are not entitled to call themselves legal executives and in principle are therefore not entitled to the same hourly rate as a legal executive.

Unqualified clerks who are fee earners of equivalent experience may be entitled to similar rates and in this regard it should be borne in mind that Fellows of the Institute of Legal Executives generally spend two years in a solicitor's office before passing their Part 1 general examinations, spend a further two years before passing the Part 2 specialist examinations and then complete a further two years in practice before being able to become Fellows. Fellows have therefore possess considerable practical experience and academic achievement. Clerks without the equivalent experience of legal executives will be treated as being in the bottom grade of fee earner ie. trainee solicitors and fee earners of equivalent experience. Whether or not a fee earner has equivalent experience is ultimately a matter for the discretion of the court.

RATES TO ALLOW FOR SENIOR FEE EARNERS

Many High Court cases justify fee earners at a senior level. However the same may not be true of attendance at pre-trial hearings with counsel. The task of sitting behind counsel should be delegated to a more junior fee earner in all but the most important pre-trial hearings. The fact that the receiving party insisted upon the senior's attendance, or the fact that the fee earner is a sole practitioner who has no juniors to delegate to, should not be the determinative factors. As with hourly rates the costs estimate supplied by the paying party may be of assistance. What grade of fee earner did they use?

An hourly rate in excess of the guideline figures may be appropriate for Grade A fee earners in substantial and complex litigation where other factors, including the value of the litigation, the level of complexity, the urgency or importance of the matter as well as any international element would justify a significantly higher rate to reflect higher average costs.

BAND GRADE ONE GUIDELINE RATES FOR SUMMARY ASSESSMENT – JANUARY 2005

Band One Grade *	**A ****	**B**	**C**	**D**
Guideline Rates	184	163	137	100

Aldershot, Farnham, Bournemouth (including Poole)
Birmingham (Inner)
Bristol
Cambridge City, Harlow
Canterbury, Maidstone, Medway & Tunbridge Wells
Cardiff (Inner)
Chelmsford South, Essex & East Sussex
Fareham, Winchester
Hampshire, Dorset, Wiltshire, Isle of Wight
Kingston, Guildford, Reigate, Epsom
Leeds (Inner – within a 2-kilometer radius of the City Art Gallery)
Lewes
Liverpool, Birkenhead
Manchester Central
Newcastle City Centre (within a 2-mile radius of St Nicholas Cathedral)
Norwich City
Nottingham City
Oxford, Thames Valley
Southampton, Portsmouth
Swindon, Basingstoke
Watford

BAND TWO GRADE GUIDELINE RATES FOR SUMMARY ASSESSMENT – JANUARY 2005

Band Two Grade *	**A ****	**B**	**C**	**D**
Guideline Rates	173	152	126	95

Bath, Cheltenham and Gloucester, Taunton, Yeovil
Bury
Chelmsford North, Cambridge County, Peterborough, Bury St E, Norfolk,Lowestoft
Chester & North Wales
Coventry, Rugby, Nuneaton, Stratford and Warwick
Exeter, Plymouth
Hull (City)
Leeds Outer, Wakefield & Pontefract
Leigh
Lincoln
Luton, Bedford, St Albans, Hitchin, Hertford
Manchester Outer, Oldham, Bolton, Tameside
Newcastle (other than City Centre)
Nottingham & Derbyshire
Sheffield, Doncaster and South Yorkshire
Southport
St Helens
Stockport, Altrincham, Salford
Swansea, Newport, Cardiff (Outer)
Wigan
Wolverhampton, Walsall, Dudley & Stourbridge
York, Harrogate

BAND THREE GRADE GUIDELINE RATES FOR SUMMARY ASSESSMENT – JANUARY 2005

Band Three Grade *	**A ****	**B**	**C**	**D**
Guideline Rates	158	142	121	90
Birmingham Outer Bradford (Dewsbury, Halifax, Huddersfield, Keighley & Skipton) Cumbria Devon, Cornwall Grimsby, Skegness Hull Outer Kidderminster Northampton & Leicester Preston, Lancaster, Blackpool, Chorley, Accrington, Burnley, Blackburn,Rawenstall & Nelson Scarborough & Ripon Stafford, Stoke, Tamworth Teesside Worcester, Hereford, Evesham and Redditch Shrewsbury, Telford, Ludlow, Oswestry South & West Wales				

LONDON BAND GRADES GUIDELINE RATES FOR SUMMARY ASSESSMENT – JANUARY 2005

Grade *	**A ****	**B**	**C**	**D**
City of London: EC1, EC2, EC3, EC4	359	259	198	122
Central London: W1, WC1, WC2, SW1	276	210	171	110
Outer London: (All other London post codes: W, NW, N, E, SE, SW and Bromley, Croydon, Dartford, Gravesend and Uxbridge	198–232	149–198	144	105

* There are four grades of fee earner:

1 A.Solicitors with over 8 years post qualification experience including at least 8 years litigation experience.

2 B.Solicitors and legal executives with over 4 years post qualification experience including at least 4 years litigation experience.

3 C.Other solicitors and legal executives and fee earners of equivalent experience.

4 D.Trainee Solicitors, para legals and fee earners of equivalent experience.

Note: 'legal executive' means a Fellow of the Institute of Legal Executives.

** An hourly rate in excess of the guideline figures may be appropriate for Grade A fee earners in substantial and complex litigation where other factors, including the value of the litigation, the level of complexity, the urgency or importance of the matter as well as any international element would justify a significantly higher rate to reflect higher average costs.

COUNSEL'S FEES

The following table sets out figures based on Supreme Court Costs Office statistics dealing with run of the mill proceedings in the Queens Bench and Chancery Division and in the Administrative Court. The table gives figures for cases lasting up to an hour and up to half a day, in respect of counsel up to five years call, up to ten years call and over ten years call. It is emphasised that these figures are not recommended rates but it is hoped that they may provide a helpful starting point for judges when assessing counsel's fees. The appropriate fee in any particular case may be more or less than the figures appearing in the table, depending upon the circumstances.

The table does not include any figures in respect of leading counsel's fees since such cases would self evidently be exceptional. Similarly, no figures are included for the Commercial Court or the Technology & Construction Court.

TABLE OF COUNSEL'S FEES

Queen's Bench	*1 hour hearing*	*½ day hearing*
Junior up to 5 years call	£245	£425
Junior 5–10 years call	£365	£725
Junior 10+ years call	£550	£1100

Chancery Division	*1 hour hearing*	*½ day hearing*
Junior up to 5 years call	£275	£525
Junior 5–10 years call	£470	£800
Junior 10+ years call	£715	£1320

Administrative Court	*1 hour hearing*	*½ day hearing*
Junior up to 5 years call	£360	£550
Junior 5–10 years call	£660	£1100
Junior 10+ years call	£935	£1650

If the paying parties were represented by counsel, the fee paid to their counsel is an important factor but not a conclusive one on the question of fees payable to the receiving party's counsel.

In deciding upon the appropriate fee for counsel the question is not simply one of counsel's experience and seniority but also of the level of counsel which the particular case merits.

Counsel's fees should not be allowed in cases in which it was not reasonable to have instructed counsel, but it must be borne in mind that, especially in substantial hearings, it may be more economical if the advocacy is conducted by counsel rather than a solicitor. In all cases the court should consider whether or not the decision to instruct counsel has led to an increase in costs and whether that increase is justifiable.

APPENDIX 3

MODEL FORM OF STATEMENT OF COSTS

Statement of Costs (summary assessment)

In the	
Court	
Case Reference	

Judge/Master

Case Title

[Party]'s Statement of Costs for the hearing on *(date)* **(interim application/fast track trial)**

Description of fee earners*
(a) *(name) (grade) (hourly rate claimed)*
(b) *(name) (grade) (hourly rate claimed)*

Attendances on *(party)*

(a) *(number)*		hours at £		£	
(b) *(number)*		hours at £		£	

Attendances on opponents

(a) *(number)*		hours at £		£	
(b) *(number)*		hours at £		£	

Attendance on others

(a) *(number)*		hours at £		£	
(b) *(number)*		hours at £		£	

Site inspections etc

(a) *(number)*		hours at £		£	
(b) *(number)*		hours at £		£	

Work done on negotiations

(a) *(number)*		hours at £		£	
(b) *(number)*		hours at £		£	

Other work, not covered above

(a) *(number)*		hours at £		£	
(b) *(number)*		hours at £		£	

Work done on documents

(a) *(number)*		hours at £		£	
(b) *(number)*		hours at £		£	

Attendance at hearing

(a) *(number)*		hours at £		£	
(b) *(number)*		hours at £		£	
(a) *(number)*		hours travel and waiting at £		£	
(b) *(number)*		hours travel and waiting at £		£	

Sub Total £

N260 Statement of Costs (summary assessment) (10.01) *Printed on behalf of The Court Service*

Brought forward £

Counsel's fees *(name) (year of call)*

Fee for [advice/conference/documents] £

Fee for hearing £

Other expenses

[court fees] £

Others £

(give brief description)

Total **£**

Amount of VAT claimed

on solicitors and counsel's fees £

on other expenses £

Grand Total **£**

The costs estimated above do not exceed the costs which the *(party)* is liable to pay in respect of the work which this estimate covers.

Dated

Signed

Name of firm of solicitors [partner] for the *(party)*

* 4 grades of fee earner are suggested:

(A) Solicitors with over eight years post qualification experience including at least eight years litigation experience.

(B) Solicitors and legal executives with over four years post qualification experience including at least four years litigation experience.

(C) Other solicitors and legal executives and fee earners of equivalent experience.

(D) Trainee solicitors, para legals and other fee earners.

"Legal Executive" means a Fellow of the Institute of Legal Executives. Those who are not Fellows of the Institute are not entitled to call themselves legal executives and in principle are therefore not entitled to the same hourly rate as a legal executive.

In respect of each fee earner communications should be treated as attendances and routine communications should be claimed at one tenth of the hourly rate.

N260 Statement of Costs (summary assessment) (10.01) *Printed on behalf of The Court Service*

Practice Direction – Pilot Scheme for Detailed Assessment by the Supreme Court Costs Office of Costs of Civil Proceedings in London County Courts

This Practice Direction supplements CPR Part 47 (PDCostsPilot)

1 This practice direction applies, instead of paragraph 31.1 of the CPR Costs Practice Direction, to requests for a detailed assessment hearing which are filed between 6 January 2004 and 5 July 2004, pursuant to a judgment or order for the payment of costs by one party to another in civil proceedings in any of the following county courts:

Barnet, Bow, Brentford, Central London, Clerkenwell, Croydon, Edmonton, Ilford, Lambeth, Mayors and City of London, Romford, Shoreditch, Wandsworth, West London, Willesden and Woolwich.

2 Where this practice direction applies, unless the court orders otherwise –

- (1) the receiving party must file any request for a detailed assessment hearing in the Supreme Court Costs Office, Cliffords Inn, Fetter Lane, London EC4A 1DQ, DX 44454 Strand; and
- (2) the Supreme Court Costs Office is the appropriate office for the purpose of CPR 47.4(1), and therefore all applications and requests in the detailed assessment proceedings must be made to that Office.

PART 49
SPECIALIST PROCEEDINGS

49 (1) These Rules shall apply to the proceedings listed in paragraph (2) subject to the provisions of the relevant practice direction which applies to those proceedings.

(2) The proceedings referred to in paragraph (1) are –

(a)–(e) (*revoked*)

(f) proceedings under the Companies Act 1985 and the Companies Act 1989.

Amendments—SI 2001/1388; SI 2001/4015; SI 2002/3219.

Practice Direction See the following practice directions: Applications under the CA 1985 and the ICA 1982 (PD49B) at p 1180.

This Part now only applies to Companies matters. Commercial, Mercantile, Technology and Construction, Admiralty, Arbitration and Patent claims now have their own Parts – see Pts 59–63.

Practice Direction – Applications under the Companies Act 1985 and Other Legislation Relating to Companies

This Practice Direction supplements CPR Part 49 and replaces, with modifications, RSC Order 102 and CCR Order 49 Rule 3 (PD49B)

GENERAL

1 (1) In this practice direction –

'the Act' means the Companies Act 1985and includes the Act as applied to limited liability partnerships by the Limited Liability Partnerships Regulations 2001.

'the CJPA' means the Criminal Justice and Police Act 2001;

'the companies court registrar' means any officer of the High Court who is a registrar within the meaning of any rules for the time being in force relating to the winding-up of companies;

'the court' includes the companies court registrar;

'the EC Regulation' means Council Regulation (EC) No 2157/2001 of 8 October 2001 on the Statute for a European company (SE);

'the ICA' means the Insurance Companies Act 1982;

'Part VII FISMA' means Part VII of the Financial Services and Markets Act 2000;

'the Rules' means the Civil Procedure Rules 1998;

'SE' means a European public limited-liability company (Societas Europaea) within the meaning of Article 1 of the EC Regulation.

(2) Applications under the Act may be made in the county court if the county court would have jurisdiction to wind up the company in question (see the definition of 'the court' in section 744 of the Act).A company can be wound up in the county court if its paid-up capital is not more than £120,000 (s 117(2) Insolvency Act 1986).

(3) Every claim form or petition by which an application under the Act, Part VII FISMA or the ICA is begun and all affidavits, witness statements, notices and other documents in those proceedings must be entitled in the matter of the company in question and in the matter of the Act, Part VII FISMA or the ICA as the case may be.

'the companies court registrar' (para 1(1))—By virtue of Insolvency Rules 1986 (IR 1986), r 13.2(4), this expression means a registrar in bankruptcy of the High Court or, where proceedings are in the district registry of Birmingham, Bristol, Cardiff, Leeds, Liverpool, Manchester, Newcastle-upon-Tyne or Preston, a district judge.

'Part VII FISMA' (para 1(1))—Part VII of the FISMA regulates the transfer of insurance and banking business. In the case of insurance business, it superseded ICA 1982, Sch 2C with effect from 1 December 2001.

'Applications … may be made in the county court' (para 1(2))—Where a company has a paid-up capital of no more than £120,000, the bankruptcy county court of the district in which the company's registered office is situated has concurrent jurisdiction with the High Court to wind up the company (Insolvency Act 1986 (IA 1986), s 117(2)). Accordingly, while most applications under the Companies Act 1985 (CA 1985) are made in the High Court, it is often also possible to make such an application in a county court local to the relevant company's registered office.

Although para 1(2) is expressed in general terms, an application under CA 1985, s 721 should still be made in the High Court. Section 721 (which is concerned with the production and inspection of books where an offence is suspected) is stated to apply where an application is made 'to a judge of the High Court' (s 721(1)(a)).

Applications under the ICA 1982 and FISMA, Pt VII should also be made in the High Court rather than the county court. See in this connection the definitions of 'court' in ICA 1982, s 96(1) and FISMA, s 107(4).

COMMENCEMENT OF PROCEEDINGS

2 (1) Except in the case of the applications mentioned in sub-paragraph (4) below –

(a) every application under the Act, whether made in the High Court or in the county court;

(b) every application under Part VII FISMA;

(c) every application under Articles 25 and 26 of the EC Regulation; and

(d) every application under section 59 of the CJPA,

must be made by the issue of a claim form and the use of the procedure set out in CPR Part 8, subject to any modification of that procedure under this practice direction or any other practice direction relating to applications under the Act.

(2) Notice of an application under section 721 of the Act need not be given to the respondent and the claim form need not be served on him.

(3) A claim form issued under this paragraph must, in the High Court, be issued out of the office of the companies court registrar or a chancery district registry or, in the county court, out of a county court office.

(4) This paragraph does not apply to applications under sections 459 or 460 of the Act or to any of the applications specified in paragraph 4(1) of this practice direction.

3 All High Court applications to which this practice direction applies shall be assigned to the Chancery Division.

Applications under the Companies Act—Applications under the Companies Act are made either by petition or by claim form. A petition must be used for applications under CA 1985, ss 459 and 460 and the various provisions listed in para 4(1)(a)–(l) below. Other applications under the Companies Act, formerly made by originating summons or originating motion, will be issued by a claim form under the CPR Pt 8 procedure, provided that they are not made in conjunction with an application for winding up. Part 8 procedure is also to be adopted in the case of an application for a meeting of creditors to be summoned pursuant to CA 1985, s 425(1). In contrast, an application for a scheme to be sanctioned under CA 1985, s 425(2) must be made by petition (para 4(1)(f) below). With regard to applications under CA 1985, s 425, see further the notes to paras 6 and 7 below.

Applications under the Financial Services and Markets Act—All applications under FISMA, Pt VII must be made by claim form. The applications mentioned in para 2(4) are all applications under CA 1985, not FISMA, Pt VII.

'section 721' (para 2(2))—Companies Act 1985, s 721 empowers the court to make orders for the production and inspection of books or papers where there is reasonable cause to believe that an officer of a company has committed an offence in connection with the management of the company's affairs.

'the respondent' (para 2(2))—CPR Pt 8, which applies to applications under CA 1985, s 721, refers to *defendants* rather than *respondents*.

'This paragraph does not apply' (para 2(4))—The applications referred to in para 2(4) must be made by petition, not claim form. See para 4(1) below.

'applications under sections 459 or 460 of the Act' (para 2(4))—Applications under these provisions (which relate to the protection of company members against unfair prejudice) are dealt with in the Companies (Unfair Prejudice Applications) Proceedings Rules 1986. Those Rules have yet to be amended to take account of the CPR. Rule 2(2) continues to provide for the RSC to apply to proceedings within the scope of the Rules.

In *North Holdings Ltd v Southern Tropics Ltd* [1999] BCC 746, the Court of Appeal indicated (at 769) that the CPR would require 'a new approach by the registrar' in s 459 cases. In particular, 'ample use should be made of the power to require a joint expert or the appointment of an assessor' (per Aldous LJ at 769G).

In *Re Rotadata Ltd* [2000] BCC 686, Neuberger J observed (at 690G-H) that:

> 'when a s 459 petition comes before the registrar, there would be a great deal to be said for the registrar to consider giving directions requiring the parties and/or their advisers to meet with a view to narrowing the issues, identifying what issues are really important, what issues are really in dispute, how those issues are to be resolved or proved, and resolving and narrowing any other matters which in the context of the particular petition could reasonably be expected to be narrowed'.

The Chancery Guide observes that cases under CA 1985, s 459 are liable to involve extensive factual enquiry and that many of the measures summarised in Section A of the Guide (dealing with, among other things, case management powers) are particularly relevant to them (see para 20.21 of the Guide).

'High Court applications' (para 3)—High Court applications under the Companies Act are allocated to the Companies Court. The Companies Court is part of the Chancery Division rather than a distinct entity (*Re Shilena Hosiery Co Ltd* [1980] Ch 219 at 224) but nevertheless has an administrative procedure of its own. Proceedings are issued in the Companies Court General Office. See generally Chancery Guide, Ch 20.

Having regard to para 2(3), applications under FISMA, Pt VII will also be allocated to the Companies Court.

Until recently, applications to the judge in Companies Court matters were generally listed for a Monday morning. Such applications can now, however, be issued for hearing on any day of the week during term time, when they will normally come before the applications judge. See *Practice Direction (company matters: hearings)* [2000] 1 WLR 209.

Proceedings in the Companies Court under a particular statute should refer to the statute in the title (Chancery Guide, para 20.5). Thus, an application under CA 1985 should be headed:
'In the matter of the Companies Act 1985
And in the matter of *name and registration number of the company*'.

APPLICATIONS UNDER PART VII FISMA

3A (1) From 1 December 2001 applications to sanction insurance business transfer schemes or banking business transfer schemes must be made under Part VII FISMA. Schedule 2C of the ICA, subject to minor modifications, will continue to apply to applications to sanction or approve transfers of insurance business which are made up to and including 30 November 2001 (see the Financial Services and Markets Act 2000 (Transitional Provisions and Savings) (Business Transfers) Order 2001).

(2) Any application under Part VII FISMA must comply with the requirements of the Control of Business Transfers (Requirements on Applicants) Regulations 2001.

(3) In relation to insurance business transfer schemes, the Supervision Manual of the Financial Services Authority ('FSA') available on the FSA's website (http://www.fsa.gov.uk), contains rules and guidance with regard to the operation of Part VII FISMA and the FSA's role thereunder which should be referred to before any application under Part VII FISMA is made.

(4) Paragraphs 10 to 13 of this practice direction apply to applications under Part VII FISMA.

'the requirements of the Control of Business Transfers (Requirements on Applicants) Regulations 2001' (para 3A(2))—The Regulations in question are evidently the Financial Services and Markets Act 2000 (Control of Business Transfers) (Requirements on Applicants) Regulations 2001, SI 2001/3625.

Regulation 3 of these Regulations requires a person applying for an order sanctioning an insurance business transfer scheme to give notice of the application in various newspapers and to policyholders. The regulation also provides for certain documents to be supplied to the Financial Services Authority (the Authority) and to anyone who requests them.

Regulation 4 bars the court from sanctioning an insurance business transfer scheme where the requirements in reg 3 have not been complied with and until 21 days after the Authority has been given specified documents.

Regulations 5 and 6 contain similar provisions relating to banking business transfer schemes.

APPLICATIONS UNDER THE EC REGULATION

3B (1) An application for a certificate under Article 25(2) of the EC Regulation must –

(a) be issued in the Chancery Division of the High Court;

(b) identify the pre-merger acts and formalities applicable to the applicant company, and be accompanied by evidence that those acts and formalities have been completed;

(c) be accompanied by copies of:

(i) the draft terms of merger as provided for in Article 20 of the EC Regulation;

(ii) the entry in the Gazette containing the particulars specified in Article 21 of the EC Regulation;

(iii) a report drawn up and adopted by the directors of the applicant company containing the same information as would be required by paragraph 4 of Schedule 15B to the Act if there were to be a scheme of arrangement under sections 425 and 427A of the Act;

(vi) the expert's report to the members of the applicant company drawn up in accordance with paragraph 5 of Schedule 15B to the Act or Article 22 of the EC Regulation; and

(v) the resolution of the applicant company approving the draft terms of merger in accordance with Article 23 of the EC Regulation.

(2) Attention is drawn to Article 26(2) of the EC Regulation. Where it is proposed that the registered office of an SE should be in England or Wales, each of the merging companies is required, within 6 months

after a certificate is issued in respect of that company under Article 25(2), to submit the certificate to the High Court in order that it may scrutinise the legality of the merger.

(3) Where a merging company is required to submit a certificate to the High Court under Article 26(2) of the EC Regulation, if no other merging company has commenced proceedings under Article 26, that company shall commence such proceedings by issuing a claim form in the Chancery Division.

(4) The claim form must –
   (a) identify the SE and all of the merging companies;
   (b) be accompanied by the documents referred to in paragraph 3B(6); and
   (c) be served on each of the other merging companies.

(5) Where a merging company is required to submit a certificate to the High Court under Article 26(2) of the EC Regulation and proceedings under Article 26 have already been commenced, that company shall –
   (a) file an acknowledgment of service not more than 14 days after service of the claim form, and serve the acknowledgment of service on each of the other merging companies; and
   (b) file the documents referred to in paragraph 3B(6) within the time limit specified in Article 26(2), and serve copies of those documents on each of the other merging companies.

(6) Each merging company must file and serve the following documents in proceedings under Article 26 of the EC Regulation –
   (a) the certificate issued under Article 25(2) in respect of that company;
   (b) a copy of the draft terms of merger approved by that company;
   (c) evidence that arrangements for employee involvement have been determined by that company pursuant to Council Directive 2001/86/EC of 8 October 2001 supplementing the Statute for a European company with regard to the involvement of employees; and
   (d) evidence that the SE has been formed in accordance with the requirements of Article 26(4) of the EC Regulation.

(7) Proceedings under Article 25 and Article 26 of the EC Regulation will be heard by a High Court judge.

(8) Paragraphs 10 to 13 of this practice direction apply to proceedings under Article 25 and 26 of the EC Regulation.

APPLICATIONS MADE BY PETITION

4 (1) The following applications under the Act in addition to applications under sections 459 and 460 of the Act and applications under the ICA must be made by petition, namely, applications:
   (a) under section 5 to cancel the alteration of a company's objects,
   (b) under section 17 to cancel the alteration of a condition contained in a company's memorandum,
   (c) under section 130 to confirm a reduction of the share premium account of a company,
   (d) under section 136 to confirm a reduction of the share capital of a company,
   (e) under section 127 to cancel any variation or abrogation of the rights attached to any class of shares in a company,
   (f) under section 425 to sanction a compromise or arrangement

between a company and its creditors or any class of them or between a company and its members or any class of them,

(g) under section 653 for an order restoring the name of a company to the register, where the application is made in conjunction with an application for the winding up of the company,

(h) under section 690 to cancel the alteration of the form of a company's constitution,

(i) under section 727 for relief from liability of an officer of a company or a person employed by a company as auditor,

(j) under section 54(1) to cancel a special resolution to which that section applies,

(k) under sections 157(2) or 176(1) to cancel a special resolution to which either of those sections applies, and

(l) under section 170 in relation to the reduction of capital redemption reserve.

(2) Paragraphs 5 to 14 of this practice direction apply to the applications specified in sub-paragraph (1).

5 (1) After the presentation of a petition by which any application mentioned in paragraph 4 is made, the petitioner, except where his application is one of those mentioned in sub-paragraph (2), must apply for directions by filing an application notice.

(2) The exceptions referred to in sub-paragraph (1) are:

(a) an application under section 425 of the Act to sanction a compromise or arrangement unless there is included in the petition for such sanction an application for an order under section 427 of the Act,

(b) an application under section 653 of the Act for an order restoring the name of a company to the register,

(c) an application under section 54(1) of the Act for an order cancelling a special resolution to which that section applies, and

(d) an application under section 157(2) or 176(1) of the Act for an order cancelling a special resolution to which those sections apply.

(3) At the directions hearing the court may by order give such directions for the hearing of the application as it thinks fit including, in particular, directions for the publication of notices and the making of any inquiry .

(4) Where the application made by the petition is to confirm a reduction of the share capital, the share premium account, or the capital redemption reserve, of a company the court may give directions:

(a) for an inquiry to be made as to the debts of, and claims against, the company or as to any class or classes of such debts or claims,

(b) as to the proceedings to be taken for settling the list of creditors entitled to object to the reduction and fixing the date by reference to which the list is to be made,

and the power of the court under section 136(6) of the Act to direct that section 136(3) to (5) thereof shall not apply as regards any class of creditors may be exercised at any directions hearing.

General note—The applications listed in para 4(1) were also made by petition before the CPR were introduced. The provisions of the former RSC dealing with petitions (RSC Ord 5, r 5, Ord 9, Ord 10, r 5, and Ord 11, r 9) have no precise equivalents in the CPR. There is thus no specific guidance in either this practice direction or the CPR as to the form or content of a petition.

'applications under the ICA' (para 4(1))—Sections 53 and 54 of the ICA 1982 give the court powers to wind up insurance companies on the petition of policy holders or the Secretary of State for Trade and Industry.

'section 653' (para 4(1)(g))—An application for a 'double-barrelled' order (both restoring the name of a company to the register and winding the company up) is made by petition. In the case of other applications under s 653, the Pt 8 procedure will apply.

'section 54(1)' (para 4(1)(j))—Companies Act 1985, s 54(1) applies where a public company has passed a special resolution to be re-registered under CA 1985, s 53 as a private company.

'sections 157(2) or 176(1)' (para 4(1)(k))—Companies Act 1985, s 157(2) relates to companies giving financial assistance for the purchase of their own shares, s 176(1) relates to companies redeeming or purchasing their own shares.

'Paragraphs 5 to 14' (para 4(2))—There is no para 14.

Although para 4(2) provides only for paras 5–14 to apply to the applications specified in para 4(1), paras 10–13 are surely intended to apply to applications under the CA 1985 generally, as well as to applications under FISMA, Pt VII – as to which see para 3A(4).

'application notice' (para 5(1))—See CPR Pt 23.

'section 427 of the Act' (para 5(2)(a))—Companies Act 1985, s 427 serves to facilitate reconstructions and amalgamations. It allows the court to make provision for a variety of matters when sanctioning a compromise or arrangement under s 425 of the Act.

General note to para 5(4)—Companies Act 1985, ss 136(3)–(5) provides for the court to settle a list of creditors and envisages that there will be an inquiry as to creditors. However, s 136(6) allows the court to direct that s 136(3)–(5) should not apply if 'having regard to any special circumstances of the case it thinks proper to do so'. In reality, companies invariably take steps to ensure that no inquiry as to creditors is needed. Such inquiries are not in practice directed.

REDUCTION OF CAPITAL AND SCHEMES OF ARRANGEMENT

6 (1) The consent of a creditor to such reduction as is mentioned in paragraph 5(4) may be proved in such manner as the court thinks sufficient.

(2) The evidence in support of a petition to confirm a reduction of capital need not show as regards any issue of shares made since 1900 for a consideration other than cash that the statutory requirements as to registration were complied with. It is sufficient to state in the petition the extent to which any issued shares (other than shares issued otherwise than for cash before 1901) are or are deemed to be paid up.

(3) The existing practice will remain unaltered in respect of issues of shares otherwise than for cash made before 1901 whilst s 25 of the Companies Act 1867 remained in operation.

7 (1) This paragraph applies to:

(a) schemes of arrangement under sections 425 to 427A of the Companies Act 1985, whether made with creditors or members,

(b) schemes for the transfer of the whole or part of the long-term business of an insurance company to which schedule 2C to the ICA applies, and

(c) reductions of capital, share premium account or capital redemption reserve.

References in this and subsequent paragraphs to 'schemes' are to schemes falling within (a) or (b) above, and references to 'reductions' are to reductions falling within (c) above.

(2) Petitions to sanction schemes will be heard by the Companies Court Judge.

(3) Petitions to confirm reductions will be heard by the Companies Court

Registrar unless otherwise ordered. The Registrar will hear petitions to confirm reductions in open court on a Wednesday each week after completion of the list of winding up petitions.

'schemes of arrangement under sections 425 to 427A of the Companies Act 1985' (para 7(1)(a))—There are three stages in the process by which a compromise or arrangement becomes binding on a company and its creditors. Per Chadwick LJ in *Re Hawk Insurance Co Ltd* [2001] EWCA Civ 241, [2001] 2 BCLC 480 at 510–511:

> 'First, there must be an application to the court under s 425(1) of the 1985 Act for an order that a meeting or meetings be summoned … Second, the scheme proposals are put to the meeting or meetings held in accordance with the order that has been made; and are approved (or not) by the requisite majority in number and value of those present and voting in person or by proxy. Third, if approved at the meeting or meetings, there must be a further application to the court under s 425(2) of the 1985 Act to obtain the court's sanction to the compromise or arrangement.'

The initial application under CA 1985, s 425(1) should be made by a claim form using the CPR Pt 8 procedure. The application at the third stage under CA 1985, s 425(2) must, however, be made by petition (see para 4(1)(f) above).

Practice Statement (Companies: Schemes of Arrangement) [2002] 1 WLR 1345 makes the following, among other, points:

(a) It is the responsibility of the applicant to determine whether more than one meeting of creditors is required by a scheme and, if so, to ensure that those meetings are properly constituted by a class of creditor so that each meeting consists of creditors whose rights against the company are not so dissimilar as to make it impossible for them to consult together with a view to their common interest.
(b) Applications in respect of substantial schemes will be listed before a judge rather than a registrar.
(c) It is the responsibility of the applicant by evidence in support of the application or otherwise to draw to the attention of the court as soon as possible any issues which may arise as to the constitution of meetings of creditors or which may affect the conduct of those meetings.

SCHEMES AND REDUCTIONS IN THE LONG VACATION

8 (1) The following requirements must be satisfied for a hearing to be fixed to sanction a scheme and/or confirm a reduction in the Long Vacation:

(a) The application is one in which for financial, commercial or economic reasons a hearing before the end of the Long Vacation is desirable. This category will include cases of mergers and takeovers which arise in the summer and are likely to be affected by market fluctuations.

(b) The application is one which could not with reasonable diligence have been made and prosecuted in time to be heard before the Long Vacation begins.

(2) An informal application in chambers, to the Court Manager, accompanied by an advocate's certificate that requirements (a) and (b) are satisfied, must be made as soon as possible so that a suitable timetable may be settled, including a date for hearing.

(3) In the case of reductions to be heard by the Registrar, certain applications which do not fall within the above categories will be heard provided (i) that there is an urgent need for a hearing or (ii) that there is sufficient time available after the Registrar has disposed of the urgent applications.

(4) Applications to the Registrar in chambers for orders convening meetings to consider schemes and for directions on reduction applications will continue to be heard during the Long Vacation. Provided notice is given to the court before the Long Vacation begins, a timetable will be fixed which will enable any necessary documents to be settled in chambers and enable the Registrar to hear the application.

(5) The Vacation Judge will be available to hear petitions to sanction schemes and any petitions to confirm reductions which require to be heard by a judge on one Wednesday in August and two Wednesdays in September on dates to be arranged and subsequently notified in the Long Vacation Notice which is printed in the Daily Cause List.

(6) The Vacation Judge may also hear petitions to sanction schemes or confirm reductions on other days if he thinks fit.

9 (1) Attention is drawn to the undesirability of asking as a matter of course for a winding up order as an alternative to an order under s 459 Companies Act 1985. The petition should not ask for a winding up order unless that is the relief which the petitioner prefers or it is thought that it may be the only relief to which the petitioner is entitled.

(2) Whenever a winding up order is asked for in a contributory's petition, the petition must state whether the petitioner consents or objects to an order under s 127 of the Act in the standard form. If he objects, the written evidence in support must contain a short statement of his reasons.

(3) If the petitioner objects to a s 127 order in the standard form but consents to such an order in a modified form, the petition must set out the form of order to which he consents, and the written evidence in support must contain a short statement of his reasons for seeking the modification.

(4) If the petition contains a statement that the petitioner consents to a s 127 order, whether in the standard or a modified form, but the petitioner changes his mind before the first hearing of the petition, he must notify the respondents and may apply on notice to a judge for an order directing that no s 127 order or a modified order only (as the case may be) shall be made by the Registrar, but validating dispositions made without notice of the order made by the judge.

(5) If the petition contains a statement that the petitioner consents to a s 127 order, whether in the standard or a modified form, the Registrar shall without further enquiry make an order in such form at the first hearing unless an order to the contrary has been made by the judge in the meantime.

(6) If the petition contains a statement that the petitioner objects to a s 127 order in the standard form, the company may apply (in the case of urgency, without notice) to the judge for an order.

(7) Section 127 Order – Standard Form:

(Title etc)

ORDER that notwithstanding the presentation of the said Petition

(1) payments made into or out of the bank accounts of the Company in the ordinary course of the business of the Company and

(2) dispositions of the property of the Company made in the ordinary course of its business for proper value between the date of presentation of the Petition and the date of judgment on the Petition or further order in the meantime

shall not be void by virtue of the provisions of section 127 of the Insolvency Act 1986 in the event of an Order for the winding up of the Company being made on the said Petition Provided that (the relevant bank) shall be under no obligation to verify for itself whether any transaction through the company's bank accounts is in the ordinary course of business, or that it represents full market value for the relevant transaction.

This form of Order may be departed from where the circumstances of the case require.

'scheme' (para 8(1))—Defined in para 7(1).

'reduction' (para 8(1))—Defined in para 7(1).

General note to para 9(1)—A shareholder seeking relief from unfairly prejudicial conduct under CA 1985, s 459 should not automatically ask for a winding up order in the alternative.

Role of the Insolvency Rules 1986—Where a contributory petitions for a winding up order, Insolvency Rules 1986, rr 4.22–4.24 will apply.

's 127 of the Act' (para 9(2))—Although 'the Act' is defined to mean the Companies Act for the purpose of this practice direction (see para 1(1) above), para 9(2) is evidently referring to IA 1986, s 127. That provision strikes down dispositions of property of a company made after the commencement of its winding up.

'standard form' (para 9(2))—The standard form order is set out in para 9(7) below.

'written evidence in support' (para 9(2))—It is not in fact the practice to serve or file evidence in support of a just and equitable petition at the outset.

CASE MANAGEMENT

10 Every application under the Act or under Part VII FISMA shall be allocated to the multi-track and the CPR relating to allocation questionnaires and track allocation will not apply.

Case Management—With regard to case management of applications under Companies Act 1985, s 459, see *North Holdings Ltd v Southern Tropics Ltd* [1999] BCC 746, CA (at 769) and *Re Rotadata Ltd* [2000] BCC 686 (at 690) and para 20.21 of the Chancery Guide.

Allocation—The intention is doubtless that all applications under FISMA, Pt VII and the CA 1985, whether brought by claim form or petition, should automatically be allocated to the multi-track. Despite para 4(2), which states that paras 5–14 are to apply to the applications specified in para 4(1), para 10 presumably extends to all CA 1985 applications. It plainly applies to all applications under FISMA, Pt VII.

SERVICE

11 Service of documents in proceedings in the High Court to which this practice direction applies will be the responsibility of the parties and will not be undertaken by the court. Subject to that CPR Part 6 applies.

FILING OF DOCUMENTS

12 (1) Where an application to which this practice direction relates is proceeding in any Chancery district registry, all affidavits and witness statements made in connection with the application must be filed in that registry.

(2) Where an application to which this practice direction relates is proceeding in any county court, all affidavits and witness statements made in connection with the application must be filed in the office of that county court.

DRAWING UP OF ORDERS

13 The court will draw up all orders with the following exceptions –

(a) orders by the Registrar on the application of the Official Receiver or for which the Treasury Solicitor is responsible under the existing practice,

(b) orders by the court in relation to reductions or schemes.

APPLICATIONS UNDER SECTION 59 OF THE CJPA

14 (1) This paragraph applies to applications under section 59 of the CJPA in respect of property seized in the exercise of the power conferred by section 448(3) of the Act (including any additional powers of seizure conferred by section 50 of the CJPA which are exercisable by reference to that power).

(2) An application to which this paragraph applies should be made to a judge of the Chancery Division.

(3) The defendant to an application under section 59(2) or 59(5)(c) of the CJPA shall be the person for the time being having possession of the property to which the application relates.

(4) On an application under section 59(2) or 59(5)(c) of the CJPA, the claim form and the claimant's evidence must be served on –

(a) the person for the time being having possession of the property to which the application relates;

(b) in the case of an application under section 59(2) for the return of seized property, the person specified as the person to whom notice of such an application should be given by any notice served under section 52 of the CJPA when the property was seized;

(c) in the case of an application under section 59(5)(c), the person from whom the property was seized (if not the claimant); and

(d) in all cases, any other person appearing to have a relevant interest in the property within the meaning of section 59(11) of the CJPA.

(5) An application under section 59(2) or 59(5)(c) of the CJPA must be supported by evidence –

(a) that the claimant has a relevant interest in the property to which the application relates within the meaning of section 59(11) of the CJPA; and

(b) in the case of an application under section 59(2), that one or more of the grounds set out in section 59(3) of the CJPA is satisfied in relation to the property.

(6) The defendants to an application under section 59(5)(b) of the CJPA by a person for the time being in possession of seized property shall be –

(a) the person from whom the property was seized; and

(b) any other person appearing to have a relevant interest in the property to which the application relates within the meaning of section 59(11) of the CJPA.

(7) If an application to which this paragraph applies would not otherwise be served on the person who seized the property, and the identity of that person is known to the applicant, notice of the application shall be given to the person who seized the property.

(8) In all applications to which this paragraph applies, when the court issues the claim form it will fix a date for the hearing.

PART 50
APPLICATION OF THE SCHEDULES

50 (1) The Schedules to these Rules set out, with modifications, certain provisions previously contained in the Rules of the Supreme Court 1965 and the County Court Rules 1981.

(2) These Rules apply in relation to the proceedings to which the Schedules apply subject to the provisions in the Schedules and the relevant practice directions.

(3) A provision previously contained in the Rules of the Supreme Court 1965 –

(a) is headed 'RSC';
(b) is numbered with the Order and rule numbers it bore as part of the RSC; and
(c) unless otherwise stated in the Schedules or the relevant practice direction, applies only to proceedings in the High Court.

(4) A provision previously contained in the County Court Rules 1981 –

(a) is headed 'CCR';
(b) is numbered with the Order and rule numbers it bore as part of the CCR; and
(c) unless otherwise stated in the Schedules or the relevant practice direction, applies only to proceedings in the county court.

(5) A reference in a Schedule to a rule by number alone is a reference to the rule so numbered in the Order in which the reference occurs.

(6) A reference in a Schedule to a rule by number prefixed by 'CPR' is a reference to the rule with that number in these Rules.

(7) In the Schedules, unless otherwise stated, 'the Act' means –

(a) in a provision headed 'RSC', the Supreme Court Act 1981; and
(b) in a provision headed 'CCR', the County Courts Act 1984.

PART 51
TRANSITIONAL ARRANGEMENTS AND PILOT SCHEMES

51.1 A practice direction shall make provision for the extent to which these Rules shall apply to proceedings issued before 26 April 1999.

Amendments—SI 2001/2792.

Practice Direction—See generally PD51 at p 1192.

Scope of provision—The practice direction to which this Part refers deals with the extent to which, between 26 April 1999 and 25 April 2000, the CPR apply to cases issued on or before 23 April 1999. PD51, para 19, states that (with four exceptions) cases which have not come before a judge (whether at a hearing or on paper) between 26 April 1999 and 25 April 2000 are stayed thereafter. See PD51 and the notes thereto for the details.

51.2 Practice directions may modify or disapply any provision of these Rules –

(a) for specified periods; and
(b) in relation to proceedings in specified courts,

during the operation of pilot schemes for assessing the use of new practices and procedures in connection with proceedings.

Amendments—Inserted by SI 2001/2792.

Practice Direction – Transitional Arrangements

This Practice Direction supplements CPR Part 51 (PD51)

CONTENTS OF THIS PRACTICE DIRECTION

1 (1) This practice direction deals with the application of the Civil Procedure Rules ('CPR') to proceedings issued before 26 April 1999 ('existing proceedings').

(2) In this practice direction 'the previous rules' means, as appropriate the Rules of the Supreme Court 1965 ('RSC') or County Court Rules 1981 ('CCR') in force immediately before 26 April 1999.

GENERAL SCHEME OF TRANSITIONAL ARRANGEMENTS

2 The general scheme is:

(a) to apply the previous rules to undefended cases, allowing them to progress to their disposal, but
(b) to apply the CPR to defended cases so far as is practicable.

Scope of provision—The intention of the practice direction, in relation to cases issued on or before 25 April 1999, was to apply the RSC/CCR in their pre-26 April 1999 form to undefended cases on or after 26 April 1999, but to apply the CPR to defended cases. By now, undefended cases will have passed through the court system and, therefore, all extant pre-26 April 1999 cases will be subject to the CPR. The only paragraphs of this practice direction of continuing relevance are paras 18 and 19.

General presumption that the CPR will apply—The Court of Appeal have in several cases since 26 April 1999 stressed that there is a general presumption that the CPR will apply to cases coming before the courts after that date (see, for instance *Biguzzi v Rank Leisure plc* [1999] 1 WLR 1926,

CA; *Stanway v HM Attorney-General & ors* (1999) *The Times*, 25 November, Lloyd J and *Westriding Automobile Co Ltd & ors v The West Yorkshire Passenger Transport & anor* (1999) Lawtel, 28 October, Bernard Livesey QC).

Where the Previous Rules will Normally Apply

GENERAL PRINCIPLE

3 Where an initiating step has been taken in a case before 26 April 1999, in particular one that uses forms or other documentation required by the previous rules, the case will proceed in the first instance under the previous rules. Any step which a party must take in response to something done by another party in accordance with the previous rules must also be in accordance with those rules.

RESPONDING TO OLD PROCESS

4 A party who is served with an old type of originating process (writ, summons etc) on or after 26 April 1999 is required to respond in accordance with the previous rules and the instructions on any forms received with the originating process.

FILING AND SERVICE OF PLEADINGS WHERE OLD PROCESS SERVED

5 Where a case has been begun by an old type of originating process (whether served before or after 26 April 1999), filing and service of pleadings will continue according to the previous rules.

AUTOMATIC DIRECTIONS/DISCOVERY

HIGH COURT

6 (1) Where the timetable for automatic directions under RSC Order 25, rule 8 or automatic discovery under RSC Order 24 has begun to apply to proceedings before 26 April 1999, those directions will continue to have effect on or after 26 April 1999.

COUNTY COURT

(2) Where automatic directions under CCR Order 17, rule 11 have begun to apply to existing proceedings before 26 April 1999 or the court has sent out notice that automatic directions under CCR Order 17, rule 11 (Form N450) will apply (even if the timetable will not begin until 26 April 1999 or after), those directions will continue to have effect on or after 26 April 1999.

(3) However CCR Order 17, rule 11(9) will not apply and therefore proceedings will not be struck out where there has been no request for a hearing to be fixed within 15 months of the date when pleadings were deemed to close. (But see paragraph 19.)

HIGH COURT AND COUNTY COURT

(4) However, if the case comes before the court on or after 26 April 1999, the new rules may apply. (See paragraph 15.)

'CCR Order 17, rule 11(9) will not apply' (para 6(3))—See, however, para 9 below and the note thereto.

SECTION 2 Civil Procedure Rules and Practice Directions

DEFAULT JUDGMENT

7 (1) If a party wishes default judgment to be entered in existing proceedings, he must do so in accordance with the previous rules.

(2) Where default judgment has been entered and there are outstanding issues to be resolved (eg damages to be assessed), the court officer may refer the proceedings to the judge, so that case management decisions about the proceedings and the conduct of the hearing can be made in accordance with the practice set out in paragraph 15.

(3) If a party needs to apply for permission to enter default judgment, he must make that application under CPR Part 23 (general rules about applications for court orders).

(4) An application to set aside judgment entered in default must be made under CPR Part 23 (general rules about applications for court orders) and CPR Part 13 (setting aside or varying default judgment) will apply to the proceedings as it would apply to default judgment entered under the CPR.

(5) CPR rule 15.11 (claims stayed if it is not defended or admitted) applies to these proceedings.

JUDGMENT ON ADMISSION IN THE COUNTY COURT

8 (1) If a party to existing proceedings in the county court wishes to request judgment to be entered on an admission, he must do so in accordance with the previous rules.

(2) Where judgment has been entered and there are outstanding issues to be resolved (eg damages to be assessed), the court officer may refer the proceedings to the judge, so that case management decisions about the proceedings and the conduct of the hearing can be made in accordance with the practice set out in paragraph 15.

(3) If a party needs to apply for permission to enter judgment, he must make that application under CPR Part 23 (general rules about applications for court orders).

ORDER INCONSISTENT WITH CPR

9 Where a court order has been made before 26 April 1999, that order must still be complied with on or after 26 April 1999.

CCR Ord 17, r 11(9)—Where an order imposing a strike-out sanction to replace that in CCR Ord 17, r 11(9) is not complied with, the claim will still be struck out despite the provisions of para 6(3) above. It is not clear whether an order merely extending the period mentioned in the rule would result in a similar effect.

STEPS TAKEN BEFORE 26 APRIL 1999

10 (1) Where a party has taken any step in the proceedings in accordance with the previous rules that step will remain valid on or after 26 April 1999.

(2) A party will not normally be required to take any action that would amount to taking that step again under the CPR. For example if discovery has been given, a party will not normally be required to provide disclosure under CPR Part 31.

Where the CPR will Normally Apply

GENERAL PRINCIPLE

11 Where a new step is to be taken in any existing proceedings on or after 26 April 1999, it is to be taken under the CPR.

PART 1 (OVERRIDING OBJECTIVE) TO APPLY

12 Part 1 (overriding objective) will apply to all existing proceedings from 26 April 1999 onwards.

A new procedural code—Case law prior to 26 April 1999 is not binding on a court nor persuasive on the judge's exercise of discretion under the CPR when considering an appeal from a decision reached prior to that date but rather the CPR are to be interpreted as a new self-contained regime (*Biguzzi v Rank Leisure plc* [1999] 1 WLR 1926, CA; *Thorn plc v McDonald* (1999) *The Times*, 15 October, CA; and *Axa Insurance Co Ltd v Swire Fraser Ltd (formerly Robert Fraser Insurance Brokers Ltd)* (2000) *The Times*, 19 January, CA). Decisions, even on identical wording under the RSC or CCR will not necessarily be followed when interpreting the CPR (*Lombard Natwest Factors Ltd v Sebastian Arbis* (1999) Lawtel, 1 November, ChD, Hart J). See also *Bank of England v Vagliano Brothers* [1893] AC 107 on the relevance of previous legislation to the construction of a new code.

ORIGINATING PROCESS

13 (1) Only claim forms under the CPR will be issued by the court on or after 26 April 1999.

(2) If a request to issue an old type of originating process (writ, summons etc) is received at the court on or after 26 April 1999 it will be returned unissued.

(3) An application made on or after 26 April 1999 to extend the validity of originating process issued before 26 April 1999 must be made in accordance with CPR Part 23 (general rules about applications for court orders), but the court will decide whether to allow the application in accordance with the previous law.

APPLICATION TO THE COURT

14 (1) Any application to the court made on or after 26 April 1999 must be made in accordance with CPR Part 23 (general rules about applications for court orders).

(2) Any other relevant CPR will apply to the substance of the application, unless this practice direction provides otherwise. (See paragraphs 13(3) (application to extend the validity of originating process) and 18(2) (costs).)

(3) For example, a party wishing to apply for summary judgment must do so having regard to the test in CPR Part 24. A party wishing to apply for an interim remedy must do so under CPR Part 25 etc

(4) Any other CPR will apply as necessary. For example, CPR Part 4 will apply as to forms and CPR Part 6 will apply to service of documents.

(5) If the pleadings have not been filed at court, the applicant must file all pleadings served when he files his application notice.

FIRST TIME BEFORE A JUDGE ON OR AFTER 26 APRIL 1999

15 (1) When proceedings come before a judge (whether at a hearing or on paper) for the first time on or after 26 April 1999, he may direct how

the CPR are to apply to the proceedings and may disapply certain provisions of the CPR. He may also give case management directions (which may include allocating the proceedings to a case management track).

(2) The general presumption will be that the CPR will apply to the proceedings from then on unless the judge directs or this practice direction provides otherwise. (See paragraphs 13(3) (application to extend the validity of originating process) and 18(2) (costs).)

(3) If an application has been issued before 26 April 1999 and the hearing of the application has been set for a date on or after 26 April 1999, the general presumption is that the application will be decided having regard to the CPR. (For example an application for summary judgment issued before 26 April 1999, with a hearing date set for 1 May 1999, will be decided having regard to the test in CPR Part 24 (summary judgment).)

(4) When the first occasion on which existing proceedings are before a judge on or after 26 April 1999 is a trial or hearing of a substantive issue, the general presumption is that the trial or hearing will be conducted having regard to the CPR.

'The general presumption' (para 15(2))—See also the notes to para 2 above.

Appeals—The Court of Appeal will not after 26 April 1999 interfere with the decision of the court below made before that date if it would not have done so had the appeal been heard before 26 April 1999 (*McPhilemy v The Times* [1999] 3 All ER 775, CA; see also *Biguzzi v Rank Leisure plc* [1999] 1 WLR 1926, CA). But if the decision under appeal is one which would have been interfered with by the Court of Appeal prior to the implementation of the CPR then the Court of Appeal will apply the full rigour of the CPR in deciding what order to make.

WHERE PLEADINGS DEEMED TO CLOSE ON OR AFTER 26 APRIL 1999

16 (1) This paragraph applies to existing proceedings where pleadings are deemed to close on or after 26 April 1999. However, this paragraph does not apply to those county court proceedings where notice that automatic directions apply (Form N450) has been sent (in which case the automatic directions will apply – see paragraph 6).

(2) CPR Part 26 (case management – preliminary stage) applies to these proceedings.

(3) If a defence is filed at court on or after 26 April 1999, the court will serve an allocation questionnaire where CPR rule 26.3 would apply, unless it dispenses with the need for one.

(4) If pleadings have not been filed at court (this will normally be the case in the Queen's Bench Division) the claimant must file copies of all the pleadings served within 14 days of the date that pleadings are deemed to close.

(5) Unless it dispenses with the need for one, the court will then serve an allocation questionnaire.

(6) In the previous rules pleadings are deemed to close –

(a) High Court –

(i) 14 days after service of any reply, or

(ii) if there is no reply, 14 days after service of the defence to counterclaim; or

(iii) if there is no reply or defence to counterclaim, 14 days after the service of the defence.

(b) county court –
14 days after the delivery of a defence or, where a counterclaim is served with the defence, 28 days after the delivery of the defence.

(7) Where there are 2 or more defendants the court will normally wait until the claimant has filed copies of all the pleadings before serving an allocation questionnaire. However, the court may (in cases where there is a delay) serve allocation questionnaires despite the fact that pleadings have not closed in respect of any other defendant.

(8) The court will then allocate the proceedings in accordance with CPR rule 26.5.

(9) The CPR will then apply generally to the proceedings.

AGREEMENT TO APPLY THE CPR

17 The parties may agree in writing that the CPR will apply to any proceedings from the date of the agreement. When they do so:

(a) all those who are parties at that time must agree,
(b) the CPR must apply in their entirety,
(c) the agreement is irrevocable,
(d) the claimant must file a copy of the agreement at court.

COSTS

18 (1) Any assessment of costs that takes place on or after 26 April 1999 will be in accordance with CPR Parts 43 to 48.

(2) However, the general presumption is that no costs for work undertaken before 26 April 1999 will be disallowed if those costs would have been allowed in a costs taxation before 26 April 1999.

(3) The decision as to whether to allow costs for work undertaken on or after 26 April will generally be taken in accordance with CPR Parts 43 to 48.

(The costs practice direction contains more information on the operation of the transitional arrangements in relation to costs)

Costs—An assessment of costs after 26 April 1999 is in accordance with CPR Pts 43–48 as modified by PDCosts, Section 57. However:

(a) the general presumption is that no costs for work undertaken before 26 April 1999 will be disallowed on assessment if such costs would have been allowed in a taxation before 26 April 1999 (para 18(2)). To that extent, therefore, CPR r 44.5 and in particular the issue of proportionality is modified by PD51, para 18(2).

(b) PDCosts, paras 57.1–57.9 contain further transitional arrangements in respect of costs where:
   (i) a county court order was made before 26 April 1999 on scale I or the lower scale (PDCosts, para 57.3). Note: this provision does not apply where the order is made on or after 26 April 1999 although the costs were incurred before that date; such costs are assessed without the restrictions of scale I applying;
   (ii) there is a rehearing of an application to set aside a judgment given before 26 April 1999 (PDCosts, para 57.4) and fixed costs apply;
   (iii) there is a challenge to a bill provisionally taxed before 26 April 1999 (PDCosts, para 57.5);
   (iv) objections are carried in where a taxation took place before 26 April 1999 (PDCosts, para 57.6).

(c) for further specific transitional provisions relating to taxation proceedings commenced before 26 April 1999 also note PDCosts, para 57.7.

EXISTING PROCEEDINGS AFTER ONE YEAR

19 (1) If any existing proceedings have not come before a judge, at a hearing or on paper, between 26 April 1999 and 25 April 2000, those proceedings shall be stayed.

(2) Any party to those proceedings may apply for the stay to be lifted.

(3) Proceedings of the following types will not be stayed as a result of this provision:

(a) where the case has been given a fixed trial date which is after 25 April 2000,

(b) personal injury cases where there is no issue on liability but the proceedings have been adjourned by court order to determine the prognosis,

(c) where the court is dealing with the continuing administration of an estate or a trust or receivership,

(d) applications relating to funds in court.

(4) For the purposes of this paragraph proceedings will not be 'existing proceedings' once final judgment has been given.

'Existing proceedings after one year'—Subject to four exceptions (PD51, para 19(3)), if a case issued before 26 April 1999 has not been considered by a judge (either at a hearing or on paper) by 25 April 2000 then the case is stayed (PD51, para 19(1)). This provision does not apply to the enforcement of judgments nor to other final judgments such as a possession order suspended on terms as to the payment of current rent or current monthly mortgage instalment together with regular payments in respect of the arrears. On the other hand, where a judgment was entered for damages to be assessed before 26 April 1999, para 19 would impose a stay unless para 3(a) or (b) apply.

A party may apply under CPR Pt 23, supported by evidence, to lift the stay (para 19(2)). The court will consider the overriding objective (Pt 1) which remains paramount (see for instance *Flaxman-Binns v Lincolnshire County Council (Practice Note)* [2004] EWCA Civ 424, [2004] 1 WLR 2232, [2004] All ER (D) 88 (Apr), [2004] TLR 289, CA). Previously, however, the Court of Appeal has in addition held in *Audergon v La Baguette Ltd* [2002] EWCA Civ 10, [2002] CP Rep 27, CA and in *Woodhouse v Consignia plc* [2002] EWCA Civ 275, [2002] 2 All ER 737, CA that it is incumbent on judges to consider all the factors set out in r 3.9(1) (note *Bansal v Cheema* [2001] CP Rep 6, CA) and to carry out the necessary balancing exercise in a methodical and properly reasoned manner. Having done so, the court should then stand back and assess the significance and weight of all the relevant circumstances to arrive at the most just, or least unjust, solution (*Flaxman-Binns v Lincolnshire County Council (Practice Note)* [2004] EWCA Civ 424, [2004] 1 WLR 2232, [2004] All ER (D) 88 (Apr), [2004] TLR 289, CA); see also *B v B* [2005] EWCA Civ 237, where the Court of Appeal held that the major concern was to ensure that the claimant's undetermined claims should be justly tried and that due weight must be given to the overriding objective when applying the r 3.9 factors. An additional factor, not present in earlier decisions on para 19, has been the implementation of HRA 1998: maintaining a stay would deprive the defaulting party from access to the courts but an approach within the general framework provided by CPR rr 3.9 and 1.1 is unlikely to fall foul of the ECHR.

It was subsequently held that proceedings which had been stayed under PD51, para 19 should not be struck out, unless an unequivocal affirmative answer could be given to the question of whether there was a substantial risk that a fair trial was impossible (*Taylor v Anderson & ors* [2002] EWCA Civ 1680, [2002] TLR 488, CA). Considerable doubt that a fair trial is possible is not enough to justify striking out the claim; what is required to strike out is a substantial risk of an unfair trial. Even in cases of inordinate and inexcusable delay, the court will only strike out a claim as an abuse of process where there is a real risk that the matter can no longer be fairly tried and the interests of justice so require. Even where some heads of claim would be struck out had they not been withdrawn, claims which can still be tried should be tried (*Fay v Chief Constable of Bedfordshire Police* [2003] TLR 82, QBD, Davies J). On the other hand, the Court of Appeal subsequently held that, whilst there will be many cases where the possibility of a fair trial is highly important to the exercise of the court's discretion under r 3.9, it does not follow that where a fair trial is still possible, relief will nevertheless be granted. The correct approach under r 3.9 is to stand back and assess the significance and weight of all relevant circumstances (*Hansom v E Rex Makin & anor* [2003] EWCA Civ 1801).

For a case where hearings to suspend a warrant of possession were held not to be existing proceedings, but a counterclaim within the same proceedings was caught by PD51, para 19, see *National Westminster Bank plc v Feeney & anor* [2003] EWCA Civ 950, (2003) Lawtel, 12 June, CA.

'have not come before a judge, at a hearing or on paper' (para 19(1))—The Court of Appeal has held (*Reliance National Insurance Co (Europe) Ltd & anor v Ropner Insurance Services Ltd* (2000) Lawtel, 1 December) that the writing of a letter to the court, even if that letter was brought to the attention of the judge and he responded to it, did not mean that the proceedings had 'come before the court … on paper' for the purposes of para 19. The phrase was intended to denote an occasion on which the judge considered exercising his powers in accordance with the rules, whether that was in response to a CPR Pt 23 application or of the court's own initiative under CPR r 3.3.

'Any party … may apply for the stay to be lifted' (para 19(2))—David Steel J in *Bank of Credit and Commerce v Sheikh Ali Abdullah Bugshan* [2001] All ER (D) 149, Comm Ct held that the key point was whether there had been a good reason for the matter not being brought before a judge in the 12-month period to 25 April 2000. The burden of proof was upon the party seeking to have the stay lifted to show such good reason. If he did so, the burden shifted to the other party to establish that the stay should nevertheless remain.

Where a claim has been stayed under para 19(1), it remains open to the defendant to apply for an order for the stay to be lifted, for the action to be struck out and for an order for costs against the claimant.

'final judgment' (para 19(4))—Following the addition of para 19(4) to this practice direction it is clear that enforcement of a pre-26 April 1999 judgment or an application for an order for sale to enforce a pre-26 April 1999 charging order will not be caught by the provisions of para 19. On the other hand, for instance, mortgage possession proceedings that were adjourned generally prior to 26 April 1999 will be caught by the provision. So will an assessment of damages following an interim judgment in 1992 for damages to be assessed (*Duggan v Wood* (2001) Lawtel, 23 November, CA, where the Court of Appeal upheld the striking out of a claim for special damages).

PART 52
APPEALS

CONTENTS OF THIS PART

Procedural Guides—See Guides 58 and 59, set out in Section 1 of this work.

I General Rules about Appeals

52.1 Scope and interpretation

(1) The rules in this Part apply to appeals to –

(a) the civil division of the Court of Appeal;
(b) the High Court; and
(c) a county court.

(2) This Part does not apply to an appeal in detailed assessment proceedings against a decision of an authorised court officer.

(Rules 47.21 to 47.26 deal with appeals against a decision of an authorised court officer in detailed assessment proceedings)

(3) In this Part –

(a) 'appeal' includes an appeal by way of case stated;
(b) 'appeal court' means the court to which an appeal is made;
(c) 'lower court' means the court, tribunal or other person or body from whose decision an appeal is brought;
(d) 'appellant' means a person who brings or seeks to bring an appeal;
(e) 'respondent' means –
  (i) a person other than the appellant who was a party to the proceedings in the lower court and who is affected by the appeal; and
  (ii) a person who is permitted by the appeal court to be a party to the appeal; and
(f) 'appeal notice' means an appellant's or respondent's notice.

(4) This Part is subject to any rule, enactment or practice direction which sets out special provisions with regard to any particular category of appeal.

Amendments—Inserted by SI 2000/221; amended by SI 2000/2092.

Practice Direction—See generally PD52 at p 1217.

Scope of provision—Part 52 and PD52 lay down rules and requirements for appeals. Subject to certain exceptions, they apply to all appeals to the Court of Appeal, appeals to the High Court (eg an appeal from a master or a district judge sitting in the High Court, appeals in those cases where appeal now lies from a circuit judge to a High Court judge (see below)), and appeals in the county court from a district judge to a circuit judge (see r 52.1(1)) and also statutory appeals to both the High Court and a county court (eg an appeal under HA 1996, s 204).

The principal exceptions where Pt 52 does not apply are –

(i) appeals against decisions of authorised court officials in detailed assessment proceedings (r 52.1(2)); and
(ii) appeals (other than appeals to the Court of Appeal) in family, insolvency, probate and Mental Health Act proceedings (r 2.1(2)).

Thus, Pt 52 does not apply to an appeal from a district judge to a circuit judge in family proceedings; such appeals are governed by the Family Proceedings Rules 1991. But Pt 52 (and PD52) do apply to appeals to the Court of Appeal in family proceedings (see PD52, para 2.2), whether the appeal is from a High Court judge or a circuit judge.

Until 2 October 2000 Pt 52 did not apply to appeals in cases allocated to the small claims track, but with effect from that date small claims track appeals were brought within its scope (see below).

Part 52 (supplemented by PD52) made major changes to the rules and procedures governing appeals to which it applies; for an account of the main changes see the judgment of Brooke LJ in *Tanfern v Cameron-MacDonald* [2000] 2 All ER 801.

Commencement—Part 52 came into effect on 2 May 2000.

Types of forms and terminology—Part 52 uses the expression 'appeal notice' as a generic term covering an 'appellant's notice' and a 'respondent's notice' (r 52.1(3)(f)).

'Appellant' means a person who brings an appeal (ie permission to appeal has been granted or is not required) or seeks to bring an appeal (ie is applying for permission to appeal and/or an extension of time for appealing) (r 52.1(3)(d)). All appellant's notices must be in Form N161 (PD52, para 5.1). (For filing and service of appellant's notices see r 52.4.)

A 'respondent' is a person (other than the appellant) who was a party to the proceedings below and is affected by the appeal, or a person whom the appeal court has allowed to be a party to the appeal (r 52.1(3)(e)). A respondent's notice should be in Form N162. (For filing and service of respondent's notices see r 52.5.)

'Lower court' means the court, tribunal, body or person whose decision is being appealed (r 52.1(3)(c)). The expression 'appeal court' does not mean just the Court of Appeal, but it is used to denote whichever is the court to which the appeal concerned is being made (see r 52.1(3)(b)). Thus, if there is an appeal in a county court against a decision of a district judge in proceedings to which Pt 52 applies, the district judge is the 'lower court' and the circuit judge is the 'appeal court'.

Routes of appeal—The Access to Justice Act 1999 (Destination of Appeals) Order 2000, which came into force on the same date as Pt 52, made changes to the routes for certain types of appeal. It was amended from 1 April 2003 by the Civil Procedure (Modification of Enactments) Order 2003. The effect of the 2000 Order as amended is summarised in PD52, para 2A; however, where there is a dispute or doubt as to the correct avenue of appeal the matter must be resolved by considering the provisions of the Order itself. The principal change is that certain appeals against decisions of circuit judges now lie to a High Court judge and not the Court of Appeal. Appeal lies to a High Court judge from a first instance decision of a circuit judge in the following cases:

(i) any order (whether interim or final) in any case which has not been assigned to the multi-track (eg fast track cases, possession claims and cases which have not been assigned to any track at all); and
(ii) orders in multi-track cases which are not final orders.

Appeals against final decisions made by circuit judges and district judges in Pt 7 claims allocated to the multi-track or made in specialist proceedings lie to the Court of Appeal.

Where the decision to be appealed is a final decision in a Pt 8 claim treated as allocated to the multi-track under r 8.9(c), unless the appeal would lie to the Court of Appeal in any event, the court giving permission should consider whether the appeal should be transferred to the Court of Appeal under r 52.14 (see PD52, para 2A.6).

An appeal against an order made in committal proceedings by a circuit judge has not been affected by the 2000 Order and is to the Court of Appeal. This is the effect of Administration of

Justice Act 1960, s 13 (*Barnet LBC v Hurst* [2002] 1 WLR 722, [2002] 4 All ER 457). Technically the same route is available in relation to an order in such proceedings made by a district judge (see *King v Read and Slack* [1999] 1 FLR 425) but in *Barnet LBC v Hurst* the Court of Appeal made it clear that the normal route of appeal to a circuit judge should be used unless there are exceptional circumstances.

There can be a further appeal to the Court of Appeal against the High Court judge's decision given on appeal from the circuit judge, but the restrictions on second tier appeals (AJA 1999, s 55) will apply (see further below). Where the decision of the circuit judge was given on appeal, then any appeal against it will lie to the Court of Appeal, but the restrictions on second tier appeals will apply.

Appeals against all orders made by High Court master (or district judge exercising his High Court jurisdiction) lie to a High Court judge with one exception. Where a final decision is made by a master (or by a district judge exercising his High Court jurisdiction) in a Pt 7 claim allocated to the multi-track, the appeal will lie directly to the Court of Appeal (see the Access to Justice Act 1999 (Destination of Appeals) Order 2000, art 4 as amended). The appeal lies to the Court of Appeal against the decision of the master/district judge on the incidence of costs on the making of a final order in such a case, but not an appeal against a detailed assessment of such costs (*Dooley v Parker* [2002] EWCA Civ 96, [2002] CPLR 251, CA).

Final decision—In practice, considerable confusion has arisen as to what is or is not a final decision. It is defined in Access to Justice (Destination of Appeals) Order 2000, art 1(2)(c) as a decision that would finally determine (subject to any possible appeal or detailed assessment of costs) the entire proceedings whichever way the court decided the issues before it. Article 1(3) provides further that a decision will be treated as a final decision where it is made at the conclusion of part of a hearing or trial which has been split into parts and it would, if made at the conclusion of that hearing or trial, be a final decision under para (2)(c). These provisions are repeated in PD52, paras 2A.3 and 2A.4 (see the judgment of Brooke LJ in *Tanfern v Cameron-MacDonald* [2000] 2 All ER 801 at [17] and [18] for a further exposition and also his judgment in *Scribes West Ltd v Relsa Anstalt & anor (No 2)* [2004] 4 All ER 653 where he returned to the subject and expressed disappointment that difficulties of interpretation were still arising).

Small claims track appeals—Such cases are governed by the same procedural requirements as other appeals to which Pt 52 applies, save that the documentation which has to be lodged with the appellant's notice in a small claims track case is less extensive than in the case of other appeals (see PD52, para 5.8A).

Special provisions relating to the Court of Appeal—For provisions which lay down special rules for appeals to the Court of Appeal see PD52, paras 6.4–6.6 and 15.1–15.21. For a summary of the Court of Appeal listing system see the notes to PD52, paras 15.7–15.9.

Second tier appeals—There are stringent statutory restrictions on bringing a second appeal against a decision of a High Court judge or circuit judge that was itself given on appeal to that judge (usually referred to as a 'second tier appeal'), see further the notes to r 52.13.

52.2 Parties to comply with the practice direction

All parties to an appeal must comply with the relevant practice direction.

Amendments—Inserted by SI 2000/221.

Practice Direction—See generally PD52 at p 1217.

The practice direction—The relevant practice direction is PD52. It contains a considerable body of detailed provisions relating to appeals, and is divided into four sections –

(1) Section I (PD52, paras 2.1–15.21) contains provisions relating to appeals generally, though certain of them (in particular paras 6.4, 6.5 and 15) apply only to appeals to the Court of Appeal and para 8 deals with appeals to the High Court.
(2) Section II (PD52, paras 16.1–18.20) deals with statutory appeals and appeals by way of case stated.
(3) Section III (PD52, paras 20.1–24.1) contains provisions dealing with the specific types of appeal listed in para 20;
(4) Section IV (PD52, para 25.1–25.7) deals with reopening appeals.

Substantial changes were made to the practice direction in June 2004, particularly in relation to appeals in the Court of Appeal. For an exposition of the changes affecting that court, see *Scribes West Ltd v Relsa Anstalt* (No 1) [2004] EWCA Civ 835 and *Jeyapragash v Secretary of State for the Home Department* [2004] EWCA Civ 1260.

52.3 Permission

(1) An appellant or respondent requires permission to appeal –

(a) where the appeal is from a decision of a judge in a county court or the High Court, except where the appeal is against –

(i) a committal order;

(ii) a refusal to grant habeas corpus; or

(iii) a secure accommodation order made under section 25 of the Children Act 1989; or

(b) as provided by the relevant practice direction.

(Other enactments may provide that permission is required for particular appeals)

(2) An application for permission to appeal may be made –

(a) to the lower court at the hearing at which the decision to be appealed was made; or

(b) to the appeal court in an appeal notice.

(Rule 52.4 sets out the time limits for filing an appellant's notice at the appeal court. Rule 52.5 sets out the time limits for filing a respondent's notice at the appeal court. Any application for permission to appeal to the appeal court must be made in the appeal notice (see rules 52.4(1) and 52.5(3))

(Rule 52.13(1) provides that permission is required from the Court of Appeal for all appeals to that court from a decision of a county court or the High Court which was itself made on appeal)

(3) Where the lower court refuses an application for permission to appeal, a further application for permission to appeal may be made to the appeal court.

(4) Where the appeal court, without a hearing, refuses permission to appeal, the person seeking permission may request the decision to be reconsidered at a hearing.

(5) A request under paragraph (4) must be filed within 7 days after service of the notice that permission has been refused.

(6) Permission to appeal will only be given where –

(a) the court considers that the appeal would have a real prospect of success; or

(b) there is some other compelling reason why the appeal should be heard.

(7) An order giving permission may –

(a) limit the issues to be heard; and

(b) be made subject to conditions.

(Rule 3.1(3) also provides that the court may make an order subject to conditions)

(Rule 25.15 provides for the court to order security for costs of an appeal)

Amendments—Inserted by SI 2000/221.

Practice Direction—See generally PD52 at p 1217.

Permission to appeal—Under r 52.3(1)(a) permission to appeal is required in respect of all appeals to which Pt 52 applies, save in the three excepted cases. In respect of appeals to the Court of Appeal this reproduces the same almost universal requirement of permission to appeal which applied under the old rules (the former RSC Ord 59, r 1B). The exception in relation to a committal order applies only to a sentence of imprisonment (which includes a suspended sentence). Any other order made by a court in the exercise of its jurisdiction to punish for contempt requires permission to appeal (*Barnet LBC v Hurst* [2002] 1 WLR 722, [2002] 4 All ER 457).

In addition, there are a considerable number of statutory provisions which impose a requirement of permission to appeal in respect of specific types of appeal to which r 52.3(1)(a) does not apply. In some cases the statute also provides that any appeal is confined to questions of law, eg appeals against decisions of the Employment Appeal Tribunal (Industrial Tribunals Act 1986, s 37(1), (2)(a)), the Social Security Commissioners (Social Security Act, s 14), and the Immigration Appeals Tribunal (Asylum and Immigration Appeals Act, s 9).

Notwithstanding its wording, Paragraph 17.2 of PD52 does not have the effect of imposing a requirement of permission to appeal under r 52.3(1)(b) in the case of a statutory appeal where the statute concerned does not impose such a requirement (*Colley v Council for Licensed Conveyancers* [2001] EWCA Civ 1137, [2001] 4 All ER 998, CA).

For the new restrictive provisions governing second tier appeals see AJA 1999, s 55 and the notes to r 52.13.

Action by a respondent in relation to an appellant's application for permission to appeal—Unless the appeal court otherwise directs, a respondent need take no action on being served with an appellant's notice applying for permission to appeal, unless and until the respondent is notified that permission to appeal has been granted (PD52, para 5.22). Generally, the application for permission to appeal will be dealt with on paper and, if there is an oral hearing, it will (unless the appeal court otherwise directs) be without attendance by the respondent (see PD52, para 4.22). A respondent who files written submissions, or attends, or is represented at any oral hearing, without having been requested to do so by the appeal court, will not normally get any order for his costs (PD52, para 4.23). Where the appeal court requests submissions from or attendance by the respondent, or the application is listed with the appeal to follow if permission is granted, the respondent will normally be allowed his costs if permission is refused (PD52, para 4.24).

For the circumstances where a respondent requires permission to appeal see below, and for filing and service of a respondent's notice see the notes to r 52.5.

The application for permission to appeal—Where an appeal is contemplated, permission to appeal should normally be sought from the lower court judge (or the tribunal) as soon as the judgment or decision has been given. If the lower court refuses permission to appeal (or if the application is not made to it), a (further) application for permission can be made to the appeal court (r 52.3(3)) and that application must be included in the appellant's notice (Form N161) (see r 52.4(1)). To determine which is the relevant appeal court, see PD52, paras 2A.1–2A.6. For the time limit for filing an appellant's notice see r 52.4.

Determination by the appeal court of an application for permission to appeal—The appeal court has power to determine applications for permission to appeal on paper without a hearing (PD52, para 4.11). This continues a long-standing practice in the Court of Appeal. Most applications to the Court of Appeal are dealt with initially by a single Lord Justice on paper. If the single Lord Justice grants permission to appeal, then the case will proceed to a full appeal hearing (unless it is one of those rare cases where the Court of Appeal sets aside the grant of permission to appeal on the application of the respondent, see r 52.9(1)(b) and (2)). If the single Lord Justice refuses permission on paper, the appellant can request that the decision be reconsidered at a hearing by filing with the Civil Appeals Office a request to that effect within seven days after receipt of notification that permission to appeal was refused on paper (r 52.3(4) and (5)). The appellant must serve a copy of that request on the respondent(s), but respondents will not be given notice of the oral hearing unless the appeal court otherwise directs; the usual circumstance where the respondent will be given notice of the hearing is where the appellant is seeking a remedy pending appeal (PD52, para 4.15). Renewed applications will usually be listed before a single Lord Justice, but may sometimes be heard by a two-judge court. If the appeal court grants permission to appeal at the oral hearing, then the case will proceed to a full hearing (unless it is one of those rare cases where the Court of Appeal sets aside the grant of permission to appeal on the application of the respondent, see r 52.9(1)(b) and (2)).

The same procedure applies in the case of appeals in the High Court and the county court. There remains a discretion, however, to hold an oral hearing without prior consideration on paper. In that case, the judge will consider directing that, if permission is given, the appeal will be heard forthwith, as this may result in a significant saving in costs.

Where a legally represented appellant seeks reconsideration at an oral hearing of refusal of permission to appeal, the advocate must comply with PD52, para 4.14A.

For the steps which have to be taken after permission to appeal has been granted by the appeal court see PD52, paras 6.1–6.6.

The test for granting permission to appeal—The general test to be applied is laid down in r 52.3(6)(a). Permission to appeal will be granted if there is a realistic, as opposed to fanciful, prospect of success on the appeal (*Tanfern Ltd v Cameron-MacDonald & ors* [2000] 2 All ER 801, 808). Even if the test in r 52.3(6)(a) is not satisfied, permission to appeal can nevertheless be granted under r 52.3(6)(b) if there is some other compelling reason why the appeal should be heard. Such cases are likely to be rare and in practice the power would probably be exercised only by the appeal court. Specific factors to be considered when considering an application for permission to appeal a case management decision are identified in PD52, para 4.5.

Where on an application to a master to amend a statement of case, he refused some amendments but did not consider others for lack of time, and on appeal the judge refused the amendments not previously considered, as the proposed amendments raised common issues, the Court of Appeal held that the applicable test for granting permission to appeal was the test under r 52.3(6) and not the higher test for a second appeal under r 52.13. (*Convergence Group plc & anor v Chantrey Vellacott* [2005] EWCA Civ 290).

Limited permission and permission on terms—Under r 52.3(7)(a) the court granting permission to appeal (whether it is the lower court or the appeal court) can limit the grant of permission to a particular issue or issues. Where the court exercises that power, it will either refuse permission to appeal on any remaining issues or reserve the question of permission on any remaining issues for determination by the court hearing the appeal (PD52, para 4.18). If any remaining issues are reserved, the appellant's side must, within 14 days after service of the court's order, inform the court and the respondent(s) in writing whether it is intended to pursue the reserved issues (PD52, para 4.19). If the lower court refuses permission to appeal on any issue(s), the appellant can make a further application to the appeal court under r 52.3(3) for permission in respect of those issues. Where permission on any remaining issues is refused by the appeal court without a hearing, the appellant may, within the time limit prescribed by r 52.3(5), ask for that decision to be reconsidered at an oral hearing (PD52, para 4.20). If, however, the appeal court refuses permission to appeal on remaining issues following an oral hearing, that decision is final (see PD52, para 4.21).

Where there are good reasons for doing so, the court – particularly the appeal court – will consider imposing conditions on the grant of permission to appeal. Where the grounds of appeal, although satisfying the test are not strong, there may be a case for imposing a condition requiring the appellant to pay into court (or otherwise provide security for) the judgment debt and/or costs, by analogy with the practice of making a conditional order on an application for summary judgment where the defence is 'shadowy'. It would not be proper to impose a condition which the appellant cannot meet because that would amount to granting permission to appeal with one hand and taking it away with the other. It would be appropriate for the court to adopt the same approach as in *Yorke (MV) Motors v Edwards* [1982] 1 WLR 444, [1982] 1 All ER 1204, HL and impose such a condition where the appellant either has the resources to make the payment in, or is able to raise a loan or otherwise provide suitable security. There is also a case for imposing a condition as to payment in, or provision of security, where there is evidence that the appellant is likely to resist enforcement if the appeal fails (applying the same approach as was adopted by the Court of Appeal in *Bell Electric Ltd v Appliance Systems GmbH and Co KG* [2002] EWCA Civ 1501, [2003] 1 All ER 344 in relation to imposition of a condition under r 52.9(1)(c)).

When a respondent requires permission to appeal—Where a respondent seeks to cross-appeal, ie is asking the appeal court to vary the decision of the lower court in some respect, the respondent needs permission to appeal, unless it is one of the three excepted cases (r 52.3(1)) and must apply for such permission in the same way as an appellant. Permission should normally be sought as soon as the lower court's decision has been granted and, if that court refuses permission to appeal or no application was made to it, the respondent must apply for permission in a respondent's notice (r 52.5(2)(a) and (3)).

Finality of decisions of an appeal court on applications for permission to appeal—Where any appeal court (not just the Court of Appeal) refuses permission to appeal after a hearing, that decision cannot be further appealed (AJA 1999, s 54(4) and see also the observations of the Court of Appeal in *Foenander v Bond Lewis & Co* [2001] EWCA Civ 759, [2002] 1 WLR 525, CA). (Where permission to appeal is refused by the lower court, the appellant has the right to make a further application to the appeal court (see r 52.3(3) and commentary above); and where the appeal court refuses permission on paper, the appellant has the right to ask for the decision reconsidered at an oral hearing (see r 52.3(4) and the commentary above); both those rights are preserved by the words in brackets in s 54(4).) Section 54(4) applies where a judge in the High Court makes an order on paper dismissing an appellant's application for permission to appeal by reason of failure to lodge documents (*Hyams v Plender* [2001] 1 WLR 32, CA). (In such a case it would be open to the appellant lodge a request with the High Court for that decision to be reconsidered at an oral hearing under r 52.3(4) and, if necessary, an extension of the 7-day time limit for making such a request.)

In exceptional circumstances, the refusal by the county court of permission to appeal after a hearing may be amenable to judicial review (*R (Sivasubramaniam) v Wandsworth County Court* [2002] EWCA Civ 1738).

There is a right of appeal in relation to any other order made at such a hearing (*Riniker v University College London* [2001] 1 WLR 13). Section 54(4) does not apply to an application for an extension of time for appealing and neither does s 55 (*Foenander v Bond Lewis & Co* [2001] EWCA Civ 759, [2002] 1 WLR 525, CA). Thus, where permission to appeal is either not required or has been granted by the lower court, and a first-tier appeal court refuses an application for an extension of time for appealing, there can be an appeal to the Court of Appeal against that decision (subject only to the grant of permission to appeal) and the stringent restrictions on second-tier appeals do not apply. There cannot, however, be an appeal against the *grant* of an extension of time for appealing (Supreme Court Act 1981, s 18(1)(b)). Where both an extension of time and permission to appeal are required and the appeal is unmeritorious, the first-tier appeal court should deal with the case by granting the extension of time and then refusing permission to appeal, because that brings the appellate proceedings to an end, as s 54(4) will preclude any further appeal (*Foenander v Bond Lewis & Co*, see above).

Section 54(4) also applies to the grant of permission to appeal. Thus, a respondent cannot appeal against the grant of permission to appeal. If the appeal court has granted permission to appeal either on paper, or at a hearing without notice, the respondent can apply to the appeal court (under r 52.9(1)(b)) for that grant of permission to be set aside, but the court will only exercise that power where there is a compelling reason for doing so. Where permission to appeal is granted at a hearing at which the respondent was present or represented, he cannot apply for the permission to be set aside (r 52.9(3)).

52.4 Appellant's notice

(1) Where the appellant seeks permission from the appeal court it must be requested in the appellant's notice.

(2) The appellant must file the appellant's notice at the appeal court within –

- (a) such period as may be directed by the lower court; or
- (b) where the court makes no such direction, 14 days after the date of the decision of the lower court that the appellant wishes to appeal.

(3) Unless the appeal court orders otherwise, an appeal notice must be served on each respondent –

- (a) as soon as practicable; and
- (b) in any event not later than 7 days,

after it is filed.

Amendments—Inserted by SI 2000/221.

Practice Direction—See generally PD52 at p 1217.

Instituting an appeal—The first step is the filing of an appellant's notice with the office of the relevant appeal court and the second step is service of the appellant's notice on the respondent(s). The procedure and the forms are the same whether it is an appeal to the Court of Appeal, a High Court judge or a circuit judge.

For a step-by-step account of the steps necessary to institute and progress an appeal see Guides 58 and 59 set out in Section 1 of this work.

Filing of the appellant's notice—To determine which is the relevant appeal court, see PD52, paras 2A.1–2A.6. Form N161 must be used (PD52, para 5.1). If permission to appeal is required and has not been granted by the court below it must be applied for in the Form N161.

For the documents that must be filed with the appellant's notice and included in the appeal bundle, see PD52, paras 5.6(2) and 5.6A.

If it is not possible to file any of those items with the appellant's notice the appellant's solicitor (or the appellant, if in person) must set out in section 11 of the appellant's notice which of the required documents have not been filed, why they are currently not available and when they are expected to be available (see generally PD52, para 5.7). Note also the requirement in PD 52, para 5.6A(2) and (3) to exclude documents which are not relevant to the subject matter of the appeal and for the appellant's legal representative to certify that he has read understood and complied with this obligation.

Place of filing—In the case of appeals to the Court of Appeal the appellant's notice and other documents must be filed in the Civil Appeals Office Registry, Room E307, at the Royal Courts of Justice, Strand, London WC2A 2LL. Where the appeal lies to the High Court, the place of filing is the relevant High Court Appeal Centre (see PD52, paras 8.2 and 8.3). In the case of appeals to a circuit judge, the appellant's notice and other documents must be filed at the office of the county court concerned.

Time limit for filing the appellant's notice and accompanying documents—Unless the lower court sets some different timetable, the time limit for filing an appellant's notice is 14 days after the date on which the lower court gave its decision (r 52.4(2)(b)). That time limit runs in all cases from the date on which the decision sought to be appealed was given, not the date on which the order was sealed or issued. If the lower court exercises its power under r 52.4(2)(a) to set a different time limit, it should not normally be more than 28 days (PD52, para 5.19). Where the judge in the lower court announces the result at the conclusion of the hearing, but reserves his reasons until a later date, he should exercise his power under r 52.4(2)(a) and fix a time limit for filing an appellant's notice which takes that into account (PD52, para 5.20), ie he should set a time limit which runs from the date on which his reasoned judgment is made available.

Notwithstanding the wording of r 52.3(2)(a) and r 52.6 a two-judge court of the Court of Appeal held in *Aujla v Sanghera* (2004) EWCA Civ 121 that the lower court can give a direction under r 52.4(2)(a) not only on the date of its decision but also at a later date.

For guidance as to what constitutes the date that the decision of the lower court was made, see *Sayers v Clarke Walker* [2002] 1 WLR 3095, [2002] 3 All ER 490 and *Owusu v Jackson* [2002] EWCA Civ 877.

Service of appellant's notice—Unless the appeal court directs otherwise, an appellant's notice must be served on each separately represented respondent (or respondent in person) as soon as practicable and in any event not later than seven days after it was filed. In the case of appeals to the Court of Appeal, service must always be effected by the appellant's solicitor (or the appellant in person); the Civil Appeals Office does not serve documents (PD52, para 15.1(2)). In other cases the court may serve the documents, or give them to the appellant's solicitor (or the appellant) to serve.

In cases where permission to appeal has been granted, or is not required, the appellant's solicitor (or the appellant, if in person) must also serve on each separately represented respondent (or respondent in person) all the other documentation which was filed with the appellant's notice (the appeal bundle, skeleton argument, and transcripts) (PD52, para 5.24). If any of those documents were not filed with the appellant's notice, copies must be served on the respondent(s) when the documents are subsequently filed with the court.

Where, however, the appellant is applying for permission to appeal, only a sealed copy of the appellant's notice and the skeleton argument need be served on the respondent(s) and at that stage the appeal bundle and other documentation need not be served (PD52, para 5.24). Unless otherwise directed by the appeal court, a respondent on whom an appellant's notice applying for permission to appeal has been served should take no action in respect of it unless and until he receives notification that permission to appeal has been granted (PD52, para 5.22). If a respondent does take any action before notification of the grant of permission to appeal and without having been directed by the appeal court to take that action, he will not be entitled to recover any costs for such work. See further note **'Action to be taken by the respondent'** under r 52.3.

52.5 Respondent's notice

(1) A respondent may file and serve a respondent's notice.

(2) A respondent who –

(a) is seeking permission to appeal from the appeal court; or

(b) wishes to ask the appeal court to uphold the order of the lower court for reasons different from or additional to those given by the lower court,

must file a respondent's notice.

(3) Where the respondent seeks permission from the appeal court it must be requested in the respondent's notice.

(4) A respondent's notice must be filed within –

(a) such period as may be directed by the lower court; or

(b) where the court makes no such direction, 14 days, after the date in paragraph (5).

(5) The date referred to in paragraph (4) is –

(a) the date the respondent is served with the appellant's notice where –
(i) permission to appeal was given by the lower court; or
(ii) permission to appeal is not required;

(b) the date the respondent is served with notification that the appeal court has given the appellant permission to appeal; or

(c) the date the respondent is served with notification that the application for permission to appeal and the appeal itself are to be heard together.

(6) Unless the appeal court orders otherwise a respondent's notice must be served on the appellant and any other respondent –

(a) as soon as practicable; and
(b) in any event not later than 7 days,

after it is filed.

Amendments—Inserted by SI 2000/221.

Practice Direction—See generally PD52 at p 1217.

A respondent's notice—A respondent may file and serve a respondent's notice in the case of any appeal (r 52.5(1)). A respondent's notice should be in Form N162. In two instances a respondent's notice is obligatory –

(1) where a respondent is seeking permission to appeal (r 52.5(2)(a)), ie where the respondent is seeking to have the order of the lower court set aside or varied in some respect; and
(2) where the respondent wishes to ask the appeal court to uphold the lower court's order for reasons different from or additional to those given by the lower court (r 52.5(2)(b)), ie what used to be called a respondent's notice to affirm under the old rules.

When does a respondent require permission to appeal—A respondent who wishes to ask the appeal court to vary the order of the lower court in any way requires permission to appeal on the same basis as an appellant would require it (r 52.3(1) and PD52, para 7.1). A respondent who only wishes to seek to uphold the lower court's order does not require permission to appeal (PD52, para 7.2).

Filing of a respondent's notice—Under r 52.5(4), unless the lower court has set down a different timetable, a respondent's notice must be filed with the appeal court within 14 days of the date prescribed by r 52.5(5). Where permission to appeal was granted to the appellant by the lower court, or was not required, the time limit for filing the respondent's notice runs from the date on which the respondent was served with the appellant's notice (r 52.5(5)(a)). Where the appellant has been granted permission to appeal by the appeal court, it runs from the date on which the respondent was served with notification of that grant of permission to appeal (r 52.5(5)(b)). Where the appeal court directs that the application for permission and the appeal are to be heard together (ie that the application for permission to appeal be listed with the appeal to follow, if permission is granted), it runs from the date on which the respondent was served with notification to that effect (r 52.5(5)(c)).

Service of a respondent's notice—Unless the appeal court directs otherwise, a respondent's notice must be served on the appellant and any other separately represented respondent (or respondent in person) as soon as practicable and in any event not later than seven days after it was filed. In the case of appeals to the Court of Appeal service must always be effected by the respondent's solicitor (or the respondent in person); the Civil Appeals Office does not serve documents (PD52, para 15.1(2)). In the case of other appeal courts, the court may serve the documents, or give them to the respondent's solicitor (or the respondent in person) to serve.

52.6 Variation of time

(1) An application to vary the time limit for filing an appeal notice must be made to the appeal court.

(2) The parties may not agree to extend any date or time limit set by –

(a) these Rules;

(b) the relevant practice direction; or
(c) an order of the appeal court or the lower court.

(Rule 3.1(2)(a) provides that the court may extend or shorten the time for compliance with any rule, practice direction or court order (even if an application for extension is made after the time for compliance has expired))

(Rule 3.1(2)(b) provides that the court may adjourn or bring forward a hearing)

Amendments—Inserted by SI 2000/221.

Practice Direction—See generally PD52 at p 1217.

Effect of the rule—This rule prevents the parties from simply agreeing to an extension of any time limit set by the rules, PD52, or any order of the appeal court or the lower court. Application for any such extension must be made to the appeal court.

Any application for an extension of time for filing an appellant's notice must be made in the appellant's notice itself, and the reasons for the delay and the steps taken prior to the application being made must be set out (see PD52, paras 5.2–5.4). For the approach to applications for extensions of time for appealing see *Sayers v Clarke Walker (Practice Note)* [2002] EWCA Civ 645, [2002] 1 WLR 3095, CA and the note **'Extension of time for appealing'** under PD52, para 5.4.

52.7 Stay(GL)

Unless –

(a) the appeal court or the lower court orders otherwise; or
(b) the appeal is from the Immigration Appeal Tribunal,

an appeal shall not operate as a stay of any order or decision of the lower court.

Amendments—Inserted by SI 2000/221.

Practice Direction—See generally PD52 at p 1217.

Stay pending appeal—Save in the case of an appeal from the Immigration Appeal Tribunal, instituting an appeal (whether to the Court of Appeal, the High Court, or a judge of a county court) does not operate as an automatic stay on the order or decision of the lower court (r 52.7). If a stay is sought it must be expressly applied for either to the lower court or the appeal court.

In deciding whether or not to grant a stay, the court must conduct a balancing exercise considering the potential prejudice to both parties. In *Hammond Suddards v Agrichem International Holdings Ltd* [2001] EWCA Civ 2065 (a money order) the Court of Appeal identified three particular issues which require consideration. The approach based on prejudice to the parties was approved in relation to a non-money order in *Moat Housing Group South Ltd v Harris and Hartless* (2005) *The Times*, 13 January, CA).

52.8 Amendment of appeal notice

An appeal notice may not be amended without the permission of the appeal court.

Amendments—Inserted by SI 2000/221.

Practice Direction—See generally PD52 at p 1217.

Amendment of appeal notice—The application for permission to amend must be made by application notice. Generally it will be dealt with at the main appeal hearing and will only be heard in advance of that if waiting until the main appeal hearing would cause unnecessary expense or delay (PD52, para 5.25).

52.9 Striking out(GL) appeal notices and setting aside or imposing conditions on permission to appeal

(1) The appeal court may –

(a) strike out the whole or part of an appeal notice;
(b) set aside[(GL)] permission to appeal in whole or in part;
(c) impose or vary conditions upon which an appeal may be brought.

(2) The court will only exercise its powers under paragraph (1) where there is a compelling reason for doing so.

(3) Where a party was present at the hearing at which permission was given he may not subsequently apply for an order that the court exercise its powers under sub-paragraphs (1)(b) or (1)(c).

Amendments—Inserted by SI 2000/221.

Practice Direction—See generally PD52 at p 1217.

Striking out an appeal notice—Rule 52.9(1)(a) is suitable to be used where the appeal is manifestly without merit. It is also available as a sanction for non-compliance with a rule or order (see as an example *Taiga v Taiga* (2004) EWCA Civ 1399). It confers the power to strike out on all appeal courts and extends it to respondent's notices as well. Rule 52.9(2) makes it clear that this power, like the inherent jurisdiction, will be sparingly exercised. Where the notice is struck out as totally without merit the court must record that fact in the order and consider whether to make a civil restraint order (see r 52.10(6) below), which was one of a number of amendments introduced following the decision in *Bhamjee v Forsdick (No 2)* [2004] 1 WLR 88, [2003] EWCA Civ 1113.

Setting aside the grant of permission to appeal—Under r 52.9(1)(b) a respondent may apply for the grant of permission to appeal to be set aside in whole or in part; but a respondent who was represented or present in person at the hearing of the permission to appeal application cannot make such an application (r 52.9(3)). Again, this power will be sparingly exercised (r 52.9(2)). For an example where the Court of Appeal exercised this power see *Athletic Union of Constantinople v National Basketball Association (No 2)* [2002] EWCA Civ 830, [2002] 1 WLR 2863, CA. In this case the grant of permission to appeal by the single Lord Justice was set aside on the grounds that, by reason of AA 1996, s 67(4), the Court of Appeal had no jurisdiction to entertain the appeal. In *Nathan v Smilovitch & anor* [2002] EWCA Civ 759 Longmore LJ said:

> 'For my part, unless the nature of the application shows that some decisive authority or decisive statutory provision has been overlooked by the Lord Justice granting permission to appeal, an applicant would normally have to show that the single Lord Justice had actually been misled.'

Imposition or variation of conditions on which an appeal may be brought—This power can only be exercised if there is a compelling reason for doing so (r 52.9(2)). The Court of Appeal exercised it in *Bell Electric Ltd v Appliance Systems GmbH and Co KG* [2003] 1 All ER 344 by making an order requiring the appellant to furnish security for the judgment debt and an amount on account of costs ordered by the judge in the lower court.

52.10 Appeal court's powers

(1) In relation to an appeal the appeal court has all the powers of the lower court.

(Rule 52.1(4) provides that this Part is subject to any enactment that sets out special provisions with regard to any particular category of appeal – where such an enactment gives a statutory power to a tribunal, person or other body it may be the case that the appeal court may not exercise that power on an appeal)

(2) The appeal court has power to –

(a) affirm, set aside or vary any order or judgment made or given by the lower court;
(b) refer any claim or issue for determination by the lower court;
(c) order a new trial or hearing;
(d) make orders for the payment of interest;
(e) make a costs order.

(3) In an appeal from a claim tried with a jury the Court of Appeal may, instead of ordering a new trial –

(a) make an order for damages[(GL)]; or
(b) vary an award of damages made by the jury.

(4) The appeal court may exercise its powers in relation to the whole or part of an order of the lower court.

(Part 3 contains general rules about the court's case management powers)

[(5) If the appeal court –

(a) refuses an application for permission to appeal;
(b) strikes out an appellant's notice; or
(c) dismisses an appeal,

and it considers that the application, the appellant's notice or the appeal is totally without merit, the provisions of paragraph (6) must be complied with.

(6) Where paragraph (5) applies –

(a) the court's order must record the fact that it considers the application, the appellant's notice or the appeal to be totally without merit; and
(b) the court must at the same time consider whether it is appropriate to make a civil restraint order.

Amendments—Inserted by SI 2000/221; SI 2004/2072.

Practice Direction—See generally PD52 at p 1217.

Powers of the appeal court—These are very wide. It may be necessary on occasions to remit the case back to the lower court, but time and expense will be saved if this can be avoided.

52.11 Hearing of appeals

(1) Every appeal will be limited to a review of the decision of the lower court unless –

(a) a practice direction makes different provision for a particular category of appeal; or
(b) the court considers that in the circumstances of an individual appeal it would be in the interests of justice to hold a re-hearing.

(2) Unless it orders otherwise, the appeal court will not receive –

(a) oral evidence; or
(b) evidence which was not before the lower court.

(3) The appeal court will allow an appeal where the decision of the lower court was –

(a) wrong; or
(b) unjust because of a serious procedural or other irregularity in the proceedings in the lower court.

(4) The appeal court may draw any inference of fact which it considers justified on the evidence.

(5) At the hearing of the appeal a party may not rely on a matter not contained in his appeal notice unless the appeal court gives permission.

Amendments—Inserted by SI 2000/221.

Practice Direction—See generally PD52 at p 1217.

Nature of an appeal—The effect of this rule is that, in the case of all appeals, whether to the Court of Appeal, the High Court, or a judge of a county court, the appeal will not be by way of a complete re-hearing, unless the appeal court exercises its power under r 52.11(1)(b), but will be 'limited to a review of the decision of the lower court.' Under r 52.11(1)(b) the appeal court has power to hold a re-hearing if it considers that it would be in the interests of justice to do so.

The expression 'limited to a review of the decision of the lower court' is intended to mean that all appeal courts will apply the same approach to appeals as was applied by the Court of Appeal before this Part was introduced. In particular, the appeal court will not interfere with the exercise of any discretion by the judge of the lower court unless there was an error of law in the exercise of the discretion or the decision reached was outside the generous ambit within which a reasonable disagreement is possible. Likewise, the appeal court will not interfere with findings of fact by the lower court save in the limited circumstances in which the Court of Appeal would have done so under its established practice in relation to appeals on fact.

Appeals against interlocutory orders made by masters and district judges are no longer complete re-hearings with discretion being exercised afresh by the High Court judge or circuit judge. Instead the High Court judge or circuit judge will only be able to interfere with the exercise of discretion by the master or district judge in the limited circumstances set out above. In *Tanfern v Cameron-MacDonald* [2000] 2 All ER 801 at [32] Brooke LJ adopted the observations of Lord Fraser of Tullybelton in *G v G* [1985] 1 WLR 647, [1985] 2 All ER 225.

The Court of Appeal (as well as other appeal courts) is now empowered to conduct a complete re-hearing where the interests of justice require it (it is doubtful whether the Court of Appeal previously had that power). In *Audergon v La Baguette Ltd & ors* [2002] EWCA Civ 10, the Court of Appeal declined to formulate criteria to be applied in deciding whether to hold a rehearing, but concluded that in the circumstances of the case the judge hearing the appeal below had erred in proceeding by way of rehearing. In *Asiansky Television plc & anor v Bayer-Rosin* [2001] EWCA Civ 1792, Dyson LJ gave as a two possible examples of the need for a rehearing: (a) where the judgment of the lower court was so inadequately reasoned; or (b) where there had been a serious procedural irregularity. On failure to give reasons see *Flannery v Halifax Estate Agencies Ltd* [2000] 1 WLR 377 and *English v Emery Reimbold and Strick Ltd* [2002] 1 WLR 2409.

In *Assicurazioni General SpA v Arab Insurance Group (BSC)* [2002] EWCA Civ 1642, [2002] TLR 504, CA helpful guidance was given as to the approach to an appeal based on alleged errors of fact, but note that while Clarke J observed that the approach of the court in relation to challenges to findings of fact is the same whether it is conducting a review or a re-hearing, this view was not shared by Ward LJ.

Further evidence—Further evidence cannot be adduced on the appeal unless the appeal court grants permission to do so (r 52.11(2)(b)). This is consistent with the appeal being generally by way of review. The principles set out in *Ladd v Marshall* [1954] 1 WLR 1489, [1954] All ER 745 remain of relevance, but they must be applied in the context of the overriding objective (*Hertfordshire Investments Ltd v Bubb* [2000] 1 WLR 2318 and *Gillingham v Gillingham* [2001] EWCA Civ 906). In *Woodhouse v Consignia plc* [2002] 1 WLR 2558, [2002] 2 All ER 737 Brooke LJ drew attention to the risks run by practitioners in relying on inadequate evidence at the first hearing:

> 'The moral of this story is that greater attention needs to be paid to the quality of the evidence adduced at the first hearing, because there may not be a second chance on appeal.'

Generally the appeal court will not hear oral evidence (r 52.11(2)(a)).

The basis on which appeals will be allowed—Rule 52.11(3) seeks to specify the grounds on which the appeal court will allow an appeal. It is expressed in general terms, but it does not appear to be intended to alter the established practice in relation to the circumstances in which an appeal will be allowed, in particular appeals against the exercise of discretion and appeals on questions of fact (see above).

52.12 Non-disclosure of Part 36 offers and payments

(1) The fact that a Part 36 offer or Part 36 payment has been made must not be disclosed to any judge of the appeal court who is to hear or determine –

(a) an application for permission to appeal; or
(b) an appeal,

until all questions (other than costs) have been determined.

(2) Paragraph (1) does not apply if the Part 36 offer or Part 36 payment is relevant to the substance of the appeal.

(3) Paragraph (1) does not prevent disclosure in any application in the appeal proceedings if disclosure of the fact that a Part 36 offer or Part 36 payment has been made is properly relevant to the matter to be decided.

Amendments—Inserted by SI 2000/221; amended by SI 2003/3361.

Practice Direction—See generally PD52 at p 1217.

II Special Provisions applying to the Court of Appeal

52.13 Second appeals to the court

(1) Permission is required from the Court of Appeal for any appeal to that court from a decision of a county court or the High Court which was itself made on appeal.

(2) The Court of Appeal will not give permission unless it considers that –

(a) the appeal would raise an important point of principle or practice; or

(b) there is some other compelling reason for the Court of Appeal to hear it.

Amendments—Inserted by SI 2000/221.

Practice Direction—See generally PD52 at p 1217.

Second-tier appeals—Access to Justice Act 1999, s 55 imposes severe restrictions on second-tier appeals, ie appeals against decisions of a High Court judge or judge of a county court given in an appellate capacity. This rule covers the same topic, but adds nothing to the statutory provision. Indeed the statutory provision is of wider scope than r 52.13, because s 55 applies to appeals to which Part 52 does not apply.

Section 55 applies not only to appeals to a High Court judge, or circuit judge, from the decision of a judge below that (eg a master or a district judge), but also to statutory appeals to the High Court (eg an appeal to the High Court in a tax case from a decision of the general or special commissioners or a VAT tribunal, see *Clark (Inspector of Taxes) v Perks (Permission to Appeal)* [2001] 1 WLR 17, CA), and statutory appeals to a county court (eg an appeal under HA 1999, s 204, see *Azimi v Newham London Borough* (2001) 33 HLR 51, CA).

A second-tier appeal will only be allowed to proceed to the Court of Appeal if that court considers that either –

(i) the appeal would raise an important point of law or practice; or

(ii) there is some other compelling reason for the Court of Appeal to hear it (AJA 1999, s 55).

An appeal on an important point of law, or the interpretation of a rule or some other point of practice which is of wide general application would fall within (i). Proviso (ii) was inserted to provide an ultimate safety valve. It would allow the Court of Appeal to entertain an appeal notwithstanding that the point was a 'one-off' of no general import, if, for example, the decision sought to be appealed was so grossly erroneous or unfair that it would be an affront to justice to allow it to stand.

In *Uphill v BRB (Residuary) Ltd* [2005] EWCA Civ 60, [2005] 3 All ER 264 the Court of Appeal held that where the appeal raises an important point of principle that has not yet been determined, permission can be given but permission should be refused where the appeal seeks to raise the correct application of a principle or practice whose meaning or scope has already been defined by a higher court. 'Some other compelling reason' contemplates an appeal which does not raise an important point of principle or practice. 'Compelling' indicates the truly exceptional nature of the jurisdiction.

Section 55 does not apply to orders of the first-tier appeal court made in respect of an application for permission to appeal other than the grant or refusal of permission, eg s 55 does not apply to the order for costs made on the permission application, or the refusal of an adjournment of that application (*Clark (Inspector of Taxes) v Perks (Permission to Appeal)* [2001] 1 WLR 17, CA, at [20]), but permission to appeal would be required under r 52.3(1)(a). Also the section does not apply to an appeal to the Court of Appeal against a decision of a first-tier appeal court refusing an extension of time for appealing (see note **'Finality of decisions of an appeal court on applications for permission to appeal'** under r 52.3).

In *Henry Boot Construction (UK) Ltd v Malmaison Hotel (Manchester) Ltd* [2001] QB 388, CA) Swinton Thomas and Waller LJJ expressed the view *obiter* that AJA 1999, s 55 does not apply to cases governed by AA 1996, s 69 (appeals against arbitration awards). Their Lordships said that, if the High Court judge grants permission to appeal to the Court of Appeal under s 69(8), then the appeal can proceed to the Court of Appeal and AJA 1999, s 55 does not interpose an additional hurdle.

The Court of Appeal is the sole arbiter of whether a second-tier appeal should be allowed to proceed. It follows that, where it would be a second-tier appeal, permission to appeal cannot be granted by the High Court judge or circuit judge, and any application for permission to appeal in such a case must be made to the Court of Appeal (see PD52, paras 4.9 and 4.10).

Any such purported grant of permission to appeal by a judge or court other than the Court of Appeal is a nullity (*Clark (Inspector of Taxes) v Perks (Permission to Appeal)* [2001] 1 WLR 17, CA; *Moyse v Regal Mortgages Limited Partnership* [2004] EWCA Civ 1269, an unreported case which Brooke LJ expressly declared could be cited in court).

On its wording, s 55 clearly does not apply to second-tier appeals to the Court of Appeal from decisions of tribunals (eg the Employment Appeal Tribunal, the Social Security and Child Support Commissioners and the Immigration Appeals Tribunal, all of which hear appeals from other lower tribunals). But an approach similar to s 55 should be applied to applications for permission to appeal against decisions of the Social Security and Child Support Commissioners (*Cooke v Secretary of State for Social Security* [2001] EWCA Civ 734, [2002] 3 All ER 279 CA).

52.14 Assignment of appeals to the Court of Appeal

(1) Where the court from or to which an appeal is made or from which permission to appeal is sought ('the relevant court') considers that –

(a) an appeal which is to be heard by a county court or the High Court would raise an important point of principle or practice; or

(b) there is some other compelling reason for the Court of Appeal to hear it,

the relevant court may order the appeal to be transferred to the Court of Appeal.

(The Master of the Rolls has the power to direct that an appeal which would be heard by a county court or the High Court should be heard instead by the Court of Appeal – see section 57 of the Access to Justice Act 1999)

(2) The Master of the Rolls or the Court of Appeal may remit an appeal to the court in which the original appeal was or would have been brought.

Amendments—Inserted by SI 2000/221.

Practice Direction—See generally PD52 at p 1217.

Referral of appeals directly to the Court of Appeal—This rule makes provision for there to be a leap-frog of an appeal which would otherwise be heard by the High Court or a judge of a county court straight to the Court of Appeal, if it raises an important point of principle or practice or there is some other compelling reason to do so. This is a useful provision where there are conflicting decisions between judges in different parts of the country and authoritative guidance is required urgently. For an example of a leapfrog appeal, see *North British Housing Association v Matthews* [2004] EWCA Civ 1736. While the rule gives the lower court the power to transfer, that court will consult the Court of Appeal first. In the county court this is done via the designated civil judge.

52.15 Judicial review appeals

(1) Where permission to apply for judicial review has been refused at a hearing in the High Court, the person seeking that permission may apply to the Court of Appeal for permission to appeal.

(2) An application in accordance with paragraph (1) must be made within 7 days of the decision of the High Court to refuse to give permission to apply for judicial review.

(3) On an application under paragraph (1), the Court of Appeal may, instead of giving permission to appeal, give permission to apply for judicial review.

(4) Where the Court of Appeal gives permission to apply for judicial review in accordance with paragraph (3), the case will proceed in the High Court unless the Court of Appeal orders otherwise.

Amendments—Inserted by SI 2000/221.

Practice Direction—See generally PD52 at p 1217.

Appeals against refusal of permission to proceed in judicial review cases—Before a person can pursue a claim for judicial review permission to proceed must be obtained (see r 54.4 and SCA 1981, s 31(3)). The request for permission to proceed will be dealt with at first instance in the High Court by the Administrative Court. It will usually be dealt with initially on paper without a hearing. If permission to proceed is refused on paper, then, at that stage, the claimant is not allowed to appeal, but may request that the decision be reconsidered at an oral hearing (r 54.12(3)). If permission to proceed is refused after an oral hearing, the claimant can apply to the Court of Appeal (see r 52.15(1)).

The procedure for taking the matter to the Court of Appeal is different from the procedure under the former RSC. (Under the old rules the procedure was that the applicant renewed his application for leave to move for judicial review by making a fresh ex parte application to the Court of Appeal under RSC Ord 59, r 14(3)). The procedure under the new rules is that the claimant files with the Civil Appeal Office an appellant's notice applying to the Court of Appeal for permission to appeal against the refusal of permission to proceed (see r 52.15(1) coupled with r 52.4(1)).

Time limit for filing the appellant's notice—The appellant's notice (in which the application for permission to appeal must be made) must be filed with the Civil Appeals Office within seven days of the decision of the High Court refusing permission to proceed (r 52.15(2)).

Service on the respondent(s)—A sealed copy of the appellant's notice must be served on each separately represented respondent, and any respondent in person (see PD52, para 5.21). Unless the Court of Appeal otherwise orders, the appellant's notice must be served on the respondent(s) as soon as practicable and, in any event, not later than 7 days after the appellant's notice was filed with the Civil Appeals Office (r 52.4(3)).

Powers of the Court of Appeal—On an application under r 52.15(1) the Court of Appeal may, instead of granting permission to appeal, grant permission to proceed (ie permission to proceed with the claim for judicial review) (r 52.15(3)). In that event (unless the Court of Appeal otherwise directs) the substantive claim for judicial review will then proceed in the High Court (r 52.15(4)), and those appellate proceedings will come to an end without any main appeal hearing. In almost all cases where the Court of Appeal considers that the claim for judicial review should be allowed to proceed, the Court is likely to exercise its power under r 52.15(3) and then send the case back for the substantive claim to be dealt with by the Administrative Court.

If the Court of Appeal considers that the claim for judicial review should not be allowed to proceed, it will refuse permission to appeal against the refusal of permission to proceed and that decision cannot be further challenged because an appeal against the refusal of permission to appeal is precluded by statute (AJA 1999, s 54(4) and see also *R v Secretary of State for Trade and Industry ex p Eastaway* [2000] 1 WLR 2222). If the Court of Appeal gives permission to appeal but then refuses permission to apply for judicial review, the ability to appeal to the House of Lords is not lost (*R (Werner) v Commissioners of Inland Revenue* [2002] EWCA Civ 979).

52.16 Who may exercise the powers of the Court of Appeal

(1) A court officer assigned to the Civil Appeals Office who is –

- (a) a barrister; or
- (b) a solicitor

may exercise the jurisdiction of the Court of Appeal with regard to the matters set out in paragraph (2) with the consent of the Master of the Rolls.

(2) The matters referred to in paragraph (1) are –

- (a) any matter incidental to any proceedings in the Court of Appeal;
- (b) any other matter where there is no substantial dispute between the parties; and
- (c) the dismissal of an appeal or application where a party has failed to comply with any order, rule or practice direction.

(3) A court officer may not decide an application for –

(a) permission to appeal;
(b) bail pending an appeal;
(c) an injunction(GL);
(d) a stay(GL) of any proceedings, other than a temporary stay of any order or decision of the lower court over a period when the Court of Appeal is not sitting or cannot conveniently be convened.

(4) Decisions of a court officer may be made without a hearing.

(5) A party may request any decision of a court officer to be reviewed by the Court of Appeal.

(6) At the request of a party, a hearing will be held to reconsider a decision of –

(a) a single judge; or
(b) a court officer,

made without a hearing.

(6A) A request under paragraph (5) or (6) must be filed within 7 days after the party is served with the notice of the decision.

(7) A single judge may refer any matter for a decision by a court consisting of two or more judges.

(Section 54(6) of the Supreme Court Act 1981 provides that there is no appeal from the decision of a single judge on an application for permission to appeal)

(Section 58(2) of the Supreme Court Act 1981 provides that there is no appeal to the House of Lords from decisions of the Court of Appeal that –

(a) are taken by a single judge or any officer or member of staff of that court in proceedings incidental to any cause or matter pending before the civil division of that court; and

(b) do not involve the determination of an appeal or of an application for permission to appeal,

and which may be called into question by rules of court. Rules 52.16(5) and (6) provide the procedure for the calling into question of such decisions)

Amendments—Inserted by SI 2000/221; amended by SI 2003/3361.

Practice Direction—See generally PD52 at p 1217.

Exercise of certain powers of the Court of Appeal by court officials—This rule enables certain of the powers of the Court of Appeal in matters incidental to appeals to be exercised by court officials who are barristers or solicitors with the consent of the Master of the Rolls (r 52.16(1)). This empowers the Head of the Civil Appeals Office (who is called the Master when exercising judicial functions) and those who act as his Deputies to exercise certain judicial functions. Principally they are dealing with extensions of time (where permission to appeal has already been granted or is not required), listing and other directions, making orders for dismissal of appeals by consent and other forms of consent orders and conducting the weekly dismissal list. Appeals and applications where the appellant has failed to lodge appeal bundles or other requisite documents or failed to remedy defects in them are listed for the appellant to show cause why they should not be dismissed. Those hearings (which normally take place on Wednesdays are known as the 'Dismissal List' and are conducted by the Master or one of his Deputies). The Master and his Deputies cannot deal with permission to appeal, bail pending appeal, or injunctions, and they cannot grant a stay pending appeal, save a temporary stay when the Court of Appeal is not sitting and cannot conveniently be convened (r 52.16(3)). There is a review as of right against any decision of a Master or Deputy Master (r 52.16(5)); such a review is usually heard by a single Lord Justice.

III Provisions about Reopening Appeals

52.17 Reopening of final appeals

(1) The Court of Appeal or the High Court will not reopen a final determination of any appeal unless –

(a) it is necessary to do so in order to avoid real injustice;
(b) the circumstances are exceptional and make it appropriate to reopen the appeal; and
(c) there is no alternative effective remedy.

(2) In paragraphs (1), (3), (4) and (6), 'appeal' includes an application for permission to appeal.

(3) This rule does not apply to appeals to a county court.

(4) Permission is needed to make an application under this rule to reopen a final determination of an appeal even in cases where under rule 52.3(1) permission was not needed for the original appeal.

(5) There is no right to an oral hearing of an application for permission unless, exceptionally, the judge so directs.

(6) The judge will not grant permission without directing the application to be served on the other party to the original appeal and giving him an opportunity to make representations.

(7) There is no right of appeal or review from the decision of the judge on the application for permission, which is final.

(8) The procedure for making an application for permission is set out in the practice direction.

Amendments—Inserted by SI 2003/2113.

Reopening appeals—This rule was added following the decisions of the Court of Appeal in *Taylor v Lawrence* [2003] QB 528, [2002] 2 All ER 353 and *Seray-Wurie v Hackney LBC* [2003] 1 WLR 257, [2002] 3 All ER 448. It should be noted that it does not apply to appeals in the county court. The three conditions, all of which must be satisfied, are stringent. For an example where the application was granted, see *Couwenbergh v Valkova* [2004] EWCA Civ 676.

Practice Direction – Appeals

This Practice Direction supplements CPR Part 52 (PD52)

Procedural Guide—See Guides 58 and 59, set out in Section 1 of this work.

CONTENTS OF THIS PRACTICE DIRECTION

1.1 This practice direction is divided into four sections –

- Section I – General provisions about appeals
- Section II – General provisions about statutory appeals and appeals by way of case stated
- Section III – Provisions about specific appeals
- Section IV – Provisions about reopening appeals

SECTION I – GENERAL PROVISIONS ABOUT APPEALS

2.1 This practice direction applies to all appeals to which Part 52 applies except where specific provision is made for appeals to the Court of Appeal.

2.2 For the purpose only of appeals to the Court of Appeal from cases in family proceedings this Practice Direction will apply with such modifications as may be required.

ROUTES OF APPEAL

2A.1 Subject to paragraph 2A.2, the following table sets out to which court or judge an appeal is to be made (subject to obtaining any necessary permission):

Decision of:	Appeal made to:
District judge of a county court	Circuit judge
Master or district judge of the High Court	High Court judge
Circuit judge	High Court judge
High Court judge	Court of Appeal

2A.2 Where the decision to be appealed is a final decision –

(1) in a Part 7 claim allocated to the multi-track; or
(2) made in specialist proceedings (under the Companies Acts 1985 or 1989 or to which Sections I, II or III of Part 57 or any of Parts 58 to 63 apply),

the appeal is to be made to the Court of Appeal (subject to obtaining any necessary permission).

2A.3 A 'final decision' is a decision of a court that would finally determine (subject to any possible appeal or detailed assessment of costs) the entire proceedings whichever way the court decided the issues before it.

2A.4 A decision of a court is to be treated as a final decision for routes of appeal purposes where it:

(1) is made at the conclusion of part of a hearing or trial which has been split into parts; and
(2) would, if it had been made at the conclusion of that hearing or trial, have been a final decision.

2A.5 An order made:

(a) on a summary or detailed assessment of costs; or
(b) on an application to enforce a final decision,

is not a 'final decision' and any appeal from such an order will follow the appeal routes set out in the table in paragraph 2A.1.

(Section 16(1) of the Supreme Court Act 1981 (as amended); section 77(1) of the County Courts Act 1984 (as amended); and the Access to Justice Act 1999 (Destination of Appeals) Order 2000 set out the provisions governing routes of appeal)

2A.6

(1) Where the decision to be appealed is a final decision in a Part 8 claim

treated as allocated to the multi-track under rule 8.9(c), the court to which the permission application is made should, if permission is given, and unless the appeal would lie to the Court of Appeal in any event, consider whether to order the appeal to be transferred to the Court of Appeal under rule 52.14.

(2) An appeal against a final decision on a point of law in a case which did not involve any substantial dispute of fact would normally be a suitable appeal to be so transferred.

(See also paragraph 10.1)

GROUNDS FOR APPEAL

3.1 Rule 52.11(3)(a) and (b) sets out the circumstances in which the appeal court will allow an appeal.

3.2 The grounds of appeal should –

(1) set out clearly the reasons why rule 52.11(3)(a) or (b) is said to apply; and
(2) specify, in respect of each ground, whether the ground raises an appeal on a point of law or is an appeal against a finding of fact.

PERMISSION TO APPEAL

4.1 Rule 52.3 sets out the circumstances when permission to appeal is required.

4.2 The permission of –

(a) the Court of Appeal; or
(b) where the lower court's rules allow, the lower court,

is required for all appeals to the Court of Appeal except as provided for by statute or rule 52.3.

(The requirement of permission to appeal may be imposed by a practice direction – see rule 52.3(b))

4.3 Where the lower court is not required to give permission to appeal, it may give an indication of its opinion as to whether permission should be given.

(Rule 52.1(3)(c) defines 'lower court')

Appeals from case management decisions

4.4 Case management decisions include decisions made under rule 3.1(2) and decisions about –

(1) disclosure
(2) filing of witness statements or experts reports
(3) directions about the timetable of the claim
(4) adding a party to a claim
(5) security for costs.

4.5 Where the application is for permission to appeal from a case management decision, the court dealing with the application may take into account whether –

(1) the issue is of sufficient significance to justify the costs of an appeal;
(2) the procedural consequences of an appeal (eg loss of trial date) outweigh the significance of the case management decision;
(3) it would be more convenient to determine the issue at or after trial.

Court to which permission to appeal application should be made

4.6 An application for permission should be made orally at the hearing at which the decision to be appealed against is made.

4.7 Where:

(a) no application for permission to appeal is made at the hearing; or
(b) the lower court refuses permission to appeal,

an application for permission to appeal may be made to the appeal court in accordance with rules 52.3(2) and (3).

4.8 There is no appeal from the decision of the appeal court to allow or refuse permission to appeal to that court (although where the appeal court, without a hearing, refuses permission to appeal, the person seeking permission may request that decision to be reconsidered at a hearing). See section 54(4) of the Access to Justice Act and rule 52.3(2), (3), (4) and (5).

Application to the lower court—Where the request for permission is made to the lower court, the judge should complete Form N460 whether giving or refusing permission. The person seeking permission should ensure that this is done and should obtain a copy of the form as completed by the judge, since it is a document which is required to be filed in connection with an appeal.

Second appeals

4.9 An application for permission to appeal from a decision of the High Court or a county court which was itself made on appeal must be made to the Court of Appeal.

4.10 If permission to appeal is granted the appeal will be heard by the Court of Appeal.

Consideration of Permission without a hearing

4.11 Applications for permission to appeal may be considered by the appeal court without a hearing.

4.12 If permission is granted without a hearing the parties will be notified of that decision and the procedure in paragraphs 6.1 to 6.6 will then apply.

4.13 If permission is refused without a hearing the parties will be notified of that decision with the reasons for it. The decision is subject to the appellant's right to have it reconsidered at an oral hearing. This may be before the same judge.

4.14 A request for the decision to be reconsidered at an oral hearing must be filed at the appeal court within 7 days after service of the notice that permission has been refused. A copy of the request must be served by the appellant on the respondent at the same time.

Permission hearing

4.14A

(1) This paragraph applies where an appellant, who is represented, makes a request for a decision to be reconsidered at an oral hearing.
(2) The appellant's advocate must, at least 4 days before the hearing, in a brief written statement –
    (a) inform the court and the respondent of the points which he proposes to raise at the hearing;

(b) set out his reasons why permission should be granted notwithstanding the reasons given for the refusal of permission; and
(c) confirm, where applicable, that the requirements of paragraph 4.17 have been complied with (appellant in receipt of services funded by the Legal Services Commission).

4.15 Notice of a permission hearing will be given to the respondent but he is not required to attend unless the court requests him to do so.

4.16 If the court requests the respondent's attendance at the permission hearing, the appellant must supply the respondent with a copy of the appeal bundle (see paragraph 5.6A) within 7 days of being notified of the request, or such other period as the court may direct. The costs of providing that bundle shall be borne by the appellant initially, but will form part of the costs of the permission application.

Appellants in receipt of services funded by the Legal Services Commission applying for permission to appeal

4.17 Where the appellant is in receipt of services funded by the Legal Services Commission (or legally aided) and permission to appeal has been refused by the appeal court without a hearing, the appellant must send a copy of the reasons the appeal court gave for refusing permission to the relevant office of the Legal Services Commission as soon as it has been received from the court. The court will require confirmation that this has been done if a hearing is requested to re-consider the question of permission.

Limited permission

4.18 Where a court under rule 52.3(7) gives permission to appeal on some issues only, it will –

(1) refuse permission on any remaining issues; or
(2) reserve the question of permission to appeal on any remaining issues to the court hearing the appeal.

4.19 If the court reserves the question of permission under paragraph 4.18(2), the appellant must, within 14 days after service of the court's order, inform the appeal court and the respondent in writing whether he intends to pursue the reserved issues. If the appellant does intend to pursue the reserved issues, the parties must include in any time estimate for the appeal hearing, their time estimate for the reserved issues.

4.20 If the appeal court refuses permission to appeal on the remaining issues without a hearing and the applicant wishes to have that decision reconsidered at an oral hearing, the time limit in rule 52.3(5) shall apply. Any application for an extension of this time limit should be made promptly. The court hearing the appeal on the issues for which permission has been granted will not normally grant, at the appeal hearing, an application to extend the time limit in rule 52.3(5) for the remaining issues.

4.21 If the appeal court refuses permission to appeal on remaining issues at or after an oral hearing, the application for permission to appeal on those issues cannot be renewed at the appeal hearing. See section 54(4) of the Access to Justice Act 1999.

Respondents' costs of permission applications

4.22 In most cases, applications for permission to appeal will be determined without the court requiring –

(1) submissions from, or
(2) if there is an oral hearing, attendance by

the respondent.

4.23 Where the court does not request submissions from or attendance by the respondent, costs will not normally be allowed to a respondent who volunteers submissions or attendance.

4.24 Where the court does request –

(1) submissions from or attendance by the respondent; or
(2) attendance by the respondent with the appeal to follow if permission is granted,

the court will normally allow the respondent his costs if permission is refused.

APPELLANT'S NOTICE

5.1 An appellant's notice must be filed and served in all cases. Where an application for permission to appeal is made to the appeal court it must be applied for in the appellant's notice.

Human Rights

5.1A

(1) This paragraph applies where the appellant seeks –
  (a) to rely on any issue under the Human Rights Act 1998; or
  (b) a remedy available under that Act,

for the first time in an appeal.

(2) The appellant must include in his appeal notice the information required by paragraph 15.1 of the practice direction supplementing Part 16.
(3) Paragraph 15.2 of the practice direction supplementing Part 16 applies as if references to a statement of case were to the appeal notice.

5.1B CPR rule 19.4A and the practice direction supplementing it shall apply as if references to the case management conference were to the application for permission to appeal.

(The practice direction to Part 19 provides for notice to be given and parties joined in certain circumstances to which this paragraph applies)

Extension of time for filing appellant's notice

5.2 If an appellant requires an extension of time for filing his notice the application must be made in the appellant's notice. The notice should state the reason for the delay and the steps taken prior to the application being made.

5.3 Where the appellant's notice includes an application for an extension of time and permission to appeal has been given or is not required the respondent has the right to be heard on that application. He must be served with a copy of the appeal bundle (see paragraph 5.6A). However, a respondent who unreasonably opposes an extension of time runs the risk of being ordered to pay the appellant's costs of that application.

5.4 If an extension of time is given following such an application the procedure at paragraphs 6.1 to 6.6 applies.

Extension of time for appealing—The application must be made in Section 10 of Form 161 (appellant's notice) and be supported by evidence, either in Part C of Section 10 or a separate witnesses statement.

In many cases the judge will be able to decide whether or not to grant an extension by considering the matters set out in PD52, para 5.2 (namely the reasons for the delay and the steps taken by the appellant's side prior to the application for an extension being made). However, in more complex cases a more sophisticated approach will be required. In such cases the judge will take into account the checklist in CPR r 3.9 (which deals with relief from sanctions) and, in cases where the arguments for and against the grant of an extension are otherwise evenly balanced, the court will have to evaluate the merits of the appeal. In order to secure an extension of time the appellant may have to show a case on the merits stronger than the threshold for the grant of permission to appeal (*Sayers v Clarke Walker (Practice Note)* 2002] EWCA Civ 645, 2002] 1 WLR 3095, CA).

As to the position where the appellant is applying to the appeal court both for permission to appeal and an extension of time for appealing, see note **'Finality of decisions of an appeal court on applications for permission to appeal'** under CPR r 52.3.

Applications

5.5 Notice of an application to be made to the appeal court for a remedy incidental to the appeal (eg an interim remedy under rule 25.1 or an order for security for costs) may be included in the appeal notice or in a Part 23 application notice.

(Rule 25.15 deals with security for costs of an appeal)

(Paragraph 11 of this practice direction contains other provisions relating to applications)

Documents

5.6 (1) This paragraph applies to every case except where the appeal –
- (a) relates to a claim allocated to the small claims track; and
- (b) is being heard in a county court or the High Court.

(Paragraph 5.8 applies where this paragraph does not apply)

(2) The appellant must file the following documents together with an appeal bundle (see paragraph 5.6A) with his appellant's notice –
- (a) two additional copies of the appellant's notice for the appeal court; and
- (b) one copy of the appellant's notice for each of the respondents;
- (c) one copy of his skeleton argument for each copy of the appellant's notice that is filed (see paragraph 5.9);
- (d) a sealed copy of the order being appealed;
- (e) a copy of any order giving or refusing permission to appeal, together with a copy of the judge's reasons for allowing or refusing permission to appeal;
- (f) any witness statements or affidavits in support of any application included in the appellant's notice.

Documents—The documentation required is substantial. The reasons for the judge's decision giving or refusing permission will ordinarily be contained in Form N460. There are also very specific directions about bundles in the Court of Appeal – see PD52, paras 15.2–15.4 and the commentary after para 5.6A below.

5.6A

(1) An appellant must include in his appeal bundle the following documents:

(a) a sealed copy of the appellant's notice;
(b) a sealed copy of the order being appealed;
(c) a copy of any order giving or refusing permission to appeal, together with a copy of the judge's reasons for allowing or refusing permission to appeal;
(d) any affidavit or witness statement filed in support of any application included in the appellant's notice;
(e) a copy of his skeleton argument;
(f) a transcript or note of judgment (see paragraph 5.12), and in cases where permission to appeal was given by the lower court or is not required those parts of any transcript of evidence which are directly relevant to any question at issue on the appeal;
(g) the claim form and statements of case (where relevant to the subject of the appeal);
(h) any application notice (or case management documentation) relevant to the subject of the appeal;
(i) in cases where the decision appealed was itself made on appeal (eg from district judge to circuit judge), the first order, the reasons given and the appellant's notice used to appeal from that order;
(j) in the case of judicial review or a statutory appeal, the original decision which was the subject of the application to the lower court;
(k) in cases where the appeal is from a Tribunal, a copy of the Tribunal's reasons for the decision, a copy of the decision reviewed by the Tribunal and the reasons for the original decision and any document filed with the Tribunal setting out the grounds of appeal from that decision;
(l) any other documents which the appellant reasonably considers necessary to enable the appeal court to reach its decision on the hearing of the application or appeal; and
(m) such other documents as the court may direct.

(2) All documents that are extraneous to the issues to be considered on the application or the appeal must be excluded. The appeal bundle may include affidavits, witness statements, summaries, experts' reports and exhibits but only where these are directly relevant to the subject matter of the appeal.

(3) Where the appellant is represented, the appeal bundle must contain a certificate signed by his solicitor, counsel or other representative to the effect that he has read and understood paragraph (2) above and that the composition of the appeal bundle complies with it.

Appeal bundles—Appeal bundles now have to be lodged at the initial stage when the appellant's notice is filed (see notes to CPR r 52.4).

PD52, paras 5.6–5.8 (documents) and paras 5.12–5.18 (record of the judgment and, where necessary, record of the evidence) specify what documents must be included in appeal bundles.

As regards the form of appeal bundles, PD52 does not expressly provide that they be bound, indexed and paginated; but, in the case of appeals (and applications) to the Court of Appeal, the standard letters from the Civil Appeals Office (issued with the authority of the Master) do so require. In the case of appeals from district judge to circuit judge, the circuit judge to whom the appeal is referred for directions may well issue a specific order that such a bundle be lodged.

There should be continuous pagination from the top of the bundle through to the end, not separate sections or tabs each with its own system of pagination beginning at page 1 (see also PD39, para 3.5). If there are too many documents to fit into one lever arch file, then each file should be lettered A, B, C etc, but the continuous pagination should run on from File A into File B and so on. There should be one overall index at the beginning of File A, not separate indices for each file.

Core bundles—Where the appeal bundle to be put before the court exceeds 500, there is an obligation to file a core bundle (see PD52, paras 15.2 and 15.3).

5.7 Where it is not possible to file all the above documents, the appellant must indicate which documents have not yet been filed and the reasons why they are not currently available. The appellant must then provide a reasonable estimate of when the missing document or documents can be filed and file them as soon as reasonably practicable.

Small claims

5.8 (1) This paragraph applies where –
(a) the appeal relates to a claim allocated to the small claims track; and
(b) the appeal is being heard in a county court or the High Court.
(1A) An appellant's notice must be filed and served in Form N164.
(2) The appellant must file the following documents with his appellant's notice –
(a) a sealed copy of the order being appealed; and
(b) any order giving or refusing permission to appeal, together with a copy of the reasons for that decision.
(3) The appellant may, if relevant to the issues to be determined on the appeal, file any other document listed in paragraph 5.6 or 5.6A in addition to the documents referred to in sub-paragraph (2).
(4) The appellant need not file a record of the reasons for judgment of the lower court with his appellant's notice unless sub-paragraph (5) applies.
(5) The court may order a suitable record of the reasons for judgment of the lower court (see paragraph 5.12) to be filed –
(a) to enable it to decide if permission should be granted; or
(b) if permission is granted to enable it to decide the appeal.

Skeleton arguments

5.9 (1) The appellant's notice must, subject to (2) and (3) below, be accompanied by a skeleton argument. Alternatively the skeleton argument may be included in the appellant's notice. Where the skeleton argument is so included it will not form part of the notice for the purposes of rule 52.8.
(2) Where it is impracticable for the appellant's skeleton argument to accompany the appellant's notice it must be filed and served on all respondents within 14 days of filing the notice.
(3) An appellant who is not represented need not file a skeleton argument but is encouraged to do so since this will be helpful to the court.

Content of skeleton arguments

5.10 (1) A skeleton argument must contain a numbered list of the points which the party wishes to make. These should both define and confine the areas of controversy. Each point should be stated as concisely as the nature of the case allows.
(2) A numbered point must be followed by a reference to any document on which the party wishes to rely.
(3) A skeleton argument must state, in respect of each authority cited –
(a) the proposition of law that the authority demonstrates; and

(b) the parts of the authority (identified by page or paragraph references) that support the proposition.

(4) If more than one authority is cited in support of a given proposition, the skeleton argument must briefly state the reason for taking that course.

(5) The statement referred to in sub-paragraph (4) should not materially add to the length of the skeleton argument but should be sufficient to demonstrate, in the context of the argument –

(a) the relevance of the authority or authorities to that argument; and

(b) that the citation is necessary for a proper presentation of that argument.

(6) The cost of preparing a skeleton argument which –

(a) does not comply with the requirements set out in this paragraph; or

(b) was not filed within the time limits provided by this Practice Direction (or any further time granted by the court),

will not be allowed on assessment except to the extent that the court otherwise directs.

5.11 The appellant should consider what other information the appeal court will need. This may include a list of persons who feature in the case or glossaries of technical terms. A chronology of relevant events will be necessary in most appeals.

Suitable record of the judgment

5.12 Where the judgment to be appealed has been officially recorded by the court, an approved transcript of that record should accompany the appellant's notice. Photocopies will not be accepted for this purpose. However, where there is no officially recorded judgment, the following documents will be acceptable –

Written judgments

(1) Where the judgment was made in writing a copy of that judgment endorsed with the judge's signature.

Note of judgment

(2) When judgment was not officially recorded or made in writing a note of the judgment (agreed between the appellant's and respondent's advocates) should be submitted for approval to the judge whose decision is being appealed. If the parties cannot agree on a single note of the judgment, both versions should be provided to that judge with an explanatory letter. For the purpose of an application for permission to appeal the note need not be approved by the respondent or the lower court judge.

Advocates' notes of judgments where the appellant is unrepresented

(3) When the appellant was unrepresented in the lower court it is the duty of any advocate for the respondent to make his/her note of judgment promptly available, free of charge to the appellant where there is no officially recorded judgment or if the court so directs. Where the appellant was represented in the lower court it is the duty of his/her own former advocate to make his/her note available in these circumstances. The appellant should submit the note of judgment to the appeal court.

Reasons for Judgment in Tribunal cases

(4) A sealed copy of the tribunal's reasons for the decision.

5.13 An appellant may not be able to obtain an official transcript or other suitable record of the lower court's decision within the time within which the appellant's notice must be filed. In such cases the appellant's notice must still be completed to the best of the appellant's ability on the basis of the documentation available. However, it may be amended subsequently with the permission of the appeal court.

Record of the judgment—Unless the judge has delivered a written judgment, the primary source is the approved transcript. It is a commonly encountered misapprehension that the court will obtain this automatically. It is in fact the responsibility of the appellant to attend to this: there is a form of request (Ex 107) which must be completed and handed to the court. There is a panel of approved transcribers with an agreed scale of charges, and it is for the appellant to select the transcriber, who is an independent contractor and not an employee of Her Majesty's Courts Service.

All hearings are supposed to be recorded, but this does not always happen and, even where it does, tape malfunctions can occur. In such circumstances, recourse must be had to the note taken by the legal representatives, who have an obligation to take an adequate note. The note must be agreed with the respondent and approved by the judge, except for the purposes of an application for permission to appeal. Litigants in person are not expected to take a note, hence the obligation where one party is represented and the other is not for the advocate to make his/her note available to the party acting in person.

In a claim allocated to the small claims track, a suitable record of the judgment is not required unless the court orders such record to be obtained to enable it to decide whether or not to give permission or to determine the appeal.

Advocates' notes of judgments

5.14 Advocates' brief (or, where appropriate, refresher) fee includes –

(1) remuneration for taking a note of the judgment of the court;
(2) having the note transcribed accurately;
(3) attempting to agree the note with the other side if represented;
(4) submitting the note to the judge for approval where appropriate;
(5) revising it if so requested by the judge;
(6) providing any copies required for the appeal court, instructing solicitors and lay client; and
(7) providing a copy of his note to an unrepresented appellant.

Transcripts or Notes of Evidence

5.15 When the evidence is relevant to the appeal an official transcript of the relevant evidence must be obtained. Transcripts or notes of evidence are generally not needed for the purpose of determining an application for permission to appeal.

Notes of evidence

5.16 If evidence relevant to the appeal was not officially recorded, a typed version of the judge's notes of evidence must be obtained.

Transcripts at public expense

5.17 Where the lower court or the appeal court is satisfied that an unrepresented appellant is in such poor financial circumstances that the cost of a transcript would be an excessive burden the court may certify that the cost of obtaining one official transcript should be borne at public expense.

5.18 In the case of a request for an official transcript of evidence or proceedings to be paid for at public expense, the court must also be satisfied that there are reasonable grounds for appeal. Whenever possible a request for a transcript at public expense should be made to the lower court when asking for permission to appeal.

Public expense—That the appellant is exempt from court fees does not mean that there is an automatic entitlement to the transcript at public expense. Some people entitled to benefits may have capital. Proper information as to means is required and some courts have adapted a form used in the Court of Appeal for that purpose. There is no scheme of partial remission: the judge considering the request must either refuse it or allow it. It should be noted that where a transcript of the full hearing rather than just the judgment is requested, the judge must apply a merits test as well as a financial one. Where the appellant is in person and the other party was legally represented, the cost of a transcript can be avoided by directing the advocate to furnish his/her note of judgment under para 5.12(3). The advocate is not entitled to further payment for providing it (para 5.14).

An appellant who fails to supply grounds of appeal is not entitled to a transcript at public expense (*Perotti v Westminster CC* [2005] EWCA Civ 581).

Filing and service of appellant's notice

5.19 Rule 52.4 sets out the procedure and time limits for filing and serving an appellant's notice. The appellant must file the appellant's notice at the appeal court within such period as may be directed by the lower court which should not normally exceed 28 days or, where the lower court directs no such period, within 14 days of the date of the decision that the appellant wishes to appeal.

(Rule 52.15 sets out the time limit for filing an application for permission to appeal against the refusal of the High Court to grant permission to apply for judicial review)

5.20 Where the lower court judge announces his decision and reserves the reasons for his judgment or order until a later date, he should, in the exercise of powers under rule 52.4(2)(a), fix a period for filing the appellant's notice at the appeal court that takes this into account.

5.21(1) Except where the appeal court orders otherwise a sealed copy of the appellant's notice, including any skeleton arguments must be served on all respondents in accordance with the timetable prescribed by rule 52.4(3) except where this requirement is modified by paragraph 5.9(2) in which case the skeleton argument should be served as soon as it is filed.

(2) The appellant must, as soon as practicable, file a certificate of service of the documents referred to in paragraph (1).

5.22 Unless the court otherwise directs a respondent need not take any action when served with an appellant's notice until such time as notification is given to him that permission to appeal has been given.

5.23 The court may dispense with the requirement for service of the notice on a respondent. Any application notice seeking an order under rule 6.9 to dispense with service should set out the reasons relied on and be verified by a statement of truth.

5.24(1) Where the appellant is applying for permission to appeal in his appellant's notice, he must serve on the respondents his appellant's notice and skeleton argument (but not the appeal bundle), unless the appeal court directs otherwise.

(2) Where permission to appeal –

(a) has been given by the lower court; or

(b) is not required,

the appellant must serve the appeal bundle on the respondents with the appellant's notice.

Amendment of Appeal Notice

5.25 An appeal notice may be amended with permission. Such an application to amend and any application in opposition will normally be dealt with at the hearing unless that course would cause unnecessary expense or delay in which case a request should be made for the application to amend to be heard in advance.

PROCEDURE AFTER PERMISSION IS OBTAINED

6.1 This paragraph sets out the procedure where –

- (1) permission to appeal is given by the appeal court; or
- (2) the appellant's notice is filed in the appeal court and –
  - (a) permission was given by the lower court; or
  - (b) permission is not required.

6.2 If the appeal court gives permission to appeal, the appeal bundle must be served on each of the respondents within 7 days of receiving the order giving permission to appeal.

(Part 6 (service of documents) provides rules on service)

6.3 The appeal court will send the parties –

- (1) notification of –
  - (a) the date of the hearing or the period of time (the 'listing window') during which the appeal is likely to be heard; and
  - (b) in the Court of Appeal, the date by which the appeal will be heard (the 'hear by date');
- (2) where permission is granted by the appeal court a copy of the order giving permission to appeal; and
- (3) any other directions given by the court.

6.3A

- (1) Where the appeal court grants permission to appeal, the appellant must add the following documents to the appeal bundle –
  - (a) the respondent's notice and skeleton argument (if any);
  - (b) those parts of the transcripts of evidence which are directly relevant to any question at issue on the appeal;
  - (c) the order granting permission to appeal and, where permission to appeal was granted at an oral hearing, the transcript (or note) of any judgment which was given; and
  - (d) any document which the appellant and respondent have agreed to add to the appeal bundle in accordance with paragraph 7.11.
- (2) Where permission to appeal has been refused on a particular issue, the appellant must remove from the appeal bundle all documents that are relevant only to that issue.

Appeal Questionnaire in the Court of Appeal

6.4 The Court of Appeal will send an Appeal Questionnaire to the appellant when it notifies him of the matters referred to in paragraph 6.3.

6.5 The appellant must complete and file the Appeal Questionnaire within 14 days of the date of the letter of notification of the matters in paragraph 6.3. The Appeal Questionnaire must contain:

(1) if the appellant is legally represented, the advocate's time estimate for the hearing of the appeal;
(2) where a transcript of evidence is relevant to the appeal, confirmation as to what parts of a transcript of evidence have been ordered where this is not already in the bundle of documents;
(3) confirmation that copies of the appeal bundle are being prepared and will be held ready for the use of the Court of Appeal and an undertaking that they will be supplied to the court on request. For the purpose of these bundles photocopies of the transcripts will be accepted;
(4) confirmation that copies of the Appeal Questionnaire and the appeal bundle have been served on the respondents and the date of that service.

Time estimates

6.6 The time estimate included in an Appeal Questionnaire must be that of the advocate who will argue the appeal. It should exclude the time required by the court to give judgment. If the respondent disagrees with the time estimate, the respondent must inform the court within 7 days of receipt of the Appeal Questionnaire. In the absence of such notification the respondent will be deemed to have accepted the estimate proposed on behalf of the appellant.

RESPONDENT

7.1 A respondent who wishes to ask the appeal court to vary the order of the lower court in any way must appeal and permission will be required on the same basis as for an appellant.

(Paragraph 3.2 applies to grounds of appeal by a respondent)

7.2 A respondent who wishes only to request that the appeal court upholds the judgment or order of the lower court whether for the reasons given in the lower court or otherwise does not make an appeal and does not therefore require permission to appeal in accordance with rule 52.3(1).

(Paragraph 7.6 requires a respondent to file a skeleton argument where he wishes to address the appeal court)

7.3 (1) A respondent who wishes to appeal or who wishes to ask the appeal court to uphold the order of the lower court for reasons different from or additional to those given by the lower court must file a respondent's notice.
(2) If the respondent does not file a respondent's notice, he will not be entitled, except with the permission of the court, to rely on any reason not relied on in the lower court.

7.3A Paragraphs 5.1A, 5.1B and 5.2 of this practice direction (Human Rights and extension for time for filing appellant's notice) also apply to a respondent and a respondent's notice.

Time limits

7.4 The time limits for filing a respondent's notice are set out in rule 52.5 (4) and (5).

7.5 Where an extension of time is required the extension must be requested in the respondent's notice and the reasons why the respondent failed to act within the specified time must be included.

7.6 Except where paragraph 7.7A applies, the respondent must file a skeleton argument for the court in all cases where he proposes to address arguments to the court. The respondent's skeleton argument may be included within a respondent's notice. Where a skeleton argument is included within a respondent's notice it will not form part of the notice for the purposes of rule 52.8.

7.7 (1) A respondent who –
(a) files a respondent's notice; but
(b) does not include his skeleton argument within that notice,
must file and serve his skeleton argument within 14 days of filing the notice.
(2) A respondent who does not file a respondent's notice but who files a skeleton argument must file and serve that skeleton argument at least 7 days before the appeal hearing.

(Rule 52.5(4) sets out the period for filing and serving a respondent's notice)

7.7A
(1) Where the appeal relates to a claim allocated to the small claims track and is being heard in a county court or the High Court, the respondent may file a skeleton argument but is not required to do so.
(2) A respondent who is not represented need not file a skeleton argument but is encouraged to do so in order to assist the court.

7.7B The respondent must –
(1) serve his skeleton argument on –
(a) the appellant; and
(b) any other respondent,
at the same time as he files it at the court; and
(2) file a certificate of service.

Content of skeleton arguments

7.8 A respondent's skeleton argument must conform to the directions at paragraphs 5.10 and 5.11 with any necessary modifications. It should, where appropriate, answer the arguments set out in the appellant's skeleton argument.

Applications within respondent's notices

7.9 A respondent may include an application within a respondent's notice in accordance with paragraph 5.5 above.

Filing respondent's notices and skeleton arguments

7.10(1) The respondent must file the following documents with his respondent's notice in every case:
(a) two additional copies of the respondent's notice for the appeal court; and
(b) one copy each for the appellant and any other respondents.
(2) The respondent may file a skeleton argument with his respondent's notice and –
(a) where he does so he must file two copies; and
(b) where he does not do so he must comply with paragraph 7.7.

7.11 If the respondent wishes to rely on any documents which he reasonably considers necessary to enable the appeal court to reach its decision on the appeal in addition to those filed by the appellant, he must make every effort to agree amendments to the appeal bundle with the appellant.

7.12

(1) If the representatives for the parties are unable to reach agreement, the respondent may prepare a supplemental bundle.

(2) If the respondent prepares a supplemental bundle he must file it, together with the requisite number of copies for the appeal court, at the appeal court –

(a) with the respondent's notice; or

(b) if a respondent's notice is not filed, within 21 days after he is served with the appeal bundle.

7.13 The respondent must serve –

(1) the respondent's notice;

(2) his skeleton argument (if any); and

(3) the supplemental bundle (if any),

on –

(a) the appellant; and

(b) any other respondent,

at the same time as he files them at the court.

APPEALS TO THE HIGH COURT

Application

8.1 This paragraph applies where an appeal lies to a High Court judge from the decision of a county court or a district judge of the High Court.

8.2 The following table sets out the following venues for each circuit –

(a) Appeal centres – court centres where appeals to which this paragraph applies may be filed, managed and heard. Paragraphs 8.6 to 8.8 provide for special arrangements in relation to the South Eastern Circuit.

(b) Hearing only centres – court centres where appeals to which this paragraph applies may be heard by order made at an appeal centre (see paragraph 8.10).

Circuit	Appeal Centres	Hearing Only Centres
Midland Circuit	Birmingham Nottingham	Lincoln Leicester Northampton Stafford
North Eastern Circuit	Leeds Newcastle Sheffield	Teesside
Northern Circuit	Manchester Liverpool Preston	Carlisle

Circuit	Appeal Centres	Hearing Only Centres
Wales and Chester Circuit	Cardiff Swansea Chester	
Western Circuit	Bristol Exeter Winchester	Truro Plymouth
South Eastern Circuit	Royal Courts of Justice Lewes Luton Norwich Reading Chelmsford St Albans Maidstone Oxford	

Venue for appeals and filing of notices on circuits other than the South Eastern Circuit

8.3 Paragraphs 8.4 and 8.5 apply where the lower court is situated on a circuit other than the South Eastern Circuit.

8.4 The appellant's notice must be filed at an appeal centre on the circuit in which the lower court is situated. The appeal will be managed and heard at that appeal centre unless the appeal court orders otherwise.

8.5 A respondent's notice must be filed at the appeal centre where the appellant's notice was filed unless the appeal has been transferred to another appeal centre, in which case it must be filed at that appeal centre.

Venue for appeals and filing of notices on the South Eastern Circuit

8.6 Paragraphs 8.7 and 8.8 apply where the lower court is situated on the South Eastern Circuit.

8.7 The appellant's notice must be filed at an appeal centre on the South Eastern Circuit. The appeal will be managed and heard at the Royal Courts of Justice unless the appeal court orders otherwise. An order that an appeal is to be managed or heard at another appeal centre may not be made unless the consent of the Presiding Judge of the circuit in charge of civil matters has been obtained.

8.8 A respondent's notice must be filed at the Royal Courts of Justice unless the appeal has been transferred to another appeal centre, in which case it must be filed at that appeal centre.

General provisions

8.9 The appeal court may transfer an appeal to another appeal centre (whether or not on the same circuit). In deciding whether to do so the court will have regard to the criteria in rule 30.3 (criteria for a transfer order). The appeal court may do so either on application by a party or of its own initiative. Where an appeal is transferred under this paragraph, notice of transfer must be served on every person on whom the appellant's notice has been served. An appeal may not be transferred to an appeal centre on another circuit, either for management or hearing, unless the consent of the Presiding Judge of that circuit in charge of civil matters has been obtained.

8.10 Directions may be given for –

(a) an appeal to be heard at a hearing only centre; or
(b) an application in an appeal to be heard at any other venue,

instead of at the appeal centre managing the appeal.

8.11 Unless a direction has been made under 8.10, any application in the appeal must be made at the appeal centre where the appeal is being managed.

8.12 The appeal court may adopt all or any part of the procedure set out in paragraphs 6.4 to 6.6.

8.13 Where the lower court is a county court:

(1) subject to paragraph (1A), appeals and applications for permission to appeal will be heard by a High Court Judge or by a person authorised under paragraphs (1), (2) or (4) of the Table in section 9(1) of the Supreme Court Act 1981 to act as a judge of the High Court;
(1A) an appeal or application for permission to appeal from the decision of a Recorder in the county court may be heard by a Designated Civil Judge who is authorised under paragraph (5) of the Table in section 9(1) of the Supreme Court Act 1981 to act as a judge of the High Court; and
(2) other applications in the appeal may be heard and directions in the appeal may be given either by a High Court Judge or by any person authorised under section 9 of the Supreme Court Act 1981 to act as a judge of the High Court.

8.14 In the case of appeals from Masters or district judges of the High Court, appeals, applications for permission and any other applications in the appeal may be heard and directions in the appeal may be given by a High Court Judge or by any person authorised under section 9 of the Supreme Court Act 1981 to act as a judge of the High Court.

Appeals to a judge of a county court from a district judge

8A.1 The Designated Civil Judge in consultation with his Presiding Judges has responsibility for allocating appeals from decisions of district judges to circuit judges.

Re-hearings

9.1 The hearing of an appeal will be a re-hearing (as opposed to a review of the decision of the lower court) if the appeal is from the decision of a minister, person or other body and the minister, person or other body –

(1) did not hold a hearing to come to that decision; or
(2) held a hearing to come to that decision, but the procedure adopted did not provide for the consideration of evidence.

Appeals Transferred to the Court of Appeal

10.1 Where an appeal is transferred to the Court of Appeal under rule 52.14 the Court of Appeal may give such additional directions as are considered appropriate.

Applications

11.1 Where a party to an appeal makes an application whether in an appeal notice or by Part 23 application notice, the provisions of Part 23 will apply.

11.2 The applicant must file the following documents with the notice

(1) one additional copy of the application notice for the appeal court and one copy for each of the respondents;
(2) where applicable a sealed copy of the order which is the subject of the main appeal;
(3) a bundle of documents in support which should include:
  (a) the Part 23 application notice; and
  (b) any witness statements and affidavits filed in support of the application notice.

DISPOSING OF APPLICATIONS OR APPEALS BY CONSENT

Dismissal of applications or appeals by consent

12.1 These paragraphs do not apply where any party to the proceedings is a child or patient.

12.2 Where an appellant does not wish to pursue an application or an appeal, he may request the appeal court for an order that his application or appeal be dismissed. Such a request must contain a statement that the appellant is not a child or patient. If such a request is granted it will usually be on the basis that the appellant pays the costs of the application or appeal.

12.3 If the appellant wishes to have the application or appeal dismissed without costs, his request must be accompanied by a consent signed by the respondent or his legal representative stating that the respondent is not a child or patient and consents to the dismissal of the application or appeal without costs.

12.4 Where a settlement has been reached disposing of the application or appeal, the parties may make a joint request to the court stating that none of them is a child or patient, and asking that the application or appeal be dismissed by consent. If the request is granted the application or appeal will be dismissed.

Allowing unopposed appeals or applications on paper

13.1 The appeal court will not normally make an order allowing an appeal unless satisfied that the decision of the lower court was wrong, but the appeal court may set aside or vary the order of the lower court with consent and without determining the merits of the appeal, if it is satisfied that there are good and sufficient reasons for doing so. Where the appeal court is requested by all parties to allow an application or an appeal the court may consider the request on the papers. The request should state that none of the parties is a child or patient and set out the relevant history of the proceedings and the matters relied on as justifying the proposed order and be accompanied by a copy of the proposed order.

Unopposed appeals—For an example of the appeal court refusing to allow an appeal, see *Stevens v Gullis* [2000] 1 All ER 527 where the judge below had concluded that an expert witness had disregarded his duty to the court to such an extent as to render him unfit to give evidence.

Procedure for consent orders and agreements to pay periodical payments involving a child or patient

13.2 Where one of the parties is a child or patient –

(1) a settlement relating to an appeal or application; or
(2) in a personal injury claim for damages for future pecuniary loss, an agreement reached at the appeal stage to pay periodical payments,

requires the court's approval.

Child

13.3 In cases involving a child a copy of the proposed order signed by the parties' solicitors should be sent to the appeal court, together with an opinion from the advocate acting on behalf of the child.

Patient

13.4 Where a party is a patient the same procedure will be adopted, but the documents filed should also include any relevant reports prepared for the Court of Protection and a document evidencing formal approval by that court where required.

Periodical payments

13.5 Where periodical payments for future pecuniary loss have been negotiated in a personal injury case which is under appeal, the documents filed should include those which would be required in the case of a personal injury claim for damages for future pecuniary loss dealt with at first instance. Details can be found in the Practice Direction which supplements Part 21.

SUMMARY ASSESSMENT OF COSTS

14.1 Costs are likely to be assessed by way of summary assessment at the following hearings:

(1) contested directions hearings;
(2) applications for permission to appeal at which the respondent is present;
(3) dismissal list hearings in the Court of Appeal at which the respondent is present;
(4) appeals from case management decisions; and
(5) appeals listed for one day or less.

14.2 Parties attending any of the hearings referred to in paragraph 14.1 should be prepared to deal with the summary assessment.

OTHER SPECIAL PROVISIONS REGARDING THE COURT OF APPEAL

Filing of Documents

15.1(1) The documents relevant to proceedings in the Court of Appeal, Civil Division must be filed in the Civil Appeals Office Registry, Room E307, Royal Courts of Justice, Strand, London, WC2A 2LL.

(2) The Civil Appeals Office will not serve documents and where service is required by the CPR or this practice direction it must be effected by the parties.

Core Bundles

15.2 In cases where the appeal bundle comprises more than 500 pages, exclusive of transcripts, the appellant's solicitors must, after consultation with the respondent's solicitors, also prepare and file with the court, in addition to copies of the appeal bundle (as amended in accordance with paragraph 7.11) the requisite number of copies of a core bundle.

15.3(1) The core bundle must be filed within 28 days of receipt of the order giving permission to appeal or, where permission to appeal was granted by the lower court or is not required, within 28 days of the date of service of the appellant's notice on the respondent.

(2) The core bundle –

(a) must contain the documents which are central to the appeal; and

(b) must not exceed 150 pages.

Preparation of bundles

15.4 The provisions of this paragraph apply to the preparation of appeal bundles, supplemental respondents' bundles where the parties are unable to agree amendments to the appeal bundle, and core bundles.

(1) **Rejection of bundles**. Where documents are copied unnecessarily or bundled incompletely, costs may be disallowed. Where the provisions of this Practice Direction as to the preparation or delivery of bundles are not followed the bundle may be rejected by the court or be made the subject of a special costs order.

(2) **Avoidance of duplication**. No more than one copy of any document should be included unless there is a good reason for doing otherwise (such as the use of a separate core bundle – see paragraph 15.2).

(3) **Pagination**

(a) Bundles must be paginated, each page being numbered individually and consecutively. The pagination used at trial must also be indicated. Letters and other documents should normally be included in chronological order. (An exception to consecutive page numbering arises in the case of core bundles where it may be preferable to retain the original numbering).

(b) Page numbers should be inserted in bold figures at the bottom of the page and in a form that can be clearly distinguished from any other pagination on the document.

(4) **Format and presentation**

(a) Where possible the documents should be in A4 format. Where a document has to be read across rather than down the page, it should be so placed in the bundle as to ensure that the text starts nearest the spine.

(b) Where any marking or writing in colour on a document is important, the document must be copied in colour or marked up correctly in colour.

- (c) Documents which are not easily legible should be transcribed and the transcription marked and placed adjacent to the document transcribed.
- (d) Documents in a foreign language should be translated and the translation marked and placed adjacent to the document translated. The translation should be agreed or, if it cannot be agreed, each party's proposed translation should be included.
- (e) The size of any bundle should be tailored to its contents. A large lever arch file should not be used for just a few pages nor should files of whatever size be overloaded.
- (f) Where it will assist the Court of Appeal, different sections of the file may be separated by cardboard or other tabbed dividers so long as these are clearly indexed. Where, for example, a document is awaited when the appeal bundle is filed, a single sheet of paper can be inserted after a divider, indicating the nature of the document awaited. For example, 'Transcript of evidence of Mr J Smith (to follow)'.

(5) **Binding**

- (a) All documents, with the exception of transcripts, must be bound together. This may be in a lever arch file, ring binder or plastic folder. Plastic sleeves containing loose documents must not be used. Binders and files must be strong enough to withstand heavy use.
- (b) Large documents such as plans should be placed in an easily accessible file. Large documents which will need to be opened up frequently should be inserted in a file larger than A4 size.

(6) **Indices and labels**

- (a) An index must be included at the front of the bundle listing all the documents and providing the page references for each. In the case of documents such as letters, invoices or bank statements, they may be given a general description.
- (b) Where the bundles consist of more than one file, an index to all the files should be included in the first file and an index included for each file. Indices should, if possible, be on a single sheet. The full name of the case should not be inserted on the index if this would waste space. Documents should be identified briefly but properly.

(7) **Identification**

- (a) Every bundle must be clearly identified, on the spine and on the front cover, with the name of the case and the Court of Appeal's reference. Where the bundle consists of more than one file, each file must be numbered on the spine, the front cover and the inside of the front cover.
- (b) Outer labels should use large lettering eg ' Appeal Bundle A' or 'Core Bundle'. The full title of the appeal and solicitors' names and addresses should be omitted. A label should be used on the front as well as on the spine.

(8) **Staples etc**. All staples, heavy metal clips etc, must be removed.

(9) **Statements of case**

- (a) Statements of case should be assembled in 'chapter' form – ie claim followed by particulars of claim, followed by further information, irrespective of date.
- (b) Redundant documents, eg particulars of claim overtaken by

amendments, requests for further information recited in the answers given, should generally be excluded.

(10) **New Documents**

(a) Before a new document is introduced into bundles which have already been delivered to the court, steps should be taken to ensure that it carries an appropriate bundle/page number so that it can be added to the court documents. It should not be stapled and it should be prepared with punch holes for immediate inclusion in the binders in use.

(b) If it is expected that a large number of miscellaneous new documents will from time to time be introduced, there should be a special tabbed empty loose-leaf file for that purpose. An index should be produced for this file, updated as necessary.

(11) **Inter-solicitor correspondence**. Since inter-solicitor correspondence is unlikely to be required for the purposes of an appeal, only those letters which will need to be referred to should be copied.

(12) **Sanctions for non-compliance**. If the appellant fails to comply with the requirements as to the provision of bundles of documents, the application or appeal will be referred for consideration to be given as to why it should not be dismissed for failure to so comply.

Master in the Court of Appeal, Civil Division

15.5 When the Head of the Civil Appeals Office acts in a judicial capacity pursuant to rule 52.16, he shall be known as Master. Other eligible officers may also be designated by the Master of the Rolls to exercise judicial authority under rule 52.16 and shall then be known as Deputy Masters.

Respondent to notify Civil Appeals Office whether he intends to file respondent's notice

15.6 A respondent must, no later than 21 days after the date he is served with notification that –

(1) permission to appeal has been granted; or
(2) the application for permission to appeal and the appeal are to be heard together,

inform the Civil Appeals Office and the appellant in writing whether –

(a) he proposes to file a respondent's notice appealing the order or seeking to uphold the order for reasons different from, or additional to, those given by the lower court; or
(b) he proposes to rely on the reasons given by the lower court for its decision.

(Paragraph 15.11B requires all documents needed for an appeal hearing, including a respondent's skeleton argument, to be filed at least 7 days before the hearing)

Listing and hear-by dates

15.7 The management of the list will be dealt with by the listing officer under the direction of the Master.

15.8 The Civil Appeals List of the Court of Appeal is divided as follows:

- *The applications list* – applications for permission to appeal and other applications.
- *The appeals list* – appeals where permission to appeal has been given or where an appeal lies without permission being required where a hearing date is fixed in advance. (Appeals in this list which require special listing arrangements will be assigned to the special fixtures list)
- *The expedited list* – appeals or applications where the Court of Appeal has directed an expedited hearing. The current practice of the Court of Appeal is summarised in *Unilever plc v Chefaro Proprietaries Ltd* (Practice Note) [1995] 1 WLR 243.
- *The stand-out list* – Appeals or applications which, for good reason, are not at present ready to proceed and have been stood out by judicial direction.
- *The second fixtures list* – see paragraph 15.9A(1) below.
- *The second fixtures list* – if an appeal is designated as a 'second fixture' it means that a hearing date is arranged in advance on the express basis that the list is fully booked for the period in question and therefore the case will be heard only if a suitable gap occurs in the list.
- *The short-warned list* – appeals which the court considers may be prepared for the hearing by an advocate other than the one originally instructed with a half day's notice, or such other period as the court may direct.

Special provisions relating to the short-warned list

15.9(1) Where an appeal is assigned to the short-warned list, the Civil Appeals Office will notify the parties' solicitors in writing. The court may abridge the time for filing any outstanding bundles in an appeal assigned to this list.

(2) The solicitors for the parties must notify their advocate and their client as soon as the Civil Appeals Office notifies them that the appeal has been assigned to the short-warned list.

(3) The appellant may apply in writing for the appeal to be removed from the short-warned list within 14 days of notification of its assignment. The application will be decided by a Lord Justice, or the Master, and will only be granted for the most compelling reasons.

(4) The Civil Appeals Listing Officer may place an appeal from the short-warned list 'on call' from a given date and will inform the parties' advocates accordingly.

(5) An appeal which is 'on call' may be listed for hearing on half a day's notice or such longer period as the court may direct.

(6) Once an appeal is listed for hearing from the short warned list it becomes the immediate professional duty of the advocate instructed in the appeal, if he is unable to appear at the hearing, to take all practicable measures to ensure that his lay client is represented at the hearing by an advocate who is fully instructed and able to argue the appeal.

Listing in the Court of Appeal—Subject to any direction of the full court or a single Lord Justice, Court of Appeal listing is under the overall direction of the Head of Civil Appeals Office (known as the Master when acting in his judicial capacity); the day-to-day management of the list is dealt with by the senior listing officer (PD52, para 15.7). The Civil Appeals Listing Office is in Room E306, RCJ; the direct-dial telephone numbers are 020 7947 6195 and 6917.

Each appeal is given a hear-by date and a hearing window. The aim is that each appeal should be listed for hearing within its hearing window and should not be heard significantly later than its hear-by date, unless there is a judicial direction expediting or postponing the hearing. The hear-by dates vary according to the type of appeal. The appellant's solicitor (or the appellant, if in person) will be sent a computer-generated letter which sets out how the case will be progressed and gives the hear-by date. It is the duty of the appellant's solicitor (or appellant in person) to send a copy of that letter to the respondent(s).

Hearing dates for appeals are arranged by the listing officers with counsel's clerks, either by the clerks attending the Listing Office or by telephone. It is the responsibility of counsel's clerks to inform the instructing solicitors of the hearing date(s). Appellants and respondents in person are notified of hearing dates by letter from the Listing Office.

Fixtures—In the case of appeals which are given first or second fixtures, hearing dates are arranged with counsel's clerks in advance (for the description of a second fixture see PD52, para 15.8).

The short-warned list—Where the court considers that an appeal can be mastered by an advocate with no previous knowledge of the case, on half a day's notice, or such longer period as the court may direct, it will be assigned to the short-warned list (SWL). The purpose of the SWL is to have cases available to be dealt with when gaps occur in the Court of Appeal List. The practice relating to the SWL is set out in the *Court of Appeal Practice Direction 20 February* [2001] 2 All ER 701. The parties' solicitors will be notified by the Court of Appeals Office that the appeal has been assigned to the SWL and it is the duty of the solicitors to inform their clients and advocates of that.

Any application to remove a case from the SWL and give it some form of fixture must be made within 14 days of that notification. Such an application will be considered by a supervising Lord Justice or the Master, but will only be granted if there are compelling reasons for doing so.

The listing officer will put SWL cases on call from a given date and will notify the advocates' clerks. An appeal which is on call will be listed for hearing on half a day's notice (or such longer period as the court has prescribed in the individual case). If the party's advocate of first choice is not available a substitute advocate must be instructed immediately and it is the professional duty of the advocate of first choice to do all in his power to ensure that it is effectively done (PD52, para 15.9).

In addition to the *February 2001 Practice Direction*, the Court of Appeal issued further *Practice Directions* on 4 July 2001 [2001] 3 All ER 479 and 10 March 2003 [2003] 2 All ER 399, reviewing listing windows and hear-by dates.

The special fixtures list—This list was set up in 2001 and is used to deal with cases which require special listing arrangements, eg appeals which are 'test cases' and where there are large numbers of appeals dealing with the same subject matter. Such cases will normally be listed before the same constitution within a particular period (see the *Court of Appeal Practice Direction 20 February* [2001] 2 All ER 701).

The special fixtures list is a subdivision within the fixtures list. Where appeals are assigned to it, the parties' legal representatives (and any party acting in person) will be notified of the special arrangements for the appeals concerned and the period during which they are scheduled to be heard. Although the court will do all it can to accommodate counsel's availability, in the case of appeals assigned to the special fixtures list, it may not always be possible to do so, because of the need to have cases heard by the same constitution within the scheduled period and, in some cases, in a particular order.

Applications—In the case of applications which are to be heard separately from the appeals to which they relate, in particular applications to the Court of Appeal for permission to appeal, the usual practice is for hearing dates to be notified to the appellant's solicitor (or appellant in person) by a letter from the Civil Appeals Listing Office; if the application is being listed on notice to the other side, a similar letter will be sent to the respondent's solicitor (or respondent in person). Save in cases where there are very good reasons to the contrary, hearing dates for applications are not arranged with counsel's clerks and will not be adjourned because counsel of first choice is not available; substitute counsel must be instructed.

Special provisions relating to the special fixtures list

15.9A

(1) The special fixtures list is a sub-division of the appeals list and is used to deal with appeals that may require special listing arrangements, such as the need to list a number of cases before the same constitution, in a particular order, during a particular period or at a given location.

(2) The Civil Appeals Office will notify the parties' representatives, or the parties if acting in person, of the particular arrangements that will apply. The notice –
  (a) will give details of the specific period during which a case is scheduled to be heard; and
  (b) may give directions in relation to the filing of any outstanding documents.

(3) The listing officer will notify the parties' representatives of the precise hearing date as soon as practicable. While every effort will be made to accommodate the availability of counsel, the requirements of the court will prevail.

Requests for directions

15.10 To ensure that all requests for directions are centrally monitored and correctly allocated, all requests for directions or rulings (whether relating to listing or any other matters) should be made to the Civil Appeals Office. Those seeking directions or rulings must not approach the supervising Lord Justice either directly, or via his or her clerk.

Bundles of authorities

15.11

(1) Once the parties have been notified of the date fixed for the hearing, the appellant's advocate must, after consultation with his opponent, file a bundle containing photocopies of the authorities upon which each side will rely at the hearing.

(2) The bundle of authorities should, in general –
  (a) have the relevant passages of the authorities marked;
  (b) not include authorities for propositions not in dispute; and
  (c) not contain more than 10 authorities unless the scale of the appeal warrants more extensive citation.

(3) The bundle of authorities must be filed –
  (a) at least 7 days before the hearing; or
  (b) where the period of notice of the hearing is less than 7 days, immediately.

(4) If, through some oversight, a party intends, during the hearing, to refer to other authorities the parties may agree a second agreed bundle. The appellant's advocate must file this bundle at least 48 hours before the hearing commences.

(5) A bundle of authorities must bear a certification by the advocates responsible for arguing the case that the requirements of sub-paragraphs (3) to (5) of paragraph 5.10 have been complied with in respect of each authority included.

Supplementary skeleton arguments

15.11A

(1) A supplementary skeleton argument on which the appellant wishes to rely must be filed at least 14 days before the hearing.

(2) A supplementary skeleton argument on which the respondent wishes to rely must be filed at least 7 days before the hearing.

(3) All supplementary skeleton arguments must comply with the requirements set out in paragraph 5.10.

(4) At the hearing the court may refuse to hear argument from a party not contained in a skeleton argument filed within the relevant time limit set out in this paragraph.

Papers for the appeal hearing

15.11B

(1) All the documents which are needed for the appeal hearing must be filed at least 7 days before the hearing. Where a document has not been filed 10 days before the hearing a reminder will be sent by the Civil Appeals Office.

(2) Any party who fails to comply with the provisions of paragraph (1) may be required to attend before the Presiding Lord Justice to seek permission to proceed with, or to oppose, the appeal.

Disposal of bundles of documents

15.11C

(1) Where the court has determined a case, the official transcriber will retain one set of papers. The Civil Appeals Office will destroy any remaining sets of papers not collected within 21 days of –
   (a) where one or more parties attend the hearing, the date of the court's decision;
   (b) where there is no attendance, the date of the notification of court's decision.

(2) The parties should ensure that bundles of papers supplied to the court do not contain original documents (other than transcripts). The parties must ensure that they –
   (a) bring any necessary original documents to the hearing; and
   (b) retrieve any original documents handed up to the court before leaving the court.

(3) The court will retain application bundles where permission to appeal has been granted. Where permission is refused the arrangements in sub-paragraph (1) will apply.

(4) Where a single Lord Justice has refused permission to appeal on paper, application bundles will not be destroyed until after the time limit for seeking a hearing has expired.

Availability of Reserved judgments before hand down

15.12 This section applies where the presiding Lord Justice is satisfied that the result of the appeal will attract no special degree of confidentiality or sensitivity.

15.13 A copy of the written judgment will be made available to the parties' legal advisers by 4 p.m. on the second working day before judgment is due to be pronounced or such other period as the court may direct. This can be shown, in confidence, to the parties but only for the purpose of obtaining instructions and on the strict understanding that the judgment, or its effect, is not to be disclosed to any other person. A working day is any day on which the Civil Appeals Office is open for business.

15.14 The appeal will be listed for judgment in the cause list and the judgment handed down at the appropriate time.

Attendance of advocates on the handing down of a reserved judgment

15.15 Where any consequential orders are agreed, the parties' advocates need not attend on the handing down of a reserved judgment. Where an advocate does attend the court may, if it considers such attendance unnecessary, disallow the costs of the attendance. If the parties do not indicate that they intend to attend, the judgment may be handed down by a single member of the court.

Agreed orders following judgment

15.16 The parties must, in respect of any draft agreed orders –

(a) fax a copy to the clerk to the presiding Lord Justice; and
(b) file four copies in the Civil Appeals Office,

no later than 12 noon on the working day before the judgment is handed down.

15.17 A copy of a draft order must bear the Court of Appeal case reference, the date the judgment is to be handed down and the name of the presiding Lord Justice.

Corrections to the draft judgment

15.18 Any proposed correction to the draft judgment should be sent to the clerk to the judge who prepared the draft with a copy to any other party.

Application for leave to appeal

15.19 Where a party wishes to apply for leave to appeal to the House of Lords under section 1 of the Administration of Justice (Appeals) Act 1934 the court may deal with the application on the basis of written submissions.

15.20 A party must, in relation to his submission –

(a) fax a copy to the clerk to the presiding Lord Justice; and
(b) file four copies in the Civil Appeals Office,

no later than 12 noon on the working day before the judgment is handed down.

15.21 A copy of a submission must bear the Court of Appeal case reference, the date the judgment is to be handed down and the name of the presiding Lord Justice.

SECTION II – GENERAL PROVISIONS ABOUT STATUTORY APPEALS AND APPEALS BY WAY OF CASE STATED

16.1 This section of this practice direction contains general provisions about statutory appeals (paragraphs 17.1–17.6) and appeals by way of case stated (paragraphs 18.1–18.20).

16.2 Where any of the provisions in this section provide for documents to be filed at the appeal court, these documents are in addition to any documents required under Part 52 or section I of this practice direction.

STATUTORY APPEALS

17.1 This part of this section –

(1) applies where under any enactment an appeal (other than by way of case stated) lies to the court from a Minister of State, government department, tribunal or other person ('statutory appeals'); and

(2) is subject to any provision about a specific category of appeal in any enactment or Section III of this practice direction.

Part 52

17.2 Part 52 applies to statutory appeals with the following amendments –

Filing of appellant's notice

17.3 The appellant must file the appellant's notice at the appeal court within 28 days after the date of the decision of the lower court he wishes to appeal.

17.4 Where a statement of the reasons for a decision is given later than the notice of that decision, the period for filing the appellant's notice is calculated from the date on which the statement is received by the appellant.

Service of appellant's notice

17.5 In addition to the respondents to the appeal, the appellant must serve the appellant's notice in accordance with rule 52.4(3) on the chairman of the tribunal, Minister of State, government department or other person from whose decision the appeal is brought.

Right of Minister etc to be heard on the appeal

17.6 Where the appeal is from an order or decision of a Minister of State or government department, the Minister or department, as the case may be, is entitled to attend the hearing and to make representations to the court.

Permission to appeal—Paragraph 17.2 does not have the effect of imposing a requirement of permission to appeal under CPR r 52.3(1)(b) (see *Colley v Council for Licensed Conveyancers* [2001] EWCA Civ 1137, [2001] 4 All ER 998, CA and the note **'Permission to appeal'** under r 52.3). Accordingly, permission to appeal will not be required in respect of a statutory appeal unless the statute imposes such a requirement or permission to appeal is required under CPR r 52.3(1)(a).

APPEALS BY WAY OF CASE STATED

18.1 This part of this section –

(1) applies where under any enactment –

(a) an appeal lies to the court by way of case stated; or

(b) a question of law may be referred to the court by way of case stated; and

(2) is subject to any provision about to a specific category of appeal in any enactment or Section III of this practice direction.

Part 52

18.2 Part 52 applies to appeals by way of case stated subject to the following amendments.

Permission to appeal—Paragraph 18.2 does not have the effect of imposing a requirement of permission to appeal (see note 'Permission to appeal' under CPR r 52.3).

Case stated by Crown Court or Magistrates' Court

Application to state a case

18.3 The procedure for applying to the Crown Court or a magistrates' court to have a case stated for the opinion of the High Court is set out in the Crown Court Rules 1982 and the Magistrates' Courts Rules 1981 respectively.

Filing of appellant's notice

18.4 The appellant must file the appellant's notice at the appeal court within 10 days after he receives the stated case.

Documents to be lodged

18.5 The appellant must lodge the following documents with his appellant's notice –

(1) the stated case;
(2) a copy of the judgment, order or decision in respect of which the case has been stated; and
(3) where the judgment, order or decision in respect of which the case has been stated was itself given or made on appeal, a copy of the judgment, order or decision appealed from.

Service of appellant's notice

18.6 The appellant must serve the appellant's notice and accompanying documents on all respondents within 4 days after they are filed or lodged at the appeal court.

Case stated by Minister, government department, tribunal or other person

Application to state a case

18.7 The procedure for applying to a Minister, government department, tribunal or other person ('Minister or tribunal etc') to have a case stated for the opinion of the court may be set out in –

(1) the enactment which provides for the right of appeal; or
(2) any rules of procedure relating to the Minister or tribunal etc.

Signing of stated case by Minister or tribunal etc

18.8 A case stated by a tribunal must be signed by the chairman or president of the tribunal. A case stated by any other person must be signed by that person or by a person authorised to do so.

Service of stated case by Minister or tribunal etc

18.9 The Minister or tribunal etc must serve the stated case on –

(1) the party who requests the case to be stated; or
(2) the party as a result of whose application to the court, the case was stated.

18.10 Where an enactment provides that a Minister or tribunal etc may state a case or refer a question of law to the court by way of case stated without a request being made, the Minister or tribunal etc must –

(1) serve the stated case on those parties that the Minister or tribunal etc considers appropriate; and
(2) give notice to every other party to the proceedings that the stated case has been served on the party named and on the date specified in the notice.

Filing and service of appellant's notice

18.11 The party on whom the stated case was served must file the appellant's notice and the stated case at the appeal court and serve copies of the notice and stated case on –

(1) the Minister or tribunal etc who stated the case; and
(2) every party to the proceedings to which the stated case relates,

within 14 days after the stated case was served on him.

18.12 Where paragraph 18.10 applies the Minister or tribunal etc must –

(1) file an appellant's notice and the stated case at the appeal court; and
(2) serve copies of those documents on the persons served under paragraph 18.10,

within 14 days after stating the case.

18.13 Where –

(1) a stated case has been served by the Minister or tribunal etc in accordance with paragraph 18.9; and
(2) the party on whom the stated case was served does not file an appellant's notice in accordance with paragraph 18.11, any other party may file an appellant's notice with the stated case at the appeal court and serve a copy of the notice and the case on the persons listed in paragraph 18.11 within the period of time set out in paragraph 18.14.

18.14 The period of time referred to in paragraph 18.13 is 14 days from the last day on which the party on whom the stated case was served may file an appellant's notice in accordance with paragraph 18.11.

Amendment of stated case

18.15 The court may amend the stated case or order it to be returned to the Minister or tribunal etc for amendment and may draw inferences of fact from the facts stated in the case.

Right of Minister etc to be heard on the appeal

18.16 Where the case is stated by a Minister or government department, that Minister or department, as the case may be, is entitled to appear on the appeal and to make representations to the court.

Application for order to state a case

18.17 An application to the court for an order requiring a minister or tribunal etc to state a case for the decision of the court, or to refer a question of law to the court by way of case stated must be made to the court which would be the appeal court if the case were stated.

18.18 An application to the court for an order directing a Minister or tribunal etc to –

(1) state a case for determination by the court; or
(2) refer a question of law to the court by way of case stated,

must be made in accordance with CPR Part 23.

18.19 The application notice must contain –

(1) the grounds of the application;
(2) the question of law on which it is sought to have the case stated; and
(3) any reasons given by the minister or tribunal etc for his or its refusal to state a case.

18.20 The application notice must be filed at the appeal court and served on –

(1) the minister, department, secretary of the tribunal or other person as the case may be; and
(2) every party to the proceedings to which the application relates,

within 14 days after the appellant receives notice of the refusal of his request to state a case.

SECTION III – PROVISIONS ABOUT SPECIFIC APPEALS

20.1 This section of this practice direction provides special provisions about the appeals to which the following table refers. This Section is not exhaustive and does not create, amend or remove any right of appeal.

20.2 Part 52 applies to all appeals to which this section applies subject to any special provisions set out in this section.

20.3 Where any of the provisions in this section provide for documents to be filed at the appeal court, these documents are in addition to any documents required under Part 52 or Sections I or II of this practice direction.

APPEALS TO THE COURT OF APPEAL	Paragraph
Articles 81 and 82 of the EC Treaty and Chapters I and II of Part I of the Competition Act 1998	21.10A
Civil Partnership – conditional order for dissolution or nullity	21.1
Competition Appeal Tribunal	21.10
Contempt of Court	21.4
Decree nisi of divorce	21.1
Immigration Appeal Tribunal	21.7
Lands Tribunal	21.9
Nullity of marriage	21.1
Patents Court on appeal from Comptroller	21.3
Revocation of patent	21.2
Social Security Commissioners	21.5

APPEALS TO THE COURT OF APPEAL	**Paragraph**
Special Commissioner (where the appeal is direct to the Court of Appeal)	21.8
Value Added Tax and Duties Tribunals (where the appeal is direct to the Court of Appeal)	21.6

APPEALS TO THE HIGH COURT	**Paragraph**
Agricultural Land Tribunal	22.7
Architects Act 1997, s 22	22.3
Charities Act 1993	23.8A
Chiropractors Act 1994, s 31	22.3
Clergy Pensions Measure 1961, s 38(3)	23.2
Commons Registration Act 1965	23.9
Consumer Credit Act 1974	22.4
Dentists Act 1984, s 20 or s 44	22.3
Extradition Act 2003	22.6A
Friendly Societies Act 1974	23.7
Friendly Societies Act 1992	23.7
Industrial and Provident Societies Act 1965	23.2, 23.7
Industrial Assurance Act 1923	23.2, 23.7
Industrial Assurance Act 1923, s 17	23.6
Inheritance Tax Act 1984, s 222	23.3
Inheritance Tax Act 1984, s 225	23.5
Inheritance Tax Act 1984, ss 249(3) and 251	23.4
Land Registration Act 1925	23.2
Land Registration Act 2002	23.2, 23.8B
Law of Property Act 1922, para 16 of Sch 15	23.2
Medical Act 1983, s 40	22.3
Medicines Act 1968, ss 82(3) and 83(2)	22.3
Mental Health Review Tribunal	22.8

APPEALS TO THE HIGH COURT	Paragraph
Merchant Shipping Act 1995	22.2
Nurses, Midwives and Health Visitors Act 1997, s 12	22.3
Opticians Act 1989, s 23	22.3
Osteopaths Act 1993, s 31	22.3
Pensions Act 1995, s 97	23.2
Pension Schemes Act 1993, ss 151 and 173	23.2
Pensions Appeal Tribunal Act 1943	22.5
Pharmacy Act 1954	22.3
Social Security Administration Act 1992	22.6
Stamp Duty Reserve Tax Regulations 1986, reg 10	23.5
Taxes Management Act 1970, ss 53 and 100C(4)	23.4
Taxes Management Act 1970, s 56A	23.5
Value Added Tax and Duties Tribunal	23.8
Water Resources Act 1991, s 205(4)	23.2

APPEALS TO COUNTY COURT	Paragraph
Local Government (Miscellaneous Provisions) Act 1976	24.1
Housing Act 1996, ss 204 and 204A	24.2
Immigration and Asylum Act 1999, Part II	24.3

APPEALS TO THE COURT OF APPEAL

Appeal against decree nisi of divorce or nullity of marriage

21.1(1) The appellant must file the appellant's notice at the Court of Appeal within 28 days after the date on which the decree was pronounced or conditional order made.

(2) The appellant must file the following documents with the appellant's notice –

(a) the decree or conditional order; and

(b) a certificate of service of the appellant's notice.

(3) The appellant's notice must be served on the appropriate district judge (see sub-paragraph (6)) in addition to the persons to be served under rule 52.4(3) and in accordance with that rule.

(4) The lower court may not alter the time limits for filing of the appeal notices.

(5) Where an appellant intends to apply to the Court of Appeal for an extension of time for serving or filing the appellant's notice he must give notice of that intention to the appropriate district judge (see sub-paragraph 6) before the application is made.

(6) In this paragraph 'the appropriate district judge' means, where the lower court is –

(a) a county court, the district judge of that court;

(b) a district registry, the district judge of that registry;

(c) the Principal Registry of the Family Division, the senior district judge of that division.

Appeal against order for revocation of patent

21.2(1) This paragraph applies where an appeal lies to the Court of Appeal from an order for the revocation of a patent.

(2) The appellant must serve the appellant's notice on the Comptroller-General of Patents, Designs and Trade Marks (the 'Comptroller') in addition to the persons to be served under rule 52.4(3) and in accordance with that rule.

(3) Where, before the appeal hearing, the respondent decides not to oppose the appeal or not to attend the appeal hearing, he must immediately serve notice of that decision on –

(a) the Comptroller; and

(b) the appellant

(4) Where the respondent serves a notice in accordance with paragraph (3), he must also serve copies of the following documents on the Comptroller with that notice –

(a) the petition;

(b) any statements of claim;

(c) any written evidence filed in the claim.

(5) Within 14 days after receiving the notice in accordance with paragraph (3), the Comptroller must serve on the appellant a notice stating whether or not he intends to attend the appeal hearing.

(6) The Comptroller may attend the appeal hearing and oppose the appeal –

(a) in any case where he has given notice under paragraph (5) of his intention to attend; and

(b) in any other case (including, in particular, a case where the respondent withdraws his opposition to the appeal during the hearing) if the Court of Appeal so directs or permits.

Appeal from Patents Court on appeal from Comptroller

21.3 Where the appeal is from a decision of the Patents Court which was itself made on an appeal from a decision of the Comptroller-General of Patents, Designs and Trade Marks, the appellant must serve the appellant's notice on the Comptroller in addition to the persons to be served under rule 52.4(3) and in accordance with that rule.

Appeals in cases of contempt of court

21.4 In an appeal under section 13 of the Administration of Justice Act 1960 (appeals in cases of contempt of court), the appellant must serve the appellant's notice on the court from whose order or decision the appeal is brought in addition to the persons to be served under rule 52.4(3) and in accordance with that rule.

Appeals from Social Security or Child Support Commissioners

21.5(1) This paragraph applies to appeals under the following provisions (appeals from the decision of a Social Security Commissioner or a Child Support Commissioner on a question of law) –

(a) section 6C of the Pensions Appeal Tribunals Act 1943;

(b) section 25 of the Child Support Act 1991;

(c) section 15 of the Social Security Act 1998;

(d) paragraph 9 of Schedule 7 to the Child Support, Pensions and Social Security Act 2000.

(2) The appellant must file the appellant's notice within 6 weeks after the date on which the Commissioner's decision on permission to appeal to the Court of Appeal was given in writing to the appellant.

(3) In an appeal brought under paragraph 9 of Schedule 7 to the Child Support, Pensions and Social Security Act 2000 by a party other than the Secretary of State, the appellant must serve the appellant's notice on the Secretary of State in addition to the persons to be served under rule 52.4(3) and in accordance with that rule.

(4) Where, after a Commissioner has given a decision, responsibility for the subject matter of the appeal has been transferred from a government department or the Commissioners for HM Revenue and Customs or a local authority ('the first body') to another such body ('the second body') and an appeal is brought by a party other than the second body –

(a) the second body shall be a respondent in place of the first body and the second body shall notify the court accordingly;

(b) if the appellant serves the appellant's notice or any other document on the first body, or if the court sends to the first body any communication in relation to the appeal, the first body shall forthwith send the notice, document or communication to the second body and the date on which the appellant's notice or other document was served on the first body shall be treated as the date on which it was served on the second body.

(5) his sub-paragraph applies where the appellant is the Secretary of State, the Commissioners of the Inland Revenue or a local authority. The appellant must serve the appellant's notice on any person appointed by the appellant to proceed with a claim, or an appeal arising out of a claim, in addition to the persons to be served under rule 52.4(3) and in accordance with that rule.

(Sub-paragraph (5) applies where the Secretary of State, the Commissioners of the Inland Revenueor a local authority is the appellant and that appellant appoints a person to proceed, in effect, on behalf of a respondent who is not himself able to proceed. An example is regulation 33 of the Social Security (Claims and Payments) Regulations 1987 which authorises the Secretary of State to appoint a person to proceed with the claim of another person who is unable for the time being to act.)

Appeals from Value Added Tax and Duties Tribunals

21.6(1) An application to the Court of Appeal for permission to appeal from a value added tax and duties tribunal direct to that court must be made within 28 days after the date on which the tribunal certifies that its decision involves a point of law relating wholly or mainly to the construction of –

(a) an enactment or of a statutory instrument; or

(b) any of the Community Treaties or any Community Instrument,

which has been fully argued before and fully considered by it.

(2) The application must be made by the parties jointly filing at the Court of Appeal an appellant's notice that –

(a) contains a statement of the grounds for the application; and

(b) is accompanied by a copy of the decision to be appealed, endorsed with the certificate of the tribunal.

(3) The court will notify the appellant of its decision and –

(a) where permission to appeal to the Court of Appeal is given, the appellant must serve the appellant's notice on the chairman of the tribunal in addition to the persons to be served under rule 52.4(3) within 14 days after that notification.

(b) where permission to appeal to the Court of Appeal is refused, the period for appealing to the High Court is to be calculated from the date of the notification of that refusal.

Asylum and Immigration Appeals

21.7(1) This paragraph applies to appeals –

(a) from the Immigration Appeal Tribunal under section 103 of the Nationality, Immigration and Asylum Act 2002 ('the 2002 Act'); and

(b) from the Asylum and Immigration Tribunal under the following provisions of the 2002 Act –

(i) section 103B (appeal from the Tribunal following reconsideration); and

(ii) section 103E (appeal from the Tribunal sitting as a panel).

(2) The appellant is not required to file an appeal bundle in accordance with paragraph 5.6A of this practice direction, but must file the documents specified in paragraphs 5.6(2)(a) to (f) together with a copy of the Tribunal's determination.

(3) The appellant's notice must be filed at the Court of Appeal within 14 days after the appellant is served with written notice of the decision of the Tribunal to grant or refuse permission to appeal.

(4) The appellant must serve the appellant's notice in accordance with rule 52.4(3) on –

(a) the persons to be served under that rule; and

(b) the Asylum and Immigration Tribunal.

(5) On being served with the appellant's notice, the Asylum and Immigration Tribunal must send to the Court of Appeal copies of the documents which were before the relevant Tribunal when it considered the appeal.

21.7A(1) This paragraph applies to appeals from the Asylum and Immigration Tribunal referred to the Court of Appeal under section 103C of the Nationality, Immigration and Asylum Act 2002.

(2) On making an order referring an appeal to the Court of Appeal, the High Court shall send to the Court of Appeal copies of –
 (a) that order and any other order made in relation to the application for reconsideration; and
 (b) the application notice, written submissions and other documents filed under rule 54.29

(3) Unless the court directs otherwise, the application notice filed under rule 54.29 shall be treated as the appellant's notice.

(4) The respondent may file a respondent's notice within 14 days after the date on which the respondent is served with the order of the High Court referring the appeal to the Court of Appeal.

(5) The Court of Appeal may give such additional directions as are appropriate.

Appeal from Special Commissioners

21.8(1) An application to the Court of Appeal for permission to appeal from the Special Commissioners direct to that court under section 56A of the Taxes Management Act 1970 must be made within 28 days after the date on which the Special Commissioners certify that their decision involves a point of law relating wholly or mainly to the construction of an enactment which has been fully argued before and fully considered before them.

(2) The application must be made by the parties jointly filing at the Court of Appeal an appellant's notice that –
 (a) contains a statement of the grounds for the application; and
 (b) is accompanied by a copy of the decision to be appealed, endorsed with the certificate of the tribunal.

(3) The court will notify the parties of its decision and –
 (a) where permission to appeal to the Court of Appeal is given, the appellant must serve the appellant's notice on the Clerk to the Special Commissioners in addition to the persons to be served under rule 52.4(3) within 14 days after that notification.
 (b) where permission to appeal to the Court of Appeal is refused, the period for appealing to the High Court is to be calculated from the date of the notification of that refusal.

Appeal from Lands Tribunal

21.9 The appellant must file the appellant's notice at the Court of Appeal within 28 days after the date of the decision of the tribunal.

Appeal from Competition Appeal Tribunal

21.10

(1) Where the appellant applies for permission to appeal at the hearing at which the decision is delivered by the tribunal and –
 (a) permission is given; or
 (b) permission is refused and the appellant wishes to make an application to the Court of Appeal for permission to appeal,

 the appellant's notice must be filed at the Court of Appeal within 14 days after the date of that hearing.

(2) Where the appellant applies in writing to the Registrar of the tribunal for permission to appeal and –

(a) permission is given; or
(b) permission is refused and the appellant wishes to make an application to the Court of Appeal for permission to appeal,

the appellant's notice must be filed at the Court of Appeal within 14 days after the date of receipt of the tribunal's decision on permission.

(3) Where the appellant does not make an application to the tribunal for permission to appeal, but wishes to make an application to the Court of Appeal for permission, the appellant's notice must be filed at the Court of Appeal within 14 days after the end of the period within which he may make a written application to the Registrar of the tribunal.

APPEALS RELATING TO THE APPLICATION OF ARTICLES 81 AND 82 OF THE EC TREATY AND CHAPTERS I AND II OF PART I OF THE COMPETITION ACT 1998

21.10A

(1) This paragraph applies to any appeal to the Court of Appeal relating to the application of –
  (a) Article 81 or Article 82 of the Treaty establishing the European Community; or
  (b) Chapter I or Chapter II of Part I of the Competition Act 1998.

(2) In this paragraph –
  (a) 'the Act' means the Competition Act 1998;
  (b) 'the Commission' means the European Commission;
  (c) 'the Competition Regulation' means Council Regulation (EC) No 1/2003 of 16 December 2002 on the implementation of the rules on competition laid down in Articles 81 and 82 of the Treaty;
  (d) 'national competition authority' means –
    (i) the Office of Fair Trading; and
    (ii) any other person or body designated pursuant to Article 35 of the Competition Regulation as a national competition authority of the United Kingdom;
  (e) 'the Treaty' means the Treaty establishing the European Community.

(3) Any party whose appeal notice raises an issue relating to the application of Article 81 or 82 of the Treaty, or Chapter I or II of Part I of the Act, must –
  (a) state that fact in his appeal notice; and
  (b) serve a copy of the appeal notice on the Office of Fair Trading at the same time as it is served on the other party to the appeal (addressed to the Director of Competition Policy Co-ordination, Office of Fair Trading, Fleetbank House, 2-6 Salisbury Square, London EC4Y 8JX).

(4) Attention is drawn to the provisions of article 15.3 of the Competition Regulation, which entitles competition authorities and the Commission to submit written observations to national courts on issues relating to the application of Article 81 or 82 and, with the permission of the court in question, to submit oral observations to the court.

(5) A national competition authority may also make written observations to the Court of Appeal, or apply for permission to make oral observations, on issues relating to the application of Chapter I or II.

(6) If a national competition authority or the Commission intends to make

written observations to the Court of Appeal, it must give notice of its intention to do so by letter to the Civil Appeals Office at the earliest opportunity.

(7) An application by a national competition authority or the Commission for permission to make oral representations at the hearing of an appeal must be made by letter to the Civil Appeals Office at the earliest opportunity, identifying the appeal and indicating why the applicant wishes to make oral representations.

(8) If a national competition authority or the Commission files a notice under sub-paragraph (6) or an application under sub-paragraph (7), it must at the same time serve a copy of the notice or application on every party to the appeal.

(9) Any request by a national competition authority or the Commission for the court to send it any documents relating to an appeal should be made at the same time as filing a notice under sub-paragraph (6) or an application under sub-paragraph (7).

(10) When the Court of Appeal receives a notice under sub-paragraph (6) it may give case management directions to the national competition authority or the Commission, including directions about the date by which any written observations are to be filed.

(11) The Court of Appeal will serve on every party to the appeal a copy of any directions given or order made –

(a) on an application under sub-paragraph (7); or

(b) under sub-paragraph (10).

(12) Every party to an appeal which raises an issue relating to the application of Article 81 or 82, and any national competition authority which has been served with a copy of a party's appeal notice, is under a duty to notify the Court of Appeal at any stage of the appeal if they are aware that –

(a) the Commission has adopted, or is contemplating adopting, a decision in relation to proceedings which it has initiated; and

(b) the decision referred to in (a) above has or would have legal effects in relation to the particular agreement, decision or practice in issue before the court.

(13) Where the Court of Appeal is aware that the Commission is contemplating adopting a decision as mentioned in sub-paragraph (12)(a), it shall consider whether to stay the appeal pending the Commission's decision.

(14) Where any judgment is given which decides on the application of Article 81 or 82, the court shall direct that a copy of the transcript of the judgment shall be sent to the Commission.

Judgments may be sent to the Commission electronically to comp-amicus@cec.eu.int or by post to the European Commission – DG Competition, B–1049, Brussels.

APPEAL FROM PROSCRIBED ORGANISATIONS APPEAL COMMISSION

21.11

(1) The appellant's notice must be filed at the Court of Appeal within 14 days after the date when the Proscribed Organisations Appeal Commission –

(a) granted; or

(b) where section 6(2)(b) of the Terrorism Act 2000 applies, refused permission to appeal.

APPEALS TO THE HIGH COURT – QUEEN'S BENCH DIVISION

22.1 The following appeals are to be heard in the Queen's Bench Division.

Statutory Appeals

Appeals under the Merchant Shipping Act 1995

22.2(1) This paragraph applies to appeals under the Merchant Shipping Act 1995 and for this purpose a re-hearing and an application under section 61 of the Merchant Shipping Act 1995 are treated as appeals.

(2) The appellant must file any report to the Secretary of State containing the decision from which the appeal is brought with the appellant's notice.

(3) Where a re-hearing by the High Court is ordered under sections 64 or 269 of the Merchant Shipping Act 1995, the Secretary of State must give reasonable notice to the parties whom he considers to be affected by the re-hearing.

Appeals against decisions affecting the registration of architects and health care professionals

22.3(1) This paragraph applies to an appeal to the High Court under –

- (a) section 22 of the Architects Act 1997;
- (b) section 82(3) and 83(2) of the Medicines Act 1968;
- (c) section 12 of the Nurses, Midwives and Health Visitors Act 1997;
- (cc) article 38 of the Nursing and Midwifery Order 2001;
- (d) section 10 of the Pharmacy Act 1954;
- (e) section 40 of the Medical Act 1983;
- (f) section 29 or section 40 of the Dentists Act 1984;
- (g) section 23 of the Opticians Act 1989;
- (h) section 31 of the Osteopaths Act 1993; and
- (i) section 31 of the Chiropractors Act 1994.

(2) Every appeal to which this paragraph applies must be supported by written evidence and, if the court so orders, oral evidence and will be by way of re-hearing.

(3) The appellant must file the appellant's notice within 28 days after the decision that the appellant wishes to appeal.

(4) In the case of an appeal under an enactment specified in column 1 of the following table, the persons to be made respondents are the persons specified in relation to that enactment in column 2 of the table and the person to be served with the appellant's notice is the person so specified in column 3.

1 Enactment	2 Respondents	3 Person to be served
Architects Act 1997, s 22	The Architects' Registration Council of the United Kingdom	The registrar of the Council

1 Enactment	2 Respondents	3 Person to be served
Medicines Act 1968, s 82(3) and s 83(2)	The Pharmaceutical Society of Great Britain	The registrar of the Society
Nurses, Midwives and Health Visitors Act 1997, s 12	The United Kingdom Central Council for Nursing, Midwifery and Health Visiting	The registrar of the Council
Pharmacy Act 1954, s 10	The Pharmaceutical Society of Great Britain	The registrar of the Society
Medical Act 1983, s 40	The General Medical Council	The Registrar of the Council
Dentists Act 1984, s 29 or s 44	The General Dental Council	The Registrar of the Council
Opticians Act 1989, s 23	The General Optical Council	The Registrar of the Council
Osteopaths Act 1993, s 31	The General Osteopathic Council	The Registrar of the Council
Chiropractors Act 1994, s 31	The General Chiropractic Council	The Registrar of the Council

Consumer Credit Act 1974: appeal from Secretary of State

22.4(1) A person dissatisfied in point of law with a decision of the Secretary of State on an appeal under section 41 of the Consumer Credit Act 1974 from a determination of the Office of Fair Trading who had a right to appeal to the Secretary of State, whether or not he exercised that right, may appeal to the High Court.

(2) The appellant must serve the appellant's notice on –

(a) the Secretary of State;

(b) the original applicant, if any, where the appeal is by a licensee under a group licence against compulsory variation, suspension or revocation of that licence; and

(c) any other person as directed by the court.

(3) The appeal court may remit the matter to the Secretary of State to the extent necessary to enable him to provide the court with such further information as the court may direct.

(4) If the appeal court allows the appeal, it shall not set aside or vary the decision but shall remit the matter to the Secretary of State with the opinion of the court for hearing and determination by him.

The Pensions Appeal Tribunal Act 1943

22.5(1) In this paragraph 'the judge' means the judge nominated by the Lord Chancellor under section 6(2) of the Pensions Appeal Tribunals Act 1943 ('the Act').

(2) An application to the judge for permission to appeal against a decision of a Pensions Appeal Tribunal –
   (a) may not be made unless an application was made to the tribunal and was refused; and
   (b) must be made within 28 days after the date of the tribunal's refusal.

(3) The appellant's notice seeking permission to appeal from the judge must contain –
   (a) the point of law as respects which the appellant alleges that the tribunal's decision was wrong; and
   (b) the date of the tribunal's decision refusing permission to appeal.

(4) The court officer shall request the chairman of the tribunal to give the judge a written statement of the reasons for the tribunal's decision to refuse permission to appeal, and within 7 days after receiving the request, the chairman must give the judge such a statement.

(5) Where permission to appeal was given by –
   (a) the tribunal, the appellant must file and serve the appellant's notice;
   (b) the judge, the appellant must serve the appellant's notice, within 28 days after permission to appeal was given.

(6) Within 28 days after service of the notice of appeal on him, the chairman of the tribunal must –
   (a) state a case setting out the facts on which the decision appealed against was based;
   (b) file the case stated at the court; and
   (c) serve a copy of the case stated on the appellant and the respondent.

(7) A copy of the judge's order on the appeal must be sent by the court officer to the appellant, the respondent and the chairman of the tribunal.

The Social Security Administration Act 1992

22.6(1) Any person who by virtue of section 18 or 58(8) of the Social Security Administration Act 1992 ('the Act') is entitled and wishes to appeal against a decision of the Secretary of State on a question of law must, within the prescribed period, or within such further time as the Secretary of State may allow, serve on the Secretary of State a notice requiring him to state a case setting out –
   (a) his decision; and
   (b) the facts on which his decision was based.

(2) Unless paragraph (3) applies the prescribed period is 28 days after receipt of the notice of the decision.

(3) Where, within 28 days after receipt of notice of the decision, a request is made to the Secretary of State in accordance with regulations made under the Act to furnish a statement of the grounds of the decision, the prescribed period is 28 days after receipt of that statement.

(4) Where under section 18 or section 58(8) of the Act, the Secretary of State refers a question of law to the court, he must state that question together with the relevant facts in a case.

(5) The appellant's notice and the case stated must be filed at the appeal court and a copy of the notice and the case stated served on –
   (a) the Secretary of State; and

(b) every person as between whom and the Secretary of State the question has arisen,

within 28 days after the case stated was served on the party at whose request, or as a result of whose application to the court, the case was stated.

(6) Unless the appeal court otherwise orders, the appeal or reference shall not be heard sooner than 28 days after service of the appellant's notice.

(7) The appeal court may order the case stated by the Secretary of State to be returned to the Secretary of State for him to hear further evidence.

APPEALS UNDER THE EXTRADITION ACT 2003

22.6A (1) In this paragraph, 'the Act' means the Extradition Act 2003.

(2) Appeals to the High Court under the Act must be brought in the Administrative Court of the Queen's Bench Division.

(3) Where an appeal is brought under section 26 or 28 of the Act –

(a) the appellant's notice must be filed and served before the expiry of 7 days, starting with the day on which the order is made;

(b) the appellant must endorse the appellant's notice with the date of the person's arrest;

(c) the High Court must begin to hear the substantive appeal within 40 days of the person's arrest; and

(d) the appellant must serve a copy of the appellant's notice on the Crown Prosecution Service, if they are not a party to the appeal, in addition to the persons to be served under rule 52.4(3) and in accordance with that rule.

(4) The High Court may extend the period of 40 days under paragraph (3)(c) if it believes it to be in the interests of justice to do so.

(5) Where an appeal is brought under section 103 of the Act, the appellant's notice must be filed and served before the expiry of 14 days, starting with the day on which the Secretary of State informs the person under section 100(1) or (4) of the Act of the order he has made in respect of the person.

(6) Where an appeal is brought under section 105 of the Act, the appellant's notice must be filed and served before the expiry of 14 days, starting with the day on which the order for discharge is made.

(7) Where an appeal is brought under section 108 of the Act the appellant's notice must be filed and served before the expiry of 14 days, starting with the day on which the Secretary of State informs the person that he has ordered his extradition.

(8) Where an appeal is brought under section 110 of the Act the appellant's notice must be filed and served before the expiry of 14 days, starting with the day on which the Secretary of State informs the person acting on behalf of a category 2 territory, as defined in section 69 of the Act, of the order for discharge.

(Section 69 of the Act provides that a category 2 territory is that designated for the purposes of Part 2 of the Act).

(9) Subject to paragraph (10), where an appeal is brought under section 103, 105, 108 or 110 of the Act, the High Court must begin to hear the substantive appeal within 76 days of the appellant's notice being filed.

(10) Where an appeal is brought under section 103 of the Act before the Secretary of State has decided whether the person is to be extradited –

(a) the period of 76 days does not start until the day on which the Secretary of State informs the person of his decision; and
(b) the Secretary of State must, as soon as practicable after he informs the person of his decision, inform the High Court –
(i) of his decision; and
(ii) of the date on which he informs the person of his decision.

(11) The High Court may extend the period of 76 days if it believes it to be in the interests of justice to do so.

(12) Where an appeal is brought under section 103, 105, 108 or 110 of the Act, the appellant must serve a copy of the appellant's notice on –
(a) the Crown Prosecution Service; and
(b) the Home Office,
if they are not a party to the appeal, in addition to the persons to be served under rule 52.4(3) and in accordance with that rule.

Appeals under section 49 of the Solicitors Act 1974

22.6B(1) This paragraph applies to appeals from the Solicitors Disciplinary Tribunal ('the Tribunal') to the High Court under section 49(1)(b) of the Solicitors Act 1974 ('the Act'). The procedure for appeals to the Master of the Rolls under section 49(1)(a) of the Act is set out in the Master of the Rolls (Appeals and Applications) Regulations 2001.

(2) Appeals to the High Court under section 49(1)(b) of the Act must be brought in the Administrative Court of the Queen's Bench Division.

(3) The appellant's notice –
(a) must state in the heading that the appeal relates to a solicitor, or a solicitor's clerk, and is made under section 49 of the Act;
(b) must be filed within 14 days after the date on which the Tribunal's statement of its findings was filed with the Law Society in accordance with section 48(1) of the Act; and
(c) must be accompanied by copies of the order appealed against and the statement of the Tribunal's findings required by section 48(1) of the Act; and
(d) unless the court orders otherwise, must be served by the appellant on –
(i) every party to the proceedings before the Tribunal; and
(ii) the Law Society.

(4) The court –
(a) may order an appellant to give security for the costs of an appeal only if he was the applicant in the proceedings before the tribunal; and
(b) may not order any other party to give security for costs.

(5) The court may direct the Tribunal to provide it with a written statement of their opinion on the case, or on any question arising in it. If the court gives such a direction, the clerk to the Tribunal must as soon as possible –
(a) file the statement; and
(b) serve a copy on each party to the appeal.

(6) The court may give permission for any person to intervene to be heard in opposition to the appeal.

(7) An appellant may at any time discontinue his appeal by –
(a) serving notice of discontinuance on the clerk to the Tribunal and every other party to the appeal; and

(b) filing a copy of the notice.

(8) Unless the court orders otherwise, an appellant who discontinues is liable for the costs of every other party to the appeal.

Appeals by way of case stated

Reference of question of law by Agriculture Land Tribunal

22.7(1) A question of law referred to the High Court by an Agricultural Land Tribunal under section 6 of the Agriculture (Miscellaneous Provisions) Act 1954 shall be referred by way of case stated by the Tribunal.

(2) Where the proceedings before the tribunal arose on an application under section 11 of the Agricultural Holdings Act 1986, an –

(a) application notice for an order under section 6 that the tribunal refers a question of law to the court; and

(b) appellant's notice by which an appellant seeks the court's determination on a question of law,

must be served on the authority having power to enforce the statutory requirement specified in the notice in addition to every other party to those proceedings and on the secretary of the tribunal.

(3) Where, in accordance with paragraph (2), a notice is served on the authority mentioned in that paragraph, that authority may attend the appeal hearing and make representations to the court.

Case stated by Mental Health Review Tribunal

22.8(1) In this paragraph 'the Act' means the Mental Health Act 1983 and 'party to proceedings' means –

(a) the person who initiated the proceedings; and

(b) any person to whom, in accordance with rules made under section 78 of the Act, the tribunal sent notice of the application or reference or a request instead notice of reference.

(2) A party to proceedings shall not be entitled to apply to the High Court for an order under section 78(8) of the Act directing the tribunal to state a case for determination by court unless –

(a) within 21 days after the decision of the tribunal was communicated to him in accordance with rules made under section 78 of the Act he made a written request to the tribunal to state a case; and

(b) either the tribunal

(i) failed to comply with that request within 21 days after it was made; or

(ii) refused to comply with it.

(3) The period for filing the application notice for an order under section 78(8) of the Act is –

(a) where the tribunal failed to comply with the applicant's request to state a case within the period mentioned in paragraph (2)(b)(i), 14 days after the expiration of that period;

(b) where the tribunal refused that request, 14 days after receipt by the applicant of notice of the refusal of his request.

(4) A Mental Health Review Tribunal by whom a case is stated shall be entitled to attend the proceedings for the determination of the case and make representations to the court.

(5) If the court allows the appeal, it may give any direction which the tribunal ought to have given under Part V of the Act.

APPEALS TO THE HIGH COURT – CHANCERY DIVISION

23.1 The following appeals are to be heard in the Chancery Division

Determination of appeal or case stated under various Acts

23.2 Any appeal to the High Court, and any case stated or question referred for the opinion of that court under any of the following enactments shall be heard in the Chancery Division –

(1) paragraph 16 of Schedule 15 to the Law of Property Act 1922;
(2) the Industrial Assurance Act 1923;
(3) the Land Registration Act 1925;
(4) section 205(4) of the Water Resources Act 1991;
(5) section 38(3) of the Clergy Pensions Measure 1961;
(6) the Industrial and Provident Societies Act 1965;
(7) section 151 of the Pension Schemes Act 1993;
(8) section 173 of the Pension Schemes Act 1993; and
(9) section 97 of the Pensions Act 1995;
(10) the Charities Act 1993;
(11) section 13 and 13B of Stamp Act 1891;
(12) section 705A of the Income and Corporation Taxes Act 1988;
(13) regulation 22 of the General Commissioners (Jurisdiction and Procedure) Regulations 1994;
(14) section 53, 56A or 100C(4) of the Taxes Management Act 1970;
(15) section 222(3), 225, 249(3) or 251 of the Inheritance Tax Act 1984;
(16) regulation 8(3) or 10 of the Stamp Duty Reserve Tax Regulations 1986;
(17) the Land Registration Act 2002;
(18) regulation 74 of the European Public Limited-Liability Company Regulations 2004.

(This list is not exhaustive)

Statutory appeals

Appeal under section 222 of the Inheritance Tax Act 1984

23.3(1) This paragraph applies to appeals to the High Court under section 222(3) of the Inheritance Tax Act 1984 (the '1984 Act') and regulation 8(3) of the Stamp Duty Reserve Tax Regulations 1986 (the '1986 Regulations').

(2) The appellant's notice must –

(a) state the date on which the Commissioners for HM Revenue and Customs (the 'Board') gave notice to the appellant under section 221 of the 1984 Act or regulation 6 of the 1986 Regulations of the determination that is the subject of the appeal;

(b) state the date on which the appellant gave to the Board notice of appeal under section 222(1) of the 1984 Act or regulation 8(1) of the 1986 Regulations and, if notice was not given within the time permitted, whether the Board or the Special Commissioners have given their consent to the appeal being brought out of time, and, if they have, the date they gave their consent; and

(c) either state that the appellant and the Board have agreed that the appeal may be to the High Court or contain an application for permission to appeal to the High Court.

(3) The appellant must file the following documents with the appellant's notice –

(a) Two copies of the notice referred to in paragraph 2(a);

(b) Two copies of the notice of appeal (under section 222(1) of the 1984 Act or regulation 8(1) of the 1986 Regulations) referred to in paragraph 2(b); and

(c) where the appellant's notice contains an application for permission to appeal, written evidence setting out the grounds on which it is alleged that the matters to be decided on the appeal are likely to be substantially confined to questions of law.

(4) The appellant must –

(a) file the appellant's notice at the court; and

(b) serve the appellant's notice on the Board,

within 30 days of the date on which the appellant gave to the Board notice of appeal under section 222(1) of the 1984 Act or regulation 8(1) of the 1986 Regulations or, if the Board or the Special Commissioners have given consent to the appeal being brought out of time, within 30 days of the date on which such consent was given.

(5) The court will set a date for the hearing of not less than 40 days from the date that the appellant's notice was filed.

(6) Where the appellant's notice contains an application for permission to appeal –

(a) a copy of the written evidence filed in accordance with paragraph (3)(c) must be served on the Board with the appellant's notice; and

(b) the Board –

(i) may file written evidence; and

(ii) if it does so, must serve a copy of that evidence on the appellant,

within 30 days after service of the written evidence under paragraph (6)(a).

(7) The appellant may not rely on any grounds of appeal not specified in the notice referred to in paragraph (2)(b) on the hearing of the appeal without the permission of the court.

Appeals under section 53 and 100C(4) of the Taxes Management Act 1970 and section 249(3) or 251 of the Inheritance Tax Act 1984

23.4(1) The appellant must serve the appellant's notice on –

(a) the General or Special Commissioners against whose decision, award or determination the appeal is brought; and

(b) (i) in the case of an appeal brought under section 100C(4) of the Taxes Management Act 1970 or section 249(3) of the Inheritance Tax Act 1984 by any party other than the defendant in the proceedings before the Commissioners, that defendant; or

(ii) in any other case, the Commissioners for HM Revenue and Customs.

(2) The appellant must file the appellant's notice at the court within 30 days after the date of the decision, award or determination against which the appeal is brought.

(3) Within 30 days of the service on them of the appellant's notice, the General or Special Commissioners, as the case may be, must –
   (a) file two copies of a note of their findings and of the reasons for their decision, award or determination at the court; and
   (b) serve a copy of the note on every other party to the appeal.

(4) Any document to be served on the General or Special Commissioners may be served by delivering or sending it to their clerk.

Appeals under section 56A of the Taxes Management Act 1970, section 225 of the Inheritance Tax Act 1984 and regulation 10 of the Stamp Duty Reserve Tax Regulations 1986

23.5(1) The appellant must file the appellant's notice –
   (a) where the appeal is made following the refusal of the Special Commissioners to issue a certificate under section 56A(2)(b) of the Taxes Management Act 1970, within 28 days from the date of the release of the decision of the Special Commissioners containing the refusal;
   (b) where the appeal is made following the refusal of permission to appeal to the Court of Appeal under section 56A(2)(c) of that Act, within 28 days from the date when permission is refused; or
   (c) in all other cases within 56 days after the date of the decision or determination that the appellant wishes to appeal.

Appeal under section 17 of the Industrial Assurance Act 1923

23.6 The appellant must file the appellant's notice within 21 days after the date of the Commissioner's refusal or direction under section 17(3) of the Industrial Assurance Act 1923.

Appeals affecting industrial and provident societies etc

23.7(1) This paragraph applies to all appeals under –
   (a) the Friendly Societies Act 1974;
   (b) the Friendly Societies Act 1992;
   (c) the Industrial Assurance Act 1923; and
   (d) the Industrial and Provident Societies Act 1965.

(2) At any stage on an appeal, the court may –
   (a) direct that the appellant's notice be served on any person;
   (b) direct that notice be given by advertisement or otherwise of –
      (i) the bringing of the appeal;
      (ii) the nature of the appeal; and
      (iii) the time when the appeal will or is likely to be heard; or
   (c) give such other directions as it thinks proper to enable any person interested in –
      (i) the society, trade union, alleged trade union or industrial assurance company; or
      (ii) the subject matter of the appeal,
   to appear and be heard at the appeal hearing.

Appeal from Value Added Tax and Duties Tribunal

23.8(1) A party to proceedings before a Value Added Tax and Duties Tribunal who is dissatisfied in point of law with a decision of the tribunal may appeal under section 11(1) of the Tribunals and Inquiries Act 1992 to the High Court.

(2) The appellant must file the appellant's notice –
  (a) where the appeal is made following the refusal of the Value Added Tax and Duties Tribunal to grant a certificate under article 2(b) of the Value Added Tax and Duties Tribunal Appeals Order 1986, within 28 days from the date of the release of the decision containing the refusal;
  (b) in all other cases within 56 days after the date of the decision or determination that the appellant wishes to appeal.

Appeal against an order or decision of the Charity Commissioners

23.8A

(1) In this paragraph –
'the Act' means the Charities Act 1993; and
'the Commissioners' means the Charity Commissioners for England and Wales.

(2) The Attorney-General, unless he is the appellant, must be made a respondent to the appeal.

(3) The appellant's notice must state the grounds of the appeal, and the appellant may not rely on any other grounds without the permission of the court.

(4) Sub-paragraphs (5) and (6) apply, in addition to the above provisions, where the appeal is made under section 16(12) of the Act.

(5) If the Commissioners have granted a certificate that it is a proper case for an appeal, a copy of the certificate must be filed with the appellant's notice.

(6) If the appellant applies in the appellant's notice for permission to appeal under section 16(13) of the Act –
  (a) the appellant's notice must state –
    (i) that the appellant has requested the Commissioners to grant a certificate that it is a proper case for an appeal, and they have refused to do so;
    (ii) the date of such refusal;
    (iii) the grounds on which the appellant alleges that it is a proper case for an appeal; and
    (iv) if the application for permission to appeal is made with the consent of any other party to the proposed appeal, that fact;
  (b) if the Commissioners have given reasons for refusing a certificate, a copy of the reasons must be attached to the appellant's notice;
  (c) the court may, before determining the application, direct the Commissioners to file a written statement of their reasons for refusing a certificate;
  (d) the court will serve on the appellant a copy of any statement filed under sub-paragraph (c).

Appeal against a decision of the adjudicator under section 111 of the Land Registration Act 2002

23.8B

(1) A person who is aggrieved by a decision of the adjudicator and who wishes to appeal that decision must obtain permission to appeal.

(2) The appellant must serve on the adjudicator a copy of the appeal court's decision on a request for permission to appeal as soon as reasonably practicable and in any event within 14 days of receipt by the appellant of the decision on permission.

(3) The appellant must serve on the adjudicator and the Chief Land Registrar a copy of any order by the appeal court to stay a decision of the adjudicator pending the outcome of the appeal as soon as reasonably practicable and in any event within 14 days of receipt by the appellant of the appeal court's order to stay.

(4) The appellant must serve on the adjudicator and the Chief Land Registrar a copy of the appeal court's decision on the appeal as soon as reasonably practicable and in any event within 14 days of receipt by the appellant of the appeal court's decision.

Appeals under regulation 74 of the European Public Limited-Liability Company Regulations 2004

23.8C

(1) In this paragraph –
   (a) 'the 2004 Regulations' means the European Public Limited-Liability Company Regulations 2004;
   (b) 'the EC Regulation' means Council Regulation (EC) No 2157/2001 of 8 October 2001 on the Statute for a European company (SE);
   (c) 'SE' means a European public limited-liability company (Societas Europaea) within the meaning of Article 1 of the EC Regulation.

(2) This paragraph applies to appeals under regulation 74 of the 2004 Regulations against the opposition –
   (a) of the Secretary of State or national financial supervisory authority to the transfer of the registered office of an SE under Article 8(14) of the EC Regulation; and
   (b) of the Secretary of State to the participation by a company in the formation of an SE by merger under Article 19 of the EC Regulation.

(3) Where an SE seeks to appeal against the opposition of the national financial supervisory authority to the transfer of its registered office under Article 8(14) of the EC Regulation, it must serve the appellant's notice on both the national financial supervisory authority and the Secretary of State.

(4) The appellant's notice must contain an application for permission to appeal.

(5) The appeal will be a review of the decision of the Secretary of State and not a re-hearing. The grounds of review are set out in regulation 74(2) of the 2004 Regulations.

(6) The appeal will be heard by a High Court judge.

Appeals by way of case stated

Proceedings under the Commons Registration Act 1965

23.9 A person aggrieved by the decision of a Commons Commissioner who requires the Commissioner to state a case for the opinion of the High Court under section 18 of the Commons Registration Act 1965 must file the appellant's notice within 42 days from the date on which notice of the decision was sent to the aggrieved person.

APPEALS TO A COUNTY COURT

Local Government (Miscellaneous Provisions) Act 1976

24.1 Where one of the grounds upon which an appeal against a notice under sections 21, 23 or 35 of the Local Government (Miscellaneous Provisions) Act 1976 is brought is that –

(a) it would have been fairer to serve the notice on another person; or
(b) that it would be reasonable for the whole or part of the expenses to which the appeal relates to be paid by some other person,

that person must be made a respondent to the appeal, unless the court, on application of the appellant made without notice, otherwise directs.

Appeals under sections 204 and 204A of the Housing Act 1996

24.2(1) An appellant should include appeals under section 204 and section 204A of the Housing Act 1996 in one appellant's notice.

(2) If it is not possible to do so (for example because an urgent application under section 204A is required) the appeals may be included in separate appellant's notices.

(3) An appeal under section 204A may include an application for an order under section 204A(4)(a) requiring the authority to secure that accommodation is available for the applicant's occupation.

(4) If, exceptionally, the court makes an order under section 204A(4)(a) without notice, the appellant's notice must be served on the authority together with the order. Such an order will normally require the authority to secure that accommodation is available until a hearing date when the authority can make representations as to whether the order under section 204A(4)(a) should be continued.

Appeal under Part II of the Immigration and Asylum Act 1999 (carriers' liability)

24.3(1) A person appealing to a county court under section 35A or section 40B of the Immigration and Asylum Act 1999 ('the Act') against a decision by the Secretary of State to impose a penalty under section 32 or a charge under section 40 of the Act must, subject to paragraph (2), file the appellant's notice within 28 days after receiving the penalty notice or charge notice.

(2) Where the appellant has given notice of objection to the Secretary of State under section 35(4) or section 40A(3) of the Act within the time prescribed for doing so, he must file the appellant's notice within 28 days after receiving notice of the Secretary of State's decision in response to the notice of objection.

(3) Sections 35A and 40B of the Act provide that any appeal under those sections shall be a re-hearing of the Secretary of State's decision to impose a penalty or charge, and therefore rule 52.11(1) does not apply.

Jurisdiction of the district judge—Unless a statute, rule or practice direction provides otherwise (for example, PD2B, para 9 in relation to homelessness appeals under Housing Act 1996, ss 204 and 204A), it would appear that a district judge can hear statutory appeals to the county court. It will be a matter for the designated civil judge to decide whether the district judge should exercise that jurisdiction.

SECTION IV – PROVISIONS ABOUT REOPENING APPEALS

REOPENING OF FINAL APPEALS

25.1 This paragraph applies to applications under rule 52.17 for permission to reopen a final determination of an appeal.

25.2 In this paragraph, 'appeal' includes an application for permission to appeal.

25.3 Permission must be sought from the court whose decision the applicant wishes to reopen.

25.4 The application for permission must be made by application notice and supported by written evidence, verified by a statement of truth.

25.5 A copy of the application for permission must not be served on any other party to the original appeal unless the court so directs.

25.6 Where the court directs that the application for permission is to be served on another party, that party may within 14 days of the service on him of the copy of the application file and serve a written statement either supporting or opposing the application.

25.7 The application for permission, and any written statements supporting or opposing it, will be considered on paper by a single judge, and will be allowed to proceed only if the judge so directs.

PART 53
DEFAMATION CLAIMS

CONTENTS OF THIS PART

53.1 Scope of this Part

This Part contains rules about defamation claims.

Amendments—Inserted by SI 2000/221.

Practice Direction—See generally PD53 at p 1272.

Introduction—When embarking on a defamation claim, one should first comply with the Defamation Pre-Action Protocol (set out in Section 4 of this work).

This Part itself (which is brief) contains only rules made under Defamation Act 1996, s 10 for summary disposal of defamation claims and a provision to protect a defendant's source of information. Its Practice Direction – PD53 – not only supplements r 53.2 on summary disposal. It also conveniently brings together in one place the outline requirements for pleading a defamation statement of case, the rules for making an offer of amends under ss 2–4 of the Act, guidance on rulings on meaning and the entitlement to a statement in open court on the acceptance of a settlement offer or payment. It replaces the former RSC Ord 82 and the now revoked parts of Pt 16 which related to defamation.

53.2 Summary disposal under the Defamation Act 1996

(1) This rule provides for summary disposal in accordance with the Defamation Act 1996 ('the Act').

(2) In proceedings for summary disposal under sections 8 and 9 of the Act, rules 24.4 (procedure), 24.5 (evidence) and 24.6 (directions) apply.

(3) An application for summary judgment under Part 24 may not be made if –

- (a) an application has been made for summary disposal in accordance with the Act, and that application has not been disposed of; or
- (b) summary relief has been granted on an application for summary disposal under the Act.

(4) The court may on any application for summary disposal direct the defendant to elect whether or not to make an offer to make amends under section 2 of the Act.

(5) When it makes a direction under paragraph (4), the court will specify the time by which and the manner in which –

- (a) the election is to be made; and
- (b) notification of it is to be given to the court and the other parties.

Amendments—Inserted by SI 2000/221.

Practice Direction—See generally PD53 at p 1272.

'in accordance with the Defamation Act 1996' (r 53.2(1))—Section 10(1) of the Act authorises the rule.

'proceedings for summary disposal' (r 53.2(2))—The summary disposal regime was intended to introduce a swift means for a defamed person to obtain vindication of his reputation and an opportunity for a defendant who had mistakenly published defamatory allegations to escape a protracted claim. At any stage of defamation proceedings, on the application of either party, the court can consider the strength of the claim and defences raised and dispose of the claim on a summary basis in favour of either the claimant or the defendant.

The court can dismiss the claim on the defendant's application if it has no realistic prospect of success and there is no reason why it should be tried (s 8(2) of the Act), for example if the words complained of do not bear a defamatory meaning (*Gillick v Brook Advisory Centres* (2002) (unreported) March 12, Gray J), there is no reference to the claimant (*Mosley v Focus Magazin Verlay GmbH* [2001] EWCA Civ 1030) or there is no prospect of a claimant establishing malice in reply to a qualified privilege defence (*Fox v Wokingham District Council* [2003] EWCA Civ 499). Alternatively, on a claimant's application, the Court can give judgment and grant:

(a) a declaration that the statement was false and defamatory of the plaintiff;
(b) an order that the defendant publish or cause to be published a suitable correction and apology;
(c) damages not exceeding £10,000; and/or
(d) an order restraining the defendant from publishing or further publishing the matter complained of,

if it appears there is no defence to the claim and no reason why it should be tried (s 9 of the Act), for example where the defendants have refused to take part in the proceedings and the claimant's evidence stands unchallenged (*Mahfouz v Brisard & ors* [2004] EWHC 1735 (QB)). The £10,000 damages figure may be but has not yet been revised by the Lord Chancellor.

The summary disposal procedure has been used more frequently by defendants than claimants, possibly because by adopting the procedure a claimant restricts the possible damages he can recover to a maximum of £10,000.

Nevertheless, where a defendant is in default, a claimant seeking vindication may prefer to apply under this provision than to apply for default judgment, given the availability of a declaration of falsity.

'An application for summary judgment under Part 24 may not be made' (r 53.2(3))—In addition, Pt 24 cannot be used to determine questions of fact which should, in defamation claims (SCA 1981, s 69(1)), be decided by a jury (*Safeway v Tate* [2002] EWCA Civ 335). Whether words are nor are not defamatory is a question of fact. However, if there is not a material issue of fact fit to go to a jury then there is no reason why the judge should not give summary judgment. So if the words complained of can bear no interpretation other than a defamatory meaning, then there is not a material issue for a jury to determine and the judge could, therefore, give summary judgment (*Alexander v Arts Council of Wales* [2001] EWCA Civ 514). While a claimant can obtain summary relief under the summary disposal procedure, under the summary judgment procedure he cannot obtain an order for a correction and apology but there is no limit on the damages he can be awarded if judgment is given in his favour. In those circumstances, the claimant can then proceed to have his damages assessed by a jury at a separate hearing.

In practice, defendants are increasingly using the Pt 24 procedure to strike out or dismiss defamation claims where an allegation of malice has no real prospect of success (for example, *Crossland v Wilkinson Hardware Stores Ltd* [2005] EWHC 481 (QB)). This underlines the importance of a claimant advancing only properly constructed malice pleas based on evidence.

'direct the defendant to elect' (r 53.2(4))—Section 10(2)(f) of the Act authorises the rule. However, presumably the court could not direct a defendant to make such an election if the application for summary disposal is made after service of the defence, since s 2(5) of the Act stipulates that an offer of amends cannot be made after service of the defence.

53.3 Sources of information

Unless the court orders otherwise, a party will not be required to provide further information about the identity of the defendant's sources of information.

(Part 18 provides for requests for further information)

Amendments—Inserted by SI 2000/221.

Practice Direction—See generally PD53 at p 1272.

'Part 18 provides' (r 53.3)—The court's power to order a party to provide additional information is subject to any rule of law to the contrary (r 18.1(2)). There are a number of ways in which the law protects sources of information, namely, the Data Protection Act 1998, Contempt of Court Act 1981, s 10, Art 10, ECHR and the long established common law 'newspaper rule' (whereby disclosure will not be ordered in libel actions against newspapers so as to force them to disclose their sources of information before trial). The newspaper rule is apparently still alive (see *Gaddafi v Telegraph Group (No 1)* [2000] EMLR 431 at 455–488 per Hirst LJ).

Rule 53.3 does not sit particularly comfortably with the factors identified by Lord Nicholls in *Reynolds v Times Newspapers Ltd* [2001] 2AC 127, as being important for a newspaper to establish common law qualified privilege. These include the source of a newspaper's information, the status of that information and the steps taken to verify it. How can a claimant challenge a defendant over the extent to which it satisfied these factors if he is prohibited from requiring the defendant to reveal the identity of its sources? There is at least an inbuilt discretion given to the court in this rule so that the issue can be canvassed at a hearing if appropriate.

Practice Direction – Defamation Claims

This Practice Direction supplements CPR Part 53 (PD53)

GENERAL

1 This practice direction applies to defamation claims.

STATEMENTS OF CASE

2.1 Statements of case should be confined to the information necessary to inform the other party of the nature of the case he has to meet. Such information should be set out concisely and in a manner proportionate to the subject matter of the claim.

2.2 (1) In a claim for libel the publication the subject of the claim must be identified in the claim form.
(2) In a claim for slander the claim form must so far as possible contain the words complained of, and identify the person to whom they were spoken and when.

2.3 (1) The claimant must specify in the particulars of claim the defamatory meaning which he alleges that the words or matters complained of conveyed, both
(a) as to their natural and ordinary meaning; and
(b) as to any innuendo meaning (that is a meaning alleged to be conveyed to some person by reason of knowing facts extraneous to the words complained of).
(2) In the case of an innuendo meaning, the claimant must also identify the relevant extraneous facts.

2.4 In a claim for slander the precise words used and the names of the persons to whom they were spoken and when must, so far as possible, be set out in the particulars of claim, if not already contained in the claim form.

2.5 Where a defendant alleges that the words complained of are true he must –
(1) specify the defamatory meanings he seeks to justify; and
(2) give details of the matters on which he relies in support of that allegation.

2.6 Where a defendant alleges that the words complained of are fair comment on a matter of public interest he must –
(1) specify the defamatory meaning he seeks to defend as fair comment on a matter of public interest; and
(2) give details of the matters on which he relies in support of that allegation.

2.7 Where a defendant alleges that the words complained of were published on a privileged occasion he must specify the circumstances he relies on in support of that contention.

2.8 Where a defendant alleges that the words complained of are true, or are fair comment on a matter of public interest, the claimant must serve a reply specifically admitting or denying the allegation and giving the facts on which he relies.

2.9 If the defendant contends that any of the words or matters are fair comment on a matter of public interest, or were published on a privileged occasion, and the claimant intends to allege that the defendant acted with malice, the claimant must serve a reply giving details of the facts or matters relied on.

2.10(1) A claimant must give full details of the facts and matters on which he relies in support of his claim for damages.

(2) Where a claimant seeks aggravated or exemplary damages he must provide the information specified in rule 16.4(1)(c).

2.11 A defendant who relies on an offer to make amends under section 2 of the Defamation Act 1996, as his defence must –

(1) state in his defence –

(a) that he is relying on the offer in accordance with section 4(2) of the Defamation Act 1996; and

(b) that it has not been withdrawn by him or been accepted, and

(2) attach a copy of the offer he made with his defence.

'In a claim for libel the publication' (para 2.2(1))—Publication, for the purposes of defamation, means the words complained of must have been communicated to at least one person other than the claimant. On a libel claim form, it is enough to identify the published document.

'In a claim for slander' (para 2.2(2))—The claimant is required to disclose on a court document that will be available for public inspection, the very words that have damaged him, which can then be reported with the protection of privilege – something he is unlikely to welcome. Intended or not, this provision may act as a deterrent to slander claims generally.

'the defamatory meaning' (para 2.3(1))—The meaning of the words complained of lies at the heart of every defamation claim. The importance of getting the level and extent of one's pleaded meaning right cannot be over-emphasised (see, for example, *Miller v Associated Newspapers Ltd (No 3)* [2005] EWHC 557 (QB)).

'any innuendo meaning' (para 2.3(2)(b))—Some words have technical or slang meanings which depend on some special knowledge possessed by a limited number of persons. Also, ordinary words can sometimes bear a special meaning because of some extrinsic fact or circumstance. The claimant's particulars of claim must set out the facts and matters he relies on to attribute an innuendo meaning to the words complained of. This means including a special definition of any words known only to a limited class of persons, or facts, not inherent in the libel, which enable the defamatory nature of the words complained of to be understood. The appropriate special facts and matters need to be pleaded separately in relation to each allegation to which it is contended an innuendo meaning applies (*Federal Capital Press v Edwards* [1992] 108 FLR 118 (Federal Court of Australia)). It is generally also necessary to identify those people to whom the words were published who knew the special facts and matters and so derived from the words the defamatory meaning.

'In a claim for slander the precise words used … so far as possible' (para 2.4)—It has long been required at common law that the actual words spoken be set out (*Cook v Cox* (1814) 3 M&S 110), including of course the words which carry the defamatory sting. The transitory nature of a slander means it may not always be possible to plead the exact words used. However, it is not permissible for a claimant to plead no more than the effect or gist of the words in the hope that disclosure may help him to 'cure the inadequacies of the pleading' (*Best v Charter Medical of England* [2001] EWCA Civ 1588).

'specify the defamatory meanings he seeks to justify' (para 2.5(1))—If the defendant can prove the words complained of are true, then it provides an absolute defence to a defamation claim. The defendant is entitled to contend in his defence that the words bear a different defamatory meaning than the claimant's interpretation and that this alternative meaning is true. The justification must be pleaded so as to inform the claimant and the court precisely what meaning the defendant will seek to justify (*Lucas Box v News Group Newspapers Ltd* [1986] 1 WLR 147, CA; *Viscount de l'Isle v Times Newspapers Ltd* [1987] 3 All ER 499 per Mustill LJ at 507). In *Elaine Chase v News Group Newspapers Ltd* [2002] EWCA Civ. 1772, Brooke LJ identified the three tiers of meaning, namely, grounds to investigate, grounds to suspect, and guilt.

'give details of the matters on which he relies' (para 2.5(2))—These are known as the 'particulars of justification' and will be headed as such in the defence.

'the defamatory meaning he seeks to defend as fair comment' (para 2.6(1))—As with a justification defence, a defendant must set out the meaning which he contends is capable of being defended as fair comment. It is not sufficient that the defendant merely identifies the passage which he seeks to defend as fair comment; he must formulate the defamatory meaning of the words.

'give details of the matters on which he relies in support' (para 2.6(2))—The defendant must plead particulars of all the facts on which he claims the comment is honestly based. It is also essential that the defendant identifies in his defence the matters which he contends to be of public interest since this is a fundamental element of the defence of fair comment (see *Henry Fook v John Lee* [1976] 1 Malayan LJ 231, FC).

'were published on a privileged occasion' (para 2.7)—The defendant must plead the facts and circumstances which allow him the protection of privilege. These may include his duty to publish and the corresponding interest on the part of the recipients of the publication to receive the words complained of, or that the publication was a legitimate response to a previous attack by the claimant (see *Vassiliev v Frank Cass & Co Ltd* [2003] EWCH 1428 (QB)). In the leading case of *Reynolds v Times Newspapers Ltd* [2001] 2 AC 127, Lord Nicholls set out a non-exhaustive list of factors which the court would need to consider to determine whether a defendant could successfully argue qualified privilege. These factors can be collectively categorised as a requirement of responsible journalism, including such matters as the seriousness of the allegation, the source of the information, the steps taken to verify the story, the urgency of the matter, and whether the claimant's comment on the allegations was sought and then incorporated in the publication. Although not confined to claims against media defendants, in practice the factors have most application and relevance to them.

'Where a defendant alleges that the words are true or fair comment ... the claimant must serve a reply' (para 2.8)—This requirement prevents a claimant choosing not to plead to particulars of justification, leaving everything in issue and consequent uncertainty about the true nature of his case. However, this does not change the burden of proving the allegations, which falls on the defendant (*Morrell v International Thompson Publishing Ltd* (1990) (unreported) 18 July, CA).

'If the claimant intends to allege ... malice, the claimant must serve a reply' (para 2.9)—Malice will only appear as a plea in the particulars of claim where the claimant relies on it as aggravating the damage caused. Otherwise, the facts and particulars which give rise to an inference of malice will appear in a claimant's reply to a fair comment or qualified privilege defence.

In fair comment cases, a defendant will only be found to be acting with malice where 'he does not genuinely hold the view he expressed. In other words, when making the defamatory comment the defendant acted dishonestly' (*Tse Wai Chun Paul v Cheng* [2001] EMLR 777).

To defeat qualified privilege by proof of malice, a claimant needs to show the defendant did not believe the words were true, or did not care whether they were true or false, or had a dominant improper motive for their publication (*Horrocks v Lowe* [1975] AC 135, HL)

'where a claimant seeks aggravated or exemplary damages' (para 2.10(2))—The law presumes damage in libel (see *Ratcliffe v Evans* [1892] 2 QB 524). However, if a claimant claims to have suffered injury beyond the normal presumed damage, then the supporting facts and matters must be pleaded, including any conduct by the defendant said to have increased the claimant's suffering and any loss peculiar to his particular circumstances. Alleged financial loss must be specifically pleaded. A claim for damages for personal injury may be included (*Suttin v Nationwide News Pty* (1996) 39 NSWLR 32) – although experience shows that such a claim has little prospect of success.

'offer to make amends' (para 2.11)—Under s 4(3) of the Act, an offer of amends cannot stand as a defence if the defendant knew, or had reason to believe, that the words complained of as a defamatory allegation:

(a) referred to the claimant, or was likely to be understood as referring to him; and
(b) was both false and defamatory of him.

The proper interpretation of s 4(3) is that the journalist has to have been malicious at the time of publication (in the sense of being recklessly indifferent to the truth) (*Milne v Express Newspapers* [2004] EWCA Civ 664). It is most unlikely the claimant will be able to prove the circumstances in which a defamatory article came to be published in a way which persuades a court that the newspaper or journalist fulfils the criteria for malice. Thus it may be virtually impossible for a claimant to reject an offer of amends from a media defendant.

COURT'S POWERS IN CONNECTION WITH AN OFFER OF AMENDS

3.1 Sections 2 to 4 of the Defamation Act 1996 make provision for a person who has made a statement which is alleged to be defamatory to make an offer to make amends. Section 3 provides for the court to assist in the process of making amends.

3.2 A claim under section 3 of the Defamation Act 1996 made other than in existing proceedings may be made under CPR Part 8 –

- (1) where the parties agree on the steps to make amends, and the sole purpose of the claim is for the court to make an order under section 3(3) for an order that the offer be fulfilled; or
- (2) where the parties do not agree –
  - (a) on the steps to be taken by way of correction, apology and publication (see section 3(4));
  - (b) on the amount to be paid by way of compensation (see section 3(5)); or
  - (c) on the amount to be paid by way of costs (see section 3(6)).

(Applications in existing proceedings made under section 3 of the Defamation Act 1996 must be made in accordance with CPR Part 23)

3.3 (1) A claim or application under section 3 of the Defamation Act 1996 must be supported by written evidence.

- (2) The evidence referred to in paragraph (1) must include –
  - (a) a copy of the offer of amends;
  - (b) details of the steps taken to fulfil the offer of amends;
  - (c) a copy of the text of any correction and apology;
  - (d) details of the publication of the correction and apology;
  - (e) a statement of the amount of any sum paid as compensation;
  - (f) a statement of the amount of any sum paid for costs;
  - (g) why the offer is unsatisfactory.
- (3) Where any step specified in section 2(4) of the Defamation Act 1996 has not been taken, then the evidence referred to in paragraph (2)(c) to (f) must state what steps are proposed by the party to fulfil the offer of amends and the date or dates on which each step will be fulfilled and, if none, that no proposal has been made to take that step.

'an offer to make amends' (para 3.1)—The offer must be in writing and expressed to be made under s 2 of the Act. It should also state whether or not it is a qualified offer, in other words, whether it is limited to a specific defamatory meaning which the defendant accepts the words complained of bear, or whether it applies to the whole of the claim. It will be taken to include an offer to make a suitable correction of the statement complained of and a sufficient apology and to publish the correction and apology in a reasonable and practicable manner and to pay such compensation and costs as it is agreed or determined be payable (s 2(4)).

'A claim or application under s 3 of the Defamation Act 1996' (para 3.3)—Section 3 of the Act governs what happens if an offer of amends is accepted. The claim is stayed or, if proceedings have not yet commenced, the claimant cannot then start court action. If the parties can agree the essential terms under s 2(4), then the claimant can apply to the court to require the defendant to comply with the terms (s 3(3)). Alternatively, the defendant can make its correction and apology by way of statement in open court in terms approved by the court and give an undertaking as to the manner of publication.

If the parties cannot agree the terms, then the onus is on the defendant so far as the correction and apology is concerned. If a wholly unsuitable correction and inadequate apology are produced and published, then this does not invalidate the offer of amends procedure; it just means the court will take this into account when assessing compensation on the claimant's ensuing application.

The court will determine the quantum of damages on the same principles as in defamation proceedings (s 3(5) and see *Abu v MGN Ltd* [2002] EWHC 2345 (QB)). The determination is before a judge alone. The making of an offer of amends will usually result in a substantial discount on the damages figure, but each case turns on its own facts (see *Nail v News Group Newspapers Ltd & ors* [2004] EWCA Civ 1708). There is no lower scale of compensation in offer of amends cases. Guidance on the need for parties to conduct informal discussions to avoid applications to court is found in *Cleese v Clark* [2003] EWHC 137 (QB) which also suggests that a judge should not be told about the damages figures which the parties may have exchanged in without prejudice correspondence.

If the offer is not accepted then an unqualified offer of amends stands as a defence to the claim and a qualified offer provides a partial defence (s 4). A defendant whose offer has been rejected and who then chooses to plead a different defence cannot then rely on his offer of amends as a defence. See also note **'offer to make amends'** under para 2 as to the circumstances in which under s 4(3) an offer of amends cannot stand as a defence.

RULING ON MEANING

4.1 At any time the court may decide –

(1) whether a statement complained of is capable of having any meaning attributed to it in a statement of case;
(2) whether the statement is capable of being defamatory of the claimant;
(3) whether the statement is capable of bearing any other meaning defamatory of the claimant.

4.2 An application for a ruling on meaning may be made at any time after the service of particulars of claim. Such an application should be made promptly.

(This provision disapplies for these applications the usual time restriction on making applications in rule 24.4.1)

4.3 Where an application is made for a ruling on meaning, the application notice must state that it is an application for a ruling on meaning made in accordance with this practice direction.

4.4 The application notice or the evidence contained or referred to in it, or served with it, must identify precisely the statement, and the meaning attributed to it, that the court is being asked to consider.

(Rule 3.3 applies where the court exercises its powers of its own initiative)

(Following a ruling on meaning the court may exercise its power under rule 3.4)

(Section 7 of the Defamation Act 1996 applies to rulings on meaning)

'At any time the court may decide' (para 4.1)—This jurisdiction enables the court to fix in advance the ground rules on permissible meanings which are of such cardinal importance in defamation claims, not only for the purpose of assessing the degree of injury to the claimant's reputation but also for the purpose of evaluating any defences raised, in particular, justification or fair comment (*Mapp v News Group Newspapers Ltd* [1998] QB 520, CA, at 526).

'whether a statement … is capable of' (paras 4.1(1)–(3))—The question of whether the words complained of are capable of bearing a particular meaning is a matter of law determined by the judge. The jury, at trial, determines whether the words actually bear that meaning. When called upon to determine the range of meanings words are capable of bearing and to rule out meanings outside that range, the judge conducts 'an exercise in generosity not parsimony' (per Sedley LJ, *Berezovsky v Forbes* [2001] EWCA Civ 1251). The principles guiding the judge when conducting this exercise are based on 'the natural and ordinary meaning … conveyed to the ordinary reasonable reader reading the article once' (*Gillick v Brook Advisory Centres* [1996] EMLR 267; see also *Skuse v Granada* [1996] EMLR 139).

'An application for a ruling on meaning' (para 4.2)—Either the claimant or the defendant can make an application so, for example, a claimant can apply for a determination regarding a defendant's Lucas-Box meaning in its defence (see 'specify the defamatory meanings he seeks to justify' under para 2). It should, however, be made as soon as possible after the service of the relevant statement of case. Such an application will invariably be released by the master in the case to the judge in charge of the jury list at the request of the parties because it requires a substantive ruling which will bind the parties.

SUMMARY DISPOSAL

5.1 Where an application is made for summary disposal, the application notice must state –

(1) that it is an application for summary disposal made in accordance with section 8 of the Defamation Act 1996.
(2) the matters set out in paragraph 2(3) of the practice direction to Part 24; and
(3) whether or not the defendant has made an offer to make amends under section 2 of the Act and whether or not it has been withdrawn.

5.2 An application for summary disposal may be made at any time after the service of particulars of claim.

(This provision disapplies for these applications the usual time restriction on making applications in rule 24.4.1)

5.3 (1) This paragraph applies where –
(a) the court has ordered the defendant in defamation proceedings to agree and publish a correction and apology as summary relief under section 8(2) of the Defamation Act 1996; and
(b) the parties are unable to agree its content within the time specified in the order.

(2) Where the court grants this type of summary relief under the Act, the order will specify the date by which the parties should reach agreement about the content, time, manner, form and place of publication of the correction and apology.
(3) Where the parties cannot agree the content of the correction and apology by the date specified in the order, then the claimant must prepare a summary of the judgment given by the court and serve it on all the other parties within 3 days following the date specified in the order.
(4) Where the parties cannot agree the summary of the judgment prepared by the claimant they must within 3 days of receiving the summary –
(a) file with the court and serve on all the other parties a copy of the summary showing the revisions they wish to make to it; and
(b) apply to the court for the court to settle the summary.
(5) The court will then itself settle the summary and the judge who delivered the judgment being summarised will normally do this.

'Where an application is made for summary disposal' (para 5.1)—See 'proceedings for summary disposal' under r 53.2. Section 8(4) of the Act sets out the matters the court should have regard to in considering whether a claim should be tried and disposed of summarily.

At one end of the time spectrum, a claimant could make an application for summary disposal even before an acknowledgment of service has been filed (provided the particulars of claim have been served). At the other end, there has been an example of summary disposal even after judgment on liability has been given (*Loutchansky v Times Newspapers Ltd (Nos 2–5)* [2002] QB 783).

Since the summary relief available under s 9 of the Act includes an order for a suitable correction and apology and an order restraining a defendant from further publication, the application should be heard by a judge since a master does not have jurisdiction to grant this relief.

'where … the court has ordered … and … the parties are unable to agree' (para 5.3)—This sets out the mechanism for enforcement of an order for the publication of a correction and apology as part of summary relief under s 9. Logically, the powers under this section must also extend to publication of a summary of the judgment either agreed or settled by the court.

STATEMENTS IN OPEN COURT

6.1 This paragraph only applies where a party wishes to accept a Part 36 offer, Part 36 payment or other offer of settlement in relation to a claim for –

(1) libel;
(2) slander.

6.2 A party may apply for permission to make a statement in open court before or after he accepts the Part 36 offer or the Part 36 payment in accordance with rule 36.8(5) or other offer to settle the claim.

6.3 The statement that the applicant wishes to make must be submitted for the approval of the court and must accompany the notice of application.

6.4 The court may postpone the time for making the statement if other claims relating to the subject matter of the statement are still proceeding.

(Applications must be made in accordance with Part 23)

'permission to make a statement in open court' (para 6.2)—A statement in court is an important device whereby a claimant can obtain a measure of vindication of his reputation. A statement read in court can be reported freely by the media since it is a court proceeding and consequently a fair and accurate report of it will attract privilege.

The paragraph applies only to statements which follow acceptance of a Pt 36 offer or payment or as a term of some other settlement arrangement. It is unclear whether a defendant wishing to make a statement in court where an offer of amends has been accepted would apply for permission and approval under this paragraph or under the offer of amends procedure

An agreed statement in court in which the defendant participates is an extremely common term of settlements in defamation actions. Less satisfactory, so far as a claimant is concerned, is a unilateral statement, which he is entitled to make if he accepts a Pt 36 offer or payment. Whether the application is for a unilateral statement or a joint statement, it is for permission to make a statement in terms approved by the court. The judge: 'must first decide whether it was appropriate to permit a statement to be made, and if so, whether the statement should be made in the terms proposed. When the parties are agreed about the terms of the statement, the judge will not readily interfere with what they have agreed, but he nevertheless remains entitled, and if he thinks appropriate, obliged to require the proposed statement to be amended, or to refuse to approve it.' (*Williamson v The Commissioner of the Metropolitan Police* (1997) (unreported) 23 July, CA, per Judge LJ).

If the claimant applies to make a unilateral statement, the defendant has the right to be heard and to object to the wording of the statement. However, only in exceptional circumstances would the court refuse permission for the making of a reasonable and proportionate statement (see *Phillips v Associated Newspapers Ltd* [2004] EWHC 190). In deciding what a reasonable and proportionate statement is, the court is likely to be principally influenced by the sum of damages which the claimant has accepted. The costs of an application to make a unilateral statement and of the reading of the statement itself will generally fall to be paid by the defendant as part of the costs of the claim.

TRANSITIONAL PROVISION RELATING TO SECTION 4 OF THE DEFAMATION ACT 1952

7 Paragraph 3 of this practice direction applies, with any necessary modifications to an application to the court to determine any question as to the steps to be taken to fulfil an offer made under section 4 of the Defamation Act 1952.

(Section 4 of the Defamation Act 1952 is repealed by the Defamation Act 1996. The commencement order bringing in the repeal makes transitional provision for offers which have been made at the date the repeal came into force)

PART 54
JUDICIAL REVIEW AND STATUTORY REVIEW

CONTENTS OF THIS PART

Practice Direction—See generally PD54 at p 1300.

Procedural Guide—See Guide 60, set out in Section 1 of this work.

General note—Claims for judicial review are governed by Pt 54, which replaced RSC Ord 53 with effect from 2 October 2000 (Civil Procedure (Amendment No 4) Rules, SI 2000/2092, rr 1, 22, 23). Where the application for permission to apply for judicial review was filed before 2 October 2000, RSC Ord 53 and not Pt 54 applies (SI 2000/2092, r 30).

Section I – Judicial Review

54.1 Scope and interpretation

(1) This Section of this Part contains rules about judicial review.

(2) In this Section –

(a) a 'claim for judicial review' means a claim to review the lawfulness of –

(i) an enactment; or

(ii) a decision, action or failure to act in relation to the exercise of a public function.

(b)–(d)

(e) 'the judicial review procedure' means the Part 8 procedure as modified by this Section;

(f) 'interested party' means any person (other than the claimant and defendant) who is directly affected by the claim; and

(g) 'court' means the High Court, unless otherwise stated.

(Rule 8.1(6)(b) provides that a rule or practice direction may, in relation to a specified type of proceedings, disapply or modify any of these rules set out in Part 8 as they apply to those proceedings)

Amendments—Inserted by SI 2000/2092; amended by SI 2003/364; SI 2003/3361.

'claim for judicial review' (r 54.1(2)(a))—This rule gives a definition of a claim for judicial review. This definition is based on what is to be reviewed. By contrast, SCA, s 31(1) defines an application for judicial review by reference to the remedy sought.

Traditionally, judicial review has been concerned with the decision making process rather than with the merits of decisions made by public bodies (*Chief Constable of North Wales v Evans* [1982] 1 WLR 1155, 1160d–1161b, 1173f). On an application for judicial review the court considers whether the public body has acted lawfully (in the sense of directing itself properly on the law), fairly and reasonably (*Council of Civil Service Unions v Minister for the Civil Service* [[1985] AC 374, 410c–411c; *Associated Provincial Picture Houses v Wednesbury Corporation* [1948] 1 KB 233, 229, CA). The more substantial the interference with human rights, the more the courts have required by way of justification before being satisfied that the decision is reasonable (*R v Ministry of Defence ex parte Smith* [1996] QB 517, 554, 563–565, CA).

The coming into force of HRA 1998 on 2 October 2000 has had an important impact on the courts' approach to judicial review, the full consequences of which have yet to be established, but the distinction between review and appeal remains. The courts are mindful not to usurp discretions which have been given to the democratically accountable executive. But the principle of proportionality will in many cases require the court to undertake a closer scrutiny of the facts than was the case under the *Wednesbury* approach. Context, however, is everything (see *R (Daly) v Home Secretary* [2001] 2 AC 532; *Brown v Stott* [2001] 2 WLR 817, PC; *R v Director of Public Prosecutions ex parte Kebilene* [2000] 2 AC 326, 380–381; *Matadeen v Pointu* [1999] 1 AC 98, 116c–d, PC). Similarly, it has been held that in practice there is no a great difference between proportionality in European Community law and *Wednesbury* unreasonableness (*R v Chief Constable of Sussex ex parte International Trader's Ferry Ltd* [1999] 2 AC 415, 439).

In certain cases, a statute confers powers on a public body only if certain facts exist. If an application for judicial review is brought in such a case, the court itself determines whether those facts exist (*R v Home Secretary ex parte Khawaja* [1984] AC 74).

A claim to review the lawfulness of an enactment may be made on two grounds. First, that the enactment contravenes directly applicable European Community law (*R v Secretary of State for Transport ex parte Factortame* [1991] 1 AC 603, ECJ and HL). Secondly, that the enactment is incompatible with one or more of the provisions of the European Convention for the Protection of Human Rights and Fundamental Freedoms (Rome, 4 November 1950; Cmnd 8969) which are in HRA 1998, Sch 1 (see s 4 of that Act). The lawfulness of an enactment, including a private Act, cannot be reviewed on other grounds (*British Railways Board v Pickin* [1974] AC 765).

A Pt 54 claim may also be made to review the lawfulness of a decision, action or failure to act in relation to the exercise of a public function. 'Public function' is a new phrase. The following discussion is based on the case law under RSC Ord 53. It remains to be seen whether the scope of judicial review will be altered significantly by the wording of r 54.1(2)(a). In claims under the HRA

1998 the courts have tended to identify a public authority with a body subject to judicial review (eg *Poplar Housing and Regeneration Community Association Ltd v Donoghue* [2001] EWCA Civ 595, [2001] 3 WLR 183, CA).

Bodies subject to judicial review—Traditionally these were bodies created by statute or the prerogative. But in *R v Panel on Takeovers and Mergers ex parte Datafin* [1987] QB 815 the Court of Appeal entertained a judicial review of a self-regulatory organisation, holding that judicial review could be available where there was 'public element' or the exercise of public law functions or duties (pp 838e–f, 847c, 852c–d). Similarly, a private psychiatric hospital registered under the Registered Homes Act 1984, and consequently under statutory duties as to standards of care relating to persons detained under Mental Health Act 1983, s 3, was held by the Administrative Court to be a 'functional public authority' for the purposes of the 1998 Act, and the decisions of its managers were amenable to judicial review (*R (A) v Partnerships in Care Ltd* [2002] EWHC 529 (Admin), [2002] 1 WLR 2610). By contrast, bodies whose power is derived solely from a contractual submission to their jurisdiction have been held not to be subject to judicial review (*R v Disciplinary Committee of the Jockey Club ex parte Aga Khan* [1993] 1 WLR 909, CA).

Decisions of the Supreme Court are not subject to judicial review (SCA, s 1), but decisions of the Crown Court 'other than its jurisdiction in matters relating to trial on indictment' are amenable to judicial review (SCA, s 29(3)). This phrase has generated a wealth of case law, which is analysed in *R v Crown Court at Maidstone ex parte Harrow London Borough Council* [2000] QB 719, DC. Decisions of inferior courts and tribunals are amenable to judicial review, but a claimant may have an alternative remedy by way of appeal, in which case he should pursue this rather than seek judicial review (see note **'Alternative remedies'** below).

Decisions subject to judicial review—Not every decision of a public body is amenable to judicial review. Public bodies may have private law obligations which need to be enforced in private law proceedings. Where a claimant wishes to challenge the exercise of a public power (as opposed to its consequences, such as damage to the applicant's property), judicial review is likely to be the appropriate procedure (*O'Rourke v Camden London Borough Council* [1998] AC 188).

Delegated legislation may be challenged in a claim for judicial review (eg *R v Secretary of State for Social Security ex parte Joint Council for the Welfare of Immigrants* [1997] 1 WLR 275, CA; *R v Lord Chancellor ex parte Witham* [1998] QB 575, DC).

Decisions which are advisory, rather than determinative, may be subject to judicial review. It depends on whether the court considers the advice sufficiently authoritative to justify judicial supervision (*Gillick v West Norfolk and Wisbech Area Health Authority* [1986] AC 112).

If a public body creates a legitimate expectation that it will act in a particular way, a subsequent act which defeats that legitimate expectation my be amenable to judicial review. A legitimate expectation is now generally regarded as more than merely an aspect of the duty to act fairly and reasonably. It can be based on the principle of abuse of power and may create substantive rights (*Council of Civil Service Unions v Minister for the Civil Service* [1985] AC 374, 408e–409b; *In re Preston* [1985] AC 835; *R v Home Secretary ex parte Ruddock* [1987] 1 WLR 1482; *R v Inland Revenue Commissioners ex parte Matrix-Securities Ltd* [1994] 1 WLR 334, HL; *R v Home Secretary ex parte Hargreaves* [1997] 1 WLR 906, CA; *R v North East Devon Health Authority ex parte Coughlan* [2001] QB 213, CA).

An exercise of the Royal Prerogative is amenable to judicial review if the subject matter of the decision is of a nature which the courts are qualified to adjudicate upon, for example the refusal to issue a passport is reviewable but the conduct of foreign relations is not (*Council of Civil Service Unions v Minister for the Civil Service* [1985] AC 374; *R v Secretary of State for Foreign and Commonwealth Affairs ex parte Everett* [1989] QB 811, CA; *R v Home Secretary ex parte Bentley* [1994] QB 349, DC).

Overlap between judicial review and private law actions—In *O'Reilly v Mackman* [1983] 2 AC 237 the House of Lords held that it was generally an abuse of the process of the court for a claimant complaining of an infringement of public law rights to seek redress in a private law action, as this would circumvent the safeguards which Ord 53 provided to public bodies, particularly the time limit for bringing proceedings. More recent cases have acknowledged that an action may contain elements of both public and private law, and have held that, where this is so, a claimant should generally be able to choose which procedure to adopt (*Roy v Kensington and Chelsea and Westminster Family Practitioner Committee* [1992] 1 AC 624; *Mercury Communications Ltd v Director General of Telecommunications* [1996] 1 WLR 48, HL; *Clark v University of Lincolnshire* [2000] 1 WLR 1988, [2000] 3 All ER 752, CA).

A defendant in a private law action is entitled to raise a public law defence in that action if the point could have been raised in an application for judicial review (*Boddington v British Transport Police* [1999] 2 AC 143).

Alternative remedies—Judicial review is a discretionary remedy and a person complaining of an infringement of a public law right should generally pursue an alternative remedy if one is available, otherwise the court is likely to exercise its discretion against entertaining the application for judicial review (*R v Home Secretary ex parte Swati* [1986] 1 WLR 477, CA; *R v Birmingham City Council ex parte Ferrero Ltd* [1993] 1 ALL ER 530, CA; *R v Home Secretary ex parte Capti-Mehmet* [1997] COD 61). In an exceptional case it may be appropriate to proceed with a judicial review without pursuing the alternative remedy (*R v Chief Constable of Merseyside ex parte Calveley* [1986] QB 424, CA). But in some cases, statute may indicate that the statutory appeal is the only procedure available (*R v Wicks* [1998] AC 92). This approach is followed in the Pre-Action Protocol for Judicial Review, paras 3–4.

'is called' (r 54.1(2)(b), (c), (d))—The Latin terms *mandamus*, *prohibition* and *certiorari* survive in SCA, s 31(1). But they have been renamed in the CPR. The new names are helpfully self-explanatory. Further provision in respect of quashing orders is made by r 54.19.

'the judicial review procedure' (r 54.1(2)(e))—Judicial review has been assimilated in part with private law claims, but substantial differences remain. Perhaps the most important are the short time limits for judicial review and the need for permission to bring a Pt 54 claim. Other important differences are:

- the discretionary nature of the remedy;
- the general absence of disclosure and oral evidence;
- the limited circumstances in which damages may be awarded; and
- the use of special claim and acknowledgment of service forms.

'directly affected' (r 54.1(2)(f))—For the purposes of judicial review, this is interpreted narrowly to mean persons who will be directly affected by the decision of the court itself. It does not cover those who will be affected only by the consequences of the court's decision, however grave and however likely those consequences may be (*R v Rent Officer Service ex parte Muldoon* [1996] 1 WLR 1103, HL). Paragraph 5.2 of PD54 gives as an example of an interested person the prosecution in a claim by a defendant for judicial review of a decision of a magistrates' court. Persons not directly affected may seek the permission of the court to file evidence and/or make representations (r 54.17).

'the High Court' (r 54.1(2)(g))—Claims for judicial review must be heard in the High Court (SCA, ss 29–31; CLSA 1990, s 1(10); CCA 1984, s 38(3)). The only exception is where the Court of Appeal grants permission to apply for judicial review and, exceptionally, decides to hear the substantive application itself (r 52.15(4)).

Claims for judicial review should be commenced in the Administrative Court, Royal Courts of Justice, London. Where the claim raises a devolution issue under the Government of Wales Act 1998, or involves a Welsh public body, the proceedings may be commenced in the Administrative Court at the Law Courts, Cathays Park, Cardiff, CF10 3PG. If, in an urgent case, it is thought necessary to issue proceedings outside these venues, the Administrative Court Office should be consulted first (RCJ Room C315, Tel: 020 7947 6653).

Protective costs orders—In *R (Corner House Research) v Secretary of State for Trade and Industry* [2005] EWCA Civ 192, the Court of Appeal gave detailed guidance on the circumstances in which such orders are likely to be made. In that case, such an order was made in favour of the claimant, though it was said that the claimant should expect a cost capping order in all such cases, which would restrict it to solicitors' fees and a modest fee for one junior counsel. The recipient of a protective costs order could not expect the order to permit anything more than modest representation. By contrast, and largely because the claimant there had a claim for damages and hence a financial interest in the outcome, such an order was refused in *R (Weir & ors) v Secretary of State for Transport* (2005) (unreported) 21 April, Lindsay J.

54.2 When this Section must be used

The judicial review procedure must be used in a claim for judicial review where the claimant is seeking –

(a) a mandatory order;
(b) a prohibiting order;
(c) a quashing order; or
(d) an injunction under section 30 of the Supreme Court Act 1981 (restraining a person from acting in any office in which he is not entitled to act).

Amendments—Inserted by SI 2000/2092; amended by SI 2003/364.

'must be used' (r 54.2)—Mandatory, prohibiting and quashing orders may be made only in a claim for judicial review (SCA, s 31(1)).

'section 30' (r 54.2(d))—An application under SCA, s 30 is the successor to the obsolete writ of quo warranto. The section applies to substantive offices of a public nature and permanent character which are held under the Crown or which have been created by statutory provision or Royal Charter (SCA, s 30(2)).

54.3 When this Section may be used

(1) The judicial review procedure may be used in a claim for judicial review where the claimant is seeking –

(a) a declaration; or
(b) an injunction(GL).

(Section 31(2) of the Supreme Court Act 1981 sets out the circumstances in which the court may grant a declaration or injunction in a claim for judicial review)

(Where the claimant is seeking a declaration or injunction in addition to one of the remedies listed in rule 54.2, the judicial review procedure must be used)

(2) A claim for judicial review may include a claim for damages, restitution or the recovery of a sum due but may not seek such a remedy alone.

(Section 31(4) of the Supreme Court Act 1981 sets out the circumstances in which the court may award damages, restitution or the recovery of a sum due on a claim for judicial review)

Amendments—Inserted by SI 2000/2092; amended by SI 2003/364; SI 2003/3361.

'may be used' (r 54.3(1))—A declaration may be made or an injunction granted in a claim for judicial review where it would be just and convenient to do so, having regard to the nature of the matters in respect of which relief may be granted by mandatory, prohibiting or quashing orders, the nature of the persons and bodies against whom relief may be granted by such orders and all the circumstances of the case (SCA, s 31(2)).

The court cannot grant an injunction against the Crown (Crown Proceedings Act 1947, s 21). But in practice this causes no problems, as an injunction may be granted against a named minister (*M v Home Office* [1994] AC 377). Alternatively, the court could make a declaration. It is now possible to obtain an interim declaration (r 25.1(1)(b)).

'a claim for damages' (r 54.3(2))—A claim for judicial review may include such a claim if:
(a) this is not the sole relief claimed; and
(b) the court is satisfied that, if the claim had been made in a private law action, the claimant would have been awarded damages.

With two exceptions, conduct which is unlawful as a matter of public law does not as such give rise to an action for damages (*Bourgoin v Ministry of Agriculture, Fisheries and Food* [1986] QB 716, CA). The first exception is the wrongful failure to implement European Community legislation (*Francovich v Italian Republic* [1991] ECR I–5357, [1995] ICR 722, ECJ). 'Wrongful' in this context means that:
(i) the provision of Community law was intended to confer rights on individuals;
(ii) the breach was sufficiently serious, ie amounted to a manifest and grave disregard of the limits on the Member State's discretion; and
(iii) there is a direct causal link between the breach and the damage sustained (*Brasserie du Pêcheur v Federal Republic of Germany* [1996] ECR I–1029, [1996] QB 404, ECJ; *R v Secretary of State for Transport ex parte Factortame (No 5)* [2000] 1 AC 524).

The second exception is that damages may be awarded in respect of acts of public authorities which are contrary to the rights set out in HRA 1998, Sch 1 (ss 6–8 of the Act). Damages may not be awarded under the 1998 Act in respect of a judicial act done in good faith, otherwise than to compensate a person to the extent required by art 5(5) of the Convention (s 9(3) of the Act).

Conduct which is a breach of a public law duty may also amount to breach of a private law duty, in which case damages could be awarded on an application for judicial review. The most common of such causes of action are false imprisonment and misfeasance in public office. A public officer is guilty of misfeasance if he acts in bad faith, either intending to injure the claimant or in the knowledge of, or with reckless indifference to, the illegality of his act and in the knowledge of, or with reckless indifference to, the probability of causing injury to the claimant or persons of a class of which the claimant was a member (*Three Rivers District Council v Bank of England (No 3)* [2000] 2 WLR 1220, HL).

If there is no live public law issue, it is inappropriate to bring a claim for damages by means of an application for judicial review (*R v Home Secretary ex parte Vafi* [1996] IAR 169, CA; cf *R v Northavon District Council ex parte Palmer* [1994] Admin LR 195).

54.4 Permission required

The court's permission to proceed is required in a claim for judicial review whether started under this Section or transferred to the Administrative Court.

Amendments—Inserted by SI 2000/2092; amended by SI 2003/364.

Threshold—The court will not grant permission unless the applicant has an arguable case on the legal merits (*R v Inland Revenue Commissioners ex parte National Federation of Self-Employed and Small Businesses Ltd* [1982] AC 617). There is inevitably an element of subjectivity in deciding whether an application is arguable. Some cases can very quickly be seen to be good or bad. Others, particularly where the factual or legal framework is complex or where not all the material facts are before the court, take more time. If there is extended argument on an application for permission, the court may adopt a higher threshold for the grant of permission (*Mass Energy Ltd v Birmingham City Council* [1994] Env LR 298, CA). In an urgent but complex case the parties may ask the court and the court may agree to treat the permission application as the substantive hearing.

Standing—Under RSC Ord 53 only a person with 'sufficient interest' could bring an application for judicial review (RSC Ord 53, r 3(7)). The court looked at all the circumstances, including the importance of decision under challenge and the legal strength of that challenge, when deciding whether an applicant had sufficient interest (*R v Inland Revenue Commissioners ex parte National Federation of Self-Employed and Small Businesses Ltd* [1982] AC 617; *R v HM Treasury ex parte Smedley* [1985] QB 657, CA). Sometimes the question of standing was considered on the application for permission, sometimes at the substantive hearing. In recent years the courts have adopted a more generous approach to challenges brought by campaigners in the public interest (*R v Secretary of State for Foreign and Commonwealth Affairs ex parte World Development Movement* [1995] 1 WLR 386, DC; *R v Somerset County Council et al ex parte Dixon* [1998] Env LR 111). However, a public interest claimant will be unlikely to obtain a pre-emptive order that he will not be liable for costs if his claim fails (*R v Lord Chancellor ex parte Child Poverty Action Group* [1998] 2 All ER 755).

Part 54 and its practice direction do not mention standing. It is unclear how far, if at all, the old rules on standing will apply to the new procedure. Insofar as a claim is made under HRA 1998, the claimant must be a 'victim' (HRA 1998, s 7(1)). Section 7(2) of that Act, which was enacted while RSC Ord 53 was in force, provides that only victims have sufficient interest to apply for judicial review in reliance on a Convention right. It is possible that the concept of sufficient interest will be applied to Pt 54 by deploying r 1.1.

The court will generally consider the application for permission on the papers in the first instance (PD54, para 8.4).

Wasted costs—There are conflicting decisions on whether it is (*R v Immigration Appeal Tribunal ex parte Gulsen* [1997] COD 430) or is not (*R v Camden London Borough Council ex parte Martin* [1997] 1 WLR 359) possible for a putative defendant to obtain a wasted costs order where permission to apply for judicial review is refused.

54.5 Time limit for filing claim form

(1) The claim form must be filed –

(a) promptly; and

(b) in any event not later than 3 months after the grounds to make the claim first arose.

(2) The time limit in this rule may not be extended by agreement between the parties.

(3) This rule does not apply when any other enactment specifies a shorter time limit for making the claim for judicial review.

Amendments—Inserted by SI 2000/2092.

Time limits—Permission or relief may be refused if the court considers that there has been undue delay in making the application (SCA, s 31(6)). This needs to be read in the light of the more specific words of this rule. And the time limit stated in r 54.5(1) is not 3 months, subject to extension for good reason. It is 'promptly and in any event not later than' 3 months after the grounds to make the claim first arose.

A claimant who waits for more than 3 months before filing his Form 86A is automatically guilty of undue delay. However, time may be extended if the claimant shows good reason for his delay (*R v Dairy Produce Quota Tribunal for England and Wales ex parte Caswell* [1989] 1 WLR 1089, HL; *R v Stratford-on-Avon District Council ex parte Jackson* [1985] 1 WLR 1319, CA). But undue delay may occur well within the 3 month period (*R v Independent Television Commission ex parte TV NI* (1991) *The Times*, 30 December, CA).

What constitutes acting promptly, or good reason for extending time, depends on all the circumstances of the case, including the nature of the decision which it is sought to challenge and the conduct of the claimant. The relevance of matters such as legal aid delays and the incompetence of legal advisers varies in the cases, and it is not possible to state any general principles. Moreover, the House of Lords expressed doubt in *R (Burkett) v Hammersmith and Fulham London Borough Council & anor* [2002] UKHL 23 that the requirement to act 'promptly' is 'sufficiently certain to comply with European Community law and the Convention for the Protection of Human Rights and Fundamental Freedoms'.

Time was said to run from the date when grounds for the application first arose. In ascertaining this time, the court will look at the substance, rather than the form, of what is being challenged (*R v Secretary of State for Trade and Industry ex parte Greenpeace* [1998] Env LR 415). That approach, however, was rejected as being too uncertain by the House of Lords in *R (Burkett) v Hammersmith and Fulham London Borough Council & anor* [2002] UKHL 23, and *Greenpeace* itself was overruled. What matters is the decision which is challenged, and the mere fact that an earlier step (there a resolution by a planning authority) could have been challenged, but was not, does not deprive the applicant of the right to challenge the later, binding decision (there, the actual grant of planning permission).

Where the claim is for a quashing order in respect of a judgment, order or conviction, the date when the grounds to make the claim first arose is the date of that judgment, order or conviction (PD54, para 4.1).

The Pre-Action Protocol for Judicial Review requires a prospective claimant to write a detailed letter before claim, allowing 14 days for a response, unless this would be impractical on the facts of the particular case. The protocol also requires a detailed letter of response from the prospective defendant. The protocol makes it clear that this correspondence does not affect the time limits for issuing proceedings for judicial review. Under RSC Ord 53 failure to write a letter before claim could result in a wasted costs order being made against the applicant (*R v Horsham District Council ex parte Wenman* [1995] 1 WLR 680). The protocol confirms this (see Judicial Review Protocol, paras 8–17). Similarly, when a claimant discontinued in circumstances where the defendant had not followed the Protocol, the liability to pay the defendant's costs was reduced in consequence (*Aegis Group v Inland Revenue*, sub nom *Re Aegis* [2005] All ER (D) 209 (May), Park J)

Effect of delay on defendant—Delay is a ground for refusing permission (SCA, s 31(6)(a)). It is also a ground for refusing relief at the substantive hearing (SCA, s 31(6)(b)). A claimant who is guilty of undue delay and who cannot show good reason for extending time will be refused permission to apply for judicial review. At this stage, the fact that the delay may not have prejudiced the proposed defendant is not itself a sufficient reason for extending time. But if, notwithstanding the delay, the court grants permission, a defendant who wishes to rely on delay at the substantive hearing will have to show that the grant of relief would be likely to cause substantial hardship to, or substantially prejudice the rights of, any person or would be detrimental to good administration (SCA, s 31(6); *R v Criminal Injuries Compensation Board ex parte A* [1999] 2 AC 330).

54.6 Claim form

(1) In addition to the matters set out in rule 8.2 (contents of the claim form) the claimant must also state –

(a) the name and address of any person he considers to be an interested party;
(b) that he is requesting permission to proceed with a claim for judicial review; and
(c) any remedy (including any interim remedy) he is claiming.

(Part 25 sets out how to apply for an interim remedy)

(2) The claim form must be accompanied by the documents required by the relevant practice direction.

Amendments—Inserted by SI 2000/2092.

'Claim form' (r 54.6)—The required form is N461. It must set out the issue raised and, if the claim is being made under any enactment, what that enactment is (r 8.2, (c)). It must state the name and address of any interested party (see note **'directly affected'** under r 54.1(2)(f) above).

The claim form must state the remedy sought, including any interim remedy (see the notes under rr 54.2 and 54.3 above).

Bail—Once seised of the proceedings, the court may grant bail. But it cannot grant bail once it has refused permission. If the applicant can renew his application, or apply for permission to appeal, the court to which the renewed application may be made may grant bail (*R v Home Secretary ex parte Turkoglu* [1988] QB 398, CA).

It is possible to bring an application for judicial review against a refusal by the executive or an inferior court or tribunal to grant bail. But before doing so the claimant should exhaust any alterative remedies. For example, in immigration officer may refuse bail, but in many cases the detainee can apply to an adjudicator for bail (Immigration and Asylum Act 1999, Part III, ss 44–50).

The claim form must include or be accompanied by:
(i) a detailed statement of the claimant's grounds for bringing the claim for judicial review;
(ii) a statement of the facts relied on;
(iii) any application to extend the time limit for filing the claim form;
(iv) any application for directions; and
(v) a time estimate for the hearing (PD54, para 5.6).

It should be accompanied by:
(a) any written evidence relied on;
(b) a copy of any order that the claimant seeks to have quashed;
(c) where the claim for judicial review relates to a decision of a court or tribunal, an approved copy of the reasons for reaching that decision;
(d) copies of any documents on which the claimant proposes to rely;
(e) copies of any relevant statutory material;
(f) a list of essential documents for advance reading by the court (with page references to the passages relied on) (PD54, para 5.7).

Insofar as any of the above are not available, the claim form should give reasons why they are unavailable (PD54, para 5.8). The claim form should also give details of the claimant's solicitors.

Where the claimant seeks to raise any issue under HRA 1998, PD54, para 5.3 requires that the claim form give the particulars required by PD16, para 16, namely:
(1) that the claimant is seeking a remedy under the 1998 Act;
(2) precise details of the Convention right which it is alleged has been infringed and details of the alleged infringement;
(3) the specific relief sought;
(4) whether the relief sought includes a declaration of incompatibility or damages in respect of a judicial act;
(5) precise details of any legislative provision alleged to be incompatible with the Convention and details of the alleged incompatibility;
(6) where the claim is founded on a finding of unlawfulness by a another court or tribunal, details of the finding;
(7) where the claim is founded on a judicial act, the judicial act complained of and the court or tribunal which is alleged to have made it.

Where the claimant seeks to raise a devolution issue, the claim form must say so and must specify the relevant statutory provision and the relevant facts (PD54, para 5.4).

Claimant's duty to make full disclosure—Under RSC Ord 53 the applicant was under a duty to put before the court all material matters of fact and law, including those adverse to his case, as the application for permission was made without notice (though in practice the proposed respondent often was notified). Failure to do so could of itself be grounds for setting aside the grant of permission (*R v Jockey Club Licensing Committee ex parte Wright* [1991] COD 306 (facts); *R v Home Secretary ex parte Li Bin Shi* [1995] COD 135 (case law); *R v Cornwall County Council ex parte Huntington* [1992] 3 All ER 566, DC (statute)). Equally, non-disclosure is a ground for refusing relief at a substantive hearing (*R v General Commissioners ex parte de Polignac* [1917] 1 KB 486, CA). Now that the defendant and any interested party have the opportunity to summarise their grounds for contesting the claim before the court decides whether to grant permission (r 54.8(4)(a)), it may be that the consequences of non-disclosure will in some cases be less severe. The pre-action protocol (see para 6) states that it does not alter the common law or statutory requirements relating to disclosure, but it makes an adverse costs order more likely if a party fails to make appropriate disclosure.

54.7 Service of claim form

The claim form must be served on –

(a) the defendant; and

(b) unless the court otherwise directs, any person the claimant considers to be an interested party, within 7 days after the date of issue.

Amendments—Inserted by SI 2000/2092.

Time—Time starts to run on the day after issue (r 2.8(2), (3)(iii)). Weekends are included in the calculation of the period (r 2.8(4)). The methods of service are set out at r 6.2.

54.8 Acknowledgment of service

(1) Any person served with the claim form who wishes to take part in the judicial review must file an acknowledgment of service in the relevant practice form in accordance with the following provisions of this rule.

(2) Any acknowledgment of service must be –

(a) filed not more than 21 days after service of the claim form; and

(b) served on –

(i) the claimant; and

(ii) subject to any direction under rule 54.7(b), any other person named in the claim form, as soon as practicable and, in any event, not later than 7 days after it is filed.

(3) The time limits under this rule may not be extended by agreement between the parties.

(4) The acknowledgment of service –

(a) must –

(i) where the person filing it intends to contest the claim, set out a summary of his grounds for doing so; and

(ii) state the name and address of any person the person filing it considers to be an interested party; and

(b) may include or be accompanied by an application for directions.

(5) Rule 10.3(2) does not apply.

Amendments—Inserted by SI 2000/2092.

Time for acknowledgment —For the calculation of time, see note **'Service'** under r 54.7.

Forms—Acknowledgment of service should be made on Form N462.

54.9 Failure to file acknowledgment of service

(1) Where a person served with the claim form has failed to file an acknowledgment of service in accordance with rule 54.8, he –

- (a) may not take part in a hearing to decide whether permission should be given unless the court allows him to do so; but
- (b) provided he complies with rule 54.14 or any other direction of the court regarding the filing and service of –
  - (i) detailed grounds for contesting the claim or supporting it on additional grounds; and
  - (ii) any written evidence,

may take part in the hearing of the judicial review.

(2) Where that person takes part in the hearing of the judicial review, the court may take his failure to file an acknowledgment of service into account when deciding what order to make about costs.

(3) Rule 8.4 does not apply.

Amendments—Inserted by SI 2000/2092.

54.10 Permission given

(1) Where permission to proceed is given the court may also give directions.

(2) Directions under paragraph (1) may include a stay[(GL)] of proceedings to which the claim relates.

(Rule 3.7 provides a sanction for the non-payment of the fee payable when permission to proceed has been given)

Amendments—Inserted by SI 2000/2092.

'Where permission to proceed is given' (r 54.10(1))—A person served with the claim form may not apply to set aside the grant of permission (r 54.13).

Disclosure—There is no automatic disclosure in a claim for judicial review (PD54, para 12.1). Defendants usually serve reasonably comprehensive evidence, so an order for disclosure is rarely necessary. Generally, disclosure will be ordered in judicial review proceedings only when there is before the court evidence that the defendant's own evidence is materially inaccurate or misleading (*R v Secretary of State for Foreign and Commonwealth Affairs ex parte World Development Movement* [1995] 1 WLR 386, 396c–397h, 403d, DC).

For disclosure by the Crown, see Crown Proceedings Act 1947, s 28 and Sch 1; RSC Ord 77, r 12, which provide for public interest immunity in an appropriate case.

Cross-examination—An application for cross-examination will be granted where the justice of the case requires it. But the nature of public law is such that it is rarely necessary for the court hearing an application for judicial review to have oral evidence and cross-examination (*O'Reilly v Mackman* [1983] 2 AC 237, 282b–283a; *Roy v Kensington and Chelsea and Westminster Family Practitioner Committee* [1992] 1 AC 624, 647b–d). Even where the court is determining an issue of precedent fact, cross-examination is uncommon (*R v Home Secretary ex parte Khawaja* [1984] AC 74, 124e–125c).

54.11 Service of order giving or refusing permission

The court will serve –

- (a) the order giving or refusing permission; and
- (b) any directions,

on –

- (i) the claimant;
- (ii) the defendant; and

(iii) any other person who filed an acknowledgment of service.

Amendments—Inserted by SI 2000/2092.

54.12 Permission decision without a hearing

(1) This rule applies where the court, without a hearing –

(a) refuses permission to proceed; or
(b) gives permission to proceed –
(i) subject to conditions; or
(ii) on certain grounds only.

(2) The court will serve its reasons for making the decision when it serves the order giving or refusing permission in accordance with rule 54.11.

(3) The claimant may not appeal but may request the decision to be reconsidered at a hearing.

(4) A request under paragraph (3) must be filed within 7 days after service of the reasons under paragraph (2).

(5) The claimant, defendant and any other person who has filed an acknowledgment of service will be given at least 2 days' notice of the hearing date.

Amendments—Inserted by SI 2000/2092.

'request the decision to be reconsidered' (r 54.12(3))—Where the court considers an application for permission on the papers and refuses permission or grants permission subject to conditions or on certain grounds only, the claimant can renew his application for permission at an oral hearing. If permission is refused at the oral hearing, the claimant may seek permission to appeal to the Court of Appeal (r 52.15). The application for permission to appeal should be made using Form N161. If the Court of Appeal grants permission, the case will proceed in the High Court unless the Court of Appeal orders otherwise (r 52.15(4)). If the Court of Appeal refuses permission, no further appeal lies to the House of Lords (AJA 1999, s 54; *R v Secretary of State for Trade and Industry ex parte Eastaway* [2000] 1 WLR 2222, HL).

The time limits for these renewed applications are tight. The application for a renewed hearing in the Administrative Court must be filed within 7 days after service of the court's reasons for refusing (simple) permission (r 54.12(4)). The application for permission to appeal to the Court of Appeal must be made within 7 days of the Administrative Court's decision (r 52.15(2)). For the calculation of time, see note **'Service'** under r 54.7.

Where the court refuses to grant (simple) permission, it will give reasons for its decision (r 54.12(2)). These reasons are likely to carry weight with the court at a renewed hearing.

Neither the defendant nor any interested party need attend an oral permission hearing unless the court directs otherwise (PD54, para 8.5). Where the defendant or an interested does attend such a hearing, the court will not generally make an order for costs against the claimant (PD54, para 8.6).

54.13 Defendant etc may not apply to set aside[(GL)]

Neither the defendant nor any other person served with the claim form may apply to set aside[(GL)] an order giving permission to proceed.

Amendments—Inserted by SI 2000/2092.

Scope of provision—This is a new provision, that is to say no similar provision appeared in RSC Ord 53. It would not seem to preclude an application under Pt 24 to strike out the claim as an abuse of the process of the court. Such an application should be made only in the clearest of cases.

54.14 Response

(1) A defendant and any other person saved with the claim form who wishes to contest the claim or support it on additional grounds must file and serve –

(a) detailed grounds for contesting the claim or supporting it on additional grounds; and

(b) any written evidence,

within 35 days after service of the order giving permission.

(2) The following rules do not apply –

(a) rule 8.5(3) and 8.5(4) (defendant to file and serve written evidence at the same time as acknowledgment of service); and

(b) rule 8.5(5) and 8.5(6) (claimant to file and serve reply within 14 days).

Amendments—Inserted by SI 2000/2092.

Evidence—The respondent's evidence should be full and frank (*R v Lancashire County Council ex parte Huddleston* [1986] 2 All ER 941, CA). However, the court is very wary of evidence which is inconsistent with, or which takes points not made in, the decision under challenge: ex-post-factual rationalisation can occur innocently (*R v Westminster City Council ex parte Ermakov* [1996] 2 All ER 302, CA; *R v Home Secretary ex parte Lillycrop et al* (1996) *The Times*, 13 December, DC).

A party who does not comply with the time limits for filing evidence will not be able to rely on (further) evidence unless the court gives permission (r 54.16).

Judicial respondents—Judicial respondents often serve evidence to explain to the court what has occurred but by convention they do not adopt a partisan approach or appear at the hearing. If they limit their involvement in this way, they will not have costs awarded against them even if the applicant is successful (*R v Newcastle-under-Lyme Justices ex parte Massey* [1994] 1 WLR 1684, DC).

54.15 Where claimant seeks to rely on additional grounds

The court's permission is required if a claimant seeks to rely on grounds other than those for which he has been given permission to proceed.

Amendments—Inserted by SI 2000/2092.

'The court's permission'—Where a claimant seeks at the substantive hearing to raise a point for which permission has been refused at the first stage, there is a discretion to permit that to occur (*R (Smith) v Parole Board* [2003] EWCA Civ 1014, [2003] 1 WLR 2548). Per Lord Woolf CJ:

> 'As long as a judge recognises the need for there to be good reason for altering the view of the single judge taken at the permission stage, no further sensible guidance can be provided. The circumstances which can occur are capable of varying almost without limit, and so each case must be considered having regard to its circumstances. The idea that there has to be a new situation for the permission to be extended is one which I would regard as wrong.'

54.16 Evidence

(1) Rule 8.6(1) does not apply.

(2) No written evidence may be relied on unless –

(a) it has been served in accordance with any –

(i) rule under this Section; or

(ii) direction of the court; or

(b) the court gives permission.

Amendments—Inserted by SI 2000/2092; amended by SI 2002/2058; SI 2003/364.

54.17 Court's powers to hear any person

(1) Any person may apply for permission –

(a) to file evidence; or

(b) make representations at the hearing of the judicial review.

(2) An application under paragraph (1) should be made promptly.

Amendments—Inserted by SI 2000/2092.

'Any person' (r 54.17(1))—A person may apply for permission to file evidence or make representations because he is an interested party (see r 54.1(2)(f)) who, for whatever reason, was not served with the claim form. Providing he acts promptly (see r 54.17(2)), the court is likely to permit him to become a party. This gives him full scope to participate in the proceedings and in any appeal (see the definition of 'party' in SCA, s 151(1)).

A person who is not an interested party may nevertheless apply to intervene in a claim for judicial review. The courts, particularly at appellate level, are increasingly sympathetic to intervention by bodies that are recognised as having a particular expertise in a field relevant to the proceedings (eg *R v Home Secretary ex parte Sivakumaran* [1988] AC 958; *R v Bow Street Metropolitan Stipendiary Magistrate ex parte Pinochet Ugarte* [2000] 1 AC 61; *R v Bournewood Community and Mental Health NHS Trust ex parte L* [1999] 1 AC 458). It is more common for the intervener to be permitted to make written than oral submissions (*R v North East Devon Health Authority ex parte Coughlan* [2000] 2 WLR 622, CA; *Re A (children)(conjoined twins: surgical separation)* [2001] Fam 147, CA).

Where all the parties consent, the court may deal with an application under r 54.17 without a hearing (PD54, para 13.1). Where the court gives permission under r 54.17 it may do so on conditions and may give case management directions (PD54, para 13.2).

A person who is granted permission under r 54.17 to intervene is not automatically a party. Therefore he has no right to appeal against the substantive decision on the claim for judicial review, or to join in an appeal by those who are parties, unless the court otherwise orders (*R v Rent Officer Service ex parte Muldoon* [1996] 1 WLR 1103, HL; *R v Licensing Authority ex parte Smith Kline & French Laboratories* [1988] COD 62, CA; *R v North East Devon Health Authority ex parte Coughlan* [2000] 2 WLR 622, CA).

54.18 Judicial review may be decided without a hearing

The court may decide the claim for judicial review without a hearing where all the parties agree.

Amendments—Inserted by SI 2000/2092.

Consent resolution—Where the parties agree the final order to be made, the claimant must file at the court a document (with two copies) signed by all the parties setting out the terms of the proposed agreed order together with a short statement of the matters relied on as justifying the proposed agreed order and copies of any authorities or statutory provision relied on (PD54, para 17.1). If the court is satisfied with the proposed order, it may make it without a hearing (PD54, para 17.2). If the court is not satisfied with the proposed order, a hearing date will be set (PD54, para 17.3). The parties are not required to file a statement of reasons where the agreement relates to an order for costs only (PD54, para 17.4).

54.19 Court's powers in respect of quashing orders

(1) This rule applies where the court makes a quashing order in respect of the decision to which the claim relates.

(2) The court may –

(a) remit the matter to the decision-maker; and
(b) direct it to reconsider the matter and reach a decision in accordance with the judgment of the court.

(3) Where the court considers that there is no purpose to be served in remitting the matter to the decision-maker it may, subject to any statutory provision, take the decision itself.

(Where a statutory power is given to a tribunal, person or other body it may be the case that the court cannot take the decision itself)

Amendments—Inserted by SI 2000/2092.

54.20 Transfer

The court may –

(a) order a claim to continue as if it had not been started under this Section; and

(b) where it does so, give directions about the future management of the claim.

(Part 30 (transfer) applies to transfers to and from the Administrative Court)

Amendments—Inserted by SI 2000/2092; amended by SI 2003/364.

Scope of provision—See note **'Overlap between judicial review and private law actions'** under r 54.1.

Where proceedings are commenced in the wrong court, they can be transferred to or from the Administrative Court (r 30.5; r 54.20; PD54, paras 14.1, 14.2; CCA 1984, ss 41, 42). In deciding whether a claim is suitable for transfer to the Administrative Court, the court will consider whether it raises issues of public law to which Pt 54 should apply (PD54 para 14.2).

However, the court has the power to prevent claimants from seeking to bypass the time limits on judicial review by issuing private law actions and then seeking to have the proceedings transferred to the Administrative Court (*Heywood v Board of Visitors of Hull Prison* [1980] 1 WLR 1386).

Section II – Statutory Review under the Nationality, Immigration and Asylum Act 2002

Scope of provision—After this Section, there is inserted – by Update 39 – a new Section III, setting out the procedure for applications to the High Court under new Nationality, Immigration and Asylum Act 2002, s 103A. Both Sections relate to statutory appeals rather than judicial review at large.

An application may now be made under that section for an order that the new Asylum and Immigration Tribunal (AIT) reconsider its decision on an appeal, on the ground that the AIT made an error of law. This is part of the wider reforms contained in the Asylum and Immigration (Treatment of Claimants etc) Act 2004 which also created the AIT in place of the former immigration adjudicators and Immigration Appeal Tribunal. Consequential amendments are made to Section II, which relates to applications under s 101(2) of the 2002 Act. In particular, there are very short and stringent time limits (see notes to r 54.28) and restrictions on the AIT's powers to extend time (see r 54.30). This is a field where the non-specialist should tread warily.

54.21 Scope and interpretation

(1) This Section of this Part contains rules about applications to the High Court under section 101(2) of the Nationality, Immigration and Asylum Act 2002 for a review of a decision of the Immigration Appeal Tribunal on an application for permission to appeal from an adjudicator.

(2) In this Section –

(a) 'the Act' means the Nationality, Immigration and Asylum Act 2002;

(b) 'adjudicator' means an adjudicator appointed for the purposes of Part 5 of the Act;

(c) 'applicant' means a person applying to the High Court under section 101(2) of the Act;

(d) 'other party' means the other party to the proceedings before the Tribunal; and

(e) 'Tribunal' means the Immigration Appeal Tribunal.

Amendments—Inserted by SI 2003/364.

54.22 Application for review

(1) An application under section 101(2) of the Act must be made to the Administrative Court.

(2) The application must be made by filing an application notice.

(3) The applicant must file with the application notice –

- (a) the immigration or asylum decision to which the proceedings relate, and any document giving reasons for that decision;
- (b) the grounds of appeal to the adjudicator;
- (c) the adjudicator's determination;
- (d) the grounds of appeal to the Tribunal together with any documents sent with them;
- (e) the Tribunal's determination on the application for permission to appeal; and
- (f) any other documents material to the application which were before the adjudicator.

(4) The applicant must also file with the application notice written submissions setting out –

- (a) the grounds upon which it is contended that the Tribunal made an error of law; and
- (b) reasons in support of those grounds.

(5) (*revoked*)

Amendments—Inserted by SI 2003/364; amended by SI 2003/1329.

54.23 Time limit for application

(1) The application notice must be filed not later than 14 days after the applicant is deemed to have received notice of the Tribunal's decision in accordance with rules made under section 106 of the Act.

(2) The court may extend the time limit in paragraph (1) in exceptional circumstances.

(3) An application to extend the time limit must be made in the application notice and supported by written evidence verified by a statement of truth.

Amendments—Inserted by SI 2003/364.

54.24 Service of application

(1) The applicant must serve on the Asylum and Immigration Tribunal copies of the application notice and written submissions.

(2) Where an application is for review of a decision by the Tribunal to grant permission to appeal, the applicant must serve on the other party copies of –

- (a) the application notice;
- (b) the written submissions; and
- (c) all the documents filed in support of the application, except for documents which come from or have already been served on that party.

(3) Where documents are required to be served under paragraphs (1) and (2), they must be served as soon as practicable after they are filed.

Amendments—Inserted by SI 2003/364; amended by SI 2005/352.

54.25 Determining the application

(1) The application will be determined by a single judge without a hearing, and by reference only to the written submissions and the documents filed with them.

(2) If the applicant relies on evidence which was not submitted to the adjudicator or the Tribunal, the court will not consider that evidence unless it is satisfied that there were good reasons why it was not submitted to the adjudicator or the Tribunal.

(3) The court may –

(a) affirm the Tribunal's decision to refuse permission to appeal;
(b) reverse the Tribunal's decision to grant permission to appeal; or
(c) order the Asylum and Immigration Tribunal to reconsider the adjudicator's decision on the appeal.

(4) Where the Tribunal refused permission to appeal, the court will order the Asylum and Immigration Tribunal to reconsider the adjudicator's decision on the appeal only if it is satisfied that –

(a) the Tribunal may have made an error of law; and
(b) there is a real possibility that the Asylum and Immigration Tribunal would make a different decision from the adjudicator on reconsidering the appeal (which may include making a different direction under section 87 of the 2002 Act).

(5) Where the Tribunal granted permission to appeal, the court will reverse the Tribunal's decision only if it is satisfied that there is no real possibility that the Asylum and Immigration Tribunal, on reconsidering the adjudicator's decision on the appeal, would make a different decision from the adjudicator.

(6) The court's decision shall be final and there shall be no appeal from that decision or renewal of the application.

Amendments—Inserted by SI 2003/364; amended by .SI 2005/352.

Sub-rule (3)—This is new as at Update 39. It sets out the three possibilities for the court under the new regime, including the new order to remit the decision 'back' to the AIT for reconsideration. The previous rule allowed the court to 'affirm or reverse the Tribunal's decision'.

Sub-rule (4)—This is new as at Update 39. The court can no longer reverse a refusal by the Tribunal to grant permission to appeal (which was formerly the case); it can only now order a reconsideration. The criteria are not the same: the former rule required an error of law plus either a real prospect of success or some other compelling reason for the appeal to be heard. The first sub-limb is in different terms, the second has gone altogether.

Sub-rule (5)—This is new as at Update 39. The former rule required the court to reverse such a decision only if satisfied that the appeal would have no prospect of success and there was no other compelling reason why the appeal should be heard. Again, this last element has gone altogether.

Sub-rule (6)—This is new as at Update 39 in that, although it is in identical terms to the former sub-rule (7), it replaces the former sub-rule (6), which dealt with the (now impermissible) reversal by the court of a decision to refuse permission to appeal.

54.26 Service of order

(1) The court will send copies of its order to –

(a) the applicant, except where paragraph (2) applies;
(b) the other party; and
(c) the Asylum and Immigration Tribunal.

(2) Where –

(a) the application relates, in whole or in part, to a claim for asylum;

(b) the Tribunal refused permission to appeal; and
(c) the court affirms the Tribunal's decision,

the court will send a copy of its order to the Secretary of State, who must serve the order on the applicant.

(3) Where the Secretary of State has served an order in accordance with paragraph (2), he must notify the court on what date and by what method the order was served.

(4) If the court issues a certificate under section 101(3)(d) of the Act, it will send a copy of the certificate together with the order to –

(a) the persons to whom it sends the order under paragraphs (1) and (2); and
(b) if the applicant is in receipt of public funding, the Legal Services Commission.

Amendments—Inserted by SI 2003/364; amended by .SI 2005/352.

54.27 Costs

The court may reserve the costs of the application to be determined by the Asylum and Immigration Tribunal.

Amendments—Inserted by SI 2003/364.

Section III – Applications for Statutory Review under section 103A of the Nationality, Immigration and Asylum Act 2002

Amendments—Inserted by SI 2005/352.

General note—See the notes under Section II above. These new provisions, introduced by Update 39, are supplemented by the new PD54B.

54.28 Scope and interpretation

(1) This Section of this Part contains rules about applications to the High Court under section 103A of the Nationality, Immigration and Asylum Act 2002 for an order requiring the Asylum and Immigration Tribunal to reconsider its decision on an appeal.

(2) In this Section –

(a) 'the 2002 Act' means the Nationality, Immigration and Asylum Act 2002;
(b) 'the 2004 Act' means the Asylum and Immigration (Treatment of Claimants, etc.) Act 2004;
(c) 'appellant' means the appellant in the proceedings before the Tribunal;
(d) 'applicant' means a person applying to the High Court under section 103A;
(e) 'asylum claim' has the meaning given in section 113(1) of the 2002 Act;
(f) 'filter provision' means paragraph 30 of Schedule 2 to the 2004 Act;
(g) 'order for reconsideration' means an order under section 103A(1) requiring the Tribunal to reconsider its decision on an appeal;
(h) 'section 103A' means section 103A of the 2002 Act;
(i) 'Tribunal' means the Asylum and Immigration Tribunal.

(3) Any reference in this Section to a period of time specified in –

(a) section 103A(3) for making an application for an order under section 103A(1); or
(b) paragraph 30(5)(b) of Schedule 2 to the 2004 Act for giving notice under that paragraph,

includes a reference to that period as varied by any order under section 26(8) of the 2004 Act.

(4) Rule 2.8 applies to the calculation of the periods of time specified in –

(a) section 103A(3); and
(b) paragraph 30(5)(b) of Schedule 2 to the 2004 Act.

(5) Save as provided otherwise, the provisions of this Section apply to an application under section 103A regardless of whether the filter provision has effect in relation to that application.

Amendments—Inserted by SI 2005/352.

'periods of time specified' (r 54.28(4))—Generally, 5 days (28 days if the appellant is outside the United Kingdom) from when the appellant is treated as receiving notice of the Tribunal's decision. However, it is advisable to refer to the underlying primary and secondary legislation, including Commencement Orders. The time limits are far more stringent than the general time limits for judicial review.

'the filter provision' (r 54.28(5))—This is official shorthand for transitional arangements, whereby initially applications for review under s 103A(1) of the 2002 Act will first be considered by a member of the Tribunal. See PD54B, paras 2.1 and 2.2

54.29 Application for review

(1) Subject to paragraph (4), an application for an order for reconsideration must be made by filing an application notice –

(a) during a period in which the filter provision has effect, with the Tribunal at the address specified in the relevant practice direction; and
(b) at any other time, at the Administrative Court Office.

(2) The applicant must file with the application notice –

(a) the notice of the immigration, asylum or nationality decision to which the appeal related;
(b) any other document which was served on the appellant giving reasons for that decision;
(c) the grounds of appeal to the Tribunal;
(d) the Tribunal's determination on the appeal; and
(e) any other documents material to the application which were before the Tribunal.

(3) The applicant must also file with the application notice written submissions setting out –

(a) the grounds upon which it is contended that the Tribunal made an error of law which may have affected its decision; and
(b) reasons in support of those grounds.

(4) Where the applicant –

(a) was the respondent to the appeal; and
(b) was required to serve the Tribunal's determination on the appellant,

the application notice must contain a statement of the date on which, and the means by which, the determination was served.

(5) Where the applicant is in detention under the Immigration Acts, the application may be made either –

(a) in accordance with paragraphs (1) to (3); or
(b) by serving the documents specified in paragraphs (1) to (3) on the person having custody of him.

(6) Where an application is made in accordance with paragraph (5)(b), the person on whom the application notice is served must –

(a) endorse on the notice the date that it is served on him;
(b) give the applicant an acknowledgment in writing of receipt of the notice; and
(c) forward the notice and documents within 2 days –
   (i) during a period in which the filter provision has effect, to the Tribunal; and
   (ii) at any other time, to the Administrative Court Office.

Amendments—Inserted by SI 2005/352.

'the grounds of appeal' (r 54.29(2)(c))—The appeal must be on a point of law. As the Court of Appeal said in *Mlauzi* [2005] EWCA Civ 128, that 'it is … incumbent on all those who practise in this jurisdiction to understand that supremacy is now given, and will be given, to the original judge's decision on fact, so that it will be important to identify clearly what facts were placed before him/her, and what argument was adduced to him/her if there is to be an appeal on law. Appeals on fact are matters now very firmly in the past.'

54.30 Application to extend time limit

An application to extend the time limit for making an application under section 103A(1) must –

(a) be made in the application notice;
(b) set out the grounds on which it is contended that the application notice could not reasonably practicably have been filed within the time limit; and
(c) be supported by written evidence verified by a statement of truth.

Amendments—Inserted by SI 2005/352.

'could not reasonably practicably have been filed within the time limit' (r 54.30(b))—This is a form of words sharply limiting the Tribunal's discretion, familiar from the Employment Tribunal jurisdiction, which the Court of Appeal has considered in *Sealy v Consignia plc* [2002] EWCA Civ 878, [2002] 3 All ER 801, explaining *Dedman v British Building and Engineering Appliances* [1974] 1 WLR 171. In *Sealy* it was said that an applicant was entitled to rely on the ordinary course of the post, but that the strict deeming provisions of r 6.7 did not apply.

54.31 Procedure while filter provision has effect

(1) This rule applies during any period in which the filter provision has effect.

(2) Where the applicant receives notice from the Tribunal that it –

(a) does not propose to make an order for reconsideration; or
(b) does not propose to grant permission for the application to be made outside the relevant time limit,

and the applicant wishes the court to consider the application, the applicant must file a notice in writing at the Administrative Court Office in accordance with paragraph 30(5)(b) of Schedule 2 to the 2004 Act.

(3) Where the applicant –

(a) was the respondent to the appeal; and
(b) was required to serve the notice from the Tribunal mentioned in paragraph (2) on the appellant,

the notice filed in accordance with paragraph 30(5)(b) of Schedule 2 to the 2004 Act must contain a statement of the date on which, and the means by which, the notice from the Tribunal was served.

(4) A notice which is filed outside the period specified in paragraph 30(5)(b) must –

(a) set out the grounds on which it is contended that the notice could not reasonably practicably have been filed within that period; and
(b) be supported by written evidence verified by a statement of truth.

(5) If the applicant wishes to respond to the reasons given by the Tribunal for its decision that it –

(a) does not propose to make an order for reconsideration; or
(b) does not propose to grant permission for the application to be made outside the relevant time limit,

the notice filed in accordance with paragraph 30(5)(b) of Schedule 2 to the 2004 Act must be accompanied by written submissions setting out the grounds upon which the applicant disputes any of the reasons given by the Tribunal and giving reasons in support of those grounds.

Amendments—Inserted by SI 2005/352.

54.32 Procedure in fast track cases while filter provision does not have effect

(1) This rule applies only during a period in which the filter provision does not have effect.

(2) Where a fast track order applies to an application under section 103A –

(a) the court will serve copies of the application notice and written submissions on the other party to the appeal; and
(b) the other party to the appeal may file submissions in response to the application not later than 2 days after being served with the application.

(3) In this Rule, a 'fast track order' means an order made under section 26(8) of the 2004 Act which replaces a period of time specified in section 103A(3) of the 2002 Act with a period shorter than 5 days.

Amendments—Inserted by SI 2005/352.

'fast track order' (r 54.32(2))—Where such an order is made, PD54B, para 2.2 as to the address for filing does not apply (see ibid para 2.3).

54.33 Determination of the application by the Administrative Court

(1) This rule, and rules 54.34 and 54.35, apply to applications under section 103A which are determined by the Administrative Court.

(2) The application will be considered by a single judge without a hearing.

(3) Unless it orders otherwise, the court will not receive evidence which was not submitted to the Tribunal.

(4) Subject to paragraph (5), where the court determines an application for an order for reconsideration, it may –

(a) dismiss the application;

(b) make an order requiring the Tribunal to reconsider its decision on the appeal under section 103A(1) of the 2002 Act; or
(c) refer the appeal to the Court of Appeal under section 103C of the 2002 Act.

(5) The court will only make an order requiring the Tribunal to reconsider its decision on an appeal if it thinks that –

(a) the Tribunal may have made an error of law; and
(b) there is a real possibility that the Tribunal would make a different decision on reconsidering the appeal (which may include making a different direction under section 87 of the 2002 Act).

(6) Where the Court of Appeal has restored the application to the court under section 103C(2)(g) of the 2002 Act, the court may not refer the appeal to the Court of Appeal.

(7) The court's decision shall be final and there shall be no appeal from that decision or renewal of the application.

Amendments—Inserted by SI 2005/352.

'refer the appeal to the Court of Appeal under section 103C of the 2002 Act' (r 54.33(4)(c))—In this case, the court's order will set out the question of law raised by the appeal which is of such importance that it should be decided by the Court of Appeal, and PD52, para 21.7A makes provision relating to such appeals (see PD54B, para 4.1 and 4.2).

54.34 Service of order

(1) The court will send copies of its order to –

(a) the applicant and the other party to the appeal, except where paragraph (2) applies; and
(b) the Tribunal.

(2) Where the application relates, in whole or in part, to an asylum claim, the court will send a copy of its order to the Secretary of State.

(3) Where the court sends an order to the Secretary of State under paragraph (2), the Secretary of State must –

(a) serve the order on the appellant; and
(b) immediately after serving the order, notify the court on what date and by what method the order was served.

(4) The Secretary of State must provide the notification required by paragraph (3)(b) no later than 28 days after the date on which the court sends him a copy of its order.

(5) If, 28 days after the date on which the court sends a copy of its order to the Secretary of State in accordance with paragraph (2), the Secretary of State has not provided the notification required by paragraph (3)(b), the court may serve the order on the appellant.

(6) If the court makes an order under section 103D(1) of the 2002 Act, it will send copies of that order to –

(a) the appellant's legal representative; and
(b) the Legal Services Commission.

(7) Where paragraph (2) applies, the court will not serve copies of an order under section 103D(1) of the 2002 Act until either –

(a) the Secretary of State has provided the notification required by paragraph (3)(b); or

(b) 28 days after the date on which the court sent a copy of its order to the Secretary of State,

whichever is the earlier.

Amendments—Inserted by SI 2005/352.

'to the Secretary of State' (r 54.34(2))—Where the court sends a copy of its s 103A order to the Secretary of State, but not the appellant, under this sub-rule, then rr 5.4(3)(b) and 5.4(5)(a)(ii) (which deal with access to court documents) are modified as set out at PD54B, para 3.2 – see ibid para 3.1.

54.35 Costs

The court shall make no order as to the costs of an application under this Section except, where appropriate, an order under section 103D(1) of the 2002 Act.

Amendments—Inserted by SI 2005/352.

Practice Direction– Judicial Review

This Practice Direction supplements CPR Part 54 (PD54)

1.1 In addition to Part 54 and this practice direction attention is drawn to –

- section 31 of the Supreme Court Act 1981; and
- the Human Rights Act 1998.

THE COURT

2.1 Part 54 claims for judicial review are dealt with in the Administrative Court.

2.2 Where the claim is proceeding in the Administrative Court in London, documents must be filed at the Administrative Court Office, the Royal Courts of Justice, Strand, London, WC2A 2LL.

2.3 Where the claim is proceeding in the Administrative Court in Wales (see paragraph 3.1), documents must be filed at the Civil Justice Centre, 2 Park Street, Cardiff, CF10 1ET.

Urgent applications

2.4 Where urgency makes it necessary for the claim for judicial review to be made outside London or Cardiff, the Administrative Court Office in London should be consulted (if necessary, by telephone) prior to filing the claim form.

JUDICIAL REVIEW CLAIMS IN WALES

3.1 A claim for judicial review may be brought in the Administrative Court in Wales where the claim or any remedy sought involves –

(1) a devolution issue arising out of the Government of Wales Act 1998; or
(2) an issue concerning the National Assembly for Wales, the Welsh executive, or any Welsh public body (including a Welsh local authority) (whether or not it involves a devolution issue).

3.2 Such claims may also be brought in the Administrative Court at the Royal Courts of Justice.

RULE 54.5 – TIME LIMIT FOR FILING CLAIM FORM

4.1 Where the claim is for a quashing order in respect of a judgment, order or conviction, the date when the grounds to make the claim first arose, for the purposes of rule 54.5(1)(b), is the date of that judgment, order or conviction.

RULE 54.6 – CLAIM FORM

Interested parties

5.1 Where the claim for judicial review relates to proceedings in a court or tribunal, any other parties to those proceedings must be named in the claim form as interested parties under rule 54.6(1)(a) (and therefore served with the claim form under rule 54.7(b)).

5.2 For example, in a claim by a defendant in a criminal case in the Magistrates' or Crown Court for judicial review of a decision in that case, the prosecution must always be named as an interested party.

Human rights

5.3 Where the claimant is seeking to raise any issue under the Human Rights Act 1998, or seeks a remedy available under that Act, the claim form must include the information required by paragraph [15] of the practice direction supplementing Part 16.

Devolution issues

5.4 Where the claimant intends to raise a devolution issue, the claim form must –

(1) specify that the applicant wishes to raise a devolution issue and identify the relevant provisions of the Government of Wales Act 1998, the Northern Ireland Act 1998 or the Scotland Act 1998; and
(2) contain a summary of the facts, circumstances and points of law on the basis of which it is alleged that a devolution issue arises.

5.5 In this practice direction 'devolution issue' has the same meaning as in paragraph 1, schedule 8 to the Government of Wales Act 1998; paragraph 1, schedule 10 to the Northern Ireland Act 1998; and paragraph 1, schedule 6 of the Scotland Act 1998.

Claim form

5.6 The claim form must include or be accompanied by –

(1) a detailed statement of the claimant's grounds for bringing the claim for judicial review;
(2) a statement of the facts relied on;
(3) any application to extend the time limit for filing the claim form;
(4) any application for directions

5.7 In addition, the claim form must be accompanied by –

(1) any written evidence in support of the claim or application to extend time;
(2) a copy of any order that the claimant seeks to have quashed;
(3) where the claim for judicial review relates to a decision of a court or tribunal, an approved copy of the reasons for reaching that decision;

(4) copies of any documents on which the claimant proposes to rely;
(5) copies of any relevant statutory material;
(6) a list of essential documents for advance reading by the court (with page references to the passages relied on); and

5.8 Where it is not possible to file all the above documents, the claimant must indicate which documents have not been filed and the reasons why they are not currently available.

Bundle of documents

5.9 The claimant must file two copies of a paginated and indexed bundle containing all the documents referred to in paragraphs [5.6] and [5.7].

5.10 Attention is drawn to rules 8.5(1) and 8.5(7).

RULE 54.7 – SERVICE OF CLAIM FORM

6.1 Except as required by rules 54.11 or 54.12(2), the Administrative Court will not serve documents and service must be effected by the parties.

RULE 54.8 – ACKNOWLEDGMENT OF SERVICE

7.1 Attention is drawn to rule 8.3(2) and the relevant practice direction and to rule 10.5.

RULE 54.10 – PERMISSION GIVEN

Directions

8.1 Case management directions under rule 54.10(1) may include directions about serving the claim form and any evidence on other persons.

8.2 Where a claim is made under the Human Rights Act 1998, a direction may be made for giving notice to the Crown or joining the Crown as a party. Attention is drawn to rule 19.4A and paragraph 6 of the Practice Direction supplementing Section I of Part 19.

8.3 A direction may be made for the hearing of the claim for judicial review to be held outside London or Cardiff. Before making any such direction the judge will consult the judge in charge of the Administrative Court as to its feasibility.

Permission without a hearing

8.4 The court will generally, in the first instance, consider the question of permission without a hearing.

Permission hearing

8.5 Neither the defendant nor any other interested party need attend a hearing on the question of permission unless the court directs otherwise.

8.6 Where the defendant or any party does attend a hearing, the court will not generally make an order for costs against the claimant.

RULE 54.11 – SERVICE OF ORDER GIVING OR REFUSING PERMISSION

9.1 An order refusing permission or giving it subject to conditions or on certain grounds only must set out or be accompanied by the court's reasons for coming to that decision.

RULE 54.14 – RESPONSE

10.1 Where the party filing the detailed grounds intends to rely on documents not already filed, he must file a paginated bundle of those documents when he files the detailed grounds.

RULE 54.15 – WHERE CLAIMANT SEEKS TO RELY ON ADDITIONAL GROUNDS

11.1 Where the claimant intends to apply to rely on additional grounds at the hearing of the claim for judicial review, he must give notice to the court and to any other person served with the claim form no later than 7 clear days before the hearing (or the warned date where appropriate).

RULE 54.16 – EVIDENCE

12.1 Disclosure is not required unless the court orders otherwise.

RULE 54.17 – COURT'S POWERS TO HEAR ANY PERSON

13.1 Where all the parties consent, the court may deal with an application under rule 54.17 without a hearing.

13.2 Where the court gives permission for a person to file evidence or make representations at the hearing of the claim for judicial review, it may do so on conditions and may give case management directions.

13.3 An application for permission should be made by letter to the Administrative Court office, identifying the claim, explaining who the applicant is and indicating why and in what form the applicant wants to participate in the hearing.

13.4 If the applicant is seeking a prospective order as to costs, the letter should say what kind of order and on what grounds.

13.5 Applications to intervene must be made at the earliest reasonable opportunity, since it will usually be essential not to delay the hearing.

RULE 54.20 – TRANSFER

14.1 Attention is drawn to rule 30.5.

14.2 In deciding whether a claim is suitable for transfer to the Administrative Court, the court will consider whether it raises issues of public law to which Part 54 should apply.

Skeleton arguments

15.1 The claimant must file and serve a skeleton argument not less than 21 working days before the date of the hearing of the judicial review (or the warned date).

15.2 The defendant and any other party wishing to make representations at the hearing of the judicial review must file and serve a skeleton argument not less than 14 working days before the date of the hearing of the judicial review (or the warned date).

15.3 Skeleton arguments must contain –

(1) a time estimate for the complete hearing, including delivery of judgment;
(2) a list of issues;
(3) a list of the legal points to be taken (together with any relevant authorities with page references to the passages relied on);
(4) a chronology of events (with page references to the bundle of documents (see paragraph 16.1);
(5) a list of essential documents for the advance reading of the court (with page references to the passages relied on) (if different from that filed with the claim form) and a time estimate for that reading; and
(6) a list of persons referred to.

Bundle of documents to be filed

16.1 The claimant must file a paginated and indexed bundle of all relevant documents required for the hearing of the judicial review when he files his skeleton argument.

16.2 The bundle must also include those documents required by the defendant and any other party who is to make representations at the hearing.

Agreed final order

17.1 If the parties agree about the final order to be made in a claim for judicial review, the claimant must file at the court a document (with 2 copies) signed by all the parties setting out the terms of the proposed agreed order together with a short statement of the matters relied on as justifying the proposed agreed order and copies of any authorities or statutory provisions relied on.

17.2 The court will consider the documents referred to in paragraph 17.1 and will make the order if satisfied that the order should be made.

17.3 If the court is not satisfied that the order should be made, a hearing date will be set.

17.4 Where the agreement relates to an order for costs only, the parties need only file a document signed by all the parties setting out the terms of the proposed order.

Practice Direction – Applications for Statutory Review under section 103A of the Nationality, Immigration and Asylum Act 2002

This Practice Direction supplements Section III of CPR Part 54 (PD54B)

1 Attention is drawn to:

- Sections 103A, 103C and 103D of the Nationality, Immigration and

Asylum Act 2002 (inserted by section 26(6) of the Asylum and Immigration (Treatment of Claimants, etc.) Act 2004); and

- Paragraph 30 of Schedule 2 to the 2004 Act.

THE COURT

2.1 Applications for review under section 103A(1) of the 2002 Act are dealt with in the Administrative Court, subject to the transitional filter provision in paragraph 30 of Schedule 2 of the 2004 Act which provides that they shall initially be considered by a member of the Tribunal.

2.2 During any period in which the filter provision has effect, the address for filing section 103A applications shall be the Asylum and Immigration Tribunal, P.O. Box 6987, Leicester LE1 6ZX.

2.3 Where a fast track order within the meaning of Rule 54.32(3) applies to a section 103A application, paragraph 2.2 shall not apply and the address for filing the application shall be the address specified in the Tribunal's determination of the appeal.

ACCESS TO COURT ORDERS SERVED ON THE APPELLANT BY THE SECRETARY OF STATE

3.1 Where the court sends a copy of its order on a section 103A application to the Secretary of State but not the appellant in accordance with Rule 54.34(2), then Rules 5.4(3)(b) and 5.4(5)(a)(ii) are modified as follows.

3.2 Neither the appellant nor any other person may obtain from the records of the court a copy of the court's order on the section 103A application, or of any order made under section 103D(1) of the 2002 Act in relation to that application, until either the Secretary of State has given the court the notification required by Rule 54.34(3)(b) or 28 days after the date on which the court sent a copy of the order to the Secretary of State, whichever is the earlier.

REFERRAL TO COURT OF APPEAL

4.1 Where the court refers an appeal to the Court of Appeal, its order will set out the question of law raised by the appeal which is of such importance that it should be decided by the Court of Appeal.

4.2 Paragraph 21.7A of the practice direction supplementing Part 52 makes provision about appeals which are referred to the Court of Appeal.

PART 55
POSSESSION CLAIMS

CONTENTS OF THIS PART

Procedural Guide—See Guides 45, 46, 50, 51, 52, 53, and 54, set out in Section 1 of this work.

Practice Direction—See generally PD55 at p 1325.

General note—This Part must be used whenever a claim for possession of land is brought by a landlord, mortgagee or licensor or whenever a claim is brought against a trespasser (r 55.2); Section II of Pt 55 deals with accelerated possession claims of property let on an assured shorthold tenancy. As from 2 December 2002, the former provisions of Sch 2, CCR Ord 24, Pt II (dealing with interim possession orders) were revoked and replaced, with minor amendments, in Section III of this Part.

Possession Claims Online ('PCOL')—HM Courts Service intends to establish a scheme for possession claims (based on arrears of rent or mortgage payments) to be made electronically online. See generally r 55.10A and the extensive practice direction supplementing it, namely PD55B. At the time of going to print no date has been given for the commencement of PCOL.

Proceedings relating to anti-social behaviour and harassment—See generally Pt 65 and PD65. However, Pt 55, Section I must be used where a landlord seeks a demotion order as an alternative to a possession order. The accelerated possession procedure set out in Pt 55, Section II may be used to claim possession against the tenant of a demoted assured shorthold tenancy, ie a demoted tenancy where the landlord is a registered social landlord.

Stamp duty—With effect from 1 December 2003 and following the introduction of Stamp Duty Land Tax, Stamp Act 1891, s 14 (which prevented the use in court of an unstamped instrument relating to land) is disregarded except where the transaction in question was pursuant to a contract entered into prior to 10 July 2003. This removes from the court any obligation it otherwise may have had to ensure that stamp duty had been paid. Furthermore, with effect from 1 January 2000, leases granted by registered social landlords are exempted from stamp duty.

If stamp duty were applicable and if the document relied upon is not impressed with the payment of stamp duty, the practice is to allow the unstamped document to be used upon the personal undertaking of the claimant's solicitors to stamp it and to produce it so stamped before the order is drawn up (*In re Coolgardie Goldfields Ltd* [1900] 1 Ch 475).

Form N206B – Notice of Issue (possession claim) – contains a note stating that where the claimant seeks to rely in evidence on a tenancy agreement on which stamp duty was payable but had not been paid, the claim may be adjourned or dismissed. Tenancies granted after 28 March 2000 for indefinite terms (eg periodic tenancies) or for terms of less than 7 years without a premium where the rent was less than £5,000 per annum did not attract stamp duty. If the annual rent was more than £5,000, duty was payable. The position is different with furnished tenancies. There was a fixed duty of £5 on a furnished letting of a house or apartment let for less than one year if the rent payable in that period was more than £5,000. If the rent was less than £5,000 for the period, no duty was chargeable. If the tenancy was for a term of one year or more, the position is the same as for unfurnished tenancies. If duty was payable and there are two copies (lease and counterpart), there was a fixed duty of £5 on the landlord's counterpart.

Jurisdiction—Claims under Pt 55 may be heard by, in the county court, a circuit judge or a district judge or, in the High Court, a judge or a master.

Forms—These are available on the HM Courts Service website at *www.hmcourts-service.gov.uk*.

55.1 Interpretation

In this Part –

(a) 'a possession claim' means a claim for the recovery of possession of land (including buildings or parts of buildings);

(b) 'a possession claim against trespassers' means a claim for the recovery of land which the claimant alleges is occupied only by a person or persons who entered or remained on the land without the consent of a person entitled to possession of that land but does not include a claim against a tenant or sub-tenant whether his tenancy has been terminated or not;

(c) 'mortgage' includes a legal or equitable mortgage and a legal or equitable charge and 'mortgagee' is to be interpreted accordingly;

(d) ['the 1985 Act' means the Housing Act 1985;

[(e) 'the 1988 Act' means the Housing Act 1988;

(f) 'a demotion claim' means a claim made by a landlord for an order under section 82A of the 1985 Act or section 6A of the 1988 Act ('a demotion order');

(g) 'a demoted tenancy' means a tenancy created by virtue of a demotion order; and

(h) 'a suspension claim' means a claim made by a landlord for an order under section 121A of the 1985 Act.

Amendments—Inserted by SI 2001/256; amended by SI 2004/1306; SI 2005/2292.

' **"a demotion claim"** ' (r 55.1(f))—Where a demotion order is claimed in the alternative to a possession order, the claimant must use the Pt 55 procedure (r 65.12). Where a demotion claim is made other than in a possession claim, rr 65.14–65.19 apply (r 65.13).

' **"a suspension claim"** ' (r 55.1(h))—A local housing authority may also, at the same time as an application for a demotion order, apply for an order under Housing Act 1985, s 121 suspending the tenant's right to exercise the right to buy in relation to the property (see also r 65.12).

I General Rules

55.2 Scope

(1) The procedure set out in this Section of this Part must be used where the claim includes –

- (a) a possession claim brought by a –
  - (i) landlord (or former landlord);
  - (ii) mortgagee; or
  - (iii) licensor (or former licensor);
- (b) a possession claim against trespassers; or
- (c) a claim by a tenant seeking relief from forfeiture.

(2) This Section of this Part –

- (a) is subject to any enactment or practice direction which sets out special provisions with regard to any particular category of claim;
- (b) does not apply where the claimant uses the procedure set out in Section II of this Part[; and
- (c) does not apply where the claimant seeks an interim possession order under Section III of this Part except where the court orders otherwise or that Section so provides.

(Where a demotion claim or a suspension claim (or both) is made in the same claim form in which a possession claim is started, this Section of this Part applies as modified by rule 65.12. Where the claim is a demotion claim or a suspension claim only, or a suspension claim made in addition to a demotion claim, Section III of Part 65 applies)

Amendments—Inserted by SI 2001/256; amended by SI 2002/2058; SI 2004/1306; SI 2005/2292.

'trespassers' (r 55.2(1)(b))—A judgment or order of a county court for possession of land against trespassers under this Part may be enforced in the High Court or in the county court (see High Court and County Courts (Amendment No 2) Order 2001, SI 2001/2685).

Claims against a tenant of a demoted tenancy—Such claims must also be brought under the Pt 55 procedure (PD65, para 10.1).

55.3 Starting the claim

(1) The claim must be started in the county court for the district in which the land is situated unless paragraph (2) applies or an enactment provides otherwise.

(2) The claim may be started in the High Court if the claimant files with his claim form a certificate stating the reasons for bringing the claim in that court verified by a statement of truth in accordance with rule 22.1(1).

(3) The practice direction refers to circumstances which may justify starting the claim in the High Court.

(4) Where, in a possession claim against trespassers, the claimant does not know the name of a person in occupation or possession of the land, the claim must be brought against 'persons unknown' in addition to any named defendants.

(5) The claim form and form of defence sent with it must be in the forms set out in the relevant practice direction.

Amendments—Inserted by SI 2001/256.

'The claim must be started' (r 55.3(1))—The general rule is that a possession claim must be started in the county court where the land is situated, ie in the defendant's county court. This equally applies to demotion claims brought under Pt 55 (PD55, para 1.9 and r 65.12). However, a possession order would not be invalidated solely because a claim were issued in the wrong court (r 3.10(b)) although if the error was noticed before a final order was made the proper course would be to transfer the claim to the correct court (r 30.2(2)(a)). See generally PD55, paras 1.1–1.5 as well as note **'circumstances may justify starting a claim in the High Court'** below.

'the land' (r 55.3(1))—The court has power to make an order for possession of the whole of premises owned by the claimant even though trespassers are occupying only part of the land, particularly where there is a threat of further trespass (*University of Essex v Djemal* [1980] 2 All ER 742, CA). Such an order is enforceable against any person occupying any part of the land whether named in the order or not (*R v Wandsworth County Court ex parte Wandsworth London Borough Council* [1975] 1 WLR 1314, [1975] 3 All ER 390).

'a certificate' (r 55.3(2))—No particular form of certificate is required; a letter would suffice, provided it is verified by a statement of truth.

'circumstances which may justify starting the claim in the High Court' (r 55.3(3))—See PD55, para 1.3 save that where a demotion claim is brought as an alternative to a claim for possession (PD55, para 1.9 and r 65.12) or where proceedings are brought against the tenant of a demoted tenancy (PD65, para 10.1), the claim must be brought in a county court. If proceedings are erroneously commenced in the High Court, the costs incurred are not recoverable (HA 1996, s 143N(4) and PD65, para 12.1).

The court may strike out a claim wrongly issued in the High Court or transfer it to the county court of its own initiative. The claimant may be ordered to pay the costs involved (PD55, para 1.2). The value of the property and the amount of any financial claim may be relevant circumstances in deciding where to issue a claim, but these factors alone will not normally justify starting the claim in the High Court (PD55, para 1.4). A typical situation where issuing in the High Court would be justified would be where the developed expertise of the High Court Sheriff's Officers was considered necessary to enforce any order that might be granted.

Mortgage claim—Outside Greater London such a claim, if it relates to a dwelling-house, may only be heard and determined in the county court unless the claim is for foreclosure or sale in which a claim for possession is also made (CCA 1984, s 21).

Time of issue—A Pt 55 claim is commenced on the day it is actually issued by the court and not on any previous day when the papers were lodged at court (*Salford County Council v Garner (Mark)* [2004] EWCA Civ 364, [2004] All ER (D) 465 (Feb), [2004] TLR 160, (2004) *The Times*, 10 March, CA).

Forms—Claim Form N5 coupled with, where applicable, whichever of the Particulars of Claim N119 (rent cases), N120 (mortgage cases) or N121 (claim against trespassers) is appropriate. N119A comprises guidance to claimants when completing the N119. When seeking relief from forfeiture, use form N5A. Failure to use the correct form can be remedied under r 3.10.

When the claim relates to possession of residential property, whether rented or mortgaged, the Court Service will on issue include with the Form N5 appropriate guidance notes for the defendant. There are three separate sets of such guidance notes, namely:

(1) mortgaged residential premises – N7;
(2) rented residential premises – N7A;
(3) claim by landlord for forfeiture of a lease – N7B.

When issuing a claim for a demotion of a tenancy as an alternative to a claim for possession, the Claim Form N5 and Particulars of Claim Form N119 are still used. Any claim for an injunction is on Form N16A. Note also the requirements of PD65, para 5.1 in relation to the particulars of claim.

There are no defendant's guidance notes for use with Form N5A (claim for relief against forfeiture), or for use where Form N5 is used against trespassers.

55.4 Particulars of claim

The particulars of claim must be filed and served with the claim form.

(The relevant practice direction and Part 16 provide details about the contents of the particulars of claim)

Amendments—Inserted by SI 2001/256.

'the contents of the particulars of claim' (Explanation to r 55.4)—The general requirements are set out in PD55, para 2.1, although there are additional requirements in relation to demotion claims (PD65, para 5.1).

Residential property—In addition to the general information, PD55, paras 2.3, 2.4 and, if the claim relates to the conduct of the tenant, para 2.4A set out additional requirements where the claim is for possession of residential property let on a tenancy. If the claim is a possession claim under HA 1996, s 143D (possession claim in relation to a demoted tenancy where the landlord is a housing action trust or a local housing authority), then the particulars of claim must have attached to them a copy of the notice to the tenant served under s 143E of the 1996 Act (PD55, para 2.7). The requirements are reflected in Form N119.

Land subject to a mortgage—In addition to the general information, PD55, para 2.5 sets out additional requirements where the claim is for possession of property subject to a mortgage. The requirements in the case of residential premises are reflected in Form N120.

The value of any mortgaged property—It is not a requirement for the claimant to give an indication of the probable value of the property but the court may wish to take a view of the probable equity. If the claimant does not provide it, the court may be left with relying on the information of a defendant seeking to oppose a possession order being made.

Possession claim against trespassers—In addition to the general information, PD55, para 2.6 sets out additional requirements where the claim is for possession of property against trespassers. The requirements are reflected in Form N121.

Evidence—If a case is not allocated to track or it is allocated to the small claims track, any fact that requires to be proved may be proved by evidence in writing (see r 55.8(3)). This is a particularly useful provision as cases are most unlikely to be allocated to track prior to the first hearing. It may be done by attaching copies of all the relevant documents to the particulars of claim (which will be endorsed with a statement of truth). By this means, the attendance of live witnesses at the first hearing may be avoided. If the defendant then disputes material evidence contained in the particulars, the court will normally adjourn the hearing so that oral evidence can be given (PD55, para 5.4).

Conduct—If the claim for possession relates to the conduct of the tenant, the particulars of claim must state details of the conduct alleged (PD55, para 2.4A).

Particulars of Claim N119—This form does not include a paragraph enabling the claimant to seek interest on any rent arrears. If he makes such a claim, it will have to be written into the form.

55.5 Hearing date

(1) The court will fix a date for the hearing when it issues the claim form.

(2) In a possession claim against trespassers the defendant must be served with the claim form, particulars of claim and any witness statements –

(a) in the case of residential property, not less than 5 days; and
(b) in the case of other land, not less than 2 days,

before the hearing date.

(3) In all other possession claims –

(a) the hearing date will be not less than 28 days from the date of issue of the claim form;
(b) the standard period between the issue of the claim form and the hearing will be not more than 8 weeks; and
(c) the defendant must be served with the claim form and particulars of claim not less than 21 days before the hearing date.

(Rule 3.1(2)(a) provides that the court may extend or shorten the time for compliance with any rule)

Amendments—Inserted by SI 2001/256.

'The court will fix a date for the hearing' (r 55.5(1))—The general rules are set out in r 55.5(2) in relation to claims against trespassers and in r 55.5(3) in all other possession claims. But the court may use its power under r 3.1(2)(a) to shorten these time periods. Examples of circumstances in which the court will exercise this power are given in PD55, para 3.2.

'the defendant must be served' (r 55.5(2))—See generally Pt 6. Save in relation to service on trespassers, for which special rules are prescribed in r 55.6, the normal rules as to service in Pt 6 apply and service by any of the methods specified in Pt 6 will suffice. Irregularities in service may be waived under r 3.10 provided the defendants are aware of the proceedings.

'the standard period ... will be not more than 8 weeks' (r 55.5(3)(b))—The combined effect of this and r 55.5(3)(a) is that the first hearing should take place in the 4-week window 5–8 weeks after the date of issue, unless time is abridged by the court using its powers under r 3.1(2)(a) (see note **'The court will fix a date for the hearing'** above).

55.6 Service of claims against trespassers

Where, in a possession claim against trespassers, the claim has been issued against 'persons unknown', the claim form, particulars of claim and any witness statements must be served on those persons by –

(a) (i) attaching copies of the claim form, particulars of claim and any witness statements to the main door or some other part of the land so that they are clearly visible; and

(ii) if practicable, inserting copies of those documents in a sealed transparent envelope addressed to 'the occupiers' through the letter box; or

(b) placing stakes in the land in places where they are clearly visible and attaching to each stake copies of the claim form, particulars of claim and any witness statements in a sealed transparent envelope addressed to 'the occupiers'.

Amendments—Inserted by SI 2001/256.

'stakes and a sealed transparent envelope' (r 55.6(b))—The claimant must provide the court with the required stakes and transparent envelopes, if the court is asked to effect service (PD55, para 4.1).

55.7 Defendant's response

(1) An acknowledgment of service is not required and Part 10 does not apply.

(2) In a possession claim against trespassers rule 15.2 does not apply and the defendant need not file a defence.

(3) Where, in any other possession claim, the defendant does not file a defence within the time specified in rule 15.4, he may take part in any hearing but the court may take his failure to do so into account when deciding what order to make about costs.

(4) Part 12 (default judgment) does not apply in a claim to which this Part applies.

Amendments—Inserted by SI 2001/256.

'Where ... the defendant does not file a defence' (r 55.7(3))—The form of defence which accompanies the claim form in a possession claim against a tenant or a mortgagor is Form N11R or Form N11M, respectively. Although headed 'Defence', they allow the defendant to admit alleged arrears, to propose instalments to discharge them, and to give information on his means in support of his proposal. Notes served with the claim urge defendants to complete and return the form. Rule 45.1(2)(d) makes it clear that, unless the court orders otherwise, fixed costs apply in relation to the claimant's solicitor's charges. For the details see Pt 45, Table 2 and r 45.4A(1). Where the defendant does wish to raise a substantial defence or counterclaim, failure to file and serve it in time may result in a costs order against the defendant, the costs being summarily assessed.

'Part 12 (default judgment)' (r 55.7(4))—This rule continues the procedure under which it is not possible to obtain a default judgment where the defendant fails to file a defence. The claimant must seek his possession order at the hearing.

Time order (CCA 1974, s 129)—An application by the defendant for a time order may be made in his defence. Alternatively it may be made by application notice in the proceedings – see Pt 23 (PD55, para 7.1). Time orders enable the court to order a debtor to pay instalments to the creditor for amounts less than the periodic amounts due under the contract between the parties provided that the debtor is able, over a period of time, to pay all the moneys due to the creditor. Time orders should not be made if there is no realistic prospect of the debtor's financial position improving (*First National Bank plc v Syed* [1991] 2 All ER 250, CA).

Forms—As from 15 October 2001 new Defence Forms N11, N11R (rented residential premises) and N11M (mortgaged residential premises) are in use. The defendant is sent the appropriate defence form by the court along with Guidance Notes N7 (rented residential premises), N7A (mortgaged residential premises) or N7B (forfeiture of the lease) as applicable. Where the claim for possession is issued by a local authority against a defendant who is an introductory tenant Form N11R (although it will have been sent by the court) is not appropriate to record such defence as he may have and either Form N11 or a separately prepared defence should be used. Where the claim is for a demotion of tenancy as an alternative to a claim for possession, the Defence Form is still Form N11R.

55.8 The hearing

(1) At the hearing fixed in accordance with rule 55.5(1) or at any adjournment of that hearing, the court may –

(a) decide the claim; or
(b) give case management directions.

(2) Where the claim is genuinely disputed on grounds which appear to be substantial, case management directions given under paragraph (1)(b) will include the allocation of the claim to a track or directions to enable it to be allocated.

(3) Except where –

(a) the claim is allocated to the fast track or the multi-track; or
(b) the court orders otherwise,

any fact that needs to be proved by the evidence of witnesses at a hearing referred to in paragraph (1) may be proved by evidence in writing.

(Rule 32.2(1) sets out the general rule about evidence. Rule 32.2(2) provides that rule 32.2(1) is subject to any provision to the contrary)

(4) Subject to paragraph (5), all witness statements must be filed and served at least 2 days before the hearing.

(5) In a possession claim against trespassers all witness statements on which the claimant intends to rely must be filed and served with the claim form.

(6) Where the claimant serves the claim form and particulars of claim, he must produce at the hearing a certificate of service of those documents and rule 6.14(2)(a) does not apply.

Amendments—Inserted by SI 2001/256.

'may ... decide the claim' (r 55.8(1)(a))—Where the defendant has entered unlawfully, the court must order possession forthwith unless the claimant agrees to possession on a later date (*McPhail v Persons Unknown* [1973] 3 WLR 71, [1973] 3 All ER 393, CA).

'allocation of the claim to a track' (r 55.8(2))—See r 55.9 below. However, the emphasis is on the court only allocating to track those cases where the claim is 'genuinely disputed on grounds which appear to be substantial'. Cases where, for instance, there are outstanding housing benefit queries or where there is a dispute as to the amount of the mortgage arrears will be adjourned and relisted for hearing without being allocated to track.

'evidence in writing' (r 55.8(3))—The rule contains a fundamental change to present practice and provides a steer in favour of written, rather than oral, evidence being placed before the court. Each party should wherever possible include all the evidence he wishes to present in his statement of case, verified by a statement of truth (for which see Pt 22 generally). Attention must also be given to r 55.10(2) which requires mortgagees seeking possession to give the occupiers of the premises notice of the hearing at least 14 days before the date fixed for it; rule 55.10(4) requires the claimant to produce both a copy of the occupiers' notice and evidence of service of it at the hearing.

'rule 6.14(2)(a) does not apply' (r 55.8(6))—Where the claimant himself serves the defendant, this rule requires the claimant to produce a certificate of service of both claim form and particulars of claim at the hearing. By disapplying r 6.14(2)(a) the court does not require the certificate of service to be lodged within 7 days of service. It is also unlikely that a court would require a certificate of service where the defendant attends the hearing himself.

Evidence up to the date of the hearing—The evidence of the amount of any rent or mortgage arrears and interest on those arrears should, if possible, be up to date to the date of the hearing (if necessary by specifying a daily rate of arrears and interest) (PD55, para 5.2). However, r 55.8(4) does not prevent such evidence being brought up to date orally or in writing on the day of the hearing if necessary.

Mortgagees' evidence—As from 13 October 2003, HM Land Registry has ceased to issue charge certificates. By virtue of Land Registration Act 2002, s 67(1) official copies of the register of title are admissible in evidence to the same extent as the original. Existing charge certificates have ceased to have any legal significance.

Defendant's evidence—If relevant the defendant should give evidence of –
(1) the amount of any outstanding social security or housing benefit payments relevant to rent or mortgage arrears; and
(2) the status of –
  (a) any claims for social security or housing benefit about which a decision has not yet been made; and
  (b) any applications to appeal or review a social security or housing benefit decision where that appeal or review has not yet concluded (PD55, para 5.3).

Consumer Credit Act claims relating to the recovery of land—If the defendant has made an application for a time order (either in his defence or by application notice – see note **'Time order (CCA 1974, s 129)'** under r 55.7 above) it will normally be heard on the hearing of the possession claim. Even if he has not done so, the judge may be prepared to entertain an application then, dispensing with notice.

Failure of a witness to attend a hearing—If the maker of a witness statement does not attend a hearing and the other party disputes material evidence contained in his statement, the court will normally adjourn the hearing so that oral evidence can be given (PD55, para 5.4).

Trespassers—Where the defendant has entered unlawfully, the court must order possession forthwith unless the claimant agrees to possession on a later date (*McPhail v Persons Unknown* [1973] Ch 447, [1973] 3 WLR 71, CA). The court has power to make an order for possession of the whole of land owned by the claimant even though trespassers may be occupying only part of the land, particularly where there is a threat of further trespass (*University of Essex v Djemal* [1980] 1 WLR 1301, CA). The court may even grant an order for possession not just in respect of the land actually occupied by the trespassers but also in respect of land to which the trespassers may go (*Secretary of State for the Environment, Food and Rural Affairs v Drury* [2004] EWCA Civ 200, [2004] 1 WLR 1906, [2004] 37 EG 142, [2004] 2 All ER 1056, CA). Orders against trespassers are enforceable against *any* person occupying any part of the land whether named in the order or not (*R v Wandsworth County Court ex parte Wandsworth London Borough Council* [1975] 1 WLR 1314).

Evidence in mortgage possession claim—Section 113 of the Land Registration Act 1925 provides that office copies of the register and of documents filed in the Land Registry, including original charges, are admissible in evidence to the same extent as the originals.

Application by an occupier to be joined as a party—This is usually done by the court of its own initiative at the hearing if a person in occupation wishes to be heard. An unnamed person who wishes to oppose the making of an order must first be joined as a defendant. However, the court then has the power to make an order for costs against him, an order that cannot be made against a person unknown.

Person with disability—The court may not find it reasonable to make an order for possession where the landlord has failed to carry out a proper review under the Disability Discrimination Act 1995 (*Manchester CC v Romano & anor* [2004] EWCA Civ 834, [2004] All ER (D) 349 (Jun), [2004] TLR 384, (2004) *The Times*, 27 July, CA, where the interface between that Act and the Housing Act 1985 is discussed in detail).

Area possession orders—Where there is compelling evidence that the defendants, or people associated with them, will occupy other land of the claimant when they are evicted from the land the subject of the proceedings, the court may make a possession order covering both the land presently occupied and other land owned by the claimant (*Secretary of State for the Environment, Food and Rural Affairs v Drury* [2004] EWCA Civ 200, 2004] 1 WLR 1906, [2004] 37 EG 142, [2004] 2 All ER 1056, CA).

Costs—See note **'Where … the defendant does not file a defence'** under r 55.7 above.

Orders—The appropriate forms to be used are:

- N26 – Order for possession;
- N27 – Order for possession on forfeiture (for rent arrears);
- N27(2) – Order for possession on forfeiture (for rent arrears) (suspended);
- N28 – Order for possession (rented premises) (suspended);
- N31 – Order for possession (mortgaged premises) (suspended);
- N24 – General form of order – is used in cases for relief against forfeiture and for demotion of tenancy.

N26 is used when outright possession is given immediately, or within a specified period of time, and regardless of whether the order is made in respect of rented or mortgaged property or land, or in respect of trespassers.

Practitioners should ask, where possession is ordered on one of the mandatory grounds, that the ground is stated on the face of the order or at least recorded in the judge's note of his order. Otherwise, the position may later be uncertain and the court would assume that it had discretion to permit a suspension (*Diab v Countrywide Rentals 1 plc* (2001) *The Independent*, 5 November, ChD).

55.9 Allocation

(1) When the court decides the track for a possession claim, the matters to which it shall have regard include –

(a) the matters set out in rule 26.8 as modified by the relevant practice direction;

(b) the amount of any arrears of rent or mortgage instalments;

(c) the importance to the defendant of retaining possession of the land;

(d) the importance of vacant possession to the claimant[; and

(e) if applicable, the alleged conduct of the defendant.

(2) The court will only allocate possession claims to the small claims track if all the parties agree.

(3) Where a possession claim has been allocated to the small claims track the claim shall be treated, for the purposes of costs, as if it were proceeding on the fast track except that trial costs shall be in the discretion of the court and shall not exceed the amount that would be recoverable under rule 46.2 (amount of fast track costs) if the value of the claim were up to £3000.

(4) Where all the parties agree the court may, when it allocates the claim, order that rule 27.14 (costs on the small claims track) applies and, where it does so, paragraph (3) does not apply.

Amendments—Inserted by SI 2001/256; amended by SI 2004/1306.

'When the court decides the track for a possession claim' (r 55.9(1))—The financial value of the property will not necessarily be the most important factor in deciding the track for a possession claim and the court may direct a possession claim to be allocated to the fast track even though the value of the property is in excess of £15,000. It is the value of the *claim* (on which the value of the property will have a bearing, limited in most cases) which the court must assess under r 26.8. Probably the main determining factor when allocating a case to track will be the anticipated length of the final hearing, the court usually allocating to the fast track those cases which can be heard within a day and to the multi-track cases which genuinely will take more than a day to be heard. Other factors will include the amount of the rent or mortgage payments in arrear and any particular importance to the parties in obtaining or retaining possession of the property.

Allocation to the small claims track—It would be unusual to allocate disputed claims for possession and/or demotion claims to the small claims track (PD26, para 8.1(1)(c)).

Transfer to a Civil Trial Centre—The practice of requiring all defended multi-track possession cases to be transferred to Civil Trial Centres has been relaxed. Cases of up to 2 days' length will normally be retained at the local feeder court (see PD26, paras 10.1 and 10.2 and the notes to para 10.2).

55.10 Possession claims relating to mortgaged residential property

(1) This rule applies where a mortgagee seeks possession of land which consists of or includes residential property.

(2) Not less than 14 days before the hearing the claimant must send a notice to the property addressed to 'the occupiers'.

(3) The notice referred to in paragraph (2) must –

- (a) state that a possession claim for the property has started;
- (b) show the name and address of the claimant, the defendant and the court which issued the claim form; and
- (c) give details of the hearing.

(4) The claimant must produce at the hearing –

- (a) a copy of the notice; and
- (b) evidence that he has served it.

Amendments—Inserted by SI 2001/256.

55.10A Electronic issue of certain possession claims

(1) A practice direction may make provision for a claimant to start certain types of possession claim in certain courts by requesting the issue of a claim form electronically.

(2) The practice direction may, in particular –

- (a) provide that only particular provisions apply in specific courts;
- (b) specify –
  - (i) the type of possession claim which may be issued electronically;
  - (ii) the conditions that a claim must meet before it may be issued electronically;
- (c) specify the court where the claim may be issued;
- (d) enable the parties to make certain applications or take further steps in relation to the claim electronically;
- (e) specify the requirements that must be fulfilled in relation to such applications or steps;
- (f) enable the parties to correspond electronically with the court about the claim;
- (g) specify the requirements that must be fulfilled in relation to electronic correspondence;
- (h) provide how any fee payable on the filing of any document is to be paid where the document is filed electronically.

(3) The Practice Direction may disapply or modify these Rules as appropriate in relation to possession claims started electronically.

Amendments—Inserted by SI 2005/2292.

II Accelerated Possession Claims of Property Let on an Assured Shorthold Tenancy

55.11 When this section may be used

(1) The claimant may bring a possession claim under this Section of this Part where –

- (a) the claim is brought under section 21 of the 1988 Act to recover possession of residential property let under an assured shorthold tenancy; and
- (b) subject to rule 55.12(2), all the conditions listed in rule 55.12(1) are satisfied.

(2) The claim must be started in the county court for the district in which the property is situated.

(3) In this Section of this Part, a 'demoted assured shorthold tenancy' means a demoted tenancy where the landlord is a registered social landlord.

(By virtue of section 20B of the 1988 Act, a demoted assured shorthold tenancy is an assured shorthold tenancy)

Amendments—Inserted by SI 2001/256; amended by SI 2004/1306.

Scope of provision—This Section of Pt 55 provides an accelerated procedure where residential premises are or have been let under an assured shorthold tenancy. All private tenancies (with certain exceptions) entered into after 28 February 1997 (when the provisions of the Housing Act 1996 came into force) became assured shorthold tenancies.

Hearings—The court will fix a hearing date where the claimant does not satisfy the court that the claim form was served or that he is entitled to possession under HA 1988, s 21 (see r 55.16(2)). The court will also fix a hearing where the defendant seeks postponement of possession on the ground of exceptional hardship and the claimant has not in the claim form stated that he is willing for such a claim for postponement to be dealt with in his absence (see r 55.18). Save for these provisions the court will usually determine the claim for possession without a hearing.

Human Rights Act 1998—In *Donoghue v Poplar Housing and Regeneration Community Association Ltd* [2001] Civ 595, [2001] 2 FLR 284, CA it was argued unsuccessfully that the mandatory right of a claimant landlord to possession of property let on an assured shorthold tenancy after service of 2 months' notice is incompatible with HRA 1998, Sch 1, Pt I, Arts 6 and 8 (right to family life).

'section 21 of the Housing Act 1988' (r 55.11(1)(a))—Under this section (set out in full on the *Civil Court Service* CD-ROM) the court shall make an order for possession if it is satisfied:

- '(a) that the assured shorthold tenancy has come to an end and no further assured tenancy (whether shorthold or not) is for the time being in existence, other than an assured shorthold periodic tenancy (whether statutory or not); and
- (b) the landlord or, in the case of joint landlords, at least one of them has given to the tenant not less than two months' notice in writing stating that he requires possession of the dwelling-house.' (HA 1988, s 21(1)).

A notice under (b) above may be given before or on the day on which the tenancy comes to an end, notwithstanding that on the coming to the end of the fixed term tenancy a statutory periodic tenancy arises (see HA 1988, s 21(2)).

Where a court makes an order for possession by virtue of s 21(1) above, any statutory periodic tenancy which has arisen on the coming to an end of the assured shorthold tenancy shall end (without further notice and regardless of the period) on the day on which the order takes effect (see HA 1988, s 21(3)).

A court shall make an order for possession of a property let on an assured shorthold tenancy which is a periodic tenancy if it is satisfied:

- '(a) that the landlord or, in the case of joint landlords, at least one of them has given to the tenant a notice in writing stating that, after a date specified in the notice, being the last day of a period of the tenancy and not earlier than two months after the date the notice was given, possession of the dwelling-house is required by virtue of this section; and
- (b) that the date specified in the notice under paragraph (a) above is not earlier than the

earliest day on which, apart from section 5(1) above, the tenancy could be brought to an end by a notice to quit given by the landlord on the same date as the notice under paragraph (a) above.' (HA 1988, s 21(4)).

In *Lower Street Properties v Jones* (1996) 28 HLR 877, [1996] 2 EGLR 67, [1996] NPC 29, CA, a claim for possession was dismissed because proceedings were started the day before the s 21 notice expired. It was held that the landlord could not bring proceedings until after the date specified in the notice. However, the Court of Appeal rejected two other challenges by the tenant, namely that the s 21 notice did not specify the date on which possession was required (the wording used was 'at the end of your period of tenancy which will end next after the expiration of two months from the service upon you of this notice') and that, although dated, the notice did not state the date on which it was served. It was held that no date need be specified in a s 21 notice provided that the tenant knows or can easily ascertain the date referred to. Subsequently, the Court of Appeal has reaffirmed that s 21(4)(a) is to be construed strictly in holding that a notice under that subsection must end on the last day of a period of the tenancy (McDonald v Fernandez [2003] EWCA Civ 1219, [2003] 42 EG 128, CA).

55.12 Conditions

(1) The conditions referred to in rule 55.11(1)(b) are that –

- (a) the tenancy and any agreement for the tenancy were entered into on or after 15 January 1989;
- (b) the only purpose of the claim is to recover possession of the property and no other claim is made;
- (c) the tenancy did not immediately follow an assured tenancy which was not an assured shorthold tenancy;
- (d) the tenancy fulfilled the conditions provided by section 19A or 20(1)(a) to (c) of the 1988 Act;
- (e) the tenancy –
  - (i) was the subject of a written agreement;
  - (ii) arises by virtue of section 5 of the 1988 Act but follows a tenancy that was the subject of a written agreement; or
  - (iii) relates to the same or substantially the same property let to the same tenant and on the same terms (though not necessarily as to rent or duration) as a tenancy which was the subject of a written agreement; and
- (f) a notice in accordance with sections 21(1) or 21(4) of the 1988 Act was given to the tenant in writing.

(2) If the tenancy is a demoted assured shorthold tenancy, only the conditions in paragraph (1)(b) and (f) need be satisfied.

Amendments—Inserted by SI 2001/256; amended by SI 2004/1306.

'no other claim is made' (r 55.12(b))—These words do not, however, prevent a claimant from seeking his costs of the application. The intention of the rule is to prevent a landlord claiming rent arrears when applying under Section II of this Part. A landlord seeking to recover rent arrears as well as possession may either bring proceedings under Section I of this Part or alternatively use the Section II procedure to obtain a possession order and claim separately under Pt 7 for judgment for the rent arrears.

'conditions provided by ss 19A or 20(1)(a)–(c) of the 1988 Act' (r 55.12(d))—Prior to 28 February 1997 it was necessary, before the creation of the assured shorthold tenancy, for the landlord to give the tenant a prescribed written notice under HA 1988, s 20 stating that the assured tenancy to which it related was to be a shorthold tenancy. Failure to do so would otherwise result in the unintentional creation of an assured tenancy. However, from 28 February 1997 s 19A of the Act provides that a new assured tenancy is an assured shorthold tenancy and, therefore, it is no longer necessary to give a prospective tenant a notice under s 20. Furthermore, from 28 February 1997, it has also no longer been necessary for the fixed term tenancy to be for a term certain of not less than 6 months, or for the landlord to have no power to determine the tenancy at any time earlier than 6 months from the beginning of the tenancy. However the court cannot make a possession order which takes effect earlier than 6 months from the start of the tenancy (HA 1988, s 21(5)).

'arises by virtue of section 5 of the 1988 Act' (r 55.12(e)(ii))—This section creates a periodic tenancy on the expiry by effluxion of time of a fixed term tenancy, the periodic tenancy being subject to the same terms as the previous fixed term tenancy.

'notice in accordance with s 21(1) or 21(4) of the 1988 Act' (r 55.12(f))—See note **'section 21 of the Housing Act 1988'** at r 55.11 above. Proceedings may be commenced based on a notice given under HA 1988, s 21(4) before the expiry of the first 6 months of the tenancy, but any order for possession made does not take effect until the 6-month date has passed, save in relation to demoted assured shorthold tenancies (HA 1988, s 21(5), (5A)).

55.13 Claim form

(1) The claim form must –

(a) be in the form set out in the relevant practice direction; and
(b) (i) contain such information; and
(ii) be accompanied by such documents,

as are required by that form.

(2) All relevant sections of the form must be completed.

(3) The court will serve the claim form by first class post.

Amendments—Inserted by SI 2001/256.

Costs—The amount allowed for the claimant's solicitor's charges for preparing and filing the claim form, the documents to accompany the claim form and the request for possession is £79.50 (see r 45.4A(2)).

Forms—Form N5B and the Notes for the Claimant N5C have been revised with effect from 15 October 2001. Form N206A – Notice of Issue has been revised to explain more about the procedure following issue.

55.14 Defence

(1) A defendant who wishes to –

(a) oppose the claim; or
(b) seek a postponement of possession in accordance with rule 55.18,

must file his defence within 14 days after service of the claim form.

(2) The defence should be in the form set out in the relevant practice direction.

Amendments—Inserted by SI 2001/256.

Forms—Form N11B and the 'Notes for the defendant' have been revised with effect from 15 October 2001.

55.15 Claim referred to judge

(1) On receipt of the defence the court will –

(a) send a copy to the claimant; and
(b) refer the claim and defence to a judge.

(2) Where the period set out in rule 55.14 has expired without the defendant filing a defence –

(a) the claimant may file a written request for an order for possession; and
(b) the court will refer that request to a judge.

(3) Where the defence is received after the period set out in rule 55.14 has expired but before a request is filed in accordance with paragraph (2), paragraph (1) will still apply.

(4) Where –

- (a) the period set out in rule 55.14 has expired without the defendant filing a defence; and
- (b) the claimant has not made a request for an order for possession under paragraph (2) within 3 months after the expiry of the period set out in rule 55.14,

the claim will be stayed.

Amendments—Inserted by SI 2001/256.

'the claim will be stayed' (r 55.15(4))—If the tenant does not file a defence yet the claimant does not within 3 months of service file a written request for an order for possession, the claim will be automatically stayed. Removal of the stay will necessitate an application (incurring the appropriate fee). The claimant may invite the court to consider it without a hearing and without notice to the defendant. The court will require evidence as to the reasons for the delay.

55.16 Consideration of the claim

(1) After considering the claim and any defence, the judge will –

- (a) make an order for possession under rule 55.17;
- (b) where he is not satisfied as to any of the matters set out in paragraph (2) –
  - (i) direct that a date be fixed for a hearing; and
  - (ii) give any appropriate case management directions; or
- (c) strike out the claim if the claim form discloses no reasonable grounds for bringing the claim.

(2) The matters referred to in paragraph (1)(b) are that –

- (a) the claim form was served; and
- (b) the claimant has established that he is entitled to recover possession under section 21 of the 1988 Act against the defendant.

(3) The court will give all parties not less than 14 days' notice of a hearing fixed under paragraph (1)(b)(i).

(4) Where a claim is struck out under paragraph (1)(c) –

- (a) the court will serve its reasons for striking out the claim with the order; and
- (b) the claimant may apply to restore the claim within 28 days after the date the order was served on him.

Amendments—Inserted by SI 2001/256.

'direct that a date be fixed' (r 55.16(1)(b)(i))—Not less than 14 days' notice must be given (see r 55.16(3)).

'strike out the claim' (r 55.16(1)(c))—One of the more common reasons to strike out a claim would be that the s 21 notice was invalid (see note **'section 21 of the Housing Act 1988'** under r 55.11 above). When striking out the case the court will give its reasons (r 55.16(4)(a)). The claimant then has 28 days in which to apply to have the claim restored (r 55.16(4)(b)). The practice direction is silent as to whether the application can be dealt with without notice to the defendant and/or without a hearing. Practice may vary between courts.

55.17 Possession order

Except where rules 55.16(1)(b) or (c) apply, the judge will make an order for possession without requiring the attendance of the parties.

Amendments—Inserted by SI 2001/256.

Forms—The Order for Possession is in Form N26A.

55.18 Postponement of possession

(1) Where the defendant seeks postponement of possession on the ground of exceptional hardship under section 89 of the Housing Act 1980, the judge may direct a hearing of that issue.

(2) Where the judge directs a hearing under paragraph (1) –

(a) the hearing must be held before the date on which possession is to be given up; and

(b) the judge will direct how many days' notice the parties must be given of that hearing.

(3) Where the judge is satisfied, on a hearing directed under paragraph (1), that exceptional hardship would be caused by requiring possession to be given up by the date in the order of possession, he may vary the date on which possession must be given up.

Amendments—Inserted by SI 2001/256.

Practice Direction—The detail of the procedure is given by PD55, paras 8.1 to 8.4, which make it clear that if the judge is satisfied as to the matters set out in r 55.16(2), he will make an order for possession whether or not the defendant seeks a postponement. Normally, as he will not have considered the question, he will not have found that exceptional hardship would be caused and the order must require possession within a period not exceeding 14 days (HA 1980, s 89). At the same time, the court will give notice of a hearing within that period at which it will consider whether to vary the order to require possession by a later date (but no more than 6 weeks from the date of the original order). The exception is where the judge is satisfied that the defendant has shown exceptional hardship, he considers that possession should be given up 6 weeks after the date of the order (or earlier, if that is what the defendant seeks) and the claimant indicated on his claim form that he would be content for the court to make such an order without a hearing. In such a case, the judge may fix at the outset a date for possession up to 6 weeks from the date of the order.

'section 89 of the Housing Act 1980' (r 55.18(1))—Section 89(1) (set out in full on the *Civil Court Service* CD-ROM) provides that:

> 'Where a court makes an order for the possession of any land in a case not falling within the exceptions mentioned in s 89(2), the giving up of possession shall not be postponed … to a date later than fourteen days after the making of the order, unless it appears to the court that exceptional hardship would be caused by requiring possession to be given up by that date; and shall not in any event be postponed to a date later than six weeks after the making of the order.'

55.19 Application to set aside or vary

The court may –

(a) on application by a party within 14 days of service of the order; or

(b) of its own initiative,

set aside or vary any order made under rule 55.17.

Amendments—Inserted by SI 2001/256.

III Interim Possession Orders

55.20 When this Section may be used

(1) This Section of this Part applies where the claimant seeks an Interim Possession Order.

(2) In this section –

(a) 'IPO' means Interim Possession Order; and
(b) 'premises' has the same meaning as in section 12 of the Criminal Law Act 1977.

(3) Where this Section requires an act to be done within a specified number of hours, rule 2.8(4) does not apply.

Amendments—Inserted by SI 2002/2058.

Scope of provision—The claimant has a choice of remedy against a trespasser. Proceedings can be commenced using either the procedure set out in Pt 55, Section I and set out in Guide 52, or the IPO procedure to be found in this Section and set out in Guide 45.

As an alternative to the IPO procedure, and particularly where the conditions for applying under Pt 55, Section III are not present but where nevertheless there is a real emergency, practitioners may wish to consider the use of the procedure in Pt 55, Section I coupled with an application to abridge time for service (see rr 55.5 and 3.1(2)(a)). Furthermore, under the IPO procedure there is the expense of two court hearings (rather than just the one under the standard procedure in Pt 55, Section I) and the claimant is required to give undertakings in damages as a condition of the grant of an IPO.

55.21 Conditions for IPO application

(1) An application for an IPO may be made where the following conditions are satisfied –

(a) the only claim made is a possession claim against trespassers for the recovery of premises;
(b) the claimant –
 (i) has an immediate right to possession of the premises; and
 (ii) has had such a right throughout the period of alleged unlawful occupation; and
(c) the claim is made within 28 days of the date on which the claimant first knew, or ought reasonably to have known, that the defendant (or any of the defendants), was in occupation.

(2) An application for an IPO may not be made against a defendant who entered or remained on the premises with the consent of a person who, at the time consent was given, had an immediate right to possession of the premises.

Amendments—Inserted by SI 2002/2058.

'trespassers' (r 55.21(1)(a))—Note the definition at r 55.1(b).

55.22 The application

(1) Rules 55.3(1) and (4) apply to the claim.

(2) The claim form and the defendant's form of witness statement must be in the form set out in the relevant practice direction.

(3) When he files his claim form, the claimant must also file –

(a) an application notice in the form set out in the relevant practice direction; and

(b) written evidence.

(4) The written evidence must be given –

(a) by the claimant personally; or
(b) where the claimant is a body corporate, by a duly authorised officer.

(Rule 22.1(6)(b) provides that the statement of truth must be signed by the maker of the witness statement)

(5) The court will –

(a) issue –
(i) the claim form; and
(ii) the application for the IPO; and
(b) set a date for the hearing of the application.

(6) The hearing of the application will be as soon as practicable but not less than 3 days after the date of issue.

Amendments—Inserted by SI 2002/2058.

'Rule 55.3(1)' (r 55.22(1))—The claim must be started in the county court where the land is situated.

'Rule 55.3 … (4)' (r 55.22(1))—Where the claimant does not know the name of a person in occupation of the land, the claim must be brought against 'persons unknown' in addition to any named defendants.

Forms—The forms referred to in r 55.22(2), (3)(a) are:
(a) claim form – N5;
(b) defendant's witness statement – N133;
(c) application notice – N130.

55.23 Service

(1) Within 24 hours of the issue of the application, the claimant must serve on the defendant –

(a) the claim form;
(b) the application notice together with the written evidence in support; and
(c) a blank form for the defendant's witness statement (as set out in the relevant practice direction) which must be attached to the application notice.

(2) The claimant must serve the documents listed in paragraph (1) in accordance with rule 55.6(a).

(3) At or before the hearing the claimant must file a certificate of service in relation to the documents listed in paragraph (1) and rule 6.14(2)(a) does not apply.

Amendments—Inserted by SI 2002/2058.

Forms—Certificate of service – N215.

55.24 Defendant's response

(1) At any time before the hearing the defendant may file a witness statement in response to the application.

(2) The witness statement should be in the form set out in the relevant practice direction.

Amendments—Inserted by SI 2002/2058.

Forms—Witness statement – N133.

55.25 Hearing of the application

(1) In deciding whether to grant an IPO, the court will have regard to whether the claimant has given, or is prepared to give, the following undertakings in support of his application –

(a) if, after an IPO is made, the court decides that the claimant was not entitled to the order to –
 (i) reinstate the defendant if so ordered by the court; and
 (ii) pay such damages as the court may order; and
(b) before the claim for possession is finally decided, not to –
 (i) damage the premises;
 (ii) grant a right of occupation to any other person; and
 (iii) damage or dispose of any of the defendant's property.

(2) The court will make an IPO if –

(a) the claimant has –
 (i) filed a certificate of service of the documents referred to in rule 55.23(1); or
 (ii) proved service of those documents to the satisfaction of the court; and
(b) the court considers that –
 (i) the conditions set out in rule 55.21(1) are satisfied; and
 (ii) any undertakings given by the claimant as a condition of making the order are adequate.

(3) An IPO will be in the form set out in the relevant practice direction and will require the defendant to vacate the premises specified in the claim form within 24 hours of the service of the order.

(4) On making an IPO the court will set a date for the hearing of the claim for possession which will be not less than 7 days after the date on which the IPO is made.

(5) Where the court does not make an IPO –

(a) the court will set a date for the hearing of the claim;
(b) the court may give directions for the future conduct of the claim; and
(c) subject to such directions, the claim shall proceed in accordance with Section I of this Part.

Amendments—Inserted by SI 2002/2058.

Forms—Certificate of service – N215;
Interim Possession Order – N134.

55.26 Service and enforcement of the IPO

(1) An IPO must be served within 48 hours after it is sealed.

(2) The claimant must serve the IPO on the defendant together with copies of –

(a) the claim form; and
(b) the written evidence in support,

in accordance with rule 55.6(a).

(3) CCR Order 26, rule 17 does not apply to the enforcement of an IPO.

(4) If an IPO is not served within the time limit specified by this rule, the claimant may apply to the court for directions for the claim for possession to continue under Section I of this Part.

Amendments—Inserted by SI 2002/2058.

55.27 After IPO made

(1) Before the date for the hearing of the claim, the claimant must file a certificate of service in relation to the documents specified in rule 55.26(2).

(2) The IPO will expire on the date of the hearing of the claim.

(3) At the hearing the court may make any order it considers appropriate and may, in particular –

(a) make a final order for possession;
(b) dismiss the claim for possession;
(c) give directions for the claim for possession to continue under Section I of this Part; or
(d) enforce any of the claimant's undertakings.

(4) Unless the court directs otherwise, the claimant must serve any order or directions in accordance with rule 55.6(a).

(5) CCR Order 24, rule 6 applies to the enforcement of a final order for possession.

Amendments—Inserted by SI 2002/2058.

Forms—Certificate of service – N215;
Final Order for Possession – N136.

55.28 Application to set aside IPO

(1) If the defendant has left the premises, he may apply on grounds of urgency for the IPO to be set aside before the date of the hearing of the claim.

(2) An application under paragraph (1) must be supported by a witness statement.

(3) On receipt of the application, the court will give directions as to –

(a) the date for the hearing; and
(b) the period of notice, if any, to be given to the claimant and the method of service of any such notice.

(4) No application to set aside an IPO may be made under rule 39.3.

(5) Where no notice is required under paragraph (3)(b), the only matters to be dealt with at the hearing of the application to set aside are whether –

(a) the IPO should be set aside; and
(b) any undertaking to reinstate the defendant should be enforced,

and all other matters will be dealt with at the hearing of the claim.

(6) The court will serve on all the parties –

(a) a copy of the order made under paragraph (5); and
(b) where no notice was required under paragraph (3)(b), a copy of the defendant's application to set aside and the witness statement in support.

(7) Where notice is required under paragraph (3)(b), the court may treat the hearing of the application to set aside as the hearing of the claim.

Amendments—Inserted by SI 2002/2058.

'If the defendant has left the premises' (r 55.28(1))—There is no provision for a defendant to appeal the making of an IPO without the defendant first having vacated the premises in question. Where a defendant appears to have a meritorious defence he would have to vacate the premises and apply the same day to the court, without notice to the claimant, for an order setting aside the IPO.

Practice Direction – Possession Claims

This Practice Direction supplements CPR Part 55 (PD55)

SECTION I – GENERAL RULES

55.3 – STARTING THE CLAIM

1.1 Except where the county court does not have jurisdiction, possession claims should normally be brought in the county court. Only exceptional circumstances justify starting a claim in the High Court.

1.2 If a claimant starts a claim in the High Court and the court decides that it should have been started in the county court, the court will normally either strike the claim out or transfer it to the county court on its own initiative. This is likely to result in delay and the court will normally disallow the costs of starting the claim in the High Court and of any transfer.

1.3 Circumstances which may, in an appropriate case, justify starting a claim in the High Court are if –

(1) there are complicated disputes of fact;
(2) there are points of law of general importance; or
(3) the claim is against trespassers and there is a substantial risk of public disturbance or of serious harm to persons or property which properly require immediate determination.

1.4 The value of the property and the amount of any financial claim may be relevant circumstances, but these factors alone will not normally justify starting the claim in the High Court.

1.5 The claimant must use the appropriate claim form and particulars of claim form set out in Table 1 to Part 4 Practice Direction. The defence must be in form N11, N11B, N11M or N11R, as appropriate.

1.6 High Court claims for the possession of land subject to a mortgage will be assigned to the Chancery Division.

1.7 A claim which is not a possession claim may be brought under the procedure set out in Section I of Part 55 if it is started in the same claim form as a possession claim which, by virtue of rule 55.2(1) must be brought in accordance with that Section.

(Rule 7.3 provides that a claimant may use a single claim form to start all claims which can be conveniently disposed of in the same proceedings)

1.8 For example a claim under paragraphs 4, 5 or 6 of Part I of Schedule 1 to the Mobile Homes Act 1983 may be brought using the procedure set out in Section I of Part 55 if the claim is started in the same claim form as a claim enforcing the rights referred to in section 3(1)(b) of the Caravan Sites Act 1968 (which, by virtue of rule 55.2(1) must be brought under Section I of Part 55).

1.9 Where the claim form includes a demotion claim, the claim must be started in the county court for the district in which the land is situated.

55.4 – PARTICULARS OF CLAIM

2.1 In a possession claim the particulars of claim must:

(1) identify the land to which the claim relates;
(2) state whether the claim relates to residential property;
(3) state the ground on which possession is claimed;
(4) give full details about any mortgage or tenancy agreement; and
(5) give details of every person who, to the best of the claimant's knowledge, is in possession of the property;

Residential property let on a tenancy

2.2 Paragraphs 2.3, 2.4 and 2.4A apply if the claim relates to residential property let on a tenancy.

2.3 If the claim includes a claim for non-payment of rent the particulars of claim must set out:

(1) the amount due at the start of the proceedings;
(2) in schedule form, the dates and amounts of all payments due and payments made under the tenancy agreement for a period of two years immediately preceding the date of issue, or if the first date of default occurred less than two years before the date of issue from the first date of default and a running total of the arrears;
(3) the daily rate of any rent and interest;
(4) any previous steps taken to recover the arrears of rent with full details of any court proceedings; and
(5) any relevant information about the defendant's circumstances, in particular:
    (a) whether the defendant is in receipt of social security benefits; and
    (b) whether any payments are made on his behalf directly to the claimant under the Social Security Contributions and Benefits Act 1992.

2.3A If the claimant wishes to rely on a history of arrears which is longer than two years, he should state this in his particulars and exhibit a full (or longer) schedule to a witness statement.

2.4 If the claimant knows of any person (including a mortgagee) entitled to claim relief against forfeiture as underlessee under section 146(4) of the Law of Property Act 1925 (or in accordance with section 38 of the Supreme Court Act 1981, or section 138(9C) of the County Courts Act 1984):

(1) the particulars of claim must state the name and address of that person; and
(2) the claimant must file a copy of the particulars of claim for service on him.

2.4A If the claim for possession relates to the conduct of the tenant, the particulars of claim must state details of the conduct alleged.

Land subject to a mortgage

2.5 If the claim is a possession claim by a mortgagee, the particulars of claim must also set out:

(1) if the claim relates to residential property whether:
  (a) a land charge of Class F has been registered under section 2(7) of the Matrimonial Homes Act 1967;
  (b) a notice registered under section 2(8) or 8(3) of the Matrimonial Homes Act 1983 has been entered and on whose behalf; or
  (c) a notice under section 31(10) of the Family Law Act 1996 has been registered and on whose behalf; and

  if so, that the claimant will serve notice of the claim on the persons on whose behalf the land charge is registered or the notice or caution entered.

(2) the state of the mortgage account by including:
  (a) the amount of:
    (i) the advance;
    (ii) any periodic repayment; and
    (iii) any payment of interest required to be made;
  (b) the amount which would have to be paid (after taking into account any adjustment for early settlement) in order to redeem the mortgage at a stated date not more than 14 days after the claim started specifying the amount of solicitor's costs and administration charges which would be payable;
  (c) if the loan which is secured by the mortgage is a regulated consumer credit agreement, the total amount outstanding under the terms of the mortgage; and
  (d) the rate of interest payable:
    (i) at the commencement of the mortgage;
    (ii) immediately before any arrears referred to in paragraph (3) accrued;
    (iii) at the commencement of the proceedings.

(3) if the claim is brought because of failure to pay the periodic payments when due:
  (a) in schedule form, the dates and amounts of all payments due and payments made under the mortgage agreement or mortgage deed for a period of two years immediately preceding the date of issue, or if the first date of default occurred less than two years before the date of issue from the first date of default and a running total of the arrears;
  (b) give details of:
    (i) any other payments required to be made as a term of the mortgage (such as for insurance premiums, legal costs, default interest, penalties, administrative or other charges);
    (ii) any other sums claimed and stating the nature and amount of each such charge; and
    (iii) whether any of these payments is in arrears and whether or not it is included in the amount of any periodic payment.

(4) whether or not the loan which is secured by the mortgage is a regulated

consumer credit agreement and, if so, specify the date on which any notice required by sections 76 or 87 of the Consumer Credit Act 1974 was given;

(5) if appropriate details that show the property is not one to which section 141 of the Consumer Credit Act 1974 applies;

(6) any relevant information about the defendant's circumstances, in particular:
   (a) whether the defendant is in receipt of social security benefits; and
   (b) whether any payments are made on his behalf directly to the claimant under the Social Security Contributions and Benefits Act 1992;

(7) give details of any tenancy entered into between the mortgagor and mortgagee (including any notices served); and

(8) state any previous steps which the claimant has taken to recover the money secured by the mortgage or the mortgaged property and, in the case of court proceedings, state:
   (a) the dates when the claim started and concluded; and
   (b) the dates and terms of any orders made.

2.5A If the claimant wishes to rely on a history of arrears which is longer than two years, he should state this in his particulars and exhibit a full (or longer) schedule to a witness statement.

Possession claim against trespassers

2.6 If the claim is a possession claim against trespassers, the particulars of claim must state the claimant's interest in the land or the basis of his right to claim possession and the circumstances in which it has been occupied without licence or consent.

Possession claim in relation to a demoted tenancy by a housing action trust or a local housing authority

2.7 If the claim is a possession claim under section 143D of the Housing Act 1996 (possession claim in relation to a demoted tenancy where the landlord is a housing action trust or a local housing authority), the particulars of claim must have attached to them a copy of the notice to the tenant served under section 143E of the 1996 Act.

55.5 – HEARING DATE

3.1 The court may exercise its powers under rules 3.1(2)(a) and (b) to shorten the time periods set out in rules 55.5(2) and (3).

3.2 Particular consideration should be given to the exercise of this power if:

(1) the defendant, or a person for whom the defendant is responsible, has assaulted or threatened to assault:
   (a) the claimant;
   (b) a member of the claimant's staff; or
   (c) another resident in the locality;

(2) there are reasonable grounds for fearing such an assault; or

(3) the defendant, or a person for whom the defendant is responsible, has caused serious damage or threatened to cause serious damage to the property or to the home or property of another resident in the locality.

3.3 Where paragraph 3.2 applies but the case cannot be determined at the first hearing fixed under rule 55.5, the court will consider what steps are needed to finally determine the case as quickly as reasonably practicable.

55.6 – SERVICE IN CLAIMS AGAINST TRESPASSERS

4.1 If the claim form is to be served by the court and in accordance with rule 55.6(b) the claimant must provide sufficient stakes and transparent envelopes.

55.8 – THE HEARING

5.1 Attention is drawn to rule 55.8(3). Each party should wherever possible include all the evidence he wishes to present in his statement of case, verified by a statement of truth.

5.2 If relevant the claimant's evidence should include the amount of any rent or mortgage arrears and interest on those arrears. These amounts should, if possible, be up to date to the date of the hearing (if necessary by specifying a daily rate of arrears and interest). However, rule 55.8(4) does not prevent such evidence being brought up to date orally or in writing on the day of the hearing if necessary.

5.3 If relevant the defendant should give evidence of:

(1) the amount of any outstanding social security or housing benefit payments relevant to rent or mortgage arrears; and
(2) the status of:
  (a) any claims for social security or housing benefit about which a decision has not yet been made; and
  (b) any applications to appeal or review a social security or housing benefit decision where that appeal or review has not yet concluded.

5.4 If:

(1) the maker of a witness statement does not attend a hearing; and
(2) the other party disputes material evidence contained in his statement,

the court will normally adjourn the hearing so that oral evidence can be given.

CONSUMER CREDIT ACT CLAIMS RELATING TO THE RECOVERY OF LAND

7.1 Any application by the defendant for a time order under section 129 of the Consumer Credit Act 1974 may be made:

(1) in his defence; or
(2) by application notice in the proceedings.

ENFORCEMENT OF CHARGING ORDER BY SALE

7.2 A party seeking to enforce a charging order by sale should follow the procedure set out in rule 73.10 and the Part 55 procedure should not be used.

SECTION II – ACCELERATED POSSESSION CLAIMS OF PROPERTY LET ON AN ASSURED SHORTHOLD TENANCY

55.18 – POSTPONEMENT OF POSSESSION

8.1 If the judge is satisfied as to the matters set out in rule 55.16(2), he will make an order for possession in accordance with rule 55.17, whether or not the defendant seeks a postponement of possession on the ground of exceptional hardship under section 89 of the Housing Act 1980.

8.2 In a claim in which the judge is satisfied that the defendant has shown exceptional hardship, he will only postpone possession without directing a hearing under rule 55.18(1) if –

(1) he considers that possession should be given up 6 weeks after the date of the order or, if the defendant has requested postponement to an earlier date, on that date; and
(2) the claimant indicated on his claim form that he would be content for the court to make such an order without a hearing.

8.3 In all other cases if the defendant seeks a postponement of possession under section 89 of the Housing Act 1980, the judge will direct a hearing under rule 55.18(1).

8.4 If, at that hearing, the judge is satisfied that exceptional hardship would be caused by requiring possession to be given up by the date in the order of possession, he may vary that order under rule 55.18(3) so that possession is to be given up at a later date. That later date may be no later than 6 weeks after the making of the order for possession on the papers (see section 89 of the Housing Act 1980).

SECTION III – INTERIM POSSESSION ORDERS

9.1 The claim form must be in Form N5, the application notice seeking the interim possession order must be in Form N130 and the defendant's witness statement must be in Form N133.

9.2 The IPO will be in Form N134 (annexed to this practice direction).

Forms—Also note that the Order for Possession is Form N136.

Practice Direction – Possession Claims Online

This Practice Direction supplements CPR Part 55.10A (PD55b)

SCOPE OF THIS PRACTICE DIRECTION

1.1 This practice direction provides for a scheme ('Possession Claims Online') to operate in specified county courts –

(1) enabling claimants and their representatives to start certain possession claims under CPR Part 55 by requesting the issue of a claim form electronically via the PCOL website; and

(2) where a claim has been started electronically, enabling the claimant or defendant and their representatives to take further steps in the claim electronically as specified below.

1.2 In this practice direction –

(1) 'PCOL website' means the website www.possessionclaim.gov.uk which may be accessed via Her Majesty's Courts Service website (www.hmcourts-service.gov.uk) and through which Possession Claims Online will operate; and

(2) 'specified court' means a county court specified on the PCOL website as one in which Possession Claims Online is available.

INFORMATION ON THE PCOL WEBSITE

2.1 The PCOL website contains further details and guidance about the operation of Possession Claims Online.

2.2 In particular the PCOL website sets out –

(1) the specified courts; and

(2) the dates from which Possession Claims Online will be available in each specified court.

2.3 The operation of Possession Claims Online in any specified court may be restricted to taking certain of the steps specified in this practice direction, and in such cases the PCOL website will set out the steps which may be taken using Possession Claims Online in that specified court.

SECURITY

3.1 Her Majesty's Courts Service will take such measures as it thinks fit to ensure the security of steps taken or information stored electronically. These may include requiring users of Possession Claims Online –

(1) to enter a customer identification number or password;

(2) to provide personal information for identification purposes; and

(3) to comply with any other security measures,

before taking any step online.

FEES

4.1 A step may only be taken using Possession Claims Online on payment of the prescribed fee where a fee is payable. Where this practice direction provides for a fee to be paid electronically, it may be paid by –

(1) credit card;

(2) debit card; or

(3) any other method which Her Majesty's Courts Service may permit.

4.2 A defendant who wishes to claim exemption from payment of fees must do so through an organisation approved by Her Majesty's Courts Service before taking any step using PCOL which attracts a fee. If satisfied that the defendant is entitled to fee exemption, the organisation will submit the fee exemption form through the PCOL website to Her Majesty's Courts Service. The defendant may then use PCOL to take such a step.

(Her Majesty's Courts Service website contains guidance as to when the entitlement to claim an exemption from payment of fees arises. The PCOL website will contain a list of organisations through which the defendant may claim an exemption from fees).

CLAIMS WHICH MAY BE STARTED USING POSSESSION CLAIMS ONLINE

5.1 A claim may be started online if –

(1) it is brought under Section I of Part 55;
(2) it includes a possession claim for residential property by –
   (a) a landlord against a tenant, solely on the ground of arrears of rent (but not a claim for forfeiture of a lease); or
   (b) a mortgagee against a mortgagor, solely on the ground of default in the payment of sums due under a mortgage,
   relating to land within the district of a specified court;
(3) it does not include a claim for any other remedy except for payment of arrears of rent or money due under a mortgage, interest and costs;
(4) the defendant has an address for service in England and Wales; and
(5) the claimant is able to provide a postcode for the property.

5.2 A claim must not be started online if a defendant is known to be a child or patient.

STARTING A CLAIM

6.1 A claimant may request the issue of a claim form by –

(1) completing an online claim form at the PCOL website;
(2) paying the appropriate issue fee electronically at the PCOL website or by some other means approved by Her Majesty's Courts Service.

6.2 The particulars of claim must be included in the online claim form and may not be filed separately. It is not necessary to file a copy of the tenancy agreement, mortgage deed or mortgage agreement with the particulars of claim.

6.3 The particulars of claim must include a history of the rent or mortgage account, in schedule form setting out –

(1) the dates and amounts of all payments due and payments made under the tenancy agreement, mortgage deed or mortgage agreement either from the first date of default if that date occurred less than two years before the date of issue or for a period of two years immediately preceding the date of issue; and
(2) a running total of the arrears.

6.4 If the claimant wishes to rely on a history of arrears which is longer than two years, he should state this in his particulars and exhibit a full (or longer) schedule to a witness statement.

6.5 When an online claim form is received, an acknowledgment of receipt will automatically be sent to the claimant. The acknowledgment does not constitute notice that the claim form has been issued or served.

6.6 When the court issues a claim form following the submission of an online claim form, the claim is 'brought' for the purposes of the Limitation Act 1980 and any other enactment on the date on which the online claim form is received by the court's computer system. The court will keep a record, by electronic or other means, of when online claim forms are received.

6.7 When the court issues a claim form it will –

(1) serve a printed version of the claim form and a defence form on the defendant; and
(2) send the claimant notice of issue by post or, where the claimant has supplied an e-mail address, by electronic means.

6.8 The claim shall be deemed to be served on the fifth day after the claim was issued irrespective of whether that day is a business day or not.

6.9 Where the period of time within which a defence must be filed ends on a day when the court is closed, the defendant may file his defence on the next day that the court is open.

6.10 The claim form shall have printed on it a unique customer identification number or a password by which the defendant may access the claim on the PCOL website.

6.11 PCOL will issue the proceedings in the appropriate county court by reference to the post code provided by the claimant and that court shall have jurisdiction to hear and determine the claim and to carry out enforcement of any judgment irrespective of whether the property is within or outside the jurisdiction of that court.

(CPR 30.2(1) authorises proceedings to be transferred from one county court to another.)

DEFENCE

7.1 A defendant wishing to file –

(1) a defence; or
(2) a counterclaim (to be filed together with a defence) to a claim which has been issued through the PCOL system,
may, instead of filing a written form, do so by –
(a) completing the relevant online form at the PCOL website; and
(b) if the defendant is making a counterclaim, paying the appropriate fee electronically at the PCOL website or by some other means approved by Her Majesty's Courts Service.

7.2 Where a defendant files a defence by completing the relevant online form, he must not send the court a hard copy.

7.3 When an online defence form is received, an acknowledgment of receipt will automatically be sent to the defendant. The acknowledgment does not constitute notice that the defence has been served.

7.4 The online defence form will be treated as being filed –

(1) on the day the court receives it, if it receives it before 4 p.m. on a working day; and
(2) otherwise, on the next working day after the court receives the online defence form.

7.5 A defence is filed when the online defence form is received by the court's computer system. The court will keep a record, by electronic or other means, of when online defence forms are received.

STATEMENT OF TRUTH

8.1 CPR Part 22 requires any statement of case to be verified by a statement of truth. This applies to any online claims and defences and application notices.

8.2 CPR Part 22 also requires that if an applicant wishes to rely on matters set out in his application notice as evidence, the application notice must be verified by a statement of truth. This applies to any application notice completed online that contains matters on which the applicant wishes to rely as evidence.

8.3 Attention is drawn to –

(1) paragraph 2 of the practice direction supplementing CPR Part 22, which stipulates the form of the statement of truth; and
(2) paragraph 3 of the practice direction supplementing CPR Part 22, which provides who may sign a statement of truth; and
(3) CPR 32.14, which sets out the consequences of making, or causing to be made, a false statement in a document verified by a statement of truth, without an honest belief in its truth.

SIGNATURE

9.1 Any provision of the CPR which requires a document to be signed by any person is satisfied by that person entering his name on an online form.

COMMUNICATION WITH THE COURT ELECTRONICALLY BY THE MESSAGING SERVICE

10.1 If the PCOL website specifies that a court accepts electronic communications relating to claims brought using Possession Claims Online the parties may communicate with the court using the messaging service facility, available on the PCOL website ('the messaging service').

10.2 The messaging service is for brief and straightforward communications only. The PCOL website contains a list of examples of when it will not be appropriate to use the messaging service.

10.3 Parties must not send to the court forms or attachments via the messaging service.

10.4 The court shall treat any forms or attachments sent via the messaging service as not having been filed or received.

10.5 The court will normally reply via the messaging service where –

(1) the response is to a message transmitted via the messaging service; and
(2) the sender has provided an e-mail address.

ELECTRONIC APPLICATIONS

11.1 Certain applications in relation to a possession claim started online may be made electronically ('online applications'). An online application may be made if a form for that application is published on the PCOL website ('online application form') and the application is made at least five clear days before the hearing.

11.2 If a claim for possession has been started online and a party wishes to make an online application, he may do so by –

(1) completing the appropriate online application form at the PCOL website; and

(2) paying the appropriate fee electronically at the PCOL website or by some other means approved by Her Majesty's Courts Service.

11.3 When an online application form is received, an acknowledgment of receipt will automatically be sent to the applicant. The acknowledgment does not constitute a notice that the online application form has been issued or served.

11.4 Where an application must be made within a specified time, it is so made if the online application form is received by the court's computer system within that time. The court will keep a record, by electronic or other means, of when online application forms are received.

11.5 When the court receives an online application form it shall –

(1) serve a copy of the online application endorsed with the date of the hearing by post on the claimant at least two clear days before the hearing; and
(2) send the defendant notice of service and confirmation of the date of the hearing by post; provided that
(3) where either party has provided the court with an e-mail address for service, service of the application and/or the notice of service and confirmation of the hearing date may be effected by electronic means.

REQUEST FOR ISSUE OF WARRANT

12.1 Where –

(1) the court has made an order for possession in a claim started online; and
(2) the claimant is entitled to the issue of a warrant of possession without requiring the permission of the court

the claimant may request the issue of a warrant by completing an online request form at the PCOL website and paying the appropriate fee electronically at the PCOL website or by some other means approved by Her Majesty's Courts Service.

12.2 A request under paragraph 12.1 will be treated as being filed –

(1) on the day the court receives the request, if it receives it before 4 p.m. on a working day; and
(2) otherwise, on the next working day after the court receives the request.

(CCR Order 26 rule 5 sets out certain circumstances in which a warrant of execution may not be issued without the permission of the court. CCR Order 26 rule 17(6) applies rule 5 of that Order with necessary modifications to a warrant of possession.)

APPLICATION TO SUSPEND WARRANT OF POSSESSION

13.1 Where the court has issued a warrant of possession, the defendant may apply electronically for the suspension of the warrant, provided that:

(1) the application is made at least five clear days before the appointment for possession; and
(2) the defendant is not prevented from making such an application without the permission of the court.

13.2 The defendant may apply electronically for the suspension of the warrant, by –

(1) completing an online application for suspension at the PCOL website; and
(2) paying the appropriate fee electronically at the PCOL website or by some other means approved by Her Majesty's Courts Service.

13.3 When an online application for suspension is received, an acknowledgment of receipt will automatically be sent to the defendant. The acknowledgment does not constitute a notice that the online application for suspension has been served.

13.4 Where an application must be made within a specified time, it is so made if the online application for suspension is received by the court's computer system within that time. The court will keep a record, by electronic or other means, of when online applications for suspension are received.

13.5 When the court receives an online application for suspension it shall –

(1) serve a copy of the online application for suspension endorsed with the date of the hearing by post on the claimant at least two clear days before the hearing; and
(2) send the defendant notice of service and confirmation of the date of the hearing by post; provided that
(3) where either party has provided the court with an e-mail address for service, service of the application and/or the notice of service and confirmation of the hearing date may be effected by electronic means.

VIEWING THE CASE RECORD

14.1 A facility will be provided on the PCOL website for parties or their representatives to view –

(1) an electronic record of the status of claims started online, which will be reviewed and, if necessary, updated at least once each day; and
(2) all information relating to the case that has been filed by the parties electronically.

14.2 In addition, where the PCOL website specifies that the court has the facility to provide viewing of such information by electronic means, the parties or their representatives may view the following information electronically –

(1) court orders made in relation to the case; and
(2) details of progress on enforcement and subsequent orders made.

PART 56
LANDLORD AND TENANT CLAIMS AND MISCELLANEOUS PROVISIONS ABOUT LAND

CONTENTS OF THIS PART

Practice Direction—This Part is supplemented by a practice direction – PD56 – which is set out at p 1340.

I Landlord and Tenant Claims

56.1 Scope and interpretation

(1) In this Section of this Part 'landlord and tenant claim' means a claim under –

(a) the Landlord and Tenant Act 1927;
(b) the Leasehold Property (Repairs) Act 1938;
(c) the Landlord and Tenant Act 1954;
(d) the Landlord and Tenant Act 1985; or
(e) the Landlord and Tenant Act 1987.

(2) A practice direction may set out special provisions with regard to any particular category of landlord and tenant claim.

Amendments—Inserted by SI 2001/256.

Scope of provision—This new Part replaces Sch 1, RSC Ord 97 and Sch 2, CCR Ord 43 as to applications under the Landlord and Tenant Acts 1927, 1954, 1985 and 1987; Sch 2, CCR Ord 49, r 1 as to those under the Access to Neighbouring Land Act 1992; Sch 2, CCR Ord 49, r 8 as to those under the Leasehold Reform Act 1967; and Sch 2, CCR Ord 49, r 9 as to those under the Leasehold Reform, Housing and Urban Development Act 1993. Certain other landlord and tenant provisions are also covered. No forms are intended to be prescribed for proceedings under Pt 56. The new provisions take effect on the 15 October 2001. The Part is supplemented by a practice direction, PD56.

56.2 Starting the claim

(1) The claim must be started in the county court for the district in which the land is situated unless paragraph (2) applies or an enactment provides otherwise.

(2) The claim may be started in the High Court if the claimant files with his claim form a certificate stating the reasons for bringing the claim in that court verified by a statement of truth in accordance with rule 22.1(1).

(3) The practice direction refers to circumstances which may justify starting the claim in the High Court.

(4) (*revoked*)

Amendments—Inserted by SI 2001/256; amended by SI 2004/1306.

Scope of provision—Proceedings under this Part must normally be issued in the county court and only in the High Court in exceptional circumstances or if it has exclusive jurisdiction. Complicated disputes of fact or points of law of general importance may justify the use of the High Court (PD56, para 2.4).

Changes in procedure for opting out—Changes to LTA 1954, Pt II were introduced on 1 June 2004 by the Regulatory Reform (Business Tenancies) (England and Wales) Order 2003, SI 2003/3096 and this rule has been amended to take account of the changes. The previous court-based scheme requiring parties to apply jointly to the court for an order excluding the protection provisions of the Act under s 38(4) ceased to apply on that date. A new procedure for opting out is now in place, which may be summarised as follows –

- Prior to the parties being bound by the contract, the landlord must give the tenant a notice in the form set out in Sch 1 to the 2003 Order.
- If the notice is given 14 days or more before the parties become legally bound, the tenant (or someone duly authorised to do so on his behalf) must make a declaration in the form set out in Sch 2, para 7 of the 2003 Order.
- If the notice is given less than 14 days before the parties become legally bound, the tenant (or someone duly authorised to do so on his behalf) must make a statutory declaration in the form set out in Sch 2, para 8 of the Order.
- In either case, the instrument creating the tenancy must contain a reference to the notice, the requisite declaration and the agreement under the new LTA 1954, s 38A(1).

If any of these requirements are not met, the tenancy will not be excluded from the protection provisions of the Act. Similar provisions for the surrender of tenancies already protected by the Act are set out in Schs 3 and 4 to the Order.

56.3 Claims for a new tenancy under section 24 and for the termination of a tenancy under section 29(2) of the Landlord and Tenant Act 1954

(1) This rule applies to a claim for a new tenancy under section 24 and to a claim for the termination of a tenancy under section 29(2) of the 1954 Act.

(2) In this rule –

(a) 'the 1954 Act' means the Landlord and Tenant Act 1954;
(b) 'an unopposed claim' means a claim for a new tenancy under section 24 of the 1954 Act in circumstances where the grant of a new tenancy is not opposed;
(c) 'an opposed claim' means a claim for –
(i) a new tenancy under section 24 of the 1954 Act in circumstances where the grant of a new tenancy is opposed; or
(ii) the termination of a tenancy under section 29(2) of the 1954 Act.

(3) Where the claim is an unopposed claim –

(a) the claimant must use the Part 8 procedure, but the following rules do not apply –
(i) rule 8.5; and
(ii) rule 8.6;
(b) the claim form must be served within 2 months after the date of issue and rules 7.5 and 7.6 are modified accordingly; and
(c) the court will give directions about the future management of the claim following receipt of the acknowledgment of service.

(4) Where the claim is an opposed claim –

(a) the claimant must use the Part 7 procedure; but
(b) the claim form must be served within 2 months after the date of issue, and rules 7.5 and 7.6 are modified accordingly.

(The practice direction to this Part contains provisions about evidence, including expert evidence in opposed claims)

Amendments—Inserted by SI 2001/256; substituted by SI 2004/1306.

New procedures for terminating a tenancy and asking for a new one—This rule has been amended to take account of the changes to LTA 1954, Pt II introduced on 1 June 2004 by the Regulatory Reform (Business Tenancies) (England and Wales) Order 2003, SI 2003/3096. New provisions apply where a s 25 notice terminating a tenancy or a s 26 request for a new tenancy is given on or after 1 June 2004. The main features of the new procedure may be summarised as follows –

- There are two new s 25 notices – one where the landlord has no objection to a new tenancy and the other where he has.
- There is a new form of s 26 request.
- The tenant is not obliged to give a counter-notice to a landlord's s 25 notice.
- If a landlord wishes to object to a tenant having a new tenancy on one of the grounds set out in s 30(1) of the Act, he still needs to serve a counter-notice to a tenant's s 26 request.
- Either the landlord or the tenant may apply to the court for a tenancy within the same time constraints as applied previously (not less than 2 months or later than 4 months from the giving of the s 25 notice or s 26 request).
- The landlord may apply to the court for the termination of the tenancy where it has objected on one of the statutory grounds.
- A permitted application must be made before the end of the 'statutory period', which is the date specified in the s 25 notice or the day before the date specified in the s 26 notice. That period can be extended by written agreement entered into before the end of the statutory period and there can be further similar extension agreements.
- Applications for interim rent will be capable of being made by either the landlord or the tenant with new provisions concerning the date from which the interim rent is to be paid and the amount of it.

Where a s 25 notice or s 26 request was served before 1 June 2004, the old procedure and the former version of the rule continue to apply. The reader concerned in such a case should refer to the previous edition of this work.

'Landlord and Tenant Act 1954' (r 56.3 generally)—Part II of this Act enables a business tenant to apply for a new tenancy and there are important time constraints to be observed.

'Part 8 procedure' (r 56.3(2))—The exceptions to the Pt 8 procedure referred to in r 56.3(2) are the requirement for an acknowledgment of service (r 8.3(1)) and filing and serving written evidence (rr 8.5 and 8.6(1)). Details of what is required to be in the claim form are contained in PD56, para 3.2.

Staying a claim—The previous provisions providing for an automatic stay of proceedings for 3 months for settlement if requested have now been removed. Parties are expected instead to rely on their right to agree an extension of the time within which proceedings must be started (see above). If the claim is an opposed claim, the Pt 7 procedure is followed. This provides for, among other things, allocation questionnaires. These in turn allow each of the parties to request a stay for settlement.

Allocation—As the Pt 8 procedure applies to this claim, the claim will be treated as allocated to the multi-track (r 8.9(c)).

Forms—Claim Form – N208. Acknowledgment of Service – N210.

II Miscellaneous Provisions about Land

56.4 Scope

A practice direction may set out special provisions with regard to claims under the following enactments –

(a) the Chancel Repairs Act 1932;
(b) the Leasehold Reform Act 1967;
(c) the Access to Neighbouring Land Act 1992;
(d) the Leasehold Reform, Housing and Urban Development Act 1993; and
(e) the Commonhold and Leasehold Reform Act 2002.

Amendments—Inserted by SI 2001/256; amended by SI 2002/3219.

Practice Direction – Landlord and Tenant Claims and Miscellaneous Provisions about Land

This Practice Direction supplements CPR Part 56 (PD56)

SECTION I – LANDLORD AND TENANT CLAIMS

1.1 In this section of this practice direction –

(1) 'the 1927 Act' means the Landlord and Tenant Act 1927;
(2) 'the 1954 Act' means the Landlord and Tenant Act 1954; and
(3) 'the 1985 Act' means the Landlord and Tenant Act 1985; and
(4) 'the 1987 Act' means the Landlord and Tenant Act 1987.

56.2 – STARTING THE CLAIM

2.1 Subject to paragraph 2.1A, the claimant in a landlord and tenant claim must use the Part 8 procedure as modified by Part 56 and this practice direction.

2.1A Where the landlord and tenant claim is a claim for –

(1) a new tenancy under section 24 of the 1954 Act in circumstances where the grant of a new tenancy is opposed; or
(2) the termination of a tenancy under section 29(2) of the 1954 Act,

the claimant must use the Part 7 procedure as modified by Part 56 and this practice direction.

2.2 Except where the county court does not have jurisdiction, landlord and tenant claims should normally be brought in the county court. Only exceptional circumstances justify starting a claim in the High Court.

2.3 If a claimant starts a claim in the High Court and the court decides that it should have been started in the county court, the court will normally either strike the claim out or transfer it to the county court on its own initiative. This is likely to result in delay and the court will normally disallow the costs of starting the claim in the High Court and of any transfer.

2.4 Circumstances which may, in an appropriate case, justify starting a claim in the High Court are if –

(1) there are complicated disputes of fact; or
(2) there are points of law of general importance.

2.5 The value of the property and the amount of any financial claim may be relevant circumstances, but these factors alone will not normally justify starting the claim in the High Court.

2.6 A landlord and tenant claim started in the High Court must be brought in the Chancery Division.

CLAIMS FOR A NEW TENANCY UNDER SECTION 24 AND TERMINATION OF A TENANCY UNDER SECTION 29(2) OF THE 1954 ACT

3.1 This paragraph applies to a claim for a new tenancy under section 24 and termination of a tenancy under section 29(2) of the 1954 Act where rule 56.3 applies and in this paragraph –

(1) 'an unopposed claim' means a claim for a new tenancy under section 24 of the 1954 Act in circumstances where the grant of a new tenancy is not opposed;
(2) 'an opposed claim' means a claim for –
  (a) a new tenancy under section 24 of the 1954 Act in circumstances where the grant of a new tenancy is opposed; or
  (b) the termination of a tenancy under section 29(2) of the 1954 Act; and
(3) 'grounds of opposition' means –
  (a) the grounds specified in section 30(1) of the 1954 Act on which a landlord may oppose an application for a new tenancy under section 24(1) of the 1954 Act or make an application under section 29(2) of the 1954 Act; or
  (b) any other basis on which the landlord asserts that a new tenancy ought not to be granted.

PRECEDENCE OF CLAIM FORMS WHERE THERE IS MORE THAN ONE APPLICATION TO THE COURT UNDER SECTION 24(1) OR SECTION 29(2) OF THE 1954 ACT

3.2 Where more than one application to the court under section 24(1) or section 29(2) of the 1954 Act is made, the following provisions shall apply –

(1) once an application to the court under section 24(1) of the 1954 Act has been served on a defendant, no further application to the court in respect of the same tenancy whether under section 24(1) or section 29(2) of the 1954 Act may be served by that defendant without the permission of the court;
(2) if more than one application to the court under section 24(1) of the 1954 Act in respect of the same tenancy is served on the same day, any landlord's application shall stand stayed until further order of the court;
(3) if applications to the court under both section 24(1) and section 29(2) of the 1954 Act in respect of the same tenancy are served on the same day, any tenant's application shall stand stayed until further order of the court; and
(4) if a defendant is served with an application under section 29(2) of the 1954 Act ('the section 29(2) application') which was issued at a time when an application to the court had already been made by that defendant in respect of the same tenancy under section 24(1) of the 1954 Act ('the section 24(1) application'), the service of the section 29(2) application shall be deemed to be a notice under rule 7.7 requiring service or discontinuance of the section 24(1) application within a period of 14 days after the service of the section 29(2) application.

DEFENDANT WHERE THE CLAIMANT IS THE TENANT MAKING A CLAIM FOR A NEW TENANCY UNDER SECTION 24 OF THE 1954 ACT

3.3 Where a claim for a new tenancy under section 24 of the 1954 Act is made by a tenant, the person who, in relation to the claimant's current tenancy, is the landlord as defined in section 44 of the 1954 Act must be a defendant.

CONTENTS OF THE CLAIM FORM IN ALL CASES

3.4 The claim form must contain details of –

(1) the property to which the claim relates;
(2) the particulars of the current tenancy (including date, parties and duration), the current rent (if not the original rent) and the date and method of termination;
(3) every notice or request given or made under sections 25 or 26 of the 1954 Act; and
(4) the expiry date of –
  (a) the statutory period under section 29A(2) of the 1954 Act; or
  (b) any agreed extended period made under section 29B(1) or 29B(2) of the 1954 Act.

CLAIM FORM WHERE THE CLAIMANT IS THE TENANT MAKING A CLAIM FOR A NEW TENANCY UNDER SECTION 24 OF THE 1954 ACT

3.5 Where the claimant is the tenant making a claim for a new tenancy under section 24 of the 1954 Act, in addition to the details specified in paragraph 3.4, the claim form must contain details of –

(1) the nature of the business carried on at the property;
(2) whether the claimant relies on section 23(1A), 41 or 42 of the 1954 Act and, if so, the basis on which he does so;
(3) whether the claimant relies on section 31A of the 1954 Act and, if so, the basis on which he does so;
(4) whether any, and if so what part, of the property comprised in the tenancy is occupied neither by the claimant nor by a person employed by the claimant for the purpose of the claimant's business;
(5) the claimant's proposed terms of the new tenancy; and
(6) the name and address of –
  (a) anyone known to the claimant who has an interest in the reversion in the property (whether immediate or in not more than 15 years) on the termination of the claimant's current tenancy and who is likely to be affected by the grant of a new tenancy; or
  (b) if the claimant does not know of anyone specified by sub-paragraph (6)(a), anyone who has a freehold interest in the property.

3.6 The claim form must be served on the persons referred to in paragraph 3.5(6)(a) or (b) as appropriate.

CLAIM FORM WHERE THE CLAIMANT IS THE LANDLORD MAKING A CLAIM FOR A NEW TENANCY UNDER SECTION 24 OF THE 1954 ACT

3.7 Where the claimant is the landlord making a claim for a new tenancy under section 24 of the 1954 Act, in addition to the details specified in paragraph 3.4, the claim form must contain details of –

(1) the claimant's proposed terms of the new tenancy;

(2) whether the claimant is aware that the defendant's tenancy is one to which section 32(2) of the 1954 Act applies and, if so, whether the claimant requires that any new tenancy shall be a tenancy of the whole of the property comprised in the defendant's current tenancy or just of the holding as defined by section 23(3) of the 1954 Act; and

(3) the name and address of –

(a) anyone known to the claimant who has an interest in the reversion in the property (whether immediate or in not more than 15 years) on the termination of the claimant's current tenancy and who is likely to be affected by the grant of a new tenancy; or

(b) if the claimant does not know of anyone specified by sub-paragraph (3)(a), anyone who has a freehold interest in the property.

3.8 The claim form must be served on the persons referred to in paragraph 3.7(3)(a) or (b) as appropriate.

CLAIM FORM WHERE THE CLAIMANT IS THE LANDLORD MAKING AN APPLICATION FOR THE TERMINATION OF A TENANCY UNDER SECTION 29(2) OF THE 1954 ACT

3.9 Where the claimant is the landlord making an application for the termination of a tenancy under section 29(2) of the 1954 Act, in addition to the details specified in paragraph 3.4, the claim form must contain –

(1) the claimant's grounds of opposition;

(2) full details of those grounds of opposition; and

(3) the terms of a new tenancy that the claimant proposes in the event that his claim fails.

ACKNOWLEDGMENT OF SERVICE WHERE THE CLAIM IS AN UNOPPOSED CLAIM AND WHERE THE CLAIMANT IS THE TENANT

3.10 Where the claim is an unopposed claim and the claimant is the tenant, the acknowledgment of service is to be in form N210 and must state with particulars –

(1) whether, if a new tenancy is granted, the defendant objects to any of the terms proposed by the claimant and if so –

(a) the terms to which he objects; and

(b) the terms that he proposes in so far as they differ from those proposed by the claimant;

(2) whether the defendant is a tenant under a lease having less than 15 years unexpired at the date of the termination of the claimant's current tenancy and, if so, the name and address of any person who, to the knowledge of the defendant, has an interest in the reversion in the

property expectant (whether immediate or in not more than 15 years from that date) on the termination of the defendant's tenancy;

(3) the name and address of any person having an interest in the property who is likely to be affected by the grant of a new tenancy; and

(4) if the claimant's current tenancy is one to which section 32(2) of the 1954 Act applies, whether the defendant requires that any new tenancy shall be a tenancy of the whole of the property comprised in the claimant's current tenancy.

ACKNOWLEDGMENT OF SERVICE WHERE THE CLAIM IS AN UNOPPOSED CLAIM AND THE CLAIMANT IS THE LANDLORD

3.11 Where the claim is an unopposed claim and the claimant is the landlord, the acknowledgment of service is to be in form N210 and must state with particulars –

(1) the nature of the business carried on at the property;

(2) if the defendant relies on section 23(1A), 41 or 42 of the 1954 Act, the basis on which he does so;

(3) whether any, and if so what part, of the property comprised in the tenancy is occupied neither by the defendant nor by a person employed by the defendant for the purpose of the defendant's business;

(4) the name and address of –

  (a) anyone known to the defendant who has an interest in the reversion in the property (whether immediate or in not more than 15 years) on the termination of the defendant's current tenancy and who is likely to be affected by the grant of a new tenancy; or

  (b) if the defendant does not know of anyone specified by sub-paragraph (4)(a), anyone who has a freehold interest in the property; and

(5) whether, if a new tenancy is granted, the defendant objects to any of the terms proposed by the claimant and, if so –

  (a) the terms to which he objects; and

  (b) the terms that he proposes in so far as they differ from those proposed by the claimant.

ACKNOWLEDGMENT OF SERVICE AND DEFENCE WHERE THE CLAIM IS AN OPPOSED CLAIM AND WHERE THE CLAIMANT IS THE TENANT

3.12 Where the claim is an opposed claim and the claimant is the tenant –

(1) the acknowledgment of service is to be in form N9; and

(2) in his defence the defendant must state with particulars –

  (a) the defendant's grounds of opposition;

  (b) full details of those grounds of opposition;

  (c) whether, if a new tenancy is granted, the defendant objects to any of the terms proposed by the claimant and if so –

    (i) the terms to which he objects; and

    (ii) the terms that he proposes in so far as they differ from those proposed by the claimant;

  (d) whether the defendant is a tenant under a lease having less than 15 years unexpired at the date of the termination of the claimant's current tenancy and, if so, the name and address of any person who, to the knowledge of the defendant, has an interest in the reversion in the property expectant (whether immediately or in not more than 15 years from that date) on the termination of the defendant's tenancy;

(e) the name and address of any person having an interest in the property who is likely to be affected by the grant of a new tenancy; and

(f) if the claimant's current tenancy is one to which section 32(2) of the 1954 Act applies, whether the defendant requires that any new tenancy shall be a tenancy of the whole of the property comprised in the claimant's current tenancy.

ACKNOWLEDGMENT OF SERVICE AND DEFENCE WHERE THE CLAIMANT IS THE LANDLORD MAKING AN APPLICATION FOR THE TERMINATION OF A TENANCY UNDER SECTION 29(2) OF THE 1954 ACT

3.13 Where the claim is an opposed claim and the claimant is the landlord –

(1) the acknowledgment of service is to be in form N9; and

(2) in his defence the defendant must state with particulars –

(a) whether the defendant relies on section 23(1A), 41 or 42 of the 1954 Act and, if so, the basis on which he does so;

(b) whether the defendant relies on section 31A of the 1954 Act and, if so, the basis on which he does so; and

(c) the terms of the new tenancy that the defendant would propose in the event that the claimant's claim to terminate the current tenancy fails.

EVIDENCE IN AN UNOPPOSED CLAIM

3.14 Where the claim is an unopposed claim, no evidence need be filed unless and until the court directs it to be filed.

EVIDENCE IN AN OPPOSED CLAIM

3.15 Where the claim is an opposed claim, evidence (including expert evidence) must be filed by the parties as the court directs and the landlord shall be required to file his evidence first.

GROUNDS OF OPPOSITION TO BE TRIED AS A PRELIMINARY ISSUE

3.16 Unless in the circumstances of the case it is unreasonable to do so, any grounds of opposition shall be tried as a preliminary issue.

APPLICATIONS FOR INTERIM RENT UNDER SECTION 24A TO 24D OF THE 1954 ACT

3.17 Where proceedings have already been commenced for the grant of a new tenancy or the termination of an existing tenancy, the claim for interim rent under section 24A of the 1954 Act shall be made in those proceedings by –

(1) the claim form;

(2) the acknowledgment of service or defence; or

(3) an application on notice under Part 23.

3.18 Any application under section 24D(3) of the 1954 Act shall be made by an application on notice under Part 23 in the original proceedings.

3.19 Where no other proceedings have been commenced for the grant of a new tenancy or termination of an existing tenancy or where such proceedings have been disposed of, an application for interim rent under section 24A of the 1954 Act shall be made under the procedure in Part 8 and the claim form shall include details of –

(1) the property to which the claim relates;
(2) the particulars of the relevant tenancy (including date, parties and duration) and the current rent (if not the original rent);
(3) every notice or request given or made under sections 25 or 26 of the 1954 Act;
(4) if the relevant tenancy has terminated, the date and mode of termination; and
(5) if the relevant tenancy has been terminated and the landlord has granted a new tenancy of the property to the tenant –
    (a) particulars of the new tenancy (including date, parties and duration) and the rent; and
    (b) in a case where section 24C(2) of the 1954 Act applies but the claimant seeks a different rent under section 24C(3) of that Act, particulars and matters on which the claimant relies as satisfying section 24C(3).

OTHER CLAIMS UNDER PART II OF THE 1954 ACT

4.1 The mesne landlord to whose consent a claim for the determination of any question arising under paragraph 4(3) of Schedule 6 to the 1954 Act shall be made a defendant to the claim.

4.2 If any dispute as to the rateable value of any holding has been referred under section 37(5) of the 1954 Act to the Commissioners for HM Revenue and Customs for decision by a valuation officer, any document purporting to be a statement of the valuation officer of his decision is admissible as evidence of the matters contained in it.

CLAIM FOR COMPENSATION FOR IMPROVEMENTS UNDER PART I OF THE 1927 ACT

5.1 This paragraph applies to a claim under Part I of the 1927 Act.

The claim form

5.2 The claim form must include details of :

(1) the nature of the claim or the matter to be determined;
(2) the property to which the claim relates;
(3) the nature of the business carried on at the property;
(4) particulars of the lease or agreement for the tenancy including:
    (a) the names and addresses of the parties to the lease or agreement;
    (b) its duration;
    (c) the rent payable;
    (d) details of any assignment or other devolution of the lease or agreement;
(5) the date and mode of termination of the tenancy;

(6) if the claimant has left the property, the date on which he did so;
(7) particulars of the improvement or proposed improvement to which the claim relates; and
(8) if the claim is for payment of compensation, the amount claimed;

5.3 The court will fix a date for a hearing when it issues the claim form.

Defendant

5.4 The claimant's immediate landlord must be a defendant to the claim.

5.5 The defendant must immediately serve a copy of the claim form and any document served with it and of his acknowledgment of service on his immediate landlord. If the person so served is not the freeholder, he must serve a copy of these documents on his landlord and so on from landlord to landlord.

Evidence

5.6 Evidence need not be filed with the claim form or acknowledgment of service.

Certification under section 3 of the 1927 Act

5.7 If the court intends to certify under section 3 of the 1927 Act that an improvement is a proper improvement or has been duly executed, it shall do so by way of an order.

Compensation under section 1 or 8 of the 1927 Act

5.8 A claim under section 1(1) or 8(1) of the 1927 Act must be in writing, signed by the claimant, his solicitor or agent and include details of –

(1) the name and address of the claimant and of the landlord against whom the claim is made;
(2) the property to which the claim relates;
(3) the nature of the business carried on at the property;
(4) a concise statement of the nature of the claim;
(5) particulars of the improvement, including the date when it was completed and costs; and
(6) the amount claimed.

5.9 A mesne landlord must immediately serve a copy of the claim on his immediate superior landlord. If the person served is not the freeholder, he must serve a copy of the document on his landlord and so on from landlord to landlord.

(Paragraphs 5.8 and 5.9 provide the procedure for making claims under section 1(1) and 8(1) of the 1927 Act – these 'claims' do not, at this stage, relate to proceedings before the court)

TRANSFER TO LEASEHOLD VALUATION TRIBUNAL UNDER 1985 ACT

6.1 If a question is ordered to be transferred to a leasehold valuation tribunal for determination under section 31C of the 1985 Act the court will:

(1) send notice of the transfer to all parties to the claim; and
(2) send to the leasehold valuation tribunal:

(a) copies certified by the district judge of all entries in the records of the court relating to the question;
(b) the order of transfer; and
(c) all documents filed in the claim relating to the question.

(Paragraph 6.1 no longer applies to proceedings in England but continues to apply to proceedings in Wales)

CLAIM TO ENFORCE OBLIGATION UNDER PART I OF THE 1987 ACT

7.1 A copy of the notice served under section 19(2)(a) of the 1987 Act must accompany the claim form seeking an order under section 19(1) of that Act.

CLAIM FOR ACQUISITION ORDER UNDER SECTION 28 OF THE 1987 ACT

8.1 This paragraph applies to a claim for an acquisition order under section 28 of the 1987 Act.

Claim form

8.2 The claim form must:

(1) identify the property to which the claim relates and give details to show that section 25 of the 1987 Act applies;
(2) give details of the claimants to show that they constitute the requisite majority of qualifying tenants;
(3) state the names and addresses of the claimants and of the landlord of the property, or, if the landlord cannot be found or his identity ascertained, the steps taken to find him or ascertain his identity;
(4) state the name and address of:
  (a) the person nominated by the claimants for the purposes of Part III of the 1987 Act; and
  (b) every person known to the claimants who is likely to be affected by the application, including (but not limited to), the other tenants of flats contained in the property (whether or not they could have made a claim), any mortgagee or superior landlord of the landlord, and any tenants' association (within the meaning of section 29 of the 1985 Act); and
(5) state the grounds of the claim.

Notice under section 27

8.3 A copy of the notice served on the landlord under section 27 of the 1987 Act must accompany the claim form unless the court has dispensed with the requirement to serve a notice under section 27(3) of the 1987 Act.

Defendants

8.4 The landlord of the property (and the nominated person, if he is not a claimant) must be defendants.

Service

8.5 A copy of the claim form must be served on each of the persons named by the claimant under paragraph 8.2(4)(b) together with a notice that he may apply to be made a party.

Payment into court by nominated person

8.6 If the nominated person pays money into court in accordance with an order under section 33(1) of the 1987 Act, he must file a copy of the certificate of the surveyor selected under section 33(2)(a) of that Act.

CLAIM FOR AN ORDER VARYING LEASES UNDER THE 1987 ACT

9.1 This paragraph applies to a claim for an order under section 38 or section 40 of the 1987 Act.

Claim form

9.2 The claim form must state:

(1) the name and address of the claimant and of the other current parties to the lease or leases to which the claim relates;
(2) the date of the lease or leases, the property to which they relate, any relevant terms and the variation sought;
(3) the name and address of every person known to the claimant who is likely to be affected by the claim, including (but not limited to), the other tenants of flats contained in premises of which the relevant property forms a part, any previous parties to the lease, any mortgagee or superior landlord of the landlord, any mortgagee of the claimant and any tenants' association (within the meaning of section 29 of the 1985 Act); and
(4) the grounds of the claim.

Defendants

9.3 The other current parties to the lease must be defendants.

Service

9.4 A copy of the claim form must be served on each of the persons named under paragraph 9.2(3).

9.5 If the defendant knows of or has reason to believe that another person or persons are likely to be affected by the variation, he must serve a copy of the claim form on those persons, together with a notice that that they may apply to be made a party.

Defendant's application to vary other leases

9.6 If a defendant wishes to apply to vary other leases under section 36 of the 1987 Act:

(1) he must make the application in his acknowledgment of service;
(2) paragraphs 9.2 to 9.5 apply as if the defendant were the claimant; and
(3) Part 20 does not apply.

(Paragraphs 9.1–9.6 no longer apply to proceedings in England but continue to apply to proceedings in Wales)

SERVICE OF DOCUMENTS IN CLAIMS UNDER THE 1987 ACT

10.1 All documents must be served by the parties.

10.2 If a notice is to be served in or before a claim under the 1987 Act, it must be served –

(1) in accordance with section 54, and
(2) in the case of service on a landlord, at the address given under section 48(1).

SECTION II – MISCELLANEOUS PROVISIONS ABOUT LAND

ACCESS TO NEIGHBOURING LAND ACT 1992

11.1 The claimant must use the Part 8 procedure.

11.2 The claim form must set out:

(1) details of the dominant and servient land involved and whether the dominant land includes or consists of residential property;
(2) the work required;
(3) why entry to the servient land is required with plans (if applicable);
(4) the names and addresses of the persons who will carry out the work;
(5) the proposed date when the work will be carried out; and
(6) what (if any) provision has been made by way of insurance in the event of possible injury to persons or damage to property arising out of the proposed work.

11.3 The owner and occupier of the servient land must be defendants to the claim.

CHANCEL REPAIRS ACT 1932

12.1 The claimant in a claim to recover the sum required to put a chancel in proper repair must use the Part 8 procedure.

12.2 A notice to repair under section 2 of the Chancel Repairs Act 1932 must –

(1) state –
   (a) the responsible authority by whom the notice is given;
   (b) the chancel alleged to be in need of repair;
   (c) the repairs alleged to be necessary; and
   (d) the grounds on which the person to whom the notice is addressed is alleged to be liable to repair the chancel; and
(2) call upon the person to whom the notice is addressed to put the chancel in proper repair.

12.3 The notice must be served in accordance with Part 6.

LEASEHOLD REFORM ACT 1967

13.1 In this paragraph a section or schedule referred to by number means the section or schedule so numbered in the Leasehold Reform Act 1967.

13.2 If a tenant of a house and premises wishes to pay money into court under sections 11(4), 13(1) or 13(3) –

(1) he must file in the office of the appropriate court an application notice containing or accompanied by evidence stating –
   (a) the reasons for the payment into court,
   (b) the house and premises to which the payment relates;
   (c) the name and address of the landlord; and
   (d) so far as they are known to the tenant, the name and address of every person who is or may be interested in or entitled to the money;

(2) on the filing of the witness statement the tenant must pay the money into court and the court will send notice of the payment to the landlord and every person whose name and address are given in the witness statement;
(3) any subsequent payment into court by the landlord under section 11(4) must be made to the credit of the same account as the payment into court by the tenant and subparagraphs (1) and (2) will apply to the landlord as if he were a tenant;
(4) the appropriate court for the purposes of paragraph (a) is the county court for the district in which the property is situated or, if the payment into court is made by reason of a notice under section 13(3), any other county court as specified in the notice.

13.3 If an order is made transferring an application to a leasehold valuation tribunal under section 21(3), the court will:

(1) send notice of the transfer to all parties to the application; and
(2) send to the tribunal copies of the order of transfer and all documents filed in the proceedings.

(Paragraph 13.3 no longer applies to proceedings in England but continues to apply to proceedings in Wales)

13.4 A claim under section 17 or 18 for an order for possession of a house and premises must be made in accordance with Part 55.

13.5 In a claim under section 17 or 18, the defendant must:

(1) immediately after being served with the claim form, serve on every person in occupation of the property or part of it under an immediate or derivative sub-tenancy, a notice informing him of the claim and of his right under paragraph 3(4) of Schedule 2 to take part in the hearing of the claim with the permission of the court; and
(2) within 14 days after being served with the claim form, file a defence stating the ground, if any, on which he intends to oppose the claim and giving particulars of every such sub-tenancy.

13.6 An application made to the High Court under section 19 or 27 shall be assigned to the Chancery Division.

LEASEHOLD REFORM, HOUSING AND URBAN DEVELOPMENT ACT 1993

14.1 In this paragraph:

(1) 'the 1993 Act' means the Leasehold Reform, Housing and Urban Development Act 1993; and
(2) a section or schedule referred to by number means the section or schedule so numbered in the 1993 Act.

14.2 If a claim is made under section 23(1) by a person other than the reversioner:

(1) on the issue of the claim form in accordance with Part 8, the claimant must send a copy to the reversioner; and
(2) the claimant must promptly inform the reversioner either:
    (a) of the court's decision; or
    (b) that the claim has been withdrawn.

14.3 Where an application is made under section 26(1) or (2) or section 50(1) or (2):

(1) it must be made by the issue of a claim form in accordance with the Part 8 procedure which need not be served on any other party; and
(2) the court may grant or refuse the application or give directions for its future conduct, including the addition as defendants of such persons as appear to have an interest in it.

14.4 An application under section 26(3) must be made by the issue of a claim form in accordance with the Part 8 procedure and:

(1) the claimants must serve the claim form on any person who they know or have reason to believe is a relevant landlord, giving particulars of the claim and the hearing date and informing that person of his right to be joined as a party to the claim;
(2) the landlord whom it is sought to appoint as the reversioner must be a defendant, and must file an acknowledgment of service;
(3) a person on whom notice is served under paragraph (1) must be joined as a defendant to the claim if he gives notice in writing to the court of his wish to be added as a party, and the court will notify all other parties of the addition.

14.5 If a person wishes to pay money into court under section 27(3), section 51(3) or paragraph 4 of Schedule 8 –

(1) he must file in the office of the appropriate court an application notice containing or accompanied by evidence stating –
    (a) the reasons for the payment into court,
    (b) the interest or interests in the property to which the payment relates or where the payment into court is made under section 51(3), the flat to which it relates;
    (c) details of any vesting order;
    (d) the name and address of the landlord; and
    (e) so far as they are known to the tenant, the name and address of every person who is or may be interested in or entitled to the money;
(2) on the filing of the witness statement the money must be paid into court and the court will send notice of the payment to the landlord and every person whose name and address are given in the witness statement;
(3) any subsequent payment into court by the landlord must be made to the credit of the same account as the earlier payment into court;
(4) the appropriate court for the purposes of paragraph (1) is –
    (a) where a vesting order has been made, the county court that made the order; or
    (b) where no such order has been made, the county court in whose district the property is situated.

14.6 If an order is made transferring an application to a leasehold valuation tribunal under section 91(4), the court will:

(1) send notice of the transfer to all parties to the application; and
(2) send to the tribunal copies of the order of transfer and all documents filed in the proceedings.

(Paragraph 14.6 no longer applies to proceedings in England but continues to apply to proceedings in Wales)

14.7 If a relevant landlord acts independently under Schedule 1, paragraph 7, he is entitled to require any party to claims under the 1993 Act (as described in paragraph 7(1)(b) of Schedule 1) to supply him, on payment of the reasonable costs of copying, with copies of all documents which that party has served on the other parties to the claim.

COMMONHOLD AND LEASEHOLD REFORM ACT 2002

15.1 If a question is ordered to be transferred to a leasehold valuation tribunal for determination under paragraph 3 of Schedule 12 to the Commonhold and Leasehold Reform Act 2002 the court will –

(1) send notice of the transfer to all parties to the claim; and
(2) send to the leasehold valuation tribunal –
  (a) the order of transfer; and
  (b) all documents filed in the claim relating to the question.

(Paragraph 15.1 applies to proceedings in England but does not apply to proceedings in Wales)

PART 57
PROBATE AND INHERITANCE

CONTENTS OF THIS PART

Practice Direction—See generally PD57 at p 1364.

57.1 Scope of this Part and definitions

(1) This Part contains rules about –

- (a) probate claims;
- (b) claims for the rectification of wills;
- (c) claims and applications to –
  - (i) substitute another person for a personal representative; or
  - (ii) remove a personal representative; and
- (d) claims under the Inheritance (Provision for Family and Dependants) Act 1975.

(2) In this Part:

- (a) 'probate claim' means a claim for –
  - (i) the grant of probate of the will, or letters of administration of the estate, of a deceased person;
  - (ii) the revocation of such a grant; or
  - (iii) a decree pronouncing for or against the validity of an alleged will;

  not being a claim which is non-contentious (or common form) probate business;

(Section 128 of the Supreme Court Act 1981 defines non-contentious (or common form) probate business)

- (b) 'relevant office' means –
  - (i) in the case of High Court proceedings in a Chancery district registry, that registry;

(ii) in the case of any other High Court proceedings, Chancery Chambers at the Royal Courts of Justice, Strand, London, WC2A 2LL; and

(iii) in the case of county court proceedings, the office of the county court in question;

(c) 'testamentary document' means a will, a draft of a will, written instructions for a will made by or at the request of, or under the instructions of, the testator, and any document purporting to be evidence of the contents, or to be a copy, of a will which is alleged to have been lost or destroyed;

(d) 'will' includes a codicil.

Amendments—Inserted by SI 2001/1388; amended by SI 2002/2058.

'This Part contains' (r 57.1(1))—The Part does *not* contain rules governing non-contentious probate claims and the reader is referred to the Non-Contentious Probate Rules 1987, SI 1987/2024 (NCPR 1987), as amended (see PD57, para 1.2).

'section 128 of the Supreme Court Act 1981' (cross-reference under r 57.1(2)(a))—The definition contained in this section reads:

> ' "non-contentious or common form probate business" means the business of obtaining probate and administration where there is no contention as to the right thereto, including –
>
> (a) the passing of probates and administrations through the High Court in contentious cases where the contest has been terminated,
>
> (b) all businesses of a non-contentious nature in matters of testacy and intestacy not being proceedings in any action, and
>
> (c) the business of lodging caveats against the grant of probate or administration;'.

'probate claim' (r 57.1(2)(a))—See Guide 55A.

'rectification of wills' (r 57.1(1)(b))—The reader is particularly referred to AJA 1982 and NCPR 1987.

'substitute … or … remove a personal representative' (r 57.1(1)(c))—Again, the reader is particularly referred to AJA 1982 and NCPR 1987.

Section I – Probate Claims

57.2 General

(1) This Section contains rules about probate claims.

(2) Probate claims in the High Court are assigned to the Chancery Division.

(3) Probate claims in the county court must only be brought in –

(a) a county court where there is also a Chancery district registry; or

(b) the Central London County Court.

(4) All probate claims are allocated to the multi-track.

Amendments—Inserted by SI 2001/1388; amended by SI 2003/2113.

Jurisdiction—While the Chancery Division of the High Court is the usual venue in which to bring a probate claim, the county court does have jurisdiction of the High Court so long as the value of the deceased's net estate does not exceed the county court limit (see CCA 1984, s 32 and PD57, para 2.2; see also *Re Thomas (dec'd), Davies v Davies* [1949] P 336, [1949] 1 All ER 1048). The current limit is £30,000 (CCJO 1981). The 'net estate' of the deceased is 'the estate of that person exclusive of any property he was possessed of or entitled to as a trustee and not beneficially, and after making allowances for funeral expenses and for debts and liabilities' (CCA 1984, s 32(2)).

'there is also a Chancery district registry' (r 57.2(3))—There are Chancery district registries at Birmingham, Bristol, Cardiff, Leeds, Liverpool, Manchester, Newcastle-upon-Tyne and Preston.

57.3 How to start a probate claim

A probate claim must be commenced –

(a) in the relevant office; and
(b) using the procedure in Part 7.

Amendments—Inserted by SI 2001/1388.

'relevant office' (r 57.3(a))—See r 57.1(2)(b).

'the procedure in Part 7' (r 57.3(b))—The procedure is modified by this Part. The requirements as to acknowledgment of service differ (r 57.4). With his claim form the claimant must file evidence (r 57.5).

Effect of starting claim—Unless the court otherwise directs, the commencement of a probate claim will prevent any grant of probate or letters of administration being made until the claim has been disposed of (PD57, para 2.4).

Forms—The form to be used for starting a claim is N1P (PD4, Table 1). The form and all subsequent documents relating to the claim must be marked 'In the estate of [*name*] deceased (Probate)' (PD57, para 2.1).

57.4 Acknowledgment of service and defence

(1) A defendant who is served with a claim form must file an acknowledgment of service.

(2) Subject to paragraph (3), the period for filing an acknowledgment of service is –

(a) if the defendant is served with a claim form which states that particulars of claim are to follow, 28 days after service of the particulars of claim; and
(b) in any other case, 28 days after service of the claim form.

(3) If the claim form is served out of the jurisdiction under rule 6.19, the period for filing an acknowledgment of service is 14 days longer than the relevant period specified in rule 6.22 or the practice direction supplementing Section 3 of Part 6.

(4) Rule 15(4) (which provides the period for filing a defence) applies as if the words 'under Part 10' were omitted from rule 15.4(1)(b).

Amendments—Inserted by SI 2001/1388.

'A defendant … must file an acknowledgment of service' (r 57.4(1))—This differs from the normal Pt 7 procedure by which a defendant may file an acknowledgment of service if:
(a) he is unable to file a defence in time; or
(b) he wishes to dispute the court's jurisdiction (r 10.1(3)).

The form of acknowledgment of service to be used is N3 (PD4, Table 1).

Time limit for filing the acknowledgment of service—The extended period of 28 days accommodates the requirement that, when acknowledging service, a defendant must file at the relevant office any testamentary document of the deceased in his possession or control (r 57.5).

Time limit for filing defence—The period for filing a defence is 28 days after service of the particulars of claim.

57.5 Lodging of testamentary documents and filing of evidence about testamentary documents

(1) Any testamentary document of the deceased person in the possession or control of any party must be lodged with the court.

(2) Unless the court directs otherwise, the testamentary documents must be lodged in the relevant office –

(a) by the claimant when the claim form is issued; and

(b) by a defendant when he acknowledges service.

(3) The claimant and every defendant who acknowledges service of the claim form must in written evidence –

(a) describe any testamentary document of the deceased of which he has any knowledge or, if he does not know of any such testamentary document, state that fact, and

(b) if any testamentary document of which he has knowledge is not in his possession or under his control, give the name and address of the person in whose possession or under whose control it is or, if he does not know the name or address of that person, state that fact.

(A specimen form for the written evidence about testamentary documents is annexed to the practice direction)

(4) Unless the court directs otherwise, the written evidence required by paragraph (3) must be filed in the relevant office –

(a) by the claimant, when the claim form is issued; and

(b) by a defendant when he acknowledges service.

(5) Except with the permission of the court, a party shall not be allowed to inspect the testamentary documents or written evidence lodged or filed by any other party until he himself has lodged his testamentary documents and filed his evidence.

(6) The provisions of paragraphs (2) and (4) may be modified by a practice direction under this Part.

Amendments—Inserted by SI 2001/1388.

'testamentary documents' (r 57.5 generally)—See r 57.1(2)(c).

'Any testamentary document of the deceased person … must be lodged with the court' (r 57.5(1))—This facilitates the court in understanding the matters in issue, deciding whether the claim is correctly brought and determining which parties should be added to the proceedings. When giving case management directions in a probate claim the court will consider whether any person who may be affected by the claim and is not joined as a party should be so joined or given notice of the claim, whether under r 19.8A or otherwise, and whether to make a representation order under r 19.6 or r 19.7.

Where a claimant needs to commence a probate claim urgently, for instance where he needs to commence the claim in order to apply for an administrator pending the determination of the claim, the court may direct that the claimant shall be allowed to issue the claim form upon his giving an undertaking to the court to lodge the documents and file the testamentary evidence within such time as the court may specify.

'specimen form for the written evidence' (cross-reference under r 57.5(3))—The written evidence should be in the form annexed to PD57 and must be signed by the party personally. If the party is a child or patient, the written evidence about testamentary documents must be signed by his litigation friend (PD57, para 3.2).

When a claim is issued, the relevant office will send a notice to the Leeds District Probate Registry requesting that all testamentary documents, grants of representation and other relevant documents held at any probate registry are sent to the relevant office – as defined by r 57.1(2)(b) (PD57, para 2.3).

57.6 Revocation of existing grant

(1) In a probate claim which seeks the revocation of a grant of probate or letters of administration every person who is entitled, or claims to be entitled, to administer the estate under that grant must be made a party to the claim.

(2) If the claimant is the person to whom the grant was made, he must lodge the probate or letters of administration in the relevant office when the claim form is issued.

(3) If a defendant has the probate or letters of administration under his control, he must lodge it in the relevant office when he acknowledges service.

(4) Paragraphs (2) and (3) do not apply where the grant has already been lodged at the court, which in this paragraph includes the Principal Registry of the Family Division or a district probate registry.

Amendments—Inserted by SI 2001/1388.

General note—A claim for the revocation of a grant of probate may be commenced in a number of instances, such as where:

(a) a party contends that the will already admitted to probate is for some reason invalid;
(b) the testator's subsequent marriage to the proven will is discovered, so that it was revoked;
(c) a will of a later date to the proven will is discovered, which revokes the proven will;
(d) any other form of duly executed revocatory instrument is found revoking the proven will;
(e) it is claimed that the grant was obtained by a person who in fact was not entitled to obtain such a grant.

57.7 Contents of statements of case

(1) The claim form must contain a statement of the nature of the interest of the claimant and of each defendant in the estate.

(2) If a party disputes another party's interest in the estate he must state this in his statement of case and set out his reasons.

(3) Any party who contends that at the time when a will was executed the testator did not know of and approve its contents must give particulars of the facts and matters relied on.

(4) Any party who wishes to contend that –

(a) a will was not duly executed;
(b) at the time of the execution of a will the testator was not of sound mind, memory and understanding; or
(c) the execution of a will was obtained by undue influence or fraud,

must set out the contention specifically and give particulars of the facts and matters relied on.

(5)

(a) A defendant may give notice in his defence that he does not raise any positive case, but insists on the will being proved in solemn form and, for that purpose, will cross-examine the witnesses who attested the will.
(b) If a defendant gives such a notice, the court will not make an order for costs against him unless it considers that there was no reasonable ground for opposing the will.

Amendments—Inserted by SI 2001/1388.

57.8 Counterclaim

(1) A defendant who contends that he has any claim or is entitled to any remedy relating to the grant of probate of the will, or letters of administration of the estate, of the deceased person must serve a counterclaim making that contention.

(2) If the claimant fails to serve particulars of claim within the time allowed, the defendant may, with the permission of the court, serve a counterclaim and the probate claim shall then proceed as if the counterclaim were the particulars of claim.

Amendments—Inserted by SI 2001/1388.

57.9 Probate counterclaim in other proceedings

(1) In this rule 'probate counterclaim' means a counterclaim in any claim other than a probate claim by which the defendant claims any such remedy as is mentioned in rule 57.1(2)(a).

(2) Subject to the following paragraphs of this rule, this Part shall apply with the necessary modifications to a probate counterclaim as it applies to a probate claim.

(3) A probate counterclaim must contain a statement of the nature of the interest of each of the parties in the estate of the deceased to which the probate counterclaim relates.

(4) Unless an application notice is issued within 7 days after the service of a probate counterclaim for an order under rule 3.1(2)(e) or 3.4 for the probate counterclaim to be dealt with in separate proceedings or to be struck out, and the application is granted, the court shall order the transfer of the proceedings to either –

- (a) the Chancery Division (if it is not already assigned to that Division) and to either the Royal Courts of Justice or a Chancery district registry (if it is not already proceeding in one of those places); or
- (b) if the county court has jurisdiction, to a county court where there is also a Chancery district registry or the Central London County Court.

(5) If an order is made that a probate counterclaim be dealt with in separate proceedings, the order shall order the transfer of the probate counterclaim as required under paragraph (4).

Amendments—Inserted by SI 2001/1388; amended by SI 2003/3361.

57.10 Failure to acknowledge service or to file a defence

(1) A default judgment cannot be obtained in a probate claim and rule 10.2 and Part 12 do not apply.

(2) If any of several defendants fails to acknowledge service the claimant may –

- (a) after the time for acknowledging service has expired; and
- (b) upon filing written evidence of service of the claim form and (if no particulars of claim were contained in or served with the claim form) the particulars of claim on that defendant;

proceed with the probate claim as if that defendant had acknowledged service.

(3) If no defendant acknowledges service or files a defence then, unless on the application of the claimant the court orders the claim to be discontinued, the claimant may, after the time for acknowledging service or for filing a defence (as the case may be) has expired, apply to the court for an order that the claim is to proceed to trial.

(4) When making an application under paragraph (3) the claimant must file written evidence of service of the claim form and (if no particulars of claim were contained in or served with the claim form) the particulars of claim on each of the defendants.

(5) Where the court makes an order under paragraph (3), it may direct that the claim be tried on written evidence.

Amendments—Inserted by SI 2001/1388.

57.11 Discontinuance and dismissal

(1) Part 38 does not apply to probate claims.

(2) At any stage of a probate claim the court, on the application of the claimant or of any defendant who has acknowledged service, may order that –

(a) the claim be discontinued or dismissed on such terms as to costs or otherwise as it thinks just; and

(b) a grant of probate of the will, or letters of administration of the estate, of the deceased person be made to the person entitled to the grant.

Amendments—Inserted by SI 2001/1388.

Section II – Rectification of Wills

57.12 (1) This Section contains rules about claims for the rectification of a will.

(Section 20 of the Administration of Justice Act 1982 provides for rectification of a will. Additional provisions are contained in rule 55 of the Non-Contentious Probate Rules 1987)

(2) Every personal representative of the estate shall be joined as a party.

(3) The practice direction makes provision for lodging the grant of probate or letters of administration with the will annexed in a claim under this Section.

Amendments—Inserted by SI 2001/1388.

Practice Direction—See specifically PD57, para 9 at p 1367, para 10 at p 1367 and para 11 at p 1368 in respect of claims for rectification of wills.

'Section 20 of the Administration of Justice Act 1982' (cross-reference under r 57.12(1))—Section 20(1) provides that if a court is satisfied that a will is so expressed that it fails to carry out the testator's intentions, in consequence of a clerical error or because of a failure to understand his instructions, it may order that the will be rectified so as to carry out his intentions.

Time limit for claims—Section 20(2) of AJA 1982 stipulates that an application for rectification of a will shall not be made, except with the permission of the court, more than 6 months from the date on which representation with respect to the estate of the deceased is first taken out.

Section 20(4) of AJA 1982 makes clear that in considering when representation with respect to the estate of a deceased person was first taken out, a grant limited to settled land or to trust property shall be left out of account and a grant limited to real estate or to personal estate shall be left out of account, unless a grant limited to the remainder of the estate has previously been made or been made at the same time.

Section III – Substitution and Removal of Personal Representatives

57.13 (1) This Section contains rules about claims and applications for substitution or removal of a personal representative.

(2) Claims under this Section must be brought in the High Court and are assigned to the Chancery Division.

(Section 50 of the Administration of Justice Act 1985 gives the High Court power to appoint a substitute for, or to remove, a personal representative)

(3) Every personal representative of the estate shall be joined as a party.

(4) The practice direction makes provision for lodging the grant of probate or letters of administration in a claim under this Section.

(5) If substitution or removal of a personal representative is sought by application in existing proceedings, this rule shall apply with references to claims being read as if they referred to applications.

Amendments—Inserted by SI 2001/1388.

Practice Direction—See specifically PD57, para 12 at p 1368, para 13 at p 1368 and para 14 at p 1368 in respect of claims for substitution and removal of personal representatives.

'Section 50 of the Administration of Justice Act 1985' (cross-reference under r 57.13(2))—Section 50(1) reads:

> 'Where an application relating to the estate of a deceased person is made to the High Court under this subsection by or on behalf of a personal representative of the deceased or a beneficiary of the estate, the court may in its discretion –
> (a) appoint a person (in this section called a substituted personal representative) to act as personal representative of the deceased in place of the existing personal representative of the deceased or any of them; or
> (b) if there are two or more existing personal representatives of the deceased, terminate the appointment of one or more, but not all, of those persons.'

Section IV – Claims under the Inheritance (Provision for Family and Dependants) Act 1975

57.14 Scope of this Section

This Section contains rules about claims under the Inheritance (Provision for Family and Dependants) Act 1975 ('the Act').

Amendments—Inserted by SI 2002/2058.

General note—Under the Inheritance (Provision for Family and Dependants) Act 1975, the court has power to order provision, in favour of the persons listed in s 1 of that Act, out of the estate of a deceased person.

'claims under … ("the Act")'—See Guide 55.

57.15 Proceedings in the High Court

(1) Proceedings in the High Court under the Act shall be issued in either –

(a) the Chancery Division; or
(b) the Family Division.

(2) The Civil Procedure Rules apply to proceedings under the Act which are brought in the Family Division, except that the provisions of the Family Proceedings Rules 1991 relating to the drawing up and service of orders apply instead of the provisions in Part 40 and its practice direction.

SECTION 2 Civil Procedure Rules and Practice Directions

Amendments—Inserted by SI 2002/2058.

57.16 Procedure for claims under section 1 of the Act

(1) A claim under section 1 of the Act must be made by issuing a claim form in accordance with Part 8.

(2) Rule 8.3 (acknowledgment of service) and rule 8.5 (filing and serving written evidence) apply as modified by paragraphs (3) to (5) of this rule.

(3) The written evidence filed and served by the claimant with the claim form must have exhibited to it an official copy of –

- (a) the grant of probate or letters of administration in respect of the deceased's estate; and
- (b) every testamentary document in respect of which probate or letters of administration were granted.

(4) Subject to paragraph (4A), the time within which a defendant must file and serve –

- (a) an acknowledgment of service; and
- (b) any written evidence,

is not more than 21 days after service of the claim form on him.

(4A) If the claim form is served out of the jurisdiction under rule 6.19, the period for filing an acknowledgment of service and any written evidence is 7 days longer than the relevant period specified in rule 6.22 or the practice direction supplementing Section III of Part 6.

(5) A defendant who is a personal representative of the deceased must file and serve written evidence, which must include the information required by the practice direction.

Amendments—Inserted by SI 2002/2058; amended by SI 2004/1306.

Who can apply—Section 1(1) of the Act sets out those persons who may apply to the court for an order that provision be made out of the estate of the deceased. They are:

'(a) the wife or husband of the deceased;
(b) a former wife or former husband of the deceased who has not remarried;
(ba) any person (not being a person included in paragraph (a) or (b) above) to whom subsection (1A) … applies;
(c) a child of the deceased;
(d) any person (not being a child of the deceased) who, in the case of any marriage to which the deceased was at any time a party, was treated by the deceased as a child of the family in relation to that marriage;
(e) any person (not being a person included in the foregoing paragraphs) who immediately before the death of the deceased was being maintained, either wholly or partly, by the deceased;'.

Section 1(1A) of the Act applies to a person if the deceased died on or after 1 January 1996 and, during the whole of the period of 2 years ending immediately before the date when the deceased died, the person was living in the same household as the deceased and as the husband or wife of the deceased.

The fact that the claimant has already taken out representation in relation to the deceased's estate does not prevent him making a claim under the Act.

Death of the claimant—If the claimant dies before the hearing of his application under the Act then his claim ceases, and cannot be carried on by his personal representatives (*Whytte v Ticehurst* [1986] 1 FLR 83).

Minors and mental patients—Where the claimant is a minor or mental patient, a litigation friend will be required under Pt 21.

The application—An application is made by Pt 8 claim form (r 57.16) and is, thus, automatically allocated to the multi-track.

In *Hannigan v Hannigan* [2000] 2 FCR 650, (2000) *The Independent*, 23 May, the Court of Appeal refused to uphold a strike-out under r 3.4(2)(c) of Inheritance Act proceedings issued using the wrong form (ie N208, rather than Form 208, the standard Pt 8 claim form). Amongst other technical errors, there was a failure to include the Royal Coat of Arms, and the witness statement was not verified by a statement of truth. However, the form and witness statement had been properly issued and served at the same time, and expressly referred to the proceedings being issued under Pt 8. The defendants had been given all of the information that they required in order to be able to understand what the claimant was seeking from the court and why she was seeking it. The Court of Appeal concluded that to strike out such a claim would be a disproportionate response to the procedural irregularities that had occurred.

Time limit for claims—Section 4 of the 1975 Act provides that an application for an order under s 2 should be made within 6 months of a grant of representation being made in relation to the deceased's estate. Where a grant of probate is replaced by letters of administration, or vice versa, the 6-month period runs from the date of the later grant (*Re Freeman (dec'd), Weston v Freeman* [1984] 1 WLR 1419). If the claim form is issued within the 6-month period, then it does not matter that it is served outside the period (*Re Miller, Miller v De Courcey* [1969] 1 WLR 583).

The 6-month period can be extended by the court. A claim form issued outside the period should expressly request the court's permission to make the application out of time (*Practice Note: Procedure: Commencement of Proceedings: Family Provision* [1976] 1 WLR 418). The court's power to extend time is discretionary and in considering the application it will look at all of the circumstances of the case including:

(a) the explanation given for the delay;
(b) any efforts made to reduce or mitigate the effects of the delay;
(c) whether any negotiations are being carried out;
(d) whether the estate has been distributed and, if so, whether this distribution was made before or after notice was given that an application under the 1975 Act was to be made;
(e) whether the claimant would have a claim against his solicitors if the court refused to allow the application to be made out of time;
(f) whether refusal would cause hardship and operate unfairly against the claimant and in particular whether it would leave the claimant without redress against anyone; and
(g) whether the claimant has an arguable case under the 1975 Act (see *Re Salmon (dec'd), Coard v National Westminster Bank* [1981] Ch 167).

An application for leave to apply out of time is usually heard separately from the substantive application under the Act.

Proceedings under the Act cannot be commenced prior to a grant of representation being taken out in relation to the estate (*Re McBroom* [1992] 2 FLR 49, although *Re Searle, Searle v Siems* [1949] Ch 73 – a decision under the old 1938 Act – suggests otherwise).

Content of the claim form—The claim form should be entitled 'In the estate of XY deceased' and 'In the matter of the Inheritance (Provision for Family and Dependants) Act 1975' (r 8.2(c)). The claim form will usually ask for the court to make such provision as it thinks fit without particularising the exact provision sought. However, the claim form should contain details of any application to the court:

(a) to extend the 6-month time limit in s 4;
(b) for an interim order under s 5;
(c) for the treatment of nominated property as part of the net estate of the deceased under s 8;
(d) for an order under s 9 that the deceased's severable share of property in which he was a beneficial joint tenant be treated as part of his net estate;
(e) for an order under s 10 that dispositions made by the deceased and intended to defeat an application under the Act be set aside;
(f) for an order under s 11 frustrating the effect of a contract made by the deceased to leave his property by will;
(g) for a representation order under r 19.7.

Evidence in support—The claim form is supported by a witness statement by the claimant. Both the claim form and evidence in support must be served together. The written evidence filed and served by the claimant with the claim form must have exhibited to it an official copy of the grant of probate or letters of administration in respect of the deceased's estate and also every testamentary document in respect of which probate or letters of administration were granted.

Although not specifically provided for in the rules, the claimant's witness statement should include the following:

(a) Any evidence of the claimant's entitlement to bring a claim under s 1 of the Act, such as marriage and birth certificates. If the claimant was judicially separated or divorced from the deceased, then the appropriate orders should also be exhibited.

(b) Details of the matters to which the court is to have regard in exercising its powers under the Act, as set out in s 3. These include the financial resources and needs of the claimant, any obligations or responsibilities that he was owed by the deceased, any physical or mental disabilities of the claimant, and the size and nature of the estate. Under s 3 of the Act the court must also have regard to the position of those entitled under the deceased's will or the relevant intestacy provisions.

Note that, whilst only the personal representative is obliged by r 57.16(5) to lodge written evidence in response to the claimant's application, any other defendant who chooses not to file evidence may be prejudiced as a result. For example, under s 3 of the Act the factors relevant to the court's decision include the financial position and health of the beneficiaries of the estate, about which the beneficiary may want to provide information in the form of a witness statement.

Parties to the application—All beneficiaries who may be affected by an order made by the court under the Act must be joined as defendants. This will depend to some extent upon the size and nature of the estate and the extent of the provision sought by the claimant. For example, where there is a large residuary estate from which the court will be able to order provision, there should be no need to join those entitled to only small pecuniary legacies. Similarly, it is rarely necessary to join specific legatees entitled to items such as furniture or jewellery, save where those items are valuable in the context of the size of the estate. In contrast, if the legacies are substantial and the residuary estate is small, then it might be appropriate to join the legatees as parties.

The personal representatives of the deceased's estate should also be joined. However, it is important to remember that they have no power to represent the beneficiaries or settle the claim on their behalf, and should take a neutral stance in the litigation.

It may be appropriate to seek representation orders in relation to any beneficiaries with the same interest (r 19.7). Under such an order a defendant is appointed to represent the absent beneficiaries in a particular class or with a particular interest.

Where a child or mental patient is either a claimant or one of the defendants a litigation friend will be required (Pt 21). Any settlement of the application that affects their interest in the estate will require the court's approval.

Practice Direction – Probate

This Practice Direction supplements CPR Part 57 (PD57)

I PROBATE CLAIMS

General

1.1 This Section of this practice direction applies to contentious probate claims.

1.2 The rules and procedure relating to non-contentious probate proceedings (also known as 'common form') are the Non-Contentious Probate Rules 1987 as amended.

How to start a probate claim

2.1 A claim form and all subsequent court documents relating to a probate claim must be marked at the top 'In the estate of [*name*] deceased (Probate)'.

2.2 The claim form must be issued out of –

(1) Chancery Chambers at the Royal Courts of Justice; or
(2) one of the Chancery district registries; or
[(3) if the claim is suitable to be heard in the county court –
  (a) a county court in a place where there is also a Chancery district registry; or
  (b) the Central London County Court.

There are Chancery district registries at Birmingham, Bristol, Cardiff, Leeds, Liverpool, Manchester, Newcastle upon Tyne and Preston.

(Section 32 of the County Courts Act 1984 identifies which probate claims may be heard in a county court)

2.3 When the claim form is issued, the relevant office will send a notice to Leeds District Probate Registry, Coronet House, Queen Street, Leeds, LS1 2BA, DX 26451 Leeds (Park Square), telephone 0113 243 1505, requesting that all testamentary documents, grants of representation and other relevant documents currently held at any probate registry are sent to the relevant office.

2.4 The commencement of a probate claim will, unless a court otherwise directs, prevent any grant of probate or letters of administration being made until the probate claim has been disposed of.

(Rule 45 of the Non-Contentious Probate Rules 1987 makes provision for notice of the probate claim to be given, and section 117 of the Supreme Court Act 1981 for the grant of letters of administration pending the determination of a probate claim. Paragraph 8 of this practice direction makes provision about an application for such a grant)

Testamentary documents and evidence about testamentary documents

3.1 Unless the court orders otherwise, if a testamentary document is held by the court (whether it was lodged by a party or it was previously held at a probate registry) when the claim has been disposed of the court will send it to the Leeds District Probate Registry.

3.2 The written evidence about testamentary documents required by this Part –

(1) should be in the form annexed to this practice direction; and
(2) must be signed by the party personally and not by his solicitor or other representative (except that if the party is a child or patient the written evidence must be signed by his litigation friend).

3.3 In a case in which there is urgent need to commence a probate claim (for example, in order to be able to apply immediately for the appointment of an administrator pending the determination of the claim) and it is not possible for the claimant to lodge the testamentary documents or to file the evidence about testamentary documents in the relevant office at the same time as the claim form is to be issued, the court may direct that the claimant shall be allowed to issue the claim form upon his giving an undertaking to the court to lodge the documents and file the evidence within such time as the court shall specify.

Case management

4 In giving case management directions in a probate claim the court will give consideration to the questions –

(1) whether any person who may be affected by the claim and who is not joined as a party should be joined as a party or given notice of the claim, whether under rule 19.8A or otherwise; and
(2) whether to make a representation order under rule 19.6 or rule 19.7.

Summary judgment

5.1 If an order pronouncing for a will in solemn form is sought on an application for summary judgment, the evidence in support of the application must include written evidence proving due execution of the will.

5.2 If a defendant has given notice in his defence under rule 57.7(5) that he raises no positive case but –

(1) he insists that the will be proved in solemn form; and
(2) for that purpose he will cross-examine the witnesses who attested the will;

any application by the claimant for summary judgment is subject to the right of that defendant to require those witnesses to attend court for cross-examination.

Settlement of a probate claim

6.1 If at any time the parties agree to settle a probate claim, the court may –

(1) order the trial of the claim on written evidence, which will lead to a grant in solemn form;
(2) order that the claim be discontinued or dismissed under rule 57.11, which will lead to a grant in common form; or
(3) pronounce for or against the validity of one or more wills under section 49 of the Administration of Justice Act 1985.

(For a form of order which is also applicable to discontinuance and which may be adapted as appropriate, see Practice Form No CH38)

(Section 49 of the Administration of Justice Act 1985 permits a probate claim to be compromised without a trial if every 'relevant beneficiary', as defined in that section, has consented to the proposed order. It is only available in the High Court)

6.2 Applications under section 49 of the Administration of Justice Act 1985 may be heard by a master or district judge and must be supported by written evidence identifying the relevant beneficiaries and exhibiting the written consent of each of them. The written evidence of testamentary documents required by rule 57.5 will still be necessary.

Application for an order to bring in a will, etc

7.1 Any party applying for an order under section 122 of the Supreme Court Act 1981 ('the 1981 Act') must serve the application notice on the person against whom the order is sought.

(Section 122 of the 1981 Act empowers the court to order a person to attend court for examination, and to answer questions and bring in documents, if there are reasonable grounds for believing that such person has knowledge of a testamentary document. Rule 50(1) of the Non-Contentious Probate Rules 1987 makes similar provision where a probate claim has not been commenced)

7.2 An application for the issue of a witness summons under section 123 of the 1981 Act –

(1) may be made without notice; and
(2) must be supported by written evidence setting out the grounds of the application.

(Section 123 of the 1981 Act empowers the court, where it appears that any person has in his possession, custody or power a testamentary document, to issue a witness summons ordering such person to bring in that document. Rule 50(2) of the Non-Contentious Probate Rules makes similar provision where a probate claim has not been commenced)

7.3 An application under section 122 or 123 of the 1981 Act should be made to a master or district judge.

7.4 A person against whom a witness summons is issued under section 123 of the 1981 Act who denies that the testamentary document referred to in the witness summons is in his possession or under his control may file written evidence to that effect.

Administration pending the determination of a probate claim

8.1 An application under section 117 of the Supreme Court Act 1981 for an order for the grant of administration pending the determination of a probate claim should be made by application notice in the probate claim.

8.2 If an order for a grant of administration is made under section 117 of the 1981 Act –

(1) [Rules 69.4 to 69.7 shall apply as if the administrator were a receiver appointed by the court;
(2) if the court allows the administrator remuneration under [rule 69.7, it may make an order under section 117(3) of the 1981 Act assigning the remuneration out of the estate of the deceased; and
(3) every application relating to the conduct of the administration shall be made by application notice in the probate claim.

8.3 An order under section 117 may be made by a master or district judge.

8.4 If an order is made under section 117 an application for the grant of letters of administration should be made to the Principal Registry of the Family Division, First Avenue House, 42–49 High Holborn, London WC1V 6NP.

8.5 The appointment of an administrator to whom letters of administration are granted following an order under section 117 will cease automatically when a final order in the probate claim is made but will continue pending any appeal.

II RECTIFICATION OF WILLS

Scope of this Section

9 This Section of this practice direction applies to claims for the rectification of a will.

Lodging the grant

10.1 If the claimant is the person to whom the grant was made in respect of the will of which rectification is sought, he must, unless the court orders otherwise, lodge the probate or letters of administration with the will annexed with the court when the claim form is issued.

10.2 If a defendant has the probate or letters of administration in his possession or under his control, he must, unless the court orders otherwise, lodge it in the relevant office within 14 days after the service of the claim form on him.

Orders

11 A copy of every order made for the rectification of a will shall be sent to the Principal Registry of the Family Division for filing, and a memorandum of the order shall be endorsed on, or permanently annexed to, the grant under which the estate is administered.

III SUBSTITUTION AND REMOVAL OF PERSONAL REPRESENTATIVES

Scope of this Section

12 This Section of this practice direction applies to claims and applications for substitution or removal of a personal representative. If substitution or removal of a personal representative is sought by application in existing proceedings, this Section shall apply with references to the claim, claim form and claimant being read as if they referred to the application, application notice and applicant respectively.

Starting the claim

13.1 The claim form must be accompanied by:

- (1) a sealed or certified copy of the grant of probate or letters of administration; and
- (2) written evidence containing the grounds of the claim and the following information so far as it is known to the claimant –
  - (a) brief details of the property comprised in the estate, with an approximate estimate of its capital value and any income that is received from it;
  - (b) brief details of the liabilities of the estate;
  - (c) the names and addresses of the persons who are in possession of the documents relating to the estate;
  - (d) the names of the beneficiaries and their respective interests in the estate; and
  - (e) the name, address and occupation of any proposed substituted personal representative;

13.2 If the claim is for the appointment of a substituted personal representative, the claim form must be accompanied by –

- (1) a signed or (in the case of the Public Trustee or a corporation) sealed consent to act; and
- (2) written evidence as to the fitness of the proposed substituted personal representative, if an individual, to act.

Production of the grant

14.1 On the hearing of the claim the personal representative must produce to the court the grant of representation to the deceased's estate.

14.2 If an order is made substituting or removing the personal representative, the grant (together with a sealed copy of the order) must be sent to and remain in the custody of the Principal Registry of the Family Division until a memorandum of the order has been endorsed on or permanently annexed to the grant.

IV CLAIMS UNDER THE INHERITANCE (PROVISION FOR FAMILY AND DEPENDANTS) ACT 1975

Acknowledgment of service by personal representative – rule 57.16(4)

15 Where a defendant who is a personal representative wishes to remain neutral in relation to the claim, and agrees to abide by any decision which the court may make, he should state this in Section A of the acknowledgment of service form.

Written evidence of personal representative – rule 57.16(5)

16 The written evidence filed by a defendant who is a personal representative must state to the best of that person's ability –

(1) full details of the value of the deceased's net estate, as defined in section 25(1) of the Act;
(2) the person or classes of persons beneficially interested in the estate, and –
 (a) the names and (unless they are parties to the claim) addresses of all living beneficiaries; and
 (b) the value of their interests in the estate so far as they are known.
(3) whether any living beneficiary (and if so, naming him) is a child or patient within the meaning of rule 21.1(2); and
(4) any facts which might affect the exercise of the court's powers under the Act.

Separate representation of claimants

17 If a claim is made jointly by two or more claimants, and it later appears that any of the claimants have a conflict of interests –

(1) any claimant may choose to be represented at any hearing by separate solicitors or counsel, or may appear in person; and
(2) if the court considers that claimants who are represented by the same solicitors or counsel ought to be separately represented, it may adjourn the application until they are.

Production of the grant

18.1 On the hearing of a claim the personal representative must produce to the court the original grant of representation to the deceased's estate.

18.2 If the court makes an order under the Act, the original grant (together with a sealed copy of the order) must be sent to the Principal Registry of the Family Division for a memorandum of the order to be endorsed on or permanently annexed to the grant in accordance with section 19(3) of the Act.

18.3 Every final order embodying terms of compromise made in proceedings under the Act, whether made with or without a hearing, must contain a direction that a memorandum of the order shall be endorsed on or permanently annexed to the probate or letters of administration and a copy of the order shall be sent to the Principal Registry of the Family Division with the relevant grant of probate or letters of administration for endorsement.

Annex

A FORM OF WITNESS STATEMENT OR AFFIDAVIT ABOUT TESTAMENTARY DOCUMENTS

(CPR Rule 57.5)

(*Title of the claim*)

I [*name and address*] the claimant/defendant in this claim state [on oath] that I have no knowledge of any document –

(i) being or purported to be or having the form or effect of a will or codicil of [*name of deceased*] whose estate is the subject of this claim;

(ii) being or purporting to be a draft or written instructions for any such will or codicil made by or at the request of or under the instructions of the deceased;

(iii) being or purporting to be evidence of the contents or a copy of any such will or codicil which is alleged to have been lost or destroyed,

except ___ [*describe any testamentary document of the deceased, and if any such document is not in your control, give the name and address of the person who you believe has possession or control of it, or state that you do not know the name and address of that person*] ___

[I believe that the facts stated in this witness statement are true] [*or jurat for affidavit*]

(*NOTE: 'testamentary document' is defined in CPR rule 57.1*)

PART 58
COMMERCIAL COURT

CONTENTS OF THIS PART

Practice Direction—See generally PD58 at p 1375. See also the new Admiralty and Commercial Courts Guide.

General note—This Part – and its practice direction – represent for the most part practice already encouraged by the former Commercial Court Guide. The primary difference is that major departures from other CPR Parts are now 'properly' enshrined in the Rules and the PD, although they are amplified in them. Curiously and unlike its predecessor the new PD, however, makes no reference to the Admiralty and Commercial Courts Guide, which is essential reading for a detailed understanding of all aspects of Commercial Court practice.

58.1 Scope of this Part and interpretation

(1) This Part applies to claims in the Commercial Court of the Queen's Bench Division.

(2) In this Part and its practice direction, 'commercial claim' means any claim arising out of the transaction of trade and commerce and includes any claim relating to –

- (a) a business document or contract;
- (b) the export or import of goods;
- (c) the carriage of goods by land, sea, air or pipeline;
- (d) the exploitation of oil and gas reserves or other natural resources;
- (e) insurance and re-insurance;
- (f) banking and financial services;
- (g) the operation of markets and exchanges;
- (h) the purchase and sale of commodities;
- (i) the construction of ships;
- (j) business agency; and
- (k) arbitration.

Amendments—Inserted by SI 2001/4015.

58.2 Specialist list

(1) The commercial list is a specialist list for claims proceeding in the Commercial Court.

(2) One of the judges of the Commercial Court shall be in charge of the commercial list.

Amendments—Inserted by SI 2001/4015.

58.3 Application of the Civil Procedure Rules

These Rules and their practice directions apply to claims in the commercial list unless this Part or a practice direction provides otherwise.

Amendments—Inserted by SI 2001/4015.

58.4 Proceedings in the commercial list

(1) A commercial claim may be started in the commercial list.

(2) Rule 30.5(3) applies to claims in the commercial list, except that a Commercial Court judge may order a claim to be transferred to any other specialist list.

(Rule 30.5(3) provides that an application for the transfer of proceedings to or from a specialist list must be made to a judge dealing with claims in that list)

Amendments—Inserted by SI 2001/4015.

58.5 Claim form and particulars of claim

(1) If, in a Part 7 claim, particulars of claim are not contained in or served with the claim form –

- (a) the claim form must state that, if an acknowledgment of service is filed which indicates an intention to defend the claim, particulars of claim will follow;
- (b) when the claim form is served, it must be accompanied by the documents specified in rule 7.8(1);
- (c) the claimant must serve particulars of claim within 28 days of the filing of an acknowledgment of service which indicates an intention to defend; and
- (d) rule 7.4(2) does not apply.

(2) A statement of value is not required to be included in the claim form.

(3) If the claimant is claiming interest, he must –

- (a) include a statement to that effect; and
- (b) give the details set out in rule 16.4(2),

in both the claim form and the particulars of claim.

Amendments—Inserted by SI 2001/4015.

58.6 Acknowledgment of service

(1) A defendant must file an acknowledgment of service in every case.

(2) Unless paragraph (3) applies, the period for filing an acknowledgment of service is 14 days after service of the claim form.

(3) Where the claim form is served out of the jurisdiction, or on the agent of a defendant who is overseas, the time periods provided by rules 6.16(4), 6.21(4) and 6.22 apply after service of the claim form.

Amendments—Inserted by SI 2001/4015.

58.7 Disputing the court's jurisdiction

(1) Part 11 applies to claims in the commercial list with the modifications set out in this rule.

(2) An application under rule 11(1) must be made within 28 days after filing an acknowledgment of service.

(3) If the defendant files an acknowledgment of service indicating an intention to dispute the court's jurisdiction, the claimant need not serve particulars of claim before the hearing of the application.

Amendments—Inserted by SI 2001/4015.

58.8 Default judgment

(1) If, in a Part 7 claim in the commercial list, a defendant fails to file an acknowledgment of service, the claimant need not serve particulars of claim before he may obtain or apply for default judgment in accordance with Part 12.

(2) Rule 12.6(1) applies with the modification that paragraph (a) shall be read as if it referred to the claim form instead of the particulars of claim.

Amendments—Inserted by SI 2001/4015.

58.9 Admissions

(1) Rule 14.5 does not apply to claims in the commercial list.

(2) If the defendant admits part of a claim for a specified amount of money, the claimant may apply under rule 14.3 for judgment on the admission.

(3) Rule 14.14(1) applies with the modification that paragraph (a) shall be read as if it referred to the claim form instead of the particulars of claim.

Amendments—Inserted by SI 2001/4015.

58.10 Defence and reply

(1) Part 15 (defence and reply) applies to claims in the commercial list with the modification to rule 15.8 that the claimant must –

(a) file any reply to a defence; and
(b) serve it on all other parties,

within 21 days after service of the defence.

(2) Rule 6.23 (period for filing a defence where the claim form is served out of the jurisdiction) applies to claims in the commercial list, except that if the particulars of claim are served after the defendant has filed an acknowledgment of service the period for filing a defence is 28 days from service of the particulars of claim.

Amendments—Inserted by SI 2001/4015.

58.11 Statements of case

The court may at any time before or after the issue of the claim form order a claim in the commercial list to proceed without the filing or service of statements of case.

Amendments—Inserted by SI 2001/4015.

58.12 Part 8 claims

Part 8 applies to claims in the commercial list, with the modification that a defendant to a Part 8 claim who wishes to rely on written evidence must file and serve it within 28 days after filing an acknowledgment of service.

Amendments—Inserted by SI 2001/4015.

58.13 Case management

(1) All proceedings in the commercial list are treated as being allocated to the multi-track and Part 26 does not apply.

(2) The following parts only of Part 29 apply –

- (a) rule 29.3(2) (legal representative to attend case management conferences and pre-trial reviews);
- (b) rule 29.5 (variation of case management timetable) with the exception of rule 29.5(1)(c).

(3) As soon as practicable the court will hold a case management conference which must be fixed in accordance with the practice direction.

(4) At the case management conference or at any hearing at which the parties are represented the court may give such directions for the management of the case as it considers appropriate.

Amendments—Inserted by SI 2001/4015.

58.14 Disclosure – ships papers

(1) If, in proceedings relating to a marine insurance policy, the underwriters apply for specific disclosure under rule 31.12, the court may –

- (a) order a party to produce all the ships papers; and
- (b) require that party to use his best endeavours to obtain and disclose documents which are not or have not been in his control.

(2) An order under this rule may be made at any stage of the proceedings and on such terms, if any, as to staying the proceedings or otherwise, as the court thinks fit.

Amendments—Inserted by SI 2001/4015.

58.15 Judgments and orders

(1) Except for orders made by the court on its own initiative and unless the court orders otherwise, every judgment or order will be drawn up by the parties, and rule 40.3 is modified accordingly.

(2) An application for a consent order must include a draft of the proposed order signed on behalf of all the parties to whom it relates.

(3) Rule 40.6 (consent judgments and orders) does not apply.

Amendments—Inserted by SI 2001/4015.

Practice Direction – Commercial Court

This Practice Direction supplements CPR Part 58 (PD58)

Admiralty and Commercial Courts Guide—Reference to this Court Guide is essential for a full understanding of Commercial Court practice.

GENERAL

1.1 This practice direction applies to commercial claims proceeding in the commercial list of the Queen's Bench Division. It supersedes all previous practice directions and practice statements in the Commercial Court.

1.2 All proceedings in the commercial list, including any appeal from a judgment, order or decision of a master or district judge before the proceedings were transferred to the Commercial Court, will be heard or determined by a Commercial Court judge, except that –

- (1) another judge of the Queen's Bench Division or Chancery Division may hear urgent applications if no Commercial Court judge is available; and
- (2) unless the court otherwise orders, any application relating to the enforcement of a Commercial Court judgment or order for the payment of money will be dealt with by a master of the Queen's Bench Division or a district judge.

1.3 Provisions in other practice directions which refer to a master or district judge are to be read, in relation to claims in the commercial list, as if they referred to a Commercial Court judge.

1.4 The Admiralty and Commercial Registry in the Royal Courts of Justice is the administrative office of the court for all proceedings in the commercial list.

STARTING PROCEEDINGS IN THE COMMERCIAL COURT

2.1 Claims in the Commercial Court must be issued in the Admiralty and Commercial Registry.

2.2 When the Registry is closed, a request to issue a claim form may be made by fax, using the procedure set out in Appendix A to this practice direction. If a request is made which complies with that procedure, the claim form is issued when the fax is received by the Registry.

2.3 The claim form must be marked in the top right hand corner 'Queen's Bench Division, Commercial Court'.

2.4 A claimant starting proceedings in the commercial list, other than an arbitration claim, must use practice form N1(CC) for Part 7 claims or practice form N208(CC) for Part 8 claims.

APPLICATIONS BEFORE PROCEEDINGS ARE ISSUED

3.1 A party who intends to bring a claim in the commercial list must make any application before the claim form is issued to a Commercial Court judge.

3.2 The written evidence in support of such an application must state that the claimant intends to bring proceedings in the commercial list.

3.3 If the Commercial Court judge hearing the application considers that the proceedings should not be brought in the commercial list, he may adjourn the application to be heard by a master or by a judge who is not a Commercial Court judge.

TRANSFERRING PROCEEDINGS TO OR FROM THE COMMERCIAL COURT

4.1 If an application is made to a court other than the Commercial Court to transfer proceedings to the commercial list, the other court may –

(1) adjourn the application to be heard by a Commercial Court judge; or
(2) dismiss the application.

4.2 If the Commercial Court orders proceedings to be transferred to the commercial list –

(1) it will order them to be transferred to the Royal Courts of Justice; and
(2) it may give case management directions.

4.3 An application by a defendant, including a Part 20 defendant, for an order transferring proceedings from the commercial list should be made promptly and normally not later than the first case management conference.

[4.4 A party applying to the Commercial Court to transfer a claim to the commercial list must give notice of the application to the court in which the claim is proceeding, and the Commercial Court will not make an order for transfer until it is satisfied that such notice has been given.

ACKNOWLEDGMENT OF SERVICE

5.1 For Part 7 claims, a defendant must file an acknowledgment of service using practice form N9 (CC).

5.2 For Part 8 claims, a defendant must file an acknowledgment of service using practice form N210 (CC).

DEFAULT JUDGMENT AND ADMISSIONS

6 The practice directions supplementing Parts 12 and Part 14 apply with the following modifications –

(1) paragraph 4.1(1) of the practice direction supplementing Part 12 is to be read as referring to the service of the claim form; and
(2) the references to 'particulars of claim' in paragraphs 2.1, 3.1 and 3.2 of the practice direction supplementing Part 14 are to be read as referring to the claim form.

VARIATION OF TIME LIMITS

7.1 If the parties, in accordance with rule 2.11, agree in writing to vary a time limit, the claimant must notify the court in writing, giving brief written reasons for the agreed variation.

7.2 The court may make an order overriding an agreement by the parties varying a time limit.

AMENDMENTS

8 Paragraph 2.2 of the practice direction supplementing Part 17 is modified so that amendments to a statement of case must show the original text, unless the court orders otherwise.

SERVICE OF DOCUMENTS

9 Unless the court orders otherwise, the Commercial Court will not serve documents or orders and service must be effected by the parties.

CASE MANAGEMENT

10.1 The following parts only of the practice direction supplementing Part 29 apply –

(1) paragraph 5 (case management conferences), excluding paragraph 5.9 and modified so far as is made necessary by other specific provisions of this practice direction; and
(2) paragraph 7 (failure to comply with case management directions).

10.2 If the proceedings are started in the commercial list, the claimant must apply for a case management conference –

(a) for a Part 7 claim, within 14 days of the date when all defendants who intend to file and serve a defence have done so; and
(b) for a Part 8 claim, within 14 days of the date when all defendants who intend to serve evidence have done so.

10.3 If the proceedings are transferred to the commercial list, the claimant must apply for a case management conference within 14 days of the date of the order transferring them, unless the judge held, or gave directions for, a case management conference when he made the order transferring the proceedings.

10.4 Any party may, at a time earlier than that provided in paragraphs 10.2 or 10.3, apply in writing to the court to fix a case management conference.

10.5 If the claimant does not make an application in accordance with paragraphs 10.2 or 10.3, any other party may apply for a case management conference.

10.6 The court may fix a case management conference at any time on its own initiative. If it does so, the court will give at least 7 days notice to the parties, unless there are compelling reasons for a shorter period of notice.

10.7 Not less than 7 days before a case management conference, each party must file and serve –

(1) a completed case management information sheet; and
(2) an application notice for any order which that party intends to seek at the case management conference, other than directions referred to in the case management information sheet.

10.8 Unless the court orders otherwise, the claimant, in consultation with the other parties, must prepare –

(1) a case memorandum, containing a short and uncontroversial summary of what the case is about and of its material case history;

(2) a list of issues, with a section listing important matters which are not in dispute; and

(3) a case management bundle containing –

(a) the claim form;

(b) all statements of case (excluding schedules), except that, if a summary of a statement of case has been filed, the bundle should contain the summary, and not the full statement of case;

(c) the case memorandum;

(d) the list of issues;

(e) the case management information sheets and, if a pre-trial timetable has been agreed or ordered, that timetable;

(f) the principal orders of the court; and

(g) any agreement in writing made by the parties as to disclosure,

and provide copies of the case management bundle for the court and the other parties at least 7 days before the first case management conference or any earlier hearing at which the court may give case management directions.

10.9 The claimant, in consultation with the other parties, must revise and update the documents referred to in paragraph 10.8 appropriately as the case proceeds. This must include making all necessary revisions and additions at least 7 days before any subsequent hearing at which the court may give case management directions.

PRE-TRIAL REVIEW

11.1 At any pre-trial review or case management hearing, the court will ensure that case management directions have been complied with and give any further directions for the trial that are necessary.

11.2 Advocates who are to represent the parties at the trial should represent them at the pre-trial review and any case management hearing at which arrangements for the trial are to be discussed.

11.3 Before the pre-trial review, the parties must discuss and, if possible, agree a draft written timetable for the trial.

11.4 The claimant must file a copy of the draft timetable for the trial at least 2 days before the hearing of the pre-trial review. Any parts of the timetable which are not agreed must be identified and short explanations of the disagreement must be given.

11.5 At the pre-trial review, the court will set a timetable for the trial, unless a timetable has already been fixed or the court considers that it would be inappropriate to do so or appropriate to do so at a later time.

CASE MANAGEMENT WHERE THERE IS A PART 20 CLAIM

12 Paragraph 5 of the practice direction supplementing Part 20 applies, except that, unless the court otherwise orders, the court will give case management directions for Part 20 claims at the same case management conferences as it gives directions for the main claim.

EVIDENCE FOR APPLICATIONS

13.1 The general requirement is that, unless the court orders otherwise –

(1) evidence in support of an application must be filed and served with the application (see rule 23.7(3));
(2) evidence in answer must be filed and served within 14 days after the application is served; and
(3) evidence in reply must be filed and served within 7 days of the service of evidence in answer.

13.2 In any case in which the application is likely to require an oral hearing of more than half a day the periods set out in paragraphs 13.1(2) and (3) will be 28 days and 14 days respectively.

13.3 If the date fixed for the hearing of an application means that the times in paragraphs 13.1(2) and (3) cannot both be achieved, the evidence must be filed and served –

(1) as soon as possible; and
(2) in sufficient time to ensure that the application may fairly proceed on the date fixed.

13.4 The parties may, in accordance with rule 2.11, agree different periods from those in paragraphs 13.1(2) and (3) provided that the agreement does not affect the date fixed for the hearing of the application.

JUDGMENTS AND ORDERS

14.1 An application for a consent order must include a draft of the proposed order signed on behalf of all parties to whom it relates (see paragraph 10.4 of the practice direction supplementing Part 23).

14.2 Judgments and orders are generally drawn up by the parties (see rule 58.15). The parties are not therefore required to supply draft orders on disk (see paragraph 12.1 of the practice direction supplementing Part 23).

APPENDIX A

PROCEDURE FOR ISSUE OF CLAIM FORM WHEN REGISTRY IS CLOSED – PARAGRAPH 2.2

1 A request to issue a claim form may be made by fax when the Registry is closed, provided that –

(a) the claim form is signed by a solicitor acting on behalf of the claimant; and
(b) it does not require the permission of the court for its issue (unless such permission has already been given).

2 The solicitor requesting the issue of the claim form ('the issuing solicitor') must –

(a) endorse on the claim form and sign the endorsement set out below;
(b) send a copy of the claim form so endorsed to the Registry by fax for issue under paragraph 2.2 of this practice direction; and
(c) complete and sign a certificate in the form set out below, certifying that he has received a transmission report confirming that the fax has been transmitted in full, and stating the time and date of transmission.

3 When the Registry is next open to the public after the issue of a claim form in accordance with this procedure, the issuing solicitor or his agent must attend and deliver to the Registry –

(a) the original of the claim form which was sent by fax (including the endorsement and the certificate) or, if the claim form has been served, a true and certified copy of it;
(b) as many copies of the claim form as the Registry requires; and
(c) the transmission report.

4 When a court officer at the Registry has checked that –

(a) the claim form delivered under paragraph 3 matches the claim form received by fax; and
(b) the correct issue fee has been paid,

he will allocate a number to the case, and seal, mark as 'original' and date the claim form with the date of issue (being the date when the fax is recorded at the Registry as having been received).

5 If the issuing solicitor has served the unsealed claim form on any person, he must as soon as practicable –

(a) inform that person of the case number; and
(b) if requested, serve him with a copy of the sealed and dated claim form at any address in England and Wales.

6 Any person served with a claim form issued under this procedure may, without paying a fee, inspect and take copies of the documents lodged at the Registry under paragraphs 2 and 3 above.

7 The issue of a claim form in accordance with this procedure takes place when the fax is recorded at the Registry as having been received, and the claim form has the same effect for all purposes as a claim form issued under Part 7 or 8. Unless the court otherwise orders, the sealed version of the claim form retained by the Registry is conclusive proof that the claim form was issued at the time and on the date stated.

8 If the procedure set out in this Appendix is not complied with, the court may declare that a claim form shall be treated as not having been issued.

ENDORSEMENT

A claim form issued pursuant to a request by fax must be endorsed as follows:

'(1) This claim form is issued under paragraph 2.2 of the Commercial Court practice direction and may be served notwithstanding that it does not bear the seal of the Court.

(2) A true copy of this claim form and endorsement has been sent to the Admiralty and Commercial Registry, Royal Courts of Justice, Strand, London WC2A 2LL, at the time and date certified below by the solicitor whose name appears below ('the issuing solicitor').

(3) It is the duty of the issuing solicitor or his agent to attend at the Registry when it is next open to the public for the claim form to be sealed.

(4) Any person served with this unsealed claim form –
(a) will be notified by the issuing solicitor of the case number;
(b) may require the issuing solicitor to serve him with a copy of the sealed claim form at an address in England and Wales; and

(c) may inspect without charge the documents lodged at the Registry by the issuing solicitor.

(5) I, the issuing solicitor, undertake [to the Court, to the defendants named in this claim form, and to any other person served with this claim form –

(a) that the statement in paragraph 2 above is correct;

(b) that the time and date given in the certificate with this endorsement are correct;

(c) that this claim form is a claim form which may be issued under paragraph 2.2 and Appendix A of the Commercial Court practice direction;

(d) that I will comply in all respects with the requirements of Appendix A of the Commercial Court practice direction; and

(e) that I will indemnify any person served with the claim form before it is sealed against any loss suffered as a result of the claim form being or becoming invalid as a result of any failure to comply with Appendix A of the Commercial Court practice direction.

(*Signed*)

Solicitor for the claimant'

[**Note:** the endorsement may be signed in the name of the firm of solicitors rather than an individual solicitor, or by solicitors' agents in their capacity as agents acting on behalf of their professional clients.]

CERTIFICATE

The issuing solicitor must sign a certificate in the following form –

'I certify that I have received a transmission report confirming that the transmission of a copy of this claim form to the Registry by fax was fully completed and that the time and date of transmission to the Registry were [*enter the time and date shown on the transmission report.*

Dated

(*Signed*)

Solicitor for the claimant'

[**Note:** the certificate must be signed in the name of the firm of solicitors rather than an individual solicitor, or by solicitors' agents in their capacity as agents acting on behalf of their professional clients.]

PART 59
MERCANTILE COURTS

CONTENTS OF THIS PART

Practice Direction—This Part is supplemented by a practice direction – PD59 – which is set out at p 1385. See also the Mercantile Courts Guide, subject to the caveat set out in note '**Mercantile Courts Guide**' below.

General note—This Part and its practice direction – for the most part setting out practice already encouraged by the Mercantile Courts Guide – are very similar but not identical to Pt 58 and PD58, which govern practice in the Commercial Court.

Mercantile Courts Guide—Each of the seven mercantile courts (Birmingham, Bristol, Cardiff, Chester, Central London, Leeds, Liverpool & Manchester) has its own guide. For the most part, the contents of the guides apply uniformly to all the mercantile courts in England and Wales. The differences arise from the need to insert information that is peculiar to the court in question, such as how to contact those with special responsibility for a mercantile list. The mercantile list in the Central London County Court enjoys a particular status, which is dealt with in the relevant guide. All the guides are available on HM Courts Service's website at *www.hmcourts-service.gov.uk*.

59.1 Scope of this Part and interpretation

(1) This Part applies to claims in mercantile courts.

(2) A claim may only be started in a mercantile court if it –

(a) relates to a commercial or business matter in a broad sense; and
(b) is not required to proceed in the Chancery Division or in another specialist list.

(3) In this Part and its practice direction –

(a) 'mercantile court' means a specialist list established within –
(i) the district registries listed in the practice direction; and
(ii) the Central London County Court,

to hear mercantile claims;
(b) 'mercantile claim' means a claim proceeding in a mercantile court; and
(c) 'mercantile judge' means a judge authorised to sit in a mercantile court.

Amendments—Inserted by SI 2001/4015.

59.2 Application of the Civil Procedure Rules

These Rules and their practice directions apply to mercantile claims unless this Part or a practice direction provides otherwise.

Amendments—Inserted by SI 2001/4015.

59.3 Transfer of proceedings

Rule 30.5(3) applies with the modifications that –

(a) a mercantile judge may transfer a mercantile claim to another mercantile court; and
(b) a Commercial Court judge may transfer a claim from the Commercial Court to a mercantile court.

(Rule 30.5(3) provides that an application for the transfer of proceedings to or from a specialist list must be made to a judge dealing with claims in that list)

Amendments—Inserted by SI 2001/4015.

59.4 Claim form and particulars of claim

(1) If particulars of claim are not contained in or served with the claim form –

(a) the claim form must state that, if an acknowledgment of service is filed which indicates an intention to defend the claim, particulars of claim will follow;
(b) when the claim form is served, it must be accompanied by the documents specified in rule 7.8(1);
(c) the claimant must serve particulars of claim within 28 days of the filing of an acknowledgment of service which indicates an intention to defend; and
(d) rule 7.4(2) does not apply.

(2) If the claimant is claiming interest, he must –

(a) include a statement to that effect; and
(b) give the details set out in rule 16.4(2),

in both the claim form and the particulars of claim.

(3) Rules 12.6(1)(a) and 14.14(1)(a) apply with the modification that references to the particulars of claim shall be read as if they referred to the claim form.

Amendments—Inserted by SI 2001/4015.

59.5 Acknowledgment of service

(1) A defendant must file an acknowledgment of service in every case.

(2) Unless paragraph (3) applies, the period for filing an acknowledgment of service is 14 days after service of the claim form.

(3) Where the claim form is served out of the jurisdiction, or on the agent of a defendant who is overseas, the time periods provided by rules 6.16(4), 6.21(4) and 6.22 apply after service of the claim form.

Amendments—Inserted by SI 2001/4015.

59.6 Disputing the court's jurisdiction

(1) Part 11 applies to mercantile claims with the modifications set out in this rule.

(2) An application under rule 11(1) must be made within 28 days after filing an acknowledgment of service.

(3) If the defendant files an acknowledgment of service indicating an intention to dispute the court's jurisdiction, the claimant need not serve particulars of claim before the hearing of the application.

Amendments—Inserted by SI 2001/4015.

59.7 Default judgment

(1) Part 12 applies to mercantile claims, except that rules 12.10 and 12.11 apply as modified by paragraphs (2) and (3) of this rule.

(2) If, in a Part 7 claim –

(a) the claim form has been served but no particulars of claim have been served; and

(b) the defendant has failed to file an acknowledgment of service,

the claimant must make an application if he wishes to obtain a default judgment.

(3) The application may be made without notice, but the court may direct it to be served on the defendant.

Amendments—Inserted by SI 2001/4015.

59.8 Admissions

(1) Rule 14.5 does not apply to mercantile claims.

(2) If the defendant admits part of a claim for a specified amount of money, the claimant may apply under rule 14.3 for judgment on the admission.

Amendments—Inserted by SI 2001/4015.

59.9 Defence and reply

(1) Part 15 (Defence and Reply) applies to mercantile claims with the modification to rule 15.8 that the claimant must –

(a) file any reply to a defence; and

(b) serve it on all other parties,

within 21 days after service of the defence.

(2) Rule 6.23 (period for filing a defence where the claim form is served out of the jurisdiction) applies to mercantile claims, except that if the particulars of claim are served after the defendant has filed an acknowledgment of service the period for filing a defence is 28 days from service of the particulars of claim.

Amendments—Inserted by SI 2001/4015.

59.10 Statements of case

The court may at any time before or after issue of the claim form order a mercantile claim to proceed without the filing or service of statements of case.

Amendments—Inserted by SI 2001/4015.

59.11 Case management

(1) All mercantile claims are treated as being allocated to the multi-track, and Part 26 does not apply.

(2) The following parts only of Part 29 apply –

(a) rule 29.3(2) (appropriate legal representative to attend case management conferences and pre-trial reviews); and

(b) rule 29.5 (variation of case management timetable) with the exception of rule 29.5(1)(c).

(3) As soon as practicable the court will hold a case management conference which must be fixed in accordance with the practice direction.

(4) At the case management conference or at any hearing at which the parties are represented the court may give such directions for the management of the case as it considers appropriate.

Amendments—Inserted by SI 2001/4015.

59.12 Judgments and orders

(1) Except for orders made by the court of its own initiative and unless the court otherwise orders every judgment or order will be drawn up by the parties, and rule 40.3 is modified accordingly.

(2) An application for a consent order must include a draft of the proposed order signed on behalf of all the parties to whom it relates.

(3) Rule 40.6 (consent judgments and orders) does not apply.

Amendments—Inserted by SI 2001/4015.

Practice Direction – Mercantile Courts

This Practice Direction supplements CPR Part 59 (PD59)

Important—This practice direction came into force on 25 March 2002. For provisions governing court procedure before that date see PD49H, set out in the 2002 edition of this work.

General note—See also the Mercantile Courts Guide (although this is now very much out of date).

GENERAL

1.1 This practice direction applies to mercantile claims.

1.2 Mercantile courts are established in –

(1) the following district registries of the High Court – Birmingham, Bristol, Cardiff, Chester, Leeds, Liverpool, Manchester and Newcastle; and

(2) the Central London County Court (previously called the Business List and now called the Mercantile List).

1.3 All mercantile claims will be heard or determined by a mercantile judge, except that –

(1) an application may be heard and determined by any other judge who, if the claim were not a mercantile claim, would have jurisdiction to determine it, if –

(a) the application is urgent and no mercantile judge is available to hear it; or

(b) a mercantile judge directs it to be heard by another judge; and

(2) unless the court otherwise orders, all proceedings for the enforcement of a mercantile court judgment or order for the payment of money will be dealt with by a district judge.

1.4 Provisions in other practice directions which refer to a master or district judge are to be read, in relation to mercantile claims, as if they referred to a mercantile judge.

STARTING PROCEEDINGS IN A MERCANTILE COURT

2.1 A claim should only be started in a mercantile court if it will benefit from the expertise of a mercantile judge.

2.2 The claim form must be marked in the top right hand corner 'Queen's Bench Division, __________ District Registry, Mercantile Court' or 'Central London County Court, Mercantile List' as appropriate.

2.3 A claim having a value less than £15,000 may not be issued in the Mercantile List at the Central London County Court without permission of the court.

2.4 A claim may be issued in the Mercantile List at the Central London County Court provided it has some connection with the South Eastern Circuit, for example, because –

(1) it is convenient for the claim to be dealt with in that court;
(2) the claim arises out of a transaction which took place within that circuit; or
(3) one of the parties resides or carries on business within that circuit.

APPLICATIONS BEFORE PROCEEDINGS ARE ISSUED

3.1 A party who intends to bring a claim in a mercantile court must make any application before the claim form is issued to a judge of that court.

3.2 The written evidence in support of such an application should show why the claim is suitable to proceed as a mercantile claim.

TRANSFER OF PROCEEDINGS TO OR FROM A MERCANTILE COURT

4.1 If a claim which has not been issued in a mercantile court is suitable to continue as a mercantile claim –

(1) any party wishing the claim to be transferred to a mercantile court may make an application for transfer to the court to which transfer is sought;
(2) if all parties consent to the transfer, the application may be made by letter to the mercantile listing officer of the court to which transfer is sought, stating why the case is suitable to be transferred to that court and enclosing the written consents of the parties, the claim form and statements of case.

4.2 If an application for transfer is made to a court which does not have power to make the order, that court may –

(1) adjourn the application to be heard by a mercantile judge; or
(2) dismiss the application.

4.3 A mercantile judge may make an order under rule 59.3 of his own initiative.

DEFAULT JUDGMENT AND ADMISSIONS

5 The practice directions supplementing Parts 12 and Part 14 apply with the following modifications –

(1) paragraph 4.1(1) of the practice direction supplementing Part 12 is to be read as referring to the service of the claim form; and
(2) the references to 'particulars of claim' in paragraphs 2.1, 3.1 and 3.2 of the practice direction supplementing Part 14 are to be read as referring to the claim form.

VARIATION OF TIME LIMITS BY AGREEMENT

6.1 If the parties, in accordance with rule 2.11, agree in writing to vary a time limit, the claimant must notify the court in writing, giving brief written reasons for the agreed variation.

6.2 The court may make an order overriding an agreement by the parties varying a time limit.

CASE MANAGEMENT

7.1 The following parts only of the practice direction supplementing Part 29 apply –

(1) paragraph 5 (case management conferences), excluding paragraph 5.9 and modified so far as is made necessary by other specific provisions of this practice direction; and
(2) paragraph 7 (failure to comply with case management directions).

7.2 If proceedings are started in a mercantile court, the claimant must apply for a case management conference –

(1) for a Part 7 claim, within 14 days of the date when all defendants who intend to file and serve a defence have done so; and
(2) for a Part 8 claim, within 14 days of the date when all defendants who intend to serve evidence have done so.

7.3 If proceedings are transferred to a mercantile court, the claimant must apply for a case management conference within 14 days of receiving an acknowledgment of the transfer from the receiving court, unless the judge held, or gave directions for, a case management conference when he made the order transferring the proceedings.

7.4 Any party may, at a time earlier than that provided in paragraphs 7.2 or 7.3, apply in writing to the court to fix a case management conference.

7.5 If the claimant does not make an application in accordance with paragraphs 7.2 or 7.3, any other party may apply for a case management conference.

7.6 The court may fix a case management conference at any time on its own initiative. If it does so, the court will give at least 7 days' notice to the parties, unless there are compelling reasons for a shorter period of notice.

7.7 Not less than 7 days before a case management conference –

(1) each party shall file and serve –
    (a) a case management information sheet substantially in the form set out at Appendix A to this practice direction; and
    (b) an application notice for any order which that party intends to seek

at the case management conference, other than directions referred to in the case management information sheet; and

(2) the claimant (or other party applying for the conference) shall in addition file and serve –
 (a) a case management file containing –
  – the claim form;
  – the statements of case (excluding schedules of more than 15 pages);
  – any orders already made;
  – the case management information sheets; and
  – a short list of the principal issues to be prepared by the claimant; and
 (b) a draft order substantially in the form set out at Appendix B to this practice direction, setting out the directions which that party thinks appropriate.

7.8 In appropriate cases –

(1) the parties may, not less than 7 days before the date fixed for the case management conference, submit agreed directions for the approval of the judge;
(2) the judge will then either –
 (a) make the directions proposed; or
 (b) make them with alterations; or
 (c) require the case management conference to proceed; but
(3) the parties must assume that the conference will proceed until informed to the contrary.

7.9 If the parties submit agreed directions and the judge makes them with alterations, any party objecting to the alterations may, within 7 days of receiving the order containing the directions, apply to the court for the directions to be varied.

7.10 The directions given at the case management conference –

(1) will normally cover all steps in the case through to trial, including the fixing of a trial date or window, or directions for the taking of steps to fix the trial date or window; and
(2) may include the fixing of a progress monitoring date or dates, and make provision for the court to be informed as to the progress of the case at the date or dates fixed.

7.11 If the court fixes a progress monitoring date, it may after that date fix a further case management conference or a pre-trial review on its own initiative if –

(1) no or insufficient information is provided by the parties; or
(2) it is appropriate in view of the information provided.

PRE-TRIAL REVIEW AND QUESTIONNAIRE

8.1 The court may order a pre-trial review at any time.

8.2 Each party must file and serve a completed pre-trial check list substantially in the form set out in Appendix C to this practice direction –

(1) if a pre-trial review has been ordered, not less than 7 days before the date of the review; or

(2) if no pre-trial review has been ordered, not less than 6 weeks before the trial date.

8.3 When pre-trial check lists are filed under paragraph 8.2(2) –

(1) the judge will consider them and decide whether to order a pre-trial review; and
(2) if he does not order a pre-trial review, he may on his own initiative give directions for the further preparation of the case or as to the conduct of the trial.

8.4 At a pre-trial review –

(1) the parties should if possible be represented by the advocates who will be appearing at the trial;
(2) any representatives appearing must be fully informed and authorised for the purposes of the review; and
(3) the court will give such directions for the conduct of the trial as it sees fit.

EVIDENCE FOR APPLICATIONS

9.1 The general requirement is that, unless the court orders otherwise –

(1) evidence in support of an application must be filed and served with the application: see rule 23.7(3);
(2) evidence in answer must be filed and served within 14 days after the application is served;
(3) evidence in reply must be filed and served within 7 days of the service of the evidence in answer.

9.2 In any case in which the application is likely to require an oral hearing of more than half a day the periods set out in paragraphs 9.1(2) and (3) will be 28 days and 14 days respectively.

9.3 If the date fixed for the hearing of the application means that the times in paragraphs 9.1(2) and (3) cannot both be achieved, the evidence must be filed and served –

(1) as soon as possible; and
(2) in sufficient time to ensure that the application may fairly proceed on the date fixed.

9.4 The parties may, in accordance with rule 2.11, agree different periods from those provided above, provided that the agreement does not affect the ability to proceed on the date fixed for the hearing of the application.

FILES FOR APPLICATIONS

10 Before the hearing of any application, the applicant must –

(1) provide to the court and each other party an appropriate indexed file for the application with consecutively numbered pages; and
(2) attach to the file an estimate of the reading time required by the judge.

JUDGMENTS AND ORDERS

11.1 After any hearing the claimant must draw up a draft order, unless the decision was made on the application of another party in which case that party must do so.

11.2 A draft order must be submitted by the party responsible for drawing it up within 3 clear days of the decision, with sufficient copies for each party and for one to be retained by the court.

11.3 The sealed orders will be returned to the party submitting them, who will be responsible for serving the order on the other parties.

11.4 Orders must be dated with the date of the decision, except for consent orders submitted for approval, which must be left undated.

FORMS

****

Appendices—The Appendices mentioned in this practice direction are available on the *Civil Court Service* CD-ROM or the Department for Constitutional Affairs' website at *www.lcd.gov.uk*.

PART 60
TECHNOLOGY AND CONSTRUCTION COURT CLAIMS

CONTENTS OF THIS PART

Procedural Guide—See Guide 57, set out in Section 1 of this work.

Practice Direction—See generally PD60 at p 1393.

Important—By virtue of the Civil Procedure (Amendment No 5) Rules 2001, SI 2001/4015, this Part came into force on 25 March 2002.

Forms of address—The nomenclature 'Official Referee' is now obsolete: judges of the TCC in the High Court, whilst known as 'His/Her Honour Judge …', are addressed as 'My Lord/My Lady'. In the county court the correct form of address is 'Your Honour' as in other cases.

60.1 General

(1) This Part applies to Technology and Construction Court claims ('TCC claims').

(2) In this Part and its practice direction –

- (a) 'TCC claim' means a claim which –
  - (i) satisfies the requirements of paragraph (3); and
  - (ii) has been issued in or transferred into the specialist list for such claims;
- (b) 'Technology and Construction Court' means any court in which TCC claims are dealt with in accordance with this Part or its practice direction; and
- (c) 'TCC judge' means any judge authorised to hear TCC claims.

(3) A claim may be brought as a TCC claim if –

- (a) it involves issues or questions which are technically complex; or
- (b) a trial by a TCC judge is desirable.

(The practice direction gives examples of types of claims which it may be appropriate to bring as TCC claims)

(4) TCC claims include all official referees' business referred to in section 68(1)(a) of the Supreme Court Act 1981.

(5) TCC claims will be dealt with –

- (a) in a Technology and Construction Court; and
- (b) by a TCC judge, unless –
  - (i) this Part or its practice direction permits otherwise; or
  - (ii) a TCC judge directs otherwise.

Amendments—Inserted by SI 2001/4015.

Scope of provision—There are several points to note regarding this Part:

(1) 'TCC claim' means a claim which can be dealt with by the TCC having regard to the criteria in r 60.1(3) and PD60, para 2.1.

(2) The TCC sits in both the Queen's Bench Division of the High Court and certain designated county courts (see PD60, para 3.4).
(3) The TCC is a specialist list for the purposes of r 30.5(2) (see r 60.2(2)). This means that applications for transfer to and from the TCC must be made to the TCC. In the case of an 'arbitration claim' as defined in Pt 62 a TCC judge has the power to transfer the claim to any other court or specialist list (r 62.3(4)).

In the High Court judges of the TCC are circuit judges appointed under SCA 1981, s 68, which has not been formally amended to adopt the new terminology.

In *Saunders v Williams* [2003] BLR 125, the Court of Appeal considered whether a High Court judge had been authorised to hear a TCC case under the wording of the then current practice direction, similar to r 60.1(5). For a case where a judgment was upheld when the judge was authorised to sit as a TCC judge but no order had been made transferring the case to the TCC see *Fawdry & Co v Murfitt* [2002] EWCA Civ 643, [2003] QB 104, [2002] 3 WLR 1354, [2003] 4 All ER 61.

60.2 Specialist list

(1) TCC claims form a specialist list.

(2) A judge will be appointed to be the judge in charge of the TCC specialist list.

Amendments—Inserted by SI 2001/4015.

'specialist list' (r 60.2(1))—Rule 2.3(2) defines this expression by reference to a list designated as such by a rule or a practice direction. Hence, the scope and content of each specialist list, including the TCC, are defined by the applicable CPR Parts and practice directions. In the case of the TCC these are Pt 60 and its associated practice direction – PD60. Specialist lists do have certain limited common characteristics. First, under r 30.5(2) and (3) applications for transfer to and from a specialist list must be made to a judge dealing with claims in that list. Secondly, under PD52, para 2A.2(b) appeals from final decisions in proceedings to which Pts 57–62 apply lie to the Court of Appeal. These cover a number of specialist jurisdictions, although not all are designated specialist lists.

60.3 Application of the Civil Procedure Rules

These Rules and their practice directions apply to TCC claims unless this Part or a practice direction provides otherwise.

Amendments—Inserted by SI 2001/4015.

60.4 Issuing a TCC claim

A TCC claim must be issued in –

(a) the High Court in London;
(b) a district registry of the High Court; or
(c) a county court specified in the practice direction.

Amendments—Inserted by SI 2001/4015.

'a county court' (r 60.4(c))—See PD60, para 3.4 for designated county courts.

Pre-action protocol—A pre-action protocol for construction and engineering disputes came into force on 2 October 2000. The text is set out in Section 4 of this work.

60.5 Reply

Part 15 (Defence and Reply) applies to TCC claims with the modification to rule 15.8 that the claimant must –

(a) file any reply to a defence; and

(b) serve it on all other parties,

within 21 days after service of the defence.

Amendments—Inserted by SI 2001/4015.

60.6 Case management

(1) All TCC claims are treated as being allocated to the multi-track and Part 26 does not apply.

(2) Part 29 and its practice direction apply to the case management of TCC claims, except where they are varied by or inconsistent with the practice direction to this Part.

Amendments—Inserted by SI 2001/4015.

Arbitration claims—Arbitration claims may be started in the TCC (PD62, para 2.3). The provisions of Pt 60 are subject to Pt 62 in relation to such claims (r 62.1(3)). Rule 62.2(1) defines an 'arbitration claim'.

60.7 Judgments and Orders

(1) Except for orders made by the court of its own initiative and unless the court otherwise orders, every judgment or order made in claims proceeding in the Technology and Construction Court will be drawn up by the parties, and rule 40.3 is modified accordingly.

(2) An application for a consent order must include a draft of the proposed order signed on behalf of all the parties to whom it relates.

(3) Rule 40.6 (consent judgments and orders) does not apply.

Amendments—Inserted by SI 2005/2292.

Practice Direction – Technology and Construction Court Claims

This Practice Direction supplements CPR Part 60 (PD60)

Technology and Construction Court Guide—In addition to this Practice Direction, TCC users should be aware of the contents of the relevant Court Guide, issued by the TCC and last updated in October 2005. It is printed in Section 5 of this work. Both the Technology and Construction Bar Association and the Technology and Construction Solicitors Association (TecSA), also publish rules for use in mediations and adjudications under the Housing Grants Construction and Regeneration Act 1996, Part II.

TCC Judges sitting as an Arbitrator—A short guide to TCC judges sitting as arbitrators published in April 2003 is available in pdf format via the TCC section of the court service website *www.hmcourts-service.gov.uk* Access to the TCC section is through the link 'information about'.

Pre-Action Protocol for Construction and Engineering Disputes—This is set out in Section 4 of this work and requires certain steps to be taken by the parties before proceedings are commenced. For an example of a case where failure to comply with the protocol had adverse consequences to the defaulting party see *Paul Thomas Construction Ltd v Hyland* (2002) 18 Const LJ 345 (failure to provide details of claim, refusal to participate in adjudication without undertaking as to costs, reluctance to cooperate with defendant's surveyor). The protocol does not apply to certain situations, such as proceedings to enforce an adjudicator's award, and proceedings which will be the subject of a claim for summary judgment.

GENERAL

1 This practice direction applies to Technology and Construction Court claims ('TCC claims').

TCC CLAIMS

2.1 The following are examples of the types of claim which it may be appropriate to bring as TCC claims –

(a) building or other construction disputes, including claims for the enforcement of the decisions of adjudicators under the Housing Grants, Construction and Regeneration Act 1996;
(b) engineering disputes;
(c) claims by and against engineers, architects, surveyors, accountants and other specialised advisers relating to the services they provide;
(d) claims by and against local authorities relating to their statutory duties concerning the development of land or the construction of buildings;
(e) claims relating to the design, supply and installation of computers, computer software and related network systems;
(f) claims relating to the quality of goods sold or hired, and work done, materials supplied or services rendered;
(g) claims between landlord and tenant for breach of a repairing covenant;
(h) claims between neighbours, owners and occupiers of land in trespass, nuisance etc;
(i) claims relating to the environment (for example, pollution cases);
(j) claims arising out of fires;
(k) claims involving taking of accounts where these are complicated; and
(l) challenges to decisions of arbitrators in construction and engineering disputes including applications for permission to appeal and appeals.

2.2 A claim given as an example in paragraph 2.1 will not be suitable for this specialist list unless it demonstrates the characteristics in rule 60.1(3). Similarly, the examples are not exhaustive and other types of claim may be appropriate to this specialist list.

'types of claim' (para 2.1)—The list is not exhaustive, but the fact that the dispute is of a kind in the list will not per se qualify it as a TCC case. It must also comply with CPR r 60.1(3). In practice a key test is complexity. Hence, simple complaints relating, for example, to repair works to single dwellings are less likely to qualify as TCC cases. The normal rules relating to allocation of cases to the High Court and county court – laid down in PD7 – apply to the TCC.

HOW TO START A TCC CLAIM

3.1 TCC claims must be issued in the High Court or in a county court specified in this practice direction.

Appropriate Venue—The TCC Guide at para 1.4 suggests that, depending on the complexity of the case and the availability of a judge, claims for less than £50,000 should normally be started in the appropriate county court.

3.2 The claim form must be marked in the top right hand corner 'Technology and Construction Court' below the words 'The High Court, Queen's Bench Division' or 'The _____ County Court'.

3.3 TCC claims brought in the High Court outside London may be issued in any District Registry, but it is preferable that wherever possible they should be issued in one of the following District Registries, in which a TCC judge will usually be available –

Birmingham, Bristol, Cardiff, Chester, Exeter, Leeds, Liverpool, Newcastle, Nottingham and Salford.

3.4 The county courts in which a TCC claim may be issued are the following –

Birmingham, Bristol, Cardiff, Central London, Chester, Exeter, Leeds, Liverpool, Newcastle, Nottingham and Salford.

Genral note—On 7 June 2005, the Lord Chief Justice made a statement regarding the TCC. This announced interim arrangements pending a longer term reivew of the future of the TCC. Under the interim arrangements

(i) The High Court Judge in charge of the TCC will be based principally in the TCC.

(ii) The judge in charge of the TCC will consider every new case started in or transferred into the London TCC. Cases will be classified as 'HCJ' or 'SCJ'. The most complex and heavy cases, classified HCJ, will be managed and tried either by the judge in charge of the TCC or by another suitable High Court judge. The majority of cases, classified SCJ may be allocated to a named senior circuit judge by the judge in charge of the TCC; alternatively, they will be allocated by operation of the rota.

(iii) If in the case of TCC cases commenced in or transferred to court centres outside London, it appears to require management and trial by a High Court judge, the full time or principal TCC judge at that court centre should refer the case to the judge in charge of the TCC for a decision as to its future maangement and trial.

(iv) When proceedings are commenced in, or transferred to, the London TCC, any party to those proceedings may make brief representations by letter as to the appropriate classification.

The provisions of the practice direction should be read subject to the Lord Chief Justice's statement.

APPLICATIONS BEFORE PROCEEDINGS ARE ISSUED

4.1 A party who intends to issue a TCC claim must make any application before the claim form is issued to a TCC judge.

4.2 The written evidence in support of such an application must state that the proposed claim is a TCC claim.

Pre-action applications—Applications (such as those for interim injunctions, or for pre-action disclosure under CPR r 31.16) may in urgent cases have to be made before proceedings are commenced (see generally CPR r 25.2(a)). Freezing injunctions and search orders (defined in CPR r 25.1(1)(d) and (h) respectively) may generally only be granted by a High Court judge or other authorised judge. Accordingly, even where it is intended to issue a TCC claim in a county court, applications of this nature must be made to such a judge.

TRANSFER OF PROCEEDINGS

5.1 Where no TCC judge is available to deal with a claim which has been issued in a High Court District Registry or one of the county courts listed in paragraph 3.4 above, the claim may be transferred –

(1) if it has been issued in a District Registry, to another District Registry or to the High Court in London; or

(2) if it has been issued in a county court, to another county court where a TCC judge would be available.

Transfer generally—See TCC Guide, para 4.5.

5.2 Paragraph 5.1 is without prejudice to the court's general powers to transfer proceedings under Part 30.

(Rule 30.5(3) provides that an application for the transfer of proceedings to or from a specialist list must be made to a judge dealing with claims in that list)

Applications to transfer—See generally TCC Guide, para 4.4.

5.3 A party applying to a TCC judge to transfer a claim to the TCC specialist list must give notice of the application to the court in which the claim is proceeding, and a TCC judge will not make an order for transfer until he is satisfied that such notice has been given.

ASSIGNMENT OF CLAIM TO A TCC JUDGE

6.1 When a TCC claim is issued or an order is made transferring a claim to the TCC specialist list, the court will assign the claim to a named TCC judge ('the assigned TCC judge') who will have the primary responsibility for the case management of that claim.

6.2 All documents relating to the claim must be marked in similar manner to the claim form with the words 'Technology and Construction Court' and the name of the assigned TCC judge.

APPLICATIONS

7.1 An application should normally be made to the assigned TCC judge. If the assigned TCC judge is not available, or the court gives permission, the application may be made to another TCC judge.

7.2 If an application is urgent and there is no TCC judge available to deal with it, the application may be made to any judge who, if the claim were not a TCC claim, would be authorised to deal with the application.

Applications generally—See CPR Pt 23 and the annotations thereto.

Interim payments and payments into court—Where an interim payment or payment into court is made, that fact should not generally be disclosed to the trial judge (CPR rr 25.9 and 36.19(2)). The effect of assigning a TCC claim to a particular judge (who will normally be expected to try the case) involves a risk that he could become aware of such a payment. For example, where an application is made for interim payment, not only may the judge be aware thereafter of any order made, he is entitled to be told and take account of any payment made into court in deciding whether to order an interim payment (*Fryer v London Transport Executive* (1982) *The Times*, 4 December, CA). Accordingly, it is appropriate for such applications to be made to another judge, unless the defendant is prepared to waive the point.

Summary enforcement of adjudicator's decision—Part 24 of the CPR governs summary disposal of claims. Housing Grants, Construction and Regeneration Act 1996 (HGCRA), Pt II provides for reference to adjudication of disputes under construction contracts. The decision of the adjudicator is binding until the dispute is finally determined by proceedings or arbitration. Enforcement of an adjudicator's decision is normally sought in the TCC. Compliance with the pre-action protocol is not necessary. The correct procedure is normally to seek summary judgment (*Macob Civil Engineering Ltd v Morrison Construction Ltd* [1999] CLC 739, [1999] BLR 93, [1999] 3 EGLR 7, QBD). An adjudicator's decision which appears on its face to have been properly issued will be binding and enforceable in the courts whether or not the merits or validity of the decision are challenged (see *Macob* above). Errors made by the adjudicator but within his jurisdiction will not invalidate the decision (*Bouyges (UK) Ltd v Dahl-Jensen (UK) Ltd* [2001] All ER (Comm) 1041, [2000] BLR 522, CA). Applications to enforce an adjudicator's decision are comparable to the process of recovering an apparently undisputed debt. The court has power to abridge time limits accordingly (*Outwing Construction Ltd v H Randell & Sons Ltd* [1999] 1 BLR 156, 64 Con LR 59, QBD). The decision of an adjudicator that money must be paid gives rise to a second contractual obligation on the paying party to comply with that decision within the stipulated period. This obligation will usually preclude the paying party from making witholdings, deductions, set-offs or cross-claims against that sum (*Ferson Contractors Ltd v Levolux AT Ltd* [2003] BLR 118, CA). A stay of summary judgment, based on an adjudicator's decision on the ground that the successful party may be unable to repay the sum ordered to be paid in the event of the unsuccessful party ultimately showing in subsequeant arbitration or litigation that the decision was wrong, will rarely be granted (*Herschel Engineering Ltd v Breen Property Ltd* [2000] BLR 272, (2000) 2 TCLR 473, 70 Con LR 1, QBD; *Wimbledon Construction Company 200 Ltd v Vago* [2005] EWHC 1086 (TCC)). However, decisions which are arguably in excess of the adjudicator's jurisdiction or where there have arguably occurred breaches of the rules of natural justice will not be summarily enforced. See for example *KNS Industrial*

Services (Birmingham) Ltd v Sindall Ltd (2001) 75 Con LR 71, (2001) 3 TCLR 10, (2001) 17 Const LJ 170, QBD; *London and Amsterdam Properties Ltd v Waterman Partnership Ltd* [2004] BLR 179; *AMEC Capital Projects Ltd v Whitefriars City Estates Ltd* [2005] BLR 1, CA.

Summary assessment of costs—See paras 13–14 of PDCosts and the notes thereto. The guideline rates for summary assessment in Appendix 2 of the *Guide to Summary Assessment of Costs* (set out below PDCosts in Section 2 of this work) and the general principles in that Guide will be taken into account.

CASE MANAGEMENT CONFERENCE

8.1 The court will fix a case management conference within 14 days of the earliest of these events –

(1) the filing of an acknowledgment of service;
(2) the filing of a defence; or
(3) the date of an order transferring the claim to a TCC.

8.2 When the court notifies the parties of the date and time of the case management conference, it will at the same time send each party a case management information sheet and a case management directions form.

(The case management information sheet and the case management directions form are in the form set out in Appendixes A and B to this practice direction)

8.3 Not less than two days before the case management conference, each party must file and serve on all other parties –

(1) completed copies of the case management information sheet and case management directions form; and
(2) an application notice for any order which that party intends to seek at the case management conference, other than directions referred to in the case management directions form.

8.4 The parties are encouraged to agree directions to propose to the court by reference to the case management directions form.

8.5 If any party fails to file or serve the case management information sheet and the case management directions form by the date specified, the court may –

(1) impose such sanction as it sees fit; and
(2) either proceed with or adjourn the case management conference.

8.6 The directions given at the case management conference will normally include the fixing of dates for –

(1) any further case management conferences;
(2) a pre-trial review;
(3) the trial of any preliminary issues that it orders to be tried; and
(4) the trial.

Time for CMC—The CMC can be heard before the defence has been filed. There is in principle no reason why it should not be heard before the particulars of claim have been served in unusual circumstances, for example if there was a preliminary issue which could dispose of the claim without the need for full statements of case.

Directions—The parties are sent a case management directions form. They will be expected to complete and return case management information sheets in Form TCC/CM1. Copies of the form can be downloaded in pdf format from the TCC section of the HM Courts Service website *www.hmcourts-service.gov.uk*. Access to the TCC section is through the link 'information about'. All directions, whether or not agreed, will have to be justified to the judge to obtain his approval. The court is not limited to the agenda proposed by the parties and may raise other matters. The parties must be properly represented so as to provide the court with all that it needs for case management purposes. The directions are not mere formalities. The parties' representatives owe a duty to the court to inform the judge of all matters that might affect the decisions which are to be taken (CPR r 1.3). Where a party has a legal representative a representative familiar with the case and with sufficient authority to deal with any issues that are likely to arise must attend the CMC (CPR r 29.3(2)). Failure to comply with this may lead to a wasted costs order (PD29, para 5.2(3)). The legal representative must be in a position, therefore, to have answers to all the questions the court is likely to ask. For example, if there is an issue as to whether an exclusion clause applies, the court may need to be told whether it is a primary defence, and whether or not it justifies a preliminary issue. If a reply is to be served, the legal representative will have to be able to tell the court what it is likely to contain.

Separate trials of different issues or of liability and quantum—It will sometimes be convenient in the interest of saving costs for certain issues to be determined at an early stage, where the resolution of these may remove the need to reach decisions on other matters, or for issues of liabllity to be determined in advance of the assessment of the financial consequences. Generally, an order separating liability from quantum is not always a very meaningful exercise. In construction cases there are often extensive arguments about causation. That is particularly true of cases in which there are allegations of delay. Orders splitting the trial will usually require that any causation issues be dealt with at the first hearing, because it is typically an integral part of any proper consideration of liability.

Alternative dispute resolution—Parties are encouraged to settle disputes by ADR. Section A of the First Case Management Questionnaire relates to this. An unreasonable rejection of ADR may lead to adverse costs consequences (*Dunnett v Railtrack plc* [2002] EWCA Civ 303, [2002] 2 All ER 850, CA; *Hurst v Leeming* [2003] 1 Lloyds Rep 379). The court has power to impose a stay for ADR to be attempted even against the will of a party (*Shirayama Shokusan Co Ltd v Danovo Ltd* [2004] 1 WLR 2985). But there are cases where refusal to accept ADR is reasonable, if the other party's request is simply an attempt to extract a payment for an unmeritorious claim (*Société Internationale de Télécommunications Aéronautiques v Wyatt & Co (UK) Ltd* [2002] EWHC 2401 (Ch), [2002] All ER (D) 189 (Nov), (2002) 147 SJLB 27, ChD, *Halsey v Milton Keynes General NHS Trust* [2004] EWCA Civ 576, [2004] All ER (D) 125 (May), [2004] TLR 292, (2004) *The Times*, 27 May, CA). Admiralty and Commercial Courts Guide, App 7 (February 2002) contains a form of order which may be used (with adaptations as required) to provide for ADR.

Where ADR is attempted prior to proceedings being commenced and this, though unsuccessful, results in the potential claimant abandoning some issues, the court cannot order the claimant to pay the costs of the abandoned issues if they are not included in the proceedings (*McGlinn v Waltham Contractors Ltd* [2005] EWHC 1419 (TCC)).

TeCSA has published an ADR Protocol, Mediation Rules and a Model Mediation Agreement. Further information and the full text of the documents can be obtained from TeCSA at *www.tecsa.org.uk*. The secretary of TeCSA is currently Dominic Helps, Shadbolt & Co, Chatham Court, Lesbourne Road, Reigate, Surrey RH2 7LD, tel 01737 226277, fax 01737 226165. Various other bodies, such as the Centre for Dispute Resolution (CEDR), provide mediators and support for ADR.

Expert evidence—See CPR Pt 35 and annotations thereto. The court may debar expert evidence where the expert fails to comply with the requirements of CPR Pt 35 (*Stevens v Gullis* [2000] 1 All ER 527, CA), or if the expert is not impartial (*Liverpool Roman Catholic Archdiocesan Trustees Inc v Goldberg (No 3)* [2001] 1 WLR 2337). Rule 35.12(1) (meetings between the experts to identify the issues) has particular relevance in TCC cases.

In order to make effective use of expert evidence, a judge at the CMC will wish to be satisfied that a given issue can only be resolved by expert evidence and, if practicable, will define the issue with greater precision when giving permission for expert evidence. It will be necessary to explain the issue for which expert evidence is needed. Under CPR r 35.5(1), expert evidence is to be given in a written report unless the court directs otherwise. Therefore, a party wishing to call an expert to give oral evidence at trial or who wishes to cross-examine his opponent's experts, should seek a direction to the effect that the experts attend trial to give oral evidence, and should give reasons on the case management information sheet why he contends this direction should be made.

Directions may well be given that experts report on that issue on the basis of agreed terms of reference drawn up by the parties' advisers and approved by the court. Relevant points of fact should be ascertained before experts' reports.

Where expert evidence is required on a matter of pure scientific and other opinion, the court may be more ready to order a single expert than in other cases.

TeCSA have now produced an Expert Witness Protocol. As with their ADR Protocol – see note **'Alternative dispute resolution'** above – this can be found on the TeCSA website at *www.tecsa.org.uk*.

Information technology—The court may order in a complex case that documents such as schedules, pleadings and submissions be produced in computer-readable form as well as hard copy. A protocol dealing with this and related matters is in the course of preparation.

Trial date and time—A trial date will normally be fixed at the first CMC. The TCC operates a common list. Very long trials will only start in January and October. Trials will not be fixed across a vacation unless too long to be heard in that term even if started in January or October. No trials of 15 days or less will be listed together for a mid-term week set aside for urgent business or for long applications. All trials will be fixed to start on a Monday.

The court is likely to fix a timetable for trial based on the estimate of hearing time. This will normally be a detailed programme for each stage, ie opening, evidence in chief, cross-examination and reexamination of each witness of fact, likewise for each expert, and closing submissions.

Costs—The information sheet requires an estimate of the amount of costs, limited to the costs of legal representatives. But costs of experts and others in TCC cases may be important and estimates should be given in a case summary provided before the CMC. The objective of the CPR is to provide an overall budget for the proceedings. In substantial cases the estimates should be prepared in accordance with CPR Pt 43 with a skeleton bill in the form specified in PDCosts, Section 4. Information about funding arrangements (see CPR r 44.15) should be included.

Case summary—Paragraphs 5.6 and 5.7 of PD29 deal with the case summaries. The case summary should identify the principal issues, the evidence each party is likely to call and whether there are matters suitable for disposal as preliminary or separate issues. The case summary should be delivered not less than 2 days before the CMC. Frequently each party will submit its own skeleton argument setting out its proposals for further conduct of the case.

Disclosure and inspection of documents—This is a particularly important matter in TCC cases, where arguably relevant documentation may be very voluminous and costly to assemble. See CPR r 31.6 and annotations thereto.

The ambit of standard disclosure is likely in practice to be wide. However, in the TCC orders are made frequently to limit the ambit of disclosure in the first instance to documents that are relevant only to the case of one party, without prejudice to an application for specific disclosure.

Under CPR r 31.3 inspection may be restricted. This may be invoked where, of a series of numerous documents, only a few are in reality in issue. The court will consider ways in which excessive inspection can be avoided through informal provision of information, for example an index of relevant documents annexed to an expert's report based on the primary information. In practice many routine documents are unlikely to require formal production, provided the basic information derived from them is accurately summarised.

PRE-TRIAL REVIEW

9.1 When the court fixes the date for a pre-trial review it will send each party a pre-trial review questionnaire.

(The pre-trial review questionnaire is in the form set out in Appendix C to this practice direction).

Pre-trial review questionnaire and directions form—These, the first of which is designated TCC/PTR1, may be downloaded in pdf format from the HM Courts Service, Department of Constitutional Affairs and TecSA websites. Addresses are listed at the end of the practice direction below.

9.2 Each party must file and serve on all other parties completed copies of the questionnaire not less than two days before the date fixed for the pre-trial review.

9.3 The parties are encouraged to agree directions to propose to the court….

9.4 If any party fails to return or exchange the questionnaire by the date specified the court may –

(1) impose such sanction as it sees fit; and
(2) either proceed with or adjourn the pre-trial review.

9.5 At the pre-trial review, the court will give such directions for the conduct of the trial as it sees fit.

Purpose of pre-trial review—See generally TCC Guide, paras 9.1–9.3. The purposes of a pre-trial review (PTR) is to ensure that all necessary steps are taken to ensure the case will be ready for trial on the date fixed. The court, in making orders, will take account of the following points:

(a) Are all the issues now known and have they been clearly defined in the pleadings?
(b) Are the pleadings therefore complete; if not, what more needs to be done (for example, if it is not known whether quantum is agreed, subject to liability/ causation, then an appropriate order should be sought)?
(c) Are there any issues which are no longer relevant or not important? What is to be done about them?
(d) Are there any issues which ought to be heard before others either as preliminary issues or by scheduling the trial?
(e) Have all witness statements and expert reports and statements of matters agreed/ not agreed been served? Are any additional or supplemental statements or reports required? If so, from whom and by when? Are there any objections to any part of a statement which ought now to be decided?
(f) Has disclosure been given of all necessary documents? If not, has notice been given of the application and the affidavit in support delivered?
(g) Have documents to be obtained by means of a witness summons? If so, has it been served and a notional trial date fixed (as the documents will not be produced voluntarily)?
(h) Is the original estimate of the length of the trial still valid? If not what is the estimate and how is it justified? How many of the witnesses are in fact now to be called? How long will be required for the cross-examination of witnesses of fact and expert witnesses?
(i) Is a transcript/live note or equivalent to be provided? Will any other equipment be needed? How large a court room will be needed? Would a view be useful and should allowance be made for reading days – if so, when (in each case).
(j) Is there any way in which the court could assist to avoid the whole or any part of the trial? (For example, would an encouragement to use ADR be helpful?)
(k) Has written notice been given to every other party of everything to be raised at the PTR and has it been discussed and agreement not been reached?
(l) Has the claimant's counsel circulated an agreed list of the issues and of his/her proposals and has it and the other parties' proposals been lodged with the clerk to the judge?

Timing of PTR and practice—The following should be noted regarding these:

(1) *Timing*: A PTR should be timed for about 2 months before trial if possible to enable any slippages in the timetable to be corrected and/or further steps taken prior to trial.
(2) *Practice*: It is incumbent on all parties to adopt a proactive approach to the further steps required. Particular attention needs to be given to justifying the estimated length of trial and suggesting steps to achieve this, eg by limiting cross-examination or appointment of a joint expert. Attention also needs to be focused on whether examination in chief of witnesses can be avoided (if allowed for) by applying for leave to serve supplementary statements or statements in rebuttal. The court is normally reluctant to order split trials or mini-trials at the PTR stage, unless there is a real prospect that this course will dispose of large areas of the dispute more quickly than would otherwise be the case.

LISTING

10 The provisions about listing questionnaires and listing in Part 29 and its practice direction do not apply to TCC claims.

TRIAL

11.1 Whenever possible the trial of a claim will be heard by the assigned TCC judge.

11.2 A TCC claim may be tried at any place where there is a TCC judge available to try the claim.

FORMS

****

Appendices A–C—The Appendices mentioned in this practice direction are available on the *Civil Court Service* CD-ROM and Online services, the HM Courts Service, the Department for Constitutional Affairs' and the TecSA websites.

Useful websites—

- HM Courts Service: *www.hmcourts-service.gov.uk*
- Department of Constitutional Affairs: *www.dca.gov.uk*
- Technology and Construction Bar Association: *www.tecbar.org.uk*
- Technology and Construction Solicitors' Association: *www.tecsa.org.uk*

PART 61
ADMIRALTY CLAIMS

CONTENTS OF THIS PART

Practice Direction—See generally PD61 at p 1412. See also PD58 which, by virtue of PD61, para 1.1, applies to Admiralty claims unless inconsistent with Pt 61 or PD61.

Commercial and Admiralty Courts Guide—Reading this Court Guide is essential, though not by itself sufficient, if Admiralty Court practice is to be understood.

61.1 Scope and interpretation

(1) This Part applies to admiralty claims.

(2) In this Part –

(a) 'admiralty claim' means a claim within the Admiralty jurisdiction of the High Court as set out in section 20 of the Supreme Court Act 1981;
(b) 'the Admiralty Court' means the Admiralty Court of the Queen's Bench Division of the High Court of Justice;
(c) 'claim in rem' means a claim in an admiralty action in rem;
(d) 'collision claim' means a claim within section 20(3)(b) of the Supreme Court Act 1981;
(e) 'limitation claim' means a claim under the Merchant Shipping Act 1995 for the limitation of liability in connection with a ship or other property;
(f) 'salvage claim' means a claim –
   (i) for or in the nature of salvage;
   (ii) for special compensation under Article 14 of Schedule 11 to the Merchant Shipping Act 1995;
   (iii) for the apportionment of salvage; and
   (iv) arising out of or connected with any contract for salvage services;
(g) 'caution against arrest' means a caution entered in the Register under rule 61.7;
(h) 'caution against release' means a caution entered in the Register under rule 61.8;
(i) 'the Register' means the Register of cautions against arrest and release which is open to inspection as provided by the practice direction;
(j) 'the Marshal' means the Admiralty Marshal;
(k) 'ship' includes any vessel used in navigation; and

(l) 'the Registrar' means the Queen's Bench Master with responsibility for Admiralty claims.

(3) Part 58 (Commercial Court) applies to claims in the Admiralty Court except where this Part provides otherwise.

(4) The Registrar has all the powers of the Admiralty judge except where a rule or practice direction provides otherwise.

Amendments—Inserted by SI 2001/4015.

61.2 Admiralty claims

(1) The following claims must be started in the Admiralty Court –

(a) a claim –
   (i) in rem;
   (ii) for damage done by a ship;
   (iii) concerning the ownership of a ship;
   (iv) under the Merchant Shipping Act 1995;
   (v) for loss of life or personal injury specified in section 20(2)(f) of the Supreme Court Act 1981;
   (vi) by a master or member of a crew for wages;
   (vii) in the nature of towage; or
   (viii) in the nature of pilotage;
(b) a collision claim;
(c) a limitation claim; or
(d) a salvage claim.

(2) Any other admiralty claim may be started in the Admiralty Court.

(3) Rule 30.5(3) applies to claims in the Admiralty Court except that the Admiralty Court may order the transfer of a claim to –

(a) the Commercial list;
(b) a mercantile court;
(c) the mercantile list at the Central London County Court; or
(d) any other appropriate court.

Amendments—Inserted by SI 2001/4015.

61.3 Claims in rem

(1) This rule applies to claims in rem.

(2) A claim in rem is started by the issue of an in rem claim form as set out in the practice direction.

(3) Subject to rule 61.4, the particulars of claim must –

(a) be contained in or served with the claim form; or
(b) be served on the defendant by the claimant within 75 days after service of the claim form.

(4) An acknowledgment of service must be filed within 14 days after service of the claim form.

(5) The claim form must be served –

(a) in accordance with the practice direction; and
(b) within 12 months after the date of issue and rules 7.5 and 7.6 are modified accordingly.

(6) If a claim form has been issued (whether served or not), any person who wishes to defend the claim may file an acknowledgment of service.

Amendments—Inserted by SI 2001/4015.

61.4 Special provisions relating to collision claims

(1) This rule applies to collision claims.

(2) A claim form need not contain or be followed by particulars of claim and rule 7.4 does not apply.

(3) An acknowledgment of service must be filed.

(4) A party who wishes to dispute the court's jurisdiction must make an application under Part 11 within 2 months after filing his acknowledgment of service.

(5) Every party must –

(a) within 2 months after the defendant files the acknowledgment of service; or

(b) where the defendant applies under Part 11, within 2 months after the defendant files the further acknowledgment of service,

file at the court a completed collision statement of case in the form specified in the practice direction.

(6) A collision statement of case must be –

(a) in the form set out in the practice direction; and

(b) verified by a statement of truth.

(7) A claim form in a collision claim may not be served out of the jurisdiction unless –

(a) the case falls within section 22(2)(a), (b) or (c) of the Supreme Court Act 1981; or

(b) the defendant has submitted to or agreed to submit to the jurisdiction;

and the court gives permission in accordance with Section III of Part 6.

(8) Where permission to serve a claim form out of the jurisdiction is given, the court will specify the period within which the defendant may file an acknowledgment of service and, where appropriate, a collision statement of case.

(9) Where, in a collision claim in rem ('the original claim') –

(a) (i) a Part 20 claim; or

(ii) a cross claim in rem

arising out of the same collision or occurrence is made; and

(b) (i) the party bringing the original claim has caused the arrest of a ship or has obtained security in order to prevent such arrest; and

(ii) the party bringing the Part 20 claim or cross claim is unable to arrest a ship or otherwise obtain security,

the party bringing the Part 20 claim or cross claim may apply to the court to stay the original claim until sufficient security is given to satisfy any judgment that may be given in favour of that party.

(10) The consequences set out in paragraph (11) apply where a party to a claim to establish liability for a collision claim (other than a claim for loss of life or personal injury) –

(a) makes an offer to settle in the form set out in paragraph (12) not less than 21 days before the start of the trial;
(b) that offer is not accepted; and
(c) the maker of the offer obtains at trial an apportionment equal to or more favourable than his offer.

(11) Where paragraph (10) applies the parties will, unless the court considers it unjust, be entitled to the following costs –

(a) the maker of the offer will be entitled to –
  (i) all his costs from 21 days after the offer was made; and
  (ii) his costs before then in the percentage to which he would have been entitled had the offer been accepted; and
(b) all other parties to whom the offer was made –
  (i) will be entitled to their costs up to 21 days after the offer was made in the percentage to which they would have been entitled had the offer been accepted; but
  (ii) will not be entitled to their costs thereafter.

(12) An offer under paragraph (10) must be in writing and must contain –

(a) an offer to settle liability at stated percentages;
(b) an offer to pay costs in accordance with the same percentages;
(c) a term that the offer remain open for 21 days after the date it is made; and
(d) a term that, unless the court orders otherwise, on expiry of that period the offer remains open on the same terms except that the offeree should pay all the costs from that date until acceptance.

Amendments—Inserted by SI 2001/4015.

61.5 Arrest

(1) In a claim in rem –

(a) a claimant; and
(b) a judgment creditor

may apply to have the property proceeded against arrested.

(2) The practice direction sets out the procedure for applying for arrest.

(3) A party making an application for arrest must –

(a) request a search to be made in the Register before the warrant is issued to determine whether there is a caution against arrest in force with respect to that property; and
(b) file a declaration in the form set out in the practice direction.

(4) A warrant of arrest may not be issued as of right in the case of property in respect of which the beneficial ownership, as a result of a sale or disposal by any court in any jurisdiction exercising admiralty jurisdiction in rem, has changed since the claim form was issued.

(5) A warrant of arrest may not be issued against a ship owned by a State where by any convention or treaty, the United Kingdom has undertaken to minimise the possibility of arrest of ships of that State until –

(a) notice in the form set out in the practice direction has been served on a consular officer at the consular office of that State in London or the port at which it is intended to arrest the ship; and

(b) a copy of that notice is attached to any declaration under paragraph (3)(b).

(6) Except –

(a) with the permission of the court; or

(b) where notice has been given under paragraph (5),

a warrant of arrest may not be issued in a claim in rem against a foreign ship belonging to a port of a State in respect of which an order in council has been made under section 4 of the Consular Relations Act 1968, until the expiration of 2 weeks from appropriate notice to the consul.

(7) A warrant of arrest is valid for 12 months but may only be executed if the claim form –

(a) has been served; or

(b) remains valid for service at the date of execution.

(8) Property may only be arrested by the Marshal or his substitute.

(9) Property under arrest –

(a) may not be moved unless the court orders otherwise; and

(b) may be immobilised or prevented from sailing in such manner as the Marshal may consider appropriate.

(10) Where an in rem claim form has been issued and security sought, any person who has filed an acknowledgment of service may apply for an order specifying the amount and form of security to be provided.

Amendments—Inserted by SI 2001/4015.

61.6 Security in claim in rem

(1) This rule applies if, in a claim in rem, security has been given to –

(a) obtain the release of property under arrest; or

(b) prevent the arrest of property.

(2) The court may order that the –

(a) amount of security be reduced and may stay the claim until the order is complied with; or

(b) claimant may arrest or re-arrest the property proceeded against to obtain further security.

(3) The court may not make an order under paragraph (2)(b) if the total security to be provided would exceed the value of the property at the time –

(a) of the original arrest; or

(b) security was first given (if the property was not arrested).

Amendments—Inserted by SI 2001/4015.

61.7 Cautions against arrest

(1) Any person may file a request for a caution against arrest.

(2) When a request under paragraph (1) is filed the court will enter the caution in the Register if the request is in the form set out in the practice direction and –

(a) the person filing the request undertakes –

(i) to file an acknowledgment of service; and

(ii) to give sufficient security to satisfy the claim with interest and costs; or

(b) where the person filing the request has constituted a limitation fund in accordance with Article 11 of the Convention on Limitation of Liability for Maritime Claims 1976 he –
  (i) states that such a fund has been constituted; and
  (ii) undertakes that the claimant will acknowledge service of the claim form by which any claim may be begun against the property described in the request.

(3) A caution against arrest –

(a) is valid for 12 months after the date it is entered in the Register; but
(b) may be renewed for a further 12 months by filing a further request.

(4) Paragraphs (1) and (2) apply to a further request under paragraph (3)(b).

(5) Property may be arrested if a caution against arrest has been entered in the Register but the court may order that –

(a) the arrest be discharged; and
(b) the party procuring the arrest pays compensation to the owner of or other persons interested in the arrested property.

Amendments—Inserted by SI 2001/4015.

61.8 Release and cautions against release

(1) Where property is under arrest –

(a) an in rem claim form may be served upon it; and
(b) it may be arrested by any other person claiming to have an in rem claim against it.

(2) Any person who –

(a) claims to have an in rem right against any property under arrest; and
(b) wishes to be given notice of any application in respect of that property or its proceeds of sale,

may file a request for a caution against release in the form set out in the practice direction.

(3) When a request under paragraph (2) is filed, a caution against release will be entered in the Register.

(4) Property will be released from arrest if –

(a) it is sold by the court;
(b) the court orders release on an application made by any party;
(c) (i) the arresting party; and
  (ii) all persons who have entered cautions against release

file a request for release in the form set out in the practice direction; or

(d) any party files –
  (i) a request for release in the form set out in the practice direction (containing an undertaking); and
  (ii) consents to the release of the arresting party and all persons who have entered cautions against release.

(5) Where the release of any property is delayed by the entry of a caution against release under this rule any person who has an interest in the property may apply for an order that the person who entered the caution pay damages for losses suffered by the applicant because of the delay.

(6) The court may not make an order under paragraph (5) if satisfied that there was good reason to –

(a) request the entry of; and
(b) maintain

the caution.

(7) Any person –

(a) interested in property under arrest or in the proceeds of sale of such property; or
(b) whose interests are affected by any order sought or made,

may be made a party to any claim in rem against the property or proceeds of sale.

(8) Where –

(a) (i) a ship is not under arrest but cargo on board her is; or
(ii) a ship is under arrest but cargo on board her is not; and
(b) persons interested in the ship or cargo wish to discharge the cargo,

they may, without being made parties, request the Marshal to authorise steps to discharge the cargo.

(9) If –

(a) the Marshal considers a request under paragraph (8) reasonable; and
(b) the applicant gives an undertaking in writing acceptable to the Marshal to pay –
(i) his fees; and
(ii) all expenses to be incurred by him or on his behalf

on demand,

the Marshal will apply to the court for an order to permit the discharge of the cargo.

(10) Where persons interested in the ship or cargo are unable or unwilling to give an undertaking as referred to in paragraph (9)(b), they may –

(a) be made parties to the claim; and
(b) apply to the court for an order for –
(i) discharge of the cargo; and
(ii) directions as to the fees and expenses of the Marshal with regard to the discharge and storage of the cargo.

Amendments—Inserted by SI 2001/4015.

61.9 Judgment in default

(1) In a claim in rem (other than a collision claim) the claimant may obtain judgment in default of –

(a) an acknowledgment of service only if –
(i) the defendant has not filed an acknowledgment of service; and
(ii) the time for doing so set out in rule 61.3(4) has expired; and
(b) defence only if –
(i) a defence has not been filed; and
(ii) the relevant time limit for doing so has expired.

(2) In a collision claim, a party who has filed a collision statement of case within the time specified by rule 61.4(5) may obtain judgment in default of a collision statement of case only if –

(a) the party against whom judgment is sought has not filed a collision statement of case; and

(b) the time for doing so set out in rule 61.4(5) has expired.

(3) An application for judgment in default –

(a) under paragraph (1) or paragraph (2) in an in rem claim must be made by filing –

(i) an application notice as set out in the practice direction;

(ii) a certificate proving service of the claim form; and

(iii) evidence proving the claim to the satisfaction of the court; and

(b) under paragraph (2) in any other claim must be made in accordance with Part 12 with any necessary modifications.

(4) An application notice seeking judgment in default and, unless the court orders otherwise, all evidence in support, must be served on all persons who have entered cautions against release on the Register.

(5) The court may set aside or vary any judgment in default entered under this rule.

(6) The claimant may apply to the court for judgment against a party at whose instance a notice against arrest was entered where –

(a) the claim form has been served on that party;

(b) the sum claimed in the claim form does not exceed the amount specified in the undertaking given by that party in accordance with rule 61.7(2)(a)(ii); and

(c) that party has not fulfilled that undertaking within 14 days after service on him of the claim form.

Amendments—Inserted by SI 2001/4015.

61.10 Sale by the court, priorities and payment out

(1) An application for an order for the survey, appraisement or sale of a ship may be made in a claim in rem at any stage by any party.

(2) If the court makes an order for sale, it may –

(a) set a time within which notice of claims against the proceeds of sale must be filed; and

(b) the time and manner in which such notice must be advertised.

(3) Any party with a judgment against the property or proceeds of sale may at any time after the time referred to in paragraph (2) apply to the court for the determination of priorities.

(4) An application notice under paragraph (3) must be served on all persons who have filed a claim against the property.

(5) Payment out of the proceeds of sale will be made only to judgment creditors and –

(a) in accordance with the determination of priorities; or

(b) as the court orders.

Amendments—Inserted by SI 2001/4015.

61.11 Limitation claims

(1) This rule applies to limitation claims.

(2) A claim is started by the issue of a limitation claim form as set out in the practice direction.

(3) The –

(a) claimant; and
(b) at least one defendant

must be named in the claim form, but all other defendants may be described.

(4) The claim form –

(a) must be served on all named defendants and any other defendant who requests service upon him; and
(b) may be served on any other defendant.

(5) The claim form may not be served out of the jurisdiction unless –

(a) the claim falls within section 22(2)(a), (b) or (c) of the Supreme Court Act 1981;
(b) the defendant has submitted to or agreed to submit to the jurisdiction of the court; or
(c) the Admiralty Court has jurisdiction over the claim under any applicable Convention; and

the court grants permission in accordance with Section III of Part 6.

(6) An acknowledgment of service is not required.

(7) Every defendant upon whom a claim form is served must –

(a) within 28 days of service file –
 (i) a defence; or
 (ii) a notice that he admits the right of the claimant to limit liability; or
(b) if he wishes to –
 (i) dispute the jurisdiction of the court; or
 (ii) argue that the court should not exercise its jurisdiction,

file within 14 days of service (or where the claim form is served out of the jurisdiction, within the time specified in rule 6.22) an acknowledgment of service as set out in the practice direction.

(8) If a defendant files an acknowledgment of service under paragraph (7)(b) he will be treated as having accepted that the court has jurisdiction to hear the claim unless he applies under Part 11 within 14 days after filing the acknowledgment of service.

(9) Where one or more named defendants admits the right to limit –

(a) the claimant may apply for a restricted limitation decree in the form set out in the practice direction; and
(b) the court will issue a decree in the form set out in the practice direction limiting liability only against those named defendants who have admitted the claimant's right to limit liability.

(10) A restricted limitation decree –

(a) may be obtained against any named defendant who fails to file a defence within the time specified for doing so; and
(b) need not be advertised, but a copy must be served on the defendants to whom it applies.

(11) Where all the defendants upon whom the claim form has been served admit the claimant's right to limit liability –

(a) the claimant may apply to the Admiralty Registrar for a general limitation decree in the form set out in the practice direction; and
(b) the court will issue a limitation decree.

(12) Where one or more of the defendants upon whom the claim form has been served do not admit the claimant's right to limit, the claimant may apply for a general limitation decree in the form set out in the practice direction.

(13) When a limitation decree is granted the court –

(a) may –
(i) order that any proceedings relating to any claim arising out of the occurrence be stayed;
(ii) order the claimant to establish a limitation fund if one has not been established or make such other arrangements for payment of claims against which liability is limited; or
(iii) if the decree is a restricted limitation decree, distribute the limitation fund; and
(b) will, if the decree is a general limitation decree, give directions as to advertisement of the decree and set a time within which notice of claims against the fund must be filed or an application made to set aside the decree.

(14) When the court grants a general limitation decree the claimant must –

(a) advertise it in such manner and within such time as the court directs; and
(b) file –
(i) a declaration that the decree has been advertised in accordance with paragraph (a); and
(ii) copies of the advertisements.

(15) No later than the time set in the decree for filing claims, each of the defendants who wishes to assert a claim must file and serve his statement of case on –

(a) the limiting party; and
(b) all other defendants except where the court orders otherwise.

(16) Any person other than a defendant upon whom the claim form has been served may apply to the court within the time fixed in the decree to have a general limitation decree set aside.

(17) An application under paragraph (16) must be supported by a declaration –

(a) stating that the applicant has a claim against the claimant arising out of the occurrence; and
(b) setting out grounds for contending that the claimant is not entitled to the decree, either in the amount of limitation or at all.

(18) The claimant may constitute a limitation fund by making a payment into court.

(19) A limitation fund may be established before or after a limitation claim has been started.

(20) If a limitation claim is not commenced within 75 days after the date the fund was established –

(a) the fund will lapse; and
(b) all money in court (including interest) will be repaid to the person who made the payment into court.

(21) Money paid into court under paragraph (18) will not be paid out except under an order of the court.

(22) A limitation claim for –

(a) a restricted decree may be brought by counterclaim; and
(b) a general decree may only be brought by counterclaim with the permission of the court.

Amendments—Inserted by SI 2001/4015.

61.12 Stay of proceedings

Where the court orders a stay of any claim in rem –

(a) any property under arrest in the claim remains under arrest; and
(b) any security representing the property remains in force,

unless the court orders otherwise.

Amendments—Inserted by SI 2001/4015.

61.13 Assessors

The court may sit with assessors when hearing –

(a) collision claims; or
(b) other claims involving issues of navigation or seamanship, and

the parties will not be permitted to call expert witnesses unless the court orders otherwise.

Amendments—Inserted by SI 2001/4015.

Practice Direction – Admiralty Claims

This Practice Direction supplements CPR Part 61 (PD61)

Important—This practice direction came into force on 25 March 2002. For provisions governing court procedure before that date see PD49F and, unless inapplicable, the former Commercial Court Guide (now superseded by the new Admiralty and Commercial Courts Guide), set out in the 2002 edition of this work.

General note—For relevant commentary see the notes to CPR Pt 61.

Admiralty and Commercial Courts Guide—Reference to Chapter N of this Court Guide is essential for a fuller understanding of Admiralty Court practice.

61.1 – SCOPE

1.1 The practice direction supplementing Part 58 (Commercial Claims) also applies to Admiralty claims except where it is inconsistent with Part 61 or this practice direction.

CASE MANAGEMENT

2.1 After a claim form is issued the Registrar will issue a direction in writing stating –

(1) whether the claim will remain in the Admiralty Court or be transferred to another court; and

(2) if the claim remains in the Admiralty Court –
 (a) whether it will be dealt with by –
  (i) the Admiralty judge; or
  (ii) the Registrar; and
 (b) whether the trial will be in London or elsewhere.

2.2 In making these directions the Registrar will have regard to –

(1) the nature of the issues and the sums in dispute; and
(2) the criteria set in rule 26.8 so far as they are applicable.

2.3 Where the Registrar directs that the claim will be dealt with by the Admiralty judge, case management directions will be given and any case management conference or pre-trial review will be heard by the Admiralty judge.

61.3 – CLAIMS IN REM

3.1 A claim form in rem must be in Form ADM1.

3.2 The claimant in a claim in rem may be named or may be described, but if not named in the claim form must identify himself by name if requested to do so by any other party.

3.3 The defendant must be described in the claim form.

3.4 The acknowledgment of service must be in Form ADM2. The person who acknowledges service must identify himself by name.

3.5 The period for acknowledging service under rule 61.3(4) applies irrespective of whether the claim form contains particulars of claim.

3.6 A claim form in rem may be served in the following ways:

(1) on the property against which the claim is brought by fixing a copy of the claim form –
 (a) on the outside of the property in a position which may reasonably be expected to be seen; or
 (b) where the property is freight, either –
  (i) on the cargo in respect of which the freight was earned; or
  (ii) on the ship on which the cargo was carried;
(2) if the property to be served is in the custody of a person who will not permit access to it, by leaving a copy of the claim form with that person;
(3) where the property has been sold by the Marshal, by filing the claim form at the court;
(4) where there is a notice against arrest, on the person named in the notice as being authorised to accept service;
(5) on any solicitor authorised to accept service;
(6) in accordance with any agreement providing for service of proceedings; or
(7) in any other manner as the court may direct under rule 6.8 provided that the property against which the claim is brought or part of it is within the jurisdiction of the court.

3.7 In claims where the property –

(1) is to be arrested; or
(2) is already under arrest in current proceedings,

the Marshal will serve the in rem claim form if the claimant requests the court to do so.

3.8 In all other cases in rem claim forms must be served by the claimant.

3.9 Where the defendants are described and not named on the claim form (for example as 'the Owners of the Ship X'), any acknowledgment of service in addition to stating that description must also state the full names of the persons acknowledging service and the nature of their ownership.

3.10 After the acknowledgment of service has been filed, the claim will follow the procedure applicable to a claim proceeding in the Commercial list except that the claimant is allowed 75 days to serve the particulars of claim.

3.11 A defendant who files an acknowledgment of service to an in rem claim does not lose any right he may have to dispute the jurisdiction of the court (see rule 10.1(3)(b) and Part 11).

3.12 Any person who pays the prescribed fee may, during office hours, search for, inspect and take a copy of any claim form in rem whether or not it has been served.

61.4 – COLLISION CLAIMS

4.1 A collision statement of case must be in form ADM3.

4.2 A collision statement of case must contain –

- (1) in Part 1 of the form, answers to the questions set out in that Part; and
- (2) in Part 2 of the form, a statement –
  - (a) of any other facts and matters on which the party filing the collision statement of case relies;
  - (b) of all allegations of negligence or other fault which the party filing the collision statement of case makes; and
  - (c) of the remedy which the party filing the collision statement of case claims.

4.3 When he files his collision statement of case each party must give notice to every other party that he has done so.

4.4 Within 14 days after the last collision statement of case is filed each party must serve a copy of his collision statement of case on every other party.

4.5 Before the coming into force of Part 61, a collision statement of case was known as a Preliminary Act and the law relating to Preliminary Acts will continue to apply to collision statements of case.

61.5 – ARREST

5.1 An application for arrest must be –

- (1) in form ADM4 (which must also contain an undertaking); and
- (2) accompanied by a declaration in form ADM5.

5.2 When it receives an application for arrest that complies with the rules and the practice direction the court will issue an arrest warrant.

5.3 The declaration required by rule 61.5(3)(b) must be verified by a statement of truth and must state –

- (1) in every claim –

(a) the nature of the claim or counterclaim and that it has not been satisfied and if it arises in connection with a ship, the name of that ship;
(b) the nature of the property to be arrested and, if the property is a ship, the name of the ship and her port of registry; and
(c) the amount of the security sought, if any.

(2) in a claim against a ship by virtue of section 21(4) of the Supreme Court Act 1981 –
(a) the name of the person who would be liable on the claim if it were not commenced in rem;
(b) that the person referred to in sub-paragraph (a) was, when the right to bring the claim arose –
(i) the owner or charterer of; or
(ii) in possession or in control of,
the ship in connection with which the claim arose; and
(c) that at the time the claim form was issued the person referred to in sub-paragraph (a) was either –
(i) the beneficial owner of all the shares in the ship in respect of which the warrant is required; or
(ii) the charterer of it under a charter by demise;

(3) in the cases set out in rules 61.5(5) and (6) that the relevant notice has been sent or served, as appropriate; and

(4) in the case of a claim in respect of liability incurred under section 153 of the Merchant Shipping Act 1995, the facts relied on as establishing that the court is not prevented from considering the claim by reason of section 166(2) of that Act.

5.4 The notice required by rule 61.5(5)(a) must be in form ADM6.

5.5 Property is arrested –

(1) by service on it of an arrest warrant in form ADM9 in the manner set out at paragraph 3.6(1); or

(2) where it is not reasonably practicable to serve the warrant, by service of a notice of the issue of the warrant –
(a) in the manner set out in paragraph 3.6(1) on the property; or
(b) by giving notice to those in charge of the property.

5.6 When property is arrested the Registrar will issue standard directions in form ADM10.

5.7 The Marshal does not insure property under arrest.

61.7 – CAUTIONS AGAINST ARREST

6.1 The entry of a caution against arrest is not treated as a submission to the jurisdiction of the court.

6.2 The request for a caution against arrest must be in form ADM7.

6.3 On the filing of such a request, a caution against arrest will be entered in the Register.

6.4 The Register is open for inspection when the Admiralty and Commercial Registry is open.

61.8 – RELEASE AND CAUTIONS AGAINST RELEASE

7.1 The request for a caution against release must be in form ADM11.

7.2 On the filing of such a request, a caution against release will be entered in the Register.

7.3 The Register is open for inspection when the Admiralty and Commercial Registry is open.

7.4 A request for release under rule 61.8(4)(c) and (d) must be in form ADM12.

7.5 A withdrawal of a caution against release must be in form ADM12A.

61.9 – JUDGMENT IN DEFAULT

8.1 An application notice for judgment in default must be in form ADM13.

61.10 – SALE BY THE COURT AND PRIORITIES

9.1 Any application to the court concerning –

(1) the sale of the property under arrest; or
(2) the proceeds of sale of property sold by the court

will be heard in public and the application notice served on –

(a) all parties to the claim;
(b) all persons who have requested cautions against release with regard to the property or the proceeds of sale; and
(c) the Marshal.

9.2 Unless the court orders otherwise an order for sale will be in form ADM14.

9.3 An order for sale before judgment may only be made by the Admiralty judge.

9.4 Unless the Admiralty judge orders otherwise, a determination of priorities may only be made by the Admiralty judge.

9.5 When –

(1) proceeds of sale are paid into court by the Marshal; and
(2) such proceeds are in a foreign currency,

the funds will be placed on one day call interest bearing account unless the court orders otherwise.

9.6 Unless made at the same time as an application for sale, or other prior application, an application to place foreign currency on longer term deposit may be made to the Registrar.

9.7 Notice of the placement of foreign currency in an interest bearing account must be given to all parties interested in the fund by the party who made the application under paragraph 9.6.

9.8 Any interested party who wishes to object to the mode of investment of foreign currency paid into court may apply to the Registrar for directions.

61.11 – LIMITATION CLAIMS

10.1 The claim form in a limitation claim must be –

(1) in form ADM15; and
(2) accompanied by a declaration –
    (a) setting out the facts upon which the claimant relies; and

(b) stating the names and addresses (if known) of all persons who, to the knowledge of the claimant, have claims against him in respect of the occurrence to which the claim relates (other than named defendants),

verified by a statement of truth.

10.2 A defence to a limitation claim must be in form ADM16A.

10.3 A notice admitting the right of the claimant to limit liability in a limitation claim must be in form ADM16.

10.4 An acknowledgment of service in a limitation claim must be in form ADM16B.

10.5 An application for a restricted limitation decree must be in form ADM17 and the decree issued by the court on such an application must be in form ADM18.

10.6 An application for a general limitation decree must be in form ADM17A.

10.7 Where –

(1) the right to limit is not admitted; and
(2) the claimant seeks a general limitation decree in form ADM17A,

the claimant must, within 7 days after the date of the filing of the defence of the defendant last served or the expiry of the time for doing so, apply for an appointment before the Registrar for a case management conference.

10.8 On an application under rule 61.11(12) the Registrar may –

(1) grant a general limitation decree; or
(2) if he does not grant a decree –
   (a) order service of a defence;
   (b) order disclosure by the claimant; or
   (c) make such other case management directions as may be appropriate.

10.9 The fact that a limitation fund has lapsed under rule 61.11(20)(a) does not prevent the establishment of a new fund.

10.10 Where a limitation fund is established, it must be –

(1) the sterling equivalent of the number of special drawing rights to which [the claimant] claims to be entitled to limit his liability under the Merchant Shipping Act 1995; together with
(2) interest from the date of the occurrence giving rise to his liability to the date of payment into court.

10.11 Where the claimant does not know the sterling equivalent referred to in paragraph 10.10(1) on the date of payment into court he may –

(1) calculate it on the basis of the latest available published sterling equivalent of a special drawing right as fixed by the International Monetary Fund; and
(2) in the event of the sterling equivalent of a special drawing right on the date of payment into court being different from that used for calculating the amount of that payment into court the claimant may -
   (a) make up any deficiency by making a further payment into court which, if made within 14 days after the payment into court, will be

treated, except for the purpose of the rules relating to the accrual of interest on money paid into court, as if made on the date of that payment into court; or

(b) apply to the court for payment out of any excess amount (together with any interest accrued) paid into court.

10.12 An application under paragraph 10.11(2)(b) –

(1) may be made without notice to any party; and
(2) must be supported by evidence proving, to the satisfaction of the court, the sterling equivalent of the appropriate number of special drawing rights on the date of payment into court.

10.13 The claimant must give notice in writing to every named defendant of –

(1) any payment into court specifying –
  (a) the date of the payment in;
  (b) the amount paid in;
  (c) the amount and rate of interest included; and
  (d) the period to which it relates; and
(2) any excess amount (and interest) paid out to him under paragraph 10.11(2)(b).

10.14 A claim against the fund must be in form ADM20

10.15 A defendant's statement of case filed and served in accordance with rule 61.11(15) must contain particulars of the defendant's claim.

10.16 Any defendant who is unable to file and serve a statement of case in accordance with rule 61.11(15) and paragraph 10.15 must file a declaration, verified by a statement of truth, in form ADM21 stating the reason for his inability.

10.17 No later than 7 days after the time for filing claims [or declarations], the Registrar will fix a date for a case management conference at which directions will be given for the further conduct of the proceedings.

10.18 Nothing in rule 61.11 prevents limitation being relied on by way of defence.

PROCEEDING AGAINST OR CONCERNING THE INTERNATIONAL OIL POLLUTION COMPENSATION FUND

11.1 For the purposes of section 177 of the Merchant Shipping Act 1995 ('the Act') and the corresponding provision of Schedule 4 to the Act, the Fund may be given notice of proceedings by any party to a claim against an owner or guarantor in respect of liability under –

(1) section 153 or section 154 of the Act; or
(2) the corresponding provisions of Schedule 4 to the Act

by that person serving a notice in writing on the Fund together with copies of the claim form and any statements of case served in the claim.

11.2 The Fund may intervene in any claim to which paragraph 11.1 applies, (whether or not served with the notice), by serving notice of intervention on the –

(1) owner;
(2) guarantor; and
(3) court.

11.3 Where a judgment is given against the Fund in any claim under –

(1) section 175 of the Act; or
(2) the corresponding provisions of Schedule 4 to the Act,

the Registrar will arrange for a stamped copy of the judgment to be sent to the Fund by post.

11.4 Notice to the Registrar of the matters set out in –

(1) section 176(3)(b) of the Act; or
(2) the corresponding provisions of Schedule 4 to the Act,

must be given by the Fund in writing and sent to the court.

OTHER CLAIMS

12.1 This section applies to Admiralty claims which, before the coming into force of Part 61, would have been called claims in personam. Subject to the provisions of Part 61 and this practice direction relating to limitation claims and to collision claims, the following provisions apply to such claims.

12.2 All such claims will proceed in accordance with Part 58 (Commercial Court).

12.3 The claim form must be in Form ADM1A and must be served by the claimant.

12.4 The claimant may be named or may be described, but if not named in the claim form must identify himself by name if requested to do so by any other party.

12.5 The defendant must be named in the claim form.

12.6 Any person who files a defence must identify himself by name in the defence.

REFERENCES TO THE REGISTRAR

13.1 The court may at any stage in the claim refer any question or issue for determination by the Registrar (a 'reference').

13.2 Unless the court orders otherwise, where a reference has been ordered –

(1) if particulars of claim have not already been served, the claimant must file and serve particulars of claim on all other parties within 14 days after the date of the order; and
(2) any party opposing the claim must file a defence to the claim within 14 days after service of the particulars of claim on him.

13.3 Within 7 days after the defence is filed, the claimant must apply for an appointment before the Registrar for a case management conference.

UNDERTAKINGS

14.1 Where, in Part 61 or this practice direction, any undertaking to the Marshal is required it must be given –

(1) in writing and to his satisfaction; or
(2) in accordance with such other arrangements as he may require.

14.2 Where any party is dissatisfied with a direction given by the Marshal in this respect he may apply to the Registrar for a ruling.

FORMS

****

Forms—Forms ADM1–ADM22, which are appended to this practice direction, are available on the *Civil Court Service* CD-ROM or on the Court Service website at *www.courtservice.gov.uk*.

PART 62
ARBITRATION CLAIMS

CONTENTS OF THIS PART

Important—By virtue of the Civil Procedure (Amendment No 5) Rules 2001, SI 2001/4015, this Part came into force on 25 March 2002. For provisions governing court procedure before that date see PD49G, set out in the 2002 edition of this work.

Practice Direction—See generally PD62 at p 1438.

Introduction—This Part deals with the procedure to be followed where relief is sought from the court in relation to matters connected with arbitrations. Arbitrations are principally governed by AA 1996, Pt 1 (the 1996 Act) which applies to arbitration agreements in writing, and most of this Part and the practice direction deals with this. However, where –

(a) an arbitration was commenced before the 1996 Act came into force (ie 31 January 1997);
(b) an arbitration application was made before this date; or
(c) an arbitration application was made after this date in relation to an arbitration commenced before this date,

the 'old law' continues to apply, by virtue of the Arbitration Act 1996 (Commencement No 1) Order 1996. The old law means, by virtue of the Commencement Order, the Arbitration Acts of 1950, 1975 and 1979.

Venue—Paragraph 2.1 of PD62 explains in which courts an arbitration claim may be started. An arbitration claim under the AA 1996 (other than under s 9 of that Act) must be started in accordance with the HCCC(AAP)O (which provides that, subject to specific exceptions, proceedings under the Act must be commenced in the High Court) by the issue of the arbitration claim form. Where an arbitration claim form is issued in one of the specialist lists, in addition to this Part reference should also be made to the relevant CPR Part and the associated practice direction, namely Pt 58 (Commercial Court), Pt 59 (Mercantile Courts), Pt 60 (Technology and Construction Court Claims) and Pt 61 (Admiralty Claims). Furthermore, where an arbitration claim form relates to commercial or Admiralty proceedings, reference should also be made to the Admiralty and Commercial Courts Guide (published in February 2002), in particular Section O, which deals specifically with arbitrations.

Applications under s 9 of the 1996 Act must be issued in the court in which the proceedings of which a stay is sought are ongoing.

Scheme of the Part—The procedure to be used in relation to arbitration applications differs according to whether or not the AA 1996 or the old law applies. This Part is divided into three separate Sections: Section I (rr 62.2–62.10) applies to all matters that are governed by the 1996 Act; Section II (rr 62.11–62.16) governs all applications relating to arbitrations covered by the old law, namely the Arbitration Acts of 1950, 1975 and 1979; and Section III (rr 62.17–62.21) relates to the enforcement of all arbitration awards, irrespective of when the arbitration was commenced, other than by a claim on the award.

Arbitration claim form—As a general rule, an arbitration claim is started by the issue of an arbitration claim form which is to be issued in accordance with the Pt 8 procedure (see rr 62.3 and 62.13). The most important exception to that general rule is an application under AA 1996, s 9 for a stay of legal proceedings, where the application must be made by way of an application notice to the court dealing with those existing proceedings (see r 62.3(2)).

62.1 Scope of this Part and interpretation

(1) This Part contains rules about arbitration claims.

(2) In this Part –

- (a) 'the 1950 Act' means the Arbitration Act 1950;
- (b) 'the 1975 Act' means the Arbitration Act 1975;
- (c) 'the 1979 Act' means the Arbitration Act 1979;
- (d) 'the 1996 Act' means the Arbitration Act 1996;
- (e) references to –
  - (i) the 1996 Act; or
  - (ii) any particular section of that Act

  include references to that Act or to the particular section of that Act as applied with modifications by the ACAS Arbitration Scheme (England and Wales) Order 2001; and
- (f) 'arbitration claim form' means a claim form in the form set out in the practice direction.

(3) Part 58 (Commercial Court) applies to arbitration claims in the Commercial Court, Part 59 (Mercantile Court) applies to arbitration claims in the mercantile court and Part 60 (Technology and Construction Court claims) applies to arbitration claims in the Technology and Construction Court, except where this Part provides otherwise.

Amendments—Inserted by SI 2001/4015.

I Claims under the 1996 Act

The general principles of the Arbitration Act 1996—The equivalent section of the former Practice Direction – Arbitrations (PD49G, Section I) expressly provided that it was to be construed in accordance with the general principles as set out in AA 1996, s 1. Although this no longer appears in Pt 62, these general principles continue to be relevant to exercise of the court's powers under this Part.

The general principles as set out at AA 1996, s 1 are as follows:

'(a) the object of arbitration is to obtain the fair resolution of disputes by an impartial tribunal without unnecessary delay or expense;

(b) the parties should be free to agree how their disputes are resolved, subject only to such safeguards as are necessary in the public interest;

(c) in matters governed by this Part [ie Arbitrations pursuant to an arbitration agreement the court should not intervene except as provided by this Part.'

Powers of court under AA 1996—The 1996 Act confers various powers on the court in support of the arbitral process. The main provisions and the principles which are applied are summarised below.

Stay of legal proceedings—See AA 1996, s 9. The court will grant a stay where there is a dispute covered by an arbitration agreement. On that basis, s 9(4) excludes the court's jurisdiction to grant summary judgment on an application for a stay (*Halki Shipping Corp v Sopex Oils Ltd* [1998] 1 WLR 726, CA). Where there is a dispute as to whether there is an applicable arbitration agreement, the correct approach is normally in the interests of good litigation management and the saving of costs to determine the matter on written evidence (*Al-Naimi (t/a Buildmaster Construction Services) v Islamic Press Services Agency Inc* [2000] BLR 150, CA). But the court may alternatively stay the proceedings, leaving the arbitral tribunal to determine the issue under AA 1996, s 30 (*Birse Construction Ltd v St David Ltd* [2000] BLR 57).

A stay will be granted of a Pt 20 (third-party) claim that is started in existing proceedings, where there is in force an arbitration agreement between the Pt 20 claimant and the Pt 20 defendant and the third party (*Wealands v CLC Contractors Ltd* [2000] 1 All ER (Comm) 30, [1999] 2 Lloyd's Rep 739, [1999] CLC 1821, CA).

A dispute as to whether a claim in arbitration is time-barred involving complex contractual issues may be stayed under s 9 to be determined by the tribunal, rather than dealt with by the court under AA 1996, s 12 (*Grimaldi Compagnia di Navigazione SpA v Sekihyo Lines Ltd* [1999] 1 WLR 708, [1998] 3 All ER 943, [1998] 2 Lloyd's Rep 638, QBD).

Section 9(3) precludes the grant of a stay where the party applying for it has taken any step in those proceedings to answer the substantive claim. The issuing of a summons to set aside a default judgment and seeking leave to defend is not a 'step in the proceedings to answer the substantive claim' within s 9(3) (*Patel (Jitendra) v Patel (Dilesh)* [1999] 3 WLR 322, [1999] 1 All ER (Comm) 923, (1999) BLR 227, CA). See also *Capital Trust Investments Ltd v Radio Design TJAB* [2002] 2 All ER 159, CA), where on the facts of the case it was held that an application for summary judgment did not amount to a step in the proceedings as the applicant had made it clear that it was only being made in the event that its application for a stay of the proceedings was unsuccessful.

A stay will be refused if the arbitration agreement is null and void, inoperative, or incapable of being performed. Where one party asserted there was no contractual relationship, and in response the other treated this assertion as a repudiatory breach and issued a claim for damages, the first party was refused a stay under s 9 since the other party had accepted the repudiation by it and the arbitration agreement was accordingly no longer capable of being performed (*Downing v Al Tameer Establishment* [2002] BLR 323, CA).

A stay will be refused if the court finds the arbitration agreement contravenes the Unfair Terms in Consumer Contracts Regulations 1999, SI 1999/2083 (*Zealander v Laing Homes* [2000] 2 TCLR 724).

The court may also stay proceedings under its inherent jurisdiction to allow a dispute to be resolved by the method contractually agreed by the parties where this does not fall under AA 1996, s 9 (*Cott v FE Barber Ltd* [1997] 3 All ER 540; *Channel Tunnel Group Ltd v Balfour Beatty Construction Ltd* [1993] AC 334).

An appeal lies to the Court of Appeal against the grant or refusal of a stay (*Inco Europe Ltd v First Choice Distribution* [2000] 1 WLR 586, HL).

Extension of time for commencement of arbitration—See AA 1996, s 12. This relates to contractual time limits on commencement of arbitration or other dispute resolution procedures. There are two situations where the court can extend time.

The first is where the circumstances are outside the reasonable contemplation of the parties when the provision was agreed, and the second is where the conduct of one party makes it unjust to hold the other to the strict terms of the provision in question. On the first situation, the relevant circumstances are those at the time the provision was agreed, and the court will consider matters relevant to those (*Cathiship SA v Allansons Ltd* [1998] 2 Lloyd's Rep 511; *Fox and Widley v Guram* [1998] 3 EG 142; *Grimaldi Compagnia di Navigazione SpA v Sekihyo Lines Ltd* [1999] 1 WLR 908). Simple failure to observe a time limit will not be enough, even if the financial consequences may be serious. So in the *Fox and Widley* case, failure by tenants to serve a counter-notice disputing the landlord's proposed high rent for the premises within a contractual 3-month time limit was held not to ground an application for extension of time. See also *Monella v Pizza Express (Restaurants) Ltd* [2003] EWHC 1656 (change of law rendering time limit of essence held to be within the reasonable contemplation of the parties). On the other hand, in *Union Trans-Pacific Co Ltd v Orient Shipping Rotterdam BV* [2002] EWHC 1451 (Comm) an extension was granted when the claimant company had accidentally allowed itself to be struck off the companies register.

In the second situation, what is required to be shown is some conduct by the other party which leads the claimant not to start the claim or give notice in time. Silence or omission to alert the claimant to the time bar is not sufficient.

An appeal against a decision of the court under this section can only be brought with the leave of the court. The decision to grant or refuse leave cannot be appealed, nor can a fresh application for permission to appeal be made to the Court of Appeal (*Athletic Union of Constantinople v National*

Basketball Association [2002] 1 WLR 2863, a decision under AA 1996, s 67). The same principle applies to other provisions of AA 1996 where the same wording occurs.

Removal of arbitrator—See AA 1996, s 24. The four grounds on which the court can intervene may be summarised as –
(1) bias on the part of the arbitrator;
(2) lack of the required qualifications;
(3) physical or mental incapacity; and
(4) misconduct of the proceedings.

As to bias, the test is whether, considering the case as a reasonable man, there is a a real danger of of bias, conscious or unconscious (*AT& T Corporation v Saudi Cable Company* [2000] BLR 93).

As to misconduct, failure to comply with the duty on the tribunal to act fairly and impartially under AA 1996, s 33 would be a ground for removal under this rubric, as would many matters amounting to a serious irregularity under s 68. Indeed, in practice applications are often made under s 68 and s 24 where an interim award has been issued, with the arbitration still ongoing. Where the application is made on the ground of misconduct, the appropriate test is whether due to serious irregularity it could be reasonably concluded that there was a serious risk that the arbitrator's future conduct of the proceedings would not comply with his duties under s 33 of the 1996 Act (*AOOT Kalmneft v Glencore International AG* [2002] 1 All ER 76). In *Miller Construction Ltd v James Moore Earthmoving* [2001] BLR 10 an arbitrator issued an interim award on quantum without giving one party the opportunity to be heard. The other party, who had not been prejudiced by this, successfully applied to have the arbitrator removed on the ground that his conduct was sufficient to establish a loss of confidence in him.

Determination of preliminary point of jurisdiction—This is governed by AA 1996, s 32. See generally *Al-Naimi (t/a Buildmaster Construction Services) v Islamic Press Services Inc* [2000] BLR 150, CA. The conditions imposed by the section are restrictive.

Enforcement of peremptory orders of tribunal—See AA 1996, s 42.

Securing the attendance of witnesses—See AA 1996, s 43. A court has no power under this provision to order third-party disclosure (*BNP Paribas v Deloitte & Touche LLP* [2004] 1 Lloyd's Rep 233).

Interim remedies—See AA 1996, s 44. As to the extent of the court's powers under s 44(2)(e) (see *Hiscox Underwriting Ltd v Dickson Manchester & Co Ltd* [2004] EWHC 479 (Comm)). Under s 44(3) the court has power to make a freezing order and a mandatory injunction for the production of documents (*Cetelem SA v Roust Holdings Ltd* [2005] EWCA Civ 618).

Determination of preliminary point of law—See AA 1996, s 45. No application can be made unless the court is satisfied it would substantially affect the rights of one or more of the parties. Further, either the written agreement of all the other parties is required, or permission of the tribunal together with the court being satisfied that the determination of the issue is likely to produce substantial savings in costs and that the application is made without delay.

The arbitration claim form must identify the question of law to be determined and, unless made with the agreement of the other parties, must state the grounds on which it is said the question should be decided by the court. Where the claim is made with the written agreement of the other parties to the arbitration or with the permission of the tribunal, the evidence in support must establish the necessary agreement or pemission, exhibiting the relevant documents. Where the application is made pursuant to permission from the tribunal, evidence is required to support the contentions that the determination of the issue is likely to produce substantial savings in costs and that the application is made without delay. The court will consider these matters before deciding whether a hearing is required on them.

Extension of time for award—Section 50 of the 1996 Act allows the court to extend time for an award where the rules of the arbitration require the award to be made within a certain period. However, the applicant must first have exhausted any available procedures. For example, the ICC arbitration rules enable the ICC to grant an extension for delivery of the award. Further, the court must be satisfied that refusal to extend time would result in substantial injustice. Clearly, in many cases the possibility of the whole procedure having to be gone through again would be sufficient to persuade a court to grant a reasonable extension of time, at least where this would not seriously prejudice another party.

Enforcement of award as a judgment—See AA 1996, s 66. There are two procedures. First, subject to permission being granted, an award may be enforced as a judgment. Secondly, the award may in effect be converted into a judgment. For either procedure to apply the award must be in a form which is suitable for a judgment, cogent and free from ambiguity. Neither procedure is available for purely declaratory relief. The court has discretion whether to grant relief, and, under subs (3), must refuse it if it is shown the tribunal lacked substantive jurisdiction. Grounds on which enforcement might be refused would include if the award was defective in form or unclear, so as to be incapable of enforcement, if it purported to affect the property or rights of non-parties, or if its enforcement would be contrary to public policy. An application for permission can be made without notice, supported by evidence. A party wishing to enforce an award is entitled to apply to the Commercial Court Registry to ascertain whether a claim form applying for permission to appeal the award has been filed (*Advance Specialist Treatment Engineering Ltd v Cleveland Structural Engineering (Hong Kong) Ltd* [2000] 1 WLR 558).

Challenging jurisdiction—Section 67 of the 1996 Act. This and ss 68 and 69 are subject to s 70, which requires amongst other things that an application must be made within 28 days of the award, under s 70(3). This is subject to the power of the court to extend time under s 80(5). An application under this section is a rehearing so that new evidence can be adduced (*Electrosteel Castings Ltd v Scan Trans Shipping and Chartering Sdn Bhd* [2003] 1 Lloyd's Rep 190; *Peterson Farms Inc v C & M Farming Ltd* [2004] EWHC 121 (Comm)).

Where a tribunal has ruled on its own jurisdiction under s 31(4) it is not appropriate to seek to challenge that decision by an application under s 67 (*AOOT Kalmneft v Glencore International AG* [2002] 1 All ER 76). It is incumbent on a party seeking relief under s 67 to raise the points relied on before the tribunal (*JSC Zestafoni G Nikoladze Ferroalloy Plant v Ronly Holdings Ltd* [2004] 2 Lloyd's Rep 335).

Challenging the award for serious irregularity—Section 68 of the AA 1996. The matters are listed in subs (2). It is a requirement that the matters complained of have caused or will cause substantial injustice to the applicant. In regard to the latter point the test is not what would have happened had the matter been litigated, but whether the tribunal has gone so wrong in its conduct of the arbitration that justice calls out for it to be corrected (*Egmatra AG v Marco Trading Corporation* [1999] 1 Lloyd's Rep 862). The mere fact that there may have been an error in an award which is unfair to a party does not mean that there must have been a serious irregularity under s 68(2) (*Weldon Plant v The Commission for New Towns* [2000] BLR 496; *World Trade Corporation Ltd v C Czarnikow Sugar Ltd* [2004] 2 All ER (Comm)).

With regard to s 66(2)(d), the tribunal is not required to deal with every point of dispute in its award. The award need only deal with the very disputes that the arbitration has to resolve (*Checkpoint Ltd v Strathclyde Pension Fund* [2003] EWCA Civ 84).

Appeal on point of law—This governed by AA 1996, s 69. A party intending to appeal must first exhaust any available arbitral procedures. The time limit of 28 days in s 70(3) applies unless extended. The claim form must be issued and all written evidence filed by the expiry of the time limit. The party intending to appeal must obtain either the agreement of all the other parties or the permission of the court. The claimant must demonstrate –

(a) the existence of a point of law;
(b) that it will substantially affect the rights of one or more of the parties;
(c) which the arbitrator was asked to determine;
(d) on which the arbitrator was obviously wrong or which was one of general public importance; and
(e) which it is just and proper for the court to determine.

Where the court refuses permission, it is not bound to give reasons, but should at the very least tell an unsuccessful applicant which of the threshold tests in s 69(3) it has failed. There is no requirement for the judge to explain why the relevant test has been failed. Where it is necessary to give reasons, these have only to be brief so as to show the losing party why it has failed (*North Range Shipping Ltd v Seatrans Shipping Corporation* [2002] 4 All ER 390, CA).

An error of law arises where the arbitrator errs in ascertaining the legal principle to be applied to the facts, but not where the arbitrator, having identified the correct principle, goes on to apply it incorrectly (*Northern Elevator Manufacturing v United Engineers (Singapore)* [2004] 2 SLR 494). There can be no error of law if the actual decision is one of mixed fact and law and does not fall outside the permissible range of solutions (*The Matthew* [1992] Lloyds Rep 323). Whether or not there is sufficient evidential basis for a finding is a question of law. But no error occurs where a finding is based on little but not no evidence (*Fencegate v NEL Construction* (2001) 82 Con LR 41).

A point of law may not be just and proper for the court to determine if the arbitrator is highly skilled and/or distinguished so that a decision is entitled to a high degree of respect (*Reliance Industries v Enron Oil & Gas India Ltd* [2002] All ER Comm 59; *Keydon Estates v Western Power Distribution (South Wales) Ltd* [2004] EWHC 996).

The court's jurisdiction under AA 1996, s 69 is only to determine questions of English law, as defined by s 82 of that Act (*Sanghi Polyesters (India) Ltd v The International Investor KCFC (Kuwait)* [2000] 1 Lloyd's Rep 480, D Mackie QC, where one of the grounds upon which permission was refused was that the application raised issues of Shari'ah law and not English law).

No appeal to Court of Appeal—Where the court, having decided the substantive appeal, refuses permission to appeal against its decision under s 69(8), the Court of Appeal has no jurisdiction to grant permission, and the same applies to the decision whether to grant permission to appeal under s 69(6) (*Henry Boot Construction (UK) Ltd v Malmaison Hotel (Manchester) Ltd* [2000] BLR 509, CA; *Athletic Union of Constantinople v National Basketball Association* [2002] 1 WLR 2863, a decision under s 67). Neither in this nor in the case of an initial refusal of permssion to appeal do the provisions of s 69(5) contravene HRA 1998, Sch 1, Pt 1, Art 6(1) (*BLCT (13096) Ltd v J Sainsbury plc* [2004] 2 P & CR 3, CA). However, the Court of Appeal has a residual jurisdiction to set aside a decision where there has been unfairness (*North Range Shipping Ltd v Seatrans Shipping Corporation* [2002] 4 All ER 390 CA).

Service of documents—Section 77 of AA 1996 gives power to the court to allow service of documents as it thinks fit, or to dispense with service where the contractual methods of service or those provided under s 76 are not reasonably practicable. The application can be made without notice. The evidence must establish that any available arbitral process has been exhausted.

Extension of time limits—See AA 1996, ss 79 and 80(5) relating to applications to extend time under the CPR.

62.2 Interpretation

(1) In this Section of this Part 'arbitration claim' means –

(a) any application to the court under the 1996 Act;
(b) a claim to determine –
(i) whether there is a valid arbitration agreement;
(ii) whether an arbitration tribunal is properly constituted; or
what matters have been submitted to arbitration in accordance with an arbitration agreement;
(c) a claim to declare that an award by an arbitral tribunal is not binding on a party; and
(d) any other application affecting –
(i) arbitration proceedings (whether started or not); or
(ii) an arbitration agreement.

(2) This Section of this Part does not apply to an arbitration claim to which Sections II or III of this Part apply.

Amendments—Inserted by SI 2001/4015.

62.3 Starting the claim

(1) Except where paragraph (2) applies an arbitration claim must be started by the issue of an arbitration claim form in accordance with the Part 8 procedure.

(2) An application under section 9 of the 1996 Act to stay legal proceedings must be made by application notice to the court dealing with those proceedings.

(3) The courts in which an arbitration claim may be started are set out in the practice direction.

(4) Rule 30.5(3) applies with the modification that a judge of the Technology and Construction Court may transfer the claim to any other court or specialist list.

Amendments—Inserted by SI 2001/4015.

'in accordance with the Part 8 procedure' (r 62.3(1))—Since the arbitration claim form must be served in accordance with the Pt 8 procedure, any evidence on which the claimant relies must be served together with the claim form (r 8.5 and *Icon Navigation Corporation v Sinochem International Petroleum (Bahamas) Co Ltd* [2002] EWHC 2812; [2003] 1 All ER (Comm) 405).

'The courts in which an arbitration claim may be started' (r 62.3(3))—See PD62, paras 2.1 and 2.3 for further guidance.

62.4 Arbitration claim form

(1) An arbitration claim form must –

- (a) include a concise statement of –
  - (i) the remedy claimed; and
  - (ii) any questions on which the claimant seeks the decision of the court;
- (b) give details of any arbitration award challenged by the claimant, identifying which part or parts of the award are challenged and specifying the grounds for the challenge;
- (c) show that any statutory requirements have been met;
- (d) specify under which section of the 1996 Act the claim is made;
- (e) identify against which (if any) defendants a costs order is sought; and
- (f) specify either –
  - (i) the persons on whom the arbitration claim form is to be served, stating their role in the arbitration and whether they are defendants; or
  - (ii) that the claim is made without notice under section 44(3) of the 1996 Act and the grounds relied on.

(2) Unless the court orders otherwise an arbitration claim form must be served on the defendant within 1 month from the date of issue and rules 7.5 and 7.6 are modified accordingly.

(3) Where the claimant applies for an order under section 12 of the 1996 Act (extension of time for beginning arbitral proceedings or other dispute resolution procedures), he may include in his arbitration claim form an alternative application for a declaration that such an order is not needed.

Amendments—Inserted by SI 2001/4015.

The form of the arbitration claim form—The arbitration claim form must be substantially in the form set out in PD62, App A (see PD62, para 2.2). The Admiralty and Commercial Courts Guide, s O3.2 states that a reference in the arbitration claim form to a witness statement or affidavit filed in support of the arbitration claim is not sufficient to comply with r 62.4(1).

Service of the arbitration claim form—See PD62, paras 3.1–3.2. An arbitration claim form issued in the Admiralty and Commercial Registry must be served by the claimant (Admiralty and Commercial Courts Guide, s O4.1).

Procedural timetable—There is a procedural timetable set out at PD62, paras 6.1–6.7 that applies to all arbitration claims unless the court orders otherwise. The Admiralty and Commercial Courts Guide, s O6.2 provides that a claimant should apply for a hearing date as soon as possible after issuing an arbitration claim form or (in the case of an appeal) obtaining permission to appeal. An application for directions in a pending arbitration claim should be made by an ordinary application notice under Pt 23 (Admiralty and Commercial Courts Guide, s O6.5).

62.5 Service out of the jurisdiction

(1) The court may give permission to serve an arbitration claim form out of the jurisdiction if –

- (a) the claimant seeks to –
  - (i) challenge; or
  - (ii) appeal on a question of law arising out of,

  an arbitration award made within the jurisdiction;

(The place where an award is treated as made is determined by section 53 of the 1996 Act)

(b) the claim is for an order under section 44 of the 1996 Act; or

(c) the claimant –

(i) seeks some other remedy or requires a question to be decided by the court affecting an arbitration (whether started or not), an arbitration agreement or an arbitration award; and

(ii) the seat of the arbitration is or will be within the jurisdiction or the conditions in section 2(4) of the 1996 Act are satisfied.

(2) An application for permission under paragraph (1) must be supported by written evidence –

(a) stating the grounds on which the application is made; and

(b) showing in what place or country the person to be served is, or probably may be found.

(3) Rules 6.24 to 6.29 apply to the service of an arbitration claim form under paragraph (1).

(4) An order giving permission to serve an arbitration claim form out of the jurisdiction must specify the period within which the defendant may file an acknowledgment of service.

Amendments—Inserted by SI 2001/4015.

'affecting ... an arbitration agreement' (r 62.5(1)(c)(i))—Read literally, these words would allow an arbitration claim form to be served out of the jurisdiction on a person who was not in fact a party to the arbitration. However, it is properly to be read as being referable solely to an application that is to be made between the parties to the arbitration agreement, or persons alleged to be parties (*Vale Do Rio Doce Navegacao SA v Shanghai Bao Steel Ocean Shipping Co Ltd* [2000] 2 All ER (Comm) 70, [2000] 2 Lloyd's Rep 1, [2000] CLC 1200, QBD).

62.6 Notice

(1) Where an arbitration claim is made under section 24, 28 or 56 of the 1996 Act, each arbitrator must be a defendant.

(2) Where notice must be given to an arbitrator or any other person it may be given by sending him a copy of –

(a) the arbitration claim form; and

(b) any written evidence in support.

(3) Where the 1996 Act requires an application to the court to be made on notice to any other party to the arbitration, that notice must be given by making that party a defendant.

Amendments—Inserted by SI 2001/4015.

'section 24, 28 and 56 of the 1996 Act' (r 62.6(1))—These deal with the following matters respectively: the court's power to remove an arbitrator; joint and several liability of parties to arbitrators for fees and expenses; and the power of an arbitrator to withhold an award in the case of non-payment.

62.7 Case management

(1) Part 26 and any other rule that requires a party to file an allocation questionnaire does not apply.

(2) Arbitration claims are allocated to the multi-track.

(3) Part 29 does not apply.

(4) The automatic directions set out in the practice direction apply unless the court orders otherwise.

Amendments—Inserted by SI 2001/4015.

'automatic directions' (r 62.7(4))—See PD62, paras 6.1–6.7.

62.8 Stay of legal proceedings

(1) An application notice seeking a stay of legal proceedings under section 9 of the 1996 Act must be served on all parties to those proceedings who have given an address for service.

(2) A copy of an application notice under paragraph (1) must be served on any other party to the legal proceedings (whether or not he is within the jurisdiction) who has not given an address for service, at –

- (a) his last known address; or
- (b) a place where it is likely to come to his attention.

(3) Where a question arises as to whether –

- (a) an arbitration agreement has been concluded; or
- (b) the dispute which is the subject matter of the proceedings falls within the terms of such an agreement,

the court may decide that question or give directions to enable it to be decided and may order the proceedings to be stayed pending its decision.

Amendments—Inserted by SI 2001/4015.

Questions of fact—Rule 62.8(3) gives the court a discretion to determine whether an arbitration agreement has been concluded (see *Al-Naimi (t/a Buildmaster Construction Services) v Islamic Press Agency Inc* [2000] BLR 150, CA). The correct approach in the interests of good litigation management and the saving of costs is for the court to resolve the matter on written evidence. But the court can alternatively stay the proceedings and allow the arbitral tribunal to decide the issue itself under AA 1996, s 30 (*Birse Construction Ltd v St David Ltd* [2000] BLR 57, 70 Con LR 10, CA; [1999] BLR 194, QBD, pp 196–197).

Appeal—No appeal from any decision of the High Court under AA 1996, Pt I lies to the Court of Appeal, except as provided by Pt I of the 1996 Act (Supreme Court Act 1981, s 18(1)(g)). Notwithstanding the fact that nowhere in Pt I is it provided that a decision under AA 1996, s 9 may be appealed to the Court of Appeal, it has been held that such a decision as to whether or not to stay litigation covered by an arbitration clause may, nevertheless, be appealed – with permission (*Inco Europe Ltd v First Choice Distribution (a firm)* [2000] 1 WLR 586, [2000] 2 All ER 109, [2000] 1 All ER (Comm) 674, HL).

62.9 Variation of time

(1) The court may vary the period of 28 days fixed by section 70(3) of the 1996 Act for –

- (a) challenging the award under section 67 or 68 of the Act; and
- (b) appealing against an award under section 69 of the Act.

(2) An application for an order under paragraph (1) may be made without notice being served on any other party before the period of 28 days expires.

(3) After the period of 28 days has expired –

- (a) an application for an order extending time under paragraph (1) must –
  - (i) be made in the arbitration claim form; and
  - (ii) state the grounds on which the application is made;
- (b) any defendant may file written evidence opposing the extension of time within 7 days after service of the arbitration claim form; and

(c) if the court extends the period of 28 days, each defendant's time for acknowledging service and serving evidence shall start to run as if the arbitration claim form had been served on the date when the court's order is served on that defendant.

Amendments—Inserted by SI 2001/4015.

'section 70(3) of the 1996 Act' (r 62.9(1))—This provides for a 28-day time limit for an application to challenge an award under ss 67 or 68 of the 1996 Act or to appeal under s 69.

'section 67 or 68 of the Act' (r 62.9(1)(a))—An award may be challenged on the grounds that the tribunal lacked substantive jurisdiction in the matter (AA 1996, s 67) or on the basis of a serious irregularity affecting the tribunal, the proceedings or the award itself (AA 1996, s 68).

'extending time' (r 62.9(3)(a))—Whilst the court has a discretion to vary the 28-day time limit, the Admiralty and Commercial Courts Guide, s O9.2 explains that it is important for any challenge to an award to be pursued without delay, and that the court will require cogent reasons for extending time. The application to vary the 28 days will normally be determined without a hearing and prior to the consideration of the substantive application (PD62, para 10.2). Relevant considerations will include –

(a) the extent of the delay;
(b) whether a party has acted reasonably in allowing a time limit to expire and accruing subsequent delay;
(c) whether the respondent or the arbitrator has caused or contributed to the delay;
(d) whether irremediable prejudice will be caused to the respondent because of delay if the application is permitted to proceed;
(e) whether the arbitration has continued in the interim and if so what impact determination of the application will have on it;
(f) the strength of the application; and
(g) whether in all the circumstances it would be unfair to the applicant to refuse the opportunity of a determination (*AOOT Kalmneft v Glencore International AG* [2002] 1 All ER 76).

62.10 Hearings

(1) The court may order that an arbitration claim be heard either in public or in private.

(2) Rule 39.2 does not apply.

(3) Subject to any order made under paragraph (1) –

(a) the determination of –
(i) a preliminary point of law under section 45 of the 1996 Act; or
(ii) an appeal under section 69 of the 1996 Act on a question of law arising out of an award,

will be heard in public; and

(b) all other arbitration claims will be heard in private.

(4) Paragraph (3)(a) does not apply to –

(a) the preliminary question of whether the court is satisfied of the matters set out in section 45(2)(b); or
(b) an application for permission to appeal under section 69(2)(b).

Amendments—Inserted by SI 2001/4015.

Hearing in public or in private—As to the factors the court should consider in deciding whether the hearing should be in public or in private see *Department of Economic Policy and Development of the City of Moscow v Bankers Trust Co* [2004] 3 WLR 533, CA.

'a preliminary point of law under section 45 of the 1996 Act' (r 62.10(3)(a)(i))—Prior to entertaining such an application, the court must first be satisfied that:

(i) the determination of the question is likely to produce substantial savings in costs (AA 1996, s 45(2)(b)(i)); and
(ii) the application was made without delay (AA 1996, s 45(2)(b)(ii)).

Rule 62.10(4) disapplies r 62.10(3) in respect of the consideration of these preliminary requirements.

II Other Arbitration Claims

General note—Paragraph 14.1 of PD62 provides that all arbitration claims made under Pt 62, Section II must be started in the Commercial Court and, where required to be heard by a judge, be heard by a judge of that court unless he directs otherwise. Thus, where the subject matter of the application does not involve commercial matters and/or matters of arbitration law, there is a discretion to refer the application to a more suitable court.

62.11 Scope of this Section

(1) This Section of this Part contains rules about arbitration claims to which the old law applies.

(2) In this Section –

- (a) 'the old law' means the enactments specified in Schedules 3 and 4 of the 1996 Act as they were in force before their amendment or repeal by that Act; and
- (b) 'arbitration claim' means any application to the court under the old law and includes an appeal (or application for permission to appeal) to the High Court under section 1(2) of the 1979 Act.

(3) This Section does not apply to –

- (a) a claim to which Section III of this Part applies; or
- (b) a claim on the award.

Amendments—Inserted by SI 2001/4015.

'the old law' (r 62.11(2)(a))—In other words, AA 1950, AA 1975 and AA 1979.

62.12 Applications to judge

A claim –

- (a) seeking permission to appeal under section 1(2) of the 1979 Act;
- (b) under section 1(5) of that Act (including any claim seeking permission); or
- (c) under section 5 of that Act,

must be made in the High Court and will be heard by a judge of the Commercial Court unless any such judge directs otherwise.

Amendments—Inserted by SI 2001/4015.

General note—As PD62, para 14.1 makes clear, the starting point for an application under Pt 62, Section II is the Commercial Court. Indeed, it is of paramount importance that an application required to be heard by a judge of the Commercial Court is in fact made to that court. However, where the notice of application to set aside an arbitration award had been issued in the Chancery Division, it was held that it would be wrong to transfer the application to the Commercial Court, since that would constitute an extension of time for the appeal (*Ashbank Property Co Ltd v Department of Transport* (1994) *The Times*, 25 July).

'section 1(2) of the 1979 Act' (r 62.12(a))—This section provides that an appeal shall lie to the court on any question of law arising out of the award. The normal practice in the Commercial Court is for one judge to hear the application under s 1(2) and for another judge to hear the appeal itself, although the appropriate procedure for any particular case is a matter for the court's discretion (*Hiscox v Outhwaite (No 2)* [1991] 1 WLR 545, CA).

'section 1(5) of the 1979 Act' (r 62.12(b))—This section allows a court to order that the arbitrator or umpire state the reasons for his award in sufficient detail to enable a court to consider any questions arising, where one of the parties seeks to appeal the award on a point of law.

'section 5 of the 1979 Act' (r 62.12(c))—This section allows an arbitrator to continue with a reference in circumstances where one party has failed to acknowledge service or has failed to comply with an order made by an arbitrator.

62.13 Starting the claim

(1) Except where paragraph (2) applies an arbitration claim must be started by the issue of an arbitration claim form in accordance with the Part 8 procedure.

(2) Where an arbitration claim is to be made in existing proceedings –

(a) it must be made by way of application notice; and

(b) any reference in this Section of this Part to an arbitration claim form includes a reference to an application notice.

(3) The arbitration claim form in an arbitration claim under section 1(5) of the 1979 Act (including any claim seeking permission) must be served on –

(a) the arbitrator or umpire; and

(b) any other party to the reference.

Amendments—Inserted by SI 2001/4015.

'an arbitration claim form' (r 62.13(1))—The arbitration claim form must be substantially in the form set out in PD62, App A.

Service of the arbitration claim form—An arbitration claim form issued in the Admiralty and Commercial Registry must be served by the claimant. Where the arbitration claim form is served by the claimant he must file a certificate of service within 7 days of service of the arbitration claim form in accordance with r 6.10. In contrast to the position under PD62, Section I (see PD62, para 3.1), Section II of PD62 does not expressly provide that the court may exercise its powers under r 6.8 to permit service of an arbitration claim form on a party at the address of the solicitor or other representative acting for him in the arbitration. However, the Admiralty and Commercial Courts Guide, s O12.4 states that the court does have the power to do so in an appropriate case.

62.14 Claims in district registries

If –

(a) a claim is to be made under section 12(4) of the 1950 Act for an order for the issue of a witness summons to compel the attendance of the witness before an arbitrator or umpire; and

(b) the attendance of the witness is required within the district of a District Registry,

the claim may be started in that Registry.

Amendments—Inserted by SI 2001/4015.

62.15 Time limits and other special provisions about arbitration claims

(1) An arbitration claim to –

(a) remit an award under section 22 of the 1950 Act;

(b) set aside an award under section 23(2) of that Act or otherwise; or

(c) direct an arbitrator or umpire to state the reasons for an award under section 1(5) of the 1979 Act,

must be made, and the arbitration claim form served, within 21 days after the award has been made and published to the parties.

(2) An arbitration claim to determine any question of law arising in the course of a reference under section 2(1) of the Arbitration Act 1979 must be made, and the arbitration claim form served, within 14 days after –

(a) the arbitrator or umpire gave his consent in writing to the claim being made; or

(b) the other parties so consented.

(3) An appeal under section 1(2) of the 1979 Act must be filed, and the arbitration claim form served, within 21 days after the award has been made and published to the parties.

(4) Where reasons material to an appeal under section 1(2) of the 1979 Act are given on a date subsequent to the publication of the award, the period of 21 days referred to in paragraph (3) will run from the date on which reasons are given.

(5) In every arbitration claim to which this rule applies –

(a) the arbitration claim form must state the grounds of the claim or appeal;

(b) where the claim or appeal is based on written evidence, a copy of that evidence must be served with the arbitration claim form; and

(c) where the claim or appeal is made with the consent of the arbitrator, the umpire or the other parties, a copy of every written consent must be served with the arbitration claim form.

(6) In an appeal under section 1(2) of the 1979 Act –

(a) a statement of the grounds for the appeal specifying the relevant parts of the award and reasons; and

(b) where permission is required, any written evidence in support of the contention that the question of law concerns –

(i) a term of a contract; or

(ii) an event,

which is not a 'one-off' term or event,

must be filed and served with the arbitration claim form.

(7) Any written evidence in reply to written evidence under paragraph (6)(b) must be filed and served on the claimant not less than 2 days before the hearing.

(8) A party to a claim seeking permission to appeal under section 1(2) of the 1979 Act who wishes to contend that the award should be upheld for reasons not expressed or fully expressed in the award and reasons must file and serve on the claimant, a notice specifying the grounds of his contention not less than 2 days before the hearing.

Amendments—Inserted by SI 2001/4015.

General note—Where a party seeks to challenge an award made by an arbitrator the procedure to be adopted is as set out at r 62.15(3)–(8) which is elaborated upon in the Admiralty and Commercial Courts Guide, ss O.16 and O.17. The court has power under r 3.1(2) to vary the prescribed time limits. However, cogent reasons will be required before a court does so (Admiralty and Commercial Courts Guide, s O17.1(c)).

'within 21 days after the award has been made and published' (r 62.15(1))—Once the arbitrator notifies the parties that the award is ready, time begins to run. A party cannot extend the time limit by delaying in taking up the award (*Bulk Transport Corp v Sissy Steamship Co Ltd ('The Archipelagos & The Delfi')* [1979] 2 Lloyd's Law Rep 289). Failure to comply with the 21-day time limit is an irregularity which may be excused and does not necessarily invalidate service; the 21-day period is unrealistic when service out of the jurisdiction is required (*Nagusina Naviera v Allied Maritime Inc* [2002] CLC 385).

'grounds of the claim or appeal' (r 62.15(5)(a))—The Admiralty and Commercial Courts Guide, s O11.2 states that a reference in the arbitration claim form to a witness statement or affidavit filed in support of the arbitration claim is not sufficient to comply with r 62.15(5)(a).

'not less than 2 days before the hearing' (r 62.15(8))—The time limit is to be applied strictly (*Acada Chemicals Ltd v Empresa Nacional Pesquera SA* [1994] 1 Lloyd's Rep 428). However, the court does have jurisdiction in exceptional circumstances to grant an extension of time (*PT Putrabali Adyamulia v Société Est Epices* [2003] Loyd's Rep 700, QBD (Comm Ct)).

62.16 Service out of the jurisdiction

(1) Subject to paragraph (2) –

(a) any arbitration claim form in an arbitration claim under the 1950 Act or the 1979 Act; or

(b) any order made in such a claim,

may be served out of the jurisdiction with the permission of the court if the arbitration to which the claim relates –

(i) is governed by the law of England and Wales; or

(ii) has been, is being, or will be, held within the jurisdiction.

(2) An arbitration claim form seeking permission to enforce an award may be served out of the jurisdiction with the permission of the court whether or not the arbitration is governed by the law of England and Wales.

(3) An application for permission to serve an arbitration claim form out of the jurisdiction must be supported by written evidence –

(a) stating the grounds on which the application is made; and

(b) showing in what place or country the person to be served is, or probably may be found.

(4) Rules 6.24 to 6.29 apply to the service of an arbitration claim form under paragraph (1).

(5) An order giving permission to serve an arbitration claim form out of the jurisdiction must specify the period within which the defendant may file an acknowledgment of service.

Amendments—Inserted by SI 2001/4015.

Scope of rule—The practice under this rule is essentially the same as under Pt 6. It should be noted that r 62.16 permits service out of the jurisdiction only on parties to the arbitration reference itself and not on non-parties (*Unicargo v Flotec Maritime S de RL and Cienvik Shipping Company Ltd (The 'Cienvik')* [1996] 2 Lloyd's Rep 395, [1996] CLC 434, (1996) *The Independent*, 1 January, QBD). Some useful observations and comparisons between the former RSC Ord 11 and RSC Ord 73 (the predecessors to Pt 6 and r 62.16 respectively) are made in *Mayer Newman Co Ltd v Al Ferro Commodities Corporation SA* [1990] 2 Lloyd's Rep 290 at 293.

III Enforcement

62.17 Scope of this Section

This Section of this Part applies to all arbitration enforcement proceedings other than by a claim on the award.

Amendments—Inserted by SI 2001/4015.

62.18 Enforcement of awards

(1) An application for permission under –

(a) section 66 of the 1996 Act;

(b) section 101 of the 1996 Act;
(c) section 26 of the 1950 Act; or
(d) section 3(1)(a) of the 1975 Act,

to enforce an award in the same manner as a judgment or order may be made without notice in an arbitration claim form.

(2) The court may specify parties to the arbitration on whom the arbitration claim form must be served.

(3) The parties on whom the arbitration claim form is served must acknowledge service and the enforcement proceedings will continue as if they were an arbitration claim under Section I of this Part.

(4) With the permission of the court the arbitration claim form may be served out of the jurisdiction irrespective of where the award is, or is treated as, made.

(5) Where the applicant applies to enforce an agreed award within the meaning of section 51(2) of the 1996 Act –

(a) the arbitration claim form must state that the award is an agreed award; and
(b) any order made by the court must also contain such a statement.

(6) An application for permission must be supported by written evidence –

(a) exhibiting –
(i) where the application is made under section 66 of the 1996 Act or under section 26 of the 1950 Act, the arbitration agreement and the original award (or copies);
(ii) where the application is under section 101 of the 1996 Act, the documents required to be produced by section 102 of that Act; or
(iii) where the application is under section 3(1)(a) of the 1975 Act, the documents required to be produced by section 4 of that Act;
(b) stating the name and the usual or last known place of residence or business of the claimant and of the person against whom it is sought to enforce the award; and
(c) stating either –
(i) that the award has not been complied with; or
(ii) the extent to which it has not been complied with at the date of the application.

(7) An order giving permission must –

(a) be drawn up by the claimant; and
(b) be served on the defendant by –
(i) delivering a copy to him personally; or
(ii) sending a copy to him at his usual or last known place of residence or business.

(8) An order giving permission may be served out of the jurisdiction –

(a) without permission; and
(b) in accordance with rules 6.24 to 6.29 as if the order were an arbitration claim form.

(9) Within 14 days after service of the order or, if the order is to be served out of the jurisdiction, within such other period as the court may set –

(a) the defendant may apply to set aside the order; and
(b) the award must not be enforced until after –
(i) the end of that period; or

(ii) any application made by the defendant within that period has been finally disposed of.

(10) The order must contain a statement of –

(a) the right to make an application to set the order aside; and

(b) the restrictions on enforcement under rule 62.18(9)(b).

(11) Where a body corporate is a party any reference in this rule to place of residence or business shall have effect as if the reference were to the registered or principal address of the body corporate.

Amendments—Inserted by SI 2001/4015.

Security for costs—In appropriate circumstances, the applicant may be ordered to make a payment as security for costs (*Dardana Ltd v Yukos Oil Company* [2002] EWCA Civ 543, [2002] 1 All ER (Comm) 819, [2002] TLR 55, (2002) *The Times*, 4 February, CA).

62.19 Interest on awards

(1) Where an applicant seeks to enforce an award of interest the whole or any part of which relates to a period after the date of the award, he must file a statement giving the following particulars –

(a) whether simple or compound interest was awarded;

(b) the date from which interest was awarded;

(c) where rests were provided for, specifying them;

(d) the rate of interest awarded; and

(e) a calculation showing –

(i) the total amount claimed up to the date of the statement; and

(ii) any sum which will become due on a daily basis.

(2) A statement under paragraph (1) must be filed whenever the amount of interest has to be quantified for the purpose of –

(a) obtaining a judgment or order under section 66 of the 1996 Act (enforcement of the award); or

(b) enforcing such a judgment or order.

Amendments—Inserted by SI 2001/4015.

62.20 Registration in High Court of foreign awards

(1) Where –

(a) an award is made in proceedings on an arbitration in any part of a United Kingdom Overseas Territory (within the meaning of rule 6.18(f)) or other territory to which Part I of the Foreign Judgments (Reciprocal Enforcement) Act 1933 ('the 1933 Act') extends;

(b) Part II of the Administration of Justice Act 1920 extended to that part immediately before Part I of the 1933 Act was extended to that part; and

(c) an award has, under the law in force in the place where it was made, become enforceable in the same manner as a judgment given by a court in that place,

rules 74.1 to 74.7 and 74.9 apply in relation to the award as they apply in relation to a judgment given by the court subject to the modifications in paragraph (2).

(2) The modifications referred to in paragraph (1) are as follows –

(a) for references to the State of origin are substituted references to the place where the award was made; and
(b) the written evidence required by rule 74.4 must state (in addition to the matters required by that rule) that to the best of the information or belief of the maker of the statement the award has, under the law in force in the place where it was made, become enforceable in the same manner as a judgment given by a court in that place.

Amendments—Inserted by SI 2001/4015; amended by SI 2002/2058.

62.21 Registration of awards under the Arbitration (International Investment Disputes) Act 1966

(1) In this rule –

(a) 'the 1966 Act' means the Arbitration (International Investment Disputes) Act 1966;
(b) 'award' means an award under the Convention;
(c) 'the Convention' means the Convention on the settlement of investment disputes between States and nationals of other States which was opened for signature in Washington on 18 March 1965;
(d) 'judgment creditor' means the person seeking recognition or enforcement of an award; and
(e) 'judgment debtor' means the other party to the award.

(2) Subject to the provisions of this rule, the following provisions of Part 74 apply with such modifications as may be necessary in relation to an award as they apply in relation to a judgment to which Part I of the Foreign Judgments (Reciprocal Enforcement) Act 1933 applies –

(a) rule 74.1;
(b) rule 74.3;
(c) rule 74.4(1), (2)(a) to (d), and (4);
(d) rule 74.6 (except paragraph (3)(c) to (e)); and
(e) rule 74.9(2).

(3) An application to have an award registered in the High Court under section 1 of the 1966 Act must be made in accordance with the Part 8 procedure.

(4) The written evidence required by rule 74.4 in support of an application for registration must –

(a) exhibit the award certified under the Convention instead of the judgment (or a copy of it); and
(b) in addition to stating the matters referred to in rule 74.4(2)(a) to (d), state whether –
    (i) at the date of the application the enforcement of the award has been stayed (provisionally or otherwise) under the Convention; and
    (ii) any, and if so what, application has been made under the Convention, which, if granted, might result in a stay of the enforcement of the award.

(5) Where, on granting permission to register an award or an application made by the judgment debtor after an award has been registered, the court considers –

(a) that the enforcement of the award has been stayed (whether provisionally or otherwise) under the Convention; or

SECTION 2 Civil Procedure Rules and Practice Directions

(b) that an application has been made under the Convention which, if granted, might result in a stay of the enforcement of the award,

the court may stay the enforcement of the award for such time as it considers appropriate.

Amendments—Inserted by SI 2001/4015; amended by SI 2002/2058.

Practice Direction – Arbitration

This Practice Direction supplements CPR Part 62 (PD62)

Important—This practice direction came into force on 25 March 2002. For provisions governing court procedure before that date see PD49G, set out in the 2002 edition of this work.

SECTION I

1.1 This Section of this Practice Direction applies to arbitration claims to which Section I of Part 62 applies.

1.2 In this Section 'the 1996 Act' means the Arbitration Act 1996.

1.3 Where a rule provides for a document to be sent, it may be sent –

(1) by first class post;
(2) through a document exchange; or
(3) by fax, electronic mail or other means of electronic communication.

62.3 – STARTING THE CLAIM

2.1 An arbitration claim under the 1996 Act (other than under section 9) must be started in accordance with the High Court and County Courts (Allocation of Arbitration Proceedings) Order 1996 by the issue of an arbitration claim form.

2.2 An arbitration claim form must be substantially in the form set out in Appendix A to this practice direction.

[2.3 Subject to paragraph 2.1, an arbitration claim form –

(1) may be issued at the courts set out in column 1 of the table below and will be entered in the list set out against that court in column 2;
(2) relating to a landlord and tenant or partnership dispute must be issued in the Chancery Division of the High Court.

Court	List
Admiralty and Commercial Registry at the Royal Courts of Justice, London	Commercial list
Technology and Construction Court Registry, St. Dunstan's House, London	TCC list
District Registry of the High Court (where mercantile court established)	Mercantile list

District Registry of the High Court (where arbitration claim form marked 'Technology and Construction Court' in top right hand corner)	TCC list
Central London County Court	Mercantile list

2.3A An arbitration claim form must, in the case of an appeal, or application for permission to appeal, from a judge-arbitrator, be issued in the Civil Division of the Court of Appeal. The judge hearing the application may adjourn the matter for oral argument before two judges of that court.

General note—Applications to stay proceedings under AA 1996, s 9 must be made to the court seized of the proceedings.

62.4 – ARBITRATION CLAIM FORM

SERVICE

3.1 The court may exercise its powers under rule 6.8 to permit service of an arbitration claim form at the address of a party's solicitor or representative acting for him in the arbitration.

3.2 Where the arbitration claim form is served by the claimant he must file a certificate of service within 7 days of service of the arbitration claim form.

(Rule 6.10 specifies what a certificate of service must show)

ACKNOWLEDGMENT OF SERVICE OR MAKING REPRESENTATIONS BY ARBITRATOR OR ACAS

4.1 Where –

(1) an arbitrator; or
(2) ACAS (in a claim under the 1996 Act as applied with modifications by the ACAS Arbitration Scheme (England and Wales) Order 2001)

is sent a copy of an arbitration claim form (including an arbitration claim form sent under rule 62.6(2)), that arbitrator or ACAS (as the case may be) may –

(a) apply to be made a defendant; or
(b) make representations to the court under paragraph 4.3.

4.2 An application under paragraph 4.1(2)(a) to be made a defendant –

(1) must be served on the claimant; but
(2) need not be served on any other party.

4.3 An arbitrator or ACAS may make representations by filing written evidence or in writing to the court.

SUPPLY OF DOCUMENTS FROM COURT RECORDS

5.1 An arbitration claim form may only be inspected with the permission of the court.

Supply of documents—In *Advance Specialist Treatment Engineering Ltd v Cleveland Structural Engineering (Hong Kong) Ltd* [2000] 1 WLR 558 it was held that a party wishing to enforce an award under AA 1996, s 66 could apply to the court to ascertain whether a claim form for permission to appeal had been filed in the commercial court registry, under CPR Pt 5.

62.7 – CASE MANAGEMENT

6.1 The following directions apply unless the court orders otherwise.

6.2 A defendant who wishes to rely on evidence before the court must file and serve his written evidence –

(1) within 21 days after the date by which he was required to acknowledge service; or,
(2) where a defendant is not required to file an acknowledgment of service, within 21 days after service of the arbitration claim form.

6.3 A claimant who wishes to rely on evidence in reply to written evidence filed under paragraph 6.2 must file and serve his written evidence within 7 days after service of the defendant's evidence.

6.4 Agreed indexed and paginated bundles of all the evidence and other documents to be used at the hearing must be prepared by the claimant.

6.5 Not later than 5 days before the hearing date estimates for the length of the hearing must be filed together with a complete set of the documents to be used.

6.6 Not later than 2 days before the hearing date the claimant must file and serve –

(1) a chronology of the relevant events cross-referenced to the bundle of documents;
(2) (where necessary) a list of the persons involved; and
(3) a skeleton argument which lists succinctly –
    (a) the issues which arise for decision;
    (b) the grounds of relief (or opposing relief) to be relied upon;
    (c) the submissions of fact to be made with the references to the evidence; and
    (d) the submissions of law with references to the relevant authorities.

6.7 Not later than the day before the hearing date the defendant must file and serve a skeleton argument which lists succinctly –

(1) the issues which arise for decision;
(2) the grounds of relief (or opposing relief) to be relied upon;
(3) the submissions of fact to be made with the references to the evidence; and
(4) the submissions of law with references to the relevant authorities.

SECURING THE ATTENDANCE OF WITNESSES

7.1 A party to arbitral proceedings being conducted in England or Wales who wishes to rely on section 43 of the 1996 Act to secure the attendance of a witness must apply for a witness summons in accordance with Part 34.

7.2 If the attendance of the witness is required within the district of a district registry, the application may be made at that registry.

7.3 A witness summons will not be issued until the applicant files written evidence showing that the application is made with –

(1) the permission of the tribunal; or
(2) the agreement of the other parties.

INTERIM REMEDIES

8.1 An application for an interim remedy under section 44 of the 1996 Act must be made in an arbitration claim form.

APPLICATIONS UNDER SECTIONS 32 AND 45 OF THE 1996 ACT

9.1 This paragraph applies to arbitration claims for the determination of –

(1) a question as to the substantive jurisdiction of the arbitral tribunal under section 32 of the 1996 Act; and
(2) a preliminary point of law under section 45 of the 1996 Act.

9.2 Where an arbitration claim is made without the agreement in writing of all the other parties to the arbitral proceedings but with the permission of the arbitral tribunal, the written evidence or witness statements filed by the parties must set out any evidence relied on by the parties in support of their contention that the court should, or should not, consider the claim.

9.3 As soon as practicable after the written evidence is filed, the court will decide whether or not it should consider the claim and, unless the court otherwise directs, will so decide without a hearing.

DECISIONS WITHOUT A HEARING

10.1 Having regard to the overriding objective the court may decide particular issues without a hearing. For example, as set out in paragraph 9.3, the question whether the court is satisfied as to the matters set out in section 32(2)(b) or section 45(2)(b) of the 1996 Act.

10.2 The court will generally decide whether to extend the time limit under section 70(3) of the 1996 Act without a hearing. Where the court makes an order extending the time limit, the defendant must file his written evidence within 21 days from service of the order.

62.9 – VARIATION OF TIME

11.1 An application for an order under rule 62.9(1) –

(1) before the period of 28 days has expired, must be made in a Part 23 application notice; and
(2) after the period of 28 days has expired, must be set out in a separately identified part in the arbitration claim form.

APPLICATIONS FOR PERMISSION TO APPEAL

12.1 Where a party seeks permission to appeal to the court on a question of law arising out of an arbitration award, the arbitration claim form must –

(1) identify the question of law; and
(2) state the grounds

on which the party alleges that permission should be given.

12.2 The written evidence in support of the application must set out any evidence relied on by the party for the purpose of satisfying the court –

(1) of the matters referred to in section 69(3) of the 1996 Act; and
(2) that permission should be given.

12.3 The written evidence filed by the respondent to the application must –

(1) state the grounds on which the respondent opposes the grant of permission;
(2) set out any evidence relied on by him relating to the matters mentioned in section 69(3) of the 1996 Act; and

(3) specify whether the respondent wishes to contend that the award should be upheld for reasons not expressed (or not fully expressed) in the award and, if so, state those reasons.

12.4 The court will normally determine applications for permission to appeal without an oral hearing.

12.5 Where the court refuses an application for permission to appeal without an oral hearing, it must provide brief reasons.

12.6 Where the court considers that an oral hearing is required, it may give such further directions as are necessary.

'question of law' (para 12.1)—The court's jurisdiction under AA 1996, s 69 is only to determine questions of *English* law, as defined by s 82 of that Act (*Sanghi Polyesters (India) Ltd v The International Investor KCFC (Kuwait)* [2000] 1 Lloyd's Rep 480, D Mackie QC, where one of the grounds upon which permission was refused was that the application raised issues of Shari'ah law and not English law).

'section 69(3) of the 1996 Act' (para 12.2(1))—The affidavit or witness statement filed by the respondent must set out any evidence relating to the matters mentioned in AA 1996, s 69(3), namely:

(a) that the determination of the question will substantially affect the rights of one or more of the parties;

(b) that the question is one which the tribunal was asked to determine;

(c) that, on the basis of the findings of fact in the award –

  (i) the decision of the tribunal on the question is obviously wrong; or

  (ii) the question is one of general public importance and the decision of the tribunal is at least open to serious doubt; and

(d) that despite the agreement of the parties to resolve the matter by arbitration, it is just and proper in all the circumstances for the court to determine the question. See the notes to CPR Pt 62 above.

Upholding the award on alternative grounds (para 12.3)—As formerly under RSC Ord 73, the respondent to an application for permission to appeal to the High Court can request that the High Court should not set aside the award, even if the appellant was right on the question of law addressed and argue that the award be upheld on grounds not expressed in the award.

Where a respondent contends that the question of law being relied on by the applicant was not properly raised in the course of the arbitration with the result that – by allowing it to be relied on at the appeal stage – it would give rise to a serious irregularity, the correct approach is not for the respondent to rely on that irregularity as an alternative ground for upholding the award. A complaint of irregularity is not to be regarded as a 'reason not expressed in the award'. Rather, the correct approach is for the respondent to rely on the irregularity as a ground for opposing the application for permission to appeal (see *Icon Navigation Corporation v Sinochem International Petroleum (Bahamas) Co Ltd* [2002] EWCH 2812; [2003] 1 All ER (Comm) 405).

Although the alternative ground for upholding the award should be included in the respondent's written evidence, the court does have jurisdiction in exceptional circumstances to grant an extension of time so as to allow the alternative ground to be advanced at a later stage (*PT Putrabali Adyamulia v Société Est Epices* [2003] 2 Lloyd's Rep 700).

Oral hearing required (para 12.6)—Where the court directs that the application for permission to appeal requires an oral hearing, there is nothing to prevent the court from directing that, if permission is granted, the substantive appeal should follow immediately after the permission hearing and should be determined at the same hearing (*Hok Sport Limited (formerly Lobb Partnership Ltd) v Aintree Racecourse Company Ltd* [2002] EWHC 3094, [2003] BLR 155).

SECTION II

13.1 This Section of this Practice Direction applies to arbitration claims to which Section II of Part 62 applies.

62.13 – STARTING THE CLAIM

14.1 An arbitration claim must be started in the Commercial Court and, where required to be heard by a judge, be heard by a judge of that court unless he otherwise directs.

SECTION III

15.1 This Section of this Practice Direction applies to enforcement proceedings to which Section III of Part 62 applies.

62.21 – REGISTRATION OF AWARDS UNDER THE ARBITRATION (INTERNATIONAL INVESTMENT DISPUTES) ACT 1966

16.1 Awards ordered to be registered under the 1966 Act and particulars will be entered in the Register kept for that purpose at the Admiralty and Commercial Registry.

Appendix A

FORMS

****

Appendix A—This Appendix sets out four forms. These are available on the *Civil Court Service* CD-ROM or the HM Courts Service website at *www.hmcourts-service.gov.uk*.

PART 63
PATENTS AND OTHER INTELLECTUAL PROPERTY CLAIMS

CONTENTS OF THIS PART

General note—This Part and its supplementing PD63 replace the former RSC Ords 93 (certain applications relating to copyrights, performers' rights and design rights), 100 (trade marks) and 104 (patents and registered designs) and the former Practice Direction – Patents, etc but with a number of changes.

Many of the substantive provisions are to be found in PD63 rather than in Pt 63 itself. Even then, the provisions do not form a complete procedural code for all intellectual property claims, most being concerned with specific aspects of patent, registered design and (registered) trade mark claims. Even in those fields they do not contain a complete code. The practitioner will need to refer to relevant statutes, a substantial body of case law and the Patents Court Guide. Such matters are dealt with in the leading practitioner texts, for which the commentary here is not a substitute.

63.1 Scope of this Part and interpretation

(1) This Part applies to all intellectual property claims including –

- (a) registered intellectual property rights such as –
  - (i) patents;
  - (ii) registered designs; and
  - (iii) registered trade marks; and
- (b) unregistered intellectual property rights such as –
  - (i) copyright;
  - (ii) design right;
  - (iii) the right to prevent passing off; and
  - (iv) the other rights set out in the practice direction.

(2) In this Part –

- (a) 'the 1977 Act' means the Patents Act 1977;
- (b) 'the 1988 Act' means the Copyright, Designs and Patents Act 1988;

(c) 'the 1994 Act' means the Trade Marks Act 1994;
(d) 'the Comptroller' means the Comptroller General of Patents, Designs and Trade Marks;
(e) 'patent' means a patent under the 1977 Act and includes any application for a patent or supplementary protection certificate granted under –
  (i) the Patents (Supplementary Protection Certificates) Rules 1997;
  (ii) the Patents (Supplementary Protection Certificate for Medicinal Products) Regulations 1992; and
  (iii) the Patents (Supplementary Protection Certificate for Plant Protection Products) Regulations 1996;
(f) 'Patents Court' means the Patents Court of the High Court constituted as part of the Chancery Division by section 6(1) of the Supreme Court Act 1981;
(g) 'Patents County Court' means a county court designated as a Patents County Court under section 287(1) of the 1988 Act;
(gg) 'patents judge' means a person nominated under section 291(1) of the 1988 Act as the patents judge of a patents county court;
(h) 'the register' means whichever of the following registers is appropriate –
  (i) patents maintained by the Comptroller under section 32 of the 1977 Act;
  (ii) designs maintained by the registrar under section 17 of the Registered Designs Act 1949;
  (iii) trade marks maintained by the registrar under section 63 of the 1994 Act;
  (iv) Community trade marks maintained by the Office for Harmonisation in the Internal Market under Article 83 of Council Regulation (EC) 40/94; and
  (v) Community designs maintained by the Office for Harmonisation in the Internal Market under Article 72 of Council Regulation (EC) 6/2002; and
(i) 'the registrar' means –
  (i) the registrar of trade marks; or
  (ii) the registrar of registered designs,

whichever is appropriate.

Amendments—Inserted by SI 2002/3219; amended by SI 2005/2292.

'the other rights set out in the practice direction' (r 63.1(1)(b)(iv))—This refers to PD63, para 18.1, which lists fourteen types of claim. Note that the list includes technical trade secrets litigation. Other claims for breach of confidence are not covered by Pt 63.

'any application for a patent or supplementary protection certification granted under' (r 63.1(2)(e))—Note the extended definition.

63.2 Application of the Civil Procedure Rules

These Rules and their practice directions apply to intellectual property claims unless this Part or a practice direction provides otherwise.

Amendments—Inserted by SI 2002/3219.

'otherwise provides' (r 63.2)—Neither Pt 63 nor PD63 contains any wholesale disapplication of the CPR, but they do make certain modifications of them.

I Patents and Registered Designs

63.3 Scope of Section I

(1) This Section of this Part applies to claims in –

(a) the Patents Court; and
(b) a Patents County Court.

(2) Claims in the court include any claim relating to matters arising out of –

(a) the 1977 Act;
(b) the Registered Designs Act 1949; and
(c) the Defence Contracts Act 1958.

Amendments—Inserted by SI 2002/3219.

'include any claim' (r 63.3(2))—This definition is not exhaustive. Paragraph 2.2 of PD63 contains a list of types of claim that must be dealt with by the Patent Courts or the Patents County Court. That includes claims involving Community registered designs and semiconductor topography rights (a species of design right). Trade mark claims (over which the Patents County Court now has jurisdiction by virtue of the High Court and County Courts Jurisdiction (Amendment) Order 2005, SI 2005/587) are dealt with in Section II.

63.4 Specialist list

Claims in the Patents Court and a Patents County Court form specialist lists for the purpose of rule 30.5.

Amendments—Inserted by SI 2002/3219.

'for the purposes of rule 30.5' (r 63.4)—That is, for the purposes of the court's powers to transfer such cases to and from specialist lists. It does not appear that the Patents Court and Patents County Court lists are themselves specialist lists for other purposes (see r 2.3(2)).

Applications for transfer from or to the Patents County Court—Rules 63.4 and 30.5 need to be read in the light of CDPA 1988, s 289. The High Court may not make any order under CCA 1984, s 41 transferring claims within the special jurisdiction of a Patents County Court from such a court to itself (s 289(1). In considering in relation to such claims whether an order should be made for transfer from or to the High Court under CCA 1984, ss 40 or 42 of , the court must have regard to the financial position of the parties (s 289(2)). Furthermore, it may order transfer to the Patents County Court or refrain from ordering transfer to the High Court notwithstanding that the proceedings are likely to raise an important question of fact or law.

A court considering an application for transfer from or to the Patents County Court must also have regard to the longer list of factors contained in r 30.3(2).

The Patents County Court was intended to provide a forum for smaller, shorter, less complex, less important and less financially-significant cases than the Patents Court, and thereby to make it easier for small and medium-sized enterprises and private individuals to litigate patent disputes (*Chapman Patents Holdings Co plc v Group Lotus plc* (1994) *The Times*, 12 January). However, it is not easy to differentiate between cases which are suitable for one forum rather than the other, given that the jurisdiction of the Patents County Court is co-extensive with that of the Patents Court, that the CPR and in particular Pt 63 apply to both courts and that to a considerable extent the same (deputy) judges sit in both courts. As a result, there is a substantial inertia factor on an application for transfer, meaning that claimants are frequently able to dictate the choice of forum (*Wesley Jessen Corp v Coopervision Ltd* (2001) *The Times*, 31 July). In *Halliburton Energy Services, Inc v Smith International (North Sea) Ltd* [2005] EWHC 1623 (Pat) Pumfrey J deprecated the fact that a long and technically complex claim under two patents had originally been brought in the Patents County Court.

Costs in the Patents County Court—The fact that its jurisdiction and procedure are the same as the Patents Court makes it difficult for the Patents County Court to provide a truly low-cost forum except where a party takes advantage of the different rights of audience, in particular by instructing patent attorneys to conduct proceedings (see *Memminger-IRO GmbH v Trip-Lite Ltd* [1992] RPC 210). In *Warheit v Olympia Tools Ltd* [2003] FSR 6 the Court of Appeal observed that a claim by a patentee for costs in respect of a 2-day trial in the Patents County Court of nearly £250,000 was far in excess of what had been envisaged when the Patents County Court had been set up. Nevertheless it is by no means uncommon for costs of that magnitude to be incurred in Patents County Court cases.

63.4A Patents judge

(1) Subject to paragraph (2), proceedings in the patents county court shall be dealt with by the patents judge.

(2) When a matter needs to be dealt with urgently and it is not practicable or appropriate for the patents judge to deal with such matter, the matter may be dealt with by another judge with appropriate specialist experience who shall be nominated by the Vice-Chancellor.

Amendments—Inserted by SI 2005/2292.

63.5 Starting the claim

Claims to which this Section of this Part applies must be started –

(a) by issuing a Part 7 claim form; or
(b) in existing proceedings under Part 20.

Amendments—Inserted by SI 2002/3219.

'must be started' (r 63.5)—Claims relating to patents and registered designs may not be brought under Pt 8.

Statements of case—Are dealt with out of sequence in r 63.9.

63.6 Defence and reply

Part 15 applies with the modification –

(a) to rule 15.4 that in a claim for infringement under rule 63.9, the defence must be filed within 42 days of service of the claim form; and
(b) to rule 15.8 that the claimant must –
  (i) file any reply to a defence; and
  (ii) serve it on all other parties,

within 21 days of service of the defence.

Amendments—Inserted by SI 2002/3219.

'defence must be filed' (r 63.6(a))—The extended period for filing the defence applies only to claims for infringement. Curiously this provision is repeated in r 63.9(2).

'reply to a defence' (r 63.6(b))—The extended period for filing and serving any reply applies to any claim to which Section I applies.

63.7 Case management

(1) Claims under this Section of this Part are allocated to the multi-track.

(2) Part 26 and any other rule that requires a party to file an allocation questionnaire do not apply.

(3) The following provisions only of Part 29 apply –

(a) rule 29.3(2) (legal representatives to attend case management conferences);
(b) rule 29.4 (the court's approval of agreed proposals for the management of proceedings); and

(c) rule 29.5 (variation of case management timetable) with the exception of paragraph (1)(b) and (c).

(4) As soon as practicable the court will hold a case management conference which must be fixed in accordance with the practice direction.

Amendments—Inserted by SI 2002/3219; amended by SI 2003/3361.

'The following provisions only' (r 63.7(3))—Rule 29.3(2) provides that parties' legal representatives at a case management conference should be familiar with the case and have sufficient authority to deal with any issue that is likely to arise. Rule 29.4 provides for the court to approve agreed case management proposals if it thinks fit, thereby avoiding the need for a hearing. Rule 29.5 (except for para (1)(b) and (c)) provides that a party must apply to the court if he wishes to vary the date which the court has fixed for a case management conference, trial or trial period or wishes to vary any other dates set by the court or CPR if that would necessitate such a variation.

Similarly PD63, para 4.1 provides that only certain provisions of PD29 apply, namely paras 5 (except para 5.9) and 7.

'as soon as practicable ... in accordance with the practice direction' (r 63.7(4))—See PD63, paras 4.3–4.7.

Applications at case management conferences—An application notice for any order to be sought at the case management conference must be filed and served not less than 4 days beforehand (rather than the normal 3 days under r 23.7(1)(b)) (PD63, para 4.8). A standard form, providing a template for most of the orders that may need to be made in a patent case at a case management conference is annexed to the Patents Court Guide.

Case management bundle—Copies of this bundle, prepared by the applicant, must be provided to the court and the other parties at least 4 days before the case management conference. PD63, para 4.9 sets out the requirements and para 4.12 requires this bundle to be updated as the case proceeds.

Experts—Neither Pt 63 nor PD63PD63 contains any provisions regarding expert evidence. Accordingly, Pt 35 applies as it does to other proceedings.

In patent cases, questions can sometimes arise as to the number and qualifications of expert witnesses. The general rule is a party should not call more than one expert in each technical field (*Gerber Garment Technology Inc v Lectra Systems Ltd* [1994] FSR 471). The standard form of order for directions provides for the names of experts to be provided a certain time before exchange of experts' reports. One purpose of this is to enable each party to satisfy itself that it has the combination of experts required to meet the other side's case.

In registered design cases concerning ordinary consumer articles, expert evidence may not be necessary and, therefore, the court will be cautious about admitting it (*Thermos Ltd v Aladdin Sales & Marketing Ltd* [2000] FSR 402).

Experiments—This important subject is dealt with, not in Pt 63, but in PD63, para 9. Please refer to the commentary there.

Models, apparatus, drawings, photographs, films and videos—Where a party intends to rely upon any model or apparatus, he must apply to the court for directions at the case management conference (PD63, para 10). The standard form order deals with models and apparatus together with drawings, photographs, films and videos. It provides for the party intending to rely upon them to give notice and to permit inspection and for the other party or parties to serve notice of any models etc in reply.

Scientific advisors and primers—The court may direct the appointment of a scientific advisor and/or a document setting out basic undisputed technology (usually referred to as a 'primer') (PD63, para 4.10). Appointments of scientific advisors are surprisingly rare, although the Patents Court (*Chiron Corp v Organon Teknika Ltd (No 3)* [1994] FSR 202), the Court of Appeal (*Genentech Inc's Patent* [1989] RPC 147) and the House of Lords (*Kirin Amgen Inc v Hoechst Marion Roussel Ltd* [2004] UKHL 46, [2005] RPC 9) have all been assisted by scientific advisors in genetic engineering cases. Primers are more common, but the court and the parties need to ensure that the benefit of preparing one is not outweighed by the costs, since experience shows that primers can be the occasion for considerable wrangling between the parties. See in this regard *Evans Medical Ltd's Patent* [1998] RPC 517 and *Hoechst Celanese Corp v BP Chemicals Ltd* [1998] FSR 586.

Notices to admit—The standard form of order makes provision for each party to serve notices to admit. The reason for this is that statements of case in patent cases tend to be rather uninformative, and notices to admit are a useful way of narrowing the issues. Thus, the patentee alleging infringement will typically serve a notice seeking admissions in respect of each of the integers of the claims alleged to be infringed with a view to ascertaining which are disputed. Similarly a party challenging validity will typically serve a similar notice in respect of the disclosure of each item of prior art.

Independent validity of claims—Although not provided for in Pt 63 or PD63 or even the standard form of order, it is usual for the patentee to be requested to identify the claims of the patent which he contends are independently valid, following *Unilever plc v Chefaro Proprietaries Ltd* [1994] RPC 567. If the patentee does not do so voluntarily, the court will order him to do so.

Amendment of grounds of invalidity—There are no special provisions in Pt 63 or the practice direction concerning amendments to grounds of invalidity. Nevertheless, the subject merits comment as one which was formerly the subject of rather unusual principles. In the past, the order commonly made where the defendant amended his particulars of objections was that made in *Baird v Moule's Patent Earth Closet Co Ltd* (1881) LR 17 Ch D 139, which gave the patentee an election as to whether to discontinue the claim and, if he did so, his costs since service of the original pleading; or, more usually, that made in *See v Scott-Paine* (1933) 50 RPC 56, which required the patentee to consent to revocation of the patent if he elected to discontinue but with the same costs consequences. These forms of order were approved by the Court of Appeal in *Williamson v Moldline Ltd* [1986] RPC 556. Nevertheless, in recent years patent judges have increasingly taken the view that such orders are capable of working injustice, and refused them (see in particular *GEC Alsthom Ltd's Patent* [1996] FSR 415 and *Hewitt v P McCann Ltd* [1998] FSR 688). After the coming into force of the CPR, it was held the key question in deciding whether to grant such an order was whether the defendant had acted deligently, and that if the defendant had done so the order should be refused (*CIL International Ltd v Vitrashop Ltd* [2002] FSR 4.

Cause of action estoppel—Where a party challenges the validity of a patent or registered design or trade mark, he is under a duty to bring his full case before the court at trial, and if he is unsuccessful he will be barred by cause of action estoppel from attacking the patent or registered design or trade mark again whether on the same or different grounds (see *Hormel Food Corp v Antilles Landscape NV* [2005] EWHC 13 (Ch), [2005] RPC 28 and cases cited therein).

Certificates for fixing trial dates—Unless the court hearing the case management conference fixes the trial date then and there (which sometimes happens), any party may apply for a trial date by filing a certificate (PD63, para 4.11, which prescribes the contents).

Streamlined procedure—Paragraph 10 of the Patents Court Guide outlines a streamlined procedure in which –

(1) all factual and expert evidence is in writing;
(2) there is no disclosure;
(3) there are no experiments;
(4) cross-examination is only permitted on topics where it is necessary and confined to those topics; and
(5) the total duration of the trial is no more than a day.

This procedure can be a very useful way of obtaining a speedy ruling upon disputes, particularly infringement disputes, which turn upon short points of construction of patent claims, as in *Mayne Pharma Pty Ltd v Pharmacia Italia SpA* [2005] EWCA Civ 137. It is rarely likely to be suitable for the determination of an issue as to validity. The court will order the streamlined procedure by agreement or, in the absence of agreement, where the application of the overriding objective under r 1.1 indicates that it is appropriate.

63.8 Disclosure and inspection

Part 31 is modified to the extent set out in the practice direction.

Amendments—Inserted by SI 2002/3219.

'to the extent set out in the practice direction' (r 63.8)—Paragraphs 5.1 and 5.2 of PD63 substitute for the normal rule requiring standard disclosure a unique regime for disclosure in patent cases.

Inspection of documents containing technical or commercial confidential information—See the commentary to PD63, para 5.

63.9 Claim for infringement and challenge to validity

(1) In a claim for infringement or an application in which the validity of a patent or registered design is challenged, the statement of case must contain particulars as set out in the practice direction.

(2) In a claim for infringement, the period for service of the defence or Part 20 claim is 42 days after service of the claim form.

Amendments—Inserted by SI 2002/3219; amended by SI 2003/3361.

'set out in the practice direction' (r 63.9(1))—As to claims for infringement see PD63, para 11.1. As to claims in which the validity of patents and registered designs is challenged, see PD63, paras 11.2–11.5.

63.10 Application to amend a patent specification in existing proceedings

(1) An application under section 75 of the 1977 Act for permission to amend the specification of a patent by the proprietor of the patent must be made by application notice.

(2) The application notice must –

- (a) give particulars of –
  - (i) the proposed amendment sought; and
  - (ii) the grounds upon which the amendment is sought;
- (b) state whether the applicant will contend that the claims prior to amendment are valid; and
- (c) be served by the applicant on all parties and the Comptroller within 7 days of its issue.

(3) The application notice must, if it is reasonably possible, be served on the Comptroller electronically.

(4) Unless the court otherwise orders, the Comptroller will forthwith advertise the application to amend in the journal.

(5) The advertisement will state that any person may apply to the Comptroller for a copy of the application notice.

(6) Within 14 days of the first appearance of the advertisement any person who wishes to oppose the application must file and serve on all parties and the Comptroller a notice opposing the application which must include the grounds relied on.

(7) Within 28 days of the first appearance of the advertisement the applicant must apply to the court for directions.

(8) Unless the court otherwise orders, the applicant must within 7 days serve on the Comptroller any order of the court on the application.

(9) In this rule, 'the journal' means the journal published pursuant to rules made under section 123(6) of the 1977 Act.

Amendments—Inserted by SI 2002/3219.

General note—This rule sets out the procedure for making an application to amend a patent where proceedings concerning the patent are pending before the court.

'electronically' (r 63.10(3))—The Comptroller's fax number is 01633 813600 and his e-mail address is *enquiries@patent.go.uk* See PD6, paras 3.2 and 3.4. Consideration of PD5B, although not strictly pertinent, may be helpful.

'will forthwith advertise' (r 63.10(4))—That is in the next available issue of the Official Journal. The advertisement will give details of the amendments sought.

'apply to the court for directions' (r 63.10(7))—Not less than 2 days before the return date of the application, all parties must file and serve a document setting out the directions they seek (PD63, para 12.1). It is usual for the application to amend to be directed to be heard at the same time as the trial of the proceedings concerning the patent, but this is not an inflexible rule. The order for directions will normally provide for standard disclosure and the service of witness statements. It will frequently also contain a provision preventing the patentee from asserting the patent against non-parties pending resolution of the application.

Disclosure—A patentee who applies to amend his patent is under a duty to give full and candid details of the reasons for the application. At one time it was thought that this required the patentee to waive privilege in respect of documents relating to the reasons for amendment that are subject to legal professional privilege, but it is now clear that this is not the case (*Oxford Gene Technology Ltd v Affymetrix Inc (No 2)* [2001] RPC 18).

Post-trial applications—An application to amend may be made after trial where the nature of the amendment sought is (as a matter of substance rather than form) to delete invalid claims or invalid combinations of claims (see in particular *Hallen Co v Brabantia (UK) Ltd* [1990] FSR 134 approved in *Lubrizol Corp v Esso Petroleum Co Ltd* [1998] RPC 727). Where, however, the purpose of the amendment is to validate an invalid claim by re-writing it, an application to amend after trial will generally be struck out as an abuse of process unless it raises no new issues to validity (see *Windsurfing International Inc v Tabor Marine (GB) Ltd* [1985] RPC 59; *Procter & Gamble Co v Peaudouce (UK) Ltd* [1989] FSR 614; *Lubrizol v Esso* (above) and *Nikken Kosakusho Works v Pioneer Trading Co* [2005] EWCA Civ 906; and cf *Merrell Dow Pharmaceuticals Inc v H H Norton & Co Ltd (No 2)* (1996) (unreported), 1 October, Jacob J). It appears that the correct course where the patentee considers that the subsidiary claims of the patent do not provide him with adequate fall-back positions against a challenge to validity is for him to apply to amend before trial. It is also appears that it is not possible to make a contingent application (ie an application to amend only if the existing claims are held invalid), although it is difficult to see why not.

63.11 Court's determination of question or application

Where the Comptroller –

(a) declines to deal with a question under section 8(7), 12(2), 37(8) or 61(5) of the 1977 Act;

(b) declines to deal with an application under section 40(5) of the 1977 Act; or

(c) certifies under section 72(7)(b) of the 1977 Act that the court should determine the question whether a patent should be revoked,

any person seeking the court's determination of that question or application must issue a claim form within 14 days of the Comptroller's decision.

Amendments—Inserted by SI 2002/3219.

'any person … must issue' (r 63.11)—The rule does not state what happens if this is not done, but presumably the relevant claim or application would be deemed abandoned (compare PD63, para 20.1).

63.12 Application by employee for compensation

(1) An application by an employee for compensation under section 40(1) or (2) of the 1977 Act must be made –

(a) in a claim form; and

(b) within the period prescribed by paragraphs (2) and (3).

(2) The prescribed period begins on the date of the grant of the patent and ends 1 year after the patent has ceased to have effect.

(3) Where a patent has ceased to have effect as a result of failure to pay the renewal fees within the period prescribed under rule 39 of the Patents Rules

1995, and an application for restoration is made to the Comptroller under section 28 of the 1977 Act, the period prescribed under paragraph (2) –

(a) if restoration is ordered, continues as if the patent had remained continuously in effect; or

(b) if restoration is refused, is treated as expiring 1 year after the patent ceased to have effect, or 6 months after the refusal, whichever is the later.

Amendments—Inserted by SI 2002/3219.

'in a claim form' (r 63.12(1)(a))—That is, under Pt 7.

'within the period' (r 63.12(1)(b))—Note the special limitation period set by r 63.12(2), which is subject to modification under r 63.12(3).

Directions—The court must at the case management conference give directions as to the manner in which evidence, and in particular any accounts of expenditure or receipts relating to the claim, is to be given and the provision to the claimant of reasonable facilities for inspecting and taking extracts from accounts relied on (PD63, para 13.1).

II Registered Trade Marks and Other Intellectual Property Rights

63.13 Allocation

(1) This Section of this Part applies to –

(a) claims relating to matters arising out of the 1994 Act; and

(b) other intellectual property rights as set out in the practice direction.

(2) (*revoked*)

(3) Claims to which this Section of this Part applies must be brought in –

(a) the Chancery Division;

(b) a Patents County Court; or

(c) a county court where there is also a Chancery district registry.

Amendments—Inserted by SI 2002/3219; amended by SI 2004/3419.

'applies to ... other intellectual property rights' (r 63.13(1))—See the list in PD63, para 18.1.

'a county court where there is also a Chancery district registry' (r 63.13(3)(c))—Note that the list in PD63, para 18.2 does not include Preston.

63.14 Claims under the 1994 Act

In a claim under the 1994 Act, the claim form or application notice must be served on the registrar where the relief sought would, if granted, affect an entry in the United Kingdom register.

Amendments—Inserted by SI 2002/3219.

63.15 Claim for infringement of registered trade mark

(1) In a claim for infringement of a registered trade mark the defendant may –

(a) in his defence, challenge the validity of the registration of the trade mark; and

(b) apply by Part 20 claim for –

(i) revocation of the registration;

(ii) a declaration that the registration is invalid; or

(iii) rectification of the register.

(2) Where a defendant applies under paragraph (1)(b) and the relief sought would, if granted, affect an entry in the United Kingdom register, he must serve on the registrar a copy of his claim form.

Amendments—Inserted by SI 2002/3219.

III Service

63.16 Service

(1) Subject to paragraph (2), Part 6 applies to service of a claim form and any document under this Part.

(2) A claim form relating to a registered right may be served –

(a) on a party who has registered the right at the address for service given for that right in the United Kingdom Patent Office register, provided the address is within the jurisdiction; or

(b) in accordance with rule 6.19(1) or (1A) on a party who has registered the right at the address for service given for that right in the appropriate register at –

(i) the United Kingdom Patent Office; or

(ii) the Office for Harmonisation in the Internal Market.

Amendments—Inserted by SI 2002/3219; amended by SI 2003/3361.

General note—The rule provides additional addresses for service of a claim form to those permitted under Pt 6 where the claim relates to a registered intellectual property right.

IV Appeals

63.17 Appeals from the Comptroller

(1) Part 52 applies to appeals from the Comptroller.

(2) Patent appeals are to be made to the Patents Court, and other appeals to the Chancery Division.

(3) Where Part 52 requires a document to be served, it must also be served on the Comptroller or registrar, as appropriate.

Amendments—Inserted by SI 2002/3219.

Exceptions—There are two exceptions to r 63.17 which are not apparent on its face. First, appeals from the registrar to an appointed person under ss 76 and 77 of the 1994 Act are not governed by Pt 63 or Pt 52 but by Trade Marks Rules 2000, SI 2000/136 (as amended), rr 63–65. Secondly, appeals from the Registrar of Designs lie to the Registered Designs Appeal Tribunal and are governed by the Registered Designs Appeal Tribunal Rules 1950, SI 1950/430 (as amended). In both cases the appellate tribunal is a specialist tribunal, which is a creature of the particular rules rather than a part of the court system.

Practice Direction – Patents and Other Intellectual Property Claims

This Practice Direction supplements CPR Part 63 (PD63)

General note—The practice direction contains a number of provisions that do not really tie in with CPR Pt 63 but rather are additional substantive rules.

CONTENTS OF THIS PRACTICE DIRECTION

1.1 This practice direction is divided into three sections –

- Section I – Provisions about patents and registered designs
- Section II – Provisions about registered trade marks and other intellectual property rights
- Section III – Provisions about appeals

General note—Notwithstanding its description, Section I contains some provisions that are relevant only to patent cases and not to registered designs, even though they may appear on their face to apply to both (see, for example, paras 4.10 and 4.11).

SECTION I – PROVISIONS ABOUT PATENTS AND REGISTERED DESIGNS

2.1 This Section of this practice direction applies to claims in the Patents Court and a Patents county court.

2.2 The following claims must be dealt with in the court –

(1) any matter arising out of the 1977 Act, including –
  (a) infringement actions;
  (b) revocation actions;
  (c) threats under section 70 of the 1977 Act; and
  (d) disputes as to ownership;
(2) registered designs;
(3) Community registered designs; and
(4) semiconductor topography rights.

Starting the claim (rule 63.5)

3.1 A claim form to which this Section of this Part applies must be marked in the top right hand corner 'Patents Court' below the title of the court in which it is issued.

'must be marked' (para 3.1)—On its face, this requirement applies even if the claim form is issued in the Patents County Court, although it is difficult to see that this can have been intended.

Case management (rule 63.7)

4.1 The following parts only of the practice direction supplementing Part 29 apply –

(1) paragraph 5 (case management conferences) –
  (a) excluding paragraph 5.9; and
  (b) modified so far as is made necessary by other specific provisions of this practice direction; and
(2) paragraph 7 (failure to comply with case management directions).

4.2 Case management shall be dealt with by –

(1) a judge of the court; or
(2) a master or district judge where a judge of the court so directs.

'shall be dealt with by' (para 4.2)—In practice, case management conferences are almost always heard by a judge. Masters and district judges normally only deal with the matters listed in para 8 below, namely –

(1) orders by way of settlement;
(2) applications for extensions of time;
(3) applications for permission to serve out of the jurisdiction;
(4) applications for security for costs; and
(5) enforcement of money judgments,

in respect of which a direction of the judge is not required.

4.3 The claimant must apply for a case management conference within 14 days of the date when all defendants who intend to file and serve a defence have done so.

4.4 Where the claim has been transferred, the claimant must apply for a case management conference within 14 days of the date of the order transferring the claim, unless the court –

(1) held; or
(2) gave directions for

a case management conference, when it made the order transferring the claim.

4.5 Any party may, at a time earlier than that provided in paragraphs 4.3 and 4.4, apply in writing to the court to fix a case management conference.

4.6 If the claimant does not make an application in accordance with paragraphs 4.3 and 4.4, any other party may apply for a case management conference.

4.7 The court may fix a case management conference at any time on its own initiative.

4.8 Not less than 4 days before a case management conference, each party must file and serve an application notice for any order which that party intends to seek at the case management conference.

4.9 Unless the court orders otherwise, the claimant, or the party who makes an application under paragraph 4.6, in consultation with the other parties, must prepare a case management bundle containing –

(1) the claim form;
(2) all statements of case (excluding schedules), except that, if a summary of a statement of case has been filed, the bundle should contain the summary, and not the full statement of case;
(3) a pre-trial timetable, if one has been agreed or ordered;
(4) the principal orders of the court; and
(5) any agreement in writing made by the parties as to disclosure,

and provide copies of the case management bundle for the court and the other parties at least 4 days before the first case management conference or any earlier hearing at which the court may give case management directions.

4.10 At the case management conference the court may direct that –

(1) a scientific adviser under section 70(3) of the Supreme Court Act 1981 be appointed; and
(2) a document setting out basic undisputed technology should be prepared.

(Rule 35.15 applies to scientific advisers)

4.11 Where a trial date has not been fixed by the court, a party may apply for a trial date by filing a certificate which must –

(1) state the estimated length of the trial, agreed if possible by all parties;
(2) detail the time required for the judge to consider the documents;
(3) identify the area of technology; and
(4) assess the complexity of the technical issues involved by indicating the complexity on a scale of 1 to 5 (with 1 being the least and 5 the most complex).

'area of technology … complexity of the technical issues' (para 4.11(3) and (4))—The purpose of these two requirements is to assist in the listing of the case: the more technically complex cases will normally be listed in front of an assigned judge who is a specialist in patents.

4.12 The claimant, in consultation with the other parties, must revise and update the documents referred to in paragraph 4.9 appropriately as the case proceeds. This must include making all necessary revisions and additions at least 7 days before any subsequent hearing at which the court may give case management directions.

Disclosure and inspection (rule 63.8)

5.1 Standard disclosure does not require the disclosure of documents where the documents relate to –

(1) the infringement of a patent by a product or process if, before or at the same time as serving a list of documents, the defendant has served on the claimant and any other party –
  (a) full particulars of the product or process alleged to infringe; and
  (b) drawings or other illustrations, if necessary;
(2) any ground on which the validity of a patent is put in issue, except documents which came into existence within the period –
  (a) beginning 2 years before the earliest claimed priority date; and
  (b) ending 2 years after that date; and
(3) the issue of commercial success.

Disclosure generally—Older cases on disclosure need to be treated with considerable caution. The availability of disclosure in patent cases has been considerably restricted by this paragraph and its predecessors. Further, it is now well appreciated by the patent judges that the cost of extensive disclosure is frequently disproportionate to its probative value (if any), and accordingly courts tend nowadays to be more reluctant to order disclosure than was formerly the case.

'full particulars … drawings or other illustrations' (para 5.1(1))—Such particulars are normally referred to as a 'product (or process) description'. Their function is equivalent to that of disclosure and the duties of the parties and their advisors is the same in relation to the provision of a product (or process) description as it would be in relation to disclosure (*Taylor v Ishida (Europe) Ltd* [2000] FSR 224). The product (or process) description must contain sufficient details to enable the court to decide any issues of infringement that may arise, and so it should not be framed in general terms or include tendentious assertions (*Consafe (UK) Ltd v Emtunga UK Ltd* [1999] RPC 154).

'validity of a patent is put in issue' (para 5.1(2))—Disclosure is only required of documents that relate to a pleaded ground of invalidity (*Avery Ltd v Ashworth, Son & Co Ltd* (1915) 32 RPC 561; *VISX Inc v Nidek Co Ltd* [1999] FSR 91).

Nowadays, the courts take a critical view of whether documents relate to pleaded grounds of invalidity and, hence, are disclosable if within the 4-year window. For example, it is common for patentees to seek disclosure of the defendant's research work with a view to arguing that the patented invention was not obvious to the defendant's researchers. Such documents are only relevant, however, if the defendant's researchers correspond reasonably approximately to the addressee of the patent and were aware of the cited prior art. If they were not aware of the cited prior art, what they did in ignorance of it is irrelevant. On the other hand, disclosure of the defendant's work may be relevant and persuasive where the defendant's researchers were persons skilled in the art and aware of the prior art, particularly where an attack of obviousness over common general knowledge alone is being run.

'commercial success' (para 5.1(3))—Where the patentee relies upon commercial success in answer to an allegation of obviousness (the grounds for which must be pleaded in his statement of case pursuant to para 11.5(1) below), standard disclosure as to that issue is replaced by the requirements of para 5.2 below.

Specific disclosure—Even where a product (or process) description is served, or where documents relating to validity fall outside the 4-year window, it is open to a party to seek an order for specific disclosure of such documents. An example is where a prior use by the patentee more than 2 years before the priority date is pleaded: in such a case specific disclosure of documents relating to that prior use would be likely to be ordered if not volunteered.

Inspection of documents containing technical or commercial confidential information—A situation which frequently arises in patent litigation is that disclosable documents – or product/process descriptions (see *Intel Corp v VIA Techologies Ltd* [2002] EWHC 1434) – contain information which the disclosing party contends is technical or commercially confidential and which it is reluctant to disclose to a competitor. This situation calls for the court to balance three conflicting interests:

(1) the interest of the disclosing party in maintaining the confidentiality of its information;
(2) the interest of the opposing party in prosecuting or defending the claim; and
(3) the public interest in open justice.

There are a number of cases which indicate the principles to be applied in this situation (see in particular *Warner-Lambert & Co v Glaxo Laboratories Ltd* [1975] RPC 354; *Roussel Uclaf v Imperial Chemical Industries plc* [1989] RPC 59; *Helitune Ltd v Stewart Hughes Ltd* [1994] FSR 422 and *Dyson Ltd v Hoover Ltd (No 3)* [2002] RPC 42). These show that how the balance comes down depends on the particular circumstances of the individual case, but that two important factors are the sensitivity of the information in question and the safeguards proposed or sought to protect it. Technical secrets are usually regarded as more deserving of protection than commercial information. The safeguards commonly imposed include restricting inspection to a 'confidentiality club' and requiring express undertakings of confidentiality to be entered into by members of the confidentiality club. Where the inspecting party offers safeguards of this kind, the onus lies on the disclosing party to show that inspection should be further restricted. Another important factor is the stage which the proceedings have reached: the court may sanction restrictions during the pre-trial stages that it is not prepared to countenance at trial.

5.2 Where the issue of commercial success arises, the patentee must, within such time limit as the court may direct, serve a schedule containing –

(1) where the commercial success relates to an article or product –
   (a) an identification of the article or product (for example by product code number) which the patentee asserts has been made in accordance with the claims of the patent;
   (b) a summary by convenient periods of sales of any such article or product;
   (c) a summary for the equivalent periods of sales, if any, of any equivalent prior article or product marketed before the article or product in subparagraph (a); and
   (d) a summary by convenient periods of any expenditure on advertising and promotion which supported the marketing of the articles or products in subparagraphs (a) and (c); or
(2) where the commercial success relates to the use of a process –
   (a) an identification of the process which the patentee asserts has been used in accordance with the claims of the patent;
   (b) a summary by convenient periods of the revenue received from the use of such process;
   (c) a summary for the equivalent periods of the revenues, if any, received from the use of any equivalent prior art process; and
   (d) a summary by convenient periods of any expenditure which supported the use of the process in subparagraphs (a) and (c).

Short applications

6.1 Where any application is listed for a short hearing, the parties must file all necessary documents, skeleton arguments and drafts of any orders sought, by no later than 3.00 pm on the preceding working day.

6.2 A short hearing is any hearing which is listed for no more than 1 hour.

Timetable for trial

7.1 Not less than 1 week before the beginning of the trial, each party must inform the court in writing of the estimated length of its –

(1) oral submissions;
(2) examination in chief, if any, of its own witnesses; and
(3) cross-examination of witnesses of any other party.

7.2 At least 4 days before the date fixed for the trial, the claimant must file –

(1) the trial bundle; and
(2) a Reading Guide for the judge.

7.3 The Reading Guide filed under paragraph 7.2 must –

(1) be short and, if possible, agreed;
(2) set out the issues, the parts of the documents that need to be read on each issue and the most convenient order that they should be read;
(3) identify the relevant passages in text books and cases, if appropriate; and
(4) not contain argument.

Jurisdiction of masters

8.1 A master may deal with –

(1) orders by way of settlement, except settlement of procedural disputes;
(2) orders on applications for extension of time;
(3) applications for leave to serve out of the jurisdiction;
(4) applications for security for costs;
(5) other matters as directed by a judge of the court; and
(6) enforcement of money judgments.

Experiments

9.1 Where a party seeks to establish any fact by experimental proof conducted for the purpose of litigation he must, at least 21 days before service of the application notice for directions under paragraph 9.3, or within such other time as the court may direct, serve on all parties a notice –

(1) stating the facts which he seeks to establish; and
(2) giving full particulars of the experiments proposed to establish them.

9.2 A party served with notice under paragraph 9.1 –

(1) must within 21 days after such service, serve on the other party a notice stating whether or not he admits each fact; and
(2) may request the opportunity to inspect a repetition of all or a number of the experiments identified in the notice served under paragraph 9.1.

9.3 Where any fact which a party seeks to establish by experimental proof is not admitted, he must apply to the court for permission and directions by application notice.

'experimental proof' (para 9.1)—As to what constitutes an experiment for the purpose of para 9, the courts take a fairly broad view. In essence, anything which involves the carrying out of a physical act (as opposed to the expression of something in words, such as an opinion of an expert) may constitute an experiment for this purpose. This is particularly so if the act in question involves the selection of materials and/or conditions and it would be instructive to witness the performance of the act. Thus, in *Consafe (UK) Ltd v Emtunga UK Ltd* [1999] RPC 154 it was held that the computer modelling technique known as finite element analysis constituted an experiment. On the other hand, it has been held that the requirement to serve a notice of experiments only applies to experiments performed for the purposes of the litigation; it does not apply to experiments carried out in the ordinary course of research (*Richardson-Vicks Inc's Patent* [1995] RPC 568 and *Patents Court Practice Explanation* [1997] RPC 166).

'a notice' (para 9.1)—This is usually referred to as a 'notice of experiments'. The time for service of such notices, if the need for them is envisaged, is normally stipulated in the order for directions made at the case management conference. In practice, more time is required between service of the notice and any application to the court for directions under para 9.3 than the minimum 21 days mentioned in para 9.1, since para 9.2 gives the party on whom the notice is served 21 days to respond.

'full particulars of the experiments proposed' (para 9.1(2))—If insufficient particulars are provided, a party may be ordered to give further particulars. The requirement to give full particulars does not necessarily mean that results have to be included. Thus, a party may serve a notice of experiments 'blind', that is to say, without having carrying out the experiments privately first. Normally, however, a party will have carried out the experiments privately before serving the notice. In such circumstances it is usual to include the results in the notice. If this is not done, then that party may be ordered to provide the results (*Société Française Hoechst v Allied Colloids Ltd* [1991] RPC 245).

'opportunity to inspect a repetition of ... the experiments' (para 9.2(2))—The party may, of course, seek the opportunity to inspect the carrying of them out, if they have not been performed before.

Results of repetitions—Where an experiment is repeated, the normal rule is that it is the results obtained on the repeat that are relied on at trial. Nevertheless, the results of experiments which the party relying upon the experiments conducted privately are admissible if proved: the fact that those results were obtained in the absence of the other side goes to weight not admissibility (*Electrolux Northern Ltd v Black & Decker* [1996] FSR 595). If no request is made for a repeat, the general rule is the method and results set out in the notice are taken to be proved (see *Electrolux Northern Ltd v Black & Decker* above).

Reports—In a case where an experiment has been repeated, it is usual, and good practice, to draw up an agreed report of the repetition which can then form the basis of comment in the experts' reports.

'permission' (para 9.3)—Since experiments, and the evidence relating to them, can be very costly and since it is not infrequent for experiments to be carried out which are found at trial not to be relevant or at least useful, it is preferable for the court to consider the relevance and cost-benefit ratio of experiments before they are carried out. In practice this is difficult, however, since the court and the parties rarely have a sufficient grasp of the issues at the case management conference to enable properly-informed decisions to be made. Usually, therefore, the only deterrence against conducting irrelevant or unhelpful experiments is the prospect that the trial judge will make an order disallowing the costs of such experiments (as does sometimes happen – see *Pall Corp v Commercial Hydraulics (Bedford) Ltd* [1990] FSR 329).

On an application for permission (ie permission to adduce the experimental evidence) and directions, it is usual for permission to be granted unless it is manifest that the experiments sought to be relied upon are irrelevant. Normally the dispute, if any, is as to the terms. The normal terms are that the party on whom the notice has been served has the right to inspect a repetition (or the carrying out) of the experiments and to serve a notice of experiments in reply. In an appropriate case, however, a party may be permitted to rely upon experiments without repeating them for the benefit of the other party (*American Cyanamid Co v Ethicon Ltd* [1978] RPC 667).

Late applications—Problems not infrequently arise as a result of late applications to rely on experiments. Such applications fall to be decided according to the principles applicable to late applications under the CPR generally. A key question is whether the admission of the late evidence will jeopardise an existing trial date. If it will, then the evidence may well be excluded. If not, then it may well be admitted. There is no universal formula, however, everything depends on the particular circumstances obtaining in the individual case.

Experiments not put in evidence—It may emerge that a party has conducted experiments for the purposes of the litigation that it has not put in evidence. The general rule is that such experiments are privileged and accordingly (a) no disclosure may be ordered in respect of them and (b) no adverse inference may be drawn from that party's failure to put them in evidence (*Electrolux Northern Ltd v Black & Decker* [1996] FSR 595). An expert's report should, however, include the statement 'I know of no experiment which is inconsistent with my evidence' (*Patents Court Practice Explanation* [1997] RPC 166).

Use of models or apparatus

10.1 Where a party intends to rely on any model or apparatus, he must apply to the court for directions at the first case management conference.

Claim for infringement and challenge to validity (rule 63.9)

11.1 In a claim for infringement of a patent –

(1) the statement of case must –
  (a) show which of the claims in the specification of the patent are alleged to be infringed; and
  (b) give at least one example of each type of infringement alleged; and

(2) a copy of each document referred to in the statement of case, and where necessary a translation of the document, must be served with the statement of case.

'each type of infringement' (para 11.1)—These words refer to types of infringing act, namely acts such as manufacture or sale, and the words 'at least one instance' require particularisation of at least one instance when such type of infringement is alleged to have occurred (*Lubrizol Corp v Esso Petroleum Co Ltd (No 3)* [1993] FSR 59). The degree of particularisation required depends on the circumstances: thus fewer particulars are needed as against a manufacturer than as against a mere vendor (*Lubrizol Corp v Esso Petroleum Co Ltd (No 3)* above).

It is conventional to serve a separate document entitled 'particulars of infringements' together with the particulars of claim, but nothing in Pt 63 or PD63 requires this (contrast the position regarding grounds of invalidity described below).

Claims for registered design infringement—Contrary to what might be supposed from r 63.9, PD63 contains no specific requirements for statements of case in claims for registered design infringement.

11.2 Where the validity of a patent or registered design is challenged –

(1) the statement of case must contain particulars of –
  (a) the relief sought; and
  (b) the issues except those relating to validity of the patent or registered design;

(2) the statement of case must have a separate document annexed to it headed 'Grounds of Invalidity' specifying the grounds on which validity of the patent is challenged;

(3) a copy of each document referred to in the Grounds of Invalidity, and where necessary a translation of the document, must be served with the Grounds of Invalidity; and

(4) the Comptroller must be sent a copy of the Grounds of Invalidity and where any such Grounds of Invalidity are amended, a copy of the amended document, at the same time as the Grounds of Invalidity are served or amended.

'except those relating to validity' (para 11.2(1)(b))—Such particulars are instead placed in the separate document required by para 11.2(2).

11.3 Where, in an application in which the validity of a patent or a registered design is challenged, the Grounds of Invalidity include an allegation –

(1) that the invention is not a patentable invention because it is not new or does not involve an inventive step, the particulars must specify such details of the matter in the state of art relied on, as set out in paragraph 11.4;

(2) that the specification of the patent does not disclose the invention clearly enough and completely enough for it to be performed by a person skilled in the art, the particulars must state, if appropriate,

which examples of the invention cannot be made to work and in which respects they do not work or do not work as described in the specification; or

(3) that the registered design is not new, the particulars must specify such details of the matter in the state of art relied on, as set out in paragraph 11.4.

'clearly enough and completely enough for it to be performed by a person skilled in the art' (para 11.3(2))—In an appropriate case the patentee may be ordered to specify the parts of the specification relied upon as disclosing the invention and state what the skilled person would do in the light of them (*Polaroid Corp's Patent* [1977] FSR 233), but usually such order would not be appropriate before experiments (*Halcon International Inc v Shell Transport & Trading Co* [1977] FSR 458).

11.4 The details required under paragraphs 11.3(1) and 11.3(3) are –

(1) in the case of matter or a design made available to the public by written description the date on which and the means by which it was so made available, unless this is clear from the face of the matter; and

(2) in the case of matter or a design made available to the public by use –

(a) the date or dates of such use;

(b) the name of all persons making such use;

(c) any written material which identifies such use;

(d) the existence and location of any apparatus employed in such use; and

(e) all facts and matters relied on to establish that such matter was made available to the public.

'the details required' (para 11.4)—Where the prior art consists of matter made available to the public by oral disclosure (eg a lecture), there are no specified details. So far as possible, details analogous to those required in respect of prior uses should be given.

11.5 In any proceedings in which the validity of a patent is challenged –

(1) on the ground that the invention did not involve an inventive step, a party who wishes to rely on the commercial success of the patent must state the grounds on which he so relies in his statement of case; and

(2) the court may order inspection of machinery or apparatus where a party alleges such machinery or apparatus was used before the priority date of the claim.

Generally—Although the requirements specified in the practice direction are expressed in mandatory terms, in an appropriate case the court may allow a ground of invalidity to be pleaded even though the defendant is unable to give full particulars prior to disclosure, provided that the pleading does not amount to a fishing expedition (*VISX Inc v Nidek Co Ltd* [1999] FSR 91).

Where common general knowledge is relied on, it should be distinctly pleaded (*Philips v Ivel Cycle Co Ltd* (1890) 7 RPC 77). The general rule is the particulars of common general knowledge need not be given, but sometimes particulars are ordered as in (*Solaflex Signs Amalgamated Ltd v Allen Manufacturing Co Ltd* (1931) 48 RPC 577). Particulars are more likely to be ordered where the defendant is alleging obviousness over common general knowledge alone or where it appears for some other reason that the defendant intends to advance a specific case based on common general knowledge.

It is important that every ground of invalidity relied on be properly pleaded. As noted above, disclosure is only required in respect of pleaded grounds. At trial the court may refuse to allow the admission of evidence or cross-examination relating to an insufficiently particularised plea of invalidity (*British Thomson-Houston Co Ltd v Tunstalite Ltd* (1940) 57 RPC 271). Furthermore the court will not consider unpleaded objections even if they appear on the evidence (*Alsop Flour Process Co v Flour Oxidising Co* (1908) 25 RPC 490; *British United Shoe Machinery Co v Fussell & Co* (1908) 25 RPC 631).

Application to amend a patent specification in existing proceedings (rule 63.10)

12.1 Not later than 2 days before the first hearing date the applicant, the Comptroller if he wishes to be heard, the parties to the proceedings and any other opponent, must file and serve a document stating the directions sought.

12.2 Where the application notice is served on the Comptroller electronically under rule 63.10(3), it must comply with any requirements for the sending of electronic communications to the Comptroller.

Application by employee for compensation (rule 63.12)

13.1 Where an employee applies for compensation under section 40(1) or (2) of the 1977 Act, the court must at the case management conference give directions as to –

(1) the manner in which the evidence, including any accounts of expenditure and receipts relating to the claim, is to be given at the hearing of the claim and if written evidence is to be given, specify the period within which witness statements or affidavits must be filed; and
(2) the provision to the claimant by the defendant or a person deputed by him, of reasonable facilities for inspecting and taking extracts from the accounts by which the defendant proposes to verify the accounts in subparagraph (1) or from which those accounts have been derived.

General note—The purpose of this provision is to ensure that a cost-effective way is provided to deal with the financial evidence required for claims under s 40 of the 1977 Act.

Communication of information to the European Patent Office

14.1 The court may authorise the communication of any such information in the court files as the court thinks fit to –

(1) the European Patent Office; or
(2) the competent authority of any country which is a party to the European Patent convention.

'may authorise' (para 14.1)—If the information in question is contained in disclosure documents, this provision needs to be considered together with r 31.22 and cases such as *Halcon International Inc v Shell Transport & Trading Co* [1979] RPC 97 and *Crest Homes plc v Marks* [1987] AC 829.

14.2 Before authorising the disclosure of information under paragraph 14.1, the court shall permit any party who may be affected by the disclosure to make representations, in writing or otherwise, on the question of whether the information should be disclosed.

Order affecting entry in the register of patents or designs

15.1 Where any order of the court affects the validity of an entry in the register, the court and the party in whose favour the order is made, must serve a copy of such order on the Comptroller within 14 days.

15.2 Where the order is in favour of more than one party, a copy of the order must be served by such party as the court directs.

Claim for rectification of the register of patents or designs

16.1 Where a claim is made for the rectification of the register of patents or designs, the claimant must at the same time as serving the other parties, serve a copy of –

(1) the claim form; and
(2) accompanying documents

on the Comptroller or registrar, as appropriate.

16.2 Where documents under paragraph 16.1 are served on the Comptroller or registrar, he shall be entitled to take part in the proceedings.

European Community designs

17.1 The Patents Court and the Central London County Court are the designated Community design courts under Article 80(5) of Council Regulation (EC) 6/2002.

'Central London County Court'—The Central London County Court is currently the only Patents County Court (Patents County Court (Designation and Jurisdiction) Order 1994, SI 1994/1609). Obviously, Community design claims should go into the Patents County Court list and not the ordinary lists of the Central London County Court.

17.2 Where a counterclaim is filed at the Community design court, for a declaration of invalidity of a registered Community design, the Community design court shall inform the Office for Harmonisation in the Internal Market of the date on which the counterclaim was filed, in accordance with Article 86(2) of Council Regulation (EC) 6/2002.

17.3 On filing a counterclaim under paragraph 17.2, the party filing it must inform the Community design court in writing that it is a counterclaim to which paragraph 17.2 applies and that the Office for Harmonisation in the Internal Market needs to be informed of the date on which the counterclaim was filed.

17.4 Where a Community design court has given a judgment which has become final on a counterclaim for a declaration of invalidity of a registered Community design, the Community design court shall send a copy of the judgment to the Office for Harmonisation in the Internal Market, in accordance with Article 86(4) of Council Regulation (EC) 6/2002.

17.5 The party in whose favour judgment is given under paragraph 17.4 must inform the Community design court at the time of judgment that paragraph 17.4 applies and that the Office for Harmonisation in the Internal Market needs to be sent a copy of the judgment.

SECTION II – PROVISIONS ABOUT REGISTERED TRADE MARKS AND OTHER INTELLECTUAL PROPERTY RIGHTS

Allocation (rule 63.13)

18.1 Any of the following claims must be brought in the Chancery Division, a Patents county court or a county court where there is also a Chancery district registry –

(1) copyright;
(2) rights in performances;
(3) rights conferred under Part VII of the 1988 Act;
(4) design right;

(5) Community design right;
(6) Olympic symbols;
(7) plant varieties;
(8) moral rights;
(9) database rights;
(10) unauthorised decryption rights;
(11) hallmarks;
(12) technical trade secrets litigation;
(13) passing off;
(14) geographical indications;
(15) registered trade marks; and
(16) Community registered trade marks.

18.2 There are Chancery district registries at Birmingham, Bristol, Cardiff, Leeds, Liverpool, Manchester and Newcastle upon Tyne.

Starting the claim

19.1 A claim form to which this Section of this Part applies must be marked in the top right hand corner 'Chancery Division, Intellectual Property' below the title of the court in which it is issued.

'Chancery Division' (para 19.1)—It cannot be intended that these words are to be used in the Patents County Court, where the claim should simply be marked 'Intellectual Property'.

Claims under the 1994 Act (rule 63.14)

20.1 Where the registrar refers to the court an application made to him under the 1994 Act, then unless within 1 month of receiving notification of the decision to refer, the applicant makes the application to the court, he shall be deemed to have abandoned it.

20.2 The period prescribed under paragraph 20.1 may be extended by –

(1) the registrar; or
(2) the court

where a party so applies, even if such application is not made until after the expiration of the period prescribed.

20.3 Where an application is made under section 19 of the 1994 Act, the applicant must serve his claim form or application notice on all identifiable persons having an interest in the goods, materials or articles within the meaning of section 19 of the 1994 Act.

Claim for infringement of registered trade mark (rule 63.15)

21.1 Where a document under rule 63.15(2) is served on the registrar, he –

(1) may take part in the proceedings; and
(2) need not serve a defence or other statement of case, unless the court otherwise orders.

'a document is served' (para 21.1)—Claims for a declaration of invalidity or revocation of a trade mark or rectification of the register are required to be served on the registrar, whether brought by original claim (r 63.14) or Pt 20 claim (r 61.15). There is a lacuna in that para 21.1 does not apply where such a claim is brought by way of original claim since it does not refer to r 63.14. As it obviously should do so, the court is likely in practice to allow the registrar to take part, if he wishes, and not to require a defence from him, in either case. In fact, the registrar does not normally appear unless some aspect of his practice is in question.

Order affecting entry in the register of trade marks

22.1 Where any order of the court affects the validity of an entry in the register, the provisions of paragraphs 15.1 and 15.2 shall apply.

Claim for rectification of the register of trade marks

23.1 Where a claim is made for the rectification of the register of trade marks, the provisions of paragraphs 16.1 and 16.2 shall apply.

European Community trade marks

24.1 The Chancery Division of the High Court, a Patents County Court or a county court where there is also a Chancery district registry are designated Community trade mark courts under Article 91(1) of Council Regulation (EC) 40/94.

General note—The paragraph has not yet been revised to reflect the designation of the Court of Session, the High Court of Northern Ireland, the Patents County Court and the county courts at Birmingham, Bristol, Cardiff, Leeds, Liverpool, Manchester and Newcastle as Community trade marks courts (Community Trade Mark (Designation of Community Trade Mark Courts) Regulations 2005, SI 2005/440).

24.2 Where a counterclaim is filed at the Community trade mark court, for revocation or for a declaration of invalidity of a Community trade mark, the Community trade mark court shall inform the Office for Harmonisation in the Internal Market of the date on which the counterclaim was filed, in accordance with Article 96(4) of Council Regulation (EC) 40/94.

24.3 On filing a counterclaim under paragraph 24.2, the party filing it must inform the Community trade mark court in writing that it is a counterclaim to which paragraph 24.2 applies and that the Office for Harmonisation in the Internal Market needs to be informed of the date on which the counterclaim was filed.

24.4 Where the Community trade mark court has given a judgment which has become final on a counterclaim for revocation or for a declaration of invalidity of a Community trade mark, the Community trade mark court shall send a copy of the judgment to the Office for Harmonisation in the Internal Market, in accordance with Article 96(6) of Council Regulation (EC) 40/94.

24.5 The party in whose favour judgment is given under paragraph 24.4 must inform the Community trade mark court at the time of judgment that paragraph 24.4 applies and that the Office for Harmonisation in the Internal Market needs to be sent a copy of the judgment.

Claim for additional damages under section 97(2) or section 229(3) of the 1988 Act

25.1 Where a claimant seeks to recover additional damages under section 97(2) or section 229(3) of the 1988 Act, the particulars of claim must include –

(1) a statement to that effect; and
(2) the grounds for claiming them.

'sections 97(2) or 229(3) of the 1988 Act' (para 25.1)—The paragraph does not refer to a claim for additional damages under s 191J(2) of the 1988 Act, but presumably the same rule is intended to apply.

Application for delivery up or forfeiture under the 1988 Act

26.1 Where a claimant applies under sections 99, 114, 195, 204, 230 or 231 of the 1988 Act for delivery up or forfeiture he must serve –

(1) the claim form; or
(2) application notice, where appropriate,

on all identifiable persons who have an interest in the goods, material or articles within the meaning of sections 114 or 204 of the 1988 Act.

Olympic symbols

27.1 In this practice direction 'the Olympic Symbol Regulations' means the Olympic Association Right (Infringement Proceedings) Regulations 1995.

27.2 Where an application is made under regulation 5 of the Olympic Symbol Regulations, the applicant must serve his claim form or application notice on all identifiable persons having an interest in the goods, materials or articles within the meaning of regulation 5 of the Olympic Symbol Regulations.

SECTION III – PROVISIONS ABOUT APPEALS

Appeals and references from the Comptroller (rule 63.17)

28.1 Where –

(1) a person appointed by the Lord Chancellor to hear and decide appeals under section 77 of the 1994 Act, refers an appeal to the the Chancery Division of the High Court under section 76(3) of the 1994 Act; or
(2) the Comptroller refers the whole proceedings or a question or issue to the the Chancery Division of the High Court under section 251(1) of the 1988 Act,

the appeal or reference must be brought within 14 days of the reference.

'must be brought within 14 days' (para 28.1)—Like CPR r 63.11, the paragraph does not state what happens if this is not done, but presumably the relevant claim or application would be deemed abandoned (compare PD63, para 20.1).

PART 64
ESTATES, TRUSTS AND CHARITIES

CONTENTS OF THIS PART

Practice Direction—This Part is supplemented by a practice direction – PD64 – which is set out at p 1469.

64.1 General

(1) This Part contains rules –

(a) in Section I, about claims relating to –
(i) the administration of estates of deceased persons, and
(ii) trusts; and
(b) in Section II, about charity proceedings.

(2) In this Part and its practice directions, where appropriate, references to trustees include executors and administrators.

(3) All proceedings in the High Court to which this Part applies must be brought in the Chancery Division.

Amendments—Inserted by SI 2002/2058.

Section I – Claims relating to the Administration of Estates and Trusts

64.2 Scope of this Section

This Section of this Part applies to claims –

(a) for the court to determine any question arising in –
(i) the administration of the estate of a deceased person; or
(ii) the execution of a trust;
(b) for an order for the administration of the estate of a deceased person, or the execution of a trust, to be carried out under the direction of the court ('an administration order');
(c) under the Variation of Trusts Act 1958; or
(d) under section 48 of the Administration of Justice Act 1985.

Amendments—Inserted by SI 2002/2058.

64.3 Claim form

A claim to which this Section applies must be made by issuing a Part 8 claim form.

Amendments—Inserted by SI 2002/2058.

64.4 Parties

(1) In a claim to which this Section applies, other than an application under section 48 of the Administration of Justice Act 1985 –

(a) all the trustees must be parties;
(b) if the claim is made by trustees, any of them who does not consent to being a claimant must be made a defendant; and
(c) the claimant may make parties to the claim any persons with an interest in or claim against the estate, or an interest under the trust, who it is appropriate to make parties having regard to the nature of the order sought.

(2) In addition, in a claim under the Variation of Trusts Act 1958, unless the court directs otherwise any person who –

(a) created the trust; or
(b) provided property for the purposes of the trust,

must, if still alive, be made a party to the claim.

(The court may, under rule 19.2, order additional persons to be made parties to a claim)

Amendments—Inserted by SI 2002/2058.

Section II – Charity Proceedings

64.5 Scope of this Section and interpretation

(1) This Section applies to charity proceedings.

(2) In this Section –

(a) 'the Act' means the Charities Act 1993;
(b) 'charity proceedings' has the same meaning as in section 33(8) of the Act; and
(c) 'the Commissioners' means the Charity Commissioners for England and Wales.

Amendments—Inserted by SI 2002/2058.

64.6 Application for permission to take charity proceedings

(1) An application to the High Court under section 33(5) of the Act for permission to start charity proceedings must be made within 21 days after the refusal by the Commissioners of an order authorising proceedings.

(2) The application must be made by issuing a Part 8 claim form, which must contain the information specified in the practice direction.

(3) The Commissioners must be made defendants to the claim, but the claim form need not be served on them or on any other person.

(4) The judge considering the application may direct the Commissioners to file a written statement of their reasons for their decision.

(5) The court will serve on the applicant a copy of any statement filed under paragraph (4).

(6) The judge may either –

(a) give permission without a hearing; or
(b) fix a hearing.

Amendments—Inserted by SI 2002/2058.

Practice Direction – Estates, Trusts and Charities

This Practice Direction supplements CPR Part 64 (PD64)

I CLAIMS RELATING TO THE ADMINISTRATION OF ESTATES AND TRUSTS

Examples of claims under rule 64.2(a)

1 The following are examples of the types of claims which may be made under rule 64.2(a) –

- (1) a claim for the determination of any of the following questions –
  - (a) any question as to who is included in any class of persons having –
    - (i) a claim against the estate of a deceased person;
    - (ii) a beneficial interest in the estate of such a person; or
    - (iii) a beneficial interest in any property subject to a trust;
  - (b) any question as to the rights or interests of any person claiming –
    - (i) to be a creditor of the estate of a deceased person;
    - (ii) to be entitled under a will or on the intestacy of a deceased person; or
    - (iii) to be beneficially entitled under a trust;
- (2) a claim for any of the following remedies –
  - (a) an order requiring a trustee –
    - (i) to provide and, if necessary, verify accounts;
    - (ii) to pay into court money which he holds in that capacity; or
    - (iii) to do or not to do any particular act;
  - (b) an order approving any sale, purchase, compromise or other transaction by a trustee; or
  - (c) an order directing any act to be done which the court could order to be done if the estate or trust in question were being administered or executed under the direction of the court.

Applications by trustees for directions

2 A separate practice direction contains guidance about applications by trustees for directions.

Administration orders – rule 64.2(b)

3.1 The court will only make an administration order if it considers that the issues between the parties cannot properly be resolved in any other way.

3.2 If, in a claim for an administration order, the claimant alleges that the trustees have not provided proper accounts, the court may –

- (1) stay the proceedings for a specified period, and order them to file and serve proper accounts within that period; or
- (2) if necessary to prevent proceedings by other creditors or persons

claiming to be entitled to the estate or fund, make an administration order and include in it an order that no such proceedings are to be taken without the court's permission.

3.3 Where an administration order has been made in relation to the estate of a deceased person, and a claim is made against the estate by any person who is not a party to the proceedings –

(1) no party other than the executors or administrators of the estate may take part in any proceedings relating to the claim without the permission of the court; and
(2) the court may direct or permit any other party to take part in the proceedings, on such terms as to costs or otherwise as it thinks fit.

3.4 Where an order is made for the sale of any property vested in trustees, those persons shall have the conduct of the sale unless the court directs otherwise.

Applications under the Variation of Trusts Act 1958 – rule 64.2(c)

4.1 Where children or unborn beneficiaries will be affected by a proposed arrangement under the Act, the evidence filed in support of the application must –

(1) show that their litigation friends or the trustees support the arrangements as being in the interests of the children or unborn beneficiaries; and
(2) unless paragraph 4.3 applies or the court orders otherwise, be accompanied by a written opinion to this effect by the advocate who will appear on the hearing of the application.

4.2 A written opinion filed under paragraph 4.1(2) must –

(1) if it is given on formal instructions, be accompanied by a copy of those instructions; or
(2) otherwise, state fully the basis on which it is given.

4.3 No written opinion needs to be filed in support of an application to approve an arrangement under section 1(1)(d) of the Act (discretionary interests under protective trusts).

4.4 Where the interests of two or more children, or two or more of the children and unborn beneficiaries, are similar, only a single written opinion needs to be filed.

Applications under section 48 of the Administration of Justice Act 1985 – rule 64.2(d)

5 A Part 8 claim form for an application by trustees under section 48 of the Administration of Justice Act 1985 (power of High Court to authorise action to be taken in reliance on legal opinion) may be issued without naming a defendant, under rule 8.2A. No separate application for permission under rule 8.2A need be made.

Prospective costs orders

6.1 These paragraphs are about the costs of applications under [rule 64.2(a).

6.2 Where trustees have power to agree to pay the costs of a party to such an application, and exercise such a power, rule 48.3 applies. In such a case, an order is not required and the trustees are entitled to recover out of the trust fund any costs which they pay pursuant to the agreement made in the exercise of such power.

6.3 Where the trustees do not have, or decide not to exercise, a power to make such an agreement, the trustees or the party concerned may apply to the court at any stage of proceedings for an order that the costs of any party (including the costs of the trustees) shall be paid out of the fund (a 'prospective costs order').

6.4 The court, on an application for a prospective costs order, may –

(a) in the case of the trustees' costs, authorise the trustees to raise and meet such costs out of the fund;

(b) in the case of the costs of any other party, authorise or direct the trustees to pay such costs (or any part of them, or the costs incurred up to a particular time) out of the trust fund to be assessed, if not agreed by the trustees, on the indemnity basis or, if the court directs, on the standard basis, and to make payments from time to time on account of such costs. A model form of order is annexed to this Practice Direction.

6.5 The court will always consider whether it is possible to deal with the application for a prospective costs order on paper without a hearing and in an ordinary case would expect to be able to do so. The trustees must consider whether a hearing is needed for any reason. If they consider that it is they should say so and explain why in their evidence. If any party to the application referred to in paragraph 6.1 above (or any other person interested in the trust fund) considers that a hearing is necessary (for instance because he wishes to oppose the making of a prospective costs order) this should be stated, and the reasons explained, in his evidence, if any, or otherwise in a letter to the court.

6.6 If the court would be minded to refuse the application on a consideration of the papers alone, the parties will be notified and given the opportunity, within a stated time, to ask for a hearing.

6.7 The evidence in support of an application for a prospective costs order should be given by witness statement. The trustees and the applicant (if different) must ensure full disclosure of the relevant matters to show that the case is one which falls within the category of case where a prospective costs order can properly be made.

6.8 The model form of order is designed for use in the more straightforward cases, where a question needs to be determined which has arisen in the administration of the trust, whether the claimants are the trustees or a beneficiary. The form may be adapted for use in less straightforward cases, in particular where the proceedings are hostile, but special factors may also have to be reflected in the terms of the order in such a case.

II CHARITY PROCEEDINGS

Role of Attorney-General

7 The Attorney-General is a necessary party to all charity proceedings, other than any commenced by the Charity Commissioners, and must be joined as a defendant if he is not a claimant.

Service on Charity Commissioners or Attorney-General

8 Any document required or authorised to be served on the Commissioners or the Attorney-General must be served on the Treasury Solicitor in accordance with RSC Order 77, rule 4(2).

Applications for permission to take charity proceedings – rule 64.6

9.1 The claim form for an application under section 33(5) of the Act must state –

(1) the name, address and description of the applicant;
(2) details of the proceedings which he wishes to take;
(3) the date of the Commissioners' refusal to grant an order authorising the taking of proceedings;
(4) the grounds on which the applicant alleges that it is a proper case for taking proceedings; and
(5) if the application is made with the consent of any other party to the proposed proceedings, that fact.

9.2 If the Commissioners have given reasons for refusing to grant an order, a copy of their reasons must be filed with the claim form.

Appeals against orders of the Charity Commissioners

10 Part 52 applies to any appeal against an order of the Charity Commissioners. Section III of the practice direction supplementing Part 52 contains special provisions about such appeals.

APPENDIX

MODEL FORM OF PROSPECTIVE COSTS ORDER

UPON THE APPLICATION etc.

AND UPON HEARING etc.

AND UPON READING etc.

AND UPON the Solicitors for the .... Defendant undertaking to make the repayments mentioned in paragraph 2 below in the circumstances there mentioned

IT IS [BY CONSENT] ORDERED THAT:

1. The Claimants as trustees of .... ('the [Settlement/Scheme]') do –
   (a) pay from the assets of the [Settlement/Scheme] the costs of and incidental to these proceedings incurred by the .... Defendant such costs to be subject to a detailed assessment on the indemnity basis if not agreed and (for the avoidance of doubt) to –
      (i) include costs incurred by the .... Defendant from and after [*date*] in anticipation of being appointed to represent any class of persons presently or formerly beneficially interested under the trusts of the [Settlement/Scheme] irrespective of whether [he/she] is in fact so appointed; and
      (ii) exclude (in the absence of any further order) costs incurred in prosecuting any Part 20 claim or any appeal;

(b) indemnify the .... Defendant in respect of any costs which he may be ordered to pay to any other party to these proceedings in connection therewith.

2. Until the outcome of the detailed assessment (or the agreement regarding costs) contemplated in paragraph 1 above, the Claimants as trustees do pay from the assets of the [Settlement/Scheme] to the Solicitors for the .... Defendant monthly (or at such other intervals as may be agreed) such sums on account of the costs referred to in paragraph 1(a) of this Order as the Solicitors for the .... Defendant shall certify –

(i) to have been reasonably and properly incurred and not to exceed such amount as is likely in their opinion to be allowed on a detailed assessment on the indemnity basis; and

(ii) to have accrued on account of the present proceedings in the period prior to the date of such certificate and not to have been previously provided for under this Order.

PROVIDED ALWAYS that the Solicitors for the .... Defendant shall repay such sums (if any) as, having been paid to them on account, are disallowed on a detailed assessment or are otherwise agreed to be repaid and any such sums shall be repaid together with interest at 1% above the base rate for the time being of [Barclays] Bank plc from and including the date of payment to those Solicitors up to and including the date of repayment, such interest to accrue daily.

3. Any party may apply to vary or discharge paragraphs 1 and 2 of this Order but only in respect of costs to be incurred after the date of such application.

Note: this form of order assumes that the trustees are the claimants. If the claimant is a beneficiary and the trustees are defendants, references to the parties need to be adapted accordingly.

Practice Direction – Applications to the Court for Directions by Trustees in Relation to the Administration of the Trust

This Practice Direction supplements Section I of CPR Part 64 (PD64B)

1 This Practice Direction is about applications to the court for directions by trustees in relation to the administration of the trust.

CONTENTS OF THE CLAIM FORM

2 If confidentiality of the directions sought is important (for example, where the directions relate to actual or proposed litigation with a third party who could find out what directions the trustees are seeking through access to the claim form under CPR rule 5.4) the statement of the remedy sought, for the purposes of CPR rule 8.2(b), may be expressed in general terms. The trustees must, in that case, state specifically in the evidence what it is that they seek to be allowed to do.

PROCEEDINGS IN PRIVATE

3 The proceedings will in the first instance be listed in private (see paragraph 1.5 of the Practice Direction supplementing Part 39 and rule 39.2(3)(f)). Accordingly the order made, as well as the other documents among the court records (apart from a claim form which has been served), will not be open to inspection by third parties without the court's permission (rule 5.4(2)). If the matter is disposed of without a hearing, the order made will be expressed to have been made in private.

JOINING DEFENDANTS OR GIVING NOTICE TO THOSE INTERESTED

4.1 Rule 64.4(1)(c) deals with the joining of beneficiaries as defendants. Often, especially in the case of a private trust, it will be clear that some, and which, beneficiaries need to be joined as defendants. Sometimes, if there are only two views of the appropriate course, and one is advocated by one beneficiary who will be joined, it may not be necessary for other beneficiaries to be joined since the trustees may be able to present the other arguments. Equally, in the case of pension trust, it may not be necessary for a member of every possible different class of beneficiaries to be joined.

4.2 In some cases the court may be able to assess whether or not to give the directions sought, or what directions to give, without hearing from any party other than the trustees. If the trustees consider that their case is in that category they may apply to the court to issue the claim form without naming any defendants under rule 8.2A. They must apply to the court before the claim form is issued (rule 8.2A(2)) and include a copy of the claim form that they propose to issue (rule 8.2A(3)(b)).

4.3 In other cases the trustees may know that beneficiaries need to be joined as defendants, or to be given notice, but may be in doubt as to which. Examples could include a case concerning a pension scheme with many beneficiaries and a number of different categories of interest, especially if they may be differently affected by the action for which directions are sought, or a private trust with a large class of discretionary beneficiaries. In those cases the trustees may apply to issue the claim form without naming any defendants under rule 8.2A. The application may be combined with an application to the court for directions as to which persons to join as parties or to give notice to under rule 19.8A.

4.4 In the case of a charitable trust the Attorney-General is always the appropriate defendant, and almost always the only one.

CASE MANAGEMENT DIRECTIONS

5.1 The claim will be referred to the master or district judge once a defendant has acknowledged service, or otherwise on expiry of the period for acknowledgment of service, (or, if no defendant is named, as soon as the claimants' evidence has been filed) to consider directions for the management of the case. Such directions may be given without a hearing in some cases; these might include directions as to parties or as to notice of proceedings, as mentioned in paragraph 4 above.

PROCEEDING WITHOUT A HEARING

6.1 The court will always consider whether it is possible to deal with the application on paper without a hearing. The trustees must always consider whether a hearing is needed for any reason. If they consider that it is they should say so and explain why in their evidence. If a defendant considers that a hearing is needed, this should be stated, and the reasons explained, in his evidence, if any, or otherwise in a letter to the court.

6.2 If the court would be minded to refuse to give the directions asked for on a consideration of the papers alone, the parties will be notified and given the opportunity, within a stated time, to ask for a hearing.

6.3 In charity cases, the master or district judge may deal with the case without a hearing on the basis of a letter by or on behalf of the Attorney-General that sets out his attitude to the application.

EVIDENCE

7.1 The trustees' evidence should be given by witness statement. In order to ensure that, if directions are given, the trustees are properly protected by the order, they must ensure full disclosure of relevant matters, even if the case is to proceed with the participation of beneficiaries as defendants.

7.2 Applications for directions whether or not to take or defend or pursue litigation should be supported by evidence including the advice of an appropriately qualified lawyer as to the prospects of success and other matters relevant to be taken into account, including a cost estimate for the proceedings and any known facts concerning the means of the opposite party to the proceedings, and a draft of any proposed statement of case. There are cases in which it is likely to be so clear that the trustees ought to proceed as they wish that the costs of making the application, even on a simplified procedure without a hearing and perhaps without defendants, are not justified in comparison with the size of the fund or the matters at issue.

7.3 References in this practice direction to an appropriately qualified lawyer mean one whose qualifications and experience are appropriate to the circumstances of the case. The qualifications should be stated. If the advice is given on formal instructions, the instructions should always be put in evidence as well, so that the court can see the basis on which the advice was given. If it is not, the advice must state fully the basis on which it is given.

7.4 All applications for directions should be supported by evidence showing the value of the trust assets, the significance of the proposed litigation or other course of action for the trust, and why the court's directions are needed. In the case of a pension trust the evidence should include the latest actuarial valuation, and should describe the membership profile and, if a deficit on winding up is likely, the priority provisions and their likely effect.

7.5 On an application for directions about actual or possible litigation the evidence should also state whether (i) any relevant Pre-Action Protocol has been followed; and (ii) the trustees have proposed or undertaken, or intend to propose, mediation by ADR, and (in each case) if not why not.

7.6 If a beneficiary of the trust is a party to the litigation about which directions are sought, with an interest opposed to that of the trustees, that beneficiary should be a defendant to the trustees' application, but any material which would be privileged as regards that beneficiary in the litigation should be put in evidence as exhibits to the trustees' witness statement, and should not be served on the beneficiary. However if the trustees' representatives consider that no harm would be done by the disclosure of all or some part of the material, then that material should be served on that defendant. That defendant may also be excluded from part of the hearing, including that which is devoted to discussion of the material withheld.

CONSULTATION WITH BENEFICIARIES

7.7 The evidence must explain what, if any, consultation there has been with beneficiaries, and with what result. In preparation for an application for directions in respect of litigation, the following guidance is to be followed:

(1) If the trust is a private trust where the beneficiaries principally concerned are not numerous and are all or mainly adult, identified and traceable, the trustees will be expected to have canvassed with all the adult beneficiaries the proposed or possible courses of action before applying for directions.

(2) If it is a private trust with a larger number of beneficiaries, including those not yet born or identified, or children, it is likely that there will nevertheless be some adult beneficiaries principally concerned, with whom the trustees must consult.

(3) In relation to a charitable trust the trustees must have consulted the Attorney-General, through the Treasury Solicitor, as well as the Charity Commissioners whose consent to the application will have been needed under section 33 of the Charities Act 1993.

(4) In relation to a pension trust, unless the members are very few in number, no particular steps by way of consultation with beneficiaries (including, where relevant, employers) or their representatives are required in preparation for the application, though the trustees' evidence should describe any consultation that has in fact taken place. If no consultation has taken place, the court could in some cases direct that meetings of one or more classes of beneficiaries be held to consider the subject matter of the application, possibly as a preliminary to deciding whether a member of a particular class ought to be joined as a defendant, though in a case concerning actual or proposed litigation, steps would need to be considered to protect privileged material from too wide disclosure.

7.8 (1) If the court gives directions allowing the trustees to take, defend or pursue litigation it may do so up to a particular stage in the litigation, requiring the trustees, before they carry on beyond that point, to renew their application to the court. What stage that should be will depend on the likely management of the litigation under the CPR. If the application is to be renewed after disclosure of documents, and disclosed documents need to be shown to the court, it may be necessary to obtain permission to do this from the court in which the other litigation is proceeding.

(2) In such a case the court may sometimes direct that the case be dealt with at that stage without a hearing if the beneficiaries obtain and lodge the written advice of an appropriately qualified lawyer stating that he or they support the continuation of the directions. Any such advice will

be considered by the court and, if thought fit, the trustees will be given a direction allowing them to continue pursuing the proceedings without a hearing.

7.9 In a case of urgency, such as where a limitation period or period for service of proceedings is about to expire, the court may be able to give directions on a summary consideration of the evidence to cover the steps which need to be taken urgently, but limiting those directions so that the application needs to be renewed on fuller consideration at an early stage.

7.10 In any application for directions where a child is a defendant, the court will expect to have put before it the instructions to and advice of an appropriately qualified lawyer as to the benefits and disadvantages of the proposed, and any other relevant, course of action from the point of view of the child beneficiary.

7.11 The master or district judge may give the directions sought though, if the directions relate to actual or proposed litigation, only if it is a plain case, and therefore the master or district judge may think it appropriate to give the directions without a hearing: see the Practice Direction supplementing Part 2: Allocation of Cases to Levels of the Judiciary, para 4.1 and para. 5.1(e), and see also paragraph 6 above. Otherwise the case will be referred to the judge.

7.12 Where a hearing takes place, if the advice of a lawyer has been put in evidence in accordance with paragraph 7.2 or 7.10, that lawyer should if possible appear on the hearing.

PART 65
PROCEEDINGS RELATING TO ANTI-SOCIAL BEHAVIOUR AND HARASSMENT

CONTENTS OF THIS PART

65.1 Scope of this Part

This Part contains rules –

(a) in Section I, about injunctions under the Housing Act 1996;
(b) in Section II, about applications by local authorities under section 91(3) of the Anti-social Behaviour Act 2003 for a power of arrest to be attached to an injunction;
(c) in Section III, about claims for demotion orders under the Housing Act 1985 and Housing Act 1988 and proceedings relating to demoted tenancies;
(d) in Section IV, about anti-social behaviour orders under the Crime and Disorder Act 1998;
(e) in Section V, about claims under section 3 of the Protection from Harassment Act 1997.

Amendments—Inserted by SI 2004/1306.

Practice Direction—See generally PD65 at p 1490.

General note—This Part gathers together in one convenient place the procedural rules which apply to proceedings under various different statutes that have the objective of controlling anti-social behaviour. These fall broadly into three separate categories: ASBOs, breach of which is a criminal offence; anti-social behaviour injunctions, breach of which will be dealt with under the normal procedures for contempt of court; and demoted tenancy orders under the Housing Acts of 1985 and 1998 as amended by ASBA 2003.

If a person against whom an order is sought is a party to existing proceedings, a relevant authority may apply for an ASBO against him and for that purpose may apply if necessary to be joined in the proceedings as a party (Crime and Disorder Act 1998 as amended by Police Reform Act 2002). Under ASBA 2003, the relevant authority may now apply to join a person against whom an order is sought as an additional defendant to existing proceedings, provided that there is some factual connection between the behaviour complained of and the existing proceedings. These provisions are limited to adult defendants but pilot schemes may be introduced from late 2004 in certain courts under which persons under 18 years may be joined as defendants to existing proceedings.

ASBA 2003 introduces new ss 153A to 153E to replace HA 1988, ss 152 and 153 in England only from 30 June 2004. The Welsh Assembly is expected to make the necessary commencement order in September 2004 for proceedings in Wales. These sections enable the county court to make anti-social behaviour injunctions which can include powers of arrest and orders excluding a defendant from a particular area which may include his normal residence.

The provisions covering the new demoted tenancy orders came into force in England on 30 June 2004 but are not expected to come into force in Wales until the end of 2004. The effect of a demotion order is to deprive the tenant who has been guilty of anti-social behaviour of any security which he may have enjoyed for a basic period of one year effectively putting him on probation.

Jurisdiction—Apart from dealing with those brought before the court following arrest under the Protection from Harassment Act 1997 and contempt proceedings under that Act, district judges have jurisdiction to deal with all matters covered by this Part including the making of ASBOs and anti-social behaviour injunctions and dealing with those who have been arrested under either a power of arrest or a warrant of arrest issued by the court.

I Housing Act 1996 Injunctions

65.2 Scope of this Section and interpretation

(1) This Section applies to applications for an injunction and other related proceedings under Chapter III of Part V of the Housing Act 1996 (injunctions against anti-social behaviour).

(2) In this Section 'the 1996 Act' means the Housing Act 1996.

Amendments—Inserted by SI 2004/1306.

65.3 Applications for an injunction

(1) An application for an injunction under Chapter III of Part V of the 1996 Act shall be subject to the Part 8 procedure as modified by this rule and the relevant practice direction.

(2) The application must be –

- (a) made by a claim form in accordance with the relevant practice direction;
- (b) commenced in the court for the district in which the defendant resides or the conduct complained of occurred; and
- (c) supported by a witness statement which must be filed with the claim form.

(3) The claim form must state –

- (a) the matters required by rule 8.2; and
- (b) the terms of the injunction applied for.

(4) An application under this rule may be made without notice and where such an application without notice is made –

- (a) the witness statement in support of the application must state the reasons why notice has not been given; and
- (b) the following rules do not apply –
  - (i) 8.3;
  - (ii) 8.4;
  - (iii) 8.5(2) to (6);
  - (iv) 8.6(1);
  - (v) 8.7; and
  - (vi) 8.8.

(5) In every application made on notice, the application notice must be served, together with a copy of the witness statement, by the claimant on the defendant personally.

(6) An application made on notice may be listed for hearing before the expiry of the time for the defendant to file an acknowledgment of service under rule 8.3, and in such a case –

- (a) the claimant must serve the application notice and witness statement on the defendant not less than two days before the hearing; and
- (b) the defendant may take part in the hearing whether or not he has filed an acknowledgment of service.

Amendments—Inserted by SI 2004/1306; amended by SI 2004/2072.

'relevant practice direction' (r 65.3(1))—See PD65, para 1.1. Form N16A must be used in place of the Pt 8 claim form in any case where no other relief is claimed. If the injunction forms part of a claim for possession, the Pt 55 claim form must be used suitably amended to include the information required by Form N16A.

'supported by a witness statement' (r 65.3(2)(c))—Note that use of an affidavit is no longer mandatory following the Civil Procedure (Amendment No 2) Rules 2004. The normal witness statement supported by a statement of truth is now acceptable.

'without notice applications' (r 65.3(4))—Whenever possible, a draft of the proposed order must be lodged with the application (PD25, para 2.4). See also *Manchester CC v Lee* [2003] EWCA Civ 1256, [2004] 1 WLR 349, [2004] HLR 161, CA and, in particular, the comments of Chadwick and Mummery LLJ for the importance of precision and clarity in the drafting of orders under these sections.

65.4 Injunction containing provisions to which a power of arrest is attached

(1) In this rule 'relevant provision' means a provision of an injunction to which a power of arrest is attached.

(Sections 153C(3) and 153D(4) of the 1996 Act confer powers to attach a power of arrest to an injunction)

(2) Where an injunction contains one or more relevant provisions –

- (a) each relevant provision must be set out in a separate paragraph of the injunction; and
- (b) subject to paragraph (3), the claimant must deliver a copy of the relevant provisions to any police station for the area where the conduct occurred.

(3) Where the injunction has been granted without notice, the claimant must not deliver a copy of the relevant provisions to any police station for the area where the conduct occurred before the defendant has been served with the injunction containing the relevant provisions.

(4) Where an order is made varying or discharging any relevant provision, the claimant must –

- (a) immediately inform the police station to which a copy of the relevant provisions was delivered under paragraph (2)(b); and
- (b) deliver a copy of the order to any police station so informed.

Amendments—Inserted by SI 2004/1306.

'a copy of the relevant provisions' (r 65.4(2)(b))—This requirement follows similar provisions for Family Law Act 1996 injunctions but is not identical. A separate copy of the order containing only those provisions to which a power of arrest has been attached must be prepared for delivery to the appropriate police station.

Service of the order—Service by an alternative method or dispensing with service altogether under r 6.8 or r 6.9 are both possible, although the court will exercise considerable caution in making such an order. Note that the requirement in r 65.4(3) to serve the defendant before delivering a copy to the police station only applies where the order has been made without notice, but it is good practice to apply this procedure to any order made at a hearing at which the defendant was not present.

65.5 Application for warrant of arrest under section 155(3) of the 1996 Act

(1) An application for a warrant of arrest under section 155(3) of the 1996 Act must be made in accordance with Part 23 and may be made without notice.

(2) An applicant for a warrant of arrest under section 155(3) of the 1996 Act must –

- (a) file an affidavit setting out grounds for the application with the application notice; or
- (b) give oral evidence as to the grounds for the application at the hearing.

Amendments—Inserted by SI 2004/1306.

Warrant of arrest—See PD65, para 2.1 for evidential requirements before a warrant can be issued.

65.6 Proceedings following arrest

(1) This rule applies where a person is arrested pursuant to –

- (a) a power of arrest attached to a provision of an injunction; or

(b) a warrant of arrest.

(2) The judge before whom a person is brought following his arrest may –

(a) deal with the matter; or

(b) adjourn the proceedings.

(3) Where the proceedings are adjourned the judge may remand the arrested person in accordance with section 155(2)(b) or (5) of the 1996 Act.

(4) Where the proceedings are adjourned and the arrested person is released –

(a) the matter must be dealt with (whether by the same or another judge) within 28 days of the date on which the arrested person appears in court; and

(b) the arrested person must be given not less than 2 days' notice of the hearing.

(5) An application notice seeking the committal for contempt of court of the arrested person may be issued even if the arrested person is not dealt with within the period mentioned in paragraph (4)(a).

(6) CCR Order 29, rule 1 shall apply where an application is made in a county court to commit a person for breach of an injunction, as if references in that rule to the judge included references to a district judge.

(For applications in the High Court for the discharge of a person committed to prison for contempt of court see RSC Order 52, rule 8. For such applications in the county court see CCR Order 29, rule 3)

Amendments—Inserted by SI 2004/1306.

Procedure on arrest—The rule gives disappointingly little guidance as to the proper procedure to be followed on arrest, which has serious Human Rights Act implications under Arts 5 and 6 of the Convention. The arrested person is entitled to have written notice of the precise breach for which he has been arrested (*Newman v Modern Bookbinders* (2000) [2000] 2 All ER 814) but there is no clear provision whether it is the claimant, the court, or the arresting officer who bears the responsibility for preparing the notice. If the arrested person is likely to be imprisoned in case the breach is proved, he must be offered the chance to obtain legal representation (*King v Read* [1999] 1 FLR 425, [1999] Fam Law 90, CA).

Remand (r 65.6(3))—The rules for remand in custody as set out in HA 1996, Sch 15 are as follows –

(a) remand to police custody for a maximum of 3 days;

(b) remand to prison for a maximum of 8 days at a time;

(c) remand for medical examination and report under s 156 a maximum of three weeks at a time.

The power to remand either on bail or in custody can only be exercised once the court has been satisfied that the arrested person has been lawfully arrested. If the lawfulness of the arrest cannot be established, for example because the arresting officer is not present to give evidence, the arrested person must be discharged. The claimant may then bring proceedings for contempt (see the notes to Sch 2, CCR Ord 29).

Although the Act and PD65, para 3 contain elaborate provisions for remand on bail, there are effectively no provisions for applying any sanction for breach of bail. If the arrested person is not remanded in custody the better course is simply to adjourn to a fixed date (notified to the arrested person there and then) and the court can simply proceed in the arrested person's absence if he fails to attend the adjourned hearing.

Completion of the proceedings—It is not clear whether the provisions of r 3.1(2)(a) would allow the time of 28 days specified in r 65.6(4)(a) to be extended.

65.7 Recognizance

(1) Where, in accordance with paragraph 2(2)(b) of Schedule 15 to the 1996 Act, the court fixes the amount of any recognizance with a view to it being taken subsequently, the recognizance may be taken by –

(a) a judge;
(b) a justice of the peace;
(c) a justices' clerk;
(d) a police officer of the rank of inspector or above or in charge of a police station; or
(e) where the arrested person is in his custody, the governor or keeper of a prison,

with the same consequences as if it had been entered into before the court.

(2) The person having custody of an applicant for bail must release him if satisfied that the required recognizances have been taken.

Amendments—Inserted by SI 2004/1306.

II Applications by Local Authorities for Power of Arrest to be Attached to Injunction

65.8 Scope of this Section and interpretation

(1) This Section applies to applications by local authorities under section 91(3) of the Anti-social Behaviour Act 2003 for a power of arrest to be attached to an injunction.

(Section 91 of the 2003 Act applies to proceedings in which a local authority is a party by virtue of section 222 of the Local Government Act 1972 (power of local authority to bring, defend or appear in proceedings for the promotion or protection of the interests of inhabitants in their area)

(2) In this Section 'the 2003 Act' means the Anti-social Behaviour Act 2003.

Amendments—Inserted by SI 2004/1306.

65.9 Applications under section 91(3) of the 2003 Act for a power of arrest to be attached to any provision of an injunction

(1) An application under section 91(3) of the 2003 Act for a power of arrest to be attached to any provision of an injunction must be made in the proceedings seeking the injunction by –

(a) the claim form;
(b) the acknowledgment of service;
(c) the defence or counterclaim in a Part 7 claim; or
(d) application under Part 23.

(2) Every application must be supported by written evidence.

(3) Every application made on notice must be served personally, together with a copy of the written evidence, by the local authority on the person against whom the injunction is sought not less than 2 days before the hearing.

(Attention is drawn to rule 25.3(3) – applications without notice)

Amendments—Inserted by SI 2004/1306.

General power to apply for injunctions—Local Government Act 1972, s 222 gives a local authority a wide general power to apply for injunctions. A power of arrest may now be added to an injunction granted under this section but this must be specifically applied for in the proceedings seeking the injunction.

'written evidence' (r 65.9(2))—Affidavits are not required for applications under this rule.

65.10 Injunction containing provisions to which a power of arrest is attached

(1) Where a power of arrest is attached to a provision of an injunction on the application of a local authority under section 91(3) of the 2003 Act, the following rules in Section I of this Part shall apply –

(a) rule 65.4; and
(b) paragraphs (1), (2), (4) and (5) of rule 65.6.

(2) CCR Order 29, rule 1 shall apply where an application is made in a county court to commit a person for breach of an injunction.

Amendments—Inserted by SI 2004/1306.

Procedure—See the notes to rr 65.4 and 65.6.

III Demotion Claims, Proceedings Related to Demoted Tenancies and Applications to Suspend the Right to Buy

65.11 Scope of this Section and interpretation

(1) This Section applies to –

(a) claims by a landlord for an order under section 82A of the Housing Act 1985 or under section 6A of the Housing Act 1988 ('a demotion order');
(aa) claims by a landlord for an order under section 121A of the Housing Act 1985 ('a suspension order'); and
(b) proceedings relating to a tenancy created by virtue of a demotion order.

(2) In this Section –

(a) 'a demotion claim' means a claim made by a landlord for a demotion order;
(b) 'a demoted tenancy' means a tenancy created by virtue of a demotion order;
(c) 'suspension claim' means a claim made by a landlord for a suspension order; and
(d) 'suspension period' means the period during which the suspension order suspends the right to buy in relation to the dwelling house.

Amendments—Inserted by SI 2004/1306; amended by SI 2005/2292.

'a demoted tenancy' (r 65.11(2)(b))—Under HA 1985, s 82A, local housing authorities, housing action trusts and registered social landlords may apply to a county court to convert a secure tenancy into a demoted tenancy. The court may only make a demotion order if both satisfied that –

(a) the tenant or any person residing in or visiting the property has engaged, or threatened to engage, in anti-social behaviour or has used the property for unlawful purposes; and
(b) that it is reasonable to make the order.

The effect of the demotion order is to convert the secure/assured tenancy into a demoted tenancy lacking security of tenure. To end a demoted tenancy, the landlord must merely serve notice and provide a procedure for an internal review of the decision to seek possession; in such circumstances the court must grant an order for possession. If, however, no claim for possession is made, then after a period of 12 months the demoted tenancy reverts back to a secure tenancy. Similar provisions under HA 1996, s 6A apply generally to assured tenancies.

65.12 Demotion claims or suspension claims made in the alternative to possession claims

Where a demotion order or suspension order (or both) is claimed in the alternative to a possession order, the claimant must use the Part 55 procedure and Section I of Part 55 applies, except that the claim must be made in the county court for the district in which the property to which the claim relates is situated.

Amendments—Inserted by SI 2004/1306; amended by SI 2005/2292.

'Part 55 procedure'—See generally Pt 55, Section I.

65.13 Other demotion or suspension claims

Where a demotion claim or suspension claim (or both) is made other than in a possession claim, rules 65.14 to 65.19 apply.

Amendments—Inserted by SI 2004/1306; amended by SI 2005/2292.

65.14 Starting a demotion or suspension claim

(1) The claim must be made in the county court for the district in which the property to which the claim relates is situated.

(2) The claim form and form of defence sent with it must be in the forms set out in the relevant practice direction.

(The relevant practice direction and Part 16 provide details about the contents of the particulars of claim)

Amendments—Inserted by SI 2004/1306; amended by SI 2005/2292.

'relevant practice direction' (r 65.14(2))—See generally PD65, paras 6 and 7.

Forms—The following forms are relevant:
- Claim form for a demotion of tenancy – N6;
- Particulars of claim – N122;
- Notice of Issue – N206D;
- Application for injunction (if applicable) – N16A;
- Notes to defendant – N7D;
- Defence form to a claim for demotion of tenancy – N11D.

Costs—See rr 45.2A and 45.4A which apply 'unless the court orders otherwise' (r 45.1(1)).

65.15 Particulars of claim

The particulars of claim must be filed and served with the claim form.

Amendments—Inserted by SI 2004/1306.

'The particulars of claim'—These are in Form N122, and note PD65, para 7.

65.16 Hearing date

(1) The court will fix a date for the hearing when it issues the claim form.

(2) The hearing date will be not less than 28 days from the date of issue of the claim form.

(3) The standard period between the issue of the claim form and the hearing will be not more than 8 weeks.

(4) The defendant must be served with the claim form and the particulars of claim not less than 21 days before the hearing date.

(Rule 3.1(2)(a) provides that the court may extend or shorten the time for compliance with any rule and rule 3.1(2)(b) provides that the court may adjourn or bring forward a hearing)

Amendments—Inserted by SI 2004/1306.

'The court will fix a date for the hearing' (r 65.16(1))—There is scope, by the application of r 3.1(2)(a), for the court to shorten the time between issue and hearing date. See also generally PD65, para 8.

Costs—Unless the court orders otherwise, fixed costs apply in relation to the claimant's solicitor's charges. For the details see Pt 45, Table 2 and r 45.4A(1).

65.17 Defendant's response

(1) An acknowledgment of service is not required and Part 10 does not apply.

(2) Where the defendant does not file a defence within the time specified in rule 15.4 he may take part in any hearing but the court may take his failure to do so into account when deciding what order to make about costs.

(3) Part 12 (default judgment) does not apply.

Amendments—Inserted by SI 2004/1306; amended by SI 2005/2292.

65.18 The hearing

(1) At the hearing fixed in accordance with rule 65.16(1) or at any adjournment of that hearing the court may –

(a) decide the claim; or
(b) give case management directions.

(2) Where the claim is genuinely disputed on grounds which appear to be substantial, case management directions given under paragraph (1)(b) will include the allocation of the claim to a track or directions to enable it to be allocated.

(3) Except where –

(a) the claim is allocated to the fast track or the multi-track; or
(b) the court directs otherwise,

any fact that needs to be proved by the evidence of witnesses at a hearing referred to in paragraph (1) may be proved by evidence in writing.

(Rule 32.2(1) sets out the general rule about evidence. Rule 32.2(2) provides that rule 32.2(1) is subject to any provision to the contrary)

(4) All witness statements must be filed and served at least two days before the hearing.

(5) Where the claimant serves the claim form and particulars of claim, he must produce at the hearing a certificate of service of those documents and rule 6.14(2)(a) does not apply.

Amendments—Inserted by SI 2004/1306; amended by SI 2005/2292.

'At the hearing' (r 65.18(1))—Note also generally the provisions of PD65, para 9.

Allocation of cases to levels of judiciary—Demotion claims may be heard by either circuit judges or by district judges (PD2B, para 11.1(b)).

Costs—See rr 45.2A and 45.4A which apply 'unless the court orders otherwise' (r 45.1(1)).

65.19 Allocation

When the court decides the track for the claim, the matters to which it shall have regard include –

(a) the matters set out in rule 26.8; and
(b) the nature and extent of the conduct alleged.

Amendments—Inserted by SI 2004/1306; amended by SI 2005/2292.

Allocation to the small claims track—It would be unusual to allocate a disputed demotion claim to the small claims track (PD26, para 8.1(1)(c)).

Transfer to a Civil Trial Centre—A disputed demotion claim does not have to be transferred to the local Civil Trial Centre (PD26, para 10.1 and see the notes to para 10.2)

65.20 Proceedings relating to demoted tenancies

A practice direction may make provision about proceedings relating to demoted tenancies.

Amendments—Inserted by SI 2004/1306.

IV Anti-Social Behaviour Orders under the Crime and Disorder Act 1998

65.21 Scope of this Section and interpretation

(1) This Section applies to applications in proceedings in a county court under sub-sections (2), (3) or (3B) of section 1B of the Crime and Disorder Act 1998 by a relevant authority, and to applications for interim orders under section 1D of that Act.

(2) In this Section –

(a) 'the 1998 Act' means the Crime and Disorder Act 1998;
(b) 'relevant authority' has the same meaning as in section 1(1A) of the 1998 Act; and
(c) 'the principal proceedings' means any proceedings in a county court.

Amendments—Inserted by SI 2004/1306.

General note—A county court has no power to grant an ASBO, unless either the party against whom the order is sought is already a party to existing proceedings or the court orders him to be added to existing proceedings in any case where there is a factual connection between the behaviour complained of and the issues arising in those proceedings. Thus, where a relevant authority brings proceedings for possession based upon the behaviour of a person for whom the tenant is responsible under the terms of the tenancy agreement, it may now apply for that person to be joined in the proceedings for the purpose of obtaining an ASBO against him. The facts upon which the order is based as set out in HA 1998, s 1(1) must be proved to the criminal standard (*R (McCann & ors) v Crown Court at Manchester* [2002] UKHL 39, [2002] 3 WLR 1313, [2002] 4 All ER 593, HL).

65.22 Application where the relevant authority is a party in principal proceedings

(1) Subject to paragraph (2) –

(a) where the relevant authority is the claimant in the principal proceedings, an application under section 1B(2) of the 1998 Act for an order under section 1B(4) of the 1998 Act must be made in the claim form; and
(b) where the relevant authority is a defendant in the principal proceedings, an application for an order must be made by application notice which must be filed with the defence.

(2) Where the relevant authority becomes aware of the circumstances that lead it to apply for an order after its claim is issued or its defence filed, the application must be made by application notice as soon as possible thereafter.

(3) Where the application is made by application notice, it should normally be made on notice to the person against whom the order is sought.

Amendments—Inserted by SI 2004/1306.

General note—This rule covers the situation where both the relevant authority and the defendant are parties to proceedings, but there must be a separate cause of action between the parties before a claim for an ASBO can be included in those proceedings.

65.23 Application by a relevant authority to join a person to the principal proceedings

(1) An application under section 1B(3B) of the 1998 Act by a relevant authority which is a party to the principal proceedings to join a person to the principal proceedings must be made –

(a) in accordance with Section I of Part 19;
(b) in the same application notice as the application for an order under section 1B(4) of the 1998 Act against the person; and
(c) as soon as possible after the relevant authority considers that the criteria in section 1B(3A) of the 1998 Act are met.

(2) The application notice must contain –

(a) the relevant authority's reasons for claiming that the person's anti-social acts are material in relation to the principal proceedings; and
(b) details of the anti-social acts alleged.

(3) The application should normally be made on notice to the person against whom the order is sought.

Amendments—Inserted by SI 2004/1306.

General note—See the note to r 65.21 above.

65.24 Application where the relevant authority is not party in principal proceedings

(1) Where the relevant authority is not a party to the principal proceedings –

(a) an application under section 1B(3) of the 1998 Act to be made a party must be made in accordance with Section I of Part 19; and
(b) the application to be made a party and the application for an order under section 1B(4) of the 1998 Act must be made in the same application notice.

(2) The applications –

(a) must be made as soon as possible after the authority becomes aware of the principal proceedings; and
(b) should normally be made on notice to the person against whom the order is sought.

Amendments—Inserted by SI 2004/1306.

General note—This rule covers the situation where the parties to the existing proceedings are the person against whom the ASBO is sought and some other party. Such proceedings might relate to an entirely separate matter such as a road traffic accident. Although there is no formal requirement that there should be some factual connection between the existing proceedings and the behaviour which gives rise to the application for an ASBO, the court has a discretion as to whether or not to grant the application and will apply the overriding objective set out in r 1.1 in deciding whether to do so. The closer the connection between the behaviour complained of and the existing proceedings the more likely it is that the application will succeed.

65.25 Evidence

An application for an order under section 1B(4) of the 1998 Act must be accompanied by written evidence, which must include evidence that section 1E of the 1998 Act has been complied with.

Amendments—Inserted by SI 2004/1306.

'section 1E of the 1998 Act'—This section imposes a specific obligation on applicants to consult with other interested parties before commencing proceedings for an ASBO.

65.26 Application for an interim order

(1) An application for an interim order under section 1D of the 1998 Act must be made in accordance with Part 25.

(2) The application should normally be made –

- (a) in the claim form or application notice seeking the order; and
- (b) on notice to the person against whom the order is sought.

Amendments—Inserted by SI 2004/1306.

General note—The court has power to make an interim order either on notice or without notice if it considers that it is just to do so, see s 1D(2) of the 1998 Act. Schedule 1, Art 6 of HRA 1998 is not engaged at this stage of the proceedings (*R (M) v Secretary of State for Constitutional Affairs and the Lord Chancellor* [2004] EWCA Civ 312, [2004] 1 WLR 2298, [2004] 2 All ER 531, [2004] TLR 197, CA). Interim Orders must be for a fixed period, may be varied, renewed or discharged, and if still in force, end with the determination of the main application (HRA 1998, s 1D(4)).

Service of orders and interim orders—Paragraph 13.1 of PD65 provides for personal service of an interim or final order. The provisions of rr 6.8 and 6.9 dealing with service by an alternative method and dispensing with service are not specifically disapplied to ASBOs. However, a final order must run for at least 2 years from the date of service of the order (HRA 1998, s 1(7)), which would indicate that an order dispensing with service is not possible and any order for service by an alternative method should clearly specify the date upon which service is deemed to have been made.

V Proceedings under the Protection from Harassment Act 1997

65.27 Scope of this Section

This Section applies to proceedings under section 3 of the Protection from Harassment Act 1997 ('the 1997 Act').

Amendments—Inserted by SI 2004/1306.

65.28 Claims under section 3 of the 1997 Act

A claim under section 3 of the 1997 Act –

- (a) shall be subject to the Part 8 procedure; and
- (b) must be commenced –
  - (i) if in the High Court, in the Queen's Bench Division;
  - (ii) if in the county court, in the court for the district in which the defendant resides or carries on business or the court for the district in which the claimant resides or carries on business.

Amendments—Inserted by SI 2004/1306.

Standard of proof—The facts upon which the order under s 3 of the 1997 Act is based must be proved to the criminal standard (*R (McCann & ors) v Crown Court at Manchester* [2002] UKHL 39, [2002] 3 WLR 1313, [2002] 4 All ER 593, HL). Breach of an order made under s 3 is both a criminal offence and a contempt of court.

65.29 Applications for issue of a warrant of arrest under section 3(3) of the 1997 Act

(1) An application for a warrant of arrest under section 3(3) of the 1997 Act –

(a) must be made in accordance with Part 23; and
(b) may be made without notice.

(2) The application notice must be supported by affidavit evidence which must –

(a) set out the grounds for the application;
(b) state whether the claimant has informed the police of the conduct of the defendant as described in the affidavit; and
(c) state whether, to the claimant's knowledge, criminal proceedings are being pursued.

Amendments—Inserted by SI 2004/1306.

'criminal proceedings' (r 65.29(2)(c))—The Act as amended by ASBA 2003 now provides that a defendant who is in breach of an order made under PHA 1997, s 3 may either be dealt with for contempt of court or for the criminal offence, but not both.

65.30 Proceedings following arrest

(1) The judge before whom a person is brought following his arrest may –

(a) deal with the matter; or
(b) adjourn the proceedings.

(2) Where the proceedings are adjourned and the arrested person is released –

(a) the matter must be dealt with (whether by the same or another judge) within 28 days of the date on which the arrested person appears in court; and
(b) the arrested person must be given not less than 2 days' notice of the hearing.

Amendments—Inserted by SI 2004/1306.

Procedure on arrest—See note to r 65.6 above.

Practice Direction – Anti-Social Behaviour and Harassment

This Practice Direction supplements CPR Part 65 (PD65)

SECTION I – HOUSING ACT 1996 INJUNCTIONS

Issuing the claim

1.1 An application for an injunction under Chapter III of Part V of the 1996 Act must be made by form N16A and for the purposes of applying the practice direction that supplements Part 8 to applications under Section I of Part 65, form N16A shall be treated as the Part 8 claim form.

Warrant of arrest on an application under section 155(3) of the 1996 Act

2.1 In accordance with section 155(4) of the 1996 Act, a warrant of arrest on an application under section 155(3) of that Act shall not be issued unless –

(1) the application is substantiated on oath; and
(2) the judge has reasonable grounds for believing that the defendant has failed to comply with the injunction.

Application for bail

3.1 An application for bail by a person arrested under –

(1) a power of arrest attached to an injunction under Chapter III of Part V of the 1996 Act; or
(2) a warrant of arrest issued on an application under section 155(3) of that Act,

may be made either orally or in an application notice.

3.2 An application notice seeking bail must contain –

(1) the full name of the person making the application;
(2) the address of the place where the person making the application is detained at the time when the application is made;
(3) the address where the person making the application would reside if he were to be granted bail;
(4) the amount of the recognizance in which he would agree to be bound; and
(5) the grounds on which the application is made and, where previous application has been refused, full details of any change in circumstances which has occurred since that refusal.

3.3 A copy of the application notice must be served on the person who obtained the injunction.

Remand for medical examination and report

4.1 Section 156(4) of the 1996 Act provides that the judge has power to make an order under section 35 of the Mental Health Act 1983 in certain circumstances. If he does so attention is drawn to section 35(8) of that Act, which provides that a person remanded to hospital under that section may obtain at his own expense an independent report on his mental condition from a registered medical practitioner chosen by him and apply to the court on the basis of it for his remand to be terminated under section 35(7).

SECTION II – DEMOTION OR SUSPENSION

(Suspension claims may be made in England, but may not be made in Wales).

SUSPENSION CLAIMS MADE IN THE ALTERNATIVE TO POSSESSION CLAIMS

5A.1 If the claim relates to a residential property let on a tenancy and if the claim includes a suspension claim, the particulars of claim must –

(1) state that the suspension claim is a claim under section 121A of the 1985 Act;
(2) state which of the bodies the claimant's interest belongs to in order to comply with the landlord condition under section 80 of the 1985 Act;
(3) state details of the conduct alleged; and
(4) explain why it is reasonable to make the suspension order, having regard in particular to the factors set out in section 121A(4) of the 1985 Act.

Demotion claims made in the alternative to possession claims

5.1 If the claim relates to residential property let on a tenancy and if the claim includes a demotion claim, the particulars of claim must –

(1) state whether the demotion claim is a claim under section 82A(2) of the 1985 Act or under section 6A(2) of the 1988 Act;
(2) state whether the claimant is a local housing authority, a housing action trust or a registered social landlord;
(3) provide details of any statement of express terms of the tenancy served on the tenant under section 82A(7) of the 1985 Act or under section 6A(10) of the 1988 Act, as applicable; and
(4) state details of the conduct alleged.

'a claim under section 82A(2) of the (Housing Act) 1985' (para 5.1(1))—That is, a secure tenancy where the landlord is a local housing authority, housing action trust or a registered social landlord.

'a claim under section 6A(2) of the Housing Act 1988' (para 5.1(1))—That is, an assured tenancy where the landlord is a registered social landlord.

'a statement of express terms' (para 5.1(3))—That is, a landlord's statement of the express terms which are to apply to any demoted tenancy ordered by the court.

Other Demotion or Suspension Claims

6.1 Demotion or suspension claims, other than those made in the alternative to possession claims, must be made in the county court for the district in which the property to which the claim relates is situated.

6.2 The claimant must use the appropriate claim form and particulars of claim form set out in Table 1 to the Part 4 practice direction. The defence must be in form N11D as appropriate.

6.3 The claimant's evidence should include details of the conduct alleged, and any other matters relied upon.

Particulars of claim

7.1 In a demotion claim the particulars of claim must –

(1) state whether the demotion claim is a claim under section 82A(2) of the 1985 Act or under section 6A(2) of the 1988 Act;
(2) state whether the claimant is a local housing authority, a housing action trust or a registered social landlord;
(3) identify the property to which the claim relates;
(4) provide the following details about the tenancy to which the demotion claim relates –
 (a) the parties to the tenancy;
 (b) the period of the tenancy;
 (c) the amount of the rent;

(d) the dates on which the rent is payable; and
(e) any statement of express terms of the tenancy served on the tenant under section 82A(7) of the 1985 Act or under section 6A(10) of the 1988 Act, as applicable; and

(5) state details of the conduct alleged.

'a claim under section 82A(2) of the Housing Act 1985' (para 7.1(1))—That is, a secure tenancy where the landlord is a local housing authority, housing action trust or a registered social landlord.

'a claim under section 6A(2) of the Housing Act 1988' (para 7.1(1))—That is, an assured tenancy where the landlord is a registered social landlord.

7.2 In a suspension claim, the particulars of claim must –

(1) state that the suspension claim is a claim under section 121A of the 1985 Act;
(2) state which of the bodies the claimant's interest belongs to in order to comply with the landlord condition under section 80 of the 1985 Act;
(3) identify the property to which the claim relates;
(4) state details of the conduct alleged; and
(5) explain why it is reasonable to make the order, having regard in particular to the factors set out in section 121A(4) of the 1985 Act.

Hearing date

8.1 The court may use its powers under rules 3.1(2)(a) and (b) to shorten the time periods set out in rules 65.16(2), (3) and (4).

8.2 Particular consideration should be given to the exercise of this power if –

(1) the defendant, or a person for whom the defendant is responsible, has assaulted or threatened to assault –
  (a) the claimant;
  (b) a member of the claimant's staff; or
  (c) another resident in the locality;
(2) there are reasonable grounds for fearing such an assault; or
(3) the defendant, or a person for whom the defendant is responsible, has caused serious damage or threatened to cause serious damage to the property or to the home or property of another resident in the locality.

8.3 Where paragraph 8.2 applies but the case cannot be determined at the first hearing fixed under rule 65.16, the court will consider what steps are needed to finally determine the case as quickly as reasonably practicable.

The hearing

9.1 Attention is drawn to rule 65.18(3). Each party should wherever possible include all the evidence he wishes to present in his statement of case, verified by a statement of truth.

9.2 The claimant's evidence should include details of the conduct to which section 153A or 153B of the 1996 Act applies and in respect of which the claim is made.

9.3 If –

(1) the maker of a witness statement does not attend a hearing; and
(2) the other party disputes material evidence contained in the statement,

the court will normally adjourn the hearing so that oral evidence can be given.

'the conduct to which section 153A … of the Housing Act 1996 … applies' (para 9.2)—That is, conduct which is either capable of causing nuisance or annoyance to any person or, alternatively, directly or indirectly relates to or affects the housing management functions of a relevant landlord.

'the conduct to which section … 153B of the Housing Act 1996 … applies' (para 9.2)—That is, conduct which consists of or involves using or threatening to use housing accommodation owned or managed by a relevant landlord for an unlawful purpose.

SECTION III – PROCEEDINGS RELATING TO DEMOTED TENANCIES

Proceedings for the possession of a demoted tenancy

10.1 Proceedings against a tenant of a demoted tenancy for possession must be brought under the procedure in Part 55 (Possession Claims).

Proceedings in relation to a written statement of demoted tenancy terms

11.1 Proceedings as to whether a statement supplied in pursuance to section 143M(4)(b) of the 1996 Act (written statement of certain terms of tenancy) is accurate must be brought under the procedure in Part 8.

Recovery of costs

12.1 Attention is drawn to section 143N(4) of the 1996 Act which provides that if a person takes proceedings under Chapter 1A of the 1996 Act in the High Court which he could have taken in the county court, he is not entitled to recover any costs.

SECTION IV – ANTI-SOCIAL BEHAVIOUR ORDERS UNDER THE CRIME AND DISORDER ACT 1998

Service of an order under sections 1B(4) or 1D of the 1998 Act

13.1 An order under section 1B(4) or an interim order under section 1D of the 1998 Act must be served personally on the defendant.

APPLICATION TO JOIN A PERSON TO THE PRINCIPAL PROCEEDINGS

13.2 Except as provided in paragraph 13.3, an application by a relevant authority under section 1B(3B) of the 1998 Act to join a person to the principal proceedings may only be made against a person aged 18 or over.

PILOT SCHEME: APPLICATION TO JOIN A CHILD TO THE PRINCIPAL PROCEEDINGS

13.3

(1) A pilot scheme shall operate from 1 October 2004 to 31 March 2006 in the county courts specified below, under which a relevant authority may –
   (a) apply under section 1B(3B) of the 1998 Act to join a child to the principal proceedings; and
   (b) if that child is so joined, apply for an order under section 1B(4) of the 1998 Act against him.

(2) In this paragraph, 'child' means a person aged under 18.

(3) The county courts in which the pilot scheme shall operate are Bristol,

Central London, Clerkenwell, Dewsbury, Huddersfield, Leicester, Manchester, Oxford, Tameside, Wigan and Wrexham.

(4) Attention is drawn to the provisions of Part 21 and its practice direction: in particular as to the requirement for a child to have a litigation friend unless the court makes an order under rule 21.2(3), and as to the procedure for appointment of a litigation friend. The Official Solicitor may be invited to act as litigation friend where there is no other willing and suitable person.

(5) Rule 21.3(2)(b) shall not apply to an application under the pilot scheme, and sub-paragraph (6) shall apply instead.

(6) A relevant authority may not, without the permission of the court, take any step in an application to join a child to the principal proceedings, except –

(a) filing and serving its application notice; and

(b) applying for the appointment of a litigation friend under rule 21.6, unless the child has a litigation friend.

SECTION V – PROCEEDINGS UNDER THE PROTECTION FROM HARASSMENT ACT 1997

Warrant of arrest on application under section 3(3) of the 1997 Act

14.1 In accordance with section 3(5) of the 1997 Act, a warrant of arrest on an application under section 3(3) of that Act may only be issued if –

(1) the application is substantiated on oath; and

(2) the judge has reasonable grounds for believing that the defendant has done anything which he is prohibited from doing by the injunction.

PART 66
CROWN PROCEEDINGS

CONTENTS OF THIS PART

66.1 Scope of this Part and interpretation

(1) This Part contains rules for civil proceedings by or against the Crown, and other civil proceedings to which the Crown is a party.

(2) In this Part –

(a) 'the Act' means the Crown Proceedings Act 1947;
(b) 'civil proceedings by the Crown' means the civil proceedings described in section 23(1) of the Act, but excluding the proceedings described in section 23(3);
(c) 'civil proceedings against the Crown' means the civil proceedings described in section 23(2) of the Act, but excluding the proceedings described in section 23(3);
(d) 'civil proceedings to which the Crown is a party' has the same meaning as it has for the purposes of Parts III and IV of the Act by virtue of section 38(4).

Amendments—Inserted by SI 2005/2292.

66.2 Application of the Civil Procedure Rules

These Rules and their practice directions apply to civil proceedings by or against the Crown and to other civil proceedings to which the Crown is a party unless this Part, a practice direction or any other enactment provides otherwise.

Amendments—Inserted by SI 2005/2292.

66.3 Action on behalf of the Crown

(1) Where by reason of a rule, practice direction or court order the Crown is permitted or required –

(a) to make a witness statement,
(b) to swear an affidavit,
(c) to verify a document by a statement of truth;
(d) to make a disclosure statement; or
(e) to discharge any other procedural obligation,

that function shall be performed by an appropriate officer acting on behalf of the Crown.

(2) The court may if necessary nominate an appropriate officer.

Amendments—Inserted by SI 2005/2292.

66.4 Counterclaims, other Part 20 claims, and set-off

(1) In a claim by the Crown for taxes, duties or penalties, the defendant cannot make a counterclaim or other Part 20 claim or raise a defence of set-off.

(2) In any other claim by the Crown, the defendant cannot make a counterclaim or other Part 20 claim or raise a defence of set-off which is based on a claim for repayment of taxes, duties or penalties.

(3) In proceedings by or against the Crown in the name of the Attorney-General, no counterclaim or other Part 20 claim can be made or defence of set-off raised without the permission of the court.

(4) In proceedings by or against the Crown in the name of a government department, no counterclaim or other Part 20 claim can be made or defence of set-off raised without the permission of the court unless the subject-matter relates to that government department.

Amendments—Inserted by SI 2005/2292.

66.5 Applications in revenue matters

(1) This rule sets out the procedure under section 14 of the Act, which allows the Crown to make summary applications in the High Court in certain revenue matters.

(2) The application must be made in the High Court using the Part 8 procedure.

(3) The title of the claim form must clearly identify the matters which give rise to the application.

Amendments—Inserted by SI 2005/2292.

66.6 Enforcement against the Crown

(1) The following rules do not apply to any order against the Crown –

- (a) Parts 69 to 73;
- (b) RSC Orders 45 to 47 and 52; and
- (c) CCR Orders 25 to 29.

(2) In paragraph (1), 'order against the Crown' means any judgment or order against the Crown, a government department, or an officer of the Crown as such, made –

- (a) in civil proceedings by or against the Crown;
- (b) in proceedings in the Administrative Court;
- (c) in connection with an arbitration to which the Crown is a party; or
- (d) in other civil proceedings to which the Crown is a party.

(3) An application under section 25(1) of the Act for a separate certificate of costs payable to the applicant may be made without notice.

Amendments—Inserted by SI 2005/2292.

66.7 Money due from the Crown

(1) None of the following orders –

- (a) a third party debt order under Part 72;
- (b) an order for the appointment of a receiver under Part 69; or
- (c) an order for the appointment of a sequestrator under RSC Order 45,

may be made or have effect in respect of any money due from the Crown.

(2) In paragraph (1), 'money due from the Crown' includes money accruing due, and money alleged to be due or accruing due.

(3) An application for an order under section 27 of the Act –

(a) restraining a person from receiving money payable to him by the Crown; and

(b) directing payment of the money to the applicant or another person,

may be made under Part 23.

(4) The application must be supported by written evidence setting out the facts on which it is based, and in particular identifying the debt from the Crown.

(5) Where the debt from the Crown is money in a National Savings Bank account, the witness must if possible identify the number of the account and the name and address of the branch where it is held.

(6) Notice of the application, with a copy of the written evidence, must be served –

(a) on the Crown, and

(b) on the person to be restrained,

at least 7 days before the hearing.

(7) Rule 72.8 applies to an application under this rule as it applies to an application under rule 72.2 for a third party debt order, except that the court will not have the power to order enforcement to issue against the Crown.

Amendments—Inserted by SI 2005/2292.

Practice Direction – Crown Proceedings

This Practice Direction supplements CPR Part 66 (PD66)

TRANSFER

1.1 Rule 30.3(2) sets out the circumstances to which the court must have regard when considering whether to make an order under section 40(2), 41(1) or 42(2) of the County Courts Act 1984 (transfer between the High Court and County Court), rule 30.2(1) (transfer between county courts) or rule 30.2(4) (transfer between the Royal Courts of Justice and the district registries).

1.2 From time to time the Attorney General will publish a note concerning the organisation of the Government Legal Service and matters relevant to the venue of Crown proceedings, for the assistance of practitioners and judges. When considering questions of venue under rule 30.3(2), the court should have regard to the Attorney General's note in addition to all the other circumstances of the case.

SERVICE OF DOCUMENTS

2.1 In civil proceedings by or against the Crown, documents required to be served on the Crown must be served in accordance with rule 6.5(8).

(The list published under section 17 of the Crown Proceedings Act 1947 of the solicitors acting for the different government departments on whom service is to be effected, and of their addresses is annexed to this Practice Direction).

Annex

List of Authorised Government Departments

CABINET OFFICE

CROWN PROCEEDINGS ACT 1947

List of Authorised Government Departments and the names and addresses for service of the person who is, or is acting for the purposes of the Act as, Solicitor for such Departments, published by the Minister for the Civil Service in pursuance of Section 17 of the Crown Proceedings Act 1947.

This list supersedes the list published on 23 November 2001

AUTHORISED GOVERNMENT DEPARTMENTS	SOLICITOR AND ADDRESSES FOR SERVICE
Advisory, Conciliation and Arbitration Service Assets Recovery Agency Board of Trade Cabinet Office Central Office of Information Crown Prosecution Service Ministry of Defence Department for Education and Skills Director General of Electricity Supply for Northern Ireland Department for Transport Export Credits Guarantee Department Director General of Fair Trading Department for International Development Foreign and Commonwealth Office Director General of Gas for Northern Ireland Government Actuary's Department Health and Safety Executive Her Majesty's Chief Inspector of Schools in England Her Majesty's Chief Inspector of Schools in Wales Home Office Lord Chancellor's Department Department for Culture, Media and Sport National Savings and Investments Northern Ireland Office Office for National Statistics Office of the Deputy Prime Minister Office of HM Paymaster General Ordnance Survey Privy Council Office Public Record Office Public Works Loan Board The Rail Regulator The International Rail Regulator Royal Mint Serious Fraud Office Director General of Telecommunications Department of Trade and Industry Her Majesty's Treasury Wales Office (Office of the Secretary of State for Wales) (see Note (3))	The Treasury Solicitor Queen Anne's Chambers 28 Broadway Westminster London SW1H 9JS (see Notes (1) and (2))

AUTHORISED GOVERNMENT DEPARTMENTS	SOLICITOR AND ADDRESSES FOR SERVICE
Department for Environment, Food and Rural Affairs (see Note (3)) Forestry Commissioners	The Solicitor to the Department for Environment, Food and Rural Affairs Nobel House 17 Smith Square London SW1P 3JR
Commissioners of Customs and Excise	The Solicitor for the Customs and Excise New King's Beam House 22 Upper Ground London SE1 9PJ
Commissioners of Inland Revenue	The Solicitor of Inland Revenue Somerset House The Strand London WC2R 1LB
Crown Estate Commissioners	The Solicitor to the Crown Estate Commissioners Crown Estate Office 16 Carlton House Terrace London SW1Y 5AH
Department of Health Department for Work and Pensions Food Standards Agency	The Solicitor to the Department for Work and Pensions and the Department of Health New Court 48 Carey Street London WC2A 2LS
Director General of Water Services	Head of Legal Services The Office of Water Services Centre City Tower 7 Hill Street Birmingham B5 4UA
National Assembly for Wales	The Counsel General to the National Assembly for Wales Cathays Park Cardiff CF10 3NQ
Gas and Electricity Markets Authority	General Counsel Office of Gas and Electricity Markets 9 Millbank London SW1P 3GE
Postal Services Commission	The Chief Legal Adviser Postal Services Commission Hercules House 6 Hercules Road London SE1 7DB

NOTES

(1) Section 17(3) and section 18 of the Crown Proceedings Act 1947 provide as follows:

17(3) Civil proceedings against the Crown shall be instituted against the appropriate authorised Government department, or, if none of the authorised Government departments is appropriate or the person instituting the proceedings has any reasonable doubt whether any and if so which of those departments is appropriate, against the Attorney General.

18 All documents required to be served on the Crown for the purpose of or in connection with any civil proceedings by or against the Crown shall, if those proceedings are by or against an authorised Government department, be served on the solicitor, if any, for that department, or the person, if any, acting for the purposes of this Act as solicitor for that department, or if there is no such solicitor and no person so acting, or if the proceedings are brought by or against the Attorney General, on the Solicitor for the affairs of His Majesty's Treasury.

(2) The above-mentioned provisions do not apply to Scotland, where in accordance with the Crown Suits (Scotland) Act 1857, as amended by the Scotland Act 1998, civil proceedings against the Crown (other than the Scottish Administration) or any Government Department (other than the Scottish Executive) may be directed against the Advocate General for Scotland. The Advocate General's address for service is the Office of the Solicitor to the Advocate General for Scotland, Victoria Quay, Edinburgh EH6 6QQ. Civil proceedings against the Scottish Administration may be directed against the Scottish Ministers at St.Andrew's House, Edinburgh EH1 3DG, or against the Lord Advocate for and on behalf of the Scottish Executive. The Lord Advocate's address for service is 25 Chambers Street, Edinburgh, EH1 1LA.

(3) The Solicitor and address for service for the purposes of or in connection with civil proceedings brought by or against the Crown which relate to those matters for which the Secretary of State is responsible in Wales and for which the Secretary of State for Environment, Food and Rural Affairs is responsible is the Solicitor to the Department for Environment, Food and Rural Affairs, Nobel House, 17 Smith Square, London, SW1P 3JR.

The Treasury Solicitor is the Solicitor acting for the Wales Office (Office of the Secretary of State for Wales) in all other civil proceedings affecting that Office.

CABINET OFFICE
WHITEHALL
LONDON SW1

Andrew Turnbull

(Signed) SIR ANDREW TURNBULL
5 April **2003**

PART 67
PROCEEDINGS RELATING TO SOLICITORS

CONTENTS OF THIS PART

67.1 Scope and interpretation

(1) This Part contains rules about the following types of proceedings relating to solicitors –

(a) proceedings to obtain an order for a solicitor to deliver a bill or cash account and proceedings in relation to money or papers received by a solicitor (rule 67.2);
(b) proceedings under Part III of the Solicitors Act 1974 relating to the remuneration of solicitors (rule 67.3); and
(c) proceedings under Schedule 1 to the Solicitors Act 1974 arising out of the Law Society's intervention in a solicitor's practice (rule 67.4).

(2) In this Part –

'the Act' means the Solicitors Act 1974; and
'LLP' means limited liability partnership.

(Part 48 and Section 56 of the Costs Practice Direction contain provisions about the procedure and basis for the detailed assessment of solicitor and client costs under Part III of the Act)

(The practice direction supplementing Part 52 contains provisions about appeals to the High Court from the Solicitors Disciplinary Tribunal under section 49 of the Act)

Amendments—Inserted by SI 2004/3419.

Derivation—This Part replaces the former Sch 1, RSC Ord 106 concerning the courts' exercise of jurisdiction in relation to solicitors.
Reference should also be made to rr 48.8 and 48.10 and to PDCosts, Section 56.

Forms—Relevant to Solicitors Act detailed assessments are Precedents J, K, L, M and P of the Schedule to PDCosts.

67.2 Power to order solicitor to deliver cash account etc

(1) Where the relationship of solicitor and client exists or has existed, the orders which the court may make against the solicitor, on the application of the client or his personal representatives, include any of the following –

(a) to deliver a bill or cash account;
(b) to pay or deliver up any money or securities;
(c) to deliver a list of the moneys or securities which the solicitor has in his possession or control on behalf of the applicant;
(d) to pay into or lodge in court any such money or securities.

(2) An application for an order under this rule must be made –

(a) by Part 8 claim form; or

(b) if the application is made in existing proceedings, by application notice in accordance with Part 23.

(3) If the solicitor alleges that he has a claim for costs against the applicant, the court may make an order for –

(a) the detailed assessment and payment of those costs; and

(b) securing the payment of the costs, or protecting any solicitor's lien.

Amendments—Inserted by SI 2004/3419.

67.3 Proceedings under Part III of the Act

(1) A claim for an order under Part III of the Act for the assessment of costs payable to a solicitor by his client –

(a) which –

(i) relates to contentious business done in a county court; and

(ii) is within the financial limit of the county court's jurisdiction specified in section 69(3) of the Act,

may be made in that county court;

(b) in every other case, must be made in the High Court.

(Rule 30.2 makes provision for any county court to transfer the proceedings to another county court for detailed assessment of costs)

(Provisions about the venue for detailed assessment proceedings are contained in rule 47.4, Section 31 of the Costs Practice Direction and the Costs Pilot Scheme Practice Direction supplementing Part 47)

(2) A claim for an order under Part III of the Act must be made –

(a) by Part 8 claim form; or

(b) if the claim is made in existing proceedings, by application notice in accordance with Part 23.

(A model form of claim form is annexed to the Costs Practice Direction)

(3) A claim in the High Court under Part III of the Act may be determined by –

(a) a High Court judge;

(b) a Master, a costs judge or a district judge of the Principal Registry of the Family Division; or

(c) a district judge, if the costs are for –

(i) contentious business done in proceedings in the district registry of which he is the district judge;

(ii) contentious business done in proceedings in a county court within the district of that district registry; or

(iii) non-contentious business.

Amendments—Inserted by SI 2004/3419.

67.4 Proceedings under Schedule 1 to the Act

(1) Proceedings in the High Court under Schedule 1 to the Act must be brought –

(a) in the Chancery Division; and

(b) by Part 8 claim form, unless paragraph (4) below applies.

(2) The heading of the claim form must state that the claim relates to a solicitor and is made under Schedule 1 to the Act.

(3) Where proceedings are brought under paragraph 6(4) or 9(8) of Schedule 1 to the Act, the court will give directions and fix a date for the hearing immediately upon issuing the claim form.

(4) If the court has made an order under Schedule 1 to the Act, any subsequent application for an order under that Schedule which has the same parties may be made by a Part 23 application in the same proceedings.

(5) The table below sets out who must be made a defendant to each type of application under Schedule 1.

Defendants to applications under Schedule 1 to the Act

Paragraph of Schedule 1 under which the application is made	*Defendant to application*
Paragraph 5	if the application relates to money held on behalf of an individual solicitor, the solicitor if the application relates to money held on behalf of a firm, every partner in the firm if the application relates to money held on behalf of a LLP or other corporation, the LLP or other corporation
Paragraph 6(4) or 9(8)	the Law Society
Paragraph 8, 9(4), 9(5) or 9(6)	the person against whom the Law Society is seeking an order
Paragraph 9(10)	the person from whom the Law Society took possession of the documents which it wishes to dispose of or destroy
Paragraph 10	if the application relates to postal packets addressed to an individual solicitor, the solicitor if the application relates to postal packets addressed to a firm, every partner in the firm if the application relates to postal packets addressed to a LLP or other corporation, the LLP or other corporation
Paragraph 11	the trustee whom the Law Society is seeking to replace and, if he is a co-trustee, the other trustees of the trust

(6) At any time after the Law Society has issued an application for an order under paragraph 5 of Schedule 1 to the Act, the court may, on an application by the Society –

(a) make an interim order under that paragraph to have effect until the hearing of the application; and

(b) order the defendant, if he objects to the order being continued at the hearing, to file and serve written evidence showing cause why the order should not be continued.

Amendments—Inserted by SI 2004/3419.

Practice Direction – Proceedings Relating to Solicitors

This Practice Direction supplements CPR Part 67 (PD67)

GENERAL

1 This Practice Direction applies to proceedings under Rule 67.2 and to the following types of claim under Rule 67.3 and Part III of the Solicitors Act 1974 ('the Act'):

(1) an application under section 57(5) of the Act for a costs officer to enquire into the facts and certify whether a non-contentious business agreement should be set aside or the amount payable under it reduced;

(2) a claim under section 61(1) of the Act for the court to enforce or set aside a contentious business agreement and determine questions as to its validity and effect;

(3) a claim by a client under s 61(3) of the Act for a costs officer to examine a contentious business agreement as to its fairness and reasonableness;

(4) where the amount agreed under a contentious business agreement has been paid, a claim under section 61(5) of the Act for the agreement to be re-opened and the costs assessed;

(5) proceedings under section 62 of the Act for the examination of a contentious business agreement, where the client makes the agreement as a representative of a person whose property will be chargeable with the amount payable;

(6) proceedings under section 63 of the Act where, after some business has been done under a contentious business agreement, but before the solicitor has wholly performed it:
   (a) the solicitor dies or becomes incapable of acting; or
   (b) the client changes solicitor;

(7) where an action is commenced on a gross sum bill, an application under section 64(3) of the Act for an order that the bill be assessed;

(8) a claim under section 68 of the Act for the delivery by a solicitor of a bill of costs and for the delivery up of, or otherwise in relation to, any documents;

(9) an application under section 69 of the Act for an order that the solicitor be at liberty to commence an action to recover his costs within one month of delivery of the bill;

(10) a claim under section 70(1) of the Act, by the party chargeable with the solicitor's bill, for an order that the bill be assessed and that no action be taken on the bill until the assessment is completed;

(11) a claim under section 70(2) of the Act, by either party, for an order that the bill be assessed and that no action be commenced or continued on the bill until the assessment is completed;

(12) a claim under section 70(3) of the Act, by the party chargeable with the bill, for detailed assessment showing special circumstances;

(13) a claim under section 71(1) of the Act, by a person other than the party chargeable with the bill, for detailed assessment;

(14) a claim under section 71(3) of the Act, by any person interested in any property out of which a trustee, executor or administrator has paid or is entitled to pay a solicitor's bill, for detailed assessment; and

(15) a claim by a solicitor under section 73 of the Act for a charging order.

PROCEEDINGS IN THE SUPREME COURT COSTS OFFICE

2.1 Where a claim to which this practice direction applies is made by Part 8 claim form in the High Court in London –

(1) if the claim is of a type referred to in paragraphs 1(1) to (5), it must be issued in the Supreme Court Costs Office;

(2) in any other case, the claim may be issued in the Supreme Court Costs Office.

2.2 A claim which is made by Part 8 claim form in a district registry or by Part 23 application notice in existing High Court proceedings may be referred to the Supreme Court Costs Office.

JURISDICTION AND ALLOCATION OF CLAIMS BETWEEN JUDICIARY

3.1 Rule 67.3(3) makes provision about jurisdiction to determine claims under Part III of the Act.

3.2 Claims for any of the orders listed in paragraph 1 should normally be made to a Master, costs judge or district judge. Only exceptional circumstances will justify making the claim directly to a High Court Judge.

3.3 Paragraph 1 of the practice direction supplementing Part 23 sets out the circumstances in which a matter may be referred to a judge.

EVIDENCE IN PROCEEDINGS FOR ORDER FOR DETAILED ASSESSMENT

4 Where a Part 8 claim is brought for an order for the detailed assessment of a solicitor's bill of costs, the parties are not required to comply with Rule 8.5 unless:

(1) the claim will be contested; or

(2) the court directs that the parties should comply with Rule 8.5.

DRAWING UP AND SERVICE OF ORDERS

5 Unless the court orders otherwise, an order in proceedings in the Supreme Court Costs Office to which this practice direction applies shall be drawn up and served by the party who made the relevant claim or application.

PART 68
REFERENCES TO THE EUROPEAN COURT

CONTENTS OF THIS PART

Practice Direction—This Part is supplemented by a practice direction – PD68 – which is set out at p 1510.

68.1 Interpretation

In this Part –

(a) 'the court' means the court making the order;
(b) 'the European Court' means the Court of Justice of the European Communities;
(c) 'order' means an order referring a question to the European Court for a preliminary ruling under –
  (i) article 234 of the Treaty establishing the European Community;
  (ii) article 150 of the Euratom Treaty;
  (iii) article 41 of the ECSC Treaty;
  (iv) the Protocol of 3 June 1971 on the interpretation by the European Court of the Convention of 27 September 1968 on Jurisdiction and the Enforcement of Judgments in Civil and Commercial Matters; or
  (v) the Protocol of 19 December 1988 on the interpretation by the European Court of the Convention of 19 June 1980 on the Law applicable to Contractual Obligations.

Amendments—Inserted by SI 2002/2058.

68.2 Making of order of reference

(1) An order may be made at any stage of the proceedings –

(a) by the court of its own initiative; or
(b) on an application by a party in accordance with Part 23.

(2) An order may not be made –

(a) in the High Court, by a Master or district judge;
(b) in a county court, by a district judge.

(3) The request to the European Court for a preliminary ruling must be set out in a schedule to the order, and the court may give directions on the preparation of the schedule.

Amendments—Inserted by SI 2002/2058.

68.3 Transmission to the European Court

(1) The Senior Master will send a copy of the order to the Registrar of the European Court.

(2) Where an order is made by a county court, the proper officer will send a copy of it to the Senior Master for onward transmission to the European Court.

(3) Unless the court orders otherwise, the Senior Master will not send a copy of the order to the European Court until –

- (a) the time for appealing against the order has expired; or
- (b) any application for permission to appeal has been refused, or any appeal has been determined.

Amendments—Inserted by SI 2002/2058.

68.4 Stay of proceedings

Where an order is made, unless the court orders otherwise the proceedings will be stayed until the European Court has given a preliminary ruling on the question referred to it.

Amendments—Inserted by SI 2002/2058.

Practice Direction – References to the European Court

This Practice Direction supplements CPR Part 68 (PD68)

WORDING OF REFERENCES

1.1 Where the court intends to refer a question to the European Court it will welcome suggestions from the parties for the wording of the reference. However the responsibility for settling the terms of the reference lies with the English court and not with the parties.

1.2 The reference should identify as clearly and succinctly as possible the question on which the court seeks the ruling of the European Court. In choosing the wording of the reference, it should be remembered that it will need to be translated into many other languages.

1.3 The court will incorporate the reference in its order. Scheduled to the order should be a document –

- (1) giving the full name of the referring court;
- (2) identifying the parties;
- (3) summarising the nature and history of the proceedings, including the salient facts, indicating whether these are proved or admitted or assumed;
- (4) setting out the relevant rules of national law;
- (5) summarising the relevant contentions of the parties;
- (6) explaining why a ruling of the European Court is sought; and
- (7) identifying the provisions of Community law which it is being requested to interpret.

1.4 Where, as will often be convenient, some of these matters are in the form of a judgment, passages of the judgment not relevant to the reference should be omitted.

TRANSMISSION TO THE EUROPEAN COURT

2.1 The order containing the reference, and the document scheduled to it, should be sent to The Senior Master, Room E115, Queen's Bench Division, Royal Courts of Justice, Strand, London WC2A 2LL, for onward transmission to the European Court.

2.2 The relevant court file should also be sent to the Senior Master at the above address.

EUROPEAN COURT INFORMATION NOTE

3 There is annexed to this Practice Direction an Information Note issued by the European Court. The reference in the opening passage to Article 177 of the EC Treaty should now be read as a reference to Article 234.

COURT OF JUSTICE OF THE EUROPEAN COMMUNITIES

INFORMATION NOTE ON REFERENCES BY NATIONAL COURTS FOR PRELIMINARY RULINGS

The development of the Community legal order is largely the result of cooperation established between the Court of Justice of the European Communities and the national courts and tribunals through the preliminary ruling procedure provided for in Article 177 of the EC Treaty and the corresponding provisions of the ECSC and Euratom Treaties.

1 A preliminary ruling procedure is also provided for by the protocols to several conventions concluded by the Member States, in particular the Brussels Convention on Jurisdiction and the Enforcement of Judgments in Civil and Commercial Matters.

In order to make this cooperation more effective, and thus to enable the Court of Justice to meet the expectations of national courts more suitably by providing answers to preliminary questions which are of assistance to them, this Note provides information for all interested parties, in particular the national courts.

The Note is for information only and does not have any regulatory or interpretative effect in relation to the provisions which govern the preliminary ruling procedure. It merely contains practical information which, in the light of experience accumulated in the application of the preliminary ruling procedure, may help to prevent the kind of difficulties which the Court has sometimes encountered.

1. Any court or tribunal of a Member State may ask the Court of Justice to interpret a rule of Community law, whether contained in the Treaties or in acts of secondary law, if it considers that that is necessary for it to give judgment in a case pending before it.

Courts against whose decisions there is no judicial remedy under national law must refer questions of interpretation arising before them to the Court of Justice, unless the Court has already ruled on the point or unless the correct application of the rule of Community law is obvious.

1 Judgment in Case 283/81 *CILFIT v Ministry of Health* [1982] ECR 3415.

2. The Court of Justice has jurisdiction to rule on the validity of acts of the Community institutions. National courts may reject a pleas challenging the

validity of an act. All national courts – even those whose decisions are still open to appeal – raising the question of the validity of a Community act must refer that question to the Court of Justice.

1 Judgment in Case 314/85 *Foto-Frost v Hauptzollamt Lübeck-Ost* [1987] ECR 4199.

However, if a national court has serious doubts about the validity of a Community act on which a national measure is based, it may exceptionally suspend application of that measure temporarily or grant other interim relief with respect to it. It must then refer the question of validity to the Court of Justice, stating the reasons for which it considers that the Community act is not valid.

1 Judgments in Joined Cases C-143/88 and C-92/89 *Zuckerfabrik Süderdithmarschen and Zuckerfabrik Soest* [1991] ECR I-415 and in Case C-465/93 *Atlanta Fruchthandelsgesellschaft* [1995] ECR I-3761.

3. Questions referred for a preliminary ruling must concern the interpretation or validity of a provision of Community law only, since the Court of Justice does not have jurisdiction to interpret national law or assess its validity. It is for the referring court to apply the relevant provision of Community law in the specific case pending before it.

4. The decision by which a national court or tribunal refers a question to the Court of Justice for a preliminary ruling may be in any form allowed by national law as regards procedural steps. The reference of a question or questions to the Court of Justice generally causes the national proceedings to be stayed until the Court gives its ruling, but the decision to stay proceedings is one which the national court alone must take in accordance with its own national law.

5. The decision making the reference and containing the question or questions referred to the Court will have to be translated by the Court's translators into the other official languages of the Community. Questions concerning the interpretation or validity of Community law are frequently of general interest and the Member States and Community institutions are entitled to submit observations. It is therefore desirable that the decision making the reference should be drafted as clearly and precisely as possible.

6. It must contain a statement of reasons which is succinct but sufficiently complete to give the Court, and those to whom the decision must be notified (the Member States, the Commission, and in certain cases the Council and the European Parliament), a clear understanding of the factual and legal context of the main proceedings.

1 Judgment in Joined Cases C-320/90, C-321/90 and C-322/90 *Telemarsicabruzzo* [1993] ECR I-393.

In particular, it must include an account of the facts which are essential for understanding the full legal significance of the main proceedings, an account of the points of law which may apply, a statement of the reasons which prompted the national court to refer the question or questions to the Court of Justice and, if need be, a summary of the arguments of the parties. The purpose of all this is to put the Court of Justice in a position to give the national court an answer which will be of assistance to it.

The decision making the reference must also be accompanied by copies of the documents needed for a proper understanding of the case, especially the text of the applicable national provisions. However, as the case-file or documents annexed to the decision making the reference are not always translated in full into the other official languages of the Community, the national court must make sure that its decision includes all the relevant information.

7. A national court or tribunal may refer a question to the Court of Justice for a preliminary ruling as soon as it finds that a ruling on the point or points of interpretation or validity is necessary to enable it to give judgment. It must be stressed, however, that it is not for the Court of Justice to decide issues of fact or differences of opinion as to the interpretation or application of rules of national law. It is therefore desirable that a decision to make a reference should not be taken until the national proceedings have reached a stage where the national court is able to define, if only hypothetically, the factual and legal context of the question. In any event, the administration of justice may well be best served by waiting to refer a question for a preliminary ruling until both sides have been heard.

1 Judgment in Case 70/77 *Simmenthal v Amministrazione delle Finanze dello Stato* [1978] ECR 1453.

8. The decision making the reference and the relevant documents are to be sent by the national court directly to the Court of Justice, by registered post (addressed to the Registry of the Court of Justice of the European Communities, L-2925 Luxembourg, telephone 352-43031). The Court Registry will stay in contact with the national court until judgment is given, and will send it copies of the various documents (written observations, Report for the Hearing, Opinion of the Advocate General). The Court will also send its judgment to the national court. It would be grateful to receive word that its judgment has been applied in the national proceedings and a copy of the national court's final decision.

9. Proceedings for a preliminary ruling before the Court of Justice are free of charge. The Court does not rule on costs.

PART 69
COURT'S POWER TO APPOINT A RECEIVER

CONTENTS OF THIS PART

Practice Direction—This Part is supplemented by a practice direction – PD69 – which is set out at p 1517.

69.1 Scope of this Part

(1) This Part contains provisions about the court's power to appoint a receiver.

(2) In this Part 'receiver' includes a manager.

Amendments—Inserted by SI 2002/2058.

69.2 Court's power to appoint receiver

(1) The court may appoint a receiver –

(a) before proceedings have started;
(b) in existing proceedings; or
(c) on or after judgment.

(2) A receiver must be an individual.

(3) The court may at any time –

(a) terminate the appointment of a receiver; and
(b) appoint another receiver in his place.

(The practice direction describes the powers for the court to appoint a receiver)

Amendments—Inserted by SI 2002/2058.

69.3 How to apply for the appointment of a receiver

An application for the appointment of a receiver –

(a) may be made without notice; and
(b) must be supported by written evidence.

Amendments—Inserted by SI 2002/2058.

69.4 Service of order appointing receiver

An order appointing a receiver must be served by the party who applied for it on –

(a) the person appointed as receiver;
(b) unless the court orders otherwise, every other party to the proceedings; and
(c) such other persons as the court may direct.

Amendments—Inserted by SI 2002/2058.

69.5 Security

(1) The court may direct that before a receiver begins to act or within a specified time he must either –

(a) give such security as the court may determine; or
(b) file and serve on all parties to the proceedings evidence that he already has in force sufficient security,

to cover his liability for his acts and omissions as a receiver.

(2) The court may terminate the appointment of the receiver if he fails to –

(a) give the security; or
(b) satisfy the court as to the security he has in force,

by the date specified.

Amendments—Inserted by SI 2002/2058.

69.6 Receiver's application for directions

(1) The receiver may apply to the court at any time for directions to assist him in carrying out his function as a receiver.

(2) The court, when it gives directions, may also direct the receiver to serve on any person –

(a) the directions; and
(b) the application for directions.

(The practice direction makes provision for the form of applications by, and directions to, a receiver)

Amendments—Inserted by SI 2002/2058.

69.7 Receiver's remuneration

(1) A receiver may only charge for his services if the court –

(a) so directs; and
(b) specifies the basis on which the receiver is to be remunerated.

(2) The court may specify –

(a) who is to be responsible for paying the receiver; and
(b) the fund or property from which the receiver is to recover his remuneration.

(3) If the court directs that the amount of a receiver's remuneration is to be determined by the court –

(a) the receiver may not recover any remuneration for his services without a determination by the court; and
(b) the receiver or any party may apply at any time for such a determination to take place.

(4) Unless the court orders otherwise, in determining the remuneration of a receiver the court shall award such sum as is reasonable and proportionate in all the circumstances and which takes into account –

(a) the time properly given by him and his staff to the receivership;
(b) the complexity of the receivership;
(c) any responsibility of an exceptional kind or degree which falls on the receiver in consequence of the receivership;
(d) the effectiveness with which the receiver appears to be carrying out, or to have carried out, his duties; and
(e) the value and nature of the subject matter of the receivership.

(5) The court may refer the determination of a receiver's remuneration to a costs judge.

Amendments—Inserted by SI 2002/2058.

69.8 Accounts

(1) The court may order a receiver to prepare and serve accounts.

(The practice direction contains provisions about directions for the preparation and service of accounts)

(2) A party served with such accounts may apply for an order permitting him to inspect any document in the possession of the receiver relevant to those accounts.

(3) Any party may, within 14 days of being served with the accounts, serve notice on the receiver –

(a) specifying any item in the accounts to which he objects;
(b) giving the reason for such objection; and
(c) requiring the receiver, within 14 days of receipt of the notice, either –
    (i) to notify all the parties who were served with the accounts that he accepts the objection; or
    (ii) if he does not accept the objection, to apply for an examination of the accounts in relation to the contested item.

(4) When the receiver applies for the examination of the accounts he must at the same time file –

(a) the accounts; and
(b) a copy of the notice served on him under this rule.

(5) If the receiver fails to comply with paragraph (3)(c) of this rule, any party may apply to the court for an examination of the accounts in relation to the contested item.

(6) At the conclusion of its examination of the accounts the court will certify the results.

(The practice direction supplementing Part 40 provides for inquiries into accounts)

Amendments—Inserted by SI 2002/2058.

69.9 Non-compliance by receiver

(1) If a receiver fails to comply with any rule, practice direction or direction of the court the court may order him to attend a hearing to explain his non-compliance.

(2) At the hearing the court may make any order it considers appropriate, including –

- (a) terminating the appointment of the receiver;
- (b) reducing the receiver's remuneration or disallowing it altogether; and
- (c) ordering the receiver to pay the costs of any party.

(3) Where –

- (a) the court has ordered a receiver to pay a sum of money into court; and
- (b) the receiver has failed to do so,

the court may order him to pay interest on that sum for the time he is in default at such rate as it considers appropriate.

Amendments—Inserted by SI 2002/2058.

69.10 Application for discharge of receiver

(1) A receiver or any party may apply for the receiver to be discharged on completion of his duties.

(2) The application notice must be served on the persons who were required under rule 69.4 to be served with the order appointing the receiver.

Amendments—Inserted by SI 2002/2058; amended by SI 2004/1306.

69.11 Order discharging or terminating appointment of receiver

(1) An order discharging or terminating the appointment of a receiver may –

- (a) require him to pay into court any money held by him; or
- (b) specify the person to whom he must pay any money or transfer any assets still in his possession; and
- (c) make provision for the discharge or cancellation of any guarantee given by the receiver as security.

(2) The order must be served on the persons who were required under rule 69.4 to be served with the order appointing the receiver.

Amendments—Inserted by SI 2002/2058.

Practice Direction – Court's Power to Appoint a Receiver

This Practice Direction supplements CPR Part 69 (PD69)

COURT'S POWER TO APPOINT RECEIVER

1.1 The court's powers to appoint a receiver are set out in –

- (1) section 37 of the Supreme Court Act 1981 (powers of the High Court with respect to injunctions and receivers);

(2) section 38 of the County Courts Act 1984 (remedies available in county courts); and
(3) section 107 of the County Courts Act 1984 (receivers by way of equitable execution.

APPLICATIONS BEFORE PROCEEDINGS ARE STARTED – RULE 69.2(1)(A)

2.1 The court will normally only consider an application for the appointment of a receiver before proceedings are started after notice of the application has been served.

2.2 Rule 25.2(2) contains provisions about the grant of an order before proceedings are started.

RELATED INJUNCTIONS

3.1 If a person applies at the same time for –

(1) the appointment of a receiver; and
(2) a related injunction,

he must use the same claim form or application notice for both applications.

3.2 The second practice direction supplementing Part 2 (Allocation of Cases to Levels of Judiciary) sets out who may grant injunctions. Among other things, it provides that a master or a district judge may grant an injunction related to an order appointing a receiver by way of equitable execution.

EVIDENCE IN SUPPORT OF AN APPLICATION – RULE 69.3

4.1 The written evidence in support of an application for the appointment of a receiver must –

(1) explain the reasons why the appointment is required;
(2) give details of the property which it is proposed that the receiver should get in or manage, including estimates of –
    (a) the value of the property; and
    (b) the amount of income it is likely to produce;
(3) if the application is to appoint a receiver by way of equitable execution, give details of –
    (a) the judgment which the applicant is seeking to enforce;
    (b) the extent to which the debtor has failed to comply with the judgment;
    (c) the result of any steps already taken to enforce the judgment; and
    (d) why the judgment cannot be enforced by any other method; and
(4) if the applicant is asking the court to allow the receiver to act –
    (a) without giving security; or
    (b) before he has given security or satisfied the court that he has security in place,

    explain the reasons why that is necessary.

4.2 In addition, the written evidence should normally identify an individual whom the court is to be asked to appoint as receiver ('the nominee'), and should –

(1) state the name, address and position of the nominee;
(2) include written evidence by a person who knows the nominee, stating

that he believes the nominee is a suitable person to be appointed as receiver, and the basis of that belief; and
(3) be accompanied by written consent, signed by the nominee, to act as receiver if appointed.

4.3 If the applicant does not nominate a person to be appointed as receiver, or if the court decides not to appoint the nominee, the court may –

(1) order that a suitable person be appointed as receiver; and
(2) direct any party to nominate a suitable individual to be appointed.

4.4 A party directed to nominate a person to be appointed as receiver must file written evidence containing the information required by paragraph 4.2 and accompanied by the written consent of the nominee.

APPOINTMENT OF RECEIVER TO ENFORCE A JUDGMENT

5 Where a judgment creditor applies for the appointment of a receiver as a method of enforcing a judgment, in considering whether to make the appointment the court will have regard to –

(1) the amount claimed by the judgment creditor;
(2) the amount likely to be obtained by the receiver; and
(3) the probable costs of his appointment.

COURT'S DIRECTIONS

6.1 The court may give directions to the receiver when it appoints him or at any time afterwards.

6.2 The court will normally, when it appoints a receiver, give directions in relation to security – see paragraph 7 below.

6.3 Other matters about which the court may give directions include –

(1) whether, and on what basis, the receiver is to be remunerated for carrying out his functions;
(2) the preparation and service of accounts – see rule 69.8(1) and paragraph 10 below;
(3) the payment of money into court; and
(4) authorising the receiver to carry on an activity or incur an expense.

DIRECTIONS RELATING TO SECURITY – RULE 69.5

7.1 An order appointing a receiver will normally specify the date by which the receiver must –

(1) give security; or
(2) file and serve evidence to satisfy the court that he already has security in force.

7.2 Unless the court directs otherwise, security will be given –

(1) if the receiver is a licensed insolvency practitioner, by the bond provided by him under the Insolvency Practitioner Regulations 1990 extended to cover appointment as a court appointed receiver; or
(2) in any other case, by a guarantee.

7.3 Where the court has given directions about giving security, then either –

(1) written evidence of the bond, the sufficiency of its cover and that it includes appointment as a court appointed receiver must be filed at court; or
(2) a guarantee should be prepared in a form, and entered into with a clearing bank or insurance company, approved by the court.

RECEIVER'S APPLICATION FOR DIRECTIONS – RULE 69.6

8.1 An application by a receiver for directions may be made by filing an application notice in accordance with Part 23.

8.2 If the directions sought by the receiver are unlikely to be contentious or important to the parties, he may make the application by letter, and the court may reply by letter. In such cases the receiver need not serve his letter or the court's reply on the parties, unless the court orders him to do so.

8.3 Where a receiver applies for directions by letter, the court may direct him to file and serve an application notice.

RECEIVER'S REMUNERATION – RULE 69.7

9.1 A receiver may only charge for his services if the court gives directions permitting it and specifying how the remuneration is to be determined.

9.2 The court will normally determine the amount of the receiver's remuneration on the basis of the criteria in rule 69.7(4). Parts 43 to 48 (costs) do not apply to the determination of the remuneration of a receiver.

9.3 Unless the court orders otherwise, the receiver will only be paid or be able to recover his remuneration after the amount of it has been determined.

9.4 An application by a receiver for the amount of his remuneration to be determined must be supported by –

(1) written evidence showing –
 (a) on what basis the remuneration is claimed; and
 (b) that it is justified and in accordance with this Part; and
(2) a certificate signed by the receiver that he considers that the remuneration he claims is reasonable and proportionate.

9.5 The court may, before determining the amount of a receiver's remuneration –

(1) require the receiver to provide further information in support of his claim; and
(2) appoint an assessor under rule 35.15 to assist the court.

9.6 Paragraphs 9.1 to 9.5 do not apply to expenses incurred by a receiver in carrying out his functions. These are accounted for as part of his account for the assets he has recovered, and not dealt with as part of the determination of his remuneration.

ACCOUNTS – RULE 69.8

10.1 When the court gives directions under rule 69.8(1) for the receiver to prepare and serve accounts, it may –

(1) direct the receiver to prepare and serve accounts either by a specified date or at specified intervals; and
(2) specify the persons on whom he must serve the accounts.

10.2 A party should not apply for an order under rule 69.8(2) permitting him to inspect documents in the possession of the receiver, without first asking the receiver to permit such inspection without an order.

10.3 Where the court makes an order under rule 69.8(2), it will normally direct that the receiver must –

(1) permit inspection within 7 days after being served with the order; and
(2) provide a copy of any documents the subject of the order within 7 days after receiving a request for a copy from the party permitted to inspect them, provided that party has undertaken to pay the reasonable cost of making and providing the copy.

PART 70
GENERAL RULES ABOUT ENFORCEMENT OF JUDGMENTS AND ORDERS

CONTENTS OF THIS PART

Practice Direction—This Part is supplemented by a practice direction – PD70 – which is set out at p 1524.

70.1 Scope of this Part and interpretation

(1) This Part contains general rules about enforcement of judgments and orders.

(Rules about specific methods of enforcement are contained in Parts 71 to 73, Schedule 1 RSC Orders 45 to 47 and 52 and Schedule 2 CCR Orders 25 to 29)

(2) In this Part and in Parts 71 to 73 –

(a) 'judgment creditor' means a person who has obtained or is entitled to enforce a judgment or order;

(b) 'judgment debtor' means a person against whom a judgment or order was given or made;

(c) 'judgment or order' includes an award which the court has –

(i) registered for enforcement;

(ii) ordered to be enforced; or

(iii) given permission to enforce

as if it were a judgment or order of the court, and in relation to such an award, 'the court which made the judgment or order' means the court which registered the award or made such an order; and

(d) 'judgment or order for the payment of money' includes a judgment or order for the payment of costs, but does not include a judgment or order for the payment of money into court.

Amendments—Inserted by SI 2001/2792; amended by SI 2002/2058.

70.2 Methods of enforcing judgments or orders

(1) The relevant practice direction sets out methods of enforcing judgments or orders for the payment of money.

(2) A judgment creditor may, except where an enactment, rule or practice direction provides otherwise –

(a) use any method of enforcement which is available; and

(b) use more than one method of enforcement, either at the same time or one after another.

Amendments—Inserted by SI 2001/2792.

Practice Direction—See PD70, paras 7.1 at p 1526 and 7.2 at p 1527.

'at the same time' (r 70.2(2)(b))—Although concurrent enforcement by different methods is normally permitted, judgment creditors are obliged by PD70, paras 7.1 and 7.2 to notify in writing either the court, or the Sheriff's Officer in the case of a High Court writ of execution, if any payment is made by the judgment debtor in the period between issue and hearing or execution.

70.3 Transfer of proceedings for enforcement

(1) A judgment creditor wishing to enforce a High Court judgment or order in a county court must apply to the High Court for an order transferring the proceedings to that county court.

(2) A practice direction may make provisions about the transfer of proceedings for enforcement.

(CCR Order 25 rule 13 contains provisions about the transfer of county court proceedings to the High Court for enforcement)

Amendments—Inserted by SI 2001/2792.

Practice Direction—See PD70, paras 2.1–2.4 at p 1525.

70.4 Enforcement of judgment or order by or against non-party

If a judgment or order is given or made in favour of or against a person who is not a party to proceedings, it may be enforced by or against that person by the same methods as if he were a party.

Amendments—Inserted by SI 2001/2792.

70.5 Enforcement of awards of bodies other than the High Court and county courts

(1) This rule applies, subject to paragraph (2), if –

- (a) an award of a sum of money [or other decision is made by any court, tribunal, body or person other than the High Court or a county court; and
- (b) an enactment provides that the award may be enforced as if payable under a court order[, or that the decision may be enforced as if it were a court order.

(2) This rule does not apply to –

- (a) any judgment to which Part 74 applies;
- (b) arbitration awards; or
- (c) any order to which RSC Order 115 applies.

(Part 74 provides for the registration in the High Court for the purposes of enforcement of judgments from other jurisdictions and European Community judgments)

(RSC Order 115 provides for the registration in the High Court for the purposes of enforcement of certain orders made in connection with criminal proceedings and investigations)

(3) If the enactment provides that [an award of a sum of money is enforceable if a court so orders, an application for such an order must be made in accordance with paragraphs (4) to (7) of this rule.

(4) An application for an order that an award may be enforced as if payable under a court order –

(a) may be made without notice; and
(b) must be made to the court for the district where the person against whom the award was made resides or carries on business, unless the court otherwise orders.

(5) The application notice must –

(a) be in the form; and
(b) contain the information

required by the relevant practice direction.

(6) A copy of the award must be filed with the application notice.

(7) The application may be dealt with by a court officer without a hearing.

[(8) If an enactment provides that an award or decision may be enforced in the same manner as an order of the High Court if it is registered, any application to the High Court for registration must be made in accordance with the relevant practice direction.

Amendments—Inserted by SI 2001/2792; amended by SI 2001/4015; SI 2002/2058; SI 2003/2113.

Practice Direction—See PD70, paras 4.1–4.3 at p 1526 as to application notices (r 70.5(5)) and PD70, paras 5.1–5.3 at p 1526 as to applications to register decisions of VAT and duties Tribunals (r 70.5(8)).

70.6 Effect of setting aside judgment or order

If a judgment or order is set aside, any enforcement of the judgment or order shall cease to have effect unless the court otherwise orders.

Amendments—Inserted by SI 2001/2792.

'unless the court otherwise orders'—This provision enables the court to preserve the security and priority of a charging order obtained by the judgment creditor as a condition for setting aside judgment.

Practice Direction – Enforcement of Judgments and Orders …

This Practice Direction supplements CPR Part 70 (PD70)

METHODS OF ENFORCING MONEY JUDGMENTS – RULE 70.2

1.1 A judgment creditor may enforce a judgment or order for the payment of money by any of the following methods:

(1) a writ of fieri facias or warrant of execution (see RSC Orders 46 and 47 and CCR Order 26);
(2) a third party debt order (see Part 72);
(3) a charging order, stop order or stop notice (see Part 73);
(4) in a county court, an attachment of earnings order (see CCR Order 27);
(5) the appointment of a receiver (see Part 69);

1.2 In addition the court may make the following orders against a judgment debtor –

(1) an order of committal, but only if permitted by –
 (a) a rule; and
 (b) the Debtors Acts 1869 and 1878

(see RSC Order 45, rule 5 and CCR Order 29. The practice direction on committal applications applies to an application for committal of a judgment debtor); and

(2) in the High Court, a writ of sequestration, but only if permitted by RSC Order 45, rule 5.

1.3 The enforcement of a judgment or order may be affected by –

(1) the enactments relating to insolvency; and
(2) county court administration orders.

'permitted by a rule' (para 1.2(1)(a))—The judgment summons procedure is now only available for non-payment of certain kinds of tax and social security contributions. The procedure is governed by CPR Sch 2, CCR Ord 28.

TRANSFER OF COUNTY COURT PROCEEDINGS TO ANOTHER COURT FOR ENFORCEMENT – RULE 70.3

2.1 If a judgment creditor is required by a rule or practice direction to enforce a judgment or order of one county court in a different county court, he must first make a request in writing to the court in which the case is proceeding to transfer the proceedings to that other court.

2.2 On receipt of such a request, a court officer will transfer the proceedings to the other court unless a judge orders otherwise.

2.3 The court will give notice of the transfer to all the parties.

2.4 When the proceedings have been transferred, the parties must take any further steps in the proceedings in the court to which they have been transferred, unless a rule or practice direction provides otherwise.

(Part 52 and its practice direction provide to which court or judge an appeal against the judgment or order, or an application for permission to appeal, must be made)

ENFORCEMENT OF HIGH COURT JUDGMENT OR ORDER IN A COUNTY COURT – RULE 70.3

3.1 If a judgment creditor wishes to enforce a High Court judgment or order in a county court, he must file the following documents in the county court with his application notice or request for enforcement –

(1) a copy of the judgment or order;
(2) a certificate verifying the amount due under the judgment or order;
(3) if a writ of execution has previously been issued in the High Court to enforce the judgment or order, a copy of the relevant enforcement officer's return to the writ; and
(4) a copy of the order transferring the proceedings to the county court.

3.2 In this paragraph and paragraph 7 –

(1) 'enforcement officer' means an individual who is authorised to act as an enforcement officer under the Courts Act 2003; and
(2) 'relevant enforcement officer' means –
    (a) in relation to a writ of execution which is directed to a single enforcement officer, that officer;
    (b) in relation to a writ of execution which is directed to two or more enforcement officers, the officer to whom the writ is allocated.

ENFORCEMENT OF AWARDS OF BODIES OTHER THAN THE HIGH COURT OR A COUNTY COURT – RULE 70.5

4.1 An application under rule 70.5 for an order to enforce an award as if payable under a court order must be made by filing an application notice in practice form N322A.

4.2 The application notice must state –

(1) the name and address of the person against whom it is sought to enforce the award; and
(2) how much of the award remains unpaid.

4.3 Rule 70.5(6) provides that a copy of the award must be filed with the application notice.

REGISTRATION OF AWARDS AND DECISIONS IN THE HIGH COURT FOR ENFORCEMENT – RULE 70.5(8)

5.1 An application to the High Court under an enactment to register a decision for enforcement must be made in writing to the head clerk of the Action Department at the Royal Courts of Justice, Strand, London WC2A 2LL.

5.2 The application must –

(1) specify the statutory provision under which the application is made;
(2) state the name and address of the person against whom it is sought to enforce the decision;
(3) if the decision requires that person to pay a sum of money, state the amount which remains unpaid.

INTEREST ON JUDGMENT DEBTS

6 If a judgment creditor is claiming interest on a judgment debt, he must include in his application or request to issue enforcement proceedings in relation to that judgment details of –

(1) the amount of interest claimed and the sum on which it is claimed;
(2) the dates from and to which interest has accrued; and
(3) the rate of interest which has been applied and, where more than one rate of interest has been applied, the relevant dates and rates.

(Interest may be claimed on High Court judgment debts under section 17 of the Judgments Act 1838. The County Courts (Interest on Judgment Debts) Order 1991 specifies when interest may be claimed on county court judgment debts)

'Interest may be claimed' (para 6 cross-reference)—In the county court, interest may be claimed on relevant 'judgments'. These are judgments which are not for a sum of money payable under a regulated agreement within the meaning of the Consumer Credit Act 1974, and are either:

(a) for a sum of money not less than £5000; or
(b) for a debt owed to a small business by a large business or public authority under the Late Payment of Commercial Debts (Interest) Act 1998.

PAYMENT OF DEBT AFTER ISSUE OF ENFORCEMENT PROCEEDINGS

7.1 If a judgment debt or part of it is paid –

(1) after the judgment creditor has issued any application or request to enforce it; but

(2) before –
 (a) any writ or warrant has been executed; or
 (b) in any other case, the date fixed for the hearing of the application;
 the judgment creditor must, unless paragraph 7.2 applies, immediately notify the court in writing.

7.2 If a judgment debt or part of it is paid after the judgment creditor has applied to the High Court for a writ of execution, paragraph 7.1 does not apply, and the judgment creditor must instead immediately notify the relevant enforcement officer in writing.

PART 71
ORDERS TO OBTAIN INFORMATION FROM JUDGMENT DEBTORS

CONTENTS OF THIS PART

Practice Direction—This Part is supplemented by a practice direction – PD71 – which is set out at p 1531.

General note—This Part replaces the procedure for oral examination of a judgment debtor formerly to be found in Sch 1, RSC Ord 48 and Sch 2, CCR Ord 25 rr 3 and 4 with a unified code which applies to all judgment debts.

71.1 Scope of this Part

This Part contains rules which provide for a judgment debtor to be required to attend court to provide information, for the purpose of enabling a judgment creditor to enforce a judgment or order against him.

Amendments—Inserted by SI 2001/2792.

71.2 Order to attend court

(1) A judgment creditor may apply for an order requiring –

(a) a judgment debtor; or
(b) if a judgment debtor is a company or other corporation, an officer of that body;

to attend court to provide information about –

(i) the judgment debtor's means; or
(ii) any other matter about which information is needed to enforce a judgment or order.

(2) An application under paragraph (1) –

(a) may be made without notice; and
(b) (i) must be issued in the court which made the judgment or order which it is sought to enforce, except that
(ii) if the proceedings have since been transferred to a different court, it must be issued in that court.

(3) The application notice must –

(a) be in the form; and
(b) contain the information

required by the relevant practice direction.

(4) An application under paragraph (1) may be dealt with by a court officer without a hearing.

(5) If the application notice complies with paragraph (3), an order to attend court will be issued in the terms of paragraph (6).

(6) A person served with an order issued under this rule must –

- (a) attend court at the time and place specified in the order;
- (b) when he does so, produce at court documents in his control which are described in the order; and
- (c) answer on oath such questions as the court may require.

(7) An order under this rule will contain a notice in the following terms –

'You must obey this order. If you do not, you may be sent to prison for contempt of court.'

Amendments—Inserted by SI 2001/2792.

Practice Direction—See PD71, para 1.2 at p 1531 (r 71.2(3)).

'to provide information' (r 71.2(1))—The purpose of the rule is to enable the judgment creditor to obtain information as to the best means of satisfying his judgment debt. The judgment debtor is under a duty to make full and frank disclosure of his means.

'will be issued' (r 71.2(5))—In contrast to the previous provisions it appears that the judgment creditor will be entitled to an order as of right if any part of a judgment debt remains outstanding. Subrule (4) merely permits the order to be issued by a court officer rather than a judge but does not confer any discretion on the court.

'answer on oath such questions' (r 71.2(6)(c))—The judgment creditor may cross-examine the debtor vigorously as to his assets (*Republic of Costa Rica v Strousberg* (1880) 16 ChD 8), including those overseas (*Interpool Ltd v Galani* [1987] 3 WLR 1042, CA) and as to any means by which the judgment debt may be satisfied, but not for some other purpose (*Watkins v Ross* (1893) 68 LT 423).

71.3 Service of order

(1) An order to attend court must, unless the court otherwise orders, be served personally on the person ordered to attend court not less than 14 days before the hearing.

(2) If the order is to be served by the judgment creditor, he must inform the court not less than 7 days before the date of the hearing if he has been unable to serve it.

Amendments—Inserted by SI 2001/2792.

'unless the court otherwise orders' (r 71.3(1))—Normally there must be an attempt at personal service before the court will order service by an alternative method under r 6.8.

'served personally' (r 71.3(1))—In county court proceedings where the judgment creditor is an individual litigant in person, personal service will be done by the court bailiff (PD71, para 3).

71.4 Travelling expenses

(1) A person ordered to attend court may, within 7 days of being served with the order, ask the judgment creditor to pay him a sum reasonably sufficient to cover his travelling expenses to and from court.

(2) The judgment creditor must pay such a sum if requested.

Amendments—Inserted by SI 2001/2792.

71.5 Judgment creditor's affidavit

(1) The judgment creditor must file an affidavit(GL) or affidavits –

(a) by the person who served the order (unless it was served by the court) giving details of how and when it was served;
(b) stating either that –
(i) the person ordered to attend court has not requested payment of his travelling expenses; or
(ii) the judgment creditor has paid a sum in accordance with such a request; and
(c) stating how much of the judgment debt remains unpaid.

(2) The judgment creditor must either –

(a) file the affidavit(GL) or affidavits not less than 2 days before the hearing; or
(b) produce it or them at the hearing.

Amendments—Inserted by SI 2001/2792.

'unless it was served by the court' (r 71.5(1)(a))—In which case service will be proved by a certificate under CCA 1984, s 133. Such certificate is not conclusive but merely evidence of service (*Maher v Gower formerly Kubilius* (1981) 3 FLR 287).

71.6 Conduct of the hearing

(1) The person ordered to attend court will be questioned on oath.

(2) The questioning will be carried out by a court officer unless the court has ordered that the hearing shall be before a judge.

(3) The judgment creditor or his representative –

(a) may attend and ask questions where the questioning takes place before a court officer; and
(b) must attend and conduct the questioning if the hearing is before a judge.

Amendments—Inserted by SI 2001/2792.

'hearing is before a judge' (r 71.6(3)(b))—The hearing will only take place before a judge if there are compelling reasons to make such an order (PD71, para 2.2).

71.7 Adjournment of the hearing

If the hearing is adjourned, the court will give directions as to the manner in which notice of the new hearing is to be served on the judgment debtor.

Amendments—Inserted by SI 2001/2792.

'notice of service of adjourned hearing'—Where the judgment debtor is present and can be given personal notice then and there of the date and time of the new hearing, the court will normally dispense with personal service of notice of the new hearing in accordance with r 1.1(2)(c).

71.8 Failure to comply with order

(1) If a person against whom an order has been made under rule 71.2 –

(a) fails to attend court;
(b) refuses at the hearing to take the oath or to answer any question; or
(c) otherwise fails to comply with the order;

the court will refer the matter to a High Court judge or circuit judge.

(2) That judge may, subject to paragraphs (3) and (4), make a committal order against the person.

(3) A committal order for failing to attend court may not be made unless the judgment creditor has complied with rules 71.4 and 71.5.

(4) If a committal order is made, the judge will direct that –

- (a) the order shall be suspended provided that the person –
  - (i) attends court at a time and place specified in the order; and
  - (ii) complies with all the terms of that order and the original order; and
- (b) if the person fails to comply with any term on which the committal order is suspended, he shall be brought before a judge to consider whether the committal order should be discharged.

Amendments—Inserted by SI 2001/2792; amended by SI 2001/4015.

'High Court or circuit judge' (r 71.8(1))—Although suspended committal orders can only be made by judges at this level, the hearing at which the decision is made whether the committal order should be discharged may take place before a master or district judge (PD71, para 8.4).

'shall be suspended' (r 71.8(4)(a))—See PD71, para 7.1 for the detailed provisions as to the suspended order.

'he shall be brought before a judge' (r 71.8(4)(b))—The procedure for dealing with a judgment debtor who fails to comply with a suspended committal order raises serious issues under HRA 1998, Sch 1, Pt I, Art 6. See PD71, para 8 and the notes thereto for details of the problems which may arise. On the arrest of the judgment debtor, the judgment creditor is likely to have to be prepared to attend court at very short notice in order to conduct the hearing to decide whether the committal order should be discharged, or the hearing will have to be adjourned. It will be for the judgment creditor to prove to the criminal standard that the judgment debtor has been served both with the original order to attend court and the suspended committal order, and that he has failed to comply with the terms of the suspended committal order (PD71, para 8.5).

Practice Direction – Orders to Obtain Information from Judgment Debtors

This Practice Direction supplements CPR Part 71 (PD71)

APPLICATION NOTICE – RULE 71.2

1.1 An application by a judgment creditor under rule 71.2(1) must be made by filing an application notice in Practice Form N316 if the application is to question an individual judgment debtor, or N316A if the application is to question an officer of a company or other corporation.

1.2 The application notice must –

- (1) state the name and address of the judgment debtor;
- (2) identify the judgment or order which the judgment creditor is seeking to enforce;
- (3) if the application is to enforce a judgment or order for the payment of money, state the amount presently owed by the judgment debtor under the judgment or order;
- (4) if the judgment debtor is a company or other corporation, state –
  - (a) the name and address of the officer of that body whom the judgment creditor wishes to be ordered to attend court; and
  - (b) his position in the company;
- (5) if the judgment creditor wishes the questioning to be conducted before a judge, state this and give his reasons;

(6) if the judgment creditor wishes the judgment debtor (or other person to be questioned) to be ordered to produce specific documents at court, identify those documents; and

(7) if the application is to enforce a judgment or order which is not for the payment of money, identify the matters about which the judgment creditor wishes the judgment debtor (or officer of the judgment debtor) to be questioned.

1.3 The court officer considering the application notice –

(1) may, in any appropriate case, refer it to a judge (rule 3.2); and

(2) will refer it to a judge for consideration, if the judgment creditor requests the judgment debtor (or officer of the judgment debtor) to be questioned before a judge.

'amount presently owed' (para 1.2(3))—If part of the judgment debt has been paid the judgment creditor should state the date and amount of the last payment which has been taken into account in arriving at the balance due.

'before a judge' (para 1.2(5))—Note that the judgment creditor or his representative must attend the hearing to conduct the questioning (para 5.1).

'give his reasons' (para 1.2(5))—The judgment creditor must show compelling reasons for a hearing before a judge (see para 2.2 below).

ORDER TO ATTEND COURT – RULE 71.2

2.1 The order will provide for the judgment debtor (or other person to be questioned) to attend the county court for the district in which he resides or carries on business, unless a judge decides otherwise.

2.2 The order will provide for questioning to take place before a judge only if the judge considering the request decides that there are compelling reasons to make such an order.

SERVICE OF ORDER TO ATTEND COURT – RULE 71.3

3 Service of an order to attend court for questioning must be carried out by the judgment creditor (or someone acting on his behalf), except that in county court proceedings if the judgment creditor is an individual litigant in person the order will be served by the court bailiff.

'individual litigant in person'—This expression is not defined but is intended to exclude unrepresented business organisations which, it is assumed, will not need the assistance of the court bailiff.

'will be served'—The individual litigant in person does not initially have the option to arrange for personal service but may apply for permission to serve by another method if the bailiff is unable to serve.

ATTENDANCE AT COURT: NORMAL PROCEDURE – RULE 71.6

4.1 The court officer will ask a standard series of questions, as set out in the forms in Appendixes A and B to this practice direction. The form in Appendix A will be used if the person being questioned is the judgment debtor, and the form in Appendix B will be used if the person is an officer of a company or other corporation.

4.2 The judgment creditor or his representative may either –

(1) attend court and ask questions himself; or

(2) request the court officer to ask additional questions, by attaching a list of proposed additional questions to his application notice.

4.3 The court officer will –

(1) make a written record of the evidence given, unless the proceedings are tape recorded;
(2) at the end of the questioning, read the record of evidence to the person being questioned and ask him to sign it; and
(3) if the person refuses to sign it, note that refusal on the record of evidence.

'list of proposed additional questions' (para 4.2(2))—The list should allow sufficient space for the answer to each question to be recorded immediately after the question.

'make a written record' (para 4.3(1))—Although both CPR Pt 71 and the practice direction are silent the court will send a copy of the record to the judgment creditor.

'unless the proceedings are tape recorded' (para 4.3(1))—Presumably tape recording is envisaged when the judgment creditor is present or represented and elects to make his own written note of the evidence. Subparagraph (2) cannot apply when the proceedings have been recorded. It is difficult to see what benefit a recording will be to the judgment creditor until the court is in a position to e-mail the digital recording to the judgment creditor as a file, except as a record in case of subsequent dispute about what was said.

'refuses to sign' (para 4.3(3))—The debtor signs to confirm that his replies have been accurately recorded. There is no sanction for a refusal to sign.

ATTENDANCE AT COURT: PROCEDURE WHERE THE ORDER IS TO ATTEND BEFORE A JUDGE – RULE 71.6

5.1 Where the hearing takes places before a judge, the questioning will be conducted by the judgment creditor or his representative, and the standard questions in the forms in Appendixes A and B will not be used.

5.2 The proceedings will be tape recorded and the court will not make a written record of the evidence.

'will not be used' (para 5.1)—Some questions in the standard forms may still be relevant and can be asked.

'will be tape recorded' (para 5.2)—The judgment creditor must take a note of the answers given or request a transcript at his (considerable) expense.

FAILURE TO COMPLY WITH ORDER: REFERENCE TO JUDGE – RULE 71.8(1)

6 If a judge or court officer refers to a High Court judge or circuit judge the failure of a judgment debtor to comply with an order under rule 71.2, he shall certify in writing the respect in which the judgment debtor failed to comply with the order.

'certify in writing'—Surprisingly the practice direction makes no provision for a copy of the certificate to be sent either to the judgment creditor or judgment debtor. The failure to provide for the judgment debtor to receive a copy of the certificate at any stage of the proceedings may give rise to challenge to this procedure under HRA 1998, Sch 1, Pt I, Art 6 (see *Newman v Modern Bookbinders* [2001] 1 WLR 2559, [2000] 2 All ER 814, CA). The usual form of suspended committal order (Form N79A) does, however, recite the breach found by the judge in reliance on the certificate and will be served on the debtor.

SUSPENDED COMMITTAL ORDER – RULE 71.8(2) AND (4)(A)

7.1 A committal order will be suspended provided that the person attends court at a time and place specified in the order (rule 71.8(4)(a)(i)). The appointment specified will be –

(1) before a judge, if –

(a) the original order under rule 71.2 was to attend before a judge; or
(b) the judge making the suspended committal order so directs; and
(2) otherwise, before a court officer.

7.2 Rule 71.3 and paragraph 3 of this practice direction (service of order), and rule 71.5(1)(a) and (2) (affidavit of service), apply with the necessary changes to a suspended committal order as they do to an order to attend court.

'service of order' (para 7.2)—Judgment creditors may wish to serve a copy of the certificate under para 6 with the suspended committal order to reduce the risk of the particular HRA challenge mentioned in the note to para 6 above.

BREACH OF TERMS ON WHICH COMMITTAL ORDER IS SUSPENDED – RULE 71.8(4)(B)

8.1 If –

(1) the judgment debtor fails to attend court at the time and place specified in the suspended committal order; and
(2) it appears to the judge or court officer that the judgment debtor has been duly served with the order,

the judge or court officer will certify in writing the debtor's failure to attend.

8.2 If the judgment debtor fails to comply with any other term on which the committal order was suspended, the judge or court officer will certify in writing the non-compliance and set out details of it.

8.3 A warrant to bring the judgment debtor before a judge may be issued on the basis of a certificate under paragraph 8.1 or 8.2.

8.4 The hearing under rule 71.8(4)(b) may take place before a master or district judge.

8.5 At the hearing the judge will discharge the committal order unless he is satisfied beyond reasonable doubt that –

(1) the judgment debtor has failed to comply with –
  (a) the original order to attend court; and
  (b) the terms on which the committal order was suspended; and
(2) both orders have been duly served on the judgment debtor.

8.6 If the judge decides that the committal order should not be discharged, a warrant of committal shall be issued immediately.

'certify in writing' (para 8.2)—See the note **'certify in writing'** to para 6 above.

'certificate' (para 8.3)—See the note **'certify in writing'** to para 6 above.

'A warrant' (para 8.3)—In a county court, the warrant (Form N40A) authorises the court bailiff to arrest the judgment debtor (and, in order to be effective, impliedly in so doing to use such force as is necessary) and bring him before a judge.

'At the hearing' (para 8.5)—On its face, this provision bristles with potential HRA pitfalls. First, there is no specific requirement that the judgment debtor must have received a copy of the certificates under paras 6 and 8.1 or para 8.2. This was held to be a mandatory requirement in *Newman v Modern Bookbinders* (see note **'certify in writing'** under para 6 above). Secondly, the judgment debtor is likely to be unrepresented. Since he is alleged to be in breach of a suspended committal order may be sent to prison. He must therefore be offered an adjournment and the opportunity to apply for legal aid or to take legal advice. Thirdly, if the judgment debtor wishes to challenge the evidence of service or the contents of either certificate he must be given an opportunity for cross examination of witnesses. Fourth even if the judgment debtor is found to be in contempt of court he must be given a chance to address the court in mitigation before sentence is passed (*Shoreditch County Court v De Madeiros* (1988) *The Times*, 24 February, CA).

In practice, however, if the judgment debtor submits to the original order for questioning, the committal order will be discharged.

'shall be issued immediately' (para 8.6)—Again, if read literally with para 8.5, there are serious HRA problems with this provision. First the original committal order will have specified a term of imprisonment which appeared appropriate to the contempt on the information available to the judge at the time. There appears to be no power to vary the term, in clear breach of HRA 1998, Sch 1, Art 6, to take account of proper mitigation advanced by the judgment debtor. Even more serious breaches of Art 6 may arise if the original committal was for non-attendance and the judgment debtor subsequently attends and commits a breach of a different term of the original order, eg by neglecting to produce a document. The sentence which was passed for failure to attend could, at least in theory, then be put into effect as a result of a less serious breach.

The court will in practice do everything possible to obtain the information required without sending the judgment debtor to prison. Thus, a judge before whom a judgment debtor is brought may use the general powers contained in CPR r 3.1(2) and (3) to adjourn the hearing for a short time to allow the judgment debtor a final opportunity to purge his apparent contempt. Paragraph 8.5 should not be interpreted as limiting the judge's power to discharge the order to the matters specified in that paragraph, and if the judgment debtor complies the committal order will be discharged. If a full hearing has to take place the judge will first consider the matters set out in the note **'At the hearing'** above, if necessary adjourning the hearing on terms as to the judgment debtor's attendance. The judge will further make sure that the judgment debtor is aware of the adjourned hearing before leaving the court building, so that service of the notice of the adjourned hearing can be dispensed with, and warn him that if he fails to attend the court will proceed in his absence. Ultimately the court retains a discretion whether or not to activate the terms of a suspended committal order (*Re W(B)* [1969] 1 All ER 594).

****

Appendices—Appendices A and B to this practice direction contain Records of Examination EX140 and EX141. These can be accessed on the *Civil Court Service* CD-ROM and on the Department for Constitutional Affairs' website at *www.lcd.gov.uk*.

PART 72
THIRD PARTY DEBT ORDERS

CONTENTS OF THIS PART

Practice Direction—This Part is supplemented by a practice direction – PD72 – which is set out at p 1542.

General note—This Part replaces, with a new name and important amendments, provisions relating to garnishee orders which were formerly to be found in Sch 1, RSC Ord 49 and Sch 2, CCR Ord 30, both of which have been wholly repealed. Where garnishee proceedings have been issued before 25 March 2002 the old rules will continue to apply.

72.1 Scope of this Part and interpretation

(1) This Part contains rules which provide for a judgment creditor to obtain an order for the payment to him of money which a third party who is within the jurisdiction owes to the judgment debtor.

(2) In this Part, 'bank or building society' includes any person carrying on a business in the course of which he lawfully accepts deposits in the United Kingdom.

Amendments—Inserted by SI 2001/2792; amended by SI 2001/4015.

72.2 Third party debt order

(1) Upon the application of a judgment creditor, the court may make an order (a 'final third party debt order') requiring a third party to pay to the judgment creditor –

- (a) the amount of any debt due or accruing due to the judgment debtor from the third party; or
- (b) so much of that debt as is sufficient to satisfy the judgment debt and the judgment creditor's costs of the application.

(2) The court will not make an order under paragraph 1 without first making an order (an 'interim third party debt order') as provided by rule 72.4(2).

(3) In deciding whether money standing to the credit of the judgment debtor in an account to which section 40 of the Supreme Court Act 1981 or section 108 of the County Courts Act 1984 relates may be made the subject of a third party debt order, any condition applying to the account that a receipt for money deposited in the account must be produced before any money is withdrawn will be disregarded.

(Section 40(3) of the Supreme Court Act 1981 and section 108(3) of the County Courts Act 1984 contain a list of other conditions applying to accounts that will also be disregarded)

Amendments—Inserted by SI 2001/2792.

'final third party debt order' (r 72.2(1))—This expression replaces the former 'garnishee order absolute'.

'any debt' (r 72.2(1)(a))—There must be in existence something recognised in law as a debt, notwithstanding that it may be payable on a future date (*O'Driscoll v Manchester Insurance Committee* [1915] 3 KB 499). Thus, a cause of action in damages is not attachable (*Johnson v Diamond* (1855) 11 Exch 73), until judgment is pronounced (*Holtby v Hodgson* (1889) 24 QBD 103). Once an order is made, a subsequent cross-claim by the third party against the judgment debtor does not reduce the third party's liability under the order (*Wolfe v Marshall and Harding (Garnishee)* (1997) (unreported) 25 March, CA). In the case of a foreign debt, the court has no jurisdiction to make a third party debt order unless compliance with the order will be recognised as discharging the debt owed by the third party to the judgment debtor under the law which governs that debt (*Société Eram Shipping Co Ltd v Compagnie Internationale de Navigation & ors* [2003] UKHL 30, [2003] TLR 351, HL).

'interim third party debt order' (r 72.2(2))—This expression replaces the former 'garnishee order nisi'.

'any condition applying to the account' (r 72.2(3))—If a liability is conditional, there may be no debt if the condition is not satisfied. In the case of balances held for the debtor by banks, building societies and the like, this difficulty is removed by SCA 1981, s 40, and CCA 1984, s 108, which provide that requirements for notice, personal application and production of a passbook are to be disregarded.

The Crown—This procedure is not available against the Crown as third party. An equivalent procedure is provided by Crown Proceedings Act 1947, s 27 and Sch 1, RSC Ord 77, r 16 and Sch 2, CCR Ord 42, r 14. This restriction includes the National Savings Bank and, although SCA 1981, s 139(2) enables the Lord Chancellor to make an order removing the restriction, no such order has been made.

72.3 Application for third party debt order

(1) An application for a third party debt order –

- (a) may be made without notice; and
- (b) (i) must be issued in the court which made the judgment or order which it is sought to enforce; except that
  - (ii) if the proceedings have since been transferred to a different court, it must be issued in that court.

(2) The application notice must –

- (a) (i) be in the form; and
  - (ii) contain the information

required by the relevant practice direction; and

- (b) be verified by a statement of truth.

Amendments—Inserted by SI 2001/2792.

Practice Direction—See PD72, paras 1.1 at p 1542 and 1.2 at p 1542 as to the application notice (r 72.3(2)(a)).

'statement of truth' (r 72.3(2)(b))—See Pt 22.

72.4 Interim third party debt order

(1) An application for a third party debt order will initially be dealt with by a judge without a hearing.

(2) The judge may make an interim third party debt order –

(a) fixing a hearing to consider whether to make a final third party debt order; and
(b) directing that until that hearing the third party must not make any payment which reduces the amount he owes the judgment debtor to less than the amount specified in the order.

(3) An interim third party debt order will specify the amount of money which the third party must retain, which will be the total of –

(a) the amount of money remaining due to the judgment creditor under the judgment or order; and
(b) an amount for the judgment creditor's fixed costs of the application, as specified in the relevant practice direction.

(4) An interim third party debt order becomes binding on a third party when it is served on him.

(5) The date of the hearing to consider the application shall be not less than 28 days after the interim third party debt order is made.

Amendments—Inserted by SI 2001/2792.

Practice Direction—See PD72, para 2 at p 1543.

Time for making interim order—If the order requires payment by a stated date, then the interim third party debt order will not be made before that date. An interim order is analogous to execution against goods and will not be made where such execution would not issue (*White, Son & Pill v Stennings* [1911] 2 KB 418).

'the judge may make' (r 72.4(2))—The court has a discretion as to whether to make the interim order and may decline to do so where, for example, the judgment debt is so small that the costs would be disproportionately burdensome.

'relevant practice direction' (r 72.4(3)(b))—In addition to PD72, para 2, see r 45.6.

72.5 Service of interim order

(1) Copies of an interim third party debt order, the application notice and any documents filed in support of it must be served –

(a) on the third party, not less than 21 days before the date fixed for the hearing; and
(b) on the judgment debtor not less than –
  (i) 7 days after a copy has been served on the third party; and
  (ii) 7 days before the date fixed for the hearing.

(2) If the judgment creditor serves the order, he must either –

(a) file a certificate of service not less than 2 days before the hearing; or
(b) produce a certificate of service at the hearing.

Amendments—Inserted by SI 2001/2792.

Documents to be served—Note that the rule now requires the third party to be served not only with the order, but also with the application notice and any documents filed in support.

'must be served' (r 72.5(1))—The general rules as to service set out in Pt 6 apply. Where the third party is a deposit-taking institution the best practice will be to effect service at the branch where the judgment debtor's account is believed to be held as being a place of business which has a real connection with the claim under r 6.5(6), as well as at the head office.

72.6 Obligations of third parties served with interim order

(1) A bank or building society served with an interim third party debt order must carry out a search to identify all accounts held with it by the judgment debtor.

(2) The bank or building society must disclose to the court and the creditor within 7 days of being served with the order, in respect of each account held by the judgment debtor –

- (a) the number of the account;
- (b) whether the account is in credit; and
- (c) if the account is in credit –
  - (i) whether the balance of the account is sufficient to cover the amount specified in the order;
  - (ii) the amount of the balance at the date it was served with the order, if it is less than the amount specified in the order; and
  - (iii) whether the bank or building society asserts any right to the money in the account, whether pursuant to a right of set-off or otherwise, and if so giving details of the grounds for that assertion.

(3) If –

- (a) the judgment debtor does not hold an account with the bank or building society; or
- (b) the bank or building society is unable to comply with the order for any other reason (for example, because it has more than one account holder whose details match the information contained in the order, and cannot identify which account the order applies to),

the bank or building society must inform the court and the judgment creditor of that fact within 7 days of being served with the order.

(4) Any third party other than a bank or building society served with an interim third party debt order must notify the court and the judgment creditor in writing within 7 days of being served with the order, if he claims –

- (a) not to owe any money to the judgment debtor; or
- (b) to owe less than the amount specified in the order.

Amendments—Inserted by SI 2001/2792; amended by SI 2001/4015.

'must disclose to the court and the creditor' (r 72.6(2))—Note that unlike other third parties, banks and building societies are not required to make disclosure in writing, presumably opening the way to allow fax or e-mail communication with the court and judgment creditor.

Effect of interim third party order—There seems to be no reason why the relevant law which applied to garnishee orders should not continue to apply to third party debt orders. Thus, the third party's debt to the debtor is not transferred to the judgment creditor, but an equitable charge is created (to the extent stated in the interim order) so that, if a third party who has been served with the interim order makes payment otherwise than to the judgment creditor, he risks having to pay twice (*Galbraith v Grimshaw & Baxter* [1910] AC 508). The judgment creditor can be in no better position against the third party than was the judgment debtor (*Levene v Maton* (1907) 51 SJ 532). If, for example, the judgment debtor assigned the debt to a fourth party before the interim order was served, then there will be no debt due to him for the interim order to attach, even though it was served before the third party had notice of the assignment (*Holt v Heatherfield* [1942] 2 KB 1). If the third party is aware that a fourth party claims the debt, he must so inform the court or the fact that he paid the judgment creditor under a third party debt order will not provide a defence to the fourth party's claim (*The Leader* (1868) LR 2 A&E 314). The third party is not protected if he pays the judgment creditor upon receipt of the interim order but before it is made final (*Re Webster* [1907] 1 KB 623).

72.7 Arrangements for debtors in hardship

(1) If –

(a) a judgment debtor is an individual;
(b) he is prevented from withdrawing money from his account with a bank or building society as a result of an interim third party debt order; and
(c) he or his family is suffering hardship in meeting ordinary living expenses as a result,

the court may, on an application by the judgment debtor, make an order permitting the bank or building society to make a payment or payments out of the account ('a hardship payment order').

(2) An application for a hardship payment order may be made –

(a) in High Court proceedings, at the Royal Courts of Justice or to any district registry; and
(b) in county court proceedings, to any county court.

(3) A judgment debtor may only apply to one court for a hardship payment order.

(4) An application notice seeking a hardship payment order must –

(a) include detailed evidence explaining why the judgment debtor needs a payment of the amount requested; and
(b) be verified by a statement of truth.

(5) Unless the court orders otherwise, the application notice –

(a) must be served on the judgment creditor at least 2 days before the hearing; but
(b) does not need to be served on the third party.

(6) A hardship payment order may –

(a) permit the third party to make one or more payments out of the account; and
(b) specify to whom the payments may be made.

Amendments—Inserted by SI 2001/2792.

Practice Direction—See PD72, para 5.2 at p 1544 and paras 5.4–5.5 at p 1544.

Scope of provision—This rule, which is entirely new, has been introduced to meet possible challenges to the third party debt order either under HRA 1998, Sch 1, Pt I, Art 8 or Art 1 of the First Protocol. It will require a very high degree of communication and co-operation between the court in which the interim order is made and any court which deals with an application for a hardship payment order. It is most likely to be used when the credit balance which has been frozen by the interim order is one which the judgment debtor reasonably expected would be available to fund essential payments for living expenditure, such as rent or mortgage instalments.

'suffering hardship' (r 72.7(1)(c))—The test is ordinary and not exceptional hardship. A judgment debtor is likely to establish hardship if the interim order prevents him from having sufficient money to cover his rent or mortgage, the cost of travel to work and at least the weekly basic DSS entitlement for himself and his family.

Venue—Although the application is made in the proceedings, it does not have to be made to the court which made the interim order and will not be transferred to that court for hearing (see PD72, para 5.2).

'statement of truth' (r 72.7(4)(b))—See Pt 22.

'must be served' (r 72.7(5)(a))—See PD72, paras 5.4 and 5.5 for the procedure where the application is dealt with without the required notice to the judgment creditor.

72.8 Further consideration of the application

(1) If the judgment debtor or the third party objects to the court making a final third party debt order, he must file and serve written evidence stating the grounds for his objections.

(2) If the judgment debtor or the third party knows or believes that a person other than the judgment debtor has any claim to the money specified in the interim order, he must file and serve written evidence stating his knowledge of that matter.

(3) If –

(a) the third party has given notice under rule 72.6 that he does not owe any money to the judgment debtor, or that the amount which he owes is less than the amount specified in the interim order; and

(b) the judgment creditor wishes to dispute this,

the judgment creditor must file and serve written evidence setting out the grounds on which he disputes the third party's case.

(4) Written evidence under paragraphs (1), (2) or (3) must be filed and served on each other party as soon as possible, and in any event not less than 3 days before the hearing.

(5) If the court is notified that some person other than the judgment debtor may have a claim to the money specified in the interim order, it will serve on that person notice of the application and the hearing.

(6) At the hearing the court may –

(a) make a final third party debt order;

(b) discharge the interim third party debt order and dismiss the application;

(c) decide any issues in dispute between the parties, or between any of the parties and any other person who has a claim to the money specified in the interim order; or

(d) direct a trial of any such issues, and if necessary give directions.

Amendments—Inserted by SI 2001/2792.

'may make a final ... order' (r 72.8(6)(a))—There is a general discretion as to whether to make an order. Relevant considerations will include the size of the judgment debt, the existence of an instalment order in respect of that debt, the amount of the debt due from the third party, the existence of an instalment order or agreement in respect of the debt attached and the burden of costs resulting from an order. The interests of any other creditors of the judgment debtor are also material (*Roberts Petroleum Ltd v Bernard Kenney Ltd* [1983] 2 AC 192, CA). If there is doubt whether the judgment debtor is solvent, the court may order the third party to pay the money into court pending its decision (*George Lee & Sons (Builders) Ltd v Olink* [1972] 1 WLR 214, CA, a case where the debtor was deceased and his estate was possibly insolvent).

'any issues in dispute' (r 72.8(6)(c))—Primarily, the issue is between the judgment creditor and the third party and the judgment debtor is not a party to it. However, if there is a question as to whether another party is interested in or entitled to the fund, that other party may be joined to the proceedings under r 72.8(5). If the judgment creditor prefers not to contest the issue raised, he may abandon his application, but he may be liable in costs (*Wintle v Williams* (1858) 3 H&N 288).

72.9 Effect of final third party order

(1) A final third party debt order shall be enforceable as an order to pay money.

(2) If –

(a) the third party pays money to the judgment creditor in compliance with a third party debt order; or

(b) the order is enforced against him,

the third party shall, to the extent of the amount paid by him or realised by enforcement against him, be discharged from his debt to the judgment debtor.

(3) Paragraph (2) applies even if the third party debt order, or the original judgment or order against the judgment debtor, is later set aside.

Amendments—Inserted by SI 2001/2792.

72.10 Money in court

(1) If money is standing to the credit of the judgment debtor in court –

(a) the judgment creditor may not apply for a third party debt order in respect of that money; but

(b) he may apply for an order that the money in court, or so much of it as is sufficient to satisfy the judgment or order and the costs of the application, be paid to him.

(2) An application notice seeking an order under this rule must be served on –

(a) the judgment debtor; and

(b) the Accountant General at the Court Funds Office.

(3) If an application notice has been issued under this rule, the money in court must not be paid out until the application has been disposed of.

Amendments—Inserted by SI 2001/2792.

Scope of provision—The court cannot itself be the subject of third party debt order proceedings. Accordingly, this rule provides a procedure for the judgment creditor to apply for payment out to himself where the court is holding money to which the judgment debtor is entitled.

72.11 Costs

If the judgment creditor is awarded costs on an application for an order under rule 72.2 or 72.10 –

(a) he shall, unless the court otherwise directs, retain those costs out of the money recovered by him under the order; and

(b) the costs shall be deemed to be paid first out of the money he recovers, in priority to the judgment debt.

Amendments—Inserted by SI 2001/2792.

Scope of provision—The judgment debt is reduced by the net amount received under the third party debt order proceedings after deducting the costs of those proceedings, unless the court otherwise directs. Such a direction may be given, for example, following the trial of an issue.

Practice Direction – Third Party Debt Orders

This Practice Direction supplements CPR Part 72 (PD72)

APPLICATION NOTICE – RULE 72.3

1.1 An application for a third party debt order must be made by filing an application notice in Practice Form N349.

1.2 The application notice must contain the following information –

(1) the name and address of the judgment debtor;
(2) details of the judgment or order sought to be enforced;
(3) the amount of money remaining due under the judgment or order;
(4) if the judgment debt is payable by instalments, the amount of any instalments which have fallen due and remain unpaid;
(5) the name and address of the third party;
(6) if the third party is a bank or building society –
   (a) its name and the address of the branch at which the judgment debtor's account is believed to be held; and
   (b) the account number;
   or, if the judgment creditor does not know all or part of this information, that fact;
(7) confirmation that to the best of the judgment creditor's knowledge or belief the third party –
   (a) is within the jurisdiction; and
   (b) owes money to or holds money to the credit of the judgment debtor;
(8) if the judgment creditor knows or believes that any person other than the judgment debtor has any claim to the money owed by the third party –
   (a) his name and (if known) his address; and
   (b) such information as is known to the judgment creditor about his claim;
(9) details of any other applications for third party debt orders issued by the judgment creditor in respect of the same judgment debt; and
(10) the sources or grounds of the judgment creditor's knowledge or belief of the matters referred to in (7), (8) and (9).

1.3 The court will not grant speculative applications for third party debt orders, and will only make an interim third party debt order against a bank or building society if the judgment creditor's application notice contains evidence to substantiate his belief that the judgment debtor has an account with the bank or building society in question.

'judgment debtor's account' (para 1.2(6)(a))—Paragraphs 3.1 and 3.2 below make clear that a bank or building society will not normally search for accounts which are not in the sole name of the judgment debtor. A specific order must be requested to freeze any such account supported by evidence that the judgment debtor is the sole beneficial owner of the money in that account.

'speculative applications' (para 1.3)—Paragraph 1.3 offers a stern reminder that forms of application must be informative, accurate and so far as possible supported by positive evidence before the court will grant relief.

'bank or building society' (para 1.3)—As a matter of practicality deposit-taking institutions are unlikely to be able to identify accounts holders or accounts without information about the particular branch at which the account is held.

INTERIM THIRD PARTY DEBT ORDER – RULE 72.4

2 An interim third party debt order will specify the amount of money which the third party must retain (rule 72.4(3)). This will include, in respect of the judgment creditor's fixed costs of the application, the amount which would be allowed to the judgment creditor under rule 45.6 if the whole balance of the judgment debt were recovered.

'amount which would be allowed'—See CPR r 45.6. The present figure is £98.50, assuming the unpaid balance of the judgment debt exceeds £150.

INTERIM ORDERS RELATING TO BANK OR BUILDING SOCIETY ACCOUNTS – RULE 72.6(1)–(3)

3.1 A bank or building society Obligations of the third party served with an interim third party debt order is only required by rule 72.6, unless the order states otherwise –

(1) to retain money in accounts held solely by the judgment debtor (or, if there are joint judgment debtors, accounts held jointly by them or solely by either or any of them); and
(2) to search for and disclose information about such accounts.

3.2 The bank or building society is not required, for example, to retain money in, or disclose information about –

(1) accounts in the joint names of the judgment debtor and another person; or
(2) if the interim order has been made against a firm, accounts in the names of individual members of that firm.

Scope of provision—Paragraphs 3.1 and 3.2 explain the scope of the enquiries expected to be carried out by a bank or building society unless the court otherwise orders. In practice such accounts as those mentioned in para 3.2 are unlikely to be capable of being made subject to third party debt orders.

TRANSFER

4 The court may, on an application by a judgment debtor who wishes to oppose an application for a third party debt order, transfer it to the court for the district where the judgment debtor resides or carries on business, or to another court.

APPLICATIONS FOR HARDSHIP PAYMENT ORDERS – RULE 72.7

5.1 The court will treat an application for a hardship payment order as being made –

(1) in the proceedings in which the interim third party debt order was made; and
(2) under the same claim number,

regardless of where the judgment debtor makes the application.

5.2 An application for a hardship payment order will be dealt with by the court to which it is made.

(Rule 72.7(2) provides that an application may be made –
- in High Court proceedings, in the Royal Courts of Justice or to any district registry; and
- in county court proceedings, to any county court.)

5.3 If the application is made to a different court from that dealing with the application for a third party debt order –

(1) the application for a third party debt order will not be transferred; but
(2) the court dealing with that application will send copies of –
    (a) the application notice; and
    (b) the interim third party debt order

    to the court hearing the application for a hardship payment order.

5.4 Rule 72.7(3) requires an application for a hardship payment order to be served on the judgment creditor at least 2 days before the court is to deal with the application, unless the court orders otherwise. In cases of exceptional urgency the judgment debtor may apply for a hardship payment order without notice to the judgment creditor and a judge will decide whether to –

(1) deal with the application without it being served on the judgment creditor; or
(2) direct it to be served.

5.5 If the judge decides to deal with the application without it being served on the judgment creditor, where possible he will normally –

(1) direct that the judgment creditor be informed of the application; and
(2) give him the opportunity to make representations,

by telephone, fax or other appropriate method of communication.

5.6 The evidence filed by a judgment debtor in support of an application for a hardship payment order should include documentary evidence, for example (if appropriate) bank statements, wage slips and mortgage statements, to prove his financial position and need for the payment.

Scope of provision (para 5.1)—The concept of allowing an application to be conducted in a different court without transferring the proceedings is entirely novel. Since there is no provision requiring the judgment debtor to lodge a copy of the interim third party debt order or the application notice these documents will have to be obtained immediately by the court dealing with the hardship payment application (see para 5.3(2) below).

'to which it is made' (para 5.2)—This mandatory provision appears to preclude the transfer of the application to another court under CPR r 30.2

'without notice to the judgment creditor' (para 5.4)—Although a hearing without notice is possible para 5.5 contains special provisions to allow the judgment creditor an opportunity to be heard. on such applications.

'by telephone' (para 5.5)—This provision differs from those about telephone hearings set out in PD23, para 6 in that a telephone conference hearing may take place without the consent of the judgment creditor and while one party, the judgment debtor, is present before the judge.

FINAL ORDERS RELATING TO BUILDING SOCIETY ACCOUNTS

6 A final third party debt order will not require a payment which would reduce to less than £1 the amount in a judgment debtor's account with a building society or credit union.

PART 73
CHARGING ORDERS, STOP ORDERS AND STOP NOTICES

CONTENTS OF THIS PART

Practice Direction—This Part is supplemented by a practice direction – PD73 – which is set out at p 1555.

Procedural Guide—See Guides 36 and 47 set out in Section 1 of this work.

General note—This Part introduces a new regime to harmonise and replace provisions formerly contained in Sch 1, RSC Ord 50 and Sch 2, CCR Ord 31 which have been completely revoked, except where proceedings for a charging order or stop notice or for enforcement of a charging order by sale have been commenced before 25 March 2002, in which case the old rules will continue to apply (Civil Procedure (Amendment No 4) Rules 2001, SI 2001/2792, r 24).

73.1 Scope of this Part and interpretation

(1) This Part contains rules which provide for a judgment creditor to enforce a judgment by obtaining –

- (a) a charging order (Section I);
- (b) a stop order (Section II); or
- (c) a stop notice (Section III),

over or against the judgment debtor's interest in an asset.

(2) In this Part –

- (a) 'the 1979 Act' means the Charging Orders Act 1979;
- (b) 'the 1992 Regulations' means the Council Tax (Administration and Enforcement) Regulations 1992;
- (c) 'funds in court' includes securities held in court;
- (d) 'securities' means securities of any of the kinds specified in section 2(2)(b) of the 1979 Act.

Amendments—Inserted by SI 2001/2792.

Section I – Charging Orders

73.2 Scope of this Section

This Section applies to an application by a judgment creditor for a charging order under –

(a) section 1 of the 1979 Act; or
(b) regulation 50 of the 1992 Regulations.

Amendments—Inserted by SI 2001/2792.

73.3 Application for charging order

(1) An application for a charging order may be made without notice.

(2) An application for a charging order must be issued in the court which made the judgment or order which it is sought to enforce, unless –

(a) the proceedings have since been transferred to a different court, in which case the application must be issued in that court;
(b) the application is made under the 1992 Regulations, in which case it must be issued in the county court for the district in which the relevant dwelling (as defined in regulation 50(3)(b) of those Regulations) is situated;
(c) the application is for a charging order over an interest in a fund in court, in which case it must be issued in the court in which the claim relating to that fund is or was proceeding; or
(d) the application is to enforce a judgment or order of the High Court and it is required by section 1(2) of the 1979 Act to be made to a county court.

(3) Subject to paragraph (2), a judgment creditor may apply for a single charging order in respect of more than one judgment or order against the same debtor.

(4) The application notice must –

(a) (i) be in the form; and
(ii) contain the information,

required by the relevant practice direction; and
(b) be verified by a statement of truth.

Amendments—Inserted by SI 2001/2792.

Practice Direction—See PD73, para 1.2 at p 1555 as to the application notice (r 73.3(4)(a)).

Jurisdiction—Under COA 1979, s 1(2)(a), (b) and (c) the jurisdiction of the High Court is limited to the following situations:
(a) where the property to be charged is a fund in court lodged in the High Court;
(b) where the order to be enforced is a maintenance order of the High Court;
(c) where the judgment or order to be enforced is a judgment of the High Court for a sum of more than £5000. This includes a county court judgment which has been transferred to the High Court for enforcement.

'statement of truth' (r 73.3(4)(b))—See Pt 22.

73.4 Interim charging order

(1) An application for a charging order will initially be dealt with by a judge without a hearing.

(2) The judge may make an order (an 'interim charging order') –

(a) imposing a charge over the judgment debtor's interest in the asset to which the application relates; and

(b) fixing a hearing to consider whether to make a final charging order as provided by rule 73.8(2)(a).

Amendments—Inserted by SI 2001/2792.

Practice Direction—See PD73, para 1.3 at p 1555.

'may make an order' (r 73.4(2))—An interim order is not granted automatically. It may be refused not only if the application notice fails to comply with PD73, para 1.2 but also if the debt is too small to justify the remedy or the application appears otherwise oppressive. An order will not be made where there is a county court instalment order in force, under which there are no arrears (*Mercantile Credit Co Ltd v Ellis* (1987) *The Times*, 1 April, CA).

'an interim charging order' (r 73.4(2))—A charging order is made initially in the form of an interim order, to be confirmed by a final charging order or discharged on the hearing. Any Land Registry notice or caution or Land Charges Registry entry is properly effected pursuant to COA, s 3(2) or (3) on the making of the interim order and should not be repeated when a final charging order is made. Any such entry should be removed promptly if the interim order is discharged.

'asset to which the application relates' (r 73.4(2)(a))—More than one asset belonging to the judgment debtor may be included in a single application but a separate interim order will be drawn in respect of each asset (PD73, para 1.3).

73.5 Service of interim order

(1) Copies of the interim charging order, the application notice and any documents filed in support of it must, not less than 21 days before the hearing, be served on the following persons –

(a) the judgment debtor;

(b) such other creditors as the court directs;

(c) if the order relates to an interest under a trust, on such of the trustees as the court directs;

(d) if the interest charged is in securities other than securities held in court, then –

(i) in the case of stock for which the Bank of England keeps the register, the Bank of England;

(ii) in the case of government stock to which (i) does not apply, the keeper of the register;

(iii) in the case of stock of any body incorporated within England and Wales, that body;

(iv) in the case of stock of any body incorporated outside England and Wales or of any state or territory outside the United Kingdom, which is registered in a register kept in England and Wales, the keeper of that register;

(v) in the case of units of any unit trust in respect of which a register of the unit holders is kept in England and Wales, the keeper of that register; and

(e) if the interest charged is in funds in court, the Accountant General at the Court Funds Office.

(2) If the judgment creditor serves the order, he must either –

(a) file a certificate of service not less than 2 days before the hearing; or
(b) produce a certificate of service at the hearing.

Amendments—Inserted by SI 2001/2792.

'Service of interim order' (r 73.5 generally)—The normal procedure is for the interim order to be served by the court by first-class post. Judgment creditors should take care to supply the court with the names and addresses of all persons required to be served under r 73.5(1), together with sufficient copies of the application for service.

'other creditors' (r 73.5(1)(b))—The court will usually direct service on all known creditors (see COA, s 1(5)(b)) although service on prior chargees appears not to be necessary for their protection on the basis that they cannot be prejudiced by the making of the order. The former rule, requiring persons interested in the asset sought to be charged to be served at this stage of the proceedings, has not been reproduced. The expression 'creditor' may be given a purposive interpretation to include spouses or former spouses where the asset sought to be charged is or was a matrimonial home, particularly where rights of occupation have been registered under Family Law Act 1996, s 30 or where an application for ancillary relief has been registered as a pending action against the property. The form of application notice Form N379 (or N380) requires all persons interested to be identified. A direction is likely to be given that any such person identified be served (*Harman v Glencross* [1986] Fam 81, CA). Alternatively, such persons may apply after the event under r 73.9 below for the final charging order to be varied or discharged.

73.6 Effect of interim order in relation to securities

(1) If a judgment debtor disposes of his interest in any securities, while they are subject to an interim charging order which has been served on him, that disposition shall not, so long as that order remains in force, be valid as against the judgment creditor.

(2) A person served under rule 73.5(1)(d) with an interim charging order relating to securities must not, unless the court gives permission –

(a) permit any transfer of any of the securities; or
(b) pay any dividend, interest or redemption payment relating to them.

(3) If a person acts in breach of paragraph (2), he will be liable to pay to the judgment creditor –

(a) the value of the securities transferred or the amount of the payment made (as the case may be); or
(b) if less, the amount necessary to satisfy the debt in relation to which the interim charging order was made.

Amendments—Inserted by SI 2001/2792.

73.7 Effect of interim order in relation to funds in court

If a judgment debtor disposes of his interest in funds in court while they are subject to an interim charging order which has been served on him and on the Accountant General in accordance with rule 73.5(1), that disposition shall not, so long as that order remains in force, be valid as against the judgment creditor.

Amendments—Inserted by SI 2001/2792.

73.8 Further consideration of the application

(1) If any person objects to the court making a final charging order, he must –

(a) file; and
(b) serve on the applicant,

written evidence stating the grounds of his objections, not less than 7 days before the hearing.

(2) At the hearing the court may –

(a) make a final charging order confirming that the charge imposed by the interim charging order shall continue, with or without modification;
(b) discharge the interim charging order and dismiss the application;
(c) decide any issues in dispute between the parties, or between any of the parties and any other person who objects to the court making a final charging order; or
(d) direct a trial of any such issues, and if necessary give directions.

(3) If the court makes a final charging order which charges securities other than securities held in court, the order will include a stop notice unless the court otherwise orders.

(Section III of this Part contains provisions about stop notices)

(4) Any order made at the hearing must be served on all the persons on whom the interim charging order was required to be served.

Amendments—Inserted by SI 2001/2792.

'the court may' (r 73.8(2))—For the principles on which the court will exercise its discretion see *Roberts Petroleum Ltd v Bernard Kenney Ltd* [1983] 2 AC 192, CA at 690.

'final charging order' (r 73.8(2)(a))—The charge is effective from the day the interim order was made (*Haley v Barry* (1868) 3 Ch App 452). The fact that an instalment order has been made after the interim order does not prevent it from being confirmed (*Robaigealach v Allied Irish Bank plc* (2001) (unreported) 12 November, CA).

'with or without modification' (r 73.8(2)(a))—As there remains only one charging order, it cannot be modified to extend to property which was not included in the interim order. Modifications may include the imposition of conditions on enforcement under COA, s 3(1) (see note **'Conditions'** below).

'discharge the interim charging order' (r 73.8(2)(b))—All the factors which are relevant in the exercise of the court's discretion whether to grant an interim order under r 73.4(2) above apply also in considering whether to make a final charging order or discharge the interim order and dismiss the application. The interim order should be discharged if the debtor had no interest in the property when the interim order was made; or if the debtor has since parted with it and passed it on to someone who would not be affected by a mere equitable charge, such as a *bona fide* purchaser for value without notice (*Howell v Montey* (1990) *The Times*, 17 March, CA).

Adjournment—The court does have power to adjourn a hearing to another date under r 3.1(2)(b). Any adjournment should either be to a fixed date or to a particular event, eg the hearing of an application for ancillary relief. It is usual when adjourning to direct specifically that the interim order remain in force.

Conditions—Charging Orders Act 1979, s 3(1) enables the order to be made subject to conditions. Where the order is against the judgment debtor's interest in a family home, conditions delaying execution may now be more frequently used to comply with HRA 1998, Sch 1, Pt I, Art 8.

Costs—Fixed costs of £110 are specified in r 45.6. Courts may also (and normally will) allow Land Registry fees as disbursements. In practice, minor disbursements such as oath fees necessarily incurred are sometimes allowed in addition.

73.9 Discharge or variation of order

(1) Any application to discharge or vary a charging order must be made to the court which made the charging order.

(Section 3(5) of the 1979 Act and regulation 51(4) of the 1992 Regulations provide that the court may at any time, on the application of the debtor, or of any person interested in any property to which the order relates, or (where the 1992 Regulations apply) of the authority, make an order discharging or varying the charging order)

(2) The court may direct that –

(a) any interested person should be joined as a party to such an application; or

(b) the application should be served on any such person.

(3) An order discharging or varying a charging order must be served on all the persons on whom the charging order was required to be served.

Amendments—Inserted by SI 2001/2792.

'to discharge or vary' (r 73.9(1))—See note **'discharge the interim charging order'** to r 73. 8(2)(b) above.

'any interested person' (r 73.9(2)(a))—In particular, interested persons who did not receive notice of the making of an interim order may apply under this rule to be joined as parties to the application and for the order to be discharged or varied. Such applications may become inextricably linked with ancillary relief applications under the Matrimonial Causes Act 1973 to the extent that they must be heard together. The competing interests of judgment creditor, judgment debtor and former spouse can then all be decided on a single occasion.

73.10 Enforcement of charging order by sale

(1) Subject to the provisions of any enactment, the court may, upon a claim by a person who has obtained a charging order over an interest in property, order the sale of the property to enforce the charging order.

(2) A claim for an order for sale under this rule should be made to the court which made the charging order, unless that court does not have jurisdiction to make an order for sale.

(A claim under this rule is a proceeding for the enforcement of a charge, and section 23(c) of the County Courts Act 1984 provides the extent of the county court's jurisdiction to hear and determine such proceedings)

(3) The claimant must use the Part 8 procedure.

(4) A copy of the charging order must be filed with the claim form.

(5) The claimant's written evidence must include the information required by the relevant practice direction.

Amendments—Inserted by SI 2001/2792.

Practice Direction—See PD73, paras 4.1–4.5 at p 1555.

'interest in property' (r 73.10(1))—Application under this rule is likely to be useful only where the legal estate of the judgment debtor has been charged. Where the charge has been imposed on the judgment debtor's beneficial interest, sale of that interest alone may be difficult or impossible to achieve.

'jurisdiction to make an order for sale' (r 73.10(2))—A county court has jurisdiction to make orders for sale where the amount of the charge at the date of commencement of the proceedings does not exceed £30,000 (CCA 1984, s 23(c) and *Shields, Whitley and District Amalgamated Model Building Society v Richards* (1901) 84 LT 587), or where the amount exceeds £30,000 and both parties consent under CCA 1984, s 24.

Section II – Stop Orders

73.11 Interpretation

In this Section, 'stop order' means an order of the High Court not to take, in relation to funds in court or securities specified in the order, any of the steps listed in section 5(5) of the 1979 Act.

Amendments—Inserted by SI 2001/2792.

73.12 Application for stop order

(1) The High Court may make –

- (a) a stop order relating to funds in court, on the application of any person –
  - (i) who has a mortgage or charge on the interest of any person in the funds; or
  - (ii) to whom that interest has been assigned; or
  - (iii) who is a judgment creditor of the person entitled to that interest; or
- (b) a stop order relating to securities other than securities held in court, on the application of any person claiming to be beneficially entitled to an interest in the securities.

(2) An application for a stop order must be made –

- (a) by application notice in existing proceedings; or
- (b) by Part 8 claim form if there are no existing proceedings in the High Court.

(3) The application notice or claim form must be served on –

- (a) every person whose interest may be affected by the order applied for; and
- (b) either –
  - (i) the Accountant General at the Court Funds Office, if the application relates to funds in court; or
  - (ii) the person specified in rule 73.5(1)(d), if the application relates to securities other than securities held in court.

Amendments—Inserted by SI 2001/2792.

73.13 Stop order relating to funds in court

A stop order relating to funds in court shall prohibit the transfer, sale, delivery out, payment or other dealing with –

- (a) the funds or any part of them; or
- (b) any income on the funds.

Amendments—Inserted by SI 2001/2792.

73.14 Stop order relating to securities

(1) A stop order relating to securities other than securities held in court may prohibit all or any of the following steps –

- (a) the registration of any transfer of the securities;
- (b) the making of any payment by way of dividend, interest or otherwise in respect of the securities; and

(c) in the case of units of a unit trust, any acquisition of or other dealing with the units by any person or body exercising functions under the trust.

(2) The order shall specify –

(a) the securities to which it relates;
(b) the name in which the securities stand;
(c) the steps which may not be taken; and
(d) whether the prohibition applies to the securities only or to the dividends or interest as well.

Amendments—Inserted by SI 2001/2792.

73.15 Variation or discharge of order

(1) The court may, on the application of any person claiming to have a beneficial interest in the funds or securities to which a stop order relates, make an order discharging or varying the order.

(2) An application notice seeking the variation or discharge of a stop order must be served on the person who obtained the order.

Amendments—Inserted by SI 2001/2792.

Section III – Stop Notices

73.16 General

In this Section –

(a) 'stop notice' means a notice issued by the court which requires a person or body not to take, in relation to securities specified in the notice, any of the steps listed in section 5(5) of the 1979 Act, without first giving notice to the person who obtained the notice; and
(b) 'securities' does not include securities held in court.

Amendments—Inserted by SI 2001/2792.

73.17 Request for stop notice

(1) The High Court may, on the request of any person claiming to be beneficially entitled to an interest in securities, issue a stop notice.

(A stop notice may also be included in a final charging order, by either the High Court or a county court, under rule 73.8(3))

(2) A request for a stop notice must be made by filing –

(a) a draft stop notice; and
(b) written evidence which –
    (i) identifies the securities in question;
    (ii) describes the applicant's interest in the securities; and
    (iii) gives an address for service for the applicant.

(A sample form of stop notice is annexed to the relevant practice direction)

(3) If a court officer considers that the request complies with paragraph (2), he will issue a stop notice.

(4) The applicant must serve copies of the stop notice and his written evidence on the person to whom the stop notice is addressed.

Amendments—Inserted by SI 2001/2792.

73.18 Effect of stop notice

(1) A stop notice –

- (a) takes effect when it is served in accordance with rule 73.17(4); and
- (b) remains in force unless it is withdrawn or discharged in accordance with rule 73.20 or 73.21.

(2) While a stop notice is in force, the person on whom it is served –

- (a) must not –
  - (i) register a transfer of the securities described in the notice; or
  - (ii) take any other step restrained by the notice,

without first giving 14 days' notice to the person who obtained the stop notice; but

- (b) must not, by reason only of the notice, refuse to register a transfer or to take any other step, after he has given 14 days' notice under paragraph (2)(a) and that period has expired.

Amendments—Inserted by SI 2001/2792.

73.19 Amendment of stop notice

(1) If any securities are incorrectly described in a stop notice which has been obtained and served in accordance with rule 73.17, the applicant may request an amended stop notice in accordance with that rule.

(2) The amended stop notice takes effect when it is served.

Amendments—Inserted by SI 2001/2792.

73.20 Withdrawal of stop notice

(1) A person who has obtained a stop notice may withdraw it by serving a request for its withdrawal on –

- (a) the person or body on whom the stop notice was served; and
- (b) the court which issued the stop notice.

(2) The request must be signed by the person who obtained the stop notice, and his signature must be witnessed by a practising solicitor.

Amendments—Inserted by SI 2001/2792.

73.21 Discharge or variation of stop notice

(1) The court may, on the application of any person claiming to be beneficially entitled to an interest in the securities to which a stop notice relates, make an order discharging or varying the notice.

(2) An application to discharge or vary a stop notice must be made to the court which issued the notice.

(3) The application notice must be served on the person who obtained the stop notice.

Amendments—Inserted by SI 2001/2792.

Practice Direction – Charging Orders, Stop Orders and Stop Notices

This Practice Direction supplements CPR Part 73 (PD73)

SECTION I – CHARGING ORDERS

APPLICATION NOTICE – RULE 73.3

1.1 An application for a charging order must be made by filing an application notice in Practice Form N379 if the application relates to land, or N380 if the application relates to securities.

1.2 The application notice must contain the following information –

- (1) the name and address of the judgment debtor;
- (2) details of the judgment or order sought to be enforced;
- (3) the amount of money remaining due under the judgment or order;
- (4) if the judgment debt is payable by instalments, the amount of any instalments which have fallen due and remain unpaid;
- (5) if the judgment creditor knows of the existence of any other creditors of the judgment debtor, their names and (if known) their addresses;
- (6) identification of the asset or assets which it is intended to charge;
- (7) details of the judgment debtor's interest in the asset; and
- (8) the names and addresses of the persons on whom an interim charging order must be served under rule 73.5(1).

1.3 A judgment creditor may apply in a single application notice for charging orders over more than one asset, but if the court makes interim charging orders over more than one asset, it will draw up a separate order relating to each asset.

'details of the judgment' (para 1.2(2))—There is no reason in principle why a judgment debt and an order for costs as assessed or the sums due under two separate judgments should not be included in a single application provided the identity of the judgment creditor and judgment debtor are the same in each case.

'more than one asset' (para 1.3)—Where the judgment debtor owns a large number of properties all of which are to be included in the interim order it may be more convenient to list these with their title numbers in a separate schedule to the application notice.

HIGH COURT AND COUNTY COURT JURISDICTION

2 The jurisdiction of the High Court and the county court to make charging orders is set out in section 1(2) of the 1979 Act.

'jurisdiction'—See note **'Jurisdiction'** to COA 1979, s 1(2).

TRANSFER

3 The court may, on an application by a judgment debtor who wishes to oppose an application for a charging order, transfer it to the court for the district where the judgment debtor resides or carries on business, or to another court.

'application'—See CPR Pt 23 for the procedure on making applications. The court may also be invited to make such an order of its own initiative under CPR r 3.3.

ENFORCEMENT OF CHARGING ORDERS BY SALE – RULE 73.10

4.1 A county court has jurisdiction to determine a claim under rule 73.10 for the enforcement of a charging order if the amount owing under the charge does not exceed the county court limit.

4.2 A claim in the High Court for an order for sale of land to enforce a charging order must be started in Chancery Chambers at the Royal Courts of Justice, or a Chancery district registry.

(There are Chancery district registries at Birmingham, Bristol, Cardiff, Leeds, Liverpool, Manchester, Newcastle upon Tyne and Preston)

4.3 The written evidence in support of a claim under rule 73.10 must –

- (1) identify the charging order and the property sought to be sold;
- (2) state the amount in respect of which the charge was imposed and the amount due at the date of issue of the claim;
- (3) verify, so far as known, the debtor's title to the property charged;
- (4) state, so far as the claimant is able to identify –
  - (a) the names and addresses of any other creditors who have a prior charge or other security over the property; and
  - (b) the amount owed to each such creditor; and
- (5) give an estimate of the price which would be obtained on sale of the property.
- (6) if the claim relates to land, give details of every person who to the best of the claimant's knowledge is in possession of the property; and
- (7) if the claim relates to residential property –
  - (a) state whether –
    - (i) a land charge of Class F; or
    - (ii) a notice under section 31(10) of the Family Law Act 1996, or under any provision of an Act which preceded that section,

    has been registered; and
  - (b) if so, state –
    - (i) on whose behalf the land charge or notice has been registered; and
    - (ii) that the claimant will serve notice of the claim on that person.

4.4 The claimant must take all reasonable steps to obtain the information required by paragraph 4.3(4) before issuing the claim.

4.5 Sample forms of orders for sale are set out in Appendix A to this practice direction for guidance. These are not prescribed forms of order and they may be adapted or varied by the court to meet the requirements of individual cases.

'county court limit' (para 4.1)—The present figure is £30,000 which may be exceeded only if both parties consent under CCA 1984, s 24.

'verify … the debtor's title'(para 4.3(3))—If the charging order affects registered land office copy entries of the title should be filed.

SECTION II – STOP NOTICES

5 A sample form of stop notice is set out in Appendix B to this practice direction.

APPENDIX A

ORDER FOR SALE **In the** **Claim No**
following a charging order **Appn No**
[(property solely owned by judgment debtor)]

Claimant

Defendant

On the 20 , sitting at
heard
The claimant is entitled to an equitable charge upon the defendant's interest in the property
[registered at HM Land Registry under Title No]
('the property')
under a charging order made on the
in the in Claim No
and the court orders that

1 The remainder of this order will not take effect if the defendant by 4.00 pm on the 20 pays to the claimant the judgment debt of £ secured by the charge and his costs to date of this application assessed at £ , making together £ [together with interest at the rate of £ per day from the date of this order until payment is received by the claimant].

2 The property shall be sold without further reference to the court at a price not less than £ , unless that figure is changed by a further order of the court.

3 The [claimant] [claimant's solicitor] will have conduct of the sale.

4 To enable the claimant to carry out the sale, there be created and vested in the claimant pursuant to section 90 of the Law of Property Act 1925 a legal term in the property of [3000 years] [one day less than the remaining period of the term created by the lease under which the defendant holds the property].

5 The defendant must deliver possession of the property to the claimant [on or before the 20] [within [ ] days of this order being served on him].

6 The claimant shall first apply the proceeds of sale of the property –
(i) to pay the costs and expenses of effecting the sale; and
(ii) to discharge any charges or other securities over the property which have priority over the charging order.

7 Out of the remaining proceeds of sale the claimant shall –
(i) retain the amount due to him as stated in paragraph 1; and
(ii) pay the balance (if any) [to the Defendant] [to] [into court].

8 Either party may apply to the court to vary any of the terms of this order, or for further directions about the sale or the application of the proceeds of sale, or otherwise.

ORDER FOR SALE following a charging order (property owned by judgment debtor and another person)

In the
Claim No

Claimant

Defendants

On the 20 , sitting at
heard
The claimant is entitled to an equitable charge upon the first defendant's interest in the property
[registered at HM Land Registry under Title No]
('the property')
under a charging order made on the
in the in Claim No
and the court orders that

1 The remainder of this order will not take effect if the defendant by 4.00 pm on the 20 pays to the claimant the judgment debt of £ secured by the charge and his costs to date of this application assessed at £ , making together £ [together with interest at the rate of £ per day from the date of this order until payment is received by the claimant].

2 The property shall be sold without further reference to the court at a price not less than £ , unless that figure is changed by a further order of the court.

3 The [claimant] [claimant's solicitor] will have conduct of the sale.

4 The court pursuant to section 50 of the Trustee Act 1925 appoints the [claimant] [claimant's solicitor] to convey the property.

5 The defendant must deliver possession of the property to the claimant [on or before the 20] [within [ ] days of this order being served on him].

6 The claimant shall first apply the proceeds of sale of the property –
(i) to pay the costs and expenses of effecting the sale; and
(ii) to discharge any charges or other securities over the property which have priority over the charging order.

7 The claimant shall then divide the remaining proceeds of sale into two equal shares and –
(i) pay one equal share to the second defendant; and
(ii) out of the other equal share, retain the amount due to him stated in paragraph 1, and pay the balance (if any) [to the first defendant] [to] [into court].

8 Any party may apply to the court to vary any of the terms of this order, or for further directions about the sale or the application of the proceeds of sale, or otherwise.

APPENDIX B

STOP NOTICE

CPR rule 73.17

To [*insert name of person or body to whom the notice is addressed*]

TAKE NOTICE that
[*insert name and address*]

claims to be beneficially entitled to an interest in the following securities –
[*specify the securities, giving the name(s) in which they stand*]
This Notice requires you to refrain from–
(1) registering a transfer of the securities specified above; or
(2) paying any dividend or interest in respect of the securities [*delete if inappropriate*];
without first giving 14 days' notice in writing to the said [*insert name*] of the above address.

PART 74
ENFORCEMENT OF JUDGMENTS IN DIFFERENT JURISDICTIONS

CONTENTS OF THIS PART

Practice Direction—This Part is supplemented by a practice direction – PD74 – which is set out at p 1574.

General note—Section I of Pt 74, together with its practice direction, is a valiant attempt to bring order out of the chaos which the former RSC Ord 71 had become. It can only be understood if the legal background is briefly examined.

A judgment of a foreign court cannot be directly enforced in England and Wales. However, it can be made the basis of an action in the English courts, in which summary judgment will be granted (see *Colt Industries Inc v Sarlie (No 2)* [1966] 1 WLR 1287) unless the defendant can establish one of a limited number of defences.

Special arrangements have been made for the reciprocal enforcement of foreign maintenance orders. Arrears under such orders can generally not be the subject of an action in England (*Harrop v Harrop* [1920] 3 KB 386) but the order can be registered in the appropriate magistrates' court under the Maintenance Orders (Reciprocal Enforcement) Act 1972, for details of which see *The Family Court Practice* (Family Law).

Four pieces of legislation – the 1920, 1933 and 1982 Acts and the Judgments Regulation – allow foreign judgments to be registered in the High Court for enforcement, without the claimant needing to bring a fresh action. Unless the case falls within the scope of one of them, there is no power to register a foreign judgment for enforcement. Note particularly that there is at present no provision for the registration of judgments from the United States of America, although attempts have been made to negotiate one.

74.1 Scope of this Part and interpretation

(1) Section I of this Part applies to the enforcement in England and Wales of judgments of foreign courts.

(2) Section II applies to the enforcement in foreign countries of judgments of the High Court and of county courts.

(3) Section III applies to the enforcement of the United Kingdom judgments in other parts of the United Kingdom.

(4) Section IV applies to the enforcement in England and Wales of European Community judgments and Euratom inspection orders.

(4A) Section V applies to –

- (a) the certification of judgments and court settlements in England and Wales as European Enforcement Orders; and
- (b) the enforcement in England and Wales of judgments, court settlements and authentic instruments certified as European Enforcement Orders by other Member States.

(5) In this Part –

- (a) 'the 1920 Act' means the Administration of Justice Act 1920;
- (b) 'the 1933 Act' means the Foreign Judgments (Reciprocal Enforcement) Act 1933;
- (c) 'the 1982 Act' means the Civil Jurisdiction and Judgments Act 1982;
- (d) 'the Judgments Regulation' means Council Regulation (EC) No 44/2001 of 22 December 2000 on jurisdiction and the recognition and enforcement of judgments in civil and commercial matters;
- (e) 'the EEO Regulation' means Council Regulation (EC) No 805/2004 creating a European Enforcement Order for uncontested claims.

(A copy of the EEO Regulation is annexed to Practice Direction 74B European Enforcement Orders and can be found at http://europa.eu.int/eur-lex/pri/en/oj/dat/2004/l_143/l_14320040430en00150039.pdf)

Amendments—Inserted by SI 2002/2058; amended by SI 2005/2292.

'the 1920 Act' (r 74.1(5)(a))—This Act provides for reciprocal enforcement of judgments of the superior courts in countries to which the Act had been applied by Order in Council before the 1933 Act came into force. The consolidated list is as follows:

Anguilla, Antigua and Barbuda, Bahamas, Barbados, Belize, Bermuda, Botswana, British Indian Ocean Territory, British Virgin Islands, Cayman Islands, Christmas Island, Cocos (Keeling) Islands, Republic of Cyprus, Dominica, Falkland Islands, Fiji, The Gambia, Ghana, Grenada, Guyana, Jamaica, Kenya, Kiribati, Lesotho, Malawi, Malaysia, Malta, Mauritius, Montserrat, New Zealand, Nigeria, Territory of Norfolk Island, Papua New Guinea, St Christopher and Nevis, St Helena, St Lucia, St Vincent and the Grenadines, Seychelles, Sierra Leone, Singapore, Solomon Islands, Sovereign Base Area of Akrotiri and Dhekelia in Cyprus, Sri Lanka, Swaziland, Tanzania, Tasmania, Trinidad and Tobago, Turks and Caicos Islands, Tuvalu, Uganda, Zambia, Zimbabwe.

The 1920 Act no longer applies to Hong Kong or Gibraltar; Gibraltar is now subject to the Brussels Convention.

See s 9(2) of the Act for limitations on the judgments which may be registered. It should be noted that registration under this Act is discretionary. As the 1920 Act is based on reciprocity it may well be that at the present time registration of judgments from Zimbabwe should be refused (compare *Habib Bank v Ahmed* (2000) 97 (43) LSG 37, (2000) *The Times*, 2 November, QBD).

'the 1933 Act' (r 74.1(5)(b))—This Act made further provision for reciprocal enforcement of judgments with a number of countries. The only non-Commonwealth countries to which the 1933 Act is still relevant are Israel, Surinam and Tonga. All the other countries formerly covered by the Act are now parties to the Brussels or Lugano conventions and applications should be made under the 1982 Act or the Judgments Regulation as appropriate. The list of Commonwealth countries to which the Act has been applied is as follows:

Australia including the Australian Capital Territory, the Federal Court of Canada and courts of all provinces except Quebec, Island of Guernsey, Isle of Man, Bailiwick of Jersey, certain territories of the Republic of India named in the Schedule to the Reciprocal Enforcement of Judgments (India) Order 1958, SI 1958/425, and Pakistan.

A judgment which is capable of being registered under the 1933 Act cannot be made the subject of an action (see s 6 of the Act and *Yukon Consolidated Gold Corporation Ltd v Clark* [1938] 2 KB 241).

'the 1982 Act' (r 74.1(5)(c))—This Act gives effect to the Brussels Convention (to which the EEC countries were parties) and the similar Lugano Convention signed by the Member States of EFTA. As with the 1933 Act, a registrable judgment cannot be made the subject of an action. The grounds on which registration may be set aside are very limited.

'the Judgments Regulation' (r 74.1(5)(d))—This Regulation applies a uniform regime, similar though not identical to that under the Brussels Convention, to all the Member States of the European Union with the exception of Denmark (to which the Brussels Convention continues to apply).

I Enforcement in England and Wales of Judgments of Foreign Courts

74.2 Interpretation

(1) In this Section –

- (a) 'Contracting State' has the meaning given in section 1(3) of the 1982 Act;
- (b) 'Regulation State' has the same meaning as 'Member State' in the Judgments Regulation, that is all Member States except Denmark;
- (c) 'judgment' means, subject to any other enactment, any judgment given by a foreign court or tribunal, whatever the judgment may be called, and includes –
  - (i) a decree;
  - (ii) an order;
  - (iii) a decision;
  - (iv) a writ of execution; and
  - (v) the determination of costs by an officer of the court;
- (d) 'State of origin', in relation to any judgment, means the State in which that judgment was given.

(2) For the purposes of this Section, 'domicile' is to be determined –

- (a) in an application under the 1982 Act, in accordance with sections 41 to 46 of that Act;
- (b) in an application under the Judgments Regulation, in accordance with paragraphs 9 to 12 of Schedule 1 to the Civil Jurisdiction and Judgments Order 2001.

Amendments—Inserted by SI 2002/2058.

'Contracting State' (r 74.2(1)(a))—This includes all states which are signatories to the Brussels Convention (which includes Denmark) or the Lugano Convention (which includes Norway, Poland and Switzerland).

74.3 Applications for registration

(1) This Section provides rules about applications under –

- (a) section 9 of the 1920 Act, in respect of judgments to which Part II of that Act applies;
- (b) section 2 of the 1933 Act, in respect of judgments to which Part I of that Act applies;
- (c) section 4 of the 1982 Act; and
- (d) the Judgments Regulation,

for the registration of foreign judgments for enforcement in England and Wales.

(2) Applications –

- (a) must be made to the High Court; and
- (b) may be made without notice.

Amendments—Inserted by SI 2002/2058.

'must be made to the High Court' (r 74.3(2)(a))—The draftsman regarded it as too obvious to need stating, but subsequent enforcement proceedings are submitted to the Central Office (at the Royal Courts of Justice), not the district registry or county court in whose area the defendant resides.

74.4 Evidence in support

(1) An application for registration of a judgment under the 1920, 1933 or 1982 Act must be supported by written evidence exhibiting –

- (a) the judgment or a verified or certified or otherwise authenticated copy of it; and
- (b) where the judgment is not in English, a translation of it into English –
  - (i) certified by a notary public or other qualified person; or
  - (ii) accompanied by written evidence confirming that the translation is accurate.

(2) The written evidence in support of the application must state –

- (a) the name of the judgment creditor and his address for service within the jurisdiction;
- (b) the name of the judgment debtor and his address or place of business, if known;
- (c) the grounds on which the judgment creditor is entitled to enforce the judgment;
- (d) in the case of a money judgment, the amount in respect of which it remains unsatisfied; and
- (e) where interest is recoverable on the judgment under the law of the State of origin –
  - (i) the amount of interest which has accrued up to the date of the application, or
  - (ii) the rate of interest, the date from which it is recoverable, and the date on which it ceases to accrue.

(3) Written evidence in support of an application under the 1920 Act must also state that the judgment is not a judgment –

- (a) which under section 9 of that Act may not be ordered to be registered; or
- (b) to which section 5 of the Protection of Trading Interests Act 1980 applies.

(4) Written evidence in support of an application under the 1933 Act must also –

- (a) state that the judgment is a money judgment;
- (b) confirm that it can be enforced by execution in the State of origin;
- (c) confirm that the registration could not be set aside under section 4 of that Act;
- (d) confirm that the judgment is not a judgment to which section 5 of the Protection of Trading Interests Act 1980 applies;
- (e) where the judgment contains different provisions, some but not all of which can be registered for enforcement, set out those provisions in respect of which it is sought to register the judgment; and
- (f) be accompanied by any further evidence as to –
  - (i) the enforceability of the judgment in the State of origin, and
  - (ii) the law of that State under which any interest has become due under the judgment,

which may be required under the relevant Order in Council extending Part I of the 1933 Act to that State.

(5) Written evidence in support of an application under the 1982 Act must also exhibit –

- (a) documents which show that, under the law of the State of origin, the judgment is enforceable on the judgment debtor and has been served;
- (b) in the case of a judgment in default, a document which establishes that the party in default was served with the document instituting the proceedings or with an equivalent document; and
- (c) where appropriate, a document showing that the judgment creditor is in receipt of legal aid in the State of origin.

(6) An application for registration under the Judgments Regulation must, in addition to the evidence required by that Regulation, be supported by the evidence required by paragraphs (1)(b) and (2)(e) of this rule.

Amendments—Inserted by SI 2002/2058.

'An application' (r 74.4(1))—The application is made without notice to a master in the Queen's Bench Division. An application notice under Pt 23 should be issued in the Action Department at the Royal Courts of Justice, not in a district registry.

'amount in respect of which it remains unsatisfied' (r 74.4(2)(d))—The amount outstanding under a foreign currency judgment must not be converted into sterling as it will be registered in the currency in which it is expressed (*Miliangos v George Frank (Textiles) Ltd* [1976] AC 443, HL). For the proper method of conversion on enforcement see *Practice Direction (Judgment: Foreign Currency)* [1976] 1 WLR 83.

74.5 Security for costs

(1) Subject to paragraphs (2) and (3), section II of Part 25 applies to an application for security for the costs of –

- (a) the application for registration;
- (b) any proceedings brought to set aside the registration; and
- (c) any appeal against the granting of the registration

as if the judgment creditor were a claimant.

(2) A judgment creditor making an application under the 1982 Act or the Judgments Regulation may not be required to give security solely on the ground that he is resident out of the jurisdiction.

(3) Paragraph (1) does not apply to an application under the 1933 Act where the relevant Order in Council otherwise provides.

Amendments—Inserted by SI 2002/2058.

'security for costs' (r 74.5(1))—The procedures under the 1920 and 1933 Acts effectively require security to be given by claimants residing in countries to which those Acts apply (*Kohn v Rinson & Stafford (Brod) Ltd* [1948] 1 KB 327).

74.6 Registration orders

(1) An order granting permission to register a judgment ('a registration order') must be drawn up by the judgment creditor and served on the judgment debtor –

- (a) by delivering it to him personally;
- (b) as provided by section 725 of the Companies Act 1985; or
- (c) in such other manner as the court may direct.

(2) Permission is not required to serve a registration order out of the jurisdiction, and rules 6.24, 6.25, 6.26 and 6.29 apply to such an order as they apply to a claim form.

(3) A registration order must state –

- (a) full particulars of the judgment registered;
- (b) the name of the judgment creditor and his address for service within the jurisdiction;
- (c) the right of the judgment debtor –
  - (i) in the case of registration following an application under the 1920 or the 1933 Act, to apply to have the registration set aside;
  - (ii) in the case of registration following an application under the 1982 Act or under the Judgments Regulation, to appeal against the registration order;
- (d) the period within which such an application or appeal may be made; and
- (e) that no measures of enforcement will be taken before the end of that period, other than measures ordered by the court to preserve the property of the judgment debtor.

Amendments—Inserted by SI 2002/2058.

74.7 Applications to set aside registration

(1) An application to set aside registration under the 1920 or the 1933 Act must be made within the period set out in the registration order.

(2) The court may extend that period; but an application for such an extension must be made before the end of the period as originally fixed or as subsequently extended.

(3) The court hearing the application may order any issue between the judgment creditor and the judgment debtor to be tried.

Amendments—Inserted by SI 2002/2058.

74.8 Appeals

(1) An appeal against the granting or the refusal of registration under the 1982 Act or the Judgments Regulation must be made in accordance with Part 52, subject to the following provisions of this rule.

(2) Permission is not required –

(a) to appeal; or
(b) to put in evidence.

(3) If –

(a) the judgment debtor is not domiciled within a Contracting State or a Regulation State, as the case may be, and
(b) an application to extend the time for appealing is made within two months of service of the registration order

the court may extend the period for filing an appellant's notice against the order granting registration, but not on grounds of distance.

(4) The appellant's notice must be served –

(a) where the appeal is against the granting of registration, within –
   (i) one month; or
   (ii) where service is to be effected on a party not domiciled within the jurisdiction, two months

of service of the registration order;

(b) where the appeal is against the refusal of registration, within one month of the decision on the application for registration.

Amendments—Inserted by SI 2002/2058.

'appeal' (r 74.8(1))—A purported application to a master to set aside a registration under the 1982 Act or the Judgments Regulation is a nullity (*Maronier v Larmer* [2002] EWCA Civ 774, [2003] QB 620, CA).

There is a strong presumption that a judgment from another European Union State will be compliant with Art 6 ECHR (see eg *TSN Kunststoffrecycling GmbH v Jürgens* [2002] EWCA Civ 11, [2002] 1 WLR 2459, CA) but the presumption can be rebutted (*Maronier v Larmer* [2002] EWCA Civ 774, [2003] QB 620, CA, where an action had been stayed for 12 years and it was accepted that the defendant only became aware of the revival of the proceedings after the time for appealing in the Netherlands had expired).

Even if it is clear that the original court acted without jurisdiction, the receiving court cannot, under European law, refuse to recognise the judgment on that ground (*Bamberski v Krombach (C-7/98)* [2001] QB 709, ECJ).

'within one month' (r 74.8(4)(a)(i))—There appears to be power under r 3.1(2)(a) to extend the time for appealing (*Citibank NA v Rafidian Bank* [2003] All ER (D) 23 (Aug), Tugendhat J) but on the facts of that case an extension of time was refused and the burden of showing that time should be extended will be heavy).

74.9 Enforcement

(1) No steps may be taken to enforce a judgment –

(a) before the end of the period specified in accordance with rule 74.6(3)(d), or that period as extended by the court; or
(b) where there is an application under rule 74.7 or an appeal under rule 74.8, until the application or appeal has been determined.

(2) Any party wishing to enforce a judgment must file evidence of the service on the judgment debtor of –

(a) the registration order; and
(b) any other relevant order of the court.

(3) Nothing in this rule prevents the court from making orders to preserve the property of the judgment debtor pending final determination of any issue relating to the enforcement of the judgment.

Amendments—Inserted by SI 2002/2058.

74.10 Recognition

(1) Registration of a judgment serves as a decision that the judgment is recognised for the purposes of the 1982 Act and the Judgments Regulation.

(2) An application for recognition of a judgment is governed by the same rules as an application for registration of a judgment under the 1982 Act or under the Judgments Regulation, except that rule 74.4(5)(a) and (c) does not apply.

Amendments—Inserted by SI 2002/2058.

74.11 Authentic instruments and court settlements

The rules governing the registration of judgments under the 1982 Act or under the Judgments Regulation apply as appropriate and with any necessary modifications for the enforcement of –

- (a) authentic instruments which are subject to –
  - (i) article 50 of Schedule 1 to the 1982 Act;
  - (ii) article 50 of Schedule 3C to the 1982 Act; and
  - (iii) article 57 of the Judgments Regulation; and
- (b) court settlements which are subject to –
  - (i) article 51 of Schedule 1 to the 1982 Act;
  - (ii) article 51 of Schedule 3C to the 1982 Act; and
  - (iii) article 58 of the Judgments Regulation.

Amendments—Inserted by SI 2002/2058.

II Enforcement in Foreign Countries of Judgments of the High Court and County Courts

74.12 Application for a certified copy of a judgment

(1) This Section applies to applications –

- (a) to the High Court under section 10 of the 1920 Act;
- (b) to the High Court or to a county court under section 10 of the 1933 Act;
- (c) to the High Court or to a county court under section 12 of the 1982 Act; or
- (d) to the High Court or to a county court under article 54 of the Judgments Regulation.

(2) A judgment creditor who wishes to enforce in a foreign country a judgment obtained in the High Court or in a county court must apply for a certified copy of the judgment.

(3) The application may be made without notice.

Amendments—Inserted by SI 2002/2058.

'the High Court' (r 74.12(1)(a))—It will be recalled that the 1920 Act applies only to judgments of the superior courts. It has no application to county court judgments.

'enforce in a foreign country' (r 74.12(2))—Before deciding whether to issue in the High Court or the county court, it may be prudent to ascertain from local advisers whether the foreign country will enforce county court judgments. The courts of Jersey, for example, have declined to enforce a county court judgment under the 1933 Act even where it has been transferred to the High Court under CCA 1984, s 42 (*Re Hardwick* [1995] Jersey LR 245, see *www.jerseylegalinfo.je*); and in *Fawdry & Co v Murfitt* [2002] EWCA Civ 643, [2003] QB 104, [2002] 3 WLR 1354, [2003] 4 All ER 61 a claim for £19,340 was retained in the High Court rather than being transferred to the county court because the claimant wished to be able to enforce in Jersey, see per Hale LJ at 62.

74.13 Evidence in support

(1) The application must be supported by written evidence exhibiting copies of –

- (a) the claim form in the proceedings in which judgment was given;
- (b) evidence that it was served on the defendant;
- (c) the statements of case; and
- (d) where relevant, a document showing that for those proceedings the applicant was an assisted person or an LSC funded client, as defined in rule 43.2(1)(h) and (i).

(2) The written evidence must –

- (a) identify the grounds on which the judgment was obtained;
- (b) state whether the defendant objected to the jurisdiction and, if he did, the grounds of his objection;
- (c) show that the judgment –
  - (i) has been served in accordance with Part 6 and rule 40.4, and
  - (ii) is not subject to a stay of execution;
- (d) state –
  - (i) the date on which the time for appealing expired or will expire;
  - (ii) whether an appeal notice has been filed;
  - (iii) the status of any application for permission to appeal; and
  - (iv) whether an appeal is pending;
- (e) state whether the judgment provides for the payment of a sum of money, and if so, the amount in respect of which it remains unsatisfied;
- (f) state whether interest is recoverable on the judgment, and if so, either –
  - (i) the amount of interest which has accrued up to the date of the application, or
  - (ii) the rate of interest, the date from which it is recoverable, and the date on which it ceases to accrue.

Amendments—Inserted by SI 2002/2058.

III Enforcement of United Kingdom Judgments in Other Parts of the United Kingdom

74.14 Interpretation

In this Section –

- (a) 'money provision' means a provision for the payment of one or more sums of money in a judgment whose enforcement is governed by section 18 of, and Schedule 6 to, the 1982 Act; and
- (b) 'non-money provision' means a provision for any relief or remedy not requiring payment of a sum of money in a judgment whose enforcement is governed by section 18 of, and Schedule 7 to, the 1982 Act.

Amendments—Inserted by SI 2002/2058.

74.15 Registration of money judgments in the High Court

(1) This rule applies to applications to the High Court under paragraph 5 of Schedule 6 to the 1982 Act for the registration of a certificate for the enforcement of the money provisions of a judgment –

(a) which has been given by a court in another part of the United Kingdom, and

(b) to which section 18 of that Act applies.

(2) The certificate must within six months of the date of its issue be filed in the Central Office of the Supreme Court, together with a copy certified by written evidence to be a true copy.

Amendments—Inserted by SI 2002/2058.

'to the High Court' (r 74.15(1))—Subsequent enforcement proceedings should be taken in the Central Office (at Royal Courts of Justice), not a district registry or county court.

'another part of the United Kingdom' (r 74.15(1)(a))—Note that this includes only Scotland and Northern Ireland. It does not include, for example, the Isle of Man or the Channel Islands.

74.16 Registration of non-money judgments in the High Court

(1) This rule applies to applications to the High Court under paragraph 5 of Schedule 7 to the 1982 Act for the registration for enforcement of the non-money provisions of a judgment –

(a) which has been given by a court in another part of the United Kingdom, and

(b) to which section 18 of that Act applies.

(2) An application under paragraph (1) may be made without notice.

(3) An application under paragraph (1) must be accompanied –

(a) by a certified copy of the judgment issued under Schedule 7 to the 1982 Act; and

(b) by a certificate, issued not more than six months before the date of the application, stating that the conditions set out in paragraph 3 of Schedule 7 are satisfied in relation to the judgment.

(4) Rule 74.6 applies to judgments registered under Schedule 7 to the 1982 Act as it applies to judgments registered under section 4 of that Act.

(5) Rule 74.7 applies to applications to set aside the registration of a judgment under paragraph 9 of Schedule 7 to the 1982 Act as it applies to applications to set aside registrations under the 1920 and 1933 Acts.

Amendments—Inserted by SI 2002/2058.

74.17 Certificates of High Court and county court money judgments

(1) This rule applies to applications under paragraph 2 of Schedule 6 to the 1982 Act for a certificate to enable the money provisions of a judgment of the High Court or of a county court to be enforced in another part of the United Kingdom.

(2) The judgment creditor may apply for a certificate by filing at the court where the judgment was given or has been entered written evidence stating –

(a) the name and address of the judgment creditor and, if known, of the judgment debtor;

(b) the sums payable and unsatisfied under the money provisions of the judgment;
(c) where interest is recoverable on the judgment, either –
  (i) the amount of interest which has accrued up to the date of the application, or
  (ii) the rate of interest, the date from which it is recoverable, and the date on which it ceases to accrue;
(d) that the judgment is not stayed;
(e) the date on which the time for appealing expired or will expire;
(f) whether an appeal notice has been filed;
(g) the status of any application for permission to appeal; and
(h) whether an appeal is pending.

Amendments—Inserted by SI 2002/2058.

74.18 Certified copies of High Court and county court non-money judgments

(1) This rule applies to applications under paragraph 2 of Schedule 7 to the 1982 Act for a certified copy of a judgment of the High Court or of a county court to which section 18 of the Act applies and which contains non-money provisions for enforcement in another part of the United Kingdom.

(2) An application under paragraph (1) may be made without notice.

(3) The applicant may apply for a certified copy of a judgment by filing at the court where the judgment was given or has been entered written evidence stating –

(a) full particulars of the judgment;
(b) the name and address of the judgment creditor and, if known, of the judgment debtor;
(c) that the judgment is not stayed;
(d) the date on which the time for appealing expired or will expire;
(e) whether an appeal notice has been filed;
(f) the status of any application for permission to appeal; and
(g) whether an appeal is pending.

Amendments—Inserted by SI 2002/2058.

IV Enforcement in England and Wales of European Community Judgments

74.19 Interpretation

In this Section –

(a) 'Community judgment' means any judgment, decision or order which is enforceable under –
  (i) article 244 or 256 of the Treaty establishing the European Community;
  (ii) article 18, 159 or 164 of the Euratom Treaty;
  (iii) article 44 or 92 of the ECSC Treaty;
  (iv) article 82 of Council Regulation (EC) 40/94 of 20 December 1993 on the Community trade mark; or
  (v) article 71 of Council Regulation (EC) 6/2002 of 12 December 2001 on Community designs;

(b) 'Euratom inspection order' means an order made by the President of the European Court, or a decision of the Commission of the European Communities, under article 81 of the Euratom Treaty;
(c) 'European Court' means the Court of Justice of the European Communities;
(d) 'order for enforcement' means an order under the authority of the Secretary of State that the Community judgment to which it is appended is to be registered for enforcement in the United Kingdom.

Amendments—Inserted by SI 2002/2058; amended by SI 2003/3361.

74.20 Application for registration of a Community judgment

An application to the High Court for the registration of a Community judgment may be made without notice.

Amendments—Inserted by SI 2002/2058.

74.21 Evidence in support

(1) An application for registration must be supported by written evidence exhibiting –

(a) the Community judgment and the order for its enforcement, or an authenticated copy; and
(b) where the judgment is not in English, a translation of it into English –
   (i) certified by a notary public or other qualified person; or
   (ii) accompanied by written evidence confirming that the translation is accurate.

(2) Where the application is for registration of a Community judgment which is a money judgment, the evidence must state –

(a) the name of the judgment creditor and his address for service within the jurisdiction;
(b) the name of the judgment debtor and his address or place of business, if known;
(c) the amount in respect of which the judgment is unsatisfied; and
(d) that the European Court has not suspended enforcement of the judgment.

Amendments—Inserted by SI 2002/2058.

74.22 Registration orders

(1) A copy of the order granting permission to register a Community judgment ('the registration order') must be served on every person against whom the judgment was given.

(2) The registration order must state the name and address for service of the person who applied for registration, and must exhibit –

(a) a copy of the registered Community judgment; and
(b) a copy of the order for its enforcement.

(3) In the case of a Community judgment which is a money judgment, the registration order must also state the right of the judgment debtor to apply within 28 days for the variation or cancellation of the registration under rule 74.23.

Amendments—Inserted by SI 2002/2058.

74.23 Application to vary or cancel registration

(1) An application to vary or cancel the registration of a Community judgment which is a money judgment on the ground that at the date of registration the judgment had been partly or wholly satisfied must be made within 28 days of the date on which the registration order was served on the judgment debtor.

(2) The application must be supported by written evidence.

Amendments—Inserted by SI 2002/2058.

74.24 Enforcement

No steps may be taken to enforce a Community judgment which is a money judgment –

(a) before the end of the period specified in accordance with rule 74.23(1); or

(b) where an application is made under that rule, until it has been determined.

Amendments—Inserted by SI 2002/2058.

74.25 Application for registration of suspension order

(1) Where the European Court has made an order that the enforcement of a registered Community judgment should be suspended, an application for the registration of that order in the High Court is made by filing a copy of the order in the Central Office of the Supreme Court.

(2) The application may be made without notice.

Amendments—Inserted by SI 2002/2058.

74.26 Registration and enforcement of a Euratom inspection order

(1) Rules 74.20, 74.21(1), and 74.22(1) and (2), which apply to the registration of a Community judgment, also apply to the registration of a Euratom inspection order but with the necessary modifications.

(2) An application under article 6 of the European Communities (Enforcement of Community Judgments) Order 1972 to give effect to a Euratom inspection order may be made on written evidence, and –

(a) where the matter is urgent, without notice;

(b) otherwise, by claim form.

Amendments—Inserted by SI 2002/2058.

V European Enforcement Orders

74.27 Interpretation

In this Section –

(a) 'European Enforcement Order' has the meaning given in the EEO Regulation;

(b) 'EEO' means European Enforcement Order;

(c) 'judgment', 'authentic instrument', 'member state of origin', 'member state of enforcement', and 'court of origin' have the meanings given by Article 4 of the EEO Regulation; and

(d) 'Regulation State' has the same meaning as 'Member State' in the EEO Regulation, that is all Member States except Denmark.

Amendments—Inserted by SI 2005/2292.

74.28 Certification of Judgments of the Courts of England and Wales

An application for an EEO certificate must be made by filing the relevant practice form in accordance with Article 6 of the EEO Regulation.

Amendments—Inserted by SI 2005/2292.

74.29 Applications for a certificate of lack or limitation of enforceability

An application under Article 6(2) of the EEO Regulation for a certificate indicating the lack or limitation of enforceability of an EEO certificate must be made to the court of origin by application in accordance with Part 23.

Amendments—Inserted by SI 2005/2292.

74.30 Applications for rectification or withdrawal

An application under Article 10 of the EEO Regulation for rectification or withdrawal of an EEO certificate must be made to the court of origin and may be made by application in accordance with Part 23.

Amendments—Inserted by SI 2005/2292.

74.31 Enforcement of European Enforcement Orders in England and Wales

(1) A person seeking to enforce an EEO in England and Wales must lodge at the court in which enforcement proceedings are to be brought the documents required by Article 20 of the EEO Regulation.

(2) Where a person applies –

(a) to the High Court for a charging order, a writ of fieri facias or an attachment of earnings order; or

(b) to the county court for a warrant of execution or an attachment of earnings order,

to enforce an EEO expressed in a foreign currency, the application must contain a certificate of the sterling equivalent of the judgment sum at the close of business on the date nearest preceding the date of issue of the application.

(Section 1 of the Charging Orders Act 1979 provides that the High Court only has jurisdiction to make a charging order where the amount of the original judgment exceeds the county court limit.)

(Article 8 of the High Court and County Courts Jurisdiction Order 1991 provides that (1) judgments in excess of £5,000 shall only be enforced by execution against goods in the High Court (2) those in excess of £600 may be enforced in the High Court and (3) those for less than £600 shall only be enforced in the county court.)

Amendments—Inserted by SI 2005/2292.

74.32 Refusal of Enforcement

(1) An application under Article 21 of the EEO Regulation that the court should refuse to enforce an EEO must be made by application in accordance with Part 23 to the court in which the EEO is being enforced.

(2) The judgment debtor must, as soon as practicable, serve copies of any order made under Article 21(1) on –

- (a) all other parties to the proceedings and any other person affected by the order; and
- (b) any court in which enforcement proceedings are pending in England and Wales.

(3) Upon service of the order on those persons all enforcement proceedings in England and Wales under the EEO, in respect of those persons upon whom, and those courts at which, the order has been served in accordance with paragraph (2), will cease.

Amendments—Inserted by SI 2005/2292.

74.33 Stay or limitation of enforcement

(1) Where an EEO certificate has been lodged and the judgment debtor applies to stay or limit the enforcement proceedings under Article 23 of the EEO Regulation, such application must be made by application in accordance with Part 23 to the court in which the EEO is being enforced.

(2) The judgment debtor shall, as soon as practicable, serve a copy of any order made under the Article on –

- (a) all other parties to the proceedings and any other person affected by the order; and
- (b) any court in which enforcement proceedings are pending in England and Wales;

and the order will not have effect on any person until it has been served in accordance with this rule and they have received it.

Amendments—Inserted by SI 2005/2292.

Practice Direction – Enforcement of Judgments in Different Jurisdictions

This Practice Direction supplements CPR Part 74 (PD74)

1 This practice direction is divided into two sections –

- (1) Section I – Provisions about the enforcement of judgments
- (2) Section II – The Merchant Shipping (Liner Conferences) Act 1982

SECTION I – ENFORCEMENT OF JUDGMENTS

Meaning of 'judgment'

2 In rule 74.2(1)(c), the definition of 'judgment' is 'subject to any other enactment'. Such provisions include –

(1) section 9(1) of the 1920 Act, which limits enforcement under that Act to judgments of superior courts;
(2) section 1(1) of the 1933 Act, which limits enforcement under that Act to judgments of those courts specified in the relevant Order in Council;
(3) section 1(2) of the 1933 Act, which limits enforcement under that Act to money judgments.

Registers

3 There will be kept in the Central Office of the Supreme Court at the Royal Courts of Justice, under the direction of the Senior Master –

(1) registers of foreign judgments ordered by the High Court to be enforced following applications under –
   (a) section 9 of the 1920 Act;
   (b) section 2 of the 1933 Act;
   (c) section 4 of the 1982 Act; or
   (d) the Judgments Regulation;
(2) registers of certificates issued for the enforcement in foreign countries of High Court judgments under the 1920, 1933 and 1982 Acts, and under article 54 of the Judgments Regulation;
(3) a register of certificates filed in the Central Office of the High Court under rule 74.15(2) for the enforcement of money judgments given by the courts of Scotland or Northern Ireland;
(4) a register of certificates issued under rule 74.16(3) for the enforcement of non-money judgments given by the courts of Scotland or Northern Ireland;
(5) registers of certificates issued under rules 74.17 and 74.18 for the enforcement of High Court judgments in Scotland or Northern Ireland under Schedule 6 or Schedule 7 to the 1982 Act; and
(6) a register of Community judgments and Euratom inspection orders ordered to be registered under article 3 of the European Communities (Enforcement of Community Judgments) Order 1972.

Making an application

4.1 Applications for the registration for enforcement in England and Wales of –

(1) foreign judgments under rule 74.3;
(2) judgments of courts in Scotland or Northern Ireland under rule 74.15 or 74.16; and
(3) European Community judgments under rule 74.20,

are assigned to the Queen's Bench Division and may be heard by a master.

4.2 An application under rule 74.12 for a certified copy of a High Court or county court judgment for enforcement abroad must be made –

(1) in the case of a judgment given in the Chancery Division or the Queen's Bench Division of the High Court, to a master or district judge;

(2) in the case of a judgment given in the Family Division of the High Court, to a district judge of that Division;
(3) in the case of a county court judgment, to a district judge.

4.3 An application under rule 74.17 or 74.18 for a certificate or a certified copy of a High Court or county court judgment for enforcement in Scotland or Northern Ireland must be made –

(1) in the case of a judgment given in the Chancery Division or the Queen's Bench Division of the High Court, to a master or district judge;
(2) in the case of a judgment given in the Family Division of the High Court, to a district judge of that Division;
(3) in the case of a county court judgment, to a district judge.

4.4 The following applications must be made under Part 23 –

(1) applications under rule 74.3 for the registration of a judgment;
(2) applications under rule 74.7 to set aside the registration of a judgment;
(3) applications under rule 74.12 for a certified copy of a judgment;
(4) applications under Section III for a certificate for enforcement of a judgment;
(5) applications under rule 74.20 for the registration of a Community judgment;
(6) applications under rule 74.23 to vary or cancel the registration of a Community judgment; and
(7) applications under rule 74.25 for the registration of an order of the European Court that the enforcement of a registered Community judgment should be suspended.

Applications under the 1933 Act

5 Foreign judgments are enforceable in England and Wales under the 1933 Act where there is an agreement on the reciprocal enforcement of judgments between the United Kingdom and the country in which the judgment was given. Such an agreement may contain particular provisions governing the enforcement of judgments (for example limiting the categories of judgments which are enforceable, or the courts whose judgments are enforceable). Any such specific limitations will be listed in the Order in Council giving effect in the United Kingdom to the agreement in question, and the rules in Section I of Part 74 will take effect subject to such limitations.

Evidence in support of an application under the Judgments Regulation: rule 74.4(6)

6.1 Where a judgment is to be recognised or enforced in a Regulation State, Council Regulation (EC) No 44/2001 of 22 December 2000 on jurisdiction and the recognition and enforcement of judgments in civil and commercial matters applies.

6.2 As a consequence of article 38(2) of the Judgments Regulation, the provisions in Chapter III of that Regulation relating to declaring judgments enforceable are the equivalent, in the United Kingdom, of provisions relating to registering judgments for enforcement.

6.3 Chapter III of, and Annex V to, the Judgments Regulation are annexed to this practice direction. They were originally published in the official languages of the European Community in the Official Journal of the European Communities by the Office for Official Publications of the European Communities.

6.4 Sections 2 and 3 of Chapter III of the Judgments Regulation (in particular articles 40, 53, 54 and 55, and Annex V) set out the evidence needed in support of an application.

6.5 The Judgments Regulation is supplemented by the Civil Jurisdiction and Judgments Order 2001, SI 2001 No 3929. The Order also makes amendments, in respect of that Regulation, to the Civil Jurisdiction and Judgments Act 1982.

Certified copies of judgments issued under rule 74.12

7.1 In an application by a judgment creditor under rule 74.12 for the enforcement abroad of a High Court judgment, the certified copy of the judgment will be an office copy, and will be accompanied by a certificate signed by a judge. The judgment and certificate will be sealed with the Seal of the Supreme Court.

7.2 In an application by a judgment creditor under rule 74.12 for the enforcement abroad of a county court judgment, the certified copy will be a sealed copy, and will be accompanied by a certificate signed by a judge.

7.3 In applications under the 1920, 1933 or 1982 Acts, the certificate will be in Form 110, and will have annexed to it a copy of the claim form by which the proceedings were begun.

7.4 In an application under the Judgments Regulation, the certificate will be in the form of Annex V to the Regulation.

Certificates under Section III of Part 74

8.1 A certificate of a money judgment of a court in Scotland or Northern Ireland must be filed for enforcement under rule 74.15(2) in the Action Department of the Central Office of the Supreme Court, Royal Courts of Justice, Strand, London WC2A 2LL. The copy will be sealed by a court officer before being returned to the applicant.

8.2 A certificate issued under rule 74.17 for the enforcement in Scotland or Northern Ireland of a money judgment of the High Court or of a county court will be in Form 111.

8.3 In an application by a judgment creditor under rule 74.18 for the enforcement in Scotland or Northern Ireland of a non-money judgment of the High Court or of a county court, the certified copy of the judgment will be a sealed copy to which will be annexed a certificate in Form 112.

Material additional to Section IV of Part 74

9.1 Enforcement of Community judgments and of Euratom inspection orders is governed by the European Communities (Enforcement of Community Judgments) Order 1972, SI 1972 No 1590.

9.2 The Treaty establishing the European Community is the Treaty establishing the European Economic Community (Rome, 1957); relevant amendments are made by the Treaty of Amsterdam (1997, Cm 3780).

9.3 The text of the Protocol of 3 June 1971 on the interpretation by the European Court of the Convention of 27 September 1968 on Jurisdiction and the Enforcement of Judgments in Civil and Commercial Matters is set out in Schedule 2 to the Civil Jurisdiction and Judgments Act 1982.

9.4 The text of the Protocol of 19 December 1988 on the interpretation by the European Court of the Convention of 19 June 1980 on the Law applicable to Contractual Obligations is set out in Schedule 3 to the Contracts (Applicable Law) Act 1990.

SECTION II – THE MERCHANT SHIPPING (LINER CONFERENCES) ACT 1982

Content of this Section

10 The Merchant Shipping (Liner Conferences) Act 1982 ('the Act') contains provisions for the settlement of disputes between liner conferences, shipping lines and shippers. This Section of the Practice Direction deals with the enforcement by the High Court under section 9 of the Act of recommendations of conciliators, and determinations and awards of costs.

Exercise of powers under the Act

11 The powers of the High Court under the Act are exercised by the Commercial Court.

Applications for registration

12.1 An application under section 9 of the Act for the registration of a recommendation, determination or award is made under Part 23.

12.2 An application for the registration of a recommendation must be supported by written evidence exhibiting –

- (1) a verified or certified or otherwise authenticated copy of –
  - (a) the recommendation;
  - (b) the reasons for it; and
  - (c) the record of settlement;
- (2) where any of those documents is not in English, a translation of it into English –
  - (a) certified by a notary public or other qualified person; or
  - (b) accompanied by written evidence confirming that the translation is accurate; and
- (3) copies of the acceptance of the recommendation by the parties on whom it is binding, or otherwise verifying the acceptance where it is not in writing.

12.3 The evidence in support of the application must –

- (1) give particulars of the failure to implement the recommendation; and
- (2) confirm that none of the grounds which would render it unenforceable is applicable.

12.4 An application for the registration of a determination of costs or an award of costs must be supported by written evidence –

- (1) exhibiting a verified or certified or otherwise authenticated copy of the recommendation or other document containing the determination or award; and
- (2) stating that the costs have not been paid.

Order for registration

13.1 The applicant must draw up the order giving permission to register the recommendation, determination or award.

13.2 The order must include a provision that the reasonable costs of the registration should be assessed.

Register of recommendations

14 There will be kept in the Admiralty and Commercial Registry at the Royal Courts of Justice, under the direction of the Senior Master, a register of the recommendations, determinations and awards ordered to be registered under section 9 of the Act, with particulars of enforcement.

ANNEX

CHAPTER III
RECOGNITION AND ENFORCEMENT

ARTICLE 32

For the purposes of this Regulation, 'judgment' means any judgment given by a court or tribunal of a Member State, whatever the judgment may be called, including a decree, order, decision or writ of execution, as well as the determination of costs or expenses by an officer of the court.

SECTION 1
RECOGNITION

ARTICLE 33

1 A judgment given in a Member State shall be recognised in the other Member States without any special procedure being required.

2 Any interested party who raises the recognition of a judgment as the principal issue in a dispute may, in accordance with the procedures provided for in Sections 2 and 3 of this Chapter, apply for a decision that the judgment be recognised.

3 If the outcome of proceedings in a court of a Member State depends on the determination of an incidental question of recognition that court shall have jurisdiction over that question.

ARTICLE 34

A judgment shall not be recognised:

1 if such recognition is manifestly contrary to public policy in the Member State in which recognition is sought;

2 where it was given in default of appearance, if the defendant was not served with the document which instituted the proceedings or with an equivalent document in sufficient time and in such a way as to enable him to arrange for his defence, unless the defendant failed to commence proceedings to challenge the judgment when it was possible for him to do so;

3 if it is irreconcilable with a judgment given in a dispute between the same parties in the Member State in which recognition is sought;

4 if it is irreconcilable with an earlier judgment given in another Member State or in a third State involving the same cause of action and between the same parties, provided that the earlier judgment fulfils the conditions necessary for its recognition in the Member State addressed.

ARTICLE 35

1 Moreover, a judgment shall not be recognised if it conflicts with Sections 3, 4 or 6 of Chapter II, or in a case provided for in Article 72.

2 In its examination of the grounds of jurisdiction referred to in the foregoing paragraph, the court or authority applied to shall be bound by the findings of fact on which the court of the Member State of origin based its jurisdiction.

3 Subject to the paragraph 1, the jurisdiction of the court of the Member State of origin may not be reviewed. The test of public policy referred to in point 1 of Article 34 may not be applied to the rules relating to jurisdiction.

ARTICLE 36

Under no circumstances may a foreign judgment be reviewed as to its substance.

ARTICLE 37

1 A court of a Member State in which recognition is sought of a judgment given in another Member State may stay the proceedings if an ordinary appeal against the judgment has been lodged.

2 A court of a Member State in which recognition is sought of a judgment given in Ireland or the United Kingdom may stay the proceedings if enforcement is suspended in the State of origin, by reason of an appeal.

SECTION 2
ENFORCEMENT

ARTICLE 38

1 A judgment given in a Member State and enforceable in that State shall be enforced in another Member State when, on the application of any interested party, it has been declared enforceable there.

2 However, in the United Kingdom, such a judgment shall be enforced in England and Wales, in Scotland, or in Northern Ireland when, on the application of any interested party, it has been registered for enforcement in that part of the United Kingdom.

ARTICLE 39

1 The application shall be submitted to the court or competent authority indicated in the list in Annex II.

2 The local jurisdiction shall be determined by reference to the place of domicile of the party against whom enforcement is sought, or to the place of enforcement.

ARTICLE 40

1 The procedure for making the application shall be governed by the law of the Member State in which enforcement is sought.

2 The applicant must give an address for service of process within the area of jurisdiction of the court applied to. However, if the law of the Member State in which enforcement is sought does not provide for the furnishing of such an address, the applicant shall appoint a representative *ad litem*.

3 The documents referred to in Article 53 shall be attached to the application.

ARTICLE 41

The judgment shall be declared enforceable immediately on completion of the formalities in Article 53 without any review under Articles 34 and 35. The party against whom enforcement is sought shall not at this stage of the proceedings be entitled to make any submissions on the application.

ARTICLE 42

1 The decision on the application for a declaration of enforceability shall forthwith be brought to the notice of the applicant in accordance with the procedure laid down by the law of the Member State in which enforcement is sought.

2 The declaration of enforceability shall be served on the party against whom enforcement is sought, accompanied by the judgment, if not already served on that party.

ARTICLE 43

1 The decision on the application for a declaration of enforceability may be appealed against by either party.

2 The appeal is to be lodged with the court indicated in the list in Annex III.

3 The appeal shall be dealt with in accordance with the rules governing procedure in contradictory matters.

4 If the party against whom enforcement is sought fails to appear before the appellate court in proceedings concerning an appeal brought by the applicant, Article 26(2) to (4) shall apply even where the party against whom enforcement is sought is not domiciled in any of the Member States.

5 An appeal against the declaration of enforceability is to be lodged within one month of service thereof. If the party against whom enforcement is sought is domiciled in a Member State other than that in which the declaration of enforceability was given, the time for appealing shall be two months and shall run from the date of service, either on him in person or at his residence. No extension of time may be granted on account of distance.

ARTICLE 44

The judgment given on the appeal may be contested only by the appeal referred to in Annex IV.

ARTICLE 45

1 The court with which an appeal is lodged under Article 43 or Article 44 shall refuse or revoke a declaration of enforceability only on one of the grounds specified in Articles 34 and 35. It shall give its decision without delay.

2 Under no circumstances may the foreign judgment be reviewed as to its substance.

ARTICLE 46

1 The court with which an appeal is lodged under Article 43 or Article 44 may, on the application of the party against whom enforcement is sought, stay the proceedings if an ordinary appeal has been lodged against the judgment in the Member State of origin or if the time for such an appeal has not yet expired; in the latter case, the court may specify the time within which such an appeal is to be lodged.

2 Where the judgment was given in Ireland or the United Kingdom, any form of appeal available in the Member State of origin shall be treated as an ordinary appeal for the purposes of paragraph 1.

3 The court may also make enforcement conditional on the provision of such security as it shall determine.

ARTICLE 47

1 When a judgment must be recognised in accordance with this Regulation, nothing shall prevent the applicant from availing himself of provisional, including protective, measures in accordance with the law of the Member State requested without a declaration of enforceability under Article 41 being required.

2 The declaration of enforceability shall carry with it the power to proceed to any protective measures.

3 During the time specified for an appeal pursuant to Article 43(5) against the declaration of enforceability and until any such appeal has been determined, no measures of enforcement may be taken other than protective measures against the property of the party against whom enforcement is sought.

ARTICLE 48

1 Where a foreign judgment has been given in respect of several matters and the declaration of enforceability cannot be given for all of them, the court or competent authority shall give it for one or more of them.

2 An applicant may request a declaration of enforceability limited to parts of a judgment.

ARTICLE 49

A foreign judgment which orders a periodic payment by way of a penalty shall be enforceable in the Member State in which enforcement is sought only if the amount of the payment has been finally determined by the courts of the Member State of origin.

ARTICLE 50

An applicant who, in the Member State of origin has benefited from complete or partial legal aid or exemption from costs or expenses, shall be entitled, in the procedure provided for in this Section, to benefit from the most favourable legal aid or the most extensive exemption from costs or expenses provided for by the law of the Member State addressed.

ARTICLE 51

No security, bond or deposit, however described, shall be required of a party who in one Member State applies for enforcement of a judgment given in another Member State on the ground that he is a foreign national or that he is not domiciled or resident in the State in which enforcement is sought.

ARTICLE 52

In proceedings for the issue of a declaration of enforceability, no charge, duty or fee calculated by reference to the value of the matter at issue may be levied in the Member State in which enforcement is sought.

SECTION 3

COMMON PROVISIONS

ARTICLE 53

1 A party seeking recognition or applying for a declaration of enforceability shall produce a copy of the judgment which satisfies the conditions necessary to establish its authenticity.

2 A party applying for a declaration of enforceability shall also produce the certificate referred to in Article 54, without prejudice to Article 55.

ARTICLE 54

The court or competent authority of a Member State where a judgment was given shall issue, at the request of any interested party, a certificate using the standard form in Annex V to this Regulation.

ARTICLE 55

1 If the certificate referred to in Article 54 is not produced, the court or competent authority may specify a time for its production or accept an equivalent document or, if it considers that it has sufficient information before it, dispense with its production.

2 If the court or competent authority so requires, a translation of the documents shall be produced. The translation shall be certified by a person qualified to do so in one of the Member States.

ARTICLE 56

No legalisation or other similar formality shall be required in respect of the documents referred to in Article 53 or Article 55(2), or in respect of a document appointing a representative *ad litem*.

ANNEX V

CERTIFICATE REFERRED TO IN ARTICLES 54 AND 58 OF THE REGULATION ON JUDGMENTS AND COURT SETTLEMENTS

(English, inglés, anglais, inglese, ___)

1. Member State of origin
2. Court or competent authority issuing the certificate
   2.1. Name
   2.2. Address
   2.3. Tel./fax/e-mail
3. Court which delivered the judgment/approved the court settlement(*)
   3.1. Type of court
   3.2. Place of court
4. Judgment/court settlement(*)
   4.1. Date
   4.2. Reference number
   4.3. The parties to the judgment/court settlement(*)
      4.3.1. Name(s) of plaintiff(s)
      4.3.2. Name(s) of defendant(s)
      4.3.3. Name(s) of other party(ies), if any
   4.4. Date of service of the document instituting the proceedings where judgment was given in default of appearance
   4.5. Text of the judgment/court settlement(*) as annexed to this certificate
5. Names of parties to whom legal aid has been granted

The judgment/court settlement(*) is enforceable in the Member State of origin (Articles 38 and 58 of the Regulation) against:

Name:

Done at ___ , date ___

Signature and/or stamp ___

(*) Delete as appropriate.

Practice Direction – European Enforcement Orders

This Practice Direction supplements CPR Part 74B (PD74B)

COUNCIL REGULATION

1.1 Certification and enforcement of European Enforcement Orders is governed by Council Regulation (EC) No 805/2004 creating a European Enforcement Order for uncontested claims.

1.2 The EEO Regulation is annexed to this practice direction and can be found at http://europa.eu.int/eur-lex/pri/en/oj/dat/2004/l_143/l_14320040430en00150039.pdf It was originally published in the official languages of the European Community in the Official Journal of the European Communities by the Office for Official Publications of the European Communities.

1.3 Section V of Part 74 sets out the procedure for enforcement under the EEO Regulation. A claim that does not meet the requirements of the EEO Regulation, or which the judgment creditor does not wish to enforce using the EEO Regulation, may be enforceable using another method of enforcement.

Rule 74.28 – Certification of Judgments of the Courts of England and Wales

2.1 An application under rule 74.28 for a certificate of a High Court or county court judgment for enforcement in another Regulation State must be made using Form N219 or Form N219A –

(1) in the case of a judgment given in the Chancery or Queen's Bench Division of the High Court, or in a district registry, to a Master or district judge; or

(2) in the case of a county court judgment, to a district judge.

2.2 Where the application is granted, the court will send the EEO certificate and a sealed copy of the judgment to the person making the application. Where the court refuses the application, the court will give reasons for the refusal and may give further directions.

Rule 74.29 – Applications for a certificate of lack of enforceability

3.1 An application must be supported by written evidence in support of the grounds on which the judgment has ceased to be enforceable or its enforceability has been suspended or limited.

Rule 74.30 – Application for rectification or withdrawal

4.1 An application must be supported by written evidence in support of the grounds on which it is contended that the EEO should be rectified or withdrawn.

Rule 74.31 – Enforcement of European Enforcement Orders in England and Wales

5.1 When an EEO is lodged at the court in which enforcement proceedings are to be brought, it will be assigned a case number.

5.2 A copy of a document will satisfy the conditions necessary to establish its authenticity if it is an official copy of the courts of the member state of origin.

5.3 The judgment creditor must notify all courts in which enforcement proceedings are pending in England and Wales under the EEO if judgment is set aside in the court of origin, as soon as reasonably practicable after the order is served on the judgment creditor. Notification may be by any means available including fax, e-mail, post or telephone.

Rule 74.32 – Refusal of Enforcement

6.1 An application must be accompanied by an official copy of the earlier judgment, any other documents relied upon and any translations required by the EEO Regulation and supported by written evidence stating –

(1) why the earlier judgment is irreconcilable; and
(2) why the irreconcilability was not, and could not have been, raised as an objection in the proceedings in the court of origin.

Rule 74.33 – Stay or limitation of enforcement

7.1 An application must, unless the court orders otherwise, be accompanied by evidence of the application in the court of origin, including –

(1) the application (or equivalent foreign process) or a copy of the application (or equivalent foreign process) certified by an appropriate officer of the court of origin; and
(2) where that document is not in English, a translation of it into English –
    (a) certified by a notary public or person qualified to certify a translation in the Member State of the court of origin under Article 20(2)(c) of the EEO Regulation; or
    (b) accompanied by written evidence confirming that the translation is accurate.

7.2 The written evidence in support of the application must state –

(1) that an application has been brought in the member state of origin;
(2) the nature of that application, including the grounds on which the application is made and the order sought; and
(3) the date on which the application was filed, the state of the proceedings and the date by which it is believed that the application will be determined.

7.3 If on the application of a debtor under rule 74.32 the court makes a conditional order under Article 23(b), the order shall be effective to bar enforcement until the creditor has lodged evidence at court that he has complied with such conditions. In cases other than where the order is conditional upon the creditor making a payment into court, the evidence lodged should be referred to the Master or district judge.

ANNEX

European Enforcement Order Regulation

30.4.2004 EN Official Journal of the European Union L 143/15

REGULATION (EC) No 805/2004 OF THE EUROPEAN PARLIAMENT AND OF THE COUNCIL

of 21 April 2004

creating a European Enforcement Order for uncontested claims

THE EUROPEAN PARLIAMENT AND THE COUNCIL OF THE EUROPEAN UNION,

Having regard to the Treaty establishing the European Community, and in particular Articles 61(c) and the second indent of Article 67(5) thereof,

Having regard to the proposal from the Commission ([1]),

Having regard to the Opinion of the European Economic and Social Committee ([2]),

Acting in accordance with the procedure laid down in Article 251 of the Treaty ([3]),

Whereas:

(1) The Community has set itself the objective of maintaining and developing an area of freedom, security and justice, in which the free movement of persons is ensured. To this end, the Community is to adopt, inter alia, measures in the field of judicial cooperation in civil matters that are necessary for the proper functioning of the internal market.

(2) On 3 December 1998, the Council adopted an Action Plan of the Council and the Commission on how best to implement the provisions of the Treaty of Amsterdam on an area of freedom, security and justice ([4]) (the Vienna Action Plan).

(3) The European Council meeting in Tampere on 15 and 16 October 1999 endorsed the principle of mutual recognition of judicial decisions as the cornerstone for the creation of a genuine judicial area.

(4) On 30 November 2000, the Council adopted a programme of measures for implementation of the principle of mutual recognition of decisions in civil and commercial matters ([5]). This programme includes in its first stage the abolition of exequatur, that is to say, the creation of a European Enforcement Order for uncontested claims.

(5) The concept of 'uncontested claims' should cover all situations in which a creditor, given the verified absence of any dispute by the debtor as to the nature or extent of a pecuniary claim, has obtained either a court decision against that debtor or an enforceable document that requires the debtor's express consent, be it a court settlement or an authentic instrument.

(6) The absence of objections from the debtor as stipulated in Article 3(1)(b) can take the shape of default of appearance at a court hearing or of failure to comply with an invitation by the court to give written notice of an intention to defend the case.

(7) This Regulation should apply to judgments, court settlements and authentic instruments on uncontested claims and to decisions delivered following challenges to judgments, court settlements and authentic instruments certified as European Enforcement Orders.

(8) In its Tampere conclusions, the European Council considered that access to enforcement in a Member State other than that in which the judgment has been given should be accelerated and simplified by dispensing with any intermediate measures to be taken prior to enforcement in the Member State in which enforcement is sought. A judgment that has been certified as a European Enforcement Order by the court of origin should, for enforcement purposes, be treated as if it had been delivered in the Member State in which enforcement is sought. In the United Kingdom, for example, the registration of a certified foreign judgment will therefore follow the same rules as the registration of a judgment from another part of the United Kingdom and is not to imply a review as to the substance of the foreign judgment. Arrangements for the enforcement of judgments should continue to be governed by national law.

(9) Such a procedure should offer significant advantages as compared with the exequatur procedure provided for in Council Regulation (EC) No 44/2001 of 22 December 2000 on jurisdiction and the recognition and enforcement of judgments in civil and commercial matters ([6]), in that there is no need for approval by the

([1]) OJ C 203 E, 27.8.2002, p. 86.
([2]) OJ C 85, 8.4.2003, p. 1.
([3]) Opinion of the European Parliament of 8 April 2003 (OJ C 64 E, 12.3.2004, p. 79), Council Common Position of 6.2.2004 (not yet published in the Official Journal) and Position of the European Parliament of 30.3.2004 (not yet published in the Official Journal).
([4]) OJ C 19, 23.1.1999, p. 1.
([5]) OJ C 12, 15.1.2001, p. 1.

([6]) OJ L 12, 16.1.2001, p. 1. Regulation as last amended by Commission Regulation (EC) No 1496/2002 (OJ L 225, 22.8.2002, p. 13).

judiciary in a second Member State with the delays and expenses that this entails.

(10) Where a court in a Member State has given judgment on an uncontested claim in the absence of participation of the debtor in the proceedings, the abolition of any checks in the Member State of enforcement is inextricably linked to and dependent upon the existence of a sufficient guarantee of observance of the rights of the defence.

(11) This Regulation seeks to promote the fundamental rights and takes into account the principles recognised in particular by the Charter of Fundamental Rights of the European Union. In particular, it seeks to ensure full respect for the right to a fair trial as recognised in Article 47 of the Charter.

(12) Minimum standards should be established for the proceedings leading to the judgment in order to ensure that the debtor is informed about the court action against him, the requirements for his active participation in the proceedings to contest the claim and the consequences of his non-participation in sufficient time and in such a way as to enable him to arrange for his defence.

(13) Due to differences between the Member States as regards the rules of civil procedure and especially those governing the service of documents, it is necessary to lay down a specific and detailed definition of those minimum standards. In particular, any method of service that is based on a legal fiction as regards the fulfilment of those minimum standards cannot be considered sufficient for the certification of a judgment as a European Enforcement Order.

(14) All the methods of service listed in Articles 13 and 14 are characterised by either full certainty (Article 13) or a very high degree of likelihood (Article 14) that the document served has reached its addressee. In the second category, a judgment should only be certified as a European Enforcement Order if the Member State of origin has an appropriate mechanism in place enabling the debtor to apply for a full review of the judgment under the conditions set out in Article 19 in those exceptional cases where, in spite of compliance with Article 14, the document has not reached the addressee.

(15) Personal service on certain persons other than the debtor himself pursuant to Article 14(1)(a) and (b) should be understood to meet the requirements of those provisions only if those persons actually accepted/received the document in question.

(16) Article 15 should apply to situations where the debtor cannot represent himself in court, as in the case of a legal person, and where a person to represent him is determined by law as well as situations where the debtor has authorised another person, in particular a lawyer, to represent him in the specific court proceedings at issue.

(17) The courts competent for scrutinising full compliance with the minimum procedural standards should, if satisfied, issue a standardised European Enforcement Order certificate that makes that scrutiny and its result transparent.

(18) Mutual trust in the administration of justice in the Member States justifies the assessment by the court of one Member State that all conditions for certification as a European Enforcement Order are fulfilled to enable a judgment to be enforced in all other Member States without judicial review of the proper application of the minimum procedural standards in the Member State where the judgment is to be enforced.

(19) This Regulation does not imply an obligation for the Member States to adapt their national legislation to the minimum procedural standards set out herein. It provides an incentive to that end by making available a more efficient and rapid enforceability of judgments in other Member States only if those minimum standards are met.

(20) Application for certification as a European Enforcement Order for uncontested claims should be optional for the creditor, who may instead choose the system of recognition and enforcement under Regulation (EC) No 44/2001 or other Community instruments.

(21) When a document has to be sent from one Member State to another for service there, this Regulation and in particular the rules on service set out herein should apply together with Council Regulation (EC) No 1348/2000 of 29 May 2000 on the service in the Member States of judicial and extrajudicial documents in civil or commercial matters ([1]), and in particular Article 14 thereof in conjunction with Member States declarations made under Article 23 thereof.

(22) Since the objectives of the proposed action cannot be sufficiently achieved by the Member States and can therefore, by reason of the scale or effects of the action, be better achieved at Community level, the Community

([1]) OJ L 160, 30.6.2000, p. 37.

may adopt measures, in accordance with the principle of subsidiarity as set out in Article 5 of the Treaty. In accordance with the principle of proportionality, as set out in that Article, this Regulation does not go beyond what is necessary in order to achieve those objectives.

(23) The measures necessary for the implementation of this Regulation should be adopted in accordance with Council Decision 1999/468/EC of 28 June 1999 laying down the procedures for the exercise of implementing powers conferred on the Commission ([1]).

(24) In accordance with Article 3 of the Protocol on the position of the United Kingdom and Ireland annexed to the Treaty on European Union and the Treaty establishing the European Community, the United Kingdom and Ireland have notified their wish to take part in the adoption and application of this Regulation.

(25) In accordance with Articles 1 and 2 of the Protocol on the position of Denmark annexed to the Treaty on European Union and the Treaty establishing the European Community, Denmark does not take part in the adoption of this Regulation, and is therefore not bound by it or subject to its application.

(26) Pursuant to the second indent of Article 67(5) of the Treaty, the codecision procedure is applicable from 1 February 2003 for the measures laid down in this Regulation,

HAVE ADOPTED THIS REGULATION:

CHAPTER I

SUBJECT MATTER, SCOPE AND DEFINITIONS

Article 1

Subject matter

The purpose of this Regulation is to create a European Enforcement Order for uncontested claims to permit, by laying down minimum standards, the free circulation of judgments, court settlements and authentic instruments throughout all Member States without any intermediate proceedings needing to be brought in the Member State of enforcement prior to recognition and enforcement.

([1]) OJ L 184, 17.7.1999, p. 23.

Article 2

Scope

1. This Regulation shall apply in civil and commercial matters, whatever the nature of the court or tribunal. It shall not extend, in particular, to revenue, customs or administrative matters or the liability of the State for acts and omissions in the exercise of State authority ('acta iure imperii').

2. This Regulation shall not apply to:

(a) the status or legal capacity of natural persons, rights in property arising out of a matrimonial relationship, wills and succession;

(b) bankruptcy, proceedings relating to the winding-up of insolvent companies or other legal persons, judicial arrangements, compositions and analogous proceedings;

(c) social security;

(d) arbitration.

3. In this Regulation, the term 'Member State' shall mean Member States with the exception of Denmark.

Article 3

Enforcement titles to be certified as a European Enforcement Order

1. This Regulation shall apply to judgments, court settlements and authentic instruments on uncontested claims.

A claim shall be regarded as uncontested if:

(a) the debtor has expressly agreed to it by admission or by means of a settlement which has been approved by a court or concluded before a court in the course of proceedings; or

(b) the debtor has never objected to it, in compliance with the relevant procedural requirements under the law of the Member State of origin, in the course of the court proceedings; or

(c) the debtor has not appeared or been represented at a court hearing regarding that claim after having initially objected to the claim in the course of the court proceedings, provided that such conduct amounts to a tacit admission of the claim or of the facts alleged by the creditor under the law of the Member State of origin; or

(d) the debtor has expressly agreed to it in an authentic instrument.

2. This Regulation shall also apply to decisions delivered following challenges to judgments, court settlements or authentic instruments certified as European Enforcement Orders.

Article 4

Definitions

For the purposes of this Regulation, the following definitions shall apply:

1. 'judgment': any judgment given by a court or tribunal of a Member State, whatever the judgment may be called, including a decree, order, decision or writ of execution, as well as the determination of costs or expenses by an officer of the court;

2. 'claim': a claim for payment of a specific sum of money that has fallen due or for which the due date is indicated in the judgment, court settlement or authentic instrument;

3. 'authentic instrument':

   (a) a document which has been formally drawn up or registered as an authentic instrument, and the authenticity of which:

      (i) relates to the signature and the content of the instrument; and

      (ii) has been established by a public authority or other authority empowered for that purpose by the Member State in which it originates;

   or

   b) an arrangement relating to maintenance obligations concluded with administrative authorities or authenticated by them;

4. 'Member State of origin': the Member State in which the judgment has been given, the court settlement has been approved or concluded or the authentic instrument has been drawn up or registered, and is to be certified as a European Enforcement Order;

5. 'Member State of enforcement': the Member State in which enforcement of the judgment, court settlement or authentic instrument certified as a European Enforcement Order is sought;

6. 'court of origin': the court or tribunal seised of the proceedings at the time of fulfilment of the conditions set out in Article 3(1)(a), (b) or (c);

7. in Sweden, in summary proceedings concerning orders to pay (betalningsföreläggande), the expression 'court' includes the Swedish enforcement service (kronofogdemyndighet).

CHAPTER II

EUROPEAN ENFORCEMENT ORDER

Article 5

Abolition of exequatur

A judgment which has been certified as a European Enforcement Order in the Member State of origin shall be recognised and enforced in the other Member States without the need for a declaration of enforceability and without any possibility of opposing its recognition.

Article 6

Requirements for certification as a European Enforcement Order

1. A judgment on an uncontested claim delivered in a Member State shall, upon application at any time to the court of origin, be certified as a European Enforcement Order if:

(a) the judgment is enforceable in the Member State of origin; and

(b) the judgment does not conflict with the rules on jurisdiction as laid down in sections 3 and 6 of Chapter II of Regulation (EC) No 44/2001; and

(c) the court proceedings in the Member State of origin met the requirements as set out in Chapter III where a claim is uncontested within the meaning of Article 3(1)(b) or (c); and

(d) the judgment was given in the Member State of the debtor's domicile within the meaning of Article 59 of Regulation (EC) No 44/2001, in cases where

   — a claim is uncontested within the meaning of Article 3(1)(b) or (c); and

   — it relates to a contract concluded by a person, the consumer, for a purpose which can be regarded as being outside his trade or profession; and

   — the debtor is the consumer.

2. Where a judgment certified as a European Enforcement Order has ceased to be enforceable or its enforceability has been suspended or limited, a certificate indicating the lack or limitation of enforceability shall, upon application at any time to the court of origin, be issued, using the standard form in Annex IV.

3. Without prejudice to Article 12(2), where a decision has been delivered following a challenge to a judgment certified as a European Enforcement Order in accordance with paragraph 1 of this Article, a replacement certificate shall, upon application at any time, be issued, using the standard form in Annex V, if that decision on the challenge is enforceable in the Member State of origin.

Article 7

Costs related to court proceedings

Where a judgment includes an enforceable decision on the amount of costs related to the court proceedings, including the interest rates, it shall be certified as a European Enforcement Order also with regard to the costs unless the debtor has specifically objected to his obligation to bear such costs in the course of the court proceedings, in accordance with the law of the Member State of origin.

Article 8

Partial European Enforcement Order certificate

If only parts of the judgment meet the requirements of this Regulation, a partial European Enforcement Order certificate shall be issued for those parts.

Article 9

Issue of the European Enforcement Order certificate

1. The European Enforcement Order certificate shall be issued using the standard form in Annex I.

2. The European Enforcement Order certificate shall be issued in the language of the judgment.

Article 10

Rectification or withdrawal of the European Enforcement Order certificate

1. The European Enforcement Order certificate shall, upon application to the court of origin, be

(a) rectified where, due to a material error, there is a discrepancy between the judgment and the certificate;

(b) withdrawn where it was clearly wrongly granted, having regard to the requirements laid down in this Regulation.

2. The law of the Member State of origin shall apply to the rectification or withdrawal of the European Enforcement Order certificate.

3. An application for the rectification or withdrawal of a European Enforcement Order certificate may be made using the standard form in Annex VI.

4. No appeal shall lie against the issuing of a European Enforcement Order certificate.

Article 11

Effect of the European Enforcement Order certificate

The European Enforcement Order certificate shall take effect only within the limits of the enforceability of the judgment.

CHAPTER III

MINIMUM STANDARDS FOR UNCONTESTED CLAIMS PROCEDURES

Article 12

Scope of application of minimum standards

1. A judgment on a claim that is uncontested within the meaning of Article 3(1)(b) or (c) can be certified as a European Enforcement Order only if the court proceedings in the Member State of origin met the procedural requirements as set out in this Chapter.

2. The same requirements shall apply to the issuing of a European Enforcement Order certificate or a replacement certificate within the meaning of Article 6(3) for a decision following a challenge to a judgment where, at the time of that decision, the conditions of Article 3(1)(b) or (c) are fulfilled.

Article 13

Service with proof of receipt by the debtor

1. The document instituting the proceedings or an equivalent document may have been served on the debtor by one of the following methods:

(a) personal service attested by an acknowledgement of receipt, including the date of receipt, which is signed by the debtor;

(b) personal service attested by a document signed by the competent person who effected the service stating that the debtor has received the document or refused to receive it without any legal justification, and the date of the service;

(c) postal service attested by an acknowledgement of receipt including the date of receipt, which is signed and returned by the debtor;

(d) service by electronic means such as fax or e-mail, attested by an acknowledgement of receipt including the date of receipt, which is signed and returned by the debtor.

2. Any summons to a court hearing may have been served on the debtor in compliance with paragraph 1 or orally in a previous court hearing on the same claim and stated in the minutes of that previous court hearing.

Article 14

Service without proof of receipt by the debtor

1. Service of the document instituting the proceedings or an equivalent document and any summons to a court hearing on the debtor may also have been effected by one of the following methods:

(a) personal service at the debtor's personal address on persons who are living in the same household as the debtor or are employed there;

(b) in the case of a self-employed debtor or a legal person, personal service at the debtor's business premises on persons who are employed by the debtor;

(c) deposit of the document in the debtor's mailbox;

(d) deposit of the document at a post office or with competent public authorities and the placing in the debtor's mailbox of written notification of that deposit, provided that the written notification clearly states the character of the document as a court document or the legal effect of the notification as effecting service and setting in motion the running of time for the purposes of time limits;

(e) postal service without proof pursuant to paragraph 3 where the debtor has his address in the Member State of origin;

(f) electronic means attested by an automatic confirmation of delivery, provided that the debtor has expressly accepted this method of service in advance.

2. For the purposes of this Regulation, service under paragraph 1 is not admissible if the debtor's address is not known with certainty.

3. Service pursuant to paragraph 1, (a) to (d), shall be attested by:

(a) a document signed by the competent person who effected the service, indicating:

(i) the method of service used; and

(ii) the date of service; and

(iii) where the document has been served on a person other than the debtor, the name of that person and his relation to the debtor,

or

b) an acknowledgement of receipt by the person served, for the purposes of paragraphs 1(a) and (b).

Article 15

Service on the debtor's representatives

Service pursuant to Articles 13 or 14 may also have been effected on a debtor's representative.

Article 16

Provision to the debtor of due information about the claim

In order to ensure that the debtor was provided with due information about the claim, the document instituting the proceedings or the equivalent document must have contained the following:

(a) the names and the addresses of the parties;

(b) the amount of the claim;

(c) if interest on the claim is sought, the interest rate and the period for which interest is sought unless statutory interest is automatically added to the principal under the law of the Member State of origin;

(d) a statement of the reason for the claim.

Article 17

Provision to the debtor of due information about the procedural steps necessary to contest the claim

The following must have been clearly stated in or together with the document instituting the proceedings, the equivalent document or any summons to a court hearing:

(a) the procedural requirements for contesting the claim, including the time limit for contesting the claim in writing or the time for the court hearing, as applicable, the name and the address of the institution to which to respond or before which to appear, as applicable, and whether it is mandatory to be represented by a lawyer;

(b) the consequences of an absence of objection or default of appearance, in particular, where applicable, the possibility that a judgment may be given or enforced against the debtor and the liability for costs related to the court proceedings.

Article 18

Cure of non-compliance with minimum standards

1. If the proceedings in the Member State of origin did not meet the procedural requirements as set out in Articles 13 to 17, such non-compliance shall be cured and a judgment may be certified as a European Enforcement Order if:

(a) the judgment has been served on the debtor in compliance with the requirements pursuant to Article 13 or Article 14; and

(b) it was possible for the debtor to challenge the judgment by means of a full review and the debtor has been duly informed in or together with the judgment about the procedural requirements for such a challenge, including the name and address of the institution with which it must be lodged and, where applicable, the time limit for so doing; and

(c) the debtor has failed to challenge the judgment in compliance with the relevant procedural requirements.

2. If the proceedings in the Member State of origin did not comply with the procedural requirements as set out in Article 13 or Article 14, such non-compliance shall be cured if it is proved by the conduct of the debtor in the court proceedings that he has personally received the document to be served in sufficient time to arrange for his defence.

Article 19

Minimum standards for review in exceptional cases

1. Further to Articles 13 to 18, a judgment can only be certified as a European Enforcement Order if the debtor is entitled, under the law of the Member State of origin, to apply for a review of the judgment where:

(a) (i) the document instituting the proceedings or an equivalent document or, where applicable, the summons to a court hearing, was served by one of the methods provided for in Article 14; and

(ii) service was not effected in sufficient time to enable him to arrange for his defence, without any fault on his part;

or

(b) the debtor was prevented from objecting to the claim by reason of force majeure, or due to extraordinary circumstances without any fault on his part,

provided in either case that he acts promptly.

2. This Article is without prejudice to the possibility for Member States to grant access to a review of the judgment under more generous conditions than those mentioned in paragraph 1.

CHAPTER IV

ENFORCEMENT

Article 20

Enforcement procedure

1. Without prejudice to the provisions of this Chapter, the enforcement procedures shall be governed by the law of the Member State of enforcement.

A judgment certified as a European Enforcement Order shall be enforced under the same conditions as a judgment handed down in the Member State of enforcement.

2. The creditor shall be required to provide the competent enforcement authorities of the Member State of enforcement with:

(a) a copy of the judgment which satisfies the conditions necessary to establish its authenticity; and

(b) a copy of the European Enforcement Order certificate which satisfies the conditions necessary to establish its authenticity; and

(c) where necessary, a transcription of the European Enforcement Order certificate or a translation thereof into the official language of the Member State of enforcement or, if there are several official languages in that Member State, the official language or one of the official languages of court proceedings of the place where enforcement is sought, in conformity with the law of that Member State, or into another language that the Member State of enforcement has indicated it can accept. Each Member State may indicate the official language or languages of the institutions of the European Community other than its own which it can accept for the completion of the certificate. The translation shall be certified by a person qualified to do so in one of the Member States.

3. No security, bond or deposit, however described, shall be required of a party who in one Member State applies for enforcement of a judgment certified as a European Enforcement Order in another Member State on the ground that he is a foreign national or that he is not domiciled or resident in the Member State of enforcement.

Article 21

Refusal of enforcement

1. Enforcement shall, upon application by the debtor, be refused by the competent court in the Member State of enforcement if the judgment certified as a European Enforcement Order is irreconcilable with an earlier judgment given in any Member State or in a third country, provided that:

(a) the earlier judgment involved the same cause of action and was between the same parties; and

(b) the earlier judgment was given in the Member State of enforcement or fulfils the conditions necessary for its recognition in the Member State of enforcement; and

(c) the irreconcilability was not and could not have been raised as an objection in the court proceedings in the Member State of origin.

2. Under no circumstances may the judgment or its certification as a European Enforcement Order be reviewed as to their substance in the Member State of enforcement.

Article 22

Agreements with third countries

This Regulation shall not affect agreements by which Member States undertook, prior to the entry into force of Regulation (EC) No 44/2001, pursuant to Article 59 of the Brussels Convention on jurisdiction and the enforcement of judgments in civil and commercial matters, not to recognise judgments given, in particular in other Contracting States to that Convention, against defendants domiciled or habitually resident in a third country where, in cases provided for in Article 4 of that Convention, the judgment could only be founded on a ground of jurisdiction specified in the second paragraph of Article 3 of that Convention.

Article 23

Stay or limitation of enforcement

Where the debtor has

— challenged a judgment certified as a European Enforcement Order, including an application for review within the meaning of Article 19, or

— applied for the rectification or withdrawal of a European Enforcement Order certificate in accordance with Article 10,

the competent court or authority in the Member State of enforcement may, upon application by the debtor:

(a) limit the enforcement proceedings to protective measures; or

(b) make enforcement conditional on the provision of such security as it shall determine; or

(c) under exceptional circumstances, stay the enforcement proceedings.

CHAPTER V

COURT SETTLEMENTS AND AUTHENTIC INSTRUMENTS

Article 24

Court settlements

1. A settlement concerning a claim within the meaning of Article 4(2) which has been approved by a court or concluded before a court in the course of proceedings and is enforceable in the Member State in which it was approved or concluded shall, upon application to the court that approved it or before which it was concluded, be certified as a European Enforcement Order using the standard form in Annex II.

2. A settlement which has been certified as a European Enforcement Order in the Member State of origin shall be enforced in the other Member States without the need for a declaration of enforceability and without any possibility of opposing its enforceability.

3. The provisions of Chapter II, with the exception of Articles 5, 6(1) and 9(1), and of Chapter IV, with the exception of Articles 21(1) and 22, shall apply as appropriate.

Article 25

Authentic instruments

1. An authentic instrument concerning a claim within the meaning of Article 4(2) which is enforceable in one Member State shall, upon application to the authority designated by the Member State of origin, be certified as a European Enforcement Order, using the standard form in Annex III.

2. An authentic instrument which has been certified as a European Enforcement Order in the Member State of origin shall be enforced in the other Member States without the need for a declaration of enforceability and without any possibility of opposing its enforceability.

3. The provisions of Chapter II, with the exception of Articles 5, 6(1) and 9(1), and of Chapter IV, with the exception of Articles 21(1) and 22, shall apply as appropriate.

CHAPTER VI

TRANSITIONAL PROVISION

Article 26

Transitional provision

This Regulation shall apply only to judgments given, to court settlements approved or concluded and to documents formally drawn up or registered as authentic instruments after the entry into force of this Regulation.

CHAPTER VII

RELATIONSHIP WITH OTHER COMMUNITY INSTRUMENTS

Article 27

Relationship with Regulation (EC) No 44/2001

This Regulation shall not affect the possibility of seeking recognition and enforcement, in accordance with Regulation (EC) No 44/2001, of a judgment, a court settlement or an authentic instrument on an uncontested claim.

Article 28

Relationship with Regulation (EC) No 1348/2000

This Regulation shall not affect the application of Regulation (EC) No 1348/2000.

CHAPTER VIII

GENERAL AND FINAL PROVISIONS

Article 29

Information on enforcement procedures and authorities

The Member States shall cooperate to provide the general public and professional circles with information on:

(a) the methods and procedures of enforcement in the Member States; and

(b) the competent authorities for enforcement in the Member States,

in particular via the European Judicial Network in civil and commercial matters established in accordance with Decision 2001/470/EC [1].

Article 30

Information relating to redress procedures, languages and authorities

1. The Member States shall notify the Commission of:

(a) the procedures for rectification and withdrawal referred to in Article 10(2) and for review referred to in Article 19(1);

(b) the languages accepted pursuant to Article 20(2)(c);

(c) the lists of the authorities referred to in Article 25;

and any subsequent changes thereof.

2. The Commission shall make the information notified in accordance with paragraph 1 publicly available through publication in the *Official Journal of the European Union* and through any other appropriate means.

[1] OJ L 174, 27.6.2001, p. 25.

Article 31

Amendments to the Annexes

Any amendment to the standard forms in the Annexes shall be adopted in accordance with the advisory procedure referred to in Article 32(2).

Article 32

Committee

1. The Commission shall be assisted by the committee provided for by Article 75 of Regulation (EC) No 44/2001.

2. Where reference is made to this paragraph, Articles 3 and 7 of Decision 1999/468/EC shall apply, having regard to the provisions of Article 8 thereof.

3. The Committee shall adopt its Rules of Procedure.

Article 33

Entry into force

This Regulation shall enter into force on 21 January 2004.

It shall apply from 21 October 2005, with the exception of Articles 30, 31 and 32, which shall apply from 21 January 2005.

This Regulation shall be binding in its entirety and directly applicable in the Member States in accordance with the Treaty establishing the European Community.

Done at Strasbourg, 21 April 2004.

For the European Parliament	*For the Council*
The President	*The President*
P. COX	D. ROCHE

30.4.2004 EN Official Journal of the European Union L 143/25

ANNEX I

EUROPEAN ENFORCEMENT ORDER CERTIFICATE — JUDGMENT

1. Member State of origin: AT ☐ BE ☐ DE ☐ EL ☐ ES ☐ FI ☐ FR ☐
IE ☐ IT ☐ LU ☐ NL ☐ PT ☐ SE ☐ UK ☐

2. Court/Tribunal issuing the certificate

2.1. Name:

2.2. Address:

2.3. Tel./fax/e-mail:

3. If different, Court/Tribunal giving the judgment

3.1. Name:

3.2. Address:

3.3. Tel./fax/e-mail:

4. Judgment

4.1. Date:

4.2. Reference number:

4.3. The parties

4.3.1. Name and address of creditor(s):

4.3.2. Name and address of debtor(s):

5. Monetary claim as certified

5.1. Principal Amount :

5.1.1. Currency
Euro ☐
Swedish Kronor ☐
Pounds Sterling ☐
other (explain) ☐

5.1.2. If the claim is for periodical payments

5.1.2.1. Amount of each instalment:

5.1.2.2. Due date of first instalment:

5.1.2.3. Due dates of following instalments

weekly ☐ monthly ☐ other (explain) ☐

SECTION 2 Civil Procedure Rules and Practice Directions

5.1.2.4. Period of the claim

5.1.2.4.1. Currently indefinite ☐ or

5.1.2.4.2. Due date of last instalment:

5.2. Interest

5.2.1. Interest rate

5.2.1.1. ... % or

5.2.1.2. ... % above the base rate of the ECB ([1])

5.2.1.3. Other (explain)

5.2.2. Interest to be collected as from:

5.3. Amount of reimbursable costs if specified in the judgment:

6. Judgment is enforceable in the Member State of origin ☐

7. Judgment is still subject to the possibility of a challenge
Yes ☐ No ☐

8. Judgment is on an uncontested claim under Article 3(1) ☐

9. Judgment is in compliance with Article 6(1) (b) ☐

10. The judgment concerns matters relating to consumer contracts
Yes ☐ No ☐

10.1. If yes:

The debtor is the consumer
Yes ☐ No ☐

10.2. If yes:

The debtor is domiciled in the Member State of origin (within the meaning of Article 59 of Regulation (EC) 44/2001) ☐

11. Service of the document instituting the proceedings under Chapter III, where applicable
Yes ☐ No ☐

11.1. Service was effected in compliance with Article 13 ☐

or service was effected in compliance with Article 14 ☐

or it is proved in accordance with Article 18(2) that the debtor has received the document ☐

([1]) Interest rate applied by the European Central Bank to its main refinancing operations.

11.2. Due information

The debtor was informed in compliance with Articles 16 and 17 ☐

12. Service of summons, where applicable

Yes ☐ No ☐

12.1. Service was effected in compliance with Article 13 ☐

or service was effected in compliance with Article 14 ☐

or it is proved in accordance with Article 18(2) that the debtor has received the summons ☐

12.2. Due information

The debtor was informed in compliance with Article 17 ☐

13. Cure of non-compliance with procedural minimum standards pursuant to Article 18(1)

13.1. Service of the judgment was effected in compliance with Article 13 ☐

or service of the judgment was effected in compliance with Article 14 ☐

or it is proved in accordance with Article 18(2) that the debtor has received the judgment ☐

13.2. Due information

The debtor was informed in compliance with Article 18(1)(b) ☐

13.3. It was possible for the debtor to challenge the judgment

Yes ☐ No ☐

13.4. The debtor failed to challenge the judgment in compliance with the relevant procedural requirements

Yes ☐ No ☐

Done at . . . . date . . . .

. . . .

Signature and/or stamp

L 143/28 EN Official Journal of the European Union 30.4.2004

ANNEX II

EUROPEAN ENFORCEMENT ORDER CERTIFICATE — COURT SETTLEMENT

1. Member State of origin: AT ☐ BE ☐ DE ☐ EL ☐ ES ☐ FI ☐ FR ☐
IE ☐ IT ☐ LU ☐ NL ☐ PT ☐ SE ☐ UK ☐

2. Court issuing the certificate

2.1. Name:

2.2. Address:

2.3. Tel./fax/e-mail:

3. If different, Court approving the settlement or before which it was concluded

3.1. Name:

3.2. Address:

3.3. Tel./fax/e-mail:

4. Court settlement

4.1. Date:

4.2. Reference number:

4.3. The parties

4.3.1. Name and address of creditor(s):

4.3.2. Name and address of debtor(s):

5. Monetary claim as certified

5.1. Principal Amount:

5.1.1. Currency
Euro ☐
Swedish Kronor ☐
Pounds Sterling ☐
other (explain) ☐

5.1.2. If the claim is for periodical payments

5.1.2.1. Amount of each instalment:

5.1.2.2. Due date of first instalment:

5.1.2.3. Due dates of following instalments

weekly ☐ monthly ☐ other (explain) ☐

5.1.2.4. Period of the claim

5.1.2.4.1. Currently indefinite ☐ or

5.1.2.4.2. Due date of last instalment:

5.2. Interest

5.2.1. Interest rate

5.2.1.1. ... % or

5.2.1.2. ... % above the base rate of the ECB [1]

5.2.1.3. Other (explain)

5.2.2. Interest to be collected as from:

5.3. Amount of reimbursable costs if specified in the court settlement:

6. The court settlement is enforceable in the Member State of origin ☐

Done at .... date ....

....
Signature and/or stamp

[1] Interest rate applied by the European Central Bank to its main refinancing operations.

L 143/30 EN Official Journal of the European Union 30.4.2004

ANNEX III

EUROPEAN ENFORCEMENT ORDER CERTIFICATE — AUTHENTIC INSTRUMENT

1. Member State of origin: AT ☐ BE ☐ DE ☐ EL ☐ ES ☐ FI ☐ FR ☐
IE ☐ IT ☐ LU ☐ NL ☐ PT ☐ SE ☐ UK ☐

2. Court/Authority issuing the certificate

2.1. Name:

2.2. Address:

2.3. Tel./fax/e-mail:

3. If different, Court/Authority drawing up or registering the authentic instrument

3.1. Name:

3.2. Address:

3.3. Tel./fax/e-mail:

4. Authentic instrument

4.1. Date:

4.2. Reference number:

4.3. The parties

4.3.1. Name and address of creditor(s):

4.3.2. Name and address of debtor(s):

5. Monetary claim as certified

5.1. Principal Amount:

5.1.1. Currency
Euro ☐
Swedish Kronor ☐
Pounds Sterling ☐
other (explain) ☐

5.1.2. If the claim is for periodical payments

5.1.2.1. Amount of each instalment:

5.1.2.2. Due date of first instalment:

5.1.2.3. Due dates of following instalments

weekly ☐ monthly ☐ other (explain) ☐

5.1.2.4. Period of the claim

5.1.2.4.1. Currently indefinite ☐ or

5.1.2.4.2. Due date of last instalment

5.2. Interest

5.2.1. Interest rate

5.2.1.1. ... % or

5.2.1.2. ... % above the base rate of the ECB [1]

5.2.1.3. Other (explain)

5.2.2. Interest to be collected as from:

5.3. Amount of reimbursable costs if specified in the authentic instrument:

6. The authentic instrument is enforceable in the Member State of origin ☐

Done at .... date ....

....
Signature and/or stamp

[1] Interest rate applied by the European Central Bank to its main refinancing operations.

L 143/32 EN Official Journal of the European Union 30.4.2004

ANNEX IV

CERTIFICATE OF LACK OR LIMITATION OF ENFORCEABILITY
(Article 6(2))

1. Member State of origin: AT ☐ BE ☐ DE ☐ EL ☐ ES ☐ FI ☐ FR ☐
IE ☐ IT ☐ LU ☐ NL ☐ PT ☐ SE ☐ UK ☐

2. Court/Authority issuing the certificate

2.1. Name:

2.2. Address:

2.3. Tel./fax/e-mail:

3. If different, Court/Authority issuing the judgment/Court settlement/Authentic Instrument (*)

3.1. Name:

3.2. Address:

3.3. Tel./fax/e-mail:

4. Judgment/Court settlement/Authentic Instrument (*)

4.1. Date:

4.2. Reference number:

4.3. The parties

4.3.1. Name and address of creditor(s):

4.3.2. Name and address of debtor(s):

5. This judgment/court settlement/authentic instrument (*) was certified as a European Enforcement Order but

5.1. the judgment/court settlement/authentic instrument (*)is no longer enforceable ☐

5.2. Enforcement is temporarily

5.2.1. stayed ☐

5.2.2. limited to protective measures ☐

(*) Delete as appropriate.

30.4.2004 EN Official Journal of the European Union L 143/33

5.2.3. conditional upon the provision of a security which is still outstanding ☐

5.2.3.1. Amount of the security:

5.2.3.2. Currency
- Euro ☐
- Swedish Kronor ☐
- Pounds Sterling ☐
- other(explain) ☐

5.2.4. Other (explain) ☐

Done at . . . . date . . . .

. . . .
Signature and/or stamp

L 143/34 EN Official Journal of the European Union 30.4.2004

ANNEX V

EUROPEAN ENFORCEMENT ORDER REPLACEMENT CERTIFICATE FOLLOWING A CHALLENGE
(Article 6(3))

A. The following judgment/court settlement/authentic instrument (*) certified as a European Enforcement Order was challenged

1. Member State of origin: AT ☐ BE ☐ DE ☐ EL ☐ ES ☐ FI ☐ FR ☐
IE ☐ IT ☐ LU ☐ NL ☐ PT ☐ SE ☐ UK ☐

2. Court/Authority issuing the certificate

2.1. Name:

2.2. Address:

2.3. Tel./fax/e-mail:

3. If different, Court/Authority issuing the judgment/Court settlement/Authentic Instrument (*)

3.1. Name:

3.2. Address:

3.3. Tel./fax/e-mail:

4. Judgment/Court settlement/Authentic Instrument (*)

4.1. Date:

4.2. Reference number:

4.3. The parties

4.3.1. Name and address of creditor(s):

4.3.2. Name and address of debtor(s):

B. Upon that challenge the following decision has been handed down and is hereby certified as a European Enforcement Order replacing the original European Enforcement Order.

1. Court

1.1. Name:

1.2. Address:

1.3. Tel./fax/e-mail:

(*) Delete as appropriate.

30.4.2004 EN Official Journal of the European Union L 143/35

2. Decision

2.1. Date:

2.2. Reference number:

3. Monetary claim as certified

3.1. Principal Amount

3.1.1. Currency Euro ☐
Swedish Kronor ☐
Pounds Sterling ☐
Other (explain) ☐

3.1.2. If the claim is for periodic payments

3.1.2.1. Amount of each instalment:

3.1.2.2. Due date of first instalment:

3.1.2.3. Due dates of following instalments

weekly ☐ monthly ☐ other (explain) ☐

3.1.2.4. Period of the claim

3.1.2.4.1. Currently indefinite ☐ or

3.1.2.4.2. Due date of last instalment:

3.2. Interest

3.2.1. Interest rate

3.2.1.1. ... % or

3.2.1.2. ... % above the base rate of the ECB (1)

3.2.1.3. Other (explain)

3.2.2. Interest to be collected as from:

3.3. Amount of reimbursable costs if specified in the decision:

4. Decision is enforceable in the Member State of origin ☐

5. Decision is still subject to the possibility of a further appeal

Yes ☐ No ☐

6. Decision is in compliance with Article 6(1)(b) ☐

(1) Interest rate applied by the European Central Bank to its main refinancing operations.

7. The decision concerns matters relating to consumer contracts

Yes ☐ No ☐

7.1. If yes:

The debtor is the consumer

Yes ☐ No ☐

7.2. If yes:

The debtor is domiciled in the Member State of origin in the meaning of Article 59 of Regulation (EC) No 44/2001 ☐

8. At the time of the decision following the challenge, the claim is uncontested within the meaning of Article 3(1)(b) or (c)

Yes ☐ No ☐

If yes:

8.1. Service of the document instituting the challenge.

Did the creditor lodge the challenge?

Yes ☐ No ☐

If yes:

8.1.1. Service was effected in compliance with Article 13 ☐

or service was effected in compliance with Article 14 ☐

or it is proved in accordance with Article 18(2) that the debtor has received the document ☐

8.1.2. Due information

The debtor was informed in compliance with Articles 16 and 17 ☐

8.2. Service of summons, where applicable

Yes ☐ No ☐

If yes:

8.2.1. Service was effected in compliance with Article 13 ☐

or service was effected in compliance with Article ☐

or it is proved in accordance with Article 18(2) that the debtor has received the summons ☐

8.2.2. Due information

The debtor was informed in compliance with Article 17 ☐

8.3. Cure of non-compliance with procedural minimum standards pursuant to Article 18(1)

8.3.1. Service of the decision was effected in compliance with Article 13 ☐

or Service of the decision was effected in compliance with Article 14 ☐

or it is proved in accordance with Article 18(2) that the debtor has received the decision ☐

8.3.2. Due information

The debtor was informed in compliance with Article 18(1)(b) ☐

Done at . . . . date . . . .

. . . .
Signature and/or stamp

L 143/38 EN Official Journal of the European Union 30.4.2004

ANNEX VI

APPLICATION FOR RECTIFICATION OR WITHDRAWAL OF THE EUROPEAN ENFORCEMENT ORDER CERTIFICATE (Article 10(3))

THE FOLLOWING EUROPEAN ENFORCEMENT ORDER CERTIFICATE

1. Member State of origin: AT ☐ BE ☐ DE ☐ EL ☐ ES ☐ FI ☐ FR ☐
IE ☐ IT ☐ LU ☐ NL ☐ PT ☐ SE ☐ UK ☐

2. Court/Authority issuing the certificate

2.1. Name:

2.2. Address:

2.3. Tel./fax/e-mail:

3. If different, Court/Authority issuing the judgment/Court settlement/Authentic Instrument (*)

3.1. Name:

3.2. Address:

3.3. Tel./fax/e-mail:

4. Judgment/Court settlement/Authentic Instrument

4.1. Date:

4.2. Reference number:

4.3. The parties

4.3.1. Name and address of creditor(s):

4.3.2. Name and address of debtor(s):

HAS TO BE

5. RECTIFIED as due to a material error there is the following discrepancy between the European Enforcement Order certificate and the underlying judgment/court settlement/authentic instrument (explain) ☐

(*) Delete as appropriate.

6. WITHDRAWN because:

6.1. the certified judgment was related to a consumer contract but was given in a Member State where the consumer is not domiciled within the meaning of Article 59 of Regulation (EC) No 44/2001 ☐

6.2. the European Enforcement Order certificate was clearly wrongly granted for another reason (explain) ☐

Done at . . . . date . . . .

. . . .
Signature and/or stamp

PART 75
TRAFFIC ENFORCEMENT

CONTENTS OF THIS PART

Important—By virtue of the Civil Procedure (Amendment) Rules 2002, SI 2002/2058, this Part came into force on 1 October 2002. For provisions governing court procedure before that date see Sched 2, CCR Ord 48B (set out in the 2002 edition of this work) which is revoked as of that date.

Practice Direction—See generally PD75 at p 1616.

75.1 Scope and interpretation

(1) The practice direction –

(a) sets out the proceedings to which this Part applies; and
(b) may apply this Part with modifications in relation to any particular category of those proceedings.

(2) In this Part –

(a) 'the Centre' means the Traffic Enforcement Centre established under the direction of the Lord Chancellor;
(b) 'no relevant return to the warrant' means that –
  (i) the bailiff has been unable to seize goods because he has been denied access to premises occupied by the defendant or because the goods have been removed from those premises;
  (ii) any goods seized under a warrant of execution are insufficient to satisfy the debt and the cost of execution; or
  (iii) the goods are insufficient to cover the cost of their removal and sale.
(c) 'the 1993 Order' means the Enforcement of Road Traffic Debts Order 1993;
(d) 'relevant period', in relation to any particular case, means –
  (i) the period allowed for serving a statutory declaration under any enactment which applies to that case; or
  (ii) where an enactment permits the court to extend that period, the period as extended;
(e) 'specified debts' means the debts specified in article 2 of the 1993 Order or treated as so specified by any other enactment; and
(f) 'the authority', 'notice of the amount due', 'order' and 'the respondent' have the meaning given by the practice direction.

Amendments—Inserted by SI 2002/2058.

75.2 The Centre

(1) Proceedings to which this Part applies must be started in the Centre.

(2) For any purpose connected with the exercise of the Centre's functions –

(a) the Centre shall be deemed to be part of the office of the court whose name appears on the documents to which the functions relates or in whose name the documents are issued; and

(b) any officer of the Centre, in exercising its functions, is deemed to act as an officer of that court.

Amendments—Inserted by SI 2002/2058.

75.3 Request

(1) The authority must file a request in the appropriate form scheduling the amount claimed to be due.

(2) The authority must, in that request or in another manner approved by the court officer –

(a) certify –

(i) that 14 days have elapsed since service of the notice of the amount due;

(ii) the date of such service;

(iii) the number of the notice of the amount due; and

(iv) that the amount due remains unpaid;

(b) specify the grounds (whether by reference to the appropriate code or otherwise), as stated in the notice, on which the authority claims to be entitled to claim that amount; and

(c) state –

(i) the name, title and address of the respondent;

(ii) the registration number of the vehicle concerned;

(iii) the authority's address for service;

(iv) the court fee; and

(v) such other matters as required by the practice direction.

(3) On receipt of a request that meets the requirements of paragraphs (1) and (2), the court officer will order that the amount due may be recovered as if it were payable under a county court order by sealing the request and returning it to the authority.

(4) On receipt of a sealed request the authority may draw up an order and must attach to it a form of statutory declaration for the respondent's use.

(5) Within 14 days of receipt of the sealed request, the authority must serve the order (and the form of statutory declaration) on the respondent in accordance with Part 6.

(6) Where an order is served by first class post rule 6.7 is modified so that the date of service will be deemed to be the seventh day after the date on which the order was sent to the respondent.

Amendments—Inserted by SI 2002/2058.

75.4 Electronic delivery of documents

(1) Where the authority is required to file any document other than the request, that requirement is satisfied if the information which would be contained in the document is delivered in computer-readable form.

(2) For the purposes of paragraph (1), information which would be contained in a document relating to one case may be combined with information of the same nature relating to another case.

(3) Where a document is required to be produced, that requirement will be satisfied if a copy of the document is produced from computer records.

Amendments—Inserted by SI 2002/2058.

75.5 Functions of court officer

(1) The practice direction sets out circumstances in which a court officer may exercise the functions of the court or a district judge.

(2) Any party may request any decision of a court officer to be reviewed by a district judge.

(3) Such a request must be made within 14 days of service of the decision.

Amendments—Inserted by SI 2002/2058.

75.6 Enforcement of orders

Subject to the 1993 Order and this rule the following rules apply to the enforcement of specified debts –

- (a) Parts 70 to 73;
- (b) CCR Order 25, rules 1 and 9;
- (c) CCR Order 26, rule 5; and
- (d) CCR Order 27, rules 1 to 7, 7A, 7B, 9 to 16 and 18 to 22.

(Rule 30.2 provides for the transfer between courts in order to enforce a judgment)

Amendments—Inserted by SI 2002/2058.

75.7 Warrant of execution

(1) An authority seeking the issue of a warrant of execution must file a request –

- (a) certifying the amount remaining due under the order;
- (b) specifying the date of service of the order on the respondent; and
- (c) certifying that the relevant period has elapsed.

(2) The court will seal the request and return it to the authority.

(3) Within 7 days of the sealing of the request the authority must prepare the warrant in the appropriate form.

(4) No payment under a warrant will be made to the court.

(5) For the purposes of execution a warrant will be valid for 12 months beginning with the date of its issue.

(6) An authority may not renew a warrant issued in accordance with this Part.

Amendments—Inserted by SI 2002/2058.

75.8 Revocation of order

Where, in accordance with any enactment, an order is deemed to have been revoked following the filing of a statutory declaration –

(a) the court will serve a copy of the statutory declaration on the authority;
(b) any execution issued on the order will cease to have effect; and
(c) if appropriate, the authority must inform any bailiff instructed to levy execution of the withdrawal of the warrant as soon as possible.

Amendments—Inserted by SI 2002/2058.

75.9 Transfer for enforcement

If an authority requests the transfer of proceedings to another county court for enforcement, the request must –

(a) where the authority has not attempted to enforce by execution, give the reason why no such attempt was made;
(b) certify that there has been no relevant return to the warrant of execution;
(c) specify the date of service of the order on the respondent; and
(d) certify that the relevant period has elapsed.

Amendments—Inserted by SI 2002/2058.

75.10 Further information required

An application for –

(a) an attachment of earnings order;
(b) an order to obtain information from a debtor;
(c) a third party debt order; or
(d) a charging order,

must, in addition to the requirements of Parts 71, 72 or 73 or CCR Order 27 –

(i) where the authority has not attempted to enforce by execution, give the reasons no such attempt was made;
(ii) certify that there has been no relevant return to the warrant of execution;
(iii) specify the date of service of the order on the respondent; and
(iv) certify that the relevant period has elapsed.

Amendments—Inserted by SI 2002/2058.

75.11 Combining requests

If the court officer allows, an authority may combine information relating to different orders against the same defendant in any request or application made under rules 75.9 or 75.10.

Amendments—Inserted by SI 2002/2058.

Practice Direction – Traffic Enforcement

This Practice Direction supplements CPR Part 75 (PD75)

INTERPRETATION AND SCOPE

1.1 In this Practice Direction –

(1) 'the 1991 Act' means the Road Traffic Act 1991;
(2) 'the 1996 Act' means the London Local Authorities Act 1996;
(3) 'the Road User Charging Regulations' means the Road User Charging (Enforcement and Adjudication) (London) Regulations 2001;
(4) 'the Vehicle Emissions (England) Regulations' means the Road Traffic (Vehicle Emissions) (Fixed Penalty) (England) Regulations 2002;
(5) 'the Vehicle Emissions (Wales) Regulations' means the Road Traffic (Vehicle Emissions) (Fixed Penalty) (Wales) Regulations 2003;
(6) 'the 2003 Act' means the London Local Authorities and Transport for London Act 2003.

1.2 Part 75 applies to proceedings for the recovery of –

(1) increased penalty charges provided for in parking charge certificates issued under paragraph 6 of Schedule 6 to the 1991 Act;
(2) amounts payable by a person other than an authority under an adjudication of a parking adjudicator pursuant to section 73 of the 1991 Act;
(3) increased penalty charges provided for in a charge certificate issued under paragraph 8 of Schedule 1 to the 1996 Act (relating to a contravention or failure to comply with an order made under a provision referred to in section 4(2) of that Act reserving all or part of a carriageway of a road as a bus lane); and
(4) increased fixed penalties to which regulation 17(6) of the Vehicle Emissions (England) Regulations refer;
(5) amounts payable by a person other than an authority under an adjudication of an adjudicator pursuant to the Schedule to the Road User Charging Regulations;
(6) increased penalty charges provided for in charge certificates issued under regulation 17 of the Road User Charging Regulations; and.
(7) increased fixed penalty charges to which regulation 17(6) of the Vehicle Emissions (Wales) Regulations refer.

1.3 In Part 75 and this practice direction –

(1) 'authority' means the authority entitled to recover amounts due under the enactments referred to in paragraph 1.2;
(2) 'notice of the amount due' means, as the case may be –
    (a) a parking charge certificate issued under paragraph 6 of Schedule 6 to the 1991 Act;
    (b) a charge certificate issued under paragraph 8 of Schedule 1 to the 1996 Act;
    (c) a fixed penalty notice issued under regulations 10 or 13 of the Vehicle Emissions (England) Regulations; …
    (d) a charge certificate issued under regulation 17 of the Road User Charging Regulations; or
    (e) a fixed penalty notice issued under regulations 10 or 13 of the Vehicle Emissions (Wales) Regulations.

(3) 'order' means an order made under –
  (a) paragraph 7 of Schedule 6 to the 1991 Act;
  (b) paragraph 9 of Schedule 1 to the 1996 Act;
  (c) section 73(15) of the 1991 Act;
  (d) regulation 21 of the Vehicle Emissions (England) Regulations;
  (e) regulation 7 of the Road User Charging Regulations;
  (f) regulation 18 of the Road User Charging Regulations; or
  (g) regulation 21 of the Vehicle Emissions (Wales) Regulations; and

(4) 'respondent' means –
  (a) the person on whom the notice of the amount due was served; or
  (b) the person (other than an authority) by whom the amount due under an adjudication is payable.

TRAFFIC ENFORCEMENT CENTRE

2.1 All claims to which Part 75 applies must be started in the Traffic Enforcement Centre ('the Centre') at Northampton County Court.

REQUEST

3.1 Where an order in respect of amounts payable by a person other than an authority under an adjudication pursuant to section 73 of the 1991 Act or the Schedule to the Road User Charging Regulations is sought, rule 75.3 applies with the necessary modifications and, in addition, the request must –

(1) state the date on which the adjudication was made;
(2) provide details of the order made on the adjudication; and
(3) certify the amount awarded by way of costs and that the amount remains unpaid.

FUNCTIONS OF COURT OFFICER

4.1 A court officer may exercise the functions of –

(1) the district judge under –
  (a) paragraph 8(4) and (5)(d) of Schedule 6 to the 1991 Act;
  (b) paragraphs 10(4) and (5)(d) of Schedule 1 to the 1996 Act; and
  (c) regulations 19(4) and 19(5)(d) of the Road User Charging Regulations; and

(2) the court under–
  (a) paragraph 23(3)of the Vehicle Emissions (England) Regulations; and
  (b) paragraph 23(3)of the Vehicle Emissions (Wales) Regulations.

APPLICATION FOR LONGER PERIOD FOR FILING OF STATUTORY DECLARATION

5.1 Paragraphs 5.2 to 5.5 apply where the respondent applies under –

(1) paragraph 8(3) of Schedule 6 to the Road Traffic Act 1991;
(2) paragraph 10(3) of Schedule 1 to the London Local Authorities Act 1996;
(3) regulation 23(3) of the Vehicle Emissions (England) Regulations; …
(4) regulation 19(3) of the Road User Charging Regulations; or
(5) regulation 23(3) of the Vehicle Emissions (Wales) Regulations,

SECTION 2 Civil Procedure Rules and Practice Directions

for an order allowing a longer period than 21 days for service of the statutory declaration.

5.2 The respondent must send to the Centre –

(1) a completed application notice (Form PE2 may be used); and
(2) a completed statutory declaration in Form PE3.

(Forms PE2 and PE3 can be obtained from the Centre at Northampton County Court, Bulk Centre, 21/27 St Katherine's Street, Northampton NN1 2LH. (Telephone number: 08457 045007))

5.3 The court will serve a copy of the application notice and a copy of the statutory declaration on the authority that obtained the court order seeking representations on the application.

5.4 A court officer will deal with the application without a hearing. The matter will not be dealt with until at least 14 days after the date on which the application notice and statutory declaration were served on the authority.

5.5 If the proceedings have been transferred to another court the Centre will transfer the application to that court.

5.6 Paragraphs 5.3 to 5.5 shall not apply where the court receives an application notice that is accompanied by a statutory declaration that is invalid by virtue of paragraph 8(2A) of Schedule 6 to the 1991 Act as inserted by section 15 of the 2003 Act.

APPLICATION TO REVIEW ORDER MADE BY COURT OFFICER

6.1 Where any order is made by a court officer it will contain a statement of the right of either party to request a review of the decision by a district judge at a hearing.

6.2 Attention is drawn to rule 75.5 paragraphs (2) and (3).

HEARING

7.1 When a hearing is to be held, the proceedings will be transferred to the county court for the district in which the respondent's address for service is situated. This transfer is only for the purposes of holding the hearing and serving any orders made as a result of the hearing.

7.2 The respondent's address for service is his address for service shown on the last of the following documents filed at court by the respondent –

(1) the application notice or, if more than one, the latest application notice; and
(2) the appellant's notice.

7.3 The court where the hearing is held will serve any orders made as a result of the hearing before returning the papers to the Centre, or, if the proceedings have been transferred, to the court where the proceedings have been transferred.

7.4 Evidence at any hearing may be given orally or by witness statement.

APPLICATIONS TO SUSPEND A WARRANT OF EXECUTION

8.1 Where –

(1) the respondent makes an application under paragraph 5; and
(2) before that application is determined, a warrant of execution is issued,

the local authority must suspend enforcement of the warrant of execution until the application for an extension order is determined.

(Rule 75.8(b) provides that, where a court order is deemed to have been revoked following the filing of a statutory declaration, any execution issued on the order will cease to have effect)

PART 76
PROCEEDINGS UNDER THE PREVENTION OF TERRORISM ACT 2005

CONTENTS OF THIS PART

Section I – Application of this Part

76.1 Scope and interpretation

(1) This Part contains rules about –

(a) control order proceedings in the High Court; and
(b) appeals to the Court of Appeal against an order of the High Court in such proceedings.

(2) In the case of proceedings brought by virtue of section 11(2) of the Act, the rules in this Part shall apply with any modification which the court considers necessary.

(3) In this Part –

- (a) 'the Act' means the Prevention of Terrorism Act 2005;
- (b) 'closed material' means any relevant material that the Secretary of State objects to disclosing to a relevant party;
- (c) 'control order proceedings' has the same meaning as in section 11(6) of the Act;
- (d) 'controlled person', has the same meaning as in section 15(1) of the Act;
- (e) 'legal representative' is to be construed in accordance with paragraph 11 of the Schedule to the Act;
- (f) 'open material' means any relevant material that the Secretary of State does not object to disclosing to a relevant party;
- (g) 'relevant law officer' has the same meaning as in paragraph 7(6) of the Schedule to the Act;
- (h) 'relevant material' has the same meaning as in paragraph 4(5) of the Schedule to the Act;
- (i) 'relevant party' has the same meaning as in paragraph 11 of the Schedule to the Act;
- (j) 'special advocate' means a person appointed under paragraph 7 of the Schedule to the Act.

(4) For the purposes of this Part, disclosure is contrary to the public interest if it is made contrary to the interests of national security, the international relations of the United Kingdom, the detection and prevention of crime, or in any other circumstances where disclosure is likely to harm the public interest.

Amendments—Inserted by SI 2005/656.

76.2 Modification to the overriding objective

(1) Where this Part applies, the overriding objective in Part 1, and so far as relevant any other rule, must be read and given effect in a way which is compatible with the duty set out in paragraph (2).

(2) The court must ensure that information is not disclosed contrary to the public interest.

(3) Subject to paragraph (2), the court must satisfy itself that the material available to it enables it properly to determine proceedings.

Amendments—Inserted by SI 2005/656.

Section II – Applications to the High Court relating to derogating control orders

76.3 Scope of this section

(1) This section of this Part contains rules about applications relating to derogating control orders.

(2) Part 23 does not apply to an application made under this section of this Part.

Amendments—Inserted by SI 2005/656.

76.4 Applications for the making of a derogating control order

An application for the making of a derogating control order under section 4(1) of the Act must be made by the Secretary of State by filing with the court –

(a) a statement of reasons to support the application for –
  (i) making such an order, and
  (ii) imposing each of the obligations to be imposed by that order;
(b) all relevant material;
(c) any written submissions; and
(d) a draft of the order sought.

Amendments—Inserted by SI 2005/656.

76.5 Directions for a full hearing on notice

(1) When the court makes a derogating control order under section 4(3) of the Act it must –

(a) immediately fix a date, time and place for a further hearing at which the controlled person, his legal representative and a special advocate (if one has been appointed) can be present; and
(b) unless the court otherwise directs, that date must be no later than 7 days from the date that the order is made.

(2) At the hearing referred to in paragraph (1)(a) the court must give directions –

(a) for the holding of a full hearing under section 4(1)(b) of the Act to determine whether to confirm the control order (with or without modifications) or to revoke it; and
(b) specifying the date and time by which the parties and special advocate must file and serve any written evidence or written submissions in accordance with rule 76.30.

(3) When giving directions under paragraph (2), the court must have regard to the need to expedite the full hearing.

Amendments—Inserted by SI 2005/656.

76.6 Applications on notice

(1) An application under section 4(9) for the renewal, or under section 7(4) of the Act, for the revocation of a control order or for the modification of obligations imposed by such an order, must be made in accordance with this rule.

(2) An application by the Secretary of State must be made by –

(a) filing with the court –
  (i) a statement of reasons to support the application,
  (ii) all relevant material,
  (iii) any written submissions, and
  (iv) a draft of the order sought; and
(b) serving on the controlled person or his legal representative any open material.

(3) An application by the controlled person must be made by filing with the court and serving on the Secretary of State –

(a) a statement of reasons to support the application;

(b) any written evidence upon which he relies;
(c) any written submissions; and
(d) where appropriate, a draft of the order sought.

(4) If the controlled person wishes to oppose an application made under this rule, he must as soon as practicable file with the court, and serve on the Secretary of State, any written evidence and any written submissions upon which he relies.

(5) If the Secretary of State wishes to oppose an application made under this rule, he must as soon as practicable –

(a) file with the court –
  (i) all relevant material, and
  (ii) any written submissions; and
(b) serve on the controlled person any open material.

(Attention is drawn to rule 76.18 relating to the address for issuing proceedings in the High Court. Rules 76.28 and 76.29 will apply where any closed material is filed by the Secretary of State).

Amendments—Inserted by SI 2005/656.

Section III – Permission applications, references and appeals to the High Court relating to non-derogating control orders

76.7 Scope of this section

This section of this Part contains rules about –

(a) applications under section 3(1)(a) of the Act (application for permission to make a non-derogating control order);
(b) references under section 3(3) of the Act (reference of a non-derogating control order made without permission); and
(c) appeals to the High Court under section 10 of the Act (appeals relating to non-derogating control orders).

Amendments—Inserted by SI 2005/656.

76.8 Application for permission to make non-derogating control order

An application under section 3(1)(a) for permission to make a non-derogating control order must be made by the Secretary of State by filing with the court –

(a) a statement of reasons to support the application;
(b) all relevant material;
(c) any written submissions; and
(d) the proposed control order.

Amendments—Inserted by SI 2005/656.

76.9 References under section 3(3) of the Act

(1) This rule applies where the Secretary of State makes a reference under section 3(3) of the Act (reference of a non-derogating control order).

(2) The Secretary of State must promptly file with the court –

(a) a statement of the reasons for –

(i) making the control order,
(ii) imposing the obligations imposed by that order;

(b) all relevant material; and

(c) any written submissions.

Amendments—Inserted by SI 2005/656.

76.10 Directions for hearing on application for permission or on a reference

(1) This rule applies where the court gives directions under section 3(2)(c) or (6)(b) or (c) of the Act.

(2) The court must immediately –

(a) fix a date, time and place for a further hearing at which the controlled person, his legal representative and a special advocate (if one has been appointed) can be present; and

(b) unless the court otherwise directs, that date must be no later than 7 days from the date that the order is made.

(3) At the hearing referred to in paragraph (2), the court must give directions –

(a) for a hearing under section 3(10); and

(b) specifying the date and time by which the parties and special advocate must file and serve any written evidence or written submissions in accordance with rule 76.30.

(4) When giving directions under paragraph (3), the court must have regard to the need to expedite that hearing.

(Rules 76.28 and 76.29 will apply where any closed material is filed by the Secretary of State).

Amendments—Inserted by SI 2005/656.

76.11 Appeals under section 10 of the Act

This rule and rules 76.12 to 76.15 apply to an appeal under section 10 of the Act (appeals relating to a non-derogating control order).

Amendments—Inserted by SI 2005/656.

76.12 Modification of Part 52 (appeals)

(1) Part 52 (appeals) applies to an appeal under section 10 of the Act, subject to –

(a) rule 76.2;

(b) the rules in section 5 of this Part; and

(c) the modifications set out in paragraphs (2) and (3) of this rule.

(2) The following rules do not apply to appeals under section 10 of the Act –

(a) rule 52.3 (permission);

(b) rule 52.4 (appellant's notice);

(c) rule 52.5 (respondent's notice); and

(d) rule 52.11 (hearing of appeals).

(3) Rule 52.2 (all parties to comply with the practice direction) applies, but the parties shall not be required to comply with paragraphs 5.6, 5.6A, 5.7, 5.9 and 5.10 of that practice direction.

Amendments—Inserted by SI 2005/656.

76.13 Notice of appeal

(1) The controlled person must give notice of appeal by –

(a) filing it with the court; and
(b) serving a copy of the notice and any accompanying documents on the Secretary of State.

(2) The notice of appeal must –

(a) set out the grounds of the appeal; and
(b) state the name and address of –
    (i) the controlled person, and
    (ii) any legal representative of that person.

(3) A notice of appeal may include an application for an order under rule 76.19 requiring anonymity.

(4) The notice of appeal must be filed with –

(a) a copy of the order that is the subject of the appeal;
(b) a copy of the Secretary of State's decision on an application for the revocation of the control order, or for the modification of an obligation imposed by such an order.

(Attention is drawn to rule 76.18 relating to the address for issuing proceedings in the High Court).

Amendments—Inserted by SI 2005/656.

76.14 Time limit for appealing

(1) Subject to paragraph (2), the controlled person must give notice of appeal no later than 28 days after receiving notice of –

(a) the order that is the subject of the appeal; or
(b) the decision by the Secretary of State on an application for the revocation of the control order, or for the modification of an obligation imposed by such an order.

(2) In a case where the Secretary of State has failed to determine an application for the revocation of the control order, or for the modification of an obligation imposed by such an order, the controlled person must file the notice of appeal –

(a) no earlier than 28 days; and
(b) no later than 42 days;

after the date the application was made.

Amendments—Inserted by SI 2005/656.

76.15 Secretary of State's reply

If the Secretary of State wishes to oppose an appeal made under section 10 of the Act, he must no later than 14 days after he is served with the notice of appeal –

(a) file with the court –
    (i) all relevant material, and
    (ii) any written submissions; and
(b) serve on the controlled person any open material.

Amendments—Inserted by SI 2005/656.

Section IV – Appeals to the Court of Appeal

76.16 Modification of Part 52 (appeals)

(1) Part 52 (appeals) applies to an appeal to the Court of Appeal against an order of the High Court in control order proceedings, subject to –

(a) rule 76.2;
(b) the rules in section 5 of this Part; and
(c) paragraphs (2) and (3) of this rule.

(2) The following rules do not apply to appeals to the Court of Appeal –

(a) rule 52.4(1) (appellant's notice); and
(b) rule 52.5 (respondent's notice); but

the provisions of rules 76.13 and 76.15 shall apply with appropriate modifications.

(3) Rule 52.2 (all parties to comply with the practice direction) applies, but the parties shall not be required to comply with paragraphs 5.6, 5.6A, 5.7, 6.3A, 15.2, 15.3, 15.4 and 15.6 of that practice direction.

Amendments—Inserted by SI 2005/656.

Section V – General provisions

76.17 Scope of this section

This section of this Part applies to –

(a) control order proceedings in the High Court; and
(b) appeals to the Court of Appeal against an order of the High Court in such proceedings.

Amendments—Inserted by SI 2005/656.

76.18 Address for issuing proceedings in the High Court

Any control order proceedings must be issued at the Administrative Court Office, Room C315, Royal Courts of Justice, Strand, London, WC2A 2LL.

Amendments—Inserted by SI 2005/656.

76.19 Applications for anonymity

(1) The controlled person or the Secretary of State may apply for an order requiring the anonymity of the controlled person.

(2) An application under paragraph (1) may be made at any time, irrespective of whether any control order proceedings have been commenced.

(3) An application may be made without notice to the other party.

(4) References in this rule to an order requiring anonymity for the controlled person are to be construed in accordance with paragraph 5(3) of the Schedule to the Act.

Amendments—Inserted by SI 2005/656.

76.20 Notification of hearing

Unless the court orders otherwise, it must serve notice of the date, time and place fixed for any hearing on –

(a) every party, whether or not entitled to attend that hearing; and
(b) if one has been appointed for the purposes of the hearing, the special advocate or those instructing him.

Amendments—Inserted by SI 2005/656.

76.21 Hearings

(1) The following proceedings must be determined at a hearing –

(a) a hearing pursuant to directions given under section 4(1)(b) of the Act (derogating control orders);
(b) a hearing pursuant to directions given under sections 3(2)(c) or (6)(b) or (c) of the Act (non-derogating control orders);
(c) an appeal under section 10 of the Act (appeal relating to a non-derogating control order);
(d) an appeal to the Court of Appeal from an order of the High Court made in any of the above proceedings; and
(e) a hearing under rule 76.29(2) (consideration of Secretary of State's objection).

(2) Paragraph (1)(c) and (d) do not apply where –

(a) the appeal is withdrawn by the controlled person;
(b) the Secretary of State consents to the appeal being allowed; or
(c) the controlled person is outside the United Kingdom or it is impracticable to give him notice of a hearing and, in either case, he is unrepresented.

Amendments—Inserted by SI 2005/656.

76.22 Hearings in private

(1) If the court considers it necessary for any relevant party and his legal representative to be excluded from a hearing or part of a hearing in order to secure that information is not disclosed contrary to the public interest, it must –

(a) direct accordingly; and
(b) conduct the hearing, or that part of it from which the relevant party and his legal representative are excluded, in private.

(2) The court may conduct a hearing or part of a hearing in private for any other good reason.

Amendments—Inserted by SI 2005/656.

76.23 Appointment of a special advocate

(1) Subject to paragraph (2), the Secretary of State must immediately give notice of the proceedings to the relevant law officer upon –

(a) making an application under section 4(1) of the Act (relating to a derogating control order);
(b) making an application under section 3(1)(a) of the Act (application for permission to make a non-derogating control order);

(c) making a reference under section 3(3) of the Act (reference of a non-derogating control order made without permission); or
(d) being served with a copy of any application, claim, or notice of appeal in proceedings to which this Part applies.

(2) Paragraph (1) applies unless –

(a) the Secretary of State does not intend to –
(i) oppose the appeal or application; or
(ii) withhold closed material from a relevant party; or
(b) a special advocate has already been appointed to represent the interests of the relevant party in the proceedings and that special advocate is not prevented from communicating with that party by virtue of rule 76.25.

(3) Where notice is given to the relevant law officer under paragraph (1), the relevant law officer may appoint a special advocate to represent the interests of the relevant party in the proceedings.

(4) Where any proceedings to which this Part apply are pending but no special advocate has been appointed, a relevant party or the Secretary of State may request the relevant law officer to appoint a special advocate.

Amendments—Inserted by SI 2005/656.

76.24 Functions of special advocate

The functions of a special advocate are to represent the interests of a relevant party by –

(a) making submissions to the court at any hearings from which the relevant party and his legal representatives are excluded;
(b) cross-examining witnesses at any such hearings; and
(c) making written submissions to the court.

Amendments—Inserted by SI 2005/656.

76.25 Special advocate: communicating about proceedings

(1) The special advocate may communicate with the relevant party or his legal representative at any time before the Secretary of State serves closed material on him.

(2) After the Secretary of State serves closed material on the special advocate, the special advocate must not communicate with any person about any matter connected with the proceedings, except in accordance with paragraph (3) or a direction of the court pursuant to a request under paragraph (4).

(3) The special advocate may, without directions from the court, communicate about the proceedings with –

(a) the court;
(b) the Secretary of State, or any person acting for him;
(c) the relevant law officer, or any person acting for him; or
(d) any other person, except for the relevant party or his legal representative, with whom it is necessary for administrative purposes for him to communicate about matters not connected with the substance of the proceedings.

(4) The special advocate may request directions from the court authorising him to communicate with the relevant party or his legal representative or with any other person.

(5) Where the special advocate makes a request for directions under paragraph (4) –

(a) the court must notify the Secretary of State of the request; and
(b) the Secretary of State must, within a period specified by the court, file with the court and serve on the special advocate notice of any objection which he has to the proposed communication, or to the form in which it is proposed to be made.

(6) Paragraph (2) does not prohibit the relevant party from communicating with the special advocate after the Secretary of State has served material on him as mentioned in paragraph (1), but –

(a) the relevant party may only communicate with the special advocate through a legal representative in writing; and
(b) the special advocate must not reply to the communication other than in accordance with directions of the court, except that he may without such directions send a written acknowledgment of receipt to the legal representative of the relevant party.

Amendments—Inserted by SI 2005/656.

76.26 Modification of the general rules of evidence and disclosure

(1) Part 31 (disclosure and inspection of documents), Part 32 (evidence) and Part 33 (miscellaneous rules about evidence) do not apply to any proceedings to which this Part applies.

(2) Subject to the other rules in this Part, the evidence of a witness may be given either –

(a) orally, before the court; or
(b) in writing, in which case it shall be given in such manner and at such time as the court directs.

(3) The court may also receive evidence in documentary or any other form.

(4) The court may receive evidence that would not, but for this rule, be admissible in a court of law.

(5) Every party shall be entitled to adduce evidence and to cross-examine witnesses during any part of a hearing from which he and his legal representative are not excluded.

(6) The court may require a witness to give evidence on oath.

Amendments—Inserted by SI 2005/656.

76.27 Filing and service of relevant material

The Secretary of State is required to make a reasonable search for relevant material and to file and serve that material in accordance with the rules in this Part.

Amendments—Inserted by SI 2005/656.

76.28 Closed material

(1) The Secretary of State –

(a) must apply to the court for permission to withhold closed material from a relevant party or his legal representative in accordance with this rule; and
(b) may not rely on closed material at a hearing on notice unless a special advocate has been appointed to represent the interests of the relevant party.

(2) The Secretary of State must file with the court and serve, at such time as the court directs, on the special advocate –

(a) the closed material;
(b) a statement of his reasons for withholding that material from the relevant party; and
(c) if he considers it possible to summarise that material without disclosing information contrary to the public interest, a summary of that material in a form which can be served on the relevant party.

(3) The Secretary of State may at any time amend or supplement material filed under this rule, but only with –

(a) the agreement of the special advocate; or
(b) the permission of the court.

Amendments—Inserted by SI 2005/656.

76.29 Consideration of Secretary of State's objection

(1) This rule applies where the Secretary of State has –

(a) objected under rule 76.25(5)(b) to a proposed communication by the special advocate; or
(b) applied under rule 76.28 for permission to withhold closed material.

(2) The court must fix a hearing for the Secretary of State and the special advocate to make oral representations, unless –

(a) the special advocate gives notice to the court that he does not challenge the objection or application;
(b) the court has previously considered –
 (i) an objection under rule 76.25(5)(b), or
 (ii) an application under rule 76.28(1) for permission to withhold the same or substantially the same material, and

is satisfied that it would be just to uphold that objection or to give permission without a hearing; or

(c) the Secretary of State and the special advocate consent to the court deciding the issue without a hearing.

(3) If the special advocate does not challenge the objection or the application, he must give notice of that fact to the court and the Secretary of State within 14 days, or such other period as the court may direct, after the Secretary of State serves on him a notice under rule 76.25(5)(b) or material under rule 76.28(2).

(4) Where the court fixes a hearing under this rule, the Secretary of State and the special advocate must before the hearing file with the court a schedule identifying the issues which cannot be agreed between them, which must –

(a) list the items or issues in dispute;
(b) give brief reasons for their contentions on each; and

(c) set out any proposals for the court to resolve the issues in contention.

(5) A hearing under this rule shall take place in the absence of the relevant party and his legal representative.

(6) Where the court gives permission to the Secretary of State to withhold closed material, the court must –

(a) consider whether to direct the Secretary of State to serve a summary of that material on the relevant party or his legal representative; but

(b) ensure that no such summary contains information or other material the disclosure of which would be contrary to the public interest.

(7) Where the court has not given permission to the Secretary of State to withhold closed material from, or has directed the Secretary of State to serve a summary of that material on, a relevant party or his legal representative –

(a) the Secretary of State shall not be required to serve that material or summary; but

(b) if he does not do so, at a hearing on notice the court may –

(i) if it considers that the material or anything that is required to be summarised might be of assistance to the relevant party in relation to a matter under consideration by the court, direct that the matter be withdrawn from its consideration, and

(ii) in any other case, direct that the Secretary of State shall not rely in the proceedings on that material or (as the case may be) on what is required to be summarised.

(8) The court must give permission to the Secretary of State to withhold closed material where it considers that the disclosure of that material would be contrary to the public interest.

Amendments—Inserted by SI 2005/656.

76.30 Order of filing and serving material and written submissions

Subject to any directions given by the court, the parties must file and serve any material and written submissions, and the special advocate must file and serve any written submissions, in the following order –

(a) the Secretary of State must file with the court all relevant material;

(b) the Secretary of State must serve on –

(i) the relevant party or his legal representative; and

(ii) the special advocate (as soon as one is appointed) or those instructing him,

any open material;

(c) the relevant party must file with the court and serve on the Secretary of State and special advocate (if one is appointed) or those instructing him any written evidence which he wishes the court to take into account at the hearing;

(d) the Secretary of State must file with the court any further relevant material;

(e) the Secretary of State must serve on –

(i) the relevant party or his legal representative, and

(ii) the special advocate (as soon as one is appointed) or those instructing him,

any open material filed with the court under paragraph (d);

(f) the Secretary of State must serve on the special advocate (if one has been appointed) any closed material;

(g) the parties and the special advocate (if one has been appointed) must file and serve any written submissions as directed by the court.

(Rules 76.28 and 76.29 will apply where any closed material is filed by the Secretary of State).

Amendments—Inserted by SI 2005/656.

76.31 Failure to comply with directions

(1) Where a party or the special advocate fails to comply with a direction of the court, the court may serve on him a notice which states –

(a) the respect in which he has failed to comply with the direction;

(b) a time limit for complying with the direction; and

(c) that the court may proceed to determine the proceedings before it, on the material available to it, if the party or the special advocate fails to comply with the relevant direction within the time specified.

(2) Where a party or special advocate fails to comply with such a notice, the court may proceed in accordance with paragraph (1)(c).

Amendments—Inserted by SI 2005/656.

76.32 Judgments

(1) When the court gives judgment in any proceedings to which this Part applies, it may withhold any or part of its reasons if and to the extent that it is not possible to give reasons without disclosing information contrary to the public interest.

(2) Where the judgment of the court does not include the full reasons for its decision, the court must serve on the Secretary of State and the special advocate a separate written judgment including those reasons.

Amendments—Inserted by SI 2005/656.

76.33 Application by Secretary of State for reconsideration of decision

(1) This rule applies where the court proposes, in any proceedings to which this Part applies, to serve notice on a relevant party of any –

(a) order or direction made or given in the absence of the Secretary of State; or

(b) any judgment.

(2) Before the court serves any such notice on the relevant party, it must first serve notice on the Secretary of State of its intention to do so.

(3) The Secretary of State may, within 5 days of being served with notice under paragraph (2), apply to the court to reconsider the terms of the order or direction or to review the terms of the proposed judgment if he considers that –

(a) his compliance with the order or direction; or

(b) the notification to the relevant party of any matter contained in the judgment, order or direction;

would cause information to be disclosed contrary to the public interest.

(4) Where the Secretary of State makes an application under paragraph (3), he must at the same time serve a copy of it on the special advocate, if one has been appointed.

(5) Rule 76.29 (except for paragraphs (6) and (7)) shall, if a special advocate has been appointed, apply with any necessary modifications to the consideration of an application under paragraph (3) of this rule.

(6) The court must not serve notice on the relevant party as mentioned in paragraph (1) before the time for the Secretary of State to make an application under paragraph (3) has expired.

Amendments—Inserted by SI 2005/656.

76.34 Supply of court documents

Unless the court otherwise directs, rule 5.4 (supply of court documents – general) does not apply to any proceedings to which this Part applies.

Amendments—Inserted by SI 2005/656.

GLOSSARY

Scope

This glossary is a guide to the meaning of certain legal expressions as used in these Rules, but it does not give the expressions any meaning in the Rules which they do not otherwise have in the law.

Expression	**Meaning**
Affidavit	A written, sworn statement of evidence.
Alternative dispute resolution	Collective description of methods of resolving disputes otherwise than through the normal trial process.
Base rate	The interest rate set by the Bank of England which is used as the basis for other banks' rates.
Contribution	A right of someone to recover from a third person all or part of the amount which he himself is liable to pay.
Counterclaim	A claim brought by a defendant in response to the claimant's claim, which is included in the same proceedings as the claimant's claim.
Cross-examination (and see 'evidence in chief')	Questioning of a witness by a party other than the party who called the witness.
Damages	A sum of money awarded by the court as compensation to the claimant.
– aggravated damages	Additional damages which the court may award as compensation for the defendant's objectionable behaviour.
– exemplary damages	Damages which go beyond compensating for actual loss and are awarded to show the court's disapproval of the defendant's behaviour.
Defence of tender before claim	A defence that, before the claimant started proceedings, the defendant unconditionally offered to the claimant the amount due or, if no specified amount is claimed, an amount sufficient to satisfy the claim.
Evidence in chief (and see 'cross-examination')	The evidence given by a witness for the party who called him.
Indemnity	A right of someone to recover from a third party the whole amount which he himself is liable to pay.
Injunction	A court order prohibiting a person from doing something or requiring a person to do something.
Joint liability (and see 'several liability')	Parties who are jointly liable share a single liability and each party can be held liable for the whole of it.

Expression	Meaning
Limitation period	The period within which a person who has a right to claim against another person must start court proceedings to establish that right. The expiry of the period may be a defence to the claim.
List	Cases are allocated to different lists depending on the subject matter of the case. The lists are used for administrative purposes and may also have their own procedures and judges.
Official copy	A copy of an official document, supplied and marked as such by the office which issued the original.
Practice form	Form to be used for a particular purpose in proceedings, the form and purpose being specified by a practice direction.
Pre-action protocol	Statements of understanding between legal practitioners and others about pre-action practice and which are approved by a relevant practice direction.
Privilege	The right of a party to refuse to disclose a document or produce a document or to refuse to answer questions on the ground of some special interest recognised by law.
Seal	A seal is a mark which the court puts on a document to indicate that the document has been issued by the court.
Service	Steps required by rules of court to bring documents used in court proceedings to a person's attention.
Set aside	Cancelling a judgment or order or a step taken by a party in the proceedings.
Several liability (and see 'joint liability')	A person who is severally liable with others may remain liable for the whole claim even where judgment has been obtained against the others.
Stay	A stay imposes a halt on proceedings, apart from taking any steps allowed by the Rules or the terms of the stay. Proceedings can be continued if a stay is lifted.
Strike out	Striking out means the court ordering written material to be deleted so that it may no longer be relied upon.
Without prejudice	Negotiations with a view to a settlement are usually conducted 'without prejudice' which means that the circumstances in which the content of those negotiations may be revealed to the court are very restricted.

SCHEDULE 1
RSC RULES

Rule 50(3)

****

RSC ORDER 15

****

Amendments—The whole Order was revoked by SI 2002/2058, with effect from 1 October 2002. Provisions about representation of beneficiaries by trustees are now to be found in CPR Pt 19.

RSC ORDER 17
INTERPLEADER

1 Entitlement to relief by way of interpleader

(1) Where –

(a) a person is under a liability in respect of a debt or in respect of any money, goods or chattels and he is, or expects to be, sued for or in respect of that debt or money or those goods or chattels by two or more persons making adverse claims thereto; or

(b) claim is made to any money, goods or chattels taken or intended to be taken by a sheriff in execution under any process, or to the proceeds or value of any such goods or chattels, by a person other than the person against whom the process is issued,

the person under liability as mentioned in sub-paragraph (a) or (subject to rule 2) the sheriff, may apply to the court for relief by way of interpleader.

(2) References in this Order to a sheriff shall be construed as [including references to –

(a) an individual authorised to act as an enforcement officer under the Courts Act 2003; and

(b) any other officer charged with the execution of process by or under the authority of the High Court..

Amendments—SI 2003/3361.

'interpleader' (r 1)—The essential feature of interpleader is that a person is in possession of property which does not belong to him and he is faced with claims by two or more persons each claiming ownership or at least the right to possession of that property. Under this rule he can compel the competing claimants to come before the court to establish who is entitled to ownership or possession of the property. Special rules apply to goods taken in execution by a sheriff but the general principles are the same, the claimants being (a) almost always a person other than the debtor who asserts entitlement to those goods and (b) the execution creditor.

'is, or expects to be, sued' (r 1(1)(a))—Relief cannot be obtained after one claimant has obtained judgment (*Stevenson & Son v Brownell* [1912] 2 Ch 344).

'adverse claims' (r 1(1)(a))—The claims need not have a common origin but must be to the same property (*Ex parte Mersey Docks and Harbour Board* [1899] 1 QB 546), so relief may be granted where one person faces a claim from an agent and his undisclosed principal (*Meynell v Angel* (1863) 32 LJQB14) but relief was refused where two agents claimed commission under separate contracts for the sale of the same house (*Smith v Saunders* (1877) 37 LT 359).

The claimants may be husband and wife (*De La Rue v Hernu Ltd* [1936] 2 KB 164). Where judgment has been entered against one partner of a partnership and another partner claims that goods taken in execution are partnership property relief may be granted (*Peake v Carter* [1916] 1 KB 652).

'proceeds or value' (r 1(1)(b))—If the goods have been sold by the sheriff the proceeds become the subject of the claim. The claimant may be ordered to pay money into court or give security, or he may pay money to the sheriff under protest, in return for the goods being handed over to him. The money paid or security becomes the value of the goods within this rule (*Smith v Critchfield* (1885) 14 QBD 873, CA)

'may apply to the court' (r 1(1))—See r 2(3), 2(4) and 3(1) below.

2 Claim to goods, etc, taken in execution

(1) Any person making a claim to or in respect of any money, goods or chattels taken or intended to be taken in execution under process of the court, or to the proceeds or value of any such goods or chattels, must give notice of his claim to the sheriff charged with the execution of the process and must include in his notice a statement of his address, and that address shall be his address for service.

(2) On receipt of a claim made under this rule the sheriff must forthwith give notice thereof to the execution creditor and the execution creditor must, within 7 days after receiving the notice, give notice to the sheriff informing him whether he admits or disputes the claim. An execution creditor who gives notice in accordance with this paragraph admitting a claim shall only be liable to the sheriff for any fees and expenses incurred by the sheriff before receipt of that notice.

(3) Where –

(a) the sheriff receives a notice from an execution creditor under paragraph (2) disputing a claim, or the execution creditor fails, within the period mentioned in that paragraph, to give the required notice; and

(b) the claim made under this rule is not withdrawn,

the sheriff may apply to the court for relief under this Order.

(4) A sheriff who receives a notice from an execution creditor under paragraph (2) admitting a claim made under this rule shall withdraw from possession of the money, goods or chattels claimed and may apply to the court for relief under this Order of the following kind, that is to say, an order restraining the bringing of a claim against him for or in respect of his having taken possession of that money or those goods or chattels.

'money … taken in execution' (r 2(1))—Supreme Court Act 1981, s 138(3A) abolishes the old common law rule that money could not be taken in execution.

'must give notice' (r 2(1))—Notice under r 2(1) must follow PF23QB. Notice under r 2(2) must follow PF24QB.

'address for service' (r 2(1))—See CPR r 6.5(2) and (3) for provisions on the address which a party may use as his address for service.

'may apply to the court' (rr 2(3) and 2(4))—The form is PF26QB.

2A Claim in respect of goods protected from seizure

(1) Where a judgment debtor whose goods have been seized, or are intended to be seized, by a sheriff under a writ of execution claims that such goods are not liable to execution by virtue of section 138(3A) of the Act, he must within 5

days of the seizure give notice in writing to the sheriff identifying all those goods in respect of which he makes such a claim and the grounds of such claim in respect of each item.

(2) Upon receipt of a notice of claim under paragraph (1), the sheriff must forthwith give notice thereof to the execution creditor and to any person who has made a claim to, or in respect of, the goods under rule 2(1) and the execution creditor and any person who has made claim must, within 7 days of receipt of such notice, inform the sheriff in writing whether he admits or disputes the judgment debtor's claim in respect of each item.

(3) The sheriff shall withdraw from possession of any goods in respect of which the judgment debtor's claim is admitted or if the execution creditor or any person claiming under rule 2(1) fails to notify him in accordance with paragraph (2) and the sheriff shall so inform the parties in writing.

(4) Where the sheriff receives notice from –

(a) the execution creditor; or
(b) any such person to whom notice was given under paragraph (2),

that the claim or any part thereof is disputed, he must forthwith seek the directions of the court and may include therein an application for an order restraining the bringing of any claim against him for, or in respect of, his having seized any of those goods or his having failed so to do.

(5) The sheriff's application for directions under paragraph (4) shall be made by an application in accordance with CPR Part 23 and, on the hearing of the application, the court may –

(a) determine the judgment debtor's claim summarily; or
(b) give such directions for the determination of any issue raised by such claim as may be just.

(6) A master and a district judge of a district registry shall have power to make an order of the kind referred to in paragraph (4) and the reference to master shall be construed in accordance with rule 4.

'not liable to execution' (r 2A(1))—Supreme Court Act 1981, s 138(3A)(a) lists the judgment debtor's goods which are protected from execution.

3 Mode of application

(1) An application for relief under this Order must be made by claim form unless made in an existing claim, in which case it must be made by accordance with CPR Part 23.

(2) Where the applicant is a sheriff who has withdrawn from possession of money, goods or chattels taken in execution and who is applying for relief under rule 2(4) the claim form must be served on any person who made a claim under that rule to or in respect of that money or those goods or chattels, and that person may attend the hearing of the application.

(4) Subject to paragraph (5) a claim form or application notice under this rule must be supported by evidence that the applicant –

(a) claims no interest in the subject-matter in dispute other than for charges or costs;
(b) does not collude with any of the claimants to that subject-matter; and
(c) is willing to pay or transfer that subject-matter into court or to dispose of it as the court may direct.

(5) Where the applicant is a sheriff, he shall not provide such evidence as is referred to in paragraph (4) unless directed by the court to do so.

(6) Any person who makes a claim under rule 2 and who is served with a claim form under this rule shall within 14 days serve on the execution creditor and the sheriff a witness statement or affidavit specifying any money and describing any goods and chattels claimed and setting out the grounds upon which such claim is based.

(7) Where the applicant is a sheriff a claim form under this rule must give notice of the requirement in paragraph (6).

'claim form' (r 3(1))—These proceedings are listed in PD8, Section A, Table 1 so PD8, para 3.2 applies where the proceedings are commenced by claim form.

Service—CPR Pt 6 sets out the general rules as to service.

'supported by evidence' (r 3(4))—The evidence may be contained in the application notice itself if it is verified by a statement of truth, or by witness statement or affidavit. The additional costs of using an affidavit will not usually be allowed (CPR r 32.15(2). Any delay in making the application should be explained.

'charges or costs' (r 3(4)(a))—This may include a lien for storage or repairs (*De Rothschild Frères v Morrison Kekwich & Co* (1890) 24 QBD 750, CA).

'does not collude' (r 3(4)(b))—The applicant must show that he is not taking sides in the dispute between the claimants (*Fredericks and Pelhams Timber Buildings v Wilkins, Read (Claimant)* [1971] 3 All ER 545).

4 To whom Sheriff may apply for relief

An application to the court for relief under this Order may, if the applicant is a sheriff, be made –

(a) where the claim in question is proceeding in the Royal Courts of Justice, to a master or, if the execution to which the application relates has been or is to be levied in the district of a district registry, either to a master or to the district judge of that registry;

(b) where the claim in question is proceeding in a district registry, to the district judge of that registry or, if such execution has been or is to be levied in the district of some other district registry or outside the district of any district registry, either to the said district judge or to the district judge of that other registry or to a master as the case may be.

Where the claim in question is proceeding in the Admiralty Court or the Family Division, references in this rule to a master shall be construed as references to the Admiralty Registrar or to a Registrar of that Division.

5 Powers of court hearing claim

(1) Where on the hearing of a claim under this Order all the persons by whom adverse claims to the subject-matter in dispute (hereafter in this Order referred to as 'the interpleader claimants') appear, the court may order –

(a) that any interpleader claimant be made a defendant in any claim pending with respect to the subject-matter in dispute in substitution for or in addition to the applicant for relief under this Order; or

(b) that an issue between the interpleader claimants be stated and tried and may direct which of the interpleader claimants is to be claimant and which defendant.

(2) Where –

(a) the applicant under this Order is a sheriff; or
(b) all the interpleader claimants consent or any of them so requests; or
(c) the question at issue between the interpleader claimants is a question of law and the facts are not in dispute,

the court may summarily determine the question at issue between the interpleader claimants and make an order accordingly on such terms as may be just.

(3) Where an interpleader claimant, having been duly served with a claim form under this Order, does not appear at the hearing or, having appeared, fails or refuses to comply with an order made in the proceedings, the court may make an order declaring the interpleader claimant, and all persons claiming under him, for ever barred from prosecuting his claim against the applicant for such relief and all persons claiming under him, but such an order shall not affect the rights of the interpleader claimants as between themselves.

'an issue … be stated and tried' (r 5(1)(b))—See PF31QB and PF32QB for the normal form of order. Such issues are normally tried before a master or district judge. Case management directions will normally be given at the first hearing.

'which … is to be claimant and which defendant' (r 5(1)(b))—Since the burden of proof rests on the claimant this may have important consequences. In the case of sheriff's interpleader the established rule is that the interpleader claimant becomes the claimant and the execution judgment creditor the defendant (*Chase v Goble* (1841) 2 M&G 930). However where the goods in the possession of the interpleader claimant have been taken in execution the execution judgment creditor will normally be made claimant. In other interpleaders the normal rule is that the person from whom the applicant received the goods will normally be the defendant. So where the police hold money taken from a person in custody and apply for relief the person in custody will be made defendant (*Gordon v Commissioner of Metropolitan Police* (1935) 79 SJ 921, CA).

'summarily determine' (r 5(2))—Where a sheriff applies for relief this course is commonly used in order to avoid unnecessary costs of possession being incurred. See PF34 for the form of order on summary disposal.

6 Power to order sale of goods taken in execution

Where an application for relief under this Order is made by a sheriff who has taken possession of any goods or chattels in execution under any process, and an interpleader claimant alleges that he is entitled, under a bill of sale or otherwise, to the goods or chattels by way of security for debt, the court may order those goods or chattels or any part thereof to be sold and may direct that the proceeds of sale be applied in such manner and on such terms as may be just and as may be specified in the order.

'order those goods … to be sold'—Sale will be ordered where the value of the goods clearly exceeds the amount of the security (*Stern v Tegner* [1898] 1 QB 37).

'on such terms as may be just'—The court has a complete discretion and may for example limit the interest payable to the secured creditor to that accrued to the date of sale (*West v Diprose* [1900] 1 Ch 337).

7 Power to stay proceedings

Where a defendant to a claim applies for relief under this Order in the claim, the court may by order stay all further proceedings in the claim.

8 Other powers

(1) Subject to the foregoing rules of this Order, the court may in or for the purposes of any interpleader proceedings make such order as to costs or any other matter as it thinks just.

(2) Where the interpleader claimant fails to appear at the hearing, the court may direct that the sheriff's and the execution creditor's costs shall be assessed by a master or, where the hearing was heard in a district registry, by a district judge of that registry and the following CPR rules shall apply –

- (a) 44.4 (basis of assessment);
- (b) 44.5 (factors to be taken into account in deciding the amount of costs);
- (c) 48.4 (limitations on court's power to award costs in favour of trustee or personal representative); and
- (d) 48.6 (litigants in person).

(3) Where the claim in question is proceeding in the Admiralty Court or the Family Division, references in this rule to a master shall be construed as references to the Admiralty Registrar or to a Registrar of that Division.

Amendments—SI 1999/1008.

'such order as to costs' (r 8(1))—See CPR r 44.3 for the matters to be taken into account in the exercise of the court's discretion.

'any other matter' (r 8(1))—The court has power under this rule to follow the procedure contained in CCA 1984, s 100 of requiring the interpleader claimant to pay into court the value of the goods seized by the sheriff or the amount for which execution has been levied and the sheriff's costs if less. This procedure has the advantage of allowing the claimant possession of the goods immediately and limiting the sheriff's possession fees. An order may be made even if it affects property rights (*BP Benzin und Petroleum AG v European American Banking Corp* [1978] 1 Lloyd's Rep 364) and may have retrospective effect (*PBJ Davis Manufacturing Co v Fahn, Fahn (Claimant)* [1967] 2 All ER 1274, CA)

9 One order in several proceedings

Where the court considers it necessary or expedient to make an order in any interpleader proceedings in several proceedings pending in several Divisions, or before different judges of the same Division, the court may make such an order; and the order shall be entitled in all those causes or matters and shall be binding on all the parties to them.

10 Disclosure

CPR Parts 31 and 18 shall, with the necessary modifications, apply in relation to an interpleader issue as they apply in relation to any other proceedings.

11 Trial of interpleader issue

(1) CPR Part 39 shall, with the necessary modifications, apply to the trial of an interpleader issue as it applies to the trial of a claim.

(2) The court by whom an interpleader issue is tried may give such judgment or make such order as finally to dispose of all questions arising in the interpleader proceedings.

Appeals—Where the court has directed the trial of an issue by a master or district judge, appeal from the judgment on that issue is to the Court of Appeal. Permission is required, see CPR r 52.3, either from the master or district judge or from the Court of Appeal.

****

RSC ORDER 30

****

Amendments—The whole Order was revoked by SI 2002/2058, with effect from 1 October 2002. Provisions about receivers are now to be found in CPR Pt 69.

****

RSC ORDER 44

****

Amendments—The whole Order was revoked by SI 2002/2058, with effect from 1 October 2002.

RSC ORDER 45
ENFORCEMENT OF JUDGMENTS AND ORDERS: GENERAL

1A Interpretation

In this Order, and in RSC Orders 46 and 47 –

(a) 'enforcement officer' means an individual who is authorised to act as an enforcement officer under the Courts Act 2003; and

(b) 'relevant enforcement officer' means –

(i) in relation to a writ of execution which is directed to an single enforcement officer, that officer;

(ii) in relation to a writ of execution which is directed to two or more enforcement officers, the officer to whom the writ is allocated.

Amendments—Inserted by SI 2003/3361.

1 Enforcement of judgment, etc, for payment of money

(1)–(3) (*revoked*)

(4) In this Order references to any writ shall be construed as including references to any further writ in aid of the first mentioned writ.

Amendments—SI 2001/2792.

Judgments or order for payment of money (r 1 generally)—Following the amendments made by SI 2001/2792, the various methods by which a successful party may enforce his judgment in the High Court are now to be found both in the new CPR Pts 70–73 and what remains of RSC Ords 45–52. CPR Pt 70 contains general rules about enforcement; Pt 71 covers obtaining information from judgment debtors (replacing oral examination); Pt 72 covers third party debt orders (replacing garnishee proceedings), and Pt 73 covers charging orders and stop notices. None of these rules applies to proceedings against the Crown, see Ord 77, r 15(1) below. These rules do apply to an order for the payment of costs, but execution cannot issue until a costs certificate has been issued under CPR Pt 47, or costs have been summarily assessed.

2 Notice of seizure

When first executing a writ of fieri facias, the Sheriff or his officer [or the relevant enforcement officer shall deliver to the debtor or leave at each place where execution is levied a notice in Form No 55 in the relevant practice direction informing the debtor of the execution.

Amendments—SI 2003/3361.

3 Enforcement of judgment for possession of land

(1) Subject to the provisions of these rules, a judgment or order for the giving of possession of land may be enforced by one or more of the following means, that is to say –

(a) writ of possession;
(b) in a case in which rule 5 applies, an order of committal;
(c) in such a case, writ of sequestration.

(2) A writ of possession to enforce a judgment or order for the giving of possession of any land shall not be issued without the permission of the court except where the judgment or order was given or made in proceedings by a mortgagee or mortgagor or by any person having the right to foreclose or redeem any mortgage, being proceedings in which there is a claim for –

(a) payment of moneys secured by the mortgage;
(b) sale of the mortgaged property;
(c) foreclosure;
(d) delivery of possession (whether before or after foreclosure or without foreclosure) to the mortgagee by the mortgagor or by any other person who is alleged to be in possession of the property;
(e) redemption;
(f) reconveyance of the land or its release from the security; or
(g) delivery of possession by the mortgagee.

(2A) In paragraph (2) 'mortgage' includes a legal or equitable mortgage and a legal or equitable charge, and reference to a mortgagor, a mortgagee and mortgaged land is to be interpreted accordingly.

(3) Such permission [as is referred to in paragraph (2) shall not be granted unless it is shown –

(a) that every person in actual possession of the whole or any part of the land has received such notice of the proceedings as appears to the court sufficient to enable him to apply to the court for any relief to which he may be entitled; and
(b) if the operation of the judgment or order is suspended by subsection (2) of section 16 of the Landlord and Tenant Act 1954, that the applicant has not received notice in writing from the tenant that he desires that the provisions of paragraphs (a) and (b) of that subsection shall have effect.

(4) A writ of possession may include provision for enforcing the payment of any money adjudged or ordered to be paid by the judgment or order which is to be enforced by the writ.

Amendments—SI 2001/256.

'permission of the court' (r 3(2))—See Ord 46, r 4 below for the procedure to be followed where permission is required.

Restitution—If, after a writ of possession has been executed, possession is unlawfully regained, the plaintiff may obtain a writ of restitution to have the occupants again evicted. Such a writ is in aid of the original writ (see Ord 46, rr 3 and 4 below).

Forms—Evidence in support of application to enforce judgment for possession: Form PF91. Writ of possession: No 66. Writ of restitution: No 68.

4 Enforcement of judgment for delivery of goods

(1) Subject to the provisions of these rules, a judgment or order for the delivery of any goods which does not give a person against whom the judgment is given or order made the alternative of paying the assessed value of the goods may be enforced by one or more of the following means, that is to say –

- (a) writ of delivery to recover the goods without alternative provision for recovery of the assessed value thereof (hereafter in this rule referred to as a 'writ of specific delivery');
- (b) in a case in which rule 5 applies, an order of committal;
- (c) in such a case, writ of sequestration.

(2) Subject to the provisions of these rules, a judgment or order for the delivery of any goods or payment of their assessed value may be enforced by one or more of the following means, that is to say –

- (a) writ of delivery to recover the goods or their assessed value;
- (b) by order of the court, writ of specific delivery;
- (c) in a case in which rule 5 applies, writ of sequestration.

An application for an order under sub-paragraph (b) shall be made in accordance with CPR Part 23, which must be served on the defendant against whom the judgment or order sought to be enforced was given or made.

(3) A writ of specific delivery, and a writ of delivery to recover any goods or their assessed value, may include provision for enforcing the payment of any money adjudged or ordered to be paid by the judgment or order which is to be enforced by the writ.

(4) A judgment or order for the payment of the assessed value of any goods may be enforced by the same means as any other judgment or order for the payment of money.

'alternative of paying the assessed value' (r 4(1))—A judgment for the return of goods may be in one of two forms. An order for specific return of goods requires the judgment debtor to hand over particular goods. If he fails to do so the judgment creditor may use any of the enforcement methods specified in r 4(1). Alternatively, the order may be for return of goods or payment of their value as assessed. If the judgment creditor then wishes to apply for a writ of specific delivery he must obtain permission of the court under r 4(2)(b).

Forms—Writ of specific delivery: No 64 writ of delivery of goods or assessed value: No 65.

5 Enforcement of judgment to do or abstain from doing any act

(1) Where –

- (a) a person required by a judgment or order to do an act within a time specified in the judgment or order refuses or neglects to do it within that time or, as the case may be, within that time as extended or abridged under a court order or CPR rule 2.11; or
- (b) a person disobeys a judgment or order requiring him to abstain from doing an act,

then, subject to the provisions of these rules, the judgment or order may be enforced by one or more of the following means, that is to say –

(i) with the permission of the court, a writ of sequestration against the property of that person;

(ii) where that person is a body corporate, with the permission of the court, a writ of sequestration against the property of any director or other officer of the body;

(iii) subject to the provisions of the Debtors Act 1869 and 1878, an order of committal against that person or, where that person is a body corporate, against any such officer.

(2) Where a judgment or order requires a person to do an act within a time therein specified and an order is subsequently made under rule 6 requiring the act to be done within some other time, references in paragraph (1) of this rule to a judgment or order shall be construed as references to the order made under rule 6.

(3) Where under any judgment or order requiring the delivery of any goods the person liable to execution has the alternative of paying the assessed value of the goods, the judgment or order shall not be enforceable by order of committal under paragraph (1), but the court may, on the application of the person entitled to enforce the judgment or order, make an order requiring the first mentioned person to deliver the goods to the applicant within a time specified in the order, and that order may be so enforced.

'may be enforced' (r 5(1))—Disobedience of an injunction (see below), is a contempt of court which may be punished. See notes to Ord 52 below for further details. An injunction which is irregular or thought to be oppressive must be obeyed until it is set aside (*Isaac v Robertson* [1985] AC 97). Application to set aside an order made without notice should be made to the court which granted the order and not by way of appeal (*G v G (Ouster: Ex parte Application)* [1990] 1 FLR 395). An injunction which is unfairly oppressive may be reviewed by the court which granted it (*Jordan v Norfolk CC* [1994] 1 WLR 1353).

'Debtors Act 1869 and 1878' (r 5(1)(iii))—With very limited exceptions an order for payment of money cannot now be enforced by committal. See AJA 1970, s 11 for details.

Undertakings—An undertaking to the court to do or refrain from doing some act is enforceable as if it were an order and may be enforced by committal if an order in those terms could have been enforced in that way (*Gandolfo v Gandolfo (Standard Chartered Bank, Garnishee)* [1981] QB 359). It follows that an undertaking to pay money cannot be enforced by committal except as permitted by Debtors Act 1869, s 5 (*Backley v Crawford* [1893] 1 QB 105).

6 Judgment, etc requiring act to be done: order fixing time for doing it

(1) Notwithstanding that a judgment or order requiring a person to do an act specifies a time within which the act is to be done, the court shall, have power to make an order requiring the act to be done within another time, being such time after service of that order, or such other time, as may be specified therein.

(2) Where a judgment or order requiring a person to do an act does not specify a time within which the act is to be done, the court shall have power subsequently to make an order requiring the act to be done within such time after service of that order, or such other time, as may be specified therein.

(3) An application for an order under this rule must be made in accordance with CPR Part 23 and the application notice must, be served on the person required to do the act in question.

'specifies a time' (r 6(1))—CPR r 2.9 provides that wherever practicable a calendar date and time of day must be specified.

7 Service of copy of judgment, etc, prerequisite to enforcement under rule 5

(1) In this rule references to an order shall be construed as including references to a judgment.

(2) Subject to paragraphs (6) and (7) of this rule, an order shall not be enforced under rule 5 unless –

(a) a copy of the order has been served personally on the person required to do or abstain from doing the act in question; and
(b) in the case of an order requiring a person to do an act, the copy has been so served before the expiration of the time within which he was required to do the act.

(3) Subject as aforesaid, an order requiring a body corporate to do or abstain from doing an act shall not be enforced as mentioned in rule 5(1)(b)(ii) or (iii) unless –

(a) a copy of the order has also been served personally on the officer against whose property permission is sought to issue a writ of sequestration or against whom an order of committal is sought; and
(b) in the case of an order requiring the body corporate to do an act, the copy has been so served before the expiration of the time within which the body was required to do the act.

(4) There must be prominently displayed on the front of the copy of an order served under this rule a warning to the person on whom the copy is served that disobedience to the order would be a contempt of court punishable by imprisonment, or (in the case of an order requiring a body corporate to do or abstain from doing an act) punishable by sequestration of the assets of the body corporate and by imprisonment of any individual responsible.

(5) With the copy of an order required to be served under this rule, being an order requiring a person to do an act, there must also be served a copy of any order or agreement under CPR rule 2.11 extending or abridging the time for doing the act and, where the first-mentioned order was made under rule 5(3) or 6 of this Order, a copy of the previous order requiring the act to be done.

(6) An order requiring a person to abstain from doing an act may be enforced under rule 5 notwithstanding that service of a copy of the order has not been effected in accordance with this rule if the court is satisfied that pending such service, the person against whom or against whose property is sought to enforce the order has had notice thereof either –

(a) by being present when the order was made; or
(b) by being notified of the terms of the order, whether by telephone, telegram or otherwise.

(7) The court may dispense with service of a copy of an order under this rule if it thinks it just to do so.

'prominently displayed … a warning' (r 7(4))—The warning notice should be in the following words or words to the same effect:

(a) In the case of an order requiring a person to do an act within a specified time:

'If you, the within named AB, neglect to obey this order by the time stated you may be held to be in contempt of court and liable to imprisonment.'

(b) In the case of an order requiring a person to abstain from doing an act:

'If you, the within named AB, disobey this order you may be held to be in contempt of court and liable to imprisonment.'

(c) In the case of an order requiring a body corporate to do an act within a specified time:

'If you, the within named AB Ltd, neglect to obey this order by the time stated you may be held to be in contempt of court and liable to sequestration of your assets.'

(d) In the case of an order requiring a body corporate to abstain from doing an act:

'If you, the within named AB Ltd, disobey this order you may be held to be in contempt of court and liable to sequestration of your assets'

(e) In the case where an order has been made against a body corporate and the order is sought to be enforced against a director or officer of that body:

'If AB Ltd disobeys this order, you, XY (a director or officer of AB Ltd), may be held to be in contempt of court and liable to imprisonment.'

The court has no discretion to dispense with the requirement that this warning be prominently displayed on the order served (*Moerman-Lenglet v Henshaw* (1992) *The Times*, November 23). If, however, the order served is defective in this way service may be dispensed with under r 7(7) (*Davy International & ors v Tazzyman & ors* [1997] 3 All ER 183, CA).

8 Court may order act to be done at expense of disobedient party

If a mandatory order, an injunction or a judgment or order for the specific performance of a contract is not complied with, then, without prejudice to its powers under section 39 of the Act and its powers to punish the disobedient party for contempt, the court may direct that the act required to be done may, so far as practicable, be done by the party by whom the order or judgment was obtained or some other person appointed by the court, at the cost of the disobedient party, and upon the act being done the expenses incurred may be ascertained in such manner as the court may direct and execution may issue against the disobedient party for the amount so ascertained and for costs.

Amendments—SI 2003/3361.

Scope of provision—Rather than coerce the defendant into doing the required act himself, the court may, if it is practicable to do so, authorise it to be done by the claimant (or someone else) at the defendant's expense. If the act is not one which requires the defendant's personal attention and a fund is available from which the expense can be met, it will be preferable to proceed under this rule. Although the rule gives powers additional to, not in substitution for, those of committal and sequestration, if the object of the order can be achieved under this rule the court will be reluctant also to commit, save in the case of blatant, contumelious contempt. In cases where large sums are at stake, the rule may be used as an adjunct to sequestration.

Undertakings—This rule does not apply in the case of a breach of an undertaking, but the court may be prepared to exercise its inherent powers to similar effect (*Mortimer v Wilson* [1885] 33 WR 927). It may be prudent to apply in the alternative for an order in the terms of the undertaking, which order could be enforced subsequently under this rule if it is not complied with.

Execution of documents—A similar but specific remedy is available, where a person has been ordered to execute a document but neglects or refuses to do so or cannot be found, under SCA, s 39.

****

11 Matters occurring after judgment: stay of execution, etc

Without prejudice to Order 47, rule 1, a party against whom a judgment has been given or an order made may apply to the court for a stay of execution of the judgment or order or other relief on the ground of matters which have occurred since the date of the judgment or order, and the court may by order grant such relief, and on such terms, as it thinks just.

Scope of provision—This rule gives the court extremely wide powers to control the execution of a judgment or order if some occurrence *since* it was given or made makes that appropriate. The rule is not confined to cases of inability to pay, nor indeed to money judgments.

'Order 47, rule 1'—This rule enables the court to stay execution of a money judgment against the debtor's goods by reason of inability to pay (whenever arising) or in other special circumstances.

12 Forms of writs

(1) A writ of fieri facias must be in such of the Forms Nos 53 to 63 in the relevant practice direction as is appropriate in the particular case.

(2) A writ of delivery must be in Form No 64 or 65 in the relevant practice direction, whichever is appropriate.

(3) A writ of possession must be in Form No 66 or 66A in the relevant practice direction, whichever is appropriate.

(4) A writ of sequestration must be in Form No 67 in the relevant practice direction.

****

RSC ORDER 46
WRITS OF EXECUTION: GENERAL

Practice Direction—See PDExecution, para 1.1 at p 1653 which forbids execution on a Sunday, Good Friday or Christmas Day unless the court orders otherwise.

1 Definition

In this Order, unless the context otherwise requires, 'writ of execution' includes a writ of fieri facias, a writ of possession, a writ of delivery, a writ of sequestration and any further writ in aid of any of the aforementioned writs.

'writ in aid'—The only writ in aid likely to be encountered in practice is the writ of restitution (see note, **Restitution**, under Ord 45, r 3 above).

2 When permission to issue any writ of execution is necessary

(1) A writ of execution to enforce a judgment or order may not issue without the permission of the court in the following cases, that is to say –

- (a) where 6 years or more have elapsed since the date of the judgment or order;
- (b) where any change has taken place, whether by death or otherwise, in the parties entitled or liable to execution under the judgment or order;
- (c) where the judgment or order is against the assets of a deceased person coming to the hands of his executors or administrators after the date of the judgment or order, and it is sought to issue execution against such assets;
- (d) where under the judgment or order any person is entitled to a remedy subject to the fulfilment of any condition which it is alleged has been fulfilled;
- (e) where any goods sought to be seized under a writ of execution are in the hands of a receiver appointed by the court or a sequestrator.

(2) Paragraph (1) is without prejudice to section 2 of the Reserve and Auxiliary Forces (Protection of Civil Interests) Act 1951, or any other enactment or rule by virtue of which a person is required to obtain the permission of the court for the issue of a writ of execution or to proceed to execution on or otherwise to the enforcement of a judgment or order.

(3) Where the court grants permission, whether under this rule or otherwise, for the issue of a writ of execution and the writ is not issued within one year after the date of the order granting such permission, the order shall cease to have effect, without prejudice, however, to the making of a fresh order.

'6 years or more have elapsed' (r 2(1)(a))—The delay should be explained in the witness statement or affidavit (see r 4(2)). The court may be reluctant to allow a stale judgment or order to be enforced and will not do so if the debtor is prejudiced by the delay.

'any change … in the parties' (r 2(1)(b))—The alternative is to apply to change the party under CPR Pt 19.

It is not thought that, following an order under that rule, permission would also be required under this rule. An order under CPR Pt 19 would still be needed before other enforcement proceedings were taken following a (presumably abortive) writ of execution issued with permission under this rule.

'assets of a deceased person' (r 2(1)(c))—Where r 2(1)(c) applies, a summons to service of an application notice upon the personal representatives will always be required (*Re Shephard* (1890) 43 Ch D 131).

'within one year' (r 2(3))—The limitation on the time within which the writ of execution must be issued does not apply only to cases where permission is required by virtue of this rule but to all cases where permission is required.

3 Permission required for issue of writ in aid of other writ

A writ of execution in aid of any other writ of execution shall not issue without the permission of the court.

4 Application for permission to issue writ

(1) An application for permission to issue a writ of execution may be made in accordance with CPR Part 23 but the application notice need not be served on the respondent unless the court directs.

(2) Such an application must be supported by a witness statement or affidavit –

(a) identifying the judgment or order to which the application relates and, if the judgment or order is for the payment of money, stating the amount originally due thereunder and the amount due thereunder at the date the application notice is filed;

(b) stating, where the case falls within rule 2(1)(a), the reasons for the delay in enforcing the judgment or order;

(c) stating where the case falls within rule 2(1)(b), the change which has taken place in the parties entitled or liable to execution since the date of the judgment or order;

(d) stating, where the case falls within rule 2(1)(c) or (d), that a demand to satisfy the judgment or order was made on the person liable to satisfy it and that he has refused or failed to do so;

(e) giving such other information as is necessary to satisfy the court that the applicant is entitled to proceed to execution on the judgment or order in question and that the person against whom it is sought to issue execution is liable to execution on it.

(3) The court hearing such application may grant permission in accordance with the application or may order that any issue or question, a decision on which is necessary to determine the rights of the parties, be tried in any manner in which any question of fact or law arising in proceedings may be tried and, in either case, may impose such terms as to costs or otherwise as it thinks just.

'a demand to satisfy' (r 4(2)(d))—Where it is sought to enforce against the assets of a deceased debtor or where the creditor has to satisfy some condition before enforcing, demand must be made of the personal representatives or the debtor, as the case may be, before application is made under this rule.

5 Application for permission to issue writ of sequestration

(1) Notwithstanding anything in rules 2 and 4, an application for permission to issue a writ of sequestration must be made in accordance with CPR Part 23 and be heard by a judge.

(2) Subject to paragraph (3), the application notice, stating the grounds of the application and accompanied by a copy of the witness statement or affidavit in support of the application, must be served personally on the person against whose property it is sought to issue the writ.

(3) The court may dispense with service of the application notice under this rule if it thinks it just to do so.

(4) The judge hearing an application for permission to issue a writ of sequestration may sit in private in any case in which, if the application were for an order of committal, he would be entitled to do so by virtue of Order 52, rule 6 but, except in such a case, the application shall be heard in public.

Sequestration—Sequestration is a process corresponding to contempt of court. In general terms, all the considerations which apply to committal apply to sequestration (see Ord 45, rr 5 and 7 and below), save that the restrictions imposed on the court's power to commit for non-compliance with a money judgment by Debtors Acts 1869 and 1878 do not apply. It is an expensive process and by application of the overriding objective permission is unlikely to be given unless the contemnor's assets are considerable; permission is also unlikely to be given if the contempt can appropriately be met by a fine, or if the judgment or order can readily be enforced by execution against goods, garnishee proceedings or the like.

Sequestration is available to enforce a restraining order or an order requiring an act to be done ('a positive order'), provided, in the latter case, that the time for doing the act is stated and has passed (see Ord 45, r 5(1)). An order to pay money (including a periodical payments order) is a positive order and, in family proceedings, will often state the time for payment. If it does not, a further order may be sought under Ord 45, r 6; however, an application for such a further order may be refused if its sole object is to found an application under this rule, unless it is shown that the debtor is wilfully neglecting or refusing to pay.

Subject to the court's power to dispense with service, which is rarely exercised, particularly in the case of a positive order, the order (bearing an appropriate 'penal' notice) must have been personally served on the contemnor before the date specified so that he has had the opportunity to comply with it (see Ord 45, r 7).

Dispensing with service (r 5(3))—In view of the draconian nature of the remedy, the court exercises this power only in cases of extreme urgency (ie where it appears that the assets to be sequestrated are about to be removed from the reach of the proposed sequestrators or are being dissipated). If personal service is impracticable, the court prefers to order service by an alternative method under CPR r 6.8. If service is dispensed with, ie if the order giving leave/permission is made without notice, the order may be made subject to terms which provide some protection for the defendant (eg an undertaking as to damages), and the contemnor is entitled to have the matter reconsidered.

Effect of writ of sequestration—The writ requires the four sequestrators named to take possession of the contemnor's land and collect in his other property and hold them until further order. It does not itself automatically vest the property in them but gives them authority to demand and receive it (*Bucknell v Bucknell* 1969] 1 WLR 1204). A mortgagee under a mortgage given after issue of the writ is not affected by it unless he had notice of the sequestration when the mortgage was given (*Ward v Booth* (1872) LR 14 Eq 195). The writ should be registered as a land charge (Land Charges Act 1972, s 6).

Application of property—The court may authorise the sale of sequestered property and payment out of the proceeds of sale (as well as out of any ready money received) of the costs and expenses of the sequestration and the judgment debt and costs due to the claimant/judgment creditor.

Discharge—The contemnor may, on purging his contempt, apply for the sequestration to be discharged. The order, if made, will require the sequestrators to pass their final accounts, authorise payment of their outstanding costs and expenses and discharge them from liability on their paying the balance in their hands to the contemnor.

Forms—Writ of sequestration: No 67.

6 Issue of writ of execution

(1) Issue of a writ of execution takes place on its being sealed by a court officer of the appropriate office.

(2) Before such a writ is issued, a praecipe for its issue must be filed.

(3) The praecipe must be signed by or on behalf of the solicitor of the person entitled to execution or, if that person is acting in person, by him.

(4) No such writ shall be sealed unless at the time of the tender thereof for sealing –

- (a) the person tendering it produces –
  - (i) the judgment or order on which the writ is to issue, or an office copy thereof;
  - (ii) where the writ may not issue without the permission of the court, the order granting such permission or evidence of the granting of it;
  - (iii) where judgment on failure to acknowledge service has been entered against a State, as defined in section 14 of the State Immunity Act 1978, evidence that the State has been served in accordance with CPR rule 40.10 and that the judgment has taken effect; and
- (b) the court officer authorised to seal it is satisfied that the period, if any, specified in the judgment or order for the payment of any money or the doing of any other act thereunder has expired.

(5) Every writ of execution shall bear the date of the day on which it is issued.

(6) In this rule 'the appropriate office' means –

- (a) where the proceedings in which execution is to issue are in a district registry, that registry;
- (b) where the proceedings are in the Principal Registry of the Family Division, that registry;
- (c) where the proceedings are Admiralty proceedings or commercial proceedings which are not in a district registry, the Admiralty and Commercial Registry;
- (ca) where the proceedings are in the Chancery Division, Chancery Chambers;
- (d) in any other case, the Central Office of the Supreme Court.

Forms—Writ of fieri facias: Nos 53–63, praecipe: PF86; writ of specific delivery: No 64, praecipe: PF90; writ of delivery of goods or value: No 65, praecipe: PF90; writ of possession: No 66, praecipe: PF88 or 89; writ of restitution: No 68; writ of sequestration: No 67, praecipe: PF87.

8 Duration and renewal of writ of execution

(1) For the purpose of execution, a writ of execution is valid in the first instance for 12 months beginning with the date of its issue.

(2) Where a writ has not been wholly executed the court may by order extend the validity of the writ from time to time for a period of 12 months at any one time beginning with the day on which the order is made, if an application for extension is made to the court before the day next following that on which the writ would otherwise expire or such later day, if any, as the court may allow.

(3) Before a writ the validity of which had been extended under paragraph (2) is executed either the writ must be sealed with the seal of the office out of which it was issued showing the date on which the order extending its validity was made or the applicant for the order must serve a notice (in Form No 71 in the relevant practice direction) sealed as aforesaid, on the sheriff to whom the writ is directed or the relevant enforcement officer informing him of the making of the order and the date thereof.

(4) The priority of a writ, the validity of which has been extended under this rule, shall be determined by reference to the date on which it was originally delivered to the sheriff or relevant enforcement officer.

(5) The production of a writ of execution, or of such a notice as is mentioned in paragraph (3) purporting in either case to be sealed as mentioned in that paragraph, shall be evidence that the validity of that writ, or, as the case may be, of the writ referred to in that notice, has been extended under paragraph (2).

(6) If, during the validity of a writ of execution, an interpleader summons is issued in relation to an execution under that writ, the validity of the writ shall be extended until the expiry of 12 months from the conclusion of the interpleader proceedings.

Amendments—SI 2003/3361.

Order to extend validity (r 8(2))—The extension is for a period of 12 months. It commences with the date of the order so that, strangely, there may be a gap in the writ's validity if the order is made after the original date of expiry.

Priority—Once extended, the writ retains its original priority date. If necessary, the court will direct that an application notice be served on other execution creditors whose position may be prejudiced if the writ is extended. Preservation of priority will be important if there are protracted interpleader proceedings (Practice Direction of 1 December 1981).

Procedure on application for extension—The application is initially made by application notice without a hearing under CPR r 23.8(c). The application must be supported by a witness statement or affidavit, which should specify the reason for preferring not to proceed by issuing a fresh writ, give the reason why (if applicable) the application is made beyond the writ's expiry and indicate the steps taken to ascertain the views of any other execution creditors, exhibiting their responses.

9 Return to writ of execution

(1) Any party at whose instance or against whom a writ of execution was issued may serve a notice on the sheriff to whom the writ was directed or the relevant enforcement officer requiring him, within such time as may be specified in the notice, to indorse on the writ a statement of the manner in which he has executed it and to send to that party a copy of the statement.

(2) If a sheriff or enforcement officer on whom such a notice is served fails to comply with it the party by whom it was served may apply to the court for an order directing the sheriff or enforcement officer to comply with the notice.

Amendments—SI 2003/3361.

Practice Direction – Execution

This Practice Direction supplements RSC Order 46 (Schedule 1 to the CPR) and CCR Order 26 (Schedule 2 to the CPR) (PDExecution)

LEVYING EXECUTION ON CERTAIN DAYS

1.1 Unless the court orders otherwise, a writ of execution or a warrant of execution to enforce a judgment or order must not be executed on a Sunday, Good Friday or Christmas Day.

1.2 Paragraph 1.1 does not apply to an Admiralty claim in rem.

RSC ORDER 47
WRITS OF FIERI FACIAS

1 Power to stay execution by writ of fieri facias

(1) Where a judgment is given or an order made for the payment by any person of money, and the court is satisfied, on an application made at the time of the judgment or order, or at any time thereafter, by the judgment debtor or other party liable to execution –

(a) that there are special circumstances which render it inexpedient to enforce the judgment or order; or

(b) that the applicant is unable from any cause to pay the money,

then, notwithstanding anything in rule 2 or 3, the court may by order stay the execution of the judgment or order by writ of fieri facias either absolutely or for such period and subject to such conditions as the court thinks fit.

(2) An application under this rule, if not made at the time the judgment is given or order made, must be made in accordance with CPR Part 23 and may be so made notwithstanding that the party liable to execution did not acknowledge service of the claim form or serve a defence or take any previous part in the proceedings.

(3) The grounds on which an application under this rule is made must be set out in the application notice and be supported by a witness statement or affidavit made by or on behalf of the applicant substantiating the said grounds and, in particular, where such application is made on the grounds of the applicant's inability to pay, disclosing his income, the nature and value of any property of his and the amount of any other liabilities of his.

(4) The application notice and a copy of the supporting witness statement or affidavit must, not less than 4 clear days before the hearing, be served on the party entitled to enforce the judgment or order.

(5) An order staying execution under this rule may be varied or revoked by a subsequent order.

Procedure on application for stay—The application may be made at any hearing at which the judgment or order is given or made. It may also be made subsequently by application notice under CPR Pt 23, which must be supported by a witness statement or affidavit containing the information described in r 1(3). The court has a wide discretion which must be exercised from the starting point that there must be good reason to deny the creditor the fruits of his judgment (*Winchester Cigarette Machinery Ltd v Payne (No 2)* (1993) *The Times*, December 15, CA). If the debtor has other assets, such as property, which may provide security for the judgment debt the court may grant a stay conditional upon the debtor agreeing to an immediate charging order absolute over that property without going through the formalities required by Ord 50.

'special circumstances' (r 1(1)(a))—Special circumstances do not include the fact of a pending appeal, as an application for a stay in those circumstances would be made under the rule governing the appeal (CPR r 52.7). It may include a pending application to set aside the judgment or order. For the factors to be considered in an application under this paragraph, see *Burnett v Francis Industries plc* [1987] 2 All ER 323.

Effect of order—The order stays execution against goods only. While it may now make an instalment order on giving judgment in default (CPR Pt 12) or on admission (CPR Pt 14), the High Court does not, after judgment, except on a judgment summons under Debtors Act 1869, s 5 make an order staying the judgment or order generally on terms of instalment payments. However, other enforcement remedies are available only in the court's discretion, and it seems likely that that discretion would be influenced by the same factors which justify stay of execution under this rule.

****

3 Separate writs to enforce payment of costs, etc

(1) Where only the payment of money, together with costs to be assessed in accordance with CPR Part 47 (detailed costs assessment), is adjudged or ordered, then, if when the money becomes payable under the judgment or order the costs have not been assessed, the party entitled to enforce that judgment or order may issue a writ of fieri facias to enforce payment of the sum (other than for costs) adjudged or ordered and, not less than 8 days after the issue of that writ, he may issue a second writ to enforce payment of the assessed costs.

(2) A party entitled to enforce a judgment or order for the delivery of possession of any property (other than money) may, if he so elects, issue a separate writ of fieri facias to enforce payment of any damages or costs awarded to him by that judgment or order.

4 No expenses of execution in certain cases

Where a judgment or order is for less than £600 and does not entitle the claimant to costs against the person against whom the writ of fieri facias to enforce the judgment or order is issued, the writ may not authorise the sheriff or enforcement officer to whom it is directed to levy any fees, poundage or other costs of execution.

Amendments—SI 2003/3361.

5 Writ of fieri facias de bonis ecclesiasticis, etc

(1) Where it appears upon the return of any writ of fieri facias that the person against whom the writ was issued has no goods or chattels in the county of the sheriffs to whom the writ was directed or the district of the relevant enforcement officer but that he is the incumbent of a benefice named in the return, then, after the writ and return have been filed, the party by whom the writ of fieri facias

was issued may issue a writ of fieri facias de bonis ecclesiasticis or a writ of sequestrari de bonis ecclesiasticis directed to the bishop of the diocese within which that benefice is.

(2) Any such writ must be delivered to the bishop to be executed by him.

(3) Only such fees for the execution of any such writ shall be taken by or allowed to the bishop or any diocesan officer as are for the time being authorised by or under any enactment, including any measure of the General Synod.

Amendments—SI 2003/3361.

6 Order for sale otherwise than by auction

(1) An order of the court under paragraph 10 of Schedule 7 to the Courts Act 2003 that a sale of goods seized under an execution may be made otherwise than by public auction may be made on the application of –

- (a) the person at whose instance the writ of execution under which the sale is to be made was issued;
- (b) the person against whom that writ was issued (in this rule referred to as 'the judgment debtor');
- (c) if the writ was directed to a sheriff, that sheriff; and
- (d) if the writ was directed to one or more enforcement officers, the relevant enforcement officer.

(2) Such an application must be made in accordance with CPR Part 23 and the application notice must contain a short statement of the grounds of the application.

(3) Where the applicant for an order under this rule is not the sheriff or enforcement officer, the sheriff or enforcement officer must, on the demand of the applicant, send to the applicant a list stating –

- (a) whether he has notice of the issue of another writ or writs of execution against the goods of the judgment debtor; and
- (b) so far as is known to him, the name and address of every creditor who has obtained the issue of another such writ of execution,

and where the sheriff or enforcement officer is the applicant, he must prepare such a list.

(4) Not less than 4 clear days before the hearing the applicant must serve the application notice on each of the other persons by whom the application might have been made and on every person named in the list under paragraph (3).

(5) Service of the application notice on a person named in the list under paragraph (3) is notice to him for the purpose of paragraph 10(3) of Schedule 7 to the Courts Act 2003.

> (Paragraph 10(3) provides that if the person who seized the goods has notice of another execution or other executions, the court must not consider an application for leave to sell privately until the notice prescribed by Civil Procedure Rules has been given to the other execution creditor or creditors)

(6) The applicant must produce the list under paragraph (3) to the court on the hearing of the application.

(7) Every person on whom the application notice was served may attend and be heard on the hearing of the application.

Amendments—SI 2003/3361.

Scope of provision—Bankruptcy Act 1883, s 145 requires a sale of goods seized in execution to be by public auction (if the execution is for more than £20), unless the court otherwise orders. This rule provides the procedure for an application for such an order.

Applicant (r 6(1))—The application may be made by either party or by the sheriff.

Procedure on application—The application is by application notice under CPR Pt 23 which must be served on any party who is not the applicant, on the sheriff if he is not the applicant and on any other known execution creditor.

Private sale—The advantage of seeking a private sale is that a better price may be obtained than at auction, to the benefit of both debtor and creditors. It is preferable for the order to authorise a particular sale, and the application should be specific as to the actual sale proposed. The purchaser may be the execution creditor (*Ex parte Villars* (1874) LR 9 Ch 432). If the point is contentious the applicant must be prepared to compare the proposed sale price with what is likely to be achieved at auction. The procedure may be particularly useful where the creditor has an intimate knowledge of the debtor's leviable assets, and therefore some idea of the best market for them, or where the goods are of a specialised nature for which there is no ready market.

RSC ORDER 48

****

Amendments—The whole Order was revoked by SI 2001/2792 with effect from 25 March 2002. Provisions about orders to obtain information from judgment debtors are now to be found in CPR Pt 71.

RSC ORDER 49

****

Amendments—The whole Order was revoked by SI 2001/2792 with effect from 25 March 2002. Provisions about third party debt orders are now to be found in CPR Pt 72.

RSC ORDER 50

****

Amendments—The whole Order was revoked by SI 2001/2792 with effect from 25 March 2002. Provisions about charging orders, stop orders and stop notices are now to be found in CPR Pt 73.

RSC ORDER 51

****

Amendments—The whole Order was revoked by SI 2002/2058 with effect from 2 December 2002. Provisions about the court's power to appoint receivers are now to be found in CPR Pt 69.

RSC ORDER 52
COMMITTAL

Procedural Guide—See Guide 44, set out in Section 1 of this work.

Practice Direction—See generally PDCommittal at p 1661.

1 Committal for contempt of court

(1) The power of the High Court or Court of Appeal to punish for contempt of court may be exercised by an order of committal.

(2) Where contempt of court –

(a) is committed in connection with –

(i) any proceedings before a Divisional Court of the Queen's Bench Division; or

(ii) criminal proceedings, except where the contempt is committed in the face of the court or consists of disobedience to an order of the court or a breach of an undertaking to the court; or

(iii) proceedings in an inferior court; or

(b) is committed otherwise than in connection with any proceedings, then, subject to paragraph (4), an order of committal may be made only by a Divisional Court of the Queen's Bench Division.

This paragraph shall not apply in relation to contempt of the Court of Appeal.

(3) Where contempt of court is committed in connection with any proceedings in the High Court, then, subject to paragraph (2), an order of committal may be made by a single judge of the Queen's Bench Division except where the proceedings were assigned or subsequently transferred to some other Division, in which case the order may be made only by a single judge of that other Division.

The reference in this paragraph to a single judge of the Queen's Bench Division shall, in relation to proceedings in any court the judge or judges of which are, when exercising the jurisdiction of that court, deemed by virtue of any enactment to constitute a court of the High Court, be construed as a reference to a judge of that court.

(4) Where by virtue of any enactment the High Court has power to punish or take steps for the punishment of any person charged with having done anything in relation to a court, tribunal or person which would, if it had been done in relation to the High Court, have been a contempt of that court, an order of committal may be made –

(a) on an application under section 88 of the Charities Act 1993, by a single judge of the Chancery Division; and

(b) in any other case, by a single judge of the Queen's Bench Division.

Amendments—SI 2002/2058.

Jurisdiction—This Order deals with contempts which fall to be dealt with in the High Court. County courts have jurisdiction over alleged contempt of an order of the county court or alleged contempt of that court (PDCommittal, para 1.2). The procedure is governed by CCR Ord 29 in Sch 2 below.

Venue—Each division of the High Court has jurisdiction to deal with contempts arising from its own orders or proceedings in that division. The Divisional Court has jurisdiction not only over contempt of its own orders, for example disobedience of a prerogative order, but also original jurisdiction to punish other behaviour which has been held to constitute a contempt, for example acts or words calculated to interfere with the course of justice, and also statutory contempts under the Contempt of Court Act 1981.

2 Application to Divisional Court

(1) No application to a Divisional Court for an order of committal against any person may be made unless permission to make such an application has been granted in accordance with this rule.

(2) An application for such permission must be made without notice to a Divisional Court, except in vacation when it may be made to a judge in chambers and must be supported by a statement setting out the name and

description of the applicant, the name, description and address of the person sought to be committed and the grounds on which his committal is sought, and by an affidavit, to be filed before the application is made, verifying the facts relied on.

(3) The applicant must give notice of the application for permission not later than the preceding day to the Crown Office and must at the same time lodge in that office copies of the statement and affidavit.

(4) Where an application for permission under this rule is refused by a judge in chambers, the applicant may make a fresh application for such permission to a Divisional Court.

(5) An application made to a Divisional Court by virtue of paragraph (4) must be made within 8 days after the judge's refusal to give permission or, if a Divisional Court does not sit within that period, on the first day on which it sits thereafter.

The application for permission—This is made by application notice (see PDCommittal, para 2.4).

3 Application for order after leave to apply granted

(1) When permission has been granted under rule 2 to apply for an order of committal, the application for the order must be made to a Divisional Court and, unless the court or judge granting permission has otherwise directed, there must be at least 14 clear days between the service of the claim form and the day named therein for the hearing.

(2) Unless within 14 days after such permission was granted, the claim form is issued the permission shall lapse.

(3) Subject to paragraph 4, the claim form, accompanied by a copy of the statement and affidavit in support of the application for permission, must be served personally on the person sought to be committed.

(4) Without prejudice to the powers of the court or judge under Part 6 of the CPR, the court or judge may dispense with service under this rule if it or he thinks it just to do so.

The application for the order—Contempts of this nature should always be dealt with under the CPR Pt 8 procedure.

Part 6 of the CPR—Where personal service is impractical, CPR r 6.8 allows service by an alternative method for example by posting through the letter box at an address with which the respondent has some real connection.

4 Application to court other than Divisional Court

(1) Where an application for an order of committal may be made to a court other than a Divisional Court, the application must be made by claim form or application notice and be supported by an affidavit.

(2) Subject to paragraph (3) the claim form or application notice, stating the grounds of the application and accompanied by a copy of the affidavit in support of the application, must be served personally on the person sought to be committed.

(3) Without prejudice to its powers under Part 6 of the CPR, the court may dispense with service under this rule if it thinks it just to do so.

(4) This rule does not apply to committal applications which under rules 1(2) and 3(1) should be made to a Divisional Court but which, in vacation, have been properly made to a single judge in accordance with RSC Order 64, rule 4.

Claim form or application notice—Paragraph 2.2 of PDCommittal sets out the rule for deciding whether to use a CPR Pt 8 claim form or application notice in existing proceedings. It may sometimes be difficult to determine whether or not final judgment has been given within the meaning of PDCommittal, para 2.2(c). Procedural challenges based upon the use of the wrong form will have to overcome the saving provision in PDCommittal, para 10 and the overriding objective in CPR Pt 1. See also *R v Immigration Appeal Tribunal ex parte Jeyeanthan* [1999] 3 All ER 231 for the modern approach to procedural irregularities.

Affidavit—Paragraphs 2–16 of PD32 set out the requirements for the form and content of affidavits.

The grounds of the application—See PDCommittal, paras 2.5(2) and 2.6(2) for detailed requirements.

Part 6 of the CPR—See note to r 3 above.

5 Saving for power to commit without application for purpose

Nothing in the foregoing provisions of this Order shall be taken as affecting the power of the High Court or Court of Appeal to make an order of committal of its own initiative against a person guilty of contempt of court.

'committal of its own initiative'—These powers will normally be used to deal with contempts in the face of the court. A person accused of such contempt should be allowed the opportunity to obtain legal representation before being dealt with by the court.

6 Provisions as to hearing

(1) Subject to paragraph (2), the court hearing an application for an order of committal may sit in private in the following cases, that is to say –

- (a) where the application arises out of proceedings relating to the wardship or adoption of an infant or wholly or mainly to the guardianship, custody, maintenance or upbringing of an infant, or rights of access to an infant;
- (b) where the application arises out of proceedings relating to a person suffering or appearing to be suffering from mental disorder within the meaning of the Mental Health Act 1983;
- (c) where the application arises out of proceedings in which a secret process, discovery or invention was in issue;
- (d) where it appears to the court that in the interests of the administration of justice or for reasons of national security the application should be heard in private;

but, except as aforesaid, the application shall be heard in public.

(2) If the court hearing an application in private by virtue of paragraph (1) decides to make an order of committal against the person sought to be committed, it shall in public state –

- (a) the name of that person;
- (b) in general terms the nature of the contempt of court in respect of which the order of committal is being made; and
- (c) the length of the period for which he is being committed.

(3) Except with the permission of the court hearing an application for an order of committal, no grounds shall be relied upon at the hearing except the grounds set out in the statement under rule 2 or, as the case may be, in the claim form or application notice under rule 4.

(4) If on the hearing of the application the person sought to be committed expresses a wish to give oral evidence on his own behalf, he shall be entitled to do so.

Amendments—SI 1999/1008.

Evidence—The normal rule is that witnesses who have sworn affidavits in committal proceedings must be tendered for cross examination. Cross-examination may be refused if it is simply for a collateral purpose (*Comet Products UK Ltd v Hawkex Plastics Ltd* [1971] 1 All ER 1141). The court has a discretion whether or not to allow in evidence the affidavit of a witness who fails to attend for cross examination (*Re a Debtor No 2283 of 1976* [1979] 1 All ER 434).

'he shall be entitled to do so' (r 6(4))—Although a respondent to a committal application may be directed to swear an affidavit there would appear to be no power to compel him to do so. Any interpretation of para (4) must now accord with Human Rights Act 1998, Sch 1, Art 6.

Committal—If an order for immediate committal is made it will be executed by the tipstaff who will convey the person in contempt to prison. The order is in Form No 85.

7 Power to suspend execution of committal order

(1) The court by whom an order of committal is made may by order direct that the execution of the order of committal shall be suspended for such period or on such terms or conditions as it may specify.

(2) Where execution of an order of committal is suspended by an order under paragraph (1), the applicant for the order of committal must, unless the court otherwise directs, serve on the person against whom it was made a notice informing him of the making and terms of the order under that paragraph.

Suspended committal—If a contemnor is in breach of the terms of a suspended order the court retains a discretion whether or not to activate the order (*Re W(B)* [1969] 1 All ER 594). The court has no power to activate a suspended sentence of imprisonment unless the contemnor has been properly served with a copy of the order drawn on the proper Form No 85 (*Couzens v Couzens* [2001] EWCA Civ 992, [2001] 2 FLR 701, [2001] 3 FCR 289, CA).

Appeals—Appeal to the Court of Appeal can be made without leave from any order made in committal proceedings. The principles laid down in *Williams v Fawcett* [1986] QB 604 must now be treated with great caution in the light of *Nichols v Nichols* [1997] 2 All ER 97 which sets out the modern approach of the Court of Appeal. In the absence of prejudice or injustice to the person in contempt, procedural defects in the proceedings or the order itself will now be rectified under CPR rr 52.10 and 52.11(3) or AJA 1960, s 13(3).

7A Warrant for arrest

A warrant for the arrest of a person against whom an order of committal has been made shall not, without further order of the court, be enforced more than 2 years after the date on which the warrant is issued.

Amendments—Inserted by SI 2003/3361.

8 Discharge of person committed

(1) The court may, on the application of any person committed to prison for any contempt of court, discharge him.

(2) Where a person has been committed for failing to comply with a judgment or order requiring him to deliver any thing to some other person or to deposit it in court or elsewhere, and a writ of sequestration has also been issued to enforce that judgment or order, then, if the thing is in the custody or power of the person committed, the commissioners appointed by the writ of sequestration may take possession of it as if it were the property of that person and, without prejudice to the generality of paragraph (1), the court may discharge the person committed and may give such directions for dealing with the thing taken by the commissioners as it thinks fit.

(RSC Order 46, rule 5 contains rules relating to writs of sequestration)

Procedure—Application is made by application notice under CPR Pt 23.

9 Saving for other powers

Nothing in the foregoing provisions of this Order shall be taken as affecting the power of the court to make an order requiring a person guilty of contempt of court, or a person punishable by virtue of any enactment in like manner as if he had been guilty of contempt of the High Court, to pay a fine or to give security for his good behaviour, and those provisions, so far as applicable, and with the necessary modifications, shall apply in relation to an application for such an order as they apply in relation to an application for an order of committal.

Practice Direction – Committal Applications

This Practice Direction is supplemental to RSC Order 52 (Schedule 1 to the CPR) and CCR Order 29 (Schedule 2 to the CPR) (PDCommittal)

Procedural Guide—See Guide 44, set out in Section 1 of this work.

GENERAL

1.1 Part I of this practice direction applies to any application for an order for committal of a person to prison for contempt of court (a 'committal application'). Part II makes additional provision where the committal application relates to a contempt in the face of the court.

1.2 Where the alleged contempt of court consists of or is based upon disobedience to an order made in a county court or breach of an undertaking given to a county court or consists of an act done in the course of proceedings in a county court, or where in any other way the alleged contempt is a contempt which the county court has power to punish, the committal application may be made in the county court in question.

1.3 In every other case (other than one within Part II of this practice direction), a committal application must be made in the High Court.

1.4 In all cases the Convention rights of those involved should particularly be borne in mind. It should be noted that the burden of proof, having regard to the possibility that a person may be sent to prison, is that the allegation be proved beyond reasonable doubt.

(Section 1 of the Human Rights Act defines 'the Convention rights')

'may be made in the county court in question' (para 1.2)—Although the wording appears to be permissive, statutory contempts under CCA 1984, ss 14 or 118 must be dealt with in the county court. Where the committal application is made in separate proceedings under CPR Pt 8, it will normally be more convenient to commence them in the court which dealt with the original proceedings.

Legal Aid—In these proceedings, the court has power to grant Legal Aid to respondents under Legal Aid Act 1988, s 29.

PART I

COMMENCEMENT OF COMMITTAL PROCEEDINGS

2.1 A committal application must, subject to paragraph 2.2, be commenced by the issue of a Part 8 claim form. The Part 8 claim form must be used (see paragraph 2.5).

2.2 (1) If the committal application is made in existing proceedings it must be commenced by the filing of an application notice in those proceedings.
(2) An application to commit for breach of an undertaking or order must be commenced by the filing of an application notice in the proceedings in which the undertaking was given or the order was made.
(3) The application notice must state that the application is made in the proceedings in question and its title and reference number must correspond with the title and reference number of those proceedings.

2.3 If the committal application is one which cannot be made without permission, the claim form or application notice, as the case may be, may not be issued or filed until the requisite permission has been granted.

2.4 If the permission of the court is needed in order to make a committal application –

(1) the permission must be applied for by filing an application notice (see CPR rule 23.2(4));
(2) the application notice need not be served on the respondent;
(3) the date on which and the name of the judge by whom the requisite permission was granted must be stated on the claim form or application notice by which the committal application is commenced;
(4) the permission may only be granted by a judge who, under paragraph 11, would have power to hear the committal application if permission were granted; and
(5) CPR rules 23.9 and 23.10 do not apply.

2.5 If the committal application is commenced by the issue of a claim form, CPR Part 8 shall, subject to the provisions of this practice direction, apply as though references to 'claimant' were references to the person making the committal application and references to 'defendant' were references to the person against whom the committal application is made (in this practice direction referred to as 'the respondent') but:

(1) the claim form together with copies of all written evidence in support must, unless the court otherwise directs, be served personally on the respondent,
(2) the claim form must set out in full the grounds on which the committal

application is made and must identify, separately and numerically, each alleged act of contempt including, if know, the date of each alleged act,

(3) an amendment to the claim form can be made with the permission of the court but not otherwise,

(4) CPR rule 8.4 does not apply, and

(5) the claim form must contain a prominent notice stating the possible consequences of the court making a committal order and of the respondent not attending the hearing. A form of notice, which may be used is annexed to this practice direction.

2.6 If a committal application is commenced by the filing of an application notice, CPR Part 23 shall, subject to the provisions of this practice direction, apply, but:

(1) the application notice together with copies of all written evidence in support must, unless the court otherwise directs, be served personally on the respondent,

(2) the application notice must set out in full the grounds on which the committal application is made and must identify, separately and numerically, each alleged act of contempt including, if known, the date of each of the alleged acts,

(3) an amendment to the application notice can be made with the permission of the court but not otherwise, and

(4) the court may not dispose of the committal application without a hearing.

(5) the application notice must contain a prominent notice stating the possible consequences of the court making a committal order and of the respondent not attending the hearing. A form of notice, which may be used, is annexed to this practice direction.

'served personally' (para 2.6(1))—The court has power to order service by an alternative method under CPR r 6.8(1) or exceptionally to dispense with service under CPR r 6.9. In order to comply with HRA 1998, Sch 1, Pt I, Art 6, any committal order made in the defendant's absence must provide for the debtor to be brought before the court before being conveyed to prison. See *Newman v Modern Bookbinders* [2000] 1 WLR 2559, [2000] 2 All ER 814, CA for a full discussion of the procedural safeguards to which any alleged contemnor is entitled.

'separately and numerically' (para 2.6(2))—The purpose of particulars is to enable the respondent to know the case he has to meet. Where possible, dates and times should always be given. If the claimant alleges that a number of acts taken together amount to a contempt, for example harassment, the claimant should use numbered subparagraphs to set out the individual acts which, taken together, are alleged to amount to an act of contempt.

'amendment' (para 2.6(3))—Permission to amend may be sought by adding further breaches of the order alleged to have occurred after the issue of the committal application. The court will balance the advantage of disposing of all issues between the parties at a single hearing in accordance with the overriding objective against any prejudice which may be caused to the respondent. A short adjournment may be necessary to avoid injustice.

WRITTEN EVIDENCE

3.1 Written evidence in support of or in opposition to a committal application must be given by affidavit.

3.2 Written evidence served in support of or in opposition to a committal application must, unless the court otherwise directs, be filed.

3.3 A respondent may give oral evidence at the hearing, whether or not he has filed or served any written evidence. If he does so, he may be cross-examined.

3.4 A respondent may, with the permission of the court, call a witness to give oral evidence at the hearing whether or not the witness has sworn an affidavit.

'written evidence ... must be given by affidavit' (para 3.1)—This paragraph must be taken to override CPR r 8.5(7).

'with the permission of the court' (para 3.4)—A refusal to permit the respondent to call witnesses may amount to a breach of Human Rights Act 1998, Sch 1, Art 6.

CASE MANAGEMENT AND DATE OF HEARING

4.1 The applicant for the committal order must, when lodging the claim form or application notice with the court for issuing or filing, as the case may be, obtain from the court a date for the hearing of the committal application.

4.2 Unless the court otherwise directs, the hearing date of a committal application shall be not less than 14 clear days after service of the claim form or of the application notice, as the case may be, on the respondent. The hearing date must be specified in the claim form or application notice or in a Notice of Hearing or Application attached to and served with the claim form or application notice.

4.3 The court may, however, at any time give case management directions, including directions for the service of written evidence by the respondent and written evidence in reply by the applicant, or may convene and hold a directions hearing.

4.4 The court may on the hearing date –

(1) give case management directions with a view to a hearing of the committal application on a future date, or
(2) if the committal application is ready to be heard, proceed forthwith to hear it.

4.5 In dealing with any committal application, the court will have regard to the need for the respondent to have details of the alleged acts of contempt and the opportunity to respond to the committal application.

4.6 The court should also have regard to the need for the respondent to be –

(1) allowed a reasonable time for responding to the committal application including, if necessary, preparing a defence;
(2) made aware of the availability of assistance from the Community Legal Service and how to contact the Service;
(3) given the opportunity, if unrepresented, to obtain legal advice; and
(4) if unable to understand English, allowed to make arrangements, seeking the assistance of the court if necessary, for an interpreter to attend the hearing.

'Unless the court otherwise directs' (para 4.2)—CPR r 3.1(2)(a) allows the court to reduce the time between service and hearing. An application to shorten the time should be made by application notice verified by statement of truth under CPR r 23.8(c).

'14 clear days' (para 4.2)—See CPR r 2.8. In selecting the return date upon issue of the application, sufficient time should be allowed for service.

'written evidence by the respondent' (para 4.3)—Although the court may direct service of written evidence it is clear from RSC Ord 52, r 6(4) and para 3.3 above that he cannot be compelled to do so. The only available sanction would lie in the exercise of the court's discretion as to costs.

'Notice of Hearing or Application' (sic) (para 4.2)—'or' must be a typographical error for 'of'. The form is N244A.

STRIKING OUT

5 The court may, on application by the respondent or on its own initiative, strike out a committal application if it appears to the court:

(1) that the committal application and the evidence served in support of it disclose no reasonable ground for alleging that the respondent is guilty of a contempt of court,

(2) that the committal application is an abuse of the court's process or, if made in existing proceedings, is otherwise likely to obstruct the just disposal of those proceedings, or

(3) that there has been a failure to comply with a rule, practice direction or court order.

(CPR Part 3 contains general powers for the management by the court.)

'application by the respondent'—This will be by application notice under CPR Pt 23.

'on its own initiative'—CPR r 3.3 will apply to any such order.

'failure to comply with a rule' (para 5(3))—See however para 10 below.

MISCELLANEOUS

6 CPR Rules 35.7 (Court's power to direct that evidence is to be given by a single joint expert), 35.8 (Instructions to single joint expert) and 35.9 (Power of court to direct a party to provide information) do not apply to committal applications.

7 An order under CPR rule 18.1 (Order for a party to give additional information) may not be made against a respondent to a committal application.

8 A committal application may not be discontinued without the permission of the court.

9 A committal application should normally be heard in public (see CPR rule 39.2), but if it is heard in private and the court finds the respondent guilty of contempt of court, the judge shall, when next sitting in public, state:

(1) the name of the respondent,

(2) in general terms the nature of the contempt or contempts found proved, and,

(3) the penalty (if any) imposed.

10 The court may waive any procedural defect in the commencement or conduct of a committal application if satisfied that no injustice has been caused to the respondent by the defect.

11 Except where under an enactment a master or district judge has power to make a committal order[1], a committal order can only be made:

(1) in High Court proceedings, by a High Court judge or a person authorised to act as such[2],

(2) in county court proceedings by a circuit judge or a person authorised to act or capable by virtue of his office of acting as such[3].

1 Eg ss 14 and 118, County Courts Act 1984.
2 See s 9(1), Supreme Court Act 1981.
3 See s 5(3), County Courts Act 1984.

'procedural defect'—Paragraph 10 describes the position stated in *Nichols v Nichols* [1997] 2 All ER 97.

Appeals—AJA 1960, s 13(1) gives a right of appeal to the Court of Appeal without leave against any committal order.

PART II

12 Where the committal application relates to a contempt in the face of the court the following matters should be given particular attention. Normally, it will be appropriate to defer consideration of the behaviour to allow the respondent time to reflect on what has occurred. The time needed for the following procedures should allow such a period of reflection.

13 A Part 8 claim form and an application notice are not required for Part II, but other provisions of this practice direction should be applied, as necessary, or adapted to the circumstances. In addition the judge should:

(1) tell the respondent of the possible penalty he faces;
(2) inform the respondent in detail, and preferably in writing, of the actions and behaviour of the respondent which have given rise to the committal application;
(3) if he considers that an apology would remove the need for the committal application, tell the respondent;
(4) have regard to the need for the respondent to be –
  (a) allowed a reasonable time for responding to the committal application, including, if necessary, preparing a defence;
  (b) made aware of the availability of assistance from the Community Legal Service and how to contact the Service;
  (c) given the opportunity, if unrepresented, to obtain legal advice;
  (d) if unable to understand English, allowed to make arrangements, seeking the court's assistance if necessary, for an interpreter to attend the hearing; and
  (e) brought back before the court for the committal application to be heard within a reasonable time.
(5) allow the respondent an opportunity to –
  (a) apologise to the court;
  (b) explain his actions and behaviour; and,
  (c) if the contempt is proved, to address the court on the penalty to be imposed on him;
(6) if there is a risk of the appearance of bias, ask another judge to hear the committal application.
(7) where appropriate, nominate a suitable person to give the respondent the information.

(It is likely to be appropriate to nominate a person where the effective communication of information by the judge to the respondent was not possible when the incident occurred)

14 Where the committal application is to be heard by another judge, a written statement by the judge before whom the actions and behaviour of the respondent which have given rise to the committal application took place may be submitted as evidence of those actions and behaviour.

Annex

IMPORTANT NOTICE

The court has power to send you to prison and to fine you if it finds that any of the allegations made against you are true and amount to a contempt of court.

You must attend court on the date shown on the front of this form. It is in your own interest to do so. You should bring with you any witnesses and documents which you think will help you put your side of the case.

If you consider the allegations are not true you must tell the court why. If it is established that they are true, you must tell the court of any good reason why they do not amount to a contempt of court, or, if they do, why you should not be punished.

If you need advice you should show this document at once to your solicitor or go to a Citizens' Advice Bureau.

****

RSC ORDER 54
APPLICATIONS FOR WRIT OF HABEAS CORPUS

Procedural Guide—See Guide 56, set out in Section 1 of this work.

Habeas corpus—There are three forms of the writ. All of them require that a person being detained be produced to a court or other tribunal.

- Habeas corpus ad subjiciendum enables an applicant to have the court rule upon the lawfulness of his detention and to direct his release.
- Habeas corpus ad testificandum requires the detainee to be brought before a court to give evidence.
- Habeas corpus ad respondendum requires the detainee to be produced for trial or examination.

The writ is now used less often than previously, because of the widening of the scope of judicial review. Habeas corpus still plays an important role in safeguarding the liberty of the subject, in recognition of which it has priority over other court business (*R v Home Secretary ex parte Cheblak* [1991] 1 WLR 890, 894a–b, CA). Nevertheless, habeas corpus would benefit from being updated and incorporated into CPR Pt 54, which would provide a single procedure for all the prerogative orders, not least because the European Court of Human Rights has held that judicial review generally does (*D v UK* (1997) 24 EHRR 423) whereas habeas corpus does not (*X v UK* (1982) 4 EHRR 188, ECHR) provide adequate scrutiny of executive discretion. But the Law Commission has not recommended this: Judicial Review and Statutory Appeals (1994) (Law Com No 226).

1 Application for writ of habeas corpus ad subjiciendum

(1) Subject to rule 11, an application for a writ of habeas corpus ad subjiciendum shall be made to a judge in court, except that –

(a) it shall be made to a Divisional Court of the Queen's Bench Division if the court so directs;

(b) it may be made to a judge otherwise than in court at any time when no judge is sitting in court; and

(c) any application on behalf of a child must be made in the first instance to a judge otherwise than in court.

(2) An application for such writ may be made without notice being served on any other party and, subject to paragraph (3) must be supported by a witness statement or affidavit by the person restrained showing that it is made at his instance and setting out the nature of the restraint.

(3) Where the person restrained is unable for any reason to make the witness statement or affidavit required by paragraph (2) the witness statement or affidavit may be made by some other person on his behalf and that witness

statement or affidavit must state that the person restrained is unable to make the witness statement or affidavit himself and for what reason.

Practice Direction—See generally PDRSC54 at p 1672.

Habeas corpus ad subjiciendum: scope of the writ—The applicant must be the subject of a current restraint on his liberty (*Bernardo v Ford* [1892] AC 326). This includes a person who is on bail (*In re Amand* [1941] 2 KB 239, DC).

The applicant must generally be in the jurisdiction, ie England and Wales (*R v Cowle* (1759) 2 Burr 834, 97 ER 587 (Scotland); *Re Keenan* [1972] 1 QB 533, CA (Northern Ireland); Habeas Corpus Act 1862 s 1 (colonies and foreign dominions which have their own courts). The respondent must also be in the jurisdiction (*R v Pinckney* [1904] 2 KB 84, CA).

The writ is not discretionary, in that, if the detention is unlawful, the court will order the applicant's release. But the court will generally not entertain applications by persons convicted by a competent court. They must challenge their convictions by means of appeal (*In re Wring* [1960] 1 WLR 138, DC; cf where the applicant argues that his trial was a nullity, *R v Governor of Spring Hill Prison ex parte Sohi* [1988] 1 WLR 596, DC).

Distinction between habeas corpus and judicial review—Habeas corpus is appropriate where there is no power to detain the applicant. Judicial review is appropriate where there is power to detain the applicant but that power has been exercised unlawfully, eg unfairly, irrationally or pursuant to a misdirection on the law. In the latter case, the detention is lawful until the defective decision to detain is quashed. In the former case, the detention is already unlawful (*R v Home Secretary ex parte Cheblak* [1991] 1 WLR 890, 894d–f; *R v Home Secretary ex parte Muboyayi* [1992] QB 244, CA; *In re S-C (mental patient: habeas corpus)* [1996] QB 599, CA). Where the court has to determine a question of precedent fact, either procedure may be appropriate (*R v Home Secretary ex parte Khawaja* [1984] AC 74). The trend is to favour proceeding by judicial review, as this gives the court greater flexibility (*R v Oldham Justices ex parte Cawley* [1997] QB 1, DC; *R v Barking Havering & Brentwood Community Health Care NHS Trust* [1999] 1 FLR 106, [1999] Lloyd's Med Rep 101, (1999) 47 BMLR 112, CA).

A detention which is initially lawful may become unlawful if the original purpose of the detention, eg to secure the deportation of the applicant, cannot be achieved in a reasonable time. When this occurs, habeas corpus is the appropriate procedure (*R v Governor of Durham Prison ex parte Hardial Singh* [1984] 1 WLR 740; *Tan Te Lam v Superintendent of Tai A Chau Detention Centre* [1997] AC 97, PC).

Application for the writ—The application should be made in the Queen's Bench Division of the High Court, unless it is by a parent or guardian concerning the custody care or control of a child, in which case it must be made in the Family Division (SCA, s 61, Sch 1, para 2(a); RSC Ord 54, rr 1(1), 11). The Court of Appeal has no original jurisdiction to issue the writ (*Re Carroll* [1931] 1 KB 104, CA).

2 Power of court to whom application made without notice being served on any other party

(1) The court or judge to whom an application under rule 1 is made without notice being served on any other party may make an order forthwith for the writ to issue, or may –

- (a) where the application is made to a judge otherwise than in court, direct the issue of a claim form seeking the writ, or that an application therefor be made by claim form to a Divisional Court or to a judge in court;
- (b) where the application is made to a judge in court, adjourn the application so that notice thereof may be given, or direct that an application be made by claim form to a Divisional Court;
- (c) where the application is made to a Divisional Court, adjourn the application so that notice thereof may be given.

(2) The claim form must be served on the person against whom the issue of the writ is sought and on such other persons as the court or judge may direct, and,

unless the court or judge otherwise directs, there must be at least 8 clear days between the service of the claim form and the date named therein for the hearing of the application.

Practice Direction—See generally PDRSC54 at p 1672.

The initial hearing—The application is formally without notice. In practice, the applicant often notifies the respondent.

The court may grant the application at the initial hearing. But it will do so only if it has heard full argument and the case is clear. This is rare. The court may adjourn the application, to give the respondent the opportunity to appear and serve evidence. In a criminal cause or matter, the application is generally adjourned to be heard by a Divisional Court. Alternatively, the court may dismiss the application. Even in a criminal cause or matter, a single judge can now dismiss the application (Administration of Justice Act 1960, s 14(1), repealed by Access to Justice Act 1999, s 65).

A criminal cause or matter includes extradition proceedings (*R v Governor of Brixton Prison ex parte Levin* [1997] AC 741; *Cuoghi v Governor of Brixton Prison* [1998] 1 WLR 1513, CA).

A prisoner will generally not be produced at the hearing. The prison authorities may produce him at court, but generally will not do so unless he pays for his escort (Criminal Justice Act 1961, s 29; *Becker v Home Office* [1972] 2 QB 407, CA; *R v Home Secretary ex parte Wynne* [1992] QB 407, HL). The court prefers applications for habeas corpus to be made by counsel (*In re Wring* [1960] 1 WLR 138, DC).

Where the court directs the claimant to serve a claim form, Form 87 should be used (PDRSC54, para 3).

Service of the claim form—The claim form should be served on the person having custody of the applicant.

Respondent's evidence—The respondent may rely on matters which would not be admissible evidence in a court of law (*R v Home Secretary ex parte Rahman* [1998] QB 136, CA).

Renewed applications—If the application is refused, it may not be renewed on the same grounds unless there is fresh evidence (Administration of Justice Act 1960, s 14(2). If an applicant seeks to manipulate matters by making a series of applications, proceedings will be struck out as an abuse of the process of the court (*R v Governor of Pentonville Prison ex parte Tarling* [1979] 1 WLR 1417, DC; *R v Governor of Brixton Prison ex parte Osman (No 4)* [1992] 1 All ER 579, DC). It will generally be an abuse of the process of the court to bring an application for habeas corpus on the same grounds as a previously unsuccessful application for judicial review (*Sheikh, the Queen on the application of v Secretary of State for the Home Department* [2001] Imm AR 219, CA).

Appeals—If the application is refused, the applicant can appeal, subject to the grant of leave. In a non-criminal cause or matter, the appeal is to the Court of Appeal. In a criminal cause or matter it is directly to the House of Lords and, although leave is required, it is not necessary for the Divisional Court to certify a question of general public importance. See Administration of Justice Act 1960, ss 1, 15(1), (3).

If the application is granted, the respondent may appeal, subject to the grant of leave. In a criminal cause or matter, the court may order the applicant to be detained or released on bail pending the prosecutor's appeal. Subject to this, an applicant is not liable to be detained even if the respondent succeeds in his appeal (Administration of Justice Act 1960, ss 5, 15(1), (4); *R v Home Secretary ex parte Virk* [1996] COD 134).

3 Copies of witness statements or affidavits to be supplied

Every party to an application under rule 1 must supply to every other party on demand and on payment of the proper charges copies of the witness statements or affidavits which he proposes to use at the hearing of the application.

Practice Direction—See generally PDRSC54 at p 1672.

4 Power to order release of person restrained

(1) Without prejudice to rule 2(1), the court or judge hearing an application for a writ of habeas corpus ad subjiciendum may in its or his discretion order that

the person restrained be released, and such order shall be a sufficient warrant to any governor of a prison, constable or other person for the release of the person under restraint.

(2) Where such an application in criminal proceedings is heard by a judge and the judge does not order the release of the person restrained, he shall direct that the application be made by claim form to a Divisional Court of the Queen's Bench Division.

Practice Direction—See generally PDRSC54 at p 1672.

Release of the applicant—If the court directs the release of the applicant, the Master of the Crown Office may write to the respondent, directing him to release the applicant. In such a case, there is no need for the writ to issue. Sometimes the writ is issued, as a formality, after the applicant's release has been directed. It is rare for the writ to issue before the court has ruled on the lawfulness of the applicant's detention.

5 Directions as to return to writ

Where a writ of habeas corpus ad subjiciendum is ordered to issue, the court or judge by whom the order is made shall give directions as to the court or judge before whom, and the date on which, the writ is returnable.

Practice Direction—See generally PDRSC54 at p 1672.

6 Service of writ and notice

(1) Subject to paragraphs (2) and (3), a writ of habeas corpus ad subjiciendum must be served personally on the person to whom it is directed.

(2) If it is not possible to serve such writ personally, or if it is directed to a governor of a prison or other public official, it must be served by leaving it with a servant or agent of the person to whom the writ is directed at the place where the person restrained is confined or restrained.

(3) If the writ is directed to more than one person, the writ must be served in manner provided by this rule on the person first named in the writ, and copies must be served on each of the other persons in the same manner as the writ.

(4) There must be served with the writ a notice (in Form No 90 in the relevant practice direction) stating the court or judge before whom and the date on which the person restrained is to be brought and that in default of obedience proceedings for committal of the party disobeying will be taken.

Practice Direction—See generally PDRSC54 at p 1672.

7 Return to the writ

(1) The return to a writ of habeas corpus ad subjiciendum must be indorsed on or annexed to the writ and must state all the causes of the detainer of the person restrained.

(2) The return may be amended, or another return substituted therefor, by permission of the court or judge before whom the writ is returnable.

Practice Direction—See generally PDRSC54 at p 1672.

Return to the writ—The court may enquire into the truth of the facts stated in the return to the writ (Habeas Corpus Act 1816, ss 3, 4). The respondent too can go behind the wording of the return to the writ (*In re Shahid Iqbal* [1979] QB 264, DC).

8 Procedure at hearing of writ

When a return to a writ of habeas corpus ad subjiciendum is made, the return shall first be read, and motion then made for discharging or remanding the person restrained or amending or quashing the return, and where that person is brought up in accordance with the writ, his counsel shall be heard first, then the counsel for the Crown, and then one counsel for the person restrained in reply.

Practice Direction—See generally PDRSC54 at p 1672.

9 Bringing up prisoner to give evidence, etc

(1) An application for a writ of habeas corpus ad testificandum or of habeas corpus ad respondendum must be made on witness statement or affidavit to a judge.

(2) An application for an order to bring up a prisoner, otherwise than by writ of habeas corpus, to give evidence in any proceedings, civil or criminal, before any court, tribunal or justice, must be made on witness statement or affidavit to a judge.

Amendments—SI 1999/1008.

Practice Direction—See generally PDRSC54 at p 1672.

Habeas corpus ad testificandum—This enables a judge of the High Court to require a prisoner to be produced to give evidence before a court or before an arbitrator or umpire (Habeas Corpus Act 1804, s 1; Arbitration Act 1950, s 12(5); Agricultural Holdings Act 1986, Sch 11, para 13).

For the costs of the prisoner's attendance, see note **'The initial hearing'** under r 2 above.

Habeas corpus ad respondendum—This enables a judge of the High Court to require a prisoner to be produced to answer certain charges (eg in a court-martial) or be examined (eg in insolvency proceedings) (Habeas Corpus Act 1803, s 1).

10 Form of writ

A writ of habeas corpus must be in Form No 89, 91 or 92 in the relevant practice direction, whichever is appropriate.

Practice Direction—See generally PDRSC54 at p 1672.

11 Applications relative to the custody, etc, of child

An application by a parent or guardian of a child for a writ of habeas corpus ad subjiciendum relative to the custody, care or control of the child must be made in the Family Division, and this Order shall accordingly apply to such applications with the appropriate modifications.

Practice Direction—See generally PDRSC54 at p 1672.

Family Division—Applications for habeas corpus relative to the custody care or control of a child must be made in the Family Division. In all other cases, the application is made in the Queen's Bench Division (SCA, s 61, Sch 1, paras 2(a), 3).

Practice Direction – Application for Writ of Habeas Corpus

This Practice Direction supplements RSC Order 54 and CPR Part 50 (PDRSC54)

Procedural Guide—See Guide 56, set out in Section 1 of this work.

General note—See also the notes to RSC Ord 54 for relevant commentary.

TERMINOLOGY

1.1 In this practice direction –

(1) 'Order 54' means those provisions contained in Schedule 1, RSC Order 54 which were previously contained in the Rules of the Supreme Court (1965);
(2) a reference to a rule or Part prefixed with CPR is a reference to a rule or Part contained in the CPR rules; and
(3) a reference to a rule number alone is a reference to the rule so numbered in Order 54.

SCOPE

2.1 This practice direction supplements Order 54 (which sets out how to apply for a writ of habeas corpus) by providing further detail about the application.

2.2 This practice direction must be read together with Order 54.

2.3 It also lists at paragraph 7 other practice directions which governed procedure relating to Order 54 before 26 April 1999 and which will continue to do so.

FORM TO BE USED WHERE COURT DIRECTS CLAIM FORM TO BE USED

3.1 Where the court directs that an application be made by claim form, under –

(1) rule 2 (on hearing application under rule 1); or
(2) rule 4(2) (application in criminal proceedings ordered to be made to Divisional Court of the Queen's Bench Division),

the claimant must use Form 87 modified in accordance with the guidance set out in the Forms practice direction.

FORM TO BE USED FOR NOTICE OF ADJOURNED APPLICATION DIRECTED BY COURT

4.1 Where the court directs under rule 2(1)(c) that an application made under rule 1 is adjourned to allow for service of notice of the application, such notice must be given in modified Form 88.

SERVICE

5.1 The party seeking the writ must serve –

(1) the claim form in accordance with rule 2.2; and
(2) the writ of habeas corpus ad subjiciendum and notice in Form 90, as modified, in accordance with rule 6.

(CPR rule 6.3 provides that the court will normally serve a document which it has issued or prepared)

THE CROWN OFFICE LIST

6.1 When the court directs that an application is to be made by claim form under –

(1) rule 2(1) (powers of court to whom application made under rule 1); or
(2) rule 4(2) (power of court in where application made in criminal proceedings)

the application must be entered in the Administrative Court List in accordance with Practice Direction (Crown Office List) 1987 1 WLR 232, [1987] 1 All ER 368.

(In Schedule 1, RSC Order 57, rule 2 provides for the entry of claims in the appropriate office and for the filing of copy documents for the use of the court)

PRACTICE DIRECTIONS ETC, WHICH APPLY TO ORDER 54

7.1 On and after 26 April 1999, the practice directions, Statements and Practice Notes set out in Table 1 continue to apply to proceedings under Order 54.

Table 1 **Practice Direction etc**	Content
Practice Note [1983] 2 All ER 1020	Urgent matters outside London – consultation of Crown Office and continuation in London
Practice Note (Crown Office List) [1987] 1 All ER 1184	Need for accuracy in time estimates
Practice Direction (Crown Office List) [1987] 1 WLR 232, [1987] 1 All ER 368	Parts of the List
Practice Direction (Crown Office List: Preparation for hearings) [1994] 4 All ER 671, [1994] 1 WLR 1551 (18th November 1994)	Preparation for hearings; Documentation; Time limits; Skeleton arguments: amendment of grounds
Practice Direction (Crown Office List; Consent Orders) [1997] 1 WLR 825	Consent orders
Practice Statement (Supreme Court; Judgments) [1998] 1 WLR 825, [1998] 2 All ER 638	Judgments

****

RSC ORDER 62

****

Amendments—The whole Order was revoked by SI 2004/3419, with effect from 1 April 2005. Provisions about costs on judgment for possession of land are now to be found in CPR Pt 45.

RSC ORDER 64
SITTINGS, VACATIONS AND OFFICE HOURS

4 Divisional Court business during vacation

Proceedings which require to be immediately or promptly heard and which by virtue of the following provisions must be brought in a Divisional Court may, in vacation, be brought before a single judge –

(a) Order 52, rules 1(2) and 3(1);
(b) (*revoked*)
(c) (*revoked*)
(d) (*revoked*)

Amendments—SI 2000/221; SI 2000/2092.

'following provisions'—The provisions referred to deal with matters of committal (Ord 52).

RSC ORDER 69

****

Amendments—The whole Order was revoked by SI 2002/2058 with effect from 2 December 2002. Provisions about service of foreign process are now to be found in CPR Pt 6.

RSC ORDER 70

****

Amendments—The whole Order was revoked by SI 2002/2058 with effect from 2 December 2002. Provisions about evidence for foreign courts are now to be found in CPR Pt 34.

RSC ORDER 71

****

Amendments—The whole Order was revoked by SI 2002/2058 with effect from 2 December 2002. Provisions about enforcement of judgments in different jurisdictions are now to be found in CPR Pt 74.

RSC ORDER 74

****

Amendments—This Order was revoked by SI 2001/4015 with effect from 25 March 2002. Provisions relating to applications under the Merchant Shipping Act 1995 are now to be found in CPR Pt 61 – Admiralty Claims.

RSC ORDER 77

****

Amendments—The whole Order was revoked by SI 2002/2058 with effect from 2 December 2002. Provisions about the court's power to appoint receivers are now to be found in CPR Pt 69.

RSC ORDER 79
CRIMINAL PROCEEDINGS

8 Estreat of recognizances

(1) No recognizance acknowledged in or removed into the Queen's Bench Division shall be estreated without the order of a judge.

(2) Every application to estreat a recognizance in the Queen's Bench Division must be made by claim form and will be heard by a judge and must be supported by a witness statement or affidavit showing in what manner the breach has been committed and proving that the claim form was duly served.

(2A) When it issues the claim form the court will fix a date for the hearing of the application.

(3) A claim form under this rule must be served at least 2 clear days before the day named therein for the hearing.

(4) On the hearing of the application the judge may, and if requested by any party shall, direct any issue of fact in dispute to be tried by a jury.

(5) If it appears to the judge that a default has been made in performing the conditions of the recognizance, the judge may order the recognizance to be estreated.

Amendments—SI 1999/1008.

9 Bail

(1) Subject to the provisions of this rule, every application to the High Court in respect of bail in any criminal proceeding –

- (a) where the defendant is in custody, must be made by claim form to a judge to show cause why the defendant should not be granted bail;
- (b) where the defendant has been admitted to bail, must be made by claim form to a judge to show cause why the variation in the arrangements for bail proposed by the applicant should not be made.

(2) Subject to paragraph (5), the claim form (in Form No 97 or 97A in the relevant practice direction) must, at least 24 hours before the day named therein for the hearing, be served –

- (a) where the application was made by the defendant, on the prosecutor and on the Director of Public Prosecutions, if the prosecution is being carried on by him;
- (b) where the application was made by the prosecutor or a constable under section 3(8) of the Bail Act 1976, on the defendant.

(3) Subject to paragraph (5), every application must be supported by witness statement or affidavit.

(4) Where a defendant in custody who desires to apply for bail is unable through lack of means to instruct a solicitor, he may give notice in writing to the court stating his desire to apply for bail and requesting that the Official Solicitor shall act for him in the application, and the court may assign the Official Solicitor to act for the applicant accordingly.

(5) Where the Official Solicitor has been so assigned the court may dispense with the requirements of paragraphs (1) to (3) and deal with the application in a summary manner.

(6) Where the court grants the defendant bail, the order must be in Form No 98 in the relevant practice direction and a copy of the order shall be transmitted forthwith –

- (a) where the proceedings in respect of the defendant have been transferred to the Crown Court for trial or where the defendant has been committed to the Crown Court to be sentenced or otherwise dealt with, to the appropriate officer of the Crown Court;
- (b) in any other case, to the justices' chief executive for the court which committed the defendant.

(6A) The recognizance of any surety required as a condition of bail granted as aforesaid may, where the defendant is in a prison or other place of detention, be entered into before the governor or keeper of the prison or place as well as before the persons specified in section 8(4) of the Bail Act 1976.

(6B) Where under section 3(5) or (6) of the Bail Act 1976 the court imposes a requirement to be complied with before a person's release on bail, it may give directions as to the manner in which and the person or persons before whom the requirement may be complied with.

(7) A person who in pursuance of an order for the grant of bail made by the court under this rule proposes to enter into a recognizance or give security must, unless the court otherwise directs, give notice (in Form No 100 in the relevant practice direction) to the prosecutor at least 24 hours before he enters into the recognizance or complies with the requirements as aforesaid.

(8) Where in pursuance of such an order as aforesaid a recognizance is entered into or requirement complied with before any person, it shall be the duty of that person to cause the recognizance or, as the case may be, a statement of the requirement complied with to be transmitted forthwith –

- (a) where the proceedings in respect of the defendant have been transferred to the Crown Court for trial or where the defendant has been committed to the Crown Court to be sentenced or otherwise dealt with, to the appropriate officer of the Crown Court;
- (b) in any other case, to the justices' chief executive for the court which committed the defendant;

and a copy of such recognizance or statement shall at the same time be sent to the governor or keeper of the prison or other place of detention in which the defendant is detained, unless the recognizance was entered into or the requirement complied with before such governor or keeper.

(10) An order varying the arrangements under which the defendant has been granted bail shall be in Form 98A in the relevant practice direction and a copy of the order shall be transmitted forthwith –

- (a) where the proceedings in respect of the defendant have been transferred to the Crown Court for trial or where the defendant has been committed to the Crown Court to be sentenced or otherwise dealt with, to the appropriate officer of the Crown Court;

(b) in any other case, to the justices' chief executive for the court which committed the defendant.

(11) Where in pursuance of an order of the High Court or the Crown Court a person is released on bail in any criminal proceeding pending the determination of an appeal to the High Court or House of Lords or an application for a quashing order, then, upon the abandonment of the appeal or application, or upon the decision of the High Court or House of Lords being given, any justice (being a justice acting for the same petty sessions area as the magistrates' court by which that person was convicted or sentenced) may issue process for enforcing the decision in respect of which such appeal or application was brought or, as the case may be, the decision of the High Court or House of Lords.

(12) If an applicant to the High Court in any criminal proceedings is refused bail, the applicant shall not be entitled to make a fresh application for bail to any other judge or to a Divisional Court.

(13) The record required by section 5 of the Bail Act 1976 to be made by the High Court shall be made by including in the file relating to the case in question a copy of the relevant order of the court and shall contain the particulars set out in Form No 98 or 98A in the relevant practice direction, whichever is appropriate, except that in the case of a decision to withhold bail the record shall be made by inserting a statement of the decision on the court's copy of the relevant claim form and including it in the file relating to the case in question.

(14) In the case of a person whose return or surrender is sought under the Extradition Act 1989, this rule shall apply as if references to the defendant were references to that person and references to the prosecutor were references to the state seeking the return or surrender of that person.

Amendments—SI 1999/1008; SI 2001/256; SI 2003/3361.

****

RSC ORDER 81
PARTNERS

1 Claims by and against firms within jurisdiction

Subject to the provisions of any enactment, any two or more persons claiming to be entitled, or alleged to be liable, as partners in respect of a cause of action and carrying on business within the jurisdiction may sue, or be sued, in the name of the firm (if any) of which they were partners at the time when the cause of action accrued.

2 Disclosure of partners' names

(1) Any defendant to a claim brought by partners in the name of a firm may serve on the claimants or their solicitor a notice requiring them or him forthwith to furnish the defendant with a written statement of the names and places of residence of all the persons who were partners in the firm at the time when the cause of action accrued; and if the notice is not complied with the court may

order the claimants or their solicitor to furnish the defendant with such a statement and to verify it on oath or otherwise as may be specified in the order, or may order that further proceedings in the claim be stayed on such terms as the court may direct.

(2) When the names of the partners have been declared in compliance with a notice or order given or made under paragraph (1) the proceedings shall continue in the name of the firm but with the same consequences as would have ensued if the persons whose names have been so declared had been named as claimants in the claim form.

(3) Paragraph (1) shall have effect in relation to a claim brought against partners in the name of a firm as it has effect in relation to a claim brought by partners in the name of a firm but with the substitution, for references to the defendant and the claimants, of references to the claimant and the defendants respectively, and with the omission of the words 'or may order' to the end.

4 Acknowledgment of service in a claim against firm

(1) Where persons are sued as partners in the name of their firm, service may not be acknowledged in the name of the firm but only by the partners thereof in their own names, but the claim shall nevertheless continue in the name of the firm.

(2) Where in a claim against a firm the claim form by which the claim is begun is served on a person as a partner, that person, if he denies that he was a partner or liable as such at any material time, may acknowledge service of the claim form and state in his acknowledgment that he does so as a person served as a partner in the defendant firm but who denies that he was a partner at any material time.

An acknowledgment of service given in accordance with this paragraph shall, unless and until it is set aside, be treated as an acknowledgment by the defendant firm.

(3) Where an acknowledgment of service has been given by a defendant in accordance with paragraph (2) then –

(a) the claimant may either apply to the court to set it aside on the ground that the defendant was a partner or liable as such at a material time or may leave that question to be determined at a later stage of the proceedings;

(b) the defendant may either apply to the court to set aside the service of the claim form on him on the ground that he was not a partner or liable as such at a material time or may at the proper time serve a defence on the claimant denying in respect of the claimant's claim either his liability as a partner or the liability of the defendant firm or both.

(4) The court may at any stage of the proceedings in a claim in which a defendant has acknowledged service in accordance with paragraph (2) on the application of the claimant or of that defendant, order that any question as to the liability of that defendant or as to the liability of the defendant firm be tried in such manner and at such time as the court directs.

(5) (*revoked*)

Amendments—SI 1999/1008.

5 Enforcing judgment or order against firm

(1) Where a judgment is given or order made against a firm, execution to enforce the judgment or order may, subject to rule 6, issue against any property of the firm within the jurisdiction.

(2) Where a judgment is given or order made against a firm, execution to enforce the judgment or order may, subject to rule 6 and to the next following paragraph, issue against any person who –

(a) acknowledged service of the claim form as a partner; or
(b) having been served as a partner with the claim form, failed to acknowledge service of it; or
(c) admitted in his statement of case that he is a partner; or
(d) was adjudged to be a partner.

(3) Execution to enforce a judgment or order given or made against a firm may not issue against a member of the firm who was out of the jurisdiction when the claim form was issued unless he –

(a) acknowledged service of the claim form as a partner; or
(b) was served within the jurisdiction with the claim form as a partner; or
(c) was, with the permission of the court given under Section III of CPR Part 6, served out of the jurisdiction with the claim form, as a partner,

and, except as provided by paragraph (1) and by the foregoing provisions of this paragraph, a judgment or order given or made against a firm shall not render liable, release or otherwise affect a member of the firm who was out of the jurisdiction when the claim form was issued.

(4) Where a party who has obtained a judgment or order against a firm claims that a person is liable to satisfy the judgment or order as being a member of the firm, and the foregoing provisions of this rule do not apply in relation to that person, that party may apply to the court for permission to issue execution against that person, the application to be made in accordance with CPR Part 23 and the application notice must be served personally on that person.

(5) Where the person against whom an application under paragraph (4) is made does not dispute his liability, the court hearing the application may, subject to paragraph (3) give permission to issue execution against that person, and, where that person disputes his liability, the court may order that the liability of that person be tried and determined in any manner in which any issue or question in a claim may be tried and determined.

Amendments—SI 2000/221.

6 Enforcing judgment or order in actions between partners, etc

(1) Execution to enforce a judgment or order given or made in –

(a) a claim by or against a firm in the name of the firm against or by a member of the firm; or
(b) a claim by a firm in the name of the firm against a firm in the name of the firm where those firms have one or more members in common,

shall not issue except with the permission of the court.

(2) The court hearing an application under this rule may give such directions, including directions as to the taking of accounts and the making of inquiries, as may be just.

7 Attachment of debts owed by firm

(1) An order may be made under CPR rule 72.2, in relation to debts due or accruing due from a firm carrying on business within the jurisdiction notwithstanding that one or more members of the firm is resident out of the jurisdiction.

(2) An interim third party debt order under CPR rule 72.4(2) relating to such debts as aforesaid must be served on a member of the firm within the jurisdiction or on some other person having the control or management of the partnership business.

(3) Where an order made under the said rules 72.2 or 72.4(2) requires a firm to appear before the court, an appearance by a member of the firm constitutes a sufficient compliance with the order.

Amendments—SI 2001/2792.

9 Application to person carrying on business in another name

An individual carrying on business within the jurisdiction in a name or style other than his own name, may whether or not he is within the jurisdiction be sued in that name or style as if it were the name of a firm, and rules 2 to 8 shall, so far as applicable, apply as if he were a partner and the name in which he carries on business were the name of his firm.

10 Applications for orders charging partner's interest in partnership property, etc

(1) Every application to the court by a judgment creditor of a partner for an order under section 23 of the Partnership Act 1890 (which authorises the High Court or a judge thereof to make certain orders on the application of a judgment creditor of a partner, including an order charging the partner's interest in the partnership property) and every application to the court by a partner of the judgment debtor made in consequence of the first mentioned application must be made in accordance with CPR Part 23.

(2) A master or the Admiralty Registrar or a district judge may exercise the powers conferred on a judge by the said section 23.

(3) Every application notice issued by a judgment creditor under this rule, and every order made on such an application, must be served on the judgment debtor and on such of his partners as are within the jurisdiction or, if the partnership is a cost book company, on the judgment debtor and the purser of the company.

(4) Every application notice issued by a partner of a judgment debtor under this rule, and every order made on such an application, must be served –

- (a) on the judgment creditor; and
- (b) on the judgment debtor; and
- (c) on such of the other partners of the judgment debtor as do not join in the application and are within the jurisdiction or, if the partnership is a cost book company, on the purser of the company.

(5) An application notice or order served in accordance with this rule on the purser of a cost book company or, in the case of a partnership not being such a company, on some only of the partners thereof, shall be deemed to have been served on that company or on all the partners of that partnership, as the case may be.

Amendments—SI 1999/1008.

****

RSC ORDER 85

****

Amendments—The whole Order was revoked by SI 2002/2058 with effect from 2 December 2002. Provisions about administration of estates are now to be found in CPR Pt 64.

RSC ORDER 87

****

Amendments—The whole Order was revoked by SI 2002/2058 with effect from 2 December 2002. Provisions about the court's power to appoint receivers are now to be found in CPR Pt 69.

RSC ORDER 88

****

Amendments—Rules 1–5 and 7 of this Order were revoked by SI 2001/256 with effect from 15 October 2001. Provisions about claims for possession of land are now to be found in CPR Pt 55.

Rule 5A was revoked by SI 2001/2792 with effect from 25 March 2002. Provisions about charging orders are now to be found in CPR Pt 73.

RSC ORDER 91

****

Amendments—The whole Order was revoked by SI 2003/2113 with effect from 6 October 2003.

RSC ORDER 92

****

Amendments—The whole Order was revoked by SI 2002/2058 with effect from 2 December 2002.

RSC ORDER 93
APPLICATIONS AND APPEALS TO HIGH COURT UNDER VARIOUS ACTS: CHANCERY DIVISION

1 Notice of petition under section 55 of the National Debt Act 1870

Where a petition is presented under section 55 of the National Debt Act 1870, the petitioner must, before the petition is heard, apply to a judge of the Chancery Division for directions with respect to giving notice of the claim to which the petition relates, and the judge may direct that notice thereof be given by advertisement or in such other manner as he may direct or may dispense with the giving of such notice.

Amendments—SI 1999/1008.

2 Application under the Public Trustee Act 1906

Without prejudice to sections 10(2) and 13(7) of the Public Trustee Act 1906, the jurisdiction of the High Court under that Act shall be exercised by a judge of the Chancery Division sitting in private.

4 Proceedings under the Trustee Act 1925

All proceedings brought in the High Court under the Trustee Act 1925, shall be assigned to the Chancery Division.

5 Application under section 2(3) of the Public Order Act 1936

(1) Proceedings by which an application is made to the High Court under section 2(3) of the Public Order Act 1936, shall be assigned to the Chancery Division.

(2) Such an application shall be made by claim form and the persons to be made defendants to the claim shall be such persons as the Attorney-General may determine.

(3) In the absence of other sufficient representation the court may appoint the Official Solicitor to represent any interests which in the opinion of the court ought to be represented on any inquiry directed by the court under the said section 2(3).

****

Amendments—Rule 6 was revoked by SI 2002/2058 with effect from 2 December 2002. Provisions about trusts are now to be found in CPR Pt 64.

9 Right of appeal under the Law of Property Act

An appeal shall lie to the High Court against a decision of the Minister of Agriculture, Fisheries and Food under paragraph 16 of Schedule 15 to the Law of Property Act 1922.

10 Determination of appeal or case stated under various Acts

(1) An appeal to the High Court against an order of a county court made under the Land Registration Act 1925, shall be heard and determined by a Divisional Court of the Chancery Division.

(2) (*revoked*)

(3) (*revoked*)

****

16 Proceedings under the Commons Registration Act 1965

(1) Proceedings in the High Court under section 14 or 18 of the Commons Registration Act 1965 shall be assigned to the Chancery Division.

(2) (*revoked*)

(3) (*revoked*)

Amendments—SI 2000/221.

17 Proceedings under section 21 or 25 of the Law of Property Act 1969

Proceedings in the High Court under section 21 or 25 of the Law of Property Act 1969 shall be assigned to the Chancery Division.

18 Proceedings under section 86 of the Civil Aviation Act 1982

(1) Proceedings in the High Court for the amendment of any register of aircraft mortgages kept pursuant to an Order in Council made under section 86 of the Civil Aviation Act 1982 shall be assigned to the Chancery Division.

(2) Such proceedings shall be brought by claim form and every person, other than the claimant, appearing in the register as mortgagee or mortgagor of the aircraft in question shall be made a defendant to the claim.

(3) A copy of the claim form shall also be sent to the Civil Aviation Authority and the Authority shall be entitled to be heard in the proceedings.

19 Proceedings under section 85(7) of the Fair Trading Act 1973 and the Control of Misleading Advertisements Regulations 1988

(1) Proceedings to which this rule applies shall be assigned to the Chancery Division and may be begun by claim form.

(2) This rule applies to any application to the High Court for an order under section 85(7) of the Fair Trading Act 1973, or under any provision to which that section applies or under the Control of Misleading Advertisements Regulations 1988.

****

Amendments—Rule 21 was revoked by SI 2002/2058 with effect from 2 December 2002. Provisions about trusts are now to be found in CPR Pt 64.

22 Proceedings under the Financial Services and Marketing Act 2000]

(1) In this rule 'the Act' means the Financial Services and Marketing Act 2000 and a section referred to by number means the section so numbered in that Act.

(2) Proceedings in the High Court under the Act (other than applications for a mandatory order) and actions for damages for breach of a statutory duty imposed by the Act shall be assigned to the Chancery Division.

(3) Such proceedings and actions shall be begun by claim form except for applications by petition by the Financial Services Authority under section 367.

(4) Where there is a question of the construction of any rule or other instrument made by or with the approval or consent of the Financial Services Authority under the Act, that Authority may make representations to the court.

Amendments—SI 2001/4015; SI 2003/3361.

****

RSC ORDER 94
APPLICATIONS AND APPEALS TO HIGH COURT UNDER VARIOUS ACTS: QUEEN'S BENCH DIVISION

1 Jurisdiction of High Court to quash certain orders, schemes, etc

(1) Where by virtue of any enactment the High Court has jurisdiction, on the application of any person, to quash or prohibit any order, scheme, certificate or plan, any amendment or approval of a plan, any decision of a Minister or government department or any action on the part of a Minister or government department, the jurisdiction shall be exercisable by a single judge of the Queen's Bench Division.

(2) The application must be made by claim form which must state the grounds of the application.

2 Filing and service of claim form

(1) A claim form under rule 1 must be filed at the Crown Office, and served, within the time limited by the relevant enactment for making the application.

(2) Subject to paragraph (4) the claim form must be served on the appropriate Minister or government department, and –

- (a) if the application relates to a compulsory purchase order made by an authority other than the appropriate Minister or government department, or to a clearance order under the Housing Act 1985, on the authority by whom the order was made;
- (b) if the application relates to a scheme or order to which Schedule 2 to the Highways Act 1980, applies made by an authority other than the Secretary of State, on that authority;
- (c) if the application relates to a structure plan, local plan or other development plan within the meaning of the Town and Country Planning Act 1990, on the local planning authority who prepared the plan;
- (d) if the application relates to any decision or order, or any action on the part of a Minister of the Crown to which section 21 of the Land Compensation Act 1961, or section 288 of the Town and Country Planning Act 1990, applies, on the authority directly concerned with such decision, order or action or, if that authority is the applicant, on every person who would, if he were aggrieved by the decision, order or action, be entitled to apply to the High Court under the said section 21 or the said section 245, as the case may be;
- (e) if the application relates to a scheme to which Schedule 32 to the Local Government, Planning and Land Act 1980 applies, on the body which adopted the scheme.

(3) In paragraph (2) 'the appropriate Minister or government department' means the Minister of the Crown or government department by whom the order, scheme, certificate, plan, amendment, approval or decision in question was or may be made, authorised, confirmed, approved or given or on whose part the action in question was or may be taken.

(4) Where the application relates to an order made under the Road Traffic Regulation Act 1984, the claim form must be served –

(a) if the order was made by a Minister of the Crown, on that Minister;
(b) if the order was made by a local authority with the consent, or in pursuance of a direction, of a Minister of the Crown, on that authority and also on that Minister;
(c) in any other case, on the local authority by whom the order was made.

3 Filing of witness statement or affidavits, etc

(1) Evidence at the hearing of an application under rule 1 shall be by witness statement or affidavit.

(2) Any witness statement or affidavit in support of the application must be filed by the applicant in the Crown Office within 14 days after service of the claim form and the applicant must, at the time of filing, serve a copy of the witness statement or affidavit and of any exhibit thereto on the respondent.

(3) Any witness statement or affidavit in opposition to the application must be filed by the respondent in the Crown Office within 21 days after the service on him under paragraph (2) of the applicant's witness statement or affidavit and the respondent must, at the time of filing, serve a copy of his witness statement or affidavit and of any exhibit thereto on the applicant.

(4) When filing a witness statement or affidavit under this rule a party must leave a copy thereof and of any exhibit thereto at the Crown Office for the use of the court.

(5) Unless the court otherwise orders, an application under rule 1 shall not be heard earlier than 14 days after the time for filing a witness statement or affidavit by the respondent has expired.

4 Rectification of register of deeds of arrangement

(1) Every application to the court under section 7 of the Deeds of Arrangement Act 1914, for an order –

(a) that any omission to register a deed of arrangement within the time prescribed by that Act be rectified by extending the time for such registration; or
(b) that any omission or mis-statement of the name, residence or description of any person be rectified by the insertion in the register of his true name, residence or description,

must be made by witness statement or affidavit without notice being served on any other party to a master of the Queen's Bench Division.

(2) The witness statement or affidavit must set out particulars of the deed of arrangement and of the omission or mis-statement in question and must state the grounds on which the application is made.

5 Exercise of jurisdiction under Representation of the People Acts

(1) Proceedings in the High Court under the Representation of the People Acts shall be assigned to the Queen's Bench Division.

(2) Subject to paragraphs (3) and (4) the jurisdiction of the High Court under the said Acts in matters relating to parliamentary and local government elections shall be exercised by a Divisional Court.

(3) Paragraph (2) shall not be construed as taking away from a single judge or a master any jurisdiction under the said Acts which, but for that paragraph, would be exercisable by a single judge or, as the case may be, by a master.

(4) Where the jurisdiction of the High Court under the said Acts is by a provision of any of those Acts made exercisable in matters relating to parliamentary elections by a single judge, that jurisdiction in matters relating to local government elections shall also be exercisable by a single judge.

(5) (*revoked*)

Amendments—SI 1999/1008.

****

8 Tribunals and Inquiries Act 1992: appeal from tribunal

(1) A person who was a party to proceedings before any such tribunal as is mentioned in section 11(1) of the Tribunals and Inquiries Act 1992 and is dissatisfied in point of law with the decision of the tribunal may appeal to the High Court.

(2) The appellant's notice must be served –

- (a) on the chairman of the tribunal;
- (b) in the case of a tribunal which has no chairman or member who acts as a chairman, on the member or members of that tribunal; or
- (c) in the case of any such tribunal as is specified in paragraph 16 of Schedule 1 to the said Act of 1992, on the secretary of the tribunal.

(3) Where an appeal is against the decision of the tribunal constituted under section 46 of the National Health Service Act 1977 the appellant's notice must be filed at the High Court within 14 days after the date of that decision.

(4) Where an appeal is against the decision of a tribunal established under section 1 of the Industrial Tribunals Act 1996 the appellant's notice must be filed at the High Court within 42 days after the date of that decision.

Amendments—Substituted by SI 2000/221.

9 Tribunals and Inquiries Act 1992: case stated by tribunal

(1) Any such tribunal as is mentioned in section 11(1) of the Tribunals and Inquiries Act 1992 may, of its own initiative or at the request of any party to proceedings before it, state in the course of proceedings before it in the form of a special case for the decision of the High Court any question of law arising in the proceedings.

(2) Any party to proceedings before any such tribunal who is aggrieved by the tribunal's refusal to state such a case may apply to the High Court for an order directing the tribunal to do so.

(3) A case stated by any such tribunal which has no chairman or member who acts as a chairman must be signed by the member or members of the tribunal.

****

12 Applications for permission under section 289(6) of the Town and Country Planning Act 1990 and section 65(5) of the Planning (Listed Buildings and Conservation Areas) Act 1990

(1) An application for permission to appeal to the High Court under section 289 of the Town and Country Planning Act 1990 or section 65 of the Planning (Listed Buildings and Conservation Areas) Act 1990 shall be made within 28 days after the date on which notice of the decision was given to the applicant.

(2) An application shall –

- (a) include, where necessary, any application to extend the time for applying;
- (b) be in writing setting out the reasons why permission should be granted, and if the time for applying has expired, the reasons why the application was not made within that time;
- (c) be made by filing it in the Crown Office together with the decision, a draft [appellant's notice, and a witness statement or affidavit verifying any facts relied on;
- (d) before being filed under sub-paragraph (c), be served together with the draft [appellant's notice and a copy of the witness statement or affidavit to be filed with the application, upon the persons who are referred to in rule 13(5); and
- (e) be accompanied by a witness statement or affidavit giving the names and addresses of, and the places and dates of service on, all persons who have been served with the application and, if any person who ought to be served has not been served, the witness statement or affidavit must state that fact and the reason for it.

(3) An application shall be heard –

- (a) by a single judge;
- (b) unless the court otherwise orders, not less than 21 days after it was filed at the Crown Office.

Any person served with the application shall be entitled to appear and be heard.

(4) If on the hearing of an application the court is of opinion that any person who ought to have been served has not been served, the court may adjourn the hearing on such terms (if any) as it may direct in order that the application may be served on that person.

(5) If the court grants permission –

- (a) it may impose such terms as to costs and as to giving security as it thinks fit;
- (b) it may give directions; and
- (c) the [appellant's notice by which the appeal is to be brought shall be served and filed within 7 days of the grant.

(6) Any respondent who intends to use a witness statement or affidavit at the hearing shall file it in the Crown Office and serve a copy thereof on the applicant as soon as is practicable and in any event, unless the court otherwise allows, at least 2 days before the hearing. The court may allow the applicant to use a further witness statement or affidavit.

Amendments—SI 1999/1008; SI 2000/221.

13 Proceedings under sections 289 and 290 of the Town and Country Planning Act 1990 and under section 65 of the Planning (Listed Buildings and Conservation Areas) Act 1990

(1) In this rule a reference to 'section 65' is a reference to section 65 of the Planning (Listed Buildings and Conservation Areas) Act 1990, but, save as aforesaid, a reference to a section by number is a reference to the section so numbered in the Town and Country Planning Act 1990.

(2) An appeal shall lie to the High Court on a point of law against a decision of the Secretary of State under subsection (1) or (2) of section 289 or under subsection (1) of section 65 at the instance of any person or authority entitled to appeal under any of those subsections respectively.

(3) In the case of a decision to which section 290 applies, the person who made the application to which the decision relates, or the local planning authority, if dissatisfied with the decision in point of law, may appeal against the decision to the High Court.

(4) Any appeal under section 289(1) or (2), section 65(1) or section 290, and any case stated under section 289(3) or section 65(2), shall be heard and determined by a single judge unless the court directs that the matter shall be heard and determined by a Divisional Court.

(5) The persons to be served with the [appellant's notice by which an appeal to the High Court is brought by virtue of section 289(1) or (2), section 65(1) or section 290 are –

- (a) the Secretary of State;
- (b) the local planning authority who served the notice or gave the decision, as the case may be, or, where the appeal is brought by that authority, the appellant or applicant in the proceedings in which the decision appealed against was given;
- (c) in the case of an appeal brought by virtue of section 289(1) or section 65(1), any other person having an interest in the land to which the notice relates, and;
- (d) in the case of an appeal brought by virtue of section 289(2), any other person on whom the notice to which those proceedings related was served.

(6) The court hearing any such appeal may remit the matter to the Secretary of State to the extent necessary to enable him to provide the court with such further information in connection with the matter as the court may direct.

(7) Where the court is of opinion that the decision appealed against was erroneous in point of law, it shall not set aside or vary that decision but shall remit the matter to the Secretary of State with the opinion of the court for rehearing and determination by him.

(8) (*revoked*)

(9) The court may give directions as to the exercise, until an appeal brought by virtue of section 289(1) is finally concluded and any re-hearing and determination by the Secretary of State has taken place, of the power to serve, and institute proceedings (including criminal proceedings) concerning –

- (a) a stop notice under section 183; and
- (b) a breach of condition notice under section 187A.

Amendments—SI 2000/221.

14 Applications under section 13 of the Coroners Act 1988

(1) Any application under section 13 of the Coroners Act 1988 shall be heard and determined by a Divisional Court.

(2) The application must be made by claim form and the claim form must state the grounds of the application and, unless the application is made by the Attorney-General, shall be accompanied by his fiat.

(3) The claim form must be filed in the Crown Office and served upon all persons directly affected by the application within 6 weeks after the grant of the fiat.

15 Applications under section 42 of the Supreme Court Act 1981

(1) Every application to the High Court by the Attorney-General under section 42 of the Supreme Court Act 1981 shall be heard and determined by a Divisional Court.

(2) The application must be made by claim form which, together with a witness statement or affidavit in support, shall be filed in the Crown Office and served on the person against whom the order is sought.

16

****

RSC ORDER 95

BILLS OF SALE ACTS 1878 AND 1882 AND THE INDUSTRIAL AND PROVIDENT SOCIETIES ACT 1967

Introduction—There are many different kinds of bill of sale. By far the commonest in practice is a written instrument whereby the vendor of goods, while transferring possession of the goods to the buyer, secures payment (or the fulfilment of some other condition) by retaining title to the goods. The resulting situation, in which the buyer appears to own goods in reality belonging to another, creates an obvious danger for third parties. In order to protect the latter, the legislation requires that any such instrument (1) be in proper form and (2) be registered. Any failure to comply will render such an instrument void, whether wholly or partly. The most important of the relevant statutes are: Bills of Sale Act 1878 ('the 1878 Act') and Bills of Sale Act (1878) Amendment Act 1882 ('the 1882 Act'). *Reference should be made to those Acts and to the practitioners' books for a fuller treatment of this highly technical part of the law.*

1 Rectification of register

(1) Every application to the court under section 14 of the Bills of Sale Act 1878, for an order –

- (a) that any omission to register a bill of sale or a witness statement or affidavit of renewal thereof within the time prescribed by that Act be rectified by extending the time for such registration; or
- (b) that any omission or mis-statement of the name, residence or occupation of any person be rectified by the insertion in the register of his true name, residence or occupation,

must be made by witness statement or affidavit to a master of the Queen's Bench Division, and a copy of the witness statement or affidavit need not be served on any other person.

(2) Every application for such an order as is described in paragraph (1) shall be supported by a witness statement or affidavit setting out particulars of the bill of sale and of the omission or mis-statement in question and stating the grounds on which the application is made.

General note—The masters of the Queen's Bench Division are authorised to deal with matters of registration: 1878 Act, s 13. In practice, the task is allotted to a named master in order to help promote consistency of practice in this field. The overwhelming majority of bills of sale are bills to secure the payment of money, and are governed by the 1882 Act. All other bills, for example those to secure the fulfilment of a condition other than the payment of money, are known as 'absolute bills', and are governed by the 1878 Act. For most purposes, a bill of sale in either category must be properly attested and must be registered within 7 days after being made, or it is deemed void. Bills of sale relating to the same chattels have priority in order of their respective dates of registration. Any registration must be renewed before the expiry of 5 years, whether from registration or from any subsequent renewal, or the bill of sale is deemed void. If an extension of time is needed, the master must be satisfied that the omission to register (or re-register, or otherwise as the case may be) in the permitted time was accidental or due to inadvertence, and may impose terms. If the master does grant an extension of time, he will invariably conclude the endorsement with the formula, 'This Order to be without prejudice to the rights of parties acquired prior to the time when such bill of sale shall be actually registered (or re-registered)', abbreviated to 'UT' ('Usual terms'). Similar considerations apply where rectification is sought. The Filing Department of the Central Office is required by statute to maintain a register of bills of sale, and there are facilities for searching and for obtaining office copies of any registered bill of sale or affidavit on payment of the prescribed fee. If the affidavit of registration indicates that the grantor of the bill of sale is or the goods the subject of it are outside London, the Filing Department is required to provide copies of the bill of sale to the local county court.

Forms—PF179QB to PF182QB.

2 Entry of satisfaction

(1) Every application under section 15 of the Bills of Sale Act 1878, to a master of the Queen's Bench Division for an order that a memorandum of satisfaction be written on a registered copy of a bill of sale must be made by claim form.

(1A) If a consent to the satisfaction signed by the person entitled to the benefit of the bill of sale can be obtained, the claim form and the documents set out in paragraph (2) must not be served on any other person.

(2) Where paragraph (1A) applies, the claim form must be supported by –

- (a) particulars of the consent referred to in that paragraph; and
- (b) a witness statement or affidavit by a witness who attested the consent verifying the signature on it.

(3) Where paragraph (1A) does not apply, the claim form must be served on the person entitled to the benefit of the bill of sale and must be supported by evidence that the debt (if any) for which the bill of sale was made has been satisfied or discharged.

Amendments—SI 1999/1008.

'Every application … must be made by claim form' (r 2(1))—If the consent of the person entitled to the benefit of the bill can be obtained, the application may be made without a claim form, but instead by affidavit or witness statement without notice (PDRSC95).

'If a consent … can be obtained' (r 2(1A))—See note to r 2(1) above.

Forms—PF183QB to PF185QB.

3 Restraining removal on sale of goods seized

An application to the court under the proviso to section 7 of the Bills of Sale Act (1878) Amendment Act 1882 must be made by the issue of a claim form.

'**An application**'—This application is made to the judge.

4 Search of register

Any master of the Queen's Bench Division shall, on a request in writing giving sufficient particulars, and on payment of the prescribed fee, cause a search to be made in the register of bills of sale and issue a certificate of the result of the search.

5 Application under section 1(5) of the Industrial and Provident Societies Act 1967

Every application to the court under section 1(5) of the Industrial and Provident Societies Act 1967 for an order –

(a) that the period for making an application for recording a charge be extended; or

(b) that any omission from or mis-statement in such an application be rectified,

must be made to a master of the Queen's Bench Division by witness statement or affidavit setting out particulars of the charge and of the omission or mis-statement in question and stating the grounds of the application, and need not be served on any other person.

'**Industrial and Provident Societies Act 1967**'—Under the Act, any charge on the assets of a registered society must be registered within 14 days beginning with the date of its execution, or within such extended period as may be allowed by the court. To obtain an extension, the applicant must show inadvertence or other sufficient cause for failing to register within 14 days, or for the omission or misstatement, as the case may be. The applicant may be either the society or any other person claiming the benefit of the charge: see s 1(5). The practice is the same as for bills of sale.

6 Assignment of book debts

(1) There shall continue to be kept in the Central Office, under the supervision of the registrar, a register of assignments of book debts.

(2) Every application for registration of an assignment of a book debt under section 344 of the Insolvency Act 1986 shall be made by producing at the Filing and Record Department of the Central Office –

(a) a true copy of the assignment, and of every schedule thereto; and

(b) a witness statement or affidavit verifying the date and the time, and the due execution of the assignment in the presence of the witness, and setting out the particulars of the assignment and the parties thereto.

(3) On an application being made in accordance with the preceding paragraph, the documents there referred to shall be filed, and the particulars of the assignment, and of the parties to it, shall be entered in the register.

(4) In this rule, 'the registrar' has the meaning given in section 13 of the Bills of Sale Act 1878.

'**Assignments of book debts**'—An assignment of book-debts by a person subsequently adjudicated bankrupt will be void as against the trustee in bankruptcy unless the assignment has been registered as if it were an absolute bill of sale (see above).

Forms—PF186QB.

Practice Direction – Bills of Sale

This Practice Direction supplements RSC Order 95 (Schedule 1 to the CPR) (PDRSC95)

ENTRY OF SATISFACTION

1 Notwithstanding the provisions of RSC Order 95, rule 2(1), (1A) and (2), if a consent to the satisfaction signed by the person entitled to the benefit of the bill of sale can be obtained, the application under RSC Order 95, rule 2(1) can be made by affidavit or witness statement instead of by claim form.

2 If paragraph 1 applies and the application is made by affidavit or witness statement –

1 CPR Part 23 will apply to the application;
2 the affidavit or witness statement will constitute the application notice;
3 the affidavit or witness statement need not be served on any other person; and
4 the application will normally be dealt with without a hearing.

3 Where the consent of the person entitled to the benefit of the bill of sale cannot be obtained, the application under RSC Order 95, rule 2(1) must be made by claim form in accordance with CPR Part 8 and RSC Order 95, rule 2(3) will apply.

RSC ORDER 96
THE MINES (WORKING FACILITIES AND SUPPORT) ACT 1966, ETC

1 Assignment to Chancery Division

Any proceedings in which the jurisdiction conferred on the High Court by section 1 of the Railway and Canal Commission (Abolition) Act 1949 is invoked shall be assigned to the Chancery Division and be begun by claim form which need not be served on any other party.

2 Reference by Secretary of State of certain applications

Where under any provision of the Mines (Working Facilities and Support) Act 1966, the Secretary of State refers any application to the High Court, he shall –

(a) file the reference, signed by him or by an officer authorised by him for the purpose, in Chancery Chambers, together with all documents and plans deposited with him by the applicant; and
(b) within 3 days after doing so give notice to the applicant of the filing of the reference.

3 Issue of claim form

Within 10 days after receipt of the notice mentioned in rule 2(b) the applicant must issue a claim form which need not be served on any other party which must state the application of the applicant under the said Act of 1966 and any other relief sought.

4 Appointment for directions

(1) Within 7 days after issue of the claim form the applicant, having applied at Chancery Chambers for the name of the master assigned to hear the claim, must take an appointment before that master for the hearing of the claim and must forthwith serve notice of the appointment on the Secretary of State.

(2) Not less than 2 clear days before the day appointed for the first hearing of the claim, the applicant must leave at Chancery Chambers –

- (a) a witness statement or affidavit of facts in support of the claim, giving particulars of all persons known to the applicant to be interested in or affected by the application; and
- (b) a draft of any proposed advertisement or notice of the application.

(3) On the appointment the master shall –

- (a) fix a time within which any notice of objection under rule 5 must be given,
- (b) fix a date for the further hearing of the claim; and
- (c) direct what, if any, advertisements and notices of the application and of the date fixed for the further hearing of the claim are to be inserted and given, and what persons, if any, are to be served with a copy of the application and of any other document in the proceedings.

(4) Any such advertisement or notice must include a statement of the effect of rule 5.

5 Objections to application

(1) Any person wishing to oppose the application must, within the time fixed by the master under rule 4(3), serve on the applicant a notice of objection stating –

- (a) his name and address and the name and address of his solicitor, if any;
- (b) the grounds of his objection and any alternative methods of effecting the objects of the application which he alleges may be used; and
- (c) the facts on which he relies.

(2) Any notice required to be served on a person who has given notice of objection (hereafter in this Order referred to as 'the objector') may be served by delivering it or sending it by prepaid post –

- (a) where the name and address of a solicitor is stated in the notice of objection, to the solicitor at that address; and
- (b) in any other case, to the objector at his address stated in the notice of objection.

(3) An objector shall be entitled to appear in person or by a solicitor or counsel at the further hearing of the claim and to take such part in the proceedings as the master or judge thinks fit; but if he does not so appear his notice of objection shall be of no effect and he shall not be entitled to take any part in the proceedings unless the master or judge otherwise orders.

6 List of objectors

Not less than 2 clear days before the day fixed for the further hearing of the claim, the applicant must leave at Chancery Chambers any notices of objection served on the applicant together with a list arranged in 3 columns stating –

(a) in column 1, the names and addresses of the objectors;
(b) in column 2, the names and addresses of their respective solicitors, if any; and
(c) in column 3, short summaries of their respective grounds of objection.

7 Directions on further hearing

At the further hearing of the claim the master shall –

(a) give directions as to the procedure to be followed before the claim is set down for hearing, including, if he thinks fit, a direction –
  (i) that further particulars be given of any of the grounds or facts relied on in support of or in opposition to the application made by the claim;
  (ii) that the applicant may serve a reply to any notice of objection;
  (iii) that any particular fact be proved by witness statement or affidavit;
  (iv) that statements of case or points of claim or defence be served; and
[(b) adjourn the claim for hearing before the judge in such manner as he shall think best adapted to secure the just, expeditious and economical disposal of the proceedings.

Amendments—SI 1999/1008.

8 Other applications

Rules 2 to 7 shall, so far as applicable and with the necessary adaptations, apply in relation to any other application to the High Court falling within rule 1 as they apply in relation to an application under the Mines (Working Facilities and Support) Act 1966.

****

RSC ORDER 98

****

Amendments—The whole Order was revoked by SI 2004/1306, with effect from 30 June 2004.

RSC ORDER 99

****

Amendments—The whole Order was revoked by SI 2002/2058 with effect from 2 December 2002. Provisions about claims under the Inheritance (Provision for Family and Dependants) Act 1975 are now to be found in CPR Pt 57.

****

RSC ORDER 106

****

Amendments—The whole Order was revoked by SI 2004/3419, with effect from 1 April 2005. Provisions about proceedings relating to solicitors are now to be found in CPR Pt 67.

RSC ORDER 108

****

Amendments—The whole Order was revoked by SI 2002/2058 with effect from 2 December 2002. Provisions about charity proceedings are now to be found in CPR Pt 64.

RSC ORDER 109
THE ADMINISTRATION OF JUSTICE ACT 1960

1 Applications under Act

(1) Any of the following applications, that is to say –

- (a) an application under section 2 of the Administration of Justice Act 1960, or under that section as applied by section 13 of that Act, to extend the time within which an application may be made to a Divisional Court for permission to appeal to the House of Lords under section 1 of that Act, or section 13 thereof, from an order or decision of that court, and
- (b) an application by a defendant under section 9(3) of that Act to a Divisional Court for permission to be present on the hearing of any proceedings preliminary or incidental to an appeal to the House of Lords under section 1 of that Act from a decision of that court

must be made to a Divisional Court except in vacation when it may be made to a judge.

(2) Any such application to a Divisional Court, if not made in the proceedings before the Divisional Court from whose order or decision the appeal in question is brought, must be made by the issue of a claim form.

(3) Any such application to a judge must, in the case of such an application as is referred to in paragraph (1)(a) be made by the issue of a claim form and, in the case of such an application as is referred to in paragraph (1)(b) need not be served on any other person unless, in the latter case, the judge otherwise directs.

(4) No application notice or copy of the claim form (as the case may be) by which such an application as is referred to in paragraph (1)(b) is made, need be given to any party affected thereby unless the Divisional Court otherwise directs.

(5) Where any application to which this rule applies is made in vacation to a single judge and the judge refuses the application, the applicant shall be entitled to have the application determined by a Divisional Court.

Amendments—SI 1999/1008.

2 Appeals under section 13 of Act

(1) An appeal to a Divisional Court of the High Court under section 13 of the Administration of Justice Act 1960, shall be heard and determined by a Divisional Court of the Queen's Bench Division.

(3) (*revoked*)

(4) Unless the court gives permission, there shall be not more than 4 clear days between the date on which the order or decision appealed against was made and the day named in the notice of appeal for the hearing of the appeal.

(5) The notice must be served, and the appeal entered, not less than one clear day before the day named in the notice for the hearing of the appeal.

Amendments—SI 2000/221.

3 Release of appellant on bail

(1) Where, in the case of an appeal under section 13 of the Administration of Justice Act 1960, to a Divisional Court or to the House of Lords from a Divisional Court, the appellant is in custody, the High Court may order his release on his giving security (whether by recognizance, with or without sureties, or otherwise and for such reasonable sum as the court may fix) for his appearance, within 10 days after the judgment of the Divisional Court or, as the case may be, of the House of Lords, on the appeal before the court from whose order or decision the appeal is brought unless the order or decision is reversed by that judgment.

(2) Order 79, rule 9(1) to (6) and (8) shall apply in relation to an application to the High Court for bail pending an appeal under the said section 13 to which this rule applies, and to the admission of a person to bail in pursuance of an order made on the application, as they apply in relation to an application to that court for bail in criminal proceedings, and to the admission of a person to bail in pursuance of an order made on the application, but with the substitution, for references to the defendant, of references to the appellant, and, for references to the prosecutor, of references to the court officer of the court from whose order or decision the appeal is brought and to the parties to the proceedings in that court who are directly affected by the appeal.

4 Release of appellant on bail by the Court of Appeal

(1) Where, in the case of an appeal under section 13 of the Administration of Justice Act 1960 to the Court of Appeal or to the House of Lords from the Court of Appeal, the appellant is in custody, the Court of Appeal may order his release on his giving security (whether by recognisance, with or without sureties, or otherwise and for such reasonable sum as that court may fix) for his appearance within 10 days after the judgment of the Court of Appeal or, as the case may be, of the House of Lords on the appeal shall have been given, before the court from whose order or decision the appeal is brought unless the order or decision is reversed by that judgment.

(2) An application for the release of a person under paragraph (1) pending an appeal to the Court of Appeal or House of Lords under the said section 13 must be made in accordance with CPR Part 23, and the application notice must, at least 24 hours before the day named therein for the hearing, be served on the

court from whose order or decision the appeal is brought and on all parties to the proceedings in that court who are directly affected by the appeal.

(3) Order 79, rules 9(6), (6A), (6B) and (8) shall apply in relation to the grant of bail under this rule by the Court of Appeal in a case of criminal contempt of court as they apply in relation to the grant of bail in criminal proceedings by the High Court, but with the substitution for references to a judge of references to the Court of Appeal and for references to the defendant of references to the appellant.

(4) When granting bail under this rule in a case of civil contempt of court, the Court of Appeal may order that the recognisance or other security to be given by the appellant or the recognisance of any surety shall be given before any person authorised by virtue of section 119(1) of the Magistrates' Courts Act 1980 to take a recognisance where a magistrates' court having power to take it has, instead of taking it, fixed the amount in which the principal and his sureties, if any, are to be bound. An order by the Court of Appeal granting bail as aforesaid must be in Form 98 in the relevant practice direction with the necessary adaptations.

(5) Where in pursuance of an order of the Court of Appeal under paragraph (4) of this rule a recognisance is entered into or other security given before any person, it shall be the duty of that person to cause the recognisance of the appellant or any surety or, as the case may be, a statement of the other security given, to be transmitted forthwith to the justices' chief executive for the court which committed the appellant; and a copy of such recognisance or statement shall at the same time be sent to the governor or keeper of the prison or other place of detention in which the appellant is detained, unless the recognisance or security was given before such governor or keeper.

(6) The powers conferred on the Court of Appeal by paragraphs (1), (3) and (4) of this rule may be exercised by a single judge.

Amendments—Inserted by SI 2000/221; amended by SI 2001/256.

RSC ORDER 110
ENVIRONMENTAL CONTROL PROCEEDINGS

1 Injunctions to prevent environmental harm

(1) An injunction under –

(a) section 187B or 214A of the Town and Country Planning Act 1990;
(b) section 44A of the Planning (Listed Buildings and Conservation Areas) Act 1990; or
(c) section 26AA of the Planning (Hazardous Substances) Act 1990

may be granted against a person whose identity is unknown to the applicant; and in the following provisions of this rule such an injunction against such a person is referred to as 'an injunction under paragraph (1)' and the person against whom it is sought is referred to as 'the defendant'.

(2) An applicant for an injunction under paragraph (1) shall, in the claim form, describe the defendant by reference to –

(a) a photograph,
(b) a thing belonging to or in the possession of the defendant, or

(c) any other evidence,

with sufficient particularity to enable service to be effected.

(3) An applicant for an injunction under paragraph (1) shall file in support of the application evidence by witness statement or affidavit –

(a) verifying that he was unable to ascertain, within the time reasonably available to him, the defendant's identity,
(b) setting out the action taken to ascertain the defendant's identity, and
(c) verifying the means by which the defendant has been described in the application and that the description is the best that the applicant is able to provide.

(4) Paragraph (2) is without prejudice to the power of the court to make an order for service by an alternative method or dispensing with service.

Amendments—SI 1999/1008.

****

RSC ORDER 112
APPLICATIONS FOR USE OF SCIENTIFIC TESTS IN DETERMINING PARENTAGE

1 Interpretation

In this Order –

'the Act' means Part III of the Family Law Reform Act 1969;

'Bodily samples' and 'scientific tests' have the meanings assigned to them by section 25 of the Act;

'direction' means a direction for the use of scientific tests under section 20(1) of the Act;

'the court officer' means the officer of the court who draws up a direction.

Amendments—SI 2001/256.

2 Application for direction

(1) Except with the permission of the court, an application in any proceedings for a direction shall be in accordance with CPR Part 23 and a copy of the application notice shall be served on every party to the proceedings (other than the applicant) and to any other person from whom the direction involves the taking of bodily samples.

(3) Any notice required by this rule to be served on a person who is not a party to the proceedings shall be served on him personally.

Amendments—SI 2001/256.

3 Applications involving children under 16 and patients

Where an application is made for a direction in respect of a person who is either –

(a) under 16; or

(b) suffering from a mental disorder within the meaning of the Mental Health Act 1983 and incapable of understanding the nature and purpose of scientific tests,

the application notice shall state the name and address of the person having the care and control of the person under disability and shall be served on him instead of on the person under disability.

Amendments—SI 1999/1008; SI 2001/256.

4 Addition as a party of person to be tested

Where an application is made for a direction involving the taking of bodily samples from a person who is not a party to the proceedings in which the application is made, the court may at any time direct that person to be made a party to the proceedings.

Amendments—SI 2001/256.

5 Service of direction and adjournment of proceedings

Where the court gives a direction in any proceedings, the court officer shall send a copy to every party to the proceedings and to every other person from whom the direction involves the taking of bodily samples and, unless otherwise ordered, further consideration of the proceedings shall be adjourned until the court receives a report pursuant to the direction.

Amendments—SI 2001/256.

6 Service of copy report

On receipt by the court of a report made pursuant to a direction, the proper officer shall send a copy to every party to the proceedings and to every other person from whom the direction involved the taking of bodily samples.

Amendments—SI 2001/256.

RSC ORDER 113
SUMMARY PROCEEDINGS FOR POSSESSION OF LAND

****

7 Writ of possession

(1) Order 45, rule 3(2) shall not apply in relation to an order for possession [in a possession claim against trespassers under Part 55 but no writ of possession to enforce such an order shall be issued after the expiry of 3 months from the date of the order without the permission of the court.

An application for permission may be made without notice being served on any other party unless the court otherwise directs.

(2) The writ of possession shall be in Form No 66A.

Amendments—SI 2001/256.

'permission of the court' (r 7(1))—A witness statement or affidavit should be filed explaining the reason for the delay.

'writ of possession' (r 7(2))—In the case of land a proper plan should always be attached.

Re-entry by respondents—A writ of restitution may be issued with the permission of the court under Ord 46, r 3 where the original respondent has re-entered the claimant's property after eviction. Re-entry may sometimes be made by one or some only of those who were originally in occupation accompanied by others. The claimant may then proceed by way of restitution rather than fresh proceedings if there is a clear and sufficient connection between the original recovery of possession and the need to effect recovery again of the same land (*Wiltshire County Council v Frazer* [1986] 1 All ER 65). This is one good reason for a proper plan to be supplied by the claimant to be attached to any order for possession of land as opposed to residential premises. No specific time-limit is prescribed. In practice if the re-entry occurs within 6 months of the original eviction the claimant may be allowed to issue a writ of restitution instead of issuing fresh proceedings. The procedure is set out in Ord 46, r 4.

****

RSC ORDER 114

****

Amendments—The whole Order was revoked by SI 2002/2058 with effect from 2 December 2002. Provisions about references to the European Court are now to be found in CPR Pt 68.

RSC ORDER 115
CONFISCATION AND FORFEITURE IN CONNECTION WITH CRIMINAL PROCEEDINGS

I Drug Trafficking Act 1994 and Criminal Justice (International Co-operation) Act 1990

1 Interpretation

(1) In this Part of this Order, 'The Act' means the Drug Trafficking Act 1994 and a section referred to by number means the section so numbered in the Act.

(2) Expressions used in this Part of this Order which are used in the Act have the same meanings in this Part of this Order as in the Act and include any extended meaning given by the Criminal Justice (Confiscation) (Northern Ireland) Order 1990.

2 Assignment of proceedings

Subject to rule 12, the jurisdiction of the High Court under the Act shall be exercised by a judge of the Chancery Division or of the Queen's Bench Division.

2A Title of proceedings

An application made in accordance with CPR Part 23, or a claim form issued in relation to proceedings under this Part of this Order shall be entitled in the matter of the defendant, naming him, and in the matter of the Act, and all subsequent documents in the matter shall be so entitled.

2B Application for confiscation order

(1) An application by the prosecutor for a confiscation order under section 19 shall be made in accordance with CPR Part 23 where there have been proceedings against the defendant in the High Court, and shall otherwise be made by the issue of a claim form.

(2) The application shall be supported by a witness statement or affidavit giving full particulars of the following matters –

(a) the grounds for believing that the defendant has died or absconded;
(b) the date or approximate date on which the defendant died or absconded;
(c) where the application is made under section 19(2), the offence or offences of which the defendant was convicted, and the date and place of conviction;
(d) where the application is made under section 19(4), the proceedings which have been initiated against the defendant (including particulars of the offence and the date and place of institution of those proceedings); and
(e) where the defendant is alleged to have absconded, the steps taken to contact him.

(3) The prosecutor's statement under section 11 shall be exhibited to the witness statement or affidavit and shall include the following particulars –

(a) the name of the defendant;
(b) the name of the person by whom the statement is given;
(c) such information known to the prosecutor as is relevant to the determination whether the defendant has benefited from drug trafficking and to the assessment of the value of his proceeds of drug trafficking.

(4) Unless the court otherwise orders, a witness statement or affidavit under paragraph (2) may contain statements of information and belief, with their sources and grounds.

(5) The application and the witness statement or affidavit in support shall be served not less than 7 days before the date fixed for the hearing of the application on –

(a) the defendant (or on the personal representatives of a deceased defendant);
(b) any person who the prosecutor reasonably believes is likely to be affected by the making of a confiscation order; and
(c) the receiver, where one has been appointed in the matter.

3 Application for restraint order or charging order

(1) An application for a restraint order under section 26 or for a charging order under section 27 (to either of which may be joined an application for the appointment of a receiver) may be made by the prosecutor by the issue of a claim form notice of which need not be served on any other party.

(2) An application under paragraph (1) shall be supported by a witness statement or affidavit, which shall –

(a) give the grounds for the application; and

(b) to the best of the witness's ability, give full particulars of the realisable property in respect of which the order is sought and specify the person or persons holding such property.

(3) Unless the court otherwise directs, a witness statement or affidavit under paragraph (2) may contain statements of information or belief with the sources and grounds thereof.

4 Restraint order and charging order

(1) A restraint order may be made subject to conditions and exceptions, including but not limited to conditions relating to the indemnifying of third parties against expenses incurred in complying with the order, and exceptions relating to living expenses and legal expenses of the defendant, but the prosecutor shall not be required to give an undertaking to abide by any order as to damages sustained by the defendant as a result of the restraint order.

(2) Unless the court otherwise directs, a restraint order made where notice of it has not been served on any person shall have effect until a day which shall be fixed for the hearing where all parties may attend on the application and a charging order shall be an order to show cause, imposing the charge until such day.

(3) Where a restraint order is made the prosecutor shall serve copies of the order and of the witness statement or affidavit in support on the defendant and on all other named persons restrained by the order and shall notify all other persons or bodies affected by the order of its terms.

(4) Where a charging order is made the prosecutor shall serve copies of the order and of the witness statement or affidavit in support on the defendant and, where the property to which the order relates is held by another person, on that person and shall serve a copy of the order on such of the persons or bodies specified in CPR rule 73.5(1)(c) to (e) as shall be appropriate.

Amendments—SI 2001/2792.

5 Discharge or variation of order

(1) Any person or body on whom a restraint order or a charging order is served or who is notified of such an order may make an application in accordance with CPR Part 23 to discharge or vary the order.

(2) The application notice and any witness statement or affidavit in support shall be lodged with the court and served on the prosecutor and, where he is not the applicant, on the defendant, not less than 2 clear days before the date fixed for the hearing of the application.

(3) Upon the court being notified that proceedings for the offences have been concluded or that the amount, payment of which is secured by a charging order has been paid into court, any restraint order or charging order, as the case may be, shall be discharged.

(4) The court may also discharge a restraint order or a charging order upon receiving notice from the prosecutor that it is no longer appropriate for the restraint order or the charging order to remain in place.

Amendments—SI 1999/1008.

6 Further application by prosecutor

(1) Where a restraint order or a charging order has been made the prosecutor may apply by an application in accordance with CPR Part 23 with notice or, where the case is one of urgency or the giving of notice would cause a reasonable apprehension of dissipation of assets, without notice –

- (a) to vary such order; or
- (b) for a restraint order or a charging order in respect of other realisable property; or
- (c) for the appointment of a receiver.

(2) An application under paragraph (1) shall be supported by a witness statement or affidavit which, where the application is for a restraint order or a charging order, shall to the best of the witness's ability give full particulars of the realisable property in respect of which the order is sought and specify the person or persons holding such property.

(3) The application and witness statement or affidavit in support shall be lodged with the court and served on the defendant and, where one has been appointed in the matter, on the receiver, not less than 2 clear days before the date fixed for the hearing of the application.

(4) Rule 4(3) and (4) shall apply to the service of restraint orders and charging orders respectively made under this rule on persons other than the defendant.

Amendments—SI 1999/1008.

7 Realisation of property

(1) An application by the prosecutor under section 29 shall, where there have been proceedings against the defendant in the High Court, be made by an application in accordance with CPR Part 23 and shall otherwise be made by the issue of a claim form.

(2) The application notice or claim form, as the case may be, shall be served with the evidence in support not less than 7 days before the date fixed for the hearing of the application or claim on –

- (a) the defendant;
- (b) any person holding any interest in the realisable property to which the application relates; and
- (c) the receiver, where one has been appointed in the matter.

(3) The application shall be supported by a witness statement or affidavit, which shall, to the best of the witness's ability, give full particulars of the realisable property to which it relates and specify the person or persons holding such property, and a copy of the confiscation order, of any certificate issued by the Crown Court under section 5(2) and of any charging order made in the matter shall be exhibited to such witness statement or affidavit.

(4) The court may, on an application under section 29 –

- (a) exercise the power conferred by section 30(2) to direct the making of payments by a receiver;
- (b) give directions in respect of the property interests to which the application relates; and
- (c) make declarations in respect of those interests.

8 Receivers

(1) Subject to the provisions of this rule, the provisions of CPR Part 69 shall apply where a receiver is appointed in pursuance of a charging order or under sections 26 or 29.

(2) Where the receiver proposed to be appointed has been appointed receiver in other proceedings under the Act, it shall not be necessary for a witness statement or affidavit of fitness to be sworn or for the receiver to give security, unless the court otherwise orders.

(3) Where a receiver has fully paid the amount payable under the confiscation order and any sums remain in his hands, he shall make an application to the court for directions in accordance with CPR Part 23, as to the distribution of such sums.

(4) An application under paragraph (3) shall be served with any evidence in support not less than 7 days before the date fixed for the hearing of the application on –

(a) the defendant; and

(b) any other person who held property realised by the receiver.

(5) A receiver may apply for an order to discharge him from his office by making an application in accordance with CPR Part 23, which shall be served, together with any evidence in support, on all persons affected by his appointment not less than 7 days before the day fixed for the hearing of the application.

Amendments—SI 2002/2058.

9 Certificate of inadequacy

(1) The defendant or a receiver appointed under section 26 or 29 or in pursuance of a charging order may apply in accordance with CPR Part 23 for a certificate under section 17(1).

(2) An application under paragraph (1) shall be served with any supporting evidence not less than 7 days before the date fixed for the hearing of the application on the prosecutor and, as the case may be, on either the defendant or the receiver (where one has been appointed).

9A Certificate under section 16

An application under section 16(2) (increase in realisable property) shall be served with any supporting evidence not less than 7 days before the date fixed for the hearing of the application on the defendant and, as the case may be, on either the prosecutor or (where one has been appointed in the matter) on the receiver.

10 Compensation

An application for an order under section 18 shall be made in accordance with CPR Part 23, which shall be served, with any supporting evidence, on the person alleged to be in default and on the relevant authority under section 18(5) not less than 7 days before the date fixed for the hearing of the application.

11 Disclosure of information

(1) An application by the prosecutor under section 59 shall be made in accordance with CPR Part 23 and the application notice shall state the nature of the order sought and whether material sought to be disclosed is to be disclosed to a receiver appointed under section 26 or 29 or in pursuance of a charging order or to a person mentioned in section 59(8).

(2) The application notice and witness statement or affidavit in support shall be served on the authorised Government Department in accordance with Order 77, rule 4 not less than 7 days before the date fixed for the hearing of the application.

(3) The witness statement or affidavit in support of an application under paragraph (1) shall state the grounds for believing that the conditions in section 59(4) and, if appropriate, section 59(7) are fulfilled.

11A Compensation for, discharge and variation of confiscation order

(1) An application under section 21, 22 or 23 shall be made in accordance with CPR Part 23 which, together with any evidence in support, shall be lodged with the court and served on the prosecutor not less than 7 days before the day fixed for the hearing of the application.

(2) Notice shall also be served on any receiver appointed in pursuance of a charging order or under section 26 or 29.

(3) An application for an order under section 22 shall be supported by a witness statement or affidavit giving details of –

(a) the confiscation order made under section 19(4);
(b) the acquittal of the defendant;
(c) the realisable property held by the defendant; and
(d) the loss suffered by the applicant as a result of the confiscation order.

(4) An application for an order under section 23 shall be supported by a witness statement or affidavit giving details of –

(a) the confiscation order made under section 19(4);
(b) the date on which the defendant ceased to be an absconder;
(c) the date on which proceedings against the defendant were instituted and a summary of the steps taken in the proceedings since then; and
(d) any indication given by the prosecutor that he does not intend to proceed against the defendant.

(5) An application made under section 21 shall be supported by a witness statement or affidavit giving details of –

(a) the confiscation order made under section 19(4);
(b) the circumstances in which the defendant ceased to be an absconder; and
(c) the amounts referred to in section 21(2).

(6) Where an application is made for an order under section 23(3) or 24(2)(b), the witness statement or affidavit shall also include –

(a) details of the realisable property to which the application relates; and
(b) details of the loss suffered by the applicant as a result of the confiscation order.

(7) Unless the court otherwise orders, a witness statement or affidavit under paragraphs (3) to (6) may contain statements of information and belief, with the sources and grounds thereof.

12 Exercise of powers under sections 37 and 40

The powers conferred on the High Court by sections 37 and 40 may be exercised by a judge or a master of the Queen's Bench Division.

13 Application for registration

An application for registration of an order specified in an Order in Council made under section 37 or of an external confiscation order under section 40(1) must be made in accordance with CPR Part 23, and may be made without notice.

14 Evidence in support of application under section 37

An application for registration of an order specified in an Order in Council made under section 37 must be made in accordance with CPR Part 23, and be supported by a witness statement or affidavit –

(i) exhibiting the order or a certified copy thereof; and

(ii) stating, to the best of the witness's knowledge, particulars of what property the person against whom the order was made holds in England and Wales, giving the source of the witness's knowledge.

15 Evidence in support of application under section 40(1)

(1) An application for registration of an external confiscation order must be made in accordance with CPR Part 23, and be supported by a witness statement or affidavit –

(a) exhibiting the order or a verified or certified or otherwise duly authenticated copy thereof and, where the order is not in the English language, a translation thereof into English certified by a notary public or authenticated by witness statement or affidavit; and

(b) stating –

(i) that the order is in force and is not subject to appeal;

(ii) where the person against whom the order was made did not appear in the proceedings, that he received notice thereof in sufficient time to enable him to defend them;

(iii) in the case of money, either that at the date of the application the sum payable under the order has not been paid or the amount which remains unpaid, as may be appropriate, or, in the case of other property, the property which has not been recovered; and

(iv) to the best of the witness's knowledge, particulars of what property the person against whom the order was made holds in England and Wales, giving the source of the witness's knowledge.

(2) Unless the court otherwise directs, a witness statement or affidavit for the purposes of this rule may contain statements of information or belief with the sources and grounds thereof.

16 Register of orders

(1) There shall be kept in the Central Office under the direction of the Master of the Crown Office a register of the orders registered under the Act.

(2) There shall be included in such register particulars of any variation or setting aside of a registration and of any execution issued on a registered order.

17 Notice of registration

(1) Notice of the registration of an order must be served on the person against whom it was obtained by delivering it to him personally or by sending it to him at his usual or last known address or place of business or in such other manner as the court may direct.

(2) Permission is not required to serve such a notice out of the jurisdiction and CPR rules 6.24, 6.25 and 6.29 shall apply in relation to such notice as they apply in relation to a claim form.

Amendments—SI 2000/221.

18 Application to vary or set aside registration

An application made in accordance with CPR Part 23 by the person against whom an order was made to vary or set aside the registration of an order must be made to a judge and be supported by witness statement or affidavit.

19 Enforcement of order

(2) If an application is made under rule 18, an order shall not be enforced until after such application is determined.

20 Variation, satisfaction and discharge of registered order

Upon the court being notified by the applicant for registration that an order which has been registered has been varied, satisfied or discharged, particulars of the variation, satisfaction or discharge, as the case may be, shall be entered in the register.

21 Rules to have effect subject to Orders in Council

Rules 12 to 20 shall have effect subject to the provisions of the Order in Council made under section 37 or, as the case may be, of the Order in Council made under section 39.

21A Criminal Justice (International Co-operation) Act 1990: external forfeiture orders

The provisions of this Part of this Order shall, with such modifications as are necessary and subject to the provisions of any Order in Council made under section 9 of the Criminal Justice (International Co-operation) Act 1990, apply to proceedings for the registration and enforcement of external forfeiture orders as they apply to such proceedings in relation to external confiscation orders.

For the purposes of this rule, an external forfeiture order is an order made by a court in a country or territory outside the United Kingdom which is enforceable in the United Kingdom by virtue of any such Order in Council.

II Part VI of the Criminal Justice Act 1988

22 Interpretation

(1) In this Part of this Order, 'the 1988 Act' means the Criminal Justice Act 1988 and a section referred to by number means the section so numbered in that Act.

(2) Expressions which are used in this Part of this Order which are used in the Act have the same meanings in this Part of this Order as in the Act and include any extended meaning given by the Criminal Justice (Confiscation) (Northern Ireland) Order 1990.

23 Application of Part I of Order 115

Part I of Order 115 (except rule 11) shall apply for the purposes of proceedings under Part VI of the Act with the necessary modifications and, in particular –

(a) references to drug trafficking offences and to drug trafficking shall be construed as references to offences to which Part VI of the Act applies and to committing such an offence;

(b) references to the Drug Trafficking Act 1994 shall be construed as references to the Act and references to sections 5(2), 26, 27, 29, 30(2), 17(1), 18, 18(5), 39 and 40 of the 1994 Act shall be construed as references to sections 73(6), 77, 78, 80, 81, 81(1), 83(1), 89, 89(5), 96 and 97 of the Act respectively;

(c) rule 3(2) shall have effect as if the following sub-paragraphs were substituted for sub-paragraphs (a) and (b) –

'(a) state, as the case may be, either that proceedings have been instituted against the defendant for an offence to which Part VI of the Act applies (giving particulars of the offence) and that they have not been concluded or that, whether by the laying of an information or otherwise, a person is to be charged with such an offence;

(b) state, as the case may be, either that a confiscation order has been made or the grounds for believing that such an order may be made;'

(d) rule 7(3) shall have effect as if the words 'certificate issued by a magistrates' court or the Crown Court' were substituted for the words 'certificate issued by the Crown Court';

(e) rule 8 shall have effect as if the following paragraph were added at the end –

'(6) Where a receiver applies in accordance with CPR Part 23 for the variation of a confiscation order, the application notice shall be served, with any supporting evidence, on the defendant and any other person who may be affected by the making of an order under section 83 of the Act, not less than 7 days before the date fixed for the hearing of the application.';

(f) rule 11 shall apply with the necessary modifications where an application is made under section 93J of the Act for disclosure of information held by government departments.

III Terrorism Act 2000

24 Interpretation

In this Part of this Order –

(a) 'the Act' means the Terrorism Act 2000;
(b) 'Schedule 4' means Schedule 4 to the Act;
(ba) 'the prosecutor' means the person with conduct of proceedings which have been instituted in England and Wales for an offence under any of sections 15 to 18 of the Act, or the person who the High Court is satisfied will have the conduct of any proceedings for such an offence; and
(c) other expressions used have the same meanings as they have in Schedule 4 to the Act.

Amendments—SI 2001/1388; SI 2001/4016.

25 Assignment of proceedings

(1) Subject to paragraph (2), the jurisdiction of the High Court under the Act shall be exercised by a judge of the Queen's Bench Division or of the Chancery Division.

(2) The jurisdiction conferred on the High Court by paragraph 9 of Schedule 4 may also be exercised by a master of the Queen's Bench Division.

Amendments—SI 1999/1008.

26 Application for restraint order

(1) An application for a restraint order under paragraph 5 of Schedule 4 may be made by the prosecutor by a claim form, which need not be served on any person.

(2) An application under paragraph (1) shall be supported by a witness statement or affidavit, which shall –

(a) state, as the case may be, either –
  (i) that proceedings have been instituted against a person for an offence under any of sections 15 to 18 of the Act and that they have not been concluded; or
  (ii) that a criminal investigation has been started in England and Wales with regard to such an offence,

and in either case give details of the alleged or suspected offence and of the defendant's involvement;
(b) where proceedings have been instituted state, as the case may be, that a forfeiture order has been made in the proceedings or the grounds for believing that such an order may be made;
(ba) where proceedings have not been instituted –
  (i) indicate the state of progress of the investigation and when it is anticipated that a decision will be taken on whether to institute proceedings against the defendant;

(ii) state the grounds for believing that a forfeiture order may be made in any proceedings against the defendant; and

(iii) verify that the prosecutor is to have the conduct of any such proceedings;

(c) to the best of the witness's ability, give full particulars of the property in respect of which the order is sought and specify the person or persons holding such property and any other persons having an interest in it;

(d), (e) (*revoked*)

(3) A claim form under paragraph (1) shall be entitled in the matter of the defendant, naming him, and in the matter of the Act, and all subsequent documents in the matter shall be so entitled.

(4) Unless the court otherwise directs, a witness statement or affidavit under paragraph (2) may contain statements of information or belief with the sources and grounds thereof.

Amendments—SI 2001/1388; SI 2001/4016.

27 Restraint order

(1) A restraint order may be made subject to conditions and exceptions, including but not limited to conditions relating to the indemnifying of third parties against expenses incurred in complying with the order, and exceptions relating to living expenses and legal expenses of the defendant, but the prosecutor shall not be required to give an undertaking to abide by any order as to damages sustained by the defendant as a result of the restraint order.

(2) Unless the court otherwise directs, a restraint order made without notice of the application for it being served on any person shall have effect until a day which shall be fixed for the hearing where all parties may attend on the application.

(3) Where a restraint order is made the prosecutor shall serve copies of the order and unless the court otherwise orders of the witness statement or affidavit in support on the defendant and on all other persons affected by the order.

Amendments—SI 2001/1388; SI 2001/4016.

28 Discharge or variation of order

(1) Subject to paragraph (2), an application to discharge or vary a restraint order shall be made in accordance with CPR Part 23.

(2) Where the case is one of urgency, an application under this rule by the prosecutor may be made without notice.

(3) The application and any witness statement or affidavit in support shall be lodged with the court and, where the application is made in accordance with CPR Part 23 the application notice shall be served on the following persons (other than the applicant) –

(a) the prosecutor;

(b) the defendant; and

(c) all other persons restrained or otherwise affected by the order;

not less than 2 clear days before the date fixed for the hearing of the application.

(4) Where a restraint order has been made and has not been discharged, the prosecutor shall notify the court when proceedings for the offence have been concluded, and the court shall thereupon discharge the restraint order.

(5) Where an order is made discharging or varying a restraint order, the applicant shall serve copies of the order of discharge or variation on all persons restrained by the earlier order and shall notify all other persons affected of the terms of the order of discharge or variation.

29 Compensation

An application for an order under paragraph 9 or 10 of Schedule 4 shall be made in accordance with CPR Part 23, and the application notice, shall be served, with any supporting evidence, on the person alleged to be in default and on the person or body by whom compensation, if ordered, will be payable under paragraph 9(6) or 10(4) not less than 7 days before the date fixed for the hearing of the application.

Amendments—SI 2001/1388.

30 Application for registration

An application for registration of a Scottish order, a Northern Ireland order or an Islands order must be made in accordance with CPR Part 23 and may be made without notice.

31 Evidence in support of application

(1) An application for registration of any such order as is mentioned in rule 30 must be supported by a witness statement or affidavit –

(a) exhibiting the order or a certified copy thereof; and
(b) which shall, to the best of the witness's ability, give particulars of such property in respect of which the order was made as is in England and Wales, and specify the person or persons holding such property.

(2) Unless the court otherwise directs, a witness statement or affidavit for the purposes of this rule may contain statements of information or belief with the sources and grounds thereof.

32 Register of orders

(1) There shall be kept in the Central Office under the direction of the Master of the Administrative Court a register of the orders registered under the Act.

(2) There shall be included in such register particulars of any variation or setting aside of a registration, and of any execution issued on a registered order.

Amendments—SI 2001/1388.

33 Notice of registration

(1) Notice of the registration of an order must be served on the person or persons holding the property referred to in rule 31(1)(b) and any other persons appearing to have an interest in that property.

(2) Permission is not required to serve such a notice out of the jurisdiction and CPR rules 6.24, 6.25 and 6.29 shall apply in relation to such notice as they apply in relation to a claim form.

Amendments—SI 2000/221.

34 Application to vary or set aside registration

An application to vary or set aside the registration of an order must be made to a judge in accordance with CPR Part 23 and be supported by a witness statement or affidavit.

This rule does not apply to a variation or cancellation under rule 36.

35 Enforcement of order

(2) If an application is made under rule 34, an order shall not be enforced until after such application is determined.

(3) This rule does not apply to the taking of steps under paragraph 7 or 8 of Schedule 4, as applied by paragraph 13(6) of that Schedule.

Amendments—SI 2001/1388.

36 Variation and cancellation of registration

If effect has been given (whether in England or Wales or elsewhere) to a Scottish, Northern Ireland or Islands order, or if the order has been varied or discharged by the court by which it was made, the applicant for registration shall inform the court and –

(a) if such effect has been given in respect of all the money or other property to which the order applies, or if the order has been discharged by the court by which it was made, registration of the order shall be cancelled;

(b) if such effect has been given in respect of only part of the money or other property, or if the order has been varied by the court by which it was made, registration of the order shall be varied accordingly.

IV International Criminal Court Act 2001: Fines, Forfeitures and Reparation Orders

37 Interpretation

In this Part of this Order –

(a) 'the Act' means the International Criminal Court Act 2001;

(b) 'the ICC' means the International Criminal Court;

(c) 'an order of the ICC' means –

  (i) a fine or forfeiture ordered by the ICC; or

  (ii) an order by the ICC against a person convicted by the ICC specifying a reparation to, or in respect of, a victim.

Amendments—Inserted by SI 2003/2113.

38 Registration of ICC orders for enforcement

(1) An application to the High Court to register an order of the ICC for enforcement, or to vary or set aside the registration of an order, may be made to a judge or a Master of the Queen's Bench Division.

(2) Rule 13 and rules 15 to 20 in Part I of this Order shall, with such modifications as are necessary and subject to the provisions of any regulations made under section 49 of the Act, apply to the registration for enforcement of an order of the ICC as they apply to the registration of an external confiscation order.

Amendments—Inserted by SI 2003/2113.

Practice Direction – Restraint Orders and Appointment of Receivers in Connection with Criminal Proceedings and Investigations

This Practice Direction supplements RSC Order 115 (Schedule 1 to the CPR) (PDRSC115)

Scope and interpretation

1.1 This practice direction applies to applications to the High Court for a restraint order or the appointment of a receiver under –

(1) Part VI of the Criminal Justice Act 1988 ('the 1988 Act');
(2) Part I of the Drug Trafficking Act 1994 ('the 1994 Act'); or
(3) Schedule 4 to the Terrorism Act 2000 ('the 2000 Act').

(Part VI of the 1988 Act and Part I of the 1994 Act are repealed by the Proceeds of Crime Act 2002 from a day to be appointed, but will continue to apply to pending and transitional cases. Following their repeal, applications for a restraint order or the appointment of a receiver which would previously have been made under those Acts will instead be made to the Crown Court under Part 2 of the 2002 Act)

1.2 In this practice direction –

(1) 'the prosecutor' means the person applying for a restraint order or the appointment of a receiver; and
(2) 'the defendant' means the person against whom criminal proceedings have been brought or a criminal investigation is taking place, and against whom a confiscation order or forfeiture order has been or might be made.

SECTION I – RESTRAINT ORDERS

Form of restraint order

2 An example of a restraint order is annexed to this practice direction. This example may be modified as appropriate in any particular case.

Amount under restraint

3.1 A restraint order may, where appropriate, apply to –

(1) all of the defendant's realisable property;
(2) the defendant's realisable property up to a specified value; or

(3) one or more particular specified assets.

3.2 Where –

(1) a confiscation order or forfeiture order has already been made against the defendant in a particular amount; or
(2) the prosecutor is able to make a reasonably accurate estimate of the amount of any confiscation order or forfeiture order that might be made against him,

and, in either case, it is clear that the defendant's realisable property is greater in value than the amount or estimated amount of that order, the court will normally limit the application of the restraint order in accordance with paragraph 3.1(2) or (3).

3.3 In such cases the prosecutor's draft order should normally either include an appropriate financial limit or specify the particular assets to which the order should apply.

Living expenses and legal fees

4 A restraint order will normally, unless it is clear that a person restrained has sufficient assets which are not subject to the order, include an exception to the order permitting that person to spend assets –

(1) in the case of an individual, for reasonable living expenses; and
(2) in the case of either an individual or a company, to pay reasonable legal fees so that they may take advice in relation to the order and if so advised apply for its variation or discharge.

Restraint orders against third parties

5.1 Where a restraint order applies to property held in the name of a person other than the defendant –

(1) the order must be addressed to that person in addition to the defendant; and
(2) in applying for the order, the prosecutor must consider the guidance given in the matter of G (restraint order) [2001] EWHC Admin 606.

5.2 Examples of additional persons to whom an order must, where appropriate, be addressed include –

(1) a person who has a joint bank account with the defendant;
(2) in proceedings under the 1988 Act or the 1994 Act, a person to whom the defendant is alleged to have made a gift which may be treated as realisable property of the defendant under the provisions of the relevant Act; or
(3) a company, where the prosecutor alleges that assets apparently belonging to the company are in reality those of the defendant.

5.3 However, an order should not normally be addressed –

(1) to a bank with whom a defendant has an account; or
(2) to the business name of a defendant who carries on an unincorporated business (such business not being a separate legal entity from the defendant).

Restraint orders against businesses

6 If an application for a restraint order is made against a company, partnership or individual apparently carrying on a legitimate business –

(1) the court will take into account the interests of the employees, creditors and customers of the business and, in the case of a company, any shareholders other than the defendant, before making an order which would or might prevent the business from being continued; and

(2) any restraint order made against that person will normally contain an exception enabling it to deal with its assets in the ordinary course of business.

Duration of order made on application without notice – rules 4(2) and 27(2)

7.1 RSC Order 115 rules 4(2) and 27(2) provide that, unless the court otherwise directs, a restraint order made without notice shall have effect until a day which shall be fixed for a further hearing where all parties may attend ('the return date').

7.2 Where a return date is fixed, it will normally be no more than 14 days after the date of the order.

7.3 Where no return date is fixed, the court will always include in the order a provision giving the defendant or anyone affected by the order permission to apply to vary or discharge the order (see paragraph 14 of the sample form of order).

SECTION II – APPOINTMENT OF RECEIVER

8.1 CPR Part 69, and the practice direction supplementing that Part, apply to the appointment of a receiver under the 1988, 1994 or 2000 Act, subject to the provisions of RSC Order 115 rule 8 and rule 23(e) where applicable.

8.2 In particular, CPR rule 69.7, and paragraph 9 of the practice direction supplementing Part 69, apply in relation to the remuneration of the receiver.

8.3 Where no confiscation or forfeiture order has been made –

(1) an application for the appointment of a receiver should not be made without notice, unless the application is urgent or there is some other good reason for not giving notice to the defendant; and

(2) if the application is made without notice, the prosecutor's written evidence should explain the reasons for doing so.

8.4 Where the court appoints a receiver on an application without notice in the circumstances set out in paragraph 8.3, the order will normally limit the receiver's powers to manage, deal with or sell property (other than with the defendant's consent) to the extent that is shown to be urgently necessary. If the receiver seeks further powers, he should apply on notice for further directions.

APPENDIX

RESTRAINT ORDER PROHIBITING DISPOSAL OF ASSETS

****

Draft order—The draft restraint order appended to this practice direction can be accessed either on the *Civil Court Service* CD-ROM or via the Internet at the Department for Constitutional Affairs' website at *www.lcd.gov.uk*.

RSC ORDER 116
THE CRIMINAL PROCEDURE AND INVESTIGATIONS ACT 1996

1 Application

This Order shall apply in relation to acquittals in respect of offences alleged to be committed on or after 15 April 1997.

Amendments—Inserted by SI 1999/1008.

2 Interpretation

In this Order, unless the context otherwise requires –

'the Act' means the Criminal Procedure and Investigations Act 1996;

'acquitted person' means a person whose acquittal of an offence is the subject of a certification under section 54(2) of the Act, and 'acquittal' means the acquittal of that person of that offence;

'magistrates' court' has the same meaning as in section 148 of the Magistrates' Courts Act 1980;

'prosecutor' means the individual or body which acted as prosecutor in the proceedings which led to the acquittal;

'record of court proceedings' means –

(a) (where the proceedings took place in the Crown Court) a transcript of the evidence, or

(b) a note of the evidence made by the justices' clerk,

in the proceedings which led to the conviction for the administration of justice offence referred to in section 54(1)(b) of the Act or, as the case may be, the proceedings which led to the acquittal;

'single judge' means a judge of the Queen's Bench Division;

'witness' means a witness whose evidence is contained in a witness statement or affidavit filed under rule 5, 7, 8 or 9.

Amendments—Inserted by SI 1999/1008.

3 Assignment of proceedings

The jurisdiction of the High Court under section 54(3) of the Act shall be exercised by a single judge.

Amendments—Inserted by SI 1999/1008.

4 Time limit for making application

An application under section 54(3) of the Act shall be made not later than 28 days after –

(a) the expiry of the period allowed for appealing (whether by case stated or otherwise), or making an application for leave to appeal, against the conviction referred to in section 54(1)(b) of the Act; or

(b) where notice of appeal or application for leave to appeal against the conviction is given, the determination of the appeal or application for leave to appeal and, for this purpose, 'determination' includes abandonment (within the meaning of rule 10 of the Criminal Appeal Rules 1968 or, as the case may be, rule 11 of the Crown Court Rules 1982).

Amendments—Inserted by SI 1999/1008.

5 Application

(1) An application under section 54(3) of the Act shall be made by claim form which shall be issued out of the Crown Office by the prosecutor.

(2) The application shall be accompanied by –

(a) a witness statement or affidavit which deals with the conditions in section 55(1), (2), and (4) of the Act and which exhibits any relevant documents (which may include a copy of any record of court proceedings);

(b) a copy of the certification under section 54(2) of the Act.

Amendments—Inserted by SI 1999/1008.

6 Notice to the acquitted person

(1) The prosecutor shall, within 4 days of the issue of the application, serve written notice on the acquitted person that the application has been issued.

(2) The notice given under paragraph (1) shall –

(a) specify the date on which the application was issued;

(b) be accompanied by a copy of the application and of the documents which accompanied it;

(c) inform the acquitted person that –

(i) the result of the application may be the making of an order by the High Court quashing the acquittal, and

(ii) if he wishes to respond to the application, he must, within 28 days of the date of service on him of the notice, file in the Crown Office any witness statement or affidavit on which he intends to rely.

Amendments—Inserted by SI 1999/1008.

7 Witness statement or affidavit of service on an acquitted person

The prosecutor shall, as soon as practicable after service of the notice under rule 6, file at the Crown Office a witness statement or affidavit of service which exhibits a copy of the notice.

Amendments—Inserted by SI 1999/1008.

8 Response of acquitted person

(1) If the acquitted person wishes to respond to the application, he shall, within 28 days of service on him of notice under rule 6, file in the Crown Office a witness statement or affidavit which –

(a) deals with the conditions in section 55(1), (2), and (4) of the Act; and

(b) exhibits any relevant documents (which may include a copy of any record of court proceedings).

(2) The acquitted person shall, within 4 days of the filing of the documents mentioned in paragraph (1), serve copies of them on the prosecutor.

Amendments—Inserted by SI 1999/1008.

9 Evidence

(1) A witness statement or affidavit filed under rule 5, 7, 8 or this rule may contain statements of information or belief with the sources and grounds thereof.

(2) The prosecutor may, not later than 10 days after expiry of the period allowed under rule 8(1), apply for an order granting permission to file further evidence without notice being served on any other party.

(3) If the single judge grants permission, the order shall specify a period within which further evidence or records are to be filed, and the Crown Office shall serve a copy of the order on the prosecutor and on the acquitted person.

(4) The prosecutor shall, within 4 days of filing further evidence in the Crown Office, serve a copy of that evidence on the acquitted person.

Amendments—Inserted by SI 1999/1008.

10 Determination of the application

(1) Subject to paragraph (3), the single judge shall determine whether or not to make an order under section 54(3) of the Act on the basis of the written material provided under rules 5, 7, 8 and 9 in the absence of the prosecutor, the acquitted person, or of any witness.

(2) The determination shall not be made, and any hearing under paragraph (3) shall not take place, before the expiry of –

(a) 10 days after the expiry of the period allowed under rule 8(1), or

(b) 10 days after the expiry of the period allowed by any order made under rule 9(3).

(3) The single judge may, of his own initiative or on the application of the prosecutor or acquitted person, order a hearing of the application if he thinks fit.

(4) An application under paragraph (3) shall state whether a hearing is desired in order for a deponent for the other party to attend and be cross-examined, and, if so, the reasons for wishing the witness to attend.

(5) An application under paragraph (3) shall be made no later than 7 days after the expiry of the period allowed –

(a) under rule 8(1) or

(b) by any order made under rule 9(3).

(6) Where a hearing is ordered, the single judge may, of his own initiative or on the application of the prosecutor or acquitted person, order a witness to attend in order to be cross-examined.

(7) The prosecutor or the acquitted person, as the case may be, shall within 4 days after filing the application under paragraph (3), serve a copy of it on the other party, and file in the Crown Office a witness statement or affidavit of service.

(8) A party served under paragraph (7) shall, within 5 days of service, file any representations he wishes to make as to whether or not a hearing should be ordered.

(9) Subject to paragraph (10) below –

(a) the single judge shall not determine an application for a hearing under paragraph (3) unless –
   (i) a witness statement or affidavit of service has been filed as required by paragraph (7), and
   (ii) the period for filing representations allowed under paragraph (8) has elapsed; or
   (iii) representations have been filed under paragraph (8).

(b) The requirements imposed by sub-paragraph (a)(i) and (iii) are satisfied even though the witness statement or affidavit of service or, as the case may be, the representations are filed outside the time limits allowed.

(10) Where after an application for a hearing has been made –

(a) no witness statement or affidavit of service has been filed, and
(b) no representations under paragraph (8) have been received after the expiry of 7 days from the filing of the application,

the single judge may reject the application.

(11) Where after a hearing is ordered, either the prosecutor or the acquitted person desires a witness for the other party to attend the hearing in order to be cross-examined, he must apply for an order under paragraph (5) giving his reasons without notice being served on any other party.

(12) The Crown Office shall serve notice on the prosecutor and the acquitted person of any order made under the foregoing paragraphs of this rule and, where a hearing is ordered, the notice shall –

(a) set out the date, time and place of the hearing, and
(b) give details of any witness ordered to attend for cross-examination.

(13) A hearing ordered under paragraph (3) above shall be in public unless the single judge otherwise directs.

(14) The Crown Office shall serve notice of any order made under section 54(3) of the Act quashing the acquittal or of a decision not to make such an order on the prosecutor, the acquitted person and –

(a) where the court before which the acquittal or conviction occurred was a magistrates' court, on the justices' chief executive;
(b) where the court before which the acquittal or conviction occurred was the Crown Court, on the appropriate officer of the Crown Court sitting at the place where the acquittal or conviction occurred.

Amendments—Inserted by SI 1999/1008; amended by SI 2001/256.

SCHEDULE 2
CCR RULES

Rule 50(4)

CCR ORDER 1
CITATION, APPLICATION AND INTERPRETATION

6 Application of RSC to county court proceedings

Where by virtue of these rules or section 76 of the Act or otherwise any provision of the RSC is applied in relation to proceedings in a county court, that provision shall have effect with the necessary modifications and in particular –

(b) any reference in that provision to a master, district judge of the Principal Registry of the Family Division, the Admiralty registrar, or a district judge or taxing officer shall be construed as a reference to the district judge of the county court; and

(d) any reference in that provision to an office of the Supreme Court having the conduct of the business of a division or court or a district registry shall be construed as a reference to the county court office.

****

CCR ORDER 4

****

Amendments—Rule 3 was revoked by SI 2003/2113 with effect from 6 October 2003.

CCR ORDER 5
CAUSES OF ACTION AND PARTIES

General note—This provisions in this rule are similar to RSC Ord 15 in Sch 1 with some closely corresponding provisions. The following table summarises such provisions contained in the two orders as survive after 2 May 2000:

Rule Title	CCR Ord 5	RSC Ord 15	Notes
Claims by and against partners	r 9	–	See RSC Ord 81, rr 1 and 2
Defendant carrying on business in another name	r 10	–	
Notice of claims to non-parties	–	r 13A	Estates and property in trust
Representation of beneficiaries by trustees	–	r 14	

Rule Title	CCR Ord 5	RSC Ord 15	Notes
Declaratory judgments	–	r 16	

****

9 Partners may sue and be sued in firm name

(1) Subject to the provisions of any enactment, any two or more persons claiming to be entitled, or alleged to be liable, as partners in respect of a cause of action and carrying on business within England or Wales may sue or be sued in the name of the firm of which they were partners when the cause of action arose.

(2) Where partners sue or are sued in the name of the firm, the partners shall, on demand made in writing by any other party, forthwith deliver to the party making the demand and file a statement of the names and places of residence of all the persons who were partners in the firm when the cause of action arose.

(3) If the partners fail to comply with such a demand, the court, on application by any other party, may order the partners to furnish him with such a statement and to verify it on oath and may direct that in default –

- (a) if the partners are claimants, the proceedings be stayed on such terms as the court thinks fit; or
- (b) if the partners are defendants, they be debarred from defending the claim.

(4) When the names and places of residence of the partners have been stated in compliance with a demand or order under this rule, the proceedings shall continue in the name of the firm.

Claims by and against partners—RSC Ord 81, rr 1–2 carry the corresponding provisions.

'carrying on business within England or Wales' (r 9(1))—Parties living outside the jurisdiction but carrying on business as partners within England or Wales still qualify under this provision.

10 Defendant carrying on business in another name

(1) A person carrying on business in England or Wales in a name other than his own name may, whether or not he is within the jurisdiction, be sued –

- (a) in his own name, followed by the words 'trading as A.B.', or
- (b) in his business name, followed by the words '(a trading name)'.

(2) Where a person is sued in his business name in accordance with paragraph (1)(b), the provisions of these rules relating to claims against firms shall, subject to the provisions of any enactment, apply as if he were a partner and the name in which he carried on business were the name of his firm.

****

Amendments—Rules 12–14 were revoked by SI 2002/2058 with effect from 2 December 2002.

CCR ORDER 6

****

Amendments—Rule 6 was revoked by SI 2003/1242 with effect from 2 June 2003.

****

CCR ORDER 16
TRANSFER OF PROCEEDINGS

7 Interpleader proceedings under execution

(1) This rule applies to interpleader proceedings under an execution which are ordered to be transferred from the High Court.

(1A) In this rule references to the sheriff shall be interpreted as including references to an individual authorised to act as an enforcement officer under the Courts Act 2003.

(2) Notice of the hearings or pre-trial review of the proceedings shall be given by the court officer to the sheriff as well as to every other party to the proceedings.

(3) The interpleader claimant shall, within 8 days of the receipt by him of the notice referred to in paragraph (2), file in triplicate particulars of any goods alleged to be his property and the grounds of his interpleader claim and the court officer shall send a copy to the execution creditor and to the sheriff, but the judge may hear the proceedings or, as the case may be, the district judge may proceed with the pre-trial review, if he thinks fit, notwithstanding that the particulars have not been filed.

(4) Subject to any directions in the order of the High Court, damages may be claimed against the execution creditor in the same manner as in interpleader proceedings commenced in a county court.

(5) On any day fixed for the pre-trial review of the proceedings or for the hearing of any application by the sheriff or other party for directions the court may order the sheriff –

- (a) to postpone the sale of the goods seized;
- (b) to remain in possession of such goods until the hearing of the proceedings; or
- (c) to hand over possession of such goods to the district judge,

and, where a direction is given under sub-paragraph (c), the district judge shall be allowed reasonable charges for keeping possession of the goods, not exceeding those which might be allowed to the sheriff, and, if the district judge is directed to sell the goods, such charges for the sale as would be allowed under an execution issued by the county court.

(6) No order made in the proceedings shall prejudice or affect the rights of the sheriff to any proper charges and the judge may make such order with respect to them as may be just.

(7) The charges referred to in paragraphs (5) and (6) shall ultimately be borne in such manner as the judge shall direct.

(8) The order made at the hearing of the proceedings shall direct how any money in the hands of the sheriff is to be disposed of.

Amendments—SI 2003/3361.

'transferred from the High Court' (r 7(1))—Proceedings are transferred under CCA 1984, s 40(2).

'the pre-trial review' (r 7(3) and (5))—If the matter is not dealt with summarily, the court will give case management directions under CPR Pt 3 or allocation directions under CPR Pt 26.

CCR ORDER 19

****

Amendments—The whole Order was revoked by SI 2002/2058 with effect from 2 December 2002. Provisions about references to the European Court are now to be found in CPR Pt 68.

CCR ORDER 22
JUDGMENTS AND ORDERS

8 Certificate of judgment

(1) Any person who wishes to have a certificate of any judgment or order given or made in a claim shall make a request in writing to the court stating –

- (a) if he is a party to the claim whether the certificate –
  - (i) is required for the purpose of taking proceedings on the judgment or order in another court;
  - (ii) is required for the purpose of enforcing the judgment or order in the High Court; or
  - (iii) is for the purpose of evidence only;
- (b) if he is not a party to the claim, the purpose for which the certificate is required, the capacity in which he asks for it and any other facts showing that the certificate may properly be granted.

(1A) Where the certificate is required for the purpose of enforcing the judgment or order in the High Court, the applicant shall also either –

- (a) state that –
  - (i) it is intended to enforce the judgment or order by execution against goods; or
  - (ii) the judgment or order to be enforced is an order for possession of land made in a possession claim against trespassers; or
- (b) confirm that an application has been made for an order under section 42 of the Act (transfer to High Court by order of a county court) and attach a copy of the application to the request for a certificate.

(2) Where the request is made by a person who is not a party to the claim, the request shall be referred to the district judge, who may, if he thinks fit, refer it to the judge.

(3) Without prejudice to paragraph (2), for the purposes of section 12(2) of the Act a certificate under this rule may be signed by the court manager or any other officer of the court acting on his behalf.

Amendments—SI 2001/2792.

Forms—The certificate is based on Form N293 (see PD4, Table 3).

10 Variation of payment

(1) Where a judgment or order has been given or made for the payment of money, the person entitled to the benefit of the judgment or order or, as the case may be, the person liable to make the payment (in this rule referred to as 'the

judgment creditor' and 'the debtor' respectively) may apply in accordance with the provisions of this rule for a variation in the date or rate of payment.

(2) The judgment creditor may apply in writing, without notice being served on any other party, for an order that the money, if payable in one sum, be paid at a later date than that by which it is due or by instalments or, if the money is already payable by instalments, that it be paid by the same or smaller instalments, and the court officer may make an order accordingly unless no payment has been made under the judgment or order for 6 years before the date of the application in which case he shall refer the application to the district judge.

(3) The judgment creditor may apply to the district judge on notice for an order that the money, if payable in one sum, be paid at an earlier date than that by which it is due or, if the money is payable by instalments, that it be paid in one sum or by larger instalments, and any such application shall be made in writing stating the proposed terms and the grounds on which it is made.

(4) Where an application is made under paragraph (3) –

- (a) the proceedings shall be automatically transferred to the debtor's home court if the judgment or order was not given or made in that court; and
- (b) the court officer shall fix a day for the hearing of the application before the district judge and give to the judgment creditor and the debtor not less than 8 days' notice of the day so fixed,

and at the hearing the district judge may make such order as seems just.

(5) The debtor may apply for an order that the money, if payable in one sum, be paid at a later date than that by which it is due or by instalments or, if the money is already payable by instalments, that it be paid by smaller instalments, and any such application shall be in the appropriate form stating the proposed terms, the grounds on which it is made and including a signed statement of the debtor's means.

(6) Where an application is made under paragraph (5), the court officer shall –

- (a) send the judgment creditor a copy of the debtor's application (and statement of means); and
- (b) require the judgment creditor to notify the court in writing, within 14 days of service of notification upon him, giving his reasons for any objection he may have to the granting of the application.

(7) If the judgment creditor does not notify the court of any objection within the time stated, the court officer shall make an order in the terms applied for.

(8) Upon receipt of a notice from the judgment creditor under paragraph (6), the court officer may determine the date and rate of payment and make an order accordingly.

(9) Any party affected by an order made under paragraph (8) may, within 14 days of service of the order on him and giving his reasons, apply on notice for the order to be re-considered and, where such an application is made –

- (a) the proceedings shall be automatically transferred to the debtor's home court if the judgment or order was not given or made in that court; and
- (b) the court officer shall fix a day for the hearing of the application before the district judge and give to the judgment creditor and the debtor not less than 8 days' notice of the day so fixed.

(10) On hearing an application under paragraph (9), the district judge may confirm the order or set it aside and make such new order as he thinks fit and the order so made shall be entered in the records of the court.

(11) Any order made under any of the foregoing paragraphs may be varied from time to time by a subsequent order made under any of those paragraphs.

Stay of enforcement pending application—It is a common misconception that enforcement is automatically stayed pending the hearing of an application to vary payment. An application to stay must be made separately and to the court where the order or judgment originated.

Forms—N294 Claimants Application for a Variation Order, (PD4, Table 1); N245 – Application for Suspension of a Warrant and/or Variation of an Instalment Order, (PD4, Table 3); N246 – Claimant's Reply to Defendant's Application to Vary Instalment Order; N35 – Variation Order.

11 Set-off of cross-judgments

(1) An application under section 72 of the Act for permission to set off any sums, including costs, payable under several judgments or orders each of which was obtained in a county court shall be made in accordance with this rule.

(2) Where the judgments or orders have been obtained in the same county court, the application may be made to that court on the day when the last judgment or order is obtained, if both parties are present, and in any other case shall be made on notice.

(3) Where the judgments or orders have been obtained in different county courts, the application may be made to either of them on notice, and notice shall be given to the other court.

(4) The district judge of the court to which the application is made and the district judge of any other court to which notice is given under paragraph (3) shall forthwith stay execution on any judgment or order in his court to which the application relates and any money paid into court under the judgment or order shall be retained until the application has been disposed of.

(5) The application may be heard and determined by the court and any order giving permission shall direct how any money paid into court is to be dealt with.

(6) Where the judgments or orders have been obtained in different courts, the court in which an order giving permission is made shall send a copy of the order to the other court, which shall deal with any money paid into that court in accordance with the order.

(7) The court officer or, as the case may be, each of the court officers affected shall enter satisfaction in the records of his court for any sums ordered to be set off, and execution or other process for the enforcement of any judgment or order not wholly satisfied shall issue only for the balance remaining payable.

(8) Where an order is made by the High Court giving permission to set off sums payable under several judgments and orders obtained respectively in the High Court and a county court, the court officer of the county court shall, on receipt of a copy of the order, proceed in accordance with paragraph (7).

13 Order of appellate court

Where the Court of Appeal or High Court has heard and determined an appeal from a county court, the party entitled to the benefit of the order of the Court of Appeal or High Court shall deposit the order or an office copy thereof in the office of the county court.

CCR ORDER 24
SUMMARY PROCEEDINGS FOR THE RECOVERY OF LAND

Part I – Land

****

6 Warrant of possession

(1) Subject to paragraphs (2) and (3), a warrant of possession to enforce an order for possession in a possession claim against trespassers under Part 55 may be issued at any time after the making of the order and subject to the provisions of Order 26, rule 17, a warrant of restitution may be issued in aid of the warrant of possession.

(2) No warrant of possession shall be issued after the expiry of 3 months from the date of the order without the permission of the court, and an application for such permission may be made without notice being served on any other party unless the court otherwise directs.

(3) Nothing in this rule shall authorise the issue of a warrant of possession before the date on which possession is ordered to be given.

Amendments—SI 2001/256.

'permission of the court' (r 6(2))—A witness statement or affidavit should be filed explaining the reason for the delay.

****

Amendments—Rules 8–15 were revoked by SI 2002/2058 with effect from 2 December 2002. Provisions about interim possession orders are now to be found in CPR Pt 55.

CCR ORDER 25
ENFORCEMENT OF JUDGMENTS AND ORDERS: GENERAL

1 Judgment creditor and debtor

In this Order and Orders 26 to 29 'judgment creditor' means the person who has obtained or is entitled to enforce a judgment or order and 'debtor' means the person against whom it was given or made.

****

Amendments—Rules 2, 3, 4, 5 and 5A were revoked by SI 2001/2792 with effect from 25 March 2002. Provisions about enforcement of judgments and orders are now to be found in CPR Pts 70–73.

6 Description of parties

Where the name or address of the judgment creditor or the debtor as given in the request for the issue of a warrant of execution or delivery, judgment summons or warrant of committal differs from his name or address in the judgment or order sought to be enforced and the judgment creditor satisfies the court officer that the name or address as given in the request is applicable to the person concerned, the judgment creditor or the debtor, as the case may be, shall be described in the warrant or judgment summons as 'CD of [name and address as given in the request] suing [or sued] as AD of [name and address in the judgment or order]'.

7 Recording and giving information as to warrants and orders

(1) Subject to paragraph (1A), every district judge by whom a warrant or order is issued or received for execution shall from time to time state in the records of his court what has been done in the execution of the warrant or order.

(1A) Where a warrant of execution issued by a court ('the home court') is sent to another court for execution ('the foreign court'), paragraph (1) shall not apply to the district judge of the home court, but when such a warrant is returned to the home court under paragraph (7), the court officer of the home court shall state in the records of his court what has been done in the execution of the warrant or order.

(2) If the warrant or order has not been executed within one month from the date of its issue or receipt by him, the court officer of the court responsible for its execution shall, at the end of that month and every subsequent month during which the warrant remains outstanding, send notice of the reason for non-execution to the judgment creditor and, if the warrant or order was received from another court, to that court.

(3) The district judge responsible for executing a warrant or order shall give such information respecting it as may reasonably be required by the judgment creditor and, if the warrant or order was received by him from another court, by the district judge of that court.

(4) Where money is received in pursuance of a warrant of execution or committal sent by one court to another court, the foreign court shall, subject to paragraph (5) and to section 346 of Insolvency Act 1986 and section 326 of the Companies Act 1948, send the money to the judgment creditor in the manner prescribed by the Court Funds Rules 1987 and, where the money is received in pursuance of a warrant of committal, make a return to the home court.

(5) Where interpleader proceedings are pending, the court shall not proceed in accordance with paragraph (4) until the interpleader proceedings are determined and the district judge shall then make a return showing how the money is to be disposed of and, if any money is payable to the judgment creditor, the court shall proceed in accordance with paragraph (4).

(6) Where a warrant of committal has been received from another court, the foreign court shall, on the execution of the warrant, send notice thereof to the home court.

(7) Where a warrant of execution has been received from another court, either –

(a) on the execution of the warrant; or

(b) if the warrant is not executed –
(i) on the making of a final return to the warrant; or
(ii) on suspension of the warrant under rule 8 (suspension of judgment or execution) or Order 26, rule 10 (withdrawal and suspension of warrant at creditor's request),

the foreign court shall return the warrant to the home court.

Scope of provision—This rule sets out the duties of the court in which a warrant is issued and (if different) the court by which it is executed to record and provide information.

'such information … as may reasonably be required' (r 7(3))—Rule 7(3) has to be read subject to the constraints of practicability (*Polentz v Roberts* (1900) 110 LT Jo 376). Resources expended on dealing with enquiries are necessarily diverted from dealing with the process itself.

8 Suspension of judgment or execution

(1) The power of the court to suspend or stay a judgment or order or to stay execution of any warrant may be exercised by the district judge or, in the case of the power to stay execution of a warrant of execution and in accordance with the provisions of this rule, by the court officer.

(2) An application by the debtor to stay execution of a warrant of execution shall be in the appropriate form stating the proposed terms, the grounds on which it is made and including a signed statement of the debtor's means.

(3) Where the debtor makes an application under paragraph (2), the court shall –

(a) send the judgment creditor a copy of the debtor's application (and statement of means); and
(b) require the creditor to notify the court in writing, within 14 days of service of notification upon him, giving his reasons for any objection he may have to the granting of the application.

(4) If the judgment creditor does not notify the court of any objection within the time stated, the court officer may make an order suspending the warrant on terms of payment.

(5) Upon receipt of a notice by the judgment creditor under paragraph (3)(b), the court officer may, if the judgment creditor objects only to the terms offered, determine the date and rate of payment and make an order suspending the warrant on terms of payment.

(6) Any party affected by an order made under paragraph (5) may, within 14 days of service of the order on him and giving his reasons, apply on notice for the order to be reconsidered and the court shall fix a day for the hearing of the application before the district judge and give to the judgment creditor and the debtor not less than 8 days' notice of the day so fixed.

(7) On hearing an application under paragraph (6), the district judge may confirm the order or set it aside and make such new order as he thinks fit and the order so made shall be entered in the records of the court.

(8) Where the judgment creditor states in his notice under paragraph (3)(b) that he wishes the bailiff to proceed to execute the warrant, the court shall fix a day for a hearing before the district judge of the debtor's application and give to the judgment creditor and to the debtor not less than 2 days' notice of the day so fixed.

(9) Subject to any directions given by the district judge, where a warrant of execution has been suspended, it may be re-issued on the judgment creditor's filing a request showing that any condition subject to which the warrant was suspended has not been complied with.

(10) Where an order is made by the district judge suspending a warrant of execution, the debtor may be ordered to pay the costs of the warrant and any fees or expenses incurred before its suspension and the order may authorise the sale of a sufficient portion of any goods seized to cover such costs, fees and expenses and the expenses of sale.

Amendments—SI 2001/2792.

Scope of provision—This rule covers applications to suspend or stay judgments or orders or to stay execution. In the case of warrants of execution where the only question is the terms of payment of the stay, the order is made in the first instance by the proper officer or an officer of the court on his behalf, subject to review on application to the district judge.

'power of the court to suspend or stay' (r 8(1))—Power to stay a judgment on terms is given by County Courts Act 1984, s 71(2) and that to stay execution by s 88. In each case the ground is the debtor's inability to pay. The proper officer's authority does not extend to applications to stay on any other ground as he can make an order suspending the warrant only on terms as to payment.

'may make an order' (r 8(4))—The proper officer is not obliged to exercise his powers under this rule. If he declines to do so, the application will be listed before a district judge in the same way as an application where the creditor opposes any suspension.

Costs (r 8(10))—The proper officer has no power to deal with the question of costs. Where it seems that an order for costs may be appropriate, the application will be listed for hearing before a district judge.

9 Enforcement of judgment or order against firm

(1) Subject to paragraph (2), a judgment or order against a firm may be enforced against –

- (a) any property of the firm;
- (b) any person who admitted in the proceedings that he was a partner or was adjudged to be a partner;
- (c) any person who was served as a partner with the claim form if –
  - (i) judgment was entered under CPR Part 12, in default of defence or under CPR Part 14 on admission; or
  - (iii) the person so served did not appear at the trial or hearing of the proceedings.

(2) A judgment or order may not be enforced under paragraph (1) against a member of the firm who was out of England and Wales when the claim form was issued unless he –

- (a) was served within England and Wales with the claim form as a partner; or
- (b) was, with the [permission of the court under CPR rule 6.20 served out of England and Wales with the claim form as a partner,

and, except as provided by paragraph (1)(a) and by the foregoing provisions of this paragraph, a judgment or order obtained against a firm shall not render liable, release or otherwise affect a member of the firm who was out of England and Wales when the claim form was issued.

(3) A judgment creditor who claims to be entitled to enforce a judgment or order against any other person as a partner may apply to the court for permission to do so by filing an application notice in accordance with CPR Part 23.

(4) An application notice under paragraph (3) shall be served on the alleged partner, not less than 3 days before the hearing of the application, in the manner [set out in CPR rule 6.2 and on the hearing of the application, if the alleged partner does not dispute his liability, the court may, subject to paragraph (2), give permission to enforce the judgment or order against him and, if he disputes liability, the court may order that the question of his liability be tried and determined in such a manner as the court thinks fit.

(5) The foregoing provisions of this rule shall not apply where it is desired to enforce in a county court a judgment or order of the High Court, or a judgment, order, decree or award of any court or arbitrator which is or has become enforceable as if it were a judgment or order of the High Court, and in any such case the provisions of the RSC relating to the enforcement of a judgment or order against a firm shall apply.

Amendments—SI 2000/221; SI 2001/2792.

'judgment or order against a firm' (r 9(1))—Partnership Act 1890, s 23(1) specifically prohibits execution against partnership property unless the judgment is in the name of the firm. This rule extends to all forms of enforcement and sets out the limitations on enforcement which apply where judgment has been given against a firm.

'any other person' (r 9(3))—This rule may be used where the creditor seeks to enforce a judgment against a person who has held himself out as being a partner in a firm against which judgment has obtained (*Davis v Hyman & Co* [1903] 1 KB 854).

'judgment ... of the High Court' (r 9(5))—This rule preserves the application of RSC Ord 81, r 5 to judgments which have been transferred to the county court for enforcement.

10 Enforcing judgment between a firm and its members

(1) Execution to enforce a judgment or order given or made in –

- (a) proceedings by or against a firm, in the name of the firm against or by a member of the firm; or
- (b) proceedings by a firm in the name of the firm against a firm in the name of the firm where those firms have one or more members in common,

shall not issue without the permission of the court.

(2) On an application for permission the court may give such directions, including directions as to the taking of accounts and the making of inquiries, as may be just.

****

Amendments—Rules 11 and 12 were revoked by SI 2001/2792 with effect from 25 March 2002. Provisions about enforcement of judgments and orders are now to be found in CPR Pts 70–73.

13 Transfer to High Court for enforcement

(1) Where the judgment creditor makes a request for a certificate of judgment under Order 22, rule 8(1) for the purpose of enforcing the judgment or order in the High Court –

- (a) by execution against goods; or
- (b) where the judgment or order to be enforced is an order for possession of land made in a possession claim against trespassers,

the grant of a certificate by the court shall take effect as an order to transfer the proceedings to the High Court and the transfer shall have effect on the grant of that certificate.

(2) On the transfer of proceedings in accordance with paragraph (1), the court shall give notice to the debtor [or the person against whom the possession order was made that the proceedings have been transferred and shall make an entry of that fact in the records of his court.

(3) In a case where a request for a certificate of judgment is made under Order 22, rule 8(1) for the purpose of enforcing a judgment or order in the High Court and –

(a) an application for a variation in the date or rate of payment of money due under a judgment or order;
(b) an application under either CPR rule 39.3(3) or CPR rule 13.4;
(c) a request for an administration order; or
(d) an application for a stay of execution under section 88 of the Act,

is pending, the request for the certificate shall not be dealt with until those proceedings are determined.

Amendments—SI 2001/2792.

Jurisdiction—This is now governed by High Court and County Courts Jurisdiction Order 1991, art 8. A practice direction relating to the enforcement of county court judgments in the High Court issued by the Senior Master is set out at [1998] 4 All ER 63.

CCR ORDER 26
WARRANTS OF EXECUTION, DELIVERY AND POSSESSION

Procedural Guide—See Guides 37 (Issue of a Writ or Warrant of Delivery) and 38 (Issue of Execution against Goods), set out in Section 1 of this work.

Practice Direction—See PDExecution at p 1653 which forbids execution on a Sunday, Good Friday or Christmas Day unless the court orders otherwise.

1 Application for warrant of execution

(1) A judgment creditor desiring a warrant of execution to be issued shall file a request in that behalf certifying –

(a) the amount remaining due under the judgment or order; and
(b) where the order made is for payment of a sum of money by instalments –
  (i) that the whole or part of any instalment due remains unpaid; and
  (ii) the amount for which the warrant is to be issued.

(1A) The court officer shall discharge the functions –

(a) under section 85(2) of the Act of issuing a warrant of execution;
(b) under section 85(3) of the Act of entering in the record mentioned in that subsection and on the warrant the precise time of the making of the application to issue the warrant; and
(c) under section 103(1) of the Act of sending the warrant of execution to another county court.

(2) Where the court has made an order for payment of a sum of money by instalments and default has been made in payment of such an instalment, a warrant of execution may be issued for the whole of the said sum of money and costs then remaining unpaid or, subject to paragraph (3), for such part as the

judgment creditor may request, not being in the latter case less than £50 or the amount of one monthly instalment or, as the case may be, 4 weekly instalments, whichever is the greater.

(3) In any case to which paragraph (2) applies no warrant shall be issued unless at the time when it is issued –

- (a) the whole or part of an instalment which has already become due remains unpaid; and
- (b) any warrant previously issued for part of the said sum of money and costs has expired or has been satisfied or abandoned.

(4) Where a warrant is issued for the whole or part of the said sum of money and costs, the court officer shall, unless the district judge responsible for execution of the warrant directs otherwise, send a warning notice to the person against whom the warrant is issued and, where such a notice is sent, the warrant shall not be levied until 7 days thereafter.

(5) Where judgment is given or an order made for payment otherwise than by instalments of a sum of money and costs to be assessed in accordance with CPR Part 47 (detailed assessment procedure) and default is made in payment of the sum of money before the costs have been assessed, a warrant of execution may issue for recovery of the sum of money and a separate warrant may issue subsequently for the recovery of the costs if default is made in payment of them.

Scope of provision—This and the following rules set out the regulatory framework for the issue of a warrant of execution against goods. This rule prescribes the method of application for a warrant.

Considerations affecting issue of warrant—The power to enforce judgments by execution against goods and to issue a warrant of execution to the like effect as a writ of fieri facias is given by County Courts Act 1984, s 85 and controlled by ss 86–104. Practical considerations include:

- (a) *Priority* – The court records the time the warrant is applied for (s 85(3)) and the warrant 'binds the property in the goods' (and therefore has priority over later executions) from that time (s 99(1)), unless it is used to levy on goods in another county court district, in which case the time of its receipt by that county court is recorded and governs its priority as regards those goods (s 103(2)).
- (b) *Instalment judgments* – Execution may not be issued unless the debtor is in arrear (s 86).
- (c) *Suspension* – The court may suspend or stay the execution (on terms if it thinks fit) if the debtor is unable to pay (s 88 – see also Ord 25, r 8). Where the warrant has been sent to another court, both courts have this power (s 103(5)).
- (d) *Goods* – Section 89 exempts certain goods from execution. Cash and valuable securities may be taken in the execution of the warrant.
- (e) *Rescue* – The rescue by any person of goods seized in execution is punishable by up to one month's imprisonment or a fine of up to £1000 (s 92).
- (f) *Sale* – Goods seized must be sold by public auction unless the court otherwise orders (s 97 – see also r 15).

Availability of warrant of execution—High Court and County Courts Jurisdiction Order 1991, art 8 prohibits enforcement by execution of county court judgments for £5000 or more in the county court or under £2000 in the High Court.

It is no longer possible to enforce a High Court judgment or order immediately by execution in the county court following the repeal of CCA 1984, s 105. The action must now first be transferred to the county court under CCA 1984, s 40.

Insolvency of debtor—Note Insolvency Act 1986, s 285(3), which prevents enforcement of provable debts against a bankrupt.

'file a request' (r 1(1))—Form N323 should be used as it contains space for recording of information by the court staff.

Warning notice (r 1(4))—The usual form of warning notice is set out in Practice Form N326, which informs the debtor that extra costs may be incurred if goods are seized and sold and that further interest will accrue (if the judgment is for more than £5000) unless the warrant and any balance of the judgment debt are paid off. Courts' practices on sending this notice vary. If there is any particular reason to fear that the debtor may hide goods if warned, the court should be advised of this at the time of issue and requested not to use the notice.

2 Execution of High Court judgment

(1) Where it is desired to enforce by warrant of execution a judgment or order of the High Court, or a judgment, order, decree or award which is or has become enforceable as if it were a judgment of the High Court, the request referred to in rule 1(1) may be filed in any court in the district of which execution is to be levied.

(2) Subject to Order 25, rule 9(5), any restriction imposed by these rules on the issue of execution shall apply as if the judgment, order, decree or award were a judgment or order of the county court, but permission to issue execution shall not be required if permission has already been given by the High Court.

(3) Notice of the issue of the warrant shall be sent by the county court to the High Court.

3 Execution against farmer

If after the issue of a warrant of execution the district judge for the district in which the warrant is to be executed has reason to believe that the debtor is a farmer, the execution creditor shall, if so required by the district judge, furnish him with an official certificate, dated not more than 3 days beforehand, of the result of a search at the Land Registry as to the existence of any charge registered against the debtor under the Agricultural Credits Act 1928.

Scope of provision—This rule enables the court to call for a search under Agricultural Credits Act 1928 where the debtor is a farmer. It is unlikely to do so unless goods are in fact seized. The search will reveal whether a charge over the farmer's assets exists under the Act. If there is a charge, the chargee is informed of the levy in case he wishes to claim the goods on the ground that the charge has crystallised.

4 Concurrent warrants

Two or more warrants of execution may be issued concurrently for execution in different districts, but –

(a) no more shall be levied under all the warrants together than is authorised to be levied under one of them; and

(b) the costs of more than one such warrant shall not be allowed against the debtor except by order of the court.

Scope of provision—This rule provides for the possibility that the debtor may have goods in more than one county court district, and allows the concurrent issue of warrants for execution in several districts.

Costs—The fixed costs of one warrant only will be allowed against the debtor unless the creditor, on application to the district judge, can justify the use of concurrent warrants.

5 Permission to issue certain warrants

(1) A warrant of execution shall not issue without the permission of the court where –

(a) six years or more have elapsed since the date of the judgment or order;

(b) any change has taken place, whether by death or otherwise in the parties entitled to enforce the judgment or order or liable to have it enforced against them;

(c) the judgment or order is against the assets of a deceased person coming into the hands of his executors or administrators after the date of the judgment or order and it is sought to issue execution against such assets; or

(d) any goods to be seized under a warrant of execution are in the hands of a receiver appointed by a court.

(2) An application for permission shall be supported by a witness statement or affidavit establishing the applicant's right to relief and may be made without notice being served on any other party in the first instance but the court may direct the application notice to be served on such persons as it thinks fit.

(3) Where, by reason of one and the same event, a person seeks permission under paragraph (1)(b) to enforce more judgments or orders than one, he may make one application only, specifying in a schedule all the judgments or orders in respect of which it is made, and if the application notice is directed to be served on any person, it need set out only such part of the application as affects him.

(4) Paragraph (1) is without prejudice to any enactment, rule or direction by virtue of which a person is required to obtain the permission of the court for the issue of a warrant or to proceed to execution or otherwise to the enforcement of a judgment or order.

Scope of provision—This rule sets out four cases in which leave is needed before a warrant of execution (or delivery or possession) may be issued and the procedure by which the application is made.

'six years ... have elapsed' (r 5(1)(a))—The court will require the applicant to show good reason before permitting execution on a stale judgment and will take into account any prejudice to the debtor caused by the delay.

Change of party (r 5(1)(b))—The alternative is to apply to change the party under CPR Pt 19. It is not thought that following an order under that rule leave would also be required under this rule. A mere change of description does not call for leave under this rule if the proper officer is satisfied under Ord 25, r 6.

Procedure (r 5(2))—The application may be made by application notice without serving a copy under CPR r 23.4(2). The district judge may however require notice to be given (and indeed must do so in the case of an application under r 5(1)(c) (*Re Shephard* (1890) 43 Ch D 131, CA). In a case where he clearly will so require, time may be saved by making the application on notice supported by witness statement or affidavit in the first instance.

Duration of leave—In the High Court leave to issue execution (whether granted under the equivalent rule or in any other case where leave is required) ceases to have effect if the authorised process is not issued within one year (RSC Ord 46, r 2(3)). The High Court practice applies in the county court by virtue of County Courts Act 1984, s 76.

Other cases where leave is required (r 5(4))—See for example Ord 24, r 6(2) which requires leave to issue a possession warrant once 3 months have passed from the date of the order.

6 Duration and renewal of warrant

(1) A warrant of execution shall, for the purpose of execution, be valid in the first instance for 12 months beginning with the date of its issue, but if not wholly executed, it may be renewed from time to time, by order of the court, for a period of 12 months at any one time, beginning with the day next following that on which it would otherwise expire, if an application for renewal is made before that day or such later day (if any) as the court may allow.

(2) A note of any such renewal shall be indorsed on the warrant and it shall be entitled to priority according to the time of its original issue or, where appropriate, its receipt by the district judge responsible for its execution.

Defined terms—'warrant of execution': County Courts Act 1984, s 85(2).

Scope of provision—This rule provides that a warrant is valid for 12 months but may be extended.

Extension—The extension covers the period of 12 months immediately following the original period of validity (or previous extension). Only one extension may be granted at a time. An extension may be granted after a warrant has expired, but the period of 12 months will run from the expiry date, not from the date of the order (the converse of the position in the High Court: see RSC Ord 46, r 8(2)). Thus an extension given more than 12 months after expiry would be ineffective and will not be granted (cf *Rolph v Zolan* [1993] 1 WLR 1305, CA).

Priority—Rule 6(2) preserves the existing priority of the warrant (see note **'Considerations affecting issue of warrant'**, (a) *Priority* under r 1). Extension therefore prejudices any other execution creditors who would have achieved a higher priority on the expiry of the applicant's warrant.

Procedure for application for renewal—Note that the rule does not specify the use of the application notice procedure under CPR Pt 23. In practice, courts often allow the application to be made by letter. The grounds of the application, including any reason for allowing the warrant to expire, should be given. The High Court practice is to extend only if priority is important (as fresh execution can be issued if it is not) and accordingly to require the applicant to identify any other execution creditors and give them the opportunity to make representations. In the county court, the delay will usually have occurred because the warrant has been suspended (with consequent loss of priority) and, in such a case, the court will be the more ready to extend. Nevertheless, if it appears to the proper officer that other execution creditors would be significantly prejudiced, he may require the application to be made on notice to them, by analogy with the High Court practice under RSC Ord 46, r 8.

7 Notice on levy

Any bailiff upon levying execution shall deliver to the debtor or leave at the place where execution is levied a notice of the warrant.

Scope of provision—The rule requires the bailiff to give the debtor formal written notice of the effect of the warrant.

Forms—A form of notice is incorporated into the warrant document as a slip to be torn off and handed to the debtor. Similar information is provided to the debtor in the warning notice Form N326 (see r 1), if used.

8 Bankruptcy or winding up of debtor

(1) Where the district judge responsible for the execution of a warrant is required by any provision of the Insolvency Act 1986 or any other enactment relating to insolvency to retain the proceeds of sale of goods sold under the warrant or money paid in order to avoid a sale, the court shall, as soon as practicable after the sale or the receipt of the money, send notice to the execution creditor and, if the warrant issued out of another court, to that court.

(2) Where the district judge responsible for the execution of a warrant –

(a) receives notice that a bankruptcy order has been made against the debtor or, if the debtor is a company, that a provisional liquidator has been appointed or that an order has been made or a resolution passed for the winding up of the company; and
(b) withdraws from possession of goods seized or pays over to the official receiver or trustee in bankruptcy or, if the debtor is a company, to the

liquidator the proceeds of sale of goods sold under the warrant or money paid in order to avoid a sale or seized or received in part satisfaction of the warrant,

the court shall send notice to the execution creditor and, if the warrant issued out of another court, to that court.

(3) Where the court officer of a court to which a warrant issued out of another court has been sent for execution receives any such notice as is referred to in paragraph (2)(a) after he has sent to the home court any money seized or received in part satisfaction of the warrant, he shall forward the notice to that court.

Scope of provision—This rule requires the court to give notices where the proceeds of execution are retained under Insolvency Act 1986.

Insolvency Act 1986 (r 8(1))—At the time when a bankruptcy order is made, Insolvency Act 1986, s 346(1) passes to the trustee in bankruptcy the benefit of execution against goods (or payment made to avoid it) begun before the bankruptcy order was made, unless the goods are seized and sold (or the payment is made) before then. Further, where execution against goods is issued but before it is completed the bailiff receives notice that a bankruptcy order has been made against the debtor, s 346(2) requires him to pass the fruits of the execution to the trustee in bankruptcy. Where the amount levied for (not the amount of the judgment: *Re Grubb ex parte Sims* (1877) 5 Ch D 375; *Re Hinks ex parte Berthier* (1878) 7 Ch D 882) exceeds £500, the bailiff within 14 days after sale or payment receives notice that a bankruptcy petition has been presented against the debtor, and a bankruptcy order is made on it, then again the proceeds go to the bankrupt's estate. Accordingly, the bailiff is required to retain the amount received for 14 days in case such a notice is received. However s 346(6) enables the bankruptcy court to set aside the trustee's rights under s 346; a creditor's special position must be considered in relation to an Insolvent Voluntary Arrangement under that Act (*Re a Debtor* No 488 IO of 1996, 12 November 1998).

10 Withdrawal and suspension of warrant at creditor's request

(1) Where an execution creditor requests the district judge responsible for executing a warrant to withdraw from possession, he shall, subject to the following paragraphs of this rule, be treated as having abandoned the execution, and the court shall mark the warrant as withdrawn by request of the execution creditor.

(2) Where the request is made in consequence of a claim having been made under Order 33, rule 1, to goods seized under the warrant, the execution shall be treated as being abandoned in respect only of the goods claimed.

(3) If the district judge responsible for executing a warrant is requested by the execution creditor to suspend it in pursuance of an arrangement between him and the debtor, the court shall mark the warrant as suspended by request of the execution creditor and the execution creditor may subsequently apply to the district judge holding the warrant for it to be re-issued and, if he does so, the application shall be deemed for the purpose of section 85(3) of the Act to be an application to issue the warrant.

(4) Nothing in this rule shall prejudice any right of the execution creditor to apply for the issue of a fresh warrant or shall authorise the re-issue of a warrant which has been withdrawn or has expired or has been superseded by the issue of a fresh warrant.

Scope of provision—A distinction must be made between withdrawal or abandonment of a warrant by the creditor on the one hand and its suspension by him on the other. This rule deals with the consequences of both.

Suspension by court—This rule does not apply to suspension by the court; Ord 25, r 8 applies in such circumstances.

Priority—The effect of r 10(3) is that on suspension the priority of the warrant is lost and on re-issue it is accorded priority as if issued on the re-issue date, or presumably its re-delivery to the foreign court (see note, **'Considerations affecting issue of warrant'**, (a) *Priority* under r 1). It is otherwise if the bailiff maintains the levy, by taking 'walking possession', for example so as to allow the debtor time to raise money to pay. However the creditor is not entitled to require the bailiff to proceed thus, and in view of the heavy burden which it places upon the court he may well decline to maintain 'walking possession' for any great length of time.

11 Suspension of part warrant

Where a warrant issued for part of a sum of money and costs payable under a judgment or order is suspended on payment of instalments, the judgment or order shall, unless the court otherwise directs, be treated as suspended on those terms as respects the whole of the sum of money and costs then remaining unpaid.

Scope of provision—A 'part warrant' may be issued only if there is already an instalment order in force (r 1(2)). This rule sets out the position where such a warrant is itself suspended on instalments; the underlying instalment order is treated as varied in the same terms (unless otherwise ordered). This rule is taken to apply only to suspensions by order (see Ord 25, r 8), not those effected by arrangement under r 10(3). Presumably the 'arrangement' between creditor and debtor will provide for payment of the whole debt, not merely the amount recoverable under the part warrant.

12 Inventory and notice where goods removed

(1) Where goods seized in execution are removed, the court shall forthwith deliver or send to the debtor a sufficient inventory of the goods removed and shall, not less than 4 days before the time fixed for the sale, give him notice of the time and place at which the goods will be sold.

(2) The inventory and notice shall be given to the debtor by delivering them to him personally or by sending them to him by post at his place of residence or, if his place of residence is not known, by leaving them for him, or sending them to him by post, at the place from which the goods were removed.

13 Account of sale

Where goods are sold under an execution, the court shall furnish the debtor with a detailed account in writing of the sale and of the application of the proceeds.

14 Notification to foreign court of payment made

Where, after a warrant has been sent to a foreign court for execution but before a final return has been made to the warrant, the home court is notified of a payment made in respect of the sum for which the warrant is issued, the home court shall send notice of the payment to the foreign court.

15 Order for private sale

(1) Subject to paragraph (6), an order of the court under section 97 of the Act that a sale under an execution may be made otherwise than by public auction may be made on the application of the execution creditor or the debtor or the district judge responsible for the execution of the warrant.

(2) Where he is not the applicant for an order under this rule, the district judge responsible for the execution of the warrant shall, on the demand of the

applicant, furnish him with a list containing the name and address of every execution creditor under any other warrant or writ of execution against the goods of the debtor of which the district judge has notice, and where the district judge is the applicant, he shall prepare such a list.

(3) Not less than 4 days before the day fixed for the hearing of the application, the applicant shall give notice of the application to each of the other persons by whom the application might have been made and to every person named in the list referred to in paragraph (2).

(4) The applicant shall produce the list to the court on the hearing of the application.

(5) Every person to whom notice of the application was given may attend and be heard on the hearing of the application.

(6) Where the district judge responsible for the execution of the warrant is the district judge by whom it was issued and he has no notice of any other warrant or writ of execution against the goods of the debtor, an order under this rule may be made by the court of its own motion with the consent of the execution creditor and the debtor or after giving them an opportunity of being heard.

Scope of provision—CCA 1984, s 97 requires a sale of goods seized in execution to be by public auction (if the execution is for more than £20) unless the court otherwise orders. This rule provides the procedure for making such an order.

'court' (r 15(1))—The order must be made by the court which issued the warrant. In family proceedings this will normally be the court in which the cause or matter is proceeding. The warrant may of course have been sent to some other (possibly non-divorce) county court for execution.

Applicant (r 15(2))—The application may be made by either party or (in effect) by the bailiff.

Procedure—Notice must be given to any party who is not the applicant and to any other known execution creditor. Only if there is no such other creditor can the order be made without a hearing, provided the parties consent or, having been given an opportunity to be heard, do not object.

Private sale—The advantage of seeking a private sale is that a better price may be obtained than at auction, to the benefit of both debtor and creditors. The order authorises 'a sale' so that the application should be specific as to the actual sale proposed. If the point is contentious the applicant must be prepared to compare the proposed sale price with what is likely to be achieved at auction. The procedure may be particularly useful where the creditor has an intimate knowledge of the debtor's leviable assets and therefore some idea of the best market for them, or where the goods taken in execution are of such a specialised or perishable nature that sale by auction is either impracticable or would not attract the best price obtainable.

16 Warrant of delivery

(1) Except where an Act or rule provides otherwise, a judgment or order for the delivery of any goods shall be enforceable by warrant of delivery in accordance with this rule.

(2) If the judgment or order does not give the person against whom it was given or made the alternative of paying the value of the goods, it may be enforced by a warrant of specific delivery, that is to say, a warrant to recover the goods without alternative provision for recovery of their value.

(3) If the judgment or order is for the delivery of the goods or payment of their value, it may be enforced by a warrant of delivery to recover the goods or their value.

(4) Where a warrant of delivery is issued, the judgment creditor shall be entitled, by the same or a separate warrant, to execution against the debtor's goods for any money payable under the judgment or order which is to be enforced by the warrant of delivery.

(4A) Where a judgment or order is given or made for the delivery of goods or payment of their value and a warrant is issued to recover the goods or their value, money paid into court under the warrant shall be appropriated first to any sum of money and costs awarded.

(5) The foregoing provisions of this Order, so far as applicable, shall have effect, with the necessary modifications, in relation to warrants of delivery as they have effect in relation to warrants of execution.

Scope of provision—This rule provides the procedure whereby an order for delivery of goods may be enforced by a warrant requiring the bailiff physically to take the goods from the debtor and hand them to the judgment creditor.

Form of warrant (r 16(2), (3))—There are two forms of warrant, one requires the return of the goods or payment of their value (Form N48) and the other simply requires delivery of the goods (Form N46). In the case of the former, the bailiff will levy execution for the value if the goods cannot be found; in the case of the latter, if the bailiff cannot recover the goods, application may be made for the order to be enforced by committal (see note **'Delivery of goods'** under r 18). It is therefore important to seek at the hearing the form of order appropriate to the case. In either case the warrant may provide also for execution for any money judgment or order and will provide for execution for the costs of the warrant.

Application of other rules to warrants of delivery (r 16(5))—Rules 1–15 apply, so far as applicable, to delivery warrants as they apply to warrants of execution.

Forms—N324 (request for warrant of goods – specific delivery or return or value), N46 (specific return of goods), N48 (return of goods or value).

17 Warrant of possession

(1) A judgment or order for the recovery of land shall be enforceable by warrant of possession.

(2) Without prejudice to paragraph (3A), the person desiring a warrant of possession to be issued shall file a request in that behalf certifying that the land has not been vacated in accordance with the judgment or order for the recovery of the said land.

(3) Where a warrant of possession is issued, the judgment creditor shall be entitled, by the same or a separate warrant, to execution against the debtor's goods for any money payable under the judgment or order which is to be enforced by the warrant of possession.

(3A) In a case to which paragraph (3) applies or where an order for possession has been suspended on terms as to payment of a sum of money by instalments, the judgment creditor shall in his request certify –

(a) the amount of money remaining due under the judgment or order; and
(b) that the whole or part of any instalment due remains unpaid.

(4) A warrant of restitution may be issued, with the permission of the court, in aid of any warrant of possession.

(5) An application for permission under paragraph (4) may be made without notice being served on any other party and shall be supported by evidence of wrongful re-entry into possession following the execution of the warrant of possession and of such further facts as would, in the High Court, enable the judgment creditor to have a writ of restitution issued.

(6) Rules 5 and 6 shall apply, with the necessary modifications, in relation to a warrant of possession and any further warrant in aid of such a warrant as they apply in relation to a warrant of execution.

Scope of provision—This rule provides the primary method of enforcing a judgment or order for the recovery of land (including of course any building or part).

Enforcement of suspended orders—The procedure set out in r 17(3A) may not comply with HRA 1998, Sch 1, Pt II, Art 1 (First Protocol to the Human Rights Convention), for example where a claimant local authority (as Housing Benefit Authority) is responsible for ensuring that the necessary credits are applied to the defendant's rent account. Given its own duty under HRA 1998, s 3(1), the court may now have to include a direction in any suspended order requiring the claimant to apply on notice for leave to issue a warrant for possession. Such a direction, which is clearly envisaged by Ord 26, r 5(4), would bring county court procedure into line with that of the High Court.

Issue—The warrant cannot be issued until the date for possession in the order has passed; however, where the order requires possession 'forthwith', the warrant can be issued immediately. Normal administrative processes mean that several days or weeks may elapse before the eviction takes place. Fixing the actual date is a matter of administrative process which may be controlled by the court in appropriate cases (*Air Ministry v Harris* [1951] 2 All ER 862, CA). If it is thought necessary, a direction to this effect should be sought from the judge either when the order is made or subsequently.

Effect—When enforcing a warrant of possession, the bailiff need not remove chattels (County Courts Act 1984, s 111(1)) but may evict any person on the premises even though not a party (*R v Wandsworth County Court ex parte Wandsworth London Borough Council* [1975] 1 WLR 1314). An occupier who claims the right to stay may apply to be added as a defendant (CPR r 19.3) in order to apply for the judgment to be set aside.

Warrant of restitution (r 17(4), (5))—If after possession has been recovered the land or premises are re-occupied, application may be made ex parte for a warrant of restitution to eject the occupier. There must be a sufficient connection between the original eviction and the re-occupation, but it may be that restitution is effective against someone other than those originally evicted (*Wiltshire County Council v Frazer* [1986] 1 WLR 109, where however there had been a summary order for possession against trespassers). See also notes to RSC Ord 46, r 3.

Application of other rules to warrants of possession (r 17(6))—Only rr 5 (leave to issue certain warrants) and 6 (duration and renewal of warrant) apply to possession warrants.

18 Saving for enforcement by committal

Nothing in rule 16 or 17 shall prejudice any power to enforce a judgment or order for the delivery of goods or the recovery of land by an order of committal.

Scope of provision—This rule preserves the power to enforce delivery and possession orders by committal.

Delivery of goods—By analogy with the High Court practice (see RSC Ord 45, r 4), an order for delivery of goods or their value will not be enforced by committal. However, County Courts Act 1984, s 76 no doubt enables the court in a proper case to apply RSC Ord 45, r 5(3) and in effect substitute a specific delivery order, which would be enforceable by committal.

Committal generally—The court will be reluctant to commit where the order could well have been enforced by the less draconian (and much less expensive) option of a warrant (*Danchevsky v Danchevsky* [1974] 3 All ER 934, CA). The applicant for committal should therefore be prepared to show that a warrant has been issued but has proved ineffective or that that method of enforcement is for some reason inappropriate.

CCR ORDER 27
ATTACHMENT OF EARNINGS

Procedural Guide—See Guide 35, set out in Section 1 of this work.

Part I – General

1 Interpretation

(1) In this Order –

'the Act of 1971' means the Attachment of Earnings Act 1971 and, unless the context otherwise requires, expressions used in that Act have the same meanings as in that Act.

2 Index of orders

(1) The court officer of every court shall keep a nominal index of the debtors residing within the district of his court in respect of whom there are in force attachment of earnings orders which have been made by that court or of which the court officer has received notice from another court.

(2) Where a debtor in respect of whom a court has made an attachment of earnings order resides within the district of another court, the court officer of the first-mentioned court shall send a copy of the order to the court officer of the other court for entry in his index.

(3) The court officer shall, on the request of any person having a judgment or order against a person believed to be residing within the district of the court, cause a search to be made in the index of the court and issue a certificate of the result of the search.

Searching the index (r 2(3))—Form N336 is the composite form which covers both the request and certificate of search.

3 Appropriate court

(1) Subject to paragraphs (2) and (3), an application for an attachment of earnings order may be made to the court for the district in which the debtor resides.

(2) If the debtor does not reside within England or Wales, or the creditor does not know where he resides, the application may be made to the court in which, or for the district in which, the judgment or order sought to be enforced was obtained.

(3) Where the creditor applies for attachment of earnings orders in respect of two or more debtors jointly liable under a judgment or order, the application may be made to the court for the district in which any of the debtors resides, so however that if the judgment or order was given or made by any such court, the application shall be made to that court.

4 Mode of applying

(1) A judgment creditor who desires to apply for an attachment of earnings order shall file his application certifying the amount of money remaining due under the judgment or order and that the whole or part of any instalment due remains unpaid and, where it is sought to enforce an order of a magistrates' court –

(a) a certified copy of the order; and

(b) a witness statement or affidavit verifying the amount due under the order or, if payments under the order are required to be made to the [justices' chief executive for the magistrates' court, a certificate by that [chief executive to the same effect.

(2) On the filing of the documents mentioned in paragraph (1) the court officer shall, where the order to be enforced is a maintenance order, fix a day for the hearing of the application.

Amendments—SI 2001/256.

High Court judgments—These can be enforced by attachment without any order for transfer under CCA 1984, s 40 (COA, s 1). The documents to be lodged are specified in Ord 25, r 11(1)(a)–(c).

Forms—The application is made on Form N337.

5 Service and reply

[(1) Notice of the application together with a form of reply in the appropriate form, shall be served on the debtor in the manner set out in CPR rule 6.2.

(2) The debtor shall, within 8 days after service on him of the documents mentioned in paragraph (1), file a reply in the form provided, and the instruction to that effect in the notice to the debtor shall constitute a requirement imposed by virtue of section 14(4) of the Act of 1971:

Provided that no proceedings shall be taken for an offence alleged to have been committed under section 23(2)(c) or (f) of the Act of 1971 in relation to the requirement unless the said documents have been served on the debtor personally or the court is satisfied that they came to his knowledge in sufficient time for him to comply with the requirement.

(2A) Nothing in paragraph (2) shall require a defendant to file a reply if, within the period of time mentioned in that paragraph, he pays to the judgment creditor the money remaining due under the judgment or order and, where such payment is made, the judgment creditor shall so inform the court officer.

(3) On receipt of a reply the court officer shall send a copy to the applicant.

Amendments—SI 2000/221; SI 2001/2792.

'Order 25, rule 3' (r 5(1))—Service will be by first-class post unless the creditor chooses personal service.

'the form provided' (r 5(2))—The debtor replies on Form N56.

Failure to reply—If the debtor does not return the Form N56, the court will automatically issue a Form N61 endorsed with a penal notice for personal service on the debtor, see r 7A below.

'served on the debtor personally' (r 5(2))—If personal service is impractical, the court may order service by another method (CPR r 6.8).

'an offence' (r 5(2))—The combined effect of this rule and r 15 below is that the debtor does not actually commit an offence until he has been served either personally or by another method with an order in Form N61 endorsed with a penal notice.

6 Notice to employer

Without prejudice to the powers conferred by section 14(1) of the Act of 1971, the court officer may, at any stage of the proceedings, send to any person appearing to have the debtor in his employment a notice requesting him to give to the court, within such period as may be specified in the notice, a statement of the debtor's earnings and anticipated earnings with such particulars as may be so specified.

Statement of earnings—The form is N338. A creditor who knows the name of the debtor's employer should always request the issue of Form N338 when applying for attachment of earnings. If the debtor then fails to return the Form N56, the court may proceed to make an order without further delay, on the basis of the information given by the employer. The debtor retains the right to apply for reconsideration of the order under r 7(2) below.

7 Attachment of earnings order

(1) On receipt of the debtor's reply, the court officer may, if he has sufficient information to do so, make an attachment of earnings order and a copy of the order shall be sent to the parties and to the debtor's employer.

(2) Where an order is made under paragraph (1), the judgment creditor or the debtor may, within 14 days of service of the order on him and giving his reasons, apply on notice for the order to be re-considered and the court officer shall fix a day for the hearing of the application and give to the judgment creditor and the debtor not less than 2 days' notice of the day so fixed.

(3) On hearing an application under paragraph (2), the district judge may confirm the order or set it aside and make such new order as he thinks fit and the order so made shall be entered in the records of the court.

(4) Where an order is not made under paragraph (1), the court officer shall refer the application to the district judge who shall, if he considers that he has sufficient information to do so without the attendance of the parties, determine the application.

(5) Where the district judge does not determine the application under paragraph (4), he shall direct that a day be fixed for the hearing of the application whereupon the court officer shall fix such a day and give to the judgment creditor and the debtor not less than 8 days' notice of the day so fixed.

(6) Where an order is made under paragraph (4), the judgment creditor or the debtor may, within 14 days of service of the order on him and giving his reasons, apply on notice for the order to be re-considered; and the court officer shall fix a day for the hearing of the application and give to the judgment creditor and the debtor not less than 2 days' notice of the day so fixed.

(7) On hearing an application under paragraph (6), the district judge may confirm the order or set it aside and make such new order as he thinks fit and the order so made shall be entered in the records of the court.

(8) If the creditor does not appear at the hearing of the application under paragraph (5) but –

- (a) the court has received a witness statement or affidavit of evidence from him; or
- (b) the creditor requests the court in writing to proceed in his absence,

the court may proceed to hear the application and to make an order thereon.

(9) An attachment of earnings order may be made to secure the payment of a judgment debt if the debt is –

- (a) of not less than £50; or
- (b) for the amount remaining payable under a judgment for a sum of not less than £50.

Procedure—The making of attachment orders is now a paper procedure handled by the court staff subject to the right to refer cases to the district judge who may either determine the application or fix a hearing. Any order made without a hearing can be reconsidered under r 7(2) or r 7(6).

Suspended orders may be made under CCA 1984, s 71(2).

7A Failure by debtor

(1) If the debtor has failed to comply with rule 5(2) or to make payment to the judgment creditor, the court officer may issue an order under section 14(1) of the Act of 1971 which shall –

(a) be indorsed with or incorporate a notice warning the debtor of the consequences of disobedience to the order;
(b) be served on the debtor personally; and
(c) direct that any payments made thereafter shall be paid into the court and not direct to the judgment creditor.

(2) Without prejudice to rule 16, if the person served with an order made pursuant to paragraph (1) fails to obey it or to file a statement of his means or to make payment, the court officer shall issue a notice calling on that person to show good reason why he should not be imprisoned and any such notice shall be served on the debtor personally not less than 5 days before the hearing.

(3) Order 29, rule 1 shall apply, with the necessary modifications and with the substitution of references to the district judge for references to the judge, where a notice is issued under paragraph (2) or (4) of that rule.

(4) In this rule 'statement of means' means a statement given under section 14(1) of the Act of 1971.

Notice to show good reason (r 7A(2))—The form is N63. A district judge may exercise all the powers of the court.

'served on the debtor personally' (r 7A(1)(b) and (2))—See note to r 5 above.

7B Suspended committal order

(1) If the debtor fails to attend at an adjourned hearing of an application for an attachment of earnings order and a committal order is made, the judge or district judge may direct that the committal order shall be suspended so long as the debtor attends at the time and place specified in the committal order and paragraphs (2), (4) and (5) of Order 28, rule 7 shall apply, with the necessary modifications, where such a direction is given as they apply where a direction is given under paragraph (1) of that rule.

(2) Where a committal order is suspended under paragraph (1) and the debtor fails to attend at the time and place specified under paragraph (1), a certificate to that effect given by the court officer shall be sufficient authority for the issue of a warrant of committal.

8 Failure by debtor – maintenance orders

(1) An order made under section 23(1) of the Act of 1971 for the attendance of the debtor at an adjourned hearing of an application for an attachment of earnings order to secure payments under a maintenance order shall –

(a) be served on the debtor personally not less than 5 days before the day fixed for the adjourned hearing; and
(b) direct that any payments made thereafter shall be paid into the court and not direct to the judgment creditor.

(2) An application by a debtor for the revocation of an order committing him to prison and, if he is already in custody, for his discharge under subsection (7) of the said section 23 shall be made to the judge or district judge in writing without notice to any other party showing the reasons for the debtor's failure to attend the court or his refusal to be sworn or to give evidence, as the case may be, and containing an undertaking by the debtor to attend the court or to be sworn or to give evidence when next ordered or required to do so.

(3) The application shall, if the debtor has already been lodged in prison, be attested by the governor of the prison (or any other officer of the prison not below the rank of principal officer) and in any other case be made on witness statement or affidavit.

(4) Before dealing with the application the judge or district judge may, if he thinks fit, cause notice to be given to the judgment creditor that the application has been made and of a day and hour when he may attend and be heard.

'maintenance order' (r 8(1))—Although such orders are made only in family proceedings (outside the scope of this work), the rule is reproduced here as providing a model for the procedure likely to be followed in other cases where the debtor is ordered to attend an adjourned hearing of the application (for which no express provision is made).

9 Costs

(1) Where costs are allowed to the judgment creditor on an application for an attachment of earnings order, there may be allowed –

(a) a charge of a solicitor for attending the hearing and, if the court so directs, for serving the application;
(b) if the court certifies that the case is fit for counsel, a fee to counsel; and
(c) the court fee on the issue of the application.

(2) For the purpose of paragraph (1)(a) a solicitor who has prepared on behalf of the judgment creditor a witness statement or affidavit or request under rule 7(8) shall be treated as having attended the hearing.

(3) The costs may be fixed and allowed without detailed assessment under CPR Part 47.

Costs—The power to order detailed assessment is likely to be reserved to those rare cases which involve some substantial issue, eg under s 16 of the Act. Fixed costs are normally allowed under Ord 38, App B.

10 Contents and service of order

(1) An attachment of earnings order shall contain such of the following particulars relating to the debtor as are known to the court, namely –

(a) his full name and address;
(b) his place of work; and
(c) the nature of his work and his works number, if any,

and those particulars shall be the prescribed particulars for the purposes of section 6(3) of the Act of 1971.

(2) An attachment of earnings order and any order varying or discharging such an order shall be served on the debtor and on the person to whom the order is directed, and CPR Part 6 and CPR rules 40.4 and 40.5 shall apply with the further modification that where the order is directed to a corporation which has requested the court that any communication relating to the debtor or to the class

of persons to whom he belongs shall be directed to the corporation at a particular address, service may, if the district judge thinks fit, be effected on the corporation at that address.

(3) Where an attachment of earnings order is made to enforce a judgment or order of the High Court or a magistrates' court, a copy of the attachment of earnings order and of any order discharging it shall be sent by the court officer of the county court to the court officer of the High Court, or, as the case may be, the [justices' chief executive for the magistrates' court.

Amendments—SI 2001/256.

11 Application to determine whether particular payments are earnings

An application to the court under section 16 of the Act of 1971 to determine whether payments to the debtor of a particular class or description are earnings for the purpose of an attachment of earnings order may be made to the district judge in writing and the court officer shall thereupon fix a date and time for the hearing of the application by the court and give notice thereof to the persons mentioned in the said section 16(2)(a), (b) and (c).

'in writing'—Note that the rule does not require the use of a formal application notice under CPR Pt 23.

12 Notice of cesser

Where an attachment of earnings order ceases to have effect under section 8(4) of the Act of 1971, the court officer of the court in which the matter is proceeding shall give notice of the cesser to the person to whom the order was directed.

13 Variation and discharge by court of own motion

(1) Subject to paragraph (9), the powers conferred by section 9(1) of the Act of 1971 may be exercised by the court of its own motion in the circumstances mentioned in the following paragraphs.

(2) Where it appears to the court that a person served with an attachment of earnings order directed to him has not the debtor in his employment, the court may discharge the order.

(3) Where an attachment of earnings order which has lapsed under section 9(4) of the Act of 1971 is again directed to a person who appears to the court to have the debtor in his employment, the court may make such consequential variations in the order as it thinks fit.

(4) Where, after making an attachment of earnings order, the court makes or is notified of the making of another such order in respect of the same debtor which is not to secure the payment of a judgment debt or payments under an administration order, the court may discharge or vary the first-mentioned order having regard to the priority accorded to the other order by paragraph 8 of Schedule 3 to the Act of 1971.

(5) Where, after making an attachment of earnings order, the court makes an order under section 4(1)(b) of the Act of 1971 or makes an administration order,

the court may discharge the attachment of earnings order or, if it exercises the power conferred by section 5(3) of the said Act, may vary the order in such manner as it thinks fit.

(6) On making a consolidated attachment of earnings order the court may discharge any earlier attachment of earnings order made to secure the payment of a judgment debt by the same debtor.

(7) Where it appears to the court that a bankruptcy order has been made against a person in respect of whom an attachment of earnings order is in force to secure the payment of a judgment debt, the court may discharge the attachment of earnings order.

(8) Where an attachment of earnings order has been made to secure the payment of a judgment debt and the court grants permission to issue execution for the recovery of the debt, the court may discharge the order.

(9) Before varying or discharging an attachment of earnings order of its own motion under any of the foregoing paragraphs of this rule, the court shall, unless it thinks it unnecessary in the circumstances to do so, give the debtor and the person on whose application the order was made an opportunity of being heard on the question whether the order should be varied or discharged, and for that purpose the court officer may give them notice of a date, time and place at which the question will be considered.

14 Transfer of attachment order

(1) Where the court by which the question of making a consolidated attachment order falls to be considered is not the court by which any attachment of earnings order has been made to secure the payment of a judgment debt by the debtor, the district judge of the last-mentioned court shall, at the request of the district judge of the first-mentioned court, transfer to that court the matter in which the attachment of earnings order was made.

(2) Without prejudice to paragraph (1), if in the opinion of the judge or district judge of any court by which an attachment of earnings order has been made, the matter could more conveniently proceed in some other court, whether by reason of the debtor having become resident in the district of that court or otherwise, he may order the matter to be transferred to that court.

(3) The court to which proceedings arising out of an attachment of earnings are transferred under this rule shall have the same jurisdiction in relation to the order as if it has been made by that court.

15 Exercise of power to obtain statement of earnings etc

(1) An order under section 14(1) of the Act of 1971 shall be indorsed with or incorporate a notice warning the person to whom it is directed of the consequences of disobedience to the order and shall be served on him personally.

(2) Order 34, rule 2, shall apply, with the necessary modifications, in relation to any penalty for failure to comply with an order under the said section 14(1) or, subject to the proviso to rule 5(2), any penalty for failure to comply with a requirement mentioned in that rule, as it applies in relation to a fine under section 55 of the County Courts Act 1984.

'a notice warning' (r 15(1))—The endorsement or incorporation of this notice commonly called a penal notice is necessary before any further enforcement action can be taken.

'Order 34, rule 2' (r 15(2))—This rule deals with the procedure where a person fails to attend court after service of a witness summons.

16 Offences

(1) Where it is alleged that a person has committed any offence mentioned in section 23(2)(a), (b), (d), (e) or (f) of the Act of 1971 in relation to proceedings in, or to an attachment of earnings order made by, a county court, the district judge shall, unless it is decided to proceed against the alleged offender summarily, issue a summons calling upon him to show cause why he should not be punished for the alleged offence.

The summons shall be served on the alleged offender personally not less than 14 days before the return day.

(2) Order 34, rules 3 and 4, shall apply, with the necessary modifications, to proceedings for an offence under section 23(2) of the Act of 1971 as they apply to proceedings for offences under the County Courts Act 1984.

Section 23(2) (r 16(1))—Note that offences under s 23(2)(c) are dealt with under r 7A above. For offences under the paragraphs listed the court will either issue a summons in Form N62 or a notice to show cause in Form N63.

'to proceed ... summarily' (r 16(1))—This procedure may be appropriate where the debtor attends court but refuses to give details of his employment or earnings. See the notes to CCA 1984, s 118 for the proper procedure to be followed.

'Order 34, rules 3 and 4' (r 16(2))—These rules relate to fines imposed by the court.

17 Maintenance orders

(1) The foregoing rules of this Order shall apply in relation to maintenance payments as they apply in relation to a judgment debt, subject to the following paragraphs.

(2) An application for an attachment of earnings order to secure payments under a maintenance order made by a county court shall be made to that county court.

(3) Any application under section 32 of the Matrimonial Causes Act 1973 for permission to enforce the payment of arrears which became due more than 12 months before the application for an attachment of earnings order shall be made in that application.

[(3A) Notice of the application together with a form of reply in the appropriate form, shall be served on the debtor in the manner set out in CPR rule 6.2.

[(3B) Service of the notice shall be effected not less than 21 days before the hearing, but service may be effected at any time before the hearing on the applicant satisfying the court by witness statement or affidavit that the respondent is about to remove from his address for service.

[(3C) ... Rule 5(2A) shall not apply.

(4) An application by the debtor for an attachment of earnings order to secure payments under a maintenance order may be made on the making of the maintenance order or an order varying the maintenance order, and rules 4 and 5 shall not apply.

(5) Rule 7 shall have effect as if for paragraphs (1) to (8) there were substituted the following paragraph –

> '(1) An application for an attachment of earnings order may be heard and determined by the district judge, who shall hear the application in private.'

(6) Rule 9 shall apply as if for the reference to the amount payable under the relevant adjudication there were substituted a reference to the arrears due under the related maintenance order.

(7) Where an attachment of earnings order made by the High Court designates the court officer of a county court as the collecting officer, that officer shall, on receipt of a certified copy of the order from the court officer of the High Court, send to the person to whom the order is directed a notice as to the mode of payment.

(8) Where an attachment of earnings order made by a county court to secure payments under a maintenance order ceases to have effect and –

- (a) the related maintenance order was made by that court; or
- (b) the related maintenance order was an order of the High Court and –
  - (i) the court officer of the county court has received notice of the cessation from the court officer of the High Court; or
  - (ii) a committal order has been made in the county court for the enforcement of the related maintenance order,

the court officer of the county court shall give notice of the cessation to the person to whom the attachment of earnings order was directed.

(9) Where an attachment of earnings order has been made by a county court to secure payments under a maintenance order, notice under section 10(2) of the Act of 1971 to the debtor and to the person to whom the district judge is required to pay sums received under the order shall be in the form provided for that purpose, and if the debtor wishes to request the court to discharge the attachment of earnings order or to vary it otherwise than by making the appropriate variation, he shall apply to the court, within 14 days after the date of the notice, for the remedy desired.

(10) Rule 13 shall have effect as if for paragraphs (4) to (7) there were substituted the following paragraph –

> '(4) Where it appears to the court by which an attachment of earnings order has been made that the related maintenance order has ceased to have effect, whether by virtue of the terms of the maintenance order or under section 28 of the Matrimonial Causes Act 1973 or otherwise, the court may discharge or vary the attachment of earnings order.'

Amendments—SI 1999/1008; SI 2000/221; SI 2001/2792.

Part II – Consolidated Attachment of Earnings Orders

18 Cases in which consolidated order may be made

Subject to the provisions of rules 19 to 21, the court may make a consolidated attachment order where –

- (a) two or more attachment of earnings orders are in force to secure the payment of judgment debts by the same debtor; or

(b) on an application for an attachment of earnings order to secure the payment of a judgment debt, or for a consolidated attachment order to secure the payment of two or more judgment debts, it appears to the court that an attachment of earnings order is already in force to secure the payment of a judgment debt by the same debtor.

Consolidated attachment order—The form used is N66.

19 Application for consolidated order

(1) An application for a consolidated attachment order may be made –

(a) by the debtor in respect of whom the order is sought; or
(b) by any person who has obtained or is entitled to apply for an attachment of earnings order to secure the payment of a judgment debt by that debtor.

(2) An application under paragraph (1) may be made in the proceedings in which any attachment of earnings order (other than a priority order) is in force and rules 3, 4 and 5 of this Order shall not apply.

(3) Where the judgment which it is sought to enforce was not given by the court which made the attachment of earnings order, the judgment shall be automatically transferred to the court which made the attachment of earnings order.

(3A) An application under paragraph (1)(b) shall certify the amount of money remaining due under the judgment or order and that the whole or part of any instalment due remains unpaid.

(3B) Where an application for a consolidated attachment of earnings order is made, the court officer shall –

(a) notify any party who may be affected by the application of its terms; and
(b) require him to notify the court in writing, within 14 days of service of notification upon him, giving his reasons for any objection he may have to the granting of the application.

(3C) If notice of any objection is not given within the time stated, the court officer shall make a consolidated attachment of earnings order.

(3D) If any party objects to the making of a consolidated attachment of earnings order, the court officer shall refer the application to the district judge who may grant the application after considering the objection made and the reasons given.

(3E) In the foregoing paragraphs of this rule, a party affected by the application means –

(a) where the application is made by the debtor, the creditor in the proceedings in which the application is made and any other creditor who has obtained an attachment of earnings order which is in force to secure the payment of a judgment debt by the debtor;
(b) where the application is made by the judgment creditor, the debtor and every person who, to the knowledge of the applicant, has obtained an attachment of earnings order which is in force to secure the payment of a judgment debt by the debtor.

(4) A person to whom two or more attachment of earnings orders are directed to secure the payment of judgment debts by the same debtor may request the court in writing to make a consolidated attachment order to secure the payment

of those debts, and on receipt of such a request paragraphs (3B) to (3E) shall apply, with the necessary modifications, as if the request were an application by the judgment creditor.

'other than a priority order' (r 19(2))—An order to secure payment of maintenance is a priority order.

20 Making of consolidated order by court of its own motion

Where an application is made for an attachment of earnings order to secure the payment of a judgment debt by a debtor in respect of whom an attachment of earnings order is already in force to secure the payment of another judgment debt and no application is made for a consolidated attachment order, the court officer may make such an order of his own motion after giving all persons concerned an opportunity of submitting written objections.

21 Extension of consolidated order

(1) Where a consolidated attachment order is in force to secure the payment of two or more judgment debts, any creditor to whom another judgment debt is owed by the same judgment debtor may apply to the court by which the order was made for it to be extended so as to secure the payment of that debt as well as the first-mentioned debts and, if the application is granted, the court may either vary the order accordingly or may discharge it and make a new consolidated attachment order to secure payment of all the aforesaid judgment debts.

(2) An application under this rule shall be treated for the purposes of rules 19 and 20 as an application for a consolidated attachment order.

'may apply to the court' (r 21(1))—Although the creditor making the application will not be a party to the proceedings in which the existing order was made, r 21(2) has the effect of permitting the application to be made by application notice. Information about existing orders can be obtained by searching the index maintained under r 2 above.

22 Payments under consolidated order

Instead of complying with section 13 of the Act of 1971, a court officer who receives payments made to him in compliance with a consolidated attachment order shall, after deducting such court fees, if any, in respect of proceedings for or arising out of the order as are deductible from those payments, deal with the sums paid as he would if they had been paid by the debtor to satisfy the relevant adjudications in proportion to the amounts payable thereunder, and for that purpose dividends may from time to time be declared and distributed among the creditors entitled thereto.

CCR ORDER 28
JUDGMENT SUMMONSES

General note—This Order and the associated forms have been substantially amended to take account of the decision of the Court of Appeal in *Mubarak v Mubarak* [2001] 1 FLR 698 and the Human Rights Act deficiencies in the previous regime identified in the case.

1 Application for judgment summons

(1) An application for the issue of a judgment summons may be made to the court for the district in which the debtor resides or carries on business or, if the summons is to issue against two or more persons jointly liable under the judgment or order sought to be enforced, in the court for the district in which any of the debtors resides or carries on business.

(2) The judgment creditor shall make his application by filing a request in that behalf certifying the amount of money remaining due under the judgment or order, the amount in respect of which the judgment summons is to issue and that the whole or part of any instalment due remains unpaid.

(3) The judgment creditor must file with the request all written evidence on which he intends to rely.

Amendments—SI 2001/4015.

Judgment summons—The expression is defined in CCA 1984, s 147(1). By virtue of AJA 1970, s 11 the power of the court to commit a defendant to prison under Debtors Act 1869, s 5 may only be exercised to enforce:

(a) a High Court or county court maintenance order;
(b) a judgment or order for payment of income tax, any tax recoverable under Taxes Management Act 1970, ss 65, 66 or 68, national insurance contributions, or state scheme pensions recoverable under Social Security Contributions and Benefits Act 1992, Pt I.

A committal order may only be made by a circuit judge or his deputy.

Forms—The form of request is N342. The judgment summons is in Form N67.

2 Mode of service

(1) Subject to paragraph (2), a judgment summons shall be served personally on every debtor against whom it is issued.

(2) Where the judgment creditor or his solicitor gives a certificate for postal service in respect of a debtor residing or carrying on business within the district of the court, the judgment summons shall, unless the district judge otherwise directs, be served on that debtor by an officer of the court sending it to him by first-class post at the address stated in the request for the judgment summons and, unless the contrary is shown, the date of service shall be deemed to be the seventh day after the date on which the judgment summons was sent to the debtor.

(3) Where a judgment summons has been served on a debtor in accordance with paragraph (2), no order of commitment shall be made against him unless –

(a) he appears at the hearing; or
(b) it is made under section 110(2) of the Act.

(4) The written evidence on which the judgment creditor intends to rely must be served with the judgment summons.

Amendments—SI 2001/4015.

'certificate for postal service' (r 2(2))—The normal procedure is to use postal service in the first instance and then proceed under r 4 below if the debtor fails to attend on the first hearing.

3 Time for service

(1) The judgment summons and written evidence must be served not less than 14 days before the day fixed for the hearing.

(2) A notice of non-service shall be sent pursuant to CPR rule 6.11 in respect of a judgment summons which has been sent by post under rule 2(2) and has been returned to the court office undelivered.

(3) CPR rules 7.5 and 7.6 shall apply, with the necessary modifications, to a judgment summons as they apply to a claim form.

Amendments—SI 2001/4015.

'CPR rules 7.5 and 7.6' (r 3(3))—The application of these rules means that a judgment summons must be served within 4 months after issue but this time may be extended by the court.

4 Enforcement of debtor's attendance

(1) Order 27, rules 7B and 8, shall apply, with the necessary modifications, to an order made under section 110(1) of the Act for the attendance of the debtor at an adjourned hearing of a judgment summons as they apply to an order made under section 23(1) of the Attachment of Earnings Act 1971 for the attendance of the debtor at an adjourned hearing of an application for an attachment of earnings order.

(1A) An order made under section 110(1) of the Act must be served personally on the judgment debtor.

(1B) Copies of –

(a) the judgment summons; and
(b) the written evidence,

must be served with the order.

(2) At the time of service of the order there shall be paid or tendered to the debtor a sum reasonably sufficient to cover his expenses in travelling to and from the court, unless such a sum was paid to him at the time of service of the judgment summons.

Amendments—SI 2001/4015.

Order for attendance (r 4(1))—The consequence of failure to attend on the original hearing is not that the court may commit the debtor but that, pursuant to CCA 1984, s 110(1), it may order his attendance at an adjourned hearing. Failure to comply with that order is punishable by committal for up to 14 days. There is also a power to order the debtor to be arrested and brought before the court (s 110(3)). Conduct money must have been paid or tendered (s 110(4)) and there is power to revoke or discharge the committal (s 110(5)). There is a close parallel with the procedure on failure to attend an attachment of earnings application, but in the case of a judgment summons the court's powers are not exercisable by the district judge.

Forms—The order to attend is in Form N69; the form of committal for failure to attend is Form N70; the order revoking such committal is Form N71; and the order for arrest is Form N112.

5 Evidence

(1) No person may be committed on an application for a judgment summons unless –

(a) the order is made under section 110(2) of the Act; or
(b) the judgment creditor proves that the debtor –
  (i) has or has had since the date of the judgment or order the means to pay the sum in respect of which he has made default; and
  (ii) has refused or neglected or refuses or neglects to pay that sum.

(2) The debtor may not be compelled to give evidence.

Amendments—Substituted by SI 2001/4015.

Scope of provision—This new paragraph makes clear that a judgment debtor will only be committed to prison when:

(a) he has been duly served with an order made under s 110(2) of the Act and failed to attend the subsequent hearing; or

(b) the judgment creditor has discharged the burden of proving beyond reasonable doubt that the judgment debtor has or has had the means to pay and has refused or neglected to do so.

Since a committal order under s 110(2) will be made only in the absence of the judgment debtor, the order will provide for the judgment debtor to be brought before a judge before being conveyed to prison when he will have the opportunity either to purge his contempt or to apply to set aside the committal order on the basis of any procedural defect that he wishes to raise.

7 Suspension of committal order

(1) If on the hearing of a judgment summons a committal order is made, the judge may direct execution of the order to be suspended to enable the debtor to pay the amount due.

(2) A note of any direction given under paragraph (1) shall be entered in the records of the court and notice of the suspended committal order shall be sent to the debtor.

(3) Where a judgment summons is issued in respect of one or more but not all of the instalments payable under a judgment or order for payment by instalments and a committal order is made and suspended under paragraph (1), the judgment or order shall, unless the judge otherwise orders, be suspended for so long as the execution of the committal order is suspended.

(4) Where execution of a committal order is suspended under paragraph (1) and the debtor subsequently desires to apply for a further suspension, the debtor shall attend at or write to the court office and apply for the suspension he desires, stating the reasons for his inability to comply with the terms of the original suspension, and the court shall fix a day for the hearing of the application by the judge and give at least 3 days' notice thereof to the judgment creditor and the debtor.

(5) The district judge may suspend execution of the committal order pending the hearing of an application under paragraph (4).

'on the hearing' (r 7(1))—As an alternative to a committal order or a new order (see r 8 below) the court may make an attachment of earnings order under Attachment of Earnings Act 1971, s 3(4) and (6).

Forms—The notice of suspended committal order is in Form N72.

8 New order on judgment summons

(1) Where on the hearing of a judgment summons, the judge makes a new order for payment of the amount of the judgment debt remaining unpaid, there shall be included in the amount payable under the order for the purpose of any enforcement proceedings, otherwise than by judgment summons, any amount in respect of which a committal order has already been made and the debtor imprisoned.

(2) No judgment summons under the new order shall include any amount in respect of which the debtor was imprisoned before the new order was made, and any amount subsequently paid shall be appropriated in the first instance to the amount due under the new order.

Scope of provision—A new order will include any amounts in respect of which the debtor has been previously committed, but he is not thereby rendered liable to committal again in respect of such amounts.

New order—The making of a simple instalment order is authorised by Debtors Act 1869, s 5 itself.

No judgment summons under the new order—Debtors Act 1869, s 5 permits a term of imprisonment in respect of any debt or instalment under any judgment or order, and this means one term only (*Evans v Wills* (1876) 1 CPD 229). This rule prohibits a second judgment summons for the same debt or instalment notwithstanding that it has become due under a different order, namely the new order.

Forms—A new order on a judgment summons is in Form N73.

9 Notification of order on judgment of High Court

(1) Notice of the result of the hearing of a judgment summons on a judgment or order of the High Court shall be sent by the county court to the High Court.

If a committal order or a new order for payment is made on the hearing, the office copy of the judgment or order filed in the county court shall be deemed to be a judgment or order of the court in which the judgment summons is heard.

Amendments—SI 2001/2792.

Forms—The form of notice to the High Court is Form N343.

10 Costs on judgment summons

(1) No costs shall be allowed to the judgment creditor on the hearing of a judgment summons unless –

- (a) a committal order is made; or
- (b) the sum in respect of which the judgment summons was issued is paid before the hearing.

(2) Where costs are allowed to the judgment creditor,

- (a) there may be allowed –
  - (i) a charge of the judgment creditor's solicitor for attending the hearing and, if the judge so directs, for serving the judgment summons;
  - (ii) a fee to counsel if the court certifies that the case is fit for counsel;
  - (iii) any travelling expenses paid to the debtor; and
  - (iv) the court fee on the issue of the judgment summons;
- (b) the costs may be fixed and allowed without detailed assessment under CPR Part 47.

(3) (*revoked*)

Amendments—SI 2001/4015.

'No costs shall be allowed … unless' (r 10(1))—Not only is the creditor deprived of costs if the debt is not paid and no committal order is made, he is also at risk as to the debtor's costs if he fails to prove means and refusal or neglect. The request for the judgment summons (Form N342) includes an acknowledgment of this risk.

'may be fixed and allowed without detailed assessment' (r 10(2)(b))—The successful creditor does not have the right to elect.

Amount of costs—See CCR Ord 38, App C, Pt III, Item 6.

11 Issue of warrant of committal

(1) A judgment creditor desiring a warrant to be issued pursuant to a committal order shall file a request in that behalf.

(2) Where two or more debtors are to be committed in respect of the same judgment or order, a separate warrant of committal shall be issued for each of them.

(3) Where a warrant of committal is sent to a foreign court for execution, that court shall indorse on it a notice as to the effect of section 122(3) of the Act addressed to the governor of the prison of that court.

Nature of warrant—The warrant requires the district judge to take the body of the person against whom it is issued, the police to assist the district judge and the governor of the prison to receive and keep the person until discharged (CCA 1984, s 119).

Forms—The request for warrant is in Form N344; the warrant in Form N74; and the indorsement to a foreign court is in Form N75.

12 Notification to foreign court of part payment before debtor lodged in prison

Where, after a warrant of committal has been sent to a foreign court for execution but before the debtor is lodged in prison, the home court is notified that an amount which is less than the sum on payment of which the debtor is to be discharged has been paid, the home court shall send notice of the payment to the foreign court.

Forms—The form of notification is Form N335.

13 Payment after debtor lodged in prison

(1) Where, after the debtor has been lodged in prison under a warrant of committal, payment is made of the sum on payment of which the debtor is to be discharged, then –

- (a) if the payment is made to the court responsible for the execution of the warrant, the court officer shall make and sign a certificate of payment and send it by post or otherwise to the gaoler;
- (b) if the payment is made to the court which issued the warrant of committal after the warrant has been sent to a foreign court for execution, the home court shall send notice of the payment to the foreign court, and the court officer at the foreign court shall make and sign a certificate of payment and send it by post or otherwise to the gaoler;
- (c) if the payment is made to the gaoler, he shall sign a certificate of payment and send the amount to the court which made the committal order.

(2) Where, after the debtor has been lodged in prison under a warrant of committal, payment is made of an amount less than the sum on payment of which the debtor is to be discharged, then subject to paragraph (3), paragraph (1)(a) and (b) shall apply with the substitution of references to a notice of payment for the references to a certificate of payment and paragraph (1)(c) shall apply with the omission of the requirement to make and sign a certificate of payment.

(3) Where, after the making of a payment to which paragraph (2) relates, the balance of the sum on payment of which the debtor is to be discharged is paid, paragraph (1) shall apply without the modifications mentioned in paragraph (2).

Amendments—SI 1999/1008.

Discharge—The purpose of this seemingly cumbersome and obvious rule is to provide the mechanism for discharge on payment which is required by Debtors Act 1869, s 5.

Forms—The certificate of payment is Form N345.

14 Discharge of debtor otherwise than on payment

(1) Where the judgment creditor lodges with the district judge a request that a debtor lodged in prison under a warrant of committal may be discharged from custody, the district judge shall make an order for the discharge of the debtor in respect of the warrant of committal and the court shall send the gaoler a certificate of discharge.

(2) Where a debtor who has been lodged in prison under a warrant of committal desires to apply for his discharge under section 121 of the Act, the application shall be made to the judge in writing and without notice showing the reasons why the debtor alleges that he is unable to pay the sum in respect of which he has been committed and ought to be discharged and stating any offer which he desires to make as to the terms on which his discharge is to be ordered, and Order 27, rule 8(3) and (4), shall apply, with the necessary modifications, as it applies to an application by a debtor for his discharge from custody under section 23(7) of the Attachment of Earnings Act 1971.

(3) If in a case to which paragraph (2) relates the debtor is ordered to be discharged from custody on terms which include liability to re-arrest if the terms are not complied with, the judge may, on the application of the judgment creditor if the terms are not complied with, order the debtor to be re-arrested and imprisoned for such part of the term of imprisonment as remained unserved at the time of discharge.

(4) Where an order is made under paragraph (3), a duplicate warrant of committal shall be issued, indorsed with a certificate signed by the court officer as to the order of the judge.

Scope of provision—This rule enables the creditor to request, and the debtor to apply for, the debtor's discharge from custody, and provides in the latter case that the discharge may be on terms.

'section 121 of the Act' (r 14(2))—CCA 1984, s 121 provides that while a committal order may be made if it is proved that the debtor *has had* the means to pay, the judge may order his discharge if satisfied that he is now unable to pay (and that he ought to be discharged).

Forms—The form of creditor's request to discharge is Form N346; the form of certificate of discharge on the creditor's request is Form N347; the certificate of discharge following the debtor's application is Form N348; and the form of indorsement on the duplicate committal warrant is Form N76.

CCR ORDER 29
COMMITTAL FOR BREACH OF ORDER OR UNDERTAKING

Procedural Guide—See Guide 44, set out in Section 1 of this work.

Practice Direction—See generally PDCommittal at p 1661.

1 Enforcement of judgment to do or abstain from doing any act

(1) Where a person required by a judgment or order to do an act refuses or neglects to do it within the time fixed by the judgment or order or any subsequent order, or where a person disobeys a judgment or order requiring him to abstain from doing an act, then, subject to the Debtors Acts 1869 and 1878 and to the provisions of these rules, the judgment or order may be enforced, by order of the judge, by a committal order against that person or, if that person is a body corporate, against any director or other officer of the body.

(2) Subject to paragraphs (6) and (7), a judgment or order shall not be enforced under paragraph (1) unless –

- (a) a copy of the judgment or order has been served personally on the person required to do or abstain from doing the act in question and also, where that person is a body corporate, on the director or other officer of the body against whom a committal order is sought; and
- (b) in the case of a judgment or order requiring a person to do an act, the copy has been so served before the expiration of the time within which he was required to do the act and was accompanied by a copy of any order, made between the date of the judgment or order and the date of service, fixing that time.

(3) Where a judgment or order enforceable by committal order under paragraph (1) has been given or made, the court officer shall, if the judgment or order is in the nature of an injunction, at the time when the judgment or order is drawn up, and in any other case on the request of the judgment creditor, issue a copy of the judgment or order, indorsed with or incorporating a notice as to the consequences of disobedience, for service in accordance with paragraph (2).

(4) If the person served with the judgment or order fails to obey it, the judgment creditor may issue a claim form or, as the case may be, an application notice seeking the committal for contempt of court of that person and subject to paragraph (7), the claim form or application notice shall be served on him personally.

(4A) The claim form or application notice (as the case may be) shall –

- (a) identify the provisions of the injunction or undertaking which it is alleged have been disobeyed or broken;
- (b) list the ways in which it is alleged that the injunction has been disobeyed or the undertaking has been broken;
- (c) be supported by an affidavit stating the grounds on which the application is made,

and unless service is dispensed with under paragraph (7), a copy of the affidavit shall be served with the claim form or application notice.

(5) If a committal order is made, the order shall be for the issue of a warrant of committal and, unless the judge otherwise orders –

- (a) a copy of the order shall be served on the person to be committed either before or at the time of the execution of the warrant; or
- (b) where the warrant has been signed by the judge, the order for issue of the warrant may be served on the person to be committed at any time within 36 hours after the execution of the warrant.

[(5A) A warrant of committal shall not, without further order of the court, be enforced more than 2 years after the date on which the warrant is issued.

(6) A judgment or order requiring a person to abstain from doing an act may be enforced under paragraph (1) notwithstanding that service of a copy of the judgment or order has not been effected in accordance with paragraph (2) if the judge is satisfied that, pending such service, the person against whom it is sought to enforce the judgment or order has had notice thereof either –

- (a) by being present when the judgment or order was given or made; or
- (b) by being notified of the terms of the judgment or order whether by telephone, telegram or otherwise.

(7) Without prejudice to its powers under Part 6 of the CPR, the court may dispense with service of a copy of a judgment or order under paragraph (2) or a claim form or application notice under paragraph (4) if the court thinks it just to do so.

(8) Where service of the claim form or application notice has been dispensed with under paragraph (7) and a committal order is made in the absence of the respondent, the judge may on his own initiative fix a date and time when the person to be committed is to be brought before him or before the court.

Amendments—SI 2003/3361.

Jurisdiction—The county court has concurrent jurisdiction to deal with contempts of an order of the county court, with breaches of undertakings given to the county court (by the application of r 1A below) and with contempts of the county court itself (PDCommittal, para 2.1).

Venue—Whenever possible the application should be made in the county court in which the original order was made or undertaking given.

Related criminal proceedings—It is not a breach of the HRA 1998 for a defendant to face concurrent proceedings for civil contempt and criminal proceedings arising out of the same incident. The court has a discretion to adjourn the contempt proceedings but should only do so where there is a real risk of prejudice which might lead to injustice (*Barnet LBC v Hurst* [2002] EWCA Civ 1009, [2002] 4 All ER 457).

'committal order' (r 1(8))—The court may deal with a person in contempt in a number of different ways:

- (a) an immediate order for committal for up to 2 years (Contempt of Court Act 1981, s 14(1)). If the person in contempt has to be sentenced for more than one contempt, consecutive terms may be imposed (*Lee v Walker* [1985] QB 1191, CA) but the total period of imprisonment must not *exceed* 2 years (*Villiers v Villiers* [1994] 1 FLR 647);
- (b) a suspended order for committal (*Brewer v Brewer* [1989] 2 FLR 251, CA). The court may impose terms which must be clearly set out in the order. The suspension must be for a finite period (*Pidduck v Molloy* [1992] 2 FLR 202, CA). The court has no power to activate a suspended sentence of imprisonment unless the contemnor has been properly served with a copy of the order drawn on the proper Form N79 (*Couzens v Couzens* [2001] EWCA Civ 992, [2001] 2 FLR 701, [2001] 3 FCR 289, CA);
- (c) an unlimited fine;
- (d) taking security for good behaviour (*Skipworth and the Defendant's Case* (1873) LR 9 QB 230, p 241);
- (e) an injunction order. This may also be made against persons who are not parties to the action who have aided a breach (*Elliot v Klinger* [1967] 3 All ER 1141);
- (f) adjournment of sentence. As with a suspended committal this may be on terms and should specify a period after which the person in contempt will no longer be punished;
- (g) no order. This will be appropriate in cases of purely technical breach or where the court considers that some other remedy should have been used in order to achieve justice.

Alternative remedies—Committal proceedings should not be used where other remedies would be equally effective (*Danchevsky v Danchevsky* [1974] 3 WLR 709, CA). These include writs of execution, delivery or possession, a vesting order under Trustee Act 1925, the appointment of a person to execute a document under SCA 1981, s 39, sequestration under Sch 1, RSC Ord 46, r 5, or an order under Sch 1, RSC Ord 45, r 8 authorising the breach to be remedied at the contemnor's expense.

'Part 6 of the CPR' (r 1(7))—Where personal service is impractical, CPR r 6.8 allows service by an alternative method for example by posting through the letter box at an address with which the

Respondent has some real connection. However where a committal order is made after service by an alternative method the order may be set aside and a new trial ordered if the person in contempt was unaware of the hearing (*Duo v Osborne, formerly Duo* [1992] 3 All ER 121, CA).

'dispense with service' (r 1(7))—This is a wholly exceptional course and an order made will be provisional in the sense that the person in contempt is entitled to apply for its discharge (*Wright v Jess* [1987] 1 WLR 1070, CA and see CPR r 23.10). The court will then rehear the application (*Aslam v Singh* [1987] 1 FLR 122, CA) but the court may not increase the sentence (*Lamb v Lamb* [1984] FLR 278, CA).

Human Rights Act 1998—Committal proceedings are criminal proceedings as defined by HRA 1998, Sch 1, Art 6. Any respondent is entitled to the full protection of Art 6.3, including the offer of legal representation if he faces the prospect of imprisonment for any breach found proved. The court has no power to grant legal aid for this purpose so an adjournment may be necessary. Where a committal order has been made in the respondent's absence, for whatever reason, the order should direct that he be produced to the court immediately after arrest and before being conveyed to prison. The court then has an opportunity to set aside or vary the order.

1A Undertaking given by party

Rule 1 (except paragraph (6)) shall apply to undertakings as it applies to orders with the necessary modifications and as if –

(a) for paragraph (2) of that rule there were substituted the following –

'(2) A copy of the document recording the undertaking shall be delivered by the court officer to the party giving the undertaking –

(a) by handing a copy of the document to him before he leaves the court building; or

(b) where his place of residence is known, by posting a copy to him at his place of residence; or

(c) through his solicitor,

and, where delivery cannot be effected in this way, the court officer shall deliver a copy of the document to the party for whose benefit the undertaking is given and that party shall cause it to be served personally as soon as is practicable'.

(b) in paragraph (7), the words from 'a copy of' to 'paragraph (2) or' were omitted.

'shall apply to undertakings as it applies to orders' (r 1)—The court has no greater powers to deal with breach of an undertaking than it has to deal with breach of an order. So where the undertaking given is outside the power of the court to have ordered it may not be enforced by committal. Such an undertaking may give rise to contractual obligations and if it is an undertaking to pay money may be directly enforced by garnishee (now third party debt order) proceedings (*Gandolfo v Gandolfo (Standard Chartered Bank, Garnishee)* [1981] QB 359, CA). Otherwise an undertaking to pay money may be enforced by committal only where permitted under Debtors Act 1869, s 5 (*Buckley v Crawford* (1893) 1 QB 105) – see note **'Judgment summons'** under CCR Ord 28, r 1.

2 Solicitor's undertaking

(1) An undertaking given by a solicitor in relation to any proceeding in a county court may be enforced, by order of the judge of that court, by committal order against the solicitor.

(2) Where it appears to the judge that a solicitor has failed to carry out any such undertaking, he may of his own initiative direct the court officer to issue a notice calling on the solicitor to show cause why he should not be committed to prison.

(3) Where any party to the proceedings desires to have the undertaking enforced by committal order, the court officer shall, on the application of the party supported by an affidavit setting out the facts on which the application is based, issue such a notice as is referred to in paragraph (2).

3 Discharge of person in custody

(1) Where a person in custody under a warrant or order, other than a warrant of committal to which Order 27, rule 8, or Order 28, rule 4 or 14, relates, desires to apply to the court for his discharge, he shall make his application in writing attested by the governor of the prison (or any other officer of the prison not below the rank of principal officer) showing that he has purged or is desirous of purging his contempt and shall, not less than 1 day before the application is made, serve notice of it on the party, if any, at whose instance the warrant or order was issued.

(2) If the committal order –

(a) does not direct that any application for discharge shall be made to a judge; or

(b) was made by the district judge under section 118 of the Act,

any application for discharge may be made to the district judge.

(3) Nothing in paragraph (1) shall apply to an application made by the Official Solicitor in his official capacity for the discharge of a person in custody.

Procedure for 'application in writing' (r 3(1))—Application is made by application notice under CPR Pt 23, as modified by the provisions of this rule.

CCR ORDER 30

****

Amendments—The whole Order was revoked by SI 2001/2792 with effect from 25 March 2002. Provisions about enforcement of judgments and orders are now to be found in CPR Pts 70–73.

CCR ORDER 31

****

Amendments—The whole Order was revoked by SI 2001/2792 with effect from 25 March 2002. Provisions about charging orders are now to be found in CPR Pt 73.

CCR ORDER 33
INTERPLEADER PROCEEDINGS

Part I – Under Execution

1 Notice of claim

(A1) In this Part of this Order 'the interpleader claimant' means any person making a claim to or in respect of goods seized in execution or the proceeds or value thereof and 'the interpleader claim' means that claim.

(1) The interpleader claimant shall deliver to the bailiff holding the warrant of execution, or file in the office of the court for the district in which the goods were seized, notice of his claim stating –

(a) the grounds of the interpleader claim or, in the case of a claim for rent, the particulars required by section 102(2) of the Act; and
(b) the interpleader claimant's full name and address.

(2) On receipt of an interpleader claim made under this rule, the court shall –

(a) send notice thereof to the execution creditor; and
(b) except where the interpleader claim is to the proceeds or value of the goods, send to the interpleader claimant a notice requiring him to make a deposit or give security in accordance with section 100 of the Act.

'notice of his claim' (r 1(1))—The claimant must give the best particulars he can of his claim to the goods. A bare assertion that the goods belong to the claimant without any supporting information is not sufficient (*R v Chilton* (1850) 15 QB 220). The purpose of the notice is to enable the court to make a proper decision which of the possible orders under CCA 1984, s 100 is appropriate and also to enable the execution creditor to make a proper decision whether or not to admit the claim. Copies of documentary evidence to the claimant's title such as receipts should be attached to the notice. The High Court form PF23QB may be adapted for use under this rule.

'a claim for rent' (r 1(1)(a))—CCA 1984, s 102 permits a landlord whose rent is in arrears to give notice to the bailiff within 5 days of goods being seized. Within the limits set out in s 102(4)(b) he then becomes entitled to payment of the arrears out of the sale proceeds of the goods in preference to the execution creditor.

'full name and address' (r 1(1)(b))—This will become the claimant's address for service and the provisions in CPR r 6.5 will apply.

'to make a deposit or give security' (r 1(2)(b))—The procedure under CCA 1984, s 100(1)(a)(i) or (b) is preferable as it enables the court to release the goods to the claimant immediately. The procedure under s 100(1)(a)(ii) offers more limited relief to the execution creditor as it only covers the bailiff's possession costs.

2 Reply to interpleader claim

(1) Within 4 days after receiving notice of an interpleader claim under rule 1(2) the execution creditor shall give notice to the court informing him whether he admits or disputes the interpleader claim or requests the district judge to withdraw from possession of the goods or money claimed.

(2) If, within the period aforesaid, the execution creditor gives notice to the court admitting the interpleader claim or requesting the district judge to withdraw from possession of the goods or money claimed, the execution creditor shall not be liable to the district judge for any fees or expenses incurred after receipt of the notice.

'shall give notice' (r 2(1))—If the execution creditor fails to respond and the claimant fails to make a deposit or give security as ordered, the bailiff must proceed with the sale of the goods under CCA 1984, s 100(3). The High Court form PF24QB may be adapted for use under this rule.

3 Order protecting district judge

Where the execution creditor gives the court such a notice as is mentioned in rule 2(2), the district judge shall withdraw from possession of the goods or money claimed and may apply to the judge, on notice to the interpleader claimant, for an order restraining the bringing of a claim against the district judge for or in respect of his having taken possession of the goods or money and on the hearing of the application the judge may make such order as may be just.

'such order as may be just'—The judge has a wide discretion but before relief is refused the claimant must show a fairly arguable case that he will succeed in overcoming the statutory defences available to the district judge under CCA 1984, s 98 (*Observer Ltd v Gordon* [1983] 2 All ER 945).

Relief was held to have been properly granted where the claimant with a good title delayed in bringing his claim and failed to show that the goods had been sold at a gross undervalue (*Neumann v Bakeway Ltd* [1983] 2 All ER 935).

4 Issue of interpleader proceedings

(1) Where the execution creditor gives notice under rule 2(1) disputing an interpleader claim made under rule 1 or fails, within the period mentioned in rule 2(1), to give the notice required by that rule, the district judge shall, unless the interpleader claim is withdrawn, issue an interpleader notice to the execution creditor and the interpleader claimant.

(2) On the issue of an interpleader notice under paragraph (1) the court officer shall enter the proceedings in the records of the court, fix a day for the hearing by the judge and prepare sufficient copies of the notice for service under this rule.

(3) Subject to paragraph (4) the notice shall be served on the execution creditor and the interpleader claimant in the manner [set out in CPR rule 6.2.

(4) Service shall be effected not less than 14 days before the return day.

Amendments—SI 2000/221; SI 2001/2792.

'shall … issue an interpleader notice' (r 4(1))—Notice is in Form N88 and N88(1).

5 Claim for damages

Where in interpleader proceedings under an execution the interpleader claimant claims from the execution creditor or the district judge, or the execution creditor claims from the district judge, damages arising or capable of arising out of the execution –

- (a) the party claiming damages shall, within 8 days after service of the notice on him under rule 4(3), give notice of this claim to the court and to any other party against whom the claim is made, stating the amount and the grounds of the claim; and
- (b) the party from whom damages are claimed may pay money into court in satisfaction of the claim as if the interpleader proceedings were a claim brought in accordance with CPR Part 7 by the person making the claim.

'damages arising … out of the execution'—The district judge may be liable if he has sold goods at a gross undervalue. Sale by public auction is not conclusive (*Observer Ltd v Gordon,* see above). Section 98 of CCA 1984 affords the district judge a measure of statutory protection.

Part II – Otherwise than under Execution

6 Application for relief

(1) Where a person (in this Part of this Order called 'the applicant') is under a liability in respect of a debt or any money or goods and he is, or expects to be, sued for or in respect of the debt, money or goods by two or more persons making adverse claims thereto ('the interpleader claimants'), he may apply to the court, in accordance with these rules, for relief by way of interpleader.

(2) The application shall be made to the court in which the claim is pending against the applicant or, if no claim is pending against him, to the court in which he might be sued.

(3) The application shall be made by filing a witness statement or affidavit showing that –

(a) the applicant claims no interest in the subject-matter in dispute other than for charges or costs;
(b) the applicant does not collude with any of the interpleader claimants ; and
(c) the applicant is willing to pay or transfer the subject-matter into court or to dispose of it as the court may direct,

together with as many copies of the witness statement or affidavit as there are interpleader claimants.

'is, or expects to be, sued' (r 6(1))—Relief cannot be obtained after one claimant has obtained judgment (*Stevenson & Son v Brownell* [1912] 2 Ch 344).

'adverse claims' (r 6(1))—The claims need not have a common origin but must be to the same property (*Ex parte Mersey Docks and Harbour Board* [1899] 1 QB 546), so relief may be granted where one person faces claims from an agent and his undisclosed principal (*Meynell v Angel* (1863) 32 LJQB 14) but relief was refused where two agents claimed commission under separate contracts for the sale of the same house (*Smith v Saunders* (1877) 37 LT 359). The claimants may be husband and wife (*De La Rue v Hernu Ltd* [1936] 2 KB 164). Where judgment has been entered against one partner of a partnership and another partner claims that goods taken in execution are partnership property relief may be granted (*Peake v Carter* [1916] 1 KB 652).

'he may apply to the court' (r 6(1))—See rr 7 and 8 below.

'relief by way of interpleader' (r 6(1))—The essential feature of interpleader is that a person is in possession of property which does not belong to him and he is faced with claims by two or more persons each claiming ownership or at least the right to possession of that property. Under this rule he can compel the competing claimants to come before the court to establish who is entitled to ownership or possession of the property.

'witness statement or affidavit' (r 6(3))—See PD32, paras 17–22 for rules as to the form and contents of witness statements. The additional costs of using an affidavit will not usually be allowed (CPR r 32.15(2)).

'charges or costs' (r 6(3)(a))—This may include a lien for storage or repairs (*De Rothschild Frères v Morrison Kekwich & Co* (1890) 24 QBD 750, CA).

'does not collude' (r 6(3)(b))—The applicant must show that he is not taking sides in the dispute between the claimants (*Fredericks and Pelhams Timber Buildings v Wilkins, Read (Claimant)* [1971] 3 All ER 545, CA).

7 Relief in pending claim

Where the applicant is a defendant in a pending claim –

(a) the witness statement or affidavit and copies required by rule 6(3) shall be filed within 14 days after service on him of the claim form;
(b) the return day of the application shall be a day fixed for the pre-trial review of the claim including the interpleader proceedings and, if a day has already been fixed for the pre-trial review or hearing of the claim, the court shall, if necessary, postpone it;
(c) the interpleader claimant , the applicant and the claimant in the claim shall be given notice of the application, which shall be prepared by the court together with sufficient copies for service;
(d) the notice to the interpleader claimant shall be served on him, together with a copy of the witness statement or affidavit filed under rule 6(3) and of the claim form and particulars of claim in the claim, not less than 21 days before the return day in the same manner as an interpleader notice in accordance with rule 4(3);

(e) the notices to the applicant and the claimant shall be sent to them by the court and the notice to the claimant shall be accompanied by a copy of the said witness statement or affidavit.

'pre-trial review' (r 7(b))—Under the CPR there will normally be no date fixed for pre-trial review. Since the application is not a defence the court will not send out an allocation questionnaire on receipt of the application. Instead the court will fix a hearing and give notice to all parties in Form N361.

8 Relief otherwise than in pending claim

Where the applicant is not a defendant in a pending claim –

(a) the court shall enter the proceedings in the records of the court;
(b) the court shall fix a day for the pre-trial review or, if the court so directs, a day for the hearing of the proceedings and shall prepare and issue an interpleader notice, together with sufficient copies for service;
(c) the notice together with a copy of the witness statement or affidavit filed under rules 6(3), shall be served on each of the claimants not less than 21 days before the return day in the same manner as an interpleader notice to be served under rule 4(3); and
(d) the court shall deliver or send a notice of issue to the applicant .

'not a defendant in a pending claim'—No CPR Pt 8 claim form is required. The applicant simply files a witness statement or affidavit and the court then prepares and issues a notice in Form N89 directed to the claimants.

9 Payment into court etc

Before or after the court officer proceeds under rule 7 or 8 the district judge may direct the applicant to bring the subject-matter of the proceedings into court, or to dispose of it in such manner as the district judge thinks fit, to abide the order of the court.

'Before … the court officer proceeds'—This rule enables the court to grant summary relief to the applicant where for example he is a stakeholder. Once the applicant has paid the money into court he may be dismissed from the proceedings.

10 Reply by interpleader claimant

(1) An interpleader claimant shall, within 14 days after service on him of the notice under rule 7(c) or the interpleader notice under rule 8(c), file –

(a) a notice that he makes no interpleader claim; or
(b) particulars stating the grounds of his interpleader claim to the subject-matter,

together in either case with sufficient copies for service under paragraph (2).

(2) The court shall send to each of the other parties a copy of any notice or particulars filed under paragraph (1).

(3) The court may, if it thinks fit, hear the proceedings although no notice or particulars have been filed.

11 Order barring interpleader claim etc

(1) Where an interpleader claimant does not appear on any day fixed for a pre-trial review or the hearing of interpleader proceedings, or fails or refuses to comply with an order made in the proceedings, the court may make an order barring his interpleader claim.

(2) If, where the applicant is a defendant in a pending claim, the claimant does not appear on any day fixed for a pre-trial review or the hearing of the interpleader proceedings, the claim including the interpleader proceedings may be struck out.

(3) In any other case where a day is fixed for the hearing of interpleader proceedings, the court shall hear and determine the proceedings and give judgment finally determining the rights and claims of the parties.

(4) Where the court makes an order barring the interpleader claim of an interpleader claimant, the order shall declare the interpleader claimant , and all persons claiming under him, forever barred from prosecuting his interpleader claim against the applicant and all persons claiming under him, but unless the interpleader claimant has filed a notice under rule 10 that he makes no interpleader claim, such an order shall not affect the rights of the interpleader claimants as between themselves.

'the court shall hear and determine' (r 11(3))—At the hearing the court may grant interpleader relief to the applicant and if necessary give directions for the issue between the various claimants to be resolved. See Sch 1, RSC Ord 17, rr 5–8 and notes thereto for the procedure which may be adopted.

CCR ORDER 34
PENAL AND DISCIPLINARY PROVISIONS

1 Issue and service of summons for offence under section 14, 92 or 124 of the Act

Where –

(a) it is alleged that any person has committed an offence under section 14[, 92 or 118 of the Act by assaulting an officer of the court while in the execution of his duty, or by rescuing or attempting to rescue any goods seized in execution, [or by wilfully insulting a judge, juror, witness or any officer of the court and the alleged offender has not been taken into custody and brought before the judge; or

(b) a complaint is made against an officer of the court under section 124 of the Act for having lost the opportunity of levying execution,

the court officer shall issue a summons, which shall be served on the alleged offender personally not less than 8 days before the return day appointed in the summons.

Amendments—SI 2001/4015.

General note—The amendments made by SI 2001/4015 now permit the issue of a summons for an alleged breach of s 118 in line with the procedure under ss 14 and 92.

'issue a summons'—The defendant is entitled to notice in writing setting out clearly what he is alleged to have done wrong. On the hearing, if there is a chance that he may be sent to prison, he must be offered legal representation and the court has power to grant legal aid if the complaint is made under CCA 1984, s 14 or 92 (*Newman v Modern Bookbinders* [2000] 2 All ER 814, CA).

1A Committal under section 14, 92 or 118 of the Act

Rule 1(5) of Order 29 shall apply, with the necessary modifications, where an order is made under section 14, 92 or 118 of the Act committing a person to prison.

2 Notice to show cause before or after fine under section 55 of the Act

Before or after imposing a fine on any person under section 55 of the Act for disobeying a witness summons or refusing to be sworn or give evidence, the judge may direct the court officer to give to that person notice that if he has any cause to show why a fine should not be or should not have been imposed on him, he may show cause in person or by witness statement or affidavit or otherwise on a day named in the notice, and the judge after considering the cause shown may make such order as he thinks fit.

3 Non-payment of fine

(1) If a fine is not paid in accordance with the order imposing it, the court officer shall forthwith report the matter to the judge.

(2) Where by an order imposing a fine, the amount of the fine is directed to be paid by instalments and default is made in the payment of any instalment, the same proceedings may be taken as if default had been made in payment of the whole of the fine.

(3) If the judge makes an order for payment of a fine to be enforced by warrant of execution, the order shall be treated as an application made to the district judge for the issue of the warrant at the time when the order was received by him.

4 Repayment of fine

If, after a fine has been paid, the person on whom it was imposed shows cause sufficient to satisfy the judge that, if it had been shown at an earlier date, he would not have imposed a fine or would have imposed a smaller fine or would not have ordered payment to be enforced, the judge may order the fine or any part thereof to be repaid.

CCR ORDER 35

****

Amendments—The whole Order was revoked by SI 2002/2058 with effect from 2 December 2002. Provisions about enforcement in different jurisdictions are now to be found in CPR Pt 74.

CCR ORDER 37

****

Amendments—The whole Order was revoked by SI 2002/2058 with effect from 2 December 2002. Refer to the 2002 Reissue of this work for the text of the Order prior to its revocation.

General note—The Court now has power to vary or revoke its order under r 3.1(7); nevertheless a judge of co-extensive jurisdiction still has jurisdiction to entertain such an application under Order

37 made prior to its repeal (*Paragon Finance plc (formerly the National Home Loans Corporation plc) v Pender* [2003] EWHC 2834 (Ch) applying *RS and M Engineering Ltd* [1999] 2 BCLC 485, CA).

CCR ORDER 38

****

Amendments—The whole Order was revoked by SI 2004/3419, with effect from 1 April 2005. Provisions about costs on judgment for possession of land are now to be found in CPR Pt 45.

CCR ORDER 39
ADMINISTRATION ORDERS

1 Exercise of powers by district judge

Any powers conferred on the court by Part VI of the Act, section 4 of the Attachment of Earnings Act 1971 or this Order may be exercised by the district judge or, in the circumstances mentioned in this Order, by the court officer.

2 Request and list of creditors

(1) A debtor who desires to obtain an administration order under Part VI of the Act shall file a request in that behalf in the court for the district in which he resides or carries on business.

(2) Where on his examination under set out in CPR Part 71, or otherwise, a debtor furnishes to the court on oath a list of his creditors and the amounts which he owes to them respectively and sufficient particulars of his resources and needs, the court may proceed as if the debtor had filed a request under paragraph (1).

(3) Where a debtor is ordered to furnish a list under section 4(1)(b) of the said Act of 1971, then, unless otherwise directed, the list shall be filed within 14 days after the making of the order.

Amendments—SI 2001/2792.

'Order 25, rule 3' (r 2(2))—This refers to oral examination of the debtor.

Forms—Request for order Form N92, list of creditors Form N93.

3 Verification on oath

The statements in the request mentioned in rule 2(1) and the list mentioned in rule 2(3) shall be verified by the debtor on oath.

5 Orders made by the court officer

(1) The question whether an administration order should be made, and the terms of such an order, may be decided by the court officer in accordance with the provisions of this rule.

(2) On the filing of a request or list under rule 2, the court officer may, if he considers that the debtor's means are sufficient to discharge in full and within a

reasonable period the total amount of the debts included in the list, determine the amount and frequency of the payments to be made under such an order ('the proposed rate') and –

(a) notify the debtor of the proposed rate requiring him to give written reasons for any objection he may have to the proposed rate within 14 days of service of notification upon him;

(b) send to each creditor mentioned in the list provided by the debtor a copy of the debtor's request or of the list together with the proposed rate;

(c) require any such creditor to give written reasons for any objection he may have to the making of an administration order within 14 days of service of the documents mentioned in sub-paragraph (b) upon him.

Objections under sub-paragraph (c) may be to the making of an order, to the proposed rate or to the inclusion of a particular debt in the order.

(3) Where no objection under paragraph (2)(a) or (c) is received within the time stated, the court officer may make an administration order providing for payment in full of the total amount of the debts included in the list.

(4) Where the debtor or a creditor notifies the court of any objection within the time stated, the court officer shall fix a day for a hearing at which the district judge will decide whether an administration order should be made and the court officer shall give not less than 14 days' notice of the day so fixed to the debtor and to each creditor mentioned in the list provided by the debtor.

(5) Where the court officer is unable to fix a rate under paragraph (2) (whether because he considers that the debtor's means are insufficient or otherwise), he shall refer the request to the district judge.

(6) Where the district judge considers that he is able to do so without the attendance of the parties, he may fix the proposed rate providing for payment of the debts included in the list in full or to such extent and within such a period as appears practicable in the circumstances of the case.

(7) Where the proposed rate is fixed under paragraph (6), paragraphs (2) to (4) shall apply with the necessary modifications as if the rate had been fixed by the court officer.

(8) Where the district judge does not fix the proposed rate under paragraph (6), he shall direct the court officer to fix a day for a hearing at which the district judge will decide whether an administration order should be made and the court officer shall give not less than 14 days' notice of the day so fixed to the debtor and to each creditor mentioned in the list provided by the debtor.

(9) Where an administration order is made under paragraph (3), the court officer may exercise the power of the court under section 5 of the Attachment of Earnings Act 1971 to make an attachment of earnings order to secure the payments required by the administration order.

'providing for payment in full' (r 5(3))—CCA 1984, s 112(6) empowers the court to make an order for payment by the debtor of part of the total of his debts. Such an order can only be made by the district judge.

6 Notice of objection by creditor

(1) Any creditor to whom notice has been given under rule 5(8) and who objects to any debt included in the list furnished by the debtor shall, not less

than 7 days before the day of hearing, give notice of his objection, stating the grounds thereof, to the court officer, to the debtor and to the creditor to whose debt he objects.

(2) Except with the permission of the court, no creditor may object to a debt unless he has given notice of his objection under paragraph (1).

7 Procedure on day of hearing

On the day of the hearing –

(a) any creditor, whether or not he is mentioned in the list furnished by the debtor, may attend and prove his debt or, subject to rule 6, object to any debt included in that list;
(b) every debt included in that list shall be taken to be proved unless it is objected to by a creditor or disallowed by the court or required by the court to be supported by evidence;
(c) any creditor whose debt is required by the court to be supported by evidence shall prove his debt;
(d) the court may adjourn proof of any debt and, if it does so, may either adjourn consideration of the question whether an administration order should be made or proceed to determine the question, in which case, if an administration order is made, the debt, when proved, shall be added to the debts scheduled to the order;
(e) any creditor whose debt is admitted or proved, and, with the permission of the court, any creditor the proof of whose debt has been adjourned, shall be entitled to be heard and to adduce evidence on the question whether an administration order should be made and, if so, in what terms.

8 Direction for order to be subject to review

(1) The court may, on making an administration order or at any subsequent time, direct that the order shall be subject to review at such time or at such intervals as the court may specify.

(2) Where the court has directed that an administration order shall be subject to review, the court officer shall give to the debtor and to every creditor who appeared when the order was made not less than 7 days' notice of any day appointed for such a review.

(3) Nothing in this rule shall require the court officer to fix a day for a review under rule 13A.

9 Service of order

Where an administration order is made, the court officer shall send a copy to –

(a) the debtor;
(b) every creditor whose name was included in the list furnished by the debtor;
(c) any other creditor who has proved his debt; and
(d) every other court in which, to the knowledge of the district judge, judgment has been obtained against the debtor or proceedings are pending in respect of any debt scheduled to the order.

Forms—Administration Order Form N94.

10 Subsequent objection by creditor

(1) After an administration order has been made, a creditor who has not received notice under rule 5 and who wishes to object to a debt scheduled to the order, or to the manner in which payment is directed to be made by instalments, shall give notice to the court officer of his objection and of the grounds thereof.

(2) On receipt of such notice the court shall consider the objection and may –

- (a) allow it;
- (b) dismiss it; or
- (c) adjourn it for hearing on notice being given to such persons and on such terms as to security for costs or otherwise as the court thinks fit.

(3) Without prejudice to the generality of paragraph (2), the court may dismiss an objection if it is not satisfied that the creditor gave notice of it within a reasonable time of his becoming aware of the administration order.

11 Subsequent proof by creditor

(1) Any creditor whose debt is not scheduled to an administration order, and any person who after the date of the order became a creditor of the debtor, shall, if he wishes to prove his debt, send particulars of his claim to the court officer, who shall give notice of it to the debtor and to every creditor whose debt is so scheduled.

(2) If neither the debtor nor any creditor gives notice to the court officer, within 7 days after receipt of notice under paragraph (1), that he objects to the claim, then, unless it is required by the court to be supported by evidence, the claim shall be taken to be proved.

(3) If the debtor or a creditor gives notice of objection within the said period of 7 days or the court requires the claim to be supported by evidence, the court officer shall fix a day for consideration of the claim and give notice of it to the debtor, the creditor by whom the claim was made and the creditor, if any, making the objection, and on the hearing the court may either disallow the claim or allow it in whole or in part.

(4) If a claim is taken to be proved under paragraph (2) or allowed under paragraph (3), the debt shall be added to the schedule to the order and a copy of the order shall then be sent to the creditor by whom the claim was made.

12 Permission to present bankruptcy petition

An application by a creditor under section 112(4) of the Act for permission to present or join in a bankruptcy petition shall be made on notice to the debtor in accordance with CPR Part 23, but the court may, if it thinks fit, order that notice be given to any other creditor whose debt is scheduled to the administration order.

13 Conduct of order

(1) The court manager or such other officer of the court as the court making an administration order shall from time to time appoint shall have the conduct of

the order and shall take all proper steps to enforce the order (including exercising the power of the court under section 5 of the Attachment of Earnings Act 1971 to make an attachment of earnings order to secure payments required by the administration order) or to bring to the attention of the court any matter which may make it desirable to review the order.

(2) Without prejudice to section 115 of the Act, any creditor whose debt is scheduled to the order may, with the permission of the court, take proceedings to enforce the order.

(3) The debtor or, with the permission of the court, any such creditor may apply to the court to review the order.

(4) When on a matter being brought to its attention under paragraph (1) the court so directs or the debtor or a creditor applies for the review of an administration order, rule 8(2) shall apply as if the order were subject to review under that rule.

(5) Nothing in this rule shall require the court officer to fix a day for a review under rule 13A.

13A Review by court officer in default of payment

(1) Where it appears that the debtor is failing to make payments in accordance with the order, the court officer shall (either of his own initiative or on the application of a creditor whose debt is scheduled to the administration order) send a notice to the debtor –

- (a) informing him of the amounts which are outstanding; and
- (b) requiring him (within 14 days of service of the notice upon him) to;
  - (i) make the payments as required by the order; or
  - (ii) explain his reasons for failing to make the payments; and
  - (iii) make a proposal for payment of the amounts outstanding; or
  - (iv) make a request to vary the order.

(2) If the debtor does not comply with paragraph (1)(b) within the time stated, the court officer shall revoke the administration order.

(3) The court officer shall refer a notice given by a debtor under paragraph (1)(b)(ii), (iii) or (iv) to the district judge who may –

- (a) without requiring the attendance of the parties –
  - (i) revoke the administration order or vary it so as to provide for payment of the debts included in the order in full or to such extent and within such a period as appears practicable in the circumstances of the case; or
  - (ii) suspend the operation of the administration order for such time and on such terms as he thinks fit; or
- (b) require the court officer to fix a day for the review of the administration order and to give to the debtor and to every creditor whose debt is scheduled to the administration order not less than 8 days' notice of the day so fixed.

(4) Any party affected by an order made under paragraph (2) or (3)(a) may, within 14 days of service of the order on him and giving his reasons, apply on notice for the district judge to consider the matter afresh and the court officer shall fix a day for the hearing of the application before the district judge and

give to the debtor and to every creditor whose debt is scheduled to the administration order not less than 8 days' notice of the day so fixed.

(5) On hearing an application under paragraph (4), the district judge may confirm the order or set it aside and make such new order as he thinks fit and the order so made shall be entered in the records of the court.

Revocation of administration orders—The procedure which regulates administration orders made under CCA 1984, Pt VI is contained in CCR Ord 39. In r 13A(2) there is provision for 'the court officer' to revoke an administration order, and in r 14(1)(c) for 'the court' to do so. In most instances, such revocation will be as a result of the debtor failing to make the required payments.

Pursuant to IA 1986, s 429, where a person fails to make any payment which he is required to make by virtue of an administration order, the court which is administering that person's estate under the order may, if it thinks fit, (a) revoke the order, and (b) make an order that IA 1986, s 429 and CDDA 1986, s 12 shall apply to him for such period, not exceeding 1 year, as may be specified in the order.

The effect of IA 1986, s 429 is to make it an offence, punishable by fine or imprisonment, if a person to whom it applies obtains credit (which is further defined) either alone or jointly with another person of or exceeding the amount prescribed for the purposes of IA 1986, s 360(1)(a) under the Insolvency Proceedings (Monetary Limits) Order 1986. The same applies if he enters into any transaction in the course of or for the purpose of any business in which he is directly or indirectly engaged, without disclosing to the person from whom he obtains credit, or (as the case may be) with whom the transaction is entered into, that the section applies to him.

Section 12 of the CDDA 1986 provides that a person to whom it applies shall not – except with the leave of the court which made the order – act as a director, or liquidator of, or directly or indirectly take part or be concerned in the promotion, formation or management of a company. Section 13 of the CDDA 1986 provides that a person who acts in contravention of this restriction commits an offence punishable as there stated.

14 Review of order

(1) On the review of an administration order the court may –

(a) if satisfied that the debtor is unable from any cause to pay any instalment due under the order, suspend the operation of the order for such time and on such terms as it thinks fit;

(b) if satisfied that there has been a material change in any relevant circumstances since the order was made, vary any provision of the order made by virtue of section 112(6) of the Act;

(c) if satisfied that the debtor has failed without reasonable cause to comply with any provision of the order or that it is otherwise just and expedient to do so, revoke the order, either forthwith or on failure to comply with any condition specified by the court; or

(d) make an attachment of earnings order to secure the payments required by the administration order or vary or discharge any such attachment of earnings order already made.

(2) The court officer shall send a copy of any order varying or revoking an administration order to the debtor, to every creditor whose debt is scheduled to the administration order and, if the administration order is revoked, to any other court to which a copy of the administration order was sent pursuant to rule 9.

'revoke the order' (r 14(1)(c))—See note **'Revocation of administration orders'** under r 13A above.

16 Discharge of attachment of earnings order

On the revocation of an administration order any attachment of earnings order made to secure the payments required by the administration order shall be discharged.

17 Declaration of dividends

(1) The officer having the conduct of an administration order shall from time to time declare dividends and distribute them among the creditors entitled to them.

(2) When a dividend is declared, notice shall be sent by the officer to each of the creditors.

18 Creditors to rank equally

All creditors scheduled under section 113(d) of the Act before an administration order is superseded under section 117(2) of the Act shall rank equally in proportion to the amount of their debts subject to the priority given by the said paragraph (d) to those scheduled as having been creditors before the date of the order, but no payment made to any creditor by way of dividend or otherwise shall be disturbed by reason of any subsequent proof by any creditor under the said paragraph (d).

19 Change of debtor's address

(1) A debtor who changes his residence shall forthwith inform the court of his new address.

(2) Where the debtor becomes resident in the district of another court, the court in which the administration order is being conducted may transfer the proceedings to that other court.

CCR ORDER 42

****

Amendments—The whole Order was revoked by SI 2005/2292 with effect from 1 October 2005. Provisions about Crown proceedings are now to be found in CPR Pt 66.

****

CCR ORDER 44
THE AGRICULTURAL HOLDINGS ACT 1986

1 Order to arbitrator to state case

(1) An application under paragraph 26 of Schedule 11 to the Agricultural Holdings Act 1986 for an order directing an arbitrator to state, in the form of a special case for the opinion of the court, a question of law arising in the course of the arbitration shall include a concise statement of the question of law.

(2) The arbitrator shall not be made a respondent to the application, but if the judge grants the application, a copy of the order shall be served on the arbitrator.

2 Special case stated by arbitrator

(1) Where, pursuant to the said paragraph 26, an arbitrator states, in the form of a special case for the opinion of the court, any question of law arising in the course of the arbitration, the case shall contain a statement of such facts and reference to such documents as may be necessary to enable the judge to decide the question of law.

(2) The case shall be signed by the arbitrator and shall be lodged in the court office by the arbitrator or any party to the arbitration, together with a copy for the use of the judge.

(3) The court officer shall fix a day for the hearing of the special case and give notice thereof to the parties.

(4) On the hearing the judge shall be at liberty to draw any inferences of fact from the case and the documents referred to therein.

(5) The judge may remit the case to the arbitrator for restatement or further statement.

(6) A copy of the order made by the judge on the hearing shall be served on the parties to the arbitration and on the arbitrator.

3 Removal of arbitrator or setting aside award

(1) An application under paragraph 27 of Schedule 11 to the said Act of 1986 for the removal of an arbitrator on the ground of his misconduct or for an order setting aside an award on the ground that the arbitrator has misconducted himself or that an arbitration or award has been improperly procured or that there is an error of law on the face of the award shall be made within 21 days after the date of the award.

(2) The arbitrator and all parties to the arbitration, other than the applicant, shall be made respondents.

Application—This is by claim form (N208) under CPR Pt 8 – see PD8, Section B, Table 2 and Guide 3, set out in Section 1 of this work.

4 Enforcement of order imposing penalty

(1) When taking any proceedings for the enforcement in a county court of an order under section 27 of the Agricultural Holdings Act 1986, the party in whose favour the order was made shall file –

- (a) a certified copy of the order; and
- (b) a certificate specifying the amount due under the order and stating whether any previous proceedings have been taken for its enforcement and, if so, the nature of the proceedings and their result.

(2) Where it is desired to enforce the order by warrant of execution, the proceedings may be taken in any court in the district of which execution is to be levied.

CCR ORDER 45
THE REPRESENTATION OF THE PEOPLE ACT 1983

1 Application for detailed assessment of returning officer's account

(1) An application by the Secretary of State under section 30 of the Representation of the People Act 1983 for the detailed assessment of a returning officer's account shall be made by claim form and on issuing the claim form the court will fix a day for the hearing which shall be a day for proceeding with the detailed assessment if the application is granted.

(2) Where on the application the returning officer desires to apply to the court to examine any claim made against him in respect of matters charged in the account, the application shall be made in writing and filed, together with a copy thereof, within 7 days after service on the returning officer of the copy of the application for detailed assessment.

(3) On the filing of an application under paragraph (2) the court officer shall fix a day for the hearing and give notice thereof to the returning officer, and a copy of the application and of the notice shall be served on the claimant in the manner set out in CPR rule 6.2.

(4) The examination and detailed assessment may, if the court thinks fit, take place on the same day, but the examination shall be determined before the detailed assessment is concluded.

(5) The application for detailed assessment and any application under paragraph (2) may be heard and determined by the district judge and a copy of the order made on the application shall be served on the Secretary of State and the returning officer and, in the case of an application under paragraph (2), on the claimant.

Amendments—SI 2000/221; SI 2001/2792.

2 Appeal from decision of registration officer

(1) Where notice of appeal from a decision of a registration officer is given pursuant to regulations made under section 53 of the said Act of 1983, the registration officer shall, within 7 days after receipt of the notice by him, forward the notice by post to the court in which the appeal is required to be brought, together with the statement mentioned in those regulations.

(2) The appeal shall be brought in the court for the district in which the qualifying premises are situated.

In this paragraph 'qualifying premises' means the premises in respect of which –

- (a) the person whose right to be registered in the register of electors is in question on the appeal is entered on the electors' list or is registered or claims to be entitled to be registered; or
- (b) the person whose right to vote by proxy or by post is in question on the appeal is or will be registered in the register of electors; or
- (c) the elector whose proxy's right to vote by post is in question on the appeal is or will be registered in the register of electors,

as the case may be.

(3) The respondents to the appeal shall be the registration officer and the party (if any) in whose favour the decision of the registration officer was given.

(4) On the hearing of the appeal –

(a) the statement forwarded to the court by the registration officer and any document containing information furnished to the court by the registration officer pursuant to the regulations mentioned in paragraph (1) shall be admissible as evidence of the facts stated therein; and

(b) the judge shall have power to draw all inferences of fact which might have been drawn by the registration officer and to give any decision and make any order which ought to have been given or made by the registration officer.

(5) A respondent to an appeal other than the registration officer shall not be liable for or entitled to costs, unless he appears before the court in support of the decision of the registration officer.

3 Selected appeals

(1) Where two or more appeals to which rule 2 relates involve the same point of law, the judge may direct that one appeal shall be heard in the first instance as a test case and thereupon the court shall send a notice of the direction to the parties to the selected appeal and the parties to the other appeals.

(2) If within 7 days after service of such notice on him any party to an appeal other than the selected appeal gives notice to the court that he desires the appeal to which he is a party to be heard –

(a) the appeal shall be heard after the selected appeal is disposed of;

(b) the court shall give the parties to the appeal notice of the day on which it will be heard;

(c) the party giving notice under this paragraph shall not be entitled to receive any costs occasioned by the separate hearing of the appeal to which he is a party, unless the judge otherwise orders.

(3) If no notice is given under paragraph (2) within the time limited –

(a) the decision on the selected appeal shall bind the parties to each other appeal without prejudice to their right to appeal to the Court of Appeal;

(b) an order similar to the order in the selected appeal shall be made in each other appeal without further hearing;

(c) the party to each other appeal who is in the same interest as the unsuccessful party to the selected appeal shall be liable for the costs of the selected appeal in the same manner and to the same extent as the unsuccessful party to that appeal and an order directing him to pay such costs may be made and enforced accordingly.

CCR ORDER 46
THE LEGITIMACY ACT 1976

1 Manner of application

(1) An application to a county court under section 45(2) of the Matrimonial Causes Act 1973 for a declaration of legitimation by virtue of the Legitimacy Act 1976 shall be made by claim form stating –

(a) the grounds on which the applicant relies;
(b) the date and place of birth of the applicant and the maiden name of his mother and, if it be the case, that the applicant is known by a name other than that which appears in the certificate of his birth; and
(c) particulars of every person whose interest may be affected by the proceedings and his relationship, if any, to the applicant, including any person other than the applicant's father to whom his mother was married at the date of his birth.

(2) The application may be filed in the court for the district in which the applicant resides or the marriage leading to the legitimation was celebrated, or if neither the residence of the applicant nor the place of the marriage is in England or Wales, then in the Westminster County Court.

(3) The applicant shall file with the claim form –

(a) a witness statement or affidavit by him (or, if he is a child, by his litigation friend) verifying the application; and
(b) any birth, death or marriage certificate intended to be relied on at the hearing.

2 Preliminary consideration and service

(1) On the filing of the documents mentioned in rule 1, the court officer shall fix a day for a case management hearing and give notice thereof to the Attorney-General.

(2) It shall not be necessary to serve the application on the Attorney-General otherwise than by delivering a copy of it to him in accordance with section 45(6) of the Matrimonial Causes Act 1973.

(3) At the case management hearing the court shall give directions as to the persons, if any, other than the Attorney-General, who are to be made respondents to the application.

(4) Where in the opinion of the court it is impracticable to serve a respondent other than the Attorney-General in accordance with the rules relating to service or it is otherwise necessary or expedient to dispense with service of the claim form on any such respondent, the court may make an order dispensing with service on him.

3 Answer

(1) The Attorney-General may file an answer to the application within 14 days after directions have been given at the case management hearing.

(2) Any other respondent who wishes to oppose the application or to dispute any of the facts alleged in it shall, within 14 days after service of the application on him, file an answer to the application.

(3) A respondent who files an answer shall file with it as many copies as there are other parties to the proceedings and the court shall send one of the copies to each of those parties.

CCR ORDER 47
DOMESTIC AND MATRIMONIAL PROCEEDINGS

5 Family Law Reform Act 1969

(1) In this rule –

'bodily samples' and 'scientific tests' have the meanings assigned to them by section 25 of the Family Law Reform Act 1969; and

'direction' means a direction for the use of scientific tests under section 20(1) of that Act.

(2) Except with the permission of the court, an application in any proceedings for a direction shall be made on notice to every party to the proceedings (other than the applicant) and to any other person from whom the direction involves the taking of bodily samples.

(3) Where an application is made for a direction involving the taking of bodily samples from a person who is not a party to the proceedings in which the application is made, the application notice shall be served on him personally and the court may at any time direct him to be made a party to the proceedings.

(4) Where an application is made for a direction in respect of a person (in this paragraph referred to as a person under disability) who is either –

(a) under 16; or
(b) suffering from mental disorder within the meaning of the Mental Health Act 1983 and incapable of understanding the nature and purpose of scientific tests,

the notice of application shall state the name and address of the person having the care and control of the person under disability and shall be served on him instead of on the person under disability.

(5) Where the court gives a direction in any proceedings, the court officer shall send a copy to every party to the proceedings and to every other person from whom the direction involves the taking of bodily samples, and, unless otherwise ordered, the proceedings shall stand adjourned until the court receives a report pursuant to the direction.

(6) On receipt by the court of a report made pursuant to a direction, the court officer shall send a copy to every party to the proceedings and to every other person from whom the direction involved the taking of bodily samples.

Amendments—SI 2001/256.

CCR ORDER 48B

****

Amendments—The whole Order was revoked by SI 2002/2058, with effect from 1 October 2002. Provisions about enforcement of traffic penalties are now to be found in CPR Pt 75.

CCR ORDER 48D

****

Amendments—The whole Order was revoked by SI 2003/2113, with effect from 6 October 2003.

CCR ORDER 49
MISCELLANEOUS STATUTES

****

6B

****

7 Injunctions to prevent environmental harm: Town and Country Planning Act 1990 etc

(1) An injunction under –

(a) section 187B or 214A of the Town and Country Planning Act 1990;
(b) section 44A of the Planning (Listed Buildings and Conservation Areas) Act 1990; or
(c) section 26AA of the Planning (Hazardous Substances) Act 1990,

may be granted against a person whose identity is unknown to the applicant; and in the following provisions of this rule such an injunction against such a person is referred to as 'an injunction under paragraph (1)', and the person against whom it is sought is referred to as 'the respondent'.

(2) An applicant for an injunction under paragraph (1) shall describe the respondent by reference to –

(a) a photograph;
(b) a thing belonging to or in the possession of the respondent; or
(c) any other evidence,

with sufficient particularity to enable service to be effected, and the form of the claim form used shall be modified accordingly.

(3) An applicant for an injunction under paragraph (1) shall file evidence by witness statement or affidavit –

(a) verifying that he was unable to ascertain, within the time reasonably available to him, the respondent's identity;
(b) setting out the action taken to ascertain the respondent's identity; and
(c) verifying the means by which the respondent has been described in the claim form and that the description is the best that the applicant is able to provide.

(4) Paragraph (2) is without prejudice to the power of the court to make an order in accordance with CPR Part 6 for service by an alternative method or dispensing with service.

****

12 Mental Health Act 1983

(1) In this rule –

a section referred to by number means the section so numbered in the Mental Health Act 1983 and 'Part II' means Part II of that Act;

'place of residence' means, in relation to a patient who is receiving treatment as an in-patient in a hospital or other institution, that hospital or institution;

'hospital authority' means the managers of a hospital as defined in section 145(1).

(2) An application to a county court under Part II shall be made by a claim form filed in the court for the district in which the patients' place of residence is situated or, in the case of an application made under section 30 for the discharge or variation of an order made under section 29, in that court or in the court which made the order.

(3) Where an application is made under section 29 for an order that the functions of the nearest relative of the patient shall be exercisable by some other person –

(a) the nearest relative shall be made a respondent to the application unless the application is made on the grounds set out in subsection (3)(a) of the said section or the court otherwise orders; and
(b) the court may order that any other person shall be made a respondent.

(4) On the hearing of the application the court may accept as evidence of the facts stated therein any report made by a medical practitioner and any report made in the course of his official duties by –

(a) a probation officer; or
(b) an officer of a local authority or of a voluntary organisation exercising statutory functions on behalf of a local authority; or
(c) an officer of a hospital authority,

provided that the respondent shall be told the substance of any part of the report bearing on his fitness or conduct which the judge considers to be material for the fair determination of the application.

(5) Unless otherwise ordered, an application under Part II shall be heard and determined by the court sitting in private.

(6) For the purpose of determining the application the judge may interview the patient either in the presence of or separately from the parties and either at the court or elsewhere, or may direct the district judge to interview the patient and report to the judge in writing.

****

17 Sex Discrimination Act 1975, Race Relations Act 1976, Disability Discrimination Act 1995 and Disability Rights Commission Act 1999

(1) In this rule –

(a) 'the Act of 1975', 'the Act of 1976', 'the Act of 1995' and 'the Act of 1999' mean respectively the Sex Discrimination Act 1975, the Race Relations Act 1976, the Disability Discrimination Act 1995 and the Disability Rights Commission Act 1999;
(aa) 'the Religion or Belief Regulations' means the Employment Equality (Religion or Belief) Regulations 2003 and 'the Sexual Orientation Regulations' means the Employment Equality (Sexual Orientation) Regulations 2003;
(b) in relation to proceedings under any of those Acts or Regulations, expressions which are used in the Act or Regulations concerned have the same meaning in this rule as they have in that Act or those Regulations;

(c) in relation to proceedings under the Act of 1976 'court' means a designated county court and 'district' means the district assigned to such a court for the purposes of that Act.

(2) A claimant who brings a claim under section 66 of the Act of 1975, section 57 of the Act of 1976 or section 25 of the Act of 1995 shall forthwith give notice to the Commission of the commencement of the proceedings and file a copy of the notice.

(3) CPR Rule 35.15 shall have effect in relation to an assessor who is to be appointed in proceedings under section 66(1) of the Act of 1975.

(4) Proceedings under section 66, 71 or 72 of the Act of 1975, section 57, 62 or 63 of the Act of 1976, regulation 31 of the Religion or Belief Regulations or regulation 31 of the Sexual Orientation Regulations, section 17B or 25 of the Act of 1995 or section 6 of the Act of 1999 may be commenced –

(a) in the court for the district in which the defendant resides or carries on business; or

(b) in the court for the district in which the act or any of the acts in respect of which the proceedings are brought took place.

(5) An appeal under section 68 of the Act of 1975, section 59 of the Act of 1976 or paragraph 10 of Schedule 3 to the Act of 1999 against a requirement of a non-discrimination notice shall be brought in the court for the district in which the acts to which the requirement relates were done.

(6) Where the claimant in any claim alleging discrimination has questioned the defendant under section 74 of the Act of 1975, section 65 of the Act of 1976, section 56 of the Act of 1995, regulation 33 of the Religion or Belief Regulations or regulation 33 of the Sexual Orientation Regulations or –

(a) either party may make an application to the court in accordance with CPR Part 23 to determine whether the question or any reply is admissible under that section; and

(b) CPR Rule 3.4 shall apply to the question and any answer as it applies to any statement of case.

(7) Where in any claim the Commission claim a charge for expenses incurred by them in providing the claimant with assistance under section 75 of the Act of 1975, section 66 of the Act of 1976 or section 7 of the Act of 1999 –

(a) the Commission shall, within 14 days after the determination of the claim, give notice of the claim to the court and the claimant and thereafter no money paid into court for the benefit of the claimant, so far as it relates to any costs or expenses, shall be paid out except in pursuance of an order of the court; and

(b) the court may order the expenses incurred by the Commission to be assessed whether by the summary or detailed procedure as if they were costs payable by the claimant to his own solicitor for work done in connection with the proceedings.

(8) Where an application is made for the removal or modification of any term of a contract to which section 77(2) of the Act of 1975, section 72(2) of the Act of 1976, section 26 of or Schedule 3A to the Act of 1995, paragraph 1(1) or (2) of Schedule 4 to the Religion or Belief Regulations or paragraph 1(1) or (2) of Schedule 4 to the Sexual Orientation Regulations applies, all persons affected shall be made respondents to the application, unless in any particular case the court otherwise directs, and the proceedings may be commenced –

(a) in the court for the district in which the respondent or any of the respondents resides or carries on business; or
(b) in the court for the district in which the contract was made.

Amendments—SI 2000/1317; SI 2003/3361; SI 2004/2072; SI 2005/2292.

****

18A Telecommunications Act 1984

(1) CPR Rule 35.15 applies to proceedings under paragraph 5 of Schedule 2 to the Telecommunications Act 1984.

****

19 Trade Union and Labour Relations Consolidation Act 1992

(1) Where a complainant desires to have an order of the Certification Officer under section 82 of the Trade Union and Labour Relations Consolidation Act 1992 recorded in the county court, he shall produce the order and a copy thereof to the court for the district in which he resides or the head or main office of the trade union is situate.

(2) The order shall be recorded by filing it, and the copy shall be sealed and dated and returned to the complainant.

(3) The sealed copy shall be treated as if it were the notice of issue in a claim begun by the complainant.

(4) The costs, if any, allowed for recording the order shall be recoverable as if they were payable under the order.

(5) The order shall not be enforced until proof is given to the satisfaction of the court that the order has not been obeyed and, if the order is for payment of money, of the amount remaining unpaid.

****

Amendments—Rule 20 was revoked by SI 2002/2058 with effect from 2 December 2002. Provisions about trusts are now to be found in CPR Pt 64.

SECTION 3

Other Practice Directions

SECTION 3: Other Practice Directions

Contents

Practice Direction – Competition Law – Claims Relating to the Application of Articles 81 and 82 of the EC Treaty and Chapters I and II of Part I of the Competition Act 1998

Scope and Interpretation

1.1 This practice direction applies to any claim relating to the application of –

(a) Article 81 or Article 82 of the Treaty establishing the European Community; or
(b) Chapter I or Chapter II of Part I of the Competition Act 1998.

1.2 In this practice direction –

(a) 'the Act' means the Competition Act 1998;
(b) 'the Commission' means the European Commission;
(c) 'the Competition Regulation' means Council Regulation (EC) No 1/2003 of 16 December 2002 on the implementation of the rules on competition laid down in Articles 81 and 82 of the Treaty;
(d) 'national competition authority' means –
   (i) the Office of Fair Trading; and
   (ii) any other person or body designated pursuant to Article 35 of the Competition Regulation as a national competition authority of the United Kingdom;
(e) 'the Treaty' means the Treaty establishing the European Community.

Venue

2.1 A claim to which this Practice Direction applies –

(a) must be commenced in the High Court at the Royal Courts of Justice; and
(b) will be assigned to the Chancery Division, unless it comes within the scope of rule 58.1(2), in which case it will be assigned to the Commercial Court of the Queen's Bench Division.

2.2 Any party whose statement of case raises an issue relating to the application of Article 81 or 82 of the Treaty, or Chapter I or II of Part I of the Act, must –

(a) state that fact in his statement of case; and
(b) apply for the proceedings to be transferred to the Chancery Division at the Royal Courts of Justice, if they have not been commenced there, or in the Commercial or Admiralty Courts; or
(c) apply for the transfer of the proceedings to the Commercial Court, in accordance with rules 58.4(2) and 30.5(3). If such application is refused, the proceedings must be transferred to the Chancery Division of the High Court at the Royal Courts of Justice.

2.3 Rule 30.8 provides that where proceedings are taking place in the Queen's Bench Division (other than proceedings in the Commercial or Admiralty Courts), a district registry of the High Court or a county court, the court must transfer the proceedings to the Chancery Division at the Royal Courts of Justice if the statement of case raises an issue relating to the application of Article 81 or 82, or Chapter I or II. However, if any such proceedings which have been commenced in the Queen's Bench Division or a Mercantile Court fall within the scope of rule 58.1(2), any party to those proceedings may apply for the transfer of the proceedings to the Commercial Court, in accordance with rules 58.4(2) and 30.5(3). If the application is refused, the proceedings must be transferred to the Chancery Division of the High Court at the Royal Courts of Justice.

2.4 Where proceedings are commenced in or transferred to the Chancery Division at the Royal Courts of Justice in accordance with this paragraph, that court may transfer the proceedings or any part of the proceedings to another court if –

(a) the issue relating to the application of Article 81 or 82, or Chapter I or II, has been resolved; or
(b) the judge considers that the proceedings or part of the proceedings to be transferred does not involve any issue relating to the application of Article 81 or 82, or Chapter I or II.

(Rule 30.3 sets out the matters to which the court must have regard when considering whether to make a transfer order.)

Notice of proceedings

3 Any party whose statement of case raises or deals with an issue relating to the application of Article 81 or 82, or Chapter I or II, must serve a copy of the statement of case on the Office of Fair Trading at the same time as it is served on the other parties to the claim (addressed to the Director of Competition Policy Co-ordination, Office of Fair Trading, Fleetbank House, 2-6 Salisbury Square, London EC4Y 8JX).

Case management

4.1 Attention is drawn to the provisions of article 15.3 of the Competition Regulation (co-operation with national courts), which entitles competition authorities and the Commission to submit written observations to national courts on issues relating to the application of Article 81 or 82 and, with the permission of the court in question, to submit oral observations to the court.

4.1A A national competition authority may also make written observations to the court, or apply for permission to make oral observations, on issues relating to the application of Chapter I or II.

4.2 If a national competition authority or the Commission intends to make written observations to the court, it must give notice of its intention to do so by letter to Chancery Chambers at the Royal Courts of Justice (including the claim number and addressed to the Court Manager, Room TM 6.06, Royal Courts of Justice, Strand, London WC2A 2LL) at the earliest reasonable opportunity.

4.3 An application by a national competition authority or the Commission for permission to make oral representations at the hearing of a claim must be made by letter to Chancery Chambers (including the claim number and addressed to the Court Manager, Room TM 6.06, Royal Courts of Justice, Strand, London WC2A 2LL) at the earliest reasonable opportunity, identifying the claim and indicating why the applicant wishes to make oral representations.

4.4 If a national competition authority or the Commission files a notice under paragraph 4.2 or an application under paragraph 4.3, it must at the same time serve a copy of the notice or application on every party to the claim.

4.5 Any request by a national competition authority or the Commission for the court to send it any documents relating to a claim should be made at the same time as filing a notice under paragraph 4.2 or an application under paragraph 4.3.

4.6 Where the court receives a notice under paragraph 4.2 it may give case management directions to the national competition authority or the Commission, including directions about the date by which any written observations are to be filed.

4.7 The court will serve on every party to the claim a copy of any directions given or order made –

(a) on an application under paragraph 4.3; or
(b) under paragraph 4.6.

4.8 In any claim to which this practice direction applies, the court shall direct a pre-trial review to take place shortly before the trial, if possible before the judge who will be conducting the trial.

Avoidance of conflict with Commission decisions

5.1 In relation to claims which raise an issue relating to the application of Article 81 or 82 of the Treaty, attention is drawn to the provisions of article 16 of the Competition Regulation (uniform application of Community competition law).

5.2 Every party to such a claim, and any national competition authority which has been served with a copy of a party's statement of case, is under a duty to notify the court at any stage of the proceedings if they are aware that –

(a) the Commission has adopted, or is contemplating adopting, a decision in relation to proceedings which it has initiated; and
(b) the decision referred to in (a) above has or would have legal effects in relation to the particular agreement, decision or practice in issue before the court.

5.3 Where the court is aware that the Commission is contemplating adopting a decision as mentioned in paragraph 5.2(a), it shall consider whether to stay the claim pending the Commission's decision.

Judgments

6 Where any judgment is given which decides on the application of Article 81 or Article 82 of the Treaty, the judge shall direct that a copy of the transcript of the judgment shall be sent to the Commission.

Judgments may be sent to the Commission electronically to comp-amicus@cec.eu.int or by post to the European Commission – DG Competition, B–1049, Brussels.

Practice Direction – Application for a Warrant under the Competition Act 1998

Interpretation

1.1 In this practice direction –

(1) 'the Act' means the Competition Act 1998;
(2) 'the Commission' means the European Commission;
(3) 'Commission official' means a person authorised by the Commission for any of the purposes set out in section 62(10), 62A(12) or 63(10) of the Act;
(4) 'the OFT' means the Office of Fair Trading;
(5) 'officer' means an officer of the OFT;
(6) 'named officer' means the person identified in a warrant as the principal officer in charge of executing that warrant, and includes a named authorised officer under section 63 of the Act; and
(7) 'warrant' means a warrant under section 28, 28A, 62, 62A, 63, 65G or 65H of the Act.

1.2 In relation to an application for a warrant by a regulator entitled pursuant to section 54 and Schedule 10 of the Act to exercise the functions of the OFT, references to the OFT shall be interpreted as referring to that regulator.

Application for a warrant

2.1 An application by the OFT for a warrant must be made to a High Court judge using the Part 8 procedure as modified by this practice direction.

2.2 The application should be made to a judge of the Chancery Division at the Royal Courts of Justice (if available).

2.3 The application is made without notice and the claim form may be issued without naming a defendant. Rules 8.1(3), 8.3, 8.4, 8.5(2)-(6), 8.6(1), 8.7 and 8.8 do not apply.

Confidentiality of court documents

3.1 The court will not effect service of any claim form, warrant, or other document filed or issued in an application to which this practice direction applies, except in accordance with an order of the judge hearing the application.

3.2 CPR rule 5.4 does not apply, and paragraphs 3.3 and 3.4 have effect in its place.

3.3 When a claim form is issued the court file will be marked 'Not for disclosure' and, unless a High Court judge grants permission, the court records relating to the application (including the claim form and documents filed in support and any warrant or order that is issued) will not be made available by the court for any person to inspect or copy, either before or after the hearing of the application.

3.4 An application for permission under paragraph 3.3 must be made on notice to the OFT in accordance with Part 23.

(Rule 23.7(1) requires a copy of the application notice to be served as soon as practicable after it is filed, and in any event at least 3 days before the court is to deal with the application.)

Contents of claim form, affidavit and documents in support

4.1 The claim form must state –

(1) the section of the Act under which the OFT is applying for a warrant;
(2) the address or other identification of the premises to be subject to the warrant; and
(3) the anticipated date or dates for the execution of the warrant.

4.2 The application must be supported by affidavit evidence, which must be filed with the claim form.

4.3 The evidence must set out all the matters on which the OFT relies in support of the application, including all material facts of which the court should be made aware. In particular it must state –

(1) the subject matter (ie the nature of the suspected infringement of the Chapter I or II prohibitions in the Act, or of Articles 81 or 82 of the Treaty establishing the European Community) and purpose of the investigation to which the application relates;
(2) the identity of the undertaking or undertakings suspected to have committed the infringement;
(3) the grounds for applying for the issue of the warrant and the facts relied upon in support;
(4) details of the premises to be subject to the warrant and of the possible occupier or occupiers of those premises;
(5) the connection between the premises and the undertaking or undertakings suspected to have committed the infringement;
(6) the name and position of the officer who it is intended will be the named officer;
(7) if it is intended that the warrant may pursuant to a relevant provision of the Act authorise any person (other than an officer or a Commission official) to accompany the named officer in executing the warrant, the name and job title of each such person and the reason why it is intended that he may accompany the named officer.

4.4 There must be exhibited to an affidavit in support of the application –

(1) the written authorisation of the OFT containing the names of –
 (a) the officer who it is intended will be the named officer;
 (b) the other persons who it is intended may accompany him in executing the warrant; and
(2) in the case of an application under section 62, 62A or 63 of the Act, if it is intended that Commission officials will accompany the named officer in executing the warrant, the written authorisations of the Commission containing the names of the Commission officials.

4.5 There must also be filed with the claim form –

(1) drafts of –
 (a) the warrant; and
 (b) an explanatory note to be produced and served with it; and
(2) the written undertaking by the named officer required by paragraph 6.2 of this practice direction.

(Examples of forms of warrant under sections 28 and 62 of the Act, and explanatory notes to be produced and served with them, are annexed to this practice direction. These forms and notes should be used with appropriate modifications in applications for warrants under other sections of the Act.)

4.6 If possible the draft warrant and explanatory note should also be supplied to the court on disk in a form compatible with the word processing software used by the court.

Listing

5 The application will be listed by the court on any published list of cases as 'An application by D'.

Hearing of the application

6.1 An application for a warrant will be heard and determined in private, unless the judge hearing it directs otherwise.

6.2 The court will not issue a warrant unless there has been filed a written undertaking, signed by the named officer, to comply with paragraph 8.1 of this practice direction.

The warrant

7.1 The warrant must –

- (1) contain the information required by section 29(1), 64(1) or 65I(1) of the Act;
- (2) state the address or other identification of the premises to be subject to the warrant;
- (3) state the names of –
  - (a) the named officer; and
  - (b) any other officers, Commission officials or other persons who may accompany him in executing the warrant;
- (4) set out the action which the warrant authorises the persons executing it to take under the relevant section of the Act;
- (5) give the date on which the warrant is issued;
- (6) include a statement that the warrant continues in force until the end of the period of one month beginning with the day on which it issued; and
- (7) state that the named officer has given the undertaking required by paragraph 6.2.

7.2 Rule 40.2 applies to a warrant.

(Rule 40.2 requires every judgment or order to state the name and judicial title of the person making it, to bear the date on which it is given or made, and to be sealed by the court.)

7.3 Upon the issue of a warrant the court will provide to the OFT –

- (1) the sealed warrant and sealed explanatory note; and
- (2) a copy of the sealed warrant and sealed explanatory note for service on the occupier or person in charge of the premises subject to the warrant.

Execution of warrant

8.1 A named officer attending premises to execute a warrant must, if the premises are occupied –

- (1) produce the warrant and an explanatory note on arrival at the premises; and

(2) as soon as possible thereafter personally serve a copy of the warrant and the explanatory note on the occupier or person appearing to him to be in charge of the premises.

8.2 The named officer must also comply with any order which the court may make for service of any other documents relating to the application.

8.3 Unless the court otherwise orders –

(1) the initial production of a warrant and entry to premises under the authority of the warrant must take place between 9.30 am and 5.30 pm Monday to Friday; but

(2) once persons named in the warrant have entered premises under the authority of a warrant, they may, whilst the warrant remains in force –

(a) remain on the premises; or

(b) re-enter the premises to continue executing the warrant,

outside those times.

8.4 If the persons executing a warrant propose to remove any items from the premises pursuant to the warrant they must, unless it is impracticable –

(1) make a list of all the items to be removed;

(2) supply a copy of the list to the occupier or person appearing to be in charge of the premises; and

(3) give that person a reasonable opportunity to check the list before removing any of the items.

Application to vary or discharge warrant

9.1 The occupier or person in charge of premises in relation to which a warrant has been issued may apply to vary or discharge the warrant.

9.2 An application under paragraph 9.1 to stop a warrant from being executed must be made immediately upon the warrant being served.

9.3 A person applying to vary or discharge a warrant must first inform the named officer that he is making the application.

9.4 The application should be made to the judge who issued the warrant, or, if he is not available, to another High Court judge.

Application under s.59 Criminal Justice and Police Act 2001

10.1 Attention is drawn to section 59 of the Criminal Justice and Police Act 2001, which makes provision about applications relating to property seized in the exercise of the powers conferred by (among other provisions) section 28(2) of the Act.

10.2 An application under section 59 –

(1) must be made by application notice in accordance with CPR Part 23; and

(2) should be made to a judge of the Chancery Division at the Royal Courts of Justice (if available).

****

Form—The warrant under CA 1998, ss 28 and 29 appended to this practice direction can be accessed on the *Civil Court Service* CD-ROM or on the Court Service website at *www.courtservice.gov.uk*.

EXPLANATORY NOTE TO WARRANT UNDER SECTIONS 28 AND 29 OF THE COMPETITION ACT 1998 ('THE ACT')

This Explanatory Note is provided for information only. It is not a detailed note of the powers under the Act which are subject to interpretation by the courts.

Subject matter and powers

Officers of the Office of Fair Trading ('the OFT') [[if the Judge so orders pursuant to section 28(3A), insert the following here and elsewhere as indicated] and other persons] have been authorised under Warrant to enter and search the premises identified in the Warrant in connection with an investigation under the Act. The subject matter of this investigation is set out in paragraph 2 of the Warrant. The officers [and other persons] will not elaborate on this.

Paragraph 4 of the Warrant sets out the powers of the named officer[1] and other officers [and other persons] under section 28 of the Act for the purposes of the present investigation. On entering the premises, the named officer will, as a matter of practice, produce evidence of the identity of the other officers in addition to his identity when producing the Warrant.

1 The named officer is the principal officer of the OFT who, together with the other officers [and other persons], is authorised by the Warrant to exercise the powers under section 28 of the Act. His name and the names of the other officers [and other persons] are set out in Schedule B to the Warrant.

Unless the Court has ordered otherwise, the initial production of the Warrant and entry to premises must take place between 9.30 am and 5.30 pm Monday to Friday and, once officers [and other persons] have entered premises under the authority of the Warrant, they may outside those times and whilst the Warrant remains in force, remain on the premises or re-enter the premises to continue executing the Warrant.

Access to legal advice

You are advised to seek legal advice. If the named officer and other officers consider it reasonable in the circumstances to do so and if they are satisfied that you are complying with, or will comply with, such conditions as they consider it appropriate to impose, the named officer and other officers will grant a request to allow a reasonable time for your legal adviser to arrive at the premises before the inspection continues.

If you decide to seek legal advice you should do so promptly and this must not unduly delay or impede the inspection. Any delay must be kept to a strict minimum.

If you have an in-house legal adviser on the premises, or if you have received prior notice of the inspection, the named officer and other officers [and other persons] will not wait for your external legal adviser to arrive.

Self-incrimination

The named officer and other officers [and other persons] have powers, among other matters, to search and take copies of, or extracts from, documents covered by the Warrant, to require you to produce relevant information which is stored in any electronic form and to require you to provide an explanation of any such documents (which the Act defines as including information recorded in any form). However, if your undertaking is suspected of having committed an infringement of the Act, they cannot require you to provide answers or statements that might involve an admission on your part of the existence of that infringement.

You should note also that, any statement made by a person in response to a requirement imposed by the named officer or other officers [or other persons] in exercise of their powers under paragraph 4 of the Warrant, may not be used in evidence against him on a prosecution for an offence under section 188 of the Enterprise Act 2002 (the cartel offence) unless, in the proceedings –

(a) in giving evidence, he makes a statement inconsistent with it, and

(b) evidence relating to it is adduced, or a question relating to it is asked, by him or on his behalf.

Legally privileged communications

The powers under section 28 of the Act to search, take copies etc. (set out in paragraph 4(b) onwards in the Warrant) do not apply in respect of any 'privileged communication'. This is defined in section 30 of the Act to mean a communication

(a) between a professional legal adviser and his client, or

(b) made in connection with, or in contemplation of, legal proceedings and for the purposes of those proceedings,

which would be protected from disclosure in proceedings in the High Court on grounds of legal professional privilege.

For the purposes of section 30, a 'professional legal adviser' includes both an external and an in-house qualified legal adviser.

If you consider that a document or information is privileged, you should provide the named officer or other officer [or other person] with material of such a nature as to demonstrate to his satisfaction that the document or information, or parts of it, for which privilege is claimed, fulfil the conditions for it being privileged.

If you fail to do so, you should gather together the items for which privilege is claimed. These items will not be examined or copied unless you reach an agreement with the named officer that they may be examined or copied. If no agreement is reached on the day of the inspection, the named officer will request that you make a copy of the items and place this in a sealed envelope or package in his presence. The named officer will then discuss with you appropriate arrangements for the safe-keeping of these items pending resolution of the issue of privilege. For example, such arrangements may include a request that your legal adviser should give (or if no legal adviser is present, that you give), a written undertaking that the envelope or package will be retained safely and that its contents will not be concealed, removed, tampered with or destroyed until the issue of privilege is resolved.

Listing of items

Unless it is impracticable in all the circumstances, no item may be removed from the premises by the named officer or other officers [or other persons] until they have prepared a list of all the items to be removed, a copy of the list has been supplied to you, and you have been given a reasonable opportunity to check that the list relates to all the items concerned, and only to those items.

This does not entitle you or your legal adviser to insist that the list or its contents should take any particular form.

Confidentiality

You should note that, subject to the safeguards in relation to self-incrimination and legal privilege, you are not entitled to withhold a document or information by claiming that it is confidential.

Where it is possible to do so, it is suggested that after the inspection on the premises you should identify any part or parts of any information or document copied or taken that you consider to be confidential and provide a written explanation as to why it should be treated as such. For these purposes information is confidential if it is:

(i) commercial information the disclosure of which would, or might, significantly harm the legitimate business interests of the undertaking to which it relates; or

(ii) information relating to the private affairs of an individual the disclosure of which would, or might, significantly harm his interests[1].

1 SI 2000/293, The Competition Act 1998 (Director's rules) Order 2000, rule 30(1)(c).

A document will be treated as confidential to the extent that it contains confidential information.

It is for the OFT to determine whether or not the information is to be disclosed in accordance with Part 9 of the Enterprise Act 2002 and any applicable obligation or power to disclose information pursuant to Council Regulation (EC) No 1/2003[1].

1 Council Regulation (EC) No 1/2003 of 16 December 2002 on the implementation of the rules on competition laid down in Articles 81 and 82 of the Treaty, OJ L 1, 4.1.2003, p.1.

Application to vary or discharge the Warrant

You are entitled to apply to the Court to vary or discharge the Warrant. If you intend to make such an application, you must first inform the named officer. An application to stop the Warrant from being executed must be made immediately upon it being served.

The application must be made to the judge who issued the Warrant, or if he is not available, to another High Court judge.

If you are making an immediate application to stop the Warrant from being executed, the named officer will delay starting or continuing a search of the premises for a reasonable period (not exceeding two hours) while you make your application, provided that you

(1) permit the named officer and other officers [and other persons] to enter and remain on the premises;

(2) keep the named officer informed of the steps you are taking in relation to the application; and

(3) comply with any other conditions that the named officer imposes.

Examples of conditions that the named officer may impose pursuant to (3) above include: that you do not disturb or move any document or information that is the subject of the Warrant; and/or you do not tell anyone other than your legal adviser about the Warrant or the investigation.

Application under section 59 Criminal Justice and Police Act 2001

Your attention is drawn to section 59 of the Criminal Justice and Police Act 2001, which makes provision about applications relating to property seized in the exercise of the powers conferred by (among other provisions) section 28(2) of the Act.

An application under section 59 –

(1) must be made by application notice in accordance with Part 23 of the Civil Procedure Rules; and

(2) should be made to a judge of the Chancery Division at the Royal Courts of Justice (if available).

****

Form—The warrant under CA 1998, ss 62 and 64 appended to this practice direction can be accessed on the *Civil Court Service* CD-ROM or on the Court Service website at *www.courtservice.gov.uk*.

EXPLANATORY NOTE TO WARRANT UNDER SECTIONS 62 AND 64 OF THE COMPETITION ACT 1998 ('THE ACT')

This Explanatory Note is provided for information only. It is not a detailed note of the powers under the Act or of the European Commission's powers of enquiry and investigation which are subject to interpretation respectively by the courts and the Court of Justice of the European Communities.

Subject matter and powers

Officers of the Office of Fair Trading (the 'OFT') [[if the Judge so orders pursuant to section 62(5A), insert the following here and elsewhere as indicated], other persons] and European Commission officials ('Commission officials') have been authorised under Warrant to enter and search the premises identified in the Warrant in connection with an investigation under the EC competition rules. The inspection of the premises has been ordered by a decision of the European Commission. The subject matter of this inspection is set out in paragraph 1 of the Warrant and in the European Commission's decision. The officers [, other persons] and Commission officials will not elaborate on this.

Paragraph 3 of the Warrant sets out the powers of the named officer[1], the other officers [, other persons] and the Commission officials under section 62 of the Act for the purposes of the present inspection. On entering the premises, the named officer and the Commission officials will, as a matter of practice, produce evidence of the identity of the other officers in addition to their identity when producing the Warrant.

1 The named officer is the principal officer of the OFT who, together with the other officers [, other persons] and Commission officials, is authorised by the Warrant to exercise the powers under section 62 of the Act. His name and the names of the other officers [, other persons] and Commission officials are set out in Schedule B to the Warrant.

Unless the Court has ordered otherwise, the initial production of the Warrant and entry to premises must take place between 9.30 am and 5.30 pm Monday to Friday and, once the officers [, the other persons] and Commission officials have entered premises under the authority of the Warrant, they may outside those times and whilst the Warrant remains in force, remain on the premises or re-enter the premises to continue executing the Warrant.

Access to legal advice

You are advised to seek legal advice as explained in the European Commission's explanatory note to their Authorisation to Investigate, a copy of which will be produced to you by the Commission officials.

Self-incrimination

You may be requested to provide explanations on facts or documents relating to the subject matter and purpose of the inspection. However, if your undertaking is suspected of having committed an infringement of EC competition laws, or you have committed the offence of intentional obstruction under section 65 of the Act[1], you cannot be compelled to provide answers or statements that might involve an admission on your part of the existence of that infringement or offence.

1 The relevant terms of this offence are set out in Schedule C to the Warrant.

Legally privileged communications

The powers under section 62 of the Act (set out in paragraph 3(b) onwards in the Warrant) do not apply in respect of documents or information that are legally privileged. The Court of Justice of the European Communities has recognised that correspondence between a client and an external legal adviser, entitled to practise in one of the Member States, is privileged where

(a) the correspondence follows the initiation of proceedings by the European Commission and concerns the defence of the client; or

(b) the correspondence existed before the initiation of proceedings but is closely linked with the subject matter of the proceedings.

Correspondence between a client and an external legal adviser who is not entitled to practise in one of the Member States or between a client and an in-house legal adviser is not recognised by the Court of Justice as being protected by legal privilege. However, where the in-house legal adviser is simply reporting the statement of an external legal adviser who is entitled to practise in one of the Member States, privilege will apply.

If you consider that a document or information is privileged, you should provide the Commission officials with material of such a nature as to demonstrate to their satisfaction that the document or information, or parts of it, for which privilege is claimed, fulfil the conditions for it being privileged.

If you fail to do so, you should gather together the items for which privilege is claimed. These items will not be examined or copied unless you reach an agreement with the named officer or the Commission officials that they may be examined or copied. If no agreement is reached on the day of the inspection, the named officer or the Commission officials will request that you make a copy of the items and place this in a sealed envelope or package in his or their presence. They will then discuss with you appropriate arrangements for the safe-keeping of these items pending resolution of the issue of privilege. For example, such arrangements may include a request that your legal adviser should give (or if no legal adviser is present, that you give), a written undertaking that the envelope or package will be retained safely and that its contents will not be concealed, removed, tampered with or destroyed until the issue of privilege is resolved. The European Commission may adopt a decision requiring the documents to be handed over. You can challenge this by bringing proceedings for review of that decision before the Court of First Instance of the European Communities.

Listing of items

Unless it is impracticable in all the circumstances, no item may be removed from the premises by the named officer or the Commission officials until they have prepared a list of all the items to be removed, a copy of the list has been supplied to you, and you have been given a reasonable opportunity to check that the list relates to all the items concerned, and only to those items. This does not entitle you or your legal adviser to insist that the list or its contents should take any particular form.

Confidentiality

You should note that, subject to the safeguards in relation to self-incrimination and legal privilege, you are not entitled to withhold a document or information by claiming that it is confidential.

Where it is possible to do so, it is suggested that after the inspection on the premises you should identify any information or document copied that you consider to be confidential and provide a written explanation to the European Commission as to why it should be treated as such.

A document will be treated as confidential to the extent that it contains confidential information.

It is for the European Commission to determine, subject to review by the Court of Justice, whether or not the information is to be disclosed, subject to the duty not to disclose information of the kind covered by the obligation of professional secrecy (Article 287 (ex 214) of the Treaty establishing the European Community and Article 28 of Council Regulation (EC) No 1/2003[1]).

1 Council Regulation (EC) No 1/2003 of 16 December 2002 on the implementation of the rules on competition laid down in Articles 81 and 82 of the Treaty, OJ L 1, 4.1.2003, p.1.

Application to vary or discharge the Warrant

You are entitled to apply to the Court to vary or discharge the Warrant. If you intend to make such an application, you must first inform the named officer. An application to stop the Warrant from being executed must be made immediately upon it being served.

The application must be made to the judge who issued the Warrant, or if he is not available, to another High Court judge.

If you are making an immediate application to stop the Warrant from being executed, the named officer will delay starting or continuing a search of the premises for a reasonable period (not exceeding two hours) while you make your application, provided that you

(1) permit the named officer, the other officers [, other persons] and the Commission officials to enter and remain on the premises;

(2) keep the named officer informed of the steps you are taking in relation to the application; and

(3) comply with any other conditions that the named officer imposes.

Examples of conditions that the named officer may impose pursuant to (3) above include: that you do not disturb or move any document or information that is the subject of the Warrant; and/or you do not tell anyone other than your legal adviser about the Warrant, the inspection or the investigation.

In issuing the Warrant the judge was satisfied that the applicable statutory grounds were met, in particular that the measures authorised by the Warrant are neither arbitrary nor excessive having regard to the subject matter of the inspection ordered by the European Commission's decision specified in paragraph 1 of the Warrant. The Court cannot question the need for the inspection or the investigation, nor the lawfulness of the assessments of fact and law made by the European Commission in adopting the decision to order the inspection. Such issues may be raised only in proceedings for review of that decision brought before the Court of First Instance of the European Communities.

Practice Direction –
Proceeds of Crime Act 2002 Parts 5 and 8: Civil Recovery

Scope and Interpretation

1.1 Section I of this practice direction contains general provisions about proceedings in the High Court under Parts 5 and 8 of the Proceeds of Crime Act 2002.

1.2 Section II contains provisions about applications to the High Court under Part 5 of the Act for –

(a) a recovery order; and
(b) an interim receiving order.

1.3 Section III contains provisions about applications to the High Court under Part 8 of the Act for any of the following types of order or warrant in connection with a civil recovery investigation –

(a) a production order;
(b) a search and seizure warrant;
(c) a disclosure order;
(d) a customer information order; and
(e) an account monitoring order.

1.4 Section IV of this practice direction contains further provisions about applications for each of the specific types of order and warrant listed in paragraph 1.3 above.

1.5 In this practice direction –

(1) 'the Act' means the Proceeds of Crime Act 2002;
(2) 'the Director' means the Director of the Assets Recovery Agency, or any person authorised by him to act on his behalf in accordance with section 1(6) of the Act; and
(3) other expressions used have the same meaning as in the Act.

SECTION I – GENERAL PROVISIONS

Venue

2.1 A claim or application to the High Court under Part 5 or Part 8 of the 2002 Act must be issued in the Administrative Court.

2.2 The Administrative Court will thereupon consider whether to transfer the claim or application to another Division or Court of the High Court.

Use of pseudonyms by Agency staff

3.1 If a member of staff of the Assets Recovery Agency gives written or oral evidence in any proceedings using a pseudonym in accordance with section 449 of the Act –

(1) the court must be informed that the witness is using a pseudonym; and
(2) a certificate under section 449(3) of the Act must be filed or produced.

SECTION II – PROCEEDINGS UNDER PART 5 OF THE ACT

Claim for a recovery order

4.1 A claim by the Director for a recovery order must be made using the CPR Part 8 procedure.

4.2 The claim form must –

(1) identify the property in relation to which a recovery order is sought;
(2) state, in relation to each item or description of property –
  (a) whether the property is alleged to be recoverable property or associated property; and
  (b) either –
    (i) who is alleged to hold the property; or
    (ii) where the Director is unable to identify who holds the property, the steps that have been taken to try to establish their identity;
(3) set out the matters relied upon in support of the claim; and
(4) give details of the person nominated by the Director to act as trustee for civil recovery in accordance with section 267 of the Act.

4.3 The evidence in support of the claim must include the signed, written consent of the person nominated by the Director to act as trustee for civil recovery if appointed by the court.

Application for an interim receiving order

5.1 An application for an interim receiving order must be made –

(1) to a High Court judge; and
(2) in accordance with Part 23.

5.2 The application may be made without notice in the circumstances set out in section 246(3) of the Act.

5.3 Part 69 (court's power to appoint a receiver) and its practice direction apply to an application for an interim receiving order with the following modifications –

(1) paragraph 2.1 of the practice direction supplementing Part 69 does not apply;
(2) the Director's written evidence must, in addition to the matters required by paragraph 4.1 of that practice direction, also state in relation to each item or description of property in respect of which the order is sought –
  (a) whether the property is alleged to be –
    (i) recoverable property; or
    (ii) associated property,
  and the facts relied upon in support of that allegation; and
  (b) in the case of any associated property –
    (i) who is believed to hold the property; or
    (ii) if the Director is unable to establish who holds the property, the steps that have been taken to establish their identity; and
(3) the Director's written evidence must always identify a nominee and include the information in paragraph 4.2 of that practice direction.

5.4 There must be filed with the application notice a draft of the order sought. This should if possible also be supplied to the court on disk in a form compatible with the word processing software used by the court.

Application for directions

6.1 An application for directions as to the exercise of the interim receiver's functions may, under section 251 of the Act, be made at any time by –

(1) the interim receiver;
(2) any party to the proceedings; and
(3) any person affected by any action taken by the interim receiver, or who may be affected by any action proposed to be taken by him.

6.2 The application must always be made by application notice, which must be served on –

(1) the interim receiver (unless he is the applicant);
(2) every party to the proceedings; and
(3) any other person who may be interested in the application.

Application to vary or discharge an interim receiving order

7.1 An application to vary or discharge an interim receiving order may be made at any time by –

(1) the Director; or
(2) any person affected by the order.

7.2 A copy of the application notice must be served on –

(1) every party to the proceedings;
(2) the interim receiver; and
(3) any other person who may be affected by the court's decision.

SECTION III – APPLICATIONS UNDER PART 8 OF THE ACT

How to apply for an order or warrant

8.1 An application by the Director for an order or warrant under Part 8 of the Act in connection with a civil recovery investigation must be made –

(1) to a High Court judge;

(2) by filing an application notice.

8.2 The application may be made without notice.

Confidentiality of court documents

9.1 CPR rule 5.4 does not apply to an application under Part 8 of the Act, and paragraphs 9.2 and 9.3 below have effect in its place.

9.2 When an application is issued, the court file will be marked 'Not for disclosure' and, unless a High Court judge grants permission, the court records relating to the application (including the application notice, documents filed in support, and any order or warrant that is made) will not be made available by the court for any person to inspect or copy, either before or after the hearing of the application.

9.3 An application for permission under paragraph 9.2 must be made on notice to the Director in accordance with Part 23.

(Rule 23.7(1) requires a copy of the application notice to be served as soon as practicable after it is filed, and in any event at least 3 days before the court is to deal with the application.)

Application notice and evidence

10.1 The application must be supported by written evidence, which must be filed with the application notice.

10.2 The evidence must set out all the matters on which the Director relies in support of the application, including any matters required to be stated by the relevant sections of the Act, and all material facts of which the court should be made aware.

10.3 There must also be filed with the application notice a draft of the order sought. This should if possible also be supplied to the court on disk in a form compatible with the word processing software used by the court.

Hearing of the application

11.1 The application will be heard and determined in private, unless the judge hearing it directs otherwise.

Variation or discharge of order or warrant

12.1 An application to vary or discharge an order or warrant may be made by –

(1) the Director; or
(2) any person affected by the order or warrant.

12.2 An application under paragraph 12.1 to stop an order or warrant from being executed must be made immediately upon it being served.

12.3 A person applying to vary or discharge a warrant must first inform the Director that he is making the application.

12.4 The application should be made to the judge who made the order or issued the warrant or, if he is not available, to another High Court judge.

SECTION IV – FURTHER PROVISIONS ABOUT SPECIFIC APPLICATIONS UNDER PART 8 OF THE ACT

Production order

13.1 The application notice must name as a respondent the person believed to be in possession or control of the material in relation to which a production order is sought.

13.2 The application notice must specify –

(1) whether the application is for an order under paragraph (a) or (b) of section 345(4) of the Act;
(2) the material, or description of material, in relation to which the order is sought; and
(3) the person who is believed to be in possession or control of the material.

13.3 An application under section 347 of the Act for an order to grant entry may be made either –

(1) together with an application for a production order; or
(2) by separate application, after a production order has been made.

13.4 An application notice for an order to grant entry must –

(1) specify the premises in relation to which the order is sought; and
(2) be supported by written evidence explaining why the order is needed.

13.5 A production order, or an order to grant entry, must contain a statement of the right of any person affected by the order to apply to vary or discharge the order.

Search and seizure warrant

14.1 The application notice should name as respondent the occupier of the premises to be subject to the warrant, if known.

14.2 The evidence in support of the application must state –

(1) the matters relied on by the Director to show that one of the requirements in section 352(6) of the Act for the issue of a warrant is satisfied;
(2) details of the premises to be subject to the warrant, and of the possible occupier or occupiers of those premises;
(3) the name and position of the member of the staff of the Agency who it is intended will execute the warrant.

14.3 There must be filed with the application notice drafts of –

(1) the warrant; and
(2) a written undertaking by the person who is to execute the warrant to comply with paragraph 13.8 of this practice direction.

14.4 A search and seizure warrant must –

(1) specify the statutory power under which it is issued and, unless the court orders otherwise, give an indication of the nature of the investigation in respect of which it is issued;
(2) state the address or other identification of the premises to be subject to the warrant;

(3) state the name of the member of staff of the Agency who is authorised to execute the warrant;
(4) set out the action which the warrant authorises the person executing it to take under the relevant sections of the Act;
(5) give the date on which the warrant is issued;
(6) include a statement that the warrant continues in force until the end of the period of one month beginning with the day on which it is issued;
(7) contain a statement of the right of any person affected by the order to apply to discharge or vary the order.

14.5 An example of a search and seizure warrant is annexed to this practice direction. This example may be modified as appropriate in any particular case.

14.6 Rule 40.2 applies to a search and seizure warrant.

(Rule 40.2 requires every judgment or order to state the name and judicial title of the person making it, to bear the date on which it is given or made, and to be sealed by the court.)

14.7 Upon the issue of a warrant the court will provide to the Director –

(1) the sealed warrant; and
(2) a copy of it for service on the occupier or person in charge of the premises subject to the warrant.

14.8 A person attending premises to execute a warrant must, if the premises are occupied produce the warrant on arrival at the premises, and as soon as possible thereafter personally serve a copy of the warrant and an explanatory notice on the occupier or the person appearing to him to be in charge of the premises.

14.9 The person executing the warrant must also comply with any order which the court may make for service of any other documents relating to the application.

Disclosure order

15.1 The application notice should normally name as respondents the persons on whom the Director intends to serve notices under the disclosure order sought.

15.2 A disclosure order must –

(1) give an indication of the nature of the investigation for the purposes of which the order is made;
(2) set out the action which the order authorises the Director to take in accordance with section 357(4) of the Act;
(3) contain a statement of –
 (a) the offences relating to disclosure orders under section 359 of the Act; and
 (b) the right of any person affected by the order to apply to discharge or vary the order.

15.3 Where, pursuant to a disclosure order, the Director gives to any person a notice under section 357(4) of the Act, he must also at the same time serve on that person a copy of the disclosure order.

Customer information order

16.1 The application notice should normally (unless it is impracticable to do so because they are too numerous) name as respondents the financial institution or institutions to which it is proposed that an order should apply.

16.2 A customer information order must –

(1) specify the financial institution, or description of financial institutions, to which it applies;
(2) state the name of the person in relation to whom customer information is to be given, and any other details to identify that person;
(3) contain a statement of –
   (a) the offences relating to disclosure orders under section 366 of the Act; and
   (b) the right of any person affected by the order to apply to discharge or vary the order.

16.3 Where, pursuant to a customer information order, the Director gives to a financial institution a notice to provide customer information, he must also at the same time serve a copy of the order on that institution.

Account monitoring order

17.1 The application notice must name as a respondent the financial institution against which an account monitoring order is sought.

17.2 The application notice must –

(1) state the matters required by section 370(2) and (3) of the Act; and
(2) give details of –
   (a) the person whose account or accounts the application relates to;
   (b) each account or description of accounts in relation to which the order is sought, including if known the number of each account and the branch at which it is held;
   (c) the information sought about the account or accounts;
   (d) the period for which the order is sought;
   (e) the manner in which, and the frequency with which, it is proposed that the financial institution should provide account information during that period.

17.3 An account monitoring order must contain a statement of the right of any person affected by the order to apply to vary or discharge the order.

Annex

****

Annex—The draft search and seizure warrant annexed to this practice direction is available on the *Civil Court Service* CD-ROM or on the Department for Constitutional Affairs' website at *www.dca.gov.uk*.

Practice Direction – Devolution Issues

This practice direction is divided into 4 parts:

Part I	Introduction
Part II	Directions applicable to all proceedings
Part III	Directions applicable to specific proceedings
Part IV	Appeals

PART I
INTRODUCTION

DEFINITIONS

1 In this practice direction –

'the Assembly' means the National Assembly for Wales or Cynulliad Cenedlaethol Cymru;

'the GWA' means the Government of Wales Act 1998;

'the NIA' means the Northern Ireland Act 1998;

'the SA' means the Scotland Act 1998;

'the Acts' mean the GWA, the NIA and the SA;

'the Judicial Committee' means the Judicial Committee of the Privy Council;

'the CPR' means the Civil Procedure Rules 1998;

'the FPR' means the Family Proceedings Rules 1991

'the FPC' means the Family Proceedings Courts (Children Act 1989) Rules 1991;

'devolution issue' has the same meaning as in paragraph 1, schedule 8 to the GWA; paragraph 1, schedule 10 to the NIA; and paragraph 1, schedule 6 of the SA;

'devolution issue notice' means a notice that a devolution issue has arisen in proceedings;

SCOPE

2.1 This practice direction supplements the provisions dealing with devolution issues in the Acts. It deals specifically with the position if a devolution issue arises under the GWA. If a devolution issue arises under the NIA or the SA the procedure laid down in this practice direction should be adapted as required.

THE DEVOLUTION LEGISLATION

3.1 Schedule 8 to the GWA contains provisions dealing with devolution issues arising out of the GWA; schedule 10 to the NIA contains provisions dealing with devolution issues arising out of the NIA; and schedule 6 to the SA contains provisions dealing with devolution issues arising out of the SA.

3.2 Broadly a devolution issue will involve a question whether a devolved body has acted or proposes to act within its powers (which includes not acting incompatibly with Convention rights[1] and Community law[2]) or has failed to comply with a duty imposed on it. Reference should be made to the Acts where 'devolution issue' is defined.

1 The rights and fundamental freedoms set out in – (a) Articles 2 to 12 and 14 of the European

Convention on Human Rights ('ECHR'), (b) Articles 1 to 3 of the First Protocol (agreed at Paris on 20 March 1952), and (c) Articles 1 and 2 of the Sixth Protocol (agreed at Strasbourg on 11 May 1994), as read with Articles 16 and 18 of the ECHR (Section 1 Human Rights Act 1998; s 107(1) and (5) GWA; sections 6(2); 24(1) and 98(1) NIA; sections 29(2); 57(2) and 126 (1) SA).

2 All the rights, powers, liabilities, obligations and restrictions from time to time created or arising by or under the Community Treaties; and all the remedies and procedures from time to time provided for by or under the Community Treaties (sections 106(7) and 155(1), GWA; sections 6(2); 24(1) and 98(1), NIA; sections 29(2); 57(2) and 126(9) SA).

3.3 (1) If a devolution issue under the GWA arises in proceedings, the court must order notice of it to be given to the Attorney General and the Assembly if they are not already a party. They have a right to take part as a party in the proceedings so far as they relate to a devolution issue, if they are not already a party (paragraph 5, schedule 8 to the GWA.) If they do take part, they may require the court to refer the devolution issue to the Judicial Committee (paragraph 30, schedule 8 to the GWA)[1].

(2) There are similar provisions in the NIA and the SA although the persons to be notified are different (paragraphs 135, 146, and 33, schedule 10 to the NIA; paragraphs 165, 176 and 33, schedule 6 to the SA).

1 If the Attorney General or the Assembly had become a party to the original proceedings but did not exercise their right to require the devolution issue to be referred to the Judicial Committee and the court decided the case, they would have the same rights of appeal as parties. These would not allow them to appeal a decision made in proceedings on indictment, although the Attorney General has a power under section 36 of the Criminal Justice Act 1972 to refer a point of law to the Court of Appeal where the defendant has been acquitted in a trial on indictment.
Paragraph 31, schedule 8 to the GWA, allows the Attorney General and Assembly to refer to the Judicial Committee any devolution issue which is not the subject of proceedings. This power could possibly be used if a court reached a decision where they had not been parties and so had no rights of appeal but such a reference could not affect the decision of the court.

3.4 Under all the Acts the court may refer a devolution issue to another court as follows:

(1) The Crown Court or a magistrates' court may refer a devolution issue arising in civil or summary proceedings to the High Court (paragraphs 6 and 9, schedule 8 to the GWA; paragraphs 15 and 18, schedule 10 to the NIA; and paragraphs 18 and 21, schedule 6 to the SA).

(2) The Crown Court may refer a devolution issue arising in summary proceedings to the High Court and a devolution issue arising in proceedings on indictment to the Court of Appeal (paragraph 9, schedule 8 to the GWA; paragraph 18, schedule 10 to the NIA; paragraph 21, schedule 6 to the SA).

(3) A county court, the High Court (unless the devolution issue has been referred to the High Court)[1], and the Crown Court[2] may refer a devolution issue arising in civil proceedings to the Court of Appeal (paragraph 7, schedule 8 to the GWA; paragraph 16, schedule 10 to the NIA; paragraph 19, schedule 6 to the SA).

(4) A tribunal from which there is no appeal must, and any other tribunal may, refer a devolution issue to the Court of Appeal (paragraph 8, schedule 8 to the GWA; paragraph 17, schedule 10 to the NIA; paragraph 20, schedule 6 to the SA).

(5) The Court of Appeal may refer a devolution issue to the Judicial Committee, unless the devolution issue was referred to it by another

court (paragraph 10, schedule 8 to the GWA; paragraph 19, schedule 10 to the NIA; paragraph 22, schedule 6 to the SA).

(6) An appeal against the determination of a devolution issue by the High Court or the Court of Appeal on a reference lies to the Judicial Committee with the leave permission of the court concerned, or, failing such leave, with special leave of the Judicial Committee (paragraph 11, schedule 8 to the GWA; paragraph 20, schedule 10 to the the NIA; paragraph 23, schedule 6 to the SA).

1 If an appeal by way of case stated in criminal proceedings goes to the Divisional Court there appears to be no power for the Divisional Court to refer a devolution issue to the Court of Appeal.

2 Eg in appeals from a magistrates' court in a licensing matter.

3.5 A court may take into account additional expense which the court considers that a party has incurred as a result of the participation of the Attorney General or the Assembly in deciding any question as to costs (paragraph 35, schedule 8 to the GWA).

PART II
DIRECTIONS APPLICABLE TO ALL PROCEEDINGS

SCOPE

4 Paragraphs 5 to 13 apply to proceedings in England and Wales in the magistrates' courts, the county courts, the Crown Court, the High Court and the Court of Appeal (Civil and Criminal Division). Paragraph 10 also applies to the form and procedure for a reference to the Court of Appeal by a tribunal.

RAISING THE QUESTION AS TO WHETHER A DEVOLUTION ISSUE ARISES

5.1 Where a party to any form of proceedings wishes to raise an issue which may be a devolution issue whether as a claim (or part of a claim) to enforce or establish a legal right or to seek a remedy or as a defence (or part of a defence), the provisions of this practice direction apply in addition to the rules of procedure applicable to the proceedings in which the issue arises.

5.2 A court may, of its own volition, require the question of whether a devolution issue arises to be considered, if the materials put before the court indicate such an issue may arise, even if the parties have not used the term 'devolution issue'.

DETERMINATION BY A COURT OF WHETHER A DEVOLUTION ISSUE ARISES

6.1 The court may give such directions as it considers appropriate to obtain clarification or additional information to establish whether a devolution issue arises.

6.2 In determining whether a devolution issue arises the court, notwithstanding the contention of a party to the proceedings, may decide that a devolution issue shall not be taken to arise if the contention appears to the court to be frivolous or vexatious (paragraph 2 of schedule 8 to the GWA).

6.3 If the court determines that a devolution issue arises it must state what that devolution issue is clearly and concisely.

NOTICE OF DEVOLUTION ISSUE TO THE ATTORNEY GENERAL AND THE ASSEMBLY

7.1 If a court determines that a devolution issue arises in the proceedings, it must order a devolution issue notice substantially in the form numbered 'DI 1' in Annex 1 to be given to the Attorney General and the Assembly unless they are already a party to the proceedings (paragraph 5(1), schedule 8 to the GWA).

7.2 A court receiving a reference does not have to serve a devolution issue notice unless it determines that a devolution issue that was not identified by the court making the reference has arisen. In that case the court receiving the reference must serve a devolution issue notice which must:

(1) state what devolution issue has been referred to it;
(2) state what further devolution issue has arisen; and
(3) identify the referring court.

7.3 If the devolution issue has arisen in criminal proceedings, the devolution issue notice must state:

(1) whether the proceedings have been adjourned;
(2) whether the defendant is remanded in custody; and
(3) if the defendant has been remanded in custody and his trial has not commenced, when the custody time limit expires.[1]

1 Custody time limits are imposed by the Prosecution of Offences (Custody Time Limits) Regulations 1987 as amended.

7.4 If the devolution issue arises in an appeal, the devolution issue notice must:

(1) state that the devolution issue arises in an appeal;
(2) identify the court whose decision is being appealed; and
(3) state whether the devolution issue is raised for the first time on appeal; or, if it is not, state that the devolution issue was raised in the court whose decision is being appealed, what decision was reached by that court, and the date of the previous notice to the Attorney General and the Assembly.

7.5 The devolution issue notice will specify a date which will be 14 days, or such longer period as the court may direct (see below), after the date of the devolution issue notice as the date by which the Attorney General or the Assembly must notify the court that he or it wishes to take part as a party to the proceedings, so far as they relate to a devolution issue.

7.6 The court may, in exceptional circumstances, specify a date longer than 14 days after the date of the devolution issue notice as the date by which the Attorney General and the Assembly must notify the court that he or it wishes to take part as a party to the proceedings. The court may do this before the notice is given, or before or after the expiry of the period given in the notice.

7.7 (1) On the date of the devolution issue notice,
 (a) the devolution issue notice for the Attorney General must be faxed to him by the court[1]; and
 (b) the devolution issue notice for the Assembly must be faxed by the court to the Counsel General for the Assembly.
(2) On the same day as a fax is sent a copy of the devolution issue notice must be sent by the court by first class post to the Attorney General and the Counsel General for the Assembly.

1 See Annex 2 for information about fax numbers and addresses.

7.8 The court may, on such terms as it considers appropriate, order such additional documents to be served (eg in civil proceedings, the claim form) or additional information to be supplied with the devolution issue notice.

7.9 (1) When a court orders a devolution issue notice to be given the court may make such further orders as it thinks fit in relation to any adjournment, stay, continuance of the proceedings, or interim measures, during the period within which the Attorney General and the Assembly have to notify the court if they intend to take part as a party to the proceedings.

(2) Before ordering an adjournment in criminal proceedings, the court will consider all material circumstances, including whether it would involve delay that might extend beyond the custody time limits if the defendant is remanded in custody and his trial has not commenced.

7.10 If neither the Attorney General nor the Assembly notify the court within the specified time that he or it wishes to take part as a party to the proceedings:

(1) the proceedings should immediately continue on expiry of the period within which they had to notify the court; and

(2) the court has no duty to inform them of the outcome of the proceedings apart from the duty to notify them if the court decides to refer the devolution issue to another court (see paragraph 10.3(5))[1].

1 If there is an appeal, the court will serve a devolution issue notice on the Attorney-General and the Assembly (see paragraph 7.4).

ADDING THE ATTORNEY GENERAL OR THE ASSEMBLY TO THE PROCEEDINGS AND THEIR RIGHT TO REQUIRE REFERRAL OF A DEVOLUTION ISSUE TO THE JUDICIAL COMMITTEE

8.1 If the Attorney General or the Assembly wishes to take part as a party to the proceedings so far as they relate to a devolution issue, he or it must send to the court and the other parties (and to each other if only one of them has become a party) a notice substantially in the form numbered 'DI 2' shown in Annex 1 within the time specified in the devolution issue notice.

8.2 On receipt of this form the court may give such consequential directions as it considers necessary.

8.3 If the Attorney General or the Assembly is a party to the proceedings, and either of them wishes to require the court to refer the devolution issue to the Judicial Committee, he or it must as soon as practicable send to the court and the other parties (and to each other if only one of them has become a party) a notice substantially in the form numbered 'DI 3' shown in Annex 1.

DETERMINATION BY THE COURT OF WHETHER OR NOT TO MAKE A REFERENCE OF A DEVOLUTION ISSUE IF THE ATTORNEY GENERAL OR THE ASSEMBLY DO NOT REQUIRE A REFERENCE

9.1 If the court is not required to refer the devolution issue to the Judicial Committee, the court will decide whether it should refer the devolution issue to the relevant court as specified in paragraph 3.4.

9.2 Before deciding whether to make a reference the court may hold a directions hearing or give written directions as to the making of submissions on the question of whether to make a reference.

9.3 The court may make a decision on the basis of written submissions if its procedures permit this and it wishes to do so, or the court may have a hearing before making a decision.

9.4 In exercising its discretion as to whether to make a reference, the court will have regard to all relevant circumstances and in particular to:

(1) the importance of the devolution issue to the public in general;
(2) the importance of the devolution issue to the original parties to the proceedings;
(3) whether a decision on the reference of the devolution issue will be decisive of the matters in dispute between the parties;
(4) whether all the relevant findings of fact have been made (a devolution issue will not, unless there are exceptional circumstances, be suitable for a reference if it has to be referred on the basis of assumed facts);
(5) the delay that a reference would entail particularly in cases involving children and criminal cases (including whether the reference is likely to involve delay that would extend beyond the expiry of the custody time limits if the defendant is remanded in custody and his trial has not commenced); and
(6) additional costs that a reference might involve[1].

1 In criminal cases section 16 of the Prosecution of Offences Act 1985 does not enable a court receiving a reference to make a defendant's costs order. If the defendant is subsequently acquitted by the court who made the reference that court can make a defendant's costs order. However it would not cover the costs of the reference as 'proceedings' is defined in section 21 as including proceedings in any court below but makes no mention of proceedings on a reference.

9.5 The court should state its reasons for making or declining to make a reference.

9.6 If the court decides not to refer the case, it will give directions for the future conduct of the action, which will include directions as to the participation of the Attorney General and the Assembly if they are parties.

FORM AND PROCEDURE FOR REFERENCES

10.1 If the court or tribunal is required by the Attorney General or the Assembly (in relation to any proceedings before the court to which he or it is a party) to refer the devolution issue to the Judicial Committee:

(1) the court or tribunal will make the reference as soon as practicable after receiving the notice from the Attorney General or the Assembly substantially in the form numbered 'DI 3' shown in Annex 1, and follow the procedure for references in the Judicial Committee (Devolution Issues) Rules Order 1999; and
(2) the court or tribunal may order the parties, or any of them, to draft the reference.

10.2 If the Court of Appeal decides to refer the devolution issue to the Judicial Committee:

(1) a higher court it will follow the procedure in the Judicial Committee (Devolution Issues) Rules Order 1999; and
(2) the court may order the parties, or any of them, to draft the reference.

10.3 If any other court or tribunal decides, or if a tribunal is required, to refer the devolution issue to another court:

(1) the reference must be substantially in the form numbered 'DI 4' shown in Annex 1 and must set out the following:
   (a) the question referred;
   (b) the addresses of the parties, except in the case of family proceedings, for which see paragraphs 15.2–4;
   (c) a concise statement of the background of the matter including –
      (i) the facts of the case, including any relevant findings of fact by the referring court or lower courts; and
      (ii) the main issues in the case and the contentions of the parties with regard to them;
   (d) the relevant law, including the relevant provisions of the GWA;
   (e) the reasons why an answer to the question is considered necessary for the purpose of disposing of the proceedings;

(2) all judgments already given in the proceedings will be annexed to the reference;

(3) the court may order the parties, or any of them, to draft the reference;

(4) the court or tribunal will transmit the reference to:
   (a) the Civil Appeals Office Registry if the reference is to the Court of Appeal from a county court, the High Court or the Crown Court in civil proceedings, or from a tribunal;
   (b) the Registrar of Criminal Appeals if the reference is to the Court of Appeal from the Crown Court in proceedings on indictment; and
   (c) the [Administrative Court Office if the reference is to the High Court from a magistrates' court in civil or summary proceedings or from the Crown Court in summary proceedings[1].

If the reference is transmitted to Cardiff an additional copy of the reference must be filed so that it can be retained by the Cardiff Office. The original reference will be forwarded to the Crown Office in London.

(5) at the same time as the reference is transmitted to the court receiving the reference a copy of the reference will be sent by first class post to:
   (a) the parties;
   (b) the Attorney General if he is not already a party; and
   (c) the Assembly if it is not already a party;

(6) each person on whom a copy of the reference is served must within 21 days notify the court to which the reference is transmitted and the other persons on whom the reference is served whether they wish to be heard on the reference;

(7) the court receiving the reference (either the Court of Appeal or the High Court) will give directions for the conduct of the reference, including the lodging of cases or skeleton arguments; and transmit a copy of the determination on the reference to the referring court; and

(8) if there has been an appeal to the Judicial Committee against a decision of the High Court or the Court of Appeal on a reference, and a copy of the Judicial Committee's decision on that appeal has been sent to the High Court or Court of Appeal (as the case may be), that court will send a copy to the court which referred the devolution issue to it.

1 See Annex 2 for the relevant addresses. It shows The Law Courts, Cathays Park, Cardiff, CF10 3PG and the Royal Courts of Justice, Strand, London WC2A 2LL as alternative addresses for transmitting documents to the Crown Office. If the order is transmitted to Cardiff, the additional copy will be forwarded by the Cardiff Office to the Crown Office in London.

10.4 When a court receives notification of the decision on a reference, it will determine how to proceed with the remainder of the case.

POWER OF THE COURT TO DEAL WITH PENDING PROCEEDINGS IF A REFERENCE IS MADE (WHETHER BY THE ATTORNEY GENERAL, THE ASSEMBLY OR THE COURT).

11 If a reference is made the court will adjourn or stay the proceedings in which the devolution issue arose, unless it otherwise orders; and will make such further orders as it thinks fit in relation to any adjournment or stay.

THE WELSH LANGUAGE

12.1 If any party wishes to put forward a contention in relation to a devolution issue that involves comparison of the Welsh and English texts of any Assembly subordinate legislation, that party must give notice to the court as soon as possible.

12.2 Upon receipt of the notification, the court will consider the appropriate means of determining the issue, including, if necessary, the appointment of a Welsh speaking judicial assessor to assist the court.

12.3 Parties to any proceedings in which the Welsh language may be used must also comply with the practice direction of 16 October 1998 (relating to proceedings in the Crown Court) and the practice direction of 26 April 1999 (relating to civil proceedings). These practice directions apply, as appropriate, to proceedings involving a devolution issue in which the Welsh language may be used.

CROWN PROCEEDINGS ACT 1947 (SECTION 19)

13 Where the court has determined that a devolution issue arises, the Attorney General will give any necessary consent to:

(1) the proceedings being transferred to The Law Courts, Cathays Park, Cardiff, CF 10 3PG, or to such other district registry as shall (exceptionally) be directed by the court; and
(2) to the trial taking place at Cardiff or at such other trial location as shall (exceptionally) be directed by the court.

PART III
DIRECTIONS APPLICABLE TO SPECIFIC PROCEEDINGS

JUDICIAL REVIEW PROCEEDINGS IN WALES

14.1

The practice direction supplementing Part 54 (judicial review) contains provisions about when judicial review proceedings may be brought in the Administrative Court in Wales.

FAMILY PROCEEDINGS IN THE MAGISTRATES' COURTS, THE COUNTY COURTS AND THE HIGH COURT

15.1 In any proceedings in which any question with respect to the upbringing of a child arises, the court shall have regard to the general principle that any delay in determining the question is likely to prejudice the welfare of the child.[1]

1 Section 1(2), Children Act 1989.

15.2 If the FPR apply, the court will comply with rule 10.21[1].

1 Rule 10.21 states: (1) Subject to rule 2.3 [of the FPR] nothing in these rules shall be construed as requiring any party to reveal the address of their private residence (or that of any child) save by order of the court. (2) Where a party declines to reveal an address in reliance upon paragraph (1) above, he shall give notice of that address to the court in Form C8 and that address shall not be revealed to any person save by order of the court.

15.3 If Part IV of the FPR applies, the court will comply with rule 4.23[1].

1 Rule 4.23 states: (1) Notwithstanding any rule of court to the contrary, no document, other than a record of an order, held by the court and relating to proceedings to which [Part IV] applies shall be disclosed, other than to – (a) a party, (b) the legal representative of a party (c) the guardian ad litem, (d) the Legal Aid Board, or (e) a welfare officer, without the leave of the judge or the district judge. (2) Nothing in this rule shall prevent the notification by the court or the proper officer of a direction under section 37(1) to the authority concerned. (3) Nothing in this rule shall prevent the disclosure of a document prepared by a guardian ad litem for the purpose of – (a) enabling a person to perform functions required by regulations made under section 41(7); (b) assisting a guardian ad litem or a reporting officer (within the meaning of section 65(1)(b) of the Adoption Act 1976) who is appointed under any enactment to perform his functions.

15.4 If the FPC apply, the court will comply with Rules 23 and 33A[1].

1 Rule 23 states: (1) No document, other than a record of an order, held by the court and relating to relevant proceedings shall be disclosed, other than to – (a) a party, (b) the legal representative of a party, (c) the guardian ad litem, (d) the Legal Aid Board, or (e) a welfare officer, without leave of the justices' clerk or the court. (2) Nothing in this rule shall prevent the notification by the court or the justices' clerk of a direction under section 37(1) to the authority concerned. (3) Nothing in this rule shall prevent the disclosure of a document prepared by a guardian ad litem for the purpose of – (a) enabling a person to perform functions required by regulations made under section 41(7); (b) assisting a guardian ad litem or a reporting officer (within the meaning of section 65(1)(b) of the Adoption Act 1976) who is appointed under any enactment to perform his functions.

Rule 33A states: (1) Nothing in these Rules shall be construed as requiring any party to reveal the address of their private residence (or that of any child) except by order of the court. (2) Where a party declines to reveal an address in reliance upon paragraph (1) he shall give notice of that address to the court in Form C8 and that address shall not be revealed to any person except by order of the court.

15.5 If the proceedings are listed in column (i) of Appendix 3 to the FPR or Schedule 2 to the FPC, a copy of any notice to be given to the parties must also be given to the persons set out in column (iv) of Appendix 3 or Schedule 2 as the case may be.

15.6 A party wishing to raise a devolution issue must, wherever possible, raise it (giving full particulars of the provisions relied on) in the application or answer or at the first directions hearing where appropriate.

15.7 If a party has not raised a devolution issue as above, the party must seek the permission of the court to raise it at a later stage.

15.8 Where a court has referred the devolution issue to another court and has received notification of the decision on the reference, the matter should so far as is practicable be placed before the same judge or magistrates who dealt with the case before the reference.

CIVIL PROCEEDINGS IN THE COUNTY COURTS AND THE HIGH COURT

16.1 A party wishing to raise a devolution issue must specify in the claim form, or if he is a defendant, in the defence (or written evidence filed with the acknowledgment of service in a Part 8 claim) that the claim raises a devolution issue and the relevant provisions of the GWA.

16.2 The particulars of claim or defence if the devolution issue is raised by the defendant (or written evidence filed with the acknowledgment of service in a Part 8 claim) must contain the facts and circumstances and points of law on the basis of which it is alleged that a devolution issue arises in sufficient detail to enable the court to determine whether a devolution issue arises in the proceedings.

16.3 Whether or not the allocation rules apply, if a question is raised during the proceedings that might be a devolution issue, then a directions hearing must take place and the matter must be referred to a circuit judge (in county court actions) or a High Court judge (in High Court actions) for determination as to whether a devolution issue arises and for further directions.

16.4 If a party fails to specify in the appropriate document that a devolution issue arises but that party subsequently wishes to raise a devolution issue, that party must seek the permission of the court.

16.5 Where any party has specified that a devolution issue arises, no default judgment can be obtained.

CRIMINAL PROCEEDINGS IN THE CROWN COURT

17 If the defendant wishes to raise a devolution issue he should do so at the Plea and Directions Hearing.

CRIMINAL AND CIVIL PROCEEDINGS IN THE MAGISTRATES' COURTS

18.1(1) Where a defendant, who has been charged or has had an information laid against him in respect of a criminal offence and has entered a plea of 'Not Guilty', wishes to raise a devolution issue he should, wherever possible, give full particulars of the provisions relied on by notice in writing.

(2) Where a party to a complaint, or applicant for a licence wishes to raise a devolution issue he should, wherever possible, give full particulars of the provisions relied on by notice in writing.

(3) Such notice should be given to the prosecution (and other party if any) and the court as soon as practicable after the 'Not Guilty' plea is entered or the complaint or application is made as the case may be.

18.2 Where proceedings are to be committed or transferred to the Crown Court by the magistrates, the question as to whether a devolution issue arises shall be a matter for the Crown Court.

PART IV
APPEALS

APPEALS TO THE COURT OF APPEAL (CIVIL AND CRIMINAL DIVISION)

19.1 This paragraph applies if a devolution issue is raised in any appeal to either the Civil or the Criminal Division of the Court of Appeal.

19.2 The devolution issue may already have been raised in the court whose decision is being appealed. The devolution issue may, however, be raised for the first time on appeal.

19.3 Where an application for permission to appeal is made, or an appeal is brought where permission is not needed, the appellant must specify in the application notice (or the notice of appeal or notice of motion as the case may be):

(1) that the appeal raises a devolution issue and the relevant provisions of the GWA;
(2) the facts and circumstances and points of law on the basis of which it is alleged that a devolution issue arises in sufficient detail to enable the court to determine whether a devolution issue arises; and
(3) whether the devolution issue was considered in the court below, and, if so, provide details of the decision.

19.4 An appellant may not seek to raise a devolution issue without the permission of the court after he has filed an application notice; or a notice of appeal or notice of motion (if no application notice).

19.5 Where permission to appeal is sought and a party to the appeal wishes to raise a devolution issue which was not raised in the lower court, the court will determine if a devolution issue arises before deciding whether to grant leave to appeal.

APPEALS TO THE CROWN COURT

20 A notice of appeal from a decision of the magistrates' courts to the Crown Court must specify whether the devolution issue was considered in the court below and if so, provide details of the decision. If it was not so considered, the notice should specify:

(1) that the appeal raises a devolution issue and the relevant provisions of the GWA; and
(2) the facts and circumstances and points of law on the basis of which it is alleged that a devolution issue arises in sufficient detail to enable the court to determine whether a devolution issue arises.

Annex 1

DI 1

DEVOLUTION ISSUES

Notice of Devolution Issue to Attorney General and the National Assembly for Wales

[NAME OF CASE]
Take notice that the above mentioned case has raised a devolution issue as defined by Schedule 8 to the Government of Wales Act 1998. Details of the devolution issue are given in the attached schedule.

This notice meets the notification requirements under paragraph 5(1) of Schedule 8 to the Government of Wales Act 1998. You may take part as a party to these proceedings, so far as they relate to a devolution issue (paragraph 5(2) of Schedule 8). If you want to do this you must notify the court by completing the attached form, and returning it to the court at [address] by [date].

DATED

To: The Attorney-General

The National Assembly for Wales

Other parties (where appropriate)

DI 2

DEVOLUTION ISSUES

Notice of intention of Attorney General or the National Assembly for Wales to become party to proceedings, so far as they relate to a devolution issue, under Paragraph 5(2) Schedule 8 to the Government of Wales Act 1998

In the [name of court]
[case name]

Take notice that the [Attorney General] [the National Assembly for Wales] intends to take part as a party to proceedings so far as they relate to a devolution issue as permitted by paragraph 5(2) of Schedule 8 to the Government of Wales Act 1998 in relation to the devolution issue raised by [ ], of which notice was received by the [Attorney General] [Assembly] on [ ].

[The [ ] also gives notice that it [requires the matter to be referred to] [is still considering whether to require the matter to be referred to] the Judicial Committee of the Privy Council under paragraph 30 of Schedule 8 to the Government of Wales Act 1998.]

[DATE]

On behalf of the [Attorney General] [National Assembly for Wales]

To: The clerk of the court at [ ]
The parties to the case
[Attorney General] [National Assembly for Wales]

DI 3
DEVOLUTION ISSUES

Notice by Attorney General or National Assembly for Wales that they require devolution issue to be referred to the Judicial Committee of the Privy Council

In the [court]

[case name]

The [Attorney General] [National Assembly for Wales] gives notice that the devolution issue, which has been raised in the above case and to which [he] [it] is a party, must be referred to the Judicial Committee of the Privy Council under paragraph 30 of Schedule 8 to the Government of Wales Act 1998.

[DATE]

On behalf of the [Attorney General] [National Assembly for Wales]

To: The clerk of the court at [ ]
The parties to the case
[Attorney General] [National Assembly for Wales]

DI 4
DEVOLUTION ISSUES

Reference by the court or tribunal of devolution issue to [High Court] [Court of Appeal] [Judicial Committee of the Privy Council]

In the [court]
[case name]

It is ordered that the devolution issue(s) set out in the schedule be referred to the [High Court] [Court of Appeal] [Judicial Committee of the Privy Council] for determination in accordance with paragraph [ ] of Schedule 8 to the Government of Wales Act 1998.
It is further ordered that the proceedings be stayed until the [High Court] [Court of Appeal] Judicial Committee of the Privy Council] determine the devolution issue[s] or until further order.
DATED

Judge/clerk to the magistrates court
Chairman of the tribunal
[Address]

SKELETON REFERENCE TO BE ATTACHED TO FORM DI 4

In the [court]
[case name]

(a) [The question referred.]
(b) [The addresses of the parties]
(c) [A concise statement of the background to the matters including –
(i) The facts of the case including any relevant findings of fact by the referring court or lower courts; and
(ii) The main issues in the case and the contentions of the parties with regard to them;]
(d) [the relevant law including the relevant provisions of the Government of Wales Act 1998]
(e) [the reasons why an answer to the question is considered necessary for the purpose of disposing of the proceedings.]

[All judgments already given in the proceedings are annexed to this reference.]

Annex 2

ADDRESSES

1 Notices to the National Assembly for Wales (*Cynulliad Cenedlaethol Cymru*) must be sent to the Counsel General to the National Assembly for Wales, Crown Buildings, Cathays Park, Cardiff CF99 1NA. Fax number: [ ].

2 Notices to the Attorney General must be sent to the Attorney General's Chambers, 9 Buckingham Gate, London, SW1E 6JP. Fax number 0171 271 2433.

3 References to the Crown Office under paragraph 9.3(1)c of the practice direction may be sent to the Crown Office, Royal Courts of Justice, Strand, London WC2A 2LL; or the Law Courts, Cathays Park, Cardiff, CF10 3PG (2 copies).

EXPLANATORY NOTE

4 The addresses and fax numbers above are the best information available, however it is possible that these (particularly the fax numbers and address for Notices to the Assembly) may change, it would therefore be advisable to confirm the numbers before sending information.

Practice Direction – Directors Disqualification Proceedings

General note—In order to understand the effects of the practice direction on directors' disqualification it is necessary to give a brief account of the law and practice on the subject. The reader is referred to *Mithani: Directors' Disqualification* (looseleaf, Butterworths) for a detailed account. Unless otherwise stated, the references to section numbers are to sections of CDDA 1986 ('the Act') as principally amended by IA 2000 and EA 2002. References to 'the Disqualification Rules' are references to the Insolvent Companies (Disqualification of Unfit Directors) Proceedings Rules 1987 as amended.

Meaning of disqualification order—Section 1 defines a disqualification order as meaning an order that the person against whom it is made –

(a) shall not be a director of a company, act as a receiver of a company's property, or in any way, whether directly or indirectly, be concerned or take part in the promotion, formation or management of a company, unless (in each case) he has the leave of the court; and
(b) shall not act as an insolvency practitioner.

Where a disqualification order is made pursuant to s 1(1), the court must make an absolute disqualification applying the entirety of s 1(1), not 'pick and choose' which of the restrictions contained in s 1(1) it should impose (*Official Receiver v Hannan* [1997] 2 BCLC 473, CA).

Circumstances in which a disqualification order or some other form of disqualification can be made or imposed:

I Discretionary disqualification

The Act gives the court a discretionary power to make a disqualification order in the following circumstances –

(a) on conviction of an indictable offence (s 2);
(b) for persistent breaches of companies legislation (s 3);
(c) for fraud in the course of a winding up (s 4);
(d) on summary conviction for offences under companies legislation (s 5);
(e) for unfitness where it is in the public interest after an investigation by inspectors, or from information and documents obtained, under various statutory provisions (s 8);
(f) following the making by the court of a declaration against a person for fraudulent trading under IA 1986, s 213 or wrongful trading under IA 1986, s 214 (s 10).

II Mandatory disqualification

However, the court *must* make the disqualification order:

(a) where a company has at any time become insolvent and where the conduct of the director in question makes him unfit to be concerned in the management of a company (ss 6 and 7). In an appropriate case, the Secretary of State may accept a disqualification undertaking – which has identical effect to a disqualification order – from such a person (s 1A and see under note **'Compromises and settlements'** below);
(b) where a company, of which the person concerned is a director, commits a breach of competition law and the court considers that the conduct of such person is such as to make him unfit to be concerned in the management of a company (s 9A). Proceedings for a disqualification order under this provision can only be brought by the OFT or by one of the regulators specified in

s 9E(2). In an appropriate case, the OFT or a specified regulator may accept a disqualification undertaking from such a person (see note **'Compromises and settlements'** below).

III Other forms of disqualification

In addition, disqualification in some form (ie not necessarily in the form set out in s 1(1)) may in certain cases be either automatic or imposed by the court. These include –

(a) bankruptcy (s 11).

(b) the imposition of a bankruptcy restrictions order, subjecting a bankrupt to certain restrictions (similar to those applying during bankruptcy) for a period of not less that 2 years and not more than 15 years from the date when the order is made (IA 1986, s 281A and Sch 4A). Such an order can only be made on the application of the Secretary of State or the Official Receiver acting on a direction of the Secretary of State (IA 1986, Sch 4A, para 1). In an appropriate case, the Secretary of State may accept a bankruptcy restrictions undertaking (which has identical effect to a bankruptcy restrictions order) from a bankrupt (IA 1986, Sch 4A, para 7) (see note **'Compromises and settlements'** below);

(c) where a county court administration order made under CCA 1984, Pt VI is revoked under IA 1986, s 429 by a court (s 12) (see further note **'Revocation of administration orders'** under CPR Sch 2, CCR Ord 39, r 13A);

(d) where IA 1986, s 216 (restriction on re-use of company names) applies.

Applications for disqualification orders—In certain cases, a disqualification order can only be made upon application to a court having jurisdiction to make one. In other cases, disqualification (but not necessarily in the form of a disqualification order) may be imposed either automatically (as, for example, in a case of a bankruptcy) or ancillary to the consideration by the court of a separate matter, for example, where disqualification follows a conviction (ss 2 and 5) or a finding of fraudulent and/or wrongful trading under IA 1986, ss 213 and/or 214 (s 10).

In practice, applications for disqualification orders are most frequently brought under s 7. Accordingly, unless otherwise stated, this note deals primarily with applications under that provision.

Only the Secretary of State for Trade and Industry and (where the company, in respect of which the applications is brought, is being wound up by the court) the Official Receiver (*Re Probe Data Systems Limited (No 1)* [1989] BCLC 561; *Re NP Engineering & Security Products Limited* [1998] 1 BCLC 208) are able to bring applications under s 7. Such applications can only be brought against a director of a company which has at any time become insolvent in circumstances where that person's conduct as a director of that company (either taken alone or taken together with his conduct as a director of any other company) makes him unfit to be concerned in the management of a company. A director includes any person occupying the position of a director by whatever name called and also includes a 'shadow director', defined in s 22(5) as '... a person in accordance with whose instructions the directors of a company are accustomed to act...' (see further: *Re Hydrodam (Corby) Limited* [1994] BCC 161; *Secretary of State for Trade and Industry v Laing* [1996] 2 BCLC 324, ChD; *Re Kaytech International plc* [1999] 2 BCLC 351 and *Secretary of State for Trade and Industry v Deverell* [2000] 2 WLR 907). A limited company may be the subject of a disqualification order (*Official Receiver v Brady* [1999] BCC 258, ChD).

Operation of s 7 of the Act—Once the court finds that conduct of the director in question makes him unfit to be concerned in the management of a company, a disqualification order is mandatory under s 7 (*Re Sevenoaks Stationers (Retail) Limited* [1991] Ch 164; *Re Swift 736 Limited* [1993] BCC 312; *Secretary of State for Trade and Industry v Gray & anor* [1995] BCC 594; *Re Country Farm Inns Limited* [1997] 2 BCLC 334; *Re Westmid Packing Limited* [1998] 2 All ER 124). Section 9 requires the court to take into account certain guidelines, set out in Sch 1 to the Act, in deciding the question of unfitness. However, the guidelines are not exhaustive and the court will take into account any allegation which shows unfitness on the part of the director concerned (*Re Amaron* [1998] BCC 264; *Re Sykes (Butchers) Limited* [1998] 1 BCLC 110; *Re Migration Services Limited* [2000] 1 BCLC 666).

Period of disqualification—In cases of automatic disqualification, the period of disqualification may be prescribed by the statutory provision under which the disqualification arises. However, as a general rule, if the court makes a disqualification order, it will determine the period. The Act prescribes maximum periods. Save in the case of an order under s 7, where the minimum is 2 years, there is no minimum period prescribed for disqualification under a disqualification order. As to the principles upon which the court will act in fixing the period under s 7, see *Re Sevenoaks Stationers (Retail) Limited* [1991] Ch 164 and *Re Westmid Packing Limited* [1998] 2 All ER 124.

Reporting provisions—In order to enable the Secretary of State to consider whether to bring disqualification applications under s 7, detailed provisions requiring office holders of insolvent companies to make returns concerning directors and to report unfitness to the Secretary of State are contained in s 7(3) and in the Insolvent Companies (Report on Conduct of Directors) Rules 1996. Failure by an insolvency practitioner to submit returns to the Secretary of State when required is a criminal offence (Insolvent Companies (Reports on Conduct of Directors) Rules 1996, r 4.7). Further, failure may also result in an order requiring compliance by the office holder with his obligations to the Secretary of State (r 6 *ibid*).

Period within which proceedings should be commenced—Save in respect of applications under s 7, there is no maximum period laid down by the Act for the bringing of an application for disqualification. In cases under s 7, any application must be made before the end of 2 years beginning with the date on which the company in question became insolvent (s 7(2)). However, the court may give permission for the application to be brought out of time (s 7(2)). Section 6(2) defines when a company becomes insolvent. As to the principles upon which the court relies in deciding whether or not to give that permission, see: *Re Probe Data Systems Limited (No 3)* [1992] BCLC 405; *Re Copecrest Limited* [1993] BCC 844; *Re Polly Peck International plc (No 2)* [1992] 4 All ER 769; *Re Packaging Direct Limited* [1994] BCC 213; *Secretary of State for Trade and Industry v Davies* [1996] 4 All ER 289.

The consequences of making a disqualification order—A disqualification order once made is registered in the Register of Disqualification Orders maintained under s 18 and the Companies (Disqualification Orders) Regulations 2001. Further, a person acting in contravention of a disqualification order commits a criminal offence. The offence is committed even if the defendant is not aware that he is acting in contravention of the order (*R v Brockley* (1994) 99 Cr App R 385). Further, where a person subject to a disqualification order is involved in the management of a company in contravention of the order, he will be personally liable for all debts and other liabilities of that company incurred during his involvement in its management. The civil liability is extended under s 15(1)(b) to any person who, while not himself subject to a disqualification order, is involved in the management of a company and either acts or is willing to act on the instructions of a person whom he knows at the time is the subject of a disqualification order. The liability is for all debts and liabilities of the company incurred while he so acts or is willing to act. Discussion of the other disabilities of a person subject to a disqualification order is outside the scope of this work.

Permission to act as a director or in management—Section 1(1) enables the court to grant permission to a person who is otherwise disqualified from undertaking the activities there referred to. Section 17 deals with permission applications. As to the principles upon which the court will act, see: *Re Dicetrade Limited* [1994] 2 BCLC 113; *Re Gibson Davies Limited* [1995] BCC 11, ChD; *Re Barings plc (No 3)* [1999] 1 BCLC 226; *Re Barings plc (No 4)* [1999] 1 WLR 1985, CA; and *Re Dawes and Henderson* [1999] 2 BCLC 217. See further *Re TTL Realisations Limited* (2000) 2 BCLC 223.

Compromises and settlements—In cases where a disqualification order might be made on the ground of unfitness (ss 7 and 8), it is possible for a defendant to avoid the substantial costs of the proceedings by agreeing to enter into a 'disqualification undertaking' pursuant to s 1A instead. The effect of giving such an undertaking is identical in all respects to the making of a disqualification order. The terms of the undertaking will be a matter of negotiation between the Secretary of State and the defendant. The Secretary of State is, however, required to have regard to the matters mentioned in Sch 1 to the Act when determining whether he may accept a disqualification undertaking. The provisions relating to reporting, minimum and maximum periods, registration, consequences of breach and permission to act which apply to disqualification orders apply equally to disqualification undertakings. In addition, s 8A enables a person who has given a disqualification undertaking to apply to the court to reduce the period for which the undertaking is to be in force or provide for it to cease to be in force. The '*Carecraft* procedure' (approved in *Re Carecraft Construction Co Ltd* [1994] 1 WLR 172 and modified by *Secretary of State for Trade and Industry v Rogers* [1996] 1 WLR 1569), which involved the making of a disqualification order based on the defendant's admission of some or all of the facts alleged and his acceptance that such facts amounted to unfitness on his part, is seldom likely now to be relevant in practice.

Section 9B enables the OFT or a specified regulator to accept a disqualification undertaking (having identical effect to a disqualification order) in the terms set out in subsections (3) and (4) of that section from a person against whom disqualification proceedings for breaches of competition law have been, or might be, brought. Similarly, IA 1986, Sch 4A, para 7 permits the Secretary of State to accept a bankruptcy restrictions undertaking (having identical effect to a bankruptcy restrictions order) from a person against whom proceedings for a bankruptcy restrictions order have been, or may be, brought. Such a disqualification or bankruptcy restrictions undertaking must be identical in form and substance to a disqualification order or bankruptcy restrictions order and may only be for a period for which such an order may be made.

Application of CPR and PDs to disqualification proceedings—The procedure is governed by the Disqualification Rules, which state that CPR and 'any relevant practice direction' apply to disqualification applications under ss 7 and 8 and 9A, except where the Disqualification Rules make provision to inconsistent effect (r 2). Appeals in disqualification matters are not dealt with by the PD but by the Disqualification Rules. They are discussed in the note to PDInsolvency, para 17. Unless otherwise stated, references to paragraph numbers in the notes below are to paragraphs of the practice direction.

PART 1

1 APPLICATION AND INTERPRETATION

1.1 In this practice direction:

(1) 'the Act' means the Company Directors Disqualification Act 1986 [(as amended);

(2) 'the Disqualification Rules' means the rules for the time being in force made under section 411 of the Insolvency Act 1986 in relation to disqualification proceedings[1];

(3) 'the Insolvency Rules' means the rules for the time being in force made under sections 411 and 412 of the Insolvency Act 1986 in relation to insolvency proceedings;

(4) 'CPR' means the Civil Procedure Rules 1998 and 'CPR' followed by 'Part' or 'Rule' and a number means the part or Rule with that number in those Rules;

(5) 'disqualification proceedings' has the meaning set out in paragraph 1.3 below;

(6) 'a disqualification application' is an application under the Act for the making of a disqualification order;

(7) 'registrar' means any judge of the High Court or the county court who is a registrar within the meaning of the Insolvency Rules;

(8) 'companies court registrar' means any judge of the High Court sitting in the Royal Courts of Justice in London who is a registrar within the meaning of the Insolvency Rules;

(9) except where the context otherwise requires references to –

(a) 'company' or 'companies' shall include references to 'partnership' or 'partnerships' and to 'limited liability partnership' and 'limited liability partnerships';

(b) 'director' shall include references to an 'officer' of a partnership and to a 'member' of a limited liability partnership;

(c) 'shadow director' shall include references to a 'shadow member' of a limited liability partnership;

and, in appropriate cases, the forms annexed to this practice direction shall be varied accordingly;

(10) 'disqualification order' has the meaning set out in section 1 of the Act and 'disqualification undertaking' has the meaning set out in section 1A or section 9B of the Act (as the context requires);

(11) a 'Section 8A application' is an application under section 8A of the Act to reduce the period for which a disqualification undertaking is in force or to provide for it to cease to be in force.

(12) 'specified regulator' has the meaning set out in section 9E(2) of the Act.

1 The current rules are the Insolvent Companies (Disqualification of Unfit Directors) Proceedings

Rules 1987. [For convenience, relevant references to the Insolvent Companies (Disqualification of Unfit Directors) Proceedings Rules 1987, which apply to disqualification applications under [sections 7, 8 and 9A of the Act (see rule 1(3)), are set out in footnotes to this practice direction. This practice direction applies certain provisions contained in the Insolvent Companies (Disqualification of Unfit Directors) Proceedings Rules 1987 to disqualification proceedings other than applications under sections [7, 8 and 9A of the Act.

1.2 This practice direction shall come into effect on 26 April 1999 and shall replace all previous practice directions relating to disqualification proceedings.

1.3 This practice direction applies to the following proceedings ('disqualification proceedings'):

- (1) disqualification applications made:
  - (a) under section 2(2)(a) of the Act (after the person's conviction of an indictable offence in connection with the affairs of a company);
  - (b) under section 3 of the Act (on the ground of persistent breaches of provisions of companies legislation);
  - (c) under section 4 of the Act (on the ground of fraud etc);
  - (d) by the Secretary of State or the official receiver under section 7(1) of the Act (on the ground that the person is or has been a director of a company which has at any time become insolvent and his conduct makes him unfit to be concerned in the management of a company);
  - (e) by the Secretary of State under section 8 of the Act (on it appearing to the Secretary of State from investigative material that it is expedient in the public interest that a disqualification order should be made); or
  - (f) by the Office of Fair Trading or a specified regulator under section 9A of the Act (on the ground of breach of competition law by an undertaking and unfitness to be concerned in the management of a company);
- (2) any application made under section 7(2) or 7(4) of the Act;
- (3) any application for permission to act made under section 17 of the Act for the purposes of any of sections 1(1)(a), 1A(1)(a) or 9B(4), or made under section 12(2) of the Act;
- (4) any application for a court order made under CPR Part 23 in the course of any of the proceedings set out in sub-paragraphs (1) to (3) above.
- (5) any application under the Act to the extent provided for by subordinate legislation[1];
- (6) any section 8A application.

1 Current subordinate legislation includes the Insolvent Partnerships Order 1994 and the Limited Liability Partnerships Regulations 2001.

'disqualification proceedings' (paras 1.1(5) and 1.3)—An application by a bankrupt or a person subject to a bankruptcy restrictions order for permission to be a director or to act in the management of a company under s 11 is not included in the definition of 'disqualification proceedings'. Such application is governed by IR 1986, rr 6.202A–6.205. Nor is an application for permission to act under IA 1986, s 216. Rule 4.226 *et seq* of those rules apply to such applications.

'disqualification application' (paras 1.1(6) and 1.3(1))—The disqualification applications to which the practice direction applies are those made under ss 2(2)(a), 3, 4, 7 and 8. The practice direction therefore only applies to those applications for a disqualification order where –

(a) such application is made either to a court having jurisdiction to wind up the company or to the High Court; and

(b) the making of a disqualification order is the only or the only substantive relief sought by the applicant.

SECTION 3 Other Practice Directions

It does not therefore apply where the court making the disqualification order is a court of criminal jurisdiction or where disqualification is automatic or where it is ancillary to the consideration by the court of a separate matter (for example, under s 10, discussed above). Although the Disqualification Rules in terms apply to applications made for disqualification orders under s 9A for breaches of competition law (r 2), the practice direction has not been amended to incorporate such applications.

'registrar' (para 1.1(7))—This term is defined in IR 1986, r 13.2. It covers *in general terms* a registrar in bankruptcy of the High Court in London or district judge of any of the Chancery district registries (Bristol, Cardiff, Leeds, Liverpool, Manchester, Newcastle upon Tyne or Preston) having jurisdiction in company insolvency proceedings and a district judge of any county court exercising any relevant insolvency jurisdiction. The Chancery district registries (as opposed to county courts) do not have jurisdiction in individual insolvency proceedings.

'companies court registrar' (para 1.1(8))—This expression simply includes a registrar in bankruptcy of the High Court in London sitting in that capacity.

's 7(2) ... of the Act' (para 1.3(2))—This deals with an application for permission to bring a disqualification application out of time.

's 7(4) of the Act' (para 1.3(2))—This deals with an application brought by the Secretary of State or (as the case may be) the Official Receiver, for an order directing compliance by an office holder with his obligations to provide information and documentation to the Secretary of State under the Act to enable the Secretary of State to decide whether to bring disqualification proceedings.

's 12(2) or s 17 of the Act' (para 1.3(3))—These sections deal with an application for permission to act.

2 MULTI-TRACK

2.1 All disqualification proceedings are allocated to the multi-track. The CPR relating to allocation questionnaires and track allocation shall not apply.

'Disqualification proceedings'—See under para 1 above.

3 RIGHTS OF AUDIENCE

3.1 Official receivers and deputy official receivers have right of audience in any proceedings to which this practice direction applies, including cases where a disqualification application is made by the Secretary of State or by the official receiver at his direction, and whether made in the High Court or a county court[1].

1 Rule 10 of the Insolvent Companies (Disqualification of Unfit Directors) Proceedings Rules 1987.

Scope of provision—This provision follows the provision of Disqualification Rules, r 10 which gives Official Receivers and Deputy Official Receivers the right of audience in proceedings to which the Disqualification Rules apply where the proceedings are brought by the Secretary of State or the Official Receiver. This provision would appear to give Official Receivers and Deputy Official Receivers rights of audience in any disqualification proceedings as defined in para 1.3 above, not just in applications under ss 7 and 8. In *Re Minotaur Data Systems Limited* [1999] 1 WLR 1129, the Court of Appeal held that where the Official Receiver was empowered by law to bring proceedings in his own name without representation, he did so as *a litigant in person* and was entitled to costs as a litigant in person in accordance with the provisions of the Litigant in Person (Costs and Expenses) Act 1975 and the provisions of RSC Ord 62, r 18 (now CPR 48.6). Such costs were recoverable by him on the more generous basis set out in CPR r 48.6(2) rather than the fixed rate specified in CPR r 48.6(4) and PDCosts, para 52.4. However, where the Official Receiver exercises his right of audience on behalf of the Secretary of State in disqualification proceedings issued by the latter, the Secretary of State is not regarded as a litigant in person. In those circumstances, having regard to the definitions in PDCosts, para 1.4 of the words 'counsel' and 'solicitor', the Official Receiver may be regarded as a 'solicitor' or 'counsel' and be entitled to charge for his appearance on behalf of the Secretary of State accordingly.

PART 2
DISQUALIFICATION APPLICATIONS

4 COMMENCEMENT

4.1 Sections 2(2)(a), 3(4), 4(2), 6(3), 8(3) and 9E(3) of the Act identify the civil courts which have jurisdiction to deal with disqualification applications.

4.1A A disqualification application must be commenced by a claim form issued:

(1) in the case of a disqualification application under section 9A of the Act, in the High Court out of the office of the companies court registrar at the Royal Courts of Justice;

(2) in any other case,
   (a) in the High Court out of the office of the companies court registrar or a chancery district registry; and
   (b) in the county court, out of a county court office.

4.2 Disqualification applications shall be made by the issue of a claim form in the form annexed hereto and the use of the procedure set out in CPR Part 8[1], as modified by this practice direction and (where the application is made under sections 7, 8 or 9A of the Act) the Disqualification Rules[2]. CPR the court to order the application to continue as if the claimant had not used the Part 8 Procedure) shall not apply.

1 Rule 2(2) of the Insolvent Companies (Disqualification of Unfit Directors) Proceedings Rules 1987 as amended.

2 For convenience, relevant references to the Insolvency Companies (Disqualification of Unfit Directors) Proceedings Rules 1987, which apply to disqualification applications under sections 7 and 8 of the Act (see rule 1(3)(a) and (b)) are set out in footnotes to this practice direction.

4.3 When the claim form is issued, the claimant will be given a date for the first hearing of the disqualification application. This date is to be not less than eight weeks from the date of issue of the claim form[1]. The first hearing will be before a registrar.

1 Rule 7(1) of the Insolvent Companies (Disqualification of Unfit Directors) Proceedings Rules 1987.

'shall be made by the issue of a claim form in the form annexed hereto' (para 4.2)—It is essential that any disqualification application is made by the issue of a claim form in the form annexed to the practice direction. The power of the court to order an application under CPR Pt 8 to continue as if the claimant had not used the Pt 8 procedure (CPR r 8.1(3)) is specifically excluded. The failure to use the correct procedure may result in the disqualification application being struck out under CPR Pt 3. See for example *Re Westmid Packing Limited (No 1)* [1995] BCC 203, ChD where proceedings were struck out on account of the failure by the Secretary of State to use the then correct procedure for the bringing of an application for permission to issue proceedings out of time under s 7(2). See also *Probe Data Systems Limited (No 1)* (above) and compare *Re NP Engineering* (above). It has yet to be seen whether the court's wide powers under CPR r 3.10 would be used to save the position in these circumstances.

Paragraph 4.3—The date of the first hearing is to be not less than 8 weeks from the date of issue. The date of service (see below) can be less than 8 weeks from the date of the hearing, although the claimant will be required to serve the proceedings immediately upon issue. In practice, there is usually a gap of more than 8 weeks between service and the date of the first hearing.

5 HEADINGS

5.1 Every claim form by which an application under the Act is begun and all affidavits, notices and other documents in the proceedings must be entitled in the matter of the company or companies in question and in the matter of the Act.

In the case of any disqualification application under section 7 or 9A of the Act it is not necessary to mention in the heading any company other than that referred to in section 6(1)(a) or 9A(2) of the Act (as the case may be).

'all affidavits, notices and other documents in the proceedings'—In the case of an application under s 7, it is only necessary to mention in the heading the 'lead' company which has become insolvent within the meaning of s 6(1)(a) and in respect of which it is alleged that the defendant's 'conduct as a director of that company' (within the meaning of s 6(1)(b)) is such as to make him unfit to be concerned in the management of the company. It is possible for there to be more than one lead company (*Re Surrey Leisure Limited* [1999] 2 BCLC 457) and in such a case, all the lead companies should be referred to in the heading. See also paras 19, 21 and 25 below.

6 THE CLAIM FORM

6.1 CPR Rule 8.2 does not apply. The claim form must state:

(1) that CPR Part 8 (as modified by this practice direction) applies, and (if the application is made under sections 7, 8 or 9A of the Act) that the application is made in accordance with the Disqualification Rules[1];
(2) that the claimant seeks a disqualification order, and the section of the Act pursuant to which the disqualification application is made;
(3) the period for which, in accordance with the Act, the court has power to impose a disqualification period.

The periods are as follows –

(a) where the application is under section 2 of the Act, for a period of up to 15 years;
(b) where the application is under section 3 of the Act, for a period of up to 5 years;
(c) where the application is under section 4 of the Act, for a period of up to 15 years;
(d) where the application is under section 7 of the Act, for a period of not less than 2, and up to 15, years[2];
(e) where the application is under section 8 or 9A of the Act, for a period of up to 15 years[3].

(4) in cases where the application is made under sections 7, 8 or 9A of the Act, that on the first hearing of the application, the court may hear and determine it summarily, without further or other notice to the defendant, and that, if the application is so determined, the court may impose a period of disqualification of up to 5 years but that if at the hearing of the application the court, on the evidence then before it, is minded to impose, in the case of any defendant, disqualification for any period longer than 5 years, it will not make a disqualification order on that occasion but will adjourn the application to be heard (with further evidence, if any) at a later date that will be notified to the defendant[4];
(5) that any evidence which the defendant wishes the court to take into consideration must be filed in court in accordance with the time limits set out in paragraph 9 below (which time limits shall be set out in the notes to the Claim Form)[5].

1 Rule 4(a) of the Insolvent Companies (Disqualification of Unfit Directors) Proceedings Rules 1987.

2 Rule 4(b)(i) of the Insolvent Companies (Disqualification of Unfit Directors) Proceedings Rules 1987.

3 Rule 4(b)(ii) of the Insolvent Companies (Disqualification of Unfit Directors) Proceedings Rules 1987.

4 Rule 4(c) and (d) of the Insolvent Companies (Disqualification of Unfit Directors) Proceedings Rules 1987.

5 Rule 4(e) of the Insolvent Companies (Disqualification of Unfit Directors) Proceedings Rules 1987.

Contents of claim form—It is unlikely that the failure of a claim form to contain any of the information set out in para 6 will invalidate the proceedings. It is almost certain that the court will exercise its jurisdiction under CPR r 3.10 to remedy any error if it has not caused any prejudice to the defendant. See also under CPR r 3.10.

7 SERVICE OF THE CLAIM FORM

7.1 Service of claim forms in disqualification proceedings will be the responsibility of the parties and will not be undertaken by the court.

7.2 The claim form shall be served by the claimant on the defendant. It may be served by sending it by first class post to his last known address; and the date of service shall, unless the contrary is shown, be deemed to be the 7th day following that on which the claim form was posted[1]. CPR r 6.7(1) shall be modified accordingly. Otherwise Sections I and II of CPR Part 6 apply.[2]

1 Rule 5(1) of the Insolvent Companies (Disqualification of Unfit Directors) Proceedings Rules 1987.
2 Attention is drawn to CPR 6.14(2) regarding a certificate of service of the claim form.

7.3 Where any claim form or order of the court or other document is required under any disqualification proceedings to be served on any person who is not in England and Wales, the court may order service on him to be effected within such time and in such manner as it thinks fit, may require such proof of service as it thinks fit[1], and may give such directions as to acknowledgment of service as it thinks fit. Section III of CPR Part 6 shall not apply.

1 Rule 5(2) of the Insolvent Companies (Disqualification of Unfit Directors) Proceedings Rules 1987.

7.4 The claim form served on the defendant shall be accompanied by an acknowledgment of service.

Service—Although para 7.2 states that the claim form *may be* served by the claimant sending it by first-class post to the defendant's last known address, Disqualification Rules, r 5(1) which applies to applications under ss 7, 8 and 9A provides that a claim form *must be* served in this way. Other disqualification applications may be served by any method of service referred to in CPR Pt 6, provided it is capable of being (and is) undertaken by the claimant.

Service by an alternative method under CPR r 6.8—This will be permissible where there is good reason.

Where service is effected 'by first-class post' (para 7.2)—The date of service is, unless the contrary is shown, deemed to be the 7th day following that on which the claim form was sent by post. This is in contra-distinction to CPR r 6.7(1) (deemed service 2nd day after posting) which is modified accordingly.

Irregularity in service—In an appropriate case, the court will disregard any irregularity in service (*Secretary of State for Trade and Industry v Cash* (1998) (unreported) 27 November, CA and CPR r 3.10).

Service outside England and Wales (para 7.3)—The court has a discretion whether to order service and will not do so if it is not satisfied that there is a good and arguable case against the defendant (*Re Seagull Manufacturing Limited (No 2)* [1994] Ch 91).

8 ACKNOWLEDGMENT OF SERVICE

8.1 The form of acknowledgment of service is annexed to this practice direction. CPR rr 8.3(2) and 8.3(3)(a) do not apply to disqualification applications.

8.2 In cases brought under section 7, 8 or 9A of the Act, the form of acknowledgment of service shall state that the defendant should indicate[1]:

(1) whether he contests the application on the grounds that, in the case of any particular company –
   (a) he was not a director or shadow director of that company at a time when conduct of his, or of other persons, in relation to that company is in question; or
   (b) his conduct as director or shadow director of that company was not as alleged in support of the application for a disqualification order;
   (c) in the case of an application made under section 7 of the Act, the company has at no time become insolvent within the meaning of section 6; or
   (d) in the case of an application under section 9A of the Act, the undertaking which is a company did not commit a breach of competition law within the meaning of that section.

(2) whether, in the case of any conduct of his, he disputes the allegation that such conduct makes him unfit to be concerned in the management of a company; and

(3) whether he, while not resisting the application for a disqualification order, intends to adduce mitigating factors with a view to reducing the period of disqualification.

1 Rule 5(4) of the Insolvent Companies (Disqualification of Unfit Directors) Proceedings Rules 1987.

8.3 The defendant shall:

(1) (subject to any directions to the contrary given under paragraph 7.3 above) file an acknowledgment of service in the prescribed form not more than 14 days after service of the claim form; and

(2) serve the acknowledgment of service on the claimant and any other party.

8.4 Where the defendant has failed to file an acknowledgment of service and the time period for doing so has expired, the defendant may attend the hearing of the application but may not take part in the hearing unless the court gives permission.

Failure to file acknowledgment of service (para 8.4)—Judgment in default is not, of course, available (CPR r 12.2(b)). Although the defendant in default may not take part in the hearing without the permission of the court, the court is likely to give the defendant permission (subject to filing and serving evidence) if he files the acknowledgment of service within such further period as the court may stipulate.

9 EVIDENCE

9.1 Evidence in disqualification applications shall be by affidavit, except where the official receiver is a party, in which case his evidence may be in the form of a written report (with or without affidavits by other persons) which shall be treated as if it had been verified by affidavit by him and shall be prima facie evidence of any matter contained in it[1].

1 Rule 3(2) of the Insolvent Companies (Disqualification of Unfit Directors) Proceedings Rules 1987. Section 441 of the Companies Act 1985 makes provision for the admissibility in legal proceedings of a certified copy of a report of inspectors appointed under Part XIV of the Companies Act 1985. [Note that the requirements of paragraph 8.1(2)(c) and (d) of this practice direction are additional to the provisions in the said rule 5(4).

9.2 In the affidavits or (as the case may be) the official receiver's report in support of the application, there shall be included:

(1) a statement of the matters by reference to which it is alleged that a disqualification order should be made against the defendant[1]; and
(2) a statement of the steps taken to comply with any requirements imposed by sections 16(1) and 9C(4) of the Act

1 Rule 3(3) of the Insolvent Companies (Disqualification of Unfit Directors) Proceedings Rules 1987.

9.3 When the claim form is issued:

(1) the affidavit or report in support of the disqualification application must be filed in court;
(2) exhibits must be lodged with the court where they shall be retained until the conclusion of the proceedings; and
(3) copies of the affidavit/report and exhibits shall be served with the claim form on the defendant[1].

1 Rule 3(1) of the Insolvent Companies (Disqualification of Unfit Directors) Proceedings Rules 1987.

9.4 The defendant shall, within 28 days from the date of service of the claim form[1]:

(1) file in court any affidavit evidence in opposition to the disqualification application that he or she wishes the court to take into consideration; and
(2) lodge the exhibits with the court where they shall be retained until the conclusion of the proceedings; and
(3) at the same time, serve upon the claimant a copy of the affidavits and exhibits.

1 Rule 6(1) of the Insolvent Companies (Disqualification of Unfit Directors) Proceedings Rules 1987.

9.5 In cases where there is more than one defendant, each defendant is required to serve his evidence on the other defendants unless the court otherwise orders.

9.6 The claimant shall, within 14 days from receiving the copy of the defendant's evidence[1]:

(1) file in court any further affidavit or report in reply he wishes the court to take into consideration; and
(2) lodge the exhibits with the court where they shall be retained until the conclusion of the proceedings; and
(3) at the same time serve a copy of the affidavits/reports and exhibits upon the defendant.

1 Rule 6(2) of the Insolvent Companies (Disqualification of Unfit Directors) Proceedings Rules 1987.

9.7 Prior to the first hearing of the disqualification application, the time for serving evidence may be extended by written agreement between the parties. After the first hearing, the extension of time for serving evidence is governed by CPR rr 2.11 and 29.5.

9.8 So far as is possible all evidence should be filed before the first hearing of the disqualification application.

'shall be by affidavit' (para 9.1)—Special provision is made for the Official Receiver where he is is a party to the proceedings. Otherwise, evidence in disqualification applications must be given by affidavit (*Re Rex Williams Leisure plc* [1994] Ch 350) save that in exceptional circumstances (where for example a witness sought to be called by one party refuses to provide an affidavit), a witness's attendance and evidence may be procured by a witness summons although even in such a case a witness summary in respect of that witness would ordinarily be required, pursuant to the provisions of CPR r 32.9. Accordingly, it is not possible for a defendant simply to turn up at the hearing of the disqualification application and give his version of events from the witness box without having filed and served affidavit evidence.

Evidence in support of the application (para 9.3)—The requirement that this be filed and served with the claim form may be waived, see CPR r 3.10 and *Re Jazzgold Limited* [1994] 1 BCLC 38.

Extension of time for serving evidence (para 9.7)—In considering whether to grant any extension to the Secretary of State, the court will be influenced by the factors which it would need to take into account on an application for permission to bring proceedings out of time under s 7(2) (*Secretary of State for Trade and Industry v Davies* [1996] 4 All ER 289). The court's power to grant an extension will need to be exercised with considerable caution; see the observations of Lord Woolf, MR in *Re Westmid Packing Limited* [1998] 2 All ER 124 at p 134.

10 THE FIRST HEARING OF THE DISQUALIFICATION APPLICATION

10.1 The date fixed for the hearing of the disqualification application shall be not less than 8 weeks from the date of issue of the claim form[1].

1 Rule 7(1) of the Insolvent Companies (Disqualification of Unfit Directors) Proceedings Rules 1987.

10.2 The hearing shall in the first instance be before the registrar[1].

1 Rule 7(2) of the Insolvent Companies (Disqualification of Unfit Directors) Proceedings Rules 1987.

10.3 The registrar shall either determine the case on the date fixed or give directions and adjourn it[1].

1 Rule 7(3) of the Insolvent Companies (Disqualification of Unfit Directors) Proceedings Rules 1987.

10.4 All interim directions should insofar as possible be sought at the first hearing of the disqualification application so that the disqualification application can be determined at the earliest possible date. The parties should take all such steps as they respectively can to avoid successive directions hearings.

10.5 In the case of [a disqualification application made under sections [7, 8 or 9A of the Act, the registrar shall adjourn the case for further consideration if –

(1) he forms the provisional opinion that a disqualification order ought to be made, and that a period of disqualification longer than 5 years is appropriate[1], or
(2) he is of opinion that questions of law or fact arise which are not suitable for summary determination[2].

1 Rule 7(4)(a) of the Insolvent Companies (Disqualification of Unfit Directors) Proceedings Rules 1987.
2 Rule 7(4)(b) of the Insolvent Companies (Disqualification of Unfit Directors) Proceedings Rules 1987.

10.6 If the registrar adjourns the application for further consideration he shall –

(1) direct whether the application is to be heard by a registrar or by a judge[1]. This direction may at any time be varied by the court either on application or of its own initiative. If the court varies the direction in the absence of any of the parties, notice will be given to the parties;
(2) consider whether or not to adjourn the application to a judge so that the judge can give further directions;
(3) consider whether or not to make any direction with regard to fixing the trial date or a trial window;
(4) state the reasons for the adjournment[2].

1 Rule 7(5)(a) of the Insolvent Companies (Disqualification of Unfit Directors) Proceedings Rules 1987.
2 Rule 7(5)(b) of the Insolvent Companies (Disqualification of Unfit Directors) Proceedings Rules 1987.

'registrar' (para 10.2)—See under para 1 above.

Uncontested applications—If the defendant fails to appear or if he does appear but does not oppose the application – something which, having regard to the undertakings regime now in place (see above), is less frequently likely to arise in practice – the application may be disposed at the first hearing. However, if para 10.5 applies, the hearing will need to be adjourned. If the application is contested, the hearing will almost certainly need to be adjourned and directions given.

Exceptions to and scope of para 10.5—In the circumstances referred to in para 10.5, it is necessary for the court to adjourn the case for further consideration. It might, exceptionally, be possible for the court to determine a case to which para 10.5(1) applies if the defendant is present in court and agrees to be disqualified for a period exceeding 5 years. As para 10.5 only applies to applications under ss 7 or 8, the court will in an appropriate case be able to dispose of an application brought under any of the other provisions specified in the practice direction, regardless of whether the circumstances specified in para 10.5(1) and (2) obtain.

Varying a trial date, trial window, or other direction specified in CPR r 29.5, fixed by the registrar—If a trial date or trial window is fixed or any of the other directions specified in CPR r 29.5 are given, it will not be possible to vary the date which the court has fixed for those matters to be dealt with, without an application being made to it.

11 CASE MANAGEMENT

11.1 On the first or any subsequent hearing of the disqualification application, the registrar may also give directions as to the following matters:

(1) the filing in court and the service of further evidence (if any) by the parties[1];
(2) the time-table for the steps to be taken between the giving of directions and the hearing of the application;
(3) such other matters as the registrar thinks necessary or expedient with a view to an expeditious disposal of the application or the management of it generally[2];
(4) the time and place of the adjourned hearing[3]; and
(5) the manner in which and the time within which notice of the adjournment and the reasons for it are to be given to the parties[4].

1 Rule 7(5)(c)(ii) of the Insolvent Companies (Disqualification of Unfit Directors) Proceedings Rules 1987.
2 Rule 7(5)(c)(iii) of the Insolvent Companies (Disqualification of Unfit Directors) Proceedings Rules 1987.
3 Rule 7(5)(c)(iv) of the Insolvent Companies (Disqualification of Unfit Directors) Proceedings Rules 1987.
4 Rule 7(5)(c)(i) of the Insolvent Companies (Disqualification of Unfit Directors) Proceedings Rules 1987.

11.2 Where a case is adjourned other than to a judge, it may be heard by the registrar who originally dealt with the case or by another registrar[1].

1 Rule 7(6) of the Insolvent Companies (Disqualification of Unfit Directors) Proceedings Rules 1987.

11.3 If the companies court registrar adjourns the application to a judge, all directions having been complied with and the evidence being complete, the application will be referred to the Listing Office and any practice direction relating to listing shall apply accordingly.

11.4 In all disqualification applications, the court may direct a pre-trial review ('PTR'), a case management conference or pre-trial check lists (listing questionnaires) (in the form annexed to this practice direction) and will fix a trial date or trial period in accordance with the provisions of CPR Part 29 ('The Multi-Track') as modified by any relevant practice direction made thereunder.

11.5 At the hearing of the PTR, the registrar may give any further directions as appropriate and, where the application is to be heard in the Royal Courts of Justice in London, unless the trial date has already been fixed, may direct the parties (by Counsel's clerks if applicable), to attend the Registrar at a specified time and place in order solely to fix a trial date. The court will give notice of the date fixed for the trial to the parties.

11.6 In all cases, the parties must inform the court immediately of any material change to the information provided in a pre-trial check list.

Scope of para 11—The case management provisions set out in para 11 are consistent with the power of the court to manage cases which are dealt with in the multi-track in accordance with the provisions of CPR Pt 29 and PD29.

12 THE TRIAL

12.1 Trial bundles containing copies of –

(1) the claim form;
(2) the acknowledgment of service;
(3) all evidence filed by or on behalf of each of the parties to the proceedings, together with the exhibits thereto;
(4) all relevant correspondence; and
(5) such other documents as the parties consider necessary, shall be lodged with the court.

12.2 Skeleton arguments should be prepared by all the parties in all but the simplest cases whether the case is to be heard by a registrar or a judge. They should comply with all relevant guidelines.

12.3 The advocate for the claimant should also in all but the simplest cases provide: (a) a chronology; (b) a dramatis personae; (c) in respect of each defendant, a list of references to the relevant evidence.

12.4 The documents mentioned in paragraph 12.1–12.3 above must be delivered to the court in accordance with any order of the court and/or any relevant practice direction[1].

(1) If the case is to be heard by a judge sitting in the Royal Courts of Justice, London, but the name of the judge is not known, or the judge is a deputy judge, these documents must be delivered to the Clerk of the Lists. If the name of the judge (other than a deputy judge) is known, these documents must be delivered to the judge's clerk;
(2) If the case is to be heard by a companies court registrar, these documents must be delivered to Room 409, Thomas More Building, Royal Courts of Justice. Copies must be provided to the other party so far as possible when they are delivered to the court;
(3) If the case is to be heard in the Chancery district registries in Birmingham, Bristol, Cardiff, Leeds, Liverpool, Manchester or Newcastle, the addresses for delivery are set out in Annex 1;
(4) If the case is to be heard in a county court, the documents should be delivered to the relevant county court office.

1 Attention is drawn to the provisions of the Chancery Guide. Chapter 7 of that Guide dated September 2000 provides guidance on the preparation of trial bundles and skeleton arguments. Unless the court otherwise orders, paragraph 7.16 of the Chancery Guide requires that trial

bundles be delivered to the court 7 days before trial and paragraph 7.21 requires that skeleton arguments be delivered to the court not less than 2 clear days before trial.

12.5 Copies of documents delivered to the court must, so far as possible, be provided to each of the other parties to the claim.

12.6 The provisions in paragraphs 12.1 to 12.5 above are subject to any order of the court making different provision.

'skeleton arguments' (para 12.2)—Skeleton arguments will be required in every case save in cases where the defendant has not acknowledged service or filed evidence (and is, therefore, unlikely to appear at the hearing) or where he does not oppose the making of the disqualification order against him.

'chronology, … dramatis personae, … list of references to the relevant evidence' (para 12.3)—See note **'skeleton arguments'** above.

'Chancery district registries' (para 12.4(3))—By an oversight on the part of the draftsman, there is no reference to the Chancery district registry in Preston in this subparagraph, although Annex 1 does refer to it.

13 SUMMARY PROCEDURE

13.1 If the parties decide to invite the court to deal with the application under the procedure adopted in *Re Carecraft Construction Co Ltd* [1994] 1 WLR 172, they should inform the court immediately and obtain a date for the hearing of the application.

13.2 Whenever the *Carecraft* procedure is adopted, the claimant must:

(1) except where the court otherwise directs, submit a written statement containing in respect of each defendant any material facts which (for the purposes of the application) are either agreed or not opposed (by either party); and

(2) specify in writing the period of disqualification which the parties accept that the agreed or unopposed facts justify or the band of years (eg 4 to 6 years) or bracket (ie 2 to 5 years; 6 to 10 years; 11 to 15 years) into which they will submit the case falls.

13.3 Paragraph 12.4 of the above applies to the documents mentioned in paragraph 13.2 above unless the court otherwise directs.

13.4 Unless the court otherwise orders, a hearing under the *Carecraft* procedure will be held in private.

13.5 If the court is minded to make a disqualification order having heard the parties' representations, it will usually give judgment and make the disqualification order in public. Unless the court otherwise orders, the written statement referred to in paragraph 13.2 shall be annexed to the disqualification order.

13.6 If the court refuses to make the disqualification order under the *Carecraft* procedure, the court shall give further directions for the hearing of the application.

'specify in writing the period of disqualification' (para 13.2(2))—The court is not bound by any agreement which the parties reach (*Secretary of State for Trade and Industry v Rogers* [1996] 4 All ER 854, CA at p 858).

'*Carecraft* procedure' (para 13.6)—In view of the introduction of disqualification undertakings, the use of the *Carecraft* procedure is seldom likely to arise in practice.

14 MAKING AND SETTING ASIDE OF DISQUALIFICATION ORDER

14.1 The court may make a disqualification order against the defendant, whether or not the latter appears, and whether or not he has completed and returned the acknowledgment of service of the claim form, or filed evidence[1].

1 Rule 8(1) of the Insolvent Companies (Disqualification of Unfit Directors) Proceedings Rules 1987.

14.2 Any disqualification order made in the absence of the defendant may be set aside or varied by the court on such terms as it thinks just[1].

1 Rule 8(2) of the Insolvent Companies (Disqualification of Unfit Directors) Proceedings Rules 1987.

Failure to attend hearing—Where the defendant fails to attend a hearing, the court will need to be satisfied that he has been served and will undoubtedly enquire as to the method of service.

Setting aside disqualification order made in the absence of a defendant—This provision is cast in substantially the same terms as the old RSC Ord 35, r 2(1) which has now been superseded by CPR r 39.3. It was held in *Official Receiver v Wilson* (1996) (unreported) 17 July, Chadwick J and *Official Receiver v Wilson* (1997) (unreported) 7 March, CA that the principles applicable under RSC Ord 35, r 2(1) applied equally to an application under r 8(2) but that the court was not obliged to follow those principles and the authorities under RSC Ord 35, r 2(1) slavishly. Although the CPR introduce a new procedural code making it unnecessary for the court to follow previous authorities (*Biguzzi v Rank Leisure plc* [1999] 1 WLR 1926, CA), in practice the court is unlikely to depart from these principles as they are consistent with the overriding objective and with the requirements of CPR r 39.3. The principles which the court will apply are summarised in *Shocked v Goldschmidt* [1998] 1 All ER 372.

15 SERVICE OF DISQUALIFICATION ORDERS

15.1 Service of disqualification orders will be the responsibility of the claimant.

16 COMMENCEMENT OF DISQUALIFICATION ORDER

16.1 Unless the court otherwise orders, the period of disqualification imposed by a disqualification order shall begin at the end of the period of 21 days beginning with the date of the order[1].

1 Section 1(2) of the Act (as amended).

'Commencement' (para 16 heading)—In an appropriate case, it may be possible to extend the 21 day period, see *Re Travel Mondial (UK) Limited* [1991] BCLC 120 at p 123 and *Re Hughes Asphalt Limited* (1992) (unreported) 31 July.

PART 3
APPLICATIONS UNDER SECTIONS 7(2) AND 7(4) OF THE ACT

17 APPLICATIONS FOR PERMISSION TO MAKE A DISQUALIFICATION APPLICATION AFTER THE END OF THE PERIOD OF 2 YEARS SPECIFIED IN SECTION 7(2) OF THE ACT

17.1 Such applications shall be made by Practice Form N208 under CPR Part 8 save where it is sought to join a director or former director to existing proceedings, in which case such application shall be made by Application Notice under CPR Part 23, and the Part 23 Practice Direction shall apply save as modified below.

'application notice'—Although applications for permission to bring disqualification proceedings under s 7 out of time are originating in nature (*Re Probe Data Systems Limited (No 1)* and *(No 3)* above; *Re Westmid Packing Limited (No 1)*, above; *Re Crestjoy Products Limited* [1990] BCLC 677), they are to be made by application notice and not by claim form.

18 APPLICATIONS FOR EXTRA INFORMATION MADE UNDER SECTION 7(4) OF THE ACT

18.1 Such applications may be made:

(1) by Practice Form N208 under CPR Part 8;
(2) by Application Notice in existing disqualification proceedings; or
(3) by application under the Insolvency Rules in the relevant insolvency, if the insolvency practitioner against whom the application is made remains the officeholder.

'existing disqualification claim proceedings' (para 18.1(2))—Where disqualification proceedings are already in existence in respect of a company of which the office holder is acting or has acted in any of the offices specified in s 7(4), the application is by application notice. Otherwise it is by way of claim form.

19 PROVISIONS APPLICABLE TO APPLICATIONS UNDER SECTIONS 7(2) AND 7(4) OF THE ACT

19.1 **Headings:** Every claim form and notice by which such an application is begun and all witness statements, affidavits, notices and other documents in relation thereto must be entitled in the matter of the company or companies in question and in the matter of the Act.

19.2 **Service:**

(1) Service of claim forms and application notices seeking orders under section 7(2) or 7(4) of the Act will be the responsibility of the applicant and will not be undertaken by the court.
(2) Where any [claim form, application notice or order of the court or other document is required in any application under section 7(2) or section 7(4) of the Act to be served on any person who is not in England and Wales, the court may order service on him to be effected within such time and in such manner as it thinks fit, may require such proof of service as it thinks fit, and may make such directions as to acknowledgment of service as it thinks fit. Section III of CPR Part 6 does not apply.

Service—See paras 7 above and 26 below.

Service outside England and Wales—See para 7 above.

PART 4
APPLICATIONS FOR PERMISSION TO ACT

20 COMMENCING AN APPLICATION FOR PERMISSION TO ACT

20.1 This practice direction governs applications for permission to act made under:

(1) section 17 of the Act for the purposes of any of sections 1(1)(a), 1A(1)(a) or 9B(4); and
(2) section 12(2) of the Act.

20.2 Sections 12 and 17(2) of the Act identify the courts which have jurisdiction to deal with applications for permission to act. Subject to these sections, such applications may be made:

(1) by Practice Form N208 under CPR Part 8; or
(2) by application notice in an existing disqualification application.

20.3 In the case of a person subject to disqualification under section 12A or 12B of the Act (by reason of being disqualified in Northern Ireland), permission to act notwithstanding disqualification can only be granted by the High Court of Northern Ireland.

Applications for permission to act—Where there is an existing disqualification application, the paragraph makes it clear that it is no longer necessary to issue a fresh claim for permission.

21 HEADINGS

21.1 Every claim form or application notice by which an application for permission to act is begun, and all affidavits, notices and other documents in the application must be entitled in the matter of the company or companies in question and in the matter of the Act.

21.2 Every application notice by which an application for permission to act is made and all affidavits, notices and other documents in the application shall be entitled in the same manner as the heading of the claim form in the existing disqualification application.

'companies in question'—This must mean the companies in respect of which permission is being sought. It follows that where an application is made in an existing disqualification application, the heading will not only contain the name of the companies in respect of which the defendant's conduct is called into question (see under para 5 above and para 25 below) but also the name of the company or companies in respect of which permission is sought.

22 EVIDENCE

22.1 Evidence in support of an application for permission to act shall be by affidavit.

Evidence—It will be possible for evidence from the Official Receiver in response to the applicant's evidence to be in the form of a report (see para 9.1 above and IR 1986, r 7.9).

23 SERVICE[1]

23.1 Where a disqualification application has been made under section 9A of the Act or a disqualification undertaking has been accepted under section 9B of the Act, the claim form or application notice (as appropriate), together with the evidence in support thereof, must be served on the Office of Fair Trading or specified regulator which made the relevant disqualification application or accepted the disqualification undertaking (as the case may be).

23.2 In all other cases, the claim form or application notice (as appropriate), together with the evidence in support thereof, must be served on the Secretary of State.

Service on the Secretary of State—As it is possible for a disqualification application under the provisions of the Act set out in para 1.3(1) above (apart from applications under ss 7, 8 and 9A) to be brought by a liquidator, creditor or contributory, it follows that if a disqualification order is made pursuant to an application brought by any such person, it will be necessary for such person to be made a party to the permission application. However, as the Secretary of State has a duty to look after the public interest, he is required (also) to be served with the application for permission, in order that he can 'take over' any response to the application which needs to be made on behalf of the public and bring to the attention of the court any matters which appear relevant to him in order to protect that public interest.

1 Addresses for service on government departments are set out in the List of Authorised Government Departments issued by the Cabinet Office under section 17 of the Crown Proceedings Act 1947, which is annexed to the Practice Direction supplementing Part 66.

PART 5
APPLICATIONS

24 FORM OF APPLICATION

24.1 CPR Part 23 and the Part 23 practice direction (General Rules about Applications for Court Orders) shall apply in relation to applications governed by this practice direction (see paragraph 1.3(4) above) save as modified below.

25 HEADINGS

25.1 Every notice and all witness statements and affidavits in relation thereto must be entitled in the same manner as the Claim Form in the proceedings in which the application is made.

'Headings'—This has to be read in the light of para 21 where an application for permission is being made. In any application for permission made in existing proceedings, the application will not only refer to the headings required by para 25 but also by para 21. See also under para 5 above.

26 SERVICE

26.1 Service of application notices in disqualification proceedings will be the responsibility of the parties and will not be undertaken by the court.

26.2 Where any application notice or order of the court or other document is required in any application to be served on any person who is not in England and Wales, the court may order service on him to be effected within such time and in such manner as it thinks fit, and may also require such proof of service as it thinks fit. Section III of CPR Part 6 does not apply.

Service—See para 7 above and the annotations thereto.

PART 6
DISQUALIFICATION PROCEEDINGS OTHER THAN IN THE ROYAL COURTS OF JUSTICE

27.1 Where a disqualification application [or a section 8A application is made by a claim form issued other than in the Royal Courts of Justice this practice direction shall apply with the following modifications:

(1) Upon the issue of the claim form the court shall endorse it with the date and time for the first hearing before a district judge. The powers exercisable by a registrar under this practice direction shall be exercised by a district judge.

(2) If the district judge (either at the first hearing or at any adjourned hearing before him) directs that the disqualification claim [or section 8A application is to be heard by a High Court judge or by an authorised circuit judge he will direct that the case be entered forthwith in the list

for hearing by that judge and the court will allocate (i) a date for the hearing of the trial by that judge and (ii) unless the district judge directs otherwise a date for the hearing of a PTR by the trial judge.

'is to be heard by a High Court judge or by an authorised circuit judge' (para 27.1(2))—As the district judge is only likely to reach that view if the application is contested and he considers that complex questions of law or fact arise which are not suitable for determination by him, it is entirely appropriate that a date for the hearing of the trial by that judge be fixed at the earliest possible date and that the hearing of a PTR by that judge also take place as soon as possible.

PART 7
DISQUALIFICATION UNDERTAKINGS

28 COSTS

28.1 The general rule is that the court will order the defendant to pay –

- (1) the costs of the Secretary of State (and, in the case of a disqualification application made under section 7(1)(b) of the Act, the costs of the official receiver) if:
  - (a) a disqualification application under section 7 or 8 of the Act has been commenced; and
  - (b) that application is discontinued because the Secretary of State has accepted a disqualification undertaking under section 1A of the Act;
- (2) the costs of the Office of Fair Trading or a specified regulator if:
  - (a) a disqualification application under section 9A of the Act has been commenced; and
  - (b) that application is discontinued because the Office of Fair Trading or specified regulator (as the case may be) has accepted a disqualification undertaking under section 9B of the Act.

28.2 The general rule will not apply where the court considers that the circumstances are such that it should make another order.

Applications Under Section 8A of the Act to Reduce the Period for which a Disqualification Undertaking is in Force or to Provide for it to Cease to be in Force

29 HEADINGS

29.1 Every claim form by which a section 8A application is begun and all affidavits, notices and other documents in the proceedings must be entitled in the matter of a disqualification undertaking and its date and in the matter of the Act.

Paragraph 29—See also the notes under paras 5 and 25 above.

30 COMMENCEMENT: THE CLAIM FORM

30.1 Section 8A(3) of the Act identifies the courts which have jurisdiction to deal with section 8A applications.

30.1A A section 8A application must be commenced by a claim form issued:

- (1) in the case of a disqualification undertaking given under section 9B of the Act, in the High Court out of the office of the companies court registrar at the Royal Courts of Justice;

(2) in any other case,
 (a) in the High Court out of the office of the companies court registrar or a chancery district registry; and
 (b) in the county court, out of a county court office.

30.2 A section 8A application shall be made by the issue of a Part 8 claim form in the form annexed hereto and the use of the procedure set out in CPR Part 8, as modified by this practice direction. CPR rule 8.1(3) (power of the court to order the application to continue as if the claimant had not used the Part 8 procedure) shall not apply.

30.3 When the claim form is issued, the claimant will be given a date for the first hearing of the section 8A application. This date is to be not less than 8 weeks from the date of issue of the claim form. The first hearing will be before the registrar.

30.4 CPR rule 8.2 does not apply. The claim form must state:

(1) that CPR Part 8 (as modified by this practice direction) applies;
(2) the form of order the claimant seeks.

30.5 In the case of a disqualification undertaking given under section 9B of the Act, the defendant to the section 8A application shall be the Office of Fair Trading or specified regulator which accepted the undertaking. In all other cases, the Secretary of State shall be made the defendant to the section 8A application.

30.6 Service of claim forms in section 8A applications will be the responsibility of the claimant and will not be undertaken by the court. The claim form may be served by sending it by first class post and the date of service shall, unless the contrary is shown, be deemed to be the 7th day following that on which the claim form was posted. CPR r 6.7(1) shall be modified accordingly. Otherwise Sections I and II of CPR Part 6 apply[1].

1 Attention is drawn to CPR r 6.14(2) regarding a certificate of service of the claim form.

30.7 Where any order of the court or other document is required to be served on any person who is not in England and Wales, the court may order service on him to be effected within such time and in such manner as it thinks fit and may require such proof of service as it thinks fit. Section III of CPR Part 6 shall not apply.

30.8 The claim form served on the defendant shall be accompanied by an acknowledgment of service in the form annexed hereto.

Paragraph 30—See also the notes under paras 6 and 7 above.

31 ACKNOWLEDGMENT OF SERVICE

31.1 The defendant shall:

(1) … file an acknowledgment of service in the relevant practice form not more than 14 days after service of the claim form; and
(2) serve a copy of the acknowledgment of service on the claimant and any other party.

31.2 Where the defendant has failed to file an acknowledgment of service and the time period for doing so has expired, the defendant may nevertheless attend the hearing of the application and take part in the hearing as provided for by section 8A(2) or (2A) of the Act. However, this is without prejudice to the court's case management powers and its powers to make costs orders.

Paragraph 31.2—This is in contradistinction to para 8 above. The defendant (ie the Secretary of State) is allowed to take part in the proceedings even where no acknowledgment of service has been filed, subject to the court's case management powers and its power to make costs orders. In practice, the Secretary of State will not only file an acknowledgment of service but will also file and serve evidence in response to the application in compliance with his obligation under s 8A(2).

32 EVIDENCE

32.1 Evidence in section 8A applications shall be by affidavit. The undertaking (or a copy) shall be exhibited to the affidavit.

32.2 When the claim form is issued:

(1) the affidavit in support of the section 8A application must be filed in court;
(2) exhibits must be lodged with the court where they shall be retained until the conclusion of the proceedings; and
(3) copies of the affidavit and exhibits shall be served with the claim form on the defendant.

32.3 The defendant shall, within 28 days from the date of service of the claim form:

(1) file in court any affidavit evidence that he wishes the court to take into consideration on the application; and
(2) lodge the exhibits with the court where they shall be retained until the conclusion of the proceedings; and
(3) at the same time, serve upon the claimant a copy of the affidavits and exhibits.

32.4 The claimant shall, within 14 days from receiving the copy of the defendant's evidence:

(1) file in court any further affidavit evidence in reply he wishes the court to take into consideration; and
(2) lodge the exhibits with the court where they shall be retained until the conclusion of the proceedings; and
(3) at the same time serve a copy of the affidavits and exhibits upon the defendant.

32.5 Prior to the first hearing of the section 8(2) application, the time for serving evidence may be extended by written agreement between the parties. After the first hearing, the extension of time for serving evidence is governed by CPR rules 2.11 and 29.5.

32.6 So far as is possible all evidence should be filed before the first hearing of the section 8A application.

Paragraph 32—See also the notes under para 9 above.

33 HEARINGS AND CASE MANAGEMENT

33.1 The date fixed for the first hearing of the section 8A application shall be not less than 8 weeks from the date of issue of the claim form.

33.2 The hearing shall in the first instance be before the registrar.

33.3 The registrar shall either determine the case on the date fixed or give directions and adjourn it.

33.4 All interim directions should insofar as possible be sought at the first hearing of the section 8A application so that the section 8A application can be determined at the earliest possible date. The parties should take all such steps as they respectively can to avoid successive directions hearings.

33.5 If the registrar adjourns the application for further consideration he shall:

(1) direct whether the application is to be heard by a registrar or by a judge. This direction may at any time be varied by the court either on application or of its own initiative. If the court varies the direction in the absence of any of the parties, notice will be given to the parties;
(2) consider whether or not to adjourn the application to a judge so that the judge can give further directions;
(3) consider whether or not to make any direction with regard to fixing the trial date or a trial window.

33.6 On the first or any subsequent hearing of the section 8A application, the registrar may also give directions as to the following matters:

(1) the filing in court and the service of further evidence (if any) by the parties;
(2) the time-table for the steps to be taken between the giving of directions and the hearing of the section 8A application;
(3) such other matters as the registrar thinks necessary or expedient with a view to an expeditious disposal of the section 8A application or the management of it generally;
(4) the time and place of the adjourned hearing.

33.7 Where a case is adjourned other than to a judge, it may be heard by the registrar who originally dealt with the case or by another registrar.

33.8 If the companies court registrar adjourns the application to a judge, all directions having been complied with and the evidence being complete, the application will be referred to the Listing Office and any practice direction relating to listing shall apply accordingly.

33.9 In all section 8A applications, the court may direct a pre-trial review ('PTR'), a case management conference or pre-trial check lists (listing questionnaires) (in the form annexed to this practice direction) and will fix a trial date or trial period in accordance with the provisions of CPR Part 29: The Multi-Track, as modified by any relevant practice direction made thereunder.

33.10 At the hearing of the PTR, the registrar may give any further directions as appropriate and, where the application is to be heard in the Royal Courts of Justice in London, unless the trial date has already been fixed, may direct the parties (by Counsel's clerks, if applicable) to attend the Registrar at a specified time and place in order solely to fix a trial date. The court will give notice of the date fixed for the trial to the parties.

33.11 In all cases, the parties must inform the court immediately of any material change to the information provided in a pre-trial check list.

Paragraph 33—See also the notes under paras 10 and 11.

34 THE TRIAL

34.1 Trial bundles containing copies of:

(1) the claim form;
(2) the acknowledgment of service;
(3) all evidence filed by or on behalf of each of the parties to the proceedings, together with the exhibits thereto;

(4) all relevant correspondence; and
(5) such other documents as the parties consider necessary;

shall be lodged with the court.

34.2 Skeleton arguments should be prepared by all the parties in all but the simplest cases whether the case is to be heard by a registrar or a judge. They should comply with all relevant guidelines.

34.3 The advocate for the claimant should also in all but the simplest cases provide: (a) chronology; (b) a dramatis personae.

34.4 The documents mentioned in paragraph 34.1–34.3 above must be delivered to the court in accordance with any order of the court and/or and relevant practice direction[1].

(1) If the case is to be heard by a judge sitting in the Royal Courts of Justice, London, but the name of the judge is not known, or the judge is a deputy judge, these documents must be delivered to the clerk of the Lists. If the name of the judge (other than a deputy judge) is known, these documents must be delivered to the judge's clerk;
(2) If the case is to be heard by a companies court registrar, these documents must be delivered to Room 409, Thomas More Building, Royal Courts of Justice. Copies must be provided to the other party so far as possible when they are delivered to the court;
(3) If the case is to be heard in the Chancery district registries in Birmingham, Bristol, Cardiff, Leeds, Liverpool, Manchester, Newcastle, or Preston, the addresses for delivery are set out in Annex 1;
(4) If the case is to be heard in a county court, the documents should be delivered to the relevant county court office.

1 Attention is drawn to the provisions of the Chancery Guide. Chapter 7 of that Guide dated September 2000 provides guidance on the preparation of trial bundles and skeleton arguments. Unless the court otherwise orders, paragraph 7.16 of the Chancery Guide requires that trial bundles be delivered to the court 7 days before trial and paragraph 7.21 requires that skeleton arguments be delivered to the court not less than 2 clear days before trial. Addresses for service on government departments are set out in the List of Authorised Government Departments issued by the Cabinet Office under section 17 of the Crown Proceedings Act 1947, which is annexed to the Practice Direction supplementing Part 66.

34.5 Copies of documents delivered to the court must, so far as possible, be provided to each of the other parties to the claim.

34.6 The provisions in paragraphs 34.1–34.5 above are subject to any order of the court making different provision.

Paragraph 34—See also the notes under para 12 above.

35 APPEALS

35.1 Rules 7.47 and 7.49 of the Insolvency Rules, as supplemented by Part Four of the Insolvency Proceedings Practice Direction, apply to an appeal from, or review of, a decision made by the court in the course of:

(1) disqualification proceedings under any of sections 6 to 8A or 9A of the Act;
(2) an application made under section 17 of the Act for the purposes of any of sections 1(1)(a), 1A(1)(a) or 9B(4), for permission to act notwithstanding a disqualification order made, or a disqualification undertaking accepted, under any of sections 6 to 10.

Any such decision, and any appeal from it, constitutes 'insolvency proceedings' for the purposes of the Insolvency Proceedings Practice Direction[1].

35.2 An appeal from a decision made by the court in the course of disqualification proceedings under any of sections 2(2)(a), 3 or 4 of the Act or on an application for permission to act notwithstanding a disqualification order made under any of those sections is governed by CPR Part 52 and the practice direction supplementing that Part.

1 CPR rule 2.1(2) and section 21(2) of the Act. See also rule 2(4) of the Insolvent Companies (Disqualification of Unfit Directors) Proceedings Rules 1987 and Re Tasbian Limited, Official Receiver v. Nixon [1991] B.C.L.C. 59; [1990] B.C.C. 322; Re Probe Data Systems Limited (No 3), Secretary of State for Trade and Industry v. Desai [1992] B.C.L.C.405; [1992] BCC 110 and Re The Premier Screw & Repetition Company Ltd, Secretary of State for Trade and Industry v Paulin [2005] EWCH 888 (Ch).

Annex 1

Birmingham: The Chancery Listing Officer, The District Registry of the Chancery Division of the High Court, 33 Bull Street, Birmingham B4 6DS.

Bristol: The Chancery Listing Officer, The District Registry of the Chancery Division of the High Court, 3rd Floor, Greyfriars, Lewins Mead, Bristol BS1 2NR.

Cardiff: The Chancery Listing Officer, The District Registry of the Chancery Division of the High Court, 1st Floor, 2 Park Street, Cardiff CF1 1EE.

Leeds: The Chancery Listing Officer, The District Registry of the Chancery Division of the High Court, Leeds Combined Court Centre, The Court House, 1 Oxford Row, Leeds LS1 3BG.

Liverpool and Manchester: The Chancery Listing Officer, The District Registry of the Chancery Division of the High Court, Manchester Courts of Justice, Crown Square, Manchester M60 9DJ.

Newcastle: The Chancery Listing Officer, The District Registry of the Chancery Division of the High Court, The Law Courts, Quayside, Newcastle upon Tyne NE1 3LA.

Preston: The Chancery Listing Officer, The District Registry of the Chancery Division of the High Court, The Combined Court Centre, Ringway, Preston PR1 2LL.

Forms

****

Forms—The forms and notes annexed to this practice direction can be accessed on the *Civil Court Service* CD-ROM or via the Internet at the Court Service website *http://www.courtservice.gov.uk*.

Practice Direction – Insolvency Proceedings

Introduction—Sections 411 and 412 of IA 1986 empower the Lord Chancellor with the concurrence of the Secretary of State to make rules for the purpose of giving effect to Pts I–XI of that Act. Section 411 refers to Pts I–VII of the Act, which deal with company insolvency, and s 412 to

Pts VIII–XI of the Act which deal with individual insolvency. The provisions IA 1986 have been substantially amended principally by IA 2000 and EA 2002. Various rules have been made under the provisions of ss 411 and 412, the principal set of rules being the IR 1986 which govern both company and individual insolvency proceedings in England and Wales. Unless otherwise stated, the references in these notes to section numbers are references to sections of IA 1986, references to rule numbers are references to IR 1986 and references to paragraph numbers are references to paragraph numbers of this practice direction.

Following the coming into force of the CPR on 26 April 1999, IR 1986, r 7.51 has been amended to provide that the CPR, the practice and procedure of the High Court and of the county court (including any practice direction) apply to insolvency proceedings in the High Court and county courts as the case may be, in either case with any necessary modifications, except so far as inconsistent with IR 1986. This practice direction (PDInsolvency) came into force on 26 April 1999 and was made pursuant to the power contained in CPA, ss 1 and 5 and Sch 1, para 6, and CCA 1984, s 74A. Various amendments have been made to this practice direction since then.

PART 1

1 GENERAL

1.1 In this practice direction:

(1) 'The Act' means the Insolvency Act 1986 and includes the Act as applied to limited liability partnerships by the Limited Liability Partnerships Regulations 2001;

(2) 'The Insolvency Rules' means the rules for the time being in force and made under s 411 and s 412 of the Act in relation to insolvency proceedings;

(3) 'CPR' means the Civil Procedure Rules and 'CPR' followed by a Part or rule by number means the Part or rule with that number in those Rules;

(4) 'RSC' followed by an Order by number means the Order with that number set out in Schedule 1 to the CPR;

(5) 'Insolvency proceedings' means any proceedings under the Act, the Insolvency Rules, the Administration of Insolvent Estates of Deceased Persons Order 1986 (SI 1986 No 1999), the Insolvent Partnerships Order 1986 (SI 1986 No 2124) or the Insolvent Partnerships Order 1994 (SI 1994 No 2421).

(6) References to a 'company' shall include a limited liability partnership and references to a 'contributory' shall include a member of a limited liability partnership.

1.2 This practice direction shall come into effect on 26 April 1999 and shall replace all previous Practice Notes and practice directions relating to insolvency proceedings.

1.3 Except where the Insolvency Rules otherwise provide, service of documents in insolvency proceedings in the High Court will be the responsibility of the parties and will not be undertaken by the court.

1.4 Where CPR Part 2.4 provides for the court to perform any act, that act may be performed by a Registrar in Bankruptcy for the purpose of insolvency proceedings in the High Court.

1.5 A writ of execution to enforce any order made in insolvency proceedings in the High Court may be issued on the authority of a Registrar.

1.6 (1) This paragraph applies where an insolvency practitioner ('the outgoing office holder') holds office as a liquidator, administrator, trustee or supervisor in more than one case and dies, retires from practice as an insolvency practitioner or is otherwise unable or unwilling to continue in office.

(2) A single application may be made to a judge of the Chancery Division of the High Court by way of ordinary application in Form 7.2 for the appointment of a substitute office holder or office holders in all cases in which the outgoing office holder holds office, and for the transfer of each such case to the High Court for the purpose only of making such an order.

(3) The application may be made by any of the following:
  - (i) the outgoing office holder (if he is able and willing to do so);
  - (ii) any person who holds office jointly with the outgoing office holder:
  - (iii) any person who is proposed to be appointed as a substitute for the outgoing office holder; or
  - (iv) any creditor in the cases where the substitution is proposed to be made.

(4) The outgoing office holder (if he is not the applicant) and every person who holds office jointly with the office holder must be made a respondent to the application, but it is not necessary to join any other person as a respondent or to serve the application upon any other person unless the judge or registrar in the High Court so directs.

(5) The application should contain schedules setting out the nature of the office held, the identity of the court currently having jurisdiction over each case and its name and number.

(6) The application must be supported by evidence setting out the circumstances which have given rise to the need to make a substitution and exhibiting the written consent to act of each person who is proposed to be appointed in place of the outgoing office holder.

(7) The judge will in the first instance consider the application on paper and make such order as he thinks fit. In particular he may do any of the following:
  - (i) make an order directing the transfer to the High Court of those cases not already within its jurisdiction for the purpose only of the substantive application;
  - (ii) if he considers that the papers are in order and that the matter is straightforward, make an order on the substantive application;
  - (iii) give any directions which he considers to be necessary including (if appropriate) directions for the joinder of any additional respondents or requiring the service of the application on any person or requiring additional evidence to be provided;
  - (iv) if he does not himself make an order on the substantive application when the matter is first before him, give directions for the further consideration of the substantive application by himself or another judge of the Chancery Division or adjourn the substantive application to the registrar for him to make such order upon it as is appropriate.

(8) An order of the kind referred to in subparagraph (6)(i) shall follow the draft order in Form PDIP3 set out in the Schedule hereto and an order granting the substantive application shall follow the draft order in Form PDIP4 set out in the Schedule hereto (subject in each case to such modifications as may be necessary or appropriate).

SECTION 3 Other Practice Directions

(9) It is the duty of the applicant to ensure that a sealed copy of every order transferring any case to the High Court and of every order which is made on a substantive application is lodged with the court having jurisdiction over each case affected by such order for filing on the court file relating to that case.

(10) It will not be necessary for the file relating to any case which is transferred to the High Court in accordance with this paragraph to be sent to the High Court unless a judge or registrar so directs.

'Insolvency proceedings' (para 1.1(5))—These include all forms of insolvency proceedings under IA 1986 and IR 1986 and also include proceedings under the Administration of Insolvent Estates of Deceased Persons Order 1986, the Insolvent Partnerships Order 1994 and, where applicable, the now repealed Insolvent Partnerships Order 1986. Rule 7.51(2) of IR 1986 provides that all insolvency proceedings are allocated to the multi-track and that accordingly the provisions of the CPR relating to allocation questionnaires and track allocation do not apply.

'service of documents in insolvency proceedings' (para 1.3)—Except where IR 1986 provide otherwise, service of all documents in insolvency proceedings in the High Court will be the responsibility of the parties. Service by the court will still be possible in a county court but this is subject to any contrary provision contained in IR 1986 or any other rule or direction.

'registrar in bankruptcy' (para 1.4)—This expression is not defined. However, IR, r 13.2(3) states that in *individual* insolvency proceedings 'the registrar' means the registrar in bankruptcy of the High Court or a district judge of a county court; r 13.2(4) states that in *company* insolvency proceedings the registrar means –

(i) subject to para (ii) below, the registrar in bankruptcy of the High Court; or

(ii) where the proceedings are in the district registry of Birmingham, Bristol, Cardiff, Leeds, Liverpool, Manchester, Newcastle-upon-Tyne or Preston, the district judge.

Rule 13.2(5) provides that in company insolvency proceedings in a county court, 'the registrar' means the officer of the court whose duty it is to exercise the functions which in the High Court are exercised by a registrar.

Accordingly 'registrar' covers, *in general terms*, a registrar in bankruptcy of the High Court in London, a district judge of any of the Chancery district registries having jurisdiction in company insolvency proceedings (the Chancery district registries (as opposed to county courts) do not have jurisdiction in individual insolvency proceedings) and a district judge of any county court exercising any relevant insolvency jurisdiction.

PART 2
COMPANIES

Application—Paragraphs 2–8 of the practice direction relate to company insolvency matters. Paragraphs 9–16 relate to personal insolvency matters. The provisions relating to appeals in para 17 apply to both company and individual insolvencies.

2 ADVERTISEMENT OF WINDING UP PETITION

2.1 Insolvency Rule 4.11(2)(b) is mandatory, and designed to ensure that the class remedy of winding up by the court is made available to all creditors, and is not used as a means of putting pressure on the company to pay the petitioner's debt. Failure to comply with the rule, without good reason accepted by the court, may lead to the summary dismissal of the petition on the return date (Insolvency Rule 4.11(5)). If the court, in its discretion, grants an adjournment, this will be on condition that the petition is advertised in due time for the adjourned hearing. No further adjournment for the purpose of advertisement will normally be granted.

2.2 Copies of every advertisement published in connection with a winding up petition must be lodged with the Court as soon as possible after publication and in any event not later than the day specified in Insolvency Rule 4.14 of the

Insolvency Rules 1986. This direction applies even if the advertisement is defective in any way (eg is published at a date not in accordance with the Insolvency Rules, or omits or misprints some important words) or if the petitioner decides not to pursue the petition (eg on receiving payment).

'Insolvency Rule 4.11(2)(b)' (para 2.1)—Rule 4.11(2) requires the advertisement of the petition to appear not less than 7 business days (an expression which is defined in r 13.13) after service of the petition on the company nor less than 7 business days before the date of the hearing. Paragraph 2.1 emphasises the importance of advertising the petition timeously. Even if an adjournment is granted to enable a petition to be advertised where a good reason for not having advertised the same in accordance with the rules is given and accepted by the court, it will be on condition that the petition is advertised in due time for the adjourned hearing.

'Copies of every advertisement ... must be lodged with the court' (para 2.2)—Rule 4.14 provides that a certificate of compliance dealing with the matters referred to in r 4.14(2) must be filed in court at least 5 days before the hearing, *together with the advertisement*. However, see para 3 and the note to it, below.

3 CERTIFICATE OF COMPLIANCE – TIME FOR FILING

3.1 In the High Court in order to assist practitioners and the court the time laid down by Insolvency Rule 4.14 of the Insolvency Rules 1986, for filing a certificate of compliance and a copy of the advertisement, is hereby extended to not later than 4.30 pm on the Friday preceding the day on which the petition is to be heard. Applications to file the certificate and the copy advertisement after 4.30 pm on the Friday will only be allowed if some good reason is shown for the delay.

'time ... for the filing a certificate of compliance'—This provision appears to be focussed entirely on proceedings in the High Court in London where a winding up petition is given an initial return date on a Wednesday. In the Chancery district registries, a winding up petition may not necessarily be given a hearing date on a Wednesday. As there is no other provision in the practice direction specifically dealing with this point, the Friday extension applies regardless of which day in the week the petition is due for hearing. Thus, whenever a petition is due for hearing in a week, the certificate of compliance will need to be lodged no later than 4.30 pm on the Friday in the previous week. The variation of the rule does not apply in county courts.

4 ERRORS IN PETITIONS

4.1 Applications for leave to amend errors in petitions which are discovered subsequent to a winding up order being made should be made to the Court Manager in the High Court and to the district judge in the county court.

4.2 Where the error is an error in the name of the company, the Court Manager in the High Court and the district judge in the county court may make any necessary amendments to ensure that the winding up order is drawn with the correct name of the company inserted. If there is any doubt, eg where there might be another company in existence which could be confused with the company to be wound up, the Court Manager will refer the application to the Registrar and the district judge may refer it to the judge.

4.3 Where an error is an error in the registered office of the company and any director or member of the company claims that the company was unaware of the petition by reason of it having been served at the wrong registered office, it will be open to them to apply to rescind the winding up order in the usual way.

4.4 Where it is discovered that the company had been struck off the Register of Companies prior to the winding up order being made, the matter must be restored to the list before the order is entered to enable an order for the restoration of the name to be made as well as the order to wind up.

'Court Manager' (paras 4.1 and 4.2)—The Court Manager in the High Court in London has limited jurisdiction to amend errors in petitions which are discovered subsequent to a winding up order being made. Despite the reference to the 'Court Manager in the High Court' no Court Manager having such powers exists outside the High Court in London. Accordingly, both in any of the Chancery district registries having company winding up jurisdiction outside London and in a county court, this power can only be exercised by a district judge.

'company ... unaware of ... petition ... served at the wrong registered office' (para 4.3)—Rule 7.47 applies in respect of any such application. The application for rescission should be made within 7 days after the date on which the winding up order was made. However, the court has power to extend the 7-day time limit, see r 12.9 (which imports the provisions of CPR rr 2.8 and 3.1(2)(a) concerning computations extensions and abridgement of time for compliance with any matter required or authorised to be done by IR 1986) and *Re Virgo Systems Limited* [1990] BCLC 34.

Application for the restoration of the company to the Register of Companies (para 4.4)—In such a case, the application will be made by the same petition by which the winding up order is sought. The petition will seek the restoration of the company to the Register of Companies and an order that the company be wound up following such restoration, see PD49B, para 4(1)(g).

5 DISTRIBUTION OF BUSINESS

5.1 The following applications shall be made direct to the judge and, unless otherwise ordered, shall be heard in public –

(1) Applications to commit any person to prison for contempt;
(2) Applications for urgent interim relief (eg applications pursuant to s 127 of the Act prior to any winding up order being made);
(3) Applications to restrain the presentation or advertisement of a petition to wind up; or
(4) Applications for the appointment of a provisional liquidator;
(5) Petitions for administration orders or an interim order upon such a Petition;
(6) Applications after an administration order has been made pursuant to s 14(3) of the Act (for directions) or s 18(3) of the Act (to vary or discharge the order);
(7) Petitions to discharge administration orders and to wind up;
(8) Applications pursuant to s 5(3) of the Act (to stay a winding up or discharge an administration order or for directions) where a voluntary arrangement has been approved;
(9) Appeals from a decision made by a county court or by a Registrar of the High Court.

5.2 Subject to paragraph 5.4 below all other applications shall be made to the Registrar or the district judge in the first instance who may give any necessary directions and may, in the exercise of his discretion, either hear and determine it himself or refer it to the judge.

5.3 The following matters will also be heard in public –

(1) Petitions to wind up;
(2) Public examinations;
(3) All matters and applications heard by the judge, except those referred by the Registrar or the district judge to be heard in private or so directed by the judge to be heard.

5.4 In accordance with directions given by the Lord Chancellor the Registrar has authorised certain applications in the High Court to be dealt with by the Court Manager of the Companies Court, pursuant to Insolvency Rule 13.2(2). The applications are:

(1) To extend or abridge time prescribed by the Insolvency Rules in connection with winding up (Insolvency Rules 4.3 and 12.9);
(2) For substituted service of winding up petitions (Insolvency Rule 4.8(6));
(3) To withdraw petitions (Insolvency Rule 4.15);
(4) For the substitution of a petitioner (Insolvency Rule 4.19);
(5) By the Official Receiver for limited disclosure of a statement of affairs (Insolvency Rule 4.35);
(6) By the Official Receiver for relief from duties imposed upon him by the rules (Insolvency Rule 4.47);
(7) By the Official Receiver for permission to give notice of a meeting by advertisement only (Insolvency Rule 4.59);
(8) To transfer proceedings from the High Court to a county court (Insolvency Rule 7.11);
(9) For permission to amend any originating application.

NB In District Registries all such applications must be made to the district judge.

'Court Manager' (para 5.4)—See note to para 4 above.

6 DRAWING UP OF ORDERS

6.1 The court will draw up all orders except orders on the application of the Official Receiver or for which the Treasury Solicitor is responsible under the existing practice.

7 RESCISSION OF A WINDING UP ORDER

7.1 Any application for the rescission of a winding up order shall be made within seven days after the date on which the order was made (Insolvency Rule 7.47(4)). Notice of any such application must be given to the Official Receiver.

7.2 Applications will only be entertained if made (a) by a creditor, or (b) by a contributory, or (c) by the company jointly with a creditor or with a contributory. The application must be supported by written evidence of assets and liabilities.

7.3 In the case of an unsuccessful application the costs of the petitioning creditor, the supporting creditors and of the Official Receiver will normally be ordered to be paid by the creditor or the contributory making or joining in the application. The reason for this is that if the costs of an unsuccessful application are made payable by the company, they fall unfairly on the general body of creditors.

7.4 Cases in which the making of the winding up order has not been opposed may, if the application is made promptly, be dealt with on a statement by the applicant's legal representative of the circumstances; but apart from such cases, the court will normally require any application to be supported by written evidence.

7.5 There is no need to issue a form of application (Form 7.2) as the petition is restored before the court.

'within 7 days' (para 7.1)—The time limit of 7 days can be extended, see notes under para 4, above.

'supported by written evidence of assets and liabilities' (para 7.2)—The court will need to be satisfied that the company is solvent.

'unsuccessful application' (para 7.3)—Even if the company does have assets which would be available on a winding up for the payment of the costs of the petitioning creditor pursuant to r 4.218(1)(h), the philosophy behind this paragraph is that it should nevertheless be the creditor or contributory making or joining in the application who should be responsible for such costs, rather than the general body of creditors.

Paragraph 7.5—This provision is difficult to understand. On the basis that the winding up order will have been made and therefore the petition effectively disposed of, it is difficult to see how it is possible to state that there is no need to issue a form of application 'as the petition is restored before the court'. This provision may be compared with the position which applies on an annulment of a bankruptcy order (IR 1986, r 6.206) where the applicant needs to make a formal application for annulment. Further, it seems that this provision is inconsistent with para 7.2 requiring the application to be prosecuted by a creditor or contributory. If the petition is simply restored, it is questionable whether that involves a formal application by a creditor or contributory. It is submitted that strictly a formal application should be necessary to have the winding up order rescinded and the petition restored for hearing. However, in practice, in accordance with this provision, the petition is simply 'restored' without a formal application.

8 RESTRAINT OF PRESENTATION OF A WINDING UP PETITION

8.1 An application to restrain presentation of a winding up petition must be made to the judge by the issue of an Originating Application (Form 7.1).

'restrain presentation'—Where the petition has been issued, then the appropriate course is to make an application within those proceedings by ordinary application to restrain the advertisement of the petition. Such an application also needs to be made directly to the judge, see para 5.1(3) above.

PART 3
PERSONAL INSOLVENCY – BANKRUPTCY

9 DISTRIBUTION OF BUSINESS

9.1 The following applications shall be made direct to the judge and unless otherwise ordered shall be heard in public:

(1) Applications for the committal of any person to prison for contempt;
(2) Application for injunctions or for the modification or discharge of injunctions;
(3) Applications for interlocutory relief or directions after the matter has been referred to the judge.

9.2 All other applications shall be made to the Registrar or the district judge in the first instance. He shall give any necessary directions and may, if the application is within his jurisdiction to determine, in his discretion either hear and determine it himself or refer it to the judge.

9.3 The following matters shall be heard in public:

(1) The public examination of debtors;
(2) Opposed applications for discharge or for the suspension or lifting of the suspension of discharge;
(3) Opposed applications for permission to be a director;
(4) In any case where the petition was presented or the receiving order or order for adjudication was made before the appointed day, those matters and applications specified in Rule 8 of the Bankruptcy Rules 1952;
(5) All matters and applications heard by the judge, except matters and applications referred by the Registrar or the district judge to be heard by the judge in private or directed by the judge to be so heard.

9.4 All petitions presented will be listed under the name of the debtor.

9.5 In accordance with Directions given by the Lord Chancellor the Registrar has authorised certain applications in the High Court to be dealt with by the Court Manager of the Bankruptcy Court pursuant to Insolvency Rule 13.2(2). The applications are:

(1) by petitioning creditors: to extend time for hearing petitions (s.376 of the Act).
(2) by the Official Receiver:
   (a) To transfer proceedings from the High Court to a county court (Insolvency Rule 7.13);
   (b) to amend the full title of the proceedings (Insolvency Rules 6.35 and 6.47).

   NB In District Registries all such applications must be made to the district judge

'Court Manager' (para 9.5)—See notes under paras 4 and 5 above.

'extend time for hearing of petitions' (para 9.5(1))—See para 14 below.

10 SERVICE ABROAD OF STATUTORY DEMAND

10.1 A statutory demand is not a document issued by the court. Leave to serve out of the jurisdiction is not, therefore, required.

10.2 Insolvency Rule 6.3(2) ('Requirements as to service') applies to service of the statutory demand whether outside or within the jurisdiction.

10.3 A creditor wishing to serve a statutory demand outside the jurisdiction in a foreign country with which a civil procedure convention has been made (including the Hague Convention) may and, if the assistance of a British Consul is desired, must adopt the procedure prescribed by CPR Part 6.25. In the case of any doubt whether the country is a 'convention country', enquiries should be made of the Queen's Bench Masters' Secretary Department, Room E216, Royal Courts of Justice.

10.4 In all other cases, service of the demand must be effected by private arrangement in accordance with Insolvency Rule 6.3(2) and local foreign law.

10.5 When a statutory demand is to be served out of the jurisdiction, the time limits of 21 days and 18 days respectively referred to in the demand must be amended. For this purpose reference should be made to the table set out in the practice direction supplementing Section III of CPR Part 6.

10.6 A creditor should amend the statutory demand as follows:

(1) For any reference to 18 days there must be substituted the appropriate number of days set out in the table plus 4 days, and
(2) for any reference to 21 days there must be substituted the appropriate number of days in the table plus 7 days.

Attention is drawn to the fact that in all forms of the statutory demand the figure 18 and the figure 21 occur in more than one place.

Service of statutory demand—Rule 6.3(2) requires the creditor to do all that is reasonable for the purposes of bringing the statutory demand to the debtor's attention and, if practical in the particular circumstances, to cause personal service of the demand to be effected. This requirement applies whether the debtor is within or outside the jurisdiction.

Service of the statutory demand outside jurisdiction (para 10.5)—The time limits of 21 days and 18 days referred to in the demand must be amended on the demand where service is being effected outside England and Wales. The reference to these days will now need to be amended to accord with the provisions of PD6B, supplementing CPR Part 6, Section III. There will need to be added to the days there referred to the additional days referred to in para 10.6.

'Attention is drawn' (para 10.6)—The reference to 18 days and 21 days in the statutory demand occurs in any number of places and the last sentence of this paragraph specifically draws to the attention of the person signing the statutory demand that the amendments must be made to all the relevant provisions containing those dates in the statutory demand.

11 SUBSTITUTED SERVICE

STATUTORY DEMANDS:

11.1 The creditor is under an obligation to do all that is reasonable to bring the statutory demand to the debtor's attention and, if practicable, to cause personal service to be effected. Where it is not possible to effect prompt personal service, service may be effected by other means such as first class post or by insertion through a letter box.

11.2 Advertisement can only be used as a means of substituted service where:

(1) The demand is based on a judgment or order of any Court;
(2) The debtor has absconded or is keeping out of the way with a view to avoiding service and,
(3) There is no real prospect of the sum due being recovered by execution or other process.

As there is no statutory form of advertisement, the court will accept an advertisement in the following form:

STATUTORY DEMAND

(Debt for liquidated sum payable immediately following a judgment or order of the court)

To (Block letters)
Of
TAKE NOTICE that a statutory demand has been issued by:
Name of Creditor:
Address:
The creditor demands payment of £ the amount now due on a judgment or order of the (High Court of Justice Division)(County Court) dated the day of 199 .
The statutory demand is an important document and it is deemed to have been served on you on the date of the first appearance of this advertisement. You must deal with this demand within 21 days of the service upon you or you could be made bankrupt and your property and goods taken away from you. If you are in any doubt as to your position, you should seek advice immediately from a solicitor or your nearest Citizens' Advice Bureau. The statutory demand can be obtained or is available for inspection and collection from:
Name:
Address:
(Solicitor for) the Creditor
Tel No Reference:

You have only 21 days from the date of the first appearance of this advertisement before the creditor may present a Bankruptcy Petition. You have only 18 days from that date within which to apply to the court to set aside the demand.

11.3 In all cases where substituted service is effected, the creditor must have taken all those steps which would justify the court making an order for substituted service of a petition. The steps to be taken to obtain an order for substituted service of a petition are set out below. Failure to comply with these requirements may result in the court declining to file the petition: Insolvency Rule 6.11(9).

PETITIONS

11.4 In most cases, evidence of the following steps will suffice to justify an order for substituted service:

(1) One personal call at the residence and place of business of the debtor where both are known or at either of such places as is known. Where it is known that the debtor has more than one residential or business address, personal calls should be made at all the addresses.

(2) Should the creditor fail to effect service, a first class prepaid letter should be written to the debtor referring to the call(s), the purpose of the same and the failure to meet with the debtor, adding that a further call will be made for the same purpose on the day of 19 at hours at (place). At least two business days notice should be given of the appointment and copies of the letter sent to all known addresses of the debtor. The appointment letter should also state that

- (a) in the event of the time and place not being convenient, the debtor is to name some other time and place reasonably convenient for the purpose;
- (b) (Statutory Demands) if the debtor fails to keep the appointment the creditor proposes to serve the debtor by advertisement] post] insertion through a letter box] or as the case may be, and that, in the event of a bankruptcy petition being presented, the court will be asked to treat such service as service of the demand on the debtor;
- (c) (Petitions) if the debtor fails to keep the appointment, application will be made to the court for an order for substituted service either by advertisement, or in such other manner as the court may think fit.

(3) In attending any appointment made by letter, inquiry should be made as to whether the debtor has received all letters left for him. If the debtor is away, inquiry should also be made as to whether or not letters are being forwarded to an address within the jurisdiction (England and Wales) or elsewhere.

(4) If the debtor is represented by a Solicitor, an attempt should be made to arrange an appointment for personal service through such Solicitor. The Insolvency Rules enable a Solicitor to accept service of a statutory demand on behalf of his client but there is no similar provision in respect of service of a bankruptcy petition.

(5) The written evidence filed pursuant to Insolvency Rule 6.11 should

deal with all the above matters including all relevant facts as to the debtor's whereabouts and whether the appointment letter(s) have been returned.

11.5 Where the court makes an order for service by first class ordinary post, the order will normally provide that service be deemed to be effected on the seventh day after posting. The same method of calculating service may be applied to calculating the date of service of a statutory demand.

Substituted service of statutory demand and bankruptcy petition—These provisions deal in detail with the *substituted service* of a statutory demand and of a bankruptcy petition. Guidance is given in para 11.4 as to when it would be appropriate to serve a demand or a petition by way of substituted service.

'Advertisement … as a means of substituted service' (para 11.2)—The court will accept the form of the advertisement set out under para 11.2. While the creditor is not obliged to use that form, he is strongly advised to do so. The court will need to be satisfied that the demand is likely to have come to the notice of the debtor before service will deemed to have been effected (*Lilly v Davison* [1999] BPIR 81, ChD).

Consequences of failure by creditor to take all steps required for substituted service (para 11.3)—Where substituted service of a demand is relied on, the creditor must have taken all the steps which would justify the court making an order for substituted service of a petition. Those steps are set out in para 11.4. If there is a failure to comply with those requirements, the court may, pursuant to r 6.11(9), decline to file the petition on the ground that the creditor has not, in accordance with his obligation under r 6.3(2), done all that is reasonable to bring the demand to the attention of the debtor.

Mode of substituted service (para 11.5)—Where the court makes an order for substituted service, it will normally provide that service be effected both by first-class post and by recorded delivery. Further, the order will normally provide that the service will be deemed to be effected on the 7th day after posting.

12 SETTING ASIDE A STATUTORY DEMAND

12.1 The application (Form 6.4) and written evidence in support (Form 6.5) exhibiting a copy of the statutory demand must be filed in Court within 18 days of service of the statutory demand on the debtor. Where service is effected by advertisement in a newspaper the period of 18 days is calculated from the date of the first appearance of the advertisement. Three copies of each document must be lodged with the application to enable the court to serve notice of the hearing date on the applicant, the creditor and the person named in Part B of the statutory demand.

12.2 Where, to avoid expense, copies of the documents are not lodged with the application in the High Court, any order of the Registrar fixing a venue is conditional upon copies of the documents being lodged on the next business day after the Registrar's order otherwise the application will be deemed to have been dismissed.

12.3 Where the statutory demand is based on a judgment or order, the court will not at this stage go behind the judgment or order and inquire into the validity of the debt nor, as a general rule, will it adjourn the application to await the result of an application to set aside the judgment or order.

12.4 Where the debtor (a) claims to have a counterclaim, set off or cross demand (whether or not he could have raised it in the action in which the judgment or order was obtained) which equals or exceeds the amount of the debt or debts specified in the statutory demand or (b) disputes the debt (not being a debt subject to a judgment or order) the court will normally set aside the statutory demand if, in its opinion, on the evidence there is a genuine triable issue.

12.5 A debtor who wishes to apply to set aside a statutory demand after the expiration of 18 days from the date of service of the statutory demand must apply for an extension of time within which to apply. If the applicant wishes to apply for an injunction to restrain presentation of a petition the application must be made to the judge. Paragraphs 1 and 2 of Form 6.5 (Affidavit in Support of Application to set Aside Statutory Demand) should be used in support of the application for an extension of time with the following additional paragraphs:

'3. That to the best of my knowledge and belief the creditor(s) named in the demand has/have not presented a petition against me.

4. That the reasons for my failure to apply to set aside the demand within 18 days after service are as follows: . . ..'

If application is made to restrain presentation of a bankruptcy petition the following additional paragraph should be added:

'5. Unless restrained by injunction the creditor(s) may present a bankruptcy petition against me.'

Application and written evidence—Rule 6.4 deals with the making of the application to set aside a statutory demand and r 6.5 deals with the hearing of such an application.

It is necessary for three copies of the application and evidence in support to be lodged with the court to enable it to serve notice of the hearing date on the applicant, assuming that the court decides that it will not summarily dismiss the application under r 6.5(1). Where such documents are not lodged with the application, any order fixing a date for the hearing of the application will be conditional upon copies of the documents being lodged on the next business day after the court's order, otherwise the application will be deemed to have been dismissed (para 12.2).

Application to set aside out of time (para 12.5)—Where a debtor applies to set aside a statutory demand after the expiration of 18 days, he must apply for an extension of time within which to apply to set the demand aside. If he cannot persuade the petitioning creditor to refrain from presenting a petition until the hearing of the application, the debtor should also make an application for an injunction to restrain the presentation of the petition. Such application must be made before the judge (para 9.1 above). The requirements as to the contents of the affidavit in support of the application should be noted.

13 PROOF OF SERVICE OF A STATUTORY DEMAND

13.1 Insolvency Rule 6.11(3) provides that, if the Statutory Demand has been served personally, the written evidence must be provided by the person who effected that service. Insolvency Rule 6.11(4) provides that, if service of the demand (however effected) has been acknowledged in writing, the evidence of service must be provided by the creditor or by a person acting on his behalf. Insolvency Rule 6.11(5) provides that, if neither paragraphs (3) or (4) apply, the written evidence must be provided by a person having direct knowledge of the means adopted for serving the demand.

13.2 Form 6.11 (Evidence of personal service of the statutory demand): this form should only be used where the demand has been served personally and acknowledged in writing (see Insolvency Rule 6.11(4)). If the demand has not been acknowledged in writing, the written evidence should be provided by the Process Server and Paragraphs 2 and 3 (part of Form 6.11) should be omitted (See Insolvency Rule 6.11(3)).

13.3 Form 6.12 (Evidence of Substituted Service of the Statutory Demand): this form can be used whether or not service of the demand has been acknowledged in writing. Paragraphs 4 and 5 (part) provide for the alternatives. Practitioners are reminded, however, that the appropriate person to provide the written evidence may not be the same in both cases. If the demand has been acknowledged in writing, the appropriate person is the creditor or a person acting on his behalf. If the demand has not been acknowledged, that person must be someone having direct knowledge of the means adopted for serving the demand.

Practitioners may find it more convenient to allow process servers to carry out the necessary investigation whilst reserving to themselves the service of the demand. In these circumstances Paragraph 1 should be deleted and the following paragraph substituted:

> '1 Attempts have been made to serve the demand, full details of which are set out in the accompanying affidavit of . . .'.

13.4 'Written evidence' means an affidavit or witness statement.

14 EXTENSION OF HEARING DATE OF PETITION

14.1 Late applications for extension of hearing dates under Insolvency Rule 6.28, and failure to attend on the listed hearing of a petition, will be dealt with as follows:

(1) If an application is submitted less than two clear working days before the hearing date (for example, later than Monday for Thursday, or Wednesday for Monday) the costs of the application will not be allowed under Insolvency Rule 6.28(3).

(2) If the petition has not been served and no extension has been granted by the time fixed for the hearing of the petition, and if no one attends for the hearing, the petition will be re-listed for hearing about 21 days later. The court will notify the petitioning creditor's solicitors (or the petitioning creditor in person), and any known supporting or opposing creditors or their solicitors, of the new date and times. Written evidence should then be filed on behalf of the petitioning creditor explaining fully the reasons for the failure to apply for an extension or to appear at the hearing, and (if appropriate) giving reasons why the petition should not be dismissed.

(3) On the re-listed hearing the court may dismiss the petition if not satisfied it should be adjourned or a further extension granted.

14.2 All applications for extension should include a statement of the date fixed for the hearing of the petition.

14.3 The petitioning creditor should attend (by solicitors or in person) on or before the hearing date to ascertain whether the application has reached the file and been dealt with. It should not be assumed that an extension will be granted.

Extension of hearing date—There is a difference between extending time for the hearing of a petition (r 6.28) and adjourning the petition on the hearing date to another date (r 6.29). An adjournment is only appropriate where service on the debtor has been effected. Otherwise, the appropriate course is for the petitioning creditor to apply for an extension of the hearing date of the petition. The Court Manager (see para 4 above) in the High Court in London is authorised to extend time for the hearing of a petition. Note that if the petition has not been served, no extension has been granted and no one attends the hearing, the petition should be re-listed for hearing 21 days later. On the re-listed hearing, the court may dismiss the petition if not satisfied it should be adjourned or grant a further extension. It is not appropriate, as happens frequently in county courts in the event of non-attendance on the original date, for the petition to be 'struck out' or dismissed. The petitioning creditor is entitled to expect this provision to be applied by the court and accordingly entitled to expect that the petition will be re-listed on another date with a view to an explanation being provided by him concerning his failure to attend or to apply for an extension and to have the court consider at that hearing whether in the light of that explanation the petition should be dismissed.

15 BANKRUPTCY PETITION

To help in the completion of the form of a creditor's bankruptcy petition, attention is drawn to the following points:

15.1 The petition does not require dating, signing or witnessing.

15.2 In the title it is only necessary to recite the debtor's name eg Re John William Smith or Re J W Smith (Male). Any alias or trading name will appear in the body of the petition. This also applies to all other statutory forms other than those which require the 'full title'.

15.3 Where the petition is based on a statutory demand, only the debt claimed in the demand may be included in the petition.

15.4 In completing Paragraph 2 of the petition, attention is drawn to Insolvency Rule 6.8(1)(a) to (c), particularly where the 'aggregate sum' is made up of a number of debts.

15.5 Date of service of the statutory demand (paragraph 4 of the petition):

(1) In the case of personal service, the date of service as set out in the affidavit of service should be recited and whether service is effected *before/after* 1700 hours on Monday to Friday or at any time on a Saturday or a Sunday: see CPR Part 6.7(2) and (3).

(2) In the case of substituted service (otherwise than by advertisement), the date alleged in the affidavit of service should be recited: see '11. Substituted Service' above.

(3) In the strictly limited case of service by advertisement under Insolvency Rule 6.3, the date to be alleged is the date of the advertisement's appearance or, as the case may be, its first appearance: see Insolvency Rules 6.3(3) and 6.11(8).

15.6 There is no need to include in the petition details of the person authorised to present it.

15.7 Certificates at the end of the petition:

(1) The period of search for prior petitions has been reduced to eighteen months.

(2) Where a statutory demand is based wholly or in part on a county court judgment, the following certificate is to be added:
'I/We certify that on the day of 19 I/We attended on the County Court and was/were informed by an officer of the court that no money had been paid into Court in the action or matter v Claim No pursuant to the statutory demand.'
This certificate will not be required when the demand also requires payment of a separate debt, not based on a county court judgment, the amount of which exceeds the bankruptcy level (at present £750).

15.8 Deposit on petition: the deposit will be taken by the court and forwarded to the Official Receiver. In the High Court, the petition fee and deposit should be handed to the Supreme Court Accounts Office, Fee Stamping Room, who will record the receipt and will impress two entries on the original petition, one in respect of the court fee and the other in respect of the deposit. In the county court, the petition fee and deposit should be handed to the duly authorised officer of the court's staff who will record its receipt.

In all cases cheque(s) for the whole amount should be made payable to 'HM Paymaster General'.

15.9 On the hearing of a petition for a bankruptcy order, in order to satisfy the court that the debt on which the petition is founded has not been paid or secured or compounded the court will normally accept as sufficient a certificate signed by the person representing the petitioning creditor in the following form:

> 'I certify that I have/my firm has made enquiries of the petitioning creditor(s) within the last business day prior to the hearing/adjourned hearing and to the best of my knowledge and belief the debt on which the petition is founded is still due and owing and has not been paid or secured or compounded save as to . . . .
>
> Signed . . . . Dated . . . .'

For convenience in the High Court this certificate will be incorporated in the attendance slip, which will be filed after the hearing. A fresh certificate will be required on each adjourned hearing.

15.10 On the occasion of the adjourned hearing of a petition for a bankruptcy order, in order to satisfy the court that the petitioner has complied with Insolvency Rule 6.29, the petitioner will be required to file written evidence of the manner in which notice of the making of the order of adjournment and of the venue for the adjourned hearing has been sent to:

(i) the debtor, and

(ii) any creditor who has given notice under Insolvency Rule 6.23 but was not present at the hearing when the order for adjournment was made.

Scope of provision—This provision has to be read in conjunction with the provisions of rr 6.6–6.12.

16 ORDERS WITHOUT ATTENDANCE

16.1 In suitable cases the court will normally be prepared to make orders under Part VIII of the Act (Individual Voluntary Arrangements), without the attendance of either party, provided there is no bankruptcy order in existence and (so far as is known) no pending petition. The orders are:

(1) A fourteen day interim order with the application adjourned 14 days for consideration of the nominee's report, where the papers are in order, and the nominee's signed consent to act includes a waiver of notice of the application or a consent by the nominee to the making of an interim order without attendance.

(2) A standard order on consideration of the nominee's report, extending the interim order to a date 7 weeks after the date of the proposed meeting, directing the meeting to be summoned and adjourning to a date about 3 weeks after the meeting. Such an Order may be made without attendance if the nominee's report has been delivered to the court and complies with Section 256(1) of the Act and Insolvency Rule 5.10(2) and (3) and proposes a date for the meeting not less than 14 days from that on which the nominee's report is filed in Court under Insolvency Rule 5.10 nor more than 28 days from that on which that report is considered by the court under Insolvency Rule 5.12.

(3) A 'concertina' Order, combining orders as under (1) and (2) above. Such an order may be made without attendance if the initial application for an interim order is accompanied by a report of the nominee and the conditions set out in (1) and (2) above are satisfied.

(4) A final order on consideration of the Chairman's report. Such an order may be made without attendance if the Chairman's report has been

filed and complies with Insolvency Rule 5.22(1). The order will record the effect of the Chairman's report and may discharge the interim order.

16.2 Provided that the conditions as under 16.1(2) and (4) above are satisfied and that the appropriate report has been lodged with the court in due time the parties need not attend or be represented on the adjourned hearing for consideration of the Nominee's report or of the Chairman's report (as the case may be) unless they are notified by the court that attendance is required. Sealed copies of the order made (in all four cases as above) will be posted by the court to the applicant or his Solicitor and to the Nominee.

16.3 In suitable cases the court may also make consent orders without attendance by the parties. The written consent of the parties will be required. Examples of such orders are as follows:

(1) On applications to set aside a statutory demand, orders:
   (a) dismissing the application, with or without an order for costs as may be agreed (permission will be given to present a petition on or after the seventh day after the date of the order, unless a different date is agreed);
   (b) setting aside the demand, with or without an order for costs as may be agreed; or
   (c) giving permission to withdraw the application with or without an order for costs as may be agreed.
(2) On petitions: where there is a list of supporting or opposing creditors in Form 6.21, or a statement signed by or on behalf of the petitioning creditor that no notices have been received from supporting or opposing creditors, orders:
   (a) dismissing the petition, with or without an order for costs as may be agreed, or
   (b) if the petition has not been served, giving permission to withdraw the petition (with no order for costs).
(3) On other applications, orders:
   (a) for sale of property, possession of property, disposal of proceeds of sale
   (b) giving interim directions
   (c) dismissing the application, with or without an order for costs as may be agreed
   (d) giving permission to withdraw the application, with or without an order for costs as may be agreed.

If, (as may often be the case with orders under subparagraphs (3)(a) or (b) above) an adjournment is required, whether generally with liberty to restore or to a fixed date, the order by consent may include an order for the adjournment. If adjournment to a date is requested, a time estimate should be given and the court will fix the first available date and time on or after the date requested.

16.4 The above lists should not be regarded as exhaustive, nor should it be assumed that an order will be made without attendance as requested.

16.5 The procedure outlined above is designed to save time and costs but is not intended to discourage attendance.

16.6 Applications for consent orders without attendance should be lodged at least two clear working days (and preferably longer) before any fixed hearing date.

16.7 Whenever a document is lodged or a letter sent, the correct case number, code (if any) and year (for example 123/SD/99 or 234/99) should be quoted. A note should also be given of the date and time of the next hearing (if any).

16.8 Attention is drawn to Paragraph 4.4(4) of the practice direction relating to CPR Part 44.

Orders without attendance—Although orders of the type referred to in para 16 can be made without attendance, they do not represent an exhaustive list. Further, the procedure outlined in para 16 is designed to save time and costs. It is not intended to discourage attendance.

16A BANKRUPTCY RESTRICTIONS ORDERS

Making the application

16A.1 An application for a bankruptcy restrictions order is made as an ordinary application in the bankruptcy.

16A.2 The application must be made within one year beginning with the date of the bankruptcy order unless the court gives permission for the application to be made after that period. The one year period does not run while the bankrupt's discharge has been suspended under section 279(3) of the Insolvency Act 1986.

16A.3 An application for a bankruptcy restrictions order may be made by the Secretary of State or the Official Receiver ('the Applicant'). The application must be supported by a report which must include:

(a) a statement of the conduct by reference to which it is alleged that it is appropriate for a bankruptcy restrictions order to be made; and
(b) the evidence relied on in support of the application (r 6.241 Insolvency Rules 1986).

16A.4 The report is treated as if it were an affidavit (r 7.9(2) Insolvency Rules 1986) and is prima facie evidence of any matter contained in it (r 7.9(3)).

16A.5 The application may be supported by evidence from other witnesses which may be given by affidavit or (by reason of r 7.57(5) Insolvency Rules 1986) by witness statement verified by a statement of truth.

16A.6 The court will fix a first hearing which must be not less than 8 weeks from the date when the hearing is fixed (r 6.241(4) Insolvency Rules 1986).

16A.7 Notice of the application and the venue fixed by the court must be served by the Applicant on the bankrupt not more than 14 days after the application is made. Service of notice must be accompanied by a copy of the application together with the evidence in support and a form of acknowledgment of service.

16A.8 The bankrupt must file in court an acknowledgment of service not more than 14 days after service of the application on him, indicating whether or not he contests the application. If he fails to do so he may attend the hearing of the application but may not take part in the hearing unless the court gives permission.

Opposing the application

16A.9 If the bankrupt wishes to oppose the application, he must within 28 days of service on him of the application and the evidence in support (or such longer period as the court may allow) file in court and (within three days thereof) serve on the Applicant any evidence which he wishes the court to take into consideration. Such evidence should normally be in the form of an affidavit or a witness statement verified by a statement of truth.

16A.10 The Applicant must file any evidence in reply within 14 days of receiving the evidence of the bankrupt (or such longer period as the court may allow) and must serve it on the bankrupt as soon as reasonably practicable.

Hearings

16A.11 Any hearing of an application for a bankruptcy restrictions order must be in public (r 6.241(5) Insolvency Rules 1986). The hearing will generally be before the registrar or district judge in the first instance who may:

(1) adjourn the application and give directions;
(2) make a bankruptcy restrictions order; or
(3) adjourn the application to the judge.

Making a bankruptcy restrictions order

16A.12 When the court is considering whether to make a bankruptcy restrictions order, it must not take into account any conduct of the bankrupt prior to 1 April 2004 (art 7 Enterprise Act (Commencement No 4 and Transitional Provisions and Savings) Order 2003).

16A.13 The court may make a bankruptcy restrictions order in the absence of the bankrupt and whether or not he has filed evidence (r 6.244 Insolvency Rules 1986).

16A.14 When a bankruptcy restrictions order is made the court must send two sealed copies of the order to the Applicant (r 6.244(2) Insolvency Rules 1986), and as soon as reasonably practicable after receipt, the Applicant must send one sealed copy to the bankrupt (r 6.244(3)).

16A.15 A bankruptcy restrictions order comes into force when it is made and must specify the date on which it will cease to have effect, which must be between two and 15 years from the date on which it is made.

Interim bankruptcy restriction orders

16A.16 An application for an interim bankruptcy restrictions order may be made any time between the institution of an application for a bankruptcy restrictions order and the determination of that application (Sch 4A para 5 Insolvency Act 1986). The application is made as an ordinary application in the bankruptcy.

16A.17 The application must be supported by a report as evidence in support of the application (r 6.246(1) Insolvency Rules 1986) which must include evidence of the bankrupt's conduct which is alleged to constitute the grounds for making an interim bankruptcy restrictions order and evidence of matters relating to the public interest in making the order.

16A.18 Notice of the application must be given to the bankrupt at least two business days before the date fixed for the hearing unless the court directs otherwise (r 6.245).

16A.19 Any hearing of the application must be in public (r 6.245).

16A.20 The court may make an interim bankruptcy restrictions order in the absence of the bankrupt and whether or not he has filed evidence (r 6.247).

16A.21 The bankrupt may apply to the court to set aside an interim bankruptcy restrictions order. The application is made by ordinary application in the bankruptcy and must be supported by an affidavit or witness statement verified by a statement of truth stating the grounds on which the application is made (r 6.248(2)).

16A.22 The bankrupt must send the Secretary of State, not less than 7 days before the hearing, notice of his application, notice of the venue, a copy of his application and a copy of the supporting affidavit. The Secretary of State may attend the hearing and call the attention of the court to any matters which seem to him to be relevant, and may himself give evidence or call witnesses.

16A.23 Where the court sets aside an interim bankruptcy restrictions order, two sealed copies of the order must be sent by the court, as soon as reasonably practicable, to the Secretary of State.

16A.24 As soon as reasonably practicable after receipt of sealed copies of the order, the Secretary of State must send a sealed copy to the bankrupt.

Bankruptcy restrictions undertakings

16A.25 Where a bankrupt has given a bankruptcy restrictions undertaking, the Secretary of State must file a copy in court and send a copy to the bankrupt as soon as reasonably practicable (r 6.250).

16A.26 The bankrupt may apply to annul a bankruptcy restrictions undertaking. The application is made as an ordinary application in the bankruptcy and must be supported by an affidavit or witness statement verified by a statement of truth stating the grounds on which it is made.

16A.27 The bankrupt must give notice of his application and the venue together with a copy of his affidavit in support to the Secretary of State at least 28 days before the date fixed for the hearing.

16A.28 The Secretary of State may attend the hearing and call the attention of the court to any matters which seem to him to be relevant and may himself give evidence or call witnesses.

16A.29 The court must send a sealed copy of any order annulling or varying the bankruptcy restrictions undertaking to the Secretary of State and the bankrupt.

Bankruptcy restriction orders—Section 281A and Sch 4A of IA 1986 and IR 1986, rr 6.240–6.248 deal with bankruptcy restriction orders and undertakings and the provisions of para 16 must be read in conjunction with those provisions.

PART 4

17 APPEALS IN INSOLVENCY PROCEEDINGS

17.1 This Part shall come into effect on 2 May 2000 and shall replace and revoke Paragraph 17 of, and be read in conjunction with the Practice Direction – Insolvency Proceedings which came into effect on 26 April 1999 as amended.

17.2(1) An appeal from a decision of a county court (whether made by a district judge or a circuit judge) or of a registrar of the High Court in insolvency proceedings ('a first appeal') lies to a Judge of the High

Court pursuant to s 375(2) of the Act and Insolvency Rules 7.47(2) and 7.48(2) (as amended by s 55 of the Access to Justice Act 1999).

(2) The procedure and practice for a first appeal are governed by Insolvency Rule 7.49 which imports the procedure and practice of the Court of Appeal. The procedure and practice of the Court of Appeal is governed by CPR Part 52 and its practice direction, which are subject to the provisions of the Act, the Insolvency Rules and this practice direction: see CPR Part 52, rule 1(4).

(3) A first appeal (as defined above) does not include an appeal from a decision of a Judge of the High Court.

17.3(1) Section 55 of the Access to Justice Act 1999 has amended s 375(2) of the Act and Insolvency Rules 7.47(2) and 7.48(2) so that an appeal from a decision of a judge of the High Court made on a first appeal lies, with the permission of the Court of Appeal, to the Court of Appeal.

(2) An appeal from a judge of the High Court in insolvency proceedings which is not a decision on a first appeal lies, with the permission of the Judge or of the Court of Appeal, to the Court of Appeal (see CPR Part 52 rule 3);

(3) The procedure and practice for appeals from a decision of a judge of the High Court in insolvency proceedings (whether made on a first appeal or not) are also governed by Insolvency Rule 7.49 which imports the procedure and practice of the Court of Appeal as stated at Paragraph 17.2(2) above.

17.4 CPR Part 52 and its practice direction and Forms apply to appeals from a decision of a judge of the High Court in insolvency proceedings.

17.5 An appeal from a decision of a judge of the High Court in insolvency proceedings requires permission as set out in Paragraph 17.3(1) and (2) above.

17.6 A first appeal does not require the permission of any court.

17.7 Except as provided in this Part, CPR Part 52 and its practice direction and Forms do not apply to first appeals, but Paragraphs 17.8 to 17.23 inclusive of this Part apply only to first appeals.

17.8 Interpretation –

(a) the expressions 'appeal court', 'lower court', 'appellant', 'respondent' and 'appeal notice' have the meanings given in CPR Part 52.1(3);

(b) 'Registrar of Appeals' means in relation to an appeal filed at the Royal Courts of Justice in London a bankruptcy registrar, and in relation to an appeal filed in a district registry in accordance with Paragraph 17.10(2) and (3) below a district judge of the relevant district registry.

(c) 'appeal date' means the date fixed by the appeal court for the hearing of the appeal or the date fixed by the appeal court upon which the period within which the appeal will be heard commences.

17.9 An appellant's notice and a respondent's notice shall be in Form PDIP 1 and PDIP 2 set out in the schedule hereto.

17.10

(1) An appeal from a decision of a registrar in bankruptcy shall, or from any decision made in any county court may, be filed at the Royal Courts of Justice in London.

(2) An appeal from a decision made in the county court exercising

jurisdiction over an area within the Birmingham, Bristol, Cardiff, Leeds, Liverpool, Manchester, Newcastle Upon Tyne or Preston Chancery district registries may be filed in the Chancery district registry of the High Court appropriate to the area in which the decision was made.

17.11

(1) Where a party seeks an extension of time in which to file an appeal notice it must be requested in the appeal notice and the appeal notice should state the reason for the delay and the steps taken prior to the application being made; the court will fix a date for the hearing of the application and notify the parties of the date and place of hearing;

(2) The appellant must file the appellant's notice at the appeal court within –
   (a) such period as may be directed by the lower court; or
   (b) where the court makes no such direction, 14 days after the date of the decision of the lower court which the appellant wishes to appeal.

(3) Unless the appeal court orders otherwise, an appeal notice must be served by the appellant on each respondent –
   (a) as soon as practicable; and
   (b) in any event not later than 7 days, after it is filed.

17.12

(1) A respondent may file and serve a respondent's notice.

(2) A respondent who wishes to ask the appeal court to uphold the order of the lower court for reasons different from or additional to those given by the lower court must file a respondent's notice.

(3) A respondent's notice must be filed within –
   (a) such period as may be directed by the lower court; or
   (b) where the court makes no such direction, 14 days after the date on which the respondent is served with the appellant's notice.

(4) Unless the appeal court orders otherwise a respondent's notice must be served by the respondent on the appellant and any other respondent –
   (a) as soon as practicable; and
   (b) in any event not later than 7 days, after it is filed.

17.13

(1) An application to vary the time limit for filing an appeal notice must be made to the appeal court.

(2) The parties may not agree to extend any date or time limit set by –
   (a) this practice direction; or
   (b) an order of the appeal court or the lower court.

17.14 Unless the appeal court or the lower court orders otherwise an appeal shall not operate as a stay of any order or decision of the lower court.

17.15 An appeal notice may not be amended without the permission of the appeal court.

17.16 A Judge of the appeal court may strike out the whole or part of an appeal notice where there is compelling reason for doing so.

17.17

(1) In relation to an appeal the appeal court has all the powers of the lower court.

(2) The appeal court has power to –

(a) affirm, set aside or vary any order or judgment made or given by the lower court;
(b) refer any claim or issue for determination by the lower court;
(c) order a new trial or hearing;
(d) make a costs order.

(3) The appeal court may exercise its powers in relation to the whole or part of an order of the lower court.

17.18

(1) Every appeal shall be limited to a review of the decision of the lower court.

(2) Unless it orders otherwise, the appeal court will not receive –
(a) oral evidence; or
(b) evidence which was not before the lower court.

(3) The appeal court will allow an appeal where the decision of the lower court was –
(a) wrong; or
(b) unjust because of a serious procedural or other irregularity in the proceedings in the lower court.

(4) The appeal court may draw any inference of fact which it considers justified on the evidence.

(5) At the hearing of the appeal a party may not rely on a matter not contained in his appeal notice unless the appeal court gives permission.

17.19 The following applications shall be made to a judge of the appeal court:

(1) for injunctions pending a substantive hearing of the appeal;
(2) for expedition or vacation of the hearing date of an appeal;
(3) for an order striking out the whole or part of an appeal notice pursuant to Paragraph 17.16 above;
(4) for a final order on paper pursuant to Paragraph 17.22(8) below.

17.20

(1) All other interim applications shall be made to the Registrar of Appeals in the first instance who may in his discretion either hear and determine it himself or refer it to the judge.

(2) An appeal from a decision of a Registrar of Appeals lies to a judge of the appeal court and does not require the permission of either the Registrar of Appeals or the judge.

17.21 The procedure for interim applications is by way of ordinary application (see Insolvency Rule 12.7 and Sch 4, Form 7.2).

17.22 The following practice applies to all first appeals to a judge of the High Court whether filed at the Royal Courts of Justice in London, or filed at one of the other venues referred to in Paragraph 17.10 above –

(1) on filing an appellant's notice in accordance with Paragraph 17.11(2) above, the appellant must file –
(a) two copies of the appeal notice for the use of the court, one of which must be stamped with the appropriate fee, and a number of additional copies equal to the number of persons who are to be served with it pursuant to Paragraph 17.22(4) below;
(b) a copy of the order under appeal; and
(c) an estimate of time for the hearing.

(2) the above documents may be lodged personally or by post and shall be lodged at the address of the appropriate venue listed below –
   (a) if the appeal is to be heard at the Royal Courts of Justice in London the documents must be lodged at Room 110, Thomas More Building, The Royal Courts of Justice, Strand, London WC2A 2LL;
   (b) if the appeal is to be heard in Birmingham, the documents must be lodged at the District Registry of the Chancery Division of the High Court, 33 Bull Street, Birmingham B4 6DS;
   (c) if the appeal is to be heard in Bristol the documents must be lodged at the District Registry of the Chancery Division of the High Court, Third Floor, Greyfriars, Lewins Mead, Bristol, BS1 2NR;
   (d) if the appeal is to be heard in Cardiff the documents must be lodged at the District Registry in the Chancery Division of the High Court, First Floor, 2 Park Street, Cardiff , CF10 1ET;
   (e) if the appeal is to be heard in Leeds the documents must be lodged at the District Registry of the Chancery Division of the High Court, The Court House, 1 Oxford Row, Leeds LS1 3BG;
   (f) if the appeal is to be heard in Liverpool the documents must be lodged at the District Registry of the Chancery Division of the High Court, Liverpool Combined Court Centre, Derby Square, Liverpool L2 1XA;
   (g) if the appeal is to be heard in Manchester the documents must be lodged at the District Registry of the Chancery Division of the High Court, Courts of Justice, Crown Square, Manchester, M60 9DJ;
   (h) if the appeal is to be heard at Newcastle Upon Tyne the documents must be lodged at the District Registry of the Chancery Division of the High Court, The Law Courts, Quayside, Newcastle Upon Tyne NE1 3LA;
   (i) if the appeal is to be heard in Preston the documents must be lodged at the District Registry of the Chancery Division of the High Court, The Combined Court Centre, Ringway, Preston PR1 2LL.

(3) if the documents are correct and in order the court at which the documents are filed will fix the appeal date and will also fix the place of hearing. That court will send letters to all the parties to the appeal informing them of the appeal date and of the place of hearing and indicating the time estimate given by the appellant. The parties will be invited to notify the court of any alternative or revised time estimates. In the absence of any such notification the estimate of the appellant will be taken as agreed. The court will also send to the appellant a document setting out the court's requirement concerning the form and content of the bundle of documents for the use of the judge. Not later than 7 days before the appeal date the bundle of documents must be filed by the appellant at the address of the relevant venue as set out in sub-paragraph 17.22(2) above and a copy of it must be served by the appellant on each respondent. The bundle should include an approved transcript of the judgment of the lower court or, where there is no officially recorded judgment, the document(s) referred to in paragraph 5.12 of the practice direction to CPR Part 52.

(4) the appeal notice must be served on all parties to the proceedings in the lower court who are directly affected by the appeal. This may include the Official Receiver, liquidator or trustee in bankruptcy.

(5) the appeal notice must be served by the appellant or by the legal representative of the appellant and may be effected by –
   (a) any of the methods referred to in CPR Part 6 rule 2; or
   (b) with permission of the court, an alternative method pursuant to CPR Part 6 rule 8.

(6) service of an appeal notice shall be proved by a certificate of service in accordance with CPR Part 6, rule 10 (CPR Form N215) which must be filed at the relevant venue referred to at Paragraph 17.22(2) above immediately after service.

(7) skeleton arguments, accompanied by a written chronology of events relevant to the appeal, should be filed at the address of the appropriate venue as set out in sub-paragraph 17.22(2) above, at least 2 clear days before the date fixed for the hearing. Failure to lodge may result in an adverse costs order being made by the Judge on the hearing of the appeal.

(8) where an appeal has been settled or where an appellant does not wish to continue with the appeal, the appeal may be disposed of on paper without a hearing. It may be dismissed by consent but the appeal court will not make an order allowing an appeal unless it is satisfied that the decision of the lower court was wrong. Any consent order signed by each party or letters of consent from each party must be lodged not later than 24 hours before the date fixed for the hearing of the appeal at the address of the appropriate venue as set out in sub-paragraph 17.22(2) above and will be dealt with by the judge of the appeal court. Attention is drawn to paragraph 4.4(4) of the practice direction to CPR Part 44 regarding costs where an order is made by consent without attendance.

17.23 Only the following paragraphs of the practice direction to CPR Part 52, with any necessary modifications, shall apply to first appeals: 5.12 and 5.14 to 5.20 inclusive.

17.24

(1) Where, under the procedure relating to appeals in insolvency proceedings prior to the coming into effect of this part of this practice direction, an appeal has been set down in the High Court or permission to appeal to the Court of Appeal has been granted before 2 May 2000, the procedure and practice set out in this part of this practice direction shall apply to such an appeal after that date.

(2) Where, under the procedure relating to appeals in insolvency proceedings prior to the coming into effect of this part of this practice direction, any person has failed before 2 May 2000 either –
   (a) in the case of a first appeal, to set down in the High Court an appeal which relates to an order made (county court) or sealed (High Court) after 27 March 2000 and before 2 May 2000, or
   (b) in the case of an appeal from a decision of a judge of the High Court, to obtain any requisite permission to appeal to the Court of Appeal which relates to an order sealed in the same period, the

time for filing an appeal notice is extended to 16 May 2000 and application for any such permission should be made in the appeal notice.

17.25 This paragraph applies where a judge of the High Court has made a bankruptcy order or a winding-up order or dismissed an appeal against such an order and an application is made for a stay of proceedings pending appeal.

(1) the judge will not normally grant a stay of all proceedings but will confine himself to a stay of advertisement of the proceedings.
(2) where the judge has granted permission to appeal any stay of advertisement will normally be until the hearing of the appeal but on terms that the stay will determine without further order if an appellant's notice is not filed within the period prescribed by the rules.
(3) where the judge has refused permission to appeal any stay of advertisement will normally be for a period not exceeding 28 days. Application for any further stay of advertisement should be made to the Court of Appeal.

'first appeals' (para 17 generally)—This is defined in para 17.2. In contra-distinction to ordinary appeals, a first appeal does not require permission (see para 17.6). However a first appeal is nevertheless a proper appeal (rather than a *de novo* application) before the judge of the High Court and accordingly the appeal is limited to a review of the decision of the lower court (see para 17.18).

'appeal from … a judge of the High Court' (para 17.5)—In substance the provisions of the CPR and any relevant practice direction governing ordinary appeals apply to appeals from a judge of the High Court to the Court of Appeal. Permission to appeal can only be given by the Court of Appeal if the decision of the High Court judge is a decision given on a first appeal (para 17.3(1)). Otherwise, permission may be given either by the High Court judge or the Court of Appeal.

Requirements for filing an appeal (para 17.22)—This paragraph deals with the matters which need to be complied with in order to file an appeal. Where there is a failure to comply with the provisions, the court may direct that unless the provisions there set out are complied with, the appeal should be struck out pursuant to the provisions of CPR Pt 3.

Directors' disqualification appeals—These are not dealt with either by the Directors' Disqualification Practice Direction (PDDirectors) or this practice direction but by Insolvent Companies (Disqualification of Unfit Directors) Proceedings Rules 1987, r 2(4), as amended. This provision requires all appeals in disqualification proceedings to be subject to the appeal provisions under the IR 1986. Applications for permission to act under IA 1986, ss 1 and 17 are also subject to the appeals procedure in the IR 1986 and accordingly to the provisions of this practice direction (*Re Britannia Homes Centres Limited, SOSTI v McCahill* [2001] 2 BCLC 63).

THE SCHEDULE

Forms

****

The Schedule—The Schedule to this practice direction contains two forms and two draft orders: All of them can be accessed (and the forms can be completed) on the *Civil Court Service* CD-ROM or via the Internet at the Court Service website *http://www.courtservice.gov.uk*.

Practice Direction – The Use of the Welsh Language in Cases in the Civil Courts in Wales

The purpose of this practice direction is to reflect the principle of the Welsh Language Act 1993 that in the administration of justice in Wales, the English and Welsh languages should be treated on the basis of equality.

1 GENERAL

1.1 This practice direction applies to civil proceedings in courts in Wales.

1.2 The existing practice of conducting a hearing entirely in the Welsh language on an ad hoc basis and without notice will continue to apply when all parties and witnesses directly involved at the time consent to the proceedings being so conducted.

1.3 In every case in which it is possible that the Welsh language may be used by any party or witness or in any document which may be placed before the court], the parties or their legal representatives must inform the court of that fact so that appropriate arrangements can be made for the management and listing of the case.

1.4 If costs are incurred as a result of a party failing to comply with this direction, a costs order may be made against him or his legal representative.

1.5 Where a case is tried with a jury, the law does not permit the selection of jurors in a manner which enables the court to discover whether a juror does or does not speak Welsh or to secure a jury whose members are bilingual to try a case in which the Welsh language may be used.

2 THE ALLOCATION QUESTIONNAIRE

2.1 In any proceedings in which a party is required to complete an allocation questionnaire, he must include details relating to the possible use of Welsh i.e. details of any person wishing to give oral evidence in Welsh and of any documents in Welsh (eg documents to be disclosed under Part 31 or witness statements) which that party expects to use.

2.2 A party must include the details mentioned in paragraph 2.1 in the allocation questionnaire even if he has already informed the court of the possible use of Welsh in accordance with the provisions of section 1 above.

3 CASE MANAGEMENT

3.1 At any interlocutory hearing, the court will take the opportunity to consider whether it should give case management directions. To assist the court, a party or his legal representative should draw the court's attention to the possibility of Welsh being used in the proceedings, even where he has already done so in compliance with other provisions of this direction.

3.2 In any case where a party is required to complete a pre-trial check list (listing questionnaire) and has already intimated the intention to use Welsh, he should confirm the intended use of Welsh in the pre-trial check list and provide any details which have not been set out in the allocation questionnaire.

4 LISTING BY THE COURT

4.1 The diary manager, in consultation with the designated civil judge, will ensure that a case in which the Welsh language is to be used is listed:

(a) wherever practicable before a Welsh speaking judge; and
(b) where translation facilities are needed, at a court with simultaneous translation facilities.

5 INTERPRETERS

5.1 Whenever an interpreter is needed to translate evidence from English to Welsh or from Welsh to English, the Court Manager in whose court the case is to be heard will take steps to secure the attendance of an interpreter whose name is included in the list of approved court interpreters.

6 WITNESSES AND JURORS

6.1 When each witness is called, the court officer administering the oath or affirmation will inform the witness that he or she may be sworn or may affirm in Welsh or English as he or she wishes.

6.2 Where a case is tried with a jury, the court officer swearing in the jury will inform the jurors in open court that each juror may take the oath or may affirm in Welsh or English as he or she wishes.

7 ROLE OF THE LIAISON JUDGE

7.1 If any question or difficulty arises concerning the implementation of this practice direction, contact should in the first place be made with the Liaison Judge for the Welsh language.

Guidance for the listing of civil cases—The following guidance has been issued by Mr Justice Thomas and Mr Justice Richards, Presiding Judges of the Wales and Chester Circuit with the approval of the Head of Civil Justice:

'Guidance for the listing of civil cases where the Welsh language is to be used and which originate from North Wales

The following guidance applies to all civil cases which, after allocation, are pending in the county courts or district registries of North Wales where arrangements may be made for trial at the Civil Justice Centre at Chester. The guidance is intended formally to implement existing practice.

1 In accordance with the policy set out in the Practice Direction relating to the use of the Welsh language, it is desirable that any case pending, after allocation, in the county courts or district registries of North Wales and involving evidence to be given in the Welsh language should, where practicable, be tried in Wales. If for any reason any such case (whether fast track or multi track or whether in the High Court or the county court) cannot be tried in Wales, then the case should be referred to the Designated Civil Judge for North Wales and Chester and to one of the presiding judges. No trial in that case should take place in a court outside Wales without the express consent of the Designated Civil Judge for North Wales and Chester and one of the presiding judges. The presiding judges should be provided with:

(1) detailed information about the case;
(2) the scope of the intended use of the Welsh language;
(3) information about the view of the parties about the trial and the use of the Welsh language;
(4) the name of the judge to hear the case.

Consent to the trial of a case outside Wales will be on the basis that it is heard by the judge specifically nominated for that case; no other judge should hear that case without further reference being made to one of the presiding judges.

2 No judge other than a judge designated on the list provided by the circuit administrator as approved to try cases in the Welsh language should try any case involving the use of the Welsh language, unless the consent of one of the presiding judges or the Liaison judge for the Welsh language has been specifically obtained.

3 This guidance takes immediate effect.'

SECTION 4

Protocols

SECTION 4: Protocols

Contents

Practice Direction – Protocols

GENERAL

1.1 This Practice Direction applies to the pre-action protocols which have been approved by the Head of Civil Justice.

1.2 The pre-action protocols which have been approved are set out in para 5.1. Other pre-action protocols may subsequently be added.

1.3 Pre-action protocols outline the steps parties should take to seek information from and to provide information to each other about a prospective legal claim.

1.4 The objectives of pre-action protocols are:

(1) to encourage the exchange of early and full information about the prospective legal claim;
(2) to enable parties to avoid litigation by agreeing a settlement of the claim before the commencement of proceedings;
(3) to support the efficient management of proceedings where litigation cannot be avoided.

Scope of provision—Whilst the practice direction says that it only applies in relation to the eight categories of cases where there are specific pre-action protocols (paras 1.1 and 5.1), it is also of more general application in relation to all other claims not covered by a specific pre-action protocol (see para 4.1).

COMPLIANCE WITH PROTOCOLS

2.1 The Civil Procedure Rules enable the court to take into account compliance or non-compliance with an applicable protocol when giving directions for the management of proceedings (see CPR rules 3.1(4) and (5) and 3.9(1)(e)) and when making orders for costs (see CPR rule 44.3(5)(a)).

2.2 The court will expect all parties to have complied in substance with the terms of an approved protocol.

2.3 If, in the opinion of the court, non-compliance has led to the commencement of proceedings which might otherwise not have needed to be commenced, or has led to costs being incurred in the proceedings that might otherwise not have been incurred, the orders the court may make include:

(1) an order that the party at fault pay the costs of the proceedings, or part of those costs, of the other party or parties;
(2) an order that the party at fault pay those costs on an indemnity basis;
(3) if the party at fault is a claimant in whose favour an order for the payment of damages or some specified sum is subsequently made, an order depriving that party of interest on such sum and in respect of such period as may be specified, and/or awarding interest at a lower rate than that at which interest would otherwise have been awarded;
(4) if the party at fault is a defendant and an order for the payment of damages or some specified sum is subsequently made in favour of the claimant, an order awarding interest on such sum and in respect of such period as may be specified at a higher rate, not exceeding 10% above base rate (cf. CPR rule 36.21(2)), than the rate at which interest would otherwise have been awarded.

2.4 The court will exercise its powers under paragraphs 2.1 and 2.3 with the object of placing the innocent party in no worse a position than he would have been in if the protocol had been complied with.

3.1 A claimant may be found to have failed to comply with a protocol by, for example:

(a) not having provided sufficient information to the defendant; or
(b) not having followed the procedure required by the protocol to be followed (e.g. not having followed the medical expert instruction procedure set out in the Personal Injury Protocol).

3.2 A defendant may be found to have failed to comply with a protocol by, for example:

(a) not making a preliminary response to the letter of claim within the time fixed for that purpose by the relevant protocol (21 days under the Personal Injury Protocol, 14 days under the Clinical Negligence Protocol);
(b) not making a full response within the time fixed for that purpose by the relevant protocol (3 months of the letter of claim under the Clinical Negligence Protocol, 3 months from the date of acknowledgment of the letter of claim under the Personal Injury Protocol),
(c) not disclosing documents required to be disclosed by the relevant protocol.

3.3 The court is likely to treat this practice direction as indicating the normal, reasonable way of dealing with disputes. If proceedings are issued and the parties have not complied with this practice direction or a specific protocol, it will be for the court to decide whether sanctions should be applied.

3.4 The court is not likely to be concerned with minor infringements of the practice direction or protocols. The court is likely to look at the effect of non-compliance on the other party when deciding whether to impose sanctions.

3.5 This practice direction does not alter the statutory limits for starting court proceedings. A claimant is required to start proceedings within those time limits and to adhere to subsequent time limits required by the rules or ordered by the court. If proceedings are for any reason started before the parties have followed the procedures in this practice direction, the parties are encouraged to agree to apply to the court for a stay of the proceedings while they follow the practice direction.

'the parties are encouraged to agree' (para 3.5)—In the absence of agreement between the parties the outcome is likely to be an application by the defendant for an extension of time for delivery of its defence with a claim for costs against the claimant.

PRE-ACTION BEHAVIOUR IN OTHER CASES

4.1 In cases not covered by any approved protocol, the court will expect the parties, in accordance with the overriding objective and the matters referred to in CPR 1.1(2)(a), (b) and (c), to act reasonably in exchanging information and documents relevant to the claim and generally in trying to avoid the necessity for the start of proceedings.

4.2 Parties to a potential dispute should follow a reasonable procedure, suitable to their particular circumstances, which is intended to avoid litigation. The procedure should not be regarded as a prelude to inevitable litigation. It should normally include –

(a) the claimant writing to give details of the claim;
(b) the defendant acknowledging the claim letter promptly;
(c) the defendant giving within a reasonable time a detailed written response; and
(d) the parties conducting genuine and reasonable negotiations with a view to settling the claim economically and without court proceedings.

4.3 The claimant's letter should –

(a) give sufficient concise details to enable the recipient to understand and investigate the claim without extensive further information;
(b) enclose copies of the essential documents which the claim relies on;
(c) ask for a prompt acknowledgment of the letter, followed by a full written response within a reasonable stated period;

(For many claims, a normal reasonable period for a full response may be 1 month)

(d) state whether court proceedings will be issued if the full response is not received within the stated period;
(e) identify and ask for copies of any essential documents, not in his possession, which the claimant wishes to see;
(f) state (if this is so) that the claimant wishes to enter into mediation or another alternative method of dispute resolution; and
(g) draw attention to the court's powers to impose sanctions for failure to comply with this practice direction and, if the recipient is likely to be unrepresented, enclose a copy of this practice direction.

4.4 The defendant should acknowledge the claimant's letter in writing within 21 days of receiving it. The acknowledgment should state when the defendant will give a full written response. If the time for this is longer than the period stated by the claimant, the defendant should give reasons why a longer period is needed.

4.5 The defendant's full written response should as appropriate –

(a) accept the claim in whole or in part and make proposals for settlement; or
(b) state that the claim is not accepted.

If the claim is accepted in part only, the response should make clear which part is accepted and which part is not accepted.

4.6 If the defendant does not accept the claim or part of it, the response should –

(a) give detailed reasons why the claim is not accepted, identifying which of the claimant's contentions are accepted and which are in dispute;
(b) enclose copies of the essential documents which the defendant relies on;
(c) enclose copies of documents asked for by the claimant, or explain why they are not enclosed;
(d) identify and ask for copies of any further essential documents, not in his possession, which the defendant wishes to see; and

(The claimant should provide these within a reasonably short time or explain in writing why he is not doing so)

(e) state whether the defendant is prepared to enter into mediation or another alternative method of dispute resolution.

4.7 If the claim remains in dispute, the parties should promptly engage in appropriate negotiations with a view to settling the dispute and avoiding litigation. The courts increasingly take the view that litigation should be a last resort, and that claims should not be issued prematurely when a settlement is still likely. Therefore, the parties should consider whether some form of alternative dispute resolution procedure would be more suitable than litigation, and if so, endeavour to agree which form to adopt. The Legal Services Commission has published a booklet on 'Alternatives to Court', CLS Direct information leaflet 23 (www.clsdirect.org.uk/legalhelp/leaflet23.jsp), which lists a number of organisations that provide alternative dispute resolution services.

The parties may be required by the Court to provide evidence that alternative means of dispute resolution were considered.

4.8 Documents disclosed by either party in accordance with this practice direction may not be used for any purpose other than resolving the dispute, unless the other party agrees.

4.9 The resolution of some claims, but by no means all, may need help from an expert. If an expert is needed, the parties should wherever possible and to save expense engage an agreed expert.

4.10 Parties should be aware that, if the matter proceeds to litigation, the court may not allow the use of an expert's report, and that the cost of it is not always recoverable.

'engage an agreed expert' (para 4.9)—For guidance generally on the instruction of a single joint expert, see rr 35.7 and 35.8.

'the court may not allow the use of an expert's report' (para 4.10)—No party may call an expert or put in evidence an expert's report without the court's permission (r 35.4).

[INFORMATION ABOUT FUNDING ARRANGEMENTS

4A.1 Where a person enters into a funding arrangement within the meaning of rule 43.2(1)(k) he should inform other potential parties to the claim that he has done so.

4A.2 Paragraph 4A.1 applies to all proceedings whether proceedings to which a pre-action protocol applies or otherwise.

(Rule 44.3B(1)(c) provides that a party may not recover any additional liability for any period in the proceedings during which he failed to provide information about a funding arrangement in accordance with a rule, practice direction or court order)

Scope of provision—This section would suggest that notification of a funding arrangement should be made at an early stage and not simply on the issue of proceedings.

COMMENCEMENT

5.1 The following table sets out the protocols currently in force, the date they came into force and their date of publication:

Protocol	Coming into force	Publication
Personal Injury	26 April 1999	January 1999
Clinical Negligence	26 April 1999	January 1999

Protocol	Coming into force	Publication
Construction and Engineering Disputes	2 October 2000	September 2000
Defamation	2 October 2000	September 2000
Professional Negligence	16 July 2001	May 2001
Judicial Review	4 March 2002	3 December 2001
Disease and Illness	8 December 2003	September 2003
Housing Disrepair	8 December 2003	September 2003

5.2 The court will take compliance or non-compliance with a relevant protocol into account where the claim was started after the coming into force of that protocol but will not do so where the claim was started before that date.

5.3 Parties in a claim started after a relevant protocol came into force, who have, by work done before that date, achieved the objectives sought to be achieved by certain requirements of that protocol, need not take any further steps to comply with those requirements. They will not be considered to have not complied with the protocol for the purposes of paragraphs 2 and 3.

5.4 Parties in a claim started after a relevant protocol came into force, who have not been able to comply with any particular requirements of that protocol because the period of time between the publication date and the date of coming into force was too short, will not be considered to have not complied with the protocol for the purposes of paragraphs 2 and 3.

Pre-Action Protocol for the Resolution of Clinical Disputes

CONTENTS

General note—This protocol represents a very significant step forward in this area of litigation. As noted in the introductory remarks it is the product of a collaborative effort by parties involved on both sides of the litigation equation. The protocol was designed to lay down minimum standards for co-operation between the parties. The intention is to keep the protocol under review. The first major review was conducted by the Clinical Disputes Forum during 2001 and it is expected that revisions will be published shortly. No major change is envisaged.

The protocol has been widely disseminated across all areas of clinical practice including NHS Trusts and private providers. Hence, all healthcare providers should have full knowledge of its scope and operation.

Executive Summary

1 The Clinical Disputes Forum is a multi-disciplinary body which was formed in 1997, as a result of Lord Woolf's 'Access to Justice' inquiry. One of the aims of the Forum is to find less adversarial and more cost effective ways of resolving disputes about healthcare and medical treatment. The names and addresses of the Chairman and Secretary of the Forum can be found at Annex E.

2 This protocol is the Forum's first major initiative. It has been drawn up carefully, including extensive consultations with most of the key stakeholders in the medico-legal system.

3 The protocol –

- encourages a climate of openness when something has 'gone wrong' with a patient's treatment or the patient is dissatisfied with that treatment and/or the outcome. This reflects the new and developing requirements for clinical governance within healthcare;
- provides **general guidance** on how this more open culture might be achieved when disputes arise;
- recommends **a timed sequence** of steps for patients and healthcare providers, and their advisers, to follow when a dispute arises. This should facilitate and speed up exchanging relevant information and increase the prospects that disputes can be resolved without resort to legal action.

4 This protocol has been prepared by a working party of the Clinical Disputes Forum. It has the support of the Lord Chancellor's Department, the Department of Health and NHS Executive, the Law Society, the Legal Aid Board and many other key organisations.

1 Why this Protocol?

MISTRUST IN HEALTHCARE DISPUTES

1.1 The number of complaints and claims against hospitals, GPs, dentists and private healthcare providers is growing as patients become more prepared to question the treatment they are given, to seek explanations of what happened, and to seek appropriate redress. Patients may require further treatment, an apology, assurances about future action or compensation. These trends are unlikely to change. The Patients' Charter encourages patients to have high expectations, and a revised NHS Complaints Procedure was implemented in 1996. The civil justice reforms and new Rules of Court should make litigation quicker, more user friendly and less expensive.

1.2 It is clearly in the interests of patients, healthcare professionals and providers that patients' concerns, complaints and claims arising from their treatment are resolved as quickly, efficiently and professionally as possible. A climate of mistrust and lack of openness can seriously damage the patient/ clinician relationship, unnecessarily prolong disputes (especially litigation), and reduce the resources available for treating patients. It may also cause additional work for, and lower the morale of, healthcare professionals.

1.3 At present there is often mistrust by both sides. This can mean that patients fail to raise their concerns with the healthcare provider as early as possible. Sometimes patients may pursue a complaint or claim which has little merit, due to a lack of sufficient information and understanding. It can also mean that patients become reluctant, once advice has been taken on a potential claim, to disclose sufficient information to enable the provider to investigate that claim efficiently and, where appropriate, resolve it.

1.4 On the side of the healthcare provider this mistrust can be shown in a reluctance to be honest with patients, a failure to provide prompt clear explanations, especially of adverse outcomes (whether or not there may have been negligence) and a tendency to 'close ranks' once a claim is made.

WHAT NEEDS TO CHANGE

1.5 If that mistrust is to be removed, and a more co-operative culture is to develop –

- healthcare professionals and providers need to adopt a constructive approach to complaints and claims. They should accept that concerned patients are entitled to an explanation and an apology, if warranted, and to appropriate redress in the event of negligence. An overly defensive approach is not in the long-term interest of their main goal: patient care;
- patients should recognise that unintended and/or unfortunate consequences of medical treatment can only be rectified if they are brought to the attention of the healthcare provider as soon as possible.

1.6 A protocol which sets out 'ground rules' for the handling of disputes at their early stages should, if it is to be subscribed to, and followed –

- encourage greater openness between the parties;
- encourage parties to find the most appropriate way of resolving the particular dispute;
- reduce delay and costs;
- reduce the need for litigation.

WHY THIS PROTOCOL NOW?

1.7 Lord Woolf in his Access to Justice Report in July 1996, concluded that major causes of costs and delay in medical negligence litigation occur at the pre-action stage. He recommended that patients and their advisers, and healthcare providers, should work more closely together to try to resolve disputes co-operatively, rather than proceed to litigation. He specifically recommended a pre-action protocol for medical negligence cases.

1.8 A fuller summary of Lord Woolf's recommendations is at Annex D.

WHERE THE PROTOCOL FITS IN

1.9 Protocols serve the needs of litigation and pre-litigation practice, especially –

- predictability in the time needed for steps pre-proceedings;
- standardisation of relevant information, including records and documents to be disclosed.

1.10 Building upon Lord Woolf's recommendations, the Lord Chancellor's Department is now promoting the adoption of protocols in specific areas, including medical negligence.

1.11 It is recognised that contexts differ significantly. For example, patients tend to have an ongoing relationship with a GP, more so than with a hospital; clinical staff in the National Health Service are often employees, while those in the private sector may be contractors; providing records quickly may be relatively easy for GPs and dentists, but can be a complicated procedure in a large multi-department hospital. The protocol which follows is intended to be sufficiently broadly based, and flexible, to apply to all aspects of the health service: primary and secondary; public and private sectors.

ENFORCEMENT OF THE PROTOCOL AND SANCTIONS

1.12 The civil justice reforms will be implemented in April 1999. One new set of Court Rules and procedures is replacing the existing rules for both the High Court and county courts. This and the personal injury protocol are being published with the Rules, Practice Directions and key court forms. The courts will be able to treat the standards set in protocols as the normal reasonable approach to pre-action conduct.

1.13 If proceedings are issued it will be for the court to decide whether non-compliance with a protocol should merit sanctions. Guidance on the court's likely approach will be given from time to time in practice directions.

1.14 If the court has to consider the question of compliance after proceedings have begun it will not be concerned with minor infringements, eg failure by a short period to provide relevant information. One minor breach will not entitle the 'innocent' party to abandon following the protocol. The court will look at the effect of non-compliance on the other party when deciding whether to impose sanctions.

2 The Aims of the Protocol

2.1 The ***general*** aims of the protocol are –

- to maintain/restore the patient/healthcare provider relationship;
- to resolve as many disputes as possible without litigation.

2.2 The ***specific*** objectives are –

OPENNESS

- to encourage early communication of the perceived problem between patients and healthcare providers;
- to encourage patients to voice any concerns or dissatisfaction with their treatment as soon as practicable;
- to encourage healthcare providers to develop systems of early reporting and investigation for serious adverse treatment outcomes and to provide full and prompt explanations to dissatisfied patients;
- to ensure that sufficient information is disclosed by both parties to enable each to understand the other's perspective and case, and to encourage early resolution;

TIMELINESS

- to provide an early opportunity for healthcare providers to identify cases where an investigation is required and to carry out that investigation promptly;
- to encourage primary and private healthcare providers to involve their defence organisations or insurers at an early stage;
- to ensure that all relevant medical records are provided to patients or their appointed representatives on request, to a realistic timetable by any healthcare provider.
- to ensure that relevant records which are not in healthcare providers' possession are made available to them by patients and their advisers at an appropriate stage;
- where a resolution is not achievable to lay the ground to enable litigation to proceed on a reasonable timetable, at a reasonable and proportionate cost and to limit the matters in contention;
- to discourage the prolonged pursuit of unmeritorious claims and the prolonged defence of meritorious claims.

AWARENESS OF OPTIONS

- To ensure that patients and healthcare providers are made aware of the available options to pursue and resolve disputes and what each might involve.

2.3 This protocol does not attempt to be prescriptive about a number of related clinical governance issues which will have a bearing on healthcare providers' ability to meet the standards within the protocol. Good clinical governance requires the following to be considered –

(a) **Clinical risk management:** the protocol does not provide any detailed guidance to healthcare providers on clinical risk management or the adoption of risk management systems and procedures. This must be a matter for the NHS Executive, the National Health Service Litigation Authority, individual trusts and providers, including GPs, dentists and the private sector. However, effective co-ordinated, focused clinical risk management strategies and procedures can help in managing risk and in the early identification and investigation of adverse outcomes.

(b) **Adverse outcome reporting:** the protocol does not provide any detailed guidance on which adverse outcomes should trigger an investigation. However, healthcare providers should have in place procedures for such investigations, including recording of statements of key witnesses. These procedures should also cover when and how to inform patients that an adverse outcome has occurred.

(c) **The professional's duty to report:** the protocol does not recommend changes to the codes of conduct of professionals in healthcare, or attempt to impose a specific duty on those professionals to report known adverse outcomes or untoward incidents. Lord Woolf in his final report suggested that the professional bodies might consider this. The General Medical Council is preparing guidance to doctors about their duty to report adverse incidents and to co-operate with inquiries.

3 The Protocol

3.1 This protocol is not a comprehensive code governing all the steps in clinical disputes. Rather it attempts to set out **a code of good practice** which parties should follow when litigation might be a possibility.

3.2 The **commitments** section of the protocol summarises the guiding principles which healthcare providers and patients and their advisers are invited to endorse when dealing with patient dissatisfaction with treatment and its outcome, and with potential complaints and claims.

3.3 The **steps** section sets out in a more prescriptive form, a recommended sequence of actions to be followed if litigation is a prospect.

GOOD PRACTICE COMMITMENTS

3.4 **Healthcare providers** should –

(i) ensure that **key staff**, including claims and litigation managers, are appropriately trained and have some knowledge of healthcare law, and of complaints procedures and civil litigation practice and procedure;

(ii) develop an approach to **clinical governance** that ensures that clinical practice is delivered to commonly accepted standards and that this is routinely monitored through a system of clinical audit and clinical risk management (particularly adverse outcome investigation);

(iii) set up **adverse outcome reporting systems** in all specialties to record and investigate unexpected serious adverse outcomes as soon as possible. Such systems can enable evidence to be gathered quickly, which makes it easier to provide an accurate explanation of what happened and to defend or settle any subsequent claims;

(iv) use the results of **adverse incidents and complaints positively** as a guide to how to improve services to patients in the future;

(v) ensure **that patients receive clear and comprehensible information** in an accessible form about how to raise their concerns or complaints;

(vi) establish **efficient and effective systems of recording and storing patient records**, notes, diagnostic reports and X-rays, and to retain these in accordance with Department of Health guidance (currently for a minimum of eight years in the case of adults, and all obstetric and paediatric notes for children until they reach the age of 25);

(vii) **advise patients** of a serious adverse outcome and provide on request to the patient or the patient's representative an oral or written explanation of what happened, information on further steps open to the patient, including where appropriate an offer of future treatment to rectify the problem, an apology, changes in procedure which will benefit patients and/or compensation.

3.5 **Patients and their advisers should** –

(i) **report any concerns and dissatisfaction** to the healthcare provider as soon as is reasonable to enable that provider to offer clinical advice where possible, to advise the patient if anything has gone wrong and take appropriate action;

(ii) consider the **full range of options** available following an adverse outcome with which a patient is dissatisfied, including a request for an explanation, a meeting, a complaint, and other appropriate dispute resolution methods (including mediation) and negotiation, not only litigation;

(iii) **inform the healthcare provider when the patient is satisfied** that the matter has been concluded: legal advisers should notify the provider when they are no longer acting for the patient, particularly if proceedings have not started.

PROTOCOL STEPS

3.6 The steps of this protocol which follow have been kept deliberately simple. An illustration of the likely sequence of events in a number of healthcare situations is at Annex A.

OBTAINING THE HEALTH RECORDS

3.7 Any request for records by the **patient** or their adviser should –

- **provide sufficient information** to alert the healthcare provider where an adverse outcome has been serious or had serious consequences;
- be as **specific as possible** about the records which are required.

3.8 Requests for copies of the patient's clinical records should be made using the Law Society and Department of Health approved **standard forms** (enclosed at Annex B), adapted as necessary.

3.9 The copy records should be provided **within 40 days** of the request and for a cost not exceeding the charges permissible under the Access to Health Records Act 1990 (currently a maximum of £10 plus photocopying and postage).

3.10 In the rare circumstances that the healthcare provider is in difficulty in complying with the request within 40 days, the **problem should be explained** quickly and details given of what is being done to resolve it.

3.11 It will not be practicable for healthcare providers to investigate in detail each case when records are requested. But healthcare providers should **adopt a policy on which cases will be investigated** (see paragraph 3.5 on clinical governance and adverse outcome reporting).

3.12 If the healthcare provider fails to provide the health records within 40 days, the patient or their adviser can then apply to the court for an **order for pre-action disclosure**. The new Civil Procedure Rules should make pre-action applications to the court easier. The court will also have the power to impose costs sanctions for unreasonable delay in providing records.

3.13 If either the patient or the healthcare provider considers **additional health records are required from a third party**, in the first instance these should be requested by or through the patient. Third party healthcare providers are expected to co-operate. The Civil Procedure Rules will enable patients and healthcare providers to apply to the court for pre-action disclosure by third parties.

General note—The disclosure of records envisaged by the protocol is not intended to be restricted to those records discloseable under Access to Health Records Act 1990, Data Protection Act 1998, Supreme Court Act 1981, ss 33, 34 and County Courts Act 1984, ss 52, 53. Instead the protocol envisages that both an intended party to proceedings and a non party should, upon proper request as outlined above, provide copies of all records relevant to the case. 'Records' has a wide interpretation and will include all clinical documents, scans, test results and correspondence.

The intention is that the parties should have available all documentation necessary to enable a detailed investigation of the case.

'within 40 days' (paras 3.9 and 3.12)—This time-limit was deemed reasonable to permit a healthcare provider to assemble and copy the relevant records. In general terms, no application to court under CPR r 31.16 should be made within this time-limit. Consistent with the overriding objective flexibility maybe required; for example, in the context of a case where the limitation period is due to expire imminently, a shortened time scale maybe appropriate, or in a case where access to records is difficult because of ongoing treatment, more time may be necessary.

Access to Health Records Act 1990—This legislation has now been repealed except for sections dealing with requests for access to records relating to a deceased person. Requests for access to records of deceased persons will continue to be made under that Act but requests for access to health records relating to living individuals will now fall within the scope of the Data Protection Act 1998. This Act was implemented on 1 March 2000 and governs both manual and automated records.

Data Protection Act 1998—A guidance note on the operation of the Act was issued by the Office of the Data Protection Commissioner in August 2000 and provides helpful information on the applicability of the legislation to the subject of access to health records. It is important to note that the Data Protection Act 1998 defines a 'health record' as being any record which consists of information relating to the physical or mental health or condition of an individual and has been made by or on behalf of a health professional in connection with the care of that individual. The guidance note makes clear that this definition has a wide interpretation and will, for example, include radiographic material.

Cost—This has been a vexed issue in the past with wide discrepancies around the country. The protocol intended that a reasonable limit should be imposed in line with the charging structure thus described in the Access to Health Records Act 1990. The position has been significantly clarified by the Data Protection Act 1998 and is as follows:

(a) A maximum fee of £10 for granting access to health records which are automatically processed or are recorded with the intention that they be so processed.
(b) A maximum fee of £50 for granting access to manual records, or a mixture of manual and automated records. This fee will only be charged in respect of any request made before 24 October 2001. After that date the maximum fee will reduce to £10.
(c) There is no provision for there to be any separate or additional charge for copying or postage.
(d) There is no charge for allowing an individual to inspect records, where the request relates to recently created records – ie where at least some of the records were made within the period of 40 days prior to the date of request (thus replicating the previous provision of the Access to Health Records Act 1990).
(e) Note the position regarding records of a deceased person remains governed by the Access to Health Records Act 1990.

This statutory regulation of charging now provides consistency and will eliminate, for example, the variation of charges being requested by general practitioners.

Health records from a third party (para 3.13)—Whilst CPR r 31.16 limits disclosure before proceedings start to documents from those respondents likely to be a party to proceedings, the protocol is wider and requires third party disclosure. This may be highly relevant in clinical negligence cases to help determine issues such as causation. Hence, note the requirement for third party co-operation. Two points arise:

(a) query whether the wide power of CPR r 31.18 may be applied to support the protocol intent and, thus, in the event of non co-operation by a third party, permit a pre-action application to court; or
(b) in the alternative, if a post commencement of proceedings application for third party disclosure is made, that third party may bear a costs penalty for failure to co-operate with a protocol request.

LETTER OF CLAIM

3.14 Annex C1 to this protocol provides **a template for the recommended contents of a letter of claim**: the level of detail will need to be varied to suit the particular circumstances.

3.15 If, following the receipt and analysis of the records, and the receipt of any further advice (including from experts if necessary – see Section 4), the patient/adviser decides that there are grounds for a claim, they should then send, as soon as practicable, to the healthcare provider/potential defendant, a **letter of claim**.

3.16 This letter should contain a **clear summary of the facts** on which the claim is based, including the alleged adverse outcome, and the **main allegations**

of negligence. It should also describe the **patient's injuries**, and present condition and prognosis. The **financial loss** incurred by the plaintiff should be outlined with an indication of the heads of damage to be claimed and the scale of the loss, unless this is impracticable.

3.17 In more complex cases a **chronology** of the relevant events should be provided, particularly if the patient has been treated by a number of different healthcare providers.

3.18 The letter of claim **should refer to any relevant documents**, including health records, and if possible enclose copies of any of those which will not already be in the potential defendant's possession, eg any relevant general practitioner records if the plaintiff's claim is against a hospital.

3.19 **Sufficient information** must be given to enable the healthcare provider defendant to **commence investigations** and to put an initial valuation on the claim.

3.20 Letters of claim are **not** intended to have the same formal status as a **pleading**, nor should any sanctions necessarily apply if the letter of claim and any subsequent statement of claim in the proceedings differ.

3.21 **Proceedings should not be issued until after three months from the letter of claim**, unless there is a limitation problem and/or the patient's position needs to be protected by early issue.

3.22 The patient or their adviser may want to make an **offer to settle** the claim at this early stage by putting forward an amount of compensation which would be satisfactory (possibly including any costs incurred to date). If an offer to settle is made, generally this should be supported by a medical report which deals with the injuries, condition and prognosis, and by a schedule of loss and supporting documentation. The level of detail necessary will depend on the value of the claim. Medical reports may not be necessary where there is no significant continuing injury, and a detailed schedule may not be necessary in a low value case. The Civil Procedure Rules are expected to set out the legal and procedural requirements for making offers to settle.

Recommended contents (para 3.19)—Note paras 3.14 and 3.16 which should be read in the context of para 3.19. The level of detail to be provided will vary depending upon the complexity of the case. The protocol is not intended to be overly prescriptive; disclosure of a report on condition and prognosis is not mandated; a comprehensive schedule of financial loss is not required (in a smaller case an analysis of the financial losses maybe appropriate; in a major injury case, which will require expert analysis of quantum issues, a summary of the main heads of claim maybe sufficient). The intention is not to create a welter of case law interpreting whether a letter of claim is protocol compliant but rather to instill a sensible level of exchange of information consistent with the overall aim of the protocol.

Since the Pre-Action Protocol for the Resolution of Clinical Disputes was produced the Access to Justice Act 1999 has come into force and further extended the role of conditional fee agreements. Consequently, PDProt was amended on 3 July 2000 and paras 4A.1 and 4A.2 were added. These paragraphs imply that notification of a funding arrangement should be given during the protocol. This may mean that it would be appropriate to include details (in the letter of claim if applicable).

'not intended to have . . . formal status' (para 3.20)—This is important. The letter of claim is intended to provide adequate information to enable a respondent to understand, in general terms, the nature of the case it has to meet. It is recognised that after the submission of that letter the claimant's position may vary, for example, because of the impact of the letter of response, receipt of further information or expert advice. Hence, whilst sanctions are not expressly ruled out by para 3.20, it is intended that they should be applied only in the most appropriate of cases.

'three months' (para 3.21)—This period is intended to dovetail with the time for response – see below. It is recognised that, for example, limitation difficulties may require earlier issue. Where this arises, then consistent with both the aim of the protocol and the overriding objective, flexibility will be required so that, for example, it maybe appropriate to extend the time for delivery of full particulars of claim until after the response letter has been received; a stay may be sensible to permit the sending of a response letter and to enable the parties to discuss the case.

'offer to settle' (para 3.22)—This provision is intended to dovetail with Pt 36. Note that in the context of a clinical negligence case, a claimant wishing to make an offer before proceedings have been commenced should generally provide information in support of quantum, eg a report on condition and prognosis.

THE RESPONSE

3.23 Attached at Annex C2 is a template for the suggested contents of the **letter of response**.

3.24 The healthcare provider should **acknowledge** the letter of claim **within 14 days of receipt** and should identify who will be dealing with the matter.

3.25 The healthcare provider should, **within three months** of the letter of claim, provide a **reasoned answer –**

- if the **claim is admitted** the healthcare provider should say so in clear terms;
- if only **part of the claim is admitted** the healthcare provider should make clear which issues of breach of duty and/or causation are admitted and which are denied and why;
- it is intended that any **admissions will be binding**;
- if the claim is denied, this should include specific comments on the allegations of negligence, and if a synopsis or chronology of relevant events has been provided and is disputed, the healthcare provider's version of those events;
- where additional documents are relied upon, eg an internal protocol, copies should be provided.

3.26 If the patient has made an offer to settle, the healthcare provider should **respond to that offer** in the response letter, preferably with reasons. The provider may make its own offer to settle at this stage, either as a counter-offer to the patient's, or of its own accord, but should accompany any offer by any supporting medical evidence, and/or by any other evidence in relation to the value of the claim which is in the healthcare provider's possession.

3.27 If the parties reach agreement on liability, but time is needed to resolve the value of the claim, they should aim to agree a reasonable period.

'letter of response' (para 3.23)—The response should reciprocate the intention of the letter of claim and thus provide a detailed answer to the claim sufficient to enable the patient/patient's adviser to understand the position. A bare denial is unacceptable. Hence, note the detail required by para 3.25 and envisaged by the template letter at App C2.

'within three months' (para 3.25)—Several points arise:

(a) This time-limit starts to run from the date of receipt of the letter of claim. Thus, the 14 day period for acknowledgement of receipt falls within the 3 months.

(b) Anecdotal evidence suggests some difficulty is being encountered in responding within this period. This will be considered when the protocol is reviewed but note that –

  (i) 3 months was felt by all on the CDF to be a reasonable period – it balances the patient's desire for a speedy response against the healthcare provider's need for time to investigate and consult with those involved.

  (ii) Consistent with the Good Practice Commitments, a healthcare provider is expected pro-actively to identify adverse outcomes, report them and tell the patient. Hence, there may well be and possibly should be a level of awareness before even the request for records is received.

  (iii) The receipt of the request for records should alert as to the possibility of a claim and possibly prompt investigation.

(iv) There may well be knowledge of the position because of an internal investigation or pursuit of a formal complaint, eg under the NHS complaints system.

'admissions will be binding' (para 3.25)—This is a fundamental point. It is not intended that there should be any facility to resile from an admission. This contrasts with CPR r 14.1(5) (the facility given there is not intended to apply in the protocol situation). An admission made under the protocol will be binding when proceedings are later commenced.

This issue does not appear to have been tested in a clinical negligence case but note, by way of example, that in a personal injury case (*Hackman v Hounslow LBC* (2000) Current Law, October) the circuit judge considered whether a party could resile from an admission. The judge noted that the CPR were intended to make litigation more certain. Though CPR r 14.1(5) gives the court power to permit a party to withdraw from an admission, the burden rests on the party applying. The judge was influenced by the fact that the pre-action protocol (personal injury) indicated that admissions were expected to hold good.

'respond to that offer' (para 3.26)—Note the requirement to respond to an offer to settle in this situation (not something required by Pt 36) and note the obligation, if making a counter offer, to provide documentation in support.

4 Experts

General note—The protocol deliberately does not prescribe any procedures with regard to the use of experts in contradistinction to the Pre-Action Protocol for Personal Injury Claims. It was recognised that clinical negligence litigation involved special or unusual areas of difficulty and that, particularly on issues of breach of duty and causation, each party should be able to access experts of their own choosing. Consistent with this approach, there is no requirement to identify experts to be instructed in advance to the other side and no need to tender names.

4.1 In clinical negligence disputes **expert opinions** may be needed –

- on breach of duty and causation;
- on the patient's condition and prognosis;
- to assist in valuing aspects of the claim.

4.2 The civil justice reforms and the new **Civil Procedure Rules** will encourage economy in the use of experts and a **less adversarial expert culture**. It is recognised that in clinical negligence disputes, the parties and their advisers will require flexibility in their approach to expert evidence. Decisions on whether experts might be instructed jointly, and on whether reports might be disclosed sequentially or by exchange, should rest with the parties and their advisers. Sharing expert evidence may be appropriate on issues relating to the value of the claim. However, this protocol does not attempt to be prescriptive on issues in relation to expert evidence.

4.3 Obtaining expert evidence will often be an expensive step and may take time, especially in specialised areas of medicine where there are limited numbers of suitable experts. Patients and healthcare providers, and their advisers, will therefore need to consider carefully how best to obtain any necessary expert help quickly and cost-effectively. Assistance with locating a suitable expert is available from a number of sources.

Use of experts (para 4.2)—In *Oxley v Penwarden* (2000) (unreported) 21 July, CA the judge at first instance felt there was apparently a conflict between para 4.2 of the protocol and CPR r 35.7(1). The latter gives power to the court to direct that evidence on a particular issue be given by just one expert. The judge saw no reason to treat a clinical negligence claim differently from any other claim and imposed an order for a single expert to be used on the issue of causation. The case went to the Court of Appeal who allowed the appeal and restored an original order permitting each side to use its own expert. The court made clear there was no presumption in favour of a single joint expert. Mantell LJ felt this was eminently a case for each side to have its own expert evidence.

Note also the decision of the Court of Appeal in *Peet v Mid-Kent Healthcare NHS Trust* [2001] All ER (D) 58 in which their Lordships (notably including Lord Woolf) endorsed the use of single joint experts and the exercise of the courts powers under CPR r 35.7. The decision was in the context of the use of single joint experts on quantum issues and matters of access to such experts.

5 Alternative Approaches to Settling Disputes

5.1 It would not be practicable for this protocol to address in any detail how a patient or their adviser, or healthcare provider, might decide which method to adopt to resolve the particular problem. But, the courts increasingly expect parties to try to settle their differences by agreement before issuing proceedings.

5.2 Most disputes are resolved by **discussion and negotiation**. Parties should bear in mind that carefully planned face-to-face meetings may be particularly helpful in exploring further treatment for the patient, in reaching understandings about what happened, and on both parties' positions, in narrowing the issues in dispute and, if the timing is right, in helping to settle the whole matter.

5.3 Summarised below are some other alternatives for resolving disputes –

- The revised NHS Complaints Procedure, which was implemented in April 1996, is designed to provide patients with an explanation of what happened and an apology if appropriate. It is not designed to provide compensation for cases of negligence. However, patients might choose to use the procedure if their only, or main, goal is to obtain an explanation, or to obtain more information to help them decide what other action might be appropriate.
- Mediation may be appropriate in some cases: this is a form of facilitated negotiation assisted by an independent neutral party. It is expected that the new Civil Procedure Rules will give the court the power to stay proceedings for one month for settlement discussions or mediation.
- Other methods of resolving disputes include arbitration, determination by an expert, and early neutral evaluation by a medical or legal expert. The Legal Services Commission has published a booklet on **'Alternatives to Court', LSC August 2001, CLS information leaflet number 23, which lists a number of organisations that provide alternative dispute resolution services.**

Annex A
Illustrative Flowchart

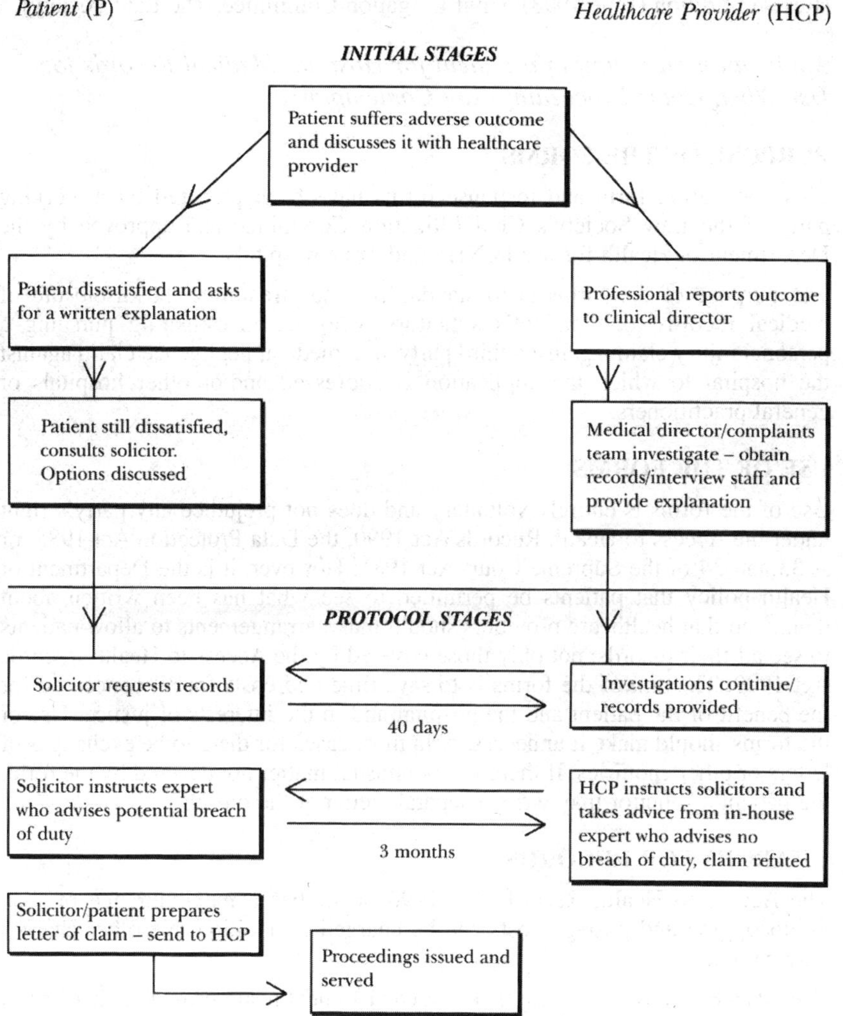

Annex B
Protocol for Obtaining Hospital Medical Records

(Revised Edition (June 1998); Civil Litigation Committee, The Law Society)

Application on Behalf of a Patient for Hospital Medical Records for Use When Court Proceedings are Contemplated

PURPOSE OF THE FORMS

This application form and response forms have been prepared by a working party of the Law Society's Civil Litigation Committee and approved by the Department of Health for use in NHS and Trust hospitals.

The purpose of the forms is to standardise and streamline the disclosure of medical records to a patient's solicitors, who are investigating pursuing a personal injury claim against a third party, or a medical negligence claim against the hospital to which the application is addressed and/or other hospitals or general practitioners.

USE OF THE FORMS

Use of the forms is entirely voluntary and does not prejudice any party's right under the Access to Health Records Act 1990, the Data Protection Act 1984, or ss 33 and 34 of the Supreme Court Act 1981. However, it is the Department of Health policy that patients be permitted to see what has been written about them, and that healthcare providers should make arrangements to allow patients to see all their records, not only those covered by the Access to Health Records Act 1990. The aim of the forms is to save time and costs for all concerned for the benefit of the patient and the hospital and in the interests of justice. Use of the forms should make it unnecessary in most cases for there to be exchanges of letters or other enquiries. If there is any unusual matter not covered by the form, the patient's solicitor may write a separate letter at the outset.

CHARGES FOR RECORDS

The Access to Health Records Act 1990 prescribes a maximum fee of £10. Photocopying and postage costs can be charged in addition. No other charges may be made.

The NHS Executive guidance makes it clear to healthcare providers that 'it is a perfectly proper use' of the 1990 Act to request records in that framework for the purpose of potential or actual litigation, whether against a third party or against the hospital or trust.

The 1990 Act does not permit differential rates of charges to be levied if the application is made by the patient, or by a solicitor on his or her behalf, or whether the response to the application is made by the healthcare provider directly (the medical records manager or a claims manager) or by a solicitor.

The NHS Executive guidance recommends that the same practice should be followed with regard to charges when the records are provided under a voluntary agreement as under the 1990 Act, except that in those circumstances the £10 access fee will not be appropriate.

The NHS Executive also advises –

- that the cost of photocopying may include 'the cost of staff time in making copies' and the costs of running the copier (but not costs of locating and sifting records);
- that the common practice of setting a standard rate for an application or charging an administration fee is not acceptable because there will be cases when this fails to comply with the 1990 Act.

RECORDS: WHAT MIGHT BE INCLUDED

X-rays and test results form part of the patient's records. Additional charges for copying X-rays are permissible. If there are large numbers of X-rays, the records officer should check with the patient/solicitor before arranging copying.

Reports on an 'adverse incident' and reports on the patient made for risk management and audit purposes may form part of the records and be discloseable: the exception will be any specific record or report made solely or mainly in connection with an actual or potential claim.

RECORDS: QUALITY STANDARDS

When copying records healthcare providers should ensure –

1 All documents are legible, and complete, if necessary by photocopying at less than 100% size.
2 Documents larger than A4 in the original, eg ITU charts, should be reproduced in A3, or reduced to A4 where this retains readability.
3 Documents are only copied on one side of paper, unless the original is two sided.
4 Documents should not be unnecessarily shuffled or bound and holes should not be made in the copied papers.

ENQUIRIES/FURTHER INFORMATION

Any enquiries about the forms should be made initially to the solicitors making the request. Comments on the use and content of the forms should be made to the Secretary, Civil Litigation Committee, The Law Society, 113 Chancery Lane, London WC2A 1PL, telephone 0171 320 5739, or to the NHS Management Executive, Quarry House, Quarry Hill, Leeds LS2 7UE.

The Law Society

May 1998

Application on Behalf of a Patient for Hospital Medical Records for Use when Court Proceedings are Contemplated

This should be completed as fully as possible

Insert Hospital Name and Address	TO: Medical Records Officer Hospital	
1 (a)	Full name of patient (including previous surnames)	
(b)	Address now	
(c)	Address at start of treatment	
(d)	Date of birth (and death, if applicable)	
(e)	Hospital ref no if available	
(f)	N.I. number, if available	
2	This application is made because the patient is considering	
(a)	a claim against your hospital as detailed in para 7 overleaf	YES/NO
(b)	pursuing an action against some one else	YES/NO
3	Department(s) where treatment was received	
4	Name(s) of consultant(s) at your hospital in charge of the treatment	

5	Whether treatment at your hospital was private or NHS, wholly or in part	
6	A description of the treatment received, with approximate dates	
7	If the answer to Q2(a) is 'Yes' details of	
	(a) the likely nature of the claim,	
	(b) grounds for the claim,	
	(c) approximate dates of the events involved	
8	If the answer to Q2(b) is 'Yes' insert	
	(a) the names of the proposed defendants	
	(b) whether legal proceedings yet begun	YES/NO
	(c) if appropriate, details of the claim and action number	
9	We confirm we will pay reasonable copying charges	
10	We request prior details of (a) photocopying and administration charges for medical records	YES/NO
	(b) number of and cost of copying x-ray and scan films	YES/NO

11	Any other relevant information, particular requirements, or any particular documents not required (eg copies of computerised records)	
	Signature of Solicitor	
	Name	
	Address	
	Ref.	
	Telephone number	
	Fax number	

Signature of patient Signature of parent or next friend if appropriate	*Please print name beneath each signature.* *Signature by child over 12 but under 18 years also requires signature by parent*
Signature of personal representative where patient has died	

First Response to Application for Hospital Records

NAME OF PATIENT Our ref Your ref		
1	Date of receipt of patient's application	
2	We intend that copy medical records will be dispatched within 6 weeks of that date	YES/NO
3	We require pre-payment of photocopying charges	YES/NO
4	If estimate of photocopying charges requested or pre-payment required the amount will be	£ / notified to you
5	The cost of x-ray and scan films will be	£ / notified to you
6	If there is any problem, we shall write to you within those 6 weeks	YES/NO
7	Any other information	
	Please address further correspondence to	
	Signed	
	Direct telephone number	
	Direct fax number	
	Dated	

Second Response Enclosing Patient's Hospital Medical Records

Address		Our Ref Your Ref
1	**NAME OF PATIENT**: We confirm that the enclosed copy medical records are all those within the control of the hospital, relevant to the application which you have made to the best of our knowledge and belief, subject to paras 2–5 below	YES/NO
2	Details of any other documents which have not yet been located	
3	Date by when it is expected that these will be supplied	
4	Details of any records which we are not producing	
5	The reasons for not doing so	
6	An invoice for copying and administration charges is attached	YES/NO
	Signed	
	Date	

Annex C
Templates for Letters of Claim and Response

C1 LETTER OF CLAIM

Essential Contents

1 **Client's name, address, date of birth, etc**

2 **Dates of allegedly negligent treatment**

3 **Events giving rise to the claim:**

- an outline of what happened, including details of other relevant treatments to the client by other healthcare providers.

4 **Allegation of negligence and causal link with injuries:**

- an outline of the allegations or a more detailed list in a complex case;

- an outline of the causal link between allegations and the injuries complained of.

5 **The client's injuries, condition and future prognosis**

6 **Request for clinical records (if not previously provided)**
- use the Law Society form if appropriate or adapt;
- specify the records required;
- if other records are held by other providers, and may be relevant, say so;
- State what investigations have been carried out to date, eg information from client and witnesses, any complaint and the outcome, if any clinical records have been seen or expert's advice obtained.

7 **The likely value of the claim**
- an outline of the main heads of damage, or, in straightforward cases, the details of loss.

Optional Information

What investigations have been carried out
An offer to settle without supporting evidence
Suggestions for obtaining expert evidence
Suggestions for meetings, negotiations, discussion or mediation

Possible Enclosures

Chronology
Clinical records request form and client's authorisation
Expert report(s)
Schedules of loss and supporting evidence

C2 LETTER OF RESPONSE

Essential Contents

1 Provide **requested records** and invoice for copying:
- explain if records are incomplete or extensive records are held and ask for further instructions;
- request additional records from third parties.

2 **Comments on events and/or chronology**:
- if events are disputed or the healthcare provider has further information or documents on which they wish to rely, these should be provided, eg internal protocol;
- details of any further information needed from the patient or a third party should be provided.

3 **If breach of duty and causation are accepted**:
- suggestions might be made for resolving the claim and/or requests for further information;
- a response should be made to any offer to settle.

4 **If breach of duty and/or causation are denied:**
- a bare denial will not be sufficient. If the healthcare provider has other explanations for what happened, these should be given at least in outline;

- suggestions might be made for the next steps, eg further investigations, obtaining expert evidence, meetings/negotiations or mediation, or an invitation to issue proceedings.

Optional Matters

An offer to settle if the patient has not made one, or a counter offer to the patient's with supporting evidence

Possible Enclosures

Clinical records
Annotated chronology
Expert reports

Annex D
Lord Woolf's Recommendations

1 Lord Woolf in his Access to Justice Report in July 1996, following a detailed review of the problems of medical negligence claims, identified that one of the major sources of **costs and delay** is **at the pre-litigation stage** because –

(a) Inadequate incident reporting and record keeping in hospitals, and mobility of staff, make it difficult to establish facts, often several years after the event.
(b) Claimants must incur the cost of an expert in order to establish whether they have a viable claim.
(c) There is often a long delay before a claim is made.
(d) Defendants do not have sufficient resources to carry out a full investigation of every incident, and do not consider it worthwhile to start an investigation as soon as they receive a request for records, because many cases do not proceed beyond that stage.
(e) Patients often give the defendant little or no notice of a firm intention to pursue a claim. Consequently, many incidents are not investigated by the defendants until after proceedings have started.
(f) Doctors and other clinical staff are traditionally reluctant to admit negligence or apologise to, or negotiate with, claimants for fear of damage to their professional reputations or career prospects.

2 Lord Woolf acknowledged that under the present arrangements **healthcare providers**, faced with possible medical negligence claims, have a number of **practical problems** to contend with –

(a) Difficulties of finding patients' records and tracing former staff, which can be exacerbated by late notification and by the health-care provider's own failure to identify adverse incidents.
(b) The healthcare provider may have only treated the patient for a limited time or for a specific complaint: the patient's previous history may be relevant but the records may be in the possession of one of several other healthcare providers.
(c) The large number of potential claims do not proceed beyond the stage of a request for medical records, or an explanation; and that it is difficult for healthcare providers to investigate fully every case whenever a patient asks to see the records.

Annex E
How to Contact the Forum

The Clinical Disputes Forum

Chairman
Dr Alastair Scotland
Medical Director and Chief Officer
National Clinical Assessment Authority
9th Floor, Market Towers
London
SW8 5NQ — Telephone: 0207 273 0850

Secretary
Sarah Leigh
c/o Margaret Dangoor
3 Clydesdale Gardens
Richmond
Surrey
TW10 5EG — Telephone: 0208 408 1012

Pre-Action Protocol for Personal Injury Claims

CONTENTS

1 Introduction

1.1 Lord Woolf in his final Access to Justice Report of July 1996 recommended the development of pre-action protocols:

> 'To build on and increase the benefits of early but well informed settlement which genuinely satisfy both parties to dispute'.

1.2 The aims of pre-action protocols are:

- more pre-action contact between the parties
- better and earlier exchange of information
- better pre-action investigation by both sides
- to put the parties in a position where they may be able to settle cases fairly and early without litigation
- to enable proceedings to run to the court's timetable and efficiently, if litigation does become necessary.

1.3 The concept of protocols is relevant to a range of initiatives for good litigation and pre-litigation practice, especially:

- predictability in the time needed for steps pre-proceedings
- standardisation of relevant information, including documents to be disclosed.

1.4 The courts will be able to treat the standards set in protocols as the normal reasonable approach to pre-action conduct. If proceedings are issued, it will be for the court to decide whether non-compliance with a protocol should merit adverse consequences. Guidance on the court's likely approach will be given from time to time in practice directions.

1.5 If the court has to consider the question of compliance after proceedings have begun it will not be concerned with minor infringements, eg failure by a short period to provide relevant information. One minor breach will not exempt the 'innocent' party from following the protocol. The court will look at the effect of non-compliance on the other party when deciding whether to impose sanctions.

2 Notes of Guidance

2.1 The protocol has been kept deliberately simple to promote ease of use and general acceptability. The notes of guidance which follow relate particularly to issues which arose during the piloting of the protocol.

SCOPE OF THE PROTOCOL

2.2 This protocol is intended to apply to all claims which include a claim for personal injury (except those claims covered by the Clinical Disputes and Disease and Illness Protocols) and to the entirety of those claims: not only to the personal injury element of a claim which also includes, for instance, property damage.

2.3 This protocol is primarily designed for those road traffic, tripping and slipping and accident at work cases which include an element of personal injury with a value of less than £15,000 which are likely to be allocated to the fast track. This is because time will be of the essence, after proceedings are issued, especially for the defendant, if a case is to be ready for trial within 30 weeks of allocation. Also, proportionality of work and costs to the value of what is in dispute is particularly important in lower value claims. For some claims within the value 'scope' of the fast track some flexibility in the timescale of the protocol may be necessary – see also paragraph 3.8.

2.4 However, the 'cards on the table' approach advocated by the protocol is equally appropriate to some higher value claims. The spirit, if not the letter of the protocol, should still be followed for multi-track type claims. In accordance with the sense of the civil justice reforms, the court will expect to see the spirit of reasonable pre-action behaviour applied in all cases, regardless of the existence of a specific protocol. In particular with regard to personal injury cases worth more than £15,000, with a view to avoiding the necessity of proceedings parties are expected to comply with the protocol as far as possible, eg in respect of letters before action, exchanging information and documents and agreeing experts.

2.5 The timetable and the arrangements for disclosing documents and obtaining expert evidence may need to be varied to suit the circumstances of the case. Where one or both parties consider the detail of the protocol is not appropriate to the case, and proceedings are subsequently issued, the court will expect an explanation as to why the protocol has not been followed, or has been varied.

'except industrial disease claims' (para 2.2)—The protocol has now been amended to clarify that it does not apply to claims for disease. A new protocol dealing with such claims has now been published and can be found in Section 4 of this work or on the Lord Chancellor's Department's website at *http://www.open.gov.uk/lcd*. It came into force on 8 December 2003.

'the court will expect to see the spirit of reasonable pre-action behaviour applied in all cases, regardless of the existence of a specific protocol' (para 2.4)—In *Ford v GKR Construction and ors* (1999) *The Times*, 5 November, the Court of Appeal confirmed that one of the aims of the new code was to enable the parties involved to know where they stood in reality at the earliest possible stage and at the lowest practicable cost, so that they might make informed decisions about their prospects and the sensible conduct of their cases. The principle that parties should conduct litigation making full and proper disclosure was even more important now that the Civil Procedure Rules 1998 had come into force. The approach reflected in the protocols should be adopted by parties generally in the conduct of their litigation. This section has been amended to amplify what is expected of parties in complying with the protocol for multi-track claims.

EARLY NOTIFICATION

2.6 The claimant's legal representative may wish to notify the defendant and/or his insurer as soon as they know a claim is likely to be made, but before they are able to send a detailed letter of claim, particularly for instance, when the defendant has no or limited knowledge of the incident giving rise to the claim or where the claimant is incurring significant expenditure as a result of the accident which he hopes the defendant might pay for, in whole or in part. If the claimant's representative chooses to do this, it will not start the timetable for responding.

THE LETTER OF CLAIM

2.7 The specimen letter of claim at Annex A will usually be sent to the individual defendant. In practice, he/she may have no personal financial interest in the financial outcome of the claim/dispute because he/she is insured. Court imposed sanctions for non-compliance with the protocol may be ineffective against an insured. This is why the protocol emphasises the importance of passing the letter of claim to the insurer and the possibility that the insurance cover might be affected. If an insurer receives the letter of claim only after some delay by the insured, it would not be unreasonable for the insurer to ask the claimant for additional time to respond.

2.8 In road traffic cases, the letter of claim should always contain the name and address of the hospital where the claimant was treated and, where available, the claimant's hospital reference number.

2.9 The priority at letter of claim stage is for the claimant to provide sufficient information for the defendant to assess liability. Sufficient information should also be provided to enable the defendant to estimate the likely size of the claim.

2.10 Once the claimant has sent the letter of claim no further investigation on liability should normally be carried out until a response is received from the defendant indicating whether liability is disputed.

'letter of claim' (para 2.7)—If the case is funded under a funding arrangement at the time of the initial letter of claim, notification of this should be given in the letter of claim (cf PDProt, para 4A).

Note the decision of *Jimaale v London Buses Ltd* (2000) 12 CL 61, where delay in notifying the defendant of the claim resulted in the case being struck out even though it was issued within the limitation period.

REASONS FOR EARLY ISSUE

2.11 The protocol recommends that a defendant be given three months to investigate and respond to a claim before proceedings are issued. This may not always be possible, particularly where a claimant only consults a solicitor close to the end of any relevant limitation period. In these circumstances, the claimant's solicitor should give as much notice of the intention to issue proceedings as is practicable and the parties should consider whether the court might be invited to extend time for service of the claimant's supporting documents and for service of any defence, or alternatively, to stay the proceedings while the recommended steps in the protocol are followed.

STATUS OF LETTERS OF CLAIM AND RESPONSE

2.12 Letters of claim and response are not intended to have the same status as a statement of case in proceedings. Matters may come to light as a result of investigation after the letter of claim has been sent, or after the defendant has responded, particularly if disclosure of documents takes place outside the recommended three-month period. These circumstances could mean that the 'pleaded' case of one or both parties is presented slightly differently than in the letter of claim and response. It would not be consistent with the spirit of the protocol for a party to 'take a point' on this in the proceedings, provided that there was no obvious intention by the party who changed their position to mislead the other party.

DISCLOSURE OF DOCUMENTS

2.13 The aim of the early disclosure of documents by the defendant is not to encourage 'fishing expeditions' by the claimant, but to promote an early exchange of relevant information to help in clarifying or resolving issues in dispute. The claimant's solicitor can assist by identifying in the letter of claim or in a subsequent letter the particular categories of documents which they consider are relevant.

EXPERTS

2.14 The protocol encourages joint selection of, and access to, experts. Most frequently this will apply to the medical expert, but on occasions also to liability experts, eg engineers. The protocol promotes the practice of the claimant obtaining a medical report, disclosing it to the defendant who then asks questions and/or agrees it and does not obtain his own report. The Protocol provides for nomination of the expert by the claimant in personal injury claims because of the early stage of the proceedings and the particular nature of such claims. If proceedings have to be issued, a medical report must be attached to these proceedings. However, if necessary after proceedings have commenced and with the permission of the court, the parties may obtain further expert reports. It would be for the court to decide whether the costs of more than one expert's report should be recoverable.

'medical expert' (para 2.11)—This section has been amended to emphasise that the usual procedure will be for the claimant to nominate the medical expert because of the nature of these claims.

The protocol is being further amended to clarify that the report obtained under the protocol is not a joint report. This was confirmed by the Court of Appeal in *Thurber Carlson (Richard) v Townsend (Karen)* [2001] EWCA Civ 511.

2.15 Some solicitors choose to obtain medical reports through medical agencies, rather than directly from a specific doctor or hospital. The defendant's prior consent to the action should be sought and, if the defendant so requests, the agency should be asked to provide in advance the names of the doctor(s) whom they are considering instructing.

NEGOTIATIONS/SETTLEMENT

2.16 Parties and their legal representatives are encouraged to enter into discussions and/or negotiations prior to starting proceedings. The protocol does not specify when or how this might be done but parties should bear in mind that the courts increasingly take the view that litigation should be a last resort, and that claims should not be issued prematurely when a settlement is in reasonable prospect.

'negotiations prior to starting proceedings' (para 2.13)—In *Taylor v KD Coach Hire Ltd* (2000) 11 CL 33 it was held that it was unreasonable for the defendants to have waited until after the issue of proceedings before negotiating.

STOCKTAKE

2.17 Where a claim is not resolved when the protocol has been followed, the parties might wish to carry out a 'stocktake' of the issues in dispute, and the evidence that the court is likely to need to decide those issues, before proceedings are started. Where the defendant is insured and the pre-action steps have been conducted by the insurer, the insurer would normally be expected to nominate solicitors to act in the proceedings and the claimant's solicitor is recommended to invite the insurer to nominate solicitors to act in the proceedings and do so 7–14 days before the intended issue date.

3 The Protocol

LETTER OF CLAIM

3.1 The claimant shall send to the proposed defendant two copies of a letter of claim, immediately sufficient information is available to substantiate a realistic claim and before issues of quantum are addressed in detail. One copy of the letter is for the defendant, the second for passing on to his insurers.

3.2 The letter shall contain a **clear summary of the facts** on which the claim is based together with an indication of the **nature of any injuries** suffered and of **any financial loss incurred**. In cases of road traffic accidents, the letter should provide the name and address of the hospital where treatment has been obtained and the claimant's hospital reference number. Where the case is funded by a conditional fee agreement (or collective conditional fee agreement), notification should be given of the existence of the agreement and where appropriate, that there is a success fee and/or insurance premium, although not the level of the success fee or premium.

3.3 Solicitors are recommended to use a **standard format** for such a letter – an example is at Annex A: this can be amended to suit the particular case.

3.4 The letter should ask for **details of the insurer** and that a copy should be sent by the proposed defendant to the insurer where appropriate. If the insurer is known a copy shall be sent directly to the insurer. Details of the claimant's

National Insurance number and date of birth should be supplied to the defendant's insurer once the Defendant has responded to the letter of claim and confirmed the identity of the insurer. This information should not be supplied in the letter of claim.

3.5 **Sufficient information** should be given in order to enable the defendant's insurer/solicitor to commence investigations and at least put a broad valuation on the 'risk'.

3.6 The **defendant should reply within 21 calendar days** of the date of posting of the letter identifying the insurer (if any). If there has been no reply by the defendant or insurer within 21 days, the claimant will be entitled to issue proceedings.

3.7 The **defendant** ('s insurers) will have a **maximum of three months** from the date of acknowledgment of the claim **to investigate**. No later than the end of that period the defendant (insurer) shall reply, stating whether liability is denied and, if so, giving reasons for their denial of liability.

3.8 Where the accident occurred outside England and Wales and/or where the defendant is outside the jurisdiction, the time periods of 21 days and three months should normally be extended up to 42 days and six months.

3.9 Where **liability is admitted**, the presumption is that the defendant will be bound by this admission for all claims with a total value of up to £15,000. Where the claimant's investigation indicates that the value of the claim has increased to more than £15,000 since the letter of claim, the claimant should notify the defendant as soon as possible.

'The letter shall contain' (para 3.2)—Allegations of negligence should be given in as much detail as possible. Every allegation should be answered by the insurers and therefore will assist in narrowing the issues.

Where the case is funded by a conditional fee agreement, notification should be given of the existence of the agreement and where appropriate that there is a success fee and insurance premium – see PDProt, paras 4A.1 and 4A.2. The level of the success fee and premium should not be disclosed.

'National Insurance number and date of birth' (para 3.4)—To prevent possible fraud this paragraph has been amended to ensure that details of the claimant's date of birth and national insurance number were not sent to individuals.

'Sufficient information' (para 3.5)—As it is not envisaged that a medical report will be available at this stage the description of injury will usually be in general terms but should be sufficiently detailed as to enable the insurers to put an approximate value on the claim. Details of time off work will also assist the insurers in making a broad evaluation.

'giving reasons for their denial of liability' (para 3.7)—The insurers should address each allegation of negligence. This will assist in clarifying the issues in dispute.

'should normally be extended' (para 3.8)—'Normally' has been substituted for 'reasonably' in this section to avoid disputes about when it would be reasonable to allow longer times.

'Where liability is admitted' (para 3.9)—The claimant must be wary of relying on an admission in a case where the valuation may rise above £15,000.

DOCUMENTS

3.10 If the **defendant denies liability**, he should enclose with the letter of reply, documents in his possession which are **material to the issues** between the parties, and which would be likely to be ordered to be disclosed by the court, either on an application for pre-action disclosure, or on disclosure during proceedings.

3.11 Attached at Annex B are **specimen**, but non-exhaustive, **lists** of documents likely to be material in different types of claim. Where the claimant's investigation of the case is well advanced, the letter of claim could indicate which classes of documents are considered relevant for early disclosure. Alternatively these could be identified at a later stage.

3.12 Where the defendant admits primary liability, but alleges contributory negligence by the claimant, the defendant should give reasons supporting those allegations and disclose those documents from Annex B which are relevant to the issues in dispute. The claimant should respond to the allegations of contributory negligence before proceedings are issued.

3.13 No charge will be made for providing copy documents under the Protocol.

'specimen . . . lists' (para 3.11)—At the time of going to press, the specimen list is being revised by the Personal Injury Pre-Action Protocol Working Party.

SPECIAL DAMAGES

3.14 The claimant will send to the defendant as soon as practicable a Schedule of Special Damages with supporting documents, particularly where the defendant has admitted liability.

EXPERTS

3.15 Before any party instructs an expert he should give the other party a list of the **name**(s) of **one or more experts** in the relevant speciality whom he considers are suitable to instruct.

3.16 Where a medical expert is to be instructed the claimant's solicitor will organise access to relevant medical records – see specimen letter of instruction at Annex C.

3.17 **Within 14 days** the other party may indicate **an objection** to one or more of the named experts. The first party should then instruct a mutually acceptable expert (which is not the same as a joint expert). It must be emphasised that if the claimant nominates an expert in the original letter of claim, the defendant has 14 days to object to one or more of the named experts after expiration of the period of 21 days within which he has to reply to the letter of claim, as set out in paragraph 3.6.

3.18 If the second party objects to all the listed experts, the parties may then instruct **experts of their own choice**. It would be for the court to decide subsequently, if proceedings are issued, whether either party had acted unreasonably.

3.19 If the **second party does not object to an expert nominated**, he shall not be entitled to rely on his own expert evidence within that particular speciality unless:

- (a) the first party agrees
- (b) the court so directs, or
- (c) the first party's expert report has been amended and the first party is not prepared to disclose the original report.

3.20 **Either party may send to an agreed expert written questions** on the report, relevant to the issues, via the first party's solicitors. The expert should send answers to the questions separately and directly to each party.

3.21 The cost of a report from an agreed expert will usually be paid by the instructing first party: the costs of the expert replying to questions will usually be borne by the party which asks the questions.

'specimen letter of instruction' (para 3.15)—The specimen letter does not comply with the requirements set out in PD35, para 1 and is being amended by the Personal Injury Pre-Action Protocol Working Party at the time of going to press.

Payment of expert's fees (para 3.20)—Note the contrast with PD35, para 4.3 where the party instructing the expert pays his fees for answering questions.

4 Rehabilitation

4.1 The claimant or the defendant or both shall consider as early as possible whether the claimant has reasonable needs that could be met by rehabilitation treatment or other measures.

4.2 The parties shall consider, in such cases, how those needs might be addressed. The Rehabilitation Code (which is attached at Annex D) may be helpful in considering how to identify the claimant's needs and how to address the cost of providing for those needs.

4.3 The time limit set out in paragraph 3.7 of this Protocol shall not be shortened, except by consent to allow these issues to be addressed.

4.4 The provision of any report obtained for the purposes of assessment of provision of a party's rehabilitation needs shall not be used in any litigation arising out of the accident, the subject of the claim, save by consent and shall in any event be exempt from the provisions of paragraphs 3.15 to 3.21 inclusive of this protocol.

5 Resolution of Issues

5.1 Where the defendant admits liability in whole or in part, before proceedings are issued, any medical reports obtained under this protocol on which a party relies should be disclosed to the other party. The claimant should delay issuing proceedings for 21 days from disclosure of the report (unless such delay would cause his claim to become time-barred), to enable the parties to consider whether the claim is capable of settlement.

5.2 The Civil Procedure Rules Part 36 permit claimants and defendants to make offers to settle pre-proceedings. Parties should always consider before issuing if it is appropriate to make Part 36 Offer. If such an offer is made, the party making the offer must always supply sufficient evidence and/or information to enable the offer to be properly considered.

5.3 Where the defendant has admitted liability, the claimant should send to the defendant schedules of special damages and loss at least 21 days before proceedings are issued (unless that would cause the claimant's claim to become time-barred).

Annex A
Letter of Claim

To

Defendant

Dear Sirs

Re: Claimant's full name

Claimant's full address

Claimant's Clock or Works Number

Claimant's Employer (*name and address*)

We are instructed by the above named to claim damages in connection with ***an accident at work/ road traffic accident / tripping accident*** on day of ***(year)*** at ***(place of accident which must be sufficiently detailed to establish location)***

Please confirm the identity of your insurers. Please note that the insurers will need to see this letter as soon as possible and it may affect your insurance cover and/or the conduct of any subsequent legal proceedings if you do not send this letter to them.

The circumstances of the accident are:-

(brief outline)

The reason why we are alleging fault is:

(simple explanation eg defective machine, broken ground)

A description of our client's injuries is as follows:-

(brief outline)

(In cases of road traffic accidents)

Our client (state hospital reference number) received treatment for the injuries at name and address of hospital).

Our client is still suffering from the effects of his/her injury. We invite you to participate with us in addressing his/her immediate needs by use of rehabilitation.

He is employed as ***(occupation)*** and has had the following time off work ***(dates of absence)***. His approximate weekly income is (***insert if known***).

If you are our client's employers, please provide us with the usual earnings details which will enable us to calculate his financial loss.

We are obtaining a police report and will let you have a copy of the same upon your undertaking to meet half the fee.

We have also sent a letter of claim to ***(name and address)*** and a copy of that letter is attached. We understand their insurers are ***(name, address and claims number if known)***.

At this stage of our enquiries we would expect the documents contained in parts ***(insert appropriate parts of standard disclosure list)*** to be relevant to this action.

Please note that we have entered into a conditional fee agreement with our client dated in relation to this claim which provides for a success fee within the meaning of section 58(2) of the Courts and Legal Services Act 1990. Our client has taken out an insurance policy with [name of insurance company] of [address of insurance company] to which section 29 of the Access Justice Act 1999 applies. The policy number is and the policy is dated . Where the funding arrangement is an insurance policy, the party must state the name and address of the insurer, the policy number and the date of the policy, and must identify the claim or claims to which it relates (including Part 20 claims if any).

A copy of this letter is attached for you to send to your insurers. Finally we expect an acknowledgment of this letter within 21 days by yourselves or your insurers.

Yours faithfully

'Letter of Claim'—The draft letter is being amended to include the information which should be given where the claim is being funded by a conditional fee agreement.

Annex B
Standard Disclosure Lists
(Fast Track Disclosure)

RTA CASES

SECTION A

In all cases where liability is at issue –

- (i) Documents identifying nature, extent and location of damage to defendants vehicle where there is any dispute about point of impact.
- (ii) MOT certificate where relevant.
- (iii) Maintenance records where vehicle defect is alleged or it is alleged by defendant that there was an unforeseen defect which caused or contributed to the accident.

SECTION B

Accident involving commercial vehicle as potential defendant –

- (i) Tachograph charts or entry from individual control book.
- (ii) Maintenance and repair records required for operators' licence where vehicle defect is alleged or it is alleged by defendants that there was an unforeseen defect which caused or contributed to the accident.

SECTION C

Cases against local authorities where highway design defect is alleged –

- (i) Documents produced to comply with Section 39 of the Road Traffic Act 1988 in respect of the duty designed to promote road safety to include studies into road accidents in the relevant area and documents relating to measures recommended to prevent accidents in the relevant area.

HIGHWAY TRIPPING CLAIMS

Documents from Highway Authority for a period of 12 months prior to the accident –

- (i) Records of inspection for the relevant stretch of highway.
- (ii) Maintenance records including records of independent contractors working in relevant area.

(iii) Records of the minutes of Highway Authority meetings where maintenance or repair policy has been discussed or decided.
(iv) Records of complaints about the state of highways.
(v) Records of other accidents which have occurred on the relevant stretch of highway.

WORKPLACE CLAIMS

(i) Accident book entry.
(ii) First aider report.
(iii) Surgery record.
(iv) Foreman/supervisor accident report.
(v) Safety representatives accident report.
(vi) RIDDOR (Reporting of Injuries, Diseases and Dangerous Occurrences Regulations) report to HSE.
(vii) Other communications between defendants and HSE.
(viii) Minutes of Health and Safety Committee meeting(s) where accident/matter considered.
(ix) Report to DSS.
(x) Documents listed above relative to any previous accident/matter identified by the claimant and relied upon as proof of negligence.
(xi) Earnings information where defendant is employer.

Documents produced to comply with requirements of the Management of Health and Safety at Work Regulations 1992 –

(i) Pre-accident Risk Assessment required by Regulation 3.
(ii) Post-accident Re-Assessment required by Regulation 3.
(iii) Accident Investigation Report prepared in implementing the requirements of Regulations 4, 6 and 9.
(iv) Health Surveillance Records in appropriate cases required by Regulation 5.
(v) Information provided to employees under Regulation 8.
(vi) Documents relating to the employees health and safety training required by Regulation 11.

WORKPLACE CLAIMS – DISCLOSURE WHERE SPECIFIC REGULATIONS APPLY

SECTION A – WORKPLACE (HEALTH SAFETY AND WELFARE) REGULATIONS 1992

(i) Repair and maintenance records required by Regulation 5.
(ii) Housekeeping records to comply with the requirements of Regulation 9.
(iii) Hazard warning signs or notices to comply with Regulation 17 (Traffic Routes).

SECTION B – PROVISION AND USE OF WORK EQUIPMENT REGULATIONS 1998

(i) Manufacturers' specifications and instructions in respect of relevant work equipment establishing its suitability to comply with Regulation 5.

(ii) Maintenance log/maintenance records required to comply with Regulation 6.

(iii) Documents providing information and instructions to employees to comply with Regulation 8.

(iv) Documents provided to the employee in respect of training for use to comply with Regulation 9.

(v) Any notice, sign or document relied upon as a defence to alleged breaches of Regulations 14 to 18 dealing with controls and control systems.

(vi) Instruction/training documents issued to comply with the requirements of Regulation 22 insofar as it deals with maintenance operations where the machinery is not shut down.

(vii) Copies of markings required to comply with Regulation 23.

(viii) Copies of warnings required to comply with Regulation 24.

SECTION C – PERSONAL PROTECTIVE EQUIPMENT AT WORK REGULATIONS 1992

(i) Documents relating to the assessment of the Personal Protective Equipment to comply with Regulation 6.

(ii) Documents relating to the maintenance and replacement of Personal Protective Equipment to comply with Regulation 7.

(iii) Record of maintenance procedures for Personal Protective Equipment to comply with Regulation 7.

(iv) Records of tests and examinations of Personal Protective Equipment to comply with Regulation 7.

(v) Documents providing information, instruction and training in relation to the Personal Protective Equipment to comply with Regulation 9.

(vi) Instructions for use of Personal Protective Equipment to include the manufacturers' instructions to comply with Regulation 10.

SECTION D – MANUAL HANDLING OPERATIONS REGULATIONS 1992

(i) Manual Handling Risk Assessment carried out to comply with the requirements of Regulation 4(1)(b)(i).

(ii) Re-assessment carried out post-accident to comply with requirements of Regulation 4(1)(b)(i).

(iii) Documents showing the information provided to the employee to give general indications related to the load and precise indications on the weight of the load and the heaviest side of the load if the centre of gravity was not positioned centrally to comply with Regulation 4(1)(b)(iii).

(iv) Documents relating to training in respect of manual handling operations and training records.

SECTION E – HEALTH AND SAFETY (DISPLAY SCREEN EQUIPMENT) REGULATIONS 1992

(i) Analysis of work stations to assess and reduce risks carried out to comply with the requirements of Regulation 2.

(ii) Re-assessment of analysis of work stations to assess and reduce risks following development of symptoms by the claimant.

(iii) Documents detailing the provision of training including training records to comply with the requirements of Regulation 6.
(iv) Documents providing information to employees to comply with the requirements of Regulation 7.

SECTION F – CONTROL OF SUBSTANCES HAZARDOUS TO HEALTH REGULATIONS 1999

(i) Risk assessment carried out to comply with the requirements of Regulation 6.
(ii) Reviewed risk assessment carried out to comply with the requirements of Regulation 6.
(iii) Copy labels from containers used for storage handling and disposal of carcinogenics to comply with the requirements of Regulation 7(2A)(h).
(iv) Warning signs identifying designation of areas and installations which may be contaminated by carcinogenics to comply with the requirements of Regulation 7(2A)(h).
(v) Documents relating to the assessment of the Personal Protective Equipment to comply with Regulation 7(3A).
(vi) Documents relating to the maintenance and replacement of Personal Protective Equipment to comply with Regulation 7(3A).
(vii) Record of maintenance procedures for Personal Protective Equipment to comply with Regulation 7(3A).
(viii) Records of tests and examinations of Personal Protective Equipment to comply with Regulation 7(3A).
(ix) Documents providing information, instruction and training in relation to the Personal Protective Equipment to comply with Regulation 7(3A).
(x) Instructions for use of Personal Protective Equipment to include the manufacturers' instructions to comply with Regulation 7(3A).
(xi) Air monitoring records for substances assigned a maximum exposure limit or occupational exposure standard to comply with the requirements of Regulation 7.
(xii) Maintenance examination and test of control measures records to comply with Regulation 9.
(xiii) Monitoring records to comply with the requirements of Regulation 10.
(xiv) Health surveillance records to comply with the requirements of Regulation 11.
(xv) Documents detailing information, instruction and training including training records for employees to comply with the requirements of Regulation 12.
(xvi) Labels and Health and Safety data sheets supplied to the employers to comply with the CHIP Regulations.

SECTION G – CONSTRUCTION (DESIGN AND MANAGEMENT) (AMENDMENT) REGULATIONS 2000

(i) Notification of a project form (HSE F10) to comply with the requirements of Regulation 7.
(ii) Health and Safety Plan to comply with requirements of Regulation 15.
(iii) Health and Safety file to comply with the requirements of Regulations 12 and 14.

(iv) Information and training records provided to comply with the requirements of Regulation 17.
(v) Records of advice from and views of persons at work to comply with the requirements of Regulation 18.

SECTION H – PRESSURE SYSTEMS AND TRANSPORTABLE GAS CONTAINERS REGULATIONS 1989

(i) Information and specimen markings provided to comply with the requirements of Regulation 5.
(ii) Written statements specifying the safe operating limits of a system to comply with the requirements of Regulation 7.
(iii) Copy of the written scheme of examination required to comply with the requirements of Regulation 8.
(iv) Examination records required to comply with the requirements of Regulation 9.
(v) Instructions provided for the use of operator to comply with Regulation 11.
(vi) Records kept to comply with the requirements of Regulation 13.
(vii) Records kept to comply with the requirements of Regulation 22.

SECTION I – LIFTING OPERATIONS AND EQUIPMENT REGULATIONS 1998

(i) Record kept to comply with the requirements of Regulation 6.

SECTION J – THE NOISE AT WORK REGULATIONS 1989

(i) Any risk assessment records required to comply with the requirements of Regulations 4 and 5.
(ii) Manufacturers' literature in respect of all ear protection made available to claimant to comply with the requirements of Regulation 8.
(iii) All documents provided to the employee for the provision of information to comply with Regulation 11.

SECTION K – CONSTRUCTION (HEAD PROTECTION) REGULATIONS 1989

(i) Pre-accident assessment of head protection required to comply with Regulation 3(4).
(ii) Post-accident re-assessment required to comply with Regulation 3(5).

SECTION L – THE CONSTRUCTION (GENERAL PROVISIONS) REGULATIONS 1961

(i) Report prepared following inspections and examinations of excavations etc to comply with the requirements of Regulation 9.

SECTION M – GAS CONTAINERS REGULATIONS 1989

(i) Information and specimen markings provided to comply with the requirements of Regulation 5.
(ii) Written statements specifying the safe operating limits of a system to comply with the requirements of Regulation 7.
(iii) Copy of the written scheme of examination required to comply with the requirements of Regulation 8.

(iv) Examination records required to comply with the requirements of Regulation 9.
(v) Instructions provided for the use of operator to comply with Regulation 11.

Annex C
Letter of Instruction

Dear Sir,

Re: ***(Name and Address)***

D.O.B.–

Telephone No. –

Date of Accident –

We are acting for the above named in connection with injuries received in an accident which occurred on the above date. The main injuries appear to have been ***(main injuries)***.

We should be obliged if you would examine our Client and let us have a full and detailed report dealing with any relevant pre-accident medical history, the injuries sustained, treatment received and present condition, dealing in particular with the capacity for work and giving a prognosis.

It is central to our assessment of the extent of our client's injuries to establish the extent and duration of any continuing disability. Accordingly, in the prognosis section we would ask you to specifically comment on any areas of continuing complaint or disability or impact on daily living. If there is such continuing disability you should comment upon the level of suffering or inconvenience caused and, if you are able, give your view as to when or if the complaint or disability is likely to resolve.

Please send our Client an appointment direct for this purpose. Should you be able to offer a cancellation appointment please contact our Client direct. We confirm we will be responsible for your reasonable fees.

We are obtaining the notes and records from our client's GP and Hospitals attended and will forward them to you when they are to hand/or please request the GP and Hospital records direct and advise that any invoice for the provision of these records should be forwarded to us.

In order to comply with Court Rules we would be grateful if you would insert above your signature a statement that the contents are true to the best of your knowledge and belief.

In order to avoid further correspondence we can confirm that on the evidence we have there is no reason to suspect we may be pursuing a claim against the hospital or its staff.

We look forward to receiving your report within   weeks. If you will not be able to prepare your report within this period please telephone us upon receipt of these instructions.

When acknowledging these instructions it would assist if you could give an estimate as to the likely time scale for the provision of your report and also an indication as to your fee.

Yours faithfully

Annex D
The Rehabilitation Code

****

Form—The Rehabilitation Code appended to this protocol can be accessed on either the *Civil Court Service* CD-ROM or the *Civil Court Service* Online at www.civilcourtservice.co.uk.

Pre-Action Protocol
for the Construction and Engineering Disputes

CONTENTS

General note—For commentary relevant to this protocol see the notes to CPR Pt 60 – Technology and Construction Court Claims – and its supplementing practice direction PD60, set out in Section 2 of this work.

1 Introduction

1.1 This pre-action protocol applies to all construction and engineering disputes (including professional negligence claims against architects, engineers and quantity surveyors).

EXCEPTIONS

1.2 A claimant shall not be required to comply with this protocol before commencing proceedings to the extent that the proposed proceedings –

(i) are for the enforcement of the decision of an adjudicator to whom a dispute has been referred pursuant to section 108 of the Housing Grants, Construction and Regeneration Act 1996 ('the 1996 Act'),
(ii) include a claim for interim injunctive relief,
(iii) will be the subject of a claim for summary judgment pursuant to Part 24 of the Civil Procedure Rules, or
(iv) relate to the same or substantially the same issues as have been the subject of recent adjudication under the 1996 Act, or some other formal alternative dispute resolution procedure.

OBJECTIVES

1.3 The objectives of this protocol are as set out in the practice direction relating to civil procedure pre-action protocols, namely –

(i) to encourage the exchange of early and full information about the prospective legal claim;

(ii) to enable parties to avoid litigation by agreeing a settlement of the claim before commencement of proceedings; and
(iii) to support the efficient management of proceedings where litigation cannot be avoided.

COMPLIANCE

1.4 If proceedings are commenced, the court will be able to treat the standards set in this protocol as the normal reasonable approach to pre-action conduct. If the court has to consider the question of compliance after proceedings have begun, it will be concerned with substantial compliance and not minor departures, eg failure by a short period to provide relevant information. Minor departures will not exempt the 'innocent' party from following the protocol. The court will look at the effect of non-compliance on the other party when deciding whether to impose sanctions. For sanctions generally, see paragraph 2 of the practice direction – Protocols 'Compliance with Protocols'.

2 Overview of Protocol

GENERAL AIM

2 The general aim of this protocol is to ensure that before court proceedings commence –

(i) the claimant and the defendant have provided sufficient information for each party to know the nature of the other's case;
(ii) each party has had an opportunity to consider the other's case, and to accept or reject all or any part of the case made against him at the earliest possible stage;
(iii) there is more pre-action contact between the parties;
(iv) better and earlier exchange of information occurs;
(v) there is better pre-action investigation by the parties;
(vi) the parties have met formally on at least one occasion with a view to
– defining and agreeing the issues between them; and
– exploring possible ways by which the claim may be resolved;
(vii) the parties are in a position where they may be able to settle cases early and fairly without recourse to litigation; and
(viii) proceedings will be conducted efficiently if litigation does become necessary.

3 The Letter of Claim

3 Prior to commencing proceedings, the claimant or his solicitor shall send to each proposed defendant (if appropriate to his registered address) a copy of a letter of claim which shall contain the following information –

(i) the claimant's full name and address;
(ii) the full name and address of each proposed defendant;
(iii) a clear summary of the facts on which each claim is based;
(iv) the basis on which each claim is made, identifying the principal contractual terms and statutory provisions relied on;
(v) the nature of the relief claimed: if damages are claimed, a breakdown showing how the damages have been quantified; if a sum is claimed

pursuant to a contract, how it has been calculated; if an extension of time is claimed, the period claimed;

(vi) where a claim has been made previously and rejected by a defendant, and the claimant is able to identify the reason(s) for such rejection, the claimant's grounds of belief as to why the claim was wrongly rejected;

(vii) the names of any experts already instructed by the claimant on whose evidence he intends to rely, identifying the issues to which that evidence will be directed.

4 Defendant's Response

THE DEFENDANT'S ACKNOWLEDGMENT

4.1 Within 14 calendar days of receipt of the letter of claim, the defendant should acknowledge its receipt in writing and may give the name and address of his insurer (if any). If there has been no acknowledgment by or on behalf of the defendant within 14 days, the claimant will be entitled to commence proceedings without further compliance with this protocol.

OBJECTIONS TO THE COURT'S JURISDICTION OR THE NAMED DEFENDANT

4.2

4.2.1 If the defendant intends to take any objection to all or any part of the claimant's claim on the grounds that (i) the court lacks jurisdiction, (ii) the matter should be referred to arbitration, or (iii) the defendant named in the letter of claim is the wrong defendant, that objection should be raised by the defendant within 28 days after receipt of the letter of claim. The letter of objection shall specify the parts of the claim to which the objection relates, setting out the grounds relied on, and, where appropriate, shall identify the correct defendant (if known). Any failure to take such objection shall not prejudice the defendant's rights to do so in any subsequent proceedings, but the court may take such failure into account when considering the question of costs.

4.2.2 Where such notice of objection is given, the defendant is not required to send a letter of response in accordance with paragraph 4.3.1 in relation to the claim or those parts of it to which the objection relates (as the case may be).

4.2.3 If at any stage before the claimant commences proceedings, the defendant withdraws his objection, then paragraph 4.3 and the remaining part of this protocol will apply to the claim or those parts of it to which the objection related as if the letter of claim had been received on the date on which notice of withdrawal of the objection had been given.

THE DEFENDANT'S RESPONSE

4.3

4.3.1 Within 28 days from the date of receipt of the letter of claim, or such other period as the parties may reasonably agree (up to a maximum of 4 months), the defendant shall send a letter of response to the claimant which shall contain the following information –

(i) the facts set out in the letter of claim which are agreed or not agreed, and if not agreed, the basis of the disagreement;

(ii) which claims are accepted and which are rejected, and if rejected, the basis of the rejection;
(iii) if a claim is accepted in whole or in part, whether the damages, sums or extensions of time claimed are accepted or rejected, and if rejected, the basis of the rejection;
(iv) if contributory negligence is alleged against the claimant, a summary of the facts relied on;
(v) whether the defendant intends to make a counterclaim, and if so, giving the information which is required to be given in a letter of claim by paragraph 3(iii) to (vi) above;
(vi) the names of any experts already instructed on whose evidence it is intended to rely, identifying the issues to which that evidence will be directed.

4.3.2 If no response is received by the claimant within the period of 28 days (or such other period as has been agreed between the parties), the claimant shall be entitled to commence proceedings without further compliance with this protocol.

CLAIMANT'S RESPONSE TO COUNTERCLAIM

4.4 The claimant shall provide a response to any counterclaim within the equivalent period allowed to the defendant to respond to the letter of claim under paragraph 4.3.1 above.

5 Pre-Action Meeting

5.1 As soon as possible after receipt by the claimant of the defendant's letter of response, or (if the claimant intends to respond to the counterclaim) after receipt by the defendant of the claimant's letter of response to the counterclaim, the parties should normally meet.

5.2 The aim of the meeting is for the parties to agree what are the main issues in the case, to identify the root cause of disagreement in respect of each issue, and to consider:

(i) whether, and if so how, the issues might be resolved without recourse to litigation, and
(ii) if litigation is unavoidable, what steps should be taken to ensure that it is conducted in accordance with the overriding objective as defined in Part 1.1 of the Civil Practice Rules.

5.3 In some circumstances, it may be necessary to convene more than one meeting. It is not intended by this protocol to prescribe in detail the manner in which the meetings should be conducted. But the court will normally expect that those attending will include –

(i) where the party is an individual, that individual, and where the party is a corporate body, a representative of that body who has authority to settle or recommend settlement of the dispute;
(ii) a legal representative of each party (if one has been instructed);
(iii) where the involvement of insurers has been disclosed, a representative of the insurer (who may be its legal representative); and
(iv) where a claim is made or defended on behalf of some other party (such as, for example, a claim made by a main contractor pursuant to a

contractual obligation to pass on subcontractor claims), the party on whose behalf the claim is made or defended and/or his legal representatives.

5.4 In respect of each agreed issue or the dispute as a whole, the parties should consider whether some form of alternative dispute resolution procedure would be more suitable than litigation, and if so, endeavour to agree which form to adopt.

5.5 If the parties are unable to agree on a means of resolving the dispute other than by litigation they should use their best endeavours to agree –

(i) whether, if there is any area where expert evidence is likely to be required, a joint expert may be appointed, and if so, who that should be; and (so far as is practicable)
(ii) the extent of disclosure of documents with a view to saving costs; and
(iii) the conduct of the litigation with the aim of minimising cost and delay.

5.6 Any party who attended any pre-action meeting shall be at liberty to disclose to the court –

(i) that the meeting took place, when and who attended;
(ii) the identity of any party who refused to attend, and the grounds for such refusal;
(iii) if the meeting did not take place, why not; and
(iv) any agreements concluded between the parties.

5.7 Except as provided in paragraph 5.6, everything said at a pre-action meeting shall be treated as 'without prejudice'.

6 Limitation of Action

6 If by reason of complying with any part of this protocol a claimant's claim may be time-barred under any provision of the Limitation Act 1980, or any other legislation which imposes a time limit for bringing an action, the claimant may commence proceedings without complying with this protocol. In such circumstances, a claimant who commences proceedings without complying with all, or any part, of this protocol must apply to the court on notice for directions as to the timetable and form of procedure to be adopted, at the same time as he requests the court to issue proceedings. The court will consider whether to order a stay of the whole or part of the proceedings pending compliance with this protocol.

Pre-Action Protocol for Defamation

CONTENTS

General note—The protocol is the product of a collaborative effort between specialist defamation practitioners representing both claimants and defendants. It gathers together the best elements of good pre-action practice and sets them out in a comprehensible form, enabling litigants in person and those not experienced in defamation claims to prepare pre-action correspondence that forms a proper platform for any future court action. It has virtually eliminated the 'shoot first and ask questions later' approach where the first notification a defendant received was service of a writ.

The protocol has undoubtedly contributed, as part of the wider civil procedure reforms, to the significant decline in the number of defamation claims issued in recent years. Meanwhile, there has been a steady growth in the use of mediation and other forms of alternative dispute resolution. The protocol has also assisted, to some extent, in the contentious area of legal costs in defamation.

1 Introduction

1.1 Lord Irvine of Lairg, in his foreword to the Pre-Action Protocol for Personal Injury Claims identified the value of creating pre-action protocols as a key part of the Civil Justice Reforms. He hoped that pre-action protocols would set effective and enforceable standards for the efficient conduct of pre-action litigation.

1.2 Lord Irvine went on to state that –

> *'The protocol aims to improve pre-action communication between the parties by establishing a timetable for the exchange of information relevant to the dispute and by setting standards for the content of correspondence. Compliance with the protocol will enable parties to make an informed judgment on the merits of their cases earlier than tends to happen today, because they will have earlier access to the information they need. This will provide every opportunity for improved communications between the parties designed to lead to an increase in the number of pre-action settlements.'*

1.3 It is against this background that a Pre-Action Protocol for Claims in Defamation is submitted. This protocol is intended to encourage exchange of information between parties at an early stage and to provide a clear framework within which parties to a claim in defamation, acting in good faith, can explore the early and appropriate resolution of that claim.

1.4 There are important features which distinguish defamation claims from other areas of civil litigation, and these must be borne in mind when both applying, and reviewing the application of, the pre-action protocol. In particular, time is always 'of the essence' in defamation claims; the limitation period is (uniquely) only 1 year, and almost invariably, a claimant will be seeking an immediate correction and/or apology as part of the process of restoring his/her reputation.

1.5 This pre-action protocol embraces the spirit of the reforms to the Civil Justice system envisaged by Lord Woolf, and now enacted in the Civil Procedure Rules. It aims to incorporate the concept of the overriding objective, as provided by the Rules at Part 1, before the commencement of any court proceedings, namely –

dealing with a case justly includes, so far as is practicable –

- ensuring that the parties are on an equal footing;
- saving expense;

dealing with the case in ways which are proportionate –

- to the amount of money involved;
- to the importance of the case;
- to the complexity of the issues; and
- to the financial position of each party;
- ensuring that it is dealt with expeditiously and fairly; and

- allotting to it an appropriate share of the court's resources, while taking into account the need to allot resources to other cases.

2 Aims of the Protocol

2 This protocol aims to set out a code of good practice which parties should follow when litigation is being considered.

- It encourages early communication of a claim.
- It aims to encourage both parties to disclose sufficient information to enable each to understand the other's case and to promote the prospect of early resolution.
- It sets a timetable for the exchange of information relevant to the dispute.
- It sets standards for the content of correspondence.
- It identifies options which either party might adopt to encourage settlement of the claim.
- Should a claim proceed to litigation, the extent to which the protocol has been followed both in practice and in spirit by the parties will assist the court in dealing with liability for costs and making other orders.
- Letters of claim and responses sent pursuant to this protocol are not intended to have the same status as a statement of case in proceedings.
- It aims to keep the costs of resolving disputes subject to this protocol proportionate.

3 Pre-Action Protocol

LETTER OF CLAIM

3.1 The claimant should notify the defendant of his/her claim in writing at the earliest reasonable opportunity.

3.2 The letter of claim should include the following information –

- name of claimant;
- sufficient details to identify the publication or broadcast which contained the words complained of;
- the words complained of and, if known, the date of publication; where possible, a copy or transcript of the words complained of should be enclosed;
- factual inaccuracies or unsupportable comment within the words complained of; the claimant should give a sufficient explanation to enable the defendant to appreciate why the words are inaccurate or unsupportable;
- the nature of the remedies sought by the claimant.
- Where relevant, the letter of claim should also include –
  - any facts or matters which make the claimant identifiable from the words complained of;
  - details of any special facts relevant to the interpretation of the words complained of and/or any particular damage caused by the words complained of.

3.3 It is desirable for the claimant to identify in the letter of claim the meaning(s) he/she attributes to the words complained of.

'meaning(s) he/she attributes to the words complained of' (para 3.3)—Given that, in defamation claims, a jury is entitled to see the pre-action correspondence, compelling a party to commit to a meaning at that stage could be a cause of embarrassment where the meaning is subsequently refined or even altered in the pleadings. The protocol does not compel the parties to commit to a meaning but states that 'it is desirable' for them to do so. Earlier settlement is no doubt assisted if parties focus on the meaning of 'the words complained of' at the earliest possible stage.

DEFENDANT'S RESPONSE TO LETTER OF CLAIM

3.4 The defendant should provide a full response to the letter of claim as soon as reasonably possible. If the defendant believes that he/she will be unable to respond within 14 days (or such shorter time limit as specified in the letter of claim), then he/she should specify the date by which he/she intends to respond.

3.5 The response should include the following –

- whether or to what extent the claimant's claim is accepted, whether more information is required or whether it is rejected;
- if the claim is accepted in whole or in part, the defendant should indicate which remedies it is willing to offer;
- if more information is required, then the defendant should specify precisely what information is needed to enable the claim to be dealt with and why;
- if the claim is rejected, then the defendant should explain the reasons why it is rejected, including a sufficient indication of any facts on which the defendant is likely to rely in support of any substantive defence;
- it is desirable for the defendant to include in the response to the letter of claim the meaning(s) he/she attributes to the words complained of.

PROPORTIONALITY OF COSTS

3.6 In formulating both the letter of claim and response and in taking any subsequent steps, the parties should act reasonably to keep costs proportionate to the nature and gravity of the case and the stage the complaint has reached.

'keep costs proportionate' (para 3.6)—Inevitably, legal costs are incurred in addressing and developing the areas identified in the protocol exchange of correspondence but, where a dispute cannot be settled, this work should enable work done subsequently to be focussed and proportionate.

ALTERNATIVE DISPUTE RESOLUTION

3.7 Both the claimant and defendant will be expected by the court to provide evidence that alternative means of resolving their dispute were considered. It is not practical in this protocol to address in detail how the parties might decide which method to adopt to resolve their particular dispute. However, summarised below are some of the options for resolving disputes without litigation.

- Determination by an independent third party (for example, a lawyer experienced in the field of defamation or an individual experienced in the subject matter of the claim) whose name and fees, along with the precise issues which are to be determined, will have been agreed by the parties in advance.
- Mediation or any other form of Alternative Dispute Resolution.
- Arbitration (which does of course carry statutory implications).

Professional Negligence Pre-Action Protocol

This Protocol Merges the two Protocols Previously Produced by the Solicitors Indemnity Fund (SIF) and Claims Against Professionals (CAP)

CONTENTS

General note—This protocol came into force on 16 July 2001 – see PDProt, para 5.1. It has not been reviewed or amended since its introduction.

A Introduction

A1 This protocol is designed to apply when a claimant wishes to claim against a professional (other than construction professionals and healthcare providers) as a result of that professional's alleged negligence or equivalent breach of contract or breach of fiduciary duty. Although these claims will be the usual situation in which the protocol will be used, there may be other claims for which the protocol could be appropriate. For a more detailed explanation of the scope of the protocol see **Guidance Note C2**.

A2 The aim of this protocol is to establish a framework in which there is an early exchange of information so that the claim can be fully investigated and, if possible, resolved without the need for litigation. This includes:

- (a) ensuring that the parties are on an equal footing
- (b) saving expense
- (c) dealing with the dispute in ways which are proportionate:
  - (i) to the amount of money involved
  - (ii) to the importance of the case
  - (iii) to the complexity of the issues
  - (iv) to the financial position of each party
- (d) ensuring that it is dealt with expeditiously and fairly.

A3 This protocol is not intended to replace other forms of pre-action dispute resolution (such as internal complaints procedures, the Surveyors and Valuers Arbitration Scheme, etc). Where such procedures are available, parties are encouraged to consider whether they should be used. If, however, these other procedures are used and fail to resolve the dispute, the protocol should be used before litigation is started, adapting it where appropriate. See also **Guidance Note C3**.

A4 The courts will be able to treat the standards set in this protocol as the normal reasonable approach. If litigation is started, it will be for the court to decide whether sanctions should be imposed as a result of substantial non-compliance with a protocol. Guidance on the courts' likely approach is given in the Protocols Practice Direction. The court is likely to disregard minor departures from this protocol and so should the parties as between themselves.

A5 Both in operating the timetable and in requesting and providing information during the protocol period, the parties are expected to act reasonably, in line with the court's expectations of them. See also **Guidance Note C1.2**.

'aim of the protocol' (para A2)—The aims of the protocol are consistent with the overriding objective in CPR Pt 1 (in fact para A2(a)–(d) of the protocol are exactly the same as CPR r 1.1(2)(a)–(d)).

The aims are unambitious when compared with the Clinical Disputes Protocol (which has been in force since the introduction of the CPR and applies to professional negligence claims against healthcare professionals). That protocol refers to the maintenance/restoration of the patient–healthcare provider relationship and goes on to encourages pro-active risk management, early reporting and investigation and communication between the professional and the client about the options available to them. The aims of the Construction Disputes Protocol (which has been in force since October 2000 and which applies specifically to professional negligence claims for architects, engineers and quantity surveyors) has a much clearer emphasis on settlement – a word missing from the introduction and aims of the Professional Negligence Protocol.

'the financial position of each party' (para A2(c)(iv))—There are broadly two issues which dominate the issue of costs in this protocol. The first is the front-loading of costs. The second is the inability of the defendant to recover costs expended during the protocol period if the claimant decides not to proceed.

As to the front-loading of costs, both parties, if they follow the protocol, will spend more on investigation, often with reference to counsel and experts, than they might otherwise have done prior to the issue of proceedings. If the protocol does not succeed in achieving the settlement of the dispute prior to issue, then it is likely that the overall costs will be greater.

As to the recovery of the defendant's protocol costs, if proceedings are issued and the claim is unsuccessful, then costs incurred before the issue of proceedings are potentially recoverable (CPR r 44.3(6)(d)). The same applies if the claimant discontinues (CPR rr 38.6, 44.12(1)(d)).

If the claimant seeks pre-action disclosure, then the defendant will ordinarily be awarded his costs of the application and of complying with the order (CPR r 48.1(2)). If the application is made only because the defendant has declined to comply with his obligation to disclose documents under the protocol (B4.3 and C5), the court is likely to take different view on costs.

There is no mechanism for the professional to recoup costs spent in the preparation of a letter of response which persuades the claimant not to issue proceedings in the absence of exceptional circumstances (*Ian McGlinn v (1) Waltham Contractors Ltd (2) Huw Thoms Associates (3) D J Hartigan & Associates Ltd* [2005] EWHC 1419 (TCC)). In contrast, the claimant will ordinarily be offered his costs as part of any pre-issue settlement (although there is no obligation for the defendant to pay those costs). That convention has been in existence in professional negligence claims for many years prior to the protocol and has survived its introduction.

B The Protocol

B1 **Preliminary Notice** (See also **Guidance Note C3.1**)

B1.1 As soon as the claimant decides there is a reasonable chance that he will bring a claim against a professional, the claimant is encouraged to notify the professional in writing.

B1.2 This letter should contain the following information:

(a) the identity of the claimant and any other parties
(b) a brief outline of the claimant's grievance against the professional
(c) if possible, a general indication of the financial value of the potential claim.

B1.3 This letter should be addressed to the professional and should ask the professional to inform his professional indemnity insurers, if any, immediately.

B1.4 The professional should acknowledge receipt of the claimant's letter within 21 days of receiving it. Other than this acknowledgement, the protocol places no obligation upon either party to take any further action.

'preliminary notice' (para B1)—A preliminary notice should be served as soon as the claimant decides that there is a reasonable chance that he will bring a claim.

The protocol does not require the professional to notify his insurer, nor to give the claimant the details of that insurance (although in claims against solicitors he is entitled to it pursuant to Part 10 of the Solicitors Indemnity Rules).

B2 Letter of Claim

B2.1 As soon as the claimant decides there are grounds for a claim against the professional, the claimant should write a detailed Letter of Claim to the professional.

B2.2 The Letter of Claim will normally be an open letter (as opposed to being 'without prejudice') and should include the following –

(a) The identity of any other parties involved in the dispute or a related dispute.
(b) A clear chronological summary (including key dates) of the facts on which the claim is based. Key documents should be identified, copied and enclosed.
(c) The allegations against the professional. What has he done wrong? What has he failed to do?
(d) An explanation of how the alleged error has caused the loss claimed.
(e) An estimate of the financial loss suffered by the claimant and how it is calculated. Supporting documents should be identified, copied and enclosed. If details of the financial loss cannot be supplied, the claimant should explain why and should state when he will be in a position to provide the details. This information should be sent to the professional as soon as reasonably possible.

If the claimant is seeking some form of non-financial redress, this should be made clear.

(f) Confirmation whether or not an expert has been appointed. If so, providing the identity and discipline of the expert, together with the date upon which the expert was appointed.
(g) A request that a copy of the Letter of Claim be forwarded immediately to the professional's insurers, if any.

B2.3 The Letter of Claim is not intended to have the same formal status as a Statement of Case. If, however, the Letter of Claim differs materially from the Statement of Case in subsequent proceedings, the court may decide, in its discretion, to impose sanctions.

B2.4 If the claimant has sent other Letters of Claim (or equivalent) to any other party in relation to this dispute or related dispute, those letters should be copied to the professional. (If the claimant is claiming against someone else to whom this protocol does not apply, please see **Guidance Note C4**.)

'should include' (para B2.2)—In addition to that listed, if the case is funded by a CFA, notification should be given of the existence of the agreement, success fee and insurance premium (PDProt, paras 4A.1 and 4A.2). The level of the success fee and insurance premium should not be disclosed, save as appropriate in advanced settlement negotiations.

There is no provision for the letter of claim to include an offer to settle (unlike the Clinical Disputes Protocol) but there is equally no prohibition on taking that step.

'differs materially' (para B2.3)—The same test is applied for the letter of response (see para B5.3). This is at subtle variance to the Clinical Disputes Protocol (at para 3.20), which states that sanctions should not 'necessarily apply if the letter of claim and any subsequent statement of claim in the proceedings differ'. It is recognised that save only in exceptional cases the claimant may amend his case after the letter of response without sanction (*Ian McGlinn v (1) Waltham Contractors Ltd (2) Huw Thoms Associates (3) D J Hartigan & Associates Ltd* [2005] EWHC 1419 (TCC)).

B3 The Letter of Acknowledgment

B3.1 The professional should acknowledge receipt of the Letter of Claim within 21 days of receiving it.

'letter of acknowledgment' (para B3.1)—By comparison the CPR allows 14 days for the filing of an acknowledgment of service. The Clinical Disputes Protocol also allows 14 days. The Construction Disputes Protocol allows 14 days and permits the claimant to immediately issue proceedings in default.

B4 **Investigations**

B4.1 The professional will have three months from the date of the Letter of Acknowledgment to investigate.

B4.2 If the professional is in difficulty in complying with the three month time period, the problem should be explained to the claimant as soon as possible. The professional should explain what is being done to resolve the problem and when the professional expects to complete the investigations. The claimant should agree to any reasonable request for an extension of the three month period.

B4.3 The parties should supply promptly, at this stage and throughout, whatever relevant information or documentation is reasonably requested. (Please see **Guidance Note C5**.)

(If the professional intends to claim against someone who is not currently a party to the dispute, please see **Guidance Note C4**.)

'three months' (para B4.1)—The protocol allows 3 months from the date of the letter of acknowledgment. That is longer than in clinical disputes, where the response is due 3 months from the letter of claim. In construction disputes the defendant has only 28 days (although this may be extended by agreement).

B5 **Letter of Response and Letter of Settlement**

B5.1 As soon as the professional has completed his investigations, the professional should send to the claimant:

(a) a Letter of Response, or
(b) a Letter of Settlement; or
(c) both.

The Letters of Response and Settlement can be contained within a single letter.

THE LETTER OF RESPONSE

B5.2 The Letter of Response will normally be an open letter (as opposed to being 'without prejudice') and should be a reasoned answer to the claimant's allegations:

(a) if the claim is admitted the professional should say so in clear terms.
(b) if only part of the claim is admitted the professional should make clear which parts of the claim are admitted and which are denied.
(c) if the claim is denied in whole or in part, the Letter of Response should include specific comments on the allegations against the professional and, if the claimant's version of events is disputed, the professional should provide his version of events.
(d) if the professional is unable to admit or deny the claim, the professional should identify any further information which is required.
(e) if the professional disputes the estimate of the claimant's financial loss, the Letter of Response should set out the professional's estimate. If an estimate cannot be provided, the professional should explain why and

should state when he will be in a position to provide an estimate. This information should be sent to the claimant as soon as reasonably possible.

(f) where additional documents are relied upon, copies should be provided.

B5.3 The Letter of Response is not intended to have the same formal status as a Defence. If, however, the Letter of Response differs materially from the Defence in subsequent proceedings, the court may decide, in its discretion, to impose sanctions.

'if the claim is admitted' (para B5.2(a))—The protocol does not explicitly refer to admissions being binding, unlike para 3.25 of the Clinical Disputes Protocol. It is, therefore, open to the defendant to apply under CPR r 14.1(5) to amend or withdraw an admission in any subsequent proceedings.

THE LETTER OF SETTLEMENT

B5.4 The Letter of Settlement will normally be a without prejudice letter and should be sent if the professional intends to make proposals for settlement. It should:

(a) set out the professional's views to date on the claim identifying those issues which the professional believes are likely to remain in dispute and those which are not. (The Letter of Settlement does not need to include this information if the professional has sent a Letter of Response.)

(b) make a settlement proposal or identify any further information which is required before the professional can formulate its proposals.

(c) where additional documents are relied upon, copies should be provided.

EFFECT OF LETTER OF RESPONSE AND/OR LETTER OF SETTLEMENT

B5.5 If the Letter of Response denies the claim in its entirety and there is no Letter of Settlement, it is open to the claimant to commence proceedings.

B5.6 In any other circumstance, the professional and the claimant should commence negotiations with the aim of concluding those negotiations within 6 months of the date of the Letter of Acknowledgment (NOT from the date of the Letter of Response).

B5.7 If the claim cannot be resolved within this period:

(a) the parties should agree within 14 days of the end of the period whether the period should be extended and, if so, by how long.

(b) the parties should seek to identify those issues which are still in dispute and those which can be agreed.

(c) if an extension of time is not agreed it will then be open to the claimant to commence proceedings.

'differs materially' (para B5.3)—The same test is applied for the letter of claim (see para B2.3).

B6 **Alternative Dispute Resolution**

B6.1 The parties can agree at any stage to take the dispute (or any part of the dispute) to mediation or some other form of alternative dispute resolution (ADR).

B6.2 In addition, any party at any stage can refer the dispute (or any part of the dispute) to an ADR agency for mediation or some other form of ADR.

B6.3 When approached by a party or an ADR agency with a proposal that ADR be used, the other party or parties should respond within 14 days stating that:

(a) they agree to the proposal; or
(b) they agree that ADR will be or may be appropriate, but they believe it has been suggested prematurely. They should state when they anticipate it would or may become appropriate; or
(c) they agree that ADR is appropriate, but not the form of ADR proposed (if any). They should state the form of ADR which they believe to be appropriate; or
(d) they do not accept that any form of ADR is appropriate. They should state their reasons.

This letter should be copied to the other party or parties and can be disclosed to the court on the issue of costs.

B6.4 It is expressly recognised that no party can or should be forced to mediate or enter into any other form of ADR.

B7 **Experts**

(The following provisions apply where the claim raises an issue of professional expertise whose resolution requires expert evidence.)

B7.1 If the claimant has obtained expert evidence prior to sending the Letter of Claim, the professional will have equal right to obtain expert evidence prior to sending the Letter of Response/Letter of Settlement.

B7.2 If the claimant has not obtained expert evidence prior to sending the Letter of Claim, the parties are encouraged to appoint a joint expert. If they agree to do so, they should seek to agree the identity of the expert and the terms of the expert's appointment.

B7.3 If agreement about a joint expert cannot be reached, all parties are free to appoint their own experts.

(For further details on experts see **Guidance Note C6**.)

B8 **Proceedings**

B8.1 Unless it is necessary (for example, to obtain protection against the expiry of a relevant limitation period) the claimant should not start court proceedings until:

(a) the Letter of Response denies the claim in its entirety and there is no Letter of Settlement (see paragraph B5.5 above); or
(b) the end of the negotiation period (see paragraphs B5.6 and B5.7 above); or

(For further discussion of statutory time limits for the commencement of litigation, please see **Guidance Note C7**.)

B8.2 Where possible 14 days written notice should be given to the professional before proceedings are started, indicating the court within which the claimant is intending to commence litigation.

B8.3 Proceedings should be served on the professional, unless the professional's solicitor has notified the claimant in writing that he is authorised to accept service on behalf of the professional.

C Guidance Notes

C1 Introduction

C1.1 The protocol has been kept simple to promote ease of use and general acceptability. The guidance notes which follow relate particularly to issues on which further guidance may be required.

C1.2 The Woolf reforms envisage that parties will act reasonably in the pre-action period. Accordingly, in the event that the protocol and the guidelines do not specifically address a problem, the parties should comply with the spirit of the protocol by acting reasonably.

C2 Scope of Protocol

C2.1 The protocol is specifically designed for claims of negligence against professionals. This will include claims in which the allegation against a professional is that they have breached a contractual term to take reasonable skill and care. The protocol is also appropriate for claims of breach of fiduciary duty against professionals.

C2.2 The protocol is not intended to apply to claims:

(a) against architects, engineers and quantity surveyors – parties should use the Construction and Engineering Disputes (CED) Protocol.
(b) against healthcare providers – parties should use the Pre-Action Protocol for the Resolution of Clinical Disputes.
(c) concerning defamation – parties should use the Pre-Action Protocol for Defamation Claims.

C2.3 'Professional' is deliberately left undefined in the protocol. If it becomes an issue as to whether a defendant is or is not a professional, parties are reminded of the overriding need to act reasonably (see paragraphs A4 and C1.2 above). Rather than argue about the definition of 'professional', therefore, the parties are invited to use this protocol, adapting it where appropriate.

C2.4 The protocol may not be suitable for disputes with professionals concerning intellectual property claims, etc. Until specific protocols are created for those claims, however, parties are invited to use this protocol, adapting it where necessary.

C2.5 Allegations of professional negligence are sometimes made in response to an attempt by the professional to recover outstanding fees. Where possible these allegations should be raised before litigation has commenced, in which case the parties should comply with the protocol before either party commences litigation. If litigation has already commenced it will be a matter for the court whether sanctions should be imposed against either party. In any event, the parties are encouraged to consider applying to the court for a stay to allow the protocol to be followed.

C3 Inter-action with other pre-action methods of dispute resolution

C3.1 There are a growing number of methods by which disputes can be resolved without the need for litigation, eg internal complaints procedures, the Surveyors and Valuers Arbitration Scheme, and so on. The Preliminary Notice procedure of the protocol (see paragraph B1) is designed to enable both parties to take stock at an early stage and to decide before work starts on preparing a Letter of Claim whether the grievance should be referred to one of these other dispute resolution procedures. (For the avoidance of doubt, however, there is no obligation on either party under the protocol to take any action at this stage other than giving the acknowledgment provided for in paragraph B1.4.)

C3.2 Accordingly, parties are free to use (and are encouraged to use) any of the available pre-action procedures in an attempt to resolve their dispute. If appropriate, the parties can agree to suspend the protocol timetable whilst the other method of dispute resolution is used.

C3.3 If these methods fail to resolve the dispute, however, the protocol should be used before litigation is commenced. Because there has already been an attempt to resolve the dispute, it may be appropriate to adjust the protocol's requirements. In particular, unless the parties agree otherwise, there is unlikely to be any benefit in duplicating a stage which has in effect already been undertaken. However, if the protocol adds anything to the earlier method of dispute resolution, it should be used, adapting it where appropriate. Once again, the parties are expected to act reasonably.

C4 **Multi-Party Disputes**

C4.1 Paragraph B2.2(a) of the protocol requires a claimant to identify any other parties involved in the dispute or a related dispute. This is intended to ensure that all relevant parties are identified as soon as possible.

C4.2 If the dispute involves more than two parties, there are a number of potential problems. It is possible that different protocols will apply to different defendants. It is possible that defendants will claim against each other. It is possible that other parties will be drawn into the dispute. It is possible that the protocol timetable against one party will not be synchronised with the protocol timetable against a different party. How will these problems be resolved?

C4.3 As stated in paragraph C1.2 above, the parties are expected to act reasonably. What is 'reasonable' will, of course, depend upon the specific facts of each case. Accordingly, it would be inappropriate for the protocol to set down generalised rules. Whenever a problem arises, the parties are encouraged to discuss how it can be overcome. In doing so, parties are reminded of the protocol's aims which include the aim to resolve the dispute without the need for litigation (paragraph A2 above).

C5 **Investigations**

C5.1 Paragraph B4.3 is intended to encourage the early exchange of relevant information, so that issues in the dispute can be clarified or resolved. It should not be used as a 'fishing expedition' by either party. No party is obliged under paragraph B4.3 to disclose any document which a court could not order them to disclose in the pre-action period.

C5.2 This protocol does not alter the parties' duties to disclose documents under any professional regulation or under general law.

Disclosure (para C5.1)—Subject to each profession's rules, the professional may seek to rely on a lien where fees remain unpaid, as is common in such claims. The protocol does not meet that situation head on but reasonable provision should be made by both sides to overcome the potential obstacle, for instance by the provision of copy, rather than original, documentation and/or the payment of some of the fees without prejudice to the outcome of the dispute.

C6 **Experts**

C6.1 Expert evidence is not always needed, although the use and role of experts in professional negligence claims is often crucial. However, the way in which expert evidence is used in, say, an insurance brokers' negligence case, is not necessarily the same as in, say, an accountants' case. Similarly, the approach to be adopted in a £10,000 case does not necessarily compare with the approach in a £10 million case. The protocol therefore is designed to be flexible and does not dictate a standard approach. On the contrary it envisages that the parties will bear the responsibility for agreeing how best to use experts.

C6.2 If a joint expert is used, therefore, the parties are left to decide issues such as: the payment of the expert, whether joint or separate instructions are used, how and to whom the expert is to report, how questions may be addressed to the expert and how the expert should respond, whether an agreed statement of facts is required, and so on.

C6.3 If separate experts are used, the parties are left to decide issues such as: whether the expert's reports should be exchanged, whether there should be an expert's meeting, and so on.

C6.4 Even if a joint expert is appointed, it is possible that parties will still want to instruct their own experts. The protocol does not prohibit this.

C7 **Proceedings**

C7.1 This protocol does not alter the statutory time limits for starting court proceedings. A claimant is required to start proceedings within those time limits.

C7.2 If proceedings are for any reason started before the parties have followed the procedures in this protocol, the parties are encouraged to agree to apply to the court for a stay whilst the protocol is followed.

'statutory time limits' (para C7.1)—It may be possible for the parties to reach a 'standstill' agreement prior to the expiry of the relevant limitation period, effectively extending that period to allow the protocol to be complied with, without the need to issue proceedings.

However, the claimant should ensure that the terms of such an agreement are clearly recorded and agreed – for an illustration of a failure to do so, where the respective advisers fatally had 'a good working relationship', see *Excel Polymers Ltd v Achillesmark Ltd* [2005] EWHC 1927, Robin Purchas QC.

Pre-Action Protocol for Judicial Review

CONTENTS

General note—This protocol came into force on 4 March 2002 – see PDProt, para 5.1.

Introduction

This protocol applies to proceedings within England and Wales only. It does not affect the time-limit specified by Rule 54.5(1) of the Civil Procedure Rules which requires that any claim form in an application for judicial

review must be filed promptly and in any event not later than 3 months after the grounds to make the claim first arose.[1]

1 Judicial review allows people with a sufficient interest in a decision or action by a public body to ask a judge to review the lawfulness of:

- an enactment; or
- a decision, action or failure to act in relation to the exercise of a public function.[2]

2 Civil Procedure Rule 54.1(2).

2 Judicial review may be used where there is no right of appeal or where all avenues of appeal have been exhausted.

3 Where alternative procedures have not been used the judge may refuse to hear the judicial review case. However, his or her decision will depend upon the circumstances of the case and the nature of the alternative remedy. Where an alternative remedy does exist a claimant should give careful consideration as to whether it is appropriate to his or her problem before making a claim for judicial review.

4 Judicial review may not be appropriate in every instance.

Claimants are strongly advised to seek appropriate legal advice when considering such proceedings and, in particular, before adopting this protocol or making a claim. Although the Legal Services Commission will not normally grant full representation before a letter before claim has been sent and the proposed defendant given a reasonable time to respond, initial funding may be available, for eligible claimants, to cover the work necessary to write this. (See Annex C for more information).

5 This protocol sets out a code of good practice and contains the steps which parties should generally follow before making a claim for judicial review.

6 This protocol does not impose a greater obligation on a public body to disclose documents or give reasons for its decision than that already provided for in statute or common law. However, where the court considers that a public body should have provided **relevant** documents and/or information, particularly where this failure is a breach of a statutory or common law requirement, it may impose sanctions.

This protocol will not be appropriate where the defendant does not have the legal power to change the decision being challenged, for example decisions issued by tribunals such as the Immigration Appeal Authorities.

This protocol will not be appropriate in urgent cases, for example, when directions have been set, or are in force, for the claimant's removal from the UK, or where there is an urgent need for an interim order to compel a public body to act where it has unlawfully refused to do so (for example, the failure of a local housing authority to secure interim accommodation for a homeless claimant) a claim should be made immediately. A letter before claim will not stop the implementation of a disputed decision in all instances.

7 All claimants will need to satisfy themselves whether they should follow the protocol, depending upon the circumstances of his or her case. Where the use of the protocol is appropriate, the court will normally expect all parties to have complied with it and will take into account compliance or non-compliance when giving directions for case management of proceedings or when making orders

for costs.[3] However, even in emergency cases, it is good practice to fax to the defendant the draft claim form which the claimant intends to issue. A claimant is also normally required to notify a defendant when an interim mandatory order is being sought.

3 Civil Procedure Rules Costs Practice Direction.

THE LETTER BEFORE CLAIM

8 Before making a claim, the claimant should send a letter to the defendant. The purpose of this letter is to identify the issues in dispute and establish whether litigation can be avoided.

9 Claimants should normally use the suggested **standard format** for the letter outlined at Annex A.

10 The letter should contain **the date and details of the decision, act or omission being challenged and a clear summary of the facts** on which the claim is based. It should also contain the **details of any relevant information** that the claimant is seeking and an explanation of why this is considered relevant.

11 The letter should normally contain the **details of any interested parties**[4] known to the claimant. They should be sent a **copy** of the letter before claim **for information. Claimants are strongly advised to seek appropriate legal advice when considering such proceedings and, in particular, before sending the letter before claim to other interested parties or making a claim.**

4 See Civil Procedure Rule 54.1(2)(f).

12 A claim should not normally be made until the proposed reply date given in the letter before claim has passed, unless the circumstances of the case require more immediate action to be taken.

THE LETTER OF RESPONSE

13 Defendants should normally respond within 14 days using the **standard format** at Annex B. Failure to do so will be taken into account by the court and sanctions may be imposed unless there are good reasons.[5]

5 See Civil Procedure Rules Pre-action Protocol Practice Direction paragraphs 2–3.

14 Where it is not possible to reply within the proposed time-limit the defendant should send an interim reply and propose a reasonable extension. Where an extension is sought, reasons should be given and, where required, additional information requested. **This will not affect the time-limit for making a claim for judicial review**[6] nor will it bind the claimant where he or she considers this to be unreasonable. However, where the court considers that a subsequent claim is made prematurely it may impose sanctions.

6 See Civil Procedure Rule 54.5(1).

15 If the **claim is being conceded in full**, the reply should say so in clear and unambiguous terms.

16 If the **claim is being conceded in part or not being conceded at all**, the reply should say so in clear and unambiguous terms, and:

(a) where appropriate, contain a new decision, clearly identifying what aspects of the claim are being conceded and what are not, or, give a clear timescale within which the new decision will be issued;

(b) provide a fuller explanation for the decision, if considered appropriate to do so;
(c) address any points of dispute, or explain why they cannot be addressed;
(d) enclose any **relevant** documentation requested by the claimant, or explain why the documents are not being enclosed; and
(e) where appropriate, confirm whether or not they will oppose any application for an interim remedy.

17 The response should be sent to **all interested parties**[7] identified by the claimant and contain details of any other parties who the defendant considers also have an interest.

7 See Civil Procedure Rule 54.1(2)(f).

Annex A
Letter before Claim

SECTION 1 – INFORMATION REQUIRED IN A LETTER BEFORE CLAIM

PROPOSED CLAIM FOR JUDICIAL REVIEW

1 **To**

(*Insert the name and address of the proposed defendant – see details in section 2*)

2 **The claimant**

(*Insert the title, first and last name and the address of the claimant*)

3 **Reference details**

(*When dealing with large organisations it is important to understand that the information relating to any particular individual's previous dealings with it may not be immediately available, therefore it is important to set out the relevant reference numbers for the matter in dispute and/or the identity of those within the public body who have been handling the particular matter in dispute – see details in section 3*)

4 **The details of the matter being challenged**

(*Set out clearly the matter being challenged, particularly if there has been more than one decision*)

5 **The issue**

(*Set out the date and details of the decision, or act or omission being challenged, a brief summary of the facts and why it is contented to be wrong*)

6 **The details of the action that the defendant is expected to take**

(*Set out the details of the remedy sought, including whether a review or any interim remedy are being requested*)

7 **The details of the legal advisers, if any, dealing with this claim**

(*Set out the name, address and reference details of any legal advisers dealing with the claim*)

8 **The details of any interested parties**

SECTION 4 Protocols

(*Set out the details of any interested parties and confirm that they have been sent a copy of this letter*)

9 **The details of any information sought**

(*Set out the details of any information that is sought. This may include a request for a fuller explanation of the reasons for the decision that is being challenged*)

10 **The details of any documents that are considered relevant and necessary**

(*Set out the details of any documentation or policy in respect of which the disclosure is sought and explain why these are relevant. If you rely on a statutory duty to disclose, this should be specified*)

11 **The address for reply and service of court documents**

(*Insert the address for the reply*)

12 **Proposed reply date**

(*The precise time will depend upon the circumstances of the individual case. However, although a shorter or longer time may be appropriate in a particular case, 14 days is a reasonable time to allow in most circumstances*)

SECTION 2 – ADDRESS FOR SENDING THE LETTER BEFORE CLAIM

Public bodies have requested that, for certain types of cases, in order to ensure a prompt response, letters before claim should be sent to specific addresses.

- **Where the claim concerns a decision in an Immigration, Asylum or Nationality case:**

The Judicial Review Management Unit
Immigration and Nationality Directorate
1st Floor
Green Park House
29 Wellesley Road
Croydon CR0 2AJ

- **Where the claim concerns a decision by the Legal Services Commission:**
  - The address on the decision letter/notification; and

Policy and Legal Department
Legal Services Commission
85 Gray's Inn Road
London WC1X 8TX

- **Where the claim concerns a decision by a local authority:**
  - The address on the decision letter/notification; and
  - Their legal department[8]
- **Where the claim concerns a decision by a department or body for whom Treasury Solicitor acts** *and Treasury Solicitor has already been involved in the case* a copy should also be sent, quoting the Treasury Solicitor's reference, to:

Treasury Solicitor
Queen Anne's Chambers
28 Broadway

London SW1H 9JS

- **In all other circumstances, the letter should be sent to the address on the letter notifying the decision.**

SECTION 3 – SPECIFIC REFERENCE DETAILS REQUIRED

Public bodies have requested that the following information should be provided in order to ensure prompt response.

- **Where the claim concerns an Immigration, Asylum or Nationality case, dependent upon the nature of the case:**
- The Home Office reference number
- The Port reference number
- The Immigration Appellate Authority reference number
- The National Asylum Support Service reference number

Or, if these are unavailable:

- The full name, nationality and date of birth of the claimant.

- **Where the claim concerns a decision by the Legal Services Commission:**
  - The certificate reference number.

Annex B
Response to a Letter before Claim

INFORMATION REQUIRED IN A RESPONSE TO A LETTER BEFORE CLAIM

PROPOSED CLAIM FOR JUDICIAL REVIEW

1 **The claimant**

(*Insert the title, first and last names and the address to which any reply should be sent*)

2 **From**

(*Insert the name and address of the defendant*)

3 **Reference details**

(*Set out the relevant reference numbers for the matter in dispute and the identity of those within the public body who have been handling the issue*)

4 **The details of the matter being challenged**

(*Set out details of the matter being challenged, providing a fuller explanation of the decision, where this is considered appropriate*)

5 **Response to the proposed claim**

(*Set out whether the issue in question is conceded in part, or in full, or will be contested. Where it is not proposed to disclose any information that has been requested, explain the reason for this. Where an interim reply is being sent and there is a realistic prospect of settlement, details should be included*)

6 **Details of any other interested parties**

(*Identify any other parties who you consider have an interest who have not already been sent a letter by the claimant*)

7 **Address for further correspondence and service of court documents**

(*Set out the address for any future correspondence on this matter*)

Annex C
Notes on Public Funding for Legal Costs in Judicial Review

Public funding for legal costs in judicial review is available from legal professionals and advice agencies which have contracts with the Legal Services Commission as part of the Community Legal Service. Funding may be provided for:

- *Legal Help* to provide initial advice and assistance with any legal problem; or
- *Legal Representation* to allow you to be represented in court if you are taking or defending court proceedings. This is available in two forms:
- *Investigative Help* is limited to funding to investigate the strength of the proposed claim. It includes the issue and conduct of proceedings only so far as is necessary to obtain disclosure of relevant information or to protect the client's position in relation to any urgent hearing or time-limit for the issue of proceedings. This includes the work necessary to write a **letter before claim** to the body potentially under challenge, setting out the grounds of challenge, and giving that body a reasonable opportunity, typically 14 days, in which to respond.
- *Full Representation* is provided to represent you in legal proceedings and includes litigation services, advocacy services, and all such help as is usually given by a person providing representation in proceedings, including steps preliminary or incidental to proceedings, and/or arriving at or giving affect to a compromise to avoid or bring to an end any proceedings. Except in emergency cases, a proper **letter before claim** must be sent and the other side must be given an opportunity to respond before *Full Representation* is granted.

Further information on the type(s) of help available and the criteria for receiving that help may be found in the Legal Service Manual Volume 3: '*The Funding Code*'. This may be found on the Legal Services Commission website at:

www.legalservices.co.uk

A list of contracted firms and Advice Agencies may be found on the Community Legal Services website at:

www.justask.org.uk

Pre-Action Protocol for Disease and Illness Claims

CONTENTS

1 Introduction

1.1 Lord Woolf in his final Access to Justice Report of July 1996 recommended the development of protocols: 'To build on and increase the benefits of early but well informed settlement which genuinely satisfy both parties to dispute.'

1.2 The aims of these protocols are:

- more contact between the parties
- better and earlier exchange of information
- better investigation by both sides
- to put the parties in a position where they may be able to settle cases fairly and early without litigation
- to enable proceedings to run to the court's timetable and efficiently, if litigation does become necessary.

1.3 The concept of protocols is relevant to a range of initiatives for good claims practice, especially:

- predictability in the time needed for steps to be taken
- standardisation of relevant information, including documents to be disclosed.

1.4 The Courts will be able to treat the standards set in protocols as the normal reasonable approach. If proceedings are issued, it will be for the court to decide whether non-compliance with a protocol should merit adverse consequences. Guidance on the court's likely approach will be given from time to time in practice directions.

1.5 If the court has to consider the question of compliance after proceedings have begun, it will not be concerned with minor infringements, eg failure by a short period to provide relevant information. One minor breach will not exempt the 'innocent' party from following the protocol. The court will look at the effect of non-compliance on the other party when deciding whether to impose sanctions.

2 Notes of Guidance

SCOPE OF THE PROTOCOL

2.1 This protocol is intended to apply to all personal injury claims where the injury is not as the result of an accident but takes the form of an illness or disease.

2.2 This protocol covers disease claims which are likely to be complex and frequently not suitable for fast-track procedures even though they may fall within fast track limits. Disease for the purpose of this protocol primarily covers any illness physical or psychological, any disorder, ailment, affliction, complaint, malady, or derangement other than a physical or psychological injury solely caused by an accident or other similar single event.

2.3 This protocol is not limited to diseases occurring in the workplace but will embrace diseases occurring in other situations for example through occupation of premises or the use of products. It is not intended to cover those cases, which are dealt with as a 'group' or 'class' action.

2.4 The 'cards on the table' approach advocated by the personal injury protocol is equally appropriate to disease claims. The spirit of that protocol, and of the clinical negligence protocol is followed here, in accordance with the sense of the civil justice reforms.

2.5 The timetable and the arrangements for disclosing documents and obtaining expert evidence may need to be varied to suit the circumstances of the case. If a party considers the detail of the protocol to be inappropriate they should communicate their reasons to all of the parties at that stage. If proceedings are subsequently issued, the court will expect an explanation as to why the protocol has not been followed, or has been varied. In a terminal disease claim with short life expectancy, for instance for a claimant who has a disease such as mesothelioma, the time scale of the protocol is likely to be too long. In such a claim, the claimant may not be able to follow the protocol and the defendant would be expected to treat the claim with urgency.

3 The Aims of the Protocol

3.1 The *general* aims of the protocol are –

- to resolve as many disputes as possible without litigation;
- where a claim cannot be resolved to identify the relevant issues which remain in dispute.

3.2 The *specific* objectives are –

OPENNESS

- to encourage early communication of the perceived problem between the parties or their insurers;
- to encourage employees to voice any concerns or worries about possible work related illness as soon as practicable;
- to encourage employers to develop systems of early reporting and investigation of suspected occupational health problems and to provide full and prompt explanations to concerned employees or former employees;

- to apply such principles to perceived problems outside the employer/employee relationship, for example occupiers of premises or land and producers of products;
- to ensure that sufficient information is disclosed by both parties to enable each to understand the other's perspective and case, and to encourage early resolution;

TIMELINESS

- to provide an early opportunity for employers (past or present) or their insurers to identify cases where an investigation is required and to carry out that investigation promptly;
- to encourage employers (past or present) or other defendants to involve and identify their insurers at an early stage;
- to ensure that all relevant records including health and personnel records are provided to employees (past or present) or their appointed representatives promptly on request, by any employer (past or present) or their insurers. This should be complied with to a realistic timetable;
- to ensure that relevant records which are in the claimant's possession are made available to the employers or their insurers by claimants or their advisers at an appropriate stage;
- to proceed on a reasonable timetable where a resolution is not achievable to lay the ground to enable litigation to proceed at a reasonable and proportionate cost, and to limit the matters in contention;
- to communicate promptly where any of the requested information is not available or does not exist;
- to discourage the prolonged pursuit of unmeritorious claims and the prolonged defence of meritorious claims.
- To encourage all parties, at the earliest possible stage, to disclose voluntarily any additional documents which will assist in resolving any issue.

4 The Protocol

This protocol is not a comprehensive code governing all the steps in disease claims. Rather it attempts to set out **a code of good practice** which parties should follow.

OBTAINING OCCUPATIONAL RECORDS INCLUDING HEALTH RECORDS

4.1 In appropriate cases, a **potential claimant** may request Occupational Records including Health Records and Personnel Records before sending a Letter of Claim.

4.2 Any request for records by the **potential claimant** or his adviser should **provide sufficient information** to alert the **potential defendant** or his insurer where a possible disease claim is being investigated; Annex A1 provides a suggested form for this purpose for use in cases arising from employment. Similar forms can be prepared and used in other situations.

4.3 The copy records should be provided **within a maximum of 40 days** of the request at no cost. Although these will primarily be occupational records, it will be good practice for a **potential defendant** to disclose product data documents identified by a **potential claimant** at this stage which may resolve a causation issue.

4.4 In the rare circumstances that the **potential defendant** or his insurer is in difficulty in providing information quickly details should be given of what is being done to resolve it with a reasonable time estimate for doing so.

4.5 If the **potential defendant** or his insurer fails to provide the records including health records within 40 days and fails to comply with paragraph 4.4 above, the **potential claimant** or his adviser may then apply to the court for an **order for pre-action disclosure**. The Civil Procedure Rules make pre-action applications to the court easier. The court also has the power to impose costs sanctions for unreasonable delay in providing records.

5 Communication

5.1 If either the **potential claimant** or his adviser considers **additional records are required from a third party**, such as records from previous employers or general practitioner records, in the first instance these should be requested by the **potential claimant** or their advisers. Third party record holders would be expected to co-operate. The Civil Procedure Rules enable parties to apply to the court for pre-action disclosure by third parties.

5.2 As soon as the records have been received and analysed, the **potential claimant** or his adviser should consider whether a claim should be made. General practitioner records will normally be obtained before a decision is reached.

5.3 If a decision is made not to proceed further at this stage against a party identified as a **potential defendant**, the **potential claimant** or his adviser should notify that **potential defendant** as soon as practicable.

6 Letter of Claim

6.1 Where a decision is made to make a claim, the claimant shall send to the proposed defendant two copies of a letter of claim, as soon as sufficient information is available to substantiate a realistic claim and before issues of quantum are addressed in detail. One copy is for the defendants, the second for passing on to his insurers.

6.2 This letter shall contain a **clear summary of the facts** on which the claim is based, including details of the illness alleged, and the **main allegations of fault**. It shall also give details of present condition and prognosis. The **financial loss** incurred by the claimant should be outlined. Where the case is funded by a conditional fee agreement, notification should be given of the existence of the agreement and where appropriate, that there is a success fee and insurance premium, although not the level of the success fee or premium.

6.3 Solicitors are recommended to use a **standard format** for such a letter – an example is at Annex B: this can be amended to suit the particular case, for example, if the client has rehabilitation needs these can also be detailed in the letter.

6.4 A **chronology** of the relevant events (eg dates or periods of exposure) should be provided. In the case of alleged occupational disease an appropriate employment history should also be provided, particularly if the claimant has been employed by a number of different employers and the illness in question has a long latency period.

6.5 The letter of claim should identify any **relevant documents**, including health records not already in the defendant's possession eg any relevant general practitioner records. These will need to be disclosed in confidence to the nominated insurance manager or solicitor representing the defendant following receipt of their letter of acknowledgement. Where the action is brought under the Law Reform Act 1934 or the Fatal Accidents Act 1976 then **relevant documents** will normally include copies of the death certificate, the post mortem report, the inquest depositions and if obtained by that date the grant of probate or letters of administration.

6.6 The letter of claim should indicate whether a claim is also being made against any **other potential defendant** and identify any known insurer involved.

6.7 Sufficient information should be given to enable the defendant's insurer/ solicitor to commence **investigations** and at least to put a broad valuation on the 'risk'.

6.8 It is not a requirement for the claimant to provide **medical evidence** with the letter of claim, but the claimant may choose to do so in very many cases.

6.9 **Letters of claim and response** are not intended to have the same **status** as a statement of case in proceedings. Matters may come to light as a result of investigation after the letter of claim has been sent, or after the defendant has responded, particularly if disclosure of documents takes place outside the recommended three-month period. These circumstances could mean that the 'pleaded' case of one or both parties is presented slightly differently than in the letter of claim or response. It would not be consistent with the spirit of the protocol for a party to 'take a point' on this in the proceedings, provided that there was no obvious intention by the party who changed their position to mislead the other party.

6.10 **Proceedings should not be issued until after three months from the date of acknowledgement** (see paragraph 7), unless there is a limitation problem and/or the claimant's position needs to be protected by early issue. (See paragraph 2.5)

7 The Response

7.1 The defendant should **send an acknowledgement within 21 calendar days** of the date of posting of the letter of claim, identifying the liability insurer (if any) who will be dealing with the matter and, if necessary, identifying specifically any significant omissions from the Letter of Claim. If there has been no acknowledgement by the defendant or insurer within 21 days, the claimant will be entitled to issue proceedings.

7.2 The identity of all relevant insurers, if more than one, should be notified to the claimant by the insurer identified in the acknowledgement letter, within one calendar month of the date of that acknowledgement.

7.3 The defendant or his representative should, **within three months of the date of the acknowledgement letter**, provide a **reasoned answer**: –

- if the **claim is admitted**, they should say so in clear terms;

- if only **part of the claim is admitted** they should make clear which issues of fault and/or causation and/or limitation are admitted and which remain in issue and why;
- if the **claim is not admitted in full**, they should explain why and should, **for example**, include comments on the employment status of the claimant, (including job description(s) and details of the department(s) where the claimant worked), the allegations of fault, causation and of limitation, and if a synopsis or chronology of relevant events has been provided and is disputed, their version of those events;
- if the **claim is not admitted in full**, the defendant should enclose with his letter of reply **documents** in his possession which are **material to the issues** between the parties and which would be likely to be ordered to be disclosed by the court, either on an application for pre-action disclosure, or on disclosure during proceedings. Reference can be made to the documents annexed to the personal injury protocol.
- where more than one defendant receives a letter of claim, the timetable will be activated for each defendant by the date on the letter of claim addressed to them. If any defendant wishes to extend the timetable because the number of defendants will cause complications, they should seek agreement to a different timetable as soon as possible.

7.4 If the parties reach agreement on liability and/or causation, but time is needed to resolve other issues including the value of the claim, they should aim to agree a reasonable period.

7.5 Where it is not practicable for the defendant to complete his investigations within 3 months, the defendant should indicate the difficulties and outline the further time needed. Any request for an extension of time should be made, with reasons, as soon as the defendant becomes aware that an extension is needed and normally before the 3 month period has expired. Such an extension of time should be agreed in circumstances where reasonable justification has been shown. Lapse of many years since the circumstances giving rise to the claim does not, by itself, constitute reasonable justification for further time.

7.6 Where the relevant negligence occurred outside England and Wales and/or where the defendant is outside the jurisdiction, the time periods of 21 days and three months should normally be extended up to 42 days and six months.

8 Special Damages

8.1 The claimant will send to the defendant as soon as practicable a Schedule of Special Damages with supporting documents, particularly where the defendant has admitted liability.

9 Experts

9.1 In disease claims expert opinions will usually be needed: –

- on knowledge, fault and causation;
- on condition and prognosis;
- to assist in valuing aspects of the claim.

9.2 The civil justice reforms and the Civil Procedure Rules encourage economy in the use of experts and a less adversarial expert culture. It is recognised that in disease claims, the parties and their advisers will require flexibility in their approach to expert evidence. Decisions on whether experts might be instructed jointly, and on whether reports might be disclosed sequentially or by exchange, should rest with the parties and their advisers. Sharing expert evidence may be appropriate on various issues including those relating to the value of the claim. However, this protocol does not attempt to be prescriptive on issues in relation to expert evidence.

9.3 Obtaining expert evidence will often be an expensive step and may take time, especially in specialised areas where there are limited numbers of suitable experts. Claimants, defendants and their advisers, will therefore need to consider carefully how best to obtain any necessary expert help quickly and cost-effectively.

9.4 The protocol recognises that a flexible approach must be adopted in the obtaining of medical reports in claims of this type. There will be very many occasions where the claimant will need to obtain a medical report before writing the letter of claim. In such cases the defendant will be entitled to obtain their own medical report. In some other instances it may be more appropriate to send the letter of claim before the medical report is obtained. Defendants will usually need to see a medical report before they can reach a view on causation.

9.5 Where the parties agree the nomination of a single expert is appropriate, before any party instructs an expert he should give the other party a list of the **name**(s) of **one or more experts** in the relevant speciality whom he considers are suitable to instruct. The parties are encouraged to agree the instruction of a single expert to deal with discrete areas such as cost of care.

9.6 **Within 14 days** the other party may indicate **an objection** to one or more of the named experts. The first party should then instruct a mutually acceptable expert. If the Claimant nominates an expert in the original letter of claim, the 14 days is in addition to the 21 days in paragraph 7.1.

9.7 If the second party objects to all the listed experts, the parties may then instruct **experts of their own choice**. It would be for the court to decide subsequently, if proceedings are issued, whether either party had acted unreasonably.

9.8 If the **second party does not object to an expert nominated**, he shall not be entitled to rely on his own expert evidence within that particular speciality unless:

- (a) the first party agrees,
- (b) the court so directs, or
- (c) the first party's expert report has been amended and the first party is not prepared to disclose the original report.

9.9 **Either party may send to an agreed expert written questions** on the report, relevant to the issues, via the first party's solicitors. The expert should send answers to the questions separately and directly to each party.

9.10 The cost of a report from an agreed expert will usually be paid by the instructing first party: the costs of the expert replying to questions will usually be borne by the party which asks the questions.

9.11 Where the defendant admits liability in whole or in part, before proceedings are issued, any medical report obtained under this protocol which **the claimant** relies upon, should be disclosed to the other party.

9.12 Where the defendant admits liability in whole or in part before proceedings are issued, any medical report obtained under this protocol which **the defendant** relies upon, should be disclosed to the claimant.

10 Resolution of Issues

10.1 The Civil Procedure Rules Part 36 enable claimants and defendants to make formal offers to settle before proceedings are started. Parties should consider making such an offer, since to do so often leads to settlement. If such an offer is made, the party making the offer must always supply sufficient evidence and/or information to enable the offer to be properly considered.

10.2 Where a claim is not resolved when the protocol has been followed, the parties might wish to carry out a 'stocktake' of the issues in dispute, and the evidence that the court is likely to need to decide those issues, before proceedings are started.

10.3 Prior to proceedings it will be usual for all parties to disclose those expert reports relating to liability and causation upon which they propose to rely.

10.4 The claimant should delay issuing proceedings for 21 days from disclosure of reports to enable the parties to consider whether the claim is capable of settlement.

10.5 Where the defendant is insured and the pre-action steps have been conducted by the insurer, the insurer would normally be expected to nominate solicitors to act in the proceedings and the claimant's solicitor is recommended to invite the insurer to nominate solicitors to act in the proceedings and to do so 7–14 days before the intended issue date.

11 Limitation

11.1 If by reason of complying with any part of this protocol a claimant's claim may be time-barred under any provision of the Limitation Act 1980, or any other legislation which imposes a time limit for bringing an action, the claimant may commence proceedings without complying with this protocol. In such circumstances, a claimant who commences proceedings without complying with all, or any part, of this protocol may apply to the court on notice for directions as to the timetable and form of procedure to be adopted, at the same time as he requests the court to issue proceedings. The court will consider whether to order a stay of the whole or part of the proceedings pending compliance with this protocol.

Annex A
Letter Requesting Occupational Records including Health Records

Dear Sirs,

We are acting on behalf of the above-named who has developed the following (***insert disease***).We are investigating whether this disease may have been caused: –

- ***during the course of his employment with you /name of employer if different***
- ***whilst at your premises at (address)***

- ***as a result of your product (name)***

We are writing this in accordance with the Protocol for Disease and Illness Claims

We seek the following records: –

(***Insert details eg personnel/occupational health***)

Please note your insurers may require you to advise them of this request.

We enclose a request form and expect to receive the records within 40 days. If you are not able to comply with this request within this time, please advise us of the reason.

Yours faithfully

Annex A1
Application on Behalf of a Potential Claimant for Use where a Disease Claim is Being Investigated

Company Name and Address		
1 (a)	Full name of claimant (including previous surnames)	
(b)	Address now	
(c)	Address at date of termination of employment, if different	
(d)	Date of birth (and death, if applicable)	
(e)	National Insurance number, if available	
2	Department(s) where claimant worked	
3	This application is made because the claimant is considering	
(a)	a claim against you as detailed in para 4	YES/NO

(b)	pursuing an action against someone else	YES/NO
4	If the answer to Q3(a) is 'Yes' details of	
	(a) the likely nature of the claim, eg dermatitis	
	(b) grounds for the claim, eg exposure to chemical	
	(c) approximate dates of the events involved	
5	If the answer to Q3(b) is 'Yes' insert	
	(a) the names of the proposed defendants	
	(b) have legal proceedings been started	YES/NO
	(c) if appropriate, details of the claim and action number	
6	Any other relevant information or documents requested	
	Signature of Solicitor	
	Name	
	Address	
	Ref.	
	Telephone number	
	Fax number	

I authorise you to disclose all of your records relating to me/the claimant to my solicitor and to your legal and insurance representatives. Signature of claimant
Signature of personal representative where patient has died

Annex B
Template for Letter of Claim

To: – Defendant

Dear Sirs

Re: Claimant's full name
Claimant's full address
Claimant's National Insurance Number
Claimant's Date of Birth
Claimant's Clock or Works Number
Claimant's Employer (name and address)

We are instructed by the above named to claim damages in connection with a claim for: –

Specify occupational disease

We are writing this letter in accordance with the pre-action protocol for disease and illness claims.

Please confirm the identity of your insurers. Please note that your insurers will need to see this letter as soon as possible and it may affect your insurance cover if you do not send this to them.

The Claimant was employed by you (***if the claim arises out of public or occupiers' liability give appropriate details***)as job description from date to date .During the relevant period of his employment he worked: –

description of precisely where the Claimant worked and what he did to include a description of any machines used and details of any exposure to noise or substances

The circumstances leading to the development of this condition are as follows: –

Give chronology of events

The reason why we are alleging fault is: –

Details should be given of contemporary and comparable employees who have suffered from similar problems if known; any protective equipment provided; complaints; the supervisors concerned, if known.

Our client's employment history is attached.

We have also made a claim against: –

Insert details

Their insurers' details are: –

Insert if known

We have the following documents in support of our client's claim and will disclose these in confidence to your nominated insurance manager or solicitor when we receive their acknowledgement letter.

eg Occupational health notes; GP notes

We have obtained a medical report from (name)and will disclose this when we receive your acknowledgement of this letter.

(This is optional at this stage)

From the information we presently have: –

(i) the Claimant first became aware of symptoms on (***insert approximate date***)
(ii) the Claimant first received medical advice about those symptoms on (***insert date***)(***give details of advice given if appropriate***)
(iii) the Claimant first believed that those symptoms might be due to exposure leading to this claim on (***insert approximate date***)

A description of our client's condition is as follows:-

This should be sufficiently detailed to allow the Defendant to put a broad value on the claim

He has the following time off work: –

Insert dates

He is presently employed as a ***job description*** and his average net weekly income is **£**

If you are our client's employers, please provide us with the usual earnings details, which will enable us to calculate his financial loss.

Please note that we have entered into a conditional fee agreement with our client dated in relation to this claim which provides for a success fee within the meaning of section 58(2) of the Courts and Legal Services Act 1990.Our client has taken out an insurance policy dated with (name of insurance company) to which section 29 of the Access to Justice Act 1999 applies in respect of this claim.

A copy of this letter is attached for you to send to your insurers. Finally we expect an acknowledgement of this letter within 21 days by yourselves or your insurers.

Yours faithfully

Pre-Action Protocol for Housing Disrepair Cases[1]

[Prepared by the Housing Disrepair Protocol Working Party]

CONTENTS

General note—This Protocol came into force on 8 December 2003 (see PDProt, para 5.1).

1 Introduction

Following a review of the problems of civil housing disrepair claims, Lord Woolf recommended in his final Access to Justice Report in July 1996 that there should be a Pre-action Protocol.

The Protocol, which covers claims in England and Wales, is intended to encourage the exchange of information between parties at an early stage and to provide a clear framework within which parties in a housing disrepair claim can attempt to achieve an early and appropriate resolution of the issues. An attempt has been made to draft the Protocol in plain English and to keep the contents straightforward in order to make the Protocol accessible and easy to use by all, including those representing themselves.

The Protocol embraces the spirit of the Woolf Reforms to the Civil Justice System. As Lord Woolf noted, landlords and tenants have a common interest in maintaining housing stock in good condition. It is generally common ground that in principle court action should be treated as a last resort, and it is hoped that the Protocol will lead to the avoidance of unnecessary litigation. Before using the Protocol tenants should therefore ensure that the landlord is aware of the disrepair. Tenants should also consider whether other options for having repairs carried out and/or obtaining compensation are more appropriate. Examples of other options are set out in paragraph 4.1(a).

Should a claim proceed to litigation, the court will expect all parties to have complied with the Protocol as far as possible. The court has the power to order parties who have unreasonably failed to comply with the Protocol to pay costs or be subject to other sanctions.

2 Aims of the Protocol

The Practice Direction on Protocols in the Civil Procedure Rules provides that the objectives of pre-action Protocols, are:

(1) *to encourage the exchange of early and full information about the prospective legal claim,*
(2) *to enable parties to avoid litigation by agreeing a settlement of the claim before the commencement of proceedings,*
(3) *to support the efficient management of proceedings where litigation cannot be avoided.*

The specific aims of this Protocol are:–

- To avoid unnecessary litigation
- To promote the speedy and appropriate carrying out of any repairs which are the landlord's responsibility
- To ensure that tenants receive any compensation to which they are entitled as speedily as possible
- To promote good pre-litigation practice, including the early exchange of information and to give guidance about the instruction of experts
- To keep the costs of resolving disputes down.

3 Protocol

When using this Protocol, please refer to the Guidance Notes in paragraph 4.

3.1 DEFINITIONS

For the purposes of this Protocol:

(a) A disrepair claim is a civil claim arising from the condition of residential premises and may include a related personal injury claim. (See paragraphs 4.4 (c), (d) and (e) of the Guidance Notes.) It does not include disrepair claims which originate as counterclaims or set-offs in other proceedings.

(b) The types of claim which this Protocol is intended to cover include those brought under Section 11 of the Landlord and Tenant Act 1985, Section 4 of the Defective Premises Act 1972, common law nuisance and negligence, and those brought under the express terms of a tenancy agreement or lease. It does not cover claims brought under Section 82 of the Environmental Protection Act 1990 (which are heard in the Magistrates' Court).

(c) This protocol covers claims by any person with a disrepair claim as referred to in paragraphs (a) and (b) above, including tenants, lessees and members of the tenant's family. The use of the term 'tenant' in this protocol is intended to cover all such people. (See also paragraph 4.4(e).)

3.2 EARLY NOTIFICATION LETTER

(a) Notice of the claim should be given to the landlord as soon as possible. In order to avoid delay in notifying the landlord it may be appropriate to send a letter notifying the landlord of the claim (Early Notification Letter) before sending a letter setting out the full details of the claim (Letter of Claim). An Early Notification letter is intended to be a helpful tool, but it will not be necessary in every case. It might be appropriate where, for example, a repair is urgent or there is likely to be some delay before enough details are available to make a claim. The Early Notification Letter to the landlord should give the following information:

(i) tenant's name, the address of the property, tenant's address if different, tenant's telephone number and when access is available

(ii) details of the defects, including any defects outstanding, in the form of a schedule, if appropriate. Attached at Annex G of paragraph 5 is a specimen schedule which can be used to inform the landlord of the disrepair
(iii) details of any notification previously given to the landlord of the need for repair or information as to why the tenant believes that the landlord has knowledge of the need for repair
(iv) proposed expert (see paragraph 3.6)
(v) proposed letter of instruction to expert (see Annex C of paragraph 5)
(vi) tenant's disclosure of such relevant documents as are readily available.

(b) The Early Notification Letter should also request the following disclosure from the landlord:–

All relevant records or documents including:–

(i) copy of tenancy agreement including tenancy conditions
(ii) documents or computerised records relating to notice given, disrepair reported, inspection reports or repair works to the property.

(c) The Early Notification Letter should include the authorisation for release of the information (except in a case where the tenant is acting in person).

(d) Specimen Early Notification Letters are attached at Annex A of paragraph 5. They may be suitably adapted as appropriate.

3.3 LETTER OF CLAIM

(a) The tenant should send to the landlord a Letter of Claim at the earliest reasonable opportunity. The Letter of Claim should contain the following details (if they have not already been provided in an Early Notification Letter):–

(i) tenant's name, the address of the property, tenant's address if different, the tenant's telephone number and when access is available
(ii) details of the defects, including any defects outstanding, in the form of a schedule, if appropriate. Attached at Annex G of paragraph 5 is a specimen schedule which can be used to inform the landlord of the disrepair
(iii) history of the defects, including attempts to rectify them
(iv) details of any notification previously given to the landlord of the need for repair or information as to why the tenant believes that the landlord has knowledge of the need for repair
(v) the effect of the defects on the tenant (see paragraphs 4.4 (c), (d) and (e) regarding personal injury claims)
(vi) details of any special damages (see form attached at Annex E of paragraph 5 and definition of 'special damages' at paragraph 4.10)
(vii) proposed expert (see paragraph 3.6)
(viii) proposed letter of instruction to the expert (See Annex C of paragraph 5)
(ix) tenant's disclosure of relevant documents.

(b) If not already requested in an Early Notification Letter, the Letter of Claim should also request the following disclosure from the landlord:–

All relevant records or documents including:–

(i) copy of tenancy agreement including tenancy conditions
(ii) tenancy file

(iii) documents relating to notice given, disrepair reported, inspection reports or requirements to the property
(iv) computerised records.

(c) If not requested in an Early Notification Letter, the Letter of Claim should also include the authorisation for release of the information (except in a case where the tenant is acting in person).

(d) Specimen Letters of Claim are attached at Annex B of paragraph 5. It will be seen that there are different versions depending on whether or not an Early Notification Letter has been sent. The letters may be suitably adapted as appropriate.

3.4 LIMITATION PERIOD

The procedures in this Protocol do not extend statutory limitation periods. If a limitation period is about to expire, the tenant may need to issue proceedings immediately unless the landlord confirms that they will not rely on limitation as a defence in subsequent proceedings. (See paragraph 4.8 for guidance about the limitation period, and paragraph 4.10 for a definition of 'limitation period'.) Alternatively the tenant can ask the landlord to agree to extend the limitation period.

3.5 LANDLORD'S RESPONSE

3.5.1 Response to First Letter

The landlord should normally reply within 20 working days of the date of receipt of the first letter from the tenant ie the Early Notification Letter or the Letter of Claim if no Early Notification Letter is sent. (See paragraph 4.10 for a definition of 'working days'). The Landlord's response to the first letter, whether an Early Notification letter or a Letter of Claim, should include the following:–

Disclosure

(a) All relevant records or documents including:–

(i) copy of tenancy agreement including tenancy conditions
(ii) documents or computerised records relating to notice given, disrepair reported, inspection reports or requirements to the property.

Expert

(b) A response to the tenant's proposals for instructing an expert including:–

(i) whether or not the proposed single joint expert is agreed
(ii) whether the letter of instruction is agreed
(iii) if the single joint expert is agreed but with separate instructions, a copy of the letter of instruction
(iv) if the appointment of a single joint expert is not agreed, whether the landlord agrees to a joint inspection.

3.5.2 Response to Letter of Claim

(a) The landlord's response to the tenant's Letter of Claim should include:

(i) whether liability is admitted and if so, in respect of which defects. If liability is disputed in respect of some or all of the defects, the reasons for this
(ii) any point which the landlord wishes to make regarding lack of notice of the repair or regarding any difficulty in gaining access
(iii) a full schedule of intended works including anticipated start and completion dates and a timetable for the works
(iv) any offer of compensation
(v) any offer in respect of costs
(vi) the information set out at 3.5.1(a) and (b), if it has not already been provided.

(b) On receipt of the Letter of Claim (whether or not an Early Notification Letter was sent), the landlord may provide a response to the issues set out at paragraph (a) above either:

(i) within 20 working days of the date of receipt of the Letter of Claim (see paragraph 4.10 for a definition of 'working days') or
(ii) within 20 working days of the date of receipt of the report of the single joint expert (see paragraph 3.6(h)) or date of receipt of the experts' agreed schedule following a joint inspection (see paragraph 3.6(g)).

3.5.3 If Landlord does not Respond

(a) If no response is received from the landlord to the Early Notification Letter within 20 working days, the tenant should send a Letter of Claim giving as many of the details outlined at paragraph 3.3 as possible, on the basis of the information the tenant has to hand.

(b) Failure to respond within the time limits set out in paragraphs 3.5.1 and 3.5.2, or at all, to the Early Notification Letter or the Letter of Claim will be a breach of the Protocol. (See paragraphs 4.7(a) and (b) regarding time limits and the power of the court if the Protocol is breached).

3.6 EXPERTS

General

See Paragraph 4.6 for guidance regarding the use of experts.

(a) Tenants should remember that in some cases it might not be necessary to instruct an expert to provide evidence of disrepair, for example, if the only issue relates to the level of any damages claimed. It may be advisable to take photographs of any defects before and after works, and consideration should be given to the use of video footage, particularly if an expert has not been instructed.

(b) The expert should be instructed to report on all items of disrepair which the landlord ought reasonably to know about, or which the expert ought reasonably to report on. The expert should be asked to provide a schedule of works, an estimate of the costs of repair, and to list any urgent works.

(c) Information is given at paragraph 4.6(a) about obtaining lists of independent experts who can be instructed in disrepair cases.

Single Joint Expert

(d) If the landlord does not raise an objection to the proposed expert or letter of instruction within 20 working days of the date of receipt of the Early Notification Letter or Letter of Claim, the expert should be instructed as a single joint expert, using the tenant's proposed letter of instruction. Attached at Annex C of paragraph 5 are specimen letters of instruction to an expert. Alternatively, if the parties cannot agree joint instructions, the landlord and tenant should send their own separate instructions to the single joint expert. If sending separate instructions, the landlord should send the tenant a copy of the landlord's letter of instruction with their response to the first letter. (The tenant has already forwarded the proposed letter of instruction to the landlord).

Joint Inspection

(e) If it is not possible to reach agreement to instruct a single joint expert, even with separate instructions, the parties should attempt to arrange a joint inspection, ie an inspection by different experts instructed by each party to take place at the same time. If the landlord wishes to send their own expert to a joint inspection, they should inform both the tenant's expert and the tenant's solicitor. If the landlord instructs their own expert to inspect then the tenant can also instruct their own expert. It will be for the court to decide subsequently, if proceedings are issued, whether or not either party has acted reasonably.

Time Limits

(f) Whether a single joint expert or a joint inspection is used, the property should be inspected within 20 working days of the date that the landlord responds to the tenant's first letter.

(g) If there is a joint inspection, the experts should produce an agreed schedule of works detailing:–

(i) the defects and required works which are agreed and a timetable for the agreed works
(ii) the areas of disagreement and the reasons for disagreement.

The agreed schedule should be sent to both the landlord and the tenant within 10 working days of the joint inspection.

(h) If there is a single joint expert, a copy of the report should be sent to both the landlord and the tenant within 10 working days of the inspection. Either party can ask relevant questions of the expert.

(i) At Annex D of paragraph 5 are flowcharts showing the time limits in the Protocol.

Urgent Cases

(j) The Protocol does not prevent a tenant from instructing an expert at an earlier stage if this is considered necessary for reasons of urgency, and the landlord should give access in such cases. Appropriate cases may include:–

(i) where the tenant reasonably considers that there is a significant risk to health and safety
(ii) where the tenant is seeking an interim injunction
(iii) where it is necessary to preserve evidence.

Access

(k) Tenants must give reasonable access to the landlord for inspection and repair in line with the tenancy agreement. The landlord should give reasonable notice of the need for access, except in the case of an emergency. The landlord must give access to common parts as appropriate, eg for the inspection of a shared heating system.

Costs

(l) Terms of appointment should be agreed at the outset and should include:

- (i) the basis of the expert's charges (either daily or hourly rates and an estimate of the time likely to be required, or a fee for the services);
- (ii) any travelling expenses and other relevant expenses;
- (iii) rates for attendance at court should this become necessary, and provisions for payment on late notice of cancellation of a court hearing;
- (iv) time for delivery of report;
- (v) time for making payment;
- (vi) whether fees are to be paid by a third party; and
- (vii) arrangements for dealing with questions for experts and discussions between experts and for providing for the cost involved.

(m) If a single joint expert is instructed, each party will pay one half of the cost of the report. If a joint inspection is carried out, each party will pay the full cost of the report from their own expert. (See paragraph 3.7).

(n) The expert should send separately and directly to both parties answers to any questions asked.

'single joint expert' (para 3.6)—For guidance generally on the instruction of a single joint expert, see rr 35.7 and 35.8.

3.7 COSTS

(a) If the tenant's claim is settled without litigation on terms which justify bringing it, the landlord will pay the tenant's reasonable costs or out of pocket expenses. (See paragraph 4.10 for a definition of 'costs' and 'out of pocket expenses'.)

(b) Attached at Annex F of paragraph 5 is a Statement of Costs Form which can be used to inform the landlord of the costs of the claim.

4 Guidance Notes

4.1 NEGOTIATIONS/SETTLEMENT

(a) Other options which should be considered before using the Protocol, include alternative dispute resolution (see paragraph 4.10 for a definition of alternative dispute resolution), and in respect of the following specific categories:–

(i) For council tenants:–

- local authority repairs, complaints and/or arbitration procedures.
- the Right to Repair Scheme. The scheme is only suitable for small, urgent repairs of less than £250 in value.
- Information and leaflets about the scheme in England can be obtained from the Office of the Deputy Prime Minister, Eland House, Bressenden Place, London SW1E 5DU. Tel: 020 7944 3672.
- Information about the scheme in Wales can be obtained from the National Assembly for Wales, Cathays Park, Cardiff, CF10 3NQ. Tel. 029 2082 5111.

- Commission for Local Administration in England. Tel. 0845 602 1983.
- the Local Government Ombudsman for Wales. Tel. 01656 661325.

(ii) For tenants of social landlords who are not council tenants, and for tenants of qualifying private landlords:

- In England, the Independent Housing Ombudsman. 3rd Floor, Norman House, 105–109 Strand, London WC2R 0AA. Tel 020 7836 3630.
- In Wales, the National Assembly for Wales, Cathays Park, Cardiff CF10 3NQ. Tel. 029 2082 5111.
- Local authority environmental health officers.

(iii) or private tenants:–

- Local authority environmental health officers.

(b) Parties and their legal representatives are encouraged to enter into discussions and/or negotiations before starting proceedings, and to consider the use of alternative dispute resolution throughout the use of the Protocol. (Further information and guidance about alternative dispute resolution is available in leaflet number 23 published by the Community Legal Service. Copies of the leaflet can be obtained free from *www.legalservices.gov.uk*). The courts increasingly take the view that litigation should be a last resort, and that claims should not be issued too early when a settlement is still likely.

(c) Information about repair rights generally is available free of charge from the following web pages: *www.shelter.org.uk/housing-advice.asp* and *www.legalservices.gov.uk/leaflets/cls/index.htm.*

(d) The former Department for Transport, Local Government and the Regions issued Good Practice Guidance on Housing Disrepair Legal Obligations in January 2002. Copies of the Guidance (ISBN 185112 523X) can be obtained from ODPM Publications Sales Centre, Cambertown House, Goldthorpe Industrial Estate, Rotherham, S63 9BL. A summary, Housing Research Summary No. 154, is available free from the Housing Support Unit, ODPM, Zone 2/C6, Eland House, Bressenden Place, London SW1E 5DU (Fax 020 7944 4527). The ODPM housing website *www.housing.odpm.gov.uk* is a general source of information for landlords and tenants.

4.2 SCOPE OF THE PROTOCOL

(a) This Protocol is intended to apply to all civil law claims which include a claim for disrepair, but not to counterclaims or set-offs in disrepair claims which originate as other proceedings. (See paragraph 4.10 for an explanation of 'counterclaim' and 'set-off'.) In cases which involve a counterclaim or set-off, the landlord and tenant will still be expected to act reasonably in exchanging information and trying to settle the case at an early stage.

(b) In practice, most disrepair cases will have a value of more than £1000 but less than £15,000 and so are likely to be allocated to the fast track if they come to court. (See paragraph 4.10 for an explanation of 'the fast track'.) The Protocol is aimed at this type of case. The need to keep costs down is especially important in claims of lower value. The approach of the Protocol is however, equally appropriate to all claims and the Protocol should also be followed in small track and multi-track claims. (See paragraph 4.10 for an explanation of 'small claims track' and 'multi-track'.) The court will expect to see reasonable pre-action behaviour applied in all cases.

4.3 EARLY NOTIFICATION LETTER

(a) The Early Notification letter is not intended to replace the direct reporting of defects to the landlord at an early stage, using any procedure the landlord may have established. The Protocol is for use in those cases where, despite the landlord's knowledge of the disrepair, the matter remains unresolved.

(b) It is recognised that disrepair cases can range from straightforward to highly complex, and that it is not always possible to obtain detailed information at an early stage. In order to avoid unnecessary delay and to ensure that notice of the claim is given to the landlord at the earliest possible opportunity, the Protocol suggests the use of two letters in some cases; an Early Notification Letter and a later Letter of Claim. (See paragraph 3.2(a) and Annexes A & B of paragraph 5).

(c) A copy of the Protocol need only be sent to the landlord if the tenant has reason to believe that the landlord will not have access to the Protocol eg because the landlord is an individual or small organisation. If in doubt, a copy should be sent.

4.4 LETTERS OF CLAIM AND LANDLORD'S RESPONSE

(a) Letters of Claim and a landlord's response are not intended to have the same status as a Statement of Case in court proceedings. Matters may come to light after the Letter of Claim has been sent, or after the landlord has responded, which could mean that the case of one or both parties is presented slightly differently than in the Letters of Claim or in the landlord's response. It would be inconsistent with the spirit of the Protocol to seek to capitalise on this in the proceedings, provided that there was no intention to mislead. In particular, advantage should not be taken regarding discrepancies relating to the general details of notice given in the Early Notification Letter.

(b) See paragraph 4.3(c) regarding the sending of a copy of the Protocol by the tenant to the landlord.

Cases with a Personal Injury Element

(c) Housing disrepair claims may contain a personal injury element. This should be set out in the Letter of Claim, as should a clear indication of the identities of all persons who plan to make a personal injury claim.

(d) There is also a Personal Injury Protocol. This Protocol should be followed for that part of the disrepair claim which forms a personal injury claim, unless it is insufficient to warrant separate procedures and would therefore be dealt with only as part of the disrepair claim and evidenced by a General Practitioner's letter. The Personal Injury Protocol should be followed for any claim which requires expert evidence other than a General Practitioner's letter. If the disrepair claim is urgent, it would be reasonable to pursue separate disrepair and personal injury claims, which could then be case managed or consolidated at a later date.

(e) Paragraph 3.3(a)(v) refers to the effect of the defects on 'the tenant'. This should be taken to include all persons who have a personal injury claim. The details of any such claim and of all likely claimants should be set out in the Letter of Claim.

4.5 DISCLOSURE OF DOCUMENTS

(a) When giving disclosure, the landlord should copy all relevant documents. In housing disrepair claims, this includes any and all documents relating in particular to the disrepair and to notice given by the tenant to the landlord of the disrepair. Notice is often given by personal attendance at the landlord's office, and copies of any notes of meetings and oral discussions should also be copied, along with other relevant documents. Documents regarding rent arrears or tenants' disputes will not normally be relevant.

(b) The aim of the early disclosure of documents by the landlord is not to encourage 'fishing expeditions' by the tenant, but to promote an early exchange of relevant information to help in clarifying or resolving issues in dispute. The tenant should assist by identifying the particular categories of documents which they consider relevant.

(c) The 20 working days time limit specified in paragraph 3.5 runs from the date of receipt of either letter. Receipt of the letter is deemed to have taken place two days after the date of the letter. If necessary, a written request for extra time should be made by the landlord to the tenant. Should a case come to court, the court will decide whether the parties have acted reasonably, and whether any sanctions, including costs orders, are appropriate. The principles regarding time limits are referred to again at paragraph 4.7.

(d) Nothing in the Protocol restricts the right of the tenant to look personally at their file or to request a copy of the whole file. Neither is the landlord prevented from sending to the tenant a copy of the whole file, should the landlord wish.

4.6 EXPERTS

(a) Information about independent experts can be obtained from:

- (i) The Chartered Institute of Environmental Health, Chadwick Court, 15 Hatfields, London SE1 8DJ Tel: 020 7928 6006. Ask for a copy of the Consultants and Trainers Directory.
- (ii) The Law Society, 113 Chancery Lane, London WC2A 1PL, Tel: 020 7831 0344. Refer to the Society's Expert Witness Directory.
- (iii) The Royal Institution of Chartered Surveyors, 12 Great George Street, Parliament Square, London SW1P 3AD, Tel: 0845 304 4111. Ask for a copy of the relevant regional directory.

(b) The Protocol encourages the use of a single joint expert. In order to make it less likely that a second expert will be necessary, the Protocol provides for the landlord to forward their own instructions directly to the single joint expert if they cannot agree joint instructions. Both parties can ask relevant questions of the expert. If the parties cannot agree on a single joint expert, either with joint or separate instructions, the Protocol suggests a joint inspection by each party's expert.

(c) The specimen letters at Annexes A and B of paragraph 5 ask for reasons to be given as to why the landlord objects to the expert proposed by the tenant. Should a case come to court, it will be for the court to decide whether the parties have acted reasonably and whether the costs of more than one expert should be recoverable.

(d) Parties should bear in mind that it may not always be necessary to obtain expert evidence of disrepair, and in view of this, the Protocol encourages the use of photos before and after works, and if appropriate, video evidence.

(e) Parties are reminded that the Civil Procedure Rules provide that expert evidence should be restricted to that which is necessary and that the court's permission is required to use an expert's report. The court may limit the amount of experts' fees and expenses recoverable from another party.

(f) When instructing an expert, regard should be had to any approved Code of Guidance for Experts and whether a copy of the Protocol should be sent to the expert.

4.7 TIME LIMITS

(a) The time scales given in the Protocol are long stops and every attempt should be made to comply with the Protocol as soon as possible. If parties are able to comply earlier than the time scales provided, they should do so.

(b) Time limits in the Protocol may be changed by agreement. However, it should always be borne in mind that the court will expect an explanation as to why the Protocol has not been followed or has been varied and breaches of the Protocol may lead to costs or other orders being made by the court.

4.8 LIMITATION PERIOD

(a) In cases where the limitation period will shortly expire, the tenant should ask in the first letter for an extension of the limitation period. The extension requested should be only so long as is necessary to avoid the cost of starting court proceedings.

(b) It will be for the court to decide whether refusal to grant the request is reasonable and whether any sanctions, including costs orders, are appropriate.

4.9 CONTACT POINT

Where a landlord is not an individual, a person should be designated to act as a point of contact for the tenant as soon as possible after the landlord receives the first letter from the tenant and (if one is involved) their solicitor. The appointee's name and contact details should be sent to the tenant and their solicitor as soon as possible after the appointment is made.

4.10 GLOSSARY

Alternative Dispute Resolution	Mediation, or other dispute resolution method, which seeks to settle disputes without the need for court proceedings.
Counterclaim	A claim that either party makes in response to an initial claim by the other.
Costs	Legal fees or, in a small track claim, out of pocket expenses incurred as a result of a claim. (See Out of Pocket Expenses below)
Damages	Money obtained as the result of a claim to compensate for inconvenience and/or distress suffered because of the condition of the property. (See also Special Damages below)
Defect/Disrepair	A fault or problem with a property, for which the landlord is responsible.

Disclosure	The making available by one party to the other of documentation relevant to the claim.
Fast Track/Multi-Track/Small Claims Track	Cases which proceed to court will be allocated to separate tracks depending on their value. The separate tracks have different rules and procedures. Housing cases worth between £1000–£15,000 where there is a claim for works to be done will usually be allocated to the **fast track**. Housing cases where the costs of the repairs and/or the damages do not exceed £1000 will usually be dealt with on the **small claims track**. Cases over £15,000 will usually be allocated to the **multi-track**.
Joint Inspection	An inspection of a property carried out at the same time by one expert instructed by the tenant and by one expert instructed by the landlord.
Limitation Period	The time limit after which a legal action cannot be started. In most housing cases it is 6 years. In personal injury cases it is 3 years.
Litigation	A court case or court proceedings. The taking of legal action by someone.
Notice	Notification of a disrepair, either directly by the tenant in writing or orally to the landlord or his employee, or indirectly, by inspection of the property by the landlord or his employee.
Out of Pocket Expenses	Expenses incurred in a small track claims as a result of the claim, such as loss of earnings and experts' fees.
Protocol	A code or procedure – in this case for dealing with housing disrepair.
Set-off	Where one party agrees with the other's claim or part of it, but sets up one which counterbalances it.
Single Joint Expert	An expert who is instructed by both the tenant and the landlord, either with joint or separate instructions.
Special Damages	Compensation for loss of or damage to specific items eg clothes, carpets, curtains, wallpaper, bedding or extra electricity costs.
Tenant	Someone who rents land (including property) owned by another. (See also the definition at paragraph 3.1(c))
Third Party	Someone other than the landlord or tenant.
Working Days	All days other than Saturdays, Sundays and Bank Holidays.

5 Annexes

SPECIMEN LETTERS

It will be noted that the attached specimen letters are in pairs for use by solicitors and by tenants acting in person respectively.

It is emphasised that they may be suitably adapted as appropriate.

The letters, with the paragraph of the Protocol to which each one relates, are as follows:–

Annex A

Early Notification Letter (see paragraph 3.2.)

Annex B

Letter of Claim (see paragraph 3.3.)

Note: There are two versions of this:–

(a) for use where an Early Notification Letter has been sent;

(b) for other cases.

Annex C

Letter of Instruction to Expert (see paragraph 3.6.)

Annex D

Early Notification Letter Flowchart

Annex E

Special Damages Form

Annex F

Statement of Costs

Annex G

Schedule

Annex A
Early Notification Letter

EARLY NOTIFICATION LETTER

(i) LETTER FROM SOLICITOR

To Landlord

Dear Sirs,

RE: TENANT'S NAME AND ADDRESS OF PROPERTY

We are instructed by your above named tenant. (*Include a sentence stating how the case is being funded.*) We are using the Housing Disrepair Protocol. *We enclose a copy of the Protocol for your information.**

Repairs

Your tenant complains of the following defects at the property (*set out nature of defects*).

*We enclose a schedule, which sets out the disrepair in each room.**

You received notice of the defects as follows: (*list details of notice relied on*).

Please arrange to inspect the property as soon as possible. Access will be available on the following dates and times:– (*list dates and times as appropriate*)

Please let us know what repairs you propose to carry out and the anticipated date for completion of the works.

Disclosure

Please also provide within 20 working days of receipt of this letter, the following:–

All relevant records or documents including:–

- (i) copy of tenancy agreement including tenancy conditions
- (ii) documents or computerised records relating to notice given, disrepair reported, inspection reports or repair works to the property.

We enclose a signed authority from our clients for you to release this information to ourselves.

We also enclose copies of the following relevant documents from our client:–

Expert

If agreement is not reached about the carrying out of repairs within 20 working days of this letter, we propose to jointly instruct a single joint expert (*insert expert's name and address*) to carry out an inspection of the property and provide a report. We enclose a copy of their CV, plus a draft letter of instruction.

Please let us know if you agree to his/her appointment. If you object, please let us know your reasons within 20 working days. If you do not object to the expert being instructed as a single joint expert, but wish to provide your own instructions, you should send those directly to (*insert expert's name*) within 20 working days of this letter. Please send to ourselves a copy of your letter of instruction. If you do not agree to a single joint expert, we will instruct (*insert expert's name*) to inspect the property in any event. In those circumstances, if you wish to instruct your expert to attend at the same time, please let ourselves and (*insert expert's name*) know within 20 working days of this letter.

Claim

Our client's disrepair claim requires further investigation. We will write to you as soon as possible with further details of the history of the defects and of notice relied on, along with details of our client's claim for general and special damages.

Yours faithfully,

* *Delete as appropriate*

(ii) LETTER FROM TENANT

To Landlord

Dear

RE: YOUR NAME AND ADDRESS OF PROPERTY

I write regarding disrepair at the above address. I am using the Housing Disrepair Protocol. *I enclose a copy of the Protocol for your information.**

Repairs

The following defects exist at the property (*set out nature of defects*).

*I enclose a schedule which sets out the disrepair in each room.**

Please arrange to inspect the property as soon as possible. Access will be available on the following dates and times:– (*list dates and time as appropriate*)

You received notice of the defects as follows: (*list details of notice relied on*).

Please let me know what repairs you propose to carry out and the anticipated date for completion of the works.

Disclosure

Please also provide within 20 working days of receipt of this letter, the following:–

All relevant records or documents including:–

(i) copy of tenancy agreement including tenancy conditions
(ii) documents or computerised records relating to notice given, disrepair reported, inspection reports or repair works to the property.

I also enclose copies of the following relevant documents:– (*list documents enclosed*)

Expert

If agreement is not reached about the carrying out of repairs within 20 working days, I propose that we jointly instruct a single joint expert (*insert expert's name and address*) to carry out an inspection of the property and provide a report. I enclose a copy of their CV, plus a draft letter of instruction. Please let me know if you agree to his/her appointment. If you object, please let me know your reasons within 20 working days.

If you do not object to the expert being appointed as a single joint expert but wish to provide your own instructions, you should send those directly to (*insert expert's name*) within 20 working days. Please send a copy of your letter of instruction to me. If you do not agree to a single joint expert I will instruct (*insert expert's name*) to inspect the property in any event. In those circumstances if you wish your expert to attend at the same time, please let me and (*insert expert's name*) know within 20 working days.

Claim

I will write to you as soon as possible with further details of the history of the defects and of notice relied on, along with details of my claim for general and special damages.

Yours sincerely,

* *Delete as appropriate*

Annex B
Letter of Claim

LETTER OF CLAIM

(a) For use where an Early Notification Letter has been sent (as set out in Annex A).

(i) LETTER FROM SOLICITOR

To Landlord

Dear Sirs,

RE: TENANT'S NAME AND ADDRESS OF PROPERTY

We write further to our letter of (*insert date*) regarding our client's housing disrepair claim. We have now taken full instructions from our client.

Repairs

The history of the disrepair is as follows:– (*set out history of defects*).

*I enclose a schedule which sets out the disrepair in each room.**

You received notice of the defects as follows (*list details of notice relied on*).

The defects at the property are causing (*set out the effects of the disrepair on the client and their family, including any personal injury element. Specify if there will be any other additional claimant*).

Please forward to us within 20 working days of receipt of this letter a full schedule of works together with the anticipated date for completion of the works proposed.

Claim

We take the view that you are in breach of your repairing obligations. Please provide us with your proposals for compensation. (*Alternatively, set out suggestions for general damages ie £x for x years*). *Our client also requires compensation for special damages, and we attach a schedule of the special damages claimed.**

Yours faithfully,

* *Delete as appropriate*

(ii) LETTER FROM TENANT

To Landlord

Dear

RE: YOUR NAME AND ADDRESS OF PROPERTY

I write further to my letter of (*insert date*) regarding my housing disrepair claim. I am now able to provide you with further details.

Repairs

The history of the disrepair is as follows:– (*set out history of defects*).

You received notice of the defects as follows (*list details of notice relied on*).

The defects at the property are causing (*set out the effects of the disrepair on you and your family, including any personal injury element. Specify if there will be any other additional claimant*).

Please forward to me within 20 working days of receipt of this letter a full schedule of works together with the anticipated date for completion of the works proposed.

Claim

I take the view that you are in breach of your repairing obligations. Please provide me with your proposals for compensation. (*Alternatively, set out suggestions for general damages ie £x for x years*). *I also require compensation for special damages, and I attach a schedule of the special damages claimed.* *

Yours sincerely,

* *Delete as appropriate*

(b) For use where an Early Notification Letter has NOT been sent.

(i) LETTER FROM SOLICITOR

To Landlord

Dear Sirs,

RE: TENANT'S NAME AND ADDRESS OF PROPERTY

We are instructed by your above named tenant. (*Insert a sentence stating how the case is being funded.*) We are using the Housing Disrepair Protocol. *We enclose a copy of the Protocol for your information.* *

Repairs

Your tenant complains of the following defects at the property (*set out nature and history of defects*).

*We enclose a schedule which sets out the disrepair in each room.**

You received notice of the defects as follows (*list details of notice relied on*).

The defects at the property are causing (*set out the effects of the disrepair on the client and their family, including any personal injury element, specifying if there are any additional claimants*).

Disclosure

Please provide within 20 working days of receipt of this letter a full schedule of the works you propose to carry out to remedy the above defects and the anticipated date for completion of the works.

Please also provide within 20 working days of this letter the following:–

All relevant records or documents including:–

(i) copy of tenancy agreement including tenancy conditions
(ii) tenancy file
(iii) documents relating to notice given, disrepair reported, inspection reports or repair works to the property.
(iv) computerised records

We enclose a signed authority from our clients for you to release this information to ourselves.

We also enclose copies of the following relevant documents:– (*list documents enclosed*)

Expert

If agreement is not reached about the carrying out of repairs within 20 working days of receipt of this letter, we propose to jointly instruct a single joint expert (*insert expert's name and address*) to carry out an inspection of the property and provide a report. We enclose a copy of their CV, plus a draft letter of instruction. Please let me know if you agree to his/her appointment. If you object, please let me know your reasons within 20 working days.

If you do not object to the expert being instructed a single joint expert, but wish to provide your own instructions, you should send those directly to (*insert expert's name*) within 20 working days. Please send to ourselves a copy of your letter of instruction to ourselves. If you do not agree to a single joint expert, we will instruct (*insert expert's name*) to inspect the property in any event. In those circumstances, if you wish to instruct your expert to attend at the same time please let ourselves and (*insert expert's name*) know within 20 working days.

Claim

We take the view that you are in breach of your repairing obligations. Please provide us with your proposals for compensation. (*Alternatively, set out suggestions for general damages ie £x for x years*). *Our client also requires compensation for the special damages, and we attach a schedule of the special damages claimed.**

Yours faithfully,

* *Delete as appropriate*

(ii) LETTER FROM TENANT

To Landlord

Dear

RE: YOUR NAME AND ADDRESS OF PROPERTY

I write regarding the disrepair at the above address. I am using the Housing Disrepair Protocol. *I enclose a copy of the Protocol for your information.**

Repairs

The property has the following defects (*set out nature and history of defects*).

*I enclose a schedule which sets out the disrepair in each room.**

You received notice of the defects as follows (*list details of notice relied on*).

The defects at the property are causing (*set out the effects of the disrepair on you and your family, including any personal injury element, specifying if there are any additional claimants*).

Please provide within 20 working days of receipt of this letter a full schedule of the works you propose to carry out to remedy the above defects and the anticipated date for completion of the works.

Disclosure

Please also provide within 20 working days of receipt of this letter the following:–

All relevant records or documents including:–

(i) copy of tenancy agreement including tenancy conditions
(ii) tenancy file
(iii) documents relating to notice given, disrepair reported, inspection reports or repair works to the property
(iv) computerised records.

I also enclose copies of the following relevant documents:– (*list documents enclosed*).

Expert

If agreement is not reached about the carrying out of repairs within 20 working days of receipt of this letter, I propose that we jointly instruct a single joint expert (*insert expert's name and address*) to carry out an inspection of the property and provide a report. I enclose a copy of their CV, plus a draft letter of instruction. Please let me know if you agree to his/her appointment. If you object, please let me know your reasons within 20 working days.

If you do not object to the expert being instructed as a single joint expert, but wish to provide your own instructions, you should send those directly to (*insert expert's name*) within 20 working days. Please also send a copy of the letter of instruction to me. If you do not agree to a single joint expert, I will instruct (*insert expert's name*) to inspect the property in any event. In those circumstances, if you wish to instruct your expert to attend at the same time please let me and (*insert expert's name*) know within 20 working days.

Claim

I take the view that you are in breach of your repairing obligations. Please provide me with your proposals for compensation. (*Alternatively, set out suggestions for general damages ie £x for x years*). *I also require compensation for special damages, and I attach a schedule of the special damages claimed.**

Yours sincerely,

* *Delete as appropriate*

Annex C
Letter of Instruction to Expert

(i) LETTER FROM SOLICITOR

Dear

RE: TENANT 'S NAME AND ADDRESS OF PROPERTY

We act for the above named in connection with a housing disrepair claim at the above property. We are using the Housing Disrepair Protocol. *We enclose a copy of the Protocol for your information.**

Please carry out an inspection of the above property by (*date*)**and provide a report covering the following points:–

(a) whether you agree that the defects are as claimed
(b) whether any of the defects is structural
(c) the cause of the defect(s)
(d) the age, character and prospective life of the property.

Access will be available on the following dates and times:– (*list dates and times as appropriate*)

*You are instructed as a single joint expert /The landlord is (landlord 's name and details)/The landlord will be providing you with their own instructions direct /The landlord will contact you to confirm that their expert will attend at the same time as you to carry out a joint inspection.**

Please provide the report within 10 working days of the inspection. Please contact us immediately if there are any works which require an interim injunction.

If the case proceeds to court, the report may be used in evidence. In order to comply with court rules we would be grateful if you would insert above your signature a statement that the contents are true to the best of your knowledge and belief. We refer you to part 35 of the Civil Procedure Rules which specifies experts ' responsibilities, the contents of any report, and the statements experts must sign.

Insert details as to cost and payment.

Yours sincerely,

* *Delete as appropriate*
** *The date to be inserted should be 20 working days from the date of the letter, in accordance with paragraph 3.6(f)of the Protocol.*

(ii) LETTER FROM TENANT

Dear

RE: YOUR NAME AND ADDRESS OF PROPERTY

I am currently in dispute with my landlord about disrepair at the above property. I am using the Housing Disrepair Protocol. *I enclose a copy of the Protocol for your information.**

Please carry out an inspection of the above property by (*date*)** and provide a report covering the following points:–

(a) whether you agree that the defects are as claimed
(b) whether any of the defects is structural

(c) the cause of the defect(s)
(d) the age, character and prospective life of the property.

Access will be available on the following dates and times:– (*list dates and times as appropriate*)

*You are instructed as a single joint expert /The landlord is (landlord 's name and details)/The landlord will be providing you with their own instructions direct /The landlord will contact you to confirm that their expert will attend at the same time as you to carry out a joint inspection.**

Please provide the report within 10 working days of the inspection. Please contact me immediately if there are any works which require an interim injunction.

If the case proceeds to court, the report may be used in evidence. In order to comply with court rules I would be grateful if you would insert above your signature a statement that the contents are true to the best of your knowledge and belief. I refer you to part 35 of the Civil Procedure Rules which specifies experts' responsibilities, the contents of any report, and the statements experts must sign.

Insert details as to cost and payment.

Yours sincerely,

* *Delete as appropriate*

** *The date to be inserted should be 20 working days from the date of the letter, in accordance with paragraph 3.6(f)of the Protocol.*

Annex D
Early Notification Letter Flowchart

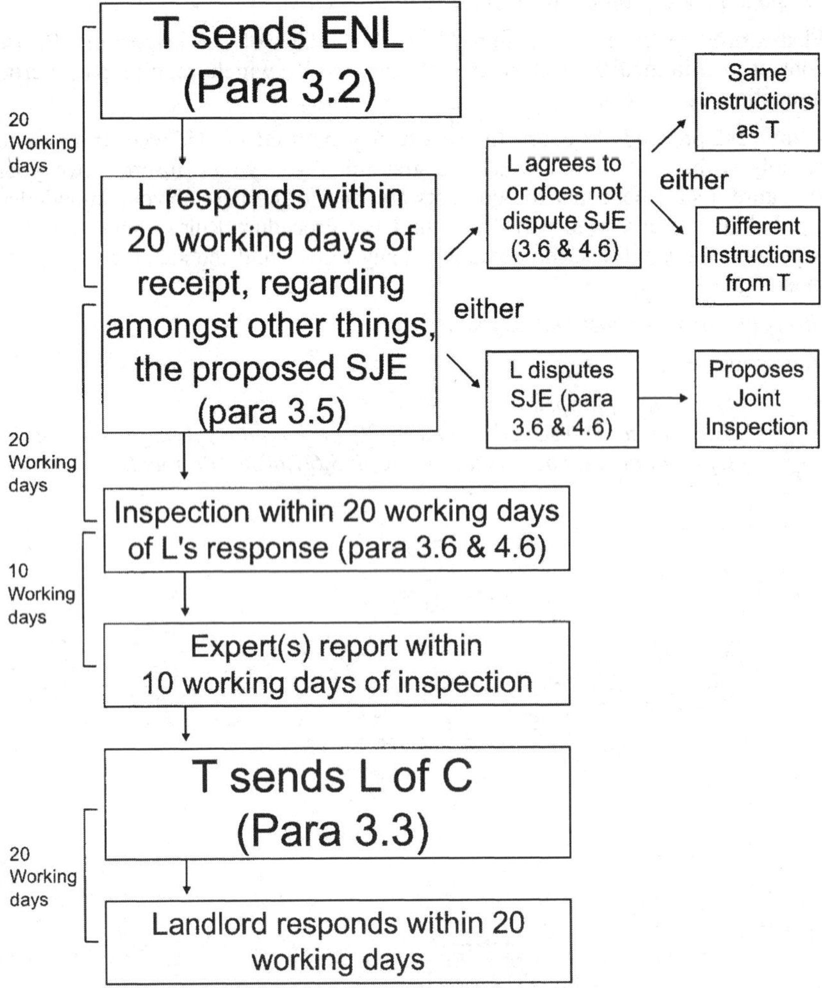
Early Notification Letter Flowchart
T sends ENL (Para 3.2)
20 Working days
L responds within 20 working days of receipt, regarding amongst other things, the proposed SJE (para 3.5)
either
L agrees to or does not dispute SJE (3.6 & 4.6)
either
Same instructions as T
Different Instructions from T
L disputes SJE (para 3.6 & 4.6)
Proposes Joint Inspection
20 Working days
Inspection within 20 working days of L's response (para 3.6 & 4.6)
10 Working days
Expert(s) report within 10 working days of inspection
T sends L of C (Para 3.3)
20 Working days
Landlord responds within 20 working days

Letter of Claim Flowchart

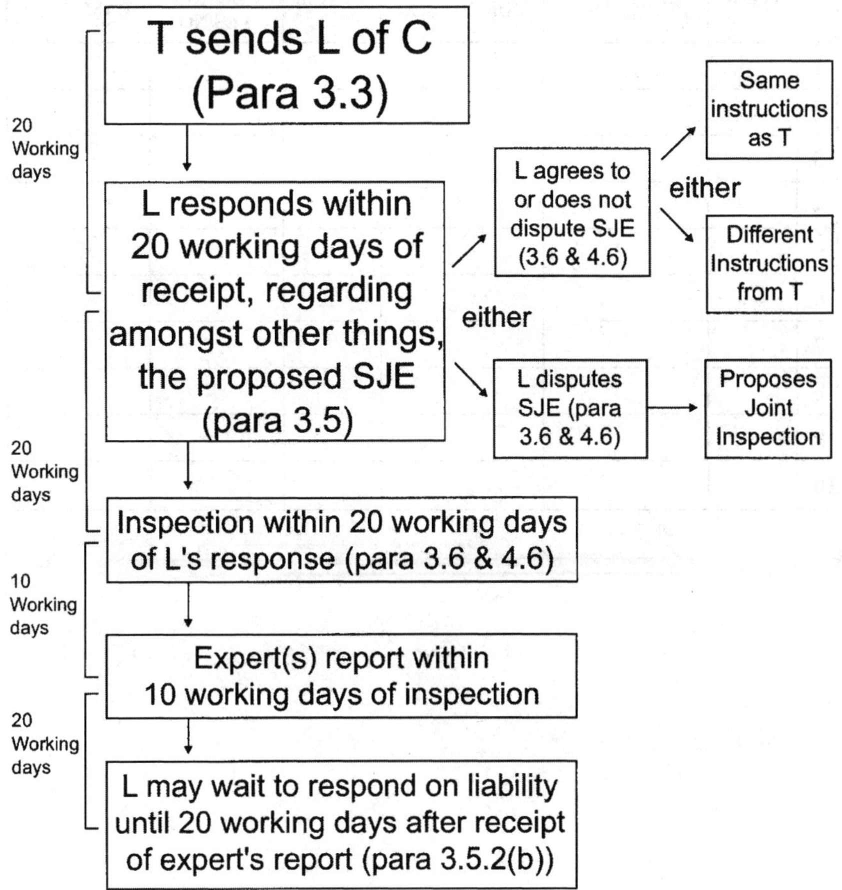

Annex E
Special Damages Form

	ITEM	DATE PURCHASED	WHERE PURCHASED	PRICE	RE-CEIPTS – YES/NO	HOW DAMAGED
1						
2						
3						
4						
5						
6						
7						
8						
9						
10						

Annex F
Statement of Costs

****

Form—The Statement of Costs form annexed to the protocol is Form N260. This form can be accessed and completed on the *Civil Court Service* CD-ROM or the Department for Constitutional Affairs' website at *www.dca.gov.uk*.

Annex G
Schedule

Schedule
Disrepair Protocol
TENANT

	Item Number	Room (tick where appropriate	Disrepair (identify briefly)	Notice given (How was the landlord made aware of the problem)	Inconvenience suffered (How has the disrepair affected you)
Exterior of premises, roof and access Comment:					
Entrance, hall and storage Comment:					
Living room (s) Comment:					
Kitchen Comment:					
Bathroom Comment:					
Bedroom 1 Comment:					
Bedroom 2 Comment:					
Bedroom 3 Comment:					
Other Comment					

SECTION 5

Court Guides

SECTION 5: Court Guides

Contents

The Admiralty and Commercial Courts Guide

ARRANGEMENT OF SECTIONS

Introduction

This edition of the Admiralty and Commercial Courts Guide is published to coincide with the introduction of Parts 58, 61 and 62 of the Civil Procedure Rules dealing with Commercial and Admiralty proceedings and proceedings relating to arbitrations respectively. Most of the provisions which have hitherto been contained in the practice directions made under Part 49 and the fifth edition of the Commercial Court Guide are now to be found in these new rules and their associated practice directions, although the Guide still contains a number of additional provisions which are necessary to ensure the efficient conduct of business in the Admiralty and Commercial Courts.

For some time now the administration of the Admiralty and Commercial Courts has been undertaken by a single Registry and Listing Office and the two courts have shared many common procedures. It seemed only natural, therefore, that this edition of the Guide should reflect that fact, both in its title and in the inclusion of a separate section dealing with admiralty proceedings.

This edition of the Guide draws heavily on its predecessor, but the introduction of the new rules has necessitated a substantial revision of the text.

Moreover, the need to describe in detail various respects in which the procedure applicable to commercial proceedings diverges from that generally applicable under the Civil Procedure Rules, has diminished in importance as practitioners have become familiar both with the operation of the Rules themselves and with the procedures applicable in the Commercial and Admiralty Courts. We have therefore taken the opportunity to remove much of the explanatory material which we consider no longer serves a useful purpose in an attempt to produce a concise manual which meets the day to day needs of those who use the courts. We have also taken the opportunity to review the courts' procedures as a whole. This has resulted in the removal of some provisions which seemed to be otiose or to have outlived their usefulness and the introduction of others which we consider will enable the courts to function more efficiently.

The fact that some provisions to be found in the fifth edition do not reappear in this edition should not necessarily be taken as an indication that they are no longer regarded as reflecting approved practice. In the interests of brevity we have not thought it necessary to reproduce all those provisions which were essentially matters of common sense or good practice, preferring in many cases to rely on the good sense and judgment of those who use the courts. The Guide is not intended to be a blueprint to which all litigation must unthinkingly conform: as in the past, it seeks to provide a modern and flexible framework within which litigation can be conducted efficiently and in the interests of justice. We would emphasise that there has been no change in the courts' approach to the business which comes before them or in their expectation that those who use the courts will display the highest professional standards.

This Guide has been produced in order to set out in a convenient manner the practice which applies in the Admiralty and Commercial Courts. It should be read in conjunction with the Civil Procedure Rules and Practice Directions. For ease of reference we have included wherever possible references to the relevant rules and practice directions to which the reader should refer as necessary. In the interests of brevity references to the Practice Directions take the form 'PD[rule number] para [paragraph number]'.

Accordingly, PD32 should be understood as meaning 'the Practice Direction supplementing Part 32' and PD58 para 15 as meaning 'paragraph 15 of the Practice Direction supplementing Part 58'.

The Hon Mr Justice David Steel
Admiralty Judge

The Hon Mr Justice Moore-Bick
Judge in Charge of the Commercial List

February 2002

A PRELIMINARY

A1 The procedural framework

A1.1 Proceedings in the Commercial Court are governed by the Civil Procedure Rules ('CPR') and Practice Directions. CPR Part 58 and its associated practice direction deal specifically with the Commercial Court. Part 61 deals with the Admiralty Court and Part 62 deals with arbitration applications. Parts 58 and 61 and their associated practice directions are set out in Appendix 1; Rule 62 and its associated practice direction is set out in Appendix 2.

A1.2 The Admiralty and Commercial Courts Guide is published with the approval of the Lord Chief Justice and the Head of Civil Justice in consultation with the judges of the Admiralty and Commercial Courts and with the advice and support of the Admiralty Court and Commercial Court Committees. It is intended to provide guidance about the conduct of proceedings in the Admiralty and Commercial Courts and, within the framework of the Civil Procedure Rules and Practice Directions, to establish the practice to be followed in those courts.

A1.3 In matters for which specific provision is not made by the Guide, the parties, their solicitors and counsel will be expected to act reasonably and in accordance with the spirit of the Guide.

A1.4 The requirements of the Guide are designed to ensure effective management of proceedings in the Admiralty and Commercial Courts. If parties fail to comply with these requirements the court may impose sanctions including orders for costs and (where appropriate) wasted costs orders.

A1.5 Pre-trial matters in the Admiralty and Commercial Courts are dealt with by the judges of those courts: 58PD para 1.2.

A1.6 The court expects a high level of co-operation and realism from the legal representatives of the parties. This applies to dealings (including correspondence) between legal representatives as well as to dealings with the court.

A1.7 In order to avoid excessive repetition, the Guide has been written by reference to proceedings in the Commercial Court. Practitioners should treat the guidance as applicable to proceedings in the Admiralty Court unless the content of Part 61 or Section N of this Guide ('Admiralty') specifically requires otherwise.

A2 The Admiralty and Commercial Registry; the Commercial Court Listing Office

A2.1 The administrative office for the Admiralty Court and the Commercial Court is the Admiralty and Commercial Registry ('the Registry') which is located at Room E200 in the Royal Courts of Justice, Strand, London WC2A 2LL. The Commercial Court Listing Office ('the Listing Office') is located at Room E201 in the Royal Courts of Justice, Strand, London WC2A 2LL.

A2.2 It is important that there is close liaison between legal representatives of the parties and both the Registry and the Listing Office.

A3 The Commercial Court Committee

A3.1 The success of the court's ability to meet the special problems and continually changing needs of the commercial community depends in part upon a steady flow of information and constructive suggestions between the court, litigants and professional advisers.

A3.2 The Commercial Court Committee has assisted in this process for many years. It is expected to play an important part in helping to ensure that the procedures of the court enable the achievement of the 'overriding objective'. All concerned with the court are encouraged to make the fullest use of this important channel of communication. Correspondence raising matters for the consideration of the Committee should be addressed to the clerk to the Commercial Court, Royal Courts of Justice, Strand, London WC2A 2LL.

A4 Specialist associations

A4.1 There are a number of associations of legal representatives which liaise closely with the Commercial Court. These will also play an important part in helping to ensure that the court remains responsive to the 'overriding objective'.

A4.2 The associations include the Commercial Bar Association ('COMBAR'), the London Common Law and Commercial Bar Association ('LCLCBA'), the City of London Law Society, the London Solicitors Litigation Association and the Admiralty Solicitors Group.

B COMMENCEMENT, TRANSFER AND REMOVAL

B1 Commercial cases

B1.1 Rule 58.1(2) describes a 'commercial claim' as follows:

> 'any claim arising out of the transaction of trade and commerce and includes any claim relating to –
>
> (a) a business document or contract;
>
> (b) the export or import of goods;
>
> (c) the carriage of goods by land, sea, air or pipeline;
>
> (d) the exploitation of oil and gas reserves or other natural resources;
>
> (e) insurance and reinsurance;
>
> (f) banking and financial services;
>
> (g) the operation of markets and exchanges;
>
> (h) the purchase and sale of commodities;
>
> (i) the construction of ships;
>
> (j) business agency; and
>
> (k) arbitration.'

B2 Starting a case in the Commercial Court

B2.1 Except for arbitration applications which are governed by the provisions of CPR Part 62 and section O of the Guide, the case will be begun by a claim form under Part 7 or Part 8.

B2.2 Save where otherwise specified, references in this Guide to a claim form are to a Part 7 claim form.

B2.3 The Commercial Court may give a fixed date for trial (see section D16), but it does not give a fixed date for a hearing when it issues a claim. Rules 7.9 and 7.10 and their associated practice directions do not apply to the Commercial Court.

B3 Part 7 claims

The form

B3.1 A claimant starting proceedings in the Commercial Court must use practice form N1(CC) for Part 7 claims: PD58 para 2.4. A copy of this practice form is included at the end of the Guide.

Marking

B3.2 In accordance with PD58 para 2.3 the claim form should be marked in the top right hand corner with the words 'Queen's Bench Division, Commercial Court', and on the issue of the claim form out of the Registry the case will be entered in the Commercial List. Marking the claim form in this way complies sufficiently with PD7 para 3.6(3).

Statement of value

B3.3 Rule 16.3, which provides for a statement of value to be included in the claim form, does not apply in the Commercial Court: rule 58.5(2).

Particulars of claim and the claim form

B3.4 Although particulars of claim may be served with the claim form, this is not a requirement in the Commercial Court. However, if the particulars of claim are not contained in or served with the claim form, the claim form must contain a statement that if an acknowledgment of service is filed indicating an intention to defend the claim, particulars of claim will follow: rule 58.5(1)(a).

B3.5 If particulars of claim do not accompany the claim form they must be served within 28 days after the defendant has filed an acknowledgment of service indicating an intention to defend the claim: rule 58.5(1)(c).

B3.6 The three forms specified in rule 7.8(1) must be served with the claim form. One of these is a form for acknowledging service: rule 58.5(1)(b).

Statement of truth

B3.7

(a) A claim form must be verified by a statement of truth: rule 22.1. Unless the court otherwise orders, any amendment to a claim form must also be verified: rule 22.1(2).
(b) The required form of statement of truth is set out at PD7 para 7.2.
(c) A claim form will remain effective even where not verified by a statement of truth, unless it is struck out: PD22 para 4.1.
(d) In certain cases the statement of truth may be signed by a person other than the party on whose behalf it is served or its legal representative: section C1.8–1.9.

Trial without service of particulars of claim or a defence

B3.8 The attention of the parties and their legal representatives is drawn to rule 58.11 which allows the court to order (before or after the issue of a claim form) that the case shall proceed without the filing or service of particulars of claim or defence or of any other statement of case.

Interest

B3.9 The claim form (and not only the particulars of claim) must comply with the requirements of rules 16.4(1)(b) and 16.4(2) concerning interest: rule 58.5(3).

B3.10 References to particulars of claim in rule 12.6(1)(a) (referring to claims for interest where there is a default judgment) and rule 14.14(1)(a) (referring to claims for interest where there is a judgment on admissions) may be treated as references to the claim form: rules 58.8(2) and 58.9(3).

Issue of a claim form when the Registry is closed

B3.11 A request for the issue of a Part 7 claim form may be made by fax at certain times when the Registry is closed to the public: PD58 para 2.2. The procedure is set out in Appendix 3. Any further details may be obtained from the Registry. The fax number is 020 7947 6667.

B4 Part 8 claims

Form

B4.1 A claimant who wishes to commence a claim under CPR Part 8 must use practice form N208(CC): PD58 para 2.4. A copy of this practice form is included at the end of this Guide.

B4.2 Attention is drawn to the requirement in rule 8.2(a) that where a claimant uses the Part 8 procedure his claim form must state that Part 8 applies. Similarly, PD7 para 3.3 requires that the claim form state (if it be the case) that the claimant wishes his claim to proceed under Part 8 or that the claim is required to proceed under Part 8.

Marking and statement of truth

B4.3 Sections B3.2 (marking) and B3.7 (statement of truth) also apply to a claim form issued under Part 8.

Issue of a claim form when the Registry is closed

B4.4 A request for the issue of a Part 8 claim form may be made by fax at certain times when the Registry is closed to the public: PD58 para 2.2. The procedure is set out in Appendix 3.

Time for filing evidence in opposition to a Part 8 claim

B4.5 A defendant to a Part 8 claim who wishes to rely on written evidence must file and serve it within 28 days after filing an acknowledgment of service: rule 58.12.

B5 Part 20 claims

Form

B5.1 Adapted versions of the Part 20 claim form and acknowledgment of service (Practice Forms no. N211 and N213) and of the related Notes to Part 20 claimant and Part 20 defendant have been approved for use in the Commercial Court. Copies of the practice forms are included at the end of the Guide.

B6 Service of the claim form

Service by the parties

B6.1 Claim forms issued in the Commercial List are to be served by the parties, not by the Registry: PD58 para 9.

Methods of service

B6.2 Methods of service are set out in CPR Part 6, which is supplemented by a Practice Direction.

B6.3 PD6 paras 2.1 and 3.1 concern service by document exchange and by fax. Service of the claim form on the legal representative of the defendant by document exchange or fax will not be effective unless that legal representative has authority to accept service. It is desirable to obtain confirmation from the legal representative in writing that he has instructions to accept service of a claim form on behalf of the defendant.

Applications for extension of time

B6.4 Applications for an extension of time in which to serve a claim form are governed by rule 7.6. Rule 7.6(3)(a), which refers to service of the claim form by the court, does not apply in the Commercial Court.

B6.5 The evidence required on an application for an extension of time is set out in PD7 para 8.2.

Certificate of service

B6.6 When the claimant has served the claim form he must file a certificate of service: rule 6.14(2). Satisfaction of this requirement is relevant, in particular, to the claimant's ability to obtain judgment in default (see Part 12) and to the right of a non-party to search for, inspect and take a copy of the claim form under rule 5.4(2)(a).

B7 Service of the claim form out of the jurisdiction

B7.1 Applications for permission to serve a claim form out of the jurisdiction are governed by rules 6.19 to 6.31. A guide to the appropriate practice is set out in Appendix 15.

B7.2 Service of process in some foreign countries may take a long time to complete; it is therefore important that solicitors take prompt steps to effect service.

B8 Acknowledgment of service

Part 7 claims

B8.1

(a) A defendant must file an acknowledgment of service in every case: rule 58.6(1). An adapted version of practice form N9 (which includes the acknowledgment of service) has been approved for use in the Commercial Court. A copy of this practice form (Form N9(CC)) is included at the end of the Guide, together with adapted versions of the notes for claimants and defendants on completing and replying to a Part 7 claim form.

(b) The period for filing an acknowledgment of service is calculated from the service of the claim form, whether or not particulars of claim are contained in or accompany the claim form or are to follow service of the claim form. Rule 9.1(2), which provides that in certain circumstances the defendant need not respond to the claim until particulars of claim have been served on him, does not apply: rule 58.6(1).

Part 8 claims

B8.2

(a) A defendant must file an acknowledgment of service in every case: rule 58.6(1). An adapted version of practice form N210 (acknowledgment of service of a Part 8 claim form) has been approved for use in the Commercial Court. A copy of this practice form (Form N210(CC)) is included at the end of the Guide, together with adapted versions of the notes for claimants and defendants on completing and replying to a Part 8 claim form.

(b) The time for filing an acknowledgment of service is calculated from the service of the claim form.

Acknowledgment of service in a claim against a firm

B8.3

(a) PD10 para 4.4 allows an acknowledgment of service to be signed on behalf of a partnership by any of the partners or a person having the control or management of the partnership business, whether he be a partner or not.

(b) However, attention is drawn to Schedule 1 to the CPR which includes, with modifications, provisions previously contained in RSC Order 81 concerning acknowledgment of service by a person served as a partner who denies his liability as such (see also the note at the end of CPR Part 10).

Time for filing acknowledgment of service

B8.4

(a) Except in the circumstances described in section B8.4(b) and B8.4(c), or is otherwise ordered by the court, the period for filing an acknowledgment of service is 14 days after service of the claim form.
(b) If the claim form has been served out of the jurisdiction without the permission of the court under rule 6.19, the time for filing an acknowledgment of service is governed by rule 6.22, save that in all cases time runs from the service of the claim form: rule 58.6(3).
(c) If the claim form has been served out of the jurisdiction with the permission of the court under rule 6.20 the time for filing an acknowledgment of service is governed by rule 6.21(4)(a), the second practice direction supplementing rule 6 and the table to which it refers, save that in all cases time runs from the service of the claim form: rule 58.6(3).

B9 Disputing the court's jurisdiction

Part 7 claims

B9.1

(a) If the defendant intends to dispute the court's jurisdiction or contend that the court should not exercise its jurisdiction he must
    (i) file an acknowledgment of service – rule 11(2); and
    (ii) issue an application notice seeking the appropriate relief.
(b) An application to dispute the court's jurisdiction must be made within 28 days of filing an acknowledgment of service: rule 58.7(2).
(c) if the defendant wishes to rely on written evidence in support of that application, he must file and serve that evidence when he issues the application.
(d) If the defendant makes an application under rule 11(1), the claimant is not bound to serve particulars of claim until that application has been disposed of: rule 58.7(3).

Part 8 claims

B9.2

(a) The provisions of section B9.1(a)–(c) also apply in the case of Part 8 claims.
(b) If the defendant makes an application under rule 11(1), he is not bound to serve any written evidence on which he wishes to rely in opposition to the substantive claim until that application has been disposed of: rule 11.9.

Effect of an application challenging the jurisdiction

B9.3 An acknowledgment of service of a Part 7 or Part 8 claim form which is followed by an application challenging the jurisdiction under Part 11 does not constitute a submission by the defendant to the jurisdiction: rules 11(3) and 11(7).

B9.4 If an application under Part 11 is unsuccessful, and the court then considers giving directions for filing and serving statements of case (in the case of a Part 7 claim) or evidence (in the case of a Part 8 claim), a defendant does not submit to the jurisdiction merely by asking for time to serve and file his statement of case or evidence, as the case may be.

B10 Default judgment

B10 Default judgment is governed by Part 12 and PD12. However, because in the Commercial Court the period for filing the acknowledgment of service is calculated from service of the claim form, the reference to 'particulars of claim' in PD12 para 4.1(1) should be read as referring to the claim form: PD58 para 6(1).

B11 Admissions

B11

(a) Admissions are governed by CPR Part 14, and PD14, except that the references to 'particulars of claim' in PD14 paras 2.1, 3.1 and 3.2 should be read as referring to the claim form: PD58 para 6(2).
(b) Adapted versions of the practice forms of admission (practice forms no N9A and no N9C) have been approved for use in the Commercial Court.

Copies of these practice forms (Forms N9A(CC) and N9C(CC)) are included at the end of the Guide.

B12 Transfer of cases into and out of the Commercial List

B12.1 The procedure for transfer and removal is set out in PD58 para 4. All such applications must be made to the Commercial Court: rule 30.5(3).

B12.2 Although an order to transfer a case to the Commercial List may be made at any stage, any application for such an order should normally be made at an early stage in the proceedings.

B12.3 Transfer to the Commercial List may be ordered for limited purposes only, but a transferred case will normally remain in the Commercial List until its conclusion.

B12.4 An order transferring a case out of the Commercial List may be made at any stage, but will not usually be made after a pre-trial timetable has been fixed at the case management conference (see section D8).

B12.5 Some commercial cases may more suitably, or as suitably, be dealt with in one of the Mercantile Courts. Parties should consider whether it would be more appropriate to begin proceedings in one of those courts and the Commercial judge may on his own initiative order the case to be transferred there.

C PARTICULARS OF CLAIM, DEFENCE AND REPLY

C1 Form, content, serving and filing

C1.1

(a) Particulars of claim, the defence and any reply must be set out in separate consecutively numbered paragraphs and be as brief and concise as possible.

(b) If it is necessary for the proper understanding of the statement of case to include substantial parts of a lengthy document the passages in question should be set out in a schedule rather than in the body of the case.

(c) The document must be signed by the individual person or persons who drafted it, not, in the case of a solicitor, in the name of the firm alone.

C1.2

(a) Particulars of claim, the defence and also any reply must comply with the provisions of rules 16.4 and 16.5, save that rules 16.5(6) and 16.5(8) do not apply.

(b) The requirements of PD16 para 8.4–9.1 (which relate to claims based upon oral agreements, agreements by conduct and Consumer Credit Agreements and to reliance upon evidence of certain matters under the Civil Evidence Act 1968) should be treated as applying to the defence and reply as well as to the particulars of claim.

(c) (i) full and specific details must be given of any allegation of fraud, dishonesty, malice or illegality; and

(ii) where an inference of fraud or dishonesty is alleged, the facts on the basis of which the inference is alleged must be fully set out.

(d) Any legislative provision upon which an allegation is based must be clearly identified and the basis of its application explained.

(e) Any provision of The Human Rights Act 1998 (including the Convention) on which a party relies in support of its case must be clearly identified and the basis of its application explained.

(f) Any principle of foreign law or foreign legislative provision upon which a party's case is based must be clearly identified and the basis of its application explained.

C1.3

(a) PD16 para 7.3 relating to a claim based upon a written agreement should be treated as also applying to the defence, unless the claim and the defence are based on the same agreement.

(b) In most cases attaching documents to or serving documents with a statement of case does not promote the efficient conduct of the proceedings and should be avoided.

(c) If documents are to be served at the same time as a statement of case they should normally be served separately from rather than attached to the statement of case.

(d) Only those documents which are obviously of critical importance and necessary for a proper understanding of the statement of case should be attached to or served with it. The statement of case must itself refer to the fact that documents are attached to or served with it.

(e) An expert's report should not be attached to the statement of case and should not be filed with the statement of case at the Registry. A party must obtain permission from the court in order to adduce expert evidence at trial and therefore any party which serves an expert's report without obtaining such permission does so at his own risk as to costs.

(f) Notwithstanding PD16 para 7.3(1), a true copy of the complete written agreement may be made available at any hearing unless the court orders otherwise.

Adapted versions of the practice forms of defence and counterclaim have been approved for use in the Commercial Court. Copies of these practice forms are included at the end of this Guide.

Summaries

C1.4 If a statement of case exceeds 25 pages (excluding schedules), a summary, not exceeding four pages, must also be filed and served. The summary should cross-refer to the paragraph numbering of the full statement of case. The summary is to be included in the case management bundle: section D7.2(ii).

Length

C1.5 Parties serving statements of case should bear in mind that the court will take into account the length of the document served when considering any application by another party for further time within which to respond.

Statement of truth

C1.6 Particulars of claim, a defence and any reply must be verified by a statement of truth: rule 22.1. So too must any amendment, unless the court otherwise orders: rule 22.1(2); see also section C5.4.

C1.7 The required form of statement of truth is as follows:

(i) for particulars of claim, as set out in PD7 para 7.2 or PD16 para 3.4;
(ii) for a defence, as set out in PD15 para 2.2 or PD16 para 12.2;
(iii) for a reply the statement of truth should follow the form for the particulars of claim, but substituting the word 'reply' for the words 'particulars of claim' (see PD22 para 2.1).

C1.8 A party may apply to the court for permission that a statement of truth be signed by a person other than one of those required by rule 22.1(6).

C1.9 If insurers are conducting proceedings on behalf of many claimants or defendants a statement of truth may be signed by a senior person responsible for the case at a lead insurer, but:

(i) the person signing must specify the capacity in which he signs;
(ii) the statement of truth must be a statement that the lead insurer believes that the facts stated in the document are true; and
(iii) the court may order that a statement of truth also be signed by one or more of the parties. See PD22 para 3.6B.

C1.10 A statement of case remains effective (although it may not be relied on as evidence) even where it is not verified by a statement of truth, unless it is struck out: PD22 paras 4.1–4.3.

Service

C1.11 All statements of case are served by the parties, not by the court: PD58 para 9.

Filing

C1.12 The statements of case filed with the court form part of the permanent record of the court.

C2 Serving and filing particulars of claim

C2.1 Subject to any contrary order of the court and unless particulars of claim are contained in or accompany the claim form:

(i) the period for serving particulars of claim is 28 days after filing an acknowledgment of service: rule 58.5(1)(c);

(ii) the parties may agree extensions of the period for serving the particulars of claim. However, any such agreement must be evidenced in writing and notified to the court, addressed to the Case Management Unit: PD58 para 7.1;

(iii) any notification of an agreed extension exceeding 6 weeks, or which when taken together with preceding extensions exceeds 6 weeks in total, must be accompanied by a brief statement of the reasons for the extension.

C2.2 The court may make an order overriding any agreement by the parties varying a time-limit: PD58 para 7.2.

C2.3 The claimant must serve the particulars of claim on all other parties. A copy of the claim form will be filed at the Registry on issue. If the claimant serves particulars of claim separately from the claim form he must file a copy within 7 days of service together with a certificate of service: rule 7.4(3).

C3 Serving and filing a defence

C3.1 The defendant must serve the defence on all other parties and must at the same time file a copy with the court.

C3.2

(a) If the defendant files an acknowledgment of service which indicates an intention to defend the period for serving and filing a defence is 28 days after service of the particulars of claim, subject to the provisions of rule 15.4(2). (See also Appendix 15 for cases where the claim form has been served out of the jurisdiction).

(b) The defendant and the claimant may agree that the period for serving and filing a defence shall be extended by up to 28 days: rule 15.5(1).

(c) An application to the court is required for any further extension. If the parties are able to agree that a further extension should be granted, a draft consent order should be provided together with a brief explanation of the reasons for the extension.

C3.3 The general power to agree variations to time-limits contained in rule 2.11 and PD58 para 7.1 enables parties to agree extensions of the period for serving and filing a defence that exceed 28 days. The length of extension must in all cases be specified. Any such agreement must be evidenced in writing and comply with the requirements of section C2.1.

C3.4

(a) Where an extension is agreed the defendant must, in accordance with rule 15.5(2), notify the court in writing; the notification should be addressed to the Case Management Unit.

(b) Any notification of an agreed extension exceeding 6 weeks, or which when taken together with preceding extensions exceeds 6 weeks in total, must be accompanied by a brief statement (agreed by the claimant and the defendant) of the reasons for the extension. The reasons will be brought to the attention of the Judge in Charge of the Commercial List.

C3.5 The claimant must notify the Case Management Unit by letter when all defendants who intend to serve a defence have done so. This information is material to the fixing of the case management conference (see section D3.1).

C4 Serving and filing a reply

C4.1 Subject to section C4.3, the period for serving and filing a reply is 21 days after service of the defence: rule 58.10(1).

C4.2

(a) A reply must be filed at the same time as it is served: rule15.8(b); rule 15.8(a) does not apply in proceedings in the Commercial List.

(b) The reply should be served before case management information sheets are provided to the court (see section D8.5). In the normal case, this will allow the parties to consider any reply before completing the case management information sheet, and allow time for the preparation of the case memorandum and the list of issues each of which is required for the case management conference (see sections D4–D7).

C4.3 In some cases, more than 21 days may be needed for the preparation, service and filing of a reply. In such cases an application should be made on paper for an extension of time and for a postponement of the case management conference. The procedure to be followed when making an application on paper is set out in section F4.

C4.4 Any reply must be served by the claimant on all other parties: rule 58.10(1).

C5 Amendment

C5.1

(a) Amendments to a statement of case must show the original text, unless the court orders otherwise: PD58 para 8.

(b) Amendments may be shown by using footnotes or marginal notes, provided they identify precisely where and when an amendment has been made.

(c) Unless the court so orders, there is no need to show amendments by colour-coding.

(d) If there have been extensive amendments it may be desirable to prepare a fresh copy of the statement of case. However, a copy of the statement of case showing where and when amendments have been made must also be made available.

C5.2 All amendments to any statement of case must be verified by a statement of truth unless the court orders otherwise: rule 22.1(2).

C5.3 Questions of amendment, and consequential amendment, should wherever possible be dealt with by consent. A party should consent to a proposed amendment unless he has substantial grounds for objecting to it.

C5.4 Late amendments should be avoided and may be disallowed.

D CASE MANAGEMENT IN THE COMMERCIAL COURT

D1 Generally

D1.1 All proceedings in the Commercial List will be subject to management by the court.

D1.2 All proceedings in the Commercial List are automatically allocated to the multi-track and consequently Part 26 and the rules relating to allocation do not apply: rule 58.13(1).

D1.3 Except for rule 29.3(2) (legal representatives to attend case management conferences and pre-trial reviews) and rule 29.5 (variation of case management timetable), Part 29 does not apply to proceedings in the Commercial List: rule 58.13(2).

D2 Key features of case management in the Commercial Court

D2 Case management is governed by rule 58.13 and PD58 para 10. In a normal commercial case commenced by a Part 7 claim form, case management will include the following 10 key features:

(1) statements of case will be exchanged within fixed or monitored time periods;

(2) a case memorandum, a list of issues and a case management bundle will be produced at an early point in the case;

(3) the case memorandum, list of issues and case management bundle will be amended and updated or revised on a running basis throughout the life of the case and will be used by the court at every stage of the case;

(4) a mandatory case management conference will be held shortly after statements of case have been served, if not before (and preceded by the parties lodging case management information sheets identifying their views on the requirements of the case);

(5) at the case management conference the court will (as necessary) discuss the issues in the case and the requirements of the case with the advocates retained in the case. The court will set a pre-trial timetable and give any other directions as may be appropriate;

(6) before the progress monitoring date the parties will report to the court, using a progress monitoring information sheet, the extent of their compliance with the pre-trial timetable;

(7) on or shortly after the progress monitoring date a judge will (without a hearing) consider progress and give such further directions as he thinks appropriate;
(8) if at the progress monitoring date all parties have indicated that they will be ready for trial, all parties will complete a pre-trial checklist;
(9) in many cases there will be a pre-trial review; in such cases the parties will be required to prepare a trial timetable for consideration by the court;
(10) throughout the case there will be regular reviews of the estimated length of trial.

D3 Fixing a case management conference

D3.1 A mandatory case management conference will normally take place on the first available date 6 weeks after all defendants who intend to serve a defence have done so. This will normally allow time for the preparation and service of any reply (see section C4).

D3.2

(a) If proceedings have been started by service of a Part 7 claim form, the claimant must take steps to fix the date for the case management conference with the Listing Office in co-operation with the other parties within 14 days of the date when all defendants who intend to file and serve a defence have done so: PD58 para 10.2(a). The parties should bear in mind the need to allow time for the preparation and service of any reply.
(b) If proceedings have been begun by service of a Part 8 claim form, the claimant must take steps to fix a date for the case management conference with the Listing Office in co-operation with the other parties within 14 days of the date when all defendants who wish to serve evidence have done so: PD58 para 10.2(b).

D3.3

(a) In accordance with section C3 the Registry will expect a defence to be served and filed by the latest of:
    (i) 28 days after service of particulars of claim (as certified by the certificate of service); or
    (ii) any extended date for serving and filing a defence as notified to the court in writing following agreement between the parties; or
    (iii) any extended date for serving and filing a defence as ordered by the court on an application.
(b) If within 28 days after the latest of these dates has passed for each defendant, the parties have not taken steps to fix the date for the case management conference, the Case Management Unit will inform the Judge in Charge of the List, and at his direction will take steps to fix a date for the case management conference without further reference to the parties.

D3.4 If the proceedings have been transferred to the Commercial List, the claimant must apply for a case management conference within 14 days of the date of the order transferring them, unless the judge held, or gave directions for, a case management conference when he made the order transferring the proceedings: PD58 para 10.3.

D3.5 If the claimant fails to make an application as required by the rules, any other party may apply for a case management conference: PD58 para 10.5.

D3.6

(a) In some cases it may be appropriate for a case management conference to take place at an earlier date.
(b) Any party may apply to the court in writing at an earlier time for a case management conference: PD58 para 10.4. A request by any party for an early case management conference should be made in writing to the Judge in Charge of the List, on notice to all other parties, at the earliest possible opportunity.

D3.7 If before the date on which the case management conference would be held in accordance with section D3 there is a hearing in the case at which the parties are represented, the business of the case management conference will normally be transacted at that hearing and there will be no separate case management conference.

D3.8 The court may fix a case management conference at any time on its own initiative. If it does so, the court will normally give at least 7 days' notice to the parties: PD58 para 10.6.

D3.9 A case management conference may not be postponed or adjourned without an order of the court.

D4 Two-judge team system

D4.1

(a) Cases which are exceptional in size or complexity or in having a propensity to give rise to numerous pre-trial applications may be allocated to a management team of two designated judges.
(b) An application for the appointment of a two-judge management team should be made in writing to the Judge in Charge of the List at the time of fixing the case management conference.
(c) If an order is made for allocation to a two-judge team, one of the designated judges will preside at the case management conference.

D4.2 Except for an application for an interim payment, all applications in the case, and the trial itself, will be heard by one or other of the designated judges.

D5 Case memorandum

D5.1 In order that the judge conducting the case management conference may be informed of the general nature of the case and the issues which are expected to arise, after service of the defence and any reply the solicitors and counsel for each party shall draft an agreed case memorandum.

D5.2 The case memorandum should contain:

(i) a short and uncontroversial description of what the case is about; and
(ii) a very short and uncontroversial summary of the material procedural history of the case.

D5.3 Unless otherwise ordered, the solicitors for the claimant are to be responsible for producing and filing the case memorandum.

D5.4 The case memorandum should not refer to any application for an interim payment, to any order for an interim payment, to any voluntary interim payment, or to any payment or offer under CPR Part 36 or Part 37.

D5.5

(a) It should be clearly understood that the only purpose of the case memorandum is to help the judge understand broadly what the case is about. The case memorandum does not play any part in the trial. It is unnecessary, therefore, for parties to be unduly concerned about the precise terms in which it is drafted, provided it contains a reasonably fair and balanced description of the case.
(b) Accordingly, in all but the most exceptional cases it should be possible for the parties to draft an agreed case memorandum. However, if it proves impossible to do so, the claimant must draft the case memorandum and send a copy to the defendant. The defendant may provide its comments to the court (with a copy to the claimant) separately.
(c) The failure of the parties to agree a case memorandum is a matter which the court may wish to take into account when dealing with the costs of the case management conference.

D6 List of issues

D6.1 After service of the defence (and any reply), the solicitors and counsel for each party shall produce an agreed list of the important issues in the case. The list should include both issues of fact and issue of law. A separate section of the document should list what is common ground between the parties (or any of them, specifying which).

D6.2 Unless otherwise ordered, the solicitors and counsel for the claimant are to have responsibility for the production and revision of the list of issues.

D7 Case management bundle

Preparation

D7.1 Before the case management conference (see sections D3 and D8), a case management bundle should be prepared by the solicitors for the claimant: PD58 para 10.8.

Contents

D7.2 The case management bundle should only contain the documents listed below (where the documents have been created by the relevant time):

(i) the claim form;
(ii) all statements of case (excluding schedules), except that, if a summary has been prepared, the bundle should contain the summary, not the full statement of case;
(iii) the case memorandum (see section D5);
(iv) the list of issues (see section D6);
(v) the case management information sheets and the pre-trial timetable if one has already been established (see sections D8.5 and D8.9);

(vi) the principal orders in the case; and

(vii) any agreement in writing made by the parties to disclose documents without making a list or any agreement in writing that disclosure (or inspection or both) shall take place in stages.

See generally PD58 para 10.8.

D7.3 The case management bundle must not include a copy of any order for an interim payment.

Lodging the case management bundle

D7.4 The case management bundle should be lodged with the Listing Office at least 7 days before the (first) case management conference (or earlier hearing at which the parties are represented and at which the business of the case management conference may be transacted: see section D3.7).

Preparation and upkeep

D7.5 The claimant (or other party responsible for the preparation and upkeep of the case management bundle), in consultation with the other parties, must revise and update the case management bundle as the case proceeds: PD58 para 10.9. The claimant should attend at the Case Management Unit for this purpose at the following stages:

(i) within 10 days of the case management conference, in order to add the pre-trial timetable (or any other order made at the case management conference) and an updated case memorandum;

(ii) within 10 days of an order being made on an application, if in the light of the order or the application it is necessary to add a copy of the order made (as a principal order in the case) or an updated case memorandum;

(iii) within 14 days of the service of any amended statement of case (or summary), in order to substitute a copy of the amended statement of case (or summary) for that which it replaces and to incorporate an updated case memorandum and (if appropriate) a revised list of issues;

(iv) within 10 days of any other revision to the case memorandum or list of issues, in order to incorporate the revised document.

D8 Case Management Conference

Application to postpone the case management conference

D8.1

(a) An application to postpone the case management conference must be made within 21 days after all defendants who intend to serve a defence have done so.

(b) The application will be dealt with on paper unless the court considers it appropriate to direct an oral hearing.

Attendance at the case management conference

D8.2 Clients need not attend a case management conference unless the court otherwise orders. A representative who has conduct of the case must attend from each firm of solicitors instructed in the case. At least one of the advocates retained in the case on behalf of each party should also attend.

D8.3 The case management conference is a very significant stage in the case. It is not simply a substitute for the summons for directions under the former Rules of the Supreme Court and although parties are encouraged to agree proposals for directions for the consideration of the court, directions will not normally be made by consent without the need for attendance.

Applications

D8.4

- (a) If by the time of the case management conference a party wishes to apply for an order in respect of a matter not covered by Questions (1)–(16) in the case management information sheet, he should make that application at the case management conference.
- (b) In some cases notice of such an application may be given in the case management information sheet itself: see section D8.5(c).
- (c) In all other cases the applicant should ensure that an application notice and any supporting evidence is filed and served in time to enable the application to be heard at the case management conference.

Materials: case management information sheet and case management bundle

D8.5

- (a) All parties attending a case management conference must complete a case management information sheet: PD58 para 10.7. A standard form of case management information sheet is set out in Appendix 6. The information sheet is intended to include reference to all applications which the parties would wish to make at a case management conference.
- (b) A completed case management information sheet must be provided by each party to the court (and copied to all other parties) at least 7 days before the case management conference.
- (c) Applications not covered by the standard questions raised in the case management information sheet should be entered under Question (17). No other application notice is necessary if written evidence will not be involved and the 7 day notice given by entering the application on the information sheet will in all the circumstances be sufficient to enable all other parties to deal with the application.

D8.6 The case management bundle must be provided to the court at least 7 days before the case management conference: PD58 para 10.8. Only where it is essential for the court on the case management conference to see the full version of a statement of case that has been summarised in accordance with section C1.4 above should a copy of that statement of case be lodged for the case management conference.

The hearing

D8.7 The court's power to give directions at the case management conference is to be found in rules 3.1 and 58.13(4). At the case management conference the judge will:

(i) discuss the issues in the case, and the requirements of the case, with the advocates retained in the case;
(ii) fix the entire pre-trial timetable, or, if that is not practicable, fix as much of the pre-trial timetable as possible; and
(iii) in appropriate cases make an ADR order.

D8.8

(a) Rules 3.1(2) and 58.13(4) enable the court at the case management conference to stay the proceedings while the parties try to settle the case by alternative means. The case management information sheet requires the parties to indicate whether a stay for such purposes is sought.
(b) In an appropriate case an ADR order may be made without a stay of proceedings. The parties should consider carefully whether it may be possible to provide for ADR in the pre-trial timetable without affecting the date of trial.
(c) Where a stay has been granted for a fixed period for the purposes of ADR the court has power to extend it. If an extension of the stay is desired by all parties, a judge will normally be prepared to deal with an application for such an extension if it is made before the expiry of the stay by letter from the legal representatives of one of the parties. The letter should confirm that all parties consent to the application.
(d) An extension will not normally be granted for more than four weeks unless clear reasons are given to justify a longer period, but more than one extension may be granted.

The pre-trial timetable

D8.9 The pre-trial timetable will normally include:

(i) a progress monitoring date (see section D12 below); and
(ii) a direction that the parties attend upon the clerk to the Commercial Court to obtain a fixed date for trial.

Variations to the pre-trial timetable

D8.10 The parties may agree minor variations to the time periods set out in the pre-trial timetable without the case needing to be brought back to the court provided that the variation:

(i) will not jeopardise the date fixed for trial;
(ii) does not relate to the progress monitoring date; and
(iii) does not provide for the completion after the progress monitoring date of any step which was previously scheduled to have been completed by that date.

D8.11 If in any case it becomes apparent that variations to the pre-trial timetable are required which do not fall within section D8.10 above, the parties should apply to have the case management conference reconvened immediately. The parties should not wait until the progress monitoring date.

D9 Case management conference: Part 8 claims

D9 In a case commenced by the issue of a Part 8 claim form, a case management conference will normally take place on the first available date 6 weeks after service and filing of the defendant's evidence. At that case management conference the court will make such pre-trial directions as are necessary, adapting (where useful in the context of the particular claim) those of the case management procedures used for a claim commenced by the issue of a Part 7 claim form.

D10 Case management conference: Part 20 claims

D10.1 Wherever possible, any party who intends to make a Part 20 claim should do so before the hearing of the case management conference dealing with the main claim.

D10.2 Where permission to make a Part 20 claim is required it should be sought at the case management conference in the main claim.

D10.3 If the Part 20 claim is a counterclaim by a defendant against a claimant alone, the court will give directions in the Part 20 claim at the case management conference in the main claim.

D10.4 If the Part 20 claim is not a counterclaim by a defendant against a claimant alone, the case management conference in the main claim will be reconvened on the first available date 6 weeks after service of the defence to the Part 20 claim.

D10.5 All parties to the proceedings (ie the parties to the main claim and the parties to the Part 20 claim) must attend the reconvened case management conference. There will not be a separate case management conference for the Part 20 claim alone.

D10.6 In any case involving a Part 20 claim the court will give case management directions at the same case management conferences as it gives directions for the main claim: PD58 para 12. The court will therefore normally only give case management directions at hearings attended by all parties to the proceedings.

D11 Management throughout the case

D11 The court will continue to take an active role in the management of the case throughout its progress to trial. Parties should be ready at all times to provide the court with such information and assistance as it may require for that purpose.

D12 Progress monitoring

Fixing the progress monitoring date

D12.1 The progress monitoring date will be fixed at the case management conference and will normally be after the date in the pre-trial timetable for exchange of witness statements and expert reports.

Progress monitoring information sheet

D12.2 At least 3 days (ie 3 clear days) before the progress monitoring date the parties must each send to the Case Management Unit (with a copy to all other parties) a progress monitoring information sheet to inform the court:

- (i) whether they have complied with the pre-trial timetable, and if they have not, the respects in which they have not; and
- (ii) whether they will be ready for a trial commencing on the fixed date specified in the pre-trial timetable, and if they will not be ready, why they will not be ready.

D12.3 A standard form of progress monitoring information sheet is set out in Appendix 12.

D13 Reconvening the case management conference

D13.1 If in the view of the court the information given in the progress monitoring sheets justifies this course, the court may direct that the case management conference be reconvened.

D13.2 At a reconvened hearing of the case management conference the court may make such orders and give such directions as it considers appropriate.

D14 Pre-trial checklist

D14 Not later than three weeks before the date fixed for trial each party must send to the Listing Office (with a copy to all other parties) a completed checklist confirming final details for trial (a 'pre-trial checklist') in the form set out in Appendix 13.

D15 Further information

D15.1

- (a) If a party declines to provide further information requested under Part 18, the solicitors or counsel for the parties concerned must communicate directly with each other in an attempt to reach agreement before any application is made to the court.
- (b) No application for an order that a party provide further information will normally be listed for hearing without prior written confirmation from the applicant that the requirements of this section D15.1(a) have been complied with.

D15.2 Because it falls within the definition of a statement of case (see rule 2.3(1)) a response providing further information under CPR Part 18 must be verified by a statement of truth.

D16 Fixed trial dates

D16.1 Most cases will be given fixed trial dates immediately after the pre-trial timetable has been set at the case management conference.

D16.2 A fixed date for trial is given on the understanding that if previous fixtures have been substantially underestimated or other urgent matters need to be heard, the trial may be delayed. Where such delay might cause particular inconvenience to witnesses or others involved in the trial, the clerk to the Commercial Court should be informed well in advance of the fixed date.

D17 Estimates of length of trial

D17.1 At the case management conference an estimate will be made of the minimum and maximum lengths of the trial. The estimate will appear in the pre-trial timetable and will be the basis on which a date for trial will be fixed.

D17.2 If a party subsequently instructs new advocate(s) to appear on its behalf at the trial, the Listing Office should be notified of that fact within 14 days. Advocates newly instructed should review the estimate of the minimum and maximum lengths of the trial, and submit to the Listing Office a signed note revising or confirming the estimate as appropriate.

D17.3 A confirmed estimate of the minimum and maximum lengths of the trial, signed by the advocates who are to appear at the trial, should be attached to the pre-trial checklist.

D17.4 It is the duty of all advocates who are to appear at the trial to seek agreement, if possible, on the estimated minimum and maximum lengths of trial.

D17.5 The provisional estimate and (after it is given) the confirmed estimate must be kept under review by the advocates who are to appear at the trial. If at any stage an estimate needs to be revised, a signed revised estimate (whether agreed or not) must be submitted by the advocates to the clerk to the Commercial Court.

D17.6 Accurate estimation of trial length is of great importance to the efficient functioning of the court. The court will be guided by, but will not necessarily accept, the estimates given by the parties.

D18 Pre-trial review and trial timetable

D18.1 The court will order a pre-trial review in any case in which it considers it appropriate to do so.

D18.2 A pre-trial review will normally take place between 8 and 4 weeks before the date fixed for trial.

D18.3 Whenever possible the pre-trial review will be conducted by the trial judge. It should be attended by the advocates who are to appear at the trial: PD58 para 11.2.

D18.4 Before the pre-trial review the parties must attempt to agree a timetable for the trial providing for oral submissions, witnesses of fact and expert evidence: PD58 para 11.3. The claimant must file a copy of the draft timetable at least 2 days before the date fixed for the pre-trial review; any differences of view should be clearly identified: PD58 para 11.4. At the pre-trial review the judge may set a timetable for the trial and give such other directions for the conduct of the trial as he considers appropriate.

D19 Orders

D19.1

- (a) Except for orders made by the court on its own initiative under rule 3.3, and unless the court otherwise orders, every judgment or order will be drawn up by the parties and rule 40.3 is modified accordingly: rule 58.15(1).
- (b) Consent orders are to be drawn up in accordance with the procedure described in section F9.
- (c) All other orders are to be drawn up in draft by the parties and dated in the draft with the date of the judge's decision. The claimant is to have responsibility for drafting the order, unless it was made on the application of another party in which case that other party is to have the responsibility.
- (d) Two copies of the draft, signed by the parties themselves, or by their solicitors or counsel, must be lodged with the Registry **within 5 days** of the decision of the court reflected in the draft.

D19.2 If the court orders that an act be done by a certain date without specifying a time for compliance, the latest time for compliance is 4.30 pm on the day in question.

D19.3 Orders that are required to be served must be served by the parties, unless the court otherwise directs.

E DISCLOSURE

E1 Generally

E1.1 The court will seek to ensure that disclosure is no wider than appropriate. Anything wider than standard disclosure (see section E3) will need to be justified.

E2 Procedure

E2.1 At the case management conference the court will normally wish to consider one or more of the following:

- (i) ordering standard disclosure: rule 31.5(1);
- (ii) dispensing with or limiting standard disclosure: rule 31.5(2);
- (iii) ordering sample disclosure;
- (iv) ordering disclosure in stages;
- (v) ordering disclosure otherwise than by service of a list of documents, for example, by service of copy documents; and
- (vi) ordering specific disclosure: rule 31.12.

E2.2 The obligations imposed by an order for disclosure continue until the proceedings come to an end. If, after a list of documents has been prepared and served, the existence (present or past) of further documents to which the order applies comes to the attention of the disclosing party, that party must prepare and serve a supplemental list.

E3 Standard disclosure

E3.1 Standard disclosure is defined by rule 31.6. Where standard disclosure is ordered a party is required to disclose only:

(i) the documents on which he relies; and
(ii) documents which –
  - adversely affect his own case;
  - adversely affect another party's case; or
  - support another party's case; and
(iii) documents which he is required to disclose by any relevant practice direction.

E3.2 A party who contends that to search for a category or class of document under rule 31.6(b) would be unreasonable must indicate this in his case management information sheet (see Appendix 6).

E3.3 In order to comply with rule 31.10(3) (which requires the list to identify the documents in a convenient order and manner and as concisely as possible) it will normally be necessary to list the documents in date order, to number them consecutively and to give each a concise description. However, where there is a large number of documents all falling within a particular category the disclosing party may (unless otherwise ordered) list those documents as a category rather than individually.

E3.4 Each party to the proceedings must serve a separate list of documents. This applies even if two or more parties are represented by the same firm of solicitors.

E3.5 If the physical structure of a file may be of evidential value (eg a placing or chartering file) solicitors should make one complete copy of the file in the form in which they received it before any documents are removed for the purpose of giving disclosure or inspection.

E3.6 Unless the court directs otherwise, the disclosure statement must comply with the requirements of rules 31.7(3) and 31.10(6). In particular, it should:

(i) expressly state that the disclosing party believes the extent of the search to have been reasonable in all the circumstances; and
(ii) draw attention to any particular limitations on the extent of the search adopted for reasons of proportionality and give the reasons why they were adopted.

E3.7 The disclosure statement for standard disclosure should begin with the following words:

> '[I/we], [name(s)] state that [I/we] have carried out a reasonable and proportionate search to locate all the documents which [I am/*here name the party* is] required to disclose under [the order made by the court or the agreement in writing made between the parties] on the [ ] day of [ ] 20[ ].'

E3.8 The disclosure statement for standard disclosure should end with the following certificate:

> '[I/we] certify that [I/we] understand the duty of disclosure and to the best of [my/our] knowledge [I have/*here name the party* has] carried out that duty.

[I/we] certify that the list above is a complete list of all documents which are or have been in [my/*here name the party*'s] control and which [I am/*here name the party* is] obliged under [the said order or the said agreement in writing] to disclose.'

E3.9 An adapted version of practice form N265 (list of documents: standard disclosure) has been approved for use in the Commercial Court. A copy of this practice form (Form N265(CC)) is included at the end of the Guide. The court may at any stage order that a disclosure statement be verified by affidavit.

E3.10

(a) For the purposes of PD31 para 4.3 the court will normally regard as an appropriate person any person who is in a position responsibly and authoritatively to search for the documents required to be disclosed by that party and to make the statements contained in the disclosure statement concerning the documents which must be disclosed by that party.
(b) A legal representative may in certain cases be an appropriate person.
(c) An explanation why the person is considered an appropriate person must still be given in the disclosure statement.
(d) A person holding an office or position in the disclosing party but who is not in a position responsibly and authoritatively to make the statements contained in the disclosure statement will not be regarded as an appropriate person to make the disclosure statement of the party.
(e) The court may of its own initiative or on application require that a disclosure statement also be signed by another appropriate person.

E4 Specific disclosure

E4.1 Specific disclosure is defined by rule 31.12(2).

E4.2 An order for specific disclosure under rule 31.12 may in an appropriate case direct a party to carry out a thorough search for any documents which it is reasonable to suppose may adversely affect his own case or support the case of the party applying for disclosure or which may lead to a train of enquiry which has either of these consequences and to disclose any documents located as a result of that search: PD31 para 5.5.

E4.3 The court may at any stage order that specific disclosure be verified by affidavit or witness statement.

E4.4 Applications for ship's papers are provided for in rule 58.14.

F APPLICATIONS

F1 Generally

F1.1

(a) Applications are governed by CPR Part 23 and PD23 as modified by rule 58 and PD58. As a result:
   (i) PD23 paras 1 and 2.3–2.6 do not apply;
   (ii) PD23 paras 2.8 and 2.10 apply only if the proposed (additional) application will not increase the time estimate already given for the hearing for which a date has been fixed; and

(iii) PD23 para 3 is subject in all cases to the judge's agreeing that the application may proceed without an application notice being served.

(b) An adapted version of practice form N244 (application notice) has been approved for use in the Commercial Court. A copy of this practice form (Form N244(CC)) is included at the end of the Guide.

F1.2 An application for a consent order must include a draft of the proposed order signed on behalf of all parties to whom it relates: PD58 para 14.1.

F1.3 The requirement in PD23 para 12.1 that a draft order be supplied on disk does not apply in the Commercial Court since orders are generally drawn up by the parties: PD58 para 14.2.

Service

F1.4 Application notices are served by the parties, not by the court: PD58 para 9.

Evidence

F1.5

(a) Particular attention is drawn to PD23 para 9.1 which points out that even where no specific requirement for evidence is set out in the Rules or Practice Directions the court will in practice often need to be satisfied by evidence of the facts that are relied on in support of, or in opposition to, the application.

(b) Where convenient the written evidence relied on in support of an application may be included in the application notice, which may be lengthened for this purpose.

Time for service of evidence

F1.6 The time allowed for the service of evidence in relation to applications is governed by PD58 para 13.

Hearings

F1.7

(a) Applications (other than arbitration applications) will be heard in public in accordance with rule 39.2, save where otherwise ordered.

(b) With certain exceptions, arbitration applications will normally be heard in private: rule 62.10(3). See section O.

(c) An application without notice for a freezing injunction or a search order will normally be heard in private.

F1.8 Parties should pay particular attention to PD23 para 2.9 which warns of the need to anticipate the court's wish to review the conduct of the case and give further management directions. The parties should be ready to give the court their assistance and should be able to answer any questions that the court may ask for this purpose.

F1.9 PD23 paras 6.1–6.5 and para 7 deal with the hearing of applications by telephone (other than an urgent application out of court hours) and the hearing of applications using video-conferencing facilities. These methods may be considered when an application needs to be made before a particular Commercial judge who is currently on circuit. In most other cases applications are more conveniently dealt with in person.

F2 Applications without notice

F2.1 All applications should be made on notice, even if that notice has to be short, unless:

(i) any rule or Practice Direction provides that the application may be made without notice; or
(ii) there are good reasons for making the application without notice, for example, because notice would or might defeat the object of the application.

F2.2 Where an application without notice does not involve the giving of undertakings to the court, it will normally be made and dealt with on paper, as, for example, applications for permission to serve a claim form out of the jurisdiction, and applications for an extension of time in which to serve a claim form.

F2.3 Any application for an interim injunction or similar remedy will require an oral hearing.

F2.4

(a) A party wishing to make an application without notice which requires an oral hearing before a judge should contact the clerk to the Commercial Court at the earliest opportunity.
(b) If a party wishes to make an application without notice at a time when no commercial judge is available he should apply to the Queen's Bench judge in chambers (see section P1.1).

F2.5 On all applications without notice it is the duty of the applicant and those representing him to make full and frank disclosure of all matters relevant to the application.

F2.6 The papers lodged for the application should include two copies of a draft of the order sought. Save in exceptional circumstances where time does not permit, all the evidence relied upon in support of the application and any other relevant documents must be lodged in advance with the clerk to the Commercial Court.

If the application is urgent, the clerk to the Commercial Court should be informed of the fact and of the reasons for the urgency.

F3 Expedited applications

F3.1 The court will expedite the hearing of an application on notice in cases of sufficient urgency and importance.

F3.2 Where a party wishes to make an expedited application a request should be made to the clerk to the Commercial Court on notice to all other parties.

F4 Paper applications

F4.1

(a) Although contested applications are usually best determined at an oral hearing, some applications may be suitable for determination on paper.

(b) Attention is drawn to the provisions of rule 23.8 and PD23 para 11. If the applicant considers that the application is suitable for determination on paper, he should ensure before lodging the papers with the court:

  (i) that the application notice together with any supporting evidence has been served on the respondent;

  (ii) that the respondent has been allowed the appropriate period of time in which to serve evidence in opposition;

  (iii) that any evidence in reply has been served on the respondent; and

  (iv) that there is included in the papers:

    (A) the written consent of the respondent to the disposal of the application without a hearing; or

    (B) a statement by the applicant of the grounds on which he seeks to have the application disposed of without a hearing, together with confirmation that a copy has been served on the respondent.

(c) Only in exceptional cases will the court dispose of an application without a hearing in the absence of the respondent's consent.

F4.2

(a) Certain applications relating to the management of proceedings may conveniently be made in correspondence without issuing an application notice.

(b) It must be clearly understood that such applications are not applications without notice and the applicant must therefore ensure that a copy of the letter making the application is sent to all other parties to the proceedings.

(c) Accordingly, the following procedure should be followed when making an application of this kind:

  (i) the applicant should first ascertain whether the application is opposed by the other parties;

  (ii) if it is, the applicant should apply to the court by letter stating the nature of the order which it seeks and the grounds on which the application is made;

  (iii) a copy the letter should be sent (by fax, where possible) to all other parties at the same time as it is sent to the court;

  (iv) any other party wishing to make representations should do so by letter within 2 days (ie 2 clear days) of the date of the applicant's letter of application. The representations should be sent (by fax, where possible) to the applicant and all other parties at the same time as they are sent to the court;

  (v) the court will advise its decision by letter to the applicant. The applicant must forthwith copy the court's letter to all other parties, by fax where possible.

F5 Ordinary applications

F5.1 Applications likely to require an oral hearing lasting half a day or less are regarded as 'ordinary' applications.

F5.2 Ordinary applications will generally be heard on Fridays, but may be heard on other days. Where possible, the Listing Office will have regard to the availability of advocates when fixing hearing dates.

F5.3 Many ordinary applications, especially those in the non-counsel list on Fridays, are very short indeed (eg applications to extend time). As in the past, it is likely that many, if not most, of such applications can be heard without evidence and on short (ie a few days') notice. The parties should however have in mind what is said in section F1.5(a) above.

F5.4

(a) The timetable for ordinary applications is set out in PD58 para 13.1 and is as follows:
   (i) evidence in support must be filed and served with the application;
   (ii) evidence in answer must be filed and served within 14 days thereafter;
   (iii) evidence in reply (if any) must be filed and served within 7 days thereafter.

(b) This timetable may be abridged or extended by agreement between the parties provided that any date fixed for the hearing of the application is not affected: PD58 para 13.4. In appropriate cases, this timetable may be abridged by the court.

F5.5 An application bundle (see section F11) must be lodged with the Listing Office by 1 pm one clear day before the date fixed for the hearing. The case management bundle will also be required on the hearing; this file will be passed by the Listing Office to the judge. Only where it is essential for the court on the hearing of the ordinary application to see the full version of a statement of case that has been summarised in accordance with section C1.4 above should a copy of that statement of case be lodged for the ordinary application.

F5.6 Save in very short and simple cases, skeleton arguments must be provided by all parties. These must be lodged with the Listing Office and served on the advocates for all other parties to the application by 1 pm on the day before the date fixed for the hearing (ie the immediately preceding day). Guidelines on the preparation of skeleton arguments are set out in Part 1 of Appendix 9.

F5.7 Thus, for an application estimated for a half day or less and due to be heard on a Friday:

(i) the application bundle must be lodged by 1 pm on Wednesday; and
(ii) skeleton arguments must be lodged by 1 pm on Thursday.

F5.8 The applicant should, as a matter of course, provide all other parties to the application with a copy of the application bundle at the cost of the receiving party. Further copies should be supplied on request, again at the cost of the receiving party.

F5.9 Problems with the lodging of bundles or skeleton arguments should be notified to the clerk to the Commercial Court as far in advance as possible. **If the application bundle or skeleton argument is not lodged by the time specified, the application may be stood out of the list without further warning.**

F6 Heavy applications

F6.1 Applications likely to require an oral hearing lasting more than half a day are regarded as 'heavy' applications.

F6.2 Heavy applications normally involve a greater volume of evidence and other documents and more extensive issues. They accordingly require a longer lead-time for preparation and exchange of evidence. Where possible the Listing Office will have regard to the availability of advocates when fixing hearing dates.

F6.3 The timetable for heavy applications is set out in PD58 para 13.2 and is as follows:

(i) evidence in support must be filed and served with the application;
(ii) evidence in answer must be filed and served within 28 days thereafter;
(iii) evidence in reply (if any) must be filed and served as soon as possible, and in any event within 14 days of service of the evidence in answer.

F6.4

(a) An application bundle (see section F11) must be lodged with the Listing Office by 4 pm 2 days (ie 2 clear days) before the date fixed for the hearing. The case management bundle will also be required on the hearing; this file will be passed by the Listing Office to the judge.
(b) Only where it is essential for the court on the hearing of the application to see the full version of a statement of case that has been summarised in accordance with section C1.4 above should a copy of that statement of case be lodged for the application.

F6.5 Skeleton arguments must be lodged with the Listing Office and served on the advocates for all other parties to the application as follows:

(i) applicant's skeleton argument (with chronology unless one is unnecessary, and with a dramatis personae if one is warranted), by 4 pm 2 days (ie 2 clear days) before the hearing;
(ii) respondent's skeleton argument, by 4 pm one day (ie one clear day) before the hearing.

Guidelines on the preparation of skeleton arguments are set out in Part 1 of Appendix 9.

F6.6 Thus, for an application estimated for more than half a day and due to be heard on a Thursday:

(i) the application bundle and the applicant's skeleton argument must be lodged by 4 pm on Monday;
(ii) the respondent's skeleton argument must be lodged by 4 pm on Tuesday.

F6.7 The applicant must, as a matter of course, provide all other parties to the application with a copy of the application bundle at the cost of the receiving party. Further copies must be supplied on request, again at the cost of the receiving party.

F6.8 Problems with the lodging of bundles or skeleton arguments should be notified to the clerk to the Commercial Court as far in advance as possible. **If the application bundle or skeleton argument is not lodged by the time specified, the application may be stood out of the list without further warning.**

F7 Evidence

F7.1 Although evidence may be given by affidavit, it should generally be given by witness statement, except where PD32 requires evidence to be given on affidavit (as, for example, in the case of an application for a freezing injunction or a search order: PD32 para 1.4). In other cases the court may order that evidence be given by affidavit: PD32 para 1.4(1) and 1.6.

F7.2 Witness statements and affidavits must comply with the requirements of PD32, save that photocopy documents should be used unless the court orders otherwise.

F7.3

(a) Witness statements must be verified by a statement of truth signed by the maker of the statement: rule 22.1.
(b) At hearings other than trial an applicant may rely on the application notice itself, and a party may rely on his statement of case, if the application notice or statement of case (as the case may be) is verified by a statement of truth: rule 32.6(2).
(c) A statement of truth in an application notice may also be signed as indicated in sections C1.8 and C1.9 above.

F7.4 Proceedings for contempt of court may be brought against a person who makes, or causes to be made, a false statement in a witness statement (or any other document verified by a statement of truth) without an honest belief in its truth: rule 32.14(1).

F8 Reading time

F8

(a) It is essential for the efficient conduct of the court's business that the parties inform the court of the reading required in order to enable the judge to dispose of the application within the time allowed for the hearing and of the time likely to be required for that purpose. Accordingly:
  (i) each party must lodge with the Listing Office by 1 pm on the day before the date fixed for the hearing of an application (ie the immediately preceding day) a reading list with an estimate of the time required to complete the reading;
  (ii) each party's reading list should identify the material **on both sides** which the court needs to read; and
  (iii) if any advocate considers that the time required for reading is likely to exceed 2.5 hours, the Listing Office must be warned of that fact **not later than 4.00 pm one clear day before the hearing of the application**.
(b) **Failure to comply with these requirements may result in the adjournment of the hearing.**

F9 Applications disposed of by consent

F9.1

(a) Consent orders may be submitted to the court in draft for approval and initialling without the need for attendance.

(b) Two copies of the draft, one of which (or a counterpart) must be signed on behalf of all parties to whom it relates, should be lodged at the Registry. The copies should be undated. The order will be dated with the date on which the judge initials it, but that does not prevent the parties acting on their agreement immediately if they wish.

(c) The parties should act promptly in lodging the copies at the Registry. If it is important that the orders are made by a particular date, that fact (and the reasons for it) should be notified in writing to the Registry.

F9.2 For the avoidance of doubt, this procedure is not normally available in relation to a case management conference or a pre-trial review. Whether or not the parties are agreed as between themselves on the directions that the court should be asked to consider giving at a case management conference or a pre-trial review, attendance will normally be required. See section D8.3.

F9.3 Where an order provides a time by which something is to be done the order should wherever possible state the particular date by which the thing is to be done rather than specify a period of time from a particular date or event: rule 2.9.

F10 Hearing dates, time estimates and time-limits

F10.1 Dates for the hearing of applications to be attended by advocates are normally fixed after discussion with the counsel's clerks or with the solicitor concerned.

F10.2 The efficient working of the court depends on accurate estimates of the time needed for the oral hearing of an application. Overestimating can be as wasteful as underestimating.

F10.3 Subject to section F10.4, the clerk to the Commercial Court will not accept or act on time estimates for the oral hearing of applications where those estimates exceed the following maxima:

Application to set aside service:	4 hours
Application for summary judgment:	4 hours
Application to set aside or vary interim remedy:	4 hours
Application to set aside or vary default judgment:	2 hours
Application to amend statement of case:	1 hour
Application for specific disclosure:	1 hour
Application for security for costs:	1 hour

F10.4 A longer listing time will only be granted upon application in writing specifying the additional time required and giving reasons why it is required. A copy of the written application should be sent to the advocates for all other parties in the case at the same time as it is sent to the Listing Office.

F10.5

(a) Not later than 5 days before the date fixed for the hearing the applicant must provide the Listing Office with his current estimate of the time required to dispose of the application.

(b) If at any time either party considers that there is a material risk that the hearing of the application will exceed the time currently allowed it must inform the Listing Office immediately.

F10.6

(a) All time estimates should be given on the assumption that the judge will have read in advance the skeleton arguments and the documents identified in the reading list. In this connection attention is drawn to section F8.

(b) A time estimate for an ordinary application should allow time for judgment and consequential matters; a time estimate for a heavy application should not.

F10.7 Save in the situation referred to at section F10.8, a separate estimate must be given for each application, including any application issued after, but to be heard at the same time as, another application.

F10.8 A separate estimate need not be given for any application issued after, but to be heard at the same time as, another application where the advocate in the case certifies in writing that:

(i) the determination of the application first issued will necessarily determine the application issued subsequently; or

(ii) the matters raised in the application issued subsequently are not contested.

F10.9 If it is found at the hearing that the time required for the hearing has been significantly underestimated, the judge hearing the application may adjourn the matter and may make any special costs orders (including orders for the immediate payment of costs and wasted costs orders) as may be appropriate.

F10.10 Failure to comply with the requirements for lodging bundles for the application will normally result in the application not being heard on the date fixed at the expense of the party in default (see further sections F5.9 and F6.8 above). An order for immediate payment of costs may be made.

F11 Application bundles

F11.1

(a) Bundles for use on applications may be compiled in any convenient manner but must contain the following documents (preferably in separate sections in the following order):
   (i) a copy of the application notice;
   (ii) a draft of the order which the applicant seeks;
   (iii) a copy of the statements of case;
   (iv) copies of any previous orders which are relevant to the application;
   (v) copies of the witness statements and affidavits filed in support of, or in opposition to, the application, together with any exhibits.

(b) Copies of the statements of case and of previous orders in the action should be provided in a separate section of the bundle. They should not be exhibited to witness statements.

(c) Witness statements and affidavits previously filed in the same proceedings should be included in the bundle at a convenient location. They should not be exhibited to witness statements.

F12 Chronologies, indices and dramatis personae

F12.1 For most applications it is of assistance for the applicant to provide a chronology. Dramatis personae are often useful as well.

F12.2 Guidelines on the preparation of chronologies and indices are set out in Part 2 of Appendix 9.

F13 Authorities

F13.1 On some applications there will be key authorities that it would be useful for the judge to read before the oral hearing of the application. Copies of these authorities should be provided with the skeleton arguments.

F13.2 It is also desirable for bundles of the authorities on which the parties wish to rely to be provided to the judge hearing the application as soon as possible after skeleton arguments have been exchanged.

F13.3 Unreported cases should only be cited where the advocate is ready to give an assurance that the transcript contains a statement of some principle of law, relevant to an issue on the application, of which the substance, as distinct from some mere choice of phraseology, is not to be found in any judgment that has appeared in one of the recognised series of law reports.

F14 Costs

F14.1 Costs are dealt with generally at section J13.

F14.2 Reference should be also be made to the rules governing the summary assessment of costs for shorter hearings contained in Parts 43 and 44.

F14.3 In carrying out a summary assessment of costs, the court may have regard amongst other matters to:

- (i) advice from a Commercial Costs Judge or from the Chief Costs Judge on costs of specialist solicitors and counsel;
- (ii) any survey published by the London Solicitors Litigation Association showing the average hourly expense rate for solicitors in London;
- (iii) any information provided to the court at its request by one or more of the specialist associations (referred to at section A4.2) on average charges by specialist solicitors and counsel.

F15 Interim injunctions

Generally

F15.1

- (a) Applications for interim injunctions are governed by CPR Part 25.
- (b) Applications must be made on notice in accordance with the procedure set out in CPR Part 23 unless there are good reasons for proceeding without notice.

F15.2 A party who wishes to make an application for an interim injunction must give the clerk to the Commercial Court as much notice as possible.

F15.3

- (a) Except when the application is so urgent that there has not been any opportunity to do so, the applicant must issue his claim form and obtain the evidence on which he wishes to rely in support of the application before making the application.

(b) On applications of any weight, and unless the urgency means that this is not possible, the applicant should provide the court at the earliest opportunity with a skeleton argument.
(c) An affidavit, and not a witness statement, is required on an application for a freezing injunction or a search order: PD25 para 3.1.

Fortification of undertakings

F15.4

(a) Where the applicant for an interim remedy is not able to show sufficient assets within the jurisdiction of the court to provide substance to the undertakings given, particularly the undertaking in damages, he may be required to reinforce his undertakings by providing security.
(b) Security will be ordered in such form as the judge decides is appropriate but may, for example, take the form of a payment into court, a bond issued by an insurance company or a first demand guarantee or standby credit issued by a first-class bank.
(c) In an appropriate case the judge may order a payment to be made to the applicant's solicitors to be held by them as officers of the court pending further order. Sometimes the undertaking of a parent company may be acceptable.

Form of order

F15.5 Standard forms of wording for freezing injunctions and search orders are set out in Appendix 5. The forms have been adapted for use in the Commercial Court and should be followed unless the judge hearing a particular application considers there is good reason for adopting a different form.

F15.6 A phrase indicating that an interim remedy is to remain in force until judgment or further order means that it remains in force until the delivery of a final judgment. If an interim remedy continuing after judgment is required, say until judgment has been satisfied, an application to that effect must be made (see further section K1).

F15.7 It is good practice to draft an order for an interim remedy so that it includes a proviso which permits acts which would otherwise be a breach of the order to be done with the written consent of the claimant's solicitors. This enables the parties to agree in effect to variations (or the discharge) of the order without the necessity of coming back to the court.

Freezing injunctions

F15.8

(a) Freezing injunctions made on an application without notice will provide for a return date, unless the judge otherwise orders: PD25 para 5.1(3). In the usual course, the return date given will be a Friday (unless a date for a case management conference has already been fixed, in which event the return date given will in the usual course be that date).

(b) If, after service or notification of the injunction, one or more of the parties considers that more than 15 minutes will be required to deal with the matter on the return date the Listing Office should be informed forthwith and in any event no later than 4 pm on the Wednesday before the Friday fixed as the return date.

(c) If the parties agree, the return date may be postponed to a later date on which all parties will be ready to deal with any substantive issues. In this event, an agreed form of order continuing the injunction to the postponed return date should be submitted for consideration by a judge and if the order is made in the terms submitted there will be no need for the parties to attend on the day originally fixed as the return date.

(d) In such a case the defendant and any other interested party will continue to have liberty to apply to vary or set aside the order.

F15.9 A provision for the defendant to give notice of any application to discharge or vary the order is usually included as a matter of convenience but it is not proper to attempt to fetter the right of the defendant to apply without notice or on short notice if need be.

F15.10 As regards freezing injunctions in respect of assets outside the jurisdiction, the standard wording in relation to effects on third parties should normally incorporate wording to enable overseas branches of banks or similar institutions which have offices within the jurisdiction to comply with what they reasonably believe to be their obligations under the laws of the country where the assets are located or under the proper law of the relevant banking or other contract relating to such assets.

F15.11 Any bank or third party served with, notified of or affected by a freezing injunction may apply to the court without notice to any party for directions, or notify the court in writing without notice to any party, in the event that the order affects or may affect the position of the bank or third party under legislation, regulations or procedures aimed to prevent money laundering.

Search orders

F15.12 Attention is drawn to the detailed requirements in respect of search orders set out in PD25 paras 7.1–8.3. The applicant for the search order will normally be required to undertake not to inform any third party of the search order or of the case until after a specified date.

Applications to discharge or vary freezing injunctions and search orders

F15.13 Applications to discharge or vary freezing injunctions and search orders are treated as matters of urgency for listing purposes. Those representing applicants for discharge or variation should ascertain before a date is fixed for the hearing whether, having regard to the evidence which they wish to adduce, the claimant would wish to adduce further evidence in opposition. If so, all reasonable steps must be taken by all parties to agree upon the earliest practicable date at which they can be ready for the hearing, so as to avoid the last minute need to vacate a fixed date. In cases of difficulty the matter should be referred to a judge who may be able to suggest temporary solutions pending the hearing.

F15.14 If a freezing injunction or search order is discharged on an application to discharge or vary, or on the return date, the judge will consider whether it is appropriate that he should assess damages at once and direct immediate payment by the applicant.

Applications under section 25 of the Civil Jurisdiction and Judgments Act 1982

F15.15 A Part 8 claim form (rather than an application notice: cf. rule 25.4(2)) must be used for an application under section 25 of the Civil Jurisdiction and Judgments Act 1982 ('Interim relief in England and Wales and Northern Ireland in the absence of substantive proceedings'). The modified Part 8 procedure used in the Commercial Court is referred to at section B4 above.

F16 Security for costs

F16.1 Applications for security for costs are governed by rules 25.12–14.

F16.2 The applicable practice is set out in Appendix 16.

G ALTERNATIVE DISPUTE RESOLUTION ('ADR')

G1 Generally

G1.1 While emphasising its primary role as a forum for deciding commercial cases, the Commercial Court encourages parties to consider the use of ADR (such as, but not confined to, mediation and conciliation) as an alternative means of resolving disputes or particular issues.

G1.2 Whilst the Commercial Court remains an entirely appropriate forum for resolving most of the disputes which are entered in the Commercial List, the view of the Commercial Court is that the settlement of disputes by means of ADR:

(i) significantly helps parties to save costs;
(ii) saves parties the delay of litigation in reaching finality in their disputes;
(iii) enables parties to achieve settlement of their disputes while preserving their existing commercial relationships and market reputation;
(iv) provides parties with a wider range of solutions than those offered by litigation; and
(v) is likely to make a substantial contribution to the more efficient use of judicial resources.

G1.3 The Commercial judges will in appropriate cases invite the parties to consider whether their dispute, or particular issues in it, could be resolved through ADR.

G1.4 Legal representatives in all cases should consider with their clients and the other parties concerned the possibility of attempting to resolve the dispute or particular issues by ADR and should ensure that their clients are fully informed as to the most cost effective means of resolving their dispute.

G1.5 Parties who consider that ADR might be an appropriate means of resolving the dispute or particular issues in the dispute may apply for directions at any stage, including before service of the defence and before the case management conference.

G1.6 At the case management conference if it should appear to the judge that the case before him or any of the issues arising in it are particularly appropriate for an attempt at settlement by means of ADR but that the parties have not previously attempted settlement by such means, he may invite the parties to use ADR.

G1.7 The judge may, if he considers it appropriate, adjourn the case for a specified period of time to encourage and enable the parties to use ADR. He may for this purpose extend the time for compliance by the parties or any of them with any requirement under the rules, the Guide or any order of the court.

G1.8 The judge may further consider in an appropriate case making an ADR Order in the terms set out in Appendix 7.

G1.9

(a) The clerk to the Commercial Court keeps some published information on individuals and bodies that offer ADR and arbitration services. If the parties are unable to agree upon a neutral individual or panel of individuals to act as a mediator, they may by consent refer to the judge for assistance in reaching such agreement.
(b) The court will not recommend any individual or body to act as a mediator or arbitrator.

G1.10 At the case management conference or at any other hearing in the course of which the judge makes an order providing for ADR he may make such order as to the costs that the parties may incur by reason of their using or attempting to use ADR as may in all the circumstances seem appropriate.

G2 Early neutral evaluation

G2.1 In appropriate cases and with the agreement of all parties the court will provide a without-prejudice, non-binding, early neutral evaluation ('ENE') of a dispute or of particular issues.

G2.2 The approval of the Judge in Charge of the List must be obtained before any ENE is undertaken.

G2.3 If, after discussion with the advocates representing the parties, it appears to a judge that an ENE is likely to assist in the resolution of the dispute or of particular issues, he will, with the agreement of the parties, refer the matter to the Judge in Charge of the List.

G2.4

(a) The Judge in Charge of the List will nominate a judge to conduct the ENE.
(b) The judge who is to conduct the ENE will give such directions for its preparation and conduct as he considers appropriate.

G2.5 The judge who conducts the ENE will take no further part in the case, either for the purpose of the hearing of applications or as the judge at trial, unless the parties agree otherwise.

H EVIDENCE FOR TRIAL

H1 Witnesses of fact

Preparation and form of witness statements

H1.1 Witness statements must comply with the requirements of PD32. The following points are also emphasised:

- (i) the function of a witness statement is to set out in writing the evidence in chief of the witness; as far as possible, therefore, the statement should be in the witness's own words;
- (ii) it should be as concise as the circumstances of the case allow without omitting any significant matters;
- (iii) it should not contain lengthy quotations from documents;
- (iv) it should not engage in argument;
- (v) it must indicate which of the statements made in it are made from the witness's own knowledge and which are made on information or belief, giving the source for any statement made on information or belief;
- (vi) it must contain a statement by the witness that he believes the matters stated in it are true; proceedings for contempt of court may be brought against a person if he makes, or causes to be made, a false statement in a witness statement without an honest belief in its truth: rule 32.14(1).

H1.2 It is improper to put pressure of any kind on a witness to give anything other than his own account of the matters with which his statement deals. It is also improper to serve a witness statement which is known to be false or which it is known the maker does not in all respects actually believe to be true.

Fluency of witnesses

H1.3 If a witness is not sufficiently fluent in English to give his evidence in English, the witness statement should be in the witness's own language and a translation provided.

H1.4 If a witness is not fluent in English but can make himself understood in broken English and can understand written English, the statement need not be in his own words provided that these matters are indicated in the statement itself. It must however be written so as to express as accurately as possible the substance of his evidence.

Witness statement as evidence in chief

H1.5

- (a) Where a witness is called to give oral evidence, his witness statement is to stand as his evidence in chief unless the court orders otherwise: rule 32.5(2).
- (b) In an appropriate case the trial judge may direct that the whole or any part of a witness's evidence in chief is to be given orally. Any application for such an order should be made at the beginning of the trial.

Additional evidence from a witness

H1.6

(a) A witness giving oral evidence at trial may with the permission of the court amplify his witness statement and give evidence in relation to new matters which have arisen since the witness statement was served: rule 32.5(3). Permission will be given only if the court considers that there is good reason not to confine the evidence of the witness to the contents of his witness statement: rule 32.5(4).

(b) A supplemental witness statement should normally be served where the witness proposes materially to add to, alter, correct or retract from what is in his original statement. Permission will be required for the service of a supplemental statement.

Notice of decision not to call a witness

H1.7

(a) A party who has decided not to call to give oral evidence at trial a witness whose statement has been served must give prompt notice of this decision to all other parties. He must at the same time state whether he proposes to put the statement in as hearsay evidence.

(b) If the party who has served the statement does not put it in as hearsay evidence, any other party may do so: rule 32.5(5).

Witness summonses

H1.8

(a) Rules 34.2–34.8 deal with witness summonses, including a summons for a witness to attend court or to produce documents in advance of the date fixed for trial.

(b) Witness summonses are served by the parties, not the court.

H2 Expert witnesses

Application for permission to call an expert witness

H2.1 Any application for permission to call an expert witness or serve an expert's report should normally be made at the case management conference.

H2.2 Parties should bear in mind that expert evidence can lead to unnecessary expense and they should be prepared to consider the use of single joint experts in appropriate cases. In many cases the use of single joint experts is not appropriate and each party will generally be given permission to call one expert in each field requiring expert evidence. These are referred to in the Guide as 'separate experts'.

H2.3 When the use of a single joint expert is contemplated, the court will expect the parties to co-operate in developing, and agreeing to the greatest possible extent, terms of reference for that expert. In most cases the terms of reference will (in particular) identify in detail what the expert is asked to do, identify any documentary materials he is asked to consider and specify any assumptions he is asked to make.

Provisions of general application in relation to expert evidence

H2.4 The provisions set out in Appendix 11 to the Guide apply to all aspects of expert evidence (including expert reports, meetings of experts and expert evidence given orally) unless the court orders otherwise. Parties should ensure that they are drawn to the attention of any experts they instruct at the earliest opportunity.

Form and content of expert's reports

H2.5 Expert's reports must comply with the requirements of PD35 paras 1 and 2.

H2.6

(a) In stating the substance of all material instructions on the basis of which his report is written as required by rule 35.10(3) and PD35 para 1.2(8) an expert witness should state the facts or assumptions upon which his opinion is based.
(b) The expert must make it clear which, if any, of the facts stated are within his own direct knowledge.
(c) If a stated assumption is, in the opinion of the expert witness, unreasonable or unlikely he should state that clearly.

H2.7 It is useful if a report contains a glossary of significant technical terms.

Statement of truth

H2.8

(a) The report must be signed by the expert and must contain a statement of truth in accordance with Part 35.
(b) Proceedings for contempt of court may be brought against a person if he makes, or causes to be made, without an honest belief in its truth, a false statement in an expert's report verified in the manner set out in this section.

Request by an expert to the court for directions

H2.9 An expert may file with the court a written request for directions to assist him in carrying out his function as expert, but:

(i) at least 7 days before he does so (or such shorter period as the court may direct) he should provide a copy of his proposed request to the party instructing him; and
(ii) at least 4 days before he does so (or such shorter period as the court may direct) he should provide a copy of his proposed request to all other parties.

Exchange of reports

H2.10 In appropriate cases the court will direct that the reports of expert witnesses be exchanged sequentially rather than simultaneously. This is an issue that the court will normally wish to consider at the case management conference.

Meetings of expert witnesses

H2.11 The court will normally direct a meeting or meetings of expert witnesses before trial. Sometimes it may be useful for there to be further meetings during the trial itself.

H2.12 The purposes of a meeting of experts are to give the experts the opportunity:

- (i) to discuss the expert issues;
- (ii) to decide, with the benefit of that discussion, on which expert issues they share or can come to share the same expert opinion and on which expert issues there remains a difference of expert opinion between them (and what that difference is).

H2.13 Subject to section H2.16 below, the content of the discussion between the experts at or in connection with a meeting is without prejudice and shall not be referred to at the trial unless the parties so agree: rule 35.12(4).

H2.14 Subject to any directions of the court, the procedure to be adopted at a meeting of experts is a matter for the experts themselves, not the parties or their legal representatives.

H2.15 Neither the parties nor their legal representatives should seek to restrict the freedom of experts to identify and acknowledge the expert issues on which they agree at, or following further consideration after, meetings of experts.

H2.16 Unless the court orders otherwise, at or following any meeting the experts should prepare a joint memorandum for the court recording:

- (i) the fact that they have met and discussed the expert issues;
- (ii) the issues on which they agree;
- (iii) the issues on which they disagree; and
- (iv) a brief summary of the reasons for their disagreement.

H2.17 If experts reach agreement on an issue that agreement shall not bind the parties unless they expressly agree to be bound by it.

Written questions to experts

H2.18

- (a) Under rule 35.6 a party may, without the permission of the court, put written questions to an expert instructed by another party (or to a single joint expert) about his report. Unless the court gives permission or the other party agrees, such questions must be for the purpose only of clarifying the report.
- (b) The court will pay close attention to the use of this procedure (especially where separate experts are instructed) to ensure that it remains an instrument for the helpful exchange of information. The court will not allow it to interfere with the procedure for an exchange of professional opinion at a meeting of experts, or to inhibit that exchange of professional opinion. In cases where (for example) questions that are oppressive in number or content are put, or questions are put for any purpose other than clarification of the report, the court will not hesitate to disallow the questions and to make an appropriate order for costs against the party putting them.

Documents referred to in experts' reports

H2.19 Unless they have already been provided on inspection of documents at the stage of disclosure, copies of any photographs, plans, analyses, measurements, survey reports or other similar documents relied on by an expert witness as well as copies of any unpublished sources must be provided to all parties at the same time as his report.

H2.20

(a) Rule 31.14(e) provides that (subject to rule 35.10(4)) a party may inspect a document mentioned in an expert's report. In a commercial case an expert's report will frequently, and helpfully, list all or many of the relevant previous papers (published or unpublished) or books written by the expert or to which the expert has contributed. Requiring inspection of this material may often be unrealistic, and the collating and copying burden could be huge.

(b) Accordingly, a party wishing to inspect a document in an expert report should (failing agreement) make an application to the court. The court will not permit inspection unless it is satisfied that it is necessary for the just disposal of the case and that the document is not reasonably available to the party making the application from an alternative source.

Trial

H2.21 At trial the evidence of expert witnesses is usually taken as a block, after the evidence of witnesses of fact has been given.

H3 Evidence by video link

H3.1 In an appropriate case permission may be given for the evidence of a witness to be given by video link. If permission is given the court will give directions for the conduct of this part of the trial.

H3.2 The party seeking permission to call evidence by video link should prepare and serve on all parties and lodge with the court a memorandum dealing with the matters outlined in the Video Conferencing Guidance contained in Annex 3 to PD32 (see Appendix 14) and setting out precisely what arrangements are proposed. Where the proposal involves transmission from a location with no existing video-link facility, experience shows that questions of feasibility, timing and cost will require particularly close investigation.

H3.3 An application for permission to call evidence by video link should be made, if possible, at the case management conference or, at the latest, at any pre-trial review. However, an application may be made at an even later stage if necessary.

H3.4 In considering whether to give permission for evidence to be given in this way the court will be concerned in particular to balance any potential savings of costs against the inability to observe the witness at first hand when giving evidence.

H4 Taking evidence abroad

H4.1 In an appropriate case permission may be given for the evidence of a witness to be taken abroad. CPR Part 34 contains provisions for the taking of evidence by deposition, and the issue of letters of request.

H4.2 In a very exceptional case, and subject in particular to all necessary approvals being obtained and diplomatic requirements being satisfied, the court may be willing to conduct part of the proceedings abroad. However, if there is any reasonable opportunity for the witness to give evidence by video link, the court is unlikely to take that course.

J TRIAL

J1 Expedited trial

J1.1 The Commercial Court is able to provide an expedited trial in cases of sufficient urgency and importance.

J1.2 A party seeking an expedited trial should apply to the Judge in Charge of the Commercial List on notice to all parties at the earliest possible opportunity. The application should normally be made after issue and service of the claim form but before service of particulars of claim.

J2 Split trials

J2.1 It will sometimes be advantageous to try liability first. Assessment of damages can be referred to a judge of the Technology and Construction Court or to a Master, or the parties may choose to ask an arbitrator to decide them. The same approach can be applied to other factual questions.

J3 Documents for trial

J3.1 Bundles of documents for the trial must be prepared in accordance with Appendix 10.

J3.2 The number, content and organisation of the trial bundles must be approved by the advocates with the conduct of the trial.

J3.3 Consideration must always be given to what documents are and are not relevant and necessary. Where the court is of the opinion that costs have been wasted by the copying of unnecessary documents it will have no hesitation in making a special order for costs against the person responsible.

J3.4 The number content and organisation of the trial bundles should be agreed in accordance with the following procedure:

- (i) the claimant must submit proposals to all other parties at least 6 weeks before the date fixed for trial; and
- (ii) the other parties must submit details of additions they require and any suggestions for revision of the claimant's proposals to the claimant at least 4 weeks before the date fixed for trial.

This information must be supplied in a form that will be most convenient for the recipient to understand and respond to. The form to be used should be discussed between the parties before the details are supplied.

J3.5

(a) It is the claimant's responsibility to prepare and lodge the agreed trial bundles.
(b) If another party wishes to put before the court a bundle that the claimant regards as unnecessary he must prepare and lodge it himself.

J3.6

(a) Preparation of the trial bundles must be completed not later than 2 weeks before the date fixed for trial unless the court orders otherwise.
(b) Any party preparing a trial bundle should, as a matter of course, provide all other parties who are to take part in the trial with a copy, at the cost of the receiving party. Further copies should be supplied on request, again at the cost of the receiving party.

J3.7 Unless the court orders otherwise, a full set of the trial bundles must be lodged with the Listing Office at least 7 days before the date fixed for trial.

J3.8 Failure to comply with the requirements for lodging bundles for the trial may result in the trial not commencing on the date fixed, at the expense of the party in default. An order for immediate payment of costs may be made.

J3.9 If oral evidence is to be given at trial, the claimant must provide a clean unmarked set of all relevant trial bundles for use in the witness box. The claimant is responsible for ensuring that these bundles are kept up to date throughout the trial.

J4 Information technology at trial

J4.1 The use of information technology at trial is encouraged where it is likely substantially to save time and cost or to increase accuracy.

J4.2 If any party considers that it might be advantageous to make use of information technology in preparation for, or at, trial, the matter should be raised at the case management conference. This is particularly important if it is considered that document handling systems would assist disclosure and inspection of documents or the use of documents at trial.

J4.3 Where information technology is to be used for the purposes of presenting the case at trial the same system must be used by all parties and must be made available to the court.

J5 Reading lists, authorities and trial timetable

J5.1 Unless the court orders otherwise, a single reading list approved by all advocates must be lodged with the Listing Office not later than 1 pm 2 days (ie 2 clear days) before the date fixed for trial together with an estimate of the time required for reading.

J5.2

(a) If any party objects to the judge reading any document in advance of the trial, the objection and its grounds should be clearly stated in a letter accompanying the trial bundles and in the skeleton argument of that party.
(b) Parties should consider in particular whether they have any objection to the judge's reading the witness statements before the trial.

(c) In the absence of objection, the judge will be free to read the witness statements and documents in advance.

J5.3

(a) A composite bundle of the authorities referred to in the skeleton arguments should be lodged with the Listing Office as soon as possible after skeleton arguments have been exchanged.
(b) Unless otherwise agreed, the preparation of the bundle of authorities is the responsibility of the claimant, who should provide copies to all other parties. Advocates should liaise in relation to the production of bundles of authorities to ensure that the same authority does not appear in more than one bundle.

J5.4 Unreported cases should normally only be cited where the advocate is ready to give an assurance that the transcript contains a statement of some relevant principle of law of which the substance, as distinct from some mere choice of phraseology, is not to be found in any judgment that has appeared in one of the general or specialised series of law reports.

J5.5

(a) When lodging the reading list the claimant should also lodge a trial timetable.
(b) A trial timetable may have been fixed by the judge at the pre-trial review (section D18.4 above). If it has not, a trial timetable should be prepared by the advocate(s) for the claimant after consultation with the advocate(s) for all other parties.
(c) If there are differences of view between the advocate(s) for the claimant and the advocate(s) for other parties, these should be shown.
(d) The trial timetable will provide for oral submissions, witness evidence and expert evidence over the course of the trial. On the first day of the trial the judge may fix the trial timetable, subject to any further order.

J6 Skeleton arguments etc at trial

J6.1 Written skeleton arguments should be prepared by each party. Guidelines on the preparation of skeleton arguments are set out in Part 1 of Appendix 9.

J6.2 Unless otherwise ordered, the skeleton arguments should be served on all other parties and lodged with the court as follows:

(i) by the claimant, not later than 1 pm 2 days (ie 2 clear days) before the start of the trial;
(ii) by each of the defendants, not later than 1 pm one day (ie one clear day) before the start of the trial.

J6.3 In heavier cases it will often be appropriate for skeleton arguments to be served and lodged at earlier times than indicated at section J6.2. The timetable should be discussed between the advocates and may be the subject of a direction in the pre-trial timetable or at any pre-trial review.

J6.4 The claimant should provide a chronology with his skeleton argument. Indices (ie documents that collate key references on particular points, or a substantive list of the contents of a particular bundle or bundles) and dramatis personae should also be provided where these are likely to be useful. Guidelines on the preparation of chronologies and indices are set out in Part 2 of Appendix 9.

J7 Trial sitting days and hearing trials in public

J7.1 Trial sitting days will not normally include Fridays.

J7.2 Where it is necessary in order to accommodate hearing evidence from certain witnesses or types of witness, the court may agree to sit outside normal hours.

J7.3 The general rule is that a hearing is to be in public: rule 39.2(1).

J8 Oral opening statements at trial

J8.1 Oral opening statements should as far as possible be uncontroversial and in any event no longer than the circumstances require. Even in a very heavy case, oral opening statements may be very short.

J8.2 At the conclusion of the opening statement for the claimant the advocates for each of the other parties will usually each be invited to make a short opening statement.

J9 Applications in the course of trial

J9.1 It will not normally be necessary for an application notice to be issued for an application which is to be made during the course of the trial, but all other parties should be given adequate notice of the intention to apply.

J9.2 Unless the judge directs otherwise the parties should prepare skeleton arguments for the hearing of the application

J10 Oral closing submissions at trial

J10.1 All parties will be expected to make oral closing submissions, whether or not closing submissions have been made in writing. It is a matter for the advocate to consider how in all the circumstances these oral submissions should be presented.

J10.2 Unless the trial judge directs otherwise, the claimant will make his oral closing submissions first, followed by the defendant(s) in the order in which they appear on the claim form with the claimant having a right of reply.

J11 Written closing submissions at trial

J11.1

- (a) In a more substantial trial, the court will normally also require closing submissions in writing before oral closing submissions.
- (b) In such a case the court will normally allow an appropriate period of time after the conclusion of the evidence to allow the preparation of these submissions.
- (c) Even in a less substantial trial the court will normally require a skeleton argument on matters of law.

J12 Judgment

J12.1

(a) When judgment is reserved the judge may deliver judgment orally or by handing down a written judgment.
(b) If the judge intends to hand down a written judgment a copy of the draft text marked 'Unapproved Judgment. No permission is granted to copy or use in Court' and bearing the rubric 'Confidential to Counsel and Solicitors, but the substance may be communicated to clients not more than one hour before the giving of judgment' will normally be supplied to the advocates one clear day before the judgment is to be delivered.
(c) Advocates should inform the judge's clerk not later than noon on the day before judgment is to be handed down of any typographical or other errors of a similar nature which the judge might wish to correct.
(d) The requirement to treat the text as confidential must be strictly observed. Failure to do so amounts to a contempt of court.

J12.2

(a) Judgment is not delivered until it is formally pronounced in open court.
(b) Copies of the approved judgment will be made available to the parties, to law reporters and to any other person wanting a copy.
(c) The judge may direct that the written judgment stand as the definitive record and that no transcript need be made. Any editorial corrections made at the time of handing down will be incorporated in an approved official text as soon as possible, and the approved official text, so marked, will be available from the Mechanical Recording Department.

J13 Costs

J13.1 The rules governing the award and assessment of costs are contained in CPR Parts 43 to 48.

J13.2 The summary assessment procedure provided for in Parts 43 and 44 also applies to trials lasting one day or less.

K AFTER TRIAL

K1 Continuation, variation and discharge of interim remedies and undertakings

K1.1

(a) Applications to continue, vary or discharge interim remedies or undertakings should be made to a Commercial judge, even after trial.
(b) If a party wishes to continue a freezing injunction after trial or judgment, care should be taken to ensure that the application is made before the existing freezing injunction has expired.

K2 Accounts and enquiries

K2.1 The court may order that accounts and inquiries be referred to a judge of the Technology and Construction Court or to a Master. Alternatively, the parties may choose to refer the matter to arbitration.

K3 Enforcement

K3.1 Unless the court orders otherwise, all proceedings for the enforcement of any judgment or order for the payment of money given or made in the Commercial Court will be referred automatically to a master of the Queen's Bench Division or a district judge: PD58 para 1.2(2).

K3.2 Applications in connection with the enforcement of a judgment or order for the payment of money should accordingly be directed to the Registry which will allocate them to the Admiralty Registrar or to one of the Queen's Bench masters as appropriate.

K4 Assessment of damages or interest after a default judgment

K4.1 Unless the court orders otherwise, the assessment of damages or interest following the entry of a default judgment for damages or interest to be assessed will be carried out by the Admiralty Registrar or one of the Queen's Bench masters to whom the case is allocated by the Registry.

L MULTI-PARTY DISPUTES

L1 Early consideration

L1.1 Cases which involve, or are expected to involve, a large number of claimants or defendants require close case management from the earliest point. The same is true where there are, or are likely to be, a large number of separate cases involving the same or similar issues. Both classes of case are referred to as 'multi-party' disputes.

L1.2

(a) The Judge in Charge of the List should be informed as soon as it becomes apparent that a multi-party dispute exists or is likely to exist and an early application for directions should be made.
(b) In an appropriate case an application for directions may be made before issue of a claim form. In some cases it may be appropriate for an application to be made without notice in the first instance.

L2 Available procedures

L2.1 In some cases it may be appropriate for the court to make a group litigation order under Part 19 of the Rules. In other cases it may be more convenient for the court to exercise its general powers of management. These include powers:

(i) to dispense with statements of case;
(ii) to direct parties to serve outline statements of case;
(iii) to direct that cases be consolidated or managed and tried together;

(iv) to direct that certain cases or issues be determined before others and to stay other proceedings in the meantime;
(v) to advance or put back the usual time for pre-trial steps to be taken (for example the disclosure of documents by one or more parties or a payment into court).

L2.2 Attention is drawn to the provisions of Section III of Part 19, rules 19.10–19.15 and the practice direction supplementing Section III of Part 19. Practitioners should note that the provisions of Section III of Part 19 give the court additional powers to manage disputes involving multiple claimants or defendants. They should also note that a group litigation order may not be made without the consent of the Lord Chief Justice: PD19B para 3.3(1).

L2.3 An application for a group litigation order should be made in the first instance to the Judge in Charge of the List: PD19B para 3.5.

M LITIGANTS IN PERSON

M1 The litigant in person

M1.1 Litigants in person appear less often in the Commercial Court than in some other courts. Their position requires special consideration.

M2 Represented parties

M2.1 Where a litigant in person is involved in a case the court will expect solicitors and counsel for other parties to do what they reasonably can to ensure that he has a fair opportunity to prepare and put his case.

M2.2 The duty of an advocate to ensure that the court is informed of all relevant decisions and legislative provisions of which he is aware (whether favourable to his case or not) and to bring any procedural irregularity to the attention of the court during the hearing is of particular importance in a case where a litigant in person is involved.

M2.3 Further, the court will expect solicitors and counsel appearing for other parties to ensure that the case memorandum, the list of issues and all necessary bundles are prepared and provided to the court in accordance with the Guide, even where the litigant in person is unwilling or unable to participate.

M2.4 If the claimant is a litigant in person the judge at the case management conference will normally direct which of the parties is to have responsibility for the preparation and upkeep of the case management bundle.

M2.5 At the case management conference the court may give directions relating to the costs of providing application bundles and trial bundles to the litigant in person.

M3 Companies without representation

M3.1 Although rule 39.6 allows a company or other corporation with the permission of the court to be represented at trial by an employee, the complexity of most cases in the Commercial Court makes that unsuitable. Accordingly, permission is likely to be given only in unusual circumstances.

N ADMIRALTY

N1 General

N1.1 Proceedings in the Admiralty Court are dealt with in Part 61 and its associated practice direction.

N1.2 The Admiralty and Commercial Courts Guide has been prepared in consultation with the Admiralty Judge. It has been adopted to provide guidance about the conduct of proceedings in the Admiralty Court. The Guide must be followed in the Admiralty Court unless the content of Part 61, its associated practice direction or the terms of this section N require otherwise.

N1.3 One significant area of difference between practice in the Commercial Court and practice in the Admiralty Court is that many interlocutory applications are heard by the Admiralty Registrar who has all the powers of the Admiralty judge save as provided otherwise: rule 61.1 (4).

N2 The Admiralty Court Committee

N2.1 The Admiralty Court Committee provides a specific forum for contact and consultation between the Admiralty Court and its users. Any correspondence should be addressed to the Deputy Admiralty Marshal, Royal Courts of Justice, Strand, WC2A 2LL.

N3 Commencement of proceedings, service of Statements of Case and associated matters

N3.1 Sections B and C of this guide apply to all Admiralty claims except:

(i) a claim in rem;
(ii) a collision claim; and
(iii) a limitation claim.

N4 Commencement and early stages of a claim in rem

N4.1 The early stages of an in rem claim differ from those of other claims. The procedure is governed generally by rule 61.3 and PD61 paras 3.1–3.11.

N4.2 In addition, the following sections of the Guide apply to claims in rem: B3.3, B3.7–B3.11, B6.4–B6.6, C1.1–C1.9, C1.11 and C2.1(ii)–C5.4.

N4.3 Subject to PD61 para 3.7, section C1.10 of the Guide also applies to claims in rem.

N4.4 After an acknowledgment of service has been filed a claim in rem follows the procedure applicable to a claim proceeding in the Commercial List, save that the claimant is allowed 75 days in which to serve his particulars of claim: PD61 para 3.10.

N5 The early stages of a collision claim

N5.1 Where a collision claim is commenced in rem, the general procedure applicable to claims in rem applies subject to rule 61.4 and PD61 paras 4.1–4.5.

N5.2 Where a collision claim is not commenced in rem the general procedure applicable to claims proceeding in the Commercial List applies subject to rule 61.4 and PD61 paras 4.1–4.5.

N5.3 Service of a claim form out of the jurisdiction in a collision claim (other than a claim in rem) is permitted in the circumstances identified in rule 61.4(7) only and the procedure set out in Appendix 15 of the Guide should be adapted accordingly.

N5.4 One particular feature of a collision action is that the parties must prepare and file a Collision Statement of Case. Prior to the coming into force of Part 61, a Collision Statement of Case was known as a Preliminary Act and the law relating to Preliminary Acts continues to apply to Collision Statements of Case: PD61 para 4.5.

N5.5 The provisions of Appendix 4 apply to Part 2 of a Collision Statement of Case (but not to Part 1).

N5.6 Every party is required, so far as it is able, to provide full and complete answers to the questions contained in Part 1 of the Collision Statement of Case. The answers should descend to a reasonable level of particularity.

N5.7 The answers to the questions contained in Part 1 are treated as admissions made by the party answering the questions and leave to amend such answers will be granted only in exceptional circumstances.

N6 The early stages of a limitation claim

N6.1 The procedure governing the early stages of a limitation claim differs significantly from the procedure relating to other claims and is contained in rule 61.11 and PD61 para 10.1.

N6.2 Service of a limitation claim form out of the jurisdiction is permitted in the circumstances identified in rule 61.11 (5) only and the procedure set out in Appendix 15 of the Guide should be adapted accordingly.

N7 Issue of documents when the Registry is closed

N7.1 When the Registry is closed (and only when it is closed) an Admiralty claim form may be issued on the following designated fax machine: 020 7947 6667 and only on that machine.

N7.2 The procedure to be followed is set out in Appendix 3 of the Guide.

N7.3 The issue of an Admiralty claim form in accordance with the procedure set out in Appendix 3 shall have the same effect for all purposes as a claim form issued in accordance with the relevant provisions of rule 61 and PD61.

N7.4 When the Registry is closed (and only when it is closed) a notice requesting a caution against release may be filed on the following designated fax machine: 020 7947 6056 and only on that machine. This machine is manned 24 hours a day by court security staff (telephone 020 7947 6260).

N7.5 The notice requesting the caution should be transmitted with a note in the following form for ease of identification by security staff:

'CAUTION AGAINST RELEASE

Please find notice requesting caution against release of the … (*name ship/identify cargo*) … for filing in the Admiralty and Commercial Registry.'

N7.6 The notice must be in Admiralty Form No. ADM11 and signed by a solicitor acting on behalf of the applicant.

N7.7 Subject to the provisions of sections N7.9 and N7.10 below, the filing of the notice takes place when the fax is recorded as having been received.

N7.8 When the Registry is next open to the public, the filing solicitor or his agent shall attend and deliver to the Registry the document which was transmitted by fax together with the transmission report. Upon satisfying himself that the document delivered fully accords with the document received by the Registry, the court officer shall stamp the document delivered with the time and date on which the notice was received, enter the same in the caution register and retain the same with the faxed copy.

N7.9 Unless otherwise ordered by the court, the stamped notice shall be conclusive proof that the notice was filed at the time and on the date stated.

N7.10 If the filing solicitor does not comply with the foregoing procedure, or if the notice is not stamped, the notice shall be deemed never to have been filed.

N8 Case Management

N8.1 The case management provisions of the Guide apply to Admiralty claims save that:

(i) in Admiralty claims the case management provisions of the Guide are supplemented by PD61 paras 2.1–2.3 which make provision for the early classification and streaming of cases;

(ii) in a collision case the claimant should apply for a case management conference within 7 days after the last Collision Statement of Case is filed;

(iii) in a limitation claim where the right to limit is not admitted and the claimant seeks a general limitation decree, the claimant must, within 7 days after the date of the filing of the defence of the defendant last served or the expiry of the time for doing so, apply to the Admiralty Registrar for a case management conference: PD61 para 10.7;

(iv) in a collision claim or a limitation claim a mandatory case management conference will normally take place on the first available date 5 weeks after the date when the claimant is required to take steps to fix a date for the case management conference;

(v) in a limitation claim, case management directions are initially given by the Registrar: PD61 para 10.8;

(vi) in the Admiralty Court, the Case Management Information Sheet should be in the form in Appendix 6 of this Guide but should also include the following questions –

1. Do any of the issues contained in the List of Issues involve questions of navigation or other particular matters of an essentially Admiralty nature which require the trial to be before the Admiralty Judge?
2. Is the case suitable to be tried before a Deputy Judge nominated by the Admiralty Judge?

3. Do you consider that the court should sit with nautical or other assessors? If you intend to ask that the court sit with one or more assessors who is not a Trinity Master, please state the reasons for such an application.

N8.2 The two judge team system referred to in section D.4 of the Guide does not apply to Admiralty claims.

N9 Evidence

N9.1 In collision claims, section H1.5 and Appendix 8 are subject to the proviso that experience has shown that it is usually desirable for the main elements of a witness' evidence in chief to be adduced orally.

Authenticity

N9.2 Where:

- (i) the authenticity of any document or entry in any document is challenged;
- (ii) it will be suggested at trial that a document or entry in a document was not made at the time or by the person stated; or
- (iii) a document or entry in a document will be in any other way challenged in a manner which may require a witness to be produced at trial to support the document or entry in a document; such challenge –
  - (i) must be raised in good time in advance of the trial to enable any such witness to be produced; and
  - (ii) must be contained in the skeleton argument.

Skeleton arguments in collision claims

N9.3 In collision claims the skeleton argument of each party must be accompanied by a plot or plots of that party's case or alternative cases as to the navigation of vessels during and leading to the collision. All plots must contain a sufficient indication of the assumptions used in the preparation of the plot.

N10 Split trials, accounts, enquiries and enforcement

N10.1 In collision claims it is usual for liability to be tried first and for the assessment of damages and interest to be referred to the Admiralty Registrar.

N10.2 Where the Admiralty Court refers an account, enquiry or enforcement, it will usually refer the matter to the Admiralty Registrar.

N11 Release of vessels out of hours

N11.1 This section makes provision for release from arrest when the Registry is closed.

N11.2 An application for release under rule 61.8(4)(c) or (d) may, when the Registry is closed, be made in, and only in, the following manner:

(i) the solicitor for the arrestor or the other party applying must telephone the security staff at the Royal Courts of Justice (020 7947 6260) and ask to be contacted by the Admiralty Marshal, who will then respond as soon as practicably possible;

(ii) upon being contacted by the Admiralty Marshal the solicitor must give oral instructions for the release and an oral undertaking to pay the fees and expenses of the Admiralty Marshal as required in Form No. ADM 12;

(iii) the arrestor or other party applying must then send a written request and undertaking on Form No. ADM 12 by fax to a number given by the Admiralty Marshal;

(iv) the solicitor must provide written consent to the release from all persons who have entered cautions against release (and from the arrestor if the arrestor is not the party applying) by sending such consents by fax to the number supplied by the Admiralty Marshal;

(v) upon the Admiralty Marshal being satisfied that no cautions against release are in force, or that all persons who have entered cautions against release, and if necessary the arrestor, have given their written consent to the release, the Admiralty Marshal shall effect the release as soon as practicable.

N11.3 Practitioners should note that the Admiralty Marshal is not formally on call and therefore at times may not be available to assist. Similarly the practicalities of releasing a ship in some localities may involve the services of others who may not be available outside court hours.

N11.4 This service is offered to practitioners for use during reasonable hours and on the basis that if the Admiralty Marshal is available and can be contacted he will use his best endeavours to effect instructions to release but without guarantee as to their success.

N12 Use of postal facilities in the Registry

N12.1 Applications together with the requisite documents may be posted to:

The Admiralty and Commercial Registry,
Room E200,
Royal Courts of Justice,
Strand,
London WC2A 2LL.

N12.2 In addition to the classes of business for which the use of postal facilities is permitted by the CPR or the Commercial Court Guide, the filing of the following classes of documents is also permitted in Admiralty matters:

(i) requests for cautions;
(ii) Collision Statements of Case.

N12.3

(a) Documents sent by post for filing must be accompanied by two copies of a list of the documents sent and an envelope properly addressed to the sender.

(b) On receipt of the documents in the Registry, the court officer will, if the circumstances are such that had the documents been presented personally they would have been filed, cause them to be filed and will, by post, notify the sender that this has been done. If the documents would not have been accepted if presented personally the court officer will not file them but will retain them in the Registry for collection by the sender and will, by post, so inform the sender.

(c) When documents received through the post are filed by the court officer they will be sealed and entered as filed on the date on which they were received in the Registry.

N13 Insurance of arrested property

N13.1 The Marshal will not insure any arrested property for the benefit of parties at any time during the period of arrest (whether before or after the lodging of an application for sale, if any).

N13.2 The Marshal will use his best endeavours (but without any legal liability for failure to do so) to advise all parties known to him as being on the record in actions in rem against the arrested property, including those who have filed cautions against release of that property, before any such property moves or is moved beyond the area covered by the usual port risks policy.

N13.3 In these circumstances, practitioners' attention is drawn to the necessity of considering the questions of insuring against port risks for the amount of their clients' interest in any property arrested in an Admiralty action and the inclusion in any policy of a 'Held Covered' clause in case the ship moves or is moved outside the area covered by the usual port risks policy. The usual port risks policy provides, among other things, for a ship to be moved or towed from one berth to another up to a distance of five miles within the port where she is lying.

N14 Assessors

N14.1 In collision claims and other cases involving issues of navigation and seamanship, the Admiralty Court usually sits with assessors. The parties are not permitted to call expert evidence on such matters without the leave of the court: rule 61.13.

N14.2 Provision is made in rule 35.15 for assessors' remuneration. The usual practice is for the court to seek an undertaking from the claimant to pay the remuneration on demand after the case has concluded.

O ARBITRATION

O1 Arbitration claims

O1.1

(a) Applications to the court under the Arbitration Acts 1950–1996 and other applications relating to arbitrations are known as 'arbitration claims'.

(b) The procedure applicable to arbitration claims is to be found in Part 62 and its associated practice direction. Separate provision is made:

  (i) by Section I for claims relating to arbitrations to which the Arbitration Act 1996 applies;

  (ii) by Section II for claims relating to arbitrations to which the Arbitration Acts 1950–1979 ('the old law') apply; and

  (iii) by Section III for enforcement proceedings.

(c) For a full definition of the expression 'arbitration claim' see rule 62.2(1) (claims under the 1996 Act) and rule 62.11(2) (claims under the old law).
(d) Part 58 applies to arbitration claims in the Commercial Court insofar as no specific provision is made by Part 62: rule 62.1(3).

Claims under the Arbitration Act 1996

O2 Starting an arbitration claim

O2.1 Subject to section O2.3 an arbitration claim must be started by the issue of an arbitration claim form in accordance with the Part 8 procedure: rule 62.3(1).

O2.2 The claim form must be substantially in the form set out in Appendix A to practice direction 62: PD62 para 2.2.

O2.3 An application to stay proceedings under section 9 of the Arbitration Act 1996 must be made by application notice in the proceedings: rule 62.3(2).

O3 The arbitration claim form

O3.1 The arbitration claim form must contain, among other things, a concise statement of the remedy claimed and, if an award is challenged, the grounds for that challenge: rule 62.4(1).

O3.2 Reference in the arbitration claim form to a witness statement or affidavit filed in support of the claim is not sufficient to comply with the requirements of rule 62.4(1).

O4 Service of the arbitration claim form

O4.1 An arbitration claim form issued in the Admiralty and Commercial Registry must be served by the claimant.

O4.2

(a) The rules governing service of the claim form are set out in Part 6 of the Civil Procedure Rules.
(b) Unless the court orders otherwise an arbitration claim form must be served on the defendant within 1 month from the date of issue: rule 62.4(2).

O4.3

(a) An arbitration claim form may be served out of the jurisdiction with the permission of the court: rule 62.5(1).
(b) Rules 6.24–6.29 apply to the service of an arbitration claim form out of the jurisdiction: rule 62.5(3).

O4.4 The court may exercise its powers under rule 6.8 to permit service of an arbitration claim form on a party at the address of the solicitor or other representative acting for him in the arbitration: PD62 para 3.1.

O4.5 The claimant must file a certificate of service within 7 days of serving the arbitration claim form: PD62 para 3.2.

O5 Acknowledgment of service

O5.1

(a) A defendant must file an acknowledgment of service of the arbitration claim form in every case: rule 58.6(1).
(b) An adapted version of practice form N210 (acknowledgment of service of a Part 8 claim form) has been approved for use in the Commercial Court.

A copy of this practice form (Form N210(CC)) is included at the end of the Guide, together with adapted versions of the notes for claimants and defendants on completing and replying to an arbitration claim form.

O5.2 The time for filing an acknowledgment of service is calculated from the service of the arbitration claim form.

O6 Standard directions

O6.1 The directions set out in PD62 paras 6.2–6.7 apply unless the court orders otherwise.

O6.2 The claimant should apply for a hearing date as soon as possible after issuing an arbitration claim form or (in the case of an appeal) obtaining permission to appeal.

O6.3 A defendant who wishes to rely on evidence in opposition to the claim must file and serve his evidence within 21 days after the date by which he was required to acknowledge service: PD62 para 6.2.

O6.4 A claimant who wishes to rely on evidence in response to evidence served by the defendant must file and serve his evidence within 7 days after the service of the defendant's evidence: PD62 para 6.3.

O6.5 An application for directions in a pending arbitration claim should be made by application notice under Part 23.

O7 Interim remedies

O7.1 An application for an interim remedy under section 44 of the Arbitration Act 1996 must be made in an arbitration claim form: PD62 para 8.1.

O8 Challenging the award

Challenge by way of appeal

O8.1 A party wishing to appeal against the award of an arbitrator or umpire must set out in the arbitration claim form

(i) the question of law on which the appeal is based; and
(ii) a succinct statement of the grounds of appeal, identifying the relevant part(s) of the award and reasons.

O8.2 If the appeal is brought with the agreement of the other parties to the proceedings, a copy of their agreement in writing must be filed with the arbitration claim form.

O8.3 A party seeking permission to appeal must:

(i) state in his arbitration claim form the grounds on which he contends that permission to appeal should be given PD62 para 12.1; and
(ii) file and serve with the arbitration claim form any written evidence on which he wishes to rely for the purposes of satisfying the court of the matters referred to in section 69(3) of the 1996 Act: PD62 para 12.2.

O8.4

(a) If the defendant wishes to oppose the claimant's application for permission to appeal he must file a witness statement setting out:
  (i) the grounds on which he opposes the grant of permission; and
  (ii) any evidence on which he relies in relation to the matters mentioned in section 69(3) of the 1996 Act: PD62 paras 12.3(1) and (2).
(b) If the defendant wishes to contend that that the award should be upheld for reasons other than those expressed in the award, he must set out those reasons in his witness statement: PD62 para 12.3(3).

O8.5 The court will normally determine applications for permission to appeal without an oral hearing. If the court considers that an oral hearing is required, it will give further directions as appropriate.

Challenging an award for serious irregularity

O8.6

(a) An arbitration claim challenging an award on the ground of serious irregularity under section 68 of the 1996 Act is appropriate only in cases where there are grounds for thinking:
  (i) that an irregularity has occurred which
  (ii) has caused or will cause **substantial** injustice to the party making the challenge.
(b) An application challenging an award on the ground of serious irregularity should therefore not be regarded as an alternative to, or a means of supporting, an application for permission to appeal.

O8.7 The challenge to the award must be supported by evidence of the circumstances on which the claimant relies as giving rise to the irregularity complained of and the nature of the injustice which has been or will be caused to him.

O8.8 If the nature of the challenge itself or the evidence filed in support of it leads the court to consider that the claim has no real prospect of success, the court may exercise its powers under rule 3.3(4) to dismiss the application summarily.

In such cases the applicant will have the right to apply to the court to set aside the order and to seek directions for the hearing of the application.

Multiple claims

O8.9 If the arbitration claim form includes both a challenge to an award by way of appeal and a challenge on the ground of serious irregularity, the applications should be set out in separate sections of the arbitration claim form and the grounds on which they are made separately identified.

O8.10 In such cases the papers will be placed before a judge to consider how the applications may most appropriately be disposed of. It is usually more appropriate to dispose of the application to set aside or remit the award before considering the application for permission to appeal.

O9 Time-limits

O9.1 An application to challenge an award under sections 67 or 68 of the 1996 Act or to appeal under section 69 of the Act must be brought within 28 days of the date of the award: see section 70(3).

O9.2 The court has power to vary the period of 28 days fixed by section 70(3) of the 1996 Act: rule 62.9(1). However, it is important that any challenge to an award be pursued without delay and the court will require cogent reasons for extending time.

O9.3 An application to extend time made **before** the expiry of the period of 28 days must be made in a Part 23 application notice, but the application notice need not be served on any other party: rule 62.9(2) and PD62 para 11.1(1).

O9.4 An application to extend time made **after** the expiry of the period of 28 days must be made in the arbitration claim form in which the applicant is seeking substantive relief: rule 62.9(3)(a).

O9.5 An application to vary the period of 28 days will normally be determined without a hearing and prior to the consideration of the substantive application: PD62 para 10.2.

Claims under the Arbitration Acts 1950–1979

O10 Starting an arbitration claim

O10.1 Subject to section O10.2 an arbitration claim must be started by the issue of an arbitration claim form in accordance with the Part 8 procedure: rule 62.13(1).

O10.2 The claim form must be substantially in the form set out in Appendix A to PD62 para 2.2.

O10.3 An application to stay proceedings on the grounds of an arbitration agreement must be made by application notice in the proceedings: rule 62.13(2).

O11 The arbitration claim form

O11.1 An arbitration claim form must state the grounds of the claim or appeal: rule 62.15(5)(a).

O11.2 Reference in the arbitration claim form to the witness statement or affidavit filed in support of the claim is not sufficient to comply with the requirements of rule 62.15(5)(a).

O12 Service of the arbitration claim form

O12.1 An arbitration claim form issued in the Admiralty and Commercial Registry must be served by the claimant.

O12.2 The rules governing service of the claim form are set out in Part 6 of the Civil Procedure Rules.

O12.3

(a) An arbitration claim form may be served out of the jurisdiction with the permission of the court: rule 62.16(1).

(b) Rules 6.24–6.29 apply to the service of an arbitration claim form out of the jurisdiction: rule 62.16(4).

O12.4 Although not expressly covered by PD62, the court may in an appropriate case exercise its powers under rule 6.8 to permit service of an arbitration claim form on a party at the address of the solicitor or other representative acting for him in the arbitration.

O12.5 The claimant must file a certificate of service within 7 days of serving the claim form.

Acknowledgment of service

O13.1

(a) A defendant must file an acknowledgment of service in every case: rule 58.6(1).

(b) An adapted version of practice form N210 (acknowledgment of service of a Part 8 claim form) has been approved for use in the Commercial Court.

A copy of this practice form (Form N210(CC)) is included at the end of the Guide, together with adapted versions of the notes for claimants and defendants on completing and replying to an arbitration claim form.

O13.2 The time for filing an acknowledgment of service is calculated from the service of the arbitration claim form.

O14 Standard directions

O14.1 Where the claim or appeal is based on written evidence, a copy of that evidence must be served with the arbitration claim form: rule 62.15(5)(b).

O14.2 Where the claim or appeal is made with the consent of the arbitrator or umpire or other parties, a copy of every written consent must be served with the arbitration claim form: rule 62.15(5)(c).

O14.3 An application for directions in a pending arbitration claim should be made by application notice under Part 23.

O15 Interim remedies

O15.1 An application for an interim remedy under section 12(6) of the 1950 Act must be made in accordance with Part 25.

O15.2 The application must be made by arbitration claim form.

O15.3 A claim under section 12(4) of the 1950 Act for an order for the issue of a witness summons to compel the attendance of a witness before an arbitrator or umpire where the attendance of the witness is required within the district of a District Registry may be started in that Registry: rule 62.14.

O16 Challenging the award

Challenge by way of appeal

O16.1 A party wishing to appeal against the award of an arbitrator or umpire must file and serve with the arbitration claim form a statement of the grounds for the appeal, specifying the relevant part(s) of the award and reasons: rule 62.15(6).

O16.2 A party seeking permission to appeal must also file and serve with the arbitration claim form any written evidence in support of the contention that the question of law concerns a term of the contract or an event which is not 'one off': rule 62.15(6).

O16.3 Any written evidence in reply must be filed and served not less than 2 days before the hearing of the application for permission to appeal: rule 62.15(7).

O16.4 A party who wishes to contend that the award should be upheld for reasons other than those set out in the award and reasons must file and serve on the claimant a notice specifying the grounds of his contention not less than 2 days before the hearing of the application for permission to appeal: rule 62.15(8).

O16.5 Applications for permission to appeal will be heard orally, but will not normally be listed for longer than half an hour. Skeleton arguments should be lodged.

Claims to set aside or remit the award

O16.6 A claim to set aside or remit an award on the grounds of misconduct should not be regarded as an alternative to, or a means of supporting, an application for permission to appeal.

O16.7 The directions set out in PD62 paras 6.2–6.7 should be followed unless the court orders otherwise.

Multiple claims

O16.8 If the arbitration claim form includes both an appeal and an application to set aside or remit the award, the applications should be set out in separate sections of the arbitration claim form and the grounds on which they are made separately identified.

O16.9 The court may direct that one application be heard before the other or may direct that they be heard together, as may be appropriate. It is usually more appropriate to dispose of the application to set aside or remit the award before considering the application for permission to appeal.

O17 Time-limits

O17.1

(a) Time-limits governing claims under the 1950 and 1979 Acts are set out in rule 62.15.

(b) Different time-limits apply to different claims. It is important to consult rule 62.15 to ensure that applications are made within the time prescribed.

(c) The court has power under rule 3.1(2) to vary the time-limits prescribed by rule 62.15, but will require cogent reasons for doing so.

Provisions applicable to all arbitrations

Enforcement of awards

O18.1 All applications for permission to enforce awards are governed by Section III of Part 62: rule 62.17.

O18.2 An application for permission to enforce an award in the same manner as a judgment may be made without notice, but the court may direct that the arbitration claim form be served, in which case the application will continue as an arbitration claim in accordance with the procedure set out in Section I: rule 62.18(1)–(3).

O18.3 An application for permission to enforce an award in the same manner as a judgment must be supported written evidence in accordance with rule 62.18(6).

O18.4

(a) Two copies of the draft order must accompany the application.

(b) If the claimant wishes to enter judgment, the form of the judgment must correspond to the terms of the award.

(c) The defendant has the right to apply to the court to set aside an order made without notice giving permission to enforce the award and the order itself must state in terms:

  (i) that the defendant may apply to set it aside within within 14 days after service of the order or, if the order is to be served out of the jurisdiction, within such other period as the court may set; and

  (ii) that it may not be enforced until after the end of that period or any application by the defendant to set it aside has been finally disposed of: rule 62.18(9) and (10).

Matters of general application

O19 Transfer of arbitration claims

O19.1 An arbitration claim which raises no significant point of arbitration law or practice will normally be transferred

(i) if a rent review arbitration, to the Chancery Division;

(ii) if a construction or engineering arbitration, to the Technology and Construction Court;

(iii) if an employment arbitration, to the Central London County Court Mercantile List.

O19.2 Salvage arbitrations will normally be transferred to the Admiralty Court.

O20 Appointment of a Commercial judge as sole arbitrator or umpire

O20.1 Section 93 of the Arbitration Act 1996 provides for the appointment of a Commercial judge as sole arbitrator or umpire. The Act limits the circumstances in which a judge may accept such an appointment.

O20.2 Enquiries should be directed to the Judge in Charge of the Commercial List or the clerk to the Commercial Court.

P MISCELLANEOUS

P1 Out of hours emergency arrangements

P1.1

(a) When the Listing Office is closed, solicitors or counsel's clerks should in an emergency contact the clerk to the Queen's Bench judge in chambers by telephone through the security desk at the Royal Courts of Justice: PD58 para 2.2.

(b) The telephone number of the security desk is included in the list of addresses and contact details at the end of the Guide.

P1.2 When the Listing Office is closed an urgent hearing will initially be dealt with by the Queen's Bench judge in chambers who may dispose of the application himself or make orders allowing the matter to come before a Commercial judge at the first available opportunity.

P2 Index of unreported decisions

P2.1 An index has been prepared on a subject matter basis of unreported Commercial Court and Admiralty Court judgments from 1995 onwards. The Index is updated regularly.

P2.2 The Index is provided as a service to litigants and to the legal profession, and to assist the Commercial Court and the Admiralty Court to maintain reasonable consistency of approach in those areas of law and procedure most frequently before them.

P2.3 The Index is available on disk to counsel and solicitors from the Listing Office, free of charge, in exchange for new unused 1.44 MB disks. Except in special circumstances no more than one disk will be issued to each set of chambers or firm of solicitors. Copies of the disk should not be made except for copies that are to be made available to members of the set of chambers or firm of solicitors to which it has been issued.

P2.4 The judgments referred to in the Index are kept in the Registry. They may be consulted there.

P2.5 Copies of the judgments referred to in the Index may be obtained from the Registry (or where there is difficulty, from the clerk to the judge) unless the judgment is in the form of a transcript, in which case copies should be obtained from the shorthand writers or other transcript agency.

****

Appendices 1 and 2—Appendix 1 contains CPR Pt 58 and PD58 (Commercial Court) as well as CPR Pt 61 and PD61 (Admiralty Claims). Appendix 2 contains CPR Pt 62 and PD62 (Arbitration). All of these CPR Parts and practice directions are set out in Section 2 of this work.

APPENDIX 3

PROCEDURE FOR ISSUE OF CLAIM FORM WHEN REGISTRY CLOSED

(See generally sections B3.11 and B4.4 of the Guide.)

Procedure

The procedure is as follows:

1 The claim form must be signed by a solicitor acting on behalf of the claimant, and must not require the permission of the court for its issue (unless such permission has already been given).

2 The solicitor causing the claim form to be issued ('the issuing solicitor') must:

- (i) endorse on the claim form the endorsement shown below and sign that endorsement;
- (ii) send a copy of the claim form so endorsed to the Registry by fax for issue under this section; and
- (iii) when he has received a transmission report stating that the transmission of the claim form to the Registry was completed in full and the time and the date of the transmission, complete and sign the certificate shown below.

3 When the Registry is next open to the public after the issue of a claim form in accordance with this procedure the issuing solicitor or his agent shall attend and deliver to the Registry the document which was transmitted by fax (including the endorsement and the certificate), or if that document has been served, a true and certified copy of it, together with as many copies as the Registry shall require and the transmission report.

4 When the proper officer at the Registry has checked and is satisfied that the document delivered under paragraph 3 fully accords with the document received under paragraph 2, and that all proper fees for issue have been paid, he shall allocate a number to the case, and seal, mark as 'original' and date the claim form with the date on which it was issued (being, as indicated below, the date when the fax is recorded at the Registry as having been received).

5 As soon as practicable thereafter the issuing solicitor shall inform any person served with the unsealed claim form of the case number, and (on request) shall serve any such person with a copy of the claim form sealed and dated under paragraph 4 above (at such address in England and Wales as the person may request) and the person may, without paying a fee, inspect and take copies of the documents lodged at the Registry under paragraphs 2 and 3 above.

Effect of issue following request by fax

The issue of a claim form in accordance with this procedure takes place when the fax is recorded at the Registry as having been received, and the claim form bearing the endorsement shall have the same effect for all purposes as a claim form issued under CPR Part 7 [or 8, as the case may be]. Unless otherwise ordered the sealed version of the claim form retained by the Registry shall be conclusive proof that the claim form was issued at the time and on the date stated. If the procedure set out in this Appendix is not complied with, the court may declare (on its own initiative or on application) that the claim form shall be treated as not having been issued.

Endorsement

A claim form issued pursuant to a request by fax must be endorsed as follows:

> '1 This claim form is issued under section B3.11/B4.4 of the Commercial Court Guide and may be served notwithstanding that it does not bear the seal of the Court.
>
> 2 A true copy of this claim form and endorsement has been transmitted to the Admiralty and Commercial Registry, Royal Courts of Justice, Strand, London WC2A 2LL, at the time and date certified below by the undersigned solicitor.
>
> 3 It is the duty of the undersigned solicitor or his agent to attend at the Registry when it is next open to the public for the claim form to be sealed.
>
> 4 Any person upon whom this unsealed claim form is served will be notified by the undersigned solicitor of the number of the case and may require the undersigned solicitor to serve a copy of the sealed claim form at an address in England and Wales and may inspect without charge the documents which have been lodged at the Registry by the undersigned solicitor.
>
> 5 I, the undersigned solicitor, undertake to the Court, to the defendants named in this claim form, and to any other person upon whom this claim form may be served:
>
> (i) that the statement in paragraph 2 above is correct;
>
> (ii) that the time and date given in the certificate at the foot of this endorsement are correct;
>
> (iii) that this claim form is a claim form which may be issued under section B3.11 (or B4.4, as the case may be) of the Commercial Court Guide;
>
> (iv) that I will comply in all respects with the requirements of section B3.11/B4.4 of the Commercial Court Guide;
>
> (v) that I will indemnify any person served with the claim form before it is sealed against any loss suffered as a result of the claim form being or becoming invalid in accordance with section B3.11/B4.4 of the Commercial Court Guide.
>
> *(Signed)*
>
> Solicitor for the claimant'

[**Note**: the endorsement may be signed in the name of the firm of solicitors rather than an individual solicitor, or by solicitors' agents in their capacity as agents acting on behalf of their professional clients.]

Certificate

A solicitor who causes a claim form to be issued pursuant to a request sent by fax must sign a certificate in the following form:

> 'I, the undersigned solicitor, certify that I have received a transmission report confirming that the transmission of a copy of this claim form to the Registry by fax was fully completed and that the time and date of transmission to the Registry were [*enter the time and date shown on the transmission report.*
>
> Dated
>
> *(Signed)*
>
> Solicitor for the claimant'

[**Note**: the certificate may be signed in the name of the firm of solicitors rather than an individual solicitor, or by solicitors' agents in their capacity as agents acting on behalf of their professional clients.]

APPENDIX 4

STATEMENTS OF CASE

The following principles apply to all statements of case and should, as far as possible, also be observed when drafting a Part 8 claim form, which will not contain, or be followed by, particulars of claim:

1 The document must be as brief and concise as possible.

2 The document must be set out in separate consecutively numbered paragraphs and sub-paragraphs.

3 So far as possible each paragraph or sub-paragraph should contain no more than one allegation.

4 The document must deal with the case on a point by point basis to allow a point by point response.

5 Where particulars are given of any allegation or reasons given for a denial, the allegation or denial should be stated first and the particulars or reasons for it listed one by one in separate numbered sub-paragraphs.

6 A party wishing to advance a positive case should set that case out in the document; a simple denial is not sufficient.

7 Any matter which, if not stated, might take another party by surprise should be stated.

8 Where they will assist:

- (i) headings should be used; and
- (ii) abbreviations and definitions should be established and used, and a glossary annexed.

9 Contentious headings, abbreviations and definitions should not be used. Every effort should be made to ensure that headings, abbreviations and definitions are in a form that will enable them to be adopted without issue by the other parties.

10 Particulars of primary allegations should be stated as particulars and not as primary allegations.

11 If it is necessary to rely upon a substantial amount of detailed factual information or lengthy particulars in support of an allegation, these should be set out in schedules or appendices.

12 Particular care should be taken to set out only those factual allegations which are necessary to support the case. Evidence should not be included.

13 A response to particulars set out in a schedule should be set out in a corresponding schedule.

14 If it is necessary for the proper understanding of the statement of case to include substantial parts of a lengthy document the passages in question should be set out in a schedule rather than in the body of the case.

15 Contentious paraphrasing should be avoided.

16 The document must be signed by the individual person or persons who drafted it, not, in the case of a solicitor, in the name of the firm alone.

APPENDIX 5

****SEARCH ORDER****
IN THE HIGH COURT OF JUSTICE
QUEEN'S BENCH DIVISION
Before The Honourable Mr Justice

COMMERCIAL COURT
[ ]

Claim No.

BETWEEN

Claimant(s)

– and –

Defendant(s)

Applicant(s)

Respondent(s)

IF YOU [ ][1] DISOBEY THIS ORDER YOU MAY BE HELD TO BE IN CONTEMPT OF COURT AND MAY BE IMPRISONED, FINED OR HAVE YOUR ASSETS SEIZED.

ANY OTHER PERSON WHO KNOWS OF THIS ORDER AND DOES ANYTHING WHICH HELPS OR PERMITS THE RESPONDENT TO BREACH THE TERMS OF THIS ORDER MAY ALSO BE HELD TO BE IN CONTEMPT OF COURT AND MAY BE IMPRISONED, FINED OR HAVE THEIR ASSETS SEIZED.

1 Insert name of Respondent.

THIS ORDER

1 This is a Search Order made against [ ] ('the Respondent') on [ ] by Mr Justice [ ] on the application of [ ] ('the Applicant'). The Judge read the Affidavits listed in Schedule F and accepted the undertakings set out in Schedules C, D and E at the end of this order.

2 This order was made at a hearing without notice to the Respondent. The Respondent has a right to apply to the court to vary or discharge the order – see paragraph 27 below.

3 There will be a further hearing in respect of this order on [ ] ('the return date').

4 If there is more than one Respondent –

(a) unless otherwise stated, references in this order to 'the Respondent' mean both or all of them; and
(b) this order is effective against any Respondent on whom it is served or who is given notice of it.

5 This order must be complied with by –

(a) the Respondent;
(b) any director, officer, partner or responsible employee of the Respondent; and
(c) if the Respondent is an individual, any other person having responsible control of the premises to be searched.

THE SEARCH

6 The Respondent must permit the following persons[1] –

(a) [ ] ('the Supervising Solicitor');
(b) [ ], a solicitor in the firm of [ ], the Applicant's solicitors; and
(c) up to [ ] other persons[2] being [*their identity or capacity*] accompanying them,

(together 'the search party'), to enter the premises mentioned in Schedule A to this order and any other premises of the Respondent disclosed under paragraph 18 below and any vehicles under the Respondent's control on or around the premises ('the premises') so that they can search for, inspect, photograph or photocopy, and deliver into the safekeeping of the Applicant's solicitors all the documents and articles which are listed in Schedule B to this order ('the listed items').

7 Having permitted the search party to enter the premises, the Respondent must allow the search party to remain on the premises until the search is complete. In the event that it becomes necessary for any of those persons to leave the premises before the search is complete, the Respondent must allow them to re-enter the premises immediately upon their seeking re-entry on the same or the following day in order to complete the search.

1 Where the premises are likely to be occupied by an unaccompanied woman and the Supervising Solicitor is a man, at least one of the persons accompanying him should be a woman.

2 None of these persons should be people who could gain personally or commercially from anything they might read or see on the premises, unless their presence is essential.

RESTRICTIONS ON SEARCH

8 This order may not be carried out at the same time as a police search warrant.

9 Before the Respondent allows anybody onto the premises to carry out this order, he is entitled to have the Supervising Solicitor explain to him what it means in everyday language.

10 The Respondent is entitled to seek legal advice and to ask the court to vary or discharge this order. Whilst doing so, he may ask the Supervising Solicitor to delay starting the search for up to 2 hours or such other longer period as the Supervising Solicitor may permit. However, the Respondent must –

(a) comply with the terms of paragraph 27 below;
(b) not disturb or remove any listed items; and
(c) permit the Supervising Solicitor to enter, but not start to search.

11 Before permitting entry to the premises by any person other than the Supervising Solicitor, the Respondent may, for a short time (not to exceed two hours, unless the Supervising Solicitor agrees to a longer period), gather together any documents he believes may be [incriminating or][1] privileged and hand them to the Supervising Solicitor for him to assess whether they are [incriminating or] privileged as claimed. If the Supervising Solicitor decides that any of the documents may be [incriminating or] privileged or is in any doubt as to their status, he will exclude them from the search and retain them in his possession pending further order of the court.

12 If the Respondent wishes to take legal advice and gather documents as permitted, he must first inform the Supervising Solicitor and keep him informed of the steps being taken.

13 No item may be removed from the premises until a list of the items to be removed has been prepared, and a copy of the list has been supplied to the Respondent, and he has been given a reasonable opportunity to check the list.

14 The premises must not be searched, and items must not be removed from them, except in the presence of the Respondent.

15 If the Supervising Solicitor is satisfied that full compliance with paragraphs 13 or 14 is not practicable, he may permit the search to proceed and items to be removed without fully complying with them.

1 References to incriminating documents should be omitted from orders made in intellectual property proceedings, where the privilege against self-incrimination does not apply – see paragraph 8.4 of the practice direction.

DELIVERY UP OF ARTICLES/DOCUMENTS

16 The Respondent must immediately hand over to the Applicant's solicitors any of the listed items, which are in his possession or under his control, save for any computer or hard disk integral to any computer. Any items the subject of a dispute as to whether they are listed items must immediately be handed over to the Supervising Solicitor for safe keeping pending resolution of the dispute or further order of the court.

17 The Respondent must immediately give the search party effective access to the computers on the premises, with all necessary passwords, to enable the computers to be searched. If they contain any listed items the Respondent must cause the listed items to be displayed so that they can be read and copied.[1] The Respondent must provide the Applicant's Solicitors with copies of all listed

items contained in the computers. All reasonable steps shall be taken by the Applicant and the Applicant's solicitors to ensure that no damage is done to any computer or data. The Applicant and his representatives may not themselves search the Respondent's computers unless they have sufficient expertise to do so without damaging the Respondent's system.

1 If it is envisaged that the Respondent's computers are to be imaged (i.e. the hard drives are to be copied wholesale, thereby reproducing listed items and other items indiscriminately), special provision needs to be made and independent computer specialists need to be appointed, who should be required to give undertakings to the court.

PROVISION OF INFORMATION

18 The Respondent must immediately inform the Applicant's Solicitors (in the presence of the Supervising Solicitor) so far as he is aware –

(a) where all the listed items are;
(b) the name and address of everyone who has supplied him, or offered to supply him, with listed items;
(c) the name and address of everyone to whom he has supplied, or offered to supply, listed items; and
(d) full details of the dates and quantities of every such supply and offer.

19 Within [ ] working days after being served with this order the Respondent must swear and serve an affidavit setting out the above information[1].

1 The period should ordinarily be longer than the period in paragraph (2) of Schedule D, if any of the information is likely to be included in listed items taken away of which the Respondent does not have copies.

PROHIBITED ACTS

20 Except for the purpose of obtaining legal advice, the Respondent must not directly or indirectly inform anyone of these proceedings or of the contents of this order, or warn anyone that proceedings have been or may be brought against him by the Applicant until 4.30 pm on the return date or further order of the court.

21 Until 4.30 pm on the return date the Respondent must not destroy, tamper with, cancel or part with possession, power, custody or control of the listed items otherwise than in accordance with the terms of this order.

22 [Insert any negative injunctions.]

23 [Insert any further order.]

COSTS

24 The costs of this application are reserved to the judge hearing the application on the return date.

RESTRICTIONS ON SERVICE

25 This order may only be served between [ ] am/pm and [ ] am/pm [and on a weekday][1].

26 This order must be served by the Supervising Solicitor, and paragraph 6 of the order must be carried out in his presence and under his supervision.

1 Normally, the order should be served in the morning (not before 9.30 am) and on a weekday to enable the Respondent more readily to obtain legal advice.

VARIATION AND DISCHARGE OF THIS ORDER

27 Anyone served with or notified of this order may apply to the court at any time to vary or discharge this order (or so much of it as affects that person), but they must first inform the Applicant's solicitors. If any evidence is to be relied upon in support of the application, the substance of it must be communicated in writing to the Applicant's solicitors in advance.

INTERPRETATION OF THIS ORDER

28 Any requirement that something shall be done to or in the presence of the Respondent means –

(a) if there is more than one Respondent, to or in the presence of any one of them; and
(b) if a Respondent is not an individual, to or in the presence of a director, officer, partner or responsible employee.

29 A Respondent who is an individual who is ordered not to do something must not do it himself or in any other way. He must not do it through others acting on his behalf or on his instructions or with his encouragement.

30 A Respondent which is not an individual which is ordered not to do something must not do it itself or by its directors, officers, partners, employees or agents or in any other way.

COMMUNICATIONS WITH THE COURT

All communications to the court about this order should be sent to Room E201, Royal Courts of Justice, Strand, London WC2A 2LL quoting the case number. The telephone number is 0207 947 6826.

The offices are open between 10 am and 4.30 pm Monday to Friday.

SCHEDULE A

THE PREMISES

SCHEDULE B

THE LISTED ITEMS

SCHEDULE C

UNDERTAKINGS GIVEN TO THE COURT BY THE APPLICANT

(1) If the court later finds that this order or carrying it out has caused loss to the Respondent, and decides that the Respondent should be compensated for that loss, the Applicant will comply with any order the court may make. Further if the carrying out of this order has been in breach of the terms of this order or otherwise in a manner inconsistent with the Applicant's solicitors' duties as officers of the court, the Applicant will comply with any order for damages the court may make.

[(2) As soon as practicable the Applicant will issue a claim form [in the form of the draft produced to the court] [claiming the appropriate relief].]

(3) The Applicant will [swear and file an affidavit] [cause an affidavit to be sworn and filed] [substantially in the terms of the draft affidavit produced to the court] [confirming the substance of what was said to the court by the Applicant's counsel/solicitors].

(4) The Applicant will not, without the permission of the court, use any information or documents obtained as a result of carrying out this order nor inform anyone else of these proceedings except for the purposes of these proceedings (including adding further Respondents) or commencing civil proceedings in relation to the same or related subject matter to these proceedings until after the return date.

[(5) The Applicant will maintain pending further order the sum of £ [ ] in an account controlled by the Applicant's solicitors.]

[(6) The Applicant will insure the items removed from the premises.]

SCHEDULE D

UNDERTAKINGS GIVEN BY THE APPLICANT'S SOLICITORS

(1) The Applicant's solicitors will provide to the Supervising Solicitor for service on the Respondent –

- (i) a service copy of this order;
- (ii) the claim form (with defendant's response pack) or, if not issued, the draft produced to the court;
- (iii) an application for hearing on the return date;
- (iv) copies of the affidavits [*or draft affidavits*] and exhibits capable of being copied containing the evidence relied upon by the applicant;
- (v) a note of any allegation of fact made orally to the court where such allegation is not contained in the affidavits or draft affidavits read by the judge; and
- (vi) a copy of the skeleton argument produced to the court by the Applicant's [counsel/solicitors].

(2) The Applicants' solicitors will answer at once to the best of their ability any question whether a particular item is a listed item.

(3) Subject as provided below the Applicant's solicitors will retain in their own safe keeping all items obtained as a result of this order until the court directs otherwise.

(4) The Applicant's solicitors will return the originals of all documents obtained as a result of this order (except original documents which belong to the Applicant) as soon as possible and in any event within [two] working days of their removal.

SCHEDULE E

UNDERTAKINGS GIVEN BY THE SUPERVISING SOLICITOR

(1) The Supervising Solicitor will use his best endeavours to serve this order upon the Respondent and at the same time to serve upon the Respondent the other documents required to be served and referred to in paragraph (1) of Schedule D.

(2) The Supervising Solicitor will offer to explain to the person served with the order its meaning and effect fairly and in everyday language, and to inform him of his right to take legal advice (such advice to include an explanation that the Respondent may be entitled to avail himself of [the privilege against self-incrimination or] [legal professional privilege]) and to apply to vary or discharge this order as mentioned in paragraph 27 above.

(3) The Supervising Solicitor will retain in the safe keeping of his firm all items retained by him as a result of this order until the court directs otherwise.

(4) Within [48] hours of completion of the search the Supervising Solicitor will make and provide to the Applicant's solicitors, the Respondent or his solicitors and to the judge who made this order (for the purposes of the court file) a written report on the carrying out of the order.

SCHEDULE F

AFFIDAVITS

The Applicant relied on the following affidavits –

[*name*]	[*number of affidavit*]	[*date sworn*]	[*filed on behalf of*]
(1)			
(2)			

NAME AND ADDRESS OF APPLICANT'S SOLICITORS

The Applicant's solicitors are –

[Name, address, reference, fax and telephone numbers both in and out of office hours.]

****FREEZING INJUNCTION****
IN THE HIGH COURT OF JUSTICE
QUEEN'S BENCH DIVISION
Before The Honourable Mr Justice

COMMERCIAL COURT
[ ]

Claim No.

BETWEEN

Claimant(s)

– and –

Defendant(s)

Applicant(s)

Respondent(s)

IF YOU [ ][1] DISOBEY THIS ORDER YOU MAY BE HELD TO BE IN CONTEMPT OF COURT AND MAY BE IMPRISONED, FINED OR HAVE YOUR ASSETS SEIZED.

ANY OTHER PERSON WHO KNOWS OF THIS ORDER AND DOES ANYTHING WHICH HELPS OR PERMITS THE RESPONDENT TO BREACH THE TERMS OF THIS ORDER MAY ALSO BE HELD TO BE IN CONTEMPT OF COURT AND MAY BE IMPRISONED, FINED OR HAVE THEIR ASSETS SEIZED.

1 Insert name of Respondent.

THIS ORDER

1 This is a Freezing Injunction made against [ ] ('the Respondent') on [ ] by Mr Justice [ ] on the application of [ ] ('the Applicant'). The Judge read the Affidavits listed in Schedule A and accepted the undertakings set out in Schedule B at the end of this Order.

2 This order was made at a hearing without notice to the Respondent. The Respondent has a right to apply to the court to vary or discharge the order – see paragraph 13 below.

3 There will be a further hearing in respect of this order on [ ] ('the return date').

4 If there is more than one Respondent –

- (a) unless otherwise stated, references in this order to 'the Respondent' mean both or all of them; and
- (b) this order is effective against any Respondent on whom it is served or who is given notice of it.

FREEZING INJUNCTION

[*For injunction limited to assets in England and Wales*]

5 Until the return date or further order of the court, the Respondent must not remove from England and Wales or in any way dispose of, deal with or diminish the value of any of his assets which are in England and Wales up to the value of £ .

[*For worldwide injunction*]

5 Until the return date or further order of the court, the Respondent must not –

- (1) remove from England and Wales any of his assets which are in England and Wales up to the value of £ ; or
- (2) in any way dispose of, deal with or diminish the value of any of his assets whether they are in or outside England and Wales up to the same value.

[*For either form of injunction*]

6 Paragraph 5 applies to all the Respondent's assets whether or not they are in his own name and whether they are solely or jointly owned. For the purpose of this order the Respondent's assets include any asset which he has the power, directly or indirectly, to dispose of or deal with as if it were his own. The Respondent is to be regarded as having such power if a third party holds or controls the asset in accordance with his direct or indirect instructions.

7 This prohibition includes the following assets in particular –

(a) the property known as [*title/address*] or the net sale money after payment of any mortgages if it has been sold;

(b) the property and assets of the Respondent's business [known as [*name*]] [carried on at [*address*]] or the sale money if any of them have been sold; and

(c) any money in the account numbered [*account number*] at [*title/ address*].

[*For injunction limited to assets in England and Wales*]

8 If the total value free of charges or other securities ('unencumbered value') of the Respondent's assets in England and Wales exceeds £ , the Respondent may remove any of those assets from England and Wales or may dispose of or deal with them so long as the total unencumbered value of his assets still in England and Wales remains above £ .

[*For worldwide injunction*]

8 (1) If the total value free of charges or other securities ('unencumbered value') of the Respondent's assets in England and Wales exceeds £ , the Respondent may remove any of those assets from England and Wales or may dispose of or deal with them so long as the total unencumbered value of the Respondent's assets still in England and Wales remains above £ .

(2) If the total unencumbered value of the Respondent's assets in England and Wales does not exceed £ , the Respondent must not remove any of those assets from England and Wales and must not dispose of or deal with any of them. If the Respondent has other assets outside England and Wales, he may dispose of or deal with those assets outside England and Wales so long as the total unencumbered value of all his assets whether in or outside England and Wales remains above £ .

PROVISION OF INFORMATION

9 (1) Unless paragraph (2) applies, the Respondent must [immediately] [within hours of service of this order] and to the best of his ability inform the Applicant's solicitors of all his assets [in England and Wales] [worldwide] [exceeding £ in value] whether in his own name or not and whether solely or jointly owned, giving the value, location and details of all such assets.

(2) If the provision of any of this information is likely to incriminate the Respondent, he may be entitled to refuse to provide it, but is recommended to take legal advice before refusing to provide the information. Wrongful refusal to provide the information is contempt of court and may render the Respondent liable to be imprisoned, fined or have his assets seized.

10 Within [ ] working days after being served with this order, the Respondent must swear and serve on the Applicant's solicitors an affidavit setting out the above information.

EXCEPTIONS TO THIS ORDER

11 (1) This order does not prohibit the Respondent from spending £ a week towards his ordinary living expenses and also £ [or a

reasonable sum] on legal advice and representation. [But before spending any money the Respondent must tell the Applicant's legal representatives where the money is to come from.]

([2) This order does not prohibit the Respondent from dealing with or disposing of any of his assets in the ordinary and proper course of business.]

(3) The Respondent may agree with the Applicant's legal representatives that the above spending limits should be increased or that this order should be varied in any other respect, but any agreement must be in writing.

(4) The order will cease to have effect if the Respondent –
   (a) provides security by paying the sum of £ into court, to be held to the order of the court; or
   (b) makes provision for security in that sum by another method agreed with the Applicant's legal representatives.

COSTS

12 The costs of this application are reserved to the judge hearing the application on the return date.

VARIATION OR DISCHARGE OF THIS ORDER

13 Anyone served with or notified of this order may apply to the court at any time to vary or discharge this order (or so much of it as affects that person), but they must first inform the Applicant's solicitors. If any evidence is to be relied upon in support of the application, the substance of it must be communicated in writing to the Applicant's solicitors in advance.

INTERPRETATION OF THIS ORDER

14 A Respondent who is an individual who is ordered not to do something must not do it himself or in any other way. He must not do it through others acting on his behalf or on his instructions or with his encouragement.

15 A Respondent which is not an individual which is ordered not to do something must not do it itself or by its directors, officers, partners, employees or agents or in any other way.

PARTIES OTHER THAN THE APPLICANT AND RESPONDENT

16 **Effect of this order**

It is a contempt of court for any person notified of this order knowingly to assist in or permit a breach of this order. Any person doing so may be imprisoned, fined or have their assets seized.

17 **Set off by banks**

This injunction does not prevent any bank from exercising any right of set off it may have in respect of any facility which it gave to the respondent before it was notified of this order.

18 **Withdrawals by the Respondent**

No bank need enquire as to the application or proposed application of any money withdrawn by the Respondent if the withdrawal appears to be permitted by this order.

[*For worldwide injunction*]

19 **Persons outside England and Wales**

(1) Except as provided in paragraph (2) below, the terms of this order do not affect or concern anyone outside the jurisdiction of this court.

(2) The terms of this order will affect the following persons in a country or state outside the jurisdiction of this court –

(a) the Respondent or his officer or agent appointed by power of attorney;

(b) any person who –

(i) is subject to the jurisdiction of this court;

(ii) has been given written notice of this order at his residence or place of business within the jurisdiction of this court; and

(iii) is able to prevent acts or omissions outside the jurisdiction of this court which constitute or assist in a breach of the terms of this order; and

(c) any other person, only to the extent that this order is declared enforceable by or is enforced by a court in that country or state.

[*For worldwide injunction*]

20 **Assets located outside England and Wales**

Nothing in this order shall, in respect of assets located outside England and Wales, prevent any third party from complying with –

(1) what it reasonably believes to be its obligations, contractual or otherwise, under the laws and obligations of the country or state in which those assets are situated or under the proper law of any contract between itself and the Respondent; and

(2) any orders of the courts of that country or state, provided that reasonable notice of any application for such an order is given to the Applicant's solicitors.

COMMUNICATIONS WITH THE COURT

All communications to the court about this order should be sent to Room E201, Royal Courts of Justice, Strand, London WC2A 2LL quoting the case number. The telephone number is 0207 947 6826.

The offices are open between 10 am and 4.30 pm Monday to Friday.

SCHEDULE A

AFFIDAVITS

The Applicant relied on the following affidavits –

[*name*]	[*number of affidavit*]	[*date sworn*]	[*filed on behalf of*]
(1)			
(2)			

SCHEDULE B

UNDERTAKINGS GIVEN TO THE COURT BY THE APPLICANT

(1) If the court later finds that this order has caused loss to the Respondent, and decides that the Respondent should be compensated for that loss, the Applicant will comply with any order the court may make.

[(2) The Applicant will –

(a) on or before [*date*] cause a written guarantee in the sum of £ to be issued from a bank with a place of business within England or Wales, in respect of any order the court may make pursuant to paragraph (1) above; and

(b) immediately upon issue of the guarantee, cause a copy of it to be served on the Respondent.]

(3) As soon as practicable the Applicant will issue and serve a claim form [in the form of the draft produced to the court] [claiming the appropriate relief].

(4) The Applicant will [swear and file an affidavit] [cause an affidavit to be sworn and filed] [substantially in the terms of the draft affidavit produced to the court] [confirming the substance of what was said to the court by the Applicant's counsel/solicitors].

(5) The Applicant will serve upon the Respondent [together with this order] [as soon as practicable] –

(i) copies of the affidavits and exhibits containing the evidence relied upon by the Applicant, and any other documents provided to the court on the making of the application;

(ii) the claim form; and

(iii) an application notice for continuation of the order.

[(6) Anyone notified of this order will be given a copy of it by the Applicant's legal representatives.]

(7) The Applicant will pay the reasonable costs of anyone other than the Respondent which have been incurred as a result of this order including the costs of finding out whether that person holds any of the Respondent's assets and if the court later finds that this order has caused such person loss, and decides that such person should be compensated for that loss, the Applicant will comply with any order the court may make.

(8) If this order ceases to have effect (for example, if the Respondent provides security or the Applicant does not provide a bank guarantee as provided for above) the Applicant will immediately take all reasonable steps to inform in writing anyone to whom he has given notice of this order, or who he has reasonable grounds for supposing may act upon this order, that it has ceased to have effect.

[(9) The Applicant will not without the permission of the court use any information obtained as a result of this order for the purpose of any civil or criminal proceedings, either in England and Wales or in any other jurisdiction, other than this claim.]

[(10) The Applicant will not without the permission of the court seek to enforce this order in any country outside England and Wales [or seek an order of a similar nature including orders conferring a charge or other security against the Respondent or the Respondent's assets].]

NAME AND ADDRESS OF APPLICANT'S LEGAL REPRESENTATIVES

The Applicant's legal representatives are –

[*Name, address, reference, fax and telephone numbers both in and out of office hours and e-mail*]

APPENDIX 6

CASE MANAGEMENT INFORMATION SHEET

Case Management Information Sheet Party lodging information sheet:

Name of solicitors:

Name(s) of advocates for trial:

[**Note:** This Sheet should normally be completed with the involvement of the advocate(s) instructed for trial. If the claimant is a litigant in person this fact should be noted at the foot of the sheet and proposals made as to which party is to have responsibility for the preparation and upkeep of the case management bundle.]

(1) By what date can you give standard disclosure?

(2) In relation to standard disclosure, do you contend in relation to any category or class of document under rule 31.6(b) that to search for that category or class would be unreasonable? If so, what is the category or class and on what grounds do you so contend?

(3) Is specific disclosure required on any issue? If so, please specify.

(4) By what dates can you (a) give specific disclosure or (b) comply with a special disclosure order?

(5) May the time periods for inspection at rule 31.15 require adjustment, and if so by how much?

(6) Are amendments to or is information about any statement of case required? If yes, please give brief details of what is required.

(7) Can you make any additional admissions? If yes, please give brief details of the additional admissions.

(8) Are any of the issues in the case suitable for trial as preliminary issues?

(9) (a) On the evidence of how many witnesses of fact do you intend to rely at trial (subject to the directions of the court)? Please give their names, or explain why this is not being done.

(b) By what date can you serve signed witness statements?

(c) How many of these witnesses of fact do you intend to call to give oral evidence at trial (subject to the directions of the court)? Please give their names, or explain why this is not being done.

(d) Will interpreters be required for any witness? (e) Do you wish any witness to give oral evidence by video link? Please give his or her name, or explain why this is not being done. Please state the country and city from which the witness will be asked to give evidence by video link.

(10) (a) On what issues may expert evidence be required?

(b) Is this a case in which the use of a single joint expert might be suitable (see rule 35.7)?

(c) On the evidence of how many expert witnesses do you intend to rely at trial (subject to the directions of the court)? Please give their names, or explain why this is not being done. Please identify each expert's field of expertise.

(d) By what date can you serve signed expert reports?

(e) When will the experts be available for a meeting or meetings of experts?

(f) How many of these expert witnesses do you intend to call to give oral evidence at trial (subject to the directions of the court)? Please give their names, or explain why this is not being done.

(g) Will interpreters be required for any expert witness?

(h) Do you wish any expert witness to give oral evidence by video link? Please give his or her name, or explain why this is not being done. Please state the country and city from which the witness will be asked to give evidence by video link.

(11) What are the advocates' present provisional estimates of the minimum and maximum lengths of the trial?

(12) What is the earliest date by which you believe you can be ready for trial?

(13) Is this a case in which a pre-trial review is likely to be useful?

(14) Is there any way in which the court can assist the parties to resolve their dispute or particular issues in it without the need for a trial or a full trial?

(15) (a) Might some form of Alternative Dispute Resolution procedure assist to resolve or narrow the dispute or particular issues in it?

(b) Has the question at (a) been considered between the client and legal representatives (including the advocate(s) retained)?

(c) Has the question at (a) been explored with the other parties in the case?

(d) Do you request that the case is adjourned while the parties try to settle the case by Alternative Dispute Resolution or other means?

(e) Would an ADR order in the form of Appendix 7 to the Commercial Court Guide be appropriate?

(f) Are any other special directions needed to allow for Alternative Dispute Resolution?

(16) What other applications will you wish to make at the Case Management Conference?

(17) Does provision need to be made in the pre-trial timetable for any application or procedural step not otherwise dealt with above? If yes, please specify the application or procedural step.

(18) Are there, or are there likely in due course to be, any related proceedings (e.g. a Part 20 claim)? Please give brief details.

[Signature of solicitors]

Note: This information sheet must be lodged with the Clerk to the Commercial Court at least 7 days before the Case Management Conference (with a copy to all other parties): see section D8.5 of the Commercial Court Guide.

APPENDIX 7

DRAFT ADR ORDER

1 On or before [*] the parties shall exchange lists of three neutral individuals who are available to conduct ADR procedures in this case prior to [*]. Each party may [in addition] [in the alternative] provide a list identifying the constitution of one or more panels of neutral individuals who are available to conduct ADR procedures in this case prior to [*].

2 On or before [*] the parties shall in good faith endeavour to agree a neutral individual or panel from the lists so exchanged and provided.

3 Failing such agreement by [*] the Case Management Conference will be restored to enable the court to facilitate agreement on a neutral individual or panel.

4 The parties shall take such serious steps as they may be advised to resolve their disputes by ADR procedures before the neutral individual or panel so chosen by no later than [*].

5 If the case is not finally settled, the parties shall inform the court by letter prior to [disclosure of documents/exchange of witness statements/exchange of experts' reports] what steps towards ADR have been taken and (without prejudice to matters of privilege) why such steps have failed. If the parties have failed to initiate ADR procedures the Case Management Conference is to be restored for further consideration of the case.

6 [Costs].

Note: The term 'ADR procedures' is deliberately used in the draft ADR order.

This is in order to emphasise that (save where otherwise provided) the parties are free to use the ADR procedure that they regard as most suitable, be it mediation, early neutral evaluation, non-binding arbitration etc.

APPENDIX 8

STANDARD PRE-TRIAL TIMETABLE

1 [Standard disclosure is to be made by [*], with inspection [*] days after notice.]

2 Signed statements of witnesses of fact, and hearsay notices where required by rule 33.2, are to be exchanged not later than [*].

3 Unless otherwise ordered, witness statements are to stand as the evidence in chief of the witness at trial.

4 Signed reports of experts

(i) are to be confined to one expert for each party from each of the following fields of expertise: [*];
(ii) are to be confined to the following issues: [*];
(iii) are to be exchanged [sequentially/simultaneously];

(iv) are to be exchanged not later than [date or dates for each report in each field of expertise].

5 Meeting of experts

(i) The meeting of experts is to be by [*];
(ii) The joint memorandum of the experts is to be completed by [*];
(iii) Any short supplemental expert reports are to be exchanged [sequentially/simultaneously] by not later than [date or dates for each supplemental report].

6 [If the experts' reports cannot be agreed, the parties are to be at liberty to call expert witnesses at the trial, limited to those experts whose reports have been exchanged pursuant to 4. above.] [Or: The parties are to be at liberty to apply to call as expert witnesses at the trial those experts whose reports they have exchanged pursuant to 4. above, such application to be made not earlier than [*] and not later than [*].]

7 Preparation of trial bundles to be completed in accordance with Appendix 10 to the Commercial Court Guide by not later than [*].

8 The provisional estimated length of the trial is [*].

9 Within [*] days the parties are to attend on the Clerk to the Commercial Court to fix the date for trial which shall be not before [*].

10 The progress monitoring date is [*]. Each party is to lodge a completed progress monitoring information sheet with the Clerk to the Commercial Court at least 3 days before the progress monitoring date (with a copy to all other parties).

11 Each party is to lodge a completed pre-trial checklist not later than 3 weeks before the date fixed for trial.

12 [There is to be a pre-trial review not earlier than [*] and not later than [*]].

13 Save as varied by this order or further order, the practice and procedures set out in the Admiralty & Commercial Courts Guide are to be followed.

14 Costs in the case.

15 Liberty to restore the Case Management Conference.

APPENDIX 9

SKELETON ARGUMENTS, CHRONOLOGIES AND INDICES

PART 1
SKELETON ARGUMENTS

1 A skeleton argument is intended to identify both for the parties and the court those points which are, and are not, in issue and the nature of the argument in relation to those points that are in issue. It is not a substitute for oral argument.

2 Skeleton arguments must therefore –

(a) identify concisely:
  (i) the nature of the case generally and the background facts insofar as they are relevant to the matter before the court;
  (ii) the propositions of law relied on with references to the relevant authorities;

(iii) the submissions of fact to be made with references to the evidence;

(b) be in numbered paragraphs and state the name of the advocate(s) who prepared them; and

(c) should avoid arguing the case at length.

PART 2
CHRONOLOGIES AND INDICES

3 As far as possible chronologies and indices should not be prepared in a tendentious form. The ideal is that the court and the parties should have a single point of reference that all find useful and are happy to work with.

4 Where there is disagreement about a particular event or description, it is useful if that fact is indicated in neutral terms and the competing versions shortly stated.

5 If time and circumstances allow its preparation, a chronology or index to which all parties have contributed and agreed can be invaluable.

6 Chronologies and indices once prepared can be easily updated and are of continuing usefulness throughout the life of the case.

APPENDIX 10
PREPARATION OF BUNDLES

1 The preparation of bundles requires a high level of co-operation between legal representatives for all parties. It is the duty of all legal representatives to co-operate to this high level.

2 Bundles should be prepared as follows:

(i) No more than one copy of any one document should be included, unless there is good reason for doing otherwise;

(ii) Contemporaneous documents, and correspondence, should be included in chronological order;

(iii) Where a contract or similar document is central to the case it may be included in a separate place provided that a page is inserted in the chronological run of documents to indicate:

(A) the place the contract or similar document would have appeared had it appeared chronologically and

(B) where it may be found instead;

(iv) Documents in manuscript, or not fully legible, should be transcribed; the transcription should be marked and placed adjacent to the document transcribed;

(v) Documents in a foreign language should be translated; the translation should be marked and placed adjacent to the document transcribed; the translation should be agreed, or, if it cannot be agreed, each party's proposed translation should be included;

(vi) If a document has to be read across rather than down the page, it should be so placed in the bundle as to ensure that the top of the text is nearest the spine;

(vii) **No bundle should contain more than 300 pages**;

(viii) Bundles should not be overfilled, and should allow sufficient room for later insertions. Subject to this, the size of file used should not be a size that is larger than necessary for the present and anticipated contents;

(ix) Bundles should be paginated, in the bottom right hand corner and in a form that can clearly be distinguished from any existing pagination on the document;

(x) Bundles should be indexed, save that a chronological bundle of contemporaneous documents need not be indexed if an index is unlikely to be useful;

(xi) Bundles should be numbered and named on the outside and on the inside front cover, the label to include the short title of the case, and a description of the bundle (including its number, where relevant).

3 Documents within bundles should be marked as follows:

(i) When copy documents from exhibits have been included in the bundle(s), then unless clearly unnecessary, the copy of the affidavit or witness statement to which the documents were exhibited should be marked in the right hand margin (in manuscript if need be) to show where the document referred to may be found in the bundle(s).

(ii) Unless clearly unnecessary, where copy documents in a bundle are taken from the disclosure of more than one party the documents should be marked in the top right hand corner (in manuscript if need be) to show from which party's disclosure the copy document has been taken;

(iii) Where there is a reference in a statement of case or witness statement to a document which is contained in the trial bundles a note should be made in the margin (if necessary in manuscript) identifying the place where that document is to be found. Unless otherwise agreed this is the responsibility of the party tendering the statement of case or witness statement.

4 For the trial a handy-sized core bundle should normally be provided containing the really important documents in the case. The documents in this bundle should be paginated, but each page should also bear its bundle and page number reference in the main bundles. It is particularly important to allow sufficient room for later insertions (see paragraph 2(viii) above).

5 Large documents, such as plans, should be placed in an easily accessible file.

6 (a) When agreeing bundles for trial, the parties should also establish through their legal representatives, and record in correspondence, whether the agreement of bundles:

(i) extends no further than agreement of the composition and preparation of the bundles; or

(ii) includes agreement that the documents in the bundles are authentic (see further rule 32.19); or

(iii) includes agreement that the documents may be treated as evidence of the facts stated in them.

(b) The court will normally expect parties to agree that the documents or at any rate the great majority of them may be treated as evidence of the facts stated in them. A party not willing so to agree should, when the trial bundles are lodged, write a letter to the court (with a copy to all other parties) stating that it is not willing so to agree, and explaining why that is so.

APPENDIX 11

EXPERT EVIDENCE – REQUIREMENTS OF GENERAL APPLICATION

1 It is the duty of an expert to help the court on the matters within his expertise: **rule 35.3(1)**. This duty is paramount and overrides any obligation to the person from whom the expert has received instructions or by whom he is paid: **rule 35.3(2)**.

2 Expert evidence presented to the court should be, and should be seen to be, the independent product of the expert uninfluenced by the pressures of litigation.

3 An expert witness should provide independent assistance to the court by way of objective unbiased opinion in relation to matters within his expertise. An expert witness should never assume the role of an advocate.

4 An expert witness should not omit to consider material facts which could detract from his concluded opinion.

5 An expert witness should make it clear when a particular question or issue falls outside his expertise.

6 If an expert's opinion is not properly researched because he considers that insufficient data is available, this must be stated in his report with an indication that the opinion is no more than a provisional one.

7 In a case where an expert witness who has prepared a report is unable to confirm that the report contains the truth, the whole truth and nothing but the truth without some qualification, that qualification must be stated in the report.

8 If, after exchange of reports, an expert witness changes his view on a material matter having read another expert's report or for any other reason, such change of view should be communicated in writing (through the party's legal representatives) to the other side without delay, and when appropriate to the court.

APPENDIX 12

PROGRESS MONITORING INFORMATION SHEET

[SHORT TITLE OF CASE and FOLIO NUMBER]

Fixed trial date/provisional range of dates for trial specified in the pre-trial timetable:

Party lodging information sheet:

Name of solicitors:

Name(s) of advocates for trial:

[**Note:** this information sheet should normally be completed with the involvement of the advocate(s) instructed for trial]

(1) Have you complied with the pre-trial timetable in all respects?

(2) If you have not complied, in what respects have you not complied?

(3) Will you be ready for a trial commencing on the fixed date (or, where applicable, within the provisional range of dates) specified in the pre-trial timetable?

(4) If you will not be ready, why will you not be ready?

[*Signature of solicitors*]

Note: This information sheet must be lodged with the Case Management Unit at least 3 days before the progress monitoring date (with a copy to all other parties): see section D12.2 of the Guide.

APPENDIX 13

PRE-TRIAL CHECKLIST

[SHORT TITLE OF CASE and FOLIO NUMBER]

a Trial date:

b Party lodging checklist:

c Name of solicitors:

d Name(s) of advocates for trial:

[**Note**: this checklist should normally be completed with the involvement of the advocate(s) instructed for trial.]

1 Have you completed preparation of trial bundles in accordance with Appendix 10 to the Commercial Court Guide?

2 If not, when will the preparation of the trial bundles be completed?

3 Which witnesses of fact do you intend to call?

4 Which expert witness(es) do you intend to call (if directions for expert evidence have been given)?

5 Will an interpreter be required for any witness and if so, have any necessary directions already been given?

6 Have directions been given for any witness to give evidence by video link? If so, have all necessary arrangements been made?

7 What are the advocates' confirmed estimates of the minimum and maximum lengths of the trial? (A confirmed estimate of length signed by the advocates should be attached).

8 What is your estimate of costs already incurred and to be incurred at trial for the purposes of section 46 of the Practice Direction supplementing CPR Part 43? (If the trial is not expected to last more than **one day** the estimate should be substantially in the form of a statement of costs as illustrated in Form H of the Schedule of Costs Forms annexed to the Practice Direction).

[Signature of solicitors]

****

Appendix 14—Appendix 14 contains Video Conferencing Guidance, which is also available at PD32, Annex 3, set out in Section 2 of this work.

APPENDIX 15

SERVICE OUT OF THE JURISDICTION: RELATED PRACTICE

Service out of the jurisdiction without permission

1 Before issuing a claim form or seeking permission to serve out of the jurisdiction, it is necessary to consider whether the jurisdiction of the English courts is affected by the Civil Jurisdiction and Judgments Act 1982. Where each claim in the claim form is a claim which the court has by virtue of the Civil Jurisdiction and Judgments Act 1982 power to hear and determine, service of the claim form out of the jurisdiction may be effected without permission provided that the requirements of rule 6.19 are satisfied and the claim form is endorsed before issue with a statement that the court has power under the Act to hear and determine the claim against the defendant, and that no proceedings involving the same claim are pending between the parties in Scotland, Northern Ireland or another convention country. Care must be taken to see that the endorsement is not made unless the statement is accurate.

Application for permission: affidavit or witness statement

2 (a) On applications for permission under rule 6.20 the written evidence must, amongst other things:

- (i) identify the paragraph or paragraphs of rule 6.20 relied on as giving the court jurisdiction to order service out, together with a summary of the facts relied on as bringing the case within each such paragraph;
- (ii) state the belief of the deponent that there is a good claim and state in what place or country the defendant is or probably may be found;
- (iii) summarise the considerations relied upon as showing that the case is a proper one in which to subject a party outside the jurisdiction to proceedings within it;
- (iv) draw attention to any features which might reasonably be thought to weigh against the making of the order sought;
- (v) state the deponent's grounds of belief and sources of information;
- (vi) exhibit copies of the documents referred to and any other significant documents.

(b) Where convenient the written evidence should be included in the form of application notice, rather than in a separate witness statement. The form of application notice may be extended for this purpose.

Application for permission: copies of draft order

3 The documents submitted with the application must include two copies of a draft of the order sought which must state the time allowed for acknowledgment of service in accordance with any applicable practice direction and paragraphs 6 and 7 below.

Application for permission: copy or draft of claim form

4 A copy or draft of the claim form which the applicant intends to issue and serve must be provided for the judge to initial. If the endorsement to the claim form includes causes of action or claims not covered by the grounds on which permission to serve out of the jurisdiction can properly be granted, permission will be refused unless the draft is amended to restrict it to proper claims. Where the application is for the issue of a concurrent claim form, the documents submitted must also include a copy of the original claim form.

Arbitration matters

5 Service out of the jurisdiction in arbitration matters is governed by Part 62. As to the 1968 Convention on Jurisdiction in the context of arbitration, see Article 1(4).

Practice under rules 6.19 and 6.20

6 (a) Although a Part 7 claim form may contain or be accompanied by particulars of claim, there is no need for it to do so and in many cases particulars of claim will be served after the claim form: rule 58.5.
(b) A defendant should acknowledge service in every case: rule 58.6(1).
(c) The period for filing acknowledgment of service will be calculated from the service of the claim form, whether or not particulars of claim are to follow: rule 58.6.
(d) The period for serving, and filing, particulars of claim (where they were not contained in the claim form and did not accompany the claim form) will be calculated from acknowledgment of service: rule 58.5(1)(c).
(e) The period for serving and filing the defence will be calculated from service of the particulars of claim: rule 58.10(2).

7 Time for serving and filing a defence is calculated as follows:

(i) where particulars of claim were included in or accompanied the claim form the period for serving and filing a defence is 21 or 31 days as prescribed by rule 6.23, or the number of days shown in the table in practice direction 6BPD, in either case plus an additional 14 days;
(ii) where particulars of claim were not included in and did not accompany the claim form, the period for serving and filing a defence is 28 days from the service of the particulars of claim.

APPENDIX 16

SECURITY FOR COSTS: RELATED PRACTICE

First applications

1 First applications for security for costs should not be made later than at the Case Management Conference and in any event any application should not be left until close to the trial date. Delay to the prejudice of the other party or the administration of justice will probably cause the application to fail, as will any use of the application to harass the other party. Where it is intended to make an

application for security at the Case Management Conference the procedure, and timetable for evidence, for an ordinary application must be followed (see section F5 of the Guide).

Successive applications

2 Successive applications for security can be granted where the circumstances warrant. If a claimant wishes to seek to preclude any further application it is incumbent on him to make that clear.

Evidence

3 An affidavit or witness statement in support of an application for security for costs should deal not only with the residence of the claimant (or other respondent to the application) and the location of his assets but also with the practical difficulties (if any) of enforcing an order for costs against him.

Investigation of the merits of the case

4 Investigation of the merits of the case on an application for security is strongly discouraged. Only in those cases where it can be shown without detailed investigation of evidence or law that the claim is certain or almost certain to succeed or fail will the merits be taken into consideration.

Undertaking by the applicant

5 In appropriate cases an order for security for costs may only be made on terms that the applicant gives an undertaking to comply with any order that the court may make if the court later finds that the order for security for costs has caused loss to the claimant and that the claimant should be compensated for such loss. Such undertakings are intended to compensate claimants in cases where no order for costs is ultimately made in favour of the applicant.

Stay of proceedings

6 It is not usually convenient or appropriate to order an automatic stay of the proceedings pending the provision of the security. It leads to delay and may disrupt the preparation of the case for trial, or other hearing.

Experience has shown that it is usually better to give the claimant (or other relevant party) a reasonable time within which to provide the security and the other party liberty to apply to the court in the event of default. This enables the court to put the claimant to his election and then, if appropriate, to dismiss the case.

Amount of security

7 Where the dispute on an application for security for costs relates to the correct evaluation of the amount of costs likely to be allowed to a successful defendant on an assessment of costs, parties should consider whether it would be advantageous for the judge hearing the application to sit with a Costs Judge as an informal assessor. The judge himself may take such an initiative.

Addresses and Contact Details

The Admiralty Marshal:

Room E203, Royal Courts of Justice, Strand, London WC2A 2LL Tel: 020 7947 6111 Fax: 020 7947 7671

The Admiralty & Commercial Registry:

Room E200, Royal Courts of Justice, Strand, London WC2A 2LL Tel: 020 7947 6112 Fax: 020 7947 6245 DX 44450 STRAND

The Admiralty and Commercial Court Listing Office:

Room E201, Royal Courts of Justice, Strand, London WC2A 2LL Tel: 020 7947 6826 Fax: 020 7947 7670 DX 44450 STRAND

The Admiralty and Commercial Case Management Unit:

Room E206, Royal Courts of Justice, Strand, London WC2A 2LL Tel: 020 7947 6256 Fax: 020 7947 7672

The Secretary to the Commercial Court Committee:

Mrs Angela Hodgson Room E201 Royal Courts of Justice Strand London WC2A 2LL Tel: 020 7947 6826 Fax: 020 7947 7670 DX 44450 STRAND

Out of hours emergency number:

(Security Office at Royal Courts of Justice): 020 7947 6000

Fax number for the procedure under sections B3.11 and B4.4 of the Guide for the issue of claim forms when the Registry is closed: 020 7947 6667.

****

Forms—The forms annexed to this Courts Guide can be accessed on the *Civil Court Service* CD-ROM or on the Court Service website at *www.courtservice.gov.uk*.

The Chancery Guide 2002

ARRANGEMENT OF CHAPTERS

Preface

The Chancery Guide was first published in April 1995. It was published again in April 1999 at the time when the Civil Procedure Rules came into force, and then republished in July 2000 to take account of the Civil Procedure Rules and Practice Directions then in force. Since then many of the surviving Rules of the Supreme Court preserved in Schedule 1 to the Civil Procedure Rules have been replaced by further Parts and Practice Directions. This, the fourth, edition takes account of those brought into force before 31 May 2002, and anticipates some due to come into force before the end of 2002.

The Chancery Guide is not a substitute for the Civil Procedure Rules or associated Practice Directions. It seeks only to give practical guidance on the conduct of cases in the Chancery Division within the framework of those Rules and Practice Directions.

This edition has been produced by or under the supervision of Sir Timothy Lloyd. I am very grateful to him for undertaking the task. The amount of work involved has been a considerable extra burden for him to bear. He has been assisted with regard to various topics by many others to whom I send my thanks. It is always dangerous to mention some lest others have been overlooked; nevertheless I would particularly thank Chief Master Winegarten, Chief Registrar James, Master Bowles, Anthony Trace QC and Andrew Ayres on behalf of the Chancery Bar Association, and Vicky Bell. I am also grateful to Roger Horne and Laurie West-Knights QC for their help in relation to the version of the Guide for the Court Service website.

Practice and procedure continuously evolve. The replacement of the former Rules of the Supreme Court proceeds and, in the light of experience, changes are made from time to time to the existing Civil Procedure Rules and Practice Directions. No doubt a fifth edition of the Chancery Guide will be needed in 2004–2005. Until then I hope and believe this edition will be of considerable use to all those who, in whatever capacity, have occasion to participate in litigation in the Chancery Division.

Andrew Morritt
Vice-Chancellor
14 June 2002

The Civil Procedure Rules (comprising Rules, Practice Directions, Pre-Action Protocols and Forms) are published by the Stationery Office. They are also published on the Lord Chancellor's Department's website: *www.lcd.gov.uk/*. This Guide will also be found on the Chancery Division section of the Court Service website: *www.courtservice.gov.uk*.

Abbreviations used in this Guide:

Civil Procedure Rules	CPR
Practice Direction supplementing a Civil Procedure Rule	PD
Rules of the Supreme Court 1965	RSC
Pre-trial review	PTR

Part 1 means CPR Part 1
rule 1.1 means CPR Part 1 rule 1.1.
PD52 means the PD supplementing CPR Part 52

Chapter 1 – Introductory

Reform of the Civil Justice System

1.1 The Civil Procedure Rules and the Practice Directions which supplement them represent a major change in the civil justice system, whose aim is to remove identified defects of the previous system, above all those of excessive delay and expense, and to improve access to justice through quicker, cheaper and more proportionate justice. As an integral part of the reforms, cases are now more closely monitored through to trial by the judiciary.

1.2 To achieve these aims, all procedural decisions under the CPR are guided by the overriding objective stated in rule 1.1. The court must deal with cases justly; dealing justly with a case includes, so far as practicable, ensuring that the parties are on an equal footing, saving expense, dealing with the case in ways which are proportionate to the sum at stake, to the importance of the case, to its complexity and to each party's financial position, ensuring expedition and fairness and allotting to each case an appropriate share of the court's resources.

About the Chancery Division

1.3 The Chancery Division is one of the three parts, or Divisions, of the High Court of Justice, the other two being the Queen's Bench Division and the Family Division. The effective head of the Chancery Division is the Vice-Chancellor. There are currently seventeen High Court judges attached to the Division. In addition, in the Royal Courts of Justice in London, there are six masters (one of whom is the Chief Master), and six Bankruptcy registrars (one of whom is the Chief Registrar). In the District Registries (see Chapter 12) the work done by masters in London is performed by district judges. References in this Guide to a master include, in the case of proceedings in a District Registry, references to a district judge. Deputies sit on a regular basis for both judges and masters. Any reference to a judge or master in the Guide includes a reference to a person sitting as a deputy.

1.4 The Chancery Division undertakes civil work of many kinds, including specialist work such as companies, patents and contentious probate. The range of cases heard in the Chancery Division is wide and varied. The major part of the case-load today involves business disputes of one kind or another. Often these are complex and involve substantial sums of money.

1.5 In many types of case (eg claims for professional negligence against solicitors, accountants, valuers or other professionals) the claimant has a choice whether to bring the claim in the Chancery Division or elsewhere in the High Court. But there are other types of case which, in the High Court, must be brought in the Chancery Division. The specialist work of the Chancery Division is dealt with in Section B of this Guide.

1.6 If a claim brought in the Chancery Division is a 'commercial claim' within the meaning of rule 58.1(2), the court will in general, and to the extent that it is consistent with the CPR and relevant PDs, adopt the same practice as the Commercial Court, which is described in the Admiralty and Commercial Courts Guide 2002. There may also be cases which are not commercial claims as so defined but where procedures can usefully be adapted from those set out in the Admiralty and Commercial Courts Guide. However, case management in Chancery Division cases will usually be carried out by the masters.

About this Guide

1.7 The aim of this Guide is to provide additional practical information not already contained in the CPR or the Practice Directions supplementing them.

1.8 Litigants and their advisers are expected to be familiar with the CPR. It is not the function of this Guide to summarise the CPR, nor should it be regarded as a substitute for them.

1.9 This Guide is published as part of a series of Guides to various civil courts. Where information is more readily available in another Guide this Guide may simply refer to it. A separate book contains Forms for use in the Chancery Division and in the Queen's Bench Division, as an Appendix to the Queen's Bench Guide. However, three Forms used in the Chancery Division are found in the Appendices to this Guide, not in the separate book.

1.10 Section A of this Guide is concerned with general civil work. Section B deals with specialist work. Some subjects are covered in more detail in the Appendices, and Appendix 8 sets out some contact details which may be useful.

1.11 Material which used to be contained in the Chancery Division Practice Directions and which remains relevant has been incorporated into either Section A or Section B of this Guide, as appropriate.

1.12 A reference in this Guide to a Part is to that Part of the CPR, to a rule is to the relevant rule in the CPR, unless otherwise stated, and to PD[*number*] is to the PD supplementing the Part so numbered, the title being given if necessary to distinguish one from another. The PD about costs, supplementing Parts 43 to 48 is called the Costs PD.

1.13 This Guide states the position as at 31 May 2002, except that it anticipates some changes to the CPR and PDs which are due to come into force before the end of 2002. During the currency of the Guide, and even in some cases before publication, there are likely to be changes in matter covered in the text, including room numbers and other contact details; these should be checked as necessary. The Guide will be kept under review in the light of practical experience and of changes to the rules and practice directions. Any comments on the text of the Guide are welcome and should be addressed to the clerk to the Vice-Chancellor.

1.14 Further copies of this Guide may be obtained from the Fees Room at the Royal Courts of Justice or from the shop at the main entrance to the Royal Courts of Justice.

1.15 The text of the Guide is also to be found, together with other Court Guides and other useful information concerning the administration of justice in the Chancery Division and elsewhere, on the Court Service website: *www.courtservice.gov.uk*.

SECTION A
GENERAL CIVIL WORK

Chapter 2 – Starting Proceedings, Service, Allocation and Statements of Case

Key Rules: CPR Parts 6, 7, 8, 9, 10, 15, 16, 18, 20 and 26 and CPR Schedule 1

How to start a claim

2.1 Claims are issued out of the High Court of Justice, Chancery Division, either in the Royal Courts of Justice (Chancery Chambers) or in a District Registry. There is no Production Centre for Chancery claims.

2.2 The claim form must be issued either as a Part 7 claim under Part 7, or as a Part 8 claim under the alternative procedure for claims in Part 8.

2.3 When issuing proceedings, the general rule is that the title of the claim should contain only the names of the parties to the proceedings. To this there are four exceptions: (a) proceedings relating to the administration of an estate, which should be entitled 'In the estate of AB deceased' (some cases relating to the estates of deceased Lloyd's names require additional wording: see paragraph 26.53 below); (b) contentious probate proceedings, which should be entitled 'In the estate of AB deceased (probate)'; (c) proceedings under the Inheritance (Provision for Family and Dependants) Act 1975, which should be entitled 'In the Matter of the Inheritance (Provision for Family and Dependants) Act 1975'; and (d) proceedings relating to pension schemes, which may be entitled 'In the Matter of the [ ] Pension Scheme'. In addition, proceedings in the Companies Court are entitled in the matter of the relevant legislation and of the relevant company or other person: see paragraph 20.5.

Service

2.4 Part 6 applies to the service of documents, including claim forms. Unless the claimant notifies the court that he or she wishes to serve the claim form, it will be served by the court. Many solicitors, however, will prefer to serve the claim form themselves and will notify the court that they wish to do so.

Allocation

2.5 The vast majority of claims issued, and all those retained, in the Chancery Division will be allocated to the multi-track. Chapter 13 deals with transfer to county courts.

Statements of case

2.6 In addition to the matters which PD16 requires to be set out specifically in the particulars of claim, a party must set out in any statement of case:

(1) full particulars of any allegation of fraud, dishonesty, malice or illegality;

(2) where any inference of fraud or dishonesty is alleged, the facts on the basis of which the inference is alleged.

2.7 A party should not set out allegations of fraud or dishonesty unless there is material admissible in evidence to support the contentions made. Setting out such matters without such material being available may result in the particular allegations being struck out and may result in wasted costs orders being made against the legal advisers responsible.

2.8 Points of law may be set out in any statement of case, and any point to be taken under the Human Rights Act 1998 must be so set out.

2.9 In the preparation of statements of case, the guidelines in Appendix 1 should be followed.

2.10 The guidelines apply to: the claim form (unless no particulars are given in it); particulars of claim; defence; Part 20 claim; reply to a defence; and a response to a request for further information under Part 18.

2.11 Parties should not attach copies of documents or any expert's report to their statement of case if they are bulky.

2.12 Notwithstanding rule 15.8, claimants should if possible serve any reply before they file their allocation questionnaire. This will enable other parties to consider the reply before they file their allocation questionnaire.

Part 8 claims

2.13 This procedure may be used where there is no substantial dispute of fact, such as where the case raises only questions of the construction of a document or a statute. Additionally, however, a large number of particular claims are also brought under Part 8 pursuant to PD8, Part 8. Of particular relevance to Chancery practitioners will be applications to enforce charging orders, applications with respect to funds in court and proceedings relating to solicitors. Subject to jurisdiction and following the coming into force of Part 73, applications to enforce charging orders are now issued in the court in which the charging order was made. Proceedings to enforce charging orders made in any division of the High Court are issued in the Chancery Division.

2.14 Provision is also made in Part 8 for a claim form to be issued without naming a defendant with the permission of the court. No separate application for permission is required where personal representatives seek permission to distribute the estate of a deceased Lloyd's name nor for applications under section 48 of the Administration of Justice Act 1985 (see further Chapter 26 – Trusts). Where permission is needed, it is to be sought by application notice under Part 23.

2.15 Part 8 claims will generally be disposed of on written evidence. The features of the Part 8 procedure are:

(1) no particulars of claim
(2) no defence
(3) no allocation questionnaire
(4) no judgment in default
(5) normally no oral evidence.

2.16 Defendants who wish to contest a Part 8 claim or to take part in the proceedings should complete and file the acknowledgment of service in form N210 which accompanies the claim form. Alternatively the information required to be contained in the acknowledgment of service can be provided by letter. It is helpful to the court if a party who does not wish to contest a claim indicates that fact on the form acknowledging service or by letter. As yet, however, form N210 contains no provision in this regard.

2.17 Claimants must file the written evidence on which they intend to rely with the claim form. Defendants are required to file and serve their evidence when they file their acknowledgment of service, namely within 14 days after service of the claim form (rule 8.5(3)). By paragraph 5.6 of PD8, Alternative Procedure for Claims, a defendant's time for filing evidence may be extended by agreement for not more than 14 days from the filing of the acknowledgment of service. Any such agreement must be filed with the court by the defendant at the same time as he or she files an acknowledgment of service. The claimant has 14 days for filing evidence in reply but this period may be extended by agreement for not more than 28 days from service of the defendant's evidence. Again, any such agreement must be filed with the court. Any longer extension either for the defendant or the claimant requires an application to the court. It is recognised that in substantial matters the provisions in Part 8 may be burdensome upon Defendants and in such matters the court will readily grant an extension. If the parties are in agreement that such an extension should be granted the application should be made in writing.

2.18 Defendants who acknowledge service but do not intend to file evidence should notify the court in writing when they file their acknowledgment of service that they do not intend to file evidence. This enables the court to know what each defendant's intention is when it considers the file.

2.19 The general rule (exceptions include, for example, some claims under the Variation of Trusts Act 1958 or where a party has made a Part 24 application) is that the court file will be considered by the court after the time for acknowledgment of service has expired, or, if the time for serving the defendant's evidence has been extended, after the expiry of that period.

2.20 In some cases if the papers are in order the court will not require any oral hearing, but will be able to deal with the matter on paper either by making the final order, or by directing a hearing before a judge. In the majority of cases, however, the court will direct that the Part 8 claim be listed either for substantive hearing or for consideration of further case management directions.

Chapter 3 – The Court's Case Management Powers

Key Rules: CPR rule 1.4, and Parts 3, 18, 19, 26, 29, 31, 39

3.1 A key feature of the CPR is that cases are closely monitored by the court. Case management by the court includes: identifying disputed issues at an early stage; fixing timetables; dealing with as many aspects of the case as possible on the same occasion; controlling costs; disposing of cases summarily where they disclose no case or defence; dealing with the case without the parties having to attend court; and giving directions to ensure that the trial of a case proceeds quickly and efficiently. The court will expect the parties to co-operate with each other. Where appropriate the court will encourage the parties to use alternative dispute resolution or otherwise help them settle the case. In particular, the court will readily grant a short stay at allocation or at any other stage to accommodate mediation or any other form of settlement negotiations. The court will not, however, normally, grant an open-ended stay for such purposes and if, for any reason, a lengthy stay is granted it will be on terms that the parties report to the court on a regular basis in respect of their negotiations.

3.2 In the Chancery Division case management is normally carried out by the master, but a judge may be nominated by the Vice-Chancellor to hear the case and to deal with the case management where it is appropriate due to the size or complexity of the case or for other reasons. A request by any or all parties for such a nomination should be addressed to the Vice-Chancellor.

Directions

3.3 It is expected that parties and their advisers will endeavour to agree proposals for management of the case at the allocation stage in accordance with rule 29.4 and paragraphs 4.6 to 4.8 of PD29. The court will approve the parties' proposals, if they are suitable, and give directions accordingly without a hearing. If it does not approve the agreed directions it may give modified directions or its own directions or direct the holding of a case management conference. If the parties cannot agree directions then each party should put forward its own proposals for the future management of the case for consideration by the court. Draft Orders commonly made by the masters on allocation and at case management conferences are set out at Appendix 6, and parties drafting proposed directions for submission to a master on allocation or at a case management conference should have regard to and make use, as appropriate, of those Draft Orders.

3.4 If parties do not, at the allocation stage, agree or attempt to agree directions and if, in consequence, the court is unable to give directions without ordering a case management conference, the parties should not expect to recover any costs in respect of such a case management conference.

3.5 In many claims the court will give directions without holding a case management conference.

3.6 Any party who considers that a case management conference should be held before any directions are given should so state in his or her allocation questionnaire (or, in the case of a Part 8 claim, inform the court in writing) and give reasons why he or she considers that a case management conference is required. The court when sending out allocation questionnaires will also send out a questionnaire inviting the parties to give their time estimate for any case management conference and to specify any dates or times inconvenient for the holding of a case management conference.

3.7 Wherever possible, the advocate(s) instructed or expected to be instructed to appear at the trial should attend any hearing at which case management directions are likely to be given. To this end the court when ordering a case management conference, otherwise than upon allocation, will normally send out questionnaires to the parties in respect of their availability. Parties must not, however, expect that a case management conference will be held in abeyance for a substantial length of time in order to accommodate the advocates' convenience.

3.8 Case management conferences are intended to deal with the general management of the case. They are not an opportunity to make controversial interim applications without appropriate notice to the opposing party. Accordingly, as provided by paragraph 5.8(1) of PD29, where a party wishes to obtain an order not routinely made at a case management conference (such as an order for specific disclosure or summary disposal) such application should be made by separate Part 23 application to be heard at the case management conference and the case management conference should be listed for a sufficient period of time to allow the application to be heard. Where parties fail to comply with this paragraph it is highly unlikely that the court will entertain, other than by consent, an application which is not of a routine nature.

3.9 Even where routine orders are sought (ie orders falling within the topics set out in paragraph 5.3 of PD29) care should be taken to ensure that the opposing party is given notice of the orders intended to be sought.

Applications for information and disclosure

3.10 Before a party applies to the court for an order that another party provides him or her with any further information or specific disclosure of documents he or she must communicate directly with the other party in an attempt to reach agreement or narrow the issues before the matter is raised with the court. If not satisfied that the parties have taken steps to reach agreement or narrow the issues, the court will normally require such steps to be taken before hearing the application.

Preliminary issues

3.11 Costs can sometimes be saved by identifying decisive issues, or potentially decisive issues, and ordering that they are tried first. The decision of one issue, although not itself decisive in law of the whole case, may enable the parties to settle the remainder of the dispute. In such cases a preliminary issue may be appropriate.

3.12 At the allocation stage, at any case management conference and again at any PTR, consideration will be given to the possibility of the trial of preliminary issues the resolution of which is likely to shorten proceedings. The court may suggest the trial of a preliminary issue, but it will rarely make an order without the concurrence of at least one of the parties.

Group Litigation Orders

3.13 Under rule 19.11, where there are likely to be a number of claims giving rise to common or related issues of fact, the court may make a Group Litigation Order ('GLO') for their case management. Such orders may be appropriate in chancery proceedings and some have already been made. An application for a GLO is made under Part 23. The procedure is set out in PD19 Group Litigation, which provides that the application should be made to the Chief Master, except for claims in a specialist list (such as the business of the Patents Court), when the application should be made to the senior judge of that list.

3.14 Claimants wishing to join in group litigation should issue proceedings in the normal way and should then apply (by letter) to be entered on the Group Register set up by a GLO. The details required for entry will be specified in the GLO. The Register is maintained either by the management court or by the lead solicitors, as specified in the GLO. Where the Register is maintained in the Chancery Division at the Royal Courts of Justice, it is kept by Mrs VC Bell, Chancery Lawyer (Room 5.06, Thomas More Building, tel. 020 7947 6080). Any initial enquiries regarding GLO's may be addressed to her.

Trial timetable

3.15 The judge at trial, or sometimes at the PTR, may determine the timetable for the trial. The advocates for the parties should be ready to assist the court in this respect if so required. The time estimate given for the trial should have been based on an approximate forecast of the trial timetable, and must be reviewed by each party at the stage of the PTR and as preparation for trial proceeds thereafter. If that review requires a change in the estimate the other parties' advocates and the court must be informed.

3.16 When a trial timetable is set by the court, it will ordinarily fix the time for the oral submissions and factual and expert evidence, and it may do so in greater or lesser detail. Trial timetables are always subject to any further order by the trial judge.

Pre-Trial Review

3.17 In cases estimated to take more than 10 days and in other cases where the circumstances warrant it, the court may direct that a PTR be held (see rule 29.7).

3.18 Such a PTR will normally be heard by a judge. The date and time should be fixed with the Clerk of the Lists. If the trial judge has already been nominated, the application will if possible be heard by that judge. The advocates' clerks must attend the Clerk of the Lists in sufficient time so that the PTR can be fixed between 4 and 8 weeks before the trial date.

3.19 A PTR should be attended by advocates who are to represent the parties at the trial.

3.20 Not less than 7 days before the date fixed for the PTR the claimant, or another party if so directed by the court, must circulate a list of matters to be considered at the PTR, including proposals as to how the case should be tried, to the other parties, who must respond with their comments at least 2 days before the PTR.

3.21 The claimant, or another party if so directed by the court, should deliver a bundle containing the lists of matters to be considered and proposals served by the parties on each other and the trial timetable, together with the results of the discussions between the parties as to those matters, and any other documents the court is likely to need in order to deal with the PTR, to the Listing Office by 10 am on the day before the day fixed for the hearing of the PTR.

3.22 At the PTR the court will review the state of preparation of the case, and deal with outstanding procedural matters, not limited to those apparent from the lists of matters lodged by the parties. The court may give directions as to how the case is to be tried, including directions as to the order in which witnesses are to be called (for example all witnesses of fact before all expert witnesses) or as to the time to be allowed for particular stages in the trial.

Chapter 4 – Disclosure of Documents and Expert Evidence

Key Rules: CPR Parts 18, 29, 31 and 35; PDs supplementing Parts 31 and 35

4.1 As part of its management of a case, the court will give directions about the disclosure of documents and any expert evidence. Attention is drawn to paragraphs 3.8 to 3.10 above. An application for specific disclosure should be made by a specific Part 23 application and is not to be regarded as a matter routinely dealt with at a case management conference.

DISCLOSURE OF DOCUMENTS

4.2 Under the CPR, the normal order for disclosure is an order for standard disclosure, which requires disclosure of:

(1) **a party's own documents** – that is, the documents on which a party relies;
(2) **adverse documents** – that is, documents which adversely affect his or her own or another party's case or support another party's case; and
(3) **required documents** – that is, documents which a practice direction requires him or her to disclose.

4.3 The court may make an order for specific disclosure going beyond the limits of standard disclosure if it is satisfied that standard disclosure is inadequate.

4.4 The court will not make such an order readily. One of the clear principles underlying the CPR is that the burden and cost of disclosure should be reduced. The court will, therefore, seek to ensure that any specific disclosure ordered is proportionate in the sense that the cost of such disclosure does not outweigh the benefits to be obtained from such disclosure. The court will, accordingly, seek to tailor the order for disclosure to the requirements of the particular case. The financial position of the parties, the importance of the case and the complexity of the issues will be taken into account when considering whether more than standard disclosure should be ordered.

4.5 If specific disclosure is sought, the parties should give careful thought to the ways in which such disclosure can be limited, for example by requiring disclosure in stages or by requiring disclosure simply of sufficient documents to show a specified matter and so on. They should also consider whether the need for disclosure could be avoided by requiring a party to provide information under Part 18.

EXPERT EVIDENCE

General

4.6 Part 35 contains particular provisions designed to limit the amount of expert evidence to be placed before the court and to reinforce the obligation of impartiality which is imposed upon an expert witness.

4.7 Fundamentally, Part 35 states that expert evidence must be restricted to what is reasonably required to resolve the proceedings and makes provision for the court to direct that expert evidence is given by a single joint expert. The key question now in relation to expert evidence is the question as to what added value such evidence will provide to the court in its determination of a given case.

Duties of an expert

4.8 It is the duty of an expert to help the court on the matters within his or her expertise; this duty overrides any obligation to the person from whom the expert has received instructions or by whom he or she is paid (rule 35.3). Attention is drawn to PD35.

4.9 In fulfilment of this duty, an expert must for instance make it clear if a particular question or issue falls outside his or her expertise or he or she considers that insufficient data is available on which to express an opinion. Any material change of view by an expert should be communicated in writing (through legal representatives) to the other parties without delay, and when appropriate to the court.

Single joint expert

4.10 The introduction to PD35 states that, where possible, matters requiring expert evidence should be dealt with by a single expert.

4.11 In very many cases it is possible for the question of expert evidence to be dealt with by a single expert. Single experts are, for example, often appropriate to deal with questions of quantum in cases where the primary issues are as to liability. Likewise, where expert evidence is required in order to acquaint the court with matters of expert fact, as opposed to opinion, a single expert will usually be appropriate. There remains, however, a substantial body of cases where liability will turn upon expert opinion evidence or where quantum is a primary issue and where it will be appropriate for the parties to instruct their own experts. For example, in cases where the issue for determination is as to whether a party acted in accordance with proper professional standards, it will often be of value to the court to hear the opinions of more than one expert as to the proper standard in order that the court becomes acquainted with the range of views existing upon the question and in order that the evidence can be tested in cross-examination.

4.12 It is not necessarily a sufficient objection to the making by the court of an order for a single joint expert that the parties have already appointed their own experts. An order for a single joint expert does not prevent a party from having his or her own expert to advise him or her, but he or she may well be unable to recover the cost of employing his or her own expert from the other party. The duty of an expert who is called to give evidence is to help the court.

4.13 When the use of a single joint expert is contemplated the court will expect the parties to co-operate in developing, and agreeing to the greatest possible extent, terms of reference for the expert. In most cases the terms of reference will (in particular) detail what the expert is asked to do, identify any documentary material he or she is asked to consider and specify any assumptions he or she is asked to make.

More than one expert – exchange of reports

4.14 In an appropriate case the court will direct that experts' reports are delivered sequentially. Sequential reports may, for example, be appropriate if the service of the first expert's report would help to define and limit the issues on which such evidence may be relevant.

Discussion between experts

4.15 The court will normally direct discussion between experts before trial. Sometimes it may be useful for there to be further discussions during the trial itself. The purpose of these discussions is to give the experts the opportunity:

(1) to discuss the expert issues; and
(2) to identify the expert issues on which they share the same opinion and those on which there remains a difference of opinion between them (and what that difference is).

4.16 Unless the court otherwise directs, the procedure to be adopted at these discussions is a matter for the experts. It may be sufficient if the discussion takes place by telephone.

4.17 Parties must not seek to restrict their expert's participation in any discussion directed by the court, but they are not bound by any agreement on any issue reached by their expert unless they expressly so agree.

Written questions to experts

4.18 It is emphasised that this procedure is only for the purpose (generally) of seeking clarification of an expert's report where the other party is unable to understand it. Written questions going beyond this can only be put with the agreement of the parties or with the permission of the court. The procedure of putting written questions to experts is not intended to interfere with the procedure for an exchange of professional opinion in discussions between experts or to inhibit that exchange of professional opinion. If questions that are oppressive in number or content are put or questions are put without permission for any purpose other than clarification of an expert's report, the court will not hesitate to disallow the questions and to make an appropriate order for costs against the party putting them.

Request by an expert to the court for directions

4.19 An expert may file with the court a written request for directions to assist him or her in carrying out his or her function as expert: rule 35.14. Copies of any such request must be provided to the parties in accordance with rule 35.14(2) save where the court orders otherwise. The expert should guard against accidentally informing the court about, or about matters connected with, communications or potential communications between the parties that are without prejudice or privileged. The expert may properly be privy to the content of these communications because he or she has been asked to assist the party instructing him or her to evaluate them.

Assessors

4.20 Under rule 35.15 the court may appoint an assessor to assist it in relation to any matter in which the assessor has skill and experience. The report of the assessor is made available to the parties. The remuneration of the assessor is determined by the court and forms part of the costs of the proceedings.

Chapter 5 – Applications

Key Rules: CPR Parts 23 and 25, PDs 23 and 25

5.1 This Chapter deals with applications to a judge, including applications for interim remedies, and applications to a master. As regards the practical arrangements for making, listing and adjourning applications, the Chapter is primarily concerned with hearings at the Royal Courts of Justice. Hearings before Chancery judges outside London are dealt with in Chapter 12.

5.2 Only applications which need to be heard by a judge (eg most applications for an injunction) should be made to a judge. Any procedural application (eg for directions) should be made to a master unless there is some special reason for making it to a judge. Otherwise the application may be dismissed with costs. If an application is to be made to a judge, the application notice should state that it is a judge's application.

5.3 Part 23 contains rules as to how an application may be made. In some circumstances it may be dealt with without a hearing, or by a telephone hearing.

Applications without notice

5.4 Generally it is wrong to make an application without giving prior notice to the respondent. There are, however, two classes of exceptions.

(1) First, there are cases where the giving of notice might frustrate the order (eg a search order) or where there is such urgency that there has not been time to give notice. Even in an urgent case, however, the applicant should notify the respondent informally of the application if possible, unless secrecy is essential.

(2) Secondly, there are in the Chancery Division some procedural applications normally made without notice relating to such matters as service out of the jurisdiction, service, extension of the validity of claim forms, permission to issue writs of possession etc. All of these are properly made without notice but will be subjected by the rules to an express provision in any order made that the absent party will be entitled to apply to set aside or vary the order provided that application is so made within a given number of days of service of the order.

An application made without giving notice which does not fall within the classes of cases where absence of notice is justified may be dismissed or adjourned until proper notice has been given.

Applications without a hearing

5.5 Part 23 makes provision for applications to be dealt with without a hearing. This is a useful provision in cases where the parties consent to the terms of the order sought or agree that a hearing is not necessary (often putting in written representations by letter or otherwise). It is also a useful provision in cases where, although the parties have not agreed to dispense with a hearing and the order is not consented to, the order sought by the application is, essentially, non-contentious. In such circumstances, the order made will, in any event, be treated as being made on the court's own initiative and will set out the right of any party affected by the application who has not been heard to apply to vary or set aside the order.

5.6 These provisions should not be used to deal with contentious matters without notice to the opposing party and without a hearing. Usually, this will result in delay since the court will simply order a hearing. It may also give rise to adverse costs orders. It will normally be wrong to seek an order which imposes sanctions in the event of non-compliance without notice and without a hearing. An application seeking such an order may well be dismissed.

Applications to a judge

5.7 If an application is made to a judge in existing proceedings, eg for an injunction, it should be made by application notice. This is called an Interim Application. Normally 3 clear days' notice to the other party is required but in an emergency or for other good reason the application can be made without giving notice, or the full 3 days' notice, to the other side. Permission to serve on short notice may be obtained on application without notice to the interim applications judge. Such permission will not be given by the master. Except in an emergency a party notifies the court of his or her wish to bring an application by delivering the requisite documents to the Listing Office and paying the appropriate fee. He or she should at the same time deliver a completed 'Judge's Application Information Form' in the form set out in Part 1 of Appendix 5. An application will only be listed if (1) two copies of the Claim Form and (2) two copies of the application notice (one stamped with the appropriate fee) are lodged in the Listing Office (Room WG4 Royal Courts of Justice) before 12 noon on the working day before the date for which notice of the application has been given.

5.8 An Interim Application, other than in the Patents Court, need not state the name of the judge to whom the application is to be made. It is sufficient to state the 'interim applications judge' or, in the case of an application in the Companies Court, 'the companies judge'. The current practice is that one judge combines the functions of interim applications judge and companies judge. His or her name will be found in the Daily Cause List and also in the Chancery Division Term List.

5.9 The interim applications judge is available to hear applications each day in term and an application notice can be served for any day in term except the last. If the volume of applications requires it, any other judge who is available to assist with Interim Applications will hear such applications as the interim applications judge may direct. Special arrangements are made for hearing applications out of hours and in vacation, for which see paras 5.28 to 5.34 below.

5.10 At the beginning of each day's hearing the interim applications judge calls on each of the applications to be made that day in turn. This enables him or her to establish the identity of the parties, their state of readiness, their estimates of the duration of the hearing, and where relevant the degree of urgency of the case. On completion of this process, the judge decides the order in which he or she will hear applications and gives any other directions that may be necessary. Sometimes cases are released to other judges at this point. If cases are likely to take 2 hours or more, the judge usually orders that they are given a subsequent fixed date for hearing (they are then called 'Interim Applications by Order') and hears any application for a court order to last until the application is heard fully.

5.11 In such a case the solicitors or the clerks to counsel concerned should apply to the Chancery Listing Officer for a date for the hearing. Before so doing there must be lodged with the Chancery Listing Office a certificate signed by the advocate stating the estimated length of the hearing. Applications by order may be entered in the Interim Hearings List and, if not fixed by arrangement with the Chancery Listing Officer, will be liable to be listed for hearing in accordance with the timetable fixed by the judge.

5.12 Parties and their representatives should arrive at least ten minutes before the court sits. This will assist the usher to take a note of the names of those proposing to address the court and of their estimate of the hearing time. This information is given to the judge before he or she sits. Parties should also allow time before the court sits to agree any form of order with any other party if this has not already been done. If the form of the order is not agreed before the court sits, the parties may have to wait until there is a convenient break in the list before they can ask the court to make any agreed order. If an application, not being an Interim Application by Order, is adjourned the Associate in attendance will notify the Chancery Listing Office of the day to which it has been adjourned and the Listing Office will list the application for that day.

Agreed Adjournment of Interim Applications

5.13 If all parties to an Interim Application agree, it can be adjourned for not more than 14 days by counsel or solicitors attending the Chancery Listing Officer in Room WG4 at any time before 4 pm on the day before the hearing of the application and producing consents signed by solicitors or counsel for all parties agreeing to the adjournment. A litigant in person must attend before the Listing Officer as well as signing a consent. This procedure may not be used for more than three successive adjournments and no adjournment may be made by this procedure to the last 2 days of any sitting.

Interim Applications by Order by agreement

5.14 This procedure should also be used where the parties agree that the hearing of the application will take 2 hours or more and that, in consequence, the application should be adjourned to be heard as an Interim Application by Order. In that event, the consents set out above should also contain an agreed timetable for the filing of evidence or confirmation that no further evidence is to be filed. Any application arising from the failure of a party to abide by the timetable and any application to extend the timetable must be made to the judge. Interim Applications by Order will, initially at least, enter the Interim Hearings warned list on the first Monday after close of evidence.

5.15 Undertakings given to the court may be continued unchanged over any adjournment. If, however, on an adjournment an undertaking is to be varied or a new undertaking given then that must be dealt with by the court.

The duty of disclosure

5.16 On all applications made in the absence of the respondent the applicant and his or her legal representatives owe a duty to the court to disclose fully all matters relevant to the application, including matters, whether of fact or law, which are, or may be, adverse to it. If there is a failure to comply with this duty and an order is made, the court may subsequently set aside the order on that ground alone. The disclosure, if made orally, must be confirmed by witness statement or affidavit. The representatives for the applicant must specifically direct the court to passages in the evidence which disclose matters adverse to the application.

5.17 A party wishing to apply urgently to a judge for remedies without notice to the Respondent must notify the clerk to the interim applications judge by telephone (the number will be set out in the Daily Cause List). Where such an urgent application is made, two copies of the order sought and an electronic copy on disk (in Word for Windows) and a completed Judge's Application Information Form in the form in Part 1 of Appendix 5 should, where possible, be included with the papers handed to the judge's clerk. Where an application is very urgent and the interim applications judge is unable to hear it promptly, it may be heard by any judge who is available, though the request for this must be made to the clerk to the interim applications judge, or, in default, to the Chancery Listing Officer. Every effort should be made to issue the claim form before the application is made. If this is not practicable, the party making the application must give an undertaking to the court to issue the claim form forthwith even if the court makes no order, unless the court orders otherwise. A party making an urgent application must ensure that all necessary fees are paid.

Freezing Injunctions and Search Orders

5.18 The grant of freezing injunctions (both domestic and world-wide) and search orders is a staple feature of the work of the interim applications judge. Applications for such orders are invariably made without notice in the first instance; and in a proper case the court will sit in private in order to hear them. Where such an application is to be listed, two copies of the order sought, together with the application notice, should be lodged with the Chancery Listing Office. If the application is to be made in private, it will be listed as 'Application without notice' without naming the parties. The judge will consider, in each case, whether publicity might defeat the object of the hearing and, if so, may hear the application in private.

5.19 Freezing injunctions and search orders are never granted as a matter of course. A strong case must be made out, and applications need to be prepared with great care. The application should always be accompanied by a draft of the order which the court is to be invited to make.

Period for which an injunction or an order appointing a receiver is granted if the application was without notice

5.20 When an application for an injunction is heard without notice, and the judge decides that an injunction should be granted, it will normally be granted for a limited period only – usually not more than 7 days. The same applies to an interim order appointing a receiver. The applicant will be required to give the respondent notice of his or her intention to apply to the court at the expiration of that period for the order to be continued. In the meantime the respondent will be entitled to apply, though generally only after giving notice to the applicant, for the order to be varied or discharged.

Opposed applications without notice

5.21 These are applications of which proper notice has not been given to the respondents but which are made in the presence of both parties in advance of a full hearing of the application. The judge may impose time limits on the parties if, having regard to the pressure of business or for any other reason, he or she considers it appropriate to do so. On these applications, the judge may, in an appropriate case, make an order which will have effect until trial or further order as if proper notice had been given.

Implied cross-undertakings in damages where undertakings are given to the court

5.22 Often the party against whom an injunction is sought gives to the court an undertaking which avoids the need for the court to grant the injunction. In these cases, there is an implied undertaking in damages by the party applying for the injunction in favour of the other. The position is less clear where the party applying for the injunction also gives an undertaking to the court. The parties should consider and, if necessary, raise with the judge whether the party in whose favour the undertaking is given must give a cross-undertaking in damages in those circumstances.

Orders on applications

5.23 The judge may direct the parties to agree, sign and deliver to the court a statement of the terms of the order made by the court (commonly still referred to as a minute of order), particularly where complex undertakings are given.

Consents by parties not attending hearing

5.24 It is commonly the case that on an Interim Application the respondent does not appear either in person or by solicitors or counsel but the applicant seeks a consent order based upon a letter of consent from the respondent or his or her solicitors or a draft statement of agreed terms signed by the respondent's solicitors. This causes no difficulty where the agreed relief falls wholly within the relief claimed in the application notice.

5.25 If, however, the agreed relief goes outside that which is claimed in the application notice or even in the Claim Form or when undertakings are offered then difficulties can arise. A procedure has been established for this purpose to be applied to all applications in the Chancery Division.

5.26 Subject always to the discretion of the court, no order will be made in such cases unless a consent signed by or on behalf of the respondent to an application is put before the court in accordance with the following provisions:

(1) Where there are solicitors on the record for the respondent the court will normally accept as sufficient a written consent signed by those solicitors on their headed notepaper.

(2) Where there are solicitors for the respondent who are not on the record, the court will normally accept as sufficient a written consent signed by those solicitors on their headed notepaper only if in the consent (or some other document) the solicitors certify that they have fully

explained to the respondent the effect of the order and that the respondent appeared to have understood the explanation.

(3) Where there is a written consent signed by a respondent acting in person the court will not normally accept it as sufficient unless the court is satisfied that the respondent understands the effect of the order either by reason of the circumstances (for example the respondent is himself a solicitor or barrister) or by means of other material (for example, the respondent's consent is given in reply to a letter explaining in simple terms the effect of the order).

(4) Where the respondent offers any undertaking to the court (a) the document containing the undertaking must be signed by the respondent personally, (b) solicitors must certify on their headed notepaper that the signature is that of the respondent and (c) if the case falls within (2) or (3) above, solicitors must certify that they have explained to the respondent the consequences of giving the undertaking and that the respondent appeared to understand the explanation.

Bundles and Skeleton Arguments

5.27 See Chapter 7

Out of hours emergency arrangements

5.28 An application should not be made out of hours unless it is essential. An explanation will be required as to why it was not made or could not be made during normal court hours. Applications made during legal vacations must also constitute vacation business.

5.29 There is always a Chancery judge available to hear urgent out of hours applications. The following is a summary of the procedure:

(1) All requests for the duty Chancery judge to hear urgent matters are to be made through the judge's clerk. There may be occasions when the duty judge is not immediately available. The clerk will be able to inform the applicant of the judge's likely availability.

(2) Initial contact should be through the Security Office at the Royal Courts of Justice (tel: 020 7947 6260), who should be requested to contact the duty Chancery judge's clerk. The applicant must give a telephone number for the return call.

(3) When the clerk contacts the applicant, he or she will need to know:
   (a) the name of the party on whose behalf the application is to be made;
   (b) the name of the person who is to make the application and his or her status (counsel or solicitor);
   (c) the nature of the application;
   (d) the degree of urgency;
   (e) the contact telephone numbers.

(4) The duty judge will indicate to his or her clerk whether he or she is prepared to deal with the matter by telephone or whether it will be necessary for the matter to be dealt with by a hearing, in court or elsewhere. The clerk will inform the applicant and make the necessary arrangements.

(5) Applications for interim remedies will (normally) be heard by telephone only where the applicant is represented by counsel or solicitors (PD25, Interim Injunctions, paragraph 4.5). If, however, an applicant not so represented indicates reasons why, exceptionally, the application should be heard by telephone, the judge may require that the applicant be attended by a responsible person who can confirm the identity of the applicant and the accuracy of what is said: see PD23 paragraphs 6.3 and 8. If satisfied that it is really necessary, the judge may grant an injunction on such an application, but it is likely to be granted for as short a time as possible pending a hearing on notice to the Respondent.

5.30 Which judge will, in appropriate cases, hear an out of hours application varies according to when the application is made.

(1) *Weekdays*. Out of hours duty, during term time, is the responsibility of the applications judge. He or she is normally available from 4.15 pm until 10.15 am Monday to Thursday.

(2) *Weekends*. A Chancery Division judge is nominated by rota for weekends, commencing 4.15 pm Friday until 10.15 am Monday.

(3) *Vacation*. The vacation judge also undertakes out of hours applications.

5.31 *Sealing orders out of hours*. In normal circumstances it is not possible to issue a sealed order out of hours. The judge may direct the applicant to lodge a draft of the order made at Chancery Chambers Registry by 10 am on the following working day.

5.32 *County court matters*. Similar arrangements exist for making urgent applications out of hours in county court matters in certain parts of England and Wales. Contact with the circuit judge on duty for the London County Courts can be made through the Security Office of the Royal Courts of Justice.

Vacation arrangements

5.33 There is a Chancery judge available to hear applications in vacation. Applications must generally constitute vacation business in that, in particular, they require to be immediately or promptly heard. Special arrangements exist, however, in the Companies Court for certain schemes of arrangement and reductions of capital to be heard in the long vacation (see para 8 of PD49 – Applications under the Companies Act 1985).

5.34 In the long vacation, the vacation judge sits each day to hear vacation business. In other vacations there are no regular sittings. Mondays and Thursdays are made available for urgent Interim Applications on notice. The judge is available on the remaining days for urgent business.

Applications to a master

5.35 Applications to a master should be made by application notice. Application notices are issued by the masters' clerks in Room TM7.09. If the master has directed a case management conference the parties should ensure that all applications in the proceedings are listed to be heard at the case management conference. It is the duty of the parties to seek to agree directions if possible and to provide a draft of the order for consideration by the master.

5.36 Applications to a master estimated to last in excess of 2 hours require the master's directions before they are listed. The master will normally give his permission to list such an application on condition that there is compliance with directions given by the master. Those directions are likely to require that the applicant agrees the time estimate with his opponent and that, if the time allowed subsequently becomes insufficient, the court is informed and a new and longer appointment given; that the parties agree an appropriate timetable for filing evidence such that the hearing will be effective on the date listed; that positive confirmation is to be given to the master 5 working days before the hearing date that the hearing remains effective; and, in the event of settlement, that the master be informed of that fact. The agreed time estimate must take into account not only the hearing time of the application but the time for the master to give any judgment at the conclusion of the hearing. It should also take into account any further time that may be required for the master to assess costs, and for any application for permission to appeal.

5.37 Failure to comply with the master's directions given in respect of the listing of an appointment in excess of 2 hours may result, depending upon the circumstances, in the application being struck out or in adverse costs orders being made.

5.38 On any matter of substance, the master will require a bundle and skeleton arguments to be provided before the hearing (see paragraphs 7.39 to 45 below). Where directions are given in respect of an application to which paragraph 5.36 applies, the provision of a bundle and skeleton arguments should form part of the agreed timetable.

5.39 The masters may also allow applications to be made to them informally. However applications by letter should not be used in place of a Part 23 application, and parties should be careful to limit any correspondence with the masters to a minimum and to ensure that opposing parties receive copies of any correspondence. Failure in this regard is likely to mean that the master will refuse to deal with the correspondence.

5.40 There is no distinction between term time and vacation so far as business before the Chancery masters is concerned. They will deal with all types of business throughout the year; when a master is on holiday, his or her list will normally be taken by a deputy master.

Chapter 6 – Listing Arrangements

Key Rules: CPR Parts 29 and 39

6.1 This Chapter deals with listing arrangements for hearings before judges and masters in the Royal Courts of Justice.

HEARINGS BEFORE JUDGES

Responsibility for listing

6.2 The Clerk of the Lists (Room WG3, Royal Courts of Justice) has overall responsibility for listing. Day-by-day management of Chancery listing is dealt with by the Chancery Listing Officer (Room WG4, Royal Courts of Justice). All applications relating to listing should, in the first instance, be made to the Chancery Listing Officer, who will refer matters, as necessary, to the Clerk of the Lists. Any party dissatisfied with any decision of the Clerk of the Lists may, on 1 clear day's notice to all other parties, apply to the judge in charge of the list. Any such application should be made within 7 days of the decision of the Clerk of the Lists and be arranged through the Chancery Listing Office.

6.3 There are three main lists in the Chancery Division: the Trial List, the General List and the Interim Hearings List. In addition there is a separate Patents List which is controlled by the judge in charge of the Patents List (see Chapter 23).

The Trial List

6.4 This comprises a list of all trials to be heard with witnesses.

The Interim Hearings List

6.5 This list comprises interim applications and appeals from masters.

The General List

6.6 This list comprises other matters including revenue, bankruptcy and pension appeals, Part 8 proceedings, applications for judgment and all company matters.

6.7 The procedure for listing Chancery cases to be heard in the Royal Courts of Justice and listed in the Trial List is that at an early stage in the claim the court will give directions with a view to fixing the period during which the case will be heard. In a Part 7 claim that period (the Trial Window) will be determined by the court either when the case is allocated or subsequently at any case management conference or other directions hearing. In a Part 8 claim covered by this procedure, that is to say a Part 8 claim to be heard with witnesses, similar directions will be given when the Part 8 claim is listed for preliminary directions or for a case management conference. It is only in a small minority of Part 8 claims that the claim is tried by a judge in the Trial List and the Trial Window procedure applies. The bulk of Part 8 claims are heard on written evidence either by the master or by the judge. Additionally, many Part 8 claims, even where oral evidence is to be called, will be heard by the master pursuant to the jurisdiction set out in para 4.1 of PD2 Allocation of Cases to Levels of Judiciary.

6.8 In determining the Trial Window the court will have regard to the listing constraints created by the existing court list and will determine a Trial Window which provides the parties with enough time to complete their preparations for trial. A Trial Window, once fixed, will not readily be altered. When determining the Trial Window the court will direct that one party, normally the claimant, makes an appointment to attend on the Listing Officer (Room WG4, Royal Courts of Justice) to fix a trial date within the Trial Window, by such date as may be specified in the order and gives notice of that appointment to all other parties. When fixing the Trial Window the court will normally dispense with the requirement of a listing questionnaire unless the Listing Officer, when fixing the trial date, directs otherwise.

6.9 At the listing appointment, the Listing Officer will take account, insofar as it is practical to do so, of any difficulties the parties may have as to the availability of counsel, experts and witnesses. The Listing Officer will, nevertheless, try to ensure the speedy disposal of the trial by arranging a firm trial date as soon as possible within the Trial Window. If a Case Summary has been prepared (see PD29 paras 5.6 and 5.7) the claimant must produce a copy at the listing appointment together with a copy of the particulars of claim and any orders relevant to the fixing of the trial date. If, exceptionally, at the listing appointment, it appears to the Listing Officer that a trial date cannot be provided by the court within the trial window, the Listing Officer may fix the trial date outside the Trial Window at the first available date.

6.10 A party wishing to appeal a date allocated by the Listing Officer must, within 7 days of the allocation, make an application to the judge nominated to hear such applications. The application notice should be filed in the Listing Office and served, giving 1 clear day's notice to the other parties.

6.11 A trial date once fixed will, like a Trial Window, only rarely be altered or vacated. An application to adjourn a trial date will normally be made to the judge nominated to hear such applications (see further para 7.38). Such an application will however be entertained by the master if, for example, on the hearing of an interim application or case management conference it becomes clear that the trial date cannot stand without injustice to one or both parties.

Warned List – General and Interim Hearings Lists

6.12 On each Friday of term and on such other days as may be appropriate, the Clerk of the Lists will publish a Warned List, showing the matters that are liable to be heard in the following week. Any matters for which no date has been arranged will be liable to appear in the list for hearing with no warning save that given by the next day's list of cases, posted each afternoon outside Room WG4. Where a case is listed in the Warned List, the parties may agree to offer the case for a specified date, in accordance with the statement of Listing Office practice on offering cases issued by the Clerk of the Lists.

Estimate of duration

6.13 If after a case is listed the estimated length of the hearing is varied, or if the case is settled, withdrawn or discontinued, the solicitors for the parties must forthwith inform the Chancery Listing Officer in writing. Failure so to do may result in an adverse costs order being made. If the case is settled but the parties wish the master to make a consent order, the solicitor must notify the Chancery Listing Officer in writing, whereupon he or she will take the case out of the list and notify the master. The master may then make the consent order.

6.14 Seven days before the date for the hearing, the claimant's solicitors must inform the Chancery Listing Officer whether there is any variation in the estimate of duration, and, in particular, whether the case is likely to be disposed of in some summary way. If the claimant is a litigant in person, this must be done by the solicitor for the first-named defendant who has instructed a solicitor. If a summary disposal is likely, the solicitor must keep the Chancery Listing Officer informed of any developments as soon as they occur.

Applications after listing

6.15 After a case has been listed, any application in the case should be made to the interim applications judge if a hearing before a master cannot be obtained in time for this not to delay the hearing of the case. Parties should not list an application before the interim applications judge without first consulting the masters' clerks as to the availability of the master or, in an appropriate case, applying to the master himself. Provision can sometimes be made for urgent applications to be dealt with by the Chief Master or a deputy (see further para 6.28).

Daily list of cases

6.16 This list, known as the Daily Cause List, is available on the Court Service website: *www.courtservice.gov.uk*.

Listing of Particular Business

6.17 Appeals from masters

Appeals from masters, where permission has been given, will appear in the Interim Hearings List. Such appeals (stamped with the appropriate fee) must be lodged with the Clerk of the Lists' Office in Room WG7. On being satisfied that the case has been placed in the Warned List, solicitors should forthwith inform the Chancery Listing Officer whether they intend to instruct counsel and, if so, the name or names of counsel.

6.18 Applications for permission to appeal from masters

Applications for permission to appeal from a decision of a master (stamped with the appropriate fee) must be lodged in the Clerk of the Lists' Office in Room WG7. If permission to appeal is granted the appeal will appear in the Interim Hearings List and the procedure set out above will apply.

6.19 Bankruptcy Appeals

Notice of appeal from the decision of a registrar or of a county court should be lodged in Room TM2.11. The appeal will be entered in the General List, usually with a fixed date. The date of the hearing will be fixed by the Chancery Listing Officer in the usual way.

6.20 Bankruptcy Applications

All originating and ordinary applications to the judge should be lodged with the Deputy Court Manager in Bankruptcy. Urgent applications without notice for (i) the committal of any person to prison for contempt or (ii) injunctions or the modification or discharge of injunctions will be passed directly to the clerk to the interim applications judge for hearing by that judge. All applications on notice for (i) and (ii) above, and applications referred to the judge by the registrar, will be listed by the Chancery Listing Officer. Applications estimated not to exceed 2 hours will be heard by the interim applications judge. The Listing Officer is to give at least 3 clear days' notice of the hearing to the applicant and to any respondent who attended before the registrar. Applications over 2 hours will be heard on a fixed or floating date by such judges as are available.

6.21 Companies Court

Matters for hearing before the companies judge, such as petitions for an administration order under Part II of the Insolvency Act 1986, petitions for approval by the court of schemes of arrangement and applications for the appointment of provisional liquidators, may be issued for hearing on any day of the week in term time (other than the last day of each term) and will be dealt with by the interim applications judge as companies judge. Applications or petitions which are estimated to exceed 2 hours are liable to be stood over to a date to be fixed by the Chancery Listing Officer. Urgent applications will also be dealt with by the interim applications judge. Applications and petitions referred to the judge by the registrar will be placed in the General List and listed accordingly.

6.22 Applications referred to the judge

Applications referred by the master to the judge will be added to the Interim Hearings List. The power to refer applications made to the master and in respect of which the master has jurisdiction is now very sparingly exercised. The proper use of judicial resources dictates that where the master has jurisdiction in respect of an interlocutory matter he should ordinarily exercise that jurisdiction.

6.23 Judge's Applications

Reference should be made to Chapter 5.

6.24 Revenue Appeals

Appeals will be entered in the General List, usually with fixed dates, and will be heard by such judges as are available. The dates for hearing are settled in the usual way on application to the Chancery Listing Officer. Where it would assist counsel and solicitor with their other commitments, the Chancery Listing Officer, if requested, will endeavour to fix two or more revenue appeals so that they will come on consecutively.

6.25 Short Applications

An application for judgment in default made to a judge (because the master has no jurisdiction) should be made to the interim applications judge.

6.26 Summary Judgment

Where an application for summary judgment includes an application for an injunction, it usually has to be made to a judge because in most cases the master cannot grant an injunction save in terms agreed by the parties. In such cases the application should be made returnable before the judge instead of the master and will be listed in the General List. The return date to be inserted in the application notice should be a Monday at least 14 clear days after the application notice has been served. The application notice should be issued in the Chancery Listing Office (Room WG4) when there must be lodged two copies of the application notice and the witness statements or affidavits in support together with their exhibits. On the return date the application will normally be adjourned to a date to be fixed if the hearing is likely to take longer than thirty minutes. The adjourned date will be fixed in the usual way through the Chancery Listing Officer, and a certificate signed by an advocate as to the estimated length of the hearing must be lodged with the Chancery Listing Officer.

6.27 Variation of Trusts: Application to a judge

Applications under the Variation of Trusts Act 1958 for a hearing before the judge may be listed for hearing in the General List without any direction by a master on the lodgment in Room WG4 of a certificate signed by advocates for all the parties, stating (i) that the evidence is complete and has been filed; (ii) that the application is ready for hearing and (iii) the estimated length of the hearing.

HEARINGS BEFORE MASTERS

Assignment of cases before masters

6.28 The general rule is that cases are assigned to the masters in accordance with the last digit of the claim number. At present cases are allocated as follows:

0 and 1	Master Bragge	6 and 7	Master Price
2 and 3	Master Bowman	8 and 9	Master Moncaster
4 and 5	Master Bowles		

In view of other commitments, the Chief Master does not take assigned cases. He will take individual cases or classes of case in his own discretion and arrangements will be made accordingly through the Court Manager. Applications by the Official Solicitor under rule 21.12 to be appointed a guardian of a minor's estate are normally dealt with by the Chief Master, as are joint applications by a landlord and a tenant under rule 56.2(4) to authorise an agreement under section 38(4) of the Landlord and Tenant Act 1954. All applications for a Group Litigation Order in the Chancery Division have to be made to the Chief Master: see para 3.13.

Where matters require to be heard at short notice, because, for example, of an imminent trial date but where the assigned master's list is already full, arrangements can often be made for the matter to be listed before the Chief Master. In such a case application should first be made to the assigned master, who will determine whether the case is one which is appropriate to release to the Chief Master.

6.29 An important exception to the general rule is that all registered trade mark claims are assigned to Master Bragge. Practitioners must, therefore, ensure, both at the date of issue of proceedings and when any application is to be made, that the court staff are aware that the claim is a registered trade mark claim and that, irrespective of the claim number, the claim and any application in the claim is assigned to and should be listed before Master Bragge. Each month in term time a day is set aside in Master Bragge's list specifically for applications in trade mark claims and practitioners should, if possible, seek to have applications listed on that day. If the provisions of this paragraph are ignored and an application in a registered trade mark claim is listed other than before Master Bragge, it is likely that the Master before whom it is listed will refuse to hear it.

6.30 In addition, from time to time, the Chief Master assigns particular classes of case to particular masters. This will normally relate to managed litigation where the particular parties will be aware that their cases have been specifically assigned.

Oral applications without notice to the masters

6.31 Masters are normally available to hear oral applications without notice between 2.15 pm and 2.45 pm on working days. Notice should be given to the master's clerk in Room TM7.09, or by telephone or fax, by 4.30 pm on the previous day (except in cases of real emergency when notice may be given at any time) so that the file will be before the master. If this procedure is not followed the master may well refuse to deal with the application.

6.32 If the assigned master is not available on any particular day, the applicant will be informed and (except in cases of emergency) asked to come when the assigned master is next available. Applications will only be heard by another master in cases of emergency or when the assigned master is on vacation.

6.33 See also Chapter 5, paragraphs 5.35 to 40 (Applications to Masters).

Chapter 7 – Preparation for Hearings

Key Rules: CPR Parts 29 and 39

7.1 This Chapter contains guidance on the preparation of cases for hearings before judges and masters. Guidelines about the conduct of trials are given in Chapter 8 of this Guide. When an affidavit or witness statement (or other document) is filed in Chancery Chambers in preparation for a hearing or for any other purpose, it should be accompanied by a written evidence lodgment form as set out in Part 2 of Appendix 5, unless it accompanies an application notice. The preparation of witness statements is covered in Chapter 8.

HEARINGS BEFORE JUDGES

7.2 To ensure court time is used efficiently there must be adequate preparation of cases prior to the hearing. This covers, among other things, the preparation and exchange of skeleton arguments, compiling bundles of documents and dealing out of court with queries which need not concern the court. The parties should also use their best endeavours to agree before any hearing what are the issues or the main issues.

Estimates

7.3 Realistic estimates of the length of time a hearing is expected to take must be given.

7.4 In estimating the length of a hearing, sufficient time must be allowed for reading any documents required to be read, the length of the speeches, the time required to examine witnesses (if any), and, if appropriate, an immediate judgment, together with the summary assessment of costs, in cases where that may arise, and any application for permission to appeal.

7.5 Except as mentioned below, a written estimate signed by the advocates for all the parties is required in the case of any hearing before a judge. This should be delivered to the Chancery Listing Officer:

(1) in the case of a trial, on the application to fix the trial date; and
(2) in any other case, as soon as possible after the application notice or case papers have been lodged with the Listing Office.

7.6 If the estimate given in the application notice for an application to the interim applications judge (other than applications by order) or for an application listed before the companies judge requires to be revised, the revised estimate should be given to the court orally when the application is called on.

Changes in Estimate

7.7 The parties must inform the court immediately of any material change in a time estimate. They should keep each other informed of any such change. In any event a further time estimate signed by the advocates to the parties must be lodged when bundles are lodged (see paragraph 7.17 below).

Inaccurate estimates

7.8 Where estimates prove inaccurate, a hearing may have to be adjourned to a later date and the party responsible for the adjournment is likely to be ordered to pay the costs thrown away.

Bundles

7.9 Bundles of documents for use in court will generally be required for all hearings if more than 25 pages are involved (and may be appropriate even if fewer pages are involved). The efficient preparation of bundles of documents is very important. Where bundles have been properly prepared, the case will be easier to understand and present, and time and costs are likely to be saved. Where documents are copied unnecessarily or bundled incompetently the cost may be disallowed.

7.10 Where the provisions of this Guide as to the preparation or delivery of bundles are not followed, the bundle may be rejected by the court or be made the subject of a special costs order.

7.11 The claimant or applicant (as the case may be) should begin his or her preparation of the bundles in sufficient time to enable:

(1) the bundles to be agreed with the other parties (so far as possible);
(2) references to the bundles to be used in skeleton arguments; and
(3) the bundles to be delivered to the court at the required time.

7.12 The representatives for all parties involved must co-operate in agreeing bundles for use in court. The court and the advocates should all have exactly the same bundles.

7.13 When agreeing bundles for trial, the parties should establish through their legal representatives, and record in correspondence, whether the agreement of bundles:

(1) extends no further than agreement of the composition and preparation of the bundles; or
(2) includes agreement that the documents in the bundles are authentic (see rule 32.19); or
(3) includes agreement that the documents may be treated as evidence of the facts stated in them.

The court will normally expect parties to agree that the documents, or at any rate the great majority of them, may be treated as evidence of the facts stated in them. A party not willing to agree should, when the trial bundles are lodged, write a letter to the court (with a copy to all other parties) stating that it is not willing to agree, and explaining why.

7.14 Documents disclosed are in general deemed to be admitted to be authentic under rule 32.19.

7.15 Detailed guidelines on the preparation of bundles are set out in Appendix 2, in addition to those in PD39, Miscellaneous Provisions relating to Hearings, para 3. These should always be followed unless there is good reason not to do so.

7.16 The general rule is that the claimant/applicant must ensure that one copy of a properly prepared bundle is delivered at the Listing Office at least 2 clear days before the hearing of an application and at least 7 days before a trial. However, the court may direct the delivery of bundles earlier than this. Where oral evidence is to be given a second copy of the bundle must be available in court for the use of the witnesses. In the case of bundles to be used on judge's applications (other than applications by order) the bundles must be delivered to the clerk to the interim applications judge by 10 am on the morning preceding the day of the hearing unless the court directs otherwise. A bundle delivered to the court should always be in final form and parties should not make a request to alter the bundle after it has been delivered to the court save for good reason.

7.17 When lodging the agreed bundles there should also be lodged a further agreed time estimate, together with an agreed reading list and an agreed time estimate in respect of that reading list. The time estimates and reading list must be signed by the advocates for the parties. Failing agreement as to the time estimates or reading list then separate reading lists and time estimates must be submitted signed by the appropriate advocate. See Appendix 3 as to reading lists.

7.18 If the case is one which does not require the preparation of a bundle, the advocate should check before the hearing starts that all the documents to which he or she wishes to refer and which ought to have been filed have been filed, and, if possible, indicate to the associate which they are.

7.19 Bundles provided for the use of the court should be removed promptly after the conclusion of the hearing unless the court directs otherwise.

Skeleton Arguments

7.20 The general rule is that for the purpose of all hearings before a judge skeleton arguments should be prepared. The exceptions to this general rule are where the application does not warrant one, for example because it is likely to be short, or where the application is so urgent that preparation of a skeleton argument is impracticable or where an application is ineffective and the order is agreed by all parties (see also paras 26.25 and 26.32).

Time for delivery of skeleton arguments

7.21 **In the more substantial matters (eg trials and applications by order)** – not less than 2 clear days before the date or first date on which the application or trial is due to come on for hearing.

7.22 **On judge's applications without notice** – with the papers which the judge is asked to read on the application.

7.23 **On all other applications to a judge, including interim applications** – as soon as possible and not later than 10 am on the day preceding the hearing.

7.24 Where a case is liable to be placed in the Warned List, consideration should be given to the preparation of skeleton arguments as soon as the case is placed in the Warned List, so that the skeleton arguments are ready to be delivered to the court on time. Preparation of skeleton arguments should not be left until notice is given that the case is to be heard. Notice may be given that the case is to be heard the next day.

Place to which skeleton arguments should be delivered

7.25 If the name of the judge is not known, or the judge is a deputy judge, skeleton arguments should be delivered to the Listing Office.

7.26 If the name of the judge (other than a deputy judge) is known, skeleton arguments should be delivered to the judge's clerk.

Content of skeleton arguments

7.27 Appendix 3 contains guidelines which should be followed on the content of skeleton arguments and chronologies, as well as indices and reading lists.

7.28 In most cases before a judge, a list of the persons involved in the facts of the case, a chronology and a list of issues will also be required. The chronology and list of issues should be agreed where possible. The claimant/applicant is responsible for preparing the list of persons involved and the chronology, and he or she should deliver these and his or her list of issues (if required) to the court with his or her skeleton argument.

7.29 Unless the court gives any other direction, the parties shall, as between themselves, arrange for the delivery, exchange, or sequential service of skeleton arguments and any list of persons involved, list of issues or chronology. Where there are no such arrangements, all such documents should, where possible, be given to the other parties (if any) in sufficient time before the hearing to enable them properly to consider them.

Failure to lodge bundles or skeleton arguments on time

7.30 Failure to lodge skeleton arguments and bundles in accordance with this Guide may result in:

(1) the matter not being heard on the date in question; and
(2) the costs of preparation being disallowed; and
(3) an adverse costs order being made.

7.31 In the Royal Courts of Justice, a log will be maintained of all late skeletons and bundles.

Authorities

7.32 Lists of authorities should be supplied to the usher by 9 am on the first day of the hearing. Where photocopies of authorities are to be provided this should be indicated on the list. Delivery of skeleton arguments does not relieve a party of his or her duty to deliver his or her list of authorities to the usher by the time stated.

7.33 Advocates should exchange lists of authorities by 4 pm on the day before the hearing. Any failure in this regard which has the effect of increasing the length of a hearing or of giving rise to delay in the hearing of an application may give rise to an adverse costs order.

7.34 Excessive citation of authority should be avoided and practitioners must have full regard to the matters contained in *Practice Note (citation of cases: restrictions and rules)* [2001] 1 WLR 1001. In particular, the citation of authority should be restricted to the expression of legal principle rather than the application of such principle to particular facts. Practitioners must also, when citing authority, seek to ensure that their citations comply with *Practice Direction (Judgments: Neutral Citations)* [2002] 1 WLR 346.

Oral Argument

7.35 The court may indicate the issues on which it wishes to be addressed and those on which it wishes to be addressed only briefly.

Documents and Authorities

7.36 Only the key part of any document or authority should be read aloud in court.

7.37 At any hearing, handing in written material designed to reduce or remove the need for the court to take a manuscript note will assist the court and save time.

Adjournments

7.38 As a timetable for the case will have been fixed at an early stage, applications for adjournment of a trial should only be necessary where there has been a change of circumstances not known when the timetable was fixed.

When to apply

(1) A party who seeks to have a hearing before a judge adjourned must inform the Chancery Listing Officer of his or her application as soon as possible.

(2) Applications for an adjournment immediately before a hearing begins should be avoided as they take up valuable time which could be used for dealing with effective business and, if successful, they may result in a loss of court time altogether.

How to apply

(3) If the application is agreed, the parties should, in writing, apply to the Chancery Listing Officer. The Officer will consult the judge nominated for such matters. The judge may grant the application on conditions and give directions as to a new hearing date. But the judge may direct that the application be listed for a hearing and that all parties attend.

(4) If the adjournment is opposed the party asking for it should apply to the judge nominated for such matters or to the judge to whom the matter has been allocated. A hearing should be arranged, at the first opportunity, through the Chancery Listing Office.

(5) A short summary of the reasons for the adjournment should be delivered to the Listing Office, where possible by 12 noon on the day before the application is made. A witness statement or affidavit is not generally required.

(6) The party requesting an adjournment will, in general, be expected to show that he or she has conducted his or her own case diligently.

Parties should take all reasonable steps to ensure that their cases are adequately prepared in sufficient time to enable a hearing before the court to proceed. Likewise, they should take reasonable steps to prepare and serve any document (including any written evidence) required to be served on any other party in sufficient time to enable the other party similarly to be adequately prepared.

(7) If a failure to take reasonable steps necessitates an adjournment, the court may disallow costs as between solicitor and client, or order the person responsible to pay the costs under rule 48.7, or dismiss the application, or make any other order (including an order for the payment of costs on an indemnity basis).

(8) A trial date may, on occasion, also be vacated by the master in the circumstances envisaged in paragraph 6.11.

HEARINGS BEFORE MASTERS

7.39 The general considerations set out in paragraph 7.2 apply to hearings before the masters as they do to hearings in court. Likewise, the matters set out in respect of time estimates in paragraphs 7.3, 7.4, 7.7 and 7.8 apply just as much to applications before the masters as to those before judges. Parties must ensure when issuing applications to be heard by the masters that time estimates are realistic and make proper allowance for the time taken to give judgment and deal with the summary assessment of costs and any application for permission to appeal.

7.40 In the case of a hearing before a master which is listed for 1 hour or more and in any other case before a master, such as a case management conference, where a bundle would assist, a bundle should be provided and lodged. Bundles must be lodged for a trial or a hearing equivalent to a trial (such as a substantial account or enquiry or a Part 8 claim with oral evidence) which is listed before a master. Bundles must comply with Appendix 2 and contain or be accompanied by a reading list and an estimate of reading time as set out in paragraph 7.17 above.

7.41 In the case of a trial or similar hearing the bundle should be lodged not less than 2 clear days before the date fixed for the trial or other hearing. In any other case where a bundle is to be lodged then, subject to any other order, it should be delivered to the master's room no later than 10 am on the day before the hearing.

7.42 If a bundle of documents is not prepared for the use of the master, but a party intends to rely on the exhibits to a witness statement or affidavit filed on behalf of that party, that party must ensure that those exhibits are also filed with the court in sufficient time to be available to be read by the master in advance of the hearing.

7.43 Skeleton arguments should be prepared in respect of any application before the master of 1 or more hour's duration and certainly for any trial or similar hearing. They are to be lodged by the same time as applies to the lodging of bundles: see para 7.41 above. The contents of the skeleton argument should be in accordance with paragraph 7.27 and Appendix 3.

7.44 Where a skeleton argument is required, photocopies of any authorities to be relied upon should be attached to the skeleton argument.

7.45 Failure to lodge skeleton arguments or bundles in accordance with this Guide is likely to result in one or more of the consequences set out in paragraph 7.30.

7.46 When matters before the masters settle, Chancery Chambers should be so informed in writing as soon as possible and no later than 4 pm on the day preceding the appointment. Failure so to do and consequent waste of court time may result in an adverse costs order being made.

Chapter 8 – Conduct of a Trial

Key Rules: CPR Parts 32 and 39

8.1 An important aim of all concerned must be to ensure that at trial court time is used as efficiently as possible. Thorough preparation of the case prior to trial is the key to this.

8.2 Chapter 7 of this Guide applies to preparation for a trial as well as for other hearings in court. This Chapter contains matters which principally affect trials.

Time limits

8.3 The court may, either at the outset of the trial or at any time thereafter, fix time limits for oral submissions, speeches and the examination and cross-examination of witnesses. (See paragraphs 3.15–16.)

Opening Speeches

8.4 The party opening the case should in general begin by making a short opening speech.

8.5 Unless notified otherwise, advocates should assume that the judge will have read their skeleton arguments and the principal documents referred to in the reading list lodged in advance of the hearing (see paragraph 7.17). The judge will state at an early stage how much he or she has read and what arrangements are to be made about reading any documents not already read, for which an adjournment of the trial after opening speeches may be appropriate. If the judge needs to read any documents additional to those mentioned in the reading list lodged in advance of the hearing, a list should be provided during the opening.

8.6 It is normally convenient for any outstanding procedural matters to be dealt with in the course of, or immediately after, the opening speech.

8.7 The judge may ask or allow the other party to make a short speech at the end of the opening speech of the party opening the case.

8.8 In a lengthy and complex case each party should provide written summaries of their opening speeches. In other cases a supplemental skeleton argument should be provided if, in opening, it is desired to cover substantive points not already dealt with in the original skeleton argument. In both cases the guidelines in Appendix 3 apply. A summary of an opening speech or any supplemental skeleton argument should be delivered to the judge and the other parties no later than the time when the opening speech commences.

Witness Statements

8.9 In the preparation of witness statements for use at trial, the guidelines in Appendix 4 should be followed.

8.10 Unless the court orders otherwise, a witness statement will stand as the witness's evidence in chief if he or she is called and confirms that he or she believes the facts stated in the statement are true: rule 32.5.

8.11 A witness may be allowed to supplement his or her witness statement orally at the trial before submitting to cross-examination, for example to deal with events occurring, or matters discovered, after his or her statement was served, or in response to matters dealt with by another party's witness, but a party seeking to examine in chief a witness who has provided a witness statement must satisfy the judge that there is good reason not to confine the evidence to the contents of his or her witness statement: see rule 32.5(3) and (4). Where practicable a supplementary witness statement should be prepared and served on the other parties, as soon as possible, to deal with matters not dealt with in the original witness statement. Permission is required to adduce a supplementary witness statement at trial if any other party objects to it. This need not be sought prior to service; it can be sought at a case management conference if convenient or, if need be, at trial.

8.12 Witnesses are expected to have re-read their witness statements shortly before they are called to give evidence.

8.13 Where a party decides not to call a witness whose witness statement has been served to give oral evidence at trial, prompt notice of this decision should be given to all other parties. The party should make plain when he or she gives this notice whether he or she proposes to put, or seek to put, the witness statement in as hearsay evidence. If he or she does not put the witness statement in as hearsay evidence, rule 32.5(5) allows any other party to put it in as hearsay evidence.

8.14 Facilities may be available to assist parties or witnesses with special needs, whether as regards access to the court, or audibility in court, or otherwise. The Listing Office should be notified of any such needs prior to the hearing. The Customer Service Officer (tel 020 7947 7731) can also assist with parking, access etc.

Cross-examination

8.15 The party cross-examining is not necessarily obliged to put his or her case to each witness even if they deal in chief with the same point. It may be sufficient if he or she puts it to one of the other side's witnesses. If that witness makes any admission or expresses any opinion or otherwise adds a qualification to his or her evidence, the party cross-examining can rely on it in argument but he or she cannot assume that other witnesses would have made the same admission or qualification and expressed the same opinion: see *Re Yarn Spinners' Agreement* [1959] 1 All ER 299 at 309 per Devlin J.

Expert Evidence

8.16 The trial judge may disallow expert evidence which either is not relevant for any reason, or which he or she regards as excessive and disproportionate in all the circumstances, even though permission for the evidence has been given.

8.17 The evidence of experts (or of the experts on a particular topic) is commonly taken together at the same time and after the factual evidence has been given. If this is to be done it should be agreed by the parties before the trial and should be raised with the judge at the PTR, if there is one, or otherwise at the start of the trial. Expert evidence should as far as possible be given by reference to the reports exchanged.

8.18 The evidence of experts must be impartial, complying with rule 35.3. If it is not it may be disregarded.

Physical exhibits

8.19 Some cases involve a number of physical exhibits. The parties should endeavour to agree the exhibits in advance and their system of labelling. Where it would be desirable, a scheme of display should be agreed (eg on a board with labels readable from a distance). Where witness statements refer to these, a note in the margin (which can be handwritten) of the exhibit number should be added.

Original documents

8.20 At the hearing of any case where a will is to be construed, the probate of the will must be in court at the opening of the case. When the construction of a document other than a will is to be considered, the original document must be similarly available. The court should not be asked to construe any document by reference to a copy.

Final speeches

8.21 The judge may direct that the parties submit summaries of their final speeches before they begin. The guidelines in Appendix 3 apply. For this purpose the court may grant an adjournment. The court may require the written summaries to set out the principal findings of fact for which the party contends.

Chapter 9 – Judgments, Orders and Proceedings after Judgment

Key Rules and PDs: PD 40, and RSC Order 44

Judgments

9.1 Where judgment is reserved, the judge may deliver his or her judgment by handing down the written text without reading it out in open court. Where this course is adopted, the advocates will be supplied with the full text of the judgment in advance of delivery. In such cases, the advocates should familiarise themselves with the text of the judgment and be ready to deal with any points which may arise when judgment is delivered. Any requirement to treat the text as confidential must be complied with. Where appropriate, arrangements analogous to those set out in *Practice Note (Court of Appeal: Handed Down Judgments)* [2002] 1 WLR 344 will apply.

9.2 The judgment does not take effect until formally delivered in court. If the judgment is to be handed down in writing copies will then be made available to the parties and, if requested and so far as practicable, to the law reporters and the press.

9.3 The judge may direct that the written judgment may be used for all purposes as the text of the judgment, and that no transcript of the judgment need be made. Where such a direction is made, copies of the judgment may be obtained from the Mechanical Recording Department.

Orders

9.4 It may often be possible for the court to prepare and seal an order more quickly if a draft of the order is handed in. Speed may be particularly important where the order involves the grant of an interim injunction or the appointment of a receiver without notice. In all but the most simple cases a draft order should be prepared and brought to the hearing.

9.5 The court may in any case direct the parties to agree and sign a statement of the terms of the order made by the court (still commonly called a minute of order). Where the proceedings are in the Royal Courts of Justice, the statement should, when agreed and signed, be delivered to Chancery Chambers Registry and Issue Section (Room TM 5.04) unless otherwise requested. In the case of any dispute or difficulty as to the contents of the order, the parties should mention the matter to the judge or master who heard the application.

9.6 Where a draft or an agreed statement of the terms of an order exists in electronic form, it is often helpful if the draft or agreed statement is provided to the court on disk as well as in hard copy, particularly if the order needs to be drawn quickly. Any disk supplied for this purpose must be new and newly-formatted before writing the material on it so as to minimise the risk of transferring a computer virus. The current word processing system used by the Chancery Associates is Word for Windows 2000. Enquiries regarding the provision of disks should be made of the associate responsible for drawing the order in question.

Drafting and Service of Orders

9.7 Where a judge directs that a statement of the terms of an order be agreed and signed, the agreed statement should be lodged in Room TM 5.04 as set out in para 9.5 above. Agreed statements will normally be adopted as the order of the court.

9.8 Orders will be drawn up by the court, unless the judge or master directs that no order be drawn. Unless a contrary order is made, or the party concerned has asked to serve the order, a sealed order will be sent to each party.

9.9 Where a particular order is required to be served personally, the party concerned (see above) will be responsible for service.

9.10 If the order is to be drawn up by a party, two engrossments of the order proposed should be lodged at or posted to:

Chancery Chambers Registry
Room TM 5.04 Thomas More Building
Royal Courts of Justice
Strand
London WC2A 2LL

Forms of Order

9.11 Recitals will be kept to a minimum and the body of the order will be confined to setting out the decision of the court and the directions required to give effect to it. If upon receipt of an order any party is of the view that it is not drawn up in such a way as to give effect to the decision of the court, prompt notice must be given to the Chancery Chambers Registry in Room TM5.04 and to all other parties setting out the reasons for dissatisfaction. If the differences cannot be resolved, the objecting party may apply on notice for the order to be amended.

Copies of Orders

9.12 Copies of orders may be obtained from Room TM5.04 upon payment of the appropriate fee.

Consent Orders

9.13 All consent orders lodged in Chancery Chambers are referred to the master for approval before the order is sealed.

Consent Orders under the Inheritance (Provision for Family and Dependants) Act 1975

9.14 Every final order embodying terms of compromise made in proceedings in the Chancery Division under the 1975 Act must contain a direction that a memorandum of the order shall be endorsed on or permanently annexed to the probate or letters of administration and a copy of the order shall be sent to the Principal Registry of the Family Division with the relevant grant of probate or letters of administration for endorsement notwithstanding that any particular order may not, strictly speaking, be an order under the 1975 Act.

Consents by parties not attending the hearing

9.15 This is covered in paragraphs 5.24–26 above.

Tomlin Orders

9.16 Where proceedings are to be stayed on agreed terms to be scheduled to the order, the draft order should be drawn so as to read, with any appropriate provision in respect of costs, as follows:

'And the parties having agreed to the terms set out in the attached schedule

IT IS BY CONSENT ORDERED

That all further proceedings in this claim be stayed except for the purpose of carrying such terms into effect

AND for that purpose the parties have permission to apply'.

This form of order is called a 'Tomlin Order'.

Proceedings after judgment

9.17 Proceedings under judgments and orders in the Chancery Division are now regulated by PD40 Accounts, Inquiries etc, PD40 Judgments and Orders, and PD40 Court's Powers in Relation to Land etc as well as RSC Order 44.

Directions

9.18 Where a judgment or order directs further proceedings, such as accounts or inquiries, it will often give directions as to how the accounts and inquiries are to be conducted, for example:

for accounts

(1) who is to lodge the account and within what period;
(2) within what period objection is to be made;
(3) arrangements for inspection of vouchers or other relevant documents;

for inquiries

(4) whether the inquiry is to proceed on written evidence or with statements of case;
(5) directions for service of such evidence or statements; and
(6) directions as to disclosure.

9.19 If directions are not given in the judgment or order an application should be made to the appropriate master as soon as possible asking for such directions. The application notice should be made in writing specifying the directions sought. Before making the application, applicants should write to the other parties setting out the directions they seek and inviting their response within 14 days. The application to the court should not be made until after the expiry of that period unless there is some special urgency. The application must state that the other parties have been consulted and have attached to it copies of the applicant's letter to the other parties and of any response from them. The master will then consider what directions are appropriate. In complex cases he or she may direct a case management conference.

9.20 If any inquiry is estimated to last more than 2 days and involves very large sums of money or strongly contested issues of fact or difficult points of law, the master may direct that it be taken by a judge. Accounts, however long they are estimated to take, will normally be taken before the master.

Chapter 10 – Appeals

Key Rules: CPR Part 52 and PD52; PD Insolvency Proceedings, Part 4, paragraph 17: appeals

General

10.1 This Chapter is concerned with the following appeals affecting the Chancery Division:

(1) Appeals within the ordinary work of the Division, from masters to High Court judges;
(2) Insolvency appeals from High Court registrars and from county courts to High Court judges;
(3) Appeals to High Court judges in the Chancery Division from orders in claims proceeding in a county court;
(4) Statutory appeals from tribunals and others to the Chancery Division.

Proceedings under the Companies Acts are specialist proceedings for the purposes of rule 49(2) and therefore as regards the destination of appeals. In those cases appeals from final decisions by a registrar of the Companies Court go direct to the Court of Appeal. Such appeals are not covered in this Chapter.

10.2 This Chapter does not deal with appeals from High Court judges of the Division, except as regards permission to appeal, and as to giving notice to the court of an appeal in a contempt case. It does not deal with appeals in the course of the detailed assessment of costs.

10.3 The detailed procedure for appeals is set out in Part 52 and in PD52, and in the PD relating to Insolvency Proceedings, to which reference should be made. This Chapter only refers to some of the salient points.

Permission to appeal

10.4 Permission to appeal is required in all cases except: (a) appeals against committal orders, (b) certain insolvency appeals and (c) certain statutory appeals.

10.5 An application for permission may be made to the lower court, but only if it is made at the hearing at which the decision to be appealed was made. Permission may be granted, or refused, or granted in part (whether as to a part of the order, a ground of appeal or an issue) and refused as to the rest. It may be granted conditionally.

10.6 If the lower court refuses permission, or if permission is not applied for to the lower court at the original hearing, an application for permission may be made to the appeal court, by appeal notice.

10.7 An application to the appeal court for permission may be dealt with without a hearing, but if refused without a hearing the applicant may request that it be reconsidered at a hearing. Notice of the hearing is often given to the respondent; the respondent may submit written representations or attend the hearing but will not necessarily be awarded any costs of so doing even if permission to appeal is refused.

10.8 Guidance for litigants in relation to appeals to the High Court is available by way of a Practice Statement which may be obtained from the High Court Appeals Office at the Royal Courts of Justice (Room WG04).

10.9 If a party who wishes to appeal cannot lodge all the documents which are required at the time when the appellant's notice is issued, the Appeals Office is able to allow some further time by way of an extension, but beyond this any further extension has to be allowed by a judge, who will consider the case on paper. If there is a delay in obtaining a transcript of the judgment to be appealed, the appellant should endeavour to obtain a note of the judgment, which the lawyers representing any party at the hearing below ought to be able to provide, at least as an interim measure before a transcript is obtained.

10.10 If the documents required for consideration of an application for permission to appeal have not been lodged, despite any extension which has been allowed, the case may be listed for oral hearing in the Dismissal List, for the appellant to show cause why the case should not be dismissed. The respondent will not normally be notified of such a hearing.

Time for appealing

10.11 The time limit for an appeal notice to be filed at the appeal court is 14 days after the decision of the lower court to be appealed, unless the lower court fixes some other period, which may be longer or shorter. The lower court can only fix a different period if it does so at the time it makes the order to be appealed from. Otherwise only the appeal court can alter the time limits.

Stay

10.12 Unless the lower court or the appeal court orders otherwise, an appeal does not operate as a stay of any order or decision of the lower court. A stay of execution may be applied for in the appellant's notice. If it is, it may be dealt with on paper. If the stay is required as a matter of great urgency, or before the appellant's notice can be filed, an application should be made to the applications judge.

Appeals from masters in cases proceeding in the Chancery Division

10.13 If permitted, an appeal from a decision of a master in a case proceeding in the Chancery Division lies to a High Court judge of the Division.

10.14 Every such appeal is limited to a review of the decision of the lower court, unless the court considers that, in the circumstances of the individual appeal, it would be in the interests of justice to hold a re-hearing. This principle applies to all appeals dealt with in this Chapter except where some other provision is made, as mentioned below. Unless the court does decide, exceptionally, to hold a re-hearing, the appeal will be allowed if the decision of the lower court was wrong or if it was unjust because of a serious procedural or other irregularity in the proceedings in the lower court.

Insolvency appeals

10.15 An appeal lies from a county court (circuit or district judge) or a High Court registrar in bankruptcy or company insolvency matters to a High Court judge of the Chancery Division, for which permission is not required.

10.16 Appeals in proceedings under the Company Directors Disqualification Act 1986 are treated as being in insolvency proceedings.

10.17 The time limit for such an appeal is the same as for ordinary Chancery appeals. An appeal is limited to a review of the decision of the lower court.

Appeals from orders made in county court claims

10.18 An appeal against a decision of a circuit judge in a claim proceeding in a county court lies to the High Court, unless, either, the decision is a final decision in a claim allocated to the multi-track or in specialist proceedings to which rule 49(2) applies, or the decision is itself on an appeal; in either of these cases the appeal lies direct to the Court of Appeal. This does not apply, however, where the allocation to the multi-track is deemed, rather than the result of a specific order, so that in cases begun by a Part 8 claim form, even though they are deemed to be so allocated, appeals lie to the High Court. The general rules as to the requirement for permission described above apply to these appeals.

Statutory appeals

10.19 The Chancery Division hears a variety of appeals and cases stated under statute from decisions of tribunals and other persons. Some of these are listed or referred to in PD52, but this is not exhaustive. Particular cases include appeals under the Taxes Management Act 1970 and the Inheritance Tax Act 1984, appeals from the Value Added Tax and Duties Tribunal, from the Pensions Ombudsman and the Occupational Pensions Regulatory Authority, from the Comptroller-General of Patents, Designs and Trade Marks, from the Chief Land Registrar, from the Commons Commissioners, and from the Charity Commissioners under the Charities Act 1993.

10.20 Tax and VAT appeals are dealt with in Chapter 25 below, and appeals in patent, design and trade mark matters in Chapter 23. For other appeals reference should be made to the relevant statute and to PD52.

10.21 In such cases, the appeal is a review of the decision appealed against unless the minister, person or other body from whom the appeal is brought did not hold a hearing to reach the decision, or not one at which evidence was or could have been considered.

Appeals to the Court of Appeal: permission to appeal

10.22 An appeal lies from a judgment of a High Court judge of the Division to the Court of Appeal (unless an enactment makes it final and unappealable), but permission is required in all cases except where the order is for committal. Permission may be granted by the High Court judge, if applied to at the hearing at which the decision to be appealed was made, unless the order of the High Court judge was itself on an appeal, in which case permission may only be granted by the Court of Appeal.

Appeals in cases of contempt of court

10.23 Appellant's notices which by paragraph 21.4 of PD52 are required to be served on 'the court from whose order or decision the appeal is brought' may be served, in the case of appeals from the Chancery Division, on the Chief Master of the Chancery Division; service may be effected by leaving a copy of the notice of appeal with the Clerk of the Lists in Room WG4, Royal Courts of Justice, Strand, London WC2A 2LL.

Dismissal by consent

10.24 The practice is as set out in paragraph 12 of PD52, for all appeals except first appeals in insolvency matters. A document signed by solicitors for all parties must be lodged with the Chancery Listing Office (Room WG7), Royal Courts of Justice, Strand, London WC2A 2LL, requesting dismissal of the appeal. The appeal can be dismissed without any hearing by an order made in the name of the Vice-Chancellor. Any orders with directions as to costs will be drawn by the Chancery Associates. In the case of a first appeal in an insolvency matter, reference should be made to paragraph 17.22(8) of the PD Insolvency Proceedings.

Chapter 11 – Costs

Key Rules: CPR Parts 43 to 48 and the PD supplementing them

11.1 This Chapter does not set out to do more than refer to some salient points on costs relevant to proceedings in the Chancery Division. In particular it does not deal with the processes of detailed assessment or appeals in relation to such assessments.

11.2 A number of provisions in respect of costs in the CPR and in the PD supplementing Parts 43 to 48 (Costs PD) are likely to be relevant to Chancery proceedings:

(1) *Informing the client of costs orders*: Solicitors have a duty to tell their clients, within 7 days, if an order for costs is made against them and they were not present at the hearing. Solicitors must also tell anyone else who has instructed them to act on the case or who is liable to pay their fees. They must inform these persons how the order came to be made (rule 44.2; Costs PD, para 7.1).

(2) *Providing the court with estimates of costs*: The court can order a party to file an estimate of costs and to serve it on the other parties. (Costs PD, para 6.3). This is to assist the court in deciding what case management orders to make and also to inform other parties as to their potential liability for costs. In addition parties must file estimates of costs when they file their allocation questionnaire or any listing questionnaire (Costs PD, para 6.4).

(3) *Summary assessment of costs*: An outline of these provisions is given below. Their effect is that in the majority of contested hearings lasting no more than a day the court will decide, at the end of the hearing, not only who is to pay the costs but also how much those costs should be, and will order them to be paid, usually within 14 days. As a result the paying party will have to pay the costs at a much earlier stage than before.

(4) *Interim orders for costs*: Where the court decides immediately who is to pay particular costs, but does not assess the costs summarily, for example after a trial lasting more than a day, so that the final amount of

SECTION 5 Court Guides

costs payable has to be fixed by a detailed assessment, the court may order the paying party to pay a sum or sums on account of the ultimate liability for costs.

(5) *Interest on costs*: The court has power to award interest on costs from a date before the date of the order, so compensating the receiving party for the delay between incurring the costs and receiving a payment in respect of them from the paying party.

Summary Assessment

11.3 The court will generally make a summary assessment of costs whenever the hearing lasts for less than 1 day. The judge or master who heard the application or other hearing (which will include a trial, or the hearing of a Part 8 Claim, lasting less than a day) carries out the summary assessment. The court may decide not to assess costs summarily either because it orders the costs to be 'costs in the case' or because it considers the case to be otherwise inappropriate for summary assessment, typically because substantial issues arise as to the amount of the costs claimed. Costs payable to a party funded by the Legal Services Commission cannot be assessed summarily.

11.4 In order that the court can assess costs summarily at the end of the hearing each party who intends to claim costs must, no later than 24 hours before the time fixed for the hearing, serve on the other party, and file with the court, his or her statement of costs. Paragraph 13.5 of the Costs PD contains requirements about the information to be included in this statement, and the form of the statement. Failure by a party to file and serve his or her statement of costs as required by para 13.5 of the Costs PD will be taken into account by the court in deciding what order to make about costs and could result in a reduced assessment, in no order being made as to costs, or in the party being penalised in respect of the costs of any further hearing or detailed assessment hearing which may be required as a result of the party's failure.

11.5 Where the *receiving* party (the party to whom the costs are to be paid) is funded by the Legal Services Commission the court cannot assess costs summarily. It is not, however, prevented from assessing costs summarily by the fact that the *paying* party (the party by whom the costs are to be paid) is so funded. A summary assessment of costs payable by a person funded by the Legal Services Commission is not by itself a determination of the amount of those costs which the funded party is to pay (as to which see section 11 of the Access to Justice Act 1999 and regulation 10 of the Community Legal Services Costs Regulations 2000). Ordinarily, where costs are summarily assessed and ordered to be paid by a funded person the order will provide that the determination of any amount which the person who is or was in receipt of services funded by the Legal Services Commission is to pay shall be dealt with in accordance with regulation 10 of the above Regulations.

11.6 The amount of costs to be paid by one person to another can be determined on the standard basis or the indemnity basis. The basis to be used is determined when the court decides that a person should pay the costs of another. The usual basis is the standard basis and this is the basis that will apply if the order does not specify the basis of assessment. Costs that are unreasonably incurred or are unreasonable in amount are not allowed on either basis.

11.7 On the standard basis the court only allows costs which are proportionate to the matters in issue. If it has any doubt as to whether the costs were reasonably incurred or reasonable and proportionate in amount, it resolves the doubt in favour of the *paying* party. The concept of proportionality will always require the court to consider whether the costs which have been incurred were warranted having regard to the issues involved. A successful party who incurs costs which are disproportionate to the issues involved and upon which he or she has succeeded will only recover an amount of costs which the court considers to have been proportionate to those issues.

11.8 On the indemnity basis the court resolves any doubt it may have as to whether the costs were reasonably incurred or were reasonable in amount in favour of the *receiving* party.

11.9 The court must take into account all the circumstances, including the parties' conduct and the other matters mentioned in rule 44.5. Indemnity costs are not confined to cases of improper or reprehensible conduct. They will not, however, usually be awarded unless there has been conduct by the paying party which the court regards as unreasonable or unless the case falls within rule 48.4 (see paragraph 11.13 below).

11.10 A party must normally pay costs which are awarded against him or her and summarily assessed within 14 days of the assessment. But the court can extend that time (rules 44.8, 3.1(2)(a)). The court may therefore direct payment by instalments, or defer the liability to pay costs until the end of the proceedings so that the costs can then be set against any costs or judgment to which the paying party then becomes entitled.

11.11 If the parties have agreed the amount of costs, they do not need to file a statement of the costs, and summary assessment is unnecessary. If the parties to an application are able to agree an order by consent without the parties attending they should also agree a figure for costs to be inserted in the order or agree that there should be no order as to costs. If the costs position cannot be agreed then the parties will have to attend on the appointment but unless good reason can be shown for the failure of the parties to deal with costs as set out above no costs will be allowed for that attendance. The court finds it most unsatisfactory if parties agree the terms of a consent order but not the provision for costs. Depending on the facts and circumstances, the court may not be able to decide on the question of costs without hearing the application fully, but it is not likely to be consistent with the overriding objective to allow the necessary amount of court time to the dispute on costs in such a case. The court may then have to decide the costs issue on a broad brush approach, making an order against one party or the other only if it is clear, without spending too much time on it, that such an order would be appropriate, and otherwise making no order as to the costs.

Conditional fee agreements

11.12 The court should be informed, on any application for the payment of costs, if any party has entered into a conditional fee agreement. The court can then consider whether, in the light of that agreement, to stay the payment of any costs which have been summarily assessed until the end of the action, or to decline to order the payment of costs on account under rule 44.3(8).

Other provisions

11.13 Parts 45 to 48, and the Costs PD, contain provisions regarding:

(1) special cases in which costs are payable;
(2) wasted costs;
(3) fixed costs (these are payable for instance if judgment for a sum of money is given in default); and
(4) detailed assessment.

In the context of Chancery litigation attention is drawn to rule 48.2 (Costs orders in favour of or against non-parties); rule 48.3 (Amount of costs where costs are payable pursuant to a contract) (see further Costs PD paragraph 50 and see also Chapter 21 – Mortgage Claims); and rule 48.4 and Costs PD para 50A (Limitations on court's power to award costs in favour of trustee or personal representative). Reference may also be made to Chapter 26 as regards costs orders in trust litigation.

Chapter 12 – District Registries

General

12.1 Many Chancery cases are heard in the District Registries. Chancery judges sit regularly in Birmingham, Bristol, Cardiff, Leeds, Liverpool, Manchester and Newcastle-upon-Tyne, and occasionally in Preston.

12.2 Outside London, county courts have exclusive jurisdiction in bankruptcy, and proceedings in bankruptcy must therefore be brought in the relevant county court which has bankruptcy jurisdiction rather than in the District Registries.

Judges

12.3 Two Chancery judges supervise the arrangements for the hearing of Chancery cases out of London. Mr Justice Lloyd, as Vice-Chancellor of the County Palatine of Lancaster (from October 2002), is concerned with Chancery hearings for the Northern and North Eastern Circuits. Mr Justice Neuberger is the Chancery Supervising Judge for Birmingham, Bristol and Cardiff and is concerned with Chancery hearings on the Western, Wales and Chester, and Midland Circuits. Both these judges regularly take substantial Chancery matters for hearing outside London. Mr Justice Lloyd sits regularly in Manchester, Liverpool, Leeds and Newcastle and, as business may require, in Preston. If appropriate he will also sit at other court centres on the two circuits (eg Carlisle, Lancaster and Sheffield). Mr Justice Neuberger sits regularly in Birmingham, Bristol and Cardiff, but if appropriate will sit elsewhere on the relevant circuit, for example in Chester.

12.4 There are also specialist circuit judges who have the authority to exercise the powers of a judge of the Chancery Division (under section 9 of the Supreme Court Act 1981, therefore known as section 9 judges) and who normally sit out of London. They exercise a general Chancery jurisdiction, subject to exceptions. Those exceptions are proceedings directly concerning revenue, and proceedings before the Patents Court constituted as part of the Chancery Division under section 96 of the Patents Act 1977.

12.5 Currently the circuit judges who sit regularly in Chancery out of London are:

Judge Weeks QC (Bristol)
Judge Norris QC (Birmingham)
Judge Moseley QC (Cardiff)
Judge Howarth (Manchester, Liverpool and Preston)
Judge Maddocks (Manchester, Liverpool and Preston)
Judge Behrens (Leeds and Newcastle)
Judge Langan QC (Leeds and Newcastle)

Judge George (who normally sits in Liverpool), Judge Cooke and Judge Gilliland QC (who normally sits in Salford hearing Technology and Construction cases) and Judges Kershaw QC and Hegarty QC (who are the local mercantile judges based in Manchester and Liverpool) also assist in the disposal of Chancery business on the Northern Circuit. So also does Judge McGonigal in Leeds and Newcastle. The Chancery, Mercantile and TCC judges assist each other in Birmingham, Bristol and Cardiff as well.

12.6 In addition certain other circuit judges and some Queen's Counsel are authorised to take Chancery cases on the same basis.

Trials

12.7 If a Chancery case is proceeding in any District Registry other than a Chancery District Registry, the case should normally be transferred to the appropriate Chancery District Registry upon the first occasion the case comes before the court.

12.8 The venue of a Chancery trial out of London will normally be one of the centres mentioned above. However in many circumstances (eg because of the number or age of local witnesses, the need for a site visit, or travel problems) arrangements can be made for the Chancery Court to sit elsewhere.

12.9 In cases of exceptional difficulty or importance the trial may be by a High Court judge. Arrangements can also be made in exceptional circumstances for a High Court judge to deal with any of the matters excepted from the jurisdiction of an authorised circuit judge. Such a judge may be one of the Chancery judges other than Lloyd or Neuberger JJ.

12.10 Where it is desired that a hearing be outside one of the normal Chancery Centres, or be taken by a High Court judge, inquiries should normally be made in the first instance to the Listing Officer for the area concerned. If the need arises, inquiries can also be made to the clerk to Mr Justice Lloyd or the clerk to Mr Justice Neuberger, as the case may be. If no relevant clerk is available, inquiries should be made to the Chancery Listing Officer at the Royal Courts of Justice in London. The clerks' contact numbers are in Appendix 8.

Applications

12.11 Subject to the following paragraphs any application should normally be made to a district judge (unless it relates to a matter which a district judge does not have power to hear).

12.12 A district judge may of his or her own initiative (for instance because of the complexity of the matter or the need for specialist attention) direct that an application be referred to a High Court or an authorised circuit judge.

12.13 If all or any of the parties consider that the matter should be dealt with by a judge (High Court or circuit), the parties or any of them may arrange that the matter be listed on one of the ordinary application days (see para 12.14 below). The district judges, who will consult where necessary with one of the judges (High Court or circuit), are usually available by post or telephone to give guidance on procedural matters, for example the court before which the matter should come or whether the matter may be dealt with in writing.

Application Days before a judge

12.14 Normally 1 day a week is reserved for the hearing of applications and short appeals, including all interim matters. All matters will be called into court at the commencement of the day in order to work out a running order. Matters will be heard without the court going into private session unless good reason is shown. Rights of audience are unaffected.

12.15 Applications days are: Monday in Birmingham, Thursday in Bristol and Friday in Cardiff. In Manchester and Liverpool application days are on either Tuesday or Thursday of each week. In Leeds and Newcastle Chancery and Mercantile application days are combined. In Leeds applications are heard every Friday, and there is an additional application day every fortnight. In Newcastle there is one application day each month.

Applications out of hours and telephone applications

12.16 These are governed by the general rules, save that in the case of applications out of hours, the party applying should contact the relevant court office. The main relevant contact numbers are set out in Appendix 8. In case of difficulty, contact the Royal Courts of Justice, on the number given in Appendix 8.

Agreed interim orders

12.17 Normally a hearing will not be necessary. The procedure is as in the general rules.

12.18 A judge is unlikely to agree to more than two consent adjournments of an interim application. Applications to vacate a trial date will require substantial justification and a hearing, normally before the trial judge.

Local Listing Arrangements

12.19 Listing arrangements may vary at different centres, depending on availability of judges and courtrooms. The current details are described below.

Birmingham: Shared Listing

12.20 The Shared List

The shared list is primarily for use by the three specialised lists of the Birmingham District Registry – those operated by the Chancery, Mercantile and Technology and Construction Courts.

The shared list is in addition to the normal lists of those Courts and allows better use to be made of judicial time. Given the settlement rate of trials in the three divisions, two additional cases, the fourth and fifth fixtures, will be listed at any one time, in addition to the three cases listed before the three specialist courts. Those two additional cases will be taken by any of the section 9 judges who become available. Cases are only entered into the shared list if there is a very strong expectation that they will be heard on the day fixed.

In order, therefore, for a case to enter the shared list it must be suitable for hearing before any of the section 9 specialist judges.

Suitability for listing a case in the shared list may be suggested by the district judge at directions stage, or by the parties when applying for the case to be listed. It is likely that fourth and fifth fixtures will be allocated an earlier trial date than a case which has to be heard by the appropriate specialist judge.

The final decision to list a case in the shared list will lie with Judge Norris QC for Chancery cases, Judge Alton for Mercantile cases, and Judge Kirkham for Technology and Construction cases.

Bristol: Reserve Listing

12.21 In order to make available earlier hearing dates than would otherwise be possible, a reserve list is operated for Chancery cases listed to be heard in the Bristol District Registry. Cases in the reserve list are given a fixed date, usually as a second fixture. A second fixture will only be given when there is a very strong expectation of the case being heard on that date. Other judges are called upon in the event of both first and second fixtures being effective.

Cardiff: Reserve Listing

12.22 Judge Moseley QC sits both as a Chancery judge and a judge of the Technology and Construction Court. His list contains both categories of case. All cases are allocated a fixed starting date but some are first and some reserve fixtures. Other judges are called upon in the event of both first and reserve fixtures being effective. All the judges who sit at the Cardiff Civil Justice Centre (Judges Jones Price QC, Masterman and Chambers QC) are authorised to sit as Chancery judges. Any discussions concerning listing should be with the Chancery Listing clerk in Cardiff.

Manchester, Liverpool and Preston

12.23 The Shared List

When sitting at the same court centre Judge Howarth and Judge Maddocks assist each other in the disposal of their respective daily lists. If necessary and if they are available at the relevant court centre, Judge Kershaw QC and Judge Hegarty QC (who are the local Mercantile Judges) and Judge George will assist in the disposal of business.

Second Fixtures

Second fixtures may be listed, but currently (2002) this is rarely necessary. Parties to such fixtures are notified not later than 3.30 pm on the working day preceding the day for which the case is listed (and frequently considerably before then) if the second fixture will not be in the list for trial.

Leeds and Newcastle

12.24 When sitting at the same time in Leeds or Newcastle any of Judge Behrens, Judge McGonigal (the principal Mercantile Judge on the North Eastern Circuit) and Judge Langan QC will assist each other in the disposal of their respective daily lists.

Chapter 13 – County Courts

Key Rules: CPR Part 30; PD7, paragraph 2

Unified procedure

13.1 A key feature of the civil justice reforms is the introduction of a unified procedure for the High Court and for county courts. The procedure to be followed in both courts is therefore the same.

Transfer to a county court

13.2 Any case which does not require to be heard by a High Court judge, and falls within the jurisdiction of the county courts, may be transferred to a county court. Where a case has been so transferred, the papers must be marked 'Chancery Business' so as to ensure, so far as possible, suitable listing.

13.3 The jurisdiction of county courts is set out in the High Court and County Court Jurisdiction Order 1991 as amended, and in enactments amended by that Order.

13.4 The jurisdiction of the High Court to transfer cases to a county court is contained in the County Courts Act 1984, section 40, as substituted by the Courts and Legal Services Act 1990, section 2(1). Under that section, the court has jurisdiction in certain circumstances to strike out actions which ought to have been begun in a county court.

13.5 A claim with an estimated value of less than £50,000 will generally be transferred to a county court, if the county court has jurisdiction, unless it is either within a specialist list or is within the criteria of Article 7(5) of the High Court and County Court Jurisdiction Order 1991.

13.6 If the case is one of a specifically Chancery nature a transfer from the Royal Courts of Justice will ordinarily be to the Central London County Court (Chancery List) ('the CLCC') where cases are heard by specialist Chancery circuit judges or recorders and a continuous Chancery List is maintained, unless the parties prefer a transfer to a local county court.

13.7 Even where the estimated value of the claim is more than £50,000 transfer to the CLCC may still be ordered if the criteria in Article 7(5) point in that direction, in particular having regard to the criteria in Article 7(5)(c), namely the complexity of the facts, legal issues, remedies or procedures involved.

13.8 If a claim is transferred to a county court at the allocation stage no other directions will usually be given and all case management will be left to the county court.

13.9 The Chancery List at the CLCC is managed by the Business Chancery & Patents Section at 26 Park Crescent W1 4HT. The telephone number of the section manager is set out in Appendix 8. A guide to the Chancery List may be obtained from the section manager.

13.10 As an alternative to starting the case in the Chancery Division and transferring to the CLCC a case (if appropriate to be started there) may be started at the CLCC and a request made there for it to be transferred to the Chancery List. The request will receive judicial consideration and a transfer will be made if appropriate.

13.11 It should be noted that only in very limited circumstances may freezing orders or search orders be granted in the county court. If necessary, an application may be made in the High Court in aid of the county court proceedings if such an order is to be sought in a case where it cannot be granted in the county court.

Patents County Court

13.12 See Chapter 23 below.

Chapter 14 – Use of Information Technology

Key Rules and PDs: CPR rule 1.4, Part 6; PD6, PD32, Annex 3

General

14.1 The CPR contain certain provisions about the use of information technology in the conduct of cases. Apart from these provisions, no standard practice has evolved or been prescribed for the use of information technology in civil cases, but it is possible to identify certain areas in which electronic techniques may be used which should encourage the efficient and economical conduct of litigation.

14.2 It must be remembered, however, that it is unlikely that the number of litigants in person will diminish, and the number may well increase, in the future and that not all solicitors have available sophisticated IT facilities. Use of IT is acceptable only if no party to the case will be unfairly prejudiced and its use will save time or money.

14.3 A number of specific applications of information technology have been well developed in recent years. The use of fax, the provision of skeleton arguments on disk, and daily transcripts on disk (with or without appropriate software) have become commonplace. Short applications may be economically heard by a conference telephone call. Taking evidence by video link has become more common, and the available technology has improved considerably. There is still little experience of the intensive use of information technology in the ordinary course of the trial by, for example, providing documents as images to be displayed.

14.4 In any case in which it is proposed to use information technology in the preparation, management and presentation of a case in a manner which is not provided for by the CPR, it may be necessary for directions to be given by the judge who is to hear the case. It is unlikely to be satisfactory for parties and their solicitors to agree to a particular application of information technology (for example, using imaging techniques to deal either with disclosure or with the preparation of documents for use in court, in effect by way of electronic bundles) without the agreement of the judge. Accordingly it is likely, particularly in heavy cases, that it will be desirable for a judge to be nominated to conduct the case. Where a nomination is desired, application should be made to the Vice-Chancellor in writing by letter addressed to his clerk for a judge to be nominated.

14.5 In every case in which it is proposed to use information technology, the first step will be for the solicitors for all parties to determine whether it is possible to establish a common protocol for the electronic exchange and management of information. It is recommended that the protocol provided by the Technology and Construction Solicitors' Association ('TeCSA') be used. The TeCSA protocol has enjoyed success and is available from TeCSA's website at *http://www.tecsa.org.uk/protocol/protocol.htm*. The CPR's underlying policy of co-operation and collaboration is particularly important in this context. In a large case the parties must facilitate the task of the judge by providing any additional help and IT know-how, including, for example, demonstrations, which he or she requires in order to control the case properly.

14.6 The judges of the Chancery Division and their clerks are equipped with IBM compatible computers running Windows (usually NT 4.0 but in some cases another version) and MS Office 97 or 2000. To avoid compatibility problems it is preferable that text files to be provided for use by a judge or clerk be provided in Rich Text Format (RTF). As an alternative to using disks, it may be possible to deliver text files to a particular judge by electronic mail. The clerk to the judge concerned should be contacted to find out whether this is possible.

Provision of information on disk

Skeleton arguments etc

14.7 Skeleton arguments, chronologies, witness statements, experts' reports and other documents (if available in electronic form) should be provided on disk (or by electronic mail) if the judge requests it. Enquiry should be made of the judge's clerk for this purpose. Where the complexity of the case justifies it, attention must be given to providing the judge with versions of the documents containing links to enable cross-references to be followed up in a convenient manner. Disks provided to judges must be checked for virus contamination and be clean.

Transcripts

14.8 The various shorthand writers provide a number of different transcript services. These range from an immediately displayed transcript which follows the evidence as it is given (usually with about 10 seconds' delay) to provision of transcripts of a day's proceedings 1 or 2 days in arrears. The use of transcripts is always of assistance if they can be justified on the ground of cost and in long cases they are a considerable advantage. If an instantaneous service is proposed, inquiries should be made of the judge's clerk, and sufficient time for the installation of the equipment necessary and for any familiarisation on the part of the judge with the system should be found. If special transcript-handling software is to be used by the parties, consideration should be given to making the software available to the judge.

14.9 If the shorthand writers make disks available (and nearly all do) the judge should be provided with disks as they appear if he or she requires them.

Fax communications

14.10 The use of fax in the service of documents is now authorised by rule 6.2(1) and PD6.

14.11 Each of the judges sitting in the Chancery Division may be reached by fax if the occasion warrants it. The respective judges' clerks' telephone and fax numbers are set out in Appendix 8. Where the name of the judge is not known, short documents may be sent to the listing office, whose fax number is also given in Appendix 8. Written evidence should not be sent by fax to this number. All fax messages should have a cover sheet setting out the name of the case, the case number and the judge's name, if known.

Telephone hearings

14.12 Applications may be heard by telephone, if the court so orders, but normally only if all parties entitled to be given notice agree, and none of them intends to be present in person. Special provisions apply where the applicant or another party is in person: see PD23 para 6.3. Guidance on other aspects of telephone hearings, and in particular how to set them up, is contained in PD23 para 6.5. When putting that guidance into practice once an order has been made for a hearing to take place by a telephone conference call, the following points may be useful:

(1) A telephone hearing may be set up by calling the BT Legal Call Centre on 0800 028 4194. The caller's name and EB account number will have to be given. Other telecommunications providers may also be able to offer the same facility.
(2) The names and telephone numbers of the participants in the hearing including the judge must be provided.
(3) The co-ordinator should be told the date, time and likely approximate duration of the hearing.
(4) The name and address of the court and the court case reference should be given, for delivery of the tape of the hearing.
(5) Then tell the court that the hearing has been arranged.

It is necessary to ensure that all participants in the hearing have all documents that it may be necessary for any of them to refer to by the time the hearing begins.

Video-conferencing

14.13 The court may allow evidence to be taken using video-conferencing facilities: rule 32.3. Experience has shown that normally taking evidence by this means is comparatively straightforward, but its suitability may depend on the particular witness, and the case, and on such matters as the volume and nature of documents which need to be referred to in the course of the evidence.

14.14 A video-link may also be used for an application, or otherwise in the course of any hearing.

14.15 Annex 3 to PD32 (Video Conferencing Guidance) provides further detail on the manner in which video conferencing facilities are to be used in civil proceedings.

14.16 Video conferencing facilities are available at the RCJ in Court 38. It is convenient that these facilities should be used if at all possible in relation to proceedings which are under way in the RCJ. Attention is drawn to the following matters:

(a) Permission to use video conferencing during a hearing should be obtained as early as possible in the proceedings. If all parties are agreed that the use of video conferencing is appropriate, then a hearing may not be necessary to obtain such permission.
(b) Before an order fixing the appointment for the use of the facilities at the RCJ is obtained their availability must be ascertained from the video managers at the RCJ (Roger Little/Norman Muller, tel 020 7947 6581, fax 020 7947 6613). When the order is made the video managers must be informed immediately so as to ensure that all necessary arrangements can be made well in advance of the hearing.
(c) If it is necessary for other facilities to be used, whether because the RCJ facilities are unavailable or for any other reason, consideration should be given to using the facilities available at the Bar Council or the Law Society. The party seeking to use the facilities will be responsible for making all the necessary arrangements.
(d) If the use of facilities other than those at the RCJ, the Bar Council or the Law Society is proposed, approval must first be obtained to the use of the particular facilities even if the parties are agreed.

Chapter 15 – Miscellaneous Matters

Key Rules: CPR Part 39; PD – Miscellaneous Provisions relating to Hearings supplementing CPR Part 39

Litigants in person

15.1 The provisions of this Guide in general apply to litigants in person. Thus, for example, litigants in person should, unless they have good reason for not doing so:

(1) prepare a written summary of their argument in the same circumstances as those in which a represented party is required to produce a skeleton argument;
(2) prepare a bundle of documents in the same way that a represented party is required to produce a bundle of documents; and
(3) be prepared to put forward their argument within a limited time if they are directed to do so by the court.

15.2 This means that litigants in person should identify in advance of the hearing those points which they consider to be their strongest points, and that they should put those points at the forefront of their oral and written submissions to the court.

15.3 It is not the function of court officials to give legal advice. However, subject to that, they will do their best to assist any litigant. Litigants in person who need further assistance should contact the Community Legal Service through their Information Points. The CLS are developing local networks of people giving legal assistance such as law centres, local solicitors or the Citizens' Advice Bureaux. CLS Information Points are being set up in libraries and other public places. Litigants can telephone the CLS to find their nearest CLS Information Point on 0845 608 1122 or can log on to the CLS website at *www.justask.org.uk* for the CLS directory and for legal information.

15.4 The RCJ Advice Bureau off the Main Hall at the Royal Courts of Justice is open from Monday to Friday from 10 am to 1 pm and from 2 pm to 5 pm. The bureau is run by lawyers in conjunction with the Citizens' Advice Bureau and is independent of the court. The Bureau operates on a 'first come first served' basis, or telephone advice is available on 0845 120 3715 (or 020 7947 6880) from Monday to Friday between 11 am and 12 noon and between 3 and 4 pm.

15.5 Where a litigant in person is the applicant, the court may ask one of the represented parties to open the matter briefly and impartially, and to summarise the issues.

15.6 It is the duty of an advocate to ensure that the court is informed of all relevant decisions and enactments of which the advocate is aware (whether favourable or not to his or her case) and to draw the court's attention to any material irregularity.

15.7 Representatives for other parties must treat litigants in person with consideration. They should where possible be given photocopies of any authorities which are to be cited before the case starts in addition to the skeleton argument. They should be asked to give their names to the usher if they have not already done so. Representatives for other parties should explain the court's order after the hearing if the litigant in person does not appear to understand it.

15.8 If a litigant in person wishes to give oral evidence he or she will generally be required to do so from the witness box in the same manner as any other witness of fact.

15.9 A litigant in person must give an address for service in England or Wales. If he or she is a claimant, the address will be in the claim form or other document by which the proceedings are brought. If he or she is a defendant, it will be in the acknowledgment of service form which he or she must send to the court on being served with the proceedings. It is essential that any change of address should be notified in writing to Chancery Chambers and to all other parties to the case. Notice of hearing dates will be given by post to litigants at the address shown in the court file. A litigant in person will generally be given a fixed date for trial on application. A litigant in person who wishes to apply for a fixed date should ask the Listing Office for a copy of its Guidance Notes for Litigants in Person.

15.10 Litigants in person may use the Supreme Court Library in the Queen's Building at the discretion of the Librarian.

Assistance to litigants in person

15.11 A litigant who is acting in person may be assisted at a hearing by another person, often referred to as a McKenzie friend (see *McKenzie v McKenzie*

[1971] P 33). The litigant must be present at the hearing. If the hearing is in private, it is a matter of discretion for the court whether such an assistant is allowed to attend the hearing. That may depend, among other things, on the nature of the proceedings.

15.12 The assistant is allowed to help by taking notes, quietly prompting the litigant and offering advice and suggestions to the litigant. The court can, and sometimes does, permit the assistant to address the court on behalf of the litigant, by making an order to that effect under section 27(2)(c) of the Courts and Legal Services Act 1990 (by reference to sections 17 and 18 of that Act), but this is an exceptional course. Some factors which may be relevant to whether this should be permitted have been discussed in reported judgments, including *Izzo v Philip Ross* [2002] BIPR 310 and *Paragon Finance v Noueiri (Practice Note)* [2001] EWCA Civ 1402 [2001] 1 WLR 2357.

Representation on behalf of companies

15.13 Rule 39.6 allows a company or other corporation to be represented at trial by an employee if the employee has been authorised by the company or corporation to appear on its behalf and the court gives permission. Paragraph 5 of PD39 describes what is needed to obtain permission from the court for this purpose and mentions some of the considerations relevant to the grant or refusal of permission.

Robed and unrobed hearings

15.14 Advocates (and judges) wear robes at hearings by High Court judges of trials (including preliminary issues) and statutory appeals or cases stated. Robes are not worn for other hearings, including appeals from masters, Bankruptcy registrars and county courts. The Daily Cause List states, in relation to each judge's list, whether the matter is to be heard robed or unrobed. Robes are not worn at hearings before masters. Robes are worn at the following hearings before Bankruptcy and Companies Court registrars: public examinations of bankrupts and of directors or other officers of companies; applications for discharge from bankruptcy or for suspension of such discharge; all proceedings under the Company Directors Disqualification Act 1986; petitions to wind up companies; final hearings of petitions for the reduction of capital of companies.

Solicitors' rights of audience

15.15 At hearings in chambers before 26 April 1999 solicitors had general rights of audience. The fact that a matter which would then have been heard in chambers is now heard in public under Part 39 does not affect rights of audience, so in such matters as would have been heard in chambers previously, the general right of audience for solicitors continues to apply. Such cases included appeals from masters, applications for summary judgment, and those concerned with pleadings, security for costs and the like, pre-trial reviews, and applications concerned with the administration of a deceased person's estate, a trust or a charity. They did not include applications in what is now the Interim Applications List or the Companies Court, nor appeals from county courts or insolvency appeals. Solicitors do, however, have general rights of audience in personal insolvency matters; this is not affected by whether the hearing is in public or private.

15.16 If a solicitor who does not have the appropriate special right of audience wishes to be heard in a case which is not one which, before 26 April 1999, would have been heard in chambers nor a personal insolvency case, an application may be made for the grant of a special right of audience before the particular court and for the particular proceedings under the Courts and Legal Services Act 1990, section 27(2)(c).

Tape recording at hearings

15.17 In the Royal Courts of Justice it is normal to record all oral evidence and any judgment delivered during a hearing before a judge. If any party wishes a recording to be made of any other part of the proceedings, this should be mentioned in advance or at the time of the hearing. At hearings before masters, it is not normally practicable to record anything other than any oral evidence and the judgment, but these will be recorded. No party or member of the public may use recording equipment without the court's permission.

Chapter 16 – Suggestions for Improvement and Court Users' Committees

16.1 Suggestions for improvements in this Guide or in the practice or procedure of the Chancery Division are welcome. Unless they fall within the remit of the committees mentioned at paras 16.3 to 16.6 below, they should be sent to the clerk to the Vice-Chancellor.

Chancery Division Court Users' Committee

16.2 The Chancery Division Court Users' Committee's function is to review, as may from time to time be required, the practice and procedure of all courts forming part of the Chancery Division, to ensure that they continue to provide a just, economical and expeditious system for the resolution of disputes. The Vice-Chancellor is the chairman. Its membership includes judges, a master, barristers, solicitors and other representatives of court staff and users. Meetings are held three times a year, and more often if necessary. Suggestions for points to be considered by the Committee should be sent to the clerk to the Vice-Chancellor.

Insolvency Court Users' Committee

16.3 Proposals for change in insolvency matters fall within the remit of the Insolvency Court Users' Committee unless they relate to the Insolvency Rules 1986. The members of the Insolvency Court Users' Committee include members of the Bar, the Law Society, the Insolvency Service and the Society of Practitioners of Insolvency. Meetings are held three times a year, and more often if necessary.

Insolvency Rules Committee

16.4 The Insolvency Rules 1986 can only be changed by the Lord Chancellor with the concurrence of the Secretary of State for Trade and Industry. The Insolvency Rules Committee must be consulted before any changes to the Rules are made. The Chairman of the Insolvency Rules Committee is Mr Justice Evans-Lombe. Proposals for changes in the Rules should be sent to The Insolvency Service, Room 502, PO Box 203, 21 Bloomsbury Street, London WC1B 3QW, with a copy to the clerk to Mr Justice Evans-Lombe.

Intellectual Property Court Users' Committee

16.5 This considers the problems and concerns of intellectual property litigation generally. Membership of the committee includes the principal Patent judges, a representative of each of the Patent Bar Association, the Intellectual Property Lawyers Association, the Chartered Institute of Patent Agents, the Institute of Trade Mark Agents and the Trade Marks Designs and Patents Federation. It will also include one or more other Chancery judges. The Chairman is Mr Justice Jacob. Anyone having views concerning the improvement of intellectual property litigation is invited to make his or her views known to the committee, preferably through the relevant professional representative on the committee.

Pension Litigation Court Users' Committee

16.6 This consists of a judge and a master, two barristers and two solicitors. Its Chairman is Mr Justice Lloyd. Any suggestions for consideration by the committee should be sent to the clerk to Mr Justice Lloyd.

Chapter 17 – Alternative Dispute Resolution

Key Rules: CPR rules 3.1 and 26.4

17.1 While emphasising the primary role of the court as a forum for deciding cases, the court encourages parties to consider the use of ADR (such as, but not confined to, mediation and conciliation) as a possible means of resolving disputes or particular issues.

17.2 The settlement of disputes by means of ADR can:

(1) significantly help litigants to save costs;
(2) save litigants the delay of litigation in reaching finality in their disputes;
(3) enable litigants to achieve settlement of their disputes while preserving their existing commercial relationships and market reputation;
(4) provide litigants with a wider range of solutions than those offered by litigation; and
(5) make a substantial contribution to the more efficient use of judicial resources.

17.3 The court will in an appropriate case invite the parties to consider whether their dispute, or particular issues in it, could be resolved through ADR. The court may also adjourn the case for a specified period of time to encourage and enable the parties to use ADR and for this purpose extend the time for compliance by the parties or any of them with any requirement under the CPR or this Guide or any order of the court. The court may make such order as to the costs that the parties may incur by reason of the adjournment or their using or attempting to use ADR as may in all the circumstances seem appropriate.

17.4 Legal representatives in all cases should consider with their clients and the other parties concerned the possibility of attempting to resolve the dispute or particular issues by ADR and they should ensure that their clients are fully informed as to the most cost effective means of resolving their dispute.

17.5 Parties who consider that ADR might be an appropriate means of resolving their dispute, or particular issues in the dispute, may apply for directions at any stage.

17.6 The clerk to the Commercial Court keeps some published information as to individuals and bodies that offer ADR services. (The list also includes individuals and bodies that offer arbitration services.) If the parties are unable to agree upon a neutral individual, or panel of individuals, for ADR, they may refer to the judge for assistance, though the court will not recommend any particular body or individual to act as mediator or arbitrator.

SECTION B
SPECIALIST WORK

Chapter 18 – Introduction to the Specialist Work of the Chancery Division

18.1 As explained in Chapter 1 of this Guide, some proceedings in the High Court must be brought in the Chancery Division. These matters include:

(1) claims for the sale, exchange or partition of land, or the raising of charges on land;
(2) mortgage claims;
(3) claims relating to the execution of trusts;
(4) claims relating to the administration of the estates of deceased persons;
(5) bankruptcy matters;
(6) claims for the dissolution of partnerships or the taking of partnership or other accounts;
(7) claims for the rectification, setting aside or cancellation of deeds or other instruments in writing;
(8) contentious probate business;
(9) claims relating to patents, trade marks, registered designs, copyright or design right;
(10) claims for the appointment of a guardian of a minor's estate;
(11) jurisdiction under the Companies Acts 1985 and the Insolvency Act 1986 relating to companies;
(12) some revenue matters;
(13) claims relating to charities;
(14) some proceedings under the Solicitors Act 1974;
(15) proceedings under the Landlord and Tenant Acts 1927 (Part I), 1954 (Part II) and 1987 and the Leasehold Reform Act 1967; and
(16) proceedings under other miscellaneous statutory jurisdictions.

18.2 There is concurrent jurisdiction with the Family Division under the Inheritance (Provision for Family and Dependants) Act 1975.

18.3 Certain appeals lie to the Chancery Division under statute. These are dealt with in paragraph 10.19. Intellectual property appeals and revenue appeals are also covered in Chapters 23 and 25 respectively.

18.4 The Chancery judges are the nominated judges of the Court of Protection but this Guide does not deal with the Court of Protection.

Chapter 19 – The Bankruptcy Court

Key Rules: PD – Insolvency Proceedings; Insolvency Rules

19.1 The Bankruptcy Court is part of the Chancery Division and disposes of proceedings relating to insolvent individuals arising under Parts VIII to XI of the Insolvency Act 1986 and related legislation. These include applications for interim orders to support an individual voluntary arrangement, applications to set aside a statutory demand, bankruptcy petitions and various applications concerned with the realisation and distribution of the assets of individuals who have been adjudged bankrupt, as well as proceedings concerning the administration in bankruptcy of the insolvent estate of a deceased person.

19.2 The procedure in the Bankruptcy Court is governed by the Insolvency Rules and the PD – Insolvency Proceedings. Appeals in bankruptcy matters are covered in Chapter 10.

19.3 Proceedings in the Bankruptcy Court are issued in the Bankruptcy Issue and Search Room and are dealt with by the registrars in Bankruptcy, not the masters. Proceedings under Parts VIII to XI of the Insolvency Act 1986 should be entitled 'IN BANKRUPTCY'.

19.4 Certain matters, such as applications for injunctions or for committal for contempt, are heard by a judge. A judge is available to hear such matters each day in term time and applications may be listed for any such day. The judge will normally also be hearing the interim applications list for the day, but one or more other judges may be available to assist if necessary.

19.5 There are prescribed forms for use in connection with all types of statutory demand and of petitions for bankruptcy orders. Every other type of application is either an *originating application* in Form 7.1 (meaning an application to the court which is not an application in pending proceedings before the court) or an *ordinary application* in Form 7.2 (meaning any other application to the court).

Statutory demands

19.6 All applications to set aside a statutory demand are referred initially to a registrar. The application may be dismissed by the court without a hearing if it fails to disclose sufficient grounds. If it is not dismissed summarily, it will be allocated a hearing date when the registrar may either dispose of it summarily or give directions for its disposal at a later date. Such directions will commonly include an order for the filing and service of written evidence and of a certificate of compliance (see para 19.13 below).

Bankruptcy petitions

19.7 The court will not normally allow more than one bankruptcy petition to be presented against an individual at any one time.

19.8 In cases where the statutory demand relied on has not been personally served on the debtor or where execution of the debt has been returned unsatisfied in whole or in part, the permission of the registrar is required before a petition may be presented to the court.

19.9 On presentation to the court a bankruptcy petition is given a distinctive number. The details of the name and address of the petitioner, of his solicitors and of the debtor are entered on a computerised record which may be searched by attendance at the Issue and Search Room. It will also be endorsed with a hearing date which may be extended on application without notice if the petitioner has been unable to serve the petition on the debtor before the hearing date.

19.10 A debtor who intends to oppose the making of a bankruptcy order should file and serve a written notice in the prescribed form stating his grounds for opposing the petition not less than 7 days before the hearing date. The court may give such further directions as to the filing of evidence and of certificates of compliance (see para 19.13 below) as it considers appropriate to the disposal of the petition.

Other applications

19.11 Many different types of application may be made to the court for the purpose of the administration of the estate and affairs of a bankrupt individual or insolvent person who is subject to an individual voluntary arrangement (IVA). These may involve such matters as the examination of the bankrupt or of persons having knowledge of his affairs, the realisation of assets in his estate and the determination of disputes regarding the validity of a creditor's claim to dividend or entitlement to vote at a creditors' meeting. Such applications will be given a hearing date when the registrar will give such directions as are appropriate to the type of case, which may include directions for the filing and service of written evidence, for the cross-examination of witnesses and for the filing of certificates of compliance (see para 19.13 below).

Orders without attendance

19.12 In suitable cases the court will normally be prepared to make orders under Part VIII of the Act (interim orders for IVAs) and consent orders without attendance by the parties. Details of these types of order are set out in paragraph 16 of the PD – Insolvency Proceedings.

Certificates of compliance

19.13 In order to prevent waste of the court's time each party to insolvency proceedings may be required by the court to file a certificate of compliance in which he will be required to certify whether the directions previously given by the court have been complied with, whether and by whom he will be represented at the final hearing, his estimate of the time required for such hearing and his and his representative's dates to avoid. On the filing of the certificates in any particular case the court will fix a date for the final hearing of the case and notify the parties.

Preparation for hearings before the registrars

19.14 Paragraphs 7.39 to 7.45 apply to hearings before the Bankruptcy registrars. Skeleton arguments and bundles should be delivered to the Bankruptcy Registry.

General information

19.15 Inspection of the court's record and court file in any insolvency proceedings is governed by Insolvency Rules 7.28 and 7.31.

19.16 The following publications regarding practice and procedure in the Bankruptcy Court are available free from the Bankruptcy Issue and Search Room and from Room TM1.10 Thomas More Building, Royal Courts of Justice:

(1) Current Practice Direction and Practice Notes;
(2) A concise Guide to procedure in the Bankruptcy Court;
(3) *'I want to set aside my statutory demand – what do I do?'*
(4) *'I have a petition against me – what do I do?'*
(5) *'I want to appeal an order made by a district judge or an order made by a Bankruptcy registrar of the High Court – what can I do?'*
(6) *'I wish to apply for my Certificate of Discharge from Bankruptcy – what do I do?'*

Chapter 20 – The Companies Court

Key Rules and PDs: PD49 – Applications under the Companies Act; PD – Insolvency; Insolvency Rules 1986; Insolvent Companies (Disqualification of Unfit Directors) Proceedings Rules 1987; PD – Directors Disqualification Proceedings

20.1 The Companies Court is a part of the Chancery Division. Applications in the High Court under the Companies Act 1985, the Insurance Companies Act 1982, the Insolvency Act 1986 in relation to companies registered in England and Wales, and the Company Directors Disqualification Act 1986, must be commenced in the Companies Court. Proceedings concerning insolvent partnerships, under the Insolvent Partnerships Order 1994, are also brought in the Companies Court (unlike proceedings against partners separately, which, if the partner is an individual, are brought in bankruptcy). Many other kinds of application are brought in the Companies Court. Appeals in Companies Court matters are dealt with in Chapter 10.

20.2 Applications, other than in insolvency, are governed by the Civil Procedure Rules and PD49 – Applications under the Companies Act 1985.

20.3 Applications in insolvency relating to companies (and to insolvent partnerships) are governed by the Insolvency Rules and PD – Insolvency Proceedings.

20.4 Proceedings under the Company Directors Disqualification Act 1986 are governed by the Insolvent Companies (Disqualification of Unfit Directors) Proceedings Rules 1987 and the PD – Directors Disqualification Proceedings.

20.5 Proceedings in the Companies Court under a particular statute should be entitled accordingly, thus:

'In the matter of the Companies Act 1985 [and of any other statute as appropriate] And in the matter of [name and registration number of the company]'

'In the matter of the Company Directors Disqualification Act 1986 And in the matter of [name of the relevant company]'

'In the matter of the Insolvency Act 1986 [and of any appropriate order, such as the Insolvent Partnerships Order 1994] And in the matter of [name of the debtor]'

20.6 The Companies Court has a separate administrative procedure. Proceedings are issued in the Companies Court General Office, and they are dealt with by the registrars.

20.7 Petitions for winding up, petitions for confirmation by the court of reduction of capital, and interim applications for directions in proceedings by shareholders are among the principal matters heard by the registrars. A registrar may direct that any case be heard by a judge even if it is a kind of application which would normally be heard by a registrar.

20.8 Certain matters such as petitions for an administration order under Part II of the Insolvency Act 1986, petitions for approval by the court of schemes of arrangement and applications for the appointment of provisional liquidators are heard by a judge. A judge is available to hear companies matters each day in term time, and applications to be heard by that judge may be listed for any such day. The judge will normally also be hearing the Interim Applications List for the day, but one or more other judges may be available to assist if necessary.

Preparation for hearings before the registrars

20.9 Paragraphs 7.39 to 7.45 apply to hearings before the registrars of the Companies Court. Skeleton arguments and bundles should be delivered to the Companies Court Issue Section.

Petitions for administration orders

20.10 An administration order is an order directing that, during the period for which the order is in force, the affairs, business and property of the company are to be managed by a person ('the administrator') appointed for the purpose by the court. A company or its directors or a creditor may apply to the court for an administration order. The court may make an administration order if it is satisfied that the company is or is likely to become unable to pay its debts and considers that the making of the order would be likely to achieve one or more of the following purposes:

(1) the survival of the company and the whole or any part of its undertaking as a going concern;
(2) the approval of a voluntary arrangement;
(3) the sanctioning of a compromise or scheme of arrangement under section 425 of the Companies Act 1985; or
(4) a more advantageous realisation of the company's assets than would be effected on a winding up.

20.11 An application of administration order must be commenced by the prescribed form of petition. The petition should be listed before a judge (see 20.8 above).

20.12 Administration orders are sometimes made for a specifically limited time, or subject to a requirement that the administrator apply to the court for directions, or report to the court, by a given date. If the order is limited in time, the administrator may apply for it to be extended. If the application is made sufficiently in advance of the date when the order would otherwise expire, it may be dealt with on paper, unless the judge considers that a hearing is needed. If the order requires a written report to the court, it may specify that the report is to be addressed to the judge making the order. Once the judge has considered any such report it will be placed on the court file.

20.13 Practice Statements explain the extent to which the proposed administrator must comply with the reporting requirement of Rule 2.2, Insolvency Rules 1986, and the circumstances in which information in the report may be withheld from creditors: see *Practice Statements (Administration Orders: Reports)* dated 17 January 1994 and 15 April 2002, printed at [1994] 1 WLR 160 and [2002] 1 WLR 1358.

Schemes of arrangement

20.14 A scheme under section 425 of the Companies Act 1985 can be proposed whether or not a company is in liquidation. It is necessary to obtain the sanction of the Court to a scheme which has been approved by the requisite majority of creditors of each class at separately convened meetings directed by the Court. If the company is insolvent the objective of the scheme can be more simply and economically achieved by a company voluntary arrangement under Part I of the Act. However, a scheme under section 425 has the advantage that the Court may approve the distribution of assets otherwise than in accordance with creditors' strict legal rights.

20.15 The petition may be listed before either the judge or a registrar, but petitions in respect of substantial schemes will be listed before a judge.

20.16 A Practice Statement sets out the procedure to be followed in respect of any issues which may arise as to the constitution of meetings of creditors or which otherwise affect the conduct of those meetings: *Practice Statement (Companies: Schemes of Arrangement)* dated 15 April 2002, printed at [2002] 1 WLR 1345.

Winding-up petitions

20.17 Proceedings to wind up a company are commenced by presenting a petition to the court. The presentation of a winding-up petition can cause substantial damage to a company. A winding-up petition should not be presented when it is known that a debt is disputed in good faith. Practitioners should make reasonable enquiries from their client as to the existence of any such dispute. The court may order a petitioner to pay the company's costs of a petition based on a disputed debt on the indemnity basis.

20.18 When a winding-up petition is presented to either the Companies Court, a Chancery District Registry or a county court having jurisdiction, particulars including the name of the company and the petitioner's solicitors are entered in a computerised register. This is called the Central Registry of Winding-Up Petitions. It may be searched by personal attendance at the Companies Court General Office, or by telephone on 020 7947 7328.

20.19 The requirement to advertise the petition (Insolvency Rule 4.11(2)(b)) is mandatory, and designed to ensure that the class remedy of winding up by the court is made available to all creditors, and is not used simply as a means of putting pressure on the company to pay the petitioner's debt. Failure to comply with the rule, without good reason accepted by the court, may lead to the summary dismissal of the petition on the return date (Insolvency Rule 4.11(5)). If the court, in its discretion, grants an adjournment, this will be on condition that the petition is advertised in due time for the adjourned hearing. No further adjournment for the purpose of advertisement will normally be granted.

20.20 If an order is made restraining advertisement while an application is made to the court to stop the proceedings, the case is listed in the Daily Cause List by number only so that the name of the company is not given.

Proceedings for relief from unfairly prejudicial conduct under the Companies Act 1985, section 459

20.21 Petitions under the Companies Act 1985, section 459, are liable to involve extensive factual enquiry and many of the measures summarised in Section A of this Guide which are designed to avoid unnecessary cost and delay are particularly relevant to them.

20.22 Where applications are brought in the Companies Court and in a related case in the Chancery Division at the same time, special arrangements can be made on request to the Listing Officer for the applications to be heard by the same judge.

General

20.23 Inspection of the court's records and the court file in any insolvency proceedings is governed by Insolvency Rules 7.28 and 7.31.

20.24 The following leaflets are available from the Companies Court General Office:

(1) Current Practice Directions and Practice Notes;
(2) 'I want to wind up a company: what do I do?'
(3) 'I want to restore a company's name to the Register: what do I do?'
(4) 'I want to apply to extend time for registration of a charge or to rectify a mis-statement or omission (in the registered particulars of a charge or of a memorandum of satisfaction): what do I do?'

Chapter 21 – Mortgage Claims

Key Rules: CPR Parts 55 and 73 and the PDs supplementing them; RSC Order 88 rule 5A

21.1 The traditional jurisdiction of the Chancery Division in respect of mortgages has been radically affected by Part 55 and to a lesser extent by Part 73.

21.2 The effect of Part 55 is to remove from the High Court all new mortgage possession claims, whether in respect of residential or commercial property, save in respect of the relatively small number of cases where either the county court has no jurisdiction or where the claimant can certify, verified by a statement of truth, his reasons for bringing the claim in the High Court.

21.3 PD55 emphasises that the latter class of cases are to be regarded as exceptional and that while the value of the property and the size of the claim may well be relevant circumstances they will not, taken alone, normally justify the issue of proceedings in the High Court. High Court proceedings may, however, be justified where there are complicated disputes of fact or where a claim gives rise to points of law of general importance. Where a mortgage possession claim is issued in the High Court it is assigned to the Chancery Division. The provisions of Part 55 will apply to it.

21.4 The most common instance where, notwithstanding Part 55, the Chancery Division will retain jurisdiction in a mortgage possession case is where proceedings are brought seeking an order for sale under an equitable charge, ordinarily that created by a charging order, but where part of the relief claimed ancillary to the order for sale is an order for possession. Although Part 73 now provides that proceedings to enforce charging orders by sale should be made in the court in which the charging order was made, that provision is expressly subject to that court having jurisdiction. The jurisdiction of a county court to enforce a charge is confined to those cases where the amount secured by the charge falls within the relevant county court limit (currently £30,000) and it follows that in many cases where judgments have been obtained in county courts and charging orders made enforcement will nonetheless require proceedings in the High Court.

21.5 Such proceedings, as well as proceedings to enforce charging orders made in other divisions of the High Court, are assigned to the Chancery Division. The evidence required in support of such proceedings is that set out in paragraph 4.3 of PD73.

21.6 In addition, RSC Order 88 rule 5A remains in force in respect of transitional cases; that is to say proceedings to enforce charging orders which were commenced in the Chancery Division, as then required by RSC Order 50, prior to 25 March 2002.

21.7 There remain in the Chancery Division a large number of mortgage possession proceedings issued prior to Part 55 coming into force (on 15 October 2001) which are still subject to RSC Order 88. Of those proceedings, some may never have been adjudicated upon and many will have given rise to suspended possession orders, in respect of which applications to issue execution are still likely to arise. In dealing with such cases practitioners should have regard to the matters set out in paras 21.13 to 21.16 below, retained from the previous edition of the Guide.

21.8 Practitioners should also have regard to the fact that 'old' proceedings which have not been adjudicated upon and which were issued prior to 26 April 1999 will fall within the 'automatic stay' provisions of paragraph 19 of PD51 so that a claimant wishing to proceed with such a claim will have to apply to lift the stay. Such an application may be made at the same time as the application for possession but the court will require sufficient evidence to allow it to determine properly whether it is appropriate to lift the stay.

21.9 The Chancery Division retains its jurisdiction in respect of redemption and foreclosure of mortgages and kindred matters.

21.10 Rule 48.3 and para 50 of the Costs PD (Amount of costs where costs are payable under a contract) are of particular relevance to mortgage claims.

21.11 In summary, where under a mortgage a mortgagee has a contractual right to his or her costs, the court's discretion in respect of costs under section 51 of the Supreme Court Act 1981 should be exercised so as to reflect that contractual right. The power of the court to disallow a mortgagee's costs sought to be added to the security stems not from section 51 but from the power of the courts of equity to fix the terms upon which redemption will be allowed. A decision by the court to refuse costs to a mortgagee litigant may be a decision in the exercise of the court's discretion under section 51, or pursuant to its power to fix the terms upon which redemption will be allowed, or a decision as to the extent of the mortgagee's contractual right, in a given case, to add costs to his or her security, or any combination of these three things. A mortgagee is not to be deprived of a contractual or equitable right to add costs to his or her security without reference to the mortgagee's contractual or equitable rights to such costs and without a proper adjudication as to whether or not the mortgagee should be deprived of his or her costs.

Suspended possession orders (pre-15 October 2001 cases)

21.12 The following paragraphs are retained from the previous edition of this Guide, as being of relevance to mortgage possession proceedings begun in the High Court before 15 October 2001, when Part 55 was brought into force. The previous rules apply to them as if they had not been amended.

21.13 A suspended possession order is an order under which a person is entitled to a remedy subject to the fulfilment of a condition for the purposes of RSC Order 46 rule 2(1)(d) (which remains in force), so that Order 46 rule 4 applies. Permission to issue execution should not be given without notice and it follows that an application for such permission must be made on notice.

21.14 Suspended possession orders are made frequently in mortgagee possession claims by virtue of section 36 of the Administration of Justice Act 1970 and in such claims the defendant is often in default of acknowledging service of the claim form.

21.15 Where a defendant has not acknowledged service no special directions as to service are needed, but a claimant requiring permission to issue execution on a suspended possession order when there has been a default in acknowledging service must send a copy of the application notice and of the witness statement in support of the application notice to each defendant in default at his or her last known address, so as to reach him not less than 3 clear days before the hearing, and lodge with the master's clerk, at least 1 day before the hearing, the witness statement in support of the application endorsed with a certificate by the claimant's solicitor in the form following or as near thereto as may be appropriate:

> 'I certify that on day the day of 20.. a copy of the application notice herein dated together with a true copy of this document was sent by pre-paid letter post addressed to the defendant at [his/her] last known address. (*signed*) Claimant's solicitor'.

No further proof of service should normally be required in default cases.

21.16 The same principles apply and the same practice should be followed where permission to issue execution is required because 6 years or more have elapsed since the date of an unsuspended possession order or because there has been a change in the party liable to execution (see RSC Order 46 rule 2).

Chapter 22 – Partnership Claims and Receivers

Key Rules and PDs: CPR Part 69, PDs 24 and 40

PARTNERSHIP CLAIMS

22.1 In claims for or arising out of the dissolution of a partnership often the only matters in dispute between the partners are matters of accounting. In such cases there will be no trial. The court will, if appropriate, make a summary order under paragraph 6 of PD24 for the taking of an account. This will be taken before the master.

22.2 Only if there is a dispute as to the existence of a partnership (whether it is claimed that there never was a partnership or that the partnership is still continuing and has not been dissolved) or if there is a material dispute as to the terms of the partnership (eg as to the profit sharing ratios) will there be a trial, at which the judge will decide those issues. In such cases there will be a two stage procedure with the judge deciding these issues at the trial and ordering the winding up of the partnership which will involve the taking of the partnership accounts by the master (see PD40 Accounts, Inquiries etc).

22.3 To avoid the expense of such a two stage procedure the parties may agree that disputes as to the terms of the partnership be determined by an inquiry by the master held at the same time as he or she takes the accounts.

22.4 The expense of taking an account in court is usually wholly disproportionate to the amount at stake. Parties are strongly encouraged to refer disputes on accounts to an accountant for determination or mediation. The master can (whether before or after the reference to the accountant) decide any matters of principle arising on the accounts (eg the method for valuation of goodwill) or any substantial factual disputes (eg as to whether a partner has made a particular drawing or not).

22.5 The functions of a receiver in a partnership action are limited. It is not his or her duty to wind up the partnership, like the liquidator of a company. His or her primary function is to get in the debts and preserve the assets pending winding up by the court and he or she has no power of sale without the permission of the court.

RECEIVERS

22.6 New rules are expected to come into force in the autumn of 2002 as regards receivers. A guide to the procedure relating to receivers appointed by the court exists, and it will be revised if the changes to the rules make that appropriate. Subject to that, copies of the guide can be obtained from an associate, or, if the order appointing the receiver is made by a master, from the master who makes the order or, in advance of the making of an order, from the Court Manager, Chancery Chambers.

Chapter 23 – The Patents Court and Trade Marks etc

Key PD: PD49 – Patents, etc

23.1 The matters assigned to the Patents Court are essentially all those concerned with patents or registered designs. PD49 Patents, etc deals with its particular procedures. A new Part 63 is expected to come into force during 2003. This will cover all forms of intellectual property. Appeals in patent, design and trade mark cases are governed by Part 52; reference should be made to Chapter 10 for the general procedure as regards such appeals.

23.2 The judges of the Patents Court are nominated by the Lord Chancellor. The following judges of the Chancery Division are currently nominated:

Mr Justice Ferris
Mr Justice Jacob
Mr Justice Laddie
Mr Justice Neuberger
Mr Justice Pumfrey

Several senior practitioners have also been appointed to sit as Deputy High Court judges to hear Patent Court matters.

23.3 Mr Justice Jacob is the judge in charge of the Patents List.

23.4 In cases of great urgency, when a nominated judge or deputy judge is not available an application can be made to any other judge of the High Court, preferably a judge of the Chancery Division.

23.5 The procedure of the Patents Court is broadly that of the Chancery Division as a whole, but there are exceptions.

23.6 The Patents Court has its own Court Guide which is available from the clerk in Charge of the Patents Court List (currently Mrs Lorraine Bennett, Clerk to Mr Justice Jacob, Room W311, Royal Courts of Justice) and on the Patents Court Website (*www.courtservice.gov.uk*). That Guide should be consulted for detailed guidance as to the procedure in the Patents Court.

23.7 The Court's diary can be accessed on its Website. The Patents Court sits in the latter part of September, in addition to term time.

Patents County Court

23.8 Special provisions relate to the transfer of cases between the Patents Court and the Patents County Court. The Patents Court has no power to order the transfer to it of cases commenced in the Patents County Court which fall within the latter court's special jurisdiction (ie matters relating to patents and designs). On the other hand it does have the power to transfer cases commenced in the High Court to the Patents County Court.

Trade marks, copyright, design right and passing off

23.9 Proceedings in the High Court under the Trade Marks Acts 1938 and 1994, the Olympic Symbol Protection Act 1995, the Olympic Association Right (Infringement Proceedings) Regulations 1995, the Copyright, Designs and Patents Act 1988, and for passing off are heard in the Chancery Division. Paragraphs 19 to 26 of PD49 Patents, etc apply to these proceedings. They will be heard by any Chancery judge save that in a suitable design right case the case may be transferred to one of the Patent judges. Among the Chancery masters trade mark cases are assigned to Master Bragge: see paragraph 6.29 above.

23.10 Appeals from decisions of the registrar of Trade Marks are brought to the Chancery Division. Until new provision for these appeals is made by Part 63, such appeals should be brought by a notice of appeal in a form adapted from that for equivalent patent appeals which is annexed to PD49, Patents etc.

Chapter 24 – Probate and Inheritance Claims

Key Rules and PD: CPR Part 57 and PD57

PROBATE

24.1 In general, contentious probate proceedings follow the same pattern as an ordinary claim but there are important differences and Part 57 and PD57 should be carefully studied. Particular regard should be had to the following:

(1) A defendant must file an acknowledgment of service. An additional 14 days is provided for doing so.

(2) Save where the court orders otherwise, the parties must at the outset of proceedings lodge all testamentary documents in their possession and control with the court. At the same time parties must file written evidence describing any testamentary document of the deceased of which they have knowledge, stating, if any such document is not in the party's possession or control, the name and address, if known, of the person in whose possession or under whose control the document is. In the case of a claimant, these materials must be lodged at the time when the Claim Form is issued. In the case of a defendant, these materials must be lodged when service is acknowledged. If these requirements are not complied with it is likely that the claim will not be issued and, correspondingly, that the acknowledgment of service will not be permitted to be lodged.

(3) The court will generally ensure that all persons with any potential interest in the proceedings are joined as parties or served with notice under Part 19.8A.

(4) A default judgment cannot be obtained in a probate claim. Where, however, no defendant acknowledges service or files a defence, the claimant may apply for an order that the claim proceed to trial and seek a direction that the claim be tried on written evidence.

(5) If an order pronouncing for a will in solemn form is sought under Part 24, the evidence in support must include written evidence proving due execution of the will. In such a case, if a defendant has given notice under rule 57.11 that he raises no positive case but requires that the will be proved in solemn form and that, to that end, he wishes to cross examine the attesting witnesses, then the Claimant's application for summary judgment is subject to the right of such a defendant to require the attesting witnesses to attend for cross-examination.

(6) A defendant who wishes to do more than test the validity of the will by cross-examining the attesting witnesses must set up by Counterclaim his positive case in order to enable the court to make an appropriate finding or declaration as to which is the valid will, or whether a person died intestate or as the case may be.

(7) The proceedings may not be discontinued without permission. Even if they are compromised, it will usually be necessary to have an order stating to whom the grant is to be made, either under rule 57.11 (leading to a grant in common form), or after a trial on written

evidence under paragraph 6.1(1) of PD57 (leading to a grant in solemn form) or under section 49 of the Administration of Justice Act 1985 and paragraph 6.1(3) of PD57 (again leading to a grant in solemn form).

24.2 When the court orders trial of a contentious probate claim on written evidence, or where the court is asked to pronounce in solemn form under Part 24, it is normally necessary for an attesting witness to sign a witness statement or swear an affidavit of due execution of any will or codicil sought to be admitted to probate. The will or codicil is at that stage in the court's possession and cannot be handed out of court for use as an exhibit to the witness statement or affidavit, so that the attesting witness has to attend at the Royal Courts of Justice.

24.3 Where an attesting witness is unable to attend the Royal Courts of Justice in order to sign his or her witness statement or swear his or her affidavit in the presence of an officer of the court, the solicitor concerned may request from Room TM7.09, Thomas More Building, a photographic copy of the will or codicil in question. This will be certified as authentic by the court and may be exhibited to the witness statement or affidavit of due execution in lieu of the original. The witness statement or affidavit must in that case state that the exhibited document is an authenticated copy of the document signed in the witness's presence.

24.4 When a probate claim is listed for trial outside London, the solicitor for the party responsible for preparing the court bundle must write to Room TM7.09 and request that the testamentary documents be forwarded to the appropriate District Registry.

INHERITANCE (PROVISION FOR FAMILY AND DEPENDANTS) ACT 1975

24.5 Claims under the Inheritance (Provision for Family and Dependants) Act 1975 in the Chancery Division are issued by way of a Part 8 claim. Ordinarily they will be heard by the master. At present they are governed by RSC Order 99, but this is to be replaced by additions to Part 57 and PD57 before the end of 2002. The following paragraphs describe the procedure as it will be under the new rules.

24.6 The written evidence filed with such a claim must exhibit an official copy of the grant of probate or letters of administration together with every testamentary document in respect of which probate or letters of administration was granted.

24.7 A defendant must file and serve acknowledgment of service not later than 21 days after service of the Part 8 claim form. Any written evidence (subject to any extension agreed or directed) must likewise be served and filed no later than 21 days after service.

24.8 The personal representatives of the deceased are necessary defendants to a claim under the 1975 Act and the written evidence filed by a defendant who is a personal representative must comply with paragraph 15 of PD57.

24.9 On the hearing of a claim under the 1975 Act, the personal representatives must produce the original grant of representation to the deceased's estate. If the court makes an order under the Act, the original grant together with a sealed copy of the order must be sent to the Principal Registry of the Family Division for a memorandum of the order to be endorsed on or permanently annexed to the grant.

24.10 Where claims under the 1975 Act are compromised the consent order lodged must comply with paragraph 9.14 of this Guide.

Chapter 25 – Revenue Proceedings

Key Rules and PD: RSC Order 91 (see CPR Schedule 1), CPR Part 52, PD52, paragraphs 23.3 to 23.8

25.1 Several kinds of revenue proceedings are heard in the Chancery Division. Usually the parties are the Inland Revenue or HM Customs and Excise on one side and a taxpayer on the other. The main examples are described below. Almost all of them are appeals, which are governed by Part 52. Reference should be made to Chapter 10 for the general procedure relating to such appeals.

Appeals from decisions of the General Commissioners relating to income tax, corporation tax or capital gains tax

25.2 The General Commissioners are a first instance appeal tribunal for cases concerning these three taxes. Appeals from their decisions, whether by the Inland Revenue or by a taxpayer, are conducted on the basis of a case stated, drawn up by the General Commissioners, which sets out the facts, the arguments, and the General Commissioners' decision. The case stated is usually backed up by whatever documents were before the Commissioners. These appeals are limited to questions of law. The judge never hears evidence, and the appeal will almost certainly fail if the appellant's real complaint is that the General Commissioners got the facts wrong.

25.3 The rules provide that, when the party who is appealing from the General Commissioners receives the case stated in its final form from the General Commissioners' clerk, the party has to transmit it to the High Court within 30 days. The court has no power to extend this time limit, which must be strictly observed if the court is to be able to hear the appeal: *Petch v Gurney* [1994] STC 689.

Appeals from decisions of the Special Commissioners relating to income tax, corporation tax, capital gains tax or inheritance tax

25.4 The Special Commissioners are the other first instance appeal tribunal for tax purposes, and hear cases relating to all four taxes mentioned above, known as the direct taxes. Appeals from their decisions, whether by the Inland Revenue or by a taxpayer, are conducted, not on the basis of a case stated, but on the basis of the Special Commissioners' decision and the papers which they had before them. Those papers may include a transcript of the evidence or the Special Commissioners' notes of the evidence, but, as with appeals from General Commissioners, appeals to the Chancery Division are limited to questions of law. The judge never hears evidence.

25.5 Exceptionally, appeals from the Special Commissioners in relation to the direct taxes may go directly to the Court of Appeal, so leapfrogging the Chancery Division.

25.6 Some inheritance tax appeals are exceptions to the normal procedure and do not start before the Special Commissioners, so that the Chancery Division is the court of first instance. These are limited to cases where the issues to be decided are wholly or mainly issues of law and there is no substantial dispute about the facts.

Stamp duty appeals

25.7 These are heard in the Chancery Division, and are conducted on the basis of a case stated drawn up by the Inland Revenue. Usually there is no oral evidence, but it has occasionally been heard.

25.8 Appeals relating to stamp duty reserve tax are also heard in the Chancery Division. Rules relating to such appeals have been made, but no such appeal has yet arisen.

Appeals from the Value Added Tax and Duties Tribunal

25.9 Most of these appeals relate to VAT. The appeal may be brought either by Customs and Excise or by the taxpayer. As with appeals from the Special Commissioners relating to the direct taxes, exceptionally leapfrog appeals may lie direct to the Court of Appeal, but normally the appeal will be to the Chancery Division.

25.10 As with appeals from the Special Commissioners, VAT appeals are based on the Tribunal's decision and the documents in the case. The judge never hears evidence. The documents usually include a transcript of the evidence before the Tribunal or the Tribunal's notes of the evidence. Nevertheless, like appeals from the Special Commissioners concerning the direct taxes, an appeal lies only on a point of law.

Chapter 26 – Trusts

Key Rules and PDs: CPR Part 8; Part 19; RSC Order 85; from December 2002 Part 64 and PD64

Introduction

26.1 This Chapter contains material about a number of aspects of proceedings concerning trusts, the estates of deceased persons (other than probate claims) and charities. It incorporates some material previously set out in Chancery Division Practice Direction 12. At present the relevant rules are mainly to be found in RSC Orders 85, 93 (rule 21) and 108 (charities), all preserved in Sch 1 to the CPR, supplemented as regards Order 85 and CPR rule 8.2A by a PD. This material is expected to be replaced with effect from a date before the end of 2002 by a new Part 64 and one or more PDs. Reference is therefore made in this Chapter to Part 64 rather than to the RSC rules, where relevant, but without specific reference as the rules and PDs were not in final form at the date on which the text of the Guide had to be settled.

26.2 The topics covered in this Chapter are, in order, (a) applications by trustees for directions and related matters, (b) the Variation of Trusts Act 1958, (c) section 48 of the Administration of Justice Act 1985, (d) vesting orders as regards property in Scotland, (e) trustees under a disability, (f) lodgment of funds and (g) the estates of deceased Lloyd's Names.

Trustees' applications for directions

26.3 Applications to the court by trustees for directions in relation to the administration of a trust or charity, or by personal representatives in relation to a deceased person's estate, are to be brought by Part 8 claim form, and are governed by Part 64, and its PDs; rule 8.2A is also relevant.

26.4 If confidentiality of the directions sought is important (for example, where the directions relate to actual or proposed litigation with a third party who could find out what directions the claimants are seeking through access to the claim form under rule 5.4) the statement of the remedy sought, for the purposes of rule 8.2(b), may be expressed in general terms. The trustees must, in that case, state specifically in the evidence what it is that they seek to be allowed to do.

26.5 The proceedings will normally be listed and heard in private: rule 39.2(3)(f) and paragraph 1.5 of PD39. Accordingly the order made, and the other documents among the court records (apart from a claim form which has been served), will not be open to inspection by third parties without the court's permission: rule 5.4(2). If the matter is disposed of without a hearing, the order made will be expressed to have been made in private.

26.6 Part 64 deals with the joining of beneficiaries as defendants. Often, especially in the case of a private trust, it will be clear that some, and which, beneficiaries need to be joined as defendants. Sometimes, if there are only two views as to the appropriate course, and one is advocated by one beneficiary who will be joined, it may not be necessary for other beneficiaries to be joined since the trustees may be able to present the other arguments. Equally, in the case of a pension trust, it may not be necessary for a member of every possible different class of beneficiaries to be joined.

26.7 In some cases, it may be that the court will or might be able to assess whether or not to give the directions sought, or what directions to give, without hearing from any party other than the trustees. If the trustees consider that their case is in that category they may apply to the court under rule 8.2A for permission to issue the claim form without naming any defendants. They must apply to the court before the claim form is issued, and include a copy of the claim form that they propose to issue.

26.8 In other cases the trustees may know that beneficiaries need to be joined as defendants, or to be given notice, but may be in doubt as to which. Examples could include a case concerning a pension scheme with many beneficiaries and a number of different categories of interest, especially if they may be differently affected by the action for which directions are sought, or a private trust with a large class of discretionary beneficiaries. In those cases the trustees may apply for permission to issue the claim form without naming any defendants under rule 8.2A. The application may be combined with an application for directions as to which persons to join as parties or to give notice to under rule 19.8A.

26.9 In the case of a charitable trust the Attorney-General is always the appropriate defendant, and almost always the only one.

Case management directions

26.10 The claim will be referred to the master once a defendant has acknowledged service, or otherwise on expiry of the period for acknowledgment of service, (or, if no defendant is named, as soon as the claimants' evidence has been filed) to consider directions for the management of the case. Such directions may be given without a hearing in some cases; these might include directions as to parties or as to notice of proceedings, as mentioned in paragraph 26.8 above.

26.11 Case management directions will be given where the court grants an application to issue the claim form without naming a defendant under rule 8.2A.

Proceeding without a hearing

26.12 The court will always consider whether it is possible to deal with the application on paper without a hearing. The trustees must always consider whether a hearing is needed for any reason. If they consider that it is they should say so and explain why in their evidence. If a defendant considers that a hearing is needed, this should be stated, and the reasons explained, in his evidence, if any, or otherwise in a letter to the court.

26.13 If the court would be minded to refuse to give the directions asked for on a consideration of the papers alone, the parties will be notified and given the opportunity, within a stated time, to ask for a hearing.

26.14 In charity cases, the master may deal with the case without a hearing on the basis of a letter from or on behalf of the Attorney-General setting out his attitude to the application.

26.15 Cases in which the directions can be given without a hearing include those where personal representatives apply to be allowed to distribute the estate of a deceased Lloyd's name, following the decision in *Re Yorke deceased* [1997] 4 All ER 907 (see paragraphs 26.50–55 below), as well as applications under section 48 of the Administration of Justice Act 1985 (see paragraphs 26.37–42 below).

Evidence

26.16 The trustees' evidence should be given by witness statement. In order to ensure that, if directions are given, the trustees are properly protected by the order, they must ensure full disclosure of relevant matters, even if the case is to proceed with the participation of beneficiaries as defendants.

26.17 Applications for directions whether or not to take or defend or pursue litigation (see *Re Beddoe* [1893] 1 Ch 547) should be supported by evidence including the advice of an appropriately qualified lawyer as to the prospects of success and other matters relevant to be taken into account, including a cost estimate for the proceedings and any known facts concerning the means of the opposite party to the proceedings, and a draft of any proposed statement of case. There are cases in which it is likely to be so clear that the trustees ought to proceed as they wish that the costs of making the application, even on a simplified procedure without a hearing and perhaps without defendants, are not justified in comparison with the size of the fund or the matters at issue.

26.18 References to an appropriately qualified lawyer mean one whose qualifications and experience are appropriate to the circumstances of the case. The qualifications should be stated. If the advice is given on formal instructions, the instructions should always be put in evidence as well, so that the court can see the basis on which the advice was given. If it is not, the advice must state fully the basis on which it is given. If a hearing is necessary the lawyer whose opinion is relied on should if possible be the advocate at the hearing.

26.19 All applications for directions should be supported by evidence showing the value of the trust assets, the significance of the proposed litigation or other course of action for the trust, and why the court's directions are needed. In the case of a pension trust the evidence should include the latest actuarial valuation, and should describe the membership profile and, if a deficit on winding up is likely, the priority provisions and their likely effect.

26.20 On an application for directions about actual or possible litigation, the evidence should also state (i) whether any relevant Pre-Action Protocol has been followed, and (ii) whether the trustees have proposed or undertaken, or intend to propose, ADR, and (in each case) if not why not.

26.21 If a beneficiary of the trust is a party to the litigation about which directions are sought, with an interest opposed to that of the trustees, that beneficiary should be a defendant to the trustees' application, but any material which would be privileged as regards that beneficiary in the litigation should be put in evidence as exhibits to the trustees' witness statement, and should not be served on the beneficiary. However, if the claimant's representatives consider that no harm would be done by the disclosure of all or some part of the material then that material should be served on that defendant. That defendant may also be excluded from part of the hearing, including that which is devoted to discussion of the material withheld: see *Re Moritz* [1960] Ch 251; *Re Eaton* [1964] 1 WLR 1269.

Consultation with beneficiaries

26.22 The evidence must explain what, if any, consultation there has been with beneficiaries, and with what result. In preparation for an application for directions in respect of litigation, the following guidance is to be followed.

(1) If the trust is a private trust where the beneficiaries principally concerned are not numerous and are all or mainly adult, identified and traceable, the trustees will be expected to have canvassed with all the adult beneficiaries the proposed or possible courses of action before applying for directions.
(2) If it is a private trust with a larger number of beneficiaries, including those not yet born or identified, or children, it is likely that there will nevertheless be some adult beneficiaries principally concerned, with whom the trustees must consult.
(3) In relation to a charitable trust the trustees must have consulted the Attorney-General, through the Treasury Solicitor, as well as the Charity Commissioners, whose consent to the application will have been needed under section 33 of the Charities Act 1993.
(4) In relation to a pension trust, unless the members are very few in number, no particular steps by way of consultation with beneficiaries (including, where relevant, employers) or their representatives are

required in preparation for the application, though the trustees' evidence should describe any consultation that has in fact taken place. If no consultation has taken place, the court could in some cases direct that meetings of one or more classes of beneficiaries be held to consider the subject-matter of the application, possibly as a preliminary to deciding whether a member of a particular class ought to be joined as a defendant, though in a case concerning actual or proposed litigation, steps would need to be considered to protect privileged material from too wide disclosure.

26.23 If the court gives directions allowing the claimant to take, defend or pursue litigation it may do so up to a particular stage in the litigation, requiring the trustees, before they carry on beyond that point, to renew their application to the court. What stage that should be will depend on the likely management of the litigation under the CPR. If the application is to be renewed after disclosure of documents, and disclosed documents need to be shown to the court, it may be necessary to obtain permission to do this from the court in which the other litigation is proceeding. However, the implied undertaking limiting the use of documents disclosed by another party to the litigation does not preclude their use on an application by trustee parties for directions, since that is use for the purposes of the litigation: *White v Biddulph*, Hart J, unreported 22 May 1998.

26.24 In such a case the court may sometimes direct that the case be dealt with at that stage without a hearing if the beneficiaries obtain and lodge an opinion of an appropriately qualified lawyer supporting the continuation of the directions. Any such opinion will be considered by the court and, if thought fit, the trustees will be given a direction allowing them to continue pursuing the proceedings without a hearing.

26.25 In a case of urgency, such as where a limitation period or period for service of proceedings is about to expire, the court may give directions on a summary consideration of the evidence to cover the steps which need to be taken urgently, but limiting those directions so that the application needs to be renewed for fuller consideration at an early stage.

26.26 On any application for directions where a child is a defendant, the court will expect to have put before it the instructions to and advice of an appropriately qualified lawyer as to the benefits and disadvantages of the proposed, and any other relevant, course of action from the point of view of the child beneficiary. Where the matters to be drawn to the attention of the court are fully covered in the instructions and written opinion, it should not be necessary for a separate skeleton argument to be lodged, but the court needs to be informed that this is the case. The opinion should be given by the lawyer who is to be the advocate at the hearing.

Hearing

26.27 The master may give the directions sought though, if the directions relate to actual or proposed litigation, only if it is a plain case, and the master may be prepared to proceed without a hearing: see PD2 Allocation of Cases to Levels of Judiciary, paragraph 4.1 and paragraph 5.1(e), and see also paragraphs 26.12 to 26.15 above. Otherwise the case will be referred to the judge.

Representation Orders

26.28 It is not necessary to make representation orders under rule 19.7 on an application for directions, and sometimes it would not be possible, for lack of separate representatives among the parties of all relevant classes of beneficiaries, but such orders can be useful in an appropriate case and they are sometimes made.

Costs

26.29 Normally the trustees' costs of a proper application will be allowed out of the trust fund, on an indemnity basis, as will the assessed (or agreed) costs of beneficiaries joined as defendants, subject to their conduct of the proceedings having been proper and reasonable.

Prospective costs orders

26.30 In proceedings brought by one or more beneficiaries against trustees, the court has power to direct that the beneficiaries be indemnified out of the trust fund in any event for any costs incurred by them and any costs which they may be ordered to pay to any other party, known as a prospective costs order: see *McDonald v Horn* [1995] 1 All ER 961. Such an order may provide for payments out of the trust fund from time to time on account of the indemnity so that the beneficiaries' costs may be paid on an interim basis. Applications for prospective costs orders should be made on notice to the trustees. The court will require to be satisfied that there are matters which need to be investigated. How far the court will wish to go into that question, and in what way it should be done, will depend on the circumstances of the particular case. The order may be expressed to cover costs incurred only up to a particular stage in the proceedings, so that the application has to be renewed, if necessary, in the light of what has occurred in the proceedings in the meantime. See *Practice Statement (Trust Proceedings: Prospective Costs Orders)* 1 May 2001 [2001] 1 WLR 1082, [2001] 3 All ER 574, which includes a model form of order.

Charity trustees' applications for permission to bring proceedings

26.31 In the case of a charitable trust, if the Charity Commissioners refuse their consent to the trustees applying to the court for directions, under Charities Act 1993 section 33(2), and also refuse to give the trustees the directions under their own powers, under sections 26 or 29, the trustees may apply to the court under section 33(5). On such an application, which may be dealt with on paper, the judge may call for a statement from the Charity Commissioners of their reasons for refusing permission, if not already apparent from the papers. The court may require the trustees to attend before deciding whether to grant permission for the proceedings. It is possible to require notice of the hearing to be given to the Attorney-General, but this would not normally be appropriate.

Variation of Trusts Act 1958

26.32 An application under the Variation of Trusts Act 1958 should be made by a Part 8 claim form. As to listing of such applications see para 6.27. The master will not consider the file without an application.

26.33 Where any children or unborn beneficiaries will be affected by an arrangement under the Variation of Trusts Act 1958, evidence must normally be before the court which shows that their litigation friends or the trustees support the arrangements as being in the interests of the children or unborn beneficiaries, and exhibits a written opinion to this effect. In complicated cases a written opinion is usually essential to the understanding of the litigation friends and the trustees, and to the consideration by the court of the merits and fiscal consequences of the arrangement. If the written opinion was given on formal instructions, those instructions must be exhibited. Otherwise the opinion must state fully the basis on which it was given. The opinion must be given by the advocate who will appear on the hearing of the application. A skeleton argument may not be needed where a written opinion has been put in evidence and no matters not appearing from the instructions or the opinion are to be relied on: see para 26.26 above.

26.34 Where the interests of two or more children, or two or more of the children and unborn beneficiaries, are similar, a single written opinion will suffice; and no written opinion is required in respect of those who fall within the proviso to section 1(1) of the Act (Discretionary interests under protective trusts). Further, in proper cases the requirement of a written opinion may at any stage be dispensed with by the master or the judge.

Stamp Duty

26.35 An undertaking by solicitors with regard to stamping is not required to be included in an order under the Variation of Trusts Act 1958 whether made by a judge or master.

26.36 The Commissioners of Inland Revenue consider that the stamp duty position of duplicate orders is as follows:

(1) Orders confined to the lifting of protective trusts. These orders are not liable for duty at all and should not be presented to a stamp office.

(2) Orders effecting voluntary dispositions *inter vivos*. These orders may be certified under the Stamp Duty (Exempt Instruments) Regulations 1987 (SI 1987 No 516), as within category L in the schedule to those regulations, in which case they should not be presented to a stamp office. Without such a certificate they attract 50p duty under the head 'Conveyance or transfer of any kind not hereinbefore described.'

(3) Orders outside those described at paragraphs (1) and (2) above that contain declarations of the trust, ie that effect no disposition of trust property. These orders attract 50p fixed duty under the head 'Declaration of trust.' They may be presented for stamping at any stamp office in the usual way, or sent for adjudication if preferred.

Applications under section 48 of the Administration of Justice Act 1985

26.37 Applications under section 48 of the Administration of Justice Act 1985 should be made by Part 8 Claim Form without naming a defendant, under rule 8.2A. No separate application for permission under rule 8.2A need be made. The claim should be supported by a witness statement or affidavit to which are exhibited: (a) copies of all relevant documents, (b) instructions to a person with a 10-year High Court qualification within the meaning of the Courts and Legal Services Act 1990 ('the qualified person'), (c) the qualified person's opinion, (d) draft terms of the desired order.

26.38 The witness statement or affidavit (or exhibits thereto) should state: (a) the names of all persons who are, or may be, affected by the order sought, (b) all surrounding circumstances admissible and relevant in construing the document, (c) the date of qualification of the qualified person and his or her experience in the construction of trust documents, (d) the approximate value of the fund or property in question, (e) whether it is known to the applicant that a dispute exists and, if so, details of such dispute.

26.39 When the file is placed before the master he will consider whether the evidence is complete and if it is send the file to the judge.

26.40 The judge will consider the papers and, if necessary, direct service of notices under rule 19.8A or request such further information as he or she may desire. If the judge is satisfied that the order sought is appropriate, the order will be made and sent to the claimant.

26.41 If following service of notices under rule 19.8A any acknowledgment of service is received, the claimant must apply to the master (on notice to the parties who have so acknowledged service) for directions. If the claimant desires to pursue the application to the court, in the ordinary case the master will direct that the case proceeds as a Part 8 claim.

26.42 If on the hearing of the claim the judge is of the opinion that any party who entered an acknowledgment of service has no reasonably tenable argument contrary to the qualified person's opinion, in the exercise of his or her discretion he or she may order such party to pay any costs thrown away, or part thereof.

Vesting orders – property in Scotland

26.43 In applications for vesting orders under the Trustee Act 1925 any investments or property situate in Scotland should be set out in a separate schedule to the claim form, and the claim form should ask that the trustees may have permission to apply for a vesting order in Scotland in respect thereto.

26.44 The form of the order to be made in such cases will (with any necessary variation) be as follows:

> 'It is ordered that the as Trustees have permission to take all steps that may be necessary to obtain a vesting order in Scotland relating to [the securities] specified in the schedule herein.'

Disability of Trustee

26.45 There must be medical evidence showing incapacity to act as a trustee at the date of issue of the claim form and that the incapacity is continuing at the date of signing the witness statement or swearing the affidavit. The witness statement or affidavit should also show incapacity to execute transfers, where a vesting order of stocks and shares is asked for.

26.46 The trustee under disability should be made a defendant to the claim but need not be served unless he or she is sole trustee or has a beneficial interest.

Lodgment of Funds

26.47 Lodgment into the High Court of amounts of cash or securities of less than £500 under section 63 of the Trustee Act 1925, and rule 14(1) of the Court Funds Rules 1987 will not be accepted by the Accountant-General unless the Chief Master so signifies in writing.

26.48 The Accountant-General will refer the applicant to the Chief Master who will consider whether there is a more economical method of preserving the fund than lodging it in the High Court or, failing that, may suggest that the money be lodged in a county court (which has power to accept sums of up to £30,000 lodged under section 63 of the Trustee Act 1925).

26.49 If the Chief Master decides that a particular lodgment should be made in the High Court, he will so signify on the back of the request (in respect of applications under rule 14(1)(ii)(a)) or the office copy schedule to the affidavit (in respect of applications under rule 14(1)(ii)(b)).

Estates of Deceased Lloyd's Names

26.50 The following paragraphs describe a procedure concerning the estates of deceased Lloyd's names which used to be in section G of Chancery Division Practice Direction 12, and was originally promulgated in a Practice Direction dated 21 November 1997. This has now been replaced by a Practice Statement dated 25 May 2001, printed at [2001] 3 All ER 765.

26.51 Personal representatives who wish to apply to the court for permission to distribute the estate of a deceased Lloyd's Name following the decision of Lindsay J in *Re Yorke (deceased)* [1997] 4 All ER 907, or trustees who wish to administer any will trusts arising in such an estate, may, until further notice and if appropriate in the particular estate, adopt the following procedure.

26.52 The procedure will be appropriate where:

(1) the only, or only substantial, reason for delaying distribution of the estate is the possibility of personal liability to Lloyd's creditors and
(2) all liabilities of the estate in respect of syndicates of which the Name was a member have for the years 1992 and earlier (if any) been reinsured (whether directly or indirectly) into the Equitas group and
(3) all liabilities of the estate in respect of syndicates of which the Name was a member have for the years 1993 and later (if any) arisen in respect of syndicates which have closed by reinsurance in the usual way or are protected by the terms of an Estate Protection Plan issued by Centrewrite Limited or are protected by the terms of EXEAT insurance cover provided by Centrewrite Limited.

26.53 In these circumstances personal representatives (and, if applicable, trustees) may apply by a Part 8 Claim Form headed 'In the Matter of the Estate of [ ] deceased (a Lloyd's Estate) and In the Matter of the Practice Direction dated May 25 2001' for permission to distribute the estate (and, if applicable, to administer the will trusts) on the footing that no or no further provision need be made for Lloyd's creditors. Ordinarily, the claim form need not name any other party. It may be issued in this form without a separate application for permission under rule 8.2A.

26.54 The claim should be supported by a witness statement or an affidavit substantially in the form set out in Appendix 7, adapted as necessary to the particular circumstances and accompanied by a draft of the desired order substantially in the form also set out in Appendix 7. If the amount of costs has been agreed with the residuary beneficiaries (or, if the costs are not to be taken from residue, with the beneficiaries affected) their signed consent to those costs should also be submitted. If the Claimants are inviting the Court to make a summary assessment they should submit a statement of costs in the form specified in the Costs PD. If in his discretion the master (or outside London the district judge) thinks fit, he will summarily assess the costs but with permission for the paying party to apply within 14 days of service of the order on him to vary or discharge the summary assessment. Subject to the foregoing, the order will provide for a detailed assessment unless subsequently agreed.

26.55 The application will be considered in the first instance by the master who, if satisfied that the order should be made, may make the order without requiring the attendance of the applicants, and the court will send it to them. If not so satisfied, the master may give directions for the further disposal of the application.

APPENDICES

APPENDIX 1

GUIDELINES ON STATEMENTS OF CASE

1 The document must be as brief and concise as possible.

2 The document must be set out in separate consecutively numbered paragraphs and subparagraphs.

3 So far as possible each paragraph or subparagraph should contain no more than one allegation.

4 The document should deal with the case on a point by point basis, to allow a point by point response.

5 Where the CPR require a party to give particulars of an allegation or reasons for a denial (see rule 16.5(2)), the allegation or denial should be stated first and then the particulars or reasons listed one by one in separate numbered subparagraphs.

6 A party wishing to advance a positive case must identify that case in the document; a simple denial is not sufficient.

7 Any matter which if not stated might take another party by surprise should be stated.

8 Where they will assist, headings, abbreviations and definitions should be used and a glossary annexed.

9 Contentious headings, abbreviations, paraphrasing and definitions should not be used; every effort should be made to ensure that headings, abbreviations and definitions are in a form that will enable them to be adopted without issue by the other parties.

10 Particulars of primary allegations should be stated as particulars and not as primary allegations.

11 Schedules or appendices should be used if this would be helpful, for example where lengthy particulars are necessary.

12 The names of any witness to be called may be given, and necessary documents (including an expert's report) can be attached or served contemporaneously if not bulky (PD16; Guide paragraph 2.11). Otherwise evidence should not be included.

13 A response to particulars stated in a schedule should be stated in a corresponding schedule.

14 A party should not set out lengthy extracts from a document in his or her statement of case. If an extract has to be included, it should be placed in a schedule.

15 The document must be signed by the individual person or persons who drafted it not, in the case of a solicitor, in the name of the firm only.

APPENDIX 2

GUIDELINES ON BUNDLES

Bundles of documents must comply with paragraph 3 of PD39 Miscellaneous Provisions relating to Hearings. These guidelines are additional to those requirements, and they should be followed wherever possible.

1 The preparation of bundles requires co-operation between the legal representatives for all parties, and in many cases a high level of co-operation. It is the duty of all legal representatives to co-operate to the necessary level. Where a party is acting in person it is also that party's duty to co-operate as necessary with the other parties' legal representatives.

2 Bundles should be prepared in accordance with the following guidance.

Avoidance of duplication

3 No more than one copy of any one document should be included, unless there is good reason for doing otherwise. One such reason may be the use of a separate core bundle.

4 If the same document is included in the chronological bundles and is also an exhibit to an affidavit or witness statement, it should be included in the chronological bundle and where it would otherwise appear as an exhibit a sheet should instead be inserted. This sheet should state the page and bundle number in the chronological bundles where the document can be found.

5 Where the court considers that costs have been wasted by copying unnecessary documents, a special costs order may be made against the relevant person.

Chronological order and organisation

6 In general documents should be arranged in date order starting with the earliest document.

7 If a contract or other transactional document is central to the case it may be included in a separate place provided that a page is inserted in the chronological run of documents to indicate where it would have appeared chronologically and where it is to be found instead. Alternatively transactional documents may be placed in a separate bundle as a category.

Pagination

8 This is covered by paragraph 3 of the PD, but it is permissible, instead of numbering the whole bundle, to number documents separately within tabs. An exception to consecutive page numbering arises in the case of the core bundle. For this it may be preferable to retain the original numbering with each bundle represented by a separate divider.

9 Page numbers should be inserted in bold figures, at the bottom of the page and in a form that can clearly be distinguished from any other pagination on the document.

Format and presentation

10 Where possible, the documents should be in A4 format. Where a document has to be read across rather than down the page, it should so be placed in the bundle as to ensure that the top of the text starts nearest the spine.

11 Where any marking or writing in colour on a document is important, for example on a conveyancing plan, the document must be copied in colour or marked up correctly in colour.

12 Documents in manuscript, or not easily legible, should be transcribed; the transcription should be marked and placed adjacent to the document transcribed.

13 Documents in a foreign language should be translated; the translation should be marked and placed adjacent to the document translated; the translation should be agreed or, if it cannot be agreed, each party's proposed translation should be included.

14 The size of any bundle should be tailored to its contents. There is no point having a large lever-arch file with just a few pages inside. On the other hand bundles should not be overloaded as they tend to break. **No bundle should contain more than 300 pages.**

15 Binders and files must be strong enough to withstand heavy use.

16 Large documents, such as plans, should be placed in an easily accessible file. If they will need to be opened up often, it may be sensible for the file to be larger than A4 size.

Indices and labels

17 Indices should, if possible, be on a single sheet. It is not necessary to waste space with the full heading of the action. Documents should be identified briefly but properly, eg 'AGS3 – Defendants Accounts'.

18 Outer labels should use large lettering, eg 'A. Pleadings.' The full title of the action and solicitors' names and addresses should be omitted. A label should be used on the front as well as on the spine.

19 A label should also be stuck on to the front inside cover of a file at the top left, in such a way that it can be seen even when the file is open.

Staples etc

20 All staples, heavy metal clips etc should be removed.

Statements of case

21 Statements of case should be assembled in 'chapter' form, ie claim form followed by particulars of claim, followed by further information, irrespective of date.

22 Redundant documents, eg particulars of claim overtaken by amendments, requests for further information recited in the answers given, should generally be excluded. Backsheets to statements of case should also be omitted.

Witness statements, affidavits and expert reports

23 Where there are witness statements, affidavits and/or expert reports from two or more parties, each party's witness statements etc should, in large cases, be contained in separate bundles.

24 The copies of the witness statements, affidavits and expert reports in the bundles should have written on them, next to the reference to any document, the reference to that document in the bundles. This can be done in manuscript.

25 Documents referred to in, or exhibited to, witness statements, affidavits and expert reports should be put in a separate bundle and not placed behind the statement concerned, so that the reader can see both the text of the statement and the document referred to at the same time.

26 Backsheets to affidavits and witness statements should be omitted.

New Documents

27 Before a new document is introduced into bundles which have already been delivered to the court – indeed before it is copied – steps should be taken to ensure that it carries an appropriate bundle/page number, so that it can be added to the court documents. It should not be stapled, and it should be prepared with punch holes for immediate inclusion in the binders in use.

28 If it is expected that a large number of miscellaneous new documents will from time to time be introduced, there should be a special tabbed empty loose-leaf file for that purpose. An index should be produced for this file, updated as necessary.

Inter-Solicitor Correspondence

29 It is seldom that all inter-solicitor correspondence is required. Only those letters which are likely to be referred to should be copied. They should normally be placed in a separate bundle.

Core bundle

30 Where the volume of documents needed to be included in the bundles, and the nature of the case, makes it sensible, a separate core bundle should be prepared for the trial, containing those documents likely to be referred to most frequently.

Basis of agreement of bundles

31 See Chapter 7, paragraph 13.

Photocopy authorities

32 If authorities, extracts from text-books etc are photocopied for convenience for use in court, the photocopies should be placed in a separate bundle with an index and dividers. Reduced size copies (ie two pages of original to each A4 sheet) should not be used. Where only a short passage from a long case is needed, the headnote and key pages only should be copied and the usher should be asked to have the full volume in court. Whenever possible the parties' advocates should liaise about these bundles in order to avoid duplication of copies.

APPENDIX 3

GUIDELINES ON SKELETON ARGUMENTS, CHRONOLOGIES, INDICES AND READING LISTS

Skeleton arguments

1 A skeleton argument is intended to identify both for the parties and the court those points which are, and those that are not, in issue, and the nature of the argument in relation to those points which are in issue. It is not a substitute for oral argument.

2 Every skeleton argument should therefore:

- (1) identify concisely:
  - (a) the nature of the case generally, and the background facts insofar as they are relevant to the matter before the court;
  - (b) the propositions of law relied on with references to the relevant authorities;
  - (c) the submissions of fact to be made with reference to the evidence;
- (2) be as brief as the nature of the issues allows – it should not normally exceed 20 pages of double-spaced A4 paper and in many cases it should be much shorter than this;
- (3) be in numbered paragraphs and state the name (and contact details) of the advocate(s) who prepared it;
- (4) avoid arguing the case at length;
- (5) avoid formality and make use of abbreviations, eg C for Claimant, A/345 for bundle A page 345, 1.1.95 for 1 January 1995 etc.

3 Paragraph 1 also applies to written summaries of opening speeches and final speeches. Even though in a large case these may necessarily be longer, they should still be as brief as the case allows.

Reading lists

4 The documents which the judge should if possible read before the hearing may be identified in a skeleton argument, but must in any event be listed in a

separate reading list, if possible agreed between the advocates, which must be lodged with the agreed bundles, together with an estimate, if possible agreed, of the time required for the reading.

Chronologies and indices

5 Chronologies and indices should be non-contentious and agreed with the other parties if possible. If there is a material dispute about any event stated in the chronology, that should be stated in neutral terms and the competing versions shortly stated.

6 If time and circumstances allow its preparation, a chronology or index to which all parties have contributed and agreed can be invaluable.

7 Chronologies and indices once prepared can be easily updated and may be of continuing usefulness throughout the case.

APPENDIX 4

GUIDELINES ON WITNESS STATEMENTS

1 The function of a witness statement is to set out in writing the evidence in chief of the maker of the statement. Accordingly witness statements should, so far as possible, be expressed in the witness's own words. This guideline applies unless the perception or recollection of the witness of the events in question is not in issue.

2 Witness statements should be as concise as the circumstances of the case allow. They should be written in consecutively numbered paragraphs. They should present the evidence in an orderly and readily comprehensible manner. They must be signed by the witness, and contain a statement that he or she believes that the facts stated in his or her witness statement are true. They must indicate which of the statements made are made from the witness's own knowledge and which are made on information and belief, giving the source of the information or basis for the belief.

3 Inadmissible material should not be included. Irrelevant material should likewise not be included.

4 Any party on whom a witness statement is served who objects to the relevance or admissibility of material contained in a witness statement should notify the other party of his or her objection within 28 days after service of the witness statement in question and the parties concerned should attempt to resolve the matter as soon as possible. If it is not possible to resolve the matter, the party who objects should make an appropriate application, normally at the PTR, if there is one, or otherwise at trial.

5 It is incumbent on solicitors and counsel not to allow the costs of preparation of witness statements to be unnecessarily increased by over-elaboration of the statements. Any unnecessary elaboration may be the subject of a special order as to costs.

6 Witness statements must contain the truth, the whole truth and nothing but the truth on the issues covered. Great care must be taken in the preparation of witness statements. No pressure of any kind should be placed on a witness to give other than a true and complete account of his or her evidence. It is improper to serve a witness statement which is known to be false or which the maker does

not in all respects actually believe to be true. In addition, a professional adviser may be under an obligation to check where practicable the truth of facts stated in a witness statement if he or she is put on enquiry as to their truth. If a party discovers that a witness statement which he or she has served is incorrect he or she must inform the other parties immediately.

7 A witness statement should simply cover those issues, but only those issues, on which the party serving the statement wishes that witness to give evidence in chief. Thus it is not, for example, the function of a witness statement to provide a commentary on the documents in the trial bundle, nor to set out quotations from such documents, nor to engage in matters of argument. Witness statements should not deal with other matters merely because they may arise in the course of the trial.

8 Witness statements very often refer to documents. If there could be any doubt as to what document is being referred to, or if the document has not previously been made available on disclosure, it may be helpful for the document to be exhibited to the witness statement. If, to assist reference to the documents, the documents referred to are exhibited to the witness statement, they should nevertheless not be included in trial bundles in that form: see Appendix 2 paragraph 4. If (as is normally preferable) the documents referred to in the witness statement are not exhibited, care should be taken in identifying them, for example by reference to the lists of documents exchanged on disclosure. In preparation for trial, it will be necessary to insert cross-references to the trial bundles so as to identify the documents: see Appendix 2 paragraph 24.

9 If a witness is not sufficiently fluent in English to give his evidence in English, the witness statement should be in the witness's own language and a translation provided. If a witness is not fluent in English but can make himself understood in broken English and can understand written English, the statement need not be in his own words provided that these matters are indicated in the statement itself. It must however be written so as to express as accurately as possible the substance of his evidence.

APPENDIX 5

PART 1
JUDGE'S APPLICATION INFORMATION FORM

Title as in claim form

Application Information

1. [– DATE APPLICATION TO BE HEARD –]

2. DETAILS OF SOLICITOR/PARTY LODGING THE APPLICATION

   a. [Name]
   b. [Address]
   c. [Telephone No.]
   d. [Reference]
   e. [Acting for Claimant(s)/Defendant(s)]

3. DETAILS OF COUNSEL/OR OTHER ADVOCATE

   a. [Name]
   b. [Address of Chambers/Firm]
   c. [Telephone No.]

4. DETAILS OF OTHER PART(Y'S)(IES') SOLICITORS

   a. [Name]
   b. [Address]
   c. [Telephone No.]
   d. [Reference]

[Acting for Claimant(s)/Defendant(s)]

PART 2
WRITTEN EVIDENCE LODGMENT FORM

CHANCERY CHAMBERS

TO FILING SECTION – ROOM TM3.07

CLAIM NO:

SHORT TITLE:

Herewith Affidavit or witness statement of . . . .
. . ..

/or if other document specify . . . .
. . . .

filed in respect of:

	Tick
1. Application before Judge on	
2. Application before Master on	
3. Charging Order	
4. Garnishee Order	
5. Permission to issue [claim for] possession	
6. Service by alternative method	
7. Service out of Jurisdiction	
8. Evidence	
9. Oral examination of debtor	
10. To enable a Master's order to be drawn	
11. Other (Specify)	

Signed:

Solicitors for Claimant/Defendant
other (please specify)
Telephone No:
Ref:

APPENDIX 6

CASE MANAGEMENT DIRECTIONS

Draft orders for use on allocation or at case management conferences

Claim No.

IT IS ORDERED

1 Allocation to multi-track

( ) that this claim is allocated to the multi-track.

2 Transfer of claims, including transfer from Part 8

( ) that the claim be transferred to:

(a) the .... Division of the High Court;
(b) the .... District Registry;
(c) the .... [Central London] County Court [Chancery List].

( ) that the issue(s) .... (*define issue(s)*) be transferred to .... (*one of (a) to (c) above*) for determination.

( ) that the .... (*party*) apply by .... (*date*) to a Judge of the Technology and Construction Court [*or other Specialist List*] for an Order to transfer the claim to that Court.

( ) that the claim .... (*title and claim number*) commenced in [the .... County Court] [the District Registry of ....], be transferred from that Court to the Chancery Division of the High Court.

( ) that this claim shall continue as if commenced under Part 7 and shall be allocated to the multi-track.

3 Alternative dispute resolution

This claim be stayed until .... [*one month*] for the parties to try to settle the dispute by alternative dispute resolution or other means. The parties shall notify the Court in writing at the end of that period whether settlement has been reached. The parties shall at the same time lodge *either*:

(a) (if a settlement has been reached) a draft consent Order signed by all parties; *or*

(b) (if no settlement has been reached) a statement of agreed directions signed by all parties or (in the absence of agreed directions) statements of the parties' respective proposed directions.

4 Probate cases only

( ) that the .... [*party*] file [his] [her] witness statement or affidavit of testamentary scripts and lodge any testamentary script at Room TM7.09, Thomas More Building, Royal Courts of Justice, Strand, London WC2A 2LL [.................. District Registry] by .... (*date*).

5 Case summary

( ) that [each party] [the .... (*party*)] by .... (*date*) prepare and serve a case summary [not exceeding .... words] on all other parties, to be agreed by .... (*date*) and filed by .... (*date*) and if it is not agreed by that date the parties shall file their own case summaries.

6 Trial date

( ) that the trial of the claim/issue(s) take place between .... (*date*) and .... (*date*) ('the trial window').

( ) that the . . . . (*party*) shall make an appointment to attend on the Listing Officer (Room WG4, Royal Courts of Justice, Strand, London WC2A 2LL; Tel. 020 7947 6816; Fax No. 020 7947 7352) to fix a trial date within the trial window, such appointment to be not later than . . . . (*date*) and give notice of the appointment to all other parties.

( ) that the Court dispenses with the requirement for a listing questionnaire unless the Listing Officer directs otherwise.

( ) that
(i) the claim be entered in the [Trial List] [General List], with a listing category of [A] [B] [C], with a time estimate of . . . . days/weeks
(ii) the trial take place in London (*or* identify venue).

7 Pre Trial Review

( ) [the trial being estimated to last more than 10 days] that there be a Pre Trial Review on a date to be arranged by the Listing Officer [in conjunction with the parties] [to take place shortly before the trial and, if possible, in front of the Judge who will be conducting the trial] at which, except for urgent matters in the meantime, the Court will hear any further applications for Orders.

8 All directions agreed

( ) The parties having agreed directions it is by consent ordered: [Set out all the directions by reference to parties' draft Order on file].

9 Some directions agreed

( ) The parties having agreed the following directions it is by consent ordered: [Set out the agreed directions by reference to parties' draft Order on file as above, and any further directions to be given at this stage].

10 Case management conference etc

( ) that there be a [further] case management conference before the Master in Room TM . . . ., Thomas More Building, Royal Courts of Justice, Strand, London WC2A 2LL on . . . . (*date*) at . . . . o'clock (of . . . . hours/minutes duration).

( ) that there shall be a case management conference (of . . . . hours/minutes duration). In order for the Court to fix a date the parties are to complete the accompanying questionnaire and file it by . . . . (*date*).

( ) that the . . . . (*party*) apply for an appointment for a [further] case management conference by . . . . (*date*).

( ) At the case management conference, except for urgent matters in the meantime, the Court will hear any further applications for Orders and any party must file an Application Notice for any such Orders and serve it and supporting evidence (if any) by . . . . (*date*).

11 Failure to file allocation questionnaire

( ) that, ***no allocation questionnaire having been received from [the Claimant] [the Defendant],*** if [the Claimant] [the Defendant] [does not file [his] [her] allocation questionnaire within 3 days after service of this Order upon [him] [her], the [claim] [counterclaim] shall be struck out without further Order [*or as the case may be*]. [Add Order as to costs].

12 Amendments to statement of case

( ) that the .... (*party*) has permission to amend [his] [her] statement of case as in the copy on the Court file [initialled by the Master].

( ) that the amended statement of case be verified by a statement of truth.

( ) that the amended statement of case be filed by .... (*date*).

( ) that [the amended statement of case be served by .... (*date*).] [service of the amended statement of case be dispensed with].

( ) that any consequential amendments to other statements of case be filed and served by .... (*date*)

( ) that the costs of and consequential to the amendment to the statement of case [shall be paid by .... (*party*) in any event] [are assessed in the sum of £.................. and are to be paid by .... (*party*)] [within .... (*time*)].

13 Addition of parties etc

( ) that the .... (*party*) has permission:
(a) to [add] [substitute] [remove] .... (*name of party*) as a .... (*party*) and
(b) to amend [his] [her] statement of case in accordance with the copy on the Court file [initialled by the Master].
and that the amended statement of case be verified by a statement of truth.

( ) that the amended statement of case be:
(a) filed by .... (*date*);
(b) served on .... (*new party, existing parties or removed party, as appropriate*), by .... (*date*).

( ) that a copy of this Order be served on .... (*new party, existing parties or removed party, as appropriate*), by .... (*date*).

( ) that any consequential amendments to other statements of case be filed and served by .... (*date*).

( ) that the costs of and consequential to the amendment to the statement of case [shall be paid by the .... (*party*) in any event] [are assessed in the sum of £.................. and are to be paid by the .... (*party*)].

14 Consolidation

( ) that this claim be consolidated with claim number .... (*number and title of claim*), the lead claim to be claim number .... [The title to the consolidated case shall be as set out in the Schedule to this Order].

15 Trial of issue

( ) that the issue of .... (*define issue*) be tried as follows:

(a) with the consent of the parties, before a Master
  - (i) on .... (*date*) in Room TM .... Thomas More Building, Royal Courts of Justice, Strand, London WC2A 2LL;
  - (ii) with a time estimate of .... (hours),
  - (iii) with the filing of listing questionnaires dispensed with, *or*

(b) before a Judge
  - (i) with the trial of the issue to take place between .... (*date*) and .... (*date*) ('the trial window')
  - (ii) with the .... (*party*) to make an appointment to attend on the Listing Officer (Room WG4, Royal Courts of Justice, Strand, London WC2A 2LL; Tel. 020 7947 6778/6690; Fax No. 020 7947 7345) to fix a trial date within the trial window, such appointment to be not later than .... (*date*) and to give notice of the appointment to all other parties.
  - (iii) with the issue to be entered in the [Trial List] [General List], with a listing category of [A] [B] [C], and a time estimate of .... days/weeks and to take place in London (*or* identify venue).
  - (iv) with the filing of listing questionnaires dispensed with unless the Listing Officer directs otherwise.

16 Further information

( ) that the .... (*party*) provide by .... (*date*) the [further information] [clarification] sought in the request dated .... (*date*) [initialled by the Master].

( ) that any request for [further information] [clarification] shall be served by .... [*date*].

17 Disclosure of documents

( ) that each party give by .... (*date*) standard disclosure to every other party by list [by categories].

( ) that the .... (*party/parties*) give specific disclosure of documents [limited to the issues of ....] described in the Schedule to this Order [initialled by the Master] by list [by categories] by .... (*date*).

( ) that the . . . . (*party*) give by . . . . (*date*) standard disclosure by list [by categories] to . . . . (*party*) of documents limited to the issue(s) of . . . . (*define issues*) by list.

18 Inspection of documents

( ) that any requests for inspection or copies of disclosed documents shall be made within . . . . days after service of the list.

19 Preservation of property

( ) that the . . . . (*party*) preserve . . . . (*give details of relevant property*) until trial of the claim or further Order *or other remedy under rule 25.1(1).*

20 Witness statements

( ) that each party serve on every other party the witness statement of the oral evidence which the party serving the statement intends to rely on in relation to [any issues of fact] [the following issues of fact . . . . (*define issues*)] to be decided at the trial, those statements [and any notices of intention to rely on hearsay evidence] to be
(a) exchanged by . . . . (*date*) or
(b) served by . . . . (*party*) by . . . . (*date*) and by . . . . (*party*) by . . . . (*date*) provided that before exchange the parties shall liaise with a view to agreeing a method of identification of any documents referred to in any such witness statement.

( ) that the . . . . (*party*) has permission to serve a witness summary relating to the evidence of . . . . (*name*) of . . . . (*address*) [on every other party by] [to be served on . . . . (*party*)/exchanged at the same time as exchange of witness statements].

21 No expert evidence

( ) no expert evidence being necessary, that [no party has permission to call or rely on expert evidence] [permission to call or rely on expert evidence is refused].

22 Single expert

( ) that evidence be given by the report of a single expert in the field of . . . . (*define field*) instructed jointly by the parties, on the issue of . . . . (*define issue*) [and [his] [her] fees shall be limited to £ . . . .].

( ) that if the parties are unable to agree [by . . . . (*date*)] who that expert is to be and about the payment of [his] [her] fees any party may apply for further directions.

( ) that unless the parties agree in writing or the Court orders otherwise, the fees and expenses of the single expert shall be paid to [him] [her] by the parties equally.

( ) that each party give [his] [her] instructions to the single expert by . . . . (*date*).

( ) that the report of the single expert be filed and served by [him] [her] on the parties by . . . . (*date*).

( ) that no party may recover from another party more than £. . . . . for the fees and expenses of the expert.

( ) that the evidence of the expert be given at the trial by [written report] [oral evidence] of the expert.

23 Separate experts

( ) that each party has permission to adduce [oral] expert evidence in the field of . . . . (*specify*) [limited to . . . . expert(s) [per party] [on each side].

( ) that the experts' reports shall be exchanged by . . . . (*date*).

( ) that the experts shall hold a discussion for the purpose of:
(a) identifying the issues, if any, between them; and
(b) where possible, reaching agreement on those issues.

( ) that the experts shall by . . . . [*specify date after discussion*] prepare and file a statement for the Court showing:
(a) those issues on which they are agreed; and
(b) those issues on which they disagree and a summary of their reasons for disagreeing.

( ) No party shall be entitled to recover by way of costs from any other party more than £. . . . . for the fees or expenses of an expert.

24 Definition and reduction of issues

( ) that by . . . . (*date*) the parties list and discuss the issues in the claim [including the experts' reports and statements] and attempt to define and narrow the issues [including those issues the subject of discussion by the experts].

25 Trial bundle and skeleton arguments

( ) that not earlier than 7 days or later than 3 days before the date fixed for trial or of the claim entering the Warned List the Claimant shall file with the Chancery Listing Office a trial bundle for the use of the Judge in accordance with Appendix 2 of the Chancery Guide.

( ) that skeleton arguments and chronologies shall be filed not less than 2 clear days before the date fixed for trial or of the claim entering the Warned List, in accordance with Appendix 3 of the Chancery Guide.

26 Settlement

( ) that if the claim or part of the claim is settled the parties must immediately inform the Court, whether or not it is then possible to file a draft Consent Order to give effect to the settlement.

27 Compliance with Directions

( ) that the parties shall by .... (*date*) notify the Court in writing that they have fully complied with all directions or state:
(a) with which directions they have not complied;
(b) why they have not complied; and
(c) what steps they are taking to comply with the outstanding directions in time for the trial.

If the Court does not receive such notification or if the steps proposed to comply with outstanding directions are considered by the Court unsatisfactory, the Court may order a hearing (and may make appropriate orders as to costs against a party in default).

28 Costs

( ) that the costs of this application be:
(a) costs in the case;
(b) summarily assessed at £.................. and paid by .... (*party*); *or*
(c) the [party/parties]'[s] in any event, to be subject to detailed assessment.

Notes

NOTE 1: The attention of the parties is drawn to the importance of seeking to agree at an early stage directions for the management of the case as emphasised in the Practice Direction to Part 29 of the Civil Procedure Rules.

NOTE 2: The parties may, subject to any agreement being in accordance with the provisions of the Civil Procedure Rules, agree to extend the time periods given in the directions above provided this does not affect the date given for any case management conference or pre-trial review or the date of the trial or trial period.

NOTE 3: If you fail to attend a hearing that has been ordered, the Court may order you to pay the costs of the other party, or parties, that do attend. Failure to pay those costs within the time stated may lead to your statement of case (claim or defence) being struck out.

NOTE 4: If you do not comply with these directions, any other party to the claim will be entitled to apply to the Court for an order that your statement of case (claim or defence) be struck out.

APPENDIX 7

LLOYD'S NAMES' ESTATE APPLICATIONS: FORMS

Form of witness statement

[Heading as in claim form]

1 We are the personal representatives of the estate of the above-named Deceased ('the Deceased') who died on [ ]. We obtained [a grant of probate] [letters of administration] out of the [ ] Registry on [ ] and a copy of the grant [and the Deceased's will dated [ ]] is now produced and shown to us marked ' .1'. We make this witness statement in support of our application for permission to distribute the Deceased's estate [and to administer the will trusts of which we will be the Trustees following administration]. This witness statement contains facts and matters which, unless otherwise stated, are within our own knowledge obtained in acting in the administration of the estate. We believe them to be true.

2 The Deceased was before his death an underwriting member of Lloyd's of London whose underwriting activities are treated as having ceased on [ ]. The estate was sworn for probate purposes at £[ ]. We are now in a position to complete the administration of the estate and to distribute it to the beneficiaries but we do not wish to do so [or to constitute the will trusts] without the authority of the Court because of the existence of possible contingent claims arising out of the Deceased's underwriting liabilities for which we might be liable.

3 The position concerning the Deceased's Lloyd's liabilities is as follows:

3.1 [The Deceased's liabilities in respect of the years of account 1992 and earlier were reinsured into Equitas as part of the Lloyd's settlement. There is now produced and shown to us marked ' .2' a copy of the certificate or statement of reinsurance into Equitas].

3.2 [The syndicates in which the Deceased participated in the years of account 1993 and later have [closed by reinsurance in the usual way] [are the subject of an Estate Protection Plan issued to the Deceased by Centrewrite Limited] [are protected by an EXEAT policy obtained by the Claimants from Centrewrite Limited].

4 There is now produced and shown to us marked ' .3' a copy of a letter dated [ ] from the estate's Lloyd's agents confirming that [all] the syndicates have been reinsured to close [with the exception of [ ] which syndicate is protected by [the Estate Protection Plan] [the EXEAT policy]] and confirming that in the case of failure of a reinsuring syndicate to honour its obligations, the primary liability to a creditor will fall on Lloyd's Central Fund. [A copy of the [Estate Protection Plan and Annual Certificate] [EXEAT policy] is now produced and shown to us marked ' .4'.]

5 The Claimants believe that the interests of any Lloyd's claimant are reasonably secured by virtue of the fact that all the Lloyd's syndicates in which the Deceased participated have either been closed ultimately by reinsurance to close (in respect of any open years prior to 1992 into the Equitas group) or, in respect of subsequent years [have all closed by reinsurance] [are protected by the Estate Protection Plan] [are protected by the EXEAT policy.] Equitas remains licensed

to conduct insurance business and there is presently no reason to doubt its solvency. A copy of the latest report and accounts of Equitas Holdings Limited is now produced and shown to us marked '   .5'. [The [Estate Protection Plan] [EXEAT policy] is provided by Centrewrite Limited which is a wholly-owned subsidiary of Lloyd's and the beneficiary of an undertaking by Lloyd's to maintain its solvency. We have no reason to doubt the solvency of Centrewrite. A copy of the latest report and accounts of Centrewrite Limited is now produced and shown to us marked '   .6'.]

6 As appears from the schedule now produced and shown to us marked '   .7' in which we summarise the assets and liabilities of the estate, we have paid all the debts of the Deceased known to us (apart from the costs and expenses associated with the final administration of the estate) and we have also advertised for and dealt with all claimants in accordance with s.27 of the Trustee Act 1925 [*or if not explain why*].

7 We know of no special reason or circumstance which might give rise to doubt whether the provision described above can reasonably be regarded as adequate provision for potential claims against the estate and we ask for permission to distribute accordingly.

Form of order

[Heading as in claim form]

ON THE APPLICATION of the Claimants by Part 8 Claim Form dated [   ]

UPON READING the documents recorded on the Court file as having been read

IT IS ORDERED THAT:

1 the Claimants as [the personal representatives of the estate ('the Estate') of the above named deceased ('the Deceased')] [and] [the trustees of the trusts of the Deceased's will dated [   ]('the Will')] have permission to [distribute the Estate] [and] [administer the trusts of the Will and distribute capital and income in accordance with such trusts] without making any retention or further provision in respect of any contract of insurance or reinsurance under-written by the Deceased in the course of his business as an underwriting member of Lloyd's of London

2 the costs of the Claimants of this application [*either* in the agreed sum of £[   ] [*or* summarily assessed in the sum of £ [assessed in the sum of £ . . ..] (with permission to [the residuary beneficiaries] [*name beneficiaries*] to apply within 14 days after service of this order on them for the variation or discharge of this summary assessment] [*or* subject to detailed assessment on the indemnity basis if not agreed by or on behalf of [the residuary beneficiaries] *name beneficiaries*]] be raised and paid or retained out of the Estate in due course of administration.

APPENDIX 8

ADDRESSES AND OTHER CONTACT DETAILS

1 Clerks to the Chancery Judges

(all numbers to be preceded by 020 7947)

Clerk to	*Telephone*	*Fax*
The Vice-Chancellor	6412	6572
Mr Justice Ferris	7419	6572
Mr Justice Lindsay	6253	7185
Mr Justice Evans-Lombe	6657	6719
Mr Justice Jacob	6771	6650
Mr Justice Blackburne	6589	7379
Mr Justice Lightman	6671	6291
Mr Justice Rimer	6418	6649
Mr Justice Laddie	6518	6439
Mr Justice Lloyd	6794	6197
Mr Justice Neuberger	7280	6894
Mr Justice Park	6741	6196
Mr Justice Pumfrey	7482	6593
Mr Justice Hart	6419	6062
Mr Justice Lawrence Collins	7467	7298
Mr Justice Patten	7617	6693
Mr Justice Etherton	6116	6165
Mr Justice Peter Smith	6183	6133

2 At the Royal Courts of Justice, Thomas More Building

(All telephone extension numbers and fax numbers should be prefixed by 020 7947 unless otherwise specified)

1ST FLOOR

TM1.10.	Bankruptcy Registrars' Clerks, applications without notice, Registrars' hearings and orders	(6444)
	Bankruptcy Registrars' Chambers	(6444/7387)
	Bankruptcy Court fax number	(6378)

2ND FLOOR

TM2.04.	Deputy Court Manager	(6812)
TM2.07.	Court Manager, Companies, Bankruptcy Courts	(6870)
TM2.09.	Companies Court General Office: issue of all winding-up petitions and all other Companies Court applications; filing of documents	(6294)
	Central Index	(7328)
TM2.11.	Bankruptcy Issue and Search Room; issue of all petitions presented by creditors and debtors and applications to set aside statutory demand and applications for interim orders; search room	(6448)
	Setting down appeals from Registrars and District and Circuit Judges	(6863)
	Companies Court Fax number:	(6958)

3RD FLOOR

TM3.08.	Bankruptcy and Companies Registry. Filing affidavits, witness statements and documents and requesting bankruptcy and company files for applications without notice to be made in Chambers; requests for office copies, lodging applications for certificates of discharge in bankruptcy	(6441)
4TH FLOOR		
TM4.04.	Companies Schemes and reductions of capital	(6727)
TM4.05.	Companies Orders Section: Winding up Court Registrars' Orders and disqualification of directors	(6780) (6822)
5TH FLOOR		
TM5.04.	Chancery Chambers Registry and Issue Section: issue and amendment of all Chancery process, filing affidavits and witness statements (save those lodged within 2 days of a hearing before a Master which are to be filed in Room TM7.09); filing acknowledgments of service, searches of cause book; applications for office copy documents, including orders; transfers in and out	(6148/6167)
TM5.05.	Deputy Court Manager, Chancery Chambers. Certification of documents for use abroad	(6754)
TM5.06.	Lawyer, Chancery Chambers	(6080)
TM5.07.	Orders and Accounts Section. Associates: preparation of all Chancery Orders and Companies and Bankruptcy Court Orders; small payments; bills of costs for assessment; settlement of payment and lodgment schedules; accounts of receivers, judicial trustees, guardians and administrators; applications relating to security set by the court; matters arising out of accounts and inquiries ordered by the court	(6855)
	Chancery Orders and Accounts Fax number:	(7049)
6TH FLOOR		
Court 78.		
TM6.04.	Chancery Masters' Library	
TM6.05.	Master Bowman	
TM6.06.	Court Manager, Chancery Chambers	(6075)
TM6.07.	Master Bowles	
TM6.08.	Secretary to Masters	(6777)
TM6.09.	Master Bragge	
7TH FLOOR		
TM7.05.	Master Price	
TM7.06.	Master Moncaster	
TM7.08.	Chief Master Winegarten	

TM7.09.	Masters' Appointments. Issue of Masters' applications, including applications without notice to Masters; filing affidavits and witness statements in proceedings before Masters (only if filed within 2 working days of hearing before the Master); applications to serve out of jurisdiction; filing stop notices; filing testamentary documents in contested probate cases; filing grants lodged under O.99, r.7; filing affidavits relating to funds paid into court under the Trustee Act 1925, Compulsory Purchase Act 1965 and the Lands Clauses Consolidation Act 1845. Executive officer in charge (6095). Clerks to Chancery Masters	(6702/7391)
	Masters' Appointments Fax no:	(7422)

3 At the Royal Courts of Justice but outside Thomas More Building

(Prefaced by 020 7947 unless otherwise specified).

RCJ Switchboard	(6000)
RCJ Security Office	(6260)
Fees Office (Room E01)	(6527)
Clerk of the Lists, Room WG3	(6778)
Chancery Judges' Listing Office, Room WG4	(6690)
High Court Appeals Office, Room WG7	(7518)
Chancery Judges' Listing Office Fax number*:	(7345) (**See paragraph 14.11*)
Officer in charge of mechanical recording	(Room WB.14) (6154)
Head Usher: Fax number	(6668)
Customer Service Officer	(7731)
Video-conferencing managers	(6581, fax 6613)
Citizens Advice Bureau at Royal Courts of Justice	(0845 120 3715, or 020 7947 6880, fax 020 7947 7167)

4 London, outside the Royal Courts of Justice

Central London County Court
Civil Trial Centre, Chancery List, 26–29 Park Crescent, London W1N 4HT
DX 97325 Regents Park 2

Business Chancery and Patents section	(020 7917 7821/7887) Fax 0207 917 7935/794

5 Outside London

The following are the Court addresses, telephone and fax numbers for the courts at which there are regular Chancery sittings outside London:

	Address	Telephone	Fax
Birmingham:	The Priory Courts, 33 Bull Street, Birmingham B4 6DS	0121 681 3033	0121 681 3121
Bristol:	The Law Courts, Small Street, Bristol BS1 1DA	0117 976 3098	0117 976 3074
Cardiff:	The Civil Justice Centre, 2 Park Street, Cardiff CF1 1ET	01222 376402	01222 376470
Leeds:	The Court House, 1 Oxford Row, Leeds LS1 3BG	0113 283 0040	0113 244 8507
Liverpool:	Queen Elizabeth II Law Courts, Derby Square, Liverpool L2 1XA	0151 473 7373	0151 227 2806
Manchester:	The Courts of Justice, Crown Square, Manchester M3 3FL	0161 954 1800	0161 832 5179
Newcastle:	The Law Courts, Quayside, Newcastle-upon-Tyne NE1 3LB	0191 201 2000	0191 201 2001
Preston:	The Law Courts, Openshaw Place, Ringway, Preston PR1 2LL	01772 832300	01772 832476

In some centres resources do not permit the listing telephone numbers to be attended personally at all times. In cases of urgency, solicitors, counsel and counsel's clerks may come into the Chancery Court and leave messages with the member of staff sitting in Court.

Urgent Court business officer pager numbers for out of hours applications:

Birmingham (Midland Circuit):	
West Side:	07699 618079
East Side:	07699 618078
Bristol:	07699 618088
Cardiff:	07699 618086
Manchester and Liverpool:	07699 618080
Preston:	07699 618081
Newcastle:	01399 618083
Leeds and Bradford:	01399 618082

In case of difficulty out of hours, contact the Royal Courts of Justice on 020 7947 6260.

Patents Court Guide

(applicable on and after 1/4/2003)

ARRANGEMENT OF PARAGRAPHS

1 Introduction

The general guidance applicable to matters in the Chancery Division, as set out in the Chancery Guide, also applies to patent actions unless specifically mentioned below. 'PD63' refers to the Practice Direction – Patents and Other Intellectual Property Claims which supplements CPR Part 63. This Guide applies as appropriate to both the Patents Court and the Patents County Court.

2 General

Actions proceeding in the Patents Court are allocated to the multi-track (CPR 63.7(1)). Attention is drawn to CPR 63(7) and its associated PD (case management).

3 Clerk in Charge of the Patents List of the Patents Court

The clerk to one of the principal assigned Patent judges is in charge of the patents list. The clerk in charge of the Patents list is the clerk to Jacob J, Mrs Lorraine Bennett who is located in Room W311 in the Royal Courts of Justice (telephone 020 7947 6771, fax 020 7947 6650, Email: *lorraine.bennett@gtnet.gov.uk*). Applications to fix both trials and interim or procedural matters within the court should be made to her. It is possible to fix at any time. Normally the other parties should first be contacted to discuss available dates.

The three principal Patent judges (Jacob, Laddie and Pumfrey JJ) sit in turn for one term at a time (October–December, January–Easter, Easter–August) in the main Patents list. Cases within that list are given fixed dates. Additionally, cases are set down in the general Chancery list where they are given a trial window to be heard by a Patent judge. A case so set down may be transferred to the Patents list if the case there settles. The clerk in charge of the Patents list works in close liaison with the Chancery listing officer. In the absence of the clerk in charge (for instance in vacation) application for listing may be made to the clerk to another Patent judge (if available) or the Chancery listing office. However such applications should only be made in an emergency. The clerks to the other principal Patents judges are:

Peter Smith (Clerk to Laddie J) telephone 020 7947 6518, fax 020 7947 6439
e-mail: *peter.smith@courtservice.gsi.gov.uk*
Bob Glen (Clerk to Pumfrey J) telephone 020 7947 7482, fax 020 7947 6593
e-mail: *robert.glen@courtservice.gsi.gov.uk*
The other two assigned Patents judges are:
Ferris J (Clerk: Lionel Duffield – telephone 020 7947 7419, fax 020 7947 6572)
e-mail: *lionel.duffield@courtservice.gsi.gov.uk*
Neuberger J (Clerk: Don Bennett – telephone 020 7947 7280, fax 020 7947 6894)
e-mail: *donald.bennett@courtservice.gsi.gov.uk*

4 Patents County Court

The Patents County Court judge is HHJ Fysh QC. All written communications to his court must be clearly marked 'Patents'. The court details are as follows:

The Patents County Court
Central London Civil Justice Centre
13/14 Park Crescent
London W1B 1HT
Telephone 020 7917 7821/7889

Fax 020 7917 7935

5 Short Applications

These are listed for hearing before the normal court day starts at 10.30, for instance at 9.30 or 10 am. Attention is drawn to PD63.6. Accurate time estimates are essential and a guillotine may be imposed on oral submissions if estimates show signs of being exceeded.

6 September Sittings

Although the previous experiment of the court sitting in September for routine business is not being continued, the Patents Court will endeavour, if the parties so desire and the case is urgent, to sit in September.

7 Appeals from the Comptroller General of Patents, Trade Marks and Designs

Patents

By virtue of statute these lie only to the High Court and not the Patents County Court. They are now governed by CPR Part 52 (see CPR 63.17). Permission to appeal is not required. Note that the Comptroller must be served with a Notice of Appeal (CPR 63.17(3)). The appellant has the conduct of the appeal and he or his representative should within 2 weeks of lodging the appeal, contact the clerk in charge of the Patents List with a view to arranging a hearing date. The appellant shall ensure that the appeal is set down as soon as is reasonably practicable after service of the notice of appeal. Parties are reminded that the provisions about the service of skeleton arguments apply to appeals from the Comptroller.

Trade Marks

These are assigned to the Chancery Division as a whole, not the Patents Court (CPR 63.17(2)). Permission to appeal is not required.

Appeals on Paper only

The court will hear appeals on the papers only if that is what the parties desire. If the appellant is willing for the appeal to be heard on paper only, he should contact the respondent and the Patent office at the earliest opportunity to discover whether such a way of proceeding is agreed. If it is, the clerk to the Patents judge should be informed as soon as possible. The parties (and the office if it so desires) should liaise amongst themselves for early preparation of written submissions and bundles and provide the court with all necessary materials.

Appeals concerning Registered Designs

These go to the Registered Designs Appeal Tribunal. This consists of one of the Patents judges sitting as a tribunal. The CPR and PD do not apply to such appeals. Where such an appeal is desired, contact should be made direct to the clerk in charge of the Patents List.

8 Applications without Notice

A party wishing to apply without notice to the respondent(s) should contact the clerk in charge of the Patents Court list, or in her absence the clerk to one of the other principal Patents judges, failing that absence Chancery listing. In cases of emergency in vacation or out of normal court hours the application should be made to the duty Chancery judge. In the Patents County Court, contact should be made with the court office.

9 Documents

(a) Bundling is of considerable importance and should be approached intelligently. The general guidance given in Appendix 2 of the Chancery Guide should be followed. Solicitors or patent agents who fail to do so may be required to explain why and may be penalised personally in costs.

(b) Copies of documents referred to in a statement of case (eg an advertisement referred to in a claim of infringement form or documents cited in Grounds of Invalidity) should be served with the statement of case. Where any such document requires translation, a translation should be served at the same time.

(c) If it is known which judge will be taking the case, papers for the case should be lodged directly with that judge's clerk. Faxed documents of significance (and particularly skeleton arguments) should be followed up by clean direct prints. By agreement documents may also be sent by e-mail to the clerk of the judge concerned.

(d) It is the responsibility of both parties to ensure that all relevant documents are lodged with the clerk of the judge who will be taking the case by noon 2 days before the date fixed for hearing unless some longer or shorter period has been ordered by the judge or is prescribed by this Guide.

(e) The judges request that all important documents also be supplied to them on disk in a format convenient for the judge's use (normally Microsoft Word 7 for Windows). These will include skeleton arguments, the witness statements and expert reports.

10 Streamlined Procedure

(a) Nature of a streamlined procedure.

A streamlined procedure is one in which, save and to the extent that it is otherwise ordered:

- (i) all factual and expert evidence is in writing;
- (ii) there is no requirement to give disclosure of documents;
- (iii) there are no experiments;
- (iv) cross-examination is only permitted on any topic or topics where it is necessary and is confined to those topics;
- (v) the total duration of the trial fixed is and will normally be not more than one day;
- (vi) the date for trial will be fixed when the Order for a streamlined trial is made and will normally be about 6 months thereafter.

A streamlined procedure also includes minor variants of the above (eg disclosure confined to a limited issue).

(b) Criteria for a streamlined procedure

The court will order a streamlined procedure by agreement or, in the absence of agreement, where application of the overriding objective indicates that it is appropriate. Particular emphasis will be placed on proportionality, the financial position of each of the parties, degree of complexity and the importance of the case.

(c) When to apply for streamlined procedure

Any party may apply at any time after commencement of the action for a streamlined procedure. Any such application should be made at the earliest time reasonably possible, which will generally be at the case management conference required by PD63 within 14 days after service of the defence.

(d) How to apply for a streamline procedure

A party wishing for a streamlined procedure should, in the first instance, invite the other party(ies) to agree, setting out the proposed procedural steps in a draft Order. If there is agreement, the court will normally make the Order on a written application signed on behalf of each party. The parties should liaise with each other and the clerk to the Patents Court or the Patents County court concerning a date for trial so that this can be fixed.

If there is no agreement, the party wishing for a streamlined procedure must make an application for it, setting forth the proposed procedural directions in his application notice and requesting that the application be determined on paper. He should support the application by a witness statement addressing the criteria in CPR Rule 1(2). The opposing party must, unless he obtains an extension of time (by consent or from the court) make and serve on the opposite party a witness statement in response within 10 days of service upon him of the application notice.

The court will determine the matter provisionally on paper alone and make a provisional judgment and order accordingly. Unless either side seeks an oral hearing the provisional order will come into effect 7 days after its service on the parties.

If a party is desirous of an oral hearing, it must, within 7 days of service upon it of the provisional order, seek an oral hearing in the immediate future by contacting the clerk to the judge in charge of the patent list. Such an oral hearing will be fixed as soon as is practicable, either by way of a telephone hearing or a short application.

(e) Duty to inform clients

The parties' legal advisers must draw their clients' attention to the availability of a streamlined procedure in the Patents Court and the Patents County Court.

11 Timetable for trial, Reading Guide, Time Estimates, common general knowledge

Attention is drawn to PD63.7. Further the parties should endeavour to produce a composite document setting forth the matters alleged to form part of the common general knowledge and, where they disagree, what that disagreement is.

12 Narrowing of Issues

As early as possible the patentee should identify which of the claims of its patent are contended to have independent validity and which of those claims are said to be infringed and should communicate a list of those claims to the other party.

This position should be kept under constant review. If there is any alteration in the number of claims said to have independent validity the patentee must forthwith notify the other parties.

13 Admissions

With a view to early elimination of non-issues, practitioners are reminded of the necessity of making admissions in accordance with CPR Rule 32.18 at an early stage. It should be done as early as possible, for instance, in a defence or reply. Thus in a defence a party may admit the acts complained of or that his article/process has certain of the features of a claim. In a reply a patentee may be able to admit prior publication of cited documents.

Parties should also consider making a request to identify points not in dispute. Technically a request seeking admissions in respect of particular integers of a claim may involve a mixed question of fact and law and so not be within the rules about admissions. By asking whether or not the defendant disputes that his article/process has certain features of the claim the real dispute can be narrowed. Thus the ambit of disclosure and of witness and expert statements will be narrowed.

14 Skeleton Arguments, Pre-Trial and after the Evidence

In addition to the Reading Guide parties should lodge skeleton arguments in time for the judge to read them before trial. That should normally be at least 2 days before commencement of the trial, but in substantial cases a longer period (to be discussed with the clerk to the judge concerned) may be needed. It is desirable that each party should summarise what it contends to be the common general knowledge of the man skilled in the art.

Following the evidence in a substantial trial a short adjournment may be granted to enable the parties to summarise their arguments in writing before oral argument.

In trials where a transcript of evidence is being made and supplied to the judge, the transcript should be accompanied by a version on disk.

15 Jurisdiction of Masters

Masters have only a limited jurisdiction in patent matters (see PD63.8). Generally it is more convenient for consent orders (on paper or in court) to be made by a judge even where a master has jurisdiction to do so.

Where a master makes a consent order disposing of an action which has been fixed, it is the duty of all the parties' representatives to inform both the clerk in charge of the Patents list and the listing office that the case has settled.

16 Agreed Orders

The court is normally willing to make consent orders without the need for the attendance of any parties. A draft of the agreed order and the written consent of all the parties' respective solicitors or counsel should be supplied to the clerk in charge of the Patents list. Where a draft has been substantially amended by hand, it is helpful for a disk of the unamended version to be supplied in accordance with paragraph 9.6 of the Chancery Guide. Unless the judge considers a hearing is needed he will make the order in the agreed terms by initialling it. It will be drawn up accordingly and sent to the parties.

17 Telephone Applications

For short (20 minutes or less) matters, the Patents judges are willing, unless a matter of general public importance is involved, to hear applications by telephone conference in accordance with the Practice Direction under CPR Part 23.

It is possible for the application to be recorded, and if recording by the Patents Court rather than by British Telecom (or other service provider) is requested arrangements should be made with the clerk in charge of the Patents list. The recording will not be transcribed. The tape will be kept for a period of 6 months. Arrangements for transcription, if needed, must be made by the parties.

This procedure should be used where it will save costs.

18 Patents judges able and willing to sit out of London

If the parties so desire, for the purpose of saving time or costs, the Patents Court will sit out of London. Before any approach is made to the clerk in charge of the Patents list, the parties should discuss between themselves the desirability of such course. If there is a dispute as to venue the court will resolve the matter on an application. Where there is no dispute, the clerk should be contacted as soon as possible so that arrangements can be put in place well before the date of the proposed hearing. The Patents County Court may also be able to sit out of London.

19 Intellectual Property Court Users' Committee

This considers the problems and concerns of intellectual property litigation generally. Membership of the committee includes the principal Patents judges, the Patents County Court judge, a representative of each of the Patent Bar Association, the Intellectual Property Lawyers Association, the Chartered Institute of Patent Agents, the Institute of Trade Mark Agents and the Trade Marks Designs and Patents Federation. It will also include one or more other Chancery judges. Anyone having views concerning the improvement of intellectual property litigation is invited to make his or her views known to the committee, preferably through the relevant professional representative on the committee. The Patents County Court also has a Users' Committee.

20 Orders following judgment

Where a judgment is made available in draft before being given in open court the parties should, in advance of that occasion, exchange drafts of the desired consequential order. It is highly undesirable that one party should spring a proposal on the other for the first time when judgment is given. Where the parties are agreed as to the consequential order and have supplied a copy of the same signed by all parties or their representatives, attendance at the handing down of the judgment is not necessary.

21 Applications for interim remedies: trial dates

When an application for an interim remedy is made the claimant should, where practicable, make prior investigations as to the estimated length of trial and possible trial dates.

22 Specimen minute of order for directions

The general form minute of order for directions annexed to this practice direction has the approval of the Patents judges. It is intended only as a guide and may need adaptation for particular circumstances.

ANNEX

STANDARD FORM OF ORDER FOR DIRECTIONS

(* indicates a provision which may be necessary when a rule has not been complied with, for example, standard disclosure in accordance with the Practice Direction supplementing CPR Part 63.)

[RECITALS AS NECESSARY]

Transfer

1 [This Action and Counterclaim be transferred to the Patents County Court.] (If this order is made, no other Order will generally be necessary, though it will generally be desirable for procedural orders to be made at this time to save the costs of a further conference in the County Court.)

Proof of Documents

2 Legible copies of the specification of the Patent in suit [and any patent specifications or other documents cited in the Particulars of Objections] may be used at the trial without further proof thereof or of their contents.

Amendments to Pleadings

3 The Claimants have leave to amend their Claim Form shown in red on the copy [annexed to the Application Notice/as signed by the solicitors for the parties/annexed hereto] and [to re-serve the same on or before [date]/and that re-service be dispensed with] and that the Defendants have leave to serve a consequentially amended Defence within [number] days [thereafter/hereafter]

and that the Claimants have leave to serve a consequentially amended Reply (if so advised) within [number] days thereafter.

4 (a) The Defendants have leave to amend their Defence [and Part 20 Claim and Grounds of Invalidity] as shown in red on the copy [annexed to the Application notice/as signed by the solicitors for the parties/annexed hereto] and [to reserve the same within [number] days/on or before-[date]] [and that re-service be dispensed with] and that the Claimants have leave to serve a consequentially amended Reply (if so advised) within [number] days thereafter.

(b) The Claimants do on or before [date] elect whether they will discontinue this Claim and withdraw their Defence to Part 20 Claim and consent to an Order for the revocation of Patent No. … ('the patent in suit') AND IF the Claimants shall so elect and give notice thereof in the time aforesaid IT IS ORDERED THAT the patent in suit be revoked [and that it be referred to the Costs Judge to assess the costs of the Defendants and this Action and Grounds of Invalidity up to and including [date] being the date of service of the [amended] Grounds of Invalidity and Part 20 Claim to the date of this Order [except so far as the same have been increased by the failure of the Defendants originally to deliver the Defence and Grounds of Invalidity in its amended form], and to assess the costs of the Claimants in this Action and Part 20 Claim from [date] [insofar as they have been increased by the failure of the Defendants aforesaid] AND IT IS ORDERED that the said Costs Judge is to set off the costs of the Defendants and of the Claimants when so assessed as aforesaid and to certify to which of them the balance after such set-off is due.]/[Order for payment of sums determined by the court on a summary assessment].

Further Information and Clarification

5 (a) The [Claimants/Defendants] do on or before [date] serve on the [Defendants/Claimants] the Further Information or Clarification of the [specify Statement of case] as requested by the [Claimants/Defendants] by their Request served on the [Defendants/Claimants] on [date] [and/or]

(b) The [Claimants/Defendants] do on or before [date] serve on the [Defendants/Claimants] a response to their Request for Further Information or Clarification of the [identify statement of case] served on the [Defendants/Claimants] on [date].

Admissions*

6 The [Claimants/Defendants] do on or before [date] state in writing whether or not they admit the facts specified in the [Defendants'/Claimants'] Notice to Admit facts dated [date].

Security

7 The Claimants do provide security for the Defendants' costs in the sum of £[state sum] by [specify manner in which security to be given] and that in the meantime all further proceedings be stayed.

Lists of Documents*

8 (a) The Claimants and the Defendants respectively do on or before [state date] make and serve on the other of them a list in accordance with form N265 of the documents in their control which they are required to disclose in accordance with the obligation of standard disclosure in accordance with CPR Part 31 as modified by paragraph 5 of the Practice Direction – Patents etc supplementing CPR Part 63.

(b) In respect of those issues identified in Schedule [number] hereto disclosure shall be limited to those [documents/categories of documents] listed in Schedule [number].

Inspection*

9 If any party wishes to inspect or have copies of such documents as are in another party's control it shall give notice in writing that it wishes to do so and such inspection shall be allowed at all reasonable times upon reasonable notice and any copies shall be provided within [number] working days of the request upon the undertaking of the party requesting the copies to pay the reasonable copying charges.

Experiments*

10 (a) Where a party desires to establish any fact by experimental proof, including an experiment conducted for the purposes of litigation or otherwise not being an experiment conducted in the normal course of research, that party shall on or before [date] serve on all the other parties a notice stating the facts which it desires to establish and giving full particulars of the experiments proposed to establish them.

(b) A party upon whom a notice is served under the preceding subparagraph shall within [number] days, serve on the party serving the notice a notice stating in respect of each fact whether or not that party admits it.

(c) Where any fact which a party wishes to establish by experimental proof is not admitted that party shall apply to the court for further directions in respect of such experiments.

[Or where paragraph 9 of the Practice Direction – Patents etc supplementing CPR Part 63 has been complied with.]

11 (a) The Claimants/Defendants are to afford to the other parties an opportunity, if so requested, of inspecting a repetition of the experiments identified in paragraphs [specify them] of the Notice[s] of Experiments served on [date]. Any such inspection must be requested within [number] days of the date of this Order and shall take place within [number] days of the date of the request.

(b) If any party shall wish to establish any fact in reply to experimental proof that party shall on or before [date] serve on all the other parties a notice stating the facts which it desires to establish and giving full particulars of the experiments proposed to establish them.

(c) A party upon whom a notice is served under the preceding subparagraph shall within [number] days serve on the party serving the notice a notice stating in respect of each fact whether or not that party admits it.
(d) Where any fact which a party wishes to establish by experimental proof in reply is not admitted the party may apply to the court for further directions in respect of such experiments.

Notice of Models, etc

12 (a) If any party wishes to rely at the trial of this action upon any model, apparatus, drawing, photograph, cinematograph or video film whether or not the same is contained in a witness statement, affidavit or expert's report that party shall on or before [date] give notice thereof to all the other parties; shall afford the other parties an opportunity within [number] days of the service of such notice of inspecting the same and shall, if so requested, furnish the other party with copies of any such drawing or photograph and a sufficient drawing photograph or other illustration of any model or apparatus.
(b) If any party wishes to rely upon any such materials in reply to any matter of which notice was given under subparagraph (a) of this paragraph, that party shall within [number] days after the last inspection to be made in pursuance of the said subparagraph (a) give to the other parties a like notice, and if so requested within [number] days of delivery of such notice shall afford like opportunities of inspection which shall take place within [number] days of such request; and shall in like manner furnish copies of any drawing or photograph and illustration of any such model or apparatus.
(c) No further or other model apparatus drawing photograph cinematograph or video film shall be relied upon in evidence by either party save with consent or by leave of the court.

Written Evidence

13 (a) Each party may call up to [number] expert witnesses in this Action and Part 20 Claim provided that the said party:
(i) supplies the name of such expert to the other parties and to the court on or before [date]; and
(ii) no later than [date/[number days] before the date set for the hearing of this Action and Part 20 Claim] serve upon the other parties a report of each such expert comprising the evidence which that expert intends to give at trial.
(b) Each party shall on or before [date] serve on the other parties [signed] written statements of the oral evidence which the party intends to lead on any issues of fact to be decided at the trial, such statements to stand as the evidence in chief of the witness unless the court otherwise directs.
(c) The parties shall [here insert the particular directions sought, eg within 21 days after service of the other party's expert reports and written statements state in writing the facts and matters in those reports and statements which are admitted].

Admissibility of Evidence

14 A party who objects to any statements of any witness being read by the judge prior to the hearing of the trial, shall serve upon each other party a notice in writing to that effect setting out the grounds of the objection.

Non-Compliance

15 Where either party fails to comply with the directions relating to experiments and written evidence it shall not be entitled to adduce evidence to which such directions relate without the leave of the court.

Trial Bundles

16 Each party shall no later than [number] days before the date fixed for the trial of this Action and Counterclaim serve upon the parties a list of all the documents to be included in the trial bundles. The Claimants shall no later than [number] days before the date fixed for trial serve upon the Defendants … sets of the bundles for use at trial.

Trial

17 The trial of these proceedings shall be before an Assigned Judge alone in [London], estimated length [number] days and a pre-reading estimate for the Judge of [number] days.

Liberty to Apply

18 The parties are to be at liberty on 2 days' notice to apply for further directions and generally.

Costs

19 The costs of this Application are to be costs in the Action and Part 20 Claim.

The Queen's Bench Guide

ARRANGEMENT OF PARAGRAPHS

A GUIDE TO THE WORKING PRACTICES OF THE QUEEN'S BENCH DIVISION WITHIN THE ROYAL COURTS OF JUSTICE

May 2000
Foreword by The Rt Hon Lord Bingham of Cornhill
The Lord Chief Justice of England and Wales

We live in a new procedural world. Old landmarks have disappeared from view. New features have taken their place. And everyone seems to be speaking a different language. It is easy to become disoriented.

This Guide, prepared for those litigating in the Queen's Bench Division of the High Court, particularly in the Central Office, provides a clear and detailed road-map for those who have lost, or are not sure of, the way. The Guide draws on the unrivalled expertise and experience of the Senior Master, who takes the opportunity to give much wise advice along the route.

I am sure this Guide will prove invaluable to the many who will, I hope, use it. In preparing the Guide, the Senior Master has rendered a notable public service.

AN APPRECIATION

With the support and encouragement of Lord Bingham of Cornhill during his tenure of office as Lord Chief Justice of England & Wales, this Guide has been prepared for the assistance of all who practice or litigate in the Queen's Bench Division.

The contributions made by the Queen's Bench masters and the staff of the Central Office have been invaluable but this Guide would not have been completed without the hard work and diligence of Bryony Young, formerly Chief Associate, to whom I am indebted.

However, all errors and omissions are mine and I would welcome any comments and suggestions from the profession and all using this Guide for its improvement.

Senior Master and
Queen's Remembrancer
18 May 2000

1 INTRODUCTION

1.1 The Guide

1.1.1 This Guide has been prepared by the Senior Master, acting under the authority of the Lord Chief Justice, and provides a general explanation of the work and practice of the Queen's Bench Division with particular regard to proceedings started in the Central Office, and is designed to make it easier for parties to use and proceed in the Queen's Bench Division.

1.1.2 The Guide must be read with the Civil Procedure Rules ('the CPR') and the supporting Practice Directions. Litigants and their advisers are responsible for acquainting themselves with the CPR; it is not the task of this Guide to summarise the CPR, nor should anyone regard it as a substitute for the CPR. It is intended to bring the Guide up to date at regular intervals as necessary.

1.1.3 The Guide does not have the force of law, but parties using the Queen's Bench Division will be expected to act in accordance with this Guide. Further guidance as to the practice of the Queen's Bench Division may be obtained from the Practice Master (see paragraph 6.1 below).

1.1.4 It is assumed throughout the Guide that the litigant intends to proceed in the Royal Courts of Justice. For all essential purposes, though, the Guide is equally applicable to the work of the district registries, which deal with the work of the Queen's Bench Division outside London, but it should be borne in mind that there are some differences.

1.1.5 The telephone numbers and room numbers quoted in the Guide are correct at the time of going to press. However, the room numbers quoted for the Clerk of the Lists and the Listing Office are effective as from 2 October 2000.

1.2 The Civil Procedure Rules

1.2.1 The Overriding Objective set out in Part 1 of the CPR is central to the new culture which enables the court to deal with cases justly. To further this aim the work is allocated to one of three tracks – the small claims track, the fast track and the multi-track – so as to dispose of the work in the most appropriate and effective way combined with active case management by the court.

1.2.2 The CPR are divided into Parts. A particular Part is referred to in the Guide as Part 7, etc, as the case may be. Any particular rule within a Part is referred to as rule 6.4(2), and so on.

1.3 The Practice Directions

1.3.1 Each Part – or almost each Part – has an accompanying practice direction or directions, and other practice directions deal with matters such as the Pre-Action Protocols and the former Rules of the Supreme Court and the County Court Rules which are scheduled to Part 50.

1.3.2 The Practice Directions are made pursuant to statute, and have the same authority as do the CPR themselves[1]. However, in case of any conflict between a rule and a practice direction, the rule will prevail[2]. Each practice direction is referred to in the Guide with the number of any Part that it supplements preceding it; for example, the Practice Direction supplementing Part 6 is referred to as the Part 6 Practice Direction. But where there is more than one practice direction supplementing a Part it will also be described either by topic, for example, Part 25 Practice Direction – Interim Payments, or where appropriate, the Part 40B Practice Direction.

1 Civil Procedure Act 1997, ss 1 and 5, and Sch 1, paras 3 and 6.
2 There is one exception: Part 8.

1.4 The forms

1.4.1 The Practice Direction supplementing Part 4 (Forms) lists the practice forms that are required by or referred to in the CPR, and also those referred to in such of the Rules of the Supreme Court and the County Court Rules as are still in force (see Part 50 of the CPR; Schedules 1 and 2).

1.4.2 Those listed in Table 1 with a number prefixed by the letter N are new forms, a number of these forms have been published with the CPR. Those listed in Table 2 are forms still in use in the High Court but altered so as to conform to the CPR. They may be used as precedents and are set out in a separate Appendix to this Guide and include:

(1) Forms that were previously prescribed forms; these are listed under the same numbers that previously identified them.
(2) Former practice forms common to both the Chancery and Queen's Bench Divisions; these forms have been given numbers starting with the letters PF.
(3) Former practice forms used mainly in the Queen's Bench Division; these forms have been given numbers ending with the letters QB.
(4) Former practice forms used mainly in the Chancery Division; these forms have been given numbers ending with the letters CH.

1.4.3 The forms may be modified as circumstances in individual cases require[3], but it is essential that a modified form contains at least as full information or guidance as would have been given if the original form had been used.

3 See rule 4.3.

1.4.4 Where the Royal Arms appears on any listed form it must appear on any modification of that form. The same format for the Royal Arms as is used on the listed forms need not be used. All that is necessary is that there is a complete Royal Arms.

1.5 The Queen's Bench Division

1.5.1 The Queen's Bench Division is one of the three divisions of the High Court, together with the Chancery Division and Family Division. The Lord Chief Justice is President of the Queen's Bench Division, and certain High Court judges and masters are assigned to it. A Lord Justice of Appeal (currently Lord Justice Kennedy) has been appointed by the Lord Chief Justice to be the Vice-President of the Division; a High Court judge is appointed as judge in charge of the Jury List (currently Mr Justice Moreland); another is appointed as judge in charge of the Trial List (currently Mr Justice Buckley).

1.5.2 Outside London, the work of the Queen's Bench Division is administered in provincial offices known as district registries. In London, the work is administered in the Central Office at the Royal Courts of Justice. The work in the Central Office of the Queen's Bench Division is the responsibility of the Senior Master, acting under the authority of the Lord Chief Justice.

1.5.3 The work of the Queen's Bench Division is (with certain exceptions) governed by the CPR. The Divisional Court, the Admiralty Court, the Commercial Court and the Technology and Construction Court are all part of the Queen's Bench Division. However, each does specialised work requiring a distinct procedure that to some extent modifies the CPR. For that reason each publishes its own Guide or practice direction, to which reference should be made by parties wishing to proceed in the specialist courts.

1.5.4 The work of the Queen's Bench Division consists mainly of claims for;

(1) damages in respect of
    (a) personal injury,
    (b) negligence,
    (c) breach of contract, and
    (d) libel and slander (defamation),

(2) non-payment of a debt, and
(3) possession of land or property.

Proceedings retained to be dealt with in the Central Office of the Queen's Bench Division will almost invariably be multi-track claims.

1.5.5 In many types of claim – for example claims in respect of negligence by solicitors, accountants, etc or claims for possession of land – the claimant has a choice whether to bring the claim in the Queen's Bench Division or in the Chancery Division. However, there are certain claims that may be brought only in the Queen's Bench Division, namely:

(1) sheriff's interpleader proceedings,
(2) enrolment of deeds,
(3) registration of foreign judgments under the Civil Jurisdictions and Judgments Act 1982,
(4) applications for bail in criminal proceedings,
(5) applications under the Administration of Justice Act 1920 and the Foreign Judgments (Reciprocal Enforcement) Act 1933,
(6) registration and satisfaction of bills of sale,
(7) election petitions,
(8) obtaining evidence for foreign courts.

1.6 The Central Office

1.6.1 The information in this and the following paragraph is to be found in the Part 2 Practice Direction at paragraph 2; it is reproduced here for the convenience of litigants. The Central Office is open for business from 10 am to 4.30 pm (except during August when it is open from 10 am to 2.30 pm) on every day of the year except;

(1) Saturdays and Sundays,
(2) Good Friday and the day after Easter Monday,
(3) Christmas Day and, if that day is a Friday or Saturday, then 28 December,
(4) Bank Holidays in England and Wales (under the Banking and Financial Dealings Act 1971), and
(5) such other days as the Lord Chancellor, with the concurrence or the Lord Chief Justice, the Master of the Rolls, the President of the Family Division and the Vice-Chancellor, may direct.

1.6.2 One of the masters of the Queen's Bench Division is present at the Central Office on every day on which the office is open for the purpose of superintending the business administered there and giving any directions that may be required on questions of practice and procedure. He is normally referred to as the 'Practice Master'. (See paragraph 6.1 below for information about the Practice Master and masters in general.)

1.6.3 The Central Office consists of the Action Department, the Masters' Secretary's Department, the Queen's Bench Associates' Department, the Clerk of the Lists, the Registry of the Technology and Construction Court and the Admiralty and Commercial Registry.

1.6.4 The Action Department deals with the issue of claims, responses to claims, admissions, undefended and summary judgments, enforcement, drawing up certain orders, public searches, provision of copies of court documents, enrolment of deeds, submission of references to the Court of Justice of the European Communities and registration of foreign judgments.

1.6.5 The Masters' Secretary's Department covers three discrete areas of work;

(1) the Masters' Support Unit which provides support (a) to the masters, including assisting with case-management, and (b) to the Senior Master,
(2) Foreign Process, and
(3) Investment of Children's Funds.

1.6.6 The Queen's Bench associates sit in court with the judges during trials and certain interim hearings. The Chief Associate manages the Queen's Bench associates and also provides support to the Senior Master as the Queen's Remembrancer and as the Prescribed Officer for election petitions. The associates draw up the orders made in court at trial and those interim orders that the parties do not wish to draw up themselves.

1.6.7 The Clerk of the Lists lists all trials and matters before the judges (see paragraph 8 below).

1.6.8 The Technology and Construction Court deals with claims which involve issues or questions which are technically complex or for which a trial by a judge of that court is for any other reason desirable (see the Part 49C Practice Direction – Technology and Construction Court).

1.6.9 The Admiralty and Commercial Court deals mainly with shipping collision claims and claims concerning charters and insurance, and commercial arbitrations. See the Commercial Court Guide and the Part 49D Practice Direction – Commercial Court, the Part 49F Practice Direction – Admiralty and the Part 49G Practice Direction – Arbitrations.

1.7 The judiciary

1.7.1 The judiciary in the Queen's Bench Division consist of the High Court judges (The Honourable Mr/Mrs Justice.........and addressed in court as my Lord/my Lady) and in the Royal Courts of Justice the masters (Master.........); in the district registries the work of the masters is conducted by district judges.

1.7.2 Trial normally takes place before a High Court judge (or deputy High Court judge[4]) who may also hear pre-trial reviews and other interim applications. Wherever possible the judge before whom a trial has been fixed will hear any pre-trial review. A High Court judge will hear applications to commit for contempt of court, applications for injunctions[5] and most appeals from masters' orders. (See the Practice Direction to Part 2B Allocation of cases to levels of Judiciary, and see paragraphs 7.11 and 7.12 below for more information on hearings and applications.)

4 A deputy High Court judge may be a circuit judge or Queen's Counsel. A retired High Court judge may also sit as a High Court judge.

5 See Part 25 and the practice direction which supplements it for more information about injunctions and who may hear them, and interim remedies in general.

1.7.3 The masters deal with interim and some pre-action applications, and manage the claims so that they proceed without delay. The masters' rooms are situated in the East Block of the Royal Courts of Justice. Hearings take place in these rooms or (short hearings only) in the Bear Garden.

1.7.4 Cases are assigned on issue by a court officer in the Action Department to masters on a random basis, and that master is then known as the assigned master in relation to that case. (See paragraphs 6.2 and 6.3 below for more information about assignment and the masters' lists.)

1.7.5 General enquiries about the business dealt with by the masters should initially be made in writing to the Masters' Support Unit in Room E14.

2 GENERAL

2.1 Essential matters

2.1.1 Before bringing any proceedings, the intending claimant should think carefully about the implications of so doing. (See paragraph 3 below about steps to be taken before issuing a claim form.)

2.1.2 A litigant who is acting in person faces a heavier burden in terms of time and effort than does a litigant who is legally represented, but all litigation calls for a high level of commitment from the parties. No intending claimant should underestimate this.

2.1.3 The Overriding Objective of the CPR is to deal with cases justly, which means dealing with the claim in a way which is proportionate (amongst other things) to the amount of money involved[6]. However, in all proceedings there are winners and losers; the loser is generally ordered to pay the costs of the winner and the costs of litigation can still be large. The risk of large costs is particularly acute in cases involving expert witnesses, barristers and solicitors. Also, the costs of an interim hearing are almost always summarily assessed and made payable by the unsuccessful party usually within 14 days after the order for costs is made[7]. There may be a number of interim hearings before the trial itself is reached, so the costs must be paid as the claim progresses. (See also paragraph 2.5 Costs below.)

6 See rule 1.1.
7 See rule 44.8.

2.1.4 The intending claimant should also keep in mind that every claim must be proved, unless of course the defendant admits the allegations. There is little point in incurring the risks and expense of litigating if the claim cannot be proved. An intending claimant should therefore be taking steps to obtain statements from his prospective witnesses before starting the claim; if he delays until later, it may turn out that he is in fact unable to obtain the evidence that he needs to prove his claim. A defendant faces a similar task.

2.1.5 Any party may, if he is to succeed, need an opinion from one or more expert witnesses, such as medical practitioners, engineers, accountants, or as the case may be. However he must remember that no expert evidence may be given at trial without the permission of the court. If the claim is for compensation for personal injuries, the claimant must produce a medical report with his particulars of claim.

2.1.6 The services of such experts are in great demand, especially as in some fields of expertise there are few of them. It may take many months to obtain an opinion, and the cost may be high. (See paragraph 7.9 below for information about experts' evidence.) The claimant must remember also not to allow the time-limit for starting his claim to pass (see paragraph 2.3 below for information about time-limits).

2.1.7 Any intending claimant should also have in mind that he will usually be required to give standard disclosure of the documents on which he relies. Although rule 31.3(2) makes provision for a party not to be required to disclose documents if disclosure would be disproportionate to the value of the claim, in complex cases it may still be necessary to disclose relatively large quantities of documents, and this invariably involves much time, effort and expense. (See paragraph 7.8 below for information about disclosure.)

2.1.8 In many cases the parties will need legal assistance, whether by way of advice, drafting, representation at hearings or otherwise. It is not the function of court staff to give legal advice, however, subject to that, they will do their best to assist any litigant. Litigants in person who need assistance or funding should contact the Community Legal Service through their information points. The CLS are developing local networks of people giving legal assistance such as law centres, local solicitors or the Citizens Advice Bureaux. CLS Information Points are being set up in libraries and other public places. Litigants can telephone the CLS to find their nearest CLS Information Point on 0845 608 1122 or can log on to the CLS website at www.justask.org.uk for the CLS directory and for legal information.

2.1.9 The RCJ Advice Bureau off the Main Hall at the Royal Courts of Justice is open Monday to Friday from 10.00 am to 1.00 pm and from 2.00 pm to 5.00 pm. The Bureau is run by lawyers in conjunction with the Citizens Advice Bureau and is independent of the court. The Bureau operates on a 'first come first served' basis, or telephone advice is available on 020 7947 7604 Monday to Friday from 11.00 am to 12.00 pm and from 3.00 pm to 4.00 pm.

2.2 Inspection and copies of documents

2.2.1 Intending claimants must not expect to be able to keep the details of a claim away from public scrutiny. In addition to the right of a party to obtain copies of documents in the proceedings to which he is a party from the court record (on payment of the prescribed fee), a claim form when it has been served, and the particulars of claim where they are included in or served with the claim form, may be inspected by anyone simply on payment of the fee. Any judgment or order made in public may also be inspected on payment of the fee. Additionally, other documents may be inspected with the permission of the court[8].

8 See rule 5.4 and the practice direction supplementing Part 5.

2.2.2 Witness statements[9] used at trial are open to inspection unless the court directs otherwise[10]. Considerations of publicity are often particularly important in deciding whether to commence proceedings in respect of an alleged libel or slander; such a claim may by its attendant publicity do more damage than was ever inflicted by the original publication. In such proceedings the claimant may decide to serve his particulars of claim separately from the claim form[11].

9 See paragraph 7.10 below about evidence.

10 See rule 32.13.

11 See Part 53 and the Part 53 practice direction for matters to be included in the claim form in a defamation claim where the particulars of claim are served separately.

2.3 Time-limits

2.3.1 There are strict time-limits that apply to every claim. First, there are time-limits fixed by the Limitation Act 1980 within which proceedings must be brought. There are circumstances in which the court may extend those time-limits, but this should be regarded as exceptional. In all other cases, once the relevant time-limit has expired, it is rarely possible to start a claim.

2.3.2 Secondly, in order to try and bring the proceedings to an early trial date, a timetable will be set with which all parties must comply. Unless the CPR or a practice direction provide otherwise, or the court orders otherwise, the timetable may be varied by the written agreement of the parties[12]. However, there are certain 'milestone' events in the timetable in which the time-limits may not be varied by the parties. Examples of these are;

(1) return of the allocation questionnaire
(2) date for the case management conference
(3) return of the listing questionnaire
(4) date fixed for trial.

Where parties have extended a time-limit by agreement, the party for whom the time has been extended must advise the Masters' Support Unit in writing of the event in the proceedings for which the time has been extended and the new date by which it must be done. For example, if an extension is agreed for the filing of the defence, it is for the defendant to inform the Masters' Support Unit.

12 See rule 2.11.

2.3.3 The court has power to penalise any party who fails to comply with a time-limit. If the court considers that a prior warning should be given before a penalty is imposed, it will make an 'unless' order; in other words, the court will order that, unless that party performs his obligation by the time specified, he will be penalised in the manner set out in the order. This may involve the party in default having his claim or statement of case struck out and judgment given against him.

2.4 Legal representation

2.4.1 A party may act in person or be represented by a lawyer. A party who is acting in person may be assisted at any hearing by another person (often referred to as a McKenzie friend) subject to the discretion of the court. The McKenzie friend is allowed to help by taking notes, quietly prompting the litigant and offering advice and suggestions. The litigant however, must conduct his own case; the McKenzie friend may not represent him and may only in very exceptional circumstances be allowed to address the court on behalf of the litigant under s 27(2)(c) of the Courts and Legal Services Act 1990.

2.4.2 A written statement should be provided to the court at any hearing concerning the representation of the parties in accordance with paragraph 5.1 of the Part 39 Practice Direction.

2.4.3 At a trial, a company or corporation may be represented by an employee if the company or corporation authorise him to do so and the court gives permission. Where this is to be the case, the permission of the judge who is to hear the case may be sought informally; paragraph 5 of the Part 39 Practice Direction describes what is needed to obtain permission from the court for this purpose and mentions some of the considerations relevant to the grant or refusal of permission. A further statement concerning representation should be provided in accordance with paragraph 5.2 of the Part 39 Practice Direction.

2.4.4 The practice of allowing experienced outdoor clerks to appear before the masters will continue.

2.5 Costs

2.5.1 Costs are dealt with in Parts 43–48[13]. There are important new provisions in the costs rules, particularly with respect to;

(1) informing the client of costs orders,
(2) providing the court with estimates of costs,
(3) summary assessment of costs,
(4) interim orders for costs, and
(5) interest on costs.

13 Rule 43.2 and sections 1 and 2 of the costs practice direction contain the definitions and applications used throughout Parts 43–48 and the practice direction.

2.5.2 Solicitors now have a duty under rule 44.2 to notify their client within 7 days if an order for costs is made against him in his absence. Solicitors must also notify any other person who has instructed them to act in the proceedings or who is liable to pay their fees (such as an insurer, trade union or the Legal Services Commission (LSC)). They must also inform these persons how the order came to be made (paragraphs 7.1 and 7.2 of the Costs Practice Direction).

2.5.3 The court may at any stage order any party to file an estimate of base costs (substantially in the form of Precedent H in the Schedule of Costs Precedents annexed to the Costs Practice Direction) and serve copies on all the other parties (paragraph 6.3 of the Costs Practice Direction). This will both assist the court in deciding what case management directions to make and inform the other parties as to their potential liability for payment of costs.

2.5.4 If a party seeks an order for his costs, in order to assist the court in making a summary assessment, he must prepare a written statement of the costs he intends to claim in accordance with paragraph 13.5 of the Costs Practice Direction, following as closely as possible Form N260. In addition, when an allocation questionnaire or a listing questionnaire is filed, the party filing it must file and serve an estimate of costs on all the other parties.

2.5.5 If the parties have agreed the amount of costs, they do not need to file a statement of the costs, and summary assessment is unnecessary. Or, where the parties agree a consent order without any party attending on the application, the parties should insert either an agreed figure for costs or that there should be no order for costs in the order (paragraph 13.4 of the Costs Practice Direction).

2.5.6 Unless the court decides not to order an assessment of costs where, for example, it orders costs to be 'costs in the case'[14], it may either make a summary assessment of costs or order a detailed assessment to take place[15]. The court will generally make a summary assessment of costs at any hearing which lasts for less than one day;

(1) 'summary assessment' is where the court, when making an order for costs, assesses those costs and orders payment of a sum of money in respect of them[16], and
(2) 'detailed assessment' is the procedure by which the amount of costs is decided by a costs officer at a later date in accordance with Part 47.

The provision of summary assessment means that the paying party is likely to be paying the costs at an earlier stage than he would have done under the previous rules (and see paragraph 2.5.15 below).

14 See the table in para 8.5 of the costs practice direction for some of the most common costs orders the court may make.
15 See rule 44.7 and section 12 of the costs practice direction.
16 See sections 12 and 13 of the costs practice direction.

2.5.7 The court will not make a summary assessment of the costs of a receiving party (the party to whom the costs are to be paid) where he is;

(1) a child or patient within the meaning of Part 21 unless the solicitor acting for the child or patient has waived the right to further costs[17], or
(2) an assisted person or a person in receipt of funded services under sections 4–11 of the Access to Justice Act 1999.

The costs payable by a party who is an assisted person or a person in receipt of funded services may be summarily assessed as the assessment is not by itself a determination of the assisted person's liability to pay those costs[18].

17 See the costs practice direction paras 13.11 and 51.1.
18 See the costs practice direction para 13.10.

2.5.8 Rule 44.3A prevents the court from assessing an additional liability in respect of a funding agreement before the conclusion of the proceedings. At an interim hearing therefore, the court will assess only the base costs. (See paragraph 14.9 of the Costs Practice Direction for assessing an additional liability and Section 19 for information about funding arrangements.)

2.5.9 Interim orders for costs; where the court decides immediately who is to pay particular costs, but does not assess the costs summarily, for example after a trial lasting more than a day, so that the final amount of costs payable has to be fixed by a detailed assessment, the court may order the paying party to pay a sum or sums on account of the ultimate liability for costs[19].

19 See rule 44.3(8).

2.5.10 Interest on costs; the court has power to award interest on costs from a date before the date of the order, so compensating the receiving party for the delay between incurring the costs and receiving payment in respect of them.

2.5.11 Parties should note that where the court makes an order which does not mention costs, no party is entitled to costs in relation to that order[20].

20 See rule 44.13(1).

2.5.12 Rule 44.3 describes the court's discretion as to costs and the circumstances to be taken into account when exercising its discretion. Rules 44.4 and 44.5 set out the basis of assessment and the factors to be taken into account in deciding the amount of costs. (See also Sections 8 and 11 of the Costs Practice Direction.)

2.5.13 The amount of costs to be paid by one party to another can be assessed on the standard basis or on the indemnity basis. The basis to be used is decided when the court decides that a party should pay the costs of another. Costs that are unreasonably incurred or are unreasonable in amount are not allowed on either basis.

2.5.14 The standard basis is the usual basis for assessment, where only costs which are proportionate to the matters in issue are allowed, and any doubt as to whether the costs were reasonably incurred or reasonable and proportionate in amount is resolved in favour of the paying party. On the indemnity basis, any such doubts are resolved in favour of the receiving party.

2.5.15 A party must normally pay summarily assessed costs awarded against him within 14 days of the assessment, but the court can extend that time, direct payment by instalments, or defer the liability to pay the costs until the end of the proceedings so that they can then be set off against any costs or judgment to which the paying party becomes entitled.

2.5.16 Fixed costs relating to default judgments, certain judgments on admissions and summary judgments etc are set out in Part 45, (see also Section 25 of the Costs Practice Direction). Part 46 relates to fast track costs.

2.5.17 Part 47 and Sections 28–49 of the Costs Practice Direction contain the procedure for detailed assessment together with the default provisions. Precedents A,B,C and D set out in the Schedule of Costs Precedents annexed to the Costs Practice Direction are model forms of bills of costs for detailed assessment. Section 43 deals with costs payable out of the Community Legal Service fund, Section 44 deals with costs payable out of a fund other than the CLS fund and Section 49 deals with costs payable by the LSC. Part 48 and Sections 50–56 of the Costs Practice Direction deal with Special Cases, in particular;

(1) costs payable by or to a child or patient,
(2) litigants in person, and
(3) wasted costs orders – personal liability of the legal representative.

2.5.18 Costs-only proceedings are dealt with in rule 44.12A and Section 17 of the Costs Practice Direction. They may be brought in the High Court only where the dispute was of such a value or type that had proceedings been brought they would have been commenced in the High Court. Proceedings are brought under Part 8 by the issue of a claim form in the Supreme Court Costs Office at Clifford's Inn, Fetter Lane, London EC4A 1DQ. (See also paragraphs 4.1.16 and 6.8.13 below.)

2.6 Court fees

2.6.1 The fees payable in the High Court are set out in Schedule 1 to the Supreme Court Fees Order 1999. Fees (as amended on 25 April 2000 and 2 May 2000) relating to the Queen's Bench Division are listed in Annex 1 to the Guide.

2.6.2 In the Royal Courts of Justice fees are paid in the Fees Room E01 and are usually stamped on the document to which they relate.

2.7 Information technology

2.7.1 To support the work of the Central Office in operating the provisions of the CPR, and to facilitate effective case management, a computerised system will be introduced to provide a record of proceedings and a search facility, and to produce court forms and orders. The full system is not yet available, but an interim system has been in use since 26 April 1999.

2.7.2 A number of specific applications of information technology have been well developed in recent years; the use of fax, the provision of skeleton arguments on disk and daily transcripts on disk have become more commonplace. Short applications may be dealt with more economically by a conference telephone call, and taking evidence by video link has become more common and the available technology has improved considerably. The CPR contains certain provisions about the use of information technology, for example, Part 6 and the Part 6 Practice Direction deal with service of documents by Fax or other electronic means, the Part 23 Practice Direction refers to telephone hearings and video conferencing, rule 32.3 allows the use of evidence given by video link and the Part 5 Practice Direction refers to the filing of documents at court by Fax.

2.7.3 Parties may agree to use information technology in the preparation, management and presentation of a case, however the agreement of the judge or master should be sought before providing the court with material in electronic form. Where permission has been given, the material for use at a hearing or in support of an application can be provided on a floppy disk. The parties should check with the court which word-processing format should be used. This will normally be Word 6 for Windows or WordPerfect for DOS 5.1.

2.7.4 A protocol has been prepared as a guide to all persons who are involved in the use of video conferencing equipment in civil proceedings in the High Court. It covers its use in courtrooms where the equipment may be installed, and also the situation where the court assembles in a commercial studio or conference room containing video conferencing equipment. Copies of the Video-conferencing Protocol may be obtained from the Bar Council at a charge of £2.50 to cover expenses. A room has now been made available as an audio/video conferencing courtroom for applications to masters, as a pilot measure. More information may be obtained from the Senior Master through the Masters' Secretary's Department.

3 STEPS BEFORE ISSUE OF A CLAIM FORM

3.1 Settlement

3.1.1 So far as reasonably possible, a claimant should try to resolve his claim without litigation. The court is increasingly taking the view that litigation should be a last resort and parties may wish to consider the use of alternative dispute resolution ('ADR'). (See paragraph 6.6 below.)

3.1.2 There are codes of practice for preliminary negotiations in certain types of claim. These codes of practice are called 'Protocols' and are set out in a schedule to the Protocols Practice Direction to the CPR. At present there are protocols covering only the areas of personal injury and clinical negligence. Even if there is no protocol that applies to the claim, the parties will nonetheless be expected to comply with the spirit of the Overriding Objective[21].

21 See the Protocols practice direction paragraph 4.

3.1.3 An offer to settle a claim may be made by either party[22] whether before or after a claim is brought. The court will take account of any offer to settle made before proceedings are started when making any order as to costs after proceedings have started[23].

22 See paragraph 3.21 of the Personal Injury protocol and paragraphs 3.22 and 3.26 of the Clinical Negligence protocol.

23 See rule 36.10 and rule 44.3(4)(c).

3.2 Disclosure before proceedings are started

3.2.1 An intending claimant may need documents to which he does not yet have access. Rule 31.16 sets out the provisions for making an application for disclosure of documents before proceedings have started.

3.2.2 Essentially, the court must be satisfied that the applicant and respondent to the application are likely to be parties when proceedings are brought, that the required documents are those that the respondent would be required to disclose under rule 31.6 when proceedings are brought and that their early disclosure might dispose of or assist the disposal of anticipated proceedings or save costs.

3.3 Defamation proceedings

3.3.1 Application may be made to the court before a claim is brought for the court's assistance in accepting an offer of amends under section 3 of the Defamation Act 1996. The application is made by Part 8 claim form. For more information see paragraph 4.1.15 Part 8 procedure and paragraph 12.7 defamation below.

4 STARTING PROCEEDINGS IN THE CENTRAL OFFICE

4.1 Issuing the claim form

4.1.1 All claims must be started by issuing a claim form. The great majority of claims involve a dispute of fact, and the claim form should be issued in accordance with Part 7 of the CPR. The Part 8 procedure may be followed in the types of claim described in paragraphs 4.1.14–4.1.16 below.

4.1.2 The requirements for issuing a claim form are set out in Part 7 and the Part 7 Practice Direction, the main points of which are summarised in the following paragraphs.

4.1.3 The Practice Direction at paragraphs 2, 3 and 4 provides information as to;

(1) where a claim should be started,
(2) certain matters that must be included in the claim form, and
(3) how the heading of the claim should be set out on the claim form.

In defamation cases see Part 53 and the Part 53 Practice Direction for matters that should be included in the claim form and particulars of claim. See also paragraph 12.7 below.

4.1.4 Proceedings are started when the court issues a claim form, and a claim form is issued on the date entered on the claim form by the court[24]. However, where a claim form is received in the court office on an earlier date than the date of issue, then, for the purposes of the Limitation Act 1980, the claim is brought on the earlier date (see paragraphs 5.1–5.4 of the Part 7 Practice Direction).

24 See rule 7.2.

4.1.5 To start proceedings in the Central Office, a claimant must use form N1 or form N208 for a Part 8 claim (or a form suitably modified as permitted by Part 4), and should take or send the claim form to Room E17, Action Department, Central Office, Royal Courts of Justice, Strand, London WC2A 2LL. If the court is to serve the claim form, the claimant must provide sufficient copies for each defendant. A claimant who wishes to retain for his file a copy of the claim form as issued should provide a further copy of the claim form which the court will seal and return it to him marked 'claimant's copy'. This copy will bear any amendments which have been made to the court's copy and the copies for service. Copies of practice forms relevant to the work of the Action Department (including the claim form and response pack) are available from that office. Alternatively, claimants may produce their own forms, which may be modified as the circumstances require, provided that all essential information, especially any information or guidance that the form gives to the recipient, is included. (See Part 4 Forms.)

4.1.6 On issuing the claim form, the court will give or send the claimant a notice of issue endorsed with the date of issue of the claim form. If the claimant requires the court to serve the claim form, the date of posting and deemed date of service will also be endorsed on the notice of issue. Claimants, especially solicitors who have been accustomed to using the Action Department, are encouraged to continue to serve their own documents but must inform the court when service has been effected (see paragraph 4.2.4 in relation to service by the claimant and the certificate of service). For certain types of claims, the notice of issue contains the request for judgment. (See paragraph 5 below for information about default judgments.)

4.1.7 A claim form must be served within 4 months after the date of issue (rule 7.5) unless it is to be served out of the jurisdiction, when the period is 6 months; and rule 7.6 and paragraph 7 of the Practice Direction set out how an extension of time for service of the claim form may be sought. (See paragraph 4.2 below about service.)

4.1.8 The particulars of claim may be;

(1) included in the claim form,
(2) in a separate document served with the claim form, or
(3) in a separate document served within 14 days of service of the claim form provided that the particulars of claim are served within the latest time for serving the claim form[25].

25 See rule 7.4.

4.1.9 A claim form that does not include particulars of claim must nonetheless contain a concise statement of the nature of the claim[26]. Any claim form that;

(1) does not comply with the requirements of rule 16.2, or
(2) is garbled or abusive,

will be referred to a master and is likely to be struck out by the court[27].

26 See rule 16.2(1), and paragraph 8 of the Part 16 practice direction in respect of defamation claims.
27 See rule 3.2.

4.1.10 Where the particulars of claim are neither included in or served with the claim form;

(1) the claim form must contain a statement that particulars of claim will follow, and
(2) the particulars of claim must be served by the claimant[28].

However, where a claim form is to be served out of the jurisdiction[29], the particulars of claim must accompany the claim form. (See paragraph 4.2.13 below.)

28 See rule 7.4(1)(b).
29 See rule 2.3 for the definition of 'jurisdiction'.

4.1.11 Certain forms must accompany the particulars of claim when they are served on the defendant. These forms are listed in rule 7.8 and are included in a response pack, which is available from the Action Department.

4.1.12 A party who has entered into a funding arrangement and who wishes to claim an additional liability must give the court and any other party information about that claim if he is to recover the additional liability. Where the funding arrangement has been entered into before proceedings are commenced, the claimant should file a notice of funding in form N251 when the claim form is issued[30].

30 See rule 44.15 and section 19 of the costs practice direction.

4.1.13 Part 22 requires the particulars of claim, and where they are not included in the claim form itself, the claim form to be verified by a statement of truth; see paragraph 6 of the Part 7 Practice Direction, and the Part 22 Practice Direction.

4.1.14 Part 16 and the Part 16 Practice Direction deal with statements of case, and in particular the contents of the claim form and the particulars of claim. Part 16 does not apply to claims in respect of which the Part 8 alternative procedure for claims is being used. See paragraph 5.6 below for more about statements of case.

4.1.15 A claimant may use the Part 8 procedure where;

(1) he seeks the court's decision on a question that is unlikely to involve a substantial dispute of fact, or
(2) a rule or practice direction requires or permits the use of the Part 8 procedure[31],

however, the court may at any stage order the claim to continue as if the claimant had not used the Part 8 procedure[32].

31 See rule 8.1.
32 See rule 8.1(3).

4.1.16 Certain matters that must be included on the claim form when the Part 8 procedure is being used are set out in rule 8.2. The types of claim for which the Part 8 procedure may be used include[33];

(1) a claim by or against a child or patient that has been settled before the commencement of proceedings, the sole purpose of the claim being to obtain the approval of the court to the settlement,
(2) provided there is unlikely to be a substantial dispute of fact, a claim for a summary order for possession against named or unnamed defendants occupying land or premises without the licence or consent of the person claiming possession (Schedule 1 – RSC Ord 113),
(3) a claim for provisional damages that has been settled before the commencement of proceedings, the sole purpose of the claim being to obtain a judgment by consent,
(4) a claim under s 3 of the Defamation Act 1996 (made other than in existing proceedings), and
(5) a claim under rule 44.12A where the parties have agreed all issues before the commencement of proceedings except the amount of costs and an order for costs is required.

33 See paragraph 1.4 of the Part 8 practice direction.

4.1.17 In addition to the provisions of rule 8.1, attention is drawn also to the Part 8(B) Practice Direction which deals with proceedings brought under 'the Schedule Rules'[34].

See Paragraph 6.7 below for more information regarding the Part 8 procedure.

34 See paragraph 1.1 of the Part 8B practice direction.

4.2 Service

4.2.1 Service of documents is dealt with in Part 6; Section I (rules 6.1–6.11) contains provisions relating to service generally and Section II (rules 6.12–6.16) contains special provisions relating to service of the claim form. Section III (rules 6.17–6.31) deals with service out of the jurisdiction. Some of the more important provisions are described below.

WITHIN THE JURISDICTION

4.2.2 The methods by which a document may be served are to be found in rule 6.2. The court will serve a document that it has issued or prepared unless;

(1) the party on whose behalf it is to be served notifies the court that he wishes to serve it himself,
(2) the court orders otherwise, or
(3) a rule or practice direction provides otherwise[35].

It is anticipated that practitioners familiar with Central Office procedures will wish to continue to serve their own documents.

35 See rule 6.3.

4.2.3 Where a party has entered into a funding agreement the notice of funding (form N251) must be served on all the other parties. If a claimant files his notice of funding when his claim form is issued, the court will serve it on the other parties provided sufficient copies are provided. Otherwise the claimant must serve the notice of funding with the claim form[36]. A defendant should file his notice of funding with his first document, ie his defence or acknowledgment of service etc. Sufficient copies of the notice should be provided for the court to serve.

36 See rule 44.15 and section 19 of the costs practice direction.

4.2.4 In all other circumstances a party must serve a notice of funding within 7 days of entering into the funding agreement[37].

37 See para 19.2 of the costs practice direction.

4.2.5 Where the court has tried to serve a document but has been unable to serve it, the court will send a notice of non-service to the party on whose behalf it was to be served stating the method attempted[38]. On receipt of this notice, the party should take steps to serve the document himself, as the court is under no further duty to effect service. The method of service used by the court will normally be first-class post.

38 See rule 6.11.

4.2.6 Where a claimant has served a claim form, he must file a certificate of service that complies with the provisions of rule 6.10. The certificate of service must be filed within 7 days of service of the claim form, and the claimant may not obtain judgment in default if it has not been filed[39].

39 See rule 6.14(2)(b).

4.2.7 Information as to how personal service is to be effected and as to service by electronic means is to be found in the Part 6 Practice Direction. Rule 6.6 deals with service on a child or patient.

4.2.8 A party must give an address for service within the jurisdiction. Rule 6.5 contains information as to the address for service.

4.2.9 A party may make an application for permission to serve a document by an alternative method[40] to those set out in rule 6.2. The application may be made without notice, and paragraph 9.1 of the Practice Direction sets out the evidence that will be required in support of the application. (Paragraph 7.12 below contains information in relation to applications.)

40 See rule 6.8.

OUT OF THE JURISDICTION

4.2.10 The provisions for service out of the jurisdiction are contained in rules 6.17–6.31. Rule 6.19 sets out the provisions whereby a claim form may be served out of the jurisdiction without the permission of the court, and rule 6.20 sets out the circumstances where the court's permission is required. Parties should also see the Practice Direction on service out of the jurisdiction.

4.2.11 A claimant may issue a claim form against defendants, one or some of whom appear to be out of the jurisdiction, without first having obtained permission for service out of the jurisdiction, provided that where the claim form is not one which may be served without the permission of the court under rule 6.19, the claim form is endorsed by the court that it is 'not for service out of jurisdiction'.

4.2.12 Where a claim form is to be served in accordance with rule 6.19 it must contain a statement of the grounds on which the claimant is entitled to serve it out of the jurisdiction. The statement should be as follows;

(1) 'I, (*name*) state that the High Court of England and Wales has power under the Civil Jurisdiction and Judgments Act 1982 to hear this claim and that no proceedings are pending between the parties in Scotland, Northern Ireland or another Convention territory of any contracting state as defined by section 1(3) of the Act.', or

(2) where the proceedings are those to which Article 16 of Schedule 1, 3C or 4 to the Act refers,

'I, (*name*) state that the High Court of England and Wales has power under the Civil Jurisdiction and Judgments Act 1982, the claim having as its object rights in rem in immovable property or tenancies in immovable property (or otherwise in accordance with the provisions of Article 16 of Schedule 1, 3C or 4 to that Act) to which Article 16 of Schedule 1, 3C or 4 to that Act applies, to hear the claim and that no proceedings are pending between the parties in Scotland, Northern Ireland or another Convention territory of any contracting state as defined by section 1(3) of the Act.', or

(3) where the defendant is party to an agreement conferring jurisdiction to which Article 17 of Schedule 1, 3C or 4 to that Act applies,

'I, (*name*) state that the High Court of England and Wales has power under the Civil Jurisdiction and Judgments Act 1982, the defendant being a party to an agreement conferring jurisdiction to which Article 17 of Schedule 1, 3C or 4 to that Act applies, to hear the claim and that no proceedings are pending between the parties in Scotland, Northern Ireland or another Convention territory of any contracting state as defined by section 1(3) of the Act.'.

4.2.13 The above statement should be signed and have set out the full name of the signatory. If a claim form as specified in paragraph 4.2.10 above does not bear the above statement, the claim form will be endorsed 'not for service out of the jurisdiction'.

4.2.14 An application for an order for permission to issue a claim form for service out of the jurisdiction or to serve the claim form out of the jurisdiction should be made in accordance with Part 23 (form PF6(A) may be used). The application must be supported by written evidence, and may be made without notice. The written evidence should state the requirements set out in rule 6.21(1) and (2).

4.2.15 An order giving permission for service out of the jurisdiction will be drawn up by the court (in form PF6(B)), unless a party wishes to do so, and will;

(1) specify the country in which, or place at which, service is to be effected, and
(2) specify the number of days within which the defendant may either
 (a) file an acknowledgment of service,
 (b) file or serve an admission, or
 (c) file a defence to

the claim, and where an acknowledgment of service is filed, specify a further 14 days within which the defendant may file a defence.

4.2.16 Where service is to be effected in a country which requires a translation of the documents to be served[41], it is the claimant's responsibility to provide the translation of all the documents for each defendant. In every case, it is the claimant's duty to ensure that the response pack clearly states the appropriate period for responding to the claim form, and form N9, form N1C and other relevant forms must be modified accordingly. Every translation must be accompanied by a statement by the person making it;

(1) that it is a correct translation, and
(2) including the person's name, address and qualifications for making the translation[42].

41 See rule 6.28.
42 Rule 6.28(3).

4.2.17 The periods for acknowledging service of a claim form served out of the jurisdiction are set out in rule 6.22 and in the Table contained in the Part 6 Section III Practice Direction, and the periods for serving a defence to a claim form served out of the jurisdiction are set out in rule 6.23 and in the Table in the Practice Direction. Rule 6.24 describes the methods of service.

4.2.18 Where the claim form is to be served through;

(1) the judicial authorities of the country where the claim form is to be served,
(2) a British Consular authority in that country,
(3) the authority designated under the Hague Convention in respect of that country, or
(4) the government of that country, or
(5) where the court permits service on a State, the Foreign and Commonwealth Office,

the claimant should provide the Senior Master with the following documents by forwarding them to the Foreign Process section, Room E 02;

 (a) a request for service by the chosen method (in form PF7),

(b) a sealed copy and a duplicate copy of the claim form,
(c) the response pack as referred to in paragraph 4.2.14,
(d) a translation in duplicate, and the statement referred to in paragraph 4.2.13, and
(e) any other relevant documents.

4.2.19 Where service has been requested in accordance with paragraph 4.2.16, the particulars of claim, if not included in the claim form, must accompany the claim form (in duplicate). Where the claimant is effecting service of the claim form direct (and not as in paragraph 4.2.16) and the claim form states that particulars of claim are to follow, the permission of the court is not required to serve the particulars of claim out of the jurisdiction.

4.2.20 Where an official certificate of service[43] is received in a foreign language, it is the responsibility of the claimant to obtain a translation of the certificate. Where a defendant served out of the jurisdiction fails to attend a hearing, the official certificate of service is evidence of service. Otherwise the claimant may take no further steps against the defendant until written evidence showing that the claim form has been duly served is filed[44].

43 See rules 6.26(5) and 6.27(4).
44 See rule 6.31.

4.2.21 Further advice on service out of the jurisdiction may be obtained from the Foreign Process section, Room E 02.

5 RESPONSE TO A PART 7 CLAIM

5.1 General

5.1.1 Responding to particulars of claim is dealt with in Part 9. A defendant may respond to the service of particulars of claim by[45];

(1) filing or serving an admission in accordance with Part 14,
(2) filing a defence in accordance with Part 15,
(3) doing both if part only of the claim is admitted, or
(4) filing an acknowledgment of service in accordance with Part 10.

45 See rule 9.2.

5.1.2 Where a defendant receives a claim form that states that particulars of claim are to follow, he need not respond to the claim until the particulars of claim have been served on him[46].

46 See rule 9.1(2).

5.1.3 If a defendant fails to;

(1) file an acknowledgment of service within the time specified in rule 10.3, and
(2) file a defence within the time specified in rule 15.4, or
(3) file or serve an admission in accordance with Part 14

the claimant may obtain default judgment if Part 12 allows it[47]. (See paragraph 5.5 below for information about default judgments.)

47 See rule 10.2.

5.2 Acknowledgment of service

5.2.1 Acknowledgments of service are dealt with in Part 10. A defendant may file an acknowledgment of service if;

(1) he is unable to file a defence within the period specified in rule 15.4, or
(2) he wishes to dispute the court's jurisdiction[48].

Filing an acknowledgment of service extends the time for filing the defence by 14 days.

48 See rule 10.1(3).

5.2.2 A defendant who wishes to acknowledge service of a claim form should do so by using form N9. Rule 10.5 states that the acknowledgment of service must;

(1) be signed by the defendant or his legal representative, and
(2) include the defendant's address for service.

The Part 10 Practice Direction contains information relating to the acknowledgment of service and how it may be signed.

5.3 Admissions

5.3.1 The manner in which a defendant may make an admission of a claim or part of a claim is set out in rules 14.1 and 14.2, and rules 14.3–14.7 set out how judgment may be obtained on a written admission.

5.3.2 Included in the response pack that will accompany the particulars of claim when they are served on the defendant is an admission form (form N9A for a specified amount and form N9C for an unspecified amount). If the defendant makes an admission and requests time to pay, he should complete as fully as possible the statement of means contained in the admission form, or otherwise give in writing the same details of his means as could have been given in the admission form.

5.3.3 Where the defendant has;

(1) made an admission in respect of a specified sum and requested time to pay, or
(2) made an admission in respect of an unspecified sum, offered a sum in satisfaction (which is accepted) and requested time to pay,

and the claimant has not accepted the request for time to pay, on receipt of the claimant's notice the court will enter judgment for the amount admitted or offered (less any payments made) to be paid at the time and rate of payment determined by the court[49].

49 See rule 14.10(4).

5.3.4 Where the defendant has;

(1) made an admission for an unspecified amount, or
(2) made an admission for an unspecified amount and offered in satisfaction a sum that the claimant has not accepted,

on receipt of the claimant's request for judgment the court will enter judgment for an amount to be decided by the court and costs[50].

50 See rules 14.6(7) and 14.7(10).

5.3.5 The matters that the court will take into account when determining the time and rate of payment are set out in paragraph 5.1 of the Part 14 Practice Direction.

5.3.6 The court may determine the time and rate of payment with or without a hearing, but, where a hearing is to take place, the proceedings must, where the provisions of rule 14.12(2) apply, be transferred to the defendant's home court. Where the claim form was issued in the Royal Courts of Justice the defendant's home court will be the district registry for the district in which the defendant's address given in the admission form is situated. If there is no such district registry the proceedings will remain in the Royal Courts of Justice[51].

51 Derived from rule 2.3.

5.3.7 The procedure for an application for re-determination of a decision determining the time and rate of payment is to be found in rule 14.13 and paragraphs 5.3–5.6 of the Practice Direction.

5.3.8 Where judgment has been entered for an amount to be decided by the court and costs, the court will give any directions that it considers appropriate, which may include allocating the case to a track[52]. (See paragraph 6.5 below about allocation.)

52 See rule 14.8.

5.3.9 Judgment will not be entered on an admission where;

(1) the defendant is a child or patient, or
(2) the claimant is a child or patient and the admission is made in respect of
 (a) a specified amount of money, or
 (b) a sum offered in satisfaction of a claim for an unspecified amount of money.

See Part 21 and the Part 21 Practice Direction, and in particular rule 21.10 which provides that, where a claim is made by or on behalf of a child or patient or against a child or patient, no settlement, compromise or payment shall be valid, so far as it relates to that person's claim, without the approval of the court.

5.4 Defence

5.4.1 A defendant who wishes to defend all or part of a claim must file a defence, and if he fails to do so, the claimant may obtain default judgment if Part 12 allows it[53]. The time for filing a defence is set out in rule 15.4.

53 See rules 15.2 and 15.3.

5.4.2 A form for defending the claim[54] is included in the response pack. The form for defending the claim also contains provision for making a counterclaim[55]. Part 22 requires a defence to be verified by a statement of truth (see the Part 15 Practice Direction, paragraph 2; and see also Part 22 and the Part 22 Practice Direction).

54 Forms N9B and N9D.
55 See Part 20.

5.4.3 The parties may, by agreement, extend the period specified in rule 15.4 for filing a defence by up to 28 days[56]. If the parties do so, the defendant must notify the court in writing of the date by which the defence must be filed.

56 See rule 15.5.

5.5 Default judgment

5.5.1 A party may obtain default judgment under Part 12 except in the circumstances set out in rule 12.2 and paragraphs 1.2 and 1.3 of the Part 12 Practice Direction, which list the circumstances where default judgment may not be obtained.

5.5.2 To obtain default judgment under the circumstances set out in rules 12.4(1) and 12.9(1), a party may do so by filing a request[57]. A request is dealt with by a court officer and provided he is satisfied that the provisions of paragraph 4.1 of the Part 12 Practice Direction have been complied with, he will enter the default judgment.

57 Forms N205A, N255, N255B or N227.

5.5.3 Default judgment in respect of claims specified in rules 12.4(2)(a), 12.9 and 12.10 must be obtained by making an application to a master. The following are some of the types of claim which require an application for default judgment;

(1) against children and patients,
(2) for costs (other than fixed costs) only,
(3) by one spouse against the other on a claim in tort,
(4) for delivery up of goods where the defendant is not allowed the alternative of paying their value,
(5) against the Crown, and
(6) against persons or organisations who enjoy immunity from civil jurisdiction under the provisions of the International Organisations Acts 1968 and 1981.

Paragraph 4 of the Practice Direction provides information about the evidence required in support of an application for default judgment.

5.5.4 Where default judgment has been obtained for an amount to be decided by the court, the matter will be referred to a master for directions to be given concerning the management of the case and any date to be fixed for a hearing.

Statements of case

5.6.1 Statements of case comprise the particulars of claim and defence in the main proceedings and also in any Part 20 proceedings, and are dealt with in Part 16. (Part 16 does not apply to claims proceeding under Part 8.)

5.6.2 The particulars of claim, whether contained in the claim form or served separately, should set out the claimant's claim clearly and fully. The same principle applies to the defence.

5.6.3 Part 16 sets out certain matters which must be included in a statement of case. Paragraphs 8 and 9 of the Part 16 Practice Direction contain matters which should be included in the particulars of claim in specific types of claim, and paragraph 10 lists matters which must be set out in the particulars of claim if relied on. In addition to the matters listed in paragraph 10, full particulars of any allegation of dishonesty or malice and, where any inference of fraud or dishonesty is alleged, the basis on which the inference is alleged should also be included. Points of law may be set out in any statement of case. For information in respect of statements of case in defamation claims see the Part 53 Practice Direction.

5.6.4 In addition to the information contained in Part 16 and the Part 16 Practice Direction, the following guidelines on preparing a statement of case should be followed;

(1) a statement of case must be as brief and concise as possible,
(2) a statement of case should be set out in separate consecutively numbered paragraphs and sub-paragraphs,
(3) so far as possible each paragraph or sub-paragraph should contain no more than one allegation,
(4) the facts and other matters alleged should be set out as far as reasonably possible in chronological order,
(5) the statement of case should deal with the claim on a point by point basis, to allow a point by point response,
(6) where a party is required to give reasons[58], the allegation should be stated first and then the reasons listed one by one in separate numbered sub-paragraphs,
(7) a party wishing to advance a positive claim must identify that claim in the statement of case,
(8) any matter which if not stated might take another party by surprise should be stated,
(9) where they will assist, headings, abbreviations and definitions should be used and a glossary annexed; contentious headings, abbreviations, paraphrasing and definitions should not be used and every effort should be made to ensure that they are in a form acceptable to the other parties,
(10) particulars of primary allegations should be stated as particulars and not as primary allegations,
(11) schedules or appendices should be used if this would be helpful, for example where lengthy particulars are necessary, and any response should also be stated in a schedule or appendix,
(12) any lengthy extracts from documents should be placed in a schedule.

58 See rule 16.5(2).

5.6.5 A statement of case should be verified by a statement of truth[59]. If a party fails to verify his statement of case, it will remain effective unless struck out, but that party may not rely on the statement of case as evidence of any of the matters contained in it[60]. Any party may apply to the court for an order to strike out a statement of case which has not been verified[61].

59 See rule 22.1.
60 See rule 22.2(1).
61 See rule 22.2(2) and (3).

6 PRELIMINARY CASE MANAGEMENT

6.1 The Practice Master

6.1.1 On every working day, the Practice Master is available from 10.30 am to 1.00 pm and from 2.00 pm to 4.30 pm to answer questions about the practice of the Queen's Bench Division. Usually, one master takes the Morning Practice, and another master takes the Afternoon Practice. This will be shown on the case-lists for the day and on the notice boards in the masters' corridors. Also, a board is placed on the door of the master who is sitting as Practice Master.

6.1.2 The Practice Master cannot give advice, whether about a given case or about the law generally. He is there simply to answer general questions about the CPR and practice governing the work of the Queen's Bench Division, and can deal with any consent order, notwithstanding that the claim in which it is to be made has been assigned to another master. The Practice Master may grant stays of execution and deal with urgent applications which do not require notice to be given to the respondent. It is unnecessary to make an appointment to see the Practice Master, litigants are generally seen in order of arrival.

6.2 Assignment to masters

6.2.1 A claim issued in the Central Office will normally be assigned at the issue stage to a particular master as the procedural judge responsible for managing the claim. The Action Department will endorse the name of the assigned master on the claim form. However, assignment may be triggered at an earlier stage, for example, by one of the following events;

(1) an application for pre-action disclosure under rule 31.16,
(2) an application for an interim remedy before the commencement of a claim or where there is no relevant claim (Part 25).

It occasionally happens that a claim is assigned to a master who may have an 'interest' in the claim. In such cases the Senior Master will re-assign the claim to another master.

6.2.2 Where either an application notice or Part 8 claim form is issued which requires a hearing date to be given immediately, the Masters' Support Unit will give a hearing date and assign it to the master who has the next available date for the hearing. The Masters' Support Unit will endorse the name of that master on the application notice or Part 8 claim form at the time of entering it in the list for hearing.

6.2.3 The Senior Master may assign a particular master to a class/group of claims or may re-assign work generally. At present clinical negligence claims are assigned to Master Murray and Master Ungley. In the event of an assigned master being on leave or for any other reason temporarily absent from the Royal Courts of Justice then the Masters' Support Unit may endorse on the appropriate document the name of another master.

6.2.4 A court file will normally be opened when a defence is filed, provided that the claim is not one that will automatically be transferred (see paragraph 6.4 below). The court file will be endorsed with the name of the assigned master. Any application notice in an assigned claim for hearing before a master should have the name of the assigned master entered on it by the solicitors making the application.

6.3 Listing before masters

6.3.1 The masters' lists consist of;

(1) the ordinary list – short applications in Rooms E102 and E110 ('the Bear Garden lists'),
(2) the Floating list,
(3) private room appointments[62], and
(4) the sheriff's first return applications.

62 A private room appointment is given where the hearing will be more than 20 minutes and takes place in the master's private room rather than a Bear Garden room. The appointment must be made by the master personally.

6.3.2 Parties attending on all applications before the masters are requested to complete the court record sheet (form PF48) which will be used to record details of the claim, representation and the nature of the application, and will be used by the master for his notes. Copies of this form may be found in the writing desks in the masters' corridors and the Bear Garden.

6.3.3 Masters will sit each day at 10.30 am in the Bear Garden to hear applications in the Bear Garden lists. Applications of up to 20 minutes duration are listed at 10.30 am, 11.00 am, 11.30 am and 12 noon. Solicitors and Counsel may attend any application in these lists although the costs of being represented by Counsel may be disallowed if not fully justified. If an application is estimated to take longer than 20 minutes the applicant must request a private room appointment. To do so the applicant must complete the PRA form giving details of the parties' availability as fully as possible. Failure to do so may result in the request form being returned for further information thereby delaying the hearing date.

6.3.4 Hearing dates for the Bear Garden lists are given by the Masters' Support Unit. Hearing dates for private room appointments are given by the assigned master personally. The parties or their legal representatives must inform the Masters' Support Unit of any settlements as soon as possible. All time estimates must be updated as necessary.

6.3.5 Applications in the Bear Garden list may, by agreement or where the application notice has not been served, be transferred (in the case of a 10 minute application) to the next available 12 noon list or (in either case) for a private room appointment on a date to be specified by the master. In all other cases an application for a postponement of the hearing date must be made to the master to whom the claim has been assigned. An application may be re-listed in the Bear Garden list without permission of a master if for any reason the application has not been heard or has not been fully disposed of.

6.3.6 When an application in the Bear Garden list is adjourned by a master he will specify the date to which it is adjourned. An application for the adjournment of a private room appointment must be made to the master who gave the appointment unless the application is by agreement of all parties and the master approves. The master will usually require details of parties' availability. Any adjournment will normally now be to a new hearing date.

6.3.7 Where an application for which a master has given a private room appointment has been settled, it is the duty of the parties or their legal representatives, particularly those who obtained that appointment, to notify the master immediately.

6.3.8 If the master hearing an application considers that the result might affect the date fixed for a trial, he may refer the application to the judge in charge of the list. This possibility should be considered when making an application and a request should be included in the application notice asking the master to refer the application to the judge.

6.3.9 If the master considers that an application should more properly be heard by a judge, he may either during the hearing or before it takes place refer the application to the Interim Applications judge. Among the circumstances that may make this appropriate are;

(1) that the time required for the hearing is longer than a master could ordinarily make available,
(2) that, whatever the master's decision on the application, an appeal to the judge is considered inevitable,
(3) that the application raises issues of unusual difficulty or importance, etc or
(4) that the outcome is likely to affect the trial date or window.

However, it is emphasised that no single factor or combination of factors is necessarily decisive, and the master has a complete discretion.

6.3.10 The sheriff's first return applications are interpleader applications (under RSC Ord 17 as set out in Schedule 1 to the CPR) and are listed at monthly intervals.

6.3.11 The Floating List is run by the Masters' Support Unit. Applications in this list will usually have a time estimate of not more than 30 minutes and are released by the assigned master, if he considers them suitable, when the request for a private room appointment is made. Dates and times of hearings are allocated by staff in Room E14. The parties should assemble at Room E14 well before the appointed time in order to facilitate the allocation of the application to a master or deputy who is free.

6.4 Automatic transfer

6.4.1 Part 26 requires certain claims to be transferred automatically[63]. Where;

(1) the claim is for a specified amount of money,
(2) the claim has not been issued in a specialist list[64],
(3) the defendant, or one of the defendants is an individual,
(4) the claim has not been issued in the individual defendant's home court, and
(5) the claim has not already been transferred to another individual defendant's home court,

the claim will, on receipt of the defence, be transferred to the individual defendant's home court.

63 See rules 26.1 and 2.
64 See Part 49.

6.4.2 Where the claim form was issued in the Royal Courts of Justice the defendant's home court will be the district registry for the district in which the defendant's address for service as shown on the defence is situated. If there is no such district registry the proceedings will remain in the Royal Courts of Justice[65]. If the claim is against more than one individual defendant, the claim will be transferred to the home court of the defendant who first files his defence. (See paragraph 6.9 below about transfer following an order.)

65 See rule 2.3(1)(b).

6.5 Allocation

6.5.1 When a defence to a claim is received in the Central Office from all the defendants, or from one or more of the defendants and the time for filing a defence has expired, the Action Department Registry will send an allocation questionnaire to those defendants who have filed a defence[66], unless it has been dispensed with.

66 See Part 26 and the Part 26 practice direction.

6.5.2 The allocation questionnaire to be used in accordance with Part 26 is form N150. The allocation questionnaire will state the time within which it must be filed, which will normally be at least 14 days after the day on which it is deemed served. Where proceedings are automatically transferred to a defendant's home court, notwithstanding that the issuing court will send out the allocation questionnaire before transfer, the allocation questionnaire should nevertheless be returned to the receiving court.

6.5.3 Each party should state in his allocation questionnaire if there is any reason why the claim should be managed and tried at a court other than the Royal Courts of Justice or the trial centre for a particular district registry. Paragraph 2.6 of the Part 29 Practice Direction sets out certain types of claim which are suitable for trial in the Royal Courts of Justice. Form PF49 will be sent out to parties with the allocation questionnaire requesting the parties to state convenient dates for a case management conference, if one should be ordered, or for other hearings. Parties are encouraged to agree directions for the management of the claim.

6.5.4 Where a party fails to file his allocation questionnaire within the specified time the court officer will refer the proceedings to the master for his directions. The master's directions may include 'the standard unless order', that is that unless the defaulting party files his allocation questionnaire within 3 days, his statement of case will be struck out[67].

67 See paragraph 2.5 of the Part 26 practice direction.

6.5.5 Where one but not all of the parties has filed an allocation questionnaire the master may allocate the claim to the multi-track where he considers that he has sufficient information to do so. Alternatively, the master may order that an allocation hearing take place and that all or any particular parties must attend. The court officer will then send out a Notice of Allocation Hearing (form N153) giving reasons for the hearing and any other directions.

6.5.6 Parties requesting a stay to settle the proceedings should do so in their allocation questionnaire or otherwise in writing. The court encourages parties to consider the use of ADR (see paragraph 6.6 below). The master will normally direct the proceedings to be stayed for one month, but parties may by agreement seek an extension of the stay. Paragraph 3 of the Part 26 Practice Direction sets out the procedure for seeking an extension.

6.5.7 Parties are reminded that an estimate of costs must be filed and served when the allocation questionnaire is filed (paragraph 6.4 of the Costs Practice Direction).

6.5.8 On receipt of the allocation questionnaires or on an allocation hearing the master will allocate the claim to the multi-track or transfer the claim to the appropriate county court[68]. Rule 26.6 sets out the scope of each track. Claims proceeding in the Royal Courts of Justice must be allocated to the multi-track.

68 County Courts Act 1984, ss 40–42 and Part 30.

6.6 Alternative dispute resolution ('ADR')

6.6.1 Parties are encouraged to use ADR (such as, but not confined to, mediation and conciliation) to try to resolve their disputes or particular issues. Legal representatives should consider with their clients and the other parties the possibility of attempting to resolve the dispute or particular issues by ADR and they should ensure that their clients are fully informed as to the most cost effective means of resolving their dispute.

6.6.2 The settlement of disputes by ADR can;

(1) significantly reduce parties' costs,
(2) save parties the delay of litigation in resolving their disputes,
(3) assist parties to preserve their existing commercial relationships while resolving their disputes, and
(4) provide a wider range of remedies than those available through litigation.

The master will in an appropriate case invite the parties to consider whether their dispute, or particular issues in it, could be resolved by ADR. The master may also either adjourn proceedings for a specified period of time or extend the time for compliance with an order, a rule or practice direction to encourage and enable the parties to use ADR. Parties may apply for directions seeking a stay for ADR at any time.

6.6.3 Information concerning ADR may be obtained from the Admiralty and Commercial Court registry.

6.7 Part 8 – alternative procedure for claims

6.7.1 Paragraphs 4.1.14–4.1.16 above deal with issuing a Part 8 claim form. The alternative procedure set out in Part 8 ('the Part 8 procedure') may not be used if a practice direction disapplies it in respect of a particular type of claim. A practice direction may require or permit the Part 8 procedure and may disapply or modify any of the rules contained in Part 8. The Part 8B Practice Direction deals with commencement of proceedings under the Rules of the Supreme Court and the County Court Rules the provisions of which remain in force in Schedules 1 and 2 to the CPR ('the Schedule rules'). The Schedule rules and the practice directions supporting them may require certain proceedings to be commenced by the issue of a Part 8 claim form with appropriate modifications to the Part 8 procedure.

6.7.2 The main features of the Part 8 procedure are;

(1) Part 16 (statements of case) does not apply,
(2) Part 15 (defence and reply) does not apply,
(3) judgment in default may not be obtained (rule 12.2),
(4) Rules 14.4–14.7 (judgment by request on an admission) do not apply,
(5) a Part 8 claim shall be treated as being allocated to the multi-track[69]

69 Rule 8.9.

6.7.3 A master may give directions for managing the claim as soon as the Part 8 claim form is issued. In certain circumstances this may include fixing a hearing date. Where a hearing date is fixed, notice of the hearing date must be served with the claim form[70]. Where the master does not fix a hearing date when the claim form is issued he will give directions for the disposal of the claim as soon as practicable after the receipt of the acknowledgment of service or as the case may be, the expiry of the period for acknowledging service.

70 See paragraph 4 of the Part 8 practice direction (alternative procedure) about managing the claim.

6.7.4 Where a Part 8 claim form has been issued for the purpose of giving effect to a consent order for an award of damages to a child or patient or an award of provisional damages as in paragraph 4.1.15 (1) and (2) above, a draft of the order sought should be attached to the claim form. For more information see paragraphs 6.8.1–6.8.8 and 9.3.8–9.3.10 below about children and patients, and paragraphs 6.8.12, 9.3.11 and 9.3.12 below about provisional damages.

6.7.5 A defendant who wishes to respond to a Part 8 claim form should acknowledge service of it and may do so either by using form N210 or otherwise in writing giving the following information;

(1) whether he contests the claim, and
(2) where he is seeking a different remedy from that set out in the claim form, what that remedy is.

If a defendant does not acknowledge service of the claim form within the specified time, he may attend the hearing of the claim but may not take part in the hearing unless the court gives permission[71].

71 See rule 8.4.

6.7.6 Rules 8.5 and 8.6 and paragraph 5 of the Part 8 Practice Direction (alternative procedure) deal with evidence to be relied on in Part 8 proceedings; the claimant's evidence must be filed and served with the claim form, and the defendant's evidence (if any) must be filed with his acknowledgment of service. If the defendant files written evidence he must at the same time serve it on the other parties. It is helpful to the court if, where the defendant does not intend to rely on written evidence, he notifies the court in writing to that effect.

6.7.7 Where a defendant contends that the Part 8 procedure should not be used, he should state the reasons for his contention on his acknowledgment of service. On receipt of the acknowledgment of service, the master will give appropriate directions for the future management of the claim.

6.8 Specific matters which may be dealt with under the Part 8 procedure

SETTLEMENTS ON BEHALF OF CHILDREN AND PATIENTS

6.8.1 Part 21 and the Part 21 Practice Direction set out the requirements for litigation by or against children and patients. References in Part 21, the Part 21 Practice Direction and in this guide to;

(1) 'child' means a person under 18, and
(2) 'patient' means a person who by reason of mental disorder within the meaning of the Mental Health Act 1983 is incapable of managing and administering his own affairs[72].

No settlement or compromise of a claim by or against a child or patient will be binding unless and until it has been approved by the court. In addition, a party may not obtain a default judgment against a child or patient without the permission of the court, and may not enter judgment on an admission against a child or patient.

72 See rule 21.1(2).

6.8.2 A patient must have a litigation friend to conduct proceedings on his behalf, and so must a child unless the court makes an order permitting the child to act on his own behalf. A litigation friend is someone who can fairly and competently conduct proceedings on behalf of the child or patient. He must have no interest in the proceedings adverse to that of the child or patient, and all steps he takes in the proceedings must be taken for the benefit of the child or patient. Rules 21.5–21.8 and paragraphs 2 and 3 of the Practice Direction set out how a person may become a litigation friend.

6.8.3 Applications for the approval of settlements or compromises of claims by or against a child or patient proceeding in the Central Office are heard by a master. If the purpose of starting the claim is for the approval of a settlement, a Part 8 claim form should be issued in accordance with form PF170(A) which must contain a request for approval of the settlement (or compromise) and, in addition to the details of the claim, must set out the terms of the settlement (or compromise) or must have attached to it a draft consent order. The draft consent order should be in form N292. See paragraph 6 of the Practice Direction for further information which the master will require.

6.8.4 Where parties reach a settlement (or compromise) in proceedings started by the issue of a Part 7 claim form (where the trial has not started) an application may be made to the master in accordance with Part 23 for the approval of the settlement. The application notice should be in form PF170(B) and should have attached to it a draft consent order in form N292. The application notice should be filed in Room E16. (See paragraph 7.12 below for information about applications.) However, where the trial hearing has been listed, the application notice should be filed in Room WG5. If the trial has started, oral application may be made to the trial judge. Applications for approval of a settlement on behalf of a child or patient will normally be heard in public unless the judge or master orders otherwise[73]. If a settlement is approved in private, the terms of settlement can be announced in public.

73 See rule 39.2.

6.8.5 Paragraph 8 of the Practice Direction gives information about control of money recovered by or on behalf of a child or patient. Paragraph 10 deals with investment of money on behalf of a child and paragraph 11 deals with investment on behalf of a patient. Enquiries concerning investment for a child are dealt with in Room E13.

6.8.6 In respect of investment on behalf of a child, the litigation friend or his legal representative should provide the master with form PF172 (request for investment) for completion by the master. The child's birth certificate should also be provided. The PF172 will then be forwarded to the Court Funds Office for their investment managers to make the appropriate investment. The Court of Protection is responsible for the administration of patients' funds (unless they are small). Paragraph 11 of the Practice Direction gives full information about procedure for investment by the Court of Protection. These procedures may also be used for investment of money on behalf of a child or patient following an award of damages at trial.

6.8.7 Damages may also be paid to a child or patient by way of a structured settlement. A structured settlement on behalf of a child or patient must be approved by a judge or master. A structured settlement on behalf of a patient must also be approved by the Court of Protection. (For more information about structured settlements see the Part 40C Practice Direction – Structured Settlements.)

6.8.8 Control of a child's fund, provided he is not also a patient, passes to him when he reaches the age of 18 (see paragraph 12.2 of the Practice Direction).

SUMMARY ORDER FOR POSSESSION

6.8.9 Where there is unlikely to be a substantial dispute of fact, a claim for a summary order for possession against named or unnamed defendants occupying land or premises without the licence or consent of the person claiming possession under RSC Ord 113 (Schedule 1 to the CPR) may be started by the issue of a Part 8 claim form.

6.8.10 When the claim form has been issued in the Action Department it will be passed to the Masters' Support Unit who will assign a master to the claim and fix a hearing date. Parties should check that they have sufficient time for service.

6.8.11 At the hearing the master may make the order sought or such other order as appropriate including directions for the management of the claim.

SETTLEMENT OF A PROVISIONAL DAMAGES CLAIM

6.8.12 A claim for provisional damages may proceed under Part 8 where the claim form is issued solely for the purpose of obtaining a consent judgment[74]. The claimant must state in his claim form in addition to the matters set out in paragraph 4.4 of the Part 16 Practice Direction that the parties have reached agreement and request a consent judgment. A draft order in accordance with paragraph 4.2 of the Part 41 Practice Direction should be attached to the claim form. The claimant or his legal representative must lodge the case file documents (set out in the draft order) in Room E14 for the case file to be compiled and preserved by the court. For more information about provisional damages claims and orders see Part 41 and the Part 41 Practice Direction, and paragraph 9.3 below.

74 See paragraph 1.4(2) of the Part 8 practice direction.

COSTS-ONLY PROCEEDINGS

6.8.13 Proceedings may be brought under Part 8 where the parties to a dispute have reached a written agreement before proceedings have been started but have been unable to agree an amount of costs. The costs-only proceedings may be started by the issue of a claim form in the Supreme Court Costs Office at Clifford's Inn, Fetter Lane, London EC4A 1DQ. The Costs Practice Direction at Section 17 sets out in detail the provisions for issue and proceeding with the claim.

6.9 Transfer

6.9.1 Part 30 and the Part 30 Practice Direction deal with transfer of proceedings, within the High Court, and between county courts. The jurisdiction of the High Court to transfer proceedings to the county courts is contained in s 40 of the County Courts Act 1984 as substituted by s 2(1) of the Courts and Legal Services Act 1990. Under that section the court has jurisdiction in certain circumstances to strike out claims which should have been started in a county court.

6.9.2 Rule 30.2 sets out the provisions for the transfer of proceedings between;

(1) county courts,
(2) the Royal Courts of Justice and a district registry of the High Court, and
(3) between district registries.

Rule 30.3 sets out the criteria to which the court will have regard when making an order for transfer. The High Court may order proceedings in any Division of the High Court to be transferred to another Division or to or from a specialist list. An application for the transfer of proceedings to or from a specialist list must be made to a judge dealing with claims in that list[75]. (See paragraph 6.4 above about automatic transfer.)

75 See rule 30.5.

6.9.3 A claim with an estimated value of less than £50,000 will generally be transferred to a county court, if the county court has jurisdiction, unless it is to proceed in the High Court under an enactment or in a specialist list.

6.9.4 An order for transfer takes effect from the date it is made[76]. When an order for transfer is made the court officer will immediately send notice of the transfer to the receiving court. The notice will contain the title of the proceedings and the claim number. At the same time, the court officer will also notify all parties of the transfer.

76 See paragraph 3 of the Part 30 practice direction.

6.9.5 Paragraph 5 of the Practice Direction sets out the procedure for appealing an order for transfer. Where an order for transfer is made in the absence of a party, that party may apply to the court which made the order to have it set aside[77]. The transferring court will normally retain the court file until the time for appealing the order or applying to set it aside has expired, whereupon the court officer will send the court file to the court manager of the receiving court. If, at the time an order for transfer is made a court file has not been compiled, the court officer will send to the receiving court those documents which have been filed at that time.

77 See paragraph 6 of the practice direction.

6.9.6 Where money has been paid into court before an order for transfer is made, the court may direct transfer of the money to the control of the receiving court.

6.10 Part 20 proceedings

6.10.1 Part 20 deals with (a) counterclaims and (b) other additional claims, being claims for contribution or indemnity and what were formerly called 'third party' claims. A Part 20 claim is treated as a claim for the purpose of the CPR with certain exceptions, for which see rule 20.3.

6.10.2 A defendant may make a counterclaim by completing the defence and counterclaim form provided in the response pack. If the counterclaim is not filed with the defence, the permission of the court is required[78]. Where a counterclaim brings in a new party, the defendant (Part 20 claimant) must apply to the court for an order in form PF21A adding the new party as defendant[79].

78 Rule 20.4.
79 Rule 20.5.

6.10.3 A defendant claiming contribution or indemnity from another defendant may do so by filing a notice, in form PF22, containing a statement of the nature and grounds of his claim and serving the notice on the other defendant[80].

80 Rule 20.6.

6.10.4 Any other additional claim may be brought by the issue of a Part 20 claim form, N211. If the Part 20 claim form is issued at a time other than when the defence is filed, the permission of the court is required. Rule 20.8 deals with service of a Part 20 claim form and rule 20.12 sets out the forms which must accompany the Part 20 claim form.

6.11 Summary judgment

6.11.1 The court may give summary judgment under Part 24 against a claimant or defendant;

(1) if it considers that (a) the claimant has no real prospect of succeeding on the claim or issue, or (b) the defendant has no real prospect of successfully defending the claim, and
(2) there is no other reason why the claim or issue should be disposed of at a trial.

6.11.2 The court may give summary judgment against a claimant in any type of proceedings, and against a defendant in any type of proceedings except (a) proceedings for possession of residential premises against a mortgagor, or a tenant or person holding over after the end of his tenancy where occupancy is protected within the meaning of the Rent Act 1977 or the Housing Act 1988, (b) proceedings for an Admiralty claim in Rem, and (c) contentious probate proceedings[81]. For information about summary disposal of defamation claims see Part 53, the Part 53 Practice Direction and paragraph 12.7 below.

81 See rule 24.3 but see also Schedule 1 RSC Ord 77, r 7(1).

6.11.3 An application for summary judgment should be made in accordance with Part 23 and the application notice should contain the information set out in paragraph 2 of the Part 24 Practice Direction (parties may use forms PF11 and PF12 as precedents). The application notice should be filed and served on the respondent giving at least 14 days notice of the date fixed for the hearing and the issues to be decided at the hearing. Unless the application notice contains all the evidence on which the applicant relies, the application notice should identify that evidence. In claims which include a claim for;

(1) specific performance of an agreement,
(2) rescission of such an agreement, or
(3) forfeiture or return of a deposit made under such an agreement,

the application notice and any evidence in support must be served on the defendant not less than 4 days before the hearing[82].

82 See the Part 24 practice direction paragraph 7.

6.11.4 The application will normally be listed before a master unless for example, an injunction is also sought. In that case the application notice should state that the application is intended to be made to a judge.

6.11.5 Where an order made on an application for summary judgment does not dispose of the claim or issue, the court will give case management directions in respect of the claim or issue.

6.12 Offers to settle and payments into and out of court

6.12.1 A party may offer to settle a claim at any time. Part 36 deals with offers to settle and payments into court. An offer to settle made in accordance with Part 36 will have the costs and other consequences specified in that Part and may be made at any time after proceedings have started. Paragraph 1 of the Part 36 Practice Direction defines an offer made in accordance with Part 36. See also paragraph 5 of the Part 36 Practice Direction which contains general provisions concerning Part 36 offers and Part 36 payments.

6.12.2 A Part 36 offer may be made by any party, but to comply with Part 36 a defendant who makes an offer to settle for a specified sum must do so by way of a Part 36 payment into court. Paragraph 4.1(2) of the Part 36 Practice Direction sets out the requirements for making a Part 36 payment in respect of a claim proceeding in the Royal Courts of Justice. If a defendant has made a pre-action offer to settle and proceedings are then started, in order for the court to take account of his offer he must make a Part 36 payment of not less than the amount offered within 14 days of service of the claim form. See also paragraph 10 of the Part 36 Practice Direction which deals with compensation recovery in respect of Part 36 payments.

6.12.3 The times for accepting a Part 36 offer or Part 36 payment are set out in rules 36.11 and 36.12; the general rule is that a Part 36 offer or Part 36 payment made more than 21 days before the start of the trial may be accepted without the permission of the court, within 21 days after it was made. Otherwise, the permission of the court must be obtained. A Part 36 offer is made when received by the offeree. A Part 36 payment is made when the Part 36 payment notice (form N242A) is served on the claimant.

6.12.4 A party may accept a Part 36 offer or Part 36 payment by serving on the offeror a notice of acceptance (form N243 may be used to accept a Part 36 payment) within the times set out in rules 36.11 and 36.12. When a Part 36 offer or Part 36 payment is accepted within those times, the general rule is that the claimant will be entitled to his costs up to the date of service of the notice of acceptance.

6.12.5 To obtain money out of court on acceptance of a Part 36 payment, the claimant should file a request for payment (form N243) in the Action Department of the Central Office, and file a completed Court Funds Office form 201 in the Court Funds Office. See paragraph 8 of the Part 36 Practice Direction for more information about obtaining payment out of court.

6.12.6 The court's permission is required for acceptance of a Part 36 offer or Part 36 payment;

(1) which is not made or accepted within the times set out in rules 36.11 and 36.12,
(2) where acceptance is by or on behalf of a child or patient[83], or
(3) where a defence of tender has been put forward, or
(4) otherwise as mentioned in rule 36.17.

83 See rule 21.10.

6.12.7 Where a Part 36 offer or Part 36 payment is not accepted and a trial of the claim takes place, rule 36.20 sets out the costs consequences where a claimant fails to do better than the Part 36 offer or Part 36 payment, and rule 36.21 sets out the costs and other consequences where a claimant does better than he proposed in his Part 36 offer.

7 CASE MANAGEMENT AND INTERIM REMEDIES

7.1 Case management – general

7.1.1 The CPR require the court to provide a high degree of case management. Case management includes; identifying disputed issues at an early stage; fixing timetables; dealing with as many aspects of the claim as possible on the same occasion; controlling costs; disposing of proceedings summarily where appropriate; dealing with the applications without a hearing where appropriate; and giving directions to ensure that the trial of a claim proceeds quickly and efficiently. The court will expect the parties to co-operate with each other, and where appropriate, will encourage the parties to use ADR or otherwise help them settle the case.

7.1.2 Parties and their legal representatives will be expected to do all that they can to agree proposals for the management of the claim in accordance with rule 29.4 and paragraphs 4.6–4.8 of the Part 29 Practice Direction. There is provision in the allocation questionnaire for proposing certain directions to be made, otherwise parties may use form PF50 for making the application (attaching to it the draft form of order in form PF52) and file it for the master's approval. If the master approves the proposals he will give directions accordingly.

7.1.3 Parties should consider whether a case summary would assist the master in dealing with the issues before him. Paragraph 5.7 of the Part 29 Practice Direction sets out the provisions for preparation of a case summary.

7.2 The case management conference

7.2.1 Parties who are unable to agree proposals for the management of the case, should notify the court of the matters which they are unable to agree.

7.2.2 Where;

(1) the parties proposed directions are not approved, or
(2) parties are unable to agree proposed directions, or
(3) the master wishes to make further directions,

the master will generally either consult the parties or direct that a case management conference be held.

7.2.3 In relatively straightforward claims, the court will give directions without holding a case management conference.

7.2.4 Any party who considers that a case management conference should be held before any directions are given should so state in his allocation questionnaire, (or in a Part 8 claim should notify the master in writing), giving his reasons and supplying a realistic time estimate for the case management conference, with a list of any dates or times convenient to all parties, or most of them, in form PF49.

7.2.5 Where a case management conference has been fixed, parties should ensure that any other applications are listed or made at that hearing. A party applying for directions at the case management conference should use form PF50 for making their application and attach to it the draft order for directions (form PF52).

7.2.6 The advocates instructed or expected to be instructed to appear at the trial should attend any hearing at which case management directions are likely to be given. In any event, the legal representatives who attend the case management conference must be familiar with the case and have sufficient authority to deal with any issues which may arise. Where necessary, the court may order the attendance of a party[84].

84 See rule 3.1(c).

7.3 Preliminary issues

7.3.1 Costs can sometimes be saved by identifying decisive issues, or potentially decisive issues, and by the court ordering that they be tried first. The decision of one issue, although not necessarily itself decisive of the claim as a whole, may enable the parties to settle the remainder of the dispute. In such a case, the trial of a preliminary issue may be appropriate.

7.3.2 At the allocation stage, at any case management conference and again at any pre-trial review, the court will consider whether the trial of a preliminary issue may be helpful. Where such an order is made, the parties and the court should consider whether the costs of the issue should be in the issue or in the claim as a whole.

7.3.3 Where there is an application for summary judgment, and issues of law or construction may be determined in the respondent's favour, it will usually be in the interests of the parties for such issues to be determined conclusively, rather than that the application should simply be dismissed.

7.4 Trial timetable

7.4.1 To assist the court to set a trial timetable[85], a draft timetable should be prepared by the claimant's advocate(s) after consulting the other parties advocates. If there are differing views, those differences should be clearly indicated in the timetable. The draft timetable should be filed with the trial bundle.

85 See rules 29.8 and 39.4.

7.4.2 The trial timetable will normally include times for giving evidence (whether of fact or opinion) and for oral submissions during the trial.

7.4.3 The trial timetable may be fixed at the case management conference, at any pre-trial review or at the beginning of the trial itself.

7.5 Listing questionnaire

7.5.1 The court may send out a listing questionnaire (N170) to all parties for completion, specifying the date by which it must be returned. The master will then fix the trial date or period ('the trial window'). It is likely however, that the master will already have sufficient information to enable him to fix a trial window, and will dispense with the need for a listing questionnaire subject to any requirement of the Clerk of the Lists for one to be filed. Instead, the master will direct the parties within a specified time to attend before the Clerk of the Lists to fix a trial date within that window.

7.5.2 Paragraph 6.4 of the Costs Practice Direction requires an estimate of costs to be filed and served with the listing questionnaire. If the filing of a listing questionnaire has been dispensed with, the estimate of costs should be filed on attendance before the Clerk of the Lists.

7.6 Pre-trial review

7.6.1 Where the trial of a claim is estimated to last more than 10 days, or where the circumstances require it, the master may direct that a pre-trial review ('PTR') should be held[86]. The PTR may be heard by a master, but more usually is heard by a judge.

86 See rule 29.7.

7.6.2 Application should normally be made to the Clerk of the Lists for the PTR to be heard by the trial judge (if known), and the applicant should do all that he can to ensure that it is heard between 8 and 4 weeks before the trial date, and in any event long enough before the trial date to allow a realistic time in which to complete any outstanding matters.

7.6.3 The PTR should be attended by the advocates who are to represent the parties at the trial.

7.6.4 At least 7 days before the date fixed for the PTR, the applicant must serve the other parties with a list of matters to be considered at the PTR, and those other parties must serve their responses at least 2 days before the PTR. Account must be taken of the answers in any listing questionnaires filed. Realistic proposals must be put forward and if possible agreed as to the time likely to be required for each stage of the trial and as to the order in which witnesses are to be called.

7.6.5 The applicant should lodge a properly indexed bundle containing the listing questionnaires (if directed to be filed) and the lists of matters and the proposals, together with the results of discussions between the parties, and any other relevant material, in the Listing Office, Room WG5, by no later than 10.00 am on the day before the day fixed for the hearing of the PTR. If the PTR is to take place before a master and he asks for the bundle in advance, it should be lodged in the Masters' Support Unit, Room E14. Otherwise it should be lodged at the hearing.

7.6.6 At the PTR, the court will review the parties' state of preparation, deal with any outstanding matters, and give any directions or further directions that may be necessary.

7.7 Requests for further information

7.7.1 A party seeking further information or clarification under Part 18 should serve a written request on the party from whom the information is sought before making an application to the court. Paragraph 1 of the Part 18 Practice Direction deals with how the request should be made, and paragraph 2 deals with the response. A response should be verified by a statement of truth[87]. Parties may use form PF56 for a combined request and reply, if they so wish.

87 See Part 22.

7.7.2 If a party who has been asked to provide further information or clarification objects or is unable to do so, he must notify the party making the request in writing[88].

88 See paragraph 4 of the Part 18 practice direction.

7.7.3 Where it is necessary to apply for an order for further information or clarification the party making the application should set out in or have attached to his application notice;

(1) the text of the order sought specifying the matters on which further information or clarification is sought, and

(2) whether a request has been made and, if so, the result of that request[89].

Applicants may use form PF57 for their application notice.

89 See paragraph 5 of the Part 18 practice direction.

7.8 Disclosure

7.8.1 Under Part 31, there is no longer any general duty to disclose documents. Instead, a party is prevented from relying on any document that he has not disclosed, and is required to give inspection of any document to which he refers in his statement of case or in any witness statement, etc[90]. The intention is that disclosure should be proportionate to the value of the claim.

90 Rules 31.14 and 31.21.

7.8.2 If an order for disclosure is made, unless the contrary is stated, the court will order standard disclosure, namely disclosure of only;

(1) the documents on which a party relies,

(2) the documents that adversely affect his own or another party's case,

(3) the documents that support another party's case, and

(4) the documents required to be disclosed by a relevant practice direction.

Parties should give standard disclosure by completing form N265 but may also list documents by category[91].

91 See paragraph 3.2 of the Part 31 practice direction.

7.8.3 The court may either limit or dispense with disclosure (and the parties may agree to do likewise). The court may also order disclosure of specified documents or specified classes of documents. In deciding whether to make any such order for specific disclosure, the court will want to be satisfied that the disclosure is necessary, that the cost of disclosure will not outweigh the benefits of disclosure and that a party's ability to continue the litigation would not be impaired by any such order.

7.8.4 The court will therefore seek to ensure that any specific disclosure ordered is appropriate to the particular case, taking into account the financial position of the parties, the importance of the case and the complexity of the issues.

7.8.5 If specific disclosure is sought, a separate application for specific disclosure should be made in accordance with Part 23; it is not a matter that would be routinely dealt with at the CMC. The parties should give careful thought to ways of limiting the burdens of such disclosure, whether by giving disclosure in stages, by dispensing with the need to produce copies of the same document, by requiring disclosure of documents sufficient merely for a limited purpose, or otherwise. They should also consider whether the need for disclosure could be reduced or eliminated by a request for further information.

7.8.6 A party who has the right to inspect a document[92] should give written notice of his wish to inspect to the party disclosing the document. That party must permit inspection not more than 7 days after receipt of the notice.

92 See rules 31.3 and 31.15.

7.9 Experts and assessors

7.9.1 The parties in a claim must bear in mind that under Part 35 no party may call an expert or put in evidence an expert's report without the court's express permission, and the court is under a duty to restrict such evidence to what is reasonably required.

7.9.2 The duty of an expert called to give evidence is to assist the court. This duty overrides any obligation to the party instructing him or by whom he is being paid (see the Part 35 Practice Direction). In fulfilment of this duty, an expert must for instance make it clear if a particular question or issue falls outside his expertise or if he considers that insufficient information is available on which to express an opinion.

7.9.3 Before the master gives permission, he must be told the field of expertise of the expert on whose evidence a party wishes to rely and where practicable the identity of the expert. Even then, he may, before giving permission, impose a limit on the extent to which the cost of such evidence may be recovered from the other parties in the claim[93].

93 Rule 35.4.

7.9.4 Parties should always consider whether a single expert could be appointed in a particular claim or to deal with a particular issue. Before giving permission for the parties to call separate experts, the master will always consider whether a single joint expert ought to be used, whether in relation to the issues as a whole or to a particular issue[94].

94 Rule 35.7.

7.9.5 In very many cases it is possible for the question of expert evidence to be dealt with by a single expert. Single experts are, for example, often appropriate to deal with questions of quantum in cases where primary issues are as to liability. Likewise, where expert evidence is required in order to acquaint the court with matters of expert fact, as opposed to opinion, a single expert will usually be appropriate. There remain, however, a body of cases where liability will turn upon expert opinion evidence and where it will be appropriate for the parties to instruct their own experts. For example, in cases where the issue for determination is as to whether a party acted in accordance with proper professional standards, it will often be of value to the court to hear the opinions of more than one expert as to the proper standard in order that the court becomes acquainted with a range of views existing upon the question and in order that the evidence can be tested in cross-examination.

7.9.6 It will not be a sufficient ground for objecting to an order for a single joint expert that the parties have already chosen their own experts. An order for a single joint expert does not prevent a party from having his own expert to advise him, though that is likely to be at his own cost, regardless of the outcome.

7.9.7 When the use of a single joint expert is being considered, the master will expect the parties to co-operate in agreeing terms of reference for the expert. In most cases, such terms of reference will include a statement of what the expert is asked to do, will identify any documents that he will be asked to consider and will specify any assumptions that he is asked to make.

7.9.8 The court will generally also order that experts in the same field confer on a 'without prejudice' basis, and then report in writing to the parties and the court on the extent of any agreement, giving reasons at least in summary for any continuing disagreement. A direction to 'confer' gives the experts the choice of discussing the matter by telephone or in any other convenient way, as an alternative to attending an actual meeting. Any material change of view of an expert should be communicated in writing to the other parties through their legal representatives, and when appropriate, to the court.

7.9.9 Written questions may be put to an expert within 28 days after service of his report, but are for purposes of clarification of the expert's report when the other party does not understand it. Questions going beyond this can only be put with the agreement of the parties or the master's permission. The procedure of putting written questions to experts is not intended to interfere with the procedure for an exchange of professional opinion in discussions between experts or to inhibit that exchange of professional opinion. If questions that are oppressive in number or content are put without permission for any purpose other than clarification of the expert's report, the court is likely to disallow the questions and make an appropriate order for costs against the party putting them. (See paragraph 4.3 of the Part 35 Practice Direction with respect to payment of an expert's fees for answering questions under rule 35.6.)

7.9.10 An expert may file with the court a written request for directions to assist him in carrying out his function as an expert[95]. The expert should guard against accidentally informing the court about, or about matters connected with, communications or potential communications between the parties that are without prejudice or privileged. The expert may properly be asked to be privy to the content of these communications because he has been asked to assist the party instructing him to evaluate them.

95 See rule 35.14.

7.9.11 Under rule 35.15 the court may appoint an assessor to assist it in relation to any matter in which the assessor has skill and experience. The report of the assessor is made available to the parties. The remuneration of the assessor is decided by the court and forms part of the costs of the proceedings.

7.10 Evidence

7.10.1 Evidence is dealt with in the CPR in Parts 32, 33 and 34.

7.10.2 The most common form of written evidence is a witness statement. The Part 32 Practice Direction at paragraphs 17, 18 and 19 contains information about the heading, body (what it must contain) and format of a witness statement. The witness must sign a statement of truth to verify the witness statement; the wording of the statement of truth is set out in paragraph 20.2 of the Practice Direction.

7.10.3 A witness statement may be used as evidence in support of an interim application and, where it has been served on any other party to a claim, it may be relied on as a statement of the oral evidence of the witness at the trial. Part 33 contains provisions relating to the use of hearsay evidence in a witness statement.

7.10.4 In addition to the information and provisions for making a witness statement mentioned in paragraph 7.10.2, the following matters should be borne in mind;

(1) a witness statement must contain the truth, the whole truth and nothing but the truth on the issues it covers,

(2) those issues should consist only of the issues on which the party serving the witness statement wishes that witness to give evidence in chief and should not include commentary on the trial bundle or other matters which may arise during the trial,
(3) a witness statement should be as concise as the circumstances allow, inadmissible or irrelevant material should not be included,
(4) the cost of preparation of an over-elaborate witness statement may not be allowed,
(5) Rule 32.14 states that proceedings for contempt of court may be brought against a person if he makes, or causes to be made, a false statement in a document verified by a statement of truth without an honest belief in its truth,
(6) if a party discovers that a witness statement which they have served is incorrect they must inform the other parties immediately.

7.10.5 Evidence may also be given by affidavit[96] but unless an affidavit is specifically required either in compliance with a court order, a rule or practice direction, or an enactment, the party putting forward the affidavit may not recover from another party the cost of making an affidavit unless the court so orders[97].

96 See rule 32.15(2).
97 See rule 32.15(1) and (2).

7.10.6 The Part 32 Practice Direction at paragraphs 3–6 contains information about the heading, body, jurat (the sworn statement which authenticates the affidavit) and the format of an affidavit. The court will normally give directions as to whether a witness statement or, where appropriate, an affidavit is to be filed[98].

98 See rule 32.4(3)(b).

7.10.7 A statement of case which has been verified by a statement of truth and an application notice containing facts which have been verified by a statement of truth may also stand as evidence other than at the trial.

7.10.8 Evidence by deposition is dealt with in Part 34. A party may apply to a master for an order for a person to be examined before a hearing takes place (rule 34.8). Evidence obtained on an examination under that rule is referred to as a deposition. The master may order the person to be examined before either a judge, an examiner of the court or such other person as the court appoints. The Part 34 Practice Direction at paragraph 4 sets out in detail how the examination should take place.

7.10.9 Provisions relating to applications for evidence by deposition to be taken either;

(1) in this country for use in a foreign court[99], or
(2) abroad for use in proceedings within the jurisdiction[100]

are set out in detail in the Part 34 Practice Direction at paragraphs 5 and 6.

99 See RSC Ord 70 (Schedule 1 to Part 50).
100 See rule 34.13.

7.10.10 The procedure for issuing a witness summons is also dealt with in Part 34 and the Practice Direction. A witness summons may require a witness to;

(1) attend court,
(2) produce documents to the court, or
(3) both,

on either a date fixed for the hearing or another date as the court may direct[101] (but see also rule 31.17 which may be used when there are areas of contention).

101 See rule 34.2(4).

7.10.11 The court may also issue a witness summons in aid of a court or tribunal which does not have the power to issue a witness summons in relation to the proceedings before it (and see the Part 34 Practice Direction at paragraphs 1, 2 and 3).

7.10.12 To issue a witness summons, two copies should be filed in the Action Department, Room E14 for sealing; one copy will be retained on the court file.

7.11 Hearings

HEARINGS GENERALLY

7.11.1 All hearings are in principle open to the public, even though in practice most of the hearings until the trial itself will be attended only by the parties and their representatives. However, in an appropriate case the court may decide to hold a hearing in private. Rule 39.2 lists the circumstances where it may be appropriate to hold a hearing in private. In addition, paragraph 1.5 of the Part 39 Practice Direction sets out certain types of hearings which may be listed in private.

7.11.2 The court also has the power under section 11 of the Contempt of Court Act 1981 to make an order forbidding publication of any details that might identify one or more of the parties. Such orders are granted only in exceptional cases.

7.11.3 References in the CPR and Practice Directions to hearings being in public or private do not restrict any existing rights of audience or confer any new rights of audience in respect of applications or proceedings which under the rules previously in force would have been heard in court or chambers respectively[102]. Advocates (and judges) do not wear robes at interim hearings before High Court judges, including appeals from masters, district judges and the county courts. Robes are worn for trials and certain other proceedings such as preliminary issues, committals etc. It is not intended that the new routes of appeal should restrict the advocate's right of audience, in that a solicitor who appeared in a county court matter which is the subject of an appeal to a High Court judge would normally be allowed to appear at the appeal hearing.

102 See paragraph 1.14 of the Part 39 practice direction.

7.11.4 Parties are reminded that they are expected to act with courtesy and respect for the other parties present and for the proceedings of the court. Punctuality is particularly important; being late for hearings is unfair to the other parties and other court users, as well as being discourteous to them and to the court.

PREPARATION FOR HEARINGS

7.11.5 To ensure court time is used efficiently there must be adequate preparation prior to the hearing. This includes the preparation and exchange of skeleton arguments, the compilation of bundles of documents and giving realistic time estimates. Where estimates prove inaccurate, a hearing may have to be adjourned to a later date, and the party responsible for the adjournment is likely to be ordered to pay the costs thrown away.

7.11.6 The parties should use their best endeavours to agree beforehand the issues, or main issues between them, and must co-operate with the court and each other to enable the court to deal with claims justly; parties may expect to be penalised for failing to do so.

7.11.7 A bundle of documents must be compiled for the court's use at the trial, and also for hearings before the Interim Applications judge or a master where the documents to be referred to total 25 pages or more. The party lodging a trial bundle should supply identical bundles to all parties and for the use of witnesses. The efficient preparation of bundles is very important. Where bundles have been properly prepared, the claim will be easier to understand and present, and time and costs are likely to be saved. Where documents are copied unnecessarily or bundled incompetently, the costs may be disallowed. Paragraph 3 of the Part 39 Practice Direction sets out in full the requirements for compiling bundles of documents for hearings or trial.

7.11.8 The trial bundle must be filed not more than 7 and not less than 3 days before the start of the trial. Bundles for a master's hearing should be brought to the hearing unless the master directs otherwise. The contents of the trial bundle should be agreed where possible, and it should be made clear whether in addition, they are agreeing that the documents in the bundle are authentic even if not previously disclosed and are evidence of the facts stated in them even if a notice under the Civil Evidence Act 1995 has not been served.

7.11.9 Lists of authorities for use at trial or at substantial hearings before a judge should be provided to the usher by 9.00 am on the first day of the hearing. For other applications before a judge, or applications before a master, copies of the authorities should be included in the bundle.

7.11.10 For trial and most hearings before a judge, and substantial hearings before a master, a chronology, a list of the persons involved and a list of the issues should be prepared and filed with the skeleton argument. A chronology should be non-contentious and agreed with the other parties if possible. If there is a material dispute about any event stated in the chronology, that should be stated.

7.11.11 Skeleton arguments should be prepared and filed;

(1) for trials, not less than 2 days before the trial in the Listing Office, and
(2) for substantial applications or appeals, not later than 1 day before the hearing in the Listing Office and, where the master has requested papers in advance of the hearing, in the Masters' Support Unit Room E16.

7.11.12 A skeleton argument should;

(1) concisely summarise the party's submissions in relation to each of the issues,
(2) cite the main authorities relied on, which may be attached,
(3) contain a reading list and an estimate of the time it will take the judge to read,
(4) be as brief as the issues allow and not normally be longer than 20 pages of double-spaced A4 paper,
(5) be divided into numbered paragraphs and paged consecutively,
(6) avoid formality and use understandable abbreviations, and
(7) identify any core documents which it would be helpful to read beforehand.

7.11.13 Where a party decides not to call a witness whose witness statement has been served, to give oral evidence at trial, prompt notice of this decision should be given to all other parties. The party should also indicate whether he proposes to put, or seek to put, the witness statement in as hearsay evidence. If he does not, any other party may do so[103].

103 Rule 32.5(5).

RECORDING OF PROCEEDINGS

7.11.14 At any hearing, including the trial, any oral evidence, the judgment or decision (including reasons) and any summing up to a jury will be recorded. At hearings before masters, it is not normally practicable to record anything other than oral evidence and any judgment, but these will be recorded. A party to the proceedings may obtain a transcript of the proceedings on payment of the appropriate charge, from the Mechanical Recording Department, Room WG5. A person who is not a party to the proceedings may not obtain a transcript of a hearing which took place in private without the permission of the court.

7.11.15 No person or party may use unofficial recording equipment at a hearing without the permission of the court; to do so constitutes a contempt of court[104].

104 Section 9, Contempt of Court Act 1981.

7.12 Applications

7.12.1 Applications for court orders are governed by Part 23 and the Part 23 Practice Direction. Rule 23.6 and paragraph 2 of the Part 23 Practice Direction set out the matters an application notice must include. The Part 23 Practice Direction states that form N244 may be used, however, parties may prefer to use form PF244 which is available for use in the Royal Courts of Justice only. To make an application the applicant must file an application notice unless a rule or practice direction permits otherwise or the court dispenses with the requirement for an application notice[105]. Except in cases of extreme urgency, or where giving notice might frustrate the order (as with a search order), an application notice must be served on every party unless a rule or practice direction or a court order dispenses with service[106] (see paragraph 7.12.3 below).

105 See rule 23.3.
106 See rule 23.4.

7.12.2 Applications for remedies which a master has jurisdiction to grant should ordinarily be made to a master. The Part 2 Practice Direction (Allocation of cases to levels of Judiciary) contains information about the types of applications which may be dealt with by masters and judges. An application notice for hearing by;

(1) a judge should be issued in the Listing Office, Room WG5, and
(2) a master should be issued in the Masters' Support Unit, Room E16,

and wherever possible should be accompanied by a draft in double spacing of the order sought.

7.12.3 The following are examples of applications which may be heard by a master where service of the application notice is not required;

(1) service by an alternative method (rule 6.8),
(2) service of a claim form out of the jurisdiction (section III of Part 6),
(3) default judgment under rule 12.11(4) or (5),
(4) substituting a party under rule 19.1(4),

(5) permission to issue a witness summons under rule 34.3(2),
(6) deposition for use in a foreign court (Schedule 1 to the CPR – RSC Ord 70),
(7) charging order to show cause (Schedule 1 to the CPR – RSC Ord 50, r 1(2)), and
(8) garnishee order to show cause (Schedule 1 to the CPR – RSC Ord 49, r 2(1).

7.12.4 Paragraph 3 of the Part 23 Practice Direction states in addition that an application may be made without serving an application notice;

(1) where there is exceptional urgency,
(2) where the overriding objective is best furthered by doing so,
(3) by consent of all parties, and
(4) where a date for a hearing has been fixed and a party wishes to make an application at that hearing but does not have sufficient time to serve an application notice[107].

With the court's permission an application may also be made without serving an application notice where secrecy is essential.

107 See paragraph 2.10 of the Part 23 practice direction.

7.12.5 Where an application is heard in the absence of one or more of the parties, it is the duty of the party attending to disclose fully all matters relevant to the application, even those matters adverse to the applicant. Failure to do so may result in the order being set aside. Any party who does not attend a hearing may apply to have the order set aside[108].

108 See rule 23.11.

7.12.6 Where notice of an application is to be given, the application notice should be served as soon as practicable after issue and, if there is to be a hearing, at least 3 clear days before the hearing date[109]. Where there is insufficient time to serve an application notice, informal notice of the application should be given unless the circumstances of the application require secrecy.

109 See rule 23.7(1)(b).

7.12.7 The court may deal with an application without a hearing if;

(1) the parties agree the terms of the order sought,
(2) the parties agree that the application should be dealt with without a hearing, or
(3) the court does not consider that a hearing would be appropriate[110].

110 See rule 23.8.

7.12.8 The court may deal with an application or part of an application by telephone where it is convenient to do so or in matters of extreme urgency. See paragraph 6 of the Part 23 Practice Direction and paragraph 4.5 of the Part 25 Practice Direction (Interim Injunctions).

7.12.9 Applications of extreme urgency may be made out of hours and will be dealt with by the duty judge. An explanation will be required as to why it was not made or could not be made during normal court hours.

7.12.10 Initial contact should be made through the Security Office on 020 7947 6260 who will require the applicants phone number. The clerk to the duty judge will then contact the applicant and will require the following information;

(1) the name of the party on whose behalf the application is to be made,
(2) the name and status of the person making the application,

(3) the nature of the application,
(4) the degree of urgency, and
(5) the contact telephone number(s).

7.12.11 The duty judge will indicate to his clerk if he thinks it appropriate for the application to be dealt with by telephone or in court. The clerk will inform the applicant and make the necessary arrangements. Where the duty judge decides to deal with the application by telephone, and the facility is available, it is likely that the judge will require a draft order to be faxed to him. An application for an injunction will be dealt with by telephone only where the applicant is represented by counsel or solicitors.

7.12.12 It is not normally possible to seal an order out of hours. The judge is likely to order the applicant to file the application notice and evidence in support on the same or next working day, together with two copies of the order for sealing.

7.13 Interim remedies

7.13.1 Interim remedies which the court may grant are listed in rule 25.1. An order for an interim remedy may be made at any time including before proceedings are started and after judgment has been given[111]. Some of the most commonly sought remedies are injunctions, most of which are heard by the Interim Applications judge.

111 See rule 25.2(1).

7.13.2 An application notice for an injunction should be filed in the Listing Office, Room WG5, and may be made without giving notice to the other parties in the first instance. This is most likely to be appropriate in applications for search orders and freezing injunctions which may also be heard in private if the judge thinks it appropriate to do so. Where the injunction is granted without the other party being present it will normally be for a limited period, seldom more than 7 days. The Part 25 (Interim Injunctions) Practice Direction at paragraph 4 deals fully with making urgent applications and those without notice, and paragraphs 6, 7 and 8 deal specifically with search orders and freezing injunctions, examples of which are annexed to the Practice Direction.

7.13.3 Applications for interim payments are heard by a master. The application notice should be filed in the Masters' Support Unit, Room E14. The requirements for obtaining an order for an interim payment are fully dealt with in the Part 25 (Interim Payments) Practice Direction.

8 LISTING BEFORE JUDGES

8.1 Responsibility for listing

8.1.1 The Clerk of the Lists (Room WG3, Royal Courts of Justice) is in general responsible for listing. All applications relating to listing should in the first instance be made to him. Any party dissatisfied with any decision of the Clerk of the Lists may, on one day's notice to all other parties, apply to the judge in charge of the list.

8.1.2 The application should be made within 7 days of the decision of the Clerk of the Lists and should be arranged through the Queen's Bench Listing Office, Room WG5.

8.2 The lists

8.2 There are three lists, namely;

(1) the Jury List
(2) the Trial List, and
(3) the Interim Hearings List.

The lists are described below.

8.3 The Jury List

8.3.1 Claims for damages for libel and slander (defamation), fraud, malicious prosecution and false imprisonment will be tried by a judge and jury unless the court orders trial by a judge alone.

8.3.2 Where a claim is being tried by a judge and jury it is vitally important that the jury should not suffer hardship and inconvenience by having been misled by an incorrect time estimate. It is therefore essential that time estimates given to the court are accurate and realistic.

8.3.3 Dates for the trial of substantial claims will be fixed by the Listing Office after consideration of the parties' views. In such cases the Listing Office may, in addition, impose an alternative reserve date several weeks or months in advance of the trial date, in an endeavour to dispose of claims more quickly and to fill gaps in the list created by frequent settlements. When a reserve date is so allocated a 'cut off' date will be stated by the Clerk of the Lists again, after consideration of any views expressed by the parties and having regard to the complexity of the claim and the commitments of counsel and expert witnesses. On the cut off date a decision will be made by the Clerk of the Lists to break or confirm the reserved date for trial.

8.3.4 If a party considers that he will suffer significant prejudice as the result of the decision of the Clerk of the Lists relating to either a reserved date or the cut off date he may apply to the judge in charge of the Jury List for reversal or variation of the decision, as set out in paragraph 8.1.1 above.

8.3.5 Jury applications will enter the Interim Warned List not less than two weeks from the date the application notice is filed. Parties may 'offer' a date for hearing the application within the week for which they are warned. Subject to court availability, the application will be listed on the offered date. Any application not reached on the offered date will return to the current Warned List and will be taken from that list as and when required.

8.3.6 Applications in defamation claims in respect of 'meaning' (for an explanation of 'meaning' see paragraph 4.1 of the Part 53 Practice Direction) may be listed in private on a specific day allocated for such matters.

8.3.7 Jury applications of length and/or complexity may be fixed by the same manner as set out in paragraph 8.3.6 above. (See the section below on the Trial List for general information about fixing trials).

8.3.8 Applications for directions and other applications within the master's jurisdiction should firstly be made to a master unless;

(1) a direction has been given for the arranging of a trial date, or
(2) a date has been fixed or a window given for the trial.

Interim applications made after (1) or (2) above should be made to the judge. The master will use his discretion to refer a matter to the judge if he thinks it right to do so.

8.3.9 If a party believes that the master is very likely to refer the application to the judge, for example where there is a substantial application to strike out, the matter should first be referred to the master or Practice Master on notice to the other parties without waiting for a private room appointment. The master will then decide whether the application should be referred to the judge.

8.4 The Trial List

8.4.1 This list consists of trials (other than Jury trials), preliminary questions or issues ordered to be tried and proceedings to commit for contempt of court.

8.4.2 The Royal Courts of Justice presents unique problems in terms of fixing trial dates. The number of judges and masters involved and their geographical location has caused, for the time being at least, a different approach to the fixing of trials in the Chancery and Queen's Bench Divisions.

8.4.3 The requirement of judges to go on circuit, sit in the Criminal Division of the Court of Appeal, deal with cases in the Crown Office and other lists make it difficult to fix dates for trials before particular judges. Accordingly the following will only apply to the Listing Offices in the Royal Courts of Justice.

8.4.4 At as early an interim stage as practicable, the court will give directions with a view to fixing the trial date, week, or other short period within which the trial is to begin (the trial window).

8.4.5 For that purpose the court may;

(1) direct that the trial do not begin earlier than a specified date calculated to provide enough time for the parties to complete any necessary preparations for trial, and/or
(2) direct that the trial date be within a specified period, and/or
(3) specify the trial date or window.

8.4.6 If directions under 8.4.5(1) or (2) are given the court will direct the parties to attend upon the Clerk of the Lists in Room WG5 in order to fix the trial date or trial window.

8.4.7 The claimant must, unless some other party agrees to do so, take out an appointment with the Clerk of the Lists within 7 days of obtaining the direction in paragraph 8.4.6 above. If an appointment is not taken out within the 7 days, the Listing Office will appoint a date for a listing hearing and give notice of the date to all parties.

8.4.8 At the listing hearing the Clerk of the Lists will take account, in so far as it is practical to do so, of any difficulties the parties may have as to availability of counsel, experts and witnesses. The Clerk of the Lists will, nevertheless, try to ensure the speedy disposal of the trial by arranging a firm trial date as soon as possible within the trial period or, as the case may be, after the 'not before' date directed by the court under paragraph 8.4.5 above. If exceptionally it appears to the Clerk of the Lists at the listing hearing that a trial date cannot be provided within a trial window, he may fix the trial date outside the trial period at the first available date. (If a case summary has been prepared (see the Part 29 Practice Direction The Multi-track, paragraphs 5.6 and 5.7) the claimant must produce a copy at the listing hearing together with a copy of particulars of claim and any orders relevant to the fixing of the trial date.)

8.4.9 The Listing Office will notify the Masters' Support Unit of any trial date or trial window given. In accordance with rule 29.2(3) notice will also be given to all the parties.

8.4.10 A party who wishes to appeal a date or window allocated by the Listing Officer must, within 7 days of the notification, make an application to the judge nominated by each Division to hear such applications. The application notice should be filed in the Listing Office and served, giving one days notice, on the other parties.

8.5 The Interim Hearings List

8.5.1 This list consists of interim applications, appeals and applications for judgment.

8.5.2 On each Thursday of Term and on such other days as may be appropriate, the Clerk of the Lists will publish a Warned List showing the matters in the Interim Hearings List that are liable to be heard in the following week. Any matters for which no date has been arranged will be liable to appear in the list for hearing with no warning save that given by the Cause List for the following day, posted each afternoon outside Room WG5.

8.5.3 Fixtures will only be given in exceptional circumstances. The parties may by agreement 'offer' preferred dates for their matter to be heard, to be taken from the list on designated days, within the week following entry into the Warned List in accordance with Listing Office practice. Matters lasting less than a day are usually offered for two preferred consecutive days and matters lasting more than a day are usually offered for three preferred consecutive days.

8.6 General

8.6.1 In addition to the matters listed to be heard by individual judges, the Daily Cause List for each day may list 'unassigned cases'. These are matters from the two lists to be heard that day but not assigned to a particular judge. If on any day a matter assigned to a particular judge proves to be ineffective, he will hear an unassigned case. It is hoped that the great majority of unassigned cases will be heard on the day that they are listed but this cannot be absolutely guaranteed. Parties engaged in matters listed as unassigned should attend outside the court where the matter is listed. The Clerk of the Lists will notify them as soon as possible which judge is to hear the matter. It is not the practice to list cases as unassigned unless the parties consent and there are no witnesses.

8.6.2 Appeals from masters' decisions will appear in the Interim Hearings List. The appeal notice (stamped with the appropriate fee) must be filed in Room WG7. On filing the appeal notice the solicitors should inform the Clerk of the Lists whether they intend to instruct counsel and, if so, the names of counsel.

8.7 Listing before the Interim Applications judge

8.7.1 All interim applications on notice to the Interim Applications judge will initially be entered in a list for hearing. They will be listed for hearing in Room

E101 or some other nominated venue on any day of the week. Any matter which cannot be disposed of with within one hour will not be taken on the date given for the listed hearing.

8.7.2 If the parties agree that a matter cannot be disposed of within one hour, the applicant/appellant;

(1) may, on filing the application notice/notice of appeal, seek to have the matter placed directly into the Interim Hearings Warned List, or
(2) must as soon as practicable and in any event not later than 24 hours before the hearing date transfer the matter into the Interim Hearings List.

If the parties do not so agree, or agree less than 24 hours before the hearing date, the parties must attend on that date.

8.7.3 Matters in the Interim Hearings List will be listed by the Clerk of the Lists in Room WG3, and the parties will be notified by the Listing Office (Room WG5) of the date on which the matter will enter the Warned List. Matters in the Warned List may be listed for hearing at any time on or after that date.

8.7.4 In order to ensure that a complete set of papers in proper order is available for the judge to read before the hearing, the parties must in advance of the hearing lodge in room WG4 a bundle, properly paginated in date order, and indexed, containing copies of the following documents;

(1) the application notice or notice of appeal,
(2) any statements of case,
(3) copies of all written evidence (together with copy exhibits) on which any party intends to rely, and
(4) any relevant order made in the proceedings.

8.7.5 The bundle should be agreed if possible. In all but simple cases a skeleton argument and, where that would be helpful, a chronology should also be lodged. (See paragraph 8.9.1 and 8.9.2 below in respect of skeleton arguments.)

8.7.6 Where a date for the hearing has been arranged the bundle must be lodged not later than 3 clear days before the fixed date. For application or appeals where there is no fixed date for hearing, the bundle must be lodged not later than 48 hours after the parties have been notified that the matter is to appear in the Warned List. (For information concerning trial bundles see the Part 39 Practice Direction.)

8.7.7 Except with the permission of the judge no document may be used in evidence or relied on unless a copy of it has been included in the bundle referred to in paragraph 8.7.6 above. If any party seeks to rely on written evidence which has not been included in the bundle, that party should lodge the original (with copy exhibits) in Room WG5 in advance of the hearing, or otherwise with the court associate before the hearing commences.

8.7.8 In appeals from circuit and district judges the provisions of paragraphs 8.7.4, 8.7.5, 8.7.6 and 8.7.7 should be complied with. In addition, the notes (if any) of reasons given by the circuit judge or district judge, prepared by the judge, counsel or solicitors should be lodged.

8.7.9 Subject to the discretion of the judge, any application or appeal normally made to the Interim Applications judge may be made in the month of September. In the month of August, except with the permission of a judge, only appeals in respect of orders;

(1) to set aside a claim form, or service of a claim form,
(2) to set aside judgment,
(3) for stay of execution,
(4) for any order by consent,
(4) for permission to enter judgment,
(5) for approval of settlements or for interim payment,
(6) for relief from forfeiture,
(7) for a charging order,
(8) for a garnishee order,
(9) for appointment or discharge of a receiver,
(10) for relief by way of sheriff's interpleader,
(11) for transfer to a county court or for trial by master, or
(12) for time where time is running in the month of August,

may be heard, and only applications of real urgency will be dealt with, for example, urgent applications in respect of injunctions, or for possession (under RSC Ord 113 in Schedule 1 to Part 50).

8.7.10 It is desirable, where this is practical, that application notices or appeal notices are submitted to the Practice Master or a judge prior to the hearing of the application or appeal so that they can be marked 'fit for August' or 'fit for vacation'. If they are so marked, then normally the judge will be prepared to hear the application or appeal in August, if marked 'fit for August' or in September if marked 'fit for vacation'. The application to a judge to have the papers so marked should normally be made in writing, the application shortly setting out the nature of the application or appeal and the reasons why it should be dealt with in August or in September, as the case may be.

8.8 The lists generally

8.8.1 Where a fixed date has been given it is the duty of the parties to keep the Clerk of the Lists fully informed as to the current position of the matter with regard to negotiations for settlement, whether all aspects of the claim are being proceeded with, an estimate of the length of the hearing, and so on.

8.8.2 Applications for adjournments will not be granted except for the most cogent reasons. If an application is made because solicitors were unaware of the state of the list they may be ordered personally to pay the costs of the application.

8.8.3 A party who seeks to have a hearing before a judge adjourned must inform the Clerk of the Lists of his application as soon as possible. Applications for an adjournment immediately before a hearing begins should be avoided as they take up valuable time which could be used for dealing with effective matters and, if successful, may result in court time being wasted.

8.8.4 If the application is made by agreement, the parties should, in writing, apply to the Clerk of the Lists who will consult the judge nominated to deal with such matters. The judge may grant the application on conditions which may include giving directions for a new hearing date.

8.8.5 If the application is opposed the applicant should apply to either the nominated judge or the judge to whom the matter has been allocated. A hearing should then be arranged through the Clerk of the Lists. A short summary of the reasons for the adjournment should be lodged with the Listing Office where possible by 10.30 am on the day before the application is to be made. Formal written evidence is not normally required.

8.8.6 The applicant will be expected to show that he has conducted his own case diligently. Any party should take all reasonable steps;

(1) to ensure his case is adequately prepared in sufficient time to enable the hearing to proceed, and
(2) to prepare and serve any document (including any evidence) required to be served on any other party in sufficient time to enable that party also to be prepared.

8.8.7 If a party or his solicitor's failure to take reasonable steps necessitates an adjournment, the court may dismiss the application or make any other order including an order penalising the defaulting party in costs.

8.9 Listing Office – general matters

8.9.1 To facilitate the efficient listing of proceedings, parties are reminded that skeleton arguments concisely summarising each party's submissions must be prepared and filed with the Listing Office;

(1) for trials, not less than 3 days before the trial, and
(2) for substantial applications or appeals, not later than 1 day before the hearing.

8.9.2 If it is anticipated that a skeleton argument will be filed late, a letter of explanation should accompany it which will be shown to the judge before whom the trial or hearing is to take place.

8.9.3 For parties' information, the following targets for the disposal of matters in the lists have been agreed as set out below:

Interim Hearings Warned List	within 4 weeks
From date of fixing;	
Trials under 5 days	within 4 months
Trials over 5 but under 10 days	within 6 months
Trials over 10 but under 20 days	within 9 months
Trials over 20 days	within 12 months.

9 TRIAL, JUDGMENTS AND ORDERS

9.1 General

9.1.1 The trial of a claim in the Royal Courts of Justice normally takes place before a High Court judge or a deputy sitting as a High Court judge. A master may assess the damages or sum due to a party under a judgment and, subject to any practice direction, may try a claim which is

(1) treated as being allocated to the multi-track because it is proceeding under Part 8, or
(2) with the consent of the parties, allocated to the multi-track under Part 26[112].

112 See paragraph 4 of the Part 2B practice direction.

9.1.2 Claims for defamation, malicious prosecution or false imprisonment will be tried by a judge sitting with a Jury unless the court orders otherwise.

9.2 The trial

9.2.1 See paragraphs 2.4.2 and 2.4.3 above about representation at the trial, and paragraphs 7.11.14 and 7.11.15 above about recording of proceedings.

9.2.2 Rule 39.3 sets out the consequences of a party's failure to attend the trial and see also paragraph 2 of the Part 39 Practice Direction.

9.2.3 The judge may fix a timetable for evidence and submissions if it has not already been fixed. The claimant's advocate will normally begin the trial with a short opening speech, and the judge may then allow the other party to make a short speech. Each party should provide written summaries of their opening speeches if the points are not covered in their skeleton arguments.

9.2.4 It is normally convenient for any outstanding procedural matters or applications to be dealt with in the course of, or immediately after, the opening speech. In a jury trial such matters would normally be dealt with before the jury is sworn in.

9.2.5 Unless the court orders otherwise, a witness statement will stand as the evidence in chief of the witness, provided he is called to give oral evidence. With the court's permission, a witness may amplify his witness statement or give evidence in relation to new matters which have arisen since the witness statement was served on the other parties[113].

113 Rule 32.5.

9.2.6 The court associate will be responsible for any exhibits produced as evidence during the trial. After the trial, the exhibits are the responsibility of the party who produced them. Where a number of physical exhibits are involved, it is desirable, if possible, for the parties to agree a system of labelling and the manner of display, beforehand. The associate will normally draw the judgment or order made at the trial.

9.2.7 At a jury trial, it is the parties' responsibility to provide sufficient bundles of documents for the use of the jury.

9.2.8 Facilities are available to assist parties or witnesses with special needs. The Listing Office should be notified of any needs or requirements prior to the trial.

9.3 Judgments and orders

9.3.1 Part 40 deals with judgments and orders. Rule 40.2 contains the standard requirements of a judgment or order and rule 40.3 contains provisions about drawing them up, see also paragraph 1 of the Part 40B Practice Direction for more information.

9.3.2 Provisions concerning consent orders are contained in rule 40.6 which sets out in paragraph (3) the types of consent judgments and orders that may be sealed and entered by a court officer, provided;

(1) that none of the parties is a litigant in person, and
(2) the approval of the court is not required by a rule, a practice direction or an enactment.

Other types of consent order require an application to be made to a master or judge for approval. It is common for a respondent to a consent order not to attend the hearing but to provide a written consent. The consent may either be written on the document or contained in a letter, and must be signed by the respondent, or where there are solicitors on record as acting for him, by his solicitors. Paragraph 3 of the Part 40B Practice Direction contains further information about consent orders.

9.3.3 Rule 40.11 sets out the time for complying with a judgment or order, which is 14 days unless the judgment or order specifies otherwise (for example by instalments), or a rule specifies a different time, or the judgment or proceedings have been stayed.

9.3.4 The Part 40B Practice Direction contains further information about the effect of non-compliance with a judgment or order (and sets out the penal notice), adjustment of the final judgment sum in respect of interim payments and compensation recovery, and refers to various precedents for types of judgments and orders. See also;

(1) the Part 40 Practice Direction – Accounts and Enquiries, and
(2) the Part 40C Practice Direction – Structured Settlements which sets out the procedure to be followed both on settlement and after trial. Precedents for structured settlement orders, Parts 1 and 2, are annexed to the Practice Direction.

9.3.5 Where judgment is reserved, the judge may deliver his judgment by handing down the written text without reading it out in open court. Where this is the case, the advocates will be supplied with the full text of the judgment in advance of delivery. The advocates should then familiarise themselves with the contents and be ready to deal with any points which may arise when the judgment is delivered. Any direction or requirement as to confidentiality must be complied with.

9.3.6 The judgment does not take effect until formally delivered in court. If the judgment is to be handed down in writing copies will then be made available to the parties and, if requested and so far as practicable, to the law reporters and the press.

9.3.7 The judge will usually direct that the written judgment may be used for all purposes as the text of the judgment, and that no transcript need be made. Where such a direction is made, a copy will be provided to the Mechanical Recording Department from where further copies may be obtained (and see paragraph 7.11.14 above).

JUDGMENT OR ORDER FOR PAYMENT OF MONEY ON BEHALF OF A CHILD OR PATIENT

9.3.8 The usual order made at trial will make provision for any immediate payment to the litigation friend or his legal representative and for the balance of the award to be placed to a special investment account pending application to a master or district judge (in the case of a child) or the Court of Protection (in the case of a patient) for investment directions. The order will specify the time within which the application should be made.

9.3.9 The litigation friend or his legal representative should then write to or make an appointment with;

(1) in the case of a child, the master or district judge in accordance with paragraph 6.8.6 above and the Part 21 Practice Direction, or
(2) in the case of a patient, the Court of Protection in accordance with paragraph 11 of the Part 21 Practice Direction.

9.3.10 Where after trial the judge has found in favour of a child or patient, instead of judgment being given, the proposed award of damages may be paid by way of a structured settlement. The structure must be approved by the judge, and in the case of a patient must also be approved by the Court of Protection. (See also the Part 40C Practice Direction – Structured Settlements.)

PROVISIONAL DAMAGES

9.3.11 Rule 41.1 defines an award of provisional damages. Where there is a chance that a claimant may in the future develop a particular disease or deterioration as a result of the event giving rise to the claim, he can seek an award of damages for personal injury on the assumption that he will not develop the disease or deterioration, with provision for him to make a further application within the time specified in the order, if he does so develop the disease or deterioration.

9.3.12 The Part 41 Practice Direction gives further information about provisional damages awards and, in particular, about the preservation of the case file for the time specified in the order for making a further application, and the documents to be included in the case file. A precedent for a provisional damages judgment is annexed to the Practice Direction.

10 APPEALS

10.1 General

10.1.1 Appeals are governed by Part 52 and the Part 52 Practice Direction. The contents of Part 52 are divided into two sections; General rules about Appeals and Special Provisions applying to the Court of Appeal. The Practice Direction is divided into three sections; General Provisions about Appeals, General Provisions about Statutory Appeals and Appeals by way of Case Stated, and Provisions about Specific Appeals. The following paragraphs apply to orders made after 2 May 2000 and are intended only to draw parties' attention to the basic provisions for making an appeal in or from the Queen's Bench Division. For further information about these procedures and about other specific types of appeal, parties should refer to the Part 52 Practice Direction and the Civil Appeals Guide.

10.1.2 In the Queen's Bench Division an appeal from a master will lie to a High Court judge unless it is a final decision in a claim allocated to the multi-track or in specialist proceedings referred to in Part 49 in which case the appeal will lie to the Court of Appeal. An appeal from a High Court judge will lie to the Court of Appeal.

10.1.3 Unless the lower court or the appeal court orders otherwise, an appeal does not operate as a stay of any order or decision of the lower court.

10.2 Permission to appeal

10.2.1 Permission is required to appeal from a decision of a judge in a county court or the High Court, except where the appeal is in respect of;

(1) a committal order,
(2) a refusal to grant habeas corpus,
(3) certain insolvency appeals, and
(4) certain statutory appeals.

For the purposes of Part 52 and the Part 52 Practice Direction, the term 'judge' includes a master or district judge.

(For more information see rule 52.3).

10.2.2 Permission should be sought at the hearing at which the decision to be appealed against is made. If it is not, or if it is sought and refused, permission should be sought from the court appealed to ('the appeal court'). Where permission is sought from the appeal court it must be requested in the appellant's notice. Permission may be granted, or refused, or granted in part (whether as to a part of the order, a ground of appeal or an issue) and refused as to the rest. Paragraphs 4.1–4.12 of the Practice Direction deal with permission to appeal including the matters to be stated in the notice and the documents to be filed with it.

10.2.3 An application to the appeal court for permission may be dealt with without a hearing, but if refused without a hearing the applicant may request that it be reconsidered at a hearing; the court need not require that notice of the hearing be given to the respondent.

10.3 Notices

10.3.1 Rule 52.4 and paragraph 5 of the Practice Direction deal with the appellant's notice. The appellant must file his notice at the appeal court either within a period specified by the court appealed from ('the lower court') or, if no such period is specified, within 14 days of the date of the decision appealed from. The notice must be served on each respondent as soon as practicable and in any event not later than 7 days after it is filed.

10.3.2 A respondent must file a notice where;

(1) he also wishes to appeal the lower court's decision,
(2) he wishes to uphold the decision of the lower court for different or additional reasons to those given by the lower court, or
(3) he is seeking permission to appeal from the appeal court.

10.3.3 The respondent's notice must be filed either within a period specified by the lower court or, if no such period is specified, within 14 days of;

(1) the date the respondent is served with the appellant's notice where
  (a) permission to appeal was given by the lower court or
  (b) permission to appeal is not required,
(2) the date the respondent is served with notification that the appeal court has given the appellant permission to appeal, or
(3) the date the respondent is served with notification that the application for permission to appeal and the appeal itself are to be heard together.

(Paragraph 7 of the Practice Direction deals with the respondent's notice of appeal.)

10.3.4 The notices to be used are as follows;

(1) the Appellant's Notice is form N161, and
(2) the Respondent's Notice is form N162.

There is a leaflet available from the Listing Office, Room WG5 entitled 'I want to appeal', which provides information about appealing other than to the Court of Appeal.

10.4 Appeals in cases of contempt of court

10.4.1 Appellant's notices which by paragraph 21.4 of the Part 52 Practice Direction are required to be served on 'the court from whose order or decision the appeal is brought' may be served, in the case of appeals from the Queen's Bench Division, on the Senior Master of the Queen's Bench Division; service may be effected by leaving a copy of the notice of appeal with the Clerk of the Lists in Room WG5, Royal Courts of Justice, Strand, London WC2A 2LL.

11 ENFORCEMENT

11.1 General

11.1.1 Enforcement in the High Court is still governed by RSC Orders 17, 45–52 and 71 as in Schedule 1 to the CPR.

11.1.2 RSC Ord 45 deals with enforcement generally. A judgment or order for payment of money (other than into court) may be enforced by a writ of fieri facias, garnishee proceedings, a charging order or the appointment of a receiver[114]. A judgment or order to do or abstain from doing an act may be enforced by a writ of sequestration (with the permission of the court) or an order of committal[115]. A judgment or order for possession of land may be enforced by a writ of possession[116], and a judgment or order for delivery of goods without the alternative of paying their value by a writ of specific delivery[117]. In each case, where RSC Ord 45, r 5 applies enforcement may also be by a writ of sequestration or an order of committal.

114 RSC Ord 45, r 1.
115 RSC Ord 45, r 5.
116 RSC Ord 45, r 3.
117 RSC Ord 45, r 4.

11.2 Writs of execution

11.2.1 RSC Ord 46 deals with writs of execution generally. Rules 2 and 3 set out the circumstances when permission to issue a writ is necessary[118]. Rule 4 contains provisions for making an application for permission. Rule 5 deals with applications for permission to issue a writ of sequestration. RSC Ord 47 contains provisions concerning writs of fieri facias. Forms of writs of execution may be used as follows:

(1) writs of fieri facias in form Nos 53–63,
(2) writs of delivery in form Nos 64 and 65,
(3) writs of possession in form Nos 66 and 66A,
(4) writ of sequestration in form No 67,
(5) writ of restitution in form No 68,
(6) writ of assistance in form No 69.

118 See also RSC Ord 45, r 3.

11.2.2 With certain exceptions, writs of execution issued in the Royal Courts of Justice are executed by the sheriff of the county in which the debtor has assets, or his officer. RSC Ord 46, r 6 sets out the provisions for issue of writs of execution. In the Queen's Bench Division writs of execution are issued in the Central Office in Room E17. Before the Writ can be sealed for issue, a signed praecipe for its issue must be filed[119] in one of forms PF86–90, as appropriate, stamped with the appropriate fee. A copy of the judgment or order requiring enforcement should also be provided.

119 RSC Ord 46, r 6(3).

11.2.3 On an application for permission to issue a writ of possession under RSC Ord 45, r 3(2), if the property consists of a house of which various parts are sublet to, or in the occupation of, different persons, the evidence in support should show the nature and length of the notice which has been given to the various occupiers. Where the defendant or any other persons are in actual possession of the premises of which possession is sought, the evidence must contain the following information:

- (1) whether the premises or any part of it is residential,
- (2) if so,
  - (a) what is the rateable value of the residential premises, and
  - (b) whether it is let furnished or unfurnished and, if furnished, the amount of furniture it contains, and
- (3) any other matters that will assist the master in deciding whether any occupier is protected by the Rent Acts.

11.2.4 Where a party wishes to enforce a judgment or order expressed in a foreign currency by the issue of a writ of fieri facias, the praecipe must be endorsed with the following certificate:

> 'I/We certify that the rate current in London for the purchase of (*state the unit of foreign currency in which the judgment is expressed*) at the close of business on (*state the nearest preceding date to the date of issue of the writ of fieri facias*) was (   ) to the £ sterling and at this rate the sum of (*state amount of the judgment debt in the foreign currency*) amounts to £   .'

The schedule to the writ of fieri facias should be amended;

- (1) showing the amount of the judgment or order in the foreign currency at paragraph 1.
- (2) inserting a new paragraph 2 as follows:

  > '2 Amount of the sterling equivalent as appears from the certificate endorsed on the praecipe for issue of the writ £   '

- (3) renumbering the remaining paragraphs accordingly.

11.2.5 County court judgments or orders to which Article 8(1) of the High Court and County Courts Jurisdiction Order 1991 applies may be enforced in the High Court, and since 26 April 1999, any county court judgment for over £600 may be transferred to the High Court sheriff for enforcement (except where it is a judgment arising from a regulated agreement under the Consumer Credit Act).

11.2.6 The party seeking enforcement should obtain from the appropriate county court a certificate of judgment of the county court in compliance with CCR Ord 22, r 8(1A) (in Schedule 2 to the CPR), setting out details of the judgment or order to be enforced, sealed with the seal of that court and dated and signed by an officer of that court and stating on its face that it is granted for the purpose of enforcing the judgment or order by execution against goods in the High Court. Form N293A is a 'Combined Certificate of Judgment and Request for Writ of Fieri Facias' and should be used.

11.2.7 A correctly completed form N293A together with a copy should be filed in Room E17 where the court officer will;

(1) allocate a reference number,
(2) date seal the certificate and copy, returning the original to the party and retaining the copy, and
(3) enter the proceedings in a register kept for that purpose.

The certificate shall be treated for enforcement purposes as a High Court judgment and interest at the appropriate rate shall run from the date of the certificate.

11.2.8 The title of all subsequent documents shall be set out as follows:

'

QUEEN'S BENCH DIVISION
IN THE HIGH COURT OF JUSTICE
High Court Claim No
County Court Claim No

(Sent from the [ ] County Court by certificate dated (*date*))

Claimant

Defendant

'

When the writ of fieri facias is issued, the certificate of judgment retained by the party shall be date sealed by the court officer on the bottom left hand corner and endorsed with the designation of the Sheriff to whom the writ is directed.

11.2.9 The Sheriffs Lodgment Centre at 2 Serjeant's Inn, Fleet Street, London EC4Y 1NX provides a service for arranging transfer up of county court judgments, and will complete the required forms and take all the above steps on behalf of the judgment creditor. (A helpline is provided on 020 7353 3640.)

11.2.10 It is important to remember in these cases that although any application for a stay of execution may be made to a master in the High Court by application notice filed in accordance with Part 23, all other applications for enforcement or other relief must be made to the issuing county court. This practice is followed in the district registries with such variations as circumstances require.

11.2.11 When a writ of execution has been issued in the Royal Courts of Justice it may then be delivered to the Sheriffs Lodgment Centre. Value Added Tax is payable in addition to the sheriff's fee on the services for which the fee is payable, and must be paid at the time of delivery. If the goods, chattels and property to be seized in execution are not within Greater London, the sheriff will direct the writ to the sheriff of the appropriate county. Goods which may not be seized in execution of a writ are set out in s 138(3A) of the Supreme Court Act 1981 as follows:

(1) such tools, books, vehicles and other items of equipment as are necessary to that person for use personally by him in his employment, business or vocation,
(2) such clothing, bedding, furniture, household equipment and provisions as are necessary for satisfying the basic domestic needs of that person and his family,
(3) any money, bank notes, bills of exchange, promissory notes, bonds, specialties or securities for money belonging to that person.

11.2.12 When first executing a writ of fieri facias the sheriff will deliver to the debtor or leave at each place where execution is levied a notice of seizure in form No 55[120]. This is commonly known as 'walking possession' and the notice explains to the debtor the situation with regard to the goods seized and what he then has to do.

120 RSC Ord 45, r 2.

11.2.13 After execution of a writ of execution, the sheriff will endorse on the writ a statement of the manner in which he has executed it and will send a copy of the statement to the party issuing the writ.

11.3 Interpleader proceedings (RSC Ord 17)

11.3.1 Where a person is under liability in respect of a debt or property and has been, or expects to be claimed against by two or more persons claiming the same debt or property, if the person under liability does not dispute the debt or claim the property, he may apply to the court for relief by way of interpleader, ie for the entitlement of the persons claiming the same debt or property to be established in separate proceedings between them.

11.3.2 Where the sheriff has seized goods in execution and a person other than the person against whom the writ of execution was issued wishes to claim the goods seized, he must give notice of his claim to the sheriff, including in his notice a statement of his address which will be his address for service. The sheriff will then give notice of that claim to the claimant on whose behalf the goods were seized, in form PF23. The notice requires the claimant to state whether he admits or disputes the claim. The claimant must do so within 7 days of receipt of the sheriff's notice and may use form PF24 to do so.

11.3.3 Where the claimant admits the claim, the sheriff will withdraw from possession of the goods and may apply under RSC Ord 17, r 2(4) for an order to restrain a claim being brought against him for having taken possession of the goods. Where the claimant disputes the claim, the sheriff may apply for interpleader relief. An application for interpleader relief if made in existing proceedings is made by an application in accordance with Part 23, otherwise it is made by the issue of a Part 8 claim form.

11.3.4 The master may deal with the claims summarily, or may direct an issue to be tried between the parties in dispute (see RSC Ord 17, r 5) or make such other order as is appropriate.

11.4 Examination of judgment debtor (RSC Ord 48)

11.4.1 Where a person ('the judgment creditor') has obtained a judgment or order for payment of a sum of money against a person ('the judgment debtor'), the judgment creditor may apply for an order requiring the judgment debtor to attend to be orally examined concerning his assets and means[121]. If the judgment debtor is a company or corporation, the court will order an officer of the company or corporation to attend for examination. In the case of a judgment or order which is not for payment of a sum of money, the court may make an order for the attendance of the party liable for his examination on such questions as may be specified in the order.

121 RSC Ord 48, r 1.

11.4.2 An application for an order under RSC Ord 48, r 1 should be made in accordance with Part 23 without notice to any other party. The application must be supported by evidence giving details of the judgment or order, including the amount still owing, and showing that the judgment creditor is entitled to enforce the judgment or order. Where the judgment debtor is a company or corporation the evidence must give details of the officer to be examined. Form PF98 may be used as a precedent for the evidence in support. Where a judgment creditor has obtained judgments in several different proceedings against the same judgment debtor, only one application need be made, setting out in the body of the application details of all the judgments on which examination is sought.

11.4.3 The examination will take place before a master, registrar, district judge or nominated officer, as may be ordered, and will normally be at the court where the least expense will be incurred, usually the county court for the area where the judgment debtor lives. If a different court is requested the reason why should be given.

11.4.4 The application notice/evidence should be filed in the Masters' Support Unit Room E16 for consideration by a master who will, if satisfied, make the order sought. Where the examination is to take place in a county court, the judgment creditor should lodge a copy of the order with the county court and obtain an appointment for the examination. If the examination is to take place in the Royal Courts of Justice, the order should be taken to Room E17 where the appointment will be endorsed on the order. In the Central Office the nominated officer is nominated at the discretion of the Senior Master and their names may be obtained from Room E17.

11.4.5 The order (endorsed with the penal notice as set out in paragraph 9.1 of the Part 40B Practice Direction) together with details of the appointment must be served personally on the judgment debtor or on the officer of the judgment debtor company or corporation to be examined. A judgment debtor should be offered his conduct money, ie expenses of travelling to and from the examination and of attending to give evidence.

11.4.6 The officer conducting the examination will take down, or arrange to have taken down in writing the judgment debtor's statement. The officer will read the statement to the judgment debtor and will ask him to sign it. If he refuses to do so the officer will sign the statement. If the judgment debtor refuses to answer any question or if any other difficulties arise, the matter will be referred to the Senior Master or the Practice Master who will give such direction as he thinks fit.

11.5 Garnishee proceedings (RSC Ord 49)

11.5.1 Where a judgment creditor has obtained a judgment or order for payment of a sum of money of at least £50 against a judgment debtor, and another person ('the garnishee') is indebted to the judgment debtor, the judgment creditor may apply to the master for an order that the garnishee pays to the judgment creditor the amount of the debt due to the judgment debtor, or sufficient of it to satisfy the judgment debt.

11.5.2 The application should be made in accordance with Part 23 but the application notice need not be served on the judgment debtor. The application will normally be dealt with without a hearing and must be supported by evidence as set out in RSC Ord 49, r 2. Parties may use form PF100 for their evidence in support. If the master is satisfied that such an order is appropriate, he will make an order in form No 72 specifying the debt attached and appointing a time for the garnishee to attend and show cause why the order should not be made absolute.

11.5.3 The garnishee order to show cause must be served personally on the garnishee, and served on the judgment debtor, in accordance with RSC Ord 49, r 3. Where the garnishee fails to attend the hearing or attends but does not dispute the debt, the master may make a garnishee order absolute against the garnishee under RSC Ord 49, r 1. The order absolute may be enforced in the same manner as any other order for the payment of money[122]. Where the garnishee disputes the debt, the master may dispose of the matter as set out in RSC Ord 49, r 5.

122 RSC Ord 49, r 4(2).

11.5.4 Where the judgment creditor seeks to enforce a judgment expressed in a foreign currency by garnishee proceedings, the evidence in support of the application must contain words to the following effect:

> 'The rate current in London for the purchase of (*state the unit of foreign currency in which the judgment is expressed*) at the close of business on (*state the nearest preceding date to the date of verifying the evidence*) was (   ) to the £ sterling, and at this rate the sum of (*state the amount of the judgment debt in the foreign currency*) amounts to £   . I have obtained this information from (*state source*) and believe it to be true.'

11.6 Charging Orders (RSC Ord 50)

11.6.1 A judgment creditor may apply for a charging order on the property or assets of the judgment debtor, which will have the effect of providing him with security over the property of the judgment debtor. The High Court has jurisdiction to impose a charging order in the following cases:

(1) where the property is a fund lodged in the High Court,
(2) where the order to be enforced is a maintenance order[123] of the High Court, and
(3) where the judgment or order is made in the High Court and exceeds £5000[124].

The property and assets of the judgment debtor on which a charge may be imposed by a charging order are specified by s 2 of the Charging Orders Act 1979.

123 See s 2(a) Attachment of Earnings Act 1971.
124 In the case of subparas (2) and (3) the county court also has jurisdiction.

11.6.2 A charging order to show cause imposing a charge on land will be drawn in respect of the judgment debtors interest in the land and not the land itself, unless the court orders otherwise. If a charging order to show cause is made on stocks or shares in more than one company, a separate order must be drawn in respect of each company. If the judgment debt is expressed in a foreign currency, the evidence in support of any application for a charging order should contain a similar provision to that set out in paragraph 11.5.4 above.

11.6.3 The application for a charging order is made to a master and should be made in accordance with Part 23 but the application is made without being served on the judgment debtor. The application will normally be dealt with without a hearing and must be supported by evidence as set out in RSC Ord 50, r 3. Parties may use form PF101 for their evidence in support. If the master is satisfied that such an order is appropriate, he will make an order in form No 75 appointing a time for the judgment debtor to attend and show cause why the order should not be made absolute.

11.6.4 The order to show cause and the evidence in support should be served in accordance with RSC Ord 50, r 2, or otherwise as directed by the master. After further consideration at the hearing the master will either make the order absolute (with or without modifications) as in form No 76, or discharge it. Where the order is discharged, the order of discharge must be served in accordance with RSC Ord 50, r 7.

11.6.5 See RSC Ord 50, r 4 for provisions concerning imposing a charge on an interest held by a trustee. RSC Ord 50, r 5 deals with the effects of a charging order in relation to securities out of court, and RSC Ord 50, r 6 with funds in court. Proceedings for the enforcement of a charging order by sale of the property charged must be begun by a Part 8[125] claim form issued out of Chancery Chambers or a Chancery district registry (RSC Ord 50, r 9A).

125 See Table 1, Part 8B practice direction.

11.7 Receivers; equitable execution (RSC Ord 51)

11.7.1 Equitable execution is a process which enables a judgment creditor to obtain payment of the judgment debt where the interest of the judgment debtor in property cannot be reached by ordinary execution.

11.7.2 An application for appointment of a receiver by way of equitable execution may be made to a master, who also has jurisdiction to grant an injunction if, and only so far as, the injunction is ancillary or incidental to the order. The procedure follows that set out in RSC Ord 30, rr 1–6, and the application should be made in accordance with Part 23 and the Part 23 Practice Direction as described in the following paragraphs.

11.7.3 If the judgment creditor seeks an injunction (as in 11.7.2 above) he should file his application notice based on form No 82 but setting out in addition the injunction sought, together with a witness statement or affidavit in support stating:

(1) the date and particulars of the judgment, and that it remains wholly unsatisfied, or to what extent it remains unsatisfied,
(2) the particulars and result of any execution which has been issued, and the nature of the sheriff's return (if any),
(3) that the judgment debtor has no property which can be taken by the ordinary process of execution, (*if he has, give reasons showing that legal execution would be futile*),
(4) particulars of the property in respect of which it is proposed to appoint a receiver,
(5) the name and address of the receiver proposed to be appointed, and that in the deponent's judgment he is a fit and proper person to be appointed receiver, and
(6) that the judgment debtor is in financial difficulties [that the immediate appointment of a receiver without the delay of giving security is of great importance] and that the deponent believes that the judgment debtor may assign or dispose of his estate or interest in (*give details of property*) unless restrained from doing so by the order and injunction of the court.

11.7.4 The judgment creditor need not give notice of this application which will normally be dealt with without a hearing. If the master is satisfied with the evidence he will make an order in form No 83 for a hearing to take place in respect of the application for the appointment of the receiver and granting an injunction meanwhile.

11.7.5 If the judgment creditor does not seek an injunction, the application notice should be filed and served together with the evidence in support (as in paragraph 11.7.3 above but without paragraph (6)).

11.7.6 At the hearing of the application to appoint the receiver, the master will, if he thinks fit, make an order in form No 84. A copy of the order appointing the receiver shall be served by the judgment creditor on the receiver and all other parties to the proceedings[126].

126 RSC Ord 30, r 4.

11.7.7 Where a receiver has been ordered to give security under RSC Ord 30, r 2, the judgment creditor should obtain an appointment before the master who made the order appointing the receiver, to settle the form and amount of the security. Unless otherwise ordered, the security will be in the form of a guarantee. The judgment creditor should have prepared a draft form of guarantee for the master to approve at the appointment. Form PF30CH may be used as a precedent for the guarantee.

11.7.8 RSC Ord 30, r 3 deals with the remuneration of the receiver which may either be assessed by the master or referred to a costs judge. RSC Ord 30, r 5 contains the provisions for submitting the receiver's accounts.

11.8 Committals, etc (RSC Ord 52)

11.8.1 The court has power to punish contempt of court by an order of committal to prison or by other means. These may be by ordering the payment of a fine, by the issue of a writ of sequestration, or by making a hospital or guardianship order under certain provisions of the Mental Health Act 1983. Committal applications under RSC Ord 52, r 4 are always dealt with by a High Court judge. The following provisions apply to applications made under RSC Ord 52, r 4.

11.8.2 The application should be made in existing proceedings by filing an application notice. If not in existing proceedings, a Part 8 claim form should be issued[127] (see paragraphs 2.1 and 2.2 of the Practice Direction – Committal Applications). Evidence in support of a committal application must be by affidavit [128]and, together with the Part 8 claim form or application notice, must be served personally on the person sought to be committed. A date for the hearing must be obtained from the Listing Office, Room WG5 and endorsed on or served with the claim form or application notice.

127 See the Part 8B practice direction, Table 1.
128 RSC Ord 52, r 4(2).

11.8.3 Paragraphs 2.5, 2.6 and 3.1–3.4 of the Practice Direction deal with the content of the evidence, and serving and filing, and paragraph 4 deals with the hearing date and management of the proceedings.

11.8.4 Committal proceedings will normally be heard in public, but see RSC Ord 52, r 6 which sets out certain types of cases which may be heard in private, and see paragraph 9 of the Practice Direction.

11.8.5 Where the court makes a finding of contempt, details of the contempt and of the order or undertaking breached (where appropriate) must be set out in the order. The term of any period of committal must be stated in the order and must not exceed 2 years[129]. A fine must be expressed as payable to Her Majesty the Queen and the order must state the amount of the fine and the date and time within which it must be paid. A contemnor and his solicitors will be notified separately as to how the fine should be paid. A precedent of the order is in form No 85 and will normally be drawn by the court.

129 Contempt of Court Act 1981, s 14.

11.8.6 When an order for committal to prison is made, the court will issue a warrant to the Tipstaff authorising him to convey the contemnor to the appropriate prison. A copy of the order should be served on the prison governor. RSC Ord 52, r 8 deals with the discharge of a person committed.

11.9 Execution against property of foreign or Commonwealth States

11.9.1 In cases where judgment has been obtained against a foreign or Commonwealth State and it is sought to execute the judgment by a writ of fieri facias, a charging order or a garnishee order, the following provisions apply:

(1) Before the writ of fieri facias is issued, the master must be informed in writing and his direction sought. In cases where an application is to be made for a charging order to show cause or a garnishee order to show cause, the evidence in support of the application must include a statement that the execution sought is against a foreign or Commonwealth State.

(2) The master, having been so informed will, as soon as practicable, inform the Foreign and Commonwealth Office ('FCO') of the application and will not permit the issue of a writ of fieri facias, nor grant an order to show cause until the FCO has been so informed. The Privileges and Immunities Section of the Protocol Department of the FCO may be contacted by telephone on 020 7210 4053 or by Fax on 020 7270 4126.

(3) Having regard to all the circumstances of the case, the master may postpone the decision whether to issue the writ or grant the order to show cause for so long as he considers reasonable for the purpose of enabling the FCO to furnish further information relevant to his decision, but not for longer than 3 days from the time of his contacting the FCO. In the event that no further information is received from the FCO within 24 hours of its being informed, then the writ of fieri facias may be issued or the order to show cause may be sealed without further delay.

11.10 Recovery of enforcement costs

11.10.1 Subsection (3) of section 15 of the Courts and Legal Services Act 1990 enables a person taking steps to enforce a money judgment in the High Court to recover the costs of any previous attempt to enforce that judgment. Subsection (4) of section 15 excludes costs that the court considers to have been unreasonably incurred.

11.10.2 The application for an enforcement costs order is made to a master and should be made in accordance with Part 23 but the application notice need not be served on the judgment debtor. The application will normally be dealt with without a hearing and must be supported by evidence substantially as set out in form PF205. The deponent should exhibit sufficient vouchers, receipts or other documents as are reasonably necessary to verify the amount of the costs of previous attempts to enforce the judgment.

11.10.3 If the master is satisfied that such an order is appropriate, he will make an order for payment of the amount of such costs as he considers may be recoverable under subsection (3) of section 15. If the amount of such costs is less than that claimed by the judgment creditor, the master may either disallow the balance or give directions for a detailed assessment or other determination of the balance. If after assessment or other determination it appears that the judgment creditor is entitled to further costs beyond those originally allowed, he may issue a further writ of fieri facias or take other lawful steps to enforce those costs. Interest on the costs runs either from the date the master made the enforcement costs order or from the date of the costs certificate.

11.11 Enforcement of magistrates' courts' orders

11.11.1 The Magistrates' Courts Act 1980, s 87 provides that payment of a sum ordered to be paid on a conviction of a magistrates' court may be enforced by the High Court or a county court (otherwise than by the issue of a writ of fieri facias or other process against goods or by imprisonment or attachment of earnings) as if the sum were due to the clerk of the magistrates' court under a judgment of the High Court or county court, as the case may be.

11.11.2 In the Central Office, the application is made to a master and should be made in accordance with Part 23. Where enforcement is sought by a garnishee or charging order to show cause, the application will normally be dealt with without a hearing. Otherwise the application notice and evidence in support should be served on the defendant.

11.11.3 The application must be supported by a witness statement or affidavit in a form appropriate to the type of execution sought and must have exhibited to it the authority of the magistrates' court to take the proceedings which will recite the conviction, the amount outstanding and the nature of the proceedings authorised to be taken (Magistrates Courts Forms Rules 1981, Form 63).

11.11.4 The application notice and evidence in support together with an additional copy of the exhibit should be filed in Room E15 where it will be assigned a reference number from the register kept for that purpose. The matter will then be dealt with by the master according to the type of enforcement sought.

11.11.5 This practice will also be followed in the district registries with such variations as circumstances may render necessary.

11.12 Reciprocal enforcement of judgments and enforcement of European Community judgments and recommendations etc under the Merchant Shipping (Liner Conferences) Act 1982 (RSC Ord 71)

RECIPROCAL ENFORCEMENT; THE ADMINISTRATION OF JUSTICE ACT 1920 AND THE FOREIGN JUDGMENTS (RECIPROCAL ENFORCEMENT) ACT 1933

11.12.1 RSC Ord 71, r 2 sets out how an application under s 9 of the Act of 1920 or under s 2 of the Act of 1933 for registration of a foreign judgment in the

High Court may be made. The application should be made without notice being served on any other party, but the master may direct that a Part 8 claim form should be issued and served.

11.12.2 RSC Ord 71, r 3 sets out what the evidence in support of the application should contain or have exhibited to it. The title of the witness statement or affidavit should;

(1) expressly state whether it is made 'In the matter of the Administration of Justice Act 1920' or 'In the matter of the Foreign Judgments (Reciprocal Enforcement) Act 1933', and
(2) identify the judgment by reference to the court in which it was obtained and the date it was given.

The foreign judgment will be registered in the foreign currency in which it is expressed and must not be converted into Sterling in the evidence in support. When it comes to enforcing the foreign judgment, the amount should then be converted in accordance with the instructions set out above in paragraph 11 in respect of the type of enforcement sought.

11.12.3 The order giving permission to register the judgment must be drawn up by, or on behalf of the judgment creditor (Form PF154 may be used as a precedent) and will be entered in the Register of Judgments kept in the Central Office for that purpose[130]. The order will usually contain a direction that the costs of and caused by the application and the registration be assessed and added to the judgment as registered. Notice of registration of the judgment must state the matters set out in RSC Ord 71, r 7(3) including the right of the judgment debtor to apply, and the time within he may do so, to have the registration set aside. The notice must be served on the judgment debtor in accordance with RSC Ord 71, r 7(1).

130 RSC Ord 71, rr 5 and 6.

11.12.4 An application to set aside the registration of a judgment under RSC Ord 71, r 9 must be made in accordance with Part 23 and be supported by a witness statement or affidavit.

11.12.5 An application for a certified copy of a judgment entered in the High Court must be made without notice by witness statement or affidavit in accordance with RSC Ord 71, r 13. The certified copy will be endorsed with a certificate signed by the master in accordance with RSC Ord 71, r 13(4). Where the application was made under s 10 of the Act of 1933, an additional certificate will be issued and signed by the master as in form PF155. Judgment creditors who intend to seek enforcement abroad should ensure that their judgment is endorsed as follows:

> 'This judgment carries interest from (*date*) at the rate of 8% per annum in accordance with the provisions of the Judgments Act 1838.'.

ENFORCEMENT OF EUROPEAN COMMUNITY JUDGMENTS

11.12.6 RSC Ord 71, rr 15–24 contains provisions concerning applications for enforcement of Community judgments and Euratom inspection orders under the European Communities (Enforcement of Community Judgments) Order 1972 and for their enforcement. The application for registration may be made without notice being served on any other party and must be supported by a witness statement or affidavit containing or having exhibited to it the matters referred to in RSC Ord 71, r 18. Form PF156 may be used as a precedent.

11.12.7 The order for registration (form PF157) will be entered in the register of the Community judgments and Euratom inspection orders kept in the Central Office for that purpose. The court will serve notice of the registration in form PF158 in accordance with RSC Ord 71, r 20.

11.12.8 An application to vary or cancel a registration under the provisions of RSC Ord 71, r 22 shall be made by application notice in accordance with Part 23, supported by a witness statement or an affidavit.

RECIPROCAL ENFORCEMENT; THE CIVIL JURISDICTION AND JUDGMENTS ACT 1982

APPLICATIONS UNDER S 4 OF THE ACT OF 1982

11.12.9 The provisions concerning applications for registration of judgments of another Contracting State under s 4 of the Act of 1982 are set out in RSC Ord 71, rr 25–35. The application is made without notice being served on any other party and must be supported by evidence as set out in RSC Ord 71, r 28. Form PF159 may be used as a precedent.

11.12.10 The order for registration (form PF160) will be entered in the register of judgments ordered to be registered under s 4 of the Act of 1982 kept in the Central Office for that purpose. The notice of registration in form PF161 should be served in accordance with RSC Ord 71, r 32.

11.12.11 An appeal against registration must be made to a judge under the provisions of RSC Ord 71, r 33(2) by application notice in accordance with Part 23, and should be served in accordance with RSC Ord 71, r 33(2)(a) and (b).

APPLICATIONS UNDER S 12 OF THE ACT OF 1982

11.12.12 RSC Ord 71, r 36 deals with applications for enforcement of High Court judgments in other Contracting States under s 12 of the Act of 1982. The application for a certified copy of the judgment entered in the High Court must be made without notice being served on any other party and must be supported by evidence as set out in RSC Ord 71, r 36(2). Form PF163 may be used as a precedent.

11.12.13 The court will issue a certified copy of the judgment together with a certificate in form PF110 signed by the master, and having annexed to it a copy of the claim form by which the proceedings were begun.

APPLICATIONS UNDER S 18 OF THE ACT OF 1982; JUDGMENT CONTAINING MONEY PROVISIONS

11.12.14 RSC Ord 71, r 37 deals with applications for registration in the High Court of a certificate in respect of any money provisions contained in a judgment given in another part of the United Kingdom. The certificate may be obtained by filing a draft certificate in form No 111 together with a witness statement or affidavit in accordance with RSC Ord 71, r 37(3). Form PF164 may be used as a precedent.

11.12.15 The certificate must be filed for registration in Room E13 in the Central Office within 6 months from the date of its issue. Under paragraph 9 of schedule 6 to the Act of 1982 an application may be made to stay the enforcement of the certificate. The application may be made without notice being served on any other party supported by a witness statement or affidavit stating that the applicant is entitled and intends to apply to the judgment court to set aside or stay the judgment.

APPLICATIONS UNDER S 18 OF THE ACT OF 1982; JUDGMENT CONTAINING NON-MONEY PROVISIONS

11.12.16 RSC Ord 71, r 38 deals with applications for registration in the High Court of a judgment which contains non-money provisions, given in another part of the United Kingdom. The application should be made broadly in accordance with paragraphs 11.12.11 and 11.12.12 above, without notice being served on any other party, but the master may direct that a Part 8 claim form should be issued and served.

11.12.17 The application should be accompanied by a draft certificate in form No 112 and must be supported by a witness statement or affidavit in accordance with RSC Ord 71, r 37(3) (with the necessary modifications). Form PF165 may be used as a precedent. An application to set aside registration of a judgment under schedule 7 to the Act of 1982 may be made in accordance with RSC Ord 71, r 9 (1) and (2).

11.12.18 The certificates will be entered in the register of certificates in respect of judgments ordered to be registered under Schedules 6 or 7 of the Act of 1982 kept in the Central Office for that purpose.

ENFORCEMENT OF RECOMMENDATIONS ETC UNDER THE MERCHANT SHIPPING (LINER CONFERENCES) ACT 1982

11.12.19 Applications under s 9 of the Act of 1982 for registration of a recommendation, determination or award, are dealt with by a commercial judge and shall be made by the issue of a Part 8 claim form[131]. The application should be supported by evidence in accordance with RSC Ord 71, r 42.

131 RSC Ord 71, r 41 and the Part 8B practice direction, Table 1.

11.12.20 The order giving permission to register the recommendation, determination or award must be drawn up by or on behalf of the party making the application, and entered in the register of the recommendations, determinations and awards ordered to be registered under s 9 of the Act of 1982, directed by the Senior Master to be kept in the Admiralty and Commercial Registry.

12 MISCELLANEOUS

12.1 Service of foreign process (RSC Ord 69)

12.1.1 RSC Ord 69 applies to the service on a person in England or Wales of any process in connection with civil or commercial proceedings in a foreign court or tribunal. A request for service is made to the Senior Master from either Her Majesty's Principal Secretary of State for Foreign and Commonwealth Affairs, or where the foreign court or tribunal is in a convention country[132], from a consular or other authority of that country.

132 For definition of 'convention country' see RSC Ord 69, r 1.

12.1.2 Where the foreign court or tribunal certifies that the person to be served understands the language of the process, it is not necessary to provide a translation. RSC Ord 69, r 3 deals with the manner of service; the process may be served through the machinery of the county court and the usual practice is for the Senior Master to provide a certificate for the bailiff or county court officer to use. The Senior Master may make an order for service by an alternative method based on the bailiff's certificate.

12.1.3 When service has been effected, the Senior Master will send a certificate, together with a copy of the process served, to the authority who requested service, stating how service was effected, or why service could not be effected. There is a discretion to charge for the costs of service or attempted service, but recovery is usually sought only where the country requesting service does not provide a reciprocal free service.

12.2 Rectification of register of deeds of arrangement (RSC Ord 94, r 4)

12.2.1 Deeds of arrangement must be registered[133]. The registration office is at the Department of Trade.

133 Deeds of Arrangement Act 1914, as amended by the Administration of Justice Act 1925, s 22.

12.2.2 An application for an order as set out in RSC Ord 94, r 4(1)(a) or (b) must be made to a master of the Queen's Bench Division. Notice need not be served on any other party and the application must be supported by a witness statement or affidavit as described in rule 4(2).

12.3 Exercise of jurisdiction under the Representation of the People Acts (RSC Ord 94, r 5)

12.3.1 RSC Ord 94, r 5 describes the jurisdiction of the High Court under the above Acts. The practice is governed by the Election Petition Rules 1960 (as amended).

12.3.2 Under Part III of the Representation of the People Act 1983, the result of a parliamentary or local government election may be questioned on the grounds of some irregularity either before or during the election. The provisions of Part III have also been applied to European Parliamentary elections.

12.3.3 The challenge is made by the issue of an election petition

(a) in respect of a Parliamentary election by one or more electors or

(b) in respect of a local government election by four or more electors,

or by an unsuccessful or alleged candidate. The member/councillor whose election is complained of is a respondent to the petition as is the returning officer if his conduct is complained of. The petition is issued in the Election Petitions Office, Room E218, normally within 21 days of the election, although this may be extended in certain circumstances.

12.3.4 The petition is tried by two High Court judges of the Queen's Bench Division in respect of parliamentary elections or by a Commissioner in respect of local government elections. The Commissioner must be a lawyer of not less than 10 years standing who neither resides nor practices in the area concerned. The trial usually takes place in the constituency/local government area although preliminary matters are dealt with at the Royal Courts of Justice.

12.3.5 The election court may confirm the result of the election, or substitute another candidate as the member/councillor, or may order the election to be re-run.

12.3.6 Applications for remedies under various sections of the Representation of the People Act 1983 are also issued in the Election Petitions Office, and are usually heard by an Election Rota judge.

12.3.7 Outside the court offices' opening times, but while the building is still open to the public, election petitions and applications may be left in the letter box fixed to the door of Room E218. When the building is closed, election petitions and applications may be left with Security at the Main Entrance, up until midnight.

12.4 Bills of Sale Acts 1878 and 1882 and the Industrial and Provident Societies Act 1967 (RSC Ord 95)

12.4.1 Every bill of sale and absolute bill of sale to which the Act of 1878 applies must be registered under s 8 of that Act, within 7 clear days of its making, and, under s 11 of the Act of 1878, the registration of a bill of sale must be renewed at least once every 5 years. The register for the purpose of the Bills of Sale Acts contains the particulars of registered bills of sale and an alphabetical index of the names of the grantors, and is kept in the Action Department in Room E10.

12.4.2 An application to register a bill of sale which is made within the prescribed time should be made by filing in Room E17 the original bill of sale and any document annexed to it together with a witness statement or affidavit in form PF179 or PF180. An application to re-register a bill of sale which is made within the prescribed time should be made by filing in Room E17 a witness statement or affidavit in form PF181.

12.4.3 An application to rectify;

(1) an omission to register, by extending the time for registration, or
(2) an omission or mis-statement of the name, residence or occupation of a person in the register, by correcting the registration,

must be made by witness statement or affidavit to a master of the Queen's Bench Division. In addition to the matters set out in forms PF179 or PF180, the evidence in support must also set out the particulars of the omission and state the grounds on which the application is made.

12.4.4 Where the residence of the grantor of the bill of sale or the person against whom the process is issued is outside the London bankruptcy district, or where the bill of sale describes the goods as being in a place outside that district, the Central Office will send copies of the bill of sale to the appropriate county court district judge[134].

134 Section 11, Bills of Sale Act 1882 and the Bills of Sale (Local Registration) Rules 1960.

12.4.5 The master, on being satisfied that the omission or mis-statement of name, residence or occupation of a person in the register was accidental or due to inadvertence, may order the omission or mis-statement to be rectified by the insertion in the register of the correct name, residence or occupation of the person.

12.4.6 Where the master is satisfied that the omission to register a bill of sale or a witness statement or affidavit of renewal within the prescribed time was accidental or due to inadvertence, he may extend the time for registration on such terms as he thinks fit. In order to protect any creditors who have accrued rights of property in the assets in respect of which the bill of sale was granted between the date of the bill and its actual registration, any order to extend the time for registration will normally be made 'without prejudice' to those creditors. The order will be drawn up in form PF182.

12.4.7 An application for an order that a memorandum of satisfaction be written on a registered copy of a bill of sale, made without the consent of the person entitled to the benefit of the bill of sale, must be made by the issue of a Part 8 claim form. Where the consent of the person entitled to the benefit of the bill of sale has been obtained, the application may be made by a witness statement or affidavit[135] containing that consent and verifying the signature on it. Form PF183 contains precedents for the evidence and forms of consent. Where the application is made with consent, the evidence need not be served on any other person. If the master is satisfied on the evidence, he will endorse his approval on the witness statement or affidavit (an order is not normally drawn up) and send it to Room E17 for satisfaction to be entered. If a copy of the bill of sale has been sent to a county court district judge, a notice of satisfaction will be sent to that district judge.

135 See the practice direction – Bills of Sale.

12.4.8 Where the consent has not been obtained, the claim form must be served on the person entitled to the benefit of the bill of sale and must be supported by evidence that the debt (if any) for which the bill of sale was made has been satisfied or discharged.

12.4.9 An application to restrain removal on sale of goods seized in accordance with RSC Ord 95, r 3 and under the proviso to s 7 of the Bills of Sale Act (1878) Amendment Act 1882 must be made by the issue of a Part 8 claim form for hearing before the Interim Applications judge.

12.4.10 Under the Industrial and Provident Societies Act 1967 an application to record an instrument creating a fixed or floating charge on the assets of a registered society or to rectify any omission or mis-statement in it must be made within 14 days beginning with the date of its execution.

12.4.11 Under RSC Ord 95, r 5 and in accordance with s 1(5) of the Act of 1967 the court may order;

(1) that the period for making an application for recording a charge be extended, or

(2) an omission or mis-statement in such an application be rectified.

The procedure for obtaining an order as in (1) or (2) above is similar to that under s 14 of the Bills of Sale Act 1878 and must be made by witness statement or affidavit to a master of the Queen's Bench Division as in paragraph 12.4.3 above and must exhibit a copy of the instrument duly authenticated in the prescribed manner together with any other particulars relating to the charge.

12.4.12 RSC Ord 95, r 3 refers to the assignment of book debts; the register of assignments of book debts is kept in Room E10 in the Central Office. An application for registration under s 344 of the Insolvency Act 1986 should be made in accordance with RSC Ord 95, r 6(2). Parties may use form PF186 for their evidence in support. It is helpful if the original assignment is also produced.

12.5 Enrolment of deeds and other documents

12.5.1 Any deed or document which by virtue of any enactment is required or authorised to be enrolled in the Supreme Court may be enrolled in the Central

Office. See the Part 5 Practice Direction at paragraph 6 which fully sets out the procedure for enrolment and contains in an appendix the Enrolment of Deeds (Change of Name) Regulations 1994.

12.6 Bail (RSC Ord 79, r 9)

12.6.1 Under the provisions of subsections (1) and (2) of section 22 of the Criminal Justice Act 1967 (as amended by Schedule 2 to the Bail Act 1976) the High Court may grant bail in criminal proceedings to a defendant in custody who has been refused bail, or vary the arrangements for bail of an inferior court.

12.6.2 The application must be made to the Interim Applications judge by the issue of a Part 8 claim form in form No 97 or 97A, and supported by a witness statement or affidavit in accordance with RSC Ord 79, r 9 (1) to (3). The claim form should be issued in the Listing Office, Room WG5, and will be given a bail number from the register kept there for recording bail applications.

12.6.3 If a defendant wishing to apply for bail is unable to instruct a solicitor to act for him through lack of means, he may write to the Interim Applications judge to that effect and requesting that the Official Solicitor act for him. The letter should be addressed to the Listing Office, Room WG5, marked for the attention of the Interim Applications judge. Where the judge assigns the Official Solicitor to act for the defendant, he may dispense with the issue of a claim form and a witness statement or affidavit in support.

12.6.4 Where the judge grants bail, the order will be drawn up in form No 98 which provides for the conditions to be complied with both before release, including the provision of sureties, and after release. An order varying the arrangements for bail will be drawn up in form No 98A. Copies of those orders must be sent to the appropriate officer of the Crown Court or of the court which committed the defendant.

12.7 Defamation

12.7.1 Defamation claims are governed by Part 53 and the Part 53 Practice Direction. Paragraph 2 of the Practice Direction sets out the information which should be included in a statement of case.

OFFER TO MAKE AMENDS

12.7.2 Under section 2 of the Defamation Act 1996 a person who has published a statement alleged to be defamatory of another may offer to make amends ('a section 2 offer'). The section 2 offer must;

(1) be in writing,
(2) be expressed to be an offer to make amends under section 2 of the Act, and
(3) state whether it is a qualified offer, and if so, set out the defamatory meaning in relation to which it is made.

A section 2 offer is an offer;

(1) to make a suitable correction of the statement complained of and sufficient apology,
(2) to publish the correction and apology in a manner that is reasonable and practicable in the circumstances, and

(3) to pay to the aggrieved party compensation (if any) and costs as may be agreed or determined to be payable.

12.7.3 Where a section 2 offer is accepted by an aggrieved person he may not bring or continue defamation proceedings against the person making the offer, but he may apply to the court under section 3 of the Act for an order that the other party fulfil his offer by taking the agreed steps. If the parties are unable to agree the amount of compensation or costs, the aggrieved party may apply to the court for the amount to be decided.

12.7.4 In the event that the parties are unable to agree on the steps to be taken, the person making the offer may take such steps as he thinks appropriate, including making an application for the court's approval of the terms of a statement to be read in court containing a correction and apology. He may also give an undertaking to the court as to the manner of their publication.

12.7.5 In existing proceedings the above applications may be made in accordance with Part 23, otherwise a Part 8 claim form should be issued. The application or claim must be supported by written evidence as set out in the Part 53 Practice Direction at paragraph 3.3, and should be made to a master. If the application or claim involves the court's approval for a statement to be read in court, it should be made to the Senior Master. The claim form or application notice should be issued or filed in the Masters' Support Unit, Room E17.

RULING ON MEANING

12.7.6 An application for an order determining whether or not a statement complained of is capable of;

(1) having any meaning or meanings attributed to it in a statement of case,
(2) being defamatory of the claimant, or
(3) bearing any other meaning defamatory of the claimant,

should be made in accordance with Part 23 and may be made at any time after service of the particulars of claim. Paragraphs 4.3 and 4.4 or the Practice Direction state the information which must be included in the application notice and evidence in support.

12.7.7 The application notice should be filed in the Listing Office, Room WG5, for hearing by the judge in charge of the Jury list, or another designated judge.

SUMMARY DISPOSAL

12.7.8 Section 8 of the Act gives the court power to dispose summarily of the claimant's claim. The court may;

(1) dismiss the claim if it appears that it has no realistic prospect of success and there is no reason why it should be tried, or
(2) give judgment for the claimant and grant him summary relief.

12.7.9 Summary relief includes the following;

(1) a declaration that the statement was false and defamatory of the claimant,
(2) an order that the defendant publish or cause to be published a suitable correction and apology,
(3) damages not exceeding £10,000,
(4) an order restraining the defendant from publishing or further publishing the matter complained of.

12.7.10 Applications for summary disposal are dealt with in rule 53.2 and paragraphs 5.1–5.3 of the Part 53 Practice Direction. Substantial claims and those involving the police authorities or the media or those seeking an order restraining publication will be dealt with by the judge in charge of the Jury list or another designated judge, and the application notice should be filed in the Listing Office, Room WG5. Applications for summary disposal in other defamation claims may be made at first instance to a master.

12.7.11 An application notice for summary disposal must state;

(1) that it is an application for summary disposal made in accordance with section 8 of the Act,
(2) the matters set out in paragraph 2(3) of the Part 24 Practice Direction, and
(3) whether or not the defendant has made an offer to make amends under section 2 of the Act, and whether or not it has been withdrawn.

The application may be made at any time after service of the particulars of claim and the provisions of rule 24.4(1)(a) and (b) do not apply.

12.7.12 Where the court has made an order for summary relief as in 12.7.9(2) above (specifying the date by which the parties should agree the content, time, manner, form and place of publication of the correction and apology) and the parties are unable to comply within the specified time, the claimant must prepare a summary of the court's judgment and serve it on the other parties within 3 days following the date specified in the order for the content to be agreed by the parties[136].

136 Paragraph 5.3 of the Part 53 practice direction.

12.7.13 If the parties are unable to agree the summary, they must within 3 days of its receipt, apply to the court by;

(1) filing an application notice, and
(2) filing and serving on all the other parties a copy of the summary showing the revisions they wish to make to it.

The court (normally the judge who delivered the judgment) will then settle the summary.

STATEMENTS READ IN COURT

12.7.14 Paragraph 6 of the Practice Direction only applies where a party wishes to accept a Part 36 offer, Part 36 payment or other offer of settlement.

12.7.15 An application for permission to make the statement before a judge in court may be made before or after acceptance of the Part 36 offer, Part 36 payment or other offer to settle, and should be made in accordance with Part 23 to the Senior Master, or if he is not available, to the Practice Master. The application notice, together with a copy of the statement, should be filed in the Masters' Support Unit, Room E17.

12.7.16 Where permission has been given, the parties may take a copy of the order to the Listing Office, Room WG5 for the matter will be listed before the judge in charge of the Jury List for mention. Otherwise, the Action Department will send the court file to the Listing Office for the matter to be listed.

12.8 References to the Court of Justice of the European Communities

12.8.1 A party wishing to apply for an order[137] under RSC Ord 114 (Schedule 1 to the CPR) may do so by application before or at the trial or hearing. An application made before the trial or hearing should be made in accordance with Part 23.

137 An 'order' means an order referring a question to the European Court for a preliminary ruling under article 234 (formerly article 177) of the Treaty establishing the European Community, article 150 of the Treaty establishing the European Atomic Energy Community or article 41 of the Treaty establishing the European Coal and Steel Community, or for a ruling on the interpretation of any of the Brussels Conventions (within the meaning of s 1(1) of the Civil Jurisdiction and Judgments Act 1982) or any of the instruments referred to in s 1 of the Contracts (Applicable Law) Act 1990.

12.8.2 Before making an order for reference, the court will pay close attention to the terms of the appropriate article, to RSC Ord 114, to form PF109 and to the 'Guidance of the Court of Justice of the European Communities on References by National Courts for Preliminary Rulings' which may be found in the Practice Direction (ECJ References: Procedure) (1999) 1 WLR 260.

12.8.3 It is the responsibility of the court, rather than the parties, to settle the terms of the reference. This should identify as clearly, succinctly and simply as the nature of the case permits the question to which the British court seeks an answer and it is very desirable that language should be used which lends itself readily to translation.

12.8.4 The referring court should, in a single document scheduled to the order (in form PF109);

(1) identify the parties and summarise the nature and history of the proceedings,
(2) summarise the salient facts, indicating whether these are proved or admitted or assumed,
(3) make reference to the rules of national law (substantive and procedural) relevant to the dispute,
(4) summarise the contentions of the parties as far as relevant,
(5) explain why a ruling of the European Court is sought, identifying the EC provisions whose effect is in issue, and
(6) formulate, without avoidable complexity, the question(s) to which an answer is requested.

12.8.5 Where the document is in the form of a judgment, passages which are not relevant to the reference should be omitted from the text scheduled to the order. Incorporation of appendices, annexes or enclosures as part of the document should be avoided, unless the relevant passages lend themselves readily to translation and are clearly identified.

12.8.6 When the order of reference has been approved by the judge and sealed by the court, the order, together with any other necessary documents should be promptly passed to Room E.13 for the attention of the Senior Master of the Queen's Bench Division, for transmission to Luxembourg without avoidable delay.

12.9 Group litigation orders 'GLOs'

12.9.1 Section III of Part 19 and the Practice Direction – Group Litigation deal with claims where multiple parties are claimants.

12.9.2 When considering applying for a GLO, the applicant should contact the Law Society at 113 Chancery Lane, London WC2A 1PL, who may be able to assist in putting the applicant in contact with other parties who may also be interested in applying for a GLO in the same matter.

12.9.3 The consent of either the Lord Chief Justice or the Vice-Chancellor to the GLO is required. In the Queen's Bench Division the application should be made to the Senior Master in accordance with Part 23. If the Senior Master is minded to make the GLO he will forward a copy of the application notice and any written evidence to the Lord Chief Justice. The application notice should include the information set out in paragraph 3.2 of the Practice Direction.

12.9.4 A group register will be set up and maintained in the court of all the parties to the group of claims to be managed under the GLO. In order to publicise the GLO when it has been made, a copy should be supplied to the Law Society and to the Senior Master. A record of each GLO made will be maintained in the Central Office.

12.9.5 The Practice Direction sets out how the group litigation will be managed. In particular, a managing judge will be appointed. The case management directions are likely to direct;

(1) that a 'group particulars of claim' containing the various claims of the claimants on the group register are served,
(2) that one claim proceed as a 'test' claim, and
(3) a cut-off date after which no additions may be made to the group register.

****

ANNEX 2

The following is a list of the abbreviations commonly used by masters on endorsements of orders, though there may be some variation as between individual masters.

ADR	Alternative dispute resolution
Aff	Affidavit
AM-T	Allocate to multi-track
AN	Appointment Notice
App	Application
AQ	Allocation questionnaire
AS	Assessed summarily
BNLT	By no later than
CC	County court
CIA	Costs in the application
CIAE	Costs in any event
CIC	Costs in the case
Cl	Claimant
Col	Certificate for counsel
CMC	Case management conference

COA	Charging order absolute
COCB	Costs of and caused by
COSC	Charging order to show cause
CR	Costs reserved
CTR	Costs of today reserved
D/Def	Defendant/Defence
DAI/NA	Detailed assessment if not agreed
Disc	Disclosure
Dism	Dismissed
Disp C/S	Dispense with requirement of certificate of service
FC	Fixed costs
FI	Further information
FO	Further order
FOD	First open date
GOA	Garnishee order absolute
GOSC	Garnishee order to show cause
IAE	In any event
IB	Indemnity basis
Insp	Inspection
J	Judgment (as in Part 24 applications)
LA	Legal aid
LAA	Legal aid assessment
LQ	Listing questionnaire
O	Order
On CServ	On producing certificate of service
O Exam	Oral examination
P/C	Particulars of claim
PD	Practice direction
Pm	Permission
Pm A	Permission to apply
Pm R	Permission to restore
Pm RFD	Permission to restore for further directions
Pt	Part
PRA	Private room appointment
R	Rule
SA	Set aside/Special allowance
SOJ	Service out of the jurisdiction
S/C	Statement of case
SB	Standard basis
S/T	Statement of truth
Tfr	Transfer
WN	Without notice
WCO	Wasted costs order
WS	Witness statement

The Technology and Construction Court Guide

SECOND EDITION OF THE TCC GUIDE

(coming into effect on 3 October 2005)

ARRANGEMENT OF SECTIONS

SECTION 1 – INTRODUCTION

1.1 Purpose of Guide

1.1.1 This new edition of the Technology and Construction Court ('TCC') Guide is intended to provide straightforward, practical guidance to the conduct of litigation in the TCC. Whilst it is intended to be comprehensive, it naturally concentrates on the most important aspects of such litigation. It therefore cannot cover all the procedural points that may arise. It does, however, describe the main elements of the practice that is likely to be followed in most TCC cases.

1.1.2 The Guide reflects the flexible framework within which litigation in the TCC is habitually conducted. The requirements set out in the Guide are designed to ensure effective management of proceedings in the TCC. It must always be remembered that, if parties fail to comply with these requirements, the court may impose sanctions including orders for costs.

1.1.3 In respect of those procedural areas for which specific provision is not made in this Guide, the parties, together with their advisors, will be expected to act reasonably and in accordance with both the spirit of the Guide and the overriding objective at CPR Rule 1.1

1.1.4 It is not the function of the Guide to summarise the Civil Procedure Rules ('the CPR'), and it should not be regarded as a substitute for the CPR. The parties and their advisors are expected to familiarise themselves with the CPR and, in particular, to understand the importance of the 'overriding objective' of the CPR. The TCC endeavours to ensure that all its cases are dealt with justly and with proper proportionality. This includes ensuring that the parties are on an equal footing; taking all practicable steps to save expenditure; dealing with the dispute in ways which are proportionate to the size of the claim and cross-claim and the importance of the case to the parties; and managing the case throughout in a way that takes proper account of its complexity and the different financial positions of the parties. The court will also endeavour to ensure expedition, and to allot to each case an appropriate share of the court's resources.

1.1.5 This new edition of the TCC Guide has been prepared in consultation with the judges of the TCC in London, Cardiff, Birmingham, Manchester and Leeds, and with the advice and support of TECBAR, TeCSA, the Society for Computers and Law and the TCC Users' Committees in London, Cardiff, Birmingham, Manchester, Liverpool and Leeds. The TCC Guide is published with the approval of the Head of Civil Justice and the deputy Head of Civil Justice.

1.2 The CPR

1.2.1 Proceedings in the TCC are governed by the CPR and the supplementary Practice Directions. CPR Part 60 and its associated Practice Direction deal specifically with the practice and procedure of the TCC.

1.2.2 Other parts of the CPR that frequently arise in TCC cases include Part 8 (Alternative Procedure for Claims); Parts 12 and 13 (Default Judgment and Setting Aside); Part 17 (Amendments); Part 20 (Counterclaims and Other Additional Claims); Part 24 (Summary Judgment); Part 25 (Interim Remedies and Security for Costs); Part 26 (Case Management); Part 32 (Evidence); Part 35 (Experts and Assessors) and Part 62 (Arbitration Claims).

1.3 The TCC

1.3.1 What are TCC Claims? CPR Rules 60.1(2) and (3) provide that a TCC claim is a claim which (i) involves technically complex issues or questions (or for which trial by a TCC judge is desirable) and (ii) has been issued in or transferred into the TCC specialist list. Paragraph 2.1 of the TCC Practice Direction identifies the following as examples of the types of claim which it may be appropriate to bring as TCC claims –

(a) building or other construction disputes, including claims for the enforcement of the decisions of adjudicators under the Housing Grants, Construction and Regeneration Act 1996;
(b) engineering disputes;
(c) claims by and against engineers, architects, surveyors, accountants and other specialised advisors relating to the services they provide;

(d) claims by and against local authorities relating to their statutory duties concerning the development of land or the construction of buildings;
(e) claims relating to the design, supply and installation of computers, computer software and related network systems;
(f) claims relating to the quality of goods sold or hired, and work done, materials supplied or services rendered;
(g) claims between landlord and tenant for breach of a repairing covenant;
(h) claims between neighbours, owners and occupiers of land in trespass, nuisance, etc.
(i) claims relating to the environment (for example, pollution cases);
(j) claims arising out of fires;
(k) claims involving taking of accounts where these are complicated; and
(l) challenges to decisions of arbitrators in construction and engineering disputes including applications for permission to appeal and appeals.

It should be noted that this list is not exhaustive and other types of claim may well be appropriate for the TCC.

1.3.2 The Court. Both the High Court and the county courts deal with TCC business. Circuit judges and recorders only have jurisdiction to manage and try TCC cases if they have been nominated by the Lord Chancellor pursuant to section 68(1)(a) of the Supreme Court Act 1981. It should be noted that those circuit judges who have been nominated pursuant to section 68(1) of the Supreme Court Act 1981 fall into two categories: 'full time' TCC judges and 'part time' TCC judges. 'Full time' TCC judges spend most of their time dealing with TCC business, although they will do other work when there is no TCC business requiring their immediate attention. 'Part time' TCC judges are circuit judges who are only available to sit in the TCC for part of their time. They have substantial responsibilities outside the TCC.

In respect of a court centre where there is no full time TCC judge, the term 'principal TCC judge' is used in this Guide to denote the circuit judge who has principal responsibility for TCC work.

The phrase 'Technology and Construction Court' or 'TCC' or 'the court' is used in this Guide to denote any court which deals with TCC claims. All of the courts which deal with TCC claims form a composite group of courts. When those courts are dealing with TCC business, CPR Part 60, its accompanying Practice Direction and this Guide govern the procedures of those courts. The High Court judge in charge of the TCC('the Judge in Charge'), although based principally in London, has overall responsibility for the judicial supervision of TCC business in those courts.

1.3.3 The TCC in London. The principal centre for TCC work is the High Court in London at St Dunstan's House, 133-137 Fetter Lane, London, EC4A 1HD. The Judge in Charge of the TCC sits principally at St Dunstan's House together with five full time TCC judges. Subject to paragraph 3.7.1 below, any communication or enquiry concerning a TCC case, which is proceeding at St Dunstan's House, should be directed to the clerk of the judge who is assigned to that case. The various contact details for the judges' clerks are set out in Appendix D.

The TCC judges who are based at St Dunstan's House will, when appropriate, sit at court centres outside London.

TCC county court cases in London are brought in (or transferred to) the Central London Civil Justice Centre, 13–14 Park Crescent, London W1N 4HT.

1.3.4 District Registries. TCC claims can be brought in the High Court outside London in any District Registry, although the Practice Direction states that it is preferable that, wherever possible, such claims should be issued in one of the following District Registries: Birmingham, Bristol, Cardiff, Chester, Exeter, Leeds, Liverpool, Newcastle, Nottingham and Salford (Manchester). There are full-time TCC Judges in Birmingham, Liverpool and Salford (Manchester). Contact details are again set out in Appendix D. There are part time TCC judges and/or recorders nominated to deal with TCC business available at most court centres throughout England and Wales.

In a number of regions a 'TCC liaison district judge' has been appointed. It is the function of the TCC liaison district judge:

(a) To keep other district judges in that region well informed about the role and remit of the TCC (in order that appropriate cases may be transferred to the TCC at an early, rather than late, stage).

(b) To deal with any queries from colleagues concerning the TCC or cases which might merit transfer to the TCC.

(c) To deal with any subsidiary matter which a TCC judge directs should be determined by a district judge pursuant to rule 60.1(5)(b)(ii).

(d) To deal with urgent applications in TCC cases pursuant to paragraph 7.2 of the Practice Direction (ie no TCC judge is available and the matter is of a kind that falls within the district judge's jurisdiction).

1.3.5 County Courts outside London. TCC claims may also be brought in those county courts which are specified in the Part 60 Practice Direction. The specified county courts are: Birmingham, Bristol, Cardiff, Chester, Exeter, Leeds, Liverpool, Newcastle, Nottingham and Salford (Manchester). Contact details are again set out in Appendix D.

Where TCC proceedings are brought in a county court, statements of case and applications should be headed:

'In the ... County Court
Technology and Construction Court'

This heading is important because in TCC cases (subject to the limited exceptions mentioned in paragraph 1.3.4 above) district judges do not have jurisdiction to hear applications or make orders.

1.3.6 The division between High Court and county court TCC cases. As a general rule TCC claims for more than £50,000 are brought in the High Court, whilst claims for lower sums are brought in the county court. However, this is not a rigid dividing line. The monetary threshold for High Court TCC claims tends to be higher in London than in the regions. Regard must also be had to the complexity of the case and all other circumstances. Arbitration claims and claims to enforce or challenge adjudicators' awards are generally (but not invariably) brought in the High Court. The scale of fees differs in the High Court and the county court. This is a factor which should be borne in mind in borderline cases.

1.4 The TCC Users' Committees

1.4.1 The continuing ability of the TCC to meet the changing needs of all those involved in TCC litigation depends in large part upon a close working relationship between the TCC and its users.

1.4.2 London. The Judge in Charge chairs two meetings a year of the London TCC Users' Committee. The judge's clerk acts as secretary to the Committee and takes the minutes of meetings. That Committee is made up of representatives of the London TCC judges, the barristers and solicitors who regularly use the Court, the professional bodies, such as architects, engineers and arbitrators, whose members are affected by the decisions of the Court, and representatives of both employers and contractors' groups.

1.4.3 Outside London. There are similar meetings of TCC Users' Committees in Birmingham, Salford (Manchester), Liverpool, Cardiff and Leeds. Each Users' Committee is chaired by the full time TCC judge or the principal TCC judge in that location.

1.4.4 The TCC regards these channels of communication as extremely important and all those who are concerned with the work of the Court are encouraged to make full use of these meetings. Any suggestions or other correspondence raising matters for consideration by the Users' Committee should, in the first instance, be addressed to the clerk to the Judge in Charge at St. Dunstan's House or to the clerk to the appropriate TCC judge outside London.

1.5 Specialist Associations

1.5.1 There are a number of associations of legal representatives which are represented on the Users' Committees and which also liaise closely with the Court. These contacts ensure that the Court remains responsive to the opinions and requirements of the professional users of the Court.

1.5.2 The relevant professional organisations are the TCC Bar Association ('TECBAR') and the TCC Solicitors Association ('TeCSA'). Details of the relevant contacts at these organisations are set out on their respective websites, namely www.tecbar.org and www.tecsa.org.

SECTION 2 – PRE-ACTION PROTOCOL

2.1 Introduction

2.1.1 There is a Pre-Action Protocol for Construction and Engineering Disputes. Where the dispute involves a claim against architects, engineers or quantity surveyors, this Protocol prevails over the Professional Negligence Pre-Action Protocol: see paragraph 1.1 of the Protocol for Construction and Engineering Disputes and paragraph A.1 of the Professional Negligence Pre-Action Protocol. The current version of the Construction and Engineering Pre-Action Protocol ('the Protocol') is set out in volume 1 of the White Book at section C.

2.1.2 The purpose of the Protocol is to encourage the frank and early exchange of information about the prospective claim and any defence to it; to enable parties to avoid litigation by agreeing a settlement of the claim before the commencement of proceedings; and to support the efficient management of proceedings where litigation cannot be avoided.

2.1.3 Proportionality. The overriding objective (CPR rule 1.1) applies to the pre-action period. The Protocol must not be used as a tactical device to secure advantage for one party or to generate unnecessary costs. In small TCC claims (such as those likely to proceed in the county court), the letter of claim and the response should be simple and the costs of both sides should be kept to a modest level. In all cases the costs incurred at the Protocol stage should be proportionate to the complexity of the case and the amount of money which is at stake. The Protocol does not impose a requirement on the parties to marshal and disclose all the supporting details and evidence that may ultimately be required if the case proceeds to litigation.

2.2 To Which Claims Does The Protocol Apply?

2.2.1 The court will expect all parties to have complied in substance with the provisions of the Protocol in all construction and engineering disputes. The only exceptions to this are identified in paragraph 2.3 below.

2.2.2 The court regards the Protocol as setting out normal and reasonable pre-action conduct. Accordingly, whilst the Protocol is not mandatory for a number of the claims noted by way of example in paragraph 1.3.1 above, such as computer cases or dilapidations claims, the court would, in the absence of a specific reason to the contrary, expect the Protocol generally to be followed in such cases prior to the commencement of proceedings in the TCC.

2.3 What Are The Exceptions?

2.3.1 A claimant does not have to comply with the Protocol if his claim:

(a) is to enforce the decision of an adjudicator;
(b) includes a claim for interim injunctive relief;
(c) will be the subject of a claim for summary judgment pursuant to Part 24 of the CPR; or
(d) relates to the same or substantially the same issues as have been the subject of a recent adjudication or some other formal alternative dispute resolution procedure.

2.3.2 In addition, a claimant need not comply with any part of the Protocol if, by so doing, his claim may become time-barred under the Limitation Act 1980. In those circumstances, a claimant should commence proceedings without complying with the Protocol and must, at the same time, apply for specific directions as to the timetable and form of procedure to be adopted. The court may order a stay of those proceedings pending completion of the steps set out in the Protocol.

2.4 What Are The Essential Ingredients Of The Protocol?

2.4.1 The Letter of Claim. The letter of claim must comply with Section 3 of the Protocol. Amongst other things, it must contain a clear summary of the facts on which each claim is based; the basis on which each claim is made; and details of the relief claimed, including a breakdown showing how any damages have been quantified. The claimant must also provide the names of experts already instructed and on whom he intends to rely.

2.4.2 The Defendant's Response. The defendant has 14 days to acknowledge the letter of claim and 28 days (from receipt of the letter of claim) either to take any jurisdiction objection or to respond in substance to the letter of claim. Paragraph 4.3.1 of the Protocol enables the parties to agree an extension of the 28 day period up to a maximum of 4 months. In any case of substance it is quite usual for an extension of time to be agreed for the defendant's response. The letter of response must comply with section 4 of the Protocol. Amongst other things, it must state which claims are accepted, which claims are rejected and on what basis. It must set out any counterclaim to be advanced by the defendant. The defendant should also provide the names of experts who have been instructed and on whom he intends to rely. If the defendant fails either to acknowledge or to respond to the letter of claim in time, the claimant is entitled to commence proceedings.

2.4.3 Pre-action Meeting. The Construction and Engineering Protocol is the only Protocol under the CPR that generally requires the parties to meet, without prejudice, at least once, in order to identify the main issues and the root causes of their disagreement on those issues. The purpose of the meeting is to see whether, and if so how, those issues might be resolved without recourse to litigation or, if litigation is unavoidable, what steps should be taken to ensure that it is conducted in accordance with the overriding objective. At or as a result of the meeting, the parties should consider whether some form of alternative dispute resolution ('ADR') would be more suitable than litigation and if so, they should endeavour to agree which form of ADR to adopt. Although the meeting is 'without prejudice', any party who attended the meeting is at liberty to disclose to the Court at a later stage that the meeting took place; who attended and who refused to attend, together with the grounds for their refusal; and any agreements concluded between the parties.

2.5 What Happens To The Material Generated By The Protocol?

2.5.1 The letter of claim, the defendant's response, and the information relating to attendance (or otherwise) at the meeting are not confidential or 'without prejudice' and can therefore be referred to by the parties in any subsequent litigation. The detail of any discussion at the meeting(s) and/or any note of the meeting cannot be referred to the court unless all parties agree.

2.5.2 Normally the parties should include in the bundle for the first case management conference: (a) the letter of claim, (b) the response, and (c) any agreed note of the pre-action meeting: see Section 5 below. The documents attached to or enclosed with the letter and the response should not be included in the bundle.

2.6 What If One Party Has Not Complied With The Protocol?

2.6.1 There can often be a complaint that one or other party has not complied with the Protocol. The court will consider any such complaints once proceedings have been commenced. If the court finds that the claimant has not complied with one part of the Protocol, then the court may stay the proceedings until the steps set out in the Protocol have been taken.

2.6.2 Paragraph 2.3 of the Practice Direction in respect of Protocols (section C of volume 1 of the White Book) makes plain that the court may make adverse costs orders against a party who has failed to comply with the Protocol. The court will exercise any sanctions available with the object of placing the innocent party in no worse a position than he would have been if the Protocol had been complied with.

2.6.3 The court is unlikely to be concerned with minor infringements of the Protocol or to engage in lengthy debates as to the precise quality of the information provided by one party to the other during the Protocol stages. The court will principally be concerned to ensure that, as a result of the Protocol stage, each party to any subsequent litigation has a clear understanding of the nature of the case that it has to meet at the commencement of those proceedings.

2.7 Costs of compliance with the Protocol.

2.7.1 If compliance with the Protocol results in settlement, the costs incurred will not be recoverable from the paying party, unless this is specifically agreed.

2.7.2 If compliance with the Protocol does not result in settlement, then the costs of the exercise cannot be recovered as costs, unless:

- those costs fall within the principles stated by Sir Robert Megarry V-C in Re Gibson's Settlement Trusts [1981] Ch 179; or
- the steps taken in compliance with the Protocol can properly be attributable to the conduct of the action.

SECTION 3 – COMMENCEMENT AND TRANSFER

3.1 Claim Forms

3.1.1 All proceedings must be started using a claim form under CPR Part 7 or CPR Part 8. All claims allocated to the TCC are assigned to the Multi-Track: see CPR Rule 60.6(1).

3.2 Part 7 Claims

3.2.1 The Part 7 claim form must be marked 'Technology and Construction Court' in the appropriate place on the form.

3.2.2. Particulars of Claim may be served with the claim form, but this is not a mandatory requirement. If the Particulars of Claim are not contained in or served with the claim form, they must be served within 14 days after service of the claim form.

3.2.3 A claim form must be verified by a statement of truth, and this includes any amendment to a claim form, unless the court otherwise orders.

3.3 Part 8 Claims

3.3.1 The Part 8 claim form must be marked 'Technology and Construction Court' in the appropriate place on the form.

3.3.2 A Part 8 claim form will normally be used where there is no substantial dispute of fact, such as the situation where the dispute turns on the construction of the contract or the interpretation of statute. For example, claims challenging the jurisdiction of an adjudicator or the validity of his decision are sometimes brought under Part 8. In those cases the relevant primary facts are often not in dispute. Part 8 claims will generally be disposed of on written evidence and oral submissions.

3.3.3 It is important that, where a claimant uses the Part 8 procedure, his claim form states that Part 8 applies and that the claimant wishes the claim to proceed under Part 8.

3.3.4 A statement of truth is again required on a Part 8 claim form.

3.4 Service

3.4.1 Claim forms issued in the TCC at St Dunstan's House in London are to be served by the claimant, not by the Registry. In some other court centres claim forms are served by the court, unless the claimant specifically requests otherwise.

3.4.2 The different methods of service are set out in CPR Part 6 and the accompanying Practice Direction.

3.4.3 Applications for an extension of time in which to serve a claim form are governed by CPR Rule 7.6. The evidence required on an application for an extension of time is set out in paragraph 8.2 of Practice Direction A supplementing CPR Part 7.

3.4.4 When the claimant has served the claim form, he must file a certificate of service: Rule 6.14(2). This is necessary if, for instance, the claimant wishes to obtain judgment in default (CPR Part 12).

3.4.5 Applications for permission to serve a claim form out of the jurisdiction are subject to Rules 6.19-6.31 inclusive.

3.5 Acknowledgment of Service

3.5.1 A defendant must file an acknowledgment of service in response to both Part 7 and Part 8 claims. Save in the special circumstances that arise when the claim form has been served out of the jurisdiction, the period for filing an acknowledgment of service is 14 days after service of the claim form.

3.6 Transfer

3.6.1 Proceedings may be transferred from any Division of the High Court or from any specialist list to the TCC pursuant to CPR rule 30.5. The order made by the transferring court should be expressed as being subject to the approval of a TCC judge. The decision whether to accept such a transfer must be made by a TCC judge: see rule 30.5(3). Many of these applications are uncontested, and may conveniently be dealt with on paper. Transfers from the TCC to other Divisions of the High Court or other specialist lists are also governed by CPR rule 30.5. In London there are quite often transfers between the Commercial Court and the TCC, in order to ensure that cases are dealt with by the most appropriate judge. Outside London there are quite often transfers between the TCC and the mercantile courts.

3.6.2 A TCC claim may be transferred from the High Court to one of the county courts noted above, and from any county court to the High Court, if the criteria stated in CPR Rule 30.3 are satisfied. In ordinary circumstances, proceedings will be transferred from the TCC in the High Court to the TCC in an appropriate county court if the amount of the claim does not exceed £50,000.

3.6.3 Where no TCC judge is available to deal with a TCC claim which has been issued in a district registry or one of the county courts noted above, the claim may be transferred to another district registry or county court or to the High Court TCC in London (depending upon which court is appropriate).

3.7 Assignment

3.7.1 Where a claim has been issued at or transferred to the TCC at St Dunstan's House in London, the Judge in Charge of the TCC ('the Judge in Charge') shall with the assistance of court staff classify the case either 'HCJ' or 'SCJ'.

(i) If the case is classified 'HCJ', it shall be managed and tried either by the Judge in Charge or by another High Court judge, who will be identified after consultation between the Judge in Charge and the Vice-President of the Queen's Bench Division. The clerical administration of 'HCJ' cases will be carried out by the Case Administration Unit ('CAU') of the TCC at St Dunstan's House. The CAU will also deal with the listing of all applications and trials in such cases.

(ii) If the case is classified 'SCJ', it shall be managed and tried by one of the senior circuit judges, who is a full time TCC judge in London. Cases in the latter category will either (a) be assigned by the Judge in Charge to a specific senior circuit judge or (b) be assigned to a senior circuit judge by operation of the rota. The assigned judge will have primary responsibility for the management of that case.

(iii) Although continuity of judge is regarded as important, it will sometimes be necessary for there to be a change of assigned judge. If no judge is available during the period fixed for trial, then the case may be tried by one of the deputy judges or recorders who has been nominated by the Lord Chancellor under section 68(1) (a) of the Supreme Court Act 1981.

3.7.2 When classifying a case 'HCJ' or 'SCJ', the Judge in Charge will take into account the following matters, as well as all the circumstances of the case:

1. The size and complexity of the case.
2. The nature and importance of any points of law arising.
3. The amount of money which is at stake.
4. Whether the case is one of public importance.
5. Whether the case has an international element or involves overseas parties.
6. The limited number of High Court judges and the needs of other court users, both civil and criminal.

Most TCC cases in London will be classified 'SCJ'. The Judge in Charge may change the classification of any case from 'HCJ' to 'SCJ' or from 'SCJ' to 'HCJ', if it becomes appropriate to do so. There will be a band of cases near the borderline between 'HCJ' and 'SCJ', where the classification will be liable to change depending upon the settlement rate of other cases and the availability of judges.

3.7.3 When proceedings are commenced in, or transferred to, the TCC at St Dunstan's House in London, any party to those proceedings may write to the court setting out matters relevant to classification. Any such letter must be clear and concise. It will seldom need to exceed one page and must never exceed two pages.

3.7.4 When a case has been assigned to a named senior circuit judge in the TCC at St Dunstan's House, all communications to the court about the case (save for communications in respect of fees) shall be made to that judge's clerk. When a TCC case has been assigned to a named High Court judge, all such communications shall be made to the CAU or to the judge's clerk as appropriate. All communications in respect of fees, however, should be sent to the Registry. All statements of case and applications should be marked with the name of the assigned judge.

3.7.5 There are full time TCC judges at Birmingham, Liverpool and Salford (Manchester). There are principal TCC judges at other court centres outside London. TCC cases at these court centres are assigned to judges either (a) by direction of the full time or principal TCC judge or (b) by operation of a rota. It will not generally be appropriate for the Judge in Charge (who is based in London) to consider TCC cases which are commenced in, or transferred to, court centres outside London. Nevertheless, if any TCC case brought in a court centre outside London appears to require management and trial by a High Court judge, then the full time or principal TCC judge at that court centre should refer the case to the Judge in Charge for a decision as to its future management and trial.

3.7.6 When a TCC case has been assigned to a named circuit judge at a court centre other than St Dunstan's House, all communications to the court about the case (save for communications in respect of fees) shall be made to that judge's clerk. All communications in respect of fees should be sent to the relevant registry. All statements of case and applications should be marked with the name of the assigned judge.

SECTION 4 – ACCESS TO THE COURT

4.1 General Approach

4.1.1 There may be a number of stages during the case management phase when the parties will make applications to the court for particular orders: see Section 6 below. There will also be the need for the court to give or vary directions, so as to enable the case to progress to trial.

4.1.2 The court is acutely aware of the costs that may be incurred when both parties prepare for an oral hearing in respect of such interlocutory matters and is always prepared to consider alternative, and less expensive, ways in which the parties may seek the court's assistance.

4.1.3 There are certain stages in the case management phase when it will generally be better for the parties to appear before the assigned judge. Those are identified at Section 4.2 below. But there are other stages, and/or particular applications which a party may wish to make, which could conveniently be dealt with by way of a telephone hearing (Section 4.3 below) or by way of a paper application (Section 4.4 below).

4.2 Hearings in Court

4.2.1 First Case Management Conference. The court will normally require the parties to attend an oral hearing for the purposes of the first Case Management Conference. This is because there may be matters which the judge would wish to raise with the parties arising out of the answers to the case management information sheets and the parties' proposed directions: see section 5.4 below. Even in circumstances where the directions and the case management timetable may be capable of being agreed by the parties and the court, the assigned judge may still wish to consider a range of case management matters face-to-face with the parties, including the possibility of ADR. See paragraphs 7.2.3, 7.3.2, 8.1.3, 11.1, 13.3, 13.4 and 16.3.2 below.

4.2.2 Whilst the previous paragraph sets out the ideal position, it is recognised that in low value cases the benefits of personal attendance might be outweighed by the costs involved. This is particularly so at court centres outside London, where the parties may have to travel substantial distances to court. Ultimately, the question whether personal attendance should be dispensed with at any particular case management conference must be decided by the judge, after considering any representations made and the circumstances of that particular case.

4.2.3 Pre-trial Review. It will normally be helpful for the parties to attend before the judge on a Pre-trial Review ('PTR'). It is always preferable for Counsel or other advocates who will be appearing at the trial to attend the PTR. Again, even if the parties can agree beforehand any outstanding directions and the detailed requirements for the management of the trial, it is still of assistance for the judge to raise matters of detailed trial management with the parties at an oral hearing. In appropriate cases, eg where the amount in issue is disproportionate to the costs of a full trial, the judge may wish to consider with the parties whether there are other ways in which the dispute might be resolved.

4.2.4 Whether or not other interlocutory applications require to be determined at an oral hearing will depend on the nature and effect of the application being made. Disputed applications for interim payments, summary judgment and security for costs will almost always require an oral hearing. Likewise, the resolution of a contested application to enforce an adjudicator's decision will normally be heard orally. At the other end of the scale, applications for extensions of time for the service of pleadings or to comply with other orders of the court can almost always be dealt with by way of a telephone hearing or in writing.

4.3 Telephone Hearings

4.3.1 Depending on the nature of the application and the extent of any dispute between the parties, the Court is content to deal with many case management matters and other interlocutory applications by way of a telephone conference.

4.3.2 Whilst it is not possible to lay down mandatory rules as to what applications should be dealt with in this way (rather than by way of an oral hearing in court), it may be helpful to identify certain situations which commonly arise and which can conveniently be dealt with by way of a telephone conference.

(a) If the location of the court is inconvenient for one or more of the parties, or the value of the claim is low, then the CMC and the PTR could, in the alternative to the procedure set out in Section 4.2 above, take place by way of a telephone conference. The judge's permission for such a procedure would have to be sought in advance.

(b) If the parties are broadly agreed on the orders to be made by the court, but they are in dispute in respect of one or two particular matters, then a telephone hearing is a convenient way in which those outstanding matters can be dealt with by the parties and the assigned judge.

(c) Similarly, specific arguments about costs, once a substantive application has been disposed of, or arguments consequential on a particular judgment or order having been handed down, may also conveniently be dealt with by way of telephone hearing.

(d) Other applications which, depending on their size and importance, may conveniently be dealt with by way of a telephone hearing include limited applications in respect of disclosure and specific applications as to the scope and content of factual or expert evidence exchanged by the parties.

4.3.3 Telephone hearings are not generally suitable for matters which are likely to last for more than an hour, although the judge may be prepared, in an appropriate case, to list a longer application for a telephone hearing.

4.3.4 Practical matters. Telephone hearings can be listed at any time between 8.30 a.m. and 5.30 p.m., subject to the convenience of the parties and the availability of the judge. Any party, who wishes to have an application dealt with by telephone, should make such request by letter or e-mail to the judge's clerk, sending copies to all other parties. Except in cases of urgency, the judge will allow a period of three days for the other parties to comment upon that request before deciding whether to deal with the application by telephone.

4.3.5 If permission is given for a telephone hearing, the court will normally indicate which party is to make all the necessary arrangements. In most cases, it will be the applicant. The procedure to be followed in setting up and holding a telephone hearing is that set out in section 6 of the Practice Direction supplementing CPR Part 23. The party making arrangements for the telephone hearing must ensure that all parties and the judge have a bundle for that hearing with identical pagination.

It is vital that the judge has all the necessary papers, in good time before the telephone conference, in order that it can be conducted efficiently and effectively.

4.4 Paper Applications

4.4.1 CPR rule 23.8 and section 11 of the accompanying Practice Direction enable certain applications to be dealt with in writing. Parties in a TCC case are encouraged to deal with applications in writing, whenever practicable. Applications for both abridgments of time and extensions of time can generally be dealt with in writing, as well as all other variations to existing directions which are wholly or largely agreed. Disputes over particular aspects of disclosure and evidence may also be capable of being resolved in this way.

4.4.2 If a party wishes to make an application to the court, it should ask itself the question: 'Can this application be conveniently dealt with in writing?' If it can, then the party should issue the application and make its (short) written submissions both in support of its application and why it should be dealt with on paper. The application, any supporting evidence and the written submissions should be provided to all parties, as well as the court. These must include a draft of the precise order sought.

4.4.3 The party against whom the application is made, and any other interested party, should respond within 3 days dealing both with the substantive application and the request for it to be dealt with in writing.

4.4.4 The court can then decide whether or not to deal with the application in writing. If the parties are agreed that the court should deal with it in writing, it will be rare for the court to take a different view. If the parties disagree as to whether or not the application should be dealt with in writing, the court can decide that issue and, if it decides to deal with it in writing can go on to resolve the substantive point on the basis of the parties' written submissions.

4.4.5 Further guidance in respect of paper applications is set out in Section 6.7 below.

4.4.6 It is important for the parties to ensure that all documents provided to the court are also provided to all the other parties, so as to ensure that both the court and the parties are working on the basis of the same documentation. The pagination of any bundle which is provided to the court and the parties must be identical.

4.5 E-mail Communications

4.5.1 The general rules relating to communication and filing of documents by e-mail are set out in CPR Part 5, Practice Direction B.

4.5.2 The judges' clerks all have e-mail addresses identified in Appendix D. They welcome communication from the parties electronically. By agreement with the judge's clerk, it may also be possible to provide documents to the Court in this way. However, it should be noted that HM Court Service has imposed a blanket restriction of 2MB on the length of any e-mail, including its attachments. This equates to approximately 40 pages of normal typescript.

4.5.3 Depending on the particular circumstances of an individual trial, the assigned judge may ask for an e-mail contact address for each of the parties and may send e-mail communications to that address. In addition, the judge may provide a direct contact e-mail address so that the parties can communicate directly with him out of court hours. In such circumstances, the judge and the parties should agree the times at which the respective e-mail addresses can be used.

4.5.4 Every e-mail communication to and from the judge must be simultaneously copied to all the other parties.

4.5.5 The procedure for e-mail communication with the court and for filing documents by e-mail is described in the 'E-mail Court User Guidance'. This is available on a website maintained by HM Court Service at: http://www.hmcourts-service.gov.uk/infoabout/email_guidance/index.htm .

4.6 Video Conferencing

4.6.1 In appropriate cases, particularly where there are important matters in dispute and the parties' representatives are a long distance from one another and/or the court, the hearing may be conducted by way of a Video Conference ('VC'). Prior arrangements will be necessary for any such hearing.

4.6.2 In London, a VC can be arranged through the VC suite at the Royal Courts of Justice. However, this facility is popular and will need to be booked well in advance of the hearing. Alternatively, there are a number of other VC suites in the Strand/Fleet Street area which would be suitable. Details of these facilities are available from the judges' clerks.

4.6.3 Outside London, a VC can be arranged at the following TCC courts with the requisite facilities: Birmingham, Bristol, Cardiff, Central London, Chester, Exeter, Leeds, Liverpool, Newcastle-upon-Tyne, Nottingham and Salford (Manchester).

4.7 Contacting the court out of hours

4.7.1 Occasionally it is necessary to contact a TCC judge out of hours. For example, it may be necessary to apply for an injunction to prevent the commencement of building works which will damage adjoining property; or for an order to preserve evidence. A case may have settled and it may be necessary to inform the judge, before he/she spends an evening or a weekend reading the papers.

4.7.2 At St Dunstan's House. RCJ Security has been provided with the telephone numbers and other contact information of all the TCC judges based at St Dunstan's House and of the court manager. If contact is required with a judge out of hours, the initial approach should be to RCJ Security on 0207-947-6000. Security will then contact the judge and/or the court manager and pass on the message or other information. If direct contact with the judge or court manager is required, RCJ Security must be provided with an appropriate contact number. This number will then be passed to the judge and/or the court manager, who will decide whether it is appropriate for him or her to speak directly to the contacting party.

4.7.3 At other court centres. At the Central London Civil Justice Centre and at all court centres outside London there is a court officer who deals with out of hours applications.

SECTION 5 – CASE MANAGEMENT AND THE FIRST CMC

5.1 General

5.1.1 The general approach of the TCC to case management is to give directions at the outset and then throughout the proceedings to serve the overriding objective of dealing with cases justly. The judge to whom the case has been assigned has wide case management powers, which will be exercised to ensure that:

- the real issues are identified early on and remain the focus of the ongoing proceedings;
- a realistic timetable is ordered which will allow for the fair and prompt resolution of the action;
- costs are properly controlled and reflect the value of the issues to the parties and their respective financial positions.

5.1.2 In order to assist the judge in the exercise of his case management functions, the parties will be expected to co-operate with one another at all times. See CPR rule 1.3. Costs sanctions may be applied, if the judge concludes that one party is not reasonably co-operating with the other parties.

5.1.3 A hearing at which the judge gives general procedural directions is a case management conference ('CMC'). CMCs are relatively informal and business-like occasions. Counsel are not robed. Representatives sit when addressing the judge.

5.1.4 The following procedures apply in order to facilitate effective case management:

- Upon commencement of a case in the TCC, it is allocated automatically to the multi-track. The provisions of CPR Part 29 apply to all TCC cases.
- The TCC encourages a structured exchange of proposals and submissions for CMCs in advance of the hearing, so as to enable the parties to respond on an informed basis to proposals made.
- The judges of the TCC operate pro-active case management. In order to avoid the parties being taken by surprise by any judicial initiative, the judge will consider giving prior notification of specific or unusual case management proposals to be raised at a case management conference.

5.1.5 The TCC's aim is to ensure that the trial of each case takes place before the judge who has managed the case since the first CMC. Whilst continuity of judge is not always possible, because of the need to double- or triple-book judges, or because cases can sometimes overrun their estimated length through no fault of the parties, this remains an aspiration of case management within the TCC.

5.2 The Fixing of the First CMC

5.2.1 Where a claim has been started in the TCC, or where it has been transferred into the TCC, paragraph 8.1 of the Part 60 Practice Direction requires the court to fix the first CMC within 14 days of the earliest of

- the filing by the defendant of an acknowledgement of service or
- the filing by the defendant of the defence or
- the date of the order transferring the case to the TCC.

5.2.2 This means that the first CMC takes place relatively early, sometimes before the defendant has filed a defence. However, if, as will usually be the case, the parties have complied with the protocol (Section 2 above) they will have a good idea of each other's respective positions, and an effective CMC can take place. If, on the other hand, there has been a failure to comply with the protocol, or there are other reasons why the issues are not clearly defined at the outset, then it may be important for the judge to be involved at an early stage.

5.2.3 Despite the foregoing considerations, it is sometimes apparent to the parties that it will be more cost effective to postpone the first CMC until after service of the defence or the defences. If any of the parties wishes to delay the first CMC until then, they can write to the judge's clerk explaining why a delayed CMC is appropriate. If such a request is agreed by the other party or parties, it is likely that the judge will grant the request.

5.3 The Case Management Information Sheet and Other Documents

5.3.1 All parties are expected to complete a detailed response to the case management information sheet sent out by the Registry when the case is commenced/transferred. A copy of a blank case management information sheet is attached as Appendix A. It is important that all parts of the form are completed, particularly those sections (eg concerned with estimated costs) that enable the judge to give directions in accordance with the overriding objective.

5.3.2 The Registry will also send out a blank standard directions form to each party. A copy is attached at Appendix B. This sets out the usual directions made on the first CMC. The parties should fill them in, indicating the directions and timetable sought. The parties should return both the questionnaire and the directions form to the court, so that the areas (if any) of potential debate at the CMC can be identified. The parties are encouraged to exchange proposals for directions and the timetable sought, with a view to agreeing the same before the CMC for consideration by the court.

5.3.3 If the case is large or complex, it is helpful for the advocates to prepare a Note to be provided to the judge the day before the CMC which can address the issues in the case, the suggested directions, and the principal areas of dispute between the parties. If such a Note is provided, it is unnecessary for the claimant also to prepare a Case Summary as well.

5.3.4 In smaller cases, a Case Summary for the CMC, explaining briefly the likely issues, can be helpful. Such Case Summaries should be non-contentious and should (if this is possible without incurring disproportionate cost) be agreed between the parties in advance of the hearing.

5.4 Checklist of Matters likely to be considered at the first CMC

5.4.1 The following checklist identifies the matters which the judge is likely to want to consider at the first CMC, although it is not exhaustive:

- The need for, and content of, any further pleadings. This is dealt with in Section 5.5 below.
- The outcome of the Protocol process, and the possible further need for ADR. ADR is dealt with in Section 7 below.
- The desirability of dealing with particular disputes by way of a Preliminary Issue hearing. This is dealt with in Section 8 below.
- Whether the trial should be in stages (eg stage 1 liability and causation, stage 2 quantum). In very heavy cases this may be necessary in order to make the trial manageable. In more modest cases, where the quantum evidence will be extensive, a staged trial may be in the interest of all parties.
- The appropriate orders in respect of the disclosure of documents. This is dealt with in Section 11 below.
- The appropriate orders as to the exchange of written witness statements. This is dealt with in Section 12 below. It should be noted that, although it is normal for evidence-in-chief to be given by way of the written statements in the TCC, the judge may direct that evidence about particular disputes (such as what was said at an important meeting) should be given orally without reference to such statements.
- Whether it is appropriate for the parties to rely on expert evidence and, if so, what disciplines of experts should give evidence, and on what issues. This may be coupled with an order relating to the carrying out of inspections, the obtaining of samples, the conducting of experiments, or the performance of calculations. Considerations relating to expert evidence are dealt with in Section 13 below. The parties must be aware that, in accordance with the overriding objective, the judge will only give the parties permission to rely on expert evidence if it is both necessary and appropriate, and, even then, will wish to ensure that the scope of any such evidence is limited as far as possible.

- In certain cases the possibility of making a costs cap order. See section 16.3 below.
- The appropriate timetable for the taking of the various interlocutory steps noted above, and the fixing of dates for both the PTR and the trial itself (subject to paragraph 5.4.2 below). The parties will therefore need to provide the judge with an estimate for the length of the trial, assuming all issues remain in dispute. Unless there is good reason not to, the trial date will generally be fixed at the first CMC (although this may be more difficult at court centres with only one TCC judge). Therefore, to the extent that there are any relevant concerns as to availability of either witnesses or legal representatives, they need to be brought to the attention of the court on that occasion. The length of time fixed for the trial will depend on the parties' estimates, and also the judge's own view.

If the parties' estimate of trial length subsequently changes, they should inform the clerk of the assigned judge immediately.

5.4.2 The fixing of the trial date at the CMC is usually as a provisional fixture. Therefore no trial fee is payable at this stage. The court should at the same time specify a date upon which the fixture will cease to be 'provisional' and, therefore, the trial fee will become payable. This should ordinarily be two months before the trial date. It should be noted that:

- if the trial fee is not paid within 14 days of the due date, then the whole claim will be struck out: see CPR rule 3.7(1)(a) and (4);
- if the court is notified at least 14 days before the trial date that the case is settled or discontinued, then the trial fee, which has been paid, shall be refunded: see fee 2.2 in Schedule 1 to the Civil Proceedings Fees Order 2004.

For all other purposes other than payment of the trial fee, the provisional date fixed at the CMC shall be regarded as a firm date.

5.4.3 Essentially, the judge's aim at the first CMC is to set down a detailed timetable which, in the majority of cases, will ensure that the parties need not return to court until the PTR.

5.5 Further Pleadings

5.5.1 Defence. If no defence has been served prior to the first CMC, then (except in cases where judgment in default is appropriate) the court will usually make an order for service of the defence within a specified period. The defendant must plead its positive case. Bare denials and non-admissions are, save in exceptional circumstances, unacceptable.

5.5.2 Further Information. If the defendant wants to request further information of the Particulars of Claim, the request should, if possible, be formulated prior to the first CMC, so that it can be considered on that occasion. All requests for further information should be kept within reasonable limits, and concentrate on the important parts of the case.

5.5.3 Reply. A reply to the defence is not always necessary. However, where the defendant has raised a positive defence on a particular issue, it may be appropriate for the claimant to set out in a reply how it answers such a defence.

If the defendant makes a counterclaim, the claimant's defence to counterclaim and its reply (if any) should be in the same document.

5.5.4 Part 20 Claims. The defendant should, at the first CMC, indicate (so far as possible) any Part 20 claims that it is proposing to make, whether against the claimant or any other party. Part 20 claims are required to be pleaded in the same detail as the original claim. They are a very common feature of TCC cases, because the widespread use of sub-contractors in the UK construction industry often makes it necessary to pass claims down a contractual chain. Defendants are encouraged to start any necessary Part 20 proceedings as soon as possible. It is undesirable for applications to join Part 20 defendants, to be made late in the proceedings.

5.6 Scott Schedules

5.6.1 It can sometimes be appropriate for elements of the claim, or any Part 20 claim, to be set out by way of a Scott Schedule. For example, claims involving a final account or numerous alleged defects or items of disrepair, may be best formulated in this way, which then allows for a detailed response from the defendant. Sometimes, even where all the damage has been caused by one event, such as a fire, it can be helpful for the individual items of loss and damage to be set out in a Scott Schedule. The secret of an effective Scott Schedule lies in the information that is to be provided. This is defined by the column headings. The judge may give directions for the relevant column headings for any Schedule ordered by the court. It is important that the defendant's responses to any such Schedule are as detailed as possible. Each party's entries on a Scott Schedule should be supported by a statement of truth.

5.6.2 Nevertheless, before any order is made or agreement is reached for the preparation of a Scott Schedule, both the parties and the court should consider whether this course (a) will genuinely lead to a saving of cost and time or (b) will lead to a wastage of costs and effort (because the Scott Schedule will simply duplicating earlier schedules, pleadings or expert reports). A Scott Schedule should only be ordered by the court, or agreed by the parties, in those cases where it is appropriate and proportionate.

5.6.3 When a Scott Schedule is ordered by the court or agreed by the parties, the format must always be specified. The parties must co-operate in the physical task of preparation. Electronic transfer between the parties of their respective entries in the columns will enable a clear and user-friendly Scott Schedule to be prepared, for the benefit of all involved in the trial.

5.7 Agreement Between the Parties

5.7.1 Many, perhaps most, of the required directions at the first CMC may be agreed by the parties. If so, the judge will endeavour to make orders in the terms which have been agreed, unless he considers that the agreed terms fail to take into account important features of the case as a whole, or the principles of the CPR. The agreed terms will always, at the very least, form the starting-point of the judge's consideration of the orders to be made at the CMC.

5.7.2 The approach outlined in paragraph 5.7.1 above is equally applicable to all other occasions when the parties come before the court with a draft order that is wholly or partly agreed.

5.8 Drawing Up of Orders

5.8.1 Unless the court itself draws up the order, it will direct one party (usually the claimant or applicant) to do so within a specified time. That party must draw up the order and lodge it with the court for approval. Once approved, the order will be stamped by the court and returned to that party for service upon all other parties.

5.9 Further CMC

5.9.1 In an appropriate case, the judge will fix a review CMC, to take place part way through the timetable that has been set down, in order to allow the court to review progress, and to allow the parties to raise any matters arising out of the steps that have been taken up to that point. This will not, however, be ordered automatically.

5.9.2 Each party will be required to give notice in writing to the other parties and the court of any order which it will be seeking at the review CMC, two days in advance of the hearing..

5.10 The Permanent Case Management Bundle

5.10.1 In conjunction with the judge's clerk, the claimant's solicitor is responsible for ensuring that, for the first CMC and at all times thereafter, there is a permanent bundle of copy documents available to the judge, which contains:

- any relevant documents resulting from the Pre-Action Protocol;
- the claim form and all statements of case;
- all orders;
- all completed case management information sheets.

5.10.2 The permanent case management bundle can then be supplemented by the specific documents relevant to any particular application that may be made. Whether these supplementary documents should (a) become a permanent addition to the case management bundle or (b) be set on one side, will depend upon their nature. The permanent case management bundle may remain at court and be marked up by the judge; alternatively, the judge may direct that the permanent case management bundle be maintained at the offices of the claimant's solicitors and provided to the court when required.

SECTION 6 – APPLICATIONS AFTER THE FIRST CMC

6.1 Relevant parts of the CPR

6.1.1 The basic rules relating to all applications that any party may wish to make are set out in CPR Part 23 and its accompanying Practice Directions.

6.1.2 Part 7 of the Practice Direction accompanying CPR Part 60 is also of particular relevance.

6.2 Application Notice

6.2.1 As a general rule, any party to proceedings in the TCC wishing to make an application of any sort must file an application notice (rule 23.3) and serve that application notice on all relevant parties as soon as practicable after it has been filed (rule 23.4). Application notices should be served by the parties, unless (as happens in some court centres outside London) service is undertaken by the court.

6.2.2 The application notice must set out in clear terms what order is sought and, more briefly, the reasons for seeking that order: see rule 23.6.

6.2.3 The application notice must be served at least 3 days before the hearing at which the Court deals with the application: rule 23.7(1). Such a short notice period is only appropriate for the most straight-forward type of application.

6.2.4 Most applications, in particular applications for summary judgment under CPR Part 24 or to strike out a statement of case under CPR rule 3.4, will necessitate a much longer notice period than 3 days. In such cases, it is imperative that the applicant obtain a suitable date and time for the hearing of the application from the assigned judge's clerk before the application notice is issued. The applicant must then serve his application notice and evidence in support sufficiently far ahead of the date fixed for the hearing of the application for there to be time to enable the respondent to serve evidence in response. Save in exceptional circumstances, there should be a minimum period of 10 working days between the service of the notice (and supporting evidence) and the hearing date. If any party considers that there is insufficient time before the hearing of the application or if the time estimate for the application itself is too short, that party must notify the Judge's clerk and the hearing may then be refixed by agreement.

6.2.5 When considering the application notice, the judge may give directions in writing as to the dates for the provision or exchange of evidence and any written submissions or skeleton arguments for the hearing.

6.3 Evidence in Support

6.3.1 The application notice when it is served must be accompanied by all evidence in support: rule 23.7(2).

6.3.2 Unless the CPR expressly requires otherwise, evidence will be given by way of witness statements. Such statements must be verified by a statement of truth signed by the maker of the statement: rule 22.1.

6.4 Evidence in opposition and Evidence in reply

6.4.1 Likewise, any evidence in opposition to the application should, unless the rules expressly provide otherwise, be given by way of witness statement verified by a statement of truth.

6.4.2 It is important to ensure that the evidence in opposition to the application is served in good time before the hearing so as to enable:

- the court to read and note up the evidence;
- the applicant to put in any further evidence in reply that may be considered necessary.

Such evidence should be served at least 5 working days before the hearing.

6.4.3 Any evidence in reply should be served not less than 3 working days before the hearing. Again, if there are disputes as to the time taken or to be taken for the preparation of evidence prior to a hearing, or any other matters in respect of a suitable timetable for that hearing, the court will consider the written positions of both parties and decide such disputes on paper. It will not normally be necessary for either a separate application to be issued or a hearing to be held for such a purpose.

6.4.4 If the hearing of an application has to be adjourned because of delays by one or other of the parties in serving evidence, the court is likely to order that party to pay the costs straight away, and to make a summary assessment of those costs.

6.5 Application Bundle

6.5.1 The bundle for the hearing of anything other than the most simple and straightforward application should consist of:

- the permanent case management bundle (see Section 5.8 above);
- the witness statements provided in support of the application, together with any exhibits;
- the witness statements provided in opposition to the application together with exhibits;
- any witness statements in reply, together with exhibits.

6.5.2 The permanent case management bundle will either be with the court or with the claimant's solicitors, depending on the order made at the first CMC: see paragraph 5.9 above. If it is with the claimant's solicitors, it should be provided to the court not less than 2 working days before the hearing. In any event, a paginated bundle (see paragraph 6.5.4 below) containing any material specific to the application should also be provided to the court not less than 2 working days before the hearing, unless otherwise directed by the judge. A failure to comply with this deadline may result in the adjournment of the hearing, and the costs thrown away being paid by the defaulting party.

6.5.3 In all but the simplest applications, the court will expect the parties to provide skeleton arguments and copies of any authorities to be relied on. The form and content of the skeleton argument is principally a matter for the author, although the judge will expect it to identify the issues that arise on the application, the important parts of the evidence relied on, and the applicable legal principles. For detailed guidance as to the form, content and length of skeleton arguments, please see paragraph 7.11.12 of the Queen's Bench Guide; Appendix 3 of the Chancery Guide; and Appendix 9 of the Commercial Court Guide.

6.5.4 For an application that is estimated to last ½ day or less, the skeleton should be provided no later than 1 pm on the last working day before the hearing. It should be accompanied by photocopies of the authorities relied on.

6.5.5 For an application that is estimated to last more than ½ day, the skeleton should be provided no later than 4 pm one clear working day before the hearing. It should be accompanied by photocopies of the authorities relied on.

6.5.6 The time limits at paragraphs 6.5.4 and 6.5.5 above will be regarded as the latest times by which such skeletons should be provided to the court. Save in exceptional circumstances, no extension to these periods will be permitted.

6.5.7 Pagination. It is generally necessary for there to be a paginated bundle for the hearing. Where the parties have produced skeleton arguments, these should be cross-referred to the bundle page numbers.

6.6 Hearings

6.6.1 Arbitration applications may be heard in private: see CPR rule 62.10. All other applications will be heard in public in accordance with CPR rule 39.2, save where otherwise ordered.

6.6.2 Provided that the application bundle and the skeletons have been lodged in accordance with the time limits set out above, the parties can assume that the court will have a good understanding of the points in issue. However, the court will expect to be taken to particular documents relied on by the parties and will also expect to be addressed on any important legal principles that arise.

6.6.3 It is important that the parties ensure that every application is dealt with in the estimated time period. Since many applications are dealt with on Fridays, it causes major disruption if application hearings are not disposed of within the estimated period. If the parties take too long in making their submissions, the application may be adjourned, part heard, and the Court may impose appropriate costs sanctions.

6.6.4 At the conclusion of the hearing, unless the court itself draws up the order, it will direct the applicant's solicitor to do so within a specified period.

6.7 Paper Applications

6.7.1 Contested applications are usually best disposed of at an oral hearing (either in court or by telephone). However, as noted in Section 4 above, some applications may be suitable for determination on paper. The procedure for dealing with paper applications is outlined in paragraph 4.4 above.

6.7.2 In addition, certain simple applications (particularly in lower value cases) arising out of the management of the proceedings may be capable of being dealt with by correspondence without the need for any formal application or order of the court. This is particularly true of applications to vary procedural orders, which variations are wholly or largely agreed, or proposals to vary the estimated length of the trial. In such cases, the applicant should write to the other parties indicating the nature of its application and to seek their agreement to it. If, however, it emerges that there is an issue to be resolved by the court, then a formal application must be issued and dealt with in the normal manner.

6.8 Consent Orders

6.8.1 Consent Orders may be submitted to the Court in draft for approval and initialling without the need for attendance.

6.8.2 Two copies of the draft order should be lodged, at least one of which should be signed. The copies should be undated.

6.8.3 As noted above, whilst the parties can agree between themselves the orders to be made either at the Case Management Conference or the Pre-Trial Review, it is normally necessary for the Court to consider the case with the parties (either at an oral hearing or by way of a telephone conference) on those occasions in any event.

6.8.4 Generally, when giving directions, the court will endeavour to identify the date by which the relevant step must be taken, and will not simply provide a period during which that task should be performed. The parties should therefore ensure that any proposed consent order also identifies particular dates, rather then periods, by which the relevant steps must be taken.

6.9 Costs

6.9.1 Costs are dealt with generally at Section 16 below.

6.9.2 The costs of any application which took a day or less to be heard and disposed of will be dealt with summarily, unless there is a good reason for the court not to exercise its powers as to the summary assessment of costs.

6.9.3 Accordingly, it is necessary for parties to provide to the court and to one another their draft statements of costs no later than 24 hours before the start of the application hearing. Any costs which are incurred after these draft statements have been prepared, but which have not been allowed for (eg because the hearing has exceeded its anticipated length), can be mentioned at the hearing.

SECTION 7 – ADR

7.1 General

7.1.1 The court will provide encouragement to the parties to use alternative dispute resolution ('ADR') and will, whenever appropriate, facilitate the use of such a procedure. In this Guide, ADR is taken to mean any process through which the parties attempt to resolve their dispute, which is voluntary. In most cases, ADR takes the form of mediation conducted by a neutral mediator. Alternative forms of ADR include formal inter-party negotiations or (occasionally) early neutral evaluations. In an early neutral evaluation either a judge or some other neutral person receives a concise presentation from each party and then states his own evaluation of the case.

7.1.2 Although the TCC is an appropriate forum for the resolution of all IT and construction/engineering disputes, the use of ADR can lead to a significant saving of costs and may result in a settlement which is satisfactory to all parties.

7.1.3 Legal representatives in all TCC cases should ensure that their clients are fully aware of the benefits of ADR and that the use of ADR has been carefully considered prior to the first CMC.

7.2 Timing

7.2.1 ADR may be appropriate before the proceedings have begun or at any subsequent stage.

7.2.2 The TCC Pre-Action Protocol (Section 2 above) itself provides for a type of ADR, because it requires there to be at least one face-to-face meeting between the parties before the commencement of proceedings. At this meeting, there should be sufficient time to discuss and resolve the dispute. As a result of this procedure having taken place, the court will not necessarily grant a stay of proceedings upon demand and it will always need to be satisfied that an adjournment is actually necessary to enable ADR to take place.

7.2.3 However, at the first CMC, the court will want to be addressed on the parties' views as to the likely efficacy of ADR, the appropriate timing of ADR, and the advantages and disadvantages of a short stay of proceedings to allow ADR to take place. Having considered the representations of the parties, the court may order a short stay to facilitate ADR at that stage. Alternatively, the court may simply encourage the parties to seek ADR and allow for it to occur within the timetable for the resolution of the proceedings set down by the court.

7.2.4 At any stage after the first CMC and prior to the commencement of the trial, the court, will, either on its own initiative or if requested to do so by one or both of the parties, consider afresh the likely efficacy of ADR and whether or not a short stay of the proceedings should be granted, in order to facilitate ADR.

7.3 Procedure

7.3.1 In an appropriate case, the court may indicate the type of ADR that it considers suitable, but the decision in this regard must be made by the parties. In most cases, the appropriate ADR procedure will be mediation.

7.3.2 If at any stage in the proceedings the court considers it appropriate, an ADR order in the terms of Appendix E may be made. If such an order is made at the first CMC, the court may go on to give directions for the conduct of the action up to trial (in the event that the ADR fails). Such directions may include provision for a review CMC.

7.3.3 The court will not ordinarily recommend any individual or body to act as mediator or to perform any other ADR procedure. In the event that the parties fail to agree the identity of a mediator or other neutral person pursuant to an order in the terms of Appendix E, the court may select such a person from the lists provided by the parties. To facilitate this process, the court would also need to be furnished with the CV's of each of the individuals on the lists.

7.3.4 Information as to the types of ADR procedures available and the individuals able to undertake such procedures is available from TeCSA, TECBAR, the Civil Mediation Council, and from some TCC court centres outside London.

7.4 Non-Cooperation

7.4.1 Generally. At the end of the trial, there may be costs arguments on the basis that one or more parties unreasonably refused to take part in ADR. The court will determine such issues having regard to all the circumstances of the particular case. In *Halsey v Milton Keynes General NHS Trust* [2004] EWCA Civ 576; [2004] 1 WLR 3002, the Court of Appeal identified six factors that may be relevant to any such consideration:

a) the nature of the dispute;
b) the merits of the case;
c) the extent to which other settlement methods have been attempted;
d) whether the costs of the ADR would be disproportionately high;
e) whether any delay in setting up and attending the ADR would have been prejudicial;
f) whether the ADR had a reasonable prospect of success.

7.4.2 If an ADR Order Has Been Made. The court will expect each party to co-operate fully with any ADR which takes place following an order of the court. If any other party considers that there has not been proper co-operation in relation to arrangements for the mediation, the complaint will be considered by the court and cost orders and/or other sanctions may be ordered against the defaulting party in consequence. However, nothing in this paragraph should be understood as modifying the rights of all parties to a mediation to keep confidential all that is said or done in the course of that mediation.

7.5 Early Neutral Evaluation

7.5.1 An early neutral evaluation ('ENE') may be carried out by any appropriately qualified person, whose opinion is likely to be respected by the parties. In an appropriate case, and with the consent of all parties, a TCC judge may provide an early neutral evaluation either in respect of the full case or of particular issues arising within it. Such an ENE will not, save with the agreement of the parties, be binding on the parties.

7.5.2 If the parties would like an ENE to be carried out by the court, then they can seek an appropriate order from the assigned judge either at the first CMC or at any time prior to the commencement of the trial.

7.5.3 The assigned judge may choose to do the ENE himself. In such instance, the judge will take no further part in the proceedings once he has produced the ENE, unless the parties expressly agree otherwise. Alternatively, the assigned judge will select another available TCC judge to undertake the ENE.

7.5.4 The judge undertaking the ENE will give appropriate directions for the preparation and conduct of the ENE. This may include a stay of the substantive proceedings whilst the ENE is carried out. The ENE may be carried out entirely on paper. Alternatively, there may be an oral hearing (either with or without evidence). The parties should agree whether the entire ENE procedure is to be without prejudice, or whether it can be referred to at any subsequent trial or hearing.

SECTION 8 – PRELIMINARY ISSUES

8.1 General

8.1.1 The hearing of Preliminary Issues ('PI'), at which the court considers and delivers a binding judgment on particular issues in advance of the main trial, can be an extremely cost-effective and efficient way of narrowing the issues between the parties and, in certain cases, of resolving disputes altogether.

8.1.2 Some cases listed in the TCC lend themselves particularly well to this procedure. A PI hearing can address particular points which may be decisive of the whole proceedings; even if that is not the position, it is often possible for a PI hearing to cut down significantly on the scope (and therefore the costs) of the main trial.

8.1.3 At the first CMC the court will expect to be addressed on whether or not there are matters which should be taken by way of Preliminary Issues in advance of the main trial. Subject to paragraph 8.5 below, it is not generally appropriate for the court to make an order for the trial of preliminary issues until after the defence has been served. After the first CMC, and at any time during the litigation, any party is at liberty to raise with any other party the possibility of a PI hearing and the court will consider any application for the hearing of such Preliminary Issues. In many cases, although not invariably, a PI order will be made with the support of all parties.

8.1.4 Whilst, for obvious reasons, it is not possible to set out hard and fast rules for what is and what is not suitable for a PI hearing, the criteria set out in Section 8.2 below should assist the parties in deciding whether or not some or all of the disputes between them will be suitable for a PI hearing.

8.1.5 Drawbacks of preliminary issues in inappropriate cases. If preliminary issues are ordered inappropriately, they can have adverse effect. Evidence may be duplicated. The same witnesses may give evidence before different judges, in the event that there is a switch of assigned judge. Findings may be made at the PI hearing, which are affected by evidence called at the main hearing. The prospect of a PI hearing may delay the commencement of ADR or settlement negotiations. Also two trials are more expensive than one. For all these reasons, any proposal for preliminary issues needs to be examined carefully, so that the benefits and drawbacks can be evaluated. Also the court should give due weight to the views of the parties when deciding whether a PI hearing would be beneficial.

8.1.6 Staged trials. The breaking down of a long trial into stages should be differentiated from the trial of preliminary issues. Sometimes it is sensible for liability (including causation) to be tried before quantum of damages. Occasionally the subject matter of the litigation is so extensive that for reasons of case management the trial needs to be broken down into separate stages.

8.2 Guidelines

8.2.1 The Significance of the Preliminary Issues. The court would expect that any issue proposed as a suitable PI would, if decided in a particular way, be capable of:

- resolving the whole proceedings or a significant element of the proceedings; or
- significantly reducing the scope, and therefore the costs, of the main trial; or
- significantly improving the possibility of a settlement of the whole proceedings.

8.2.2 Oral Evidence. The court would ordinarily expect that, if issues are to be dealt with by way of a PI hearing, there would be either no or relatively limited oral evidence. If extensive oral evidence was required on any proposed PI, then it may not be suitable for a PI hearing. Although it is difficult to give specific guidance on this point, it is generally considered that a PI hearing in a smaller case should not take more than about 2 days, and in a larger and more complex case, should not take more than about 4 days.

8.3 Common Types of Preliminary Issue

The following are commonly resolved by way of a PI hearing:

(a) Disputes as to whether or not there was a binding contract between the parties.
(b) Disputes as to what documents make up or are incorporated within the contract between the parties and disputes as to the contents or relevance of any conversations relied on as having contractual status or effect.
(c) Disputes as to the proper construction of the contract documents or the effect of an exclusion or similar clause.
(d) Disputes as to the correct application of a statute or binding authority to a situation where there is little or no factual dispute.
(e) Disputes as to the existence and/or scope of a statutory duty.
(f) Disputes as to the existence and/or scope of a duty of care at common law in circumstances where there is no or little dispute about the relevant facts.

8.4 Other Possible Preliminary Issues

The following can sometimes be resolved by way of a preliminary issue hearing, although a decision as to whether or not to have such a hearing will always depend on the facts of the individual case:

8.4.1 A Limitation Defence. It is often tempting to have limitation issues resolved in advance of the main trial. This can be a good idea because, if a complex claim is statute-barred, a decision to that effect will lead to a significant saving of costs. However, there is also a risk that extensive evidence relevant to the limitation defence (relating to matters such as when the damage occurred or whether or not there has been deliberate concealment) may also be relevant to the liability issues within the main trial. In such a case, a preliminary issue hearing may lead to a) extensive duplication of evidence and therefore costs and b) give rise to difficulty if the main trial is heard by a different judge.

8.4.2 Causation and 'No Loss' Points. Causation and 'No Loss' points may be suitable for a PI hearing, but again their suitability will diminish if it is necessary for the court to resolve numerous factual disputes as part of the proposed PI hearing. The most appropriate disputes of this type for a PI hearing are those where the defendant contends that, even accepting all the facts alleged by the claimant, the claim must fail by reason of causation or the absence of recoverable loss.

8.4.3 'One-Off' Issues. Issues which do not fall into any obvious category, like economic duress, or misrepresentation, may be suitable for resolution by way of a PI hearing, particularly if the whole case can be shown to turn on them.

8.5 Use of PI as an adjunct to ADR

8.5.1 Sometimes parties wish to resolve their dispute by ADR, but there is one major issue which is a sticking point in any negotiation or mediation. The parties may wish to obtain the court's decision on that single issue, in the expectation that after that they can resolve their differences without further litigation.

8.5.2 In such a situation the parties may wish to bring proceedings under CPR Part 8, in order to obtain the court's decision on that issue. Such proceedings can be rapidly progressed. Alternatively, if the issue is not suitable for Part 8 proceedings, the parties may bring proceedings under Part 7 and then seek determination of the critical question as a preliminary issue. At the first CMC the position can be explained and the judge can be asked to order early trial of the proposed preliminary issue, possibly without the need for a defence or any further pleadings.

8.6 Precise Wording of PI

8.6.1 If a party wishes to seek a PI hearing, either at the first CMC or thereafter, that party must circulate a precise draft of the proposed preliminary issues to the other parties and to the court well in advance of the relevant hearing.

8.6.2 If the court orders a PI hearing, it is likely to make such an order only by reference to specific and formulated issues, in order to avoid later debate as to the precise scope of the issues that have been ordered. Of course, the parties are at liberty to propose amendments to the issues before the PI hearing itself, but if such later amendments are not agreed by all parties, they are unlikely to be ordered.

8.7 Appeals

8.7.1 When considering whether or not to order a PI hearing, the court will take into account the effect of any possible appeal against the PI judgment, and the concomitant delay caused.

8.7.2 At the time of ordering preliminary issues, both the parties and the court should specifically consider whether, in the event of an appeal against the PI judgment, it is desirable that the trial of the main action should (a) precede or (b) follow such appeal. It should be noted, however, that the first instance court has no power to control the timetable for an appeal. A first instance court's power to extend time under CPR rule 52.4(2) (a) for filing an appellant's notice is effectively limited to 14 days (see paragraph 5.19 of the Practice direction supplementing Part 52). The question whether an appeal should be (a) expedited or (b) stayed is entirely a matter for the Court of Appeal. Nevertheless, the Court of Appeal will take notice of any 'indication' given by the lower court in this regard.

SECTION 9 – ADJUDICATION BUSINESS

9.1 Introduction

9.1.1 The TCC is ordinarily the court in which the enforcement of an adjudicator's decision and any other business connected with adjudication is undertaken. Adjudicators' decisions predominantly arise out of adjudications which are governed by the mandatory provisions of the Housing Grants, Construction and Regeneration Act 1996 ('HGCRA'). These provisions apply automatically to any construction contract as defined in the legislation. Some Adjudicators' decisions arise out of standard form contracts which contain adjudication provisions, and others arise from ad-hoc agreements to adjudicate. The TCC enforcement procedure is the same for all three kinds of adjudication.

9.1.2 In addition to enforcement applications, declaratory relief is sometimes sought in the TCC at the outset of an adjudication in respect of matters such as the jurisdiction of the adjudicator or the validity of the adjudication. This kind of application is dealt with in Paragraph 9.4 below.

9.1.3 The HGCRA provides for a mandatory 28-day period within which the entire adjudication process must be completed, unless a) the referring party agrees to an additional 14 days, or b) both parties agree to a longer period. In consequence, the TCC has moulded a rapid procedure for enforcing an adjudication decision that has not been honoured. Other adjudication proceedings are ordinarily subject to similar rapidity.

9.2 Procedure In Enforcement Proceedings

9.2.1 Unlike arbitration business, there is neither a practice direction nor a claim form concerned with adjudication business. The enforcement proceedings normally seek a monetary judgment so that CPR Part 7 proceedings are usually appropriate. However, if the enforcement proceedings are known to raise a question which is unlikely to involve a substantial dispute of fact and no monetary judgment is sought, CPR Part 8 proceedings may be used instead.

9.2.2 The TCC has fashioned a procedure whereby enforcement applications are dealt with promptly. The details of this procedure are set out below.

9.2.3 The claim form should identify the construction contract, the jurisdiction of the adjudicator, the procedural rules under which the adjudication was conducted, the adjudicator's decision, the relief sought and the grounds for seeking that relief.

9.2.4 The claim form should be accompanied by an application notice that sets out the procedural directions that are sought. Commonly, the claimant's application will seek an abridgement of time for the various procedural steps, and summary judgment under CPR Part 24. The claim form and the application should be accompanied by a witness statement or statements setting out the evidence relied on in support of both the adjudication enforcement claim and the associated procedural application. This evidence should ordinarily include a copy of the adjudicator's decision.

9.2.5 The claim form, application notice and accompanying documents should be lodged in the appropriate registry or court centre clearly marked as being a 'paper without notice adjudication enforcement claim and application for the urgent attention of a TCC judge'. The parties will be informed that the enforcement proceedings will be assigned to a named judge. That judge will then manage the proceedings up to and including any hearing. He will ordinarily provide his directions made in connection with the procedural application within 3 working days of the receipt of the application notice at the courts.

9.2.6 The procedural application is dealt with by a TCC judge on paper, without notice. The paper application and the consequent directions should deal with:

(a) the abridged period of time in which the defendant is to file an acknowledgement of service;
(b) the time for service by the defendant of any witness statement in opposition to the relief being sought;
(c) an early return date for the hearing of the summary judgment application and a note of the time required or allowed for that hearing; and
(d) identification of the judgment, order or other relief being sought at the hearing of the adjudication claim.

The order made at this stage will always give the defendant liberty to apply.

9.2.7 A direction providing for a date by which the claim form, supporting evidence and court order providing for the hearing are to be served on the defendant should ordinarily also be given when the judge deals with the paper procedural application.

9.2.8 The directions will ordinarily provide for an enforcement hearing within 28 days of the directions being made and for the defendant to be given at least 14 days from the date of service for the serving of any evidence in opposition to the adjudication application. In more straightforward cases, the abridged periods may be less.

9.2.9 Draft standard directions of the kind commonly made by the court on a procedural application by the claimant in an action to enforce the decision of an adjudicator are attached as Appendix F.

9.2.10 The claimant should, with the application, provide an estimate of the time needed for the hearing of the application. This estimate will be taken into account by the judge when fixing the date and length of the hearing. The parties should, if possible jointly, communicate any revised time estimate to the court promptly and the judge to whom the case has been allocated will consider whether to refix the hearing date or alter the time period that has been allocated for the hearing.

9.2.11 If the parties cannot agree on the date or time fixed for the hearing, a paper application must be made to the judge to whom the hearing has been allocated for directions.

9.3 The Enforcement Hearing

9.3.1 Where there is any dispute to be resolved at the hearing, the judge should be provided with copies of the relevant sections of the HGCRA, the adjudication procedural rules under which the adjudication was conducted, the adjudicator's decision and copies of any adjudication provisions in the contract underlying the adjudication.

9.3.2 The parties should lodge, 24 hours before the hearing, a bundle containing the documents that will be required at the hearing, copies of any authorities which are to be relied on and short skeletons summarising their respective contentions as to why the adjudicator's decision is or is not enforceable or as to any other relief being sought.

9.3.3 The parties should be ready to address the court on the limited grounds on which a defendant may resist an application seeking to enforce an adjudicator's decision or on which a court may provide any other relief to any party in relation to an adjudication or an adjudicator's decision.

9.4 Other Proceedings Arising Out Of Adjudication

9.4.1 As noted above, the TCC will also hear any applications for declaratory relief arising out of the commencement of a disputed adjudication. Commonly, these will concern:

a) Disputes over the jurisdiction of an adjudicator. It can sometimes be appropriate to seek a declaration as to jurisdiction at the outset of an adjudication, rather than both parties incurring considerable costs in the adjudication itself, only for the jurisdiction point to emerge again at the enforcement hearing.
b) Disputes over whether there is a written contract between the parties or, in appropriate cases, whether there is a construction contract within the meaning of the Act.
c) Disputes over the permissible scope of the adjudication, and, in particular, whether the matters which the claimant seeks to raise in the adjudication are the subject of a pre-existing dispute between the parties.

9.4.2 Any such application will be immediately assigned to a named judge. In such circumstances, given the probable urgency of the application, the judge will usually require the parties to attend a CMC within 2 working days of the assignment of the case to him, and he will then give the necessary directions to ensure the speedy resolution of the dispute.

9.4.3 It sometimes happens that one party to an adjudication commences enforcement proceedings, whilst the other commences proceedings under Part 8, in order to challenge the validity of the adjudicator's award. This duplication of effort is unnecessary and it involves the parties in extra costs, especially if the two actions are commenced at different court centres. Accordingly there should be sensible discussions between the parties or their lawyers, in order to agree the appropriate venue and also to agree who shall be claimant and who defendant. All the issues raised by each party can and should be raised in a single action.

SECTION 10 – ARBITRATION

10.1 Arbitration Claims in the TCC

10.1.1 'Arbitration claims' are any application to the court under the Arbitration Act 1996 and any other claim concerned with an arbitration that is referred to in CPR 62.2(1). Common examples of arbitration claims are challenges to an award on grounds of jurisdiction under section 67, challenges to an award for serious irregularity under section 68 or appeals on points of law under section 69 of the Arbitration Act 1996. Arbitration claims may be started in the TCC, as is provided for in paragraph 2.3 of the Practice Direction – Arbitration which supplements CPR Part 62.

10.1.2 In practice, arbitration claims arising out of or connected with a construction or engineering arbitration (or any other arbitration where the subject matter involved one or more of the categories of work set out in paragraph 1.3.1 above) should be started in the TCC. The only arbitration claims that must be started in the Commercial Court are those (increasingly rare) claims to which the old law (ie the pre-1996 Act provisions) apply: see CPR rule 62.12.

10.1.3 The TCC follows the practice and procedure for arbitration claims established by CPR Part 62 and (broadly) the practice of the Commercial Court as summarised by Section O of the Admiralty and Commercial Court Guide. In the absence of any specific directions given by the court, the automatic directions set out in section 6 of the Practice Direction supplementing CPR Part 62 govern the procedures to be followed in any arbitration claim from the date of service up to the substantive hearing.

10.2 Leave to appeal

10.2.1 Where a party is seeking to appeal a question of law arising out of an award pursuant to section 69 of the Arbitration Act 1996 and the parties have not in their underlying contract agreed that such an appeal may be brought, the party seeking to appeal must apply for leave to appeal pursuant to sections 69(2), 69(3) and 69(4) of that Act. That application must be included in the arbitration claim form as explained in paragraph 12 of the Practice Direction.

10.2.2 In conformity with the practice of the Commercial Court, the TCC will normally consider any application for permission to appeal on paper after the defendant has had an appropriate opportunity to answer in writing the application being raised.

10.2.3 The claimant must include within the claim form an application for permission to appeal . No separate application notice is required.

10.2.4 The claim form and supporting documents must be served on the defendant. The judge will not consider the application for permission to appeal until (a) a certificate of service has been filed at the appropriate TCC registry or court centre and (b) a further 28 days have elapsed, so as to enable the defendant to file written evidence in opposition. Save in exceptional circumstances, the only material admissible on an application for permission to appeal is (a) the award itself and any documents annexed to the award and (b) evidence relevant to the issue whether any identified question of law is of general public importance.

10.2.5 If necessary, the judge dealing with the application will direct an oral hearing with a date for the hearing. That hearing will, ordinarily, consist of brief submissions by each party. The judge dealing with the application will announce his decision in writing or, if a hearing has been directed, at the conclusion of the hearing with brief reasons if the application is refused.

10.2.6 Where the permission has been allowed in part and refused in part:

(a) Only those questions for which permission has been granted may be raised at the hearing of the appeal.
(b) Brief reasons will be given for refusing permission in respect of the other questions.

10.2.7 If the application is granted, the judge will fix the date for the appeal, and direct whether the same judge or a different judge shall hear the appeal.

10.3 Appeals where leave to appeal is not required

10.3.1 Parties to a construction contract should check whether they have agreed in the underlying contract that an appeal may be brought without leave, since some construction and engineering standard forms of contract so provide. If that is the case, the appeal may be set down for a substantive hearing without leave being sought. The arbitration claim form should set out the clause or provision which it is contended provides for such agreement and the claim form should be marked 'Arbitration Appeal – Leave not required'.

10.3.2 Where leave is not required, the claimant should identify each question of law that it is contended arises out of the award and which it seeks to raise in an appeal under section 69. If the defendant does not accept that the questions thus identified are questions of law or maintains that they do not arise out of the award or that the appeal on those questions may not be brought for any other reason, then the defendant should notify the claimant and the court of its contentions and apply for a directions hearing before the judge nominated to hear the appeal on a date prior to the date fixed for the hearing of the appeal. Unless the judge hearing the appeal otherwise directs, the appeal will be confined to the questions of law identified in the arbitration claim form.

10.3.3 In an appropriate case, the judge may direct that the question of law to be raised and decided on the appeal should be reworded, so as to identify more accurately the real legal issue between the parties.

10.4 The hearing of the appeal

10.4.1 Parties should ensure that the court is provided only with material that is relevant and admissible to the point of law. Again, save in exceptional circumstances, this will be limited to the award and any documents annexed to the award: see *Hok Sport Ltd v Aintree Racecourse Ltd* [2003] BLR 155 at 160.

10.4.2 On receiving notice of permission being granted, or on issuing an arbitration claim form in a case where leave to appeal is not required, the parties should notify the court of their joint estimate or differing estimates of the time needed for the hearing of the appeal.

10.4.3 The hearing of the appeal is to be in open court unless an application (with notice) has previously been made that the hearing should be wholly or in part held in private and the court has directed that this course should be followed.

10.5 Section 68 applications – Serious Irregularity

10.5.1 In some arbitration claims arising out of construction and engineering arbitrations, a party will seek to appeal a question of law and, at the same time, seek to challenge the award under section 68 of the Arbitration Act 1996 on the grounds of serious irregularity. This raises questions of procedure, since material may be admissible in a section 68 application which is inadmissible on an application or appeal under section 69. Similarly, it may not be appropriate for all applications to be heard together. A decision is needed as to the order in which the applications should be heard, whether there should be one or more separate hearings to deal with them and whether or not the same judge should deal with all applications. Where a party intends to raise applications under both sections of the Arbitration Act 1996, they should be issued in the same arbitration claim form or in separate claim forms issued together. The court should be informed that separate applications are intended and asked for directions as to how to proceed.

10.5.2 The court will give directions as to how the section 68 and section 69 applications will be dealt with before hearing or determining any application. These directions will normally be given in writing but, where necessary or if such is applied for by a party, the court will hold a directions hearing at which directions will be given. The directions will be given following the service of any documentation by the defendant in answer to all applications raised by the claimant.

10.6 Successive awards and successive applications

10.6.1 Some construction and engineering arbitrations give rise to two or more separate awards issued at different times. Where arbitration applications arise under more than one of these awards, any second or subsequent application, whether arising from the same or a different award, should be referred to the same judge who has heard previous applications. Where more than one judge has heard previous applications, the court should be asked to direct to which judge any subsequent application is to be referred.

10.7 Other applications and Enforcement

10.7.1 All other arbitration claims, and any other matter arising in an appeal or an application concerning alleged serious irregularity, will be dealt with by the TCC in the same manner as is provided for in CPR Part 62, Practice Direction – Arbitration and Section O of The Admiralty and Commercial Courts Guide.

10.7.2 All applications for permission to enforce arbitration awards are governed by Section III of Part 62 (rules 62.17- 62.19).

10.7.3 An application for permission to enforce an award in the same manner as a judgment or order of the court may be made in an arbitration claim form without notice and must be supported by written evidence in accordance with rule 62.18(6). Two copies of the draft order must accompany the application, and the form of the order sought must correspond to the terms of the award.

10.7.4 An order made without notice giving permission to enforce the award:

(a) must give the defendant 14 days after service of the order (or longer, if the order is to be served outside the jurisdiction) to apply to set it aside;
(b) must state that it may not be enforced until after the expiry of the 14 days (or any longer period specified) or until any application to set aside the order has been finally disposed of: rule 62.18(9) and(10).

10.7.5 On considering an application to enforce without notice, the judge may direct that, instead, the arbitration claim form must be served on specified parties, with the result that the application will then continue as an arbitration claim in accordance with the procedure set out in Section I of Part 62: see rule 62.18(1)–(3).

SECTION 11 – DISCLOSURE

11.1 Standard Disclosure

11.1.1 The appropriate disclosure and inspection orders to be made will normally be considered and made at the first case management conference. This is governed by CPR Part 31 and the Practice Direction supplementing it. This procedure provides for standard disclosure, being disclosure and inspection in accordance with CPR Part 31 of:

(a) the documents upon which a party relies;
(b) the documents which adversely affect his or another party's case or support another party's case; and
(c) the documents which a party is required to disclose by any relevant practice direction.

11.2 Limiting disclosure and the cost of disclosure

11.2.1 In many cases being conducted in the TCC, standard disclosure will not be appropriate. This may for any one or more of the following reasons:

(a) The amount of documentation may be considerable, given the complexity of the dispute and the underlying contract or contracts, and the process of giving standard disclosure may consequently be disproportionate to the issues and sums in dispute.
(b) The parties may have many of the documents in common from their previous dealings so that disclosure is not necessary or desirable.

(c) The parties may have provided informal disclosure and inspection of the majority of these documents, for example when complying with the pre-action Protocol.
(d) The cost of providing standard disclosure may be disproportionate.

In such cases, the parties should seek to agree upon a more limited form of disclosure or to dispense with formal disclosure altogether. Such an agreement could limit disclosure to specified categories of documents or to such documents as may be specifically applied for.

11.2.2 Where disclosure is to be provided, the parties should consider whether it is necessary for lists of documents to be prepared or whether special arrangements should be agreed as to the form of listing and identifying disclosable documents, the method, timing and location of inspection and the manner of copying or providing copies of documents. Where documents are scattered over several locations, or are located overseas or are in a foreign language, special arrangements will also need to be considered. Thought should also be given to providing disclosure in stages or to reducing the scope of disclosure by providing the relevant material in other forms.

11.2.3 Electronic data and documents give rise to particular problems as to searching, preserving, listing, inspecting and other aspects of discovery and inspection. These problems should be considered and, if necessary made the subject of special directions. Furthermore, in appropriate cases, disclosure, inspection and the provision of copies of hard copies may be undertaken using information technology. Attention is drawn to the relevant provisions in CPR Part 31, to the Admiralty and Commercial Courts Guide concerned with Electronic Disclosure, and to the TeCSA IT Protocol which provide guidance in relation to these matters. In appropriate cases the TCC will order that the provisions concerning electronic disclosure contained in section E of the Admiralty and Commercial Courts Guide shall apply.

11.2.4 All these matters should be agreed between the parties. If it is necessary to raise any of these matters with the court they should be raised, if possible, at the first CMC. If points arise on disclosure after the first CMC, they may well be capable of being dealt with by the court on paper.

11.3 Service using information technology

11.3.1 The parties should consult with each other before the first CMC with a view to arranging the service and (where required) filing of pleadings, schedules, witness statements, experts' reports, disclosure lists and other documents in computer readable form as well as in hard copy. The parties should also consider whether to maintain a common running index, so that every document which has been exchanged between the parties has a unique reference number. Any agreement reached on these matters should be recorded and made the subject of an order for directions. Where agreement is not possible, the parties should raise these matters for decision at a CMC.

SECTION 12 – WITNESS STATEMENTS AND FACTUAL EVIDENCE FOR USE AT TRIAL

12.1 Witness statements

12.1.1 Witness statements should be prepared generally in accordance with CPR Part 22.1 (documents verified by a statement of truth) and CPR Part 32 (provisions governing the evidence of witnesses) and their practice directions, particularly paragraphs 17 to 22 of the Practice Direction supplementing CPR Part 32.

12.1.2 Unless otherwise directed by the court, witness statements should not have annexed to them copies of other documents and should not reproduce or paraphrase at length passages from other documents. The only exception arises where a specific document needs to be annexed to the statement in order to make that statement reasonably intelligible.

12.1.3 When preparing witness statements, attention should be paid to the following matters:

- (a) Even when prepared by a legal representative or other professional, the witness statement should be, so far as practicable, in the witness's own words.
- (b) The witness statement should indicate which matters are within the witness's own knowledge and which are matters of information and belief. Where the witness is stating matters of hearsay or of either information or belief, the source of that evidence should also be stated.
- (c) The witness statement must include a statement by the witness that he believes the facts stated to be true.
- (d) A witness statement should be no longer than necessary and should not be argumentative.

12.2 Other matters concerned with witness statements

12.2.1 Foreign language. If a witness is not sufficiently fluent in English to give his evidence in English, the witness statement should be in his or her own language and an authenticated translation provided. Where the witness has a broken command of English, the statement may be drafted by others so as to express the witness's evidence as accurately as possible. In that situation, however, the witness statement should indicate that this process of interpolation has occurred and also should explain the extent of the witness's command of English and how and to what parts of the witness statement the process of interpolation has occurred.

12.2.2 Reluctant witness. Sometimes a witness is unwilling or not permitted or is unavailable to provide a witness statement before the trial. The party seeking to adduce this evidence should comply with the provisions of CPR rule 32.9 concerned with the provision of witness summaries.

12.2.3 Hearsay. Parties should keep in mind the need to give appropriate notice of their intention to rely on hearsay evidence or the contents of documents without serving a witness statement from their maker or from the originator of the evidence contained in those documents. The appropriate procedure is contained in CPR rules 33.1–33.5.

12.3 Cross-referencing

12.3.1 Where a substantial number of documents will be adduced in evidence or contained in the trial bundles, it is of considerable assistance to the court and to all concerned if the relevant page references are annotated in the margins of the copy witness statements. It is accepted that this is a time-consuming exercise, the need for which will be considered at the PTR, and it will only be ordered where it is both appropriate and proportionate to do so. See further paragraphs 14.5.1 and 15.2.3 below.

12.4 Video link

12.4.1 If any witness (whose witness statement has been served and who is required to give oral evidence) is located outside England and Wales or would find a journey to court inconvenient or impracticable, his evidence might be given via a video link. Thought should be given before the PTR to the question whether this course would be appropriate and proportionate. Such evidence is regularly received by the TCC and facilities for its reception, whether in appropriate court premises or at a convenient venue outside the court building, are now readily available.

12.4.2 Any application for a video link direction and any question relating to the manner in which such evidence is to be given should be dealt with at the PTR. Attention is drawn to the Video-conferencing Protocol set out at Annex 3 to the Practice Direction – Witness Evidence. The procedure described in Annex 3 is followed by the TCC.

SECTION 13 – EXPERT EVIDENCE

13.1 Nature of expert evidence

13.1.1 Expert evidence is evidence as to matters of a technical or scientific nature and will generally include the opinions of the expert. The quality and reliability of expert evidence will depend upon (a) the experience and the technical or scientific qualifications of the expert and (b) the accuracy of the factual material that is used by the expert for his assessment. Expert evidence is dealt with in detail in CPR Part 35 ('Experts and Assessors') and in the Practice Direction supplementing Part 35. Particular attention should be paid to all these provisions, given the detailed reliance on expert evidence in most TCC actions. Particular attention should also be paid to the 'Protocol for the instruction of experts to give evidence in civil claims' published by the Civil Justice Council in June 2005. This protocol has been approved by the Master of the Rolls.

13.1.2 The provisions in CPR Part 35 are concerned with the terms upon which the court may receive expert evidence. These provisions are principally applicable to independently instructed expert witnesses. In cases where a party is a professional or a professional has played a significant part in the subject matter of the action, opinion evidence will almost inevitably be included in the witness statements. Any points arising from such evidence (if they cannot be resolved by agreement) can be dealt with by the judge on an application or at the PTR.

13.2 Control of expert evidence

13.2.1 Expert evidence is frequently needed and used in TCC cases. Experts are often appointed at an early stage. Most types of case heard in the TCC involve more than one expertise and some, even when the dispute is concerned with relatively small sums, involve several different experts. Such disputes include those concerned with building failures and defects, delay and disruption, dilapidations, subsidence caused by tree roots and the supply of software systems. However, given the cost of preparing such evidence, the parties and the court must, from the earliest pre-action phase of a dispute until the conclusion of the trial, seek to make effective and proportionate use of experts. The scope of any expert evidence must be limited to what is necessary for the requirements of the particular case.

13.2.2 At the first CMC, or thereafter, the court may be asked to determine whether the cost of instructing experts is proportionate to the amount at issue in the proceedings, and the importance of the case to the parties. In dealing with any issues of proportionality, the court should be provided with estimates of the experts' costs.

13.2.3 The parties should also be aware that the court has the power to limit the amount of the expert's fees that a party may recover pursuant to CPR 35.4(4).

13.3 Prior to and at the first CMC

13.3.1 There is an unresolved tension arising from the need for parties to instruct and rely on expert opinions from an early pre-action stage and the need for the court to seek, wherever possible, to reduce the cost of expert evidence by dispensing with it altogether or by encouraging the appointment of jointly instructed experts. This tension arises because the court can only consider directing joint appointments or limiting expert evidence long after a party may have incurred the cost of obtaining expert evidence and have already relied on it. Parties should be aware of this tension. So far as possible, the parties should avoid incurring the costs of expert evidence on uncontroversial matters or matters of the kind referred to in paragraph 13.4.3 below, before the first CMC has been held.

13.3.2 In cases where it is not appropriate for the court to order a single joint expert, it is imperative that, wherever possible, the parties' experts co-operate fully with one another. This is particularly important where tests, surveys, investigations, sample gathering or other technical methods of obtaining primary factual evidence are needed. It is often critical to ensure that any laboratory testing or experiments are carried out by the experts together, pursuant to an agreed procedure. Alternatively, the respective experts may agree that a particular firm or laboratory shall carry out specified tests or analyses on behalf of all parties.

13.3.3 Parties should, where possible, disclose initial or preliminary reports to opposing parties prior to any pre-action protocol meeting, if only on a without prejudice basis. Such early disclosure will assist in early settlement or mediation discussions and in helping the parties to define and confine the issues in dispute with a corresponding saving in costs.

13.3.4 Before and at the first CMC and at each subsequent pre-trial stage of the action, the parties should give careful thought to the following matters:

(a) The number, disciplines and identity of the expert witnesses they are considering instructing as their own experts or as single joint experts.

(b) The precise issues which each expert is to address in his/her reports, to discuss without prejudice with opposing parties' experts and give evidence about at the trial.
(c) The timing of any meeting, agreed statement or report.
(d) Any appropriate or necessary tests, inspections, sampling or investigations that could be undertaken jointly or in collaboration with other experts. Any such measures should be preceded by a meeting of relevant experts at which an appropriate testing or other protocol is devised. This would cover (i) all matters connected with the process in question and its recording and (ii) the sharing and agreement of any resulting data or evidence.
(e) Any common method of analysis, investigation or reporting where it is appropriate or proportionate that such should be adopted by all relevant experts. An example of this would be an agreement as to the method to be used to analyse the cause and extent of any relevant period of delay in a construction project, where such is in issue in the case.
(f) The availability and length of time that experts will realistically require to complete the tasks assigned to them.

13.3.5 In so far as the matters set out in the previous paragraph cannot be agreed, the court will give appropriate directions. In giving permission for the reception of any expert evidence, the court will ordinarily order the exchange of such evidence, with a definition of the expert's area of expertise and a clear description of the issues about which that expert is permitted to give evidence. It is preferable that, at the first CMC or as soon as possible thereafter, the parties should provide the court with the name(s) of their expert(s).

13.4 Single joint experts

13.4.1 An order may be made, at the first CMC or thereafter, that a single joint expert should address particular issues between the parties. Such an order would be made pursuant to CPR Parts 35.7 and 35.8.

13.4.2 Single joint experts are not usually appropriate for the principal liability disputes in a large case, or in a case where considerable sums have been spent on an expert in the pre-action stage. They are generally inappropriate where the issue involves questions of risk assessment or professional competence.

13.4.3 On the other hand, single joint experts can often be appropriate:

(a) in low value cases, where technical evidence is required but the cost of adversarial expert evidence may be prohibitive;
(b) where the topic with which the single joint expert's report deals is a separate and self-contained part of the case, such as the valuation of particular heads of claim;
(c) where there is a subsidiary issue, which requires particular expertise of a relatively uncontroversial nature to resolve;
(d) where testing or analysis is required, and this can conveniently be done by one laboratory or firm on behalf of all parties.

13.4.4 Where a single joint expert is to be appointed or is to be directed by the court, the parties should attempt to devise a protocol covering all relevant aspects of the appointment (save for those matters specifically provided for by CPR rules 35.6, 35.7 and 35.8).

13.4.5 The matters to be considered should include: any ceiling on fees and disbursements that are to be charged and payable by the parties; how, when and by whom fees will be paid to the expert on an interim basis pending any costs order in the proceedings; how the expert's fees will be secured; how the terms of reference are to be agreed; what is to happen if terms of reference cannot be agreed; how and to whom the jointly appointed expert may address further enquiries and from whom he should seek further information and documents; the timetable for preparing any report or for undertaking any other preparatory step; the possible effect on such timetable of any supplementary or further instructions. Where these matters cannot be agreed, an application to the court, which may often be capable of being dealt with as a paper application, will be necessary.

13.4.6 The usual procedure for a single joint expert will involve:

(a) The preparation of the expert's instructions. These instructions should clearly identify those issues or matters where the parties are in conflict, whether on the facts or on matters of opinion. If the parties can agree joint instructions, then a single set of instructions should be delivered to the expert. However, rule 35.8 expressly permits separate instructions and these are necessary where joint instructions cannot be agreed
(b) The preparation of the agreed bundle, which is to be provided to the expert. This bundle must include CPR Part 35, the Practice Direction supplementing Part 35 and the section 13 of the TCC Guide.
(c) The preparation and production of the expert's report.
(d) The provision to the expert of any written questions from the parties, which the expert must answer in writing.

13.4.7 In most cases the single joint expert's report, supplemented by any written answers to questions from the parties, will be sufficient for the purposes of the trial. Sometimes, however, it is necessary for a single joint expert to be called to give oral evidence. In those circumstances, the usual practice is for the judge to call the expert and then allow each party the opportunity to cross-examine. Such cross-examination should be conducted with appropriate restraint, since the witness has been instructed by the parties. Where the expert's report is strongly in favour of one party's position, it may be appropriate to allow only the other party to cross-examine.

13.5 Meetings of experts

13.5.1 The desirability of holding without prejudice meetings between experts at all stages of the pre-trial preparation should be kept in mind. The desired outcome of such meetings is to produce a document whose contents are agreed and which defines common positions or each expert's differing position. The purpose of such meetings includes the following:

(a) to define a party's technical case and to inform opposing parties of the details of that case;
(b) to clear up confusion and to remedy any lack of information or understanding of a party's technical case in the minds of opposing experts;
(c) to identify the issues about which any expert is to give evidence;
(d) to narrow differences and to reach agreement on as many 'expert' issues as possible; and

(e) to assist in providing an agenda for the trial and for cross examination of expert witnesses, and to limit the scope and length of the trial as much as possible.

13.5.2 In many cases it will be helpful for the parties' respective legal advisors to provide assistance as to the agenda and topics to be discussed at an experts' meeting. However, (save in exceptional circumstances and with the permission of the judge) the legal advisors must not attend the meeting. They must not attempt to dictate what the experts say at the meeting.

13.5.3 Experts' meetings can sometimes usefully take place at the site of the dispute. Thought is needed as to who is to make the necessary arrangements for access, particularly where the site is occupied or in the control of a non-party. Expert meetings are often more productive, if (a) the expert of one party (usually the claimant) is appointed as chairman and (b) the experts exchange in advance agendas listing the topics each wishes to raise and identifying any relevant material which they intend to introduce or rely on during the meeting.

13.5.4 It is generally sensible for the experts to meet at least once before they exchange their reports.

13.6 Experts' Joint Statements

13.6.1 Following the experts' meetings, and pursuant to CPR 35.12(3), the judge will almost always require the experts to produce a signed statement setting out the issues which have been agreed, and those issues which have not been agreed, together with a short summary of the reasons for their disagreement. In any TCC case in which expert evidence has an important role to play, this statement is a critical document and it must be as clear as possible.

13.6.2 It should be noted that, even where experts have been unable to agree very much, it is of considerable importance that the statement sets out their disagreements and the reasons for them. Such disagreements as formulated in the joint statement are likely to form an important element of the agenda for the trial of the action.

13.6.3 Whilst the parties' legal advisors may assist in identifying issues which the statement should address, those legal advisors must not be involved in either negotiating or drafting the experts' joint statement.

13.7 Experts' Reports

13.7.1 It is the duty of an expert to help the court on matters within his expertise. This duty overrides any duty to his client: CPR rule 35.3. Each expert's report must be independent and unbiased.

13.7.2 The parties must identify the issues with which each expert should deal in his report. Thereafter, it is for the expert to draft and decide upon the detailed contents and format of his report, so as to conform with section 2 of the Part 35 Practice Direction. It is appropriate, however, for the party instructing an expert to indicate that the report (a) should be as short as is reasonably possible; (b) should not set out copious extracts from other documents; (c) should identify the source of any opinion or data relied upon; and (d) should not annex or exhibit more than is reasonably necessary to support the opinions expressed in the report.

SECTION 14 – THE PRE-TRIAL REVIEW

14.1 Timing and Attendance

14.1.1 The Pre-Trial Review ('PTR') will usually be fixed for a date that is 4-6 weeks in advance of the commencement of the trial itself. It is vital that the advocates, who are going to conduct the trial, should attend the PTR and every effort should be made to achieve this. It is usually appropriate for the PTR to be conducted by way of an oral hearing or, at the very least, a telephone conference.

14.2 Documents

14.2.1 The parties must complete the PTR Questionnaire (a copy of which is at Appendix C attached) and return it in good time to the court. In addition, the judge may order the parties to provide other documents for the particular purposes of the PTR.

14.2.2 In an appropriate case, the advocates for each party should prepare a Note for the PTR, which addresses:

- any outstanding directions or interlocutory steps still to be taken;
- the issues for determination at the trial;
- the most efficient way in which those issues might be dealt with at the trial, including all questions of timetabling of witnesses.

These Notes should be provided to the court by 4 p.m. one clear day before the PTR.

14.2.3 The parties should also ensure that, for the PTR, the court has an up-to-date permanent case management bundle, together with a bundle of the evidence (factual and expert) that has been exchanged. This Bundle should also be made available to the court by 4 p.m. one clear day before the PTR.

14.3 Outstanding Directions

14.3.1 It can sometimes be the case that there are still outstanding interlocutory steps to be taken at the time of the PTR. That will usually mean that one, or more, of the parties has not complied with an earlier direction of the court. In that event, the court is likely to require prompt compliance, and may make costs orders to reflect the delays.

14.3.2 Sometimes a party will wish to make an application to be heard at the same time as the PTR. Such a practice is unsatisfactory, because it uses up time allocated for the PTR, and it gives rise to potential uncertainty close to the trial date. It is always better for a party, if it possibly can, to make all necessary applications well in advance of the PTR. If that is not practicable, the court should be asked to allocate additional time for the PTR, in order to accommodate specific applications. If additional time is not available, such applications will not generally be entertained.

14.4 Issues

14.4.1 The parties should, if possible, provide the judge at the PTR with an agreed list of the Issues for the forthcoming trial (including, where appropriate, a separate list of technical issues to be covered by the experts).

14.4.2 If the parties are unable to agree the precise formulation of the issues, they should provide to the court their respective contentions as to what the issues are, and why.

14.4.3 In order to determine the best way to deal with the trial, it is necessary for the issues to be identified. If the precise formulation of the issues is a matter of dispute between the parties, the judge will note the parties' respective contentions, but is unlikely to give a ruling on this matter at the PTR.

14.5 Timetabling and Trial Logistics

14.5.1 Much of the PTR will be devoted to a consideration of the appropriate timetable for the trial, and other logistical matters. These will commonly include:

- Directions in respect of oral and written openings.
- Sequence of oral evidence; for example, whether all the factual evidence should be called before the expert evidence.
- Timetabling of oral evidence. (To facilitate this exercise, the advocates should tell the judge which witnesses need to be cross-examined and which evidence can be agreed.)
- Whether any form of time limits should be imposed. (Since the purpose of time limits is to ensure that that the costs incurred and the resources devoted to the trial are proportionate, this is for the benefit of the parties. The judge will endeavour to secure agreement to any time limits imposed.)
- Directions in respect of the trial bundle: when it should be agreed and lodged; the contents and structure of the bundle; avoidance of duplication; whether witness statements and/or expert reports should be annotated with cross references to page numbers in the main bundle (see paragraph 12.3 above); and similar matters.
- Whether there should be a core bundle; if so how it should be prepared and what it should contain. (The court will order a core bundle in any case where (a) there is substantial documentation and (b) having regard to the issues it is appropriate and proportionate to put the parties to cost of preparing a core bundle).
- Rules governing any email communication during trial between the parties and the court.
- Any directions relating to the use of simultaneous transcription at trial (this subject to agreement between the parties).

14.5.2 The topics identified in paragraph 14.5.1 are discussed in greater detail in section 15 below.

SECTION 15 – THE TRIAL

15.1 Arrangements prior to the trial – witnesses

15.1.1 Prior to the trial the parties' legal representatives should seek to agree on the following matters, in so far as they have not been resolved at the PTR: the order in which witnesses are to be called to give evidence; which witnesses are not required for cross examination and whose evidence in consequence may be adduced entirely from their witness statements; the timetable for the trial and the length of time each advocate is to be allowed for a brief opening speech.

When planning the timetable, it should be noted that trials normally take place on Mondays to Thursdays, since Fridays are reserved for applications.

15.1.2 The witnesses should be notified in advance of the trial as to: (a) when each is required to attend court and (b) the approximate period of time for which he or she will be required to attend.

15.1.3 It is the parties' responsibility to ensure that their respective witnesses are ready to attend court at the appropriate time. It is never satisfactory for witnesses to be interposed, out of their proper place. It would require exceptional circumstances for the trial to be adjourned for any period of time because of the unavailability of a witness.

15.2 Opening notes, trial bundle and oral openings

15.2.1 Opening notes. Unless the court has ordered otherwise, each party's advocate should provide an opening note, which outlines that party's case in relation to each of the issues identified at the PTR. Each opening note should indicate which documents (giving their page numbers in the trial bundle) that party considers that the judge should pre-read. The claimant's opening note should include a neutral summary of the background facts, as well as a chronology and cast list. The other parties' opening notes should be shorter and should assume familiarity with the factual background. In general terms, all opening notes should be of modest length and proportionate to the size and complexity of the case. Subject to any specific directions at the PTR, the claimant's opening note should be served two working days before the start of the trial; the other parties opening notes should be served by 12 noon on the last working day before the trial.

15.2.2 Trial bundles. Subject to any specific directions at the PTR, the trial bundles should be delivered to court at least three working days before the hearing. It is helpful for the party delivering the trial bundles to liaise in advance with the judge's clerk, in order to discuss practical arrangements, particularly when a large number of bundles are to be delivered. The parties should provide for the court an agreed index of all trial bundles. There should also be an index at the front of each bundle. This should be a helpful guide to the contents of that bundle. (An interminable list, itemising every letter or sheet of paper is not a helpful guide. Nor are bland descriptions, such as 'exhibit 'JT3', of much help to the bundle user.) The spines of bundles should be clearly labelled.

15.2.3 As a general rule the trial bundles should be clearly divided between statements of case, orders, contracts, witness statements, expert reports and correspondence/ minutes of meetings. The correspondence/ minutes of meetings should be in a separate bundle or bundles and in chronological order. Documents should only be included, if they are relevant to the issues in the case or helpful as background material. Documents should not be duplicated. Exhibits to witness statements should generally be omitted, since the documents to which the witnesses are referring will be found elsewhere in the bundles. The bundles of contract documents and correspondence/ minutes of meetings should be paginated, so that every page has a discrete number. The other bundles could be dealt with in one of two ways:

- The statements of case, witness statements and expert reports could be placed in bundles and continuously paginated.

- Alternatively, the statements of case, witness statements and expert reports could be placed behind tabbed divider cards, and then the internal numbering of each such document can be used at trial. If the latter course is adopted, it is vital that the internal page numbering of each expert report continues sequentially through the appendices to that report.

The ultimate objective is to create trial bundles, which are user friendly and in which any page can be identified with clarity and brevity (eg 'bundle G page 273' or 'defence page 3' or 'Dr Smith page 12'). The core bundle, if there is one (as to which see paragraph 14.5.1 above), will be a separate bundle with its own pagination

15.2.4 Opening speeches. Subject to any directions made at the PTR, each party will be permitted to make an opening speech. These speeches should be prepared and presented on the basis that the judge will have pre-read the opening notes and the documents identified by the parties for pre-reading. The claimant's advocate may wish to highlight the main features of the claimant's case and/or to deal with matters raised in the other parties' opening notes. The other parties' advocates will then make shorter opening speeches, emphasising the main features of their own cases and/or responding to matters raised in the claimant's opening speech.

15.2.5 It is not usually necessary or desirable to embark upon legal argument during opening speeches. It is, however, helpful to foreshadow those legal arguments which (a) explain the relevance of particular parts of the evidence or (b) will assist the judge in following a party's case that is to be presented during the trial.

15.2.6 Narrowing of issues. Experience shows that often that the issues between the parties progressively narrow as the trial advances. Sometimes this process begins during the course of opening speeches. Weaker contentions may be abandoned and responses to those contentions may become irrelevant. The advocates will co-operate in focussing their submissions and the evidence on the true issues between the parties, as those issues are thrown into sharper relief by the adversarial process.

15.3 Simultaneous transcription

15.3.1 Many trials in the TCC, including the great majority of the longer trials, are conducted with simultaneous transcripts of the evidence being provided. There are a number of transcribing systems available. It is now common for a system to be used involving simultaneous transcription onto screens situated in court. However, systems involving the production of the transcript in hard or electronic form at the end of the day or even after a longer period of time are also used. The parties must make the necessary arrangements with one of the companies who provide this service. The court can provide a list, on request, of all companies who offer such a service.

15.3.2 In long trials or those which involve any significant amount of detailed or technical evidence, simultaneous transcripts are helpful. Furthermore, they enable all but the shortest trials to be conducted so as to reduce the overall length of the trial appreciably, since the judge does not have to note the evidence or submissions in longhand as the trial proceeds. Finally, a simultaneous transcript makes the task of summarising a case in closing submissions and preparing the judgment somewhat easier. It reduces both the risk of error or omission and the amount of time needed to prepare a reserved judgment.

15.3.3 If possible, the parties should have agreed at or before the PTR whether a simultaneous transcript is to be employed. It is usual for parties to agree to share the cost of a simultaneous transcript as an interim measure pending the assessment or agreement of costs, when this cost is assessable and payable as part of the costs in the case. Sometimes, a party cannot or will not agree to an interim cost sharing arrangement. If so, it is permissible for one party to bear the cost, but the court cannot be provided with a transcript unless all parties have equal access to the transcript. Unlike transcripts for use during an appeal, there is no available means of obtaining from public funds the cost of a transcript for use at the trial.

15.4 Time limits

15.4.1 Generally trials in the TCC are conducted under some form of time limit arrangement. Several variants of time limit arrangements are available, but the TCC has developed the practice of imposing flexible guidelines in the form of directions as to the sharing of the time allotted for the trial. These are not mandatory but an advocate should ordinarily be expected to comply with them.

15.4.2 The practice is, in the usual case, for the court to fix, or for the parties to agree, at the PTR or before trial an overall length of time for the trial and overall lengths of time within that period for the evidence and submissions. The part of those overall lengths of time that will be allocated to each party must then be agreed or directed.

15.4.3 The amount of time to be allotted to each party will not usually be the same. The guide is that each party should have as much time as is reasonably needed for it to present its case and to test and cross examine any opposing case, but no longer.

15.4.4 Before the trial, the parties should agree a running order of the witnesses and the approximate length of time required for each witness. A trial timetable should be provided to the court when the trial starts and, in long trials, regularly updated.

15.4.5 The practice of imposing a strict guillotine on the examination or cross examination of witnesses, is not normally appropriate. Flexibility is encouraged, but the agreed or directed time limits should not ordinarily be exceeded without good reason. It is unfair on a party, if that party's advocate has confined cross-examination to the agreed time limits, but an opposing party then greatly exceeds the corresponding time limits that it has been allocated.

15.4.6 An alternative form of time limit, which is sometimes agreed between the parties and approved by the court, is the 'chess clock arrangement'. The available time is divided equally between the parties, to be used by the parties as they see fit. Thus each side has X hours. One representative on each side operates the chess clock. The judge has discretion 'to stop the clock' in exceptional circumstances. A chess clock arrangement is only practicable in a two-party case.

15.5 Oral evidence

15.5.1 Evidence in chief is ordinarily adduced by the witness confirming on oath the truth and accuracy of the previously served witness statement or statements. A limited number of supplementary oral questions will usually be allowed (a) to give the witness an opportunity to become familiar with the procedure and (b) to cover points omitted by mistake from the witness statement or which have arisen subsequent to its preparation.

15.5.2 In some cases, particularly those involving allegations of dishonest, disreputable or culpable conduct or where significant disputes of fact are not documented or evidenced in writing, it is desirable that the core elements of a witness's evidence-in-chief are given orally. The giving of such evidence orally will often assist the court in assessing the credibility or reliability of a witness.

15.5.3 If any party wishes such evidence to be given orally, a direction should be sought either at the PTR or during the openings to that effect. Where evidence in chief is given orally, the rules relating to the use of witness statements in cross-examination and to the adducing of the statement in evidence at any subsequent stage of the trial remain in force and may be relied on by any party.

15.5.4 It is usual for all evidence of fact from all parties to be adduced before expert evidence and for the experts to give evidence in groups with all experts in a particular discipline giving their evidence in sequence. Usually, but not invariably, the order of witnesses will be such that the claimant's witnesses give their evidence first, followed by all the witnesses for each of the other parties in turn. If a party wishes a different order of witnesses to that normally followed, the agreement of the parties or a direction from the judge must be obtained in advance.

15.5.5 In a multi-party case, attention should be given (when the timetable is being discussed) to the order of cross-examination and to the extent to which particular topics will be covered by particular cross-examiners. Where these matters cannot be agreed, the order of cross-examination will (subject to any direction of the judge) follow the order in which the parties are set out in the pleadings. The judge will seek to limit cross examination on a topic which has been covered in detail by a preceding cross examination.

15.5.6 The coaching of witnesses or the suggestion of answers that may be given, before that witness starts to give evidence, is not permitted. Any prior discussion between the lawyers and the witness about the giving of evidence should be confined to factual information about the evidence-giving process. In short, witness familiarisation is permissible, but witness coaching is not. The boundary between witness familiarisation and witness coaching is discussed by the Court of Appeal in *R v Momodou* [2005] EWCA Crim 177 at [61]–[62]. Once a witness has started giving evidence, he cannot discuss the case or his evidence either with the lawyers or with anyone else until he has finally left the witness box. Occasionally a dispensation is needed (for example, an expert may need to participate in an experts' meeting about some new development). In those circumstances the necessary dispensation will either be agreed between the advocates or ordered by the judge.

15.6 Submissions during the trial

15.6.1 Submissions and legal argument should be kept to a minimum during the course of the trial. Where these are necessary, (a) they should, where possible, take place when a witness is not giving evidence and (b) the judge should be given forewarning of the need for submissions or legal argument. Where possible, the judge will fix a time for these submissions outside the agreed timetable for the evidence.

15.7 Closing submissions

15.7.1 The appropriate form of closing submissions can be determined during the course of the trial. Those submissions may take the form of (a) oral closing speeches or (b) written submission alone or (c) written submissions supplemented by oral closing speeches. In shorter or lower value cases, oral closing speeches immediately after the evidence may be the most cost effective way to proceed. Alternatively, if the evidence finishes in the late afternoon, a direction for written closing submissions to be delivered by specified (early) dates may avoid the cost of a further day's court hearing. In longer and heavier cases the judge may (in consultation with the advocates) set a timetable for the delivery of sequential written submissions (alternatively, an exchange of written submissions) followed by an oral hearing. In giving directions for oral and/or written closing submissions, the judge will have regard to the circumstances of the case and the overriding objective.

15.7.2 It is helpful if, in advance of preparing closing submissions, the parties can agree on the principal topics or issues that are to be covered. It is also helpful for the written and oral submissions of each party to be structured so as to cover those topics in the same order.

15.7.3 It is both customary and helpful for the judge to be provided with a photocopy of each authority and statutory provision that is to be cited in closing submissions.

15.8 Views

15.8.1 It is sometimes necessary or desirable for the judge to be taken to view the subject-matter of the case. In normal circumstances, such a view is best arranged to take place immediately after the openings and before the evidence is called. However, if the subject matter of the case is going to be covered up or altered prior to the trial, the view must be arranged earlier. In that event, it becomes particularly important to avoid a change of judge. Accordingly, the court staff will note on the trial diary the fact that the assigned judge has attended a view. In all subsequent communications between the parties and court concerning trial date, the need to avoid a change of judge must be borne firmly in mind.

15.8.2 The matters viewed by the judge form part of the evidence that is received and may be relied on in deciding the case. However, nothing said during the view to (or in the earshot of) the judge, has any evidential status, unless there has been an agreement or order to that effect.

15.8.3 The parties should agree the arrangements for the view and then make those arrangements themselves. The judge will ordinarily travel to the view unaccompanied and, save in exceptional circumstances when the cost will be shared by all parties, will not require any travelling costs to be met by the parties.

15.9 Judgments

15.9.1 Depending on the length and complexity of the trial, the judge may (a) give judgment orally immediately after closing speeches; (b) give judgment orally on the following day or soon afterwards; or (c) deliver a reserved judgment in writing at a later date.

15.9.2 Where judgment is reserved. The judge will normally indicate at the conclusion of the trial what arrangements will be followed in relation to (a) the making available of any draft reserved judgment and (b) the handing down of the reserved judgment in open court. If a judgment is reserved, it will be handed down as soon as possible. Save in exceptional circumstances, any reserved judgment will be handed down within 3 months of the conclusion of the trial. Any enquiries as to the progress of a reserved judgment should be addressed in the first instance to the judge's clerk, with notice of that enquiry being given to other parties. If concerns remain following the judge's response to the parties, further enquiries or communication should be addressed to the judge in charge of the TCC.

15.9.3 If the judge decides to release a draft judgment in advance of the formal hand down, this draft judgment will be confidential to the parties and their legal advisers. Solicitors and counsel on each side should send to the judge a note (if possible, agreed) of any clerical errors or slips which they note in the judgment. However, this is not to be taken as an opportunity to re-argue the issues in the case.

15.10 Disposal of judge's bundle after conclusion of the case

15.10.1 The judge will have made notes and annotations on the bundle during the course of the trial. Accordingly, the normal practice is that the entire contents of the judge's bundle are disposed of as confidential waste. The empty ring files can be recovered by arrangement with the judge's clerk.

15.10.2 If any party wishes to retrieve from the judge's bundle any particular items of value which it has supplied (eg plans or photographs), a request for these items should be made to the judge's clerk promptly at the conclusion of the case. If the judge has not made annotations on those particular items, they will be released to the requesting party.

SECTION 16 – COSTS

16.1 General

16.1.1 All disputes as to costs will be resolved in accordance with CPR Part 44, and in particular CPR rule 44.3.

16.1.2 The judge's usual approach will be to determine which party can be properly described as 'the successful party', and then to investigate whether there are any good reasons why that party should be deprived of some or all of their costs.

16.1.3 It should be noted that, in view of the complex nature of TCC cases, a consideration of the outcome on particular issues or areas of dispute can sometimes be an appropriate starting point for any decision on costs.

16.2 Summary Assessment of Costs

16.2.1 Interlocutory hearings that last one day or less will usually be the subject of a summary assessment of costs in accordance with CPR 44.7 and section 13 of the Costs Practice Direction. The parties must ensure that their statements of costs, on which the summary assessment will be based, are provided to each other party, and the Court, no later than 24 hours before the hearing in question: see paragraph 6.9.3 above.

16.2.2 The Supreme Court Costs Office Guide to the Summary Assessment of Costs sets out clear advice and guidance as to the principles to be followed in any summary assessment. Generally summary assessment proceeds on the standard basis. In making an assessment on the standard basis, the court will only allow a reasonable amount in respect of costs reasonably incurred and any doubts must be resolved in favour of the paying party.

16.2.3 In arguments about the hourly rates claimed, the judge will have regard to the principles set out by the Court of Appeal in *Wraith v Sheffield Forgemasters Ltd* [1998] 1 WLR 132: ie the judge will consider whether the successful party acted reasonably in employing the solicitors who had been instructed and whether the costs they charged were reasonable compared with the broad average of charges made by similar firms practising in the same area.

16.2.4 In addition, when considering hourly rates, the judge in the TCC may have regard to the guideline rates published from time to time by TecSA.

16.2.5 The court will also consider whether unnecessary work was done or an unnecessary amount of time was spent on the work.

16.2.6 It may be that, because of pressures of time, and/or the nature and extent of the disputes about the level of costs incurred, the court is unable to carry out a satisfactory summary assessment of the costs. In those circumstances, the court will direct that costs be assessed on the standard (or indemnity) basis and will order an amount to be paid on account of costs under CPR Rule 44.3(8).

16.3 Costs Cap Orders

16.3.1 In exercising case management powers, the judge may make costs cap orders which, in normal circumstances, will be prospective only. He should only do so, however, where there is a real and substantial risk that, without such an order:

(a) costs will be disproportionately or unreasonably incurred and
(b) such costs cannot be controlled by conventional case management and a detailed assessment of costs after a trial, and
(c) it is just to make such an order.

See CPR rule 3.1 and the notes to that rule in the White Book headed 'Prospective costs cap orders'.

16.3.2 The possibility of a costs cap order should be considered at the first CMC. The later such an order is sought, the more difficult it may be to impose an effective costs cap.

16.4 Costs: Miscellaneous

16.4.1 The court may at any stage order any party to file and serve on the other parties an estimate of costs: see CPR rule 3.1(2) (ll) and section 6 of the Costs Practice Direction. The case management information sheet for the first CMC requires such costs information. This information allows the court properly to exercise its case management functions. In appropriate cases (and where it is proportionate to do so) the judge will exercise his power under paragraph 3 of the Costs Practice Direction to direct the parties to file estimates of costs prepared in such a way as to demonstrate the likely effects of giving or not giving or not giving a particular case management direction.

16.4.2 Pursuant to CPR Rule 44.2 and Section 7 of the Costs Practice Direction, solicitors have a duty to tell their clients within 7 days if an order for costs was made against the clients and they were not present at the hearing, explaining how the order came to be made. They must also give the same information to anyone else who has instructed them to act on the case or who is liable to pay their fees.

SECTION 17 – ENFORCEMENT

17.1 General

17.1.1 The TCC is concerned with the enforcement of judgments and orders given by the TCC and with the enforcement of adjudicators' decisions and arbitrators' awards. Adjudication and arbitration enforcement have been dealt with in, respectively, sections 9 and 10 above.

17.2 High Court

17.2.1 London. A party wishing to make use of any provision of the CPR concerned with the enforcement of judgments and orders made in the TCC in London can use the TCC Registry in London or any other convenient TCC District Registry listed in Appendix A.

17.2.2 Outside London. Where the judgment or order in respect of which enforcement is sought was made by a judge of the TCC out of London, the party seeking enforcement should use the Registry of the court in which the judgment or order was made.

17.2.3 Where orders are required or sought to support enforcement of a TCC judgment or order, a judge of the TCC is the appropriate judge for that purpose. If available, the judge who gave the relevant judgment or made the relevant order is the appropriate judge to whom all applications should be addressed.

17.3 County Court

17.3.1 A TCC county court judgment (like any other county court judgment):

(a) if for less than £600, must be enforced in the county court;
(b) if for between £600 and £4999, can be enforced in either the county court or the High Court, at the option of the judgment creditor;
(c) if for £5,000 or more, must be enforced in the High Court.

17.3.2 If a judgment creditor in a TCC county court wishes to transfer any enforcement proceedings to any other county court (whether a TCC county court or not), he must make a written request to do so pursuant to section 2 of the Practice Direction supplementing Part 70. Alternatively, at the end of the trial the successful party may make an oral application to the trial judge to transfer the proceedings to some other specified county court for the purposes of enforcement.

17.4 Enforcement on paper

17.4.1 Where the application or order is unopposed or does not involve any substantial dispute, the necessary order should be sought by way of a paper application.

SECTION 18 – THE TCC JUDGE AS ARBITRATOR

18.1 General

18.1.1 Section 93(1) of the Arbitration Act 1996 provides that a judge of the TCC (previously an Official Referee) may 'if in all the circumstances he thinks fit, accept appointment as a sole arbitrator or as an umpire by or by virtue of an arbitration agreement.' Judges of the TCC may accept appointments as arbitrators or umpires pursuant to these statutory provisions. A judge of the TCC may also accept an appointment as a member of a three-member panel of arbitrators pursuant to these provisions.

18.1.2 A TCC judge cannot accept such an appointment unless the Lord Chief Justice 'has informed him that, having regard to the state of (TCC) business, he can be made available': see section 93(3) of the 1996 Act.

18.1.3 Application should be made in the first instance to the judge whose acceptance of the appointment is sought. If the judge is willing to accept the appointment, he will make application on behalf of the appointing party or parties, through the judge in charge of the TCC, to the Lord Chief Justice for his necessary approval. He will inform the party or parties applying for his appointment once the consent or refusal of consent has been obtained.

18.1.4 Subject to the workload of the court, such requests for judge arbitrators will generally be accepted. Particular advantages have been noted by both TECBAR and TeCSA in the appointment of a TCC judge to act as arbitrator where the dispute centres on the proper interpretation of a clause or clauses within one of the standard forms of building and engineering contracts.

18.2 Arbitration Management and Fees

18.2.1 Following the appointment of the judge arbitrator, the rules governing the arbitration will be decided upon, or directed, at the First Preliminary Meeting, when other appropriate directions will be given. The judge arbitrator will manage the reference to arbitration in a similar way to a TCC case.

18.2.2 The judge sitting as an arbitrator will sit in a TCC court room (suitably rearranged) unless the parties and the judge arbitrator agree to some other arrangement.

18.2.3 Fees are payable to the Court Service for the judge arbitrator's services and for any accommodation provided. The appropriate fee for the judge arbitrator, being a daily rate, is published in the Fees Order and should be paid through the TCC Registry.

18.3 Appeals

18.3.1 Section 2 of Schedule 2 to the Arbitration Act 1996 provides that any appeal from a judge arbitrator is to be heard, in the first instance, by the Court of Appeal.

APPENDIX A

CASE MANAGEMENT INFORMATION SHEET

This Appendix is the same as Appendix A to the Part 60 Practice Direction. In electronic versions of the TCC Guide it is not possible to copy this Appendix. Practitioners should refer either to the Part 60 Practice Direction or to published hard copies of this Guide.

APPENDIX B

CASE MANAGEMENT DIRECTIONS FORM

Action no HT–...........

Delete or amend the following directions, as appropriate to the circumstances of the case.

1. Trial date .... For the purposes of payment of the trial fee, but for no other purposes, this date is provisional. This date will cease to be provisional and the trial fee will become payable on … [usually be 2 months before the trial date].

2. Estimated length of trial ....

3. Directions, if appropriate, (a) for the trial of any preliminary issues or (b) for the trial to be divided into stages …

4. This action is to be [consolidated] [managed and tried with] action no … The lead action shall be … All directions given in the lead action shall apply to both actions, unless otherwise stated.

5. Further statements of case shall be filed and served as follows:

- Defence and any counterclaim by 4 p.m. on …
- Reply (if any) and defence to counterclaim (if any) by 4 p.m. on …

6. Permission to make the following amendments …

7. Disclosure of documents by 5 p.m. on … [Standard disclosure dispensed with/ limited/ varied as follows …]. Specific directions in respect of electronic disclosure …

8. There shall be a Scott Schedule in respect of defects/ items of damage/ other …

- The column headings shall be as follows …
- Claimant/ defendant to serve Scott Schedule by 5 p.m. on …
- Defendant/ claimant to respond to Scott Schedule by 5 p.m. on …

9. Signed statements of witnesses of fact to be served by 5 p.m. on …

[Supplementary statements of witnesses of fact to be served by 5 p.m. on …]

10. The parties have permission to call the following expert witnesses in respect of the following issues:

- …

- …
- …

11. In respect of any expert evidence permitted under paragraph 10:
    - Directions for carrying out inspections/ taking samples/ conducting experiments/ performance of calculations shall be …
    - Experts in like fields to hold discussions in accordance with rule 35.12 by …
    - Experts' statements rule 35.12(3) to be prepared and filed by 5 pm on …
    - Experts' reports to be served by 5 p.m. on …

12. A single joint expert shall be appointed by the parties to report on the following issue(s) …. The following directions shall govern the appointment of the single joint expert:

- ….
- ….

13. The following documents shall be provided to the court electronically or in computer readable form, as well as in hard copy …

14. A review case management conference shall be held on … at …am/pm. Time allowed …

15. The pre-trial review shall be held on … at . . . am/pm. Time allowed …

16. The above dates and time limits may be extended by agreement between the parties. Nevertheless:

- The dates and time limits specified in paragraphs … may not be extended by more than … days without the permission of the court.
- The dates specified in paragraph 1 (trial) and paragraph 15 (pre-trial review) cannot be varied without the permission of the court.

16. Liberty to restore.

17. Costs in the case.

18. Claimant's solicitors to draw up this order by … [Delete if order is to be drawn up by the court.]

APPENDIX C

PRE-TRIAL REVIEW QUESTIONNAIRE

This Appendix is the same as Appendix C to the Part 60 Practice Direction. In electronic versions of the TCC Guide it is not possible to copy this Appendix. Practitioners should refer either to the Part 60 Practice Direction or to published hard copies of this Guide.

APPENDIX D

CONTACT DETAILS FOR TECHNOLOGY AND CONSTRUCTION COURT

The High Court of Justice, Queen's Bench Division,
Technology and Construction Court
St Dunstan's House
133–137 Fetter Lane
London EC4A 1HD

(a) Management
Court Manager: Kevin Johnson
Case Administration Unit Manager/Registry Manager: Sharon Rowand (Sharon.Rowand@hmcourts-service.gsi.gov.uk)
Registry: Tel: 020 7947 6022/7427
Fax: 020 7947 7428
Case Administration Unit: Tel: 020 7947 7156
Fax: 020 7947 6465

(b) TCC Judges
Mr Justice Rupert Jackson
Clerk: Mrs Pembe Overson (Pembe.Overson@hmcourts-service.gsi.gov.uk)
Tel: 020 7947 6484
Fax: 020 7947 6803
His Honour Judge Richard Havery QC
Clerk: Ms Sarah Landau (Sarah.Landau@hmcourts-service.gsi.gov.uk)
Tel: 020 7947 7445
His Honour Judge Anthony Thornton QC
Clerk: Ms Anne Farrelly (Anne.Farrelly@hmcourts-service.gsi.gov.uk)
Tel: 020 7947 6457
His Honour David Wilcox
Clerk: Ms Pam Gilham (Pamela.Gilham@hmcourts-service.gsi.gov.uk)
Tel: 020 7947 6450
His Honour Judge John Toulmin CMG QC
Clerk: Ms Kim Andrews (Kim.Andrews@hmcourts-service.gsi.gov.uk)
Tel: 020 7947 6456
His Honour Judge Peter Coulson QC
Clerk: Mr Steve Jones (Stephen.Jones3@hmcourts-service.gsi.gov.uk)
Tel: 020 7947 6547

– The following five High Court Judges will be available, when necessary and by arrangement with the Vice-President of the Queen's Bench Division, to sit in the TCC:
Mr Justice Elias
Mr Justice Field
Mr Justice Ouseley
Mr Justice Simon
Mr Justice Christopher Clarke

– The Case Administration Unit, headed by Sharon Rowand administers cases classified as 'HCJ' (see section 3.7 of guide).
Birmingham District Registry: Birmingham County Court
33 Bull Street
Birmingham B4 6DS
TCC listing and clerk to HH Judge Kirkham: Peter Duke (Peter.Duke@hmcourts-service.gsi.gov.uk)
Tel: 0121 681 3181
Fax: 0121 681 3121

TCC Judges
Her Honour Judge Frances Kirkham (full time TCC Judge)
Her Honour Judge Caroline Alton (Mercantile Judge)
His Honour Judge Alastair Norris QC (Chancery Judge)
Each judge has his or her own diary with a first fixture. If the first fixture settles, the Judge in question will take a case from a shared list (which includes TCC, Mercantile and Chancery work).

Other judges in Birmingham who have been nominated to deal with TCC business are: His Honour Judge MacDuff QC and His Honour Judge Patrick McCahill QC

Bristol District Registry: Bristol County Court

TCC Listing Office
The Law Courts
Small Street
Bristol BS1 1DA
TCC Listing officers: Liz Bodman and Louise Piotrowski
(Louise.Piotrowski@hmcourts-service.gsi.gov.uk)
Tel: 0117 976 3098
Fax: 0117 976 3074

TCC Judges

His Honour Judge Mark Havelock-Allan QC (principal TCC judge)
His Honour Judge Rupert Bursell QC

Cardiff District Registry: Cardiff County Court

Cardiff Civil Justice Centre
2 Park Street
Cardiff CF10 1 ET
Main switchboard: 02920 376 400
Fax: 02920 376 475
Listing office: 02920 376 412

TCC Judges

His Honour Judge Gary Hickinbottom (principal TCC judge)
His Honour Judge Nicholas Chambers QC
His Honour Judge Wyn Williams QC

Central London Civil Justice Centre

13-14 Park Crescent,
London WIN 4HT
Listing office for TCC, Chancery and Mercantile Courts
Tel: 0207 917 7889/ 7821
Fax: 0207 917 7935

TCC Judges

His Honour Judge Brian Knight QC (principal TCC judge)
His Honour Judge Michael Dean QC
His Honour Judge Michael Rich QC
His Honour Judge David Mackie QC

Chester District Registry: Chester County Court

The Chester Civil Justice Centre
Trident House
Little St John Street
Chester CH1 1SN
Tel: 01244 404200
Fax: 01244 404300

TCC Judge

His Honour Judge Derek Halbert

Leeds Combined Court Centre

The Courthouse
1 Oxford Row
Leeds LS1 3BG
High Court Civil Listing Officers: Chris Waring and Ms Sam Cox
Tel: 0113 254 2607

Fax: 0113 242 6380
e-mail: Chris.Waring@hmcourts-service.gsi.gov.uk
TCC Judges
His Honour Judge John Cockroft (principal TCC judge)
His Honour Judge John Behrens
His Honour Judge Peter Langan QC
His Honour Judge Simon Grenfell
His Honour Judge Simon Hawkesworth QC
Leicester District Registry: Leicester County Court
PO Box 3
90 Wellington Street
Leicester LE1 6ZZ
Tel : 0116 222 5700
TCC Judges
His Honour Judge David Brunning
His Honour Judge Hugh Mayor QC
Liverpool Combined Court Centre
QE 11 Law Court
Derby Square
Liverpool L2 1XA
TCC listing officer: Joseph Kelly
Tel: 0151 471 1069/ 1091
Fax: 0151 471 1095
The Chancery and Mercantile listing officer, Helen Davidson, on the same telephone and fax numbers also assists with TCC matters when necessary.
TCC Judges
His Honour Judge David Mackay (full time TCC judge)
His Honour Judge David Harris QC
His Honour Judge Stephen Stewart QC
His Honour Judge Nigel Gilmour QC
Newcastle upon Tyne Combined Court Centre
The Law Courts
Quayside
Newcastle upon Tyne NE1 3LA
Tel: 0191 201 2000
TCC Judge
His Honour Judge Christopher Walton
Nottingham District Registry: Nottingham County Court
60 Canal Street
Nottingham NG1 7EJ

Tel: 0115 910 3500
Fax: 0115 910 3510
TCC Judge
His Honour Judge Richard Inglis
Plymouth Combined Court Centre
The Law Courts
10 Armada Way
Plymouth
Devon PL1 2ER
Tel: 01752 677 400
TCC Judge

His Honour Judge Sean Overend
Salford District Registry: SalfordCounty Court
Prince William House
Peel Cross Road
Salford M5 4RR
TCC clerks: Isobel Rich and Colette Worthington
Tel: 0161 745 7511
Fax: 0161 745 7202
e-mail: Hearings@salford.countycourt.gsi.gov.uk
TCC Judges
His Honour Judge David Gilliland QC (full time TCC judge)
His Honour Judge Phillip Raynor QC
The following judges at Manchester are nominated to deal with TCC business: His Honour Judge Brian Hegarty QC and His Honour Judge Michael Kershaw QC
Sheffield Combined Court Centre
The Law Courts
50 West Bar
Sheffield S3 8PH
Tel: 0114 281 2419
Fax: 0114 281 2585
TCC Judge
His Honour Judge John Bullimore
Southampton Combined Court Centre
Courts of Justice
London Road
Southampton SO15 2XQ
Diary Manager: Mr Wayne Hacking
Tel: 023 8021 3254
Fax: 023 8021 3232
TCC Judge
His Honour Judge Hughes QC

APPENDIX E

DRAFT ADR ORDER

1. By [ ] the parties shall exchange lists of three neutral individuals who have indicated their availability to conduct a mediation/ENE in this case prior to [ ].

2. By [ ] the parties shall agree an individual from the exchanged lists to conduct the mediation/ENE by [ ]. If the parties are unable to agree on the neutral individual, they will apply to the Court in writing by [ ] and the Court will choose one of the listed individuals to conduct the mediation/ENE.

3. There will be a stay of the proceedings until [ ] to allow the mediation/ENE to take place. On or before that date, the Court shall be informed as to whether or not the case has been finally settled. If it has not been finally settled, the parties will:

   a) comply with all outstanding directions made by the Court;
   b) attend for a review CMC on [ ].

APPENDIX F

DRAFT DIRECTIONS IN ADJUDICATION ENFORCEMENT PROCEEDINGS

Upon reading the Claim Form, Particulars of Claim, the Claimant's without notice application dated the day of 200 and the evidence in support thereof

IT IS ORDERED THAT:

1. The Claimant's solicitor shall [as soon as practicable after receipt of this Order/ by 4pm on day of] serve upon the Defendant

    a. The Claim Form and Response Pack
    b. This Order
    c. The Claimant's Application Pursuant to Part 24 and the Claimant's evidence in support.

2. The time for the Defendant to file its acknowledgement of service is abridged to [ ] days.

3. The Claimant hereby has permission to issue an application pursuant to CPR Part 24 without an acknowledgement of service or Defence having been filed.

4. The Part 24 application will be heard on the day of at am/pm at .Estimated Length of Hearing hours]

5. Any further evidence in relation to the Part 24 Application shall be served and filed

    a. By the Defendant, [14 days after the service of the documents in Paragraph 1 above/ at least 5 working days before the date fixed for the hearing of the Application] [on day the day of]
    b. By the Claimant, in response to that of the Defendant, [at least 3 working days before the date fixed for the hearing of the Application] [on day the day of 200]

and in either case no later than 4.00pm upon that day.

6. The Claimant's solicitor shall file a paginated bundle comprising

    a. The witness statements provided in support of the application, together with any exhibits;
    b. The witness statements provided in opposition to the application together with exhibits;
    c. Any witness statements in reply, together with exhibits;
    d. Photocopies of relevant authorities.

This bundle is to be provided no later than [2 working days before the hearing of the Application] [on day of].

7. The parties shall file and serve skeleton arguments by no later than [4.00pm one clear working day before the hearing/ 1pm the last working day before the hearing]* [on day the day of]

8. The costs of and incidental to these directions are reserved to the Part 24 hearing. Permission to apply in respect of such costs in the absence of such hearing.

9. The parties have permission to apply to the court on 48 hours written notice to the other to seek to set aside or vary these directions.

* Depending whether the hearing is estimated to last in excess of ½ day or not

SECTION 6

Fees

SECTION 6: Fees

Contents

Civil Proceedings Fees Order 2004 , SI 2004/3121

1 Citation, commencement and interpretation

(1) This Order may be cited as the Civil Proceedings Fees Order 2004 and shall come into force on 4 January 2005.

(2) In this Order –

- (a) a fee referred to by number means the fee so numbered in Schedule 1 to this Order;
- (b) 'CCBC' means County Court Bulk Centre;
- (c) 'CPC' means Claim Production Centre;
- (d) 'the CPR' means the Civil Procedure Rules 1998;
- (e) expressions also used in the CPR have the same meaning as in those Rules; and
- (f) 'family proceedings' means family proceedings in the High Court or in any county court as appropriate;
- (g) 'LSC' means the Legal Services Commission established under section 1 of the Access to Justice Act 1999.
- (h) 'Funding Code' means the code approved under section 9 of the Access to Justice Act 1999.
- (i) 'GLO' means Group Litigation Order.

2 Fees to be taken

The fees set out in column 2 of Schedule 1 to this Order shall be taken in the Supreme Court and in county courts respectively in respect of the items described in column 1 in accordance with and subject to the directions specified in column 1.

3 The provisions of this Order shall not apply to –

- (a) non-contentious probate business;
- (b) proceedings in the Court of Protection, except in so far as fees 1, 2, 3, 6, 9 and 10 in Schedule 1 (High Court only) are applicable;
- (c) the enrolment of documents;
- (d) criminal proceedings (except proceedings on the Crown side of the Queen's Bench Division to which the fees contained in Schedule 1 are applicable);
- (e) proceedings by sheriffs, under-sheriffs, deputy-sheriffs or other officers of the sheriff; and
- (f) family proceedings.

4 Exemptions, reductions and remissions

(1) No fee shall be payable under this Order by a party who, at the time when a fee would otherwise become payable –

- (a) is in receipt of any qualifying benefit, and
- (b) is not in receipt of, as appropriate, either –
  - (i) representation under Part IV of the Legal Aid Act 1988 for the purposes of the proceedings; or

(ii) funding provided by the LSC for the purposes of the proceedings and for which a certificate has been issued under the Funding Code certifying a decision to fund services for that party.

(2) The following are qualifying benefits for the purposes of paragraph (1)(a) above –

(a) income support under the Social Security Contributions and Benefits Act 1992;

(b) working tax credit, provided that –

(i) child tax credit is being paid to the party, or otherwise following a claim for child tax credit made jointly by the members of a married couple or an unmarried couple (as defined respectively in section 3(5) and (6) of the Tax Credits Act 2002) which includes the party; or

(ii) there is a disability element or severe disability element (or both) to the tax credit received by the party;

and that the gross annual income taken into account for the calculation of the working tax credit is £15,050 or less;

(c) income-based jobseeker's allowance under the Jobseekers Act 1995; and

(d) guarantee credit under the State Pensions Credit Act 2002.

(3) In the county courts paragraph (1) shall not apply to fee 7.8 (fee payable on a consolidated attachment of earnings order or an administration order).

Amendments—SI 2005/473.

5 Where it appears to the Lord Chancellor that the payment of any fee prescribed by this Order would, owing to the exceptional circumstances of the particular case, involve undue financial hardship, he may reduce or remit the fee in that case.

6 (1) Subject to paragraph (2), where a fee has been paid at a time –

(a) when, under article 4, it was not payable, the fee shall be refunded;

(b) where the Lord Chancellor, if he had been aware of all the circumstances, would have reduced the fee under article 5, the amount by which the fee would have been reduced shall be refunded; and

(c) where the Lord Chancellor, if he had been aware of all the circumstances, would have remitted the fee under article 5, the fee shall be refunded.

(2) No refund shall be made under paragraph (1) unless the party who paid the fee applies within 6 months of paying the fee.

(3) The Lord Chancellor may extend the period of 6 months referred to in paragraph (2) if he considers that there is good reason for an application being made after the end of the period of 6 months.

7 Where by any convention entered into by Her Majesty with any foreign power it is provided that no fee shall be required to be paid in respect of any proceedings, the fees specified in this Order shall not be taken in respect of those proceedings.

8 Revocations

The Orders specified in Schedule 2, in so far as they were made under sections 414 and 415 of the Insolvency Act 1986 and section 128 of the Finance Act 1990, shall be revoked.

SCHEDULE 1

FEES TO BE TAKEN

Article 2

Column 1 Number & description of fee	*Column 2* Amount of fee
1 Commencement of proceedings (High Court and county court)	
1.1 On the commencement of originating proceedings in the High Court (including originating proceedings issued after leave to issue is granted) to recover a sum of money where the sum claimed:	
(a) does not exceed £50,000	£400
(b) exceeds £50,000 but does not exceed £100,000	£700
(c) exceeds £100,000 but does not exceed £150,000	£900
(d) exceeds £150,000 but does not exceed £200,000	£1,100
(e) exceeds £200,000 but does not exceed £250,000	£1,300
(f) exceeds £250,000 but does not exceed £300,000	£1,500
(g) exceeds £300,000 or is not limited	£1,700
1.2 On the commencement of originating proceedings in the county court (including originating proceedings issued after leave to issue is granted) to recover a sum of money, except in CPC cases brought by Centre users, where the sum claimed:	
(a) does not exceed £300	£30
(b) exceeds £300 but does not exceed £500	£50
(c) exceeds £500 but does not exceed £1,000	£80
(d) exceeds £1,000 but does not exceed £5,000	£120
(e) exceeds £5,000 but does not exceed £15,000	£250
(f) exceeds £15,000 but does not exceed £50,000	£400
(g) exceeds £50,000 but does not exceed £100,000	£700
(h) exceeds £100,000 but does not exceed £150,000	£900
(i) exceeds £150,000 but does not exceed £200,000	£1,100
(j) exceeds £200,000 but does not exceed £250,000	£1,300
(k) exceeds £250,000 but does not exceed £300,000	£1,500
(l) exceeds 300,000 or is not limited	£1,700

Column 1 Number & description of fee	*Column 2* Amount of fee
1.3 On the commencement of originating proceedings in the county court to recover a sum of money in Claim Production Centre cases brought by Centre users, where the sum claimed:	
(a) does not exceed £300	£20
(b) exceeds £300 but does not exceed £500	£40
(c) exceeds £500 but does not exceed £1,000	£70
(d) exceeds £1,000 but does not exceed £5,000	£110
(e) exceeds £5,000 but does not exceed £15,000	£240
(f) exceeds £15,000 but does not exceed £50,000	£390
(g) exceeds £50,000 but does not exceed £100,000	£690
Fee 1.3 Claims above £99,999.99 cannot be issued through the Claim Production Centre. Parties should issue the claim in the relevant court.	
1.4 On the commencement of originating proceedings for any other remedy or relief (including originating proceedings issued after leave to issue is granted):	
– in the High Court	£400
– in the county court	£150
Fees 1.1, 1.2 and 1.4 Recovery of land or goods Where a claim for money is additional or alternative to a claim for recovery of land or goods, only fee 1.4 shall be payable. Fees 1.1, 1.2 and 1.4 Claims other than recovery of land or goods Where a claim for money is additional to a non money claim (other than a claim for recovery of land or goods), then fee 1.1 or fee 1.2 as appropriate shall be payable in addition to fee 1.4. Where a claim for money is alternative to a non money claim (other than a claim for recovery of land or goods), only fee 1.1 shall be payable in the High Court, and, in the county court, fee 1.2 or fee 1.4 shall be payable, whichever is the greater. Fees 1.1 or 1.2 as appropriate and 1.4 – Generally Where more than one non money claim is made in the same proceedings, fee 1.4 shall be payable once only, in addition to any fee which may be payable under fees 1.1 or fee 1.2 as appropriate. Fees 1.1 or fee 1.2 as appropriate and fee 1.4 shall not be payable where fee 1.7(b), fee 1.8(a) (in the High Court only), fee 9.1 (in the High Court only) or fee 3 apply.	

Column 1 Number & description of fee	*Column 2* Amount of fee
Fees 1.1or 1.2 as appropriate and 1.4 – Amendment of claim or counterclaim	
Where the claim or counterclaim is amended, and the fee paid before amendment is less than that which would have been payable if the document, as amended, had been so drawn in the first instance, the party amending the document shall pay the difference.	
1.5 On the filing of proceedings against a party or parties not named in the originating proceedings:	
– in the High Court	£50
– in the county court	£30
Fee 1.5	
Fee 1.5 shall be payable by a defendant who adds or substitutes a party or parties to the proceedings or by a claimant who adds or substitutes a defendant or defendants.	
1.6 On the filing of a counterclaim	The same fee as if the relief or remedy sought were the subject of separate proceedings
Fee 1.6	
No fee is payable on a counterclaim which a defendant is required to make under the CPR because he contends that he has any claim or is entitled to any remedy relating to a grant of probate of a will, or letters of administration of an estate, of a deceased person.	
1.7(a) On an application for leave to issue originating proceedings	
– in the High Court	£50
– in the county court	£30
1.7(b) On an application for an order under Part III of the Solicitors Act 1974 for the assessment of costs payable to a solicitor by his client or on the commencement of costs-only proceedings	
– in the High Court	£50
– in the county court	£30
1.8(a) On the commencement of the judicial review procedure (applies to High Court only)	£50
Where the court has made an order giving permission to proceed with a claim for judicial review, there shall be payable by the claimant within 7 days of service on the claimant of that order:	

SECTION 6 Fees

Column 1 Number & description of fee	*Column 2* Amount of fee
1.8(b) if the judicial review procedure has been commenced	£180
1.8(c) if the claim for judicial review was commenced otherwise than by using the judicial review procedure	£50
2. General Fees (High Court and county court)	
2.1 On the claimant filing an allocation questionnaire; or • where the court dispenses with the need for an allocation questionnaire, within 14 days of the date of despatch of the notice of allocation to track; or • where the CPR or a Practice Direction provide for automatic allocation or provide that the rules on allocation shall not apply, within 28 days of the filing of the defence (or the filing of the last defence if there is more than one defendant), or within 28 days of the expiry of the time permitted for filing all defences if sooner	
– in the High Court	£200
– in the county court	£100
Fee 2.1 Fee 2.1 shall be payable by the claimant except where the action is proceeding on the counterclaim alone, when it shall be payable by the defendant – • on the defendant filing an allocation questionnaire; or • where the court dispenses with the need for an allocation questionnaire, within 14 days of the date of despatch of the notice of allocation to track; or • where the CPR or a Practice Direction provide for automatic allocation or provide that the rules on allocation shall not apply, within 28 days of the filing of the defence to the counterclaim (or the filing of the last defence to the counterclaim if there is more than one party entitled to file a defence to a counterclaim), or within 28 days of the expiry of the time permitted for filing all defences to the counterclaim if sooner	
2.2 On the claimant filing a listing questionnaire; or where the court fixes the trial date or trial week without the need for a listing questionnaire, within 14 days of the date of despatch of the notice (or the date when oral notice is given if no written notice is given) of the trial week or the trial date if no trial week is fixed	
– in the High Court	£600

Column 1 Number & description of fee	*Column 2* Amount of fee
– in the county court if the case is on the multi-track	£500
– in the county court in any other case	£275
Fee 2.2 Fee 2.2 shall be payable by the claimant except where the action is proceeding on the counterclaim alone, when it shall be payable by the defendant – – on the defendant filing a listing questionnaire; or – where the court fixes the trial date or trial week without the need for a listing questionnaire, within 14 days of the date of despatch of the notice (or the date when oral notice is given if no written notice is given) of the trial week or the trial date if no trial week is fixed. Where the court receives notice in writing – – before the trial date has been fixed or, – where a trial date has been fixed, at least 14 days before the trial date, from the party who paid Fee 2.2 that the case is settled or discontinued, Fee 2.2 shall be refunded. Fees 2.1 and 2.2 Generally in the High Court Fees 2.1 and 2.2 shall be payable as appropriate where the court allocates a case to track for a trial of the assessment of damages. Fees 2.1 and 2.2 shall not be payable in relation to claims managed under a GLO after that GLO is made. Fees 2.1 and 2.2 shall be payable once only in the same proceedings. Fee 2.1 shall not be payable where the procedure in Part 8 of the CPR is used. Fees 2.1 and 2.2 Generally in the county court Fees 2.1 and 2.2 shall be payable once only in the same proceedings. Fees 2.1 and 2.2 shall be payable as appropriate where the court allocates a case to a track for a trial of the assessment of damages. Fees 2.1 and 2.2 shall not be payable in relation to claims managed under a GLO after that GLO is made. Fee 2.1 shall not be payable where the procedure in Part 8 of the CPR is used. Fee 2.1 shall not be payable in proceedings where the only claim is a claim to recover a sum of money and the sum claimed does not exceed £1,500. Fee 2.2 shall not be payable in respect of a small claims hearing.	

Column 1 Number & description of fee	*Column 2* Amount of fee
2.3 In the High Court on filing: – an appellant's notice, or – a respondent's notice where the respondent is appealing or wishes to ask the appeal court to uphold the order of the lower court for reasons different from or additional to those given by the lower court.	£200
2.4 In the county court on filing – – an appellant's notice, or – a respondent's notice where the respondent is appealing or wishes to ask the appeal court to uphold the order of the lower court for reasons different from or additional to those given by the lower court: –	
(a) in a claim allocated to the small claims track	£80
(b) in all other claims	£100
Fee 2.3 and 2.4 Fee 2.3 and 2.4 do not apply on appeals against a decision made in detailed assessment proceedings.	
2.5 On an application on notice where no other fee is specified	
– in the High Court	£100
– in the county court	£60
2.6 On an application by consent or without notice for a judgment or order where no other fee is specified	
– in the High Court	£50
– in the county court	£30
For the purpose of Fee 2.6 a request for a judgment or order on admission or in default shall not constitute an application and no fee shall be payable. Fee 2.6 shall not be payable in relation to an application by consent for an adjournment of a hearing where the application is received by the court at least 14 days before the date set for that hearing. Fees 2.5 and 2.6 Fees 2.5 and 2.6 shall not be payable when an application is made in an appeal notice or is filed at the same time as an appeal notice.	
2.7 On an application for a summons or order for a witness to attend court to be examined on oath or an order for evidence to be taken by deposition, other than an application for which Fee 6.2 enforcement in the High Court or for which Fee 7.3 is payable	

Column 1 Number & description of fee	*Column 2* Amount of fee
– in the High Court	£50
– in the county court	£30
2.8 On an application to vary a judgment or suspend enforcement (where more than one remedy is sought in the same application only one fee shall be payable)	
– in the High Court	£50
– in the county court	£30
3. Companies Act 1985 and Insolvency Act 1986 (High Court and county court)	
3.1 On entering a bankruptcy petition:	
(a) if presented by a debtor or the personal representative of a deceased debtor	£150
(b) if presented by a creditor or other person	£190
3.2 On entering a petition for an administration order	£150
3.3 On entering any other petition	£190
One fee only is payable where more than one petition is presented in relation to a partnership.	
3.4(a) On a request for a certificate of discharge from bankruptcy	£60
3.4(b) and after the first certificate for each copy	£1
3.5 On an application under the Companies Act 1985 or the Insolvency Act 1986 other than one brought by petition and where no other fee is specified.	£130
Fee 3.5	
Fee 3.5 is not payable where the application is made in existing proceedings.	
3.6 On an application for the conversion of a voluntary arrangement into a winding up or bankruptcy under Article 37 of Council Regulation (EC) No 1346/2000.	£130
3.7 On an application, for the purposes of Council Regulation (EC) No 1346/2000, for an order confirming creditors' voluntary winding up (where the company has passed a resolution for voluntary winding up, and no declaration under section 89 of the Insolvency Act 1986 has been made).	£30
3.8 On filing	
• a notice of intention to appoint an administrator under paragraph 14 of Schedule B1 to the Insolvency Act 1986 or in accordance with paragraph 27 of that Schedule; or	£30

Column 1 Number & description of fee	*Column 2* Amount of fee
• a notice of appointment of an administrator in accordance with paragraphs 18 or 29 of that Schedule.	
Fee 3.8	
Where a person pays Fee 3.8 on filing a notice of intention to appoint an administrator, no fee shall be payable on that same person filing a notice of appointment of that administrator.	
3.9 On submitting a nominee's report under section 2(2) of the Insolvency Act 1986 or	£30
3.10 On filing documents in accordance with paragraph 7(1) of Schedule A1 to the Insolvency Act 1986	£30
3.11 On an application by consent or without notice within existing proceedings where no other fee is specified	£30
3.12 On an application with notice within existing proceedings where no other fee is specified	£60
Requests and applications with no fee:	
No fee is payable on a request or on an application to the Court by the Official Receiver when applying only in the capacity of Official Receiver to the case (and not as trustee or liquidator), or on an application to set aside a statutory demand.	
4. Copy Documents (High Court, Court of Appeal and county court)	
4.1 On a request for a copy of any document (other than where Fee 4.2 applies):	
(a) for the first page (except the first page of a subsequent copy of the same document supplied at the same time)	£1
(b) per page in any other case	20p
Fee 4.1	
Fee 4.1 shall be payable for a faxed copy or for examining a plain copy and marking it as an examined copy.	
Fee 4.1 shall be payable whether or not the copy is issued as an office copy.	
4.2 On a request for a copy of a document required in connection with proceedings and supplied by the party making the request at the time of copying, for each page.	20p
4.3 On a request for a copy of a document on a computer disk or in other electronic form, for each such copy.	£3

Column 1 Number & description of fee	*Column 2* Amount of fee
5. Determination of costs (Supreme Court and county court)	
Transitional Provision	
Where a bill of costs or a request for detailed assessment or a request for a detailed assessment hearing is filed pursuant to an order made by the court before the coming into operation of this Order, or an application is made to review a taxing officer's decision (in the Supreme Court) or taxation (in the county court) made before the coming into operation of this Order, the fees payable shall be those which applied immediately before this Order came into force.	
5.1 On the filing of a request for detailed assessment where the party filing the request is legally aided or is funded by the LSC and no other party is ordered to pay the costs of the proceedings	
– in the Supreme Court	£120
– in the county court	£100
5.2 On the filing of a request for a detailed assessment hearing in any case where Fee 5.1 does not apply; or on the filing of a request for a hearing date for the assessment of costs payable to a solicitor by his client pursuant to an order under Part III of the Solicitors Act 1974	
– in the Supreme Court	£600
– in the county court	£300
Where there is a combined party and party and legal aid, or a combined party and party and LSC, or a combined party and party, legal aid and LSC determination of costs, Fee 5.2 shall be attributed proportionately to the party and party, legal aid, or LSC (as the case may be) portions of the bill on the basis of the amount allowed.	
5.3 On a request for the issue of a default costs certificate	
– Supreme Court	£50
– county court	£40
5.4 On an appeal against a decision made in detailed assessment proceedings	
– Supreme Court	£200
– county court	£100
5.5 On applying for the court's approval of a certificate of costs payable from the Community Legal Service Fund.	
– Supreme Court	£50

SECTION 6 Fees

Column 1 Number & description of fee	*Column 2* Amount of fee
– county court	£30
Fee 5.5	
Fee 5.5 is payable at the time of applying for the court's approval and is recoverable only against the Community Legal Service Fund.	
5.6 On a request or application to set aside a default costs certificate	
– Supreme Court	£100
– county court	£60
6. Enforcement in the High Court	
6.1 On sealing a writ of execution/possession/delivery	£50
Where the recovery of a sum of money is sought in addition to a writ of possession and delivery, no further fee is payable.	
6.2 On an application for an order requiring a judgment debtor or other person to attend court to provide information in connection with enforcement of a judgment or order.	£50
6.3(a) On an application for a third party debt order or the appointment of a receiver by way of equitable execution	£100
6.3(b) On an application for a charging order	£100
Fee 6.3(a) and (b)	
Fee 6.3(a) shall be payable in respect of each third party against whom the order is sought.	
Fee 6.3(b) shall be payable in respect of each application issued.	
6.4 On an application for a judgment summons	£100
6.5 On a request or application to register a judgment or order, or for leave to enforce an arbitration award, or for a certificate or a certified copy of a judgment or order for use abroad	£50
7. Enforcement in the county court	
7.1 On an application for or in relation to enforcement of a judgment or order of a county court or through a county court:	
In cases other than CCBC cases brought by Centre users, by the issue of a warrant of execution against goods except a warrant to enforce payment of a fine;	(a) Where the amount for which the warrant issues does not exceed £125 . . . .£30

Column 1 Number & description of fee	*Column 2* Amount of fee
In CCBC cases brought by Centre users, by the issue of a warrant of execution against goods except a warrant to enforce payment of a fine	(b) Where the amount for which the warrant issues exceeds £125 . . . .£50 (c) Where the amount for which the warrant issues does not exceed £125 . . . .£25 (d) Where the amount for which the warrant issues exceeds £125 . . . .£45
7.2 On a request for a further attempt at execution of a warrant at a new address following a notice of the reason for non-execution (except a further attempt following suspension and CCBC cases brought by Centre users)	£20
7.3 On an application for an order requiring a judgment debtor or other person to attend court to provide information in connection with enforcement of a judgment or order	£40
7.4(a) On an application for a third party debt order or the appointment of a receiver by way of equitable execution	£50
7.4(b) On an application for a charging order Fee 7.4(a) and (b) Fee 7.4(a) shall be payable in respect of each third party against whom the order is sought. Fee 7.4(b) shall be payable in respect of each application issued.	£50
7.5 On an application for a judgment summons	£90
7.6 On the issue of a warrant of possession or a warrant of delivery Where the recovery of a sum of money is sought in addition, no further fee is payable.	£90
7.7 On an application for an attachment of earnings order (other than a consolidated attachment of earnings order) to secure payment of a judgment debt Fee 7.7	£60

Column 1 Number & description of fee	*Column 2* Amount of fee
Fee 7.7 is payable for each defendant against whom an order is sought. Fee 7.7 is not payable where the attachment of earnings order is made on the hearing of a judgment summons.	
7.8 On a consolidated attachment of earnings order or on an administration order	For every £1 or part of a £1 of the money paid into court in respect of debts due to creditors 10p
Fee 7.8 Fee 7.8 shall be calculated on any money paid into court under any order at the rate in force at the time when the order was made (or, where the order has been amended, at the time of the last amendment before the date of payment).	
7.9 On the application for the recovery of a tribunal award	£30
7.10 On a request for an order to recover a sum that is: • a specified debt within the meaning of the Enforcement of Road Traffic Debts Order 1993 as amended from time to time; or • pursuant to an enactment, treated as a specified debt for the purposes of that Order No fee is payable on: • an application for an extension of time to serve a statutory declaration in connection with any such order; or • a request to issue a warrant of execution to enforce any such order	£5
8. Sale (county court only)	
8.1 For removing or taking steps to remove goods to a place of deposit Fee 8.1 is to include the reasonable expenses of feeding and caring for any animals.	The reasonable expenses incurred
8.2 For advertising a sale by public auction pursuant to section 97 of the County Courts Act 1984	The reasonable expenses incurred
8.3 For the appraisement of goods	5p in the £1 or part of a £1 of the appraised value

Column 1 Number & description of fee	*Column 2* Amount of fee
8.4 For the sale of goods (including advertisements, catalogues, sale and commission and delivery of goods)	15p in the £1 or part of a £1 on the amount realised by the sale or such other sum as the district judge may consider to be justified in the circumstances
8.5 Where no sale takes place by reason of an execution being withdrawn, satisfied or stopped	(a)10p in the £1 or part of a £1 on the value of the goods seized, the value to be the appraised value where the goods have been appraised or such other sum as the district judge may consider to be justified in the circumstances; and in addition (b) any sum payable under Fee 8.1,8.2 or 8.3
FEES PAYABLE IN HIGH COURT ONLY	
9. Miscellaneous proceedings or matters (High Court only)	
Bills of Sale	
9.1 On filing any document under the Bills of Sale Acts 1878 and the Bills of Sale Act (1878) Amendment Act 1882 or on an application under section 15 of the Bills of Sale Act 1878 for an order that a memorandum of satisfaction be written on a registered copy of the bill	£10
Searches	
9.2 For an official certificate of the result of a search for each name, in any register or index held by the court; or in the Court Funds Office, for an official certificate of the result of a search of unclaimed balances for a specified period of up to 50 years	£5
9.3 On a search in person of the bankruptcy and companies records, including inspection, for each 15 minutes or part of 15 minutes	£5
Judge sitting as arbitrator	

Column 1 Number & description of fee	*Column 2* Amount of fee
9.4 On the appointment of –	
(a) a judge of the Commercial Court as an arbitrator or umpire under section 93 of the Arbitration Act 1996; or	£1,800
(b) a judge of the Technology and Construction Court as an arbitrator or umpire under section 93 of the Arbitration Act 1996	£1,400
9.5 For every day or part of a day (after the first day) of the hearing before –	
(a) a judge of the Commercial Court; or	£1,800
(b) a judge of the Technology and Construction Court, so appointed as arbitrator or umpire	£1,400
Where Fee 9.4 has been paid on the appointment of a judge of the Commercial Court or a judge of the Technology and Construction Court as an arbitrator or umpire but the arbitration does not proceed to a hearing or an award, the fee shall be refunded.	
10. Fees payable in Admiralty Matters (High Court only)	
In the Admiralty Registrar and Marshal's Office –	
10.1 On the issue of a warrant for the arrest of a ship or goods	£100
10.2 On the sale of a ship or goods –	
Subject to a minimum fee of £200,	
(a) for every £100 or fraction of £100 of the price up to £100,000	£1
(b) for every £100 or fraction of £100 of the price exceeding £100,000	50p
Where there is sufficient proceeds of sale in court, Fee 10.2 shall be taken by transfer from the proceeds of sale in court.	
10.3 On entering a reference for hearing by the Registrar	£50
FEES PAYABLE IN HIGH COURT AND COURT OF APPEAL ONLY	
11. Affidavits	
11.1 On taking an affidavit or an affirmation or attestation upon honour in lieu of an affidavit or a declaration except for the purpose of receipt of dividends from the Accountant General and for a declaration by a shorthand writer appointed in insolvency proceedings	
– for each person making any of the above	£5
11.2 For each exhibit referred to in an affidavit, affirmation, attestation or declaration for which Fee 11.1 is payable	£2

Column 1 Number & description of fee	*Column 2* Amount of fee
FEES PAYABLE IN COURT OF APPEAL ONLY	
12. Fees payable in appeals to the Court of Appeal	
12.1(a) Where in an appeal notice permission to appeal or an extension of time for appealing is applied for (or both are applied for) –	£200
on filing an appellant's notice, or	
where the respondent is appealing, on filing a respondent's notice	
12.1(b) Where permission to appeal is not required or has been granted by the lower court –	£400
on filing an appellant's notice, or	
on filing a respondent's notice where the respondent is appealing	
12.1(c) On the appellant filing an appeal questionnaire (unless the appellant has paid Fee 12.1(b), or on the respondent filing an appeal questionnaire (unless the respondent has paid Fee 12.1(b))	£400
12.2 On filing a respondent's notice where the respondent wishes to ask the appeal court to uphold the order of the lower court for reasons different from or additional to those given by the lower court	£200
12.3 On filing an application notice	£200
Fee 12.3	
Fee 12.3 shall not be payable for an application made in an appeal notice.	
FEES PAYABLE IN COUNTY COURT ONLY	
13. Registry of County Court Judgments	
13.1 On a request for the issue of a certificate of satisfaction or on a request for cancellation of the entry of a judgment in the Register where the judgment is satisfied in full within one month of the date of its entry	£10

Amendments—SI 2005/473.

SCHEDULE 2
ORDERS REVOKED

Article 8

Title	*Reference*
The Supreme Court Fees Order 1999	SI 1999/687
The Supreme Court Fees (Amendment) Order 1999	SI 1999/2569
The Supreme Court Fees (Amendment) Order 2000	SI 2000/641
The Supreme Court Fees (Amendment) Order 2003	SI 2003/646
The Supreme Court Fees (Amendment) Order 2004	SI 2004/2100
The Supreme Court Fees (Amendment No. 2) Order 2000	SI 2000/937
The Supreme Court Fees (Amendment No. 2) Order 2003	SI 2003/717
The County Court Fees Order 1999	SI 1999/689
The County Court Fees (Amendment) Order 1999	SI 1999/2548
The County Court Fees (Amendment) Order 2000	SI 2000/639
The County Court Fees (Amendment) Order 2003	SI 2003/648
The County Court Fees (Amendment) Order 2004	SI 2004/2098
The County Court Fees (Amendment No. 2) Order 2000	SI 2000/939
The County Court Fees (Amendment No. 2) Order 2003	SI 2003/718
The County Court Fees (Amendment No. 4) Order 2000	SI 2000/2310

SECTION 7

Other Statutory Material

SECTION 7: Other Statutory Material

Contents

Attachment of Earnings Act 1971

Cases in which attachment is available

1 Courts with power to attach earnings

(1) The High Court may make an attachment of earnings order to secure payments under a High Court maintenance order.

(2) A county court may make an attachment of earnings order to secure –

(a) payments under a High Court or a county court maintenance order;
(b) the payment of a judgment debt, other than a debt of less than £5 or such other sum as may be prescribed by county court rules; or
(c) payments under an administration order.

(3) A magistrates' court may make an attachment of earnings order to secure–

(a) payments under a magistrates' court maintenance order;
(b) the payment of any sum adjudged to be paid by a conviction or treated (by any enactment relating to the collection and enforcement of fines, costs, compensation or forfeited recognisances) as so adjudged to be paid; or
(c) the payment of any sum required to be paid by an order under section 17(2) of the Access to Justice Act 1999.

(4) The following provisions of this Act apply, except where otherwise stated, to attachment of earnings orders made, or to be made, by any court.

(5) Any power conferred by this Act to make an attachment of earnings order includes a power to make such an order to secure the discharge of liabilities arising before the coming into force of this Act.

Amendments—Access to Justice Act 1999, s 24, Sch 4, para 8.

Introduction—This Act sets out a method of enforcement by which a creditor may obtain payment of a judgment debt through direct deduction by the employer from the debtor's wages. The Act covers both maintenance orders, orders of magistrates' courts and judgment debts. Maintenance Orders are not covered in this volume and readers are referred to *The Family Court Practice* for further guidance. Orders made by magistrates courts, except orders for payment of money to be recoverable as a civil debt, are also outside the scope of this volume and are not covered here.The county court has exclusive jurisdiction to make attachment of earnings orders. Any judgment creditor and any person whose debt is included in an administration order may apply provided the debtor has failed to make at least one payment due under the judgment or order. The debtor must complete a form (N56) sent to him by the court giving particulars of his income and expenditure, and may be arrested or committed to prison if he fails or refuses to do so. If the debtor has other debts the court is obliged to consider whether to make an Administration Order. The court may also obtain up to date information about the debtors earnings direct from the employer. Once the court has confirmation that the debtor is employed and has sufficient information about his means an order may be made. The order must specify the amount to be deducted (the normal deduction rate) and the amount below which the debtors earnings must not fall (the protected earnings rate). This will not be below the debtor's income support entitlement unless the debtor has other means of support. Where more than one debt is to be paid by attachment the court will usually make a consolidated order. Part II of Sch 3 set out the rules for priority between various debts.

The Act imposes duties on employers and contains penal sanctions which may be invoked against those who fail to carry out these duties.

'a debt of less than £5' (s 1(2)(b))—The minimum (in the case of a county court judgment debt) is now £50 or the balance (including costs and interest) of a judgment which was for £50 or more (CCR Ord 27, r 7(9)).

2 Principal definitions

In this Act –

(a) 'maintenance order' means any order specified in Schedule 1 to this Act and includes such an order which has been discharged if any arrears are recoverable thereunder;
(b) 'High Court maintenance order', 'county court maintenance order' and 'magistrates' court maintenance order' mean respectively a maintenance order enforceable by the High Court, a county court and a magistrates' court;
(c) 'judgment debt' means a sum payable under –
  (i) a judgment or order enforceable by a court in England and Wales (not being a magistrates' court);
  (ii) an order of a magistrates' court for the payment of money recoverable summarily as a civil debt; or
  (iii) an order of any court which is enforceable as if it were for the payment of money so recoverable;

but does not include any sum payable under a maintenance order or an administration order;

(d) 'the relevant adjudication', in relation to any payment secured or to be secured by an attachment of earnings order, means the conviction, judgment, order or other adjudication from which there arises the liability to make the payment; and
(e) 'the debtor', in relation to an attachment of earnings order, or to proceedings in which a court has power to make an attachment of earnings order, or to proceedings arising out of such an order, means the person by whom payment is required by the relevant adjudication to be made.

3 Application for order and conditions of court's power to make it

(1) The following persons may apply for an attachment of earnings order –

(a) the person to whom payment under the relevant adjudication is required to be made (whether directly or through an officer of any court);
(b) where the relevant adjudication is an administration order, any one of the creditors scheduled to the order;
(c) without prejudice to paragraph (a) above, where the application is to a magistrates' court for an order to secure maintenance payments, and there is in force an order under section 59 of the Magistrates' Courts Act 1980 or section 19(2) of the Maintenance Orders Act 1950, that those payments be made to the designated officer for a magistrates' court, that officer;
(d) in the following cases the debtor–
  (i) where the application is to a magistrates' court; or
  (ii) where the application is to the High Court or a county court for an order to secure maintenance payments.

(2) (*repealed*)

(3) Subject to subsection (3A) below for an attachment of earnings order to be made on the application of any person other than the debtor it must appear to the court that the debtor has failed to make one or more payments required by the relevant adjudication.

(3A) Subsection (3) above shall not apply where the relevant adjudication is a maintenance order.

(3B) Where–

(a) a magistrates' court imposes a fine on a person in respect of an offence, and

(b) that person consents to an order being made under this subsection,

the court may at the time it imposes the fine, and without the need for an application, make an attachment of earnings order to secure the payment of the fine.

(3C) Where—

(a) a magistrates' court makes in the case of a person convicted of an offence an order under section 130 of the Powers of Criminal Courts (Sentencing) Act 2000 (a compensation order) requiring him to pay compensation or to make other payments, and

(b) that person consents to an order being made under this subsection,

the court may at the time it makes the compensation order, and without the need for an application, make an attachment of earnings order to secure the payment of the compensation or other payments.

(4) Where proceedings are brought–

(a) in the High Court or a county court for the enforcement of a maintenance order by committal under section 5 of the Debtors Act 1869; or

(b) in a magistrates' court for the enforcement of a maintenance order under section 76 of the Magistrates' Courts Act 1980 (distress or committal),

then, the court may make an attachment of earnings order to secure payments under the maintenance order, instead of dealing with the case under section 5 of the said Act of 1869 or, as the case may be, section 76 of the said Act of 1980.

(5) (*repealed*)

(6) Where proceedings are brought in a county court for an order of committal under section 5 of the Debtors Act 1869 in respect of a judgment debt for any of the taxes, contributions or liabilities specified in Schedule 2 to this Act, the court may, in any circumstances in which it has power to make such an order, make instead an attachment of earnings order to secure the payment of the judgment debt.

(7) A county court shall not make an attachment of earnings order to secure the payment of a judgment debt if there is in force an order or warrant for the debtor's committal, under section 5 of the Debtors Act 1869, in respect of that debt; but in any such case the court may discharge the order or warrant with a view to making an attachment of earnings order instead.

Amendments—Magistrates' Courts Act 1980, s 154, Sch 7, para 97; Maintenance Enforcement Act 1991, s 11(1), Sch 2, para 1; Criminal Procedure and Investigations Act 1996, s 53; Access to Justice Act 1999, s 90, Sch 13, paras 64, 65; Powers of Criminal Courts (Sentencing) Act 2000, s 165(1), Sch 9, para 44; Courts Act 2003, s 109(1), Sch 8, para 141.

'failed to make ... payments'—If a judgment is payable by instalments a late payment is not a failure for this purpose provided the payments are up to date at the date on which the order falls to be made.

Administration orders—For the power to make an administration order see CCA 1984, s 112, set out in Section 6 of this work and see Section 2 for the procedure under CCR Ord 39, Pt I

Administration orders in the county court

4 Extension of power to make administration order

(1) Where, on an application to a county court for an attachment of earnings order to secure the payment of a judgment debt, it appears to the court that the debtor also has other debts, the court –

- (a) shall consider whether the case may be one in which all the debtor's liabilities should be dealt with together and that for that purpose an administration order should be made; and
- (b) if of opinion that it may be such a case, shall have power (whether or not it makes the attachment of earnings order applied for), with a view to making an administration order, to order the debtor to furnish to the court a list of all his creditors and the amounts which he owes to them respectively.

(2) If, on receipt of the list referred to in subsection (1)(b) above, it appears to the court that the debtor's whole indebtedness amounts to not more than the amount which for the time being is the county court limit for the purposes of s 112 of the County Courts Act 1984 (limit of total indebtedness governing county court's power to make administration order on application of debtor), the court may make such an order in respect of the debtor's estate.

(2A) Subsection (2) above is subject to s 112(3) and (4) of the County Courts Act 1984 (which require that, before an administration order is made, notice is to be given to all the creditors and thereafter restrict the right of any creditor to institute bankruptcy proceedings).

(3) (*repealed*)

(4) Nothing in this section is to be taken as prejudicing any right of a debtor to apply, under section 112 of the County Courts Act 1984, for an administration order.

Amendments—Insolvency Act 1976, ss 13, 14(4), Sch 3; County Courts Act 1984, s 148(1), Sch 2, para 40.

'order the debtor to furnish ... a list of ... creditors' (s 4(1)(b))—Once this order has been made the collecting officer must retain any money paid over by the employer until the court has decided whether or not to make an order, see s 13(3) below.

Procedure—The Act provides no sanction for a debtor's failure to provide the information about his debts. If he fails to co-operate, the court must decide to make no order so that sums retained by the collecting officer under s 13(3) can be released to the creditor.

Limit of total indebtedness—The current figure is £5000.

5 Attachment of earnings to secure payments under administration order

(1) Where a county court makes an administration order in respect of a debtor's estate, it may also make an attachment of earnings order to secure the payments required by the administration order.

(2) At any time when an administration order is in force a county court may (with or without an application) make an attachment of earnings order to secure the payments required by the administration order, if it appears to the court that the debtor has failed to make any such payment.

(3) The power of a county court under this section to make an attachment of earnings order to secure the payments required by an administration order shall, where the debtor is already subject to an attachment of earnings order to secure the payment of a judgment debt, include power to direct that the last-mentioned order shall take effect (with or without variation under section 9 of this Act) as an order to secure the payments required by the administration order.

Consequences of attachment order

6 Effect and contents of order

(1) An attachment of earnings order shall be an order directed to a person who appears to the court to have the debtor in his employment and shall operate as an instruction to that person –

- (a) to make periodical deductions from the debtor's earnings in accordance with Part I of Schedule 3 to this Act; and
- (b) at such times as the order may require, or as the court may allow, to pay the amounts deducted to the collecting officer of the court, as specified in the order.

(2) For the purposes of this Act, the relationship of employer and employee shall be treated as subsisting between two persons if one of them, as a principal and not as a servant or agent, pays to the other any sums defined as earnings by section 24 of this Act.

(3) An attachment of earnings order shall contain prescribed particulars enabling the debtor to be identified by the employer.

(4) Except where it is made to secure maintenance payments, the order shall specify the whole amount payable under the relevant adjudication (or so much of that amount as remains unpaid), including any relevant costs.

(5) The order shall specify –

- (a) the normal deduction rate, that is to say, the rate (expressed as a sum of money per week, month or other period) at which the court thinks it reasonable for the debtor's earnings to be applied to meeting his liability under the relevant adjudication; and
- (b) the protected earnings rate, that is to say the rate (so expressed) below which, having regard to the debtor's resources and needs, the court thinks it reasonable that the earnings actually paid to him should not be reduced.

(6) In the case of an order made to secure payments under a maintenance order (not being an order for the payment of a lump sum), the normal deduction rate–

- (a) shall be determined after taking account of any right or liability of the debtor to deduct income tax when making the payments; and
- (b) shall not exceed the rate which appears to the court necessary for the purpose of–
  - (i) securing payment of the sums falling due from time to time under the maintenance order, and

(ii) securing payment within a reasonable period of any sums already due and unpaid under the maintenance order.

(7) For the purposes of an attachment of earnings order, the collecting officer of the court shall be (subject to later variation of the order under section 9 of this Act) –

(a) in the case of an order made by the High Court, either–
   (i) the proper officer of the High Court, or
   (ii) the appropriate officer of such county court as the order may specify;

(b) in the case of an order made by a county court, the appropriate officer of that court; and

(c) in the case of an order made by a magistrates' court, the designated officer for that court or for another magistrates' court specified in the order.

(8) In subsection (7) above 'appropriate officer' means an officer designated by the Lord Chancellor.

(9)–(12) *(not yet in force)*

Amendments—Administration of Justice Act 1977, s 19(5); Courts and Legal Services Act 1990, s 125(2), Sch 17 (not yet in force); Access to Justice Act 1999, s 90, Sch 13, paras 64, 66; Courts Act 2003, s 109(1), Sch 8, para 142.

Earnings—These are defined by s 24. Section 16 and CCR Ord 27, r 11 set out the procedure for resolving disputes as to what payments may be included in the debtor's earnings for the purpose of operating any order.

Prescribed particulars—These are set out in CCR Ord 27, r 10.

Relevant costs—See s 25(2) below. Costs awarded in the original proceedings and costs awarded in the application for attachment are both included.

7 Compliance with order by employer

(1) Where an attachment of earnings order has been made, the employer shall, if he has been served with the order, comply with it; but he shall be under no liability for non-compliance before seven days have elapsed since the service.

(2) Where a person is served with an attachment of earnings order directed to him and he has not the debtor in his employment, or the debtor subsequently ceases to be in his employment, he shall (in either case), within ten days from the date of service or, as the case may be, the cesser, give notice of that fact to the court.

(3) Part II of Schedule 3 to this Act shall have effect with respect to the priority to be accorded as between two or more attachment of earnings orders directed to a person in respect of the same debtor.

(4) On any occasion when the employer makes, in compliance with the order, a deduction from the debtor's earnings –

(a) he shall be entitled to deduct, in addition, £1.00, or such other sum as may be prescribed by order made by the Lord Chancellor, towards his clerical and administrative costs; and

(b) he shall give to the debtor a statement in writing of the total amount of the deduction.

(5) An order of the Lord Chancellor under subsection (4)(a) above –

(a) may prescribe different sums in relation to different classes of cases;

(b) may be varied or revoked by a subsequent order made under that paragraph; and
(c) shall be made by statutory instrument subject to annulment by resolution of either House of Parliament.

Amendments—SI 1991/356.

Non-compliance—An employer who fails to comply with either subs (1) or (2) commits an offence under s 23, (see below).

8 Interrelation with alternative remedies open to creditor

(1) Where an attachment of earnings order has been made to secure maintenance payments, no order or warrant of commitment shall be issued in consequence of any proceedings for the enforcement of the related maintenance order begun before the making of the attachment of earnings order.

(2) Where a county court has made an attachment of earnings order to secure the payment of a judgment debt –

(a) no order or warrant of commitment shall be issued in consequence of any proceedings for the enforcement of the debt begun before the making of the attachment of earnings order; and
(b) so long as the order is in force, no execution for the recovery of the debt shall issue against any property of the debtor without the leave of the county court.

(3) An attachment of earnings order made to secure maintenance payments shall cease to have effect upon the making of an order of commitment or the issue of a warrant of commitment for the enforcement of the related maintenance order, or upon the exercise for that purpose of the power conferred on a magistrates' court by section 77(2) of the Magistrates' Courts Act 1980 to postpone the issue of such a warrant.

(4) An attachment of earnings order made to secure the payment of a judgment debt shall cease to have effect on the making of an order of commitment or the issue of a warrant of commitment for the enforcement of the debt.

(5) An attachment of earnings order made to secure any payment specified in section 1(3)(b) or (c) of this Act shall cease to have effect on the issue of a warrant committing the debtor to prison for default in making that payment.

Amendments—Magistrates' Courts Act 1980, s 154, Sch 7, para 98.

Subsequent proceedings

9 Variation, lapse and discharge of orders

(1) The court may make an order discharging or varying an attachment of earnings order.

(2) Where an order is varied, the employer shall, if he has been served with notice of the variation, comply with the order as varied; but he shall be under no liability for non-compliance before seven days have elapsed since the service.

(3) Rules of court may make provision –

(a) as to the circumstances in which an attachment of earnings order may be varied or discharged by the court of its own motion:
(b) in the case of an attachment of earnings order made by a magistrates' court, for enabling a single justice, on an application made by the

debtor on the ground of a material change in his resources and needs since the order was made or last varied, to vary the order for a period of not more than four weeks by an increase of the protected earnings rate.

(4) Where an attachment of earnings order has been made and the person to whom it is directed ceases to have the debtor in his employment, the order shall lapse (except as respects deduction from earnings paid after the cesser and payment to the collecting officer of amounts deducted at any time) and be of no effect unless and until the court again directs it to a person (whether the same as before or another) who appears to the court to have the debtor in his employment.

(5) The lapse of an order under subsection (4) above shall not prevent its being treated as remaining in force for other purposes.

Non Compliance—An employer who fails to comply with subs (2) commits an offence under s 23, (see below).

Lapse of order—Note that if a debtor becomes unemployed or changes employment the order is not discharged but simply lapses until it is revived by being directed to the new employer.

****

12 Termination of employer's liability to make deductions

(1) Where an attachment of earnings order ceases to have effect under section 8 or 11 of this Act, the proper officer of the prescribed court shall give notice of the cesser to the person to whom the order was directed.

(2) Where, in the case of an attachment of earnings order made other wise than to secure maintenance payments, the whole amount payable under the relevant adjudication has been paid, and also any relevant costs, the court shall give notice to the employer that no further compliance with the order is required.

(3) Where an attachment of earnings order –

(a) ceases to have effect under section 8 or 11 of this Act; or
(b) is discharged under section 9,

the person to whom the order has been directed shall be under no liability in consequence of his treating the order as still in force at any time before the expiration of seven days from the date on which the notice required by subsection (1) above or, as the case may be, a copy of the discharging order is served on him.

Administrative provisions

13 Application of sums received by collecting officer

(1) Subject to subsection (3) below, the collecting officer to whom a person makes payments in compliance with an attachment of earnings order shall, after deducting such court fees, if any, in respect of proceedings for or arising out of the order, as are deductible from those payments, deal with the sums paid in the same way as he would if they had been paid by the debtor to satisfy the relevant adjudication.

(2) Any sums paid to the collecting officer under an attachment of earnings order made to secure maintenance payments shall, when paid to the person entitled to receive those payments, be deemed to be payments made by the

debtor (with such deductions, if any, in respect of income tax as the debtor is entitled or required to make) so as to discharge–

(a) first, any sums for the time being due and unpaid under the related maintenance order (a sum due at an earlier date being discharged before a sum due at a later date); and

(b) secondly, any costs incurred in proceedings relating to the related maintenance order which were payable by the debtor when the attachment of earnings order was made or last varied.

(3) When a county court makes an attachment of earnings order to secure the payment of a judgment debt and also, under section 4(1) of this Act, orders the debtor to furnish to the court a list of his creditors, sums paid to the collecting officer in compliance with the attachment of earnings order shall not be dealt with by him as mentioned in subsection (1) above, but shall be retained by him pending the decision of the court whether or not to make an administration order and shall then be dealt with by him as the court may direct.

Insolvency of debtor—As soon as money has been paid to the collecting officer it belongs to the creditor who, at least until he has notice that an insolvency petition has been presented, is protected by Insolvency Act 1986, s 284(4) and is entitled to be paid in preference to the Trustee in Bankruptcy (*Re Green, a bankrupt ex parte Official Receiver v Cutting* [1979] 1 All ER 832).

Insolvency of Employer—The position regarding the entitlement to money deducted by an employer and not paid over before he becomes insolvent is less clear. The better view is that by invoking the Attachment of Earnings procedure, the creditor has constituted the employer his agent for receiving payment by the debtor. Once the deduction has been made, payment has effectively been made to the creditor, who will be able to claim against the employer's Trustee in Bankruptcy.

14 Power of court to obtain statement of earnings etc

(1) Where in any proceedings a court has the power to make an attachment of earnings order, it may –

(a) order the debtor to give to the court, within a specified period, a statement signed by him of –

(i) the name and address of any person by whom earnings are paid to him;

(ii) specified particulars as to his earnings and anticipated earnings, and as to his resources and needs; and

(iii) specified particulars for the purpose of enabling the debtor to be identified by any employer of his;

(b) order any person appearing to the court to have the debtor in his employment to give to the court, within a specified period, a statement signed by him or on his behalf of specified particulars of the debtor's earnings and anticipated earnings.

(2) Where an attachment of earnings has been made, the court may at any time thereafter while the order is in force –

(a) make such an order as is described in subsection (1)(a) or (b) above; and

(b) order the debtor to attend before it on a day and at a time specified in the order to give the information described in subsection (1)(a) above.

(3) In the case of an application to a magistrates' court for an attachment of earnings order, or for the variation or discharge of such an order, the power to make an order under subsection (1) or (2) above shall be exercisable also, before the hearing of the application, by a single justice.

(4) Without prejudice to subsections (1) to (3) above, rules of court may provide that where notice of application for an attachment of earnings order is served on the debtor it shall include a requirement that he shall give to the court, within such period and in such manner as may be prescribed, a statement in writing of the matters specified in subsection (1)(a) above and of any other prescribed matters which are, or may be, relevant under section 6 of this Act to the determination of the normal deduction rate and the protected earnings rate to be specified in any order made on the application.

(5) In any proceedings in which a court has the power to make an attachment of earnings order, and in any proceedings for the making, variation or discharge of such an order, a document purporting to be a statement given to the court in compliance with an order under subsection (1)(a) or (b) above, or with any such requirement of a notice of application for an attachment of earnings order as is mentioned in subsection (4) above, shall, in the absence of proof to the contrary, be deemed to be a statement so given and shall be evidence of the facts stated therein.

Amendments—Administration of Justice Act 1982, s 53(1).

'any person appearing to the Court to have the debtor in his employment' (s 14(1)(b))—Where the creditor knows the name of the debtor's employer, he should request the court to make an order under s 14(1)(b) as soon as he applies for an attachment of earning order. This will enable the court (a) to verify the earnings figures disclosed by the debtor in his form N56 and (b) to make an order forthwith if the debtor fails to return his Form N56.

Non-compliance—Section 23 below sets out the penalties for non-compliance with orders under subss (1), (2)(b) and (4)

15 Obligation of debtor and his employers to notify changes of employment and earnings

While an attachment of earnings order is in force –

- (a) the debtor shall from time to time notify the court in writing of every occasion on which he leaves any employment, or becomes employed or re-employed, not later (in each case) than seven days from the date on which he did so;
- (b) the debtor shall, on any occasion when he becomes employed or re-employed, include in his notification under paragraph (a) above particulars of his earnings and anticipated earnings from the relevant employment; and
- (c) any person who becomes the debtor's employer and knows that the order is in force and by what court it was made shall, within seven days of his becoming the debtor's employer or of acquiring that knowledge (whichever is the later) notify that court in writing that he is the debtor's employer, and include in his notification a statement of the debtor's earnings and anticipated earnings.

Non-compliance—Any person who fails to comply with this section commits an offence under s 23, (see below).

16 Power of court to determine whether particular payments are earnings

(1) Where an attachment of earnings order is in force, the court shall, on application of a person specified in subsection (2) below, determine whether

payments to the debtor of a particular class or description specified by the application are earnings for the purposes of the order; and the employer shall be entitled to give effect to any determination for the time being in force under this section.

(2) The persons referred to in subsection (1) above are –

- (a) the employer;
- (b) the debtor;
- (c) the person to whom payment under the relevant adjudication is required to be made (whether directly or through the officer of any court); and
- (d) without prejudice to paragraph (c) above, where the application is in respect of an attachment of earnings order made to secure payments under a magistrates' court maintenance order, the collecting officer.

(3) Where an application under this section is made by the employer, he shall not incur any liability for non-compliance with the order as respects any payments of the class or description specified by the application which are made by him to the debtor while the application, or any appeal in consequence thereof, is pending; but this subsection shall not, unless the court otherwise orders, apply as respects such payments if the employer subsequently withdraws the application or, as the case may be, abandons the appeal.

Procedure—See CCR Ord 27, r 11. The application should be made to the district judge.

17 Consolidated attachment orders

(1) The powers of a county court under sections 1 and 3 of this Act shall include power to make an attachment of earnings order to secure the payment of any number of judgment debts; and the powers of a magistrates' court under those sections shall include power to make an attachment of earnings order to secure the discharge of any number of such liabilities as are specified in section 1(3).

(2) An attachment of earnings order made by virtue of this section shall be known as a consolidated attachment order.

(3) The power to make a consolidated attachment order shall be exercised subject to and in accordance with rules of court; and rules made for the purposes of this section may provide –

- (a) for the transfer from one court to another –
  - (i) of an attachment of earnings order, or any proceedings for or arising out of such an order; and
  - (ii) of functions relating to the enforcement of any liability capable of being secured by attachment of earnings;
- (b) for enabling a court to which any order, proceedings or functions have been transferred under the rules to vary or discharge an attachment of earnings order made by another court and to replace it (if the court thinks fit) with a consolidated attachment order;
- (c) for the cases in which any power exercisable under this section or the rules may be exercised by a court of its own motivation or on the application of a prescribed person;

(d) for requiring the officer of a court who receives payments made to him in compliance with an attachment of earnings order, instead of complying with section 13 of this Act, to deal with them as directed by the court or the rules; and

(e) for modifying or excluding provisions of this Act or Part III of the Magistrates' Courts Act 1980, but only so far as may be necessary or expedient for securing conformity with the operation of rules made by virtue of paragraphs (a) to (d) of this subsection.

Amendments—Magistrates' Courts Act 1980, s 154, Sch 7, para 99; Access to Justice Act 1999, s 90, Sch 13, paras 64, 67.

Rules of court—These are set out at CCR Ord 27, rr 18–22.

****

Miscellaneous provisions

22 Persons employed under the Crown

(1) The fact that an attachment of earnings order is made at the suit of the Crown shall not prevent its operation at any time when the debtor is in the employment of the Crown.

(2) Where a debtor is in the employment of the Crown and an attachment of earnings order is made in respect of him, then for the purposes of this Act –

(a) the chief officer for the time being of the department, office or other body in which the debtor is employed shall be treated as having the debtor in his employment (any transfer of the debtor from one department, office or body to another being treated as a change of employment); and

(b) any earnings paid by the Crown or a Minister of the Crown, or out of the public revenue of the United Kingdom, shall be treated as paid by the said chief officer.

(3) If any question arises, in the proceedings for or arising out of an attachment of earnings order, as to what department, office or other body is concerned for the purposes of this section, or as to who for those purposes is the chief officer thereof, the question shall be referred to and determined by the Minister for the Civil Service; but that Minister shall not be under any obligation to consider a reference under this subsection unless it is made by the court.

(4) A document purporting to set out a determination of the said Minister under subsection (3) above and to be signed by an official of the Office of Public Service shall, in any such proceedings as are mentioned in that subsection, be admissible in evidence and be deemed to contain an accurate statement of such a determination unless the contrary is shown.

(5) This Act shall have effect notwithstanding any enactment passed before 29 May 1970 and preventing or avoiding the attachment or diversion of sums due to a person in respect of service under the Crown, whether by way of remuneration, pension or otherwise.

Amendments—SI 1992/1296; SI 1995/2985.

Service personnel—The earnings of service personnel cannot be attached, s 24(2)(b) below. However there are special provisions in Armed Forces Act 1971, ss 59 and 61 for judgments to be satisfied by administrative deduction from service pay.

23 Enforcement provisions

(1) If, after being served with notice of an application to a county court for an attachment of earnings order or for the variation of such an order or with an order made under section 14(2)(b) above, the debtor fails to attend on the day and at the time specified for any hearing of the application or specified in the order, the court may adjourn the hearing and order him to attend at a specified time on another day; and if the debtor –

(a) fails to attend at that time on that day; or
(b) attends, but refuses to be sworn or give evidence,

he may be ordered by the judge to be imprisoned for not more than fourteen days.

(1A) In any case where the judge has the power to make an order of imprisonment under subsection (1) for failure to attend, he may, in lieu of or in addition to making that order, order the debtor to be arrested and brought to the court either forthwith or at such time as the judge may direct.

(2) Subject to this section, a person commits an offence if –

(a) being required by section 7(1) or 9(2) of this Act to comply with an attachment of earnings order, he fails to do so; or
(b) being required by section 7(2) of this Act to give a notice for the purposes of that subsection, he fails to give it, or fails to give it within the time required by that subsection; or
(c) he fails to comply with an order under section 14(1) of this Act or with any such requirement of a notice of application for an attachment of earnings order as is mentioned in section 14(4), or fails (in either case) to comply within the time required by the order or notice; or
(d) he fails to comply with section 15 of this Act; or
(e) he gives notice for the purposes of section 7(2) of this Act, or a notification for the purposes of section 15, which he knows to be false in a material particular, or recklessly gives such a notice or notification which is false in a material particular, or
(f) in purported compliance with section 7(2) or 15 of this Act, or with an order under section 14(1), or with any such requirement of a notice of application for an attachment of earnings order as is mentioned in section 14(4), he makes any statement which he knows to be false in a material particular, or recklessly makes any statement which is false in a material particular.

(3) Where a person commits an offence under subsection (2) above in relation to proceedings in, or to an attachment of earnings order made by, the High Court or a county court, he shall be liable on summary conviction to a fine of not more than level 2 on the standard scale or he may be ordered by a judge of the High Court or the county court judge (as the case may be) to pay a fine of not more than £250 or, in the case of an offence specified in subsection (4) below, to be imprisoned for not more than fourteen days; and where a person commits an offence under subsection (2) otherwise than as mentioned above in this subsection, he shall be liable on summary conviction to a fine of not more than level 2 on the standard scale.

(4) The offences referred to above in the case of which a judge may impose imprisonment are –

(a) an offence under subsection (2)(c) or (d), if committed by the debtor; and

(b) an offence under subsection (2)(e) or (f), whether committed by the debtor or any other person.

(5) It shall be a defence –

(a) for a person charged with an offence under subsection (2)(a) above to prove that he took all reasonable steps to comply with the attachment of earnings order in question;

(b) for a person charged with an offence under subsection (2)(b) to prove that he did not know, and could not reasonably be expected to know, that the debtor was not in his employment, or (as the case may be) had ceased to be so, and that he gave the required notice as soon as reasonably practicable after the fact came to his knowledge.

(6) Where a person is convicted or dealt with for an offence under subsection (2)(a), the court may order him to pay, to whoever is the collecting officer of the court for the purposes of the attachment of earnings order in question, any sums deducted by that person from the debtor's earnings and not already paid to the collecting officer.

(7) Where under this section a person is ordered by a judge of the High Court or a county court judge to be imprisoned, the judge may at any time revoke the order and, if the person is already in custody, order his discharge.

(8) Any fine imposed by a judge of the High Court under subsection (3) above and any sums ordered by the High Court to be paid under subsection (6) above shall be recoverable in the same way as a fine imposed by that court in the exercise of its jurisdiction to punish for contempt of court; section 129 of the County Courts Act 1984 (enforcement of fines) shall apply to payment of a fine imposed by a county court judge under subsection (3) and of any sums ordered by a county court judge to be paid under subsection (6); and any sum ordered by a magistrates' court to be paid under subsection (6) shall be recoverable as a sum adjudged to be paid on a conviction by that court.

(9) For the purposes of section 13 of the Administration of Justice Act 1960 (appeal in cases of contempt of court), subsection (3) above shall be treated as an enactment enabling the High Court or a county court to deal with an offence under subsection (2) above as if it were contempt of court.

(10) In this section references to proceedings in a court are to proceedings in which that court has power to make an attachment of earnings order or has made such an order.

(11) A district judge, assistant district judge or deputy district judge shall have the same powers under this section as a judge of a county court.

Amendments—Contempt of Court Act 1981, s 41(5), Sch 2; Administration of Justice Act 1982, s 53(2); Criminal Justice Act 1982, ss 37, 38, 46; County Courts Act 1984, s 148(1), Sch 2, para 41; Courts and Legal Services Act 1990, s 125(2), Sch 17; Criminal Justice Act 1991, s 17, Sch 4, Pt I.

Imprisonment under s 23(1) and s 23(3)—Section 23(1) only applies where the district judge has directed a hearing under CCR Ord 27, r 7(4) and the debtor fails to attend the adjourned hearing despite having been personally served. with notice in Form N58. In these cases only, the court may use the alternative of ordering arrest under s 23(1)(A) or making a suspended committal order under CCR Ord 27, r 7A.

Much more commonly, the debtor fails to complete a Form N56 giving details of his earnings. He then fails to comply with an order in Form N61 requiring him under s 14(1)(a) to give these details. This failure is an offence under s 23(2)(c). In that event, the judge cannot order arrest under s 23(1)(A). The debtor is served with a notice to show cause in Form N63 and may be fined or imprisoned under s 23(3). Any offence under s 23(2) is in the nature of a contempt of court. Any sentence of imprisonment may be therefore be suspended (*Lee v Walker* [1985] 1 All ER 781, CA). All offences committed by employers fall within s 23(2) and can be dealt with by fine or imprisonment under s 23(3).

'level 2 on the standard scale'(s 23(3))—The present figure is £500 (Criminal Justice Act 1991, s 17(1)).

'It shall be a defence' (s 23(5))—A defendant who relies upon one of the defences in s 23(5) carries the burden of proof but to the civil standard only.

Appeals—If the order is made by the district judge there is a general right of appeal to a Circuit Judge under CCR Ord 37, r 6. Additionally, Administration of Justice Act 1960, s 13(2)(b) provides for a direct right of appeal to the Court of Appeal against any order made under s 23(3). Leave to appeal is not required. There is no direct right of appeal to the Court of Appeal against orders made under s 23(1).

24 Meaning of 'earnings'

(1) For the purposes of this Act, but subject to the following subsection, 'earnings' are any sums payable to a person –

(a) by way of wages or salary (including any fees, bonus, commission, overtime pay or other emoluments payable in addition to wages or salary or payable under a contract of service);

(b) by way of pension (including an annuity in respect of past services, whether or not rendered to the person paying the annuity, and including periodical payments by way of compensation for the loss, abolition or relinquishment, or diminution in emoluments, of any office or employment);

(c) by way of statutory sick pay.

(2) The following shall not be treated as earnings –

(a) sums payable by any department of the Government of Northern Ireland or of a territory outside the United Kingdom;

(b) pay or allowances payable to the debtor as a member of Her Majesty's forces other than pay or allowances payable by his employer to him as a special member of a reserve force (within the meaning of the Reserve Forces Act 1996);

(ba) a tax credit (within the meaning of the Tax Credits Act 2002);

(c) pension, allowances or benefit payable under any enactment relating to social security;

(d) pension or allowances payable in respect of disablement or disability;

(e) except in relation to a maintenance order wages payable to a person as a seaman, other than wages payable to him as a seaman of a fishing boat;

(f) guaranteed minimum pension within the meaning of the Pension Schemes Act 1993.

(3) In subsection (2)(e) above –

'fishing boat' means a vessel of whatever size, and in whatever way propelled, which is for the time being employed in sea fishing or in the sea-fishing service;

'seaman' includes every person (except masters and pilots) employed or engaged in any capacity on board any ship; and

'wages' includes emoluments.

Amendments—Social Security Pensions Act 1975, s 65(1), Sch 4, para 15; Merchant Shipping Act 1979, s 39(1); Social Security Act 1985, s 21, Sch 4, para 1; Social Security Act 1986, s 86(1),

Sch 10, Pt VI, para 102; Pension Schemes Act 1993, s 190, Sch 8, para 4; Merchant Shipping Act 1995, s 314(2), Sch 13, para 46; SI 1998/3086; Tax Credits Act 2002, s 47, Sch 3, para 1.

Pension payable in respect of disablement—Any pension payable to a debtor who retires on grounds of disablement does not fall within s 24(2)(d) if the pension is calculated solely by reference ot his length of service (*Miles v Miles* [1979] 1 All ER 865).

Service personnel—In contrast to service pay (see note to s 22 above), service pensions may be attached.

25 General interpretation

(1) In this Act, except where the context otherwise requires –

'administration order' means an order made under, and so referred to in, Part VI of the County Courts Act 1984;

'the court', in relation to an attachment of earnings order, means the court which made the order, subject to rules of court as to the venue for, and the transfer of, proceedings in county courts and magistrates' courts;

'debtor' and 'relevant adjudication' have the meanings given by section 2 of this Act;

'the employer', in relation to the attachment of earnings order, means the person who is required by the order to make deductions from earnings paid by him to the debtor;

'judgment debt' has the meaning given by section 2 of this Act;

'maintenance order' has the meaning given by section 2 of this Act;

'maintenance payments' means payments required under a maintenance order;

'prescribed' means prescribed by rules of court;

(*revoked*)

(2) Any reference in this Act to sums payable under a judgment or order, or to the payment of such sums, includes a reference to costs and the payment of them; and the references in sections 6(4) and 12(2) to relevant costs are to any costs of the proceedings in which the attachment of earnings order in question was made, being costs which the debtor is liable to pay.

(3) References in sections 6(5)(b), 9(3)(b) and 14(1)(a) of this Act to the debtor's needs include references to the needs of any person for whom he must, or reasonably may, provide.

(4) (*repealed*)

(5) Any power to make rules which is conferred by this Act is without prejudice to any other power to make rules of court.

(6) This Act, so far as it relates to magistrates' courts, and Part III of the Magistrates' Courts Act 1980 shall be construed as if this Act were contained in that Part.

(7) References in this Act to any enactment include references to that enactment amended by or under any other enactment, including this Act.

Amendments—Magistrates' Courts Act 1980, s 154, Sch 7, para 101; County Courts Act 1984, s 148(1), Sch 2, para 42; Legal Aid Act 1988, Sch 5, para 3; Dock Work Act 1989, Sch 1, Pt I; Access to Justice Act 1999, s 106, Sch 15, Pts I, V; Courts Act 2003, s 109(1), (3), Sch 8, para 145.

****

29 Citation, repeal, extent and commencement

(1) This Act may be cited as the Attachment of Earnings Act 1971.

(2) The enactments specified in Schedule 6 to this Act are hereby repealed to the extent specified in the third column of that Schedule.

(3) This Act, except section 20(2), does not extend to Scotland and, except section 20(2) does not extend to Northern Ireland.

(4) This Act shall come into force on the day appointed under section 54 of the Administration of Justice Act 1970 for the coming into force of Part II of that Act.

Amendments—Northern Ireland Constitution Act 1973, s 41(1), Sch 6, Pt I.

****

SCHEDULE 2

TAXES, SOCIAL SECURITY CONTRIBUTIONS ETC RELEVANT FOR PURPOSES OF SECTION 3(6)

1 Income tax or any other tax or liability recoverable under section 65, 66 or 68 of the Taxes Management Act 1970.

2 (*repealed*)

3 Contributions equivalent premiums under Part III of the Pension Schemes Act 1993.

3A Class 1, 2 and 4 contributions under Part I of the Social Security Contributions and Benefits Act 1992

4 (*repealed*)

Amendments—Social Security Act 1973, s 100(2), Sch 28, Pt I; Social Security Pensions Act 1975, s 65(1), Sch 4, para 16; Social Security (Consequential Provisions) Act 1975, s 1(3), Sch 2, para 42; Statute Law (Repeals) Act 1989; Social Security (Consequential Provisions) Act 1992, s 4, Sch 2, para 6; Pension Schemes Act 1993, s 190, Sch 8, para 4; Pensions Act 1995, s 151, Sch 5, para 3.

SCHEDULE 3

DEDUCTIONS BY EMPLOYER UNDER ATTACHMENT OF EARNINGS ORDER

PART I
SCHEME OF DEDUCTIONS

Preliminary definitions

1 The following three paragraphs have effect for defining and explaining, for purposes of this Schedule, expressions used therein.

2 'Pay-day', in relation to earnings paid to a debtor, means an occasion on which they are paid.

3 'Attachable earnings', in relation to a pay-day, are the earnings which remain payable to the debtor on that day after deduction by the employer of –

- (a) income tax;
- (b) (*repealed*)
- (bb) Primary Class I contributions under Part I of the Social Security Act 1975;
- (c) amounts deductible under any enactment, or in pursuance of a request in writing by the debtor, for the purposes of a superannuation scheme, namely any enactment, rules, deed or other instrument providing for the payment of annuities or lump sums –
  - (i) to the persons with respect to whom the instrument has effect on their retirement at a specified age or on becoming incapacitated at some earlier age, or
  - (ii) to the personal representatives or the widows, relatives or dependants of such persons on their death or otherwise,

whether with or without any further or other benefits.

4 (1) On any pay-day –

- (a) 'the normal deduction' is arrived at by applying the normal deduction rate (as specified in the relevant attachment of earnings order) with respect to the relevant period; and
- (b) 'the protected earnings' are arrived at by applying the protected earnings rate (as so specified) with respect to the relevant period.

(2) For the purposes of this paragraph the relevant period in relation to any pay-day is the period beginning –

- (a) if it is the first pay-day of the debtor's employment with the employer, with the first day of employment; or
- (b) if on the last pay-day earnings were paid in respect of a period falling wholly or partly after that pay-day, with the first day after the end of that period; or
- (c) in any other case, with the first day after the last pay-day, and ending –

(i) where earnings are paid in respect of a period falling wholly or partly after the pay-day, with the last day of that period; or
(ii) in any other case, with the pay-day.

5 Employer's deduction (judgment debts and administration orders)

In the case of an attachment of earnings order made to secure the payment of a judgment debt or payments under an administration order, the employer shall on any pay-day –

(a) if the attachable earnings exceed the protected earnings, deduct from the attachable earnings the amount of the excess or the normal deduction, whichever is the less;
(b) make no deduction if the attachable earnings are equal to, or less than, the protected earnings.

6 Employer's deduction (other cases)

(1) The following provision shall have effect in the case of an attachment of earnings order to which paragraph 5 above does not apply.

(2) If on a pay-day the attachable earnings exceed the sum of –

(a) the protected earnings; and
(b) so much of any amount by which the attachable earnings on any previous pay-day fell short of the protected earnings as has not been made good by virtue of this sub-paragraph on another previous pay-day,

then, in so far as the excess allows, the employer shall deduct from the attachable earnings the amount specified in the following sub-paragraph.

(3) The said amount is the sum of –

(a) the normal deduction; and
(b) so much of the normal deduction on any previous pay-day as was not deducted on that day and has not been paid by virtue of this sub-paragraph on any other previous pay-day.

(4) No deduction shall be made on any pay-day when the attachable earnings are equal to, or less than, the protected earnings.

PART II
PRIORITY AS BETWEEN ORDERS

7 Where the employer is required to comply with two or more attachment of earnings orders in respect of the same debtor, all or none of which orders are made to secure either the payment of judgment debts or payments under an administration order, then on any pay-day the employer shall, for the purpose of complying with Part I of this Schedule, –

(a) deal with the orders according to the respective dates on which they were made, disregarding any later order until an earlier one has been dealt with;

(b) deal with any later order as if the earnings to which it relates were the residue of the debtor's earnings after the making of deduction to comply with any earlier order.

8 Where the employer is required to comply with two or more attachment of earnings orders, and one or more (but not all) of those orders are made to secure either the payment of judgment debts or payments under an administration order, then on any pay-day the employer shall, for the purpose of complying with Part I of this Schedule –

(a) deal first with any order which is not made to secure the payment of a judgment debt or payments under an administration order (complying with paragraph 7 above if there are two or more such orders); and
(b) deal thereafter with any order which is made to secure the payment of a judgment debt or payments under an administration order as if the earnings to which it relates were the residue of the debtor's earnings after the making of any deduction to comply with an order having priority by virtue of sub-paragraph (a) above; and
(c) if there are two or more orders to which sub-paragraph (b) above applies, comply with paragraph 7 above in respect of those orders.

Amendments—Social Security Pensions Act 1975, s 65(3), Sch 5; Social Security (Consequential Provisions) Act 1975, s 1(3), Sch 2, para 43; Administration of Justice Act 1982, s 54; Wages Act 1986, s 32(1), Sch 4, para 4; Employment Rights Act 1996, s 240, Sch 1, para 3.

Priority as between creditors—Paragraphs 7 and 8 establish the following priority as between creditors. Maintenance orders come first, ranking in date order. Other judgment debts come next, again ranking in date order.

****

Charging Orders Act 1979

General—This Act offers what is effectively a two stage method of enforcement of judgment debts where the debtor has an interest in any property of the kind specified in s 2. The first stage is the making of the charging order on the property which has the same effect as an equitable charge made by the debtor (s 3(4)). The order gives the creditor security for the ultimate payment of the debt. If necessary this is followed by the second stage, an order for sale of the property and the debt is then satisfied out of the sale proceeds. This second order is made in separate proceedings by the creditor under CPR Pt 8. The order will be made under the general law of equitable mortgages if the debtor is entitled to the whole beneficial interest in the property charged, or under Trusts of Land and Appointment of Trustees Act 1996, s 14 if the debtor is simply entitled to a beneficial interest in the property for example a jointly owned home. (*Midland Bank plc v Pike* [1988] 2 All ER 434). At this stage, the court has a wide discretion and will consider the competing interests of the creditor and any other person interested in the property before deciding whether or not to order a sale (*Mortgage Corporation v Shaire* [2001] 3 WLR 639, Ch D).

What debts are covered?—Any judgment or order for payment of a sum of money where the debtor has failed to pay in accordance with the terms of the judgment (*Mercantile Credit Co Ltd v Ellis* (1987) *The Times*, 1 April, CA). Arbitration awards and awards of various tribunals are included once the procedure set out in CPR r 70.5 has been completed, (s 6(2)). The amount of any order for costs made against a legally-aided party cannot be enforced by charging order until the court has determined the amount which it would be reasonable for the debtor to pay under AJA 1999, s 11(1).

Nature of the relief—The court has a discretion whether or not to make an order. For the applicable principles see *Roberts Petroleum Ltd v Bernard Kenny Ltd* [1983] 2 AC 192. The burden is on the debtor to show why an order should not be made.

Special considerations apply where:
(a) the property to be charged is a matrimonial home which is jointly owned; and

(b) the debtor and his or her spouse are joint beneficial owners; and
(c) divorce or judicial separation proceedings have been commenced between the spouses before the hearing of the application for a charging order.

In these cases CPR Pt 73 does not expressly provide for notice of the interim order to be given to a spouse or former spouse as an interested party, although such a spouse may be served as a trustee of any jointly owned property. However, the form of application notice requires details of those known to have an interest in the property or to be in occupation, and the court has a general power to add any person as respondent to an application (CPR r 23.1). Unless the circumstances are so clear that it is proper to refuse the order forthwith, the court will direct service of the interim order on the spouse or former spouse as a trustee (or any other person it identifies as having an interest which may be prejudiced), thereby giving an opportunity to object to the making of a final order under CPR r 73.8(1). The court may adjourn the hearing, for example to allow it to be heard with the application for ancillary relief (*Harman v Glencross* [1986] 1 All ER 545, cf *First National Securities v Hegarty* [1984] 3 All ER 640).

The order may be made subject to conditions. For an example of a conditional order where enforcement was postponed until the majority of minor children of the debtor, see *Austin-Fell v Austin-Fell and Midland Bank plc* [1990] 2 All ER 455. Where the property to be charged is one debtor's jointly owned family home, the court may impose a condition that the order is not to be enforced so long as the debtor pays the judgment debt by specified instalments. These may be varied from time to time under CCA 1984, s 88.

1 Charging orders

(1) Where, under a judgment or order of the High Court or a county court, a person (the 'debtor') is required to pay a sum of money to another person (the 'creditor') then, for the purpose of enforcing that judgment or order, the appropriate court may make an order in accordance with the provisions of this Act imposing on any such property of the debtor as may be specified in the order a charge for securing the payment of any money due or to become due under the judgment or order.

(2) The appropriate court is –

(a) in a case where the property to be charged is a fund in court, the court in which that fund is lodged;
(b) in a case where paragraph (a) above does not apply and the order to be enforced is a maintenance order of the High Court, the High Court or a county court;
(c) in a case where neither paragraph (a) nor paragraph (b) above applies and the judgment or order to be enforced is a judgment or order of the High Court for a sum exceeding the county court limit, the High Court or a county court; and
(d) in any other case, a county court.

In this section 'county court limit' means the county court limit for the time being specified in an Order in Council under section 145 of the County Courts Act 1984 as the county court limit for the purposes of this section and 'maintenance order' has the same meaning as in section 2(a) of the Attachment of Earnings Act 1971.

(3) An order under subsection (1) above is referred to in this Act as a 'charging order'.

(4) Where a person applies to the High Court for a charging order to enforce more than one judgment or order, that court shall be the appropriate court in relation to the application if it would be the appropriate court, apart from this subsection, on an application relating to one or more of the judgments or orders concerned.

(5) In deciding whether to make a charging order the court shall consider all the circumstances of the case and, in particular, any evidence before it as to –

(a) the personal circumstances of the debtor, and
(b) whether any other creditor of the debtor would be likely to be unduly prejudiced by the making of the order.

Amendments—Administration of Justice Act 1982, s 34(3); County Courts Act 1984, s 148(1), Sch 2, para 71.

Scope of provision—This section creates the jurisdiction to make a charging order on property of the description specified in s 2.

Jurisdiction—Except where s 1(2)(a) applies, any county court has jurisdiction to make a charging order to enforce any judgment order or award as defined by s 6(2).

The High Court also has concurrent jurisdiction to make a charging order to enforce:

(a) High Court maintenance orders and High Court judgments or orders where the order or judgment originally exceeded £5000; and
(b) more than one judgment where one of the judgments falls within paragraph (a).

'a sum of money' (s 1(1)—The sum must be specified or at least capable of mathematical calculation. So a charging order cannot be made in respect of costs which have not yet been assessed (*A & M Records v Darajdjian* [1975] 3 All ER 983). The order can however include interest and costs of enforcement even where not specified in the original order (*Ezekiel v Orakpo* [1997] 1 WLR 340).

'to another person' (s 1(1))—A charging order cannot be made to secure an order to pay into court (*Ward v Shakeshaft* [1860] 1 Dr & Sm 269).

'due or to become due' (s 1(1))—A charging order may secure amounts which have not yet fallen due for payment under the judgment, but the court may exercise its discretion not to include such payments in an order (see **'consider all the circumstances'** below).

'maintenance order' (s 1(2)(b))—As to the extended meaning of this expression, see Attachment of Earnings Act 1971, Sch 1.

County court limit (s 1(2))—The relevant limit is currently £5000, notwithstanding the increase in the jurisdiction of the county court which took place on 1 July 1991.

'consider all the circumstances' (s 1(5))—The court has a general discretion. A charging order will not lightly be made where the costs of and consequent on doing so (including the costs of discharging the charge in due course) would be disproportionate in comparison with the judgment debt. A charging order will not be made where the creditor would gain security in the face of a pending liquidation or bankruptcy (*Roberts Petroleum Ltd v Bernard Kenny Ltd* [1983] AC 192).

The position of the debtor's spouse must be considered. In the absence of divorce proceedings, her interests will not prevent the order being made as her beneficial interest is not affected and the creditor will be in no better position than the debtor would be (on, for example, an application under Trusts of Land and Appointment of Trustees Act 1996, s 14); however, the interests of the debtor's resident family must be taken into account (*Lloyds Bank plc v Byrne* [1993] 1 FLR 369). Where a divorce petition has been issued, the spouse's expectation of financial provision and of security of accommodation must be balanced against the creditor's expectation of payment so that it may be appropriate to hear the applications for ancillary relief and for the charging order together (*Harman v Glencross* [1986] Fam 81, [1986] 2 FLR 241; *Austin-Fell v Austin-Fell and Midland Bank plc* [1990] 2 All ER 455).

If the judgment debt is subject to an instalment order, a charging order should not be made while the payments are up to date (*Mercantile Credit Co Ltd v Ellis* (1987) *The Times*, 1 April, CA where it was also stated obiter that in the county court there is no power to make a charging order in such circumstances). Similar considerations would no doubt apply to an instalment agreement. However, where an instalment order is made between the dates of the interim order and the hearing, the court has jurisdiction to make a final order even when the instalments are up to date (*Robaigealach v Allied Irish Bank plc* (2001) (unreported) 12 November, CA).

2 Property which may be charged

(1) Subject to subsection (3) below, a charge may be imposed by a charging order only on –

(a) any interest held by the debtor beneficially –
(i) in any asset of a kind mentioned in subsection (2) below, or
(ii) under any trust; or
(b) any interest held by a person as trustee of a trust ('the trust'), if the interest is in such an asset or is an interest under another trust and –
(i) the judgment or order in respect of which a charge is to be imposed was made against that person as trustee of the trust, or
(ii) the whole beneficial interest under the trust is held by the debtor unencumbered and for his own benefit, or
(iii) in a case where there are two or more debtors all of whom are liable to the creditor for the same debt, they together hold the whole beneficial interest under the trust unencumbered and for their own benefit.

(2) The assets referred to in subsection (1) above are –
(a) land,
(b) securities of any of the following kinds –
(i) government stock,
(ii) stock of any body (other than a building society) incorporated within England and Wales,
(iii) stock of any body incorporated outside England and Wales or of any state or territory outside the United Kingdom, being stock registered in a register kept at any place within England and Wales, or
(c) funds in court.

(3) In any case where a charge is imposed by a charging order on any interest in an asset of a kind mentioned in paragraph (b) or (c) of subsection (2) above, the court making the order may provide for the charge to extend to any interest or dividend payable in respect of the asset.

Scope of provision—This section identifies the nature of the interests which may be charged and the assets in which the interest may subsist.

Partnerships—A debtor's share in a partnership may also be made the subject of a charging order by virtue of Partnership Act 1890, s 23.

The debtor's interest (s 2(1))—If the debtor is the sole beneficial owner of the property, the charging order is made under s 2(1)(a)(i).

If the debtor's interest is as one of two or more proprietors of land, the charging order is made under s 2(1)(a)(ii).

If joint debtors hold property on trust for themselves as beneficial owners, the charging order is made under s 2(1)(b)(iii).

3 Provisions supplementing sections 1 and 2

(1) A charging order may be made absolutely or subject to conditions as to notifying the debtor or as to the time when the charge is to become enforceable, or as to other matters.

(2) The Land Charges Act 1972 and the Land Registration Act 2002 shall apply in relation to charging orders as they apply in relation to other orders or writs issued or made for the purpose of enforcing judgments.

(3) (*repealed*)

(4) Subject to the provisions of this Act, a charge imposed by a charging order shall have the like effect and shall be enforceable in the same courts and in the same manner as an equitable charge created by the debtor by writing under his hand.

(5) The court by which a charging order was made may at any time, on the application of the debtor or of any person interested in any property to which the order relates, make an order discharging or varying the charging order.

(6) Where a charging order has been protected by an entry registered under the Land Charges Act 1972 or the Land Registration Act 2002, an order under subsection (5) above discharging the charging order may direct that the entry be cancelled.

(7) The Lord Chancellor may by order made by statutory instrument amend section 2(2) of this Act by adding to, or removing from, the kinds of asset for the time being referred to there, any asset of a kind which in his opinion ought to be so added or removed.

(8) Any order under subsection (7) above shall be subject to annulment in pursuance of a resolution of either House of Parliament.

Amendments—Land Registration Act 2002, ss 133, 135, Sch 11, para 15, Sch 13.

Scope of provision—This section contains provisions as to the terms on which a charging order may be made, its protection by Land Registry entry, its effect and its discharge.

'enforceable' (s 3(4))—As to enforcement by order for sale, see CPR r 73.10.

'person interested' (s 3(5))—The interest need not be a beneficial interest in the property charged (*Harman v Glencross* [1986] Fam 81).

'a charging order' (s 3(6))—To ensure effective registration, the order must specify precisely the nature of the debtor's interest in the property charged. Wherever possible, creditors should make clear in their application the nature of the interest over which the order is sought to be made. The utmost flexibility in the terms of the order tailored to the circumstances of the case is permitted.

Registration—The distinction between legal and beneficial interests is crucial when it comes to protecting the creditor's position by registration.

****

5 Stop orders and notices

(1) In this section –

'stop order' means an order of the court prohibiting the taking, in respect of any of the securities specified in the order, of any of the steps mentioned in subsection (5) below;

'stop notice' means a notice requiring any person or body on whom it is duly served to refrain from taking, in respect of any of the securities specified in the notice, any of those steps without first notifying the person by whom, or on whose behalf, the notice was served; and

'prescribed securities' means securities (including funds in court) of a kind prescribed by rules of court made under this section.

(2) The power to make rules of court under section 1 of, and Schedule 1 to, the Civil Procedure Act 1997 shall include power by any such rules to make provision –

(a) for the High Court to make a stop order on the application of any person claiming to be entitled to an interest in prescribed securities; and

(b) for the service of a stop notice by any person claiming to be entitled to an interest in prescribed securities.

(3) (*repealed*)

(4) Rules of court made by virtue of subsection (2) above shall prescribe the person or body on whom a copy of any stop order or a stop notice is to be served.

(5) The steps mentioned in subsection (1) above are –

(a) the registration of any transfer of the securities;

(b) in the case of funds in court, the transfer, sale, delivery out, payment or other dealing with the funds, or of the income thereon;

(c) the making of any payment by way of dividend, interest or otherwise in respect of the securities; and

(d) in the case of a unit trust, any acquisition of or other dealing with the units by any person or body exercising functions under the trust.

(6) Any rules of court made by virtue of this section may include such incidental, supplemental and consequential provisions as the authority making them consider necessary or expedient, and may make different provision in relation to different cases or classes of case.

Amendments—Supreme Court Act 1981, s 152(1), Sch 5; County Courts Act 1984, s 148(1), Sch 2, para 72; SI 2002/439.

'rules of court' (s 5 generally)—See CPR rr 73.11–73.15 for stop orders and rr 73.16–73.21 for stop notices. See CPR r 73.17(4) for service of stop notices.

6 Interpretation

(1) In this Act –

'building society' has the same meaning as in the Building Societies Act 1986;

'charging order' means an order made under section 1(1) of this Act;

'debtor' and 'creditor' have the meanings given by section 1(1) of this Act;

'dividend' includes any distribution in respect of any unit of a unit trust;

'government stock' means any stock issued by Her Majesty's government in the United Kingdom or any funds of, or annuity granted by, that government;

'stock' includes shares, debentures and any securities of the body concerned, whether or not constituting a charge on the assets of that body;

'unit trust' means any trust established for the purpose, or having the effect, of providing, for persons having funds available for investment, facilities for the participation by them, as beneficiaries under the trust, in any profits or income arising from the acquisition, holding, management or disposal of any property whatsoever.

(2) For the purposes of section 1 of this Act references to a judgment or order of the High Court or a county court shall be taken to include references to a judgment, order, decree or award (however called) of any court or arbitrator (including any foreign court or arbitrator) which is or has become enforceable (whether wholly or to a limited extent) as if it were a judgment or order of the High Court or a county court.

(3) References in section 2 of this Act to any securities include references to any such securities standing in the name of the Accountant General.

Amendments—Building Societies Act 1986, s 120(1), Sch 18, Pt I, para 14.

****

Civil Procedure Act 1997

ARRANGEMENT OF SECTIONS

Rules and directions

1 Civil Procedure Rules

(1) There are to be rules of court (to be called 'Civil Procedure Rules') governing the practice and procedure to be followed in –

(a) the civil division of the Court of Appeal,
(b) the High Court, and
(c) county courts.

(2) Schedule 1 (which makes further provision about the extent of the power to make Civil Procedure Rules) is to have effect.

(3) The power to make Civil Procedure Rules is to be exercised with a view to securing that the civil justice system is accessible, fair and efficient.

2 Rule Committee

(1) Civil Procedure Rules are to be made by a committee known as the Civil Procedure Rule Committee, which is to consist of –

(aa) the Head of Civil Justice,
(ab) the Deputy Head of Civil Justice (if there is one),
(a) the Master of the Rolls (unless he holds an office mentioned in paragraph (aa) or (ab)), and
(b) the Vice-Chancellor, and
(c) the persons currently appointed by the Lord Chancellor under subsection (2).

(2) The Lord Chancellor must appoint –

(a) either two or three judges of the Supreme Court,
(b) one Circuit judge,
(c) one district judge,
(d) one person who is a Master referred to in Part II of Schedule 2 to the Supreme Court Act 1981,
(e) three persons who have a Supreme Court qualification (within the meaning of section 71 of the Courts and Legal Services Act 1990), including at least one with particular experience of practice in county courts,
(f) three persons who have been granted by an authorised body, under Part II of that Act, the right to conduct litigation in relation to all proceedings in the Supreme Court, including at least one with particular experience of practice in county courts,
(g) two persons with experience in and knowledge of the lay advice sector or consumer affairs.

(3) Before appointing a judge of the Supreme Court under subsection (2)(a), the Lord Chancellor must consult the Lord Chief Justice.

(4) Before appointing a person under paragraph (e) or (f) of subsection (2), the Lord Chancellor must consult any body which –

(a) has members who are eligible for appointment under that paragraph, and
(b) is an authorised body for the purposes of section 27 or 28 of the Courts and Legal Services Act 1990.

(5) The Lord Chancellor may reimburse the members of the Civil Procedure Rule Committee their travelling and out-of-pocket expenses.

(6) The Civil Procedure Rule Committee must, before making or amending Civil Procedure Rules –

(a) consult such persons as they consider appropriate, and
(b) meet (unless it is inexpedient to do so).

(7) The Civil Procedure Rule Committee must, when making Civil Procedure Rules, try to make rules which are both simple and simply expressed.

(8) Rules made by the Civil Procedure Rule Committee must be signed by at least eight members of the Committee and be submitted to the Lord Chancellor, who may allow or disallow them.

Amendments—Courts Act 2003, s 83(1), (2), (3).

2A Power to change certain requirements relating to Committee

(1) The Lord Chancellor may by order –

(a) amend section 2(2) (persons to be appointed to Committee by Lord Chancellor), and
(b) make consequential amendments in any other provision of section 2.

(2) Before making an order under this section the Lord Chancellor must consult –

(a) the Head of Civil Justice,
(b) the Deputy Head of Civil Justice (if there is one), and
(c) the Master of the Rolls (unless he holds an office mentioned in paragraph (a) or (b)).

(3) The power to make an order under this section is exercisable by statutory instrument.

(4) A statutory instrument containing such an order is subject to annulment in pursuance of a resolution of either House of Parliament.

Amendments—Inserted by Courts Act 2003, s 84.

3 Section 2: supplementary

(1) Rules made and allowed under section 2 are to –

(a) come into force on such day as the Lord Chancellor may direct, and
(b) be contained in a statutory instrument to which the Statutory Instruments Act 1946 is to apply as if it contained rules made by a Minister of the Crown.

(2) A statutory instrument containing Civil Procedure Rules shall be subject to annulment in pursuance of a resolution of either House of Parliament.

4 Power to make consequential amendments

(1) The Lord Chancellor may by order amend, repeal or revoke any enactment to the extent he considers necessary or desirable in consequence of –

(a) section 1 or 2, or
(b) Civil Procedure Rules.

(2) The Lord Chancellor may by order amend, repeal or revoke any enactment passed or made before the commencement of this section to the extent he considers necessary or desirable in order to facilitate the making of Civil Procedure Rules.

(3) Any power to make an order under this section is exercisable by statutory instrument.

(4) A statutory instrument containing an order under subsection (1) shall be subject to annulment in pursuance of a resolution of either House of Parliament.

(5) No order may be made under subsection (2) unless a draft of it has been laid before and approved by resolution of each House of Parliament.

5 Practice directions

(1) Practice directions may provide for any matter which, by virtue of paragraph 3 of Schedule 1, may be provided for by Civil Procedure Rules.

(2) …

Civil Justice Council

6 Civil Justice Council

(1) The Lord Chancellor is to establish and maintain an advisory body, to be known as the Civil Justice Council.

(2) The Council must include –

(a) members of the judiciary,
(b) members of the legal professions,
(c) civil servants concerned with the administration of the courts,
(d) persons with experience in and knowledge of consumer affairs,
(e) persons with experience in and knowledge of the lay advice sector, and
(f) persons able to represent the interests of particular kinds of litigants (for example, businesses or employees).

(3) The functions of the Council are to include –

(a) keeping the civil justice system under review,
(b) considering how to make the civil justice system more accessible, fair and efficient,
(c) advising the Lord Chancellor and the judiciary on the development of the civil justice system,
(d) referring proposals for changes in the civil justice system to the Lord Chancellor and the Civil Procedure Rule Committee, and
(e) making proposals for research.

(4) The Lord Chancellor may reimburse the members of the Council their travelling and out-of-pocket expenses.

Court orders

7 Power of courts to make orders for preserving evidence, etc

(1) The court may make an order under this section for the purpose of securing, in the case of any existing or proposed proceedings in the court –

(a) the preservation of evidence which is or may be relevant, or
(b) the preservation of property which is or may be the subject-matter of the proceedings or as to which any question arises or may arise in the proceedings.

(2) A person who is, or appears to the court likely to be, a party to proceedings in the court may make an application for such an order.

(3) Such an order may direct any person to permit any person described in the order, or secure that any person so described is permitted –

(a) to enter premises in England and Wales, and
(b) while on the premises, to take in accordance with the terms of the order any of the following steps.

(4) Those steps are –

(a) to carry out a search for or inspection of anything described in the order, and
(b) to make or obtain a copy, photograph, sample or other record of anything so described.

(5) The order may also direct the person concerned –

(a) to provide any person described in the order, or secure that any person so described is provided, with any information or article described in the order, and
(b) to allow any person described in the order, or secure that any person so described is allowed, to retain for safe keeping anything described in the order.

(6) An order under this section is to have effect subject to such conditions as are specified in the order.

(7) This section does not affect any right of a person to refuse to do anything on the ground that to do so might tend to expose him or his spouse to proceedings for an offence or for the recovery of a penalty.

(8) In this section –

'court' means the High Court, and
'premises' includes any vehicle;

and an order under this section may describe anything generally, whether by reference to a class or otherwise.

8 Disclosure etc of documents before action begun

(1) The Lord Chancellor may by order amend the provisions of section 33(2) of the Supreme Court Act 1981, or section 52(2) of the County Courts Act 1984 (power of court to order disclosure etc of documents where claim may be made in respect of personal injury or death), so as to extend the provisions –

(a) to circumstances where other claims may be made, or
(b) generally.

(2) The power to make an order under this section is exercisable by statutory instrument which shall be subject to annulment in pursuance of a resolution of either House of Parliament.

General

9 Interpretation

(1) A court the practice and procedure of which is governed by Civil Procedure Rules is referred to in this Act as being 'within the scope' of the rules; and references to a court outside the scope of the rules are to be read accordingly.

(2) In this Act –

'enactment' includes an enactment contained in subordinate legislation (within the meaning of the Interpretation Act 1978), and
'practice directions' means directions as to the practice and procedure of any court within the scope of Civil Procedure Rules.

10 Minor and consequential amendments

Schedule 2 (which makes minor and consequential amendments) is to have effect.

11 Short title, commencement and extent

(1) This Act may be cited as the Civil Procedure Act 1997.

(2) Sections 1 to 10 are to come into force on such day as the Lord Chancellor may by order made by statutory instrument appoint, and different days may be appointed for different purposes.

(3) This Act extends to England and Wales only.

SCHEDULE 1

CIVIL PROCEDURE RULES

1 Matters dealt with by the former rules

Among the matters which Civil Procedure Rules may be made about are any matters which were governed by the former Rules of the Supreme Court or the former county court rules (that is, the Rules of the Supreme Court (Revision) 1965 and the County Court Rules 1981).

2 Exercise of jurisdiction

Civil Procedure Rules may provide for the exercise of the jurisdiction of any court within the scope of the rules by officers or other staff of the court.

3 Removal of proceedings

(1) Civil Procedure Rules may provide for the removal of proceedings at any stage –

- (a) within the High Court (for example, between different divisions or different district registries), or
- (b) between county courts.

(2) In sub-paragraph (1) –

- (a) 'provide for the removal of proceedings' means –
  - (i) provide for transfer of proceedings, or
  - (ii) provide for any jurisdiction in any proceedings to be exercised (whether concurrently or not) elsewhere within the High Court or, as the case may be, by another county court without the proceedings being transferred, and
- (b) 'proceedings' includes any part of proceedings.

4 Evidence

Civil Procedure Rules may modify the rules of evidence as they apply to proceedings in any court within the scope of the rules.

5 Application of other rules

(1) Civil Procedure Rules may apply any rules of court which relate to a court which is outside the scope of Civil Procedure Rules.

(2) Any rules of court, not made by the Civil Procedure Rule Committee, which apply to proceedings of a particular kind in a court within the scope of Civil Procedure Rules may be applied by Civil Procedure Rules to other proceedings in such a court.

(3) In this paragraph 'rules of court' includes any provision governing the practice and procedure of a court which is made by or under an enactment.

(4) Where Civil Procedure Rules may be made by applying other rules, the other rules may be applied –

(a) to any extent,
(b) with or without modification, and
(c) as amended from time to time.

6 Practice directions

Civil Procedure Rules may, instead of providing for any matter, refer to provision made or to be made about that matter by directions.

7 Different provision for different cases etc

The power to make Civil Procedure Rules includes power to make different provision for different cases or different areas, including different provision –

(a) for a specific court or specific division of a court, or
(b) for specific proceedings, or a specific jurisdiction,

specified in the rules.

****

County Courts Act 1984

ARRANGEMENT OF SECTIONS

PART I
CONSTITUTION AND ADMINISTRATION

County courts and districts

1 County courts to be held for districts

(1) For the purposes of this Act, England and Wales shall be divided into districts, and a court shall be held under this Act for each district at one or more places in it; and each court shall have such jurisdiction and powers as are conferred by this Act and any other enactment for the time being in force.

(2) Every court so held shall be called a county court and shall be a court of record and shall have a seal.

(3) Nothing in this section affects the operation of section 42 of the Courts Act 1971 (City of London).

Amendments—Civil Procedure Act 1997, s 10, Sch 2, para 2(4).

2 County court districts etc

(1) The Lord Chancellor may by order specify places at which county courts are to be held and the name by which the court held at any place so specified is to be known.

(2) Any order under this section shall be made by statutory instrument, which shall be laid before Parliament after being made.

(3) The districts for which county courts are to be held shall be determined in accordance with directions given by or on behalf of the Lord Chancellor.

(4) Subject to any alterations made by virtue of this section, county courts shall continue to be held for the districts and at the places and by the names appointed at the commencement of this Act.

Places and times of sittings of courts

3 Places and times of sittings

(1) In any district the places at which the court sits, and the days and times when the court sits at any place, shall be determined in accordance with directions given by or on behalf of the Lord Chancellor.

(2) A judge may from time to time adjourn any court held by him, and a district judge may from time to time adjourn –

(a) any court held by him, or

(b) in the absence of the judge, any court to be held by the judge.

(3) (*repealed*)

(4) References in this Act to sittings of the court shall include references to sittings by any district judge in pursuance of any provision contained in, or made under, this Act.

Amendments—CPA 1997, s 10, Sch 2, para 2(5).

4 Use of public buildings for courts

(1) Where, in any place in which a county court is held, there is a building, being a town hall, court-house or other public building belonging to any local or other public authority, that building shall, with all necessary rooms, furniture and fittings in it, be used for the purpose of holding the court, without any charge for rent or other payment, except the reasonable and necessary charges for lighting, heating and cleaning the building when used for that purpose.

(2) Where any such building is used for the purpose of holding any court, the sittings of the court shall be so arranged as not to interfere with the business of the local or other public authority usually transacted in the building or with any purpose for which the building may be used by virtue of any local Act.

(3) This section shall not apply to any place in which a building was erected before 1st January 1889 for the purpose of holding and carrying on the business of a county court.

Judges

5 Judges of county courts

(1) Every Circuit judge shall, by virtue of his office, be capable of sitting as a judge for any county court district in England and Wales, and the Lord Chancellor shall assign one or more Circuit judges to each district and may from time to time vary the assignment of Circuit judges among the districts.

(2) Subject to any directions given by or on behalf of the Lord Chancellor, in any case where more than one Circuit judge is assigned to a district under subsection (1), any function conferred by or under this Act on the judge for a district may be exercised by any of the Circuit judges for the time being assigned to that district.

(3) The following, that is –

every judge of the Court of Appeal,
every judge of the High Court,
every Recorder,

shall, by virtue of his office, be capable of sitting as a judge for any county court district in England and Wales and, if he consents to do so, shall sit as such a judge at such times and on such occasions as the Lord Chancellor considers desirable.

(4) Notwithstanding that he is not for the time being assigned to a particular district, a Circuit judge –

- (a) shall sit as a judge of that district at such times and on such occasions as the Lord Chancellor may direct; and
- (b) may sit as a judge of that district in any case where it appears to him that the judge of that district is not, or none of the judges of that district is, available to deal with the case.

District judges, assistant district judges and deputy district judges

6 District judges

(1) Subject to the provisions of this section, there shall be a district judge for each district, who shall be appointed by the Lord Chancellor and paid such salary as the Lord Chancellor may, with the concurrence of the Treasury, direct.

(2) The Lord Chancellor may, if he thinks fit, appoint a person to be district judge for two or more districts.

(3) The Lord Chancellor may, if he thinks fit, appoint two or more persons to execute jointly the office of district judge for a district and may, in any case where joint district judges are appointed, give directions with respect to the division between them of the duties of the office.

(4) The Lord Chancellor may, as he thinks fit, on the death, resignation or removal of a joint district judge, either appoint another person to be joint district judge in his place or give directions that the continuing district judge shall act as sole district judge or, as the case may be, that the continuing district judges shall execute jointly the office of district judge.

(5) The district judge for any district shall be capable of acting in any other district for the district judge of that other district.

Amendments—Courts and Legal Services Act 1990, s 125(3), Sch 18, para 42.

****

8 Deputy district judges

(1) If it appears to the Lord Chancellor that it is expedient as a temporary measure to make an appointment under this subsection in order to facilitate the disposal of business in county courts, he may appoint a person to be deputy district judge for any county court district during such period or on such occasions as the Lord Chancellor thinks fit; and a deputy district judge, while acting under his appointment, shall have the same powers and be subject to the same liabilities as if he were the district judge.

(1A) Any appointment of a person as a deputy district judge –

(a) if he has previously held office as a district judge, shall not be such as to extend beyond the day on which he attains the age of 75 years; and

(b) in any other case, shall not be such as to extend beyond the day on which he attains the age of 70 years, but subject to section 26(4) to (6) of the Judicial Pensions and Retirement Act 1993 (power to authorise continuance in office up to the age of 75).

(2) (*repealed*)

(3) The Lord Chancellor may pay to any person appointed under this section as deputy district judge such remuneration and allowances as he may, with the approval of the Treasury, determine.

Amendments—CLSA 1990, s 125(3), Sch 18, para 42; Judicial Pensions and Retirement Act 1993, ss 26, 31, Sch 6, para 17(1), Sch 9.

9 Qualifications

No person shall be appointed a district judge, or deputy district judge unless he has a 7 year general qualification, within the meaning of section 71 of the Courts and Legal Services Act 1990.

Amendments—CLSA 1990, ss 71(2), 125(3), Sch 10, para 57, Sch 18, para 42; JPRA 1993, s 31, Sch 8, para 17(b), Sch 9.

****

11 Tenure of office

(1) This subsection applies to the office of district judge.

(2) Subject to the following provisions of this section and to subsections (4) to (6) of section 26 of the Judicial Pensions and Retirement Act 1993 (Lord Chancellor's power to authorise continuance in office up to the age of 75), a person who holds an office to which subsection (1) applies shall vacate his office on the day on which he attains the age of 70 years.

(3) (*repealed*)

(4) A person appointed to an office to which subsection (1) applies shall hold that office during good behaviour.

(5) The power to remove such a person from his office on account of misbehaviour shall be exercisable by the Lord Chancellor.

(6) The Lord Chancellor may also remove such a person from his office on account of inability to perform the duties of his office.

Amendments—JPRA 1993, ss 26(10), 31(4), Sch 6, para 17(2)–(4), Sch 9.

12 Records of proceedings to be kept by district judges

(1) The district judge for every district shall keep or cause to be kept such records of and in relation to proceedings in the court for that district as the Lord Chancellor may by regulations made by statutory instrument prescribe.

(2) Any entry in a book or other document required by the said regulations to be kept for the purposes of this section, or a copy of any such entry or document purporting to be signed and certified as a true copy by the district judge, shall at all times without further proof be admitted in any court or place whatsoever as evidence of the entry and of the proceeding referred to by it and of the regularity of that proceeding.

Amendments—CLSA 1990, s 125(3), Sch 18, para 42.

Miscellaneous provisions as to officers

13 Officers of court not to act as solicitors in that court

(1) Subject to the provisions of this section, no officer of a court shall, either by himself or his partner, be directly or indirectly engaged as legal representative or agent for any party in any proceedings in that court.

(2) Every person who contravenes this section shall for each offence be liable on summary conviction to a fine of an amount not exceeding level 3 on the standard scale.

(3) Subsection (1) does not apply to a person acting as district judge by virtue of section 6(5).

(4) Subsection (1) does not apply to a deputy district judge; but a deputy district judge shall not act as such in relation to any proceedings in which he is, either by himself or his partner, directly or indirectly engaged as legal representative or agent for any party.

Amendments—CLSA 1990, s 125(3), Sch 18, para 49.

14 Penalty for assaulting officers

(1) If any person assaults an officer of a court while in the execution of his duty, he shall be liable –

- (a) on summary conviction, to imprisonment for a term not exceeding 3 months or to a fine of an amount not exceeding level 5 on the standard scale, or both; or
- (b) on an order made by the judge in that behalf, to be committed for a specified period not exceeding 3 months to prison or to such a fine as aforesaid, or to be so committed and to such a fine,

and a bailiff of the court may take the offender into custody, with or without warrant, and bring him before the judge.

(2) The judge may at any time revoke an order committing a person to prison under this section and, if he is already in custody, order his discharge.

(3) A district judge, assistant district judge or deputy district judge shall have the same powers under this section as a judge.

Amendments—Statute Law (Repeals) Act 1986; CLSA 1990, s 74(4).

Entitlements of party—Both at common law and in order to comply with the HRA 1998, any person who is brought before the judge under this section is entitled to minimum safeguards. He must be given in writing details of the charge against him at the outset of any hearing. He must also be offered the opportunity to obtain legal advice and offered legal aid, which the court has power to grant of its own initiative under LAA 1988, s 29, immediately it becomes apparent to the judge that a sentence of imprisonment may be imposed for the particular offence (*Newman v Modern Bookbinders* [2000] 2 All ER 814, CA).

PART II
JURISDICTION AND TRANSFER OF PROCEEDINGS

Actions of contract and tort

15 General jurisdiction in actions of contract and tort

(1) Subject to subsection (2), a county court shall have jurisdiction to hear and determine any action founded on contract or tort.

(2) A county court shall not, except as in this Act provided, have jurisdiction to hear and determine –

- (a) (*repealed*)
- (b) any action in which the title to any toll, fair, market or franchise is in question; or
- (c) any action for libel or slander.

(3) (*repealed*)

Amendments—SI 1991/724.

16 Money recoverable by statute

A county court shall have jurisdiction to hear and determine an action for the recovery of a sum recoverable by virtue of any enactment for the time being in force, if –

- (a) it is not provided by that or any other enactment that such sums shall only be recoverable in the High Court or shall only be recoverable summarily;
- (b) (*repealed*)

Amendments—SI 1991/724.

17 Abandonment of part of claim to give court jurisdiction

(1) Where a plaintiff has a cause of action for more than the county court limit in which, if it were not for more than the county court limit, a county court would have jurisdiction, the plaintiff may abandon the excess, and thereupon a county court shall have jurisdiction to hear and determine the action, but the plaintiff shall not recover in the action an amount exceeding the county court limit.

(2) Where the court has jurisdiction to hear and determine an action by virtue of this section, the judgment of the court in the action shall be in full discharge of all demands in respect of the cause of action, and entry of the judgment shall be made accordingly.

18 Jurisdiction by agreement in certain actions

If the parties to any action, other than an action which, if commenced in the High Court, would have been assigned to the Chancery Division or to the Family Division or have involved the exercise of the High Court's Admiralty jurisdiction, agree, by a memorandum signed by them or by their respective legal representatives, that a county court specified in the memorandum shall have jurisdiction in the action, that court shall have jurisdiction to hear and determine the action accordingly.

Amendments—CLSA 1990, s 125(3), Sch 18, para 49.

****

Recovery of land and cases where title in question

21 Actions for recovery of land and actions where title is in question

(1) A county court shall have jurisdiction to hear and determine any action for the recovery of land.

(2) A county court shall have jurisdiction to hear and determine any action in which the title to any hereditament comes in question.

(3) Where a mortgage of land consists of or includes a dwelling-house and no part of the land is situated in Greater London then, subject to subsection (4), if a county court has jurisdiction by virtue of this section to hear and determine an action in which the mortgagee under that mortgage claims possession of the mortgaged property, no court other than a county court shall have jurisdiction to hear and determine that action.

(4) Subsection (3) shall not apply to an action for foreclosure or sale in which a claim for possession of the mortgaged property is also made.

(5), (6) (*repealed*)

(7) In this section –

'dwelling-house' includes any building or part of a building which is used as a dwelling;

'mortgage' includes a charge and 'mortgagor' and 'mortgagee' shall be construed accordingly;

'mortgagor' and 'mortgagee' includes any person deriving title under the original mortgagor or mortgagee.

(8) The fact that part of the premises comprised in a dwelling-house is used as a shop or office or for business, trade or professional purposes shall not prevent the dwelling-house from being a dwelling-house for the purposes of this section.

(9) This section does not apply to a mortgage securing an agreement which is a regulated agreement within the meaning of the Consumer Credit Act 1974.

Amendments—SI 1991/724.

****

Equity proceedings

23 Equity jurisdiction

A county court shall have all the jurisdiction of the High Court to hear and determine –

- (a) proceedings for the administration of the estate of a deceased person, where the estate does not exceed in amount or value the county court limit;
- (b) proceedings –
  - (i) for the execution of any trust, or
  - (ii) for a declaration that a trust subsists, or
  - (iii) under section 1 of the Variation of Trusts Act 1958,

where the estate or fund subject, or alleged to be subject, to the trust does not exceed in amount or value the county court limit;

- (c) proceedings for foreclosure or redemption of any mortgage or for enforcing any charge or lien, where the amount owing in respect of the mortgage, charge or lien does not exceed the county court limit;
- (d) proceedings for the specific performance, or for the rectification, delivery up or cancellation, of any agreement for the sale, purchase or lease of any property, where, in the case of a sale or purchase, the purchase money, or in the case of a lease, the value of the property, does not exceed the county court limit;
- (e) proceedings relating to the maintenance or advancement of a minor, where the property of the minor does not exceed in amount or value the county court limit;
- (f) proceedings for the dissolution or winding-up of any partnership (whether or not the existence of the partnership is in dispute), where the whole assets of the partnership do not exceed in amount or value the county court limit;
- (g) proceedings for relief against fraud or mistake, where the damage sustained or the estate or fund in respect of which relief is sought does not exceed in amount or value the county court limit.

24 Jurisdiction by agreement in certain equity proceedings

(1) If, as respects any proceedings to which this section applies, the parties agree, by a memorandum signed by them or by their respective legal representatives or agents, that a county court specified in the memorandum shall have jurisdiction in the proceedings, that court shall, notwithstanding anything in any enactment, have jurisdiction to hear and determine the proceedings accordingly.

(2) Subject to subsection (3), this section applies to any proceedings in which a county court would have jurisdiction by virtue of –

- (a) section 113(3) of the Settled Land Act 1925,
- (b) section 63A of the Trustee Act 1925,
- (c) sections 3(7), 49(4), 66(4), 89(7), 90(3), 91(8), 92(2), 136(3), 181(2), 188(2) of, and paragraph 3A of Part III and paragraph 1(3A) and (4A) of Part IV of Schedule 1 to, the Law of Property Act 1925,
- (d) sections 17(2), 38(4), 41(1A), and 43(4) of the Administration of Estates Act 1925,
- (e) section 6(1) of the Leasehold Property (Repairs) Act 1938,

(f) sections 1(6A) and 5(11) of the Land Charges Act 1972, and
(g) section 23 of this Act,

but for the limits of the jurisdiction of the court provided in those enactments.

(3) This section does not apply to proceedings under section 1 of the Variation of Trusts Act 1958.

Amendments—CLSA 1990, s 125(3), Sch 18, para 49; SI 1991/724; Statute Law (Repeals) Act 2004, s 1(1), Sch 1, Pt 1.

Family provision proceedings

25 Jurisdiction under Inheritance (Provision for Family and Dependants) Act 1975

A county court shall have jurisdiction to hear and determine any application for an order under section 2 of the Inheritance (Provision for Family and Dependants) Act 1975 (including any application for permission to apply for such an order and any application made, in the proceedings on an application for such an order, for an order under any other provision of that Act).

Amendments—SI 1991/724.

Admiralty proceedings

26 Districts for Admiralty purposes

(1) If at any time it appears expedient to the Lord Chancellor that any county court should have Admiralty jurisdiction, it shall be lawful for him, by order –

(a) to appoint that court to have, as from such date as may be specified in the order, such Admiralty jurisdiction as is provided in this Act; and
(b) to assign to that court as its district for Admiralty purposes any part or parts of any county court district or of two or more county court districts.

(2) Where a district has been so assigned to a court as its district for Admiralty purposes, the parts of the sea (if any) adjacent to that district to a distance of 3 miles from the shore thereof shall be deemed to be included in that district, and the judge and all officers of the court shall have jurisdiction and authority for those purposes throughout that district as if it were the district for the court for all purposes.

(3) Where an order is made under this section for the discontinuance of the Admiralty jurisdiction of any county court, whether wholly or within a part of the district assigned to it for Admiralty purposes, provision may be made in the order with respect to any Admiralty proceedings commenced in that court before the order comes into operation.

(4) The power to make orders under this section shall be exercisable by statutory instrument.

27 Admiralty jurisdiction

(1) Subject to the limitations of amount specified in subsection (2), an Admiralty county court shall have the following Admiralty jurisdiction, that is to say, jurisdiction to hear and determine –

(a) any claim for damage received by a ship;
(b) any claim for damage done by a ship;

(c) any claim for loss of life or personal injury sustained in consequence of any defect in a ship or in her apparel or equipment, or in consequence of the wrongful act, neglect or default of –
   (i) the owners, charterers or persons in possession or control of a ship; or
   (ii) the master or crew of a ship, or any other person for whose wrongful acts, neglects or defaults the owners, charterers or persons in possession or control of a ship are responsible,

being an act, neglect or default in the navigation or management of the ship, in the loading, carriage or discharge of goods on, in or from the ship, or in the embarkation, carriage or disembarkation of persons on, in or from the ship;

(d) any claim for loss of or damage to goods carried in a ship;
(e) any claim arising out of any agreement relating to the carriage of goods in a ship or to the use or hire of a ship;
(f) any claim –
   (i) under the Salvage Convention 1989;
   (ii) under any contract for or in relation to salvage services; or
   (iii) in the nature of salvage not falling within (i) or (ii) above;

or any corresponding claim in connection with an aircraft;

(g) any claim in the nature of towage in respect of a ship or an aircraft;
(h) any claim in the nature of pilotage in respect of a ship or an aircraft;
(j) any claim in respect of goods or materials supplied to a ship for her operation or maintenance;
(k) any claim in respect of the construction, repair or equipment of a ship or dock charges or dues;
(l) any claim by a master or member of the crew of a ship for wages (including any sum allotted out of wages or adjudged by a superintendent to be due by way of wages);
(m) any claim by a master, shipper, charterer or agent in respect of disbursements made on account of a ship.

(2) The limitations of amount referred to in subsection (1) are that the court shall not have jurisdiction to hear and determine –

(a) a claim falling within paragraph (f) of that subsection where the value of the property saved exceeds £15,000; or
(b) any other claim mentioned in that subsection for an amount exceeding £5,000.

(3) In subsection (1)(f) –

(a) the 'Salvage Convention 1989' means the International Convention on Salvage, 1989 as it has effect under section 224 of the Merchant Shipping Act 1995;
(b) the reference to salvage services includes services rendered in saving life from a ship and the reference to any claim under any contract for or in relation to salvage services includes any claim arising out of such a contract whether or not arising during the provision of the services;
(c) the reference to a corresponding claim in connection with an aircraft is a reference to any claim corresponding to any claim mentioned in sub-paragraph (i) or (ii) of paragraph (f) which is available under section 87 of the Civil Aviation Act 1982.

(4) Subject to subsection (5), subsections (1) to (3) apply –

(a) in relation to all ships or aircraft whether British or not and whether registered or not and wherever the residence or domicile of their owners may be, and

(b) in relation to all claims, wheresoever arising (including, in the case of cargo or wreck salvage, claims in respect of cargo or wreck found on land).

(5) Nothing in subsection (4) shall be construed as extending the cases in which money or property is recoverable under any of the provisions of the Merchant Shipping Act 1995.

(6) If, as regards any proceedings as to any such claim as is mentioned in subsection (1), the parties agree, by a memorandum signed by them or by their respective legal representatives or agents, that a particular county court specified in the memorandum shall have jurisdiction in the proceedings, that court shall, notwithstanding anything in subsection (2) or in rules of court for prescribing the courts in which proceedings shall be brought, have jurisdiction to hear and determine the proceedings accordingly.

(7) Nothing in this section shall be taken to affect the jurisdiction of any county court to hear and determine any proceedings in which it has jurisdiction by virtue of section 15 or 17.

(8) Nothing in this section, or in section 26 or in any order made under that section, shall be taken to confer on a county court the jurisdiction of a prize court within the meaning of the Naval Prize Acts 1864 to 1916.

(9) No county court shall have jurisdiction to determine any claim or question certified by the Secretary of State to be a claim or question which, under the Rhine Navigation Convention, falls to be determined in accordance with the provisions of that Convention; and any proceedings to enforce such a claim which are commenced in a county court shall be set aside.

(10) In subsection (9) 'the Rhine Navigation Convention' means the Convention of the 7th October 1868 as revised by any subsequent Convention.

(11) (*repealed*)

Amendments—CLSA 1990, s 125(3), Sch 18, para 49; Merchant Shipping (Salvage and Pollution) Act 1994, ss 1(6), s 314(1), 314(2), Sch 2, para 7(2), (3), (4), Sch 12, Sch 13, para 72(2)(a), (b); CPA 1997, s 10, Sch 2, para 2(2).

28 Mode of exercise of Admiralty jurisdiction

(1) The following provisions of this section shall apply to cases within the Admiralty jurisdiction of a county court.

(2) Subject to the following provisions of this Part of this Act, an action in personam may be brought in all such cases.

(3) In any case in which there is a maritime lien or other charge on any ship, aircraft or other property for the amount claimed, an action in rem may be brought in a county court against that ship, aircraft or property.

(4) In the case of any such claim as is mentioned in paragraphs (b) to (m) of section 27(1), where –

(a) the claim arises in connection with a ship; and

(b) the person who would be liable on the claim in an action in personam ('the relevant person') was, when the cause of action arose, the owner or charterer of, or in possession of or in control of, the ship,

an action in rem may (whether or not the claim gives rise to a maritime lien on that ship) be brought in a county court against –

(i) that ship if at the time when the action is brought the relevant person is either the beneficial owner of that ship as respects all the shares in it or the charterer of it under a charter by demise; or

(ii) any other ship of which, at the time when the action is brought, the relevant person is the beneficial owner as respects all the shares in it.

(5) In the case of a claim in the nature of towage or pilotage in respect of an aircraft, an action in rem may be brought in a county court against that aircraft if, at the time when the action is brought, it is beneficially owned by the person who would be liable on the claim in an action in personam.

(6) Where, in the exercise of its Admiralty jurisdiction, a county court orders any ship, aircraft or other property to be sold, the court shall have jurisdiction to hear and determine any question arising as to the title to the proceeds of sale.

(7) In determining for the purposes of subsections (4) and (5) whether a person would be liable on a claim in an action in personam it shall be assumed that he has his habitual residence or a place of business within England or Wales.

(8) Where, as regards any such claim as is mentioned in section 27(1)(b) to (m), a ship has been served with a summons or arrested in an action in rem brought to enforce that claim, no other ship may be served with a summons or arrested in that or any other action in rem brought to enforce that claim; but this subsection does not prevent the issue, in respect of any one such claim, of a summons naming more than one ship or of two or more summonses each naming a different ship.

(9) A county court may issue a warrant for the arrest and detention of any vessel, aircraft or property to which an action in rem brought in the court relates unless or until bail to the amount of the claim made in the action and the reasonable costs of the plaintiff in the action be entered into and perfected by or on behalf of the defendant.

(10) Except as provided by subsection (9), no vessel, aircraft or property shall be arrested or detained in Admiralty proceedings in a county court otherwise than in execution.

(11) Where –

(a) a vessel, aircraft or other property would or might be sold under an execution to enforce a judgment or order given or made by a county court in Admiralty proceedings; and

(b) the owner of the vessel, aircraft or property desires that the sale should be conducted in the High Court instead of in the county court,

he shall be entitled, on giving security for costs, and subject to such other provisions as may be prescribed, to obtain an order of the county court for transfer of the proceedings for sale, with or without (as the judge of the county court thinks fit) the transfer of any subsequent proceedings to the High Court.

(12) On an appeal by a party to any Admiralty proceedings, the Court of Appeal, if it appears to it expedient that any sale ordered to be made of the vessel, aircraft or other property to which the proceedings relate should be

conducted in the High Court instead of in the county court, may direct the transfer of the proceedings for sale, with or without the transfer of the subsequent proceedings, to the High Court.

(13) Where an action is transferred to a county court under section 40, any vessel, aircraft or other property which has been arrested in the action before the transfer shall, notwithstanding the transfer, remain in the custody of the Admiralty Marshal who shall, subject to any directions of the High Court, comply with any orders made by the county court with respect to that vessel, aircraft or property.

****

30 Restrictions on entertainment of actions in personam in collision and other similar cases

(1) The claims to which this section applies are claims for damage, loss of life or personal injury arising –

- (a) out of a collision between ships;
- (b) out of the carrying out of or omission to carry out a manoeuvre in the case of one or more of two or more ships; or
- (c) out of the non-compliance, on the part of one or more of two or more ships with safety regulations under section 85 of the Merchant Shipping Act 1995.

(2) No county court shall entertain an action in personam to enforce a claim to which this section applies unless –

- (a) the defendant has his habitual residence or a place of business within England and Wales; or
- (b) the cause of action arose within inland waters of England and Wales or within the limits of a port of England and Wales; or
- (c) an action arising out of the same incident or series of incidents is proceeding in the court or has been heard and determined in the court.

(3) In subsection (2) –

'inland waters' includes any part of the sea adjacent to the coast of the United Kingdom certified by the Secretary of State to be waters falling by international law to be treated as within the territorial sovereignty of Her Majesty apart from the operation of that law in relation to territorial waters; and

'port' means any port, harbour, river, estuary, haven, dock, canal or other place so long as a person or body of persons is empowered by or under an Act to make charges in respect of ships entering it or using the facilities in it, and 'limits of a port' means the limits thereof as fixed by or under the Act in question or, as the case may be, by the relevant charter or custom;

'charges' means any charges with the exception of light dues, local light dues and any other charges in respect of lighthouses, buoys or beacons and of charges in respect of pilotage.

(4) No county court shall entertain an action in personam to enforce a claim to which this section applies until any proceedings previously brought by the

plaintiff in any court outside England and Wales against the same defendant in respect of the same incident or series of incidents have been discontinued or otherwise come to an end.

(5) Subsections (1) to (4) shall apply to counterclaims (except counterclaims in proceedings arising out of the same incident or series of incidents) as they apply to actions in personam, but as if the references to the plaintiff and the defendant were respectively references to the plaintiff on the counterclaim and the defendant to the counterclaim.

(6) Subsections (1) to (5) shall not apply to any action or counterclaim if the defendant submits or has agreed to submit to the jurisdiction of the court.

(7) Nothing in this section shall prevent an action or counterclaim which is brought in accordance with the provisions of this section in a county court being transferred, in accordance with the enactments in that behalf, to some other court (whether a county court or not).

(8) This section applies in relation to the jurisdiction of any county court not being Admiralty jurisdiction, as well as in relation to its Admiralty jurisdiction, if any.

Amendments—Merchant Shipping Act 1995, s 314(2), Sch 13, para 72(3).

31 Admiralty – interpretation

(1) In the provisions of this Part of this Act relating to Admiralty proceedings, unless the context otherwise requires, –

'goods' includes baggage;

'master' has the same meaning as in the Merchant Shipping Act 1995, and accordingly includes every person (except a pilot) having command or charge of a ship;

'towage' and 'pilotage', in relation to an aircraft, mean towage and pilotage while the aircraft is waterborne.

(2) Nothing in those provisions shall –

(a) be construed as limiting the jurisdiction of a county court to refuse to entertain an action for wages by the master or a member of the crew of a ship, not being a British ship;

(b) affect section 226 of the Merchant Shipping Act 1995 (power of receiver of wreck to detain a ship in respect of a salvage claim);

(c) authorise proceedings in rem in respect of any claim against the Crown, or the arrest, detention or sale of any of Her Majesty's ships or Her Majesty's aircraft, or of any cargo or other property belonging to the Crown.

(3) In subsection (2) 'Her Majesty's ships' and 'Her Majesty's aircraft' have the meanings given by section 38(2) of the Crown Proceedings Act 1947.

Amendments—MSA 1995, s 314(2), Sch 13, para 72(4).

Probate proceedings

32 Contentious probate jurisdiction

(1) Where –

(a) an application for the grant or revocation of probate or administration has been made through the principal registry of the Family Division or a district probate registry under section 105 of the Supreme Court Act 1981; and

(b) it is shown to the satisfaction of a county court that the value at the date of the death of the deceased of his net estate does not exceed the county court limit,

the county court shall have the jurisdiction of the High Court in respect of any contentious matter arising in connection with the grant or revocation.

(2) In subsection (1) 'net estate', in relation to a deceased person, means the estate of that person exclusive of any property he was possessed of or entitled to as a trustee and not beneficially, and after making allowances for funeral expenses and for debts and liabilities.

Amendments—Substituted by Administration of Justice Act 1985, s 51(1).

33 Effect of order of judge in probate proceedings

Where an order is made by a county court for the grant or revocation of probate or administration, in pursuance of any jurisdiction conferred upon the court by section 32 –

(a) the district judge of the county court shall transmit to the principal registry of the Family Division or a district probate registry, as he thinks convenient, a certificate under the seal of the court certifying that the order has been made; and

(b) on the application of a party in favour of whom the order has been made, probate or administration in compliance with the order shall be issued from the registry to which the certificate was sent or, as the case may require, the probate or letters of administration previously granted shall be recalled or varied by, as the case may be, a district judge of the principal registry of the Family Division or the district probate registrar according to the effect of the order.

Amendments—Administration of Justice Act 1985, s 67, Sch 7, para 7, Sch 8, Pt III.

Miscellaneous provisions as to jurisdiction

****

35 Division of causes of action

It shall not be lawful for any plaintiff to divide any cause of action for the purpose of bringing two or more actions in one or more of the county courts.

36 No action on judgment of High Court

No action shall be brought in a county court on any judgment of the High Court.

Exercise of jurisdiction and ancillary jurisdiction

37 Persons who may exercise jurisdiction of court

(1) Any jurisdiction and powers conferred by this or any other Act –

(a) on a county court; or

(b) on the judge of a county court,

may be exercised by any judge of the court.

(2) Subsection (1) applies to jurisdiction and powers conferred on all county courts or judges of county courts or on any particular county court or the judge of any particular county court.

38 Remedies available in county courts

(1) Subject to what follows, in any proceedings in a county court the court may make any order which could be made by the High Court if the proceedings were in the High Court.

(2) Any order made by a county court may be –

(a) absolute or conditional;

(b) final or interlocutory.

(3) A county court shall not have power –

(a) to order mandamus, certiorari or prohibition; or

(b) to make any order of a prescribed kind.

(4) Regulations under subsection (3) –

(a) may provide for any of their provisions not to apply in such circumstances or descriptions of case as may be specified in the regulations;

(b) may provide for the transfer of the proceedings to the High Court for the purpose of enabling an order of a kind prescribed under subsection (3) to be made;

(c) may make such provision with respect to matters of procedure as the Lord Chancellor considers expedient; and

(d) may make provision amending or repealing any provision made by or under any enactment, so far as may be necessary or expedient in consequence of the regulations.

(5) In this section 'prescribed' means prescribed by regulations made by the Lord Chancellor under this section.

(6) The power to make regulations under this section shall be exercised by statutory instrument.

(7) No such statutory instrument shall be made unless a draft of the instrument has been approved by both Houses of Parliament.

Amendments—Substituted by CLSA 1990, s 3.

****

Transfer of proceedings

40 Transfer of proceedings to county court

(1) Where the High Court is satisfied that any proceedings before it are required by any provision of a kind mentioned in subsection (8) to be in a county court it shall –

(a) order the transfer of the proceedings to a county court; or

(b) if the court is satisfied that the person bringing the proceedings knew, or ought to have known, of that requirement, order that they be struck out.

(2) Subject to any such provision, the High Court may order the transfer of any proceedings before it to a county court.

(3) An order under this section may be made either on the motion of the High Court itself or on the application of any party to the proceedings.

(4) Proceedings transferred under this section shall be transferred to such county court as the High Court considers appropriate, having taken into account the convenience of the parties and that of any other persons likely to be affected and the state of business in the courts concerned.

(5) The transfer of any proceedings under this section shall not affect any right of appeal from the order directing the transfer.

(6) Where proceedings for the enforcement of any judgment or order of the High Court are transferred under this section –

(a) the judgment or order may be enforced as if it were a judgment or order of a county court; and
(b) subject to subsection (7), it shall be treated as a judgment or order of that court for all purposes.

(7) Where proceedings for the enforcement of any judgment or order of the High Court are transferred under this section –

(a) the powers of any court to set aside, correct, vary or quash a judgment or order of the High Court, and the enactments relating to appeals from such a judgment or order, shall continue to apply; and
(b) the powers of any court to set aside, correct, vary or quash a judgment or order of a county court, and the enactments relating to appeals from such a judgment or order, shall not apply.

(8) The provisions referred to in subsection (1) are any made –

(a) under section 1 of the Courts and Legal Services Act 1990; or
(b) by or under any other enactment.

(9) This section does not apply to family proceedings within the meaning of Part V of the Matrimonial and Family Proceedings Act 1984.

Amendments—Substituted by CLSA 1990, s 2(1).

41 Transfer to High Court by Order of High Court

(1) If at any stage in proceedings commenced in a county court or transferred to a county court under section 40, the High Court thinks it desirable that the proceedings, or any part of them, should be heard and determined in the High Court, it may order the transfer to the High Court of the proceedings or, as the case may be, of that part of them.

(2) The power conferred by subsection (1) is without prejudice to section 29 of the Supreme Court Act 1981 (power of High Court to issue prerogative orders) but shall be exercised in relation to family proceedings (within the meaning of Part V of the Matrimonial and Family Proceedings Act 1984) in accordance with any directions given under section 37 of that Act (directions as to distribution and transfer of family business and proceedings).

(3) The power conferred by subsection (1) shall be exercised subject to any provision made –

(a) under section 1 of the Courts and Legal Services Act 1990; or
(b) by or under any other enactment.

Amendments—Matrimonial and Family Proceedings Act 1984, s 46(1), Sch 1, para 30; CLSA 1990, s 2(2).

42 Transfer to High Court by order of a county court

(1) Where a county court is satisfied that any proceedings before it are required by any provision of a kind mentioned in subsection (7) to be in the High Court, it shall –

- (a) order the transfer of the proceedings to the High Court; or
- (b) if the court is satisfied that the person bringing the proceedings knew, or ought to have known, of that requirement, order that they be struck out.

(2) Subject to any such provision, a county court may order the transfer of any proceedings before it to the High Court.

(3) An order under this section may be made either on the motion of the court itself or on the application of any party to the proceedings.

(4) The transfer of any proceedings under this section shall not affect any right of appeal from the order directing the transfer.

(5) Where proceedings for the enforcement of any judgment or order of a county court are transferred under this section –

- (a) the judgment or order may be enforced as if it were a judgment or order of the High Court; and
- (b) subject to subsection (6), it shall be treated as a judgment or order of that court for all purposes.

(6) Where proceedings for the enforcement of any judgment or order of a county court are transferred under this section –

- (a) the powers of any court to set aside, correct, vary or quash a judgment or order of a county court, and the enactments relating to appeals from such a judgment or order, shall continue to apply; and
- (b) the powers of any court to set aside, correct, vary or quash a judgment or order of the High Court, and the enactments relating to appeals from such a judgment or order, shall not apply.

(7) The provisions referred to in subsection (1) are any made –

- (a) under section 1 of the Courts and Legal Services Act 1990; or
- (b) by or under any other enactment.

(8) This section does not apply to family proceedings within the meaning of Part V of the Matrimonial and Family Proceedings Act 1984.

Amendments—Substituted by CLSA 1990, s 2(3).

****

45 Costs in transferred cases

(1) Where an action, counterclaim or matter is ordered to be transferred –

- (a) from the High Court to a county court; or
- (b) from a county court to the High Court; or
- (c) from one county court to another county court,

the costs of the whole proceedings both before and after the transfer shall, subject to any order of the court which ordered the transfer, be in the discretion of the court to which the proceedings are transferred; and that court shall have power to make orders with respect to the costs, and the costs of the whole proceedings shall be taxed in that court.

(2) (*repealed*)

Amendments—CLSA 1990, s 125(7), Sch 20.

PART III
PROCEDURE

Parties

46 Proceedings by the Crown

(1) Subject to the provisions of any enactment limiting the jurisdiction of a county court, whether by reference to the subject matter of the proceedings to be brought or the amount sought to be recovered in the proceedings or otherwise, proceedings by the Crown may be instituted in a county court.

(2) Subject to section 40(5), all rules of law and enactments regulating the removal or transfer of proceedings from a county court to the High Court and the transfer of proceedings in the High Court to a county court shall apply respectively to the removal or transfer of proceedings by the Crown in a county court and to the transfer of proceedings by the Crown in the High Court.

(3) Nothing in this section shall apply to proceedings affecting Her Majesty in Her private capacity.

****

48 Persons jointly liable

(1) Where a plaintiff has a demand recoverable under this Act against two or more persons jointly liable, it shall be sufficient to serve any of those persons with process, and judgment may be obtained and execution issued against any person so served, notwithstanding that others jointly liable may not have been served or sued or may not be within the jurisdiction of the court.

(2) Where judgment is so obtained against any person by virtue of subsection (1) and is satisfied by that person, he shall be entitled to recover in the court contribution from any other person jointly liable with him.

49 Bankruptcy of plaintiff

(1) The bankruptcy of the plaintiff in any action in a county court which the trustee might maintain for the benefit of the creditors shall not cause the action to abate if, within such reasonable time as the court orders, the trustee elects to continue the action and to give security for the costs of the action.

(2) The hearing of the action may be adjourned until such an election is made.

(3) Where the trustee does not elect to continue the action and to give such security as is mentioned in subsection (1) within the time limited by the order, the defendant may avail himself of the bankruptcy as a defence to the action.

Interim payments in pending proceedings

50 Orders for interim payments

(1) Provision may be made by rules of court for enabling the court, in such circumstances as may be prescribed, to make an order requiring a party to the proceedings to make an interim payment of such amount as may be specified in the order, with provision for the payment to be made to such other party to the proceedings as may be so specified or, if the order so provides, by paying it into court.

(2) Any rules of court which make provision in accordance with subsection (1) may include provision for enabling a party to any proceedings who, in pursuance of such an order, has made an interim payment to recover the whole or part of the amount of the payment in such circumstances, and from such other party to the proceedings, as may be determined in accordance with the rules.

(3) Any rules made by virtue of this section may include such incidental, supplementary and consequential provisions as the Civil Procedure Rule Committee may consider necessary or expedient.

(4) Nothing in this section shall be construed as affecting the exercise of any power relating to costs, including any power to make rules of court relating to costs.

(5) In this section 'interim payment', in relation to a party to any proceedings, means a payment on account of any damages, debt or other sum (excluding any costs) which that party may be held liable to pay to or for the benefit of another party to the proceedings if a final judgment or order of the court in the proceedings is given or made in favour of that other party; and any reference to a party to any proceedings includes a reference to any person who for the purposes of the proceedings acts as next friend or guardian of a party to the proceedings.

Amendments—CPA 1997, s 10, Sch 2, para 2(2), (3).

Provisional damages for personal injuries

51 Orders for provisional damages for personal injuries

(1) This section applies to an action for damages for personal injuries in which there is proved or admitted to be a chance that at some definite or indefinite time in the future the injured person will, as a result of the act or omission which gave rise to the cause of action, develop some serious disease or suffer some serious deterioration in his physical or mental condition.

(2) Subject to subsection (4), as regards any action for damages to which this section applies in which a judgment is given in the county court, provision may be made by rules of court for enabling the court, in such circumstances as may be prescribed, to award the injured person –

- (a) damages assessed on the assumption that the injured person will not develop the disease or suffer the deterioration in his condition; and
- (b) further damages at a future date if he develops the disease or suffers the deterioration.

(3) Any rules made by virtue of this section may include such incidental, supplementary and consequential provisions as the Civil Procedure Rule Committee may consider necessary or expedient.

(4) Nothing in this section shall be construed –

(a) as affecting the exercise of any power relating to costs, including any power to make rules of court relating to costs; or

(b) as prejudicing any duty of the court under any enactment or rule of law to reduce or limit the total damages which would have been recoverable apart from any such duty.

(5) In this section 'personal injuries' includes any disease and any impairment of a person's physical or mental condition.

Amendments—CPA 1997, s 10, Sch 2, para 2(2), (3).

Discovery and related procedures

52 Powers of court exercisable before commencement of action

(1) On the application of any person in accordance with rules of court, a county court shall, in such circumstances as may be prescribed, have power to make an order providing for any one or more of the following matters, that is to say –

(a) the inspection, photographing, preservation, custody and detention of property which appears to the court to be property which may become the subject-matter of subsequent proceedings in the court, or as to which any question may arise in any such proceedings; and

(b) the taking of samples of any such property as is mentioned in paragraph (a), and the carrying out of any experiment on or with any such property.

(2) On the application, in accordance with rules of court, of a person who appears to a county court to be likely to be a party to subsequent proceedings in that court the county court shall, in such circumstances as may be prescribed, have power to order a person who appears to the court to be likely to be a party to the proceedings and to be likely to have or to have had in his possession, custody or power any documents which are relevant to an issue arising or likely to arise out of that claim –

(a) to disclose whether those documents are in his possession, custody or power; and

(b) to produce such of those documents as are in his possession, custody or power to the applicant or on such conditions as may be specified in the order, –

(i) to the applicant's legal advisers; or

(ii) to the applicant's legal advisers and any medical or other professional adviser of the applicant; or

(iii) if the applicant has no legal adviser, to any medical or other professional adviser of the applicant.

(3) This section is subject to any provision made under section 38.

Amendments—CLSA 1990, s 125(3), Sch 18, para 43; CPA 1997, s 10, Sch 2, para 2(2); SI 1998/2940.

53 Power of court to order disclosure of documents, inspection of property etc in proceedings for personal injuries or death

(1) (*repealed*)

(2) On the application, in accordance with rules of court, of a party to any proceedings, a county court shall, in such circumstances as may be prescribed,

have power to order a person who is not a party to the proceedings and who appears to the court to be likely to have in his possession, custody or power any documents which are relevant to any issue arising out of the said claim –

(a) to disclose whether those documents are in his possession, custody or power; and

(b) to produce such of those documents as are in his possession, custody or power to the applicant or, on such conditions as may be specified in the order, –

(i) to the applicant's legal advisers; or

(ii) to the applicant's legal advisers and any medical or other professional adviser of the applicant; or

(iii) if the applicant has no legal adviser, to any medical or other professional adviser of the applicant.

(3) On the application, in accordance with rules of court, of a party to any proceedings, a county court shall, in such circumstances as may be prescribed, have power to make an order providing for any one or more of the following matters, that is to say –

(a) the inspection, photographing, preservation, custody and detention of property which is not the property of, or in the possession of, any party to the proceedings but which is the subject-matter of the proceedings or as to which any question arises in the proceedings;

(b) the taking of samples of any such property as is mentioned in paragraph (a) and the carrying out of any experiment on or with any such property.

(4) The preceding provisions of this section are without prejudice to the exercise by a county court of any power to make orders which is exercisable apart from those provisions.

(5) This section is subject to any provision made under section 38.

Amendments—CLSA 1990, s 125(3), Sch 18, para 44; CPA 1997, s 10, Sch 2, para 2(2); SI 1998/2940.

54 Provisions supplementary to sections 52 and 53

(1) A county court shall not make an order under section 52 or 53 if it considers that compliance with the order, if made, would be likely to be injurious to the public interest.

(2) Rules of court may make provision as to the circumstances in which an order under section 52 or 53 can be made; and any rules making such provision may include such incidental, supplementary and consequential provisions as the Civil Procedure Rule Committee may consider necessary or expedient.

(3) Without prejudice to the generality of subsection (2), rules of court shall be made for the purpose of ensuring that the costs of and incidental to proceedings for an order under section 52(2) or 53 incurred by the person against whom the order is sought shall be awarded to that person unless the court otherwise directs.

(4) Sections 52(2) and 53 and this section bind the Crown; and section 52(1) binds the Crown so far as it relates to property as to which it appears to the court that it may become the subject-matter of subsequent proceedings involving a claim in respect of personal injuries to a person or in respect of a person's death.

In this subsection references to the Crown do not include references to Her Majesty in Her private capacity or to Her Majesty in right of Her Duchy of Lancaster or to the Duke of Cornwall.

(5) In sections 52 and 53 and this section –

'property' includes any land, chattel or other corporeal property of any description;

'personal injuries' includes any disease and any impairment of a person's physical or mental condition.

(6) This section is subject to any provision made under section 38.

Amendments—CLSA 1990, s 125(3), Sch 18, para 45; CPA 1997, s 10, Sch 2, para 2(2), (3).

Witnesses and evidence

55 Penalty for neglecting or refusing to give evidence

(1) Subject to subsections (2) and (3), any person who –

(a) having been summoned in pursuance of rules of court as a witness in a county court refuses or neglects, without sufficient cause, to appear or to produce any documents required by the summons to be produced; or

(b) having been so summoned or being present in court and being required to give evidence, refuses to be sworn or give evidence,

shall forfeit such fine as the judge may direct.

(2) A judge shall not have power under subsection (1) to direct that a person shall forfeit a fine of an amount exceeding £1,000.

(3) No person summoned in pursuance of rules of court as a witness in a county court shall forfeit a fine under this section unless there has been paid or tendered to him at the time of the service of the summons such sum in respect of his expenses (including, in such cases as may be prescribed, compensation for loss of time) as may be prescribed for the purposes of this section.

(4) The judge may at his discretion direct that the whole or any part of any such fine, after deducting the costs, shall be applicable towards indemnifying the party injured by the refusal or neglect.

(4A) A district judge, assistant district judge or deputy district judge shall have the same powers under this section as a judge.

(5) This section does not apply to a debtor summoned to attend by a judgment summons.

Amendments—CLSA 1990, s 74(5); Criminal Justice Act 1991, ss 17(3), 101(1), Sch 4, Pt I, Sch 12, para 6; CPA 1997, s 10, Sch 2, para 2(2).

56 Examination of witnesses abroad

The High Court shall have the same power to issue a commission, request or order to examine witnesses abroad for the purpose of proceedings in a county court as it has for the purpose of an action or matter in the High Court.

57 Evidence of prisoners

(1) Subject to subsection (2), in any proceedings pending before a county court, the judge may, if he thinks fit, upon application on affidavit by any party, issue

an order under his hand for bringing up before the court any person (in this section referred to as a 'prisoner') confined in any place under any sentence or under committal for trial or otherwise, to be examined as a witness in the proceedings.

(2) No such order shall be made with respect to a person confined under process in any civil action or matter.

(3) Subject to subsection (4), the prisoner mentioned in any such order shall be brought before the court under the same custody, and shall be dealt with in the same manner in all respects, as a prisoner required by a writ of habeas corpus to be brought before the High Court and examined there as a witness.

(4) The person having the custody of the prisoner shall not be bound to obey the order unless there is tendered to him a reasonable sum for the conveyance and maintenance of a proper officer or officers and of the prisoner in going to, remaining at, and returning from, the court.

58 Persons who may take affidavits for use in county courts

(1) An affidavit to be used in a county court may be sworn before –

(a) the judge or district judge of any court; or
(b) any justice of the peace; or
(c) an officer of any court appointed by the judge of that court for the purpose,

as well as before a commissioner for oaths or any other person authorised to take affidavits under the Commissioners for Oaths Acts 1889 and 1891.

(2) An affidavit sworn before a judge or district judge or before any such officer may be sworn without the payment of any fee.

Amendments—AJA 1985, s 67, Sch 7, para 8, Sch 8, Pt II.

59 Evidence in Admiralty proceedings

(1) In any Admiralty proceedings, evidence taken before a district judge of an Admiralty county court, in accordance with the directions of a judge or pursuant to rules of court, may be received as evidence in any other Admiralty county court.

(2) The district judge of any Admiralty county court shall, for the purpose of the examination of any witness within the district assigned to that court for Admiralty purposes, have all the power of an examiner of the High Court, and evidence taken by him in that capacity may be received as evidence in the High Court.

Amendments—CPA 1997, s 10, Sch 2, para 2(2).

Right of audience

60 Right of audience

(1) (*repealed*)

(2) Where an action is brought in a county court by a local authority for either or both of the following –

(a) the recovery of possession of a house belonging to the authority;

(b) the recovery of any rent, mesne profits, damages or other sum claimed by the authority in respect of the occupation by any person of such a house,

then, in so far as the proceedings in the action are heard by the district judge, any officer of the authority authorised by the authority in that behalf, may address the district judge.

(3) In this section –

'local authority' means a county council, a district council, the Broads Authority any National Park authority, a London borough council, a police authority established under section 3 of the Police Act 1996, the Metropolitan Police Authority, a joint authority established by Part IV of the Local Government Act 1985, the London Fire and Emergency Planning Authority or the Common Council of the City of London; and

'house' includes a part of a house, a flat or any other dwelling and also includes any yard, garden, outhouse or appurtenance occupied with a house or part of a house or with a flat or other dwelling,

and any reference to the occupation of a house by a person includes a reference to anything done by that person, or caused or permitted by him to be done, in relation to the house as occupier of the house, whether under a tenancy or licence or otherwise.

Amendments—Local Government Act 1985, ss 84, 102, Sch 14, para 63, Sch 17; Education Reform Act 1988, s 237, Sch 13, Pt I; Norfolk and Suffolk Broads Act 1988, s 21, Sch 6, para 24; CLSA 1990, s 125(7), Sch 20; Police and Magistrates' Courts Act 1994, s 43, Sch 4, Pt II, para 57; Environment Act 1995, s 78, Sch 10, para 23; Police Act 1996, s 103, Sch 7, para 1(2)(u); Police Act 1997, s 134(1), Sch 9, para 45; Greater London Authority Act 1999, ss 325, 328, Sch 27, para 49, Sch 29, Pt I, para 38; Criminal Justice and Police Act 2001, ss 128(1), 137, Sch 6, Pt 3, para 66, Sch 7, Pt 5(1).

61 Right of audience by direction of Lord Chancellor

(1) The Lord Chancellor may at any time direct that such categories of persons in relevant legal employment as may be specified in the direction may address the court in any proceedings in a county court, or in proceedings in a county court of such description as may be so specified.

(2) In subsection (1), 'relevant legal employment' means employment which consists of or includes giving assistance in the conduct of litigation to a legal representative whether in private practice or not.

(3) A direction under this section may be given subject to such conditions and restrictions as appear to the Lord Chancellor to be necessary or expedient, and may be expressed to have effect as respects every county court or as respects a specified county court or as respects one or more specified places where a county court sits.

(4) The power to give directions conferred by this section includes a power to vary or rescind any direction given under this section.

Amendments—CLSA 1990, s 125(3), Sch 18, para 49.

Mode of trial

62 General power of judge to determine questions of law and fact

Subject to the provisions of this Act and of rules of court, the judge of a county court shall be the sole judge in all proceedings brought in the court, and shall determine all questions of fact as well as of law.

Amendments—CPA 1997, s 10, Sch 2, para 2(2).

63 Assessors

(1) In any proceedings the judge may, if he thinks fit, summon to his assistance, in such manner as may be prescribed, one or more persons of skill and experience in the matter to which the proceedings relate who may be willing to sit with the judge and act as assessors.

(2) (*repealed*)

(3) Subject to subsection (4), the remuneration of assessors for sitting under this section shall be determined by the judge and shall be costs in the proceedings unless otherwise ordered by the judge.

(4) Where one or more assessors are summoned for the purposes of assisting the judge in reviewing the taxation by the district judge of the costs of any proceedings the remuneration of any such assessor –

- (a) shall be at such rate as may be determined by the Lord Chancellor with the approval of the Treasury; and
- (b) shall be payable out of moneys provided by Parliament.

(5) Where any person is proposed to be summoned as an assessor, objection to him, either personally or in respect of his qualification, may be taken by any party in the prescribed manner.

Amendments—SI 1998/2940.

Prospective amendment by Courts and Legal Services Act 1990—By virtue of CLSA 1990, ss 14(2), (3), 125(7), Sch 20 (when in force), this section is amended.

64 Reference to arbitration

(1) Rules of court –

- (a) may prescribe cases in which proceedings are (without any order of the court) to be referred to arbitration, and
- (b) may prescribe the manner in which and the terms on which cases are to be so referred, and
- (c) may, where cases are so referred, require other matters within the jurisdiction of the court in dispute between the parties also to be referred to arbitration.

(2) Rules of court –

- (a) may prescribe cases in which proceedings may be referred to arbitration by order of the court, and
- (b) may authorise the court also to order other matters in dispute between the parties and within the jurisdiction of the court to be so referred.

(2A) Rules of court may prescribe the procedures and rules of evidence to be followed on any reference under subsection (1) or (2).

(2B) Rules made under subsection (2A) may, in particular, make provision with respect to the manner of taking and questioning evidence.

(3) On a reference under subsection (1) or (2) the award of the arbitrator, arbitrators or umpire shall be entered as the judgment in the proceedings and shall be as binding and effectual to all intents, subject to subsection (4), as if it had been given by the judge.

(4) The judge may, if he thinks fit, on application made to him within such time as may be prescribed, set aside the award, or may, with the consent of the parties, revoke the reference or order another reference to be made in the manner specified in this section.

(5) In this section 'award' includes an interim award.

Amendments—CLSA 1990, s 6; CPA 1997, s 10, Sch 2, para 2(2).

65 Power of judge to refer to district judge or referee

(1) Subject to rules of court, the judge may refer to the district judge or a referee for inquiry and report –

- (a) any proceedings which require any prolonged examination of documents or any scientific or local investigation which cannot, in the opinion of the judge, conveniently be made before him;
- (b) any proceedings where the question in dispute consists wholly or in part of matters of account;
- (c) with the consent of the parties, any other proceedings;
- (d) subject to any right to have particular cases tried with a jury, any question arising in any proceedings.

(2) In such cases as may be prescribed by, and subject to, rules of court the district judge may refer to a referee for inquiry and report any question arising in any proceedings.

(3) Where any proceedings or question are referred under subsection (1) or (2), the judge or, as the case may be, the district judge may direct how the reference shall be conducted, and may remit any report for further inquiry and report, and on consideration of any report or further report may give such judgment or make such order in the proceedings as may be just.

(4) The judge may, after deciding or reserving any question of liability, refer to the district judge any mere matter of account which is in dispute between the parties and, after deciding the question of liability, may give judgment on the district judge's report.

Amendments—CPA 1997, s 10, Sch 2, para 2(2).

Juries

66 Trial by jury

(1) n the following proceedings in a county court the trial shall be without a jury –

- (a) Admiralty proceedings;
- (b) proceedings arising –
  - (i) under Part I, II or III of the Rent (Agriculture) Act 1976, or
  - (ii) under any provision of the Rent Act 1977 other than a provision contained in Part V, sections 103 to 106 or Part IX, or

(iii) under Part I of the Protection from Eviction Act 1977 or
(iv) under Part I of the Housing Act 1988;

(c) any appeal to the county court under the Housing Act 1985.

(2) In all other proceedings in a county court the trial shall be without a jury unless the court otherwise orders on an application made in that behalf by any party to the proceedings in such manner and within such time before the trial as may be prescribed.

(3) Where, on any such application, the court is satisfied that there is in issue –

(a) a charge of fraud against the party making the application; or
(b) a claim in respect of libel, slander, malicious prosecution or false imprisonment; or
(c) any question or issue of a kind prescribed for the purposes of this paragraph,

the action shall be tried with a jury, unless the court is of opinion that the trial requires any prolonged examination of documents or accounts or any scientific or local investigation which cannot conveniently be made with a jury.

(4) There shall be payable, in respect of the trial with a jury of proceedings in a county court, such fees as may be prescribed by an order under section 92 of the Courts Act 2003 (fees).

Amendments—Housing (Consequential Provisions) Act 1985, s 4, Sch 2, para 57; Housing Act 1988, s 140, Sch 17, Pt I; Courts Act 2003, s 109(1), Sch 8, para 271(a).

67 Impanelling and swearing of jury

At any county court where proceedings are to be tried with a jury, eight jurymen shall be impanelled and sworn as occasion requires to give their verdicts in the proceedings brought before them, and being once sworn need not be re-sworn in each trial.

68 Duty of judge to determine foreign law in jury trials

Where, for the purpose of disposing of any proceedings which are being tried in a county court by the judge with a jury, it is necessary to ascertain the law of any other country which is applicable to the facts of the case, any question as to the effect of the evidence given with respect to that law shall, instead of being submitted to the jury, be decided by the judge alone.

Interest on debts and damages

69 Power to award interest on debts and damages

(1) Subject to rules of court, in proceedings (whenever instituted) before a county court for the recovery of a debt or damages there may be included in any sum for which judgment is given simple interest, at such rate as the court thinks fit or as may be prescribed, on all or any part of the debt or damages in respect of which judgment is given, or payment is made before judgment, for all or any part of the period between the date when the cause of action arose and –

(a) in the case of any sum paid before judgment, the date of the payment; and
(b) in the case of the sum for which judgment is given, the date of the judgment.

(2) In relation to a judgment given for damages for personal injuries or death which exceed £200 subsection (1) shall have effect –

(a) with the substitution of 'shall be included' for 'may be included'; and
(b) with the addition of 'unless the court is satisfied that there are special reasons to the contrary' after 'given', where first occurring.

(3) Subject to rules of court, where –

(a) there are proceedings (whenever instituted) before a county court for the recovery of a debt; and
(b) the defendant pays the whole debt to the plaintiff (otherwise than in pursuance of a judgment in the proceedings),

the defendant shall be liable to pay the plaintiff simple interest, at such rate as the court thinks fit or as may be prescribed, on all or any part of the debt for all or any part of the period between the date when the cause of action arose and the date of the payment.

(4) Interest in respect of a debt shall not be awarded under this section for a period during which, for whatever reason, interest on the debt already runs.

(5) Interest under this section may be calculated at different rates in respect of different periods.

(6) In this section 'plaintiff' means the person seeking the debt or damages and 'defendant' means the person from whom the plaintiff seeks the debt or damages and 'personal injuries' includes any disease and any impairment of a person's physical or mental condition.

(7) Nothing in this section affects the damages recoverable for the dishonour of a bill of exchange.

(8) In determining whether the amount of any debt or damages exceeds that prescribed by or under any enactment, no account shall be taken of any interest payable by virtue of this section except where express provision to the contrary is made by or under that or any other enactment.

Amendments—CLSA 1990, s 125(3), Sch 18, para 46; CPA 1997, s 10, Sch 2, para 2(2).

Rates of statutory interest in commercial cases—The CPR give no real guidance as to rates of interest. Previously in commercial cases a rate of 1% over base rate has commonly been used unless for some reason that would be unfair to one party or the other. There is no reason why that measure should not continue to be used, or be used in the county court dealing with a commercial dispute such as a claim under an insurance policy (*Adcock v Co-operative Insurance Society Ltd* [2000] EWCA Civ 117, [2000] All ER (D) 505, [2000] Lloyd's Rep IR 657, *The Times*, 26 April, CA).

Judgments and orders

70 Finality of judgments and orders

Every judgment and order of a county court shall, except as provided by this or any other Act or as may be prescribed, be final and conclusive between the parties.

71 Satisfaction of judgments and orders for payment of money

(1) Where a judgment is given or an order is made by a county court under which a sum of money of any amount is payable, whether by way of satisfaction of the claim or counterclaim in the proceedings or by way of costs or otherwise, the court may, as it thinks fit, order the money to be paid either –

(a) in one sum, whether forthwith or within such period as the court may fix; or

(b) by such instalments payable at such times as the court may fix.

(2) If at any time it appears to the satisfaction of the court that any party to any proceedings is unable from any cause to pay any sum recovered against him (whether by way of satisfaction of the claim or counterclaim in the proceedings or by way of costs or otherwise) or any instalment of such a sum, the court may, in its discretion, suspend or stay any judgment or order given or made in the proceedings for such time and on such terms as the court thinks fit, and so from time to time until it appears that the cause of inability has ceased.

72 Set-off in cases of cross judgments in county courts and High Court

(1) Where one person has obtained a judgment or order in a county court against another person, and that other person has obtained a judgment or order against the first-mentioned person in the same or in another county court or in the High Court, either such person may, in accordance with rules of court, give notice in writing to the court or the several courts as the case may be, and may apply to the court or any of the said courts in accordance with rules of court for leave to set off any sums, including costs, payable under the several judgments or orders.

(2) Upon any such application, the set-off may be allowed in accordance with the practice for the time being in force in the High Court as to the allowance of set-off and in particular in relation to any solicitor's lien for costs.

(3) Where the cross judgments or orders have not been obtained in the same court, a copy of the order made on any such application shall be sent by the proper officer of the court to which the application is made to the proper officer of the other court.

73 Register of judgments and orders

(1) A register of every –

(a) judgment entered in a county court;

(b) administration order made under section 112; and

(c) order restricting enforcement made under section 112A,

shall be kept in such manner and in such place as may be prescribed.

(2) The Lord Chancellor may, by statutory instrument, make regulations as to the keeping of the register, and in this section 'prescribed' means prescribed by those regulations.

(3) Regulations under this section may –

(a) prescribe circumstances in which judgments or orders are to be exempt from registration or in which the registration of any judgment or order is to be cancelled;

(b) provide for any specified class of judgments or orders to be exempt from registration.

(4) Regulations under this section shall be subject to annulment in pursuance of a resolution of either House of Parliament.

(5) The Lord Chancellor may, with the concurrence of the Treasury, fix the fees to be paid in respect of –

(a) the making of any information contained in an entry in the register available for inspection in visible and legible form;
(b) the carrying out of any official search of the register;
(c) the supply of a certified copy of any information contained in an entry in the register.

(6) The proceeds of the fees shall be applied in such manner as the Treasury may direct in paying the expenses incurred in maintaining the register, and any surplus, after providing for the payment of those expenses, shall be paid to the credit of the Consolidated Fund.

Amendments—AJA 1985, s 54; CLSA 1990, s 125(2), Sch 17, para 14.

73A Provision for register under s 73 to be kept by body under contract to Lord Chancellor

(1) If –

(a) there is in force an agreement between the Lord Chancellor and a body corporate relating to the keeping by that body corporate of the register under section 73 ('the register'); and
(b) provision is made by regulations under that section for the register to be kept in accordance with such an agreement,

the register shall be kept by that body corporate.

(2) Where the register is kept by a body corporate in pursuance of subsection (1) –

(a) the Lord Chancellor may recover from that body any expenses incurred by the Lord Chancellor in connection with the supply of information to that body for the purposes of the register;
(b) subsection (5) of section 73 shall have effect as if the words 'maximum amounts in relation to' were inserted after the word 'fix'; and
(c) subsection (6) of that section shall not apply.

(3) Where subsection (1) of this section ceases to apply to a body corporate as a result of the termination (for any reason), of the agreement in question, the Lord Chancellor may require the information for the time being contained in the entries in the register to be transferred to such person as he may direct.

Amendments—Inserted by AJA 1985, s 54(5).

74 Interest on judgment debts etc

(1) The Lord Chancellor may by order made with the concurrence of the Treasury provide that any sums to which this subsection applies shall carry interest at such rate and between such times as may be prescribed by the order.

(2) The sums to which subsection (1) applies are –

(a) sums payable under judgments or orders given or made in a county court, including sums payable by instalments; and
(b) sums which by virtue of any enactment are, if the county court so orders, recoverable as if payable under an order of that court, and in respect of which the county court has so ordered.

(3) The payment of interest due under subsection (1) shall be enforceable as a sum payable under the judgment or order.

(4) The power conferred by subsection (1) includes power –

(a) to specify the descriptions of judgment or order in respect of which interest shall be payable;
(b) to provide that interest shall be payable only on sums exceeding a specified amount;
(c) to make provision for the manner in which and the periods by reference to which the interest is to be calculated and paid;
(d) to provide that any enactment shall or shall not apply in relation to interest payable under subsection (1) or shall apply to it with such modifications as may be specified in the order; and
(e) to make such incidental or supplementary provisions as the Lord Chancellor considers appropriate.

(5) Without prejudice to the generality of subsection (4), an order under subsection (1) may provide that the rate of interest shall be the rate specified in section 17 of the Judgments Act 1838 as that enactment has effect from time to time.

(5A) The power conferred by subsection (1) includes power to make provision enabling a county court to order that the rate of interest applicable to a sum expressed in a currency other than sterling shall be such rate as the court thinks fit (instead of the rate otherwise applicable).

(6) The power to make an order under subsection (1) shall be exercisable by statutory instrument subject to annulment in pursuance of a resolution of either House of Parliament.

Amendments—Private International Law (Miscellaneous Provisions) Act 1995, s 2.

Practice directions

74A Practice directions

(1) Directions as to the practice and procedure of county courts may be made by the Lord Chancellor.

(2) Directions as to the practice and procedure of county courts may not be made by any other person without the approval of the Lord Chancellor.

(3) The power of the Lord Chancellor to make directions under subsection (1) includes power –

(a) to vary or revoke directions made by him or any other person, and
(b) to make different provision for different cases or different areas, including different provision –
  (i) for a specific court, or
  (ii) for specific proceedings, or a specific jurisdiction,

specified in the directions.

(4) References in this section to the Lord Chancellor include any person authorised by him to act on his behalf.

Amendments—Inserted by CPA 1997, s 5(2).

General rules of procedure

****

76 Application of practice of High Court

In any case not expressly provided for by or in pursuance of this Act, the general principles of practice in the High Court may be adopted and applied to proceedings in a county court.

PART IV
APPEALS ETC

Appeals

77 Appeals: general provisions

(1) Subject to the provisions of this section and the following provisions of this Part of this Act and to any order made by the Lord Chancellor under section 56(1) of the Access to Justice Act 1999, if any party to any proceedings in a county court is dissatisfied with the determination of the judge or jury, he may appeal from it to the Court of Appeal in such manner and subject to such conditions as may be provided by the Civil Procedure Rules.

(1A) Without prejudice to the generality of the power to make rules of court under section 75, such rules may make provision for any appeal from the exercise by a district judge, assistant district judge or deputy district judge of any power given to him by virtue of any enactment to be to a judge of a county court.

(2)–(4) (*repealed*)

(5) Subject to the provisions of this section and the following provisions of this Part of this Act, where an appeal is brought under subsection (1) in any action, an appeal may be brought under that subsection in respect of any claim or counterclaim in the action notwithstanding that there could have been no such appeal if that claim had been the subject of a separate action.

(6) In proceedings in which either the plaintiff or the defendant is claiming possession of any premises this section shall not confer any right of appeal on any question of fact if by virtue of –

- (a) section 13(4) of the Landlord and Tenant Act 1954; or
- (b) Cases III to IX in Schedule 4 to the Rent (Agriculture) Act 1976; or
- (c) section 98 of the Rent Act 1977, as it applies to Cases 1 to 6 and 8 and 9 in Schedule 15 to that Act, or that section as extended or applied by any other enactment; or
- (d) section 99 of the Rent Act 1977, as it applies to Cases 1 to 6 and 9 in Schedule 15 to that Act; or
- (e) section 84(2)(a) of the Housing Act 1985; or
- (ee) section 7 of the Housing Act 1988, as it applies to the grounds in Part II of Schedule 2 to that Act; or
- (f) any other enactment,

the court can only grant possession on being satisfied that it is reasonable to do so.

(7) This section shall not –

- (a) confer any right of appeal from any judgment or order where a right of appeal is conferred by some other enactment; or

(b) take away any right of appeal from any judgment or order where a right of appeal is so conferred,

and shall have effect subject to any enactment other than this Act.

(8) In this section –

'enactment' means an enactment whenever passed.

Amendments—Housing (Consequential Provisions) Act 1985, s 4, Sch 2, para 57; Housing Act 1988, s 140, Sch 17, Pt I; CLSA 1990, s 125(2), Sch 17, para 15; CPA 1997, s 10, Sch 2, para 2(2), (7); Access to Justice Act 1999, s 106, Sch 15, Pt III; SI 2000/1071.

78 Assistance of Trinity masters for Court of Appeal in Admiralty proceedings

Where, on an appeal by a party to any Admiralty proceedings which have been heard in a county court with the assistance of assessors, any party makes application to the Court of Appeal in that behalf, the court shall summon Trinity masters to assist on the hearing of the appeal if the court is of opinion that such assistance is necessary or desirable.

79 Agreement not to appeal

(1) No appeal shall lie from any judgment, direction, decision or order of a judge of county courts if, before the judgment, direction, decision or order is given or made, the parties agree, in writing signed by themselves or their legal representatives or agents, that it shall be final.

(2) (*repealed*)

Amendments—Statute Law (Repeals) Act 1986; CLSA 1990, s 125(3), Sch 18, para 49.

80 Judge's note on appeal

(1) At the hearing of any proceedings in a county court in which there is a right of appeal or from which an appeal may be brought with leave, the judge shall, at the request of any party, make a note –

(a) of any question of law raised at the hearing; and
(b) of the facts in evidence in relation to any such question; and
(c) of his decision on any such question and of his determination of the proceedings.

(2) Where such a note has been taken, the judge shall (whether notice of appeal has been served or not), on the application of any party to the proceedings, and on payment by that party of such fee as may be prescribed by an order under section 92 of the Courts Act 2003 (fees), furnish him with a copy of the note, and shall sign the copy, and the copy so signed shall be used at the hearing of the appeal.

Amendments—Courts Act 2003, s 109(1), Sch 8, para 271(b).

81 Powers of Court of Appeal on appeal from county court

(1) On the hearing of an appeal, the Court of Appeal may draw any inference of fact and either –

(a) order a new trial on such terms as the court thinks just; or

(b) order judgment to be entered for any party; or
(c) make a final or other order on such terms as the court thinks proper to ensure the determination on the merits of the real question in controversy between the parties.

(2) Subject to Civil Procedure Rules, on any appeal from a county court the Court of Appeal may reverse or vary, in favour of a party seeking to support the judgment or order of the county court in whole or in part, any determinations made in the county court on questions of fact, notwithstanding that the appeal is an appeal on a point of law only, or any such determinations on points of law, notwithstanding that the appeal is an appeal on a question of fact only.

(3) Subsection (2) shall not enable the Court of Appeal to reverse or vary any determination, unless the party dissatisfied with the determination would have been entitled to appeal in respect of it if aggrieved by the judgment or order.

Amendments—CPA 1997, s 10, Sch 2, para 2(8).

82 Decision of Court of Appeal on probate appeals to be final

No appeal shall lie from the decision of the Court of Appeal on any appeal from a county court in any probate proceedings.

Certiorari and prohibition

83 Stay of proceedings in case of certiorari or prohibition

(1) The grant by the High Court of leave to make an application for an order of certiorari or prohibition to a county court shall, if the High Court so directs, operate as a stay of the proceedings in question until the determination of the application, or until the High Court otherwise orders.

(2) Where any proceedings are so stayed, the judge of the county court shall from time to time adjourn the hearing of the proceedings to such day as he thinks fit.

84 Prohibition

(1) Where an application is made to the High Court for an order of prohibition addressed to any county court, the matter shall be finally disposed of by order.

(2) Upon any such application, the judge of the county court shall not be served with notice of it, and shall not, except by the order of a judge of the High Court –

(a) be required to appear or be heard; or
(b) be liable to any order for the payment of the costs of the application;

but the application shall be proceeded with and heard in the same manner in all respects as an appeal duly brought from a decision of the judge, and notice of the application shall be given to or served upon the same parties as in the case of an order made or refused by a judge in a matter within his jurisdiction.

PART V
ENFORCEMENT OF JUDGMENTS AND ORDERS

Execution against goods

85 Execution of judgments or orders for payment of money

(1) Subject to article 8 of the High Court and County Courts Jurisdiction Order 1991, any sum of money payable under a judgment or order of a county court may be recovered, in case of default or failure of payment, forthwith or at the time or times and in the manner thereby directed, by execution against the goods of the party against whom the judgment or order was obtained.

(2) The district judge, on the application of the party prosecuting any such judgment or order, shall issue a warrant of execution in the nature of a writ of fieri facias whereby the district judge shall be empowered to levy or cause to be levied by distress and sale of the goods, wherever they may be found within the district of the court, the money payable under the judgment or order and the costs of the execution.

(3) The precise time of the making of the application to the district judge to issue such a warrant shall be entered by him in the record prescribed for the purpose under section 12 and on the warrant.

(4) It shall be the duty of every constable within his jurisdiction to assist in the execution of every such warrant.

Amendments—SI 1991/724.

86 Execution of orders for payment by instalments

(1) Where the court has made an order for payment of any sum of money by instalments, execution on the order shall not be issued until after default in payment of some instalment according to the order.

(2) Rules of court may prescribe the cases in which execution is to issue if there is any such default and limit the amounts for which and the times at which execution may issue.

(3) Except so far as may be otherwise provided by rules of court made for those purposes, execution or successive executions may issue if there is any such default for the whole of the said sum of money and costs then remaining unpaid or for such part as the court may order either at the time of the original order or at any subsequent time; but except so far as may be otherwise provided by such rules, no execution shall issue unless at the time when it issues the whole or some part of an instalment which has already become due remains unpaid.

Amendments—CPA 1997, s 10, Sch 2, para 2(2).

87 Execution to be superseded on payment

(1) In or upon every warrant of execution issued from a county court against the goods of any person, the district judge shall cause to be inserted or indorsed the total amount to be levied, inclusive of the fee for issuing the warrant but exclusive of the fees for its execution.

(2) If the person against whom the execution is issued, before the actual sale of the goods, pays or causes to be paid or tendered to the district judge of the court

from which the warrant is issued, or to the bailiff holding the warrant, the amount inserted in, or indorsed upon, the warrant under subsection (1), or such part as the person entitled agrees to accept in full satisfaction, together with the amount stated by the officer of the court to whom the payment or tender is made to be the amount of the fees for the execution of the warrant, the execution shall be superseded, and the goods shall be discharged and set at liberty.

88 Power to stay execution

If at any time it appears to the satisfaction of the court that any party to any proceedings is unable from any cause to pay any sum recovered against him (whether by way of satisfaction of the claim or counterclaim in the proceedings or by way of costs or otherwise), or any instalment of such a sum, the court may, in its discretion, stay any execution issued in the proceedings for such time and on such terms as the court thinks fit, and so from time to time until it appears that the cause of inability has ceased.

Seizure and custody of goods etc

89 Goods which may be seized

(1) Every bailiff or officer executing any warrant of execution issued from a county court against the goods of any person may by virtue of it seize –

- (a) any of that person's goods except –
  - (i) such tools, books, vehicles and other items of equipment as are necessary to that person for use personally by him in his employment, business or vocation;
  - (ii) such clothing, bedding, furniture, household equipment and provisions as are necessary for satisfying the basic domestic needs of that person and his family;
- (b) any money, banknotes, bills of exchange, promissory notes, bonds, specialties or securities for money belonging to that person.

(2) Any reference to the goods of an execution debtor in this Part of this Act includes a reference to anything else of his that may lawfully be seized in execution.

(3) (*repealed*)

Amendments—CLSA 1990, ss 15(2), 125(7), Sch 20.

90 Custody of goods seized

Goods seized in execution under process of a county court shall, until sale, –

- (a) be deposited by the bailiff in some fit place; or
- (b) remain in the custody of a fit person approved by the district judge to be put in possession by the bailiff; or
- (c) be safeguarded in such other manner as the district judge directs.

91 Disposal of bills of exchange, etc, seized

The district judge shall hold any bills of exchange, promisory notes, bonds, specialties or other securities for money seized in execution under process of a county court as security for the amount directed to be levied by the execution, or for so much of that amount as has not been otherwise levied or raised, for the benefit of the plaintiff, and the plaintiff may sue in the name of the defendant, or in the name of any person in whose name the defendant might have sued, for the recovery of the sum secured or made payable thereby, when the time of payment arrives.

92 Penalty for rescuing goods seized

(1) If any person rescues or attempts to rescue any goods seized in execution under process of a county court, he shall be liable –

(a) on summary conviction, to imprisonment for a term not exceeding one month or to a fine of an amount not exceeding level 4 on the standard scale, or both; or

(b) on an order made by the judge in that behalf, to be committed for a specified period not exceeding one month to prison or to a fine of an amount not exceeding level 4 on the standard scale or to be so committed and to such a fine,

and a bailiff of the court may take the offender into custody, with or without warrant, and bring him before the judge.

(2) The judge may at any time revoke an order committing a person to prison under this section and, if he is already in custody, order his discharge.

Amendments—SL(R)A 1986.

Entitlements of party—Both at common law and in order to comply with the HRA 1998, any person who is brought before the judge under this section is entitled to minimum safeguards. He must be given in writing details of the charge against him at the outset of any hearing. He must also be offered the opportunity to obtain legal advice and offered legal aid, which the court has power to grant of its own initiative under LAA 1988, s 29, immediately it becomes apparent to the judge that a sentence of imprisonment may be imposed for the particular offence (*Newman v Modern Bookbinders* [2000] 2 All ER 814, CA).

Sale of goods seized

93 Period to elapse before sale

No goods seized in execution under process of a county court shall be sold for the purpose of satisfying the warrant of execution until the expiration of a period of at least 5 days next following the day on which the goods have been so seized unless –

(a) the goods are of a perishable nature; or

(b) the person whose goods have been seized so requests in writing.

94 Goods not to be sold except by brokers or appraisers

No goods seized in execution under process of a county court shall be sold for the purpose of satisfying the warrant of execution except by one of the brokers or appraisers appointed under this Part of this Act.

95 Appointment of brokers, appraisers etc

(1) The district judge may from time to time as he thinks fit appoint such number of persons for keeping possession, and such number of brokers and

appraisers for the purpose of selling or valuing any goods seized in execution under process of the court, as appears to him to be necessary.

(2) The district judge may direct security to be taken from any broker, appraiser or other person so appointed for such sum and in such manner as he thinks fit for the faithful performance of his duties without injury or oppression.

(3) The judge or district judge may dismiss any broker, appraiser or other person so appointed.

(4) There shall be payable to brokers and appraisers so appointed in respect of their duties, out of the produce of goods distrained or sold, such fees as may be prescribed by an order under section 92 of the Courts Act 2003 (fees).

Amendments—Courts Act 2003, s 109(1), Sch 8, para 271(c).

96 Power to appoint bailiffs to act as brokers and appraisers

(1) The judge may appoint in writing any bailiff of the court to act as a broker or appraiser for the purpose of selling or valuing any goods seized in execution under process of the court.

(2) A bailiff so appointed may, without other licence in that behalf, perform all the duties which brokers or appraisers appointed under section 95 may perform under this Act.

97 Sales under executions to be public unless otherwise ordered

(1) Where any goods are to be sold under execution for a sum exceeding £20 (including legal incidental expenses), the sale shall, unless the court from which the warrant of execution issued otherwise orders, be made by public auction and not by bill of sale or private contract, and shall be publicly advertised by the district judge on, and during 3 days next preceding, the day of sale.

(2) Where any goods are seized in execution and the district judge has notice of another execution or other executions, the court shall not consider an application for leave to sell privately until the prescribed notice has been given to the other execution creditor or creditors, who may appear before the court and be heard upon the application.

98 Protection of district judge selling goods under execution without notice of claim by third party

(1) Where any goods in the possession of an execution debtor at the time of seizure by a district judge or other officer charged with the enforcement of a warrant or other process of execution issued from a county court are sold by that district judge or other officer without any claims having been made to them –

- (a) the purchaser of the goods so sold shall acquire a good title to those goods; and
- (b) no person shall be entitled to recover against the district judge or other officer, or anyone lawfully acting under his authority –
  - (i) for any sale of the goods, or
  - (ii) for paying over the proceeds prior to the receipt of a claim to the goods,

unless it is proved that the person from whom recovery is sought had notice, or might by making reasonable inquiry have ascertained, that the goods were not the property of the execution debtor.

(2) Nothing in this section shall affect the right of any claimant, who may prove that at the time of sale he had a title to any goods so seized and sold, to any remedy to which he may be entitled against any person other than the district judge or other officer.

(3) The provisions of this section have effect subject to those of sections 183, 184 and 346 of the Insolvency Act 1986.

Amendments—Insolvency Act 1986, s 439(2), Sch 14; Courts Act 2003, s 109(1), Sch 8, para 273.

Claims in respect of goods seized

99 Effect of warrants of execution

(1) Subject –

(a) to subsection (2); and
(b) to section 103(2),

a warrant of execution against goods issued from a county court shall bind the property in the goods of the execution debtor as from the time at which application for the warrant was made to the district judge of the county court.

(2) Such a warrant shall not prejudice the title to any goods of the execution debtor acquired by a person in good faith and for valuable consideration unless he had at the time when he acquired his title –

(a) notice that an application for the issue of a warrant of execution against the goods of the execution debtor had been made to the district judge of a county court and that the warrant issued on the application either –
  (i) remained unexecuted in the hands of the district judge of the court from which it was issued; or
  (ii) had been sent for execution to, and received by, the district judge of another county court, and remained unexecuted in the hands of the district judge of that court; or
(b) notice that a writ of fieri facias or other writ of execution by virtue of which the goods of the execution debtor might be seized or attached had been delivered to an enforcement officer or other officer charged with the execution of the writ and remained unexecuted in the hands of that person.

(3) It shall be the duty of the district judge (without fee) on application for a warrant of execution being made to him to endorse on its back the hour, day, month and year when he received the application.

(4) For the purposes of this section –

(za) 'enforcement officer' means an individual who is authorised to act as an enforcement officer under the Courts Act 2003;
(a) 'property' means the general property in goods, and not merely a special property;
(b) (*repealed*)
(c) a thing shall be treated as done in good faith if it is in fact done honestly whether it is done negligently or not.

Amendments—Courts Act 2003, s 109(1), Sch 8, para 274(1), (2)(a), (b), (3)(a), (b).

100 Sale of goods to which claim is made

(1) Where a claim is made to or in respect of any goods seized in execution under process of a county court, the claimant may –

(a) deposit with the bailiff either –
 (i) the amount of the value of the goods claimed; or
 (ii) the sum which the bailiff is allowed to charge as costs for keeping possession of the goods until the decision of the judge can be obtained on the claim; or
(b) give the bailiff in the prescribed manner security for the value of the goods claimed.

(2) For the purpose of this section, the amount of the value of the goods claimed shall, in case of dispute, be fixed by appraisement, and where that amount is deposited it shall be paid by the bailiff into court to abide the decision of the judge upon the claim.

(3) Subject to subsection (4), in default of the claimant's complying with this section, the bailiff shall sell the goods as if no such claim had been made, and shall pay into court the proceeds of the sale to abide the decision of the judge.

(4) The goods shall not be sold if the district judge decides that, in all the circumstances, the decision of the judge on the claim made to or in respect of them ought to be awaited.

101 Interpleader by district judge

(1) If a claim is made to or in respect of any goods seized in execution under process of a county court, or in respect of the proceeds or value of any such goods, the district judge may, as well before as after any action brought against him, issue a summons calling before the court the party at whose instance the process issued and the party making the claim.

(2) Upon the issue of the summons, any action brought in any county court or other court in respect of the claim or of any damage arising out of the execution of the warrant shall be stayed.

(3) On the hearing of the summons, the judge shall adjudicate upon the claim, and shall also adjudicate between the parties or either of them and the district judge upon any claim to damages arising or capable of arising out of the execution of the warrant by the district judge, and shall make such order in respect of any such claim and the costs of the proceedings as he thinks fit.

102 Claims for rent where goods seized in execution

(1) Section 1 of the Landlord and Tenant Act 1709 shall not apply to goods seized in execution under process of a county court, but the following provisions of this section shall apply in substitution.

(2) The landlord of any tenement in which any goods are seized may claim the rent of the tenement in arrear at the date of the seizure, at any time within the 5 days next following that date, or before the removal of the goods, by delivering to the bailiff or officer making the levy a claim in writing, signed by himself or his agent, stating –

(a) the amount of rent claimed to be in arrear; and
(b) the period in respect of which the rent is due.

(3) Where such a claim is made, the bailiff or officer making the levy shall in addition distrain for the rent so claimed and the cost of the distress, and shall not, within 5 days next after the distress, sell any part of the goods seized, unless –

(a) the goods are of a perishable nature; or
(b) the person whose goods have been seized so requests in writing.

(4) The bailiff shall afterwards sell under the execution and distress such of the goods as will satisfy –

(a) first, the costs of and incidental to the sale;
(b) next, the claim of the landlord not exceeding –
  (i) in a case where the tenement is let by the week, 4 weeks' rent;
  (ii) in a case where the tenement is let for any other term less than a year, the rent of two terms of payment;
  (iii) in any other case, one year's rent; and
(c) lastly, the amount for which the warrant of execution issued.

(5) If any replevin is made of the goods seized, the bailiff shall nevertheless sell such portion of them as will satisfy the costs of and incidental to the sale under the execution and the amount for which the warrant of execution issued.

(6) In any event the surplus of the sale, if any, and the residue of the goods shall be returned to the execution debtor.

(7) The fees of the district judge and broker for keeping possession, appraisement and sale under any such distress shall be the same as would have been payable if the distress had been an execution of the court, and no other fees shall be demanded or taken in respect thereof.

(8) Nothing in this section affects section 346 of the Insolvency Act 1986.

Amendments—IA 1986, s 439(2), Sch 14.

Execution out of jurisdiction of court

103 Execution out of jurisdiction of court

(1) Where a warrant of execution has been issued from a county court (hereafter in this section referred to as a 'home court') against the goods of any person and the goods are out of the jurisdiction of that court, the district judge of that court may send the warrant of execution to the district judge of any other county court within the jurisdiction of which the goods are or are believed to be, with a warrant endorsed on it or annexed to it requiring execution of the original warrant.

(2) The original warrant shall bind the property in goods of the execution debtor which are within the jurisdiction of the court to which it is sent as from the time when it is received by the district judge of that court.

(3) It shall be the duty of the district judge of the court to which the warrant is sent (without fee) on receipt of the warrant to endorse on its back the hour, day, month and year when he received it.

(4) On the receipt of the warrant, the district judge of the other county court shall act in all respects as if the original warrant of execution had been issued by the court of which he is district judge and shall within the prescribed time –

(a) report to the district judge of the home court what he has done in the execution of the warrant; and

(b) pay over all moneys received in pursuance of the warrant.

(5) Where a warrant of execution is sent by the district judge of a home court to the district judge of another court for execution under this section, that other court shall have the same power as the home court of staying the execution under section 88 as respects any goods within the jurisdiction of that other court.

(6) Rules of court may make provision for the suspension of any judgment or order, on terms, in connection with any warrant issued with respect to any instalment payable under the judgment or order.

Amendments—CLSA 1990, s 125(2), Sch 17, para 16; CPA 1997, s 10, Sch 2, para 2(2).

104 Information as to writs and warrants of execution

(1) Where a writ against the goods of any person issued from the High Court is delivered to an enforcement officer who is under a duty to execute the writ or to a sheriff, then on demand from the district judge of a county court that person shall –

(a) in the case of an enforcement officer, by writing signed by that officer or a person acting under his authority, and

(b) in the case of a sheriff, by writing signed by any clerk in the office of the under-sheriff,

inform the district judge of the precise time the writ was delivered to him.

(2) A bailiff of a county court shall on demand show his warrant to any enforcement officer, any person acting under the authority of an enforcement officer and any sheriff's officer.

(3) Any writing purporting to be signed as mentioned in subsection (1) and the endorsement on any warrant issued from a county court shall respectively be sufficient justification to any district judge, or enforcement officer or sheriff, acting on it.

(4) In this section 'enforcement officer' means an individual who is authorised to act as an enforcement officer under the Courts Act 2003.

Amendments—Substituted by Courts Act 2003, s 109(1), Sch 8, para 274(1), (2)(a), (b), (3)(a), (b).

****

Receivers and attachment of debts

107 Receivers

(1) The power of the county court to appoint a receiver by way of equitable execution shall operate in relation to all legal estates and interests in land.

(2) The said power may be exercised in relation to an estate or interest in land whether or not a charge has been imposed on that land under section 1 of the Charging Orders Act 1979 for the purpose of enforcing the judgment, decree, order or award in question, and the said power shall be in addition to and not in derogation of any power of any court to appoint a receiver in proceedings for enforcing such a charge.

(3) Where an order under section 1 of the Charging Orders Act 1979 imposing a charge for the purpose of enforcing a judgment, decree, order or award has been registered under section 6 of the Land Charges Act 1972, subsection (4) of that section (which provides that, amongst other things, an order appointing a

receiver and any proceedings pursuant to the order or in obedience to it, shall be void against a purchaser unless the order is for the time being registered under that section) shall not apply to an order appointing a receiver made either in proceedings for enforcing the charge or by way of equitable execution of the judgment, decree, order or award or, as the case may be, of so much of it as requires payment of moneys secured by the charge.

108 Attachment of debts

(1) Subject to any order for the time being in force under subsection (4), this section applies to any deposit account, and any withdrawable share account, with a deposit-taker.

(2) In determining whether, for the purposes of the jurisdiction of the county court to attach debts for the purpose of satisfying judgments or orders for the payment of money, a sum standing to the credit of a person in an account to which this section applies is a sum due or accruing to that person and, as such, attachable in accordance with rules of court, any condition mentioned in subsection (3) which applies to the account shall be disregarded.

(3) Those conditions are –

- (a) any condition that notice is required before any money or share is withdrawn;
- (b) any condition that a personal application must be made before any money or share is withdrawn;
- (c) any condition that a deposit book or share-account book must be produced before any money or share is withdrawn; or
- (d) any other prescribed condition.

(4) The Lord Chancellor may by order make such provision as he thinks fit, by way of amendment of this section or otherwise, for all or any of the following purposes, namely –

- (a) including in, or excluding from, the accounts to which this section applies accounts of any description specified in the order;
- (b) excluding from the accounts to which this section applies all accounts with any particular deposit-taker so specified or with any deposit-taker of a description so specified.

(5) An order under subsection (4) shall be made by statutory instrument subject to annulment in pursuance of a resolution of either House of Parliament.

Amendments—CPA 1997, s 10, Sch 2, para 2(2); SI 2001/3649.

109 Administrative and clerical expenses of garnishees

(1) Where an interim third party debt order made in the exercise of the jurisdiction mentioned in subsection (2) of the preceding section is served on a deposit-taker, it may, subject to the provisions of this section, deduct from the relevant debt or debts an amount not exceeding the prescribed sum towards its administrative and clerical expenses in complying with the order; and the right to make a deduction under this subsection shall be exercisable as from the time the interim third party debt order is served on it.

(1A) In subsection (1) 'the relevant debt or debts', in relation to an interim third party debt order served on a deposit-taker, means the amount, as at the time the order is served on it, of the debt or debts of which the whole or a part is expressed to be attached by the order.

(1B) A deduction may be made under subsection (1) in a case where the amount referred to in subsection (1A) is insufficient to cover both the amount of the deduction and the amount of the judgment debt and costs in respect of which the attachment was made, notwithstanding that the benefit of the attachment to the creditor is reduced as a result of the deduction.

(2) An amount may not in pursuance of subsection (1) be deducted or, as the case may be, retained in a case where by virtue of section 346 of the Insolvency Act 1986 or section 325 of the Companies Act 1948 or otherwise, the creditor is not entitled to retain the benefit of the attachment.

(3) In this section 'prescribed' means prescribed by an order made by the Lord Chancellor.

(4) An order under this section –

(a) may make different provision for different cases;
(b) without prejudice to the generality of paragraph (a) may prescribe sums differing according to the amount due under the judgment or order to be satisfied.
(c) may provide for this section not to apply to deposit-takers of any prescribed description.

(5) Any such order shall be made by statutory instrument subject to annulment in pursuance of a resolution of either House of Parliament.

Amendments—AJA 1985, ss 52, (4), 67(2), 69(5), Sch 8, Pt II, Sch 9, para 11(2); IA 1985, s 235, Sch 8, para 38; IA 1986, s 439(2), Sch 14; SI 2001/3649; SI 2002/439.

Miscellaneous provisions as to enforcement of judgments and orders

110 Penalty for non-attendance on judgment summons

(1) If a debtor summoned to attend a county court by a judgment summons fails to attend on the day and at the time fixed for any hearing of the summons, the judge may adjourn or further adjourn the summons to a specified time on a specified day and order the debtor to attend at that time on that day.

(2) If –

(a) a debtor, having been ordered under subsection (1) to attend at a specified time on a specified day, fails to do so;

the judge may make an order committing him to prison for a period not exceeding 14 days in respect of the failure or refusal.

(3) In any case where the judge has power to make an order of committal under subsection (2) for failure to attend, he may in lieu of or in addition to making that order, order the debtor to be arrested and brought before the court either forthwith or at such time as the judge may direct.

(4) A debtor shall not be committed to prison under subsection (2) for having failed to attend as required by an order under subsection (1) unless there was paid to him at the time of the service of the judgment summons, or paid or tendered to him at the time of the service of the order, such sum in respect of his expenses as may be prescribed for the purposes of this section.

(5) The judge may at any time revoke an order committing a person to prison under this section and, if he is already in custody, order his discharge.

Amendments—SI 2002/439.

111 Provisions as to warrants of possession

(1) For the purpose of executing a warrant to give possession of any premises, it shall not be necessary to remove any goods from those premises.

(2) The duration of any warrant of possession issued by a county court to enforce a judgment or order for the recovery of land or for the delivery of possession of land shall be such as may be fixed by or in accordance with rules of court.

Amendments—CPA 1997, s 10, Sch 2, para 2(2).

PART VI
ADMINISTRATION ORDERS

112 Power to make administration order

(1) Where a debtor –

- (a) is unable to pay forthwith the amount of a judgment obtained against him; and
- (b) alleges that his whole indebtedness amounts to a sum not exceeding the county court limit, inclusive of the debt for which the judgment was obtained;

a county court may make an order providing for the administration of his estate.

(2) In this Part of this Act –

'administration order' means an order under this section; and

'the appropriate court', in relation to an administration order, means the court which has the power to make the order.

(3) Before an administration order is made, the appropriate court shall, in accordance with rules of court, send to every person whose name the debtor has notified to the appropriate court as being a creditor of his, a notice that that person's name has been so notified.

(4) So long as an administration order is in force, a creditor whose name is included in the schedule to the order shall not, without the leave of the appropriate court, be entitled to present, or join in, a bankruptcy petition against the debtor unless –

- (a) his name was so notified; and
- (b) the debt by virtue of which he presents, or joins in, the petition, exceeds £1,500; and
- (c) the notice given under subsection (3) was received by the creditor within 28 days immediately preceding the day on which the petition is presented.

(5) An administration order shall not be invalid by reason only that the total amount of the debts is found at any time to exceed the county court limit, but in that case the court may, if it thinks fit, set aside the order.

(6) An administration order may provide for the payment of the debts of the debtor by instalments or otherwise, and either in full or to such extent as appears practicable to the court under the circumstances of the case, and subject to any conditions as to his future earnings or income which the court may think just.

(7) The Secretary of State may by regulations increase or reduce the sum for the time being specified in subsection (4)(b); but no such increase in the sum so specified shall affect any case in which the bankruptcy petition was presented before the coming into force of the increase.

(8) The power to make regulations under subsection (7) shall be exercisable by statutory instrument; and no such regulations shall be made unless a draft of them has been approved by resolution of each House of Parliament.

Amendments—IA 1985, s 220(2); CPA 1997, s 10, Sch 2, para 2(2).

Prospective amendment by Courts and Legal Services Act 1990—By virtue of CLSA 1990, ss 13(1), (2), (3), (4), 125(7), Sch 20 (when in force), this section is extensively amended.

113 Notice of order and proof of debts

Where an administration order has been made –

(a) notice of the order –
  (i) (*repealed*)
  (ii) shall be posted in the office of the county court for the district in which the debtor resides, and
  (iii) shall be sent to every person whose name the debtor has notified to the appropriate court as being a creditor of his or who has proved;

(b) any creditor of the debtor, on proof of his debt before the district judge, shall be entitled to be scheduled as a creditor of the debtor for the amount of his proof;

(c) any creditor may object in the prescribed manner to any debt scheduled, or to the manner in which payment is directed to be made by instalments;

(d) any person who, after the date of the order, becomes a creditor of the debtor shall, on proof of his debt before the district judge, be scheduled as a creditor of the debtor for the amount of his proof, but shall not be entitled to any dividend under the order until the creditors who are scheduled as having been creditors before the date of the order have been paid to the extent provided by the order.

Amendments—AJA 1985, s 67(2), Sch 8, Pt II.

114 Effect of administration order

(1) Subject to sections 115 and 116, when an administration order is made, no creditor shall have any remedy against the person or property of the debtor in respect of any debt –

(a) of which the debtor notified the appropriate court before the administration order was made; or

(b) which has been scheduled to the order,

except with the leave of the appropriate court, and on such terms as that court may impose.

(2) Subject to subsection (3), any county court in which proceedings are pending against the debtor in respect of any debt so notified or scheduled shall,

on receiving notice of the administration order, stay the proceedings, but may allow costs already incurred by the creditor, and such costs may, on application, be added to the debt.

(3) The requirement to stay proceedings shall not operate as a requirement that a county court in which proceedings in bankruptcy against the debtor are pending shall stay those proceedings.

115 Execution by district judge

(1) Where it appears to the district judge of the appropriate court at any time while an administration order is in force that property of the debtor exceeds in value the minimum amount, he shall, at the request of any creditor, and without fee, issue execution against the debtor's goods.

(1A) In subsection (1) above 'the minimum amount' means £50 or such other amount as the Lord Chancellor may by order specify instead of that amount or the amount for the time being specified in such an order; and an order under this subsection shall be made by statutory instrument subject to annulment in pursuance of a resolution of either House of Parliament.

(2) Section 89 applies on an execution under this section as it applies on an execution under Part V.

Amendments—IA 1985, s 220.

116 Right of landlord to distrain notwithstanding order

A landlord or other person to whom any rent is due from a debtor in respect of whom an administration order is made, may at any time, either before or after the date of the order, distrain upon the goods or effects of the debtor for the rent due to him from the debtor, with this limitation, that if the distress for rent is levied after the date of the order, it shall be available only for six months' rent accrued due prior to the date of the order and shall not be available for rent payable in respect of any period subsequent to the date when the distress was levied, but the landlord or other person to whom the rent may be due from the debtor may prove under the order for the surplus due for which the distress may not have been available.

117 Appropriation of money paid under order and discharge of order

(1) Money paid into court under an administration order shall be appropriated –

- (a) first in satisfaction of the costs of administration (which shall not exceed 10 pence in the pound on the total amount of the debts); and
- (b) then in liquidation of debts in accordance with the order.

(2) Where the amount received is sufficient to pay –

- (a) each creditor scheduled to the order to the extent provided by the order;
- (b) the costs of the plaintiff in the action in respect of which the order was made; and
- (c) the costs of the administration,

the order shall be superseded, and the debtor shall be discharged from his debts to the scheduled creditors.

PART VII
COMMITTALS

118 Power to commit for contempt

(1) If any person –

(a) wilfully insults the judge of a county court, or any juror or witness, or any officer of the court during his sitting or attendance in court, or in going to or returning from the court; or
(b) wilfully interrupts the proceedings of a county court or otherwise misbehaves in court;

any officer of the court, with or without the assistance of any other person, may, by order of the judge, take the offender into custody and detain him until the rising of the court, and the judge may, if he thinks fit, –

(i) make an order committing the offender for a specified period not exceeding one month to prison; or
(ii) impose upon the offender, for every offence, a fine of an amount not exceeding £2,500, or may both make such an order and impose such a fine.

(2) The judge may at any time revoke an order committing a person to prison under this section and, if he is already in custody, order his discharge.

(3) A district judge, assistant district judge or deputy district judge shall have the same powers under this section in relation to proceedings before him as a judge.

Amendments—SL(R)A 1986; CLSA 1990, s 74(6); Criminal Justice Act 1991, ss 17(3), 101(1), Sch 4, Pt I, Sch 12, para 6.

Entitlements of party—Both at common law and in order to comply with the HRA 1998, any person who is brought before the judge under this section is entitled to minimum safeguards. He must be given in writing details of the charge against him at the outset of any hearing. He must also be offered the opportunity to obtain legal advice and offered legal aid, which the court has power to grant of its own initiative under LAA 1988, s 29, immediately it becomes apparent to the judge that a sentence of imprisonment may be imposed for the particular offence (*Newman v Modern Bookbinders* (2000) 2 All ER 814, CA).

119 Issue and execution of orders of committal

(1) Whenever any order or warrant for the committal of any person to prison is made or issued by a county court (whether in pursuance of this or any other Act or of rules of court), the order or warrant shall be directed to the district judge of the court, who shall thereby be empowered to take the body of the person against whom the order is made or warrant issued.

(2) It shall be the duty of every constable within his jurisdiction to assist in the execution of every such order or warrant.

(3) The governor of the prison mentioned in any such order or warrant shall be bound to receive and keep the person mentioned in it until he is lawfully discharged.

Amendments—CPA 1997, s 10, Sch 2, para 2(2).

120 Prisons to which committals may be made

Any person committed to prison by the judge of any county court, in pursuance of this or any other Act or of rules of court, shall be committed to such prison as may from time to time be directed in the case of that court by order of the Secretary of State.

Amendments—CPA 1997, s 10, Sch 2, para 2(2).

121 Power of judge to order discharge

(1) If at any time it appears to the satisfaction of a judge of a county court that any debtor arrested or confined in prison by order of the court is unable from any cause to pay any sum recovered against him (whether by way of satisfaction of a claim or counterclaim or by way of costs or otherwise), or any instalment thereof, and ought to be discharged, the judge may order his discharge upon such terms (including liability to re-arrest if the terms are not complied with) as the judge thinks fit.

122 Execution of committal orders out of jurisdiction of court

(1) Where any order or warrant for the committal of any person to prison has been made or issued (whether in pursuance of this or any other Act or of rules of court) by a county court (hereafter in this section referred to as a 'home court') and that person is out of the jurisdiction of that court, the district judge may send the order or warrant to the district judge of any other county court within the jurisdiction of which that person is or is believed to be, with a warrant endorsed on it or annexed to it requiring execution of the original order or warrant.

(2) On receipt of the warrant, the district judge of the other county court shall act in all respects as if the original order or warrant had been issued by the court of which he is district judge and shall within the prescribed time –

- (a) report to the district judge of the home court what he has done in the execution of the order or warrant; and
- (b) pay over all moneys received in pursuance of the order or warrant.

(3) Where a person is apprehended under the order or warrant, he shall be forthwith conveyed, in custody of the officer apprehending him, to the prison of the court within the jurisdiction of which he was apprehended and kept there, unless sooner discharged by law, until the expiration of the period mentioned in the order or warrant.

(4) It shall be the duty of every constable within his jurisdiction to assist in the execution of every such order or warrant.

(5) Where an order of committal –

- (a) under the Debtors Act 1869; or
- (b) under section 110,

is sent by the district judge of a home court to the district judge of another court for execution under this section, the judge of that other court shall have the same powers to order the debtor's discharge as the judge of the home court would have under section 110 or 121.

Amendments—CPA 1997, s 10, Sch 2, para 2(2).

PART VIII
RESPONSIBILITY AND PROTECTION OF OFFICERS

123 District judge to have same responsibilities as sheriff

Every district judge shall be responsible for the acts and defaults of himself and of the bailiffs appointed to assist him in like manner as the sheriff of any county in England and Wales is responsible for the acts and defaults of himself and his officers.

124 Liability of bailiff for neglect to levy execution

(1) Where a bailiff of a county court, being employed to levy any execution against goods, loses the opportunity of levying the execution by reason of neglect, connivance or omission, any party aggrieved thereby may complain to the judge of that court.

(2) On any such complaint the judge, if the neglect, connivance or omission is proved to his satisfaction, shall order the bailiff to pay such damages as it appears that the complainant has sustained by reason of it, not exceeding in any case the sum for which the execution issued.

125 Irregularity in executing warrants

(1) No officer of a county court in executing any warrant of a court, and no person at whose instance any such warrant is executed, shall be deemed a trespasser by reason of any irregularity or informality –

(a) in any proceeding on the validity of which the warrant depends; or
(b) in the form of the warrant or in the mode of executing it;

but any person aggrieved may bring an action for any special damage sustained by him by reason of the irregularity or informality against the person guilty of it.

(2) No costs shall be recovered in such an action unless the damages awarded exceed £2.

126 Actions against bailiffs acting under warrants

(1) No action shall be commenced against any bailiff for anything done in obedience to a warrant issued by the district judge, unless –

(a) a demand for inspection of the warrant and for a copy of it is made or left at the office of the bailiff by the party intending to bring the action, or his legal representative or agent; and
(b) the bailiff refuses or neglects to comply with the demand within six days after it is made.

(2) The demand must be in writing and signed by the person making it.

(3) If an action is commenced against a bailiff in a case where such a demand has been made and not complied with, judgment shall be given for the bailiff if the warrant is produced or proved at the trial, notwithstanding any defect of jurisdiction or other irregularity in the warrant; but the district judge who issued the warrant may be joined as a defendant in the action, and if the district judge

is so joined and judgment is given against him, the costs to be recovered by the plaintiff against the district judge shall include such costs as the plaintiff is liable to pay to the bailiff.

(4) In this section (except in paragraph (a) of subsection (1)) 'bailiff' includes any person acting by the order and in aid of a bailiff.

Amendments—CLSA 1990, s 125(3), Sch 18, para 49.

127 Warrants evidence of authority

In any action commenced against a person for anything done in pursuance of this Act, the production of the warrant of the county court shall be deemed sufficient proof of the authority of the court previous to the issue of the warrant.

PART IX
MISCELLANEOUS AND GENERAL

Financial provisions

128

(*repealed*)

129 Enforcement of fines

Payment of any fine imposed by any court under this Act may be enforced upon the order of the judge in like manner –

(a) as payment of a debt adjudged by the court to be paid may be enforced under this Act; or

(b) as payment of a sum adjudged to be paid by a conviction of a magistrates' court may be enforced under the Magistrates' Courts Act 1980 (disregarding section 81(1) of that Act).

130 Payment and application of fees, fines, etc

(1) Subject to subsection (2), all fees, forfeitures and fines payable under this Act and any penalty payable to an officer of a county court under any other Act shall be paid to officers designated by the Lord Chancellor and dealt with by them in such manner as the Lord Chancellor, after consultation with the Treasury, may direct.

(2) Subsection (1) does not apply to fines imposed on summary conviction or to so much of a fine as is applicable under section 55(4) to indemnify a party injured.

(3) The Lord Chancellor, with the concurrence of the Treasury, shall from time to time make such rules as he thinks fit for securing the balances and other sums of money in the hands of any officers of a county court, and for the due accounting for and application of those balances and sums.

131 Appointment of auditors and other officers

The Lord Chancellor may, subject to the consent of the Treasury as to numbers and salaries, appoint as officers in his department such auditors and other officers as he may consider necessary for the purpose of controlling the accounts of county courts.

132 Payment of salaries and expenses

There shall be paid out of money provided by Parliament –

(a) all salaries, remuneration and other sums payable under Part I of this Act or under section 131;
(b) the expenses of supplying the courts and offices with law and office books and stationery and postage stamps;
(c) expenses incurred in conveying to prison persons committed by the courts; and
(d) all other expenses arising out of any jurisdiction for the time being conferred on the courts or any officer of the courts.

Summonses and other documents

133 Proof of service of summonses etc

(1) Where any summons or other process issued from a county court is served by an officer of a court, the service may be proved by a certificate in a prescribed form showing the fact and mode of the service.

(2) Any officer of a court wilfully and corruptly giving a false certificate under subsection (1) in respect of the service of a summons or other process shall be guilty of an offence and, on conviction thereof, shall be removed from office and shall be liable –

(a) on conviction on indictment, to imprisonment for any term not exceeding 2 years; or
(b) on summary conviction, to imprisonment for any term not exceeding 6 months or to a fine not exceeding the statutory maximum or to both such imprisonment and fine.

Amendments—SI 1998/2940

****

135 Penalty for falsely pretending to act under authority of court

Any person who –

(a) delivers or causes to be delivered to any other person any paper falsely purporting to be a copy of any summons or other process of a county court, knowing it to be false; or
(b) acts or professes to act under any false colour or pretence of the process or authority of a county court;

shall be guilty of an offence and shall for each offence be liable on conviction on indictment to imprisonment for a term not exceeding 7 years.

136 Penalty for falsely representing document to have been issued from county court

(1) It shall not be lawful to deliver or cause to be delivered to any person any document which was not issued under the authority of a county court but which, by reason of its form or contents or both, has the appearance of having been issued under such authority.

(2) If any person contravenes this section, he shall for each offence be liable on summary conviction to a fine of an amount not exceeding level 3 on the standard scale.

(3) Nothing in this section shall be taken to prejudice section 135.

137 Lessee to give notice of summons for recovery of land

(1) Every lessee to whom there is delivered any summons issued from a county court for the recovery of land demised to or held by him, or to whose knowledge any such summons comes, shall forthwith give notice of the summons to his lessor or his bailiff or receiver.

(2) If a lessee fails to give notice as required by subsection (1), he shall be liable to forfeit to the person of whom he holds the land an amount equal to the value of 3 years' improved or rack rent of the land to be recovered by action in any county court or other court having jurisdiction in respect of claims for such an amount.

Forfeiture for non-payment of rent

138 Provisions as to forfeiture for non-payment of rent

(1) This section has effect where a lessor is proceeding by action in a county court (being an action in which the county court has jurisdiction) to enforce against a lessee a right of re-entry or forfeiture in respect of any land for non-payment of rent.

(2) If the lessee pays into court or to the lessor not less than 5 clear days before the return day all the rent in arrear and the costs of the action, the action shall cease, and the lessee shall hold the land according to the lease without any new lease.

(3) If –

(a) the action does not cease under subsection (2); and
(b) the court at the trial is satisfied that the lessor is entitled to enforce the right of re-entry or forfeiture,

the court shall order possession of the land to be given to the lessor at the expiration of such period, not being less than 4 weeks from the date of the order, as the court thinks fit, unless within that period the lessee pays into court or to the lessor all the rent in arrear and the costs of the action.

(4) The court may extend the period specified under subsection (3) at any time before possession of the land is recovered in pursuance of the order under that subsection.

(5) If –

(a) within the period specified in the order; or
(b) within that period as extended under subsection (4),

the lessee pays into court or to the lessor –

(i) all the rent in arrear; and

(ii) the costs of the action,

he shall hold the land according to the lease without any new lease.

(6) Subsection (2) shall not apply where the lessor is proceeding in the same action to enforce a right of re-entry or forfeiture on any other ground as well as for non-payment of rent, or to enforce any other claim as well as the right of re-entry or forfeiture and the claim for arrears of rent.

(7) If the lessee does not –

(a) within the period specified in the order; or

(b) within that period as extended under subsection (4),

pay into court or to the lessor –

(i) all the rent in arrear; and

(ii) the costs of the action,

the order shall be enforceable in the prescribed manner and so long as the order remains unreversed the lessee shall, subject to subsections (8) and (9A), be barred from all relief.

(8) The extension under subsection (4) of a period fixed by a court shall not be treated as relief from which the lessee is barred by subsection (7) if he fails to pay into court or to the lessor all the rent in arrear and the costs of the action within that period.

(9) Where the court extends a period under subsection (4) at a time when –

(a) that period has expired; and

(b) a warrant has been issued for the possession of the land, the court shall suspend the warrant for the extended period; and, if, before the expiration of the extended period, the lessee pays into court or to the lessor all the rent in arrear and all the costs of the action, the court shall cancel the warrant.

(9A) Where the lessor recovers possession of the land at any time after the making of the order under subsection (3) (whether as a result of the enforcement of the order or otherwise) the lessee may, at any time within six months from the date on which the lessor recovers possession, apply to the court for relief; and on any such application the court may, if it thinks fit, grant to the lessee such relief, subject to such terms and conditions, as it thinks fit.

(9B) Where the lessee is granted relief on an application under subsection (9A) he shall hold the land according to the lease without any new lease.

(9C) An application under subsection (9A) may be made by a person with an interest under a lease of the land derived (whether immediately or otherwise) from the lessee's interest therein in like manner as if he were the lessee; and on any such application the court may make an order which (subject to such terms and conditions as the court thinks fit) vests the land in such a person, as lessee of the lessor, for the remainder of the term of the lease under which he has any such interest as aforesaid, or for any lesser term.

In this subsection any reference to the land includes a reference to a part of the land.

(10) Nothing in this section or section 139 shall be taken to affect –

(a) the power of the court to make any order which it would otherwise have power to make as respects a right of re-entry or forfeiture on any ground other than non-payment of rent; or
(b) section 146(4) of the Law of Property Act 1925 (relief against forfeiture).

Amendments—AJA 1985, ss 55(2), (3), (4), 67(2), Sch 8, Pt III; CLSA 1990, s 125(2), Sch 17, para 17.

139 Service of summons and re-entry

(1) In a case where section 138 has effect, if –

(a) one-half-year's rent is in arrear at the time of the commencement of the action; and
(b) the lessor has a right to re-enter for non-payment of that rent; and
(c) no sufficient distress is to be found on the premises countervailing the arrears then due,

the service of the summons in the action in the prescribed manner shall stand in lieu of a demand and re-entry.

(2) Where a lessor has enforced against a lessee, by re-entry without action, a right of re-entry or forfeiture as respects any land for non-payment of rent, the lessee may at any time within six months from the date on which the lessor re-entered apply to the county court for relief, and on any such application the court may, if it thinks fit, grant to the lessee such relief as the High Court could have granted.

(3) Subsections (9B) and (9C) of section 138 shall have effect in relation to an application under subsection (2) of this section as they have effect in relation to an application under subsection (9A) of that section.

Amendments—AJA 1985, s 55; SI 1991/724.

140 Interpretation of sections 138 and 139

For the purposes of sections 138 and 139 –

'lease' includes –

(a) an original or derivative under-lease;

(b) an agreement for a lease where the lessee has become entitled to have his lease granted; and

(c) a grant at a fee farm rent, or under a grant securing a rent by condition;

'lessee' includes –

(a) an original or derivative under-lessee;

(b) the persons deriving title under a lessee;

(c) a grantee under a grant at a fee farm rent, or under a grant securing a rent by condition; and

(d) the persons deriving title under such a grantee;

'lessor' includes –

(a) an original or derivative under-lessor;

(b) the persons deriving title under a lessor;

(c) a person making a grant at a fee farm rent, or a grant securing a rent by condition; and

(d) the persons deriving title under such a grantor;

'under-lease' includes an agreement for an under-lease where the under-lessee has become entitled to have his underlease granted; and

'under-lessee' includes any person deriving title under an under-lessee.

Solicitors

141 No privilege allowed to solicitors

No privilege shall be allowed to any solicitor to exempt him from the jurisdiction of the court.

142 Power to enforce undertakings of solicitors

A county court shall have the same power to enforce an undertaking given by a solicitor in relation to any proceedings in that court as the High Court has to enforce an undertaking so given in relation to any proceedings in the High Court.

143 Prohibition on persons other than solicitors receiving remuneration for business done in county courts

(1) No person other than –

(a) a legal representative; or

(b) a person exercising a right of audience or a right to conduct litigation by virtue of an order made under section 11 of the Courts and Legal Services Act 1990 (representation in county courts),

shall be entitled to have or recover any fee or reward for acting on behalf of a party in proceedings in a county court.

(2) (*repealed*)

Amendments—CLSA 1990, ss 125(3), (7), Sch 18, para 48, Sch 20.

Replevin

144 Replevin

Schedule 1 to this Act shall have effect.

Power to raise monetary limits

145 Power to raise monetary limits

(1) If it appears to Her Majesty in Council –

(a) that the county court limit for the purposes of any enactment referring to that limit, or

(b) that the higher limit or the lower limit referred to in section 20 of this Act,

should be increased, Her Majesty may by Order in Council direct that the limit in question shall be such amount as may be specified in the Order.

(2) An Order under subsection (1) may contain such incidental or transitional provisions as Her Majesty considers appropriate.

(3) No recommendation shall be made to Her Majesty in Council to make an Order under this section unless a draft of the Order has been laid before Parliament and approved by resolution of each House of Parliament.

General

146 Lords Commissioners to represent Lord Chancellor when Great Seal in commission

When the Great Seal is in commission, the Lords Commissioners shall represent the Lord Chancellor for the purposes of this Act; but the powers vested in him by this Act in relation to the appointment of officers may be exercised by the senior Lord Commissioners for the time being.

147 Interpretation

(1) In this Act, unless the context otherwise requires –

'action' means any proceedings in a county court which may be commenced as prescribed by plaint;

'Admiralty county court' means a county court appointed to have Admiralty jurisdiction by order under this Act;

'Admiralty proceedings' means proceedings in which the claim would not be within the jurisdiction of a county court but for sections 26 and 27;

'bailiff' includes a district judge;

'the county court limit' means –

(a) in relation to any enactment contained in this Act for which a limit is for the time being specified by an Order under section 145, that limit,

(b) (*repealed*)

(c) in relation to any enactment contained in this Act and not within paragraph (a), the county court limit for the time being specified by any other Order in Council or order defining the limit of county court jurisdiction for the purposes of that enactment;

'court' and 'county court' mean a court held for a district under this Act;

'deposit-taking institution' means any person who may, in the course of his business, lawfully accept deposits in the United Kingdom;

'district' and 'county court district' mean a district for which a court is to be held under section 2;

(*repealed*)

'hearing' includes trial, and 'hear' and 'heard' shall be construed accordingly;

'hereditament' includes both a corporeal and an incorporeal hereditament;

'judge', in relation to a county court, means a judge assigned to the district of that court under subsection (1) of section 5 and any person sitting as a judge for that district under subsection (3) or (4) of that section;

'judgment summons' means a summons issued on the application of a person entitled to enforce a judgment or order under section 5 of the Debtors Act 1869 requiring a person, or where two or more persons are liable under the judgment or order, requiring any one or more of them, to attend court;

'landlord', in relation to any land, means the person entitled to the immediate reversion or, if the property therein is held in joint tenancy, any of the persons entitled to the immediate reversion;

'legal representative' means an authorised advocate or authorised litigator, as defined by section 119(1) of the Courts and Legal Services Act 1990;

(*repealed*)

'matter' means every proceeding in a county court which may be commenced as prescribed otherwise than by plaint;

'officer', in relation to a court, means any district judge, deputy district judge or assistant district judge of that court, and any clerk, bailiff, usher or messenger in the service of that court;

'part-time district judge' and 'part-time assistant district judge' have the meaning assigned to them by section 10(3);

'party' includes every person served with notice of, or attending, any proceeding, whether named as a party to that proceeding or not;

'prescribed' means prescribed by rules of court;

'probate proceedings' means proceedings brought in a county court by virtue of section 32 or transferred to that court under section 40;

'proceedings' includes both actions and matters;

'district judge' and 'district judge of a county court' mean a district judge appointed for a district under this Act, or, in a case where two or more district judges are appointed jointly, either or any of those district judges;

'return day' means the day appointed in any summons or proceeding for the appearance of the defendant or any other day fixed for the hearing of any proceedings;

'ship' includes any description of vessel used in navigation;

'solicitor' means solicitor of the Supreme Court;

(*repealed*)

(*repealed*)

(1A) The definition of 'deposit-taking institution' in subsection (1) must be read with –

(a) section 22 of the Financial Services and Markets Act 2000;
(b) any relevant order under that section; and
(c) Schedule 2 to that Act.

(2), (3) (*repealed*)

Amendments—Matrimonial and Family Proceedings Act 1984, s 46(3), Sch 3; Banking Act 1987, s 108(1), Sch 6, para 15; CLSA 1990, s 125(3), Sch 18, para 49; SI 1990/776; SI 1991/724; SL(R)A 1993; CPA 1997, s 10, Sch 2, para 2(2), (9); SI 2001/3649; SI 2002/439; Courts Act 2003, s 109(1), (3), Sch 8, para 277.

148 Amendments of other Acts, transitory provisions, transitional provisions, savings and repeals

(1) The enactments specified in Schedule 2 shall have effect subject to the amendments there specified.

(2) This Act shall have effect subject to the transitory provisions and transitional provisions and savings contained in Schedule 3.

(3) The enactments specified in Schedule 4 are hereby repealed to the extent specified in the third column of that Schedule.

149 Extent

(1) Section 148(1) and Schedule 2 extend to Scotland so far as they amend enactments extending to Scotland.

(2) Section 148(1) and Schedule 2 extend to Northern Ireland so far as they amend enactments extending to Northern Ireland.

(3) Subject to subsections (1) and (2), this Act extends to England and Wales only.

150 Commencement

This Act shall come into force on 1 August 1984.

151 Short title

This Act may be cited as the County Courts Act 1984.

SCHEDULE 1

REPLEVIN

1 (1) The sheriff shall have no power or responsibility with respect to replevin bonds or replevins.

(2) The district judge for the district in which any goods subject to replevin are taken shall have power, subject to the provisions of this Schedule, to approve of replevin bonds and to grant replevins and to issue all necessary process in relation to them, and any such process shall be executed by a bailiff of the court.

(3) The district judge shall, at the instance of the party whose goods have been seized, cause the goods to be replevied to that party on his giving such security as is provided in this Schedule.

2 (1) It shall be a condition of any security given under paragraph 1 that the replevisor will –

- (a) commence an action of replevin against the seizor in the High Court within one week from the date when the security is given; or
- (b) commence such an action in a county court within one month from that date.

(2) In either case –

- (a) the replevisor shall give security, to be approved by the district judge having power in the matter, for such an amount as the district judge thinks sufficient to cover both the probable costs of the action and either –
  - (i) the alleged rent or damage in respect of which the distress has been made; or
  - (ii) in a case where the goods replevied have been seized otherwise than under colour of distress, the value of the goods; and
- (b) it shall be a further condition of the security that the replevisor will –
  - (i) prosecute the action with effect and without delay; and

(ii) make a return of the goods, if a return of them is ordered in the action.

(3) (*repealed*)

Amendments—CLSA 1990, s 125(2), (7), Sch 17, para 18, Sch 20.

****

SCHEDULE 3

TRANSITORY AND TRANSITIONAL PROVISIONS AND SAVINGS

****

4 Administration Orders

(1) Any reference in Part VI of this Act to an administration order includes a reference to an administration order made under an enactment repealed by this Act.

(2) (*repealed*)

5 County court

References in any enactment or document to a county court constituted under the County Courts Act 1888 or the County Courts Act 1934 or the County Courts Act 1959 shall be construed as references to a county court constituted under this Act and anything done or proceedings taken in respect of any action or matter whatsoever before the commencement of this Act in a county court under any of the enactments mentioned above shall be deemed to have been done or taken in a county court constituted under this Act.

6 Former enactments

Any document referring to any former enactment relating to county courts shall be construed as referring to the corresponding enactment in this Act. In this paragraph 'former enactment relating to county courts' means any enactment repealed by the County Courts Act 1959, by the County Courts Act 1934 or by the County Courts Act 1888.

7 High bailiffs

References to a high bailiff in any enactment, Order in Council, order, rule, regulation or any document whatsoever shall be construed as a reference to a district judge.

8 Periods of time

Where a period of time specified in an enactment repealed by this Act is current at the coming into force of this Act, this Act shall have effect as if the corresponding provision of it had been in force when that period began to run.

9 Offences

Nothing in this Act renders a person liable to punishment by way of fine or imprisonment for an offence committed before the coming into force of this Act which differs from the punishment to which he would have been liable if this Act had not been passed.

10

(*repealed*)

11 General

Without prejudice to any express amendment made by this Act, a reference in an enactment or other document, whether express or implied, to an enactment repealed by this Act shall, unless the context otherwise requires, be construed as, or as including, a reference to this Act or to the corresponding provisions of this Act.

12 Nothing in this Schedule shall be taken as prejudicing the operation of the provisions of the Interpretation Act 1978 as respects the effect of repeals.

Amendments—SL(R)A 1989.

****

Courts and Legal Services Act 1990

PART I
PROCEDURE ETC IN CIVIL COURTS

Allocation and transfer of business

1 Allocation of business between High Court and county courts

(1) The Lord Chancellor may by order make provision –

- (a) conferring jurisdiction on the High Court in relation to proceedings in which county courts have jurisdiction;
- (b) conferring jurisdiction on county courts in relation to proceedings in which the High Court has jurisdiction;
- (c) allocating proceedings to the High Court or to county courts;
- (d) specifying proceedings which may be commenced only in the High Court;
- (e) specifying proceedings which may be commenced only in a county court;
- (f) specifying proceedings which may be taken only in the High Court;
- (g) specifying proceedings which may be taken only in a county court.

(2) Without prejudice to the generality of section 120(2), any such order may differentiate between categories of proceedings by reference to such criteria as the Lord Chancellor sees fit to specify in the order.

(3) The criteria so specified may, in particular, relate to –

(a) the value of an action (as defined by the order);
(b) the nature of the proceedings;
(c) the parties to the proceedings;
(d) the degree of complexity likely to be involved in any aspect of the proceedings; and
(e) the importance of any question likely to be raised by, or in the course of, the proceedings.

(4) An order under subsection (1)(b), (e) or (g) may specify one or more particular county courts in relation to the proceedings so specified.

(5) Any jurisdiction exercisable by a county court, under any provision made by virtue of subsection (4), shall be exercisable throughout England and Wales.

(6) Rules of court may provide for a matter –

(a) which is pending in one county court; and
(b) over which that court has jurisdiction under any provision made by virtue of subsection (4),

to be heard and determined wholly or partly in another county court which also has jurisdiction in that matter under any such provision.

(7) Any such order may –

(a) amend or repeal any provision falling within subsection (8) and relating to –
  (i) the jurisdiction, practice or procedure of the Supreme Court; or
  (ii) the jurisdiction, practice or procedure of any county court,

so far as the Lord Chancellor considers it to be necessary, or expedient, in consequence of any provision made by the order; or

(b) make such incidental or transitional provision as the Lord Chancellor considers necessary, or expedient, in consequence of any provision made by the order.

(8) A provision falls within this subsection if it is made by any enactment other than this Act or made under any enactment.

(9) Before making any such order the Lord Chancellor shall consult the Lord Chief Justice, the Master of the Rolls, the President of the Family Division, the Vice-Chancellor and the Senior Presiding Judge (appointed under section 72).

(10) No such order shall be made so as to confer jurisdiction on any county court to hear any application for judicial review.

(11) For the purposes of this section the commencement of proceedings may include the making of any application in anticipation of any proceedings or in the course of any proceedings.

(12) (*repealed*)

Amendments—Courts Act 2003, s 109(1), (3), Sch 8, para 348, Sch 10.

****

5 Witness statements

(1) Rules of court may make provision –

(a) requiring, in specified circumstances, any party to civil proceedings to serve on the other parties a written statement of the oral evidence which he intends to adduce on any issue of fact to be decided at the trial;

(b) enabling the court to direct any party to civil proceedings to serve such a statement on the other party; and

(c) prohibiting a party who fails to comply with such a requirement or direction from adducing oral evidence on the issue of fact to which it relates.

(2) Where a party to proceedings has refused to comply with such a requirement or direction, the fact that his refusal was on the ground that the required statement would have been a document which was privileged from disclosure shall not affect any prohibition imposed by virtue of subsection (1)(c).

(3) This section is not to be read as prejudicing in any way any other power to make rules of court.

****

8 Powers of Court of Appeal to award damages

(1) In this section 'case' means any case where the Court of Appeal has power to order a new trial on the ground that damages awarded by a jury are excessive or inadequate.

(2) Rules of court may provide for the Court of Appeal, in such classes of case as may be specified in the rules, to have power, in place of ordering a new trial, to substitute for the sum awarded by the jury such sum as appears to the court to be proper.

(3) This section is not to be read as prejudicing in any way any other power to make rules of court.

****

Rights of audience and rights to conduct litigation

27 Rights of audience

(1) The question whether a person has a right of audience before a court, or in relation to any proceedings, shall be determined solely in accordance with the provisions of this Part.

(2) A person shall have a right of audience before a court in relation to any proceedings only in the following cases –

(a) where –

(i) he has a right of audience before that court in relation to those proceedings granted by the appropriate authorised body; and

(ii) that body's qualification regulations and rules of conduct have been approved for the purposes of this section, in relation to that right;

(b) where paragraph (a) does not apply but he has a right of audience before that court in relation to those proceedings granted by or under any enactment;

(c) where paragraph (a) does not apply but he has a right of audience granted by that court in relation to those proceedings;
(d) where he is a party to those proceedings and would have had a right of audience, in his capacity as such a party, if this Act had not been passed; or
(e) where –
  (i) he is employed (whether wholly or in part), or is otherwise engaged, to assist in the conduct of litigation and is doing so under instructions given (either generally or in relation to the proceedings) by a qualified litigator; and
  (ii) the proceedings are being heard in chambers in the High Court or a county court and are not reserved family proceedings.

(2A) Every person who exercises before any court a right of audience granted by an authorised body has –

(a) a duty to the court to act with independence in the interests of justice; and
(b) a duty to comply with rules of conduct of the body relating to the right and approved for the purposes of this section;

and those duties shall override any obligation which the person may have (otherwise than under the criminal law) if it is inconsistent with them.

(3) (*repealed*)

(4) Nothing in this section affects the power of any court in any proceedings to refuse to hear a person (for reasons which apply to him as an individual) who would otherwise have a right of audience before the court in relation to those proceedings.

(5) Where a court refuses to hear a person as mentioned in subsection (4) it shall give its reasons for refusing.

(6) (*repealed*)

(7) Where, immediately before the commencement of this section, no restriction was placed on the persons entitled to exercise any right of audience in relation to any particular court or in relation to particular proceedings, nothing in this section shall be taken to place any such restriction on any person.

(8) Where –

(a) immediately before the commencement of this section; or
(b) by virtue of any provision made by or under an enactment passed subsequently,

a court does not permit the appearance of advocates, or permits the appearance of advocates only with leave, no person shall have a right of audience before that court, in relation to any proceedings, solely by virtue of the provisions of this section.

(8A) But a court may not limit the right to appear before the court in any proceedings to only some of those who have a right by virtue of the provisions of this section.

(9) In this section –

'advocate', in relation to any proceedings, means any person exercising a right of audience as a representative of, or on behalf of, any party to the proceedings;

'authorised body' means –

(a) the General Council of the Bar;

(b) the Law Society; and

(c) any professional or other body which has been designated by Order in Council as an authorised body for the purposes of this section;

'appropriate authorised body', in relation to any person claiming to be entitled to any right of audience by virtue of subsection (2)(a), means the authorised body –

(a) granting that right; and

(b) of which that person is a member;

'family proceedings' has the same meaning as in the Matrimonial and Family Proceedings Act 1984 and also includes any other proceedings which are family proceedings for the purposes of the Children Act 1989;

'qualification regulations', in relation to an authorised body, means regulations (however they may be described) as to the education and training which members of that body must receive in order to be entitled to, or to exercise, any right of audience granted by it;

'qualified litigator' means –

(i) any practising solicitor (that is, one who has a practising certificate in force or is employed wholly or mainly for the purpose of providing legal services to his employer);

(ii) any recognised body; and

(iii) any person who is exempt from the requirement to hold a practising certificate by virtue of section 88 of the Solicitors Act 1974 (saving for solicitors to public departments and the City of London);

'recognised body' means any body recognised under section 9 of the Administration of Justice Act 1985 (incorporated practices);

'reserved family proceedings' means such category of family proceedings as the Secretary of State may, after consulting the President of the Law Society and with the concurrence of the President of the Family Division, by order prescribe; and

'rules of conduct', in relation to an authorised body, means rules (however they may be described) as to the conduct required of members of that body in exercising any right of audience granted by it.

(10) Section 20 of the Solicitors Act 1974 (unqualified person not to act as a solicitor), section 22 of that Act (unqualified person not to prepare certain documents etc) and section 25 of that Act (costs where an unqualified person acts as a solicitor), shall not apply in relation to any act done in the exercise of a right of audience.

Amendments—Access to Justice Act 1999, ss 42(1), 43, 106, Sch 6, paras 4, 6, Sch 15, Pt II; SI 2003/1887.

Scope of provision—Section 27 purports to be an exclusive code for the determination of rights of audience, but it is clear that it is concerned with ad hoc *permissions* as well as *rights*. And see CPR r 39.6 and PD39 which make provision for hearing authorised employees of companies. *Avinue Ltd v Sunrule Ltd* [2003] EWCA Civ 1942, [2004] 1 WLR 634, CA established that in small claims hearings companies are entitled to appear by lay representatives whether or not duly authorised officers or employees.

Section 27(2)(a) refers to rights properly so called, conferred by membership of appropriate professional bodies. The Bar Council and the Law Society are specifically mentioned. Solicitors need certification for open court trial advocacy in the High Court. The Institute of Legal Executives and the Chartered Institute of Patent Agents are authorised bodies whose members have limited rights of audience. Where they have been approved by the Institute, Fellows of the Institute of Legal Executives are able to conduct open court trials before district judges. As at November 2004, 22 Legal Executives had certificates of approval.

McKenzie friends (*McKenzie v McKenzie* [1971] P 33, CA) do not have a right of audience, by definition. Their role, reiterated in *Noueiri v Paragon Finance plc* [2001] EWCA Civ 1402, [2001] 1 WLR 2357, CA reflects the right of a litigant to have reasonable assistance unless the judge is satisfied that fairness and the interests of justice do not so require. Where the *McKenzie* friend impedes the efficient administration of justice the judge may prevent him from continuing to act.

Noueiri gives guidance about the increasingly common phenomenon of unqualified persons who put themselves forward regularly to conduct litigation on behalf of others. The CA emphasised the statement of Lord Woolf MR in *D v S (Rights of Audience)* (1997) 1 FLR 724 that the discretion to grant rights of audience to individuals who did not meet the stringent requirements of the 1990 Act ought only to be exercised in exceptional circumstances and that the courts should pause before granting rights to individuals who made a practice of seeking to represent otherwise unrepresented litigants.

In *Clarkson v Gilbert* [2000] Fam Law 808, CA Lord Woolf CJ determined the question of whether a husband should be allowed to represent his wife in accordance with the overriding objective, having regard to the wife's ill health and lack of means. There is nothing in any decision of the Court of Appeal on this subject which suggests that anything other than close scrutiny and careful consideration should be given to the grant of ad hoc rights of audience to those who are not otherwise qualified. On the other hand there is no presumption against such grant.

It is common practice in the county courts to allow housing officers to conduct cases on behalf of local authorities and social landlords. Inspectors of taxes have statutory rights of audience. The practice in hearings in the small claims track is informal – under CPR r 27.8(1) '[t]he court may adopt any method of proceeding at a hearing that it considers to be fair'. Family members and friends are frequently allowed to speak for litigants in person in such hearings.

A litigant in person is not entitled to costs for the work done in assisting him by an acquaintance who is not legally qualified (*United Building and Plumbing Contractors v Kajla* [2002] EWCA Civ 628, (2002) Lawtel, 29 April, CA). *Gregory v Turner* [2003] EWCA Civ 183 decided that the right to appear in person could not be delegated by power of attorney, stopping a gap through which many have attempted to pass.

****

63 Legal Professional Privilege

(1) This section applies to any communication made to or by a person who is not a barrister or solicitor at any time when that person is –

(a) providing advocacy or litigation services as an authorised advocate or authorised litigator;

(b) providing conveyancing services as an authorised practitioner; or

(c) providing probate services as a probate practitioner.

(2) Any such communication shall in any legal proceedings be privileged from disclosure in like manner as if the person in question had at all material times been acting as his client's solicitor.

****

113 Administration of Oaths and taking of Affidavits

(1) In this section –

'authorised person' means –

(a) any authorised advocate or authorised litigator, other than one who is a solicitor (in relation to whom provision similar to that made by this section is made by section 81 of the Solicitors Act 1974); or

(b) any person who is a member of a professional or other body prescribed by the Secretary of State for the purposes of this section; and

'general notary' means any public notary other than –

(a) an ecclesiastical notary.

(2) Section 1(1) of the Commissioners for Oaths Act 1889 (appointment of commissioners by Lord Chancellor) shall cease to have effect.

(3) Subject to the provisions of this section, every authorised person shall have the powers conferred on a commissioner for oaths by the Commissioners for Oaths Act 1889 and 1891 and section 24 of the Stamp Duties Management Act 1891; and any reference to such commissioner in an enactment or instrument (including an enactment passed or instrument made after the commencement of this Act) shall include a reference to a authorised person unless the context otherwise requires.

(4) Subject to the provisions of this section, every general notary shall have the powers conferrred on a commissioner for oaths by the Commissioners for Oaths Acts 1889 and 1891; and any reference to such a commissioner in an enactment or instrument (including an enactment passed or instrument made after the commencement of this Act) shall include a reference to a general notary unless the context otherwise requires.

(5) No person shall exercise the powers conferred on them by this section in any proceedings in which he is interested.

(6) A person exercising such powers and before whom any oath or affidavit is taken or made shall state in the jurat or attestation at which place and on what date the oath or affidavit is taken or made.

(7) A document containing such a statement and purporting to be sealed or signed by an authorised person or general notary shall be admitted in evidence without proof of the seal or signature, and without proof that he is an authorised person or general notary.

(8) The Secretary of State may, with the concurrence of the Lord Chief Justice and the Master of the Rolls, by order prescribe the fees to be charged by authorised persons exercising the powers of commmissioners for oaths by virtue of this section in respect of the administration of an oath or the taking of an affidavit.

(9) In this section 'affidavit' has the same meaning as in the Commissioners for Oaths Act 1889.

(10) Every –

(a) solicitor who holds a practising certificate which is in force;
(b) authorised person;
(c) general notary

shall have the right to use the title 'Commissioner for Oaths.'

Amendments—Access to Justice Act 1999, s 106, Sch 15, Pt II; SI 2003/1887.

****

119 Interpretation

(1) In this Act –

'administration', in relation to letters of administration, has the same meaning as in section 128 of the Supreme Court Act 1981;

'advocacy services' means any services which it would be reasonable to expect a person who is exercising, or contemplating exercising, a right of audience in relation to any proceedings, or contemplated proceedings, to provide;

'authorised advocate' means any person (including a barrister or solicitor) who has a right of audience granted by an authorised body in accordance with the provisions of this Act;

'authorised body' and 'appropriate authorised body' –

(a) in relation to any right of audience or proposed right of audience, have the meanings given in section 27; and

(b) in relation to any right to conduct litigation or proposed right to conduct litigation, have the meanings given in section 28;

'authorised litigator' means any person (including a solicitor) who has a right to conduct litigation granted by an authorised body in accordance with the provisions of this Act;

'authorised practitioner' has the same meaning as in section 37;

'Consultative Panel' means the Legal Services Consultative Panel;

'conveyancing services' means the preparation of transfers, conveyances, contracts and other documents in connection with, and other services ancillary to, the disposition or acquisition of estates or interests in land;

'court' includes –

(a) any tribunal which the Council on Tribunals is under a duty to keep under review;

(b) any court-martial; and

(c) a statutory inquiry within the meaning of section 16(1) of the Tribunals and Inquiries Act 1992;

'designated judge' means the Lord Chief Justice, the Master of the Rolls, the President of the Family Division or the Vice-Chancellor;

(*repealed*)

'duly certificated notary public' has the same meaning as it has in the Solicitors Act 1974 by virtue of section 87(1) of that Act;

'the general principle' has the meaning given in section 17(4);

'licensed conveyancer' has the same meaning as it has in the Administration of Justice Act 1985 by virtue of section 11 of that Act;

'litigation services' means any services which it would be reasonable to expect a person who is exercising, or contemplating exercising, a right to conduct litigation in relation to any proceedings, or contemplated proceedings, to provide;

'member', in relation to any professional or other body (other than any body established by this Act), includes any person who is not a member of that body but who may be subject to disciplinary sanctions for failure to comply with any of that body's rules;

'multi-national partnership' has the meaning given by section 89(9);
'officer', in relation to a limited liability partnership, means a member of the limited liability partnership;
'OFT' means the Office of Fair Trading;
'probate services' means the drawing or preparation of any papers on which to found or oppose a grant of probate or a grant of letters of administration and the administration of the estate of a deceased person;
'prescribed' means prescribed by regulations under this Act;
'proceedings' means proceedings in any court;
'qualification regulations' and 'rules of conduct' –

(a) in relation to any right of audience or proposed right of audience, have the meanings given in section 27; and

(b) in relation to any right to conduct litigation or proposed right to conduct litigation, have the meanings given in section 28;

'qualified person' has the meaning given in section 36(6);
'registered foreign lawyer' has the meaning given by section 89(9);
'right of audience' means the right to appear before and address a court including the right to call and examine witnesses;

'right to conduct litigation' means the right –

(a) to issue proceedings before any court; and

(b) to perform any ancillary functions in relation to proceedings (such as entering appearances to actions);

'solicitor' means solicitor of the Supreme Court; and
'the statutory objective' has the meaning given in section 17(2).

(2) For the purposes of the definition of 'conveyancing services' in subsection (1) –

'disposition' –

(i) does not include a testamentary disposition or any disposition in the case of such a lease as is referred to in section 54(2) of the Law of Property Act 1925 (short leases); but

(ii) subject to that, includes in the case of leases both their grant and their assignment; and

'acquisition' has a corresponding meaning.

(3) In this Act any reference (including those in sections 27(9) and 28(5)) to rules of conduct includes a reference to rules of practice.

Amendments—Tribunals and Inquiries Act 1992, s 18(1), Sch 3, para 35; Access to Justice Act 1999, ss 36, 43, Sch 6, para 10(2); SI 2001/1090; Enterprise Act 2002, s 278, Sch 25, para 23(1), (9)(a), (b), Sch 26.

****

Supreme Court Act 1981

ARRANGEMENT OF SECTIONS

PART I
CONSTITUTION OF SUPREME COURT

The Supreme Court

1 The Supreme Court

(1) The Supreme Court of England and Wales shall consist of the Court of Appeal, the High Court of Justice and the Crown Court, each having such jurisdiction as is conferred on it by or under this or any other Act.

(2) The Lord Chancellor shall be president of the Supreme Court.

The Court of Appeal

2 The Court of Appeal

(1) The Court of Appeal shall consist of ex-officio judges and not more than thirty-seven ordinary judges.

(2) The following shall be ex-officio judges of the Court of Appeal –

- (a) the Lord Chancellor;
- (b) any person who has been Lord Chancellor;
- (c) any Lord of Appeal in Ordinary who at the date of his appointment was, or was qualified for appointment as, an ordinary judge of the Court of Appeal or held an office within paragraphs (d) to (g);
- (d) the Lord Chief Justice;
- (e) the Master of the Rolls;
- (f) the President of the Queen's Bench Division;
- (g) the President of the Family Division;
- (h) the Chancellor of the High Court;

but a person within paragraph (b) or (c) shall not be required to sit and act as a judge of the Court of Appeal unless at the Lord Chancellor's request he consents to do so.

(3) An ordinary judge of the Court of Appeal (including the vice-president, if any, of either division) shall be styled 'Lord Justice of Appeal' or 'Lady Justice of Appeal'.

(4) Her Majesty may by Order in Council from time to time amend subsection (1) so as to increase or further increase the maximum number of ordinary judges of the Court of Appeal.

(5) No recommendation shall be made to Her Majesty in Council to make an Order under subsection (4) unless a draft of the Order has been laid before Parliament and approved by resolution of each House of Parliament.

(6) The Court of Appeal shall be taken to be duly constituted notwithstanding any vacancy in the office of Lord Chancellor, Lord Chief Justice, Master of the Rolls, President of the Queen's Bench Division, President of the Family Division or Chancellor of the High Court.

Amendments—SI 1996/1142; SI 2002/2837; Courts Act 2003, s 63(1); Constitutional Reform Act 2005, s 15(1), Sch 4, Pt 1, paras 114, 115(1), (2)(c), (5)(b).

3 Divisions of Court of Appeal

(1) There shall be two divisions of the Court of Appeal, namely the criminal division and the civil division.

(2) The Lord Chief Justice shall be president of the criminal division of the Court of Appeal, and the Master of the Rolls shall be president of the civil division of that court.

(3) The Lord Chancellor may appoint one of the ordinary judges of the Court of Appeal as vice-president of both divisions of that court, or one of those judges as vice-president of the criminal division and another of them as vice-president of the civil division.

(4) When sitting in a court of either division of the Court of Appeal in which no ex-officio judge of the Court of Appeal is sitting, the vice-president (if any) of that division shall preside.

(5) Any number of courts of either division of the Court of Appeal may sit at the same time.

The High Court

4 The High Court

(1) The High Court shall consist of –

(a) the Lord Chancellor;
(b) the Lord Chief Justice;
(ba) the President of the Queen's Bench Division;
(c) the President of the Family Division;
(d) the Chancellor of the High Court;
(dd) the Senior Presiding Judge;
(ddd) the vice-president of the Queen's Bench Division; and
(e) not more than 108 puisne judges of that court.

(2) The puisne judges of the High Court shall be styled 'Justices of the High Court'.

(3) All the judges of the High Court shall, except where this Act expressly provides otherwise, have in all respects equal power, authority and jurisdiction.

(4) Her Majesty may by Order in Council from time to time amend subsection (1) so as to increase or further increase the maximum number of puisne judges of the High Court.

(5) No recommendation shall be made to Her Majesty in Council to make an Order under subsection (4) unless a draft of the Order has been laid before Parliament and approved by resolution of each House of Parliament.

(6) The High Court shall be taken to be duly constituted notwithstanding any vacancy in the office of Lord Chancellor, Lord Chief Justice, President of the Queen's Bench Division, President of the Family Division, Chancellor of the High Court or Senior Presiding Judge and whether or not an appointment has been made to the office of vice-president of the Queen's Bench Division.

Amendments—Courts and Legal Services Act 1990, s 72(6); Access to Justice Act 1999, s 69(2); SI 1999/3138; SI 2003/775; Constitutional Reform Act 2005, s 15(1), Sch 4, Pt 1, paras 114, 117(1), (2)(b), (4)(b).

5 Divisions of High Court

(1) There shall be three divisions of the High Court namely –

(a) the Chancery Division, consisting of the Lord Chancellor, who shall be president thereof, the Vice-Chancellor, who shall be vice-president thereof, and such of the puisne judges as are for the time being attached thereto in accordance with this section;
(b) the Queen's Bench Division, consisting of the Lord Chief Justice, the President of the Queen's Bench Division, the vice-president of the Queen's Bench Division and such of the puisne judges as are for the time being so attached thereto; and

(c) the Family Division, consisting of the President of the Family Division and such of the puisne judges as are for the time being so attached thereto.

(2) The puisne judges of the High Court shall be attached to the various Divisions by direction of the Lord Chancellor; and any such judge may with his consent be transferred from one Division to another by direction of the Lord Chancellor, but shall be so transferred only with the concurrence of the senior judge of the Division from which it is proposed to transfer him.

(3) Any judge attached to any Division may act as an additional judge of any other Division at the request of the Lord Chief Justice made with the concurrence of the President of the Family Division or the Vice-Chancellor, or both, as appropriate.

(4) Nothing in this section shall be taken to prevent a judge of any Division (whether nominated under section 6(2) or not) from sitting, whenever required, in a divisional court of another Division or for any judge of another Division.

(5) Without prejudice to the provisions of this Act relating to the distribution of business in the High Court, all jurisdiction vested in the High Court under this Act shall belong to all the Divisions alike.

Amendments—CLSA 1990, s 125(2), Sch 17, para 12; Access to Justice Act 1999, s 69(3); Constitutional Reform Act 2005, s 15(1), Sch 4, Pt 1, paras 114, 118(1), (3).

6 The Patents, Admiralty and Commercial Courts

(1) There shall be –

(a) as part of the Chancery Division, a Patents Court; and
(b) as parts of the Queen's Bench Division, an Admiralty Court and a Commercial Court.

(2) The judges of the Patents Court, of the Admiralty Court and of the Commercial Court shall be such of the puisne judges of the High Court as the Lord Chancellor may from time to time nominate to be judges of the Patents Court, Admiralty Judges and Commercial Judges respectively.

7 Power to alter Divisions or transfer certain courts to different Divisions

(1) Her Majesty may from time to time, on a recommendation of the judges mentioned in subsection (2), by Order in Council direct that –

(a) any increase or reduction in the number of Divisions of the High Court; or
(b) the transfer of any of the courts mentioned in section 6(1) to a different Division,

be carried into effect in pursuance of the recommendation.

(2) Those judges are the Lord Chancellor, the Lord Chief Justice, the Master of the Rolls, the President of the Queen's Bench Division, the President of the Family Division and the Chancellor of the High Court.

(3) An Order in Council under this section may include such incidental, supplementary or consequential provisions as appear to Her Majesty necessary or expedient, including amendments of provisions referring to particular Divisions contained in this Act or any other statutory provision.

(4) Any Order in Council under this section shall be subject to annulment in pursuance of a resolution of either House of Parliament.

Amendments—Constitutional Reform Act 2005, s 15(1), Sch 4, Pt 1, paras 114, 120(1), (3)(b).

****

Other provisions

9 Assistance for transaction of judicial business of Supreme Court

(1) A person within any entry in column 1 of the following Table may, subject to the proviso at the end of that Table, at any time, at the request of the appropriate authority, act –

(a) as a judge of a relevant court specified in the request; or
(b) if the request relates to a particular division of a relevant court so specified, as a judge of that court in that division.

TABLE

1 Judge or ex-judge	**2 Where competent to act on request**
1 A judge of the Court of Appeal.	The High Court and the Crown Court.
2 A person who has been a judge of the Court of Appeal.	The Court of Appeal, the High Court and the Crown Court.
3 A puisne judge of the High Court.	The Court of Appeal.
4 A person who has been a puisne judge of the High Court.	The Court of Appeal, the High Court and the Crown Court.
5 A Circuit judge.	The High Court and the Court of Appeal.
6 A Recorder	The High Court.

The entry in column 2 specifying the Court of Appeal in relation to a Circuit judge only authorises such a judge to act as a judge of a court in the criminal division of the Court of Appeal.

(1A) A person shall not act as a judge by virtue of subsection (1) after the day on which he attains the age of 75.

(2) In subsection (1) –

'the appropriate authority' –

(a) in the case of a request to a judge of the High Court or a Circuit judge to act in the criminal division of the Court of Appeal as a judge of that court, means the Lord Chief Justice or, at any time when the Lord Chief Justice is unable to make such a request himself or there is a vacancy in the office of Lord Chief Justice, the Master of the Rolls;

(b) in any other case means the Lord Chancellor;

'relevant court', in the case of a person within any entry in column 1 of the Table, means a court specified in relation to that entry in column 2 of the Table,

but no request shall be made to a Circuit judge to act as a judge of a court in the criminal division of the Court of Appeal unless he is approved for the time being by the Lord Chancellor for the purpose of acting as a judge of that division.

(3) In the case of –

(a) a request under subsection (1) to a Lord Justice of Appeal to act in the High Court; or
(b) any request under that subsection to a puisne judge of the High Court or a Circuit judge,

it shall be the duty of the person to whom the request is made to comply with it.

(4) Without prejudice to section 24 of the Courts Act 1971 (temporary appointment of deputy Circuit judges and assistant Recorders), if it appears to the Lord Chancellor that it is expedient as a temporary measure to make an appointment under this subsection in order to facilitate the disposal of business in the High Court or the Crown Court, he may appoint a person qualified for appointment as a puisne judge of the High Court to be a deputy judge of the High Court during such period or on such occasions as the Lord Chancellor thinks fit; and during the period or on the occasions for which a person is appointed as a deputy judge under this subsection, he may act as a puisne judge of the High Court.

(4A) No appointment of a person as a deputy judge of the High Court shall be such as to extend beyond the day on which he attains the age of 70, but this subsection is subject to section 26(4) to (6) of the Judicial Pensions and Retirement Act 1993 (Lord Chancellor's power to authorise continuance in office up to the age of 75).

(5) Every person while acting under this section shall, subject to subsections (6) and (6A), be treated for all purposes as, and accordingly may perform any of the functions of, a judge of the court in which he is acting.

(6) A person shall not by virtue of subsection (5) –

(a) be treated as a judge of the court in which he is acting for the purposes of section 98(2) or of any statutory provision relating to –
   (i) the appointment, retirement, removal or disqualification of judges of that court;
   (ii) the tenure of office and oaths to be taken by such judges; or
   (iii) the remuneration, allowances or pensions of such judges; or
(b) subject to section 27 of the Judicial Pensions and Retirement Act 1993 be treated as having been a judge of a court in which he has acted only under this section.

(6A) A Circuit judge or Recorder shall not by virtue of subsection (5) exercise any of the powers conferred on a single judge by sections 31, 31B, 31C and 44 of the Criminal Appeal Act 1968 (powers of single judge in connection with appeals to the Court of Appeal and appeals from the Court of Appeal to the House of Lords).

(7) (*repealed*)

(8) Such remuneration and allowances as the Lord Chancellor may, with the concurrence of the Minister for the Civil Service, determine may be paid out of money provided by Parliament –

- (a) to any person who has been –
  - (i) a Lord of Appeal in Ordinary; or
  - (ii) a judge of the Court of Appeal; or
  - (iii) a judge of the High Court,

and is by virtue of subsection (1) acting as mentioned in that subsection;

- (b) to any deputy judge of the High Court appointed under subsection (4).

Amendments—Administration of Justice Act 1982, s 58; Judicial Pensions and Retirement Act 1993, ss 26(10), 31(4), Sch 6, para 5(1)–(3), Sch 9; Criminal Justice and Public Order Act 1994, s 52(1)–(5); Courts Act 2003, s 109(1), Sch 8, para 260.

10 Appointment of judges of Supreme Court

(1) Whenever the office of Lord Chief Justice, Master of the Rolls, President of the Queen's Bench Division, President of the Family Division or Chancellor of the High Court is vacant, Her Majesty may by letters patent appoint a qualified person to that office.

(2) Subject to the limits on numbers for the time being imposed by sections 2(1) and 4(1), Her Majesty may from time to time by letters patent appoint qualified persons as Lords Justices of Appeal or as puisne judges of the High Court.

(3) No person shall be qualified for appointment –

- (a) as Lord Chief Justice, Master of the Rolls, President of the Queen's Bench Division, President of the Family Division or Chancellor of the High Court, unless he is qualified for appointment as a Lord Justice of Appeal or is a judge of the Court of Appeal;
- (b) as a Lord Justice of Appeal unless –
  - (i) he has a 10 year High Court qualification within the meaning of section 71 of the Courts and Legal Services Act 1990; or
  - (ii) he is a judge of the High Court;

or

- (c) as a puisne judge of the High Court unless –
  - (i) he has a 10 year High Court qualification, within the meaning of section 71 of the Courts and Legal Services Act 1990; or
  - (ii) he is a Circuit judge who has held that office for at least two years.

(4) Every person appointed to an office mentioned in subsection (1) or as a Lord Justice of Appeal or puisne judge of the High Court shall, as soon as may be after his acceptance of office, take the oath of allegiance and the judicial oath, as set out in the Promissory Oaths Act 1868, in the presence of the Lord Chancellor.

Amendments—Courts and Legal Services Act 1990, s 71(1); Constitutional Reform Act 2005, s 15(1), Sch 4, Pt 1, paras 114, 122(1), (2)(a), (4).

11 Tenure of office of judges of Supreme Court

(1) This section applies to the office of any judge of the Supreme Court except the Lord Chancellor.

(2) A person appointed to an office to which this section applies shall vacate it on the day on which he attains the age of seventy years unless by virtue of this section he has ceased to hold it before then.

(3) A person appointed to an office to which this section applies shall hold that office during good behaviour, subject to a power of removal by Her Majesty on an address presented to Her by both Houses of Parliament.

(4) A person holding an office within section 2(2)(d) to (g) shall vacate that office on becoming Lord Chancellor or a Lord of Appeal in Ordinary.

(5) A Lord Justice of Appeal shall vacate that office on becoming an ex-officio judge of the Court of Appeal.

(6) A puisne judge of the High Court shall vacate that office on becoming a judge of the Court of Appeal.

(7) A person who holds an office to which this section applies may at any time resign it by giving the Lord Chancellor notice in writing to that effect.

(8) The Lord Chancellor, if satisfied by means of a medical certificate that a person holding an office to which this section applies –

- (a) is disabled by permanent infirmity from the performance of the duties of his office; and
- (b) is for the time being incapacitated from resigning his office,

may, subject to subsection (9), by instrument under his hand declare that person's office to have been vacated; and the instrument shall have the like effect for all purposes as if that person had on the date of the instrument resigned his office.

(9) A declaration under subsection (8) with respect to a person shall be of no effect unless it is made –

- (a) in the case of any of the Lord Chief Justice, the Master of the Rolls, the President of the Queen's Bench Division, the President of the Family Division and the Chancellor of the High Court, with the concurrence of two others of them;
- (b) in the case of a Lord Justice of Appeal, with the concurrence of the Master of the Rolls;
- (c) in the case of a puisne judge of any Division of the High Court, with the concurrence of the senior judge of that Division.

(10) (*repealed*)

Amendments—Statute Law (Repeals) Act 1989, Sch 1; JPRA 1993, s 26(10), Sch 6, para 4; Constitutional Reform Act 2005, s 15(1), Sch 4, Pt 1, paras 114, 123(1), (4).

12 Salaries etc of judges of Supreme Court

(1) Subject to subsections (2) and (3), there shall be paid to judges of the Supreme Court, other than the Lord Chancellor, such salaries as may be determined by the Lord Chancellor with the concurrence of the Minister for the Civil Service.

(2) Unless otherwise determined under this section, there shall be paid to the judges mentioned in subsection (1) the same salaries as at the commencement of this Act.

(3) Any salary payable under this section may be increased, but not reduced, by a determination or further determination under this section.

(4) (*repealed*)

(5) Salaries payable under this section shall be charged on and paid out of the Consolidated Fund.

(6) There shall be paid out of money provided by Parliament to any judge of the Court of Appeal or of the High Court, in addition to his salary, such allowances as may be determined by the Lord Chancellor with the concurrence of the Minister for the Civil Service.

(7) Pensions shall be payable to or in respect of the judges mentioned in subsection (1) in accordance with section 2 of the Judicial Pensions Act 1981 or in the case of a judge who is a person to whom Part I of the Judicial Pensions and Retirement Act 1993 applies, in accordance with that Act.

Amendments—CLSA 1990, s 84, Sch 20; JPRA 1993, Sch 8 para 15(1).

13 Precedence of judges of Supreme Court

(1) When sitting in the Court of Appeal –

(a) the Lord Chief Justice and the Master of the Rolls shall rank in that order; and

(b) Lords of Appeal in Ordinary and persons who have been Lord Chancellor shall rank next after the Master of the Rolls and, among themselves, according to the priority of the dates on which they respectively became Lords of Appeal in Ordinary or Lord Chancellor, as the case may be.

(2) Subject to subsection (1)(b), the President of the Queen's Bench Division shall rank next after the Master of the Rolls.

(2A) The President of the Family Division shall rank next after the President of the Queen's Bench Division.

(3) The Chancellor of the High Court shall rank next after the President of the Family Division.

(4) The vice-president or vice-presidents of the divisions of the Court of Appeal shall rank next after the Chancellor of the High Court; and if there are two vice-presidents of those divisions, they shall rank, among themselves, according to the priority of the dates on which they respectively became vice-presidents.

(5) The Lords Justices of Appeal (other than the vice-president or vice-presidents of the divisions of the Court of Appeal) shall rank after the ex-officio judges of the Court of Appeal and, among themselves, according to the priority of the dates on which they respectively became judges of that court.

(6) The puisne judges of the High Court shall rank next after the judges of the Court of Appeal and, among themselves, according to the priority of the dates on which they respectively became judges of the High Court.

Amendments—Constitutional Reform Act 2005, s 15(1), Sch 4, Pt 1, paras 114, 125(1)–(3).

14 Power of judge of Supreme or Crown Court to act in cases relating to rates and taxes

(1) A judge of the Supreme Court or of the Crown Court shall not be incapable of acting as such in any proceedings by reason of being, as one of a class of ratepayers, taxpayers or persons of any other description, liable in common with

others to pay, or contribute to, or benefit from, any rate or tax which may be increased, reduced or in any way affected by those proceedings.

(2) In this section 'rate or tax' means any rate, tax, duty or liability, whether public, general or local, and includes –

(a) any fund formed from the proceeds of any such rate, tax, duty or liability; and

(b) any fund applicable for purposes the same as, or similar to, those, for which the proceeds of any such rate, tax, duty or liability are or might be applied.

PART II
JURISDICTION

The Court of Appeal

15 General jurisdiction of Court of Appeal

(1) The Court of Appeal shall be a superior court of record.

(2) Subject to the provisions of this Act, there shall be exercisable by the Court of Appeal –

(a) all such jurisdiction (whether civil or criminal) as is conferred on it by this or any other Act; and

(b) all such other jurisdiction (whether civil or criminal) as was exercisable by it immediately before the commencement of this Act.

(3) For all purposes of or incidental to –

(a) the hearing and determination of any appeal to the civil division of the Court of Appeal; and

(b) the amendment, execution and enforcement of any judgment or order made on such an appeal,

the Court of Appeal shall have all the authority and jurisdiction of the court or tribunal from which the appeal was brought.

(4) It is hereby declared that any provision in this or any other Act which authorises or requires the taking of any steps for the execution or enforcement of a judgment or order of the High Court applies in relation to a judgment or order of the civil division of the Court of Appeal as it applies in relation to a judgment or order of the High Court.

16 Appeals from High Court

(1) Subject as otherwise provided by this or any other Act (and in particular to the provision in section 13(2)(a) of the Administration of Justice Act 1969 excluding appeals to the Court of Appeal in cases where leave to appeal from the High Court directly to the House of Lords is granted under Part II of that Act), or as provided by any order made by the Lord Chancellor under section 56(1) of the Access to Justice Act 1999, the Court of Appeal shall have jurisdiction to hear and determine appeals from any judgment or order of the High Court.

(2) An appeal from a judgment or order of the High Court when acting as a prize court shall not be to the Court of Appeal, but shall be to Her Majesty in Council in accordance with the Prize Acts 1864 to 1944.

Amendments—SI 2000/1071.

17 Applications for new trial

(1) Where any cause or matter, or any issue in any cause or matter, has been tried in the High Court, any application for a new trial thereof, or to set aside a verdict, finding or judgment therein, shall be heard and determined by the Court of Appeal except where rules of court made in pursuance of subsection (2) provide otherwise.

(2) As regards cases where the trial was by a judge alone and no error of the court at the trial is alleged, or any prescribed class of such cases, rules of court may provide that any such application as is mentioned in subsection (1) shall be heard and determined by the High Court.

(3) Nothing in this section shall alter the practice in bankruptcy.

18 Restrictions on appeals to Court of Appeal

(1) No appeal shall lie to the Court of Appeal –

- (a) except as provided by the Administration of Justice Act 1960, from any judgment of the High Court in any criminal cause or matter;
- (b) from any order of the High Court or any other court or tribunal allowing an extension of time for appealing from a judgment or order;
- (c) from any order, judgment or decision of the High Court or any other court or tribunal which, by virtue of any provision (however expressed) of this or any other Act, is final;
- (d) from a decree absolute of divorce or nullity of marriage, by a party who, having had time and opportunity to appeal from the decree nisi on which that decree was founded, has not appealed from the decree nisi;
- (e), (f) (*repealed*)
- (g) except as provided by Part I of the Arbitration Act 1996, from any decision of the High Court under that Part;
- (h) (*repealed*)

(1A), (1B), (2) (*repealed*)

Amendments—CLSA 1990, ss 7(1)–(3), 125(7), Sch 20; Arbitration Act 1996, s 107(1), Sch 3, para 37(1),(2); Civil Procedure Act 1997, s 10, Sch 2, para 1(2); Access to Justice Act 1999, s 106, Sch 15.

General jurisdiction

19 General jurisdiction

(1) The High Court shall be a superior court of record.

(2) Subject to the provisions of this Act, there shall be exercisable by the High Court –

- (a) all such jurisdiction (whether civil or criminal) as is conferred on it by this or any other Act; and

(b) all such other jurisdiction (whether civil or criminal) as was exercisable by it immediately before the commencement of this Act (including jurisdiction conferred on a judge of the High Court by any statutory provision).

(3) Any jurisdiction of the High Court shall be exercised only by a single judge of that court, except in so far as it is –

(a) by or by virtue of rules of court or any other statutory provision required to be exercised by a divisional court; or

(b) by rules of court made exercisable by a master, registrar or other officer of the court, or by any other person.

(4) The specific mention elsewhere in this Act of any jurisdiction covered by subsection (2) shall not derogate from the generality of that subsection.

20 Admiralty jurisdiction of High Court

(1) The Admiralty jurisdiction of the High Court shall be as follows, that is to say –

(a) jurisdiction to hear and determine any of the questions and claims mentioned in subsection (2);

(b) jurisdiction in relation to any of the proceedings mentioned in subsection (3);

(c) any other Admiralty jurisdiction which it had immediately before the commencement of this Act; and

(d) any jurisdiction connected with ships or aircraft which is vested in the High Court apart from this section and is for the time being by rules of court made or coming into force after the commencement of this Act assigned to the Queen's Bench Division and directed by the rules to be exercised by the Admiralty Court.

(2) The questions and claims referred to in subsection (1)(a) are –

(a) any claim to the possession or ownership of a ship or to the ownership of any share therein;

(b) any question arising between the co-owners of a ship as to possession, employment or earnings of that ship;

(c) any claim in respect of a mortgage of or charge on a ship or any share therein;

(d) any claim for damage received by a ship;

(e) any claim for damage done by a ship;

(f) any claim for loss of life or personal injury sustained in consequence of any defect in a ship or in her apparel or equipment, or in consequence of the wrongful act, neglect or default of -

(i) the owners, charterers or persons in possession or control of a ship; or

(ii) the master or crew of a ship, or any other person for whose wrongful acts, neglects or defaults the owners, charterers or persons in possession or control of a ship are responsible.

being an act, neglect or default in the navigation or management of a ship, in the loading, carriage or discharge of goods on, in or from the ship, or in the embarkation, carriage or disembarkation of persons on, in or from the ship;

(g) any claim for loss of or damage to goods carried in a ship;

(h) any claim arising out of any agreement relating to the carriage of goods in a ship or to the use or hire of a ship;
(j) any claim –
(i) under the Salvage Convention 1989;
(ii) under any contract for or in relation to salvage services; or
(iii) in the nature of salvage not falling within (i) or (ii) above;
or any corresponding claim in connection with an aircraft.
(k) any claim in the nature of towage in respect of a ship or an aircraft;
(l) any claim in the nature of pilotage in respect of a ship or an aircraft;
(m) any claim in respect of goods or materials supplied to a ship for her operation or maintenance;
(n) any claim in respect of the construction, repair or equipment of a ship or dock charges or dues;
(o) any claim by a master or member of the crew of a ship for wages (including any sum allotted out of wages or adjudged by a superintendent to be due by way of wages);
(p) any claim by a master, shipper, charterer or agent in respect of disbursements made on account of a ship;
(q) any claim arising out of an act which is or is claimed to be a general average act;
(r) any claim arising out of bottomry;
(s) any claim for the forfeiture or condemnation of a ship or of goods which are being or have been carried, or have been attempted to be carried, in a ship, or for the restoration of a ship or any such goods after seizure, or for droits of Admiralty.

(3) The proceedings referred to in subsection (1)(b) are –

(a) any application to the High Court under the Merchant Shipping Act 1995.
(b) any action to enforce a claim for damage, loss of life or personal injury arising out of –
(i) a collision between ships; or
(ii) the carrying out of or omission to carry out a manoeuvre in the case of one or more of two or more ships; or
(iii) non-compliance, on the part of one or more of two or more ships, with the collision regulations;
(c) any action by shipowners or other persons under the Merchant Shipping Act 1995 for the limitation of the amount of their liability in connection with a ship or other property.

(4) The jurisdiction of the High Court under subsection (2)(b) includes power to settle any account outstanding and unsettled between the parties in relation to the ship, and to direct that the ship, or any share thereof, shall be sold, and to make such other order as the court thinks fit.

(5) Subsection (2)(e) extends to –

(a) any claim in respect of a liability incurred under Chapter III of Part VI of the Merchant Shipping Act 1995; and
(b) any claim in respect of a liability falling on the International Oil Pollution Compensation Fund, or on the International Oil Pollution Compensation Fund 1992, under Chapter IV of Part VI of the Merchant Shipping Act 1995.

(6) In subsection 2(j) –

(a) the 'Salvage Convention 1989' means the International Convention on Salvage, 1989 as it has effect under section 224 of the Merchant Shipping Act 1995;

(b) the reference to salvage services includes services rendered in saving life from a ship and the reference to any claim under any contract for or in relation to salvage services includes any claim arising out of such a contract whether or not arising during the provision of the services;

(c) the reference to a corresponding claim in connection with an aircraft is a reference to any claim corresponding to any claim mentioned in sub-paragraph (i) or (ii) of paragraph (j) which is available under section 87 of the Civil Aviation Act 1982.

(7) The preceding provisions of this section apply –

(a) in relation to all ships or aircraft, whether British or not and whether registered or not and wherever the residence or domicile of their owners may be;

(b) in relation to all claims, wherever arising (including, in the case of cargo or wreck salvage, claims in respect of cargo or wreck found on land); and

(c) so far as they relate to mortgages and charges, to all mortgages or charges, whether registered or not and whether legal or equitable, including mortgages and charges created under foreign law;

Provided that nothing in this subsection shall be construed as extending the cases in which money or property is recoverable under any of the provisions of the Merchant Shipping Act 1995.

Amendments—Merchant Shipping (Salvage and Pollution) Act 1994, s 1(6), Sch 2, para 6; Merchant Shipping Act 1995, s 314(2), Sch 13, para 59(1), (2); Merchant Shipping and Maritime Security Act 1997, s 29(1), Sch 6, para 2.

21 Mode of exercise of Admiralty jurisdiction

(1) Subject to section 22, an action in personam may be brought in the High Court in all cases within the Admiralty jurisdiction of that court.

(2) In the case of any such claim as is mentioned in section 20(2)(a), (c) or (s) or any such question as is mentioned in section 20(2)(b), an action in rem may be brought in the High Court against the ship or property in connection with which the claim or question arises.

(3) In any case in which there is a maritime lien or other charge on any ship, aircraft or other property for the amount claimed, an action in rem may be brought in the High Court against that ship, aircraft or property.

(4) In the case of any such claim as is mentioned in section 20(2)(e) to (r), where –

(a) the claim arises in connection with a ship; and

(b) the person who would be liable on the claim in an action in personam ('the relevant person') was, when the cause of action arose, the owner or charterer of, or in possession or in control of, the ship,

an action in rem may (whether or not the claim gives rise to a maritime lien on that ship) be brought in the High Court against –

(i) that ship, if at the time when the action is brought the relevant person is either the beneficial owner of that ship as respects all the shares in it or the charterer of it under a charter by demise; or

(ii) any other ship of which, at the time when the action is brought, the relevant person is the beneficial owner as respects all the shares in it.

(5) In the case of a claim in the nature of towage or pilotage in respect of an aircraft, an action in rem may be brought in the High Court against that aircraft if, at the time when the action is brought, it is beneficially owned by the person who would be liable on the claim in an action in personam.

(6) Where, in the exercise of its Admiralty jurisdiction, the High Court orders any ship, aircraft or other property to be sold, the court shall have jurisdiction to hear and determine any question arising as to the title to the proceeds of sale.

(7) In determining for the purposes of subsections (4) and (5)whether a person would be liable on a claim in an action in personam it shall be assumed that he has his habitual residence or a place of business within England or Wales.

(8) Where, as regards any such claim as is mentioned in section 20(2)(e) to (r), a ship has been served with a writ or arrested in an action in rem brought to enforce that claim, no other ship may be served with a writ or arrested in that or any other action in rem brought to enforce that claim: but this subsection does not prevent the issue, in respect of any one such claim, of a writ naming more than one ship or of two or more writs each naming a different ship.

22 Restrictions on entertainment of actions in personam in collision and other similar cases

(1) This section applies to any claim for damage, loss of life or personal injury arising out of –

(a) a collision between ships; or
(b) the carrying out of, or omission to carry out, a manoeuvre in the case of one or more of two or more ships; or
(c) non-compliance, on the part of one or more of two or more ships, with the collision regulations.

(2) The High Court shall not entertain any action in personam to enforce a claim to which this section applies unless –

(a) the defendant has his habitual residence or a place of business within England or Wales; or
(b) the cause of action arose within inland waters of England or Wales or within the limits of a port of England or Wales; or
(c) an action arising out of the same incident or series of incidents is proceeding in the court or has been heard and determined in the court.

In this subsection –

'inland waters' includes any part of the sea adjacent to the coast of the United Kingdom certified by the Secretary of State to be waters falling by international law to be treated as within the territorial sovereignty of Her Majesty apart from the operation of that law in relation to territorial waters;

'port' means any port, harbour, river, estuary, haven, dock, canal or other place so long as a person or body of persons is empowered by or under an Act to make charges in respect of ships entering it or using the facilities therein, and 'limits of a port' means the limits thereof as fixed by or under the Act in question or, as the case may be, by the relevant charter or custom;

'charges' means any charges with the exception of light dues, local light dues and any other charges in respect of lighthouses, buoys or beacons and of charges in respect of pilotage.

(3) The High Court shall not entertain any action in personam to enforce a claim to which this section applies until any proceedings previously brought by the plaintiff in any court outside England and Wales against the same defendant in respect of the same incident or series of incidents have been discontinued or otherwise come to an end.

(4) Subsections (2) and (3) shall apply to counterclaims (except counterclaims in proceedings arising out of the same incident or series of incidents) as they apply to actions, the references to the plaintiff and the defendant being for this purpose read as references to the plaintiff on the counterclaim and the defendant to the counterclaim respectively.

(5) Subsections (2) and (3) shall not apply to any action or counterclaim if the defendant thereto submits or has agreed to submit to the jurisdiction of the court.

(6) Subject to the provisions of subsection (3), the High Court shall have jurisdiction to entertain an action in personam to enforce a claim to which this section applies whenever any of the conditions specified in subsections (2)(a) to (c) is satisfied, and the rules of court relating to the service of process outside the jurisdiction shall make such provision as may appear to the rule-making authority to be appropriate having regard to the provisions of this subsection.

(7) Nothing in this section shall prevent an action which is brought in accordance with the provisions of this section in the High Court being transferred, in accordance with the enactments in that behalf, to some other court.

(8) For the avoidance of doubt it is hereby declared that this section applies in relation to the jurisdiction of the High Court not being Admiralty jurisdiction, as well as in relation to its Admiralty jurisdiction.

23 High Court not to have jurisdiction in cases within Rhine Convention

The High Court shall not have jurisdiction to determine any claim or question certified by the Secretary of State to be a claim or question which, under the Rhine Navigation Convention, falls to be determined in accordance with the provisions of that Convention; and any proceedings to enforce such a claim which are commenced in the High Court shall be set aside.

24 Supplementary provisions as to Admiralty jurisdiction

(1) In sections 20 to 23 and this section, unless the context otherwise requires –

'collision regulations' means safety regulations under section 85 of the Merchant Shipping Act 1995;

'goods' includes baggage;

'master' has the same meaning as in the Merchant Shipping Act 1995, and accordingly includes every person (except a pilot) having command or charge of a ship;

'the Rhine Navigation Convention' means the Convention of the 7th October 1868 as revised by any subsequent Convention;

'ship' includes any description of vessel used in navigation and (except in the definition of 'port' in section 22(2) and in subsection (2)(c) of this section) includes, subject to section 2(3) of the Hovercraft Act 1968, a hovercraft;

'towage' and 'pilotage', in relation to an aircraft, mean towage and pilotage while the aircraft is waterborne.

(2) Nothing in sections 20 to 23 shall –

(a) be construed as limiting the jurisdiction of the High Court to refuse to entertain an action for wages by the master or a member of the crew of a ship, not being a British ship;

(b) affect the provisions of section 226 of the Merchant Shipping Act 1995 (power of a receiver of wreck to detain a ship in respect of a salvage claim); or

(c) authorise proceedings in rem in respect of any claim against the Crown, or the arrest, detention or sale of any of Her Majesty's ships or Her Majesty's aircraft, or, subject to section 2(3) of the Hovercraft Act 1968, Her Majesty's hovercraft, or of any cargo or other property belonging to the Crown.

(3) In this section –

'Her Majesty's ships' and 'Her Majesty's aircraft' have the meanings given by section 38(2) of the Crown Proceedings Act 1947;

'Her Majesty's hovercraft' means hovercraft belonging to the Crown in right of Her Majesty's Government in the United Kingdom or Her Majesty's Government in Northern Ireland.

Amendments—Merchant Shipping Act 1995, s 314(2), Sch 13, para 59(1), (2).

Other particular fields of jurisdiction

25 Probate jurisdiction of High Court

(1) Subject to the provisions of Part V, the High Court shall, in accordance with section 19(2), have the following probate jurisdiction, that is to say all such jurisdiction in relation to probates and letters of administration as it had immediately before the commencement of this Act, and in particular all such contentious and non-contentious jurisdiction as it then had in relation to –

(a) testamentary causes or matters;

(b) the grant, amendment or revocation of probates and letters of administration; and

(c) the real and personal estate of deceased persons.

(2) Subject to the provisions of Part V, the High Court shall, in the exercise of its probate jurisdiction, perform all such duties with respect to the estates of deceased persons as fell to be performed by it immediately before the commencement of this Act.

26 Matrimonial jurisdiction of High Court

The High Court shall, in accordance with section 19(2), have all such jurisdiction in relation to matrimonial causes and matters as was immediately before the commencement of the Matrimonial Causes Act 1857 vested in or exercisable by any ecclesiastical court or person in England or Wales in respect of –

(a) divorce a mensa et thoro (renamed judicial separation by that Act);
(b) nullity of marriage (*repealed*); and
(c) any matrimonial cause or matter except marriage licences.

Amendments—Family Law Act 1986, s 68(1), (2), Sch 1, para 25, Sch 2.

27 Prize jurisdiction of High Court

The High Court shall, in accordance with section 19(2), have as a prize court –

(a) all such jurisdiction as is conferred on it by the Prize Acts 1864 to 1944 (in which references to the High Court of Admiralty are by virtue of paragraph 1 of Schedule 4 to this Act to be construed as references to the High Court); and
(b) all such other jurisdiction on the high seas and elsewhere as it has as a prize court immediately before the commencement of this Act.

28 Appeals from Crown Court and inferior courts

(1) Subject to subsection (2), any order, judgment or other decision of the Crown Court may be questioned by any party to the proceedings, on the ground that it is wrong in law or is in excess of jurisdiction, by applying to the Crown Court to have a case stated by that court for the opinion of the High Court.

(2) Subsection (1) shall not apply to –

(a) a judgment or other decision of the Crown Court relating to trial on indictment; or
(b) any decision of that court under the Betting, Gaming and Lotteries Act 1963, the Licensing Act 1964, the Gaming Act 1968 or the Local Government (Miscellaneous Provisions) Act 1982 which, by any provision of any of those Acts, is to be final.

(3) Subject to the provisions of this Act and to rules of court, the High Court shall, in accordance with section 19(2), have jurisdiction to hear and determine –

(a) any application, or any appeal (whether by way of case stated or otherwise), which it has power to hear and determine under or by virtue of this or any other Act; and
(b) all such other appeals as it had jurisdiction to hear and determine immediately before the commencement of this Act.

Amendments—Local Government (Miscellaneous Provisions) Act 1982, s 2, Sch 3, para 27(6).

28A Proceedings on case stated by magistrates' court or Crown Court

(1) This section applies where a case is stated for the opinion of the High Court –

(a) by a magistrates' court under section 111 of the Magistrates' Courts Act 1980; or
(b) by the Crown Court under section 28(1) of this Act.

(2) The High Court may, if it thinks fit, cause the case to be sent back for amendment and, where it does so, the case shall be amended accordingly.

(3) The High Court shall hear and determine the question arising on the case (or the case as amended) and shall –

- (a) reverse, affirm or amend the determination in respect of which the case has been stated, or
- (b) remit the matter to the magistrates' court, or the Crown Court, with the opinion of the High Court,

and may make such other order in relation to the matter (including as to costs) as it thinks fit.

(4) Except as provided by the Administration of Justice Act 1960 (right of appeal to House of Lords in criminal cases), a decision of the High Court under this section is final.

Amendments—Inserted by Statute Law (Repeals) Act 1993, s 1(2), Sch 2, para 9; substituted by Access to Justice Act 1999, s 61.

29 Mandatory, prohibiting and quashing orders

(1) The orders of mandamus, prohibition and certiorari shall be known instead as mandatory, prohibiting and quashing orders respectively.

(1A) The High Court shall have jurisdiction to make mandatory, prohibiting and quashing orders in those classes of case in which, immediately before 1 May 2004, it had jurisdiction to make orders of mandamus, prohibition and certiorari respectively.

(2) Every such order shall be final, subject to any right of appeal therefrom.

(3) In relation to the jurisdiction of the Crown Court, other than its jurisdiction in matters relating to trial on indictment, the High Court shall have all such jurisdiction to make mandatory, prohibiting or quashing orders as the High Court possesses in relation to the jurisdiction of an inferior court.

(3A) The High Court shall have no jurisdiction to make mandatory, prohibiting or quashing orders in relation to the jurisdiction of a court-martial in matters relating to –

- (a) trial by court-martial for an offence, or
- (b) appeals from a Standing Civilian Court;

and in this subsection 'court-martial' means a court-martial under the Army Act 1955, the Air Force Act 1955 or the Naval Discipline Act 1957.

(4) The power of the High Court under any enactment to require justices of the peace or a judge or officer of a county court to do any act relating to the duties of their respective offices, or to require a magistrates' court to state a case for the opinion of the High Court, in any case where the High Court formerly had by virtue of any enactment jurisdiction to make a rule absolute, or an order, for any of those purposes, shall be exercisable by mandatory order.

(5) In any statutory provision –

- (a) references to mandamus or to a writ or order of mandamus shall be read as references to a mandatory order;
- (b) references to prohibition or to a writ or order of prohibition shall be read as references to a prohibiting order;

(c) references to certiorari or to a writ or order of certiorari shall be read as references to a quashing order; and

(d) references to the issue or award of a writ of mandamus, prohibition or certiorari shall be read as references to the making of the corresponding mandatory, prohibiting or quashing order.

(6) In subsection (3) the reference to the Crown Court's jurisdiction in matters relating to trial on indictment does not include its jurisdiction relating to orders under section 17 of the Access to Justice Act 1999.

Amendments—Access to Justice Act 1999, s 24, Sch 4, paras 21, 23; Armed Forces Act 2001, s 23; SI 2004/1033.

30 Injunctions to restrain persons from acting in offices in which they are not entitled to act

(1) Where a person not entitled to do so acts in an office to which this section applies, the High Court may –

(a) grant an injunction restraining him from so acting; and

(b) if the case so requires, declare the office to be vacant.

(2) This section applies to any substantive office of a public nature and permanent character which is held under the Crown or which has been created by any statutory provision or royal charter.

31 Application for judicial review

(1) An application to the High Court for one or more of the following forms of relief, namely –

(a) a mandatory, prohibiting or quashing order;

(b) a declaration or injunction under subsection (2); or

(c) an injunction under section 30 restraining a person not entitled to do so from acting in an office to which that section applies,

shall be made in accordance with rules of court by a procedure to be known as an application for judicial review.

(2) A declaration may be made or an injunction granted under this subsection in any case where an application for judicial review, seeking that relief, has been made and the High Court considers that, having regard to –

(a) the nature of the matters in respect of which relief may be granted by mandatory, prohibiting or quashing orders;

(b) the nature of the persons and bodies against whom relief may be granted by such orders; and

(c) all the circumstances of the case,

it would be just and convenient for the declaration to be made or the injunction to be granted, as the case may be.

(3) No application for judicial review shall be made unless the leave of the High Court has been obtained in accordance with rules of court; and the court shall not grant leave to make such an application unless it considers that the applicant has a sufficient interest in the matter to which the application relates.

(4) On an application for judicial review the High Court may award to the applicant damages, restitution or the recovery of a sum due if –

(a) the application includes a claim for such an award arising from any matter to which the application relates; and
(b) the court is satisfied that such an award would have been made if the claim had been made in an action begun by the applicant at the time of making the application.

(5) If, on an application for judicial review seeking a quashing order, the High Court quashes the decision to which the application relates, the High Court may remit the matter to the court, tribunal or authority concerned, with a direction to reconsider it and reach a decision in accordance with the findings of the High Court.

(6) Where the High Court considers that there has been undue delay in making an application for judicial review, the court may refuse to grant –

(a) leave for the making of the application; or
(b) any relief sought on the application,

if it considers that the granting of the relief sought would be likely to cause substantial hardship to, or substantially prejudice the rights of, any person or would be detrimental to good administration.

(7) Subsection (6) is without prejudice to any enactment or rule of court which has the effect of limiting the time within which an application for judicial review may be made.

Amendments—SI 2004/1033.

Powers

32 Orders for interim payment

(1) As regards proceedings pending in the High Court, provision may be made by rules of court for enabling the court, in such circumstances as may be prescribed, to make an order requiring a party to the proceedings to make an interim payment of such amount as may be specified in the order, with provision for the payment to be made to such other party to the proceedings as may be so specified or, if the order so provides, by paying it into court.

(2) Any rules of court which make provision in accordance with subsection (1) may include provision for enabling a party to any proceedings who, in pursuance of such an order, has made an interim payment to recover the whole or part of the amount of the payment in such circumstances, and from such other party to the proceedings, as may be determined in accordance with the rules.

(3) Any rules made by virtue of this section may include such incidental, supplementary and consequential provisions as the rule-making authority may consider necessary or expedient.

(4) Nothing in this section shall be construed as affecting the exercise of any power relating to costs, including any power to make rules of court relating to costs.

(5) In this section 'interim payment', in relation to a party to any proceedings, means a payment on account of any damages, debt or other sum (excluding any costs) which that party may be held liable to pay to or for the benefit of another party to the proceedings if a final judgment or order of the court in the proceedings is given or made in favour of that other party.

32A Orders for provisional damages for personal injuries

(1) This section applies to an action for damages for personal injuries in which there is proved or admitted to be a chance that at some definite or indefinite time in the future the injured person will, as a result of the act or omission which gave rise to the cause of action, develop some serious disease or suffer some serious deterioration in his physical or mental condition.

(2) Subject to subsection (4) below, as regards any action for damages to which this section applies in which a judgment is given in the High Court, provision may be made by rules of court for enabling the court, in such circumstances as may be prescribed, to award the injured person –

(a) damages assessed on the assumption that the injured person will not develop the disease or suffer the deterioration in his condition; and

(b) further damages at a future date if he develops the disease or suffers the deterioration.

(3) Any rules made by virtue of this section may include such incidental, supplementary and consequential provisions as the rule-making authority may consider necessary or expedient.

(4) Nothing in this section shall be construed –

(a) as affecting the exercise of any power relating to costs, including any power to make rules of court relating to costs; or

(b) as prejudicing any duty of the court under any enactment or rule of law to reduce or limit the total damages which would have been recoverable apart from any such duty.

Amendments—AJA 1982, ss 6(1), 73(2).

33 Powers of High Court exercisable before commencement of action

(1) On the application of any person in accordance with rules of court, the High Court shall, in such circumstances as may be specified in the rules, have power to make an order providing for any one or more of the following matters, that is to say –

(a) the inspection, photographing, preservation, custody and detention of property which appears to the court to be property which may become the subject-matter of subsequent proceedings in the High Court, or as to which any question may arise in any such proceedings; and

(b) the taking of samples of any such property as is mentioned in paragraph (a), and the carrying out of any experiment on or with any such property.

(2) On the application, in accordance with rules of court, of a person who appears to the High Court to be likely to be a party to subsequent proceedings in that court the High Court shall, in such circumstances as may be specified in the rules, have power to order a person who appears to the court to be likely to be a party to the proceedings and to be likely to have or to have had in his possession, custody or power any documents which are relevant to an issue arising or likely to arise out of that claim –

(a) to disclose whether those documents are in his possession, custody or power; and

(b) to produce such of those documents as are in his possession, custody or power to the applicant or, on such conditions as may be specified in the order –
   (i) to the applicant's legal advisers; or
   (ii) to the applicant's legal advisers and any medical or other professional adviser of the applicant; or
   (iii) if the applicant has no legal adviser, to any medical or other professional adviser of the applicant.

Amendments—County Courts Act 1984, s 148(3), Sch 4; SI 1998/2940.

34 Power of High Court to order disclosure of documents, inspection of property etc in proceedings for personal injuries or death

(1) (*repealed*)

(2) On the application, in accordance with rules of court, of a party to any proceedings, the High Court shall, in such circumstances as may be specified in the rules, have power to order a person who is not a party to the proceedings and who appears to the court to be likely to have in his possession, custody or power any documents which are relevant to an issue arising out of the said claim –

(a) to disclose whether those documents are in his possession, custody or power; and
(b) to produce such of those documents as are in his possession, custody or power to the applicant or, on such conditions as may be specified in the order –
   (i) to the applicant's legal advisers; or
   (ii) to the applicant's legal advisers and any medical or other professional adviser of the applicant; or
   (iii) if the applicant has no legal adviser, to any medical or other professional adviser of the applicant.

(3) On the application, in accordance with rules of court, of a party to any proceedings, the High Court shall, in such circumstances as may be specified in the rules, have power to make an order providing for any one or more of the following matters, that is to say –

(a) the inspection, photographing, preservation, custody and detention of property which is not the property of, or in the possession of, any party to the proceedings but which is the subject-matter of the proceedings or as to which any question arises in the proceedings;
(b) the taking of samples of any such property as is mentioned in paragraph (a) and the carrying out of any experiment on or with any such property.

(4) The preceding provisions of this section are without prejudice to the exercise by the High Court of any power to make orders which is exercisable apart from those provisions.

Amendments—County Courts Act 1984, s 148(3), Sch 4; SI 1998/2940.

35 Provisions supplementary to ss 33 and 34

(1) The High Court shall not make an order under section 33 or 34 if it considers that compliance with the order , if made, would be likely to be injurious to the public interest.

(2) Rules of court may make provision as to the circumstances in which an order under section 33 or 34 can be made; and any rules making such provision may include such incidental, supplementary and consequential provisions as the rulemaking authority may consider necessary or expedient.

(3) Without prejudice to the generality of subsection (2), rules of court shall be made for the purpose of ensuring that the costs of and incidental to proceedings for an order under subsection 33(2) or 34 incurred by the person against whom the order is sought shall be awarded to that person unless the court otherwise directs.

(4) Sections 33(2) and 34 and this section bind the Crown; and section 33(1) binds the Crown so far as it relates to property as to which it appears to the court that it may become the subject-matter of subsequent proceedings involving a claim in respect of personal injuries to a person or in respect of a person's death.

In this subsection references to the Crown do not include references to Her Majesty in Her private capacity or to Her Majesty in right of Her Duchy of Lancaster or to the Duke of Cornwall.

(5) In sections 32A, 33 and 34 and this section–

'property' includes any land, chattel or other corporeal property of any description;

'personal injuries' includes any disease and any impairment of a person's physical or mental condition.

Amendments—AJA 1982, s 6(2); County Courts Act 1984, s 148(3), Sch 4.

35A Power of High Court to award interest on debts and damages

(1) Subject to rules of court, in proceedings (whenever instituted) before the High Court for the recovery of a debt or damages there may be included in any sum for which judgment is given simple interest, at such rate as the court thinks fit or as rules of court may provide, on all or any part of the debt or damages in respect of which judgment is given, or payment is made before judgment, for all or any part of the period between the date when the cause of action arose and –

(a) in the case of any sum paid before judgment, the date of the payment; and

(b) in the case of the sum for which judgment is given, the date of the judgment.

(2) In relation to a judgment given for damages for personal injuries or death which exceed £200 subsection (1) shall have effect –

(a) with the substitution of 'shall be included' for 'may be included'; and
(b) with the addition of 'unless the court is satisfied that there are special reasons to the contrary' after 'given', where first occurring.

(3) Subject to rules of court, where –

(a) there are proceedings (whenever instituted) before the High Court for the recovery of a debt; and
(b) the defendant pays the whole debt to the plaintiff (otherwise than in pursuance of a judgment in the proceedings),

the defendant shall be liable to pay the plaintiff simple interest at such rate as the court thinks fit or as rules of court may provide on all or any part of the debt for all or any part of the period between the date when the cause of action arose and the date of the payment.

(4) Interest in respect of a debt shall not be awarded under this section for a period during which, for whatever reason, interest on the debt already runs.

(5) Without prejudice to the generality of section 84, rules of court may provide for a rate of interest by reference to the rate specified in section 17 of the Judgments Act 1838 as that section has effect from time to time or by reference to a rate for which any other enactment provides.

(6) Interest under this section may be calculated at different rates in respect of different periods.

(7) In this section 'plaintiff' means the person seeking the debt or damages and 'defendant' means the person from whom the plaintiff seeks the debt or damages and 'personal injuries' includes any disease and any impairment of a person's physical or mental condition.

(8) Nothing in this section affects the damages recoverable for the dishonour of a bill of exchange.

Amendments—Inserted by AJA 1982, s 15(1), Sch 1, Pt I.

Rates of statutory interest in commercial cases—The CPR give no real guidance as to rates of interest. Previously in commercial cases a rate of 1% over base rate has commonly been used unless for some reason that would be unfair to one party or the other. There is no reason why that measure should not continue to be used, or be used in the county court dealing with a commercial dispute such as a claim under an insurance policy (*Adcock v Co-operative Insurance Society Ltd* [2000] EWCA Civ 117, [2000] All ER (D) 505, [2000] Lloyd's Rep IR 657, *The Times*, 26 April, CA).

36 Subpoena issued by High Court to run throughout United Kingdom

(1) If in any cause or matter in the High Court it appears to the court that it is proper to compel the personal attendance at any trial of a witness who may not be within the jurisdiction of the court, it shall be lawful for the court, if in the discretion of the court it seems fit so to do, to order that a writ of subpoena ad testificandum or writ of subpoena duces tecum shall issue in special form commanding the witness to attend the trial wherever he shall be within the United Kingdom; and the service of any such writ in any part of the United Kingdom shall be as valid and effectual for all purposes as if it had been served within the jurisdiction of the High Court.

(2) Every such writ shall have at its foot a statement to the effect that it is issued by the special order of the High Court, and no such writ shall issue without such a special order.

(3) If any person served with a writ issued under this section does not appear as required by the writ, the High Court, on proof to the satisfaction of the court of the service of the writ and of the default, may transmit a certificate of the default under the seal of the court or under the hand of a judge of the court –

(a) if the service was in Scotland, to the Court of Session at Edinburgh; or
(b) if the service was in Northern Ireland, to the High Court of Justice in Northern Ireland at Belfast;

and the court to which the certificate is sent shall thereupon proceed against and punish the person in default in like manner as if that person had neglected or refused to appear in obedience to process issued out of that court.

(4) No court shall in any case proceed against or punish any person for having made such default as aforesaid unless it is shown to the court that a reasonable and sufficient sum of money to defray –

(a) the expenses of coming and attending to give evidence and of returning from giving evidence; and
(b) any other reasonable expenses which he has asked to be defrayed in connection with his evidence,

was tendered to him at the time when the writ was served upon him.

(5) Nothing in this section shall affect –

(a) the power of the High Court to issue a commission for the examination of witnesses out of the jurisdiction of the court in any case in which, notwithstanding this section, the court thinks fit to issue such a commission; or
(b) the admissibility at any trial of any evidence which, if this section had not been enacted, would have been admissible on the ground of a witness being outside the jurisdiction of the court.

(6) In this section references to attendance at a trial include references to attendance before an examiner or commissioner appointed by the High Court in any cause or matter in that court, including an examiner or commissioner appointed to take evidence outside the jurisdiction of the court.

Amendments—CLSA 1990, s 125(2), Sch 17, para 13.

37 Powers of High Court with respect to injunctions and receivers

(1) The High Court may by order (whether interlocutory or final) grant an injunction or appoint a receiver in all cases in which it appears to the court to be just and convenient to do so.

(2) Any such order may be made either unconditionally or on such terms and conditions as the court thinks just.

(3) The power of the High Court under subsection (1) to grant an interlocutory injunction restraining a party to any proceedings from removing from the jurisdiction of the High Court, or otherwise dealing with, assets located within that jurisdiction shall be exercisable in cases where that party is, as well as in cases where he is not, domiciled, resident or present within that jurisdiction.

(4) The power of the High Court to appoint a receiver by way of equitable execution shall operate in relation to all legal estates and interests in land; and that power –

(a) may be exercised in relation to an estate or interest in land whether or not a charge has been imposed on that land under section 1 of the Charging Orders Act 1979 for the purpose of enforcing the judgment, order or award in question; and
(b) shall be in addition to, and not in derogation of, any power of any court to appoint a receiver in proceedings for enforcing such a charge.

(5) Where an order under the said section 1 imposing a charge for the purpose of enforcing a judgment, order or award has been, or has effect as if, registered under section 6 of the Land Charges Act 1972, subsection (4) of the said section 6 (effect of non-registration of writs and orders registrable under that section) shall not apply to an order appointing a receiver made either –

(a) in proceedings for enforcing the charge; or

(b) by way of equitable execution of the judgment, order or award or, as the case may be, of so much of it as requires payment of moneys secured by the charge.

38 Relief against forfeiture for non-payment of rent

(1) In any action in the High Court for the forfeiture of a lease for non-payment of rent, the court shall have power to grant relief against forfeiture in a summary manner, and may do so subject to the same terms and conditions as to the payment of rent, costs or otherwise as could have been imposed by it in such an action immediately before the commencement of this Act.

(2) Where the lessee or a person deriving title under him is granted relief under this section, he shall hold the demised premises in accordance with the terms of the lease without the necessity for a new lease.

39 Execution of instrument by person nominated by High Court

(1) Where the High Court has given or made a judgment or order directing a person to execute any conveyance, contract or other document, or to indorse any negotiable instrument, then, if that person –

(a) neglects or refuses to comply with the judgment or order; or
(b) cannot after reasonable inquiry be found, the High Court may, on such terms and conditions, if any, as may be just, order that the conveyance, contract or other document shall be executed, or that the negotiable instrument shall be indorsed, by such person as the court may nominate for that purpose.

(2) A conveyance, contract, document or instrument executed or indorsed in pursuance of an order under this section shall operate, and be for all purposes available, as if it had been executed or indorsed by the person originally directed to execute or indorse it.

40 Attachment of debts

(1) Subject to any order for the time being in force under subsection (4), this section applies to any deposit account, and any withdrawable share account, with a deposit-taker.

(2) In determining whether, for the purposes of the jurisdiction of the High Court to attach debts for the purpose of satisfying judgments or orders for the payment of money, a sum standing to the credit of a person in an account to which this section applies is a sum due or accruing to that person and, as such, attachable in accordance with rules of court, any condition mentioned in subsection (3) which applies to the account shall be disregarded.

(3) Those conditions are –

(a) any condition that notice is required before any money or share is withdrawn;
(b) any condition that a personal application must be made before any money or share is withdrawn;
(c) any condition that a deposit book or share-account book must be produced before any money or share is withdrawn; or
(d) any other prescribed condition.

(4) The Lord Chancellor may by order make such provision as he thinks fit, by way of amendment of this section or otherwise, for all or any of the following purposes, namely –

(a) including in, or excluding from, the accounts to which this section applies accounts of any description specified in the order;
(b) excluding from the accounts to which this section applies all accounts with any particular deposit-taker so specified or with any deposit-taker of a description so specified.

(5) Any order under subsection (4) shall be made by statutory instrument subject to annulment in pursuance of a resolution of either House of Parliament.

(6) Deposit-taker means a person who may, in the course of his business, lawfully accept deposits in the United Kingdom.

(7) Subsection (6) must be read with –

(a) section 22 of the Financial Services and Markets Act 2000;
(b) any relevant order under that section; and
(c) Schedule 2 to that Act.

Amendments—Banking Act 1987, s 108(1), Sch 6, para 11; SI 2001/3649.

40A Administrative and clerical expenses of garnishees

(1) Where an interim third party debt order made in the exercise of the jurisdiction mentioned in subsection (2) of the preceding section is served on a deposit-taker, it may, subject to the provisions of this section, deduct from the relevant debt or debts an amount not exceeding the prescribed sum towards its administrative and clerical expenses in complying with the order; and the right to make a deduction under this subsection shall be exercisable as from the time the interim third party debt order is served on it.

(1A) In subsection (1) 'the relevant debt or debts', in relation to an interim third party debt order served on a deposit-taker, means the amount, as at the time the order is served on it, of the debt or debts of which the whole or a part is expressed to be attached by the order.

(1B) A deduction may be made under subsection (1) in a case where the amount referred to in subsection (1A) is insufficient to cover both the amount of the deduction and the amount of the judgment debt and costs in respect of which the attachment was made, notwithstanding that the benefit of the attachment to the creditor is reduced as a result of the deduction.

(2) An amount may not in pursuance of subsection (1) be deducted or, as the case may be, retained in a case where, by virtue of section 346 of the Insolvency Act 1986 or section 183 of the Insolvency Act 1986 or otherwise, the creditor is not entitled to retain the benefit of the attachment.

(3) In this section –

'deposit-taker' has the meaning given by section 40(6); and
'prescribed' means prescribed by an order made by the Lord Chancellor.

(4) An order under this section –

(a) may make different provision for different cases;
(b) without prejudice to the generality of paragraph (a) of this subsection, may prescribe sums differing according to the amount due under the judgment or order to be satisfied

(c) may provide for this section not to apply to deposit-takers of any prescribed description.

(5) Any such order shall be made by statutory instrument subject to annulment in pursuance of a resolution of either House of Parliament.

Amendments—Inserted by AJA 1982, s 55, Sch 4, Pt I; Amended by AJA 1985, ss 52(4), 67(2), 69(5), Sch 8, Pt II, Sch 9, para 11(2); Companies Consolidation (Consequential Provisions) Act 1985, s 30, Sch 2; Insolvency Act 1986, s 439(2), Sch 14; SI 2001/3649; SI 2002/439.

41 Wards of court

(1) Subject to the provisions of this section, no minor shall be made a ward of court except by virtue of an order to that effect made by the High Court.

(2) Where an application is made for such an order in respect of a minor, the minor shall become a ward of court on the making of the application, but shall cease to be a ward of court at the end of such period as may be prescribed unless within that period an order has been made in accordance with the application.

(2A) Subsection (2) does not apply with respect to a child who is the subject of a care order (as defined by section 105 of the Children Act 1989).

(3) The High Court may, either upon an application in that behalf or without such an application, order that any minor who is for the time being a ward of court shall cease to be a ward of court.

Amendments—Children Act 1989, s 108(5), (6), Sch 13, para 45(2), Sch 14, para 1.

42 Restriction of vexatious legal proceedings

(1) If, on an application made by the Attorney General under this section, the High Court is satisfied that any person has habitually and persistently and without any reasonable ground –

(a) instituted vexatious civil proceedings, whether in the High Court or any inferior court, and whether against the same person or against different persons; or

(b) made vexatious applications in any civil proceedings, whether in the High Court or any inferior court, and whether instituted by him or another, or

(c) instituted vexatious prosecutions (whether against the same person or different persons),

the court may, after hearing that person or giving him an opportunity of being heard, make a civil proceedings order, a criminal proceedings order or an all proceedings order.

(1A) In this section –

'civil proceedings order' means an order that –

(a) no civil proceedings shall without the leave of the High Court be instituted in any court by the person against whom the order is made;

(b) any civil proceedings instituted by him in any court before the making of the order shall not be continued by him without the leave of the High Court; and

(c) no application (other than one for leave under this section) shall be made by him, in any civil proceedings instituted in any court by any person, without the leave of the High Court;

'criminal proceedings order' means an order that –

(a) no information shall be laid before a justice of the peace by the person against whom the order is made without the leave of the High Court; and

(b) no application for leave to prefer a bill of indictment shall be made by him without the leave of the High Court; and

'all proceedings order' means an order which has the combined effect of the two other orders.

(2) An order under subsection (1) may provide that it is to cease to have effect at the end of a specified period, but shall otherwise remain in force indefinitely.

(3) Leave for the institution or continuance of, or for the making of an application in, any civil proceedings by a person who is the subject of an order for the time being in force under subsection (1) shall not be given unless the High Court is satisfied that the proceedings or application are not an abuse of the process of the court in question and that there are reasonable grounds for the proceedings or application.

(3A) Leave for the laying of an information or for an application for leave to prefer a bill of indictment by a person who is the subject of an order for the time being in force under subsection (1) shall not be given unless the High Court is satisfied that the institution of the prosecution is not an abuse of the criminal process and that there are reasonable grounds for the institution of the prosecution by the applicant.

(4) No appeal shall lie from a decision of the High Court refusing leave required by virtue of this section.

(5) A copy of any order made under subsection (1) shall be published in the London Gazette.

Amendments—Prosecution of Offences Act 1985, s 24.

43 Power of High Court to vary sentence on application for quashing order

(1) Where a person who has been sentenced for an offence –

(a) by a magistrates' court; or
(b) by the Crown Court after being convicted of the offence by a magistrates' court and committed to the Crown Court for sentence; or
(c) by the Crown Court on appeal against conviction or sentence,

applies to the High Court in accordance with section 31 for a quashing order to remove the proceedings of the magistrates' court or the Crown Court into the High Court, then, if the High Court determines that the magistrates' court or the Crown Court had no power to pass the sentence, the High Court may, instead of quashing the conviction, amend it by substituting for the sentence passed any sentence which the magistrates' court or, in a case within paragraph (b), the Crown Court had power to impose.

(2) Any sentence passed by the High Court by virtue of this section in substitution for the sentence passed in the proceedings of the magistrates' court

or the Crown Court shall, unless the High Court otherwise directs, begin to run from the time when it would have begun to run if passed in those proceedings; but in computing the term of the sentence, any time during which the offender was released on bail in pursuance of section 37(1)(d) of the Criminal Justice Act 1948 shall be disregarded.

(3) Subsections (1) and (2) shall, with the necessary modifications, apply in relation to any order of a magistrates' court or the Crown Court which is made on, but does not form part of, the conviction of an offender as they apply in relation to a conviction and sentence.

Amendments—SI 2004/1033.

43ZA Power of the High Court to vary committal in default

(1) Where the High Court quashes the committal of a person to prison or detention by a magistrates' court or the Crown Court for –

(a) a default in paying a sum adjudged to be paid by a conviction; or
(b) want of sufficient distress to satisfy such a sum,

the High Court may deal with the person for the default or want of sufficient distress in any way in which the magistrates' court or Crown Court would have power to deal with him if it were dealing with him at the time when the committal is quashed.

(2) If the High Court commits him to prison or detention, the period of imprisonment or detention shall, unless the High Court otherwise directs, be treated as having begun when the person was committed by the magistrates' court or the Crown Court (except that any time during which he was released on bail shall not be counted as part of that period).

Amendments—Inserted by Access to Justice Act 1999, s 62.

43A Specific powers of arbitrator exercisable by High Court

In any cause or matter proceeding in the High Court in connection with any contract incorporating an arbitration agreement which confers specific powers upon the arbitrator, the High Court may, if all parties to the agreement agree, exercise any such powers.

Amendments—Courts and Legal Services Act 1990, s 100.

Other provisions

44 Extraordinary functions of judges of High Court

(1) Subject to the provisions of this Act, every judge of the High Court shall be –

(a) liable to perform any duty not incident to the administration of justice in any court of law which a judge of the High Court was, as the successor of any judge formerly subject to that duty, liable to perform immediately before the commencement of this Act by virtue of any statute, law or custom; and
(b) empowered to exercise any authority or power not so incident which a judge of the High Court was, as the successor of any judge formerly possessing that authority or power, empowered to exercise immediately before that commencement by virtue of any statute, law or custom.

(2) Any such duty, authority or power which immediately before the commencement of this Act was imposed or conferred by any statute, law or custom on the Lord Chancellor, the Lord Chief Justice or the Master of the Rolls shall continue to be performed and exercised by them respectively.

****

GENERAL PROVISIONS

Law and equity

49 Concurrent administration of law and equity

(1) Subject to the provisions of this or any other Act, every court exercising jurisdiction in England or Wales in any civil cause or matter shall continue to administer law and equity on the basis that, wherever there is any conflict or variance between the rules of equity and the rules of the common law with reference to the same matter, the rules of equity shall prevail.

(2) Every such court shall give the same effect as hitherto –

- (a) to all equitable estates, titles, rights, reliefs, defences and counterclaims, and to all equitable duties and liabilities; and
- (b) subject thereto, to all legal claims and demands and all estates, titles, rights, duties, obligations and liabilities existing by the common law or by any custom or created by any statute,

and, subject to the provisions of this or any other Act, shall so exercise its jurisdiction in every cause or matter before it as to secure that, as far as possible, all matters in dispute between the parties are completely and finally determined, and all multiplicity of legal proceedings with respect to any of those matters is avoided.

(3) Nothing in this Act shall affect the power of the Court of Appeal or the High Court to stay any proceedings before it, where it thinks fit to do so, either of its own motion or on the application of any person, whether or not a party to the proceedings.

50 Power to award damages as well as, or in substitution for, injunction or specific performance

Where the Court of Appeal or the High Court has jurisdiction to entertain an application for an injunction or specific performance, it may award damages in addition to, or in substitution for, an injunction or specific performance.

Costs

51 Costs in civil division of Court of Appeal, High Court and county courts

(1) Subject to the provisions of this or any other enactment and to rules of court, the costs of and incidental to all proceedings in –

- (a) the civil division of the Court of Appeal;
- (b) the High Court; and
- (c) any county court,

shall be in the discretion of the court.

(2) Without prejudice to any general power to make rules of court, such rules may make provision for regulating matters relating to the costs of those proceedings including, in particular, prescribing scales of costs to be paid to legal or other representatives.

(3) The court shall have full power to determine by whom and to what extent the costs are to be paid.

(4) In subsections (1) and (2) 'proceedings' includes the administration of estates and trusts.

(5) Nothing in subsection (1) shall alter the practice in any criminal cause, or in bankruptcy.

(6) In any proceedings mentioned in subsection (1), the court may disallow, or (as the case may be) order the legal or other representative concerned to meet, the whole of any wasted costs or such part of them as may be determined in accordance with rules of court.

(7) In subsection (6), 'wasted costs' means any costs incurred by a party –

(a) as a result of any improper, unreasonable or negligent act or omission on the part of any legal or other representative or any employee of such a representative; or

(b) which, in the light of any such act or omission occurring after they were incurred, the court considers it is unreasonable to expect that party to pay.

(8) Where –

(a) a person has commenced proceedings in the High Court; but

(b) those proceedings should, in the opinion of the court, have been commenced in a county court in accordance with any provision made under section 1 of the Courts and Legal Services Act 1990 or by or under any other enactment,

the person responsible for determining the amount which is to be awarded to that person by way of costs shall have regard to those circumstances.

(9) Where, in complying with subsection (8), the responsible person reduces the amount which would otherwise be awarded to the person in question –

(a) the amount of that reduction shall not exceed 25 per cent; and

(b) on any taxation of the costs payable by that person to his legal representative, regard shall be had to the amount of the reduction.

(10) The Lord Chancellor may by order amend subsection (9)(a) by substituting, for the percentage for the time being mentioned there, a different percentage.

(11) Any such order shall be made by statutory instrument and may make such transitional or incidental provision as the Lord Chancellor considers expedient.

(12) No such statutory instrument shall be made unless a draft of the instrument has been approved by both Houses of Parliament.

(13) In this section 'legal or other representative', in relation to a party to proceedings, means any person exercising a right of audience or right to conduct litigation on his behalf.

Amendments—Substituted by CLSA 1990, s 4.

****

PART III
PRACTICE AND PROCEDURE

THE COURT OF APPEAL

Distribution of business

53 Distribution of business between civil and criminal divisions

(1) Rules of court may provide for the distribution of business in the Court of Appeal between the civil and criminal divisions, but subject to any such rules business shall be distributed in accordance with the following provisions of this section.

(2) The criminal division of the Court of Appeal shall exercise –

(a) all jurisdiction of the Court of Appeal under Parts I and II of the Criminal Appeal Act 1968;

(b) the jurisdiction of the Court of Appeal under section 13 of the Administration of Justice Act 1960 (appeals in cases of contempt of court) in relation to appeals from orders and decisions of the Crown Court;

(c) all other jurisdiction expressly conferred on that division by this or any other Act; and

(d) the jurisdiction to order the issue of writs of venire de novo.

(3) The civil division of the Court of Appeal shall exercise the whole of the jurisdiction of that court not exercisable by the criminal division.

(4) Where any class of proceedings in the Court of Appeal is by any statutory provision assigned to the criminal division of that court, rules of court may provide for any enactment relating to –

(a) appeals to the Court of Appeal under Part I of the Criminal Appeal Act 1968; or

(b) any matter connected with or arising out of such appeals,

to apply in relation to proceedings of that class or, as the case may be, to any corresponding matter connected with or arising out of such proceedings, as it applies in relation to such appeals or, as the case may be, to the relevant matter within paragraph (b), with or without prescribed modifications in either case.

Composition of court

54 Court of civil division

(1) This section relates to the civil division of the Court of Appeal; and in this section 'court', except where the context otherwise requires, means a court of that division.

(2) Subject as follows, a court shall be duly constituted for the purpose of exercising any of its jurisdiction if it consists of one or more judges.

(3) The Master of the Rolls may, with the concurrence of the Lord Chancellor, give (or vary or revoke) directions about the minimum number of judges of which a court must consist if it is to be duly constituted for the purpose of any description of proceedings.

(4) The Master of the Rolls, or any Lord Justice of Appeal designated by him, may (subject to any directions under subsection (3)) determine the number of judges of which a court is to consist for the purpose of any particular proceedings.

(4A) The Master of the Rolls may give directions as to what is to happen in any particular case where one or more members of a court which has partly heard proceedings are unable to continue.

(5) Where –

- (a) an appeal has been heard by a court consisting of an even number of judges; and
- (b) the members of the court are equally divided, the case shall, on the application of any party to the appeal, be re-argued before and determined by an uneven number of judges not less than three, before any appeal to the House of Lords.

(6), (7) (*repealed*)

(8) Subsections (1) and (2) of section 70 (assessors in the High Court) shall apply in relation to causes and matters before the civil division of the Court of Appeal as they apply in relation to causes and matters before the High Court.

(9) Subsections (3) and (4) of section 70 (scientific advisers to assist the Patents Court in proceedings under the Patents Act 1949 and the Patents Act 1977) shall apply in relation to the civil division of the Court of Appeal and proceedings on appeal from any decision of the Patents Court in proceedings under those Acts as they apply in relation to the Patents Court and proceedings under those Acts.

(10) (*repealed*)

Amendments—CLSA 1990, s 7(4); Access to Justice Act 1999, ss 59, 106, Sch 15.

****

56 Judges not to sit on appeal from their own judgments, etc

(1) No judge shall sit as a member of the civil division of the Court of Appeal on the hearing of, or shall determine any application in proceedings incidental or preliminary to, an appeal from a judgment or order made in any case by himself or by any court of which he was a member.

(2) No judge shall sit as a member of the criminal division of the Court of Appeal on the hearing of, or shall determine any application in proceedings incidental or preliminary to, an appeal against –

- (a) a conviction before himself or a court of which he was a member; or
- (b) a sentence passed by himself or such a court.

56A

(repealed)

Amendments—Inserted by CJPOA 1994, s 52(8); repealed by Courts Act 2003, ss 67, 109(3), Sch 10.

56B Allocation of cases in criminal division

(1) The appeals or classes of appeals suitable for allocation to a court of the criminal division of the Court of Appeal in which a Circuit judge is acting under section 9 shall be determined in accordance with directions given by or on behalf of the Lord Chief Justice with the concurrence of the Lord Chancellor.

(2) In subsection (1) 'appeal' includes the hearing of, or any application in proceedings incidental or preliminary to, an appeal.

Amendments—CJPOA 1994, s 52(6), (9).

Sittings and vacations

57 Sittings and vacations

(1) Sittings of the Court of Appeal may be held, and any other business of the Court of Appeal may be conducted, at any place in England or Wales.

(2) Subject to rules of court –

- (a) the places at which the Court of Appeal sits outside the Royal Courts of Justice; and
- (b) the days and times at which the Court of Appeal sits at any place outside the Royal Courts of Justice, shall be determined in accordance with directions given by the Lord Chancellor.

(3) Rules of court may make provision for regulating the vacations to be observed by the Court of Appeal and in the offices of that court.

(4) Rules of court –

- (a) may provide for securing such sittings of the civil division of the Court of Appeal during vacation as the Master of the Rolls may with the concurrence of the Lord Chancellor determine;
- (b) without prejudice to paragraph (a), shall provide for the transaction during vacation by judges of the Court of Appeal of all such business in the civil division of that court as may require to be immediately or promptly transacted; and
- (c) shall provide for securing sittings of the criminal division of that court during vacation if necessary.

Other provisions

58 Calling into question of incidental decisions in civil division

(1) Rules of court may provide that decisions of the Court of Appeal which –

- (a) are taken by a single judge or any officer or member of staff of that court in proceedings incidental to any cause or matter pending before the civil division of that court; and
- (b) do not involve the determination of an appeal or of an application for permission to appeal,

may be called into question in such manner as may be prescribed.

(2) No appeal shall lie to the House of Lords from a decision which may be called into question pursuant to rules under subsection (1).

Amendments—Substituted by Access to Justice Act 1999, s 60.

****

60 Rules of court, and decisions of Court of Appeal, as to whether judgment or order is final or interlocutory

(1) Rules of court may provide- for orders or judgments of any prescribed description to be treated for any prescribed purpose connected with appeals to the Court of Appeal as final or as interlocutory.

(2) No appeal shall lie from a decision of the Court of Appeal as to whether a judgment or order is, for any purpose connected with an appeal to that court, final or interlocutory.

THE HIGH COURT

Distribution of business

61 Distribution of business among Divisions

(1) Subject to any provision made by or under this or any other Act (and in particular to any rules of court made in pursuance of subsection (2) and any order under subsection (3)), business in the High Court of any description mentioned in Schedule 1, as for the time being in force, shall be distributed among the Divisions in accordance with that Schedule.

(2) Rules of court may provide for the distribution of business in the High Court among the Divisions; but any rules made in pursuance of this subsection shall have effect subject to any orders for the time being in force under subsection (3).

(3) Subject to subsection (5), the Lord Chancellor may by order –

- (a) direct that any business in the High Court which is not for the time being assigned by or under this or any other Act to any Division be assigned to such Division as may be specified in the order;
- (b) if at any time it appears to him desirable to do so with a view to the more convenient administration of justice, direct that any business for the time being assigned by or under this or any other Act to any Division be assigned to such other Division as may be specified in the order; and
- (c) amend Schedule 1 so far as may be necessary in consequence of provision made by order under paragraph (a) or (b).

(4) The powers conferred by subsection (2) and subsection (3) include power to assign business of any description to two or more Divisions concurrently.

(5) No order under subsection (3)(b) relating to any business shall be made without the concurrence of the senior judge of –

- (a) the Division or each of the Divisions to which the business is for the time being assigned; and
- (b) the Division or each of the Divisions to which the business is to be assigned by the order.

(6) Subject to rules of court, the fact that a cause or matter commenced in the High Court falls within a class of business assigned by or under this Act to a particular Division does not make it obligatory for it to be allocated or transferred to that Division.

(7) Without prejudice to subsections (1) to (5) and section 63, rules of court may provide for the distribution of the business (other than business required to be heard by a divisional court) in any Division of the High Court among the judges of that Division.

(8) Any order under subsection (3) shall be made by statutory instrument, which shall be laid before Parliament after being made.

62 Business of Patents, Admiralty and Commercial Courts

(1) The Patents Court shall take such proceedings relating to patents as are within the jurisdiction conferred on it by the Patents Act 1977, and such other proceedings relating to patents or other matters as may be prescribed.

(2) The Admiralty Court shall take Admiralty business, that is to say causes and matters assigned to the Queen's Bench Division and involving the exercise of the High Court's Admiralty jurisdiction or its jurisdiction as a prize court.

(3) The Commercial Court shall take such causes and matters as may in accordance with rules of court be entered in the commercial list.

63 Business assigned to specially nominated judges

(1) Any business assigned, in accordance with this or any other Act or rules of court, to one or more specially nominated judges of the High Court may –

- (a) during vacation; or
- (b) during the illness or absence of that judge or any of those judges; or
- (c) for any other reasonable cause,

be dealt with by any judge of the High Court named for that purpose by the Lord Chancellor.

(2) If at any time it appears to the Lord Chancellor desirable to do so with a view to the more convenient administration of justice, he may by order direct that business of any description which is for the time being assigned, in accordance with this or any other Act or rules of court, to one or more specially nominated judges of the High Court shall cease to be so assigned and may be dealt with by any one or more judges of the High Court.

(3) An order under subsection (2) shall not be made in respect of any business without the concurrence of the senior judge of the Division to which the business is for the time being assigned.

64 Choice of Division by plaintiff

(1) Without prejudice to the power of transfer under section 65, the person by whom any cause or matter is commenced in the High Court shall in the prescribed manner allocate it to whichever Division he thinks fit.

(2) Where a cause or matter is commenced in the High Court, all subsequent interlocutory or other steps or proceedings in the High Court in that cause or matter shall be taken in the Division to which the cause or matter is for the time being allocated (whether under subsection (1) or in consequence of its transfer under section 65).

65 Power of transfer

(1) Any cause or matter may at any time and at any stage thereof, and either with or without application from any of the parties, be transferred, by such authority and in such manner as rules of court may direct, from one Division or judge of the High Court to another Division or judge thereof.

(2) The transfer of a cause or matter under subsection (1) to a different Division or judge of the High Court shall not affect the validity of any steps or proceedings taken or order made in that cause or matter before the transfer.

Divisional courts

66 Divisional courts of High Court

(1) Divisional courts may be held for the transaction of any business in the High Court which is, by or by virtue of rules of court or any other statutory provision, required to be heard by a divisional court.

(2) Any number of divisional courts may sit at the same time.

(3) A divisional court shall be constituted of not less than two judges.

(4) Every judge of the High Court shall be qualified to sit in any divisional court.

(5) The judge who is, according to the order of precedence under this Act, the senior of the judges constituting a divisional court shall be the president of the court.

Mode of conducting business

67 Proceedings in court and in chambers

Business in the High Court shall be heard and disposed of in court except in so far as it may, under this or any other Act, under rules of court or in accordance with the practice of the court, be dealt with in chambers.

68 Exercise of High Court jurisdiction otherwise than by judges of that court

(1) Provision may be made by rules of court as to the cases in which jurisdiction of the High Court may be exercised by –

- (a) such Circuit judges, deputy Circuit judges or Recorders as the Lord Chancellor may from time to time nominate to deal with official referees' business; or
- (b) special referees; (*repealed*)
- (c) (*repealed*)

(2) Without prejudice to the generality of subsection (1), rules of court may in particular –

- (a) (*repealed*)
- (b) authorise any question arising in any cause or matter to be referred to a special referee for inquiry and report.

(3) Rules of court shall not authorise the exercise of powers of attachment and committal by a special referee or any officer or other staff of the court.

(4) Subject to subsection (5), the decision of –

(a) any such person as is mentioned in subsection (1); or
(b) any officer or other staff of the court

may be called in question in such manner as may be prescribed by rules of court, whether by appeal to the Court of Appeal, or by an appeal or application to a divisional court or a judge in court or a judge in chambers, or by an adjournment to a judge in court or a judge in chambers.

(5) Rules of court may provide either generally or to a limited extent for decisions of persons nominated under subsection (1)(a) being called in question only by appeal on a question of law.

(6) The cases in which jurisdiction of the High Court may be exercised by persons nominated under subsection (1)(a) shall be known as 'official referees' business'; and, subject to rules of court, the distribution of official referees' business among persons so nominated shall be determined in accordance with directions given by the Lord Chancellor.

(7) Any reference to an official referee in any enactment, whenever passed, or in rules of court or any other instrument or document, whenever made, shall, unless the context otherwise requires, be construed as, or (where the context requires) as including, a reference to a person nominated under subsection (1)(a).

Amendments—AJA 1982, s 59(1), (2); CPA 1997, s 10, Sch 2, para 1(1), (3)(a), (b), (c), (d)

69 Trial by jury

(1) Where, on the application of any party to an action to be tried in the Queen's Bench Division, the court is satisfied that there is in issue –

(a) a charge of fraud against that party; or
(b) a claim in respect of libel, slander, malicious prosecution or false imprisonment; or
(c) any question or issue of a kind prescribed for the purposes of this paragraph,

the action shall be tried with a jury, unless the court is of opinion that the trial requires any prolonged examination of documents or accounts or any scientific or local investigation which cannot conveniently be made with a jury.

(2) An application under subsection (1) must be made not later than such time before the trial as may be prescribed.

(3) An action to be tried in the Queen's Bench Division which does not by virtue of subsection (1) fall to be tried with a jury shall be tried without a jury unless the court in its discretion orders it to be tried with a jury.

(4) Nothing in subsections (1) to (3) shall affect the power of the court to order, in accordance with rules of court, that different questions of fact arising in any action be tried by different modes of trial; and where any such order is made, subsection (1) shall have effect only as respects questions relating to any such charge, claim, question or issue as is mentioned in that subsection.

(5) Where for the purpose of disposing of any action or other matter which is being tried in the High Court by a judge with a jury it is necessary to ascertain the law of any other country which is applicable to the facts of the case, any question as to the effect of the evidence given with respect to that law shall, instead of being submitted to the jury, be decided by the judge alone.

70 Assessors and scientific advisers

(1) In any cause or matter before the High Court the court may, if it thinks it expedient to do so, call in the aid of one or more assessors specially qualified, and hear and dispose of the cause or matter wholly or partially with their assistance.

(2) The remuneration, if any, to be paid to an assessor for his services under subsection (1) in connection with any proceedings shall be determined by the court, and shall form part of the costs of the proceedings.

(3) Rules of court shall make provision for the appointment of scientific advisers to assist the Patents Court in proceedings under the Patents Act 1949 and the Patents Act 1977 and for regulating the functions of such advisers.

(4) The remuneration of any such adviser shall be determined by the Lord Chancellor with the concurrence of the Minister for the Civil Service and shall be defrayed out of money provided by Parliament.

Sittings and vacations

71 Sittings and vacations

(1) Sittings of the High Court may be held, and any other business of the High Court may be conducted, at any place in England or Wales.

(2) Subject to rules of court –

- (a) the places at which the High Court sits outside the Royal Courts of Justice; and
- (b) the days and times when the High Court sits at any place outside the Royal Courts of Justice,

shall be determined in accordance with directions given by the Lord Chancellor.

(3) Rules of court may make provision for regulating the vacations to be observed by the High Court and in the offices of that court.

(4) Rules of court –

- (a) may provide for securing such sittings of any Division of the High Court during vacation as the senior judge of that Division may with the concurrence of the Lord Chancellor determine; and
- (b) without prejudice to paragraph (a), shall provide for the transaction during vacation by judges of the High Court of all such business in the High Court as may require to be immediately or promptly transacted.

(5) Different provision may be made in pursuance of subsection (3) for different parts of the country.

Other provisions

72 Withdrawal of privilege against incrimination of self or spouse in certain proceedings

(1) In any proceedings to which this subsection applies a person shall not be excused, by reason that to do so would tend to expose that person, or his or her spouse, to proceedings for a related offence or for the recovery of a related penalty –

- (a) from answering any questions put to that person in the first-mentioned proceedings; or

(b) from complying with any order made in those proceedings.

(2) Subsection (1) applies to the following civil proceedings in the High Court, namely –

(a) proceedings for infringement of rights pertaining to any intellectual property or for passing off;
(b) proceedings brought to obtain disclosure of information relating to any infringement of such rights or to any passing off; and
(c) proceedings brought to prevent any apprehended infringement of such rights or any apprehended passing off.

(3) Subject to subsection (4), no statement or admission made by a person –

(a) in answering a question put to him in any proceedings to which subsection (1) applies; or
(b) in complying with any order made in any such proceedings,

shall, in proceedings for any related offence or for the recovery of any related penalty, be admissible in evidence against that person or (unless they married after the making of the statement or admission) against the spouse of that person.

(4) Nothing in subsection (3) shall render any statement or admission made by a person as there mentioned inadmissible in evidence against that person in proceedings for perjury or contempt of court.

(5) In this section –

'intellectual property' means any patent, trade mark, copyright, design right, registered design, technical or commercial information or other intellectual property;

'related offence', in relation to any proceedings to which subsection (1) applies, means –

(a) in the case of proceedings within subsection (2)(a) or (b) –

(i) any offence committed by or in the course of the infringement or passing off to which those proceedings relate; or

(ii) any offence not within sub-paragraph (i) committed in connection with that infringement or passing off, being an offence involving fraud or dishonesty;

(b) in the case of proceedings within subsection (2)(c), any offence revealed by the facts on which the plaintiff relies in those proceedings;

'related penalty', in relation to any proceedings to which subsection (1) applies means –

(a) in the case of proceedings within subsection (2)(a) or (b), any penalty incurred in respect of anything done or omitted in connection with the infringement or passing off to which those proceedings relate;

(b) in the case of proceedings within subsection (2)(c), any penalty incurred in respect of any act or omission revealed by the facts on which the plaintiff relies in those proceedings.

(6) Any reference in this section to civil proceedings in the High Court of any description includes a reference to proceedings on appeal arising out of civil proceedings in the High Court of that description.

Amendments—Patents, Designs and Marks Act 1986, s 2(3), Sch 2, para 1(2)(h); Copyright, Designs and Patents Act 1988, s 303(1), Sch 7, para 28(2).

****

84 Power to make rules of court

(1) Rules of court may be made for the purpose of regulating and prescribing, except in relation to any criminal cause or matter, the practice and procedure to be followed in the Crown Court.

(2) Without prejudice to the generality of subsection (1), the matters about which rules of court may be made under this section include all matters of practice and procedure in the Supreme Court which were regulated or prescribed by rules of court immediately before the commencement of this Act.

(3) No provision of this or any other Act, or contained in any instrument made under any Act, which –

- (a) authorises or requires the making of rules of court about any particular matter or for any particular purpose; or
- (b) provides (in whatever words) that the power to make rules of court under this section is to include power to make rules about any particular matter or for any particular purpose,

shall be taken as derogating from the generality of subsection (1).

(4) *(repealed)*

(5) Special rules may apply –

- (a) any rules made under this section,
- (b) Civil Procedure Rules,
- (c) Criminal Procedure Rules, or
- (d) Family Procedure Rules,

to proceedings to which the special rules apply.

(5A) Rules made under this section may apply –

- (a) any special rules,
- (b) Civil Procedure Rules,
- (c) Criminal Procedure Rules, or
- (d) Family Procedure Rules,

to proceedings to which rules made under this section apply.

(6) Where rules may be applied under subsection (5) or (5A), they may be applied –

- (a) to any extent,
- (b) with or without modification, and
- (c) as amended from time to time.

(7) No rule which may involve an increase of expenditure out of public funds may be made under this section except with the concurrence of the Treasury, but the validity of any rule made under this section shall not be called in question in any proceedings in any court either by the court or by any party to the

proceedings on the ground only that it was a rule as to the making of which the concurrence of the Treasury was necessary and that the Treasury did not concur or are not expressed to have concurred.

(8) Rules of court under this section shall be made by statutory instrument subject to annulment in pursuance of a resolution of either House of Parliament; and the Statutory Instruments Act 1946 shall apply to a statutory instrument containing such rules in like manner as if the rules had been made by a Minister of the Crown.

(9) In this section 'special rules' means rules applying to proceedings of any particular kind in the Supreme Court, being rules made by an authority other than the Civil Procedure Rule Committee, the Family Procedure Rule Committee, the Criminal Procedure Rule Committee, or the Crown Court Rule Committee under any provision of this or any other Act which (in whatever words) confers on that authority power to make rules in relation to proceedings of that kind in the Supreme Court.

Amendments—CPA 1997, s 10, Sch 2, para 1(4)(a), (b), (c), (d); SI 2004/2035.

****

87 Particular matters for which rules of court may provide

(1), (2) (*repealed*)

(3) Rules of court made under section 84 may amend or repeal any statutory provision relating to the practice and procedure of the Crown Court (except so far as relating to criminal causes or matters) so far as may be necessary in consequence of provision made by the rules.

(4) Criminal Procedure Rules may require courts from which an appeal lies to the criminal division of the Court of Appeal to furnish that division with any assistance or information which it may request for the purpose of exercising its jurisdiction.

(5) Rules of court made under section 84 may amend or repeal any statutory provision about appeals to the Crown Court so far as it relates to the practice and procedure with respect to such appeals (except so far as relating to criminal causes or matters).

Amendments—CPA 1997, s 10, Sch 2, para 1(1), (6)(a), (b); SI 2004/2035.

PART IV
OFFICERS AND OFFICES

Appointment of certain officers of Supreme Court

88 Qualification for office

A person shall not be qualified for appointment to any office in the Supreme Court listed in column 1 of any Part of Schedule 2 unless he is a person of any description specified in relation to that office in column 2 of that Part.

89 Masters and registrars

(1) The power to make appointments to the offices in the Supreme Court listed in column 1 of Parts II and III of Schedule 2 shall be exercisable by the Lord Chancellor, with the concurrence of the Minister for the Civil Service as to numbers and salaries.

(2) The person appointed to the office of Queen's coroner and attorney and master of the Crown Office and Registrar of Criminal Appeals shall, by virtue of his appointment, be a Master of the Queen's Bench Division.

(3) The Lord Chancellor shall appoint –

- (a) one of the masters of the Queen's Bench Division as Senior Master of that Division;
- (b) one of the masters of the Chancery Division as Chief Chancery Master;
- (c) one of the taxing masters of the Supreme Court as Chief Taxing Master;
- (d) one of the registrars in bankruptcy of the High Court as Chief Bankruptcy Registrar;
- (e) one of the district judges of the Principal Registry of the Family Division as Senior District Judge of that Division; and
- (f) (*repealed*)

with, in each case, such additional salary in respect of that appointment as the Lord Chancellor may, with the concurrence of the Minister for the Civil Service, determine.

(4) The person appointed Senior Master under subsection (3)(a) shall hold and perform the duties of the offices of the Queen's Remembrancer and registrar of judgments.

(5)–(7) (*repealed*)

(8) Salaries payable under or by virtue of this section shall be paid out of money provided by Parliament.

Amendments—SI 1982/1188; Statute Law (Repeals) Act 1989, Sch 1; CLSA 1990, s 125(3), Sch 18, paras 37, 38.

90 Official Solicitor

(1) There shall continue to be an Official Solicitor to the Supreme Court, who shall be appointed by the Lord Chancellor.

(2) There shall be paid to the Official Solicitor out of money provided by Parliament such salary as the Lord Chancellor may, with the concurrence of the Minister for the Civil Service, determine.

(3) The Official Solicitor shall have such powers and perform such duties as may for the time being be conferred or imposed on the holder of that office –

- (a) by or under this or any other Act; or
- (b) by or in accordance with any direction given (before or after the commencement of this Act) by the Lord Chancellor.

(3A) The holder for the time being of the office of Official Solicitor shall have the right to conduct litigation in relation to any proceedings.

(3B) When acting as Official Solicitor a person who would otherwise have the right to conduct litigation by virtue of section 28(2)(a) of the Courts and Legal Services Act 1990 shall be treated as having acquired that right solely by virtue of subsection (3A).

(4) If –

(a) the Official Solicitor is not available because of his absence or for some other reason; or

(b) his office is vacant,

then, during such unavailability or vacancy, any powers or duties of the Official Solicitor shall be exercisable or fall to be performed by any person for the time being appointed by the Lord Chancellor as deputy to the Official Solicitor (and any property vested in the Official Solicitor may accordingly be dealt with by any such person in all respects as if it were vested in him instead).

Amendments—CLSA 1990, ss 74(1), 125(3), Sch 18, para 39.

91 Deputies and temporary appointments

(1) If it appears to the Lord Chancellor that it is expedient to do so in order to facilitate the disposal of business in the Supreme Court, he may appoint a person –

(a) to act as a deputy for any person holding an office listed in column 1 of Part II or III of Schedule 2; or

(b) to act as a temporary additional officer in any such office,

during such period or on such occasions as the Lord Chancellor thinks fit.

(2) Subject to subsection (3), a person shall not be qualified for appointment under this section if the office in which he would act by virtue of the appointment is one to which he is not qualified for permanent appointment.

(3) A person may be appointed under this section if he would, but for his age, be qualified for permanent appointment to the office in question and he has previously held a permanent appointment to that office or –

(a) where the office in question is listed in column 1 of Part II of Schedule 2, to any other office so listed; or –

(b) where the office in question is listed in column 1 of Part III of that Schedule, to any other office listed in column 1 of either Part II or Part III; or

(c) (whatever the office in question) to the office of county court registrar

but no appointment by virtue of this subsection shall be such as to extend beyond the day on which the person in question attains the age of seventy-five years.

(4) Every person, while acting under this section, shall have all the jurisdiction of a person permanently appointed to the office in which he is acting.

(5) (*repealed*)

(6) The Lord Chancellor may, out of money provided by Parliament, pay to any person appointed under this section such remuneration and allowances as he may, with the concurrence of the Minister for the Civil Service, determine.

Amendments—JPRA 1993, ss 26, 31, Sch 6, para 15, Sch 9.

92 Tenure of office

(1) Subject to the following provisions of this section and to subsections (4) to (6) of section 26 of the Judicial Pensions and Retirement Act 1993 (Lord Chancellor's power to authorise continuance in office up to the age of 75), a person who holds an office to which this subsection applies shall vacate it on the day on which he attains the age of seventy years.

(2) Subsection (1) applies to the offices listed in column 1 of Part II of Schedule 2 …

(2A) Subject to the following provisions of this section, a person who holds an office to which this subsection applies shall vacate it at the end of the completed year of service in the course of which he attains the age of sixty-two years.

(2B) Subsection (2A) applies to the offices listed in column 1 of Part I of Schedule 2 …

(2C)–(2E) (*repealed*)

(3) (*repealed*)

(3A) Where the Lord Chancellor considers it desirable in the public interest to retain in office a person who holds an office to which subsection (2A) applies after the time when he would otherwise retire in accordance with that subsection, the Lord Chancellor may from time to time authorise the continuance in office of that person until such date, not being later than the date on which he attains the age of sixty-five years, as he thinks fit.

(4) A person appointed to an office listed in column 1 of Part 1 or 2 of Schedule 2 shall hold that office during good behaviour.

(5) The power to remove such a person from his office on account of misbehaviour shall be exercisable by the Lord Chancellor.

(6) The Lord Chancellor may also remove such a person from his office on account of inability to perform the duties of his office.

(7) A person appointed to an office listed in column 1 of Part III of Schedule 2 shall hold that office during Her Majesty's pleasure.

Amendments—CLSA 1990, s 77; JPRA 1993, ss 26, 31, Sch 6, para 14, Sch 9; Courts Act 2003, ss 89(1)(a)–(c), 109(3), Sch 10.

93 Status of officers for purposes of salary and pension

(1) Subject to subsection (2), any person who holds an office listed in column 1 of any Part of Schedule 2 or the office of Accountant General of the Supreme Court and is not employed in the civil service of the State shall be deemed to be so employed for the purposes of salary and pension.

(2) Subsection (1), so far as it relates to pension, shall not apply to a person holding qualifying judicial office, within the meaning of the Judicial Pensions and Retirement Act 1993.

Amendments—Public Trustee and Administration of Funds Act 1986, s 1, Sch; JPRA 1993, s 31(3), Sch 8, para 15(2).

****

95 Property held by officers

Any property held in his official capacity by a person holding an office listed in column 1 of Part II of Schedule 2 or by the Official Solicitor shall, on his dying or ceasing to hold office, vest in the person appointed to succeed him without any conveyance, assignment or transfer.

Central Office and Accountant General

96 Central Office

(1) The Central Office of the Supreme Court shall perform such business as the Lord Chancellor may direct.

(2) Subject to any direction of the Lord Chancellor under this section, the Central Office shall perform such business as it performed immediately before the commencement of this Act.

97 Accountant General of the Supreme Court

(1) There shall continue to be an Accountant General of, and an accounting department for, the Supreme Court.

(2) The Lord Chancellor shall appoint such person as he thinks fit to the office in the Supreme Court of Accountant General of the Supreme Court, and the person so appointed shall hold and vacate office in accordance with the terms of his appointment.

(3) The Accountant General shall be paid such salary or fees as the Lord Chancellor determines with the consent of the Treasury.

(4) If one person holds office both as the Accountant General and as the Public Trustee then, if he ceases to be the Public Trustee, he shall also cease to be the Accountant General unless the Lord Chancellor otherwise directs.

(5) If a vacancy occurs in the office of Accountant General or the person appointed to hold the office is for any reason unable to act for any period such person as the Lord Chancellor appoints as deputy in that office shall, during the vacancy or that period, perform the functions of that office (and any property vested in the Accountant General may accordingly be dealt with by the deputy in all respects as if it were vested in him instead).

Amendments—Public Trustee and Administration of Funds Act 1986, s 1(3), Sch, para 3.

Judges' clerks and secretaries

98 Judges' clerks and secretaries

(1) A clerk and a secretary shall be attached to each of the following judges of the Supreme Court, namely the Lord Chief Justice, the Master of the Rolls, the President of the Queen's Bench Division, the President of the Family Division and the Chancellor of the High Court.

(2) A clerk shall be attached to each of the following judges of the Supreme Court, namely the Lords Justices of Appeal and the puisne judges of the High Court.

(3) Any clerk or secretary attached as mentioned in subsection (1) or (2) –

(a) shall be appointed by the Lord Chancellor; and

(b) if not already employed in the civil service of the State shall be deemed for all purposes to be so employed.

(4) If at any time it appears to any of the judges mentioned in subsection (1) desirable that there should be attached to him a legal secretary (that is to say a secretary with legal qualifications) in addition to the secretary provided for by that subsection, he may, with the concurrence of the Lord Chancellor, appoint a person who has a general qualification (within the meaning of s 71 of the Courts and Legal Services Act 1990) as his legal secretary.

(5) An appointment under subsection (4) may be on either a full-time or a part-time basis; and a person appointed by a judge as his legal secretary shall, except as regards remuneration, hold and vacate that office in accordance with such terms as the judge may, with the concurrence of the Lord Chancellor, determine when making the appointment.

(6) A person appointed under subsection (4) –

(a) shall not be treated as employed in the civil service of the State by reason only of that appointment; and

(b) if the Lord Chancellor so determines in his case, shall be paid out of money provided by Parliament such remuneration as the Lord Chancellor may, with the concurrence of the Minister for the Civil Service, determine.

Amendments—CLSA 1990, s 71(2), Sch 10, para 47; Constitutional Reform Act 2005, s 15(1), Sch 4, Pt 1, paras 114, 142.

99 District registries

(1) The Lord Chancellor may by order direct that there shall be district registries of the High Court at such places and for such districts as are specified in the order.

(2) Any order under this section shall be made by statutory instrument, which shall be laid before Parliament after being made.

100 District judges

(1) Subject to subsection (2), for each district registry the Lord Chancellor shall appoint a person who is a district judge for a county court district, appointed under section 6 of the County Courts Act 1984, as a district judge of the High Court.

(2) The Lord Chancellor may, if he thinks fit, appoint two or more persons who are district judges for a county court district to execute jointly the office of district judge in any district registry.

(3) Where joint district judges are appointed under subsection (2), the Lord Chancellor may –

(a) give directions with respect to the division between them of the duties of the office of district judges; and

(b) as he thinks fit, on the death, resignation or removal of one of them, either appoint in place of that person another person to be joint district judge, or give directions that the continuing district judge shall act as sole district judge or (as the case may be) that the continuing district judges shall execute jointly the office of district judge.

(4) Subsections (4) to (6) of section 92 shall apply in relation to a person appointed as a district judge as they apply in relation to a person appointed to an office to which subsection (1) of that section applies, except that he shall vacate his office as district judge at such time as, for any cause whatever, he vacates his office as district judge for a county court district.

(5) (*repealed*)

Amendments—CLSA 1990, ss 74(1), 125(3), 125(7), Sch 18, para 40, Sch 20.

101 Power of one district judge to act for another

(1) A district judge of any registry shall be capable of acting in any other district registry for a district judge of that registry; and, where a district judge is so acting, the district judge of the other registry may divide the duties of his office as he thinks fit between himself and the district judge acting for him.

(2) (*repealed*)

Amendments—CLSA 1990, ss 74(1), 125(3), (7), Sch 18, para 40, Sch 20.

102 Deputy district judges

(1) If it appears to the Lord Chancellor that it is expedient to do so in order to facilitate the disposal of business in the High Court, he may appoint a person to be a deputy district judge in any district registry during such period or on such occasions as the Lord Chancellor thinks fit.

(2) Subject to subsection (3), a person shall not be qualified for appointment as a deputy district judge unless he is, or is qualified for appointment as, district judge for a county court district.

(3) A person may be appointed as a deputy district judge if he would, but for his age, be qualified for appointment as a district judge for a county court district and he has previously held the office of district judge for a county court district; but no appointment by virtue of this subsection shall be such as to extend beyond the day on which the person in question attains the age of seventy-five years.

(4) A deputy district judge, while acting under this section, shall have the same jurisdiction as the district judge.

(5) Subsection (6) of section 91 applies in relation to a deputy district judge appointed under this section as it applies in relation to a person appointed under that section.

(6) (*repealed*)

Amendments—CLSA 1990, s 125(3), (7), Sch 18, para 40, Sch 20; JPRA 1993, ss 26, 31, Sch 6, para 16, Sch 8, para 15(3).

****

104 District probate registries

(1) The Lord Chancellor may by order direct that there shall be district probate registries of the High Court at such places and for such districts as are specified in the order.

(2) Any order under this section shall be made by statutory instrument, which shall be laid before Parliament after being made.

PART V
PROBATE CAUSES AND MATTERS

Procedure in probate registries in relation to grants of representation

105 Applications

Applications for grants of probate or administration and for the revocation of grants may be made to –

- (a) the Principal Registry of the Family Division (in this Part referred to as 'the Principal Registry'); or
- (b) a district probate registry.

106 Grants by district probate registrars

(1) Any grant made by a district probate registrar shall be made in the name of the High Court under the seal used in the registry.

(2)–(4) (*repealed*).

Amendments—AJA 1985, ss 51(2), 67(2), Sch 8, Pt III.

107 No grant where conflicting applications

Subject to probate rules, no grant in respect of the estate, or part of the estate, of a deceased person shall be made out of the Principal Registry or any district probate registry on any application if, at any time before the making of a grant, it appears to the registrar concerned that some other application has been made in respect of that estate or, as the case may be, that part of it and has not been either refused or withdrawn.

108 Caveats

(1) A caveat against a grant of probate or administration may be entered in the Principal Registry or in any district probate registry.

(2) On a caveat being entered in a district probate registry, the district probate registrar shall immediately send a copy of it to the Principal Registry to be entered among the caveats in that Registry.

109 Refusal of grant where capital transfer tax unpaid

(1) No grant shall be made, and no grant made outside the United Kingdom shall be resealed, except –

- (a) on the production of information or documents under regulations under section 256(1)(aa) of the Inheritance Tax Act 1984 (excepted estates); or
- (b) on the production of an account prepared in pursuance of that Act showing by means of such receipt or certification as may be prescribed by the Commissioners either –

(i) that the inheritance tax payable on the delivery of the account has been paid; or

(ii) that no such tax is so payable.

(2) Arrangements may be made between the President of the Family Division and the Commissioners providing for the purposes subsection (1)(b) in such cases as may be specified in the arrangements that the receipt or certification of an account may be dispensed with or that some other document may be substituted for the account required by the Inheritance Tax Act 1984.

(3) *(repealed)*

Amendments—Inheritance Tax Act 1984, s 276, Sch 8, para 20; Finance Act 2004, ss 294(1), 326, Sch 42, Pt 4(1).

110 Documents to be delivered to commissioners of Inland Revenue

Subject to any arrangements which may from time to time be made between the President of the Family Division and the Commissioners, the Principal Registry and every district probate registry shall, within such a period after a grant as the President may direct, deliver to the Commissioners or their proper officer the following documents –

(a) in the case of a grant of probate or of administration with the will annexed, a copy of the will;

(b) in every case, such certificate or note of the grant as the Commissioners may require.

111 Records of grants

(1) There shall continue to be kept records of all grants which are made in the Principal Registry or in any district probate registry.

(2) Those records shall be in such form, and shall contain such particulars, as the President of the Family Division may direct.

Powers of court in relation to personal representatives

112 Summons to executor to prove or renounce

The High Court may summon any person named as executor in a will to prove, or renounce probate of, the will, and to do such other things concerning the will as the court had power to order such a person to do immediately before the commencement of this Act.

113 Power of court to sever grant

(1) Subject to subsection (2), the High Court may grant probate or administration in respect of any part of the estate of a deceased person, limited in any way the court thinks fit.

(2) Where the estate of a deceased person is known to be insolvent, the grant of representation to it shall not be severed under subsection (1) except as regards a trust estate in which he had no beneficial interest.

114 Number of personal representatives

(1) Probate or administration shall not be granted by the High Court to more than four persons in respect of the same part of the estate of a deceased person.

(2) Where under a will or intestacy any beneficiary is a minor or a life interest arises, any grant of administration by the High Court shall be made either to a trust corporation (with or without an individual) or to not less than two individuals, unless it appears to the court to be expedient in all the circumstances to appoint an individual as sole administrator.

(3) For the purpose of determining whether a minority or life interest arises in any particular case, the court may act on such evidence as may be prescribed.

(4) If at any time during the minority of a beneficiary or the subsistence of a life interest under a will or intestacy there is only one personal representative (not being a trust corporation), the High Court may, on the application of any person interested or the guardian or receiver of any such person, and in accordance with probate rules, appoint one or more additional personal representatives to act while the minority or life interest subsists and until the estate is fully administered.

(5) An appointment of an additional personal representative under subsection (4) to act with an executor shall not have the effect of including him in any chain of representation.

115 Grants to trust corporations

(1) The High Court may –

(a) where a trust corporation is named in a will as executor, grant probate to the corporation either solely or jointly with any other person named in the will as executor, as the case may require; or

(b) grant administration to a trust corporation, either solely or jointly with another person;

and the corporation may act accordingly as executor or administrator, as the case may be.

(2) Probate or administration shall not be granted to any person as nominee of a trust corporation.

(3) Any officer authorised for the purpose by a trust corporation or its directors or governing body may, on behalf of the corporation, swear affidavits, give security and do any other act which the court may require with a view to the grant to the corporation of probate or administration; and the acts of an officer so authorised shall be binding on the corporation.

116 Power of court to pass over prior claims to grant

(1) If by reason of any special circumstances it appears to the High Court to be necessary or expedient to appoint as administrator some person other than the person who, but for this section, would in accordance with probate rules have been entitled to the grant, the court may in its discretion appoint as administrator such person as it thinks expedient.

(2) Any grant of administration under this section may be limited in any way the court thinks fit.

117 Administration pending suit

(1) Where any legal proceedings concerning the validity of the will of a deceased person, or for obtaining, recalling or revoking any grant, are pending, the High Court may grant administration of the estate of the deceased person in question to an administrator pending suit, who shall, subject to subsection (2), have all the rights, duties and powers of a general administrator.

(2) An administrator pending suit shall be subject to the immediate control of the court and act under its direction; and, except in such circumstances as may be prescribed, no distribution of the estate, or any part of the estate, of the deceased person in question shall be made by such an administrator without the leave of the court.

(3) The court may, out of the estate of the deceased, assign an administrator pending suit such reasonable remuneration as it thinks fit.

118 Effect of appointment of minor as executor

Where a testator by his will appoints a minor to be an executor, the appointment shall not operate to vest in the minor the estate, or any part of the estate, of the testator, or to constitute him a personal representative for any purpose, unless and until probate is granted to him in accordance with probate rules.

119 Administration with will annexed

(1) Administration with the will annexed shall be granted, subject to and in accordance with probate rules, in every class of case in which the High Court had power to make such a grant immediately before the commencement of this Act.

(2) Where administration with the will annexed is granted, the will of the deceased shall be performed and observed in the same manner as if probate of it had been granted to an executor.

120 Power to require administrators to produce sureties

(1) As a condition of granting administration to any person the High Court may, subject to the following provisions of this section and subject to and in accordance with probate rules, require one or more sureties to guarantee that they will make good, within any limit imposed by the court on the total liability of the surety or sureties, any loss which any person interested in the administration of the estate of the deceased may suffer in consequence of a breach by the administrator of his duties as such.

(2) A guarantee given in pursuance of any such requirement shall enure for the benefit of every person interested in the administration of the estate of the deceased as if contained in a contract under seal made by the surety or sureties with every such person and, where there are two or more sureties, as if they had bound themselves jointly and severally.

(3) No action shall be brought on any such guarantee without the leave of the High Court.

(4) Stamp duty shall not be chargeable on any such guarantee.

(5) This section does not apply where administration is granted to the Treasury Solicitor, the Official Solicitor, the Public Trustee, the Solicitor for the affairs of the Duchy of Lancaster or the Duchy of Cornwall or the Crown Solicitor for Northern Ireland, or to the consular officer of a foreign state to which section 1 of the Consular Conventions Act 1949 applies, or in such other cases as may be prescribed.

Revocation of grants and cancellation of resealing at instance of court

121 Revocation of grants and cancellation of resealing at instance of court

(1) Where it appears to the High Court that a grant either ought not to have been made or contains an error, the court may call in the grant and, if satisfied that it would be revoked at the instance of a party interested, may revoke it.

(2) A grant may be revoked under subsection (1) without being called in, if it cannot be called in.

(3) Where it appears to the High Court that a grant resealed under the Colonial Probates Acts 1892 and 1927 ought not to have been resealed, the court may call in the relevant document and, if satisfied that the resealing would be cancelled at the instance of a party interested, may cancel the resealing.

In this and the following subsection 'the relevant document' means the original grant or, where some other document was sealed by the court under those Acts, that document.

(4) A resealing may be cancelled under subsection (3) without the relevant document being called in, if it cannot be called in.

Ancillary powers of court

122 Examination of person with knowledge of testamentary document

(1) Where it appears that there are reasonable grounds for believing that any person has knowledge of any document which is or purports to be a testamentary document, the High Court may, whether or not any legal proceedings are pending, order him to attend for the purpose of being examined in open court.

(2) The court may –

- (a) require any person who is before it in compliance with an order under subsection (1) to answer any question relating to the document concerned; and
- (b) if appropriate, order him to bring in the document in such manner as the court may direct.

(3) Any person who, having been required by the court to do so under this section, fails to attend for examination, answer any question or bring in any document shall be guilty of contempt of court.

123 Subpoena to bring in testamentary document

Where it appears that any person has in his possession, custody or power any document which is or purports to be a testamentary document, the High Court may, whether or not any legal proceedings are pending, issue a subpoena requiring him to bring in the document in such manner as the court may in the subpoena direct.

Provisions as to documents

124 Place for deposit of original wills and other documents

All original wills and other documents which are under the control of the High Court in the Principal Registry or in any district probate registry shall be deposited and preserved in such places as the Lord Chancellor may direct; and any wills or other documents so deposited shall, subject to the control of the High Court and to probate rules, be open to inspection.

125 Copies of wills and grants

An office copy, or a sealed and certified copy, of any will or part of a will open to inspection under section 124 or of any grant may, on payment of the fee prescribed by an order under section 92 of the Courts Act 2003 (fees), be obtained –

(a) from the registry in which in accordance with section 124 the will or documents relating to the grant are preserved; or

(b) where in accordance with that section the will or such documents are preserved in some place other than a registry, from the Principal Registry; or

(c) subject to the approval of the Senior Registrar of the Family Division, from the Principal Registry in any case where the will was proved in or the grant was issued from a district probate registry.

Amendments—Courts Act 2003, s 109(1), Sch 8, para 262(a).

126 Depositories for wills of living persons

(1) There shall be provided, under the control and direction of the High Court, safe and convenient depositories for the custody of the wills of living persons; and any person may deposit his will in such a depository on payment of the fee prescribed by an order under section 92 of the Courts Act 2003 (fees) and subject to such conditions as may be prescribed by regulations made by the President of the Family Division with the concurrence of the Lord Chancellor.

(2) Any regulations made under this section shall be made by statutory instrument which shall be laid before Parliament after being made; and the Statutory Instruments Act 1946 shall apply to a statutory instrument containing regulations under this section in like manner as if they had been made by a Minister of the Crown.

Amendments—Courts Act 2003, s 109(1), Sch 8, para 262(b).

Probate rules

127 Probate rules

(1) The President of the Family Division may, with the concurrence of the Lord Chancellor, make rules of court (in this Part referred to as 'probate rules') for regulating and prescribing the practice and procedure of the High Court with respect to non-contentious or common form probate business.

(2) Without prejudice to the generality of subsection (1), probate rules may make provision for regulating the classes of persons entitled to grants of probate or administration in particular circumstances and the relative priorities of their claims thereto.

(3) Probate rules shall be made by statutory instrument subject to annulment in pursuance of a resolution of either House of Parliament; and the Statutory Instruments Act 1946 shall apply to a statutory instrument containing probate rules in like manner as if they had been made by a Minister of the Crown.

Interpretation of Part V and other probate provisions

128 Interpretation of Part V and other probate provisions

In this Part, and in other provisions of this Act relating to probate causes and matters, unless the context otherwise requires –

'administration' includes all letters of administration of the effects of deceased persons, whether with or without a will annexed, and whether granted for general, special or limited purposes;

'estate' means real and personal estate, and 'real estate' includes –

(a) chattels real and land in possession, remainder or reversion and every interest in or over land to which the deceased person was entitled at the time of his death, and

(b) real estate held on trust or by way of mortgage or security, but not money secured or charged on land;

'grant' means a grant of probate or administration;

'non-contentious or common form probate business' means the business of obtaining probate and administration where there is no contention as to the right thereto, including –

(a) the passing of probates and administrations through the High Court in contentious cases where the contest has been terminated,

(b) all business of a non-contentious nature in matters of testacy and intestacy not being proceedings in any action, and

(c) the business of lodging caveats against the grant of probate or administration;

'Principal Registry' means the Principal Registry of the Family Division;

'probate rules' means rules of court made under section 127;

'trust corporation' means the Public Trustee or a corporation either appointed by the court in any particular case to be a trustee or authorised by rules made under section 4(3) of the Public Trustee Act 1906 to act as a custodian trustee;

'will' includes a nuncupative will and any testamentary document of which probate may be granted.

Amendments—Trusts of Land and Appointment of Trustees Act 1996, s 25(2), Sch 4.

PART VI
MISCELLANEOUS AND SUPPLEMENTARY

Miscellaneous provisions

129 Lords Commissioners to represent Lord Chancellor when Great Seal in commission

When the Great Seal is in commission, the Lords Commissioners shall represent the Lord Chancellor for the purposes of this Act; but the powers vested in him by this Act in relation to –

(a) the appointment of officers, and
(b) any act for which the concurrence or presence of the Lord Chancellor is required by this Act,

may be exercised by the senior Lord Commissioner for the time being.

130

(*repealed*)

131 Conveyancing counsel of Supreme Court

(1) The conveyancing counsel of the Supreme Court shall be persons who have a 10 year High Court qualification, within the meaning of section 71 of the Courts and Legal Services Act 1990 who have practised as such for not less than ten years.

(2) The conveyancing counsel of the court shall be not more than six, nor less than three, in number, and shall be appointed by the Lord Chancellor.

Amendments—CLSA 1990, s 71(2), Sch 10, para 48.

132 Proof of documents bearing seal or stamp of Supreme Court or any office thereof

Every document purporting to be sealed or stamped with the seal or stamp of the Supreme Court or of any office of the Supreme Court shall be received in evidence in all parts of the United Kingdom without further proof.

133 Enrolment and engrossment of instruments

(1) The Master of the Rolls may make regulations for authorising and regulating the enrolment or filing of instruments in the Supreme Court, and for prescribing the form in which certificates of enrolment or filing are to be issued.

(2) Regulations under subsection (1) shall not affect the operation of any enactment requiring or authorising the enrolment of any instrument in the Supreme Court or prescribing the manner in which any instrument is to be enrolled there.

(3) Any instrument which is required or authorised by or under this or any other Act to be enrolled or engrossed in the Supreme Court shall be deemed to have been duly enrolled or engrossed if it is written on material authorised or required by regulations under subsection (1) and has been filed or otherwise preserved in accordance with regulations under that subsection.

(4) The Lord Chancellor may, with the concurrence of the Master of the Rolls and of the Treasury, make regulations prescribing the fees to be paid on the enrolment or filing of any instrument in the Supreme Court, including any additional fees payable on the enrolment or filing of any instrument out of time.

(5) Any regulations under this section shall be made by statutory instrument, which shall be laid before Parliament after being made; and the Statutory Instruments Act 1946 shall apply to a statutory instrument containing regulations under subsection (1) in like manner as if the regulations had been made by a Minister of the Crown.

134 Powers of attorney deposited before October 1971

(1) This section applies to any instrument creating, or verifying the execution of, a power of attorney which was deposited in the Central Office of the Supreme Court before 1st October 1971.

(2) A separate file of such instruments shall continue to be kept and, subject to payment of the fee prescribed by an order under section 92 of the Courts Act 2003 (fees) –

- (a) any person may search that file, and may inspect any such instrument; and
- (b) an office copy of any such instrument shall be issued to any person on request.

(3) A document purporting to be an office copy of any such instrument shall, in any part of the United Kingdom, without further proof be sufficient evidence of the contents of the instrument and of its having been deposited as mentioned in subsection (1).

Amendments—Courts Act 2003, s 109(1), Sch 8, para 262(c).

135 Bonds given under order of court

(1) A bond to be given by any person under or for the purposes of any order of the High Court or the civil division of the Court of Appeal shall be given in such form and to such officer of the court as may be prescribed and, if the court so requires, with one or more sureties.

(2) An officer of the court to whom a bond is given in accordance with subsection (1) shall as such have power to enforce it or to assign it, pursuant to an order of the court under subsection (4), to some other person.

(3) Where by rules of court made for the purposes of this section another officer is at any time substituted for the officer previously prescribed as the officer to whom bonds of any class are to be given, the rules may provide that bonds of that class given before the rules come into operation shall have effect as if references in the bonds to the officer previously prescribed were references to the substituted officer.

(4) Where it appears to the court that the condition of a bond given in accordance with subsection (1) has been broken, the court may, on an application in that behalf, order the bond to be assigned to such person as may be specified in the order.

(5) A person to whom a bond is ordered to be assigned under subsection (4) shall be entitled by virtue of the order to sue on the bond in his own name as if

it had been originally given to him, and to recover on it as trustee for all persons interested the full amount recoverable in respect of the breach of condition.

136 Production of documents filed in, or in custody of, Supreme Court

(1) The Lord Chancellor may, with the concurrence of the Lord Chief Justice, the Master of the Rolls, the President of the Family Division and the Vice-Chancellor, or of any three of them, make rules for providing that, in any case where a document filed in, or in the custody of, any office of the Supreme Court is required to be produced to any court or tribunal (including an umpire or arbitrator) sitting elsewhere than at the Royal Courts of Justice –

(a) it shall not be necessary for any officer, whether served with a subpoena in that behalf or not, to attend for the purpose of producing the document; but

(b) the document may be produced to the court or tribunal by sending it to the court or tribunal, in the manner prescribed in the rules, together with a certificate, in the form so prescribed, to the effect that the document has been filed in, or is in the custody of, the office;

and any such certificate shall be prima facie evidence of the facts stated in it.

(2) Rules under this section may contain –

(a) provisions for securing the safe custody and return to the proper office of the Supreme Court of any document sent to a court or tribunal in pursuance of the rules; and

(b) such incidental and supplementary provisions as appear to the Lord Chancellor to be necessary or expedient.

(3) Rules under this section shall be made by statutory instrument, which shall be laid before Parliament after being made.

137 Money paid into court under enactment subsequently repealed

Where in pursuance of any enactment, whenever passed, any money has (before or after the commencement of this Act) been paid –

(a) into the Bank of England in the name of the Accountant General of the Supreme Court; or

(b) into the Supreme Court,

then, if that enactment has been or is subsequently repealed –

(i) the Accountant General may continue to deal with the money; and

(ii) any powers of the High Court with respect to the money shall continue to be exercisable,

in all respects as if that enactment had not been repealed.

138–138B

(*repealed*)

139 Attachment of National Savings Bank deposits

(1) In section 27 of the Crown Proceedings Act 1947 (attachment of moneys payable by the Crown) –

(a) in subsection (1), paragraph (c) of the proviso (which precludes the making of orders under that subsection by the High Court or a county court in respect of money payable on account of a deposit in the National Savings Bank) shall cease to have effect; and

(b) after subsection (2) there shall be added –

> '(3) In their application to England and Wales the preceding provisions of this section shall have effect subject to any order for the time being in force under section 139(2) of the Supreme Court Act 1981.'

(2) The Lord Chancellor may by order direct that section 27(1) and (2) of the Crown Proceedings Act 1947 (attachment of moneys payable by the Crown) shall not apply in relation to any money payable by the Crown to any person on account of –

(a) any deposit in the National Savings Bank; or

(b) a deposit in that Bank of any description specified in the order.

(3) Any order under subsection (2) shall be made by statutory instrument subject to annulment in pursuance of a resolution of either House of Parliament.

(4) Without prejudice to section 153(4), this section extends to England and Wales only.

140 Enforcement of fines and forfeited recognizances

(1) Payment of a fine imposed, or sum due under a recognizance forfeited, by the High Court or the civil division of the Court of Appeal may be enforced upon the order of the court –

(a) in like manner as a judgment of the High Court for the payment of money; or

(b) in like manner as a fine imposed by the Crown Court.

(2) Where payment of a fine or other sum falls to be enforced as mentioned in paragraph (a) of subsection (1) upon an order of the High Court or the civil division of the Court of Appeal under that subsection –

(a) the court shall, if the fine or other sum is not paid in full forthwith or within such time as the court may allow, certify to Her Majesty's Remembrancer the sum payable; and

(b) Her Majesty's Remembrancer shall thereupon proceed to enforce payment of that sum as if it were due to him as a judgment debt.

(3) Where payment of a fine or other sum falls to be enforced as mentioned in paragraph (b) of subsection (1) upon an order of the High Court or the civil division of the Court of Appeal under that subsection, the provisions of sections 139 and 140 of the Powers of Criminal Courts (Sentencing) Act 2000 shall apply to that fine or other sum as they apply to a fine imposed by the Crown Court.

(4) Where payment of a fine or other sum has become enforceable by Her Majesty's Remembrancer by virtue of this section or section 16 of the Contempt of Court Act 1981, any payment received by him in respect of that fine or other sum shall be dealt with by him in such manner as the Lord Chancellor may direct.

(5) In this section, and in sections 139 and 140 of the Powers of Criminal Courts (Sentencing) Act 2000 as extended by this section, 'fine' includes a penalty imposed in civil proceedings.

Amendments—Powers of Criminal Courts (Sentencing) Act 2000, s 165(1), Sch 9, para 88.

141

(repealed)

142 Selection of judges for trial of election petitions

(1) The judges to be placed on the rota for the trial of parliamentary election petitions in England and Wales under Part III of the Representation of the People Act 1983 in each year shall be selected, in such manner as may be provided by rules of court, from the judges of the Queen's Bench Division of the High Court exclusive of any who are members of the House of Lords.

(2) Notwithstanding the expiry of the year for which a judge has been placed on the rota he may act as if that year had not expired for the purpose of continuing to deal with, giving judgment in, or dealing with any ancillary matter relating to, any case with which he may have been concerned during that year.

(3) Any judge placed on the rota shall be eligible to be placed on the rota again in the succeeding or any subsequent year.

Amendments—Representation of the People Act 1983, s 206, Sch 8, para 26.

****

Supplementary

150 Admiralty jurisdiction: provisions as to Channel Islands, Isle of Man, colonies, etc

(1) Her Majesty may by Order in Council –

- (a) direct that any of the provisions of sections 20 to 24 specified in the Order shall extend, with such exceptions, adaptations and modifications as may be so specified, to any of the Channel Islands or the Isle of Man; or
- (b) make, for any of the Channel Islands or the Isle of Man, provision for any purposes corresponding to the purposes of any of the provisions of those sections.

(2) Her Majesty may by Order in Council direct, either generally or in relation to particular courts or territories, that the Colonial Courts of Admiralty Act 1890 shall have effect as if for the reference in section 2(2) of that Act to the Admiralty jurisdiction of the High Court in England there were substituted a reference to the Admiralty jurisdiction of that court as defined by section 20 of this Act, subject, however, to such adaptations and modifications of section 20 as may be specified in the Order.

(3) Her Majesty may by Order in Council direct that any of the provisions of sections 21 to 24 shall extend, with such exceptions, adaptations and modifications as may be specified in the Order, to any colony or to any country outside Her Majesty's dominions in which Her Majesty has jurisdiction in right of the government of the United Kingdom.

(4) Subsections (1) and (3) shall each have effect as if the provisions there mentioned included section 2(2) of the Hovercraft Act 1968 (application of the law relating to maritime liens in relation to hovercraft and property connected with them.)

151 Interpretation of this Act, and rules of construction for other Acts and documents

(1) In this Act, unless the context otherwise requires –

'action' means any civil proceedings commenced by writ or in any other manner prescribed by rules of court;

'appeal', in the context of appeals to the civil division of the Court of Appeal, includes –

(a) an application for a new trial, and

(b) an application to set aside a verdict, finding or judgment in any cause or matter in the High Court which has been tried, or in which any issue has been tried, by a jury;

'arbitration agreement' has the same meaning as it has in Part I of the Arbitration Act 1996;

'cause' means any action or any criminal proceedings;

'Division', where it appears with a capital letter, means a division of the High Court;

'judgment' includes a decree;

'jurisdiction' includes powers;

'matter' means any proceedings in court not in a cause;

'party', in relation to any proceedings, includes any person who pursuant to or by virtue of rules of court or any other statutory provision has been served with notice of, or has intervened in, those proceedings;

'prescribed' means –

(a) except in relation to fees, prescribed by rules of court;...

(b) ...;

'senior judge', where the reference is to the senior judge of a Division, means –

(a) in the case of the Chancery Division, the Vice-Chancellor;

(b) in any other case, the president of the Division in question;

'solicitor' means a solicitor of the Supreme Court;

'statutory provision' means any enactment, whenever passed, or any provision contained in subordinate legislation (as defined in section 21(1) of the Interpretation Act 1978), whenever made;

'this or any other Act' includes an Act passed after this Act.

(2) Section 128 contains definitions of expressions used in Part V and in the other provisions of this Act relating to probate causes and matters.

(3) Any reference in this Act to rules of court under section 84 includes a reference to rules of court in relation to the Supreme Court under any provision of this or any other Act which confers on the Civil Procedure Rule Committee or the Crown Court Rule Committee power to make rules of court.

(4) Except where the context otherwise requires, in this or any other Act –

(*repealed*)

(*repealed*)

'divisional court' (with or without capital letters) means a divisional court constituted under section 66;

'judge of the Supreme Court' means –

(a) a judge of the Court of Appeal other than an ex-officio judge within paragraph (b) or (c) of section 2(2), or

(b) a judge of the High Court,

and accordingly does not include, as such, a judge of the Crown Court;

'official referees' business' has the meaning given by section 68(6).

(5) The provisions of Schedule 4 (construction of references to superseded courts and officers) shall have effect.

Amendments—CLSA 1990, s 125(3), Sch 18, para 41; AA 1996, s 107(1), Sch 3, para 37(1), (3); CPA 1997, s 10, Sch 2, para 1(7)(a), (b); SI 2004/2035; Courts Act 2003, s 109(1), (3), Sch 8, para 265, Sch 10.

****

153 Citation, commencement and extent

(1) This Act may be cited as the Supreme Court Act 1981.

(2) This Act, except the provisions mentioned in subsection (3), shall come into force on 1st January 1982; and references to the commencement of this Act shall be construed as references to the beginning of that day.

(3) Sections 72, 143 and 152(2) and this section shall come into force on the passing of this Act.

(4), (5) (*not reproduced*)

Application of Act to Scotland, Northern Ireland etc—Subsections (4) and (5) set out details of the application of this Act to Scotland, Northern Ireland and Courts-Martial.

SCHEDULE 1

DISTRIBUTION OF BUSINESS IN HIGH COURT

Chancery Division

1 To the Chancery Division are assigned all causes and matters relating to –

(a) the sale, exchange or partition of land, or the raising of charges on land;
(b) the redemption or foreclosure of mortgages;
(c) the execution of trusts;
(d) the administration of the estates of deceased persons;
(e) bankruptcy;
(f) the dissolution of partnerships or the taking of partnership or other accounts;
(g) the rectification, setting aside or cancellation of deeds or other instruments in writing;
(h) probate business, other than non-contentious or common form business;
(i) patents, trade marks, registered designs, copyright or design right;

(j) the appointment of a guardian of a minor's estate,

and all causes and matters involving the exercise of the High Court's jurisdiction under the enactments relating to companies.

Queen's Bench Division

2 To the Queen's Bench Division are assigned –

(a) applications for writs of habeas corpus, except applications made by a parent or guardian of a minor for such a writ concerning the custody of the minor;
(b) applications for judicial review;
(c) all causes and matters involving the exercise of the High Court's Admiralty jurisdiction or its jurisdiction as a prize court; and
(d) all causes and matters entered in the commercial list.

Family Division

3 To the Family Division are assigned –

(a) all matrimonial causes and matters (whether at first instance or on appeal);
(b) all causes and matters (whether at first instance or on appeal) relating to –
  (i) legitimacy;
  (ii) the exercise of the inherent jurisdiction of the High Court with respect to minors, the maintenance of minors and any proceedings under the Children Act 1989, except proceedings solely for the appointment of a guardian of a minor's estate;
  (iii) adoption;
  (iv) non-contentious or common form probate business;
(c) applications for consent to the marriage of a minor or for a declaration under section 27B(5) of the Marriage Act 1949;
(d) proceedings on appeal under section 13 of the Administration of Justice Act 1960 from an order or decision made under section 63(3) of the Magistrates' Courts Act 1980 to enforce an order of a magistrates' court made in matrimonial proceedings or proceedings under Part IV of the Family Law Act 1996 or with respect to the guardianship of a minor.
(e) applications under Part III of the Family Law Act 1986;
(e) proceedings under the Children Act 1989;
(f) all proceedings under –
  (i) Part IV of the Family Law Act 1996;
  (ii) the Child Abduction and Custody Act 1985;
  (iii) the Family Law Act 1986;
  (iv) section 30 of the Human Fertilisation and Embryology Act 1990;…
  (v) Council Regulation (EC) No 2201/2003 of 27th November 2003 concerning jurisdiction and the recognition and enforcement of judgments in matrimonial matters and matters of parental responsibility, so far as that Regulation relates to jurisdiction, recognition and enforcement in parental responsibility matters;
(fa) all proceedings relating to a debit or credit under section 29(1) or 49(1) of the Welfare Reform and Pensions Act 1999;

(g) all proceedings for the purpose of enforcing an order made in any proceedings of a type described in this paragraph.
(h) all proceedings under the Child Support Act 1991.
(i) all proceedings under sections 6 and 8 of the Gender Recognition Act 2004;
(i) all civil partnership causes and matters (whether at first instance or on appeal);
(j) applications for consent to the formation of a civil partnership by a minor or for a declaration under paragraph 7 of Schedule 1 to the Civil Partnership Act 2004;
(k) applications under section 58 of that Act (declarations relating to civil partnerships).

Amendments—FLA 1986, s 68(1), Sch 1, para 26; Marriage (Prohibited Degrees of Relationship) Act 1986, s 5; FLRA 1987, s 33(4), Sch 4; CDPA 1988, s 303(1), Sch 7, para 28(1), (3); CA 1989, ss 92(11), 108(5), (6), Sch 11, para 9, Sch 13, para 45(3); SI 1991/1210; SI 1993/622; FLA 1996, s 66(1), Sch 8, Pt III, para 51; Welfare Reform and Pensions Act 1999, s 84(1), Sch 12, Pt I, para 1; SI 2004/3418; SI 2005/265;

Prospective amendments–Civil Partnership Act 2004, s 261(1), Sch 27, para 70.

****

High Court and County Courts Jurisdiction Order 1991, SI 1991/724

1 Title and commencement

This Order may be cited as the High Court and County Courts Jurisdiction Order 1991 and shall come into force on 1 July 1991.

2 Jurisdiction

(1) A county court shall have jurisdiction under –

(a) sections 146 and 147 of the Law of Property Act 1925,
(b) …
(c) section 26 of the Arbitration Act 1950,
(d) section 63(2) of the Landlord and Tenant Act 1954,
(e) section 28(3) of the Mines and Quarries (Tips) Act 1969,
(f) section 66 of the Taxes Management Act 1970,
(g) section 41 of the Administration of Justice Act 1970,
(h) section 139(5)(b) of the Consumer Credit Act 1974,
(i) section 13 of the Torts (Interference with Goods) Act 1977,
(j) section 87 of the Magistrates' Courts Act 1980,
(k) sections 17 and 18 of the Audit Commission Act 1998,
(l) sections 15, 16, 21, 25 and 139 of the County Courts Act 1984,
(m) section 39(4) of, and paragraph 3(1) of Schedule 3 to, the Legal Aid Act 1988,
(n) sections 99, 102(5), 114, 195, 204, 230, 231 and 235(5) of the Copyright, Designs and Patents Act 1988,
(o) section 40 of the Housing Act 1988,

(p) sections 13 and 14 of the Trusts of Land and Appointment of Trustees Act 1996,

whatever the amount involved in the proceedings and whatever the value of any fund or asset connected with the proceedings.

(2) A county court shall have jurisdiction under –

(a) section 10 of the Local Land Charges Act 1975, and
(b) section 10(4) of the Rentcharges Act 1977,

where the sum concerned or amount claimed does not exceed £5,000.

(3) A county court shall have jurisdiction under the following provisions of the Law of Property Act 1925 where the capital value of the land or interest in land which is to be dealt with does not exceed £30,000:

(a) sections 3, 49, 66, 181, and 188;
(b) proviso (iii) to paragraph 3 of Part III of Schedule 1;
(c) proviso (v) to paragraph 1(3) of Part IV of Schedule 1;
(d) provisos (iii) and (iv) to paragraph 1(4) of Part IV of Schedule 1.

(4) A county court shall have jurisdiction under sections 89, 90, 91 and 92 of the Law of Property Act 1925 where the amount owing in respect of the mortgage or charge at the commencement of the proceedings does not exceed £30,000.

(5) A county court shall have jurisdiction under the proviso to section 136(1) of the Law of Property Act 1925 where the amount or value of the debt or thing in action does not exceed £30,000.

(6) A county court shall have jurisdiction under section 1(6) of the Land Charges Act 1972 –

(a) in the case of a land charge of Class C(i), C(ii) or D(i), if the amount does not exceed £30,000;
(b) in the case of a land charge of Class C(iii), if it is for a specified capital sum of money not exceeding £30,000 or, where it is not for a specified capital sum, if the capital value of the land affected does not exceed £30,000;
(c) in the case of a land charge of Class A, Class B, Class C(iv), Class D(ii), Class D(iii) or Class E, if the capital value of the land affected does not exceed £30,000;
(d) in the case of a land charge of Class F, if the land affected by it is the subject of an order made by the court under section 1 of the Matrimonial Homes Act 1983 or an application for an order under that section relating to that land has been made to the court;
(e) in a case where an application under section 23 of the Deeds of Arrangement Act 1914 could be entertained by the court.

(7) A county court shall have jurisdiction under sections 69, 70 and 71 of the Solicitors Act 1974 where a bill of costs relates wholly or partly to contentious business done in a county court and the amount of the bill does not exceed £5,000.

(7A) A patents county court and the county courts listed in paragraph (7B) shall have jurisdiction under the following provisions of the Trade Marks Act 1994 –

(a) sections 15, 16, 19, 23(5), 25(4)(b), 30, 31, 46, 47, 64, 73 and 74;
(b) paragraph 12 of Schedule 1; and
(c) paragraph 14 of Schedule 2,

to include jurisdiction to hear and determine any claims or matters ancillary to, or arising from proceedings brought under such provisions.

(7B) For the purposes of paragraph (7A), the county courts at –

(a) Birmingham;
(b) Bristol;
(c) Cardiff;
(d) Leeds;
(e) Liverpool;
(f) Manchester; and
(g) Newcastle upon Tyne,

shall have jurisdiction.

(8) The enactments and statutory instruments listed in the Schedule to this Order are amended as specified therein, being amendments which are consequential on the provisions of this article.

Amendments—SI 1996/3141; Audit Commission Act 1998; SI 2005/587.

3 Injunctions

The High Court shall have jurisdiction to hear an application for an injunction made in the course of or in anticipation of proceedings in a county court where a county court may not, by virtue of regulations under section 38(3)(b) of the County Courts Act 1984 or otherwise, grant such an injunction.

4 Allocation – Commencement of proceedings

Subject to articles 4A, 5, 6 and 6A proceedings in which both the county courts and the High Court have jurisdiction may be commenced either in a county court or in the High Court.

Amendments—Access to Neighbouring Land Act 1992, s 7(2); SI 1999/1014.

4A Except for proceedings to which article 5 applies, a claim for money in which county courts have jurisdiction may only be commenced in the High Court if the financial value of the claim is more than £15,000.

Amendments—Inserted by SI 1999/1014.

5 (1) Proceedings which include a claim for damages in respect of personal injuries may only be commenced in the High Court if the financial value of the claim is £50,000 or more.

(2) In this article 'personal injuries' means personal injuries to the claimant or any other person, and includes disease, impairment of physical or mental condition, and death.

(3) This article does not apply to proceedings which include a claim for damages in respect of an alleged breach of duty of care committed in the course of the provision of clinical or medical services (including dental or nursing services).

Amendments—SI 1999/1014.

6 Applications and appeals under section 17 of the Audit Commission Act 1998 and appeals under section 18 of that Act shall be commenced in the High Court.

Amendments—Audit Commission Act 1998; SI 1993/1407.

6A Applications under section 1 of the Access to Neighbouring Land Act 1992 shall be commenced in a county court.

Amendments—Inserted by Access to Neighbouring Land Act 1992, s 7(2).

****

8 Enforcement

(1) Subject to paragraph (1A) a judgment or order of a county court for the payment of a sum of money which it is sought to enforce wholly or partially by execution against goods –

- (a) shall be enforced only in the High Court where the sum which it is sought to enforce is £5,000 or more;
- (b) shall be enforced only in a county court where the sum which it is sought to enforce is less than £600;
- (c) in any other case may be enforced in either the High Court or a county court.

(1A) A judgment or order of a county court for the payment of a sum of money in proceedings arising out of an agreement regulated by the Consumer Credit Act 1974 shall be enforced only in a county court.

(2) Section 85(1) of the County Courts Act 1984 is amended by the insertion, at the beginning of the subsection, of the words 'Subject to article 8 of the High Court and County Courts Jurisdiction Order 1991,'.

Amendments—SI 1993/1407; SI 1995/205; SI 1996/3141; SI 1999/1014.

8A Enforcement of traffic penalties

(1) Proceedings for the recovery of –

- (a) increased penalty charges provided for in charge certificates issued under –
  - (i) paragraph 6 of Schedule 6 to the 1991 Act; and
  - (ii) paragraph 8 of Schedule 1 to the London Local Authorities Act 1996;
- (b) amounts payable by a person other than a local authority under an adjudication of a parking adjudicator pursuant to section 73 of the 1991 Act; and
- (c) fixed penalties payable under fixed penalty notices issued under regulation 5 of the Road Traffic (Vehicle Emissions) (Fixed Penalty) Regulations 1997,

shall be taken in Northampton County Court.

(2) In this article, 'the 1991 Act' means the Road Traffic Act 1991 and expressions which are used in the 1991 Act have the same meaning in this article as they have in that Act.

(3) In this article 'a local authority' means –

(a) in England, a London authority, a county or district council or the Council of the Isles of Scilly; and
(b) in Wales, a county or county borough council.

Amendments—Inserted by SI 1993/1407; amended by SI 1996/3141; SI 2001/1387.

8B Enforcement of possession orders against trespassers

(1) A judgment or order of a county court for possession of land made in a possession claim against trespassers may be enforced in the High Court or a county court.

(2) In this article 'a possession claim against trespassers' has the same meaning as in Part 55 of the Civil Procedure Rules 1998.

Amendments—Inserted by SI 2001/2685.

9 Financial value of claim

For the purposes of Articles 4A and 5, the financial value of the claim shall be calculated in accordance with rule 16.3(6) of the Civil Procedure Rules 1998.

Amendments—Substituted by SI 1999/1014.

****

11 Crown proceedings – transitional provisions

For a period of two years from the date upon which this Order comes into force no order shall be made transferring proceedings in the High Court to which the Crown is a party to a county court, except –

(a) when the proceedings are set down to be tried or heard; or
(b) with the consent of the Crown.

12 Savings

This Order shall not apply to:

(a) family proceedings within the meaning of Part V of the Matrimonial and Family Proceedings Act 1984;
(b) (*revoked*)

Amendments—SI 1999/1014.

****

SECTION 8

Miscellaneous

SECTION 8: Miscellaneous

Contents

Higher Courts Directory

Courts Directory	Address
Court of Appeal – Civil Division	Royal Courts of Justice Strand London WC2A 2LL Tel: 020 7947 6409 (registry) Tel: 020 7947 6195 (listings) Fax: 020 7936 6740 (registry) DX 44450 Strand WC2
High Court of Justice – Chancery Division	Royal Courts of Justice Strand London WC2A 2LL Tel: 020 7947 6000 Fax: 020 7947 7345 (listings) DX 44450 Strand WC2
High Court of Justice – Queen's Bench Division	Royal Courts of Justice Strand London WC2A 2LL Tel: 020 7947 6000 Fax: 020 7947 6802 DX 44450 Strand WC2
The House of Lords	Westminster London SW1A 0PW Tel: 020 7219 3111 Fax: 020 7219 2476
Technology and Construction Court	St Dunstan's House 133–137 Fetter Lane London EC4A 1HD Tel: 020 7947 7429 Fax: 020 7947 7428 DX 44450 Strand
High Court of Justice – Family Division	First Avenue House 42–49 High Holborn London WC1V 6NP Tel: 020 7947 7457 Fax: 020 7947 6709

Restrictive Practices Court	Thomas More Building Royal Courts of Justice Strand London WC2R 1LP Tel: 020 7947 6727 Fax: 020 7947 6958 DX 44450 Strand WC2
Supreme Court Costs Office	Clifford's Inn Fetter Lane London EC4A 1DQ Tel: 020 7947 6163 Fax: 020 7947 6344 DX 44454 Strand
Admiralty Registry and Marshal's Office	Royal Courts of Justice Strand London WC2A 2LL Tel: 020 7936 6112 Fax: 020 7936 6245
Court of Protection	Stewart House 24 Kingsway London WC2B 6JX Tel: 020 7664 7000 Fax: 020 7664 7714
Office of the Official Solicitor	81 Chancery Lane London WC2A 1DD Tel: 020 7911 7127 Fax: 020 7911 7105 DX 0012 London Chancery Lane
Official Receiver's Office	21 Bloomsbury Street London WC1B 3SS Tel: 020 7637 1110 Fax: 020 7636 4709 DX 120875 Bloomsbury

County Courts Directory

Key	Jurisdiction	Statutory Instrument etc
AC	Adoption Centre	President's Guidelines of 1 October 2001 (Adoption Proceedings: A New Approach)
B	Bankruptcy	Civil Courts Order 1983, SI 1983/713
CC	Care Centre	Children (Allocation of Proceedings) Order 1991, SI 1991/1677
CDR	Chancery District Registry	Civil Courts Order 1983, SI 1983/713
CTC	Civil Trial Centre	
DR	**District Registry**	Civil Courts Order 1983, SI 1983/713
D	Divorce	Civil Courts Order 1983, SI 1983/713
FHC	Family Hearings Centre	Children (Allocation of Proceedings) Order 1991, SI 1991/1677
MC	Mercantile Court	PD59 – Mercantile Courts
RR	Race Relations	Civil Courts Order 1983, SI 1983/713
TCC	Technology and Construction Court	PD60 – Technology and Construction Court Claims

County Court	Address	Additional Jurisdiction
Aberdare (CTC Swansea)	The Court House Cwmbach Road Aberdare Mid Glam CF44 0JE Tel: 01685 888575 Fax: 01685 883413 DX 99600 Aberdare 2	B
Aberystwyth (CTC Swansea)	Edleston House Queens Road Aberystwyth Dyfed SY23 2HP Tel: 01970 636370 Fax: 01970 625985 DX 99560 Aberystwyth 2	AC B D **DR** FHC
Accrington (CTC Burnley)	Bradshawgate House 1 Oak Street Accrington Lancs BB5 1EQ Tel: 01254 237490 Fax: 01254 393869 DX 702645 Accrington 2	D

County Court	Address	Additional Jurisdiction
Aldershot & Farnham (CTC Winchester)	78–82 Victoria Road Aldershot Hants GU11 1SS Tel: 01252 796 800 Fax: 01252 345 705 DX 98530 Aldershot 2 *Court House* 84–86 Victoria Road Aldershot Hants GU11 1SS	D
Altrincham (CTC Salford)	Trafford Courthouse PO Box 240 Ashton Lane Sale Cheshire M33 7WX Tel: 0161 975 4760 Fax: 0161 975 4761 DX 702545 Altrincham 2	D
Ashford (CTC Canterbury)	Ground Floor The Court House Tufton Street Ashford Kent TN23 1QQ Tel: 01233 632464 Fax: 01233 612786 DX 98060 Ashford (Kent) 3	
Aylesbury (CTC Luton)	2nd Floor, Heron House 49 Buckingham Street Aylesbury Bucks HP20 2NQ Tel: 01296 393498 Fax: 01296 397363 DX 97820 Aylesbury 3	B
Banbury (CTC Oxford)	The Courthouse Warwick Road Banbury Oxon OX16 2AQ Tel: 01295 452090 Fax: 01295 452051 DX 701967 Banbury 2	B

County Court	Address	Additional Jurisdiction
Barnet (CTC Central London)	St Mary's Court Regents Park Road Finchley London N3 1BO Tel: 020 8343 4272 Fax: 020 8343 1324 DX 122570 Finchley (Church End)	D FHC
Barnsley (CTC Sheffield)	12 Regent Street Barnsley S Yorks S70 2EW Tel: 01226 203471 Fax: 01226 779126 DX 702080 Barnsley 3	B D **DR** FHC
Barnstaple (CTC Exeter)	7th Floor, The Civic Centre North Walk Barnstaple Devon EX31 1DY Tel: 01271 372252 Fax: 01271 322968 DX 98560 Barnstaple 2	B D **DR** FHC
Barrow-in-Furness	Government Buildings Michaelson Road Barrow-in-Furness Cumbria LA14 2EZ Tel: 01229 820046 Fax: 01229 430039 DX 65210 Barrow-in-Furness 2	B D **DR**
Basildon (CTC Southend-on-Sea)	Basildon Combined Court Centre The Gore Basildon Essex SS14 2EU Tel: 01268 458000 Fax: 01268 458100 DX 97633 Basildon 5	

County Court	Address	Additional Jurisdiction
Basingstoke (CTC Winchester)	3rd Floor, Grosvenor House Basing View Basingstoke Hants RG21 4HG Tel: 01256 318200 Fax: 01256 318225 DX 98570 Basingstoke 3	D **DR** FHC
Bath (CTC Bristol)	3rd & 4th Floor Cambridge House Henry Street Bath BA1 1DJ Tel: 01225 310282 Fax: 01225 480915 DX 98580 Bath 2	B D **DR** FHC
Bedford (CTC Luton)	May House 29 Goldington Road Bedford MK40 3NN Tel: 01234 760400 Fax: 01234 327431 DX 97590 Bedford 3	B D **DR** FHC
Birkenhead (CTC Liverpool)	76 Hamilton Street Birkenhead Merseyside CH41 5EN Tel: 0151 666 5800 Fax: 0151 666 5873 DX 725000 Birkenhead 10	B D **DR**
Birmingham	Birmingham Civil Justice Centre The Priory Courts 33 Bull St Birmingham B4 6DS Tel: 0121 681 4441 Fax: 0121 681 3001/2 DX 701987 Birmingham 7	AC B CDR CC D **DR** FHC MC TCC RR CTC – Dudley, Kidderminster, Stourbridge

County Court	Address	Additional Jurisdiction
Bishop Auckland (CTC Middlesbrough)	Saddler House Saddler Street Bishop Auckland County Durham DL14 7HF Tel: 01388 602423 Fax: 01388 606651 DX 65100 Bishop Aukland 2	D
Blackburn (CTC Preston)	64 Victoria Street Blackburn Lancs BB1 6DJ Tel: 01254 680640 Fax: 01254 692712 DX 702650 Blackburn 4	AC B CC D **DR** FHC
Blackpool	The Law Courts Chapel Street Blackpool Lancs FY1 5RJ Tel: 01253 754020 Fax: 01253 295255 DX 724900 Blackpool 10	B D **DR**
Blackwood (CTC Cardiff)	Blackwood Road Blackwood South Wales NP2 2XB Tel: 01495 223197 Fax: 01495 220289 DX 99470 Blackwood 2	B D **DR**
Bodmin (CTC Truro)	Cockswell House Market Street Bodmin Cornwall PL31 2HJ Tel: 01208 74224/73735 Fax: 01208 77255 DX 136846 Bodmin 2	D

County Court	Address	Additional Jurisdiction
Bolton (CTC Manchester)	Bolton Combined Court Centre The Law Courts Blackhorse Street Bolton BL1 1SU Tel: 01204 392881 Fax: 01204 373706 DX 702611 Bolton 3	AC B D **DR** FHC
Boston (CTC Lincoln)	55 Norfolk Street Boston Lincs PE21 6PE Tel: 01205 366080 Fax: 01205 311692 DX 701922 Boston 2	B D **DR**
Bournemouth	Courts of Justice Deansleigh Road Bournemouth Dorset BH7 7DS Tel: 01202 502800 Fax: 01202 502801 DX 98420 Bournemouth 4	AC B CC D **DR** FHC CTC – Poole, Weymouth
Bow (CTC Central London)	96 Romford Road Stratford London E15 4EG Tel: 020 8536 5200 Fax: 020 8503 1152 DX 97490 Stratford (London) 2	AC D FHC
Bradford	Bradford Combined Court Centre Exchange Square Drake Street Bradford W Yorks BD1 1JA Tel: 01274 840274 Fax: 01274 840275 DX 702083 Bradford 3	AC B D **DR** FHC CTC – Keighley, Skipton

County Court	Address	Additional Jurisdiction
Brecknock (CTC Swansea)	Brecon Law Courts Cambrian Way Brecon Powys LD3 7HR Tel: 01970 636370 Fax: 01970 625985 DX 124340 Brecon 2 From 23 February 2004 the court is located at: Merthyr Tydfil Combined Court Centre, *see* Merthyr Tydfil	D **DR**
Brentford (CTC Central London)	Alexandra Road High Street Brentford Middx TW8 0JJ Tel: 020 8231 8940 Fax: 020 8568 2401 DX 97840 Brentford 2	AC D FHC
Bridgend (CTC Cardiff)	Crown Buildings Angel Street Bridgend Mid Glam CF31 4AS Tel: 01656 768881 Fax: 01656 647124 DX 99750 Bridgend 2	B D **DR**
Brighton	William Street Brighton BN2 2RF Tel: 01273 674421 Fax: 01273 602138 DX 98070 Brighton 3	AC B CC D **DR** FHC CTC – Chichester, Eastbourne, Hastings, Haywards Heath, Horsham, Lewes, Worthing
Bristol	Greyfriars Lewins Mead Bristol BS1 2NR Tel: 0117 929 4414 Fax: 0117 925 0912 Fax: 0117 925 6172 DX 95903 Bristol 3	AC B CDR CC D **DR** FHC MC TCC RR CTC – Bath, Weston-super-Mare

County Court	Address	Additional Jurisdiction
Bromley (CTC Croydon)	Court House College Road Bromley Kent BR1 3PX Tel: 020 8290 9620 Fax: 020 8313 9624 DX 98080 Bromley 2	AC D FHC
Burnley	Burnley Combined Court Centre The Law Courts Hammerton Street Burnley Lancs BB11 1XD Tel: 01282 416899 Fax: 01282 414911 DX 724940 Burnley 4	B D **DR** CTC – Accrington, Nelson, Rawtenstall
Burton-upon-Trent (CTC Derby)	165 Station Street Burton-Upon-Trent Staffs DE14 1BP Tel: 01283 568241 Fax: 01283 517245 DX 702044 Burton-upon-Trent 3	B D
Bury	Tenterden Street Bury Lancs BL9 0HJ Tel: 0161 764 1344 Fax: 0161 763 4995 DX 702615 Bury 2	D **DR** CTC
Bury St Edmunds (CTC Cambridge)	Triton House Entrance B St Andrews Street (North) Bury St Edmunds IP33 1TR Tel: 01284 753254 Fax: 01284 702687 DX 97640 Bury St Edmunds 3	B D **DR**

County Court	Address	Additional Jurisdiction
Buxton (CTC Derby)	1–3 Hardwick Street Buxton Derbys SK17 6DH Tel: 01298 23734 Fax: 01298 73281 DX 701970 Buxton 2	
Caernarfon (CTC Chester)	Llanberis Road Caernarfon Gwynedd LL55 2DF Tel: 01286 678911 Fax: 01286 678965 DX 702483 Caernarfon 2	B CC D **DR** FHC
Cambridge	197 East Road Cambridge CB1 1BA Tel: 01223 224500 Fax: 01223 224590 DX 97650 Cambridge 3	AC B CC D **DR** FHC RR CTC – Harlow, Bury St Edmunds
Canterbury	Canterbury Combined Court Centre The Law Courts Chaucer Road Canterbury Kent CT1 1ZA Tel: 01227 819200 Fax: 01227 819283 DX 99710 Canterbury 3	AC CC D **DR** FHC RR CTC – Ashford, Maidstone, Medway, Thanet
Cardiff	2 Park Street Cardiff CF10 1ET Tel: 029 20376400 Fax: 029 20376475 DX 99500 Cardiff 6	AC B CDR CC D **DR** FHC MC TCC RR CTC – Blackwood, Bridgend, Newport (Gwent), Pontypool

County Court	Address	Additional Jurisdiction
Carlisle	Carlisle Combined Court Centre Courts of Justice Earl Street Carlisle Cumbria CA1 1DJ Tel: 01228 520619 Fax: 01228 590588 DX 65335 Carlisle	AC B CC D **DR** FHC RR CTC – Penrith, Whitehaven
Carmarthen (CTC Swansea)	The Old Vicarage Picton Terrace Carmarthen SA31 1BJ Tel: 01267 228010 Fax: 01267 221844 DX 99570 Carmarthen 2 *Court House* Guildhall Carmarthen	B D **DR** FHC
Central London	Central London Civil Justice Centre 13–14 Park Crescent London W1N 1HT Tel: 020 7917 5000 Fax: 020 7917 5014 DX 97325 Regents Park 2 *Court House and Listing Office* Central London Civil Justice Centre 26 Park Crescent London W1N 1HT	MC TCC RR CTC – Barnet, Bow, Brentford, Clerkenwell, Edmonton, Ilford, Lambeth, Romford, Shoreditch, Wandsworth, West London, Willesden, Woolwich
Chelmsford (CTC Colchester)	London House New London Road Chelmsford Essex CM2 0QR Tel: 01245 264670 Fax: 01245 496216 DX 97660 Chelmsford 4	AC B CC D **DR** FHC

County Court	Address	Additional Jurisdiction
Cheltenham (CTC Gloucester)	The Court House County Court Road Cheltenham Glos GL50 1HB Tel: 01242 519983 Fax: 01242 252741 DX 98630 Cheltenham 4	B **DR**
Chepstow	Closed with effect from 1.4.02 *See Newport (Gwent) from this date*	
Chester	Trident House Little St John Street Chester CH1 1SN Tel: 01244 404200 Fax: 01244 404300 DX 702460 Chester 4 *Court House* 5 Civic Way Ellesmere Port Cheshire L65 0HD	AC B CC D **DR** FHC MC TCC CTC – Caernarfon, Llangefni, Conwy & Colwyn, Crewe, Macclesfield, Mold, Northwich, Rhyl, Runcorn, Warrington, Welshpool, Wrexham
Chesterfield (CTC Derby)	St Mary's Gate Chesterfield Derbys S41 7ED Tel: 01246 501200 Fax: 01246 501205 DX 703160 Chesterfield 3	B D **DR**
Chichester (CTC Brighton)	Chichester Combined Court Centre Southgate Chichester West Sussex PO19 1SX Tel: 01243 520700 Fax: 01243 533756 DX 97460 Chichester 2	D **DR** FHC

County Court	Address	Additional Jurisdiction
Chorley (CTC Preston)	59 St Thomas's Road Chorley Lancs PR7 1JE Tel: 01257 262778 Fax: 01257 232843 DX 702665 Chorley 3	D
Clerkenwell (CTC Central London)	33 Duncan Terrace Islington London N1 8AN Tel: 020 7359 7347 Fax: 020 7354 1166 DX 146640 Islington 4	
Colchester	Falkland House 25 Southway Colchester Essex CO3 3EG Tel: 01206 572743 Fax: 01206 369610 DX 97670 Colchester 3 *Court House* Falkland House 25 Southway Colchester *Trial Centre* Norfolk House 23 Southway Colchester Tel: 01206 769649 Fax: 01206 765183	B D **DR** FHC CTC – Chelmsford, Ipswich
Consett (CTC Newcastle-upon-Tyne)	Victoria Road Consett Co Durham DH8 5AU Tel: 01207 502854 Fax: 01207 582626 DX 65106 Consett 2	D
Conwy & Colwyn (CTC Chester)	36 Princes Drive Colwyn Bay North Wales LL29 8LA Tel: 01492 530807 Fax: 01492 533591 DX 702492 Colwyn Bay 2	

County Court	Address	Additional Jurisdiction
Coventry	Coventry Combined Court Centre 140 Much Park Street Coventry CV1 2SN Tel: 024 7653 6166 Fax: 024 7652 0443 DX 701580 Coventry 5	AC B CC D **DR** FHC CTC – Nuneaton, Rugby, Stratford-upon-Avon, Warwick
Crewe (CTC Chester)	The Law Courts Civic Centre Crewe Cheshire CW1 2DP Tel: 01270 212255 Fax: 01270 216344 DX 702504 Crewe 2	B D **DR** FHC
Croydon	The Law Courts Altyre Road Croydon CR9 5AB Tel: 020 8410 4797 Fax: 020 8760 0432 DX 97470 Croydon 6	AC B D **DR** FHC CTC – Bromley, Dartford, Gravesend, Tunbridge Wells
Darlington (CTC Middlesbrough)	4 Coniscliffe Road Darlington County Durham DL3 7RL Tel: 01325 463224 Fax: 01325 362829 DX 65109 Darlington 3	B D **DR** FHC
Dartford (CTC Croydon)	Court House Home Gardens Dartford Kent DA1 1DX Tel: 01322 629820 Fax: 01322 270902 DX 98090 Dartford 2	FHC

County Court	Address	Additional Jurisdiction
Derby	Derby Combined Court Centre Morledge Derby DE1 2XE Tel: 01332 622600 Fax: 01332 622543 DX 724060 Derby 21	AC B CC D **DR** FHC CTC – Burton-upon-Trent, Buxton, Chesterfield
Dewsbury (CTC Huddersfield)	Court House Eightlands Road Dewsbury W Yorks WF13 2PE Tel: 01924 466135 Fax: 01924 456419 DX 702086 Dewsbury 2	B D **DR** FHC
Doncaster	74 Waterdale Doncaster South Yorks DN1 3BT Tel: 01302 381730 Fax: 01302 768090 DX 702089 Doncaster 4	B D **DR** FHC CTC
Dudley (CTC Birmingham)	Harbour Buildings Waterfront West Brierley Hill Dudley West Midlands DY5 1LN Tel: 01384 480799 Fax: 01384 482799 DX 701949 Dudley 2	B D **DR** FHC
Durham (CTC Newcastle-upon-Tyne)	Hallgarth Street Durham DH1 3RG Tel: 0191 3865941 Fax: 0191 3861328 DX 65115 Durham 5	B D **DR** FHC
Eastbourne (CTC Brighton)	4 The Avenue Eastbourne E Sussex BN21 3SZ Tel: 01323 735195 Fax: 01323 638829 DX 98110 Eastbourne 2	B D **DR**

County Court	Address	Additional Jurisdiction
Edmonton (CTC Central London)	The Court House 59 Fore Street Edmonton London N18 2TN Tel: 020 8807 1666 Fax: 020 8803 0564 DX 136686 Edmonton 3	D FHC
Epsom (CTC Kingston-upon-Thames)	The Parade Epsom Surrey KT18 5DN Tel: 01372 721801 Fax: 01372 726588 DX 97850 Epsom 3	D
Evesham (CTC Worcester)	1st Floor 87 High Street Evesham Worcs WR11 4EE Tel: 01386 442287 Fax: 01386 49203 DX 701910 Evesham 3	
Exeter	Exeter Combined Court Centre The Castle Exeter Devon EX4 3PS Tel: 01392 210655 Fax: 01392 433546 DX 98440 Exeter 2	AC B D **DR** FHC TCC RR CTC – Barnstaple, Torquay & Newton Abbott
Gateshead (CTC Newcastle-upon-Tyne)	5th Floor, Chad House Tynegate Precinct Gateshead Tyne and Wear NE8 3HZ Tel: 0191 477 2445 Fax: 0191 477 8562 DX 65118 Gateshead 2	D

County Court	Address	Additional Jurisdiction
Gloucester	Kimbrose Way Gloucester GL1 2DE Tel: 01452 529351 Fax: 01452 386309 DX 98660 Gloucester 5	B D **DR** FHC CTC – Cheltenham
Grantham (CTC Lincoln)	Harlatton Road Grantham Lincs NG31 7SB Tel: 01476 539030 Fax: 01476 539040 DX 701931 Grantham 2	
Gravesend (CTC Croydon)	26 King Street Gravesend Kent DA12 2DU Tel: 01474 321771 Fax: 01474 534811 DX 98140 Gravesend 2	
Great Grimsby	Great Grimsby Combined Court Centre Town Hall Square Grimsby North East Lincs DN31 1HX Tel: 01472 311811 Fax: 01472 312039 DX 702007 Grimsby 3	B D **DR** FHC CTC – Scunthorpe
Guildford (CTC Kingston-upon-Thames)	The Law Courts Mary Road Guildford Surrey GU1 4PS Tel: 01483 595200 Fax: 01483 300031 DX 97860 Guildford 5	AC B CC D **DR** FHC
Halifax (CTC Huddersfield)	Prescott Street Halifax W Yorks HX1 2JJ Tel: 01422 344700 Fax: 01422 360132 DX 702095 Halifax 2	B D **DR** FHC

County Court	Address	Additional Jurisdiction
Harlow (CTC Cambridge)	Gate House The High Harlow Essex CM20 1UW Tel: 01279 443291 Fax: 01279 451110 DX 97700 Harlow 2	D **DR**
Harrogate (CTC York)	2 Victoria Avenue Harrogate N Yorks HG1 1EL Tel: 01423 503921 Fax: 01423 528679 DX 702098 Harrogate 3	B D **DR** FHC
Hartlepool (CTC Middlesbrough)	The Law Courts Victoria Road Hartlepool TS24 8BS Tel: 01429 268198 Fax: 01429 862550 DX 65121 Hartlepool 2	D **DR**
Hastings (CTC Brighton)	The Law Courts Bohemia Road Hastings East Sussex TN34 1QX Tel: 01424 435128 Fax: 01424 421585 DX 98150 Hastings 2	B D **DR**
Haverfordwest (CTC Swansea)	Penffynnon Hawthorne Rise Haverfordwest Pembs SA61 2AZ Tel: 01437 772060 Fax: 01437 769222 DX 99610 Haverfordwest 2	B D **DR** FHC
Haywards Heath (CTC Brighton)	Milton House Milton Road Haywards Heath W Sussex RH16 1YZ Tel: 01444 447970 Fax: 01444 415282 DX 98160 Haywards Heath 3	

County Court	Address	Additional Jurisdiction
Hereford (CTC Worcester)	1st Floor Barclays Bank Chambers 1–3 Broad Street Hereford HR4 9BA Tel: 01432 357233 Fax: 01432 352593 DX 701904 Hereford 2 *Court House* Shire Hall Hereford	B D **DR**
Hertford (CTC Luton)	4th Floor, Sovereign House Hale Road Hertford SG13 8DY Tel: 01992 503954 Fax: 01992 501274 DX 97710 Hertford 2	B D
High Wycombe (CTC Reading)	The Law Courts Easton Street High Wycombe HP11 1LR Tel: 01494 436374 Fax: 01494 459430 DX 97880 High Wycombe 3	
Hitchin (CTC Luton)	Park House 1–12 Old Park Road Hitchin Herts SG5 1LX Tel: 01462 443750 – 443752 Fax: 01462 443758 DX 97720 Hitchin 2	D FHC
Horsham (CTC Brighton)	The Law Courts Hurst Road Horsham W Sussex RH12 2EU Tel: 01403 252474 Fax: 01403 258844 DX 98170 Horsham 2	D

County Court	Address	Additional Jurisdiction
Huddersfield	Queensgate House Queensgate Huddersfield HD1 2RR Tel: 01484 421043 Fax: 01484 426366 DX 703013 Huddersfield 2	B D **DR** FHC CTC – Dewsbury, Halifax
Huntingdon (CTC Northampton)	Ground Floor Godwin House George Street Huntingdon Cambs PE29 3BD Tel: 01480 450932 Fax: 01480 435397 DX 96650 Huntingdon 2	
Ilford (CTC Central London)	Buckingham Road Ilford Essex IG1 1BR Tel: 020 8478 1132 Fax: 020 8553 2824 DX 97510 Ilford 3	D FHC
Ipswich (CTC Colchester)	8 Arcade Street Ipswich Suffolk IP1 1EJ Tel: 01473 214256 Fax: 01473 251797 DX 97730 Ipswich 3	AC B CC D **DR** FHC
Keighley (CTC Bradford)	Yorkshire Bank Chambers North Street Keighley W Yorks BD21 3SH Tel: 01535 602803 Fax: 01535 610549 DX 703007 Keighley 2	D **DR** FHC

County Court	Address	Additional Jurisdiction
Kendal (CTC Lancaster)	Burneside Road Kendal Cumbria LA9 4NF Tel: 01539 721218 Fax: 01539 733840 DX 63450 Kendal 2	B D **DR**
Kettering (CTC Northampton)	Dryland Street Kettering Northants NN16 0BE Tel: 01536 512471 Fax: 01536 416857 DX 701886 Kettering 2	
Kidderminster (CTC Birmingham)	10 Comberton Place Kidderminster DY10 1QR Tel: 01562 822480 Fax: 01562 827809 DX 701946 Kidderminster 2	B
King's Lynn (CTC Norwich)	Chequer House 12 King Street King's Lynn Norfolk PE30 1ES Tel: 01553 772067 Fax: 01553 769824 DX 97740 King's Lynn 2	B D **DR** FHC
Kingston-upon-Hull	Kingston-upon-Hull Combined Court Centre Lowgate Kingston-upon-Hull HU1 2EZ Tel: 01482 586161 Fax: 01482 588527 DX 703010 Hull 5	AC B CC D **DR** FHC CTC
Kingston-upon-Thames	St James' Road Kingston-upon-Thames Surrey KT1 2AD Tel: 020 8546 8843 Fax: 020 8547 1426 DX 97890 Kingston-upon-Thames 3	B D FHC CTC – Epsom, Guildford, Reigate, Staines

County Court	**Address**	**Additional Jurisdiction**
Lambeth (CTC Central London)	Cleaver St Kennington Road SE11 4DZ Tel: 020 7091 4410/4420 Fax: 020 7735 8147 DX 145020 Kennington 2	
Lancaster	2nd Floor, Mitre House Church Street Lancaster LA1 1UZ Tel: 01524 68112 Fax: 01524 846478 DX 145880 Lancaster 2	AC B CC D **DR** FHC CTC – Kendal
Leeds	Leeds Combined Court Centre The Court House 1 Oxford Row Leeds LS1 3BG Tel: 0113 283 0040 Fax: 0113 244 8507 DX 703016 Leeds 6	AC B CDR CC D **DR** FHC MC TCC RR CTC – Pontefract, Wakefield
Leicester	90 Wellington Street Leicester LE1 6HG Tel: 0116 222 2323 Fax: 0116 222 3450 DX 17401 Leicester 3	AC B CC D **DR** FHC CTC – Melton Mowbray
Leigh (CTC Liverpool)	22 Walmesley Road Leigh Greater Manchester WN7 1YF Tel: 01942 673639 Fax: 01942 681216 DX 702555 Leigh 2	D
Lewes (CTC Brighton)	Lewes Combined Court Centre The Law Courts High Street Lewes East Sussex BN7 1YB Tel: 01273 480400 Fax: 01273 485270 DX 97395 Lewes 4	

County Court	Address	Additional Jurisdiction
Lichfield	Closed 3.7.00 *See now Burton-upon-Trent County Court, Stafford County Court, Tamworth County Court or Walsall County Court*	
Lincoln	Lincoln Combined Court Centre The Court House 360 High Street Lincoln LN5 7PS Tel: 01522 883000 Fax: 01522 883003 DX 703231 Lincoln 6	AC B CC D **DR** FHC CTC – Boston, Grantham, Newark, Skegness, Worksop
Liverpool	Liverpool Combined Court Centre Queen Elizabeth II Law Courts Derby Square Liverpool L2 1XA Tel: 0151 473 7373 Fax: 0151 471 1095 DX 702600 Liverpool 5	AC B CDR CC D **DR** FHC MC TCC CTC – Birkenhead, Leigh, St Helens, Southport, Wigan
Llanelli (CTC Swansea)	2nd Floor Court Buildings Town Hall Square Llanelli Carms SA15 3AL Tel: 01554 757171 Fax: 01554 758079 DX 99510 Llanelli 2	D
Llangefni (CTC Chester)	County Court Buildings Glanhwfa Road Llangefni Gwynedd LL77 7EN Tel: 01248 750225 Fax: 01248 750778 DX 702480 Llangefni 2	AC B D **DR** FHC

County Court	Address	Additional Jurisdiction
Lowestoft (CTC Norwich)	28 Gordon Road Lowestoft Suffolk NR32 1NL Tel: 01502 586047 Fax: 01502 569319 DX 97750 Lowestoft 2	D **DR**
Ludlow (CTC Telford)	9–10 King Street Ludlow Shropshire SY8 1QW Tel: 01584 872091 Fax: 01584 877606 DX 702013 Ludlow 2	
Luton	5th Floor, Cresta House Alma Street Luton Bedfordshire LU1 2PU Tel: 01582 506700 Fax: 01582 506701 DX 97760 Luton 4	AC B CC D **DR** FHC CTC – Aylesbury, Milton Keynes, Bedford, Hertford, Hitchin, St Albans, Watford
Macclesfield (CTC Chester)	2nd Floor Silk House 32 Park Green Macclesfield Cheshire SK11 7NA Tel: 01625 412800 Fax: 01625 501262 DX 702498 Macclesfield 3 *Court House* 2nd Floor 32 Park Green Macclesfield Cheshire SK11 7NA	AC B D **DR** FHC

County Court	Address	Additional Jurisdiction
Maidstone (CTC Canterbury)	Maidstone Combined Court Centre The Law Courts Barker Road Maidstone Kent ME16 8EQ Tel: 01622 202000 Fax: 01622 202002 DX 130065 Maidstone 7	B D **DR** FHC
Manchester	Courts of Justice Crown Square Manchester M60 9DJ Tel: 0161 954 1800 Fax: 0161 954 1661 DX 702541 Manchester 11	AC B CDR CC D **DR** FHC MC RR CTC – Bolton
Mansfield (CTC Nottingham)	Beech House 58 Commercial Gate Mansfield Notts NG18 1EU Tel: 01623 656406 Fax: 01623 626561 DX 702180 Mansfield 3	D **DR** FHC
Mayor's & City of London Court	Guildhall Buildings Basinghall Street London EC2V 5AR Tel: 020 7796 5400 Fax: 020 7796 5424 DX 97520 Moorgate (EC2)	CTC
Medway (CTC Canterbury)	Anchorage House 47–67 High Street Chatham Kent ME4 4DW Tel: 01634 810720 Fax: 01634 811332 DX 98180 Chatham 4	AC B CC D **DR** FHC

County Court	Address	Additional Jurisdiction
Melton Mowbray (CTC Leicester)	The Court House Norman Way Melton Mowbray Leics LE13 1NH Tel: 01664 458100 Fax: 01664 501869 DX 701937 Melton Mowbray 2	
Merthyr Tydfil (CTC Swansea)	Merthyr Tydfil Combined Court Centre The Law Courts Glebeland Place Merthyr Tydfil Mid Glam CF47 8BH Tel: 01685 358200 Fax: 01685 359727 DX 99582 Merthyr Tydfil 2	B D **DR** FHC
Middlesbrough	Teesside Combined Court Centre The Law Courts Russell Street Middlesbrough Cleveland TS1 2AE Tel: 01642 340000 Fax: 01642 340002 DX 65152 Middlesbrough 2	AC B CC D **DR** FHC CTC – Bishop Auckland, Darlington, Hartlepool
Milton Keynes (CTC Luton)	351 Silbury Boulevard (Rear) Witan Gate East Central Milton Keynes MK9 2DT Tel: 01908 302800 Fax: 01908 230063 DX 136266 Milton Keynes 6	AC CC D **DR** FHC
Mold (CTC Chester)	Law Courts County Civic Centre Mold Flintshire CH7 1AE Tel: 01352 707330 Fax: 01352 707333 DX 702521 Mold 2	

County Court	Address	Additional Jurisdiction
Monmouth	Closed with effect from 1.4.02 *See Newport (Gwent) from this date*	
Morpeth & Berwick (CTC Newcastle-upon-Tyne)	Fountain House Newmarket Morpeth NE61 1LA Tel: 01670 512221 Fax: 01670 504188 DX 65124 Morpeth 2	D
Neath & Port Talbot (CTC Swansea)	Forster Road Neath W Glam SA11 3BN Tel: 01639 642267 Fax: 01639 633505 DX 99550 Neath 2	B D
Nelson (CTC Burnley)	Phoenix Chambers 9–13 Holme Street Nelson Lancs BB9 9SU Tel: 01282 601177 Fax: 01282 619557 DX 702560 Nelson 2	D
Newark (CTC Lincoln)	Crown Building 41 Lombard Street Newark Notts NG24 1XN Tel: 01636 703607 Fax: 01636 613726 DX 701928 Newark 2	
Newbury (CTC Reading)	Kings Road West Newbury Berks RG14 5XU Tel: 01635 40928 Fax: 01635 37704 DX 30816 Newbury 1	B

County Court	Address	Additional Jurisdiction
Newcastle-upon-Tyne	Newcastle-upon-Tyne Combined Court Centre The Law Courts Quayside Newcastle-Upon-Tyne NE1 3LA Tel: 0191 2012000 Fax: 0191 2012001 DX 65128 Newcastle-upon-Tyne 2	AC B CDR CC D **DR** FHC MC TCC RR CTC – Consett, Durham, Gateshead, Morpeth, North Shields, South Shields, Sunderland
Newport (Gwent) (CTC Cardiff)	3rd Floor, Olympia House Upper Dock Street Newport South Wales NP20 1PQ Tel: 01633 227150 Fax: 01633 263820 DX 99480 Newport (South Wales) 4 *Court House* The Concourse Clarence House Clarence Place Newport South Wales	AC B CC D **DR** FHC
Newport (Isle of Wight) (CTC Portsmouth)	Newport (Isle of Wight) Combined Court Centre 1 Quay Street Newport Isle of Wight PO30 5YT Tel: 01983 526821 Fax: 01983 821039 DX 98460 Newport (I.o.W.) 2	B D **DR**

County Court	Address	Additional Jurisdiction
Northampton	Northampton Combined Court Centre 85–87 Lady's Lane Northampton NN1 3HQ Tel: 01604 470400 Fax: 01604 232398 DX 725380 Northampton 21 *County Court Bulk Centre* 21–27 St Katherine's Street Northampton NN1 2LH Tel: 01604 601636 Fax: 01604 601631 DX 702885 Northampton 7 *Centralised Attachment of Earnings Payments (CAPS)* Tel: 01604 601555 Fax: 01604 604806 *Parking Enforcement Centre* Tel: 0345 045007 Fax: 0345 078607	AC B CC D **DR** FHC CTC – Huntingdon, Kettering, Peterborough, Wellingborough
North Shields (CTC Newcastle-upon-Tyne)	Nothumbria House Norfolk Street North Shields Tyne & Wear NE30 1EX Tel: 0191 257 5866 Fax: 0191 296 4268 DX 65137 North Shields 2	D
Northwich (CTC Chester)	25–27 High Street Northwich Cheshire CW9 5DB Tel: 01606 42554 Fax: 01606 331490 DX 702515 Northwich 3	
Norwich	Norwich Combined Court Centre The Law Courts Bishopsgate Norwich NR3 1UR Tel: 01603 728200 Fax: 01603 760863 DX 97385 Norwich 5	AC B CC D **DR** FHC CTC – King's Lynn, Lowestoft

County Court	Address	Additional Jurisdiction
Nottingham	The Law Courts 60 Canal Street Nottingham NG1 7EJ Tel: 01159 103500 Fax: 01159 103510 Fax: 01159 103524 (Listing) DX 702380 Nottingham 7	AC B CC D **DR** FHC TCC RR CTC – Mansfield
Nuneaton (CTC Coventry)	Heron House Newdegate Street Nuneaton Warks CV11 4EL Tel: 01203 386134 Fax: 01203 352769 DX 701940 Nuneaton 2	
Oldham	The County Court House New Radcliffe Street Oldham OL1 1NL Tel: 0161 290 4200 Fax: 0161 290 4222 DX 702595 Oldham 2	B D **DR** FHC CTC – Stockport, Tameside
Oswestry (CTC Telford)	2nd Floor The Guildhall Bailey Head Oswestry Shropshire SY11 2EW Tel: 01691 652127 Fax: 01691 671239 DX 701958 Oswestry 2	
Oxford	Oxford Combined Court Centre St Aldates Oxford OX1 1TL Tel: 01865 264200 Fax: 01865 790773 DX 96450 Oxford 4	AC B CC D **DR** FHC RR CTC – Banbury

County Court	Address	Additional Jurisdiction
Penrith (CTC Carlisle)	The Court House Lowther Terrace Penrith Cumbria CA11 7QL Tel: 01768 862535 Fax: 01768 899700 DX 65207 Penrith	D
Penzance (CTC Truro)	Trevear Alverton Penzance Cornwall TR18 4GH Tel: 01736 362987 Fax: 01736 330595 DX 136900 Penzance 2	D
Peterborough (CTC Northampton)	Peterborough Combined Court Centre Crown Buildings Rivergate Peterborough PE1 1EJ Tel: 01733 349161 Fax: 01733 557348 DX 702302 Peterborough 8	AC B CC D **DR** FHC
Plymouth	Plymouth Combined Court Centre The Law Courts 10 Armada Way Plymouth Devon PL1 2ER Tel: 01752 677400 Fax: 01752 208286 DX 98470 Plymouth 7	AC B CC D **DR** FHC RR CTC
Pontefract (CTC Leeds)	Horsefair House Horsefair Pontefract W Yorks WF8 1RJ Tel: 01977 702357 Fax: 01977 600204 DX 703022 Pontefract 2	D **DR** FHC

County Court	Address	Additional Jurisdiction
Pontypool (CTC Cardiff)	Park Road, Riverside Pontypool Torfaen NP4 6NZ Tel:01495 762248 Fax: 01495 762467 DX 117500 Pontypool 2	
Pontypridd (CTC Swansea)	The Courthouse Courthouse Street Pontypridd Mid Glam CF37 1JW Tel: 01443 402471 Fax: 01443 480305 DX 99620 Pontypridd 2	AC B CC D **DR** FHC
Poole (CTC Bournemouth)	The Law Courts Civic Centre Park Road Poole Dorset BH15 2NS Tel: 01202 741150 Fax: 01202 747245 DX 98700 Poole 4	
Portsmouth	Portsmouth Combined Court Centre The Courts of Justice Winston Churchill Avenue Portsmouth Hants PO1 2EB Tel: 023 9289 3000 Fax: 023 9282 6385 DX 98490 Portsmouth 5	AC B CC D **DR** FHC CTC – Newport (Isle of Wight)
Preston	Preston Combined Court Centre The Law Courts Openshaw Place Ring Way Preston PR1 2LL Tel: 01772 844700/844713 Fax: 01772 844710 DX 702660 Preston 5	B CDR D **DR** CTC – Blackburn, Chorley

County Court	Address	Additional Jurisdiction
Rawtenstall (CTC Burnley)	1 Grange Street Rawtenstall Lancs BB4 7RT Tel: 01706 214614 Fax: 01706 219814 DX 702565 Rawtenstall	D
Reading	160–163 Friar Street Reading Berks RG1 1HE Tel: 0118 987 0500 Fax: 0118 987 0555 Fax: 0118 959 9827 DX 98010 Reading 6	AC B CC D **DR** FHC CTC – Newbury, High Wycombe, Uxbridge, Slough
Redditch (CTC Worcester)	13 Church Road Redditch Worcs B97 4AB Tel: 01527 67822 Fax: 01527 65791 DX 701880 Redditch 2	
Reigate (CTC Kingston-upon-Thames)	The Law Courts Hatchlands Road Redhill Surrey RH1 6BL Tel: 01737 763637 Fax: 01737 766917 DX 98020 Redhill West	D
Rhyl (CTC Chester)	The Courthouse Clwyd Street Rhyl LL18 3LA Tel: 01745 352940 Fax: 01745 336726 DX 702489 Rhyl 2	AC B CC D **DR** FHC
Romford (CTC Central London)	2a Oaklands Avenue Romford Essex RM1 4DP Tel: 01708 775353 Fax: 01708 756653 DX 97530 Romford 2	AC B D **DR** FHC

County Court	Address	Additional Jurisdiction
Rotherham (CTC Sheffield)	Portland House Mansfield Road Rotherham S Yorks S60 2BX Tel: 01709 364786 Fax: 01709 838044 DX 703025 Rotherham 4	D FHC
Rugby (CTC Coventry)	5 Newbold Road Rugby CV21 2RN Tel: 01788 542543 Fax: 01788 550212 DX 701934 Rugby 2	
Runcorn (CTC Chester)	The Law Courts Halton Lea Runcorn Cheshire WA7 2HA Tel: 01928 716533 Fax: 01928 701692 DX 702466 Runcorn 3	D
Salford	Prince William House Peel Cross Road Salford M5 4RR Tel: 0161 745 7511 Fax: 0161 745 7202 DX 702630 Salford 5	B D **DR** TCC CTC – Altrincham
Salisbury (CTC Swindon)	Salisbury Combined Court Centre The Courts of Justice Alexandra House St John Street Salisbury Wiltshire SP1 2PN Tel: 01722 325444 Fax: 01722 412991 DX 98500 Salisbury 2	B D **DR** FHC

County Court	Address	Additional Jurisdiction
Scarborough (CTC York)	Pavilion House Valley Bridge Road Scarborough N Yorks YO11 2JS Tel: 01723 366361 Fax: 01723 501992 DX 65140 Scarborough 2	B D **DR** FHC
Scunthorpe (CTC Great Grimsby)	Crown Buildings Comforts Avenue Scunthorpe N Lincs DN15 6PR Tel: 01724 289111 Fax: 01724 291119 DX 702010 Scunthorpe 3	B D **DR**
Sheffield	Sheffield Combined Court Centre The Law Courts 50 West Bar Sheffield S3 8PH Tel: 0114 281 2400 Fax: 0114 281 2425 DX 703028 Sheffield 6	AC B CC D **DR** FHC CTC – Barnsley, Rotherham
Shoreditch (CTC Central London)	19 Leonard Street London EC2A 4AL Tel: 020 7253 0956 Fax: 020 7490 5613 DX 121000 Shoreditch 2	
Shrewsbury (CTC Telford)	4th Floor Cambrian Business Centre Chester Street Shrewsbury SY1 1NA Tel: 01743 289069 Fax: 01743 237954 DX 702047 Shrewsbury 3	B D **DR**

County Court	Address	Additional Jurisdiction
Skegness (CTC Lincoln)	*Hearings and counter services* Skegness Magistrates' Court HerefordPark Avenue Skegness *Postal address* 55 Norfolk Street Boston Lincs PE21 6PE Tel: 01205 366080 Fax: 01205 311692 DX 701922 Boston 2	
Skipton (CTC Bradford)	The Law Courts Otley Street Skipton N Yorks BD23 1RH Tel: 01756 793315 Fax: 01756 799989 DX 703031 Skipton 2	D FHC
Slough (CTC Reading)	The Law Courts Windsor Road Slough Berkshire SL1 2HE Tel: 01753 690300 Fax: 01753 575990 DX 98030 Slough 3	B D FHC
Southampton	Southampton Combined Court Centre The Courts of Justice London Road Southampton Hants SO15 2XQ Tel: 023 8021 3200 Fax: 023 8021 3222 DX 111000 Southampton 11	AC B D **DR** FHC RR CTC
Southend	Tylers House Tylers Avenue Southend-on-Sea Essex SS1 2AW Tel: 01702 601991 Fax: 01702 603090 DX 97780 Southend-on-Sea 2	B D **DR** FHC CTC – Basildon

SECTION 8 Miscellaneous

County Court	Address	Additional Jurisdiction
Southport (CTC Liverpool)	Duke's House 34 Hoghton Street Southport Merseyside PR9 0PU Tel: 01704 531541 Fax: 01704 542487 DX 702580 Southport 2	D **DR**
South Shields (CTC Newcastle-upon-Tyne)	Secretan Way South Shields Tyne & Wear NE33 1RG Tel: 0191 456 3343 Fax: 0191 427 9503 DX 65143 South Shields 3	D **DR**
St Albans (CTC Luton)	Victoria House Victoria Street St Albans Hertfordshire AL1 3TJ Tel: 01727 856925 Fax: 01727 852484 DX 97770 St Albans 2	B
St Helens (CTC Liverpool)	1st Floor, Rexmore House Cotham Street St Helens Merseyside WA10 1SE Tel: 01744 27544 Fax: 01744 20484 DX 702570 St Helens 2	D **DR**
Stafford (CTC Stoke-on-Trent)	Stafford Combined Court Centre Victoria Square Stafford ST16 2QQ Tel: 01785 610730 Fax: 01785 213250 DX 703190 Stafford 4	B D **DR** FHC

County Court	Address	Additional Jurisdiction
Staines (CTC Kingston-upon-Thames)	The Law Courts Knowle Green Staines Middx TW18 1XH Tel: 01784 459175 Fax: 01784 460176 DX 98040 Staines 2	D
Stockport (CTC Oldham)	5th Floor, Heron House Wellington Street Stockport Cheshire SK1 3DJ Tel: 01614 747707 Fax: 01614 763129 DX 702621 Stockport 4	AC B D **DR** FHC
Stoke-on-Trent	Stoke-on-Trent Combined Court Centre Bethesda Street Hanley Stoke-on-Trent Staffs ST1 3BP Tel: 01782 854000 Fax: 01782 854046 DX 703360 Hanley 3	AC B CC D **DR** FHC CTC – Stafford, Tamworth, Walsall
Stourbridge (CTC Birmingham)	7 Hagley Road Stourbridge W Mids DY8 1QL Tel: 01384 394232 Fax: 01384 441736 DX 701889 Stourbridge 2	B
Stratford-upon-Avon (CTC Coventry)	5 Elm Court Arden Street Stratford-upon-Avon Warks CV37 6PA Tel: 01789 293056 Fax: 01789 293056 DX 701998 Stratford-upon-Avon 3	

County Court	Address	Additional Jurisdiction
Sunderland (CTC Newcastle-upon-Tyne)	The Court House 44 John Street Sunderland Tyne & Wear SR1 1RB Tel: 0191 568 0750 Fax: 0191 514 3028 DX 65149 Sunderland 2	AC B CC D **DR** FHC
Swansea	Caravella House Quay West Quay Parade Swansea SA1 1SP Tel: 01792 510350 Fax: 01792 473520 DX 99740 Swansea 5	AC B CC D **DR** FHC CTC – Aberdare, Aberystwyth, Brecknock, Carmarthen, Haverfordwest, Llanelli, Merthyr Tydfil, Neath, Pontypridd
Swindon	Swindon Combined Court Centre The Law Courts Islington Street Swindon Wilts SN1 2HG Tel: 01793 690500 Fax: 01793 690555 DX 98430 Swindon 5	AC B CC D **DR** FHC CTC – Trowbridge, Salisbury
Tameside (CTC Oldham)	Scotland Street Ashton-under-Lyne Lancs OL6 6SS Tel: 01613 391711 Fax: 01613 391645 DX 702625 Ashton-under-Lyne 2	B
Tamworth (CTC Stoke-on-Trent)	The Precinct Lower Gungate Tamworth Staffs B79 7AJ Tel: 01827 62664 Fax: 01827 65289 DX 702016 Tamworth 2	

County Court	Address	Additional Jurisdiction
Taunton	Shire Hall Taunton Somerset TA1 4EU Tel: 01823 335972 Fax: 01823 351337 DX 98410 Taunton 2	AC B CC D **DR** FHC CTC – Yeovil
Telford	Telford Square Malinsgate Town Centre Telford Shropshire TF3 4JP Tel: 01952 291045 Fax: 01952 291601 DX 701976 Telford 3	AC CC D FHC CTC – Ludlow, Oswestry, Shrewsbury, Wolverhampton
Thanet (CTC Canterbury)	The Court House 2nd floor Cecil Square Margate Kent CT9 1RL Tel: 01843 221722 Fax: 01843 222730 DX 98210 Cliftonville 2	D **DR**
Torquay & Newton Abbot (CTC Exeter)	Nicholson Road Torquay Devon TQ2 7AZ Tel: 01803 616791 Fax: 01803 616795 DX 98740 Torquay 4	B D **DR**
Trowbridge (CTC Swindon)	Ground Floor, Clarks Mill Stallard Street Trowbridge Wilts BA14 8DB Tel: 01225 752101 Fax: 01225 776638 DX 98750 Trowbridge 2	D

County Court	Address	Additional Jurisdiction
Truro	Truro Combined Court Centre Courts of Justice Edward Street Truro TR1 2PB Tel: 01872 222340 Fax: 01872 222348 DX 135396 Truro 2	AC B CC D **DR** FHC CTC – Bodmin, Penzance
Tunbridge Wells (CTC Croydon)	Merevale House 42 46 London Road Tunbridge Wells Kent TN1 1DP Tel: 01892 515515 Fax: 01892 513676 DX 98220 Tunbridge Wells 3	B D **DR**
Uxbridge (CTC Reading)	501 Uxbridge Road Hayes Middx UB4 8HL Tel 020 8561 8562 Fax 020 8561 2020 DX 44658 Hayes (Middx)	D
Wakefield (CTC Leeds)	Crown House 127 Kirkgate Wakefield W Yorks WF1 1JW Tel: 01924 370268 Fax: 01924 200818 DX 703040 Wakefield 3	B D **DR** FHC
Walsall (CTC Stoke-on-Trent)	Bridge House Bridge Street Walsall W Mids WS1 1JQ Tel: 01922 728855 Fax: 01922 728891 DX 701943 Walsall 2	B D **DR** FHC

County Court	Address	Additional Jurisdiction
Wandsworth (CTC Central London)	76–78 Upper Richmond Road Putney London SW15 2SU Tel: 020 8333 4351 Fax :020 8877 9854 DX 97540 Putney 2	D FHC
Warrington (CTC Chester)	Warrington Combined Court Centre The Law Courts Legh Street Warrington WA1 1UR Tel: 01925 256700 Fax: 01925 413335 DX 702501 Warrington 3	AC B CC D **DR** FHC
Warwick (CTC Coventry)	Warwick Combined Court Centre Northgate Southside Warwick CV34 4RB Tel: 01926 492276 Fax: 01926 411855 DX 701964 Warwick 2	B
Watford (CTC Luton)	Cassiobury House 11–19 Station Road Watford Herts WD1 1EZ Tel: 01923 699400/699401 Fax: 01923 251317 DX 122740 Watford 5	AC CC D FHC
Wellingborough (CTC Northampton)	Lothersdale House West Villa Road Wellingborough Northants NN8 4NF Tel: 01933 226 168 Fax: 01933 272977 DX 701883 Wellingbrough 2	

County Court	Address	Additional Jurisdiction
Welshpool & Newtown (CTC Chester)	The Mansion House 24 Severn Street Welshpool Powys SY21 7UX Tel: 01938 552004 Fax: 01938 555395 DX 702524 Welshpool 2	B D **DR** FHC
West London (CTC Central London)	West London Courthouse Magistrates', County and Youth Courts 181 Talgarth Road Hammersmith London W6 8DN Tel: 020 8600 6868 Fax: 020 8600 6860 DX 97550 Hammersmith 2	
Weston-super-Mare (CTC Bristol)	2nd Floor, Regent House High Street Weston-super-Mare BS23 1JF Tel: 01934 626967 Fax: 01934 643028 DX 98810 Weston-super-Mare 2	D
Weymouth (CTC Bournemouth)	Weymouth & Dorchester Combined Court Centre Westwey House Westwey Road Weymouth Dorset DT4 8TE Tel: 01305 778684 Fax: 01305 788293 DX 98820 Weymouth 3	B D **DR** FHC
Whitehaven (CTC Carlisle)	Old Town Hall Duke Street Whitehaven Cumbria CA28 7NU Tel: 01946 67788 Fax: 01946 691219 DX 63990 Whitehaven 2	B D **DR**

County Court	Address	Additional Jurisdiction
Wigan (CTC Liverpool)	The Courthouse Crawford Street Wigan Lancs WN1 1NG Tel: 01942 246481 Fax: 01942 829164 DX 724820 Wigan 9	B D **DR**
Willesden (CTC Central London)	9 Acton Lane Harlesden London NW10 8SB Tel: 020 8963 8200 Fax: 020 8453 0946 DX 97560 Harlesden 2	D FHC
Winchester	Winchester Combined Court Centre The Law Courts Winchester Hants SO23 9EL Tel: 01962 814100 Fax: 01962 853821 DX 98520 Winchester 3	B D **DR** CTC – Aldershot, Basingstoke
Wolverhampton (CTC Telford)	Wolverhampton Combined Court Centre Pipers Row Wolverhampton W Mids WV1 3LQ Tel: 01902 481000 Fax: 01902 481076 DX 702019 Wolverhampton 4	AC B CC D **DR** FHC
Woolwich (CTC Central London)	The Court House 165 Powis Street Woolwich London SE18 6JW Tel: 020 8854 8048 Fax: 020 8316 4842 DX 123450 Woolwich 8	

County Court	Address	Additional Jurisdiction
Worcester	Worcester Combined Court Centre The Shirehall Foregate Street Worcester WR1 1EQ Tel: 01905 730800 Fax: 01905 730801 DX 721120 Worcester 11	AC B CC D **DR** FHC CTC – Evesham, Hereford, Redditch
Worksop (CTC Lincoln)	8 Slack Walk Worksop Notts S80 1LN Tel: 01909 472358 Fax: 01909 530181 DX 702190 Worksop 2	
Worthing (CTC Brighton)	The Law Courts Christchurch Road Worthing W Sussex BN11 1JD Tel: 01903 221920 Fax: 01903 235559 DX 98230 Worthing 4	D **DR**
Wrexham (CTC Chester)	2nd Floor Crown Buildings 31 Chester Street Wrexham LL13 8XN Tel: 01978 296140 Fax: 01978 290677 DX 721921 Wrexham 4	B D **DR** FHC RR
Yeovil (CTC Taunton)	22 Hendford Yeovil Somerset BA20 2QD Tel: 01935 382150 Fax: 01935 410004 DX 98830 Yeovil 2	B D **DR** FHC

County Court	Address	Additional Jurisdiction
York	Piccadilly House 55 Piccadilly York YO1 9WL Tel: 01904 629935 Fax: 01904 679963 DX 65165 York 4	AC B CC D **DR** FHC CTC – Harrogate, Scarborough

Holidays and Notable Dates

	2005
New Year's Day UK IRL USA CDN AUS NZ	Jan 1
New Year's Day Bank Holiday	Jan 3
St David's Day WAL	Mar 1
Mothering Sunday	Mar 6
St Patrick's Day IRL	Mar 17
Good Friday UK CDN AUS NZ	Mar 25
British Summer Time begins	Mar 27
Easter Monday UK IRL CDN AUS NZ	Mar 28
St George's Day ENG	Apr 23
May Day Holiday UK	May 2
Spring Bank Holiday UK	May 30
Father's Day	Jun 19
August Bank Holiday UK	Aug 29
British Summer Time ends	Oct 30
St Andrew's Day SCO	Nov 30
Christmas Day UK IRL USA CDN AUS NZ	Dec 25
Boxing Day/St Stephen's Day UK IRL CDN AUS NZ	Dec 26
Substitute Bank Holiday in lieu of Dec 25	Dec 27

Weights and Measures

MEASUREMENTS OF LENGTH

Imperial Units of Length		Metric Equivalents
Mil	1/1000 inch	0.0254 millimetres
Inch	1000 mils	2.54 centimetres
Link	7.92 inches	20.1168 centimetres
Foot	12 inches	0.3048 metres
Yard	3 feet	0.9144 metres
Fathom	6 feet	1.8288 metres
Cable	60 feet or 10 fathom	18.288 metres
Chain	22 yards (100 links)	20.1168 metres
Furlong	220 yards	201.168 metres
Mile	1,760 yards (8 furlongs)	1.609344 kilometres
Nautical mile	6080 feet	1.853184 kilometres

Metric Units of Length		Imperial Equivalents
Micron	1/1000 millimetre	0.03937007 mils
Millimetre	1/1000 metre	0.03937007 inches
Centimetre	1/100 metre	0.3937 inches
Decimetre	1/10 metre	3.937 inches
Metre	Metre	1.09361329 yards
Kilometre	1000 metres	0.62137712 miles 0.53961 nautical miles

MEASUREMENTS OF AREA

Imperial Units of Area		**Metric Equivalents**
Square inch	1/144 square feet	6.4516 square centimetres
Square foot	1/9 square yard	929.0304 square centimetres
Square yard	Square yard	0.83613 square metres
Square chain	484 square yards	404.685642 square metres
Rood	1,210 square yards	1011.714 square metres
Acre	4 roods 4840 square yards	4046.85642 square metres 40.4685642 ares
Square mile	640 acres	258.998811 hectares

Metric Units of Area		**Imperial Equivalents**
Square millimetre	1/100 square centimetre	0.00155 square inches
Square centimetre	1/100 square decimetre	0.155 square inches
Square decimetre	1/100 square metre	15.5 square inches
Square metre	Square metre	1.1959 square yards 10.7639 square feet
Are	100 square metres	119.599 square yards 0.09884 roods
Dekare	10 ares	0.2471 acres
Hectare	100 ares 1000 square metres	2.47105 acres
Square Kilometre	100 hectares	247.105 acres 0.3861 square miles

MEASUREMENTS OF VOLUME

Imperial Units of Volume		Metric Equivalents
Cubic inch	1000,000,000 cubic mils	16.387064 cubic centimetres
Cubic foot	1,728 cubic inches	28.3168465 decimetres
Cubic yard	27 cubic feet	0.76455485 cubic metres

Metric Units of Volume		Imperial Equivalents
Cubic centimetre	1,000 cubic millimetres	0.06102374 cubic inches
Cubic decimetre	1,000 cubic centimetres	0.03531466 cubic feet
Cubic metre	1,000 cubic decimetres	1.30795061 cubic yards 35.3147 cubic feet

MEASUREMENTS OF CAPACITY

Imperial, Apothecaries and US Units of Capacity		**Metric Equivalents**
Minim	Minim	0.0591938 millilitres
Fluid Drachm	60 minims	0.35516328 centilitres
Fluid ounce	8 fluid drachms	2.84130625 centilitres
US fluid ounce	1.0408 UK fluid ounces	29,573522656 millilitres
Gill	5 fluid ounces	1.42065312 decilitres
Pint	4 gills or 20 fluid ounces	0.56826125 litres
US pint	0.8327 UK pints 16 US fluid ounces	0.47317636 litres
Quart	2 pints 8 gills	1.1365225 litres
Gallon	4 quarts 1.20095 US gallons	4.54609 litres
US gallon	0.08327 UK gallons	3.7854109 litres
Peck	2 gallons 16 pints	9.09218 litres
Bushel	4 pecks 8 gallons	36.36872 litres
Quarter	8 bushels or 36 pecks	2.9094976 hectolitres
Chaldron	36 bushels 4 1/2 quarters	13.0927392 hectolitres

MEASUREMENTS OF CAPACTIY

Metric Units of Capacity		Imperial Equivalents
Millilitre	Millilitre	0.28156064 fluid drachms
Centilitre	10 millilitres	0.35195080 fluid ounces
Decilitre	10 centilitres	0.70390160 gills
Litre	10 decilitres	1.75975398 pints 0.21996924 UK gallons
Dekalitre	10 litres	2.1996924 UK gallons
Hectolitre	10 dekalitres 100 litres	21.996824 UK gallons

MEASUREMENTS OF WEIGHT

Imperial and Apothecaries Units of Weight		Metric Equivalents
Grain	Grain	64.79891 milligrams
Scruple	20 grains	1.2959782 grams
Pennyweight	24 grains	1.55517384 grams
Drachm	3 scruples 60 grains	3.8879346 grams
Troy ounce	8 drachms 480 grains	31.1034768 grams
Dram	1/16 ounce	1.77184519 grams
Ounce	16 drams 437.5 grains	28.3495231 grams
Troy pound (US)	12 troy ounces 5,760 grains	373.241721grams
Pound	16 ounces 7,000 grains	453.59237 grams 0.45359237 kilograms
Stone	14 pounds	6.35029318 kilograms
Quarter	28 pounds 2 stone	12.7005863 kilograms
Cental	100 pounds	45.359237 kilograms
Hundredweight	4 quarters or 112 pounds	50.8023454 kilograms
Short hundredweight (US)	100 pounds	45.359237 kilograms
Ton (UK/long ton)	20 cwt or 2,240 pounds	1.0160469 metric tonnes
Ton (US/short ton)	2,000 pounds	0.90718474 metric tonnes

MEASUREMENTS OF WEIGHT

Metric Units of Weight		Imperial Equivalents
Milligram	.001 grams	0.012432 grains
Centigram	.01 grams	0.15432 grains
Decigram	.1 grams	1.5432 grains
Gram	1 gram	0.03527396 ounces 0.03215 troy ounces
Dekagram	10 grams	0.35273961 ounces
Hectogram	100 grams	3.52739619 ounces
Kilogram	1,000 grams	2.20462262 pounds
Myriagram	10 kilograms	22.0462 pounds
Quintal	100 kilograms	1.9684 hundredweight
Tonne	1,000 kilograms	0.984207 UK tons 1.10231 US tons

CONVERSION TABLES

Length

kilometres (km)	km or miles	miles
1.609	**1**	0.621
3.219	**2**	1.243
4.828	**3**	1.864
6.437	**4**	2.485
8.047	**5**	3.107
9.656	**6**	3.728
11.265	**7**	4.350
12.875	**8**	4.971
14.484	**9**	5.592
16.093	**10**	6.214
32.187	**20**	12.427
48.280	**30**	18.641
64.374	**40**	24.855
80.467	**50**	31.069
96.561	**60**	37.282
112.654	**70**	43.496
128.758	**80**	49.710
144.841	**90**	55.923
160.934	**100**	62.137

Area

hectares (ha)	ha or acres	acres
0.405	**1**	2.471
0.809	**2**	4.942
1.214	**3**	7.413
1.619	**4**	9.884
2.023	**5**	12.355
2.428	**6**	14.826
2.833	**7**	17.297
3.237	**8**	19.769
3.642	**9**	22.240
4.047	**10**	24.711
8.094	**20**	49.421
12.140	**30**	74.132
16.187	**40**	98.842
20.234	**50**	123.553
24.281	**60**	148.263
28.328	**70**	172.974
32.375	**80**	197.684
36.422	**90**	222.395
40.469	**100**	247.105

Capacity

litres	litres or UK gallons	UK gallons
4.546	**1**	0.220
9.092	**2**	0.440
13.638	**3**	0.660
18.184	**4**	0.880
22.730	**5**	1.100
27.276	**6**	1.320
31.822	**7**	1.540
36.368	**8**	1.760
40.914	**9**	1.980
45.460	**10**	2.200
90.919	**20**	4.399
136.379	**30**	6.599
181.839	**40**	8.799
227.298	**50**	10.998
272.758	**60**	13.198
318.217	**70**	15.398
363.677	**80**	17.598
409.137	**90**	19.797
454.596	**100**	21.997

Weight

kilograms (kg)	kg or lb	pounds (lb)
0.454	**1**	2.205
0.907	**2**	4.409
1.361	**3**	6.614
1.814	**4**	8.819
2.268	**5**	11.023
2.722	**6**	13.228
3.175	**7**	15.432
3.629	**8**	17.637
4.082	**9**	19.842
4.536	**10**	22.046
9.072	**20**	44.092
13.608	**30**	66.139
18.144	**40**	88.185
22.680	**50**	110.231
27.216	**60**	132.277
31.752	**70**	154.324
36.287	**80**	176.370
40.823	**90**	198.416
45.359	**100**	220.462

Index

References are to page numbers.